CurrentLaw

STATUTORY INSTRUMENT CITATOR 1996–1999

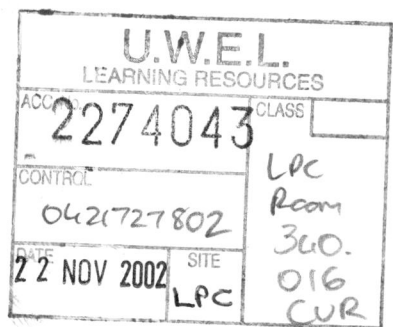

Sweet & Maxwell
·
W Green

AUSTRALIA
LBC Information Services
Brisbane ● Sydney ● Melbourne ● Perth

CANADA
Carswell
Ottawa ● Toronto ● Calgary ● Montreal ● Vancouver

Agents:
Steimatzky's Agency Ltd., Tel Aviv;
N.M. Tripathi (Private) Ltd., Bombay;
Eastern Law House (Private) Ltd., Calcutta;
M.P.P. House, Bangalore;
Universal Book Traders, Delhi;
Aditya Books, Delhi;
MacMillan Shuppan KK, Tokyo;
Pakistan Law House, Karachi, Lahore

CurrentLaw

STATUTORY INSTRUMENT CITATOR 1996–1999

Sweet & Maxwell Editorial Team
Fiona Cleaveley
Deborah Ehrenberg
Kirsty Gordon
Joanna Richards
Jean Stopford

Sweet & Maxwell
•
W Green

Published in 2000 by
Sweet & Maxwell Limited of
100 Avenue Road, London, NW3 3PF
Typeset by MFK Information Services Ltd.,
Hitchin, Herts
Printed by Antony Rowe Ltd, Reading, Berks.

A CIP catalogue record for this book is available
from The British Library

ISBN This Volume only 0–421–72780–2
With Year Book and Case Citator 0–421–72800–0

PREFACE

The Sweet & Maxwell Current Law Service

The Current Law Service began in 1947 and provides a comprehensive guide to developments in case law, primary legislation and secondary legislation in the UK and mainland Europe. The Current Law Service presently consists of the Monthly Digests, the Year Book, Current Law Statutes, the Statute Citator, the Statutory Instrument Citator, the Case Citator, Current Law Week and European Current Law.

Also available is the Current Legal Information CD Rom, which contains an archive of Year Books dating back to 1986 and the present year's cumulated Monthly Digests, as well as a range of other Sweet & Maxwell current awareness products such as the Current Law Case Citator, Current Law Statute Citator, the Legal Journals Index and the Financial Journals Index.

A booklet entitled *How to Use Current Law* is available from Sweet & Maxwell and will assist users in gaining the maximum benefit from all parts of the Current Law Service, both as current awareness tools and reference works, justice to which cannot be done here.

The Statute Citators and the Statutory Instrument Citators

The Current Law Statute Citators comprise four volumes covering the years 1947–1971, 1972–1988, 1989–1995 and 1996–1999. The Statutory Instrument Citators cover the years 1993–1995 and 1996–1999. Monthly updates to both these Citators are available in the Current Law Statutes looseleaf service and on CD Rom. The Citators list all amendments, modifications, repeals, etc. to primary and secondary legislation made in the years indicated. This volume contains the Statutory Instrument Citator 1996–1999.

The Statute Citator

The material within the Statute Citator is arranged in chronological order and the following information is provided:

(a) in respect of any Act passed between 1947 and 1959, where the Act is summarised in the Current Law Year Book, and for any Act thereafter the date of Royal Assent;

(b) in respect of any Act of any date, whether it has been repealed, amended or otherwise modified since 1947;

(c) in respect of any Act of any date, the cases in which it has been judicially considered since 1947;

v

(d) in respect of any Act of any date, the Statutory Instruments which have been made under its provisions; and
(e) in respect of any Act of any date, where it has been consolidated by an Act passed in 1996–1999.

The Statutory Instrument Citator

The material within the Statutory Instrument Citator is arranged in chronological order and the following information is provided:

(a) in respect of any Statutory Instrument of any date, whether it has been repealed, amended or otherwise modified in 1996–1999;
(b) in respect of any Statutory Instrument of any date, the cases in which it has been judicially considered in 1996–1999;
(c) in respect of any Statutory Instrument of any date, the Statutory Instruments issued in 1996–1999 which have been made under its provisions;
(d) in respect of any Statutory Instrument of any date, where it has been consolidated by an Act passed in 1996–1999.

Appendix

The Table of European Legislation implemented by Statutory Instrument details all Statutory Instruments issued from 1996 to 1999 and all Scottish Statutory Instruments issued in 1999 which give effect to European Legislation.

HOW TO USE THIS BOOK

The following fictional entries to the Statute and Statutory Instrument Citators indicate how to determine developments which have occurred to the piece of legislation in which you are interested. Entries to the Citators are arranged chronologically.

Statute Citator
12. Example Act 1993. —Chapter number, name of Act and year
Royal Assent, May 5, 1993 —Date of Royal Assent
Commencement Orders: SI 94/1234; SI 95/78 —Commencement orders bringing provisions into force
s.1, enabling SI 94/1234; SI 95/78 —Statutory Instruments made under the powers of s.1 of the Act
s.2, see *R. v Brown* [1995] Crim.L.R. 43 —Case judicially considering s.2
s.3, amended: 1996 c.3 s.2 —s.3 amended by Act (s.2 of chapter 3 of 1996) and two SIs
s.3, enabling: SI 93/82; SI 96/70
s.4, repealed: 1996 c.3 Sch. 4 —s.4 repealed by Schedule 4 of chapter 3 of 1996
s.4A added: SI 94/42 —s.4A added by SI Number 42 of 1994
Sch. 8, C. 1994 c.1 s.89 —Schedule 8 consolidated by s.89 of chapter 1 of 1994

SI Citator
1234 Example Regulations 1993. —Number, name and year of SI
Reg. 2, amended: SI 94/65 Art. 2 —reg. 2 amended by article 2 of SI number 65 of 1994
Reg. 3, revoked: 1994 c.23 Sch. 15 —reg. 3 revoked by Schedule 15 of chapter 23 of 1994
Reg. 4, see *R. v. Smith* [1994] C.O.D. 54 —Case judicially considering reg. 4
Reg. 5, C. 1996 c.7 Sch. 4 —reg. 5 consolidated by Schedule 4 of chapter 7 of 1996

CONTENTS

TABLE OF ABBREVIATIONS

Publisher's name follows reports and journals.

(S&M = Sweet & Maxwell; ICLR = Incorporated Council of Law Reporting for England and Wales; LBC = Law Book Company of Australia; OUP = Oxford University Press; Kluwer = Kluwer Law International; Cass = Frank Cass & Co Ltd; CUP = Cambridge University Press; CLP = Central Law Publishing; TSO = The Stationery Office. LLP = Lloyd's of London Press Ltd. All other names are in full.)

A. & S.L. = Air and Space Law (*Kluwer*)
A.C. = Appeal Cases (*ICLR*)
A.D.R.L.J. = Arbitration and Dispute Resolution Law Journal (*LLP*)
A.I. & L. = Artificial Intelligence and Law (*Kluwer*)
A.L.Q. = Arab Law Quarterly (*Kluwer*)
Accountancy = Accountancy (*Institute of Chartered Accountants in England and Wales*)
Ad. & Fos. = Adoption & Fostering (*British Adoption Agency Institute*)
Admin. L.R. = Administrative Law Reports (*Barry Rose*)
Adviser = Adviser (*NACAB*)
Agri. Law = Agricultural Law (*CLP*)
All E.R. = All England Law Reports (*Butterworths*)
All E.R. (Comm) = All England Law Reports (Commercial Cases) (*Butterworths*)
All E.R. (EC) = All England Law Reports European Cases (*Butterworths*)
All E.R. Rev. = All England Law Reports Annual Review (*Butterworths*)
Amicus Curiae = Amicus Curiae (*CCH Editions*)
Anglo-Am. L.R. = Anglo-American Law Review (*Barry Rose*)
A.P.L.R. = Asia Pacific Law Review (*Kluwer Law International*)
Arbitration = Arbitration (*Institute of Arbitrators*)
Arbitration Int. = Arbitration International (*Kluwer*)
Arch. News = Archbold News (*S&M*)

B.C.C. = British Company Law & Practice (*CCH Editions*)
B.C.L.C. = Butterworths Company Law Cases (*Butterworths*)
B.H.R.C. = Butterworths Human Rights Cases (*Butterworths*)
B.I.F.D. = Bulletin for International Fiscal Documentation (*IBFD Publications BV*)
B.J.I.B. & F.L. = Butterworths Journal of International Banking & Financial Law (*Butterworths*)
B.L.E. = Business Law Europe (*S&M*)
B.L.G.R. = Butterworths Local Government Reports (*Butterworths*)
B.L.R. = Building Law Reports (*LLB*)
B.M.C.R. = Butterworths Merger Control Review (*Butterworths*)
B.M.L.R. = Butterworths Medico-Legal Reports (*Butterworths*)

B.P.I.L.S. = Butterworths Personal Injury Litigation Services (*Butterworths*)
B.P.I.R. = Bankruptcy and Personal Insolvency Reports (*Jordans*)
B.P.L. = British Pension Lawyer (*Keith Wallace*)
B.T.C. = British Tax Cases (*CCH Editions*)
B.T.R. = British Tax Review (*S&M*)
B.V.C = British Value Added Tax Reporter (*CCH Editions*)
B.Y.B.I.L. = British Year Book of International Law (*OUP*)
Bracton L.J. = Bracton Law Journal (*University of Exeter*)
Brit. J. Criminol. = British Journal of Criminology (*OUP*)
Build. L.M. = Building Law Monthly (*Monitor Press*)
Bull. J.S.B. = Bulletin of the Judicial Studies Board
Bus. L.B. = Business Law Bulletin (*W. Green*)
Bus. L.R. = Business Law Review (*Kluwer*)

c. = chapter (of an Act of Parliament)
C. & E.L. = Construction & Engineering Law (*CLP*)
C. & F.L. = Credit and Finance Law (*Monitor Press*)
C. & F.L.U. = Child & Family Law Update (*SLS Legal Publications*)
C.C.L.R. = Consumer Credit Law Reports (incorporated within Consumer Credit Control—*S&M*)
C.C.L. Rep = Community Care Law Reports (*Legal Action Group*)
C.D.F.N. = Clinical Disputes Forum Newsletter (*Clinical Disputes Forum*)
C.E.C. = European Community Cases (*CCH Edition*)
C.F.L.Q. = Child and Family Law Quarterly (*Jordan*)
C.G. = Corporate Governance (*Blackwell Publishers*)
C.I.C.C. = Current Issues in Consumer Credit (incorporated within Consumer Credit Control—*S&M*)
C.I.L. = Contemporary Issues in Law (*Lawtext Publishing Ltd*)
C.I.L.L. = Construction Industry Law Letter (*Monitor Press*)
C.I.P.A.J. = Chartered Institute of Patent Agents Journal (*Chartered Institute of Patent Agents*)

TABLE OF ABBREVIATIONS

TABLE OF ABBREVIATIONS

E.E.F.N. = Eastern European Forum Newsletter (*International Bar Association*)

E.E.L.R. = European Environmental Law Review (*Kluwer*)

E.F.A. Rev. = European Foreign Affairs Review (*Kluwer Law International*)

E.F.S.L. = European Financial Services Law (*Kluwer*)

E.G. = Estates Gazette (*Estates Gazette Ltd*)

E.G.C.S. = Estates Gazette Case Summaries (*Estates Gazette Ltd*)

E.G.L.R. = Estates Gazette Law Reports (*Estates Gazette Ltd*)

E.H.L.R. = Environmental Health Law Reports (*S&M*)

E.H.R.L.R. = European Human Rights Law Review (*S&M*)

E.H.R.R. = European Human Rights Reports (*S&M*)

E.I.B. = Environment Information Bulletin (*Eclipse*)

E.I.P.R. = European Intellectual Property Review (*S&M*)

E.I.R.R. = European Industrial Relations Review (*Eclipse*)

E.J.E.L. & P. = European Journal for Educational Law and Policy (*Kluwer*)

E.J.H.L. = European Journal of Health Law (*Kluwer*)

E.J.I.L. = European Journal of International Law (*S&M*)

E.J.L.R. = European Journal of Law Reform (*Kluwer*)

E.J.S.S. = European Journal of Social Security (*Kluwer*)

E.L. = Equitable Lawyer (*Gostick Hall Publications*)

E.L.A. Briefing = Employment Lawyers Association Briefing (*S&M*)

E.L.B. = Environmental Law Brief (*Monitor Press*)

E.L.J. = European Law Journal (*Blackwell*)

E.L.L.R. = Environmental Liability Law Review (*Kluwer*)

E.L.M. = Environmental Law and Management (*Chancery Law Publishing Ltd*)

E.L.R. = Education Law Reports (*Jordans*)

E.L.Rev. = European Law Review (*S&M*)

E.M.L.R. = Entertainment and Media Law Reports (*S&M*)

E.O.R. = Equal Opportunities Review (*Eclipse*)

E.O.R. Dig. = Equal Opportunities Review and Discrimination Case Law Digest (*Eclipse*)

E.P.L. = European Public Law (*Kluwer*)

E.P.L.I. = Education, Public Law and the Individual (*John Wiley & Sons Ltd*)

E.P.O.R. = European Patent Office Reports (*S&M*)

E.R.P.L. = European Review of Private Law (*Kluwer*)

E.T.M.R. = European Trade Marks Reports (*S&M*)

E.W.C.B. = European Works Councils Bulletin (*Eclipse*)

EAT = Employment Appeal Tribunal

EC C.P.N. = European Commission Competition Policy Newsletter (*Commission of the European Communities*)

EC T.J. = EC Tax Journal (*Key Haven*)

EC T.R. = EC Tax Review (*Kluwer*)

Ecc. L.J. = Ecclesiastical Law Journal (*Ecclesiastical Law Society*)

Ed. C.R. = Education Case Reports (*S&M*)

EDI L.R. = Electronic Data Interchange Law Review (*Kluwer*)

ECJ = European Court of Justice

Eco M. & A. = Eco-Management & Auditing (*John Wiley & Sons Ltd*)

Ed. L.M. = Education Law Monitor (*Monitor Press*)

Emp. L. Brief. = Employment Law Briefing (*S&M*)

Emp. L.B. = Employment Law Bulletin (*W. Green*)

Emp L.J. = Employment Law Journal (*Legalease Ltd*)

Emp. Law. = Employment Lawyer (*CCH Editions Ltd*)

Emp. Lit. = Employment Litigation (*CLP*)

ENDS = ENDS Report (*Environmental Data Services*)

Ent. L.R. = Entertainment Law Review (*S&M*)

Env. L.B. = Environmental Law Bulletin (*W. Green*)

Env. L.M. = Environmental Law Monthly (*Monitor Press*)

Env. L.R. = Environmental Law Reports (*S&M*)

Env. Law = Environmental Law (*S&M*)

Env. Liability = Environmental Liability (*Lawtext*)

EU Focus = European Union Focus (*CCH Editions Ltd*)

Eu. L.R. = European Law Reports (*John Wiley & Sons Ltd*)

Eur. Access = European Access (*Chadwyck Healey*)

Eur. Counsel = European Counsel (*Legal & Commercial Publishing*)

Eur. J. Crime Cr. L. Cr. J. = European Journal of Crime, Criminal Law and Criminal Justice (*Kluwer*)

Euro. Env. = European Environment (*John Wiley & Sons Ltd*)

Euro. L.B. = European Legal Business (*Legalease*)

Euro. L.M. = European Law Monitor (*Monitor Press*)

Euro. Tax. = European Taxation (*IBFD*)

Expert = Expert (*Academy of Experts S&M*)

F & C.L. = Finance & Credit Law (*Monitor Press*)

F. & D.L.R. = Futures & Derivatives Law Review (*Cavendish*)

F.C.R. = Family Court Reporter (*Tolleys Ltd*)

F.D. & D.I.B. = Food, Drinks & Drugs Industry Bulletin (*Monitor*)

F.I.T.A.R. = Financial Instruments Tax & Accounting Review (*CTA Financial Publishing*)

F.L.R. = Family Law Reports (*Jordan*)

TABLE OF ABBREVIATIONS

TABLE OF ABBREVIATIONS

I.R.L.B. = Industrial Relations Law Bulletin (*Eclipse*)

I.R.L.C.T. = International Review of Law Computers & Technology (*Carfax*)

I.R.L.R. = Industrial Relations Law Reports (*Eclipse*)

I.R.T.B. = Inland Revenue Tax Bulletin (*Inland Revenue*)

I.R.V. = International Review of Victimology (*A B Academic*)

I.T. & C.L.J. = Information Technology & Communications Law Journal (*Legalease*)

IT & C.L.R. = IT & Communications Law Reports (*Legalease*)

I.T.L.J. = International Travel Law Journal (*Travel Law Centre*)

I.T.L.Q.—Internationnal Trade Law Quarterly (*LLP Ltd*)

I.T.P.J. = International Transfer Pricing Journal (*IBFD Publications BV*)

I.T.R. = Industrial Tribunal Reports

I.T.R. = International Tax Review (*Euromoney*)

I.T. Rep. = International Tax Report (*Monitor*)

I.V.M. = International VAT Monitor (*IBFD*)

IDS Brief = IDS Brief, Employment Law and Practice (*Income Data Services Ltd*)

IDS Emp. E. = IDS Employment Europe (*Income Data Services Ltd*)

IDS P.L.R. = IDS Pensions Law Reports (*Income Data Services Ltd*)

IH = Inner House of the Court of Session

IIC = International Review of Industrial Property and Copyright Law (*John Wiley & Sons Ltd*)

Imm. A.R. = Immigration Appeals Reports (*TSO*)

In Comp. = In Competition (*S&M*)

Independent = Independent Law Reports

Info. T.L.R. = Information Technology Law Reports (*Lawtext Publishing*)

Ins. L.M. = Insurance Law Monthly (*Monitor Press*)

Insolv. B. = Insolvency Bulletin (*Armstrong Information Ltd*)

Insolv. Int. = Insolvency Intelligence (*S&M*)

Insolvency = Insolvency (*Griffin Multimedia*)

Int. A.L.R. = International Arbitration Law Review (*S&M*)

Int. J. Comp. L.L.I.R. = International Journal of Comparative Labour Law and Industrial Relations (*Kluwer*)

Int. J. Law & Fam. = International Journal of Law, Policy and the Family (*OUP*)

Int. J. Soc. L. = International Journal of the Sociology of Law (*Academic Press Ltd*)

Int. M.L. = International Maritime Law (*S&M*)

Int. Rel. = International Relations (*David Davies Memorial Institute*)

Int. T.L.R. = International Trade Law & Regulation (*S&M ESC Publishing*)

Intertax = Intertax (*Kluwer*)

Ir. B.L. = Irish Business Law (*Inns Quay Publishing*)

Ir. T.R. = Irish Tax Review (*Institute of Taxation in Ireland*)

IT L.T. = IT Law Today (*Monitor Press*)

J.A.C.L. = Journal of Armed Conflict Law (*Nottingham University Press*)

J.A.L. = Journal of African Law (*OUP*)

J.B.L. = Journal of Business Law (*S&M*)

J.C. = Justiciary Cases

J. Civ. Lib. = Journal of Civil Liberties (*Northumbria Law Press*)

J. Com. Mar. St. = Journal of Common Market Studies (*Blackwell*)

J. Crim. L. = Journal of Criminal Law (*Pageant*)

J.E.L.P. = Journal of Employment Law & Practice (*Tolley*)

J. Env. L. = Journal of Environmental Law (*OUP*)

J.E.R.L. = Journal of Energy & Natural Resources Law (*Kluwer*)

J.F.C. = Journal of Financial Crime (*Henry Stewart*)

J.F.R. & C. = Journal of Financial Regulation and Compliance (*Henry Stewart*)

J.I.B.L. = Journal of International Banking Law (*S&M*)

J.I.B.R. = Journal of International Banking Regulation (*Euromoney Publications*)

J.I.E.L. = Journal of International Economic Law (*OUP*)

J.I.F.D.L. = Journal of International Franchising & Distribution Law (*Tolley*)

J.I.L.T. = Journal of Information, Law & Technology (http://elj.warwick.ac.uk/jilt)

J. Int. Arb. = Journal of International Arbitration (*Kluwer*)

J. Int. P. = Journal of International Trust and Corporate Planning (*John Wiley*)

J.L.G.L. = Journal of Local Government Law (*S&M*)

J.L.S. = Journal of Legislative Studies (*Cass*)

J.L.S.S. = Journal of the Law Society of Scotland (Law Society of Scotland)

J. Law & Soc. = Journal of Law and Society (*Blackwell*)

J. Leg. Hist. = Journal of Legal History (*Cass*)

J.M.L. & P. = Journal of Media Law & Practice (*Tolley*)

J.P. = Justice of the Peace (*Justice of the Peace Ltd*)

J.P.I.L. = Journal of Personal Injury Litigation (*S&M*)

J.P.L. = Journal of Planning & Environment Law (*S&M*)

J.P.M. & M. = Journal of Pensions Management and Marketing (*Henry Stewart*)

J.P.N. = Justice of the Peace Reports & Local Government Notes of Cases (*Justice of the Peace Ltd*)

J.P. Rep. = Justice of the Peace and Local Government Law Reports (*Justice of the Peace Ltd*)

J.S.B.J. = Judicial Studies Board Journal (*Blackstone Press*)

J.S.S.L. = Journal of Social Security Law (*S&M*)

J. Soc. Wel. & Fam. L. = Journal of Social Welfare and Family Law (*Routledge*)

Jersey L.R. = Jersey Law Review (*The Jersey Law Review*)

TABLE OF ABBREVIATIONS

Jur. Rev. = Juridical Review (*W. Green*)

K.B. = Kings Bench (Law Reports) (*ICLR*)
K.C.L.J. = Kings College Law Journal (*King's College London*)
K.I.R. = Knights Industrial Reports

L. & T. Review = Landlord & Tenant Review (*S&M*)
L. Ex. = Legal Executive (*ILEX*)
L.E. = Lawyers' Europe (*Butterworths*)
L.F. = Litigation Funding (*Law Society Publishing*)
L.G. and L. = Local Government and Law (*Monitor Press*)
L.G. Rev. = Local Government Review (*Barry Rose*)
L.G.C. Law & Admin. = Local Government Chronicle Law & Administration (*Local Government Chronicle Ltd*)
L.G.C. = Local Government Chronicle (*Local Government Chronicle Ltd*)
L.G.L.R. = Local Government Law Reports (*S&M*)
L.I.E.I. = Legal Issues of European Integration (*Kluwer*)
L.M.C.L.Q. = Lloyd's Maritime & Commercial Law Quarterly (*LLP*)
L.P. or L.V.C. = references to denote Lands Tribunal decision (*transcripts available from the Lands Tribunal*)
L.Q.R. = Law Quarterly Review (*S&M*)
L.R. App. Cas. = Law Reports Appeal Cases
L.R.L.R. = Lloyd's Reinsurance Law Reports (*LLP*)
L.S. = Legal Studies (*Butterworths*)
L.S.G. = Law Society Gazette (*The Law Society*)
L. & T.R. = Landlord and Tenant Reports (*S&M*)
Law & Crit. = Law and Critique (*Deborah Charles*)
Law & Just. = Law & Justice (*Plowden*)
Law & Pol. = Law & Policy (*Blackwell*)
Law Lib. = Law Librarian (*S&M*)
Law Teach. = Law Teacher (*S&M*)
Lawyer = Lawyer (*Centaur Communications Group*)
Legal Action = Legal Action (*Legal Action Group*)
Legal Bus. = Legal Business (*Legalease*)
Legal Ethics = Legal Ethics (*Hart Publishing Ltd*)
Legal Week = (*WDIS Ltd*)
Lit. = Litigation (*Barry Rose*)
Liverpool L.R. = Liverpool Law Review (*Deborah Charles*)
Lloyd's Rep. = Lloyd's Law Reports (*LLP*)
Lloyd's Rep. Bank. = Lloyd's Law Reports Banking (*LLP*)
Lloyd's Rep. I.R. = Lloyd's Law Reports Insurance & Reinsurance (*LLP*)
Lloyd's Rep. Med. = Lloyd's Law Report Medical (*LLP*)
Ll. Rep. = Lloyd's List Reports (*LLP*)

LVAC = Land Valuation Appeal Court

M.A.L.Q.R. = Model Arbitration Law Quarterly Review (*Simmons & Hill Publishing Ltd*)
M. Advocate = Maritime Advocate (*Merlin Legal Publishing*)
M.C.P. = Magistrates' Courts Practice (*CLP*)
M.D.U. Jour. = Medical Defence Union Journal (*Medical Defence Union*)
M.E.C.L.R. = Middle East Commercial Law Review (*S&M*)
M.I.P. = Managing Intellectual Property (*Euromoney*)
M.J. = Maastricht Journal of European and Comparative Law (*Roger Bayliss*)
M.J.L.S. = Mountbatten Journal of Legal Studies (*Southampton Institute*)
M.L.B. = Manx Law Bulletin (*Central Reference*)
M.L.J.I. = Medico-Legal Journal of Ireland (*Round Hall/S&M*)
M.L.N. = Media Lawyer Newsletter (*Tom Welsh*)
M.L.R. = Modern Law Review (*Blackwell*)
Magistrate = Magistrate (*Magistrates' Association*)
Masons C.L.R. = Masons Computer Law Reports
Med. L. Int. = Medical Law International (*A B Academic Publishing*)
Med. L. Mon. = Medical Law Monitor (*Monitor Press*)
Med. L. Rev. = Medical Law Review (*OUP*)
Med. L.R. = Medical Law Reports (*OUP*)
Med. Leg. J. = Medico-Legal Journal (*Dramrite Printers*)
Med. Lit. = Medical Litigation (*Medical Litigation Strategies*)
Med. Sci. Law = Medicine, Science & the Law (*Chiltern*)

N.I.L.Q. = Northern Ireland Legal Quarterly (*SLS Legal Publications*)
N.I.L.R. = Northern Ireland Law Reports (*Butterworths*)
N.L.J. = New Law Journal (*Butterworths*)
N.P.C. = New Property Cases (*New Property Cases Ltd*)
N.Q.H.S. = Netherlands Quarterly of Human Rights (*Kluwer*)
N.Z.L.R. = New Zealand Law Reports
Nott. L.J. = Nottingham Law Journal (*Nottingham Trent University*)

O.D. and I.L. = Ocean Development and International Law (*Taylor & Francis Ltd*)
O.J.L.S. = Oxford Journal of Legal Studies (*OUP*)
O.P.L.R. = Occupational Pensions Law Reports (*Eclipse Group*)
O.S.S. Bull. = Office for the Supervision of Solicitors Bulletin (*The Law Society's Gazette*)
O.T.R. = Offshore Taxation Review (*Key Haven*)
Occ. Pen. = Occupational Pensions (*Eclipse*)

TABLE OF ABBREVIATIONS

TABLE OF ABBREVIATIONS

S.L.P.Q. = Scottish Law & Practice Quarterly (*T & T Clark*)

S.L.R. = Student Law Review (*Cavendish*)

S.L.T. = Scots Law Times (*S&M/W. Green*)

S.L.T. (Land Ct) = Scots Law Times Land Court Reports (*S&M/W. Green*)

S.L.T. (Lands Tr) = Scots Law Times Lands Tribunal Reports (*S&M/W. Green*)

S.L.T. (Lyon Ct) = Scots Law Times Lyon Court Reports (*S&M/W. Green*)

S.L.T. News = Scots Law Times News Section (*S&M/W. Green*)

S.L.T. (Notes) = Scots Law Times Notes of Recent Decisions (1946–1981) (*S&M/W. Green*)

S.L.T. (Sh Ct) = Scots Law Times Sheriff Court Reports (*S&M/W. Green*)

S.N. = Session Notes

S.P.E.L. = Scottish Planning and Environmental Law (*Planning Exchange*)

S.P.T.L. Reporter = Society of Public Teachers of Law Reporter (*Queen Mary*)

S.T.C. = Simon's Tax Cases (*Butterworths*)

S.T.C. (SCD) = Simons Tax Cases: Special Commissioners Decisions (*Butterworths*)

S.W.T.I. = Simon's Weekly Tax Intelligence (*Butterworths*)

SCOLAG = SCOLAG (*Scottish Legal Action Group*)

SI = Statutory Instrument

S. & C.L. = Sports and Character Licensing (*Informa Publishing Group Ltd*)

Soc. L. = Socialist Lawyer (*Haldane Society*)

Stat. L.R. = Statute Law Review (*OUP*)

Sudebnik = Sudebnik (*Simmonds & Hill*)

T. & T. = Trusts & Trustees (*Gostick Hall*)

T.A.Q. = The Aviation Quarterly (*LLP*)

T.C. or Tax.Cas. = Tax Cases (*TSO*)

T.C.L.R. = Technology and Construction Law Reports (*S&M*)

T & E.L.J. = Trusts and Estates Law Journal (*Legalease*)

T.E.L.L. = Tolley's Employment Law-Line (*Tolley*)

T.L.P. = Transport Law & Policy (*Waterfront Partnership*)

T.N.I.B. = Tolley's National Insurance Brief (*Tolley*)

T.O.C. = Transnational Organized Crime (*Cass*)

T.P.I.E.U.F. = Tax Planning International European Union Focus (*BNA International Inc*)

T.P.I.R. = Tax Planning International Review (*BNA International Inc*)

T.P.I. e-commerce = Tax Planning International e-commerce (*BNA International Inc*)

T.P.T.S. = Tolley's Practical Tax Service (Tolley)

T.P.V.S. = Tolley's Practical VAT Service (Tolley)

T.S.B.P.I. = Technical Bulletin of the Society of Practitioners of Insolvency

T.W. = Trademark World (*Intellectual Property*)

TACT Review = Tolley's Practical Audit & Accounting (*The Association of Corporate Trustees*)

Tax A. = Taxation Adviser (*The Manson Group Ltd*)

Tax B. = Tax Briefing (*Office of the Revenue Commissioners*)

Tax J. = Tax Journal (*Butterworths*)

Tax. = Taxation (*Tolley*)

Theo. Crim. = Theoretical Criminology (*Sage Publications*)

Tr. & Est. = Trusts & Estates (*Monitor Press*)

Tr. L.R. = Trading Law Reports (*Barry Rose*)

Trans. ref. = Transcript reference number

Tribunals = Tribunals (*OUP*)

Tru. L.I. = Trust Law International (*Tolley*)

TSO = The Stationery Office

The Times = Times Law Reports

U.L.R. = Utilities Law Review (*Chancery Law Publishing Ltd*)

UCELNET = Universities and Colleges Education Law Network (*University of Stirling*)

UK C.L.R. = UK Competition Law Reports (*S&M*)

V. & D.R. = Value Added Tax and Duties Reports (*TSO*)

V.A.T.T.R. = Value Added Tax Tribunal Reports (*TSO*)

VAT Int. = VAT Intelligence (*Gee Publishing*)

VAT Plan. = VAT Planning (*Butterworths*)

W. Comp. = World Competition (*Kluwer*)

W.B. = Welfare Benefits (*CLP*)

W.L. = Water Law (*Chancery Law Publishing Ltd*)

W.L.R. = Weekly Law Reports (*ICLR*)

Web J.C.L.I. = Web Journal of Current Legal Issues (*Blackstone*) http://webjcli.ncl.ac.uk

Welf. R. Bull. = Welfare Rights Bulletin (*Child Poverty*)

World I.L.R. = World Internet Law Report (*BNA International Inc*)

Worldlaw Bus. = Worldlaw Business (*Euromoney Publications*)

Writ = Writ (*Northern Ireland Law Society*)

Y.E.L. = Yearbook of European Law (*OUP*)

Y.M.E.L. = Yearbook of Media & Entertainment Law (*OUP*)

Yb. Int'l Env. L. = Yearbook of International Environmental Law (*OUP*)

ALPHABETICAL TABLE OF STATUTORY INSTRUMENTS

This table lists all the Statutory Instruments cited in the Statutory Instrument Citator.

ALPHABETICAL TABLE OF STATUTORY INSTRUMENTS

ALPHABETICAL TABLE OF STATUTORY INSTRUMENTS

ALPHABETICAL TABLE OF STATUTORY INSTRUMENTS

ALPHABETICAL TABLE OF STATUTORY INSTRUMENTS

ALPHABETICAL TABLE OF STATUTORY INSTRUMENTS

Diseases of Animals (Waste Food) (Amendment) Order 1987 (S.I. 232)

Diseases of Animals (Waste Food) (Amendment) Order 1996 (S.I. 826)

Diseases of Animals (Waste Food) Order 1973 (S.I. 1936)

Diseases of Fish (Control) Regulations 1994 (S.I. 1447)

Diseases of Fish Regulations 1984 (S.I. 455)

Diseases of Poultry Order 1994 (S.I. 3141)

Disposal of Waste (Control of Beet Rhizomania Disease) Order 1988 (S.I. 45)

Disqualification for Caring for Children Regulations 1991 (S.I. 2094)

Dissolution of the Broadcasting Complaints Commission and the Broadcasting Standards Council Order 1998 (S.I. 2954)

Distress for Customs and Excise Duties and Other Indirect Taxes Regulations 1997 (S.I. 1431)

Distress for Rent Rules 1988 (S.I. 2050)

District of Alnwick (Electoral Arrangements) Order 1976 (S.I. 764)

District of Amber Valley (Electoral Arrangements) Order 1978 (S.I. 1611)

District of Bolsover (Electoral Arrangements) Order 1978 (S.I. 1494)

District of Bracknell (Electoral Arrangements) Order 1977 (S.I. 1273)

District of Chester-le-Street (Electoral Arrangements) Order 1976 (S.I. 1819)

District of Daventry (Electoral Arrangements) Order 1976 (S.I. 1704)

District of Derwentside (Electoral Arrangements) Order 1978 (S.I. 231)

District of Easington (Electoral Arrangements) Order 1978 (S.I. 1859)

District of East Devon (Electoral Arrangements) Order 1978 (S.I. 1842)

District of East Hertfordshire (Electoral Arrangements) Order 1976 (S.I. 1303)

District of East Lindsey (Electoral Arrangements) Order 1979 (S.I. 1415)

District of East Northamptonshire (Electoral Arrangements) Order 1976 (S.I. 811)

District of Eden (Electoral Arrangements) Order 1976 (S.I. 750)

District of Kennet (Electoral Arrangements) Order 1976 (S.I. 297)

District of Kingswood (Electoral Arrangements) Order 1987 (S.I. 485)

District of Mendip (Electoral Arrangements) Order 1976 (S.I. 752)

District of Mole Valley (Electoral Arrangements) Order 1975 (S.I. 2105)

District of North Devon (Electoral Arrangements) Order 1980 (S.I. 181)

District of North East Derbyshire (Electoral Arrangements) Order 1978 (S.I. 1768)

District of North Hertfordshire (Electoral Arrangements) Order 1977 (S.I. 1442)

District of North Kesteven (Electoral Arrangements) Order 1977 (S.I. 1811)

District of North Kesteven (Parishes and Electoral Changes) Order 1998 (S.I. 2338)

District of North Wiltshire (Electoral Arrangements) Order 1979 (S.I. 1015)

District of Northavon (Electoral Arrangements) Order 1975 (S.I. 2147)

District of Purbeck (Electoral Arrangements) Order 1977 (S.I. 1064)

District of Runnymede (Electoral Arrangements) Order 1975 (S.I. 1814)

District of Rutland (Electoral Arrangements) Order 1977 (S.I. 1865)

District of Salisbury (Electoral Arrangements) Order 1975 (S.I. 1815)

District of Sedgefield (Electoral Arrangements) Order 1979 (S.I. 1264)

District of Sedgemoor (Electoral Arrangements) Order 1977 (S.I. 379)

District of South Derbyshire (Electoral Arrangements) Order 1976 (S.I. 1966)

District of South Hams (Electoral Arrangements) Order 1977 (S.I. 1276)

District of South Holland (Electoral Arrangements) Order 1978 (S.I. 482)

District of South Kesteven (Electoral Arrangements) Order 1978 (S.I. 43)

District of South Lakeland (Electoral Arrangements) Order 1978 (S.I. 1665)

District of South Northamptonshire (Electoral Arrangements) Order 1976 (S.I. 285)

District of South Somerset (Electoral Arrangements) Order 1988 (S.I. 1692)

District of Tandridge (Electoral Arrangements) Order 1975 (S.I. 1817)

District of Teesdale (Electoral Arrangements) Order 1979 (S.I. 1109)

District of Teignbridge (Electoral Arrangements) Order 1978 (S.I. 47)

District of the Forest of Dean (Electoral Arrangements) Order 1980 (S.I. 43)

District of The Wrekin (Electoral Arrangements) Order 1978 (S.I. 1591)

District of Three Rivers (Electoral Arrangements) Order 1975 (S.I. 2199)

District of Three Rivers (Parishes and Electoral Changes) Order 1998 (S.I. 2556)

District of Tiverton (Electoral Arrangements) Order 1977 (S.I. 1279)

District of Torridge (Electoral Arrangements) Order 1978 (S.I. 1751)

District of Tynedale (Electoral Arrangements) Order 1976 (S.I. 182)

District of Wansbeck (Electoral Arrangements) Order 1975 (S.I. 2109)

District of Wear Valley (Electoral Arrangements) Order 1979 (S.I. 1265)

District of Welwyn Hatfield (Electoral Arrangements) Order 1976 (S.I. 65)

District of Welwyn Hatfield (Electoral Arrangements) Order 1991 (S.I. 695)

District of West Derbyshire (Electoral Arrangements) Order 1977 (S.I. 437)

District of West Devon (Electoral Arrangements) Order 1977 (S.I. 866)

District of West Lindsey (Electoral Arrangements) Order 1978 (S.I. 990)

ALPHABETICAL TABLE OF STATUTORY INSTRUMENTS

I

ALPHABETICAL TABLE OF STATUTORY INSTRUMENTS

ALPHABETICAL TABLE OF STATUTORY INSTRUMENTS

ALPHABETICAL TABLE OF STATUTORY INSTRUMENTS

Education (School Information) (Wales) Regulations 1997 (S.I. 1832)

Education (School Information) (Wales) Regulations 1999 (S.I. 1812)

Education (School Inspection) (Amendment) Regulations 1999 (S.I. 601)

Education (School Inspection) (England) (Amendment) (No.2) Regulations 1999 (S.I. 2545)

Education (School Inspection) (No.2) (Amendment) (No.2) Regulations 1996 (S.I. 3099)

Education (School Inspection) (No.2) (Amendment) Regulations 1993 (S.I. 2973)

Education (School Inspection) (No.2) (Amendment) Regulations 1996 (S.I. 1737)

Education (School Inspection) (No.2) (Amendment) Regulations 1997 (S.I. 995)

Education (School Inspection) (No.2) Regulations 1993 (S.I. 1986)

Education (School Inspection) (Wales) (Amendment) Regulations 1999 (S.I. 1440)

Education (School Inspection) (Wales) (No.2) (Amendment) Regulations 1993 (S.I. 2968)

Education (School Inspection) (Wales) (No.2) (Amendment) Regulations 1996 (S.I. 1934)

Education (School Inspection) (Wales) (No.2) (Amendment) Regulations 1997 (S.I. 1833)

Education (School Inspection) (Wales) (No.2) Regulations 1993 (S.I. 1982)

Education (School Inspection) (Wales) Regulations 1998 (S.I. 1866)

Education (School Inspection) Regulations 1997 (S.I. 1966)

Education (School Leaving Date) Order 1997 (S.I. 1970)

Education (School Meals Staff) (England) Regulations 1999 (S.I. 2258)

Education (School Meals Staff) (Wales) Regulations 1999 (S.I. 2802)

Education (School Organisation Committees) (England) Regulations 1999 (S.I. 700)

Education (School Organisation Committees) (Initial Financial Arrangements) (England) Regulations 1999 (S.I. 398)

Education (School Organisation Plans) (England) Regulations 1999 (S.I. 701)

Education (School Organisation Proposals) (England) Regulations 1999 (S.I. 2213)

Education (School Organisation Proposals) (Wales) Regulations 1999 (S.I. 1671)

Education (School Organisational Plans) (Wales) Regulations 1999 (S.I. 499)

Education (School Performance and Unauthorised Absence Targets) (Wales) Regulations 1999 (S.I. 1811)

Education (School Performance Information) (England) (Amendment) (No.2) Regulations 1997 (S.I. 2364)

Education (School Performance Information) (England) (Amendment) (No.2) Regulations 1999 (S.I. 2387)

Education (School Performance Information) (England) (Amendment) (No.3) Regulations 1997 (S.I. 2816)

Education (School Performance Information) (England) (Amendment) Regulations 1995 (S.I. 1561)

Education (School Performance Information) (England) (Amendment) Regulations 1996 (S.I. 1596)

Education (School Performance Information) (England) (Amendment) Regulations 1997 (S.I. 2060)

Education (School Performance Information) (England) (Amendment) Regulations 1998 (S.I. 3260)

Education (School Performance Information) (England) (Amendment) Regulations 1999 (S.I. 2158)

Education (School Performance Information) (England) Regulations 1994 (S.I. 1420)

Education (School Performance Information) (England) Regulations 1996 (S.I. 2577)

Education (School Performance Information) (England) Regulations 1998 (S.I. 1929)

Education (School Performance Information) (England) Regulations 1999 (S.I. 1178)

Education (School Performance Information) (Wales) (Amendment) Regulations 1996 (S.I. 1665)

Education (School Performance Information) (Wales) (Amendment) Regulations 1999 (S.I. 1470)

Education (School Performance Information) (Wales) Regulations 1995 (S.I. 1904)

Education (School Performance Information) (Wales) Regulations 1997 (S.I. 1633)

Education (School Performance Information) (Wales) Regulations 1998 (S.I. 1867)

Education (School Performance Targets) (England) Regulations 1998 (S.I. 1532)

Education (School Performance Targets) (Wales) Regulations 1998 (S.I. 2196)

Education (School Premises) (Amendment) Regulations 1989 (S.I. 1277)

Education (School Premises) (Amendment) Regulations 1990 (S.I. 2351)

Education (School Premises) Regulations 1981 (S.I. 909)

Education (School Premises) Regulations 1996 (S.I. 360)

Education (School Premises) Regulations 1999 (S.I. 2)

Education (School Sessions and Charges and Remissions Policies) (Information) (England) Regulations 1999 (S.I. 2255)

Education (School Teacher Appraisal) Regulations 1991 (S.I. 1511)

Education (School Teachers' Pay and Conditions) (No.2) Order 1995 (S.I. 1743)

Education (School Teachers' Pay and Conditions) (No.2) Order 1996 (S.I. 1816)

Education (School Teachers' Pay and Conditions) (No.2) Order 1997 (S.I. 1789)

Education (School Teachers' Pay and Conditions) (No.2) Order 1998 (S.I. 1884)

Education (School Teachers' Pay and Conditions) Order 1996 (S.I. 1003)

ALPHABETICAL TABLE OF STATUTORY INSTRUMENTS

ALPHABETICAL TABLE OF STATUTORY INSTRUMENTS

ALPHABETICAL TABLE OF STATUTORY INSTRUMENTS

Food Safety (Fishery Products) Regulations 1992 (S.I. 3163)

Food Safety (General Food Hygiene) Regulations 1995 (S.I. 1763)

Food Safety (Live Bivalve Molluscs and Other Shellfish) (Import Conditions and Miscellaneous Amendments) Regulations 1994 (S.I. 2782)

Food Safety (Live Bivalve Molluscs and Other Shellfish) Regulations 1992 (S.I. 3164)

Food Safety (Live Bivalve Molluscs) (Derogations) Regulations 1992 (S.I. 1508)

Food Safety (Northern Ireland) Order 1991 (S.I. 762)

Food Safety (Sampling and Qualifications) Regulations 1990 (S.I. 2463)

Food Safety (Temperature Control) Regulations 1995 (S.I. 2200)

Food Safety Act 1990 (Consequential Modifications) (England and Wales) Order 1990 (S.I. 2486)

Food Safety Act 1990 (Consequential Modifications) (No.2) (Great Britain) Order 1990 (S.I. 2487)

Football (Offences) (Designation of Football Matches) Order 1991 (S.I. 1565)

Football Spectators (Designation of Enforcing Authority) Order 1990 (S.I. 730)

Football Spectators (Designation of Football Matches in England and Wales) Order 1993 (S.I. 1691)

Foreign Marriage Order 1970 (S.I. 1539)

Forestry (Exceptions from Restriction of Felling) (Amendment) Regulations 1988 (S.I. 970)

Forestry (Exceptions from Restriction of Felling) Regulations 1979 (S.I. 792)

Forfeiture (Northern Ireland) Order 1982 (S.I. 1082)

Forms of Jurors Oath Order (Northern Ireland) 1996 (S.R. 268)

Forresterhill Hospitals National Health Service Trust (Establishment) Order 1991 (S.I. 2899)

Forresterhill Hospitals National Health Service Trust (Establishment) Order 1992 (S.I. 800)

Forth Valley Acute Hospitals National Health Service Trust (Establishment) Order 1998 (S.I. 2725)

Forth Valley Primary Care National Health Service Trust (Establishment) (Amendment) Order 1999 (S.I. 101)

Forth Valley Primary Care National Health Service Trust (Establishment) Order 1998 (S.I. 2713)

Fosse Health, Leicestershire Community National Health Service Trust (Establishment) Order 1994 (S.I. 3185)

Fossil Fuel Levy (Scotland) Regulations 1996 (S.I. 293)

Fossil Fuel Levy Act 1998 (Commencement) Order 1998 (S.I. 930)

Fossil Fuel Levy Regulations 1990 (S.I. 266)

Foster Placement (Children) Regulations 1991 (S.I. 910)

Fostering of Children (Scotland) Regulations 1996 (S.I. 3263)

Foundation Body Regulations 1999 (S.I. 1502)

Foyle Area (Licensing of Fishing Engines) (Amendment) Regulations 1999 (S.I. 45)

Fraserburgh Harbour Revision Order 1995 (S.I. 1527)

Free Zone (Liverpool) Designation Order 1991 (S.I. 1738)

Free Zone (Port of Sheerness) Designation Order 1994 (S.I. 2898)

Free Zone (Southampton) Designation (Variation) Order 1994 (S.I. 1410)

Free Zone (Southampton) Designation Order 1991 (S.I. 1740)

Freeman Group of Hospitals National Health Service Trust (Establishment) Order 1990 (S.I. 2416)

Freight Containers (Safety Convention) Regulations 1984 (S.I. 1890)

Frenchay Healthcare National Health Service Trust (Establishment) Order 1991 (S.I. 2349)

Fresh Meat (Beef Controls) (No.2) Regulations 1996 (S.I. 2097)

Fresh Meat (Beef Controls) Regulations 1996 (S.I. 1743)

Fresh Meat (Hygiene and Inspection) Regulations 1995 (S.I. 539)

Friendly Societies (Accounts and Related Provisions) Regulations 1994 (S.I. 1983)

Friendly Societies (Auditors) Order 1994 (S.I. 132)

Friendly Societies (General Charge and Fees) Regulations 1995 (S.I. 700)

Friendly Societies (General Charge and Fees) Regulations 1996 (S.I. 614)

Friendly Societies (General Charge and Fees) Regulations 1997 (S.I. 741)

Friendly Societies (General Charge and Fees) Regulations 1998 (S.I. 673)

Friendly Societies (Gilt-Edged Securities) (Periodic Accounting for Tax on Interest) (Amendment) Regulations 1997 (S.I. 475)

Friendly Societies (Gilt-Edged Securities) (Periodic Accounting for Tax on Interest) Regulations 1996 (S.I. 21)

Friendly Societies (Insurance Business) Regulations 1994 (S.I. 1981)

Friendly Societies (Modification of the Corporation Tax Acts) Regulations 1992 (S.I. 1655)

Friendly Societies (Modification of the Corporation Tax Acts) Regulations 1997 (S.I. 473)

Friendly Societies (Provisional Repayments for Exempt Business) (Amendment) Regulations 1997 (S.I. 474)

Friendly Societies (Provisional Repayments for Exempt Business) Regulations 1993 (S.I. 3112)

Friendly Societies (Provisional Repayments for Exempt Business) Regulations 1999 (S.I. 622)

Friendly Societies (Taxation of Transfers of Business) Regulations 1995 (S.I. 171)

Fruit Juices and Fruit Nectars (Amendment) Regulations 1982 (S.I. 1311)

Fruit Juices and Fruit Nectars (England, Wales and Scotland) (Amendment) Regulations 1991 (S.I. 1284)

ALPHABETICAL TABLE OF STATUTORY INSTRUMENTS

Merchant Shipping (Vessels in Commercial Use for Sport and Pleasure) Regulations 1993 (S.I. 1072)

Merchant Shipping (Weighing of Goods Vehicles and other Cargo) Regulations 1988 (S.I. 1275)

Merchant Shipping Act 1974 (Guernsey) Order 1981 (S.I. 225)

Merchant Shipping Act 1974 (Jersey) (Amendment) Order 1977 (S.I. 1242)

Merchant Shipping Act 1974 (Jersey) Order 1975 (S.I. 2181)

Merchant Shipping and Fishing Vessels (Health and Safety at Work) Regulations 1997 (S.I. 2962)

Merchant Shipping and Fishing Vessels (Manual Handling Operations) Regulations 1998 (S.I. 2857)

Merchant Shipping and Fishing Vessels (Medical Stores) Regulations 1995 (S.I. 1802)

Merchant Shipping and Maritime Security Act 1997 (Commencement No.1) Order 1997 (S.I. 1082)

Merchant Shipping and Maritime Security Act 1997 (Commencement No.2) Order 1997 (S.I. 1539)

Merger Reference (Universal Foods Corporation and Pointing Holdings Limited) (Interim Provision) Order 1999 (S.I. 2560)

Mersey Regional Ambulance Service National Health Service Trust (Establishment) Order 1991 (S.I. 2369)

Merseyside Development Corporation (Area and Constitution) Order 1981 (S.I. 481)

Merseyside Development Corporation (Planning Functions) (Liverpool and Wirral) Order 1988 (S.I. 1968)

Merseyside Development Corporation (Planning Functions) Order 1990 (S.I. 1568)

Merseyside Development Corporation (Vesting of Land) (British Railways Board) Order 1981 (S.I. 999)

Merseyside Development Corporation (Vesting of Land) (General) Order 1989 (S.I. 1305)

Merseyside Development Corporation (Vesting of Land) (Local Authorities) Order 1981 (S.I. 1000)

Merseyside Development Corporation (Vesting of Land) (Mersey Docks and Harbour Company No.2) Order 1981 (S.I. 1002)

Merseyside Development Corporation (Vesting of Land) (Mersey Docks and Harbour Company No.3) Order 1981 (S.I. 1003)

Merseyside Development Corporation (Vesting of Land) (Mersey Docks and Harbour Company) Order 1981 (S.I. 1001)

Merseyside Development Corporation (Vesting of Land) (Transport Land) Order 1989 (S.I. 1393)

Merton (Waiting and Loading) Order 1977 (S.I. 107)

Merton and Sutton Community National Health Service Trust (Establishment) Order 1992 (S.I. 2524)

Meters (Approval of Pattern or Construction and Method of Installation) Regulations 1990 (S.I. 791)

Meters (Certification) Order 1987 (S.I. 730)

Meters (Certification) Regulations 1990 (S.I. 792)

Microbiological Research Authority Regulations 1994 (S.I. 602)

Mid Anglia Community Health National Health Service Trust (Establishment) Order 1992 (S.I. 2573)

Mid Essex Community and Mental Health National Health Service Trust (Establishment) Order 1993 (S.I. 2856)

Mid Essex Hospital Services National Health Service Trust (Establishment) Order 1991 (S.I. 2370)

Mid Glamorgan Ambulance National Health Service Trust (Establishment) Order 1993 (S.I. 2834)

Mid-Sussex National Health Service Trust (Establishment) Order 1994 (S.I. 165)

Midlothian Educational Trust Scheme 1991

Milford Port Health Authority Order 1991 (S.I. 2913)

Milk and Dairies (General) Regulations 1959 (S.I. 277)

Milk and Dairies (Revision of Penalties) Regulations 1982 (S.I. 1703)

Milk and Dairies (Revision of Penalties) Regulations 1985 (S.I. 68)

Milk and Dairies (Scotland) Regulations 1990 (S.I. 2507)

Milk and Dairies (Standardisation and Importation) Regulations 1992 (S.I. 3143)

Milk and Milk Products (Designations) (Scotland) Regulations 1990 (S.I. 816)

Milk and Milk Products (Protection of Designations) Regulations 1990 (S.I. 607)

Milk Development Council Order 1995 (S.I. 356)

Milk Labelling (Scotland) Amendment Regulations 1990 (S.I. 2508)

Milk Labelling (Scotland) Regulations 1983 (S.I. 938)

Minced Meat and Meat Preparations (Hygiene) Regulations 1995 (S.I. 3205)

Mineral Hydrocarbons in Food (Scotland) Regulations 1966 (S.I. 1263)

Mineral Hydrocarbons in Food Regulations 1966 (S.I. 1073)

Mines (Safety of Exit) Regulations 1988 (S.I. 1729)

Mines (Safety of Exit) Regulations (Northern Ireland) 1998 (S.R. 375)

Mines (Shafts and Winding) Regulations 1993 (S.I. 302)

Mines and Quarries (Rateable Values) (Scotland) Order 1995 (S.I. 366)

Mines and Quarries (References) Rules 1956 (S.I. 1784)

Mines and Quarries (Tipping Plans) Rules 1971 (S.I. 1378)

Mines and Quarries (Tips) Regulations 1971 (S.I. 1377)

Mines and Quarries Acts 1954 to 1971 (Repeals and Modifications) Regulations 1974 (S.I. 2013)

Mines Miscellaneous Health and Safety Provisions Regulations 1995 (S.I. 2005)

Minibus and Other Section 19 Permit Buses Regulations 1987 (S.I. 1230)

Ministerial and other Salaries Order 1995 (S.I. 2984)

Ministries (Northern Ireland) Order 1973 (S.I. 2161)

Mink (Keeping) Regulations 1975 (S.I. 2223)

Mink Keeping Order 1992 (S.I. 3324)

Miscellaneous Food Additives Regulations 1995 (S.I. 3187)

Miscellaneous Food Additives Regulations (Northern Ireland) 1996 (S.R. 50)

Misuse of Drugs (Designation) Order 1986 (S.I. 2331)

Misuse of Drugs (Licence Fees) Regulations 1986 (S.I. 416)

Misuse of Drugs (Northern Ireland) Regulations 1986 (S.I. 52)

Misuse of Drugs (Notification of and Supply to Addicts) (Amendment) Regulations 1983 (S.I. 1909)

Misuse of Drugs (Notification of and Supply to Addicts) Regulations 1973 (S.I. 799)

Misuse of Drugs (Safe Custody) Regulations 1973 (S.I. 798)

Misuse of Drugs Regulations 1985 (S.I. 2066)

Money Laundering Regulations 1993 (S.I. 1933)

Money Purchase Contracted-out Schemes Regulations 1987 (S.I. 1101)

Monitoring of Advertising Regulations 1994 (S.I. 1933)

Monklands and Bellshill Hospitals National Health Service Trust (Appointment of Trustees) Order 1993 (S.I. 1139)

Monklands and Bellshill Hospitals National Health Service Trust (Establishment) (Change of Name and Amendment) Order 1998 (S.I. 922)

Monklands and Bellshill Hospitals National Health Service Trust (Establishment) Order 1992 (S.I. 3308)

Monopolies and Mergers Commission (Membership of Groups for Newspaper Merger References) Order 1982 (S.I. 1889)

Monopolies and Mergers Commission (Performance of Functions) Order 1989 (S.I. 122)

Monopoly References (Alteration of Exclusions) Order 1994 (S.I. 1922)

Montrose (Pilotage) Harbour Revision Order 1991 (S.I. 1106)

Montrose Harbour Revision Order 1974 (S.I. 348)

Montrose Harbour Revision Order 1991 (S.I. 1745)

Moorland (Livestock Extensification) (Wales) Regulations 1995 (S.I. 1159)

Moorland (Livestock Extensification) Regulations 1995 (S.I. 904)

Moray and Nairn Educational Trust Scheme 1935

Moray Health Services National Health Service Trust (Appointment of Trustees) Order 1993 (S.I. 1126)

Moray Health Services National Health Service Trust (Establishment) Order 1992 (S.I. 3309)

Morgan Trust Scheme 1963 (S.I. 1321)

Morriston Hospital National Health Service Trust (Establishment) Order 1994 (S.I. 317)

Motor Cars (Driving Instruction) Regulations 1989 (S.I. 2057)

Motor Cars (Silence Zones) (Revocation) Regulations (Northern Ireland) 1997 (S.R. 375)

Motor Cycle (EC Type Approval) (Amendment) Regulations 1997 (S.I. 2282)

Motor Cycle (EC Type Approval) Regulations 1995 (S.I. 1513)

Motor Cycles (Eye Protectors) (Amendment) Regulations 1987 (S.I. 675)

Motor Cycles (Eye Protectors) (Amendment) Regulations 1988 (S.I. 1031)

Motor Cycles (Eye Protectors) Regulations 1985 (S.I. 1593)

Motor Cycles (Protective Helmets) (Amendment) Regulations 1981 (S.I. 374)

Motor Cycles (Protective Helmets) (Amendment) Regulations 1986 (S.I. 472)

Motor Cycles (Protective Helmets) Regulations 1980 (S.I. 1279)

Motor Fuel (Composition and Content) Regulations 1994 (S.I. 2295)

Motor Vehicle Tyres (Safety) Regulations 1994 (S.I. 3117)

Motor Vehicles (Approval) Regulations 1996 (S.I. 3013)

Motor Vehicles (Authorisation of Special Types) (No.2) Order 1951 (S.I. 1963)

Motor Vehicles (Authorisation of Special Types) General Order 1979 (S.I. 1198)

Motor Vehicles (Competitions and Trials) (Scotland) Regulations 1976 (S.I. 2019)

Motor Vehicles (Compulsory Insurance) Regulations 1992 (S.I. 3036)

Motor Vehicles (Construction and Use) (Amendment No.2) Regulations (Northern Ireland) 1996 (S.R. 462)

Motor Vehicles (Construction and Use) (Amendment No.2) Regulations (Northern Ireland) 1997 (S.R. 371)

Motor Vehicles (Construction and Use) (Amendment No.2) Regulations (Northern Ireland) 1998 (S.R. 225)

Motor Vehicles (Construction and Use) (Amendment No.2) Regulations (Northern Ireland) 1999 (S.R. 103)

Motor Vehicles (Construction and Use) (Amendment No.3) Regulations (Northern Ireland) 1997 (S.R. 518)

Motor Vehicles (Construction and Use) (Amendment No.3) Regulations (Northern Ireland) 1999 (S.R. 104)

Motor Vehicles (Construction and Use) (Amendment No.4) Regulations (Northern Ireland) 1999 (S.R. 235)

Safety of Sports Grounds (Designation) (Scotland) Order 1976 (S.I. 1285)

Safety of Sports Grounds (Designation) (Scotland) Order 1977 (S.I. 1345)

Safety of Sports Grounds (Designation) (Scotland) Order 1978 (S.I. 1099)

Safety of Sports Grounds (Designation) (Scotland) Order 1979 (S.I. 1026)

Safety of Sports Grounds (Designation) (Scotland) Order 1980 (S.I. 1034)

Safety of Sports Grounds (Designation) (Scotland) Order 1984 (S.I. 1014)

Safety of Sports Grounds (Designation) (Scotland) Order 1986 (S.I. 1243)

Safety of Sports Grounds (Designation) (Scotland) Order 1989 (S.I. 2434)

Safety of Sports Grounds (Designation) (Scotland) Variation Order 1982 (S.I. 60)

Safety of Sports Grounds (Designation) Order 1976 (S.I. 1264)

Safety of Sports Grounds (Designation) Order 1978 (S.I. 1091)

Safety of Sports Grounds (Designation) Order 1986 (S.I. 1296)

Safety Representatives and Safety Committees Regulations 1977 (S.I. 500)

Safety Signs Regulations 1980 (S.I. 1471)

Salaries (Assembly Ombudsman and Commissioner for Complaints) Order (Northern Ireland) 1996 (S.R. 522)

Salaries (Assembly Ombudsman and Commissioner for Complaints) Order (Northern Ireland) 1997 (S.R. 224)

Salaries (Assembly Ombudsman and Commissioner for Complaints) Order (Northern Ireland) 1998 (S.R. 181)

Salaries (Comptroller and Auditor General) Order (Northern Ireland) 1998 (S.R. 272)

Salaries (Comptroller and Auditor-General and Others) (Northern Ireland) Order 1973 (S.I. 1086)

Sale of Dogs (Identification Tag) (Scotland) Regulations 1999 (S.S.I. 177)

Sale of Dogs (Identification Tag) Regulations 1999 (S.I. 3191)

Salford & Trafford Education Action Zone Order 1998 (S.I. 1962)

Salford Royal Hospitals National Health Service Trust (Establishment) Order 1994 (S.I. 164)

Salmon (Definition of Methods of Net Fishing and Construction of Nets) (Scotland) Regulations 1992 (S.I. 1974)

Salmon (Fish Passes and Screens) (Scotland) Regulations 1994 (S.I. 2524)

Sandwell Healthcare National Health Service Trust (Establishment) Order 1994 (S.I. 172)

Satellite Television Service Regulations 1997 (S.I. 1682)

Savings Banks (Ordinary Deposits) (Limits) Order 1969 (S.I. 939)

Savings Certificates (Children's Bonus Bonds) Regulations 1991 (S.I. 1407)

Savings Certificates (Yearly Plan) Regulations 1984 (S.I. 779)

Savings Certificates Regulations 1991 (S.I. 1031)

Savings Contracts Regulations 1969 (S.I. 1342)

Scheme for Construction Contracts (England and Wales) Regulations 1998 (S.I. 649)

Scheme for Construction Contracts (Scotland) Regulations 1998 (S.I. 687)

Scheme for the Administration of the Legacy of Robert Nicol 1984

Scheme for the Administration of the Strathclyde Schools Orchestra Trust 1979

Scholarships and Other Benefits Regulations 1977 (S.I. 1443)

School Standards and Framework Act 1998 (Admissions and Standard Numbers) (Modification) Regulations 1999 (S.I. 1064)

School Standards and Framework Act 1998 (Admissions) (Modifications No.2) Regulations 1998 (S.I. 3130)

School Standards and Framework Act 1998 (Admissions) (Modifications) Regulations 1998 (S.I. 2230)

School Standards and Framework Act 1998 (Allowances for Governors and Individual Pupil Information) (Modification) Regulations 1998 (S.I. 2916)

School Standards and Framework Act 1998 (Amendment of Commencement Orders) (England) Order 1999 (S.I. 2484)

School Standards and Framework Act 1998 (Appointed Day) (England) Order 1999 (S.I. 2221)

School Standards and Framework Act 1998 (Appointed Day) (Wales) Order 1999 (S.I. 1498)

School Standards and Framework Act 1998 (Appointed Day) Order 1998 (S.I. 2083)

School Standards and Framework Act 1998 (Appointed Day) Order 1999 (S.I. 531)

School Standards and Framework Act 1998 (Commencement No.1) Order 1998 (S.I. 2048)

School Standards and Framework Act 1998 (Commencement No.2 and Supplemental, Saving and Transitional Provisions) (Amendment) Order 1998 (S.I. 2459)

School Standards and Framework Act 1998 (Commencement No.2 and Supplemental, Saving and Transitional Provisions) Order 1998 (S.I. 2212)

School Standards and Framework Act 1998 (Commencement No.3 and Saving and Transitional Provisions) Order 1998 (S.I. 2791)

School Standards and Framework Act 1998 (Commencement No.4 and Transitional Provisions) Order 1998 (S.I. 3198)

School Standards and Framework Act 1998 (Commencement No.5 and Saving and Transitional Provisions) Order 1999 (S.I. 120)

School Standards and Framework Act 1998 (Commencement No.6 and Saving and Transitional Provisions) Order 1999 (S.I. 1016)

School Standards and Framework Act 1998 (Commencement No.7 and Saving and Transitional Provisions) Order 1999 (S.I. 2323)

Town and Country Planning (Appeals) (Written Representations Procedure) Regulations 1987 (S.I. 701)

Town and Country Planning (Assessment of Environmental Effects) (Amendment) Regulations 1990 (S.I. 367)

Town and Country Planning (Assessment of Environmental Effects) (Amendment) Regulations 1992 (S.I. 1494)

Town and Country Planning (Assessment of Environmental Effects) (Amendment) Regulations 1994 (S.I. 677)

Town and Country Planning (Assessment of Environmental Effects) Regulations 1988 (S.I. 1199)

Town and Country Planning (Atomic Energy Establishments Special Development) Order 1954 (S.I. 982)

Town and Country Planning (Atomic Energy Establishments Special Development) Order 1957 (S.I. 806)

Town and Country Planning (Atomic Energy Establishments Special Development) Order 1961 (S.I. 1295)

Town and Country Planning (Black Country Urban Development Area) Special Development Order 1987 (S.I. 1343)

Town and Country Planning (Cardiff Bay Urban Development) Special Development Order 1989 (S.I. 1180)

Town and Country Planning (Central Manchester Urban Development Area) Special Development Order 1989 (S.I. 2203)

Town and Country Planning (Churches, Places of Religious Worship and Burial Grounds) Regulations 1950 (S.I. 792)

Town and Country Planning (Compensation for Restrictions on Mineral Working and Mineral Waste Depositing) (Scotland) Regulations 1998 (S.I. 2914)

Town and Country Planning (Compensation for Restrictions on Mineral Working) (Amendment) Regulations 1990 (S.I. 803)

Town and Country Planning (Compensation for Restrictions on Mineral Working) Regulations 1985 (S.I. 689)

Town and Country Planning (Compensation for Restrictions on Mineral Workings) (Scotland) Regulations 1987 (S.I. 433)

Town and Country Planning (Control of Advertisements) (Scotland) Regulations 1984 (S.I. 467)

Town and Country Planning (Control of Advertisements) Regulations 1989 (S.I. 670)

Town and Country Planning (Control of Advertisements) Regulations 1992 (S.I. 666)

Town and Country Planning (Determination of Appeals by Appointed Persons) (Amendment) Regulations 1989 (S.I. 1087)

Town and Country Planning (Determination of Appeals by Appointed Persons) (Prescribed Classes) (Amendment) Regulations 1986 (S.I. 623)

Town and Country Planning (Determination of Appeals by Appointed Persons) (Prescribed Classes) (Amendment) Regulations 1995 (S.I. 2259)

Town and Country Planning (Determination of Appeals by Appointed Persons) (Prescribed Classes) (Scotland) Regulations 1987 (S.I. 1531)

Town and Country Planning (Determination of Appeals by Appointed Persons) (Prescribed Classes) Regulations 1981 (S.I. 804)

Town and Country Planning (Development by Planning Authorities) (Scotland) Regulations 1981 (S.I. 829)

Town and Country Planning (Development Plan) (Amendment) Regulations 1997 (S.I. 531)

Town and Country Planning (Development Plan) Regulations 1991 (S.I. 2794)

Town and Country Planning (Development Plans) (Scotland) Regulations 1966 (S.I. 1385)

Town and Country Planning (Environmental Assessment and Permitted Development) Regulations 1995 (S.I. 417)

Town and Country Planning (Environmental Assessment and Unauthorised Development) Regulations 1995 (S.I. 2258)

Town and Country Planning (Environmental Impact Assessment) (England and Wales) Regulations 1999 (S.I. 293)

Town and Country Planning (Fees for Applications and Deemed Applications) (Amendment) Regulations 1993 (S.I. 3170)

Town and Country Planning (Fees for Applications and Deemed Applications) (Scotland) Amendment (No.2) Regulations 1992 (S.I. 3137)

Town and Country Planning (Fees for Applications and Deemed Applications) (Scotland) Amendment Regulations 1990 (S.I. 2474)

Town and Country Planning (Fees for Applications and Deemed Applications) (Scotland) Amendment Regulations 1991 (S.I. 2765)

Town and Country Planning (Fees for Applications and Deemed Applications) (Scotland) Amendment Regulations 1992 (S.I. 1951)

Town and Country Planning (Fees for Applications and Deemed Applications) (Scotland) Amendment Regulations 1993 (S.I. 3211)

Town and Country Planning (Fees for Applications and Deemed Applications) (Scotland) Amendment Regulations 1994 (S.I. 3269)

Town and Country Planning (Fees for Applications and Deemed Applications) (Scotland) Regulations 1990 (S.I. 563)

Town and Country Planning (Fees for Applications and Deemed Applications) Regulations 1989 (S.I. 193)

Town and Country Planning (General Development Procedure) (Scotland) Order 1992 (S.I. 224)

Town and Country Planning (General Development Procedure) Order 1995 (S.I. 419)

Town and Country Planning (General Development) (Scotland) Order 1981 (S.I. 830)

STATUTORY INSTRUMENT CITATOR 1996–1999

This Current Law Statutory Instrument Citator covers the period 1996–1999. It comprises in a single table:

(i) Statutory Instruments affected or revoked by Statutory Instruments issued or Statutes passed in 1996–1999;
(ii) Statutory Instruments judicially considered in 1996–1999.
(iii) Statutory Instruments under the provisions of which a statutory instrument has been issued in 1996–1999;
(iv) Statutory Instruments which have been consolidated by a Statutory Instrument or Statute passed in 1996–1999.

The table also includes some Statutory Rules which have been affected by UK Statutory Instruments.

C. Indicates that the provision has been consolidated by the Act or instrument noted.

Statutory Instruments Issued by the Scottish Parliament

NO.

NO.

1999

3. **Food Protection (Emergency Prohibitions) (Amnesic Shellfish Poisoning) (No.2) Order 1999**
revoked: SSI 1999/7 Art.7
Art.3, revoked: SSI 1999/7 Art.7

13. **Food Protection (Emergency Prohibitions) (Amnesic Shellfish Poisoning) (No.2) (Scotland) Order 1999**
revoked: SSI 1999/26 Art.7, Sch.2
Art.3, revoked: SSI 1999/26 Art.7, Sch.2

14. **Food (Animals and Animal Products from Belgium) (Emergency Control) (Scotland) Order 1999**
revoked: SSI 1999/32 Art.6
Art.2, referred to: SSI 1999/15 Art.2
Art.2, revoked: SSI 1999/32 Art.6
Art.5, revoked: SSI 1999/32 Art.6
Art.6, revoked: SSI 1999/32 Art.6

15. **Animal Feedingstuffs from Belgium (Control) (Scotland) Regulations 1999**
revoked: SSI 1999/33 Reg.6
Reg.2, revoked: SSI 1999/33 Reg.6
Reg.4, revoked: SSI 1999/33 Reg.6
Reg.5, revoked: SSI 1999/33 Reg.6
Reg.6, revoked: SSI 1999/33 Reg.6

18. **Food Protection (Emergency Prohibitions) (Amnesic Shellfish Poisoning) (No.3) (Scotland) Order 1999**
revoked: SSI 1999/26 Art.7, Sch.2
Art.3, revoked: SSI 1999/26 Art.7, Sch.2

23. **Food Protection (Emergency Prohibitions) (Amnesic Shellfish Poisoning) (No.4) (Scotland) Order 1999**
revoked: SSI 1999/26 Art.7, Sch.2
Art.3, revoked: SSI 1999/26 Art.7, Sch.2

25. **Food Protection (Emergency Prohibitions) (Amnesic Shellfish Poisoning) (East Coast) (Scotland) Order 1999**
revoked: SSI 1999/41 Art.2

26. **Food Protection (Emergency Prohibitions) (Amnesic Shellfish Poisoning) (West Coast) (Scotland) Order 1999**
revoked (in part): SSI 1999/114 Art.3, SSI 1999/169 Art.3
Art.3, revoked (in part): SSI 1999/114 Art.3, SSI 1999/169 Art.3

1999—cont.

26. **Food Protection (Emergency Prohibitions) (Amnesic Shellfish Poisoning) (West Coast) (Scotland) Order 1999—cont.**
Art.7, revoked (in part): SSI 1999/114 Art.3, SSI 1999/141 Art.3, SSI 1999/169 Art.3
Sch. para.1, referred to: SSI 1999/114 Art.3
Sch. para.1, revoked (in part): SSI 1999/114 Art.3, SSI 1999/141 Art.3, SSI 1999/169 Art.3
Sch.2, revoked (in part): SSI 1999/114 Art.3, SSI 1999/141 Art.3, SSI 1999/169 Art.3

27. **Food Protection (Emergency Prohibitions) (Amnesic Shellfish Poisoning) (Orkney) (Scotland) Order 1999**
revoked (in part): SSI 1999/49 Art.2
Art.3, revoked (in part): SSI 1999/49 Art.2

32. **Food (Animals and Animal Products from Belgium) (Emergency Control) (No.2) (Scotland) Order 1999**
referred to: SSI 1999/33 Reg.2
Art.2, referred to: SSI 1999/33 Reg.2

42. **Food Protection (Emergency Prohibitions) (Amnesic Shellfish Poisoning) (Orkney) (No.2) (Scotland) Order 1999**
revoked (in part): SSI 1999/160 Art.2
Art.3, revoked (in part): SSI 1999/160 Art.2

50. **Food Protection (Emergency Prohibitions) (Amnesic Shellfish Poisoning) (West Coast) (No.2) (Scotland) Order 1999**
revoked: SSI 1999/167 Art.2
Art.3, revoked: SSI 1999/167 Art.2

71. **Food Protection (Emergency Prohibitions) (Amnesic Shellfish Poisoning) (West Coast) (No.3) (Scotland) Order 1999**
revoked: SSI 1999/168 Art.2
Art.3, revoked: SSI 1999/168 Art.2

72. **Food Protection (Emergency Prohibitions) (Amnesic Shellfish Poisoning) (East Coast) (No.2) (Scotland) Order 1999**
revoked: SSI 1999/110 Art.7
Art.3, revoked: SSI 1999/110 Art.7

73. **Food Protection (Emergency Prohibitions) (Amnesic Shellfish Poisoning) (Orkney) (No.3) (Scotland) Order 1999**
revoked (in part): SSI 1999/144 Art.2, SSI 1999/159 Art.2 (rem.)
Art.3, revoked (in part): SSI 1999/144 Art.2, SSI 1999/159 Art.2 (rem.)

NO.

1999—cont.

100. Ayshire and Arran Acute Hospitals National Health Service Trust (Establishment) Amendment Order 1999
revoked: SSI 1999/197 Art.3

101. Forth Valley Primary Care National Health Service Trust (Establishment) (Amendment) Order 1999
revoked: SSI 1999/164 Art.3

102. Ayshire and Arran Primary Care National Health Service Trust (Establishment) Order 1999
revoked: SSI 1999/165 Art.3

NO.

1999—cont.

103. Fife Acute Hospitals National Health Service Trust (Establishment) Amendment Order 1999
revoked: SSI 1999/198 Art.3

110. Food Protection (Emergency Prohibitions) (Amnesic Shellfish Poisoning) (East Coast) (No.3) (Scotland) Order 1999
revoked (in part): SSI 1999/145 Art.2
Art.3, revoked (in part): SSI 1999/145 Art.2
Art.7, revoked (in part): SSI 1999/145 Art.2

143. Food Protection (Emergency Prohibitions) (Amnesic Shellfish Poisoning) (West Coast) (No.4) (Scotland) Order 1999
revoked: SSI 1999/170 Art.2
Art.3, revoked: SSI 1999/170 Art.2

Statutory Instruments Issued by the UK Parliament

NO.

1872

Greshernish Fishery Order 1872
referred to: 1998 c.43 s.1, Sch.1 Part VII

1873

Order in Council dated September 30, 1873 Directing that the Extradition Acts shall apply in the case of the Kingdoms of Sweden and Norway 1873
revoked (in part): SI 1996/2875 Art.3, Sch.3

1874

Order in Council dated March 17, 1874 Directing that the Extradition Acts shall apply in the case of Austria and Hungary 1874
revoked (in part): SI 1996/2875 Art.3, Sch.3

1877

Evesham Order 1877
referred to: 1998 c.43 s.1, Sch.1 Part V

1878

Droitwich Gas Order 1878
referred to: 1998 c.43 s.1, Sch.1 Part V

1881

Order in Council dated May 18, 1881 Directing that the Extradition Acts shall apply in the case of Switzerland 1881
revoked (in part): SI 1996/2875 Art.3, Sch.3
Worcester Tramways Order 1881
referred to: 1998 c.43 s.1, Sch.1 Part V
Art.1, referred to: 1998 c.43 s.1, Sch.1 Part V
Art.3, referred to: 1998 c.43 s.1, Sch.1 Part V
Art.4, referred to: 1998 c.43 s.1, Sch.1 Part V
Art.9, referred to: 1998 c.43 s.1, Sch.1 Part V

1885

Worcester Tramways Order 1881 Amendment Order 1885
referred to: 1998 c.43 s.1, Sch.1 Part V

NO.

1886

Droitwich Gas Order 1886
referred to: 1998 c.43 s.1, Sch.1 Part V

1887

Worcester Tramways Order 1887
referred to: 1998 c.43 s.1, Sch.1 Part V

1890

Kent and Essex Sea Fisheries District Order 1890
Art.1, substituted: SI 1998/1212 Art.2
Art.2, substituted: SI 1998/1212 Art.2
Sch., substituted: SI 1998/1212 Art.2, Sch.
Malvern Electric Lighting Order 1890
referred to: 1998 c.43 s.1, Sch.1 Part V
Order in Council applying the Sea Fisheries Act 1883 to the International Convention of February 1, 1889 1890
revoked: 1998 c.43 s.1, Sch.1 Part X
Worcester Electric Lighting Order 1890
referred to: 1998 c.43 s.1, Sch.1 Part V
Worcester Tramways (Abandonment and Release of Deposit) Order 1890
referred to: 1998 c.43 s.1, Sch.1 Part V

1891

Kidderminster Electric Lighting Order 1891
referred to: 1998 c.43 s.1, Sch.1 Part V

1892

Canna Pier Order 1892
repealed: SSI 1999/199 Art.32

NO.

1892—cont.

Devon Sea Fisheries District Order 1892
Art.1, substituted: SI 1998/1211 Art.2
Art.2, substituted: SI 1998/1211 Art.2
Sch., substituted: SI 1998/1211 Art.2, Sch.
Ross Water Order 1892
Art.15, referred to: 1998 c.43 s.1, Sch.1 Part V
Art.16, referred to: 1998 c.43 s.1, Sch.1 Part V

1893

Sussex Sea Fisheries District Order 1893
Art.1, amended: SI 1996/847 Art.2
Sch., substituted: SI 1998/1210 Art.2, Sch.

1894

119. **Order in Council directing that the Extradition Act, shall apply in the case of Romania and of the Treaty of March 21st, 1893 1894**
revoked: SI 1998/259 Art.2

1895

County of Worcester (Dowles and Upper Arley) Order 1895
referred to: 1998 c.43 s.1, Sch.1 Part V
Upton upon Severn (Hanley Castle and Welland) Order 1895
referred to: 1998 c.43 s.1, Sch.1 Part V

1896

Evesham Joint Hospital Order 1896
referred to: 1998 c.43 s.1, Sch.1 Part V

1897

Redditch Electric Lighting Order 1897
referred to: 1998 c.43 s.1, Sch.1 Part V

1898

Hereford Electric Lighting Order 1898
referred to: 1998 c.43 s.1, Sch.1 Part V
Tewkesbury Rural Order 1898
referred to: 1998 c.43 s.1, Sch.1 Part V

1901

1027. **Worcester and District Light Railways Order 1901**
revoked (in part): 1998 c.43 s.1, Sch.1 Part V
Art.1, referred to: 1998 c.43 s.1, Sch.1 Part V
Art.2, referred to: 1998 c.43 s.1, Sch.1 Part V
Art.31, referred to: 1998 c.43 s.1, Sch.1 Part V

1902

208. **Order in Council dated 6th March 1902 directing that the Extradition Act shall apply in the case of Belgium 1902**
revoked: SI 1998/259 Art.2
616. **Prevention of Accidents Rules 1902**
revoked (in part): SI 1997/553 Reg.12, Sch Part II
737. **Order in Council Directing that the Extradition Acts shall apply in the case of Austria and Hungary 1902**
revoked (in part): SI 1996/2875 Art.3, Sch.3

NO.

1902—cont.

1023. **Worcester (Extension) Light Railways Order 1902**
revoked (in part): 1998 c.43 s.1, Sch.1 Part V
Art.1, referred to: 1998 c.43 s.1, Sch.1 Part V
Art.2, referred to: 1998 c.43 s.1, Sch.1 Part V
Art.9, referred to: 1998 c.43 s.1, Sch.1 Part V
Art.12, referred to: 1998 c.43 s.1, Sch.1 Part V

1903

Yardley Rural Order 1903
referred to: 1998 c.43 s.1, Sch.1 Part V
214. **Order in Council applying the Sea Fisheries Act 1883 to the United Kingdom - Denmark Convention of 24 June 1901 1903**
revoked: 1998 c.43 s.1, Sch.1 Part X

1905

616. **Order in Council Directing that the Extradition Acts shall apply in the case of Switzerland 1905**
revoked (in part): SI 1996/2875 Art.3, Sch.3

1906

cxiii. **Newlyn Pier and Harbour Order 1906**
Art.9, amended: SI 1996/197 Art.9
Art.10, revoked (in part): SI 1996/197 Art.11
Art.11, revoked: SI 1996/197 Art.11
Art.13, revoked: SI 1996/197 Art.11
Art.14, amended: SI 1996/197 Art.7, Art.10
Art.15, amended: SI 1996/197 Art.10
Art.17, amended: SI 1996/197 Art.7, Art.8
177. **Flax and Tow Spinning and Weaving Regulations 1906**
amended: SR 1999/150 Reg.2, Sch.
revoked: SI 1996/3022 Reg.2, Sch Part II
679. **Locomotives and Wagons (Used in Lines and Sidings) Regulations 1906**
Reg.1, revoked: SI 1997/553 Reg.12, Sch Part II
Reg.2, revoked: SI 1997/553 Reg.12, Sch Part II
Reg.5, revoked: SI 1997/553 Reg.12, Sch Part II
Reg.6, revoked: SI 1997/553 Reg.12, Sch Part II
Reg.7, revoked: SI 1997/553 Reg.12, Sch Part II
Reg.9, revoked: SI 1997/553 Reg.12, Sch Part II
Reg.10, revoked: SI 1997/553 Reg.12, Sch Part II
Reg.11, revoked: SI 1997/553 Reg.12, Sch Part II
Reg.12, revoked: SI 1997/553 Reg.12, Sch Part II
Reg.13, revoked: SI 1997/553 Reg.12, Sch Part II
Reg.14, revoked: SI 1997/553 Reg.12, Sch Part II
Reg.15, revoked: SI 1997/553 Reg.12, Sch Part II
Reg.16, revoked: SI 1997/553 Reg.12, Sch Part II
Reg.17, revoked: SI 1997/553 Reg.12, Sch Part II
Reg.18, revoked: SI 1997/553 Reg.12, Sch Part II
Reg.19, revoked: SI 1997/553 Reg.12, Sch Part II

NO.

1906—cont.

679. Locomotives and Wagons (Used in Lines and Sidings) Regulations 1906—*cont.*
Reg.20, revoked (in part): SI 1997/135 Reg.3, Sch. Part II
Reg.21, revoked: SI 1997/135 Reg.3, Sch. Part II

1907

Evesham Order 1907
referred to: 1998 c.43 s.1, Sch.1 Part V
17. Manufacture of Paints and Colours Regulations 1907
revoked: SI 1998/543 Reg.14, Sch.3
544. Order in Council of 1907 directing that the Extradition Acts shall apply in the case of Belgium, and of the Supplementing Convention of March 5, 1907
revoked: SI 1998/259 Art.2
545. Order in Council Directing that the Extradition Acts shall apply in the case of the Kingdom of Norway 1907
revoked (in part): SI 1996/2875 Art.3, Sch.3
616. Yarn (Dyed by Lead Compounds) Heading Regulations 1907
revoked: SI 1998/543 Reg.14, Sch.3
660. Hemp Spinning and Weaving Regulations 1907
amended: SR 1999/150 Reg.2, Sch.
revoked: SI 1996/3022 Reg.2, Sch Part II
696. Prevention of Accidents Rules 1907
revoked (in part): SI 1997/553 Reg.12, Sch Part II

1908

1258. Vitreous Enamelling Regulations 1908
revoked: SI 1998/543 Reg.14, Sch.3

1909

720. Tinning of Metal Hollow-ware, Iron Drums, and Harness Furniture Regulations 1909
revoked: SI 1998/543 Reg.14, Sch.3

1910

569. Post Office Savings Bank Regulations 1910
amended: SI 1998/1446 Art.17
applied: SI 1998/1446 Art.17
Reg.70, applied: SI 1998/1446 Art.18

1911

Hereford Order 1911
referred to: 1998 c.43 s.1, Sch.1 Part V
752. Lead Smelting and Manufacture Regulations 1911
revoked: SI 1998/543 Reg.14, Sch.3
793. Order in Council dated 8th August 1911 directing that the Extradition Acts shall apply in the case of Belgium in accordance with a Treaty of October 1901, and Supplementary Conventions of March 5th 1907 and March 3rd 1911
revoked: SI 1998/259 Art.2
1058. Prevention of Accidents Rules 1911
revoked (in part): SI 1997/553 Reg.12, Sch Part II

NO.

1912

Kington Order 1912
referred to: 1998 c.43 s.1, Sch.1 Part V
348. Public Trustee Rules 1912
r.27, applied: SI 1999/855 Art.27

1913

2. Manufacture and Decoration of Pottery Regulations 1913
Reg.2, applied: SI 1996/1919 (NI.16) Art.96
638. Codifying Act of Sederunt 1913
Book.L Ch.X, revoked: SI 1999/929 r.1.3, Sch.2
Book.L Ch.XI, revoked: SI 1999/929 r.1.3, Sch.2

1914

Injuries in War (Shore Employments) Compensation Scheme 1914
amended: SI 1996/573 para.2
para.3, amended: SI 1997/477 para.2, SI 1998/581 para.2, SI 1999/857 para.2

1915

769. Standing Orders and Regulations for the Constitution and Government of the Naval Medical Compassionate Fund Order in Council 1915
Art.8, amended: SI 1996/3213 Art.2
Art.9, amended: SI 1996/3213 Art.2
Art.12, substituted: SI 1996/3213 Art.2
Sch., revoked: SI 1996/3213 Art.2

1919

809. Compressed Acetylene Porous Substance Order 1919
revoked: SI 1996/2092 Reg.21, Sch.7

1922

80. Government of Ireland (Adaptation of the Taxing Acts) Order 1922
Part IV, referred to: 1998 c.36 s.150
329. Indiarubber Regulations 1922
revoked: SI 1998/543 Reg.14, Sch.3
432. Welsh Highland Railway (Light Railway) Order 1922
applied: SI 1997/2534 Art.4

1923

Hereford Order 1923
referred to: 1998 c.43 s.1, Sch.1 Part V
Stourbridge and District Water Board Order 1923
Art.8, referred to: 1998 c.43 s.1, Sch.1 Part V
Sch., referred to: 1998 c.43 s.1, Sch.1 Part V
275. Welsh Highland Railway (Light Railway) Order 1923
applied: SI 1997/2534 Art.4

1924

81. Belgium (Extradition) Order in Council 1924
revoked: SI 1998/259 Art.2

1925

28. Electric Accumulator Regulations 1925
revoked: SI 1998/543 Reg.14, Sch.3

NO.

1925—cont.

1029. Order in Council dated 12th October 1925 directing that the Extradition Acts shall apply in the case of the Republic of Latvia 1925
revoked: SI 1997/2596 Art.2

1093. Land Registration Rules 1925
Part II, amended: SI 1997/3037 r.2, Sch.1 para.10
Part III, amended: SI 1996/2975 Sch para.6
Part IV, amended: SI 1997/3037 r.2, Sch.1 para.43
r.1, amended: SI 1996/2975 Sch para.1, SI 1997/3037 r.2, Sch.1 para.1
r.3, amended: SI 1999/2097 r.2, Sch.1 para.1
r.6, amended: SI 1997/3037 r.2, Sch.1 para.2
r.8, substituted: SI 1999/2097 r.2, Sch.1 para.2
r.11, revoked: SI 1997/3037 r.3
r.16, substituted: SI 1996/2975 Sch para.2
r.19, substituted: SI 1997/3037 r.2, Sch.1 para.3
r.20, amended: SI 1997/3037 r.2, Sch.1 para.4
r.24, amended: SI 1997/3037 r.2, Sch.1 para.5
r.26, applied: SI 1997/713 Reg.4, Sch Part II
r.28, substituted: SI 1997/3037 r.2, Sch.1 para.6
r.29, substituted: SI 1997/3037 r.2, Sch.1 para.6
r.31, amended: SI 1997/3037 r.2, Sch.1 para.7
r.33, revoked: SI 1997/3037 r.3
r.35, applied: SI 1997/713 Reg.4, Sch Part II
r.36, revoked: SI 1997/3037 r.3
r.37, amended: SI 1997/3037 r.2, Sch.1 para.8
r.39, revoked: SI 1996/2975 r.3
r.42, amended: SI 1997/3037 r.2, Sch.1 para.9
r.50, amended: SI 1997/3037 r.2, Sch.1 para.11
r.51, amended: SI 1999/2097 r.2, Sch.1 para.3
r.52, amended: SI 1997/3037 r.2, Sch.1 para.12, SI 1999/2097 r.2, Sch.1 para.3
r.53, amended: SI 1999/2097 r.2, Sch.1 para.3
r.54, amended: SI 1999/2097 r.2, Sch.1 para.3
r.56, substituted: SI 1999/128 r.2, Sch.1 para.1
r.59A, added: SI 1996/2975 Sch para.3
r.60, amended: SI 1997/3037 r.2, Sch.1 para.13
r.60, substituted: SI 1996/2975 Sch para.4
r.61, amended: SI 1997/3037 r.2, Sch.1 para.14
r.61, substituted: SI 1996/2975 Sch para.4
r.62, substituted: SI 1996/2975 Sch para.4, SI 1997/3037 r.2, Sch.1 para.15
r.63, revoked: SI 1997/3037 r.3
r.64, amended: SI 1999/2097 r.2, Sch.1 para.4
r.64, substituted: SI 1997/3037 r.2, Sch.1 para.16
r.66, revoked: SI 1997/3037 r.3
r.68, amended: SI 1999/128 r.2, Sch.1 para.2, SI 1999/2097 r.2, Sch.1 para.5
r.71, revoked: SI 1997/3037 r.3
r.73, substituted: SI 1997/3037 r.2, Sch.1 para.17
r.74, substituted: SI 1997/3037 r.2, Sch.1 para.18
r.74A, added: SI 1997/3037 r.2, Sch.1 para.18
r.75, substituted: SI 1997/3037 r.2, Sch.1 para.18
r.79, amended: SI 1999/2097 r.2, Sch.1 para.6
r.80, revoked: SI 1997/3037 r.3
r.81, amended: SI 1997/3037 r.2, Sch.1 para.19
r.82, substituted: SI 1996/2975 Sch para.5
r.82A, added: SI 1996/2975 Sch para.5
r.82B, added: SI 1996/2975 Sch para.5
r.83, amended: SI 1997/3037 r.2, Sch.1 para.20
r.85A, added: SI 1997/3037 r.2, Sch.1 para.21
r.85A, amended: SI 1999/128 r.2, Sch.1 para.3
r.86, amended: SI 1997/3037 r.2, Sch.1 para.22

NO.

1925—cont.

1093. Land Registration Rules 1925—*cont.*
r.98, substituted: SI 1997/3037 r.2, Sch.1 para.23, SI 1999/128 r.2, Sch.1 para.4
r.99, substituted: SI 1999/128 r.2, Sch.1 para.5
r.101, substituted: SI 1999/128 r.2, Sch.1 para.6
r.106A, added: SI 1996/2975 Sch para.7
r.107, substituted: SI 1999/128 r.2, Sch.1 para.7
r.108, amended: SI 1997/3037 r.2, Sch.1 para.24
r.109, revoked (in part): SI 1997/3037 r.2, Sch.1 para.25, SI 1999/128 r.2, Sch.1 para.8
r.111, amended: SI 1999/128 r.2, Sch.1 para.9
r.112, amended: SI 1999/128 r.2, Sch.1 para.10
r.113, amended: SI 1999/2097 r.2, Sch.1 para.7
r.114, revoked: SI 1999/128 r.3
r.114, substituted: SI 1997/3037 r.2, Sch.1 para.26
r.115, revoked: SI 1997/3037 r.3
r.116, amended: SI 1999/128 r.2, Sch.1 para.11
r.117, amended: SI 1997/3037 r.2, Sch.1 para.27
r.118, revoked: SI 1997/3037 r.3
r.119, revoked: SI 1997/3037 r.3
r.120, revoked: SI 1997/3037 r.3
r.121, revoked: SI 1996/2975 r.3
r.122, substituted: SI 1996/2975 Sch para.8
r.123, substituted: SI 1996/2975 Sch para.8
r.124, substituted: SI 1996/2975 Sch para.8
r.125, amended: SI 1997/3037 r.2, Sch.1 para.28
r.126, amended: SI 1997/3037 r.2, Sch.1 para.28, Sch.1 para.29
r.127, amended: SI 1997/3037 r.2, Sch.1 para.28
r.128, substituted: SI 1996/2975 Sch para.9
r.131, amended: SI 1996/2975 Sch para.10
r.131, applied: SI 1997/713 Reg.4, Sch Part II
r.134, amended: SI 1996/2975 Sch para.11
r.135, substituted: SI 1997/3037 r.2, Sch.1 para.30
r.136, amended: SI 1999/128 r.2, Sch.1 para.12
r.136, substituted: SI 1997/3037 r.2, Sch.1 para.30
r.137, amended: SI 1997/3037 r.2, Sch.1 para.31
r.139, amended: SI 1997/3037 r.2, Sch.1 para.32
r.142, revoked: SI 1997/3037 r.3
r.143, revoked: SI 1997/3037 r.3
r.144, amended: SI 1997/3037 r.2, Sch.1 para.33
r.144A, added: SI 1996/2975 Sch para.12
r.151, substituted: SI 1997/3037 r.2, Sch.1 para.34, SI 1999/128 r.2, Sch.1 para.13
r.153, substituted: SI 1997/3037 r.2, Sch.1 para.35, SI 1999/128 r.2, Sch.1 para.14
r.155, amended: SI 1997/3037 r.2, Sch.1 para.36
r.158, applied: SI 1997/713 Reg.4, Sch Part II
r.159, amended: SI 1997/3037 r.2, Sch.1 para.37
r.161, amended: SI 1997/3037 r.2, Sch.1 para.38
r.167, revoked: SI 1997/3037 r.3
r.169A, added: SI 1996/2975 Sch para.13
r.170, amended: SI 1996/2975 Sch para.14, SI 1997/3037 r.2, Sch.1 para.39, SI 1999/128 r.2, Sch.1 para.15
r.170, revoked (in part): SI 1997/3037 r.2, Sch.1 para.39
r.171, amended: SI 1996/2975 Sch para.15

1925—cont.

1925—cont.

1093. Land Registration Rules 1925—*cont.*

r.186, amended: SI 1999/128 r.2, Sch.1 para.16

r.194, revoked: SI 1997/3037 r.3

r.201, substituted: SI 1999/128 r.2, Sch.1 para.17

r.202, revoked: SI 1999/128 r.2, r.3, Sch.1 para.17

r.207, amended: SI 1997/3037 r.2, Sch.1 para.40

r.213, amended: SI 1997/3037 r.2, Sch.1 para.41

r.213, substituted: SI 1996/2975 Sch para.16

r.215, amended: SI 1999/128 r.2, Sch.1 para.18

r.215, revoked (in part): SI 1999/128 r.2, Sch.1 para.18

r.216, amended: SI 1999/2097 r.2, Sch.1 para.8

r.218, referred to: SI 1997/1964 r.5

r.218, revoked (in part): SI 1999/128 r.2, Sch.1 para.19

r.220, applied: SI 1997/713 Reg.4, Reg.6, Sch Part II

r.222, amended: SI 1999/128 r.2, Sch.1 para.20

r.229, revoked: SI 1997/3037 r.3

r.230, applied: SI 1997/713 Reg.4, Sch Part II

r.233, revoked: SI 1997/3037 r.3

r.234, substituted: SI 1997/3037 r.2, Sch.1 para.42

r.235, substituted: SI 1996/2975 Sch para.17

r.236, substituted: SI 1996/2975 Sch para.17

r.236A, added: SI 1996/2975 Sch para.17

r.236B, added: SI 1996/2975 Sch para.17

r.238, amended: SI 1997/3037 r.2, Sch.1 para.44

r.247, substituted: SI 1999/3462 r.2

r.259, amended: SI 1997/3037 r.2, Sch.1 para.45

r.259, substituted: SI 1996/2975 Sch para.18

r.259A, added: SI 1996/2975 Sch para.18

r.259B, added: SI 1996/2975 Sch para.18

r.259C, added: SI 1996/2975 Sch para.18

r.259D, added: SI 1996/2975 Sch para.18

r.266, substituted: SI 1999/128 r.2, Sch.1 para.21

r.266A, added: SI 1999/128 r.2, Sch.1 para.21

r.271, applied: SI 1997/178 Sch.3 Part I, SI 1997/1710 Sch.3 Part I, SI 1998/3199 Sch.3 Part I, SI 1999/2254 Sch.3 Part I

r.273, revoked: SI 1999/2097 r.3

r.274, revoked: SI 1999/2097 r.3

r.275, revoked: SI 1999/2097 r.3

r.276, amended: SI 1999/2097 r.2, Sch.1 para.9

r.277, applied: SI 1996/187 Art.14, SI 1997/178 Art.14, SI 1997/1710 Art.14, SI 1998/3199 Art.14, SI 1999/2254 Art.14

r.277, amended: SI 1999/2097 r.2, Sch.1 para.9

r.278, amended: SI 1999/2097 r.2, Sch.1 para.9

r.279, amended: SI 1999/2097 r.2, Sch.1 para.9

r.280, substituted: SI 1999/2097 r.2, Sch.1 para.10

r.281, amended: SI 1999/2097 r.2, Sch.1 para.11

r.282, revoked: SI 1999/2097 r.3

r.283, amended: SI 1997/3037 r.2, Sch.1 para.46

r.284, revoked (in part): SI 1999/2097 r.2, Sch.1 para.12

r.285, amended: SI 1999/2097 r.2, Sch.1 para.9

r.298, applied: SI 1997/713 Reg.4, Reg.6, Sch Part II

r.300, applied: SI 1997/713 Reg.4, Sch Part II

r.303, applied: SI 1997/713 Reg.4, Sch Part II

1093. Land Registration Rules 1925—*cont.*

r.308, substituted: SI 1997/3037 r.2, Sch.1 para.47

r.308A, added: SI 1997/3037 r.2, Sch.1 para.47

r.308A, amended: SI 1999/128 r.2, Sch.1 para.22, SI 1999/2097 r.2, Sch.1 para.13

r.308B, added: SI 1997/3037 r.2, Sch.1 para.47

r.316, applied: SI 1997/713 Reg.4, Sch Part II

r.320, applied: SI 1997/713 Reg.4, Sch Part II

r.321, applied: SI 1997/713 Reg.4, Sch Part II

Sch.1, added: SI 1997/3037 r.2, Sch.2

Sch.1 Form AP1, substituted: SI 1999/128 r.2, Sch.2

Sch.1 Form AS3, added: SI 1999/128 r.2, Sch.2

Sch.1 Form CN1, added: SI 1999/128 r.2, Sch.2

Sch.1 Form CT2, added: SI 1999/128 r.2, Sch.2

Sch.1 Form DL, substituted: SI 1999/128 r.2, Sch.2

Sch.1 Form DP1, added: SI 1999/128 r.2, Sch.2

Sch.1 Form DS3, added: SI 1999/128 r.2, Sch.2

Sch.1 Form TP1, added: SI 1999/128 r.2, Sch.2

Sch.1 Form TP2, added: SI 1999/128 r.2, Sch.2

Sch.1 Form TP3, added: SI 1999/128 r.2, Sch.2

Sch.1 Form TR5, added: SI 1999/128 r.2, Sch.2

Sch.1 Form WCT, added: SI 1999/128 r.2, Sch.2

Sch.2, amended: SI 1997/3037 r.2

Sch.2 Form 1, amended: SI 1997/3037 r.2

Sch.2 Form 1, revoked: SI 1997/3037 r.3

Sch.2 Form 2, amended: SI 1997/3037 r.2

Sch.2 Form 2, revoked: SI 1997/3037 r.3

Sch.2 Form 3, amended: SI 1997/3037 r.2

Sch.2 Form 3, revoked: SI 1997/3037 r.3

Sch.2 Form 4, amended: SI 1997/3037 r.2

Sch.2 Form 4, revoked: SI 1997/3037 r.3

Sch.2 Form 5, amended: SI 1997/3037 r.2

Sch.2 Form 5, revoked: SI 1997/3037 r.3

Sch.2 Form 7, amended: SI 1997/3037 r.2

Sch.2 Form 7, revoked: SI 1997/3037 r.3

Sch.2 Form 8, amended: SI 1997/3037 r.2

Sch.2 Form 8, revoked: SI 1997/3037 r.3

Sch.2 Form 9, amended: SI 1996/2975 Sch para.19, SI 1997/3037 r.2, SI 1999/2097 r.2, Sch.2 para.1

Sch.2 Form 10, amended: SI 1996/2975 Sch para.20, SI 1997/3037 r.2

Sch.2 Form 11A, added: SI 1996/2975 Sch para.21

Sch.2 Form 11A, amended: SI 1997/3037 r.2

Sch.2 Form 11B, added: SI 1996/2975 Sch para.21

Sch.2 Form 11B, amended: SI 1997/3037 r.2

Sch.2 Form 12, amended: SI 1996/2975 Sch para.22, SI 1997/3037 r.2

Sch.2 Form 12A, amended: SI 1997/3037 r.2

Sch.2 Form 12A, revoked: SI 1996/2975 r.3

Sch.2 Form 12B, amended: SI 1997/3037 r.2

Sch.2 Form 12B, revoked: SI 1996/2975 r.3

Sch.2 Form 12C, amended: SI 1996/2975 Sch para.23, SI 1997/3037 r.2

Sch.2 Form 12D, amended: SI 1997/3037 r.2

Sch.2 Form 12D, substituted: SI 1996/2975 Sch para.24

Sch.2 Form 13, amended: SI 1997/3037 r.2

Sch.2 Form 13, revoked: SI 1997/3037 r.3

Sch.2 Form 14, amended: SI 1996/2975 Sch para.25, SI 1997/3037 r.2, Sch.3 para.1

Sch.2 Form 15, amended: SI 1997/3037 r.2, Sch.3 para.2

Sch.2 Form 16, amended: SI 1997/3037 r.2, Sch.3 para.2

NO.

1925—cont.

1093. Land Registration Rules 1925—*cont.*
Sch.2 Form 16, revoked: SI 1999/128 r.3
Sch.2 Form 17, amended: SI 1997/3037 r.2
Sch.2 Form 17, revoked: SI 1997/3037 r.3
Sch.2 Form 19, amended: SI 1997/3037 r.2
Sch.2 Form 19, revoked: SI 1997/3037 r.3
Sch.2 Form 20, revoked: SI 1999/128 r.3
Sch.2 Form 20, substituted: SI 1997/3037 r.2,
Sch.3 para.3
Sch.2 Form 21, amended: SI 1997/3037 r.2,
Sch.3 para.4
Sch.2 Form 21, revoked: SI 1999/128 r.3
Sch.2 Form 22, amended: SI 1997/3037 r.2,
Sch.3 para.4
Sch.2 Form 22, revoked: SI 1999/128 r.3
Sch.2 Form 23, amended: SI 1997/3037 r.2,
Sch.3 para.4, SI 1999/128 r.2, Sch.3 para.1
Sch.2 Form 24, amended: SI 1997/3037 r.2,
Sch.3 para.4
Sch.2 Form 24, revoked: SI 1999/128 r.3
Sch.2 Form 25, amended: SI 1997/3037 r.2,
Sch.3 para.5
Sch.2 Form 25, revoked: SI 1999/128 r.3
Sch.2 Form 26, amended: SI 1997/3037 r.2,
Sch.3 para.5
Sch.2 Form 26, revoked: SI 1999/128 r.3
Sch.2 Form 27, amended: SI 1997/3037 r.2,
Sch.3 para.5
Sch.2 Form 27, revoked: SI 1999/128 r.3
Sch.2 Form 28, amended: SI 1997/3037 r.2,
Sch.3 para.5
Sch.2 Form 28, revoked: SI 1999/128 r.3
Sch.2 Form 29, amended: SI 1997/3037 r.2,
Sch.3 para.4
Sch.2 Form 29, revoked: SI 1999/128 r.3
Sch.2 Form 30, amended: SI 1997/3037 r.2,
Sch.3 para.4
Sch.2 Form 30, revoked: SI 1999/128 r.3
Sch.2 Form 31, amended: SI 1997/3037 r.2,
Sch.3 para.4, Sch.3 para.6
Sch.2 Form 31, revoked: SI 1999/128 r.3
Sch.2 Form 32, amended: SI 1997/3037 r.2
Sch.2 Form 32, revoked: SI 1997/3037 r.3
Sch.2 Form 33, amended: SI 1997/3037 r.2
Sch.2 Form 33, revoked: SI 1997/3037 r.3
Sch.2 Form 34, amended: SI 1997/3037 r.2,
Sch.3 para.4
Sch.2 Form 34, revoked: SI 1999/128 r.3
Sch.2 Form 34A, revoked: SI 1999/128 r.3
Sch.2 Form 34B, amended: SI 1997/3037 r.2,
Sch.3 para.4
Sch.2 Form 34B, revoked: SI 1999/128 r.3
Sch.2 Form 35, amended: SI 1997/3037 r.2
Sch.2 Form 35, revoked: SI 1996/2975 r.3
Sch.2 Form 37, amended: SI 1997/3037 r.2
Sch.2 Form 37, revoked: SI 1997/3037 r.3
Sch.2 Form 38, amended: SI 1997/3037 r.2
Sch.2 Form 38, revoked: SI 1997/3037 r.3
Sch.2 Form 39, amended: SI 1997/3037 r.2
Sch.2 Form 39, revoked: SI 1997/3037 r.3
Sch.2 Form 40, amended: SI 1997/3037 r.2,
Sch.3 para.7
Sch.2 Form 41, amended: SI 1997/3037 r.2,
Sch.3 para.7, Sch.3 para.8
Sch.2 Form 42, amended: SI 1997/3037 r.2,
Sch.3 para.7
Sch.2 Form 43, amended: SI 1997/3037 r.2
Sch.2 Form 43, revoked: SI 1997/3037 r.3
Sch.2 Form 44, amended: SI 1997/3037 r.2
Sch.2 Form 44, revoked: SI 1997/3037 r.3
Sch.2 Form 45, amended: SI 1997/3037 r.2

NO.

1925—cont.

1093. Land Registration Rules 1925—*cont.*
Sch.2 Form 45, revoked: SI 1997/3037 r.3
Sch.2 Form 46, amended: SI 1997/3037 r.2
Sch.2 Form 46, revoked: SI 1997/3037 r.3
Sch.2 Form 47, amended: SI 1997/3037 r.2
Sch.2 Form 47, revoked: SI 1997/3037 r.3
Sch.2 Form 48, amended: SI 1997/3037 r.2
Sch.2 Form 48, revoked: SI 1997/3037 r.3
Sch.2 Form 49, amended: SI 1997/3037 r.2
Sch.2 Form 49, revoked: SI 1997/3037 r.3
Sch.2 Form 50, amended: SI 1997/3037 r.2
Sch.2 Form 50, revoked: SI 1997/3037 r.3
Sch.2 Form 51, amended: SI 1997/3037 r.2,
Sch.3 para.4, SI 1999/128 r.2, Sch.3 para.2
Sch.2 Form 52, amended: SI 1997/3037 r.2,
Sch.3 para.4, SI 1999/128 r.2, Sch.3 para.2
Sch.2 Form 53, amended: SI 1997/3037 r.2,
Sch.3 para.4, Sch.3 para.9
Sch.2 Form 53, revoked: SI 1999/128 r.3
Sch.2 Form 54, amended: SI 1997/3037 r.2
Sch.2 Form 54, revoked: SI 1997/3037 r.3
Sch.2 Form 55, amended: SI 1997/3037 r.2
Sch.2 Form 55, revoked: SI 1997/3037 r.3
Sch.2 Form 56, amended: SI 1996/2975 Sch
para.26, SI 1997/3037 r.2, Sch.3 para.4,
Sch.3 para.10
Sch.2 Form 56, revoked: SI 1999/128 r.3
Sch.2 Form 57, amended: SI 1997/3037 r.2,
Sch.3 para.4
Sch.2 Form 57, revoked: SI 1999/128 r.3
Sch.2 Form 58, amended: SI 1997/3037 r.2,
Sch.3 para.4, SI 1999/128 r.2, Sch.3 para.2
Sch.2 Form 59, amended: SI 1997/3037 r.2,
Sch.3 para.4, SI 1999/128 r.2, Sch.3 para.2
Sch.2 Form 62, amended: SI 1996/2975 Sch
para.27, SI 1997/3037 r.2
Sch.2 Form 63, revoked: SI 1999/128 r.3
Sch.2 Form 69, amended: SI 1997/3037 r.2,
Sch.3 para.4, SI 1999/128 r.2, Sch.3 para.2
Sch.2 Form 70, amended: SI 1997/3037 r.2,
Sch.3 para.4
Sch.2 Form 70, revoked: SI 1999/128 r.3
Sch.2 Form 71, amended: SI 1997/3037 r.2,
Sch.3 para.4
Sch.2 Form 71, revoked: SI 1999/128 r.3
Sch.2 Form 72, amended: SI 1997/3037 r.2
Sch.2 Form 72, revoked: SI 1997/3037 r.3
Sch.2 Form 73, amended: SI 1997/3037 r.2,
Sch.3 para.11
Sch.2 Form 74, amended: SI 1997/3037 r.2,
Sch.3 para.12
Sch.2 Form 75, amended: SI 1997/3037 r.2,
Sch.3 para.4, SI 1999/128 r.2, Sch.3 para.2
Sch.2 Form 75, substituted: SI 1996/2975 Sch
para.28
Sch.2 Form 76, amended: SI 1997/3037 r.2,
Sch.3 para.4, SI 1999/128 r.2, Sch.3 para.2
Sch.2 Form 76, substituted: SI 1996/2975 Sch
para.28
Sch.2 Form 77, amended: SI 1996/2975 Sch
para.29, SI 1997/3037 r.2, Sch.3 para.4, SI
1999/128 r.2, Sch.3 para.2
Sch.2 Form 78, substituted: SI 1999/2097 r.2,
Sch.2 para.2
Sch.2 Form 113, amended: SI 1997/3037 r.2,
Sch.3 para.4, SI 1999/128 r.2, Sch.3 para.2
Sch.3, added: SI 1997/3037 r.2, Sch.4
1349. Markets, Sales and Lairs Order 1925
Art.2, revoked (in part): SI 1996/3265

1926

840. Order in Council dated 28th June 1926 directing that the Extradition Acts shall apply in the case of the Republic of Estonia 1926
revoked: SI 1997/2596 Art.2

1121. South Wales Sea Fisheries District Order 1926
Art.7, substituted: SI 1996/618 Art.3
Art.17, substituted: SI 1996/618 Art.4
Sch., substituted: SI 1996/618 Art.5

1927

Hereford Order 1927
referred to: 1998 c.43 s.1, Sch.1 Part V
289. Transit of Animals Order 1927
revoked (in part): SI 1997/1480 Art.22, Sch.12 Part III
343. Coroners (Orders as to Districts) Rules 1927
applied: SI 1996/2403, SI 1997/1532, SI 1998/1799, SI 1999/1325, SI 1999/2980
referred to: SI 1996/445
399. Transit of Animals (Amendment) Order 1927
revoked: SI 1997/1480 Art.22, Sch.12 Part II
605. Order in Council dated June 27, 1927 directing that the Extradition Acts shall apply in the case of Albania 1927
revoked: SI 1999/2035 Art.2

1928

574. Belgium (Extradition) Order in Council 1928
revoked: SI 1998/259 Art.2

1929

Ross Water Order 1929
Art.46, referred to: 1998 c.43 s.1, Sch.1 Part V
Art.51, referred to: 1998 c.43 s.1, Sch.1 Part V
Upton upon Severn Order 1929
referred to: 1998 c.43 s.1, Sch.1 Part V
300. Cotton Cloth Factories Regulations 1929
revoked: SI 1996/3022 Reg.2, Sch Part II
952. Petroleum-Spirit (Motor Vehicles etc.) Regulations 1929
applied: SI 1996/2089 Reg.2, SI 1996/2092 Reg.3
Reg.15A, added: SI 1999/743 Reg.23

1930

923. Animals (Sea Transport) Order 1930
revoked: SI 1997/1480 Art.22, Sch.12 Part II

1931

Yarmouth (Isle of Wight) Pier and Harbour Order 1931
applied: SI 1996/2480 Art.3
269. Herefordshire (Ross Urban, Ross Rural and Whitchurch Rural) Order 1931
revoked: 1998 c.43 s.1, Sch.1 Part V
939. Evesham Joint Hospital Order 1931
revoked: 1998 c.43 s.1, Sch.1 Part V
1097. Treasury Solicitor (Crown's Nominee) Rules 1931
revoked: SI 1997/2870 r.1 (with savings)

1932

248. Animals (Sea Transport) Amendment Order 1932
revoked: SI 1997/1480 Art.22, Sch.12 Part II

1933

Hereford Order 1933
referred to: 1998 c.43 s.1, Sch.1 Part V
922. Employment Abroad of Persons under Eighteen, Licence and Regulations 1933
referred to: SI 1998/1678 Reg.3
revoked: SI 1998/1678 Reg.4
1243. County of Worcester Review Order 1933
revoked (in part): 1998 c.43 s.1, Sch.1 Part V
Art.1, referred to: 1998 c.43 s.1, Sch.1 Part V
Art.2, referred to: 1998 c.43 s.1, Sch.1 Part V
Art.57, referred to: 1998 c.43 s.1, Sch.1 Part V
1313. Act of Sederunt Regulating Appeals under the Pharmacy and Poisons Act 1933
revoked: SI 1999/929 r.1.3, Sch.2

1934

Robb's Trust Scheme 1934
amended: SI 1996/478 Sch
209. Poland (Extradition) Order in Council 1934
revoked (in part): SI 1996/2875 Art.3, Sch.3
1346. London Cab Order 1934
para.10, applied: SI 1996/960 Art.3
para.31, see *DPP v Computer Cab Company Ltd* [1996] R.T.R. 130 (QBD), Rose, L.J.
para.40, substituted: SI 1996/1176 Art.3, SI 1997/1116 Art.3, SI 1998/1043 Art.3, SI 1999/1117 Art.3
para.41, amended: SI 1996/1176 Art.4, SI 1999/1117 Art.4, SI 1999/3250 Art.3

1935

Angus Educational Trust Scheme 1935
amended: SI 1996/477 Sch
Moray and Nairn Educational Trust Scheme 1935
amended: SI 1996/478 Sch
426. Petroleum (Production) Regulations 1935
applied: SI 1999/160 Sch.1 Part II
Reg.2, applied: SI 1999/160 Sch.1 Part II
Reg.3, applied: SI 1999/160 Sch.1 Part II
Sch.2 Part I, referred to: 1998 c.17 Sch.1 para.1, SI 1999/160 Sch.1 para.1
Sch.2 Part III, referred to: 1998 c.17 Sch.1 para.1, SI 1999/160 Sch.1 para.1
676. Switzerland (Extradition) Order in Council 1935
revoked (in part): SI 1996/2875 Art.3, Sch.3

1936

Ayrshire Educational Trust Scheme 1936
amended: SI 1996/629 Sch
Glasgow Educational and Marshall Trust Scheme 1936
amended: SI 1996/629 Sch
Lanarkshire Educational Trust Scheme 1936
amended: SI 1996/629 Sch

1937

719. Hungary (Extradition) Order in Council 1937
revoked (in part): SI 1996/2875 Art.3, Sch.3

NO.

1938

106. Kiers Regulations 1938
revoked: SI 1996/3022 Reg.2, Sch Part II
245. Local Government Superannuation (Admin-istration) (Scotland) Regulations 1938
applied: SI 1998/366 Reg.106
574. Local Government Superannuation (Admin-istration) Regulations 1938
applied: SI 1997/1612 Reg.107
1384. Local Government Superannuation (Admin-istration) (No.2) (Scotland) Regulations 1938
applied: SI 1998/366 Reg.106

1939

501. Transit of Animals (Amendment) Order 1939
revoked: SI 1997/1480 Art.22, Sch.12 Part II
1304. Defence (Armed Forces) Regulations 1939
applied: SI 1996/2824 Reg.48
referred to: SI 1999/2864 Reg.51

1945

597. River Wye Catchment Board (River Lugg Internal Drainage District) Order 1945
amended: SI 1999/2508 Sch. para.3
636. Primary and Secondary Schools (Grants Conditions) Regulations 1945
Part IV, applied: SI 1999/2277 Sch.2 s.4
1558. Disabled Persons (General) Regulations 1945
Reg.9, applied: SI 1996/1474 Art.3

1946

36. Bretton Woods Agreements Order in Coun-cil 1946
see *Ispahani v Bank Melli Iran* [1998] Lloyd's Rep. Bank. 133 (CA), Robert Walker, L.J.
156. Operations at Unfenced Machinery (Amended Schedule) Regulations 1946
revoked: SI 1998/2306 Reg.39, Sch.4
1094. Coal Industry Nationalisation (National Coal Board) Regulations 1946
Reg.4, amended: SI 1997/1588 Reg.2
1267. Educational Development, Research and Services (Scotland) Grant Regulations 1946
revoked: SSI 1999/65 Reg.6
1331. Double Taxation Relief (Taxes on Income) (USA) Regulations 1946
Reg.2, amended: SI 1996/1781 Reg.2
1703. Collection and Disposal of Fees Under the Private Legislation Procedure (Scotland) Act 1936 Order 1946
Art.3, amended: SI 1999/1820 Art.4, Sch.2 para.134
2157. Private Legislation Procedure (Scotland) General Orders 1946
amended: SI 1999/1820 Art.4, Sch.2 para.135
Ord. 27,
amended: SI 1999/1820 Art.4, Sch.2 para.135
Ord. 27A,
amended: SI 1999/1820 Art.4, Sch.2 para.135, SSI 1999/1 Reg.63
Ord. 32,
amended: SI 1999/1820 Art.4, Sch.2 para.135
Ord. 37,
amended: SI 1999/1820 Art.4, Sch.2 para.135

NO.

1946—cont.

2157. Private Legislation Procedure (Scotland) General Orders 1946—*cont.*
Ord. 57,
amended: SI 1999/1820 Art.4, Sch.2 para.135
Ord. 98,
amended: SI 1999/1820 Art.4, Sch.2 para.135

1947

ii. Edinburgh Merchant Company Widows' Fund (Amendment) Order 1947
applied: 1996 c.xi Sch
681. Exmouth Docks (Increase of Charges) Order 1947
revoked: SI 1998/980 Art.6, Sch.
1659. Police Grant (Scotland) Order 1947
revoked: SI 1996/780 Art.7, Sch.2
1758. New Town (East Kilbride) Development Cor-poration Order 1947
referred to: SI 1996/1066 Art.1

1948

489. National Insurance (Modification of Teach-ers Pensions) Regulations 1948
applied: SI 1997/3001 Sch.10 para.2, Sch.10 para.3
1465. National Health Service (Transfer of Officers and Compensation) (Scotland) Regu-lations 1948
applied: SI 1999/1750 Art.2, Sch.1
1483. National Health Service (Superannuation) (England and Scotland) Regulations 1948
applied: SI 1999/1750 Art.2, Sch.1
1696. Jute (Safety, Health and Welfare) Regu-lations 1948
revoked: SI 1996/3022 Reg.2, Sch Part II

1949

789. Gas (Testing) Regulations 1949
Reg.1, amended: SI 1996/219 Art.11
Reg.1, applied: SI 1996/219 Art.18
Reg.1, revoked (in part): SI 1996/219 Art.12
Reg.2, amended: SI 1996/219 Art.11
Reg.2, revoked (in part): SI 1996/219 Art.13
Reg.3, revoked: SI 1996/219 Art.12
Reg.3A, amended: SI 1996/219 Art.12
Reg.4, amended: SI 1996/219 Art.14
Reg.5, amended: SI 1996/219 Art.15
1065. Act of Sederunt The Companies (Winding-up) Forms 1949
Sch. Form 111, amended: SI 1999/1820 Art.4, Sch.2 para.136
Sch. Form 112, amended: SI 1999/1820 Art.4, Sch.2 para.136

1950

65. Pottery (Health and Welfare) Special Regu-lations 1950
Reg.6, revoked: SI 1998/543 Reg.14, Sch.3
Sch.1, revoked: SI 1998/543 Reg.14, Sch.3
792. Town and Country Planning (Churches, Places of Religious Worship and Burial Grounds) Regulations 1950
Reg.16, amended: SI 1996/525 Sch para.7
1159. Chester Water Order 1950
revoked: SI 1998/281 Art.4, Sch.2 Part II

NO.

NO.

1950—cont.

1326. British Wool Marketing Scheme (Approval) Order 1950
applied: SI 1999/1747 Art.3, Sch.5 para.3
Sch. para.4, referred to: SI 1999/1319 Sch.

1951

1743. Schools Grants Regulations 1951
Part IV, applied: SI 1999/2277 Sch.2 s.4
1963. Motor Vehicles (Authorisation of Special Types) (No.2) Order 1951
revoked: SI 1998/2249 Art.4

1952

565. Prison (Scotland) Rules 1952
r.1, see *McDonald v Secretary of State for Scotland (No.2)* 1996 S.L.T. 575
776. Trafalgar Square Regulations 1952
revoked: SI 1997/1639 Reg.7
1291. Horses (Sea Transport) Order 1952
revoked (in part): SI 1997/1480 Art.22, Sch.12 Part III
1493. Argyll County Council (Allt Mor, Dervaig) Water Order 1952
revoked: SI 1997/1115 Art.8
1495. Factories (Cotton Shuttles) Special Regulations 1952
revoked: SI 1996/3022 Reg.2, Sch Part II
1899. Wireless Telegraphy (Isle of Man) Order 1952
applied: SI 1999/765
referred to: SI 1998/558, SI 1998/1510 Art.2
Sch. para.1A, added: SI 1997/285 Art.2
Sch. para.1B, added: SI 1997/285 Art.3
1900. Wireless Telegraphy (Channel Islands) Order 1952
applied: SI 1999/765
referred to: SI 1998/558, SI 1998/1511 Art.2, SI 1998/1512 Art.2
Sch. para.2A, added: SI 1997/284 Art.2
Sch. para.2B, added: SI 1997/284 Art.3

1953

884. National Insurance and Industrial Injuries (Reciprocal Agreement with Italy) Order 1953
Sch., amended: SI 1996/1928 Art.2, Sch.1
965. Cambridge Waterworks Order 1953
revoked: SI 1996/713 Art.4, Sch.2 Part II
966. Chester Water Order 1953
revoked: SI 1998/281 Art.4, Sch.2 Part II
1199. Federation of Rhodesian and Nyasaland (Constitution) Order in Council 1953
s.13, revoked (in part): 1998 c.43 s.1, Sch.1 Part IV

1954

269. Civil Defence (Gas Undertakers) Regulations 1954
amended: SI 1996/252 Art.2, Sch
488. Wireless Telegraphy (Colonial Ships and Aircraft) Order 1954
revoked: SI 1998/3148 Art.2

1954—cont.

539. Wireless Telegraphy (Colonial Ships and Aircraft) Regulations 1954
revoked: SI 1998/2970 Reg.2
540. Wireless Telegraphy (Foreign Ships and Aircraft) Regulations 1954
revoked: SI 1998/2970 Reg.2
921. Dangerous Machines (Training of Young Persons) Order 1954
revoked: SI 1997/135 Reg.3, Sch. Part II
982. Town and Country Planning (Atomic Energy Establishments Special Development) Order 1954
revoked: SI 1996/3194 Art.2
1048. Local Government Superannuation (Benefits) Regulations 1954
Reg.7, referred to: SI 1997/1612 Reg.27
Reg.13, applied: SI 1997/1612 Sch.3
1059. Local Government Superannuation (Benefits) (Scotland) Regulations 1954
applied: SI 1998/366 Reg.5
Reg.7, referred to: SI 1998/366 Reg.26
Reg.13, applied: SI 1998/366 Sch.3 para.5
Sch.2, applied: SI 1998/366 Reg.135
1192. Local Government Superannuation (Administration) Regulations 1954
applied: SI 1997/1612 Reg.107
1243. Local Government Superannuation (Administration) (Scotland) Regulations 1954
applied: SI 1998/366 Reg.106
1378. Petroleum (Production) (Amendment) Regulations 1954
referred to: 1998 c.17 Sch.1 para.1, SI 1999/160 Sch.1 para.1
1711. Youth Courts (Constitution) Rules 1954
r.1, amended: SI 1996/577 r.2, SI 1996/3068 r.3
r.12, see *R. v Birmingham Youth Court Ex p. F (A Child)* Independent, November 15, 1999 (C.S.) (QBD), Laws, L.J.
r.12, amended: SI 1998/2167 r.2
r.13, amended: SI 1998/2167 r.2
r.14, amended: SI 1996/577 r.3, SI 1996/3068 r.4

1955

Aberdeenshire Educational Trust Scheme 1955
amended: SI 1996/478 Sch
Sharpe's Trust Scheme 1955
amended: SI 1996/478 Sch
690. Potato Marketing Scheme (Approval) Order 1955
Sch. para.32, applied: SI 1997/1573 Reg.3, Reg.10, Sch. para.2
Sch. para.34, applied: SI 1997/1573 Reg.3, Reg.10, Sch. para.3
Sch. para.35, applied: SI 1997/1573 Reg.3, Reg.12, Sch. para.5
Sch. para.36, applied: SI 1997/1573 Reg.3, Reg.12, Sch. para.5
Sch. para.37, applied: SI 1997/1573 Reg.3, Reg.11, Sch. para.4
Sch. para.58, referred to: SI 1997/1573 Reg.14
Sch. para.83, applied: SI 1997/1573 Reg.3, Reg.8, Sch. para.1
Sch. para.90, applied: SI 1997/1573 Reg.3, Reg.15, Sch. para.6
874. National Insurance and Industrial Injuries (Netherlands) Order 1955
Sch., amended: SI 1996/1928 Art.2, Sch.1

NO.

1955—cont.

1041. Local Government Superannuation (Benefits) Regulations 1955
Reg.7, referred to: SI 1997/1612 Reg.27
Reg.13, applied: SI 1997/1612 Sch.3

1226. Local Government Superannuation (Benefits) (Scotland) Amendment Regulations 1955
applied: SI 1998/366 Reg.5
Reg.7, referred to: SI 1998/366 Reg.26
Reg.13, applied: SI 1998/366 Sch.3 para.5
Sch.2, applied: SI 1998/366 Reg.135

1377. Boarding-Out of Children Regulations 1955
see *H v Norfolk CC* [1997] 1 F.L.R. 384 (CA), Simon Brown, L.J.

1956

1621. South of Luton-Watford Gap-Dunchurch Special Road Scheme 1956
revoked (in part): SI 1999/2278 para.2

1771. Coal and Other Mines (Locomotives) Regulations 1956
Reg.3, amended: SI 1996/192 Reg.1, Reg.20, Sch.1
Reg.4, revoked: SI 1996/192 Reg.1, Reg.20, Sch.1
Reg.5, revoked: SI 1996/192 Reg.1, Reg.20, Sch.1

1773. Coal and Other Mines (Sidings) Regulations 1956
Reg.2, revoked (in part): SI 1997/553 Reg.12, Sch. Part II
Reg.3, revoked: SI 1997/553 Reg.12, Sch Part II
Reg.4, revoked: SI 1997/553 Reg.12, Sch Part II
Reg.5, revoked: SI 1997/553 Reg.12, Sch Part II
Reg.7, revoked: SI 1997/553 Reg.12, Sch Part II
Reg.8, revoked: SI 1997/553 Reg.12, Sch Part II
Reg.9, revoked: SI 1997/553 Reg.12, Sch Part II
Reg.10, revoked: SI 1997/553 Reg.12, Sch Part II
Reg.11, revoked: SI 1997/553 Reg.12, Sch Part II
Reg.12, revoked: SI 1997/553 Reg.12, Sch Part II
Reg.13, revoked: SI 1997/553 Reg.12, Sch Part II
Reg.14, revoked: SI 1997/553 Reg.12, Sch Part II
Reg.15, revoked: SI 1997/553 Reg.12, Sch Part II
Reg.16, revoked: SI 1997/553 Reg.12, Sch Part II
Reg.17, revoked: SI 1997/553 Reg.12, Sch Part II
Reg.18, revoked: SI 1997/553 Reg.12, Sch Part II
Reg.19, revoked: SI 1997/553 Reg.12, Sch Part II
Reg.20, revoked: SI 1997/553 Reg.12, Sch Part II

1780. Quarries (General) Regulations 1956
revoked: SI 1999/2024 Reg.48, Sch.5 Part I
Reg.13, revoked: SI 1998/2307 Reg.17, Sch.2
Reg.14, revoked: SI 1998/2307 Reg.17, Sch.2
Reg.24, revoked: SI 1997/553 Reg.12, Sch Part II
Reg.25, revoked: SI 1997/553 Reg.12, Sch Part II
Reg.26, revoked: SI 1997/553 Reg.12, Sch Part II

NO.

1956—cont.

1780. Quarries (General) Regulations 1956—*cont.*
Reg.27, revoked (in part): SI 1997/553 Reg.12, Sch Part II
Reg.28, revoked: SI 1997/553 Reg.12, Sch Part II
Reg.29, revoked: SI 1997/553 Reg.12, Sch Part II
Reg.30, revoked: SI 1997/553 Reg.12, Sch Part II
Reg.31, revoked: SI 1997/553 Reg.12, Sch Part II
Reg.32, revoked: SI 1997/553 Reg.12, Sch Part II
Reg.33, revoked: SI 1997/553 Reg.12, Sch Part II
Reg.34, revoked: SI 1997/553 Reg.12, Sch Part II
Reg.35, revoked: SI 1997/553 Reg.12, Sch Part II

1784. Mines and Quarries (References) Rules 1956
revoked: SI 1999/2024 Reg.48, Sch.5 Part I

1897. National Insurance and Industrial Injuries (Malta) Order 1956
revoked: SI 1996/1927 Art.3

1957

Clackmannanshire Educational Trust Scheme 1957
amended: SI 1996/475 Sch.

Stirlingshire Educational Trust Scheme 1957
amended: SI 1996/475 Sch.

410. China Clay and China Stone Quarries (Employment of Young People) Order 1957
revoked: SI 1999/2024 Reg.48, Sch.5 Part I

806. Town and Country Planning (Atomic Energy Establishments Special Development) Order 1957
revoked: SI 1996/3194 Art.2

1385. Agriculture (Ladders) Regulations 1957
revoked: SI 1996/3022 Reg.2, Sch Part II

1697. Petroleum (Production) (Amendment) Regulations 1957
referred to: 1998 c.17 Sch.1 para.1, SI 1999/160 Sch.1 para.1

1958

1. Jurors (Service of Summonses) Regulations (Northern Ireland) 1958
revoked: SI 1996/1141 (NI.6) s.32, Sch.5

61. Work in Compressed Air Special Regulations 1958
revoked: SI 1996/1656 Reg.22, Sch.2 Part I

358. Chester Water Order 1958
Art.3, revoked: SI 1998/281 Art.4, Sch.2 Part II
Art.4, revoked: SI 1998/281 Art.4, Sch.2 Part II
Art.5, revoked: SI 1998/281 Art.4, Sch.2 Part II
Art.6, revoked: SI 1998/281 Art.4, Sch.2 Part II
Art.7, revoked: SI 1998/281 Art.4, Sch.2 Part II
Art.8, revoked: SI 1998/281 Art.4, Sch.2 Part II
Art.9, revoked: SI 1998/281 Art.4, Sch.2 Part II
Art.10, revoked: SI 1998/281 Art.4, Sch.2 Part II
Art.15, revoked: SI 1998/281 Art.4, Sch.2 Part II

366. Agriculture (Avoidance of Accidents to Children) Regulations 1958
revoked: SI 1998/3262 Reg.6

NO.

496. Derwent Water Order 1958
Art.18, revoked: SI 1996/824 Art.3
Art.19, revoked: SI 1996/824 Art.3
Art.20, revoked: SI 1996/824 Art.3
Art.21, revoked: SI 1996/824 Art.3
Art.22, revoked: SI 1996/824 Art.3
Art.23, revoked: SI 1996/824 Art.3
Art.24, revoked: SI 1996/824 Art.3
Art.25, revoked: SI 1996/824 Art.3
Art.26, revoked: SI 1996/824 Art.3
Art.27, revoked: SI 1996/824 Art.3
Art.28, revoked: SI 1996/824 Art.3
Art.29, revoked: SI 1996/824 Art.3
Art.30, revoked: SI 1996/824 Art.3
Art.31, revoked: SI 1996/824 Art.3
Art.32, revoked: SI 1996/824 Art.3

597. National Insurance and Industrial Injuries (France) Order 1958
Sch., amended: SI 1996/1928 Art.2, Sch.1

771. Family Allowances, National Insurance and Industrial Injuries (Belgium) Order 1958
Sch., amended: SI 1996/1928 Art.2, Sch.1

772. National Insurance and Industrial Injuries (Malta) Order 1958
revoked: SI 1996/1927 Art.3

1263. Family Allowances, National Insurance and Industrial Injuries (Yugoslavia) Order 1958
Sch., amended: SI 1996/1928 Art.2, Sch.1

1272. Horses (Sea Transport) (Amendment) Order 1958
revoked: SI 1997/1480 Art.22, Sch.12 Part II

1533. Gravel and Sand Quarries (Overhanging) (Exemption) Regulations 1958
revoked: SI 1999/2024 Reg.48, Sch.5 Part I

1760. Kington Rural District Water Order 1958
Art.4, revoked (in part): 1998 c.43 s.1, Sch.1 Part V

1822. Weobley Rural District Water Order 1958
Art.4, revoked (in part): 1998 c.43 s.1, Sch.1 Part V

2110. Quarries (Ropeways and Vehicles) Regulations 1958
revoked: SI 1998/2307 Reg.17, Sch.2, SI 1999/2024 Reg.48, Sch.5 Part I

277. Milk and Dairies (General) Regulations 1959
Reg.2, amended: SI 1998/2424 Reg.10

364. Schools Regulations 1959
Reg.20, applied: SI 1999/2166 Reg.2, Sch.1 para 1, SI 1999/2817 Reg.2, Sch.1 para.1
Sch.2 para.2, applied: SI 1999/2817 Reg.2, Sch.1 para.6
Sch.2 para.2, referred to: SI 1999/2166 Reg.2, Sch.1 para 6

365. Handicapped Pupils and Special Schools Regulations 1959
Reg.15, applied: SI 1999/2166 Reg.2, Sch.1 para.1, SI 1999/2817 Reg.2, Sch.1 para.2

425. Chester Water Order 1959
revoked: SI 1998/281 Art.4, Sch.2 Part II

427. Agriculture (Circular Saws) Regulations 1959
revoked: SI 1998/2306 Reg.39, Sch.4

428. Agriculture (Safeguarding of Workplaces) Regulations 1959
revoked: SI 1996/3022 Reg.2, Sch Part II

940. Coquet Water Board Order 1959
s.14, revoked: SI 1996/824 Art.3

NO.

1131. Cambridge Waterworks Order 1959
s.3, revoked: SI 1996/713 Art.4, Sch.2 Part II
s.4, revoked (in part): SI 1996/713 Art.4, Sch.2 Part II
s.7, revoked: SI 1996/713 Art.4, Sch.2 Part II
s.8, revoked: SI 1996/713 Art.4, Sch.2 Part II
s.11, revoked: SI 1996/713 Art.4, Sch.2 Part II

1182. Direct Grant Schools Regulations 1959
Reg.4, applied: SI 1999/2277 Sch.2 s.4

1335. Diseases of Animals (Ascertainment of Compensation) Order 1959
applied: SI 1996/2007 Art.10, SI 1996/3183 Art.11, SI 1998/1645 Art.8

1375. Herefordshire Water Board Order 1959
revoked (in part): 1998 c.43 s.1, Sch.1 Part V
Art.1, referred to: 1998 c.43 s.1, Sch.1 Part V
Art.2, referred to: 1998 c.43 s.1, Sch.1 Part V
Art.19, referred to: 1998 c.43 s.1, Sch.1 Part V
Art.23, referred to: 1998 c.43 s.1, Sch.1 Part V
Art.24, referred to: 1998 c.43 s.1, Sch.1 Part V
Art.25, referred to: 1998 c.43 s.1, Sch.1 Part V
Sch.4, referred to: 1998 c.43 s.1, Sch.1 Part V

1486. Malvern Water (Revocation) Order 1959
revoked: 1998 c.43 s.1, Sch.1 Part V

1832. Direct Grant Schools Regulations 1959
revoked: SI 1998/86 Reg.2, Sch.1

1860. National Insurance (Non-participation Certificates) Regulations 1959
applied: SI 1997/664 Art.13

County of Argyll Educational Trust Scheme 1960
amended: SI 1996/629 Sch

105. Movement of Animals (Records) Order 1960
applied: SI 1997/1901 Reg.3, SI 1998/871 Reg.29
Art.2A, added: SI 1996/28 Art.15
Art.3, applied: SI 1996/3241 Reg.13

211. Family Allowances, National Insurance and Industrial Injuries (Denmark) Order 1960
Sch., amended: SI 1996/1928 Art.2, Sch.1

270. Cycle Racing on Highways (Scotland) Regulations 1960
Reg.5, amended: SI 1996/2665 Reg.2

398. Agriculture (Poisonous Substances) (Extension) Order 1960
revoked: SI 1996/3022 Reg.2, Sch Part II

421. Engineering Construction (Extension of Definition) Regulations 1960
revoked: SI 1996/1592 Reg.35, Sch.10

543. Election Petition Rules 1960
applied: SI 1999/450 Art.145
r.2, amended: SI 1999/450 Art.145, Sch.8 para.2, Sch.8 para.3, SI 1999/1352 r.2
r.4, amended: SI 1999/450 Art.145, Sch.8 para.4
r.5, amended: SI 1999/1352 r.3
r.6, amended: SI 1999/1352 r.4
r.7, amended: SI 1999/1352 r.5
r.9, amended: SI 1999/450 Art.145, Sch.8 para.5, SI 1999/1352 r.6
r.10, amended: SI 1999/450 Art.145, Sch.8 para.6, Sch.8 para.7
r.11, amended: SI 1999/1352 r.7
r.12, amended: SI 1999/450 Art.145, Sch.8 para.7, SI 1999/1352 r.8
r.13, amended: SI 1999/1352 r.9
r.14, amended: SI 1999/450 Art.145, Sch.8 para.7, SI 1999/1352 r.10

NO.

1960—cont.

543. Election Petition Rules 1960—cont.
r.16, amended: SI 1999/450 Art.145, Sch.8 para.7, SI 1999/1352 r.11
r.19, amended: SI 1999/1352 r.12
Sch. Form, amended: SI 1999/450 Art.145, Sch.8 para.8

707. National Insurance and Industrial Injuries (Republic of Ireland) Order 1960
Sch., amended: SI 1996/1928 Art.2, Sch.1

969. Ghana (Consequential Provision) (Colonial Stock Acts) Order in Council 1960
revoked: 1998 c.43 s.1, Sch.1 Part IV

1103. National Insurance (Non-participation Assurance of Equivalent Pension Benefits) Regulations 1960
Reg.2, applied: SI 1997/1613 Reg.18, SI 1998/364 Reg.18

1199. Agriculture (Threshers and Balers) Regulations 1960
revoked: SI 1996/3022 Reg.2, Sch Part II

1291. Woodside Nos 2 and 3 Mine (Diesel Vehicles) Special Regulations 1960
Reg.4, revoked: SI 1996/192 Reg.20, Sch.15 Part I
Reg.5, revoked: SI 1996/192 Reg.20, Sch.15 Part I
Reg.6, revoked: SI 1996/192 Reg.20, Sch.15 Part I

1307. Work in Compressed Air (Amendment) Regulations 1960
revoked: SI 1996/1656 Reg.22, Sch.2 Part I

1660. Israel (Extradition) Order 1960
revoked (in part): SI 1996/2875 Art.3, Sch.3

1874. Argyll County Council (Loch Lossit, Islay) Water Order 1960
Art.5, amended: SI 1998/1855 Art.2
Sch., substituted: SI 1998/1855 Art.2, Sch.

1932. Shipbuilding and Ship-repairing Regulations 1960
Reg.2, amended: SI 1998/2307 Reg.13
Reg.3, amended: SI 1998/2307 Reg.17, Sch.2
Reg.21, revoked: SI 1998/2307 Reg.17, Sch.2
Reg.31, revoked: SI 1998/2307 Reg.17, Sch.2
Reg.32, revoked: SI 1998/2307 Reg.17, Sch.2
Reg.33, revoked: SI 1998/2307 Reg.17, Sch.2
Reg.34, applied: SI 1998/2307 Reg.9
Reg.34, revoked: SI 1998/2307 Reg.17, Sch.2
Reg.35, revoked: SI 1998/2307 Reg.17, Sch.2
Reg.36, revoked: SI 1998/2307 Reg.17, Sch.2
Reg.37, applied: SI 1998/2307 Reg.9
Reg.37, revoked: SI 1998/2307 Reg.17, Sch.2
Reg.38, revoked: SI 1998/2307 Reg.17, Sch.2
Reg.39, revoked: SI 1998/2307 Reg.17, Sch.2
Reg.40, revoked: SI 1998/2307 Reg.17, Sch.2
Reg.41, revoked: SI 1998/2307 Reg.17, Sch.2
Reg.42, revoked: SI 1998/2307 Reg.17, Sch.2
Reg.43, revoked: SI 1998/2307 Reg.17, Sch.2
Reg.44, revoked: SI 1998/2307 Reg.17, Sch.2
Reg.45, revoked: SI 1998/2307 Reg.17, Sch.2
Reg.46, revoked: SI 1998/2307 Reg.17, Sch.2
Reg.47, revoked: SI 1998/2307 Reg.17, Sch.2
Reg.48, revoked: SI 1997/1713 Reg.9, Sch.
Reg.49, revoked: SI 1997/1713 Reg.9, Sch.
Reg.50, revoked: SI 1997/1713 Reg.9, Sch.
Reg.51, revoked: SI 1997/1713 Reg.9, Sch.
Reg.52, revoked: SI 1997/1713 Reg.9, Sch.
Reg.54, revoked: SI 1997/1713 Reg.9, Sch.

1934. General Optical Council (Disciplinary Committee Rules) Order of Council 1960
revoked: SI 1998/1338, SI 1998/1338 Sch. r.20

NO.

1960—cont.

1936. General Optical Council (Rules relating to Injury or Disease of the Eye) Order of Council 1960
Sch., revoked: SI 1999/3267 Sch. r.9

1961

Bute Educational Trust Scheme 1961
amended: SI 1996/629 Sch

Renfrewshire Educational Trust Scheme 1961
amended: SI 1996/629 Sch

114. Shipbuilding (Reports on Breathing Apparatus etc.) Order 1961
revoked: SI 1997/1713 Reg.9, Sch.

117. Shipbuilding (Particulars of Annealing) Order 1961
revoked: SI 1998/2307 Reg.17, Sch.2

431. Shipbuilding (Lifting Appliances, etc., Forms) Order 1961
revoked: SI 1998/2307 Reg.17, Sch.2

1202. Family Allowances, National Insurance and Industrial Injuries (Germany) Order 1961
Sch., amended: SI 1996/1928 Art.2, Sch.1

1295. Town and Country Planning (Atomic Energy Establishments Special Development) Order 1961
revoked: SI 1996/3194 Art.2

1345. Breathing Apparatus etc. (Report on Examination) Order 1961
revoked: SI 1997/1713 Reg.9, Sch.

1398. National Health Service Superannuation (Scotland) Regulations 1961
applied: SI 1998/366 Reg.135
Reg.40, referred to: SI 1998/366 Reg.135
Reg.46, applied: SI 1998/366 Reg.135
Reg.54, referred to: SI 1998/366 Reg.135
Reg.72, applied: SI 1998/1594 Reg.4, Reg.12

1441. National Health Service (Superannuation) Regulations 1961
Reg.39, referred to: SI 1997/1612 Reg.141
Reg.45, applied: SI 1997/1612 Reg.141
Reg.55, referred to: SI 1997/1612 Reg.141

1513. National Insurance (Germany) Order 1961
Sch., amended: SI 1996/1928 Art.2, Sch.1

1580. Construction (General Provisions) Regulations 1961
Reg.8, revoked: SI 1996/1592 Reg.35, Sch.10
Reg.9, revoked: SI 1996/1592 Reg.35, Sch.10
Reg.10, revoked: SI 1996/1592 Reg.35, Sch.10
Reg.11, revoked: SI 1996/1592 Reg.35, Sch.10
Reg.12, revoked: SI 1996/1592 Reg.35, Sch.10
Reg.13, revoked: SI 1996/1592 Reg.35, Sch.10
Reg.14, revoked: SI 1996/1592 Reg.35, Sch.10
Reg.15, revoked: SI 1996/1592 Reg.35, Sch.10
Reg.16, revoked: SI 1996/1592 Reg.35, Sch.10
Reg.17, revoked: SI 1996/1592 Reg.35, Sch.10
Reg.18, revoked: SI 1996/1592 Reg.35, Sch.10
Reg.19, revoked: SI 1996/1592 Reg.35, Sch.10
Reg.21, revoked: SI 1996/1592 Reg.35, Sch.10
Reg.23, revoked: SI 1996/1592 Reg.35, Sch.10
Reg.24, revoked: SI 1996/1592 Reg.35, Sch.10
Reg.25, revoked: SI 1996/1592 Reg.35, Sch.10
Reg.26, revoked: SI 1996/1592 Reg.35, Sch.10
Reg.27, revoked: SI 1996/1592 Reg.35, Sch.10
Reg.28, revoked: SI 1996/1592 Reg.35, Sch.10
Reg.29, revoked: SI 1996/1592 Reg.35, Sch.10
Reg.30, revoked: SI 1996/1592 Reg.35, Sch.10
Reg.31, revoked: SI 1996/1592 Reg.35, Sch.10
Reg.32, revoked: SI 1996/1592 Reg.35, Sch.10
Reg.33, revoked: SI 1996/1592 Reg.35, Sch.10
Reg.34, revoked: SI 1996/1592 Reg.35, Sch.10

NO.

1580. Construction (General Provisions) Regulations 1961—*cont.*
Reg.35, revoked: SI 1996/1592 Reg.35, Sch.10
Reg.36, revoked: SI 1996/1592 Reg.35, Sch.10
Reg.37, revoked: SI 1996/1592 Reg.35, Sch.10
Reg.38, revoked: SI 1996/1592 Reg.35, Sch.10
Reg.39, revoked: SI 1996/1592 Reg.35, Sch.10
Reg.40, revoked: SI 1996/1592 Reg.35, Sch.10
Reg.41, revoked: SI 1996/1592 Reg.35, Sch.10
Reg.44, see *Young v Charles Church (Southern) Ltd* (1998) 39 B.M.L.R. 146 (CA), Evans, L.J.
Reg.45, revoked: SI 1996/1592 Reg.35, Sch.10
Reg.46, revoked: SI 1996/1592 Reg.35, Sch.10
Reg.47, revoked: SI 1996/1592 Reg.35, Sch.10
Reg.48, revoked: SI 1996/1592 Reg.35, Sch.10
Reg.49, revoked: SI 1996/1592 Reg.35, Sch.10
Reg.50, revoked: SI 1996/1592 Reg.35, Sch.10
Reg.51, revoked: SI 1996/1592 Reg.35, Sch.10
Reg.53, revoked: SI 1996/1592 Reg.35, Sch.10
Reg.56, revoked: SI 1996/1592 Reg.35, Sch.10

1581. Construction (Lifting Operations) Regulations 1961
revoked: SI 1998/2307 Reg.17, Sch.2
Reg.3, amended: SI 1996/1592 Reg.34, Sch.9 para.3
Reg.3, revoked: SI 1998/2307 Reg.17, Sch.2
Reg.16, revoked: SI 1998/2307 Reg.17, Sch.2
Reg.28, applied: SI 1998/2307 Reg.9
Reg.28, revoked: SI 1998/2307 Reg.17, Sch.2
Reg.40, applied: SI 1998/2307 Reg.9
Reg.40, revoked: SI 1998/2307 Reg.17, Sch.2
Reg.46, applied: SI 1998/2307 Reg.9
Reg.46, revoked: SI 1998/2307 Reg.17, Sch.2
Reg.48A, added: SI 1996/1592 Reg.34, Sch.9 para.3
Reg.48A, revoked: SI 1998/2307 Reg.17, Sch.2
Reg.48B, added: SI 1996/1592 Reg.34, Sch.9 para.3
Reg.48B, revoked: SI 1998/2307 Reg.17, Sch.2

2192. Cambridge Waterworks Order 1961
s.5, revoked: SI 1996/713 Art.4, Sch.2 Part II
s.6, revoked: SI 1996/713 Art.4, Sch.2 Part II
s.7, revoked: SI 1996/713 Art.4, Sch.2 Part II
s.8, revoked: SI 1996/713 Art.4, Sch.2 Part II
s.9, revoked: SI 1996/713 Art.4, Sch.2 Part II

2203. Direct Grant Schools Amending Regulations No.1 1961
revoked: SI 1998/86 Reg.2, Sch.1

2444. Grimethorpe Mine (Diesel Vehicles) Special Regulations 1961
Reg.4, revoked: SI 1996/192 Reg.20, Sch.15 Part I
Reg.5, revoked: SI 1996/192 Reg.20, Sch.15 Part I
Reg.6, revoked: SI 1996/192 Reg.20, Sch.15 Part I

2445. Lynemouth Mine (Diesel Vehicles and Storage Battery Vehicles) Special Regulations 1961
Reg.4, revoked: SI 1996/192 Reg.20, Sch.15 Part I
Reg.5, revoked: SI 1996/192 Reg.20, Sch.15 Part I
Reg.6, revoked: SI 1996/192 Reg.20, Sch.15 Part I
Reg.7, revoked: SI 1996/192 Reg.20, Sch.15 Part I

NO.

2482. Stourbridge and District Water Board Order 1961
Art.11, referred to: 1998 c.43 s.1, Sch.1 Part V
Art.11, revoked: 1998 c.43 s.1, Sch.1 Part V
Sch.2, revoked: 1998 c.43 s.1, Sch.1 Part V

1962

Dunbartonshire Educational Trust Scheme 1962
amended: SI 1996/629 Sch
London Traffic (Prescribed Routes) (Lewisham) Regulations 1962
revoked: SI 1998/1705 Art.6
225. Construction (Lifting Operations) Reports Order 1962
revoked: SI 1998/2307 Reg.17, Sch.2
226. Construction (Lifting Operations) Prescribed Particulars Order 1962
revoked: SI 1998/2307 Reg.17, Sch.2
469. Chester Water (Capital) Order 1962
revoked: SI 1998/281 Art.4, Sch.2 Part II
654. Chester Water (Charges) Order 1962
revoked: SI 1998/281 Art.4, Sch.2 Part II
655. Chester Water Order 1962
Art.3, revoked (in part): SI 1998/281 Art.4, Sch.2 Part II
Art.4, revoked: SI 1998/281 Art.4, Sch.2 Part II
Art.6, revoked: SI 1998/281 Art.4, Sch.2 Part II
715. Hoists Exemption Order 1962
revoked: SI 1998/2307 Reg.17, Sch.2
717. Herefordshire Water Board Order 1962
revoked: 1998 c.43 s.1, Sch.1 Part V
931. Calverton Mine (Diesel Vehicles) Special Regulations 1962
Reg.4, revoked: SI 1996/192 Reg.20, Sch.15 Part I
Reg.5, revoked: SI 1996/192 Reg.20, Sch.15 Part I
Reg.6, revoked: SI 1996/192 Reg.20, Sch.15 Part I
1094. Brightling Mine (Diesel Vehicles) Special Regulations 1962
Reg.5, revoked: SI 1996/192 Reg.20, Sch.15 Part I
Reg.6, revoked: SI 1996/192 Reg.20, Sch.15 Part I
Reg.7, revoked: SI 1996/192 Reg.20, Sch.15 Part I
1199. Police Grant (Scotland) Order 1962
revoked: SI 1996/780 Art.7, Sch.2
1472. Agriculture (Field Machinery) Regulations 1962
revoked: SI 1996/3022 Reg.2, Sch Part II
1550. Jamaica (Constitution) Order in Council 1962
Sch.2 s.110, see *Williams (Kervin) v The Queen* [1997] A.C. 624 (PC), Lord Hutton
1561. North West Worcestershire Water Board Order 1962
revoked (in part): 1998 c.43 s.1, Sch.1 Part V
Art.1, referred to: 1998 c.43 s.1, Sch.1 Part V
Art.3, referred to: 1998 c.43 s.1, Sch.1 Part V
Art.26, referred to: 1998 c.43 s.1, Sch.1 Part V
Art.28, referred to: 1998 c.43 s.1, Sch.1 Part V
Art.30, referred to: 1998 c.43 s.1, Sch.1 Part V
Art.31, referred to: 1998 c.43 s.1, Sch.1 Part V
Sch.7, referred to: 1998 c.43 s.1, Sch.1 Part V
Sch.7, revoked (in part): 1998 c.43 s.1, Sch.1 Part V

NO.

1962—cont.

1676. Easington Mine (Diesel Vehicles) Special Regulations 1962
Reg.4, revoked: SI 1996/192 Reg.20, Sch.15 Part I
Reg.5, revoked: SI 1996/192 Reg.20, Sch.15 Part I
Reg.6, revoked: SI 1996/192 Reg.20, Sch.15 Part I

1765. Professions Supplementary to Medicine (Registration Rules) Order of Council 1962
Sch., amended: SI 1996/2945 Sch. r.2, SI 1997/2562 Sch. r.2, SI 1999/1028 Sch. r.2
Sch. r.16, amended: SI 1997/2562 Sch.r.2, SI 1999/1028 Sch. r.2

2059. Rufford Mine (Diesel Vehicles) Special Regulations 1962
Reg.4, revoked: SI 1996/192 Reg.20, Sch.15 Part I
Reg.5, revoked: SI 1996/192 Reg.20, Sch.15 Part I
Reg.6, revoked: SI 1996/192 Reg.20, Sch.15 Part I

2114. Trelewis Drift Mine (Diesel Vehicles) Special Regulations 1962
Reg.4, revoked: SI 1996/192 Reg.20, Sch.15 Part I
Reg.5, revoked: SI 1996/192 Reg.20, Sch.15 Part I
Reg.6, revoked: SI 1996/192 Reg.20, Sch.15 Part I

2130. Cambridge Waterworks (No.2) Order 1962
revoked: SI 1996/713 Art.4, Sch.2 Part II

2193. Wharncliffe Woodmoor 4 and 5 Mine (Diesel Vehicles) Special Regulations 1962
Reg.4, revoked: SI 1996/192 Reg.20, Sch.15 Part I
Reg.5, revoked: SI 1996/192 Reg.20, Sch.15 Part I
Reg.6, revoked: SI 1996/192 Reg.20, Sch.15 Part I

2512. Seaham Mine (Diesel Vehicles) Special Regulations 1962
Reg.4, revoked: SI 1996/192 Reg.20, Sch.15 Part I
Reg.5, revoked: SI 1996/192 Reg.20, Sch.15 Part I
Reg.6, revoked: SI 1996/192 Reg.20, Sch.15 Part I

1963

118. Dawdon Mine (Diesel Vehicles) Special Regulations 1963
Reg.4, revoked: SI 1996/192 Reg.20, Sch.15 Part I
Reg.5, revoked: SI 1996/192 Reg.20, Sch.15 Part I
Reg.6, revoked: SI 1996/192 Reg.20, Sch.15 Part I

262. Herefordshire Water Board Order 1963
revoked: 1998 c.43 s.1, Sch.1 Part V

373. Kincardineshire Educational Trust Scheme Order in Council 1963
amended: SI 1996/478 Sch

708. Town and Country Planning (Use Classes) Order 1963
see *Ashworth Frazer Ltd v Gloucester City Council (Consent to Assignment)* Times, April 1, 1999 (Ch D), David Donaldson Q.C.

NO.

1963—cont.

825. Thoresby Mine (Diesel Vehicles) Special Regulations 1963
Reg.4, revoked: SI 1996/192 Reg.20, Sch.15 Part I
Reg.5, revoked: SI 1996/192 Reg.20, Sch.15 Part I
Reg.6, revoked: SI 1996/192 Reg.20, Sch.15 Part I

1096. Westoe Mine (Diesel Vehicles) Special Regulations 1963
Reg.4, revoked: SI 1996/192 Reg.20, Sch.15 Part I
Reg.5, revoked: SI 1996/192 Reg.20, Sch.15 Part I
Reg.6, revoked: SI 1996/192 Reg.20, Sch.15 Part I

1136. Herefordshire Water Board (No.2) Order 1963
Art.3, revoked: 1998 c.43 s.1, Sch.1 Part V

1321. Morgan Trust Scheme 1963
amended: SI 1996/477 Sch

1379. Direct Grant Schools Amending Regulations 1963
revoked: SI 1998/86 Reg.2, Sch.1

1498. Webster and Davidson Mortification for the Blind Scheme 1963
amended: SI 1996/477 Sch

1618. Silverwood Mine (Diesel Vehicles) Special Regulations 1963
Reg.4, revoked: SI 1996/192 Reg.20, Sch.15 Part I
Reg.5, revoked: SI 1996/192 Reg.20, Sch.15 Part I
Reg.6, revoked: SI 1996/192 Reg.20, Sch.15 Part I

1918. Dockyard Port of Portland Order 1963
revoked: SI 1997/2949 Art.57

2001. Food (Preparation and Distribution of Meat) (Scotland) Regulations 1963
revoked: SI 1996/497 Reg.2

2074. Charities (Exception from Registration and Accounts) Regulations 1963
revoked: SI 1996/180 Reg.3

2085. Federation of Rhodesia and Nyasaland (Dissolution) Order in Council 1963
s.16, revoked (in part): 1998 c.43 s.1, Sch.1 Part IV

1964

Ecclesiastical Jurisdiction (Discipline) Rules 1964
r.49, applied: SI 1996/3084 Appendix para.4, SI 1997/1890 Appendix para.4, SI 1998/1712 Appendix para.4, SI 1999/2108 Appendix para.4

28. Election Petition Rules 1964
applied: SI 1996/1220 Art.3
r.1, amended: SI 1998/1287 Art.3, Sch.2
r.1, applied: SI 1996/1220 Art.3, Sch.2, SI 1998/1287 Art.3, Sch.2
r.2, amended: SI 1998/1287 Art.3, Sch.2
r.2, applied: SI 1996/1220 Art.3, Sch.2, SI 1998/1287 Art.3, Sch.2
r.3, amended: SI 1996/1220 Art.3, Sch.2, SI 1998/1287 Art.3, Sch.2
r.3, applied: SI 1998/1287 Art.3, Sch.2
r.4, amended: SI 1998/1287 Art.3, Sch.2
r.4, applied: SI 1996/1220 Art.3, Sch.2, SI 1998/1287 Art.3, Sch.2
r.5, amended: SI 1998/1287 Art.3, Sch.2
r.5, applied: SI 1996/1220 Art.3, Sch.2, SI 1998/1287 Art.3, Sch.2
r.5A, amended: SI 1998/1287 Art.3, Sch.2

NO.

NO.

1964—cont.

1964—cont.

28. Election Petition Rules 1964—*cont.*

r.5A, applied: SI 1996/1220 Art.3, Sch.2, SI 1998/1287 Art.3, Sch.2

r.6, amended: SI 1998/1287 Art.3, Sch.2

r.6, applied: SI 1996/1220 Art.3, Sch.2, SI 1998/1287 Art.3, Sch.2

r.7, amended: SI 1998/1287 Art.3, Sch.2

r.7, applied: SI 1996/1220 Art.3, Sch.2, SI 1998/1287 Art.3, Sch.2

r.8, amended: SI 1996/1220 Art.3, Sch.2, SI 1998/1287 Art.3, Sch.2

r.8, applied: SI 1998/1287 Art.3, Sch.2

r.9, amended: SI 1996/1220 Art.3, Sch.2, SI 1998/1287 Art.3, Sch.2

r.9, applied: SI 1998/1287 Art.3, Sch.2

r.10, amended: SI 1998/1287 Art.3, Sch.2

r.10, applied: SI 1996/1220 Art.3, Sch.2, SI 1998/1287 Art.3, Sch.2

r.12, amended: SI 1998/1287 Art.3, Sch.2

r.12, applied: SI 1996/1220 Art.3, Sch.2, SI 1998/1287 Art.3, Sch.2

r.13, amended: SI 1998/1287 Art.3, Sch.2

r.13, applied: SI 1996/1220 Art.3, Sch.2, SI 1998/1287 Art.3, Sch.2

r.14, amended: SI 1998/1287 Art.3, Sch.2

r.14, applied: SI 1996/1220 Art.3, Sch.2, SI 1998/1287 Art.3, Sch.2

r.15, amended: SI 1998/1287 Art.3, Sch.2

r.15, applied: SI 1996/1220 Art.3, Sch.2, SI 1998/1287 Art.3, Sch.2

r.16, amended: SI 1998/1287 Art.3, Sch.2

r.16, applied: SI 1996/1220 Art.3, Sch.2, SI 1998/1287 Art.3, Sch.2

r.17, amended: SI 1998/1287 Art.3, Sch.2

r.17, applied: SI 1996/1220 Art.3, Sch.2, SI 1998/1287 Art.3, Sch.2

r.18, amended: SI 1998/1287 Art.3, Sch.2

r.18, applied: SI 1996/1220 Art.3, Sch.2, SI 1998/1287 Art.3, Sch.2

r.19, amended: SI 1998/1287 Art.3, Sch.2

r.19, applied: SI 1996/1220 Art.3, Sch.2, SI 1998/1287 Art.3, Sch.2

r.20, amended: SI 1998/1287 Art.3, Sch.2

r.20, applied: SI 1996/1220 Art.3, Sch.2, SI 1998/1287 Art.3, Sch.2

r.21, amended: SI 1998/1287 Art.3, Sch.2

r.21, applied: SI 1996/1220 Art.3, Sch.2, SI 1998/1287 Art.3, Sch.2

r.22, amended: SI 1998/1287 Art.3, Sch.2

r.22, applied: SI 1996/1220 Art.3, Sch.2, SI 1998/1287 Art.3, Sch.2

r.23, amended: SI 1998/1287 Art.3, Sch.2

r.23, applied: SI 1996/1220 Art.3, Sch.2, SI 1998/1287 Art.3, Sch.2

r.24, amended: SI 1998/1287 Art.3, Sch.2

r.24, applied: SI 1996/1220 Art.3, Sch.2, SI 1998/1287 Art.3, Sch.2

r.25, amended: SI 1998/1287 Art.3, Sch.2

r.25, applied: SI 1996/1220 Art.3, Sch.2, SI 1998/1287 Art.3, Sch.2

r.26, amended: SI 1998/1287 Art.3, Sch.2

r.26, applied: SI 1996/1220 Art.3, Sch.2, SI 1998/1287 Art.3, Sch.2

r.27, amended: SI 1998/1287 Art.3, Sch.2

r.27, applied: SI 1996/1220 Art.3, Sch.2, SI 1998/1287 Art.3, Sch.2

Sch. A, amended: SI 1996/1220 Art.3, Sch.2, SI 1998/1287 Art.3, Sch.2

Sch. A, applied: SI 1998/1287 Art.3, Sch.2

Sch. B, amended: SI 1998/1287 Art.3, Sch.2

Sch. B, applied: SI 1996/1220 Art.3, Sch.2, SI 1998/1287 Art.3, Sch.2

388. Prison Rules 1964

applied: SI 1998/1544 r.2

revoked: SI 1999/728 r.85 (with savings), Sch. (with savings)

r.3, revoked: SI 1999/728 r.85 (with savings), Sch. (with savings)

r.4, revoked: SI 1999/728 r.85 (with savings), Sch. (with savings)

r.6, revoked: SI 1999/728 r.85 (with savings), Sch. (with savings)

r.17, amended: SI 1998/1544 r.2, Sch. r.1

r.17, revoked: SI 1999/728 r.85 (with savings), Sch. (with savings)

r.18, amended: SI 1998/1544 r.2, Sch. r.2

r.18, revoked (in part): SI 1998/1544 r.2, Sch. r.2, SI 1999/728 r.85 (with savings), Sch. (with savings)

r.20, revoked: SI 1999/728 r.85 (with savings), Sch. (with savings)

r.21, amended: SI 1998/1544 r.2, Sch. r.3

r.21, revoked (in part): SI 1998/1544 r.2, Sch. r.3, SI 1999/728 r.85 (with savings), Sch. (with savings)

r.22, amended: SI 1998/1544 r.2, Sch. r.4

r.22, revoked: SI 1999/728 r.85 (with savings), Sch. (with savings)

r.26, amended: SI 1998/1544 r.2, Sch. r.5

r.26, revoked: SI 1999/728 r.85 (with savings), Sch. (with savings)

r.27, amended: SI 1998/1544 r.2, Sch. r.6

r.27, revoked: SI 1999/728 r.85 (with savings), Sch. (with savings)

r.27, substituted: SI 1996/1663 r.2, Sch. para.1

r.27A, added: SI 1996/1663 r.2, Sch. para.1

r.27A, revoked: SI 1999/728 r.85 (with savings), Sch. (with savings)

r.28, amended: SI 1998/1544 r.2, Sch. r.7

r.28, revoked: SI 1999/728 r.85 (with savings), Sch. (with savings)

r.33, see *R. v Secretary of State for the Home Department Ex p. O'Dhuibhir* [1997] C.O.D. 315 (CA), Kennedy, L.J.; see *R. v Secretary of State for the Home Department Ex p. Simms* [1997] E.M.L.R. 261 (QBD), Latham, J.; see *R. v Secretary of State for the Home Department Ex p. Simms* [1999] 3 W.L.R. 328 (HL), Lord Steyn

r.33, revoked: SI 1999/728 r.85 (with savings), Sch. (with savings)

r.34, revoked: SI 1999/728 r.85 (with savings), Sch. (with savings)

r.37, see *R. v Secretary of State for the Home Department Ex p. O'Dhuibhir* (1996) 8 Admin. L.R. 121 (QBD), Rose, L.J.

r.37, revoked: SI 1999/728 r.85 (with savings), Sch. (with savings)

r.37A, see *R. v Governor of Whitemoor Prison Ex p. Main* Independent, May 23, 1997 (QBD), Pill, L.J.; see *R. v Secretary of State for the Home Department Ex p. Daly* [1999] C.O.D. 388 (CA), Kennedy, L.J.

r.37A, revoked: SI 1999/728 r.85 (with savings), Sch. (with savings)

r.38, revoked: SI 1999/728 r.85 (with savings), Sch. (with savings)

r.39, amended: SI 1996/1663 r.2, Sch. para.2

r.39, revoked: SI 1999/728 r.85 (with savings), Sch. (with savings)

r.43, amended: SI 1998/1544 r.2, Sch. r.8

r.43, revoked: SI 1999/728 r.85 (with savings), Sch. (with savings)

NO.

1964—cont.

388. Prison Rules 1964—*cont.*
r.43A, added: SI 1998/23 r.2
r.43A, revoked: SI 1999/728 r.85 (with savings), Sch. (with savings)
r.46, amended: SI 1998/1544 r.2, Sch. r.9
r.46, revoked: SI 1999/728 r.85 (with savings), Sch. (with savings)
r.46A, revoked: SI 1999/728 r.85 (with savings), Sch. (with savings)
r.47, see *R. v Governor of Swaleside Prison Ex p. Wynter* (1998) 10 Admin. L.R. 597 (QBD), Blofeld, J.
r.47, amended: SI 1996/1663 r.2, Sch. para.3
r.47, referred to: SI 1999/728 r.85
r.47, revoked: SI 1999/728 r.85 (with savings), Sch. (with savings)
r.49, see *R. v Governor of Swaleside Prison Ex p. Wynter* (1998) 10 Admin. L.R. 597 (QBD), Blofeld, J.
r.49, revoked: SI 1999/728 r.85 (with savings), Sch. (with savings)
r.50, revoked: SI 1999/728 r.85 (with savings), Sch. (with savings)
r.52, revoked: SI 1999/728 r.85 (with savings), Sch. (with savings)
r.53, revoked: SI 1999/728 r.85 (with savings), Sch. (with savings)
r.53, substituted: SI 1998/1544 r.2, Sch. r.10
r.92, amended: SI 1996/1663 r.2, Sch. para.4
r.92, applied: SI 1996/1663 r.3
r.92, revoked: SI 1999/728 r.85 (with savings), Sch. (with savings)
r.97, revoked: SI 1999/728 r.85 (with savings), Sch. (with savings)
r.97, substituted: SI 1996/1663 r.2, Sch. para.5
r.99, revoked: SI 1999/728 r.85 (with savings), Sch. (with savings)

539. Prince of Wales Mine (Diesel Vehicles) Special Regulations 1964
Reg.4, revoked: SI 1996/192 Reg.20, Sch.15 Part I
Reg.5, revoked: SI 1996/192 Reg.20, Sch.15 Part I
Reg.6, revoked: SI 1996/192 Reg.20, Sch.15 Part I

558. Cotton Cloth (Record of Humidity) Order 1964
revoked: SI 1996/3022 Reg.2, Sch Part II

697. Continental Shelf (Designation of Areas) Order 1964
referred to: SI 1999/2031

708. Petroleum (Production) (Continental Shelf and Territorial Sea) Regulations 1964
Sch.2, referred to: 1998 c.17 Sch.1 para.2, SI 1999/160 Sch.2 para.1

905. Herefordshire Water Board (Baron's Cross Water Tower and Pipeline) Order 1964
Art.4, revoked: 1998 c.43 s.1, Sch.1 Part V
Art.5, revoked: 1998 c.43 s.1, Sch.1 Part V

971. Prescribed Dangerous Machines Order 1964
revoked: SI 1998/2306 Reg.39, Sch.4

1003. Special Roads (Notice of Opening) (Scotland) Regulations 1964
see *Donaldson v Valentine* 1996 S.L.T. 643
applied: SI 1996/2448 Reg.1, SI 1996/2863 Reg.1

1049. Worcester Water Order 1964
Art.5, revoked: 1998 c.43 s.1, Sch.1 Part V
Sch.1, revoked (in part): 1998 c.43 s.1, Sch.1 Part V

NO.

1964—cont.

1079. Industrial Training (Construction Board) Order 1964
referred to: SI 1999/1319 Sch.

1086. Industrial Training (Engineering Board) Order 1964
referred to: SI 1999/1319 Sch.

1143. Act of Sederunt (Confirmation of Executors) 1964
applied: SI 1997/3070 Reg.3

1225. Cwmgwili Mine (Diesel Vehicles) Special Regulations 1964
Reg.4, revoked: SI 1996/192 Reg.20, Sch.15 Part I
Reg.5, revoked: SI 1996/192 Reg.20, Sch.15 Part I
Reg.6, revoked: SI 1996/192 Reg.20, Sch.15 Part I

1312. Direct Grant Schools Amending Regulations 1964
revoked: SI 1998/86 Reg.2, Sch.1

1456. British Transport Police Force Scheme 1963 (Approval) Order 1964
Sch., referred to: SI 1999/1306 Art.24

1476. Wearmouth Mine (Diesel Vehicles) Special Regulations 1964
Reg.4, revoked: SI 1996/192 Reg.20, Sch.15 Part I
Reg.5, revoked: SI 1996/192 Reg.20, Sch.15 Part I
Reg.6, revoked: SI 1996/192 Reg.20, Sch.15 Part I

1825. Charities (Exception from Registration and Accounts) Regulations 1964
revoked: SI 1996/180 Reg.3

1999. Derwent Water Order 1964
revoked: SI 1996/824 Art.3

2007. Pensions (Polish Forces) Scheme 1964
Art.14, applied: SI 1997/662 Art.2

2043. Diplomatic Privileges (Citizens of the United Kingdom and Colonies) Order 1964
revoked: SI 1999/670 Art.3, Sch.2

2058. War Pensions (Mercantile Marine) Scheme 1964
Sch.7, substituted: SI 1997/811 Art.2, Sch

1965

Territorial Waters Order in Council 1964 1965
referred to: SI 1999/1043 Art.2
Sch., referred to: SI 1999/1043 Art.2
Sch., substituted: SI 1996/1628 Art.2, SI 1998/2564 Art.2

1. Direct Grant Schools Amending Regulations 1965
revoked: SI 1998/86 Reg.2, Sch.1

4. Herefordshire Water Board (Withington) Order 1965
Art.5, revoked: 1998 c.43 s.1, Sch.1 Part V
Sch.2, revoked: 1998 c.43 s.1, Sch.1 Part V

145. Transfer of Functions (Shipping and Construction of Ships) Order 1965
Sch.1, amended: SI 1999/3445 Reg.15, Sch.4 para.2

155. Herefordshire Water Board Order 1965
revoked: 1998 c.43 s.1, Sch.1 Part V

251. Ecclesiastical Jurisdiction (Faculty Appeals) Rules 1965
applied: SI 1996/3085 Sch. Table II
revoked: SI 1998/1713 r.1

NO.

316. **Perth and Kinross Educational Trust Scheme Order in Council 1965**
amended: SI 1996/477 Sch
319. **Secretary of State for Wales and Minister of Land and Natural Resources Order 1965**
Art.6, referred to: SI 1999/672 Art.2, Sch.1
321. **Act of Sederunt (Rules of the Court, Consolidation and Amendment) 1965**
r.131, applied: SI 1996/207 Sch.8 para.43, SI 1996/2890 Sch.4 para.47
537. **Superannuation (Inner London Magistrates' Courts) Regulations 1965**
Reg.2, applied: SI 1997/1612 Reg.127
621. **London Authorities (Superannuation) Order 1965**
Art.14, applied: SI 1997/1612 Sch.5
Art.15, applied: SI 1997/1612 Sch.5
1124. **Diplomatic Privileges (Citizens of the United Kingdom and Colonies) Order 1965**
revoked: SI 1999/670 Art.3, Sch.2
1168. **Act of Sederunt (Betting, Gaming and Lotteries Act Appeals) 1965**
revoked: SI 1999/929 r.1.3, Sch.2
1194. **Bevercotes Mine (Diesel Vehicles) Special Regulations 1965**
Reg.4, revoked: SI 1996/192 Reg.20, Sch.15 Part I
Reg.5, revoked: SI 1996/192 Reg.20, Sch.15 Part I
Reg.6, revoked: SI 1996/192 Reg.20, Sch.15 Part I
1395. **Agriculture (Poisonous Substances) (Extension) Order 1965**
revoked: SI 1996/3022 Reg.2, Sch Part II
1420. **Government Stock Regulations 1965**
Reg.1, amended: SI 1997/1709 Reg.3
Reg.2, applied: SI 1998/1446 Art.25
Reg.3C, added: SI 1998/1749 Reg.3
Reg.3D, added: SI 1998/1749 Reg.3
Reg.3E, added: SI 1998/1749 Reg.3
Reg.4, amended: SI 1997/1709 Reg.4, SI 1998/1749 Reg.6
Reg.4, applied: SI 1998/1446 Art.11
Reg.6, applied: SI 1998/1446 Art.27
Reg.8, applied: SI 1998/1446 Art.11, Art.12, Art.13
Reg.10, applied: SI 1998/1446 Art.11
Reg.14, referred to: SI 1998/1446 Art.16
Reg.14, substituted: SI 1997/1709 Reg.8
Reg.16, amended: SI 1997/1709 Reg.9
Reg.17, applied: SI 1998/1446 Art.12, Art.13
Reg.18A, added: SI 1997/1709 Reg.5
Reg.23, amended: SI 1997/1709 Reg.6, SI 1998/1749 Reg.4, SI 1999/1410 Reg.2
Sch.2, revoked: SI 1997/1709 Reg.7
Sch.3, added: SI 1998/1749 Reg.5, Sch.
1441. **Power Presses Regulations 1965**
revoked: SI 1998/2306 Reg.39, Sch.4
Reg.5, applied: SI 1998/2306 Reg.32
Reg.5, revoked: SI 1998/2306 Reg.39, Sch.4
Reg.12, revoked: SI 1998/2306 Reg.39, Sch.4
1531. **Continental Shelf (Designation of Additional Areas) Order 1965**
referred to: SI 1999/2031, SI 1999/2031 Art.2, Sch.
1535. **International Headquarters and Defence Organisations (Designation and Privileges) Order 1965**
Sch. Part II, substituted: SI 1999/1735 Art.2

NO.

1536. **Visiting Forces and International Headquarters (Application of Law) Order 1965**
referred to: SI 1996/2824 Reg.48, SI 1999/2864 Reg.3, Reg.51
revoked: SI 1999/1736 Art.19, Sch.9
Art.3, amended: SI 1998/253 Art.2
Art.7, amended: SI 1998/253 Art.2
1776. **Rules of the Supreme Court 1965**
see *Manifest Shipping & Co Ltd v Uni-Polaris Shipping Co Ltd (The Star Sea)* [1997] 1 Lloyd's Rep. 360 (CA), Leggatt, L.J.; see *Mordant (A Bankrupt), Re (1993)* [1996] 1 F.L.R. 334 (Ch D), Sir Donald Nicholls, V.C.; see *Morris v Banque Arab et Internationale d'Investissement SA* Times, December 23, 1999 (Ch D), Neuberger, J.; see *Nyckeln Finance Ltd (In Administration) v Edward Symmons & Partners (A Firm)* [1996] P.N.L.R. 245 (CA), Hirst, L.J.; see *Practice Direction (Ch D: Interim Applications to Chancery Division)* [1999] B.C.C. 846 (Ch D), Neuberger, J.; see *Practice Note (Ch D: Civil Procedure Rules)* Times, May 4, 1999 (Ch D), Neuberger, J.; see *UCB Corporate Services Ltd v Halifax (SW) Ltd* Times, December 23, 1999 (CA), Lord Lloyd of Berwick
amended: SI 1998/1898 r.2
applied: SI 1998/1713 r.24
referred to: 1997 c.12 Sch.1 para.1
revoked (in part): SI 1998/3132 r.50
Appendix.A Form 8A, added: SI 1996/3219 r.6, Sch.1
Appendix.A Form 14, substituted: SI 1996/2892 r.17, Sch
Appendix.A Form 15, substituted: SI 1996/2892 r.17, Sch
Appendix.A Form 15A, added: SI 1996/3219 r.7, Sch.2
Appendix.A Form 23, amended: SI 1996/2892 r.20
Appendix.A Form 23, substituted: SI 1998/1898 r.19, Sch.1
Appendix.A Form 53, revoked (in part): SI 1996/2892 r.7
Appendix.A Form 54, revoked (in part): SI 1996/2892 r.7
Appendix.A Form 55, added: SI 1996/2892 r.9
Appendix.A Form 56, revoked (in part): SI 1996/2892 r.7
Appendix.A Form 57, revoked (in part): SI 1996/2892 r.7
Appendix.A Form 58, revoked (in part): SI 1996/2892 r.7
Ord. 1,
r.4, see *Macro (Ipswich) Ltd, Re* [1996] 1 W.L.R. 145 (Ch D), Ferris, J.
Ord. 2,
see *Kuwait Oil Tanker Co SAK v Al Bader (No.2)* [1997] 1 W.L.R. 1410 (CA), Staughton, L.J.; see *Oyston v Blaker* [1996] 2 All E.R. 106 (CA), Henry, L.J.; see *Phelps v Spon Smith & Co* Times, November 26, 1999 (Ch D), Nicholas Strauss Q.C.
r.1, see *Chohan Clothing Co (Manchester) Ltd v Fox Brooks Marshall* Times, December 9, 1997 (CA), Evans, L.J.; see *Cooke v Cooke* [1997] 2 B.C.L.C. 28 (Ch D), Chadwick, J.; see *Phelps v Spon Smith & Co* Times, November 26, 1999 (Ch D), Nicholas Strauss Q.C.; see *Riniker v University College London* Times, April 17, 1999 (CA), Evans, L.J.

NO.

1965—cont.

1776. Rules of the Supreme Court 1965—*cont.*
Ord. 3,

see *Al-Fayed v Emanouel Antiques Ltd* [1997] C.L.C. 1,335 (CA), Roch, L.J.; see *Finnegan v Parkside HA* [1998] 1 W.L.R. 411 (CA), Hirst, L.J.; see *Practice Direction (Trial: Setting Down for Trial)* [1996] 1 W.L.R. 1431 (QBD), Senior Master of the Queens Bench Division; see *Sage v South Gloucestershire CC* [1998] E.L.R. 525 (QBD), Hidden, J.

r.5, see *Sage v South Gloucestershire CC* [1999] Ed. C.R. 420 (QBD), Hidden, J.; see *Smith v Keely* [1997] B.P.I.R. 533 (CA), Millett, L.J.

Ord. 4,

see *R. v Leicester Crown Court Ex p. Phipps* (1997) 161 J.P. 505 (QBD), Collins, J.

r.1(1)(a), amended: SI 1997/415 r.6

r.9, see *R. v Leicester Crown Court Ex p. Phipps* Times, April 22, 1997 (QBD), Collins, J.

Ord. 5,

see *Crescent Oil and Shipping Services Ltd v Importang UEE* [1997] 3 All E.R. 428 (QBD (Comm Ct)), Thomas, J.; see *RH Tomlinssons (Trowbridge) Ltd v Secretary of State for the Environment, Transport and the Regions* [1999] 2 B.C.L.C. 760 (CA), Mummery L.J.

r.4, see *High Street Investments Ltd v Bellshore Property Investments Ltd* (1997) 73 P. & C.R. 143 (CA), Leggatt, L.J.

r.6, see *RH Tomlinssons (Trowbridge) Ltd v Secretary of State for the Environment, Transport and the Regions* Times, August 31, 1999 (CA), Mummery L.J.

r.6(2), see *Crescent Oil and Shipping Services Ltd v Importang UEE* [1998] 1 W.L.R. 919 (QBD (Comm Ct)), Thomas, J.

Ord. 6,

see *Crescent Oil and Shipping Services Ltd v Importang UEE* [1998] 1 W.L.R. 919 (QBD (Comm Ct)), Thomas, J.; see *Lewis v Harewood* [1997] P.I.Q.R. P58 (CA), Waite, L.J.

r.2, see *Outwing Construction Ltd v H Randell & Son Ltd* [1999] B.L.R. 156 (QBD (T&CC)), Judge Humphrey Lloyd Q.C.

Ord. 6,

r.7(1), amended: SI 1996/2892 r.2

r.8, see *Vitol Energy (Bermuda) Ltd v Pisco Shipping Co Ltd* [1998] C.L.C. 362 (CA), Hirst, L.J.

r.8(1), see *Vitol Energy (Bermuda) Ltd v Pisco Shipping Co Ltd* [1998] 1 Lloyd's Rep. 509 (CA), Hirst, L.J.

r.8(1), substituted: SI 1996/2892 r.4

r.8(1A), substituted: SI 1996/2892 r.4

Ord. 6.7A,

see *Riniker v University College London* Times April 17, 1999 (CA), Evans, L.J.

Ord. 10,

r.1, see *Robertson v Banham & Co* [1996] 1 All E.R. 79 (CA), Roch, L.J.

r.4, amended: SI 1998/3132 r.50, Sch.1

r.4, applied: SI 1998/3132 r.50, Sch.1

r.4, consolidated: SI 1998/3132 r.50, Sch.1

Ord. 11,

see *Canada Trust Co v Stolzenberg (No.2)* [1998] C.L.C. 23 (CA), Waller, L.J.; see *Citi-March Ltd v Neptune Orient Lines Ltd* [1996] 1 W.L.R. 1367 (QBD), Colman, J.;

NO.

1965—cont.

1776. Rules of the Supreme Court 1965—*cont.*
Ord. 11—*cont.*

see *Excess Insurance Co Ltd v Astra SA Insurance & Reinsurance Co* [1996] L.R.L.R. 380 (CA), Neill, L.J.; see *Firswood Ltd v Petra Bank* [1996] C.L.C. 608 (CA), Schiemann, L.J.; see *Kuwait Oil Tanker Co SAK v Al Bader (No.2)* [1997] 1 W.L.R. 1410 (CA), Staughton, L.J.; see *Ocean Marine Mutual v FAI General Insurance* Independent, October 5, 1998 (C.S.) (QBD (Comm Ct)), Tuckey, J.; see *Schiffahrtsgesellschaft Detlev Von Appen GmbH v Voest Alpine Intertrading GmbH* [1997] 2 Lloyd's Rep. 279 (CA), Hobhouse, L.J.; see *Sharp v Pereira* (1998) 148 N.L.J. Dig. 977 (CA), Lord Woolf, M.R.

applied: SI 1998/3132 r.12.11

referred to: SI 1998/3132 r.6.5

r.1, see *Amoco (UK) Exploration Co v British American Offshore Ltd* [1999] 2 All E.R. (Comm) 201 (QBD (Comm Ct)), Langley, J.; see *Canada Trust Co v Stolzenberg (No.2)* [1998] 1 W.L.R. 547 (CA), Waller, L.J.; see *Ghana Commercial Bank v C* Times, March 3, 1997 (QBD), Peter Leaver Q.C.; see *Kuwait Oil Tanker Co SAK v Al Bader (No.2)* [1997] 2 All E.R. 855 (CA), Staughton, L.J.

r.1, amended: SI 1998/3132 r.50, Sch.1

r.1, applied: SI 1998/3132 r.50, Sch.1

r.1, consolidated: SI 1998/3132 r.50, Sch.1

r.1(1), see *DR Insurance Co v Central National Insurance Co of Omaha* [1996] 1 Lloyd's Rep. 74 (QBD), Martin Moor-Bick Q.C.

r.1(1), amended: SI 1998/3132 r.50, Sch.1

r.1(1), applied: SI 1998/3132 r.6.15, r.50, Sch.1

r.1(1), consolidated: SI 1998/3132 r.50, Sch.1

r.1(1)(b)(m), see *Mercedes-Benz AG v Leiduck* [1996] 1 A.C. 284 (PC), Lord Mustill

r.1(1)(b)(m), amended: SI 1998/3132 r.50, Sch.1

r.1(1)(b)(m), applied: SI 1998/3132 r.50, Sch.1

r.1(1)(b)(m), consolidated: SI 1998/3132 r.50, Sch.1

r.1(1)(c), see *Borealis AB v Stargas Ltd (The Berge Sisar)* [1999] Q.B. 863 (CA), Millett, L.J.

r.1(1)(c), amended: SI 1998/3132 r.50, Sch.1

r.1(1)(c), applied: SI 1998/3132 r.50, Sch.1

r.1(1)(c), consolidated: SI 1998/3132 r.50, Sch.1

r.1(1)(d), see *Fetim BV v Oceanspeed Shipping Ltd (The Flechea)* [1999] 1 Lloyd's Rep. 612 (QBD (Adm Ct)), Moore-Bick, J.; see *Gan Insurance Co Ltd v Tai Ping Insurance Co Ltd* [1999] L.R.L.R. 229 (QBD (Comm Ct)), Cresswell, J.

r.1(1)(d), amended: SI 1998/3132 r.50, Sch.1

r.1(1)(d), applied: SI 1998/3132 r.50, Sch.1

r.1(1)(d), consolidated: SI 1998/3132 r.50, Sch.1

r.1(1)(f), see *Arab Business Consortium International Finance and Investment Co v Banque Franco-Tunisienne* [1996] 1 Lloyd's Rep. 485 (QBD (Comm Ct)), Waller, J.

r.1(1)(f), amended: SI 1998/3132 r.50, Sch.1

NO.

NO.

1965—cont.

1776. Rules of the Supreme Court 1965—*cont.*
Ord. 11—*cont.*

r.1(1)(f), applied: SI 1998/3132 r.50, Sch.1

r.1(1)(f), consolidated: SI 1998/3132 r.50, Sch.1

r.1(2), amended: SI 1996/2892 r.3, SI 1998/ 3132 r.50, Sch.1

r.1(2), applied: SI 1998/3132 r.6.15, r.50, Sch.1

r.1(2), consolidated: SI 1998/3132 r.50, Sch.1

r.1(2)(a), applied: SI 1998/3132 r.12.10

r.1A, amended: SI 1998/3132 r.50, Sch.1

r.1A, applied: SI 1998/3132 r.10.3, r.14.2, r.50, Sch.1

r.1A, consolidated: SI 1998/3132 r.50, Sch.1

r.1B, amended: SI 1998/3132 r.50, Sch.1

r.1B, applied: SI 1998/3132 r.15.4, r.50, Sch.1

r.1B, consolidated: SI 1998/3132 r.50, Sch.1

r.4, see *Administracion Nacional de Combustibles Alcohol Y Portland (ANCAP) v Ridgley Shipping Inc* [1996] 1 Lloyd's Rep. 570 (QBD (Comm Ct)), Longmore, J.

r.4, amended: SI 1998/3132 r.50, Sch.1

r.4, applied: SI 1998/3132 r.50, Sch.1

r.4, consolidated: SI 1998/3132 r.50, Sch.1

r.4(1)(d), amended: SI 1998/3132 r.50, Sch.1

r.4(1)(d), applied: SI 1998/3132 r.50, Sch.1

r.4(1)(d), consolidated: SI 1998/3132 r.50, Sch.1

r.4(2), amended: SI 1998/3132 r.50, Sch.1

r.4(2), applied: SI 1998/3132 r.50, Sch.1

r.4(2), consolidated: SI 1998/3132 r.50, Sch.1

r.5, amended: SI 1998/3132 r.50, Sch.1

r.5, applied: SI 1998/3132 r.50, Sch.1

r.5, consolidated: SI 1998/3132 r.50, Sch.1

r.6, amended: SI 1998/3132 r.50, Sch.1

r.6, applied: SI 1998/3132 r.50, Sch.1

r.6, consolidated: SI 1998/3132 r.50, Sch.1

r.7, amended: SI 1998/3132 r.50, Sch.1

r.7, applied: SI 1998/3132 r.50, Sch.1

r.7, consolidated: SI 1998/3132 r.50, Sch.1

r.8, amended: SI 1998/3132 r.50, Sch.1

r.8, applied: SI 1998/3132 r.50, Sch.1

r.8, consolidated: SI 1998/3132 r.50, Sch.1

r.8A, added: SI 1997/415 r.2

r.8A, amended: SI 1998/3132 r.50, Sch.1

r.8A, applied: SI 1998/3132 r.50, Sch.1

r.8A, consolidated: SI 1998/3132 r.50, Sch.1

r.9, amended: SI 1998/3132 r.50, Sch.1

r.9, applied: SI 1998/3132 r.50, Sch.1

r.9, consolidated: SI 1998/3132 r.50, Sch.1

r.9(1), amended: SI 1996/3219 r.3, SI 1998/ 3132 r.50, Sch.1

r.9(1), applied: SI 1998/3132 r.50, Sch.1

r.9(1), consolidated: SI 1998/3132 r.50, Sch.1

r.9(4), see *Union Bank of Finland Ltd v Lelakis* [1997] 1 W.L.R. 590 (CA), Henry, L.J.

r.9(4), amended: SI 1996/3219 r.3, SI 1998/ 3132 r.50, Sch.1

r.9(4), applied: SI 1998/3132 r.50, Sch.1

r.9(4), consolidated: SI 1998/3132 r.50, Sch.1

r.10, amended: SI 1998/3132 r.50, Sch.1

r.10, applied: SI 1998/3132 r.50, Sch.1

r.10, consolidated: SI 1998/3132 r.50, Sch.1

1965—cont.

1776. Rules of the Supreme Court 1965—*cont.*
Ord. 12,

see *Amoco (UK) Exploration Co v British American Offshore Ltd* [1999] 2 All E.R. (Comm) 201 (QBD (Comm Ct)), Langley, J.; see *Mohammed v Bank of Kuwait and the Middle East KSC* [1996] 1 W.L.R. 1483 (CA), Evans, L.J.; see *Robertson v Banham & Co* [1996] 1 All E.R. 79 (CA), Roch, L.J.

r.8, see *Firswood Ltd v Petra Bank* [1996] C.L.C. 608 (CA), Schiemann, L.J.; see *New Hampshire Insurance Co Ltd v Phillips Electronics North America Corp* [1998] C.L.C. 1062 (CA), Phillips, L.J.; see *Sithole v Thor Chemicals Holdings Ltd* Times, February 15, 1999 (CA), Tuckey, L.J.

Ord. 13,

see *Berliner Bank v Karageorgis* [1996] 1 Lloyd's Rep. 426 (QBD (Comm Ct)), Colman, J.; see *Day v Royal Automobile Club Motoring Services Ltd* [1999] 1 W.L.R. 2150 (CA), Ward, L.J.; see *Mullen v Conoco Ltd* [1998] Q.B. 382 (CA), Evans, L.J.

r.1, see *Bank of Credit and Commerce International (Overseas) Ltd (In Liquidation) v Habib Bank Ltd* [1999] 1 W.L.R. 42 (Ch D), Park, J.

r.9, see *Bank of Credit and Commerce International (Overseas) Ltd (In Liquidation) v Habib Bank Ltd* [1999] 1 W.L.R. 42 (Ch D), Park, J.; see *Day v RAC Motoring Services Ltd* [1999] 1 All E.R. 1007 (CA), Ward, L.J.; see *Mullen v Conoco Ltd* [1998] Q.B. 382 (CA), Evans, L.J.

Ord. 14,

see *Aetna Reinsurance Co (UK) Ltd v Central Reinsurance Corp Ltd* [1996] L.R.L.R. 165 (QBD (Comm Ct)), Longmore, J.; see *Amadeus Trading Ltd, Re* Times, April 1, 1997 (Ch D (Companies Court)), Robert Walker, J.; see *Barclays Bank Plc v Piper* [1996] 5 Bank. L.R. 9 (CA), Roch, L.J.; see *Bass Brewers Ltd v Appleby* (1997) 73 P. & C.R. 165 (CA), Millett, L.J.; see *Batjac Productions Inc v Simitar Entertainment (UK) Ltd* [1996] F.S.R. 139 (Ch D), Harman, J.; see *BBC Worldwide Ltd v Pally Screen Printing Ltd* [1998] F.S.R. 665 (Ch D), Laddie, J.; see *Bowater Windows Ltd v Aspen Windows Ltd* [1999] F.S.R. 759 (Ch D), Rimer, J.; see *Coca-Cola Financial Corp v Finsat International Ltd (The Ira)* [1998] Q.B. 43 (CA), Neill, L.J.; see *Commercial Union Assurance Co Plc v NRG Victory Reinsurance Ltd* [1998] 2 All E.R. 434 (CA), Potter, L.J.; see *Corporacion Nacional del Cobre de Chile v Metallgesellschaft AG Ltd* [1999] C.P.L.R. 309 (Ch D), Judge Colyer Q.C.; see *Demite Ltd v Protec Health Ltd* [1998] B.C.C. 638 (Ch D), Park, J.; see *DG Finance Ltd v Scott and Eagle Star Insurance Co Ltd* [1999] Lloyd's Rep. I.R. 387 (CA), Hobhouse, L.J.; see *Halki Shipping Corp v Sopex Oils Ltd (The Halki)* [1998] 1 W.L.R. 726 (CA), Henry, L.J.; see *Hill v Mercantile and General Reinsurance Co Plc* [1996] 1 W.L.R. 1239 (HL), Lord Mustill; see *Lordsvale Finance Plc v Bank of Zambia* [1996] Q.B. 752 (QBD), Colman, J.; see *McCauley v Hope*

NO.

1965—cont.

1776. Rules of the Supreme Court 1965—*cont.*
Ord. 14—*cont.*

[1999] P.I.Q.R. P185 (CA), Butler-Sloss, L.J.; see *Pacific and General Insurance Co Ltd (in liquidation) v Baltica Insurance Co (UK) Ltd* [1996] L.R.L.R. 8 (QBD (Comm Ct)), Rix, J.; see *Practice Direction (CA: Hear-by Dates)* [1998] 1 W.L.R. 1699 (CA), Lord Woolf, M.R.; see *Society of Lloyd's v Fraser* [1999] Lloyd's Rep. I.R. 156 (CA), Hobhouse, L.J.; see *Star Rider Ltd v Inntrepreneur Pub Co* [1998] 1 E.G.L.R. 53 (Ch D), Blackburne, J.; see *UPS Ltd v Lewis* Independent, February 23, 1998 (C.S.) (CA), Kennedy, L.J.

r.2, see *Petrolite Holdings Inc v Dyno Oil Field Chemicals UK Ltd* [1998] F.S.R. 190 (Ch D), Laddie, J.; see *Structural Polymer Systems Ltd v Brown (The Baltic Universal)* [1999] C.L.C. 268 (QBD (Comm Ct)), Moore-Bick, J.

r.4, see *International Asset Control Ltd (t/a IAC Films) v Films Sans Frontieres Sarl* Times, October 26, 1998 (CA), Waller, L.J.

r.4(3), see *International Asset Control Ltd (t/a IAC Films) v Films Sans Frontieres Sarl* [1999] E.M.L.R. 268 (CA), Waller, L.J.

Ord. 14A,

see *B (Deceased), Re* [1999] Ch. 206 (Ch D), Jonathan Parker, J.; see *Berkoff v Burchill* [1996] 4 All E.R. 1008 (CA), Neill, L.J.; see *Brain (Patrick John) v Ingledew Brown Bennison and Garrett (A Firm)* [1996] F.S.R. 341 (CA), Aldous, L.J.; see *Credit Lyonnais v New Hampshire Insurance Co* [1997] 1 Lloyd's Rep. 191 (QBD), Barbara Dohmann Q.C.; see *Harwood (t/a RSBS Group) v Smith* [1998] 1 E.G.L.R. 5 (CA), Hobhouse, L.J.; see *Masters v Leaver (No.2)* Times, August 5, 1999 (CA), Morritt, L.J.; see *Mohamed v Alaga & Co* [1998] 2 All E.R. 720 (Ch D), Lightman, J.; see *Practice Direction (CA: Hear-by Dates)* [1998] 1 W.L.R. 1699 (CA), Lord Woolf, M.R.; see *Ramanathan Rudra v Abbey National Plc* Independent, March 9, 1998 (C.S.) (CA), Schiemann, L.J.

Ord. 15,

see *Barings Plc v Coopers & Lybrand* Times, August 13, 1996 (Ch D), Chadwick, J.; see *Official Receiver v Pafundo* [1998] 1 B.C.L.C. 208 (CA), Morritt, L.J.; see *Mid East Trading Ltd, Re* [1997] 3 All E.R. 481 (Ch D), Evans-Lombe, J.; see *NP Engineering and Security Products Ltd, Re* [1998] 1 B.C.L.C. 208 (CA), Morritt, L.J.; see *T v T (Joinder of Third Parties)* [1996] 2 F.L.R. 357 (Fam Div), Wilson, J.; see *Wood v Perfection Travel Ltd* [1996] L.R.L.R. 233 (CA), Hirst, L.J.; see *Yorkshire RHA v Fairclough Building Ltd and Percy Thomas Partnership* [1996] 1 W.L.R. 210 (CA), Millett, L.J.

r.1, see *Cooke v Cooke* [1997] 2 B.C.L.C. 28 (Ch D), Chadwick, J.

r.2(3), see *Ernst & Young v Butte Mining Plc* [1996] 2 All E.R. 623 (Ch D), Robert Walker, J.

NO.

1965—cont.

1776. Rules of the Supreme Court 1965—*cont.*
Ord. 15—*cont.*

r.6, see *Albert v Albert* [1997] 2 F.L.R. 791 (CA), Millett, L.J.; see *Blenheim Leisure (Restaurants) Ltd, Re* Times, August 13, 1999 (CA), Aldous, L.J.; see *International Bulk Shipping and Services Ltd v Minerals and Metals Trading Corp of India* [1996] 1 All E.R. 1017 (CA), Evans, L.J.; see *Philip Powis Ltd, Re* [1998] 1 B.C.L.C. 440 (CA), Morritt, L.J.; see *Wood v Perfection Travel Ltd* [1996] L.R.L.R. 233 (CA), Hirst, L.J.

r.6(2)(b), see *Link Organisation Plc v North Derbyshire Tertiary College* [1999] Ed. C.R. 967 (CA), Buxton, L.J.; see *Myers v Dortex International Ltd* Times, March 18, 1999 (CA), Buxton, L.J.; see *Philip Powis Ltd, Re* Times, March 6, 1998 (CA), Morritt, L.J.

r.6A, amended: SI 1998/3132 r.50, Sch.1

r.6A, applied: SI 1998/3132 r.50, Sch.1

r.6A, consolidated: SI 1998/3132 r.50, Sch.1

r.7, see *Clive Brooks and Co Ltd v Baynard* Times, April 30, 1998 (CA), Roch, L.J.; see *Industrie Chimiche Italia Centrale v Alexander G Tsavliris & Sons Maritime Co (The Choko Star)* [1996] 1 W.L.R. 774 (QBD (Comm Ct)), Mance, J.; see *Ord v Belhaven Pubs Ltd* [1998] B.C.C. 607 (CA), Hobhouse, L.J.; see *Saigol v Cranley Mansions Ltd* [1996] E.G.C.S. 81 (CA), Henry, L.J.; see *Yorkshire RHA v Fairclough Building Ltd and Percy Thomas Partnership* [1996] 1 W.L.R. 210 (CA), Millett, L.J.

r.7, amended: SI 1998/3132 r.50, Sch.1

r.7, applied: SI 1998/3132 r.50, Sch.1

r.7, consolidated: SI 1998/3132 r.50, Sch.1

r.7(2), see *Global Container Lines Ltd v Bonyad Shipping Co (No.2)* [1999] 1 Lloyd's Rep. 287 (QBD (Comm Ct)), Rix, J.; see *Ord v Belhaven Pubs Ltd* [1998] 2 B.C.L.C. 447 (CA), Hobhouse, L.J.

r.7(2), amended: SI 1998/3132 r.50, Sch.1

r.7(2), applied: SI 1998/3132 r.50, Sch.1

r.7(2), consolidated: SI 1998/3132 r.50, Sch.1

r.9, amended: SI 1998/3132 r.50, Sch.1

r.9, applied: SI 1998/3132 r.50, Sch.1

r.9, consolidated: SI 1998/3132 r.50, Sch.1

r.11, amended: SI 1998/3132 r.50, Sch.1

r.11, applied: SI 1998/3132 r.50, Sch.1

r.11, consolidated: SI 1998/3132 r.50, Sch.1

r.12, amended: SI 1998/3132 r.50, Sch.1

r.12, applied: SI 1998/3132 r.50, Sch.1

r.12, consolidated: SI 1998/3132 r.50, Sch.1

r.12(1), see *Chocosuisse Union des Fabricants Suisses de Chocolat v Cadbury Ltd* [1999] E.T.M.R. 1020 (CA), Chadwick, L.J.

r.12A, see *Cooke v Cooke* [1997] 2 B.C.L.C. 28 (Ch D), Chadwick, J.

r.12A, amended: SI 1998/3132 r.50, Sch.1

r.12A, applied: SI 1998/3132 r.50, Sch.1

r.12A, consolidated: SI 1998/3132 r.50, Sch.1

r.13, amended: SI 1998/3132 r.50, Sch.1

r.13, applied: SI 1998/3132 r.50, Sch.1

r.13, consolidated: SI 1998/3132 r.50, Sch.1

r.13A, amended: SI 1998/3132 r.50, Sch.1

r.13A, applied: SI 1998/3132 r.50, Sch.1

r.13A, consolidated: SI 1998/3132 r.50, Sch.1

r.14, amended: SI 1998/3132 r.50, Sch.1

r.14, applied: SI 1998/3132 r.50, Sch.1

r.14, consolidated: SI 1998/3132 r.50, Sch.1

NO.

1965—cont.

1776. Rules of the Supreme Court 1965—*cont.*
Ord. 15—*cont.*
r.15, amended: SI 1998/3132 r.50, Sch.1
r.15, applied: SI 1998/3132 r.50, Sch.1
r.15, consolidated: SI 1998/3132 r.50, Sch.1
r.16, see *DG Finance Ltd v Scott and Eagle Star Insurance Co Ltd* [1999] Lloyd's Rep. I.R. 387 (CA), Hobhouse, L.J.; see *T v Child Support Agency* [1998] 1 W.L.R. 144 (Fam Div), Cazalet, J.
r.16, amended: SI 1998/3132 r.50, Sch.1
r.16, applied: SI 1998/3132 r.50, Sch.1
r.16, consolidated: SI 1998/3132 r.50, Sch.1
r.17, amended: SI 1998/3132 r.50, Sch.1
r.17, applied: SI 1998/3132 r.50, Sch.1
r.17, consolidated: SI 1998/3132 r.50, Sch.1
Ord. 16,
see *Waterford Wedgwood Plc v David Nagli Ltd* [1998] C.L.C. 1011 (Ch D), Charles Aldous Q.C.
r.1, see *Kinnear v Falconfilms NV* [1996] 1 W.L.R. 920 (QBD), Phillips, J.
Ord. 17,
r.1, amended: SI 1998/3132 r.50, Sch.1
r.1, applied: SI 1998/3132 r.50, Sch.1
r.1, consolidated: SI 1998/3132 r.50, Sch.1
r.1(2), amended: SI 1998/3132 r.50, Sch.1
r.1(2), applied: SI 1998/3132 r.50, Sch.1
r.1(2), consolidated: SI 1998/3132 r.50, Sch.1
r.2, amended: SI 1998/3132 r.50, Sch.1
r.2, applied: SI 1998/3132 r.50, Sch.1
r.2, consolidated: SI 1998/3132 r.50, Sch.1
r.2A, added: SI 1996/2892 r.6
r.2A, amended: SI 1998/3132 r.50, Sch.1
r.2A, applied: SI 1998/3132 r.50, Sch.1
r.2A, consolidated: SI 1998/3132 r.50, Sch.1
r.3, amended: SI 1998/3132 r.50, Sch.1
r.3, applied: SI 1998/3132 r.50, Sch.1
r.3, consolidated: SI 1998/3132 r.50, Sch.1
r.4, amended: SI 1998/3132 r.50, Sch.1
r.4, applied: SI 1998/3132 r.50, Sch.1
r.4, consolidated: SI 1998/3132 r.50, Sch.1
r.5, amended: SI 1998/3132 r.50, Sch.1
r.5, applied: SI 1998/3132 r.50, Sch.1
r.5, consolidated: SI 1998/3132 r.50, Sch.1
r.6, amended: SI 1998/3132 r.50, Sch.1
r.6, applied: SI 1998/3132 r.50, Sch.1
r.6, consolidated: SI 1998/3132 r.50, Sch.1
r.7, amended: SI 1998/3132 r.50, Sch.1
r.7, applied: SI 1998/3132 r.50, Sch.1
r.7, consolidated: SI 1998/3132 r.50, Sch.1
r.8, amended: SI 1998/3132 r.50, Sch.1
r.8, applied: SI 1998/3132 r.50, Sch.1
r.8, consolidated: SI 1998/3132 r.50, Sch.1
r.8(1), added: SI 1998/1898 r.12
r.8(1), amended: SI 1998/3132 r.50, Sch.1
r.8(1), applied: SI 1998/3132 r.50, Sch.1
r.8(1), consolidated: SI 1998/3132 r.50, Sch.1
r.8(2), added: SI 1998/1898 r.12
r.8(2), amended: SI 1998/3132 r.50, Sch.1
r.8(2), applied: SI 1998/3132 r.50, Sch.1
r.8(2), consolidated: SI 1998/3132 r.50, Sch.1
r.9, amended: SI 1998/3132 r.50, Sch.1
r.9, applied: SI 1998/3132 r.50, Sch.1
r.9, consolidated: SI 1998/3132 r.50, Sch.1
r.9(1), amended: SI 1998/3132 r.50, Sch.1
r.9(1), applied: SI 1998/3132 r.50, Sch.1
r.9(1), consolidated: SI 1998/3132 r.50, Sch.1
r.10, amended: SI 1998/3132 r.50, Sch.1
r.10, applied: SI 1998/3132 r.50, Sch.1

1965—cont.

1776. Rules of the Supreme Court 1965—*cont.*
Ord. 17—*cont.*
r.10, consolidated: SI 1998/3132 r.50, Sch.1
r.11, amended: SI 1998/3132 r.50, Sch.1
r.11, applied: SI 1998/3132 r.50, Sch.1
r.11, consolidated: SI 1998/3132 r.50, Sch.1
Ord. 18,
see *Designers Guild Ltd v Russell Williams (Textiles) Ltd (t/a Washington DC) (No.1)* [1998] F.S.R. 275 (Ch D), Lawrence Collins Q.C.
r.8, see *Brugger v Medicaid* [1996] F.S.R. 362 (Pat Ct), Jacob, J.
r.8(1)(a), see *Cooper v P&O Stena Line Ltd* [1999] 1 Lloyd's Rep. 734 (QBD (Adm Ct)), Judge Belinda Bucknall Q.C.
r.9, see *Circuit Systems Ltd (In Liquidation) v Zuken-Redac (UK) Ltd* [1996] 3 All E.R. 748 (CA), Staughton, L.J.; see *Guinness Peat Group Plc v British Land Co Plc* [1999] 2 B.C.L.C. 243 (CA), Mummery, L.J.; see *Kelley v Corston* Times, August 20, 1997 (CA), Judge, L.J.
r.12, see *Oksuzoglu v Kay* [1998] 2 All E.R. 361 (CA), Brooke, L.J.; see *Tunbridge v Buss Murton & Co* Times, April 8, 1997 (Ch D), Laddie, J.
r.15, see *Phelps v Spon Smith & Co* Times, November 26, 1999 (Ch D), Nicholas Strauss Q.C.
r.19, see *Barakot Ltd v Epiette Ltd* [1998] 1 B.C.L.C. 283 (CA), Beldam, L.J.; see *Cocking v Prudential Assurance Co Ltd* [1996] O.P.L.R. 35 (QBD), Raymond Jack, Q.C.; see *Europe Mortgage Co v Halifax Estate Agencies* [1996] E.G.C.S. 84 (QBD), May, J.; see *HR v JAPT* [1997] O.P.L.R. 123 (Ch D), Lindsay, J.; see *Jones v Vans Colina* [1996] 1 W.L.R. 1580 (CA), Nourse, L.J.; see *Kelley v Corston* [1998] Q.B. 686 (CA), Judge, L.J.; see *Petrolite Holdings Inc v Dyno Oil Field Chemicals UK Ltd* [1998] F.S.R. 190 (Ch D), Laddie, J.; see *Possfund Custodian Trustee Ltd v Diamond* [1996] 1 W.L.R. 1351 (Ch D), Lightman, J.; see *R. v Legal Aid Board Ex p. Owners Abroad (Tour Operator)* [1998] P.I.Q.R. P116 (QBD), Scott Baker, J.; see *Work Model Enterprises Ltd v Ecosystem Ltd and Clix Interiors Ltd* [1996] F.S.R. 356 (Ch D), Jacob, J.
r.19(1), see *Green v Turner* [1999] P.N.L.R. 28 (Ch D), Judge Hegarty Q.C.; see *Kelley v Corston* [1998] 3 W.L.R. 246 (CA), Judge, L.J.
r.19(1)(a), see *Hendry v Chartsearch Ltd* [1998] C.L.C. 1382 (CA), Evans, L.J.
Ord. 19,
see *Bass Holdings Ltd v Brodie* [1998] 1 E.G.L.R. 51 (QBD), Smith, J.; see *Berliner Bank v Karageorgis* [1996] 1 Lloyd's Rep. 426 (QBD (Comm Ct)), Colman, J.
r.2, see *Anson (t/a Party Planners) v Trump* [1998] 1 W.L.R. 1404 (CA), Otton, L.J.
Ord. 20,
see *Beecham Group Plc v Norton Healthcare Ltd (No.1)* [1997] F.S.R. 81 (Pat Ct), Jacob, J.; see *JFS (UK) Ltd v Dwr Cymru Cyf (No.1)* [1999] 1 W.L.R. 231 (CA), Nourse, L.J.; see *Lloyds Bank Plc v Rogers* Times, March 24, 1997 (CA), Hobhouse, L.J.; see *Murray v Hibernian Dance Club* [1997]

NO.

1776. Rules of the Supreme Court 1965—*cont.*
Ord. 20—*cont.*

P.I.Q.R. P46 (CA), Hutchison, L.J.; see *Oates v Harte Reade & Co* [1999] 1 F.L.R. 1221 (QBD), Singer, J.; see *Paragon Finance Plc v Thakerar & Co* Times, August 7, 1998 (CA), Millett, L.J.; see *Signet Group Plc v Hammerson UK Properties Ltd* Times, December 15, 1997 (CA), Lord Woolf, M.R.

r.1, see *Envis v Thakkar* [1997] B.P.I.R. 189 (CA), Kennedy, L.J.; see *Official Receiver v Hannan* Times, March 20, 1997 (CA), Morritt, L.J.

r.5, see *Beecham Group Plc v Norton Healthcare Ltd* [1997] F.S.R. 81 (Pat Ct), Jacob, J.; see *Darlington Building Society v O'Rourke James Scourfield & McCarthy* [1999] Lloyd's Rep. P.N. 33 (CA), Sir Iain Glidewell; see *International Bulk Shipping and Services Ltd v President of India* [1996] 1 All E.R. 1017 (CA), Evans, L.J.; see *JFS (UK) Ltd v Dwr Cymru Cyf* [1999] 1 W.L.R. 231 (CA), Nourse, L.J.; see *Lloyds Bank Plc v Rogers* Times, April 11, 1996 (QBD), Judge Overend Q.C.; see *Paragon Finance Plc v Thakerar & Co* [1999] 1 All E.R. 400 (CA), Millett, L.J.; see *Signet Group Plc v Hammerson UK Properties Ltd* Times, December 15, 1997 (CA), Lord Woolf, M.R.

r.5(5), see *Lloyds Bank Plc v Rogers (No.2)* [1999] 3 E.G.L.R. 83 (CA), Evans, L.J.

r.11, see *Aumac Ltd's Patent, Re* [1996] F.S.R. 843 (CA), Morritt, L.J.; see *Official Receiver v Hannan* [1997] B.C.C. 644 (CA), Morritt, L.J.

Ord. 22,

see *Black v Doncaster MBC* [1998] 3 All E.R. 631 (CA), Stuart-Smith, L.J.; see *Braben v Emap Images Ltd* [1997] 1 W.L.R. 1507 (Ch D), John Cherryman Q.C.; see *Gorse v Tinkler* [1997] P.I.Q.R. Q120 (CA), Sir Iain Glidewell

r.1, see *Braben v Emap Images Ltd* [1997] 1 W.L.R. 1507 (Ch D), John Cherryman Q.C.

r.3, see *Braben v Emap Images Ltd* [1997] 1 W.L.R. 1507 (Ch D), John Cherryman Q.C.

r.5, see *Black v Doncaster MBC* [1999] 1 W.L.R. 53 (CA), Stuart-Smith, L.J.

r.14, see *Malhotra v Dhawan* [1997] 8 Med L.R. 319 (CA), Morritt, L.J.; see *Singh v Parkfield Group Plc* [1996] P.I.Q.R. Q110 (CA), Stuart-Smith, L.J.

Ord. 23,

see *Abraham v Thompson* [1997] 4 All E.R. 362 (CA), Potter, L.J.; see *Condliffe v Hislop* [1996] 1 W.L.R. 753 (CA), Kennedy, L.J.; see *Cripps v Heritage Distribution Corp* Times, November 10, 1999 (CA), Kennedy, L.J.; see *Fitzgerald v Lloyd Williams* [1996] Q.B. 657 (CA), Sir Thomas Bingham, M.R.

r.1, amended: SI 1998/3132 r.50, Sch.1

r.1, applied: SI 1998/3132 r.50, Sch.1

r.1, consolidated: SI 1998/3132 r.50, Sch.1

r.1(1), amended: SI 1998/3132 r.50, Sch.1

r.1(1), applied: SI 1998/3132 r.50, Sch.1

r.1(1), consolidated: SI 1998/3132 r.50, Sch.1

NO.

1776. Rules of the Supreme Court 1965—*cont.*
Ord. 23—*cont.*

r.1(1)(a), see *Chequepoint Sarl v McClelland* [1997] Q.B. 51 (CA), Lord Bingham of Cornhill, L.C.J.; see *Fitzgerald v Williams* [1996] Q.B. 657 (CA), Sir Thomas Bingham, M.R.; see *Greenwich Ltd v National Westminster Bank Plc* [1999] I.L.Pr. 599 (Ch D), Blackburne, J.; see *O'Regan v Williams* Times, January 3, 1996 (CA)

r.1(1)(a), amended: SI 1998/3132 r.50, Sch.1

r.1(1)(a), applied: SI 1998/3132 r.50, Sch.1

r.1(1)(a), consolidated: SI 1998/3132 r.50, Sch.1

r.1(1)(b) see *Martin Boston & Co v Roberts* [1996] 1 P.N.L.R. 45 (CA), Simon Brown, L.J.

r.A1, amended: SI 1998/3132 r.50, Sch.1

r.A1, applied: SI 1998/3132 r.50, Sch.1

r.A1, consolidated: SI 1998/3132 r.50, Sch.1

r.2, amended: SI 1998/3132 r.50, Sch.1

r.2, applied: SI 1998/3132 r.50, Sch.1

r.2, consolidated: SI 1998/3132 r.50, Sch.1

r.3, amended: SI 1998/3132 r.50, Sch.1

r.3, applied: SI 1998/3132 r.50, Sch.1

r.3, consolidated: SI 1998/3132 r.50, Sch.1

Ord. 24,

see *Birmingham Midshires Mortgage Services Ltd v Ansell* [1998] P.N.L.R. 237 (Ch D), Jonathan Parker, J.; see *R. v Arts Council of England Ex p. Women's Playhouse Trust* [1998] C.O.D. 175 (QBD), Laws, J.

r.6, see *Manatee Towing Co Ltd v Oceanbulk Maritime SA* [1999] 1 Lloyd's Rep. 876 (QBD (Comm Ct)), Rix, J.; see *Star News Shops Ltd v Stafford Refrigeration Ltd* [1998] 1 W.L.R. 536 (CA), Otton, L.J.

r.7, see *Forrester v British Railways Board* Times, April 8, 1996 (CA), Aldous, L.J.

r.7A, see *Burns v Shuttlehurst Ltd* [1999] 2 All E.R. 27 (CA), Stuart-Smith, L.J.

r.9, see *Manatee Towing Co Ltd v Oceanbulk Maritime SA* [1999] 1 Lloyd's Rep. 876 (QBD (Comm Ct)), Rix, J.

r.10, see *Clough v Tameside and Glossop HA* [1998] 1 W.L.R. 1478 (QBD), Bracewell, J.

r.11, see *Goodridge v Chief Constable of Hampshire* [1999] 1 W.L.R. 1558 (QBD), Moore-Bick, J.; see *Secretary of State for Trade and Industry v Baker (No.2)* [1998] Ch. 356 (Ch D (Companies Court)), Sir Richard Scott, V.C.

r.13, see *Astra Holdings Plc, Re* [1998] 2 B.C.L.C. 44 (Ch D), Cresswell, J.; see *British & Commonwealth Holdings Plc (In Administration) v Barclays de Zoete Wedd Ltd (No.2)* [1999] 1 B.C.L.C. 86 (Ch D), Neuberger, J.; see *Secretary of State for Trade and Industry v Anderson* Times, December 31, 1997 (Ch D), Cresswell, J.; see *Wallace Smith Trust Co Ltd (In Liquidation) v Deloitte Haskins & Sells* [1997] 1 W.L.R. 257 (CA), Neill, L.J.

r.14A, see *Cunningham v Essex CC* Times, March 31, 1997 (QBD), Geoffrey Rivlin Q.C.; see *Mahon v Rahn* [1998] Q.B. 424 (CA), Otton, L.J.; see *Plant v Plant* [1998] 1 B.C.L.C. 38 (Ch D), Carnwath, J.; see *Smithkline Beecham Biologicals SA v Connaught Laboratories Inc* Times, January 14, 1999 (Ch D), Laddie, J.; see *SmithKline Beecham Biologicals SA v Connaught Laboratories Inc (Disclosure of Docu-*

1965—cont.

1776. Rules of the Supreme Court 1965—*cont.*
Ord. 24—*cont.*
r.14A—*cont.*
ments) [1999] 4 All E.R. 498 (CA), Lord
Bingham of Cornhill, L.C.J.
r.16, see *Star News Shops v Stafford
Refrigeration Ltd* Times, November 18,
1997 (CA), Otton, L.J.
Ord. 25,
r.8, see *Practice Direction (Trial: Setting
Down for Trial)* [1996] 1 W.L.R. 1431
(QBD), Senior Master of the Queens
Bench Division
Ord. 26,
see *Corporacion Nacional del Cobre de Chile
v Metallgesellschaft AG Ltd* [1999]
C.P.L.R. 309 (Ch D), Judge Colyer Q.C.;
see *Hall v Sevalco Ltd* [1996] P.I.Q.R.
P344 (CA), Sir Thomas Bingham, M.R.;
see *UCB Bank Plc v Halifax (SW) Ltd*
[1996] 36 E.G. 148 (QBD), Simon Goldblatt
Q.C.
Ord. 27,
see *Gale v Superdrug Stores Plc* [1996] 1
W.L.R. 1089 (CA), Waite, L.J.
Ord. 28,
r.7(4), added: SI 1997/415 r.3
Ord. 29,
r.1A, see *Belgolaise SA v Rupchandani*
[1999] Lloyd's Rep. Bank. 116 (QBD
(Comm Ct)), Colman, J.; see *Yukong Line
Ltd of Korea v Rendsburg Investments
Corp of Liberia* [1996] 2 Lloyd's Rep. 604
(CA), Phillips, L.J.
r.6, see *Ismail v Richards Butler* [1996] Q.B.
711 (QBD), Moore-Bick, J.
r.7A, see *Unicargo v Flotec Maritime S de RL
(The Cienvik)* [1996] 2 Lloyd's Rep. 395
(QBD (Adm Ct)), Clarke, J.
r.8A, added: SI 1997/415 r.4
r.11, see *Chiron Corp v Murex Diagnostics
Ltd (No.13)* [1996] F.S.R. 578 (Ch D), Robert Walker, J.; see *Sharp v Pereira* Times,
July 25, 1998 (CA), Lord Woolf, M.R.
r.11(2), see *Sharp v Pereira* [1999] 1 W.L.R.
195 (CA), Lord Woolf, M.R.
r.11(2)(a), amended: SI 1996/3219 r.10
r.11(2)(a), substituted: SI 1996/2892 r.5
Ord. 30,
see *Mirror Group Newspapers Plc v Maxwell*
[1998] 1 B.C.L.C. 638 (Ch D), Ferris, J.
r.1, amended: SI 1998/3132 r.50, Sch.1
r.1, applied: SI 1998/3132 r.50, Sch.1
r.1, consolidated: SI 1998/3132 r.50, Sch.1
r.A1, amended: SI 1998/3132 r.50, Sch.1
r.A1, applied: SI 1998/3132 r.50, Sch.1
r.A1, consolidated: SI 1998/3132 r.50, Sch.1
r.2, amended: SI 1998/3132 r.50, Sch.1
r.2, applied: SI 1998/3132 r.50, Sch.1
r.2, consolidated: SI 1998/3132 r.50, Sch.1
r.3, amended: SI 1998/3132 r.50, Sch.1
r.3, applied: SI 1998/3132 r.50, Sch.1
r.3, consolidated: SI 1998/3132 r.50, Sch.1
r.3(2)(b), see *Mirror Group Newspapers Plc v
Maxwell* [1998] 1 B.C.L.C. 638 (Ch D), Ferris, J.
r.3(2)(b), amended: SI 1998/3132 r.50, Sch.1
r.3(2)(b), applied: SI 1998/3132 r.50, Sch.1
r.3(2)(b), consolidated: SI 1998/3132 r.50,
Sch.1
r.4, amended: SI 1998/3132 r.50, Sch.1
r.4, applied: SI 1998/3132 r.50, Sch.1
r.4, consolidated: SI 1998/3132 r.50, Sch.1

1965—cont.

1776. Rules of the Supreme Court 1965—*cont.*
Ord. 30—*cont.*
r.5, amended: SI 1998/3132 r.50, Sch.1
r.5, applied: SI 1998/3132 r.50, Sch.1
r.5, consolidated: SI 1998/3132 r.50, Sch.1
r.6, amended: SI 1998/3132 r.50, Sch.1
r.6, applied: SI 1998/3132 r.50, Sch.1
r.6, consolidated: SI 1998/3132 r.50, Sch.1
r.7, amended: SI 1998/3132 r.50, Sch.1
r.7, applied: SI 1998/3132 r.50, Sch.1
r.7, consolidated: SI 1998/3132 r.50, Sch.1
r.8, amended: SI 1998/3132 r.50, Sch.1
r.8, applied: SI 1998/3132 r.50, Sch.1
r.8, consolidated: SI 1998/3132 r.50, Sch.1
Ord. 31,
see *Wicks v Wicks* [1999] Fam. 65 (CA),
Ward, L.J.
r.1, amended: SI 1998/3132 r.50, Sch.1
r.1, applied: SI 1998/3132 r.50, Sch.1
r.1, consolidated: SI 1998/3132 r.50, Sch.1
r.A1, amended: SI 1998/3132 r.50, Sch.1
r.A1, applied: SI 1998/3132 r.50, Sch.1
r.A1, consolidated: SI 1998/3132 r.50, Sch.1
r.2, amended: SI 1998/3132 r.50, Sch.1
r.2, applied: SI 1998/3132 r.50, Sch.1
r.2, consolidated: SI 1998/3132 r.50, Sch.1
r.3, amended: SI 1998/3132 r.50, Sch.1
r.3, applied: SI 1998/3132 r.50, Sch.1
r.3, consolidated: SI 1998/3132 r.50, Sch.1
r.4, amended: SI 1998/3132 r.50, Sch.1
r.4, applied: SI 1998/3132 r.50, Sch.1
r.4, consolidated: SI 1998/3132 r.50, Sch.1
r.5, amended: SI 1998/3132 r.50, Sch.1
r.5, applied: SI 1998/3132 r.50, Sch.1
r.5, consolidated: SI 1998/3132 r.50, Sch.1
r.6, amended: SI 1998/3132 r.50, Sch.1
r.6, applied: SI 1998/3132 r.50, Sch.1
r.6, consolidated: SI 1998/3132 r.50, Sch.1
r.8, amended: SI 1998/3132 r.50, Sch.1
r.8, applied: SI 1998/3132 r.50, Sch.1
r.8, consolidated: SI 1998/3132 r.50, Sch.1
Ord. 32,
r.3, see *Practice Direction (Supreme Court
Taxing Office: Taxation: Wasted Costs)
(No.1 of 1998)* [1998] 1 W.L.R. 473 (Sup Ct
Taxing Office)
r.6, see *Jones v Vans Colina* [1996] 1 W.L.R.
1580 (CA), Nourse, L.J.
Ord. 33,
r.2, see *Pavey v Ministry of Defence* [1999]
P.I.Q.R. P67 (CA), Beldam, L.J.
r.3, see *Gulf Oil (GB) Ltd v Phillis* [1998]
P.N.L.R. 166 (Ch D), Harman, J.; see
Woodford & Ackroyd v Burgess Times,
February 1, 1999 (CA), Schiemann, L.J.
Ord. 34,
r.2, see *Practice Direction (Trial: Setting
Down for Trial)* [1996] 1 W.L.R. 1431
(QBD), Senior Master of the Queens
Bench Division
r.3, see *Practice Direction (Admiralty and
Commercial Registry: Practice)* [1998] 1
W.L.R. 668 (QBD), Clarke, J.
r.3(1), see *Practice Direction (QBD: Admir-
alty and Commercial Registry: Practice)*
[1998] 1 W.L.R. 668 (QBD), Clarke, J.
r.3(5)(a), amended: SI 1997/415 r.7
Ord. 38,
see *R. v Arts Council of England Ex p. Wom-
en's Playhouse Trust* [1998] C.O.D. 175
(QBD), Laws, J.
r.2, see *R. v Arts Council of England Ex p.
Women's Playhouse Trust* Times, August
20, 1997 (QBD), Laws, J.

NO.

1965—cont.

1776. Rules of the Supreme Court 1965—*cont.*
Ord. 38—*cont.*
    r.2A, see *Gio Personal Investment Services Ltd v Liverpool and London Steamship Protection and Indemnity Association Ltd* [1999] 1 W.L.R. 984 (CA), Potter, L.J.; see *Letpak Ltd v Harris* [1997] P.N.L.R. 239 (CA), Waller, L.J.; see *Mortgage Corp Ltd v Sandoes* [1997] P.N.L.R. 263 (CA), Millett, L.J.
    r.13, see *Canada Trust Co v Stolzenberg* [1997] 1 W.L.R. 1582(CA), Millett, L.J.
    r.20, substituted: SI 1996/3219 r.8
    r.21, substituted: SI 1996/3219 r.8
    r.22, substituted: SI 1996/3219 r.8
    r.23, substituted: SI 1996/3219 r.8
    r.24, substituted: SI 1996/3219 r.8
    r.25, substituted: SI 1996/3219 r.8
    r.26, substituted: SI 1996/3219 r.8
    r.27, substituted: SI 1996/3219 r.8
    r.28, substituted: SI 1996/3219 r.8
    r.29, substituted: SI 1996/3219 r.8
    r.30, substituted: SI 1996/3219 r.8
    r.31, substituted: SI 1996/3219 r.8
    r.32, substituted: SI 1996/3219 r.8
    r.33, substituted: SI 1996/3219 r.8
    r.34, substituted: SI 1996/3219 r.8
    r.36, see *Mortgage Corp Ltd v Sandoes* [1997] P.N.L.R. 263 (CA), Millett, L.J.
Ord. 39,
    see *Batjac Productions Inc v Simitar Entertainment (UK) Ltd* [1996] F.S.R. 139 (Ch D), Harman, J.
Ord. 40,
    see *Abbey National Mortgages Plc v Key Surveyors Nationwide Ltd* [1996] 1 W.L.R. 1534 (CA), Sir Thomas Bingham
Ord. 41,
    see *Oakfame Construction Ltd, Re* [1996] B.C.C. 67 (Ch D)(Companies Court), R Reid Q.C.
    r.5, see *Debtor (No.87 of 1993) (No. 1), Re* [1996] 1 B.C.L.C. 55 (Ch D), Rimer, J.
Ord. 42,
    r.3, see *Nykredit Mortgage Bank Plc v Edward Erdman Group Ltd (No.2)* [1997] 1 W.L.R. 1627 (HL), Lord Nicholls of Birkenhead
Ord. 43,
    see *Whybro v Seymour* [1998] P.I.Q.R. P130 (CA), Otton, L.J.
Ord. 44,
    r.1, amended: SI 1998/3132 r.50, Sch.1
    r.1, applied: SI 1998/3132 r.50, Sch.1
    r.1, consolidated: SI 1998/3132 r.50, Sch.1
    r.2, amended: SI 1998/3132 r.50, Sch.1
    r.2, applied: SI 1998/3132 r.50, Sch.1
    r.2, consolidated: SI 1998/3132 r.50, Sch.1
    r.3, amended: SI 1998/3132 r.50, Sch.1
    r.3, applied: SI 1998/3132 r.50, Sch.1
    r.3, consolidated: SI 1998/3132 r.50, Sch.1
    r.4, amended: SI 1998/3132 r.50, Sch.1
    r.4, applied: SI 1998/3132 r.50, Sch.1
    r.4, consolidated: SI 1998/3132 r.50, Sch.1
    r.5, amended: SI 1998/3132 r.50, Sch.1
    r.5, applied: SI 1998/3132 r.50, Sch.1
    r.5, consolidated: SI 1998/3132 r.50, Sch.1
    r.6, amended: SI 1998/3132 r.50, Sch.1
    r.6, applied: SI 1998/3132 r.50, Sch.1
    r.6, consolidated: SI 1998/3132 r.50, Sch.1
    r.7, amended: SI 1998/3132 r.50, Sch.1
    r.7, applied: SI 1998/3132 r.50, Sch.1

NO.

1965—cont.

1776. Rules of the Supreme Court 1965—*cont.*
Ord. 44—*cont.*
    r.7, consolidated: SI 1998/3132 r.50, Sch.1
    r.8, amended: SI 1998/3132 r.50, Sch.1
    r.8, applied: SI 1998/3132 r.50, Sch.1
    r.8, consolidated: SI 1998/3132 r.50, Sch.1
    r.9, amended: SI 1998/3132 r.50, Sch.1
    r.9, applied: SI 1998/3132 r.50, Sch.1
    r.9, consolidated: SI 1998/3132 r.50, Sch.1
    r.10, amended: SI 1998/3132 r.50, Sch.1
    r.10, applied: SI 1998/3132 r.50, Sch.1
    r.10, consolidated: SI 1998/3132 r.50, Sch.1
    r.11, amended: SI 1998/3132 r.50, Sch.1
    r.11, applied: SI 1998/3132 r.50, Sch.1
    r.11, consolidated: SI 1998/3132 r.50, Sch.1
    r.12, amended: SI 1998/3132 r.50, Sch.1
    r.12, applied: SI 1998/3132 r.50, Sch.1
    r.12, consolidated: SI 1998/3132 r.50, Sch.1
Ord. 45,
    see *Davy International Ltd v Tazzyman* [1997] 1 W.L.R. 1256 (CA), Morritt, L.J.
    r.1, amended: SI 1998/3132 r.50, Sch.1
    r.1, applied: SI 1998/3132 r.50, Sch.1
    r.1, consolidated: SI 1998/3132 r.50, Sch.1
    r.2, amended: SI 1998/3132 r.50, Sch.1
    r.2, applied: SI 1998/3132 r.50, Sch.1
    r.2, consolidated: SI 1998/3132 r.50, Sch.1
    r.2, substituted: SI 1996/2892 r.7
    r.3, amended: SI 1998/3132 r.50, Sch.1
    r.3, applied: SI 1998/3132 r.50, Sch.1
    r.3, consolidated: SI 1998/3132 r.50, Sch.1
    r.4, amended: SI 1998/3132 r.50, Sch.1
    r.4, applied: SI 1998/3132 r.50, Sch.1
    r.4, consolidated: SI 1998/3132 r.50, Sch.1
    r.5, amended: SI 1998/3132 r.50, Sch.1
    r.5, applied: SI 1998/3132 r.50, Sch.1
    r.5, consolidated: SI 1998/3132 r.50, Sch.1
    r.6, amended: SI 1998/3132 r.50, Sch.1
    r.6, applied: SI 1998/3132 r.50, Sch.1
    r.6, consolidated: SI 1998/3132 r.50, Sch.1
    r.7, see *Belgolaise SA v Purchandani* Times, July 30, 1998 (QBD (Comm Ct)), Colman, J.; see *Cleveland CC v L* Times, April 8, 1996 (CA), Russell, L.J.
    r.7, amended: SI 1998/3132 r.50, Sch.1
    r.7, applied: SI 1998/3132 r.50, Sch.1
    r.7, consolidated: SI 1998/3132 r.50, Sch.1
    r.7(7), see *Belgolaise SA v Rupchandani* [1999] Lloyd's Rep. Bank. 116 (QBD (Comm Ct)), Colman, J.
    r.7(7), amended: SI 1998/3132 r.50, Sch.1
    r.7(7), applied: SI 1998/3132 r.50, Sch.1
    r.7(7), consolidated: SI 1998/3132 r.50, Sch.1
    r.8, amended: SI 1998/3132 r.50, Sch.1
    r.8, applied: SI 1998/3132 r.50, Sch.1
    r.8, consolidated: SI 1998/3132 r.50, Sch.1
    r.9, amended: SI 1998/3132 r.50, Sch.1
    r.9, applied: SI 1998/3132 r.50, Sch.1
    r.9, consolidated: SI 1998/3132 r.50, Sch.1
    r.10, amended: SI 1998/3132 r.50, Sch.1
    r.10, applied: SI 1998/3132 r.50, Sch.1
    r.10, consolidated: SI 1998/3132 r.50, Sch.1
    r.11, amended: SI 1998/3132 r.50, Sch.1
    r.11, applied: SI 1998/3132 r.50, Sch.1
    r.11, consolidated: SI 1998/3132 r.50, Sch.1
    r.12, amended: SI 1998/3132 r.50, Sch.1
    r.12, applied: SI 1998/3132 r.50, Sch.1
    r.12, consolidated: SI 1998/3132 r.50, Sch.1
    r.13, amended: SI 1998/3132 r.50, Sch.1
    r.13, applied: SI 1998/3132 r.50, Sch.1
    r.13, consolidated: SI 1998/3132 r.50, Sch.1

NO.

NO.

1965—cont.

1776. Rules of the Supreme Court 1965—*cont.*
Ord. 45—*cont.*
  r.14, amended: SI 1998/3132 r.50, Sch.1
  r.14, applied: SI 1998/3132 r.50, Sch.1
  r.14, consolidated: SI 1998/3132 r.50, Sch.1
Ord. 46,
  r.1, amended: SI 1998/3132 r.50, Sch.1
  r.1, applied: SI 1998/3132 r.50, Sch.1
  r.1, consolidated: SI 1998/3132 r.50, Sch.1
  r.2, amended: SI 1998/3132 r.50, Sch.1
  r.2, applied: SI 1998/3132 r.50, Sch.1
  r.2, consolidated: SI 1998/3132 r.50, Sch.1
  r.3, amended: SI 1998/3132 r.50, Sch.1
  r.3, applied: SI 1998/3132 r.50, Sch.1
  r.3, consolidated: SI 1998/3132 r.50, Sch.1
  r.4, amended: SI 1998/3132 r.50, Sch.1
  r.4, applied: SI 1998/3132 r.50, Sch.1
  r.4, consolidated: SI 1998/3132 r.50, Sch.1
  r.5, amended: SI 1998/3132 r.50, Sch.1
  r.5, applied: SI 1998/3132 r.50, Sch.1
  r.5, consolidated: SI 1998/3132 r.50, Sch.1
  r.6, amended: SI 1998/3132 r.50, Sch.1
  r.6, applied: SI 1998/3132 r.50, Sch.1
  r.6, consolidated: SI 1998/3132 r.50, Sch.1
  r.8, amended: SI 1998/3132 r.50, Sch.1
  r.8, applied: SI 1998/3132 r.50, Sch.1
  r.8, consolidated: SI 1998/3132 r.50, Sch.1
  r.9, amended: SI 1998/3132 r.50, Sch.1
  r.9, applied: SI 1998/3132 r.50, Sch.1
  r.9, consolidated: SI 1998/3132 r.50, Sch.1
Ord. 47,
  r.1, amended: SI 1998/3132 r.50, Sch.1
  r.1, applied: SI 1998/3132 r.50, Sch.1
  r.1, consolidated: SI 1998/3132 r.50, Sch.1
  r.2, amended: SI 1998/3132 r.50, Sch.1
  r.2, applied: SI 1998/3132 r.50, Sch.1
  r.2, consolidated: SI 1998/3132 r.50, Sch.1
  r.3, amended: SI 1998/3132 r.50, Sch.1
  r.3, applied: SI 1998/3132 r.50, Sch.1
  r.3, consolidated: SI 1998/3132 r.50, Sch.1
  r.4, amended: SI 1998/3132 r.50, Sch.1
  r.4, applied: SI 1998/3132 r.50, Sch.1
  r.4, consolidated: SI 1998/3132 r.50, Sch.1
  r.5, amended: SI 1998/3132 r.50, Sch.1
  r.5, applied: SI 1998/3132 r.50, Sch.1
  r.5, consolidated: SI 1998/3132 r.50, Sch.1
  r.6, amended: SI 1998/3132 r.50, Sch.1
  r.6, applied: SI 1998/3132 r.50, Sch.1
  r.6, consolidated: SI 1998/3132 r.50, Sch.1
Ord. 48,
  see *Union Bank of Finland Ltd v Lelakis*
    [1997] 1 W.L.R. 590 (CA), Henry, L.J.
  r.1, see *Union Bank of Finland Ltd v Lelakis*
    [1997] 1 W.L.R. 590 (CA), Henry, L.J.
  r.1, amended: SI 1998/3132 r.50, Sch.1
  r.1, applied: SI 1998/3132 r.50, Sch.1
  r.1, consolidated: SI 1998/3132 r.50, Sch.1
  r.1(3), see *Belgolaise SA v Rupchandani*
    [1999] Lloyd's Rep. Bank. 116 (QBD
    (Comm Ct)), Colman, J.
  r.1(3), amended: SI 1998/3132 r.50, Sch.1
  r.1(3), applied: SI 1998/3132 r.50, Sch.1
  r.1(3), consolidated: SI 1998/3132 r.50,
    Sch.1
  r.1(4), amended: SI 1998/1898 r.13, SI 1998/
    3132 r.50, Sch.1
  r.1(4), applied: SI 1998/3132 r.50, Sch.1
  r.1(4), consolidated: SI 1998/3132 r.50,
    Sch.1
  r.2, amended: SI 1998/3132 r.50, Sch.1
  r.2, applied: SI 1998/3132 r.50, Sch.1
  r.2, consolidated: SI 1998/3132 r.50, Sch.1

1965—cont.

1776. Rules of the Supreme Court 1965—*cont.*
Ord. 48—*cont.*
  r.3, amended: SI 1998/3132 r.50, Sch.1
  r.3, applied: SI 1998/3132 r.50, Sch.1
  r.3, consolidated: SI 1998/3132 r.50, Sch.1
Ord. 49,
  r.1, amended: SI 1998/3132 r.50, Sch.1
  r.1, applied: SI 1998/3132 r.50, Sch.1
  r.1, consolidated: SI 1998/3132 r.50, Sch.1
  r.2, amended: SI 1998/3132 r.50, Sch.1
  r.2, applied: SI 1998/3132 r.50, Sch.1
  r.2, consolidated: SI 1998/3132 r.50, Sch.1
  r.3, amended: SI 1998/3132 r.50, Sch.1
  r.3, applied: SI 1998/3132 r.50, Sch.1
  r.3, consolidated: SI 1998/3132 r.50, Sch.1
  r.4, amended: SI 1998/3132 r.50, Sch.1
  r.4, applied: SI 1998/3132 r.50, Sch.1
  r.4, consolidated: SI 1998/3132 r.50, Sch.1
  r.5, amended: SI 1998/3132 r.50, Sch.1
  r.5, applied: SI 1998/3132 r.50, Sch.1
  r.5, consolidated: SI 1998/3132 r.50, Sch.1
  r.6, amended: SI 1998/3132 r.50, Sch.1
  r.6, applied: SI 1998/3132 r.50, Sch.1
  r.6, consolidated: SI 1998/3132 r.50, Sch.1
  r.8, amended: SI 1998/3132 r.50, Sch.1
  r.8, applied: SI 1998/3132 r.50, Sch.1
  r.8, consolidated: SI 1998/3132 r.50, Sch.1
  r.9, amended: SI 1998/3132 r.50, Sch.1
  r.9, applied: SI 1998/3132 r.50, Sch.1
  r.9, consolidated: SI 1998/3132 r.50, Sch.1
  r.10, amended: SI 1998/3132 r.50, Sch.1
  r.10, applied: SI 1998/3132 r.50, Sch.1
  r.10, consolidated: SI 1998/3132 r.50, Sch.1
Ord. 50,
  r.1, amended: SI 1998/3132 r.50, Sch.1
  r.1, applied: SI 1998/3132 r.50, Sch.1
  r.1, consolidated: SI 1998/3132 r.50, Sch.1
  r.2, amended: SI 1998/3132 r.50, Sch.1
  r.2, applied: SI 1998/3132 r.50, Sch.1
  r.2, consolidated: SI 1998/3132 r.50, Sch.1
  r.3, amended: SI 1998/3132 r.50, Sch.1
  r.3, applied: SI 1998/3132 r.50, Sch.1
  r.3, consolidated: SI 1998/3132 r.50, Sch.1
  r.4, amended: SI 1998/3132 r.50, Sch.1
  r.4, applied: SI 1998/3132 r.50, Sch.1
  r.4, consolidated: SI 1998/3132 r.50, Sch.1
  r.5, amended: SI 1998/3132 r.50, Sch.1
  r.5, applied: SI 1998/3132 r.50, Sch.1
  r.5, consolidated: SI 1998/3132 r.50, Sch.1
  r.6, amended: SI 1998/3132 r.50, Sch.1
  r.6, applied: SI 1998/3132 r.50, Sch.1
  r.6, consolidated: SI 1998/3132 r.50, Sch.1
  r.7, see *Ezekiel v Orakpo* [1997] 1 W.L.R. 340
    (CA), Millett, L.J.
  r.7, amended: SI 1998/3132 r.50, Sch.1
  r.7, applied: SI 1998/3132 r.50, Sch.1
  r.7, consolidated: SI 1998/3132 r.50, Sch.1
  r.9, amended: SI 1998/3132 r.50, Sch.1
  r.9, applied: SI 1998/3132 r.50, Sch.1
  r.9, consolidated: SI 1998/3132 r.50, Sch.1
  r.9A, amended: SI 1998/3132 r.50, Sch.1
  r.9A, applied: SI 1998/3132 r.50, Sch.1
  r.9A, consolidated: SI 1998/3132 r.50, Sch.1
  r.10, amended: SI 1998/3132 r.50, Sch.1
  r.10, applied: SI 1998/3132 r.50, Sch.1
  r.10, consolidated: SI 1998/3132 r.50, Sch.1
  r.11, amended: SI 1998/3132 r.50, Sch.1
  r.11, applied: SI 1998/3132 r.50, Sch.1
  r.11, consolidated: SI 1998/3132 r.50, Sch.1
  r.12, amended: SI 1998/3132 r.50, Sch.1
  r.12, applied: SI 1998/3132 r.50, Sch.1
  r.12, consolidated: SI 1998/3132 r.50, Sch.1

NO.

NO.

1965—cont.

1776. Rules of the Supreme Court 1965—*cont.*
Ord. 50—*cont.*
r.13, amended: SI 1998/3132 r.50, Sch.1
r.13, applied: SI 1998/3132 r.50, Sch.1
r.13, consolidated: SI 1998/3132 r.50, Sch.1
r.14, amended: SI 1998/3132 r.50, Sch.1
r.14, applied: SI 1998/3132 r.50, Sch.1
r.14, consolidated: SI 1998/3132 r.50, Sch.1
r.15, amended: SI 1998/3132 r.50, Sch.1
r.15, applied: SI 1998/3132 r.50, Sch.1
r.15, consolidated: SI 1998/3132 r.50, Sch.1
Ord. 51,
r.1, amended: SI 1998/3132 r.50, Sch.1
r.1, applied: SI 1998/3132 r.50, Sch.1
r.1, consolidated: SI 1998/3132 r.50, Sch.1
r.2, amended: SI 1998/3132 r.50, Sch.1
r.2, applied: SI 1998/3132 r.50, Sch.1
r.2, consolidated: SI 1998/3132 r.50, Sch.1
r.3, amended: SI 1998/3132 r.50, Sch.1
r.3, applied: SI 1998/3132 r.50, Sch.1
r.3, consolidated: SI 1998/3132 r.50, Sch.1
Ord. 52,
r.1, amended: SI 1998/3132 r.50, Sch.1
r.1, applied: SI 1998/3132 r.50, Sch.1
r.1, consolidated: SI 1998/3132 r.50, Sch.1
r.1(2), amended: SI 1998/3132 r.50, Sch.1
r.1(2), applied: SI 1998/3132 r.50, Sch.1
r.1(2), consolidated: SI 1998/3132 r.50, Sch.1
r.2, amended: SI 1998/3132 r.50, Sch.1
r.2, applied: SI 1998/3132 r.50, Sch.1
r.2, consolidated: SI 1998/3132 r.50, Sch.1
r.3, amended: SI 1998/3132 r.50, Sch.1
r.3, applied: SI 1998/3132 r.50, Sch.1
r.3, consolidated: SI 1998/3132 r.50, Sch.1
r.4, amended: SI 1998/3132 r.50, Sch.1
r.4, applied: SI 1998/3132 r.50, Sch.1
r.4, consolidated: SI 1998/3132 r.50, Sch.1
r.5, amended: SI 1998/3132 r.50, Sch.1
r.5, applied: SI 1998/3132 r.50, Sch.1
r.5, consolidated: SI 1998/3132 r.50, Sch.1
r.6, see *B (A Minor) (Contempt: Evidence), Re* [1996] 1 W.L.R. 627 (Fam Div), Wall, J.
r.6, amended: SI 1998/3132 r.50, Sch.1
r.6, applied: SI 1998/3132 r.50, Sch.1
r.6, consolidated: SI 1998/3132 r.50, Sch.1
r.7, amended: SI 1998/3132 r.50, Sch.1
r.7, applied: SI 1998/3132 r.50, Sch.1
r.7, consolidated: SI 1998/3132 r.50, Sch.1
r.8, amended: SI 1998/3132 r.50, Sch.1
r.8, applied: SI 1998/3132 r.50, Sch.1
r.8, consolidated: SI 1998/3132 r.50, Sch.1
r.9, amended: SI 1998/3132 r.50, Sch.1
r.9, applied: SI 1998/3132 r.50, Sch.1
r.9, consolidated: SI 1998/3132 r.50, Sch.1
Ord. 53,
see *Mercury Communications Ltd v Director General of Telecommunications* [1996] 1 W.L.R. 48 (HL), Lord Slynn.; see *R. v Liverpool City Council Ex p. Muldoon* [1996] 1 W.L.R. 1103 (HL), Lord Keith of Kinkel; see *R. v Lord Saville of Newdigate Ex p. B (No.2)* Times, June 22, 1999 (QBD), Roch, L.J.; see *R. v Secretary of State for the Home Department Ex p. Arulanandam* [1996] Imm. A.R. 587 (CA), Potter, L.J.
r.1, amended: SI 1998/3132 r.50, Sch.1
r.1, applied: SI 1998/3132 r.50, Sch.1
r.1, consolidated: SI 1998/3132 r.50, Sch.1
r.1(2), amended: SI 1998/3132 r.50, Sch.1
r.1(2), applied: SI 1998/3132 r.50, Sch.1
r.1(2), consolidated: SI 1998/3132 r.50, Sch.1

1965—cont.

1776. Rules of the Supreme Court 1965—*cont.*
Ord. 53—*cont.*
r.2, amended: SI 1998/3132 r.50, Sch.1
r.2, applied: SI 1998/3132 r.50, Sch.1
r.2, consolidated: SI 1998/3132 r.50, Sch.1
r.3, see *R. v North Somerset DC and Pioneer Aggregates (UK) Ltd Ex p. Garnett* [1998] Env. L.R. 91 (QBD), Popplewell, J.
r.3, amended: SI 1998/3132 r.50, Sch.1
r.3, applied: SI 1998/3132 r.50, Sch.1
r.3, consolidated: SI 1998/3132 r.50, Sch.1
r.3(2), amended: SI 1998/3132 r.50, Sch.1
r.3(2), applied: SI 1998/3132 r.50, Sch.1
r.3(2), consolidated: SI 1998/3132 r.50, Sch.1
r.3(7), see *R. v Somerset CC Ex p. Dixon* (1998) 75 P. & C.R. 175 (QBD), Sedley, J.
r.3(7), amended: SI 1998/3132 r.50, Sch.1
r.3(7), applied: SI 1998/3132 r.50, Sch.1
r.3(7), consolidated: SI 1998/3132 r.50, Sch.1
r.4, amended: SI 1998/3132 r.50, Sch.1
r.4, applied: SI 1998/3132 r.50, Sch.1
r.4, consolidated: SI 1998/3132 r.50, Sch.1
r.4(1), see *R. v Criminal Injuries Compensation Board Ex p. A* [1998] Q.B. 659 (CA), Simon Brown, L.J.; see *R. v Criminal Injuries Compensation Board Ex p. A* [1999] 2 W.L.R. 974 (HL), Lord Slynn of Hadley; see *R. v Leeds Metropolitan University Ex p. Manders* [1998] E.L.R. 502 (QBD), Collins, J.
r.4(1), amended: SI 1998/3132 r.50, Sch.1
r.4(1), applied: SI 1998/3132 r.50, Sch.1
r.4(1), consolidated: SI 1998/3132 r.50, Sch.1
r.5, amended: SI 1998/3132 r.50, Sch.1
r.5, applied: SI 1998/3132 r.50, Sch.1
r.5, consolidated: SI 1998/3132 r.50, Sch.1
r.5(3), see *R. v Liverpool City Council Ex p. Muldoon* [1996] 1 W.L.R. 1103 (HL), Lord Keith of Kinkel
r.5(3), amended: SI 1998/3132 r.50, Sch.1
r.5(3), applied: SI 1998/3132 r.50, Sch.1
r.5(3), consolidated: SI 1998/3132 r.50, Sch.1
r.6, amended: SI 1998/3132 r.50, Sch.1
r.6, applied: SI 1998/3132 r.50, Sch.1
r.6, consolidated: SI 1998/3132 r.50, Sch.1
r.6(4), amended: SI 1998/3132 r.50, Sch.1
r.6(4), applied: SI 1998/3132 r.50, Sch.1
r.6(4), consolidated: SI 1998/3132 r.50, Sch.1
r.7, amended: SI 1998/3132 r.50, Sch.1
r.7, applied: SI 1998/3132 r.50, Sch.1
r.7, consolidated: SI 1998/3132 r.50, Sch.1
r.8, amended: SI 1998/3132 r.50, Sch.1
r.8, applied: SI 1998/3132 r.50, Sch.1
r.8, consolidated: SI 1998/3132 r.50, Sch.1
r.9, see *R. v Lord Saville of Newdigate Ex p. B* Times, April 15, 1999 (CA), Lord Woolf, M.R.
r.9, amended: SI 1998/3132 r.50, Sch.1
r.9, applied: SI 1998/3132 r.50, Sch.1
r.9, consolidated: SI 1998/3132 r.50, Sch.1
r.9(4), amended: SI 1998/3132 r.50, Sch.1
r.9(4), applied: SI 1998/3132 r.50, Sch.1
r.9(4), consolidated: SI 1998/3132 r.50, Sch.1

NO.

NO.

1965—cont.

1776. Rules of the Supreme Court 1965—*cont.*

Ord. 53—*cont.*

r.9(5), see *R. v Highgate Justices Ex p. Riley* [1996] R.T.R. 150 (QBD), Simon Brown, L.J.

r.9(5), amended: SI 1998/3132 r.50, Sch.1

r.9(5), applied: SI 1998/3132 r.50, Sch.1

r.9(5), consolidated: SI 1998/3132 r.50, Sch.1

r.10, amended: SI 1998/3132 r.50, Sch.1

r.10, applied: SI 1998/3132 r.50, Sch.1

r.10, consolidated: SI 1998/3132 r.50, Sch.1

r.11, amended: SI 1998/3132 r.50, Sch.1

r.11, applied: SI 1998/3132 r.50, Sch.1

r.11, consolidated: SI 1998/3132 r.50, Sch.1

r.12, amended: SI 1998/3132 r.50, Sch.1

r.12, applied: SI 1998/3132 r.50, Sch.1

r.12, consolidated: SI 1998/3132 r.50, Sch.1

r.13, amended: SI 1998/3132 r.50, Sch.1

r.13, applied: SI 1998/3132 r.50, Sch.1

r.13, consolidated: SI 1998/3132 r.50, Sch.1

r.14, amended: SI 1998/3132 r.50, Sch.1

r.14, applied: SI 1998/3132 r.50, Sch.1

r.14, consolidated: SI 1998/3132 r.50, Sch.1

Ord. 54,

r.1, amended: SI 1998/3132 r.50, Sch.1

r.1, applied: SI 1998/3132 r.50, Sch.1

r.1, consolidated: SI 1998/3132 r.50, Sch.1

r.2, amended: SI 1998/3132 r.50, Sch.1

r.2, applied: SI 1998/3132 r.50, Sch.1

r.2, consolidated: SI 1998/3132 r.50, Sch.1

r.3, amended: SI 1998/3132 r.50, Sch.1

r.3, applied: SI 1998/3132 r.50, Sch.1

r.3, consolidated: SI 1998/3132 r.50, Sch.1

r.4, amended: SI 1998/3132 r.50, Sch.1

r.4, applied: SI 1998/3132 r.50, Sch.1

r.4, consolidated: SI 1998/3132 r.50, Sch.1

r.5, amended: SI 1998/3132 r.50, Sch.1

r.5, applied: SI 1998/3132 r.50, Sch.1

r.5, consolidated: SI 1998/3132 r.50, Sch.1

r.6, amended: SI 1998/3132 r.50, Sch.1

r.6, applied: SI 1998/3132 r.50, Sch.1

r.6, consolidated: SI 1998/3132 r.50, Sch.1

r.7, amended: SI 1998/3132 r.50, Sch.1

r.7, applied: SI 1998/3132 r.50, Sch.1

r.7, consolidated: SI 1998/3132 r.50, Sch.1

r.8, amended: SI 1998/3132 r.50, Sch.1

r.8, applied: SI 1998/3132 r.50, Sch.1

r.8, consolidated: SI 1998/3132 r.50, Sch.1

r.9, amended: SI 1998/3132 r.50, Sch.1

r.9, applied: SI 1998/3132 r.50, Sch.1

r.9, consolidated: SI 1998/3132 r.50, Sch.1

r.10, amended: SI 1998/3132 r.50, Sch.1

r.10, applied: SI 1998/3132 r.50, Sch.1

r.10, consolidated: SI 1998/3132 r.50, Sch.1

r.11, amended: SI 1998/3132 r.50, Sch.1

r.11, applied: SI 1998/3132 r.50, Sch.1

r.11, consolidated: SI 1998/3132 r.50, Sch.1

Ord. 55,

see *Customs and Excise Commissioners v Ferrero UK Ltd* [1997] S.T.C. 881 (CA), Lord Woolf, M.R.; see *F (Time Limit for Appeals: Delay in Obtaining Legal Aid Certificate), Re* [1999] Ed. C.R. 985 (QBD), Tucker, J.; see *Northumberland and Durham Property Trust Ltd v London Rent Assessment Committee* Times, June 26, 1997 (QBD), Latham, J.; see *R. v Special Educational Needs Tribunal Ex p. South Glamorgan CC* [1996] E.L.R. 326 (CA), Rose, L.J.

r.1, amended: SI 1998/3132 r.50, Sch.1

1965—cont.

1776. Rules of the Supreme Court 1965—*cont.*

Ord. 55—*cont.*

r.1, applied: SI 1998/3132 r.50, Sch.1

r.1, consolidated: SI 1998/3132 r.50, Sch.1

r.2, amended: SI 1998/3132 r.50, Sch.1

r.2, applied: SI 1998/3132 r.50, Sch.1

r.2, consolidated: SI 1998/3132 r.50, Sch.1

r.3, amended: SI 1998/3132 r.50, Sch.1

r.3, applied: SI 1998/3132 r.50, Sch.1

r.3, consolidated: SI 1998/3132 r.50, Sch.1

r.4, amended: SI 1998/3132 r.50, Sch.1

r.4, applied: SI 1998/3132 r.50, Sch.1

r.4, consolidated: SI 1998/3132 r.50, Sch.1

r.4(2), amended: SI 1998/3132 r.50, Sch.1

r.4(2), applied: SI 1998/3132 r.50, Sch.1

r.4(2), consolidated: SI 1998/3132 r.50, Sch.1

r.5, amended: SI 1998/3132 r.50, Sch.1

r.5, applied: SI 1998/3132 r.50, Sch.1

r.5, consolidated: SI 1998/3132 r.50, Sch.1

r.6, amended: SI 1998/3132 r.50, Sch.1

r.6, applied: SI 1998/3132 r.50, Sch.1

r.6, consolidated: SI 1998/3132 r.50, Sch.1

r.6(3), see *Steinberg v McLeod Russel Holdings Plc and London Rent Assessment Panel* [1996] C.O.D. 25 (QBD), Hidden, J.

r.6(3), amended: SI 1998/3132 r.50, Sch.1

r.6(3), applied: SI 1998/3132 r.50, Sch.1

r.6(3), consolidated: SI 1998/3132 r.50, Sch.1

r.6A, amended: SI 1998/3132 r.50, Sch.1

r.6A, applied: SI 1998/3132 r.50, Sch.1

r.6A, consolidated: SI 1998/3132 r.50, Sch.1

r.7, see *Curtis v London Rent Assessment Committee* [1997] 4 All E.R. 842 (CA), Auld, L.J.; see *Knight v Dorset CC* [1997] C.O.D. 256 (QBD), Tucker, J.; see *Koca v Customs and Excise Commissioners* [1996] S.T.C. 58 (QBD), Latham, J.; see *Northumberland and Durham Property Trust Ltd v London Rent Assessment Committee* Times, June 26, 1997 (QBD), Latham, J.

r.7, amended: SI 1998/3132 r.50, Sch.1

r.7, applied: SI 1998/3132 r.50, Sch.1

r.7, consolidated: SI 1998/3132 r.50, Sch.1

r.7(2), amended: SI 1998/3132 r.50, Sch.1

r.7(2), applied: SI 1998/3132 r.50, Sch.1

r.7(2), consolidated: SI 1998/3132 r.50, Sch.1

r.7(4), see *Fisher v Hughes* [1999] Ed. C.R. 409 (QBD), Keene, J.

r.7(4), amended: SI 1998/3132 r.50, Sch.1

r.7(4), applied: SI 1998/3132 r.50, Sch.1

r.7(4), consolidated: SI 1998/3132 r.50, Sch.1

r.7(5), see *Curtis v London Rent Assessment Committee* [1999] Q.B. 92 (CA), Auld, L.J.

r.7(5), amended: SI 1998/3132 r.50, Sch.1

r.7(5), applied: SI 1998/3132 r.50, Sch.1

r.7(5), consolidated: SI 1998/3132 r.50, Sch.1

r.7(7), amended: SI 1998/3132 r.50, Sch.1

r.7(7), applied: SI 1998/3132 r.50, Sch.1

r.7(7), consolidated: SI 1998/3132 r.50, Sch.1

r.8, amended: SI 1998/3132 r.50, Sch.1

r.8, applied: SI 1998/3132 r.50, Sch.1

r.8, consolidated: SI 1998/3132 r.50, Sch.1

Ord. 56,

r.1, amended: SI 1998/3132 r.50, Sch.1

r.1, applied: SI 1998/3132 r.50, Sch.1

NO.

1965—cont.

1776. Rules of the Supreme Court 1965—*cont.*
Ord. 56—*cont.*
    r.1, consolidated: SI 1998/3132 r.50, Sch.1
    r.1(4), amended: SI 1998/3132 r.50, Sch.1
    r.1(4), applied: SI 1998/3132 r.50, Sch.1
    r.1(4), consolidated: SI 1998/3132 r.50, Sch.1
    r.4, amended: SI 1998/3132 r.50, Sch.1
    r.4, applied: SI 1998/3132 r.50, Sch.1
    r.4, consolidated: SI 1998/3132 r.50, Sch.1
    r.4A, amended: SI 1998/3132 r.50, Sch.1
    r.4A, applied: SI 1998/3132 r.50, Sch.1
    r.4A, consolidated: SI 1998/3132 r.50, Sch.1
    r.5, amended: SI 1998/3132 r.50, Sch.1
    r.5, applied: SI 1998/3132 r.50, Sch.1
    r.5, consolidated: SI 1998/3132 r.50, Sch.1
    r.6, amended: SI 1998/3132 r.50, Sch.1
    r.6, applied: SI 1998/3132 r.50, Sch.1
    r.6, consolidated: SI 1998/3132 r.50, Sch.1
    r.7, amended: SI 1998/3132 r.50, Sch.1
    r.7, applied: SI 1998/3132 r.50, Sch.1
    r.7, consolidated: SI 1998/3132 r.50, Sch.1
    r.8, amended: SI 1998/3132 r.50, Sch.1
    r.8, applied: SI 1998/3132 r.50, Sch.1
    r.8, consolidated: SI 1998/3132 r.50, Sch.1
    r.9, amended: SI 1998/3132 r.50, Sch.1
    r.9, applied: SI 1998/3132 r.50, Sch.1
    r.9, consolidated: SI 1998/3132 r.50, Sch.1
    r.10, amended: SI 1998/3132 r.50, Sch.1
    r.10, applied: SI 1998/3132 r.50, Sch.1
    r.10, consolidated: SI 1998/3132 r.50, Sch.1
    r.11, amended: SI 1998/3132 r.50, Sch.1
    r.11, applied: SI 1998/3132 r.50, Sch.1
    r.11, consolidated: SI 1998/3132 r.50, Sch.1
    r.12, amended: SI 1998/3132 r.50, Sch.1
    r.12, applied: SI 1998/3132 r.50, Sch.1
    r.12, consolidated: SI 1998/3132 r.50, Sch.1
    r.12A, amended: SI 1998/3132 r.50, Sch.1
    r.12A, applied: SI 1998/3132 r.50, Sch.1
    r.12A, consolidated: SI 1998/3132 r.50, Sch.1
    r.13, amended: SI 1998/3132 r.50, Sch.1
    r.13, applied: SI 1998/3132 r.50, Sch.1
    r.13, consolidated: SI 1998/3132 r.50, Sch.1
Ord. 57,
    r.1, amended: SI 1998/3132 r.50, Sch.1
    r.1, applied: SI 1998/3132 r.50, Sch.1
    r.1, consolidated: SI 1998/3132 r.50, Sch.1
    r.2, amended: SI 1998/3132 r.50, Sch.1
    r.2, applied: SI 1998/3132 r.50, Sch.1
    r.2, consolidated: SI 1998/3132 r.50, Sch.1
    r.3, amended: SI 1998/3132 r.50, Sch.1
    r.3, applied: SI 1998/3132 r.50, Sch.1
    r.3, consolidated: SI 1998/3132 r.50, Sch.1
    r.4, amended: SI 1998/3132 r.50, Sch.1
    r.4, applied: SI 1998/3132 r.50, Sch.1
    r.4, consolidated: SI 1998/3132 r.50, Sch.1
    r.5, amended: SI 1998/3132 r.50, Sch.1
    r.5, applied: SI 1998/3132 r.50, Sch.1
    r.5, consolidated: SI 1998/3132 r.50, Sch.1
    r.6, amended: SI 1998/3132 r.50, Sch.1
    r.6, applied: SI 1998/3132 r.50, Sch.1
    r.6, consolidated: SI 1998/3132 r.50, Sch.1
Ord. 58,
    r.1, see *Enfield LBC v P* [1996] 1 F.L.R. 629 (Fam Div), Holman, J.; see *Macro (Ipswich) Ltd, Re* [1996] 1 W.L.R. 145 (Ch D), Ferris, J.; see *Marshall v Gradon Construction Services Ltd* [1997] 4 All E.R. 880 (CA), Mummery, L.J.
    r.1, amended: SI 1998/3132 r.50, Sch.1
    r.1, applied: SI 1998/3132 r.50, Sch.1

NO.

1965—cont.

1776. Rules of the Supreme Court 1965—*cont.*
Ord. 58—*cont.*
    r.1, consolidated: SI 1998/3132 r.50, Sch.1
    r.2, amended: SI 1998/3132 r.50, Sch.1
    r.2, applied: SI 1998/3132 r.50, Sch.1
    r.2, consolidated: SI 1998/3132 r.50, Sch.1
    r.3, amended: SI 1998/3132 r.50, Sch.1
    r.3, applied: SI 1998/3132 r.50, Sch.1
    r.3, consolidated: SI 1998/3132 r.50, Sch.1
    r.4, amended: SI 1998/3132 r.50, Sch.1
    r.4, applied: SI 1998/3132 r.50, Sch.1
    r.4, consolidated: SI 1998/3132 r.50, Sch.1
    r.4(b), amended: SI 1998/3132 r.50, Sch.1
    r.4(b), applied: SI 1998/3132 r.50, Sch.1
    r.4(b), consolidated: SI 1998/3132 r.50, Sch.1
Ord. 59,
    see *Practice Direction (CA: Consolidation: Notice of Consolidation)* [1999] 2 All E.R. 490 (CA), Lord Woolf, M.R.
    r.1, amended: SI 1998/3132 r.50, Sch.1
    r.1, applied: SI 1998/3132 r.50, Sch.1
    r.1, consolidated: SI 1998/3132 r.50, Sch.1
    r.1A, see *Hughes v Jones* [1996] P.I.Q.R. P380 (CA), Henry, L.J.
    r.1A(7)(a), amended: SI 1996/3219 r.4
    r.1A(7)(b), amended: SI 1996/3219 r.4
    r.1B, see *Plumb v Ayres* Times, May 11, 1999 (CA), Brooke, L.J.; see *Yui Tong Man v Mahmood* (1997) 74 P. & C.R. 320 (CA), Leggatt, L.J.
    r.1B, amended: SI 1998/3132 r.50, Sch.1
    r.1B, applied: SI 1998/3132 r.50, Sch.1
    r.1B, consolidated: SI 1998/3132 r.50, Sch.1
    r.1B, substituted: SI 1998/3049 r.3
    r.2, amended: SI 1998/3132 r.50, Sch.1
    r.2, applied: SI 1998/3132 r.50, Sch.1
    r.2, consolidated: SI 1998/3132 r.50, Sch.1
    r.2A, amended: SI 1998/3132 r.50, Sch.1
    r.2A, applied: SI 1998/3132 r.50, Sch.1
    r.2A, consolidated: SI 1998/3132 r.50, Sch.1
    r.2B, amended: SI 1998/3132 r.50, Sch.1
    r.2B, applied: SI 1998/3132 r.50, Sch.1
    r.2B, consolidated: SI 1998/3132 r.50, Sch.1
    r.2C, amended: SI 1998/3132 r.50, Sch.1
    r.2C, applied: SI 1998/3132 r.50, Sch.1
    r.2C, consolidated: SI 1998/3132 r.50, Sch.1
    r.3, amended: SI 1998/3132 r.50, Sch.1
    r.3, applied: SI 1998/3132 r.50, Sch.1
    r.3, consolidated: SI 1998/3132 r.50, Sch.1
    r.4, amended: SI 1998/3132 r.50, Sch.1
    r.4, applied: SI 1998/3132 r.50, Sch.1
    r.4, consolidated: SI 1998/3132 r.50, Sch.1
    r.4(1), amended: SI 1998/3132 r.50, Sch.1
    r.4(1), applied: SI 1998/3132 r.50, Sch.1
    r.4(1), consolidated: SI 1998/3132 r.50, Sch.1
    r.5, amended: SI 1998/3132 r.50, Sch.1
    r.5, applied: SI 1998/3132 r.50, Sch.1
    r.5, consolidated: SI 1998/3132 r.50, Sch.1
    r.6, see *S (A Minor) (Contact: Grandparents), Re* [1996] 1 F.L.R. 158 (CA), Wall, J.
    r.6, amended: SI 1998/3132 r.50, Sch.1
    r.6, applied: SI 1998/3132 r.50, Sch.1
    r.6, consolidated: SI 1998/3132 r.50, Sch.1
    r.7, amended: SI 1998/3132 r.50, Sch.1
    r.7, applied: SI 1998/3132 r.50, Sch.1
    r.7, consolidated: SI 1998/3132 r.50, Sch.1
    r.8, amended: SI 1998/3132 r.50, Sch.1
    r.8, applied: SI 1998/3132 r.50, Sch.1
    r.8, consolidated: SI 1998/3132 r.50, Sch.1
    r.9, amended: SI 1998/3132 r.50, Sch.1

NO.

1965—cont.

1776. Rules of the Supreme Court 1965—*cont.*
Ord. 59—*cont.*

r.9, applied: SI 1998/3132 r.50, Sch.1
r.9, consolidated: SI 1998/3132 r.50, Sch.1
r.10, see *AIB Finance Ltd v Debtors* [1997] 4 All E.R. 677 (Ch D), Carnwath, J.; see *Debtor (No.214 SD of 1995), Re* [1996] 1 W.L.R. 379 (Ch D), John Weeks, Q.C.; see *Ramanathan Rudra v Abbey National Plc* Independent, March 9, 1998 (C.S.) (CA), Schiemann, L.J.; see *Zincroft Civil Engineering Ltd v Sphere Drake Insurance Plc* Times, December 13, 1996 (CA), Potter, L.J.
r.10, amended: SI 1998/3132 r.50, Sch.1
r.10, applied: SI 1998/3132 r.50, Sch.1
r.10, consolidated: SI 1998/3132 r.50, Sch.1
r.10(2), see *Natwest Lombard Factors Ltd v Arbis* Times, December 10, 1999 (Ch D), Hart, J.
r.10(2), amended: SI 1998/3132 r.50, Sch.1
r.10(2), applied: SI 1998/3132 r.50, Sch.1
r.10(2), consolidated: SI 1998/3132 r.50, Sch.1
r.10(3), amended: SI 1998/3132 r.50, Sch.1
r.10(3), applied: SI 1998/3132 r.50, Sch.1
r.10(3), consolidated: SI 1998/3132 r.50, Sch.1
r.11, see *Jones v Pollard* [1997] E.M.L.R. 233 (CA), Hirst, L.J.
r.11, amended: SI 1998/3132 r.50, Sch.1
r.11, applied: SI 1998/3132 r.50, Sch.1
r.11, consolidated: SI 1998/3132 r.50, Sch.1
r.11(4), see *Clark v Chief Constable of Cleveland* Times, May 13, 1999 (CA), Roch, L.J.
r.12, amended: SI 1998/3132 r.50, Sch.1
r.12, applied: SI 1998/3132 r.50, Sch.1
r.12, consolidated: SI 1998/3132 r.50, Sch.1
r.12A, amended: SI 1998/3132 r.50, Sch.1
r.12A, applied: SI 1998/3132 r.50, Sch.1
r.12A, consolidated: SI 1998/3132 r.50, Sch.1
r.13, see *Stabilad Ltd v Stephens & Carter Ltd* [1999] 1 W.L.R. 1201 (CA), Sir Richard Scott V.C.
r.13, amended: SI 1998/3132 r.50, Sch.1
r.13, applied: SI 1998/3132 r.50, Sch.1
r.13, consolidated: SI 1998/3132 r.50, Sch.1
r.14, see *Austintel Ltd, Re* [1997] 1 W.L.R. 616 (CA), Morritt, L.J.; see *Cliffe v Forrester* Times, September 10, 1998 (CA), Lord Woolf, M.R.; see *Dixon v Allgood (Leave to Appeal: Notices)* Times, April 30, 1999 (CA), May, L.J.
r.14, amended: SI 1998/3132 r.50, Sch.1
r.14, applied: SI 1998/3132 r.50, Sch.1
r.14, consolidated: SI 1998/3132 r.50, Sch.1
r.14(3), amended: SI 1998/3132 r.50, Sch.1
r.14(3), applied: SI 1998/3132 r.50, Sch.1
r.14(3), consolidated: SI 1998/3132 r.50, Sch.1
r.15, amended: SI 1998/3132 r.50, Sch.1
r.15, applied: SI 1998/3132 r.50, Sch.1
r.15, consolidated: SI 1998/3132 r.50, Sch.1
r.15(1), amended: SI 1998/3132 r.50, Sch.1
r.15(1), applied: SI 1998/3132 r.50, Sch.1
r.15(1), consolidated: SI 1998/3132 r.50, Sch.1
r.16, amended: SI 1998/3132 r.50, Sch.1
r.16, applied: SI 1998/3132 r.50, Sch.1
r.16, consolidated: SI 1998/3132 r.50, Sch.1
r.17, amended: SI 1998/3132 r.50, Sch.1

NO.

1965—cont.

1776. Rules of the Supreme Court 1965—*cont.*
Ord. 59—*cont.*

r.17, applied: SI 1998/3132 r.50, Sch.1
r.17, consolidated: SI 1998/3132 r.50, Sch.1
r.18, amended: SI 1998/3132 r.50, Sch.1
r.18, applied: SI 1998/3132 r.50, Sch.1
r.18, consolidated: SI 1998/3132 r.50, Sch.1
r.19, amended: SI 1998/3132 r.50, Sch.1
r.19, applied: SI 1998/3132 r.50, Sch.1
r.19, consolidated: SI 1998/3132 r.50, Sch.1
r.19(3), amended: SI 1998/3132 r.50, Sch.1
r.19(3), applied: SI 1998/3132 r.50, Sch.1
r.19(3), consolidated: SI 1998/3132 r.50, Sch.1
r.20, amended: SI 1998/3132 r.50, Sch.1
r.20, applied: SI 1998/3132 r.50, Sch.1
r.20, consolidated: SI 1998/3132 r.50, Sch.1
r.21, amended: SI 1998/3132 r.50, Sch.1
r.21, applied: SI 1998/3132 r.50, Sch.1
r.21, consolidated: SI 1998/3132 r.50, Sch.1
r.22, amended: SI 1998/3132 r.50, Sch.1
r.22, applied: SI 1998/3132 r.50, Sch.1
r.22, consolidated: SI 1998/3132 r.50, Sch.1
r.23, see *Hadfield v Knowles (Practice Note)* [1996] 1 W.L.R. 1003 (CA), Sir Thomas Bingham, M.R.
r.23, amended: SI 1998/3132 r.50, Sch.1
r.23, applied: SI 1998/3132 r.50, Sch.1
r.23, consolidated: SI 1998/3132 r.50, Sch.1
r.24, amended: SI 1998/3132 r.50, Sch.1
r.24, applied: SI 1998/3132 r.50, Sch.1
r.24, consolidated: SI 1998/3132 r.50, Sch.1
r.25, amended: SI 1998/3132 r.50, Sch.1
r.25, applied: SI 1998/3132 r.50, Sch.1
r.25, consolidated: SI 1998/3132 r.50, Sch.1
Ord. 60,
r.1, amended: SI 1998/3132 r.50, Sch.1
r.1, applied: SI 1998/3132 r.50, Sch.1
r.1, consolidated: SI 1998/3132 r.50, Sch.1
r.2, amended: SI 1998/3132 r.50, Sch.1
r.2, applied: SI 1998/3132 r.50, Sch.1
r.2, consolidated: SI 1998/3132 r.50, Sch.1
r.3, amended: SI 1998/3132 r.50, Sch.1
r.3, applied: SI 1998/3132 r.50, Sch.1
r.3, consolidated: SI 1998/3132 r.50, Sch.1
r.4, amended: SI 1998/3132 r.50, Sch.1
r.4, applied: SI 1998/3132 r.50, Sch.1
r.4, consolidated: SI 1998/3132 r.50, Sch.1
Ord. 61,
r.1, amended: SI 1998/3132 r.50, Sch.1
r.1, applied: SI 1998/3132 r.50, Sch.1
r.1, consolidated: SI 1998/3132 r.50, Sch.1
r.2, amended: SI 1998/3132 r.50, Sch.1
r.2, applied: SI 1998/3132 r.50, Sch.1
r.2, consolidated: SI 1998/3132 r.50, Sch.1
r.3, amended: SI 1998/3132 r.50, Sch.1
r.3, applied: SI 1998/3132 r.50, Sch.1
r.3, consolidated: SI 1998/3132 r.50, Sch.1
Ord. 62,
see *Enfield LBC* [1996] 1 F.L.R. 629 (Fam Div), Holman, J.; see *Malhotra v Dhawan* [1997] 8 Med L.R. 319 (CA), Morritt, L.J.
applied: SI 1999/3098 Reg.6
referred to: SI 1999/1012 r.4
r.2(4), see *Wiggins v Richard Read (Transport) Ltd* Times, January 14, 1999 (CA), Waller, L.J.
r.3, see *Penn v Bristol & West Building Society* [1997] 1 W.L.R. 1356 (CA), Waller, L.J.
r.3(3), see *Swale Storage and Distribution Services Ltd v Sittingbourne Paper Co Ltd* Times, July 30, 1998 (CA), Buxton, L.J.

1965—cont.

1776. Rules of the Supreme Court 1965—*cont.*
Ord. 62—*cont.*
r.3(4), see *Cooper v P&O Stena Line Ltd*
[1999] 1 Lloyd's Rep. 734 (QBD (Adm Ct)),
Judge Belinda Bucknall Q.C.
r.5(4), see *Kamenou (t/a Regency Developments) v Dodson* [1999] 2 All E.R. 764
(QBD (T&CC)), Judge Bowsher Q.C.
r.7, see *Mayfair Brassware Ltd v Aqualine
International Ltd (Costs Order)* [1998]
F.S.R. 135 (CA), Morritt, L.J.; see *Taylor
Made Golf Co Inc v Rata & Rata* [1996]
F.S.R. 528 (Ch D), Laddie, J.
r.7(2), revoked (in part): SI 1996/2892 r.10
r.7(4), see *Microsoft Corp v Backslash Distribution Ltd* Times, March 15, 1999 (Ch D),
Park, J.
r.9, see *Brugger v Medicaid* [1996] F.S.R.
362 (Pat Ct), Jacob, J.; see *McCaffery v
Datta (Costs)* [1997] 1 W.L.R. 870 (CA),
Stuart-Smith, L.J.; see *Singh v Parkfield
Group Plc* [1996] P.I.Q.R. Q110 (CA),
Stuart-Smith, L.J.
r.10, see *Burrows v Vauxhall Motors Ltd*
[1998] P.I.Q.R. P48 (CA), Lord Woolf, M.R.
r.11, see *Woolwich Building Society v Fineb-
erg* [1998] P.N.L.R. 216 (CA), Peter Gibson, L.J.
r.11(2), see *Tate v Hart* [1999] Lloyd's Rep.
P.N. 566 (CA), Auld, L.J.
r.12, see *L v L (Legal Aid: Taxation)* [1996] 1
F.L.R. 873 (CA), Neill, L.J.; see *L (Restraint
Order: Legal Costs), Re* Times, July 10,
1996 (QBD), Latham, J.; see *Truscott v
Truscott* Times, October 15, 1997 (CA),
Kennedy, L.J.
r.18(2), see *Minotaur Data Systems Ltd, Re*
[1999] 1 W.L.R. 1129 (CA), Aldous, L.J.
r.20(d), see *Bourns Inc v Raychem Corp
(No.3)* [1999] 3 All E.R. 154 (CA), Aldous,
L.J.
r.27, see *Practice Direction (Supreme Court
Taxing Office: Taxation: Wasted Costs)
(No.1 of 1998)* [1998] 1 W.L.R. 473 (Sup Ct
Taxing Office); see *Ross v Owners of the
Bowbelle* [1997] 1 W.L.R. 1159 (CA), Leg-
gatt, L.J.
r.28, see *Practice Direction (Supreme Court
Taxing Office: Taxation: Wasted Costs)
(No.1 of 1998)* [1998] 1 W.L.R. 473 (Sup Ct
Taxing Office)
r.28(4), see *Mainwaring v Goldtech Invest-
ments Ltd (No.2)* [1999] 1 W.L.R. 745 (CA),
Pill, L.J.; see *Southwark LBC v Nejad*
Times, January 28, 1999 (CA), Waller, L.J.;
see *Toniello v Top Deck Ski Ltd* Times,
December 7, 1998 (CA), Auld, L.J.
r.29, see *Spath Holme Ltd v Greater Manchester and Lancashire Rent Assessment
Committee (No.2)* [1998] 3 All E.R. 909
(QBD), Morland, J.
r.30(3), see *Mainwaring v Goldtech Investments Ltd (No.2)* [1999] 1 W.L.R. 745 (CA),
Pill, L.J.
r.31, see *Bromsgrove Medical Products Ltd
(Formerly Peterborough Pressure Cast-
ings Ltd) v Edgar Vaughan & Co Ltd* [1997]
1 W.L.R. 1188 (QBD), Chadwick, J.
r.33, see *Macro (Ipswich) Ltd, Re* [1996] 1
W.L.R. 145 (Ch D), Ferris, J.
r.33(3), amended: SI 1996/2892 r.11
r.34, see *Macro (Ipswich) Ltd, Re* [1996] 1
W.L.R. 145 (Ch D), Ferris, J.

1965—cont.

1776. Rules of the Supreme Court 1965—*cont.*
Ord. 62—*cont.*
r.35, see *Kawarindrasingh v White* [1997] 1
All E.R. 714 (CA), Brooke, L.J.; see *Macro
(Ipswich) Ltd, Re* [1996] 1 W.L.R. 145 (Ch
D), Ferris, J.
Appendix 3, amended: SI 1998/3132 r.50,
Sch.1
Appendix 3, applied: SI 1998/3132 r.50,
Sch.1
Appendix 3, consolidated: SI 1998/3132 r.50,
Sch.1
Ord. 63,
see *Attorney General v Limbrick* Times,
March 28, 1996 (QBD), Garland, J.
r.4(1A), added: SI 1998/1898 r.14
Ord. 64,
r.4, amended: SI 1998/3132 r.50, Sch.1
r.4, applied: SI 1998/3132 r.50, Sch.1
r.4, consolidated: SI 1998/3132 r.50, Sch.1
r.7(1)(c), revoked (in part): SI 1996/2892 r.16
Ord. 65,
r.4(1), see *Abbey National Plc v Frost* [1999]
2 All E.R. 206 (CA), Nourse, L.J.
r.4(3), see *Abbey National Plc v Frost* [1998]
2 All E.R. 321 (Ch D), Carnwath, J.; see
Abbey National Plc v Frost [1999] 2 All E.R.
206 (CA), Nourse, L.J.
r.5, see *Anson (t/a Party Planners) v Trump*
[1998] 1 W.L.R. 1404 (CA), Otton, L.J.
r.5(2B), see *Anson (t/a Party Planners) v
Trump* [1998] 1 W.L.R. 1404 (CA), Otton,
L.J.; see *Venables v Mirror Group Newspapers Ltd* Times, December 9, 1998 (CA),
Mantell, L.J.
r.13, see *Nottingham Building Society v Peter
Bennett & Co* Times, February 26, 1997
(CA), Waite, L.J.
Ord. 69,
r.1, amended: SI 1998/3132 r.50, Sch.1
r.1, applied: SI 1998/3132 r.50, Sch.1
r.1, consolidated: SI 1998/3132 r.50, Sch.1
r.2, amended: SI 1998/3132 r.50, Sch.1
r.2, applied: SI 1998/3132 r.50, Sch.1
r.2, consolidated: SI 1998/3132 r.50, Sch.1
r.3, amended: SI 1998/3132 r.50, Sch.1
r.3, applied: SI 1998/3132 r.50, Sch.1
r.3, consolidated: SI 1998/3132 r.50, Sch.1
r.4, amended: SI 1998/3132 r.50, Sch.1
r.4, applied: SI 1998/3132 r.50, Sch.1
r.4, consolidated: SI 1998/3132 r.50, Sch.1
Ord. 70,
r.1, amended: SI 1998/3132 r.50, Sch.1
r.1, applied: SI 1998/3132 r.50, Sch.1
r.1, consolidated: SI 1998/3132 r.50, Sch.1
r.2, amended: SI 1998/3132 r.50, Sch.1
r.2, applied: SI 1998/3132 r.50, Sch.1
r.2, consolidated: SI 1998/3132 r.50, Sch.1
r.3, amended: SI 1998/3132 r.50, Sch.1
r.3, applied: SI 1998/3132 r.50, Sch.1
r.3, consolidated: SI 1998/3132 r.50, Sch.1
r.4, amended: SI 1998/3132 r.50, Sch.1
r.4, applied: SI 1998/3132 r.50, Sch.1
r.4, consolidated: SI 1998/3132 r.50, Sch.1
r.5, amended: SI 1998/3132 r.50, Sch.1
r.5, applied: SI 1998/3132 r.50, Sch.1
r.5, consolidated: SI 1998/3132 r.50, Sch.1
r.6, amended: SI 1998/3132 r.50, Sch.1
r.6, applied: SI 1998/3132 r.50, Sch.1
r.6, consolidated: SI 1998/3132 r.50, Sch.1
Ord. 71,
r.1, amended: SI 1998/3132 r.50, Sch.1

NO.

1965—cont.

1776. Rules of the Supreme Court 1965—*cont.*
Ord. 71—*cont.*
r.1, applied: SI 1998/3132 r.50, Sch.1
r.1, consolidated: SI 1998/3132 r.50, Sch.1
r.2, amended: SI 1998/3132 r.50, Sch.1
r.2, applied: SI 1998/3132 r.50, Sch.1
r.2, consolidated: SI 1998/3132 r.50, Sch.1
r.3, amended: SI 1998/3132 r.50, Sch.1
r.3, applied: SI 1998/3132 r.50, Sch.1
r.3, consolidated: SI 1998/3132 r.50, Sch.1
r.4, amended: SI 1998/3132 r.50, Sch.1
r.4, applied: SI 1998/3132 r.50, Sch.1
r.4, consolidated: SI 1998/3132 r.50, Sch.1
r.5, amended: SI 1998/3132 r.50, Sch.1
r.5, applied: SI 1998/3132 r.50, Sch.1
r.5, consolidated: SI 1998/3132 r.50, Sch.1
r.6, amended: SI 1998/3132 r.50, Sch.1
r.6, applied: SI 1998/3132 r.50, Sch.1
r.6, consolidated: SI 1998/3132 r.50, Sch.1
r.7, amended: SI 1998/3132 r.50, Sch.1
r.7, applied: SI 1998/3132 r.50, Sch.1
r.7, consolidated: SI 1998/3132 r.50, Sch.1
r.9, amended: SI 1998/3132 r.50, Sch.1
r.9, applied: SI 1998/3132 r.50, Sch.1
r.9, consolidated: SI 1998/3132 r.50, Sch.1
r.10, amended: SI 1998/3132 r.50, Sch.1
r.10, applied: SI 1998/3132 r.50, Sch.1
r.10, consolidated: SI 1998/3132 r.50, Sch.1
r.11, amended: SI 1998/3132 r.50, Sch.1
r.11, applied: SI 1998/3132 r.50, Sch.1
r.11, consolidated: SI 1998/3132 r.50, Sch.1
r.12, amended: SI 1998/3132 r.50, Sch.1
r.12, applied: SI 1998/3132 r.50, Sch.1
r.12, consolidated: SI 1998/3132 r.50, Sch.1
r.13, amended: SI 1998/3132 r.50, Sch.1
r.13, applied: SI 1998/3132 r.50, Sch.1
r.13, consolidated: SI 1998/3132 r.50, Sch.1
r.15, amended: SI 1998/3132 r.50, Sch.1
r.15, applied: SI 1998/3132 r.50, Sch.1
r.15, consolidated: SI 1998/3132 r.50, Sch.1
r.16, amended: SI 1998/3132 r.50, Sch.1
r.16, applied: SI 1998/3132 r.50, Sch.1
r.16, consolidated: SI 1998/3132 r.50, Sch.1
r.17, amended: SI 1998/3132 r.50, Sch.1
r.17, applied: SI 1998/3132 r.50, Sch.1
r.17, consolidated: SI 1998/3132 r.50, Sch.1
r.18, amended: SI 1998/3132 r.50, Sch.1
r.18, applied: SI 1998/3132 r.50, Sch.1
r.18, consolidated: SI 1998/3132 r.50, Sch.1
r.19, amended: SI 1998/3132 r.50, Sch.1
r.19, applied: SI 1998/3132 r.50, Sch.1
r.19, consolidated: SI 1998/3132 r.50, Sch.1
r.20, amended: SI 1998/3132 r.50, Sch.1
r.20, applied: SI 1998/3132 r.50, Sch.1
r.20, consolidated: SI 1998/3132 r.50, Sch.1
r.21, amended: SI 1998/3132 r.50, Sch.1
r.21, applied: SI 1998/3132 r.50, Sch.1
r.21, consolidated: SI 1998/3132 r.50, Sch.1
r.22, amended: SI 1998/3132 r.50, Sch.1
r.22, applied: SI 1998/3132 r.50, Sch.1
r.22, consolidated: SI 1998/3132 r.50, Sch.1
r.23, amended: SI 1998/3132 r.50, Sch.1
r.23, applied: SI 1998/3132 r.50, Sch.1
r.23, consolidated: SI 1998/3132 r.50, Sch.1
r.24, amended: SI 1998/3132 r.50, Sch.1
r.24, applied: SI 1998/3132 r.50, Sch.1
r.24, consolidated: SI 1998/3132 r.50, Sch.1
r.25, amended: SI 1998/3132 r.50, Sch.1
r.25, applied: SI 1998/3132 r.50, Sch.1
r.25, consolidated: SI 1998/3132 r.50, Sch.1
r.26, amended: SI 1998/3132 r.50, Sch.1
r.26, applied: SI 1998/3132 r.50, Sch.1

NO.

1965—cont.

1776. Rules of the Supreme Court 1965—*cont.*
Ord. 71—*cont.*
r.26, consolidated: SI 1998/3132 r.50, Sch.1
r.27, amended: SI 1998/3132 r.50, Sch.1
r.27, applied: SI 1998/3132 r.50, Sch.1
r.27, consolidated: SI 1998/3132 r.50, Sch.1
r.28, amended: SI 1998/3132 r.50, Sch.1
r.28, applied: SI 1998/3132 r.50, Sch.1
r.28, consolidated: SI 1998/3132 r.50, Sch.1
r.29, amended: SI 1998/3132 r.50, Sch.1
r.29, applied: SI 1998/3132 r.50, Sch.1
r.29, consolidated: SI 1998/3132 r.50, Sch.1
r.30, amended: SI 1998/3132 r.50, Sch.1
r.30, applied: SI 1998/3132 r.50, Sch.1
r.30, consolidated: SI 1998/3132 r.50, Sch.1
r.31, amended: SI 1998/3132 r.50, Sch.1
r.31, applied: SI 1998/3132 r.50, Sch.1
r.31, consolidated: SI 1998/3132 r.50, Sch.1
r.32, amended: SI 1998/3132 r.50, Sch.1
r.32, applied: SI 1998/3132 r.50, Sch.1
r.32, consolidated: SI 1998/3132 r.50, Sch.1
r.33, amended: SI 1998/3132 r.50, Sch.1
r.33, applied: SI 1998/3132 r.50, Sch.1
r.33, consolidated: SI 1998/3132 r.50, Sch.1
r.34, amended: SI 1998/3132 r.50, Sch.1
r.34, applied: SI 1998/3132 r.50, Sch.1
r.34, consolidated: SI 1998/3132 r.50, Sch.1
r.35, amended: SI 1998/3132 r.50, Sch.1
r.35, applied: SI 1998/3132 r.50, Sch.1
r.35, consolidated: SI 1998/3132 r.50, Sch.1
r.36, see *Normaco Ltd v Lundman* [1999] C.P.L.R. 326 (Ch D), Carnwath, J.
r.36, amended: SI 1998/3132 r.50, Sch.1
r.36, applied: SI 1998/3132 r.50, Sch.1
r.36, consolidated: SI 1998/3132 r.50, Sch.1
r.37, amended: SI 1998/3132 r.50, Sch.1
r.37, applied: SI 1998/3132 r.50, Sch.1
r.37, consolidated: SI 1998/3132 r.50, Sch.1
r.38, amended: SI 1998/3132 r.50, Sch.1
r.38, applied: SI 1998/3132 r.50, Sch.1
r.38, consolidated: SI 1998/3132 r.50, Sch.1
r.39, amended: SI 1998/3132 r.50, Sch.1
r.39, applied: SI 1998/3132 r.50, Sch.1
r.39, consolidated: SI 1998/3132 r.50, Sch.1
r.39A, amended: SI 1998/3132 r.50, Sch.1
r.39A, applied: SI 1998/3132 r.50, Sch.1
r.39A, consolidated: SI 1998/3132 r.50, Sch.1
r.40, amended: SI 1998/3132 r.50, Sch.1
r.40, applied: SI 1998/3132 r.50, Sch.1
r.40, consolidated: SI 1998/3132 r.50, Sch.1
r.41, amended: SI 1998/3132 r.50, Sch.1
r.41, applied: SI 1998/3132 r.50, Sch.1
r.41, consolidated: SI 1998/3132 r.50, Sch.1
r.42, amended: SI 1998/3132 r.50, Sch.1
r.42, applied: SI 1998/3132 r.50, Sch.1
r.42, consolidated: SI 1998/3132 r.50, Sch.1
r.43, amended: SI 1998/3132 r.50, Sch.1
r.43, applied: SI 1998/3132 r.50, Sch.1
r.43, consolidated: SI 1998/3132 r.50, Sch.1
r.44, amended: SI 1998/3132 r.50, Sch.1
r.44, applied: SI 1998/3132 r.50, Sch.1
r.44, consolidated: SI 1998/3132 r.50, Sch.1
Ord. 72,
see *Practice Direction (Mercantile Court Lists: Leeds and Newcastle upon Tyne)* [1997] 1 W.L.R. 219, Lord Bingham of Cornhill, L.C.J.
Ord. 73,
see *Practice Note (Arbitration: New Procedure)* [1997] 1 W.L.R. 391 (QBD (Comm Ct)), Colman, J.

NO.

1965—cont.

1776. Rules of the Supreme Court 1965—*cont.*
Ord. 73—*cont.*
  amended: SI 1996/3219 r.2
  substituted: SI 1996/3219 r.5
  r.1, substituted: SI 1996/3219 r.5
  r.2, substituted: SI 1996/3219 r.5
  r.3, substituted: SI 1996/3219 r.5
  r.4, substituted: SI 1996/3219 r.5
  r.5, substituted: SI 1996/3219 r.5
  r.5(6), amended: SI 1997/415 r.8
  r.6, substituted: SI 1996/3219 r.5
  r.7, see *Unicargo v Flotec Maritime S de RL*
    [1996] 2 Lloyd's Rep. 395 (QBD (Adm Ct)),
    Clarke, J.
  r.7, substituted: SI 1996/3219 r.5
  r.8, substituted: SI 1996/3219 r.5
  r.9, substituted: SI 1996/3219 r.5
  r.10, substituted: SI 1996/3219 r.5
  r.11, substituted: SI 1996/3219 r.5
  r.12, substituted: SI 1996/3219 r.5
  r.13, substituted: SI 1996/3219 r.5
  r.14, substituted: SI 1996/3219 r.5
  r.15, substituted: SI 1996/3219 r.5
  r.16, substituted: SI 1996/3219 r.5
  r.17, substituted: SI 1996/3219 r.5
  r.18, substituted: SI 1996/3219 r.5
  r.19, substituted: SI 1996/3219 r.5
  r.20, substituted: SI 1996/3219 r.5
  r.21, substituted: SI 1996/3219 r.5
  r.22, substituted: SI 1996/3219 r.5
  r.23, substituted: SI 1996/3219 r.5
  r.24, substituted: SI 1996/3219 r.5
  r.25, substituted: SI 1996/3219 r.5
  r.26, substituted: SI 1996/3219 r.5
  r.27, substituted: SI 1996/3219 r.5
  r.28, substituted: SI 1996/3219 r.5
  r.29, substituted: SI 1996/3219 r.5
  r.30, substituted: SI 1996/3219 r.5
  r.31, substituted: SI 1996/3219 r.5
  r.31(2), amended: SI 1998/1898 r.15
  r.32, substituted: SI 1996/3219 r.5
  r.33, substituted: SI 1996/3219 r.5
  r.34, substituted: SI 1996/3219 r.5
  r.35, substituted: SI 1996/3219 r.5
Ord. 74,
  r.1, amended: SI 1998/3132 r.50, Sch.1
  r.1, applied: SI 1998/3132 r.50, Sch.1
  r.1, consolidated: SI 1998/3132 r.50, Sch.1
  r.2, amended: SI 1998/3132 r.50, Sch.1
  r.2, applied: SI 1998/3132 r.50, Sch.1
  r.2, consolidated: SI 1998/3132 r.50, Sch.1
Ord. 75,
  see *Caspian Basin Specialised Emergency
    Salvage Administration v Bouygues Off-
    shore SA (No.4)* [1997] 2 Lloyd's Rep. 507
    (QBD (Adm Ct)), Rix, J.; see *Tjaskemolen
    (Now Named Visvliet) (No.1), The* [1997] 2
    Lloyd's Rep. 465 (QBD (Adm Ct)), Clarke,
    J.
  r.26(3)(b), amended: SI 1997/415 r.7
  r.28, see *Unicargo v Flotec Maritime S de RL
    (The Cienvik)* [1996] 2 Lloyd's Rep. 395
    (QBD (Adm Ct)), Clarke, J.
Ord. 77,
  r.1, amended: SI 1998/3132 r.50, Sch.1
  r.1, applied: SI 1998/3132 r.50, Sch.1
  r.1, consolidated: SI 1998/3132 r.50, Sch.1
  r.2, amended: SI 1998/3132 r.50, Sch.1
  r.2, applied: SI 1998/3132 r.50, Sch.1
  r.2, consolidated: SI 1998/3132 r.50, Sch.1
  r.3, amended: SI 1998/3132 r.50, Sch.1
  r.3, applied: SI 1998/3132 r.50, Sch.1

NO.

1965—cont.

1776. Rules of the Supreme Court 1965—*cont.*
Ord. 77—*cont.*
  r.3, consolidated: SI 1998/3132 r.50, Sch.1
  r.4, amended: SI 1998/3132 r.50, Sch.1
  r.4, applied: SI 1998/3132 r.50, Sch.1
  r.4, consolidated: SI 1998/3132 r.50, Sch.1
  r.6, amended: SI 1998/3132 r.50, Sch.1
  r.6, applied: SI 1998/3132 r.50, Sch.1
  r.6, consolidated: SI 1998/3132 r.50, Sch.1
  r.7, amended: SI 1998/3132 r.50, Sch.1
  r.7, applied: SI 1998/3132 r.50, Sch.1
  r.7, consolidated: SI 1998/3132 r.50, Sch.1
  r.8, amended: SI 1998/3132 r.50, Sch.1
  r.8, applied: SI 1998/3132 r.50, Sch.1
  r.8, consolidated: SI 1998/3132 r.50, Sch.1
  r.8A, amended: SI 1998/3132 r.50, Sch.1
  r.8A, applied: SI 1998/3132 r.50, Sch.1
  r.8A, consolidated: SI 1998/3132 r.50, Sch.1
  r.9, amended: SI 1998/3132 r.50, Sch.1
  r.9, applied: SI 1998/3132 r.50, Sch.1
  r.9, consolidated: SI 1998/3132 r.50, Sch.1
  r.10, amended: SI 1998/3132 r.50, Sch.1
  r.10, applied: SI 1998/3132 r.50, Sch.1
  r.10, consolidated: SI 1998/3132 r.50, Sch.1
  r.11, amended: SI 1998/3132 r.50, Sch.1
  r.11, applied: SI 1998/3132 r.50, Sch.1
  r.11, consolidated: SI 1998/3132 r.50, Sch.1
  r.12, amended: SI 1998/3132 r.50, Sch.1
  r.12, applied: SI 1998/3132 r.50, Sch.1
  r.12, consolidated: SI 1998/3132 r.50, Sch.1
  r.13, amended: SI 1998/3132 r.50, Sch.1
  r.13, applied: SI 1998/3132 r.50, Sch.1
  r.13, consolidated: SI 1998/3132 r.50, Sch.1
  r.14, amended: SI 1998/3132 r.50, Sch.1
  r.14, applied: SI 1998/3132 r.50, Sch.1
  r.14, consolidated: SI 1998/3132 r.50, Sch.1
  r.15, amended: SI 1998/3132 r.50, Sch.1
  r.15, applied: SI 1998/3132 r.50, Sch.1
  r.15, consolidated: SI 1998/3132 r.50, Sch.1
  r.16, amended: SI 1998/3132 r.50, Sch.1
  r.16, applied: SI 1998/3132 r.50, Sch.1
  r.16, consolidated: SI 1998/3132 r.50, Sch.1
  r.17, amended: SI 1998/3132 r.50, Sch.1
  r.17, applied: SI 1998/3132 r.50, Sch.1
  r.17, consolidated: SI 1998/3132 r.50, Sch.1
  r.18, amended: SI 1998/3132 r.50, Sch.1
  r.18, applied: SI 1998/3132 r.50, Sch.1
  r.18, consolidated: SI 1998/3132 r.50, Sch.1
Ord. 79,
  see *R. v Croydon Crown Court Ex p. Cox*
    [1997] 1 Cr. App. R. 20 (QBD), Pill, L.J.
  r.8, amended: SI 1998/3132 r.50, Sch.1
  r.8, applied: SI 1998/3132 r.50, Sch.1
  r.8, consolidated: SI 1998/3132 r.50, Sch.1
  r.9, see *R. v Croydon Crown Court Ex p. Cox*
    [1997] 1 Cr. App. R. 20 (QBD), Pill, L.J.
  r.9, amended: SI 1998/3132 r.50, Sch.1
  r.9, applied: SI 1998/3132 r.50, Sch.1
  r.9, consolidated: SI 1998/3132 r.50, Sch.1
  r.10, amended: SI 1998/3132 r.50, Sch.1
  r.10, applied: SI 1998/3132 r.50, Sch.1
  r.10, consolidated: SI 1998/3132 r.50, Sch.1
  r.10, revoked: SI 1998/1898 r.16
  r.11, amended: SI 1998/3132 r.50, Sch.1
  r.11, applied: SI 1998/3132 r.50, Sch.1
  r.11, consolidated: SI 1998/3132 r.50, Sch.1
  r.11, revoked: SI 1998/1898 r.16
Ord. 80,
  applied: SI 1996/207 Sch.8 para.42, SI 1996/
    2890 Sch.4 para.46
  r.10, see *Abada v Gray* Times, July 9, 1997
    (CA), Lord Woolf, M.R.

1965—cont.

1776. Rules of the Supreme Court 1965—*cont.*
Ord. 80—*cont.*
  r.11, see *Griffin v Kingsmill* [1998] P.N.L.R.
  157 (QBD), Timothy Walker, J.
Ord. 81,
  r.1, amended: SI 1998/3132 r.50, Sch.1
  r.1, applied: SI 1998/3132 r.50, Sch.1
  r.1, consolidated: SI 1998/3132 r.50, Sch.1
  r.2, amended: SI 1998/3132 r.50, Sch.1
  r.2, applied: SI 1998/3132 r.50, Sch.1
  r.2, consolidated: SI 1998/3132 r.50, Sch.1
  r.3, see *Chohan Clothing Co (Manchester)
  Ltd v Fox Brooks Marshall* Times, December 9, 1997 (CA), Evans, L.J.; see *Nottingham Building Society v Peter Bennett & Co*
  Times, February 26, 1997 (CA), Waite,
  L.J.; see *Robertson v Banham & Co* Times,
  November 26, 1996 (CA), Roch, L.J.
  r.4, amended: SI 1998/3132 r.50, Sch.1
  r.4, applied: SI 1998/3132 r.50, Sch.1
  r.4, consolidated: SI 1998/3132 r.50, Sch.1
  r.5, amended: SI 1998/3132 r.50, Sch.1
  r.5, applied: SI 1998/3132 r.50, Sch.1
  r.5, consolidated: SI 1998/3132 r.50, Sch.1
  r.6, amended: SI 1998/3132 r.50, Sch.1
  r.6, applied: SI 1998/3132 r.50, Sch.1
  r.6, consolidated: SI 1998/3132 r.50, Sch.1
  r.7, amended: SI 1998/3132 r.50, Sch.1
  r.7, applied: SI 1998/3132 r.50, Sch.1
  r.7, consolidated: SI 1998/3132 r.50, Sch.1
  r.9, amended: SI 1998/3132 r.50, Sch.1
  r.9, applied: SI 1998/3132 r.50, Sch.1
  r.9, consolidated: SI 1998/3132 r.50, Sch.1
  r.10, amended: SI 1998/3132 r.50, Sch.1
  r.10, applied: SI 1998/3132 r.50, Sch.1
  r.10, consolidated: SI 1998/3132 r.50, Sch.1
Ord. 82,
  see *Coff v Berkshire CC* Independent, February 6, 1997 (QBD), Drake, J.
  r.1, amended: SI 1998/3132 r.50, Sch.1
  r.1, applied: SI 1998/3132 r.50, Sch.1
  r.1, consolidated: SI 1998/3132 r.50, Sch.1
  r.2, amended: SI 1998/3132 r.50, Sch.1
  r.2, applied: SI 1998/3132 r.50, Sch.1
  r.2, consolidated: SI 1998/3132 r.50, Sch.1
  r.3, amended: SI 1998/3132 r.50, Sch.1
  r.3, applied: SI 1998/3132 r.50, Sch.1
  r.3, consolidated: SI 1998/3132 r.50, Sch.1
  r.3A, see *Aspro Travel Ltd v Owners Abroad
  Group Plc* [1996] 1 W.L.R. 132 (CA),
  Schiemann, L.J.; see *Cruise v Express
  Newspapers Plc* [1999] Q.B. 931 (CA),
  Brooke, L.J.; see *Geenty v Channel Four
  Television Corp* [1998] E.M.L.R. 524 (CA),
  Hirst, L.J.; see *Hinduja v Asian TV Ltd*
  [1998] E.M.L.R. 516 (CA), Hirst, L.J.; see
  Mapp v News Group Newspapers Ltd
  [1998] Q.B. 520 (CA), Hirst, L.J.; see *Norman v Future Publishing Ltd* [1999]
  E.M.L.R. 325 (CA), Hirst, L.J.; see *Shah v
  Standard Chartered Bank* [1999] Q.B. 241
  (CA), Hirst, L.J.
  r.3A, amended: SI 1998/3132 r.50, Sch.1
  r.3A, applied: SI 1998/3132 r.50, Sch.1
  r.3A, consolidated: SI 1998/3132 r.50, Sch.1
  r.4, amended: SI 1998/3132 r.50, Sch.1
  r.4, applied: SI 1998/3132 r.50, Sch.1
  r.4, consolidated: SI 1998/3132 r.50, Sch.1
  r.5, amended: SI 1998/3132 r.50, Sch.1
  r.5, applied: SI 1998/3132 r.50, Sch.1
  r.5, consolidated: SI 1998/3132 r.50, Sch.1
  r.6, amended: SI 1998/3132 r.50, Sch.1

1965—cont.

1776. Rules of the Supreme Court 1965—*cont.*
Ord. 82—*cont.*
  r.6, applied: SI 1998/3132 r.50, Sch.1
  r.6, consolidated: SI 1998/3132 r.50, Sch.1
  r.8, amended: SI 1998/3132 r.50, Sch.1
  r.8, applied: SI 1998/3132 r.50, Sch.1
  r.8, consolidated: SI 1998/3132 r.50, Sch.1
Ord. 85,
  r.1, amended: SI 1998/3132 r.50, Sch.1
  r.1, applied: SI 1998/3132 r.50, Sch.1
  r.1, consolidated: SI 1998/3132 r.50, Sch.1
  r.2, amended: SI 1998/3132 r.50, Sch.1
  r.2, applied: SI 1998/3132 r.50, Sch.1
  r.2, consolidated: SI 1998/3132 r.50, Sch.1
  r.3, amended: SI 1998/3132 r.50, Sch.1
  r.3, applied: SI 1998/3132 r.50, Sch.1
  r.3, consolidated: SI 1998/3132 r.50, Sch.1
  r.5, amended: SI 1998/3132 r.50, Sch.1
  r.5, applied: SI 1998/3132 r.50, Sch.1
  r.5, consolidated: SI 1998/3132 r.50, Sch.1
  r.6, amended: SI 1998/3132 r.50, Sch.1
  r.6, applied: SI 1998/3132 r.50, Sch.1
  r.6, consolidated: SI 1998/3132 r.50, Sch.1
Ord. 87,
  r.1, amended: SI 1998/3132 r.50, Sch.1
  r.1, applied: SI 1998/3132 r.50, Sch.1
  r.1, consolidated: SI 1998/3132 r.50, Sch.1
  r.2, amended: SI 1998/3132 r.50, Sch.1
  r.2, applied: SI 1998/3132 r.50, Sch.1
  r.2, consolidated: SI 1998/3132 r.50, Sch.1
  r.2(4)(5), amended: SI 1998/3132 r.50, Sch.1
  r.2(4)(5), applied: SI 1998/3132 r.50, Sch.1
  r.2(4)(5), consolidated: SI 1998/3132 r.50,
  Sch.1
  r.3, amended: SI 1998/3132 r.50, Sch.1
  r.3, applied: SI 1998/3132 r.50, Sch.1
  r.3, consolidated: SI 1998/3132 r.50, Sch.1
  r.4, amended: SI 1998/3132 r.50, Sch.1
  r.4, applied: SI 1998/3132 r.50, Sch.1
  r.4, consolidated: SI 1998/3132 r.50, Sch.1
  r.5, amended: SI 1998/3132 r.50, Sch.1
  r.5, applied: SI 1998/3132 r.50, Sch.1
  r.5, consolidated: SI 1998/3132 r.50, Sch.1
  r.6, amended: SI 1998/3132 r.50, Sch.1
  r.6, applied: SI 1998/3132 r.50, Sch.1
  r.6, consolidated: SI 1998/3132 r.50, Sch.1
Ord. 88,
  see *National Westminster Bank Plc v Kitch*
  [1996] 1 W.L.R. 1316 (CA), Schiemann,
  L.J.
  r.1, amended: SI 1998/3132 r.50, Sch.1
  r.1, applied: SI 1998/3132 r.50, Sch.1
  r.1, consolidated: SI 1998/3132 r.50, Sch.1
  r.2, amended: SI 1998/3132 r.50, Sch.1
  r.2, applied: SI 1998/3132 r.50, Sch.1
  r.2, consolidated: SI 1998/3132 r.50, Sch.1
  r.3, amended: SI 1998/3132 r.50, Sch.1
  r.3, applied: SI 1998/3132 r.50, Sch.1
  r.3, consolidated: SI 1998/3132 r.50, Sch.1
  r.4, amended: SI 1998/3132 r.50, Sch.1
  r.4, applied: SI 1998/3132 r.50, Sch.1
  r.4, consolidated: SI 1998/3132 r.50, Sch.1
  r.5, amended: SI 1998/3132 r.50, Sch.1
  r.5, applied: SI 1998/3132 r.50, Sch.1
  r.5, consolidated: SI 1998/3132 r.50, Sch.1
  r.5A, amended: SI 1998/3132 r.50, Sch.1
  r.5A, applied: SI 1998/3132 r.50, Sch.1
  r.5A, consolidated: SI 1998/3132 r.50, Sch.1
  r.7, amended: SI 1998/3132 r.50, Sch.1
  r.7, applied: SI 1998/3132 r.50, Sch.1
  r.7, consolidated: SI 1998/3132 r.50, Sch.1

NO.

1965—cont.

1776. Rules of the Supreme Court 1965—*cont.*
Ord. 91,
  r.1, amended: SI 1998/3132 r.50, Sch.1
  r.1, applied: SI 1998/3132 r.50, Sch.1
  r.1, consolidated: SI 1998/3132 r.50, Sch.1
  r.2, amended: SI 1998/3132 r.50, Sch.1
  r.2, applied: SI 1998/3132 r.50, Sch.1
  r.2, consolidated: SI 1998/3132 r.50, Sch.1
  r.3, amended: SI 1998/3132 r.50, Sch.1
  r.3, applied: SI 1998/3132 r.50, Sch.1
  r.3, consolidated: SI 1998/3132 r.50, Sch.1
  r.4, amended: SI 1998/3132 r.50, Sch.1
  r.4, applied: SI 1998/3132 r.50, Sch.1
  r.4, consolidated: SI 1998/3132 r.50, Sch.1
  r.5, amended: SI 1998/3132 r.50, Sch.1
  r.5, applied: SI 1998/3132 r.50, Sch.1
  r.5, consolidated: SI 1998/3132 r.50, Sch.1
  r.5A, amended: SI 1998/3132 r.50, Sch.1
  r.5A, applied: SI 1998/3132 r.50, Sch.1
  r.5A, consolidated: SI 1998/3132 r.50, Sch.1
  r.6, amended: SI 1998/3132 r.50, Sch.1
  r.6, applied: SI 1998/3132 r.50, Sch.1
  r.6, consolidated: SI 1998/3132 r.50, Sch.1
  r.6(1), amended: SI 1996/2892 r.18, SI 1998/
    3132 r.50, Sch.1
  r.6(1), applied: SI 1998/3132 r.50, Sch.1
  r.6(1), consolidated: SI 1998/3132 r.50,
    Sch.1
  r.6(2), amended: SI 1998/1898 r.17, SI 1998/
    3132 r.50, Sch.1
  r.6(2), applied: SI 1998/3132 r.50, Sch.1
  r.6(2), consolidated: SI 1998/3132 r.50,
    Sch.1
Ord. 92,
  r.1, amended: SI 1998/3132 r.50, Sch.1
  r.1, applied: SI 1998/3132 r.50, Sch.1
  r.1, consolidated: SI 1998/3132 r.50, Sch.1
  r.2, amended: SI 1998/3132 r.50, Sch.1
  r.2, applied: SI 1998/3132 r.50, Sch.1
  r.2, consolidated: SI 1998/3132 r.50, Sch.1
  r.3A, amended: SI 1998/1129 Art.2, Sch.1
    para.1, SI 1998/3132 r.50, Sch.1
  r.3A, applied: SI 1998/3132 r.50, Sch.1
  r.3A, consolidated: SI 1998/3132 r.50, Sch.1
  r.4, amended: SI 1998/3132 r.50, Sch.1
  r.4, applied: SI 1998/3132 r.50, Sch.1
  r.4, consolidated: SI 1998/3132 r.50, Sch.1
  r.5, amended: SI 1998/3132 r.50, Sch.1
  r.5, applied: SI 1998/3132 r.50, Sch.1
  r.5, consolidated: SI 1998/3132 r.50, Sch.1
Ord. 93,
  r.1, amended: SI 1998/3132 r.50, Sch.1
  r.1, applied: SI 1998/3132 r.50, Sch.1
  r.1, consolidated: SI 1998/3132 r.50, Sch.1
  r.2, amended: SI 1998/3132 r.50, Sch.1
  r.2, applied: SI 1998/3132 r.50, Sch.1
  r.2, consolidated: SI 1998/3132 r.50, Sch.1
  r.4, amended: SI 1998/3132 r.50, Sch.1
  r.4, applied: SI 1998/3132 r.50, Sch.1
  r.4, consolidated: SI 1998/3132 r.50, Sch.1
  r.5, amended: SI 1998/3132 r.50, Sch.1
  r.5, applied: SI 1998/3132 r.50, Sch.1
  r.5, consolidated: SI 1998/3132 r.50, Sch.1
  r.6, amended: SI 1998/3132 r.50, Sch.1
  r.6, applied: SI 1998/3132 r.50, Sch.1
  r.6, consolidated: SI 1998/3132 r.50, Sch.1
  r.9, amended: SI 1998/3132 r.50, Sch.1
  r.9, applied: SI 1998/3132 r.50, Sch.1
  r.9, consolidated: SI 1998/3132 r.50, Sch.1
  r.10, amended: SI 1998/3132 r.50, Sch.1
  r.10, applied: SI 1998/3132 r.50, Sch.1
  r.10, consolidated: SI 1998/3132 r.50, Sch.1

NO.

1965—cont.

1776. Rules of the Supreme Court 1965—*cont.*
Ord. 93—*cont.*
  r.11, amended: SI 1998/3132 r.50, Sch.1
  r.11, applied: SI 1998/3132 r.50, Sch.1
  r.11, consolidated: SI 1998/3132 r.50, Sch.1
  r.12, amended: SI 1998/3132 r.50, Sch.1
  r.12, applied: SI 1998/3132 r.50, Sch.1
  r.12, consolidated: SI 1998/3132 r.50, Sch.1
  r.15, amended: SI 1998/3132 r.50, Sch.1
  r.15, applied: SI 1998/3132 r.50, Sch.1
  r.15, consolidated: SI 1998/3132 r.50, Sch.1
  r.16, amended: SI 1998/3132 r.50, Sch.1
  r.16, applied: SI 1998/3132 r.50, Sch.1
  r.16, consolidated: SI 1998/3132 r.50, Sch.1
  r.17, amended: SI 1998/3132 r.50, Sch.1
  r.17, applied: SI 1998/3132 r.50, Sch.1
  r.17, consolidated: SI 1998/3132 r.50, Sch.1
  r.18, amended: SI 1998/3132 r.50, Sch.1
  r.18, applied: SI 1998/3132 r.50, Sch.1
  r.18, consolidated: SI 1998/3132 r.50, Sch.1
  r.19, amended: SI 1998/3132 r.50, Sch.1
  r.19, applied: SI 1998/3132 r.50, Sch.1
  r.19, consolidated: SI 1998/3132 r.50, Sch.1
  r.20, amended: SI 1998/3132 r.50, Sch.1
  r.20, applied: SI 1998/3132 r.50, Sch.1
  r.20, consolidated: SI 1998/3132 r.50, Sch.1
  r.21, amended: SI 1998/3132 r.50, Sch.1
  r.21, applied: SI 1998/3132 r.50, Sch.1
  r.21, consolidated: SI 1998/3132 r.50, Sch.1
  r.22, amended: SI 1998/3132 r.50, Sch.1
  r.22, applied: SI 1998/3132 r.50, Sch.1
  r.22, consolidated: SI 1998/3132 r.50, Sch.1
  r.23, amended: SI 1998/1129 Art.2, Sch.1
    para.1, SI 1998/3132 r.50, Sch.1
  r.23, applied: SI 1998/3132 r.50, Sch.1
  r.23, consolidated: SI 1998/3132 r.50, Sch.1
Ord. 94,
  r.1, amended: SI 1998/3132 r.50, Sch.1
  r.1, applied: SI 1998/3132 r.50, Sch.1
  r.1, consolidated: SI 1998/3132 r.50, Sch.1
  r.2, amended: SI 1998/3132 r.50, Sch.1
  r.2, applied: SI 1998/3132 r.50, Sch.1
  r.2, consolidated: SI 1998/3132 r.50, Sch.1
  r.2(1), amended: SI 1998/3132 r.50, Sch.1
  r.2(1), applied: SI 1998/3132 r.50, Sch.1
  r.2(1), consolidated: SI 1998/3132 r.50,
    Sch.1
  r.2(2)(b), amended: SI 1998/3132 r.50, Sch.1
  r.2(2)(b), applied: SI 1998/3132 r.50, Sch.1
  r.2(2)(b), consolidated: SI 1998/3132 r.50,
    Sch.1
  r.3, amended: SI 1998/3132 r.50, Sch.1
  r.3, applied: SI 1998/3132 r.50, Sch.1
  r.3, consolidated: SI 1998/3132 r.50, Sch.1
  r.4, amended: SI 1998/3132 r.50, Sch.1
  r.4, applied: SI 1998/3132 r.50, Sch.1
  r.4, consolidated: SI 1998/3132 r.50, Sch.1
  r.5, amended: SI 1998/3132 r.50, Sch.1
  r.5, applied: SI 1998/3132 r.50, Sch.1
  r.5, consolidated: SI 1998/3132 r.50, Sch.1
  r.6, amended: SI 1998/3132 r.50, Sch.1
  r.6, applied: SI 1998/3132 r.50, Sch.1
  r.6, consolidated: SI 1998/3132 r.50, Sch.1
  r.7, amended: SI 1998/3132 r.50, Sch.1
  r.7, applied: SI 1998/3132 r.50, Sch.1
  r.7, consolidated: SI 1998/3132 r.50, Sch.1
  r.8, see *R. v Special Educational Needs Tri-*
    bunal Ex p. Brophy [1997] E.L.R. 291
    (QBD), Carnwath, J.
  r.8, amended: SI 1998/3132 r.50, Sch.1
  r.8, applied: SI 1998/3132 r.50, Sch.1
  r.8, consolidated: SI 1998/3132 r.50, Sch.1

NO.

1776. Rules of the Supreme Court 1965—*cont.*
Ord. 94—*cont.*
r.8(1), amended: SI 1996/2892 r.18, SI 1998/3132 r.50, Sch.1
r.8(1), applied: SI 1998/3132 r.50, Sch.1
r.8(1), consolidated: SI 1998/3132 r.50, Sch.1
r.8(2)(b), amended: SI 1996/2892 r.19, SI 1998/3132 r.50, Sch.1
r.8(2)(b), applied: SI 1998/3132 r.50, Sch.1
r.8(2)(b), consolidated: SI 1998/3132 r.50, Sch.1
r.9, see *R. v Special Educational Needs Tribunal Ex p. Brophy* [1997] E.L.R. 291 (QBD), Carnwath, J.
r.9, amended: SI 1998/3132 r.50, Sch.1
r.9, applied: SI 1998/3132 r.50, Sch.1
r.9, consolidated: SI 1998/3132 r.50, Sch.1
r.9(1), amended: SI 1996/2892 r.18, SI 1998/3132 r.50, Sch.1
r.9(1), applied: SI 1998/3132 r.50, Sch.1
r.9(1), consolidated: SI 1998/3132 r.50, Sch.1
r.10, amended: SI 1998/3132 r.50, Sch.1
r.10, applied: SI 1998/3132 r.50, Sch.1
r.10, consolidated: SI 1998/3132 r.50, Sch.1
r.11, amended: SI 1998/3132 r.50, Sch.1
r.11, applied: SI 1998/3132 r.50, Sch.1
r.11, consolidated: SI 1998/3132 r.50, Sch.1
r.12, amended: SI 1998/3132 r.50, Sch.1
r.12, applied: SI 1998/3132 r.50, Sch.1
r.12, consolidated: SI 1998/3132 r.50, Sch.1
r.12(2)(c), amended: SI 1998/3132 r.50, Sch.1
r.12(2)(c), applied: SI 1998/3132 r.50, Sch.1
r.12(2)(c), consolidated: SI 1998/3132 r.50, Sch.1
r.13, amended: SI 1998/3132 r.50, Sch.1
r.13, applied: SI 1998/3132 r.50, Sch.1
r.13, consolidated: SI 1998/3132 r.50, Sch.1
r.13(7)(8), amended: SI 1998/3132 r.50, Sch.1
r.13(7)(8), applied: SI 1998/3132 r.50, Sch.1
r.13(7)(8), consolidated: SI 1998/3132 r.50, Sch.1
r.14, amended: SI 1998/3132 r.50, Sch.1
r.14, applied: SI 1998/3132 r.50, Sch.1
r.14, consolidated: SI 1998/3132 r.50, Sch.1
r.16, added: SI 1998/1898 r.11
Ord. 95,
r.1, amended: SI 1998/3132 r.50, Sch.1
r.1, applied: SI 1998/3132 r.50, Sch.1
r.1, consolidated: SI 1998/3132 r.50, Sch.1
r.2, amended: SI 1998/3132 r.50, Sch.1
r.2, applied: SI 1998/3132 r.50, Sch.1
r.2, consolidated: SI 1998/3132 r.50, Sch.1
r.3, amended: SI 1998/3132 r.50, Sch.1
r.3, applied: SI 1998/3132 r.50, Sch.1
r.3, consolidated: SI 1998/3132 r.50, Sch.1
r.4, amended: SI 1998/3132 r.50, Sch.1
r.4, applied: SI 1998/3132 r.50, Sch.1
r.4, consolidated: SI 1998/3132 r.50, Sch.1
r.5, amended: SI 1998/3132 r.50, Sch.1
r.5, applied: SI 1998/3132 r.50, Sch.1
r.5, consolidated: SI 1998/3132 r.50, Sch.1
r.6, amended: SI 1998/3132 r.50, Sch.1
r.6, applied: SI 1998/3132 r.50, Sch.1
r.6, consolidated: SI 1998/3132 r.50, Sch.1
Ord. 96,
r.1, amended: SI 1998/3132 r.50, Sch.1
r.1, applied: SI 1998/3132 r.50, Sch.1
r.1, consolidated: SI 1998/3132 r.50, Sch.1

NO.

1776. Rules of the Supreme Court 1965—*cont.*
Ord. 96—*cont.*
r.2, amended: SI 1998/3132 r.50, Sch.1
r.2, applied: SI 1998/3132 r.50, Sch.1
r.2, consolidated: SI 1998/3132 r.50, Sch.1
r.3, amended: SI 1998/3132 r.50, Sch.1
r.3, applied: SI 1998/3132 r.50, Sch.1
r.3, consolidated: SI 1998/3132 r.50, Sch.1
r.4, amended: SI 1998/3132 r.50, Sch.1
r.4, applied: SI 1998/3132 r.50, Sch.1
r.4, consolidated: SI 1998/3132 r.50, Sch.1
r.5, amended: SI 1998/3132 r.50, Sch.1
r.5, applied: SI 1998/3132 r.50, Sch.1
r.5, consolidated: SI 1998/3132 r.50, Sch.1
r.6, amended: SI 1998/3132 r.50, Sch.1
r.6, applied: SI 1998/3132 r.50, Sch.1
r.6, consolidated: SI 1998/3132 r.50, Sch.1
r.7, amended: SI 1998/3132 r.50, Sch.1
r.7, applied: SI 1998/3132 r.50, Sch.1
r.7, consolidated: SI 1998/3132 r.50, Sch.1
r.8, amended: SI 1998/3132 r.50, Sch.1
r.8, applied: SI 1998/3132 r.50, Sch.1
r.8, consolidated: SI 1998/3132 r.50, Sch.1
Ord. 97,
r.1, amended: SI 1998/3132 r.50, Sch.1
r.1, applied: SI 1998/3132 r.50, Sch.1
r.1, consolidated: SI 1998/3132 r.50, Sch.1
r.2, amended: SI 1998/3132 r.50, Sch.1
r.2, applied: SI 1998/3132 r.50, Sch.1
r.2, consolidated: SI 1998/3132 r.50, Sch.1
r.3, amended: SI 1998/3132 r.50, Sch.1
r.3, applied: SI 1998/3132 r.50, Sch.1
r.3, consolidated: SI 1998/3132 r.50, Sch.1
r.4, amended: SI 1998/3132 r.50, Sch.1
r.4, applied: SI 1998/3132 r.50, Sch.1
r.4, consolidated: SI 1998/3132 r.50, Sch.1
r.5, amended: SI 1998/3132 r.50, Sch.1
r.5, applied: SI 1998/3132 r.50, Sch.1
r.5, consolidated: SI 1998/3132 r.50, Sch.1
r.6, amended: SI 1998/3132 r.50, Sch.1
r.6, applied: SI 1998/3132 r.50, Sch.1
r.6, consolidated: SI 1998/3132 r.50, Sch.1
r.6A, amended: SI 1998/3132 r.50, Sch.1
r.6A, applied: SI 1998/3132 r.50, Sch.1
r.6A, consolidated: SI 1998/3132 r.50, Sch.1
r.7, amended: SI 1998/3132 r.50, Sch.1
r.7, applied: SI 1998/3132 r.50, Sch.1
r.7, consolidated: SI 1998/3132 r.50, Sch.1
r.8, amended: SI 1998/3132 r.50, Sch.1
r.8, applied: SI 1998/3132 r.50, Sch.1
r.8, consolidated: SI 1998/3132 r.50, Sch.1
r.9, amended: SI 1998/3132 r.50, Sch.1
r.9, applied: SI 1998/3132 r.50, Sch.1
r.9, consolidated: SI 1998/3132 r.50, Sch.1
r.9A, amended: SI 1998/3132 r.50, Sch.1
r.9A, applied: SI 1998/3132 r.50, Sch.1
r.9A, consolidated: SI 1998/3132 r.50, Sch.1
r.10, amended: SI 1998/3132 r.50, Sch.1
r.10, applied: SI 1998/3132 r.50, Sch.1
r.10, consolidated: SI 1998/3132 r.50, Sch.1
r.11, amended: SI 1998/3132 r.50, Sch.1
r.11, applied: SI 1998/3132 r.50, Sch.1
r.11, consolidated: SI 1998/3132 r.50, Sch.1
r.12, amended: SI 1998/3132 r.50, Sch.1
r.12, applied: SI 1998/3132 r.50, Sch.1
r.12, consolidated: SI 1998/3132 r.50, Sch.1
r.13, amended: SI 1998/3132 r.50, Sch.1
r.13, applied: SI 1998/3132 r.50, Sch.1
r.13, consolidated: SI 1998/3132 r.50, Sch.1
r.14, amended: SI 1998/3132 r.50, Sch.1
r.14, applied: SI 1998/3132 r.50, Sch.1
r.14, consolidated: SI 1998/3132 r.50, Sch.1

NO.

1965—cont.

1776. Rules of the Supreme Court 1965—*cont.*
Ord. 97—*cont.*
r.15, amended: SI 1998/3132 r.50, Sch.1
r.15, applied: SI 1998/3132 r.50, Sch.1
r.15, consolidated: SI 1998/3132 r.50, Sch.1
r.15, revoked: SI 1998/1898 r.18
r.16, amended: SI 1998/3132 r.50, Sch.1
r.16, applied: SI 1998/3132 r.50, Sch.1
r.16, consolidated: SI 1998/3132 r.50, Sch.1
r.17, amended: SI 1998/3132 r.50, Sch.1
r.17, applied: SI 1998/3132 r.50, Sch.1
r.17, consolidated: SI 1998/3132 r.50, Sch.1
r.18, amended: SI 1998/3132 r.50, Sch.1
r.18, applied: SI 1998/3132 r.50, Sch.1
r.18, consolidated: SI 1998/3132 r.50, Sch.1
r.19, amended: SI 1998/3132 r.50, Sch.1
r.19, applied: SI 1998/3132 r.50, Sch.1
r.19, consolidated: SI 1998/3132 r.50, Sch.1
Ord. 98,
r.1, amended: SI 1998/3132 r.50, Sch.1
r.1, applied: SI 1998/3132 r.50, Sch.1
r.1, consolidated: SI 1998/3132 r.50, Sch.1
r.2, amended: SI 1998/3132 r.50, Sch.1
r.2, applied: SI 1998/3132 r.50, Sch.1
r.2, consolidated: SI 1998/3132 r.50, Sch.1
r.3, amended: SI 1998/3132 r.50, Sch.1
r.3, applied: SI 1998/3132 r.50, Sch.1
r.3, consolidated: SI 1998/3132 r.50, Sch.1
r.4, amended: SI 1998/3132 r.50, Sch.1
r.4, applied: SI 1998/3132 r.50, Sch.1
r.4, consolidated: SI 1998/3132 r.50, Sch.1
Ord. 99,
r.1, amended: SI 1998/3132 r.50, Sch.1
r.1, applied: SI 1998/3132 r.50, Sch.1
r.1, consolidated: SI 1998/3132 r.50, Sch.1
r.A1, amended: SI 1998/3132 r.50, Sch.1
r.A1, applied: SI 1998/3132 r.50, Sch.1
r.A1, consolidated: SI 1998/3132 r.50, Sch.1
r.2, amended: SI 1998/3132 r.50, Sch.1
r.2, applied: SI 1998/3132 r.50, Sch.1
r.2, consolidated: SI 1998/3132 r.50, Sch.1
r.3, amended: SI 1998/3132 r.50, Sch.1
r.3, applied: SI 1998/3132 r.50, Sch.1
r.3, consolidated: SI 1998/3132 r.50, Sch.1
r.4, amended: SI 1998/3132 r.50, Sch.1
r.4, applied: SI 1998/3132 r.50, Sch.1
r.4, consolidated: SI 1998/3132 r.50, Sch.1
r.5, amended: SI 1998/3132 r.50, Sch.1
r.5, applied: SI 1998/3132 r.50, Sch.1
r.5, consolidated: SI 1998/3132 r.50, Sch.1
r.6, amended: SI 1998/3132 r.50, Sch.1
r.6, applied: SI 1998/3132 r.50, Sch.1
r.6, consolidated: SI 1998/3132 r.50, Sch.1
r.7, amended: SI 1998/3132 r.50, Sch.1
r.7, applied: SI 1998/3132 r.50, Sch.1
r.7, consolidated: SI 1998/3132 r.50, Sch.1
r.8, amended: SI 1998/3132 r.50, Sch.1
r.8, applied: SI 1998/3132 r.50, Sch.1
r.8, consolidated: SI 1998/3132 r.50, Sch.1
r.9, amended: SI 1998/3132 r.50, Sch.1
r.9, applied: SI 1998/3132 r.50, Sch.1
r.9, consolidated: SI 1998/3132 r.50, Sch.1
r.10, amended: SI 1998/3132 r.50, Sch.1
r.10, applied: SI 1998/3132 r.50, Sch.1
r.10, consolidated: SI 1998/3132 r.50, Sch.1
Ord. 100,
r.1, amended: SI 1996/2892 r.12
r.2, amended: SI 1996/2892 r.13
r.3, amended: SI 1996/2892 r.14
Ord. 101,
r.1, amended: SI 1998/3132 r.50, Sch.1
r.1, applied: SI 1998/3132 r.50, Sch.1

NO.

1965—cont.

1776. Rules of the Supreme Court 1965—*cont.*
Ord. 101—*cont.*
r.1, consolidated: SI 1998/3132 r.50, Sch.1
r.2, amended: SI 1998/3132 r.50, Sch.1
r.2, applied: SI 1998/3132 r.50, Sch.1
r.2, consolidated: SI 1998/3132 r.50, Sch.1
r.3, amended: SI 1998/3132 r.50, Sch.1
r.3, applied: SI 1998/3132 r.50, Sch.1
r.3, consolidated: SI 1998/3132 r.50, Sch.1
r.4, amended: SI 1998/3132 r.50, Sch.1
r.4, applied: SI 1998/3132 r.50, Sch.1
r.4, consolidated: SI 1998/3132 r.50, Sch.1
Ord. 104,
r.1, amended: SI 1997/415 r.5
r.3(1)(c), amended: SI 1998/1898 r.4
r.3(1)(d), substituted: SI 1998/1898 r.5
r.3(1A), added: SI 1998/1898 r.6
r.3(1B), added: SI 1998/1898 r.6
r.3(1C), added: SI 1998/1898 r.6
r.3(1D), added: SI 1998/1898 r.6
r.3(2A), added: SI 1998/1898 r.7
r.3(2B), added: SI 1998/1898 r.7
r.3(3)(a), substituted: SI 1998/1898 r.8
r.3(3)(b), substituted: SI 1998/1898 r.8
r.3(3)(d), added: SI 1998/1898 r.9
r.4, see *Organon Teknika Ltd v Hoffmann-La-Roche AG* [1996] F.S.R. 383 (Pat Ct), Jacob, J.
r.9, substituted: SI 1996/2892 r.15
r.10, see *Practice Direction (Patents Court: Practice Explanation), Re* [1996] 1 W.L.R. 1567 (Ch D), Jacob, J.
r.11, see *Pifco Ltd v Phillips Domestic Appliances and Personal Care BV* Independent, January 18, 1999 (C.S) (Ch D), Pumfrey, J.
r.12, see *Practice Direction (Patents Court: Practice Explanation), Re* [1996] 1 W.L.R. 1567 (Ch D), Jacob, J.
r.19(17), added: SI 1998/1898 r.10
Ord. 106,
r.1, amended: SI 1998/3132 r.50, Sch.1
r.1, applied: SI 1998/3132 r.50, Sch.1
r.1, consolidated: SI 1998/3132 r.50, Sch.1
r.2, amended: SI 1998/3132 r.50, Sch.1
r.2, applied: SI 1998/3132 r.50, Sch.1
r.2, consolidated: SI 1998/3132 r.50, Sch.1
r.3, amended: SI 1998/3132 r.50, Sch.1
r.3, applied: SI 1998/3132 r.50, Sch.1
r.3, consolidated: SI 1998/3132 r.50, Sch.1
r.5A, amended: SI 1998/3132 r.50, Sch.1
r.5A, applied: SI 1998/3132 r.50, Sch.1
r.5A, consolidated: SI 1998/3132 r.50, Sch.1
r.6, amended: SI 1998/3132 r.50, Sch.1
r.6, applied: SI 1998/3132 r.50, Sch.1
r.6, consolidated: SI 1998/3132 r.50, Sch.1
r.7, amended: SI 1998/3132 r.50, Sch.1
r.7, applied: SI 1998/3132 r.50, Sch.1
r.7, consolidated: SI 1998/3132 r.50, Sch.1
r.8, amended: SI 1998/3132 r.50, Sch.1
r.8, applied: SI 1998/3132 r.50, Sch.1
r.8, consolidated: SI 1998/3132 r.50, Sch.1
r.9, amended: SI 1998/3132 r.50, Sch.1
r.9, applied: SI 1998/3132 r.50, Sch.1
r.9, consolidated: SI 1998/3132 r.50, Sch.1
r.10, amended: SI 1998/3132 r.50, Sch.1
r.10, applied: SI 1998/3132 r.50, Sch.1
r.10, consolidated: SI 1998/3132 r.50, Sch.1
r.11, amended: SI 1998/3132 r.50, Sch.1
r.11, applied: SI 1998/3132 r.50, Sch.1
r.11, consolidated: SI 1998/3132 r.50, Sch.1
r.12, see *R. v Legal Aid Board Ex p. Kaim Todner* [1999] Q.B. 966 (CA), Lord Woolf, M.R.

NO.

1965—cont.

1776. Rules of the Supreme Court 1965—*cont.*
Ord. 106—*cont.*
 r.12, amended: SI 1998/3132 r.50, Sch.1
 r.12, applied: SI 1998/3132 r.50, Sch.1
 r.12, consolidated: SI 1998/3132 r.50, Sch.1
 r.13, amended: SI 1998/3132 r.50, Sch.1
 r.13, applied: SI 1998/3132 r.50, Sch.1
 r.13, consolidated: SI 1998/3132 r.50, Sch.1
 r.14, amended: SI 1998/3132 r.50, Sch.1
 r.14, applied: SI 1998/3132 r.50, Sch.1
 r.14, consolidated: SI 1998/3132 r.50, Sch.1
 r.15, amended: SI 1998/3132 r.50, Sch.1
 r.15, applied: SI 1998/3132 r.50, Sch.1
 r.15, consolidated: SI 1998/3132 r.50, Sch.1
 r.16, amended: SI 1998/3132 r.50, Sch.1
 r.16, applied: SI 1998/3132 r.50, Sch.1
 r.16, consolidated: SI 1998/3132 r.50, Sch.1
 r.17, amended: SI 1998/3132 r.50, Sch.1
 r.17, applied: SI 1998/3132 r.50, Sch.1
 r.17, consolidated: SI 1998/3132 r.50, Sch.1
Ord. 108,
 r.1, amended: SI 1998/3132 r.50, Sch.1
 r.1, applied: SI 1998/3132 r.50, Sch.1
 r.1, consolidated: SI 1998/3132 r.50, Sch.1
 r.2, amended: SI 1998/3132 r.50, Sch.1
 r.2, applied: SI 1998/3132 r.50, Sch.1
 r.2, consolidated: SI 1998/3132 r.50, Sch.1
 r.3, amended: SI 1998/3132 r.50, Sch.1
 r.3, applied: SI 1998/3132 r.50, Sch.1
 r.3, consolidated: SI 1998/3132 r.50, Sch.1
 r.4, amended: SI 1998/3132 r.50, Sch.1
 r.4, applied: SI 1998/3132 r.50, Sch.1
 r.4, consolidated: SI 1998/3132 r.50, Sch.1
 r.5, amended: SI 1998/3132 r.50, Sch.1
 r.5, applied: SI 1998/3132 r.50, Sch.1
 r.5, consolidated: SI 1998/3132 r.50, Sch.1
 r.5(2), see *Weth v Attorney General* [1999] 1
  W.L.R. 686 (CA), Nourse, L.J.
 r.5(2), amended: SI 1998/3132 r.50, Sch.1
 r.5(2), applied: SI 1998/3132 r.50, Sch.1
 r.5(2), consolidated: SI 1998/3132 r.50,
  Sch.1
 r.6, amended: SI 1998/3132 r.50, Sch.1
 r.6, applied: SI 1998/3132 r.50, Sch.1
 r.6, consolidated: SI 1998/3132 r.50, Sch.1
Ord. 109,
 r.1, amended: SI 1998/3132 r.50, Sch.1
 r.1, applied: SI 1998/3132 r.50, Sch.1
 r.1, consolidated: SI 1998/3132 r.50, Sch.1
 r.2, amended: SI 1998/3132 r.50, Sch.1
 r.2, applied: SI 1998/3132 r.50, Sch.1
 r.2, consolidated: SI 1998/3132 r.50, Sch.1
 r.3, amended: SI 1998/3132 r.50, Sch.1
 r.3, applied: SI 1998/3132 r.50, Sch.1
 r.3, consolidated: SI 1998/3132 r.50, Sch.1
Ord. 110,
 r.1, amended: SI 1998/3132 r.50, Sch.1
 r.1, applied: SI 1998/3132 r.50, Sch.1
 r.1, consolidated: SI 1998/3132 r.50, Sch.1
Ord. 111,
 r.1, amended: SI 1998/3132 r.50, Sch.1
 r.1, applied: SI 1998/3132 r.50, Sch.1
 r.1, consolidated: SI 1998/3132 r.50, Sch.1
 r.2, amended: SI 1998/3132 r.50, Sch.1
 r.2, applied: SI 1998/3132 r.50, Sch.1
 r.2, consolidated: SI 1998/3132 r.50, Sch.1
 r.3, amended: SI 1998/3132 r.50, Sch.1
 r.3, applied: SI 1998/3132 r.50, Sch.1
 r.3, consolidated: SI 1998/3132 r.50, Sch.1
 r.4, amended: SI 1998/3132 r.50, Sch.1
 r.4, applied: SI 1998/3132 r.50, Sch.1
 r.4, consolidated: SI 1998/3132 r.50, Sch.1

NO.

1965—cont.

1776. Rules of the Supreme Court 1965—*cont.*
Ord. 111—*cont.*
 r.5, amended: SI 1998/3132 r.50, Sch.1
 r.5, applied: SI 1998/3132 r.50, Sch.1
 r.5, consolidated: SI 1998/3132 r.50, Sch.1
Ord. 112,
 r.1, amended: SI 1998/3132 r.50, Sch.1
 r.1, applied: SI 1998/3132 r.50, Sch.1
 r.1, consolidated: SI 1998/3132 r.50, Sch.1
 r.2, amended: SI 1998/3132 r.50, Sch.1
 r.2, applied: SI 1998/3132 r.50, Sch.1
 r.2, consolidated: SI 1998/3132 r.50, Sch.1
 r.3, amended: SI 1998/3132 r.50, Sch.1
 r.3, applied: SI 1998/3132 r.50, Sch.1
 r.3, consolidated: SI 1998/3132 r.50, Sch.1
 r.4, amended: SI 1998/3132 r.50, Sch.1
 r.4, applied: SI 1998/3132 r.50, Sch.1
 r.4, consolidated: SI 1998/3132 r.50, Sch.1
 r.5, amended: SI 1998/3132 r.50, Sch.1
 r.5, applied: SI 1998/3132 r.50, Sch.1
 r.5, consolidated: SI 1998/3132 r.50, Sch.1
 r.6, amended: SI 1998/3132 r.50, Sch.1
 r.6, applied: SI 1998/3132 r.50, Sch.1
 r.6, consolidated: SI 1998/3132 r.50, Sch.1
Ord. 113,
 see *McDougalls Catering Foods Ltd v BSE
  Trading Ltd* (1998) 76 P. & C.R. 312 (CA),
  Aldous, L.J.; see *R. v Brighton and Hove
  Council Ex p. Marmont* [1998] 2 P.L.R. 48
  (QBD), Tucker, J.; see *Secretary of State
  for Transport v Haughian* (1997) 73 P. &
  C.R. 85 (CA), Hutchison, L.J.; see *Southwark LBC v Logan* (1997) 19 H.L.R. 40
  (CA), Neill, L.J.
 r.1, amended: SI 1998/3132 r.50, Sch.1
 r.1, applied: SI 1998/3132 r.50, Sch.1
 r.1, consolidated: SI 1998/3132 r.50, Sch.1
 r.1A, amended: SI 1998/3132 r.50, Sch.1
 r.1A, applied: SI 1998/3132 r.50, Sch.1
 r.1A, consolidated: SI 1998/3132 r.50, Sch.1
 r.2, amended: SI 1998/3132 r.50, Sch.1
 r.2, applied: SI 1998/3132 r.50, Sch.1
 r.2, consolidated: SI 1998/3132 r.50, Sch.1
 r.3, amended: SI 1998/3132 r.50, Sch.1
 r.3, applied: SI 1998/3132 r.50, Sch.1
 r.3, consolidated: SI 1998/3132 r.50, Sch.1
 r.4, amended: SI 1998/3132 r.50, Sch.1
 r.4, applied: SI 1998/3132 r.50, Sch.1
 r.4, consolidated: SI 1998/3132 r.50, Sch.1
 r.5, amended: SI 1998/3132 r.50, Sch.1
 r.5, applied: SI 1998/3132 r.50, Sch.1
 r.5, consolidated: SI 1998/3132 r.50, Sch.1
 r.6, amended: SI 1998/3132 r.50, Sch.1
 r.6, applied: SI 1998/3132 r.50, Sch.1
 r.6, consolidated: SI 1998/3132 r.50, Sch.1
 r.7, amended: SI 1998/3132 r.50, Sch.1
 r.7, applied: SI 1998/3132 r.50, Sch.1
 r.7, consolidated: SI 1998/3132 r.50, Sch.1
 r.8, see *Seven Eight Six Properties Ltd v Gha-
  foor* [1997] B.P.I.R. 519 (CA), Hutchison,
  L.J.
 r.8, amended: SI 1998/3132 r.50, Sch.1
 r.8, applied: SI 1998/3132 r.50, Sch.1
 r.8, consolidated: SI 1998/3132 r.50, Sch.1
Ord. 114,
 see *Practice Direction (Sup Ct: References to
  the Court of Justice of the European Communities)* [1999] 1 W.L.R. 260 (Sup Ct),
  Lord Bingham of Cornhill, L.C.J.
 r.1, amended: SI 1998/3132 r.50, Sch.1
 r.1, applied: SI 1998/3132 r.50, Sch.1
 r.1, consolidated: SI 1998/3132 r.50, Sch.1

NO.

1776. Rules of the Supreme Court 1965—*cont.*
Ord. 114—*cont.*
  r.2, amended: SI 1998/3132 r.50, Sch.1
  r.2, applied: SI 1998/3132 r.50, Sch.1
  r.2, consolidated: SI 1998/3132 r.50, Sch.1
  r.3, amended: SI 1998/3132 r.50, Sch.1
  r.3, applied: SI 1998/3132 r.50, Sch.1
  r.3, consolidated: SI 1998/3132 r.50, Sch.1
  r.4, amended: SI 1998/3132 r.50, Sch.1
  r.4, applied: SI 1998/3132 r.50, Sch.1
  r.4, consolidated: SI 1998/3132 r.50, Sch.1
  r.5, amended: SI 1998/3132 r.50, Sch.1
  r.5, applied: SI 1998/3132 r.50, Sch.1
  r.5, consolidated: SI 1998/3132 r.50, Sch.1
  r.6, amended: SI 1998/3132 r.50, Sch.1
  r.6, applied: SI 1998/3132 r.50, Sch.1
  r.6, consolidated: SI 1998/3132 r.50, Sch.1
Ord. 115,
  r.1, amended: SI 1998/3132 r.50, Sch.1
  r.1, applied: SI 1998/3132 r.50, Sch.1
  r.1, consolidated: SI 1998/3132 r.50, Sch.1
  r.2, amended: SI 1998/3132 r.50, Sch.1
  r.2, applied: SI 1998/3132 r.50, Sch.1
  r.2, consolidated: SI 1998/3132 r.50, Sch.1
  r.2A, amended: SI 1998/3132 r.50, Sch.1
  r.2A, applied: SI 1998/3132 r.50, Sch.1
  r.2A, consolidated: SI 1998/3132 r.50, Sch.1
  r.2B, amended: SI 1998/3132 r.50, Sch.1
  r.2B, applied: SI 1998/3132 r.50, Sch.1
  r.2B, consolidated: SI 1998/3132 r.50, Sch.1
  r.3, amended: SI 1998/3132 r.50, Sch.1
  r.3, applied: SI 1998/3132 r.50, Sch.1
  r.3, consolidated: SI 1998/3132 r.50, Sch.1
  r.4, amended: SI 1998/3132 r.50, Sch.1
  r.4, applied: SI 1998/3132 r.50, Sch.1
  r.4, consolidated: SI 1998/3132 r.50, Sch.1
  r.5, amended: SI 1998/3132 r.50, Sch.1
  r.5, applied: SI 1998/3132 r.50, Sch.1
  r.5, consolidated: SI 1998/3132 r.50, Sch.1
  r.6, amended: SI 1998/3132 r.50, Sch.1
  r.6, applied: SI 1998/3132 r.50, Sch.1
  r.6, consolidated: SI 1998/3132 r.50, Sch.1
  r.7, amended: SI 1998/3132 r.50, Sch.1
  r.7, applied: SI 1998/3132 r.50, Sch.1
  r.7, consolidated: SI 1998/3132 r.50, Sch.1
  r.8, amended: SI 1998/3132 r.50, Sch.1
  r.8, applied: SI 1998/3132 r.50, Sch.1
  r.8, consolidated: SI 1998/3132 r.50, Sch.1
  r.9, amended: SI 1998/3132 r.50, Sch.1
  r.9, applied: SI 1998/3132 r.50, Sch.1
  r.9, consolidated: SI 1998/3132 r.50, Sch.1
  r.9A, amended: SI 1998/3132 r.50, Sch.1
  r.9A, applied: SI 1998/3132 r.50, Sch.1
  r.9A, consolidated: SI 1998/3132 r.50, Sch.1
  r.10, amended: SI 1998/3132 r.50, Sch.1
  r.10, applied: SI 1998/3132 r.50, Sch.1
  r.10, consolidated: SI 1998/3132 r.50, Sch.1
  r.11, amended: SI 1998/3132 r.50, Sch.1
  r.11, applied: SI 1998/3132 r.50, Sch.1
  r.11, consolidated: SI 1998/3132 r.50, Sch.1
  r.11A, amended: SI 1998/3132 r.50, Sch.1
  r.11A, applied: SI 1998/3132 r.50, Sch.1
  r.11A, consolidated: SI 1998/3132 r.50,
    Sch.1
  r.12, amended: SI 1998/3132 r.50, Sch.1
  r.12, applied: SI 1998/3132 r.50, Sch.1
  r.12, consolidated: SI 1998/3132 r.50, Sch.1
  r.13, amended: SI 1998/3132 r.50, Sch.1
  r.13, applied: SI 1998/3132 r.50, Sch.1
  r.13, consolidated: SI 1998/3132 r.50, Sch.1
  r.14, amended: SI 1998/3132 r.50, Sch.1
  r.14, applied: SI 1998/3132 r.50, Sch.1

NO.

1776. Rules of the Supreme Court 1965—*cont.*
Ord. 115—*cont.*
  r.14, consolidated: SI 1998/3132 r.50, Sch.1
  r.15, amended: SI 1998/3132 r.50, Sch.1
  r.15, applied: SI 1998/3132 r.50, Sch.1
  r.15, consolidated: SI 1998/3132 r.50, Sch.1
  r.16, amended: SI 1998/3132 r.50, Sch.1
  r.16, applied: SI 1998/3132 r.50, Sch.1
  r.16, consolidated: SI 1998/3132 r.50, Sch.1
  r.17, amended: SI 1998/3132 r.50, Sch.1
  r.17, applied: SI 1998/3132 r.50, Sch.1
  r.17, consolidated: SI 1998/3132 r.50, Sch.1
  r.18, amended: SI 1998/3132 r.50, Sch.1
  r.18, applied: SI 1998/3132 r.50, Sch.1
  r.18, consolidated: SI 1998/3132 r.50, Sch.1
  r.19, amended: SI 1998/3132 r.50, Sch.1
  r.19, applied: SI 1998/3132 r.50, Sch.1
  r.19, consolidated: SI 1998/3132 r.50, Sch.1
  r.20, amended: SI 1998/3132 r.50, Sch.1
  r.20, applied: SI 1998/3132 r.50, Sch.1
  r.20, consolidated: SI 1998/3132 r.50, Sch.1
  r.21, amended: SI 1998/3132 r.50, Sch.1
  r.21, applied: SI 1998/3132 r.50, Sch.1
  r.21, consolidated: SI 1998/3132 r.50, Sch.1
  r.21A, amended: SI 1998/3132 r.50, Sch.1
  r.21A, applied: SI 1998/3132 r.50, Sch.1
  r.21A, consolidated: SI 1998/3132 r.50,
    Sch.1
  r.22, amended: SI 1998/3132 r.50, Sch.1
  r.22, applied: SI 1998/3132 r.50, Sch.1
  r.22, consolidated: SI 1998/3132 r.50, Sch.1
  r.23, amended: SI 1998/3132 r.50, Sch.1
  r.23, applied: SI 1998/3132 r.50, Sch.1
  r.23, consolidated: SI 1998/3132 r.50, Sch.1
  r.24, amended: SI 1998/3132 r.50, Sch.1
  r.24, applied: SI 1998/3132 r.50, Sch.1
  r.24, consolidated: SI 1998/3132 r.50, Sch.1
  r.25, amended: SI 1998/3132 r.50, Sch.1
  r.25, applied: SI 1998/3132 r.50, Sch.1
  r.25, consolidated: SI 1998/3132 r.50, Sch.1
  r.26, amended: SI 1998/3132 r.50, Sch.1
  r.26, applied: SI 1998/3132 r.50, Sch.1
  r.26, consolidated: SI 1998/3132 r.50, Sch.1
  r.27, amended: SI 1998/3132 r.50, Sch.1
  r.27, applied: SI 1998/3132 r.50, Sch.1
  r.27, consolidated: SI 1998/3132 r.50, Sch.1
  r.28, amended: SI 1998/3132 r.50, Sch.1
  r.28, applied: SI 1998/3132 r.50, Sch.1
  r.28, consolidated: SI 1998/3132 r.50, Sch.1
  r.29, amended: SI 1998/3132 r.50, Sch.1
  r.29, applied: SI 1998/3132 r.50, Sch.1
  r.29, consolidated: SI 1998/3132 r.50, Sch.1
  r.30, amended: SI 1998/3132 r.50, Sch.1
  r.30, applied: SI 1998/3132 r.50, Sch.1
  r.30, consolidated: SI 1998/3132 r.50, Sch.1
  r.31, amended: SI 1998/3132 r.50, Sch.1
  r.31, applied: SI 1998/3132 r.50, Sch.1
  r.31, consolidated: SI 1998/3132 r.50, Sch.1
  r.32, amended: SI 1998/3132 r.50, Sch.1
  r.32, applied: SI 1998/3132 r.50, Sch.1
  r.32, consolidated: SI 1998/3132 r.50, Sch.1
  r.33, amended: SI 1998/3132 r.50, Sch.1
  r.33, applied: SI 1998/3132 r.50, Sch.1
  r.33, consolidated: SI 1998/3132 r.50, Sch.1
  r.34, amended: SI 1998/3132 r.50, Sch.1
  r.34, applied: SI 1998/3132 r.50, Sch.1
  r.34, consolidated: SI 1998/3132 r.50, Sch.1
  r.35, amended: SI 1998/3132 r.50, Sch.1
  r.35, applied: SI 1998/3132 r.50, Sch.1
  r.35, consolidated: SI 1998/3132 r.50, Sch.1
  r.36, amended: SI 1998/3132 r.50, Sch.1
  r.36, applied: SI 1998/3132 r.50, Sch.1

NO.

1776. Rules of the Supreme Court 1965—*cont.*
Ord. 115—*cont.*
r.36, consolidated: SI 1998/3132 r.50, Sch.1
Ord. 116,
added: SI 1998/1898 r.3

1823. Nuclear Installations (Insurance Certificate) Regulations 1965
Reg.2, amended: SI 1999/1820 Art.4, Sch.2 para.137

1839. Registration of Births, Still-births, Deaths and Marriages (Prescription of Forms) (Scotland) Regulations 1965
revoked: SI 1997/2348 Reg.30, Sch.27
Reg.20, revoked: SI 1997/2348 Reg.30, Sch.27
Reg.20, substituted: SI 1997/512 Reg.2
Reg.21, revoked: SI 1997/512 Reg.5, SI 1997/2348 Reg.30, Sch.27
Sch.1, revoked: SI 1997/2348 Reg.30, Sch.27
Sch.2, revoked: SI 1997/2348 Reg.30, Sch.27
Sch.5, revoked: SI 1997/2348 Reg.30, Sch.27
Sch.10, revoked: SI 1997/2348 Reg.30, Sch.27
Sch.21 Form, revoked: SI 1997/2348 Reg.30, Sch.27
Sch.21 Form, substituted: SI 1997/512 Reg.3, Sch.1
Sch.22, revoked: SI 1997/512 Reg.5, SI 1997/2348 Reg.30, Sch.27
Sch.23 Form, revoked: SI 1997/2348 Reg.30, Sch.27
Sch.23 Form, substituted: SI 1997/512 Reg.4, Sch.2

1847. Herefordshire Water Board (No.2) Order 1965
revoked: 1998 c.43 s.1, Sch.1 Part V

1871. Dockyard Port of Portland (Amendment) Order 1965
revoked: SI 1997/2949 Art.57

1932. Redundancy Payments Pensions Regulations 1965
applied: SI 1996/1680 Reg.12, SI 1996/2317 Sch.3 para.2, SI 1997/311 Reg.17, SI 1998/192 Reg.12
referred to: SI 1997/311 Reg.18

1995. Industrial and Provident Societies Regulations 1965
revoked: SI 1999/740 Reg.4
Reg.2, revoked: SI 1996/3121 Reg.13, Sch.3, SI 1999/740 Reg.4
Reg.3, revoked: SI 1996/3121 Reg.13, Sch.3, SI 1999/740 Reg.4
Reg.4, revoked: SI 1996/3121 Reg.13, Sch.3, SI 1999/740 Reg.4
Reg.5, revoked: SI 1996/3121 Reg.13, Sch.3, SI 1999/740 Reg.4
Reg.6, revoked: SI 1996/3121 Reg.13, Sch.3, SI 1999/740 Reg.4
Reg.7, revoked: SI 1996/3121 Reg.13, Sch.3, SI 1999/740 Reg.4
Reg.8, revoked: SI 1996/3121 Reg.13, Sch.3, SI 1999/740 Reg.4
Reg.9, revoked: SI 1996/3121 Reg.13, Sch.3, SI 1999/740 Reg.4
Reg.10, revoked: SI 1996/3121 Reg.13, Sch.3, SI 1999/740 Reg.4
Reg.11, revoked: SI 1996/3121 Reg.13, Sch.3, SI 1999/740 Reg.4
Reg.12, revoked: SI 1996/3121 Reg.13, Sch.3, SI 1999/740 Reg.4
Sch.1, revoked: SI 1996/3121 Reg.13, Sch.3, SI 1999/740 Reg.4
Sch.2, revoked: SI 1999/740 Reg.4
Sch.2, substituted: SI 1996/613 Reg.2, SI 1997/743 Reg.2, SI 1998/676 Reg.2

NO.

2040. Hares (Control of Importation) Order 1965
referred to: SI 1998/190 Reg.34, Sch.6

1966

94. Construction (Working Places) Regulations 1966
see *Ballantyne v John Young & Co (Kelvinhaugh)* 1996 S.L.T. 358 (OH); see *Edie v Edie* 1997 S.L.T. 1279 (OH), Lord Gill
revoked: SI 1996/1592 Reg.35, Sch.10
Reg.32, see *Nelhams v Sandells Maintenance Ltd and Gillespie (UK) Ltd* [1996] P.I.Q.R. P52 (CA), Nourse, L.J.
Reg.36, see *R. v Rhone-Poulenc Rorer Ltd* [1996] I.C.R. 1054 (CA (Crim Div)), Wright, J.

95. Construction (Health and Welfare) Regulations 1966
revoked: SI 1996/1592 Reg.35, Sch.10

357. Teachers' Superannuation (Family Benefits) Regulations 1966
Reg.27, applied: SI 1997/3001 Sch.6 para.1
Reg.28, applied: SI 1997/3001 Sch.6 para.1

645. Agriculture (Poisonous Substances) (Extension) Order 1966
revoked: SI 1996/3022 Reg.2, Sch Part II

792. River Teign Mussel Fishery Order 1966
Art.2, amended: SI 1996/61 Art.2
Art.3, amended: SI 1996/61 Art.2
Art.4, amended: SI 1996/61 Art.2
Art.7, substituted: SI 1996/61 Art.2

812. City of Dundee Educational Trust Scheme Order in Council 1966
amended: SI 1996/477 Sch

845. Act of Sederunt (Housing Appeals) 1966
revoked: SI 1999/929 r.1.3, Sch.2

881. Coal and Other Mines (Support) Regulations 1966
revoked: SI 1999/2463 Reg.18

898. Petroleum (Production) Regulations 1966
Sch.3, referred to: 1998 c.17 Sch.1 para.3, SI 1999/160 Sch.3 para.1
Sch.4, referred to: 1998 c.17 Sch.1 para.4, Sch.1 para.5, SI 1999/160 Sch.2 para.1

987. National Insurance (Industrial Injuries) (Prescribed Diseases) Amendment Regulations 1966
see *Cape Plc v Iron Trades Employers Insurance Association Ltd* [1999] P.I.Q.R. Q212 (QBD (Comm Ct)), Rix, J.

1073. Mineral Hydrocarbons in Food Regulations 1966
amended: SI 1999/1136 Reg.14

1263. Mineral Hydrocarbons in Food (Scotland) Regulations 1966
amended: SI 1999/1136 Reg.14

1375. Gas (Underground Storage) (Inquiries Procedure) Rules 1966
amended: SI 1996/252 Art.2, Sch

1385. Town and Country Planning (Development Plans) (Scotland) Regulations 1966
applied: 1997 c.8 Sch.1 para.4

1522. National Health Service Superannuation (Scotland) Regulations 1966
applied: SI 1998/366 Reg.135
Reg.40, referred to: SI 1998/366 Reg.135
Reg.46, applied: SI 1998/366 Reg.135
Reg.54, referred to: SI 1998/366 Reg.135

NO.

1966—cont.

1523. National Health Service (Superannuation) Regulations 1966
Reg.39, referred to: SI 1997/1612 Reg.141
Reg.45, applied: SI 1997/1612 Reg.141
Reg.55, referred to: SI 1997/1612 Reg.141

1610. Carry-cots (Safety) Regulations 1966
revoked: SI 1996/2756 Reg.2

1967

36. Cambridge Water Order 1967
revoked: SI 1996/713 Art.4, Sch.2 Part II

112. Work in Compressed Air (Prescribed Leaflet) Order 1967
revoked: SI 1996/1656 Reg.22, Sch.2 Part I

178. Stands for Carry-cots (Safety) Regulations (Northern Ireland) 1967
revoked: SI 1996/2756 Reg.2

296. North West Worcestershire Water Board Order 1967
Art.3, revoked: 1998 c.43 s.1, Sch.1 Part V
Art.4, revoked: 1998 c.43 s.1, Sch.1 Part V
Art.6, revoked: 1998 c.43 s.1, Sch.1 Part V
Sch.1, revoked: 1998 c.43 s.1, Sch.1 Part V

395. Veterinary Surgeons and Veterinary Practitioners (Registration Regulations) Order of Council 1967
revoked: SI 1999/2846 Art.3, Sch. Reg.22
Sch., amended: SI 1996/437 Sch
Sch., revoked: SI 1999/2846 Art.3, Sch. Reg.22
Sch. Reg.16, amended: SI 1996/437 Sch, SI 1998/270 Sch. Reg.2
Sch. Reg.16, revoked: SI 1999/2846 Art.3, Sch. Reg.22
Sch. Reg.20, amended: SI 1996/437 Sch, SI 1998/270 Sch. Reg.3
Sch. Reg.20, revoked: SI 1999/2846 Art.3, Sch. Reg.22
Sch. Reg.22, amended: SI 1996/437 Sch, SI 1998/270 Sch. Reg.4
Sch. Reg.22, revoked: SI 1999/2846 Art.3, Sch. Reg.22
Sch. Reg.23, amended: SI 1996/437 Sch, SI 1998/270 Sch. Reg.5
Sch. Reg.23, revoked: SI 1999/2846 Art.3, Sch. Reg.22

474. Diplomatic Privileges (Citizens of the United Kingdom and Colonies) Order 1967
revoked: SI 1999/670 Art.3, Sch.2

480. Carriage by Air Acts (Application of Provisions) Order 1967
Art.2, amended: SI 1999/1737 Art.2
Art.3, amended: SI 1999/1737 Art.2
Art.4, amended: SI 1998/1058 Art.2
Art.5, applied: SI 1996/244 Art.3, SI 1999/2881 Art.3
Art.5, referred to: SI 1999/1313
Art.5A, added: SI 1998/1058 Art.2
Art.5A, referred to: SI 1999/1313
Art.5B, added: SI 1998/1751 Art.4
Art.6, applied: SI 1999/2881
Art.7, amended: SI 1999/1737 Art.2
Sch.1, see *Fellowes v Clyde Helicopters Ltd* [1997] A.C. 534 (HL), Lord Mackay of Clashfern
Sch.1, substituted: SI 1999/1737 Art.2, Sch.
Sch.2, amended: SI 1999/1737 Art.2
Sch.2 para.3, amended: SI 1998/1058 Art.2
Sch.2 Art.15, revoked (in part): SI 1998/1058 Art.2
Sch.2 Art.25A, revoked: SI 1998/1058 Art.2
Sch.3, added: SI 1998/1058 Art.2
Sch.3, amended: SI 1999/1737 Art.2

NO.

1967—cont.

489. Teachers' Superannuation Regulations 1967
Part VI, applied: SI 1997/1612 Reg.142
Reg.52, applied: SI 1997/1612 Reg.142

494. Material Development Regulations 1967
Sch. para.11, amended: SI 1996/252 Art.2, Sch

524. Chester Water Order 1967
revoked: SI 1998/281 Art.4, Sch.2 Part II

599. Veterinary Surgeons (Examination of Commonwealth and Foreign Candidates) Regulations 1967
Sch. Reg.9, amended: SI 1998/271 Sch. Reg.2

759. Hoists Exemption (Amendment) Order 1967
revoked: SI 1998/2307 Reg.17, Sch.2

948. Teachers' Superannuation (Amending) Regulations 1967
applied: SI 1997/1612 Reg.142

956. Ellington Mine (Diesel Vehicles and Storage Battery Vehicles) Special Regulations 1967
Reg.4, revoked: SI 1996/192 Reg.20, Sch.15 Part I
Reg.5, revoked: SI 1996/192 Reg.20, Sch.15 Part I
Reg.6, revoked: SI 1996/192 Reg.20, Sch.15 Part I
Reg.7, revoked: SI 1996/192 Reg.20, Sch.15 Part I

1021. Police (Discipline) (Scotland) Regulations 1967
revoked: SI 1996/1642 Reg.25, Sch.2

1167. Gas (Underground Storage) (Certificates) (England and Wales) Regulations 1967
amended: SI 1996/252 Art.2, Sch

1286. Teachers' (Part-time) Superannuation Regulations 1967
applied: SI 1997/1612 Reg.142

1310. Industrial and Provident Societies Regulations 1967
Reg.3, revoked: SI 1996/3121 Reg.13, Sch.3
Reg.4, revoked: SI 1996/3121 Reg.13, Sch.3
Reg.5, amended: SI 1996/613 Reg.3, SI 1997/743 Reg.3, SI 1998/676 Reg.3
Reg.5, revoked: SI 1999/740 Reg.4
Reg.6, revoked: SI 1996/3121 Reg.13, Sch.3
Reg.7, revoked: SI 1996/3121 Reg.13, Sch.3
Reg.8, revoked: SI 1996/3121 Reg.13, Sch.3
Reg.9, revoked: SI 1996/3121 Reg.13, Sch.3
Reg.10, revoked: SI 1996/3121 Reg.13, Sch.3
Sch., revoked: SI 1996/3121 Reg.13, Sch.3

1483. Dockyard Port of Portland (Amendment) Order 1967
revoked: SI 1997/2949 Art.57

1485. Ammonium Nitrate Mixtures Exemption Order 1967
applied: SI 1996/2791 Sch.9 Part VI, SI 1997/2505 Reg.10, Sch.9 Part VI, SI 1999/645 Reg.10, Sch.9 Part VI
Art.3, applied: SI 1996/2791 Sch.9 Part V, SI 1997/2505 Reg.10, Sch.9 Part V, SI 1999/645 Reg.10, Sch.9 Part V

1507. Food (Preparation and Distribution of Meat) (Scotland) Regulations 1967
revoked: SI 1996/497 Reg.2

1768. Leasehold Reform (Notices) Regulations 1967
revoked: SI 1997/640 Reg.4 (with savings)

1807. Courts-Martial (Evidence) Regulations 1967
revoked: SI 1997/173 Reg.3

NO.

1968

208. Police Cadets (Scotland) Regulations 1968
Sch.1 Table, substituted: SI 1997/2791 Reg.2, Reg.3, Reg.4
Sch.2, amended: SI 1997/2791 Reg.5

395. North West Worcestershire Water Board (Chaddesley Corbett) Order 1968
Art.3, revoked: 1998 c.43 s.1, Sch.1 Part V
Art.5, revoked: 1998 c.43 s.1, Sch.1 Part V
Sch.1, revoked: 1998 c.43 s.1, Sch.1 Part V

414. Treasury Bills Regulations 1968
Reg.1, amended: SI 1999/2907 Reg.3
Reg.2, amended: SI 1999/2907 Reg.4
Reg.3, amended: SI 1999/2907 Reg.5
Reg.3, substituted: SI 1998/1450 Reg.2
Reg.4, amended: SI 1998/1450 Reg.2, SI 1999/2907 Reg.6
Reg.5, amended: SI 1999/2907 Reg.7
Reg.6, amended: SI 1998/1450 Reg.2, SI 1999/2907 Reg.8
Reg.6, revoked (in part): SI 1999/2907 Reg.8
Reg.9, amended: SI 1999/2907 Reg.9
Reg.9A, revoked: SI 1999/2907 Reg.10
Reg.9A, substituted: SI 1998/1450 Reg.2
Sch.1, substituted: SI 1998/1450 Reg.2, SI 1999/2907 Reg.11, Sch.

440. Prison (Amendment) Rules 1968
revoked: SI 1999/728 r.85 (with savings), Sch. (with savings)

507. Chester Water (Borrowing Powers) Order 1968
revoked: SI 1998/281 Art.4, Sch.2 Part II

717. Police (Promotion) (Scotland) Regulations 1968
revoked: SI 1996/221 Reg.10, Sch.2

849. Offices, Shops and Railway Premises (Hoists and Lifts) Regulations 1968
revoked: SI 1998/2307 Reg.17, Sch.2
Reg.3, applied: SI 1998/2307 Reg.9
Reg.3, revoked: SI 1998/2307 Reg.17, Sch.2
Reg.6, applied: SI 1998/2307 Reg.9
Reg.6, revoked: SI 1998/2307 Reg.17, Sch.2

891. Continental Shelf (Designation of Additional Areas) Order 1968
referred to: SI 1999/2031

1052. Merchant Shipping (Load Line) (Transitional Provisions) Regulations 1968
revoked: SI 1998/2241 Reg.3

1053. Merchant Shipping (Load Line) Rules 1968
applied: SI 1996/3243 Sch Part I, SI 1997/19 Reg.9
referred to: SI 1998/1609 Reg.5, Reg.6, Sch., SI 1998/2514 Reg.12
revoked: SI 1998/2241 Reg.3
r.30, applied: SI 1997/1509 Reg.16
r.30, revoked: SI 1998/2241 Reg.3
Sch.4 Part I, applied: SI 1997/1509 Reg.16
Sch.4 Part I, revoked: SI 1998/2241 Reg.3

1071. Courts-Martial Appeal Rules 1968
amended: SI 1997/580 r.2
r.2, amended: SI 1997/580 r.3
r.3, substituted: SI 1997/580 r.4
r.4, amended: SI 1997/580 r.5
r.6, amended: SI 1997/580 r.6, r.7
r.6, applied: SI 1997/580 r.13
r.14A, added: SI 1997/580 r.8
r.14B, added: SI 1997/580 r.8
r.14C, added: SI 1997/580 r.8
r.17, amended: SI 1997/580 r.9

NO.

1968—cont.

1071. Courts-Martial Appeal Rules 1968—*cont.*
r.21, substituted: SI 1997/580 r.10
Sch.1 Form 1, applied: SI 1997/580 r.13
Sch.1 Form 1, substituted: SI 1997/580 r.11, Sch.
Sch.1 Form 2, substituted: SI 1997/580 r.11, Sch.
Sch.2, revoked: SI 1997/580 r.12

1072. Merchant Shipping (Load Line) (Length of Ship) Regulations 1968
applied: SI 1996/3243 Sch Part I
referred to: SI 1998/1609 Reg.5, Reg.6, Sch.
revoked: SI 1998/2241 Reg.3

1082. Gas (Underground Storage) (Certificates) (Scotland) Regulations 1968
amended: SI 1996/252 Art.2, Sch

1089. Merchant Shipping (Load Line) (Deck Cargo) Regulations 1968
applied: SI 1996/3243 Sch Part I
referred to: SI 1998/1609 Reg.5, Reg.6, Sch.
revoked: SI 1998/2241 Reg.3

1116. Merchant Shipping (Load Line) (Exemption) Order 1968
revoked: SI 1998/2241 Reg.3

1148. Direct Grant Schools (Amendment) Regulations 1968
revoked: SI 1998/86 Reg.2, Sch.1

1170. Iron and Steel (Compensation to Employees) Regulations 1968
applied: SI 1996/3182 Sch. para.4

1262. Criminal Appeal Rules 1968
r.8, applied: SI 1997/1053 r.6
r.9, amended: SI 1997/702 r.2
r.10, applied: SI 1997/1053 r.8
r.12, see *R. v Dixon (Leon)* [1999] 3 All E.R. 889 (CA (Crim Div)), Garland, J.
r.16A, amended: SI 1997/702 r.2
r.21, applied: SI 1997/1053 r.11

1353. Teachers' Superannuation (Amending) Regulations 1968
applied: SI 1997/1612 Reg.142

1389. Patents Rules 1968
applied: SI 1996/2972 r.2, r.3, SI 1998/1778 r.3
referred to: SI 1998/1778 r.2
r.30, applied: SI 1996/2972 Sch Part B, SI 1998/1778 r.3, Sch. Part B
r.33, applied: SI 1996/2972 Sch Part B, SI 1998/1778 r.3, Sch. Part B
r.50, applied: SI 1996/2972 Sch Part B, SI 1998/1778 r.3, Sch. Part B

1405. South West Worcestershire Water Board Order 1968
revoked (in part): 1998 c.43 s.1, Sch.1 Part V
Art.1, referred to: 1998 c.43 s.1, Sch.1 Part V
Art.2, referred to: 1998 c.43 s.1, Sch.1 Part V
Art.19, referred to: 1998 c.43 s.1, Sch.1 Part V
Art.22, referred to: 1998 c.43 s.1, Sch.1 Part V
Art.23, referred to: 1998 c.43 s.1, Sch.1 Part V
Art.24, referred to: 1998 c.43 s.1, Sch.1 Part V
Sch.4, referred to: 1998 c.43 s.1, Sch.1 Part V
Sch.4, revoked (in part): 1998 c.43 s.1, Sch.1 Part V

1408. Insurance Companies (Accounts and Forms) Regulations 1968
Reg.15, applied: SI 1996/943 Reg.30

1521. Treasury Solicitor (Crown's Nominee) (Amendment) Rules 1968
revoked: SI 1997/2870 r.1

1530. Engineering Construction (Extension of Definition) (No.2) Regulations 1968
revoked: SI 1996/1592 Reg.35, Sch.10

NO.

1615. **Weights and Measures (Prescribed Stamp) Regulations 1968**
Reg.1, amended: SI 1999/504 Reg.2
Sch.1 para.(ii), amended: SI 1999/504 Reg.2
Sch.1 para.(iii), amended: SI 1999/504 Reg.2
1728. **Children (Performances) Regulations 1968**
Part VIA, added: SI 1998/1678 Reg.2
Reg.1, amended: SI 1998/1678 Reg.2
Reg.2, amended: SI 1998/1678 Reg.2
Reg.4, amended: SI 1998/1678 Reg.2
Reg.5, amended: SI 1998/1678 Reg.2
Reg.6, amended: SI 1998/1678 Reg.2
Reg.7, amended: SI 1998/1678 Reg.2
Reg.10, amended: SI 1998/1678 Reg.2
Reg.11, amended: SI 1998/1678 Reg.2
Reg.12, amended: SI 1998/1678 Reg.2
Reg.13, amended: SI 1998/1678 Reg.2
Reg.14, amended: SI 1998/1678 Reg.2
Reg.15, amended: SI 1998/1678 Reg.2
Reg.19, amended: SI 1998/1678 Reg.2
Reg.41A, added: SI 1998/1678 Reg.2
Reg.41B, added: SI 1998/1678 Reg.2
Reg.42, amended: SI 1998/1678 Reg.2
Sch.1 Part I, amended: SI 1998/1678 Reg.2
Sch.1 Part II, amended: SI 1998/1678 Reg.2
Sch.2, amended: SI 1998/1678 Reg.2
Sch.3, amended: SI 1998/1678 Reg.2
Sch.4, added: SI 1998/1678 Reg.2, Sch.
1790. **North West Worcestershire Water Board (Waresley Boreholes) Order 1968**
revoked (in part): 1998 c.43 s.1, Sch.1 Part V
Art.1, referred to: 1998 c.43 s.1, Sch.1 Part V
Art.2, referred to: 1998 c.43 s.1, Sch.1 Part V
Art.5, referred to: 1998 c.43 s.1, Sch.1 Part V
Sch.1 para.2, referred to: 1998 c.43 s.1, Sch.1 Part V
1862. **Inter-Governmental Maritime Consultative Organisation (Immunities and Privileges) Order 1968**
Art.1, amended: SI 1999/2034 Art.2, Sch.
Art.9A, added: SI 1999/2034 Art.2, Sch.
1863. **International Wheat Council (Immunities and Privileges) Order 1968**
Art.1, amended: SI 1999/2034 Art.2, Sch.
Art.10A, added: SI 1999/2034 Art.2, Sch.
1944. **Teachers' Superannuation Account (Rates of Interest) Regulations 1968**
applied: SI 1997/1612 Reg.142
2049. **Registration of Births, Deaths and Marriages Regulations 1968**
Reg.10, revoked (in part): SI 1996/1626 Reg.2
Reg.87, amended: SI 1996/2052 Reg.2, Reg.3

1969

17. **Town and Country Planning (Tree Preservation Order) Regulations 1969**
revoked: SI 1999/1892 Reg.18 (with savings)
Reg.8, revoked: SI 1999/1892 Reg.18 (with savings)
Sch., applied: SI 1998/1936 Art.22
Sch., revoked: SI 1999/1892 Reg.18 (with savings)
47. **Firearms (Dangerous Air Weapons) Rules 1969**
applied: 1997 c.5 s.48
80. **Teachers' Superannuation (Amendment) Regulations 1969**
applied: SI 1997/1612 Reg.142

NO.

103. **Exmouth Docks Order 1969**
applied: SI 1998/980 Art.3, Art.6
referred to: SI 1998/980 Art.4
270. **Firearms (Dangerous Air Weapons) (Scotland) Rules 1969**
applied: 1997 c.5 s.48
388. **Transfer of Functions (Wales) Order 1969**
applied: SI 1999/3141 Art.2
referred to: SI 1999/672 Art.2, Sch.1
592. **Civil Aviation Act 1949 (Overseas Territories) Order 1969**
referred to: SI 1997/1746
596. **Tokyo Convention Act 1967 (Guernsey) Order 1969**
revoked: SI 1997/2989 Art.2, Sch.3
601. **Herefordshire Water Board (Credenhill Camp Pipeline) Order 1969**
Art.4, revoked: 1998 c.43 s.1, Sch.1 Part V
Art.5, revoked: 1998 c.43 s.1, Sch.1 Part V
733. **International Coffee Organisation (Immunities and Privileges) Order 1969**
Art.13A, added: SI 1999/2034 Art.2, Sch.
734. **International Sugar Organisation (Immunities and Privileges) Order 1969**
Art.13A, added: SI 1999/2034 Art.2, Sch.
939. **Savings Banks (Ordinary Deposits) (Limits) Order 1969**
Art.3, amended: SI 1998/1446 Art.30, Sch.1 para.8
Art.4, referred to: SI 1998/1449 Art.3, Sch. para.1
975. **Superannuation (Local Government and Overseas Employment) Interchange Rules 1969**
Part II, applied: SI 1997/1613 Reg.24
1012. **North West Worcestershire Water Board Order 1969**
revoked: 1998 c.43 s.1, Sch.1 Part V
1342. **Savings Contracts Regulations 1969**
Reg.3, referred to: SI 1998/1449 Art.3, Sch. para.2
Reg.5, referred to: SI 1998/1449 Art.3, Sch. para.2
Reg.6, referred to: SI 1998/1449 Art.3, Sch. para.2
Reg.26, amended: SI 1997/1858 Reg.2
Reg.26, referred to: SI 1998/1449 Art.3, Sch. para.2
1377. **Prince of Wales Mine (Captive Rail Diesel Locomotives) Special Regulations 1969**
Reg.4, revoked: SI 1996/192 Reg.20, Sch.15 Part I
1409. **Chester Water (Borrowing Powers) (Amendment) Order 1969**
revoked: SI 1998/281 Art.4, Sch.2 Part II
1842. **Restrictive Trade Practices (Information Agreements) Order 1969**
Sch. Part II, amended: SI 1999/506 Art.12

1970

Lewisham (Prescribed Routes) Traffic Order 1970
revoked (in part): SI 1998/2171 Art.6
10. **Teachers' Superannuation (Amendment) Regulations 1970**
applied: SI 1997/1612 Reg.142
153. **Double Taxation Relief (Taxes on Income) (Finland) Order 1970**
Sch., amended: SI 1996/3166 Art.2
Sch. Art.2, amended: SI 1996/3166 Sch. Part I

NO.

153. **Double Taxation Relief (Taxes on Income) (Finland) Order 1970**—*cont.*
Sch. Art.6, substituted: SI 1996/3166 Sch. Part I
Sch. Art.10, substituted: SI 1996/3166 Sch. Part I
Sch. Art.11, substituted: SI 1996/3166 Sch. Part I
Sch. Art.12, amended: SI 1996/3166 Sch. Part I
Sch. Art.14, amended: SI 1996/3166 Sch. Part I
Sch. Art.16, amended: SI 1996/3166 Sch. Part I
Sch. Art.19, substituted: SI 1996/3166 Sch. Part I
Sch. Art.24, amended: SI 1996/3166 Sch. Part I
Sch. Art.25, amended: SI 1996/3166 Sch. Part I
Sch. Art.26, revoked: SI 1996/3166 Sch. Part I

168. **Quarries Vehicles Regulations 1970**
revoked: SI 1999/2024 Reg.48, Sch.5 Part I

231. **Justices' Clerks Rules 1970**
see *R. v Corby Justices Ex p. Mort* [1998] 38 R.V.R. 283 (QBD), Lord Bingham of Cornhill, L.C.J.
revoked: SI 1999/2784 r.4
r.4, amended: SI 1997/710 r.3
r.4, revoked (in part): SI 1997/710 r.3, SI 1999/2784 r.4 (rem.)
r.5, added: SI 1998/2167 r.3
r.5, revoked: SI 1999/2784 r.4
Sch. para.2A, revoked: SI 1999/2784 r.4
Sch. para.4, revoked (in part): SI 1998/2167 r.3, SI 1999/2784 r.4 (rem.)
Sch. para.4A, revoked (in part): SI 1997/710 r.4, SI 1999/2784 r.4 (rem.)
Sch. para.4B, revoked: SI 1999/2784 r.4
Sch. para.8A, revoked: SI 1999/2784 r.4
Sch. para.11, revoked: SI 1999/2784 r.4
Sch. para.11A, revoked: SI 1999/2784 r.4
Sch. para.18, revoked: SI 1999/2784 r.4
Sch. para.19, added: SI 1998/2167 r.3, SI 1999/681 r.7
Sch. para.19, revoked: SI 1999/2784 r.4
Sch. para.20, added: SI 1998/2167 r.3
Sch. para.20, revoked: SI 1999/2784 r.4
Sch. para.21, added: SI 1998/2167 r.3
Sch. para.21, revoked: SI 1999/2784 r.4
Sch. para.22, added: SI 1998/2167 r.3
Sch. para.22, revoked: SI 1999/2784 r.4
Sch. para.23, added: SI 1998/2167 r.3
Sch. para.23, revoked: SI 1999/2784 r.4
Sch. para.24, added: SI 1998/2167 r.3
Sch. para.24, revoked: SI 1999/2784 r.4
Sch. para.25, added: SI 1998/2167 r.3
Sch. para.25, revoked: SI 1999/2784 r.4
Sch. para.26, added: SI 1998/2167 r.3
Sch. para.26, revoked: SI 1999/2784 r.4
Sch. para.27, added: SI 1998/2167 r.3
Sch. para.27, revoked: SI 1999/2784 r.4
Sch. para.28, added: SI 1998/2167 r.3
Sch. para.28, revoked: SI 1999/2784 r.4
Sch. para.29, added: SI 1998/2167 r.3
Sch. para.29, revoked: SI 1999/2784 r.4
Sch. para.30, added: SI 1998/2167 r.3
Sch. para.30, revoked: SI 1999/2784 r.4

287. **Dockyard Ports (Amendment) Order 1970**
Art.6, revoked: SI 1997/2949 Art.57

294. **Merchant Shipping (Certificates of Competency as A.B.) Regulations 1970**
Reg.4, referred to: SI 1996/3243 Sch Part III
Sch.30, revoked: SI 1996/3243 Reg.2

333. **South West Worcestershire Water Board (Charges) Order 1970**
revoked: 1998 c.43 s.1, Sch.1 Part V

NO.

488. **Double Taxation Relief (Taxes on Income) (General) Regulations 1970**
Reg.2, amended: SI 1996/783 Reg.2
Reg.3, amended: SI 1996/783 Reg.2
Reg.4, amended: SI 1996/783 Reg.2

535. **Abrasive Wheels Regulations 1970**
revoked: SI 1998/2306 Reg.39, Sch.4

635. **Diplomatic Privileges (Citizens of the United Kingdom and Colonies) Order 1970**
revoked: SI 1999/670 Art.3, Sch.2

753. **Teachers' Superannuation (Amendment No.2) Regulations 1970**
applied: SI 1997/1612 Reg.142

835. **Partnerships (Unrestricted Size) No. 2 Regulations 1970**
revoked: SI 1996/262 Reg.3

862. **Teachers' Superannuation (Family Benefits) Regulations 1970**
applied: SI 1997/1612 Reg.142
Reg.27, applied: SI 1997/3001 Sch.6 para.1
Reg.28, applied: SI 1997/3001 Sch.6 para.1
Reg.29, applied: SI 1997/3001 Sch.6 para.1

1003. **Merchant Shipping (Load Line) (Amendment) Rules 1970**
referred to: SI 1998/1609 Reg.5, Reg.6, Sch.
revoked: SI 1998/2241 Reg.3

1453. **Anchors and Chain Cables Rules 1970**
referred to: SI 1998/1609 Reg.5, Reg.6, Sch.
revoked: SI 1998/2514 Reg.1

1508. **Act of Sederunt (Sheriff Court Procedure under Part IV of the Housing (Scotland) Act 1969) 1970**
revoked: SI 1999/929 r.1.3, Sch.2

1537. **Secretary of State for Trade and Industry Order 1970**
Sch.2 para.7, revoked: SI 1999/2786 Art.3

1539. **Foreign Marriage Order 1970**
Art.7, applied: SI 1997/1314 Sch. para.27, SI 1998/257 Sch. para.27, SI 1999/655 Sch. para.27, SI 1999/3132 Sch. para.27

1642. **South West Worcestershire Water Board (Warndon) Order 1970**
revoked: 1998 c.43 s.1, Sch.1 Part V

1681. **Secretary of State for the Environment Order 1970**
Sch.2, referred to: SI 1997/2971 Art.4
Sch.3 para.21, amended: SI 1999/1820 Art.4, Sch.2 para.138

1916. **Consular Relations (Merchant Shipping) (Union of Soviet Socialist Republics) Order 1970**
revoked: SI 1999/1124 Reg.2

1940. **Eurocontrol (Immunities and Privileges) Order 1970**
Art.5A, added: SI 1999/2034 Art.2, Sch.

1979. **Teachers' Superannuation (Accounts) Regulations 1970**
applied: SI 1997/1612 Reg.142

1971

British Aluminium (Saltburn Pier) Order 1971
applied: SI 1997/1953 Art.3
revoked: SI 1997/1953 Art.4

Lerwick Harbour Order 1971
s.4, applied: SI 1997/1472 Art.5
s.6, amended: SI 1997/1472 Art.5
s.6, applied: SI 1997/1472 Art.5
s.7, applied: SI 1997/1472 Art.5
s.8, applied: SI 1997/1472 Art.5
s.9, amended: SI 1997/1472 Art.5

NO.

1971—cont.

Lerwick Harbour Order 1971—cont.
s.9, applied: SI 1997/1472 Art.5
s.10, applied: SI 1997/1472 Art.5
s.11, amended: SI 1997/1472 Art.5
s.11, applied: SI 1997/1472 Art.5
s.12, amended: SI 1997/1472 Art.5
s.12, applied: SI 1997/1472 Art.5

Yarmouth (Isle of Wight) Pier and Harbour Order 1971
applied: SI 1996/2480 Art.3

92. **Act of Sederunt (Social Work) (Sheriff Court Procedure) Rules 1971**
r.10, see *M v Kennedy* 1996 S.L.T. 434 (SC)
r.10, revoked: SI 1997/291 r.1.4, Sch.2

218. **Lands Tribunal for Scotland Rules 1971**
Sch.2, amended: SI 1996/519 r.2

232. **Police Pensions Regulations 1971**
applied: SI 1999/1750 Art.2, Sch.1

234. **Special Constables (Pensions) (Scotland) Regulations 1971**
applied: SI 1999/1750 Art.2, Sch.1

246. **Police Cadets (Pensions) (Scotland) Regulations 1971**
applied: SI 1999/1750 Art.2, Sch.1

294. **Birmingham-Great Yarmouth Trunk Road (King's Lynn Southern Bypass) Order 1971**
revoked (in part): SI 1996/1802 Art.2

344. **Police (Promotion) (Scotland) Amendment Regulations 1971**
revoked: SI 1996/221 Reg.10, Sch.2

374. **Functions of Traffic Wardens (Scotland) Order 1971**
revoked: SI 1999/854 Art.4

403. **Teachers' Superannuation (Amendment) Regulations 1971**
applied: SI 1997/1612 Reg.142

450. **Road Vehicles (Registration and Licensing) Regulations 1971**
see *R. v Parking Adjudicator Ex p. Wandsworth LBC* Times, November 26, 1996 (CA), Stuart-Smith, L.J.
applied: SI 1996/1627 Art.33, SI 1996/2103 Art.19, SI 1999/2513 Art.23
Reg.3, see *R. v Parking Adjudicator Ex p. Wandsworth LBC* [1998] R.T.R. 51 (CA), Stuart-Smith, L.J.
Reg.3, amended: SI 1997/401 Reg.3
Reg.8, amended: SI 1997/401 Reg.4
Reg.12, see *R. v Parking Adjudicator Ex p. Wandsworth LBC* [1998] R.T.R. 51 (CA), Stuart-Smith, L.J.
Reg.12, amended: SI 1997/401 Reg.5
Reg.12A, added: SI 1997/401 Reg.6
Reg.17, applied: SI 1999/1851 Art.2
Reg.24, amended: SI 1997/401 Reg.7

525. **Reporter's Duties and Transmission of Information, etc. (Scotland) Rules 1971**
revoked: SI 1997/692 r.2

594. **Continental Shelf (Designation of Additional Areas) Order 1971**
referred to: SI 1999/2031, SI 1999/2031 Art.2, Sch.

679. **Teachers' Superannuation (Family Benefits) Regulations 1971**
applied: SI 1997/1612 Reg.142

778. **Town and Country Planning (Minerals) (Scotland) Regulations 1971**
revoked: SI 1998/2913 Reg.4

NO.

1971—cont.

814. **Petroleum (Production) (Amendment) Regulations 1971**
referred to: 1998 c.17 Sch.1 para.5
Sch.4, referred to: SI 1999/160 Sch.2 para.1

843. **Police (Discipline) (Scotland) Amendment Regulations 1971**
revoked: SI 1996/1642 Reg.25, Sch.2

972. **Medicines (Standard Provisions for Licences and Certificates) Regulations 1971**
Reg.2, amended: SI 1999/4 Reg.2
Reg.3, amended: SI 1996/2194 Reg.5
Sch.1 Part III, amended: SI 1996/2194 Reg.5
Sch.3 para.8, amended: SI 1999/4 Reg.3
Sch.3 para.8B, added: SI 1999/4 Reg.3

973. **Medicines (Applications for Product Licences and Clinical Trial and Animal Test Certificates) Regulations 1971**
applied: SI 1996/2194 Reg.4, Reg.5
revoked (in part): SI 1996/2194 Reg.6, Sch.3

1065. **Rent Assessment Committees (England and Wales) Regulations 1971**
Reg.2, amended: SI 1997/1854 Reg.9
Reg.2A, amended: SI 1997/3007 Reg.2

1117. **Employers' Liability (Compulsory Insurance) General Regulations 1971**
applied: SI 1998/2573 Reg.10
revoked: SI 1998/2573 Reg.10, Sch.3
Reg.2, applied: SI 1998/2573 Reg.10
Reg.2, revoked: SI 1998/2573 Reg.10, Sch.3
Reg.3, applied: SI 1998/2573 Reg.10
Reg.3, revoked: SI 1998/2573 Reg.10, Sch.3
Reg.4, applied: SI 1998/2573 Reg.10
Reg.4, revoked: SI 1998/2573 Reg.10, Sch.3
Reg.5, applied: SI 1998/2573 Reg.10
Reg.5, revoked: SI 1998/2573 Reg.10, Sch.3
Reg.6, applied: SI 1998/2573 Reg.10
Reg.6, revoked: SI 1998/2573 Reg.10, Sch.3
Sch., applied: SI 1998/2573 Reg.10
Sch., revoked: SI 1998/2573 Reg.10, Sch.3

1158. **Registration of Births, Still-births, Deaths and Marriages (Prescription of Forms) (Scotland) Amendment Regulations 1971**
revoked: SI 1997/2348 Reg.30, Sch.27

1165. **Act of Sederunt (Edictal Citations, Commissary Petitions and Petitions of Service) 1971**
para.3, revoked: SI 1996/2184 r.3, Sch.2

1253. **Indictment Rules 1971**
r.5, see *R. v Ike (Peace Nnenna)* [1996] Crim. L.R. 515 (CA (Crim Div)), Lord Taylor of Gosforth, C.J.
r.6, see *R. v Ike (Peace Nnenna)* [1996] Crim. L.R. 515 (CA (Crim Div)), Lord Taylor of Gosforth, C.J.
r.9, see *R. v Christou (George)* [1997] A.C. 117 (HL), Lord Taylor of Gosforth, C.J.; see *R. v Fenton (David George)* [1996] Crim. L.R. 259 (CA (Crim Div)), Rose, J.; see *R. v Hicks (Stuart Peter)* Independent, February 19, 1996 (C.S.) (CA (Crim Div)), Pill, L.J.; see *R. v Lockley (Simon Malcolm)* [1997] Crim. L.R. 455 (CA (Crim Div)), Forbes, J.; see *R. v White (Cindy Anne)* [1996] Crim. L.R. 512 (CA (Crim Div)), Rhys Davies, Q.C.; see *R. v Wrench (Peter)* [1996] 1 Cr. App. R. 340 (CA (Crim Div)), Roch, L.J.

1377. **Mines and Quarries (Tips) Regulations 1971**
Reg.2, amended: SI 1999/2024 Reg.48, Sch.5 Part II
Reg.3, amended: SI 1999/2024 Reg.48, Sch.5 Part II

NO.

1971—cont.

1377. **Mines and Quarries (Tips) Regulations 1971**—*cont.*
Reg.4, amended: SI 1999/2024 Reg.48, Sch.5 Part II
Reg.5, amended: SI 1999/2024 Reg.48, Sch.5 Part II
Reg.6, amended: SI 1999/2024 Reg.48, Sch.5 Part II
Reg.7, amended: SI 1999/2024 Reg.48, Sch.5 Part II
Reg.8, amended: SI 1999/2024 Reg.48, Sch.5 Part II
Reg.9, amended: SI 1999/2024 Reg.48, Sch.5 Part II
Reg.9, applied: SI 1999/2024 Reg.38
Reg.10, amended: SI 1999/2024 Reg.48, Sch.5 Part II
Reg.11, amended: SI 1999/2024 Reg.48, Sch.5 Part II
Reg.12, amended: SI 1999/2024 Reg.48, Sch.5 Part II
Reg.12, applied: SI 1999/2024 Reg.38
Reg.13, amended: SI 1999/2024 Reg.48, Sch.5 Part II
Reg.14, amended: SI 1999/2024 Reg.48, Sch.5 Part II
Reg.15, amended: SI 1999/2024 Reg.48, Sch.5 Part II
Reg.17, amended: SI 1999/2024 Reg.48, Sch.5 Part II
Reg.18, amended: SI 1999/2024 Reg.48, Sch.5 Part II
Reg.18, applied: SI 1999/2024 Reg.38
Reg.19, amended: SI 1999/2024 Reg.48, Sch.5 Part II
Reg.20, amended: SI 1999/2024 Reg.48, Sch.5 Part II
Reg.21, amended: SI 1999/2024 Reg.48, Sch.5 Part II
Reg.22, amended: SI 1999/2024 Reg.48, Sch.5 Part II
Reg.24, amended: SI 1999/2024 Reg.48, Sch.5 Part II
Reg.25, amended: SI 1999/2024 Reg.48, Sch.5 Part II

1378. **Mines and Quarries (Tipping Plans) Rules 1971**
r.3, amended: SI 1999/2024 Reg.48, Sch.5 Part II

1450. **Medicines (Exemption from Licences) (Special and Transitional Cases) Order 1971**
Art.2, applied: SI 1997/1469 Sch.1 Part I, Sch.2 para.2, SI 1998/2428 Sch.1 Part II, Sch.2 para.2

1502. **Motorways Traffic (M4) (Speed Limit) Regulations 1971**
revoked: SI 1998/1708 Reg.3

1521. **Local Authorities Traffic Orders (Exemption for Disabled Persons) (Scotland) Regulations 1971**
Reg.4, applied: SI 1999/614 Sch.6 para.1
Reg.4, referred to: SI 1999/614 Reg.19, Sch.6 para.1

1524. **Zebra Pedestrian Crossing Regulations 1971**
revoked: SI 1997/2400 Reg.2
Sch.2 Part I, applied: SI 1996/1483 Reg.4
Sch.2 Part I, revoked: SI 1997/2400 Reg.2

1526. **General Optical Council (Disciplinary Committee Rules) (Amendment) Order of Council 1971**
revoked: SI 1998/1338, SI 1998/1338 Sch. r.20

NO.

1971—cont.

1742. **National Insurance (Republic of Ireland) Order 1971**
Sch., amended: SI 1996/1928 Art.2, Sch.1

1744. **Hijacking Act 1971 (Guernsey) Order 1971**
revoked: SI 1997/2989 Art.2, Sch.3

1933. **Employers' Liability (Compulsory Insurance) Exemption Regulations 1971**
revoked: SI 1998/2573 Reg.10, Sch.3
Reg.2, revoked: SI 1998/2573 Reg.10, Sch.3
Reg.3, revoked: SI 1998/2573 Reg.10, Sch.3
Reg.4, revoked: SI 1998/2573 Reg.10, Sch.3

2019. **Prison (Amendment) Rules 1971**
revoked: SI 1999/728 r.85 (with savings), Sch. (with savings)

2084. **Indictments (Procedure) Rules 1971**
see *Practice Direction (Sup Ct: Crime: Voluntary Bills) (No.2)* [1999] 1 W.L.R. 1613 (Sup Ct), Lord Bingham of Cornhill, L.C.J.
applied: SI 1998/3045 r.2
r.2, amended: SI 1997/711 r.5, SI 1998/3045 r.2
r.5, amended: SI 1998/3045 r.2
r.8, amended: SI 1998/3045 r.2
r.9, amended: SI 1997/711 r.6, SI 1998/3045 r.2
r.11, substituted: SI 1997/711 r.7

2103. **Extradition (Tokyo Convention) Order 1971**
revoked: SI 1997/1768 Art.4

1972

Electricity Supply (Northern Ireland) Order 1972
applied: SI 1999/2450 Sch.4 para.16.2
Sch.3, applied: SI 1999/2450 Sch.4 para.10.1
Sch.3 para.1, applied: SI 1999/2450 Sch.4 para.10.1
Sch.3 para.2, applied: SI 1999/2450 Sch.4 para.10.1
Sch.3 para.3, applied: SI 1999/2450 Sch.4 para.10.1
Sch.3 para.4, applied: SI 1999/2450 Sch.4 para.10.1
Sch.3 para.5, applied: SI 1999/2450 Sch.4 para.10.1
Sch.3 para.6, referred to: SI 1999/2450 Sch.4 para.12.1
Sch.3 para.6A, referred to: SI 1999/2450 Sch.4 para.12.1

Lewisham (Prescribed Routes) (No.3) Traffic Order 1972
revoked: SI 1999/2701 Art.5

24. **Police Grant (Scotland) Order 1972**
revoked: SI 1996/780 Art.7, Sch.2

251. **South West Worcestershire Water Board Order 1972**
revoked: 1998 c.43 s.1, Sch.1 Part V

300. **Yarmouth (Isle of Wight) Harbour Revision Order 1972**
applied: SI 1996/2480 Art.3

316. **Rules of Procedure (Army) 1972**
revoked: SI 1997/169 r.90, Sch.7
r.9, amended: SI 1997/18 r.2
r.9, revoked: SI 1997/169 r.90, Sch.7
r.22, amended: SI 1996/1388 r.2, Sch. para.1
r.22, revoked: SI 1997/169 r.90, Sch.7
r.26, amended: SI 1996/1388 r.2, Sch. para.2
r.26, revoked: SI 1997/169 r.90, Sch.7
r.37, see *R. v Lisle (Graham David)* Times, February 26, 1997 (CMAC), Harrison, J.
r.37, revoked: SI 1997/169 r.90, Sch.7
r.41, amended: SI 1996/1388 r.2, Sch. para.3

NO.

1972—cont.

316. Rules of Procedure (Army) 1972—*cont.*
r.41, revoked: SI 1997/169 r.90, Sch.7
r.53A, added: SI 1996/1388 r.2, Sch. para.4
r.53A, revoked: SI 1997/169 r.90, Sch.7
r.55, amended: SI 1996/1388 r.2, Sch. para.5
r.55, revoked: SI 1997/169 r.90, Sch.7
r.71, amended: SI 1996/1388 r.2, Sch. para.6
r.71, revoked: SI 1997/169 r.90, Sch.7
r.81, amended: SI 1996/1388 r.2, Sch. para.7
r.81, revoked: SI 1997/169 r.90, Sch.7
r.90, amended: SI 1996/1388 r.2, Sch. para.8
r.90, revoked: SI 1997/169 r.90, Sch.7
Sch.1, amended: SI 1996/1388 r.2, Sch. para.9
Sch.1, revoked: SI 1997/169 r.90, Sch.7
Sch.2, amended: SI 1996/1388 r.2, Sch. para.10, Sch. para.11
Sch.2, revoked: SI 1997/169 r.90, Sch.7

360. Teachers' Superannuation (Family Benefits) (Amendment) Regulations 1972
applied: SI 1997/1612 Reg.142

382. Fire Precautions (Hotels and Boarding Houses) (Scotland) Order 1972
see *McClory v MacKinnon* 1996 S.C.C.R. 367

419. Rules of Procedure (Air Force) 1972
revoked: SI 1997/171 r.90, Sch.7
r.9, amended: SI 1997/14 r.2
r.9, revoked: SI 1997/171 r.90, Sch.7
r.22, amended: SI 1996/1389 r.2, Sch. para.1
r.22, revoked: SI 1997/171 r.90, Sch.7
r.26, amended: SI 1996/1389 r.2, Sch. para.2
r.26, revoked: SI 1997/171 r.90, Sch.7
r.36, see *R. v Lisle (Graham David)* Times, February 26, 1997 (CMAC), Harrison, J.
r.36, revoked: SI 1997/171 r.90, Sch.7
r.41, amended: SI 1996/1389 r.2, Sch. para.3
r.41, revoked: SI 1997/171 r.90, Sch.7
r.53A, added: SI 1996/1389 r.2, Sch. para.4
r.53A, revoked: SI 1997/171 r.90, Sch.7
r.55, amended: SI 1996/1389 r.2, Sch. para.5
r.55, revoked: SI 1997/171 r.90, Sch.7
r.71, amended: SI 1996/1389 r.2, Sch. para.6
r.71, revoked: SI 1997/171 r.90, Sch.7
r.81, amended: SI 1996/1389 r.2, Sch. para.7
r.81, revoked: SI 1997/171 r.90, Sch.7
r.90, amended: SI 1996/1389 r.2, Sch. para.8
r.90, revoked: SI 1997/171 r.90, Sch.7
Sch.1, amended: SI 1996/1389 r.2, Sch. para.9
Sch.1, revoked: SI 1997/171 r.90, Sch.7
Sch.5, amended: SI 1996/1389 r.2, Sch. para.10
Sch.5, revoked: SI 1997/171 r.90, Sch.7

472. Boulby Mine (Storage Battery Locomotives) Special Regulations 1972
Reg.4, revoked: SI 1996/192 Reg.20, Sch.15 Part I
Reg.5, revoked: SI 1996/192 Reg.20, Sch.15 Part I
Reg.6, revoked: SI 1996/192 Reg.20, Sch.15 Part I
Reg.7, revoked: SI 1996/192 Reg.20, Sch.15 Part I
Reg.8, revoked: SI 1996/192 Reg.20, Sch.15 Part I

538. Prosecution of Offences (Northern Ireland) Order 1972
referred to: 1998 c.32 s.58
Art.9, revoked (in part): SI 1996/1298 (NI.8) Art.21, Sch.6

568. Teachers' Superannuation (Financial Provisions) Regulations 1972
applied: SI 1997/1612 Reg.142

NO.

1972—cont.

594. Cambridge Water Order 1972
revoked: SI 1996/713 Art.4, Sch.2 Part II

674. Hovercraft (General) Order 1972
applied: SI 1997/320 Reg.6
Art.3, amended: SI 1996/3173 Art.3
Art.4, amended: SI 1996/3173 Art.4
Art.5, applied: SI 1997/320 Reg.3
Art.7A, added: SI 1996/3173 Art.5
Art.8, amended: SI 1996/3173 Art.6, Art.7
Art.9, revoked: SI 1996/3173 Art.8
Art.10, revoked: SI 1996/3173 Art.8
Art.11, amended: SI 1996/3173 Art.7, Art.9
Art.12, amended: SI 1996/3173 Art.7
Art.13, amended: SI 1996/3173 Art.7
Art.14, amended: SI 1996/3173 Art.7
Art.15, amended: SI 1996/3173 Art.7, Art.10
Art.16, amended: SI 1996/3173 Art.7, Art.11
Art.17A, added: SI 1996/3173 Art.12
Art.18, amended: SI 1996/3173 Art.13
Art.23, amended: SI 1996/3173 Art.14
Art.24, amended: SI 1996/3173 Art.15
Art.33, amended: SI 1996/3173 Art.16
Part II, applied: SI 1997/320 Reg.6
Part III, applied: SI 1997/320 Reg.6

764. National Savings Bank Regulations 1972
amended: SI 1996/1724 Reg.2, Reg.3, SI 1999/588 Reg.3
Reg.2, amended: SI 1996/1724 Reg.4, SI 1999/588 Reg.4, SI 1999/1611 Reg.3
Reg.21, referred to: SI 1998/1449 Art.3, Sch. para.3
Reg.29, amended: SI 1996/1724 Reg.5
Reg.29, referred to: SI 1998/1449 Art.3, Sch. para.3
Reg.29, substituted: SI 1996/801 Reg.2
Reg.29A, added: SI 1996/1724 Reg.6
Reg.29A, referred to: SI 1998/1449 Art.3, Sch. para.3
Reg.29B, added: SI 1996/1724 Reg.6
Reg.29C, added: SI 1996/1724 Reg.6
Reg.29D, added: SI 1996/1724 Reg.6
Reg.29E, added: SI 1996/1724 Reg.6
Reg.29F, added: SI 1996/1724 Reg.6
Reg.29G, added: SI 1996/1724 Reg.6
Reg.29G, referred to: SI 1998/1449 Art.3, Sch. para.3
Reg.29H, added: SI 1996/1724 Reg.6
Reg.29I, added: SI 1996/1724 Reg.6
Reg.29J, added: SI 1996/1724 Reg.6
Reg.29K, added: SI 1996/1724 Reg.6
Reg.29K, amended: SI 1999/588 Reg.5
Reg.29L, added: SI 1999/588 Reg.6
Reg.29L, amended: SI 1999/1611 Reg.4
Reg.29M, added: SI 1999/588 Reg.6
Reg.29N, added: SI 1999/588 Reg.6
Reg.29O, added: SI 1999/588 Reg.6
Reg.29P, added: SI 1999/588 Reg.6
Reg.29Q, added: SI 1999/588 Reg.6
Reg.29R, added: SI 1999/588 Reg.6
Reg.38, amended: SI 1998/1446 Art.30, Sch.1 para.3
Reg.38A, added: SI 1998/1446 Art.30, Sch.1 para.3
Reg.42, amended: SI 1996/1724 Reg.7, SI 1999/588 Reg.7, SI 1999/1611 Reg.5
Reg.57, amended: SI 1996/1724 Reg.8

765. Premium Savings Bonds Regulations 1972
Reg.3, referred to: SI 1998/1449 Art.3, Sch. para.4
Reg.4, amended: SI 1999/3305 Reg.2

NO.

NO.

765. Premium Savings Bonds Regulations 1972—*cont.*
Reg.7, referred to: SI 1998/1449 Art.3, Sch. para.4
Reg.8, referred to: SI 1998/1449 Art.3, Sch. para.4
Reg.19, referred to: SI 1998/1449 Art.3, Sch. para.4
Reg.30, amended: SI 1997/1862 Reg.2
Reg.30, referred to: SI 1998/1449 Art.3, Sch. para.4

862. Civil Aviation (Hovercraft) Regulations 1972
revoked: SI 1996/3231 Reg.2

917. Highly Flammable Liquids and Liquefied Petroleum Gases Regulations 1972
Reg.7, amended: SI 1996/2092 Reg.21, SI 1998/2885 Reg.2
Reg.7, applied: SI 1996/2092 Reg.22

962. Civil Aviation (Investigation of Accidents) (Guernsey) Order 1972
revoked: SI 1998/1503 Art.3 (with savings)

963. Employers' Liability (Defective Equipment and Compulsory Insurance) (Northern Ireland) Order 1972
referred to: 1998 c.32 s.51, Sch.3 para.4
Art.7, amended: 1997 c.50 s.134, Sch.9 para.25
Art.8, amended: SI 1998/2795 (NI.18) Art.6, Sch.1 para.5

971. Hovercraft (Application of Enactments) Order 1972
Sch.2 Part A, amended: SI 1998/1256 Art.2

1073. Superannuation (Northern Ireland) Order 1972
Art.3, applied: SI 1996/1919 (NI.16) Art.10, Art.212
Art.4, applied: SI 1996/1297 (NI.7) Sch.1 para.5, SI 1996/1298 (NI.8) Sch.1 para.5
Art.15, amended: 1998 c.32 s.74, Sch.4 para.6
Sch.1, amended: SI 1998/261 (NI.2) Art.15, Sch.3, SR 1999/108 Art.2
Sch.1, revoked (in part): SI 1998/261 (NI.2) Art.15, Sch.4, 1998 c.32 s.74, Sch.6
Sch.6 para.3, revoked: SI 1996/1919 (NI.16) Art.257, Sch.3

1092. Teachers' Superannuation (Financial Provisions and Family Benefits) (Amendment) Regulations 1972
applied: SI 1997/1612 Reg.142

1100. Finance (Northern Ireland) Order 1972
Art.10, applied: 1998 c.36 s.145

1139. Solicitors' Remuneration Order 1972
applied: SI 1996/3084 Appendix para.4, SI 1997/1890 Appendix para.4, SI 1998/1712 Appendix para.4, SI 1999/2108 Appendix para.4

1178. Gas Safety Regulations 1972
revoked: SI 1996/825 Reg.31, Sch.6 Part I
Reg.2, amended: SI 1996/470 Art.2
Reg.3, amended: SI 1996/470 Art.2
Reg.52, amended: SI 1996/470 Art.2

1201. Medicines (Applications for Product Licences and Clinical Trial and Animal Test Certificates) Amendment Regulations 1972
revoked (in part): SI 1996/2194 Reg.6, Sch.3

1217. Motor Vehicles (Third Party Risks) Regulations 1972
Reg.5, amended: SI 1997/97 Reg.2
Reg.9, amended: SI 1997/97 Reg.2, SI 1999/2392 Reg.3

1265. Health and Personal Social Services (Northern Ireland) Order 1972
applied: SI 1997/1830 Sch.5 Part II, 1998 c.29 Sch.12 para.6
referred to: SI 1996/3160 (NI.24) Sch.1 para.5, SI 1998/2839 (NI.20) Art.9, 1999 c.33 s.169, Sch.15 para.8
Art.2, amended: SI 1997/1177 (NI.7) Art.32, Sch.2
Art.7, amended: 1999 c.33 s.121
Art.9, amended: SI 1996/274 (NI.1) Art.43, Sch.5 Part I, SI 1998/1759 (NI.13) Art.91, Sch.5 Part I
Art.11, amended: SI 1997/1177 (NI.7) Art.32, Sch.2
Art.15, amended: 1999 c.33 s.121
Art.15A, added: SI 1996/1923 (NI.19) Art.3
Art.15B, added: SI 1997/1177 (NI.7) Art.21
Art.15C, added: SI 1997/1177 (NI.7) Art.21
Art.15D, added: SI 1997/1177 (NI.7) Art.22
Art.15E, added: SI 1997/1177 (NI.7) Art.23
Art.15F, added: SI 1997/1177 (NI.7) Art.24
Art.16, referred to: 1999 c.33 s.95, Sch.9 para.1, SI 1999/496 Reg.12, SI 1999/1001 Reg.10, SI 1999/1494 Sch.5 para.1
Art.17, amended: SI 1997/1177 (NI.7) Art.32, Sch.2
Art.17, applied: 1998 c.29 Sch.12 para.6
Art.30, applied: SI 1996/207 Sch.1 para.14, SI 1996/2745 Sch.2 para.8, SI 1996/2890 Reg.19
Art.52, amended: SI 1997/1177 (NI.7) Art.32, Sch.2
Art.56, applied: SI 1997/1177 (NI.7) Art.19
Art.56, referred to: SI 1997/1177 (NI.7) Art.3
Art.56, revoked (in part): SI 1997/1177 (NI.7) Art.32, Sch.2, Sch.3
Art.57A, added: SI 1997/1177 (NI.7) Art.25
Art.57F, added: SI 1997/1177 (NI.7) Art.24
Art.61, applied: SI 1997/1177 (NI.7) Art.5
Art.61, referred to: SI 1997/1177 (NI.7) Art.3
Art.61, revoked (in part): SI 1997/1177 (NI.7) Art.32, Sch.2, Sch.3
Art.63, amended: SI 1997/1177 (NI.7) Art.32, Sch.2
Art.63A, added: SI 1997/1177 (NI.7) Art.27
Art.63B, added: SI 1997/1177 (NI.7) Art.28
Art.64, amended: SI 1997/1177 (NI.7) Art.29, Art.32, Sch.2
Art.68, amended: SI 1997/1177 (NI.7) Art.32, Sch.2
Art.77, revoked (in part): SI 1996/1919 (NI.16) Art.257, Sch.3
Art.98, amended: SR 1999/11 Art.2
Art.105, amended: 1996 c.23 Sch.3 para.27
Part II, applied: SI 1997/1177 (NI.7) Art.3, Art.11
Part II, referred to: SI 1997/1177 (NI.7) Art.11
Part VI, applied: SI 1997/1177 (NI.7) Art.20
Part VI, referred to: SI 1997/1177 (NI.7) Art.13, Art.16
Sch.8, amended: 1998 c.32 s.44
Sch.8, applied: SI 1997/276 (NI.2) Art.65, 1998 c.32 s.44
Sch.10 para.1, amended: SI 1997/1177 (NI.7) Art.32, Sch.2
Sch.11, referred to: SI 1996/1298 (NI.8) Sch.3
Sch.11 para.5A, amended: SI 1997/1177 (NI.7) Art.32, Sch.2
Sch.15 para.1, applied: SI 1997/1177 (NI.7) Art.20
Sch.15 para.1AA, added: SI 1997/1177 (NI.7) Art.26

NO.

1265. **Health and Personal Social Services (North-ern Ireland) Order 1972**—*cont.*
Sch.15 para.2A, applied: SI 1997/1177 (NI.7) Art.20
Sch.16 Part II, revoked (in part): SI 1996/1297 (NI.7) Art.23, Sch.5, SI 1996/1298 (NI.8) Art.21, Sch.6

1298. **Pensions Increase (Annual Review) Order 1972**
applied: SI 1997/634 Art.3, SI 1998/503 Art.3, Art.4, SI 1999/522 Art.3

1339. **National Health Service (Superannuation) (Amendment) Regulations 1972**
Reg.39, referred to: SI 1997/1612 Reg.141
Reg.45, applied: SI 1997/1612 Reg.141
Reg.55, referred to: SI 1997/1612 Reg.141

1356. **National Health Service Superannuation (Scotland) Amendment Regulations 1972**
applied: SI 1998/366 Reg.135
Reg.40, referred to: SI 1998/366 Reg.135
Reg.46, applied: SI 1998/366 Reg.135
Reg.54, referred to: SI 1998/366 Reg.135

1512. **Power Presses (Amendment) Regulations 1972**
revoked: SI 1998/2306 Reg.39, Sch.4

1537. **National Health Service (Superannuation) (Amendment) (No.2) Regulations 1972**
Reg.39, referred to: SI 1997/1612 Reg.141
Reg.45, applied: SI 1997/1612 Reg.141
Reg.55, referred to: SI 1997/1612 Reg.141

1578. **European Communities Act 1972 (c.68) and the Intervention Board for Agricultural Produce Order 1972**
referred to: SI 1999/1319 Sch.

1582. **European Communities (European Schools) Order 1972**
applied: SI 1997/3001 Sch.2 para.14

1587. **National Insurance and Industrial Injuries (Jamaica) Order 1972**
revoked: SI 1997/871 Art.3

1590. **European Communities (Enforcement of Community Judgments) Order 1972**
Art.2, amended: SI 1998/1259 Art.2

1604. **National Health Service Superannuation (Scotland) Amendment (No.2) Regulations 1972**
applied: SI 1998/366 Reg.135
Reg.40, referred to: SI 1998/366 Reg.135
Reg.46, applied: SI 1998/366 Reg.135
Reg.54, referred to: SI 1998/366 Reg.135

1613. **Immigration (Exemption from Control) Order 1972**
Art.4, amended: SI 1997/1402 Art.3, SI 1997/2207 Art.3

1671. **Act of Sederunt (Social Work) (Sheriff Court Procedure Rules Amendment) 1972**
revoked: SI 1997/291 r.1.4, Sch.2

1679. **Intervention Functions (Delegation) Regulations 1972**
applied: SI 1999/672 Art.2, Sch.1

1700. **Merchant Shipping (Seamen's Wages and Accounts) Regulations 1972**
Reg.6, amended: SI 1999/3360 Reg.2

1701. **Merchant Shipping (Seamen's Wages and Accounts) (Fishing Vessels) Regulations 1972**
Reg.8, amended: SI 1999/3360 Reg.3

1705. **Railway Bridges (Load-bearing Standards) (England and Wales) Order 1972**
Art.2, amended: SI 1996/420 Sch para.9

NO.

1743. **Chester Water (Borrowing Powers) Order 1972**
revoked: SI 1998/281 Art.4, Sch.2 Part II

1789. **Trunk Roads (Speed Limits) (No.1) Order 1972**
Sch.2 para.1, amended: SI 1996/285 Art.3

1804. **Gas Quality Regulations 1972**
revoked: SI 1996/551 Reg.12

1811. **European Communities (Designation) Order 1972**
revoked: SI 1996/266 Art.3

1833. **Trunk Roads (Speed Limits) (No.2) Order 1972**
revoked: SI 1998/367 Art.5

1841. **Merchant Shipping (Load Line) (Particulars of Depth of Loading) Regulations 1972**
applied: SI 1996/3243 Sch Part I
referred to: SI 1998/1609 Reg.5, Reg.6, Sch.
revoked: SI 1998/2241 Reg.3

1847. **Special Constables (Pensions) (Scotland) (Lump Sum Payments to Widows etc.) Regulations 1972**
applied: SI 1999/1750 Art.2, Sch.1

1860. **Prison (Amendment) Rules 1972**
revoked: SI 1999/728 r.85 (with savings), Sch. (with savings)

1960. **Superannuation (Teachers and Teachers' Families) (Amendment) Regulations 1972**
applied: SI 1997/1612 Reg.142

2076. **Medicines (Data Sheet) Regulations 1972**
Reg.1, amended: SI 1996/2420 Reg.2
Reg.2, amended: SI 1996/2420 Reg.3
Reg.2A, added: SI 1996/2420 Reg.4
Reg.3, amended: SI 1996/2420 Reg.5
Reg.6, revoked: SI 1996/2420 Reg.8
Sch.1, amended: SI 1996/2420 Reg.6
Sch.2 para.10, amended: SI 1996/2420 Reg.7

1973

5. **Work in Compressed Air (Health Register) Order 1973**
revoked: SI 1996/1656 Reg.22, Sch.2 Part I

6. **Northbrook Instrument of Management Order 1973**
referred to: SI 1996/2467
Art.2, amended: SI 1996/2467 Art.2
Art.3, amended: SI 1996/2467 Art.2
Art.5, amended: SI 1996/2467 Art.2
Art.18, amended: SI 1996/2467 Art.2

36. **Employment Medical Advisory Service (Factories Act Orders etc. Amendment) Order 1973**
Sch. Part II, revoked (in part): SI 1996/1656 Reg.22, Sch.2 Part I

37. **Abstract of Special Regulations (Pottery - Health & Welfare) Order 1973**
revoked: SI 1998/543 Reg.14, Sch.3

69. **Drainage (Northern Ireland) Order 1973**
applied: SI 1999/662 (NI.6) Art.45, Art.46, Art.47
referred to: SI 1999/662 (NI.6) Art.43
Art.11, amended: SI 1999/662 (NI.6) Art.40
Art.12, amended: SI 1999/662 (NI.6) Art.45, Sch.5 para.2
Art.12, applied: SI 1999/662 (NI.6) Art.45, Sch.5 para.1
Art.12A, amended: SI 1999/662 (NI.6) Art.45, Sch.5 para.2
Art.12A, applied: SI 1999/662 (NI.6) Art.45, Sch.5 para.1

NO.

NO.

1973—cont.

69. Drainage (Northern Ireland) Order 1973—*cont.*

Art.12B, amended: SI 1999/662 (NI.6) Art.45, Sch.5 para.2

Art.12B, applied: SI 1999/662 (NI.6) Art.45, Sch.5 para.1

Art.13, amended: SI 1999/662 (NI.6) Art.45, Sch.5 para.2

Art.13, applied: SI 1999/662 (NI.6) Art.45, Sch.5 para.1

Art.14, amended: SI 1999/662 (NI.6) Art.45, Sch.5 para.2

Art.14, applied: SI 1999/662 (NI.6) Art.45, Sch.5 para.1

Art.15, amended: SI 1999/662 (NI.6) Art.45, Sch.5 para.2

Art.15, applied: SI 1999/662 (NI.6) Art.45, Sch.5 para.1

Art.15, revoked (in part): 1996 c.23 Sch.4

Art.16, amended: SI 1999/662 (NI.6) Art.45, Sch.5 para.2

Art.16, applied: SI 1999/662 (NI.6) Art.45, Sch.5 para.1

Art.17, amended: SI 1999/662 (NI.6) Art.45, Sch.5 para.2

Art.17, applied: SI 1999/662 (NI.6) Art.45, Sch.5 para.1

Art.18, amended: SI 1999/662 (NI.6) Art.45, Sch.5 para.2

Art.18, applied: SI 1999/662 (NI.6) Art.45, Sch.5 para.1

Art.19, amended: SI 1999/662 (NI.6) Art.45, Sch.5 para.2

Art.19, applied: SI 1999/662 (NI.6) Art.45, Sch.5 para.1

Art.20, amended: SI 1999/662 (NI.6) Art.45, Sch.5 para.2

Art.20, applied: SI 1999/662 (NI.6) Art.45, Sch.5 para.1

Art.25, applied: SI 1999/662 (NI.6) Art.45

Art.26, applied: SI 1999/662 (NI.6) Art.45

Art.31, amended: SI 1999/662 (NI.6) Art.45, Sch.5 para.2

Art.31, applied: SI 1999/662 (NI.6) Art.45, Sch.5 para.1

Art.32, applied: SI 1999/662 (NI.6) Art.45

Art.35, amended: SI 1999/662 (NI.6) Art.45, Sch.5 para.2

Art.35, applied: SI 1999/662 (NI.6) Art.45, Sch.5 para.1

Art.36, amended: SI 1999/662 (NI.6) Art.45, Sch.5 para.2

Art.36, applied: SI 1999/662 (NI.6) Art.45, Sch.5 para.1

Art.38, amended: SI 1999/662 (NI.6) Art.45, Sch.5 para.2

Art.38, applied: SI 1999/662 (NI.6) Art.45, Sch.5 para.1

Art.39, amended: SI 1999/662 (NI.6) Art.45, Sch.5 para.2

Art.39, applied: SI 1999/662 (NI.6) Art.45, Sch.5 para.1

Art.40, amended: SI 1999/662 (NI.6) Art.45, Sch.5 para.2

Art.40, applied: SI 1999/662 (NI.6) Art.45, Sch.5 para.1

Art.40, revoked (in part): 1996 c.23 Sch.4

Art.42, amended: SI 1999/662 (NI.6) Art.63, Sch.8 Part I

Art.45, applied: SI 1999/859 Art.5, Sch.4 para.4

Part I, amended: SI 1999/662 (NI.6) Art.45, Sch.5 para.2

1973—cont.

69. Drainage (Northern Ireland) Order 1973—*cont.*

Part I, applied: SI 1999/662 (NI.6) Art.45, Sch.5 para.1

Sch.2, amended: SI 1999/662 (NI.6) Art.45, Sch.5 para.2

Sch.2A, applied: SI 1999/662 (NI.6) Art.45, Sch.5 para.1

Sch.6 para.1, amended: SI 1999/662 (NI.6) Art.63, Sch.7

Sch.6 para.6, amended: SI 1999/662 (NI.6) Art.60

Sch.7, applied: SI 1999/662 (NI.6) Art.49, Art.50

Sch.7 para.5, amended: SI 1999/662 (NI.6) Art.40

Sch.7 para.9, revoked (in part): 1996 c.23 Sch.4

Sch.7 para.12, revoked: SI 1999/662 (NI.6) Art.63, Sch.8 Part I

Sch.7 para.13, referred to: SI 1999/662 (NI.6) Art.62

Sch.7 para.13, revoked: SI 1999/662 (NI.6) Art.63, Sch.8 Part I

Sch.7 para.13A, revoked: SI 1999/662 (NI.6) Art.63, Sch.8 Part I

Sch.8 para.13, revoked: SI 1999/662 (NI.6) Art.63, Sch.8 Part I

70. Water and Sewerage Services (Northern Ireland) Order 1973

applied: SI 1997/2777 (NI.18) Art.2, SI 1999/662 (NI.6) Art.58

referred to: SI 1996/275 (NI.2) Art.44

Art.2, amended: SI 1999/662 (NI.6) Art.63, Sch.7

Art.5, amended: SI 1999/662 (NI.6) Art.63, Sch.7

Art.6, revoked: SI 1999/662 (NI.6) Art.63, Sch.8 Part II

Art.7, referred to: SI 1996/1298 (NI.8) Sch.3

Art.8, amended: SI 1999/662 (NI.6) Art.63, Sch.7

Art.8, referred to: SI 1999/662 (NI.6) Art.32

Art.8, revoked (in part): SI 1999/662 (NI.6) Art.63, Sch.8 Part II

Art.11, amended: SI 1999/662 (NI.6) Art.63, Sch.7

Art.13, applied: SI 1997/2778 (NI.19) Art.20

Art.14, applied: SI 1997/2778 (NI.19) Art.20

Art.15, applied: SI 1997/2778 (NI.19) Art.20

Art.16, applied: SI 1997/2778 (NI.19) Art.20

Art.53, amended: SI 1999/662 (NI.6) Art.63, Sch.7

Art.56B, amended: SI 1999/662 (NI.6) Art.63, Sch.8 Part II

Art.57A, amended: SI 1996/275 (NI.2) Art.71, Sch.6

Art.57A, revoked (in part): SI 1996/275 (NI.2) Art.71, Sch.8

Part V, applied: SI 1997/2778 (NI.19) Art.70

Sch.1 para.1, amended: SI 1999/663 Art.2, Sch.1 para.19

Sch.3 para.4, revoked: SI 1999/662 (NI.6) Art.63, Sch.8 Part II

Sch.3 para.5, revoked: SI 1999/662 (NI.6) Art.63, Sch.8 Part II

Sch.3 para.6, revoked: SI 1999/662 (NI.6) Art.63, Sch.8 Part II

Sch.3 para.7, revoked: SI 1999/662 (NI.6) Art.63, Sch.8 Part II

Sch.3 para.8, revoked: SI 1999/662 (NI.6) Art.63, Sch.8 Part II

Sch.3 para.9, revoked: SI 1999/662 (NI.6) Art.63, Sch.8 Part II

1973—cont.

70. Water and Sewerage Services (Northern Ireland) Order 1973—cont.
Sch.3 para.10, revoked: SI 1999/662 (NI.6) Art.63, Sch.8 Part II
Sch.3 para.11, revoked: SI 1999/662 (NI.6) Art.63, Sch.8 Part II
Sch.3 para.12, revoked: SI 1999/662 (NI.6) Art.63, Sch.8 Part II
Sch.3 para.13, revoked: SI 1999/662 (NI.6) Art.63, Sch.8 Part II
Sch.3 para.14, revoked: SI 1999/662 (NI.6) Art.63, Sch.8 Part II

173. Value Added Tax (Terminal Markets) Order 1973
Art.2, amended: SI 1997/1836 Art.2, SI 1999/3117 Art.3, Art.4, Art.5
Art.3, amended: SI 1999/3117 Art.6, Art.7
Art.4, added: SI 1999/3117 Art.8
Art.5, added: SI 1999/3117 Art.8
Art.6, added: SI 1999/3117 Art.8
Art.7, added: SI 1999/3117 Art.8

242. National Health Service (Superannuation) (Amendment) Regulations 1973
Reg.39, referred to: SI 1997/1612 Reg.39
Reg.45, applied: SI 1997/1612 Reg.141
Reg.55, referred to: SI 1997/1612 Reg.39

293. Hounslow (Prescribed Routes) (No. 5) Traffic Order 1973
Art.3, revoked: SI 1996/69 Art.5
Art.4, revoked: SI 1996/69 Art.5
Art.5, revoked: SI 1996/69 Art.5
Sch., revoked (in part): SI 1996/69 Art.5

304. National Health Service Superannuation (Scotland) Amendment Regulations 1973
applied: SI 1998/366 Reg.135
Reg.40, referred to: SI 1998/366 Reg.135
Reg.46, applied: SI 1998/366 Reg.135
Reg.54, referred to: SI 1998/366 Reg.135

313. Local Government Superannuation (Miscellaneous Provisions) Regulations 1973
applied: SI 1997/1612 Reg.48, Reg.140, SI 1998/366 Reg.47, Sch.3 para.5
referred to: SI 1997/1612 Reg.117, Reg.119, SI 1998/366 Reg.117, Reg.119

317. Double Taxation Relief (Taxes on Income) (General) (Dividend) Regulations 1973
revoked: SI 1999/1927 Reg.2

325. Value Added Tax (Treatment of Transactions) (No.1) Order 1973
see *Allied Carpets Group Ltd v Customs and Excise Commissioners* [1998] S.T.C. 894 (QBD), Keene, J.

334. Income Tax (Employments) Regulations 1973
referred to: SI 1999/567 Reg.11, SI 1999/568 Reg.19

362. Police Grant (Scotland) Order 1973
revoked: SI 1996/780 Art.7, Sch.2

433. Special Constables (Pensions) (Scotland) Regulations 1973
applied: SI 1999/1750 Art.2, Sch.1

434. Police Cadets (Pensions) (Scotland) Regulations 1973
applied: SI 1999/1750 Art.2, Sch.1

455. Parliamentary Commissioner for Administration and Commissioner for Complaints (Pension) Order (Northern Ireland) 1973
applied: SI 1996/1297 (NI.7) Sch.1 para.2, SI 1996/1298 (NI.8) Sch.1 para.2

1973—cont.

686. Walkways Regulations 1973
Reg.3, applied: SI 1999/2106 Art.2, Sch.1 para.4
Reg.4, applied: SI 1999/2106 Art.2, Sch.1 para.4
Reg.5, applied: SI 1999/2106 Art.2, Sch.1 para.4
Reg.6, applied: SI 1999/2106 Art.2, Sch.1 para.4

731. National Health Service (Superannuation) (Amendment) (No.2) Regulations 1973
Reg.39, referred to: SI 1997/1612 Reg.141
Reg.45, applied: SI 1997/1612 Reg.141
Reg.55, referred to: SI 1997/1612 Reg.141

746. National Health Service Superannuation (Scotland) Amendment (No.2) Regulations 1973
applied: SI 1998/366 Reg.135
Reg.40, referred to: SI 1998/366 Reg.135
Reg.46, applied: SI 1998/366 Reg.135
Reg.54, referred to: SI 1998/366 Reg.135

798. Misuse of Drugs (Safe Custody) Regulations 1973
Sch.1 para.4, added: SI 1999/1403 Reg.2

799. Misuse of Drugs (Notification of and Supply to Addicts) Regulations 1973
applied: SI 1997/1001 Reg.5
revoked: SI 1997/1001 Reg.5

936. Teachers' Superannuation (Family Benefits) (Amendment) Regulations 1973
applied: SI 1997/1612 Reg.142

957. Dockyard Port of Portland (Amendment) Order 1973
revoked: SI 1997/2949 Art.57

958. African Development Fund (Immunities and Privileges) Order 1973
Art.12A, added: SI 1999/2034 Art.2, Sch.

1086. Salaries (Comptroller and Auditor-General and Others) (Northern Ireland) Order 1973
applied: SI 1996/1297 (NI.7) Art.23, SI 1996/1298 (NI.8) Art.21
revoked: SI 1996/1297 (NI.7) Art.23, Sch.5, SI 1996/1298 (NI.8) Art.21, Sch.6

1133. North West Worcestershire Water Board (Charges) Order 1973
revoked: 1998 c.43 s.1, Sch.1 Part V

1142. M66 Motorway (Bury Easterly Bypass Northern Section) and Connecting Roads Scheme 1973
Art.2, amended: SI 1996/2159 Art.1
Art.4, amended: SI 1996/2159 Art.1
Sch.2 para.1, amended: SI 1996/2159 Art.1

1228. Enterprise Ulster (Northern Ireland) Order 1973
Art.14, revoked (in part): SI 1996/1919 (NI.16) Art.257, Sch.3
Sch.1 para.9, revoked (in part): SI 1996/1297 (NI.7) Art.23, Sch.5
Sch.2, revoked: SI 1996/1919 (NI.16) Art.257, Sch.3

1311. Hydrocarbon Oil Regulations 1973
Reg.4, amended: SI 1996/2537 Reg.13
Reg.31, revoked: SI 1996/2313 Reg.2
Reg.32, revoked: SI 1996/2313 Reg.2
Reg.33, revoked: SI 1996/2313 Reg.2
Reg.34, revoked: SI 1996/2537 Reg.13
Reg.35, revoked: SI 1996/2537 Reg.13
Reg.36, revoked: SI 1996/2537 Reg.13
Reg.37, see *British Steel Plc v Customs and Excise Commissioners* [1997] 2 All E.R. 366 (CA), Sir Richard Scott, V.C.

NO.

1973—cont.

1323. Finance (Miscellaneous Provisions) (Northern Ireland) Order 1973
Art.5, applied: 1998 c.36 s.145

1327. Double Taxation Relief (Taxes on Income) (Finland) Order 1973
Sch., referred to: SI 1996/3166 Art.2

1370. Pensions Increase (Annual Review) Order 1973
applied: SI 1997/634 Art.3, SI 1998/503 Art.3, Art.4, SI 1999/522 Art.3

1377. Transit of Animals (General) Order 1973
revoked: SI 1997/1480 Art.22, Sch.12 Part II

1383. Teachers' Superannuation (Miscellaneous Amendments) Regulations 1973
applied: SI 1997/1612 Reg.142

1535. Direct Grant Schools (Amendment) Regulations 1973
revoked: SI 1998/86 Reg.2, Sch.1

1649. National Health Service (Superannuation) (Amendment) (No.3) Regulations 1973
Reg.39, referred to: SI 1997/1612 Reg.141
Reg.45, applied: SI 1997/1612 Reg.141
Reg.55, referred to: SI 1997/1612 Reg.141

1691. North West Worcestershire Water Board (Timber Lane, Stourport) Order 1973
Art.3, revoked: 1998 c.43 s.1, Sch.1 Part V
Art.5, revoked: 1998 c.43 s.1, Sch.1 Part V
Sch.1, revoked: 1998 c.43 s.1, Sch.1 Part V

1692. North West Worcestershire Water Board (Barrow Hill) Order 1973
Art.3, revoked: 1998 c.43 s.1, Sch.1 Part V
Art.5, revoked: 1998 c.43 s.1, Sch.1 Part V
Sch.1, revoked: 1998 c.43 s.1, Sch.1 Part V

1713. National Health Service Superannuation (Scotland) Amendment (No.3) Regulations 1973
applied: SI 1998/366 Reg.135
Reg.40, referred to: SI 1998/366 Reg.135
Reg.46, applied: SI 1998/366 Reg.135
Reg.54, referred to: SI 1998/366 Reg.135

1760. Protection of Aircraft Act 1973 (Guernsey) Order 1973
revoked: SI 1997/2989 Art.2, Sch.3

1776. Occupational Pensions Board (Determinations and Review Procedure) Regulations 1973
revoked: SI 1997/358 Reg.7, Sch

1822. Medicines (Pharmacies) (Applications for Registration and Fees) Regulations 1973
Reg.3, amended: SI 1996/3054 Reg.2, SI 1997/2876 Reg.2, SI 1998/3085 Reg.2, SI 1999/3295 Reg.2

1835. Special Constables (Pensions) (Scotland) (Lump Sum Payments to Widows) Regulations 1973
applied: SI 1999/1750 Art.2, Sch.1

1856. Trunk Roads (Various Routes, Hounslow) (Prescribed Routes) Order 1973
Art.5, revoked: SI 1996/1113 Art.5

1865. Church Representation Rules (Amendment) Resolution 1973
referred to: SI 1998/319, SI 1999/2112

1890. Cromarty Firth Port Authority Order 1973
Art.3, amended: SI 1996/1419 Art.3
Art.4, amended: SI 1996/1419 Art.3
Art.6, amended: SI 1996/1419 Art.3
Art.6, applied: SI 1996/1419 Art.6
Art.7, amended: SI 1996/1419 Art.3
Art.8, amended: SI 1996/1419 Art.3
Art.12, revoked: SI 1996/1419 Art.7
Art.46, amended: SI 1996/1419 Art.3
Art.48, amended: SI 1996/1419 Art.3

NO.

1973—cont.

1890. Cromarty Firth Port Authority Order 1973—cont.
Art.58, amended: SI 1996/1419 Art.3
Art.59, amended: SI 1996/1419 Art.3
Art.74, revoked: SI 1996/1419 Art.7
Art.83, substituted: SI 1996/1419 Art.3

1896. Land Acquisition and Compensation (Northern Ireland) Order 1973
amended: SI 1996/725 (NI.5) Sch.3 para.1
Art.22, amended: SI 1997/276 (NI.2) Art.75, Sch.8 para.2
Art.30A, amended: SI 1998/1071 (NI.6) Art.41, Sch.3

1920. North West Water Authority (Regional Land Drainage Committee) Order 1973
revoked: SI 1998/1637 Art.3

1923. Southern Water Authority (Regional Land Drainage Committee) Order 1973
Art.3, revoked (in part): SI 1997/1362 Art.3
Sch., revoked: SI 1997/1362 Art.3

1924. Welsh National Water Development Authority (Regional Land Drainage Committee) Order 1973
referred to: SI 1996/1007
revoked: SI 1996/1007 Art.2

1926. Yorkshire Water Authority (Regional Land Drainage Committee) Order 1973
revoked: SI 1996/1614 Art.3

1936. Diseases of Animals (Waste Food) Order 1973
applied: SI 1999/646 Art.34
revoked: SI 1999/646 Art.35, Sch.6 Part I
Art.2, amended: SI 1996/826 Art.2
Art.2, revoked: SI 1999/646 Art.35, Sch.6 Part I

1996. Local Government Superannuation (Miscellaneous Provisions) (No.2) Regulations 1973
applied: SI 1997/1612 Reg.48, Reg.140, SI 1998/366 Reg.47, Sch.3 para.5
referred to: SI 1997/1612 Reg.117, Reg.119, SI 1998/366 Reg.117, Reg.119

2001. Lake District Special Planning Board Order 1973
revoked: SI 1996/1243 Art.20, Sch.8

2014. Northumbrian Water Authority (Regional Land Drainage Committee) Order 1973
revoked: SI 1996/1617 Art.3

2061. Peak Park Joint Special Board Order 1973
revoked (in part): SI 1996/1243 Art.20, Sch.8

2136. Ipswich Port Authority Order 1973
revoked: SI 1997/948 Sch. para.12
Art.4, applied: SI 1997/948 Sch. para.11
Art.4, revoked: SI 1997/948 Sch. para.12
Art.5, applied: SI 1997/948 Sch. para.11
Art.5, revoked: SI 1997/948 Sch. para.12
Art.6, applied: SI 1997/948 Sch. para.11
Art.6, revoked: SI 1997/948 Sch. para.12
Art.7, applied: SI 1997/948 Sch. para.11
Art.7, revoked: SI 1997/948 Sch. para.12
Sch.1, applied: SI 1997/948 Sch. para.11
Sch.1, revoked: SI 1997/948 Sch. para.12

2161. Ministries (Northern Ireland) Order 1973
revoked: SI 1999/283 (NI.1) Art.9, Sch.3
Art.5, revoked (in part): SI 1996/1298 (NI.8) Art.21, Sch.6, SI 1999/283 (NI.1) Art.9, Sch.3

2163. Northern Ireland (Modification of Enactments) (No.1) Order 1973
Art.2, revoked (in part): SI 1996/1297 (NI.7) Art.23, Sch.5, SI 1996/1298 (NI.8) Art.21, Sch.6, SI 1998/1504 (NI.9) Art.65, Sch.6
Art.6, revoked (in part): 1998 c.32 s.74
Art.12, revoked: SI 1999/663 Art.2

NO.

2163. **Northern Ireland (Modification of Enactments) (No.1) Order 1973**—*cont.*
Art.13, revoked: SI 1999/663 Art.2
Art.14, applied: SI 1996/1929
Sch.1, revoked (in part): SI 1996/1141 (NI.6) s.32, Sch.5, 1998 c.32 s.74
Sch.4, revoked (in part): 1998 c.32 s.74
Sch.5 para.11, revoked: 1998 c.32 s.74
Sch.5 para.16, applied: SI 1996/1929
Sch.5 para.18, revoked: SI 1999/663 Art.2
Sch.5 para.21, revoked: 1998 c.32 s.74
Sch.5 para.24, revoked: SI 1999/663 Art.2
Sch.5 para.36, revoked: SI 1996/1141 (NI.6) Art.32, Sch.5
Sch.5 para.57, revoked (in part): SI 1998/1504 (NI.9) Art.65, Sch.6
Sch.5 para.58, revoked: SI 1996/1298 (NI.8) Art.21, Sch.6
Sch.5 para.59, revoked: SI 1996/1297 (NI.7) Art.23, Sch.5
Sch.5 para.61, revoked: 1998 c.32 s.74

1974

Veterinary Surgeons and Veterinary Practitioners Registration (Amendment) Regulations 1974
revoked: SI 1999/2846 Sch. Reg.22

15. **"Zebra" Pedestrian Crossings Regulations (Northern Ireland) 1974**
Reg.8, applied: SI 1996/1320 (NI.10) Sch.1 Part II
Reg.9, applied: SI 1996/1320 (NI.10) Sch.1 Part II
Reg.10, applied: SI 1996/1320 (NI.10) Sch.1 Part II
Reg.12, applied: SI 1996/1320 (NI.10) Sch.1 Part II

149. **General Optical Council (Education Committee Rules) Order of Council 1974**
referred to: SI 1999/1211
revoked: SI 1999/1211 Sch. para.10

182. **National Health Service Reorganisation (Retirement of Senior Officers) (Scotland) Regulations 1974**
applied: SI 1999/1750 Art.2, Sch.1

208. **Employers' Liability (Compulsory Insurance) (Amendment) Regulations 1974**
revoked: SI 1998/2573 Reg.10, Sch.3

209. **Construction (Health and Welfare) (Amendment) Regulations 1974**
revoked: SI 1996/1592 Reg.35, Sch.10

226. **Pencils and Graphic Instruments (Safety) Regulations 1974**
revoked: SI 1998/2406 Reg.2

260. **Teachers' Superannuation (Added Years and Interchange) Regulations 1974**
applied: SI 1997/1612 Reg.142, SI 1997/3001 Reg.E27

289. **Offshore Installations (Construction and Survey) Regulations 1974**
revoked: SI 1996/913 Reg.27, Sch.3
Reg.11, amended: SI 1996/913 Reg.24

302. **Kent (Coroners' Districts) Order 1974**
amended: SI 1996/445 Art.1

348. **Montrose Harbour Revision Order 1974**
Art.3, amended: SSI 1999/200 Art.8
Art.19, revoked: SSI 1999/200 Art.8

366. **Cornwall (Coroners' Districts) Order 1974**
Art.3, amended: SI 1996/2403 Art.4
Sch., substituted: SI 1996/2403 Art.4

NO.

374. **Hertfordshire (Coroners' Districts) Order 1974**
Art.3, amended: SI 1998/1799 Art.4
Sch., amended: SI 1998/1799 Art.4

390. **Teachers' Superannuation (Teacher's Contribution) Regulations 1974**
applied: SI 1997/1612 Reg.142

441. **National Health Service Superannuation (Scotland) Amendment Regulations 1974**
applied: SI 1998/366 Reg.135
Reg.40, referred to: SI 1998/366 Reg.135
Reg.46, applied: SI 1998/366 Reg.135
Reg.54, referred to: SI 1998/366 Reg.135

457. **Protection of Wrecks (Designation No.5) Order 1974**
revoked: SI 1997/1528 Art.3

468. **National Health Service (Financial Provisions) (Scotland) Regulations 1974**
applied: SI 1999/686 Art.5, Sch. Part III, SI 1999/726 Art.5, Sch. Part III

502. **Motorways Traffic (Speed Limit) Regulations 1974**
Reg.3, see *Donaldson v Valentine* 1996 S.L.T. 643

505. **National Health Service (General Dental Services) (Scotland) Regulations 1974**
revoked (in part): SI 1996/177 Reg.38, Sch.8
Reg.9, revoked: SI 1997/174 Reg.18, Sch
Reg.10, revoked: SI 1997/174 Reg.18, Sch
Reg.11, revoked: SI 1997/174 Reg.18, Sch
Reg.12, revoked: SI 1997/174 Reg.18, Sch
Reg.13, revoked: SI 1997/174 Reg.18, Sch
Reg.14, revoked: SI 1997/174 Reg.18, Sch
Reg.15, revoked: SI 1997/174 Reg.18, Sch
Reg.16, revoked: SI 1997/174 Reg.18, Sch
Reg.17, revoked: SI 1997/174 Reg.18, Sch
Reg.18, revoked: SI 1997/174 Reg.18, Sch

520. **Local Government Superannuation Regulations 1974**
applied: SI 1997/1612 Reg.48, Reg.107, Reg.139
referred to: SI 1996/1680 Reg.39, SI 1997/1612 Reg.117, Reg.119
Reg.D1, applied: SI 1997/1613 Reg.24
Reg.D6, applied: SI 1997/1613 Reg.15
Reg.D7, applied: SI 1997/1613 Reg.15
Reg.D8, applied: SI 1997/1613 Reg.15
Reg.D10, applied: SI 1997/1612 Reg.87
Reg.E19, applied: SI 1997/1613 Reg.10, SI 1997/1612 Sch.6 para.7
Reg.E19, referred to: SI 1997/1612 Sch.6 para.2
Reg.E20, applied: SI 1997/1612 Reg.6
Reg.G14, referred to: SI 1996/1680 Reg.39
Reg.J17, applied: SI 1997/1612 Reg.141
Reg.K1, applied: SI 1997/1613 Reg.24

549. **National Health Service (Professions Supplementary to Medicine) (Scotland) Regulations 1974**
applied: SI 1999/686 Art.5, Sch. Part III, SI 1999/726 Art.5, Sch. Part III

577. **Cambridgeshire (Coroners' Districts) Order 1974**
revoked: SI 1999/1325 Art.4

583. **West Midlands (Coroners' Districts) Order 1974**
Art.3, amended: SI 1999/1990 Art.4
Sch., amended: SI 1999/1990 Art.4

NO.

NO.

1974—cont.

1974—cont.

595. **Local Authorities etc. (Miscellaneous Provisions) (No.2) Order 1974**
Art.4, revoked (in part): SI 1997/325 Art.12

700. **South West Worcestershire Water Board (River Teme) Order 1974**
Art.3, revoked: 1998 c.43 s.1, Sch.1 Part V
Art.4, revoked: 1998 c.43 s.1, Sch.1 Part V
Art.5, revoked: 1998 c.43 s.1, Sch.1 Part V
Art.8, revoked: 1998 c.43 s.1, Sch.1 Part V
Art.9, revoked: 1998 c.43 s.1, Sch.1 Part V
Art.11, revoked: 1998 c.43 s.1, Sch.1 Part V
Sch., revoked: 1998 c.43 s.1, Sch.1 Part V

710. **Elsecar Main Mine (Diesel Vehicles) Special Regulations 1974**
Reg.4, revoked: SI 1996/192 Reg.20, Sch.15 Part I
Reg.5, revoked: SI 1996/192 Reg.20, Sch.15 Part I
Reg.6, revoked: SI 1996/192 Reg.20, Sch.15 Part I

713. **Prison (Amendment) Rules 1974**
revoked: SI 1999/728 r.85 (with savings), Sch. (with savings)

752. **Rules of Procedure (Air Force) (Amendment) Rules 1974**
revoked: SI 1997/171 r.90, Sch.7

761. **Rules of Procedure (Army) (Amendment) Rules 1974**
revoked: SI 1997/169 r.90, Sch.7

812. **Local Government Superannuation (Scotland) Regulations 1974**
applied: SI 1998/366 Reg.47, Reg.106, Reg.134, Reg.135
referred to: SI 1998/366 Reg.117, Reg.119
Reg.D6, applied: SI 1998/364 Reg.15, SI 1998/366 Reg.135
Reg.D7, applied: SI 1998/364 Reg.15, SI 1998/366 Reg.135
Reg.D8, applied: SI 1998/364 Reg.15
Reg.D10, referred to: SI 1998/366 Reg.86
Reg.E19, referred to: SI 1998/364 Reg.10
Reg.E21, applied: SI 1998/366 Reg.5
Reg.N12, applied: SI 1998/366 Reg.135

903. **Woodworking Machines Regulations 1974**
revoked: SI 1998/2306 Reg.39, Sch.4
Reg.4, revoked: SI 1998/2306 Reg.39, Sch.4

939. **Act of Sederunt (Maintenance Orders (Reciprocal Enforcement) Act 1972 Rules) 1974**
Part III, revoked: SI 1997/291 r.1.4, Sch.2
r.1, amended: SI 1997/291 r.1.4, Sch.2
r.2, amended: SI 1997/291 r.1.4, Sch.2
r.3, amended: SI 1997/291 r.1.4, Sch.2
r.3, revoked (in part): SI 1997/291 r.1.4, Sch.2

1251. **Asian Development Bank (Immunities and Privileges) Order 1974**
Art.13A, added: SI 1999/2034 Art.2, Sch.

1261. **United Nations and International Court of Justice (Immunities and Privileges) Order 1974**
applied: SI 1996/1296 Art.22
Art.5, applied: SI 1996/716 Art.22, SI 1997/281 Art.20, SI 1997/283 Art.20
Art.6, applied: SI 1996/716 Art.22, SI 1997/281 Art.20, SI 1997/283 Art.20
Art.7, applied: SI 1996/716 Art.22, SI 1997/281 Art.20, SI 1997/283 Art.20
Art.8, applied: SI 1996/716 Art.22, SI 1997/281 Art.20, SI 1997/283 Art.20
Art.9, applied: SI 1996/716 Art.22, SI 1997/281 Art.20, SI 1997/283 Art.20
Art.10, applied: SI 1996/716 Art.22, SI 1997/281 Art.20, SI 1997/283 Art.20

1261. **United Nations and International Court of Justice (Immunities and Privileges) Order 1974**—*cont.*
Art.11, applied: SI 1996/716 Art.22, SI 1997/281 Art.20, SI 1997/283 Art.20
Art.12, applied: SI 1996/716 Art.22, SI 1997/281 Art.20, SI 1997/283 Art.20
Art.13, applied: SI 1996/716 Art.22, SI 1997/281 Art.20, SI 1997/283 Art.20
Art.15, applied: SI 1996/716 Art.22, SI 1996/1296 Art.22, SI 1997/281 Art.20, SI 1997/283 Art.20
Art.16, applied: SI 1996/716 Art.22, SI 1996/1296 Art.22, SI 1997/281 Art.20, SI 1997/283 Art.20

1345. **Porthmadog Harbour Revision Order 1974**
revoked: SI 1998/683 Art.4 (with savings), Sch. Part I (with savings)

1357. **National Health Service Superannuation (Scotland) Amendment (No.2) Regulations 1974**
applied: SI 1998/366 Reg.135
Reg.40, referred to: SI 1998/366 Reg.135
Reg.46, applied: SI 1998/366 Reg.135
Reg.54, referred to: SI 1998/366 Reg.135

1373. **Pensions Increase (Annual Review) Order 1974**
applied: SI 1997/634 Art.3, SI 1998/503 Art.3, Art.4, SI 1999/522 Art.3

1388. **Teachers' Superannuation (Family Benefits) (Amendment) Regulations 1974**
applied: SI 1997/1612 Reg.142

1489. **Continental Shelf (Designation of Additional Areas) Order 1974**
referred to: SI 1999/2031

1565. **Valuation (Combination of Councils) (Scotland) (No.2) Order 1974**
applied: SI 1996/682 Sch.2

1735. **Radioactive Substances (Carriage by Road) (Great Britain) Regulations 1974**
revoked: SI 1996/1350 Reg.41

1838. **National Health Service (Scotland) (Injury Benefits) Regulations 1974**
applied: SI 1997/2205 Reg.2, SI 1998/1594 Reg.23
revoked: SI 1998/1594 Reg.24, Sch.

1866. **Rixey Park Mine (Storage Battery Locomotives) Special Regulations 1974**
Reg.4, revoked: SI 1996/192 Reg.20, Sch.15 Part II
Reg.5, revoked: SI 1996/192 Reg.20, Sch.15 Part II
Reg.6, revoked: SI 1996/192 Reg.20, Sch.15 Part II
Reg.7, revoked: SI 1996/192 Reg.20, Sch.15 Part II
Reg.8, revoked: SI 1996/192 Reg.20, Sch.15 Part II

1869. **National Health Service (Compensation) (Scotland) Regulations 1974**
applied: SI 1999/1750 Art.2, Sch.1

1902. **Special Constables (Pensions) (Scotland) (Lump Sum Payments to Widows) Regulations 1974**
applied: SI 1999/1750 Art.2, Sch.1

1919. **Merchant Shipping (Radio) (Fishing Vessels) Rules 1974**
applied: SI 1996/3243 Reg.5, Sch Part I
referred to: SI 1996/3243 Sch Part I
revoked (in part): SI 1999/3210 Reg.2
Part II, applied: SI 1999/3210 Reg.5
Part II, revoked (in part): SI 1999/3210 Reg.2
Part III, applied: SI 1999/3210 Reg.5

1974—cont.

1919. Merchant Shipping (Radio) (Fishing Vessels) Rules 1974—*cont.*
Part III, revoked (in part): SI 1999/3210 Reg.2
r.1, revoked (in part): SI 1999/3210 Reg.2
r.3, revoked (in part): SI 1999/3210 Reg.2
r.4, revoked (in part): SI 1999/3210 Reg.2
r.6, revoked (in part): SI 1999/3210 Reg.2
r.8, revoked (in part): SI 1999/3210 Reg.2
r.11A, revoked (in part): SI 1999/3210 Reg.2
r.12, revoked (in part): SI 1999/3210 Reg.2
r.13, revoked (in part): SI 1999/3210 Reg.2

2010. Social Security (Benefit) (Married Women and Widows Special Provisions) Regulations 1974
Reg.3, amended: SI 1996/1345 Reg.13

2013. Mines and Quarries Acts 1954 to 1971 (Repeals and Modifications) Regulations 1974
Reg.2, referred to: SI 1997/2703

2034. Agriculture (Tractor Cabs) Regulations 1974
applied: SI 1996/2791 Reg.4, Sch.3, SI 1997/2505 Reg.4, Sch.3, SI 1999/645 Reg.4, Sch.3

2040. Health and Safety Licensing Appeals (Hearings Procedure) Rules 1974
applied: SI 1996/772 Reg.14, SI 1999/3232 Reg.5, Reg.11, Sch.4 para.22

2041. Hertfordshire (Coroners' Districts) (Amendment) Order 1974
revoked: SI 1998/1799 Art.4

2048. National Health Service (General Dental Services) (Scotland) Amendment Regulations 1974
revoked (in part): SI 1996/177 Reg.38, Sch.8
Reg.2, revoked (in part): SI 1997/174 Reg.18, Sch

2057. National Insurance (Non-participation Transitional Provisions) Regulations 1974
Reg.2, applied: SI 1997/1613 Reg.18
Reg.9, referred to: SI 1997/1613 Reg.18, SI 1998/364 Reg.18

2068. Health and Safety Licensing Appeals (Hearings Procedure) (Scotland) Rules 1974
applied: SI 1996/772 Reg.14, SI 1999/3232 Reg.5, Reg.11, Sch.4 para.22

2087. Sheriffdoms Reorganisation Order 1974
revoked: SI 1996/1006 Art.4

2125. Trunk Road (Malden Way and Tolworth Rise, Kingston Upon Thames) (Prescribed Routes) Order 1974
Art.2, amended: SI 1997/153 Art.2

2141. Financial Provisions (Northern Ireland) Order 1974
Art.5, revoked: SI 1998/749 (NI.4) Art.9, Sch.

2143. Juries (Northern Ireland) Order 1974
revoked: SI 1996/1141 (NI.6) s.32, Sch.5

2211. Rabies (Importation of Dogs, Cats and Other Mammals) Order 1974
applied: SI 1998/190 Reg.34, Sch.6, SI 1999/3443 Art.9
referred to: SI 1998/190 Reg.34, Sch.6, SI 1999/3443 Art.3
Art.4, amended: SI 1999/3443 Art.13
Art.4B, added: SI 1999/3443 Art.13
Art.5A, added: SI 1999/3443 Art.13
Art.6, amended: SI 1999/3443 Art.13
Sch.1, applied: SI 1998/190 Reg.17

1975

Camden (Bus Lanes) (No.1) Traffic Order 1975
revoked (in part): SI 1998/3206 Art.6

1975—cont.

40. Pencils and Graphic Instruments (Safety) Regulations (Northern Ireland) 1975
revoked: SI 1998/2406 Reg.2

45. Agriculture (Poisonous Substances) Act 1952 (Repeals and Modifications) Regulations 1975
revoked: SI 1997/1713 Reg.9, Sch.

116. Merchant Shipping (Diving Operations) Regulations 1975
applied: SI 1996/3243 Sch Part I

148. Town and Country Planning (Tree Preservation Order) (Amendment) and (Trees in Conservation Areas) (Exempted Cases) Regulations 1975
revoked: SI 1999/1892 Reg.18 (with savings)
Reg.3, referred to: SI 1998/1936 Art.22
Reg.3, revoked: SI 1999/1892 Reg.18 (with savings)

158. European Centre for Medium-Range Weather Forecasts (Immunities and Privileges) Order 1975
Art.12A, added: SI 1999/2034 Art.2, Sch.

194. Employers' Liability (Compulsory Insurance) (Amendment) Regulations 1975
revoked: SI 1998/2573 Reg.10, Sch.3

299. Lands Tribunal Rules 1975
revoked: SI 1996/1022 r.57, Sch.2
r.38, see *Barclays Bank Plc v Kent CC* (1998) 76 P. & C.R. 1 (CA), Kennedy, L.J.
r.38, revoked: SI 1996/1022 r.57, Sch.2
r.50, see *Hepworth Building Projects Ltd v Coal Authority* [1999] 3 E.G.L.R. 99 (CA), Judge, L.J.
r.50, revoked: SI 1996/1022 r.57, Sch.2

300. Justices' Clerks (Amendment) Rules 1975
revoked: SI 1999/2784 r.4

330. Fishing Vessels (Safety Provisions) Rules 1975
applied: SI 1996/1242 para.3, SI 1997/1924 para.3, SI 1998/1011 Reg.18, SI 1999/2998 Reg.8
r.1, amended: SI 1996/2419 r.2, SI 1998/928 r.4, r.5, r.6, r.7, SI 1999/2998 Reg.3, Sch.1 para.1
r.1A, added: SI 1999/2998 Reg.3, Sch.1 para.2
r.16A, added: SI 1998/928 r.8
r.20A, added: SI 1998/928 r.9
r.41A, added: SI 1998/928 r.10
r.42A, added: SI 1998/928 r.11
r.51, amended: SI 1998/928 r.12
r.54A, added: SI 1998/928 r.13
r.54B, added: SI 1998/928 r.13
r.60A, added: SI 1998/928 r.14
r.63A, added: SI 1998/928 r.15
r.65A, added: SI 1998/928 r.16
r.65B, added: SI 1998/928 r.16
r.66, revoked: SI 1999/2998 Reg.3, Sch.1 para.8
r.67, amended: SI 1999/2998 Reg.3, Sch.1 para.3
r.67, substituted: SI 1999/2998 Reg.3, Sch.1 para.3
r.69, amended: SI 1999/2998 Reg.3, Sch.1 para.4
r.70, revoked: SI 1998/2647 Reg.1
r.71, substituted: SI 1999/2998 Reg.3, Sch.1 para.5
r.72A, added: SI 1998/928 r.17
r.76, revoked (in part): SI 1999/2998 Reg.3, Sch.1 para.8

NO.

1975—cont.

330. **Fishing Vessels (Safety Provisions) Rules 1975**—*cont.*
r.77, revoked (in part): SI 1999/2998 Reg.3, Sch.1 para.8
r.106A, added: SI 1998/928 r.18
r.119, amended: SI 1998/928 r.19
r.119, restored: SI 1999/2998 Reg.3, Sch.1 para.8
r.120, substituted: SI 1999/2998 Reg.3, Sch.1 para.6
r.125A, applied: SI 1996/3243 Reg.5, Sch Part I
r.125A, referred to: SI 1996/3243 Sch Part I
r.125A, substituted: SI 1999/3210 Reg.2
r.125B, amended: SI 1996/2419 r.2
r.125B, applied: SI 1996/3243 Reg.5, Sch Part I
r.125B, referred to: SI 1996/3243 Sch Part I
r.125C, amended: SI 1996/2419
r.125C, applied: SI 1996/3243 Reg.5, Sch Part I
r.125C, referred to: SI 1996/3243 Sch Part I
r.126B, added: SI 1999/2998 Reg.3, Sch.1 para.7
r.130, applied: SI 1996/3243 Reg.5, Sch Part I
r.130, referred to: SI 1996/3243 Sch Part I
r.131, applied: SI 1996/3243 Reg.5, Sch Part I
r.131, referred to: SI 1996/3243 Sch Part I
Sch.25, revoked: SI 1998/2647 Reg.1

411. **International Cocoa Organisation (Immunities and Privileges) Order 1975**
Art.13A, added: SI 1999/2034 Art.2, Sch.

415. **Family Allowances, National Insurance and Industrial Injuries (Spain) Order 1975**
Sch., amended: SI 1996/1928 Art.2, Sch.1

417. **Community Relations (Amendment) (Northern Ireland) Order 1975**
Art.3, revoked: SI 1999/283 (NI.1) Art.9, Sch.3
Art.4, revoked (in part): SI 1999/283 (NI.1) Art.9, Sch.3

423. **Recovery Abroad of Maintenance (Convention Countries) Order 1975**
Sch., amended: SI 1996/1925 Art.2

428. **Lord-Lieutenants Order 1975**
revoked: SI 1996/739 Art.8, Sch.3

474. **Act of Sederunt (Maintenance Orders (Reciprocal Enforcement) Act 1972 Amendment Rules) 1975**
revoked: SI 1997/291 r.1.4, Sch.2

475. **Act of Sederunt (Reciprocal Enforcement of Maintenance Orders (Republic of Ireland) Order 1974 Rules) 1975**
Part III, revoked: SI 1997/291 r.1.4, Sch.2
r.1, amended: SI 1997/291 r.1.4, Sch.2
r.2, amended: SI 1997/291 r.1.4, Sch.2
r.3, amended: SI 1997/291 r.1.4, Sch.2

487. **South Eastern Combined Fire Area Administration Scheme Order 1975**
applied: SI 1996/682 Sch.2

493. **Social Security (Benefit) (Members of the Forces) Regulations 1975**
Reg.2, amended: SI 1996/1345 Reg.14
Reg.3, amended: SI 1996/207 Reg.168
Reg.5, amended: SI 1996/1345 Reg.14

494. **Social Security (Airmen's Benefits) Regulations 1975**
Reg.3, amended: SI 1996/1345 Reg.9

496. **Social Security (Attendance Allowance) Regulations 1975**
Reg.4, see *Steane v Chief Adjudication Officer* (1996) 29 B.M.L.R. 87 (CA), Aldous, L.J.

515. **Social Security (Guardian's Allowances) Regulations 1975**
Reg.1, amended: SI 1999/1958 Art.4, Sch.2
Reg.1A, added: SI 1997/2676 Reg.7

NO.

1975—cont.

515. **Social Security (Guardian's Allowances) Regulations 1975**—*cont.*
Reg.4, amended: SI 1998/1811 Reg.2
Reg.5, applied: SI 1999/991 Reg.27, Sch.2 para.12

529. **Social Security (Mariners' Benefits) Regulations 1975**
referred to: SI 1996/2890 Reg.27
Reg.2, amended: SI 1996/207 Reg.166
Reg.4, amended: SI 1996/1345 Reg.21
Reg.4A, added: SI 1996/207 Reg.166
Reg.5, amended: SI 1996/1345 Reg.21
Reg.6, revoked (in part): SI 1997/563 Reg.6
Reg.7, amended: SI 1996/1345 Reg.21
Reg.8, revoked: SI 1996/1345 Reg.27, Sch.
Reg.9, amended: SI 1996/1345 Reg.21

536. **Trade Unions and Employers' Associations (Amalgamations, etc.) Regulations 1975**
Reg.11, amended: SI 1996/651 Reg.2, Reg.3, SI 1997/677 Reg.2, Reg.3
Reg.12, amended: SI 1996/651 Reg.4, SI 1997/677 Reg.4

555. **Social Security (Hospital In-Patients) Regulations 1975**
referred to: SI 1996/2745 Sch.2 para.8
Part III, applied: SI 1996/2567 Reg.10
Reg.2, see *Botchett v Chief Adjudication Officer* (1996) 32 B.M.L.R. 153 (CA), Evans, L.J.
Reg.2, amended: SI 1999/1326 Reg.2
Reg.2, applied: SI 1996/2890 Sch.1 Part III
Reg.6, applied: SI 1998/19 Reg.2

556. **Social Security (Credits) Regulations 1975**
amended: SI 1999/2566 Reg.2, Sch.2 Part I, Sch.2 Part II
applied: SI 1996/207 Reg.36, SI 1996/1623 Art.3, SI 1998/217 Art.2, SI 1999/779 Art.2, Sch.
Reg.2, amended: SI 1996/2367 Reg.2, SI 1999/568 Reg.20, SI 1999/2566 Reg.2, Sch.2 Part III
Reg.3, amended: SI 1996/2367 Reg.2
Reg.7A, amended: SI 1996/2367 Reg.2
Reg.7B, amended: SI 1996/2367 Reg.2, SI 1999/2566 Reg.2, Sch.2 Part II
Reg.7C, amended: SI 1996/2367 Reg.2, SI 1999/2566 Reg.2, Sch.2 Part I
Reg.8, amended: SI 1996/2367 Reg.2
Reg.8A, added: SI 1996/2367 Reg.2
Reg.8B, added: SI 1996/2367 Reg.2
Reg.9, amended: SI 1999/568 Reg.20, SI 1999/2566 Reg.2, Sch.2 Part II
Reg.9, applied: SI 1996/207 Sch.2 para.13, SI 1996/2367 Reg.4
Reg.9, substituted: SI 1996/2367 Reg.2
Reg.9A, amended: SI 1996/2367 Reg.2

561. **Social Security and Family Allowances (Polygamous Marriage) Regulations 1975**
see *Bibi v Chief Adjudication Officer* [1998] 1 F.L.R. 375 (CA), Ward, L.J.

563. **Social Security Benefit (Persons Abroad) Regulations 1975**
applied: SI 1996/2745 Sch.1 para.4
Reg.2, applied: SI 1999/991 Reg.27, Sch.2 para.21
Reg.5, amended: SI 1996/670 Reg.3
Reg.5, applied: SI 1997/576 Reg.3, SI 1998/521 Reg.3, SI 1999/858 Reg.3
Reg.9, applied: SI 1999/991 Reg.27, Sch.2 para.21
Reg.11, amended: SI 1996/207 Reg.165
Reg.12, amended: SI 1996/1345 Reg.15
Reg.13B, revoked: SI 1996/1345 Reg.27, Sch.

1975—cont.

563. Social Security Benefit (Persons Abroad) Regulations 1975—*cont.*
Reg.14, amended: SI 1996/1345 Reg.15

632. Northern Police (Amalgamation) Order 1975
applied: SI 1996/682 Sch.2

633. South-Eastern Police (Amalgamation) Order 1975
applied: SI 1996/682 Sch.2

637. Sheriff Court Districts Reorganisation Order 1975
revoked: SI 1996/1005 Art.3, Sch.2

681. Medicines (Applications for Product Licences and Clinical Trial and Animal Test Certificates) Amendment Regulations 1975
revoked (in part): SI 1996/2194 Reg.6, Sch.3

700. Merchant Shipping (Carriage of Nautical Publications) Rules 1975
revoked: SI 1998/2647 Reg.1

734. Local Government (Compensation) (Scotland) Regulations 1975
applied: SI 1999/1750 Art.2, Sch.1

829. Northern Combined Fire Area Administration Scheme Order 1975
applied: SI 1996/682 Sch.2

948. Act of Sederunt (Interest in Sheriff Court Decrees or Extracts) 1975
applied: SI 1996/2803 Reg.3

990. Trunk Road (The Parkway, Hounslow) (Prescribed Route) Order 1975
revoked: SI 1997/1503 Art.5

1023. Rehabilitation of Offenders Act 1974 (Exceptions) Order 1975
Sch.1, see *Wood v Coverage Care Ltd* [1996] I.R.L.R. 264 (EAT), Judge P Clark

1024. Transit of Animals (Road and Rail) Order 1975
revoked (in part): SI 1997/1480 Art.22, Sch.12 Part III
Sch.1 Part I, referred to: SI 1997/1480 Art.15

1034. Belgium (Extradition) (Amendment) Order 1975
revoked: SI 1998/259 Art.2

1056. Police Grant (Scotland) Order 1975
revoked: SI 1996/780 Art.7, Sch.2

1092. Colleges of Education (Compensation) Regulations 1975
applied: SI 1997/311 Reg.4
Reg.32, applied: SI 1997/311 Reg.4

1198. Direct Grant Grammar Schools (Cessation of Grant) Regulations 1975
revoked: SI 1998/86 Reg.2, Sch.1
Reg.3, applied: SI 1999/2277 Sch.2 s.4

1208. Motor Vehicles (International Circulation) Order 1975
Art.1, amended: SI 1996/1929 Art.3
Art.2, amended: SI 1996/1929 Art.4, SI 1996/1974 Reg.6, Sch.5 para.1
Art.2, applied: SI 1996/2824 Reg.16
Art.2, referred to: SI 1999/2864 Reg.18
Art.3, amended: SI 1996/1929 Art.4
Art.5, amended: SI 1996/1929 Art.5, Art.6
Art.5A, revoked: SI 1996/1929 Art.6
Sch.2, amended: SI 1996/1929 Art.3

1210. International Whaling Commission (Immunities and Privileges) Order 1975
Art.11A, added: SI 1999/2034 Art.2, Sch.

1272. Ipswich Port Authority Order 1975
revoked: SI 1997/948 Sch para.12

1349. Medicines (Feeding Stuffs Additives) Order 1975
revoked: SI 1998/1048 Reg.2 (with savings), Sch.1 (with savings)

1975—cont.

1370. Building (Third Amendment) Regulations 1975
see *Baxter v Camden LBC (No.1)* (1998) 30 H.L.R. 501 (CA), Sumner, J.

1384. Pensions Increase (Annual Review) Order 1975
applied: SI 1997/634 Art.3, SI 1998/503 Art.3, Art.4, SI 1999/522 Art.3

1433. Coal Mines (Respirable Dust) Regulations 1975
Reg.4, amended: SI 1996/2001 Reg.2

1442. Chester Water (Capital Powers) Order 1975
revoked: SI 1998/281 Art.4, Sch.2 Part II

1443. Employers' Liability (Compulsory Insurance) (Offshore Installations) Regulations 1975
referred to: SI 1998/2573 Reg.10
revoked: SI 1998/2573 Reg.10, Sch.3

1474. Police (Disposal of Property) Regulations 1975
revoked: SI 1997/1908 Reg.2

1503. Social Security Pensions (Northern Ireland) Order 1975
referred to: 1998 c.47 s.87

1539. Sheriff Court Districts (Amendment) Order 1975
revoked: SI 1996/1005 Art.3, Sch.2

1544. Police (Discipline) (Scotland) Amendment Regulations 1975
revoked: SI 1996/1642 Reg.25, Sch.2

1667. Borough of Castle Morpeth (Electoral Arrangements) Order 1975
revoked: SI 1998/2344 Art.6

1698. Borough of Southend-on-Sea (Electoral Arrangements) Order 1975
Art.9, substituted: SI 1996/1875 Art.7

1722. Spring Traps Approval (Scotland) Order 1975
revoked: SI 1996/2202 Art.3

1763. Noise Insulation Regulations 1975
applied: SI 1996/428 Reg.7

1800. Fire Services (Compensation) (Scotland) Regulations 1975
applied: SI 1999/1750 Art.2, Sch.1

1811. City of Bath (Electoral Arrangements) Order 1975
revoked: SI 1998/2700 Art.6

1812. Borough of Broxbourne (Electoral Arrangements) Order 1975
revoked: SI 1998/2551 Art.4

1814. District of Runnymede (Electoral Arrangements) Order 1975
revoked: SI 1999/2478 Art.4

1815. District of Salisbury (Electoral Arrangements) Order 1975
revoked: SI 1999/2924 Art.6

1817. District of Tandridge (Electoral Arrangements) Order 1975
revoked: SI 1999/2480 Art.4

1818. Borough of Watford (Electoral Arrangements) Order 1975
revoked: SI 1998/2559 Art.4

1913. Borough of Blackpool (Electoral Arrangements) Order 1975
applied: SI 1996/1868 Art.7

1920. Borough of Surrey Heath (Electoral Arrangements) Order 1975
revoked: SI 1999/2481 Art.4

1975—cont.

1921. **Borough of Thamesdown (Electoral Arrangements) Order 1975**
revoked: SI 1999/2927 Art.9

2019. **Borough of Corby (Electoral Arrangements) Order 1975**
revoked: SI 1998/2506 Art.3

2084. **Borough of Berwick-upon-Tweed (Electoral Arrangements) Order 1975**
revoked: SI 1998/2346 Art.6

2087. **Borough of Congleton (Electoral Arrangements) Order 1975**
revoked: SI 1998/2843 Art.10

2090. **Borough of Guildford (Electoral Arrangements) Order 1975**
revoked: SI 1999/2475 Art.5

2105. **District of Mole Valley (Electoral Arrangements) Order 1975**
revoked: SI 1999/2476 Art.4

2109. **District of Wansbeck (Electoral Arrangements) Order 1975**
revoked: SI 1998/2342 Art.3, SI 1998/2700 Art.6

2145. **Borough of Elmbridge (Electoral Arrangements) Order 1975**
revoked: SI 1999/2465 Art.4

2146. **Borough of Epsom and Ewell (Electoral Arrangements) Order 1975**
revoked: SI 1999/2474 Art.3

2147. **District of Northavon (Electoral Arrangements) Order 1975**
revoked: SI 1998/2701 Art.14

2165. **Merchant Shipping (Oil Pollution) (Bermuda) Order 1975**
revoked: SI 1997/2581 Art.3

2166. **Merchant Shipping (Oil Pollution) (Cayman Islands) Order 1975**
revoked: SI 1998/1261 Art.4

2167. **Merchant Shipping (Oil Pollution) (Falkland Islands) Order 1975**
revoked (in part): SI 1997/2584 Art.4, SI 1997/2588 Art.4

2170. **Merchant Shipping (Oil Pollution) (Montserrat) Order 1975**
revoked: SI 1998/1262 Art.3

2171. **Merchant Shipping (Oil Pollution) (Overseas Territories) Order 1975**
revoked (in part): SI 1997/2583 Art.4, SI 1997/2585 Art.4, SI 1997/2587 Art.4, SI 1998/1263 Art.4

2175. **Merchant Shipping (Oil Pollution) (Virgin Islands) Order 1975**
revoked: SI 1997/2590 Art.3

2181. **Merchant Shipping Act 1974 (Jersey) Order 1975**
revoked: SI 1997/2598 Art.5

2192. **Trial of the Pyx Order 1975**
revoked: SI 1998/1764 Art.16, Sch.3
Art.2, amended: SI 1998/264 Art.2
Art.2, revoked: SI 1998/1764 Art.16, Sch.3
Art.3, amended: SI 1998/264 Art.2
Art.3, revoked: SI 1998/1764 Art.16, Sch.3
Art.9A, added: SI 1998/264 Art.2
Art.9A, revoked: SI 1998/1764 Art.16, Sch.3
Art.10B, added: SI 1998/264 Art.2
Art.10B, revoked: SI 1998/1764 Art.16, Sch.3
Art.11, amended: SI 1998/264 Art.2
Art.11, revoked: SI 1998/1764 Art.16, Sch.3
Sch.2, amended: SI 1998/1764 Art.16, Sch.3
Sch.2, substituted: SI 1998/264 Art.2

2199. **District of Three Rivers (Electoral Arrangements) Order 1975**
revoked: SI 1998/2556 Art.10

1975—cont.

2220. **Merchant Shipping (Crew Accommodation) (Fishing Vessels) Regulations 1975**
applied: SI 1996/3243 Sch Part I
Reg.1, amended: SI 1998/929 Reg.3
Reg.2, substituted: SI 1998/929 Reg.4
Reg.3, substituted: SI 1998/929 Reg.5
Reg.6, amended: SI 1998/929 Reg.6
Reg.7, amended: SI 1998/929 Reg.7
Reg.10A, added: SI 1998/929 Reg.8
Reg.11, amended: SI 1998/929 Reg.9
Reg.14A, added: SI 1998/929 Reg.10
Reg.15A, added: SI 1998/929 Reg.11
Reg.16A, added: SI 1998/929 Reg.12
Reg.25A, added: SI 1998/929 Reg.13
Reg.25B, added: SI 1998/929 Reg.13
Reg.27A, added: SI 1998/929 Reg.14
Reg.29A, added: SI 1998/929 Reg.15
Reg.36, added: SI 1998/929 Reg.16

2223. **Mink (Keeping) Regulations 1975**
Reg.5, amended: SI 1997/2750 Reg.2

1976

City of Westminster (Bus Lanes) (No.2) Traffic Order 1976
amended: SI 1996/2165 Art.6

City of Westminster (Waiting and Loading Restriction) Order 1976
amended: SI 1996/1027 Art.5, SI 1996/1077 Art.5; SI 1996 1157 Art.5, SI 1996/1340 Art.5
revoked (in part): SI 1996/1137 Art.11, SI 1996/1223 Art.5, SI 1996/2155 Art.11, SI 1996/2166 Art.11, SI 1996/2688 Art.11, SI 1997/2002 Art.10, SI 1998/938 Art.10

Hammersmith (Waiting and Loading Restriction) Order 1976
revoked (in part): SI 1999/2345 Art.11 (with savings), SI 1999/2349 Art.11 (with savings)

Hammersmith (Waiting and Loading Restriction) (Amendment No.2) Order 1976
revoked (in part): SI 1999/2345 Art.11 (with savings), SI 1999/2349 Art.11 (with savings)

Islington (Waiting and Loading Restriction) Order 1976
revoked (in part): SI 1996/1136 Art.11, SI 1996/1137 Art.11, SI 1997/2002 Art.10, SI 1997/2326 Art.10

Southwark (Waiting and Loading Restriction) Order 1976
revoked (in part): SI 1997/3045 Art.11, SI 1999/1805 Art.10

Wandsworth (Waiting and Loading) Order 1976
revoked (in part): SI 1999/2344 Art.10, SI 1999/3103 Art.11

65. **District of Welwyn Hatfield (Electoral Arrangements) Order 1976**
revoked: SI 1998/2560 Art.6

93. **Banffshire Educational Trust Scheme 1976**
amended: SI 1996/478 Sch

98. **Restrictive Trade Practices (Services) Order 1976**
Sch. para.6A, added: SI 1998/1129 Art.2, Sch.1 para.2

114. **City of Nottingham (Electoral Arrangements) Order 1976**
applied: SI 1996/1877 Art.7

NO.

182. **District of Tynedale (Electoral Arrangements) Order 1976**
revoked: SI 1998/2343 Art.6
185. **Occupational Pensions Board (Determinations and Review Procedure) Regulations 1976**
revoked: SI 1997/358 Reg.7, Sch
197. **Borough of Ellesmere Port (Electoral Arrangements) Order 1976**
revoked: SI 1998/2844 Art.4
222. **Inter-American Development Bank (Immunities and Privileges) Order 1976**
Art.12A, added: SI 1999/2034 Art.2, Sch.
223. **Merchant Shipping (Oil Pollution) (Turks and Caicos Islands) Order 1976**
revoked: SI 1997/2589 Art.4
225. **Social Security (Reciprocal Agreements) Order 1976**
Sch.1, amended: SI 1996/1927 Art.3, SI 1997/871 Art.3
226. **Treatment of Offenders (Northern Ireland) Order 1976**
amended: 1997 c.43 Sch.1 para.12, Sch.1 para.13
Art.2, revoked (in part): SI 1996/3160 (NI.24) Sch.7
Art.3, amended: SI 1998/2798 Art.2, Sch.1 para.8, Sch.1 para.10
Art.3, applied: 1997 c.43 Sch.1 para.12, Sch.1 para.13, SI 1998/2798 Art.2, Sch.1 para.8, Sch.1 para.10, SI 1999/1748 Art.8, Sch.4 para.2
Art.4, amended: SI 1998/2798 Art.2, Sch.1 para.8, Sch.1 para.10
Art.4, applied: 1997 c.43 Sch.1 para.12, Sch.1 para.13, SI 1998/2798 Art.2, Sch.1 para.8, Sch.1 para.10, SI 1999/1748 Art.8, Sch.4 para.2
Art.5, applied: 1997 c.43 Sch.1 para.12, Sch.1 para.13, SI 1999/1748 Art.8, Sch.4 para.2
Art.6, amended: SI 1998/2798 Art.2, Sch.1 para.10
Art.6, applied: 1997 c.43 Sch.1 para.12, Sch.1 para.13, SI 1998/2798 Art.2, Sch.1 para.8, Sch.1 para.10, SI 1999/1748 Art.8, Sch.4 para.2
Part III, revoked: SI 1996/3160 (NI.24) Sch.7
Sch.2 para.7, revoked: SI 1996/1141 (NI.6) s.32, Sch.5
Sch.2 para.8, revoked: SI 1996/1141 (NI.6) s.32, Sch.5
237. **Camden and Islington (Bus Lanes) (No.1) Traffic Order 1976**
amended: SI 1996/1343 Art.6
246. **Local Government Area Changes Regulations 1976**
Reg.8, applied: SI 1996/2914 Art.5, Art.6, SI 1996/2915 Art.4, Art.5
Reg.8, referred to: SI 1999/1289 Art.5
Reg.28, amended: SI 1996/2915 Art.12
Reg.41, applied: SI 1996/494 Art.6, SI 1999/1289 Art.9
Reg.41, referred to: SI 1996/2914 Art.11
Reg.62, see *R. v Secretary of State for the Environment Ex p. Sutton LBC* [1997] C.O.D. 308 (CA), Pill, L.J.
Sch.1 Part I, amended: SI 1996/2915 Sch.2 para.1
Sch.2, amended: SI 1996/2915 Art.12
Sch.6, see *R. v Secretary of State for the Environment Ex p. Sutton LBC* [1997] C.O.D. 308 (CA), Pill, L.J.

NO.

285. **District of South Northamptonshire (Electoral Arrangements) Order 1976**
revoked: SI 1998/2509 Art.5
286. **Borough of Vale Royal (Electoral Arrangements) Order 1976**
revoked: SI 1998/2846 Art.10
288. **Borough of Woking (Electoral Arrangements) Order 1976**
revoked: SI 1999/2483 Art.4
297. **District of Kennet (Electoral Arrangements) Order 1976**
revoked: SI 1999/2922 Art.12
319. **Borough of Hertsmere (Electoral Arrangements) Order 1976**
revoked: SI 1998/2554 Art.7
374. **Act of Sederunt (Proceedings under Sex Discrimination Act 1975) 1976**
revoked: SI 1999/929 r.1.3, Sch.2
394. **London Borough of Tower Hamlets Waiting and Loading Order 1976**
revoked (in part): SI 1996/1841 Art.11, SI 1996/1891 Art.10, SI 1997/466 Art.10, SI 1998/3212 Art.11
409. **Social Security (Invalid Care Allowance) Regulations 1976**
Reg.2, amended: SI 1996/2744 Reg.2
Reg.2A, added: SI 1997/2676 Reg.11
Reg.3, amended: SI 1996/2744 Reg.2
Reg.5, amended: SI 1996/2744 Reg.2
Reg.6, amended: SI 1996/2744 Reg.2
Reg.7, amended: SI 1996/2744 Reg.2
Reg.8, amended: SI 1996/2744 Reg.2
Reg.8, applied: SI 1996/2744 Reg.3
Reg.9, amended: SI 1996/30 Reg.9, SI 1998/563 Reg.18
Reg.10, amended: SI 1996/2744 Reg.2
Reg.11, amended: SI 1996/2744 Reg.2
424. **Department of Housing, Local Government and Planning (Dissolution) (Northern Ireland) Order 1976**
Art.3, revoked (in part): SI 1999/283 (NI.1) Art.9, Sch.3
Art.5, revoked: SI 1999/283 (NI.1) Art.9, Sch.3
426. **Members' Pensions (Northern Ireland) Order 1976**
referred to: 1998 c.47 s.100, Sch.14 para.23
revoked: 1998 c.47 s.100, Sch.15
503. **Prison (Amendment) Rules 1976**
revoked: SI 1999/728 r.85 (with savings), Sch. (with savings)
509. **Specified Sugar Products Regulations 1976**
amended: SI 1999/1136 Reg.14
referred to: SI 1996/1499 Reg.4
Reg.2, amended: SI 1996/1499 Reg.49
541. **Cocoa and Chocolate Products Regulations 1976**
amended: SI 1999/1136 Reg.14
referred to: SI 1996/1499 Reg.4
Reg.7, amended: SI 1996/1499 Reg.49
Reg.22, revoked: SI 1996/1499 Reg.49, Sch.9
582. **Solicitors (Northern Ireland) Order 1976**
Art.3, revoked (in part): 1996 c.23 Sch.4
Art.42, applied: 1999 c.33 s.83, s.86, Sch.5 para.4, SI 1999/680 Art.2, Sch. Part I
Art.71H, applied: 1996 c.23 s.75
Art.71H, revoked (in part): 1996 c.23 Sch.4
Sch.1A para.39, revoked (in part): SI 1998/1071 (NI.6) Art.41, Sch.5

NO.

615. Social Security (Medical Evidence) Regulations 1976
Reg.1, amended: SI 1999/3109 Reg.5
Reg.2, amended: SI 1999/3109 Reg.5
Sch.1 para.3, amended: SI 1998/646 Reg.6
Sch.1B Part I, amended: SI 1999/3109 Reg.5
Sch.1B Part II, amended: SI 1999/3109 Reg.5
Sch.1B para.1, amended: SI 1999/3109 Reg.5
Sch.1B para.2, amended: SI 1999/3109 Reg.5
Sch.1B para.3, amended: SI 1999/3109 Reg.5

664. Wandsworth (Waiting and Loading Restriction) Order 1976
revoked (in part): SI 1996/2164 Art.10, SI 1996/2338 Art.10, SI 1996/3254 Art.11, SI 1998/939 Art.11, SI 1998/1125 Art.10, SI 1998/1150 Art.10, SI 1998/1462 Art.10
Sch.2 Item 142, revoked (in part): SI 1998/2591 Art.7
Sch.2 Item 143, revoked (in part): SI 1998/2591 Art.7

715. Conduct of Employment Agencies and Employment Businesses Regulations 1976
Reg.9, see *McMeechan v Secretary of State for Employment* [1997] I.R.L.R. 353 (CA), Waite, L.J.

721. Highways (Inquiries Procedure) Rules 1976
r.5, see *R. v Secretary of State for the Environment, Transport and the Regions Ex p. Alliance Against the Birmingham Northern Relief Road (No.2)* [1998] E.G.C.S. 146 (QBD), Latham, J.

730. Hallmarking (International Convention) Order 1976
Art.3, amended: SI 1998/2978 Reg.3, Sch. para.1
Art.5, amended: SI 1998/2978 Reg.3, Sch. para.2, Sch. para.3
Art.6, amended: SI 1998/2978 Reg.3, Sch. para.4, Sch. para.5, Sch. para.7
Art.6, revoked (in part): SI 1998/2978 Sch. para.6

750. District of Eden (Electoral Arrangements) Order 1976
revoked: SI 1998/2547 Art.5

752. District of Mendip (Electoral Arrangements) Order 1976
revoked: SI 1998/2464 Art.9

764. District of Alnwick (Electoral Arrangements) Order 1976
revoked: SI 1998/2347 Art.5

765. Borough of Blyth Valley (Electoral Arrangements) Order 1976
revoked: SI 1998/2345 Art.3

766. Employment Protection (Offshore Employment) Order 1976
applied: SI 1999/158 Art.2
referred to: SI 1996/102 Art.2
Art.3, applied: 1997 c.32 Sch.2

796. Price Marking (Pre-packed Milk in Vending Machines) Order 1976
revoked: SI 1999/3042 Art.2
Art.1, revoked: SI 1999/3042 Art.2
Art.2, revoked: SI 1999/3042 Art.2

811. District of East Northamptonshire (Electoral Arrangements) Order 1976
revoked: SI 1998/2512 Art.4

812. District of West Somerset (Electoral Arrangements) Order 1976
revoked: SI 1998/2463 Art.4

NO.

823. Borough of Kettering (Electoral Arrangements) Order 1976
revoked: SI 1998/2508 Art.6

837. Consumer Credit Licensing (Appeals) Regulations 1976
applied: SI 1998/1203 Reg.28
revoked: SI 1998/1203 Reg.27

914. Cocoa and Chocolate Products (Scotland) Regulations 1976
amended: SI 1999/1136 Reg.14
Reg.7, amended: SI 1996/1499 Reg.49
Reg.23, revoked: SI 1996/1499 Reg.49, Sch.9

946. Specified Sugar Products (Scotland) Regulations 1976
amended: SI 1999/1136 Reg.14
Reg.2, amended: SI 1996/1499 Reg.49

955. Operations at Unfenced Machinery (Amendment) Regulations 1976
revoked: SI 1998/2306 Reg.39, Sch.4

963. Child Benefit (Residence and Persons Abroad) Regulations 1976
Reg.2, amended: SI 1999/198 Reg.2
Reg.2, applied: SI 1999/198 Reg.3, SI 1999/991 Reg.27, Sch.2 para.3
Reg.7, applied: SI 1999/991 Reg.27, Sch.2 para.3

965. Child Benefit (General) Regulations 1976
applied: SI 1996/2327 Reg.3
Reg.2, applied: SI 1999/991 Reg.27, Sch.2 para.4
Reg.7C, substituted: SI 1996/1345 Reg.2
Reg.7D, amended: SI 1996/1345 Reg.2
Reg.9, amended: SI 1996/1803 Reg.3
Reg.9A, added: SI 1996/1803 Reg.4
Reg.14A, amended: SI 1999/1958 Art.4, Sch.3 para.1
Reg.14B, see *R. v Adjudication Officer Ex p. Velasquez* Times, April 30, 1999 (CA), Butler-Sloss, L.J.
Reg.14B, added: SI 1996/2327 Reg.2
Reg.14B, amended: SI 1996/2530 Reg.2, SI 1998/563 Reg.18, SI 1999/1958 Art.4, Sch.3 para.2
Reg.16, see *McLavey v Secretary of State for Social Security* [1996] 2 F.L.R. 748 (CA), Staughton, L.J.

992. Borough of Spelthorne (Electoral Arrangements) Order 1976
revoked: SI 1999/2479 Art.3

1003. Social Security (Northern Ireland Reciprocal Arrangements) Regulations 1976
Sch.1, amended: SI 1999/2227 Reg.2, Sch.
Sch.1, referred to: SI 1999/2227 Reg.2

1019. Offshore Installations (Operational Safety, Health and Welfare) Regulations 1976
see *Hegarty v EE Caledonia Ltd* [1996] 1 Lloyd's Rep. 413 (QBD), Popplewell, J.
revoked: SI 1998/2307 Reg.17, Sch.2
Reg.1, revoked (in part): SI 1997/1993 Reg.4, SI 1998/2307 Reg.17, Sch.2
Reg.2, revoked (in part): SI 1996/341 Reg.8, Sch.3 Part I, SI 1998/2307 Reg.17, Sch.2
Reg.3, revoked: SI 1998/2307 Reg.17, Sch.2
Reg.4, revoked: SI 1996/913 Reg.27, Sch.3
Reg.5, revoked: SI 1996/913 Reg.27, Sch.3
Reg.6, applied: SI 1998/2307 Reg.9
Reg.6, revoked (in part): SI 1996/913 Reg.27, Sch.3, SI 1998/2307 Reg.17, Sch.2
Reg.11, revoked: SI 1997/1993 Reg.4
Reg.14, revoked: SI 1996/913 Reg.27, Sch.3
Reg.15, revoked: SI 1996/913 Reg.27, Sch.3
Reg.17, revoked: SI 1997/1993 Reg.4

NO.

1019. Offshore Installations (Operational Safety, Health and Welfare) Regulations 1976—*cont.*
Reg.28, revoked: SI 1997/135 Reg.3, Sch. Part II
Reg.32, see *McFarlane v Wilkinson* [1997] 2 Lloyd's Rep. 259 (CA), Brooke, L.J.
Reg.32, revoked: SI 1998/2307 Reg.17, Sch.2
Reg.34, revoked: SI 1998/2307 Reg.17, Sch.2
Sch.1 Part I, revoked: SI 1996/913 Reg.27, Sch.3
Sch.1 Part II, revoked: SI 1996/913 Reg.27, Sch.3
Sch.1 Part III, applied: SI 1998/2307 Reg.9
Sch.1 Part III, revoked: SI 1998/2307 Reg.17, Sch.2
Sch.4, revoked: SI 1996/913 Reg.27, Sch.3

1035. Corn Returns Regulations 1976
revoked: SI 1997/1873 Reg.5

1037. Finland (Extradition) Order 1976
revoked (in part): SI 1996/2875 Art.3, Sch.3

1040. Animals (Northern Ireland) Order 1976
Art.10, amended: 1998 c.32 s.74, Sch.4 para.11

1041. Births and Deaths Registration (Northern Ireland) Order 1976
applied: SI 1996/1812 Reg.13, SI 1998/211 Reg.8
referred to: SI 1997/1675 Reg.13
Art.47, amended: SI 1999/663 Art.2, Sch.1 para.20
Sch.1, revoked (in part): SI 1997/2779 (NI.20) Sch.3

1042. Sex Discrimination (Northern Ireland) Order 1976
applied: SI 1996/1919 (NI.16) Art.160
referred to: SI 1996/1919 (NI.16) Art.151, SI 1998/3162 (NI.21) Art.85, SI 1999/2204 Art.3
Art.2, amended: SI 1997/1772 (NI.15) Art.25, Sch.4, 1998 c.47 s.99, Sch.13 para.2, SR 1999/311 Reg.2, Reg.4
Art.2, revoked (in part): 1998 c.47 s.100, Sch.15
Art.4A, added: SR 1999/311 Reg.2
Art.7, amended: SR 1999/311 Reg.2
Art.8, amended: SR 1999/311 Reg.3
Art.10A, added: SR 1999/311 Reg.4
Art.10B, added: SR 1999/311 Reg.4
Art.11, amended: SR 1999/311 Reg.3
Art.12, amended: SR 1999/311 Reg.4
Art.13, amended: 1998 c.17 Sch.4 para.13
Art.14, amended: SR 1999/311 Reg.4
Art.19, amended: 1997 c.50 s.134, Sch.9 para.37, 1998 c.32 s.74, Sch.4 para.12
Art.19, revoked (in part): 1998 c.32 s.74, Sch.6
Art.21, amended: SR 1999/311 Reg.5
Art.24, amended: SI 1997/1772 (NI.15) Art.25, Sch.4
Art.25, amended: SI 1997/1772 (NI.15) Art.25, Sch.4
Art.30, amended: SR 1999/311 Reg.6
Art.49, amended: SI 1998/3162 (NI.21) Art.105, Sch.3
Art.53, applied: SI 1998/3162 (NI.21) Art.105, Sch.4 para.3
Art.53, revoked (in part): SI 1998/3162 (NI.21) Art.105, Sch.4 para.3
Art.53, substituted: SI 1998/3162 (NI.21) Art.96
Art.53A, amended: SI 1998/3162 (NI.21) Art.105, Sch.3
Art.53ZA, added: SI 1998/3162 (NI.21) Art.96
Art.53ZA, applied: SI 1998/3162 (NI.21) Art.105, Sch.4 para.3
Art.53ZA, revoked (in part): SI 1998/3162 (NI.21) Art.105, Sch.4 para.3

NO.

1042. Sex Discrimination (Northern Ireland) Order 1976—*cont.*
Art.54, amended: 1998 c.47 s.99, Sch.13 para.2, SR 1999/311 Reg.7
Art.54, revoked (in part): 1998 c.47 s.99, s.100, Sch.15, Sch.13 (para.2)
Art.56A, amended: SR 1999/311 Reg.7
Art.63, amended: SI 1998/3162 (NI.21) Art.105, Sch.3
Art.63, applied: SI 1996/1921 (NI.18) Art.20
Art.63, referred to: SI 1998/3162 (NI.21) Art.85
Art.64, revoked: SI 1996/1921 (NI.18) Art.28, Sch.3
Art.74, amended: SI 1999/663 Art.2, Sch.1 para.21
Art.74, revoked (in part): SI 1999/663 Art.2, Sch.2
Art.75, amended: SI 1996/1921 (NI.18) Art.26, Sch.1 para.5
Art.76, amended: 1996 c.46 s.22
Art.77, amended: SI 1996/1921 (NI.18) Art.26, Sch.1 para.5, SI 1998/1265 (NI.8) Art.9, Art.10, Art.11, Art.16, Sch.1 para.1
Art.79, amended: SI 1999/663 Art.2, Sch.1 para.21
Art.80, amended: SI 1999/663 Art.2, Sch.1 para.21
Art.82, amended: 1996 c.46 s.22
Art.82, referred to: SI 1997/2164 Sch. para.1
Part II, referred to: SI 1997/2164 Sch. para.1
Part III, applied: SI 1998/3162 (NI.21) Art.85
Part IV, referred to: SI 1997/2164 Sch. para.1
Sch.3, revoked: 1998 c.47 s.99, s.100, Sch.13 para.2, Sch.15
Sch.4 para.1, revoked (in part): SI 1997/2777 (NI.18) Art.35, Sch.5
Sch.6 para.2, revoked: 1998 c.47 s.100, Sch.15

1043. Industrial Relations (Northern Ireland) Order 1976
revoked: SI 1996/1919 (NI.16) Art.257, Sch.3
Art.29, revoked (in part): SI 1996/1919 (NI.16) Art.257, Sch.3, SI 1996/1921 (NI.18) Art.28, Sch.3
Art.30, revoked: SI 1996/1919 (NI.16) Art.257, Sch.3, SI 1996/1921 (NI.18) Art.28, Sch.3
Art.58, revoked (in part): SI 1996/1919 (NI.16) Art.257, Sch.3, SI 1996/1921 (NI.18) Art.28, Sch.3
Art.58A, revoked: SI 1996/1919 (NI.16) Art.257, Sch.3, SI 1996/1921 (NI.18) Art.28, Sch.3
Art.59, amended: 1996 c.23 Sch.3 para.31
Art.59, revoked (in part): SI 1996/1919 (NI.16) Art.257, Sch.3, SI 1996/1921 (NI.18) Art.28, Sch.3
Art.60, revoked: SI 1996/1919 (NI.16) Art.257, Sch.3, SI 1996/1921 (NI.18) Art.28, Sch.3
Art.61, revoked: SI 1996/1919 (NI.16) Art.257, Sch.3, SI 1996/1921 (NI.18) Art.28, Sch.3
Art.62, revoked: SI 1996/1919 (NI.16) Art.257, Sch.3, SI 1996/1921 (NI.18) Art.28, Sch.3
Art.72, revoked: SI 1996/1919 (NI.16) Art.257, Sch.3, SI 1996/1921 (NI.18) Art.28, Sch.3
Art.80, revoked (in part): SI 1996/1919 (NI.16) Art.257, Sch.3, SI 1996/1921 (NI.18) Art.28, Sch.3

1073. Police (Scotland) Regulations 1976
applied: SI 1996/1642 Reg.22, SI 1996/1645 Reg.29
Reg.1, amended: SI 1996/3232 Reg.2
Reg.5, applied: SI 1996/1645 Sch.1 para.2
Reg.5, referred to: SI 1999/1074 Reg.4, Sch. para.8

1976—cont.

1073. Police (Scotland) Regulations 1976—cont.
Reg.11, amended: SI 1996/3232 Reg.3
Reg.14, amended: SI 1996/1643 Reg.22
Reg.14, revoked (in part): SI 1996/1643 Reg.22
Reg.28, substituted: SI 1996/3232 Reg.4
Reg.28ZA, added: SI 1996/3232 Reg.4
Reg.30, amended: SI 1996/3232 Reg.5
Reg.30A, amended: SI 1996/3232 Reg.6
Reg.30B, added: SI 1996/3232 Reg.7
Reg.37, amended: SI 1996/3232 Reg.8
Reg.72, revoked (in part): SI 1996/221 Reg.10, Sch.2, SI 1996/1642 Reg.25, Sch.2
Sch.1, applied: SI 1996/1645 Sch.1 para.2
Sch.1, referred to: SI 1999/1074 Reg.4, Sch. para.8
Sch.1A para.7, revoked (in part): SI 1996/3232 Reg.9
Sch.1B para.12, revoked: SI 1996/3232 Reg.10
Sch.1B para.15A, added: SI 1996/3232 Reg.10
Sch.3 para.2, amended: SI 1996/3232 Reg.11
Sch.3 para.3, amended: SI 1996/3232 Reg.11
Sch.3 para.4, amended: SI 1996/3232 Reg.11
Sch.3 para.6, amended: SI 1996/3232 Reg.11
Sch.3 para.8, amended: SI 1996/3232 Reg.11
Sch.3 para.11, amended: SI 1996/3232 Reg.11
Sch.10 para.1, amended: SI 1996/3232 Reg.12

1081. Corn Returns (Scotland) Regulations 1976
revoked: SI 1997/1873 Reg.5

1129. Petroleum (Production) Regulations 1976
Sch.4, referred to: 1998 c.17 Sch.1 para.7, Sch.1 para.8, SI 1999/160 Sch.4 para.1
Sch.5, referred to: 1998 c.17 Sch.1 para.9, Sch.1 para.10, Sch.1 para.11, Sch.1 para.12, SI 1996/2986 Art.7, SI 1996/3148 Art.7, SI 1997/1266 Art.36, Sch.10 para.1, SI 1997/1738 Art.7, SI 1997/2946 Art.4, 1996 c.8 s.87, 1996 c.53 s.54, SI 1996/275 (NI.2) Art.39, SI 1997/1612 Sch.4 para.9, SI 1998/366 Sch.4 para.9, SI 1999/160 Sch.5 para.1

1130. Borough of Medway (Electoral Arrangements) Order 1976
applied: SI 1996/1876 Art.9

1153. Continental Shelf (Designation of Additional Areas) Order 1976
referred to: SI 1999/2031, SI 1999/2031 Art.2, Sch.

1212. Financial Provisions (Northern Ireland) Order 1976
Art.15, amended: SI 1999/663 Art.2, Sch.1 para.22

1213. Pharmacy (Northern Ireland) Order 1976
applied: 1999 c.8 s.60, Sch.3 para.12
Art.19, applied: 1999 c.8 s.60, Sch.3 para.12

1214. Poisons (Northern Ireland) Order 1976
Art.5, applied: SI 1997/1830 Sch.5 Part I
Art.6, applied: SI 1997/1830 Sch.5 Part I

1238. Borough of Dacorum (Electoral Arrangements) Order 1976
revoked: SI 1998/2552 Art.5

1264. Safety of Sports Grounds (Designation) Order 1976
Sch., amended: SI 1998/1845 Art.3

1267. Child Benefit and Social Security (Fixing and Adjustment of Rates) Regulations 1976
Reg.2, amended: SI 1996/599 Art.13, SI 1996/1803 Reg.5, SI 1997/543 Art.13, SI 1998/470 Art.13, SI 1998/1581 Reg.2, SI 1999/264 Art.13
Reg.2, applied: SI 1996/207 Reg.105, SI 1996/1803 Reg.48, SI 1998/1581 Reg.3, Reg.4
Reg.2, revoked (in part): SI 1998/1581 Reg.2
Reg.4, revoked: SI 1996/1803 Reg.6

1976—cont.

1285. Safety of Sports Grounds (Designation) (Scotland) Order 1976
revoked: SI 1998/1601 Art.3, Sch.2

1303. District of East Hertfordshire (Electoral Arrangements) Order 1976
revoked: SI 1998/2553 Art.10

1356. Pensions Increase (Annual Review) Order 1976
applied: SI 1997/634 Art.3, SI 1998/503 Art.3, Art.4, SI 1999/522 Art.3

1522. Llandeilo-Carmarthen Trunk Road (Pont-ar-Gothi By-Pass) Order 1976
revoked: SI 1998/2121 Art.1

1545. Borough of Barrow-in-Furness (Electoral Arrangements) Order 1976
revoked: SI 1998/2571 Art.5

1547. Borough of Blackburn (Electoral Arrangements) Order 1976
Art.9, substituted: SI 1996/1868 Art.7

1548. Borough of Stevenage (Electoral Arrangements) Order 1976
revoked: SI 1998/2557 Art.4

1550. Borough of Thurrock (Electoral Arrangements) Order 1976
Art.9, substituted: SI 1996/1875 Art.8
Sch.2, substituted: SI 1996/1875 Art.8

1559. Compulsory Purchase by Public Authorities (Inquiries Procedure) (Scotland) Rules 1976
applied: SI 1998/2313 r.2
revoked: SI 1998/2313 r.25 (with saving)

1572. Immigration (Variation of Leave) Order 1976
Art.3, see *R. v Secretary of State for the Home Department Ex p. Jecka* [1997] Imm. A.R. 342 (QBD), Popplewell, J.

1704. District of Daventry (Electoral Arrangements) Order 1976
revoked: SI 1998/2507 Art.6

1726. Medicines (Labelling) Regulations 1976
revoked (in part): SI 1996/2194 Reg.6, Sch.3

1734. Markham Mine (Diesel Vehicles) Regulations 1976
Reg.4, revoked: SI 1996/192 Reg.20, Sch.15 Part III
Reg.5, revoked: SI 1996/192 Reg.20, Sch.15 Part III
Reg.6, revoked: SI 1996/192 Reg.20, Sch.15 Part III

1763. Borough of Reigate and Banstead (Electoral Arrangements) Order 1976
revoked: SI 1999/2477 Art.6

1767. Justices' Clerks (Amendment) Rules 1976
revoked: SI 1999/2784 r.4

1772. Rules of Procedure (Air Force) (Amendment) Rules 1976
revoked: SI 1997/171 r.90, Sch.7

1818. Honey (Scotland) Regulations 1976
Reg.15, revoked: SI 1996/1499 Reg.49, Sch.9

1819. District of Chester-le-Street (Electoral Arrangements) Order 1976
revoked: SI 1999/2503 Art.8

1832. Honey Regulations 1976
referred to: SI 1996/1499 Reg.4
Reg.14, revoked: SI 1996/1499 Reg.49, Sch.9

1851. Act of Sederunt (Proceedings under Sex Discrimination Act 1975) No.2 1976
revoked: SI 1999/929 r.1.3, Sch.2

1883. Drinking Milk Regulations 1976
revoked: SI 1998/2424 Reg.9, Sch.

NO.

1883. Drinking Milk Regulations 1976—*cont.*
Reg.5A, revoked: SI 1998/2424 Reg.9, Sch.
1888. Drinking Milk (Scotland) Regulations 1976
revoked: SI 1998/2424 Reg.9, Sch.
Reg.5A, revoked: SI 1998/2424 Reg.9, Sch.
1912. Civil Aviation Act 1971 (Overseas Territories) Order 1976
referred to: SI 1997/1746
1916. Social Security (Spain) Order 1976
Sch., amended: SI 1996/1928 Art.2, Sch.1
1961. Double Taxation Relief (Taxes on Income) (Republic of Ireland) Order 1976
Art.4, see *Wensleydale's Settlement Trustees v Inland Revenue Commissioners* [1996] S.T.C. (SCD) 241 (Sp Comm), DA Shirley
1966. District of South Derbyshire (Electoral Arrangements) Order 1976
revoked: SI 1999/2697 Art.6
1967. Barnwood and Hucclecote (as constituted by the City of Gloucester) (Electoral Arrangements) Order 1976
referred to: SI 1997/157 Art.2
1987. Teachers' Superannuation Regulations 1976
referred to: SI 1997/3001 Reg.C12
Part III, applied: SI 1997/1612 Reg.142
Reg.4, applied: SI 1997/3001 Reg.D1
Reg.4, referred to: SI 1997/3001 Reg.H12, Sch.15 para.12
Reg.7, applied: SI 1997/3001 Reg.C8, Reg.D1, Reg.E8, Reg.H12, Sch.15 para.12
Reg.24, applied: SI 1997/3001 Sch.10 para.2
Reg.26, applied: SI 1997/3001 Reg.C6, Sch.5 para.2
Reg.28, applied: SI 1997/3001 Reg.C6, Sch.5 para.5
Reg.29, applied: SI 1997/3001 Reg.C6, Sch.5 para.7
Reg.30, applied: SI 1997/3001 Reg.E3
Reg.46, applied: SI 1997/3001 Reg.E16
Reg.53, applied: SI 1997/3001 Reg.E3
Reg.72, applied: SI 1997/3001 Reg.C8, Reg.D1, Reg.H12, Sch.15 para.12
Reg.77, applied: SI 1997/1612 Reg.142
Sch.7, referred to: SI 1997/3001 Sch.12 para.3, Sch.12 para.11
Sch.9 para.2, applied: SI 1997/3001 Sch.10 para.3
Sch.9 para.2, referred to: SI 1997/3001 Sch.10 para.2
2003. Fire Certificates (Special Premises) Regulations 1976
applied: SI 1996/341 Reg.7
Sch.1 Part I, referred to: SI 1996/1592 Reg.33
2012. National Savings Stock Register Regulations 1976
amended: SI 1998/1446 Art.17
applied: SI 1998/1446 Art.6, Art.17, Art.18, Art.19, Art.26
Reg.3, revoked: SI 1998/1446 Art.30, Sch.2 Part II
Reg.4, amended: SI 1998/1446 Art.30, Sch.2 Part II
Reg.5, amended: SI 1998/1446 Art.30, Sch.2 Part II, SI 1999/2771 Reg.2
Reg.5, applied: SI 1998/1446 Art.10
Reg.5, referred to: SI 1998/1449 Art.3, Sch. para.5
Reg.5, revoked (in part): SI 1998/1446 Art.30, Sch.2 Part II
Reg.5A, revoked: SI 1998/1446 Art.30, Sch.2 Part II

NO.

2012. National Savings Stock Register Regulations 1976—*cont.*
Reg.6, referred to: SI 1998/1449 Art.3, Sch. para.5
Reg.6, revoked: SI 1998/1446 Art.30, Sch.2 Part II
Reg.7, referred to: SI 1998/1449 Art.3, Sch. para.5
Reg.7, revoked: SI 1998/1446 Art.30, Sch.2 Part II
Reg.8, referred to: SI 1998/1449 Art.3, Sch. para.5
Reg.9, referred to: SI 1998/1449 Art.3, Sch. para.5
Reg.11, applied: SI 1998/1446 Art.8
Reg.11, revoked: SI 1998/1446 Art.30, Sch.2 Part II
Reg.11A, applied: SI 1998/1446 Art.8
Reg.11A, revoked: SI 1998/1446 Art.30, Sch.2 Part II
Reg.12, amended: SI 1996/156
Reg.15, amended: SI 1998/1446 Art.30, Sch.2 Part II
Reg.16, revoked: SI 1998/1446 Art.30, Sch.2 Part II
Reg.17, applied: SI 1998/1446 Art.7, Art.13
Reg.17, revoked: SI 1998/1446 Art.30, Sch.2 Part II
Reg.19, revoked: SI 1998/1446 Art.30, Sch.2 Part II
Reg.22, referred to: SI 1998/1449 Art.3, Sch. para.5
Reg.27, applied: SI 1998/1446 Art.20
Reg.30, amended: SI 1998/1446 Art.16, Art.30, Sch.1 para.2
Reg.30, applied: SI 1998/1446 Art.16
Reg.31, amended: SI 1998/1446 Art.16
Reg.31, applied: SI 1998/1446 Art.16
Reg.36, amended: SI 1998/1446 Art.18, Art.30, Sch.1 para.5
Reg.39, amended: SI 1998/1446 Art.18, Art.30, Sch.1 para.6
Reg.39, referred to: SI 1998/1446 Art.17, Art.18
Reg.39A, added: SI 1998/1446 Art.18, Art.30, Sch.1 para.7
Reg.41, applied: SI 1998/1446 Art.27
Reg.43, applied: SI 1998/1446 Art.22, Art.24
Reg.45, applied: SI 1998/1446 Art.21
Reg.57, amended: SI 1997/1864 Reg.2
Reg.57, referred to: SI 1998/1446 Art.28, SI 1998/1449 Art.3, Sch. para.5
Sch.1, revoked: SI 1998/1446 Art.30, Sch.2 Part II
Sch.1, substituted: SI 1996/156 Sch
2019. Motor Vehicles (Competitions and Trials) (Scotland) Regulations 1976
applied: 1996 c.xii Sch s.8
2046. Bentinck Mine (Diesel Engined Stone Dusting Machine) Regulations 1976
Reg.5, revoked: SI 1996/192 Reg.20, Sch.15 Part III
Reg.6, revoked: SI 1996/192 Reg.20, Sch.15 Part III
Reg.7, revoked: SI 1996/192 Reg.20, Sch.15 Part III
2069. Borough of Gillingham (Electoral Arrangements) Order 1976
applied: SI 1996/1876 Art.9
2143. Merchant Shipping (Oil Pollution) (Falkland Islands) (Amendment) Order 1976
revoked (in part): SI 1997/2584 Art.4, SI 1997/2588 Art.4

1976—cont.

2144. United States of America (Extradition) Order 1976

see *R. v Bow Street Magistrates Court Ex p. Allison (No.2)* Times, June 2, 1998 (QBD), Kennedy, L.J.; see *R. v Bow Street Metropolitan Stipendiary Magistrate Ex p. United States (No.2)* [1999] Q.B. 847 (QBD), Kennedy, L.J.; see *R. v Bow Street Metropolitan Stipendiary Magistrates Ex p. United States (No.2)* [1999] 3 W.L.R. 620 (HL), Lord Hobhouse

Sch.1 Art.III, see *Burke, Re* Times, April 15, 1999 (QBD), Rose, L.J.

Sch.1 Art.VII, see *Burke, Re* Times, April 15, 1999 (QBD), Rose, L.J.

Sch.1 Art.VIII, see *R. v Bow Street Metropolitan Stipendiary Magistrate Ex p. Government of the United States* Times, June 5, 1997 (QBD), Pill, L.J.

2147. Industrial Relations (No.2) (Northern Ireland) Order 1976

revoked: SI 1996/1919 (NI.16) Art.257, Sch.3

Art.35, revoked (in part): SI 1996/1919 (NI.16) Art.257, Sch.3, SI 1996/1921 (NI.18) Art.28, Sch.3

Art.43, applied: SI 1996/1919 (NI.16) Sch.2 para.7

Art.56, revoked (in part): SI 1996/1919 (NI.16) Art.257, Sch.3, SI 1996/1921 (NI.18) Art.28, Sch.3

Art.57, revoked: SI 1996/1919 (NI.16) Art.257, Sch.3, SI 1996/1921 (NI.18) Art.28, Sch.3

Art.58, revoked: SI 1996/1919 (NI.16) Art.257, Sch.3, SI 1996/1921 (NI.18) Art.28, Sch.3

Sch.4 para.5, revoked (in part): SI 1996/1919 (NI.16) Art.257, Sch.3, SI 1996/1921 (NI.18) Art.28, Sch.3

2151. Double Taxation Relief (Taxes on Income) (Republic of Ireland) Order 1976

Sch. Art.5, amended: SI 1998/3151 Art.2, Sch. Art.I

Sch. Art.11, substituted: SI 1998/3151 Art.2, Sch. Art.II

Sch. Art.12, amended: SI 1998/3151 Art.2, Sch. Art.III

Sch. Art.14, substituted: SI 1998/3151 Art.2, Sch. Art.IV

Sch. Art.18, substituted: SI 1998/3151 Art.2, Sch. Art.V

Sch. Art.20, substituted: SI 1998/3151 Art.2, Sch. Art.VI

2152. Double Taxation Relief (Taxes on Income) (Republic of Ireland) (No.2) Order 1976

Sch., referred to: SI 1998/3151 Art.2

2182. Scottish Development Agency (Compensation) Regulations 1976

applied: SI 1999/1750 Art.2, Sch.1

1977

Army Pensions Warrant 1977

Appendix.VII, revoked: SI 1996/1638 Art.4, Sch.3

British Railways Board (Norfolk Railway) (Hall Lane Level Crossing) Order 1977

applied: SI 1997/2262 Art.7

British Railways Board (Norfolk Railway) (Yaxham Road Level Crossing) Order 1977

applied: SI 1997/2262 Art.7

1977—cont.

Ealing (Waiting and Loading Restrictions) Order 1977

applied: SI 1996/1088 Art.11

revoked (in part): SI 1997/2386 Art.10, SI 1999/2345 Art.11 (with savings), SI 1999/2349 Art.11 (with savings)

Greater London Council Traffic Management Order 1977

amended: SI 1996/1088 Art.11

applied: SI 1996/1088 Art.11

revoked (in part): SI 1996/63, SI 1996/1170 Art.10, SI 1997/1507 Art.10, SI 1997/2386 Art.10

7. Child Benefit (Northern Ireland Reciprocal Arrangements) Regulations 1977

Sch.1, amended: SI 1999/2225 Reg.2, Sch. Sch.1, referred to: SI 1999/2225 Reg.2

23. Croydon (Waiting and Loading Restriction) Order 1977

revoked (in part): SI 1997/1211 Art.10, SI 1997/2133 Art.11, SI 1999/414 Art.10

53. Police (Northern Ireland) Order 1977

revoked: 1998 c.32 s.74, Sch.6

86. Courts-Martial (Evidence) Regulations 1977

revoked: SI 1997/173 Reg.3

87. Courts-Martial and Standing Civilian Courts (Additional Powers on Trial of Civilians) Regulations 1977

revoked: SI 1997/579 Reg.13, Sch.3

88. Standing Civilian Courts Order 1977

revoked: SI 1997/172 Art.93, Sch.5

92. Rules of Procedure (Army) (Amendment) Rules 1977

revoked: SI 1997/169 r.90, Sch.7

94. Rules of Procedure (Air Force) (Amendment) Rules 1977

revoked: SI 1997/171 r.90, Sch.7

107. Merton (Waiting and Loading) Order 1977

revoked (in part): SI 1996/2333 Art.10, SI 1996/2334 Art.10

176. General Optical Council (Registration and Enrolment Rules) Order of Council 1977

Appendix., amended: SI 1996/3021 Sch. para.2, SI 1998/73 Sch. para.2, SI 1999/69 Sch. r.2

217. Royal and other Parks and Gardens Regulations 1977

revoked: SI 1997/1639 Reg.7

238. Enfield (Bus Lanes) (No.1) Traffic Order 1977

revoked (in part): SI 1996/1463 Art.5

289. Town and Country Planning General Development Order 1977

Art.4, see *Taunton Deane BC v Hallett* (1996) 11 P.A.D. 14

293. Local Authorities etc. (Miscellaneous Provision) Order 1977

Art.4, revoked (in part): 1996 c.56 Sch.38 Part III

343. Social Security Benefit (Dependency) Regulations 1977

Part III, applied: SI 1996/2567 Reg.10

Reg.1, amended: SI 1999/1958 Art.4, Sch.11, SI 1999/2422 Art.3, Sch.2, SI 1999/2860 Art.3, Sch.2, SI 1999/3178 Art.3, Sch.2 para.1

Reg.2, amended: SI 1996/1345 Reg.12

Reg.3, amended: SI 1996/1345 Reg.12, SI 1999/3178 Art.3, Sch.2 para.2

Reg.6, revoked: SI 1996/2745 Reg.18, Sch.4

Reg.8, amended: SI 1996/1345 Reg.12, SI 1996/2745 Reg.17

NO.

343. **Social Security Benefit (Dependency) Regulations 1977**—*cont.*
Reg.10, amended: SI 1996/1345 Reg.12
Reg.11, amended: SI 1996/1345 Reg.12
Reg.13, revoked: SI 1996/1345 Reg.27, Sch.
Sch.2 para.2B, amended: SI 1996/670 Reg.5, SI 1997/576 Reg.5, SI 1998/521 Reg.5, SI 1999/858 Reg.4
Sch.2 para.2C, amended: SI 1996/2745 Reg.17
Sch.2 para.7, applied: SI 1996/2745 Reg.7

379. **District of Sedgemoor (Electoral Arrangements) Order 1977**
revoked: SI 1998/2465 Art.6

412. **Borough of Boston (Electoral Arrangements) Order 1977**
revoked: SI 1998/2333 Art.4

426. **Criminal Damage (Northern Ireland) Order 1977**
Art.3, applied: 1996 c.22 Sch.1 para.14, 1997 c.13 s.2
Art.4, applied: 1996 c.22 Sch.1 para.14
Art.5, applied: 1996 c.22 Sch.1 para.14
Art.8, amended: 1998 c.32 s.74, Sch.4 para.13

437. **District of West Derbyshire (Electoral Arrangements) Order 1977**
revoked: SI 1999/2693 Art.4

450. **Lambeth (Restriction of Waiting at Bus Stops) (No.1 1974 and No.1 1977) Order 1977**
revoked (in part): SI 1997/2922 Art.11, SI 1999/1724 Art.10 (with saving)

500. **Safety Representatives and Safety Committees Regulations 1977**
applied: SI 1997/1840 Reg.21, SI 1997/2962 Reg.17, SI 1999/101 Reg.4, Reg.5, Sch.1 para.35, Sch.2 para.38
Reg.2, amended: SI 1999/860 Reg.3
Reg.2A, added: SI 1999/860 Reg.3
Reg.3, amended: SI 1996/1513 Reg.13
Reg.4, amended: SI 1999/860 Reg.3
Reg.4A, amended: SI 1997/1840 Reg.21, SI 1999/3242 Reg.29, Sch.2
Reg.5, amended: SI 1999/2024 Reg.48, Sch.5 Part II
Sch.1, added: SI 1999/860 Reg.3, Sch.

510. **Borough of Crewe and Nantwich (Electoral Arrangements) Order 1977**
revoked: SI 1998/2845 Art.11

546. **District of Woodspring (Electoral Arrangements) Order 1977**
revoked: SI 1998/2702 Art.10

596. **Gas (Northern Ireland) Order 1977**
revoked: SI 1996/275 (NI.2) Art.71, Sch.8
Art.13, applied: SI 1996/275 (NI.2) Sch.7 para.3
Art.14, applied: SI 1996/2911 Sch.1 Part G
Art.16, applied: SI 1996/275 (NI.2) Sch.7 para.3

599. **Transport (Northern Ireland) Order 1977**
Art.2, revoked (in part): SI 1996/1919 (NI.16) Art.257, Sch.3

610. **Social Security (Miscellaneous Provisions) (Northern Ireland) Order 1977**
Art.3, amended: SI 1998/1506 (NI.10) Art.62
Art.3, applied: SI 1998/1506 (NI.10) Art.62
Art.12, revoked: SI 1996/1921 (NI.18) Art.28, Sch.3

642. **Hounslow (Waiting and Loading Restrictions) Order 1977**
applied: SI 1996/1088 Art.11
referred to: SI 1997/2655 Art.11, SI 1997/2656 Art.10, SI 1997/2657 Art.10

NO.

642. **Hounslow (Waiting and Loading Restrictions) Order 1977**—*cont.*
revoked (in part): SI 1996/2336 Art.10, SI 1997/88 Art.10, SI 1997/1507 Art.10, SI 1997/2386 Art.10, SI 1997/2655 Art.11, SI 1997/2656 Art.10, SI 1997/2657 Art.10, SI 1998/2615 Art.10

670. **Medicines (Bal Jivan Chamcho Prohibition) (No.2) Order 1977**
Art.2, amended: SI 1997/856 Art.2

672. **Sheriff Court Districts (Amendment) Order 1977**
revoked: SI 1996/1005 Art.3, Sch.2

674. **Employment Protection (Recoupment of Unemployment Benefit and Supplementary Benefit) Regulations 1977**
revoked: SI 1996/2349 Reg.11

815. **Town and Country Planning (New Towns in Rural Wales) Special Development Order 1977**
Art.3, amended: SI 1996/525 Sch para.8
Art.8, amended: SI 1996/525 Sch para.8

827. **Medical Qualifications (EEC Recognition) Order 1977**
Art.6, see *Tattari v Private Patients Plan Ltd* [1998] I.C.R. 106 (CA), Beldam, L.J.

866. **District of West Devon (Electoral Arrangements) Order 1977**
revoked: SI 1999/2473 Art.10

867. **Employment Protection Code of Practice (Disciplinary Practice and Procedures) Order 1977**
referred to: SI 1998/44

889. **Conveyance by Rail of Military Explosives Regulations 1977**
revoked: SI 1996/2089 Reg.34

927. **Fruit Juices and Fruit Nectars Regulations 1977**
amended: SI 1999/1136 Reg.14
Reg.2, amended: SI 1996/1499 Reg.49
Reg.4, amended: SI 1996/1499 Reg.49
Reg.6, amended: SI 1996/1499 Reg.49
Reg.7, amended: SI 1996/1499 Reg.49
Reg.8, amended: SI 1996/1499 Reg.49
Reg.11, amended: SI 1997/1413 Reg.12
Reg.19, revoked: SI 1996/1499 Reg.49, Sch.9

928. **Condensed Milk and Dried Milk Regulations 1977**
amended: SI 1999/1136 Reg.14
referred to: SI 1996/1499 Reg.4
Reg.5, amended: SI 1996/1499 Reg.49
Reg.6, amended: SI 1996/1499 Reg.49

937. **Employment Protection Code of Practice (Disclosure of Information) Order 1977**
referred to: SI 1998/45

944. **Importation of Animals Order 1977**
referred to: SI 1997/757 Art.10, SI 1997/758 Art.2
Art.2, amended: SI 1996/1760 Art.2
Art.3, applied: SI 1998/190 Reg.34, Sch.6
Art.3, referred to: SI 1998/190 Reg.34, Sch.6
Art.4, referred to: SI 1998/190 Reg.34, Sch.6
Art.5, referred to: SI 1998/190 Reg.34, Sch.6
Art.7, referred to: SI 1998/190 Reg.34, Sch.6
Art.8, referred to: SI 1998/190 Reg.34, Sch.6
Art.9, referred to: SI 1998/190 Reg.34, Sch.6
Art.10, referred to: SI 1998/190 Reg.34, Sch.6
Art.11, applied: SI 1997/757 Art.10, SI 1997/758 Art.2
Art.11, referred to: SI 1998/190 Reg.34, Sch.6
Art.12, referred to: SI 1998/190 Reg.34, Sch.6
Art.13, referred to: SI 1998/190 Reg.34, Sch.6
Art.14, referred to: SI 1998/190 Reg.34, Sch.6

1977—cont.

944. Importation of Animals Order 1977—*cont.*
Art.16, referred to: SI 1998/190 Reg.34, Sch.6
Art.17, referred to: SI 1998/190 Reg.34, Sch.6
Art.18, referred to: SI 1998/190 Reg.34, Sch.6
Art.19, referred to: SI 1998/190 Reg.34, Sch.6
Art.20, referred to: SI 1998/190 Reg.34, Sch.6
Art.21, referred to: SI 1998/190 Reg.34, Sch.6
Art.23, referred to: SI 1998/190 Reg.34, Sch.6
Art.24, referred to: SI 1998/190 Reg.34, Sch.6
Art.25, referred to: SI 1998/190 Reg.34, Sch.6

956. Social Security Benefit (Persons Residing Together) Regulations 1977
Reg.2, amended: SI 1996/1345 Reg.16

973. Act of Sederunt (Proceedings under Sex Discrimination Act 1975) 1977
revoked: SI 1999/929 r.1.3, Sch.2

985. Local Land Charges Rules 1977
Sch.3, amended: SI 1998/1190 r.2, Sch.

996. Medicines (Labelling) Amendment Regulations 1977
revoked (in part): SI 1996/2194 Reg.6, Sch.3

1026. Fruit Juices and Fruit Nectars (Scotland) Regulations 1977
amended: SI 1999/1136 Reg.14
Reg.2, amended: SI 1996/1499 Reg.49
Reg.4, amended: SI 1996/1499 Reg.49
Reg.6, amended: SI 1996/1499 Reg.49
Reg.7, amended: SI 1996/1499 Reg.49
Reg.8, amended: SI 1996/1499 Reg.49
Reg.11, amended: SI 1997/1413 Reg.12
Reg.19, revoked: SI 1996/1499 Reg.49, Sch.9

1027. Condensed Milk and Dried Milk (Scotland) Regulations 1977
amended: SI 1999/1136 Reg.14
Reg.5, amended: SI 1996/1499 Reg.49
Reg.6, amended: SI 1996/1499 Reg.49

1064. District of Purbeck (Electoral Arrangements) Order 1977
revoked: SI 1998/2159 Art.6

1140. Aerosol Dispensers (EEC Requirements) Regulations 1977
Reg.2, amended: SI 1996/2421 Reg.2
Reg.3, amended: SI 1996/2421 Reg.2
Sch. para.1, substituted: SI 1996/2421 Reg.2

1148. Trunk Road (Great South West Road, Hounslow) (Prescribed Routes) Order 1977
Art.5, revoked (in part): SI 1996/69 Art.6
Art.6, revoked: SI 1996/70 Art.6
Art.11, revoked: SI 1996/70 Art.6
Art.13, revoked: SI 1996/69 Art.6
Art.14, revoked: SI 1996/69 Art.6
Art.15, revoked: SI 1996/69 Art.6
Art.16, revoked: SI 1996/70 Art.6
Art.17, revoked: SI 1996/70 Art.6
Sch.1, revoked (in part): SI 1996/69 Art.6
Sch.2, revoked (in part): SI 1996/69 Art.6

1210. National Savings Bank (Investment Deposits) (Limits) Order 1977
Art.2A, added: SI 1996/1854 Art.3
Art.2B, added: SI 1999/1056 Art.3
Art.2C, added: SI 1999/2060 Art.3
Art.3, amended: SI 1996/1854 Art.4, SI 1999/1056 Art.4
Art.3A, added: SI 1996/1854 Art.5
Art.3B, added: SI 1999/1056 Art.5
Art.3C, added: SI 1999/2060 Art.4
Art.4, amended: SI 1996/1854 Art.6, SI 1998/1446 Art.30, Sch.1 para.9, SI 1999/1056 Art.6, SI 1999/2060 Art.5

1242. Merchant Shipping Act 1974 (Jersey) (Amendment) Order 1977
revoked: SI 1997/2598 Art.5

1977—cont.

1247. Criminal Damage (Compensation) (Northern Ireland) Order 1977
applied: SI 1996/3158 (NI.22) Art.17
Art.18, revoked (in part): SI 1996/3160 (NI.24) Sch.7

1248. Criminal Injuries (Compensation) (Northern Ireland) Order 1977
Art.18, revoked (in part): SI 1996/3160 (NI.24) Sch.7

1249. Criminal Law (Amendment) (Northern Ireland) Order 1977
Art.3, applied: 1996 c.22 Sch.1 para.15

1251. Fatal Accidents (Northern Ireland) Order 1977
applied: SI 1997/2778 (NI.19) Art.45, SI 1997/2983 (NI.21) Art.10
referred to: 1996 c.48 s.3, s.7
Art.3, referred to: 1998 c.17 s.23
Sch.1 para.8, revoked: 1998 c.17 s.51, Sch.5 Part II

1273. District of Bracknell (Electoral Arrangements) Order 1977
applied: SI 1996/1879 Art.10

1276. District of South Hams (Electoral Arrangements) Order 1977
revoked: SI 1998/2487 Art.11

1279. District of Tiverton (Electoral Arrangements) Order 1977
revoked: SI 1999/2470 Art.8

1309. Heavy Goods Vehicles (Drivers' Licences) Regulations 1977
Reg.31, applied: SI 1996/2824 Reg.49, SI 1999/2864 Reg.52

1345. Safety of Sports Grounds (Designation) (Scotland) Order 1977
revoked: SI 1998/1601 Art.3, Sch.2

1387. Pensions Increase (Annual Review) Order 1977
applied: SI 1997/634 Art.3, SI 1998/503 Art.3, Art.4, SI 1999/522 Art.3

1442. District of North Hertfordshire (Electoral Arrangements) Order 1977
revoked: SI 1998/2555 Art.10

1443. Scholarships and Other Benefits Regulations 1977
Reg.4, amended: SI 1998/86 Reg.3, Sch.2
Reg.4, applied: SI 1999/120 Art.3
Reg.4, revoked (in part): SI 1998/86 Reg.2, Sch.1, SI 1999/120 Art.3 (with savings), SI 1999/229 Reg.6 (with saving), SI 1999/1727 Reg.3 (with saving)

1599. Trunk Roads (Great Western Road, Hounslow) (Prescribed Routes) Order 1977
revoked: SI 1996/1113 Art.6

1622. Act of Sederunt (Appeals under the Licensing (Scotland) Act 1976) 1977
revoked: SI 1999/929 r.1.3, Sch.2
para.3, revoked: SI 1999/929 r.1.3, Sch.2

1671. Marriage (Prescription of Forms) (Scotland) Regulations 1977
revoked: SI 1997/2349 Reg.9
Sch.1, revoked: SI 1997/2349 Reg.9
Sch.2, revoked: SI 1997/2349 Reg.9
Sch.3, revoked: SI 1997/2349 Reg.9

1753. Alcoholometers and Alcohol Hydrometers (EEC Requirements) Regulations 1977
Reg.5, referred to: SI 1998/1177 Reg.4
Reg.7, applied: SI 1998/1177 Reg.3, Sch.2 para.2

NO.

1977—cont.

1777. Grant-Aided Colleges (Compensation) (Scotland) Regulations 1977
applied: SI 1999/1750 Art.2, Sch.1

1811. District of North Kesteven (Electoral Arrangements) Order 1977
revoked: SI 1998/2338 Art.7

1820. Lands Tribunal (Amendment) Rules 1977
revoked: SI 1996/1022 r.57, Sch.2

1865. District of Rutland (Electoral Arrangements) Order 1977
applied: SI 1996/507 Art.9

1871. Continental Shelf (Designation of Additional Areas) Order 1977
referred to: SI 1999/2031

1875. Merchant Shipping (Load Lines Convention) (Various Countries) Order 1977
revoked: SI 1998/2241 Reg.3

1877. Tourism (Sleeping Accommodation Price Display) Order 1977
Art.7, applied: SI 1999/672 Art.2, Sch.1

1895. Borough of High Peak (Electoral Arrangements) Order 1977
revoked: SI 1999/2695 Art.7

2138. National Health Service (Superannuation) (War Service etc.) (Scotland) Regulations 1977
applied: SI 1999/1750 Art.2, Sch.1

2150. Social Security (Isle of Man) Order 1977
Sch., amended: SI 1996/1928 Art.2, Sch.1

2151. Agricultural Wages (Regulation) (Northern Ireland) Order 1977
applied: 1998 c.39 s.16, s.46
referred to: 1998 c.39 s.46, s.47, 1998 c.47 s.98, SI 1999/685 Art.3
Art.2, amended: 1998 c.39 s.47, Sch.2 para.22
Art.2A, added: 1998 c.39 s.47, Sch.2 para.23
Art.4, amended: 1998 c.39 s.47, Sch.2 para.24
Art.4, referred to: 1998 c.39 s.47, SI 1999/584 Reg.38
Art.6, amended: 1998 c.39 s.47, Sch.2 para.25
Art.8A, added: 1998 c.39 s.47, Sch.2 para.26
Art.8A, amended: SR 1999/172 Reg.2
Art.8A, revoked (in part): SR 1999/172 Reg.2
Art.11A, added: 1998 c.39 s.47, Sch.2 para.27
Art.15, revoked (in part): SI 1996/1919 (NI.16) Art.257, Sch.3

2157. Rates (Northern Ireland) Order 1977
Art.2, revoked: SI 1996/275 (NI.2) Art.71, Sch.8
Art.6, amended: SI 1996/3162 (NI.25) Art.3
Art.7, amended: SI 1998/3164 (NI.22) Art.10, Sch.2 para.1
Art.8, amended: SI 1998/3164 (NI.22) Art.10, Sch.2 para.2
Art.9, amended: SI 1998/3164 (NI.22) Art.10, Sch.2 para.3
Art.12, revoked: SI 1998/3164 (NI.22) Art.3, Art.12, Sch.3
Art.13, amended: SI 1996/3162 (NI.25) Art.4
Art.21, amended: SI 1998/3164 (NI.22) Art.4
Art.21, revoked (in part): SI 1998/3164 (NI.22) Art.4, Art.12, Sch.3
Art.27, amended: SI 1998/3164 (NI.22) Art.10, Sch.2 para.4
Art.31C, added: SI 1998/3164 (NI.22) Art.5
Art.33A, added: SI 1996/3162 (NI.25) Art.5
Art.34, amended: SI 1998/3164 (NI.22) Art.10, Sch.2 para.5
Art.37, amended: SI 1996/3162 (NI.25) Art.6
Art.37A, added: SI 1998/3164 (NI.22) Art.6
Art.39D, added: SI 1996/275 (NI.2) Art.71, Sch.6
Art.39E, added: SI 1996/3162 (NI.25) Art.7

NO.

1977—cont.

2157. Rates (Northern Ireland) Order 1977—*cont.*
Art.41, amended: SI 1999/1736 Art.12, Sch.6
Art.41, applied: SI 1999/1736 Art.12, Sch.6
Art.44, revoked (in part): SI 1998/3164 (NI.22) Art.12, Sch.3
Art.50, amended: SI 1996/3162 (NI.25) Art.6, SI 1998/3164 (NI.22) Art.10, Sch.2 para.6
Art.50, revoked (in part): SI 1998/3164 (NI.22) Art.12, Sch.3
Art.52, amended: SI 1998/3164 (NI.22) Art.10, Sch.2 para.7
Art.56, amended: SI 1998/3164 (NI.22) Art.10, Sch.2 para.8
Art.56, revoked (in part): SI 1998/3164 (NI.22) Art.10, Art.12, Sch.2 para.8, Sch.3
Sch.1 para.3, amended: SI 1998/3164 (NI.22) Art.7
Sch.2 para.1, amended: SI 1996/3162 (NI.25) Art.8, SI 1998/3164 (NI.22) Art.10, Sch.2 para.9
Sch.2 para.2A, added: SI 1996/3162 (NI.25) Art.8
Sch.3, amended: SI 1996/3162 (NI.25) Art.9
Sch.4 para.1, see *Newry Building Supplies Ltd v Commissioner of Valuation for Northern Ireland* [1999] R.A. 420 (Lands Tr (NI)), Michael R Curry FRICS
Sch.5 para.2, substituted: SI 1996/3162 (NI.25) Art.10
Sch.5 para.4A, added: SI 1998/3164 (NI.22) Art.8
Sch.5 para.5, amended: SI 1996/3162 (NI.25) Art.10, SI 1998/3164 (NI.22) Art.8
Sch.9A, added: SI 1998/3164 (NI.22) Art.5, Sch.1
Sch.10, amended: SI 1998/3164 (NI.22) Art.9
Sch.10, revoked (in part): SI 1998/3164 (NI.22) Art.9, Art.12, Sch.3
Sch.11, amended: SI 1996/3162 (NI.25) Art.11
Sch.11, revoked (in part): SI 1996/275 (NI.2) Art.71, Sch.8
Sch.12 Part I, amended: SI 1996/3162 (NI.25) Art.12
Sch.12 Part IA, added: SI 1998/3164 (NI.22) Art.9
Sch.12 Part III, amended: SI 1996/3162 (NI.25) Art.12
Sch.12 Part III, revoked (in part): SI 1996/275 (NI.2) Art.71, Sch.8, SI 1996/3162 (NI.25) Art.12, Sch
Sch.12 Part IV, amended: SI 1996/3162 (NI.25) Art.12
Sch.12 Part VII, revoked: SI 1996/275 (NI.2) Art.71, Sch.8
Sch.12 Part VIII, revoked: SI 1996/275 (NI.2) Art.71, Sch.8
Sch.13, amended: SI 1997/1772 (NI.15) Art.25, Sch.4, SI 1998/261 (NI.2) Art.15, Sch.3
Sch.13, revoked (in part): SI 1998/261 (NI.2) Art.15, Sch.4
Sch.14 para.2, amended: SI 1996/3162 (NI.25) Art.8
Sch.16 Part III, revoked (in part): SI 1996/3162 (NI.25) Sch

1978

Barnet (Waiting and Loading Restrictions) Order 1978
amended: SI 1996/42 Art.11
revoked (in part): SI 1996/41 Art.11

NO.

1978—cont.

Camden (Bus Lanes) (No.1) (1975) (Amendment No.1) Traffic Order 1978
revoked (in part): SI 1998/3206 Art.6

Haringey (Waiting and Loading Restrictions) Order 1978
revoked (in part): SI 1997/464 Art.10

London Borough of Havering (Waiting and Loading Restriction) Order 1978
revoked (in part): SI 1996/1894 Art.10

Property (Northern Ireland) Order 1978
amended: SI 1999/660 (NI.4) Art.8, Sch. para.1

32. **Diseases of Animals (Approved Disinfectants) Order 1978**
Art.6, amended: SI 1996/697 Art.2, SI 1997/2347 Art.2, SI 1999/919 Art.2
Sch.1, amended: SI 1996/697 Art.2
Sch.1, substituted: SI 1997/2347 Art.2, Sch.1, SI 1999/919 Art.2, Sch.1
Sch.2, amended: SI 1996/697 Art.2
Sch.2, substituted: SI 1997/2347 Art.2, Sch.2, SI 1999/919 Art.2, Sch.2
Sch.3, substituted: SI 1996/697 Art.2

43. **District of South Kesteven (Electoral Arrangements) Order 1978**
revoked: SI 1998/2337 Art.6

47. **District of Teignbridge (Electoral Arrangements) Order 1978**
revoked: SI 1999/2471 Art.9

50. **Trunk Road (M4 Motorway, Heathrow Airport Spur Road) (Prohibition of Traffic) Order 1978**
revoked: SI 1996/2157 Art.4

69. **Housing (Homeless Persons) (Appropriate Arrangements) Order 1978**
revoked: SI 1998/1578 Art.3

88. **City of Chester (Electoral Arrangements) Order 1978**
revoked: SI 1998/2866 Art.6

119. **Thoresby Mine (Cable Reel Load-Haul-Dump Vehicles) Regulations 1978**
Reg.4, revoked: SI 1996/192 Reg.20, Sch.15 Part III
Reg.5, revoked: SI 1996/192 Reg.20, Sch.15 Part III
Reg.6, revoked: SI 1996/192 Reg.20, Sch.15 Part III
Reg.7, revoked: SI 1996/192 Reg.20, Sch.15 Part III
Reg.8, revoked: SI 1996/192 Reg.20, Sch.15 Part III
Reg.9, revoked: SI 1996/192 Reg.20, Sch.15 Part III

152. **Sheriff Court Districts Amendment Order 1978**
revoked: SI 1996/1005 Art.3, Sch.2

178. **Continental Shelf (Designation of Additional Areas) Order 1978**
referred to: SI 1999/2031, SI 1999/2031 Art.2, Sch.

179. **European Patent Organisation (Immunities and Privileges) Order 1978**
Art.12A, added: SI 1999/2034 Art.2, Sch.

181. **International Rubber Study Group (Immunities and Privileges) 1978**
Art.12A, added: SI 1999/2034 Art.2, Sch.

185. **Trial of the Pyx (Amendment) Order 1978**
revoked: SI 1998/1764 Art.16, Sch.3

216. **Patents Rules 1978**
r.124, referred to: SI 1996/2972 Sch Part B, SI 1998/1778 r.3, Sch. Part B

NO.

1978—cont.

229. **Act of Sederunt (Betting and Gaming Appeals) 1978**
revoked: SI 1999/929 r.1.3, Sch.2

231. **District of Derwentside (Electoral Arrangements) Order 1978**
revoked: SI 1999/2580 Art.3

259. **Agricultural Land Tribunals (Rules) Order 1978**
Sch.1 r.21, applied: SI 1999/672 Art.2, Sch.1

272. **Transfer of Functions (Wales) (No.1) Order 1978**
applied: SI 1999/3141 Art.2, SI 1999/3142 Art.2
referred to: SI 1999/672 Art.2, Sch.1
Art.4, referred to: SI 1999/672 Art.2, Sch.1
Art.8, referred to: SI 1999/672 Art.2, Sch.1

294. **Plant Breeders' Rights Regulations 1978**
applied: SI 1998/1027 Reg.22
revoked (in part): SI 1998/1027 Reg.21 (with savings), Sch.2 (with savings)
Reg.3, referred to: SI 1998/1027 Reg.21
Reg.3, revoked (in part): SI 1998/1027 Reg.21
Reg.18, amended: SI 1998/1027 Reg.21
Reg.18, applied: SI 1998/1027 Reg.4, Reg.16, Reg.17, Reg.18, Reg.19, Reg.20, Reg.22
Reg.18, referred to: SI 1998/1027 Reg.21
Reg.18, revoked (in part): SI 1998/1027 Reg.21

329. **Perambulators and Pushchairs (Safety) Regulations (Northern Ireland) 1978**
revoked: SI 1997/2866 Reg.1

341. **Lambeth (Waiting and Loading Restriction) Order 1978**
revoked (in part): SI 1997/2922 Art.11, SI 1998/394 Art.11 (with saving), SI 1999/1724 Art.10 (with saving), SI 1999/2217 Art.10 (with saving)

374. **Social Security (Modification of Coroners (Amendment) Act 1926) Order 1978**
Art.3, applied: SI 1997/1612 Reg.131

393. **Social Security (Graduated Retirement Benefit) (No.2) Regulations 1978**
referred to: SI 1999/2422 Art.3
Reg.3, amended: SI 1997/454 Reg.5
Reg.3, referred to: SI 1996/1345 Reg.18
Sch.1, amended: SI 1997/454 Reg.5
Sch.1, referred to: SI 1996/1345 Reg.18
Sch.2, amended: SI 1996/599 Art.11, SI 1997/543 Art.11, SI 1998/470 Art.11, SI 1999/264 Art.11

436. **Fire Services (Appointments and Promotion) Regulations 1978**
Reg.4, amended: SI 1997/959 Reg.3
Reg.5, amended: SI 1997/959 Reg.4
Reg.5, revoked (in part): SI 1997/959 Reg.4
Reg.6, amended: SI 1996/2096 Reg.2

460. **Sexual Offences (Northern Ireland) Order 1978**
Art.1, amended: 1999 c.23 s.67, Sch.6
Art.1, revoked (in part): SI 1999/2789 (NI.8) Art.40, Sch.3
Art.4, referred to: SI 1999/2789 (NI.8) Art.40, Sch.2 para.4
Art.4, revoked: SI 1999/2789 (NI.8) Art.40, Sch.3
Art.5, amended: SI 1998/1504 (NI.9) Art.65, Sch.5 para.9
Art.5, revoked: SI 1999/2789 (NI.8) Art.40, Sch.3
Art.6, revoked: 1999 c.23 s.48, s.67, Sch.2 para.5, Sch.6
Art.7, revoked: 1999 c.23 s.48, s.67, Sch.2 para.5, Sch.6

NO.

1978—cont.

482. District of South Holland (Electoral Arrangements) Order 1978
revoked: SI 1998/2336 Art.4

645. Spier's Trust Scheme 1978
amended: SI 1996/629 Sch

661. Housing (Homeless Persons) (Appropriate Arrangements) (No.2) Order 1978
revoked: SI 1998/1603 Art.3 (with saving)

754. Justices' Clerks (Amendment) Rules 1978
revoked: SI 1999/2784 r.4

786. Double Taxation Relief (Taxes on Income) (Republic of Korea) Order 1978
Sch., substituted: SI 1996/3168 Sch. Part I

795. Merchant Shipping (Crew Accommodation) Regulations 1978
applied: SI 1996/3243 Sch Part I
revoked: SI 1997/1508 Reg.1
Sch.6, applied: SI 1997/1508 Reg.3
Sch.6, revoked: SI 1997/1508 Reg.1

929. Petroleum (Production) (Amendment) Regulations 1978
referred to: 1998 c.17 Sch.1 para.10, Sch.1 para.11, Sch.1 para.12, SI 1999/160 Sch.5 para.1

986. Cambridge Water (No.2) Order 1978
revoked: SI 1996/713 Art.4, Sch.2 Part II

990. District of West Lindsey (Electoral Arrangements) Order 1978
revoked: SI 1998/2366 Art.7

1006. Medicines (Administration of Radioactive Substances) Regulations 1978
Reg.3, referred to: SI 1999/1319 Sch.

1029. Continental Shelf (Designation of Additional Areas) Order 1978
referred to: SI 1999/2031

1039. Health and Safety at Work (Northern Ireland) Order 1978
amended: SI 1998/2795 (NI.18) Art.6, Sch.1 para.8
referred to: SI 1996/600 Sch.5 para.15, SI 1996/601 Sch.5 para.15, 1997 c.7 s.4, Sch para.6, SI 1997/1624 Sch.5 para.15, SI 1999/1517 Reg.12, Sch.4 para.12, SI 1999/1676 Sch.5 para.12
Art.2, amended: SI 1997/1774 (NI.16) Art.4, Art.8, SI 1998/2795 (NI.18) Art.6, Sch.1 para.9
Art.2, applied: SI 1998/1069 (NI.5) Art.5
Art.2, revoked (in part): SI 1997/1774 (NI.16) Art.4
Art.3, amended: 1998 c.17 Sch.4 para.35
Art.3, revoked (in part): 1998 c.17 Sch.4 para.35
Art.12, amended: SI 1998/2795 (NI.18) Art.3
Art.12, applied: SI 1998/2795 (NI.18) Art.3
Art.13, amended: SI 1998/2795 (NI.18) Art.4, Art.6, Sch.1 para.10, Sch.2
Art.15, amended: SI 1998/2795 (NI.18) Art.6, Sch.1 para.11
Art.16, amended: SI 1998/2795 (NI.18) Art.6, Sch.1 para.12
Art.17, referred to: SI 1998/1069 (NI.5) Art.4
Art.18, applied: SI 1996/1919 (NI.16) Art.96
Art.20, amended: SI 1998/2795 (NI.18) Art.6, Sch.1 para.13
Art.20, referred to: SI 1998/1069 (NI.5) Art.4
Art.21, amended: SI 1999/2001 Reg.24, Sch.8 para.3
Art.21, applied: SI 1997/831 Sch.15 para.3, SI 1999/2001 Reg.24, Sch.8 para.3
Art.21, referred to: 1998 c.17 s.20, SI 1998/1069 (NI.5) Art.4
Art.22, amended: SI 1997/831 Sch.15 para.3, SI 1999/2001 Reg.24, Sch.8 para.3

NO.

1978—cont.

1039. Health and Safety at Work (Northern Ireland) Order 1978—*cont.*
Art.22, applied: SI 1997/831 Sch.15 para.3, SI 1999/2001 Reg.24, Sch.8 para.3
Art.22, referred to: SI 1997/831 Reg.19, SI 1998/1069 (NI.5) Art.4, SI 1999/2001 Reg.24
Art.22, revoked (in part): SI 1999/2001 Reg.24, Sch.8 para.3
Art.23, amended: SI 1999/2001 Reg.24, Sch.8 para.3
Art.23, applied: SI 1997/831 Sch.15 para.3, SI 1999/2001 Reg.24, Sch.8 para.3
Art.23, referred to: SI 1998/1069 (NI.5) Art.4, SI 1999/1736 Art.12, Sch.5
Art.24, amended: SI 1999/2001 Reg.24, Sch.8 para.3
Art.24, applied: SI 1997/831 Sch.15 para.3, SI 1999/2001 Reg.24, Sch.8 para.3
Art.24, referred to: SI 1998/1069 (NI.5) Art.4, SI 1999/1736 Art.12, Sch.5
Art.25, amended: SI 1997/831 Sch.15 para.3, SI 1999/2001 Reg.24, Sch.8 para.3
Art.25, applied: SI 1997/831 Sch.15 para.3, SI 1999/2001 Reg.24, Sch.8 para.3
Art.25, referred to: SI 1998/1069 (NI.5) Art.4, SI 1999/1736 Art.12, Sch.5
Art.25, revoked (in part): SI 1999/2001 Reg.24, Sch.8 para.3
Art.26, amended: SI 1999/2001 Reg.24, Sch.8 para.3
Art.26, applied: SI 1997/831 Sch.15 para.3, SI 1999/2001 Reg.24, Sch.8 para.3
Art.26, referred to: SI 1998/1069 (NI.5) Art.4, SI 1999/1736 Art.12, Sch.5
Art.27, amended: SI 1999/2001 Reg.24, Sch.8 para.3
Art.27, applied: SI 1997/831 Sch.15 para.3, SI 1999/2001 Reg.24, Sch.8 para.3
Art.27, referred to: SI 1998/1069 (NI.5) Art.4, SI 1999/1736 Art.12, Sch.5
Art.28, amended: SI 1999/2001 Reg.24, Sch.8 para.3
Art.28, applied: SI 1997/831 Sch.15 para.3, SI 1999/2001 Reg.24, Sch.8 para.3
Art.28, referred to: SI 1998/1069 (NI.5) Art.4
Art.29, amended: SI 1998/2795 (NI.18) Art.6, Sch.1 para.14, Sch.2, SI 1999/2001 Reg.24, Sch.8 para.3
Art.29, applied: SI 1997/831 Sch.15 para.3, SI 1999/2001 Reg.24, Sch.8 para.3
Art.29, referred to: SI 1998/1069 (NI.5) Art.4
Art.29, revoked (in part): SI 1998/2795 (NI.18) Art.6, Sch.1 para.14
Art.30, amended: SI 1999/2001 Reg.24, Sch.8 para.3
Art.30, applied: SI 1997/831 Sch.15 para.3, SI 1999/2001 Reg.24, Sch.8 para.3
Art.30, referred to: SI 1998/1069 (NI.5) Art.4
Art.31, amended: SI 1997/831 Sch.15 para.3, SI 1999/2001 Reg.24, Sch.8 para.3
Art.31, applied: SI 1997/831 Sch.15 para.3, SI 1999/2001 Reg.24, Sch.8 para.3
Art.31, referred to: SI 1998/1069 (NI.5) Art.4, SI 1999/1736 Art.12, Sch.5
Art.31, revoked (in part): SI 1998/2795 (NI.18) Art.6, Sch.1 para.15, Sch.2, SI 1999/2001 Reg.24, Sch.8 para.3
Art.32, amended: SI 1997/831 Sch.15 para.3, SI 1999/2001 Reg.24, Sch.8 para.3
Art.32, applied: SI 1997/831 Sch.15 para.3, SI 1999/2001 Reg.24, Sch.8 para.3
Art.32, referred to: SI 1998/1069 (NI.5) Art.4, SI 1999/1736 Art.12, Sch.5

1978—cont.

1039. Health and Safety at Work (Northern Ireland) Order 1978—*cont.*

Art.32, revoked (in part): SI 1999/2001 Reg.24, Sch.8 para.3

Art.33, amended: SI 1999/2001 Reg.24, Sch.8 para.3

Art.33, applied: SI 1997/831 Sch.15 para.3, SI 1999/2001 Reg.24, Sch.8 para.3

Art.33, referred to: SI 1998/1069 (NI.5) Art.4, SI 1999/1736 Art.12, Sch.5

Art.34, applied: SI 1997/831 Sch.15 para.3, SI 1999/2001 Reg.24, Sch.8 para.3

Art.34, referred to: SI 1998/1069 (NI.5) Art.4, SI 1999/1736 Art.12, Sch.5

Art.34A, added: SI 1998/2795 (NI.18) Art.6, Sch.1 para.16

Art.35, amended: SI 1999/2001 Reg.24, Sch.8 para.3

Art.35, applied: SI 1997/831 Sch.15 para.3, SI 1999/2001 Reg.24, Sch.8 para.3

Art.35, referred to: 1998 c.17 s.20, SI 1998/1069 (NI.5) Art.4, SI 1999/1736 Art.12, Sch.5

Art.36, amended: SI 1999/2001 Reg.24, Sch.8 para.3

Art.36, applied: SI 1997/831 Sch.15 para.3, SI 1999/2001 Reg.24, Sch.8 para.3

Art.36, referred to: SI 1998/1069 (NI.5) Art.4, SI 1999/1736 Art.12, Sch.5

Art.37, referred to: SI 1998/1069 (NI.5) Art.4, SI 1999/1736 Art.12, Sch.5

Art.38, amended: SI 1999/2001 Reg.24, Sch.8 para.3

Art.38, applied: SI 1997/831 Sch.15 para.3, SI 1999/2001 Reg.24, Sch.8 para.3

Art.38, referred to: SI 1998/1069 (NI.5) Art.4, SI 1999/1736 Art.12, Sch.5

Art.39, amended: SI 1997/831 Sch.15 para.3, SI 1999/2001 Reg.24, Sch.8 para.3

Art.39, applied: SI 1997/831 Sch.15 para.3, SI 1999/2001 Reg.24, Sch.8 para.3

Art.39, referred to: SI 1998/1069 (NI.5) Art.4, SI 1999/1736 Art.12, Sch.5

Art.39, revoked (in part): SI 1999/2001 Reg.24, Sch.8 para.3

Art.41, amended: SI 1998/2795 (NI.18) Art.6, Sch.1 para.17

Art.44, applied: SI 1999/3145 Art.6

Art.46, amended: SI 1998/2795 (NI.18) Art.6, Sch.1 para.18

Art.47A, added: SI 1997/1774 (NI.16) Art.3

Art.47A, applied: SI 1997/1774 (NI.16) Art.7

Art.48, amended: SI 1998/2795 (NI.18) Art.5, Art.6, Sch.2

Art.55, amended: SI 1998/2795 (NI.18) Art.6, Sch.1 para.19

Part II, applied: SI 1997/2777 (NI.18) Art.7, SI 1999/3145 Art.6

Sch.2 para.2, revoked: SI 1998/2795 (NI.18) Art.6, Sch.1 para.20, Sch.2

Sch.2 para.4, amended: SI 1998/2795 (NI.18) Art.6, Sch.1 para.20

Sch.2 para.5, amended: SI 1998/2795 (NI.18) Art.6, Sch.1 para.20

Sch.2 para.6, amended: SI 1998/2795 (NI.18) Art.6, Sch.1 para.20

Sch.2 para.7, amended: SI 1998/2795 (NI.18) Art.6, Sch.1 para.20

Sch.2 para.8, amended: SI 1998/2795 (NI.18) Art.6, Sch.1 para.20

Sch.2 para.11, amended: SI 1998/2795 (NI.18) Art.6, Sch.1 para.20

Sch.2 para.12, amended: SI 1998/2795 (NI.18) Art.6, Sch.1 para.20

1978—cont.

1039. Health and Safety at Work (Northern Ireland) Order 1978—*cont.*

Sch.2 para.15, substituted: SI 1998/2795 (NI.18) Art.6, Sch.1 para.20

Sch.2 para.17A, added: SI 1998/2795 (NI.18) Art.6, Sch.1 para.20

Sch.2 para.18, revoked (in part): SI 1998/2795 (NI.18) Art.6, Sch.1 para.20

Sch.2 para.19, substituted: SI 1998/2795 (NI.18) Art.6, Sch.1 para.20

Sch.4, revoked: SI 1998/2795 (NI.18) Art.6, Sch.2

Sch.4 para.3, amended: 1996 c.23 Sch.3 para.35

Sch.4 para.3, revoked: SI 1998/2795 (NI.18) Art.6, Sch.2

Sch.6 para.3, revoked: SI 1998/2795 (NI.18) Art.6, Sch.2

Sch.6 para.5, revoked: SI 1996/1919 (NI.16) Art.257, Sch.3

1041. Financial Provisions (Northern Ireland) Order 1978

Art.4, revoked: SI 1998/749 (NI.4) Art.9, Sch.

1044. Licensing (Northern Ireland) Order 1978

Art.4, applied: SI 1996/3158 (NI.22) Art.2

Art.4, referred to: SI 1996/3158 (NI.22) Art.5

1045. Matrimonial Causes (Northern Ireland) Order 1978

applied: SI 1998/1071 (NI.6) Art.39, SI 1999/3147 (NI.11) Art.25, Art.45

Art.2, amended: SI 1999/3147 (NI.11) Art.18, Sch.3 para.2

Art.6, amended: SI 1998/1071 (NI.6) Art.41, Sch.6

Art.23A, added: SI 1999/3147 (NI.11) Art.18, Sch.3 para.3

Art.25, applied: 1999 c.30 s.24

Art.25, referred to: SI 1999/3147 (NI.11) Art.22

Art.26, amended: SI 1999/3147 (NI.11) Art.18, Sch.3 para.4

Art.26, applied: SI 1998/1071 (NI.6) Art.13, Sch.2 para.2, Sch.2 para.11

Art.26A, added: SI 1999/3147 (NI.11) Art.18, Sch.3 para.5

Art.26A, referred to: SI 1999/3147 (NI.11) Art.75

Art.26B, added: SI 1999/3147 (NI.11) Art.18, Sch.3 para.5

Art.26C, added: SI 1999/3147 (NI.11) Art.18, Sch.3 para.5

Art.27, amended: SI 1999/3147 (NI.11) Art.18, Sch.3 para.6

Art.27B, amended: SI 1999/3147 (NI.11) Art.19, Sch.4 para.1

Art.27B, applied: SI 1999/3147 (NI.11) Art.22

Art.27B, referred to: 1999 c.30 s.24

Art.27B, revoked (in part): SI 1999/3147 (NI.11) Art.19, Art.76, Sch.4 para.1, Sch.10 Part II

Art.27C, amended: SI 1999/3147 (NI.11) Art.19, Sch.4 para.2

Art.27C, applied: SI 1999/3147 (NI.11) Art.22

Art.27C, referred to: 1999 c.30 s.24

Art.27A, amended: SI 1999/3147 (NI.11) Art.18, Sch.3 para.7

Art.27D, amended: SI 1999/3147 (NI.11) Art.19, Art.76, Sch.4 para.3, Sch.10 Part II

Art.27D, revoked (in part): SI 1999/3147 (NI.11) Art.19, Art.76, Sch.4 para.3, Sch.10 Part II

Art.33, amended: SI 1999/3147 (NI.11) Art.18, Sch.3 para.8

Art.35A, amended: SI 1999/3147 (NI.11) Art.18, Sch.3 para.9

Art.39, amended: SI 1999/3147 (NI.11) Art.18, Sch.3 para.10

NO.

1978—cont.

1045. Matrimonial Causes (Northern Ireland) Order 1978—cont.
Art.42A, added: SI 1999/3147 (NI.11) Art.18, Sch.3 para.11
Art.47, applied: 1998 c.29 Sch.12 para.6
Part III, applied: 1999 c.30 s.23, SI 1999/3147 (NI.11) Art.21

1047. Protection of Children (Northern Ireland) Order 1978
Art.2, applied: 1997 c.51 Sch.1 para.3
Art.3, applied: 1997 c.51 Sch.1 para.3, Sch.2 para.2
Art.9, amended: SI 1998/1504 (NI.9) Art.65, Sch.5 para.10
Art.9, revoked (in part): SI 1998/1504 (NI.9) Art.65, Sch.6

1049. Pollution Control and Local Government (Northern Ireland) Order 1978
Art.2, amended: SI 1997/2777 (NI.18) Art.35, Sch.4 para.8
Art.2, revoked (in part): SI 1997/2777 (NI.18) Art.35, Sch.5
Art.3, revoked: SI 1997/2778 (NI.19) Art.83, Sch.6
Art.4, applied: SI 1997/2778 (NI.19) Art.47
Art.4, revoked: SI 1997/2778 (NI.19) Art.83, Sch.6
Art.5, applied: SI 1997/2778 (NI.19) Art.43, Art.47
Art.5, revoked: SI 1997/2778 (NI.19) Art.83, Sch.6
Art.6, applied: SI 1997/2778 (NI.19) Art.47
Art.6, revoked: SI 1997/2778 (NI.19) Art.83, Sch.6
Art.7, applied: SI 1997/2778 (NI.19) Art.5, Art.47
Art.7, revoked: SI 1997/2778 (NI.19) Art.83, Sch.6
Art.8, applied: SI 1997/2778 (NI.19) Art.47
Art.8, revoked: SI 1997/2778 (NI.19) Art.83, Sch.6
Art.9, applied: SI 1997/2778 (NI.19) Art.47
Art.9, revoked: SI 1997/2778 (NI.19) Art.83, Sch.6
Art.10, applied: SI 1997/2778 (NI.19) Art.47
Art.10, revoked: SI 1997/2778 (NI.19) Art.83, Sch.6
Art.11, applied: SI 1997/2778 (NI.19) Art.47
Art.11, revoked: SI 1997/2778 (NI.19) Art.83, Sch.6
Art.12, applied: SI 1997/2778 (NI.19) Art.47
Art.12, revoked: SI 1997/2778 (NI.19) Art.83, Sch.6
Art.13, applied: SI 1997/2778 (NI.19) Art.47
Art.13, revoked: SI 1997/2778 (NI.19) Art.83, Sch.6
Art.14, revoked: SI 1997/2778 (NI.19) Art.83, Sch.6
Art.15, revoked: SI 1997/2778 (NI.19) Art.83, Sch.6
Art.16, revoked: SI 1997/2778 (NI.19) Art.83, Sch.6
Art.17, revoked: SI 1997/2778 (NI.19) Art.83, Sch.6
Art.18, revoked: SI 1997/2778 (NI.19) Art.83, Sch.6
Art.19, amended: SI 1997/2778 (NI.19) Art.83, Sch.5 para.2
Art.21, revoked: SI 1997/2778 (NI.19) Art.83, Sch.6
Art.22, revoked: SI 1997/2778 (NI.19) Art.83, Sch.6

NO.

1978—cont.

1049. Pollution Control and Local Government (Northern Ireland) Order 1978—cont.
Art.23, revoked: SI 1997/2778 (NI.19) Art.83, Sch.6
Art.24, amended: SI 1996/275 (NI.2) Art.71, Sch.6
Art.24, revoked: SI 1997/2778 (NI.19) Art.83, Sch.6
Art.29, referred to: SI 1997/276 (NI.2) Art.54
Art.30, applied: SI 1997/276 (NI.2) Art.49, Art.53
Art.31, applied: SI 1997/276 (NI.2) Art.53, Art.54
Art.34, revoked: SI 1997/2778 (NI.19) Art.83, Sch.6
Art.35, revoked: SI 1997/2778 (NI.19) Art.83, Sch.6
Art.36, amended: SI 1997/2778 (NI.19) Art.83, Sch.5 para.3
Art.36, revoked (in part): SI 1997/2778 (NI.19) Art.83, Sch.6
Art.42, amended: SI 1999/662 (NI.6) Art.63, Sch.7
Art.42, revoked: SI 1997/2778 (NI.19) Art.83, Sch.6
Art.53, amended (in part): SI 1996/275 (NI.2) Art.71, Sch.6
Art.55, amended: SI 1997/2777 (NI.18) Art.35, Sch.4 para.9
Art.55, revoked (in part): SI 1997/2777 (NI.18) Art.35, Sch.5
Art.56, amended: SI 1997/2777 (NI.18) Art.35, Sch.4 para.10
Art.56, revoked (in part): SI 1997/2777 (NI.18) Art.35, Sch.5
Art.57, amended: SI 1997/2777 (NI.18) Art.35, Sch.4 para.11
Art.57, revoked (in part): SI 1997/2777 (NI.18) Art.35, Sch.5
Art.58, amended: SI 1997/2777 (NI.18) Art.35, Sch.4 para.12
Art.58, revoked (in part): SI 1997/2777 (NI.18) Art.35, Sch.5
Art.63, revoked (in part): SI 1997/2777 (NI.18) Art.35, Sch.5
Art.64, amended: SI 1999/662 (NI.6) Art.63, Sch.8 Part II
Art.82, revoked (in part): SI 1997/2777 (NI.18) Art.35, Sch.5
Art.85, revoked: SI 1997/2778 (NI.19) Art.83, Sch.6
Art.86, revoked (in part): SI 1997/2778 (NI.19) Art.83, Sch.6
Part II, applied: SI 1997/2777 (NI.18) Art.28, SI 1997/2778 (NI.19) Art.47
Part III, applied: SI 1997/2777 (NI.18) Art.7
Part IV, applied: SI 1997/2777 (NI.18) Art.7
Sch.3 para.1, revoked: SI 1999/662 (NI.6) Art.63, Sch.8 Part II
Sch.3 para.2, revoked: SI 1999/662 (NI.6) Art.63, Sch.8 Part II
Sch.3 para.3, revoked: SI 1999/662 (NI.6) Art.63, Sch.8 Part II
Sch.4 para.3, revoked: SI 1997/2777 (NI.18) Art.35, Sch.5
Sch.4 para.4, revoked: SI 1997/2777 (NI.18) Art.35, Sch.5
Sch.6 para.3, revoked: SI 1997/2777 (NI.18) Art.35, Sch.5

1050. Rent (Northern Ireland) Order 1978
applied: SI 1998/1071 (NI.6) Art.4
referred to: SI 1996/725 (NI.5) Art.4, Art.11

NO.

1050. Rent (Northern Ireland) Order 1978—*cont.*
Art.12, revoked (in part): SI 1996/725 (NI.5)
Sch.4
Art.14, amended: SI 1998/1071 (NI.6) Art.41,
Sch.3
Art.28, referred to: SI 1996/1298 (NI.8) Sch.3
Sch.1 para.1, referred to: SI 1998/1071 (NI.6)
Sch.2 para.8
Sch.1 para.2, referred to: SI 1998/1071 (NI.6)
Sch.2 para.8
Sch.1 para.3, referred to: SI 1998/1071 (NI.6)
Sch.2 para.8
Sch.1 para.4, referred to: SI 1998/1071 (NI.6)
Sch.2 para.8
Sch.1 para.6, referred to: SI 1998/1071 (NI.6)
Sch.2 para.8
Sch.1 para.7, referred to: SI 1998/1071 (NI.6)
Sch.2 para.8
Sch.1 para.8, referred to: SI 1998/1071 (NI.6)
Sch.2 para.8
Sch.1 para.9, referred to: SI 1998/1071 (NI.6)
Sch.2 para.8
Sch.5, applied: SI 1999/680 Art.2, Sch. Part I
Sch.8 para.7, revoked (in part): SI 1996/725
(NI.5) Sch.4

1091. Safety of Sports Grounds (Designation) Order 1978
Sch., revoked (in part): SI 1997/1676 Art.3

1096. State Awards Regulations 1978
Reg.1, applied: SI 1999/1494 Reg.12
Reg.7, applied: SI 1998/1166 Reg.12
Reg.7, referred to: SI 1997/431 Reg.12

1099. Safety of Sports Grounds (Designation) (Scotland) Order 1978
revoked: SI 1998/1601 Art.3, Sch.2

1105. European Space Agency (Immunities and Privileges) Order 1978
Art.13A, added: SI 1999/2034 Art.2, Sch.

1126. Factories (Standards of Lighting) (Revocation) Regulations 1978
revoked: SI 1998/2306 Reg.39, Sch.4

1145. Direct Grant Schools (Amendment) Regulations 1978
revoked: SI 1998/86 Reg.2, Sch.1

1211. Pensions Increase (Annual Review) Order 1978
applied: SI 1997/634 Art.3, SI 1998/503 Art.3,
Art.4, SI 1999/522 Art.3

1246. Borough of Allerdale (Electoral Arrangements) Order 1978
revoked: SI 1998/2569 Art.7

1277. New Forest (Confirmation of the Byelaws of the Verderers of the New Forest) Order 1978
revoked: SI 1999/2134 Art.3

1284. Qualifications of Directors of Social Work (Scotland) Regulations 1978
revoked: SI 1996/515 Reg.4

1299. Borough of Erewash (Electoral Arrangements) Order 1978
revoked: SI 1999/2694 Art.4

1357. Prosecution of Offences Regulations 1978
revoked: SI 1997/739 Reg.2

1372. Perambulators and Pushchairs (Safety) Regulations 1978
revoked: SI 1997/2866 Reg.1

1376. Trelewis Drift Mine (Diesel Vehicles) Regulations 1978
Reg.4, revoked: SI 1996/192 Reg.20, Sch.15
Part III
Reg.5, revoked: SI 1996/192 Reg.20, Sch.15
Part III

NO.

1376. Trelewis Drift Mine (Diesel Vehicles) Regulations 1978—*cont.*
Reg.6, revoked: SI 1996/192 Reg.20, Sch.15
Part III

1407. Theft (Northern Ireland) Order 1978
Art.3, amended: SI 1997/277 (NI.3) Art.6
Art.3, applied: SI 1996/3160 (NI.24) Art.38
Art.4, applied: SI 1996/3160 (NI.24) Art.38

1420. Coffee and Coffee Products Regulations 1978
amended: SI 1999/1136 Reg.14
referred to: SI 1996/1499 Reg.4
Reg.5, amended: SI 1996/1499 Reg.49
Reg.6, amended: SI 1996/1499 Reg.49

1437. Borough of Macclesfield (Electoral Arrangements) Order 1978
revoked: SI 1998/2847 Art.8

1465. Borough of Copeland (Electoral Arrangements) Order 1978
revoked: SI 1998/2570 Art.7

1483. Brucellosis and Tuberculosis (England and Wales) Compensation Order 1978
applied: SI 1998/3070 Reg.5
Art.3, amended: SI 1996/1352 Art.2, SI 1998/
2073 Art.2
Art.6, added: SI 1996/1352 Art.2

1485. Brucellosis and Tuberculosis (Scotland) Compensation Order 1978
applied: SI 1998/3070 Reg.5
Art.3, amended: SI 1996/1358 Art.2, SI 1998/
2181 Art.2
Art.6, added: SI 1996/1358 Art.2

1494. District of Bolsover (Electoral Arrangements) Order 1978
revoked: SI 1999/2691 Art.11

1524. State Immunity (Merchant Shipping) (Union of Soviet Socialist Republics) Order 1978
see *Guiseppe di Vittorio* [1998] 1 Lloyd's Rep.
136 (CA), Evans, L.J.; see *Guiseppe di Vittorio (No.2), The* [1998] 1 Lloyd's Rep. 661
(QBD (Adm Ct)), Clarke, J.
revoked: SI 1997/2591 Art.4

1535. Control of Off-Street Parking (England and Wales) Order 1978
Art.2, amended: SI 1996/1008 Art.2, Sch para.3

1548. 70 miles per hour, 60 miles per hour and 50 miles per hour (Temporary Speed Limit) (Continuation) Order 1978
Art.2, amended: SI 1997/2281 Art.3

1552. Borough of Chesterfield (Electoral Arrangements) Order 1978
revoked: SI 1999/2692 Art.5

1591. District of The Wrekin (Electoral Arrangements) Order 1978
applied: SI 1996/1866 Art.7

1611. District of Amber Valley (Electoral Arrangements) Order 1978
revoked: SI 1999/2690 Art.8

1623. Israel (Extradition) (Amendment) Order 1978
revoked (in part): SI 1996/2875 Art.3, Sch.3

1640. District of Wokingham (Electoral Arrangements) Order 1978
Art.6, substituted: SI 1996/1879 Art.14
Sch.2, substituted: SI 1996/1879 Art.14

1644. Licensing (Fees) Order 1978
Sch., amended: SI 1996/1063 Art.2, SI 1997/
2501 Art.2, SI 1998/115 Art.2

1664. Borough of Northampton (Electoral Arrangements) Order 1978
revoked: SI 1998/2511 Art.6

NO.

1978—cont.

1665. District of South Lakeland (Electoral Arrangements) Order 1978
revoked: SI 1998/2548 Art.9

1682. Justices of the Peace Act 1949 (Compensation) Regulations 1978
referred to: 1997 c.25 s.73, Sch.4 para.20

1689. Social Security (Categorisation of Earners) Regulations 1978
applied: SI 1998/1728 Reg.5
Reg.1, amended: SI 1998/1728 Reg.2
Sch.1 para.2, revoked (in part): SI 1998/1728 Reg.3
Sch.1 para.5A, added: SI 1998/1728 Reg.3
Sch.3 para.10, added: SI 1998/1728 Reg.4

1690. City of Durham (Electoral Arrangements) Order 1978
revoked: SI 1999/2579 Art.4

1698. Social Security Benefit (Computation of Earnings) Regulations 1978
applied: SI 1996/2745 Reg.18
revoked: SI 1996/2745 Reg.18, Sch.4
Reg.2, applied: SI 1996/2570 Reg.14
Reg.3, amended: SI 1996/1345 Reg.11
Reg.3, applied: SI 1996/2567 Reg.11, Reg.14
Reg.3, revoked: SI 1996/2745 Reg.18, Sch.4
Reg.4, applied: SI 1996/2570 Reg.14
Reg.6, applied: SI 1996/2745 Reg.16
Reg.6, revoked: SI 1996/2745 Reg.18, Sch.4

1723. Compressed Acetylene (Importation) Regulations 1978
applied: SI 1996/2791 Sch.9 Part I
referred to: SI 1997/2505 Reg.10, Sch.9 Part I, SI 1999/645 Reg.10, Sch.9 Part I
revoked: SI 1996/2092 Reg.21, Sch.7

1727. Fire Services (Appointments and Promotion) (Scotland) Regulations 1978
Reg.4, amended: SI 1997/1437 Reg.3
Reg.5, amended: SI 1997/1437 Reg.4
Reg.5, revoked (in part): SI 1997/1437 Reg.4
Reg.6, amended: SI 1996/2091 Reg.2

1750. City of Lincoln (Electoral Arrangements) Order 1978
revoked: SI 1998/2334 Art.4

1751. District of Torridge (Electoral Arrangements) Order 1978
revoked: SI 1999/2472 Art.5

1768. District of North East Derbyshire (Electoral Arrangements) Order 1978
revoked: SI 1999/2696 Art.9

1783. City of St Albans (Electoral Arrangements) Order 1978
revoked: SI 1998/2558 Art.9

1793. City of Plymouth (Electoral Arrangements) Order 1978
applied: SI 1996/1865 Art.7

1827. Contracted-out Employment (Miscellaneous Provisions) (No.2) Regulations 1978
Reg.3, revoked: SI 1997/358 Reg.7, Sch

1842. District of East Devon (Electoral Arrangements) Order 1978
revoked: SI 1999/2467 Art.6

1859. District of Easington (Electoral Arrangements) Order 1978
revoked: SI 1999/2581 Art.9

1863. Borough of Sefton (Electoral Arrangements) Order 1978
revoked: SI 1999/2782 Art.4

1893. International Lead and Zinc Study Group (Immunities and Privileges) Order 1978
Art.12A, added: SI 1999/2034 Art.2, Sch.

NO.

1978—cont.

1907. Health and Personal Social Services (Northern Ireland) Order 1978
Art.8, applied: SI 1998/5 Reg.5, Reg.8, SI 1997/1177 (NI.7) Art.4, Art.12, SI 1997/2817 Reg.5, Reg.8
Part II, referred to: SI 1997/1177 (NI.7) Art.12

1908. Rehabilitation of Offenders (Northern Ireland) Order 1978
applied: SI 1996/3159 (NI.23) Art.5, Art.8, 1997 c.50 s.126, 1998 c.29 s.56, SI 1998/1859 r.5
referred to: 1997 c.50 s.133
Art.2, revoked (in part): SI 1996/3160 (NI.24) Sch.7
Art.3, amended: SI 1996/1299 (NI.9) Art.57, Sch.3 para.4
Art.4, referred to: SI 1996/2474 Sch
Art.4, revoked (in part): 1996 c.46 s.14, Sch.7 Part III
Art.6, amended: SI 1998/1504 (NI.9) Art.65, Sch.5 para.11, Sch.6
Art.6, revoked (in part): SI 1998/1504 (NI.9) Art.65, Sch.6
Art.7, amended: 1996 c.46 s.14
Art.7, referred to: SI 1996/2474 Sch
Art.7, revoked (in part): 1996 c.46 s.14, Sch.7 Part III
Art.9, amended: 1996 c.31 s.14
Art.16, applied: SI 1996/1320 (NI.10) Art.64, Art.82
Art.30, applied: SI 1996/1320 (NI.10) Art.64, Art.82
Art.31, applied: SI 1996/1320 (NI.10) Art.64, Art.82
Art.50, applied: SI 1996/1320 (NI.10) Art.64, Art.82

1909. Shops (Northern Ireland) Order 1978
revoked: SI 1997/2779 (NI.20) Sch.3

1979

Scheme for the Administration of the Strathclyde Schools Orchestra Trust 1979
amended: SI 1996/629 Sch
Territorial Waters (Amendment) Order in Council 1979
referred to: SI 1999/1043 Art.2
revoked: SI 1996/1628 Art.4

47. Teachers' Superannuation (Policy Schemes) Regulations 1979
Reg.4, applied: SI 1997/3001 Reg.E27, Reg.E28, Reg.E32, Reg.H2

72. Isles of Scilly (Functions) Order 1979
referred to: 1999 c.28 s.40, Sch.5 para.22

82. Dick Bequest Trust Scheme 1979
amended: SI 1996/478 Sch

98. New Town (Stonehouse) Revocation of Designation) (Compensation) Regulations 1979
applied: SI 1999/1750 Art.2, Sch.1

112. General Medical Council (Constitution) Order 1979
Art.2, amended: SI 1996/1630 Art.2
Art.4, referred to: SI 1996/1630 Art.3
Art.5, amended: SI 1996/1630 Art.2
Sch., substituted: SI 1996/1630 Art.2

186. Social Security (Contributions) Regulations (Northern Ireland) 1979
applied: 1999 c.30 s.81, Sch.11 para.36, SI 1999/671 Art.3, Sch.2, SI 1999/3219 Reg.3

NO.

NO.

1979—cont.

186. Social Security (Contributions) Regulations (Northern Ireland) 1979—cont.
Reg.36, referred to: SI 1999/671 Art.3, Sch.2
Reg.37, referred to: SI 1999/671 Art.3, Sch.2
Reg.38, referred to: SI 1999/671 Art.3, Sch.2
Reg.39, referred to: SI 1999/671 Art.3, Sch.2
Reg.44, referred to: 1999 c.30 s.81, Sch.11 para.36
Sch.1 Reg.28D, substituted: SI 1999/1966 Reg.2

236. Control of Off-Street Parking outside Greater London (Appeals Procedure) (England and Wales) Regulations 1979
Reg.2, amended: SI 1996/1008 Art.2, Sch para.4

264. Juries (Divisional Jurors Lists) Regulations (Northern Ireland) 1979
Reg.4, revoked: SI 1996/1141 (NI.6) s.32, Sch.5
Reg.6, revoked: SI 1996/1141 (NI.6) s.32, Sch.5
Reg.7, revoked (in part): SI 1996/1141 (NI.6) s.32, Sch.5

290. Social Security (Reciprocal Agreements) Order 1979
Sch., amended: SI 1996/1927 Art.3, SI 1997/871 Art.3

359. Social Security (Overlapping Benefits and Miscellaneous Amendments) Regulations 1979
Reg.8, revoked: SI 1996/2745 Reg.18, Sch.4

383. Coffee and Coffee Products (Scotland) Regulations 1979
amended: SI 1999/1136 Reg.14
Reg.5, amended: SI 1996/1499 Reg.49
Reg.6, amended: SI 1996/1499 Reg.49

386. Traffic Signs Regulations (Northern Ireland) 1979
Reg.7, applied: SI 1996/1320 (NI.10) Sch.1 Part II

432. Vaccine Damage Payment Regulations 1979
Part III, revoked: SI 1999/991 Reg.59 (with savings), Sch.4 (with savings)
Part IV, substituted: SI 1999/2677 Reg.4
Reg.1, amended: SI 1999/2677 Reg.2
Reg.4, amended: SI 1999/2677 Reg.3
Reg.11, substituted: SI 1999/2677 Reg.4
Reg.12, substituted: SI 1999/2677 Reg.4

446. Act of Sederunt (Appeals under the Rating (Disabled Persons) Act 1978) 1979
revoked: SI 1999/929 r.1.3, Sch.2

453. Extradition (Internationally Protected Persons) Order 1979
revoked: SI 1997/1764 Art.4

491. Merchant Shipping (Crew Accommodation) (Amendment) Regulations 1979
revoked: SI 1997/1508 Reg.1

521. European Parliamentary Election Petition Rules 1979
r.2, amended: SI 1999/1398 r.2
r.5, amended: SI 1999/1398 r.3
r.6, amended: SI 1999/1398 r.4
r.7, amended: SI 1999/1398 r.5
r.9, amended: SI 1999/1398 r.6
r.11, amended: SI 1999/1398 r.7
r.12, amended: SI 1999/1398 r.8
r.13, amended: SI 1999/1398 r.9
r.14, amended: SI 1999/1398 r.10
r.16, amended: SI 1999/1398 r.11
r.18, amended: SI 1999/1398 r.12

1979—cont.

570. Justices' Clerks (Qualification of Assistants) Rules 1979
r.2, amended: SI 1998/3107 r.4, r.5, r.6
r.2A, added: SI 1999/2814 r.3
r.4, revoked (in part): SI 1998/3107 r.5
r.4A, added: SI 1999/2814 r.4
r.5, substituted: SI 1998/3107 r.7
Sch.1, revoked: SI 1998/3107 r.5
Sch.2, revoked: SI 1998/3107 r.5
Sch.3, revoked: SI 1998/3107 r.6

591. Social Security (Contributions) Regulations 1979
applied: 1999 c.2 s.1, Sch.2, 1999 c.30 s.81, Sch.11 para.35, SI 1999 3219 Reg.3
Part IIB, added: SI 1999/567 Reg.4
Reg.1, amended: SI 1996/2367 Reg.3, SI 1996/2407 Reg.2, SI 1996/3031 Reg.2, SI 1998/2211 Reg.2, SI 1999/561 Reg.2, SI 1999/568 Reg.2
Reg.2, amended: SI 1996/195 Reg.13
Reg.5A, amended: SI 1996/700 Reg.2, SI 1996/2407 Reg.3
Reg.6, revoked (in part): SI 1996/777 Reg.5
Reg.6A, amended: SI 1998/2211 Reg.3
Reg.7, amended: SI 1996/663 Reg.2, SI 1997/575 Reg.2, SI 1998/523 Reg.2
Reg.7, substituted: SI 1999/568 Reg.3
Reg.8, substituted: SI 1999/568 Reg.4
Reg.8A, revoked: SI 1999/568 Reg.5
Reg.9, amended: SI 1999/568 Reg.6
Reg.13, revoked (in part): SI 1996/777 Reg.5
Reg.17, substituted: SI 1999/568 Reg.7
Reg.17AB, added: SI 1998/2211 Reg.4
Reg.18, amended: SI 1996/3031 Reg.3, SI 1998/2211 Reg.5, SI 1998/2894 Reg.2, SI 1999/561 Reg.3, SI 1999/567 Reg.2, SI 1999/568 Reg.8
Reg.18, revoked (in part): SI 1999/567 Reg.2
Reg.19, amended: SI 1996/700 Reg.3, SI 1996/3031 Reg.4, SI 1997/820 Reg.2, SI 1997/1045 Reg.2, SI 1998/680 Reg.2, SI 1998/2211 Reg.6, SI 1998/2320 Reg.2, SI 1999/561 Reg.4, SI 1999/567 Reg.3, SI 1999/568 Reg.9, SI 1999/2736 Reg.3
Reg.19, referred to: SI 1998/680
Reg.19, revoked (in part): SI 1996/3031 Reg.4, SI 1998/2211 Reg.6, SI 1999/567 Reg.3
Reg.19B, amended: SI 1996/700 Reg.4
Reg.22H, added: SI 1998/2211 Reg.7
Reg.22I, added: SI 1999/567 Reg.4
Reg.22J, added: SI 1999/567 Reg.4
Reg.25, amended: SI 1999/2736 Reg.4
Reg.26, amended: SI 1996/195 Reg.13
Reg.26A, amended: SI 1996/195 Reg.13, SI 1996/2367 Reg.3, SI 1999/827 Reg.2
Reg.28, amended: SI 1999/568 Reg.10
Reg.30, amended: SI 1996/195 Reg.13, SI 1996/777 Reg.5
Reg.30A, amended: SI 1996/195 Reg.13
Reg.30B, added: SI 1996/777 Reg.5
Reg.31, amended: SI 1999/567 Reg.5
Reg.32, amended: SI 1996/1245 Reg.4, SI 1996/2407 Reg.4, SI 1999/567 Reg.6, SI 1999/568 Reg.11
Reg.32, applied: SI 1996/1245 Reg.2
Reg.32A, added: SI 1999/568 Reg.12
Reg.35, amended: SI 1996/2407 Reg.5
Reg.36, amended: SI 1999/568 Reg.13
Reg.36, referred to: 1999 c.2 s.1, Sch.2
Reg.37, referred to: 1999 c.2 s.1, Sch.2
Reg.38, amended: SI 1996/2367 Reg.3
Reg.38, referred to: SI 1997/470 Reg.15, 1999 c.2 s.1, Sch.2

NO.

591. Social Security (Contributions) Regulations 1979—*cont.*

Reg.39, amended: SI 1996/2367 Reg.3
Reg.39, applied: SI 1997/470 Reg.15
Reg.39, referred to: 1999 c.2 s.1, Sch.2
Reg.41, referred to: 1999 c.2 s.1, Sch.2
Reg.41A, referred to: 1999 c.2 s.1, Sch.2
Reg.42, referred to: 1999 c.2 s.1, Sch.2
Reg.44, amended: SI 1999/567 Reg.7
Reg.44, referred to: 1999 c.2 s.1, Sch.2, 1999 c.30 s.81, Sch.11 para.35
Reg.46, amended: SI 1999/567 Reg.8
Reg.47, substituted: SI 1999/975 Reg.2
Reg.47A, added: SI 1999/975 Reg.2
Reg.47B, added: SI 1999/975 Reg.2
Reg.47C, added: SI 1999/975 Reg.2
Reg.47D, added: SI 1999/975 Reg.2
Reg.47E, added: SI 1999/975 Reg.2
Reg.47F, added: SI 1999/975 Reg.2
Reg.47G, added: SI 1999/975 Reg.2
Reg.47H, added: SI 1999/975 Reg.2
Reg.47I, added: SI 1999/975 Reg.2
Reg.47J, added: SI 1999/975 Reg.2
Reg.47K, added: SI 1999/975 Reg.2
Reg.49, amended: SI 1999/568 Reg.14
Reg.61, amended: SI 1999/568 Reg.15
Reg.67, amended: SI 1999/568 Reg.16
Reg.69, amended: SI 1996/2407 Reg.6
Reg.98, amended: SI 1996/486 Reg.2, SI 1996/2367 Reg.3, SI 1997/545 Reg.2, SI 1998/524 Reg.2, SI 1999/361 Reg.2
Reg.115, amended: SI 1996/663 Reg.2
Reg.119, amended: SI 1999/567 Reg.9
Reg.120, amended: SI 1999/567 Reg.10
Reg.121, amended: SI 1999/568 Reg.17
Reg.132, substituted: SI 1999/975 Reg.3
Reg.134, substituted: SI 1999/568 Reg.18
Sch.1, amended: SI 1996/195 Reg.13, SI 1996/2407 Reg.7, SI 1999/567 Reg.11
Sch.1 Part IV, amended: SI 1999/567 Reg.11
Sch.1 Reg.2, amended: SI 1998/2211 Reg.8, SI 1999/568 Reg.19
Sch.1 Reg.13, amended: SI 1999/567 Reg.11, SI 1999/568 Reg.19
Sch.1 Reg.25, amended: SI 1999/568 Reg.19
Sch.1 Reg.26C, amended: SI 1999/567 Reg.11
Sch.1 Reg.26D, amended: SI 1997/820 Reg.3
Sch.1 Reg.28, substituted: SI 1999/567 Reg.11
Sch.1 Reg.28A, amended: SI 1999/567 Reg.11
Sch.1 Reg.28B, substituted: SI 1999/567 Reg.11
Sch.1 Reg.28C, substituted: SI 1999/567 Reg.11
Sch.1 Reg.28D, amended: SI 1999/567 Reg.11
Sch.1 Reg.28D, applied: SI 1999/527 Art.4
Sch.1 Reg.28D, substituted: SI 1999/1965 Reg.2
Sch.1 Reg.30, amended: SI 1999/567 Reg.11, SI 1999/568 Reg.19
Sch.1 Reg.30, revoked (in part): SI 1999/568 Reg.19
Sch.1 Reg.30A, amended: SI 1999/568 Reg.19
Sch.1 Reg.32, amended: SI 1999/567 Reg.11
Sch.1 Reg.34A, added: SI 1996/1047 Reg.2
Sch.1A para.5, amended: SI 1998/2211 Reg.9
Sch.1A para.9A, revoked: SI 1998/2211 Reg.9
Sch.1A para.9C, revoked: SI 1998/2211 Reg.9
Sch.1A para.15, revoked: SI 1998/2211 Reg.9
Sch.1A para.16, amended: SI 1998/2211 Reg.9
Sch.1A para.19, revoked: SI 1996/3031 Reg.5
Sch.1B, added: SI 1998/2211 Reg.10, Sch.
Sch.1C, added: SI 1999/561 Reg.5, Sch.

NO.

591. Social Security (Contributions) Regulations 1979—*cont.*

Sch.3 Part I, applied: SI 1996/207 Reg.18, Reg.53, Sch.6 para.9, SI 1996/2745 Sch.1 para.9, SI 1996/2890 Sch.2 para.8
Sch.3 Part I, referred to: SI 1997/932 Reg.3

597. Social Security (Overlapping Benefits) Regulations 1979

applied: SI 1996/207 Sch.1 para.8, Sch.1 para.17, SI 1996/1623 Art.3, SI 1998/217 Art.2, SI 1999/779 Art.2, Sch.
Reg.2, amended: SI 1996/1345 Reg.22
Reg.4, amended: SI 1996/1345 Reg.22, SI 1996/3207 Reg.4
Reg.8, amended: SI 1996/1803 Reg.47, SI 1999/820 Reg.2, SI 1999/1362 Reg.2
Reg.10, amended: SI 1996/1345 Reg.22
Reg.14, amended: SI 1996/1345 Reg.22
Reg.14, applied: SI 1996/2567 Reg.10
Reg.16, amended: SI 1996/1345 Reg.22
Reg.17, amended: SI 1996/1345 Reg.22
Sch.1 para.1, amended: SI 1996/1345 Reg.22

628. Social Security (Claims and Payments) Regulations 1979

Reg.2, amended: SI 1999/1958 Art.4, Sch.4 para.1
Reg.9, see *R. v Secretary of State for Social Security Ex p. Cullen* Times, May 16, 1997 (CA), Hirst, L.J.
Reg.26, amended: SI 1999/1958 Art.4, Sch.4 para.2
Reg.26, revoked (in part): SI 1999/1958 Art.4, Sch.4 para.2

642. Social Security (Widow's Benefit and Retirement Pensions) Regulations 1979

Reg.1, amended: SI 1999/2422 Art.3, Sch.3 para.1
Reg.1A, added: SI 1997/2676 Reg.15
Reg.3A, added: SI 1998/2231 Reg.7
Reg.4, amended: SI 1996/1345 Reg.26, SI 1999/2422 Art.3, Sch.3 para.2
Reg.16A, added: SI 1997/2676 Reg.15

643. Social Security (Widow's Benefit, Retirement Pensions and Other Benefits) (Transitional) Regulations 1979

Reg.2, amended: SI 1999/2422 Art.3, Sch.4 para.1
Reg.19, revoked (in part): SI 1999/2422 Art.3, Sch.4 para.2

785. Local Government (Compensation for Premature Retirement) (Scotland) Regulations 1979

applied: SI 1996/682 Art.17, SI 1998/192 Reg.52
revoked: SI 1998/192 Reg.52, Sch.2
Reg.5, amended: SI 1996/1360 Reg.14
Reg.5, applied: SI 1996/1360 Reg.8
Reg.5, revoked: SI 1998/192 Reg.52, Sch.2
Reg.14, revoked: SI 1998/192 Reg.52, Sch.2
Sch.1, amended: SI 1996/1241 Reg.3
Sch.1, revoked: SI 1998/192 Reg.52, Sch.2
Sch.1 para.K, revoked: SI 1998/192 Reg.52, Sch.2
Sch.2 Part I, applied: SI 1996/1360 Reg.4
Sch.2 Part I, revoked: SI 1998/192 Reg.52, Sch.2

792. Forestry (Exceptions from Restriction of Felling) Regulations 1979

Reg.3, amended: SI 1996/252 Art.2, Sch
Reg.4, revoked (in part): SI 1998/603 Reg.2

NO.

1979—cont.

911. **INTELSAT (Immunities and Privileges) Order 1979**
Art.11A, added: SI 1999/2032 Art.2
Art.11B, added: SI 1999/2032 Art.2
912. **International Oil Pollution Compensation Fund (Immunities and Privileges) Order 1979**
Art.13A, added: SI 1999/2034 Art.2, Sch.
913. **Norway (Extradition) Order 1979**
revoked (in part): SI 1996/2875 Art.3, Sch.3
914. **Oslo and Paris Commissions (Immunities and Privileges) Order 1979**
Art.11A, added: SI 1999/2034 Art.2, Sch.
921. **Social Security (Portugal) Order 1979**
Sch., amended: SI 1996/1928 Art.2, Sch.1
924. **Inheritance (Provision for Family and Dependants) (Northern Ireland) Order 1979**
Art.3, amended: SI 1996/3163 (NI.26) Art.4
Art.5, amended: SI 1996/3163 (NI.26) Art.4
Art.23, revoked: SI 1997/2983 (NI.21) Art.13, Sch.2
937. **Industrial and Provident Societies (Credit Unions) Regulations 1979**
Reg.16, applied: SI 1999/739 Sch. para.11
Reg.17, revoked: SI 1999/739 Reg.3
Sch.2, substituted: SI 1996/612 Reg.2, SI 1997/742 Reg.2, SI 1998/672 Reg.2
991. **Police (Promotion) Regulations 1979**
revoked: SI 1996/1685 Reg.8, Sch.3
1013. **Transit of Animals (Road and Rail) (Amendment) Order 1979**
revoked: SI 1997/1480 Art.22, Sch.12 Part II
1015. **District of North Wiltshire (Electoral Arrangements) Order 1979**
revoked: SI 1999/2923 Art.10
1016. **Borough of Waverley (Electoral Arrangements) Order 1979**
revoked: SI 1999/2482 Art.9
1026. **Safety of Sports Grounds (Designation) (Scotland) Order 1979**
revoked: SI 1998/1601 Art.3, Sch.2
1047. **Pensions Increase (Review) Order 1979**
applied: SI 1997/634 Art.3, SI 1998/503 Art.3, Art.4, SI 1999/522 Art.3
1088. **Motor Vehicles (Designation of Approval Marks) Regulations 1979**
Reg.4, applied: SI 1997/3053 Reg.13
Sch.2, applied: SI 1997/3053 Reg.13
Sch.2 Item 36B, added: SI 1997/58 Reg.3, Sch.1
Sch.2 Item 36C, added: SI 1997/58 Reg.3, Sch.1
Sch.2 Item 44C, added: SI 1997/58 Reg.3, Sch.1
Sch.2 Item 51, added: SI 1997/58 Reg.3, Sch.1
Sch.2 Item 51A, added: SI 1997/58 Reg.3, Sch.1
Sch.3 para.2A, added: SI 1997/58 Reg.4
Sch.3 para.7, substituted: SI 1997/58 Reg.4
Sch.3 para.17, amended: SI 1997/58 Reg.4
Sch.3 para.17A, added: SI 1997/58 Reg.4
Sch.4 Item 34, added: SI 1997/58 Reg.5, Sch.2
Sch.4 Item 35, added: SI 1997/58 Reg.5, Sch.2
Sch.4 Item 36, added: SI 1997/58 Reg.5, Sch.2
Sch.4 Item 37, added: SI 1997/58 Reg.5, Sch.2
Sch.5 para.16, added: SI 1997/58 Reg.6
Sch.5 para.17, added: SI 1997/58 Reg.6
Sch.5 para.18, added: SI 1997/58 Reg.6
1108. **District of West Wiltshire (Electoral Arrangements) Order 1979**
revoked: SI 1999/2926 Art.9

NO.

1979—cont.

1109. **District of Teesdale (Electoral Arrangements) Order 1979**
revoked: SI 1999/2583 Art.6
1131. **City of Carlisle (Electoral Arrangements) Order 1979**
revoked: SI 1998/2549 Art.6
1181. **Medicines (Phenacetin Prohibition) Order 1979**
revoked: SI 1996/3269 Art.2
1198. **Motor Vehicles (Authorisation of Special Types) General Order 1979**
applied: SI 1996/2186 Sch.3 para.2
Art.16, amended: SI 1998/2249 Art.3
Art.17A, added: SI 1998/2884 Art.2
Sch.5A, added: SI 1998/2884 Art.2, Sch.
Sch.5B, added: SI 1998/2884 Art.2, Sch.
1259. **Police Pensions (War Service) Regulations 1979**
applied: SI 1999/1750 Art.2, Sch.1
1264. **District of Sedgefield (Electoral Arrangements) Order 1979**
revoked: SI 1999/2582 Art.8
1265. **District of Wear Valley (Electoral Arrangements) Order 1979**
revoked: SI 1999/2584 Art.4
1267. **Merchant Shipping (Load Line) (Amendment) Rules 1979**
referred to: SI 1998/1609 Reg.5, Reg.6, Sch.
revoked: SI 1998/2241 Reg.3
1346. **Borough of Reading (Electoral Arrangements) Order 1979**
Art.9, substituted: SI 1996/1879 Art.12
1379. **Taximeters (EEC Requirements) Regulations 1979**
Reg.6, referred to: SI 1998/1177 Reg.4
1415. **District of East Lindsey (Electoral Arrangements) Order 1979**
revoked: SI 1998/2335 Art.7
1447. **Continental Shelf (Designation of Additional Areas) Order 1979**
referred to: SI 1999/2031, SI 1999/2031 Art.2, Sch.
1473. **City of Exeter (Electoral Arrangements) Order 1979**
revoked: SI 1999/2468 Art.4
1474. **City of Leicester (Electoral Arrangements) Order 1979**
applied: SI 1996/507 Art.9
1496. **Borough of Torbay (Electoral Arrangements) Order 1979**
applied: SI 1996/1865 Art.7
1532. **Boulby Mine (Diesel Vehicles) Regulations 1979**
Reg.5, revoked: SI 1996/192 Reg.20, Sch.15 Part III
Reg.6, revoked: SI 1996/192 Reg.20, Sch.15 Part III
Reg.7, revoked: SI 1996/192 Reg.20, Sch.15 Part III
Reg.8, revoked: SI 1996/192 Reg.20, Sch.15 Part III
1552. **Direct Grant Grammar Schools (Cessation of Grant) (Amendment) Regulations 1979**
revoked: SI 1998/86 Reg.2, Sch.1
1573. **Statutory Rules (Northern Ireland) Order 1979**
applied: 1996 c.23 s.91, s.105, 1996 c.vi s.10, 1997 c.24 Sch.3 para.4, 1998 c.32 s.72, 1998 c.39 s.51, 1998 c.42 s.20, 1999 c.2 s.24, 1999 c.28 s.37, SI 1999/671 Art.23, SI 1999/859

NO.

1979—cont.

1573. Statutory Rules (Northern Ireland) Order 1979—cont.
applied:—cont.
Art.5, Art.21, Sch.4 para.4, Sch.4 para.6, Sch.5 para.7
referred to: 1996 c.38 s.2, SI 1996/275 (NI.2) Art.69, SI 1997/869 (NI.6) Art.70, SI 1997/1772 (NI.15) Art.24
Art.4, amended: SI 1999/663 Art.2, Sch.1 para.23
Art.5, amended: SI 1999/663 Art.2, Sch.1 para.23
Art.7, revoked (in part): 1998 c.47 s.100, Sch.15
Art.7A, added: SI 1997/276 (NI.2) Art.74
Art.11, revoked (in part): 1998 c.47 s.100, Sch.15
Sch.1, amended: SI 1996/275 (NI.2) Sch.1 para.6
Sch.1 Part I, amended: SI 1999/283 (NI.1) Art.9, Sch.2, SI 1999/663 Art.2, Sch.1 para.23, SI 1999/859 Art.5, Art.21, Sch.4 para.5, Sch.5 para.6
Sch.1 Part II, amended: 1998 c.47 s.99, Sch.13 para.4, SI 1999/283 (NI.1) Art.9, Sch.2, SI 1999/663 Art.2, Sch.1 para.23
Sch.4 para.14, revoked: 1998 c.47 s.100, Sch.15
Sch.4 para.18, revoked: SI 1998/3162 (NI.21) Art.105, Sch.5

1587. Edinburgh Assay Office Order 1979
referred to: 1996 c.i Sch.

1596. Brucellosis (Scotland) Order 1979
revoked: SI 1997/758 Art.24, Sch.2

1644. National Health Service (Vocational Training) Regulations 1979
revoked: SI 1997/2817 Reg.20, Sch.5
Reg.2, amended: SI 1997/2787 Reg.2
Reg.2, revoked: SI 1997/2817 Reg.20, Sch.5
Reg.5, applied: SI 1997/2817 Reg.21
Reg.5, revoked: SI 1997/2817 Reg.20, Sch.5
Reg.9, applied: SI 1997/2817 Reg.21
Reg.9, revoked: SI 1997/2817 Reg.20, Sch.5
Reg.10, applied: SI 1997/2817 Reg.21
Reg.10, revoked: SI 1997/2817 Reg.20, Sch.5
Reg.11, applied: SI 1997/2817 Reg.21
Reg.11, revoked: SI 1997/2817 Reg.20, Sch.5

1678. Exchange of Securities (General) Rules 1979
r.3, amended: SI 1998/2505 r.3, r.6, SI 1999/1207 r.2
r.4, revoked: SI 1998/2505 r.6
r.5, amended: SI 1998/2505 r.4
r.6, amended: SI 1998/2505 r.3, r.5, SI 1999/1207 r.3

1695. Borough of Wellingborough (Electoral Arrangements) Order 1979
revoked: SI 1998/2510 Art.4

1702. Importation of Birds, Poultry and Hatching Eggs Order 1979
Art.4, applied: SI 1998/190 Reg.34, Sch.6
Art.4, referred to: SI 1998/190 Reg.34, Sch.6
Art.5, referred to: SI 1998/190 Reg.34, Sch.6
Art.6, referred to: SI 1996/3124 Reg.40, Sch.5 Part I, SI 1998/190 Reg.34, Sch.6
Art.7, referred to: SI 1996/3124 Reg.40, Sch.5 Part I, SI 1998/190 Reg.34, Sch.6
Art.8, referred to: SI 1996/3124 Reg.40, Sch.5 Part I
Art.9, referred to: SI 1996/3124 Reg.40, Sch.5 Part I, SI 1998/190 Reg.34, Sch.6
Art.10, referred to: SI 1998/190 Reg.34, Sch.6
Art.11, referred to: SI 1998/190 Reg.34, Sch.6
Art.12, referred to: SI 1998/190 Reg.34, Sch.6

NO.

1979—cont.

1703. Importation of Hay and Straw Order 1979
Art.5, referred to: SI 1996/3124 Reg.40, Sch.5 Part I

1709. Building Regulations (Northern Ireland) Order 1979
applied: SI 1999/3145 Art.4

1714. Perjury (Northern Ireland) Order 1979
referred to: SI 1996/725 (NI.5) Art.28, SI 1996/1299 (NI.9) Sch.2 para.6, SI 1997/1179 (NI.8) Art.43
Art.3, applied: SI 1999/2789 (NI.8) Art.17
Art.3, referred to: SI 1999/2789 (NI.8) Art.19
Art.18, amended: SI 1998/1504 (NI.9) Art.65, Sch.5 para.12
Sch.1 para.9, revoked: SI 1996/725 (NI.5) Sch.4

1746. Passenger and Goods Vehicles (Recording Equipment) Regulations 1979
Reg.1, amended: SI 1996/941 Reg.3

1980

Barking and Dagenham (Restriction on Bus Stops) No.2 Traffic Order 1980
revoked (in part): SI 1996/1896 Art.10
Camden (Bus Lane) (No.1) Traffic Order 1980
revoked (in part): SI 1998/3206 Art.6
Ealing (Waiting and Loading Restriction) (Amendment No.12) Order 1980
revoked (in part): SI 1999/2345 Art.11 (with savings), SI 1999/2349 Art.11 (with savings)

6. Insurance Companies (Accounts and Statements) Regulations 1980
applied: SI 1996/943 Reg.29

12. Importation of Embryos, Ova and Semen Order 1980
referred to: SI 1998/190 Reg.34, Sch.6
Art.4, applied: SI 1998/190 Reg.34, Sch.6

14. Importation of Animal Products and Poultry Products Order 1980
referred to: SI 1997/322 Reg.36
Art.5, referred to: SI 1996/3124 Reg.40, Sch.5 Part I
Art.6, referred to: SI 1996/3124 Reg.40, Sch.5 Part I
Art.7, referred to: SI 1996/3124 Reg.40, Sch.5 Part I

30. National Health Service (Vocational Training) (Scotland) Regulations 1980
referred to: SI 1998/5 Reg.19, Sch.4
revoked: SI 1998/5 Reg.19, Sch.4
Reg.4, revoked: SI 1998/5 Reg.19, Sch.4
Reg.8, revoked: SI 1998/5 Reg.19, Sch.4
Reg.9, applied: SI 1998/5 Reg.20
Reg.9, revoked: SI 1998/5 Reg.19, Sch.4
Reg.10, applied: SI 1998/5 Reg.20
Reg.10, revoked: SI 1998/5 Reg.19, Sch.4
Reg.11, applied: SI 1998/5 Reg.20
Reg.11, revoked: SI 1998/5 Reg.19, Sch.4

40. Colonel Maclean Trust Scheme 1980
amended: SI 1996/629 Sch

43. District of the Forest of Dean (Electoral Arrangements) Order 1980
Sch., amended: SI 1997/179 Art.5

51. Consumer Credit (Total Charge for Credit) Regulations 1980
applied: SI 1996/1812 Reg.7, SI 1998/2003 Reg.11, SI 1998/2026 Reg.11, SI 1999/496 Reg.26, SI 1999/1001 Reg.15
referred to: SI 1997/1675 Reg.7
Reg.1, amended: SI 1999/3177 Reg.3

NO.

1980—cont.

51. **Consumer Credit (Total Charge for Credit) Regulations 1980**—*cont.*
    Reg.2, see *Scarborough Building Society v Humberside Trading Standards Department* [1997] C.C.L.R. 47 (QBD), Staughton, L.J.
    Reg.2, amended: SI 1999/3177 Reg.3
    Reg.4, see *Humberclyde Finance Ltd v Thompson (t/a AG Thompson)* [1997] C.C.L.R. 23 (CA), Aldous, L.J.
    Reg.4, amended: SI 1999/3177 Reg.3
    Reg.5, amended: SI 1999/3177 Reg.3
    Reg.6, amended: SI 1999/3177 Reg.3
    Reg.6A, added: SI 1999/3177 Reg.3
    Reg.7, revoked: SI 1999/3177 Reg.3
    Reg.7, substituted: SI 1999/3177 Reg.3
    Reg.8, revoked: SI 1999/3177 Reg.3
    Reg.9, revoked: SI 1999/3177 Reg.3
    Reg.10, revoked: SI 1999/3177 Reg.3
    Reg.11, amended: SI 1999/3177 Reg.3
    Reg.15, amended: SI 1999/3177 Reg.3
    Reg.15A, amended: SI 1999/3177 Reg.3

62. **Insurance Brokers Registration Council Election Scheme Approval Order 1980**
    revoked: SI 1999/3030 Art.2
    Sch., applied: SI 1999/3030 Sch. para.5
    Sch., revoked: SI 1999/3030 Sch. para.1

79. **Enzootic Bovine Leukosis Order 1980**
    revoked: SI 1997/757 Art.15, Sch.3
    Art.3, revoked: SI 1997/757 Art.15, Sch.3
    Art.4, revoked: SI 1997/757 Art.15, Sch.3
    Art.5, revoked: SI 1997/757 Art.15, Sch.3
    Art.5A, revoked: SI 1997/757 Art.15, Sch.3

108. **Magistrates' Courts (Reciprocal Enforcement of Maintenance Orders) (Hague Convention Countries) Rules 1980**
    r.4A, amended: SI 1999/2002 r.2
    Sch.2 Part II, amended: SI 1999/2002 r.3, r.4

178. **Church Representation Rules (Amendment) Resolution 1980**
    referred to: SI 1998/319, SI 1999/2112

181. **District of North Devon (Electoral Arrangements) Order 1980**
    revoked: SI 1999/2469 Art.8

187. **INMARSAT (Immunities and Privileges) Order 1980**
    revoked: SI 1999/1125 Art.3

291. **Act of Sederunt (Reciprocal Enforcement of Maintenance Orders) (Hague Convention Countries) 1980**
    Part III, revoked: SI 1997/291 r.1.4, Sch.2
    r.2, amended: SI 1997/291 r.1.4, Sch.2
    r.3, revoked (in part): SI 1997/291 r.1.4, Sch.2
    r.4, amended: SI 1997/291 r.1.4, Sch.2
    r.4, revoked (in part): SI 1997/291 r.1.4, Sch.2

297. **City of Bristol (Electoral Arrangements) Order 1980**
    revoked: SI 1998/2699 Art.4
    Art.9, revoked: SI 1998/2699 Art.4

346. **Rules of the Supreme Court (Northern Ireland) 1980**
    Ord. 92,
        r.3A, amended: SI 1998/1129 Art.2, Sch.1 para.3
    Ord. 93,
        r.8, amended: SI 1998/1129 Art.2, Sch.1 para.3

362. **National Health Service (Superannuation) Regulations 1980**
    applied: SI 1997/1613 Reg.23
    Reg.8, applied: SI 1996/177 Reg.10
    Reg.14A, see *R. v Department of Health Ex p. Misra* [1996] 1 F.L.R. 128 (QBD), Latham, J.

NO.

1980—cont.

362. **National Health Service (Superannuation) Regulations 1980**—*cont.*
    Reg.54, applied: SI 1997/3001 Sch.10 para.37
    Reg.55, applied: SI 1997/3001 Sch.10 para.37
    Reg.56, see *Department of Health v Pensions Ombudsman* [1998] 4 All E.R. 508 (CA), Nourse, L.J.

397. **County Courts (Northern Ireland) Order 1980**
    applied: 1997 c.66 Sch.3 para.11
    Art.3, referred to: SI 1998/1071 (NI.6) Art.34, Art.39
    Art.10, applied: 1999 c.2 s.4, Sch.4 para.3
    Art.12, applied: SI 1996/725 (NI.5) Art.37
    Art.30, amended: 1996 c.23 Sch.3 para.36
    Art.31, revoked (in part): 1996 c.23 Sch.4
    Art.33, amended: SI 1998/3162 (NI.21) Art.40
    Art.33, applied: SI 1997/869 (NI.6) Art.54, SI 1998/3162 (NI.21) Art.40
    Art.42A, added: SI 1996/277 (NI.3) Art.3
    Art.42B, added: SI 1996/277 (NI.3) Art.3
    Art.42C, added: SI 1996/277 (NI.3) Art.3
    Art.60, applied: SI 1998/1071 (NI.6) Art.39
    Art.60, referred to: SI 1996/3159 (NI.23) Art.48
    Art.61, applied: SI 1996/1320 (NI.10) Art.45, SI 1996/3158 (NI.22) Art.83, SI 1996/3159 (NI.23) Art.48
    Art.61, referred to: SI 1996/3159 (NI.23) Art.48, SI 1998/1071 (NI.6) Art.34, Art.39
    Art.61A, added: 1996 c.23 Sch.3 para.36
    Art.62, applied: SI 1996/3158 (NI.22) Art.83, SI 1996/3159 (NI.23) Art.48
    Art.65, applied: SI 1996/3158 (NI.22) Art.83
    Art.65, referred to: SI 1996/3159 (NI.23) Art.48
    Part III, amended: 1999 c.2 s.4, Sch.4 para.3
    Part III, applied: SI 1998/1071 (NI.6) Art.39, 1999 c.2 s.4, Sch.4 para.3
    Part III, referred to: SI 1996/3159 (NI.23) Art.48
    Sch.1 Part II, revoked (in part): SI 1996/725 (NI.5) Sch.4, SI 1996/1297 (NI.7) Art.23, Sch.5, SI 1997/2983 (NI.21) Art.13, Sch.2

423. **Act of Sederunt (Reciprocal Maintenance Orders (America)) Rules 1980**
    revoked: SI 1997/291 r.1.4, Sch.2

429. **Borough of Slough (Electoral Arrangements) Order 1980**
    Art.9, substituted: SI 1996/1879 Art.13

456. **HMSO Trading Fund Order 1980**
    referred to: SI 1996/2483
    revoked: SI 1996/2483 Art.2

534. **Merchant Shipping (Navigational Warnings) Regulations 1980**
    revoked: SI 1996/1815 Reg.1

535. **Merchant Shipping (Passenger Ship Construction) Regulations 1980**
    applied: SI 1996/3243 Sch Part I, SI 1997/1510 Reg.11
    revoked: SI 1998/2514 Reg.1
    Reg.10, applied: SI 1997/647 Reg.6
    Reg.10, revoked: SI 1998/2514 Reg.1
    Reg.11, amended: SI 1997/647 Reg.3
    Reg.11, referred to: SI 1997/647 Reg.6
    Reg.11, revoked: SI 1998/2514 Reg.1
    Reg.11A, amended: SI 1997/647 Reg.3
    Reg.11A, revoked: SI 1998/2514 Reg.1
    Reg.128, applied: SI 1998/1011 Reg.44
    Reg.128, revoked: SI 1998/2514 Reg.1
    Reg.131, applied: SI 1998/1011 Reg.44
    Reg.131, revoked: SI 1998/2514 Reg.1

538. **Merchant Shipping (Life-Saving Appliances) Regulations 1980**
    applied: SI 1996/3243 Sch Part I, SI 1998/2070 Reg.3, Reg.11, SI 1999/2723 Reg.4

1980—cont.

538. Merchant Shipping (Life-Saving Appliances) Regulations 1980—cont.
referred to: SI 1998/1609 Reg.5, Reg.6, Sch., SI 1998/2771 Reg.4, Reg.5, Sch.1, Sch.2
revoked: SI 1999/2721 Reg.1
Reg.1, revoked: SI 1999/2721 Reg.1
Sch.15 Part III, revoked: SI 1999/2721 Reg.1

544. Merchant Shipping (Fire Appliances) Regulations 1980
applied: SI 1996/3243 Sch Part I
referred to: SI 1998/1609 Reg.5, Reg.6, Sch.
revoked: SI 1998/1012 Reg.1
Reg.1, revoked: SI 1998/1012 Reg.1
Reg.10A, revoked: SI 1998/1012 Reg.1
Reg.33, revoked: SI 1998/1012 Reg.1
Reg.37A, revoked: SI 1998/1012 Reg.1
Reg.44, revoked: SI 1998/1012 Reg.1
Reg.46, revoked: SI 1998/1012 Reg.1
Reg.51, revoked: SI 1998/1012 Reg.1
Reg.51A, revoked: SI 1998/1012 Reg.1
Reg.51B, revoked: SI 1998/1012 Reg.1
Reg.68, revoked: SI 1998/1012 Reg.1
Reg.76, revoked: SI 1998/1012 Reg.1

561. Bankruptcy Amendment (Northern Ireland) Order 1980
Art.28, referred to: SI 1996/1299 (NI.9) Sch.4 para.2
Art.30, referred to: SI 1996/1299 (NI.9) Sch.4 para.2
Art.31, amended: SI 1996/1299 (NI.9) Art.57, Sch.3 para.6

563. Domestic Proceedings (Northern Ireland) Order 1980
applied: SI 1998/1071 (NI.6) Art.41, Sch.4 para.6
Art.2, revoked (in part): SI 1998/1071 (NI.6) Art.41, Sch.5
Art.11, applied: 1998 c.29 Sch.12 para.6
Art.18, applied: SI 1998/1071 (NI.6) Art.41, Sch.4 para.2, Sch.4 para.4
Art.18, revoked: SI 1998/1071 (NI.6) Art.41, Sch.5
Art.19, revoked: SI 1998/1071 (NI.6) Art.41, Sch.5
Art.21, applied: SI 1998/1071 (NI.6) Art.41, Sch.4 para.2, Sch.4 para.4
Art.21, revoked: SI 1998/1071 (NI.6) Art.41, Sch.5
Art.30, revoked (in part): SI 1998/1071 (NI.6) Art.41, Sch.5
Art.31, revoked (in part): SI 1998/1071 (NI.6) Art.41, Sch.5
Art.33, revoked (in part): SI 1998/1071 (NI.6) Art.41, Sch.5
Sch.1, revoked: SI 1998/1071 (NI.6) Art.41, Sch.5
Sch.3 para.10, revoked: SI 1998/1504 (NI.9) Art.65, Sch.6
Sch.3 para.12, revoked: SI 1998/1071 (NI.6) Art.41, Sch.5

637. Goods Vehicles (Operators' Licences) (Temporary Use in Great Britain) Regulations 1980
revoked: SI 1996/2186 Reg.2, Sch.1

686. Merchant Shipping (Code of Safe Working Practices) Regulations 1980
applied: SI 1996/3243 Sch Part I
revoked: SI 1998/1838 Reg.1
Reg.1, revoked: SI 1998/1838 Reg.1

1980—cont.

701. Zimbabwe (Independence and Membership of the Commonwealth) (Consequential Provisions) Order 1980
Art.5, revoked: 1998 c.43 s.1, Sch.1 Part IV

703. Dental Qualifications (EEC Recognition) Order 1980
revoked: SI 1998/811 Reg.15 (with saving)

704. Criminal Justice (Northern Ireland) Order 1980
Art.8, amended: SI 1996/1320 (NI.10) Sch.3 para.34
Art.8, applied: SI 1996/1320 (NI.10) Art.29, SI 1996/3160 (NI.24) Art.4, Art.10, Art.13
Art.8, referred to: SI 1996/1320 (NI.10) Art.35, Art.40
Art.9, applied: 1997 c.51 Sch.1 para.3
Art.9, referred to: SI 1999/2789 (NI.8) Art.3
Sch.1 para.34, revoked: SI 1996/3160 (NI.24) Sch.7
Sch.1 para.48, revoked: SI 1998/1504 (NI.9) Art.65, Sch.6
Sch.1 para.58, revoked: 1998 c.32 s.74, Sch.6
Sch.1 para.61, revoked: 1996 c.25 Sch.4 para.36
Sch.1 para.71, revoked: SI 1996/1141 (NI.6) s.32, Sch.5
Sch.1 para.74, revoked: SI 1996/3160 (NI.24) Sch.7
Sch.1 para.75, revoked: SI 1996/3160 (NI.24) Sch.7
Sch.1 para.76, revoked: SI 1996/3160 (NI.24) Sch.7
Sch.1 para.77, revoked: SI 1996/3160 (NI.24) Sch.7
Sch.1 para.78, revoked: SI 1996/3160 (NI.24) Sch.7
Sch.1 para.81, revoked: SI 1996/1141 (NI.6) s.32, Sch.5

706. Double Taxation Relief (Taxes on Estates of Deceased Persons and Inheritances and on Gifts) (Netherlands) Order 1980
Sch., amended: SI 1996/730 Art.2

710. Double Taxation Relief (Taxes on Income) (Finland) Order 1980
Sch., referred to: SI 1996/3166 Art.2

721. Petroleum (Production) (Amendment) Regulations 1980
referred to: 1998 c.17 Sch.1 para.11, Sch.1 para.12, SI 1999/160 Sch.5 para.1

733. Royal Borough of Windsor and Maidenhead (Electoral Arrangements) Order 1980
applied: SI 1996/1879 Art.10

780. Double Taxation Relief (Taxes on Income) (Canadian Dividends and Interest) Regulations 1980
Reg.2, amended: SI 1996/1782 Reg.2

792. Importation of Bees Order 1980
revoked: SI 1997/310 Art.8, Sch

821. Supreme Court Fees Order 1980
revoked: SI 1999/687 Art.8 (with savings), Sch.2 (with savings)
Art.5, amended: SI 1997/2672 Art.3
Art.5, revoked (in part): SI 1996/3191 Art.3, SI 1999/687 Art.8 (with savings), Sch.2 (with savings)
Art.7, see *Scarth, Ex p.* Times, July 8, 1999 (CA), Ward, L.J.
Art.7, revoked: SI 1999/687 Art.8 (with savings), Sch.2 (with savings)
Art.7A, added: SI 1996/3191 Art.4
Art.7A, revoked: SI 1999/687 Art.8 (with savings), Sch.2 (with savings)

NO.

NO.

1980—cont.

821. Supreme Court Fees Order 1980—cont.
Sch., amended: SI 1996/3191 Art.5, Art.6, Art.7, Art.8, Art.9, Art.10, SI 1997/2672 Art.4, Art.5
Sch., revoked: SI 1999/687 Art.8 (with savings), Sch.2 (with savings)

827. Social Security Benefit (Dependency) Amendment (No.2) Regulations 1980
revoked: SI 1996/1345 Reg.27, Sch.

918. Education (Middle Schools) Regulations 1980
applied: SI 1996/889 Reg.37, SI 1997/996 Reg.39

941. General Medical Council (Legal Assessors) Rules 1980
r.1, amended: SI 1997/1861 r.2
r.4, amended: SI 1997/1861 r.3
r.5, amended: SI 1997/1861 r.3

1034. Safety of Sports Grounds (Designation) (Scotland) Order 1980
revoked: SI 1998/1601 Art.3, Sch.2

1060. Supreme Court Fees (Amendment) Order 1980
revoked: SI 1999/687 Art.8 (with savings), Sch.2 (with savings)

1084. Treatment of Offenders (Northern Ireland) Order 1980
Sch.2 para.2, revoked: SI 1998/1504 (NI.9) Art.65, Sch.6
Sch.2 para.3, revoked: SI 1998/1504 (NI.9) Art.65, Sch.6
Sch.2 para.4, revoked: SI 1998/1504 (NI.9) Art.65, Sch.6

1093. Merchant Shipping (Prevention of Pollution) (Intervention) Order 1980
revoked: SI 1997/2568 Art.2
Art.1, revoked (in part): 1997 c.28 Sch.7 Part II, SI 1997/2568 Art.2

1120. Pension Appeal Tribunals (England and Wales) Rules 1980
amended: SI 1998/1201 r.5, r.7
r.2, amended: SI 1998/1201 r.4
r.2, revoked (in part): SI 1998/1201 r.4
r.3, amended: SI 1998/1201 r.4
r.4, amended: SI 1998/1201 r.4
r.5A, added: SI 1998/1201 r.5
r.8, amended: SI 1998/1201 r.4
r.19, amended: SI 1998/1201 r.6
r.20, substituted: SI 1998/1201 r.7
r.21, amended: SI 1998/1201 r.8
r.24, amended: SI 1998/1201 r.9
r.26, amended: SI 1998/1201 r.9
Sch.1, revoked: SI 1998/1201 r.10

1177. National Health Service (Superannuation) (Scotland) Regulations 1980
Reg.10, applied: SI 1996/177 Reg.10
Reg.78, applied: SI 1998/1594 Reg.4, Reg.12

1182. Motor Vehicles (Type Approval) Regulations 1980
applied: SI 1998/2051 Reg.19
Sch.2 Part II, referred to: SI 1998/2051 Reg.19

1205. Chester Water (Capital Powers) Order 1980
revoked: SI 1998/281 Art.4, Sch.2 Part II

1220. National Health Service (General Dental Services) (Scotland) Amendment Regulations 1980
revoked: SI 1996/177 Reg.38, Sch.8

1248. Control of Lead at Work Regulations 1980
applied: SI 1996/2791 Reg.3, Reg.8, Sch.7, SI 1997/2505 Reg.3, Reg.8, Sch.7
revoked: SI 1998/543 Reg.14, Sch.3
Reg.16, applied: 1996 c.18 s.64
Reg.16, revoked: SI 1998/543 Reg.14, Sch.3

1254. Teachers' (Compensation for Premature Retirement) (Scotland) Regulations 1980
applied: SI 1996/682 Art.17, SI 1996/2317 Reg.20
revoked: SI 1996/2317 Reg.20, Sch.5

1279. Motor Cycles (Protective Helmets) Regulations 1980
revoked: SI 1998/1807 Reg.2, Sch.1

1298. Agriculture and Horticulture Development Regulations 1980
applied: SI 1999/672 Art.2, Sch.1

1302. Pensions Increase (Review) Order 1980
applied: SI 1997/634 Art.3, SI 1998/503 Art.3, Art.4, SI 1999/522 Art.3

1375. Housing (Right to Buy) (Designated Rural Areas and Designated Regions) (Wales) Order 1980
Art.1, amended: SI 1996/525 Sch para.9

1413. Land Registration (Scotland) Rules 1980
r.2, amended: SI 1998/3100 r.2
r.24, substituted: SI 1998/3100 r.3
r.24A, added: SI 1998/3100 r.4

1443. Act of Sederunt (Social Work) (Sheriff Court Procedure Rules Amendment) 1980
revoked: SI 1997/291 r.1.4, Sch.2

1471. Safety Signs Regulations 1980
amended: SI 1996/341 Reg.8, Sch.3 Part I

1474. Harworth Mine (Cable Reel Load-Haul-Dump Vehicles) Regulations 1980
Reg.4, revoked: SI 1996/192 Reg.20, Sch.15 Part III
Reg.5, revoked: SI 1996/192 Reg.20, Sch.15 Part III
Reg.6, revoked: SI 1996/192 Reg.20, Sch.15 Part III
Reg.7, revoked: SI 1996/192 Reg.20, Sch.15 Part III
Reg.8, revoked: SI 1996/192 Reg.20, Sch.15 Part III
Reg.9, revoked: SI 1996/192 Reg.20, Sch.15 Part III

1543. Licensing (Fees) (Variation) Order 1980
revoked: SI 1997/2501 Art.4

1647. Housing (Forms) (Scotland) Regulations 1980
Form 2, amended: SI 1996/632 Reg.2
Form 3, amended: SI 1996/632 Reg.2

1673. Brucellosis (Scotland) (Amendment) Order 1980
revoked: SI 1997/758 Art.24, Sch.2

1676. Town and Country Planning (Inquiries Procedure) (Scotland) Rules 1980
revoked: SI 1997/796 (with savings)
r.2, see *London and Midland Developments v Secretary of State for Scotland* 1996 S.C.L.R. 465 (IH)
r.2, revoked: SI 1997/796 (with savings)
r.13, see *London and Midland Developments v Secretary of State for Scotland* 1996 S.C.L.R. 465 (IH)
r.13, revoked: SI 1997/796 (with savings)

1677. Town and Country Planning Appeals (Determination by Appointed Person) (Inquiries Procedure) (Scotland) Rules 1980
revoked: SI 1997/750 r.25 (with savings)
r.3, amended: SI 1996/252 Art.2, Sch

1705. Point of Ayr Mine (Diesel Vehicles) Regulations 1980
Reg.5, revoked: SI 1996/192 Reg.20, Sch.15 Part III
Reg.6, revoked: SI 1996/192 Reg.20, Sch.15 Part III

NO.

1980—cont.

1709. Control of Pollution (Special Waste) Regulations 1980
revoked: SI 1996/972 Reg.26
Reg.2, referred to: SI 1997/257 Reg.2
Reg.4, see *Shanks & McEwan (Southern Waste Services) Ltd v Environment Agency* [1999] Env. L.R. 138 (QBD), Brian Smedley, J.
Reg.14, applied: SI 1996/972 Reg.16

1732. Act of Sederunt (Maintenance Orders Acts, Rules) 1980
revoked: SI 1997/291 r.1.4, Sch.2

1759. Offshore Installations (Well Control) Regulations 1980
revoked: SI 1996/913 Reg.27, Sch.3

1848. Wireless Telegraphy (Exemption) Regulations 1980
revoked: SI 1999/930 Reg.2, Sch.1

1861. Direct Grant Schools (Amendment) Regulations 1980
revoked: SI 1998/86 Reg.2, Sch.1

1873. Solent Oyster Fishery Order 1980
referred to: SI 1996/828
Art.3, amended: SI 1996/828 Art.3
Art.4, substituted: SI 1996/828 Art.4
Art.5, amended: SI 1996/828 Art.5
Art.6, amended: SI 1996/828 Art.6
Art.6A, added: SI 1996/828 Art.7
Art.7, amended: SI 1996/828 Art.8
Art.9, amended: SI 1996/828 Art.9
Art.10, amended: SI 1996/828 Art.10
Art.19, added: SI 1996/828 Art.11
Art.20, added: SI 1996/828 Art.11

1898. Legal Advice and Assistance Regulations (No.2) 1980
Reg.15, see *Joyce v Kammac (1988) Ltd* [1996] 1 W.L.R. 805 (QBD), Morland, J.

1923. Medicines (Sale or Supply) (Miscellaneous Provisions) Regulations 1980
Reg.1, amended: SI 1997/1831 Reg.2, SI 1998/1045 Reg.3
Reg.2, amended: SI 1998/1045 Reg.3
Reg.3, revoked: SI 1998/1045 Reg.3
Reg.6, amended: SI 1997/1831 Reg.3
Reg.6, applied: SI 1997/1830 Art.8
Reg.7, revoked: SI 1997/1831 Reg.5
Reg.8, amended: SI 1997/2045 Reg.2, SI 1999/644 Reg.2, SI 1999/2510 Reg.2
Reg.9, amended: SI 1997/1831 Reg.6, SI 1998/1045 Reg.3
Sch.2 para.1, applied: SI 1997/1830 Art.8
Sch.2 para.2, amended: SI 1997/1831 Reg.4

1924. Medicines (Pharmacy and General Sale - Exemption) Order 1980
Art.1, amended: SI 1997/1350 Art.2, SI 1998/2368 Art.2
Art.2, revoked (in part): SI 1998/2368 Art.2
Art.5, amended: SI 1997/1350 Art.2
Art.6A, added: SI 1998/2368 Art.2
Sch.1 Part I, amended: SI 1997/1350 Art.2, SI 1998/107 Art.2, Sch., SI 1998/2368 Art.2

1951. Gas (Metrication) Regulations 1980
Reg.3, revoked (in part): SI 1996/825 Reg.31, Sch.6 Part I

1960. Double Taxation Relief (Taxes on Income) (Denmark) Order 1980
Sch., amended: SI 1996/3165 Art.2
Sch. Art.3, amended: SI 1996/3165 Sch Part I
Sch. Art.8, substituted: SI 1996/3165 Sch Part I
Sch. Art.10, referred to: SI 1996/3165 Sch Part II
Sch. Art.10, substituted: SI 1996/3165 Sch Part I

NO.

1980—cont.

1960. Double Taxation Relief (Taxes on Income) (Denmark) Order 1980—*cont.*
Sch. Art.11, amended: SI 1996/3165 Sch Part I
Sch. Art.11, referred to: SI 1996/3165 Sch Part II
Sch. Art.12, amended: SI 1996/3165 Sch Part I
Sch. Art.12, referred to: SI 1996/3165 Sch Part II
Sch. Art.13, amended: SI 1996/3165 Sch Part I
Sch. Art.15, amended: SI 1996/3165 Sch Part I
Sch. Art.15, applied: SI 1996/3165 Sch Part I
Sch. Art.18, substituted: SI 1996/3165 Sch Part I
Sch. Art.22, amended: SI 1996/3165 Sch Part I
Sch. Art.22, referred to: SI 1996/3165 Sch Part II
Sch. Art.28, amended: SI 1996/3165 Sch Part I

1961. Double Taxation Relief (Taxes on Income) (Netherlands) Order 1980
Art.11, see *Bricom Holdings Ltd v Inland Revenue Commissioners* [1997] S.T.C. 1179 (CA), Beldam, L.J.

1967. Trial of the Pyx (Amendment) Order 1980
revoked: SI 1998/1764 Art.16, Sch.3

2037. Patrick Allan-Fraser Trust Scheme 1980
amended: SI 1996/477 Sch

1981

14. Town and Country Planning (Tree Preservation Order) (Amendment) Regulations 1981
revoked: SI 1999/1892 Reg.18 (with savings)

37. Goods Vehicles (Operators' Licences) (Temporary Use in Great Britain) (Amendment) Regulations 1981
revoked: SI 1996/2186 Reg.2, Sch.1

62. Blaenau Ffestiniog (Central Station) Light Railway Order 1981
Art.13, amended: SI 1999/2129 Art.40

70. Prison (Amendment) Rules 1981
revoked: SI 1999/728 r.85 (with savings), Sch. (with savings)

86. Police (Promotion) (Scotland) Amendment Regulations 1981
revoked: SI 1996/221 Reg.10, Sch.2

105. Lands Tribunal (Amendment) Rules 1981
revoked: SI 1996/1022 r.57, Sch.2

129. Contracting Out and Preservation (Further Provisions) Regulations 1981
Reg.4, revoked: SI 1997/358 Reg.7, Sch

154. Road Traffic (Northern Ireland) Order 1981
amended: SI 1998/1074 (NI.7) Art.7
Art.1, revoked (in part): SI 1996/1320 (NI.10) Sch.4
Art.2, amended: SI 1996/1320 (NI.10) Sch.3 para.1, SI 1997/276 (NI.2) Art.75, Sch.8 para.4
Art.2, revoked (in part): SI 1996/1320 (NI.10) Sch.4, SI 1997/276 (NI.2) Art.75, Sch.9
Art.3, applied: SI 1996/1320 (NI.10) Sch.1 Part I
Art.4, amended: SI 1996/1320 (NI.10) Sch.3 para.2, SI 1998/1074 (NI.7) Art.13, Sch.3 para.2
Art.4, applied: SI 1996/1320 (NI.10) Art.41
Art.5, amended: SI 1996/1320 (NI.10) Sch.3 para.3
Art.5, applied: SI 1996/1320 (NI.10) Art.41
Art.5, referred to: SI 1998/1074 (NI.7) Art.3
Art.9, applied: SI 1996/1320 (NI.10) Sch.1 Part I, SI 1998/1074 (NI.7) Art.6, Sch.1 para.6, Sch.1 para.9
Art.10, amended: SI 1996/1320 (NI.10) Sch.3 para.4
Art.11, amended: SI 1996/1320 (NI.10) Sch.3 para.5

NO.

NO.

1981—cont.

154. Road Traffic (Northern Ireland) Order 1981—*cont.*

Art.11, applied: SI 1996/1320 (NI.10) Art.7, Art.10, Sch.1 Part I

Art.13, amended: SI 1998/1074 (NI.7) Art.13, Sch.3 para.2

Art.13, applied: SI 1996/1320 (NI.10) Art.50, Sch.1 Part I

Art.14, amended: SI 1998/1074 (NI.7) Sch.1 para.2

Art.14, applied: SI 1996/1320 (NI.10) Sch.1 Part I, SI 1998/1071 (NI.7) Sch.1 para.9

Art.15, amended: SI 1996/1320 (NI.10) Sch.3 para.6

Art.15, applied: SI 1996/1320 (NI.10) Art.10, Sch.1 Part I

Art.19, amended: SI 1998/1074 (NI.7) Sch.2 para.2

Art.19, applied: SI 1996/1320 (NI.10) Sch.1 Part I

Art.19A, amended: SI 1996/1320 (NI.10) Sch.3 para.7

Art.19A, applied: SI 1996/1320 (NI.10) Art.57, Sch.1 Part I

Art.19A, referred to: SI 1998/1074 (NI.7) Sch.2 para.7, Sch.2 para.8

Art.19A, substituted: SI 1998/1074 (NI.7) Sch.2 para.3

Art.19B, amended: SI 1998/1074 (NI.7) Sch.2 para.4

Art.19B, applied: SI 1996/1320 (NI.10) Sch.1 Part I

Art.19C, amended: SI 1996/1320 (NI.10) Sch.3 para.8

Art.19C, applied: SI 1996/1320 Art.12, Art.27

Art.19C, revoked (in part): SI 1996/1320 (NI.10) Sch.4

Art.19D, amended: SI 1998/1074 (NI.7) Sch.2 para.5

Art.19E, amended: SI 1996/1320 (NI.10) Sch.3 para.9

Art.19E, applied: SI 1996/1320 (NI.10) Art.28, Sch.1 Part I

Art.20, applied: SI 1996/1320 (NI.10) Sch.1 Part I

Art.20, revoked: SI 1997/276 (NI.2) Art.75, Sch.9

Art.21, applied: SI 1996/1320 (NI.10) Sch.1 Part I

Art.21, revoked: SI 1997/276 (NI.2) Art.75, Sch.9

Art.22, applied: SI 1996/1320 (NI.10) Sch.1 Part I

Art.22, revoked: SI 1997/276 (NI.2) Art.75, Sch.9

Art.23, revoked: SI 1997/276 (NI.2) Art.75, Sch.9

Art.24, revoked: SI 1997/276 (NI.2) Art.75, Sch.9

Art.25, revoked: SI 1997/276 (NI.2) Art.75, Sch.9

Art.26, revoked: SI 1997/276 (NI.2) Art.75, Sch.9

Art.27, revoked: SI 1997/276 (NI.2) Art.75, Sch.9

Art.31A, amended: SI 1999/2920 Reg.19, Sch.2 para.6

Art.31A, applied: SI 1998/2051 Reg.11, SI 1999/2920 Reg.16

Art.31E, applied: SI 1996/1320 (NI.10) Sch.1 Part I, SI 1998/2051 Reg.11

Art.31E, referred to: SI 1999/2920 Reg.17

1981—cont.

154. Road Traffic (Northern Ireland) Order 1981—*cont.*

Art.31F, amended: SI 1999/2920 Reg.19, Sch.2 para.7

Art.31F, applied: SI 1996/1320 (NI.10) Sch.1 Part I

Art.31G, amended: SI 1999/2920 Reg.19, Sch.2 para.8

Art.31G, applied: SI 1996/1320 (NI.10) Sch.1 Part I, SI 1998/2051 Reg.11

Art.31G, referred to: SI 1999/2920 Reg.17

Art.50, revoked: SI 1997/276 (NI.2) Art.75, Sch.9

Art.51, revoked: SI 1997/276 (NI.2) Art.75, Sch.9

Art.52, revoked: SI 1997/276 (NI.2) Art.75, Sch.9

Art.56, applied: SI 1996/1320 (NI.10) Art.8, Sch.1 Part I

Art.56, referred to: SI 1999/1736 Art.9

Art.58, referred to: SI 1999/1736 Art.9

Art.59, applied: SI 1996/1320 (NI.10) Sch.1 Part I

Art.60, applied: SI 1996/1320 (NI.10) Sch.1 Part I

Art.61, applied: SI 1998/3094 Reg.14

Art.62, applied: SI 1996/1320 (NI.10) Sch.1 Part I

Art.62, revoked (in part): SI 1996/1320 (NI.10) Sch.4

Art.63, applied: SI 1996/1320 (NI.10) Art.8

Art.64, applied: SI 1996/1320 (NI.10) Sch.1 Part I

Art.66, applied: SI 1996/1320 (NI.10) Sch.1 Part I, SI 1998/3094 Reg.14

Art.70, applied: SI 1998/1074 (NI.7) Art.6, Sch.1 para.6, Sch.1 para.9

Art.71, applied: SI 1998/1074 (NI.7) Art.6, Sch.1 para.6, Sch.1 para.9

Art.72, applied: SI 1996/1320 (NI.10) Sch.1 Part I, SI 1998/1074 (NI.7) Art.6, Sch.1 para.6, Sch.1 para.9

Art.73, amended: SI 1996/1320 (NI.10) Sch.3 para.10

Art.73, applied: SI 1998/1074 (NI.7) Art.6, Sch.1 para.6, Sch.1 para.9

Art.74, amended: SI 1996/1320 (NI.10) Sch.3 para.11

Art.74, applied: SI 1998/1074 (NI.7) Art.6, Sch.1 para.6, Sch.1 para.9

Art.75, applied: SI 1996/1320 (NI.10) Sch.1 Part I, SI 1998/1074 (NI.7) Art.6, Sch.1 para.6, Sch.1 para.9

Art.76, applied: SI 1998/1074 (NI.7) Art.6, Sch.1 para.6, Sch.1 para.9

Art.77, applied: SI 1996/1320 (NI.10) Sch.1 Part I, SI 1998/1074 (NI.7) Art.6, Sch.1 para.6, Sch.1 para.9

Art.78, applied: SI 1998/1074 (NI.7) Art.6, Sch.1 para.6, Sch.1 para.9

Art.79, applied: SI 1998/1074 (NI.7) Art.6, Sch.1 para.6, Sch.1 para.9

Art.79A, amended: SI 1996/1632 (NI.11) Art.8

Art.79A, applied: SI 1996/1320 (NI.10) Sch.1 Part I, SI 1998/1074 (NI.7) Art.6, Sch.1 para.6, Sch.1 para.9

Art.79A, revoked (in part): SI 1996/1632 (NI.11) Art.19, Sch.6

Art.81, applied: SI 1996/1320 (NI.10) Art.8, Sch.1 Part I

Art.82, applied: SI 1996/1320 (NI.10) Sch.1 Part I

NO.

154. Road Traffic (Northern Ireland) Order 1981—*cont.*

Art.86, applied: SI 1996/1320 (NI.10) Sch.1 Part I

Art.90, applied: SI 1996/1320 (NI.10) Art.9, Art.10, Sch.1 Part I

Art.95, applied: SI 1996/1320 (NI.10) Sch.1 Part I

Art.96, applied: SI 1996/1320 (NI.10) Sch.1 Part I

Art.97, amended: SI 1996/1320 (NI.10) Sch.3 para.12

Art.97, applied: SI 1996/1320 (NI.10) Sch.1 Part I

Art.104, revoked: SI 1997/276 (NI.2) Art.75, Sch.9

Art.105, applied: SI 1996/1320 (NI.10) Sch.1 Part I

Art.105, revoked: SI 1997/276 (NI.2) Art.75, Sch.9

Art.106, revoked: SI 1997/276 (NI.2) Art.75, Sch.9

Art.107, revoked: SI 1997/276 (NI.2) Art.75, Sch.9

Art.108, revoked: SI 1997/276 (NI.2) Art.75, Sch.9

Art.109, revoked: SI 1997/276 (NI.2) Art.75, Sch.9

Art.110, revoked: SI 1997/276 (NI.2) Art.75, Sch.9

Art.111, revoked: SI 1997/276 (NI.2) Art.75, Sch.9

Art.112, revoked: SI 1997/276 (NI.2) Art.75, Sch.9

Art.113, revoked: SI 1997/276 (NI.2) Art.75, Sch.9

Art.114, revoked: SI 1997/276 (NI.2) Art.75, Sch.9

Art.115, applied: SI 1996/1320 (NI.10) Sch.1 Part I

Art.115, revoked: SI 1997/276 (NI.2) Art.75, Sch.9

Art.116, applied: SI 1996/1320 (NI.10) Sch.1 Part I

Art.116, revoked: SI 1997/276 (NI.2) Art.75, Sch.9

Art.117, revoked: SI 1997/276 (NI.2) Art.75, Sch.9

Art.118, amended: SI 1996/1320 (NI.10) Sch.3 para.13

Art.118, revoked: SI 1997/276 (NI.2) Art.75, Sch.9

Art.119, revoked: SI 1997/276 (NI.2) Art.75, Sch.9

Art.120, amended: SI 1997/276 (NI.2) Art.75, Sch.8 para.5

Art.120, revoked: SI 1996/1320 (NI.10) Sch.4

Art.121, revoked: SI 1997/276 (NI.2) Art.75, Sch.9

Art.122, revoked: SI 1997/276 (NI.2) Art.75, Sch.9

Art.123, applied: SI 1996/1320 (NI.10) Sch.1 Part I

Art.123, revoked: SI 1997/276 (NI.2) Art.75, Sch.9

Art.124, applied: SI 1996/1320 (NI.10) Sch.1 Part I

Art.124, revoked: SI 1997/276 (NI.2) Art.75, Sch.9

Art.125, revoked: SI 1997/276 (NI.2) Art.75, Sch.9

Art.126, applied: SI 1996/1320 (NI.10) Sch.1 Part I

NO.

154. Road Traffic (Northern Ireland) Order 1981—*cont.*

Art.126, revoked: SI 1997/276 (NI.2) Art.75, Sch.9

Art.127, applied: SI 1996/1320 (NI.10) Sch.1 Part I

Art.127, revoked: SI 1997/276 (NI.2) Art.75, Sch.9

Art.128, revoked: SI 1997/276 (NI.2) Art.75, Sch.9

Art.132, amended: SI 1996/1320 (NI.10) Sch.3 para.14

Art.132, applied: SI 1996/1320 (NI.10) Sch.1 Part I

Art.133, amended: SI 1996/1320 (NI.10) Sch.3 para.15

Art.133, applied: SI 1996/1320 (NI.10) Sch.1 Part I

Art.133, revoked (in part): SI 1996/1320 (NI.10) Sch.4

Art.135, applied: SI 1996/1320 (NI.10) Art.22

Art.136, applied: SI 1996/1320 (NI.10) Sch.1 Part I

Art.137, amended: SI 1996/1320 (NI.10) Sch.3 para.16

Art.137, applied: SI 1996/1320 (NI.10) Sch.1 Part I

Art.138, revoked: SI 1996/1320 (NI.10) Sch.4

Art.139, revoked: SI 1996/1320 (NI.10) Sch.4

Art.140, revoked: SI 1996/1320 (NI.10) Sch.4

Art.141, applied: SI 1996/1320 (NI.10) Art.96

Art.143, applied: SI 1996/1320 (NI.10) Art.96

Art.144, applied: SI 1996/1320 (NI.10) Art.96

Art.145, applied: SI 1996/1320 (NI.10) Art.96

Art.146, applied: SI 1996/1320 (NI.10) Art.96

Art.147, applied: SI 1996/1320 (NI.10) Art.96

Art.150, revoked: SI 1996/1320 (NI.10) Sch.4

Art.151, revoked: SI 1996/1320 (NI.10) Sch.4

Art.152, revoked: SI 1996/1320 (NI.10) Sch.4

Art.154, applied: SI 1996/1320 (NI.10) Sch.1 Part I

Art.155, applied: SI 1996/1320 (NI.10) Art.23, Sch.1 Part I

Art.155, revoked: SI 1997/276 (NI.2) Art.75, Sch.9

Art.156, applied: SI 1996/1320 (NI.10) Art.23, Sch.1 Part I

Art.156, revoked: SI 1997/276 (NI.2) Art.75, Sch.9

Art.157, revoked (in part): SI 1996/1320 (NI.10) Sch.4, SI 1997/276 (NI.2) Art.75, Sch.9

Art.166, amended: SI 1996/1320 (NI.10) Sch.3 para.17

Art.166, applied: SI 1996/1320 (NI.10) Art.10, Sch.1 Part I

Art.167, amended: SI 1996/1320 (NI.10) Sch.3 para.18

Art.167, applied: SI 1996/1320 (NI.10) Art.10, Sch.1 Part I

Art.169, revoked: SI 1996/1320 (NI.10) Sch.4

Art.171, applied: SI 1996/1320 (NI.10) Sch.1 Part I

Art.171, revoked (in part): SI 1997/276 (NI.2) Art.75, Sch.9

Art.172, referred to: SI 1996/1320 (NI.10) Art.35, Art.40, Sch.1 Part I

Art.174, amended: SI 1996/1320 (NI.10) Sch.3 para.19, SI 1998/1074 (NI.7) Art.13, Sch.3 para.3

Art.174, applied: SI 1996/1320 (NI.10) Art.10, Art.20, Sch.1 Part I

Art.174A, applied: SI 1996/1320 (NI.10) Sch.1 Part I

NO.

1981—cont.

154. Road Traffic (Northern Ireland) Order 1981—*cont.*

Art.174A, referred to: SI 1996/107 Reg.9, SI 1997/276 (NI.2) Art.1, SI 1997/2439 Art.8

Art.174A, revoked: SI 1997/276 (NI.2) Art.75, Sch.9

Art.174B, revoked: SI 1996/1320 (NI.10) Sch.4

Art.175, applied: SI 1996/1320 (NI.10) Art.9, Sch.1 Part I

Art.175, revoked (in part): SI 1996/1320 (NI.10) Sch.4

Art.176, applied: SI 1996/1320 (NI.10) Sch.1 Part I

Art.177, amended: SI 1996/1320 (NI.10) Sch.3 para.20, SI 1997/276 (NI.2) Art.75, Sch.8 para.6

Art.177, applied: SI 1996/1320 (NI.10) Art.15, Sch.1 Part I

Art.177, referred to: SI 1997/276 (NI.2) Art.44

Art.178, applied: SI 1996/1320 (NI.10) Sch.1 Part I

Art.178, referred to: SI 1997/276 (NI.2) Art.44

Art.179, applied: SI 1996/1320 (NI.10) Sch.1 Part I

Art.179, referred to: SI 1997/276 (NI.2) Art.44

Art.180, amended: SI 1996/1320 (NI.10) Sch.3 para.21

Art.180, applied: SI 1996/1320 (NI.10) Sch.1 Part I

Art.180, referred to: SI 1997/276 (NI.2) Art.44

Art.182, revoked: SI 1996/1320 (NI.10) Sch.4

Art.183, revoked: SI 1996/1320 (NI.10) Sch.4

Art.184, revoked: SI 1996/1320 (NI.10) Sch.4

Art.185, revoked: SI 1996/1320 (NI.10) Sch.4

Art.186, referred to: SI 1997/276 (NI.2) Art.66

Art.186, revoked: SI 1996/1320 (NI.10) Sch.4

Art.187, revoked: SI 1997/276 (NI.2) Art.75, Sch.9

Art.188, revoked: SI 1996/1320 (NI.10) Sch.4

Art.189, revoked: SI 1996/1320 (NI.10) Sch.4

Art.190, revoked: SI 1996/1320 (NI.10) Sch.4

Art.191, revoked: SI 1996/1320 (NI.10) Sch.4

Art.192, revoked: SI 1996/1320 (NI.10) Sch.4

Art.193, revoked: SI 1996/1320 (NI.10) Sch.4

Art.194, revoked: SI 1996/1320 (NI.10) Sch.4

Art.195, revoked: SI 1996/1320 (NI.10) Sch.4

Art.196, revoked: SI 1996/1320 (NI.10) Sch.4

Art.197, revoked: SI 1996/1320 (NI.10) Sch.4

Art.198, amended: 1997 c.16 Sch.3 para.8, SI 1997/276 (NI.2) Art.75, Sch.8 para.7

Art.198, revoked: SI 1996/1320 (NI.10) Sch.4

Art.199, revoked: SI 1996/1320 (NI.10) Sch.4

Art.200, revoked: SI 1996/1320 (NI.10) Sch.4

Art.201, revoked: SI 1996/1320 (NI.10) Sch.4

Art.202, revoked: SI 1996/1320 (NI.10) Sch.4

Art.203, revoked: SI 1996/1320 (NI.10) Sch.4

Art.204, revoked: SI 1996/1320 (NI.10) Sch.4

Art.209, applied: SI 1996/1320 (NI.10) Sch.1 Part I

Art.209, revoked: SI 1997/276 (NI.2) Art.75, Sch.9

Art.210, revoked: SI 1997/276 (NI.2) Art.75, Sch.9

Art.212, amended: SI 1996/1320 (NI.10) Sch.3 para.22

Art.212, revoked (in part): SI 1996/1320 (NI.10) Sch.4, SI 1997/276 (NI.2) Art.75, Sch.9

Art.214, amended: SI 1997/276 (NI.2) Art.75, Sch.8 para.8, SI 1999/1736 Art.9

Art.214, applied: SI 1998/2051 Reg.11

Art.214, referred to: SI 1999/2920 Reg.17

Art.215, amended: SI 1996/1320 (NI.10) Sch.3 para.23

1981—cont.

154. Road Traffic (Northern Ireland) Order 1981—*cont.*

Art.215, revoked (in part): SI 1996/1320 (NI.10) Sch.4, SI 1997/276 (NI.2) Art.75, Sch.9

Art.216, revoked: SI 1997/276 (NI.2) Art.75, Sch.9

Part II, applied: SI 1998/1074 (NI.7) Art.6, Art.7, Sch.1 para.6, Sch.1 para.9

Part IV, applied: SI 1998/2051 Reg.10, Reg.12, Reg.13, SI 1999/2920 Reg.15

Part VIII, referred to: SI 1999/1736 Art.9

Sch.4, revoked (in part): SI 1996/1320 (NI.10) Sch.4, SI 1997/276 (NI.2) Art.75, Sch.9

Sch.6 para.4, revoked: SI 1997/276 (NI.2) Art.75, Sch.9

Sch.7 para.3, revoked: SI 1996/3160 (NI.24) Sch.7

Sch.7 para.17, revoked: SI 1997/276 (NI.2) Art.75, Sch.9

Sch.7 para.21, revoked (in part): SI 1997/276 (NI.2) Art.75, Sch.9

155. Firearms (Northern Ireland) Order 1981

referred to: 1998 c.9 s.2, SI 1999/1736 Art.12, Sch.5

Art.3, referred to: 1997 c.7 s.4, Sch para.8

Art.4, applied: 1996 c.22 Sch.1 para.16

Art.4, referred to: 1997 c.7 s.4, Sch para.8

Art.5, applied: 1996 c.22 Sch.1 para.16

Art.6, applied: 1996 c.22 s.13, Sch.1 para.16

Art.6, referred to: 1997 c.7 s.4, Sch para.8

Art.7, referred to: 1997 c.7 s.4, Sch para.8

Art.12A, added: 1996 c.46 s.29

Art.17, applied: 1996 c.22 s.13, Sch.1 para.16, 1997 c.43 s.2

Art.18, applied: 1996 c.22 s.13, Sch.1 para.16, 1997 c.43 s.2

Art.18, referred to: 1997 c.7 s.4, Sch para.8

Art.19, applied: 1996 c.22 Sch.1 para.16, 1997 c.43 s.2

Art.20, applied: 1996 c.22 Sch.1 para.16

Art.20, referred to: 1997 c.7 s.4, Sch para.8

Art.21, referred to: 1997 c.7 s.4, Sch para.8

Art.22, applied: 1996 c.22 s.13, Sch.1 para.16

Art.22, referred to: 1997 c.7 s.4, Sch para.8

Art.23, applied: 1996 c.22 s.13, Sch.1 para.16

Art.23, referred to: 1997 c.7 s.4, Sch para.8

Art.26, referred to: 1997 c.7 s.4, Sch para.8

Art.43, referred to: 1997 c.7 s.4, Sch para.8

Art.57, amended: 1996 c.46 s.29, SI 1999/1736 Art.12, Sch.6

Art.57, applied: SI 1999/1736 Art.12, Sch.6

Sch.1, amended: 1998 c.32 s.74, Sch.4 para.15

Sch.1 para.4A, added: 1999 c.33 s.169, Sch.14 para.75

156. Housing (Northern Ireland) Order 1981

Art.21, applied: SI 1997/1182 (NI.11) Art.7

Art.31, revoked (in part): SI 1997/1179 (NI.8) Art.53, Sch.5

Art.155, referred to: SI 1997/2668 Art.2, Sch. Part II

Art.155, revoked: 1997 c.32 Sch.9

Sch.1 para.10, revoked: SI 1996/1297 (NI.7) Art.23, Sch.5

158. Clean Air (Northern Ireland) Order 1981

applied: SI 1999/1736 Art.15

Art.2, revoked (in part): SI 1997/2777 (NI.18) Art.35, Sch.5

Art.7, applied: SI 1997/2777 (NI.18) Art.7

Art.7, revoked: SI 1997/2777 (NI.18) Art.35, Sch.4 para.13, Sch.5

Art.8, revoked: SI 1997/2777 (NI.18) Art.35, Sch.4 para.13, Sch.5

NO.

1981—cont.

158. Clean Air (Northern Ireland) Order 1981—*cont.*
Art.9, revoked: SI 1997/2777 (NI.18) Art.35, Sch.4 para.13, Sch.5
Art.10, revoked: SI 1997/2777 (NI.18) Art.35, Sch.4 para.13, Sch.5
Art.11, revoked: SI 1997/2777 (NI.18) Art.35, Sch.4 para.13, Sch.5
Art.12, revoked: SI 1997/2777 (NI.18) Art.35, Sch.4 para.13, Sch.5
Art.13, revoked: SI 1997/2777 (NI.18) Art.35, Sch.4 para.13, Sch.5
Art.15, revoked (in part): SI 1997/2777 (NI.18) Art.35, Sch.5
Art.16, revoked (in part): SI 1997/2777 (NI.18) Art.35, Sch.5
Art.24A, added: SI 1997/2777 (NI.18) Art.35, Sch.4 para.14
Art.25, revoked: SI 1997/2777 (NI.18) Art.35, Sch.5
Art.28, revoked (in part): SI 1997/2777 (NI.18) Art.35, Sch.5
Art.39, revoked (in part): SI 1997/2777 (NI.18) Art.35, Sch.5
Art.43, revoked (in part): SI 1997/2777 (NI.18) Art.35, Sch.5
Sch.1 para.1, revoked (in part): SI 1997/2777 (NI.18) Art.35, Sch.5
Sch.4 para.2, revoked: SI 1997/2777 (NI.18) Art.35, Sch.5
Sch.4 para.3, revoked: SI 1997/2777 (NI.18) Art.35, Sch.5

215. Merchant Shipping (Oil Pollution) (Bermuda) (Amendment) Order 1981
revoked: SI 1997/2581 Art.3

216. Merchant Shipping (Oil Pollution) (British Virgin Islands) Order 1981
revoked: SI 1997/2590 Art.3

217. Merchant Shipping (Oil Pollution) (Cayman Islands) (Amendment) Order 1981
revoked: SI 1998/1261 Art.4

218. Merchant Shipping (Oil Pollution) (Falkland Islands) (Amendment) Order 1981
revoked (in part): SI 1997/2584 Art.4, SI 1997/2588 Art.4

221. Merchant Shipping (Oil Pollution) (Montserrat) Order 1981
revoked: SI 1998/1262 Art.3

222. Merchant Shipping (Oil Pollution) (Overseas Territories) (Amendment) Order 1981
revoked (in part): SI 1997/2583 Art.4, SI 1997/2585 Art.4, SI 1997/2587 Art.4, SI 1998/1263 Art.4

223. Merchant Shipping (Oil Pollution) (Turks and Caicos Islands) (Amendment) Order 1981
revoked: SI 1997/2589 Art.4

224. Merchant Shipping (Oil Pollution) Act 1971 (Guernsey) Order 1981
revoked: SI 1998/260 Art.5

225. Merchant Shipping Act 1974 (Guernsey) Order 1981
revoked: SI 1998/260 Art.5

226. Judgments Enforcement (Northern Ireland) Order 1981
applied: SI 1998/3162 (NI.21) Art.17, Art.39, Art.87
Art.4, applied: SI 1996/725 (NI.5) Art.42, SI 1997/1179 (NI.8) Art.42
Art.46, applied: SI 1997/1179 (NI.8) Art.48
Part VIII, applied: SI 1996/3159 (NI.23) Art.33
Sch.1 Part I, amended: SI 1996/1919 (NI.16) Art.255, Sch.1

NO.

1981—cont.

226. Judgments Enforcement (Northern Ireland) Order 1981—*cont.*
Sch.2 para.24, revoked: SI 1996/275 (NI.2) Art.71, Sch.8

228. Legal Aid, Advice and Assistance (Northern Ireland) Order 1981
Art.29, applied: 1996 c.22 s.4
Art.29, revoked (in part): 1996 c.25 Sch.4 para.36
Art.32, applied: 1996 c.22 s.4
Art.34, amended: SI 1998/1504 (NI.9) Art.65, Sch.5 para.14, Sch.6
Art.36, applied: 1996 c.22 s.4
Art.40, applied: 1996 c.22 s.4
Part III, applied: 1996 c.22 s.4
Sch.1 Part I, amended: SI 1998/1071 (NI.6) Art.41, Sch.3
Sch.1 Part I, revoked (in part): SI 1998/1071 (NI.6) Art.41, Sch.5
Sch.1 para.3, amended: SI 1998/1504 (NI.9) Art.65, Sch.6
Sch.1 para.8, added: SI 1999/1042 Art.3, Sch.1 para.14
Sch.3, revoked (in part): SI 1996/1297 (NI.7) Art.23, Sch.5

231. Weights and Measures (Northern Ireland) Order 1981
applied: SI 1997/1941 Sch.3 para.15
referred to: SI 1996/600 Sch.5 para.15, SI 1996/601 Sch.5 para.15, SI 1997/1624 Sch.5 para.15, SI 1999/1517 Reg.12, Sch.4 para.12, SI 1999/1676 Sch.5 para.12
Art.1, revoked (in part): SI 1996/1632 (NI.11) Art.19, Sch.6
Art.20, revoked (in part): SI 1996/1632 (NI.11) Art.4, Art.19, Sch.6
Art.22, revoked (in part): SI 1996/1632 (NI.11) Art.4, Art.19, Sch.6
Art.52, revoked: SI 1996/275 (NI.2) Art.71, Sch.8

236. Merchant Shipping (Load Lines Convention) (Countries) Order 1981
revoked: SI 1998/2241 Reg.3

239. Transfer of Functions (Treasury and Lord Advocate) Order 1981
Art.2, revoked (in part): SI 1999/1042 Art.4, Sch.2 para.12
Art.2, applied: SI 1999/678 Art.2

257. Public Service Vehicles (Conditions of Fitness, Equipment, Use and Certification) Regulations 1981
Part II, referred to: SI 1999/3413 Reg.10
Part III, referred to: SI 1999/3413 Reg.10
Part IV, referred to: SI 1999/3413 Reg.10
Part V, referred to: SI 1999/3413 Reg.10
Reg.46, amended: SI 1997/84 Reg.2, SI 1998/1670 Reg.3
Reg.50, amended: SI 1997/84 Reg.2
Reg.57, amended: SI 1997/84 Reg.2

327. Rate Product Rules 1981
r.3, see *Camden LBC v National Rivers Authority* [1997] Env. L.R. 204 (CA), Staughton, L.J.
r.10, see *Camden LBC v National Rivers Authority* [1997] Env. L.R. 204 (CA), Staughton, L.J.

374. Motor Cycles (Protective Helmets) (Amendment) Regulations 1981
revoked: SI 1998/1807 Reg.2, Sch.1

399. Diving Operations at Work Regulations 1981
applied: SI 1997/2776 Reg.17
referred to: SI 1997/1713 Reg.2

NO.

NO.

1981—cont.

399. Diving Operations at Work Regulations 1981—*cont.*
revoked: SI 1997/2776 Reg.18
Reg.2, applied: SI 1996/1656 Reg.3
Reg.2, revoked: SI 1997/2776 Reg.18
Reg.3, referred to: SI 1997/1713 Reg.2
Reg.3, revoked: SI 1997/2776 Reg.18
Reg.4, revoked: SI 1997/2776 Reg.18
Reg.7, applied: SI 1997/2776 Reg.17
Reg.7, revoked: SI 1997/2776 Reg.18

406. Merchant Shipping (Navigational Warnings) (Amendment) Regulations 1981
revoked: SI 1996/1815 Reg.1

431. Merchant Shipping (Oil Pollution) (Overseas Territories) (Amendment No.2) Order 1981
revoked (in part): SI 1997/2583 Art.4, SI 1997/2585 Art.4, SI 1997/2587 Art.4, SI 1998/1263 Art.4

432. European Communities (Medical, Dental and Nursing Professions) (Linguistic Knowledge) Order 1981
Art.3, revoked (in part): 1997 c.46 Sch.3 Part III

434. Merchant Shipping (Oil Pollution) Act 1971 (Jersey) Order 1981
revoked: SI 1997/2598 Art.5

438. Museums (Northern Ireland) Order 1981
revoked: SI 1998/261 (NI.2) Art.15, Sch.4

481. Merseyside Development Corporation (Area and Constitution) Order 1981
Art.2, revoked: SI 1998/769 Art.2
Art.3, revoked: SI 1998/769 Art.2

492. Welsh Water Authority (Alteration of Boundaries of the River Lugg Internal Drainage District) Order 1981
amended: SI 1999/2508 Sch. para.3

500. Pensions Appeal Tribunals (Scotland) Rules 1981
r.2, amended: SI 1998/1225 r.2
r.2, revoked (in part): SI 1998/1225 r.2
r.4, amended: SI 1998/1225 r.4
r.5A, added: SI 1998/1225 r.5
r.6, see *McGinley v United Kingdom* (1999) 27 E.H.R.R. 1 (ECHR), R Bernhardt (President)
r.8, amended: SI 1998/1225 r.6
r.19, amended: SI 1998/1225 r.7
r.20, substituted: SI 1998/1225 r.8
r.21, amended: SI 1998/1225 r.9
r.23, amended: SI 1998/1225 r.10
r.25, amended: SI 1998/1225 r.11
r.26, applied: SI 1999/1750 Art.5, Sch.4 para.2
r.27, applied: SI 1999/1750 Art.5, Sch.4 para.2
r.28, applied: SI 1999/1750 Art.5, Sch.4 para.2
Sch.1, revoked: SI 1998/1225 r.12

527. Goods Vehicles (Operators' Licences) (Temporary Use in Great Britain) (Amendment) Regulations 1981
revoked: SI 1996/2186 Reg.2, Sch.1

550. New Forest (Confirmation of the Byelaws of the Verderers of the New Forest) Order 1981
revoked: SI 1999/2134 Art.3

552. Magistrates' Courts Rules 1981
see *R. v Blackburn Justices Ex p. Holmes* Independent, November 29, 1999 (C.S.) (QBD), Jowitt, J.
applied: SI 1998/3046 r.2
r.2, amended: SI 1998/3046 r.2
r.4A, added: SI 1997/706 r.3
r.4A, amended: SI 1998/3046 r.2
r.4B, added: SI 1997/706 r.3
r.5, amended: SI 1997/706 r.4
r.6, amended: SI 1997/706 r.5

1981—cont.

552. Magistrates' Courts Rules 1981—*cont.*
r.6, revoked (in part): SI 1997/706 r.5
r.7, amended: SI 1997/706 r.6, r.7
r.8, substituted: SI 1997/706 r.8
r.9, amended: SI 1998/3046 r.2
r.10, amended: SI 1998/3046 r.2
r.11, amended: SI 1997/706 r.9, r.10
r.11, revoked (in part): SI 1997/706 r.10
r.11A, added: SI 1998/3046 r.2
r.21, revoked: SI 1997/706 r.11
r.28, amended: SI 1998/2167 r.4
r.33, revoked: SI 1997/706 r.12
r.41, applied: SI 1999/2784 Sch. para.37
r.44, see *A v A (Remission of Arrears: Procedure)* [1996] 1 F.C.R. 629 (Fam Div), Thorpe, J.; see *R. v Bristol Magistrates Court Ex p. Hodge* [1997] Q.B. 974 (QBD), Cazalet, J.
r.54, amended: SI 1999/2765 r.2
r.59, applied: SI 1999/2784 Sch. para.37
r.66, referred to: SI 1997/1055 r.6
r.68, see *R. v Derwentside Magistrates Court Ex p. Heaviside* [1996] R.T.R. 384 (QBD), McKinnon, J
r.70, amended: SI 1997/706 r.13, r.14
r.70, revoked (in part): SI 1997/706 r.14
r.71, see *R. v Horseferry Road Magistrates Court Ex p. Brown* Independent, October 6, 1997 (C.S.) (QBD), Rose, L.J.
r.71, amended: SI 1997/706 r.15
r.93, amended: SI 1998/3046 r.2
r.93A, applied: SI 1999/2784 Sch. para.16
r.97, see *R. v Oldham Justices Ex p. Cawley* [1997] Q.B. 1 (QBD), Simon Brown, L.J.
r.100, see *Al-Salaam, Re* Independent, April 21, 1997 (C.S.) (QBD), Auld, L.J.; see *New Southgate Metals Ltd v Islington LBC* [1996] Crim. L.R. 334 (QBD), Wright, J.; see *Thames Waste Management Ltd v Surrey CC* [1997] Env. L.R. 148 (QBD), Rose, L.J.
r.103, revoked: SI 1998/2167 r.4
r.107, amended: SI 1997/706 r.16, SI 1998/3046 r.2
r.114, added: SI 1998/2167 r.4

553. Magistrates' Courts (Forms) Rules 1981
Sch.2, amended: SI 1999/3039 r.2
Sch.2 Table, amended: SI 1999/1149 r.2
Sch.2 Form 13, amended: SI 1997/707 r.3
Sch.2 Form 14, amended: SI 1997/707 r.4
Sch.2 Form 14A, added: SI 1997/707 r.5
Sch.2 Form 16, amended: SI 1997/707 r.6
Sch.2 Form 22, revoked: SI 1997/707 r.7
Sch.2 Form 23, revoked: SI 1997/707 r.7
Sch.2 Form 24, revoked: SI 1997/707 r.8
Sch.2 Form 25, revoked (in part): SI 1997/707 r.9
Sch.2 Form 27A, added: SI 1999/1149 r.3, Sch.
Sch.2 Form 28A, added: SI 1999/1149 r.3, Sch.
Sch.2 Form 43, amended: SI 1997/2421 r.4
Sch.2 Form 44, amended: SI 1997/2421 r.4
Sch.2 Form 48, amended: SI 1999/2765 r.3
Sch.2 Form 92, amended: SI 1997/2421 r.5
Sch.2 Form 92A, amended: SI 1997/2421 r.5
Sch.2 Form 92C, amended: SI 1997/2421 r.6
Sch.2 Form 92D, amended: SI 1997/2421 r.6
Sch.2 Form 92F, amended: SI 1997/2421 r.7
Sch.2 Form 92G, amended: SI 1997/2421 r.7
Sch.2 Form 92Q, amended: SI 1997/2421 r.8
Sch.2 Form 92ZA, added: SI 1999/3039 r.3, Sch.
Sch.2 Form 92ZB, added: SI 1999/3039 r.3, Sch.

NO.

1981—cont.

553. Magistrates' Courts (Forms) Rules 1981—*cont.*
Sch.2 Form 136, amended: SI 1997/707 r.10
Sch.2 Form 137, amended: SI 1997/707 r.11
Sch.2 Form 138, amended: SI 1997/707 r.11
Sch.2 Form 139, amended: SI 1997/707 r.12

560. Town and Country Planning (Merseyside Urban Development Area) Special Development Order 1981
revoked: SI 1998/84 Art.2, Sch.

569. Merchant Shipping (Official Log Books) Regulations 1981
Reg.9, applied: SI 1998/2070 Reg.20, Reg.39, Reg.47
Sch. para.17, revoked: SI 1997/1511 Reg.2
Sch. para.19, revoked: SI 1997/1511 Reg.2
Sch. para.33, revoked: SI 1997/1511 Reg.2

570. Merchant Shipping (Official Log Books) (Fishing Vessels) Regulations 1981
Sch. para.27, revoked: SI 1997/1511 Reg.3

571. Merchant Shipping (Automatic Pilot and Testing of Steering Gear) Regulations 1981
applied: SI 1996/3243 Sch Part I

572. Merchant Shipping (Cargo Ship Construction and Survey) Regulations 1981
applied: SI 1996/3243 Sch Part I, SI 1997/1509 Reg.3
revoked: SI 1997/1509 Reg.1

573. Merchant Shipping (Cargo Ship Safety Equipment Survey) Regulations 1981
applied: SI 1996/3243 Sch Part I

574. Merchant Shipping (Fire Appliances) (Amendment) Regulations 1981
referred to: SI 1998/1609 Reg.5, Reg.6, Sch.
revoked: SI 1998/1012 Reg.1

577. Merchant Shipping (Life-Saving Appliances) (Amendment) Regulations 1981
referred to: SI 1998/1609 Reg.5, Reg.6, Sch.
revoked: SI 1999/2721 Reg.1

580. Merchant Shipping (Passenger Ship Construction) (Amendment) Regulations 1981
revoked: SI 1998/2514 Reg.1

600. Lands Tribunal (Amendment No.2) Rules 1981
revoked: SI 1996/1022 r.57, Sch.2

605. Social Security (Austria) Order 1981
Sch., amended: SI 1996/1928 Art.2, Sch.1

804. Town and Country Planning (Determination of Appeals by Appointed Persons) (Prescribed Classes) Regulations 1981
applied: SI 1997/420 Reg.6
revoked: SI 1997/420 Reg.6, Sch
Reg.2, amended: SI 1996/252 Art.2, Sch

829. Town and Country Planning (Development by Planning Authorities) (Scotland) Regulations 1981
Reg.4, applied: SSI 1999/1 Reg.22, Reg.24
Reg.4, referred to: SSI 1999/1 Reg.22
Reg.5, referred to: SSI 1999/1 Reg.25
Reg.6, applied: SSI 1999/1 Reg.25
Reg.8, applied: SSI 1999/1 Reg.24

830. Town and Country Planning (General Development) (Scotland) Order 1981
Art.3, applied: SI 1997/1952 Art.15
Sch.1 Class X, applied: SI 1997/1952 Art.15

839. Employment (Miscellaneous Provisions) (Northern Ireland) Order 1981
Art.6, amended: SI 1999/2790 (NI.9) Art.30, Sch.7 para.2
Art.6, revoked (in part): SI 1999/2790 (NI.9) Art.30, Art.40, Sch.7 para.2, Sch.9 Part 8

NO.

1981—cont.

839. Employment (Miscellaneous Provisions) (Northern Ireland) Order 1981—*cont.*
Art.7, amended: SI 1999/2790 (NI.9) Art.30, Sch.7 para.3
Art.9A, added: SI 1999/2790 (NI.9) Art.30, Sch.7 para.4
Art.9B, added: SI 1999/2790 (NI.9) Art.30, Sch.7 para.4
Art.10, amended: SI 1999/2790 (NI.9) Art.30, Sch.7 para.5
Art.11, amended: SI 1999/2790 (NI.9) Art.30, Sch.7 para.6, Sch.7 para.7

859. Traffic Signs Regulations and General Directions 1981
see *McKenzie v DPP* [1997] R.T.R. 175 (QBD), Newman, J.

861. Non-Contentious Probate Fees Order 1981
revoked: SI 1999/688 Art.6 (with savings), Sch.2 (with savings)

880. Capital Transfer Tax (Delivery of Accounts) Regulations 1981
Reg.3, amended: SI 1996/1470 Reg.2, SI 1998/1431 Reg.2

881. Capital Transfer Tax (Delivery of Accounts) (Scotland) Regulations 1981
Reg.3, amended: SI 1996/1472 Reg.2, SI 1998/1430 Reg.2

900. National Health Service Regulations (General Dental Services) (Scotland) Regulations 1981
revoked: SI 1996/177 Reg.38, Sch.8

909. Education (School Premises) Regulations 1981
revoked: SI 1996/360 Sch.1

912. Oil Pollution (Compulsory Insurance) Regulations 1981
revoked: SI 1997/1820 Reg.2

917. Health and Safety (First-Aid) Regulations 1981
Reg.6, revoked: SI 1999/3242 Reg.24
Reg.7, amended: SI 1997/2776 Reg.19, Sch.2 para.1

919. Police (Promotion) (Amendment) Regulations 1981
revoked: SI 1996/1685 Reg.8, Sch.3

934. Teachers' Superannuation (Notional Salaries) Regulations 1981
applied: SI 1997/3001 Reg.E31

936. London Docklands Development Corporation (Area and Constitution) Order 1981
Art.2, revoked: SI 1998/769 Art.2
Art.3, revoked: SI 1998/769 Art.2

937. London Docklands Development Corporation (Area and Constitution) (Amendment) Order 1981
revoked: SI 1998/769 Art.2

941. London Docklands Development Corporation (Vesting of Land) (Port of London Authority) Order 1981
revoked: SI 1998/769 Art.3, Sch.

942. London Docklands Development Corporation (Vesting of Land) (Greater London Council) Order 1981
revoked: SI 1998/769 Art.3, Sch.

959. Church Representation Rules (Amendment) Resolution 1981
referred to: SI 1998/319, SI 1999/2112

999. Merseyside Development Corporation (Vesting of Land) (British Railways Board) Order 1981
revoked: SI 1998/769 Art.3, Sch.

NO.

1981—cont.

1000. Merseyside Development Corporation (Vesting of Land) (Local Authorities) Order 1981
revoked: SI 1998/769 Art.3, Sch.

1001. Merseyside Development Corporation (Vesting of Land) (Mersey Docks and Harbour Company) Order 1981
revoked: SI 1998/769 Art.3, Sch.

1002. Merseyside Development Corporation (Vesting of Land) (Mersey Docks and Harbour Company No.2) Order 1981
revoked: SI 1998/769 Art.3, Sch.

1003. Merseyside Development Corporation (Vesting of Land) (Mersey Docks and Harbour Company No.3) Order 1981
revoked: SI 1998/769 Art.3, Sch.

1051. Export of Animals (Protection) Order 1981
referred to: SI 1997/1480 Art.22, Sch.12 Part I

1063. Jam and Similar Products Regulations 1981
amended: SI 1999/1136 Reg.14
Reg.2, amended: SI 1996/1499 Reg.49
Reg.2, referred to: SI 1999/982 Reg.3
Reg.5, amended: SI 1996/1499 Reg.49
Reg.7, amended: SI 1996/1499 Reg.49
Reg.8, amended: SI 1996/1499 Reg.49
Reg.9, amended: SI 1996/1499 Reg.49
Reg.10, amended: SI 1996/1499 Reg.49
Reg.21, revoked: SI 1996/1499 Reg.49, Sch.9
Reg.22, added: SI 1998/1398 Reg.18

1082. Town and Country Planning (London Docklands Urban Development Area) Special Development Order 1981
revoked: SI 1997/2946 Art.2

1086. Education (Schools and Further Education) Regulations 1981
Reg.10, amended: SI 1998/2792 Reg.3, Reg.4
Reg.10, revoked: SI 1999/3181 Reg.1
Sch.2 para.2, applied: SI 1997/431 Reg.4
Sch.2 para.2, referred to: SI 1999/1494 Reg.4

1089. Dangerous Substances (Conveyance by Road in Road Tankers and Tank Containers) Regulations 1981
Reg.7, applied: SI 1996/2095 Sch.3 para.2

1098. Merchant Shipping (Submersible Craft Construction and Survey) Regulations 1981
applied: SI 1996/3243 Sch Part I

1103. Non-Contentious Probate Fees (Amendment) Order 1981
revoked: SI 1999/688 Art.6 (with savings), Sch.2 (with savings)

1106. Antigua and Barbuda Constitution Order 1981
Sch.1 s.12, see *De Freitas v Permanent Secretary of Ministry of Agriculture, Fisheries, Lands and Housing* [1999] A.C. 69 (PC), Lord Clyde

1115. Diseases of Animals (Northern Ireland) Order 1981
applied: SI 1997/733 Reg.14
Art.12, applied: SI 1997/733 Reg.11
Sch.2 Part I, substituted: SR 1999/204 Art.2

1134. Hydrocarbon Oil (Amendment) Regulations 1981
Reg.3, revoked (in part): SI 1996/2313 Reg.2
Reg.7, amended: SI 1996/2537 Reg.14

1145. London Docklands Development Corporation (Vesting of Land) (Newham London Borough Council) Order 1981
revoked: SI 1998/769 Art.3, Sch.

1146. London Docklands Development Corporation (Vesting of Land) (Southwark London Borough Council) Order 1981
revoked: SI 1998/769 Art.3, Sch.

NO.

1981—cont.

1152. Kiers Regulations 1938 (Metrication) Regulations 1981
revoked: SI 1997/1713 Reg.9, Sch.

1217. Pensions Increase (Review) Order 1981
applied: SI 1997/634 Art.3, SI 1998/503 Art.3, Art.4, SI 1999/522 Art.3

1219. Rules of Procedure (Air Force) (Amendment) Rules 1981
revoked: SI 1997/171 r.90, Sch.7

1220. Rules of Procedure (Army) (Amendment) Rules 1981
revoked: SI 1997/169 r.90, Sch.7

1320. Jam and Similar Products (Scotland) Regulations 1981
amended: SI 1999/1136 Reg.14
Reg.2, amended: SI 1996/1499 Reg.49
Reg.2, referred to: SI 1999/982 Reg.3
Reg.5, amended: SI 1996/1499 Reg.49
Reg.7, amended: SI 1996/1499 Reg.49
Reg.8, amended: SI 1996/1499 Reg.49
Reg.9, amended: SI 1996/1499 Reg.49
Reg.10, amended: SI 1996/1499 Reg.49
Reg.22, revoked: SI 1996/1499 Reg.49, Sch.9
Reg.23, added: SI 1998/1398 Reg.18

1441. Capital Transfer Tax (Delivery of Accounts) (Northern Ireland) Regulations 1981
Reg.3, amended: SI 1996/1473 Reg.2, SI 1998/1429 Reg.2

1455. Brucellosis (England and Wales) Order 1981
revoked: SI 1997/758 Art.24, Sch.2

1468. Ancient Monuments (Class Consents) (Scotland) Order 1981
revoked: SI 1996/1507 Art.1

1472. Merchant Shipping (Passenger Ship Classification) Regulations 1981
applied: SI 1996/3243 Sch Part I
referred to: SI 1998/1609 Reg.5, Reg.6, Sch.
revoked: SI 1998/2514 Reg.1

1483. Postal Privilege (Suspension) Order 1981
revoked: SI 1999/1933 Art.1
Art.2, amended: SI 1999/2107 Reg.5

1489. Employers' Liability (Compulsory Insurance) (Amendment) Regulations 1981
revoked: SI 1998/2573 Reg.10, Sch.3

1499. Building (Procedure) (Scotland) Regulations 1981
Reg.3, amended: SI 1997/2157 Reg.3, SSI 1999/173 Reg.3
Sch.1 para.1, amended: SI 1997/2157 Reg.3

1558. Education (Publication and Consultation) (Scotland) Regulations 1981
Sch.2, see *King v East Ayrshire Council* Times, November 3, 1997 (1 Div), Lord Rodger L.P.

1562. Scottish Examination Board Regulations 1981
Reg.6, amended: SI 1996/579 Reg.2
Reg.13, amended: SI 1996/1970 Reg.2
Reg.14, applied: 1996 c.43 Sch.2 para.2
Reg.16, applied: 1996 c.43 Sch.2 para.2

1576. Housing (Means of Escape from Fire in Houses in Multiple Occupation) Order 1981
revoked: SI 1997/230 Art.1 (with savings)

1650. Church Representation Rules (Amendment) (No.2) Resolution 1981
referred to: SI 1998/319

1675. Magistrates' Courts (Northern Ireland) Order 1981
amended: SI 1999/450 Art.140

NO.

1675. Magistrates' Courts (Northern Ireland) Order 1981—*cont.*
applied: SI 1996/1320 (NI.10) Art.65, SI 1998/1504 (NI.9) Art.26, Art.36, SI 1999/450 Art.140
referred to: 1996 c.22 s.2, s.8, SI 1996/1320 (NI.10) Art.76
Art.2, amended: SI 1998/1504 (NI.9) Art.65, Sch.5 para.15
Art.6A, added: 1999 c.22 s.98
Art.11, applied: SI 1998/1504 (NI.9) Art.27
Art.15, amended: SI 1996/3160 (NI.24) Sch.5 para.9, SI 1998/1504 (NI.9) Art.65, Sch.6
Art.18, applied: SI 1998/1504 (NI.9) Art.17
Art.19, amended: 1996 c.53 s.123, SI 1996/1320 (NI.10) Art.69, 1997 c.22 s.21
Art.19, applied: SI 1996/1320 (NI.10) Art.79, SI 1996/3159 (NI.23) Art.41, 1997 c.22 s.21, SI 1998/1504 (NI.9) Art.17
Art.19, referred to: SI 1996/1320 (NI.10) Art.10, SI 1996/3160 (NI.24) Art.31, SI 1997/2572 Art.16, SI 1997/2592 Art.12, SI 1998/1065 Art.12, SI 1998/1752 Art.18, SI 1999/1516 Reg.9, SI 1999/3133 Art.8
Art.20, applied: SI 1996/1299 (NI.9) Art.4, SI 1996/2154 Reg.37, SI 1996/3160 (NI.24) Art.47, SI 1998/752 Art.3, 1999 c.23 s.67, Sch.7 para.6, SI 1999/2789 (NI.8) Art.40, Sch.2 para.1
Art.23, applied: SI 1996/3160 (NI.24) Art.3, Art.29
Art.24, amended: SI 1998/1504 (NI.9) Art.65, Sch.5 para.16
Art.24, applied: SI 1996/1320 (NI.10) Art.12, Art.27, SI 1996/3160 (NI.24) Art.29
Art.25, applied: SI 1996/3160 (NI.24) Art.3
Art.28, amended: SI 1998/1504 (NI.9) Art.65, Sch.5 para.17
Art.30, amended: SI 1998/1504 (NI.9) Art.65, Sch.5 para.18
Art.33, applied: SI 1996/1320 (NI.10) Art.9
Art.33, referred to: SI 1998/1504 (NI.9) Art.23
Art.45, applied: SI 1996/3160 (NI.24) Art.5, SI 1998/1504 (NI.9) Art.17, Art.23
Art.46, applied: SI 1998/1504 (NI.9) Art.17
Art.47, amended: SI 1996/3160 (NI.24) Art.35, SI 1998/1504 (NI.9) Art.65, Sch.5 para.19
Art.47, applied: SI 1999/1172 Art.2
Art.47, referred to: 1996 c.22 s.5
Art.47, revoked (in part): SI 1998/1504 (NI.9) Art.65, Sch.6
Art.53, amended: SI 1996/3160 (NI.24) Sch.3 para.2
Art.56, referred to: SI 1996/1320 (NI.10) Art.25
Art.58, referred to: SI 1996/3151 Sch.2 para.7
Art.88, amended: SI 1998/1071 (NI.6) Art.41, Sch.3
Art.91, applied: SI 1996/1299 (NI.9) Art.13, Art.14
Art.92, applied: SI 1996/3160 (NI.24) Art.32
Art.98, amended: 1999 c.33 s.169, Sch.14 para.76
Art.102, amended: SI 1996/1919 (NI.16) Art.255, Sch.1
Art.112, applied: SI 1998/1071 (NI.6) Art.27
Art.112, referred to: SI 1998/1071 (NI.6) Art.38
Art.114, applied: SI 1996/247 Art.5, SI 1996/1036 Art.5, SI 1997/883 Art.5, SI 1997/931 Art.5, SI 1997/1949 Art.5, SI 1998/268 Art.5, SI 1998/269 Art.5, SI 1999/424 Art.5, SI 1999/425 Art.5
Art.120, amended: SI 1996/3160 (NI.24) Sch.3 para.3

NO.

1675. Magistrates' Courts (Northern Ireland) Order 1981—*cont.*
Art.127, amended: SI 1998/1504 (NI.9) Art.65, Sch.5 para.20
Art.138, applied: SI 1998/1504 (NI.9) Art.6, Art.7
Art.140, amended: SI 1996/3160 (NI.24) Sch.5 para.10
Art.140, applied: SI 1996/3160 (NI.24) Art.6
Art.140, revoked (in part): SI 1996/3160 (NI.24) Sch.5 para.10, Sch.7
Art.143, applied: SI 1996/3158 (NI.22) Art.83, SI 1996/3159 (NI.23) Art.48, SI 1998/2839 (NI.20) Art.7
Art.145A, amended: 1999 c.22 s.98
Art.146, applied: SI 1996/1299 (NI.9) Art.11, SI 1996/1320 (NI.10) Art.45, SI 1996/3151 Sch.2 para.6, SI 1996/3158 (NI.22) Art.83, SI 1996/3159 (NI.23) Art.48, SI 1997/831 Sch.15 para.4, SI 1997/1624 Sch.5 para.12, SI 1997/1941 Sch.3 para.12, SI 1999/1517 Reg.12, Sch.4 para.9, SI 1999/2001 Reg.24, Sch.8 para.4
Art.146, referred to: SI 1999/1676 Sch.5 para.9
Art.154, applied: SI 1996/247 Art.5, SI 1996/1036 Art.5, SI 1997/883 Art.5, SI 1997/931 Art.5, SI 1997/1949 Art.5, SI 1998/268 Art.5, SI 1998/269 Art.5, SI 1999/424 Art.5, SI 1999/425 Art.5
Art.161, applied: SI 1996/3160 (NI.24) Art.3
Part VIII, applied: SI 1996/3158 (NI.22) Art.30, Art.43, Art.44, Art.48, Art.59, SI 1998/2839 (NI.20) Art.6
Sch.2 para.2, revoked: SI 1996/3160 (NI.24) Sch.5 para.11, Sch.7
Sch.2 para.5, amended: SI 1996/3160 (NI.24) Sch.5 para.11
Sch.5 para.4, applied: SI 1998/1504 (NI.9) Art.17
Sch.6 para.42, revoked: 1998 c.41 s.74, Sch.12 para.5, Sch.14 Part II
Sch.6 para.43, revoked: 1998 c.41 s.74, Sch.12 para.5, Sch.14 Part II
Sch.6 para.96, revoked: SI 1998/1504 (NI.9) Art.65, Sch.6
Sch.6 para.97, revoked: SI 1998/1504 (NI.9) Art.65, Sch.6
Sch.6 para.98, revoked: SI 1998/1504 (NI.9) Art.65, Sch.6
Sch.6 para.99, revoked: SI 1998/1504 (NI.9) Art.65, Sch.6
Sch.6 para.100, revoked: SI 1998/1504 (NI.9) Art.65, Sch.6
Sch.6 para.101, revoked: SI 1998/1504 (NI.9) Art.65, Sch.6
Sch.6 para.102, revoked: SI 1998/1504 (NI.9) Art.65, Sch.6
Sch.6 para.105, revoked: SI 1998/1504 (NI.9) Art.65, Sch.6
Sch.6 para.108, revoked: SI 1998/1504 (NI.9) Art.65, Sch.6
Sch.6 para.109, revoked: SI 1998/1504 (NI.9) Art.65, Sch.6
Sch.6 para.113, revoked: SI 1998/1504 (NI.9) Art.65, Sch.6
Sch.6 para.114, revoked: SI 1998/1504 (NI.9) Art.65, Sch.6
Sch.6 para.123, revoked: SI 1997/2983 (NI.21) Art.13, Sch.2
Sch.6 para.153, revoked: SI 1998/1071 (NI.6) Art.41, Sch.5
Sch.6 para.169, revoked: SI 1996/1320 (NI.10) Sch.4

NO.

1981—cont.

1675. Magistrates' Courts (Northern Ireland) Order 1981—cont.
Sch.6 para.172, revoked: SI 1996/1320 (NI.10) Sch.4
Sch.6 para.173, revoked: SI 1996/1320 (NI.10) Sch.4

1685. Company and Business Names Regulations 1981
Sch., amended: SI 1999/1820 Art.4, Sch.2 para.139

1687. County Court Rules 1981
amended: SI 1998/1899 r.6
referred to: 1997 c.12 Sch.1 para.1
revoked (in part): SI 1998/3132 r.50
Ord. 1,
r.3, amended: SI 1997/1837 r.3
r.3(b)(i), amended: SI 1996/2810 r.2
r.6, amended: SI 1998/3132 r.50, Sch.2
r.6, applied: SI 1998/3132 r.50, Sch.2
r.6, consolidated: SI 1998/3132 r.50, Sch.2
Ord. 2,
r.2(1)(d), revoked: SI 1996/2810 r.3
r.11, applied: SI 1996/2182 Art.3
Ord. 3,
r.3, applied: SI 1996/2182 Art.3
r.6, amended: SI 1998/3132 r.50, Sch.2
r.6, applied: SI 1998/3132 r.50, Sch.2
r.6, consolidated: SI 1998/3132 r.50, Sch.2
Ord. 4,
r.3, amended: SI 1998/3132 r.50, Sch.2
r.3, applied: SI 1998/3132 r.50, Sch.2
r.3, consolidated: SI 1998/3132 r.50, Sch.2
Ord. 5,
r.5, amended: SI 1998/3132 r.50, Sch.2
r.5, applied: SI 1998/3132 r.50, Sch.2
r.5, consolidated: SI 1998/3132 r.50, Sch.2
r.6, amended: SI 1998/3132 r.50, Sch.2
r.6, applied: SI 1998/3132 r.50, Sch.2
r.6, consolidated: SI 1998/3132 r.50, Sch.2
r.7, amended: SI 1998/3132 r.50, Sch.2
r.7, applied: SI 1998/3132 r.50, Sch.2
r.7, consolidated: SI 1998/3132 r.50, Sch.2
r.8, amended: SI 1998/3132 r.50, Sch.2
r.8, applied: SI 1998/3132 r.50, Sch.2
r.8, consolidated: SI 1998/3132 r.50, Sch.2
r.9, amended: SI 1998/3132 r.50, Sch.2
r.9, applied: SI 1998/3132 r.50, Sch.2
r.9, consolidated: SI 1998/3132 r.50, Sch.2
r.10, amended: SI 1998/3132 r.50, Sch.2
r.10, applied: SI 1998/3132 r.50, Sch.2
r.10, consolidated: SI 1998/3132 r.50, Sch.2
r.12, amended: SI 1998/3132 r.50, Sch.2
r.12, applied: SI 1998/3132 r.50, Sch.2
r.12, consolidated: SI 1998/3132 r.50, Sch.2
r.13, amended: SI 1998/3132 r.50, Sch.2
r.13, applied: SI 1998/3132 r.50, Sch.2
r.13, consolidated: SI 1998/3132 r.50, Sch.2
r.14, amended: SI 1998/3132 r.50, Sch.2
r.14, applied: SI 1998/3132 r.50, Sch.2
r.14, consolidated: SI 1998/3132 r.50, Sch.2
Ord. 6,
see *Croydon (Unique) Ltd v Wright* [1999] 4 All E.R. 257 (CA), Sir Christopher Staughton
r.1, see *Reed v Leeds City Council* [1996] P.I.Q.R. P59 (CA), Stuart-Smith, L.J.
r.2, see *Senyonjo v East London and the City HA* [1996] P.N.L.R. 326 (CA), Stuart-Smith, L.J.
r.3, see *Croydon (Unique) Ltd v Wright* [1999] 4 All E.R. 257 (CA), Sir Christopher Staughton

NO.

1981—cont.

1687. County Court Rules 1981—cont.
Ord. 6—cont.
r.3, amended: SI 1998/3132 r.50, Sch.2
r.3, applied: SI 1998/3132 r.50, Sch.2
r.3, consolidated: SI 1998/3132 r.50, Sch.2
r.5, amended: SI 1998/3132 r.50, Sch.2
r.5, applied: SI 1998/3132 r.50, Sch.2
r.5, consolidated: SI 1998/3132 r.50, Sch.2
r.5A, amended: SI 1998/3132 r.50, Sch.2
r.5A, applied: SI 1998/3132 r.50, Sch.2
r.5A, consolidated: SI 1998/3132 r.50, Sch.2
r.6, amended: SI 1998/3132 r.50, Sch.2
r.6, applied: SI 1998/3132 r.50, Sch.2
r.6, consolidated: SI 1998/3132 r.50, Sch.2
Ord. 7,
see *Barclays Bank Plc v Thomson* [1997] 4 All E.R. 816 (CA), Simon Brown, L.J.
r.6, applied: SI 1996/2182 Art.3
r.10, see *Senyonjo v East London and the City HA* [1996] P.N.L.R. 326 (CA), Stuart-Smith, L.J.
r.15, amended: SI 1998/3132 r.50, Sch.2
r.15, applied: SI 1998/3132 r.50, Sch.2
r.15, consolidated: SI 1998/3132 r.50, Sch.2
r.15A, amended: SI 1998/3132 r.50, Sch.2
r.15A, applied: SI 1998/3132 r.50, Sch.2
r.15A, consolidated: SI 1998/3132 r.50, Sch.2
r.20, see *Jones v Telford and Wrekin Council* Times, July 29, 1999 (CA), Lord Woolf, M.R.; see *Lewis v Harewood* [1997] P.I.Q.R. P58 (CA), Waite, L.J.
Ord. 9,
see *Greig Middleton & Co Ltd v Denderowicz (No.2)* [1998] 1 W.L.R. 1164 (CA), Saville, L.J.; see *Pearce & High Ltd v Baxter* [1999] B.L.R. 101 (CA), Evans, L.J.; see *Perrin v Short* [1997] P.I.Q.R. P426 (CA), Swinton Thomas, L.J.; see *Sullivan v Blanning* Times, October 27, 1999 (CA), Morritt, L.J.; see *Watkins v Toms* [1998] 1 W.L.R. 1376 (Note) (CA), Judge, L.J.
r.2, see *Watkins v Toms* [1998] 2 All E.R. 534 (Note) (CA), Judge, L.J.
r.2(6), see *Dialworth Ltd v TG Organisation Europe Ltd* (1998) 75 P. & C.R. 147 (CA), Henry, L.J.; see *Lightfoot v National Westminster Bank Plc* [1996] 1 W.L.R. 583 (CA), Otton, L.J.
r.6, see *Garner v Stonestreet* Times, May 28, 1999 (CA), Auld, L.J.; see *Watkins v Toms* [1998] 2 All E.R. 534 (Note) (CA), Judge, L.J.
r.6, applied: SI 1996/2182 Art.3
r.10, see *Harding v Cartwright* Times, June 9, 1997 (CA), Lord Woolf, M.R.; see *Limb v Union Jack Removals Ltd* [1998] 2 All E.R. 513 (CA), Brooke, L.J.; see *Parrott v Jackson* [1996] P.I.Q.R. P394 (CA), Hirst, L.J.; see *Watkins v Toms* [1998] 2 All E.R. 534 (Note) (CA), Judge, L.J.
r.14, see *DG Finance Ltd v Scott and Eagle Star Insurance Co Ltd* [1999] Lloyd's Rep. I.R. 387 (CA), Hobhouse, L.J.; see *Pearce & High Ltd v Baxter* [1999] B.L.R. 101 (CA), Evans, L.J.
Ord. 10,
applied: SI 1996/207 Sch.8 para.42, SI 1996/2890 Sch.4 para.46
r.10, see *C (A Minor) v Hackney LBC* [1996] 1 W.L.R. 789 (CA), Simon Brown, L.J.

NO.

1687. County Court Rules 1981—*cont.*

Ord. 11

see *Harding v Cartwright* Times, June 9, 1997 (CA), Lord Woolf, M.R.

r.1, see *Black v Doncaster MBC* [1998] 3 All E.R. 631 (CA), Stuart-Smith, L.J.; see *Hoppe v Titman* [1996] 1 W.L.R. 841 (CA), Pill, L.J.

r.1, amended: SI 1996/2181 r.3

r.1A, added: SI 1998/1899 r.2

Ord. 13,

see *Bristol City Council v Lovell* [1998] 1 W.L.R. 446 (HL), Lord Hoffmann.; see *Dodd v Chief Constable of Cheshire* Times, December 2, 1998 (CA), Cazalet, J.; see *Vandersteen (Executor of the Estate of McGuinnes, Deceased) v Agius* Times, November 14, 1997 (CA), Staughton, L.J

r.1, amended: SI 1998/3132 r.50, Sch.2

r.1, applied: SI 1998/3132 r.50, Sch.2

r.1, consolidated: SI 1998/3132 r.50, Sch.2

r.1(10), see *Toumia v Evans* Times, April 1, 1999 (CA), Brooke, L.J.

r.3, see *Kingcastle Ltd v Owen-Owen* Times, March 18, 1999 (CA), Hirst, L.J.

r.4, see *Ritchie v Ritchie* [1996] 1 F.L.R. 898 (CA), Bennett, J.; see *Tavera v Macfarlane* [1996] P.I.Q.R. P292 (CA), Hutchison, L.J.

r.5, see *Haringey LBC v Cotter* (1997) 29 H.L.R. 682 (CA), Mummery, L.J.; see *Jones v Vans Colina* [1996] 1 W.L.R. 1580 (CA), Nourse, L.J.

r.6, see *Hughes v Jones* [1996] P.I.Q.R. P380 (CA), Henry, L.J.

Ord. 15,

see *Pope (A Bankrupt), Re* [1998] B.P.I.R. 143 (Ch D), Hazel Williamson Q.C.

Ord. 16,

r.2, see *NP Engineering and Security Products Ltd, Re* [1998] 1 B.C.L.C. 208 (CA), Morritt, L.J; see *Official Receiver v Pafundo* [1998] 1 B.C.L.C. 208 (CA), Morritt, L.J.; see *St Giles Hotel Ltd v Microworld Technology Ltd* (1998) 75 P. & C.R. 380 (CA), Millett, L.J.

r.7, amended: SI 1998/3132 r.50, Sch.2

r.7, applied: SI 1998/3132 r.50, Sch.2

r.7, consolidated: SI 1998/3132 r.50, Sch.2

Ord. 17,

r.1(9), see *Carr v Northern Clubs Federation Brewery Ltd* [1996] P.I.Q.R. P315 (CA), Waite, L.J.; see *Downer & Downer Ltd v Brough* [1996] 1 W.L.R. 575 (CA), Waite, L.J.; see *Hackwell v Blue Arrow Plc (t/a Extra Staff)* Times, January 18, 1996 (CA), Waite, L.J.; see *Jackson v Slater Harrison and Co Ltd* [1996] 1 W.L.R. 597 (CA), Otton, L.J.; see *Reville v Wright* [1996] 1 W.L.R. 592 (CA), Otton, L.J.; see *Russell v Dennis* Times, January 18, 1996 (CA), Sir Thomas Bingham, M.R.; see *Williams v Globe Coaches* [1996] 1 W.L.R. 553 (CA), Sir Thomas Bingham, M.R.

r.10, see *Edmondson v Scottish and Newcastle Breweries Plc* Times, June 21, 1997 (CA), Brooke, L.J.

r.11, see *Ashworth v McKay Foods* [1996] 1 W.L.R. 542 (CA), Sir Thomas Bingham, M.R.; see *Bannister v SGB Plc* [1998] 1 W.L.R. 1123 (CA), Saville, L.J.; see *Burgess v Stratton* Times, October 15, 1996

NO.

1687. County Court Rules 1981—*cont.*

Ord. 17—*cont.*

r.11—*cont.*

(CA), Waite, L.J.; see *Cockerill v Tambrands Ltd* [1998] 1 W.L.R. 1379 (CA), Brooke, L.J.; see *Ever v WT Partnership Construction Management* Times, January 9, 1997 (CA), Aldous, L.J.; see *Ferreira v American Embassy Employees Association* [1996] 1 W.L.R. 536 (CA), Roch, L.J.; see *Figgett v Davies* [1998] 1 W.L.R. 1184 (CA), Brooke, L.J; see *Gardner v Southwark LBC (No.2)* [1996] 1 W.L.R. 561 (CA), Waite, L.J.; see *Gomes v Clark* [1997] P.I.Q.R. P219 (CA), Lord Woolf, M.R.; see *Greig Middleton & Co Ltd v Denderowicz (No.1)* [1997] 4 All E.R. 181 (CA), Saville, L.J.; see *Greig Middleton & Co Ltd v Denderowicz (No.2)* [1998] 1 W.L.R. 1164 (CA), Saville, L.J.; see *Greig Middleton & Co Ltd v Denderowicz (No.3)* Times, July 28, 1997 (CA), Saville, L.J.; see *Jones v Bayford Mining Co Ltd* Times, June 6, 1997 (CA), Lord Woolf, M.R.; see *Perry v Kang Ho Wong* [1997] 1 W.L.R. 381 (CA), Lord Bingham of Cornhill, L.C.J.; see *Segaram v Grant* (1997) 73 P. & C.R. D35 (CA), Lord Woolf, M.R.; see *Tarry v Humberclyde Finance Ltd* [1996] 1 W.L.R. 611 (CA), Sir Thomas Bingham, M.R.; see *Watkins v Toms* [1998] 1 W.L.R. 1376 (Note) (CA), Judge, L.J.; see *Whitehead v Avon CC* [1997] P.I.Q.R. P148 (CA), Waller, L.J.

r.11(3), see *Downer and Downer Ltd v Brough* [1996] 1 W.L.R. 575 (CA), Waite, L.J.

r.11(9), see *Carr v Northern Clubs Federation Brewery Ltd* Times, January 18, 1996 (CA), Waite, L.J.; see *Gardner v Southwark BC* Times, January 18, 1996 (CA), Waite, L.J.; see *Hackwell v Blue Arrow Plc t/a Extra Staff* Times, January 18, 1996 (CA), Waite, L.J.; see *Jackson v Slater Harrison and Co Ltd* Times, January 18, 1996 (CA), Otton, L.J.; see *Peters v Winfield* [1996] 1 W.L.R. 604 (CA), Sir Thomas Bingham, M.R.; see *Reville v Wright* Times, January 18, 1996 (CA), Otton, L.J.; see *Russell v Dennis* Times, January 18, 1996 (CA), Sir Thomas Bingham, M.R.

r.11(11), see *Lightfoot v National Westminster Bank Plc* [1996] 1 W.L.R. 583 (CA), Otton, L.J.

Ord. 18,

see *Gilham v Browning* [1998] 1 W.L.R. 682 (CA), May, L.J.

Ord. 19,

see *Candler v Thomas (t/a London Leisure Lines)* [1998] R.T.R. 214 (CA), Brooke, L.J.; see *Greig Middleton & Co Ltd v Denderowicz (No.1)* [1997] 4 All E.R. 181 (CA), Saville, L.J.; see *Greig Middleton & Co Ltd v Denderowicz (No.2)* [1998] 1 W.L.R. 1164 (CA), Saville, L.J.

r.4, see *Smith v Vauxhall Motors Ltd* [1997] P.I.Q.R. P19 (CA), Roch, L.J.

r.15, amended: SI 1998/3132 r.50, Sch.2

r.15, applied: SI 1998/3132 r.50, Sch.2

r.15, consolidated: SI 1998/3132 r.50, Sch.2

Ord. 20,

r.12A, see *Beachley Property Ltd v Edgar* [1997] P.N.L.R. 197 (CA), Lord Woolf, M.R.

NO.

1687. County Court Rules 1981—*cont.*
Ord. 20—*cont.*
r.14, substituted: SI 1996/3218 r.2
r.15, substituted: SI 1996/3218 r.2
r.16, substituted: SI 1996/3218 r.2
r.17, substituted: SI 1996/3218 r.2
r.18, substituted: SI 1996/3218 r.2
r.19, substituted: SI 1996/3218 r.2
r.20, substituted: SI 1996/3218 r.2
r.21, substituted: SI 1996/3218 r.2
r.22, substituted: SI 1996/3218 r.2
r.23, substituted: SI 1996/3218 r.2
r.24, substituted: SI 1996/3218 r.2
Ord. 21,
r.2(1), see *Kemmings v Sandwell MBC* Independent, February 8, 1999 (C.S.) (CA), Evans, L.J.
r.5, see *Hughes v Jones* [1996] P.I.Q.R. P380 (CA), Henry, L.J.
Ord. 22,
r.1, applied: SI 1996/2182 Art.3
r.8, amended: SI 1998/3132 r.50, Sch.2
r.8, applied: SI 1998/3132 r.50, Sch.2
r.8, consolidated: SI 1998/3132 r.50, Sch.2
r.8(1A), see *Practice Direction (QBD: County Court Order: Enforcement) (No.2)* [1998] 1 W.L.R. 1557 (QBD), RL Turner
r.8(1A), amended: SI 1998/3132 r.50, Sch.2
r.8(1A), applied: SI 1998/3132 r.50, Sch.2
r.8(1A), consolidated: SI 1998/3132 r.50, Sch.2
r.8(3), amended: SI 1997/1837 r.4, SI 1998/3132 r.50, Sch.2
r.8(3), applied: SI 1998/3132 r.50, Sch.2
r.8(3), consolidated: SI 1998/3132 r.50, Sch.2
r.10, amended: SI 1998/3132 r.50, Sch.2
r.10, applied: SI 1998/3132 r.50, Sch.2
r.10, consolidated: SI 1998/3132 r.50, Sch.2
r.10, referred to: SI 1998/3132 r.13.1
r.11, amended: SI 1998/3132 r.50, Sch.2
r.11, applied: SI 1998/3132 r.50, Sch.2
r.11, consolidated: SI 1998/3132 r.50, Sch.2
r.13, amended: SI 1998/3132 r.50, Sch.2
r.13, applied: SI 1998/3132 r.50, Sch.2
r.13, consolidated: SI 1998/3132 r.50, Sch.2
Ord. 24,
see *R. v Hillingdon LBC Ex p. McDonagh* [1999] E.H.L.R. 169 (QBD), Carnwath, J.
r.1, amended: SI 1998/3132 r.50, Sch.2
r.1, applied: SI 1998/3132 r.50, Sch.2
r.1, consolidated: SI 1998/3132 r.50, Sch.2
r.2, amended: SI 1998/3132 r.50, Sch.2
r.2, applied: SI 1998/3132 r.50, Sch.2
r.2, consolidated: SI 1998/3132 r.50, Sch.2
r.3, amended: SI 1998/3132 r.50, Sch.2
r.3, applied: SI 1998/3132 r.50, Sch.2
r.3, consolidated: SI 1998/3132 r.50, Sch.2
r.4, amended: SI 1998/3132 r.50, Sch.2
r.4, applied: SI 1998/3132 r.50, Sch.2
r.4, consolidated: SI 1998/3132 r.50, Sch.2
r.5, amended: SI 1998/3132 r.50, Sch.2
r.5, applied: SI 1998/3132 r.50, Sch.2
r.5, consolidated: SI 1998/3132 r.50, Sch.2
r.6, amended: SI 1998/3132 r.50, Sch.2
r.6, applied: SI 1998/3132 r.50, Sch.2
r.6, consolidated: SI 1998/3132 r.50, Sch.2
r.7, amended: SI 1998/3132 r.50, Sch.2
r.7, applied: SI 1998/3132 r.50, Sch.2
r.7, consolidated: SI 1998/3132 r.50, Sch.2
r.8, amended: SI 1998/3132 r.50, Sch.2
r.8, applied: SI 1998/3132 r.50, Sch.2

NO.

1687. County Court Rules 1981—*cont.*
Ord. 24—*cont.*
r.8, consolidated: SI 1998/3132 r.50, Sch.2
r.9, amended: SI 1998/3132 r.50, Sch.2
r.9, applied: SI 1998/3132 r.50, Sch.2
r.9, consolidated: SI 1998/3132 r.50, Sch.2
r.10, amended: SI 1998/3132 r.50, Sch.2
r.10, applied: SI 1998/3132 r.50, Sch.2
r.10, consolidated: SI 1998/3132 r.50, Sch.2
r.11, amended: SI 1998/3132 r.50, Sch.2
r.11, applied: SI 1998/3132 r.50, Sch.2
r.11, consolidated: SI 1998/3132 r.50, Sch.2
r.12, amended: SI 1998/3132 r.50, Sch.2
r.12, applied: SI 1998/3132 r.50, Sch.2
r.12, consolidated: SI 1998/3132 r.50, Sch.2
r.13, amended: SI 1998/3132 r.50, Sch.2
r.13, applied: SI 1998/3132 r.50, Sch.2
r.13, consolidated: SI 1998/3132 r.50, Sch.2
r.14, amended: SI 1998/3132 r.50, Sch.2
r.14, applied: SI 1998/3132 r.50, Sch.2
r.14, consolidated: SI 1998/3132 r.50, Sch.2
r.15, amended: SI 1998/3132 r.50, Sch.2
r.15, applied: SI 1998/3132 r.50, Sch.2
r.15, consolidated: SI 1998/3132 r.50, Sch.2
Ord. 25,
r.1, amended: SI 1998/3132 r.50, Sch.2
r.1, applied: SI 1998/3132 r.50, Sch.2
r.1, consolidated: SI 1998/3132 r.50, Sch.2
r.2, amended: SI 1998/3132 r.50, Sch.2
r.2, applied: SI 1998/3132 r.50, Sch.2
r.2, consolidated: SI 1998/3132 r.50, Sch.2
r.3, amended: SI 1998/3132 r.50, Sch.2
r.3, applied: SI 1998/3132 r.50, Sch.2
r.3, consolidated: SI 1998/3132 r.50, Sch.2
r.3(1), amended: SI 1997/1837 r.5, SI 1998/3132 r.50, Sch.2
r.3(1), applied: SI 1998/3132 r.50, Sch.2
r.3(1), consolidated: SI 1998/3132 r.50, Sch.2
r.4, amended: SI 1998/3132 r.50, Sch.2
r.4, applied: SI 1998/3132 r.50, Sch.2
r.4, consolidated: SI 1998/3132 r.50, Sch.2
r.5, amended: SI 1998/3132 r.50, Sch.2
r.5, applied: SI 1998/3132 r.50, Sch.2
r.5, consolidated: SI 1998/3132 r.50, Sch.2
r.5(3), applied: SI 1998/3132 r.5.2
r.5A, amended: SI 1998/3132 r.50, Sch.2
r.5A, applied: SI 1998/3132 r.50, Sch.2
r.5A, consolidated: SI 1998/3132 r.50, Sch.2
r.6, amended: SI 1998/3132 r.50, Sch.2
r.6, applied: SI 1998/3132 r.50, Sch.2
r.6, consolidated: SI 1998/3132 r.50, Sch.2
r.7, amended: SI 1998/3132 r.50, Sch.2
r.7, applied: SI 1998/3132 r.50, Sch.2
r.7, consolidated: SI 1998/3132 r.50, Sch.2
r.8, amended: SI 1998/3132 r.50, Sch.2
r.8, applied: SI 1998/3132 r.50, Sch.2
r.8, consolidated: SI 1998/3132 r.50, Sch.2
r.8(9), applied: SI 1998/3132 r.5.2
r.9, amended: SI 1998/3132 r.50, Sch.2
r.9, applied: SI 1998/3132 r.50, Sch.2
r.9, consolidated: SI 1998/3132 r.50, Sch.2
r.10, amended: SI 1998/3132 r.50, Sch.2
r.10, applied: SI 1998/3132 r.50, Sch.2
r.10, consolidated: SI 1998/3132 r.50, Sch.2
r.11, amended: SI 1998/3132 r.50, Sch.2
r.11, applied: SI 1998/3132 r.50, Sch.2
r.11, consolidated: SI 1998/3132 r.50, Sch.2
r.12, amended: SI 1998/3132 r.50, Sch.2
r.12, applied: SI 1998/3132 r.50, Sch.2
r.12, consolidated: SI 1998/3132 r.50, Sch.2
r.13, amended: SI 1998/3132 r.50, Sch.2

1981—cont.

1687. County Court Rules 1981—*cont.*
Ord. 25—*cont.*
r.13, applied: SI 1998/3132 r.50, Sch.2
r.13, consolidated: SI 1998/3132 r.50, Sch.2
Ord. 26,
r.1, amended: SI 1996/2181 r.5, SI 1998/
3132 r.50, Sch.2
r.1, applied: SI 1998/3132 r.50, Sch.2
r.1, consolidated: SI 1998/3132 r.50, Sch.2
r.2, amended: SI 1998/3132 r.50, Sch.2
r.2, applied: SI 1998/3132 r.50, Sch.2
r.2, consolidated: SI 1998/3132 r.50, Sch.2
r.3, amended: SI 1998/3132 r.50, Sch.2
r.3, applied: SI 1998/3132 r.50, Sch.2
r.3, consolidated: SI 1998/3132 r.50, Sch.2
r.4, amended: SI 1998/3132 r.50, Sch.2
r.4, applied: SI 1998/3132 r.50, Sch.2
r.4, consolidated: SI 1998/3132 r.50, Sch.2
r.5, see *Hackney LBC v White* (1996) 28
H.L.R. 219 (CA), Russell, L.J.
r.5, amended: SI 1998/3132 r.50, Sch.2
r.5, applied: SI 1998/3132 r.50, Sch.2
r.5, consolidated: SI 1998/3132 r.50, Sch.2
r.6, amended: SI 1998/3132 r.50, Sch.2
r.6, applied: SI 1998/3132 r.50, Sch.2
r.6, consolidated: SI 1998/3132 r.50, Sch.2
r.7, amended: SI 1998/3132 r.50, Sch.2
r.7, applied: SI 1998/3132 r.50, Sch.2
r.7, consolidated: SI 1998/3132 r.50, Sch.2
r.8, amended: SI 1998/3132 r.50, Sch.2
r.8, applied: SI 1998/3132 r.50, Sch.2
r.8, consolidated: SI 1998/3132 r.50, Sch.2
r.10, amended: SI 1998/3132 r.50, Sch.2
r.10, applied: SI 1998/3132 r.50, Sch.2
r.10, consolidated: SI 1998/3132 r.50, Sch.2
r.11, amended: SI 1998/3132 r.50, Sch.2
r.11, applied: SI 1998/3132 r.50, Sch.2
r.11, consolidated: SI 1998/3132 r.50, Sch.2
r.12, amended: SI 1998/3132 r.50, Sch.2
r.12, applied: SI 1998/3132 r.50, Sch.2
r.12, consolidated: SI 1998/3132 r.50, Sch.2
r.13, amended: SI 1998/3132 r.50, Sch.2
r.13, applied: SI 1998/3132 r.50, Sch.2
r.13, consolidated: SI 1998/3132 r.50, Sch.2
r.14, amended: SI 1998/3132 r.50, Sch.2
r.14, applied: SI 1998/3132 r.50, Sch.2
r.14, consolidated: SI 1998/3132 r.50, Sch.2
r.15, amended: SI 1998/3132 r.50, Sch.2
r.15, applied: SI 1998/3132 r.50, Sch.2
r.15, consolidated: SI 1998/3132 r.50, Sch.2
r.16, amended: SI 1998/3132 r.50, Sch.2
r.16, applied: SI 1998/3132 r.50, Sch.2
r.16, consolidated: SI 1998/3132 r.50, Sch.2
r.17, amended: SI 1998/3132 r.50, Sch.2
r.17, applied: SI 1998/3132 r.50, Sch.2
r.17, consolidated: SI 1998/3132 r.50, Sch.2
r.18, amended: SI 1998/3132 r.50, Sch.2
r.18, applied: SI 1998/3132 r.50, Sch.2
r.18, consolidated: SI 1998/3132 r.50, Sch.2
Ord. 27,
r.1, amended: SI 1998/3132 r.50, Sch.2
r.1, applied: SI 1998/3132 r.50, Sch.2
r.1, consolidated: SI 1998/3132 r.50, Sch.2
r.2, amended: SI 1998/3132 r.50, Sch.2
r.2, applied: SI 1998/3132 r.50, Sch.2
r.2, consolidated: SI 1998/3132 r.50, Sch.2
r.3, amended: SI 1998/3132 r.50, Sch.2
r.3, applied: SI 1998/3132 r.50, Sch.2
r.3, consolidated: SI 1998/3132 r.50, Sch.2
r.4, amended: SI 1998/3132 r.50, Sch.2
r.4, applied: SI 1998/3132 r.50, Sch.2
r.4, consolidated: SI 1998/3132 r.50, Sch.2

1981—cont.

1687. County Court Rules 1981—*cont.*
Ord. 27—*cont.*
r.5, amended: SI 1998/3132 r.50, Sch.2
r.5, applied: SI 1998/3132 r.50, Sch.2
r.5, consolidated: SI 1998/3132 r.50, Sch.2
r.6, amended: SI 1998/3132 r.50, Sch.2
r.6, applied: SI 1998/3132 r.50, Sch.2
r.6, consolidated: SI 1998/3132 r.50, Sch.2
r.7, amended: SI 1998/3132 r.50, Sch.2
r.7, applied: SI 1996/2182 Art.3, SI 1998/
3132 r.50, Sch.2
r.7, consolidated: SI 1998/3132 r.50, Sch.2
r.7A, amended: SI 1998/3132 r.50, Sch.2
r.7A, applied: SI 1998/3132 r.50, Sch.2
r.7A, consolidated: SI 1998/3132 r.50, Sch.2
r.7B, amended: SI 1998/3132 r.50, Sch.2
r.7B, applied: SI 1998/3132 r.50, Sch.2
r.7B, consolidated: SI 1998/3132 r.50, Sch.2
r.8, amended: SI 1998/3132 r.50, Sch.2
r.8, applied: SI 1998/3132 r.50, Sch.2
r.8, consolidated: SI 1998/3132 r.50, Sch.2
r.9, amended: SI 1998/3132 r.50, Sch.2
r.9, applied: SI 1998/3132 r.50, Sch.2
r.9, consolidated: SI 1998/3132 r.50, Sch.2
r.10, amended: SI 1998/3132 r.50, Sch.2
r.10, applied: SI 1998/3132 r.50, Sch.2
r.10, consolidated: SI 1998/3132 r.50, Sch.2
r.11, amended: SI 1998/3132 r.50, Sch.2
r.11, applied: SI 1998/3132 r.50, Sch.2
r.11, consolidated: SI 1998/3132 r.50, Sch.2
r.12, amended: SI 1998/3132 r.50, Sch.2
r.12, applied: SI 1998/3132 r.50, Sch.2
r.12, consolidated: SI 1998/3132 r.50, Sch.2
r.13, amended: SI 1998/3132 r.50, Sch.2
r.13, applied: SI 1998/3132 r.50, Sch.2
r.13, consolidated: SI 1998/3132 r.50, Sch.2
r.14, amended: SI 1998/3132 r.50, Sch.2
r.14, applied: SI 1998/3132 r.50, Sch.2
r.14, consolidated: SI 1998/3132 r.50, Sch.2
r.15, amended: SI 1998/3132 r.50, Sch.2
r.15, applied: SI 1998/3132 r.50, Sch.2
r.15, consolidated: SI 1998/3132 r.50, Sch.2
r.16, amended: SI 1998/3132 r.50, Sch.2
r.16, applied: SI 1998/3132 r.50, Sch.2
r.16, consolidated: SI 1998/3132 r.50, Sch.2
r.17, amended: SI 1998/3132 r.50, Sch.2
r.17, applied: SI 1998/3132 r.50, Sch.2
r.17, consolidated: SI 1998/3132 r.50, Sch.2
r.18, amended: SI 1998/3132 r.50, Sch.2
r.18, applied: SI 1998/3132 r.50, Sch.2
r.18, consolidated: SI 1998/3132 r.50, Sch.2
r.19, amended: SI 1998/3132 r.50, Sch.2
r.19, applied: SI 1998/3132 r.50, Sch.2
r.19, consolidated: SI 1998/3132 r.50, Sch.2
r.20, amended: SI 1998/3132 r.50, Sch.2
r.20, applied: SI 1998/3132 r.50, Sch.2
r.20, consolidated: SI 1998/3132 r.50, Sch.2
r.21, amended: SI 1998/3132 r.50, Sch.2
r.21, applied: SI 1998/3132 r.50, Sch.2
r.21, consolidated: SI 1998/3132 r.50, Sch.2
r.22, amended: SI 1998/3132 r.50, Sch.2
r.22, applied: SI 1998/3132 r.50, Sch.2
r.22, consolidated: SI 1998/3132 r.50, Sch.2
Ord. 28,
r.1, amended: SI 1998/3132 r.50, Sch.2
r.1, applied: SI 1998/3132 r.50, Sch.2
r.1, consolidated: SI 1998/3132 r.50, Sch.2
r.2, amended: SI 1998/3132 r.50, Sch.2
r.2, applied: SI 1998/3132 r.50, Sch.2
r.2, consolidated: SI 1998/3132 r.50, Sch.2
r.3, amended: SI 1998/3132 r.50, Sch.2
r.3, applied: SI 1998/3132 r.50, Sch.2

NO.

1981—cont.

1687. County Court Rules 1981—*cont.*

Ord. 28—*cont.*

r.3, consolidated: SI 1998/3132 r.50, Sch.2
r.4, amended: SI 1998/3132 r.50, Sch.2
r.4, applied: SI 1998/3132 r.50, Sch.2
r.4, consolidated: SI 1998/3132 r.50, Sch.2
r.5, amended: SI 1998/3132 r.50, Sch.2
r.5, applied: SI 1998/3132 r.50, Sch.2
r.5, consolidated: SI 1998/3132 r.50, Sch.2
r.7, amended: SI 1998/3132 r.50, Sch.2
r.7, applied: SI 1998/3132 r.50, Sch.2
r.7, consolidated: SI 1998/3132 r.50, Sch.2
r.8, amended: SI 1998/3132 r.50, Sch.2
r.8, applied: SI 1998/3132 r.50, Sch.2
r.8, consolidated: SI 1998/3132 r.50, Sch.2
r.9, amended: SI 1998/3132 r.50, Sch.2
r.9, applied: SI 1998/3132 r.50, Sch.2
r.9, consolidated: SI 1998/3132 r.50, Sch.2
r.10, amended: SI 1998/3132 r.50, Sch.2
r.10, applied: SI 1998/3132 r.50, Sch.2
r.10, consolidated: SI 1998/3132 r.50, Sch.2
r.11, amended: SI 1998/3132 r.50, Sch.2
r.11, applied: SI 1998/3132 r.50, Sch.2
r.11, consolidated: SI 1998/3132 r.50, Sch.2
r.11(1), applied: SI 1998/3132 r.5.2
r.12, amended: SI 1998/3132 r.50, Sch.2
r.12, applied: SI 1998/3132 r.50, Sch.2
r.12, consolidated: SI 1998/3132 r.50, Sch.2
r.13, amended: SI 1998/3132 r.50, Sch.2
r.13, applied: SI 1998/3132 r.50, Sch.2
r.13, consolidated: SI 1998/3132 r.50, Sch.2
r.14, amended: SI 1998/3132 r.50, Sch.2
r.14, applied: SI 1998/3132 r.50, Sch.2
r.14, consolidated: SI 1998/3132 r.50, Sch.2

Ord. 29,

r.1, amended: SI 1998/3132 r.50, Sch.2
r.1, applied: SI 1998/3132 r.50, Sch.2
r.1, consolidated: SI 1998/3132 r.50, Sch.2
r.1(3), amended: SI 1998/3132 r.50, Sch.2
r.1(3), applied: SI 1998/3132 r.50, Sch.2
r.1(3), consolidated: SI 1998/3132 r.50, Sch.2
r.1A, amended: SI 1998/3132 r.50, Sch.2
r.1A, applied: SI 1998/3132 r.50, Sch.2
r.1A, consolidated: SI 1998/3132 r.50, Sch.2
r.2, amended: SI 1998/3132 r.50, Sch.2
r.2, applied: SI 1998/3132 r.50, Sch.2
r.2, consolidated: SI 1998/3132 r.50, Sch.2
r.3, amended: SI 1998/3132 r.50, Sch.2
r.3, applied: SI 1998/3132 r.50, Sch.2
r.3, consolidated: SI 1998/3132 r.50, Sch.2

Ord. 30,

r.1, amended: SI 1998/3132 r.50, Sch.2
r.1, applied: SI 1998/3132 r.50, Sch.2
r.1, consolidated: SI 1998/3132 r.50, Sch.2
r.1(1), amended: SI 1996/3218 r.4, SI 1998/
3132 r.50, Sch.2
r.1(1), applied: SI 1998/3132 r.50, Sch.2
r.1(1), consolidated: SI 1998/3132 r.50, Sch.2
r.2, amended: SI 1998/3132 r.50, Sch.2
r.2, applied: SI 1998/3132 r.50, Sch.2
r.2, consolidated: SI 1998/3132 r.50, Sch.2
r.3, amended: SI 1998/3132 r.50, Sch.2
r.3, applied: SI 1998/3132 r.50, Sch.2
r.3, consolidated: SI 1998/3132 r.50, Sch.2
r.5, amended: SI 1998/3132 r.50, Sch.2
r.5, applied: SI 1998/3132 r.50, Sch.2
r.5, consolidated: SI 1998/3132 r.50, Sch.2
r.7, amended: SI 1998/3132 r.50, Sch.2
r.7, applied: SI 1998/3132 r.50, Sch.2
r.7, consolidated: SI 1998/3132 r.50, Sch.2

1687. County Court Rules 1981—*cont.*

Ord. 30—*cont.*

r.8, amended: SI 1998/3132 r.50, Sch.2
r.8, applied: SI 1998/3132 r.50, Sch.2
r.8, consolidated: SI 1998/3132 r.50, Sch.2
r.9, amended: SI 1998/3132 r.50, Sch.2
r.9, applied: SI 1998/3132 r.50, Sch.2
r.9, consolidated: SI 1998/3132 r.50, Sch.2
r.10, amended: SI 1998/3132 r.50, Sch.2
r.10, applied: SI 1998/3132 r.50, Sch.2
r.10, consolidated: SI 1998/3132 r.50, Sch.2
r.11, amended: SI 1998/3132 r.50, Sch.2
r.11, applied: SI 1998/3132 r.50, Sch.2
r.11, consolidated: SI 1998/3132 r.50, Sch.2
r.12, amended: SI 1998/3132 r.50, Sch.2
r.12, applied: SI 1998/3132 r.50, Sch.2
r.12, consolidated: SI 1998/3132 r.50, Sch.2
r.13, amended: SI 1998/3132 r.50, Sch.2
r.13, applied: SI 1998/3132 r.50, Sch.2
r.13, consolidated: SI 1998/3132 r.50, Sch.2
r.14, amended: SI 1998/3132 r.50, Sch.2
r.14, applied: SI 1998/3132 r.50, Sch.2
r.14, consolidated: SI 1998/3132 r.50, Sch.2
r.15, amended: SI 1998/3132 r.50, Sch.2
r.15, applied: SI 1998/3132 r.50, Sch.2
r.15, consolidated: SI 1998/3132 r.50, Sch.2

Ord. 31,

r.1, amended: SI 1998/3132 r.50, Sch.2
r.1, applied: SI 1998/3132 r.50, Sch.2
r.1, consolidated: SI 1998/3132 r.50, Sch.2
r.2, amended: SI 1998/3132 r.50, Sch.2
r.2, applied: SI 1998/3132 r.50, Sch.2
r.2, consolidated: SI 1998/3132 r.50, Sch.2
r.3, amended: SI 1998/3132 r.50, Sch.2
r.3, applied: SI 1998/3132 r.50, Sch.2
r.3, consolidated: SI 1998/3132 r.50, Sch.2
r.4, amended: SI 1998/3132 r.50, Sch.2
r.4, applied: SI 1998/3132 r.50, Sch.2
r.4, consolidated: SI 1998/3132 r.50, Sch.2

Ord. 33,

r.1, amended: SI 1998/3132 r.50, Sch.2
r.1, applied: SI 1998/3132 r.50, Sch.2
r.1, consolidated: SI 1998/3132 r.50, Sch.2
r.2, amended: SI 1998/3132 r.50, Sch.2
r.2, applied: SI 1998/3132 r.50, Sch.2
r.2, consolidated: SI 1998/3132 r.50, Sch.2
r.3, amended: SI 1998/3132 r.50, Sch.2
r.3, applied: SI 1998/3132 r.50, Sch.2
r.3, consolidated: SI 1998/3132 r.50, Sch.2
r.4, amended: SI 1998/3132 r.50, Sch.2
r.4, applied: SI 1998/3132 r.50, Sch.2
r.4, consolidated: SI 1998/3132 r.50, Sch.2
r.5, amended: SI 1998/3132 r.50, Sch.2
r.5, applied: SI 1998/3132 r.50, Sch.2
r.5, consolidated: SI 1998/3132 r.50, Sch.2
r.6, amended: SI 1998/3132 r.50, Sch.2
r.6, applied: SI 1998/3132 r.50, Sch.2
r.6, consolidated: SI 1998/3132 r.50, Sch.2
r.7, amended: SI 1998/3132 r.50, Sch.2
r.7, applied: SI 1998/3132 r.50, Sch.2
r.7, consolidated: SI 1998/3132 r.50, Sch.2
r.8, amended: SI 1998/3132 r.50, Sch.2
r.8, applied: SI 1998/3132 r.50, Sch.2
r.8, consolidated: SI 1998/3132 r.50, Sch.2
r.9, amended: SI 1998/3132 r.50, Sch.2
r.9, applied: SI 1998/3132 r.50, Sch.2
r.9, consolidated: SI 1998/3132 r.50, Sch.2
r.10, amended: SI 1998/3132 r.50, Sch.2
r.10, applied: SI 1998/3132 r.50, Sch.2
r.10, consolidated: SI 1998/3132 r.50, Sch.2
r.11, amended: SI 1998/3132 r.50, Sch.2
r.11, applied: SI 1998/3132 r.50, Sch.2

1981—cont.

1687. County Court Rules 1981—*cont.*
Ord. 33—*cont.*
  r.11, consolidated: SI 1998/3132 r.50, Sch.2
Ord. 34,
  r.1, see *King v Read* [1999] 1 F.L.R. 425 (CA),
    Lord Woolf, M.R.
  r.1, amended: SI 1998/3132 r.50, Sch.2
  r.1, applied: SI 1998/3132 r.50, Sch.2
  r.1, consolidated: SI 1998/3132 r.50, Sch.2
  r.1A, amended: SI 1998/3132 r.50, Sch.2
  r.1A, applied: SI 1998/3132 r.50, Sch.2
  r.1A, consolidated: SI 1998/3132 r.50, Sch.2
  r.2, amended: SI 1998/3132 r.50, Sch.2
  r.2, applied: SI 1998/3132 r.50, Sch.2
  r.2, consolidated: SI 1998/3132 r.50, Sch.2
  r.3, amended: SI 1998/3132 r.50, Sch.2
  r.3, applied: SI 1998/3132 r.50, Sch.2
  r.3, consolidated: SI 1998/3132 r.50, Sch.2
  r.4, amended: SI 1998/3132 r.50, Sch.2
  r.4, applied: SI 1998/3132 r.50, Sch.2
  r.4, consolidated: SI 1998/3132 r.50, Sch.2
Ord. 35,
  r.1, amended: SI 1998/3132 r.50, Sch.2
  r.1, applied: SI 1998/3132 r.50, Sch.2
  r.1, consolidated: SI 1998/3132 r.50, Sch.2
  r.2, amended: SI 1998/3132 r.50, Sch.2
  r.2, applied: SI 1998/3132 r.50, Sch.2
  r.2, consolidated: SI 1998/3132 r.50, Sch.2
  r.3, amended: SI 1998/3132 r.50, Sch.2
  r.3, applied: SI 1998/3132 r.50, Sch.2
  r.3, consolidated: SI 1998/3132 r.50, Sch.2
  r.4, amended: SI 1998/3132 r.50, Sch.2
  r.4, applied: SI 1998/3132 r.50, Sch.2
  r.4, consolidated: SI 1998/3132 r.50, Sch.2
  r.5, amended: SI 1998/3132 r.50, Sch.2
  r.5, applied: SI 1998/3132 r.50, Sch.2
  r.5, consolidated: SI 1998/3132 r.50, Sch.2
  r.6, amended: SI 1998/3132 r.50, Sch.2
  r.6, applied: SI 1998/3132 r.50, Sch.2
  r.6, consolidated: SI 1998/3132 r.50, Sch.2
Ord. 37,
  see *Ricketts v Hurstanger Ltd* [1998]
    C.C.L.R. 5 (CC) (Aldershot and Farnham),
    Deputy District Judge Arnold
  r.1, see *Benson v Benson (Deceased)* [1996]
    1 F.L.R. 692 (Fam Div), Bracewell, J.; see
    O'Connor v Din [1997] 1 F.L.R. 226 (CA),
    Hirst, L.J.; see *Pope (A Bankrupt), Re*
    Times, March 24, 1997 (Ch D), Hazel Wil-
    liamson Q.C.; see *T v T (Consent Order:*
    Procedure to Set Aside) [1996] 2 F.L.R.
    640 (Fam Div), Richard Anelay Q.C
  r.1, applied: SI 1998/3132 r.50, Sch.2
  r.1, consolidated: SI 1998/3132 r.50, Sch.2
  r.2, see *Kirton v Augustus Ltd* [1996] P.I.Q.R.
    P388 (CA), Peter Gibson, L.J.; see *Pope (A*
    Bankrupt), Re Times, March 24, 1997 (Ch
    D), Hazel Williamson Q.C.; see *Portman*
    Mortgage Services Ltd v Bishop (1998) 30
    H.L.R. 684 (CA), Simon Brown, L.J.
  r.3, see *Portman Mortgage Services Ltd v*
    Bishop (1998) 30 H.L.R. 684 (CA), Simon
    Brown, L.J.
  r.4, see *O'Neill v O'Brien* [1997] P.I.Q.R.
    P223 (CA), Lord Woolf, M.R.; see *Garner v*
    Stonestreet Times, May 28, 1999 (CA),
    Auld, L.J.
  r.5, see *Tavera v Macfarlane* [1996] P.I.Q.R.
    P292 (CA), Hutchison, L.J.
  r.6, see *Ritchie v Ritchie* [1996] 1 F.L.R. 898
    (CA), Bennett, J.

1981—cont.

1687. County Court Rules 1981—*cont.*
Ord. 37—*cont.*
  r.6, amended: SI 1998/3132 r.50, Sch.2
  r.6, applied: SI 1998/3132 r.50, Sch.2
  r.6, consolidated: SI 1998/3132 r.50, Sch.2
  r.6(1), amended: SI 1998/3132 r.50, Sch.2
  r.6(1), applied: SI 1998/3132 r.50, Sch.2
  r.6(1), consolidated: SI 1998/3132 r.50,
    Sch.2
  r.8, amended: SI 1998/3132 r.50, Sch.2
  r.8, applied: SI 1998/3132 r.50, Sch.2
  r.8, consolidated: SI 1998/3132 r.50, Sch.2
  r.8(1), amended: SI 1998/3132 r.50, Sch.2
  r.8(1), applied: SI 1998/3132 r.50, Sch.2
  r.8(1), consolidated: SI 1998/3132 r.50,
    Sch.2
Ord. 38,
  see *Burrows v Vauxhall Motors Ltd* [1998]
    P.I.Q.R. P48 (CA), Lord Woolf, M.R.
  applied: SI 1999/3098 Reg.6
  referred to: SI 1999/1012 r.4
  Appendix B, amended: SI 1998/3132 r.50,
    Sch.2
  Appendix B, applied: SI 1998/3132 r.50,
    Sch.2
  Appendix B, consolidated: SI 1998/3132 r.50,
    Sch.2
  r.3(3D), see *Practice Direction (Sup Ct:*
    Costs: Summary Assessment) [1999] 1
    W.L.R. 420 (QBD), Lord Bingham of Corn-
    hill, L.C.J.
  r.4, see *Brown v Commissioner of Police of*
    the Metropolis Times, April 24, 1996 (CA),
    Sir Thomas Bingham, M.R.
  r.9, see *Daniels v Lambeth LBC* Times, Octo-
    ber 18, 1996 (CA), Beldam, L.J.
  r.18, amended: SI 1998/3132 r.50, Sch.2
  r.18, applied: SI 1998/3132 r.50, Sch.2
  r.18, consolidated: SI 1998/3132 r.50, Sch.2
  r.19, see *Toniello v Top Deck Ski Ltd* Times,
    December 7, 1998 (CA), Auld, L.J.
  r.24, see *Kawarindrasingh v White* [1997] 1
    All E.R. 714 (CA), Brooke, L.J.
Ord. 39,
  r.1, amended: SI 1998/3132 r.50, Sch.2
  r.1, applied: SI 1998/3132 r.50, Sch.2
  r.1, consolidated: SI 1998/3132 r.50, Sch.2
  r.2, amended: SI 1998/3132 r.50, Sch.2
  r.2, applied: SI 1998/3132 r.50, Sch.2
  r.2, consolidated: SI 1998/3132 r.50, Sch.2
  r.3, amended: SI 1998/3132 r.50, Sch.2
  r.3, applied: SI 1998/3132 r.50, Sch.2
  r.3, consolidated: SI 1998/3132 r.50, Sch.2
  r.5, amended: SI 1998/3132 r.50, Sch.2
  r.5, applied: SI 1998/3132 r.50, Sch.2
  r.5, consolidated: SI 1998/3132 r.50, Sch.2
  r.6, amended: SI 1998/3132 r.50, Sch.2
  r.6, applied: SI 1998/3132 r.50, Sch.2
  r.6, consolidated: SI 1998/3132 r.50, Sch.2
  r.7, amended: SI 1998/3132 r.50, Sch.2
  r.7, applied: SI 1998/3132 r.50, Sch.2
  r.7, consolidated: SI 1998/3132 r.50, Sch.2
  r.8, amended: SI 1998/3132 r.50, Sch.2
  r.8, applied: SI 1998/3132 r.50, Sch.2
  r.8, consolidated: SI 1998/3132 r.50, Sch.2
  r.9, amended: SI 1998/3132 r.50, Sch.2
  r.9, applied: SI 1998/3132 r.50, Sch.2
  r.9, consolidated: SI 1998/3132 r.50, Sch.2
  r.10, amended: SI 1998/3132 r.50, Sch.2
  r.10, applied: SI 1998/3132 r.50, Sch.2
  r.10, consolidated: SI 1998/3132 r.50, Sch.2
  r.11, amended: SI 1998/3132 r.50, Sch.2

NO.

NO.

1981—cont.

1687. County Court Rules 1981—*cont.*
Ord. 39—*cont.*
 r.11, applied: SI 1998/3132 r.50, Sch.2
 r.11, consolidated: SI 1998/3132 r.50, Sch.2
 r.13, amended: SI 1998/3132 r.50, Sch.2
 r.13, applied: SI 1998/3132 r.50, Sch.2
 r.13, consolidated: SI 1998/3132 r.50, Sch.2
 r.13(1), amended: SI 1997/1837 r.4, SI 1998/
  3132 r.50, Sch.2
 r.13(1), applied: SI 1998/3132 r.50, Sch.2
 r.13(1), consolidated: SI 1998/3132 r.50,
  Sch.2
 r.13A, amended: SI 1998/3132 r.50, Sch.2
 r.13A, applied: SI 1998/3132 r.50, Sch.2
 r.13A, consolidated: SI 1998/3132 r.50,
  Sch.2
 r.14, amended: SI 1998/3132 r.50, Sch.2
 r.14, applied: SI 1998/3132 r.50, Sch.2
 r.14, consolidated: SI 1998/3132 r.50, Sch.2
 r.16, amended: SI 1998/3132 r.50, Sch.2
 r.16, applied: SI 1998/3132 r.50, Sch.2
 r.16, consolidated: SI 1998/3132 r.50, Sch.2
 r.17, amended: SI 1998/3132 r.50, Sch.2
 r.17, applied: SI 1998/3132 r.50, Sch.2
 r.17, consolidated: SI 1998/3132 r.50, Sch.2
 r.18, amended: SI 1998/3132 r.50, Sch.2
 r.18, applied: SI 1998/3132 r.50, Sch.2
 r.18, consolidated: SI 1998/3132 r.50, Sch.2
 r.19, amended: SI 1998/3132 r.50, Sch.2
 r.19, applied: SI 1998/3132 r.50, Sch.2
 r.19, consolidated: SI 1998/3132 r.50, Sch.2
Ord. 42,
 r.1, amended: SI 1998/3132 r.50, Sch.2
 r.1, applied: SI 1998/3132 r.50, Sch.2
 r.1, consolidated: SI 1998/3132 r.50, Sch.2
 r.4, amended: SI 1998/3132 r.50, Sch.2
 r.4, applied: SI 1998/3132 r.50, Sch.2
 r.4, consolidated: SI 1998/3132 r.50, Sch.2
 r.5, amended: SI 1998/3132 r.50, Sch.2
 r.5, applied: SI 1998/3132 r.50, Sch.2
 r.5, consolidated: SI 1998/3132 r.50, Sch.2
 r.5(3), amended: SI 1997/1837 r.10, SI 1998/
  3132 r.50, Sch.2
 r.5(3), applied: SI 1998/3132 r.50, Sch.2
 r.5(3), consolidated: SI 1998/3132 r.50,
  Sch.2
 r.6, amended: SI 1998/3132 r.50, Sch.2
 r.6, applied: SI 1998/3132 r.50, Sch.2
 r.6, consolidated: SI 1998/3132 r.50, Sch.2
 r.7, amended: SI 1998/3132 r.50, Sch.2
 r.7, applied: SI 1998/3132 r.50, Sch.2
 r.7, consolidated: SI 1998/3132 r.50, Sch.2
 r.8, amended: SI 1998/3132 r.50, Sch.2
 r.8, applied: SI 1998/3132 r.50, Sch.2
 r.8, consolidated: SI 1998/3132 r.50, Sch.2
 r.9, amended: SI 1998/3132 r.50, Sch.2
 r.9, applied: SI 1998/3132 r.50, Sch.2
 r.9, consolidated: SI 1998/3132 r.50, Sch.2
 r.10, amended: SI 1998/3132 r.50, Sch.2
 r.10, applied: SI 1998/3132 r.50, Sch.2
 r.10, consolidated: SI 1998/3132 r.50, Sch.2
 r.11, amended: SI 1998/3132 r.50, Sch.2
 r.11, applied: SI 1998/3132 r.50, Sch.2
 r.11, consolidated: SI 1998/3132 r.50, Sch.2
 r.12, amended: SI 1998/3132 r.50, Sch.2
 r.12, applied: SI 1998/3132 r.50, Sch.2
 r.12, consolidated: SI 1998/3132 r.50, Sch.2
 r.13, amended: SI 1998/3132 r.50, Sch.2
 r.13, applied: SI 1998/3132 r.50, Sch.2
 r.13, consolidated: SI 1998/3132 r.50, Sch.2
 r.14, amended: SI 1998/3132 r.50, Sch.2
 r.14, applied: SI 1998/3132 r.50, Sch.2
 r.14, consolidated: SI 1998/3132 r.50, Sch.2

1981—cont.

1687. County Court Rules 1981—*cont.*
Ord. 43,
 r.1, amended: SI 1998/3132 r.50, Sch.2
 r.1, applied: SI 1998/3132 r.50, Sch.2
 r.1, consolidated: SI 1998/3132 r.50, Sch.2
 r.2, amended: SI 1998/3132 r.50, Sch.2
 r.2, applied: SI 1998/3132 r.50, Sch.2
 r.2, consolidated: SI 1998/3132 r.50, Sch.2
 r.3, amended: SI 1998/3132 r.50, Sch.2
 r.3, applied: SI 1998/3132 r.50, Sch.2
 r.3, consolidated: SI 1998/3132 r.50, Sch.2
 r.4, amended: SI 1998/3132 r.50, Sch.2
 r.4, applied: SI 1998/3132 r.50, Sch.2
 r.4, consolidated: SI 1998/3132 r.50, Sch.2
 r.5, amended: SI 1998/3132 r.50, Sch.2
 r.5, applied: SI 1998/3132 r.50, Sch.2
 r.5, consolidated: SI 1998/3132 r.50, Sch.2
 r.6, amended: SI 1998/3132 r.50, Sch.2
 r.6, applied: SI 1998/3132 r.50, Sch.2
 r.6, consolidated: SI 1998/3132 r.50, Sch.2
 r.6(3), amended: SI 1998/3132 r.50, Sch.2
 r.6(3), applied: SI 1998/3132 r.50, Sch.2
 r.6(3), consolidated: SI 1998/3132 r.50,
  Sch.2
 r.7, amended: SI 1998/3132 r.50, Sch.2
 r.7, applied: SI 1998/3132 r.50, Sch.2
 r.7, consolidated: SI 1998/3132 r.50, Sch.2
 r.8, amended: SI 1998/3132 r.50, Sch.2
 r.8, applied: SI 1998/3132 r.50, Sch.2
 r.8, consolidated: SI 1998/3132 r.50, Sch.2
 r.9, amended: SI 1998/3132 r.50, Sch.2
 r.9, applied: SI 1998/3132 r.50, Sch.2
 r.9, consolidated: SI 1998/3132 r.50, Sch.2
 r.10, amended: SI 1998/3132 r.50, Sch.2
 r.10, applied: SI 1998/3132 r.50, Sch.2
 r.10, consolidated: SI 1998/3132 r.50, Sch.2
 r.11, amended: SI 1998/3132 r.50, Sch.2
 r.11, applied: SI 1998/3132 r.50, Sch.2
 r.11, consolidated: SI 1998/3132 r.50, Sch.2
 r.13, amended: SI 1998/3132 r.50, Sch.2
 r.13, applied: SI 1998/3132 r.50, Sch.2
 r.13, consolidated: SI 1998/3132 r.50, Sch.2
 r.15, amended: SI 1998/3132 r.50, Sch.2
 r.15, applied: SI 1998/3132 r.50, Sch.2
 r.15, consolidated: SI 1998/3132 r.50, Sch.2
 r.16, amended: SI 1998/3132 r.50, Sch.2
 r.16, applied: SI 1998/3132 r.50, Sch.2
 r.16, consolidated: SI 1998/3132 r.50, Sch.2
 r.16A, added: SI 1997/1837 r.6
 r.16A, amended: SI 1998/3132 r.50, Sch.2
 r.16A, applied: SI 1998/3132 r.50, Sch.2
 r.16A, consolidated: SI 1998/3132 r.50,
  Sch.2
 r.17, amended: SI 1998/3132 r.50, Sch.2
 r.17, applied: SI 1998/3132 r.50, Sch.2
 r.17, consolidated: SI 1998/3132 r.50, Sch.2
 r.18, amended: SI 1998/3132 r.50, Sch.2
 r.18, applied: SI 1998/3132 r.50, Sch.2
 r.18, consolidated: SI 1998/3132 r.50, Sch.2
 r.18, revoked: SI 1998/1899 r.3
 r.19, amended: SI 1998/3132 r.50, Sch.2
 r.19, applied: SI 1998/3132 r.50, Sch.2
 r.19, consolidated: SI 1998/3132 r.50, Sch.2
 r.20, amended: SI 1998/3132 r.50, Sch.2
 r.20, applied: SI 1998/3132 r.50, Sch.2
 r.20, consolidated: SI 1998/3132 r.50, Sch.2
 r.21, amended: SI 1998/3132 r.50, Sch.2
 r.21, applied: SI 1998/3132 r.50, Sch.2
 r.21, consolidated: SI 1998/3132 r.50, Sch.2
 r.22, amended: SI 1998/3132 r.50, Sch.2
 r.22, applied: SI 1998/3132 r.50, Sch.2

NO.

1981—cont.

1687. County Court Rules 1981—*cont.*
Ord. 43—*cont.*
r.22, consolidated: SI 1998/3132 r.50, Sch.2
Ord. 44,
r.1, amended: SI 1998/3132 r.50, Sch.2
r.1, applied: SI 1998/3132 r.50, Sch.2
r.1, consolidated: SI 1998/3132 r.50, Sch.2
r.2, amended: SI 1998/3132 r.50, Sch.2
r.2, applied: SI 1998/3132 r.50, Sch.2
r.2, consolidated: SI 1998/3132 r.50, Sch.2
r.3, amended: SI 1998/3132 r.50, Sch.2
r.3, applied: SI 1998/3132 r.50, Sch.2
r.3, consolidated: SI 1998/3132 r.50, Sch.2
r.4, amended: SI 1998/3132 r.50, Sch.2
r.4, applied: SI 1998/3132 r.50, Sch.2
r.4, consolidated: SI 1998/3132 r.50, Sch.2
Ord. 45,
r.1, amended: SI 1998/3132 r.50, Sch.2
r.1, applied: 1997 c.61 Sch.3 para.8, SI 1998/
3132 r.50, Sch.2, SI 1999/450 Art.21
r.1, consolidated: SI 1998/3132 r.50, Sch.2
r.2, amended: SI 1998/3132 r.50, Sch.2, SI
1999/450 Art.5
r.2, applied: SI 1998/3132 r.50, Sch.2, SI
1999/450 Art.5
r.2, consolidated: SI 1998/3132 r.50, Sch.2
r.3, amended: SI 1998/3132 r.50, Sch.2
r.3, applied: SI 1998/3132 r.50, Sch.2
r.3, consolidated: SI 1998/3132 r.50, Sch.2
Ord. 46,
r.1, amended: SI 1998/3132 r.50, Sch.2
r.1, applied: SI 1998/3132 r.50, Sch.2
r.1, consolidated: SI 1998/3132 r.50, Sch.2
r.2, amended: SI 1998/3132 r.50, Sch.2
r.2, applied: SI 1998/3132 r.50, Sch.2
r.2, consolidated: SI 1998/3132 r.50, Sch.2
r.3, amended: SI 1998/3132 r.50, Sch.2
r.3, applied: SI 1998/3132 r.50, Sch.2
r.3, consolidated: SI 1998/3132 r.50, Sch.2
Ord. 47,
r.5, amended: SI 1998/3132 r.50, Sch.2
r.5, applied: SI 1998/3132 r.50, Sch.2
r.5, consolidated: SI 1998/3132 r.50, Sch.2
Ord. 48,
r.1(2), amended: SI 1996/2810 r.4
r.7A, added: SI 1997/1837 r.9
Ord. 48B,
r.1, amended: SI 1998/3132 r.50, Sch.2
r.1, applied: SI 1998/3132 r.50, Sch.2
r.1, consolidated: SI 1998/3132 r.50, Sch.2
r.1(4), added: SI 1996/2810 r.4
r.1(4), amended: SI 1998/3132 r.50, Sch.2
r.1(4), applied: SI 1998/3132 r.50, Sch.2
r.1(4), consolidated: SI 1998/3132 r.50,
Sch.2
r.1A, added: SI 1996/2181 r.4
r.1A, amended: SI 1998/3132 r.50, Sch.2
r.1A, applied: SI 1998/3132 r.50, Sch.2
r.1A, consolidated: SI 1998/3132 r.50, Sch.2
r.2, amended: SI 1998/3132 r.50, Sch.2
r.2, applied: SI 1998/3132 r.50, Sch.2
r.2, consolidated: SI 1998/3132 r.50, Sch.2
r.3, amended: SI 1998/3132 r.50, Sch.2
r.3, applied: SI 1998/3132 r.50, Sch.2
r.3, consolidated: SI 1998/3132 r.50, Sch.2
r.4, amended: SI 1998/3132 r.50, Sch.2
r.4, applied: SI 1998/3132 r.50, Sch.2
r.4, consolidated: SI 1998/3132 r.50, Sch.2
r.5, amended: SI 1998/3132 r.50, Sch.2
r.5, applied: SI 1998/3132 r.50, Sch.2
r.5, consolidated: SI 1998/3132 r.50, Sch.2

1687. County Court Rules 1981—*cont.*
Ord. 48C,
r.1(1), amended: SI 1996/3218 r.5
r.1(2), amended: SI 1996/3218 r.5
r.3(2)(h), amended: SI 1996/3218 r.5
r.16, added: SI 1996/3218 r.5
Ord. 48D,
added: SI 1998/1899 r.7
Ord. 49,
r.1, amended: SI 1998/3132 r.50, Sch.2
r.1, applied: SI 1998/3132 r.50, Sch.2
r.1, consolidated: SI 1998/3132 r.50, Sch.2
r.1A, amended: SI 1998/3132 r.50, Sch.2
r.1A, applied: SI 1998/3132 r.50, Sch.2
r.1A, consolidated: SI 1998/3132 r.50, Sch.2
r.2, amended: SI 1998/3132 r.50, Sch.2
r.2, applied: SI 1998/3132 r.50, Sch.2
r.2, consolidated: SI 1998/3132 r.50, Sch.2
r.4, amended: SI 1998/3132 r.50, Sch.2
r.4, applied: SI 1998/3132 r.50, Sch.2
r.4, consolidated: SI 1998/3132 r.50, Sch.2
r.4A, amended: SI 1998/3132 r.50, Sch.2
r.4A, applied: SI 1998/3132 r.50, Sch.2
r.4A, consolidated: SI 1998/3132 r.50, Sch.2
r.5, amended: SI 1998/3132 r.50, Sch.2
r.5, applied: SI 1998/3132 r.50, Sch.2
r.5, consolidated: SI 1998/3132 r.50, Sch.2
r.6, amended: SI 1998/3132 r.50, Sch.2
r.6, applied: SI 1998/3132 r.50, Sch.2
r.6, consolidated: SI 1998/3132 r.50, Sch.2
r.6(7)(i), amended: SI 1998/1899 r.4, SI
1998/3132 r.50, Sch.2
r.6(7)(i), applied: SI 1998/3132 r.50, Sch.2
r.6(7)(i), consolidated: SI 1998/3132 r.50,
Sch.2
r.6A, amended: SI 1998/3132 r.50, Sch.2
r.6A, applied: SI 1998/3132 r.50, Sch.2
r.6A, consolidated: SI 1998/3132 r.50, Sch.2
r.6A(3)(c), amended: SI 1997/1837 r.7, SI
1998/3132 r.50, Sch.2
r.6A(3)(c), applied: SI 1998/3132 r.50, Sch.2
r.6A(3)(c), consolidated: SI 1998/3132 r.50,
Sch.2
r.6A(3)(d), amended: SI 1997/1837 r.7, SI
1998/3132 r.50, Sch.2
r.6A(3)(d), applied: SI 1998/3132 r.50, Sch.2
r.6A(3)(d), consolidated: SI 1998/3132 r.50,
Sch.2
r.6A(6)(d), amended: SI 1997/1837 r.7, SI
1998/3132 r.50, Sch.2
r.6A(6)(d), applied: SI 1998/3132 r.50, Sch.2
r.6A(6)(d), consolidated: SI 1998/3132 r.50,
Sch.2
r.6A(7)(i), amended: SI 1998/3132 r.50,
Sch.2
r.6A(7)(i), applied: SI 1998/3132 r.50, Sch.2
r.6A(7)(i), consolidated: SI 1998/3132 r.50,
Sch.2
r.6A(7)(i), substituted: SI 1998/1899 r.4
r.6A(7)(ii), amended: SI 1997/1837 r.7, SI
1998/3132 r.50, Sch.2
r.6A(7)(ii), applied: SI 1998/3132 r.50, Sch.2
r.6A(7)(ii), consolidated: SI 1998/3132 r.50,
Sch.2
r.6A(9)(d), amended: SI 1997/1837 r.7, SI
1998/3132 r.50, Sch.2
r.6A(9)(d), applied: SI 1998/3132 r.50, Sch.2
r.6A(9)(d), consolidated: SI 1998/3132 r.50,
Sch.2
r.6A(10)(b), amended: SI 1997/1837 r.7, SI
1998/3132 r.50, Sch.2

NO.

1981—cont.

1687. County Court Rules 1981—*cont.*
Ord. 49—*cont.*
r.6A(10)(b), applied: SI 1998/3132 r.50, Sch.2
r.6A(10)(b), consolidated: SI 1998/3132 r.50, Sch.2
r.6A(10)(e), amended: SI 1997/1837 r.7, SI 1998/3132 r.50, Sch.2
r.6A(10)(e), applied: SI 1998/3132 r.50, Sch.2
r.6A(10)(e), consolidated: SI 1998/3132 r.50, Sch.2
r.6A(16)(a), amended: SI 1997/1837 r.7, SI 1998/3132 r.50, Sch.2
r.6A(16)(a), applied: SI 1998/3132 r.50, Sch.2
r.6A(16)(a), consolidated: SI 1998/3132 r.50, Sch.2
r.6B, added: SI 1997/1837 r.8
r.6B, amended: SI 1998/3132 r.50, Sch.2
r.6B, applied: SI 1998/3132 r.50, Sch.2
r.6B, consolidated: SI 1998/3132 r.50, Sch.2
r.7, amended: SI 1998/3132 r.50, Sch.2
r.7, applied: SI 1998/3132 r.50, Sch.2
r.7, consolidated: SI 1998/3132 r.50, Sch.2
r.8, amended: SI 1998/3132 r.50, Sch.2
r.8, applied: SI 1998/3132 r.50, Sch.2
r.8, consolidated: SI 1998/3132 r.50, Sch.2
r.9, amended: SI 1998/3132 r.50, Sch.2
r.9, applied: SI 1998/3132 r.50, Sch.2
r.9, consolidated: SI 1998/3132 r.50, Sch.2
r.10, amended: SI 1998/3132 r.50, Sch.2
r.10, applied: SI 1998/3132 r.50, Sch.2
r.10, consolidated: SI 1998/3132 r.50, Sch.2
r.11, amended: SI 1998/3132 r.50, Sch.2
r.11, applied: SI 1998/3132 r.50, Sch.2
r.11, consolidated: SI 1998/3132 r.50, Sch.2
r.12, amended: SI 1998/3132 r.50, Sch.2
r.12, applied: SI 1998/3132 r.50, Sch.2
r.12, consolidated: SI 1998/3132 r.50, Sch.2
r.13, amended: SI 1998/3132 r.50, Sch.2
r.13, applied: SI 1998/3132 r.50, Sch.2
r.13, consolidated: SI 1998/3132 r.50, Sch.2
r.15, amended: SI 1998/3132 r.50, Sch.2
r.15, applied: SI 1998/3132 r.50, Sch.2
r.15, consolidated: SI 1998/3132 r.50, Sch.2
r.15A, added: SI 1998/1899 r.8
r.16, amended: SI 1998/3132 r.50, Sch.2
r.16, applied: SI 1998/3132 r.50, Sch.2
r.16, consolidated: SI 1998/3132 r.50, Sch.2
r.17, amended: SI 1998/3132 r.50, Sch.2
r.17, applied: SI 1998/3132 r.50, Sch.2
r.17, consolidated: SI 1998/3132 r.50, Sch.2
r.18, amended: SI 1998/3132 r.50, Sch.2
r.18, applied: SI 1998/3132 r.50, Sch.2
r.18, consolidated: SI 1998/3132 r.50, Sch.2
r.18A, amended: SI 1998/3132 r.50, Sch.2
r.18A, applied: SI 1998/3132 r.50, Sch.2
r.18A, consolidated: SI 1998/3132 r.50, Sch.2
r.18B, amended: SI 1998/3132 r.50, Sch.2
r.18B, applied: SI 1998/3132 r.50, Sch.2
r.18B, consolidated: SI 1998/3132 r.50, Sch.2
r.19, amended: SI 1998/3132 r.50, Sch.2
r.19, applied: SI 1998/3132 r.50, Sch.2
r.19, consolidated: SI 1998/3132 r.50, Sch.2
r.20, amended: SI 1998/3132 r.50, Sch.2
r.20, applied: SI 1998/3132 r.50, Sch.2
r.20, consolidated: SI 1998/3132 r.50, Sch.2

NO.

1981—cont.

1687. County Court Rules 1981—*cont.*
Ord. 50,
r.9, see *Penny v Penny* [1996] 1 W.L.R. 1204 (CA), Butler-Sloss, L.J.
Ord. 59,
r.1B(1)(d), see *Brent LBC v Carmel* (1996) 28 H.L.R. 203 (CA), Roch, L.J.

1694. Motor Vehicles (Tests) Regulations 1981
applied: SI 1996/960 Art.3
Reg.3, amended: SI 1997/81 Reg.3, SI 1998/1672 Reg.3
Reg.4 Table, amended: SI 1998/1672 Reg.4
Reg.5, amended: SI 1998/1672 Reg.5
Reg.6, amended: SI 1998/1672 Reg.6
Reg.12, amended: SI 1998/1672 Reg.7
Reg.13, amended: SI 1998/1672 Reg.8
Reg.15, amended: SI 1997/1679 Reg.3, SI 1998/1672 Reg.9
Reg.16, amended: SI 1997/1679 Reg.4, SI 1998/1672 Reg.10
Reg.16, revoked (in part): SI 1997/1679 Reg.4
Reg.20, amended: SI 1996/1751 Reg.3, SI 1997/81 Reg.4, SI 1997/1679 Reg.5, SI 1998/1672 Reg.11, SI 1999/2199 Reg.3
Reg.23, amended: SI 1998/1672 Reg.12
Reg.25, amended: SI 1996/1751 Reg.4, SI 1997/1679 Reg.5, SI 1998/1672 Reg.13
Sch.2 para.2, amended: SI 1998/1672 Reg.14
Sch.2 para.3A, added: SI 1998/1672 Reg.14
Sch.2 para.4A, added: SI 1998/1672 Reg.14
Sch.2 para.5A, added: SI 1998/1672 Reg.14
Sch.2 para.6, amended: SI 1998/1672 Reg.14

1706. Merchant Shipping (Certification of Ships Cooks) Regulations 1981
applied: SI 1996/3243 Sch Part III

1707. Farm and Horticulture Development Regulations 1981
applied: SI 1999/672 Art.2, Sch.1
Reg.4, referred to: SI 1999/672 Art.2, Sch.1

1719. London Docklands Development Corporation (Vesting of Land) (Greater London Council No.2) Order 1981
revoked: SI 1998/769 Art.3, Sch.

1720. London Docklands Development Corporation (Vesting of Land) (Tower Hamlets London Borough Council) Order 1981
revoked: SI 1998/769 Art.3, Sch.

1747. Merchant Shipping (Dangerous Goods) Regulations 1981
referred to: SI 1998/1609 Reg.5, Reg.6, Sch.

1767. Scottish Seed Potato Development Council Order 1981
revoked: SI 1997/2092 Art.9
Art.6, amended: SI 1997/2092 Art.5
Art.6, applied: SI 1997/2092 Art.5
Art.6, revoked (in part): SI 1997/2092 Art.5, Art.9
Sch.1, applied: SI 1997/2092 Art.6
Sch.1, revoked: SI 1997/2092 Art.9

1785. National Health Service (Compensation for Premature Retirement) (Scotland) Regulations 1981
applied: SI 1999/1750 Art.2, Sch.1

1788. Direct Grant Schools (Amendment) Regulations 1981
revoked: SI 1998/86 Reg.2, Sch.1

1794. Transfer of Undertakings (Protection of Employment) Regulations 1981
see *Adams v Lancashire CC* [1996] All E.R. (EC) 473 (Ch D), Robert Walker, J.; see *Addison v Denholm Ship Management (UK) Ltd* [1997] I.C.R. 770 (EAT), Lord Johnston; see

NO.

1981—cont.

1794. Transfer of Undertakings (Protection of Employment) Regulations 1981—cont.
see—cont.
Betts v Brintel Helicopters Ltd and KLM ERA Helicopters (UK) Ltd [1996] I.R.L.R. 45 (QBD), Scott Baker, J.; see Clark & Tokeley Ltd (t/a Spellbrook Ltd) v Oakes [1998] All E.R. 353 (CA), Mummery, L.J.; see ECM (Vehicle Delivery Service) Ltd v Cox [1998] I.C.R. 631 (EAT), Morison, J.; see National Union of Teachers v Governing Body of St Mary's Church of England (Aided) Junior School [1997] I.C.R. 334 (CA), Schiemann, L.J.; see Secretary of State for Trade and Industry v Cook Independent, January 15, 1997 (EAT), Morison, J.; see Sita (GB) Ltd v Burton [1998] I.C.R. 17 (EAT), Lord Johnston; see Taylor v Serviceteam Ltd [1998] P.I.Q.R. P201 (CC), Recorder W Pawlak
amended: 1999 c.9 s.12
applied: SI 1997/1613 Reg.22, 1998 c.11 Sch.4 para.2, SI 1998/364 Reg.21, Reg.22, 1999 c.9 s.12, SI 1999/2544 Art.2, Sch.2 para.5
referred to: SI 1997/456 Art.3, SI 1997/458 Art.3, SI 1997/459 Art.3, SI 1997/460 Art.3, SI 1997/461 Art.3, SI 1997/468 Art.3, SI 1997/469 Art.3, SI 1997/476 Art.3, SI 1997/478 Art.3, SI 1997/479 Art.3, SI 1997/3001 Sch.10 para.34, 1998 c.46 s.30, Sch.5 s.H1, 1998 c.v s.7, SI 1998/354 Art.3, SI 1998/442 Art.3, SI 1998/443 Art.3, SI 1998/444 Art.3, SI 1998/445 Art.3, SI 1998/446 Art.3, SI 1998/447 Art.3, SI 1998/448 Art.3, SI 1998/449 Art.3, SI 1998/450 Art.3, SI 1998/451 Art.3, SI 1999/2511 Reg.3, SSI 1999/56 Art.4
Reg.3, see Betts v Brintel Helicopters Ltd (t/a British International Helicopters) [1997] 2 All E.R. 840 (CA), Kennedy, L.J.; see Brookes v Borough Care Services [1998] I.C.R. 1198 (EAT), Kirkwood, J.; see ECM (Vehicle Delivery Services) Ltd v Cox [1999] 4 All E.R. 669 (CA), Mummery, L.J.; see Secretary of State for Trade and Industry v Cook [1997] I.R.L.R. 150 (EAT), Morison, J.
Reg.5, see Bernadone v Pall Mall Services Group Ltd [1999] I.R.L.R. 617 (QBD), Blofeld, J.; see Buchannan-Smith v Schleicher & Co International Ltd [1996] I.C.R. 613 (EAT), Mummery, J.; see Credit Suisse First Boston (Europe) Ltd v Lister [1999] 1 C.M.L.R. 710 (CA), Clarke, L.J.; see DJM International Ltd v Nicholas [1996] I.C.R. 214 (EAT), Mummery, J.; see Hay v George Hanson (Building Contractors) Ltd [1996] I.R.L.R. 427 (EAT), Lord Johnson; see MRS Environmental Services Ltd v Dyke Times, March 25, 1997 (EAT), Judge Byrt Q.C.; see Secretary of State for Trade and Industry v Cook [1997] I.R.L.R. 150 (EAT), Morison, J.; see Tsangacos v Amalgamated Chemicals Ltd [1997] I.R.L.R. 4 (EAT), Morison, J.; see Willis v McLaughlin & Harvey Plc (In Administrative Receivership and Liquidation) [1998] Eu L.R. 22 (CA (NI)), Kerr, J.; see Wilson v St Helens BC [1999] 2 A.C. 52 (HL), Lord Slynn of Hadley
Reg.8, see Cornwall County Care Ltd v Brightman [1998] I.C.R. 529 (EAT), Morison, J.; see Governing Body of Clifton Middle School v Askew [1999] I.R.L.R. 708 (CA), Peter Gibson, L.J.; see MRS Environmental Services Ltd v Marsh [1997] 1 All E.R. 92 (CA), Phillips, L.J.; see Warner v Adnet Ltd [1998] I.C.R. 1056 (CA), Mummery, L.J.; see Willis v

NO.

1981—cont.

1794. Transfer of Undertakings (Protection of Employment) Regulations 1981—cont.
Reg.8—cont.
McLaughlin & Harvey Plc (In Administrative Receivership and Liquidation) [1998] Eu L.R. 22 (CA (NI)), Kerr, J.; see Wilson v St Helens BC [1999] 2 A.C. 52 (HL), Lord Slynn of Hadley
Reg.10, amended: SI 1999/1925 Reg.8, SI 1999/2402 Reg.3
Reg.10, applied: 1996 c.18 s.47, s.61, s.103, SI 1996/1919 (NI.16) Art.70, Art.89, Art.134, SI 1999/101 Reg.4, Reg.5, Sch.1 para.35, Sch.2 para.38
Reg.10A, added: SI 1999/1925 Reg.9
Reg.11, amended: SI 1999/1925 Reg.10
Reg.11, applied: 1996 c.18 s.47, s.61, s.103, SI 1996/1919 (NI.16) Art.70, Art.89, Art.134, 1998 c.8 s.3, SI 1999/101 Reg.4, Reg.5, Sch.1 para.35, Sch.2 para.38
Reg.11A, amended: SI 1999/1925 Reg.11
Reg.11A, referred to: SI 1999/101 Reg.4, Reg.5, Sch.1 para.35, Sch.2 para.38
Reg.12, see Credit Suisse First Boston (Europe) Ltd v Lister [1999] 1 C.M.L.R. 710 (CA), Clarke, L.J.

1950. Church Representation Rules (Amendment) Resolution 1981
referred to: SI 1999/2112

1982

60. Safety of Sports Grounds (Designation) (Scotland) Variation Order 1982
revoked: SI 1998/1601 Art.3, Sch.2

91. Spring Traps Approval (Scotland) (Variation) Order 1982
revoked: SI 1996/2202 Art.3

97. Agricultural Land Tribunals (Areas) Order 1982
referred to: SI 1999/1100 Sch. Part I

106. Education (Teachers) Regulations 1982
referred to: SI 1999/2817 Reg.2, Sch.1 para.8
Reg.15, applied: SI 1999/2166 Reg.2, Sch.1 para 1, SI 1999/2817 Reg.2, Sch.1 para.1
Reg.16, applied: SI 1999/2166 Reg.2, Sch.1 para 2, SI 1999/2817 Reg.2, Sch.1 para.2
Reg.18, applied: SI 1999/2166 Reg.2, Sch.1 para 3, SI 1999/2817 Reg.2, Sch.1 para.3
Sch.4 para.4, applied: SI 1999/2166 Reg.10, Sch.2 para.1, SI 1999/2817 Reg.10, Sch.2 para.1
Sch.6 para.5, applied: SI 1999/2817 Reg.2, Sch.1 para.6
Sch.6 para.5, referred to: SI 1999/2166 Reg.2, Sch.1 para 6

107. Bee Diseases Control Order 1982
Art.8, applied: SI 1997/310 Art.4

135. Calshot Oyster Fishery Order 1982
referred to: SI 1999/697
Art.3, amended: SI 1999/697 Art.2

147. Extradition (Internationally Protected Persons) (Amendment) Order 1982
revoked: SI 1997/1764 Art.4

149. Extradition (Tokyo Convention) (Amendment) Order 1982
revoked: SI 1997/1768 Art.4

152. Health Service Commissioner for England (London Post-Graduate Teaching Hospitals) Order 1982
revoked: SI 1998/3149 Art.2

NO.

1982—cont.

192. **Under-Sheriffs (Abolition of Office and Transfer of Functions) Order (Northern Ireland) 1982**
Sch.1, revoked (in part): SI 1996/1141 (NI.6) s.32, Sch.5

209. **Commons (Schemes) Regulations 1982**
applied: SI 1996/1243 Sch.5 para.8

260. **Prison (Amendment) Rules 1982**
revoked: SI 1999/728 r.85 (with savings), Sch. (with savings)

263. **Statutory Sick Pay (General) Regulations (Northern Ireland) 1982**
Reg.9A, applied: SI 1999/671 Art.3, Sch.2
Reg.9B, applied: SI 1999/671 Art.3, Sch.2
Reg.9C, applied: SI 1999/671 Art.3, Sch.2
Reg.10, applied: SI 1999/671 Art.3, Sch.2
Reg.14, applied: SI 1999/671 Art.3, Sch.2

276. **National Health Service (Appointment of Consultants) Regulations 1982**
revoked: SI 1996/701 Art.10

338. **Departments (Northern Ireland) Order 1982**
Art.3, revoked: SI 1999/283 (NI.1) Art.9, Sch.3
Art.4, revoked (in part): SI 1999/283 (NI.1) Art.9, Sch.3
Art.6, revoked: SI 1999/283 (NI.1) Art.9, Sch.3
Art.10, revoked (in part): SI 1996/1298 (NI.8) Art.21, Sch.6
Sch.1 Part II, revoked (in part): SI 1996/725 (NI.5) Sch.4
Sch.1 Part III, revoked (in part): SI 1997/2779 (NI.20) Sch.3
Sch.3, revoked (in part): SI 1996/1298 (NI.8) Art.21, Sch.6

338. **Feeding Stuffs (Sampling and Analysis) Regulations (Northern Ireland) 1982**
Sch.1 Part I, applied: SI 1998/1049 Reg.83, Reg.84
Sch.1 Part II, amended: SI 1998/1049 Reg.83
Sch.1 Part II, applied: SI 1998/1049 Reg.83, Reg.84
Sch.1 Part V, applied: SI 1998/1049 Reg.84

365. **Courts-Martial and Standing Civilian Courts (Additional Powers on Trial of Civilians) (Amendment) Regulations 1982**
revoked: SI 1997/579 Reg.13, Sch.3

367. **Standing Civilian Courts (Amendment) Order 1982**
revoked: SI 1997/172 Art.93, Sch.5

368. **Rules of Procedure (Air Force) (Amendment) Rules 1982**
revoked: SI 1997/171 r.90, Sch.7

369. **Rules of Procedure (Army) (Amendment) Rules 1982**
revoked: SI 1997/169 r.90, Sch.7

425. **Medicines (Control of Substances for Manufacture) Order 1982**
revoked: SI 1997/1728 Art.2

498. **Fish Producers' Organisations (Formation Grants) Scheme 1982**
revoked: SI 1999/1110 Reg.9
para.5, referred to: SI 1999/1110 Reg.9
para.5, revoked: SI 1999/1110 Reg.9
para.6, referred to: SI 1999/1110 Reg.9
para.6, revoked: SI 1999/1110 Reg.9

518. **Medicines (Stilbenes and Thyrostatic Substances Prohibition) Order 1982**
revoked: SI 1997/1727 Art.2

528. **Industrial Relations (Northern Ireland) Order 1982**
revoked: SI 1996/1919 (NI.16) Art.257, Sch.3
Sch.2 Art.56, revoked: SI 1996/1919 (NI.16) Art.257, Sch.3, SI 1996/1921 (NI.18) Art.28, Sch.3

NO.

1982—cont.

555. **Town and Country Planning (Structure and Local Plans) Regulations 1982**
Reg.29, see *Gillenden Development Co Ltd v Surrey CC* (1997) 74 P. & C.R. 119 (CA), Pill, L.J.; see *Harlowbury Estates Ltd v Harlow DC* [1997] J.P.L. 541 (QBD), R Purchas Q.C.; see *Lopez De Carrizosa v Huntingdonshire DC* [1997] J.P.L. B45 (QBD), Judge Rich Q.C.
Reg.31, see *Lopez De Carrizosa v Huntingdonshire DC* [1997] J.P.L. B45 (QBD), Judge Rich Q.C.

586. **County Court (Forms) Rules 1982**
Sch., amended: SI 1997/1838 r.8
Sch. Form N.1, amended: SI 1998/3024 r.2
Sch. Form N.1(B), amended: SI 1998/3024 r.3
Sch. Form N.1(D), amended: SI 1998/3024 r.4
Sch. Form N.2, amended: SI 1998/3024 r.4
Sch. Form N.3, amended: SI 1998/3024 r.4
Sch. Form N.4, amended: SI 1998/3024 r.4
Sch. Form N.5A, substituted: SI 1997/1838 r.2, Sch.1, SI 1998/1900 r.2, Sch.1
Sch. Form N.5B, added: SI 1997/1838 r.2, Sch.1
Sch. Form N.5B, substituted: SI 1998/1900 r.2, Sch.1
Sch. Form N.8, substituted: SI 1997/1838 r.5, Sch.2
Sch. Form N.8(1), substituted: SI 1997/1838 r.5, Sch.2
Sch. Form N.8(2), substituted: SI 1997/1838 r.5, Sch.2
Sch. Form N.8(4), substituted: SI 1997/1838 r.5, Sch.2
Sch. Form N.9, amended: SI 1996/2811 r.4, SI 1997/1838 r.3
Sch. Form N.9B, amended: SI 1997/1838 r.4
Sch. Form N.10, amended: SI 1997/1838 r.3
Sch. Form N.11A, amended: SI 1998/1900 r.6
Sch. Form N.11A, substituted: SI 1997/1838 r.2, Sch.1
Sch. Form N.11B, added: SI 1997/1838 r.2, Sch.1
Sch. Form N.11B, amended: SI 1997/2171 r.2, SI 1998/1900 r.6
Sch. Form N.15, substituted: SI 1997/1838 r.5, Sch.2
Sch. Form N.16A, substituted: SI 1997/1838 r.6, Sch.3
Sch. Form N.17, substituted: SI 1997/1838 r.5, Sch.2
Sch. Form N.18, substituted: SI 1996/2811 r.2, Sch.1
Sch. Form N.18A, substituted: SI 1996/2811 r.2, Sch.1
Sch. Form N.22, amended: SI 1998/3024 r.5
Sch. Form N.23, amended: SI 1998/3024 r.5
Sch. Form N.24, substituted: SI 1997/1838 r.5, Sch.2
Sch. Form N.25, amended: SI 1998/3024 r.5
Sch. Form N.29, substituted: SI 1998/1900 r.2, Sch.1
Sch. Form N.30, amended: SI 1998/3024 r.5
Sch. Form N.30(1), amended: SI 1998/3024 r.5
Sch. Form N.30(2), amended: SI 1998/3024 r.6
Sch. Form N.30(3), amended: SI 1998/3024 r.5
Sch. Form N.31, substituted: SI 1998/1900 r.2, Sch.1
Sch. Form N.34, amended: SI 1998/3024 r.5
Sch. Form N.35, amended: SI 1998/3024 r.7
Sch. Form N.35A, amended: SI 1998/3024 r.8
Sch. Form N.37, amended: SI 1998/3024 r.9
Sch. Form N.38, amended: SI 1998/3024 r.9

NO.

586. County Court (Forms) Rules 1982—*cont.*
Sch. Form N.39, amended: SI 1998/3024 r.10
Sch. Form N.40, substituted: SI 1997/1838 r.5, Sch.2
Sch. Form N.53, substituted: SI 1997/1838 r.5, Sch.2
Sch. Form N.55, amended: SI 1998/3024 r.11
Sch. Form N.56, revoked: SI 1998/1900 r.5
Sch. Form N.60, substituted: SI 1996/2811 r.2, Sch.1
Sch. Form N.61, amended: SI 1998/3024 r.12
Sch. Form N.64, amended: SI 1998/3024 r.13
Sch. Form N.64, substituted: SI 1998/1900 r.2, Sch.1
Sch. Form N.65, substituted: SI 1996/2811 r.2, Sch.1
Sch. Form N.65A, added: SI 1996/2811 r.3, Sch.2
Sch. Form N.66, amended: SI 1998/3024 r.14
Sch. Form N.70, substituted: SI 1997/1838 r.5, Sch.2
Sch. Form N.71, substituted: SI 1997/1838 r.5, Sch.2
Sch. Form N.75, revoked: SI 1997/1838 r.5
Sch. Form N.79, substituted: SI 1998/1900 r.3, Sch.2
Sch. Form N.81, substituted: SI 1997/1838 r.5, Sch.2
Sch. Form N.84, amended: SI 1998/3024 r.15
Sch. Form N.85, amended: SI 1998/3024 r.16
Sch. Form N.86, amended: SI 1998/3024 r.16
Sch. Form N.87, amended: SI 1998/3024 r.16
Sch. Form N.88, substituted: SI 1997/1838 r.5, Sch.2
Sch. Form N.89, substituted: SI 1997/1838 r.5, Sch.2
Sch. Form N.90, substituted: SI 1996/2811 r.2, Sch.1, SI 1997/1838 r.5, Sch.2
Sch. Form N.91, substituted: SI 1997/1838 r.5, Sch.2
Sch. Form N.96, amended: SI 1998/3024 r.17
Sch. Form N.97, amended: SI 1998/3024 r.17
Sch. Form N.98, amended: SI 1998/3024 r.17
Sch. Form N.99, amended: SI 1998/3024 r.17
Sch. Form N.103, substituted: SI 1997/1838 r.5, Sch.2
Sch. Form N.104, substituted: SI 1997/1838 r.5, Sch.2
Sch. Form N.107, substituted: SI 1997/1838 r.5, Sch.2
Sch. Form N.108, amended: SI 1998/3024 r.18
Sch. Form N.109, amended: SI 1998/3024 r.18
Sch. Form N.110A, added: SI 1997/1838 r.7, Sch.4
Sch. Form N.110A, substituted: SI 1998/1900 r.2, Sch.1
Sch. Form N.112, amended: SI 1996/2811 r.5
Sch. Form N.112A, amended: SI 1996/2811 r.5
Sch. Form N.138, added: SI 1998/1900 r.4, Sch.3
Sch. Form N.140, added: SI 1998/1900 r.4, Sch.3

590. Value Added Tax Tribunal Rules 1982
see *Kwik-Fit (GB) Ltd v Customs and Excise Commissioners* 1998 S.C. 139 (Ex Div), Lord McCluskey, Lord Hamilton, Lord Johnston

626. Medicines (Stilbenes and Thyrostatic Substances) Regulations 1982
revoked: SI 1997/1729 Reg.36, Sch.2

NO.

630. Petroleum-Spirit (Plastic Containers) Regulations 1982
Reg.3, applied: SI 1996/2089 Reg.2, SI 1996/2092 Reg.3
Reg.4, applied: SI 1996/2089 Reg.2, SI 1996/2092 Reg.3
Reg.5, applied: SI 1996/2089 Reg.2, SI 1996/2092 Reg.3
Reg.6, applied: SI 1996/2089 Reg.2, SI 1996/2092 Reg.3
Reg.7, applied: SI 1996/2089 Reg.2, SI 1996/2092 Reg.3
Reg.8, added: SI 1999/743 Reg.23

712. Land Compensation (Northern Ireland) Order 1982
Art.4, applied: SI 1996/275 (NI.2) Art.67, SI 1997/2777 (NI.18) Sch.3 para.5, SI 1997/2778 (NI.19) Sch.4 para.5
Art.5, applied: SI 1996/275 (NI.2) Art.67, SI 1997/2777 (NI.18) Sch.3 para.5, SI 1997/2778 (NI.19) Sch.4 para.5
Art.6, amended: SI 1997/1179 (NI.8) Art.52
Art.18, referred to: SI 1997/2778 (NI.19) Art.7

713. Probation Board (Northern Ireland) Order 1982
Art.2, amended: SI 1996/3160 (NI.24) Sch.5 para.13
Art.4, applied: SI 1996/3160 (NI.24) Art.17
Art.14A, added: SI 1996/3160 (NI.24) Sch.5 para.14
Sch.1 para.1, revoked (in part): 1998 c.47 s.100, Sch.15
Sch.2 para.3, added: SI 1996/3160 (NI.24) Sch.5 para.15
Sch.2 para.3, revoked: SI 1996/1919 (NI.16) Art.257, Sch.3
Sch.4 para.1, revoked: SI 1996/3160 (NI.24) Sch.7
Sch.4 para.2, revoked: SI 1996/3160 (NI.24) Sch.7
Sch.4 para.3, revoked: SI 1996/3160 (NI.24) Sch.7
Sch.4 para.5, revoked: SI 1996/3160 (NI.24) Sch.7
Sch.4 para.6, revoked: SI 1996/3160 (NI.24) Sch.7
Sch.4 para.7, revoked: SI 1996/3160 (NI.24) Sch.7
Sch.4 para.8, revoked: SI 1996/3160 (NI.24) Sch.7

719. Public Lending Right Scheme 1982
referred to: SI 1996/1338
Appendix., applied: SI 1999/3304
Appendix., referred to: SI 1999/420
Appendix.Sch.2, amended: SI 1996/1338 Art.2, Appendix para.4, SI 1997/1576 Art.2, Appendix para.7, SI 1998/1218 Art.2, Appendix
Appendix.Art.4, amended: SI 1997/1576 Art.2, Appendix para.1
Appendix.Art.6, amended: SI 1999/420 Art.2, Appendix para.1
Appendix.Art.9, amended: SI 1997/1576 Art.2, Appendix para.2
Appendix.Art.20, amended: SI 1997/1576 Art.2, Appendix para.3
Appendix.Art.36, amended: SI 1997/1576 Art.2, Appendix para.4
Appendix.Art.38, amended: SI 1996/1338 Art.2, Appendix para.1
Appendix.Art.39, amended: SI 1996/1338 Art.2, Appendix para.2, SI 1997/1576 Art.2, Appendix para.5

NO.

719. Public Lending Right Scheme 1982—*cont.*
Appendix.Art.40, amended: SI 1996/1338 Art.2, Appendix para.3, SI 1997/1576 Art.2, Appendix para.5
Appendix.Art.42, amended: SI 1999/420 Art.2, Appendix para.2
Appendix.Art.44, amended: SI 1997/1576 Art.2, Appendix para.5
Appendix.Art.46, amended: SI 1996/3237 Art.2, SI 1997/1576 Art.2, Appendix para.6, SI 1999/3304 Art.2

739. Licensed Residential Establishment and Licensed Restaurant Wages Council (Variation) Order 1982
Sch.1, see *Nerva v RL&G Ltd* [1996] I.R.L.R. 461 (CA), Staughton, L.J.

841. Merchant Shipping (Tonnage) Regulations 1982
applied: SI 1996/3243 Sch Part I
revoked: SI 1997/1510 Reg.1
Sch.5, applied: SI 1996/1627 Art.16
Sch.5, revoked: SI 1997/1510 Reg.1
Sch.5 Appendix 1, applied: SI 1997/1510 Reg.12
Sch.5 Appendix 1, revoked: SI 1997/1510 Reg.1
Sch.5 Appendix 2, applied: SI 1997/1510 Reg.12
Sch.5 Appendix 2, revoked: SI 1997/1510 Reg.1
Sch.5 Appendix 3, applied: SI 1997/1510 Reg.12
Sch.5 Appendix 3, revoked: SI 1997/1510 Reg.1
Sch.5 Appendix 4, applied: SI 1997/1510 Reg.12
Sch.5 Appendix 4, revoked: SI 1997/1510 Reg.1

844. Seeds (National Lists of Varieties) Regulations 1982
Reg.5, see *R. v Secretary of State for the Environment, Transport and the Regions Ex p. Watson* [1999] Env. L.R. 310 (CA), Simon Brown, L.J.
Reg.5A, added: SI 1998/2726 Reg.2
Reg.11, see *R. v Secretary of State for the Environment, Transport and the Regions Ex p. Watson* [1999] Env. L.R. 310 (CA), Simon Brown, L.J.
Reg.11, revoked (in part): SI 1998/2726 Reg.2
Reg.11AA, added: SI 1998/2726 Reg.2

846. Departments (No.2) (Northern Ireland) Order 1982
Art.3, revoked: SI 1999/283 (NI.1) Art.9, Sch.3
Art.4, revoked (in part): SI 1999/283 (NI.1) Art.9, Sch.3

876. Merchant Shipping (Safety Officials and Reporting of Accidents and Dangerous Occurrences) Regulations 1982
applied: SI 1996/3243 Sch Part I
revoked: SI 1997/2962 Reg.1
Reg.1, revoked: SI 1997/2962 Reg.1
Reg.5, revoked: SI 1997/2962 Reg.1
Reg.9, revoked: SI 1997/2962 Reg.1
Reg.10, revoked: SI 1997/2962 Reg.1
Reg.11, revoked: SI 1997/2962 Reg.1
Reg.12, revoked: SI 1997/2962 Reg.1
Sch., revoked: SI 1997/2962 Reg.1

NO.

894. Statutory Sick Pay (General) Regulations 1982
Reg.1, amended: SI 1996/777 Reg.2
Reg.3, amended: SI 1998/2231 Reg.6
Reg.7, amended: SI 1996/777 Reg.2
Reg.9A, applied: 1999 c.2 s.1, Sch.2
Reg.9B, applied: 1999 c.2 s.1, Sch.2
Reg.9C, amended: SI 1996/672 Reg.3
Reg.9C, applied: 1999 c.2 s.1, Sch.2
Reg.10, applied: 1999 c.2 s.1, Sch.2
Reg.13, amended: SI 1996/777 Reg.2, SI 1996/3042 Reg.2
Reg.14, applied: 1999 c.2 s.1, Sch.2
Reg.15, amended: SI 1996/777 Reg.2
Reg.15A, amended: SI 1996/777 Reg.2
Reg.17, amended: SI 1999/567 Reg.13

902. Police (Discipline) (Scotland) Amendment Regulations 1982
revoked: SI 1996/1642 Reg.25, Sch.2

917. Local Government (Compensation for Premature Retirement) (Scotland) Amendment Regulations 1982
revoked: SI 1998/192 Reg.52, Sch.2

918. Teachers' (Compensation for Premature Retirement) (Scotland) Amendment Regulations 1982
revoked: SI 1996/2317 Reg.20, Sch.5

973. Town and Country Planning (Minerals) (Scotland) Regulations 1982
revoked: SI 1998/2913 Reg.4

995. Coroners' Records (Fees for Copies) Rules 1982
revoked: SI 1997/2544 r.4

1000. Petroleum (Production) Regulations 1982
Sch.4, referred to: 1998 c.17 Sch.1 para.13, SI 1999/160 Sch.4 para.1
Sch.5, referred to: 1998 c.17 Sch.1 para.14, Sch.1 para.15, SI 1999/160 Sch.6 para.1
Sch.8, referred to: 1998 c.17 Sch.1 para.16, SI 1999/160 Sch.7 para.1

1009. Local Government (Compensation for Premature Retirement) Regulations 1982
applied: SI 1996/532 Art.15
revoked: SI 1996/1680 Reg.49, Sch.5
Reg.5, revoked: SI 1996/1680 Reg.49, Sch.5
Reg.12, applied: SI 1996/1680 Sch.3 para.9
Reg.12, revoked: SI 1996/1680 Reg.49, Sch.5
Sch.1 Part I, revoked: SI 1996/1680 Reg.49, Sch.5
Sch.1 Part II, applied: SI 1996/1680 Sch.3 para.1
Sch.1 Part II, revoked: SI 1996/1680 Reg.49, Sch.5

1023. Merchant Shipping (Compensation to Seamen - War Damage to Effects) Scheme 1982
revoked: SI 1997/1674 para.2

1033. Contracting Out (Recovery of Class 1 Contributions) Regulations 1982
Reg.2, revoked: SI 1996/1172 Sch.2

1071. Commonwealth Agricultural Bureaux (Immunities and Privileges) Order 1982
Art.2, amended: SI 1999/2034 Art.2, Sch.
Art.9A, added: SI 1999/2034 Art.2, Sch.
Art.11, amended: SI 1999/2034 Art.2, Sch.

1072. Continental Shelf (Designation of Additional Areas) Order 1982
referred to: SI 1999/2031, SI 1999/2031 Art.2, Sch.
Sch., applied: SI 1997/268 Sch.

NO.

1080. Agricultural Marketing (Northern Ireland) Order 1982
Art.14, amended: 1996 c.23 Sch.3 para.39
Art.23, referred to: 1998 c.41 s.45, Sch.7 para.20
Art.29, referred to: SI 1997/733 Reg.23
Art.42, amended: SI 1999/506 Art.40
Art.42, referred to: 1998 c.41 s.45, Sch.7 para.20
Sch.2, applied: SI 1999/680 Art.2, Sch. Part I
Sch.8, amended: 1998 c.41 s.74, Sch.12 para.6, Sch.14 Part II
Sch.8 para.16, amended: 1998 c.41 s.74, Sch.12 para.6, Sch.14 Part II
Sch.8 para.16, referred to: SI 1999/505 Art.2, Sch.2

1082. Forfeiture (Northern Ireland) Order 1982
Art.6, amended: SI 1998/1506 (NI.10) Art.78, Sch.6 para.4

1083. Industrial Development (Northern Ireland) Order 1982
Art.4, amended: SI 1999/283 (NI.1) Art.9, Sch.2
Art.30, applied: SI 1997/660 Art.2, SI 1999/719 Art.2
Part III, applied: SI 1997/660 Art.2, SI 1999/719 Art.2
Sch.3 para.5, revoked: SI 1996/1919 (NI.16) Art.257, Sch.3

1084. Social Security (Northern Ireland) Order 1982
Sch.2 para.12, revoked: SI 1996/1919 (NI.16) Art.257, Sch.3

1094. Plant Breeders' Rights (Applications in Designated Countries) Order 1982
revoked: SI 1996/1811 Art.2

1101. Plant Breeders' Rights (Amendment) Regulations 1982
applied: SI 1998/1027 Reg.22
revoked: SI 1998/1027 Reg.21 (with savings), Sch.2 (with savings)

1109. Crown Court Rules 1982
see *Customs and Excise Commissioners v Brunt* (1999) 163 J.P. 161 (QBD), Mitchell, J.
applied: SI 1998/3047 r.2
r.3, amended: SI 1999/2838 r.2
r.4, amended: SI 1999/2838 r.2
r.4, revoked (in part): SI 1999/2838 r.2
r.5, amended: SI 1999/2838 r.2
r.21, amended: SI 1998/2168 r.2
r.21A, added: SI 1998/2168 r.2
r.22, substituted: SI 1997/701 r.2
r.23, substituted: SI 1999/598 r.2
r.23A, amended: SI 1998/3047 r.2
r.23B, amended: SI 1998/3047 r.2
r.23C, amended: SI 1998/3047 r.2
r.23ZA, added: SI 1999/598 r.2
r.23ZB, added: SI 1999/598 r.2
r.23ZC, added: SI 1999/598 r.2
r.24A, see *Guardian Newspapers Ltd, Ex p.* [1999] 1 W.L.R. 2130 (CA (Crim Div)), Brooke, L.J.
r.24ZA, added: SI 1998/3047 r.2
r.26, see *DPP v Coleman* [1998] 1 All E.R. 912 (QBD), Pill, L.J.
r.27, amended: SI 1998/3047 r.2
r.37, added: SI 1999/3040 r.2
Sch.11, added: SI 1999/3040 r.2, Sch.
Sch.12, added: SI 1999/3040 r.2, Sch.

1123. Registration of Overseas Births and Deaths Regulations 1982
Reg.5, amended: SI 1997/1466 Reg.2
Reg.8, amended: SI 1997/1466 Reg.2

NO.

1144. Feedingstuffs (Sampling and Analysis) Regulations 1982
revoked: SI 1999/1663 Reg.10
Sch.1 Part I, applied: SI 1998/1049 Reg.83, Reg.84
Sch.1 Part I, revoked: SI 1999/1663 Reg.10
Sch.1 Part II, amended: SI 1998/1049 Reg.83
Sch.1 Part II, applied: SI 1998/1049 Reg.83
Sch.1 Part II, revoked: SI 1999/1663 Reg.10
Sch.1 Part V, applied: SI 1998/1049 Reg.84
Sch.1 Part V, revoked: SI 1999/1663 Reg.10
Sch.2, revoked: SI 1999/1663 Reg.10

1163. Motorways Traffic (England and Wales) Regulations 1982
referred to: SI 1997/3053 Reg.18
Reg.5, amended: SI 1996/1316 Sch.
Reg.7, revoked: SI 1996/1316 Sch.
Reg.9, revoked: SI 1996/1316 Sch.
Reg.11, substituted: SI 1996/3053 Reg.2
Reg.12, referred to: SI 1999/1077 Reg.3
Reg.15, amended: SI 1996/1316 Sch.
Reg.15, applied: SI 1996/1316 Reg.10
Reg.16, amended: SI 1996/1316 Sch.
Reg.16, revoked: SI 1996/1316 Reg.10, Reg.11

1178. Pensions Increase (Review) Order 1982
applied: SI 1997/634 Art.3, SI 1998/503 Art.3, Art.4, SI 1999/522 Art.3

1230. Endangered Species (Import and Export) Act 1976 (Modification) Order 1982
revoked: SI 1996/2677 Art.5

1236. Income Tax (Interest Relief) Regulations 1982
Reg.8B, amended: SI 1996/1184 Reg.3, Reg.4

1271. Motor Vehicles (Type Approval for Goods Vehicles) (Great Britain) Regulations 1982
applied: SI 1996/3013 Reg.5, SI 1997/564 Reg.7, Reg.13, Reg.16, SI 1999/2149 Reg.5, Reg.15
referred to: SI 1997/564 Reg.10, SI 1999/2149 Reg.9
Reg.2, amended: SI 1996/2331 Reg.3, SI 1996/3014 Reg.3
Reg.3, amended: SI 1996/3014 Reg.4, Reg.5
Reg.3, referred to: SI 1996/3013 Reg.5
Reg.3A, added: SI 1996/3014 Reg.5
Reg.4, amended: SI 1996/2331 Reg.4, SI 1996/3014 Reg.6
Reg.4, applied: SI 1996/3013 Reg.6
Reg.7, applied: SI 1998/3093 Reg.4
Reg.10, applied: SI 1997/564 Reg.16
Reg.13, applied: SI 1998/3093 Reg.4
Reg.13A, amended: SI 1997/2936 Reg.2
Reg.14, applied: SI 1996/3013 Sch.1 para.1, SI 1998/3093 Reg.4
Reg.15, amended: SI 1998/3093 Reg.4
Reg.15, applied: SI 1998/3093 Reg.4
Reg.15, revoked (in part): SI 1998/3093 Reg.4
Reg.16, applied: SI 1998/3093 Reg.4
Reg.17, applied: SI 1998/3093 Reg.4
Reg.18, applied: SI 1998/3093 Reg.4
Reg.18A, added: SI 1996/3014 Reg.7
Reg.18A, amended: SI 1998/1006 Reg.2
Reg.18A, referred to: SI 1997/1365 Reg.2
Reg.19, substituted: SI 1996/3014 Reg.8
Sch.1, referred to: SI 1997/564 Reg.7
Sch.1 Part I, amended: SI 1996/2331 Reg.5
Sch.1 Item 2G, applied: SI 1997/564 Sch.1 Part II
Sch.1 Item 2H, applied: SI 1997/564 Sch.1 Part II
Sch.1 Item 2I, applied: SI 1997/564 Sch.1 Part II
Sch.1 Item 2J, applied: SI 1997/564 Sch.1 Part II

NO.

NO.

1982—cont.

1982—cont.

1271. Motor Vehicles (Type Approval for Goods Vehicles) (Great Britain) Regulations 1982—*cont.*

Sch.1 Item 3B, applied: SI 1997/564 Sch.1 Part II

Sch.1 Item 4E, applied: SI 1997/564 Sch.1 Part II

Sch.1 Item 5A, applied: SI 1997/564 Sch.1 Part II

Sch.1 Item 6E, applied: SI 1997/564 Sch.1 Part II

Sch.1 Item 6F, applied: SI 1997/564 Sch.1 Part II

Sch.1 Item 6H, applied: SI 1997/564 Sch.1 Part II

Sch.1 Item 6I, applied: SI 1997/564 Sch.1 Part II
Sch.1 Item 6J, applied: SI 1997/564 Sch.1 Part II

Sch.1 Item 9, applied: SI 1997/564 Sch.1 Part II

Sch.1 Item 14F, applied: SI 1997/564 Sch.1 Part II

Sch.1B Part I, substituted: SI 1996/2331 Reg.6
Sch.1B Part II, amended: SI 1996/2331 Reg.6
Sch.1C, added: SI 1996/2331 Reg.7
Sch.2 Part II, amended: SI 1998/3093 Reg.4
Sch.3 Part II, amended: SI 1998/3093 Reg.4

1292. Merchant Shipping (Radio) (Fishing Vessels) (Amendment) Rules 1982

revoked (in part): SI 1999/3210 Reg.2

1311. Fruit Juices and Fruit Nectars (Amendment) Regulations 1982

Reg.10, revoked: SI 1996/1499 Reg.49, Sch.9

1349. Statutory Sick Pay (Mariners, Airmen and Persons Abroad) Regulations 1982

Reg.1, amended: SI 1996/777 Reg.3
Reg.5A, added: SI 1996/777 Reg.3
Reg.10, substituted: SI 1996/777 Reg.3

1357. Notification of Installations Handling Hazardous Substances Regulations 1982

applied: 1997 c.10 s.9
Reg.3, amended: SI 1996/825 Reg.31, Sch 6 Part II
Reg.3, referred to: SI 1996/825 Reg.27
Reg.4, amended: SI 1996/825 Reg.31, Sch.6 Part II
Reg.5, amended: SI 1996/825 Reg.31, Sch.6 Part II
Sch.2 Part I, amended: SI 1996/825 Reg.31, Sch.6 Part II
Sch.2 Part II, revoked: SI 1996/825 Reg.31, Sch.6 Part II

1384. Licensing (Special Hours Certificates) Rules 1982

r.3, amended: SI 1996/978 r.2
r.3A, amended: SI 1996/978 r.2
r.7, amended: SI 1996/978 r.2
r.8, amended: SI 1996/978 r.2
Sch., substituted: SI 1996/978 r.3

1408. Social Security (General Benefit) Regulations 1982

Reg.1, amended: SI 1999/1958 Art.4, Sch.5 para.1, SI 1999/3178 Art.3, Sch.3 para.1
Reg.2, amended: SI 1996/425 Reg.4
Reg.9, amended: SI 1996/2538 Reg.5, SI 1997/454 Reg.6
Reg.11, amended: SI 1999/1958 Art.4, Sch.5 para.2, SI 1999/3178 Art.3, Sch.3 para.2
Reg.16, amended: SI 1996/670 Reg.4, SI 1997/576 Reg.4, SI 1998/521 Reg.4, SI 1999/862 Reg.2
Reg.16, applied: SI 1996/2745 Sch.1 para.8
Reg.17, applied: SI 1999/991 Reg.27, Sch.2 para.16

1408. Social Security (General Benefit) Regulations 1982—*cont.*

Reg.40, amended: SI 1999/1958 Art.4, Sch.5 para.3, SI 1999/3178 Art.3, Sch.3 para.3

1464. Horserace Betting Levy (Bookmakers' Committee) Regulations 1982

revoked: SI 1997/1604 Reg.8

1489. Workmen's Compensation (Supplementation) Scheme 1982

applied: SI 1997/731 Art.6, SI 1998/571 Art.6, SI 1999/720 Art.6
Art.1, amended: SI 1999/1958 Art.4, Sch.6 para.1
Art.5, amended: SI 1996/598 Reg.2, SI 1997/731 Art.2, SI 1998/571 Art.2, SI 1999/720 Art.2
Art.6, amended: SI 1999/1958 Art.4, Sch.6 para.2
Art.7, applied: SI 1997/731 Art.4, SI 1998/571 Art.4, SI 1999/720 Art.4
Art.12, substituted: SI 1999/1958 Art.4, Sch.6 para.3
Art.13, substituted: SI 1999/1958 Art.4, Sch.6 para.4
Art.14, substituted: SI 1999/1958 Art.4, Sch.6 para.5
Art.15, amended: SI 1999/1958 Art.4, Sch.6 para.6
Art.17, amended: SI 1999/1958 Art.4, Sch.6 para.7
Art.17, revoked (in part): SI 1999/1958 Art.4, Sch.6 para.7
Art.18, substituted: SI 1997/823 para.2
Art.26, amended: SI 1999/1958 Art.4, Sch.6 para.8
Art.33, amended: SI 1999/1958 Art.4, Sch.6 para.9
Sch.1, substituted: SI 1996/598 Reg.3, Sch, SI 1997/731 Art.3, Sch, SI 1998/571 Art.3, Sch., SI 1999/720 Art.3, Sch.
Sch.1 Part II, applied: SI 1997/731 Art.5, SI 1998/571 Art.5, SI 1999/720 Art.5
Sch.1 Part II, referred to: SI 1996/598 Reg.5
Sch.2, substituted: SI 1999/1958 Art.4, Sch.6 para.11

1513. Submarine Pipe-lines Safety Regulations 1982

revoked (in part): SI 1996/825 Reg.31, Sch.6 Part I

1535. Disabled Persons (Northern Ireland) Order 1982

Art.4, referred to: SI 1997/276 (NI.2) Art.1
Art.4, revoked (in part): SI 1996/1320 (NI.10) Sch.4, SI 1997/276 (NI.2) Art.75, Sch.9

1607. Police (Promotion) (Amendment) Regulations 1982

revoked: SI 1996/1685 Reg.8, Sch.3

1619. Fruit Juices and Fruit Nectars (Scotland) (Amendment) Regulations 1982

Reg.10, revoked: SI 1996/1499 Reg.49, Sch.9

1676. Judicial Committee (General Appellate Jurisdiction) Rules Order 1982

referred to: SI 1999/665 Art.3
Sch. B Part II, amended: SI 1996/3170 Art.1, Sch.

1697. Wireless Telegraphy (Exemption) Regulations 1982

revoked: SI 1996/316 Reg.2, Sch.1

NO.

1699. Merchant Shipping (Certification and Watchkeeping) Regulations 1982
revoked: SI 1997/1320 Reg.1

1700. Food Labelling (Amendment) Regulations 1982
revoked: SI 1996/1499 Reg.49, Sch.9

1703. Milk and Dairies (Revision of Penalties) Regulations 1982
Sch., amended: SI 1998/2424 Reg.9, Sch.

1706. County Court Fees Order 1982
revoked: SI 1999/689 Art.8 (with savings), Sch.2 (with savings)
Art.3, see *Scarth, Ex p.* Times, July 8, 1999 (CA), Ward, L.J.
Art.3, revoked: SI 1999/689 Art.8 (with savings), Sch.2 (with savings)
Art.4, amended: SI 1996/3189 Art.3, SI 1997/2670 Art.2
Art.4, revoked: SI 1999/689 Art.8 (with savings), Sch.2 (with savings)
Art.4, substituted: SI 1997/787 Art.2
Sch.1, amended: SI 1996/3189 Art.6, Art.7, Art.8, Art.9, Art.10, Art.11
Sch.1, revoked: SI 1999/689 Art.8 (with savings), Sch.2 (with savings)
Sch.1 para.1, amended: SI 1996/3189 Art.4
Sch.1 para.1, revoked: SI 1999/689 Art.8 (with savings), Sch.2 (with savings)
Sch.1 para.3, revoked: SI 1999/689 Art.8 (with savings), Sch.2 (with savings)
Sch.1 para.5, revoked: SI 1999/689 Art.8 (with savings), Sch.2 (with savings)
Sch.1 para.6, added: SI 1996/3189 Art.5
Sch.1 para.6, revoked: SI 1999/689 Art.8 (with savings), Sch.2 (with savings)

1707. Supreme Court Fees (Amendment) Order 1982
revoked: SI 1999/687 Art.8 (with savings), Sch.2 (with savings)

1713. Goods Vehicles (Operators' Licences) (Temporary Use in Great Britain) (Amendment) Regulations 1982
revoked: SI 1996/2186 Reg.2, Sch.1

1727. Food (Revision of Penalties) Regulations 1982
Sch.1, revoked (in part): SI 1996/1499 Reg.49, Sch.9

1730. Education (Particulars of Independent Schools) Regulations 1982
revoked: SI 1997/2918 Reg.3

1752. Merchant Shipping (Section 52 Inquiries) Rules 1982
r.5, applied: SI 1999/678 Sch., SI 1999/1750 Art.2, Sch.1

1779. Food Labelling (Scotland) Amendment Regulations 1982
revoked: SI 1996/1499 Reg.49, Sch.9

1854. Hull and Goole Port Health Authority Order 1982
Art.2, substituted: SI 1996/446 Art.4
Art.3, amended: SI 1996/446 Art.4
Art.4, amended: SI 1996/446 Art.4
Art.5, amended: SI 1996/446 Art.4
Art.9, amended: SI 1996/446 Art.4

1889. Monopolies and Mergers Commission (Membership of Groups for Newspaper Merger References) Order 1982
revoked: SI 1999/506 Art.45

NO.

29. Education (Special Educational Needs) Regulations 1983
Reg.4, see *R. v Commissioner for Local Administration Ex p. S* (1999) 1 L.G.L.R. 633 (QBD), Collins, J.

54. Statutory Sick Pay (Compensation of Employers) and Miscellaneous Provisions Regulations (Northern Ireland) 1983
Reg.3, applied: SI 1999/671 Art.3, Sch.2

133. Landlord and Tenant Act 1954, Part II (Notices) Regulations 1983
Sch.2, see *Sabella Ltd v Montgomery* [1998] 1 E.G.L.R. 65 (CA), Aldous, L.J.

136. Pneumoconiosis, Byssinosis and Miscellaneous Diseases Benefit Scheme 1983
Art.1, amended: SI 1999/1958 Art.4, Sch.7 para.1
Art.2, amended: SI 1999/1958 Art.4, Sch.7 para.2
Art.4, amended: SI 1999/1958 Art.4, Sch.7 para.3
Art.12, substituted: SI 1999/1958 Art.4, Sch.7 para.4
Art.13, substituted: SI 1999/1958 Art.4, Sch.7 para.5
Art.14, amended: SI 1999/1958 Art.4, Sch.7 para.6
Art.16, amended: SI 1999/1958 Art.4, Sch.7 para.7
Art.16, revoked (in part): SI 1999/1958 Art.4, Sch.7 para.7
Art.17, substituted: SI 1997/824 Art.2
Art.18, referred to: SI 1999/820 Reg.1
Art.26, substituted: SI 1999/1958 Art.4, Sch.7 para.8
Sch.1, amended: SI 1997/824 Art.3
Sch.3, substituted: SI 1999/1958 Art.4, Sch.7 para.9

142. African Development Bank (Immunities and Privileges) Order 1983
Art.13A, added: SI 1999/2034 Art.2, Sch.

143. Commonwealth Foundation (Immunities and Privileges) Order 1983
Art.8A, added: SI 1999/2034 Art.2, Sch.

144. Commonwealth Telecommunications Organisation (Immunities and Privileges) Order 1983
Art.9A, added: SI 1999/2034 Art.2, Sch.

147. Financial Provisions (Northern Ireland) Order 1983
applied: SI 1998/261 (NI.2) Art.9
Sch.3, revoked (in part): SI 1998/261 (NI.2) Art.15, Sch.4

224. Insurance (Lloyd's) Regulations 1983
Reg.3, applied: SI 1998/2842 Art.2, Sch. para.67
Reg.3, substituted: SI 1997/686 Reg.3
Reg.3A, added: SI 1997/686 Reg.3
Reg.3B, added: SI 1997/686 Reg.3
Reg.4, amended: SI 1996/3011 Reg.8
Reg.5, amended: SI 1996/3011 Reg.9
Reg.5, applied: SI 1998/2842 Art.2, Sch. para.67
Sch.1 para.2, applied: SI 1998/2842 Art.2, Sch. para.67
Sch.1A, added: SI 1997/686 Reg.3, Sch.1
Sch.1A para.4, applied: SI 1998/2842 Art.2, Sch. para.67
Sch.1A para.6, applied: SI 1998/2842 Art.2, Sch. para.67
Sch.1A para.10, applied: SI 1998/2842 Art.2, Sch. para.67

1983—cont.

224. **Insurance (Lloyd's) Regulations 1983**—*cont.*
Sch.1A para.11, applied: SI 1998/2842 Art.2, Sch. para.67
Sch.2, substituted: SI 1996/3011 Reg.8, Sch.
Sch.3, amended: SI 1996/3011 Reg.9
Sch.3 Form 1, amended: SI 1996/3011 Reg.9
Sch.3 Form 2, amended: SI 1996/3011 Reg.9
Sch.3 Form 3, amended: SI 1996/3011 Reg.9
Sch.3 Form 4, amended: SI 1996/3011 Reg.9
Sch.3 Form 4, revoked: SI 1997/686 Reg.4
Sch.3 Form 5, amended: SI 1996/3011 Reg.9
Sch.3 Form 6, amended: SI 1996/3011 Reg.9, SI 1997/686 Reg.4
Sch.3 Form 6A, added: SI 1997/686 Reg.4, Sch.2
Sch.3 Form 6B, added: SI 1997/686 Reg.4, Sch.2
Sch.3 Form 7, amended: SI 1996/3011 Reg.9
Sch.3 Form 8, amended: SI 1996/3011 Reg.9
Sch.3 Form 9, amended: SI 1996/3011 Reg.9, SI 1997/686 Reg.4
Sch.3 Form 10, amended: SI 1996/3011 Reg.9
Sch.3 para.3, substituted: SI 1996/3011 Reg.9
Sch.3 para.3A, added: SI 1997/686 Reg.4
Sch.3 para.4, amended: SI 1996/3011 Reg.9
Sch.3 para.5, substituted: SI 1996/3011 Reg.9, SI 1997/686 Reg.4

253. **Fishing Boats (European Economic Community) Designation Order 1983**
Sch., amended: SI 1996/248 Art.2

282. **Insolvency of Employer (Excluded Classes) Regulations (Northern Ireland) 1983**
revoked: SI 1996/1919 (NI.16) Art.257

363. **Gas Quality Regulations 1983**
applied: SI 1996/219 Art.2, SI 1996/551 Reg.10
revoked: SI 1996/551 Reg.12
Reg.2, amended: SI 1996/219 Art.3
Reg.2, revoked: SI 1996/551 Reg.12
Reg.3, amended: SI 1996/219 Art.4
Reg.3, applied: SI 1996/219 Art.17
Reg.3, revoked: SI 1996/551 Reg.12
Reg.4, amended: SI 1996/219 Art.4
Reg.4, applied: SI 1996/219 Art.17
Reg.4, revoked: SI 1996/551 Reg.12
Reg.5, amended: SI 1996/219 Art.4
Reg.5, applied: SI 1996/219 Art.17
Reg.5, revoked: SI 1996/551 Reg.12
Reg.6, revoked: SI 1996/219 Art.5, SI 1996 551 Reg.12
Reg.7, substituted: SI 1996/219 Art.6
Reg.7, revoked: SI 1996/551 Reg.12
Reg.9, substituted: SI 1996/219 Art.7
Reg.9, revoked: SI 1996/551 Reg.12
Reg.10, amended: SI 1996/219 Art.8
Reg.10, revoked: SI 1996/551 Reg.12
Reg.11, applied: SI 1996/219 Art.17
Reg.11, substituted: SI 1996/219 Art.9
Reg.11, revoked: SI 1996/551 Reg.12

376. **Statutory Sick Pay (Compensation of Employers) and Miscellaneous Provisions Regulations 1983**
Reg.3, applied: 1999 c.2 s.1, Sch.2

448. **Borough of Cynon Valley (Electoral Arrangements) Order 1983**
Sch.1, referred to: SI 1998/3138 Sch.

466. **Anglian Water Authority (Transfer of Powers of the Swavesey Internal Drainage Board) Order 1983**
applied: SI 1998/2227

1983—cont.

468. **Returning Officers (Parliamentary Constituencies) (England and Wales) Order 1983**
Art.3, amended: SI 1996/897 Art.3
Art.4, amended: SI 1996/897 Art.3
Art.6, amended: SI 1996/897 Art.3
Sch.1 Part II, revoked: SI 1996/897 Art.3
Sch.2 Part II, revoked: SI 1996/897 Art.3
Sch.3 Part II, revoked: SI 1996/897 Art.3

506. **Redundant Mineworkers and Concessionary Coal (Payments Schemes) Order 1983**
revoked (in part): SI 1996/1288 Art.3

514. **London Docklands Development Corporation (Vesting of Land) (Greater London Council and Southwark London Borough Council) Order 1983**
revoked: SI 1998/769 Art.3, Sch.

527. **Justices' Clerks (Amendment) Rules 1983**
revoked: SI 1999/2784 r.4

568. **Prison (Amendment) Rules 1983**
revoked: SI 1999/728 r.85 (with savings), Sch. (with savings)

603. **European Communities (Designation) Order 1983**
Sch., revoked (in part): SI 1998/1750 Art.3

612. **Trial of the Pyx (Amendment) Order 1983**
revoked: SI 1998/1764 Art.16, Sch.3

624. **Insolvency of Employer (Excluded Classes) Regulations 1983**
revoked: 1996 c.18 Sch.3 Part II

667. **Nurses, Midwives and Health Visitors (Parts of the Register) Order 1983**
Sch.1, amended: SI 1998/2623 Art.3

678. **Stonehenge Regulations 1983**
revoked: SI 1997/2038 Reg.1

684. **Gas (Meters) Regulations 1983**
Reg.4, applied: SI 1996/319 Reg.3

686. **Personal Injuries (Civilians) Scheme 1983**
applied: SI 1998/19 Reg.2
Art.14, applied: SI 1997/790 Reg.4
Art.15, applied: SI 1997/790 Reg.4
Art.16, applied: SI 1997/790 Reg.4
Art.17, substituted: SI 1997/812 Art.2
Art.18, amended: SI 1996/502 Art.2, SI 1997/812 Art.3, SI 1998/278 Art.2, SI 1999/262 Art.2
Art.21, amended: SI 1997/812 Art.3
Art.25A, amended: SI 1997/812 Art.3
Art.25A, applied: SI 1996/2890 Sch.3 para.7, SI 1997/790 Reg.4
Art.25B, substituted: SI 1999/262 Art.3
Art.26A, added: SI 1997/812 Art.4
Art.27, applied: SI 1996/207 Sch.7 para.54, SI 1996/2890 Sch.3 para.52
Art.43, applied: SI 1997/790 Reg.4
Art.44, applied: SI 1997/790 Reg.4
Art.49A, added: SI 1997/812 Art.4
Art.71, amended: SI 1997/812 Art.5
Art.71, revoked (in part): SI 1997/812 Art.5
Sch.3, substituted: SI 1996/502 Art.3, Sch.1, SI 1997/812 Art.6, Sch., SI 1998/278 Art.3, Sch., SI 1999/262 Art.4, Sch.
Sch.4, substituted: SI 1996/502 Art.3, Sch.1, SI 1997/812 Art.6, Sch., SI 1998/278 Art.3, Sch., SI 1999/262 Art.4, Sch.
Sch.4 para.1, applied: SI 1996/2890 Sch.3 para.52
Sch.5, substituted: SI 1997/812 Art.6, Sch.

708. **Merchant Shipping (Distress Signals and Prevention of Collisions) Regulations 1983**
revoked: SI 1996/75 Reg.1

1983—cont.

713. Civil Courts Order 1983
Art.4, amended: SI 1996/2579 Art.3
Art.8, revoked: SI 1999/1011 Art.3
Sch.1, amended: SI 1996/68 Art.3, SI 1996/588
  Art.3, SI 1996/2579 Art.4, Art.5, SI 1997/361
  Art.3, SI 1997/2310 Art.3, SI 1997/2762 Art.3,
  SI 1998/1880 Art.3, SI 1998/2910 Art.3, SI
  1998/216 Art.3, SI 1999/3187 Art.2, Art.3
Sch.1, revoked (in part): SI 1997/1085 Art.3
Sch.3, amended: SI 1996/68 Art.3, SI 1996/588
  Art.3, SI 1996/2579 Art.6, Art.7, SI 1997/361
  Art.4, SI 1997/2310 Art.4, SI 1997/2762 Art.4,
  SI 1998/1880 Art.4, SI 1998/2910 Art.4, SI
  1999/216 Art.4, SI 1999/1011 Art.4, SI 1999/
  3187 Art.2, Art.3
Sch.3, revoked (in part): SI 1997/1085 Art.4
Sch.4 para.3, revoked: SI 1998/2910 Art.5
Sch.4 para.10A, added: SI 1997/2762 Art.5
Sch.4 para.11A, added: SI 1996/2579 Art.8

716. Standing Civilian Courts Order (Amendment) Order 1983
revoked: SI 1997/172 Art.93, Sch.5

717. Courts-Martial and Standing Civilian Courts (Additional Powers on Trial of Civilians) (Amendment) Regulations 1983
revoked: SI 1997/579 Reg.13, Sch.3

718. Rules of Procedure (Air Force) (Amendment) Rules 1983
revoked: SI 1997/171 r.90, Sch.7

719. Rules of Procedure (Army) (Amendment) Rules 1983
revoked: SI 1997/169 r.90, Sch.7

726. Nurses, Midwives and Health Visitors (Educational Policy Advisory Committee) Order 1983
Art.2, amended: SI 1998/2623 Art.2

764. Dogs (Northern Ireland) Order 1983
Art.2, amended: SI 1996/1632 (NI.11) Art.18,
  Sch.5 para.3

808. Merchant Shipping (Medical Examination) Regulations 1983
see *P&O European Ferries (Dover) Ltd v Iverson* [1999] I.C.R. 1088 (EAT), Judge Pugsley
applied: SI 1996/3243 Sch Part III
referred to: SI 1998/2411 Reg.8

873. Nurses, Midwives and Health Visitors Rules 1983
Sch. r.7, amended: SI 1996/3101 Sch.2 para.2
Sch. r.8, amended: SI 1996/3101 Sch.2 para.2
Sch. r.9, amended: SI 1997/1723 Sch.r.2
Sch. r.14A, amended: SI 1996/3101 Sch.2
  para.2
Sch. r.22, substituted: SI 1997/1723 Sch.r.2
Sch. r.27, amended: SI 1996/3101 Sch.2
  para.2, SI 1998/2649 Sch. r.2
Sch. r.30, amended: SI 1998/2649 Sch. r.2
Sch. r.40, substituted: SI 1998/2649 Sch. r.2
Sch. r.41, substituted: SI 1998/2649 Sch. r.2

883. Naval, Military and Air Forces etc. (Disablement and Death) Service Pensions Order 1983
applied: SI 1996/1638 Art.3, Sch.2 para.3, SI
  1996/2882, SI 1996/2890 Sch.3 para.13,
  Sch.3 para.50, SI 1998/19 Reg.2
referred to: SI 1996/1638, SI 1998/262, SI
  1999/294
Art.1, amended: SI 1996/1638 Art.2, Sch.1
  para.1
Art.3, substituted: SI 1996/2882 Art.2
Art.3A, added: SI 1996/2882 Art.3
Art.3A, amended: SI 1997/286 Art.2
Art.3B, added: SI 1996/2882 Art.3

1983—cont.

883. Naval, Military and Air Forces etc. (Disablement and Death) Service Pensions Order 1983—*cont.*
Art.3C, added: SI 1996/2882 Art.3
Art.3D, added: SI 1996/2882 Art.3
Art.4, amended: SI 1996/1638 Art.2, Sch.1
  para.2
Art.5, amended: SI 1996/1638 Art.2, Sch.1
  para.2
Art.7, amended: SI 1996/1638 Art.2, Sch.1
  para.3
Art.8, amended: SI 1996/2882 Art.4
Art.9, amended: SI 1996/1638 Art.2, Sch.1
  para.4
Art.10, amended: SI 1996/1638 Art.2, Sch.1
  para.4
Art.10, applied: SI 1997/790 Reg.4
Art.11, amended: SI 1996/1638 Art.2, Sch.1
  para.4
Art.13, applied: SI 1996/1638 Art.3, Sch.2
  para.1, Sch.2 para.2, Sch.2 para.5
Art.17, amended: SI 1997/286 Art.3
Art.18, amended: SI 1996/732 Art.2, SI 1997/
  286 Art.4, SI 1998/262 Art.2, SI 1999/294
  Art.2
Art.18, applied: SI 1996/1638 Art.3, Sch.2
  para.6
Art.21, amended: SI 1996/1638 Art.2, Sch.1
  para.5, SI 1997/286 Art.4
Art.26, substituted: SI 1999/294 Art.3
Art.26A, amended: SI 1997/286 Art.4
Art.26A, applied: SI 1996/2890 Sch.3 para.7, SI
  1997/790 Reg.4
Art.27, amended: SI 1996/2882 Art.5, SI 1997/
  286 Art.5
Art.29, amended: SI 1996/732 Art.3, SI 1997/
  286 Art.6, SI 1998/262 Art.3, SI 1999/294
  Art.4
Art.29, applied: SI 1996/207 Sch.7 para.53, SI
  1996/2890 Sch.3 para.51, Sch.3 para.53
Art.30, amended: SI 1996/2882 Art.6
Art.31, amended: SI 1996/2882 Art.7
Art.32, amended: SI 1996/2882 Art.8
Art.33, applied: SI 1996/1638 Art.3, Sch.2
  para.6
Art.34, amended: SI 1996/1638 Art.2, Sch.1
  para.6
Art.35, amended: SI 1996/1638 Art.2, Sch.1
  para.7
Art.35, applied: SI 1996/1638 Art.3, Sch.2
  para.6
Art.36, applied: SI 1996/1638 Art.3, Sch.2
  para.6
Art.37, applied: SI 1996/1638 Art.3, Sch.2
  para.6
Art.38, applied: SI 1996/1638 Art.3, Sch.2
  para.1, Sch.2 para.2, Sch.2 para.5
Art.39, applied: SI 1996/1638 Art.3, Sch.2
  para.6
Art.42, amended: SI 1996/732 Art.4, SI 1997/
  286 Art.7
Art.42A, added: SI 1997/286 Art.8
Art.54, amended: SI 1996/2882 Art.9
Art.65, substituted: SI 1996/2882 Art.10, SI
  1997/286 Art.9
Art.65ZA, added: SI 1996/2882 Art.10
Art.65ZA, revoked: SI 1997/286 Art.11
Art.67, amended: SI 1996/1638 Art.2, Sch.1
  para.8
Art.69, amended: SI 1996/1638 Art.2, Sch.1
  para.9

NO.

1983—cont.

883. **Naval, Military and Air Forces etc. (Disablement and Death) Service Pensions Order 1983**—*cont.*
Sch.1 Part II, amended: SI 1996/732 Art.5, Sch.1, SI 1997/286 Art.10, Sch.1, SI 1998/262 Art.4, Sch.1, SI 1999/294 Art.5, Sch.1
Sch.1 Part III, amended: SI 1996/732 Art.5, Sch.2, Sch.3, SI 1997/286 Art.10, Sch.2, Sch.3, SI 1998/262 Art.4, Sch.2, Sch.3, SI 1999/294 Art.5, Sch.2, Sch.3
Sch.1 Part IV, substituted: SI 1996/732 Art.5, Sch.4, SI 1997/286 Art.10, Sch.4, SI 1998/262 Art.4, Sch.4, SI 1999/294 Art.5, Sch.4
Sch.2, amended: SI 1996/732 Art.5, SI 1996/1638 Art.2, Sch.1 para.11
Sch.2 Part II, amended: SI 1996/732 Art.5, Sch.5, SI 1996/1638 Art.2, Sch.1 para.11, SI 1997/286 Art.10, Sch.5, SI 1998/262 Art.4, Sch.5, SI 1999/294 Art.5, Sch.5
Sch.2 Part III, substituted: SI 1996/732 Art.5, Sch.6, SI 1997/286 Art.10, Sch.6, SI 1998/262 Art.4, Sch.6, SI 1999/294 Art.5, Sch.6
Sch.3, substituted: SI 1997/286 Art.10, Sch.7
Sch.3 para.4, substituted: SI 1996/2882 Art.11
Sch.4 Part II, amended: SI 1996/1638 Art.2, Sch.1 para.12
Sch.4 para.18A, added: SI 1996/2882 Art.12

884. **Nursing and Midwifery Qualifications (EEC Recognition) Order 1983**
revoked: 1997 c.24 s.23, Sch.6

891. **Mental Health (Nurses) Order 1983**
revoked: SI 1998/2625 Art.3
Art.2, revoked: SI 1998/2625 Art.3

892. **Mental Health Act Commission (Establishment and Constitution) Order 1983**
Art.5, added: SI 1998/1577 Art.5

893. **Mental Health (Hospital, Guardianship and Consent to Treatment) Regulations 1983**
Reg.4, amended: SI 1996/540 Reg.2
Reg.10A, added: SI 1997/801 Reg.2
Reg.14, see *S-C (Mental Patient: Habeas Corpus), Re* [1996] Q.B. 599 (CA), Sir Thomas Bingham, M.R.
Sch.1 Form 2, substituted: SI 1996/540 Reg.3, Sch
Sch.1 Form 3, substituted: SI 1996/540 Reg.3, Sch
Sch.1 Form 4, substituted: SI 1996/540 Reg.3, Sch
Sch.1 Form 7, substituted: SI 1996/540 Reg.3, Sch
Sch.1 Form 9, substituted: SI 1996/540 Reg.3, Sch
Sch.1 Form 10, substituted: SI 1996/540 Reg.3, Sch
Sch.1 Form 11, substituted: SI 1996/540 Reg.3, Sch
Sch.1 Form 12, substituted: SI 1996/540 Reg.3, Sch
Sch.1 Form 13, amended: SI 1998/2624 Reg.2
Sch.1 Form 14, substituted: SI 1996/540 Reg.3, Sch
Sch.1 Form 15, substituted: SI 1996/540 Reg.3, Sch
Sch.1 Form 21, substituted: SI 1996/540 Reg.3, Sch
Sch.1 Form 22, substituted: SI 1996/540 Reg.3, Sch
Sch.1 Form 24, substituted: SI 1996/540 Reg.3, Sch
Sch.1 Form 28, substituted: SI 1996/540 Reg.3, Sch

NO.

1983—cont.

893. **Mental Health (Hospital, Guardianship and Consent to Treatment) Regulations 1983**—*cont.*
Sch.1 Form 29, substituted: SI 1996/540 Reg.3, Sch
Sch.1 Form 30, substituted: SI 1996/540 Reg.3, Sch
Sch.1 Form 31A, added: SI 1997/801 Reg.3, Sch
Sch.1 Form 31B, added: SI 1997/801 Reg.3, Sch

894. **Mental Health Act Commission Regulations 1983**
Reg.9, substituted: SI 1996/707 Reg.17, Sch.5 para.1

921. **EEC Nursing and Midwifery Qualifications Designation Order 1983**
revoked: SI 1996/3102 Art.10

938. **Milk Labelling (Scotland) Regulations 1983**
applied: SI 1996/1499 Reg.50
revoked: SI 1996/1499 Reg.49, Sch.9

942. **Mental Health Review Tribunal Rules 1983**
see *R. v Mental Health Review Tribunal Ex p. Hall* [1999] 4 All E.R. 883 (CA), Kennedy, L.J.
r.2, amended: SI 1996/314 r.2
r.3, amended: SI 1996/314 r.3
r.6, amended: SI 1996/314 r.4
r.7, amended: SI 1996/314 r.5, SI 1998/1189 r.2
r.8, amended: SI 1996/314 r.6
r.9, amended: SI 1996/314 r.7
r.10, amended: SI 1996/314 r.8
r.11, amended: SI 1996/314 r.9
r.16, see *R. v Mental Health Review Tribunal Ex p. Hall* [1999] 3 All E.R. 132 (QBD), Scott Baker, J.
r.19, amended: SI 1996/314 r.10
r.23, amended: SI 1996/314 r.11
r.25, amended: SI 1998/1189 r.2
r.29, amended: SI 1998/1189 r.2
Sch.1, amended: SI 1996/314 r.12
Sch.1 Part E, added: SI 1996/314 r.12
Sch.1 Part F, added: SI 1996/314 r.12

1018. **Smoke Control Areas (Exempted Fireplaces) (No.3) Order 1983**
Sch., amended: SI 1997/3009 Sch.2 para.1

1026. **Quarries (Metrication) Regulations 1983**
revoked: SI 1999/2024 Reg.48, Sch.5 Part I

1028. **Sheriff Court Districts (Amendment) Order 1983**
revoked: SI 1996/1005 Art.3, Sch.2

1032. **Licensing (Fees) Order 1983**
Art.2, amended: SI 1997/2501 Art.3

1106. **Merchant Shipping (Prevention of Oil Pollution) Order 1983**
applied: SI 1996/147

1116. **Naval, Military and Air Forces etc. (Disablement and Death) Service Pensions Amendment Order 1983**
referred to: 1998 c.46 s.30, Sch.5 s.F4

1118. **Housing (Northern Ireland) Order 1983**
Art.25, referred to: SI 1998/1004 Art.4
Art.36, applied: SI 1998/1071 (NI.6) Art.41, Sch.3
Art.47, applied: SI 1998/1071 (NI.6) Art.41, Sch.3
Part II, referred to: SI 1996/2753 Reg.3
Part II Ch.II, applied: SI 1998/1071 (NI.6) Art.4, Sch.2 para.7
Sch.2 para.3A, added: 1999 c.33 s.169, Sch.14 para.78
Sch.2 para.8, amended: SI 1996/725 (NI.5) Sch.3 para.2

NO.

1983—cont.

1120. Criminal Attempts and Conspiracy (Northern Ireland) Order 1983
Art.3A, added: SI 1996/3160 (NI.24) Art.42
Art.3A, applied: SI 1996/3160 (NI.24) Art.43
Art.3A, referred to: SI 1996/3160 (NI.24) Art.40
Art.9, amended: 1998 c.40 s.9, Sch.1 para.5, Sch.2 Part II
Art.9, applied: 1996 c.29 s.4
Art.9, revoked (in part): 1998 c.40 s.9, Sch.1 para.5, Sch.2 Part II
Art.9A, added: SI 1996/3160 (NI.24) Art.42, 1998 c.40 s.6
Art.9A, applied: SI 1996/3160 (NI.24) Art.43
Art.9A, referred to: SI 1996/3160 (NI.24) Art.40
Art.10, amended: SI 1998/1504 (NI.9) Art.65, Sch.5 para.21
Art.12, amended: 1998 c.40 s.6
Part IV, applied: 1996 c.29 s.4

1140. Classification and Labelling of Explosives Regulations 1983
applied: SI 1996/2089 Reg.10, Reg.11, SI 1996/2090 Reg.28, SI 1996/2791 Reg.10, Sch.9 Part V, Sch.9 Part VI, SI 1997/2505 Reg.10, Sch.9 Part V, Sch.9 Part VI, SI 1999/645 Reg.10, Sch.9, Sch.9 Part V, Sch.9 Part VI
Reg.2, amended: SI 1999/303 Reg.2, Sch.1 para.1
Reg.4, amended: SI 1999/303 Reg.2, Sch.1 para.2
Reg.6, amended: SI 1996/2093 Reg.33, Sch.9 para.2, SI 1999/303 Reg.2, Sch.1 para.3
Reg.6, applied: SI 1996/2093 Reg.19
Reg.9, amended: SI 1996/2093 Reg.33, Sch.9 para.3, SI 1999/303 Reg.2, Sch.1 para.4
Reg.12A, added: SI 1996/2093 Reg.33, Sch.9 para.4
Sch.1, amended: SI 1996/2093 Reg.33, Sch.9 para.5
Sch.2, amended: SI 1996/2093 Reg.33, Sch.9 para.6, SI 1999/303 Reg.2, Sch.1 para.6
Sch.3, amended: SI 1996/2093 Reg.33, Sch.9 para.7
Sch.3 para.16, added: SI 1996/2093 Reg.33, Sch.9 para.7
Sch.3 para.17, added: SI 1996/2093 Reg.33, Sch.9 para.7
Sch.3 para.17, amended: SI 1999/303 Reg.2, Sch.1 para.7
Sch.4, amended: SI 1996/2093 Reg.33, Sch.9 para.8

1160. Redundancy Payments (Local Government) (Modification) Order 1983
referred to: SI 1999/2277 Art.5
revoked: SI 1999/2277 Art.4, Sch.3
Art.1, amended: SI 1996/372 Art.2
Art.1, revoked: SI 1999/2277 Art.4, Sch.3
Art.4, amended: SI 1996/372 Art.2
Art.4, revoked: SI 1999/2277 Art.4, Sch.3
Sch.1, amended: SI 1996/372 Art.2
Sch.1, revoked: SI 1999/2277 Art.4, Sch.3
Sch.2, amended: SI 1996/372 Art.2
Sch.2, revoked: SI 1999/2277 Art.4, Sch.3

1212. Medicines (Products Other Than Veterinary Drugs) (Prescription Only) Order 1983
revoked: SI 1997/1830 Art.16, Sch.6
Art.1, revoked: SI 1997/1830 Art.16, Sch.6
Art.3, amended: SI 1996/1514 Art.2
Art.3, revoked: SI 1997/1830 Art.16, Sch.6
Art.4, amended: SI 1996/1514 Art.3, SI 1996/3193 Art.2
Art.4, revoked: SI 1997/1830 Art.16, Sch.6
Sch.1 Part I, amended: SI 1996/1514 Art.4, SI 1996/3193 Art.3

NO.

1983—cont.

1212. Medicines (Products Other Than Veterinary Drugs) (Prescription Only) Order 1983—*cont.*
Sch.1 Part I, revoked: SI 1997/1830 Art.16, Sch.6
Sch.1 Part II, amended: SI 1996/1514 Art.5
Sch.1 Part II, revoked: SI 1997/1830 Art.16, Sch.6
Sch.1 Part IV, amended: SI 1996/1514 Art.6, SI 1996/3193 Art.4
Sch.1 Part IV, revoked: SI 1997/1830 Art.16, Sch.6
Sch.3 Part I, amended: SI 1996/3193 Art.5, Sch
Sch.3 Part I, revoked: SI 1997/1830 Art.16, Sch.6

1215. Education (Fees and Awards) (Scotland) Regulations 1983
revoked: SI 1997/93 Reg.14, Sch.4

1247. Measuring Instruments (EEC Requirements) (Gas Volume Meters) (Fees) Regulations 1983
revoked: SI 1996/319 Reg.4

1264. Pensions Increase (Review) Order 1983
applied: SI 1997/634 Art.3, SI 1998/503 Art.3, Art.4, SI 1999/522 Art.3

1275. National Health Service (Appointment of Consultants) (Wales) Regulations 1983
applied: SI 1996/433 Art.4
referred to: SI 1996/433 Art.3
revoked: SI 1996/1313 Reg.10
Sch.1A para.2, amended: SI 1996/433 Art.4
Sch.1A para.5, amended: SI 1996/433 Art.4
Sch.1A para.12, amended: SI 1996/433 Art.4

1398. Merchant Shipping (Prevention of Oil Pollution) Regulations 1983
revoked: SI 1996/2154 Reg.1

1399. Supplementary Benefit (Requirements) Regulations 1983
Reg.9, applied: SI 1996/207 Sch.3 para.10
Reg.19, applied: SI 1996/2890 Sch.3 para.35, Sch.4 para.28

1455. Control of Noise (Appeals) (Scotland) Regulations 1983
Reg.2, amended: SI 1996/1076 Reg.4
Reg.4, revoked (in part): SI 1996/1076 Reg.4
Reg.10, revoked (in part): SI 1996/1076 Reg.4

1486. Passenger Car Fuel Consumption Order 1983
Art.3, amended: SI 1996/1132 Sch.1 para.1
Art.4, amended: SI 1996/1132 Sch.1 para.2
Art.6, substituted: SI 1996/1132 Sch.1 para.3
Art.7, substituted: SI 1996/1132 Sch.1 para.4
Art.8, substituted: SI 1996/1132 Sch.1 para.5
Art.9, amended: SI 1996/1132 Sch.1 para.6
Art.11, amended: SI 1996/1132 Sch.1 para.7
Art.14, amended: SI 1996/1132 Sch.1 para.8
Art.17, revoked: SI 1996/1132 Sch.1 para.9
Sch.2, substituted: SI 1996/1132 Art.3, Sch.2
Sch.3, revoked: SI 1996/1132 Art.3
Sch.5, substituted: SI 1996/1132 Art.3, Sch.3

1519. Merchant Shipping (Oil Pollution) (Anguilla) Order 1983
revoked: SI 1997/2580 Art.3

1524. Social Security Adjudications (Northern Ireland) Order 1983
revoked: SI 1998/1506 (NI.10) Art.78, Sch.7

1553. Consumer Credit (Agreements) Regulations 1983
Sch.1 para.19A, added: SI 1999/3177 Reg.4
Sch.7 para.2, amended: SI 1999/3177 Reg.3
Sch.7 para.3, amended: SI 1999/3177 Reg.3
Sch.7 para.4, revoked: SI 1999/3177 Reg.4
Sch.7 para.5, revoked: SI 1999/3177 Reg.4

NO.

1983—cont.

1553. Consumer Credit (Agreements) Regulations 1983—*cont.*
Sch.8 para.19A, added: SI 1999/3177 Reg.4

1568. Consumer Credit (Realisation of Pawn) Regulations 1983
Reg.3, amended: SI 1998/998 Reg.2

1571. Consumer Credit (Increase of Monetary Amounts) Order 1983
revoked: SI 1998/997 Art.2

1573. Smoke Control Areas (Exempted Fireplaces) (Scotland) Order 1983
Sch.1, amended: SI 1997/3009 Sch.2 para.3

1575. Gas Safety (Rights of Entry) Regulations 1983
revoked: SI 1996/2535 Reg.11
Reg.2, amended: SI 1996/252 Art.2, Sch
Reg.2, revoked: SI 1996/2535 Reg.11
Reg.4, amended: SI 1996/252 Art.2, Sch
Reg.4, revoked: SI 1996/2535 Reg.11
Reg.6, amended: SI 1996/252 Art.2, Sch
Reg.6, revoked: SI 1996/2535 Reg.11
Reg.7, amended: SI 1996/252 Art.2, Sch
Reg.7, revoked: SI 1996/2535 Reg.11

1579. Hoists and Lifts (Metrication) Regulations 1983
revoked: SI 1998/2307 Reg.17, Sch.2

1590. Town and Country Planning (Structure and Local Plans) (Scotland) Regulations 1983
Reg.33, amended: SI 1996/493 Reg.6

1598. Social Security (Unemployment, Sickness and Invalidity Benefit) Regulations 1983
applied: SI 1996/1623 Art.3, SI 1998/217 Art.2
Reg.2, revoked: SI 1996/1345 Reg.27, Sch.
Reg.4, applied: SI 1996/2567 Reg.8, Reg.9, Reg.11, Reg.13
Reg.4, revoked: SI 1996/1345 Reg.27, Sch.
Reg.5, revoked: SI 1996/1345 Reg.27, Sch.
Reg.6, revoked: SI 1996/1345 Reg.27, Sch.
Reg.7, see *Secretary of State for Employment v Stewart* [1996] I.R.L.R. 334 (EAT), Lord Coulsfield
Reg.7, applied: SI 1996/2567 Reg.13
Reg.7, referred to: SI 1996/2567 Reg.15, Reg.20
Reg.7, revoked: SI 1996/1345 Reg.27, Sch.
Reg.7B, revoked: SI 1996/1345 Reg.27, Sch.
Reg.9, applied: SI 1996/2567 Reg.13
Reg.9, revoked: SI 1996/1345 Reg.27, Sch.
Reg.10, referred to: SI 1996/2567 Reg.13
Reg.10, revoked: SI 1996/1345 Reg.27, Sch.
Reg.11, referred to: SI 1996/2567 Reg.13
Reg.12, referred to: SI 1996/2567 Reg.13
Reg.13, revoked: SI 1996/1345 Reg.27, Sch.
Reg.14, revoked: SI 1996/1345 Reg.27, Sch.
Reg.16, revoked: SI 1996/1345 Reg.27, Sch.
Reg.19, revoked: SI 1996/1345 Reg.27, Sch.
Reg.20, amended: SI 1996/1345 Reg.25
Reg.23, revoked: SI 1996/1345 Reg.27, Sch.
Reg.24, revoked: SI 1996/1345 Reg.27, Sch.
Reg.25, revoked: SI 1996/1345 Reg.27, Sch.
Reg.26, revoked: SI 1996/1345 Reg.27, Sch.
Reg.27, revoked: SI 1996/1345 Reg.27, Sch.
Reg.28, revoked: SI 1996/1345 Reg.27, Sch.

1609. Endangered Species (Import and Export) Act 1976 (Modification) Order 1983
revoked: SI 1996/2677 Art.5

1621. Attachment of Debts (Expenses) Order 1983
revoked: SI 1996/3098 Art.1

1649. Asbestos (Licensing) Regulations 1983
applied: SI 1996/2791 Reg.6, Sch.5, SI 1997/2505 Reg.6, Sch.5, SI 1999/645 Reg.6, Sch.5
Reg.2, amended: SI 1998/3233 Reg.2, Sch. para.1

NO.

1983—cont.

1649. Asbestos (Licensing) Regulations 1983—*cont.*
Reg.3, amended: SI 1998/3233 Reg.2, Sch. para.2
Reg.4, amended: SI 1998/3233 Reg.2, Sch. para.3
Reg.5, amended: SI 1998/3233 Reg.2, Sch. para.4
Reg.8, amended: SI 1998/3233 Reg.2, Sch. para.5

1680. Supreme Court Fees (Amendment) Order 1983
revoked: SI 1999/687 Art.8 (with savings), Sch.2 (with savings)

1681. County Court Fees (Amendment) Order 1983
revoked: SI 1999/689 Art.8 (with savings), Sch.2 (with savings)

1698. Social Security (Cyprus) Order 1983
Sch., amended: SI 1996/1928 Art.2, Sch.1

1741. Social Security (Attendance Allowance) Amendment (No.3) Regulations 1983
see *Steane v Chief Adjudication Officer* [1996] 1 W.L.R. 1195 (HL), Lord Slynn of Hadley

1761. Accounts and Audit Regulations 1983
revoked (in part): SI 1996/590 Reg.3
Reg.3, revoked: SI 1996/590 Reg.3
Reg.4, revoked: SI 1996/590 Reg.3

1794. Equal Pay (Amendment) Regulations 1983
Reg.3, revoked (in part): 1996 c.17 Sch.3 Part II

1811. Insurance Companies (Accounts and Statements) Regulations 1983
revoked: SI 1996/943 Reg.35, Sch.7
Reg.3, amended: SI 1996/943 Reg.34, SI 1996/944 Reg.5
Reg.3, revoked: SI 1996/943 Reg.35, Sch.7
Reg.4, revoked: SI 1996/943 Reg.35, Sch.7
Reg.4, substituted: SI 1996/943 Reg.34
Reg.10, applied: SI 1996/943 Reg.33
Reg.10, revoked: SI 1996/943 Reg.35, Sch.7
Reg.22B, revoked: SI 1996/943 Reg.35, Sch.7
Reg.22B, substituted: SI 1996/943 Reg.34
Sch.1 Form 11, amended: SI 1996/943 Reg.34
Sch.1 Form 11, revoked: SI 1996/943 Reg.35, Sch.7
Sch.1 Form 12, amended: SI 1996/943 Reg.34
Sch.1 Form 12, revoked: SI 1996/943 Reg.35, Sch.7
Sch.1 Form 13, amended: SI 1996/943 Reg.34
Sch.1 Form 13, revoked: SI 1996/943 Reg.35, Sch.7
Sch.1 Form 13A, amended: SI 1996/943 Reg.34
Sch.1 Form 13A, revoked: SI 1996/943 Reg.35, Sch.7
Sch.6 Part I, amended: SI 1996/943 Reg.34
Sch.6 Part I, revoked: SI 1996/943 Reg.35, Sch.7

1831. Goods Vehicles (Authorisation of International Journeys) (Fees) Regulations 1983
revoked: SI 1996/131 Reg.4, Sch.2

1832. Goods Vehicles (Operators' Licences) (Temporary Use in Great Britain) (Amendment) Regulations 1983
revoked: SI 1996/2186 Reg.2, Sch.1

1878. Consumer Credit (Increase of Monetary Limits) Order 1983
Sch. Part II, amended: SI 1998/996 Art.2

1894. Social Security (New Zealand) Order 1983
Sch., amended: SI 1996/1928 Art.2, Sch.1

NO.

1983—cont.

1895. Access to the Countryside (Northern Ireland) Order 1983
Art.2, revoked: SI 1996/275 (NI.2) Art.71, Sch.8

1909. Misuse of Drugs (Notification of and Supply to Addicts) (Amendment) Regulations 1983
revoked: SI 1997/1001 Reg.5

1912. Secure Accommodation (Scotland) Regulations 1983
revoked: SI 1997/691 Reg.1, Sch
Reg.3, applied: SI 1997/691 Reg.2
Reg.3, revoked: SI 1997/691 Reg.1, Sch

1964. Adoption Agencies Regulations 1983
applied: SI 1996/207 Reg.78, SI 1996/2890 Reg.9
Reg.1, amended: SI 1997/649 Reg.2, SI 1997/2308 Reg.2
Reg.2, amended: SI 1997/649 Reg.2
Reg.5, substituted: SI 1997/649 Reg.2
Reg.5A, added: SI 1997/649 Reg.2
Reg.5B, added: SI 1997/649 Reg.2
Reg.8, amended: SI 1997/2308 Reg.2
Reg.8, applied: SI 1997/2308 Reg.6
Reg.8A, see *R (Adoption: Protection from Offenders Regulations)* [1999] 1 F.L.R. 472 (Fam Div), Sir Stephen Brown
Reg.8A, added: SI 1997/2308 Reg.2
Reg.9, see *R (Minors) (Adoption: Disclosure), Re* [1999] 2 F.L.R. 1123 (Fam Div), Cazalet, J.
Reg.9, amended: SI 1997/649 Reg.2
Reg.10, see *R (Minors) (Adoption: Disclosure), Re* [1999] 2 F.L.R. 1123 (Fam Div), Cazalet, J.
Reg.10, amended: SI 1997/649 Reg.2
Reg.11, amended: SI 1997/649 Reg.2
Reg.11A, added: SI 1997/649 Reg.2
Reg.11A, amended: SI 1997/2308 Reg.2
Reg.12, amended: SI 1997/649 Reg.2, SI 1997/2308 Reg.2
Reg.13, amended: SI 1997/649 Reg.2
Reg.13A, added: SI 1997/649 Reg.2
Reg.14, amended: SI 1997/649 Reg.2, SI 1997/2308 Reg.2
Reg.15, amended: SI 1997/649 Reg.2
Reg.17, substituted: SI 1997/649 Reg.2
Reg.17A, added: SI 1997/2308 Reg.2
Sch. Part I, amended: SI 1997/649 Reg.2
Sch. Part II, amended: SI 1997/649 Reg.2
Sch. Part III, amended: SI 1997/649 Reg.2
Sch. Part VIII, added: SI 1997/649 Reg.2
Sch.2, added: SI 1997/2308 Reg.2, Sch.
Sch.2 para.2, amended: SI 1999/2768 Reg.2
Sch.2 para.9, amended: SI 1999/2768 Reg.2
Sch.2 para.13, amended: SI 1999/2768 Reg.2
Sch.2 para.14, revoked: SI 1999/2768 Reg.2

1984

Barking and Dagenham (Waiting and Loading Restriction) (Amendment No.15) Order 1984
revoked (in part): SI 1996/1896 Art.10

Camden (Bus Lanes) (No.2) Traffic Order 1984
revoked (in part): SI 1998/3206 Art.6

Scheme for the Administration of the Legacy of Robert Nicol 1984
amended: SI 1996/478 Sch

12. Importation of Embryos, Ova and Semen Order 1984
Art.5, referred to: SI 1996/3124 Reg.40, Sch.5 Part I

NO.

1984—cont.

12. Importation of Embryos, Ova and Semen Order 1984—*cont.*
Art.5A, referred to: SI 1996/3124 Reg.40, Sch.5 Part I
Art.6, referred to: SI 1996/3124 Reg.40, Sch.5 Part I

16. Equal Pay (Amendment) Regulations (Northern Ireland) 1984
Reg.3, revoked (in part): SI 1996/1921 (NI.18) Art.28

41. Merchant Shipping (Crew Accommodation) (Amendment) Regulations 1984
revoked: SI 1997/1508 Reg.1

43. Registration of Births, Still-births, Deaths and Marriages (Prescription of Forms) (Scotland) Amendment Regulations 1984
revoked: SI 1997/2348 Reg.30, Sch.27

52. Feeding Stuffs (Sampling and Analysis) (Amendment) Regulations 1984
revoked: SI 1999/1663 Reg.10

70. Trunk Road (A4) (Great West Road, Hounslow) (Restriction of Traffic) Order 1984
Art.2, amended: SI 1996/357 Art.2

93. Merchant Shipping (Safety Officials and Reporting of Accidents and Dangerous Occurrences) (Amendment) Regulations 1984
revoked: SI 1997/2962 Reg.1

94. Merchant Shipping (Tankers-Officers and Ratings) Regulations 1984
revoked: SI 1997/348 Reg.1

95. Merchant Shipping (Engine Room Watch Ratings) Regulations 1984
revoked: SI 1997/348 Reg.1

96. Merchant Shipping (Navigational Watch Ratings) Regulations 1984
revoked: SI 1997/348 Reg.1

97. Merchant Shipping (Certificates of Proficiency in Survival Craft) Regulations 1984
referred to: SI 1998/1609 Reg.5, Reg.6, Sch.
revoked: SI 1997/348 Reg.1

124. Health Service Commissioner for England (Board of Governors of the Eastman Dental Hospital) Order 1984
revoked: SI 1998/3149 Art.2

125. Social Security (Finland) Order 1984
Sch., amended: SI 1996/1928 Art.2, Sch.1

129. Reciprocal Enforcement of Judgments (Administration of Justice Act 1920, Part II) (Consolidation) Order 1984
Sch.1, revoked (in part): SI 1997/2601 Art.2

144. Passenger and Goods Vehicles (Recording Equipment) (Amendment) Regulations 1984
Reg.3, amended: SI 1996/941 Reg.3

176. Goods Vehicles (Operators' Licences, Qualifications and Fees) Regulations 1984
see *Vehicle Inspectorate v TD&C Kelly Ltd* [1998] R.T.R. 297 (QBD), Collins, J.

179. Goods Vehicles (Operators' Licences) (Temporary Use in Great Britain) (Amendment) Regulations 1984
revoked: SI 1996/2186 Reg.2, Sch.1

193. Enfield and Haringey (Bus Lanes) (No.1) Traffic Order 1984
revoked: SI 1996/1459 Art.5 (with savings)

245. Amusements with Prizes (Variation of Monetary Limits) Order 1984
revoked: SI 1999/1259 Art.3, Sch.
Art.2, amended: SI 1996/3208 Art.3
Art.2, revoked: SI 1999/1259 Art.3, Sch.

NO.

247. Gaming Act (Variation of Monetary Limits) Order 1984
revoked: SI 1999/1260 Art.5, Sch.
Art.3, revoked (in part): SI 1997/1828 Art.3, SI 1999/1260 Art.5 (rem.), Sch. (rem.)

248. Gaming Clubs (Hours and Charges) Regulations 1984
Reg.5, amended: SI 1996/1109 Reg.2, SI 1998/961 Reg.2, SI 1999/1258 Reg.2, Reg.3

252. High Court of the Justiciary Fees Order 1984
Sch., amended: SI 1996/516 Art.2
Sch. Table, substituted: SI 1999/753 Art.2, Sch.

256. Court of Session etc. Fees Order 1984
revoked: SI 1997/688 Art.6, Sch.2
Sch., amended: SI 1996/514 Art.2
Sch., revoked: SI 1997/688 Art.6, Sch.2

265. Adoption Rules 1984
r.3, amended: SI 1999/1477 r.2
r.51, amended: SI 1999/1477 r.3, r.4
r.53, see *D (Minors) (Adoption Reports: Confidentiality), Re* [1996] A.C. 593 (HL), Lord Mustill

266. Registration of Births, Still-births, Deaths and Marriages (Prescription of Forms) (Scotland) Amendment Regulations 1984
revoked: SI 1997/2348 Reg.30, Sch.27

320. British Nationality (Fees) Regulations 1984
revoked: SI 1996/444 Reg.1

380. Occupational Pension Schemes (Contracting Out) Regulations 1984
applied: 1999 c.30 s.81, Sch.11 para.35
revoked: SI 1996/1172 Sch.2
Reg.18, referred to: SI 1996/1172 Reg.77
Reg.19, referred to: SI 1996/1172 Reg.77
Reg.20, referred to: SI 1996/1172 Reg.77, 1999 c.30 s.81, Sch.11 para.35, SI 1999/527 Art.2, Sch.2
Reg.21, referred to: SI 1996/1172 Reg.77
Reg.22, referred to: SI 1996/1172 Reg.77
Reg.23, referred to: SI 1996/1172 Reg.77, 1999 c.30 s.81, Sch.11 para.35
Reg.23A, referred to: 1999 c.30 s.81, Sch.11 para.35
Reg.24, referred to: SI 1996/1172 Reg.77
Reg.25, referred to: SI 1996/1172 Reg.77
Reg.26, referred to: SI 1996/1172 Reg.77
Reg.34, referred to: SI 1996/1172 Reg.77
Reg.43, amended: SI 1996/776 Reg.2
Reg.44, referred to: SI 1996/1172 Reg.77
Reg.45, referred to: SI 1996/1172 Reg.77
Reg.47, referred to: SI 1996/1172 Reg.77
Reg.48, referred to: SI 1996/1172 Reg.77
Reg.49, referred to: SI 1996/1172 Reg.77

392. Registration of Restrictive Trading Agreements Regulations 1984
Reg.10, amended: SI 1999/3446 Reg.2
Reg.11, amended: SI 1999/3446 Reg.2
Sch., amended: SI 1999/3446 Reg.2

408. Merchant Shipping (Health and Safety: General Duties) Regulations 1984
applied: SI 1996/3243 Sch Part I
revoked: SI 1997/2962 Reg.1
Reg.2, revoked: SI 1997/2962 Reg.1

418. Prevention of Terrorism (Supplemental Temporary Provisions) Order 1984
Art.4, see *Breen v Chief Constable of Dumfries and Galloway* Times, April 24, 1997 (IH), Lord Ross, L.J.C.
Art.10, see *Breen v Chief Constable of Dumfries and Galloway* Times, April 24, 1997 (IH), Lord Ross, L.J.C.

NO.

419. Offshore Installations (Application of Statutory Instruments) Regulations 1984
revoked: SI 1998/2306 Reg.39, Sch.4

455. Diseases of Fish Regulations 1984
Reg.2, referred to: SI 1996/3124 Reg.40, Sch.5 Part II, SI 1998/190 Reg.34, Sch.6
Reg.5, referred to: SI 1996/3124 Reg.40, Sch.5 Part II, SI 1998/190 Reg.34, Sch.6

457. Redundant Mineworkers and Concessionary Coal (Payments Scheme) Order 1984
revoked: SI 1996/1288 Art.3

465. Amusements with Prizes (Variation of Monetary Limits) (Scotland) Order 1984
revoked: SI 1999/1259 Art.3, Sch.
Art.2, amended: SI 1996/3273 Art.3
Art.2, revoked: SI 1999/1259 Art.3, Sch.

467. Town and Country Planning (Control of Advertisements) (Scotland) Regulations 1984
applied: 1997 c.61 Sch.3 para.3, SI 1999/787 Art.90
Reg.2, amended: SI 1996/252 Art.2, Sch
Reg.3, see *Baillie Lite Ltd v Glasgow City Council* [1999] 3 P.L.R. 64 (OH), Lord Osborne
Reg.11, applied: SI 1997/10 Reg.14
Reg.15, applied: SI 1997/10 Reg.14
Reg.24, see *Baillie Lite Ltd v Glasgow City Council* [1999] 3 P.L.R. 64 (OH), Lord Osborne

468. Gaming Act (Variation of Monetary Limits) (Scotland) Order 1984
revoked (in part): SI 1997/1828 Art.3, SI 1999/1260 Art.5 (rem.), Sch. (rem.)

470. Gaming Clubs (Hours and Charges) (Scotland) Regulations 1984
Reg.3, amended: SI 1997/942 Reg.2
Reg.5, amended: SI 1996/1144 Reg.2, SI 1997/942 Reg.3, SI 1998/961 Reg.3

516. City of Westminster (Prescribed Routes) (No.10) Traffic Order 1984
amended: SI 1996/2162 Art.5
Art.4, revoked: SI 1996/2689 Art.5
Art.11, revoked: SI 1996/2689 Art.5
Art.12, revoked: SI 1996/2689 Art.5

543. Merchant Shipping (Oil Pollution) (Overseas Territories) (Amendment) Order 1984
revoked (in part): SI 1997/2583 Art.4, SI 1997/2585 Art.4, SI 1997/2587 Art.4, SI 1998/1263 Art.4

548. European Parliamentary Constituencies (Scotland) Order 1984
revoked: SI 1996/1926 Art.3

551. Social Security (Unemployment, Sickness and Invalidity Benefit) Amendment Regulations 1984
revoked: SI 1996/1345 Reg.27, Sch.

552. Coroners Rules 1984
see *R. v HM Coroner for Birmingham Ex p. Najada* (1996) 29 B.M.L.R. 57 (CA), Auld, J.
r.2, amended: SI 1999/3325 r.3
r.9, see *Dobson v North Tyneside HA* [1997] 1 W.L.R. 596 (CA), Peter Gibson, L.J.
r.17, see *R. v Newcastle upon Tyne Coroner Ex p. A* (1998) 162 J.P. 387 (QBD), Tucker, J.
r.20, see *R. v HM Coroner for Surrey Ex p. Wright* [1997] Q.B. 786 (QBD), Tucker, J.
r.20, amended: SI 1999/3325 r.4
r.29, amended: SI 1999/3325 r.5, r.6
r.30, amended: SI 1999/3325 r.6
r.31, amended: SI 1999/3325 r.7

NO.

552. Coroners Rules 1984—*cont.*
r.32, amended: SI 1999/3325 r.8
r.33, amended: SI 1999/3325 r.9
r.35, amended: SI 1999/3325 r.10
r.37, see *R. v HM Coroner for Lincolnshire Ex p. Hay* (1999) 163 J.P. 666 (QBD), Brooke, L.J.
r.37A, added: SI 1999/3325 r.11
r.44, amended: SI 1999/3325 r.12
r.46, amended: SI 1999/3325 r.13
r.47, amended: SI 1999/3325 r.12
r.48, amended: SI 1999/3325 r.13
r.49, amended: SI 1999/3325 r.12
r.50, amended: SI 1999/3325 r.12
r.51, amended: SI 1999/3325 r.12
r.52, amended: SI 1999/3325 r.12
r.57, amended: SI 1999/3325 r.14
Sch.4 Form 5, amended: SI 1999/3325 r.15
Sch.4 Form 10, amended: SI 1999/3325 r.16
Sch.4 Form 15, amended: SI 1999/3325 r.17
Sch.4 Form 16, amended: SI 1999/3325 r.17
Sch.4 Form 22, amended: SI 1999/3325 r.18

565. Public Charitable Collections (Scotland) Regulations 1984
Reg.1, amended: SI 1996/739 Art.7, Sch.1 para.9
Reg.3, amended: SI 1996/739 Art.7, Sch.1 para.9
Reg.5, amended: SI 1996/739 Art.7, Sch.1 para.9
Reg.11, amended: SI 1996/739 Art.7, Sch.1 para.9
Reg.13, amended: SI 1996/739 Art.7, Sch.1 para.9

621. Trunk Road (A40) (Western Avenue, Ealing) (Speed Limits) Order 1984
Art.3, revoked: SI 1998/367 Art.5

647. Probation Rules 1984
r.26, see *R. v Secretary of State for the Home Department Ex p. National Association of Probation Officers* Times, February 10, 1996 (QBD), Kennedy, L.J.

648. Police (Promotion) (Scotland) Amendment Regulations 1984
revoked: SI 1996/221 Reg.10, Sch.2

702. Agriculture (Miscellaneous Provisions) (Northern Ireland) Order 1984
Art.8, revoked: SI 1999/662 (NI.6) Art.63, Sch.8 Part I
Art.12, revoked (in part): SI 1997/2984 (NI.22) Art.11, Sch.4

703. Fines and Penalties (Northern Ireland) Order 1984
Art.17, amended: SI 1996/3160 (NI.24) Sch.5 para.16
Art.17, revoked (in part): SI 1996/3160 (NI.24) Sch.7, SI 1998/1504 (NI.9) Art.65, Sch.6
Sch.2 para.5, revoked (in part): SI 1998/1504 (NI.9) Art.65, Sch.6
Sch.2 para.20, revoked: SI 1996/1320 (NI.10) Sch.4
Sch.2 para.23, revoked: SI 1998/261 (NI.2) Art.15, Sch.4
Sch.3, revoked (in part): SI 1997/2777 (NI.18) Art.35, Sch.5, 1998 c.32 s.74, Sch.6, SI 1998/1504 (NI.9) Art.65, Sch.6
Sch.4, revoked (in part): SI 1996/3160 (NI.24) Sch.7
Sch.5, amended: SI 1996/1141 (NI.6) Art.32

704. Gas (Amendment) (Northern Ireland) Order 1984
revoked: SI 1996/275 (NI.2) Art.71, Sch.8

NO.

740. Local Government (Compensation for Redundancy and Premature Retirement) Regulations 1984
revoked: SI 1996/1680 Reg.49, Sch.5

756. Medicines (Products Other Than Veterinary Drugs) (Prescription Only) Amendment Order 1984
revoked: SI 1997/1830 Art.16, Sch.6

769. Medicines (Products Other Than Veterinary Drugs) (General Sale List) Order 1984
Sch.1 Table A, amended: SI 1997/2043 Art.2, Sch.1, SI 1998/2170 Art.2, Sch.1, SI 1999/852 Art.2, Sch., SI 1999/2510 Art.2
Sch.1 Table B, amended: SI 1997/2043 Art.2, Sch.2, SI 1998/2170 Art.2, Sch.2
Sch.2 Table A, amended: SI 1998/2170 Art.3, SI 1999/852 Art.3

779. Savings Certificates (Yearly Plan) Regulations 1984
Reg.3, referred to: SI 1998/1449 Art.3, Sch. para.6
Reg.6, referred to: SI 1998/1449 Art.3, Sch. para.6
Reg.7, referred to: SI 1998/1449 Art.3, Sch. para.6
Reg.31, amended: SI 1997/1863 Reg.2
Reg.31, referred to: SI 1998/1449 Art.3, Sch. para.6

793. Lands Tribunal (Amendment) Rules 1984
revoked: SI 1996/1022 r.57, Sch.2

845. Teachers' (Compensation for Redundancy and Premature Retirement) (Scotland) Regulations 1984
revoked: SI 1996/2317 Reg.20, Sch.5
Part II, applied: SI 1996/2317 Reg.20
Part II, revoked: SI 1996/2317 Reg.20, Sch.5

846. Local Government (Compensation for Redundancy and Premature Retirement) (Scotland) Regulations 1984
revoked: SI 1998/192 Reg.52, Sch.2
Part II, applied: SI 1998/192 Reg.52
Part II, revoked: SI 1998/192 Reg.52, Sch.2

862. Prevention of Pollution (Reception Facilities) Order 1984
revoked: SI 1997/3018 Reg.16

864. Control of Pollution (Consents for Discharges) (Notices) Regulations 1984
Sch., amended: SI 1996/973 Reg.2, Sch para.7

865. Control of Pollution (Consents for Discharges) (Secretary of State Functions) Regulations 1984
applied: SI 1998/781 Art.3
Reg.2, amended: SI 1996/973 Reg.2, Sch para.8

924. City of Leicester (Electoral Arrangements) Order 1984
revoked: SI 1996/507 Art.9

960. Telecommunication (Street Works) (Northern Ireland) Order 1984
applied: SI 1999/2450 Sch.4 para.10.1, Sch.4 para.16.2
referred to: SI 1999/2450 Sch.4 para.12.1

981. Motor Vehicles (Type Approval) (Great Britain) Regulations 1984
applied: SI 1996/3013 Reg.3, SI 1997/564 Reg.7, Reg.13, SI 1998/2051 Reg.13, SI 1999/2149 Reg.5, Reg.9
referred to: SI 1997/564 Reg.10
Reg.2, amended: SI 1996/2330 Reg.3, SI 1996/3015 Reg.3

NO.

1984—cont.

981. Motor Vehicles (Type Approval) (Great Britain) Regulations 1984—*cont.*
Reg.2B, amended: SI 1996/3015 Reg.4
Reg.3, amended: SI 1996/3015 Reg.5
Reg.3, applied: SI 1998/2051 Reg.11
Reg.3, referred to: SI 1996/3013 Reg.3
Reg.3A, added: SI 1996/3015 Reg.6
Reg.4, amended: SI 1996/2330 Reg.4, SI 1996/3015 Reg.7
Reg.4, applied: SI 1996/3013 Reg.4
Reg.8, applied: SI 1998/2051 Reg.13
Reg.9, amended: SI 1997/1502 Reg.3
Reg.9, applied: SI 1996/3013 Sch.1 para.1, SI 1998/2051 Reg.11, Reg.13
Reg.13A, amended: SI 1996/3015 Reg.8, SI 1997/2933 Reg.2, SI 1998/1005 Reg.2
Reg.13A, referred to: SI 1997/1367 Reg.2
Reg.14, substituted: SI 1996/3015 Reg.9
Sch.1, referred to: SI 1997/564 Reg.7
Sch.1 Part I, amended: SI 1996/2330 Reg.5
Sch.1 Item 1, applied: SI 1997/564 Sch.1 Part II
Sch.1 Item 1A, applied: SI 1997/564 Sch.1 Part II
Sch.1 Item 2A, applied: SI 1997/564 Sch.1 Part II
Sch.1 Item 3, applied: SI 1997/564 Sch.1 Part II
Sch.1 Item 3A, applied: SI 1997/564 Sch.1 Part II
Sch.1 Item 4G, applied: SI 1997/564 Sch.1 Part II
Sch.1 Item 4H, applied: SI 1997/564 Sch.1 Part II
Sch.1 Item 4J, applied: SI 1997/564 Sch.1 Part II
Sch.1 Item 4K, applied: SI 1997/564 Sch.1 Part II
Sch.1 Item 6, applied: SI 1997/564 Sch.1 Part II
Sch.1 Item 6A, applied: SI 1997/564 Sch.1 Part II
Sch.1 Item 7, applied: SI 1997/564 Sch.1 Part II
Sch.1 Item 7A, applied: SI 1997/564 Sch.1 Part II
Sch.1 Item 8, applied: SI 1997/564 Sch.1 Part II
Sch.1 Item 8A, applied: SI 1997/564 Sch.1 Part II
Sch.1 Item 9, applied: SI 1997/564 Sch.1 Part II
Sch.1 Item 10, applied: SI 1997/564 Sch.1 Part II
Sch.1 Item 10A, applied: SI 1997/564 Sch.1 Part II
Sch.1 Item 10B, applied: SI 1997/564 Sch.1 Part II
Sch.1 Item 10C, applied: SI 1997/564 Sch.1 Part II
Sch.1 Item 11, applied: SI 1997/564 Sch.1 Part II
Sch.1 Item 11A, applied: SI 1997/564 Sch.1 Part II
Sch.1 Item 12A, applied: SI 1997/564 Sch.1 Part II
Sch.1 Item 13D, applied: SI 1997/564 Sch.1 Part II
Sch.1 Item 13E, applied: SI 1997/564 Sch.1 Part II
Sch.1 Item 13F, applied: SI 1997/564 Sch.1 Part II
Sch.1 Item 13G, applied: SI 1997/564 Sch.1 Part II
Sch.1 Item 14E, applied: SI 1997/564 Sch.1 Part II
Sch.1 Item 14G, applied: SI 1997/564 Sch.1 Part II

NO.

1984—cont.

981. Motor Vehicles (Type Approval) (Great Britain) Regulations 1984—*cont.*
Sch.1 Item 15, applied: SI 1997/564 Sch.1 Part II
Sch.1 Item 15A, applied: SI 1997/564 Sch.1 Part II
Sch.1 Item 15B, applied: SI 1997/564 Sch.1 Part II
Sch.1 Item 15C, applied: SI 1997/564 Sch.1 Part II
Sch.1 Item 16, applied: SI 1997/564 Sch.1 Part II
Sch.1 Item 17, applied: SI 1997/564 Sch.1 Part II
Sch.1 Item 17A, applied: SI 1997/564 Sch.1 Part II
Sch.1 Item 17B, applied: SI 1997/564 Sch.1 Part II
Sch.1 Item 18, applied: SI 1997/564 Sch.1 Part II
Sch.1 Item 19, applied: SI 1997/564 Sch.1 Part II
Sch.1 Item 19A, applied: SI 1997/564 Sch.1 Part II
Sch.1 Item 20, applied: SI 1997/564 Sch.1 Part II
Sch.1 Item 21, applied: SI 1997/564 Sch.1 Part II
Sch.1 Item 22, applied: SI 1997/564 Sch.1 Part II
Sch.1 Item 23, applied: SI 1997/564 Sch.1 Part II
Sch.1 Item 24, applied: SI 1997/564 Sch.1 Part II
Sch.1 Item 24A, applied: SI 1997/564 Sch.1 Part II
Sch.1B Part I, amended: SI 1996/2330 Reg.6
Sch.1B Part II, amended: SI 1996/2330 Reg.6
Sch.1B Part III, revoked: SI 1996/2330 Reg.6
Sch.1B Part IV, revoked: SI 1996/2330 Reg.6
Sch.1C, added: SI 1996/2330 Reg.7

988. Adoption Agencies (Scotland) Regulations 1984
applied: SI 1996/207 Reg.78, SI 1996/2890 Reg.9
revoked: SI 1997/691 Reg.1, Sch

994. National Health Service (Appointment of Consultants) Amendment Regulations 1984
revoked: SI 1996/701 Art.10

997. Act of Sederunt (Rules of Court Amendment No.6) (Adoption Proceedings) 1984
see *Strathclyde RC, Petitoners* 1996 S.C.L.R. 109 (Sh Ct)

1013. Act of Sederunt (Adoption of Children) 1984
revoked: SI 1997/291 r.1.4, Sch.2

1014. Safety of Sports Grounds (Designation) (Scotland) Order 1984
revoked: SI 1998/1601 Art.3, Sch.2

1039. Church Representation Rules (Amendment) (No.1) Resolution 1984
referred to: SI 1998/319, SI 1999/2112

1040. Church Representation Rules (Amendment) (No.2) Resolution 1984
referred to: SI 1998/319, SI 1999/2112

1047. Dairy Produce Quotas Regulations 1984
applied: SI 1999/680 Art.2, Sch. Part I
Reg.6, applied: SI 1997/733 Reg.34

1115. Fishing Vessels (Certification of Deck Officers and Engineer Officers) Regulations 1984
applied: SI 1996/2374 Sch.1 Part III, SI 1996/3243 Sch Part I, Sch Part IV

NO.

1984—cont.

1115. Fishing Vessels (Certification of Deck Officers and Engineer Officers) Regulations 1984—*cont.*

Reg.7, amended: SI 1998/1013 Reg.3
Reg.8, amended: SI 1998/1013 Reg.4
Reg.8, revoked (in part): SI 1998/1013 Reg.4
Reg.9, amended: SI 1998/1013 Reg.5

1148. Dockyard Port of Plymouth Order 1984
revoked: SI 1999/2029 Art.7

1159. Industrial Training (Northern Ireland) Order 1984

Art.30, applied: SI 1996/1921 (NI.18) Art.3
Art.30, referred to: SI 1996/1298 (NI.8) Sch.3
Art.30, revoked: SI 1996/1921 (NI.18) Art.28, Sch.3
Art.31, revoked: SI 1996/1921 (NI.18) Art.28, Sch.3
Sch.3 para.2, revoked: SI 1996/1921 (NI.18) Art.28, Sch.3
Sch.3 para.4, revoked (in part): SI 1996/1297 (NI.7) Art.23, Sch.5
Sch.3 para.8, revoked: SI 1996/1921 (NI.18) Art.28, Sch.3
Sch.3 para.9, revoked: SI 1996/1921 (NI.18) Art.28, Sch.3
Sch.3 para.10, revoked: SI 1996/1921 (NI.18) Art.28, Sch.3

1166. Prevention of Terrorism (Temporary Provisions) Act 1984 (Jersey) Order 1984
revoked: SI 1996/1140

1167. University of Ulster (Northern Ireland) Order 1984

Sch.1, revoked (in part): SI 1998/261 (NI.2) Art.15, Sch.4

1203. Merchant Shipping (Navigational Equipment) Regulations 1984
applied: SI 1996/3243 Sch Part I

1214. Police (Promotion) (Amendment) Regulations 1984
revoked: SI 1996/1685 Reg.8, Sch.3

1216. Merchant Shipping (Passenger Ship Construction and Survey) Regulations 1984
applied: SI 1996/3243 Sch Part I, SI 1997/1510 Reg.11, SI 1998/1012 Reg.38, SI 1998/2070 Reg.17
revoked: SI 1998/2514 Reg.1
Part III, applied: SI 1998/1011 Reg.30
Part III, revoked: SI 1998/2514 Reg.1
Reg.1, amended: SI 1996/3188 Reg.17
Reg.1, revoked: SI 1998/2514 Reg.1
Reg.10, applied: SI 1997/647 Reg.6
Reg.10, revoked: SI 1998/2514 Reg.1
Reg.11A, referred to: SI 1997/647 Reg.6
Reg.11A, revoked: SI 1998/2514 Reg.1
Reg.11B, applied: SI 1997/647 Reg.6
Reg.11B, revoked: SI 1998/2514 Reg.1
Reg.46, applied: SI 1998/1012 Reg.11
Reg.46, revoked: SI 1998/2514 Reg.1
Reg.48, applied: SI 1998/1012 Reg.68
Reg.48, revoked: SI 1998/2514 Reg.1
Reg.80, applied: SI 1998/1012 Reg.48
Reg.80, revoked: SI 1998/2514 Reg.1

1217. Merchant Shipping (Cargo Ship Construction and Survey) Regulations 1984
applied: SI 1996/3243 Sch Part I
revoked: SI 1997/1509 Reg.1
Reg.1, amended: SI 1996/3188 Reg.17
Reg.1, revoked: SI 1997/1509 Reg.1
Reg.3, applied: SI 1996/2154 Reg.30
Reg.3, revoked: SI 1997/1509 Reg.1

NO.

1984—cont.

1218. Merchant Shipping (Fire Protection) Regulations 1984
applied: SI 1996/3243 Sch Part I
revoked: SI 1998/1012 Reg.1
Reg.1, amended: SI 1996/3188 Reg.17
Reg.1, revoked: SI 1998/1012 Reg.1
Reg.9A, revoked: SI 1998/1012 Reg.1
Reg.10, revoked: SI 1998/1012 Reg.1
Reg.29, revoked: SI 1998/1012 Reg.1
Reg.35A, revoked: SI 1998/1012 Reg.1
Reg.49, revoked: SI 1998/1012 Reg.1
Reg.50, revoked: SI 1998/1012 Reg.1
Reg.51, revoked: SI 1998/1012 Reg.1
Reg.60, revoked: SI 1998/1012 Reg.1
Reg.62, revoked: SI 1998/1012 Reg.1
Reg.72A, revoked: SI 1998/1012 Reg.1
Reg.75A, revoked: SI 1998/1012 Reg.1
Reg.78, revoked: SI 1998/1012 Reg.1
Reg.82, revoked: SI 1998/1012 Reg.1
Reg.84, revoked: SI 1998/1012 Reg.1
Reg.86, revoked: SI 1998/1012 Reg.1
Reg.91A, revoked: SI 1998/1012 Reg.1
Reg.94, revoked: SI 1998/1012 Reg.1
Reg.102, revoked: SI 1998/1012 Reg.1
Reg.110, applied: SI 1998/1011 Reg.44
Reg.110, revoked: SI 1998/1012 Reg.1
Reg.112A, revoked: SI 1998/1012 Reg.1
Reg.115, revoked: SI 1998/1012 Reg.1
Reg.121, revoked: SI 1998/1012 Reg.1
Reg.128A, revoked: SI 1998/1012 Reg.1
Reg.132, revoked: SI 1998/1012 Reg.1
Reg.138, revoked: SI 1998/1012 Reg.1
Reg.143, revoked: SI 1998/1012 Reg.1
Reg.144, revoked: SI 1998/1012 Reg.1
Sch.14, revoked: SI 1998/1012 Reg.1
Sch.15, revoked: SI 1998/1012 Reg.1
Sch.16, revoked: SI 1998/1012 Reg.1

1219. Merchant Shipping (Cargo Ship Construction and Survey) Regulations 1981 (Amendment) Regulations 1984
revoked: SI 1997/1509 Reg.1

1249. General Optical Council (Education Committee Rules) (Amendment) Order of Council 1984
referred to: SI 1999/1211
revoked: SI 1999/1211 Sch. para.10

1250. General Optical Council (Disciplinary Committee Rules) Order of Council 1984
revoked: SI 1998/1338, SI 1998/1338 Sch. r.20

1259. Social Security (General Benefit) Amendment Regulations 1984
revoked: SI 1997/454 Reg.9

1285. Areas of Archaeological Importance (Forms of Notice etc.) Regulations 1984
applied: SI 1996/1243 Sch.5 para.9

1303. Social Security (Severe Disablement Allowance) Regulations 1984
Reg.2A, added: SI 1997/2676 Reg.14
Reg.3, amended: SI 1996/30 Reg.11, SI 1998/563 Reg.18
Reg.7, amended: SI 1998/2231 Reg.5
Reg.10, amended: SI 1997/1009 Reg.3, SI 1998/2231 Reg.5, SI 1999/2422 Art.3, Sch.5 para.1
Reg.10, applied: SI 1997/1009 Reg.4
Reg.10, revoked (in part): SI 1999/2422 Art.3, Sch.5 para.1
Reg.18, revoked (in part): SI 1999/2422 Art.3, Sch.5 para.2
Sch.2, revoked (in part): SI 1996/2745 Reg.18, Sch.4

NO.

1305. **Food Labelling Regulations 1984**
applied: SI 1996/1499 Reg.50
revoked: SI 1996/1499 Reg.49, Sch.9

1307. **Pensions Increase (Review) Order 1984**
applied: SI 1997/634 Art.3, SI 1998/503 Art.3, Art.4, SI 1999/522 Art.3

1325. **Importation of Bovine Semen Regulations 1984**
referred to: SI 1998/190 Reg.34, Sch.6
Reg.4, referred to: SI 1996/3124 Reg.40, Sch.5 Part I
Reg.5, referred to: SI 1996/3124 Reg.40, Sch.5 Part I

1345. **Residential Care Homes Regulations 1984**
Reg.3, amended: SI 1998/902 Reg.2
Reg.5, amended: SI 1998/902 Reg.2

1346. **Registered Homes Tribunal Rules 1984**
r.11, see *R. v Department of Health Ex p. Bhaugeerutty* Times, May 1, 1998 (QBD), Harrison, J.

1361. **Education (Fees and Awards) (Scotland) Amendment Regulations 1984**
revoked: SI 1997/93 Reg.14, Sch.4

1406. **Public Service Vehicles (Carrying Capacity) (Amendment) Regulations 1984**
Reg.5, amended: SI 1996/167 Reg.2

1431. **Cycle Tracks Regulations 1984**
Reg.2, amended: SI 1996/252 Art.2, Sch

1491. **National Health Service (General Dental Services) (Scotland) Amendment Regulations 1984**
revoked: SI 1996/177 Reg.38, Sch.8

1495. **Mental Health (Prescribed Forms) Scotland Regulations 1984**
revoked: SI 1996/743 Reg.4

1519. **Food Labelling (Scotland) Regulations 1984**
applied: SI 1996/1499 Reg.50
revoked: SI 1996/1499 Reg.49, Sch.9

1566. **Meat Products and Spreadable Fish Products Regulations 1984**
amended: SI 1999/1136 Reg.14
Reg.2, amended: SI 1996/1499 Reg.49
Reg.2, referred to: SI 1999/982 Reg.3
Reg.4, amended: SI 1996/1499 Reg.49
Reg.5, amended: SI 1996/1499 Reg.49
Reg.6, amended: SI 1996/1499 Reg.49
Reg.10, amended: SI 1996/1499 Reg.49
Reg.11, amended: SI 1996/1499 Reg.49
Reg.19, revoked: SI 1996/1499 Reg.49, Sch.9
Reg.23, added: SI 1998/1398 Reg.18

1578. **Nursing Homes and Mental Nursing Homes Regulations 1984**
Sch.1 para.1, amended: SI 1998/902 Reg.3
Sch.1 para.1, revoked (in part): SI 1998/902 Reg.3
Sch.3 para.1, amended: SI 1998/902 Reg.3
Sch.3 para.4, amended: SI 1998/902 Reg.3

1593. **Construction (Metrication) Regulations 1984**
revoked: SI 1998/2307 Reg.17, Sch.2
Reg.1, revoked (in part): SI 1996/1656 Reg.22, Sch.2 Part I, SI 1998/2307 Reg.17, Sch.2
Reg.3, revoked: SI 1996/1656 Reg.22, Sch.2 Part I
Sch.1, revoked (in part): SI 1996/1656 Reg.22, Sch.2 Part I, SI 1998/2307 Reg.17, Sch.2

1649. **Smoke Control Areas (Exempted Fireplaces) Order 1984**
Art.2, amended: SI 1997/3009 Sch.2 para.2
Sch., amended: SI 1997/3009 Sch.2 para.2

NO.

1658. **Protection of Wrecks (Designation No.2) Order 1984**
Art.2, amended: SI 1998/1746 Art.2

1670. **Rules of Procedure (Army) (Amendment) Rules 1984**
revoked: SI 1997/169 r.90, Sch.7

1671. **Standing Civilian Courts Order (Amendment) Order 1984**
revoked: SI 1997/172 Art.93, Sch.5

1697. **Social Security Benefit (Computation of Earnings) Amendment Regulations 1984**
revoked: SI 1996/2745 Reg.18, Sch.4

1714. **Meat Products and Spreadable Fish Products (Scotland) Regulations 1984**
amended: SI 1999/1136 Reg.14
Reg.2, amended: SI 1996/1499 Reg.49
Reg.2, referred to: SI 1999/982 Reg.3
Reg.4, amended: SI 1996/1499 Reg.49
Reg.5, amended: SI 1996/1499 Reg.49
Reg.6, amended: SI 1996/1499 Reg.49
Reg.10, amended: SI 1996/1499 Reg.49
Reg.11, amended: SI 1996/1499 Reg.49
Reg.19, revoked: SI 1996/1499 Reg.49, Sch.9
Reg.23, added: SI 1998/1398 Reg.18

1804. **Gaming Clubs (Hours and Charges) (Scotland) Amendment Regulations 1984**
revoked: SI 1997/942 Reg.4

1805. **Smoke Control Areas (Exempted Fireplaces) (Scotland) Order 1984**
Sch., amended: SI 1997/3009 Sch.2 para.4

1817. **Social Security (United States of America) Order 1984**
amended: SI 1997/1778 Art.2
referred to: SI 1997/1778
Sch.1 Art.1, amended: SI 1997/1778 Sch.1 Art.1
Sch.1 Art.2, amended: SI 1997/1778 Sch.1 Art.2, Sch.1 Art.3
Sch.1 Art.4, amended: SI 1997/1778 Sch.1 Art.4, Sch.1 Art.5
Sch.1 Art.7, amended: SI 1997/1778 Sch.1 Art.6
Sch.1 Art.11, amended: SI 1997/1778 Sch.1 Art.7
Sch.1 Art.14, amended: SI 1997/1778 Sch.1 Art.8
Sch.1 Art.21, amended: SI 1997/1778 Sch.1 Art.9
Sch.2 Art.2, amended: SI 1997/1778 Sch.2 Art.1
Sch.2 Art.9, amended: SI 1997/1778 Sch.2 Art.2

1821. **Fire Services (Northern Ireland) Order 1984**
Art.5, amended: SI 1998/1549 (NI.11) Art.3
Art.5, revoked (in part): 1998 c.47 s.100, Sch.15
Art.10, amended: SI 1998/1549 (NI.11) Art.4
Art.49, amended: SI 1998/2795 (NI.18) Art.6, Sch.1 para.21
Art.49, applied: SI 1999/3145 Art.5
Part III, applied: SI 1999/3145 Art.5
Sch.1 para.1, amended: SI 1998/1549 (NI.11) Art.5
Sch.1 para.2, revoked: SI 1998/1549 (NI.11) Art.6
Sch.1 para.3, amended: SI 1998/1549 (NI.11) Art.5
Sch.1 para.5, amended: SI 1998/1549 (NI.11) Art.5
Sch.1 para.6, amended: SI 1998/1549 (NI.11) Art.6
Sch.3 para.3, revoked: SI 1996/1297 (NI.7) Art.23, Sch.5

NO.

1822. General Consumer Council (Northern Ireland) Order 1984
Sch.1 para.12, applied: SI 1996/275 (NI.2) Art.34

1826. Double Taxation Relief (Taxes on Income) (China) Order 1984
Sch., amended: SI 1996/3164 Art.2
Sch. Art.2, amended: SI 1996/3164 Sch.
Sch. Art.3, amended: SI 1996/3164 Sch.
Sch. Art.4, amended: SI 1996/3164 Sch.
Sch. Art.12, amended: SI 1996/3164 Sch.
Sch. Art.13, amended: SI 1996/3164 Sch.
Sch. Art.23, amended: SI 1996/3164 Sch.
Sch. Art.30, referred to: SI 1996/3164 Sch.

1832. Petroleum (Production) (Landward Areas) Regulations 1984
Sch.1, applied: SI 1999/160 Sch.8 Cl.5
Sch.4, referred to: 1998 c.17 Sch.1 para.18
Sch.5, referred to: 1998 c.17 Sch.1 para.17, SI 1999/160 Sch.8 para.1

1835. Goods Vehicles (Operators' Licences) (Temporary Use in Great Britain) (Amendment) Regulations 1984
revoked: SI 1996/2186 Reg.2, Sch.1

1890. Freight Containers (Safety Convention) Regulations 1984
applied: SI 1996/2791 Reg.5, Sch.4, SI 1997/2505 Reg.5, Sch.4, SI 1999/645 Reg.5, Sch.4

1902. Control of Industrial Major Accident Hazards Regulations 1984
revoked: SI 1999/743 Reg.24 (with savings)
Reg.3, revoked: SI 1999/743 Reg.24 (with savings)
Reg.7, referred to: SI 1999/743 Reg.6
Reg.7, revoked: SI 1999/743 Reg.24 (with savings)
Reg.8, applied: SI 1999/743 Reg.24
Reg.8, referred to: SI 1999/743 Reg.7
Reg.8, revoked: SI 1999/743 Reg.24 (with savings)
Reg.9, applied: SI 1999/743 Reg.24
Reg.9, revoked: SI 1999/743 Reg.24 (with savings)
Reg.10, applied: SI 1999/743 Reg.9, Reg.24
Reg.10, revoked: SI 1999/743 Reg.24 (with savings)
Reg.11, applied: SI 1999/743 Reg.24
Reg.11, revoked: SI 1999/743 Reg.24 (with savings)
Reg.12, applied: SI 1999/743 Reg.24
Reg.12, revoked: SI 1999/743 Reg.24 (with savings)
Reg.13, applied: SI 1999/743 Reg.24
Reg.13, revoked: SI 1999/743 Reg.24 (with savings)
Reg.14, applied: SI 1999/743 Reg.24
Reg.14, revoked: SI 1999/743 Reg.24 (with savings)
Sch.2 Part II, revoked: SI 1999/743 Reg.24 (with savings)

1918. Imported Food Regulations 1984
referred to: SI 1996/3124 Reg.40, Sch.5 Part I, SI 1996/3125 Reg.13
Reg.6, revoked: SI 1997/2537 Reg.11
Reg.7, revoked: SI 1997/2537 Reg.11
Reg.8, revoked: SI 1997/2537 Reg.11
Reg.9, revoked: SI 1997/2537 Reg.11
Reg.10, revoked: SI 1997/2537 Reg.11

NO.

1918. Imported Food Regulations 1984—*cont.*
Reg.11, revoked: SI 1997/2537 Reg.11
Reg.15, revoked: SI 1997/2537 Reg.11
Reg.16, revoked: SI 1997/2537 Reg.11
Reg.17, revoked: SI 1997/2537 Reg.11
Reg.18, revoked: SI 1997/2537 Reg.11
Reg.19, revoked: SI 1997/2537 Reg.11
Reg.21, revoked: SI 1997/2537 Reg.11
Reg.22, revoked: SI 1997/2537 Reg.11
Reg.23, revoked: SI 1997/2537 Reg.11

1970. National Health Service (Superannuation Special Provisions) (Scotland) Regulations 1984
applied: SI 1999/1750 Art.2, Sch.1

1975. Nursing and Midwifery Qualifications (EEC Recognition) Amendment Order 1984
revoked: 1997 c.24 s.23, Sch.6

1984. Family Law (Miscellaneous Provisions) (Northern Ireland) Order 1984
applied: SI 1998/1071 (NI.6) Art.41, Sch.4 para.5, Sch.4 para.6
Art.1, revoked (in part): SI 1998/1071 (NI.6) Art.41, Sch.5
Art.4, applied: SI 1998/1071 (NI.6) Art.41, Sch.4 para.2, Sch.4 para.4, Sch.4 para.7
Art.5, applied: SI 1998/1071 (NI.6) Art.41, Sch.4 para.7
Art.13, applied: SI 1998/1071 (NI.6) Art.41, Sch.4 para.2, Sch.4 para.4
Art.20, revoked: SI 1998/1071 (NI.6) Art.41, Sch.5
Part II, applied: SI 1998/1071 (NI.6) Art.41, Sch.4 para.5
Part II, referred to: SI 1998/1071 (NI.6) Art.5
Part II, revoked: SI 1998/1071 (NI.6) Art.41, Sch.5
Sch.2 Part I, revoked (in part): SI 1998/1071 (NI.6) Art.41, Sch.5

1986. Road Traffic, Transport and Roads (Northern Ireland) Order 1984
Art.3, revoked: SI 1997/276 (NI.2) Art.75, Sch.9
Sch.1 para.1, revoked: SI 1997/276 (NI.2) Art.75, Sch.9
Sch.1 para.2, revoked: SI 1997/276 (NI.2) Art.75, Sch.9
Sch.1 para.3, revoked: SI 1997/276 (NI.2) Art.75, Sch.9
Sch.1 para.4, revoked: SI 1997/276 (NI.2) Art.75, Sch.9
Sch.1 para.5, revoked: SI 1997/276 (NI.2) Art.75, Sch.9
Sch.1 para.6, revoked: SI 1997/276 (NI.2) Art.75, Sch.9
Sch.1 para.7, revoked: SI 1996/1320 (NI.10) Sch.4
Sch.1 para.8, revoked: SI 1997/276 (NI.2) Art.75, Sch.9
Sch.1 para.9, revoked: SI 1997/276 (NI.2) Art.75, Sch.9

2024. Hill Livestock (Compensatory Allowances) Regulations 1984
applied: SI 1996/1500 Reg.3

2041. Immigration Appeals (Procedure) Rules 1984
applied: SI 1996/2070 r.39
r.42, see *Akewushola v Immigration Officer, Heathrow* [1999] Imm. A.R. 594 (CA), Sedley, L.J.

NO.

1985

City of Aberdeen Educational Endowments Scheme 1985
amended: SI 1996/478 Sch

16. Employment Tribunals (Rules of Procedure) Regulations 1985
Reg.2, see *Dattani v Trio Supermarkets Ltd* [1998] I.R.L.R. 240 (CA), Mummery, L.J.
Sch.2 r.12, see *Dattani v Trio Supermarkets Ltd* [1998] I.R.L.R. 240 (CA), Mummery, L.J.

30. Goods Vehicles (Operators' Licences) (Temporary Use in Great Britain) (Amendment) Regulations 1985
revoked: SI 1996/2186 Reg.2, Sch.1

67. Food (Revision of Penalties) Regulations 1985
Sch. Part I, revoked (in part): SI 1996/1499 Reg.49, Sch.9

68. Milk and Dairies (Revision of Penalties) Regulations 1985
revoked: SI 1998/2424 Reg.9, Sch.
Reg.2, revoked: SI 1998/2424 Reg.9, Sch.
Sch., revoked: SI 1998/2424 Reg.9, Sch.

71. Natural Mineral Waters Regulations 1985
referred to: SI 1999/1540 Reg.4, Reg.18
revoked: SI 1999/1540 Reg.21, Sch.4
Reg.28, revoked: SI 1996/1499 Reg.49, Sch.9

95. Insurance Companies (Winding Up) Rules 1985
Sch.1 para.2, see *Continental Assurance Co of London Plc (In Liquidation) (No.3), Re* [1999] 1 B.C.L.C. 751 (Ch D), Carnwath, J.

161. Landing of Carcasses and Animal Products Order (Northern Ireland) 1985
referred to: SI 1997/322 Reg.36

170. Nature (Conservation and Amenity Lands) (Northern Ireland) Order 1985
Art.9, applied: SI 1997/2844 Sch.3 Part I, Sch.4 para.3

198. Tower Hamlets (Bus Lanes) (No.2) Traffic Order 1985
Sch. Item 1, revoked (in part): SI 1999/3051 Art.6

259. Occupational Pension Schemes (Contracting Out) Regulations 1985
applied: 1999 c.30 s.81, Sch.11 para.36
Reg.19, referred to: 1999 c.30 s.81, Sch.11 para.36
Reg.22, referred to: 1999 c.30 s.81, Sch.11 para.36
Reg.22A, referred to: 1999 c.30 s.81, Sch.11 para.36

267. Local Authority Accounts (Scotland) Regulations 1985
applied: SI 1996/682 Art.3
Reg.4, amended: SI 1997/1980 Reg.2

273. Ionising Radiations Regulations (Northern Ireland) 1985
Reg.13, applied: SI 1999/3232 Reg.3
Reg.16, applied: SI 1996/1919 (N.I.16) Art.96, SI 1999/3232 Reg.3

273. Medicines (Animal Feeding Stuffs) (Enforcement) Regulations 1985
Reg.4, amended: SI 1996/1261 Reg.2

294. Motor Vehicles (Type Approval) Regulations (Northern Ireland) 1985
applied: SI 1998/2051 Reg.13
Reg.3, applied: SI 1998/2051 Reg.11
Reg.8, applied: SI 1998/2051 Reg.13
Reg.9, applied: SI 1998/2051 Reg.11, Reg.13

NO.

1985—cont.

305. Joint Consultative Committees Order 1985
revoked: SI 1996/640 Reg.23, SI 1996/2820 Art.13
Art.1, amended: SI 1996/1008 Art.2, Sch para.5
Art.1, revoked: SI 1996/2820 Art.13
Art.6, amended: SI 1996/709 Art.12
Art.7, amended: SI 1996/3019 Art.2
Art.7, substituted: SI 1996/709 Art.12
Art.8, amended: SI 1996/709 Art.12, SI 1996/3019 Art.2

315. Smoke Control Areas (Exempted Fireplaces) (Scotland) Order 1985
Sch.1, amended: SI 1997/3009 Sch.2 para.5

343. Greater London (Restriction of Goods Vehicles) Traffic Order 1985
see *TNT Express (UK) Ltd v Richmond upon Thames LBC* (1996) 160 J.P. 310 (QBD), Waller, J.

373. Public Trustee (Fees) Order 1985
revoked: SI 1999/855 Art.32, Sch.
Art.17, revoked: SI 1999/855 Art.32, Sch.
Art.20, revoked: SI 1999/855 Art.32, Sch.
Art.29A, revoked: SI 1999/855 Art.32, Sch.

415. Camden (Bus Lane) (No.1) Traffic Order 1985
amended: SI 1996/1344 Art.6

444. Falkland Islands Constitution Order 1985
Sch.1 Annex A, amended: SI 1997/864 Art.12
Sch.1 Annex B, amended: SI 1997/2974 Art.4
Sch.1 s.17, amended: SI 1997/864 Art.3
Sch.1 s.21, amended: SI 1997/864 Art.4
Sch.1 s.22, amended: SI 1997/864 Art.5
Sch.1 s.23, substituted: SI 1997/2974 Art.3
Sch.1 s.24, amended: SI 1997/864 Art.6
Sch.1 s.27, amended: SI 1997/864 Art.7
Sch.1 s.33, substituted: SI 1997/864 Art.8
Sch.1 s.37, amended: SI 1997/864 Art.9
Sch.1 s.50, amended: SI 1997/864 Art.10
Sch.1 s.51, amended: SI 1997/864 Art.11

454. Local Elections (Northern Ireland) Order 1985
Sch.2 Part I, amended: SI 1997/867 Art.3, Art.4
Sch.2 para.8, amended: SI 1998/3150 Art.2
Sch.2 para.11, amended: SI 1998/3150 Art.3

463. Traffic Signs (Temporary Obstructions) Regulations 1985
revoked: SI 1997/3053 Reg.2

518. Police (Discipline) Regulations 1985
revoked: SI 1999/730 Reg.2 (with saving)
applied: SI 1999/818 r.2
Reg.7, revoked: SI 1999/730 Reg.2 (with saving)
Reg.16, revoked: SI 1999/730 Reg.2 (with saving)
Sch.1 para.1, see *R. v Chief Constable of the British Transport Police Ex p. Farmer* Times, September 4, 1998 (QBD), Lightman, J.
Sch.1 para.1, revoked: SI 1999/730 Reg.2 (with saving)
Sch.3 para.2, revoked: SI 1999/730 Reg.2 (with saving)
Sch.3 para.4, revoked: SI 1999/730 Reg.2 (with saving)
Sch.3 para.6, revoked: SI 1999/730 Reg.2 (with saving)

519. Police (Discipline) (Senior Officers) Regulations 1985
applied: SI 1999/818 r.2
revoked: SI 1999/731 Reg.2 (with savings)

574. County Court Fees (Amendment) Order 1985
revoked: SI 1999/689 Art.8 (with savings), Sch.2 (with savings)

NO.

1985—cont.

576. Police (Appeals) Rules 1985
applied: SI 1999/818 r.2
revoked: SI 1999/818 r.2

596. Lambeth (Bus Lane) (No.5) Traffic Order 1985
revoked (in part): SI 1998/118 Art.5

660. Merchant Shipping (Passenger Ship Construction) (Amendment) Regulations 1985
revoked: SI 1998/2514 Reg.1

661. Merchant Shipping (Application of Construction and Survey Regulations to Other Ships) Regulations 1985
applied: SI 1996/3243 Sch Part I
revoked: SI 1997/1509 Reg.1, SI 1998/2514 Reg.1

663. Merchant Shipping (Cargo Ship Construction and Survey) Regulations 1981 (Amendment) Regulations 1985
revoked: SI 1997/1509 Reg.1

689. Town and Country Planning (Compensation for Restrictions on Mineral Working) Regulations 1985
referred to: SI 1997/1111 Reg.8
revoked: SI 1997/1111 Reg.8

751. Extradition (Taking of Hostages) Order 1985
revoked: SI 1997/1767 Art.4

755. Road Traffic (Type Approval) (Northern Ireland) Order 1985
Art.5, revoked: SI 1996/1320 (NI.10) Sch.4

780. Act of Sederunt (Social Work (Scotland) Act 1968) (Safeguarders) 1985
revoked: SI 1997/291 r.1.4, Sch.2

781. Act of Sederunt (Social Work) (Sheriff Court Procedure Rules 1971) (Amendment) 1985
revoked: SI 1997/291 r.1.4, Sch.2

782. Unfair Dismissal (Variation of Qualifying Period) Order 1985
see *Davidson v City Electrical Factors Ltd* [1998] I.C.R. 443 (EAT), Lord Johnston; see *R. v Secretary of State for Employment Ex p. Seymour-Smith* [1997] 1 W.L.R. 473 (HL), Lord Hoffmann; see *R. v Secretary of State for Employment Ex p. Seymour-Smith (C167/97)* [1999] 2 A.C. 554 (ECJ), GC Rodriguez Iglesias (President); see *Thomas v National Training Partnership Ltd* [1998] I.C.R. 436 (EAT), Holland, J.

826. Court of Session etc. Fees Amendment Order 1985
revoked: SI 1997/688 Art.6, Sch.2

827. Sheriff Court Fees Order 1985
Art.2, amended: SI 1996/628 Art.2
Art.2, revoked: SI 1997/687 Art.11, Sch.2
Art.5, amended: SI 1996/628 Art.2
Sch., amended: SI 1996/628 Art.2, Sch

836. Caseins and Caseinates (Scotland) Regulations 1985
Reg.5, amended: SI 1996/1499 Reg.49

886. Value Added Tax (General) Regulations 1985
Reg.23, see *Svenska International Plc v Customs and Excise Commissioners* [1999] 1 W.L.R. 769 (HL), Lord Hutton
Reg.30, see *Customs and Excise Commissioners v Dennis Rye Ltd* [1996] S.T.C. 27 (QBD), McCullough, J.; see *Customs and Excise Commissioners v Liverpool Institute for Performing Arts* [1998] S.T.C. 274 (QBD), Carnwath, J.; see *Customs and Excise Commissioners v Liverpool Institute for Performing Arts* [1999] S.T.C. 424 (CA), Nourse, L.J.;

NO.

1985—cont.

886. Value Added Tax (General) Regulations 1985—*cont.*
Reg.30—*cont.*
see *Customs and Excise Commissioners v UBAF Bank Ltd* [1996] S.T.C. 372 (CA), Neill, J.
Reg.32, see *Customs and Excise Commissioners v Liverpool Institute for Performing Arts* [1998] S.T.C. 274 (QBD), Carnwath, J.
Reg.34, see *Customs and Excise Commissioners v Svenska International Plc* [1997] S.T.C. 958 (CA), Aldous, L.J.; see *Svenska International Plc v Customs and Excise Commissioners* [1999] 1 W.L.R. 769 (HL), Lord Hutton

911. Video Recordings (Labelling) Regulations 1985
Reg.2, amended: SI 1998/852 Reg.2
Reg.4A, added: SI 1998/852 Reg.2
Reg.4B, added: SI 1998/852 Reg.2

913. Imported Food (Scotland) Regulations 1985
referred to: SI 1996/3124 Reg.40, Sch.5 Part I, SI 1996/3125 Reg.13
Reg.6, revoked: SI 1997/2537 Reg.11
Reg.7, revoked: SI 1997/2537 Reg.11
Reg.8, revoked: SI 1997/2537 Reg.11
Reg.9, revoked: SI 1997/2537 Reg.11
Reg.10, revoked: SI 1997/2537 Reg.11
Reg.11, revoked: SI 1997/2537 Reg.11
Reg.15, revoked: SI 1997/2537 Reg.11
Reg.16, revoked: SI 1997/2537 Reg.11
Reg.17, revoked: SI 1997/2537 Reg.11
Reg.18, revoked: SI 1997/2537 Reg.11
Reg.19, revoked: SI 1997/2537 Reg.11
Reg.21, revoked: SI 1997/2537 Reg.11
Reg.22, revoked: SI 1997/2537 Reg.11
Reg.23, revoked: SI 1997/2537 Reg.11

967. Social Security (Industrial Injuries) (Prescribed Diseases) Regulations 1985
Reg.1, amended: SI 1999/1958 Art.4, Sch.8 para.1
Reg.4, amended: SI 1996/425 Reg.5
Reg.6, amended: SI 1999/1958 Art.4, Sch.8 para.2
Reg.8, amended: SI 1999/1958 Art.4, Sch.8 para.3
Reg.9, amended: SI 1999/1958 Art.4, Sch.8 para.4
Reg.13, amended: SI 1999/1958 Art.4, Sch.8 para.5
Reg.15A, amended: SI 1999/1958 Art.4, Sch.8 para.6
Reg.20, amended: SI 1997/810 Reg.5, SI 1999/1958 Art.4, Sch.8 para.7
Reg.22, amended: SI 1999/1958 Art.4, Sch.8 para.8
Reg.23, amended: SI 1999/1958 Art.4, Sch.8 para.9
Reg.24, substituted: SI 1999/1958 Art.4, Sch.8 para.10
Reg.25, amended: SI 1999/1958 Art.4, Sch.8 para.11
Reg.27, amended: SI 1999/1958 Art.4, Sch.8 para.12
Reg.30, amended: SI 1999/1958 Art.4, Sch.8 para.13
Reg.31, substituted: SI 1999/1958 Art.4, Sch.8 para.14
Reg.32, substituted: SI 1999/1958 Art.4, Sch.8 para.15
Reg.34, amended: SI 1999/1958 Art.4, Sch.8 para.16

NO.

1985—cont.

967. Social Security (Industrial Injuries) (Prescribed Diseases) Regulations 1985—*cont.*
Reg.35, amended: SI 1999/1958 Art.4, Sch.8 para.17
Reg.40, amended: SI 1999/1958 Art.4, Sch.8 para.18
Sch.1 Part I, amended: SI 1996/425 Reg.5, SI 1997/810 Reg.6
Sch.8 para.A10, see *Appleby v Chief Adjudication Officer* Times, August 5, 1999 (CA), Nourse, L.J.

981. Seeds (Fees) Regulations 1985
Reg.4, added: SI 1999/1865 Reg.2
Sch.1, substituted: SI 1996/1486 Reg.2, Sch., SI 1997/1415 Reg.2, Sch., SI 1998/1396 Reg.2, Sch., SI 1999/1553 Reg.2, Sch.
Sch.2, substituted: SI 1996/1486 Reg.2, Sch., SI 1997/1415 Reg.2, Sch., SI 1998/1396 Reg.2, Sch., SI 1999/1553 Reg.2, Sch.
Sch.3, substituted: SI 1996/1486 Reg.2, Sch., SI 1997/1415 Reg.2, Sch., SI 1998/1396 Reg.2, Sch., SI 1999/1553 Reg.2, Sch.
Sch.4, substituted: SI 1996/1486 Reg.2, Sch., SI 1997/1415 Reg.2, Sch., SI 1998/1396 Reg.2, Sch., SI 1999/1553 Reg.2, Sch.
Sch.5, substituted: SI 1996/1486 Reg.2, Sch., SI 1997/1415 Reg.2, Sch., SI 1998/1396 Reg.2, Sch., SI 1999/1553 Reg.2, Sch.
Sch.6, amended: SI 1999/2698 Reg.2
Sch.6, substituted: SI 1996/1486 Reg.2, Sch., SI 1997/1415 Reg.2, Sch., SI 1998/1396 Reg.2, Sch., SI 1999/1553 Reg.2, Sch.

987. Fish Producers' Organisations (Formation Grants) (Amendment) Scheme 1985
revoked: SI 1999/1110 Reg.9

990. Chester Water (Capital Powers) (Variation) Order 1985
revoked: SI 1998/281 Art.4, Sch.2 Part II

994. Films (Certification) Regulations 1985
Reg.2, amended: SI 1999/2224 Reg.3
Reg.3, amended: SI 1997/1744 Art.2, Sch. para.3
Reg.3, applied: SI 1997/1744 Art.2, Sch. para.3
Reg.4, substituted: SI 1999/2224 Reg.4
Reg.5, amended: SI 1999/2224 Reg.5
Reg.6, amended: SI 1999/2224 Reg.6
Reg.6, revoked (in part): SI 1999/2224 Reg.6
Reg.8, added: SI 1999/2334 Reg.2

1001. Merchant Shipping (Formal Investigations) Rules 1985
r.4, applied: SI 1999/678 Sch., SI 1999/1750 Art.2, Sch.1

1063. Safety of Sports Grounds (Association Football Grounds) (Designation) Order 1985
Sch., amended: SI 1999/1930 Art.3
Sch., revoked (in part): SI 1996/2648 Art.3

1065. Building Regulations 1985
applied: SI 1997/230 Art.4

1066. Building (Approved Inspectors etc.) Regulations 1985
Reg.3, applied: SI 1998/2332 Reg.9
Reg.3, substituted: SI 1998/2332 Reg.3
Reg.4, amended: SI 1998/2332 Reg.4
Reg.4, applied: SI 1998/2332 Reg.4
Reg.5, applied: SI 1998/2332 Reg.6
Reg.6, amended: SI 1996/1906 Reg.3, SI 1998/2332 Reg.5
Reg.7, amended: SI 1998/2332 Reg.6
Reg.8A, added: SI 1996/1906 Reg.4
Reg.16, amended: SI 1998/2332 Reg.7
Reg.18, applied: SI 1998/3129 Reg.10, Reg.11
Reg.19, applied: SI 1999/672 Art.2, Sch.1

NO.

1985—cont.

1066. Building (Approved Inspectors etc.) Regulations 1985—*cont.*
Reg.28, amended: SI 1996/1906 Reg.5
Sch.2 Form 1, amended: SI 1998/2332 Reg.8
Sch.2 Form 1A, added: SI 1996/1906 Reg.6, Sch.
Sch.2 Form 1A, amended: SI 1998/2332 Reg.8
Sch.2 Form 3, amended: SI 1998/2332 Reg.8

1068. Food (Revision of Penalties and Mode of Trial) (Scotland) Regulations 1985
Sch.3, revoked (in part): SI 1996/1499 Reg.49, Sch.9

1071. International Carriage of Perishable Foodstuffs Regulations 1985
Reg.2, amended: SI 1997/1673 Reg.2
Sch. Part I, amended: SI 1996/2765 Reg.2

1092. Plant Breeders' Rights (Amendment) Regulations 1985
applied: SI 1998/1027 Reg.22
revoked: SI 1998/1027 Reg.21 (with savings), Sch.2 (with savings)

1098. Plant Breeders' Rights (Applications in Designated Countries) (Variation) Order 1985
revoked: SI 1996/1811 Art.2

1119. Feeding Stuffs (Sampling and Analysis) (Amendment) Regulations 1985
revoked: SI 1999/1663 Reg.10

1144. Stock Transfer (Gilt-Edged Securities) (CGO Service) Regulations 1985
Reg.2, amended: SI 1997/1329 Reg.3, SI 1999/1208 Reg.2
Reg.3, substituted: SI 1999/1208 Reg.3
Reg.6, amended: SI 1999/1208 Reg.4
Reg.7, amended: SI 1999/1208 Reg.5

1145. Stock Transfer (Gilt-Edged Securities) (Exempt Transfer) Regulations 1985
Reg.2, amended: SI 1999/1210 Reg.2

1155. Control of Trade in Endangered Species (Enforcement) Regulations 1985
revoked: SI 1997/1372 Reg.13
Reg.3, see *R. v Canning (Derek William)* [1996] 2 Cr. App. R. (S.) 202 (CA (Crim Div)), Lord Taylor of Gosforth, C.J.
Reg.3, revoked: SI 1997/1372 Reg.13

1176. Fire Services (Examinations) Regulations 1985
Reg.3, referred to: SI 1999/1319 Sch.

1181. Teachers (Compensation for Redundancy and Premature Retirement) Regulations 1985
Reg.4, applied: SI 1997/311 Reg.3

1193. Merchant Shipping (Fire Protection) (Amendment) Regulations 1985
revoked: SI 1998/1012 Reg.1

1194. Merchant Shipping (Fire Appliances) (Amendment) Regulations 1985
referred to: SI 1998/1609 Reg.5, Reg.6, Sch.
revoked: SI 1998/1012 Reg.1

1202. Social Security (Iceland) Order 1985
Sch., amended: SI 1996/1928 Art.2, Sch.1

1204. Betting, Gaming, Lotteries and Amusements (Northern Ireland) Order 1985
applied: SI 1996/3158 (NI.22) Art.73, Art.75, 1997 c.16 s.15
Art.2, amended: SI 1996/3159 (NI.23) Sch.7 para.2
Art.12, amended: SI 1996/3158 (NI.22) Sch.11 para.2
Art.32, amended: SI 1996/3158 (NI.22) Sch.11 para.3
Art.55, referred to: 1997 c.16 s.10
Art.96, amended: SI 1996/3159 (NI.23) Sch.7 para.3

NO.

1204. Betting, Gaming, Lotteries and Amusements (Northern Ireland) Order 1985—*cont.*

Art.99, amended: SI 1996/3159 (NI.23) Sch.7 para.4

Art.103, amended: SI 1996/3159 (NI.23) Sch.7 para.5

Art.105, amended: SI 1996/3159 (NI.23) Sch.7 para.6

Art.106, amended: SI 1997/2984 (NI.22) Art.6

Art.107, amended: SI 1996/3158 (NI.22) Sch.11 para.4

Art.108, amended: SI 1996/3158 (NI.22) Sch.11 para.5

Art.108, applied: SI 1996/3158 (NI.22) Art.7, Art.15

Art.108, referred to: 1997 c.16 s.10

Art.126, referred to: 1997 c.16 s.10

Art.153, referred to: 1997 c.16 s.10

Art.154, referred to: 1997 c.16 s.10

Art.182, amended: SI 1996/3158 (NI.22) Sch.11 para.6

Sch.8 para.3, amended: SI 1996/1632 (NI.11) Art.7

Sch.8 para.3, revoked (in part): SI 1996/1632 (NI.11) Art.19, Sch.6

Sch.15 para.5, revoked: SI 1996/725 (NI.5) Sch.4

1205. Credit Unions (Northern Ireland) Order 1985

referred to: 1998 c.47 Sch.3 para.23

Art.3, amended: SI 1997/2984 (NI.22) Art.3, Sch.1 para.1

Art.14, amended: SI 1997/2984 (NI.22) Art.3, Sch.1 para.2

Art.14, revoked (in part): SI 1997/2984 (NI.22) Art.11, Sch.4

Art.23, amended: SI 1997/2984 (NI.22) Art.3, Sch.1 para.3

Art.28, revoked (in part): SI 1997/2984 (NI.22) Art.3, Art.11, Sch.1 para.4, Sch.4

Art.28A, added: SI 1997/2984 (NI.22) Art.3, Sch.1 para.5

Art.28B, added: SI 1997/2984 (NI.22) Art.3, Sch.1 para.5

Art.28C, added: SI 1997/2984 (NI.22) Art.3, Sch.1 para.5

Art.28D, added: SI 1997/2984 (NI.22) Art.3, Sch.1 para.5

Art.72, amended: 1996 c.23 Sch.3 para.44

Art.72, revoked (in part): 1996 c.23 Sch.4

1207. Gas (Northern Ireland) Order 1985

revoked: SI 1996/275 (NI.2) Art.71, Sch.8

Art.3, applied: SI 1996/275 (NI.2) Art.42

1208. Local Government (Miscellaneous Provisions) (Northern Ireland) Order 1985

Art.5, amended: SI 1996/3158 (NI.22) Sch.11 para.7

Art.9, revoked: SI 1998/2796 (NI.19) Art.3

Art.10, revoked: SI 1998/2796 (NI.19) Art.3

Art.11, amended: SI 1998/2796 (NI.19) Art.3

Sch.1 para.10, amended: SI 1996/3158 (NI.22) Sch.11 para.8

Sch.2 para.20, applied: SI 1996/1299 (NI.9) Sch.1 Part I

Sch.2 para.21, applied: SI 1996/1299 (NI.9) Sch.1 Part I

Sch.3 para.6, revoked: SI 1997/2779 (NI.20) Sch.3

Sch.3 para.7, revoked: SI 1997/2779 (NI.20) Sch.3

Sch.3 para.8, revoked: SI 1997/2779 (NI.20) Sch.3

NO.

1208. Local Government (Miscellaneous Provisions) (Northern Ireland) Order 1985—*cont.*

Sch.3 para.9, revoked: SI 1997/2779 (NI.20) Sch.3

Sch.3 para.10, revoked: SI 1997/2779 (NI.20) Sch.3

Sch.3 para.17, revoked: SI 1997/2778 (NI.19) Art.83, Sch.6

Sch.3 para.18, revoked: SI 1997/2778 (NI.19) Art.83, Sch.6

Sch.3 para.19, revoked: SI 1997/2778 (NI.19) Art.83, Sch.6

Sch.3 para.20, revoked: SI 1997/2778 (NI.19) Art.83, Sch.6

Sch.3 para.21, revoked: SI 1997/2778 (NI.19) Art.83, Sch.6

Sch.3 para.23, revoked: SI 1997/2778 (NI.19) Art.83, Sch.6

Sch.3 para.24, revoked: SI 1997/2778 (NI.19) Art.83, Sch.6

Sch.3 para.29, revoked: SI 1997/2777 (NI.18) Art.35, Sch.5

Sch.3 para.30, revoked: SI 1997/2777 (NI.18) Art.35, Sch.5

Sch.3 para.31, revoked: SI 1997/2777 (NI.18) Art.35, Sch.5

Sch.3 para.32, revoked: SI 1997/2777 (NI.18) Art.35, Sch.5

Sch.3 para.33, revoked: SI 1997/2777 (NI.18) Art.35, Sch.5

1217. Merchant Shipping (Grain) Regulations 1985

applied: SI 1996/3243 Sch Part I

revoked: SI 1997/19 Reg.1

1218. Merchant Shipping (Fire Protection) (Ships Built Before 25th May 1980) Regulations 1985

applied: SI 1996/3243 Sch Part I

revoked: SI 1998/1012 Reg.1

Reg.1, revoked: SI 1998/1012 Reg.1

Reg.9A, revoked: SI 1998/1012 Reg.1

Reg.27, revoked: SI 1998/1012 Reg.1

Reg.28, revoked: SI 1998/1012 Reg.1

Reg.29, revoked: SI 1998/1012 Reg.1

Reg.31, revoked: SI 1998/1012 Reg.1

Reg.34A, revoked: SI 1998/1012 Reg.1

Reg.41, revoked: SI 1998/1012 Reg.1

Reg.42, revoked: SI 1998/1012 Reg.1

Reg.44, revoked: SI 1998/1012 Reg.1

Reg.47, revoked: SI 1998/1012 Reg.1

Reg.48, revoked: SI 1998/1012 Reg.1

Reg.49, revoked: SI 1998/1012 Reg.1

Reg.54, revoked: SI 1998/1012 Reg.1

Reg.60, revoked: SI 1998/1012 Reg.1

Reg.62, revoked: SI 1998/1012 Reg.1

Reg.74, revoked: SI 1998/1012 Reg.1

Sch.1, revoked: SI 1998/1012 Reg.1

Sch.1A, revoked: SI 1998/1012 Reg.1

Sch.1B, revoked: SI 1998/1012 Reg.1

1223. Education (Fees and Awards) (Scotland) Amendment Regulations 1985

revoked: SI 1997/93 Reg.14, Sch.4

1224. Sports Grounds and Sporting Events (Designation) (Scotland) Order 1985

revoked: SI 1998/2314 Art.3, Sch.3

Sch.1 Part I, amended: SI 1996/2653 Art.2, SI 1997/1787 Art.2, SI 1998/1659 Art.3

Sch.1 Part I, revoked: SI 1998/2314 Art.3, Sch.3

Sch.1 Part II, revoked: SI 1998/2314 Art.3, Sch.3

Sch.2 para.1A, added: SI 1998/1659 Art.4

Sch.2 para.1A, revoked: SI 1998/2314 Art.3, Sch.3

NO.

1985—cont.

1266. Agriculture Improvement Regulations 1985
applied: SI 1999/672 Art.2, Sch.1

1306. Merchant Shipping (Certification of Deck Officers) Regulations 1985
applied: SI 1996/2374 Sch.1 Part III, SI 1996/3243 Sch Part I, Sch Part IV
revoked: SI 1997/348 Reg.1

1319. Registration of Fish Farming and Shellfish Farming Businesses Order 1985
Sch.3 para.3, added: SI 1997/1881 Reg.23

1323. Contracting Out (Transfer) Regulations 1985
amended: SI 1996/1462 Sch.4
revoked: SI 1996/1462 Reg.14, Sch.3
Reg.1, applied: SI 1996/1462 Reg.14
Reg.2, applied: SI 1996/1462 Reg.12, Reg.14
Reg.2A, applied: SI 1996/1462 Reg.13, Reg.14
Reg.2B, applied: SI 1996/1462 Reg.14
Reg.4, revoked (in part): SI 1996/1172 Sch.2
Sch.3 para.6, applied: SI 1996/1462 Reg.14

1333. Ionising Radiations Regulations 1985
applied: SI 1996/2791 Reg.3, Reg.9, Sch.6, Sch.8, SI 1997/2505 Reg.3, Reg.7, Reg.9, Sch.6, Sch.8, SI 1999/645 Reg.3, Reg.7, Reg.9, Sch.8, SI 1999/3232 Reg.39
referred to: SI 1998/2306 Reg.12
revoked (in part): SI 1999/3232 Reg.41
Reg.2, applied: SI 1998/494 Sch.2 para.5
Reg.2, revoked (in part): SI 1999/3232 Reg.41
Reg.5, applied: SI 1997/2505 Sch.8
Reg.5, revoked (in part): SI 1999/3232 Reg.41
Reg.8, referred to: SI 1999/3232 Reg.41
Reg.8, revoked (in part): SI 1999/3232 Reg.41
Reg.13, applied: SI 1999/3232 Reg.39
Reg.13, referred to: SI 1999/3232 Reg.41
Reg.13, revoked (in part): SI 1999/3232 Reg.41
Reg.15, applied: SI 1997/2505 Sch.8, SI 1999/645 Reg.9, Sch.8, SI 1999/3232 Reg.39
Reg.15, revoked (in part): SI 1999/3232 Reg.41
Reg.16, applied: 1996 c.18 s.64
Reg.16, revoked (in part): SI 1999/3232 Reg.41
Reg.25, referred to: SI 1999/3232 Reg.41
Reg.25, revoked (in part): SI 1999/3232 Reg.41
Reg.26, applied: SI 1999/3232 Reg.41
Reg.26, revoked: SI 1999/3232 Reg.41
Reg.27, applied: SI 1999/3232 Reg.39, Reg.41
Reg.27, revoked (in part): SI 1999/3232 Reg.41
Sch.3, applied: SI 1997/2505 Sch.8, SI 1998/494 Sch.2 para.4, SI 1999/645 Reg.9, Sch.8
Sch.3, revoked (in part): SI 1999/3232 Reg.41
Sch.6, referred to: SI 1999/3232 Reg.41
Sch.6, revoked (in part): SI 1999/3232 Reg.41

1353. National Health Service (Vocational Training) Amendment Regulations 1985
revoked: SI 1997/2817 Reg.20, Sch.5

1383. Local Government (Magistrates' Courts etc.) Order 1985
Sch. para.1, revoked: 1999 c.22 s.106, Sch.15 Part V(1)
Sch. para.2, revoked: 1999 c.22 s.106, Sch.15 Part V(1)
Sch. para.3, revoked: 1997 c.25 s.73, Sch.6 Part II

1502. Endangered Species (Import and Export) Act 1976 (Variation) Order 1985
revoked: SI 1996/2677 Art.5

1516. Control of Pesticides (Advisory Committee on Pesticides) Order 1985
Art.2, amended: SI 1999/1747 Art.3, Sch.2 para.5
Art.3, referred to: SI 1999/1319 Sch.

NO.

1985—cont.

1517. Control of Pesticides (Advisory Committee on Pesticides) (Terms of Office) Regulations 1985
Reg.1, amended: SI 1999/1747 Art.3, Sch.2 para.6

1552. National Health Service (General Dental Services) (Scotland) Amendment Regulations 1985
revoked (in part): SI 1996/177 Reg.38, Sch.8
Reg.2, revoked (in part): SI 1997/174 Reg.18, Sch

1554. Langstone Harbour Revision Order 1985
Art.4, amended: SI 1999/266 Art.3

1575. Pensions Increase (Review) Order 1985
applied: SI 1997/634 Art.3, SI 1998/503 Art.3, Art.4, SI 1999/522 Art.3

1580. General Optical Council (Disciplinary Committee) (Procedure) Order of Council 1985
r.2A, added: SI 1998/1337 Sch. r.2

1593. Motor Cycles (Eye Protectors) Regulations 1985
revoked: SI 1999/535 Reg.3, Sch.

1604. Statutory Sick Pay (Medical Evidence) Regulations 1985
Sch. para.3, amended: SI 1998/646 Reg.7

1634. Belgium (Extradition) (Amendment) Order 1985
revoked: SI 1998/259 Art.2

1637. Norway (Extradition) (Amendment) Order 1985
revoked (in part): SI 1996/2875 Art.3, Sch.3

1638. Child Abduction (Northern Ireland) Order 1985
Art.3, amended: SI 1998/1504 (NI.9) Art.65, Sch.5 para.23, Sch.6
Sch. para.1, amended: SI 1998/1504 (NI.9) Art.65, Sch.6
Sch. para.2, revoked: SI 1998/1504 (NI.9) Art.65, Sch.6
Sch. para.4, amended: SI 1998/1504 (NI.9) Art.65, Sch.5 para.24

1643. Air Navigation Order 1985
Art.42, applied: SI 1997/189 Sch.4 para.1
Art.96, referred to: SI 1996/2095 Sch.2 para.10

1664. Merchant Shipping (Protective Clothing and Equipment) Regulations 1985
applied: SI 1996/3243 Sch Part I
revoked: SI 1999/2205 Art.1
Reg.2, revoked: SI 1999/2205 Art.1

1729. Radioactive Substances (Carriage by Road) (Great Britain) (Amendment) Regulations 1985
revoked: SI 1996/1350 Reg.41

1799. Boarding-Out and Fostering of Children (Scotland) Regulations 1985
revoked: SI 1997/691 Reg.1, Sch
Reg.7, applied: SI 1997/691 Reg.3
Reg.7, revoked: SI 1997/691 Reg.1, Sch
Reg.9, applied: SI 1996/207 Sch.7 para.27, SI 1996/2745 Sch.1 para.6, SI 1996/2890 Sch.3 para.23
Reg.9, revoked: SI 1997/691 Reg.1, Sch

1800. Police and Criminal Evidence Act 1984 (Application to Customs and Excise) Order 1985
Sch.2 Part I, amended: SI 1996/1860 Art.2
Sch.2 Part II, substituted: SI 1996/1860 Art.2

1807. Register of County Court Judgments Regulations 1985
amended: SI 1999/1845 Reg.3
Reg.1, amended: SI 1996/1177 Reg.2, SI 1999/1845 Reg.4
Reg.1A, added: SI 1996/1177 Reg.3

NO.

1807. Register of County Court Judgments Regulations 1985—*cont.*
Reg.5, amended: SI 1999/1845 Reg.5
Reg.6A, added: SI 1996/1177 Reg.4
Reg.8, amended: SI 1996/1177 Reg.5, SI 1999/1845 Reg.6
Reg.12, amended: SI 1999/1845 Reg.7

1808. Police (Promotion) (Amendment) Regulations 1985
revoked: SI 1996/1685 Reg.8, Sch.3

1820. Royal Air Force Terms of Service Regulations 1985
Reg.2, amended: SI 1997/231 Reg.2
Reg.3, amended: SI 1997/231 Reg.2
Reg.4, amended: SI 1997/231 Reg.2
Reg.5, amended: SI 1997/231 Reg.2
Sch.1, amended: SI 1997/231 Reg.2

1826. District of Woodspring (Electoral Arrangements) Order 1985
revoked: SI 1998/2702 Art.10

1834. County Court Fees (Amendment No.2) Order 1985
revoked: SI 1999/689 Art.8 (with savings), Sch.2 (with savings)

1852. EEC Nursing and Midwifery Qualifications Designation (Amendment) Order 1985
revoked: SI 1996/3102 Art.10

1857. Artificial Insemination of Cattle (Animal Health) (Scotland) Regulations 1985
Reg.18, amended: SI 1996/3124 Reg.41, Sch.6 para.1
Reg.21, amended: SI 1996/3124 Reg.41, Sch.6 para.1

1861. Artificial Insemination of Cattle (Animal Health) (England and Wales) Regulations 1985
Reg.18, amended: SI 1996/3124 Reg.41, Sch.6 para.2
Reg.21, amended: SI 1996/3124 Reg.41, Sch.6 para.2

1872. Redundancy Payments (Local Government) (Modification) (Amendment) Order 1985
revoked: SI 1999/2277 Art.4, Sch.3

1882. Police and Criminal Evidence Act 1984 (Application to Armed Forces) Order 1985
revoked: SI 1997/15 Art.3

1921. Service Subsidy Agreements (Tendering) Regulations 1985
Reg.3, amended: SI 1998/2197 Reg.2

1922. Local Government Superannuation (Overseas Employment) Regulations 1985
Reg.3, applied: SI 1997/1613 Reg.24, Reg.27, Sch.3 para.1

1928. Contracting Out (Transfer Premiums) Regulations 1985
revoked: SI 1996/1172 Sch.2

1929. Occupational Pension Schemes (Discharge of Liability) Regulations 1985
revoked: SI 1997/784 Reg.12, Sch.2
Reg.2, applied: SI 1996/1847 Reg.12
Reg.2, revoked: SI 1997/784 Reg.12, Sch.2
Reg.3, applied: SI 1996/1847 Reg.12
Reg.3, revoked: SI 1997/784 Reg.12, Sch.2
Reg.4, applied: SI 1996/1847 Reg.12
Reg.4, revoked: SI 1997/784 Reg.12, Sch.2
Reg.5, applied: SI 1996/1172 Reg.46
Reg.5, revoked: SI 1997/784 Reg.12, Sch.2

1930. Occupational Pension Schemes (Revaluation) Regulations 1985
Reg.9, revoked: SI 1996/1172 Sch.2

NO.

1931. Occupational Pension Schemes (Transfer Values) Regulations 1985
applied: SI 1996/1847 Reg.21
revoked: SI 1996/1847 Reg.21, Sch.3
Reg.2A, applied: SI 1996/1847 Reg.4
Reg.2A, revoked: SI 1996/1847 Reg.21, Sch.3
Reg.3, amended: SI 1996/1847 Sch.2
Reg.3, revoked: SI 1996/1847 Reg.21, Sch.3
Reg.4, amended: SI 1996/1847 Sch.2
Reg.4, revoked: SI 1996/1847 Reg.21, Sch.3

1941. National Police Records (Recordable Offences) Regulations 1985
Reg.2, amended: SI 1997/566 Reg.2

1967. Agricultural Holdings (Fee) Regulations 1985
revoked: SI 1996/337 Reg.37

1968. Construction Plant and Equipment (Harmonisation of Noise Emission Standards) Regulations 1985
applied: SI 1998/2306 Reg.10, Sch.1

1976. Act of Sederunt (Social Work) (Sheriff Court Procedure Rules 1971) (Amendment No.2) 1985
revoked: SI 1997/291 r.1.4, Sch.2

1990. Extradition (Internationally Protected Persons) (Amendment) Order 1985
revoked: SI 1997/1764 Art.4

1992. Extradition (Taking of Hostages) (Amendment) Order 1985
revoked: SI 1997/1767 Art.4

1993. Extradition (Tokyo Convention) (Amendment) Order 1985
revoked: SI 1997/1768 Art.4

1997. Double Taxation Relief (Taxes on Income) (Finland) Order 1985
Sch., referred to: SI 1996/3166 Art.2

2010. Prosecution of Offences Act 1985 (Specified Proceedings) Order 1985
revoked: SI 1999/904 Art.2

2026. Caseins and Caseinates Regulations 1985
Reg.5, amended: SI 1996/1499 Reg.49

2029. Police Pensions (War Service) (Transferees) Regulations 1985
applied: SI 1999/1750 Art.2, Sch.1

2040. Merchant Shipping (Prevention of Oil Pollution) (Amendment) Regulations 1985
revoked: SI 1996/2154 Reg.1

2047. Pushchairs (Safety) Regulations 1985
revoked: SI 1997/2866 Reg.1

2066. Misuse of Drugs Regulations 1985
Reg.2, amended: SI 1999/1404 Reg.2
Reg.4, amended: SI 1996/1597 Reg.2, SI 1999/1404 Reg.2
Reg.5, applied: SI 1997/1830 Sch.5 Part II
Reg.8, applied: SI 1997/1830 Sch.5 Part III
Reg.9, applied: SI 1997/1830 Sch.5 Part III
Reg.14, amended: SI 1999/1404 Reg.2
Reg.18, amended: SI 1999/1404 Reg.2
Reg.24A, added: SI 1999/1404 Reg.2
Sch.1 para.1, amended: SI 1998/882 Reg.2
Sch.2 para.1, amended: SI 1998/882 Reg.2
Sch.3 para.1, amended: SI 1998/882 Reg.2
Sch.4 Part I, added: SI 1996/1597 Reg.2
Sch.4 Part II, amended: SI 1996/1597 Reg.2, SI 1998/882 Reg.2
Sch.5, see *R. v Jones (Keith)* Times, April 24, 1997 (CA (Crim Div)), Rose, L.J.
Sch.5 para.2, applied: SI 1997/1001 Reg.3

2080. Security for Private Road Works (Scotland) Regulations 1985
Reg.3, amended: SI 1998/3220 Reg.2
Reg.4, amended: SI 1998/3220 Reg.2

NO.

1985—cont.

2080. Security for Private Road Works (Scotland) Regulations 1985—*cont.*
Reg.13, amended: SI 1998/3220 Reg.2
Reg.15, substituted: SI 1998/3220 Reg.2
Reg.16, amended: SI 1998/3220 Reg.2

1986

21. Registration of Births, Deaths, Marriages, etc. (Prescription of Forms) (Scotland) Regulations 1986
revoked: SI 1997/2348 Reg.30, Sch.27

24. Local Government Superannuation Regulations 1986
applied: SI 1996/1240 Reg.11, SI 1996/1680 Reg.39, SI 1997/1612 Reg.48, Reg.107
referred to: SI 1997/1612 Reg.117, Reg.119
revoked: SI 1996/1680 Reg.49, Sch.5 (rem.)
Part F, referred to: SI 1996/1680 Reg.40
Part F, revoked: SI 1996/1680 Reg.49, Sch.5
Part J, applied: SI 1996/2180 Reg.3
Part K, revoked: SI 1996/1680 Reg.49, Sch.5
Part L, see *Swansea City and County v Johnson* [1999] Ch. 189 (Ch D), Hart, J.
Part L, applied: SI 1996/1680 Sch.3 para.11
Part L, revoked: SI 1996/1680 Reg.49, Sch.5
Reg.N, see *Hutchings v Islington LBC* [1998] 3 All E.R. 445 (CA), Evans, L.J.
Reg.B1, applied: SI 1996/1680 Reg.7, S 1996 1680 Reg.40
Reg.B1, revoked: SI 1996/1680 Reg.49, Sch.5
Reg.B1A, applied: SI 1996/1680 Reg.7, Reg.40
Reg.B1A, revoked: SI 1996/1680 Reg.49, Sch.5
Reg.B1B, applied: SI 1996/1680 Reg.7
Reg.B1B, revoked: SI 1996/1680 Reg.49, Sch.5
Reg.B1C, applied: SI 1996/1680 Reg.40
Reg.B1C, revoked: SI 1996/1680 Reg.49, Sch.5
Reg.B3, applied: SI 1997/1613 Sch.4 para.6
Reg.C2, applied: SI 1997/578 Reg.16, SI 1997/1612 Reg.13, Reg.87
Reg.C3, applied: SI 1997/1612 Reg.13, Reg.87
Reg.C3A, applied: SI 1997/1612 Reg.87
Reg.C4, applied: SI 1997/1612 Reg.87
Reg.C5, applied: SI 1997/1612 Reg.87
Reg.C6, applied: SI 1997/1612 Reg.87
Reg.C6A, applied: SI 1997/1612 Reg.87
Reg.C7, applied: SI 1997/1612 Reg.87
Reg.C7A, applied: SI 1997/1612 Reg.87
Reg.C8, applied: SI 1997/1613 Reg.8, SI 1997/1612 Reg.87
Reg.C8, referred to: SI 1997/1613 Reg.15
Reg.C8A, applied: SI 1997/1612 Reg.87
Reg.D3, applied: SI 1996/2180 Reg.3
Reg.E4, applied: SI 1997/1612 Reg.6
Reg.E6, referred to: SI 1997/1613 Reg.9
Reg.E12, applied: SI 1996/1680 Sch.3 para.9, SI 1997/1613 Reg.8
Reg.E12, revoked: SI 1996/1680 Reg.49, Sch.5
Reg.E13, applied: SI 1997/1612 Sch.3
Reg.F2, referred to: SI 1996/1680 Reg.39
Reg.F2, revoked: SI 1996/1680 Reg.49, Sch.5
Reg.F3, applied: SI 1996/1680 Reg.40
Reg.F3, revoked: SI 1996/1680 Reg.49, Sch.5
Reg.F6, applied: SI 1996/1680 Reg.40, SI 1997/1612 Reg.97, Sch.3
Reg.F6, revoked: SI 1996/1680 Reg.49, Sch.5
Reg.H6, applied: SI 1997/1612 Reg.141
Reg.J2, applied: SI 1996/2180 Reg.3, Sch.
Reg.L9, applied: SI 1996/1680 Sch.3 para.11
Reg.L9, revoked: SI 1996/1680 Reg.49, Sch.5

NO.

1986—cont.

24. Local Government Superannuation Regulations 1986—*cont.*
Reg.N8, see *Hutchings v Islington LBC* [1998] 1 W.L.R. 1629 (CA), Evans, L.J.
Sch.2 Part III, applied: SI 1996/1680 Reg.7
Sch.2 Part III, revoked: SI 1996/1680 Reg.49, Sch.5
Sch.2 Part IV, applied: SI 1996/1680 Reg.7, Reg.40
Sch.2 Part IV, revoked: SI 1996/1680 Reg.49, Sch.5
Sch.9 para.4, applied: SI 1997/1612 Reg.29

26. Textile Products (Indications of Fibre Content) Regulations 1986
Sch.2 Part I, amended: SI 1998/1169 Reg.2
Sch.3, amended: SI 1998/1169 Reg.2

36. Control of Lead at Work Regulations (Northern Ireland) 1986
Reg.16, applied: SI 1996/1919 (NI.16) Art.96

37. Perambulators and Pushchairs (Safety) Regulations (Northern Ireland) 1986
revoked: SI 1997/2866 Reg.1

52. Misuse of Drugs (Northern Ireland) Regulations 1986
Reg.5, applied: SI 1997/1830 Sch.5 Part II
Reg.8, applied: SI 1997/1830 Sch.5 Part III
Reg.9, applied: SI 1997/1830 Sch.5 Part III

60. Inshore Fishing (Prohibition of Carriage of Monofilament Gill Nets) (Scotland) Order 1986
revoked: SI 1996/1907 Art.4

77. Travel Concession Schemes Regulations 1986
Reg.27, amended: SI 1996/2711 Reg.2
Sch.1 para.3, substituted: SI 1996/2711 Reg.2

103. Licensed Betting Offices Regulations 1986
Reg.4, amended: SI 1997/1071 Reg.2

120. Licensed Betting Offices (Scotland) Regulations 1986
Reg.4, amended: SI 1997/1095 Reg.2

149. General Medical Council (Registration Fees) Regulations) Order of Council 1986
Sch. Reg.3, amended: SI 1999/3189 Sch. Reg.3
Sch. Reg.4, amended: SI 1999/3189 Sch. Reg.4
Sch. Reg.5, amended: SI 1997/1884 Sch. Reg.2
Sch. Reg.6, substituted: SI 1999/3189 Sch. Reg.5
Sch. Reg.9, applied: SI 1997/1884 Sch. Reg.4
Sch. Reg.9, revoked: SI 1997/1884 Sch. Reg.3
Sch. Reg.15, substituted: SI 1999/3189 Sch. Reg.6

178. Local Authorities' Traffic Orders (Exemptions for Disabled Persons) (England and Wales) Regulations 1986
Reg.4, applied: SI 1996/2489 Sch.4 para.2

183. Removal and Disposal of Vehicles Regulations 1986
applied: SI 1996/1243 Sch.5 para.10
Reg.4B, added: SI 1999/490 Reg.3
Reg.5, amended: SI 1996/1008 Art.2, Sch para.6
Reg.5B, added: SI 1998/2019 Reg.3
Reg.6, amended: SI 1999/490 Reg.4
Reg.7, substituted: SI 1996/1316 Reg.12
Reg.12, amended: SI 1996/1008 Art.2, Sch para.6
Reg.15, amended: SI 1996/1008 Art.2, Sch para.6

NO.

1986—cont.

184. Removal and Disposal of Vehicles (Loading Area) Regulations 1986
Reg.3, amended: SI 1996/1008 Art.2, Sch para.7

237. Borough of Thamesdown (Electoral Arrangements) Order 1986
revoked: SI 1999/2927 Art.9
Art.6, revoked: SI 1999/2927 Art.9

280. Borough of Halton (Electoral Arrangements) Order 1986
Art.6, substituted: SI 1996/1863 Art.7

298. Tyne Tunnel Order 1986
applied: 1998 c.i

307. Police and Criminal Evidence Act 1984 Codes of Practice (Armed Forces) Order 1986
revoked: SI 1997/17 Art.3

317. Occupational Pension Schemes (Contracting Out) Amendment Regulations 1986
Reg.2, revoked: SI 1996/1172 Sch.2
Reg.3, revoked: SI 1996/1462 Reg.14, Sch.3

380. Local Government Superannuation (Miscellaneous Provisions) Regulations 1986
Reg.3, applied: SI 1997/1612 Reg.139
Reg.4, amended: SI 1997/1613 Reg.27, Sch.3 para.2
Reg.4, applied: SI 1997/1612 Reg.129

390. Police Grant (Scotland) (Amendment) Order 1986
revoked: SI 1996/780 Art.7, Sch.2

409. Local Government (Compensation for Premature Retirement) (Scotland) Amendment Regulations 1986
revoked: SI 1998/192 Reg.52, Sch.2

412. Teachers' (Compensation for Premature Retirement) (Scotland) Amendment Regulations 1986
revoked: SI 1996/2317 Reg.20, Sch.5

416. Misuse of Drugs (Licence Fees) Regulations 1986
Reg.3, amended: SI 1996/596 Reg.2, SI 1999/741 Reg.2

443. Town and Country Planning (Local Government Reorganisation) (Miscellaneous Amendments) Regulations 1986
Sch.1 para.7, revoked: SI 1997/420 Reg.6, Sch

451. Sheriff Court Fees Amendment Order 1986
revoked: SI 1997/687 Art.11, Sch.2

472. Motor Cycles (Protective Helmets) (Amendment) Regulations 1986
revoked: SI 1998/1807 Reg.2, Sch.1

482. Income Tax (Building Societies) Regulations 1986
see *National & Provincial Building Society v United Kingdom* [1997] S.T.C. 1466 (ECHR), R Ryssdal (President)

486. Social Security Benefit (Persons Abroad) Amendment Regulations 1986
revoked: SI 1996/1345 Reg.27, Sch.

535. Merchant Shipping (Musters and Training) Regulations 1986
Reg.4, applied: SI 1999/2721 Reg.31

545. Act of Sederunt (Mental Health (Scotland) Act 1984) 1986
revoked: SI 1996/2149 r.1

561. Peak Park Joint Planning Board Order 1986
revoked: SI 1996/1243 Art.20, Sch.8

586. Medicines (Products Other Than Veterinary Drugs) (Prescription Only) Amendment Order 1986
revoked: SI 1997/1830 Art.16, Sch.6

NO.

1986—cont.

587. National Health Service (Scotland) (Injury Benefits) Amendment Regulations 1986
revoked: SI 1998/1594 Reg.24, Sch.

590. Value Added Tax Tribunal Rules 1986
r.2, amended: SI 1997/255 r.4
r.7, amended: SI 1997/255 r.5
r.8, amended: SI 1997/255 r.5
r.8A, added: SI 1997/255 r.6
r.9, see *Kashmir Tandoori v Customs and Excise Commissioners* [1998] B.V.C. 2141 (V & DT), Theodore Wallace (Chairman)
r.9, revoked (in part): SI 1997/255 r.7
r.16, amended: SI 1997/255 r.8
r.19, see *Maharani Restaurants v Customs and Excise Commissioners* [1999] S.T.C. 295 (QBD), Turner, J.
r.19, amended: SI 1997/255 r.9
r.20, amended: SI 1997/255 r.10
r.21, amended: SI 1997/255 r.11
r.23, amended: SI 1997/255 r.12
r.29, see *University of Reading v Customs and Excise Commissioners* [1998] B.V.C. 2163 (V & DT), Stephen Oliver Q.C. (Chairman)

594. Education and Libraries (Northern Ireland) Order 1986
applied: 1998 c.29 s.30, SI 1998/1760 (NI.14) Art.2, SI 1998/1759 (NI.13) Art.40, Sch.2 para.3
referred to: SI 1996/1919 (NI.16) Art.128, SI 1997/866 (NI.5) Art.2
Art.2, amended: SI 1996/274 (NI.1) Art.30, Art.43, Sch.5 Part I, Sch.5 Part II, SI 1997/866 (NI.5) Art.2, Art.25, SI 1997/1772 (NI.15) Art.25, Sch.4, SI 1998/1759 (NI.13) Art.91, Sch.5 Part I, Sch.5 Part II
Art.2, applied: 1996 c.26 s.4, SI 1996/274 (NI.1) Art.2, 1998 c.29 Sch.11 para.8, SI 1998/1759 (NI.13) Art.2, SI 1998/1760 (NI.14) Art.2
Art.2, referred to: SI 1998/1759 (NI.13) Art.91, Sch.6 Part I
Art.2, revoked (in part): SI 1996/274 (NI.1) Art.44, Sch.6 Part I, Sch.6 Part II, SI 1997/1772 (NI.15) Art.25, Sch.5
Art.5, added: SI 1997/1772 (NI.15) Art.25, Sch.4
Art.6, revoked (in part): SI 1996/274 (NI.1) Art.44, Sch.6 Part I, SI 1998/1759 (NI.13) Art.91, Sch.6 Part I
Art.7, amended: SI 1998/1759 (NI.13) Art.91, Sch.5 Part I
Art.8, amended: SI 1997/866 (NI.5) Art.25
Art.8, revoked (in part): SI 1996/274 (NI.1) Art.44, Sch.6 Part II, SI 1998/1759 (NI.13) Art.91, Sch.6 Part II
Art.9, referred to: SI 1998/1759 (NI.13) Art.91, Sch.6 Part II
Art.9, revoked: SI 1998/1759 (NI.13) Art.91, Sch.5 Part II, Sch.6 Part II
Art.9A, revoked (in part): SI 1997/1772 (NI.15) Art.25, Sch.4, Sch.5
Art.10, referred to: SI 1998/1759 (NI.13) Art.14
Art.10, revoked (in part): SI 1997/1772 (NI.15) Art.25, Sch.4, Sch.5
Art.11, referred to: SI 1998/1759 (NI.13) Art.14
Art.11, revoked (in part): SI 1996/274 (NI.1) Art.29, Art.44, Sch.6 Part II
Art.14, applied: SI 1998/1759 (NI.13) Art.89
Art.15, revoked (in part): SI 1996/274 (NI.1) Art.43, Sch.5 Part II, Art.44, Sch.6 Part II
Art.16, amended: SI 1998/1759 (NI.13) Art.91, Sch.5 Part II
Art.16, revoked (in part): SI 1996/274 (NI.1) Art.44, Sch.6 Part II

NO.

NO.

1986—cont.

1986—cont.

594. Education and Libraries (Northern Ireland) Order 1986—*cont.*

Art.17, amended: SI 1998/1759 (NI.13) Art.91, Sch.5 Part I, Sch.6 Part I

Art.18, applied: SI 1997/866 (NI.5) Art.12

Art.21, applied: SI 1996/274 (NI.1) Art.25

Art.21, revoked (in part): SI 1996/274 (NI.1) Art.25, Art.44, Sch.6 Part I

Art.22, revoked (in part): SI 1996/274 (NI.1) Art.25, Art.44, Sch.6 Part I

Art.29, revoked: SI 1996/274 (NI.1) Art.44, Sch.6 Part I

Art.30, revoked: SI 1996/274 (NI.1) Art.44, Sch.6 Part I

Art.31, revoked: SI 1996/274 (NI.1) Art.44, Sch.6 Part I

Art.32, revoked: SI 1996/274 (NI.1) Art.44, Sch.6 Part I

Art.33, revoked: SI 1996/274 (NI.1) Art.44, Sch.6 Part I

Art.34, revoked: SI 1996/274 (NI.1) Art.44, Sch.6 Part I

Art.36, revoked: SI 1996/274 (NI.1) Art.44, Sch.6 Part I

Art.39, amended: SI 1996/274 (NI.1) Art.30

Art.40, amended: SI 1996/274 (NI.1) Art.30, Art.43, Sch.5 Part II

Art.41, amended: SI 1996/274 (NI.1) Art.43, Sch.5 Part II

Art.43, amended: SI 1996/274 (NI.1) Art.43, Sch.5 Part II

Art.46, applied: 1998 c.39 s.55

Art.46A, amended: SI 1996/274 (NI.1) Art.31

Art.46A, applied: SI 1997/866 (NI.5) Art.21

Art.48, revoked (in part): SI 1996/274 (NI.1) Art.44, Sch.6 Part I

Art.49, amended: SI 1997/1772 (NI.15) Art.25, Sch.4

Art.49A, amended: SI 1996/274 (NI.1) Art.32

Art.49A, applied: SI 1998/1759 (NI.13) Art.4

Art.50, amended: SI 1998/1760 (NI.14) Art.9, Sch.

Art.50, applied: SI 1997/1968 Reg.10

Art.50, referred to: SI 1998/1760 (NI.14) Art.6

Art.50, revoked (in part): SI 1998/1760 (NI.14) Art.9, Sch.

Art.51, substituted: SI 1996/274 (NI.1) Art.43, Sch.5 Part II

Art.52, substituted: SI 1997/866 (NI.5) Art.23

Art.55, revoked: SI 1997/1772 (NI.15) Art.25, Sch.4, Sch.5

Art.58, amended: SI 1998/1759 (NI.13) Art.91, Sch.5 Part II

Art.58, revoked (in part): SI 1997/1772 (NI.15) Art.25, Sch.4, Sch.5

Art.59, revoked (in part): SI 1997/1772 (NI.15) Art.25, Sch.4, Sch.5

Art.63, amended: SI 1998/1759 (NI.13) Art.82, Art.91, Sch.6 Part I

Art.65, revoked (in part): SI 1997/1772 (NI.15) Art.25, Sch.4, Sch.5

Art.66, applied: SI 1998/1760 (NI.14) Art.7

Art.67, revoked (in part): SI 1997/1772 (NI.15) Art.25, Sch.4, Sch.5

Art.69, referred to: SI 1998/1759 (NI.13) Art.91, Sch.6 Part II

Art.69, revoked (in part): SI 1997/1772 (NI.15) Art.25, Sch.4, Sch.5, SI 1998/1759 (NI.13) Art.43, Art.91, Sch.6 Part I

Art.69A, revoked (in part): SI 1996/274 (NI.1) Art.43, Sch.5 Part II, Art.44, Sch.6 Part II, SI 1998/1759 (NI.13) Art.91, Sch.6 Part II

594. Education and Libraries (Northern Ireland) Order 1986—*cont.*

Art.70, revoked (in part): SI 1998/1759 (NI.13) Art.91, Sch.6 Part II

Art.72, amended: SI 1996/1919 (NI.16) Art.255, Sch.1

Art.72, referred to: SI 1998/1759 (NI.13) Art.91, Sch.6 Part II

Art.72, revoked (in part): SI 1996/274 (NI.1) Art.43, Sch.5 Part II, Art.44, Sch.6 Part II, SI 1996/1919 (NI.16) Art.257, Sch.3, SI 1998/1759 (NI.13) Art.91, Sch.6 Part II

Art.73, amended: SI 1997/1772 (NI.15) Art.25, Sch.4

Art.77, revoked (in part): SI 1996/2967 Reg.11

Art.79, revoked (in part): SI 1997/1772 (NI.15) Art.25, Sch.4, Sch.5

Art.86, revoked (in part): SI 1997/1772 (NI.15) Art.25, Sch.4, Sch.5

Art.88, amended: SI 1997/866 (NI.5) Art.25, SI 1998/1759 (NI.13) Art.91, Sch.5 Part II

Art.88, applied: SI 1998/1759 (NI.13) Art.70

Art.88A, amended: SI 1997/1772 (NI.15) Art.25, Sch.4

Art.88A, referred to: SI 1998/1759 (NI.13) Sch.2 para.6

Art.97, revoked (in part): 1996 c.31 Sch.2

Art.100, amended: SI 1997/1772 (NI.15) Art.25, Sch.4

Art.101, applied: SI 1997/869 (NI.6) Art.20, SI 1997/1772 (NI.15) Art.9, Art.18

Art.102, amended: SI 1997/1772 (NI.15) Art.25, Sch.4

Art.102, applied: SI 1997/866 (NI.5) Art.7, SI 1997/1772 (NI.15) Art.18, SI 1998/1759 (NI.13) Art.14, Art.19

Art.102, substituted: SI 1996/274 (NI.1) Art.33

Art.102A, applied: SI 1997/866 (NI.5) Art.7, SI 1998/1759 (NI.13) Art.19

Art.102A, substituted: SI 1996/274 (NI.1) Art.33

Art.103, revoked (in part): SI 1997/1772 (NI.15) Art.25, Sch.4, Sch.5

Art.105, amended: SI 1997/1772 (NI.15) Art.25, Sch.4

Art.115, amended: SI 1997/1772 (NI.15) Art.25, Sch.4

Art.116, referred to: SI 1998/1759 (NI.13) Art.68

Art.116, revoked (in part): SI 1996/274 (NI.1) Art.43, Sch.5 Part II, Art.44, Sch.6 Part II, SI 1998/1759 (NI.13) Art.91, Sch.6 Part II

Art.119A, amended: SI 1998/1759 (NI.13) Art.91, Sch.5 Part II

Art.119A, revoked (in part): SI 1997/1772 (NI.15) Art.25, Sch.4, Sch.5

Part III, applied: SI 1996/274 (NI.1) Art.40

Sch.2 para.2, revoked (in part): SI 1997/1772 (NI.15) Art.25, Sch.4

Sch.2 para.4, revoked (in part): SI 1997/1772 (NI.15) Art.25, Sch.5

Sch.2 para.6, revoked (in part): SI 1997/1772 (NI.15) Art.25, Sch.4, Sch.5

Sch.4, amended: SI 1998/1759 (NI.13) Art.91, Sch.5 Part I

Sch.4 para.3, amended: SI 1997/866 (NI.5) Art.24

Sch.4 para.3, revoked (in part): SI 1997/1772 (NI.15) Art.25, Sch.4, Sch.5

Sch.4 para.4, amended: SI 1998/1759 (NI.13) Art.91, Sch.5 Part I

Sch.5 Part II, revoked: SI 1996/274 (NI.1) Art.29, Art.44, Sch.6 Part II

Sch.5 para.1, referred to: SI 1998/1759 (NI.13) Art.68

NO.

1986—cont.

594. Education and Libraries (Northern Ireland) Order 1986—*cont.*
Sch.6 para.1, referred to: SI 1998/1759 (NI.13) Art.68
Sch.8, revoked: SI 1996/274 (NI.1) Art.29, Art.44, Sch.6 Part II
Sch.11, revoked: SI 1996/274 (NI.1) Art.44, Sch.6 Part I
Sch.13 para.1, substituted: SI 1996/274 (NI.1) Art.27
Sch.13 para.1A, substituted: SI 1996/274 (NI.1) Art.27
Sch.13 para.1B, substituted: SI 1996/274 (NI.1) Art.27
Sch.13 para.2, referred to: SI 1996/274 (NI.1) Art.18
Sch.13 para.2, substituted: SI 1996/274 (NI.1) Art.27
Sch.13 para.3, amended: SI 1997/866 (NI.5) Art.23
Sch.18, revoked (in part): SI 1996/274 (NI.1) Art.44, Sch.6 Part I, SI 1996/1297 (NI.7) Art.23, SI 1996/1297 (NI.7) Sch.5, SI 1996/1919 (NI.16) Art.257, Sch.3, SI 1998/1504 (NI.9) Art.65, Sch.6, SI 1998/3162 (NI.21) Art.105, Sch.5
Sch.19 para.5, revoked: SI 1996/274 (NI.1) Art.44, Sch.6 Part I

595. Mental Health (Northern Ireland) Order 1986
applied: SI 1997/1179 (NI.8) Art.40, SI 1998/1859 r.5
referred to: SI 1996/3160 (NI.24) Art.36, SI 1999/2789 (NI.8) Art.4
Art.3, amended: 1996 c.23 Sch.3 para.48
Art.16, amended: SI 1999/1820 Art.4, Sch.2 para.140
Art.44, amended: SI 1998/1504 (NI.9) Art.65, Sch.5 para.25
Art.44, applied: SI 1998/1071 (NI.6) Art.27, SI 1998/2839 (NI.20) Art.5
Art.44, referred to: 1997 c.51 s.6
Art.45, applied: SI 1998/1071 (NI.6) Art.27
Art.49, amended: SI 1996/3160 (NI.24) Art.48
Art.49, applied: SI 1996/3160 (NI.24) Sch.6 para.3
Art.49, revoked (in part): SI 1996/3160 (NI.24) Sch.7
Art.49A, added: SI 1996/3160 (NI.24) Art.49
Art.50, amended: SI 1996/3160 (NI.24) Art.50
Art.50, applied: SI 1996/3160 (NI.24) Sch.6 para.3
Art.50, revoked (in part): SI 1996/3160 (NI.24) Sch.7
Art.50A, added: SI 1996/3160 (NI.24) Art.51
Art.50A, amended: SI 1998/1504 (NI.9) Art.65, Sch.5 para.26
Art.50A, applied: SI 1996/3160 (NI.24) Sch.6 para.3
Art.51, amended: SI 1996/3160 (NI.24) Art.51
Art.52, referred to: 1997 c.51 s.6
Art.52, revoked: 1996 c.46 Sch.7 Part III
Art.53, amended: SI 1998/1504 (NI.9) Art.65, Sch.5 para.27
Art.53, applied: SI 1998/1504 (NI.9) Sch.2 para.5, SI 1998/1859 Sch.3 Part I
Art.56, amended: SI 1998/1504 (NI.9) Art.65, Sch.5 para.28
Art.60, amended: SI 1998/1504 (NI.9) Art.65, Sch.6
Art.60, applied: SI 1996/3160 (NI.24) Sch.1 para.4

NO.

1986—cont.

595. Mental Health (Northern Ireland) Order 1986—*cont.*
Art.61, amended: SI 1998/1504 (NI.9) Art.65, Sch.5 para.29, Sch.6
Art.70, referred to: SI 1996/1298 (NI.8) Sch.3
Art.84, amended: SI 1996/3160 (NI.24) Art.51
Art.123, referred to: SI 1999/2789 (NI.8) Art.3
Part II, applied: SI 1996/3160 (NI.24) Art.22, Sch.1 para.4
Part III, applied: SI 1996/3160 (NI.24) Sch.1 para.4
Sch.2A, added: SI 1996/3160 (NI.24) Art.51, Sch.4
Sch.4 para.11, revoked: SI 1996/1297 (NI.7) Art.23, Sch.5
Sch.5, revoked (in part): SI 1996/1141 (NI.6) s.32, Sch.5
Sch.5 Part II, revoked (in part): 1998 c.47 s.100, Sch.15, SI 1998/1504 (NI.9) Art.65, Sch.6

596. Mental Health (Northern Ireland Consequential Amendments) Order 1986
Art.47, applied: 1997 c.43 Sch.3 para.3, Sch.3 para.8
Art.48, applied: 1997 c.43 Sch.3 para.3, Sch.3 para.8
Art.55, applied: 1997 c.43 Sch.3 para.3
Art.78, applied: 1997 c.43 Sch.3 para.3, Sch.3 para.8

615. Yorkshire Water Authority (Regional Land Drainage Committee) Order 1986
revoked: SI 1996/1614 Art.3

617. Northumbrian Water Authority (Regional Land Drainage Committee) Order 1986
revoked: SI 1996/1617 Art.3

623. Town and Country Planning (Determination of Appeals by Appointed Persons) (Prescribed Classes) (Amendment) Regulations 1986
revoked: SI 1997/420 Reg.6, Sch

625. Redundant Mineworkers and Concessionary Coal (Payments Schemes) Order 1986
revoked: SI 1996/1288 Art.3

633. County Court Fees (Amendment) Order 1986
revoked: SI 1999/689 Art.8 (with savings), Sch.2 (with savings)

637. Supreme Court Fees (Amendment) Order 1986
revoked: SI 1999/687 Art.8 (with savings), Sch.2 (with savings)

647. North Eastern Sea Fisheries District Order 1986
Art.3, amended: SI 1996/1034 Art.2
Sch.1, substituted: SI 1996/1034 Art.2, Sch

705. Non-Contentious Probate Fees (Amendment) Order 1986
revoked: SI 1999/688 Art.6 (with savings), Sch.2 (with savings)

751. Occupational Pension Schemes (Revaluation and Transfer Values) Amendment Regulations 1986
revoked: SI 1996/1847 Reg.21, Sch.3

833. Gaming (Bingo) Act (Fees) Order 1986
Art.2, amended: SI 1998/454 Art.2

834. Gaming Clubs (Multiple Bingo) Regulations 1986
Reg.2, substituted: SI 1998/2151 Reg.2

887. Dental Auxiliaries Regulations 1986
Reg.2, amended: SI 1999/3460 Reg.3
Reg.4, amended: SI 1999/3460 Reg.4
Reg.6, amended: SI 1996/2998 Reg.2
Reg.6, amended: SI 1999/3460 Reg.5
Reg.23, amended: SI 1999/3460 Reg.6
Reg.27, amended: SI 1999/3460 Reg.7

NO.

965. National Health Service (General Ophthalmic Services) (Scotland) Regulations 1986
applied: SI 1998/642 Reg.9
Reg.2, amended: SI 1996/843 Reg.2, SI 1996/2353 Reg.2, SI 1999/725 Reg.2, SSI 1999/55 Reg.3
Reg.3, amended: SI 1999/725 Reg.3
Reg.3, revoked (in part): SI 1999/725 Reg.3
Reg.6, amended: SI 1996/843 Reg.3, SI 1999/725 Reg.4, SSI 1999/55 Reg.4
Reg.7, amended: SI 1996/843 Reg.4, SSI 1999/55 Reg.2
Reg.8, amended: SSI 1999/55 Reg.2
Reg.9, amended: SI 1996/843 Reg.5, SSI 1999/55 Reg.2
Reg.10, amended: SSI 1999/55 Reg.2
Reg.12, amended: SSI 1999/55 Reg.5
Reg.13, amended: SI 1996/843 Reg.6, SI 1999/725 Reg.5, SSI 1999/55 Reg.6
Reg.13A, added: SI 1996/843 Reg.7
Reg.13A, amended: SI 1999/725 Reg.6, SSI 1999/55 Reg.2
Reg.14, amended: SI 1996/2353 Reg.3, SI 1999/725 Reg.7, SSI 1999/55 Reg.7
Reg.14, applied: SSI 1999/55 Reg.9
Reg.14A, amended: SSI 1999/55 Reg.2
Reg.14B, amended: SI 1999/725 Reg.8
Reg.15, amended: SI 1999/725 Reg.9
Reg.16, amended: SSI 1999/55 Reg.2
Reg.17, amended: SSI 1999/55 Reg.2
Sch.1 para.2, amended: SI 1996/843 Reg.8, SSI 1999/55 Reg.8
Sch.1 para.4, amended: SI 1999/725 Reg.10, SSI 1999/55 Reg.8
Sch.1 para.5, amended: SI 1999/725 Reg.10, SSI 1999/55 Reg.8
Sch.1 para.5, substituted: SI 1996/843 Reg.8
Sch.1 para.6, amended: SI 1999/725 Reg.10, SSI 1999/55 Reg.8
Sch.1 para.7, amended: SSI 1999/55 Reg.8
Sch.1 para.8, amended: SI 1996/843 Reg.8, SI 1999/725 Reg.10, SSI 1999/55 Reg.8
Sch.1 para.8A, added: SI 1996/843 Reg.8
Sch.1 para.8A, amended: SI 1999/725 Reg.10, SSI 1999/55 Reg.8
Sch.1 para.8B, amended: SI 1996/843 Reg.8, SSI 1999/55 Reg.8
Sch.1 para.8C, amended: SI 1996/843 Reg.8
Sch.1 para.9, amended: SI 1999/725 Reg.10
Sch.1 para.10, amended: SI 1999/725 Reg.10
Sch.1 para.10, applied: SI 1998/642 Reg.9
Sch.1 para.11, amended: SI 1996/843 Reg.8, SI 1999/725 Reg.10

975. National Health Service (General Ophthalmic Services) Regulations 1986
applied: SI 1997/818 Reg.9
Reg.2, amended: SI 1996/705 Reg.2, SI 1996/2320 Reg.2, SI 1999/2562 Reg.3, SI 1999/2841 Reg.3
Reg.3, amended: SI 1999/693 Reg.2
Reg.3, revoked (in part): SI 1999/693 Reg.2
Reg.6, amended: SI 1996/705 Reg.3
Reg.7, amended: SI 1996/705 Reg.4
Reg.9, amended: SI 1996/705 Reg.5
Reg.12, amended: SI 1996/705 Reg.6
Reg.13, amended: SI 1996/2320 Reg.3, SI 1999/693 Reg.3, SI 1999/2562 Reg.3
Sch.1 para.2, amended: SI 1996/705 Reg.8
Sch.1 para.5, substituted: SI 1996/705 Reg.8
Sch.1 para.7, amended: SI 1996/705 Reg.8
Sch.1 para.8, amended: SI 1996/705 Reg.8
Sch.1 para.8A, added: SI 1996/705 Reg.8

NO.

975. National Health Service (General Ophthalmic Services) Regulations 1986—*cont.*
Sch.1 para.8B, added: SI 1996/705 Reg.8
Sch.1 para.8C, added: SI 1996/705 Reg.8
Sch.1 para.8C, amended: SI 1998/646 Reg.8
Sch.1 para.10, applied: SI 1997/818 Reg.9

1011. Social Security (Unemployment, Sickness and Invalidity Benefit) Amendment (No.2) Regulations 1986
revoked: SI 1996/1345 Reg.27, Sch.

1032. Companies (Northern Ireland) Order 1986
applied: 1997 c.28 s.24, 1997 c.32 Sch.6, 1998 c.36 s.117, Sch.18 para.11, SI 1998/504 Sch.6 para.3, Sch.6 para.5, Sch.6 para.11, Sch.6 para.15, Sch.6 para.18
referred to: SI 1996/1299 (NI.9) Sch.4 para.3, 1998 c.36 s.42, s.117, Sch.18 para.19, 1998 c.47 Sch.3 para.23, SI 1999/727 Art.2
Art.2A, amended: SI 1996/1632 (NI.11) Art.18, Sch.5 para.4
Art.2B, amended: SI 1996/1632 (NI.11) Art.18, Sch.5 para.4
Art.4, referred to: SI 1998/3162 (NI.21) Art.69
Art.4, applied: SI 1997/470 Reg.3
Art.36, applied: SI 1996/1632 (NI.11) Sch.2 para.9
Art.148, applied: SI 1996/1632 (NI.11) Sch.2 para.2
Art.149, applied: SI 1996/1632 (NI.11) Sch.2 para.2
Art.157, applied: SI 1996/1632 (NI.11) Sch.2 para.2
Art.234, applied: SI 1996/943 Reg.29, Reg.32
Art.234, referred to: 1997 c.58 Sch.1 para.5
Art.235, applied: 1997 c.16 Sch.12 para.30
Art.235, referred to: 1997 c.58 Sch.1 para.5
Art.239, applied: SI 1996/943 Reg.31
Art.245, applied: SI 1996/943 Reg.29, Sch.6 para.10
Art.250, referred to: 1997 c.58 Sch.1 para.5
Art.252, applied: SI 1996/1632 (NI.11) Sch.2 para.9
Art.266, applied: 1997 c.16 Sch.12 para.28
Art.270, applied: 1997 c.16 Sch.12 para.30
Art.370, applied: SI 1997/1313
Art.387A, amended: SI 1997/2984 (NI.22) Art.5
Art.389A, revoked (in part): SI 1997/2984 (NI.22) Art.5, Art.11, Sch.4
Art.389B, substituted: SI 1997/2984 (NI.22) Art.5
Art.389C, amended: SI 1997/2984 (NI.22) Art.5
Art.397A, applied: SI 1996/943 Reg.29
Art.398, revoked (in part): SI 1997/2984 (NI.22) Art.5, Art.11, Sch.4
Art.427, amended: 1999 c.23 s.59, Sch.3 para.14
Art.431, applied: SI 1997/2781 Art.4
Art.440, amended: 1999 c.23 s.59, Sch.3 para.15
Art.442, amended: 1998 c.11 s.23, Sch.5 para.63
Art.645, referred to: 1997 c.28 s.10
Art.651, applied: SI 1996/1632 (NI.11) Sch.2 para.9
Art.653, amended: SI 1996/1632 (NI.11) Art.18, Sch.5 para.4
Art.654, applied: SI 1996/1632 (NI.11) Sch.2 para.2
Art.654A, applied: SI 1996/1632 (NI.11) Sch.2 para.2
Art.655, applied: SI 1996/1632 (NI.11) Sch.2 para.2

NO.

1032. Companies (Northern Ireland) Order 1986—*cont.*

Art.656, applied: SI 1996/1632 (NI.11) Sch.2 para.2

Art.658, amended: SI 1997/2983 (NI.21) Art.13, Sch.1 para.4, SI 1999/2789 (NI.8) Art.40, Sch.3

Art.658, applied: SI 1996/1632 (NI.11) Sch.2 para.2

Art.659, applied: SI 1996/1632 (NI.11) Sch.2 para.2

Art.659A, applied: SI 1996/1632 (NI.11) Sch.2 para.2

Art.673, referred to: 1997 c.28 s.10

Part II Ch.I, applied: SI 1996/1632 (NI.11) Sch.2 para.2

Part II Ch.II, applied: SI 1996/1632 (NI.11) Sch.2 para.2

Part III, applied: SI 1996/1632 (NI.11) Sch.2 para.2

Part XIII, applied: 1997 c.32 s.42

Part XV, applied: SI 1996/1299 (NI.9) Sch.2 para.7

Part XV, referred to: 1998 c.11 Sch.7 para.3

Sch.6 Part I, applied: SI 1996/943 Reg.31

Sch.9A para.50, substituted: SI 1996/946 Reg.13

Sch.14 Part I, amended: SI 1997/1313 Art.2

Sch.23, amended: SI 1997/2984 (NI.22) Art.5

1033. Business Names (Northern Ireland) Order 1986

Art.4, applied: SI 1996/1632 (NI.11) Sch.2 para.10

1035. Companies Consolidation (Consequential Provisions) (Northern Ireland) Order 1986

Sch.1, revoked (in part): SI 1996/275 (NI.2) Art.71, Sch.8

Sch.1 Part I, revoked (in part): SI 1996/725 (NI.5) Sch.4

Sch.1 Part II, amended: 1998 c.41 s.74, Sch.12 para.9, Sch.14 Part II

1046. Occupational Pension Schemes (Disclosure of Information) Regulations 1986

revoked: SI 1996/1655 Reg.12, Sch.4

Reg.6, applied: SI 1996/1676 Reg.3, Reg.4, SI 1996/1901 Reg.3

Reg.6, referred to: SI 1996/1901 Reg.4

Reg.8, applied: SI 1996/1847 Reg.8, SI 1997/664 Art.7, SI 1997/666 Reg.8

Reg.9, applied: SI 1996/1655 Reg.6, SI 1997/664 Art.7

Sch.2, applied: SI 1996/1676 Reg.3, SI 1996/1901 Reg.3

Sch.2 para.8, applied: SI 1996/1676 Reg.4

Sch.2 para.8, referred to: SI 1996/1901 Reg.4

Sch.2 para.9, applied: SI 1996/1676 Reg.4

Sch.2 para.9, referred to: SI 1996/1901 Reg.4

1066. Merchant Shipping (Life-Saving Appliances) Regulations 1986

applied: SI 1996/3243 Sch Part I, SI 1998/2070 Reg.3, Reg.11

referred to: SI 1998/1609 Reg.5, Reg.6, Sch., SI 1998/2771 Reg.4, Reg.5, Sch.1, Sch.2

revoked: SI 1999/2721 Reg.1

Reg.2, revoked: SI 1999/2721 Reg.1

Reg.4, amended: SI 1996/3188 Reg.17

Reg.4, revoked: SI 1999/2721 Reg.1

1067. Merchant Shipping (Cargo Ship Construction and Survey) Regulations 1984 (Amendment) Regulations 1986

revoked: SI 1997/1509 Reg.1

NO.

1070. Merchant Shipping (Fire Protection and Fire Appliances) (Amendment) Regulations 1986

referred to: SI 1998/1609 Reg.5, Reg.6, Sch.

revoked: SI 1998/1012 Reg.1

1071. Merchant Shipping (Masters and Training) Regulations 1986

applied: SI 1996/3243 Sch Part I, SI 1999/2722 Reg.1

revoked: SI 1999/2722 Reg.1

Reg.3, revoked: SI 1999/2722 Reg.1

Reg.4, applied: SI 1999/2721 Reg.61, Reg.82

Reg.6, revoked: SI 1999/2722 Reg.1

Reg.7, revoked: SI 1999/2722 Reg.1

1072. Merchant Shipping (Life-Saving Appliances) (Amendment) Regulations 1986

referred to: SI 1998/1609 Reg.5, Reg.6, Sch.

revoked: SI 1999/2721 Reg.1

1074. Merchant Shipping (Passenger Ship Construction) (New and Existing Ships) (Amendment) Regulations 1986

revoked: SI 1998/2514 Reg.1

1078. Road Vehicles (Construction and Use) Regulations 1986

Part IV, see *East West Transport Ltd v DPP* [1996] R.T.R. 184 (QBD), Rose, L.J.

Reg.3, amended: SI 1996/252 Art.2, Sch, SI 1996/2329 Reg.3, SI 1998/1188 Reg.3, SI 1998/3112 Reg.3

Reg.3, applied: SI 1999/2978 Reg.2

Reg.3A, added: SI 1996/3017 Reg.3

Reg.4 Table, amended: SI 1996/3133 Reg.3, SI 1997/530 Reg.3

Reg.7, amended: SI 1998/1188 Reg.4, SI 1998/3112 Reg.4

Reg.10, substituted: SI 1997/530 Reg.4, Sch.

Reg.10A, added: SI 1997/530 Reg.4, Sch.

Reg.10B, added: SI 1997/530 Reg.4, Sch.

Reg.10C, added: SI 1997/530 Reg.4, Sch.

Reg.10C, amended: SI 1998/1188 Reg.5

Reg.11, amended: SI 1998/1188 Reg.6

Reg.13, amended: SI 1998/1188 Reg.7

Reg.13A, amended: SI 1998/1188 Reg.8

Reg.13B, amended: SI 1998/1188 Reg.9

Reg.13C, amended: SI 1998/1188 Reg.10

Reg.15, amended: SI 1996/3033 Reg.3

Reg.16, amended: SI 1996/3033 Reg.4, SI 1998/2429 Reg.3

Reg.17, amended: SI 1998/2429 Reg.4

Reg.17A, added: SI 1996/3033 Reg.5

Reg.23, amended: SI 1998/3112 Reg.5

Reg.31, applied: SI 1996/3013 Sch.2 Item 14

Reg.32, applied: SI 1996/3013 Sch.2 Item 14

Reg.35, amended: SI 1998/1188 Reg.11

Reg.36A, amended: SI 1997/1340 Reg,3

Reg.36A, revoked (in part): SI 1997/1340 Reg.3

Reg.36B, amended: SI 1996/2064 Reg.3

Reg.39, applied: SI 1996/3013 Sch.2 Item 24, Sch.3 Item 7

Reg.46, amended: SI 1998/2429 Reg.6

Reg.47, amended: SI 1996/163 Reg.4, SI 1998/2429 Reg.6

Reg.47, applied: SI 1996/3013 Sch.2 Item 9

Reg.48A, added: SI 1996/163 Reg.5

Reg.49, amended: SI 1998/1188 Reg.12

Reg.53, applied: SI 1996/3013 Sch.2 Item 18

Reg.54, amended: SI 1996/2329 Reg.4

Reg.55, amended: SI 1996/2329 Reg.5

Reg.55A, added: SI 1996/2329 Reg.6

Reg.57A, amended: SI 1996/16 Reg.2

Reg.59, amended: SI 1996/2329 Reg.7

Reg.60, amended: SI 1996/2329 Reg.8

1986—cont.

1078. Road Vehicles (Construction and Use) Regulations 1986—*cont.*

Reg.61, amended: SI 1996/2085 Reg.3, SI 1996/2329 Reg.9, SI 1996/3017 Reg.4, SI 1997/2935 Reg.2, SI 1998/1000 Reg.2, SI 1998/1563 Reg.3

Reg.61, applied: SI 1996/960 Art.3, SI 1997/3058 Reg.4, Reg.5, Reg.9

Reg.61, revoked (in part): SI 1998/1563 Reg.3

Reg.61 Table II, substituted: SI 1997/1544 Reg.3, Sch.

Reg.66, amended: SI 1996/3017 Reg.5, SI 1998/3112 Reg.6

Reg.70, amended: SI 1998/3112 Reg.7

Reg.70A, amended: SI 1996/2064 Reg.4

Reg.70B, added: SI 1998/1188 Reg.13

Reg.71, amended: SI 1996/3033 Reg.6

Reg.71A, added: SI 1996/3033 Reg.7

Reg.75, amended: SI 1998/3112 Reg.8

Reg.75, applied: SI 1998/3111 Reg.4

Reg.76, applied: SI 1998/3111 Reg.4

Reg.77, applied: SI 1998/3111 Reg.4

Reg.78, applied: SI 1998/3111 Reg.4

Reg.79, applied: SI 1998/3111 Reg.4

Reg.79A, added: SI 1998/3112 Reg.9

Reg.80, amended: SI 1997/1096 Reg.3, SI 1998/3112 Reg.10

Reg.80, applied: SI 1998/3111 Reg.5

Reg.86B, added: SI 1998/1281 Reg.3

Reg.87, amended: SI 1996/3033 Reg.8

Reg.88, revoked: SI 1998/2429 Reg.7

Reg.89, amended: SI 1996/3033 Reg.9

Reg.93A, added: SI 1996/3133 Reg.4

Reg.98, amended: SI 1998/1 Reg.3

Reg.98, applied: SI 1997/3058 Reg.4, Reg.5, Reg.9

Sch.2 Table I, amended: SI 1996/2064 Reg.5, SI 1996/2329 Reg.10, SI 1996/3033 Reg.10, SI 1998/2429 Reg.8

Sch.2 Table II, amended: SI 1996/2329 Reg.10, SI 1996/3133 Reg.5

Sch.2 Item 69A, amended: SI 1998/1281 Reg.4

Sch.2 Item 74, added: SI 1998/1188 Reg.14

Sch.2 Item 75, added: SI 1998/1188 Reg.14

Sch.2 Item 76, added: SI 1998/1188 Reg.14

Sch.2 Item 77, added: SI 1998/1188 Reg.14

Sch.2A, added: SI 1996/3017 Reg.6, Sch.

Sch.7B, amended: SI 1996/2085 Reg.4

Sch.7B para.7, amended: SI 1997/1544 Reg.4, SI 1998/1563 Reg.4, SI 1999/1521 Reg.3

Sch.7XA, added: SI 1996/2329 Reg.11

Sch.11A, amended: SI 1997/1096 Reg.4

Sch.11A Part II, applied: SI 1998/3111 Reg.3

Sch.11A Part III, applied: SI 1998/3111 Reg.3

Sch.11A Part IIIA, applied: SI 1998/3111 Reg.3

Sch.11A para.2A, added: SI 1998/3112 Reg.11

Sch.11A para.8, substituted: SI 1998/3112 Reg.11

Sch.11A para.8A, added: SI 1998/3112 Reg.11

Sch.11A para.9, amended: SI 1997/1096 Reg.4

1081. Representation of the People Regulations 1986

referred to: 1997 c.61 Sch.3 Table 3, SI 1999/450 Art.4, Sch.1 para.4

Part V, applied: SI 1998/746 Art.13, Sch.2 Part III, SI 1999/450 Art.14, Sch.4 para.2

Reg.4, amended: SI 1998/746 Art.12, Sch.1 Table 4, SI 1999/1214 Reg.3, Reg.10, Reg.11, Sch.2

Reg.4, applied: 1997 c.61 Sch.3 Table 5, SI 1998/746 Art.12, Sch.1 Table 4, SI 1999/1214 Reg.3, Reg.10, Reg.11, Sch.2

1986—cont.

1081. Representation of the People Regulations 1986—*cont.*

Reg.6, amended: SI 1998/746 Art.12, Sch.1 Table 4, SI 1999/1214 Reg.3, Reg.10, Reg.11, Sch.2

Reg.6, applied: 1997 c.61 Sch.3 Table 5, SI 1998/746 Art.12, Sch.1 Table 4, SI 1999/1214 Reg.3, Reg.10, Reg.11, Sch.2

Reg.6, revoked (in part): SI 1999/1214 Reg.3, Sch.2

Reg.7, amended: SI 1998/746 Art.12, Sch.1 Table 4, SI 1999/1214 Reg.3, Reg.10, Reg.11, Sch.2

Reg.7, applied: 1997 c.61 Sch.3 Table 5, SI 1998/746 Art.12, Sch.1 Table 4, SI 1999/1214 Reg.3, Reg.10, Reg.11, Sch.2

Reg.8, amended: SI 1999/1214 Reg.3, Reg.10, Reg.11, Sch.2

Reg.8, applied: SI 1999/1214 Reg.3, Reg.10, Reg.11, Sch.2

Reg.9, amended: SI 1998/746 Art.12, Sch.1 Table 4, SI 1999/1214 Reg.3, Reg.10, Reg.11, Sch.2

Reg.9, applied: 1997 c.61 Sch.3 Table 5, SI 1998/746 Art.12, Sch.1 Table 4, SI 1999/1214 Reg.3, Reg.10, Reg.11, Sch.2

Reg.10, amended: SI 1999/1214 Reg.3, Reg.10, Reg.11, Sch.2

Reg.10, applied: SI 1999/1214 Reg.3, Reg.10, Reg.11, Sch.2

Reg.11, amended: 1997 c.61 Sch.3 Table 5, SI 1999/1214 Reg.3, Reg.10, Reg.11, Sch.2

Reg.11, applied: SI 1999/1214 Reg.3, Reg.10, Reg.11, Sch.2

Reg.12, amended: SI 1999/1214 Reg.3, Reg.10, Reg.11, Sch.2

Reg.12, applied: SI 1999/1214 Reg.3, Reg.10, Reg.11, Sch.2

Reg.12, revoked (in part): SI 1999/1214 Reg.3, Sch.2

Reg.13, amended: SI 1998/746 Art.12, Sch.1 Table 4, SI 1999/1214 Reg.3, Reg.10, Reg.11, Sch.2

Reg.13, applied: 1997 c.61 Sch.3 Table 5, SI 1998/746 Art.12, Sch.1 Table 4, SI 1999/1214 Reg.3, Reg.10, Reg.11, Sch.2

Reg.37, applied: SI 1999/450 Art.4, Sch.1 para.1

Reg.53, amended: SI 1999/1214 Reg.3, Reg.10, Reg.11, Sch.2

Reg.53, applied: SI 1999/1214 Reg.3, Reg.10, Reg.11, Sch.2

Reg.53, revoked (in part): SI 1999/1214 Reg.3, Sch.2

Reg.54, amended: SI 1999/450 Art.4, Sch.1 para.3, SI 1999/1214 Reg.3, Reg.10, Reg.11, Sch.2

Reg.54, applied: SI 1999/450 Art.4, Sch.1 para.3, SI 1999/1214 Reg.3, Reg.10, Reg.11, Sch.2

Reg.54, revoked (in part): SI 1999/1214 Reg.3, Sch.2

Reg.55, amended: SI 1999/1214 Reg.3, Reg.10, Reg.11, Sch.2

Reg.55, applied: SI 1999/450 Art.4, Sch.1 para.4, SI 1999/1214 Reg.3, Reg.10, Reg.11, Sch.2

Reg.55, revoked (in part): SI 1999/1214 Reg.3, Sch.2

Reg.56, amended: SI 1999/1214 Reg.3, Reg.10, Reg.11, Sch.2

1986—cont.

1081. Representation of the People Regulations 1986—*cont.*

Reg.56, applied: SI 1999/450 Art.4, Sch.1 para.5, SI 1999/1214 Reg.3, Reg.10, Reg.11, Sch.2

Reg.56, revoked (in part): SI 1999/1214 Reg.3, Sch.2

Reg.58, applied: SI 1999/450 Art.4, Sch.1 para.6

Reg.62, applied: SI 1999/450 Art.4, Sch.1 para.6

Reg.63, amended: SI 1998/746 Art.12, Sch.1 Table 4, SI 1999/1214 Reg.3, Reg.10, Reg.11, Sch.2

Reg.63, applied: 1997 c.61 Sch.3 Table 5, SI 1998/746 Art.12, Sch.1 Table 4, SI 1999/1214 Reg.3, Reg.10, Reg.11, Sch.2

Reg.63, revoked (in part): SI 1999/1214 Reg.3, Sch.2

Reg.63A, amended: SI 1999/1214 Reg.3, Reg.10, Reg.11, Sch.2

Reg.63A, applied: SI 1999/1214 Reg.3, Reg.10, Reg.11, Sch.2

Reg.64, amended: SI 1997/880 Reg.4, SI 1999/1214 Reg.3, Reg.10, Reg.11, Sch.2

Reg.64, applied: SI 1999/1214 Reg.3, Reg.10, Reg.11, Sch.2

Reg.64, revoked (in part): SI 1997/880 Reg.4

Reg.65, amended: SI 1999/1214 Reg.3, Reg.10, Reg.11, Sch.2

Reg.65, applied: SI 1999/1214 Reg.3, Reg.10, Reg.11, Sch.2

Reg.66, amended: SI 1997/880 Reg.5, SI 1998/746 Art.12, Sch.1 Table 4, SI 1999/1214 Reg.3, Reg.10, Reg.11, Sch.2

Reg.66, applied: 1997 c.61 Sch.3 Table 5, SI 1998/746 Art.12, Sch.1 Table 4, SI 1999/1214 Reg.3, Reg.10, Reg.11, Sch.2

Reg.67, amended: SI 1998/746 Art.12, Sch.1 Table 4, SI 1999/1214 Reg.3, Sch.2

Reg.67, applied: 1997 c.61 Sch.3 Table 5, SI 1998/746 Art.12, Sch.1 Table 4, SI 1999/1214 Reg.3, Sch.2

Reg.68, amended: SI 1998/746 Art.12, Sch.1 Table 4, SI 1999/1214 Reg.3, Sch.2

Reg.68, applied: 1997 c.61 Sch.3 Table 5, SI 1998/746 Art.12, Sch.1 Table 4, SI 1999/1214 Reg.3, Sch.2

Reg.69, amended: SI 1997/880 Reg.5, SI 1998/746 Art.12, Sch.1 Table 4, SI 1999/1214 Reg.3, Sch.2

Reg.69, applied: 1997 c.61 Sch.3 Table 5, SI 1998/746 Art.12, Sch.1 Table 4, SI 1999/1214 Reg.3, Sch.2

Reg.70, amended: SI 1998/746 Art.12, Sch.1 Table 4, SI 1999/1214 Reg.3, Sch.2

Reg.70, applied: SI 1998/746 Art.12, Sch.1 Table 4, SI 1999/1214 Reg.3, Sch.2

Reg.70, referred to: 1997 c.61 Sch.3 Table 5

Reg.71, amended: SI 1999/1214 Reg.3, Reg.10, Reg.11, Sch.2

Reg.71, applied: SI 1999/1214 Reg.3, Reg.10, Reg.11, Sch.2

Reg.72, amended: SI 1998/746 Art.12, Sch.1 Table 4, SI 1999/1214 Reg.3, Reg.10, Reg.11, Sch.2

Reg.72, applied: 1997 c.61 Sch.3 Table 5, SI 1998/746 Art.12, Sch.1 Table 4, SI 1999/1214 Reg.3, Reg.10, Reg.11, Sch.2

Reg.73, amended: SI 1999/1214 Reg.3, Reg.10, Reg.11, Sch.2

Reg.73, applied: SI 1999/1214 Reg.3, Reg.10, Reg.11, Sch.2

1986—cont.

1081. Representation of the People Regulations 1986—*cont.*

Reg.73, revoked (in part): SI 1999/1214 Reg.3, Sch.2

Reg.74, amended: SI 1998/746 Art.12, Sch.1 Table 4, SI 1999/1214 Reg.3, Reg.10, Reg.11, Sch.2

Reg.74, applied: 1997 c.61 Sch.3 Table 5, SI 1998/746 Art.12, Sch.1 Table 4, SI 1999/1214 Reg.3, Reg.10, Reg.11, Sch.2

Reg.75, amended: SI 1998/746 Art.12, Sch.1 Table 4, SI 1999/1214 Reg.3, Reg.10, Reg.11, Sch.2

Reg.75, applied: 1997 c.61 Sch.3 Table 5, SI 1998/746 Art.12, Sch.1 Table 4, SI 1999/1214 Reg.3, Reg.10, Reg.11, Sch.2

Reg.76, amended: SI 1999/1214 Reg.3, Reg.10, Reg.11, Sch.2

Reg.76, applied: SI 1999/1214 Reg.3, Reg.10, Reg.11, Sch.2

Reg.76, referred to: 1997 c.61 Sch.3 Table 5

Reg.77, amended: SI 1998/746 Art.12, Sch.1 Table 4, SI 1999/1214 Reg.3, Reg.10, Reg.11, Sch.2

Reg.77, applied: 1997 c.61 Sch.3 Table 5, SI 1998/746 Art.12, Sch.1 Table 4, SI 1999/1214 Reg.3, Reg.10, Reg.11, Sch.2

Reg.78, amended: SI 1999/1214 Reg.3, Reg.10, Reg.11, Sch.2

Reg.78, applied: SI 1999/1214 Reg.3, Reg.10, Reg.11, Sch.2

Reg.79, amended: 1997 c.61 Sch.3 Table 5, SI 1999/1214 Reg.3, Reg.10, Reg.11, Sch.2

Reg.79, applied: SI 1999/1214 Reg.3, Reg.10, Reg.11, Sch.2

Reg.80, amended: SI 1998/746 Art.12, Sch.1 Table 4, SI 1999/1214 Reg.3, Reg.10, Reg.11, Sch.2

Reg.80, applied: 1997 c.61 Sch.3 Table 5, SI 1998/746 Art.12, Sch.1 Table 4, SI 1999/1214 Reg.3, Reg.10, Reg.11, Sch.2

Reg.80, referred to: SI 1998/746 Art.13, Sch.2 Part III

Reg.80, revoked (in part): SI 1999/1214 Reg.3, Sch.2

Reg.81, amended: SI 1998/746 Art.12, Sch.1 Table 4, SI 1999/1214 Reg.3, Reg.10, Reg.11, Sch.2

Reg.81, applied: 1997 c.61 Sch.3 Table 5, SI 1998/746 Art.12, Sch.1 Table 4, SI 1999/1214 Reg.3, Reg.10, Reg.11, Sch.2

Reg.82, amended: SI 1999/1214 Reg.3, Reg.10, Reg.11, Sch.2

Reg.82, applied: SI 1999/1214 Reg.3, Reg.10, Reg.11, Sch.2

Reg.83, amended: SI 1998/746 Art.12, Sch.1 Table 4, SI 1999/1214 Reg.3, Reg.10, Reg.11, Sch.2

Reg.83, applied: 1997 c.61 Sch.3 Table 5, SI 1998/746 Art.12, Art.13, Sch.1 Table 4, Sch.2 Part III, SI 1999/1214 Reg.3, Reg.10, Reg.11, Sch.2

Reg.84, amended: SI 1998/746 Art.12, Sch.1 Table 4, SI 1999/1214 Reg.3, Reg.10, Reg.11, Sch.2

Reg.84, applied: 1997 c.61 Sch.3 Table 5, SI 1998/746 Art.12, Sch.1 Table 4, SI 1999/1214 Reg.3, Reg.10, Reg.11, Sch.2

Reg.85, amended: SI 1998/746 Art.12, Art.13, Sch.1 Table 4, Sch.2 Part III, SI 1999/1214 Reg.3, Reg.10, Reg.11, Sch.2

NO.

1081. Representation of the People Regulations 1986—*cont.*

Reg.85, applied: 1997 c.61 Sch.3 Table 5, SI 1998/746 Art.12, Art.13, Sch.1 Table 4, Sch.2 Part III, SI 1999/1214 Reg.3, Reg.10, Reg.11, Sch.2

Reg.86, amended: SI 1998/746 Art.12, Sch.1 Table 4, SI 1999/1214 Reg.3, Reg.10, Reg.11, Sch.2

Reg.86, applied: 1997 c.61 Sch.3 Table 5, SI 1998/746 Art.12, Sch.1 Table 4, SI 1999/1214 Reg.3, Reg.10, Reg.11, Sch.2

Reg.87, amended: 1997 c.61 Sch.3 Table 5, SI 1998/746 Art.12, Sch.1 Table 4, SI 1999/1214 Reg.3, Reg.10, Reg.11, Sch.2

Reg.87, applied: SI 1998/746 Art.12, Sch.1 Table 4, SI 1999/1214 Reg.3, Reg.10, Reg.11, Sch.2

Reg.88, amended: SI 1998/746 Art.12, Sch.1 Table 4, SI 1999/1214 Reg.3, Reg.10, Reg.11, Sch.2

Reg.88, applied: 1997 c.61 Sch.3 Table 5, SI 1998/746 Art.12, Sch.1 Table 4, SI 1999/1214 Reg.3, Reg.10, Reg.11, Sch.2

Reg.89, amended: SI 1998/746 Art.12, Sch.1 Table 4, SI 1999/1214 Reg.3, Reg.10, Reg.11, Sch.2

Reg.89, applied: SI 1998/746 Art.12, Art.13, Sch.1 Table 4, Sch.2 Part III, SI 1999/1214 Reg.3, Reg.10, Reg.11, Sch.2

Reg.89, revoked (in part): 1997 c.61 Sch.3 Table 5, SI 1998/746 Art.12, Sch.1 Table 4

Reg.90, amended: SI 1998/746 Art.12, Sch.1 Table 4, SI 1999/1214 Reg.3, Reg.10, Reg.11, Sch.2

Reg.90, applied: 1997 c.61 Sch.3 Table 5, SI 1998/746 Art.12, Sch.1 Table 4, SI 1999/1214 Reg.3, Reg.10, Reg.11, Sch.2

Reg.91, amended: 1997 c.61 Sch.3 Table 5, SI 1998/746 Art.12, Sch.1 Table 4, SI 1999/1214 Reg.3, Reg.10, Reg.11, Sch.2

Reg.91, applied: SI 1998/746 Art.12, Sch.1 Table 4, SI 1999/1214 Reg.3, Reg.10, Reg.11, Sch.2

Reg.91, referred to: SI 1998/746 Art.13, Sch.2 Part III

Reg.91, revoked (in part): SI 1998/746 Art.12, Sch.1 Table 4

Reg.92, amended: SI 1998/746 Art.12, Art.13, Sch.1 Table 4, Sch.2 Part III, SI 1999/1214 Reg.3, Reg.10, Reg.11, Sch.2

Reg.92, applied: 1997 c.61 Sch.3 Table 5, SI 1998/746 Art.12, Art.13, Sch.1 Table 4, Sch.2 Part III, SI 1999/1214 Reg.3, Reg.10, Reg.11, Sch.2

Reg.93, amended: SI 1998/746 Art.12, Sch.1 Table 4, SI 1999/1214 Reg.3, Reg.10, Reg.11, Sch.2

Reg.93, applied: 1997 c.61 Sch.3 Table 5, SI 1998/746 Art.12, Sch.1 Table 4, SI 1999/1214 Reg.3, Reg.10, Reg.11, Sch.2

Reg.94, amended: SI 1998/746 Art.12, Art.13, Sch.1 Table 4, Sch.2 Part III, SI 1999/1214 Reg.3, Reg.10, Reg.11, Sch.2

Reg.94, applied: 1997 c.61 Sch.3 Table 5, SI 1998/746 Art.12, Art.13, Sch.1 Table 4, Sch.2 Part III, SI 1999/1214 Reg.3, Reg.10, Reg.11, Sch.2

Reg.96, amended: 1997 c.61 Sch.3 Table 5, SI 1998/746 Art.12, Sch.1 Table 4, SI 1999/1214 Reg.3, Reg.10, Reg.11, Sch.2

Reg.96, applied: SI 1998/746 Art.12, Sch.1 Table 4, SI 1999/1214 Reg.3, Reg.10, Reg.11, Sch.2

NO.

1081. Representation of the People Regulations 1986—*cont.*

Reg.96, revoked (in part): 1997 c.61 Sch.3 Table 5, SI 1998/746 Art.12, Sch.1 Table 4

Sch.1 Table 4, referred to: SI 1998/746 Art.13, Sch.2 Part III

Sch.2 Form D, amended: SI 1998/746 Art.12, Sch.1 Table 4, SI 1999/1214 Reg.9, Sch.4 Part I, Sch.4 Part II

Sch.2 Form D, applied: SI 1998/746 Art.12, Sch.1 Table 4

Sch.2 Form E, amended: SI 1999/1214 Reg.3, Reg.10, Reg.11, Sch.2

Sch.2 Form E, applied: SI 1999/1214 Reg.3, Reg.10, Reg.11, Sch.2

Sch.2 Form F, amended: SI 1999/1214 Reg.3, Reg.10, Reg.11, Sch.2

Sch.2 Form F, applied: SI 1999/1214 Reg.3, Reg.10, Reg.11, Sch.2

Sch.2 Form G, amended: SI 1999/1214 Reg.3, Reg.10, Reg.11, Sch.2

Sch.2 Form G, applied: SI 1999/1214 Reg.3, Reg.10, Reg.11, Sch.2

Sch.2 Form H, amended: SI 1999/1214 Reg.3, Reg.10, Reg.11, Sch.2

Sch.2 Form H, applied: SI 1999/1214 Reg.3, Reg.10, Reg.11, Sch.2

Sch.2 Form J, amended: SI 1999/1214 Reg.3, Reg.10, Reg.11, Sch.2

Sch.2 Form J, applied: SI 1999/1214 Reg.3, Reg.10, Reg.11, Sch.2

Sch.2 Form K, amended: SI 1999/1214 Reg.3, Reg.10, Reg.11, Sch.2

Sch.2 Form K, applied: SI 1999/1214 Reg.3, Reg.10, Reg.11, Sch.2

Sch.2 Form N, amended: SI 1999/1214 Reg.3, Reg.10, Reg.11, Sch.2

Sch.2 Form N, applied: SI 1999/1214 Reg.3, Reg.10, Reg.11, Sch.2

1091. Representation of the People (Northern Ireland) Regulations 1986

applied: SI 1996/1220 Art.3

Reg.4, amended: SI 1996/1220 Art.3, Sch.2, SI 1998/1126 Art.6, Sch.3, SI 1998/1287 Art.3, Sch.2

Reg.4, applied: SI 1998/1126 Art.6, Sch.3, SI 1998/1287 Art.3, Sch.2

Reg.5, amended: SI 1996/1220 Art.3, Sch.2, SI 1998/1126 Art.6, Sch.3, SI 1998/1287 Art.3, Sch.2

Reg.5, applied: SI 1998/1126 Art.6, Sch.3, SI 1998/1287 Art.3, Sch.2

Reg.5, revoked (in part): SI 1998/1126 Art.6, Sch.3, SI 1998/1287 Art.3, Sch.2

Reg.6, amended: SI 1998/1126 Art.6, Sch.3, SI 1998/1287 Art.3, Sch.2

Reg.6, applied: SI 1996/1220 Art.3, Sch.2, SI 1998/1126 Art.6, Sch.3, SI 1998/1287 Art.3, Sch.2

Reg.7, amended: SI 1998/1126 Art.6, Sch.3, SI 1998/1287 Art.3, Sch.2

Reg.7, applied: SI 1996/1220 Art.3, Sch.2, SI 1998/1126 Art.6, Sch.3, SI 1998/1287 Art.3, Sch.2

Reg.8, amended: SI 1998/1126 Art.6, Sch.3, SI 1998/1287 Art.3, Sch.2

Reg.8, applied: SI 1996/1220 Art.3, Sch.2, SI 1998/1126 Art.6, Sch.3, SI 1998/1287 Art.3, Sch.2

Reg.9, amended: SI 1998/1287 Art.3, Sch.2

Reg.9, applied: SI 1996/1220 Art.3, Sch.2, SI 1998/1287 Art.3, Sch.2

Reg.10, applied: SI 1996/1220 Art.3, Sch.2

Reg.11, amended: SI 1998/1287 Art.3, Sch.2

1986—cont.

1091. Representation of the People (Northern Ireland) Regulations 1986—*cont.*
Reg.11, applied: SI 1996/1220 Art.3, Sch.2, SI 1998/1287 Art.3, Sch.2
Reg.12, amended: SI 1998/1126 Art.6, Sch.3, SI 1998/1287 Art.3, Sch.2
Reg.12, applied: SI 1996/1220 Art.3, Sch.2, SI 1998/1126 Art.6, Sch.3, SI 1998/1287 Art.3, Sch.2
Reg.53, amended: SI 1996/1220 Art.3, Sch.2, SI 1998/1287 Art.3, Sch.2
Reg.53, applied: SI 1998/1287 Art.3, Sch.2
Reg.53, revoked (in part): SI 1998/1287 Art.3, Sch.2
Reg.54, amended: SI 1996/1220 Art.3, Sch.2, SI 1998/1287 Art.3, Sch.2
Reg.54, applied: SI 1998/1287 Art.3, Sch.2
Reg.54, revoked (in part): SI 1998/1287 Art.3, Sch.2
Reg.55, amended: SI 1996/1220 Art.3, Sch.2, SI 1998/1287 Art.3, Sch.2
Reg.55, applied: SI 1998/1287 Art.3, Sch.2
Reg.55, revoked (in part): SI 1998/1287 Art.3, Sch.2
Reg.56, amended: SI 1996/1220 Art.3, Sch.2, SI 1998/1287 Art.3, Sch.2
Reg.56, applied: SI 1998/1287 Art.3, Sch.2
Reg.56, revoked (in part): SI 1998/1287 Art.3, Sch.2
Reg.63, amended: SI 1998/1126 Art.6, Sch.3, SI 1998/1287 Art.3, Sch.2
Reg.63, applied: SI 1996/1220 Art.3, Sch.2, SI 1998/1126 Art.6, Sch.3, SI 1998/1287 Art.3, Sch.2
Reg.64, amended: SI 1997/967 Reg.4, SI 1998/1287 Art.3, Sch.2
Reg.64, applied: SI 1998/1287 Art.3, Sch.2
Reg.64, revoked (in part): SI 1997/967 Reg.4
Reg.66, amended: SI 1997/967 Reg.5, SI 1998/1126 Art.6, Sch.3, SI 1998/1287 Art.3, Sch.2, SI 1998/2870 Reg.2
Reg.66, applied: SI 1996/1220 Art.3, Sch.2, SI 1998/1126 Art.6, Sch.3, SI 1998/1287 Art.3, Sch.2
Reg.67, amended: SI 1998/1126 Art.6, Sch.3, SI 1998/1287 Art.3, Sch.2
Reg.67, applied: SI 1996/1220 Art.3, Sch.2, SI 1998/1126 Art.6, Sch.3, SI 1998/1287 Art.3, Sch.2
Reg.68, amended: SI 1998/1126 Art.6, Sch.3, SI 1998/1287 Art.3, Sch.2
Reg.68, applied: SI 1996/1220 Art.3, Sch.2, SI 1998/1126 Art.6, Sch.3, SI 1998/1287 Art.3, Sch.2
Reg.69, amended: SI 1996/1220 Art.3, Sch.2, SI 1997/967 Reg.5, SI 1998/1126 Art.6, Sch.3, SI 1998/1287 Art.3, Sch.2, SI 1998/2870 Reg.3
Reg.69, applied: SI 1998/1126 Art.6, Sch.3, SI 1998/1287 Art.3, Sch.2
Reg.69, revoked (in part): SI 1998/1126 Art.6, Sch.3
Reg.70, amended: SI 1996/1220 Art.3, Sch.2, SI 1998/1126 Art.6, Sch.3, SI 1998/1287 Art.3, Sch.2
Reg.70, applied: SI 1998/1126 Art.6, Sch.3, SI 1998/1287 Art.3, Sch.2
Reg.70, revoked (in part): SI 1998/1126 Art.6, Sch.3, SI 1998/1287 Art.3, Sch.2
Reg.72, applied: SI 1996/1220 Art.3, Sch.2
Reg.74, amended: SI 1996/1220 Art.3, Sch.2, SI 1998/1126 Art.6, Sch.3, SI 1998/1287 Art.3, Sch.2

1986—cont.

1091. Representation of the People (Northern Ireland) Regulations 1986—*cont.*
Reg.74, applied: SI 1998/1126 Art.6, Sch.3, SI 1998/1287 Art.3, Sch.2
Reg.74, revoked (in part): SI 1998/1126 Art.6, Sch.3, SI 1998/1287 Art.3, Sch.2
Reg.75, amended: SI 1998/1126 Art.6, Sch.3, SI 1998/1287 Art.3, Sch.2
Reg.75, applied: SI 1996/1220 Art.3, Sch.2, SI 1998/1126 Art.6, Sch.3, SI 1998/1287 Art.3, Sch.2
Reg.76, amended: SI 1998/1126 Art.6, Sch.3, SI 1998/1287 Art.3, Sch.2
Reg.76, applied: SI 1996/1220 Art.3, Sch.2, SI 1998/1126 Art.6, Sch.3, SI 1998/1287 Art.3, Sch.2
Reg.77, amended: SI 1998/1126 Art.6, Sch.3, SI 1998/1287 Art.3, Sch.2
Reg.77, applied: SI 1996/1220 Art.3, Sch.2, SI 1998/1126 Art.6, Sch.3, SI 1998/1287 Art.3, Sch.2
Reg.78, amended: SI 1998/2870 Reg.4
Reg.78, applied: SI 1996/1220 Art.3, Sch.2
Reg.79, amended: SI 1996/1220 Art.3, Sch.2, SI 1998/1126 Art.6, Sch.3, SI 1998/1287 Art.3, Sch.2
Reg.79, applied: SI 1998/1126 Art.6, Sch.3, SI 1998/1287 Art.3, Sch.2
Reg.79, revoked (in part): SI 1998/1126 Art.6, Sch.3
Reg.80, amended: SI 1998/1126 Art.6, Sch.3, SI 1998/1287 Art.3, Sch.2
Reg.80, applied: SI 1996/1220 Art.3, Sch.2, SI 1998/1126 Art.6, Sch.3, SI 1998/1287 Art.3, Sch.2
Reg.81, amended: SI 1996/1220 Art.3, Sch.2, SI 1998/1126 Art.6, Sch.3, SI 1998/1287 Art.3, Sch.2
Reg.81, applied: SI 1998/1126 Art.6, Sch.3, SI 1998/1287 Art.3, Sch.2
Reg.82, amended: SI 1998/1126 Art.6, Sch.3, SI 1998/1287 Art.3, Sch.2
Reg.82, applied: SI 1996/1220 Art.3, Sch.2, SI 1998/1126 Art.6, Sch.3, SI 1998/1287 Art.3, Sch.2
Reg.83, amended: SI 1998/1126 Art.6, Sch.3, SI 1998/1287 Art.3, Sch.2
Reg.83, applied: SI 1996/1220 Art.3, Sch.2, SI 1998/1126 Art.6, Sch.3, SI 1998/1287 Art.3, Sch.2
Reg.84, amended: SI 1998/1126 Art.6, Sch.3, SI 1998/1287 Art.3, Sch.2
Reg.84, applied: SI 1996/1220 Art.3, Sch.2, SI 1998/1126 Art.6, Sch.3, SI 1998/1287 Art.3, Sch.2
Reg.85, amended: SI 1998/1126 Art.6, Sch.3, SI 1998/1287 Art.3, Sch.2
Reg.85, applied: SI 1996/1220 Art.3, Sch.2, SI 1998/1126 Art.6, Sch.3, SI 1998/1287 Art.3, Sch.2
Reg.86, amended: SI 1998/1126 Art.6, Sch.3, SI 1998/1287 Art.3, Sch.2
Reg.86, applied: SI 1996/1220 Art.3, Sch.2, SI 1998/1126 Art.6, Sch.3, SI 1998/1287 Art.3, Sch.2
Reg.87, amended: SI 1998/1126 Art.6, Sch.3, SI 1998/1287 Art.3, Sch.2
Reg.87, applied: SI 1996/1220 Art.3, Sch.2, SI 1998/1126 Art.6, Sch.3, SI 1998/1287 Art.3, Sch.2
Reg.88, amended: SI 1998/1126 Art.6, Sch.3, SI 1998/1287 Art.3, Sch.2

NO.

1091. Representation of the People (Northern Ireland) Regulations 1986—*cont.*

Reg.88, applied: SI 1996/1220 Art.3, Sch.2, SI 1998/1126 Art.6, Sch.3, SI 1998/1287 Art.3, Sch.2

Reg.89, amended: SI 1998/1126 Art.6, Sch.3, SI 1998/1287 Art.3, Sch.2

Reg.89, applied: SI 1996/1220 Art.3, Sch.2, SI 1998/1126 Art.6, Sch.3, SI 1998/1287 Art.3, Sch.2

Reg.90, amended: SI 1996/1220 Art.3, Sch.2, SI 1998/1126 Art.6, Sch.3, SI 1998/1287 Art.3, Sch.2

Reg.90, applied: SI 1998/1126 Art.6, Sch.3, SI 1998/1287 Art.3, Sch.2

Reg.91, amended: SI 1998/1126 Art.6, Sch.3, SI 1998/1287 Art.3, Sch.2

Reg.91, applied: SI 1996/1220 Art.3, Sch.2, SI 1998/1126 Art.6, Sch.3, SI 1998/1287 Art.3, Sch.2

Reg.92, amended: SI 1998/1126 Art.6, Sch.3, SI 1998/1287 Art.3, Sch.2

Reg.92, applied: SI 1996/1220 Art.3, Sch.2, SI 1998/1126 Art.6, Sch.3, SI 1998/1287 Art.3, Sch.2

Reg.93, amended: SI 1998/1126 Art.6, Sch.3, SI 1998/1287 Art.3, Sch.2

Reg.93, applied: SI 1996/1220 Art.3, Sch.2, SI 1998/1126 Art.6, Sch.3, SI 1998/1287 Art.3, Sch.2

Reg.94, amended: SI 1998/1287 Art.3, Sch.2

Reg.94, applied: SI 1998/1287 Art.3, Sch.2

Reg.95, amended: SI 1996/1220 Art.3, Sch.2, SI 1998/1126 Art.6, Sch.3, SI 1998/1287 Art.3, Sch.2

Reg.95, applied: SI 1998/1126 Art.6, Sch.3, SI 1998/1287 Art.3, Sch.2

Reg.95, revoked (in part): SI 1998/1126 Art.6, Sch.3

Sch.2 Form E, amended: SI 1996/1220 Art.3, Sch.2, SI 1998/1126 Art.6, Sch.3, SI 1998/1287 Art.3, Sch.2

Sch.2 Form E, applied: SI 1998/1126 Art.6, Sch.3, SI 1998/1287 Art.3, Sch.2

Sch.2 Form F, amended: SI 1996/1220 Art.3, Sch.2, SI 1998/1126 Art.6, Sch.3, SI 1998/1287 Art.3, Sch.2

Sch.2 Form F, applied: SI 1998/1126 Art.6, Sch.3, SI 1998/1287 Art.3, Sch.2

Sch.2 Form G, amended: SI 1996/1220 Art.3, SI 1998/1126 Art.6, Sch.3, SI 1998/1287 Art.3, Sch.2

Sch.2 Form G, applied: SI 1996/1220 Art.3, Sch.2, SI 1998/1126 Art.6, Sch.3, SI 1998/1287 Art.3, Sch.2

Sch.2 Form H, amended: SI 1996/1220 Art.3, Sch.2, SI 1998/1126 Art.6, Sch.3, SI 1998/1287 Art.3, Sch.2

Sch.2 Form H, applied: SI 1998/1126 Art.6, Sch.3, SI 1998/1287 Art.3, Sch.2

Sch.2 Form J, amended: SI 1996/1220 Art.3, Sch.2, SI 1998/1287 Art.3, Sch.2

Sch.2 Form J, applied: SI 1998/1287 Art.3, Sch.2

Sch.2 Form K, amended: SI 1996/1220 Art.3, Sch.2, SI 1998/1287 Art.3, Sch.2

Sch.2 Form K, applied: SI 1998/1287 Art.3, Sch.2

Sch.2 Form L, amended: SI 1998/1287 Art.3, Sch.2

Sch.2 Form L, applied: SI 1998/1287 Art.3, Sch.2

NO.

1110. Horticultural Development Council Order 1986

applied: SI 1999/672 Art.2, Sch.1, SI 1999/1747 Art.3, Sch.14 para.3

Art.3, referred to: SI 1999/1319 Sch.

1111. Representation of the People (Scotland) Regulations 1986

referred to: 1997 c.61 Sch.3 Table 3, SI 1999/787 Art.3, Sch.1 para.4

Part V, applied: SI 1999/787 Art.13, Sch.5 para.2

Reg.4, amended: SI 1996/739 Art.7, Sch.1 para.10, SI 1999/1214 Reg.3, Reg.10, Reg.11, Sch.2

Reg.4, applied: 1997 c.61 Sch.3 Table 4, SI 1999/1214 Reg.3, Reg.10, Reg.11, Sch.2

Reg.5, amended: SI 1999/1214 Reg.3, Reg.10, Reg.11, Sch.2

Reg.5, applied: 1997 c.61 Sch.3 Table 4, SI 1999/1214 Reg.3, Reg.10, Reg.11, Sch.2

Reg.5, revoked (in part): SI 1999/1214 Reg.3, Sch.2

Reg.6, amended: SI 1999/1214 Reg.3, Reg.10, Reg.11, Sch.2

Reg.6, applied: 1997 c.61 Sch.3 Table 4, SI 1999/1214 Reg.3, Reg.10, Reg.11, Sch.2

Reg.7, amended: SI 1999/1214 Reg.3, Reg.10, Reg.11, Sch.2

Reg.7, applied: SI 1999/1214 Reg.3, Reg.10, Reg.11, Sch.2

Reg.8, amended: SI 1999/1214 Reg.3, Reg.10, Reg.11, Sch.2

Reg.8, applied: 1997 c.61 Sch.3 Table 4, SI 1999/1214 Reg.3, Reg.10, Reg.11, Sch.2

Reg.9, amended: SI 1999/1214 Reg.3, Reg.10, Reg.11, Sch.2

Reg.9, applied: SI 1999/1214 Reg.3, Reg.10, Reg.11, Sch.2

Reg.10, amended: SI 1999/1214 Reg.3, Reg.10, Reg.11, Sch.2

Reg.10, applied: 1997 c.61 Sch.3 Table 4, SI 1999/1214 Reg.3, Reg.10, Reg.11, Sch.2

Reg.11, amended: SI 1999/1214 Reg.3, Reg.10, Reg.11, Sch.2

Reg.11, applied: SI 1999/1214 Reg.3, Reg.10, Reg.11, Sch.2

Reg.11, revoked (in part): SI 1999/1214 Reg.3, Sch.2

Reg.12, amended: SI 1999/1214 Reg.3, Reg.10, Reg.11, Sch.2

Reg.12, applied: 1997 c.61 Sch.3 Table 4, SI 1999/1214 Reg.3, Reg.10, Reg.11, Sch.2

Reg.43, amended: SI 1996/739 Art.7, Sch.1 para.10

Reg.43, applied: SI 1999/1512 Art.2, Sch.1 para.6

Reg.50, amended: SI 1996/739 Art.7, Sch.1 para.10

Reg.51, amended: SI 1996/739 Art.7, Sch.1 para.10, SI 1999/1214 Reg.3, Reg.10, Reg.11, Sch.2

Reg.51, applied: SI 1999/1214 Reg.3, Reg.10, Reg.11, Sch.2, SI 1999/1512 Art.2, Sch.1 para.7

Reg.51, revoked (in part): SI 1996/739 Art.7, Sch.1 para.10, SI 1999/1214 Reg.3, Sch.2

Reg.52, amended: SI 1999/787 Art.3, Sch.1 para.3, SI 1999/1214 Reg.3, Reg.10, Reg.11, Sch.2

Reg.52, applied: SI 1999/787 Art.3, Sch.1 para.3, SI 1999/1214 Reg.3, Reg.10, Reg.11, Sch.2

Reg.52, revoked (in part): SI 1999/1214 Reg.3, Sch.2

1986—cont.

1111. Representation of the People (Scotland) Regulations 1986—*cont.*

Reg.53, amended: SI 1999/1214 Reg.3, Reg.10, Reg.11, Sch.2

Reg.53, applied: SI 1999/1214 Reg.3, Reg.10, Reg.11, Sch.2

Reg.53, revoked (in part): SI 1999/1214 Reg.3, Sch.2

Reg.54, amended: SI 1999/1214 Reg.3, Reg.10, Reg.11, Sch.2

Reg.54, applied: SI 1999/1214 Reg.3, Reg.10, Reg.11, Sch.2

Reg.54, revoked (in part): SI 1999/1214 Reg.3, Sch.2

Reg.55, applied: SI 1999/1512 Art.2, Sch.1 para.6

Reg.56, amended: SI 1999/787 Art.3, Sch.1 para.6

Reg.56, applied: SI 1999/787 Art.3, Sch.1 para.6

Reg.60, amended: SI 1999/787 Art.3, Sch.1 para.6

Reg.60, applied: SI 1999/787 Art.3, Sch.1 para.6

Reg.61, amended: SI 1999/1214 Reg.3, Reg.10, Reg.11, Sch.2

Reg.61, applied: 1997 c.61 Sch.3 Table 4, SI 1999/1214 Reg.3, Reg.10, Reg.11, Sch.2

Reg.61, revoked (in part): SI 1999/1214 Reg.3, Sch.2

Reg.61A, amended: SI 1999/1214 Reg.3, Reg.10, Reg.11, Sch.2

Reg.61A, applied: SI 1999/1214 Reg.3, Reg.10, Reg.11, Sch.2

Reg.62, amended: SI 1997/979 Reg.4, SI 1999/1214 Reg.3, Reg.10, Reg.11, Sch.2

Reg.62, applied: SI 1999/1214 Reg.3, Reg.10, Reg.11, Sch.2

Reg.63, amended: SI 1999/1214 Reg.3, Reg.10, Reg.11, Sch.2

Reg.63, applied: SI 1999/1214 Reg.3, Reg.10, Reg.11, Sch.2

Reg.64, amended: SI 1997/979 Reg.5, SI 1999/1214 Reg.3, Reg.10, Reg.11, Sch.2

Reg.64, applied: 1997 c.61 Sch.3 Table 4, SI 1999/1214 Reg.3, Reg.10, Reg.11, Sch.2

Reg.65, amended: SI 1999/1214 Reg.3, Reg.10, Reg.11, Sch.2

Reg.65, applied: 1997 c.61 Sch.3 Table 4, SI 1999/1214 Reg.3, Reg.10, Reg.11, Sch.2

Reg.66, amended: SI 1999/1214 Reg.3, Reg.10, Reg.11, Sch.2

Reg.66, applied: 1997 c.61 Sch.3 Table 4, SI 1999/1214 Reg.3, Reg.10, Reg.11, Sch.2

Reg.67, amended: SI 1997/979 Reg.5, SI 1999/1214 Reg.3, Sch.2

Reg.67, applied: 1997 c.61 Sch.3 Table 4, SI 1999/1214 Reg.3, Sch.2

Reg.68, amended: SI 1999/1214 Reg.3, Sch.2

Reg.68, applied: SI 1999/1214 Reg.3, Sch.2

Reg.68, referred to: 1997 c.61 Sch.3 Table 4

Reg.69, amended: SI 1999/1214 Reg.3, Sch.2

Reg.69, applied: SI 1999/1214 Reg.3, Sch.2

Reg.70, amended: SI 1999/1214 Reg.3, Sch.2

Reg.70, applied: 1997 c.61 Sch.3 Table 4, SI 1999/1214 Reg.3, Sch.2

Reg.71, amended: SI 1999/1214 Reg.3, Reg.10, Reg.11, Sch.2

Reg.71, applied: SI 1999/1214 Reg.3, Reg.10, Reg.11, Sch.2

Reg.72, amended: SI 1999/1214 Reg.3, Reg.10, Reg.11, Sch.2

Reg.72, applied: 1997 c.61 Sch.3 Table 4, SI 1999/1214 Reg.3, Reg.10, Reg.11, Sch.2

1986—cont.

1111. Representation of the People (Scotland) Regulations 1986—*cont.*

Reg.73, amended: SI 1999/1214 Reg.3, Reg.10, Reg.11, Sch.2

Reg.73, applied: 1997 c.61 Sch.3 Table 4, SI 1999/1214 Reg.3, Reg.10, Reg.11, Sch.2

Reg.74, amended: SI 1999/1214 Reg.3, Reg.10, Reg.11, Sch.2

Reg.74, applied: 1997 c.61 Sch.3 Table 4, SI 1999/1214 Reg.3, Reg.10, Reg.11, Sch.2

Reg.75, amended: SI 1999/1214 Reg.3, Reg.10, Reg.11, Sch.2

Reg.75, applied: 1997 c.61 Sch.3 Table 4, SI 1999/1214 Reg.3, Reg.10, Reg.11, Sch.2

Reg.76, amended: SI 1999/1214 Reg.3, Reg.10, Reg.11, Sch.2

Reg.76, applied: SI 1999/1214 Reg.3, Reg.10, Reg.11, Sch.2

Reg.77, amended: SI 1999/1214 Reg.3, Reg.10, Reg.11, Sch.2

Reg.77, applied: SI 1999/1214 Reg.3, Reg.10, Reg.11, Sch.2

Reg.77, revoked (in part): 1997 c.61 Sch.3 Table 4

Reg.78, amended: SI 1999/1214 Reg.3, Reg.10, Reg.11, Sch.2

Reg.78, applied: 1997 c.61 Sch.3 Table 4, SI 1999/1214 Reg.3, Reg.10, Reg.11, Sch.2

Reg.78, revoked (in part): SI 1999/1214 Reg.3, Sch.2

Reg.79, amended: SI 1999/1214 Reg.3, Reg.10, Reg.11, Sch.2

Reg.79, applied: 1997 c.61 Sch.3 Table 4, SI 1999/1214 Reg.3, Reg.10, Reg.11, Sch.2

Reg.80, amended: SI 1999/1214 Reg.3, Reg.10, Reg.11, Sch.2

Reg.80, applied: SI 1999/1214 Reg.3, Reg.10, Reg.11, Sch.2

Reg.81, amended: SI 1999/1214 Reg.3, Reg.10, Reg.11, Sch.2

Reg.81, applied: 1997 c.61 Sch.3 Table 4, SI 1999/1214 Reg.3, Reg.10, Reg.11, Sch.2

Reg.82, amended: 1997 c.61 Sch.3 Table 4, SI 1999/1214 Reg.3, Reg.10, Reg.11, Sch.2

Reg.82, applied: SI 1999/1214 Reg.3, Reg.10, Reg.11, Sch.2

Reg.83, amended: SI 1999/1214 Reg.3, Reg.10, Reg.11, Sch.2

Reg.83, applied: 1997 c.61 Sch.3 Table 4, SI 1999/1214 Reg.3, Reg.10, Reg.11, Sch.2

Reg.84, amended: SI 1999/1214 Reg.3, Reg.10, Reg.11, Sch.2

Reg.84, applied: 1997 c.61 Sch.3 Table 4, SI 1999/1214 Reg.3, Reg.10, Reg.11, Sch.2

Reg.85, amended: 1997 c.61 Sch.3 Table 4, SI 1999/1214 Reg.3, Reg.10, Reg.11, Sch.2

Reg.85, applied: SI 1999/1214 Reg.3, Reg.10, Reg.11, Sch.2

Reg.86, amended: SI 1999/1214 Reg.3, Reg.10, Reg.11, Sch.2

Reg.86, applied: 1997 c.61 Sch.3 Table 4, SI 1999/1214 Reg.3, Reg.10, Reg.11, Sch.2

Reg.87, amended: 1997 c.61 Sch.3 Table 4, SI 1999/1214 Reg.3, Reg.10, Reg.11, Sch.2

Reg.87, applied: SI 1999/1214 Reg.3, Reg.10, Reg.11, Sch.2

Reg.87, revoked (in part): 1997 c.61 Sch.3 Table 4

Reg.88, amended: SI 1999/1214 Reg.3, Reg.10, Reg.11, Sch.2

Reg.88, applied: 1997 c.61 Sch.3 Table 4, SI 1999/1214 Reg.3, Reg.10, Reg.11, Sch.2

Reg.89, amended: 1997 c.61 Sch.3 Table 4, SI 1999/1214 Reg.3, Reg.10, Reg.11, Sch.2

NO.

NO.

1986—cont.

1986—cont.

1111. Representation of the People (Scotland) Regulations 1986—*cont.*

Reg.89, applied: SI 1999/1214 Reg.3, Reg.10, Reg.11, Sch.2

Reg.90, amended: SI 1999/1214 Reg.3, Reg.10, Reg.11, Sch.2

Reg.90, applied: 1997 c.61 Sch.3 Table 4, SI 1999/1214 Reg.3, Reg.10, Reg.11, Sch.2

Reg.91, amended: SI 1999/1214 Reg.3, Reg.10, Reg.11, Sch.2

Reg.91, applied: 1997 c.61 Sch.3 Table 4, SI 1999/1214 Reg.3, Reg.10, Reg.11, Sch.2

Reg.92, amended: SI 1999/1214 Reg.3, Reg.10, Reg.11, Sch.2

Reg.92, applied: 1997 c.61 Sch.3 Table 4, SI 1999/1214 Reg.3, Reg.10, Reg.11, Sch.2

Reg.94, amended: 1997 c.61 Sch.3 Table 4, SI 1999/1214 Reg.3, Reg.10, Reg.11, Sch.2

Reg.94, applied: SI 1999/1214 Reg.3, Reg.10, Reg.11, Sch.2

Reg.94, revoked (in part): 1997 c.61 Sch.3 Table 4

Sch.2 Form C, amended: SI 1999/1214 Reg.9, Sch.4 Part I, Sch.4 Part II

Sch.2 Form D, amended: 1997 c.61 Sch.3 Table 4, SI 1999/1214 Reg.3, Reg.10, Reg.11, Sch.2

Sch.2 Form D, applied: SI 1999/1214 Reg.3, Reg.10, Reg.11, Sch.2

Sch.2 Form E, amended: 1997 c.61 Sch.3 Table 4, SI 1999/1214 Reg.3, Reg.10, Reg.11, Sch.2

Sch.2 Form E, applied: SI 1999/1214 Reg.3, Reg.10, Reg.11, Sch.2

Sch.2 Form F, amended: 1997 c.61 Sch.3 Table 4, SI 1999/1214 Reg.3, Reg.10, Reg.11, Sch.2

Sch.2 Form F, applied: SI 1999/1214 Reg.3, Reg.10, Reg.11, Sch.2

Sch.2 Form G, amended: 1997 c.61 Sch.3 Table 4, SI 1999/1214 Reg.3, Reg.10, Reg.11, Sch.2

Sch.2 Form G, applied: SI 1999/1214 Reg.3, Reg.10, Reg.11, Sch.2

Sch.2 Form H, amended: SI 1999/1214 Reg.3, Reg.10, Reg.11, Sch.2

Sch.2 Form H, applied: SI 1999/1214 Reg.3, Reg.10, Reg.11, Sch.2

Sch.2 Form J, amended: SI 1999/1214 Reg.3, Reg.10, Reg.11, Sch.2

Sch.2 Form J, applied: SI 1999/1214 Reg.3, Reg.10, Reg.11, Sch.2

Sch.2 Form M, amended: SI 1999/1214 Reg.3, Reg.10, Reg.11, Sch.2

Sch.2 Form M, applied: SI 1999/1214 Reg.3, Reg.10, Reg.11, Sch.2

Sch.2 para.5, amended: SI 1996/739 Art.7, Sch.1 para.10

1116. Pensions Increase (Review) Order 1986

applied: SI 1997/634 Art.3, SI 1998/503 Art.3, Art.4, SI 1999/522 Art.3

1159. Child Abduction and Custody (Parties to Conventions) Order 1986

Sch.1, substituted: SI 1996/2595 Art.3, Sch., SI 1996/2874 Art.3, Sch., SI 1997/1747 Art.3, Sch., SI 1997/2575 Art.3, Sch., SI 1998/256 Art.3, Sch., SI 1999/2030 Art.3, Sch.

Sch.2, substituted: SI 1996/269 Art.3, SI 1996/2595 Art.3, Sch., SI 1996/2874 Art.3, Sch., SI 1997/1747 Art.3, Sch., SI 1997/2575 Art.3, Sch., SI 1998/256 Art.3, Sch., SI 1999/2030 Art.3, Sch.

1180. Medicines (Exemptions from Licences and Animal Test Certificates) Order 1986

revoked (in part): SI 1996/2195 Art.2, SI 1996/2197 Art.2

1201. North Western and North Wales Sea Fisheries District Order 1986

revoked: SI 1999/1043 Art.5

Art.3, amended: SI 1996/618 Art.7

Art.3, revoked: SI 1999/1043 Art.5

Art.4, revoked: SI 1999/1043 Art.5

Art.4, substituted: SI 1996/618 Art.8

Sch.1, revoked: SI 1999/1043 Art.5

Sch.1, substituted: SI 1996/618 Art.9

1241. Courts-Martial and Standing Civilian Courts (Additional Powers on Trial of Civilians) (Amendment) Regulations 1986

revoked: SI 1997/579 Reg.13, Sch.3

1243. Safety of Sports Grounds (Designation) (Scotland) Order 1986

revoked: SI 1998/1601 Art.3, Sch.2

1245. Community Bus Regulations 1986

Reg.2, amended: SI 1996/3087 Reg.2

Reg.3, amended: SI 1997/2917 Reg.2

Reg.3, substituted: SI 1996/3087 Reg.2

1248. Merchant Shipping (Fire Protection) (Non-United Kingdom) (Non-SOLAS Ships) Rules 1986

applied: SI 1996/3243 Sch Part I

revoked: SI 1998/1012 Reg.1

r.2, revoked: SI 1998/1012 Reg.1

r.4, revoked: SI 1998/1012 Reg.1

r.5, revoked: SI 1998/1012 Reg.1

r.6, revoked: SI 1998/1012 Reg.1

1271. Accounts and Audit (Amendment) Regulations 1986

revoked (in part): SI 1996/590 Reg.3

1296. Safety of Sports Grounds (Designation) Order 1986

Sch.1, amended: SI 1999/1930 Art.4

1305. Hovercraft (Civil Liability) Order 1986

Sch.3 Part B, amended: SI 1997/1257 Art.2

Sch.4 Part (3)B, amended: SI 1998/1257 Art.2

1319. Trade Marks and Service Marks Rules 1986

r.114, see *R. v Registrar of Trade Marks Ex p. SAW Co Ltd* [1996] R.P.C. 507 (QBD), Jacob, J.

1320. Weighing Equipment (Filling and Discontinuous Totalising Automatic Weighing Machines) Regulations 1986

Reg.2, amended: SI 1996/797 Reg.2

Reg.13, amended: SI 1996/797 Reg.3

Reg.24, amended: SI 1996/797 Reg.4

Reg.25, amended: SI 1996/797 Reg.5

Reg.26, amended: SI 1996/797 Reg.6

Reg.31, amended: SI 1996/797 Reg.7

Reg.32A, added: SI 1996/797 Reg.8

Reg.33, amended: SI 1996/797 Reg.9

Reg.34, amended: SI 1996/797 Reg.10

Reg.35, substituted: SI 1996/797 Reg.11

Sch.2, substituted: SI 1996/797 Reg.12

Sch.3 Table 2, amended: SI 1996/797 Reg.13

1322. Lands Tribunal (Amendment) Rules 1986

revoked: SI 1996/1022 r.57, Sch.2

1335. Costs in Criminal Cases (General) Regulations 1986

see *Solicitor (Wasted Costs Order), Re* [1996] 1 F.L.R. 40 (CA), Beldam, L.J.

amended: SI 1999/2096 Reg.3

applied: SI 1997/1051 r.8, SI 1997/1052 r.8

Reg.3C, see *Sternberg Reed Taylor & Gill, Re* Times, July 26, 1999 (CA (Crim Div)), Rose, L.J.

1986—cont.

1335. Costs in Criminal Cases (General) Regulations 1986—*cont.*
Reg.4, amended: SI 1999/2096 Reg.2
Reg.6, amended: SI 1999/2096 Reg.3
Reg.11, amended: SI 1999/2096 Reg.2
Reg.12, see *R. v North Kent Justices Ex p. McGoldrick & Co* (1996) 160 J.P. 30 (QBD), Schiemann, J.

1348. Aerodromes (Designation) (Facilities for Consultation) Order 1986
revoked: SI 1996/1392 Art.3

1375. Social Security (Unemployment Benefit) and Supplementary Benefit Amendment Regulations 1986
Reg.2, revoked: SI 1996/1345 Reg.27, Sch.

1390. General Medical Council (Constitution of Fitness to Practise Committees) Rules Order of Council 1986
revoked: SI 1996/2125 Sch. para.16, Sch. Sch.2
r.2, revoked: SI 1996/2125 Sch. para.16, Sch. Sch.1
r.6, revoked (in part): SI 1996/2125 Sch. para.16, Sch. Sch.1
r.7, revoked: SI 1996/2125 Sch. para.16, Sch. Sch.1
r.8, revoked: SI 1996/2125 Sch. para.16, Sch. Sch.1
r.9, revoked: SI 1996/2125 Sch. para.16, Sch. Sch.1

1442. Registration of Marriages Regulations 1986
Reg.3, amended: SI 1999/1621 Reg.2
Reg.3, applied: SI 1999/1621 Reg.2
Reg.4, amended: SI 1999/1621 Reg.2
Reg.4, applied: SI 1999/1621 Reg.2
Reg.5, amended: SI 1999/1621 Reg.3
Reg.5, applied: SI 1999/1621 Reg.3
Reg.6, amended: SI 1999/1621 Reg.4
Reg.6, applied: SI 1999/1621 Reg.4
Reg.7, amended: SI 1999/1621 Reg.5
Reg.7, applied: SI 1999/1621 Reg.5
Reg.8, amended: SI 1999/1621 Reg.5
Reg.8, applied: SI 1999/1621 Reg.5
Reg.10, amended: SI 1999/1621 Reg.6
Reg.10, applied: SI 1999/1621 Reg.6
Reg.11, amended: SI 1999/1621 Reg.6
Reg.11, applied: SI 1999/1621 Reg.6
Reg.12, amended: SI 1999/1621 Reg.6
Reg.12, applied: SI 1999/1621 Reg.6
Sch.1 Form 1, substituted: SI 1997/2204 Reg.2, Sch.1
Sch.1 Form 2, substituted: SI 1997/2204 Reg.2, Sch.1
Sch.1 Form 9, substituted: SI 1997/2204 Reg.2, Sch.1
Sch.1 Form 10, substituted: SI 1997/2204 Reg.2, Sch.1
Sch.1 Form 12, amended: SI 1996/2558 Reg.2
Sch.1 Form 12, substituted: SI 1997/2204 Reg.2, Sch.1

1445. Registration of Marriages (Welsh Language) Regulations 1986
revoked: SI 1999/1621 Reg.10, Sch.3
Sch.1 Form 1, revoked: SI 1999/1621 Reg.10, Sch.3
Sch.1 Form 1, substituted: SI 1997/2204 Reg.3, Sch.2
Sch.1 Form 2, revoked: SI 1999/1621 Reg.10, Sch.3
Sch.1 Form 2, substituted: SI 1997/2204 Reg.3, Sch.2
Sch.1 Form 6, revoked: SI 1999/1621 Reg.10, Sch.3

1986—cont.

1445. Registration of Marriages (Welsh Language) Regulations 1986—*cont.*
Sch.1 Form 6, substituted: SI 1997/2204 Reg.3, Sch.2
Sch.1 Form 7, revoked: SI 1999/1621 Reg.10, Sch.3
Sch.1 Form 7, substituted: SI 1997/2204 Reg.3, Sch.2
Sch.1 Form 8, amended: SI 1996/2558 Reg.3
Sch.1 Form 8, revoked: SI 1999/1621 Reg.10, Sch.3
Sch.1 Form 8, substituted: SI 1997/2204 Reg.3, Sch.2

1456. Community Drivers' Hours and Recording Equipment (Exemptions and Supplementary Provisions) Regulations 1986
Sch. para.2, amended: SI 1998/2006 Reg.3
Sch. para.7, see *Vehicle Inspectorate v Norman* [1999] R.T.R. 366 (QBD), Rose, L.J.

1460. Representation of the People (Welsh Forms) Order 1986
Sch. Part II, referred to: 1997 c.61 Sch.3 Table 5

1510. Control of Pesticides Regulations 1986
see *R. v Ministry of Agriculture, Fisheries and Food Ex p. British Agrochemicals Association Ltd* [1996] Env. L.R. D29 (QBD), Popplewell, J.; see *R. v Ministry of Agriculture, Fisheries and Food Ex p. British Agrochemicals Association Ltd (No.2)* Times, November 16, 1999 (QBD), Richards, J.; see *R. v Ministry of Agriculture, Fisheries and Food Ex p. British Agrochemicals Association Ltd (C100/96)* Times, March 30, 1999 (ECJ), PJG Kapteyn (President)
referred to: SI 1997/322 Reg.36
Reg.2, amended: SI 1997/188 Reg.3
Reg.3, substituted: SI 1997/188 Reg.4
Reg.5, amended: SI 1997/188 Reg.5
Reg.5, applied: SI 1996/2089 Reg.2, SI 1996/2094 Sch.2 Part I, SI 1996/2095 Sch.2 para.7, SI 1996/3142 Sch.2 para.20, SI 1999/1512 Art.2, Sch.2 para.7
Reg.5, referred to: SI 1999/257 Reg.3, Sch.1 para.1
Reg.6, applied: SI 1996/2089 Reg.2, SI 1996/2094 Sch.2 Part I, SI 1996/2095 Sch.2 para.7, SI 1999/1512 Art.2, Sch.2 para.8
Reg.6, referred to: SI 1999/257 Reg.3, Sch.1 para.1
Reg.6, substituted: SI 1997/188 Reg.6
Reg.7, substituted: SI 1997/188 Reg.7
Reg.8, substituted: SI 1997/188 Reg.8
Sch.1, applied: SI 1999/1512 Art.2, Sch.2 para.8
Sch.1, substituted: SI 1997/188 Reg.9, Sch.
Sch.2, applied: SI 1999/1512 Art.2, Sch.2 para.8
Sch.2, substituted: SI 1997/188 Reg.9, Sch.
Sch.3, applied: SI 1999/1512 Art.2, Sch.2 para.8
Sch.3, substituted: SI 1997/188 Reg.9, Sch.
Sch.4, applied: SI 1999/1512 Art.2, Sch.2 para.8
Sch.4, substituted: SI 1997/188 Reg.9, Sch.

1543. Economic Regulation of Airports (Expenses of the Monopolies and Mergers Commission) Regulations 1986
revoked: SI 1997/403 Reg.3

1561. Social Security (Industrial Injuries and Diseases) (Miscellaneous Provisions) Regulations 1986
Reg.2, applied: SI 1999/991 Reg.27, Sch.2 para.15

NO.   NO.

1986—cont.   *1986—cont.*

1571. National Health Service (General Dental Services) (Scotland) Amendment Regulations 1986
revoked: SI 1996/177 Reg.38, Sch.8

1622. Marriage (Prescription of Forms) (Scotland) Amendment Regulations 1986
revoked (in part): SI 1997/2349 Reg.9

1642. National Health Service (Vocational Training) Amendment Regulations 1986
revoked: SI 1997/2817 Reg.20, Sch.5

1657. National Health Service (Vocational Training) (Scotland) Amendment Regulations 1986
revoked: SI 1998/5 Reg.19, Sch.4

1682. Measuring Equipment (Measures of Length) Regulations 1986
Reg.23A, added: SI 1996/2636 Reg.2
Reg.23B, added: SI 1996/2636 Reg.2
Reg.25, substituted: SI 1996/2636 Reg.2
Sch.2, added: SI 1996/2636 Reg.2, Sch
Sch.2 para.2, amended: SI 1996/3020 Reg.2

1711. Stamp Duty Reserve Tax Regulations 1986
Reg.2, amended: SI 1997/2430 Reg.3, SI 1999/3264 Reg.3
Reg.2A, added: SI 1999/3264 Reg.4
Reg.3, amended: SI 1999/3264 Reg.5
Reg.4, amended: SI 1997/2430 Reg.4, SI 1999/3264 Reg.6
Reg.4A, added: SI 1997/2430 Reg.5
Reg.4B, added: SI 1999/3264 Reg.7
Reg.6, amended: SI 1997/2430 Reg.6, SI 1999/3264 Reg.8
Reg.7, amended: SI 1997/2430 Reg.7, SI 1999/3264 Reg.9
Reg.8, amended: SI 1997/2430 Reg.8
Reg.13, amended: SI 1997/2430 Reg.9, SI 1999/3264 Reg.10
Reg.14, amended: SI 1999/3264 Reg.11
Reg.15, amended: SI 1997/2430 Reg.10
Sch. Part I, amended: SI 1997/2430 Reg.11, SI 1999/2383 Reg.5, SI 1999/3264 Reg.12
Sch. Part II, amended: SI 1997/2430 Reg.12, SI 1999/2383 Reg.6, SI 1999/3264 Reg.13

1713. Combined Probation Areas Order 1986
amended: SI 1996/283 Art.2, SI 1997/3052 Art.2, SI 1998/782 Art.2, SI 1998/2071 Art.2, SI 1998/3264 Art.2, SI 1998/3265 Art.2, SI 1998/3267 Art.2, SI 1999/993 Art.2, SI 1999/994 Art.2, SI 1999/1507 Art.2, SI 1999/1870 Art.2
Sch.2, amended: SI 1996/284 Art.2, SI 1996/930 Art.2, SI 1996/931 Art.2, SI 1996/932 Art.2, SI 1996/933 Art.2, SI 1996/956 Art.2, SI 1996/957 Art.2, SI 1996/3209 Art.2, SI 1997/725 Art.2, SI 1997/808 Art.2, SI 1997/1059 Art.2, SI 1997/2623 Art.2, SI 1998/584 Art.2, SI 1998/1704 Art.2, SI 1998/3185 Art.2, SI 1998/3187 Art.2, SI 1998/3188 Art.2, SI 1998/3189 Art.2, SI 1999/3340 Art.2, SI 1999/3341 Art.2, SI 1999/3342 Art.2, SI 1999/3343 Art.2
Sch.2, revoked (in part): SI 1996/284 Art.3, SI 1996/957 Art.3

1716. Contracting Out (Requisite Benefits-Consequential Provisions) Regulations 1986
Reg.2, revoked: SI 1997/358 Reg.7, Sch
Reg.3, revoked: SI 1996/1172 Sch.2
Reg.5, revoked (in part): SI 1996/1462 Reg.14, Sch.3

1717. Occupational Pension Schemes (Disclosure of Information) (Amendment) Regulations 1986
revoked: SI 1996/1655 Reg.12, Sch.4

1778. Carriage by Air (Sterling Equivalent) Order 1986
revoked: SI 1996/244

1810. Restrictive Trade Practices (Gas Supply and Connected Activities) Order 1986
Art.5, amended: SI 1996/252 Art.2, Sch
Art.6, amended: SI 1996/252 Art.2, Sch
Art.7, amended: SI 1996/252 Art.2, Sch
Art.8, amended: SI 1996/252 Art.2, Sch

1883. Criminal Justice (Northern Ireland) Order 1986
Art.5, revoked: SI 1998/1504 (NI.9) Art.65, Sch.6
Art.7, revoked: SI 1996/3160 (NI.24) Sch.7

1886. Redundancy Rebates (Northern Ireland) Order 1986
revoked: SI 1996/1919 (NI.16) Art.257, Sch.3

1888. Social Security (Northern Ireland) Order 1986
Art.9, amended: SI 1999/671 Art.3, Sch.1 para.1
Art.20, applied: SI 1999/3147 (NI.11) Art.49
Art.82, amended: SI 1999/671 Art.3, Sch.1 para.2
Part III, referred to: SI 1998/1506 (NI.10) Art.12
Sch.9 Part II, revoked (in part): SI 1996/1921 (NI.18) Art.28, Sch.3

1912. Borough of Taunton Deane (Electoral Arrangements) Order 1986
revoked: SI 1998/2461 Art.6

1915. Insolvency (Scotland) Rules 1986
r.3.9, amended: SI 1999/1820 Art.4, Sch.2 para.141
r.3.10, amended: SI 1999/1820 Art.4, Sch.2 para.141
r.3.11, amended: SI 1999/1820 Art.4, Sch.2 para.141
r.4.2, amended: SI 1999/1820 Art.4, Sch.2 para.141
r.4.11, amended: SI 1999/1820 Art.4, Sch.2 para.141
r.4.18, amended: SI 1999/1820 Art.4, Sch.2 para.141
r.4.19, amended: SI 1999/1820 Art.4, Sch.2 para.141
r.4.24, amended: SI 1999/1820 Art.4, Sch.2 para.141
r.4.25, amended: SI 1999/1820 Art.4, Sch.2 para.141
r.4.26, amended: SI 1999/1820 Art.4, Sch.2 para.141
r.4.29, amended: SI 1999/1820 Art.4, Sch.2 para.141
r.4.30, amended: SI 1999/1820 Art.4, Sch.2 para.141
r.4.31, amended: SI 1999/1820 Art.4, Sch.2 para.141
r.4.36, amended: SI 1999/1820 Art.4, Sch.2 para.141
r.4.37, amended: SI 1999/1820 Art.4, Sch.2 para.141
r.4.42, amended: SI 1999/1820 Art.4, Sch.2 para.141
r.4.59, amended: SI 1999/1820 Art.4, Sch.2 para.141
r.4.63, amended: SI 1999/1820 Art.4, Sch.2 para.141
Sch.1 para.17, amended: SI 1999/1820 Art.4, Sch.2 para.141

NO.

1986—cont.

1915. Insolvency (Scotland) Rules 1986—cont.
Sch.2, amended: SI 1999/1820 Art.4, Sch.2 para.141
Sch.5 Form 3.4, amended: SI 1999/1820 Art.4, Sch.2 para.141
Sch.5 Form 4.2, amended: SI 1999/1820 Art.4, Sch.2 para.141
Sch.5 Form 4.5, amended: SI 1999/1820 Art.4, Sch.2 para.141
Sch.5 Form 4.6, amended: SI 1999/1820 Art.4, Sch.2 para.141
Sch.5 Form 4.9, amended: SI 1999/1820 Art.4, Sch.2 para.141
Sch.5 Form 4.11, amended: SI 1999/1820 Art.4, Sch.2 para.141
Sch.5 Form 4.14, amended: SI 1999/1820 Art.4, Sch.2 para.141
Sch.5 Form 4.16, amended: SI 1999/1820 Art.4, Sch.2 para.141
Sch.5 Form 4.17, amended: SI 1999/1820 Art.4, Sch.2 para.141
Sch.5 Form 4.18, amended: SI 1999/1820 Art.4, Sch.2 para.141
Sch.5 Form 4.19, amended: SI 1999/1820 Art.4, Sch.2 para.141
Sch.5 Form 4.22, amended: SI 1999/1820 Art.4, Sch.2 para.141
Sch.5 Form 4.24, amended: SI 1999/1820 Art.4, Sch.2 para.141
Sch.5 Form 4.25, amended: SI 1999/1820 Art.4, Sch.2 para.141
Sch.5 Form 4.26, amended: SI 1999/1820 Art.4, Sch.2 para.141
Sch.5 Form 4.27, amended: SI 1999/1820 Art.4, Sch.2 para.141

1916. Insolvent Companies (Reports on Conduct of Directors) (No.2) (Scotland) Rules 1986
revoked: SI 1996/1910 r.2 (with savings)
r.4, referred to: SI 1996/1910 r.7

1917. Receivers (Scotland) Regulations 1986
Reg.4, amended: SI 1999/1820 Art.4, Sch.2 para.142
Sch. Form 1, amended: SI 1999/1820 Art.4, Sch.2 para.142
Sch. Form 2, amended: SI 1999/1820 Art.4, Sch.2 para.142
Sch. Form 3, amended: SI 1999/1820 Art.4, Sch.2 para.142

1925. Insolvency Rules 1986
see *Ariyo v Sovereign Leasing Plc* [1998] B.P.I.R. 177 (CA), Nourse, L.J.; see *Company (No.62 of 1995), Re* Times, February 15, 1996 (Ch D), Laddie, J.; see *Debtor (No.26 of 1991), Re* [1996] B.C.C. 246 (Ch D), Judge Maddocks; see *Debtor (No.90 of 1997), Re* Times, July 1, 1998 (Ch D), Judge Hegarty Q.C.; see *Equity Nominees Ltd, Re* [1999] 2 B.C.L.C. 19 (Ch D (Companies Court)), Neuberger, J.; see *TSB Bank Plc v Katz* [1996] B.P.I.R. 147 (Ch D), Arden, J.; see *William Pickles Plc, Re* Times, February 13, 1996 (Ch D), Rattee, J.
Part 6 Ch.22(A), added: SI 1999/359 r.3, Sch. para.8
Part 7 Ch.6, substituted: SI 1999/1022 r.3, Sch. para.3
r.0.2, substituted: SI 1999/1022 r.3, Sch. para.1
r.1.17, see *Cancol Ltd, Re* [1996] 1 All E.R. 37 (Ch D), Knox, J.; see *Sweatfield Ltd, Re* [1997] B.C.C. 744 (Ch D), Judge Weeks Q.C.
r.4, see *Bank of Credit and Commerce International SA (In Liquidation) v Al-Saud* [1997]

NO.

1986—cont.

1925. Insolvency Rules 1986—cont.
r.4—cont.
B.C.C. 63 (CA), Neill, L.J.; see *Creditnet Ltd, Re* [1996] 1 W.L.R. 1291 (Ch D), Jonathan Parker, J.; see *Kahn v Inland Revenue Commissioners* [1999] S.T.C. 922 (Ch D (Companies Court)), Evans-Lombe, J.; see *Penrose v Official Receiver* [1996] 2 All E.R. 96 (Ch D), Chadwick, J.; see *Secretary of State for Employment v Wilson and BCCI* [1997] I.C.R. 408 (EAT), Mummery, J.
r.4.1, amended: SI 1998/1129 Art.2, Sch.1 para.4
r.4.7, amended: SI 1998/1129 Art.2, Sch.1 para.4
r.4.10, amended: SI 1998/1129 Art.2, Sch.1 para.4
r.4.11, see *Creditnet Ltd, Re* [1996] 2 B.C.L.C. 133 (Ch D), Jonathan Parker, J.; see *Practice Direction (Company: Advertisement of Compulsory Winding-up Petition)* [1996] 1 W.L.R. 1255 (Ch D) (Companies Court), Chief Bankruptcy Registrar; see *Secretary of State for Trade and Industry v North West Holdings Plc* [1999] 1 B.C.L.C. 425 (CA), Chadwick, L.J
r.4.72, amended: SI 1998/1129 Art.2, Sch.1 para.4
r.4.90, see *Bank of Credit and Commerce International SA (In Liquidation) (No.8), Re* [1998] A.C. 214 (HL), Lord Hoffmann; see *Bank of Credit and Commerce International SA (In Liquidation) (No.10), Re* [1997] Ch. 213 (Ch D (Companies Court)), Sir Richard Scott, V.C.; see *Morris v Agrichemicals Ltd* Times, January 8, 1996 (CA); see *Secretary of State for Employment v Wilson and BCCI* [1996] I.R.L.R. 330 (EAT), Mummery, J.
r.4.127, see *Tony Rowse NMC Ltd, Re* [1996] 2 B.C.L.C. 225 (Ch D), ME Mann Q.C.
r.4.130, see *Tony Rowse NMC Ltd, Re* [1996] 2 B.C.L.C. 225 (Ch D), ME Mann Q.C.
r.4.138, see *Merrygold v Horton* Times, July 11, 1997 (Ch D), James Munby Q.C.; see *Salters Hall School Ltd (In Liquidation), Re* [1998] 1 B.C.L.C. 401 (Ch D (Companies Court)), James Munby Q.C.
r.4.218, see *Exchange Travel (Holdings) Ltd (In Liquidation) (No.3), Re* [1997] 2 B.C.L.C. 579 (CA), Phillips, L.J.; see *Grey Marlin Ltd, Re* [1999] 4 All E.R. 429 (Ch D (Companies Court)), David Donaldson Q.C.; see *Katz v McNally* [1997] B.C.C. 784 (CA), Phillips, L.J.; see *Mond v Hammond Suddards (No.2)* [1999] 3 W.L.R. 697 (CA), Chadwick, L.J.
r.5, see *Debtors (Nos.400 and 401 of 1996), Re* Times, February 27, 1997 (Ch D), Rimer, J.; see *Debtor (No.488-IO of 1996), Re* [1999] 2 B.C.L.C. 571 (Ch D), Sir John Vinelott; see *Rooney v Cardona* [1999] 2 F.L.R. 1148 (Ch D), Judge Weeks Q.C.; see *Tager v Westpac Banking Corp* [1997] B.P.I.R. 543 (Ch D), John Weeks Q.C.
r.5.17, see *Debtor (No.400-IO-1996), Re* [1997] 1 W.L.R. 1319 (Ch D), Rimer, J.; see *Debtor (No.488-IO of 1996), Re* Times, February 10, 1999 (Ch D), Sir John Vinelott; see *Doorbar v Alltime Securities Ltd* [1996] 1 W.L.R. 456 (CA), Peter Gibson, L.J.; see *Emery v UCB Corporate Services Ltd* [1999] B.P.I.R. 480 (Ch D), Park, J.
r.5.23, amended: SI 1999/359 r.3, Sch. para.1
r.5.25, amended: SI 1999/359 r.3, Sch. para.2

NO.

1925. Insolvency Rules 1986—*cont.*

r.5.29, amended: SI 1999/359 r.3, Sch. para.3

r.6, see *Platts v Western Trust & Savings Ltd* [1996] B.P.I.R. 339 (CA), Nourse, L.J.

r.6.1, see *Debtor (No.106 of 1992), Re* [1996] B.P.I.R. 190 (Ch D), Evans-Lombe, J.; see *Khan v Breezevale Sarl* [1996] B.P.I.R. 190 (Ch D), Evans-Lombe, J.

r.6.4, see *McAllister v Society of Lloyd's* [1999] B.P.I.R. 548 (Ch D), Carnwath, J.

r.6.5, see *AIB Finance Ltd v Alsop* [1998] 2 All E.R. 929 (CA), Mummery, L.J.; see *Cale v Assuidoman KPS (Harrow) Ltd* [1996] B.P.I.R. 245 (Ch D), Evans-Lombe, J.; see *Debtor (No.106 of 1992), Re* [1996] B.P.I.R. 190 (Ch D), Evans-Lombe, J.; see *Debtor (No.SD 27 of 1998), Re* Independent, March 15, 1999 (C.S.) (Ch D), Neuberger, J.; see *Debtor (No.544/SD/98), Re* Independent, July 5, 1999 (C.S.) (Ch D), Jacob, J.; see *Debtor (No.87 of 1999), Re* Times, February 14, 2000 (Ch D), Rimer, J.; see *Garrow v Society of Lloyd's* Times, October 28, 1999 (CA), Robert Walker, L.J.; see *Hofer v Strawson* [1999] B.P.I.R. 501 (Ch D), Neuberger, J.; see *Khan v Breezevale Sarl* [1996] B.P.I.R. 190 (Ch D), Evans-Lombe, J.

r.6.34, amended: SI 1999/359 r.3, Sch. para.4

r.6.46, amended: SI 1999/359 r.3, Sch. para.5

r.6.176, amended: SI 1999/359 r.3, Sch. para.6

r.6.197, amended: SI 1999/1022 r.3, Sch. para.2

r.6.215, see *Jacobs v Official Receiver* [1999] 1 W.L.R. 619 (Ch D), Michael Burton Q.C.

r.6.216, amended: SI 1999/359 r.3, Sch. para.7

r.6.223(A), added: SI 1999/359 r.3, Sch. para.8

r.6.223(B), added: SI 1999/359 r.3, Sch. para.8

r.6.223(C), added: SI 1999/359 r.3, Sch. para.8

r.7, see *Bullard & Taplin Ltd, Re* [1996] B.C.C. 973 (Ch D), Knox, J.; see *Debtor (No.510 of 1997), Re* Times, June 18, 1998 (Ch D), Stanley Burnton Q.C.; see *Mid East Trading Ltd, Re* [1997] 3 All E.R. 481 (Ch D), Evans-Lombe, J.; see *Platts v Western Trust & Savings Ltd* [1996] B.P.I.R. 339 (CA), Nourse, L.J.

r.7.28, see *Austintel Ltd, Re* [1997] 1 W.L.R. 616 (CA), Morritt, L.J.; see *Creditnet Ltd, Re* [1996] 2 B.C.L.C. 133 (Ch D), Jonathan Parker, J.

r.7.33, substituted: SI 1999/1022 r.3, Sch. para.3

r.7.34, substituted: SI 1999/1022 r.3, Sch. para.3

r.7.35, substituted: SI 1999/1022 r.3, Sch. para.3

r.7.36, substituted: SI 1999/1022 r.3, Sch. para.3

r.7.37, substituted: SI 1999/1022 r.3, Sch. para.3

r.7.38, substituted: SI 1999/1022 r.3, Sch. para.3

r.7.39, substituted: SI 1999/1022 r.3, Sch. para.3

r.7.40, substituted: SI 1999/1022 r.3, Sch. para.3

r.7.41, substituted: SI 1999/1022 r.3, Sch. para.3

r.7.42, substituted: SI 1999/1022 r.3, Sch. para.3

r.7.49, substituted: SI 1999/1022 r.3, Sch. para.4

NO.

1925. Insolvency Rules 1986—*cont.*

r.7.51, substituted: SI 1999/1022 r.3, Sch. para.5

r.7.55, see *Debtor (No.340 of 1992), Re* [1996] 2 All E.R. 211 (CA), Millett, L.J.

r.7.57, substituted: SI 1999/1022 r.3, Sch. para.6

r.7.59, substituted: SI 1999/1022 r.3, Sch. para.7

r.7.60, substituted: SI 1999/1022 r.3, Sch. para.8

r.8.6, see *Cardona, Re* [1997] B.C.C. 697 (Ch D), Carnwath, J.

r.9.2, amended: SI 1999/1022 r.3, Sch. para.9

r.9.4, amended: SI 1999/1022 r.3, Sch. para.10

r.11.13, see *Park Air Services Plc, Re* [1996] 1 W.L.R. 649 (Ch D) (Companies Court), Ferris, J.; see *Park Air Services Plc, Re* [1999] 2 W.L.R. 396 (HL), Lord Millett

r.12, see *G (Children Act 1989, Sch.1), Re* [1996] 2 F.L.R. 171 (Fam Div), Singer, J.; see *Mordant (A Bankrupt), Re (1993)* [1996] 1 F.L.R. 334 (Ch D), Sir Donald Nicholls, V.C.

r.12.2, see *Exchange Travel (Holdings) Ltd (In Liquidation) (No.3), Re* [1997] 2 B.C.L.C. 579 (CA), Phillips, L.J.; see *Katz v McNally* [1997] B.C.C. 784 (CA), Phillips, L.J.

r.12.3, see *Wheatley v Wheatley* [1999] Fam. Law 375 (QBD), Judge Boggis

r.12.9, substituted: SI 1999/1022 r.3, Sch. para.11

r.12.11, substituted: SI 1999/1022 r.3, Sch. para.12

r.12.12, amended: SI 1999/1022 r.3, Sch. para.13

r.13, see *Jyske Bank (Gibraltar) Ltd v Spjeldnaes (No.1)* Times, October 10, 1998 (Ch D), Evans-Lombe, J.

r.13.13, amended: SI 1999/1022 r.3, Sch. para.14

1944. Insolvency Regulations 1986

see *Tony Rowse NMC Ltd, Re* [1996] 2 B.C.L.C. 225 (Ch D), ME Mann Q.C.

1947. Act of Sederunt (Enforcement of Judgments under the Civil Jurisdiction and Judgments Act 1982) 1986

Form 6, revoked: SI 1997/291 r.1.4, Sch.2

para.6, revoked: SI 1997/291 r.1.4, Sch.2

1954. Marriage (Prescription of Forms) (Scotland) Amendment (No.2) Regulations 1986

revoked: SI 1997/2349 Reg.9

1960. Statutory Maternity Pay (General) Regulations 1986

Reg.6, amended: SI 1996/599 Art.10, SI 1997/543 Art.10, SI 1998/470 Art.10, SI 1999/264 Art.10

Reg.7, applied: 1999 c.2 s.1, Sch.2

Reg.20, amended: SI 1999/567 Reg.12

Reg.21, amended: SI 1996/1335 Reg.2

Reg.21B, added: SI 1996/1335 Reg.3

Reg.25, applied: 1999 c.2 s.1, Sch.2

Reg.30, applied: 1999 c.2 s.1, Sch.2

Reg.31, applied: 1999 c.2 s.1, Sch.2

1984. Registration of Births, Deaths, Marriages, etc. (Prescription of Forms) (Scotland) Amendment Regulations 1986

revoked: SI 1997/2348 Reg.30, Sch.27

1985. Submarine Pipe-lines Safety (Amendment) Regulations 1986

revoked: SI 1996/825 Reg.31, Sch.6 Part I

NO.

2013. **Extradition (Internationally Protected Persons) (Amendment) Order 1986**
revoked: SI 1997/1764 Art.4

2015. **Extradition (Taking of Hostages) (Amendment) Order 1986**
revoked: SI 1997/1767 Art.4

2016. **Extradition (Tokyo Convention) (Amendment) Order 1986**
revoked: SI 1997/1768 Art.4

2021. **Financial Provisions (Northern Ireland) Order 1986**
Sch.1 para.5, revoked: SI 1998/749 (NI.4) Art.9, Sch.
Sch.1 para.7, revoked: SI 1998/749 (NI.4) Art.9, Sch.

2030. **Insolvency Fees Order 1986**
Art.8, see *R. v Lord Chancellor Ex p. Lightfoot* [1998] 4 All E.R. 764 (QBD), Laws J.

2073. **Royal Air Force Terms of Service (Amendment) Regulations 1986**
revoked: SI 1997/231 Reg.1

2090. **Sea Fishing (Enforcement of Community Conservation Measures) Order 1986**
revoked: SI 1997/1949 Art.16, Sch.2

2125. **Rules of Procedure (Air Force) (Amendment) Rules 1986**
revoked: SI 1997/171 r.90, Sch.7

2126. **Rules of Procedure (Army) (Amendment) Rules 1986**
revoked: SI 1997/169 r.90, Sch.7

2128. **Passenger and Goods Vehicles (Recording Equipment) (Approval of Fitters and Workshops) (Fees) Regulations 1986**
Reg.3, amended: SI 1997/219 Reg.2

2134. **Insolvent Companies (Reports on Conduct of Directors) No.2 Rules 1986**
revoked: SI 1996/1909 r.2 (with savings)

2143. **County Court Fees (Amendment No.2) Order 1986**
revoked: SI 1999/689 Art.8 (with savings), Sch.2 (with savings)

2144. **Supreme Court Fees (Amendment No.2) Order 1986**
revoked: SI 1999/687 Art.8 (with savings), Sch.2 (with savings)

2150. **Vickers Shipbuilding and Engineering Limited (Barrow-in-Furness) Light Railway Order 1986**
Art.8, amended: SI 1996/362 Art.5, Sch.4

2171. **Occupational Pension Schemes (Miscellaneous Amendments) Regulations 1986**
Reg.3, revoked: SI 1997/784 Reg.12, Sch.2
Reg.4, revoked: SI 1996/1847 Reg.21, Sch.3
Sch., revoked: SI 1997/784 Reg.12, Sch.2

2185. **Non-Contentious Probate Fees (Amendment) (No.2) Order 1986**
revoked: SI 1999/688 Art.6 (with savings), Sch.2 (with savings)

2194. **Housing (Right to Buy) (Prescribed Forms) Regulations 1986**
Sch.1, amended: SI 1996/2652 Reg.2

2209. **European Parliamentary Elections Regulations 1986**
applied: SI 1999/450 Art.124, Art.137
revoked: SI 1999/1214 Reg.20, Sch.5
Reg.4, revoked: SI 1999/1214 Reg.20, Sch.5
Reg.5, amended: SI 1997/874 Reg.2
Reg.5, revoked (in part): SI 1997/874 Reg.2, SI 1999/1214 Reg.20, Sch.5
Reg.8, revoked: SI 1999/1214 Reg.20, Sch.5
Sch.1, revoked: SI 1999/1214 Reg.20, Sch.5
Sch.2 Appendix, amended: SI 1999/450 Art.14, Sch.4 para.41, Sch.4 para.42, Sch.4 para.43

NO.

2209. **European Parliamentary Elections Regulations 1986**—*cont.*
Sch.2 Appendix, revoked: SI 1999/1214 Reg.20, Sch.5
Sch.2 r.1, amended: SI 1999/450 Art.14, Sch.4 para.24
Sch.2 r.1, revoked: SI 1999/1214 Reg.20, Sch.5
Sch.2 r.14, amended: SI 1999/450 Art.14, Sch.4 para.25
Sch.2 r.14, revoked: SI 1999/1214 Reg.20, Sch.5
Sch.2 r.18, amended: SI 1999/450 Art.14, Sch.4 para.26
Sch.2 r.18, revoked: SI 1999/1214 Reg.20, Sch.5
Sch.2 r.22, amended: SI 1999/450 Art.14, Sch.4 para.27
Sch.2 r.22, revoked: SI 1999/1214 Reg.20, Sch.5
Sch.2 r.23, amended: SI 1999/450 Art.14, Sch.4 para.28
Sch.2 r.23, revoked: SI 1999/1214 Reg.20, Sch.5
Sch.2 r.24, amended: SI 1999/450 Art.14, Sch.4 para.29
Sch.2 r.24, revoked: SI 1999/1214 Reg.20, Sch.5
Sch.2 r.29, amended: SI 1999/450 Art.14, Sch.4 para.30
Sch.2 r.29, revoked: SI 1999/1214 Reg.20, Sch.5
Sch.2 r.31, amended: SI 1999/450 Art.14, Sch.4 para.31
Sch.2 r.31, revoked: SI 1999/1214 Reg.20, Sch.5
Sch.2 r.32, amended: SI 1999/450 Art.14, Sch.4 para.32
Sch.2 r.32, revoked: SI 1999/1214 Reg.20, Sch.5
Sch.2 r.33, amended: SI 1999/450 Art.14, Sch.4 para.33
Sch.2 r.33, revoked: SI 1999/1214 Reg.20, Sch.5
Sch.2 r.34, amended: SI 1999/450 Art.14, Sch.4 para.34
Sch.2 r.34, revoked: SI 1999/1214 Reg.20, Sch.5
Sch.2 r.36, amended: SI 1999/450 Art.14, Sch.4 para.35
Sch.2 r.36, revoked: SI 1999/1214 Reg.20, Sch.5
Sch.2 r.37, amended: SI 1999/450 Art.14, Sch.4 para.36
Sch.2 r.37, revoked: SI 1999/1214 Reg.20, Sch.5
Sch.2 r.38, amended: SI 1999/450 Art.14, Sch.4 para.37
Sch.2 r.38, revoked: SI 1999/1214 Reg.20, Sch.5
Sch.2 r.39, amended: SI 1999/450 Art.14, Sch.4 para.38
Sch.2 r.39, revoked: SI 1999/1214 Reg.20, Sch.5
Sch.2 r.46, amended: SI 1999/450 Art.14, Sch.4 para.39
Sch.2 r.46, revoked: SI 1999/1214 Reg.20, Sch.5
Sch.2 r.49, amended: SI 1999/450 Art.14, Sch.4 para.40
Sch.2 r.49, revoked: SI 1999/1214 Reg.20, Sch.5
Sch.4 Part II, amended: SI 1996/739 Art.7, Sch.1 para.11

NO.

1986—cont.

2209. European Parliamentary Elections Regulations 1986
Sch.4 Part II, revoked: SI 1999/1214 Reg.20, Sch.5

2213. Scottish Local Elections Rules 1986
r.4, amended: SI 1996/739 Art.7, Sch.1 para.12
Sch.2, amended: SI 1996/739 Art.7, Sch.1 para.12
Sch.2 Appendix, amended: SI 1999/492 r.3, Sch., SI 1999/787 Art.13, Sch.5 para.40, Sch.5 para.41, Sch.5 para.42, Sch.5 para.43
Sch.2 r.1, amended: SI 1999/787 Art.13, Sch.5 para.23
Sch.2 r.4A, added: SI 1999/492 r.3
Sch.2 r.7, amended: SI 1999/492 r.3
Sch.2 r.13, amended: SI 1999/492 r.3, SI 1999/787 Art.13, Sch.5 para.24
Sch.2 r.17, amended: SI 1999/787 Art.13, Sch.5 para.25
Sch.2 r.21, amended: SI 1999/787 Art.13, Sch.5 para.26
Sch.2 r.22, amended: SI 1999/787 Art.13, Sch.5 para.27
Sch.2 r.23, amended: SI 1999/787 Art.13, Sch.5 para.28
Sch.2 r.28, amended: SI 1999/787 Art.13, Sch.5 para.29
Sch.2 r.30, amended: SI 1999/787 Art.13, Sch.5 para.30
Sch.2 r.31, amended: SI 1999/787 Art.13, Sch.5 para.31
Sch.2 r.32, amended: SI 1999/787 Art.13, Sch.5 para.32
Sch.2 r.33, amended: SI 1999/787 Art.13, Sch.5 para.33
Sch.2 r.35, amended: SI 1999/787 Art.13, Sch.5 para.34
Sch.2 r.36, amended: SI 1999/787 Art.13, Sch.5 para.35
Sch.2 r.37, amended: SI 1999/787 Art.13, Sch.5 para.36
Sch.2 r.38, amended: SI 1999/787 Art.13, Sch.5 para.37
Sch.2 r.45, amended: SI 1999/787 Art.13, Sch.5 para.38
Sch.2 r.48, amended: SI 1999/787 Art.13, Sch.5 para.39
Sch.3, amended: SI 1996/739 Art.7, Sch.1 para.12

2214. Local Elections (Principal Areas) Rules 1986
r.4, amended: SI 1998/578 r.3
r.5, amended: SI 1998/578 r.4
r.6, amended: SI 1998/578 r.4
Sch.2, applied: SI 1998/746 Art.13, Sch.2 Part II
Sch.2 Appendix, amended: SI 1998/578 r.5, SI 1998/746 Art.12, Art.13, Sch.1 Table 2, Sch.2 Part II, SI 1999/394 r.7, r.8, Sch.
Sch.2 Appendix, applied: SI 1998/746 Art.12, Art.13, Sch.1 Table 2, Sch.2 Part II
Sch.2 r.3, amended: SI 1998/746 Art.12, Sch.1 Table 2
Sch.2 r.3, applied: SI 1998/746 Art.12, Art.13, Sch.1 Table 2, Sch.2 Part II
Sch.2 r.4A, added: SI 1999/394 r.4
Sch.2 r.7, amended: SI 1999/394 r.5
Sch.2 r.14, amended: SI 1999/394 r.6
Sch.2 r.15, amended: SI 1998/578 r.5, SI 1998/746 Art.12, Sch.1 Table 2
Sch.2 r.15, applied: SI 1998/746 Art.12, Art.13, Sch.1 Table 2, Sch.2 Part II
Sch.2 r.17, amended: SI 1998/578 r.5, SI 1998/746 Art.12, Sch.1 Table 2

NO.

1986—cont.

2214. Local Elections (Principal Areas) Rules 1986—cont.
Sch.2 r.17, applied: SI 1998/746 Art.12, Art.13, Sch.1 Table 2, Sch.2 Part II
Sch.2 r.18, amended: SI 1998/746 Art.12, Art.13, Sch.1 Table 2, Sch.2 Part II
Sch.2 r.18, applied: SI 1998/746 Art.12, Art.13, Sch.1 Table 2, Sch.2 Part II
Sch.2 r.19, amended: SI 1998/746 Art.12, Sch.1 Table 2
Sch.2 r.19, applied: SI 1998/746 Art.12, Art.13, Sch.1 Table 2, Sch.2 Part II
Sch.2 r.20, amended: SI 1998/746 Art.12, Sch.1 Table 2
Sch.2 r.20, applied: SI 1998/746 Art.12, Art.13, Sch.1 Table 2, Sch.2 Part II
Sch.2 r.21, amended: SI 1998/746 Art.12, Sch.1 Table 2
Sch.2 r.21, applied: SI 1998/746 Art.12, Art.13, Sch.1 Table 2, Sch.2 Part II
Sch.2 r.22, amended: SI 1998/746 Art.12, Art.13, Sch.1 Table 2, Sch.2 Part II
Sch.2 r.22, applied: SI 1998/746 Art.12, Art.13, Sch.1 Table 2, Sch.2 Part II
Sch.2 r.23, amended: SI 1998/746 Art.12, Art.13, Sch.1 Table 2, Sch.2 Part II
Sch.2 r.23, applied: SI 1998/746 Art.12, Art.13, Sch.1 Table 2, Sch.2 Part II
Sch.2 r.25, amended: SI 1998/746 Art.12, Sch.1 Table 2
Sch.2 r.25, applied: SI 1998/746 Art.12, Art.13, Sch.1 Table 2, Sch.2 Part II
Sch.2 r.26, amended: SI 1998/746 Art.12, Art.13, Sch.1 Table 2, Sch.2 Part II
Sch.2 r.26, applied: SI 1998/746 Art.12, Art.13, Sch.1 Table 2, Sch.2 Part II
Sch.2 r.27, amended: SI 1998/746 Art.12, Sch.1 Table 2
Sch.2 r.27, applied: SI 1998/746 Art.12, Art.13, Sch.1 Table 2, Sch.2 Part II
Sch.2 r.28, amended: SI 1998/746 Art.12, Sch.1 Table 2
Sch.2 r.28, applied: SI 1998/746 Art.12, Art.13, Sch.1 Table 2, Sch.2 Part II
Sch.2 r.29, amended: SI 1998/746 Art.12, Sch.1 Table 2
Sch.2 r.29, applied: SI 1998/746 Art.12, Art.13, Sch.1 Table 2, Sch.2 Part II
Sch.2 r.30, amended: SI 1998/746 Art.12, Sch.1 Table 2
Sch.2 r.30, applied: SI 1998/746 Art.12, Art.13, Sch.1 Table 2, Sch.2 Part II
Sch.2 r.31, amended: SI 1998/746 Art.12, Art.13, Sch.1 Table 2, Sch.2 Part II
Sch.2 r.31, applied: SI 1998/746 Art.12, Art.13, Sch.1 Table 2, Sch.2 Part II
Sch.2 r.32, amended: SI 1998/746 Art.12, Art.13, Sch.1 Table 2, Sch.2 Part II
Sch.2 r.32, applied: SI 1998/746 Art.12, Art.13, Sch.1 Table 2, Sch.2 Part II
Sch.2 r.33, amended: SI 1998/746 Art.12, Art.13, Sch.1 Table 2, Sch.2 Part II
Sch.2 r.33, applied: SI 1998/746 Art.12, Art.13, Sch.1 Table 2, Sch.2 Part II
Sch.2 r.34, amended: SI 1998/746 Art.12, Art.13, Sch.1 Table 2, Sch.2 Part II
Sch.2 r.34, applied: SI 1998/746 Art.12, Art.13, Sch.1 Table 2, Sch.2 Part II
Sch.2 r.35, amended: SI 1998/746 Art.12, Sch.1 Table 2
Sch.2 r.35, applied: SI 1998/746 Art.12, Art.13, Sch.1 Table 2, Sch.2 Part II

NO.

2214. Local Elections (Principal Areas) Rules 1986—*cont.*

Sch.2 r.36, amended: SI 1998/746 Art.12, Sch.1 Table 2

Sch.2 r.36, applied: SI 1998/746 Art.12, Art.13, Sch.1 Table 2, Sch.2 Part II

Sch.2 r.37, amended: SI 1998/746 Art.12, Art.13, Sch.1 Table 2, Sch.2 Part II

Sch.2 r.37, applied: SI 1998/746 Art.12, Art.13, Sch.1 Table 2, Sch.2 Part II

Sch.2 r.38, amended: SI 1998/746 Art.13, Sch.2 Part II

Sch.2 r.38, applied: SI 1998/746 Art.13, Sch.2 Part II

Sch.2 r.39, amended: SI 1998/746 Art.12, Art.13, Sch.1 Table 2, Sch.2 Part II

Sch.2 r.39, applied: SI 1998/746 Art.12, Art.13, Sch.1 Table 2, Sch.2 Part II

Sch.2 r.41, amended: SI 1998/746 Art.12, Sch.1 Table 2

Sch.2 r.41, applied: SI 1998/746 Art.12, Art.13, Sch.1 Table 2, Sch.2 Part II

Sch.2 r.42, amended: SI 1998/746 Art.12, Sch.1 Table 2

Sch.2 r.42, applied: SI 1998/746 Art.12, Art.13, Sch.1 Table 2, Sch.2 Part II

Sch.2 r.45, amended: SI 1998/746 Art.12, Sch.1 Table 2

Sch.2 r.45, applied: SI 1998/746 Art.12, Art.13, Sch.1 Table 2, Sch.2 Part II

Sch.2 r.46, amended: SI 1998/746 Art.12, Sch.1 Table 2

Sch.2 r.46, applied: SI 1998/746 Art.12, Art.13, Sch.1 Table 2, Sch.2 Part II

Sch.2 r.49, amended: SI 1998/746 Art.13, Sch.2 Part II

Sch.2 r.49, applied: SI 1998/746 Art.13, Sch.2 Part II

Sch.3, amended: SI 1998/578 r.6

Sch.3 para.3, amended: SI 1998/578 r.6

Sch.3 para.4, amended: SI 1998/578 r.6

Sch.3 para.5, amended: SI 1998/578 r.6

Sch.3 para.7, amended: SI 1998/578 r.6

Sch.3 para.15, amended: SI 1998/578 r.6

Sch.3 para.18, amended: SI 1998/578 r.6

Sch.4 para.8, amended: SI 1998/578 r.7

Sch.4 para.18, amended: SI 1998/578 r.7

Sch.4 para.24, amended: SI 1998/578 r.7

2215. Local Elections (Parishes and Communities) Rules 1986

r.4, amended: SI 1998/585 r.3

r.5, amended: SI 1998/585 r.4

r.6, amended: SI 1998/585 r.4

r.7, amended: SI 1999/722 Art.4

r.8, amended: SI 1998/585 r.5, SI 1998/2366 Art.6, SI 1998/2507 Art.5, SI 1998/2548 Art.8, SI 1998/2555 Art.9, SI 1998/2558 Art.8, SI 1998/2845 Art.10, SI 1998/2847 Art.7

r.8, applied: SI 1997/776 Art.5, SI 1997/781 Art.8, SI 1997/782 Art.5, SI 1997/780 Art.11, SI 1997/777 Art.8, SI 1997/779 Art.4, SI 1998/2366 Art.6, SI 1998/2507 Art.5, SI 1998/2548 Art.8, SI 1998/2555 Art.9, SI 1998/2558 Art.8, SI 1998/2845 Art.10, SI 1998/2847 Art.7

Sch.2 Appendix, amended: SI 1999/395 r.7, r.8, Sch., SI 1999/450 Art.14, Sch.4 para.62, Sch.4 para.63, Sch.4 para.64

Sch.2 r.1, amended: SI 1999/450 Art.14, Sch.4 para.45, SI 1999/722 Art.4

Sch.2 r.4A, added: SI 1999/395 r.4

Sch.2 r.7, amended: SI 1999/395 r.5

Sch.2 r.14, amended: SI 1999/395 r.6, SI 1999/450 Art.14, Sch.4 para.46

NO.

2215. Local Elections (Parishes and Communities) Rules 1986—*cont.*

Sch.2 r.17, amended: SI 1998/585 r.6

Sch.2 r.18, amended: SI 1999/450 Art.14, Sch.4 para.47

Sch.2 r.22, amended: SI 1999/450 Art.14, Sch.4 para.48

Sch.2 r.23, amended: SI 1999/450 Art.14, Sch.4 para.49

Sch.2 r.24, amended: SI 1999/450 Art.14, Sch.4 para.50

Sch.2 r.29, amended: SI 1999/450 Art.14, Sch.4 para.51

Sch.2 r.31, amended: SI 1999/450 Art.14, Sch.4 para.52

Sch.2 r.32, amended: SI 1999/450 Art.14, Sch.4 para.53

Sch.2 r.33, amended: SI 1999/450 Art.14, Sch.4 para.54

Sch.2 r.34, amended: SI 1999/450 Art.14, Sch.4 para.55

Sch.2 r.36, amended: SI 1999/450 Art.14, Sch.4 para.56

Sch.2 r.37, amended: SI 1999/450 Art.14, Sch.4 para.57

Sch.2 r.38, amended: SI 1999/450 Art.14, Sch.4 para.58

Sch.2 r.39, amended: SI 1999/450 Art.14, Sch.4 para.59

Sch.2 r.44, amended: SI 1998/585 r.6

Sch.2 r.46, amended: SI 1998/585 r.6, SI 1999/450 Art.14, Sch.4 para.60

Sch.2 r.47, amended: SI 1998/585 r.6

Sch.2 r.48, amended: SI 1998/585 r.6

Sch.2 r.49, amended: SI 1999/450 Art.14, Sch.4 para.61

Sch.3, amended: SI 1998/585 r.7

Sch.3 para.4, amended: SI 1998/585 r.7

Sch.3 para.20, amended: SI 1998/585 r.7

Sch.4 para.22, amended: SI 1998/585 r.8

2232. Recreation and Youth Service (Northern Ireland) Order 1986

Art.3, revoked (in part): SI 1996/1297 (NI.7) Art.23, Sch.5

2243. Dockyard Services (Devonport) (Designation and Appointed Day) Order 1986

revoked: SI 1997/152 Art.2

2244. Dockyard Services (Rosyth) (Designation and Appointed Day) Order 1986

revoked: SI 1997/151 Art.2

2249. Environmentally Sensitive Areas (South Downs) Designation Order 1986

referred to: SI 1997/1443 Art.6

2250. European Parliamentary Elections (Northern Ireland) Regulations 1986

Reg.4, amended: SI 1999/1268 Reg.3

Reg.5, amended: SI 1997/969 Reg.2, SI 1999/1268 Reg.4

Reg.5, applied: SI 1999/1342, SI 1999/1342 Art.2

Reg.5, referred to: SI 1999/1342 Sch. Part B

Reg.8, added: SI 1999/1268 Reg.5

Sch.1, amended: SI 1999/1268 Reg.6

Sch.1, applied: SI 1999/1342 Art.2

Sch.1, referred to: SI 1999/1342 Sch. Part B

Sch.1 Appendix, amended: SI 1999/1268 Reg.6, Sch.

Sch.3 Part I, amended: SI 1999/1268 Reg.7

Sch.3 Part II, amended: SI 1999/1268 Reg.7

NO.

2251. Environmentally Sensitive Areas (West Penwith) Designation Order 1986
amended: SI 1998/2232 Art.3
applied: SI 1998/2232 Art.3
revoked: SI 1997/1444 Art.6 (with saving), SI 1997/1456 Reg.2 (with saving)
Art.2, amended: SI 1996/3104 Reg.2, SI 1997/1444 para.2
Art.5, amended: SI 1996/3104 Reg.2
Art.5A, added: SI 1996/3104 Reg.2
Art.5B, added: SI 1996/3104 Reg.2
Art.5C, added: SI 1996/3104 Reg.2
Art.6, amended: SI 1996/922 Art.2, SI 1997/1444 Sch.7 para.3, SI 1998/1296 Art.6

2252. Environmentally Sensitive Areas (Somerset Levels and Moors) Designation Order 1986
referred to: SI 1997/1442 Art.6

2253. Environmentally Sensitive Areas (Pennine Dales) Designation Order 1986
referred to: SI 1997/1441 Art.6

2254. Environmentally Sensitive Areas (The Broads) Designation Order 1986
referred to: SI 1997/1440 Art.6

2257. Environmentally Sensitive Areas (Cambrian Mountains) Designation Order 1986
Art.2, amended: SI 1996/3077 Reg.2, SI 1997/970 Art.2
Art.5, amended: SI 1996/3077 Reg.2
Art.5A, added: SI 1996/3077 Reg.2
Art.5B, added: SI 1996/3077 Reg.2
Art.5C, added: SI 1996/3077 Reg.2
Art.6, amended: SI 1997/970 Art.2
Art.6, revoked (in part): SI 1997/970 Art.2
Art.7, added: SI 1999/1175 Art.2
Sch.5 para.6, amended: SI 1997/970 Art.2

2265. Importation of Salmonid Viscera Order 1986
Art.4, referred to: SI 1996/3124 Reg.40, Sch.5 Part II
Art.5, referred to: SI 1996/3124 Reg.40, Sch.5 Part II
Art.6, referred to: SI 1996/3124 Reg.40, Sch.5 Part II
Art.7, referred to: SI 1996/3124 Reg.40, Sch.5 Part II
Art.8, referred to: SI 1996/3124 Reg.40, Sch.5 Part II

2291. Children's Hearings (Scotland) Rules 1986
revoked: SI 1997/692 r.2
r.6, amended: SI 1996/1199 r.2
r.6, revoked: SI 1997/692 r.2
r.14, see *L v H* 1996 S.L.T. 612
r.14, revoked: SI 1997/692 r.2

2295. Brucellosis (England and Wales) (Amendment) Order 1986
revoked: SI 1997/758 Art.24, Sch.2

2331. Misuse of Drugs (Designation) Order 1986
Sch. Part I, amended: SI 1998/881 Art.2

1987

Post Office Regulations 1987
amended: SI 1999/450 Art.66, SI 1999/787 Art.58
applied: SI 1999/450 Art.66, SI 1999/787 Art.58
Reg.1, amended: SI 1999/450 Art.66, SI 1999/787 Art.58

Strathclyde Regional Council (Ayr Road Route) (A77) (Dumbreck to City of Glasgow District Boundary) Special Road Scheme 1987
applied: SI 1996/2863 Reg.1

NO.

2. National Health Service (Food Premises) (Scotland) Regulations 1987
applied: SI 1999/686 Art.5, Sch. Part III, SI 1999/726 Art.5, Sch. Part III

6. Health Education Authority (Establishment and Constitution) Order 1987
Art.6, added: SI 1998/1577 Art.4

7. Health Education Authority Regulations 1987
Reg.4, substituted: SI 1996/707 Reg.17, Sch.5 para.2

16. Pelican Pedestrian Crossings Regulations 1987
revoked (in part): SI 1997/2400 Reg.2, Dir.2
Sch.2, applied: SI 1996/1483 Reg.4

30. Statutory Maternity Pay (General) Regulations (Northern Ireland) 1987
Reg.7, applied: SI 1999/671 Art.3, Sch.2
Reg.25, applied: SI 1999/671 Art.3, Sch.2
Reg.30, applied: SI 1999/671 Art.3, Sch.2
Reg.31, applied: SI 1999/671 Art.3, Sch.2

37. Dangerous Substances in Harbour Areas Regulations 1987
applied: SI 1996/2791 Sch.10
Part IX, applied: SI 1996/2791 Reg.12, SI 1997/2505 Reg.12, Sch.10, SI 1999/645 Reg.12, Sch.10
Reg.2, amended: SI 1996/2092 Reg.21, Sch.5 para.2, SI 1997/2367 Reg.3
Reg.3, amended: SI 1996/2092 Reg.21, Sch.5 para.3, SI 1997/2367 Reg.3
Reg.8, applied: SI 1999/2029 Art.5, Art.6, Sch.1 Reg.24, Sch.2 r.3
Reg.24, amended: SI 1996/2092 Reg.21, Sch.5 para.4, SI 1996/2095 Reg.29, SI 1998/2885 Reg.3
Reg.25, amended: SI 1996/2092 Reg.21, Sch.5 para.5, SI 1996/2095 Reg.29
Reg.33, referred to: SI 1999/2029 Art.5, Art.6, Sch.1 Reg.23
Sch.1, amended: SI 1996/2092 Reg.21, Sch.5 para.6
Sch.3, amended: SI 1996/2092 Reg.21, Sch.5 para.7

39. Sheriff Court Fees Amendment Order 1987
revoked: SI 1997/687 Art.11, Sch.2

130. Pensions Increase (Review) Order 1987
applied: SI 1997/634 Art.3, SI 1998/503 Art.3, Art.4, SI 1999/522 Art.3

135. Brucellosis (Scotland) (Amendment) Order 1987
revoked: SI 1997/758 Art.24, Sch.2

156. Police (Injury Benefit) Regulations 1987
applied: SI 1999/1750 Art.2, Sch.1
Reg.3, see *R. v Milling Ex p. West Yorkshire Police Authority* Times, December 24, 1996 (QBD), Scott Baker, J.

160. Personal and Occupational Pension Schemes (Miscellaneous Amendments) Regulations 1987
Reg.4, referred to: 1999 c.30 s.81, Sch.11 para.36

167. Education (Northern Ireland) Order 1987
Art.3, revoked (in part): SI 1996/274 (NI.1) Art.44, Sch.6 Part I
Art.6, revoked: SI 1996/274 (NI.1) Art.44, Sch.6 Part I
Art.15, revoked: SI 1996/274 (NI.1) Art.44, Sch.6 Part I
Sch.1, revoked: SI 1996/274 (NI.1) Art.44, Sch.6 Part I

NO.

179. **Trafford Park Development Corporation (Area and Constitution) Order 1987**
Art.2, revoked: SI 1998/769 Art.2
Art.3, revoked: SI 1998/769 Art.2

214. **Social Security Commissioners Procedure Regulations 1987**
applied: SI 1996/207 Reg.44
revoked (in part): SI 1999/1495 Reg.2
Reg.2, amended: SI 1997/955 Reg.7
Reg.2, revoked (in part): SI 1999/1495 Reg.2
Reg.4, amended: SI 1997/955 Reg.8
Reg.4, revoked (in part): SI 1999/1495 Reg.2
Reg.6, amended: SI 1997/955 Reg.9
Reg.6, revoked (in part): SI 1999/1495 Reg.2

232. **Diseases of Animals (Waste Food) (Amendment) Order 1987**
revoked: SI 1999/646 Art.35, Sch.6 Part I

257. **Police Pensions Regulations 1987**
applied: SI 1999/1750 Art.2, Sch.1
Reg.13A, revoked (in part): SI 1998/577 Reg.5
Reg.A9, amended: SI 1996/867 Reg.2
Reg.A11, see *R. v Kellam Ex p. South Wales Police Authority* Times, August 24, 1999 (QBD), Richards, J.
Reg.A17, amended: SI 1998/577 Reg.3
Reg.A18, amended: SI 1998/577 Reg.5
Reg.B1, amended: SI 1998/577 Reg.4, Reg.5
Reg.B5, amended: SI 1996/867 Reg.3
Reg.B6, amended: SI 1996/867 Reg.3
Reg.F3, amended: SI 1998/577 Reg.3
Reg.F8, amended: SI 1996/867 Reg.4
Reg.F8A, added: SI 1996/867 Reg.5
Reg.F8A, amended: SI 1998/577 Reg.3
Reg.F9, amended: SI 1996/867 Reg.6
Reg.F11, added: SI 1997/2852 Reg.3
Reg.G1, amended: SI 1997/1429 Reg.2
Reg.G4, amended: SI 1997/2852 Reg.4
Reg.J3A, added: SI 1998/577 Reg.3
Reg.K4, amended: SI 1998/577 Reg.3
Reg.L2, amended: SI 1996/867 Reg.7
Sch. A, amended: SI 1997/1429 Reg.3, SI 1998/577 Reg.5

260. **Local Elections (Parishes and Communities) (Amendment) Rules 1987**
r.2, revoked (in part): SI 1999/395 r.2

261. **Local Elections (Principal Areas) (Amendment) Rules 1987**
r.2, revoked (in part): SI 1999/394 r.2

281. **Occupational Pension Schemes (Contracting Out Protected Rights Premiums) Regulations 1987**
Reg.2, applied: 1999 c.30 s.81, Sch.11 para.36

289. **Personal Pension Schemes (Personal Pension Protected Rights Premiums) Regulations 1987**
applied: 1999 c.30 s.81, Sch.11 para.36
Reg.5, referred to: 1999 c.30 s.81, Sch.11 para.36
Reg.6, referred to: 1999 c.30 s.81, Sch.11 para.36

293. **Local Government Superannuation (Miscellaneous Provisions) Regulations 1987**
Reg.2, amended: SI 1997/1613 Reg.27, Sch.3 para.3
Reg.2, applied: SI 1997/1612 Reg.130
Reg.16, revoked: SI 1996/1680 Reg.49, Sch.5
Reg.25, applied: SI 1996/1680 Reg.7

293. **Personal and Occupational Pension Schemes (Incentive Payments) Regulations (Northern Ireland) 1987**
applied: SI 1999/671 Art.3, Sch.2

NO.

299. **Prosecution of Offences (Custody Time Limits) Regulations 1987**
see *R. v Manchester Crown Court Ex p. McDonald* [1999] 1 W.L.R. 841 (QBD), Lord Bingham of Cornhill, L.C.J.
applied: SI 1998/3037 Reg.20
Reg.2, amended: 1996 c.25 s.71
Reg.4, see *Najam, Re* Independent, October 19, 1998 (C.S.) (QBD), Kennedy, L.J.; see *R. v Stratford Youth Court Ex p. S* [1998] 1 W.L.R. 1758 (QBD), Schiemann, L.J.
Reg.4, amended: 1996 c.25 s.71, SI 1999/2744 Reg.2
Reg.5, amended: 1996 c.25 s.71, SI 1998/3037 Reg.2
Reg.5, revoked (in part): 1996 c.25 Sch.5 para.2
Reg.6, see *Olotu v Home Office* [1997] 1 All E.R. 385 (CA), Lord Bingham of Cornhill, L.C.J.

306. **Motor Vehicles (Type Approval) (EEC) Regulations (Northern Ireland) 1987**
applied: SI 1998/2051 Reg.19
Sch.3 Part II, referred to: SI 1998/2051 Reg.19

307. **Criminal Legal Aid (Scotland) Regulations 1987**
revoked: SI 1996/2555 Reg.3, Sch.
Reg.4, amended: SI 1996/627 Reg.3
Reg.4, revoked: SI 1996/2555 Reg.3, Sch.
Reg.7, see *McKinstry v The Law Society of Scotland* 1996 S.C.L.R. 421 (OH)
Reg.7, revoked: SI 1996/2555 Reg.3, Sch.
Reg.17, amended: SI 1996/627 Reg.4
Reg.17, revoked: SI 1996/2555 Reg.3, Sch.

309. **Colleges of Education (Scotland) Regulations 1987**
revoked (in part): SI 1998/1644 Art.8, SI 1999/442 Art.8
Sch.1, amended: SI 1996/1971 Art.2
Sch.1, revoked (in part): SI 1999/442 Art.8

311. **Merchant Shipping (Submersible Craft Operations) Regulations 1987**
applied: SI 1996/3243 Sch Part I

317. **Social Security (Unemployment, Sickness and Invalidity Benefit) Amendment Regulations 1987**
revoked: SI 1996/1345 Reg.27, Sch.

381. **Civil Legal Aid (Scotland) Regulations 1987**
revoked: SI 1996/2444 Reg.3, Sch.1
Reg.5, amended: SI 1996/812 Reg.4, Reg.5
Reg.5, revoked: SI 1996/2444 Reg.3, Sch.1
Reg.7, amended: SI 1996/812 Reg.4, Reg.5
Reg.7, revoked: SI 1996/2444 Reg.3, Sch.1
Reg.18, see *L v Kennedy* 1996 S.C.L.R. 202 (IH)
Reg.18, revoked: SI 1996/2444 Reg.3, Sch.1
Reg.23, revoked (in part): SI 1996/812 Reg.3, SI 1996/2444 Reg.3, Sch.1
Reg.46, amended: SI 1996/812 Reg.4
Reg.46, revoked: SI 1996/2444 Reg.3, Sch.1
Reg.47, amended: SI 1996/812 Reg.5
Reg.47, revoked: SI 1996/2444 Reg.3, Sch.1

382. **Advice and Assistance (Scotland) Regulations 1987**
revoked: SI 1996/2447 Reg.3, Sch.1
Reg.4, amended: SI 1996/811 Reg.3
Reg.4, revoked: SI 1996/2447 Reg.3, Sch.1
Reg.4A, added: SI 1996/811 Reg.4
Reg.4A, revoked: SI 1996/2447 Reg.3, Sch.1
Reg.5, amended: SI 1996/811 Reg.5
Reg.5, revoked: SI 1996/2447 Reg.3, Sch.1
Sch.3 Part I, amended: SI 1996/811 Reg.6
Sch.3 Part I, revoked: SI 1996/2447 Reg.3, Sch.1

NO.

1987—cont.

384. **Legal Aid (Scotland) (Children) Regulations 1987**
revoked: SI 1997/690 Reg.12 (with savings)

402. **Control of Pollution (Landed Ships' Waste) Regulations 1987**
revoked: SI 1996/972 Reg.26

403. **Public Trustee (Fees) (Amendment) Order 1987**
revoked: SI 1999/855 Art.32, Sch.

408. **Merchant Shipping (Seamen's Documents) Regulations 1987**
Reg.5, applied: SI 1996/3243 Sch Part X
Reg.18, amended: SI 1999/3281 Reg.2
Reg.18, applied: SI 1996/3243 Sch Part X
Reg.20, amended: SI 1999/3281 Reg.2
Reg.20, revoked (in part): SI 1999/3281 Reg.2
Reg.24, amended: SI 1999/3281 Reg.2
Sch.4, substituted: SI 1999/3281 Reg.2

414. **Control of Pesticides Regulations (Northern Ireland) 1987**
referred to: SI 1997/322 Reg.36

416. **Social Security (Maternity Allowance) Regulations 1987**
Reg.1A, added: SI 1997/2676 Reg.13
Reg.3, revoked (in part): SI 1997/793 Reg.18

418. **Statutory Maternity Pay (Persons Abroad and Mariners) Regulations 1987**
applied: SI 1996/777 Reg.6
Reg.1, amended: SI 1996/777 Reg.4
Reg.2A, added: SI 1996/777 Reg.4
Reg.4, revoked: SI 1996/777 Reg.4
Reg.5, amended: SI 1996/777 Reg.4
Reg.5, revoked (in part): SI 1996/777 Reg.4
Reg.9, revoked: SI 1996/777 Reg.4

427. **Act of Sederunt (Legal Aid Rules) (Children) 1987**
r.1, amended: SI 1997/1194 r.2
r.1, revoked (in part): SI 1997/1194 r.2
r.3, substituted: SI 1997/1194 r.2

431. **Civil Legal Aid (Scotland) Amendment Regulations 1987**
revoked: SI 1996/2444 Reg.3, Sch.1

433. **Town and Country Planning (Compensation for Restrictions on Mineral Workings) (Scotland) Regulations 1987**
revoked: SI 1998/2914 Reg.8
Reg.1, revoked: SI 1998/2914 Reg.8

439. **Police and Criminal Evidence Act 1984 (Application to Customs and Excise) Order 1987**
Art.4, substituted: SI 1996/1860 Art.3

458. **Agriculture (Environmental Areas) (Northern Ireland) Order 1987**
Art.3, applied: SI 1997/2844 Sch.3 Part I, Sch.4 para.3

459. **Income Support (General) Regulations (Northern Ireland) 1987**
Reg.21, amended: 1996 c.49 Sch.1 para.8

460. **Audit (Northern Ireland) Order 1987**
referred to: SI 1996/275 (NI.2) Art.44
Art.2, revoked (in part): 1998 c.47 s.100, Sch.15
Art.4, applied: 1998 c.47 s.65
Art.4, revoked (in part): 1998 c.47 s.100, Sch.15
Art.6, amended: 1998 c.47 s.99, Sch.13 para.7
Art.6, applied: 1998 c.47 s.66
Art.6, revoked (in part): 1998 c.47 s.100, Sch.15
Art.11, revoked (in part): 1998 c.47 s.100, Sch.15
Sch.1 para.4, revoked (in part): 1998 c.47 s.100, Sch.15

1987—cont.

460. **Audit (Northern Ireland) Order 1987**—*cont.*
Sch.1 para.5, revoked (in part): SI 1996/1919 (NI.16) Art.257, Sch.3
Sch.2 para.4, revoked (in part): 1998 c.47 s.100, Sch.15

461. **Housing Benefit (General) Regulations (Northern Ireland) 1987**
applied: SI 1996/3274 Art.4, SI 1998/1004 Art.5
Reg.7A, amended: 1996 c.49 Sch.1 para.9

463. **Family Credit (General) Regulations (Northern Ireland) 1987**
applied: SI 1999/3219 Reg.3
Reg.2, amended: SI 1999/2488 Reg.3, Reg.26, Sch.1, SI 1999/3188 Reg.4
Reg.2A, amended: SI 1999/2488 Reg.26, Sch.1
Reg.3, amended: SI 1999/2488 Reg.26, Sch.1, Sch.2
Reg.4, amended: SI 1999/2488 Reg.26, Sch.1, SI 1999/3188 Reg.5
Reg.4A, amended: SI 1999/2488 Reg.26, Sch.1
Reg.6, amended: SI 1999/2488 Reg.26, Sch.1
Reg.12, amended: SI 1999/2488 Reg.4
Reg.13, amended: SI 1999/2488 Reg.5, Reg.26, Sch.1
Reg.13, revoked (in part): SI 1999/2488 Reg.5
Reg.13A, amended: SI 1999/2488 Reg.6
Reg.14, amended: SI 1999/2488 Reg.26, Sch.1
Reg.19, amended: SI 1999/2488 Reg.26
Reg.20, amended: SI 1999/2488 Reg.26
Reg.22, amended: SI 1999/2488 Reg.26
Reg.26, amended: SI 1999/2488 Reg.26, Sch.1, SI 1999/3188 Reg.6
Reg.28, amended: SI 1999/2488 Reg.26, Sch.1
Reg.29, amended: SI 1999/2488 Reg.26, Sch.1
Reg.31, amended: SI 1999/3188 Reg.10
Reg.34, amended: SI 1999/2488 Reg.26, Sch.1, SI 1999/3188 Reg.7
Reg.34A, amended: SI 1999/2488 Reg.26, Sch.1
Reg.46, amended: SI 1999/2488 Reg.7, Reg.26, Sch.1
Reg.46A, added: SI 1999/2488 Reg.6
Reg.46A, amended: SI 1999/2488 Reg.8, Reg.26, Sch.1
Reg.47, amended: SI 1999/2488 Reg.9, Reg.26, Sch.1
Reg.48, amended: SI 1999/2488 Reg.10, Reg.26, Sch.1
Reg.49, amended: SI 1999/2488 Reg.26, Sch.1
Reg.49A, amended: SI 1999/2488 Reg.26, Reg.27, Sch.1
Reg.50, amended: SI 1999/2488 Reg.26, Sch.1, Sch.2
Reg.51, amended: SI 1999/2488 Reg.26, Reg.27, Sch.1, Sch.2
Reg.51A, revoked: SI 1999/2488 Reg.11
Reg.52, amended: SI 1999/2488 Reg.26, Sch.1, Sch.2
Sch.2 para.4, amended: SI 1999/2488 Reg.26, Sch.2
Sch.2 para.48, amended: SI 1999/2488 Reg.12
Sch.2 para.60, amended: SI 1999/3188 Reg.10
Sch.2 para.65, amended: SI 1999/3188 Reg.8
Sch.2 para.66, amended: SI 1999/3188 Reg.8
Sch.3 para.6, amended: SI 1999/3188 Reg.10
Sch.3 para.11, amended: SI 1999/2488 Reg.26, Sch.1
Sch.3 para.52, amended: SI 1999/3188 Reg.10
Sch.3 para.57, amended: SI 1999/3188 Reg.9
Sch.3 para.58, amended: SI 1999/3188 Reg.9
Sch.4, amended: SI 1999/2488 Reg.13, Reg.26, Sch.1

NO.

463. Public Order (Northern Ireland) Order 1987
Art.2, revoked (in part): 1998 c.2 s.18, Sch.4
Art.3, amended: SI 1997/1181 (NI.10) Art.3
Art.3, revoked: 1998 c.2 s.18, Sch.4
Art.4, amended: 1998 c.2 s.18, Sch.3 para.3
Art.4, applied: 1998 c.2 s.7
Art.4, revoked (in part): 1998 c.2 s.18, Sch.4
Art.5, amended: 1998 c.2 s.18, Sch.3 para.3
Art.5, revoked (in part): 1998 c.2 s.18, Sch.4
Art.6, revoked: 1998 c.2 s.18, Sch.4
Art.6A, added: SI 1997/1181 (NI.10) Art.4
Art.6A, revoked: 1998 c.2 s.18, Sch.4
Art.7, revoked (in part): 1998 c.2 s.18, Sch.4
Art.15, amended: SI 1999/1820 Art.4, Sch.2 para.143
Art.22, amended: 1996 c.26 s.2
Art.22, applied: 1996 c.26 s.4
Art.24, amended: 1998 c.2 s.18, Sch.3 para.3
Art.28, revoked (in part): 1998 c.2 s.18, Sch.4
Sch.1 para.4, revoked: 1998 c.2 s.18, Sch.4

465. Social Security (Claims and Payments) Regulations (Northern Ireland) 1987
Part V, amended: SI 1999/2574 Reg.16
Reg.2, amended: SI 1999/2574 Reg.3, Reg.20, Reg.24, Reg.25, Sch. Part I, Sch. Part V, Sch. Part VI
Reg.4, amended: SI 1999/2574 Reg.4, Reg.20, Reg.21, Reg.25, Sch. Part I, Sch. Part II, Sch. Part VI
Reg.5, amended: SI 1999/2574 Reg.20, Sch. Part I
Reg.6, amended: SI 1999/2574 Reg.5, Reg.24, Reg.25, Sch. Part V, Sch. Part VI
Reg.6, revoked (in part): SI 1999/2574 Reg.5
Reg.7, amended: SI 1999/2574 Reg.6, Reg.21, Reg.24, Reg.25, Sch. Part II, Sch. Part V, Sch. Part VI
Reg.8, amended: SI 1999/2574 Reg.20, Sch. Part I
Reg.9, amended: SI 1999/2574 Reg.20, Reg.22, Sch. Part I, Sch. Part III
Reg.13, amended: SI 1999/2574 Reg.7, Reg.24, Reg.25, Sch. Part V, Sch. Part VI
Reg.16, amended: SI 1999/2574 Reg.8, Reg.24, Reg.25, Sch. Part V, Sch. Part VI
Reg.17, amended: SI 1999/2574 Reg.9, Reg.24, Reg.25, Sch. Part V, Sch. Part VI
Reg.19, amended: SI 1999/2574 Reg.10, Reg.22, Reg.24, Reg.25, Sch. Part III, Sch. Part V, Sch. Part VI
Reg.20, amended: SI 1999/2574 Reg.20, Sch. Part I
Reg.20A, amended: SI 1999/2574 Reg.20, Reg.23, Sch. Part I, Sch. Part IV
Reg.21, amended: SI 1999/2574 Reg.11, Reg.20, Reg.22, Reg.23, Sch. Part I, Sch. Part III, Sch. Part IV
Reg.27, amended: SI 1999/2574 Reg.12, Reg.24, Reg.25, Sch. Part V, Sch. Part VI
Reg.29, amended: SI 1999/2574 Reg.20, Sch. Part I
Reg.30, amended: SI 1999/2574 Reg.13, Reg.20, Reg.22, Reg.24, Reg.25, Sch. Part I, Sch. Part III, Sch. Part V, Sch. Part VI
Reg.32, amended: SI 1999/2574 Reg.14, Reg.20, Sch. Part I
Reg.33, amended: SI 1999/2574 Reg.15, Reg.20, Reg.22, Reg.23, Sch. Part I, Sch. Part III, Sch. Part IV
Reg.34, amended: SI 1999/2574 Reg.20, Sch. Part I

NO.

465. Social Security (Claims and Payments) Regulations (Northern Ireland) 1987—*cont.*
Reg.35, amended: SI 1999/2574 Reg.20, Reg.24, Reg.25, Sch. Part I, Sch. Part V, Sch. Part VI
Reg.36, revoked: SI 1999/2574 Reg.17
Reg.36A, revoked: SI 1999/2574 Reg.17
Reg.36B, revoked: SI 1999/2574 Reg.17
Reg.37, amended: SI 1999/2574 Reg.18, Reg.20, Reg.23, Sch. Part I, Sch. Part IV
Reg.46, amended: SI 1999/2574 Reg.19, Reg.20, Reg.22, Sch. Part I, Sch. Part III
Sch.1 Part I, amended: SI 1999/2574 Reg.24, Reg.25, Sch. Part V, Sch. Part VI
Sch.4 para.7, amended: SI 1999/2574 Reg.24, Reg.25, Sch. Part V, Sch. Part VI
Sch.4 para.11, amended: SI 1999/2574 Reg.24, Reg.25, Sch. Part V, Sch. Part VI

470. Merchant Shipping (Prevention and Control of Pollution) Order 1987
Art.5, added: SI 1997/2569 Art.2
Art.5, amended: SI 1998/254 Art.2

481. Social Fund Maternity and Funeral Expenses (General) Regulations 1987
Reg.3, amended: SI 1996/1443 Reg.2, SI 1997/792 Reg.2, SI 1997/2538 Reg.3
Reg.4, amended: SI 1997/792 Reg.3, SI 1997/2538 Reg.4, SI 1999/3178 Art.3, Sch.4, SI 1999/3266 Reg.2
Reg.5, amended: SI 1996/1443 Reg.3, SI 1997/792 Reg.4, SI 1999/2566 Reg.2, Sch.2 Part I, Sch.2 Part II
Reg.6, amended: SI 1996/1443 Reg.4, SI 1999/2566 Reg.2, Sch.2 Part I, Sch.2 Part II
Reg.7, see *O'Flynn v Adjudication Officer (C237/94)* [1996] All E.R. (EC) 541 (ECJ), DAO Edward (President)
Reg.7, amended: SI 1996/1443 Reg.5, SI 1997/2538 Reg.5, SI 1999/2566 Reg.2, Sch.2 Part I, Sch.2 Part II, SI 1999/3266 Reg.2
Reg.7, applied: SI 1999/3266 Reg.3
Reg.7, substituted: SI 1997/792 Reg.5
Reg.7A, added: SI 1997/792 Reg.5
Reg.7A, amended: SI 1997/2538 Reg.6, SI 1999/3266 Reg.2
Reg.7A, applied: SI 1999/3266 Reg.3
Reg.8, amended: SI 1996/1443 Reg.6, SI 1997/792 Reg.6
Reg.9, amended: SI 1996/1443 Reg.7, SI 1997/792 Reg.7

485. District of Kingswood (Electoral Arrangements) Order 1987
revoked: SI 1998/2701 Art.14

492. Act of Sederunt (Civil Legal Aid Rules) 1987
r.1, amended: SI 1996/3202 r.2
r.6, amended: SI 1996/2148 r.2
r.7, added: SI 1996/2148 r.2
r.8, added: SI 1996/2148 r.2

516. Stamp Duty (Exempt Instruments) Regulations 1987
Reg.1A, added: SI 1999/2539 Reg.3
Reg.2, amended: SI 1999/2539 Reg.4
Sch., amended: SI 1999/2539 Reg.5

549. Merchant Shipping (IBC Code) Regulations 1987
applied: SI 1996/3243 Sch Part I
revoked: SI 1996/3010 Reg.1

550. Merchant Shipping (BCH Code) Regulations 1987
applied: SI 1996/3243 Sch Part I
revoked: SI 1996/3010 Reg.1

NO.   NO.

1987—cont.   *1987—cont.*

551. **Merchant Shipping (Control of Pollution by Noxious Liquid Substances in Bulk) Regulations 1987**
applied: SI 1996/3243 Sch Part I
revoked: SI 1996/3010 Reg.1

561. **Local Elections (Communities) (Welsh Forms) Order 1987**
Sch. Part I, amended: SI 1999/450 Art.14, Sch.4 para.51, Sch.4 para.64

562. **Local Elections (Principal Areas) (Welsh Forms) Order 1987**
Sch.2 Part I, amended: SI 1999/450 Art.14, Sch.4 para.43

606. **Social Security Benefit (Computation of Earnings) Amendment Regulations 1987**
revoked: SI 1996/2745 Reg.18, Sch.4

665. **Food and Environment Protection Act 1985 (Guernsey) Order 1987**
Art.3, amended: SI 1997/1770 Art.2
Sch. para.10, substituted: SI 1997/1770 Art.3
Sch. para.13, substituted: SI 1997/1770 Art.4
Sch. para.17, amended: SI 1997/1770 Art.5

667. **Food and Environment Protection Act 1985 (Jersey) Order 1987**
Art.3, amended: SI 1997/1771 Art.2
Sch. para.10, substituted: SI 1997/1771 Art.3
Sch. para.17, amended: SI 1997/1771 Art.4

670. **Carriage of Passengers and their Luggage by Sea (Domestic Carriage) Order 1987**
referred to: SI 1998/2917 Art.2

671. **Home-Grown Cereals Authority Levy Scheme (Approval) Order 1987**
applied: SI 1996/1454, SI 1997/1337, SI 1999/1577
referred to: SI 1996/2843, SI 1998/1314
para.4, amended: SI 1996/2843 Sch. para.3
para.9, amended: SI 1996/2843 Sch. para.4

674. **Medicines (Products Other Than Veterinary Drugs) (Prescription Only) Amendment Order 1987**
revoked: SI 1997/1830 Art.16, Sch.6

675. **Motor Cycles (Eye Protectors) (Amendment) Regulations 1987**
revoked: SI 1999/535 Reg.3, Sch.

701. **Town and Country Planning (Appeals) (Written Representations Procedure) Regulations 1987**
Reg.9, see *Dixon v Secretary of State for the Environment* [1997] J.P.L. 346 (QBD), George Bartlett Q.C.

716. **Crown Court (Advance Notice of Expert Evidence) Rules 1987**
r.3, amended: SI 1997/700 r.3

730. **Meters (Certification) Order 1987**
revoked: SI 1998/1566 Reg.12

738. **Town and Country Planning (Trafford Park Urban Development Area) Special Development Order 1987**
revoked: SI 1998/84 Art.2, Sch.

739. **Trafford Park Development Corporation (Planning Functions) Order 1987**
revoked: SI 1998/84 Art.2, Sch.

750. **Cambridge Water Order 1987**
revoked: SI 1996/713 Art.4, Sch.2 Part II

752. **Companies (Forms) (Amendment) Regulations 1987**
Sch.2 Form 600, amended: SI 1999/1820 Art.4, Sch.2 para.144

755. **Secure Tenancies (Notices) Regulations 1987**
Sch. Part I, amended: SI 1997/71 Reg.2, SI 1997/377 Reg.2

764. **Town and Country Planning (Use Classes) Order 1987**
see *Bromley LBC v Secretary of State for the Environment* [1996] E.G.C.S. 41 (QBD), Christopher Lockhart-Mummery Q.C.; see *Hyde Park Residence Ltd v Secretary of State for the Environment Transport and the Regions* [1999] 3 P.L.R. 1 (QBD), Lockhart-Mummery Q.C.; see *Kalra v Secretary of State for the Environment and Waltham Forest BC* [1996] 72 P. & C.R. 423 (CA), Staughton, L.J.; see *R. v Maldon DC Ex p. Pattani* [1998] 1 P.L.R. 91 (QBD), Collins, J.
Art.3, amended: SI 1999/293 Reg.35
Class A1, see *Lambeth LBC v Zedprime Ltd* (1996) 11 P.A.D. 100; see *R. v Kensington and Chelsea RLBC Ex p. Europa Foods Ltd* [1996] E.G.C.S. 5 (QBD), Macpherson, J.

773. **Patronage (Benefices) Rules 1987**
applied: SI 1996/3085 Sch. Table VI

775. **Wireless Telegraphy (Exemption) (Amendment) (Cordless Telephone Apparatus) Regulations 1987**
revoked: SI 1996/316 Reg.2, Sch.1

776. **Wireless Telegraphy (Exemption) (Amendment) (Model Control Apparatus) Regulations 1987**
revoked: SI 1999/930 Reg.2, Sch.1

821. **Court Funds Rules 1987**
amended: SI 1999/1021 r.2
applied: SI 1999/1021 r.23
r.2, amended: SI 1997/177 r.2, SI 1999/1021 r.3
r.9, amended: SI 1999/1021 r.4
r.14, amended: SI 1999/1021 r.5
r.15, amended: SI 1999/1021 r.6
r.16, amended: SI 1999/1021 r.7
r.16, revoked (in part): SI 1999/1021 r.7
r.17, amended: SI 1999/1021 r.8
r.19, substituted: SI 1999/1021 r.9
r.19A, added: SI 1999/1021 r.10
r.22, substituted: SI 1999/1021 r.50
r.22, amended: SI 1999/1021 r.11
r.23, amended: SI 1999/1021 r.12
r.24, substituted: SI 1999/1021 r.13
r.25, substituted: SI 1999/1021 r.14
r.27, applied: SI 1996/2803 Reg.3
r.27, amended: SI 1999/1021 r.16
r.28, amended: SI 1999/1021 r.15
r.31, amended: SI 1999/1021 r.17
r.32, amended: SI 1999/1021 r.18
r.32, revoked (in part): SI 1999/1021 r.18
r.34, amended: SI 1997/177 r.3
r.38, amended: SI 1999/1021 r.19
r.40, substituted: SI 1997/177 r.4
r.44, amended: SI 1997/177 r.5, r.6, SI 1999/1021 r.20
r.44, revoked (in part): SI 1999/1021 r.20
r.45, substituted: SI 1999/1021 r.21

853. **Public Order (Football Exclusion) Order 1987**
revoked: SI 1999/2460 Art.2

855. **Carriage of Passengers and their Luggage by Sea (United Kingdom Carriers) Order 1987**
revoked: SI 1998/2917 Art.2

867. **Importation of Bees (Amendment) Order 1987**
revoked: SI 1997/310 Art.8, Sch

874. **Stansted Airport Aircraft Movement Limit Order 1987**
applied: SI 1999/2120
Art.2, amended: SI 1996/1619 Art.2

NO.

874. Stansted Airport Aircraft Movement Limit Order 1987—*cont.*
Art.2, substituted: SI 1999/2120 Art.2

883. Advice and Assistance (Scotland) Amendment Regulations 1987
revoked: SI 1996/2447 Reg.3, Sch.1

884. Merchant Shipping (Certification of Deck and Marine Engineer Officers and Licensing of Marine Engine Operators) (Amendment) Regulations 1987
revoked: SI 1997/348 Reg.1

891. Building Societies Appeal Tribunal Regulations 1987
Reg.6, applied: SI 1999/678 Sch., SI 1999/1748 Art.3, Sch.1 para.23, SI 1999/1750 Art.2, Sch.1

922. Black Country Development Corporation (Area and Constitution) Order 1987
Art.2, revoked: SI 1998/769 Art.2
Art.3, revoked: SI 1998/769 Art.2

923. Teesside Development Corporation (Area and Constitution) Order 1987
Art.2, revoked: SI 1998/769 Art.2
Art.3, revoked: SI 1998/769 Art.2

924. Tyne and Wear Development Corporation (Area and Constitution) Order 1987
Art.2, revoked: SI 1998/769 Art.2
Art.3, revoked: SI 1998/769 Art.2

928. Visiting Forces and International Headquarters (Application of Law) (Amendment) Order 1987
revoked: SI 1999/1736 Art.19, Sch.9

936. Industrial Relations (Northern Ireland) Order 1987
revoked (in part): SI 1996/1919 (NI.16) Art.257, Sch.3
Sch.3 para.4, revoked (in part): SI 1996/1921 (NI.18) Art.28, Sch.3

938. Police (Northern Ireland) Order 1987
referred to: SR 1999/176 Art.3
revoked: 1998 c.32 s.74, Sch.6
Sch.1 para.16, revoked (in part): SI 1996/1919 (NI.16) Art.257, Sch.3, 1998 c.32 s.74, Sch.6

942. Financial Services Act 1986 (Delegation) Order 1987
applied: SI 1996/1669 Reg.13
referred to: SI 1996/2827 Reg.73

1088. Yorkshire Dales Light Railway Order 1987
Art.12, amended: SI 1997/102 Art.11
Art.12, applied: SI 1997/102 Art.11

1099. Contracting Out (Transfer) Amendment Regulations 1987
revoked: SI 1996/1462 Reg.14, Sch.3

1100. Contracting Out (Widowers' Guaranteed Minimum Pensions) Regulations 1987
revoked: SI 1996/1172 Sch.2

1101. Money Purchase Contracted Out Schemes Regulations 1987
revoked: SI 1996/1172 Sch.2

1103. Occupational Pension Schemes (Contracted Out Protected Rights Premiums) Regulations 1987
referred to: SI 1996/1172 Reg.77
Reg.2, applied: 1999 c.30 s.81, Sch.11 para.35
Reg.3, revoked: SI 1996/1172 Sch.2
Reg.4, revoked: SI 1996/1172 Sch.2
Reg.5, revoked: SI 1996/1172 Sch.2
Reg.6, revoked: SI 1996/1172 Sch.2
Reg.7, revoked: SI 1996/1172 Sch.2

1104. Occupational Pension Schemes (Contracting Out) Amendment Regulations 1987
revoked: SI 1996/1172 Sch.2

NO.

1105. Occupational Pension Schemes (Disclosure of Information) (Amendment) Regulations 1987
revoked: SI 1996/1655 Reg.12, Sch.4

1106. Occupational Pension Schemes (Qualifying Service - Consequential and Other Provisions) Regulations 1987
Reg.2, revoked: SI 1996/1172 Sch.2
Reg.4, revoked: SI 1997/784 Reg.12, Sch.2

1107. Occupational Pension Schemes (Transfer Values) Amendment Regulations 1987
revoked: SI 1996/1847 Reg.21, Sch.3

1108. Pension Schemes (Voluntary Contributions Requirements and Voluntary and Compulsory Membership) Regulations 1987
Reg.2, applied: SI 1997/1612 Reg.60, SI 1998/366 Reg.59

1110. Personal Pension Schemes (Disclosure of Information) Regulations 1987
applied: SI 1997/786 Reg.3, Sch.1 para.1
Reg.1, amended: SI 1996/776 Reg.4, SI 1997/786 Reg.3, Sch.1 para.1
Reg.5, amended: SI 1996/776 Reg.4, SI 1996/1435 Reg.3, SI 1997/786 Reg.3, Sch.1 para.1
Sch.1 para.5, amended: SI 1997/786 Reg.3, Sch.1 para.1
Sch.1 para.7, amended: SI 1996/776 Reg.4
Sch.2 para.2, applied: SI 1996/1676 Reg.3, Reg.4, SI 1996/1901 Reg.3
Sch.2 para.2, referred to: SI 1996/1901 Reg.4
Sch.2 para.10, amended: SI 1997/786 Reg.3, Sch.1 para.1
Sch.2 para.12, added: SI 1996/1435 Reg.3

1111. Personal Pension Schemes (Personal Pension Protected Rights Premiums) Regulations 1987
applied: 1999 c.30 s.81, Sch.11 para.35
revoked: SI 1997/786 Reg.4 (with savings), Sch.2 (with savings)
Reg.5, referred to: 1999 c.30 s.81, Sch.11 para.35
Reg.6, referred to: 1999 c.30 s.81, Sch.11 para.35

1112. Personal Pension Schemes (Transfer Values) Regulations 1987
Reg.2, amended: SI 1997/786 Reg.3, Sch.1 para.2
Reg.2A, applied: SI 1997/784 Reg.3

1113. Personal and Occupational Pension Schemes (Abatement of Benefit) Regulations 1987
Reg.2, applied: SI 1996/1461 Reg.6
Reg.3, amended: SI 1996/776 Reg.5
Reg.5, amended: SI 1996/776 Reg.5

1114. Personal and Occupational Pension Schemes (Consequential Provisions) Regulations 1987
Reg.2, revoked: SI 1997/358 Reg.7, Sch
Reg.3, revoked: SI 1997/358 Reg.7, Sch
Reg.4, revoked: SI 1996/1172 Sch.2
Reg.6, revoked: SI 1996/1462 Reg.14, Sch.3
Reg.7, revoked: SI 1997/784 Reg.12, Sch.2
Reg.8, revoked: SI 1996/1847 Reg.21, Sch.3

1115. Personal and Occupational Pension Schemes (Incentive Payments) Regulations 1987
applied: 1999 c.2 s.1, Sch.2
Reg.3, applied: SI 1996/1537 Reg.3

NO.

1117. Personal and Occupational Pension Schemes (Protected Rights) Regulations 1987
revoked: SI 1996/1537 Reg.18, Sch.
Reg.5A, added: SI 1996/776 Reg.3
Reg.5B, added: SI 1996/776 Reg.3
Reg.5B, applied: SI 1996/1311 Reg.3
Reg.6, amended: SI 1996/776 Reg.3
Reg.8, amended: SI 1996/776 Reg.3
Reg.10, amended: SI 1996/776 Reg.3
Reg.10A, added: SI 1996/776 Reg.3
Reg.13, amended: SI 1996/776 Reg.3
Reg.14, revoked: SI 1996/1172 Sch.2

1118. Protected Rights (Transfer Payment) Regulations 1987
amended: SI 1996/1461 Sch.2
revoked: SI 1996/1461 Reg.7 (with savings), Sch.1
Reg.1, applied: SI 1996/1461 Reg.7
Reg.2, applied: SI 1996/1461 Reg.6, Reg.7
Reg.3, applied: SI 1996/1461 Reg.6, Reg.7
Reg.4, applied: SI 1996/1461 Reg.7

1120. General Medical Council (Constitution of Fitness to Practise Committees) (Amendment) Rules Order of Council 1987
revoked: SI 1996/2125 Sch. para.16, Sch. Sch.2

1176. Non-Contentious Probate Fees (Amendment) Order 1987
revoked: SI 1999/688 Art.6 (with savings), Sch.2 (with savings)

1182. Direct Grant Schools (Amendment) Regulations 1987
revoked: SI 1998/86 Reg.2, Sch.1

1183. Education (Abolition of Corporal Punishment) (Independent Schools) Regulations 1987
Reg.2, revoked (in part): SI 1998/86 Reg.2, Sch.1

1229. Section 19 Minibus (Designated Bodies) Order 1987
Sch. Item 1A, added: SI 1997/535 Art.5
Sch. Item 9, substituted: SI 1997/535 Art.9
Sch. Item 10, revoked: SI 1997/535 Art.9
Sch. Item 11, revoked: SI 1997/535 Art.9
Sch. Item 13, amended: SI 1997/535 Art.7
Sch. Item 15, amended: SI 1997/535 Art.7
Sch. Item 16, amended: SI 1997/535 Art.7
Sch. Item 25, amended: SI 1997/535 Art.7
Sch. Item 30A, revoked: SI 1997/535 Art.4
Sch. Item 35, amended: SI 1997/535 Art.7
Sch. Item 42, amended: SI 1997/535 Art.6
Sch. Item 44B, amended: SI 1997/535 Art.6
Sch. Item 48, amended: SI 1997/535 Art.6
Sch. Item 50, amended: SI 1997/535 Art.6
Sch. Item 51, revoked: SI 1997/535 Art.4
Sch. Item 53, amended: SI 1997/535 Art.7
Sch. Item 59, amended: SI 1997/535 Art.6, Art.7
Sch. Item 72, revoked: SI 1997/535 Art.4
Sch. Item 73, revoked: SI 1997/535 Art.4
Sch. Item 75, amended: SI 1997/535 Art.8
Sch. Item 76, amended: SI 1997/535 Art.7
Sch. Item 80, amended: SI 1997/535 Art.7

1230. Minibus and Other Section 19 Permit Buses Regulations 1987
Reg.2, amended: SI 1996/3088 Reg.2
Reg.3, amended: SI 1997/2916 Reg.2
Reg.3, substituted: SI 1996/3088 Reg.2

1250. Medicines (Products Other Than Veterinary Drugs) (Prescription Only) Amendment (No.2) Order 1987
revoked: SI 1997/1830 Art.16, Sch.6

NO.

1256. Prison (Amendment) Rules 1987
revoked: SI 1999/728 r.85 (with savings), Sch. (with savings)

1265. Continental Shelf (Designation of Additional Areas) Order 1987
referred to: SI 1999/2031

1278. Registration of Clubs (Northern Ireland) Order 1987
applied: SI 1996/3159 (NI.23) Art.5, Art.8
referred to: SI 1996/3159 (NI.23) Sch.8 para.3
revoked: SI 1996/3159 (NI.23) Sch.9
Art.7, referred to: SI 1996/3159 (NI.23) Sch.8 para.1
Art.7, revoked: SI 1996/3159 (NI.23) Sch.9
Art.10, referred to: SI 1996/3159 (NI.23) Sch.8 para.1
Art.10, revoked: SI 1996/3159 (NI.23) Sch.9
Art.13, applied: SI 1996/3159 (NI.23) Art.3, Art.4, Art.5, Art.12
Art.13, revoked: SI 1996/3159 (NI.23) Sch.9
Art.38, applied: SI 1996/3159 (NI.23) Art.3, Art.4, Art.5, Art.12
Art.38, revoked: SI 1996/3159 (NI.23) Sch.9
Sch.2 para.1, applied: SI 1996/3159 (NI.23) Sch.8 para.2
Sch.2 para.1, revoked: SI 1996/3159 (NI.23) Sch.9

1294. Stock Transfer (Gilt-Edged Securities) (Exempt Transfer) Regulations 1987
Reg.2, amended: SI 1999/1210 Reg.2

1298. Merchant Shipping (Closing of Openings in Hulls and in Watertight Bulkheads) Regulations 1987
applied: SI 1996/3243 Sch Part I
revoked: SI 1998/2514 Reg.1

1299. Banking Appeal Tribunal Regulations 1987
amended: SI 1998/1129 Art.2, Sch.1 para.5
Reg.2, amended: SI 1998/1129 Art.2, Sch.1 para.5
Reg.20, amended: SI 1998/1129 Art.2, Sch.1 para.5

1303. Meat and Livestock Commission Levy Scheme (Confirmation) Order 1987
applied: SI 1998/3080
Sch. para.4, amended: SI 1998/3080 Sch. para.2
Sch. para.5, amended: SI 1998/3080 Sch. para.3, Sch. para.4, Sch. para.5
Sch. para.7, amended: SI 1998/3080 Sch. para.6
Sch. para.7A, added: SI 1998/3080 Sch. para.7

1332. Offshore Installations (Safety Zones) (No.48) Order 1987
revoked: SI 1997/735 Art.3, Sch.2

1336. Banking Appeal Tribunal (Scottish Appeals) Regulations 1987
amended: SI 1998/1129 Art.2, Sch.1 para.6
Reg.2, amended: SI 1998/1129 Art.2, Sch.1 para.6
Reg.6, applied: SI 1999/678 Sch., SI 1999/1750 Art.2, Sch.1
Reg.20, amended: SI 1998/1129 Art.2, Sch.1 para.6

1340. Black Country Development Corporation (Planning Functions) Order 1987
revoked: SI 1998/84 Art.2, Sch.

1341. Teesside Development Corporation (Planning Functions) Order 1987
revoked: SI 1998/84 Art.2, Sch.

NO.

1342. **Tyne and Wear Development Corporation (Planning Functions) Order 1987**
revoked: SI 1998/84 Art.2, Sch.

1343. **Town and Country Planning (Black Country Urban Development Area) Special Development Order 1987**
revoked: SI 1998/84 Art.2, Sch.
Art.6, revoked: SI 1998/84 Art.2, Sch.

1344. **Town and Country Planning (Teesside Urban Development Area) Special Development Order 1987**
revoked: SI 1998/84 Art.2, Sch.

1345. **Town and Country Planning (Tyne and Wear Urban Development Area) Special Development Order 1987**
revoked: SI 1998/84 Art.2, Sch.
Art.6, revoked: SI 1998/84 Art.2, Sch.

1356. **Advice and Assistance (Scotland) Amendment (No.2) Regulations 1987**
revoked: SI 1996/2447 Reg.3, Sch.1

1378. **Motor Vehicles (Driving Licences) Regulations 1987**
revoked: SI 1996/2824 Reg.2, Sch.1
Part III, revoked: SI 1996/2824 Reg.2, Sch.1
Part III, substituted: SI 1996/1259 Reg.6, Sch.1
Reg.3, amended: SI 1996/1259 Reg.3
Reg.3, revoked: SI 1996/2824 Reg.2, Sch.1
Reg.5, amended: SI 1996/1259 Reg.4
Reg.5, revoked: SI 1996/2824 Reg.2, Sch.1
Reg.9, amended: SI 1996/536 Reg.2, SI 1996/1259 Reg.5, SI 1996/1997 Reg.2
Reg.9, revoked: SI 1996/2824 Reg.2, Sch.1
Reg.18, revoked: SI 1996/2824 Reg.2, Sch.1
Reg.18, substituted: SI 1996/211 Reg.3
Reg.18A, added: SI 1996/211 Reg.3
Reg.18A, revoked: SI 1996/2824 Reg.2, Sch.1
Reg.18B, added: SI 1996/211 Reg.3
Reg.18B, revoked: SI 1996/2824 Reg.2, Sch.1
Reg.18C, added: SI 1996/211 Reg.3
Reg.18C, revoked: SI 1996/2824 Reg.2, Sch.1
Reg.19, amended: SI 1996/211 Reg.4
Reg.19, revoked: SI 1996/2824 Reg.2, Sch.1
Reg.19A, amended: SI 1996/211 Reg.5
Reg.19A, revoked: SI 1996/2824 Reg.2, Sch.1
Reg.20, amended: SI 1996/211 Reg.6
Reg.20, revoked: SI 1996/2824 Reg.2, Sch.1
Reg.23, revoked: SI 1996/211 Reg.7, SI 1996/2824 Reg.2, Sch.1
Reg.23A, amended: SI 1996/211 Reg.8
Reg.23A, revoked: SI 1996/2824 Reg.2, Sch.1
Reg.23B, amended: SI 1996/1259 Reg.7
Reg.23B, revoked: SI 1996/2824 Reg.2, Sch.1
Reg.29, revoked: SI 1996/2824 Reg.2, Sch.1
Reg.29, substituted: SI 1996/1259 Reg.8
Sch.2A, added: SI 1996/536 Reg.2
Sch.2A, revoked: SI 1996/2824 Reg.2, Sch.1
Sch.3, revoked: SI 1996/2824 Reg.2, Sch.1
Sch.3, substituted: SI 1996/1259 Reg.9, Sch.2
Sch.4, revoked: SI 1996/2824 Reg.2, Sch.1
Sch.4, substituted: SI 1996/1259 Reg.10, Sch.3
Sch.4A, added: SI 1996/1259 Reg.10, Sch.3
Sch.4A, revoked: SI 1996/2824 Reg.2, Sch.1
Sch.5, added: SI 1996/1259 Reg.11, Sch.4
Sch.5, revoked: SI 1996/2824 Reg.2, Sch.1
Sch.6, revoked: SI 1996/2824 Reg.2, Sch.1
Sch.6, substituted: SI 1996/1259 Reg.11, Sch.4

1383. **Education (Fees and Awards) (Scotland) Amendment Regulations 1987**
revoked: SI 1997/93 Reg.14, Sch.4

NO.

1423. **Rules of the Supreme Court (Amendment) 1987**
Ord. 11,
r.1, see *Arab Business Consortium International Finance & Investment Co v Banque Franco-Tunisienne* [1997] 1 Lloyd's Rep. 531 (CA), Neill, L.J.

1443. **Swanage Light Railway Order 1987**
Art.12, amended: SI 1996/362 Art.5, Sch.4

1522. **Town and Country Planning Appeals (Determination by Appointed Person) (Inquiries Procedure) (Scotland) Amendment Rules 1987**
revoked: SI 1997/750 r.25

1523. **Materials and Articles in Contact with Food Regulations 1987**
applied: SI 1998/1376 Reg.9, Reg.11
Reg.5, applied: SI 1998/1376 Sch.1 Part I
Reg.7, applied: SI 1998/1376 Sch.4 Part III
Reg.8, applied: SI 1998/1376 Sch.4 Part III
Reg.12, applied: SI 1998/1376 Reg.12
Reg.13, applied: SI 1998/1376 Reg.12
Reg.14, applied: SI 1998/1376 Reg.6, Sch.1 Part I
Reg.16, applied: SI 1998/1376 Reg.12
Reg.17, applied: SI 1998/1376 Reg.12
Reg.20, applied: SI 1998/1376 Reg.12
Reg.21, applied: SI 1998/1376 Reg.12

1531. **Town and Country Planning (Determination of Appeals by Appointed Persons) (Prescribed Classes) (Scotland) Regulations 1987**
Reg.2, amended: SI 1996/252 Art.2, Sch

1626. **Borough of Torbay (Electoral Arrangements) Order 1987**
revoked: SI 1996/1865 Art.7

1634. **National Health Service (General Dental Services) (Scotland) Amendment Regulations 1987**
revoked: SI 1996/177 Reg.38, Sch.8

1680. **Consumer Protection Act 1987 (Commencement No.1) Order 1987**
Art.6, applied: SI 1996/2756, SI 1997/2866, SI 1998/2406

1683. **Social Security (Hospital In-Patients) Amendment (No.2) Regulations 1987**
Reg.3, applied: SI 1996/207 Sch.7 para.40, SI 1996/2890 Sch.3 para.36

1698. **Special Constables (Injury Benefit) (Scotland) Regulations 1987**
applied: SI 1999/1750 Art.2, Sch.1

1700. **Police Cadets (Injury Benefit) (Scotland) Regulations 1987**
applied: SI 1999/1750 Art.2, Sch.1

1783. **Olive Oil (Marketing Standards) Regulations 1987**
Reg.2, amended: SI 1998/2410 Reg.2
Reg.2, applied: SI 1999/1513 Reg.6
Reg.3, applied: SI 1999/1513 Reg.6
Reg.4, amended: SI 1998/2410 Reg.2
Reg.4, revoked (in part): SI 1998/2410 Reg.2
Reg.5, applied: SI 1999/1513 Reg.6
Reg.5A, amended: SI 1998/2410 Reg.2
Reg.6, applied: SI 1999/1513 Reg.6

1799. **Bath-Lincoln Trunk Road A46 (Upper Swainswick to A420 Cold Ashton Roundabout) Order 1987**
revoked: SI 1996/1097

1800. **Bath-Lincoln Trunk Road A46 (Upper Swainswick to A420 Cold Ashton Roundabout) (Detrunking) Order 1987**
revoked: SI 1996/1097

NO.

NO.

1987—cont.

1824. Architects' Qualifications (EEC Recognition) Order 1987
revoked: 1997 c.22 s.27, Sch.3
Art.4, revoked: 1996 c.53 s.147, Sch.3 Part II

1831. Social Security (Portugal) Order 1987
Sch., amended: SI 1996/1928 Art.2, Sch.1

1850. Local Government Superannuation (Scotland) Regulations 1987
applied: SI 1996/2809 Reg.2, Reg.3, SI 1997/3048 Reg.39, SI 1998/192 Reg.20, SI 1998/364 Reg.3, Reg.4, Reg.6, Reg.19, Sch.2 para.2, Sch.2 para.5, Sch.2 para.9, Sch.4 para.5, Sch.4 para.8, SI 1998/366 Reg.47, Reg.73, Reg.93, Reg.110, Reg.111, Reg.134, Reg.135, SI 1999/1750 Art.2, Sch.1
referred to: SI 1998/364 Reg.3, Reg.10, Sch.2 para.4, Sch.2 para.6, SI 1998/366 Reg.117, Reg.119
Part E, applied: SI 1998/192 Reg.11, Reg.17, Reg.41
Part J, applied: SI 1997/3048 Reg.38, SI 1998/364 Reg.23, Sch.2 para.4, Sch.2 para.6
Part J, referred to: SI 1998/364 Reg.4, Sch.2 para.2, Sch.4 para.8
Part J, revoked: SI 1998/364 Reg.27 (with savings)
Part K, applied: SI 1998/192 Reg.52
Part K, revoked: SI 1998/192 Reg.52, Sch.2
Part L, applied: SI 1998/192 Reg.44, Reg.52
Part L, revoked: SI 1998/192 Reg.52, Sch.2
Part N, applied: SI 1998/364 Sch.2 para.4, Sch.2 para.6
Part N, referred to: SI 1998/364 Reg.4, Sch.2 para.2, Sch.4 para.8
Part N, revoked: SI 1998/364 Reg.27 (with savings)
Part P, applied: SI 1998/364 Sch.2 para.4, Sch.2 para.6
Part P, referred to: SI 1998/364 Reg.4, Sch.2 para.2, Sch.4 para.8
Part P, revoked (in part): SI 1998/364 Reg.27 (with savings)
Reg.A2, amended: SI 1997/3048 Reg.3
Reg.B1, added: SI 1997/3048 Reg.4
Reg.B2, amended: SI 1997/3048 Reg.5
Reg.B2, applied: SI 1998/192 Reg.46
Reg.B2, revoked (in part): SI 1997/3048 Reg.5
Reg.B3, applied: SI 1998/192 Reg.46
Reg.B3, revoked: SI 1997/3048 Reg.6
Reg.B4, added: SI 1997/3048 Reg.7
Reg.B4, applied: SI 1998/192 Reg.46
Reg.B4A, amended: SI 1997/3048 Reg.8
Reg.B4A, applied: SI 1998/192 Reg.46, SI 1998/364 Reg.3
Reg.B4A, revoked (in part): SI 1997/3048 Reg.8
Reg.B4B, amended: SI 1997/1373 Reg.3, SI 1997/3048 Reg.9
Reg.B4B, applied: SI 1998/192 Reg.46
Reg.B4B, referred to: SI 1998/192 Reg.34
Reg.B4ZA, added: SI 1997/3048 Reg.7
Reg.B6, amended: SI 1997/3048 Reg.10
Reg.C1, amended: SI 1996/1241 Reg.2
Reg.C1, applied: SI 1998/364 Sch.2 para.4
Reg.C1, referred to: SI 1998/364 Reg.4, Sch.2 para.2, Sch.4 para.8
Reg.C1, revoked: SI 1998/364 Reg.27 (with savings)
Reg.C2, applied: SI 1998/366 Reg.12
Reg.C2, referred to: SI 1998/366 Reg.86
Reg.C3, applied: SI 1998/364 Reg.11, SI 1998/366 Reg.12

1987—cont.

1850. Local Government Superannuation (Scotland) Regulations 1987—cont.
Reg.C3, referred to: SI 1998/364 Reg.11, SI 1998/366 Reg.86
Reg.C3A, applied: SI 1998/364 Reg.11
Reg.C3A, referred to: SI 1998/364 Reg.11, SI 1998/366 Reg.86
Reg.C4, applied: SI 1998/364 Reg.11
Reg.C4, referred to: SI 1998/364 Reg.11, SI 1998/366 Reg.86
Reg.C5, applied: SI 1998/364 Reg.22
Reg.C5, referred to: SI 1998/366 Reg.86
Reg.C6, applied: SI 1998/364 Reg.11, Reg.22, Sch.2 para.9
Reg.C6, referred to: SI 1998/364 Reg.11, SI 1998/366 Reg.86
Reg.C6A, referred to: SI 1998/366 Reg.86
Reg.C6B, added: SI 1997/3048 Reg.11
Reg.C7, referred to: SI 1998/366 Reg.86
Reg.C7A, referred to: SI 1998/366 Reg.86
Reg.C8, applied: SI 1998/364 Reg.8, Reg.9, Reg.15, Sch.2 para.9
Reg.C8, referred to: SI 1998/364 Reg.9, SI 1998/366 Reg.86
Reg.C8A, applied: SI 1998/364 Reg.9
Reg.C8A, referred to: SI 1998/364 Reg.9, SI 1998/366 Reg.86
Reg.C9, applied: SI 1998/364 Reg.15
Reg.C9, referred to: SI 1998/364 Reg.12
Reg.C9A, applied: SI 1998/364 Reg.14
Reg.C12, applied: SI 1998/364 Sch.2 para.4, SI 1998/366 Reg.115
Reg.C12, referred to: SI 1998/364 Reg.4, Sch.2 para.2, Sch.4 para.8
Reg.C12, revoked: SI 1998/364 Reg.27 (with savings)
Reg.D1, amended: SI 1997/3048 Reg.12
Reg.D1, applied: SI 1998/364 Reg.7, Reg.11
Reg.D2, applied: SI 1998/192 Reg.8
Reg.D3, amended: SI 1998/364 Sch.3 para.1
Reg.D3, applied: SI 1998/192 Reg.17
Reg.D10, applied: SI 1998/192 Reg.6, Reg.8
Reg.D11, applied: SI 1998/192 Reg.6, Reg.8
Reg.D12, applied: SI 1998/192 Reg.8
Reg.E1, amended: SI 1997/3048 Reg.13, SI 1998/364 Sch.3 para.1
Reg.E1A, substituted: SI 1997/3048 Reg.14
Reg.E2, amended: SI 1996/414 Reg.3, SI 1998/364 Sch.3 para.1
Reg.E2, applied: SI 1996/1360 Reg.7, SI 1998/192 Reg.6, Reg.9, Reg.10, Reg.11, Reg.19, Reg.21, Reg.25, SI 1998/364 Sch.2 para.6, Sch.2 para.7, SI 1998/366 Reg.31, Reg.116, Sch.3 para.2
Reg.E2, referred to: SI 1998/364 Sch.2 para.6
Reg.E2A, added: SI 1997/3048 Reg.15
Reg.E2A, applied: SI 1998/364 Reg.4, Sch.4 para.7
Reg.E3, amended: SI 1996/414 Reg.4
Reg.E4, amended: SI 1998/364 Sch.3 para.1
Reg.E4, applied: SI 1998/366 Reg.5, Reg.87
Reg.E5, amended: SI 1996/414 Reg.5
Reg.E5, applied: SI 1998/192 Reg.20
Reg.E6, amended: SI 1996/414 Reg.6
Reg.E6, applied: SI 1998/364 Reg.9, SI 1998/366 Reg.127
Reg.E6, referred to: SI 1998/364 Reg.9, Sch.2 para.5
Reg.E8, amended: SI 1996/414 Reg.7, SI 1998/364 Sch.3 para.1
Reg.E8, applied: SI 1998/192 Reg.22, Reg.24
Reg.E9, amended: SI 1996/414 Reg.8, SI 1997/3048 Reg.16, SI 1998/364 Sch.3 para.1

NO.

1850. Local Government Superannuation (Scotland) Regulations 1987—*cont.*
Reg.E9, applied: SI 1998/192 Reg.26
Reg.E11, amended: SI 1996/414 Reg.9, SI 1997/3048 Reg.17, SI 1998/364 Sch.3 para.1
Reg.E11, applied: SI 1998/364 Sch.2 para.8
Reg.E11A, added: SI 1996/414 Reg.10
Reg.E11A, applied: SI 1998/364 Sch.2 para.4, Sch.2 para.6
Reg.E11A, referred to: SI 1998/364 Reg.4, Sch.2 para.2, Sch.4 para.8
Reg.E11A, revoked: SI 1998/364 Reg.27 (with savings)
Reg.E11ZA, added: SI 1997/3048 Reg.18
Reg.E12, applied: SI 1998/364 Reg.8
Reg.E13, applied: SI 1998/366 Sch.3 para.5
Reg.E15, amended: SI 1998/192 Reg.16
Reg.E15, applied: SI 1998/192 Reg.16, SI 1998/364 Sch.2 para.3
Reg.E15, referred to: SI 1998/364 Sch.2 para.3
Reg.E16, applied: SI 1998/364 Sch.2 para.4, Sch.2 para.5, SI 1998/366 Reg.127
Reg.E16, referred to: SI 1998/364 Sch.2 para.4
Reg.E17, referred to: SI 1998/364 Sch.2 para.5
Reg.E18, applied: SI 1998/366 Reg.127
Reg.E18, referred to: SI 1998/364 Sch.2 para.5
Reg.E20, applied: SI 1998/192 Reg.19
Reg.E20, referred to: SI 1998/192 Reg.19
Reg.E21, applied: SI 1998/364 Sch.2 para.4, Sch.2 para.6
Reg.E21, referred to: SI 1998/364 Reg.4, Sch.2 para.2, Sch.4 para.8
Reg.E21, revoked: SI 1998/364 Reg.27 (with savings)
Reg.E22, amended: SI 1997/3048 Reg.19
Reg.E22, applied: SI 1998/192 Reg.41
Reg.E24, amended: SI 1997/3048 Reg.20
Reg.E28, applied: SI 1998/192 Reg.8
Reg.E29, applied: SI 1998/192 Reg.6
Reg.E30, applied: SI 1998/364 Sch.2 para.8
Reg.E33, applied: SI 1998/364 Sch.2 para.4, Sch.2 para.6
Reg.E33, referred to: SI 1998/364 Reg.4, Sch.2 para.2, Sch.4 para.8
Reg.E33, revoked: SI 1998/364 Reg.27 (with savings)
Reg.E35, amended: SI 1996/414 Reg.11
Reg.E35, applied: SI 1998/364 Sch.2 para.4, Sch.2 para.6
Reg.E35, referred to: SI 1998/364 Reg.4, Sch.2 para.2, Sch.4 para.8
Reg.E35, revoked: SI 1998/364 Reg.27 (with savings)
Reg.E35, substituted: SI 1997/3048 Reg.21
Reg.F3, applied: SI 1998/192 Reg.46
Reg.F6, applied: SI 1998/192 Reg.46, SI 1998/366 Reg.96, Sch.3 para.4
Reg.G1, applied: SI 1998/366 Reg.131, Sch.6 para.1
Reg.G3, amended: SI 1997/3048 Reg.22
Reg.G5, added: SI 1997/1143 Reg.2
Reg.G5, applied: SI 1997/1143 Reg.5
Reg.G6, added: SI 1997/1435 Reg.2
Reg.G6, applied: SI 1997/1435 Reg.4
Reg.H5, applied: SI 1998/366 Reg.135
Reg.H6, applied: SI 1998/364 Sch.4 para.4
Reg.H7, applied: SI 1998/364 Sch.4 para.4
Reg.J1, amended: SI 1997/3048 Reg.23
Reg.J2, amended: SI 1997/3048 Reg.24
Reg.J2, applied: SI 1997/3048 Reg.38
Reg.J6, referred to: SI 1998/364 Reg.23
Reg.J8, applied: SI 1997/1143 Reg.5, SI 1997/1435 Reg.4

NO.

1850. Local Government Superannuation (Scotland) Regulations 1987—*cont.*
Reg.J9, applied: SI 1997/1143 Reg.5, SI 1997/1373 Reg.4, SI 1997/1435 Reg.4, SI 1998/192 Reg.6
Reg.J13, amended: SI 1996/414 Reg.12
Reg.J14, applied: SI 1997/3048 Reg.38
Reg.J14, substituted: SI 1996/414 Reg.13
Reg.J14A, substituted: SI 1996/414 Reg.13
Reg.J14B, substituted: SI 1996/414 Reg.13
Reg.J15, added: SI 1997/1373 Reg.5
Reg.L9, applied: SI 1998/192 Reg.44
Reg.M1, amended: SI 1997/3048 Reg.25
Reg.M1, applied: SI 1998/364 Sch.2 para.4, Sch.2 para.6
Reg.M1, referred to: SI 1998/364 Reg.4, Sch.2 para.2, Sch.4 para.8
Reg.M1, revoked: SI 1998/364 Reg.27 (with savings)
Reg.M3, applied: SI 1998/364 Reg.17
Reg.N1, amended: SI 1997/674 Reg.3, SI 1997/3048 Reg.26
Reg.N2, amended: SI 1997/3048 Reg.27
Reg.N2, applied: SI 1997/3048 Reg.39
Reg.N2, revoked (in part): SI 1997/3048 Reg.27
Reg.N7, amended: SI 1997/674 Reg.4
Reg.N8, amended: SI 1997/674 Reg.5
Reg.N8, applied: SI 1997/674 Reg.9
Reg.N9, applied: SI 1997/674 Reg.9
Reg.N9, substituted: SI 1997/674 Reg.5, Reg.6
Reg.N10, added: SI 1997/674 Reg.5
Reg.N10, applied: SI 1997/674 Reg.9
Reg.N11, added: SI 1997/674 Reg.5
Reg.N11, applied: SI 1997/674 Reg.9
Reg.N12, added: SI 1997/674 Reg.5
Reg.N12, applied: SI 1997/674 Reg.9
Reg.N13, added: SI 1997/674 Reg.5
Reg.N13, applied: SI 1997/674 Reg.9
Reg.N14, added: SI 1997/674 Reg.5
Reg.N14, applied: SI 1997/674 Reg.9
Reg.P5, applied: SI 1998/364 Reg.3, Reg.4, Sch.2 para.2, Sch.4 para.2, Sch.4 para.8, SI 1998/366 Reg.80
Reg.P5, referred to: SI 1998/364 Sch.2 para.4, Sch.2 para.6
Reg.P5, revoked: SI 1998/2888 Reg.13
Reg.P6, amended: SI 1998/364 Sch.3 para.1
Reg.P6, applied: SI 1998/364 Reg.3, Reg.4, Sch.2 para.2, Sch.4 para.2, Sch.4 para.8, SI 1998/366 Reg.80
Reg.P6, referred to: SI 1998/364 Sch.2 para.4, Sch.2 para.6
Reg.P6, revoked: SI 1998/2888 Reg.13
Reg.P8, amended: SI 1997/3048 Reg.28
Reg.P12, applied: SI 1998/364 Reg.3, Reg.4, Sch.2 para.2, Sch.4 para.2, Sch.4 para.8
Reg.P12, referred to: SI 1998/364 Sch.2 para.4, Sch.2 para.6
Reg.P12, revoked (in part): SI 1998/2888 Reg.13
Reg.P13, applied: SI 1998/364 Reg.16, Reg.20
Reg.P13, referred to: SI 1998/364 Reg.20
Reg.P15, applied: SI 1998/364 Reg.3, Reg.4, Sch.2 para.2, Sch.4 para.2, Sch.4 para.8
Reg.P15, referred to: SI 1998/364 Sch.2 para.4, Sch.2 para.6
Reg.P15, revoked (in part): SI 1998/2888 Reg.13
Reg.P16, amended: SI 1997/3048 Reg.29
Reg.R1, applied: SI 1998/364 Sch.2 para.4, Sch.2 para.6
Reg.R1, referred to: SI 1998/364 Reg.4, Sch.2 para.2, Sch.4 para.8

NO.

1987—cont.

1850. Local Government Superannuation (Scotland) Regulations 1987—*cont.*
Reg.R1, revoked: SI 1998/364 Reg.27 (with savings)
Reg.R2, amended: SI 1997/674 Reg.7
Reg.R2, applied: SI 1998/364 Sch.2 para.4, Sch.2 para.6
Reg.R2, referred to: SI 1998/364 Reg.4, Sch.2 para.2
Reg.R2, revoked: SI 1998/364 Reg.27 (with savings)
Reg.R3, amended: SI 1997/674 Reg.8
Reg.R3, applied: SI 1998/364 Sch.2 para.4, Sch.2 para.6
Reg.R3, referred to: SI 1998/364 Reg.4, Sch.2 para.2, Sch.4 para.8
Reg.R3, revoked: SI 1998/364 Reg.27 (with savings)
Reg.R4, revoked (in part): SI 1997/3048 Reg.30
Reg.R5, applied: SI 1998/364 Sch.2 para.4, Sch.2 para.6
Reg.R5, referred to: SI 1998/364 Reg.4, Sch.2 para.2, Sch.4 para.8
Reg.R5, revoked: SI 1998/364 Reg.27 (with savings)
Reg.T3, referred to: SI 1996/682 Art.19
Reg.T6, applied: SI 1998/364 Sch.4 para.4
Sch.1, amended: SI 1997/1143 Reg.3, SI 1997/3048 Reg.31, SI 1998/364 Sch.3 para.1
Sch.1, referred to: SI 1998/366 Reg.86
Sch.1, revoked (in part): SI 1997/3048 Reg.31
Sch.1A, added: SI 1997/3048 Reg.32, Sch.
Sch.3, amended: SI 1997/3048 Reg.33
Sch.3 Part I, amended: SI 1996/1241 Reg.2
Sch.3 Part II, amended: SI 1997/3048 Reg.33
Sch.3 para.6, applied: SI 1998/192 Reg.32
Sch.3 para.7, applied: SI 1998/192 Reg.32
Sch.3A, referred to: SI 1996/682 Art.17
Sch.4 para.2, revoked (in part): SI 1997/3048 Reg.34
Sch.7A, referred to: SI 1998/366 Sch.4 para.7
Sch.10 para.4, applied: SI 1998/366 Reg.28
Sch.10 para.5, added: SI 1997/3048 Reg.35
Sch.13, applied: SI 1998/192 Reg.19
Sch.13 para.1, revoked (in part): SI 1997/3048 Reg.36
Sch.16, applied: SI 1997/3048 Reg.38, SI 1998/364 Sch.2 para.4, Sch.2 para.6
Sch.16, referred to: SI 1998/364 Reg.4, Sch.2 para.2, Sch.4 para.8
Sch.16, revoked: SI 1998/364 Reg.27 (with savings)
Sch.16 Part I, amended: SI 1997/3048 Reg.37
Sch.16 Part I, revoked (in part): SI 1997/3048 Reg.37
Sch.16 para.1, amended: SI 1996/414 Reg.14
Sch.16 para.4, applied: SI 1998/366 Reg.116
Sch.16A, added: SI 1997/1143 Reg.4
Sch.16B, added: SI 1997/1435 Reg.3, Sch.
Sch.16B para.5, applied: SI 1998/364 Reg.22
Sch.17 para.2, applied: SI 1997/1435 Reg.4
Sch.17 para.2, referred to: SI 1997/1143 Reg.5
Sch.17A, added: SI 1997/1373 Reg.6
Sch.18, revoked: SI 1996/414 Reg.15
Sch.19, applied: SI 1998/364 Sch.2 para.4, Sch.2 para.6
Sch.19, referred to: SI 1998/364 Reg.4, Sch.2 para.2, Sch.4 para.8
Sch.19, revoked: SI 1998/364 Reg.27 (with savings)
Sch.20, applied: SI 1998/364 Sch.2 para.4, Sch.2 para.6

NO.

1987—cont.

1850. Local Government Superannuation (Scotland) Regulations 1987—*cont.*
Sch.20, referred to: SI 1998/364 Reg.4, Sch.2 para.2, Sch.4 para.8
Sch.20, revoked: SI 1998/364 Reg.27 (with savings)
1886. Merchant Shipping (Passenger Ship Construction) (Amendment) Regulations 1987
revoked: SI 1998/2514 Reg.1
1905. Data Protection (Regulation of Financial Services etc.) (Subject Access Exemption) Order 1987
Sch.1, amended: SI 1996/2827 Reg.75, Sch.8 Part II, SI 1997/1060 Art.2, Sch., SI 1998/1129 Art.2, Sch.1 para.7
1961. Merchant Shipping (Pilot Ladders and Hoists) Regulations 1987
applied: SI 1996/3243 Sch Part I
revoked: SI 1999/17 Reg.2
Reg.3A, revoked: SI 1999/17 Reg.2
Sch., revoked: SI 1999/17 Reg.2
1967. Income Support (General) Regulations 1987
see *Chief Adjudication Officer v Webber* [1998] 1 W.L.R. 625 (CA), Hobhouse, L.J.; see *R. v Secretary of State for Social Security Ex p. Tamenene* [1997] C.O.D. 288 (QBD), Potts, J.
amended: SI 1996/206
applied: SI 1996/1307 Reg.6, SI 1996/1623 Art.3, SI 1996/1812 Reg.11, SI 1998/217 Art.2, SI 1999/779 Art.2, Sch.
referred to: SI 1998/1541 Reg.1
revoked (in part): SI 1996/206 Reg.28, Sch.3
Ch.IVA, added: SI 1998/1174 Reg.6
Part VI, applied: SI 1996/2570 Reg.5
Part VII, applied: SI 1996/2570 Reg.8
Reg.1, see *Secretary of State for Social Security v Remilien* [1997] 1 W.L.R. 1640 (HL), Lord Hoffmann
Reg.2, amended: SI 1996/206 Reg.2, SI 1996/1944 Reg.6, Reg.13, Sch. para.1, Sch. para.2, SI 1997/65 Reg.4, SI 1998/563 Reg.5, SI 1998/2231 Reg.13, SI 1998/2825 Reg.12, SI 1999/2165 Reg.2, SI 1999/2566 Reg.2, Sch.2 Part III, SI 1999/3156 Reg.12
Reg.2, applied: SI 1996/1363 Reg.1
Reg.2A, added: SI 1997/2676 Reg.10
Reg.2A, amended: SI 1997/2814 Reg.2
Reg.3, see *Bate v Chief Adjudication Officer* [1996] 1 W.L.R. 814 (HL), Lord Slynn of Hadley
Reg.3A, amended: SI 1996/206 Reg.3
Reg.3A, applied: SI 1996/207 Reg.87
Reg.4, amended: SI 1996/206 Reg.5, SI 1996/1944 Reg.6
Reg.4ZA, added: SI 1996/206 Reg.4
Reg.4ZA, amended: SI 1997/2197 Reg.5
Reg.5, see *Chief Adjudication Officer v Stafford* Times, November 9, 1999 (CA), Auld, L.J.; see *Kazantzis v Chief Adjudication Officer* Times, June 30, 1999 (CA), Peter Gibson, L.J.
Reg.5, amended: SI 1996/1944 Reg.6, SI 1999/2556 Reg.2, SI 1999/3178 Art.3, Sch.5 para.1
Reg.6, amended: SI 1996/206 Reg.6, SI 1998/2825 Reg.13, SI 1999/2165 Reg.6, SI 1999/2556 Reg.2, SI 1999/3156 Reg.13
Reg.7, revoked: SI 1996/206 Reg.28, Sch.3
Reg.8, applied: SI 1996/2567 Reg.4, Reg.12
Reg.8, revoked: SI 1996/206 Reg.28, Sch.3
Reg.9, applied: SI 1996/195 Reg.2, SI 1996/2567 Reg.15

1987—cont.

1967. Income Support (General) Regulations 1987—*cont.*

Reg.9, revoked: SI 1996/206 Reg.28, Sch.3

Reg.10, see *Driver v Chief Adjudication Officer* Independent, January 17, 1997 (CA), McCowan, L.J.

Reg.10, applied: SI 1996/1252 Reg.5, SI 1996/2567 Reg.15

Reg.10, revoked: SI 1996/206 Reg.28, Sch.3

Reg.10A, revoked: SI 1996/206 Reg.28, Sch.3

Reg.11, revoked: SI 1996/206 Reg.28, Sch.3

Reg.12, applied: SI 1999/991 Reg.13

Reg.13, amended: SI 1996/206 Reg.7

Reg.13A, revoked: SI 1996/206 Reg.28, Sch.3

Reg.14, applied: SI 1996/940 Reg.3, SI 1996/2545 Reg.10

Reg.15, applied: SI 1996/940 Reg.4

Reg.16, amended: SI 1996/206 Reg.8, SI 1996/1944 Reg.6

Reg.16, applied: SI 1996/940 Reg.5

Reg.17, amended: SI 1996/206 Reg.9, SI 1996/599 Art.18, SI 1997/543 Art.18, SI 1998/470 Art.18, SI 1999/264 Art.18

Reg.17, applied: SI 1996/207 Reg.87, SI 1996/2567 Reg.18, SI 1999/991 Reg.13, Reg.14

Reg.18, amended: SI 1996/205 Reg.10, SI 1996/599 Art.18, SI 1997/543 Art.18, SI 1998/470 Art.18, SI 1999/264 Art.18

Reg.18, applied: SI 1996/207 Reg.87, SI 1996/2567 Reg.18, SI 1999/991 Reg.13

Reg.19, amended: SI 1996/206 Reg.11, SI 1996/462 Reg.2

Reg.19, applied: SI 1998/19 Reg.2

Reg.21, see *Secretary of State for Social Security v Remilien* [1997] 1 W.L.R. 1640 (HL), Lord Hoffmann; see *Secretary of State for Social Security v Remilien* [1996] All E.R. (EC) 850 (CA), Kennedy, L.J.

Reg.21, amended: SI 1996/206 Reg.12, SI 1996/599 Art.18, SI 1996/1944 Reg.6, SI 1996/2006 Reg.4, SI 1996/2431 Reg.2, SI 1996/2614 Reg.2, SI 1997/543 Art.18, SI 1998/470 Art.18, SI 1998/563 Reg.8, Reg.18, SI 1999/264 Art.18

Reg.21, applied: SI 1996/30 Reg.8, SI 1998/19 Reg.2

Reg.21, referred to: SI 1999/3056 Reg.7

Reg.21A, applied: SI 1996/2567 Reg.12, Reg.16

Reg.21A, revoked: SI 1996/206 Reg.28, Sch.3

Reg.21ZA, added: SI 1996/2431 Reg.3

Reg.21ZA, applied: SI 1996/2890 Sch.3 para.58, Sch.4 para.51

Reg.22, amended: SI 1996/599 Sch.8

Reg.22, applied: SI 1996/2567 Reg.12, Reg.16

Reg.22, revoked: SI 1996/206 Reg.28, Sch.3

Reg.22A, added: SI 1996/206 Reg.13

Reg.22A, amended: SI 1997/543 Art.18, Sch.8, SI 1998/470 Art.18, Sch.8, SI 1999/264 Art.18, Sch.8, SI 1999/2422 Art.3, Sch.6 para.1, SI 1999/3109 Reg.6

Reg.23, amended: SI 1996/206 Reg.14

Reg.23A, added: SI 1998/1174 Reg.6

Reg.29, see *Leeves v Chief Adjudication Officer* [1999] E.L.R. 90 (CA), Potter, L.J.; see *Owen v Chief Adjudication Officer (No.2)* Independent, May 11, 1999 (CA), Mummery, L.J.

Reg.29, amended: SI 1997/65 Reg.5, SI 1998/563 Reg.12, SI 1999/2556 Reg.2

Reg.31, amended: SI 1996/206 Reg.15

Reg.32, amended: SI 1996/206 Reg.16, SI 1997/65 Reg.6

1987—cont.

1967. Income Support (General) Regulations 1987—*cont.*

Reg.35, amended: SI 1997/454 Reg.7, SI 1999/1509 Reg.2, SI 1999/2556 Reg.2

Reg.36, amended: SI 1999/2556 Reg.2

Reg.36, applied: SI 1996/2570 Reg.8

Reg.37, amended: SI 1999/2165 Reg.6

Reg.38, amended: SI 1998/1379 Reg.2, SI 1999/2556 Reg.2, SI 1999/3178 Art.3, Sch.5 para.2

Reg.38, applied: SI 1996/2570 Reg.8

Reg.39A, added: SI 1998/1174 Reg.6

Reg.39A, amended: SI 1999/3156 Reg.18

Reg.39B, amended: SI 1998/1174 Reg.6

Reg.39C, added: SI 1998/1174 Reg.6

Reg.39D, added: SI 1998/1174 Reg.6

Reg.40, amended: SI 1997/65 Reg.7, SI 1997/2197 Reg.5, SI 1998/563 Reg.13

Reg.41, amended: SI 1997/65 Reg.3, SI 1999/3178 Art.3, Sch.5 para.3

Reg.42, amended: SI 1996/206 Reg.17, SI 1996/1803 Reg.37, SI 1996/1944 Reg.13, Sch. para.3, SI 1997/2197 Reg.5, Reg.7, SI 1997/2863 Reg.17, SI 1998/563 Reg.6, Reg.13, SI 1998/2117 Reg.2, SI 1998/2825 Reg.14, SI 1999/2554 Reg.2, SI 1999/2566 Reg.2, Sch.2 Part I, Sch.2 Part II, SI 1999/2640 Reg.2, SI 1999/3156 Reg.13, SI 1999/3178 Art.3, Sch.5 para.4, SI 1999/3324 Reg.2

Reg.44, amended: SI 1999/3178 Art.3, Sch.5 para.5

Reg.45, see *Ellis v Chief Adjudication Officer* [1998] 1 F.L.R. 184 (CA), Staughton, L.J.

Reg.45, substituted: SI 1996/462 Reg.12

Reg.48, amended: SI 1998/563 Reg.14

Reg.49, amended: SI 1999/3178 Art.3, Sch.5 para.6

Reg.51, amended: SI 1997/65 Reg.9, SI 1997/2863 Reg.17, SI 1998/2117 Reg.3, SI 1998/2825 Reg.15, SI 1999/2640 Reg.2, SI 1999/3156 Reg.15

Reg.52, amended: SI 1998/2250 Reg.2

Reg.53, amended: SI 1997/65 Reg.8, SI 1997/2197 Reg.7

Reg.55, amended: SI 1996/940 Reg.6

Reg.55A, added: SI 1996/940 Reg.6

Reg.57, amended: SI 1996/1803 Reg.38

Reg.60B, amended: SI 1996/940 Reg.6

Reg.60D, amended: SI 1996/1944 Reg.6

Reg.60E, added: SI 1996/940 Reg.6

Reg.61, see *Driver v Chief Adjudication Officer* [1997] E.L.R. 145 (CA), McCowan, L.J.; see *O'Connor v Chief Adjudication Officer* [1999] 1 F.L.R. 1200 (CA), Auld, L.J.

Reg.61, amended: SI 1996/1944 Reg.6, SI 1997/2197 Reg.5, SI 1998/563 Reg.4, SI 1999/1935 Reg.3

Reg.61, referred to: SI 1996/1944 Reg.8

Reg.62, amended: SI 1996/1759 Reg.2, SI 1996/1944 Reg.6, SI 1997/1671 Reg.2, SI 1999/1935 Reg.3

Reg.65, amended: SI 1996/462 Reg.8

Reg.66, amended: SI 1999/1935 Reg.3

Reg.66A, amended: SI 1996/462 Reg.9, SI 1999/1935 Reg.3

Reg.66A, referred to: SI 1999/991 Reg.6

Reg.67, amended: SI 1996/462 Reg.10, SI 1999/1935 Reg.3

Reg.67A, added: SI 1998/563 Reg.4

Reg.67A, amended: SI 1999/1935 Reg.3

Reg.69, amended: SI 1999/3178 Art.3, Sch.5 para.7

NO.

NO.

1967. Income Support (General) Regulations 1987—*cont.*

Reg.70, see *R. v Secretary of State for the Home Department Ex p. Karaoui* Times, March 27, 1997 (QBD), Kay, J.; see *R. v Secretary of State for the Home Department Ex p. Salem* [1999] Q.B. 805 (CA), Sir John Balcombe; see *R. v Secretary of State for the Home Department Ex p. Salem* [1999] 1 A.C. 450 (HL), Lord Slynn of Hadley

Reg.70, amended: SI 1999/3178 Art.3, Sch.5 para.8

Reg.70, applied: SI 1996/30 Reg.8, SI 1996/2570 Reg.5

Reg.70, referred to: SI 1996/30 Reg.12, SI 1999/3056 Reg.7

Reg.71, amended: SI 1996/206 Reg.18, SI 1996/599 Art.18, Sch.8, SI 1997/543 Art.18, Sch.8, SI 1998/470 Art.18, Sch.8, SI 1999/264 Art.18, Sch.8, SI 1999/2422 Art.3, Sch.6 para.2

Reg.72, amended: SI 1996/2431 Reg.4, SI 1998/563 Reg.19

Reg.73, see *R. v Liverpool CC Ex p. Filla* [1996] C.O.D. 24 (QBD), Laws, J.

Reg.73, amended: SI 1996/206 Reg.19

Reg.75, amended: SI 1996/206 Reg.20

Reg.76, amended: SI 1996/206 Reg.21, SI 1999/2422 Art.3, Sch.6 para.2

Sch.1, applied: SI 1996/2567 Reg.4

Sch.1, revoked: SI 1996/206 Reg.28, Sch.3

Sch.1 para.4, applied: SI 1996/206 Reg.27

Sch.1 para.17, applied: SI 1996/2567 Reg.12

Sch.1A, revoked: SI 1996/206 Reg.28, Sch.3

Sch.1B, added: SI 1996/206 Reg.22, Sch.1

Sch.1B, referred to: SI 1996/1944 Reg.8

Sch.1B para.4, amended: SI 1996/1517 Reg.33

Sch.1B para.4, applied: SI 1996/206 Reg.27

Sch.1B para.7, applied: SI 1999/991 Reg.17

Sch.1B para.8, amended: SI 1999/2556 Reg.2

Sch.1B para.9, amended: SI 1999/2556 Reg.2

Sch.1B para.14A, added: SI 1999/3329 Reg.2

Sch.1B para.16, amended: SI 1997/827 Reg.5

Sch.1B para.24, amended: SI 1999/2422 Art.3, Sch.6 para.3

Sch.1B para.25, amended: SI 1999/2422 Art.3, Sch.6 para.3, SI 1999/3109 Reg.6

Sch.1B para.26, amended: SI 1999/2422 Art.3, Sch.6 para.3

Sch.1B para.27, amended: SI 1999/2422 Art.3, Sch.6 para.3

Sch.1B para.28, amended: SI 1999/2422 Art.3, Sch.6 para.3

Sch.2, see *Bate v Chief Adjudication Officer* [1996] 1 W.L.R. 814 (HL), Lord Slynn of Hadley

Sch.2, applied: SI 1996/2567 Reg.12

Sch.2 Part I, amended: SI 1996/599 Art.18, Sch.4, SI 1997/543 Art.18, Sch.4

Sch.2 Part I, applied: SI 1996/2444 Sch.2 para.13, SI 1996/2447 Sch.2 para.7

Sch.2 Part II, amended: SI 1996/599 Art.18, SI 1996/1803 Reg.39, SI 1997/543 Art.18

Sch.2 Part III, amended: SI 1996/599 Art.18, SI 1996/1803 Reg.39, SI 1997/543 Art.18

Sch.2 Part III, revoked (in part): SI 1996/1803 Reg.39

Sch.2 Part IV, amended: SI 1996/599 Art.18, Sch.5, SI 1996/1803 Reg.39, SI 1997/543 Art.18, Sch.5

Sch.2 para.1, amended: SI 1996/206 Reg.23, Sch.2 para.2, Sch.2 para.3, SI 1998/470 Art.18, Sch.4, SI 1999/264 Art.18, Sch.4

1967. Income Support (General) Regulations 1987—*cont.*

Sch.2 para.1A, added: SI 1996/206 Reg.23, Sch.2 para.4

Sch.2 para.2, amended: SI 1996/2545 Reg.2, SI 1997/543 Art.18, SI 1998/470 Art.18, Sch.4, SI 1998/1541 Reg.2, SI 1999/264 Art.18, Sch.4, SI 1999/2555 Reg.2

Sch.2 para.2A, amended: SI 1997/2197 Reg.7, SI 1998/470 Art.18, Sch.4, SI 1999/264 Art.18, Sch.4

Sch.2 para.2A, applied: SI 1998/19 Reg.2

Sch.2 para.3, amended: SI 1997/1790 Reg.11, SI 1998/470 Art.18, SI 1998/766 Reg.12, SI 1999/264 Art.18

Sch.2 para.3, applied: SI 1998/1581 Reg.4

Sch.2 para.9, applied: SI 1998/19 Reg.2, SI 1998/1581 Reg.4

Sch.2 para.9A, applied: SI 1996/207 Sch.2 para.1, SI 1998/19 Reg.2, SI 1998/1581 Reg.4

Sch.2 para.10, amended: SI 1998/2231 Reg.13

Sch.2 para.10, applied: SI 1998/19 Reg.2, SI 1998/1581 Reg.4

Sch.2 para.11, applied: SI 1998/1581 Reg.4

Sch.2 para.12, amended: SI 1998/2231 Reg.13, SI 1999/2556 Reg.2, SI 1999/2566 Reg.2, Sch.2 Part II

Sch.2 para.13, see *Rider v Chief Adjudication Officer* (1996) 31 B.M.L.R. 122 (CA), Nourse, L.J.

Sch.2 para.13, applied: SI 1996/2567 Reg.18, SI 1999/991 Reg.13

Sch.2 para.14, amended: SI 1998/470 Art.18, SI 1999/264 Art.18

Sch.2 para.15, amended: SI 1998/470 Art.18, Sch.5, SI 1999/264 Art.18, Sch.5

Sch.3, applied: SI 1999/991 Reg.7

Sch.3 para.1A, added: SI 1997/2305 Reg.2

Sch.3 para.4, amended: SI 1996/1944 Reg.6, SI 1997/2863 Reg.16

Sch.3 para.4, applied: SI 1996/207 Sch.2 para.4

Sch.3 para.5, amended: SI 1996/599 Sch.8, SI 1997/543 Art.18, Sch.8, SI 1998/470 Art.18, Sch.8, SI 1999/264 Art.18, Sch.8

Sch.3 para.5A, applied: SI 1996/207 Sch.2 para.4

Sch.3 para.6, amended: SI 1996/599 Sch.8, SI 1997/543 Art.18, Sch.8, SI 1997/2305 Reg.2, SI 1998/470 Art.18, Sch.8, SI 1999/264 Art.18, Sch.8

Sch.3 para.6, applied: SI 1999/991 Reg.7

Sch.3 para.7, amended: SI 1996/599 Sch.8, SI 1997/543 Art.18, Sch.8, SI 1998/470 Art.18, Sch.8, SI 1998/2231 Reg.13, SI 1999/264 Art.18, Sch.8

Sch.3 para.8, amended: SI 1996/206, SI 1996/599 Sch.8, SI 1997/543 Art.18, Sch.8, SI 1997/2305 Reg.2, SI 1998/470 Art.18, Sch.8, SI 1999/264 Art.18, Sch.8

Sch.3 para.8, applied: SI 1999/991 Reg.7

Sch.3 para.9, applied: SI 1999/991 Reg.7

Sch.3 para.10, amended: SI 1996/599 Sch.8, SI 1997/543 Art.18, Sch.8, SI 1998/470 Art.18, Sch.8, SI 1999/264 Art.18, Sch.8

Sch.3 para.11, amended: SI 1996/599 Sch.8, SI 1997/543 Art.18, Sch.8, SI 1998/470 Art.18, Sch.8, SI 1999/264 Art.18, Sch.8

NO.

1967. Income Support (General) Regulations 1987—*cont.*

Sch.3 para.12, amended: SI 1996/599 Sch.8, SI 1996/909 Reg.2, SI 1996/1363 Reg.2, SI 1996/1889 Reg.2, SI 1996/2903 Reg.2, SI 1997/543 Art.18, Sch.8, SI 1997/944 Reg.2, SI 1997/2604 Reg.2, SI 1998/470 Art.18, Sch.8, SI 1998/1128 Reg.2, SI 1998/2878 Reg.2, SI 1999/123 Reg.2, SI 1999/264 Art.18, Sch.8, SI 1999/371 Reg.2, SI 1999/907 Reg.2, SI 1999/1153 Reg.2, SI 1999/1411 Reg 2

Sch.3 para.13, amended: SI 1999/3178 Art.3, Sch.5 para.9

Sch.3 para.14, amended: SI 1996/206 Reg.24, SI 1996/1944 Reg.6, SI 1997/2863 Reg.16, SI 1998/2231 Reg.13, SI 1999/714 Reg.3, SI 1999/1921 Reg.2, SI 1999/3178 Art.3, Sch.5 para.9

Sch.3 para.15, applied: SI 1999/991 Reg.7

Sch.3 para.16, applied: SI 1999/991 Reg.7

Sch.3 para.17, applied: SI 1999/991 Reg.13

Sch.3 para.18, amended: SI 1996/599 Art.18, SI 1996/2518 Reg.4, SI 1997/543 Art.18, SI 1997/827 Reg.6, SI 1998/470 Art.18, SI 1999/264 Art.18, SI 1999/3178 Art.3, Sch.5 para.9

Sch.3 para.18, applied: SI 1999/991 Reg.13

Sch.3A, applied: SI 1996/207 Reg.87, SI 1999/991 Reg.14

Sch.3A para.1, amended: SI 1996/206 Reg.25

Sch.3B, applied: SI 1996/207 Reg.87, SI 1999/991 Reg.14

Sch.3B para.1, amended: SI 1996/206 Reg.25

Sch.3B para.3, amended: SI 1999/3178 Art.3, Sch.5 para.10

Sch.3C, amended: SI 1997/65 Reg.10

Sch.4, amended: SI 1997/543 Art.18

Sch.4 Part I, amended: SI 1997/543 Art.18

Sch.4 Part I, referred to: SI 1999/991 Reg.6

Sch.4 para.1, amended: SI 1998/470 Art.18, SI 1999/264 Art.18

Sch.4 para.2, amended: SI 1997/543 Art.18, Sch.6 Part II, SI 1998/470 Art.18, Sch.6 Part II, SI 1999/264 Art.18, Sch.6

Sch.4 para.6, amended: SI 1996/599 Art.18, SI 1997/543 Art.18, Sch.6 Part I, SI 1998/470 Art.18, Sch.6 Part I, SI 1999/264 Art.18, Sch.6

Sch.4 para.7, amended: SI 1997/543 Art.18, Sch.6 Part I, SI 1998/470 Art.18, Sch.6 Part I, SI 1999/264 Art.18, Sch.6

Sch.4 para.11, amended: SI 1997/543 Art.18, Sch.6 Part I, SI 1998/470 Art.18, Sch.6 Part I, SI 1999/264 Art.18, Sch.6

Sch.4 para.13, amended: SI 1997/543 Art.18, Sch.6 Part I, SI 1998/470 Art.18, Sch.6 Part I, SI 1999/264 Art.18, Sch.6

Sch.4 para.16, revoked: SI 1997/2197 Reg.5

Sch.4 para.17, revoked: SI 1997/2197 Reg.5

Sch.7, amended: SI 1996/599 Art.18, Sch.7

Sch.7, applied: SI 1996/2567 Reg.12

Sch.7 para.1, amended: SI 1996/1803 Reg.40, SI 1997/543 Art.18, Sch.7 Part I, SI 1998/470 Art.18, Sch.7 Part I, SI 1999/264 Art.18, Sch.7 Part I

Sch.7 para.2, amended: SI 1997/543 Art.18, Sch.7 Part I, SI 1998/470 Art.18, Sch.7 Part I, SI 1999/264 Art.18, Sch.7 Part I

Sch.7 para.2A, amended: SI 1997/543 Art.18, Sch.7 Part I, SI 1998/470 Art.18, Sch.7 Part I, SI 1998/563 Reg.8, SI 1999/264 Art.18, Sch.7 Part I

Sch.7 para.3, amended: SI 1997/543 Art.18, Sch.7 Part I, SI 1998/470 Art.18, Sch.7 Part I, SI 1999/264 Art.18, Sch.7 Part I

NO.

1967. Income Support (General) Regulations 1987—*cont.*

Sch.7 para.6, applied: SI 1998/19 Reg.2

Sch.7 para.7, amended: SI 1997/543 Art.18, Sch.7 Part II, SI 1998/470 Art.18, Sch.7 Part II, SI 1999/264 Art.18, Sch.7 Part II

Sch.7 para.8, amended: SI 1997/543 Art.18, Sch.7 Part II, SI 1998/470 Art.18, Sch.7 Part II, SI 1999/264 Art.18, Sch.7 Part II

Sch.7 para.9, applied: SI 1998/19 Reg.2

Sch.7 para.10, applied: SI 1998/19 Reg.2

Sch.7 para.10A, amended: SI 1997/543 Art.18, Sch.7 Part I, SI 1999/264 Art.18, Sch.7 Part I

Sch.7 para.10B, amended: SI 1997/543 Art.18, Sch.7 Part I, SI 1998/470 Art.18, Sch.7 Part I, SI 1999/264 Art.18, Sch.7 Part I

Sch.7 para.10B, applied: SI 1998/19 Reg.2

Sch.7 para.10C, amended: SI 1996/1803 Reg.40, SI 1997/543 Art.18, Sch.7 Part I, SI 1998/470 Art.18, Sch.7 Part I, SI 1999/264 Art.18, Sch.7 Part I

Sch.7 para.13, amended: SI 1997/543 Art.18, Sch.7 Part I, SI 1998/470 Art.18, Sch.7 Part I, SI 1999/264 Art.18, Sch.7 Part I

Sch.7 para.13, applied: SI 1998/19 Reg.2

Sch.7 para.13A, amended: SI 1997/543 Art.18, Sch.7 Part I, Sch.7 Part II, SI 1997/2197 Reg.5, SI 1998/470 Art.18, Sch.7 Part I, Sch.7 Part II, SI 1999/264 Art.18, Sch.7 Part I, Sch.7 Part II

Sch.7 para.13A, applied: SI 1998/19 Reg.2

Sch.7 para.13B, amended: SI 1997/543 Art.18, Sch.7 Part II, SI 1998/470 Art.18, Sch.7 Part II, SI 1999/264 Art.18, Sch.7 Part II

Sch.7 para.13B, applied: SI 1998/19 Reg.2

Sch.7 para.16, amended: SI 1997/543 Art.18, Sch.7 Part II, SI 1998/470 Art.18, Sch.7 Part II, SI 1999/264 Art.18, Sch.7 Part II

Sch.7 para.17, amended: SI 1997/543 Art.18, Sch.7 Part II, SI 1998/470 Art.18, Sch.7 Part II, SI 1999/264 Art.18, Sch.7 Part II

Sch.7 para.18, amended: SI 1997/543 Art.18, Sch.7 Part I, SI 1998/470 Art.18, Sch.7 Part I, SI 1999/264 Art.18, Sch.7 Part I

Sch.8 para.4, applied: SI 1996/2570 Reg.8

Sch.8 para.5, amended: SI 1996/1803 Reg.41

Sch.8 para.5, applied: SI 1996/2570 Reg.8

Sch.8 para.5, substituted: SI 1997/1790 Reg.12, SI 1998/766 Reg.13

Sch.8 para.6, applied: SI 1996/2570 Reg.8

Sch.8 para.6, substituted: SI 1996/1944 Reg.6

Sch.8 para.7, applied: SI 1996/2570 Reg.8

Sch.8 para.8, applied: SI 1996/2570 Reg.8

Sch.8 para.9, applied: SI 1996/2570 Reg.8

Sch.8 para.10, substituted: SI 1996/1944 Reg.6

Sch.8 para.15A, substituted: SI 1996/1944 Reg.6

Sch.8 para.15B, added: SI 1999/2556 Reg.2

Sch.9, amended: SI 1996/599 Art.18

Sch.9 para.5, amended: SI 1996/2431 Reg.5

Sch.9 para.7, amended: SI 1998/563 Reg.15

Sch.9 para.11, amended: SI 1997/2197 Reg.7, SI 1999/1677 Reg.2

Sch.9 para.13, amended: SI 1997/2863 Reg.17, SI 1999/2554 Reg.2

Sch.9 para.15, amended: SI 1996/462 Reg.8

Sch.9 para.15B, added: SI 1996/606 Reg.2

Sch.9 para.15B, amended: SI 1997/65 Reg.2

Sch.9 para.25, amended: SI 1998/563 Reg.15

Sch.9 para.27, substituted: SI 1998/563 Reg.7

Sch.9 para.29, referred to: SI 1999/991 Reg.7

Sch.9 para.30, amended: SI 1998/1173 Reg.4

Sch.9 para.30, referred to: SI 1999/991 Reg.7

NO.

1987—cont.

1967. Income Support (General) Regulations 1987—cont.

Sch.9 para.30ZA, added: SI 1998/1173 Reg.4
Sch.9 para.52, amended: SI 1996/2431 Reg.5
Sch.9 para.56, amended: SI 1996/2431 Reg.5
Sch.9 para.58, added: SI 1997/65 Reg.2
Sch.9 para.59, added: SI 1997/65 Reg.2
Sch.9 para.60, added: SI 1997/65 Reg.2
Sch.9 para.61, added: SI 1997/65 Reg.2
Sch.9 para.61, amended: SI 1999/1935 Reg.3
Sch.9 para.62, amended: SI 1997/2863 Reg.17
Sch.9 para.62, substituted: SI 1998/1174 Reg.7
Sch.9 para.63, amended: SI 1997/2863 Reg.17
Sch.9 para.64, added: SI 1998/563 Reg.13, SI 1998/1174 Reg.6
Sch.9 para.64, amended: SI 1999/3156 Reg.18
Sch.9 para.64, revoked: SI 1998/2117 Reg.6
Sch.9 para.65, added: SI 1998/2117 Reg.4
Sch.9 para.66, added: SI 1998/2117 Reg.6
Sch.9 para.67, amended: SI 1998/2825 Reg.16, SI 1999/3156 Reg.16
Sch.9 para.68, amended: SI 1998/2825 Reg.16, SI 1999/3156 Reg.16
Sch.9 para.69, added: SI 1999/2165 Reg.6
Sch.9 para.70, added: SI 1999/2556 Reg.2
Sch.10 para.6, amended: SI 1998/1174 Reg.7
Sch.10 para.7, amended: SI 1996/206 Reg.26, SI 1996/1944 Reg.13, Sch. para.7
Sch.10 para.44, amended: SI 1997/2197 Reg.7
Sch.10 para.45, amended: SI 1997/2197 Reg.7
Sch.10 para.46, added: SI 1996/462 Reg.11
Sch.10 para.47, added: SI 1996/2431 Reg.6
Sch.10 para.48, added: SI 1996/462 Reg.11, SI 1996/2431 Reg.6
Sch.10 para.49, added: SI 1996/462 Reg.11, SI 1996/2431 Reg.6
Sch.10 para.50, amended: SI 1997/2863 Reg.17
Sch.10 para.50, substituted: SI 1998/1174 Reg.7
Sch.10 para.51, amended: SI 1997/2863 Reg.17
Sch.10 para.52, added: SI 1998/1174 Reg.7
Sch.10 para.52, amended: SI 1999/3156 Reg.18
Sch.10 para.53, added: SI 1998/2117 Reg.5
Sch.10 para.54, amended: SI 1998/2825 Reg.17, SI 1999/3156 Reg.17
Sch.10 para.55, amended: SI 1998/2825 Reg.17, SI 1999/3156 Reg.17
Sch.10 para.56, added: SI 1999/2165 Reg.6
Sch.10 para.57, added: SI 1999/2556 Reg.2

1968. Social Security (Claims and Payments) Regulations 1987

amended: SI 1999/3178 Art.3, Sch.6 para.1
applied: SI 1996/1623 Art.3, SI 1998/217 Art.2, SI 1999/779 Art.2, Sch., SI 1999/991 Reg.27, Sch.2 para.5
Part V, amended: SI 1999/1958 Art.4, Sch.9 para.5, SI 1999/2422 Art.3, Sch.7 para.4, SI 1999/2572 Reg.16, SI 1999/2860 Art.3, Sch.3 para.8, SI 1999/3178 Art.3, Sch.6 para.11
Part V, applied: SI 1999/1958 Art.5, Sch.12 para.13, SI 1999/2860 Art.4, Sch.16 para.14, SI 1999/3178 Art.4, Sch.22 para.12
Part V, referred to: SI 1999/2422 Art.4, Sch.14 para.13, SI 1999/2739 Art.3, Sch.2 para.13
Reg.2, amended: SI 1996/1460 Reg.2, SI 1996/1803 Reg.18, SI 1996/2431 Reg.7, SI 1999/1958 Art.4, Sch.9 para.1, SI 1999/2358 Reg.2, SI 1999/2422 Art.3, Sch.7 para.1, SI

NO.

1987—cont.

1968. Social Security (Claims and Payments) Regulations 1987—cont.

Reg.2—cont.
1999/2572 Reg.3, Reg.20, Reg.24, Reg.25, Sch. Part I, Sch. Part V, Sch. Part VI, SI 1999/2860 Art.3, Sch.3 para.1, SI 1999/3108 Reg.18, Sch.3 para.2, SI 1999/3178 Art.3, Sch.6 para.2
Reg.3, amended: SI 1996/1460 Reg.2, SI 1999/2556 Reg.7, SI 1999/2860 Art.3, Sch.3 para.2, SI 1999/3178 Art.3, Sch.6 para.3
Reg.3, applied: SI 1999/991 Reg.26
Reg.4, amended: SI 1996/1460 Reg.2, SI 1996/2431 Reg.7, SI 1997/793 Reg.2, SI 1999/2572 Reg.4, Reg.20, Reg.21, Reg.25, Sch. Part I, Sch. Part II, Sch. Part VI, SI 1999/3108 Reg.18, Sch.3 para.2
Reg.4A, added: SI 1999/3108 Reg.5
Reg.4B, added: SI 1999/3108 Reg.5
Reg.5, amended: SI 1999/2572 Reg.20, Sch. Part I
Reg.6, amended: SI 1996/1460 Reg.2, SI 1996/2431 Reg.7, SI 1997/793 Reg.3, SI 1997/2290 Reg.5, SI 1999/2572 Reg.5, Reg.24, Reg.25, Sch. Part V, Sch. Part VI, SI 1999/3108 Reg.18, Sch.3 para.2
Reg.6, revoked (in part): SI 1999/2572 Reg.5
Reg.7, amended: SI 1996/1460 Reg.2, SI 1999/2572 Reg.6, Reg.21, Reg.24, Reg.25, Sch. Part II, Sch. Part V, Sch. Part VI, SI 1999/3108 Reg.18, Sch.3 para.2
Reg.7, applied: SI 1996/207 Reg.105, SI 1996/2567 Reg.7
Reg.8, amended: SI 1996/1460 Reg.2, SI 1999/2572 Reg.20, Sch. Part I
Reg.8, applied: SI 1996/1252 Reg.3, SI 1996/2567 Reg.4, Reg.20
Reg.8, revoked (in part): SI 1996/1460 Reg.2
Reg.9, amended: SI 1996/1803 Reg.19, SI 1999/2572 Reg.20, Reg.22, Sch. Part I, Sch. Part III
Reg.10, amended: SI 1997/793 Reg.4
Reg.10, revoked (in part): SI 1997/793 Reg.4
Reg.11, amended: SI 1997/793 Reg.5
Reg.13, amended: SI 1999/1958 Art.4, Sch.9 para.2, SI 1999/2422 Art.3, Sch.7 para.2, SI 1999/2572 Reg.7, Reg. 24, Reg.25, Sch. Part V, Sch. Part VI, SI 1999/2860 Art.3, Sch.3 para.3, SI 1999/3178 Art.3, Sch.6 para.4
Reg.13A, amended: SI 1999/2860 Art.3, Sch.3 para.4, SI 1999/3178 Art.3, Sch.6 para.5
Reg.13C, amended: SI 1999/2860 Art.3, Sch.3 para.5, SI 1999/3178 Art.3, Sch.6 para.5
Reg.15, revoked (in part): SI 1996/1460 Reg.2
Reg.16, amended: SI 1996/1460 Reg.2, SI 1999/2358 Reg.2, SI 1999/2572 Reg.8, Reg. 24, Reg.25, Sch. Part V, Sch. Part VI
Reg.17, amended: SI 1996/1460 Reg.2, SI 1999/1958 Art.4, Sch.9 para.3, SI 1999/2422 Art.3, Sch.7 para.3, SI 1999/2572 Reg.9, Reg. 24, Reg.25, Sch. Part V, Sch. Part VI, SI 1999/2860 Art.3, Sch.3 para.6, SI 1999/3178 Art.3, Sch.6 para.7
Reg.17, applied: SI 1996/2567 Reg.5
Reg.17, revoked (in part): SI 1996/1460 Reg.2
Reg.18, revoked: SI 1996/1460 Reg.2
Reg.19, see *Chief Adjudication Officer v Patterson* Times, July 10, 1997 (CA), Stuart-Smith, L.J.

NO.

1968. **Social Security (Claims and Payments) Regulations 1987**—*cont.*
Reg.19, amended. SI 1996/425 Reg.3, SI 1996/1460 Reg.2, SI 1996/2306 Reg.2, SI 1996/2431 Reg.7, SI 1997/2290 Reg.6, SI 1999/2572 Reg.10, Reg.20, Reg. 24, Reg.25, Sch. Part I, Sch. Part V, Sch. Part VI, SI 1999/3108 Reg.18, Sch.3 para.2
Reg.19, applied: SI 1996/2567 Reg.5, SI 1997/793 Reg.20, SI 1999/991 Reg.3
Reg.19, referred to: SI 1999/991 Reg.27, Sch.2 para.5
Reg.19, substituted: SI 1997/793 Reg.6
Reg.20, amended: SI 1999/2572 Reg.20, Sch. Part I
Reg.20A, amended: SI 1996/672 Reg.2, SI 1999/2572 Reg.20, Reg.23, Sch. Part I, Sch. Part IV
Reg.21, amended: SI 1996/672 Reg.2, SI 1999/2358 Reg.2, SI 1999/2572 Reg.11, Reg.20, Reg.22, Reg.23, Sch. Part I, Sch. Part III, Sch. Part IV
Reg.22, amended: SI 1996/2306 Reg.3
Reg.22, referred to: SI 1999/820 Reg.1
Reg.23, amended: SI 1999/2358 Reg.2
Reg.24, revoked (in part): SI 1996/1460 Reg.2
Reg.25, amended: SI 1996/1436 Reg.3
Reg.26, amended: SI 1999/3178 Art.3, Sch.6 para.8
Reg.26, applied: SI 1999/991 Reg.7
Reg.26A, added: SI 1996/1460 Reg.2
Reg.26A, amended: SI 1998/1174 Reg.8, SI 1999/2860 Art.3, Sch.3 para.7, SI 1999/3178 Art.3, Sch.6 para.9
Reg.26A, applied: SI 1999/991 Reg.7
Reg.27, amended: SI 1999/2572 Reg.12, Reg. 24, Reg.25, Sch. Part V, Sch. Part VI
Reg.29, amended: SI 1999/2572 Reg.20, Sch. Part I
Reg.29, substituted: SI 1996/672 Reg.2
Reg.30, amended: SI 1996/1460 Reg.2, SI 1999/2572 Reg.13, Reg.20, Reg.22, Reg. 24, Reg.25, Sch. Part I, Sch. Part III, Sch. Part V, Sch. Part VI
Reg.31, amended: SI 1999/1958 Art.4, Sch.9 para.4, SI 1999/3178 Art.3, Sch.6 para.10
Reg.32, amended: SI 1996/1460 Reg.2, SI 1999/2572 Reg.14, Reg.20, Sch. Part I, SI 1999/3108 Reg.18, Sch.3 para.2
Reg.32, applied: SI 1996/2567 Reg.21
Reg.32, referred to: SI 1999/991 Reg.17
Reg.33, amended: SI 1999/2572 Reg.15, Reg.20, Reg.22, Reg.23, Sch. Part I, Sch. Part III, Sch. Part IV
Reg.33, applied: SI 1999/991 Reg.25, SI 1999/1495 Reg.33
Reg.34, amended: SI 1999/2572 Reg.20, Sch. Part I
Reg.35, referred to: SI 1999/991 Reg.27, Sch.2 para.5
Reg.36, amended: SI 1999/2358 Reg.2, SI 1999/2572 Reg.20, Reg.24, Reg.25, Sch. Part I, Sch. Part V, Sch. Part VI
Reg.37, see *R. v Secretary of State for Social Security Ex p. Sherwin* (1996) 32 B.M.L.R. 1 (QBD), Kennedy, L.J.; see *R. v Secretary of State for Social Security Ex p. Sutherland* Times, January 2, 1997 (QBD), Laws, J.
Reg.37, amended: SI 1996/1460 Reg.2, SI 1996/2306 Reg.4, SI 1999/2572 Reg.20, Sch. Part I
Reg.37, revoked: SI 1999/1958 Art.4 (with savings), Sch.9 para.5 (with savings), SI 1999/2422 Art.3 (with savings), Sch.7 para.5 (with

NO.

1968. **Social Security (Claims and Payments) Regulations 1987**—*cont.*
Reg.37—*cont.*
savings), SI 1999/2572 Reg.17 (with savings), SI 1999/2860 Art.3 (with savings), Sch.3 para.9 (with savings), SI 1999/3178 Art.3 (with savings), Sch.6 para.12 (with savings)
Reg.37A, revoked: SI 1999/1958 Art.4 (with savings), Sch.9 para.5 (with savings), SI 1999/2422 Art.3 (with savings), Sch.7 para.5 (with savings), SI 1999/2572 Reg.17 (with savings), SI 1999/2860 Art.3 (with savings), Sch.3 para.9 (with savings), SI 1999/3178 Art.3 (with savings), Sch.6 para.12 (with savings)
Reg.37A, substituted: SI 1998/1381 Reg.2
Reg.37AA, amended: SI 1996/1460 Reg.2, SI 1996/2306 Reg.5
Reg.37AA, revoked: SI 1999/3178 Art.3, Sch.6 para.12
Reg.37AB, referred to: SI 1999/991 Reg.27, Sch.2 para.5
Reg.37AB, revoked: SI 1999/3178 Art.3, Sch.6 para.12
Reg.37B, revoked: SI 1999/1958 Art.4, Sch.9 para.5, SI 1999/2422 Art.3, Sch.7 para.5, SI 1999/2572 Reg.17, SI 1999/2860 Art.3, Sch.3 para.9, SI 1999/3178 Art.3, Sch.6 para.12
Reg.38, amended: SI 1996/672 Reg.2, SI 1999/2422 Art.3, Sch.7 para.6, SI 1999/2572 Reg.18, Reg.20, Reg.23, Sch. Part I, Sch. Part IV, SI 1999/2860 Art.3, Sch.3 para.10, SI 1999/3178 Art.3, Sch.6 para.13
Reg.38, referred to: SI 1999/991 Reg.27, Sch.2 para.5
Reg.47, amended: SI 1999/2572 Reg.19, Reg.20, Reg.22, Sch. Part I, Sch. Part III
Sch.1, amended: SI 1996/1460 Reg.2
Sch.1 Part I, amended: SI 1999/2572 Reg. 24, Reg.25, Sch. Part V, Sch. Part VI
Sch.1 Part II, amended: SI 1996/1803 Reg.20
Sch.2 para.1, amended: SI 1996/1460 Reg.2, SI 1999/2860 Art.3, Sch.3 para.11, SI 1999/3178 Art.3, Sch.6 para.14
Sch.3, revoked: SI 1996/1460 Reg.2
Sch.3 para.12, amended: SI 1997/2055 Reg.2, SI 1999/123 Reg.2
Sch.4, see *Chief Adjudication Officer v Patterson* Times, July 10, 1997 (CA), Stuart-Smith, L.J.
Sch.4, applied: SI 1999/991 Reg.3
Sch.4 para.1, amended: SI 1996/1460 Reg.2
Sch.4 para.2, amended: SI 1997/793 Reg.7
Sch.4 para.7, amended: SI 1999/2572 Reg.24, Reg.25, Sch. Part V, Sch. Part VI
Sch.4 para.8, amended: SI 1997/792 Reg.8
Sch.4 para.9, amended: SI 1996/2306 Reg.6
Sch.4 para.11, amended: SI 1999/2572 Reg.24, Reg.25, Sch. Part V, Sch. Part VI
Sch.5, amended: SI 1996/2306 Reg.7
Sch.5 para.1, applied: SI 1996/2567 Reg.5
Sch.5 para.1, revoked: SI 1996/1460 Reg.2
Sch.6, referred to: SI 1999/991 Reg.7, SI 1999/2860 Art.4, Sch.16 para.3
Sch.6 para.2, revoked: SI 1999/2358 Reg.2
Sch.6 para.5, referred to: SI 1999/820 Reg.1
Sch.7, amended: SI 1999/3178 Art.3, Sch.6 para.15
Sch.7 para.1, amended: SI 1996/672 Reg.2
Sch.7 para.2, revoked (in part): SI 1996/1460 Reg.2

NO.

1968. Social Security (Claims and Payments) Regulations 1987—*cont.*
Sch.7 para.2A, amended: SI 1999/3108 Reg.18, Sch.3 para.2
Sch.7 para.4, revoked (in part): SI 1996/1460 Reg.2
Sch.7 para.6, amended: SI 1996/1460 Reg.2
Sch.7 para.7, amended: SI 1998/1174 Reg.8, SI 1999/3178 Art.3, Sch.6 para.15
Sch.7 para.7, applied: SI 1996/909 Reg.1, SI 1996/1363 Reg.1, SI 1997/944 Reg.1, SI 1997/2055 Reg.1, SI 1997/2604 Reg.1, SI 1998/1128 Reg.1, SI 1998/2878 Reg.1, SI 1999/123 Reg.1, SI 1999/371 Reg.1, SI 1999/907 Reg.1, SI 1999/1153 Reg.1, SI 1999/1411 Reg.1
Sch.8 para.2, amended: SI 1996/1460 Reg.2, SI 1996/1803 Reg.21, SI 1999/2566 Reg.4
Sch.9, amended: SI 1996/3195 Reg.16
Sch.9 para.1, amended: SI 1996/672 Reg.2, SI 1996/1460 Reg.2, SI 1996/2344 Reg.25
Sch.9 para.3, amended: SI 1996/1460 Reg.2, SI 1999/2860 Art.3, Sch.3 para.12, SI 1999/3178 Art.3, Sch.6 para.16
Sch.9 para.3, referred to: SI 1999/991 Reg.27, Sch.2 para.5
Sch.9 para.4, amended: SI 1996/1460 Reg.2, SI 1999/2860 Art.3, Sch.3 para.12
Sch.9 para.4, referred to: SI 1999/991 Reg.27, Sch.2 para.5
Sch.9 para.4A, amended: SI 1996/1460 Reg.2
Sch.9 para.4A, referred to: SI 1999/991 Reg.27, Sch.2 para.5
Sch.9 para.5, amended: SI 1996/1460 Reg.2, SI 1999/2860 Art.3, Sch.3 para.12
Sch.9 para.5, referred to: SI 1999/991 Reg.27, Sch.2 para.5
Sch.9 para.6, amended: SI 1996/1460 Reg.2, SI 1999/2860 Art.3, Sch.3 para.12, SI 1999/3178 Art.3, Sch.6 para.16
Sch.9 para.6, referred to: SI 1999/991 Reg.27, Sch.2 para.5
Sch.9 para.7, amended: SI 1996/1460 Reg.2, SI 1999/2860 Art.3, Sch.3 para.12, SI 1999/3178 Art.3, Sch.6 para.16
Sch.9 para.7, referred to: SI 1999/991 Reg.27, Sch.2 para.5
Sch.9 para.7A, amended: SI 1996/481 Reg.5, SI 1999/1510 Art.4, SI 1999/2860 Art.3, Sch.3 para.12
Sch.9 para.7A, referred to: SI 1999/991 Reg.27, Sch.2 para.5
Sch.9 para.7B, added: SI 1996/2344 Reg.25
Sch.9 para.7B, amended: SI 1999/2860 Art.3, Sch.3 para.12
Sch.9 para.7B, referred to: SI 1999/991 Reg.27, Sch.2 para.5
Sch.9 para.8, amended: SI 1996/481 Reg.6, SI 1997/827 Reg.7
Sch.9 para.8, revoked (in part): SI 1997/827 Reg.7
Sch.9 para.9, amended: SI 1999/2860 Art.3, Sch.3 para.12
Sch.9 para.9, referred to: SI 1999/991 Reg.27, Sch.2 para.5
Sch.9A, amended: SI 1996/3195 Reg.16
Sch.9A para.1, amended: SI 1996/672 Reg.2, SI 1996/1460 Reg.2, SI 1997/827 Reg.7
Sch.9A para.2, amended: SI 1996/1460 Reg.2
Sch.9A para.3, amended: SI 1996/1460 Reg.2, SI 1999/2860 Art.3, Sch.3 para.13, SI 1999/3178 Art.3, Sch.6 para.17
Sch.9A para.3, revoked (in part): SI 1997/827 Reg.7

NO.

1968. Social Security (Claims and Payments) Regulations 1987—*cont.*
Sch.9A para.4, amended: SI 1996/1460 Reg.2, SI 1997/827 Reg.7
Sch.9A para.4, revoked (in part): SI 1997/827 Reg.7
Sch.9A para.5, revoked: SI 1996/672 Reg.2
Sch.9A para.7, amended: SI 1996/2988 Reg.2, SI 1997/3034 Reg.2, SI 1998/3039 Reg.2
Sch.9A para.10, see *R. v Secretary of State for Social Security Ex p. Golding* (1996) 28 H.L.R. 575 (QBD), Brooke, J.
Sch.9A para.10, amended: SI 1996/1460 Reg.2, SI 1997/2305 Reg.5
Sch.9A para.10, referred to: SI 1999/991 Reg.7
Sch.9A para.11, amended: SI 1996/1460 Reg.2

1969. Income Support (Transitional) Regulations 1987
amended: SI 1996/206
applied: SI 1996/207 Reg.87, SI 1996/1623 Art.3, SI 1998/217 Art.2, SI 1999/779 Art.2, Sch.
Part II, applied: SI 1997/431 Sch.3 para.1, SI 1999/991 Reg.14
Reg.2, amended: SI 1996/206 Reg.29
Reg.2A, amended: SI 1996/206 Reg.29
Reg.15, amended: SI 1996/599 Art.19, SI 1997/543 Art.19, SI 1998/470 Art.19, SI 1999/264 Art.19

1971. Housing Benefit (General) Regulations 1987
see *Haringey LBC v Cotter* Times, December 9, 1996 (CA), Mummery, L.J.; see *Jones v Waveney DC* Times, December 22, 1999 (CA), Pill, L.J.; see *R. v Doncaster MBC Ex p. Nortrop* (1996) 28 H.L.R. 862 (QBD), Brooke, J.
applied: SI 1996/1217 Art.11, SI 1996/1623 Art.3, SI 1996/2754 Reg.3, SI 1997/1004 Art.11, SI 1998/217 Art.2, SI 1998/562 Art.19, SI 1999/779 Art.2, Sch., SI 1999/2734 Reg.13
referred to: SI 1996/1982 Art.4
Part VII, applied: SI 1997/791 Reg.24, SI 1997/1909 Reg.24
Reg.2, amended: SI 1996/194 Reg.2, SI 1996/965 Reg.2, SI 1996/1510 Reg.2, SI 1996/1944 Reg.5, Reg.13, Sch. para.1, Sch. para.2, SI 1998/563 Reg.5, SI 1998/2825 Reg.12, SI 1999/1539 Reg.2, SI 1999/2165 Reg.2, SI 1999/2401 Reg.4, SI 1999/2566 Reg.2, Sch.2 Part III, SI 1999/2734 Reg.2, SI 1999/3108 Reg.10, Reg.12, SI 1999/3156 Reg.12, SI 1999/3178 Art.3, Sch.7 para.1
Reg.2A, added: SI 1997/2676 Reg.8
Reg.2A, revoked: SI 1999/920 Reg.2
Reg.2B, added: SI 1999/2401 Reg.3
Reg.3, amended: SI 1998/3257 Reg.2
Reg.4, amended: SI 1996/1510 Reg.3, SI 1998/2825 Reg.13, SI 1999/2165 Reg.5, SI 1999/3156 Reg.13
Reg.5, amended: SI 1997/2197 Reg.4, SI 1998/563 Reg.8
Reg.6, see *R. v Poole BC Ex p. Ross* (1996) 28 H.L.R. 351 (QBD), Sedley, J.
Reg.7, see *R. v Poole BC Ex p. Ross* (1996) 28 H.L.R. 351 (QBD), Sedley, J.; see *R. v South Gloucestershire Housing Benefit Review Board Ex p. Dadds* (1997) 29 H.L.R. 700 (QBD), George Bartlett Q.C.; see *R. v Stratford upon Avon Housing Benefit Review Board Ex p. White* (1999) 31 H.L.R. 126 (CA), Otton, L.J.; see *R. v Sutton LBC Ex p. Partridge* (1996) 28 H.L.R. 315 (QBD), Laws, J.

NO.

1971. Housing Benefit (General) Regulations 1987—*cont.*

Reg.7, amended: SI 1996/462 Reg.12, SI 1998/3257 Reg.3

Reg.7, applied: SI 1997/1984 Art.6

Reg.7, referred to: SI 1997/1995 Art.6

Reg.7A, amended: SI 1996/30 Reg.7, SI 1996/1510 Reg.4, SI 1996/1944 Reg.5, SI 1996/2006 Reg.2, SI 1996/2432 Reg.8, SI 1998/563 Reg.18

Reg.7A, referred to: SI 1996/30 Reg.12, SI 1996/2890 Reg.3, SI 1997/1004 Art.5

Reg.7B, added: SI 1996/2432 Reg.9

Reg.7B, applied: SI 1996/2890 Sch.3 para.57, Sch.4 para.50

Reg.8, amended: SI 1996/1510 Reg.5, SI 1999/2734 Reg.3

Reg.10, see *R. v Bristol City Council Ex p. Jacobs* Times, November 16, 1999 (QBD), Owen, J.; see *R. v Poole BC Ex p. Ross* (1996) H.L.R. 351 (QBD), Sedley, J.

Reg.10, amended: SI 1996/462 Reg.6, SI 1996/965 Reg.3, SI 1999/2734 Reg.4

Reg.10, applied: SI 1996/1217 Sch.6 para.10, Sch.6 para.11, SI 1997/1004 Sch.6 para.10, Sch.6 para.11, SI 1998/562 Sch.4 para.14, Sch.4 para.16

Reg.11, see *R. v Oadby and Wigston BC Ex p. Dickman* [1996] 28 H.L.R. 806 (QBD), Buxton, J.; see *R. v Waltham Forest LBC Ex p. Holder* (1997) 29 H.L.R. 71 (QBD), Brooke, J.

Reg.11, amended: SI 1996/965 Reg.4, SI 1997/852 Reg.3, SI 1998/563 Reg.9, SI 1999/2734 Reg.5

Reg.11, applied: SI 1996/1217 Art.8, Sch.6 para.5, Sch.6 para.12, SI 1997/852 Reg.4, SI 1997/1004 Art.8, Sch.6 para.5, Sch.6 para.12, SI 1998/562 Art.16, Sch.4 para.10, Sch.4 para.15

Reg.11, referred to: SI 1999/2734 Reg.11

Reg.12, amended: SI 1996/965 Reg.5, SI 1999/2734 Reg.11

Reg.12, applied: SI 1996/1217 Sch.6 para.5, SI 1997/1004 Sch.6 para.5, SI 1998/562 Sch.4 para.10

Reg.12, revoked: SI 1997/852 Reg.3 (with savings)

Reg.12A, amended: SI 1997/852 Reg.3, SI 1998/563 Reg.10, SI 1999/2401 Reg.4, SI 1999/2734 Reg.6

Reg.12A, applied: SI 1996/1217 Art.8, Sch.6 para.8, SI 1997/1004 Art.8, Sch.6 para.8, SI 1998/562 Sch.4 para.4, Sch.4 para.6

Reg.12A, revoked (in part): SI 1999/2734 Reg.6

Reg.13, amended: SI 1996/1510 Reg.6

Reg.13, applied: SI 1996/2545 Reg.10

Reg.16, amended: SI 1996/599 Art.21, SI 1996/2432 Reg.13, SI 1997/543 Art.21, SI 1998/470 Art.21, SI 1999/264 Art.21

Reg.17, amended: SI 1996/599 Art.21, SI 1996/2432 Reg.13, SI 1997/543 Art.21, SI 1998/470 Art.21, SI 1999/264 Art.21

Reg.18, amended: SI 1996/599 Art.21, SI 1996/1803 Reg.29, SI 1996/2432 Reg.13, SI 1997/543 Art.21, SI 1998/470 Art.21, SI 1999/264 Art.21

Reg.18, referred to: SI 1996/2890 Reg.19

Reg.20, amended: SI 1996/1510 Reg.7

Reg.21, amended: SI 1996/599 Art.21, SI 1997/2793 Reg.2, SI 1999/920 Reg.3

Reg.21A, amended: SI 1996/1008 Art.2, Sch para.8, SI 1996/2545 Reg.3, SI 1997/2793 Reg.2, SI 1999/920 Reg.4

NO.

1971. Housing Benefit (General) Regulations 1987—*cont.*

Reg.21A, applied: SI 1996/2745 Sch.2 para.8

Reg.28, amended: SI 1999/1509 Reg.2

Reg.30, amended: SI 1999/2165 Reg.5

Reg.34, amended: SI 1997/65 Reg.3

Reg.35, amended: SI 1996/1803 Reg.30, SI 1997/2197 Reg.7, SI 1997/2863 Reg.17, SI 1998/563 Reg.6, SI 1998/2164 Reg.2, SI 1998/2825 Reg.14, SI 1999/2640 Reg.2, SI 1999/3156 Reg.14

Reg.40, amended: SI 1998/1174 Reg.7, SI 1999/3156 Reg.18

Reg.43, amended: SI 1997/2197 Reg.7, SI 1997/2863 Reg.17, SI 1998/2164 Reg.3, SI 1998/2825 Reg.15, SI 1999/2640 Reg.2, SI 1999/3156 Reg.15

Reg.43A, amended: SI 1996/1510 Reg.8, SI 1996/1944 Reg.5, Reg.13, Sch. para.4, SI 1999/2566 Reg.2, Sch.2 Part I, Sch.2 Part II

Reg.44, amended: SI 1998/2250 Reg.2

Reg.45, amended: SI 1996/462 Reg.12

Reg.46, amended: SI 1996/1944 Reg.4, SI 1997/791 Reg.24, SI 1997/1909 Reg.24, SI 1998/563 Reg.4, SI 1998/1274 Reg.10, SI 1999/1935 Reg.5

Reg.46, applied: SI 1997/791 Reg.24

Reg.48A, amended: SI 1996/1510 Reg.9, SI 1996/1803 Reg.31, SI 1997/1790 Reg.6, SI 1998/766 Reg.7

Reg.51, amended: SI 1996/1759 Reg.3, SI 1996/1803 Reg.32, SI 1997/584 Reg.2, SI 1997/1671 Reg.3, SI 1997/1790 Reg.7, SI 1998/766 Reg.8, SI 1998/1379 Reg.3, SI 1999/1935 Reg.5

Reg.53, amended: SI 1996/1759 Reg.2, SI 1996/1944 Reg.5, SI 1997/1671 Reg.2, SI 1998/1379 Reg.2, SI 1999/1935 Reg.5

Reg.54, amended: SI 1996/1944 Reg.4

Reg.55, amended: SI 1996/1944 Reg.5

Reg.56, amended: SI 1996/462 Reg.8

Reg.57, amended: SI 1999/1935 Reg.5

Reg.57A, amended: SI 1996/462 Reg.9, SI 1999/1935 Reg.5

Reg.58, amended: SI 1996/462 Reg.10, SI 1999/1935 Reg.5

Reg.58A, added: SI 1998/563 Reg.4

Reg.58A, amended: SI 1999/1935 Reg.5

Reg.61, amended: SI 1999/3108 Reg.12

Reg.61, applied: SI 1996/1217 Art.11, SI 1997/1004 Art.11, SI 1998/562 Art.19

Reg.62, amended: SI 1999/3108 Reg.12

Reg.62A, added: SI 1996/194 Reg.3

Reg.62A, amended: SI 1999/2556 Reg.5

Reg.62B, added: SI 1999/3108 Reg.11

Reg.62C, added: SI 1999/3108 Reg.11

Reg.63, amended: SI 1996/599 Art.21, SI 1996/1510 Reg.10, SI 1996/2518 Reg.3, SI 1997/543 Art.21, SI 1998/470 Art.21, SI 1998/563 Reg.8, SI 1999/264 Art.21

Reg.63, applied: SI 1996/207 Sch.2 para.17

Reg.65, amended: SI 1999/3108 Reg.12

Reg.66, amended: SI 1996/1510 Reg.11

Reg.66, applied: SI 1996/1217 Art.10, SI 1997/852 Reg.4, SI 1997/1004 Art.10, SI 1998/562 Art.18

Reg.67, amended: SI 1996/1510 Reg.12

Reg.68, amended: SI 1999/2734 Reg.7

Reg.68, applied: SI 1996/1217 Sch.6 para.8, SI 1997/1004 Sch.6 para.8

Reg.69, amended: SI 1996/194 Reg.4

Reg.71, amended: SI 1999/3108 Reg.10

NO.

1971. Housing Benefit (General) Regulations 1987—*cont.*

Reg.72, see *R. v Aylesbury Vale DC Ex p. England* (1996) 28 H.L.R. 783 (QBD), Brooke, J.

Reg.72, amended: SI 1996/462 Reg.5, SI 1996/1510 Reg.13, SI 1996/2432 Reg.13, SI 1999/1539 Reg.3, SI 1999/2556 Reg.5, SI 1999/3108 Reg.10

Reg.72, applied: SI 1996/1217 Art.5, Art.10, Art.11, SI 1997/852 Reg.4, SI 1997/1004 Art.5, Art.10, Art.11, SI 1998/562 Art.14, Art.19

Reg.72, referred to: SI 1998/562 Art.18

Reg.72A, added: SI 1999/1539 Reg.4

Reg.72B, added: SI 1999/3108 Reg.9

Reg.72C, added: SI 1999/3108 Reg.9

Reg.73, see *R. v Winston (Winston James)* (1998) 162 J.P. 775 (QBD), Hobhouse, L.J.

Reg.73, amended: SI 1996/2432 Reg.13, SI 1999/3108 Reg.10

Reg.75, amended: SI 1996/1510 Reg.14, SI 1999/1539 Reg.5, SI 1999/3108 Reg.10

Reg.75, applied: SI 1996/1217 Art.10

Reg.76, amended: SI 1996/194 Reg.5, SI 1996/1510 Reg.15, SI 1996/2432 Reg.13, SI 1999/2556 Reg.5

Reg.76, applied: SI 1997/1004 Sch.1 para.4, SI 1998/562 Sch.2 para.2

Reg.79, see *Plymouth City Council v Gigg* (1998) 30 H.L.R. 284 (CA), Otton, L.J.; see *R. v Chorley BC Ex p. Bound* (1996) 28 H.L.R. 791 (QBD), Judge Rich Q.C.; see *R. v Lambeth LBC Ex p. Crookes (1998)* (1999) 31 H.L.R. 59 (QBD), Judge Nigel MacLeod Q.C.; see *R. v Sefton Housing Benefit Review Board Ex p. Brennan* (1997) 29 H.L.R. 735 (QBD), Dyson, J.

Reg.79, referred to: SI 1996/548 Art.2, SI 1996/549 Art.2

Reg.81, referred to: SI 1996/548 Art.2, SI 1996/549 Art.2

Reg.83, see *R. v Sefton Housing Benefit Review Board Ex p. Brennan* (1997) 29 H.L.R. 735 (QBD), Dyson, J.; see *R. v Stoke-on-Trent City Council and Secretary of State for Social Security Ex p. Highgate Projects* (1997) 29 H.L.R. 271 (CA), Simon Brown, L.J.

Reg.84, amended: SI 1999/3108 Reg.12

Reg.86, see *R. v Sefton Housing Benefit Review Board Ex p. Brennan* (1997) 29 H.L.R. 735 (QBD), Dyson, J.

Reg.88, amended: SI 1996/965 Reg.6

Reg.90, amended: SI 1996/965 Reg.7

Reg.91, see *R. v Liverpool CC Ex p. Filla* [1996] C.O.D. 24 (QBD), Laws, J.

Reg.91, applied: SI 1996/1217 Art.8, Sch.6 para.6, SI 1997/1004 Art.8, Sch.6 para.6, SI 1998/562 Art.16, Sch.4 para.11

Reg.93, see *Haringey LBC v Cotter* (1997) 29 H.L.R. 682 (CA), Mummery, L.J.

Reg.93, amended: SI 1996/1510 Reg.16, SI 1996/2432 Reg.13, SI 1997/65 Reg.12, SI 1997/2434 Reg.2

Reg.93, applied: SI 1997/2436 Reg.3

Reg.94, amended: SI 1996/965 Reg.8, SI 1996/2432 Reg.13, SI 1997/65 Reg.13, SI 1997/2434 Reg.2

Reg.94, applied: SI 1997/2436 Reg.3

Reg.95, see *R. v Kensington and Chelsea RLBC Ex p. Brandt* (1996) 28 H.L.R. 538 (QBD), Dyson, J.

NO.

1971. Housing Benefit (General) Regulations 1987—*cont.*

Reg.95, amended: SI 1996/1510 Reg.17, SI 1997/2434 Reg.2, SI 1999/3178 Art.3, Sch.7 para.2

Reg.96A, added: SI 1997/2434 Reg.3

Reg.98, see *R. v South Hams DC Ex p. Ash* Times, May 27, 1999 (QBD), Moses, J.

Reg.99, see *R. v South Hams DC Ex p. Ash* Times, May 27, 1999 (QBD), Moses, J.

Reg.99, amended: SI 1997/65 Reg.11, SI 1999/3108 Reg.10

Reg.99, applied: SI 1996/1217 Sch.6 para.6, SI 1997/1004 Sch.6 para.6, SI 1998/562 Sch.4 para.11

Reg.102, referred to: SI 1997/2435 Reg.2

Reg.105, amended: SI 1996/1510 Reg.18

Reg.105, referred to: SI 1997/2435 Reg.2

Sch. A1, added: SI 1996/2432 Reg.12

Sch. A1 para.10, amended: SI 1997/852 Reg.3

Sch. A1 para.11A, amended: SI 1997/852 Reg.3

Sch.1, see *R. v Sutton LBC Ex p. Harrison* Times, August 22, 1997 (QBD), Laws, J.; see *R. v Swansea City Council Ex p. Littler* (1998) 30 H.L.R. 800 (QBD), Laws, J.

Sch.1, applied: SI 1996/1217 Sch.6 para.11, SI 1997/1004 Sch.6 para.11, SI 1998/562 Sch.4 para.14

Sch.1 Part I, amended: SI 1996/599 Art.21, SI 1997/543 Art.21

Sch.1 Part I, applied: SI 1997/1984 Sch.1 para.7

Sch.1 Part II, amended: SI 1996/599 Art.21, SI 1997/543 Art.21

Sch.1 para.1, see *R. v Swansea City Council Ex p. Littler* (1999) 48 B.M.L.R. 24 (CA), Kennedy, L.J.

Sch.1 para.1, amended: SI 1997/1974 Reg.2, SI 1999/2734 Reg.8

Sch.1 para.1, applied: SI 1997/1984 Art.7, Sch.1 para.10, SI 1997/1995 Art.7, Sch.1 para.7, Sch.1 para.10, SI 1998/562 Art.23

Sch.1 para.1A, amended: SI 1997/65 Reg.14, SI 1998/470 Art.21, SI 1999/264 Art.21

Sch.1 para.2, amended: SI 1996/965 Reg.9

Sch.1 para.4, applied: SI 1997/1984 Sch.1 para.10, SI 1997/1995 Sch.1 para.10

Sch.1 para.5, applied: SI 1996/207 Sch.2 para.16, SI 1996/1217 Art.7

Sch.1 para.7, amended: SI 1997/1974 Reg.2, SI 1999/2734 Reg.8

Sch.1A para.1, applied: SI 1996/1217 Art.7, SI 1997/1004 Art.7

Sch.1A para.1, referred to: SI 1998/562 Art.16

Sch.1A para.2, amended: SI 1997/852 Reg.3, SI 1998/563 Reg.11

Sch.1A para.2, applied: SI 1996/1217 Art.8, SI 1997/1004 Art.8, SI 1998/562 Sch.4 para.5

Sch.1A para.2, revoked (in part): SI 1998/563 Reg.11

Sch.1A para.3, referred to: SI 1996/1217 Art.7, SI 1997/1004 Art.7, SI 1998/562 Art.16

Sch.1A para.5, applied: SI 1997/1004 Art.7

Sch.1A para.5, referred to: SI 1998/562 Art.16

Sch.1A para.6, applied: SI 1996/1217 Art.7, SI 1997/1004 Art.7

Sch.1A para.6, referred to: SI 1998/562 Art.16

Sch.1A para.7, applied: SI 1996/1217 Art.7, SI 1997/1004 Art.7

Sch.1A para.7, referred to: SI 1998/562 Art.16

Sch.1A para.8, applied: SI 1996/1217 Art.7, SI 1997/1004 Art.7

NO.

1971. Housing Benefit (General) Regulations 1987—*cont.*

Sch.1A para.8, referred to: SI 1998/562 Art.16

Sch.1A para.9, applied: SI 1996/1217 Art.7, SI 1997/1004 Art.7

Sch.1A para.9, referred to: SI 1998/562 Art.16

Sch.1A para.10, referred to: SI 1996/1217 Art.7, SI 1997/1004 Art.7, SI 1998/562 Art.16

Sch.1A para.11, referred to: SI 1998/562 Art.16

Sch.1A para.11A, referred to: SI 1998/562 Art.16

Sch.1A para.12, amended: SI 1998/563 Reg.11

Sch.1A para.12, revoked (in part): SI 1998/563 Reg.11

Sch.1B, added: SI 1999/2734 Reg.9

Sch.2 Part I, amended: SI 1996/599 Art.21, Sch.9, SI 1997/543 Art.21, Sch.9

Sch.2 Part II, amended: SI 1996/599 Art.21, SI 1996/1803 Reg.33, SI 1997/543 Art.21

Sch.2 Part III, amended: SI 1996/599 Art.21, SI 1996/1803 Reg.33, SI 1997/543 Art.21

Sch.2 Part III, revoked (in part): SI 1996/1803 Reg.33

Sch.2 Part IV, amended: SI 1996/599 Art.21, Sch.10, SI 1996/1803 Reg.33, SI 1997/543 Art.21, Sch.10

Sch.2 para.1, amended: SI 1998/470 Art.21, Sch.9, SI 1999/264 Art.21, Sch.9

Sch.2 para.2, amended: SI 1998/2545 Reg.2, SI 1997/543 Art.21, SI 1998/470 Art.21, Sch.9, SI 1998/1541 Reg.2, SI 1999/264 Art.21, Sch.9, SI 1999/2555 Reg.2

Sch.2 para.3, amended: SI 1997/1790 Reg.8, SI 1998/470 Art.21, SI 1998/766 Reg.9

Sch.2 para.10, amended: SI 1998/2231 Reg.10

Sch.2 para.10, applied: SI 1996/2745 Sch.2 para.8

Sch.2 para.12, amended: SI 1998/2231 Reg.10, SI 1999/2566 Reg.2, Sch.2 Part II

Sch.2 para.13, amended: SI 1996/462 Reg.3

Sch.2 para.14, amended: SI 1998/470 Art.21, SI 1999/264 Art.21

Sch.2 para.15, amended: SI 1996/462 Reg.3, SI 1998/470 Art.21, Sch.10, SI 1999/264 Art.21, Sch.10

Sch.3 para.4, amended: SI 1996/1803 Reg.34

Sch.3 para.4, substituted: SI 1997/1790 Reg.9, SI 1998/766 Reg.10

Sch.3 para.10, amended: SI 1996/1510 Reg.19

Sch.3 para.16, added: SI 1999/920 Reg.5

Sch.3 para.16, amended: SI 1999/2566 Reg.2, Sch.2 Part IV

Sch.4 para.4, amended: SI 1996/1510 Reg.20

Sch.4 para.6, amended: SI 1996/1510 Reg.20

Sch.4 para.10, amended: SI 1997/2197 Reg.7, SI 1999/1677 Reg.2

Sch.4 para.11, amended: SI 1997/2863 Reg.17

Sch.4 para.13, amended: SI 1996/462 Reg.8

Sch.4 para.17, amended: SI 1999/1935 Reg.5

Sch.4 para.18, amended: SI 1999/1935 Reg.5

Sch.4 para.20, amended: SI 1996/599 Art.21

Sch.4 para.23, amended: SI 1998/563 Reg.7

Sch.4 para.25, substituted: SI 1998/563 Reg.7

Sch.4 para.28, substituted: SI 1998/1173 Reg.2

Sch.4 para.33, amended: SI 1996/462 Reg.8, SI 1998/563 Reg.7

Sch.4 para.47, amended: SI 1996/1803 Reg.35

Sch.4 para.51, amended: SI 1996/2432 Reg.10

Sch.4 para.52, amended: SI 1996/1510 Reg.20

Sch.4 para.57, amended: SI 1999/920 Reg.5, SI 1999/2566 Reg.2, Sch.2 Part II, Sch.2 Part IV

NO.

1971. Housing Benefit (General) Regulations 1987—*cont.*

Sch.4 para.57, substituted: SI 1996/462 Reg.4

Sch.4 para.58, amended: SI 1999/920 Reg.5, SI 1999/2566 Reg.2, Sch.2 Part I

Sch.4 para.58, substituted: SI 1996/462 Reg.4

Sch.4 para.59, added: SI 1996/1803 Reg.35

Sch.4 para.60, amended: SI 1996/1944 Reg.13, Sch. para.6

Sch.4 para.61, added: SI 1996/2432 Reg.10

Sch.4 para.62, added: SI 1996/2432 Reg.10, SI 1997/65 Reg.2

Sch.4 para.62, revoked: SI 1997/2863 Reg.18, SI 1998/1174 Reg.8

Sch.4 para.63, added: SI 1997/65 Reg.2

Sch.4 para.64, amended: SI 1997/2863 Reg.17

Sch.4 para.64, substituted: SI 1998/1174 Reg.7

Sch.4 para.65, amended: SI 1997/2863 Reg.17

Sch.4 para.66, added: SI 1997/2863 Reg.18, SI 1998/1174 Reg.7

Sch.4 para.66, amended: SI 1999/3156 Reg.18

Sch.4 para.67, added: SI 1998/1174 Reg.8

Sch.4 para.68, added: SI 1998/2164 Reg.4

Sch.4 para.69, amended: SI 1998/2825 Reg.16, SI 1999/3156 Reg.16

Sch.4 para.70, amended: SI 1998/2825 Reg.16, SI 1999/3156 Reg.16

Sch.4 para.71, added: SI 1999/2165 Reg.5

Sch.5 para.5, amended: SI 1996/1510 Reg.21

Sch.5 para.7, amended: SI 1998/1174 Reg.7, SI 1999/3156 Reg.18

Sch.5 para.8, amended: SI 1996/1510 Reg.21, SI 1996/1944 Reg.13, Sch. para.7

Sch.5 para.45, amended: SI 1996/2432 Reg.11

Sch.5 para.46, amended: SI 1997/2197 Reg.7

Sch.5 para.47, amended: SI 1997/2197 Reg.7

Sch.5 para.49, added: SI 1996/1510 Reg.21

Sch.5 para.50, added: SI 1996/2432 Reg.11, SI 1996/3195 Reg.15

Sch.5 para.51, added: SI 1996/2432 Reg.11

Sch.5 para.53, amended: SI 1997/2863 Reg.17

Sch.5 para.53, substituted: SI 1998/1174 Reg.7

Sch.5 para.54, amended: SI 1997/2863 Reg.17

Sch.5 para.55, added: SI 1998/1174 Reg.7

Sch.5 para.55, amended: SI 1999/3156 Reg.18

Sch.5 para.56, added: SI 1998/2164 Reg.5

Sch.5 para.57, amended: SI 1998/2825 Reg.17, SI 1999/3156 Reg.17

Sch.5 para.58, amended: SI 1998/2825 Reg.17, SI 1999/3156 Reg.17

Sch.5 para.59, added: SI 1999/2165 Reg.5

Sch.5A, added: SI 1996/194 Reg.6

Sch.5A para.2, amended: SI 1996/1510 Reg.22, SI 1996/1803 Reg.36, SI 1997/1790 Reg.10, SI 1998/766 Reg.11, SI 1999/2556 Reg.5

Sch.5A para.3, amended: SI 1996/1510 Reg.22

Sch.5A para.4, amended: SI 1999/2556 Reg.5

Sch.5A para.8, amended: SI 1999/2556 Reg.5

Sch.5A para.12, amended: SI 1996/1510 Reg.22, SI 1999/2556 Reg.5

Sch.6 para.5, see *Haringey LBC v Awaritefe* Times, June 3, 1999 (CA), Roch, L.J.

Sch.6 para.9, amended: SI 1996/1510 Reg.23

Sch.6 para.10, amended: SI 1996/1510 Reg.23

Sch.6 para.11, amended: SI 1997/2434 Reg.4, SI 1997/2435 Reg.4

Sch.6 para.11A, added: SI 1997/2434 Reg.4

Sch.6 para.11A, amended: SI 1997/2435 Reg.4

Sch.6 para.13, amended: SI 1996/1510 Reg.23

Sch.6 para.14, amended: SI 1997/2435 Reg.4, SI 1997/2619 Reg.2

NO.

NO.

1987—cont.

1973. Family Credit (General) Regulations 1987
applied: SI 1996/1623 Art.3, SI 1996/2545 Reg.10, SI 1998/217 Art.2, SI 1999/779 Art.2, Sch., SI 1999/3219 Reg.3
referred to: SI 1999/2566 Reg.2
Reg.2, amended: SI 1996/1345 Reg.8, SI 1996/1944 Reg.13, Sch. para.1, SI 1998/563 Reg.5, SI 1998/2825 Reg.12, SI 1999/2165 Reg.2, SI 1999/2487 Reg.3, Reg.26, Sch.1, SI 1999/3156 Reg.12
Reg.2A, added: SI 1997/2676 Reg.6
Reg.2A, amended: SI 1999/2487 Reg.26, Sch.1
Reg.3, amended: SI 1996/30 Reg.6, SI 1998/563 Reg.18, SI 1999/2487 Reg.26, Sch.1, Sch.2
Reg.4, amended: SI 1997/806 Reg.2, SI 1998/2825 Reg.13, SI 1999/2165 Reg.4, SI 1999/2487 Reg.26, Sch.1, SI 1999/3156 Reg.13
Reg.4A, amended: SI 1999/2487 Reg.26, Sch.1
Reg.6, amended: SI 1996/1345 Reg.8, SI 1999/2487 Reg.26, Sch.1
Reg.6, applied: SI 1996/2545 Reg.10
Reg.12, amended: SI 1999/2487 Reg.4
Reg.13, amended: SI 1996/599 Art.16, SI 1997/2793 Reg.2, SI 1999/2487 Reg.26, Sch.1
Reg.13, revoked (in part): SI 1999/2487 Reg.5
Reg.13A, amended: SI 1996/1008 Art.2, Sch para.9, SI 1996/2545 Reg.4, SI 1997/2793 Reg.2, SI 1999/714 Reg.4, SI 1999/2487 Reg.6
Reg.14, amended: SI 1996/462 Reg.7, SI 1996/3137 Reg.3, SI 1999/2487 Reg.26, Sch.1
Reg.14A, amended: SI 1996/3137 Reg.3
Reg.18, amended: SI 1996/3137 Reg.3
Reg.19, amended: SI 1999/1509 Reg.2, SI 1999/2487 Reg.26
Reg.20, amended: SI 1996/3137 Reg.3
Reg.20ZA, amended: SI 1996/3137 Reg.3
Reg.21, amended: SI 1999/2165 Reg.4
Reg.22, amended: SI 1999/2487 Reg.26
Reg.23, amended: SI 1996/3137 Reg.3
Reg.25, amended: SI 1997/65 Reg.3
Reg.26, amended: SI 1997/2197 Reg.3, Reg.7, SI 1997/2863 Reg.17, SI 1998/563 Reg.6, SI 1998/2117 Reg.2, SI 1998/2825 Reg.14, SI 1999/2487 Reg.26, Sch.1, SI 1999/3156 Reg.14
Reg.28, amended: SI 1999/2487 Reg.26, Sch.1
Reg.29, amended: SI 1999/2487 Reg.26, Sch.1
Reg.31, amended: SI 1998/1174 Reg.7, SI 1999/3156 Reg.18
Reg.34, amended: SI 1997/2197 Reg.3, SI 1997/2863 Reg.17, SI 1998/2117 Reg.3, SI 1998/2825 Reg.15, SI 1999/2487 Reg.26, Sch.1, SI 1999/3156 Reg.15
Reg.34A, amended: SI 1999/2487 Reg.26, Sch.1
Reg.35, amended: SI 1998/2250 Reg.2
Reg.37, amended: SI 1998/563 Reg.4, SI 1999/1935 Reg.6
Reg.38, amended: SI 1996/1759 Reg.2, SI 1996/1944 Reg.4, SI 1997/1671 Reg.2, SI 1999/1935 Reg.6
Reg.42, amended: SI 1999/1935 Reg.6
Reg.42A, amended: SI 1996/462 Reg.9, SI 1999/1935 Reg.6
Reg.43, amended: SI 1996/462 Reg.10, SI 1999/1935 Reg.6
Reg.43A, amended: SI 1998/563 Reg.4, SI 1999/1935 Reg.6

1987—cont.

1973. Family Credit (General) Regulations 1987—cont.
Reg.46, amended: SI 1996/599 Art.16, SI 1996/2545 Reg.5, SI 1997/543 Art.16, SI 1998/470 Art.16, SI 1999/264 Art.16, SI 1999/2487 Reg.7, Reg.26, Sch.1
Reg.46, applied: SI 1996/2890 Sch.3 para.55
Reg.46A, added: SI 1999/2487 Reg.6
Reg.46A, amended: SI 1999/2487 Reg.8, Reg.26, Sch.1
Reg.47, amended: SI 1996/599 Art.16, SI 1997/543 Art.16, SI 1998/470 Art.16, SI 1999/264 Art.16, SI 1999/2487 Reg.9, Reg.26, Sch.1
Reg.48, amended: SI 1999/2487 Reg.10, Reg.26, Sch.1
Reg.49, amended: SI 1999/2487 Reg.26, Sch.1
Reg.49A, added: SI 1996/1418 Reg.2
Reg.49A, amended: SI 1999/2487 Reg.26, Reg.27, Sch.1
Reg.50, amended: SI 1996/1345 Reg.8, SI 1999/2487 Reg.26, Sch.1, Sch.2
Reg.51, amended: SI 1996/1944 Reg.4, SI 1999/2487 Reg.26, Reg.27, Sch.1, Sch.2
Reg.51A, amended: SI 1999/1510 Art.5
Reg.51A, revoked (in part): SI 1999/1510 Art.5, SI 1999/2487 Reg.11
Reg.52, amended: SI 1999/2487 Reg.26, Sch.1, Sch.2
Reg.62, amended: SI 1998/1379 Reg.2
Sch.2 para.3, amended: SI 1996/1345 Reg.8
Sch.2 para.4, amended: SI 1999/2487 Reg.26, Sch.2
Sch.2 para.5, amended: SI 1996/1345 Reg.8
Sch.2 para.9, amended: SI 1997/2197 Reg.7, SI 1999/1677 Reg.2
Sch.2 para.11, amended: SI 1997/2863 Reg.17
Sch.2 para.19, amended: SI 1996/599 Art.16
Sch.2 para.22, amended: SI 1997/65 Reg.2, SI 1998/563 Reg.7
Sch.2 para.24, substituted: SI 1998/563 Reg.7
Sch.2 para.25A, added: SI 1998/1173 Reg.3
Sch.2 para.47, amended: SI 1999/2487 Reg.12
Sch.2 para.56, amended: SI 1996/1944 Reg.13, Sch. para.5
Sch.2 para.57, added: SI 1997/65 Reg.2
Sch.2 para.58, added: SI 1997/65 Reg.2
Sch.2 para.59, amended: SI 1997/2863 Reg.17
Sch.2 para.59, substituted: SI 1998/1174 Reg.7
Sch.2 para.60, amended: SI 1997/2863 Reg.17
Sch.2 para.61, added: SI 1998/1174 Reg.7
Sch.2 para.61, added: SI 1999/3156 Reg.18
Sch.2 para.62, added: SI 1998/2117 Reg.4
Sch.2 para.63, amended: SI 1998/2825 Reg.16, SI 1999/3156 Reg.16
Sch.2 para.64, amended: SI 1998/2825 Reg.16, SI 1999/3156 Reg.16
Sch.2 para.65, added: SI 1999/2165 Reg.4
Sch.3 para.6, amended: SI 1998/1174 Reg.7, SI 1999/3156 Reg.18
Sch.3 para.8, amended: SI 1996/1345 Reg.8, SI 1996/1944 Reg.13, Sch. para.7
Sch.3 para.11, amended: SI 1999/2487 Reg.26, Sch.1
Sch.3 para.46, amended: SI 1997/2197 Reg.7
Sch.3 para.47, amended: SI 1997/2197 Reg.7
Sch.3 para.49, added: SI 1996/3195 Reg.15
Sch.3 para.50, added: SI 1996/1345 Reg.8
Sch.3 para.52, amended: SI 1997/2863 Reg.17
Sch.3 para.52, substituted: SI 1998/1174 Reg.7
Sch.3 para.53, amended: SI 1997/2863 Reg.17
Sch.3 para.54, added: SI 1998/1174 Reg.7
Sch.3 para.54, amended: SI 1999/3156 Reg.18

NO.

1973. Family Credit (General) Regulations 1987—*cont.*
Sch.3 para.55, added: SI 1998/2117 Reg.5
Sch.3 para.56, amended: SI 1998/2825 Reg.17, SI 1999/3156 Reg.17
Sch.3 para.57, amended: SI 1998/2825 Reg.17, SI 1999/3156 Reg.17
Sch.3 para.58, added: SI 1999/2165 Reg.4
Sch.4, amended: SI 1996/599 Art.16, Sch.2, SI 1997/543 Art.16, Sch.2, SI 1997/806 Reg.3, SI 1999/2487 Reg.13, Reg.26, Sch.1
Sch.4 para.1, amended: SI 1998/470 Art.16, Sch.2, SI 1999/264 Art.16, Sch.2
Sch.4 para.1A, amended: SI 1998/470 Art.16, Sch.2, SI 1999/264 Art.16, Sch.2
Sch.4 para.1A, applied: SI 1996/2890 Sch.3 para.55
Sch.4 para.2, amended: SI 1998/470 Art.16, Sch.2, SI 1998/1541 Reg.3, SI 1999/264 Art.16, Sch.2
Sch.4 para.2, substituted: SI 1996/2545 Reg.6
Sch.4 para.3, amended: SI 1998/470 Art.16, Sch.2, SI 1999/264 Art.16, Sch.2
Sch.4 para.3, substituted: SI 1996/2545 Reg.6

1986. Coffee and Coffee Products (Amendment) Regulations 1987
Reg.3, revoked: SI 1996/1499 Reg.49, Sch.9

1999. Courts-Martial and Standing Civilian Courts (Additional Powers on Trial of Civilians) (Amendment) Regulations 1987
revoked: SI 1997/579 Reg.13, Sch.3

2000. Rules of Procedure (Air Force) (Amendment) Rules 1987
revoked: SI 1997/171 r.90, Sch.7

2001. Standing Civilian Courts (Amendment) Order 1987
revoked: SI 1997/172 Art.93, Sch.5

2012. Goods Vehicles (Authorisation of International Journeys) (Fees) (Amendment) Regulations 1987
revoked: SI 1996/131 Reg.4, Sch.2

2014. Coffee and Coffee Products (Scotland) Amendment Regulations 1987
Reg.3, revoked: SI 1996/1499 Reg.49, Sch.9

2016. Offshore Installations (Safety Zones) (No.70) Order 1987
revoked: SI 1997/735 Art.3, Sch.2

2017. Offshore Installations (Safety Zones) (No.71) Order 1987
revoked: SI 1997/735 Reg.3, Sch.2

2023. Insolvent Companies (Disqualification of Unfit Directors) Proceedings Rules 1987
see *Practice Direction (No.2 of 1995) (Directors' Disqualification)* [1996] 1 All E.R. 442 (Ch D), Sir Richard Scott, V.C.; see *Secretary of State for Trade and Industry v Davies* [1996] 4 All E.R. 289 (CA), Millett, L.J.
amended: SI 1999/1023 r.3, Sch. para.1
r.1, amended: SI 1999/1023 r.3, Sch. para.2
r.2, substituted: SI 1999/1023 r.3, Sch. para.3
r.5, amended: SI 1999/1023 r.3, Sch. para.4
r.6, see *Park House Properties Ltd, Re* [1997] 2 B.C.L.C. 530 (Ch D), Neuberger, J.; see *Secretary of State for Trade and Industry v Carter* Times, August 14, 1997 (Ch D), Neuberger, J.
r.6, amended: SI 1999/1023 r.3, Sch. para.5
r.7, see *Practice Direction (Companies Court: Directors Disqualification)* [1996] 1 W.L.R. 170 (Ch D), Sir Richard Scott V.C.
r.7, amended: SI 1999/1023 r.3, Sch. para.6

NO.

2024. Non-Contentious Probate Rules 1987
amended: SI 1998/1903 r.2
r.2, amended: SI 1998/1903 r.3
r.3, substituted: SI 1999/1015 r.3
r.4, amended: SI 1998/1903 r.4
r.5, amended: SI 1998/1903 r.5, r.6
r.27, amended: SI 1998/1903 r.7
r.32, amended: SI 1998/1903 r.8
r.35, amended: SI 1998/1903 r.9
r.37, amended: SI 1998/1903 r.10
r.43, amended: SI 1998/1903 r.6
r.44, amended: SI 1998/1903 r.6, r.11
r.46, amended: SI 1998/1903 r.6
r.55, amended: SI 1998/1903 r.12
r.57, substituted: SI 1998/1903 r.13
r.62A, added: SI 1998/1903 r.14
r.66, amended: SI 1998/1903 r.15
Sch.1 Form 3, amended: SI 1998/1903 r.16
Sch.1 Form 4, amended: SI 1998/1903 r.17
Sch.1 Form 5, amended: SI 1998/1903 r.18

2025. Criminal Justice (Scotland) Act 1987 Fixed Penalty Order 1987
Art.1, revoked: SI 1996/2025 Art.6

2026. Environmentally Sensitive Areas (Cambrian Mountains - Extension) Designation Order 1987
Art.2, amended: SI 1996/3077 Reg.2, SI 1997/971 Art.2
Art.5, amended: SI 1996/3077 Reg.2
Art.5A, added: SI 1996/3077 Reg.2
Art.5B, added: SI 1996/3077 Reg.2
Art.5C, added: SI 1996/3077 Reg.2
Art.6, amended: SI 1997/971 Art.2
Art.6, revoked (in part): SI 1997/971 Art.2
Art.7, added: SI 1999/1175 Art.2
Sch.4 para.6, amended: SI 1997/971 Art.2

2027. Environmentally Sensitive Areas (Lleyn Peninsula) Designation Order 1987
Art.2, amended: SI 1996/3077 Reg.2, SI 1997/972 Art.2
Art.5, amended: SI 1996/3077 Reg.2
Art.5A, added: SI 1996/3077 Reg.2
Art.5B, added: SI 1996/3077 Reg.2
Art.5C, added: SI 1996/3077 Reg.2
Art.6, amended: SI 1997/972 Art.2
Art.6, revoked (in part): SI 1997/972 Art.2
Art.7, added: SI 1999/1175 Art.2
Sch.4 para.6, amended: SI 1997/972 Art.2

2032. Environmentally Sensitive Areas (South Downs - Western Extension) Designation Order 1987
referred to: SI 1997/1443 Art.6

2042. Extradition (Internationally Protected Persons) (Amendment) Order 1987
revoked: SI 1997/1764 Art.4

2044. Extradition (Taking of Hostages) (Amendment) Order 1987
revoked: SI 1997/1767 Art.4

2049. Consumer Protection (Northern Ireland) Order 1987
applied: SI 1997/1941 Sch.3 para.15
referred to: SI 1996/275 (NI.2) Art.44, SI 1996/600 Sch.5 para.15, SI 1996/601 Sch.5 para.15, SI 1997/1624 Sch.5 para.15, SI 1999/1517 Reg.12, Sch.4 para.12, SI 1999/1676 Sch.5 para.12
Art.29, amended: SI 1996/275 (NI.2) Art.71, Sch.6

2088. Registration of Births and Deaths Regulations 1987
Part II, amended: SI 1997/844 Reg.4
Part III, amended: SI 1997/844 Reg.2

NO.

1987—cont.

2088. Registration of Births and Deaths Regulations 1987—*cont.*
Part VIII, amended: SI 1997/844 Reg.2
Part X, amended: SI 1997/844 Reg.3
Part XII, amended: SI 1997/844 Reg.4
Reg.3, amended: SI 1997/844 Reg.4
Reg.13, amended: SI 1997/844 Reg.2
Reg.17, amended: SI 1997/1533 Reg.2
Reg.18, applied: SI 1997/962 Art.2
Reg.19, applied: SI 1997/962 Art.2
Reg.20, amended: SI 1997/1533 Reg.2
Reg.20, applied: SI 1997/962 Art.2
Reg.20, revoked (in part): SI 1997/1533 Reg.2
Reg.21, amended: SI 1997/1533 Reg.2
Reg.22, applied: SI 1997/962 Art.2
Reg.23, applied: SI 1997/962 Art.2
Reg.24, applied: SI 1997/962 Art.2
Reg.33, amended: SI 1997/844 Reg.2
Reg.34A, added: SI 1997/844 Reg.2
Reg.35, amended: SI 1997/844 Reg.2
Reg.42A, added: SI 1997/844 Reg.3
Reg.43, amended: SI 1997/844 Reg.3
Reg.44A, added: SI 1997/844 Reg.3
Reg.47, amended: SI 1997/844 Reg.3
Reg.55, amended: SI 1997/844 Reg.4, SI 1997/1533 Reg.2
Reg.55, applied: SI 1997/962 Art.2
Reg.56, applied: SI 1997/962 Art.2
Sch.2 Form 2, substituted: SI 1997/1533 Reg.2, Sch.1
Sch.2 Form 5, revoked: SI 1997/1533 Reg.2
Sch.2 Form 6, revoked: SI 1997/1533 Reg.2

2089. Registration of Births and Deaths (Welsh Language) Regulations 1987
Reg.5, amended: SI 1997/844 Reg.5
Reg.6, amended: SI 1997/844 Reg.5
Sch.2 Form 2, substituted: SI 1997/1533 Reg.3, Sch.2
Sch.2 Form 5, revoked: SI 1997/1533 Reg.3
Sch.2 Form 6, revoked: SI 1997/1533 Reg.3

2115. Control of Asbestos at Work Regulations 1987
applied: SI 1996/2791 Reg.3, Reg.7, Sch.6, SI 1997/2505 Reg.3, Reg.7, Sch.6, SI 1999/437 Reg.5, SI 1999/645 Reg.3, Reg.7, Sch.6
referred to: SI 1998/2306 Reg.12
Reg.2, amended: SI 1998/3235 Reg.2, Sch. para.1, Sch. para.2
Reg.3, amended: SI 1998/3235 Reg.2, Sch. para.3
Reg.5, amended: SI 1998/3235 Reg.2, Sch. para.4
Reg.5A, amended: SI 1998/3235 Reg.2, Sch. para.5
Reg.6, amended: SI 1998/3235 Reg.2, Sch. para.6
Reg.7, amended: SI 1998/3235 Reg.2, Sch. para.7
Reg.8, amended: SI 1998/3235 Reg.2, Sch. para.8
Reg.10, amended: SI 1998/3235 Reg.2, Sch. para.9
Reg.11, amended: SI 1998/3235 Reg.2, Sch. para.10
Reg.12, amended: SI 1998/3235 Reg.2, Sch. para.11
Reg.13, amended: SI 1998/3235 Reg.2, Sch. para.12
Reg.15A, added: SI 1998/3235 Reg.2, Sch. para.13
Reg.16, amended: SI 1998/3235 Reg.2, Sch. para.14

NO.

1987—cont.

2115. Control of Asbestos at Work Regulations 1987—*cont.*
Reg.17, amended: SI 1998/3235 Reg.2, Sch. para.15
Reg.18, amended: SI 1996/2092 Reg.21, SI 1998/3235 Reg.2, Sch. para.16
Reg.21A, added: SI 1998/3235 Reg.2, Sch. para.17
Sch.2 para.1, amended: SI 1996/2092 Reg.21

2117. Consumer Protection (Cancellation of Contracts Concluded away from Business Premises) Regulations 1987
Reg.2, amended: SI 1998/3050 Reg.2
Reg.3, amended: SI 1998/3050 Reg.2
Reg.4A, added: SI 1998/3050 Reg.2
Reg.4B, added: SI 1998/3050 Reg.2
Reg.4C, added: SI 1998/3050 Reg.2
Reg.4D, added: SI 1998/3050 Reg.2
Reg.4E, added: SI 1998/3050 Reg.2
Reg.4F, added: SI 1998/3050 Reg.2
Reg.4G, added: SI 1998/3050 Reg.2
Reg.4H, added: SI 1998/3050 Reg.2

2130. Insurance Companies (Assistance) Regulations 1987
Reg.4, revoked: SI 1996/943 Reg.35, Sch.7

2172. Rules of Procedure (Air Force) (Amendment No.2) Rules 1987
revoked: SI 1997/171 r.90, Sch.7

2173. Standing Civilian Courts (Amendment No.2) Order 1987
revoked: SI 1997/172 Art.93, Sch.5

2174. General Medical Council Health Committee (Procedure) Rules Order of Council 1987
see *Stefan v General Medical Council* [1999] 1 W.L.R. 1293 (PC), Lord Clyde
r.2, amended: SI 1996/1219 Sch. para.2, SI 1997/1529 Sch.r.33
r.5, amended: SI 1997/1529 Sch.r.33
r.8, see *R. v General Medical Council Ex p. Phillips* [1996] 7 Med. L.R. 31 (CA), Nourse, L.J.
r.28, substituted: SI 1996/1219 Sch. para.2
r.29, substituted: SI 1997/1529 Sch.r.33
r.31, amended: SI 1996/1219 Sch. para.2
r.33, amended: SI 1996/1219 Sch. para.2
r.33A, added: SI 1996/1219 Sch. para.2
r.33B, added: SI 1996/1219 Sch. para.2
r.36A, added: SI 1996/1219 Sch. para.2
Sch.2, applied: SI 1997/1529 Sch.Sch.1

2195. Coypus (Prohibition on Keeping) Order 1987
applied: SI 1997/2751

2197. Civil Jurisdiction (Offshore Activities) Order 1987
referred to: SI 1999/360 Reg.15, SI 1999/1128 Art.3
Art.1, referred to: SI 1999/160 Sch.2 para.3, Sch.2 para.4, Sch.5 para.3, Sch.5 para.4, Sch.6 para.3, Sch.6 para.4, Sch.9 para.3, Sch.9 para.4, Sch.10 para.3, Sch.10 para.4

2203. Adoption (Northern Ireland) Order 1987
applied: 1998 c.29 Sch.12 para.6, SI 1998/1071 (NI.6) Art.3
Art.16, amended: SI 1998/1504 (NI.9) Art.65, Sch.5 para.30
Art.16, applied: SI 1998/1071 (NI.6) Art.3
Art.50, applied: SI 1996/1812 Reg.13, SI 1998/211 Reg.8
Art.50, referred to: SI 1997/1675 Reg.13
Sch.4 para.1, revoked: 1998 c.47 s.100, Sch.15

2215. Police Pensions (Purchase of Increased Benefits) Regulations 1987
applied: SI 1999/1750 Art.2, Sch.1

NO.

1987—cont.

2226. Police (Discipline) (Scotland) Amendment Regulations 1987
revoked: SI 1996/1642 Reg.25, Sch.2

2233. Social Work (Residential Establishments-Child Care) (Scotland) Regulations 1987
revoked: SI 1997/691 Reg.1, Sch

2245. Local Roads Authorities Traffic Orders (Procedure) (Scotland) Regulations 1987
applied: SI 1999/614 Reg.21
revoked: SI 1999/614 Reg.22
Reg.7, see *Freight Transport Association Ltd v Lothian RC* Scotsman, March 6, 1996 (IH), Lord Kirkwood

1988

Church of England Pensions (Lump Sum Payments) Rules 1988
r.1A, added: 1997 m.1 s.10, Sch.1 para.28
r.2, revoked (in part): 1997 m.1 s.10, Sch.2 Part II
r.4, amended: 1997 m.1 s.10, Sch.1 para.29
r.5, amended: 1997 m.1 s.10, Sch.1 para.29
r.6, amended: 1997 m.1 s.10, Sch.1 para.30
r.7, amended: 1997 m.1 s.10, Sch.1 para.31
r.9, amended: 1997 m.1 s.10, Sch.1 para.32
r.10, amended: 1997 m.1 s.10, Sch.1 para.33
r.10, referred to: 1997 m.1 s.10
r.10, revoked: 1997 m.1 s.10, Sch.2 Part II
r.11, referred to: 1997 m.1 s.10
r.11, revoked: 1997 m.1 s.10, Sch.2 Part II

Logan and Johnston School Scheme 1988
amended: SI 1996/629 Sch

Oakbank School Trust Scheme 1988
amended: SI 1996/478 Sch

13. London Borough of Richmond upon Thames (Mortlake Road, Kew) (Vehicle Height Restriction) Order 1988
revoked: SI 1996/925 Art.3

16. London Borough of Hammersmith (Prescribed Routes) (No.5) Traffic Order 1988
revoked: SI 1996/1113 Art.4

34. Social Fund (Application for Review) Regulations 1988
Reg.2, amended: SI 1999/3178 Art.3, Sch.8

35. Social Fund (Recovery by Deduction from Benefits) Regulations 1988
Reg.3, amended: SI 1996/1944 Reg.9, SI 1999/2566 Reg.3
Reg.4, added: SI 1996/3195 Reg.16

38. Fishing Vessels (Life-Saving Appliances) Regulations 1988
applied: SI 1996/3243 Sch. Part I, SI 1999/2998 Reg.8
revoked (in part): SI 1999/3210 Reg.2
Reg.2, amended: SI 1998/927 Reg.3, SI 1999/2998 Reg.3, Sch.2, SI 1999/3210 Reg.2
Reg.5A, added: SI 1998/927 Reg.3
Reg.5B, added: SI 1998/927 Reg.3
Reg.5C, added: SI 1998/927 Reg.3
Reg.8, amended: SI 1998/927 Reg.3, SI 1999/3210 Reg.2

45. Disposal of Waste (Control of Beet Rhizomania Disease) Order 1988
revoked: SI 1998/2246 Art.2

88. Double Taxation Relief (Taxes on Income) (Foreign Loan Interests) Regulations 1988
revoked: SI 1999/3330 Reg.5

89. Prison (Amendment) Rules 1988
revoked: SI 1999/728 r.85 (with savings), Sch. (with savings)

NO.

1988—cont.

93. Department of Trade and Industry (Fees) Order 1988
Art.8, revoked: 1998 c.6 s.7, Sch.2 Part II
Sch.1 Part V, revoked: 1998 c.6 s.7, Sch.2 Part II

110. Act of Adjournal (Consolidation) 1988
revoked: SI 1996/513 Sch.2 r.3, Sch.3
Form 96, revoked: SI 1996/513 Sch.2 r.3, Sch.2

133. Commission for Local Authority Accounts in Scotland Regulations 1988
revoked: SI 1996/681 Reg.6

137. Personal Pension Schemes (Appropriate Schemes) Regulations 1988
Reg.1, applied: SI 1996/1435 Reg.2
Reg.1, revoked: SI 1997/470 Reg.20, Sch.3
Reg.12, amended: SI 1996/776 Reg.6
Reg.12, revoked: SI 1997/470 Reg.20, Sch.3
Reg.14, applied: SI 1996/1435 Reg.4, SI 1996/1537 Reg.3
Reg.14, revoked: SI 1997/470 Reg.20, Sch.3
Reg.14, substituted: SI 1996/1435 Reg.2
Reg.16, applied: SI 1997/470 Reg.19
Reg.16, revoked: SI 1997/470 Reg.20, Sch.3
Reg.17, applied: SI 1997/470 Reg.19
Reg.17, revoked: SI 1997/470 Reg.20, Sch.3
Reg.17A, revoked: SI 1997/470 Reg.20, Sch.3
Reg.17A, substituted: SI 1996/1435 Reg.2

142. Social Security (Payments on Account, Overpayments and Recovery) Regulations (Northern Ireland) 1988
Reg.1, amended: SI 1999/2573 Reg.3
Reg.2, amended: SI 1999/2573 Reg.4
Reg.3, amended: SI 1999/2573 Reg.5
Reg.4, amended: SI 1999/2573 Reg.6
Reg.5, amended: SI 1999/2573 Reg.7
Reg.8, revoked (in part): SI 1999/2573 Reg.8
Reg.11, amended: SI 1999/2573 Reg.9
Reg.12, amended: SI 1999/2573 Reg.10
Reg.13, amended: SI 1999/2573 Reg.11
Reg.14, amended: SI 1999/2573 Reg.12
Reg.15, revoked (in part): SI 1999/2573 Reg.13
Reg.17, amended: SI 1999/2573 Reg.14

166. London Traffic Control System (Transfer) Order 1988
Art.3, substituted: SI 1998/654 Art.2

186. Measuring Instruments (EEC Requirements) Regulations 1988
amended: SI 1996/319 Reg.2
applied: SI 1996/319 Reg.3
Reg.8, applied: SI 1998/1177 Reg.4, Sch.3 para.1
Reg.13, applied: SI 1996/319 Reg.3, SI 1998/1177 Reg.3, Sch.2 para.1
Sch.2, applied: SI 1998/1177 Reg.4
Sch.3, applied: SI 1998/1177 Reg.3

191. Merchant Shipping (Passenger Boarding Cards) Regulations 1988
revoked: SI 1999/1869 Reg.2

217. Pensions Increase (Review) Order 1988
applied: SI 1997/634 Art.3, SI 1998/503 Art.3, Art.4, SI 1999/522 Art.3

232. Stock Transfer (Gilt-Edged Securities) (Exempt Transfer) Regulations 1988
Reg.2, amended: SI 1999/1210 Reg.2

243. Carriage by Air (Parties to Convention) Order 1988
revoked: SI 1999/1313 Art.5

249. Sex Discrimination (Amendment) Order 1988
Art.3, revoked: SI 1998/3162 (NI.21) Art.105, Sch.5

NO.

260. **Police (Promotion) (Scotland) Amendment Regulations 1988**
revoked: SI 1996/221 Reg.10, Sch.2
294. **Residential Care Order (Secure Accommodation) (Scotland) Regulations 1988**
revoked: SI 1997/691 Reg.1, Sch
317. **Merchant Shipping (Closing of Openings in Enclosed Superstructures and in Bulkheads above the Bulkhead Deck) Regulations 1988**
applied: SI 1996/3243 Sch Part I
revoked: SI 1998/2514 Reg.1
361. **Construction Plant and Equipment (Harmonisation of Noise Emission Standards) Regulations 1988**
applied: SI 1998/2306 Reg.10, Sch.1
370. **International Carriage of Dangerous Goods by Road (Fees) Regulations 1988**
Reg.3, amended: SI 1997/158 Reg.2
Reg.4, amended: SI 1997/158 Reg.2
Reg.5, amended: SI 1997/158 Reg.2
Reg.6, amended: SI 1997/158 Reg.2
466. **Local Government (Superannuation and Compensation) (Amendment) Regulations 1988**
applied: SI 1996/1680 Reg.7, Sch.3 para.4
Reg.9, revoked: SI 1996/1680 Reg.49, Sch.5
Reg.10, revoked: SI 1996/1680 Reg.49, Sch.5
Reg.12, revoked: SI 1996/1680 Reg.49, Sch.5
Reg.13, revoked: SI 1996/1680 Reg.49, Sch.5
Reg.14, revoked: SI 1996/1680 Reg.49, Sch.5
Reg.15, revoked: SI 1996/1680 Reg.49, Sch.5
Reg.16, revoked: SI 1996/1680 Reg.49, Sch.5
Reg.17, revoked: SI 1996/1680 Reg.49, Sch.5
Reg.18, revoked: SI 1996/1680 Reg.49, Sch.5
Reg.19, revoked: SI 1996/1680 Reg.49, Sch.5
Reg.20, revoked: SI 1996/1680 Reg.49, Sch.5
Reg.21, revoked: SI 1996/1680 Reg.49, Sch.5
Reg.22, revoked: SI 1996/1680 Reg.49, Sch.5
474. **Personal and Occupational Pension Schemes (Tax Approval and Miscellaneous Provisions) Regulations 1988**
Reg.3, revoked: SI 1996/1847 Reg.21, Sch.3
Reg.4, revoked: SI 1996/1172 Sch.2
Reg.9, revoked: SI 1996/1537 Reg.18, Sch.
475. **Contracting Out (Miscellaneous Amendments) Regulations 1988**
Reg.2, revoked: SI 1996/1172 Sch.2
Reg.4, revoked: SI 1996/1462 Reg.14, Sch.3
476. **Occupational Pension Schemes (Miscellaneous Amendments) Regulations 1988**
Reg.3, revoked: SI 1996/1847 Reg.21, Sch.3
Reg.4, revoked: SI 1997/784 Reg.12, Sch.2
Reg.8, revoked: SI 1996/1655 Reg.12, Sch.4
489. **Advice and Assistance (Scotland) Amendment Regulations 1988**
revoked: SI 1996/2447 Reg.3, Sch.1
490. **Civil Legal Aid (Scotland) Amendment Regulations 1988**
revoked: SI 1996/2444 Reg.3, Sch.1
509. **County Court Fees (Amendment) Order 1988**
revoked: SI 1999/689 Art.8 (with savings), Sch.2 (with savings)
510. **Supreme Court Fees (Amendment) Order 1988**
revoked: SI 1999/687 Art.8 (with savings), Sch.2 (with savings)
523. **Occupational Pension Schemes (Transfer Values) Amendment Regulations 1988**
revoked: SI 1996/1847 Reg.21, Sch.3

NO.

536. **Welfare Food Regulations 1988**
applied: SI 1996/1434 Reg.24
revoked: SI 1996/1434 Reg.23, Sch.7
Reg.2, applied: SI 1996/1434 Reg.24
Reg.9, applied: SI 1996/207 Sch.7 para.48, SI 1996/2890 Sch.3 para.43, Sch.4 para.40
Reg.10, applied: SI 1996/2890 Sch.3 para.43, Sch.4 para.40
Reg.11, applied: SI 1996/207 Sch.7 para.48, SI 1996/2890 Sch.3 para.43, Sch.4 para.40
Reg.13, applied: SI 1996/207 Sch.7 para.48, SI 1996/2890 Sch.3 para.43, Sch.4 para.40
Reg.15A, applied: SI 1996/1434 Reg.24
538. **European Communities (Iron and Steel Employees Re-adaptation Benefits Scheme) (No.2) Regulations 1988**
applied: SI 1996/1623 Art.3
Sch.1, referred to: SI 1996/3182 Reg.4
Sch.1 Art.2, amended: SI 1996/3182 Reg.3
545. **Environmental Protection (Controls on Hexachloroethane) 1988**
Reg.5, amended: SI 1999/3244 Reg.6
546. **National Health Service (Travelling Expenses and Remission of Charges) (Scotland) Regulations 1988**
Reg.2, amended: SI 1996/429 Reg.2, SI 1996/2391 Reg.2, SI 1997/1012 Reg.2, SSI 1999/63 Reg.2
Reg.3, amended: SI 1998/2772 Reg.2
Reg.3, applied: SI 1996/207 Sch.7 para.47, Sch.8 para.36, SI 1996/2890 Sch.3 para.42, Sch.4 para.39
Reg.4, amended: SI 1996/429 Reg.3, SI 1996/2391 Reg.3, SI 1997/1012 Reg.3, SSI 1999/63 Reg.3
Reg.4, applied: SSI 1999/63 Reg.5
Reg.5, amended: SI 1996/429 Reg.4, SI 1998/2772 Reg.3
Reg.5, applied: SI 1996/207 Sch.7 para.47, Sch.8 para.36, SI 1996/2890 Sch.3 para.42, Sch.4 para.39
Reg.5B, added: SI 1996/429 Reg.5
Reg.6, applied: SI 1998/642 Reg.3, Reg.8
Reg.7, amended: SI 1996/429 Reg.6, SI 1996/2391 Reg.4, SI 1997/1012 Reg.4
Reg.8, amended: SI 1996/429 Reg.7
Reg.8, applied: SI 1996/207 Sch.7 para.47, Sch.8 para.36, SI 1996/2890 Sch.3 para.42, Sch.4 para.39
Reg.9, applied: SI 1996/207 Sch.8 para.37
Reg.10, applied: SI 1996/207 Sch.8 para.37
Reg.11, applied: SI 1996/207 Sch.8 para.37
Reg.13, applied: SI 1996/207 Sch.8 para.37
Sch.1, applied: SI 1998/642 Reg.3, Reg.8
Sch.1 Part I, amended: SI 1996/429 Reg.8, SI 1996/2391 Reg.5, SI 1997/1012 Reg.5, SI 1997/2455 Reg.2, SSI 1999/63 Reg.4
Sch.1 Part II, amended: SI 1996/429 Reg.9, SI 1997/1012 Reg.6, SI 1997/2455 Reg.3
Sch.1A, added: SI 1996/429 Reg.10, Sch
Sch.1A para.2, revoked: SI 1996/2391 Reg.6
Sch.1A para.8, added: SI 1996/2391 Reg.6
Sch.1A para.9, added: SI 1997/1012 Reg.7
551. **National Health Service (Travelling Expenses and Remission of Charges) Regulations 1988**
Reg.2, amended: SI 1996/410 Reg.2, SI 1996/2362 Reg.2, SI 1997/748 Reg.2, SI 1999/2507 Reg.2, SI 1999/2840 Reg.2
Reg.3, amended: SI 1998/2417 Reg.2
Reg.3, applied: SI 1996/207 Sch.7 para.47, Sch.8 para.36, SI 1996/2890 Sch.3 para.42, Sch.4 para.39

NO.

551. National Health Service (Travelling Expenses and Remission of Charges) Regulations 1988—*cont.*
Reg.4, amended: SI 1996/410 Reg.3, SI 1996/2362 Reg.3, SI 1997/748 Reg.3, SI 1999/2507 Reg.3
Reg.4, applied: SI 1999/2507 Reg.5, SI 1999/2840 Reg.3
Reg.5, amended: SI 1996/410 Reg.4, SI 1998/2417 Reg.3
Reg.5, applied: SI 1996/207 Sch.7 para.47, Sch.8 para.36, SI 1996/2890 Sch.3 para.42, Sch.4 para.39
Reg.5B, added: SI 1996/410 Reg.5
Reg.6, applied: SI 1997/818 Reg.3, Reg.8
Reg.7, amended: SI 1996/410 Reg.6, SI 1996/2362 Reg.4, SI 1997/748 Reg.4, SI 1999/767 Reg.4
Reg.8, amended: SI 1996/410 Reg.7
Reg.8, applied: SI 1996/207 Sch.7 para.47, Sch.8 para.36, SI 1996/2890 Sch.3 para.42, Sch.4 para.39
Sch.1, applied: SI 1997/818 Reg.3, Reg.8
Sch.1 Part I, amended: SI 1996/410 Reg.8, SI 1996/1346, SI 1997/748 Reg.5, SI 1997/2393 Reg.2, SI 1999/2507 Reg.4
Sch.1 Part II, amended: SI 1996/410 Reg.9, SI 1997/748 Reg.6, SI 1997/2393 Reg.3
Sch.1A, added: SI 1996/410 Reg.10
Sch.1A para.2, revoked: SI 1996/2362 Reg.5
Sch.1A para.8, added: SI 1996/2362 Reg.5
Sch.1A para.9, added: SI 1997/748 Reg.7

555. Welfare Food Amendment Regulations 1988
revoked: SI 1996/1434 Reg.23, Sch.7

566. Severn-Trent Water Authority (Regional Land Drainage Committee) Order 1988
revoked: SI 1996/1616 Art.3

571. Public Trustee (Fees) (Amendment) Order 1988
revoked: SI 1999/855 Art.32, Sch.

590. Social Security (Sweden) Order 1988
Sch., amended: SI 1996/1928 Art.2, Sch.1

591. Social Security (Reciprocal Agreements) Order 1988
Sch., amended: SI 1996/1927 Art.3, SI 1997/871 Art.3, SI 1997/1778 Art.3

613. Act of Sederunt (Rules for the Registration of Custody Orders of the Sheriff Court) 1988
revoked: SI 1997/291 r.1.4, Sch.2

625. Local Government Superannuation (Scotland) Amendment Regulations 1988
applied: SI 1998/364 Reg.4, Reg.6, Reg.19, Sch.2 para.2, Sch.2 para.5, Sch.4 para.8
referred to: SI 1998/364 Reg.3, Reg.10, Sch.2 para.4, Sch.2 para.6

630. Building Societies (Designation of Prescribed Regulatory Authorities) Order 1988
Art.5, amended: SI 1997/2302 Art.6

641. Merchant Shipping (Passenger Boarding Cards) (Application to non-UK Ships) Regulations 1988
revoked: SI 1999/1869 Reg.2

642. Merchant Shipping (Closing of Openings in Enclosed Superstructures and in Bulkheads above the Bulkhead Deck) (Application to Non-United Kingdom Ships) Regulations 1988
applied: SI 1996/3243 Sch Part I
revoked: SI 1998/2514 Reg.1

NO.

643. Department of Transport (Fees) Order 1988
applied: SI 1998/572, SI 1998/995
Sch.1 Table III, amended: SI 1996/1961 Art.2
Sch.1 Table VI, amended: SI 1998/459 Art.2, Sch.

645. Banking Act 1987 (Advertisements) Regulations 1988
Reg.2, revoked (in part): SI 1999/734 Reg.5

646. Banking Act 1987 (Exempt Transactions) Regulations 1988
revoked: SI 1997/817 Reg.16

662. Housing Benefit (Supply of Information) Regulations 1988
Reg.1, amended: SI 1996/1510 Reg.51
Reg.2, amended: SI 1996/194 Reg.7, SI 1996/1510 Reg.52
Reg.5, added: SI 1996/194 Reg.7
Reg.5, amended: SI 1999/2556 Reg.6

663. Income Support (General) Amendment Regulations 1988
Reg.6, revoked: SI 1996/206 Reg.28, Sch.3
Reg.7, revoked: SI 1996/206 Reg.28, Sch.3
Reg.11, revoked: SI 1996/206 Reg.28, Sch.3
Reg.28, revoked: SI 1996/206 Reg.28, Sch.3

664. Social Security (Payments on Account, Overpayments and Recovery) Regulations 1988
applied: SI 1999/991 Reg.27, Sch.2 para.20
Part VI, amended: SI 1999/2422 Art.3, Sch.8 para.4, SI 1999/2860 Art.3, Sch.4 para.5, SI 1999/3178 Art.3, Sch.9 para.5
Reg.1, amended: SI 1996/1345 Reg.23, SI 1999/1958 Art.4, Sch.10 para.1, SI 1999/2422 Art.3, Sch.8 para.1, SI 1999/2571 Reg.3, SI 1999/2860 Art.3, Sch.4 para.1, SI 1999/3178 Art.3, Sch.9 para.1
Reg.2, amended: SI 1996/30 Reg.10, SI 1999/1958 Art.4, Sch.10 para.2, SI 1999/2422 Art.3, Sch.8 para.2, SI 1999/2571 Reg.4, SI 1999/2860 Art.3, Sch.4 para.2, SI 1999/3178 Art.3, Sch.9 para.2
Reg.2, applied: SI 1996/193 Reg.5, SI 1996/2570 Reg.5
Reg.3, amended: SI 1999/2571 Reg.5
Reg.3, referred to: SI 1999/991 Reg.27, Sch.2 para.20
Reg.4, amended: SI 1999/2571 Reg.6
Reg.4, referred to: SI 1999/991 Reg.27, Sch.2 para.20
Reg.5, amended: SI 1996/1345 Reg.23, SI 1999/1958 Art.4, Sch.10 para.3, SI 1999/2422 Art.3, Sch.8 para.3, SI 1999/2571 Reg.7, SI 1999/2860 Art.3, Sch.4 para.3, SI 1999/3178 Art.3, Sch.9 para.3
Reg.5, referred to: SI 1999/991 Reg.27, Sch.2 para.20
Reg.7, amended: SI 1996/1345 Reg.23
Reg.8, amended: SI 1996/1345 Reg.23, SI 1999/1958 Art.4, Sch.10 para.4, SI 1999/2860 Art.3, Sch.4 para.4, SI 1999/3178 Art.3, Sch.9 para.4
Reg.8, revoked (in part): SI 1999/2571 Reg.8
Reg.11, amended: SI 1999/2571 Reg.9
Reg.11, referred to: SI 1999/991 Reg.27, Sch.2 para.20
Reg.12, amended: SI 1999/1958 Art.4, Sch.10 para.5, SI 1999/2422 Art.3, Sch.8 para.5, SI 1999/2571 Reg.10, SI 1999/2860 Art.3, Sch.4 para.6, SI 1999/3178 Art.3, Sch.9 para.6
Reg.13, amended: SI 1996/1345 Reg.23, SI 1999/2571 Reg.11

NO.

664. Social Security (Payments on Account, Overpayments and Recovery) Regulations 1988—*cont.*
Reg.13, referred to: SI 1999/991 Reg.27, Sch.2 para.20
Reg.14, amended: SI 1996/1345 Reg.23, SI 1996/2519 Reg.3, SI 1999/2571 Reg.12
Reg.14, referred to: SI 1999/991 Reg.27, Sch.2 para.20
Reg.15, amended: SI 1996/1345 Reg.23, SI 1996/2519 Reg.3
Reg.15, revoked (in part): SI 1999/2571 Reg.13
Reg.16, amended: SI 1996/672 Reg.4, SI 1996/1345 Reg.23, SI 1996/2519 Reg.3, SI 1996/3195 Reg.16
Reg.17, amended: SI 1996/1345 Reg.23, SI 1999/2571 Reg.14
Reg.19, referred to: SI 1999/991 Reg.27, Sch.2 para.20
Reg.23, amended: SI 1999/3178 Art.3, Sch.9 para.7
Reg.24, amended: SI 1999/3178 Art.3, Sch.9 para.8
Reg.24, referred to: SI 1999/991 Reg.27, Sch.2 para.20
Reg.24, revoked (in part): SI 1999/3178 Art.3, Sch.9 para.8
Reg.25, amended: SI 1999/3178 Art.3, Sch.9 para.9
Reg.26, amended: SI 1999/3178 Art.3, Sch.9 para.10

668. Pneumoconiosis etc. (Workers' Compensation) (Payment of Claims) Regulations 1988
Reg.5, amended: SI 1996/1979 Reg.2, SI 1997/1691 Reg.2, SI 1998/1840 Reg.2
Reg.6, amended: SI 1996/1979 Reg.2, SI 1997/1691 Reg.2, SI 1998/1840 Reg.2
Reg.8, amended: SI 1996/1979 Reg.2, SI 1997/1691 Reg.2, SI 1998/1840 Reg.2
Sch., substituted: SI 1996/1979 Reg.2, Sch., SI 1997/1691 Reg.2, Sch., SI 1998/1840 Reg.2, Sch.

672. Insurance Companies (Accounts and Statements) (Amendment) Regulations 1988
revoked: SI 1996/943 Reg.35, Sch.7

689. Social Security (Unemployment, Sickness and Invalidity Benefit) Amendment Regulations 1988
revoked: SI 1996/1345 Reg.27, Sch.

705. Medicines (Hormone Growth Promoters) (Prohibition of Use) Regulations 1988
revoked: SI 1997/1729 Reg.36, Sch.2

724. Financial Services Act 1986 (Occupational Pension Schemes) (No.2) Order 1988
Art.3, referred to: SI 1996/1715 Reg.3

725. Kinneil and Manuel Light Railway Order 1988
Art.10, amended: SI 1996/362 Art.5, Sch.4

747. Prison (Amendment) (No.2) Rules 1988
revoked: SI 1999/728 r.85 (with savings), Sch. (with savings)

777. Building Societies (Supplementary Capital) Order 1988
Sch. Part II, amended: SI 1996/1606 Art.3, SI 1998/1129 Art.2, Sch.1 para.8
Sch. Part III, amended: SI 1998/1129 Art.2, Sch.1 para.8

778. Ionising Radiation (Protection of Persons Undergoing Medical Examination or Treatment) Regulations 1988
Reg.11, applied: SI 1999/672 Art.2, Sch.1

NO.

785. European Communities (Designation) Order 1988
applied: SI 1999/1750 Art.3, Sch.2

793. Criminal Injuries (Compensation) (Northern Ireland) Order 1988
Art.19, revoked (in part): SI 1996/3160 (NI.24) Sch.7

796. Wages (Northern Ireland) Order 1988
revoked: SI 1996/1919 (NI.16) Art.257, Sch.3
Art.11, amended: 1996 c.14 Sch.10 para.21
Art.11, revoked: SI 1996/1919 (NI.16) Art.257, Sch.3
Sch.4 para.6, revoked: SI 1996/1919 (NI.16) Art.257, Sch.3, SI 1996/1921 (NI.18) Art.28, Sch.3

809. Excise Warehousing (etc.) Regulations 1988
Reg.16, referred to: SI 1999/1278 Reg.17

815. Transit of Animals (Amendment) Order 1988
revoked: SI 1997/1480 Art.22, Sch.12 Part II

816. Teachers' Superannuation (Miscellaneous Provisions) (No.2) Regulations 1988
Reg.10, applied: SI 1997/311 Reg.3

830. Personal Pension Schemes (Miscellaneous Amendments) Regulations 1988
Reg.3, revoked: SI 1997/470 Reg.20, Sch.3

841. Secure Accommodation (Scotland) Amendment Regulations 1988
revoked: SI 1997/691 Reg.1, Sch

849. Animals and Fresh Meat (Hormonal Substances) Regulations 1988
revoked: SI 1997/1729 Reg.36, Sch.2

854. National Health Service (General Dental Services) (Scotland) Amendment Regulations 1988
revoked: SI 1996/177 Reg.38, Sch.8

896. Pressure Vessels (Verification) Regulations 1988
Reg.10, amended: SI 1999/2001 Reg.29

907. Redundancy Payments (Local Government) (Modification) (Amendment) Order 1988
revoked: SI 1999/2277 Art.4, Sch.3

915. Control of Misleading Advertisements Regulations 1988
applied: 1998 c.41 s.74, Sch.13 para.45
referred to: SI 1996/275 (NI.2) Art.44

950. Insurance Brokers Registration Council (Conduct of Investment Business) Rules Approval Order 1988
revoked: SI 1996/1151 Art.3

957. Coast Protection (Notices) (Scotland) Regulations 1988
Reg.2, amended: SI 1996/141 Reg.2
Reg.2, revoked (in part): SI 1996/141 Reg.2
Reg.3, revoked (in part): SI 1996/141 Reg.2
Reg.5, amended: SI 1996/141 Reg.2
Sch.2, revoked: SI 1996/141 Reg.2

963. Town and Country Planning (Tree Preservation Order) (Amendment) Regulations 1988
revoked: SI 1999/1892 Reg.18 (with savings)

965. Motor Vehicles (Driving Licences) (Amendment) Regulations 1988
revoked: SI 1996/2824 Reg.2, Sch.1

966. Sheriff Court Fees Amendment Order 1988
revoked: SI 1997/687 Art.11, Sch.2

969. Court of Session etc. Fees Amendment (No.2) Order 1988
revoked: SI 1997/688 Art.6, Sch.2

970. Forestry (Exceptions from Restriction of Felling) (Amendment) Regulations 1988
revoked: SI 1998/603 Reg.4

NO.

1009. Medicines (Labelling of Medicinal Products for Incorporation in Animal Feeding Stuffs and of Medicated Animal Feeding Stuffs) Regulations 1988
revoked (in part): SI 1996/2194 Reg.6, Sch.3
Reg.2, amended: SI 1998/1048 Reg.3, Sch.2 para.1
Reg.3, amended: SI 1998/1048 Reg.3, Sch.2 para.1
Reg.4, revoked: SI 1998/1048 Reg.3, Sch.2 para.1
Reg.5, revoked: SI 1998/1048 Reg.3, Sch.2 para.1
Reg.6, substituted: SI 1998/1048 Reg.3, Sch.2 para.1
Reg.7, revoked: SI 1998/1048 Reg.3, Sch.2 para.1
Reg.8, substituted: SI 1998/1048 Reg.3, Sch.2 para.1
Reg.9, amended: SI 1998/1048 Reg.3, Sch.2 para.1
Reg.9, revoked (in part): SI 1998/1048 Reg.3, Sch.1
Reg.10, amended: SI 1998/1048 Reg.3, Sch.2 para.1
Reg.11, amended: SI 1998/1048 Reg.3, Sch.2 para.1
Reg.12, revoked: SI 1998/1048 Reg.3, Sch.2 para.1
Reg.13, amended: SI 1998/1048 Reg.3, Sch.2 para.1
Sch.1, revoked: SI 1998/1048 Reg.3, Sch.2 para.1
Sch.2, revoked: SI 1998/1048 Reg.3, Sch.2 para.1
Sch.3, revoked: SI 1998/1048 Reg.3, Sch.2 para.1
Sch.4, amended: SI 1998/1048 Reg.3, Sch.2 para.1
Sch.4 para.2, amended: SI 1998/1048 Reg.3, Sch.2 para.1
Sch.4 para.2, revoked (in part): SI 1998/1048 Reg.3, Sch.2 para.1
Sch.4 para.3, amended: SI 1998/1048 Reg.3, Sch.2 para.1
Sch.4 para.4, amended: SI 1998/1048 Reg.3, Sch.2 para.1
Sch.4 para.5, revoked: SI 1998/1048 Reg.3, Sch.2 para.1
Sch.4 para.6, amended: SI 1998/1048 Reg.3, Sch.2 para.1
Sch.4 para.7, amended (in part): SI 1998/1048 Reg.3, Sch.2 para.1
Sch.4 para.7, revoked (in part): SI 1998/1048 Reg.3, Sch.2 para.1
Sch.4 para.8, amended: SI 1998/1048 Reg.3, Sch.2 para.1
Sch.4 para.9, amended: SI 1998/1048 Reg.3, Sch.2 para.1

1012. Personal Pension Schemes (Minimum Contributions under the Social Security Act 1986) Regulations 1988
Reg.3, revoked: 1999 c.2 s.26, Sch.10 Part II
Reg.4, revoked: 1999 c.2 s.26, Sch.10 Part II
Reg.5, revoked: 1999 c.2 s.26, Sch.10 Part II
Reg.7, amended: SI 1999/671 Art.24, Sch.9 Part II
Reg.7, revoked (in part): SI 1999/671 Art.24, Sch.9 Part II

1014. Personal Pension Schemes (Transfer Payments) Regulations 1988
Reg.3, amended: SI 1997/480 Reg.2

NO.

1016. Personal and Occupational Pension Schemes (Transfer to Self-employed Pension Arrangements) Regulations 1988
Reg.2, revoked: SI 1996/1847 Reg.21, Sch.3
Reg.4, revoked (in part): SI 1997/784 Reg.12, Sch.2

1025. Amusements with Prizes (Variation of Monetary Limits) Order 1988
revoked: SI 1999/1259 Art.3, Sch.

1031. Motor Cycles (Eye Protectors) (Amendment) Regulations 1988
revoked: SI 1999/535 Reg.3, Sch.

1053. Amusements with Prizes (Variation of Monetary Limits) (Scotland) Order 1988
revoked: SI 1999/1259 Art.3, Sch.

1057. Electricity Supply Regulations 1988
Reg.3, amended: SI 1998/2971 Reg.2
Sch.4 Part IV, amended: SI 1996/252 Art.2, Sch

1062. Motor Vehicles (Driving Licences) (Amendment) (No.2) Regulations 1988
revoked: SI 1996/2824 Reg.2, Sch.1

1080. Offshore Installations (Safety Zones) Order 1988
revoked: SI 1997/735 Art.3, Sch.2

1081. Offshore Installations (Safety Zones) (No.2) Order 1988
revoked: SI 1997/735 Art.3, Sch.2

1084. Environment Protection (Overseas Territories) Order 1988
Sch.1, referred to: SI 1999/669 Art.3
Sch.2, amended: SI 1997/1748 Art.2, SI 1999/669 Art.2

1087. Employment and Training (Amendment) (Northern Ireland) Order 1988
Art.4, referred to: SI 1999/3147 (NI.11) Art.57

1091. Social Work (Residential Establishments-Child Care) (Scotland) Regulations 1988
revoked: SI 1997/691 Reg.1, Sch

1092. Residential Care Order (Secure Accommodation) (Scotland) Amendment Regulations 1988
revoked: SI 1997/691 Reg.1, Sch

1126. Criminal Legal Aid (Scotland) Amendment Regulations 1988
revoked: SI 1996/2555 Reg.3, Sch.

1131. Advice and Assistance (Scotland) Amendment (No.2) Regulations 1988
revoked: SI 1996/2447 Reg.3, Sch.1

1144. Central Manchester Development Corporation (Area and Constitution) Order 1988
revoked: SI 1996/851 Art.2 (rem.)
Art.2, revoked: SI 1996/851 Art.2
Art.3, revoked: SI 1996/851 Art.2

1146. Sheffield Development Corporation (Area and Constitution) Order 1988
revoked: SI 1997/292 Art.2
Art.2, revoked: SI 1997/292 Art.2
Art.3, revoked: SI 1997/292 Art.2

1147. Wolverhampton Urban Development Area Order 1988
revoked: SI 1998/769 Art.2

1153. Building Societies (Transfer of Business) Regulations 1988
revoked: SI 1998/212 Reg.10
Reg.9, revoked: 1997 c.32 Sch.9, SI 1998/212 Reg.10
Reg.10, revoked: 1997 c.32 Sch.9, SI 1998/212 Reg.10
Sch. Part I, revoked (in part): 1997 c.32 Sch.9, SI 1998/212 Reg.10

NO.

1153. Building Societies (Transfer of Business) Regulations 1988—*cont.*
Sch. Part III, revoked (in part): 1997 c.32 Sch.9, SI 1998/212 Reg.10

1171. Civil Legal Aid (Scotland) Amendment (No.2) Regulations 1988
revoked: SI 1996/2444 Reg.3, Sch.1

1196. Building Societies (Designation of Qualifying Bodies) Order 1988
Sch. Item 14, applied: SI 1997/470 Reg.3

1199. Town and Country Planning (Assessment of Environmental Effects) Regulations 1988
see *R. v North Yorkshire CC Ex p. Brown* [1997] Env. L.R. 391 (QBD), Hidden, J.; see *R. v North Yorkshire CC Ex p. Brown* [1999] 2 W.L.R. 452 (HL), Lord Hoffmann; see *R. v Secretary of State for the Environment, Transport and the Regions Ex p. Marson* [1998] Env. L.R. 761 (CA), Pill, L.J.
applied: SI 1999/672 Art.2, Sch.1
revoked: SI 1999/293 Reg.34, Sch.5
Reg.2, amended: SI 1996/972 Reg.21
Reg.2, revoked: SI 1999/293 Reg.34, Sch.5
Reg.3, revoked: SI 1999/293 Reg.34, Sch.5
Reg.4, see *Berkeley v Secretary of State for the Environment, Transport and the Regions (No.1)* [1998] Env. L.R. 741 (CA), Pill, L.J.
Reg.4, revoked: SI 1999/293 Reg.34, Sch.5
Reg.5, revoked: SI 1999/293 Reg.34, Sch.5
Reg.6, revoked: SI 1999/293 Reg.34, Sch.5
Reg.8, revoked: SI 1999/293 Reg.34, Sch.5
Reg.9, see *R. v St Edmundsbury BC Ex p. Walton* [1999] Env. L.R. 879 (QBD), Hooper, J
Reg.9, revoked: SI 1999/293 Reg.34, Sch.5
Reg.14, revoked: SI 1999/293 Reg.34, Sch.5
Reg.15, revoked: SI 1999/293 Reg.34, Sch.5
Reg.19, revoked: SI 1999/293 Reg.34, Sch.5
Reg.21, revoked: SI 1999/293 Reg.34, Sch.5
Sch.1, applied: SI 1999/107 Reg.3
Sch.1, revoked: SI 1999/293 Reg.34, Sch.5
Sch.2, applied: SI 1999/107 Reg.3
Sch.2, revoked: SI 1999/293 Reg.34, Sch.5
Sch.2 para.3, revoked: SI 1999/293 Reg.34, Sch.5
Sch.2 para.10, revoked: SI 1999/293 Reg.34, Sch.5
Sch.3 para.2, applied: SI 1999/107 Reg.3
Sch.3 para.2, revoked: SI 1999/293 Reg.34, Sch.5
Sch.3 para.3, revoked: SI 1999/293 Reg.34, Sch.5

1207. Environmental Assessment (Afforestation) Regulations 1988
see *Swan v Secretary of State for Scotland* [1998] Env. L.R. 251 (OH), Lord Nimmo Smith
applied: SI 1998/1731 Reg.20
revoked: SI 1998/1731 Reg.20
Reg.4, applied: SI 1998/1731 Reg.20
Reg.4, revoked: SI 1998/1731 Reg.20
Reg.5, applied: SI 1998/1731 Reg.20
Reg.5, revoked: SI 1998/1731 Reg.20
Reg.6, applied: SI 1998/1731 Reg.20
Reg.6, revoked: SI 1998/1731 Reg.20

1213. Petroleum (Production) (Seaward Areas) Regulations 1988
Reg.2, amended: SI 1996/2946 Reg.4
Reg.7, amended: SI 1996/2946 Reg.5
Reg.9, amended: SI 1996/2946 Reg.6
Sch.3 Part VI, amended: SI 1996/2946 Reg.7
Sch.3 note (A), amended: SI 1996/2946 Reg.7
Sch.3 para.5, substituted: SI 1996/2946 Reg.7
Sch.3 para.7, amended: SI 1996/2946 Reg.7

NO.

1213. Petroleum (Production) (Seaward Areas) Regulations 1988—*cont.*
Sch.3 para.9, amended: SI 1996/2946 Reg.7
Sch.3 para.11, amended: SI 1996/2946 Reg.7
Sch.4, referred to: 1998 c.17 Sch.1 para.18, Sch.1 para.19, Sch.1 para.20, Sch.1 para.21, SI 1999/160 Sch.9 para.1, Sch.10 para.1
Sch.4 cl.1, amended: SI 1996/2946 Reg.8
Sch.4 cl.2, amended: SI 1996/2946 Reg.8
Sch.4 cl.3, substituted: SI 1996/2946 Reg.8
Sch.4 cl.3A, added: SI 1996/2946 Reg.8
Sch.4 cl.4, substituted: SI 1996/2946 Reg.8
Sch.4 cl.5, substituted: SI 1996/2946 Reg.8
Sch.4 cl.6, substituted: SI 1996/2946 Reg.8
Sch.4 cl.8, substituted: SI 1996/2946 Reg.8
Sch.4 cl.12, substituted: SI 1996/2946 Reg.8
Sch.4 cl.19, referred to: SI 1996/913 Reg.18
Sch.4 cl.38, substituted: SI 1996/2946 Reg.8
Sch.5, referred to: 1998 c.17 Sch.1 para.22, Sch.1 para.23, Sch.1 para.24, SI 1999/160 Sch.10 para.1

1215. Wireless Telegraphy (Citizens' Band and Amateur Apparatus) (Various Provisions) Order 1988
revoked: SI 1998/2531 Art.2
Art.2, revoked: SI 1998/2531 Art.2
Art.3, revoked: SI 1998/2531 Art.2
Sch.2, revoked: SI 1998/2531 Art.2

1217. Land Drainage Improvement Works (Assessment of Environmental Effects) Regulations 1988
applied: SI 1999/672 Art.2, Sch.1
referred to: SI 1999/1783 Reg.15
revoked: SI 1999/1783 Reg.15 (with savings)
Reg.2, revoked: SI 1999/1783 Reg.15 (with savings)
Reg.3, applied: SI 1999/1783 Reg.15
Reg.3, revoked: SI 1999/1783 Reg.15 (with savings)
Reg.4, see *Berkeley v Secretary of State for the Environment (No.2)* Times, April 7, 1998 (CA), Nourse, L.J.
Reg.4, revoked: SI 1999/1783 Reg.15 (with savings)
Reg.5, revoked: SI 1999/1783 Reg.15 (with savings)
Reg.8, revoked: SI 1999/1783 Reg.15 (with savings)

1218. Environmental Assessment (Salmon Farming in Marine Waters) Regulations 1988
referred to: SI 1999/3445 Reg.3
revoked: SI 1999/367 Reg.16 (with savings)

1221. Environmental Assessment (Scotland) Regulations 1988
referred to: SI 1999/1672 Reg.5
Part II, applied: SSI 1999/1 Reg.64, Sch.7
Part II, revoked: SSI 1999/1 Reg.64, Sch.7
Part III, applied: SI 1999/1750 Art.2, Sch.1
Part IV, revoked: SI 1997/1870 Reg.34
Part V, applied: SSI 1999/1 Reg.64, Sch.7
Part V, revoked: SSI 1999/1 Reg.64, Sch.7
Part VI, applied: SSI 1999/1 Reg.64, Sch.7
Part VI, revoked: SSI 1999/1 Reg.64, Sch.7
Reg.2, amended: SI 1997/1870 Reg.3
Reg.2, referred to: SI 1999/1672 Reg.5
Reg.3, applied: SSI 1999/1 Reg.64, Sch.7
Reg.3, revoked: SSI 1999/1 Reg.64, Sch.7
Reg.4, amended: SI 1997/1870 Reg.4, Reg.5
Reg.4, applied: SSI 1999/1 Reg.64, Sch.7
Reg.4, revoked: SSI 1999/1 Reg.64, Sch.7
Reg.4, substituted: SI 1996/972 Reg.21
Reg.5, applied: SSI 1999/1 Reg.64, Sch.7

NO.

1988—cont.

1221. Environmental Assessment (Scotland) Regulations 1988—*cont.*
Reg.5, revoked: SSI 1999/1 Reg.64, Sch.7
Reg.6, amended: SI 1997/1870 Reg.6
Reg.6, applied: SSI 1999/1 Reg.64, Sch.7
Reg.6, revoked: SSI 1999/1 Reg.64, Sch.7
Reg.7, amended: SI 1997/1870 Reg.7, Reg.8, Reg.9, Reg.10, Reg.11, Reg.12, Reg.13, Reg.14
Reg.7, applied: SSI 1999/1 Reg.64, Sch.7
Reg.7, revoked: SSI 1999/1 Reg.64, Sch.7
Reg.8, amended: SI 1997/1870 Reg.15
Reg.8, applied: SSI 1999/1 Reg.64, Sch.7
Reg.8, revoked: SSI 1999/1 Reg.64, Sch.7
Reg.9, amended: SI 1997/1870 Reg.16, Reg.17, Reg.18, Reg.19
Reg.9, applied: SSI 1999/1 Reg.64, Sch.7
Reg.9, referred to: SI 1999/1672 Reg.5
Reg.9, revoked: SSI 1999/1 Reg.64, Sch.7
Reg.10, applied: SSI 1999/1 Reg.64, Sch.7
Reg.10, revoked: SSI 1999/1 Reg.64, Sch.7
Reg.10A, added: SI 1997/1870 Reg.20
Reg.10B, added: SI 1997/1870 Reg.20
Reg.11, amended: SI 1997/1870 Reg.21
Reg.11, applied: SSI 1999/1 Reg.64, Sch.7
Reg.11, revoked: SSI 1999/1 Reg.64, Sch.7
Reg.11A, added: SI 1997/1870 Reg.22
Reg.12, amended: SI 1997/1870 Reg.23
Reg.12, applied: SSI 1999/1 Reg.64, Sch.7
Reg.12, revoked: SSI 1999/1 Reg.64, Sch.7
Reg.13, applied: SSI 1999/1 Reg.64, Sch.7
Reg.13, revoked: SSI 1999/1 Reg.64, Sch.7
Reg.14, applied: SSI 1999/1 Reg.64, Sch.7
Reg.14, revoked: SSI 1999/1 Reg.64, Sch.7
Reg.15, applied: SSI 1999/1 Reg.64, Sch.7
Reg.15, revoked: SSI 1999/1 Reg.64, Sch.7
Reg.15A, added: SI 1997/1870 Reg.24
Reg.16, amended: SI 1997/1870 Reg.25
Reg.16, applied: SSI 1999/1 Reg.64, Sch.7
Reg.16, revoked: SSI 1999/1 Reg.64, Sch.7
Reg.17, amended: SI 1997/1870 Reg.26
Reg.17, applied: SSI 1999/1 Reg.64, Sch.7
Reg.17, revoked: SSI 1999/1 Reg.64, Sch.7
Reg.18, applied: SSI 1999/1 Reg.64, Sch.7
Reg.18, revoked: SSI 1999/1 Reg.64, Sch.7
Reg.19, applied: SSI 1999/1 Reg.64, Sch.7
Reg.19, revoked: SSI 1999/1 Reg.64, Sch.7
Reg.19A, added: SI 1997/1870 Reg.27
Reg.20, applied: SSI 1999/1 Reg.64, Sch.7
Reg.20, revoked: SSI 1999/1 Reg.64, Sch.7
Reg.21, applied: SSI 1999/1 Reg.64, Sch.7
Reg.21, revoked: SSI 1999/1 Reg.64, Sch.7
Reg.22, amended: SI 1997/1870 Reg.28, Reg.29
Reg.22, applied: SSI 1999/1 Reg.64, Sch.7
Reg.22, revoked: SSI 1999/1 Reg.64, Sch.7
Reg.23, amended: SI 1997/1870 Reg.30
Reg.23, applied: SSI 1999/1 Reg.64, Sch.7
Reg.23, revoked: SSI 1999/1 Reg.64, Sch.7
Reg.24, amended: SI 1997/1870 Reg.31
Reg.24, applied: SSI 1999/1 Reg.64, Sch.7
Reg.24, revoked: SSI 1999/1 Reg.64, Sch.7
Reg.25, amended: SI 1997/1870 Reg.32, Reg.33
Reg.25, applied: SSI 1999/1 Reg.64, Sch.7
Reg.25, revoked: SSI 1999/1 Reg.64, Sch.7
Reg.26, applied: SSI 1999/1 Reg.64, Sch.7
Reg.26, revoked: SSI 1999/1 Reg.64, Sch.7
Reg.27, applied: SSI 1999/1 Reg.64, Sch.7
Reg.27, revoked: SSI 1999/1 Reg.64, Sch.7
Reg.28, applied: SSI 1999/1 Reg.64, Sch.7
Reg.28, revoked: SSI 1999/1 Reg.64, Sch.7

NO.

1988—cont.

1221. Environmental Assessment (Scotland) Regulations 1988—*cont.*
Reg.29, applied: SSI 1999/1 Reg.64, Sch.7
Reg.29, revoked: SSI 1999/1 Reg.64, Sch.7
Reg.30, applied: SSI 1999/1 Reg.64, Sch.7
Reg.30, revoked: SSI 1999/1 Reg.64, Sch.7
Reg.31, applied: SSI 1999/1 Reg.64, Sch.7
Reg.31, revoked: SSI 1999/1 Reg.64, Sch.7
Reg.32, applied: SSI 1999/1 Reg.64, Sch.7
Reg.32, revoked: SSI 1999/1 Reg.64, Sch.7
Reg.46, revoked: SI 1997/1870 Reg.34
Reg.47, revoked: SI 1997/1870 Reg.34
Reg.48, revoked: SI 1997/1870 Reg.34
Reg.49, revoked: SI 1997/1870 Reg.34
Reg.50, revoked: SI 1997/1870 Reg.34
Reg.51, revoked: SI 1997/1870 Reg.34
Reg.52, revoked: SI 1997/1870 Reg.34
Reg.53, revoked: SI 1997/1870 Reg.34
Reg.54, revoked: SI 1997/1870 Reg.34
Reg.55, revoked: SI 1997/1870 Reg.34
Reg.56, revoked: SI 1997/1870 Reg.34
Reg.57, revoked: SI 1997/1870 Reg.34
Reg.58, revoked: SI 1997/1870 Reg.34
Reg.59, revoked: SI 1997/1870 Reg.34
Reg.60, revoked: SI 1997/1870 Reg.34
Reg.61, revoked: SI 1997/1870 Reg.34
Reg.62, revoked: SI 1997/1870 Reg.34
Reg.63, applied: SSI 1999/1 Reg.64, Sch.7
Reg.63, revoked: SSI 1999/1 Reg.64, Sch.7
Reg.64, applied: SSI 1999/1 Reg.64, Sch.7
Reg.64, revoked: SSI 1999/1 Reg.64, Sch.7
Reg.65, applied: SSI 1999/1 Reg.64, Sch.7
Reg.65, revoked: SSI 1999/1 Reg.64, Sch.7
Reg.66, applied: SSI 1999/1 Reg.64, Sch.7
Reg.66, revoked: SSI 1999/1 Reg.64, Sch.7
Reg.67, applied: SSI 1999/1 Reg.64, Sch.7
Reg.67, revoked: SSI 1999/1 Reg.64, Sch.7
Reg.68, applied: SSI 1999/1 Reg.64, Sch.7
Reg.68, revoked: SSI 1999/1 Reg.64, Sch.7
Reg.69, applied: SSI 1999/1 Reg.64, Sch.7
Reg.69, revoked: SSI 1999/1 Reg.64, Sch.7
Reg.70, applied: SSI 1999/1 Reg.64, Sch.7
Reg.70, revoked: SSI 1999/1 Reg.64, Sch.7
Reg.71, applied: SSI 1999/1 Reg.64, Sch.7
Reg.71, revoked: SSI 1999/1 Reg.64, Sch.7
Reg.72, applied: SSI 1999/1 Reg.64, Sch.7
Reg.72, revoked: SSI 1999/1 Reg.64, Sch.7
Reg.73, applied: SSI 1999/1 Reg.64, Sch.7
Reg.73, revoked: SSI 1999/1 Reg.64, Sch.7
Reg.74, applied: SSI 1999/1 Reg.64, Sch.7
Reg.74, revoked: SSI 1999/1 Reg.64, Sch.7
Sch.4, substituted: SI 1997/1870 Reg.35

1228. Income Support (General) Amendment No.3 Regulations 1988
Reg.2, revoked (in part): SI 1996/206 Reg.28, Sch.3
Reg.4, revoked: SI 1996/206 Reg.28, Sch.3
Reg.7, revoked: SI 1996/206 Reg.28, Sch.3
Reg.8, revoked: SI 1996/206 Reg.28, Sch.3
Sch., revoked: SI 1996/206 Reg.28, Sch.3

1241. Highways (Assessment of Environmental Effects) Regulations 1988
see *Secretary of State for Transport v Haughian* (1997) 73 P. & C.R. 85 (CA), Hutchison, L.J.

1251. Gaming (Records of Cheques) Regulations 1988
revoked: SI 1997/1072 Reg.8

1275. Merchant Shipping (Weighing of Goods Vehicles and other Cargo) Regulations 1988
applied: SI 1998/2514 Reg.43

NO.

1291. Farm Woodland Scheme 1988
para.3, revoked (in part): SI 1997/828 para.2
para.8, amended: SI 1997/828 para.2
para.8, revoked (in part): SI 1997/828 para.2
Sch.1, substituted: SI 1997/828 para.2, Sch.1

1298. EUMETSAT (Immunities and Privileges) Order 1988
Art.12A, added: SI 1999/2034 Art.2, Sch.

1299. EUTELSAT (Immunities and Privileges) Order 1988
Art.12A, added: SI 1999/2034 Art.2, Sch.

1308. Black Country Development Corporation (Vesting of Land) (Borough of Sandwell) Order 1988
revoked: SI 1998/769 Art.3, Sch.

1309. Black Country Development Corporation (Vesting of Land) (Borough of Walsall) Order 1988
revoked: SI 1998/769 Art.3, Sch.

1310. Black Country Development Corporation (Vesting of Land) (British Railways Board) Order 1988
revoked: SI 1998/769 Art.3, Sch.

1311. Black Country Development Corporation (Vesting of Land) (Central Electricity Generating Board) Order 1988
revoked: SI 1998/769 Art.3, Sch.

1312. Black Country Development Corporation (Vesting of Land) (General) Order 1988
revoked: SI 1998/769 Art.3, Sch.

1313. Tyne and Wear Development Corporation (Vesting of Land) (Port of Tyne Authority) Order 1988
revoked: SI 1998/769 Art.3, Sch.

1315. Tyne and Wear Development Corporation (Vesting of Land) (British Coal Corporation) Order 1988
revoked: SI 1998/769 Art.3, Sch.

1316. Tyne and Wear Development Corporation (Vesting of Land) (British Shipbuilders and British Steel Corporation) Order 1988
revoked: SI 1998/769 Art.3, Sch.

1317. Black Country Development Corporation (Vesting of Land) (British Steel Corporation) Order 1988
revoked: SI 1998/769 Art.3, Sch.

1318. Tyne and Wear Development Corporation (Vesting of Land) (City of Newcastle upon Tyne) Order 1988
revoked: SI 1998/769 Art.3, Sch.

1319. Tyne and Wear Development Corporation (Vesting of Land) (Various Local Authorities) Order 1988
revoked: SI 1998/769 Art.3, Sch.

1320. Tyne and Wear Development Corporation (Vesting of Land) (Borough of Sunderland) Order 1988
revoked: SI 1998/769 Art.3, Sch.

1321. Tyne and Wear Development Corporation (Vesting of Land) (Tyne and Wear Passenger Transport Executive) Order 1988
revoked: SI 1998/769 Art.3, Sch.

1328. Matrimonial Causes (Costs) Rules 1988
r.4, see *Pelling v Pelling* [1998] 1 F.L.R. 636 (CA), Mummery, L.J.
r.16, see *Pelling v Pelling* [1998] 1 F.L.R. 636 (CA), Mummery, L.J.

1336. Harbour Works (Assessment of Environmental Effects) Regulation 1988
revoked (in part): SI 1999/3445 Reg.1

NO.

1347. Income Tax (Interest Relief) (Housing Associations) Regulations 1988
Reg.4, amended: SI 1996/2616 Reg.3

1352. Set-Aside Regulations 1988
applied: SI 1996/1243 Sch.5 para.11

1359. Companies (Forms) (Amendment) Regulations 1988
Sch. Form 88(2), revoked: SI 1999/2356 Reg.3 (with saving)

1372. Local Government Act 1988 (Defined Activities) (Exemptions) (England) Order 1988
Art.3, amended: SI 1996/770 Art.2, SI 1997/2746 Art.2
Art.3, revoked (in part): SI 1997/176 Art.4

1373. Local Government Act 1988 (Defined Activities) (Specified Periods) (England) Regulations 1988
revoked: SI 1997/2747 Reg.2, Sch.

1386. A406 London North Circular Trunk Road (East London River Crossing (A13 to A2) Supplementary Trunk Road and Slip Roads) Order 1988
revoked: SI 1997/842 Art.2

1387. A406 London North Circular Trunk Road (East London River Crossing (A13 to A2) Trunk Road and Slip Roads) Order 1988
revoked: SI 1997/842 Art.2

1396. Merchant Shipping (Health and Safety: General Duties) (Amendment) Regulations 1988
revoked: SI 1997/2962 Reg.1

1399. Black Country Development Corporation (Planning Functions) (Wolverhampton) Order 1988
revoked: SI 1998/84 Art.2, Sch.

1400. Town and Country Planning (Wolverhampton Urban Development Area) Special Development Order 1988
revoked: SI 1998/84 Art.2, Sch.

1414. Local Government Act 1988 (Defined Activities) (Specified Periods) (Scotland) Regulations 1988
amended: SI 1996/917 Reg.4

1415. Local Government Act 1988 (Defined Activities) (Exemptions) (Scotland) Order 1988
revoked: SI 1997/198 Art.11

1416. Gaming (Records of Cheques) (Scotland) Regulations 1988
revoked: SI 1997/1072 Reg.8

1421. Prison (Amendment) (No.3) Rules 1988
revoked: SI 1999/728 r.85 (with savings), Sch. (with savings)

1422. Young Offender Institution Rules 1988
applied: SI 1998/1545 r.2, SI 1999/962 r.3
r.2, amended: SI 1996/1662 r.2, Sch. para.1
r.6, amended: SI 1996/1662 r.2, Sch. para.2, SI 1999/962 r.3, Sch. para.1
r.10, amended: SI 1999/962 r.3, Sch. para.2
r.11, amended: SI 1999/962 r.3, Sch. para.3
r.17, amended: SI 1998/1545 r.2, Sch. r.1
r.18, amended: SI 1998/1545 r.2, Sch. r.2
r.21, amended: SI 1998/1545 r.2, Sch. r.3, SI 1999/962 r.3, Sch. para.4
r.24, amended: SI 1998/1545 r.2, Sch. r.4
r.25, amended: SI 1998/1545 r.2, Sch. r.5
r.25, revoked (in part): SI 1998/1545 r.2, Sch. r.5
r.34, amended: SI 1996/1662 r.2, Sch. para.3, SI 1998/1545 r.2, Sch. r.6
r.35, amended: SI 1999/962 r.3, Sch. para.5
r.38, amended: SI 1996/1662 r.2, Sch. para.4
r.41, amended: SI 1996/1662 r.2, Sch. para.5
r.43, amended: SI 1996/1662 r.2, Sch. para.6, SI 1999/962 r.3, Sch. para.6

NO.

1422. Young Offender Institution Rules 1988—*cont.*
r.46, amended: SI 1998/1545 r.2, Sch. r.7
r.48, amended: SI 1999/962 r.3, Sch. para.7
r.49, amended: SI 1998/1545 r.2, Sch. r.8, SI 1999/962 r.3, Sch. para.8
r.50, amended: SI 1996/1662 r.2, Sch. para.7, SI 1999/962 r.3, Sch. para.9
r.50, referred to: SI 1999/962 r.4
r.53, amended: SI 1999/962 r.3, Sch. para.10
r.56, amended: SI 1998/1545 r.2, Sch. r.9
r.60, amended: SI 1999/962 r.3, Sch. para.11
r.60, revoked (in part): SI 1999/962 r.3, Sch. para.11
r.63, amended: SI 1999/962 r.3, Sch. para.12
r.67, revoked: SI 1999/962 r.3, Sch. para.13
r.70, amended: SI 1999/962 r.3, Sch. para.14
r.71A, added: SI 1999/962 r.3, Sch. para.15
r.72, substituted: SI 1999/962 r.3, Sch. para.16
r.73, amended: SI 1996/1662 r.2, Sch. para.8, SI 1999/962 r.3, Sch. para.17
r.73, applied: SI 1996/1662 r.3
r.78, substituted: SI 1996/1662 r.2, Sch. para.9
r.79A, added: SI 1997/789 r.2
r.79B, added: SI 1997/789 r.2
r.79C, added: SI 1997/789 r.2

1436. Occupational Pension Schemes (Transitional Provisions) Regulations 1988
Reg.2, amended: SI 1996/3115 Reg.3
Reg.4ZA, added: SI 1996/3115 Reg.4
Reg.4ZA, amended: SI 1996/3234 Reg.2
Reg.12, amended: SI 1996/3115 Reg.5

1445. Income Support (General) Amendment No.4 Regulations 1988
Reg.18, revoked: SI 1996/206 Reg.28, Sch.3

1462. Control of Industrial Major Accident Hazards (Amendment) Regulations 1988
revoked: SI 1999/743 Reg.24

1469. Local Government Act 1988 (Defined Activities) (Exemptions) (Wales) Order 1988
Art.3, amended: SI 1996/770 Art.2, SI 1997/2746 Art.3
Art.3, revoked (in part): SI 1997/934 Art.6, Sch.2

1470. Local Government Act 1988 (Defined Activities) (Specified Periods) (Wales) Regulations 1988
amended: SI 1996/265 Reg.4
revoked: SI 1997/2747 Reg.2, Sch.

1478. Goods Vehicles (Plating and Testing) Regulations 1988
Part III, amended: SI 1997/263 Reg.8
Part VA, added: SI 1997/263 Reg.12, Sch.
Reg.3, amended: SI 1997/82 Reg.3, SI 1997/263 Reg.3
Reg.8, amended: SI 1997/263 Reg.4, Reg.13
Reg.9, substituted: SI 1997/263 Reg.5
Reg.10, substituted: SI 1997/263 Reg.6
Reg.11, substituted: SI 1997/263 Reg.7
Reg.12, amended: SI 1997/82 Reg.4, SI 1998/1671 Reg.3
Reg.14, amended: SI 1997/82 Reg.8
Reg.14, revoked (in part): SI 1997/82 Reg.8
Reg.16, amended: SI 1997/82 Reg.5, SI 1998/1671 Reg.4
Reg.17, revoked: SI 1997/263 Reg.9
Reg.18, revoked: SI 1997/263 Reg.9
Reg.19, revoked: SI 1997/263 Reg.9
Reg.20, amended: SI 1997/263 Reg.10, SI 1998/3113 Reg.3
Reg.21, amended: SI 1997/263 Reg.13
Reg.22, substituted: SI 1997/263 Reg.13
Reg.25, amended: SI 1997/263 Reg.13

NO.

1478. Goods Vehicles (Plating and Testing) Regulations 1988—*cont.*
Reg.25A, added: SI 1997/263 Reg.11
Reg.31, substituted: SI 1997/263 Reg.13
Reg.34, amended: SI 1997/82 Reg.6
Reg.36, amended: SI 1997/263 Reg.13
Reg.37, amended: SI 1997/263 Reg.13
Reg.37A, added: SI 1997/263 Reg.12, Sch.
Reg.37B, added: SI 1997/263 Reg.12, Sch.
Reg.37C, added: SI 1997/263 Reg.12, Sch.
Reg.37D, added: SI 1997/263 Reg.12, Sch.
Reg.39, amended: SI 1997/82 Reg.7
Reg.41, amended: SI 1997/263 Reg.13
Reg.43, amended: SI 1997/263 Reg.13
Reg.46, amended: SI 1997/82 Reg.9

1481. Offshore Installations (Safety Zones) (No.3) Order 1988
revoked: SI 1997/735 Art.3, Sch.2

1482. Offshore Installations (Safety Zones) (Amendment) Order 1988
revoked: SI 1997/735 Art.3, Sch.2

1525. A406 London North Circular Trunk Road (Popes Lane (B4491) to Western Avenue (A40) Improvement, Trunk Road) Order 1988
revoked: SI 1996/3002 Art.2

1526. A406 London North Circular Trunk Road (Popes Lane (B4491) to Western Avenue (A40) Improvement, Detrunking) Order 1988
revoked: SI 1996/3002 Art.2

1535. A3 Trunk Road (Roehampton Vale, Wandsworth) (Prescribed Routes) Order 1988
Art.3, amended: SI 1997/154 Art.2

1552. Central Manchester Development Corporation (Planning Functions) Order 1988
revoked: SI 1996/232 Art.2

1553. Sheffield Development Corporation (Planning Functions) Order 1988
revoked: SI 1997/13 Art.2
Art.3, referred to: SI 1997/13 Art.3
Art.3, revoked: SI 1997/13 Art.2

1586. Electro-medical Equipment (EEC Requirements) Regulations 1988
applied: SI 1998/2306 Reg.10, Sch.1

1636. Merchant Shipping (Guarding of Machinery and Safety of Electrical Equipment) Regulations 1988
applied: SI 1996/3243 Sch Part I
Reg.3, applied: SI 1998/2306 Reg.3, SI 1998/2307 Reg.3
Reg.3, referred to: SI 1998/2306 Reg.3, SI 1998/2307 Reg.3
Reg.4, applied: SI 1998/2306 Reg.3, SI 1998/2307 Reg.3
Reg.4, referred to: SI 1998/2306 Reg.3, SI 1998/2307 Reg.3

1637. Merchant Shipping (Means of Access) Regulations 1988
applied: SI 1996/3243 Sch Part I
referred to: SI 1998/2771 Reg.4, Sch.1

1638. Merchant Shipping (Entry into Dangerous Spaces) Regulations 1988
applied: SI 1996/3243 Sch Part I

1639. Merchant Shipping (Hatches and Lifting Plant) Regulations 1988
applied: SI 1996/3243 Sch Part I
Reg.5, applied: SI 1998/2306 Reg.3, SI 1998/2307 Reg.3
Reg.5, referred to: SI 1998/2306 Reg.3, SI 1998/2307 Reg.3
Reg.6, applied: SI 1998/2306 Reg.3, SI 1998/2307 Reg.3

1988—cont.

1639. Merchant Shipping (Hatches and Lifting Plant) Regulations 1988—*cont.*
Reg.6, referred to: SI 1998/2306 Reg.3, SI 1998/2307 Reg.3
Reg.7, applied: SI 1998/2306 Reg.3, SI 1998/2307 Reg.3
Reg.7, referred to: SI 1998/2306 Reg.3, SI 1998/2307 Reg.3
Reg.8, applied: SI 1998/2306 Reg.3, SI 1998/2307 Reg.3
Reg.8, referred to: SI 1998/2306 Reg.3, SI 1998/2307 Reg.3
Reg.9, applied: SI 1998/2306 Reg.3, SI 1998/2307 Reg.3
Reg.9, referred to: SI 1998/2306 Reg.3, SI 1998/2307 Reg.3
Reg.10, applied: SI 1998/2306 Reg.3, SI 1998/2307 Reg.3
Reg.10, referred to: SI 1998/2306 Reg.3, SI 1998/2307 Reg.3

1641. Merchant Shipping (Safe Movement on Board Ship) Regulations 1988
applied: SI 1996/3243 Sch Part I

1648. Wireless Telegraphy (Cordless Telephone Apparatus) (Exemption) Regulations 1988
revoked: SI 1996/316 Reg.2, Sch.1

1652. Teachers' Superannuation (Consolidation) Regulations 1988
applied: SI 1996/1240 Reg.15, Reg.19, SI 1997/312 Reg.23, SI 1997/3001 Reg.H12, Reg.H13, Sch.15 para.2
referred to: SI 1996/1680 Reg.32, SI 1997/3001 Reg.H12, Sch.15 para.12, Sch.15 para.17
revoked: SI 1997/3001 Reg.H12, Sch.14 (with savings)
Part G, substituted: SI 1997/312 Reg.16, Sch.1
Reg.B1, applied: SI 1996/2269 Reg.26, SI 1997/311 Reg.4
Reg.B3, applied: SI 1997/3001 Reg.B2
Reg.B4, amended: SI 1996/2269 Reg.3
Reg.B4, applied: SI 1997/3001 Reg.B3
Reg.B5, amended: SI 1997/312 Reg.3
Reg.B5, applied: SI 1997/3001 Reg.B4
Reg.B6, applied: SI 1997/311 Reg.4, Reg.14, Reg.15, Sch.1 para.2, SI 1997/3001 Sch.12 para.10
Reg.C1, amended: SI 1996/2269 Reg.4
Reg.C1, applied: SI 1996/2269 Reg.26, SI 1997/3001 Reg.E7
Reg.C1, referred to: SI 1996/2269 Reg.26, SI 1997/3001 Reg.H12, Sch.15 para.10
Reg.C2, applied: SI 1997/3001 Reg.E7
Reg.C3, amended: SI 1996/2269 Reg.5
Reg.C3, applied: SI 1997/3001 Reg.H12, Sch.5 para.8, Sch.5 para.9, Sch.15 para.18
Reg.C8, amended: SI 1996/2269 Reg.6
Reg.C8A, amended: SI 1997/3001 Reg.H13, Sch.16 para.4
Reg.C8A, applied: SI 1997/3001 Reg.H13, Sch.16 para.4
Reg.C10, amended: SI 1996/2269 Reg.7
Reg.C14, amended: SI 1996/2269 Reg.8
Reg.C16, amended: SI 1996/2269 Reg.9
Reg.C16, referred to: SI 1996/2269 Reg.26
Reg.D3, amended: SI 1996/2269 Reg.10
Reg.D3, referred to: SI 1996/2269 Reg.26, SI 1997/3001 Reg.H12, Sch.15 para.11
Reg.D5, applied: SI 1997/3001 Reg.C7, Reg.D1
Reg.D5, referred to: SI 1997/3001 Reg.H12, Sch.15 para.12
Reg.D6, applied: SI 1997/3001 Reg.G2

1988—cont.

1652. Teachers' Superannuation (Consolidation) Regulations 1988—*cont.*
Reg.D6, referred to: SI 1997/3001 Reg.H12, Sch.15 para.12
Reg.E1, applied: SI 1997/311 Reg.7
Reg.E3, applied: SI 1997/312 Reg.4, SI 1997/3001 Reg.E3
Reg.E4, see *Teachers Pensions Agency v Hill* [1998] 4 All E.R. 865 (Ch D), Sullivan, J.
Reg.E4, amended: SI 1996/2269 Reg.11, SI 1997/312 Reg.4, Reg.5, Reg.6
Reg.E4, applied: SI 1996/1240 Reg.8, SI 1997/311 Reg.4, Reg.7, Reg.13
Reg.E4, referred to: SI 1997/3001 Reg.H12, Sch.15 para.13
Reg.E5, amended: SI 1997/312 Reg.7
Reg.E5, applied: SI 1997/311 Reg.7
Reg.E5, referred to: SI 1997/311 Reg.12, Reg.13
Reg.E6, amended: SI 1997/312 Reg.8
Reg.E6, applied: SI 1997/311 Reg.7
Reg.E6, referred to: SI 1997/311 Reg.12
Reg.E7, amended: SI 1997/3001 Reg.H13, Sch.16 para.5
Reg.E7, applied: SI 1997/3001 Reg.H13, Sch.16 para.5
Reg.E9, amended: SI 1997/312 Reg.9
Reg.E9, applied: SI 1997/1612 Reg.142
Reg.E10, amended: SI 1997/312 Reg.10
Reg.E11, applied: SI 1997/311 Reg.13, SI 1997/1612 Reg.142
Reg.E14, amended: SI 1997/312 Reg.11
Reg.E14, applied: SI 1997/311 Reg.8, Reg.20
Reg.E15, amended: SI 1997/312 Reg.12
Reg.E15, applied: SI 1997/311 Reg.7
Reg.E18A, added: SI 1996/2269 Reg.12
Reg.E19, amended: SI 1996/2269 Reg.13, SI 1997/312 Reg.13
Reg.E19, applied: SI 1996/2269 Reg.26
Reg.E20, amended: SI 1996/2269 Reg.13, SI 1997/312 Reg.14
Reg.E20, applied: SI 1996/2269 Reg.26, SI 1997/311 Reg.9
Reg.E23, amended: SI 1996/2269 Reg.14
Reg.E23, applied: SI 1997/311 Reg.10, Reg.14
Reg.E23, referred to: SI 1996/2269 Reg.26
Reg.E24, amended: SI 1996/2269 Reg.15, SI 1997/312 Reg.15
Reg.E24, applied: SI 1997/311 Reg.10
Reg.E24, referred to: SI 1996/2269 Reg.26
Reg.E25, applied: SI 1997/311 Reg.15
Reg.E29, added: SI 1996/2269 Reg.26
Reg.E29, amended: SI 1997/3001 Reg.H13, Sch.16 para.1, Sch.16 para.2, Sch.16 para.3
Reg.E29, applied: SI 1997/311 Reg.12, Reg.21, SI 1997/3001 Reg.H12, Sch.15 para.16
Reg.E29, referred to: SI 1997/3001 Reg.H12, Sch.15 para.15
Reg.E31, amended: SI 1996/2269 Reg.16
Reg.E31A, added: SI 1996/2269 Reg.17
Reg.F1, applied: SI 1997/3001 Sch.12 para.10
Reg.F2, applied: SI 1997/3001 Reg.G3
Reg.G1, referred to: SI 1997/3001 Reg.H12, Sch.15 para.6
Reg.G4, amended: SI 1999/607 Reg.9
Reg.G4, applied: SI 1999/607 Reg.9
Reg.G4, referred to: SI 1997/3001 Reg.H12, Sch.15 para.7
Reg.G5, referred to: SI 1997/3001 Reg.H12, Sch.15 para.8
Reg.G7, amended: SI 1999/607 Reg.9
Reg.G7, applied: SI 1999/607 Reg.9

NO.

1988—cont.

1652. Teachers' Superannuation (Consolidation) Regulations 1988—*cont.*
Reg.H1, amended: SI 1996/2269 Reg.18
Reg.H2, amended: SI 1997/312 Reg.17
Sch.1, amended: SI 1997/1652 Reg.18
Sch.2 para.1, applied: SI 1997/311 Reg.3
Sch.2 para.3, applied: SI 1997/311 Reg.3
Sch.2 para.3A, applied: SI 1997/311 Reg.3
Sch.2 para.5, applied: SI 1997/311 Reg.3
Sch.2 para.5A, applied: SI 1997/311 Reg.3
Sch.2 para.15, amended: SI 1996/2269 Reg.19
Sch.2 para.20, amended: SI 1996/2269 Reg.19
Sch.2 para.25, applied: SI 1997/311 Reg.3
Sch.2 para.26, amended: SI 1996/2269 Reg.19
Sch.4 Part III, applied: SI 1996/2269 Reg.26, SI 1997/3001 Reg.C6, Sch.5 para.8
Sch.4 Part IV, referred to: SI 1997/3001 Reg.H12, Sch.15 para.11
Sch.4 para.3, applied: SI 1997/3001 Reg.H12, Sch.15 para.18
Sch.4 para.4, applied: SI 1997/3001 Reg.H12, Sch.15 para.18
Sch.4 para.5, amended: SI 1996/2269 Reg.20
Sch.4 para.5, applied: SI 1997/3001 Reg.H12, Sch.15 para.18
Sch.4 para.8, applied: SI 1997/3001 Reg.H12, Sch.15 para.18
Sch.4 para.9, applied: SI 1997/3001 Reg.H12, Sch.15 para.18
Sch.5 para.6, amended: SI 1996/2269 Reg.21
Sch.6 para.11, amended: SI 1996/2269 Reg.22
Sch.7 para.1, amended: SI 1996/2269 Reg.23
Sch.7 para.1A, amended: SI 1996/2269 Reg.23
Sch.7 para.1A, referred to: SI 1996/2269 Reg.26
Sch.7 para.1B, added: SI 1996/2269 Reg.23
Sch.7 para.1C, added: SI 1996/2269 Reg.23
Sch.7 para.1D, added: SI 1996/2269 Reg.23
Sch.7 para.2, amended: SI 1996/2269 Reg.23
Sch.7 para.3, amended: SI 1996/2269 Reg.23
Sch.7 para.3, applied: SI 1996/2269 Reg.26
Sch.9, referred to: SI 1997/3001 Reg.E3
Sch.9 Part II, referred to: SI 1997/3001 Reg.E21
Sch.9 para.25, added: SI 1996/2269 Reg.24
Sch.9A, added: SI 1997/312 Reg.19, Sch.3
Sch.10 Part IV, amended: SI 1997/312 Reg.20
Sch.10 Part IV, applied: SI 1997/311 Sch.2 para.1
Sch.10 Part VII, added: SI 1997/312 Reg.17, Sch.2
Sch.10 para.29, applied: SI 1997/311 Sch.2 para.1
Sch.10 para.29A, applied: SI 1997/311 Sch.2 para.1
Sch.11 para.1, amended: SI 1997/312 Reg.21
Sch.11 para.1, applied: SI 1997/311 Reg.13
Sch.11 para.2, applied: SI 1997/311 Reg.13
Sch.11 para.4, applied: SI 1997/311 Reg.13
Sch.11 para.5, amended: SI 1997/312 Reg.21
Sch.11 para.5, applied: SI 1997/311 Reg.13
Sch.11 para.6, applied: SI 1997/311 Reg.13
Sch.11 para.7, applied: SI 1997/311 Reg.13
Sch.11 para.9, amended: SI 1997/312 Reg.21
Sch.11 para.9, applied: SI 1997/311 Reg.13
Sch.11 para.10, applied: SI 1997/311 Reg.13
Sch.11 para.11, applied: SI 1997/311 Reg.13
Sch.12 Part III, amended: SI 1996/2269 Reg.25
Sch.13 Part I, revoked: SI 1997/312 Reg.22
Sch.13 Part II, referred to: SI 1997/3001 Reg.H12, Sch.15 para.6
Sch.13 Part II, substituted: SI 1997/312 Reg.22, Sch.4

NO.

1988—cont.

1655. Docks Regulations 1988
Reg.13, amended: SI 1998/2307 Reg.14
Reg.14, revoked: SI 1998/2307 Reg.14
Reg.15, applied: SI 1998/2307 Reg.9
Reg.15, revoked: SI 1998/2307 Reg.14
Reg.16, revoked (in part): SI 1998/2307 Reg.14
Reg.17, revoked: SI 1998/2307 Reg.14
Reg.18, revoked: SI 1997/1713 Reg.9, Sch.

1657. Control of Substances Hazardous to Health Regulations 1988
Reg.7, see *Bilton v Fastnet Highlands Ltd* Times, November 20, 1997 (OH), Lord Nimmo Smith
Reg.11, applied: 1996 c.18 s.64

1674. Social Security (Unemployment, Sickness and Invalidity Benefit) Amendment (No.2) Regulations 1988
revoked: SI 1996/1345 Reg.27, Sch.

1691. Criminal Justice Act 1987 (Notice of Transfer) Regulations 1988
Sch. Form 1, amended: SI 1997/737 Reg.2
Sch. Form 2, amended: SI 1997/737 Reg.2

1692. District of South Somerset (Electoral Arrangements) Order 1988
revoked: SI 1998/2462 Art.10

1693. Merchant Shipping (Stability of Passenger Ships) Regulations 1988
revoked: SI 1998/2514 Reg.1

1698. Petty Sessions Areas (Divisions and Names) Regulations 1988
Reg.1, amended: SI 1996/576 Reg.2
Reg.5, amended: SI 1996/576 Reg.3
Reg.7, amended: SI 1996/576 Reg.4

1699. Criminal Justice Act 1987 (Preparatory Hearings) Rules 1988
applied: SI 1997/1051 r.12
revoked: SI 1997/1051 r.12 (with savings)
r.2, referred to: SI 1997/1051 r.12
r.2, revoked: SI 1997/1051 r.12 (with savings)
r.4, referred to: SI 1997/1051 r.12
r.4, revoked: SI 1997/1051 r.12 (with savings)

1701. Magistrates' Courts (Notices of Transfer) Rules 1988
amended: SI 1997/708 r.2
r.6, revoked: SI 1997/708 r.2
r.7, amended: SI 1997/708 r.2
Sch. Form 4, revoked: SI 1997/708 r.2

1707. Weymouth and Portland (Pilotage) Harbour Revision Order 1988
Art.3, amended: SI 1997/2949 Art.58

1715. Central Institutions (Scotland) Regulations 1988
revoked (in part): SI 1996/120 Art.19

1716. Merchant Shipping (Operations Book) Regulations 1988
revoked (in part): SI 1997/3022 Reg.2, SI 1998/1561 Reg.1

1724. Social Fund Cold Weather Payments (General) Regulations 1988
Reg.1, amended: SI 1996/2544 Reg.2, SI 1997/2311 Reg.2
Reg.1A, amended: SI 1996/2544 Reg.3
Reg.2, amended: SI 1996/2544 Reg.4, SI 1997/2311 Reg.3
Sch.1, substituted: SI 1996/2544 Reg.5, Sch.1, SI 1997/2311 Reg.4, Sch.1, SI 1998/2455 Reg.2, Sch.1, SI 1999/2781 Reg.2, Sch.1
Sch.2, substituted: SI 1996/2544 Reg.6, Sch.2, SI 1997/2311 Reg.5, Sch.2, SI 1998/2455 Reg.3, Sch.2, SI 1999/2781 Reg.3, Sch.2

NO.

1729. Mines (Safety of Exit) Regulations 1988
Reg.8, applied: SI 1999/2463 Reg.4

1771. Trade Descriptions (Place of Production) (Marking) Order 1988
revoked: SI 1996/2757 Art.2

1808. Goods Vehicles (Authorisation of International Journeys) (Fees) (Amendment) Regulations 1988
revoked: SI 1996/131 Reg.4, Sch.2

1811. Goods Vehicles (Operators' Licences) (Temporary Use in Great Britain) (Amendment) Regulations 1988
revoked: SI 1996/2186 Reg.2, Sch.1

1813. Town and Country Planning General Development Order 1988
see *Brentwood DC v Secretary of State for the Environment and Gray* (1996) P.& C.R. 61 (QBD), Lockhart-Mummery Q.C.; see *R. v King's Lynn and West Norfolk BC Ex p. Bolam* [1996] Env. L.R. D36 (QBD), Auld, L.J.; see *South Staffordshire DC v Baker* [1997] C.O.D. 153 (QBD), Simon Brown, L.J.; see *Tandridge DC v Telecom Securicor Cellular Radio* [1996] J.P.L. B128 (QBD), Sir Graham Eyre Q.C.
Art.1, see *R. v Newbury DC Ex p. Chieveley Parish Council* (1998) 10 Admin. L.R. 676 (CA), Pill, L.J.
Art.3, see *Attorney General's Reference (No.1 of 1996), Re* [1997] J.P.L. 749 (CA (Crim Div)), Lord Bingham of Cornhill, L.C.J.; see *Kent CC v Secretary of State for the Environment* (1998) 75 P. & C.R. 410 (CA), Beldam, L.J.
Art.4, see *Bolton v North Dorset DC* (1997) 74 P. & C.R. 73 (Lands Tr), JC Hill
Sch.2 Part 10, see *Doncaster BC v Secretary of State for the Environment* (1997) 74 P. & C.R. 428 (QBD), Malcolm Spence Q.C.
Sch.2 Part 17, see *Railtrack Plc v Secretary of State for Transport* (1998) 76 P. & C.R. 448 (QBD), Judge Nigel MacLeod Q.C.

1838. Bermuda (Territorial Sea) Order in Council 1988
Art.3, amended: SI 1997/1578 Art.2

1846. Criminal Justice (Serious Fraud) (Northern Ireland) Order 1988
Art.3, amended: 1996 c.25 Sch.4 para.35
Art.3, applied: SI 1996/1141 (NI.6) Art.5
Art.4, amended: 1996 c.25 Sch.4 para.18
Art.6, amended: 1996 c.25 Sch.4 para.35
Art.6, revoked (in part): 1996 c.25 Sch.4 para.36
Art.8, amended: 1996 c.25 Sch.4 para.35, SI 1996/3160 (NI.24) Art.43
Art.8, revoked (in part): 1996 c.25 Sch.4 para.36
Art.8A, added: 1996 c.25 Sch.4 para.35
Art.9, substituted: 1996 c.25 Sch.4 para.35
Art.10, substituted: 1996 c.25 Sch.4 para.35
Art.10A, substituted: 1996 c.25 Sch.4 para.35
Sch. para.3, revoked: 1996 c.25 Sch.4 para.36

1847. Criminal Justice (Evidence, etc.) (Northern Ireland) Order 1988
Art.3, revoked (in part): SI 1999/2789 (NI.8) Art.40, Sch.3
Art.4, revoked (in part): SI 1999/2789 (NI.8) Art.40, Sch.3
Art.12, revoked: SI 1998/1504 (NI.9) Art.65, Sch.6
Art.13, amended: SI 1996/3160 (NI.24) Art.45, SI 1998/1504 (NI.9) Art.65, Sch.5 para.31, SI 1999/2789 (NI.8) Art.40, Sch.1 para.2

NO.

1847. Criminal Justice (Evidence, etc.) (Northern Ireland) Order 1988—*cont.*
Art.15, applied: 1997 c.51 Sch.1 para.3
Sch.1 para.5, substituted: SI 1997/2983 (NI.21) Art.13, Sch.1 para.5

1890. Housing Benefit (Community Charge Rebates) (Scotland) Regulations 1988
Reg.59, applied: SI 1996/1217 Art.11, SI 1997/1004 Art.11, SI 1998/562 Art.19

1891. Civil Legal Aid (Scotland) Amendment (No.3) Regulations 1988
revoked: SI 1996/2444 Reg.3, Sch.1

1892. Court of Session etc. Fees Amendment (No.3) Order 1988
revoked: SI 1997/688 Art.6, Sch.2

1893. Sheriff Court Fees Amendment (No.2) Order 1988
revoked: SI 1997/687 Art.11, Sch.2

1909. Merchant Shipping (Fishing Vessels - Tonnage) Regulations 1988
Reg.2, amended: SI 1998/1916 Reg.3, SI 1999/3206 Reg.28
Reg.3, amended: SI 1998/1916 Reg.3

1910. Merchant Shipping (Tonnage) (Amendment) Regulations 1988
revoked: SI 1997/1510 Reg.1

1930. Quarries (Explosives) Regulations 1988
revoked: SI 1999/2024 Reg.48, Sch.5 Part I
Reg.2, revoked: SI 1999/2024 Reg.48, Sch.5 Part I

1955. Local Government Reorganisation (Miscellaneous Provision) Order 1988
Art.6, amended: SI 1996/1690 Art.2

1967. Liverpool and Wirral Urban Development Area Order 1988
revoked: SI 1998/769 Art.2

1968. Merseyside Development Corporation (Planning Functions) (Liverpool and Wirral) Order 1988
revoked: SI 1998/84 Art.2, Sch.

1987. Criminal Evidence (Northern Ireland) Order 1988
see *Murray v United Kingdom* (1996) 22 E.H.R.R. 29 (ECHR), R Ryssdal (President)
Art.2, amended: SI 1999/2789 (NI.8) Art.36
Art.3, amended: SI 1999/2789 (NI.8) Art.36
Art.3, revoked (in part): SI 1996/3160 (NI.24) Sch.7
Art.4, see *R. v Bingham (Graham Carlo)* [1999] 1 W.L.R. 598 (HL), Lord Lloyd of Berwick
Art.4, revoked (in part): SI 1996/3160 (NI.24) Sch.7
Art.5, amended: SI 1999/2789 (NI.8) Art.36
Art.5, revoked (in part): SI 1996/3160 (NI.24) Sch.7
Art.6, amended: SI 1999/2789 (NI.8) Art.36
Art.6, revoked (in part): SI 1996/3160 (NI.24) Sch.7

1988. Education (Academic Tenure) (Northern Ireland) Order 1988
see *Deman v Queen's University of Belfast* [1997] E.L.R. 431 (CA (NI)), Sir Brian Hutton, L.C.J.
Art.4, see *Deman v Queen's University of Belfast* [1997] E.L.R. 431 (CA (NI)), Sir Brian Hutton, L.C.J.
Art.4, amended: SI 1996/1919 (NI.16) Art.255, Sch.1

1990. Housing (Northern Ireland) Order 1988
Sch.1 para.2, revoked (in part): SI 1996/1919 (NI.16) Art.257, Sch.3

NO.

1988—cont.

2013. Act of Sederunt (Proceedings in the Sheriff Court under the Debtors (Scotland) Act 1987) 1988
r.39, amended: SI 1999/1820 Art.4, Sch.2 para.145
r.43, amended: SI 1999/1820 Art.4, Sch.2 para.145
r.68, substituted: SI 1996/2709 r.2
Sch. Form 31, amended: SI 1999/1820 Art.4, Sch.2 para.145
Sch. Form 35, amended: SI 1999/1820 Art.4, Sch.2 para.145
Sch. Form 61, substituted: SI 1996/2709 r.2, Sch.1
Sch. Form 62, substituted: SI 1996/2709 r.2, Sch.1
Sch. Form 63, substituted: SI 1996/2709 r.2, Sch.1

2017. Medicines (Products Other Than Veterinary Drugs) (Prescription Only) Amendment Order 1988
revoked: SI 1997/1830 Art.16, Sch.6

2019. Criminal Justice Act 1988 (Offensive Weapons) Order 1988
see *DPP v Hynde* [1998] 1 W.L.R. 1222 (QBD), Henry, L.J.

2022. Income Support (General) Amendment No.5 Regulations 1988
Reg.16, revoked: SI 1996/206 Reg.28, Sch.3

2050. Distress for Rent Rules 1988
amended: SI 1999/2360 r.4
applied: SI 1999/2360 r.3
Appendix.2 Form 1, amended: SI 1999/2360 r.17
Appendix.2 Form 2, substituted: SI 1999/2360 r.17, Sch.1
Appendix.2 Form 3, substituted: SI 1999/2360 r.17, Sch.1
Appendix.2 Form 4, substituted: SI 1999/2360 r.17, Sch.1
Appendix.2 Form 5, substituted: SI 1999/2360 r.17, Sch.1
Appendix.3, added: SI 1999/2360 r.18, Sch.2
Appendix.3, amended: SI 1999/2564 r.2, SI 1999/3186 r.2
r.2, amended: SI 1999/2360 r.5
r.3, revoked (in part): SI 1999/2360 r.6
r.4, amended: SI 1999/2360 r.7, r.8
r.4, revoked (in part): SI 1999/2360 r.7
r.5, amended: SI 1999/2360 r.8, r.9
r.6, amended: SI 1999/2360 r.8, r.10
r.7, revoked (in part): SI 1999/2360 r.11
r.7A, added: SI 1999/2360 r.12
r.8, amended: SI 1999/2360 r.13
r.9, amended: SI 1999/2360 r.14
r.11, amended: SI 1999/2360 r.15
r.13, amended: SI 1999/2360 r.16

2099. Veterinary Surgeons and Veterinary Practitioners Registration (Amendment) Regulations 1988
revoked: SI 1999/2846 Sch. Reg.22

2119. Social Security (Unemployment, Sickness and Invalidity Benefit) Amendment (No.3) Regulations 1988
revoked: SI 1996/1345 Reg.27, Sch.

2137. Protection of Wrecks (Designation No.2 Order 1984) (Amendment) Order 1988
revoked: SI 1998/1746 Art.3

2203. Assured Tenancies and Agricultural Occupancies (Forms) Regulations 1988
revoked: SI 1997/194 Reg.4

NO.

1988—cont.

2213. Spring Traps Approval (Scotland) (Variation) Order 1988
revoked: SI 1996/2202 Art.3

2236. Assured and Protected Tenancies (Lettings to Students) Regulations 1988
revoked: SI 1998/1967 Reg.6, Sch.3
Reg.2, revoked: SI 1998/1967 Reg.6, Sch.3
Sch.1, revoked: SI 1998/1967 Reg.6, Sch.3
Sch.2, amended: SI 1996/458 Reg.2, SI 1996/2198 Reg.2
Sch.2, revoked: SI 1998/1967 Reg.6, Sch.3

2241. Architects' Qualifications (EC Recognition) Order 1988
revoked: 1997 c.22 s.27, Sch.3

2246. Extradition (Taking of Hostages) (Amendment) Order 1988
revoked: SI 1997/1767 Art.4

2249. Health and Medicines (Northern Ireland) Order 1988
Art.10, amended: SI 1997/1177 (NI.7) Art.32, Sch.2
Art.10, referred to: SI 1997/1177 (NI.7) Art.16
Art.11, amended: SI 1996/1919 (NI.16) Art.255, Sch.1

2252. Merchant Shipping (Prevention of Pollution by Garbage) Order 1988
Art.2, amended: SI 1998/254 Art.3
Art.3, added: SI 1997/2569 Art.3
Art.3, amended: SI 1998/254 Art.3

2255. General Medical Council Preliminary Proceedings Committee and Professional Conduct Committee (Procedure) Rules Order of Council 1988
see *R. v General Medical Council Ex p. Stewart* Times, November 12, 1997 (QBD), Lightman, J.
r.2, amended: SI 1996/1218 Sch para.2, SI 1997/1529 Sch.r.34
r.4, applied: SI 1996/2125 Sch. para.3
r.12, amended: SI 1996/1218 Sch para.2
r.33, substituted: SI 1996/1218 Sch para.2
r.33A, added: SI 1996/1218 Sch para.2
r.53A, added: SI 1996/1218 Sch para.2
r.54, amended: SI 1996/1218 Sch para.2
Sch.2, amended: SI 1996/1218 Sch para.2

2256. Church of England Pensions Regulations 1988
Reg.2, amended: 1997 m.1 s.10, Sch.1 para.20, Sch.1 para.26, SI 1997/1929 Sch. para.1
Reg.2, revoked (in part): 1997 m.1 s.10, Sch.2 Part II
Reg.4, amended: 1997 m.1 s.10, Sch.1 para.21, SI 1997/1929 Sch. para.2
Reg.5, amended: 1997 m.1 s.10, Sch.1 para.26
Reg.6, amended: 1997 m.1 s.10, Sch.1 para.22, SI 1997/1929 Sch. para.3
Reg.6, revoked (in part): 1997 m.1 s.10, Sch.2 Part II
Reg.8, amended: 1997 m.1 s.10, Sch.1 para.23
Reg.12, amended: 1997 m.1 s.10, Sch.1 para.24
Reg.12, revoked (in part): 1997 m.1 s.10, Sch.2 Part II
Reg.16, amended: 1997 m.1 s.10, Sch.1 para.25, SI 1997/1929 Sch. para.4
Reg.19, amended: 1997 m.1 s.10, Sch.1 para.26, SI 1997/1929 Sch. para.5
Reg.20, amended: 1997 m.1 s.10, Sch.1 para.26, SI 1997/1929 Sch. para.6
Reg.22, amended: 1997 m.1 s.10, Sch.1 para.26

NO.

1988—cont.

2256. Church of England Pensions Regulations 1988—*cont.*
Reg.25, amended: 1997 m.1 s.10, Sch.1 para.26
Reg.26, amended: SI 1997/1929 Sch. para.7
Reg.27, amended: SI 1997/1929 Sch. para.8
Reg.27, revoked (in part): SI 1997/1929 Sch. para.8
Reg.28, amended: 1997 m.1 s.10, Sch.1 para.26
Reg.29, revoked (in part): 1997 m.1 s.10, Sch.2 Part II
Reg.30, revoked (in part): 1997 m.1 s.10, Sch.2 Part II
Sch.1 para.1, substituted: SI 1997/1929 Sch. para.9
Sch.1 para.2, substituted: SI 1997/1929 Sch. para.9
Sch.1 para.7, amended: SI 1997/1929 Sch. para.9

2264. Zoonoses Order 1988
applied: SI 1996/963, SI 1996/1192, SI 1996/1941, SI 1996/2264, SI 1996/3185, SI 1996/3268, SI 1997/617
referred to: SI 1997/2964
Sch., amended: SI 1997/2964 Art.18

2272. Merchant Shipping (Emergency Equipment Lockers for Ro/Ro Passenger Ships) Regulations 1988
applied: SI 1996/3243 Sch Part I

2290. Advice and Assistance (Assistance by Way of Representation) (Scotland) Regulations 1988
revoked: SI 1997/3070 Reg.2, Sch.
Reg.2, revoked: SI 1997/3070 Reg.2, Sch.
Reg.3, amended: SI 1996/1011 Reg.3
Reg.3, revoked: SI 1997/3070 Reg.2, Sch.
Reg.4, amended: SI 1996/1011 Reg.4
Reg.4, revoked: SI 1997/3070 Reg.2, Sch.
Reg.5, revoked: SI 1997/3070 Reg.2, Sch.
Reg.5A, amended: SI 1996/1011 Reg.5
Reg.5A, revoked: SI 1997/3070 Reg.2, Sch.

2292. Merchant Shipping (Prevention of Pollution by Garbage) Regulations 1988
revoked: SI 1998/1377 Reg.1

2293. Merchant Shipping (Reception Facilities for Garbage) Regulations 1988
revoked: SI 1997/3018 Reg.16

1989

A406 Trunk Road (South Woodford to Barking Relief Road, Redbridge, Newham, Barking and Dagenham) (Waiting and Loading) Order 1989
revoked (in part): SI 1996/1895 Art.10

Lewisham (Restriction of Waiting on Bus Stops) Order 1989
revoked (in part): SI 1997/258 Art.11

48. Act of Adjournal (Consolidation Amendment) (Reference to European Court) 1989
revoked: SI 1996/513 Sch.2 r.3, Sch.3

52. Welfare of Poultry (Transport) (Amendment) Order 1989
revoked: SI 1997/1480 Art.22, Sch.12 Part II

65. Control of Pollution (Landed Ships' Waste) (Amendment) Regulations 1989
revoked: SI 1996/972 Reg.26

76. Fire Precautions (Factories, Offices, Shops and Railway Premises) Order 1989
applied: SI 1996/1623 Art.3, SI 1998/217 Art.2, SI 1999/779 Art.2, Sch.

NO.

1989—cont.

98. Commissioner for Local Administration in Scotland (Expenses) Regulations 1989
Reg.2, amended: SI 1996/681 Reg.5
Reg.3, amended: SI 1996/681 Reg.5
Reg.4, amended: SI 1996/681 Reg.5

100. Merchant Shipping (Loading and Stability Assessment of Ro/Ro Passenger Ships) Regulations 1989
applied: SI 1996/3243 Sch Part I

102. Merchant Shipping (Provisions and Water) Regulations 1989
applied: SI 1996/3243 Sch Part I

122. Monopolies and Mergers Commission (Performance of Functions) Order 1989
revoked: SI 1999/506 Art.45

126. Fishing Vessels (Safety Training) Regulations 1989
applied: SI 1996/3243 Sch Part I

128. Farm and Conservation Grant Scheme 1989
para.7, amended: SI 1996/230 para.3, para.4

145. (Pelican) Pedestrian Crossings Regulations (Northern Ireland) 1989
Reg.6, applied: SI 1996/1320 (NI.10) Sch.1 Part II
Reg.8, applied: SI 1996/1320 (NI.10) Sch.1 Part II
Reg.12, applied: SI 1996/1320 (NI.10) Sch.1 Part II

146. Assured Tenancies and Agricultural Occupancies (Forms) (Amendment) Regulations 1989
revoked: SI 1997/194 Reg.4

147. Town and Country Planning (Use Classes) (Scotland) Order 1989
revoked: SI 1997/3061 Art.5
Art.2, revoked: SI 1997/3061 Art.5
Art.3, revoked: SI 1997/3061 Art.5
Sch., applied: SI 1997/10 Reg.6
Sch., revoked: SI 1997/3061 Art.5

184. Merchant Shipping (Crew Accommodation) (Amendment) Regulations 1989
revoked: SI 1997/1508 Reg.1

193. Town and Country Planning (Fees for Applications and Deemed Applications) Regulations 1989
Reg.1, amended: SI 1997/37 Reg.5, Sch.5
Reg.2, amended: SI 1997/37 Reg.5, Sch.5
Reg.4, amended: SI 1997/37 Reg.4
Reg.5, amended: SI 1997/37 Reg.5, Sch.5
Reg.8, amended: SI 1997/37 Reg.5, Sch.5
Reg.10, see *Geall v Secretary of State for the Environment, Transport and the Regions* (1999) 78 P. & C.R. 264 (CA), Schiemann, L.J.
Reg.10A, amended: SI 1997/37 Reg.2, Reg.3, Reg.5, Sch.5
Reg.11, amended: SI 1996/525 Sch para.11
Reg.11A, amended: SI 1997/37 Reg.2, Reg.3, Reg.5, Sch.5
Sch.1 Part I, amended: SI 1997/37 Reg.2, Reg.3
Sch.1 Part II, substituted: SI 1997/37 Reg.2, Reg.3
Sch.1 para.8, amended: SI 1996/525 Sch para.11
Sch.2, substituted: SI 1997/37 Reg.2, Reg.3

216. European Economic Interest Grouping Regulations (Northern Ireland) 1989
Reg.14, applied: SI 1996/1632 (NI.11) Sch.2 para.7

NO.

1989—cont.

216. European Economic Interest Grouping Regulations (Northern Ireland) 1989—cont.
Reg.17, applied: SI 1996/1632 (NI.11) Sch.2 para.10
Reg.18, applied: SI 1996/1632 (NI.11) Sch.2 para.8

219. Farm and Conservation Grant Regulations 1989
applied: SI 1999/672 Art.2, Sch.1

289. Small Estates (Scotland) Order 1989
revoked: SI 1999/290 Art.4

298. Teachers (Compensation for Redundancy and Premature Retirement) Regulations 1989
applied: SI 1996/330 Reg.12, SI 1996/1240 Reg.11, Reg.15, Reg.19
revoked: SI 1997/311 Reg.28
Part III, applied: SI 1996/532 Art.15
Reg.6, applied: SI 1996/1240 Reg.9
Reg.11, amended: SI 1996/2777 Reg.3
Reg.11, applied: SI 1997/311 Reg.16
Reg.11, revoked: SI 1997/311 Reg.28
Reg.12, amended: SI 1996/2777 Reg.4
Reg.12, applied: SI 1997/311 Reg.17
Reg.12, revoked: SI 1997/311 Reg.28
Reg.15, substituted: SI 1996/2777 Reg.5

299. Motor Vehicles (Construction and Use) Regulations (Northern Ireland) 1989
Reg.2, applied: SI 1999/2978 Reg.2

317. Air Quality Standards Regulations 1989
applied: SI 1999/672 Art.2, Sch.1

326. National Health Service (Charges for Drugs and Appliances) (Scotland) Regulations 1989
Reg.2, amended: SI 1996/1504 Reg.4, SI 1998/2224 Reg.6, SI 1999/612 Reg.2
Reg.3, amended: SI 1996/740 Reg.2, SI 1997/697 Reg.2, SI 1998/609 Reg.2, SI 1999/612 Reg.3
Reg.8, amended: SI 1996/740 Reg.2, SI 1997/697 Reg.2, SI 1998/609 Reg.2, SI 1999/612 Reg.3
Reg.8, applied: SI 1997/697 Reg.3, SI 1998/609 Reg.3, SI 1999/612 Reg.4
Reg.8, referred to: SI 1996/740 Reg.3
Sch.1, amended: SI 1996/740 Reg.2, Sch
Sch.1, substituted: SI 1997/697 Reg.2, Sch., SI 1998/609 Reg.2, Sch., SI 1999/612 Reg.3, Sch.
Sch.2, amended: SI 1996/740 Reg.2, Sch
Sch.2, substituted: SI 1997/697 Reg.2, Sch., SI 1998/609 Reg.2, Sch., SI 1999/612 Reg.3, Sch.
Sch.3, amended: SI 1996/740 Reg.2, Sch
Sch.3, applied: SI 1996/740 Reg.3, SI 1997/697 Reg.3, SI 1998/609 Reg.3
Sch.3, substituted: SI 1997/697 Reg.2, Sch., SI 1998/609 Reg.2, Sch., SI 1999/612 Reg.3, Sch.

330. Prison (Amendment) Rules 1989
revoked: SI 1999/728 r.85 (with savings), Sch. (with savings)

338. Civil Legal Aid (Assessment of Resources) Regulations 1989
Reg.3, amended: SI 1996/2309 Reg.3
Reg.4, amended: SI 1996/642 Reg.2, SI 1997/753 Reg.2, SI 1998/664 Reg.2, SI 1999/813 Reg.2
Reg.7A, added: SI 1996/434 Reg.4
Reg.11, amended: SI 1998/664 Reg.3
Reg.14, amended: SI 1996/2309 Reg.4
Sch.2 para.5, amended: SI 1996/2309 Reg.5

NO.

1989—cont.

338. Civil Legal Aid (Assessment of Resources) Regulations 1989—cont.
Sch.2 para.6, amended: SI 1997/753 Reg.3
Sch.2 para.6A, added: SI 1996/2309 Reg.5
Sch.2 para.9, amended: SI 1996/434 Reg.5
Sch.2 para.11, amended: SI 1998/664 Reg.4
Sch.3 para.5, amended: SI 1998/664 Reg.5
Sch.3 para.7, amended: SI 1996/2309 Reg.6
Sch.3 para.8, amended: SI 1997/753 Reg.3
Sch.3 para.8, substituted: SI 1996/2309 Reg.6
Sch.3 para.10, see *Waterford Wedgwood Plc v David Nagli Ltd (In Liquidation) (Costs)* [1999] 3 All E.R. 185 (Ch D), Charles Aldous Q.C.
Sch.3 para.10, amended: SI 1996/434 Reg.6
Sch.3 para.14A, amended: SI 1998/664 Reg.6

339. Civil Legal Aid (General) Regulations 1989
see *Tate v Hart* [1999] Lloyd's Rep. P.N. 566 (CA), Auld, L.J.; see *Willis v Redbridge HA* [1996] 1 W.L.R. 1228 (CA), Beldam, L.J.
amended: SI 1997/1079 Reg.2
applied: SI 1997/1852 Art.5
referred to: SI 1998/3132 r.42.2
Reg.3, amended: SI 1997/1079 Reg.3
Reg.17, amended: SI 1999/1113 Reg.3
Reg.26A, added: SI 1997/1079 Reg.4
Reg.33A, added: SI 1996/1257 Reg.2
Reg.46, see *Bridgewater v Griffiths* Independent, June 14, 1999 (C.S.) (QBD), Burton, J.
Reg.61, see *R. v Legal Aid Board No.15 Area Office (Liverpool) Ex p. Eccleston* [1998] 1 W.L.R. 1279 (QBD), Sedley, J.
Reg.66A, added: SI 1996/1257 Reg.2
Reg.70, amended: SI 1999/1113 Reg.4
Reg.73, amended: SI 1999/1113 Reg.5
Reg.78, see *R. v Legal Aid Board Ex p. Doran* Times, July 22, 1996 (QBD), Collins, J.; see *R. v Legal Aid Board Ex p. Parsons* [1999] 3 All E.R. 347 (CA), Beldam, L.J.
Reg.78, amended: SI 1997/416 Reg.3
Reg.79, amended: SI 1997/416 Reg.4
Reg.87, see *Debtor (No.68-SD-1997), Re* [1998] 4 All E.R. 779 (Ch D), Jonathan Parker, J.
Reg.91, see *Debtor (No.68-SD-1997), Re* [1998] 4 All E.R. 779 (Ch D), Jonathan Parker, J.
Reg.94, amended: SI 1997/416 Reg.5, SI 1999/2565 Reg.3
Reg.101, amended: SI 1996/649 Reg.2, SI 1997/416 Reg.6
Reg.103, see *Microsoft Corp v Backslash Distribution Ltd* Times, March 15, 1999 (Ch D), Park, J.
Reg.107, see *L v L (Legal Aid: Taxation)* [1996] 1 F.L.R. 873 (CA), Neill, L.J.
Reg.107A, amended: SI 1999/1113 Reg.6
Reg.107B, amended: SI 1999/1113 Reg.7
Reg.130, see *Wraith v Wraith* [1997] 1 W.L.R. 1540 (CA), Butler-Sloss, L.J.
Reg.134, see *Lancashire Fires Ltd v SA Lyons & Co Ltd (No.2)* Times, July 24, 1999 (CA), Mummery, L.J.

340. Legal Advice and Assistance Regulations 1989
amended: SI 1997/751 Reg.3
applied: SI 1997/751 Reg.2
Reg.3, amended: SI 1996/2308 Reg.3, SI 1999/2089 Reg.3
Reg.7, amended: SI 1997/751 Reg.4, SI 1998/2727 Reg.3
Reg.9, amended: SI 1996/2308 Reg.4
Reg.10, amended: SI 1996/2308 Reg.5, SI 1999/2575 Reg.4

NO.

340. Legal Advice and Assistance Regulations 1989—*cont.*

Reg.11, amended: SI 1996/641 Reg.3, SI 1997/751 Reg.5, SI 1998/663 Reg.3, SI 1999/814 Reg.2

Reg.12, amended: SI 1996/641 Reg.3, SI 1997/751 Reg.5, SI 1998/663 Reg.3, SI 1999/814 Reg.2

Reg.13, amended: SI 1996/2308 Reg.6, SI 1999/2575 Reg.5, Reg.6

Reg.15, referred to: SI 1999/3377 Reg.3

Reg.17, amended: SI 1999/2575 Reg.7

Reg.20, see *R. v Legal Aid Board Ex p. Rafina* Times, February 19, 1998 (QBD), Latham, J.

Reg.22, amended: SI 1997/751 Reg.6, SI 1998/2727 Reg.4, Reg.5, Reg.6

Reg.30, amended: SI 1998/2907 Reg.2

Reg.32, amended: SI 1999/2575 Reg.8

Sch.2 para.7, amended: SI 1996/2308 Reg.7

Sch.2 para.8, amended: SI 1996/435 Reg.4

Sch.2 para.9, amended: SI 1998/663 Reg.4

Sch.2 para.9A, amended: SI 1997/751 Reg.7

Sch.2 para.9B, added: SI 1996/2308 Reg.8

Sch.6, amended: SI 1996/641 Reg.4

Sch.6 para.3, amended: SI 1997/751 Reg.8

Sch.6 para.4, amended: SI 1997/751 Reg.8

341. Legal Advice and Assistance (Duty Solicitor) (Remuneration) Regulations 1989

applied: SI 1996/647 Reg.1

Reg.5, amended: SI 1996/647 Reg.2

342. Legal Advice and Assistance at Police Stations (Remuneration) Regulations 1989

applied: SI 1996/648 Reg.1, SI 1996/1554 Reg.1

Reg.2, amended: SI 1999/2088 Reg.3

Reg.5, amended: SI 1999/3299 Reg.3

Sch., substituted: SI 1996/648 Art.2, Sch

Sch. para.1, amended: SI 1996/1554 Reg.2

Sch. para.3, amended: SI 1996/1554 Reg.2

343. Legal Aid in Criminal and Care Proceedings (Costs) Regulations 1989

amended: SI 1996/2655 Reg.4, SI 1999/2124 Reg.2

applied: SI 1999/345 Reg.3

referred to: SI 1997/754 Reg.2

Reg.2, see *Smith Graham (A Firm) v Lord Chancellor's Department* Independent, October 7, 1999 (QBD), Hallett, J.

Reg.2, amended: SI 1996/2655 Reg.5, SI 1998/2908 Reg.3, SI 1999/2124 Reg.2

Reg.3, amended: SI 1996/2655 Reg.6, SI 1998/2908 Reg.3, SI 1999/1375 Reg.3

Reg.4E, amended: SI 1998/3154 Reg.3, SI 1998/2908 Reg.3

Reg.4F, added: SI 1996/2655 Reg.7

Reg.4F, amended: SI 1998/2908 Reg.3

Reg.4G, added: SI 1996/2655 Reg.7

Reg.4G, amended: SI 1997/1484 Reg.3

Reg.4H, amended: SI 1996/2655 Reg.7

Reg.4I, added: SI 1996/2655 Reg.7

Reg.4J, added: SI 1996/2655 Reg.7

Reg.5, amended: SI 1999/2124 Reg.3

Reg.6, see *Smith Graham (A Firm) v Lord Chancellor's Department* Independent, October 7, 1999 (QBD), Hallett, J.

Reg.6, amended: SI 1996/644 Reg.2, SI 1996/2655 Reg.8, SI 1997/1010 Reg.2, SI 1998/1191 Reg.4, SI 1998/2908 Reg.3, SI 1998/3154 Reg.4, SI 1999/345 Reg.4, SI 1999/1375 Reg.4

Reg.6, applied: SI 1998/1191 Reg.3

NO.

343. Legal Aid in Criminal and Care Proceedings (Costs) Regulations 1989—*cont.*

Reg.7, see *Smith Graham (A Firm) v Lord Chancellor's Department* Independent, October 7, 1999 (QBD), Hallett, J.

Reg.7A, amended: SI 1996/2655 Reg.9, SI 1998/3154 Reg.5

Reg.8, applied: SI 1998/1191 Reg.3

Reg.9, amended: SI 1996/644 Reg.2, SI 1996/2655 Reg.10, SI 1997/1010 Reg.2, SI 1998/1191 Reg.4

Reg.9, revoked (in part): SI 1999/1375 Reg.4

Reg.10, amended: SI 1998/3154 Reg.6

Reg.14, amended: SI 1996/2655 Reg.11, SI 1997/1484 Reg.4, SI 1998/2908 Reg.3

Reg.16, see *Lord Chancellor v Brennan* Times, February 14, 1996 (QBD), Hooper, J.

Reg.16, amended: SI 1999/2124 Reg.2

Sch.1, see *R. v Legal Aid Board Ex p. Graham Dobson & Co* Times, October 9, 1996 (QBD), Simon Brown, L.J.

Sch.1 Part I, amended: SI 1996/644 Reg.3, SI 1996/2655 Reg.12, SI 1999/345 Reg.5

Sch.1 Part II, amended: SI 1996/644 Reg.4, SI 1996/2655 Reg.13, SI 1998/2908 Reg.3, SI 1999/345 Reg.6, Reg.7

Sch.1 Part III, amended: SI 1996/644 Reg.5, SI 1997/754 Reg.3, SI 1998/2401 Reg.3

Sch.2 Part I, amended: SI 1996/644 Reg.6

Sch.2 Part I, revoked: SI 1996/2655 Reg.14

Sch.2 Part II, amended: SI 1996/644 Reg.7, SI 1996/2655 Reg.15, SI 1997/1484 Reg.5

Sch.3, added: SI 1996/2655 Reg.16

Sch.3 para.4, amended: SI 1998/1191 Reg.5

Sch.3 para.11, amended: SI 1998/1191 Reg.6, SI 1999/1375 Reg.5

Sch.3 para.11, revoked (in part): SI 1998/1191 Reg.6

Sch.3 para.19, amended: SI 1998/1191 Reg.7

Sch.3 para.19A, added: SI 1999/345 Reg.8

Sch.3 para.21, amended: SI 1998/1191 Reg.8, SI 1999/345 Reg.8, SI 1999/1375 Reg.5

Sch.3 para.24, amended: SI 1997/1484 Reg.6, Reg.7

344. Legal Aid in Criminal and Care Proceedings (General) Regulations 1989

see *R. v Welsby (John)* [1998] 1 Cr. App. R. 197 (Crown Ct) (Swansea), Ebsworth, J.

amended: SI 1997/1485 Reg.3, SI 1999/346 Reg.4

referred to: SI 1999/346 Reg.3

Reg.3, amended: SI 1996/1258 Reg.2, SI 1996/2307 Reg.3, SI 1996/2656 Reg.3, SI 1998/662 Reg.2, SI 1999/2737 Reg.4

Reg.4, amended: SI 1998/662 Reg.3, SI 1999/2123 Reg.4

Reg.11, amended: SI 1998/2909 Reg.3, SI 1999/815 Reg.2

Reg.13, amended: SI 1998/2909 Reg.4

Reg.15, amended: SI 1998/662 Reg.4, Reg.5

Reg.17, amended: SI 1998/2909 Reg.5

Reg.18, amended: SI 1998/2909 Reg.6

Reg.20, amended: SI 1998/2909 Reg.7

Reg.22, amended: SI 1998/662 Reg.6

Reg.22A, added: SI 1998/662 Reg.7

Reg.23, amended: SI 1998/662 Reg.8, SI 1998/2909 Reg.8

Reg.24, amended: SI 1996/1258 Reg.3, SI 1998/2909 Reg.9

Reg.25, amended: SI 1998/2909 Reg.10

Reg.26, amended: SI 1996/1258 Reg.4, SI 1998/662 Reg.9, SI 1998/2909 Reg.11, SI 1999/2577 Reg.4

Reg.29, amended: SI 1998/2909 Reg.12

NO.

344. Legal Aid in Criminal and Care Proceedings (General) Regulations 1989—*cont.*
Reg.31, amended: SI 1996/1258 Reg.5, SI 1998/662 Reg.10
Reg.32, amended: SI 1998/662 Reg.11
Reg.33, amended: SI 1998/662 Reg.12
Reg.35, amended: SI 1997/2647 Reg.2
Reg.37, amended: SI 1996/1258 Reg.4, SI 1999/2737 Reg.5
Reg.38, amended: SI 1998/2909 Reg.13
Reg.40, amended: SI 1998/2909 Reg.14
Reg.41, amended: SI 1996/1258 Reg.6, SI 1998/2909 Reg.15
Reg.41A, added: SI 1996/1258 Reg.7
Reg.41A, amended: SI 1996/2307 Reg.4
Reg.43, amended: SI 1998/2909 Reg.16
Reg.44, see *R. v Mills (Brett Mark)* [1997] 2 Cr. App. R. 206 (CA (Crim Div)), Swinton Thomas, L.J.; see *R. v Seale (Peter)* Times, July 17, 1997 (CA (Crim Div)), Rose, L.J.
Reg.44, amended: SI 1996/2656 Reg.4, SI 1997/1985 Reg.2
Reg.50, see *R. v Seale (Peter)* Times, July 17, 1997 (CA (Crim Div)), Rose, L.J.
Reg.54A, added: SI 1997/1485 Reg.4
Reg.54B, added: SI 1999/346 Reg.5
Reg.55, amended: SI 1999/2123 Reg.3
Reg.56, amended: SI 1996/1258 Reg.8
Sch.2, amended: SI 1996/646 Reg.2, SI 1998/662 Reg.13, SI 1999/2123 Reg.4
Sch.2 Form 1, amended: SI 1996/1258 Reg.9, Reg.10, Reg.11, SI 1998/662 Reg.14, SI 1999/2737 Reg.6
Sch.2 Form 1A, added: SI 1998/662 Reg.13, Sch.
Sch.2 Form 5, amended: SI 1996/1258 Reg.12, Reg.13, Reg.14, SI 1998/662 Reg.15, SI 1999/2737 Reg.6
Sch.2 Form 6, amended: SI 1997/752 Reg.2, SI 1998/662 Reg.16, SI 1999/815 Reg.3
Sch.2 Form 14, amended: SI 1996/1258 Reg.15
Sch.3 para.2A, added: SI 1996/436 Reg.4
Sch.3 para.2B, added: SI 1998/662 Reg.17
Sch.3 para.6, amended: SI 1997/752 Reg.4
Sch.3 para.6A, added: SI 1996/2307 Reg.5
Sch.3 para.8, amended: SI 1996/436 Reg.5
Sch.3 para.10, amended: SI 1998/662 Reg.18
Sch.3 para.15A, added: SI 1998/662 Reg.19
Sch.3 para.16, amended: SI 1996/1258 Reg.4, SI 1996/2307 Reg.6, SI 1997/752 Reg.5, SI 1999/2737 Reg.7
Sch.3 para.19, amended: SI 1996/436 Reg.6
Sch.3 para.19A, added: SI 1996/436 Reg.7
Sch.4, amended: SI 1996/646 Reg.2, SI 1997/752 Reg.3, SI 1998/662 Reg.20, SI 1999/815 Reg.4

363. National Health Service (Dental Charges) (Scotland) Regulations 1989
applied: SI 1996/177 Sch.1 para.12
Reg.1, amended: SI 1998/2258 Reg.2, SI 1999/724 Reg.14
Reg.2, substituted: SI 1998/2258 Reg.2
Reg.3, substituted: SI 1998/2258 Reg.2
Reg.4, amended: SI 1996/472 Reg.2, SI 1997/585 Reg.2, SI 1998/610 Reg.2, SI 1999/724 Reg.16
Reg.4, applied: SI 1996/177 Sch.1 para.2, SI 1997/585 Reg.3, SI 1998/610 Reg.3
Reg.4, referred to: SI 1996/472 Reg.3
Reg.4, substituted: SI 1998/2258 Reg.2
Reg.5, amended: SI 1998/2258 Reg.2
Reg.6, amended: SI 1998/2258 Reg.2
Reg.6, applied: SI 1996/177 Sch.1 para.2
Reg.8, amended: SI 1998/2258 Reg.2

NO.

363. National Health Service (Dental Charges) (Scotland) Regulations 1989—*cont.*
Reg.9, amended: SI 1998/2258 Reg.2
Reg.10, amended: SI 1998/2258 Reg.2
Reg.11, amended: SI 1999/724 Reg.17
Reg.11A, added: SI 1998/2258 Reg.2
Reg.12, revoked (in part): SI 1998/2258 Reg.2
Sch.1 para.1, amended: SI 1998/2258 Reg.2
Sch.4 para.2, amended: SI 1998/2258 Reg.2

364. National Health Service (Charges to Overseas Visitors) (Scotland) Amendment Regulations 1989
Reg.4, amended: SI 1998/251 Reg.2
Reg.4, revoked (in part): SI 1998/251 Reg.2
Sch.2, amended: SI 1998/251 Reg.3

370. Education (Pre-Scheme Financial Statements) Regulations 1989
revoked: SI 1999/711 Reg.9, Sch.2

371. Local Government Superannuation (Amendment) Regulations 1989
Reg.14, revoked: SI 1996/1680 Reg.49, Sch.5

372. Local Government (Superannuation and Compensation) (Amendment) Regulations 1989
revoked: SI 1996/1680 Reg.49, Sch.5

373. Motor Vehicles (Driving Licences) (Amendment) Regulations 1989
revoked: SI 1996/2824 Reg.2, Sch.1

378. Teachers' Superannuation (Amendment) Regulations 1989
applied: SI 1997/3001 Reg.H12, Sch.15 para.2
revoked: SI 1997/3001 Reg.H12, Sch.14

392. National Health Service (Optical Charges and Payments) (Scotland) Regulations 1989
revoked: SI 1998/642 Reg.24, Sch.4
Part VA, added: SI 1997/1013 Reg.9
Part VA, revoked: SI 1998/642 Reg.24, Sch.4
Reg.1, amended: SI 1996/2354 Reg.2, SI 1996/2556 Reg.2, SI 1997/1013 Reg.2, SI 1997/2492 Reg.2
Reg.1, revoked: SI 1998/642 Reg.24, Sch.4
Reg.4, revoked: SI 1998/642 Reg.24, Sch.4
Reg.6, applied: SI 1997/1013 Reg.12
Reg.6, revoked: SI 1998/642 Reg.24, Sch.4
Reg.6, substituted: SI 1997/1013 Reg.3
Reg.8, amended: SI 1996/2354 Reg.3
Reg.8, revoked: SI 1998/642 Reg.24, Sch.4
Reg.9, added: SI 1997/1013 Reg.12
Reg.9, amended: SI 1997/1013 Reg.3
Reg.9, revoked (in part): SI 1997/1013 Reg.3, SI 1998/642 Reg.24, Sch.4
Reg.10, amended: SI 1997/1013 Reg.4
Reg.10, applied: SI 1997/1013 Reg.12
Reg.10, revoked (in part): SI 1997/1013 Reg.4, SI 1998/642 Reg.24, Sch.4
Reg.11, amended: SI 1997/1013 Reg.5
Reg.11, applied: SI 1997/1013 Reg.12
Reg.11, revoked (in part): SI 1997/1013 Reg.5, SI 1998/642 Reg.24, Sch.4
Reg.12, applied: SI 1996/473 Reg.4, SI 1997/1013 Reg.12
Reg.12, revoked: SI 1998/642 Reg.24, Sch.4
Reg.14, applied: SI 1996/473 Reg.4, SI 1997/1013 Reg.12
Reg.14, revoked: SI 1997/1013 Reg.6, SI 1998/642 Reg.24, Sch.4
Reg.15, amended: SI 1997/1013 Reg.7
Reg.15, applied: SI 1997/1013 Reg.12
Reg.15, revoked (in part): SI 1997/1013 Reg.7, SI 1998/642 Reg.24, Sch.4
Reg.16, applied: SI 1997/1013 Reg.12

1989—cont.

1989—cont.

392. National Health Service (Optical Charges and Payments) (Scotland) Regulations 1989—*cont.*
Reg.16, revoked: SI 1998/642 Reg.24, Sch.4
Reg.17, revoked: SI 1998/642 Reg.24, Sch.4
Reg.18, applied: SI 1996/473 Reg.4, SI 1997/1013 Reg.12
Reg.18, revoked: SI 1998/642 Reg.24, Sch.4
Reg.20, amended: SI 1996/473 Reg.2, SI 1997/1013 Reg.8
Reg.20, revoked: SI 1998/642 Reg.24, Sch.4
Reg.20A, added: SI 1997/1013 Reg.9
Reg.20A, revoked: SI 1998/642 Reg.24, Sch.4
Reg.22, amended: SI 1997/1013 Reg.10
Reg.22, revoked: SI 1998/642 Reg.24, Sch.4
Sch.1, amended: SI 1996/473 Reg.3, SI 1997/1013 Reg.11
Sch.1, revoked: SI 1998/642 Reg.24, Sch.4
Sch.2, revoked: SI 1998/642 Reg.24, Sch.4
Sch.2, substituted: SI 1996/473 Reg.3, Sch, SI 1997/1013 Reg.11, Sch.
Sch.3, amended: SI 1996/473 Reg.3, SI 1997/1013 Reg.11
Sch.3, revoked: SI 1998/642 Reg.24, Sch.4
Sch.3 para.1, revoked: SI 1998/642 Reg.24, Sch.4
Sch.3 para.2, revoked: SI 1998/642 Reg.24, Sch.4

394. National Health Service (Dental Charges) Regulations 1989
Reg.1, amended: SI 1998/2221 Reg.2
Reg.2, substituted: SI 1998/2221 Reg.2
Reg.3, substituted: SI 1998/2221 Reg.2
Reg.4, amended: SI 1996/389 Reg.2, SI 1997/558 Reg.2, SI 1998/490 Reg.2, SI 1999/544 Reg.2
Reg.4, applied: SI 1996/389 Reg.4, SI 1997/558 Reg.4, SI 1998/490 Reg.4, SI 1999/544 Reg.4
Reg.4, substituted: SI 1998/2221 Reg.2
Reg.5, amended: SI 1998/2221 Reg.2
Reg.6, amended: SI 1998/2221 Reg.2
Reg.8, amended: SI 1998/2221 Reg.2
Reg.9, amended: SI 1998/2221 Reg.2
Reg.10, amended: SI 1998/2221 Reg.2
Reg.11, amended: SI 1998/2221 Reg.2
Reg.11A, added: SI 1998/2221 Reg.2
Reg.12, revoked (in part): SI 1998/2221 Reg.2
Sch.1 para.1, amended: SI 1998/2221 Reg.2
Sch.4, amended: SI 1998/2221 Reg.2
Sch.4 para.2, revoked: SI 1998/2221 Reg.2

396. National Health Service (Optical Charges and Payments) Regulations 1989
revoked: SI 1997/818 Reg.24, Sch.4
Reg.1, amended: SI 1996/2328 Reg.2, SI 1996/2574 Reg.2
Reg.1, revoked: SI 1997/818 Reg.24, Sch.4
Reg.6, applied: SI 1997/818 Reg.23
Reg.6, revoked: SI 1997/818 Reg.24, Sch.4
Reg.8, amended: SI 1996/2328 Reg.3
Reg.8, revoked: SI 1997/818 Reg.24, Sch.4
Reg.9, applied: SI 1997/818 Reg.23
Reg.9, revoked: SI 1997/818 Reg.24, Sch.4
Reg.10, applied: SI 1997/818 Reg.23
Reg.10, revoked: SI 1997/818 Reg.24, Sch.4
Reg.11, applied: SI 1997/818 Reg.23
Reg.11, revoked: SI 1997/818 Reg.24, Sch.4
Reg.12, applied: SI 1996/582 Reg.4, SI 1997/818 Reg.23
Reg.12, revoked: SI 1997/818 Reg.24, Sch.4
Reg.14, applied: SI 1996/582 Reg.4, SI 1997/818 Reg.23
Reg.14, revoked: SI 1997/818 Reg.24, Sch.4

396. National Health Service (Optical Charges and Payments) Regulations 1989—*cont.*
Reg.16, applied: SI 1997/818 Reg.23
Reg.16, revoked: SI 1997/818 Reg.24, Sch.4
Reg.18, applied: SI 1996/582 Reg.4, SI 1997/818 Reg.23
Reg.18, revoked: SI 1997/818 Reg.24, Sch.4
Reg.20, amended: SI 1996/582 Reg.2
Reg.20, revoked: SI 1997/818 Reg.24, Sch.4
Sch.1, amended: SI 1996/582 Reg.3
Sch.1, revoked: SI 1997/818 Reg.24, Sch.4
Sch.2, amended: SI 1996/582 Reg.3
Sch.2, revoked: SI 1997/818 Reg.24, Sch.4
Sch.3, revoked: SI 1997/818 Reg.24, Sch.4
Sch.3, substituted: SI 1996/582 Reg.3, Sch

398. Education (School Hours and Policies) (Information) Regulations 1989
revoked (in part): SI 1999/2255 Reg.1
Reg.2, revoked (in part): SI 1999/2255 Reg.1

419. National Health Service (Charges for Drugs and Appliances) Regulations 1989
applied: SI 1997/559 Reg.3, SI 1999/767 Reg.3
Reg.2, amended: SI 1996/583 Reg.2, SI 1998/646 Reg.9, SI 1998/2224 Reg.5, SI 1999/767 Reg.2
Reg.3, amended: SI 1996/583 Reg.3, Reg.4, Sch, SI 1997/559 Reg.2, Sch., SI 1998/491 Reg.2, Sch., SI 1998/646 Reg.9, SI 1999/767 Reg.2, Reg.3, Sch.
Reg.4, amended: SI 1996/583 Reg.3, Sch, SI 1997/559 Reg.2, Sch., SI 1998/491 Reg.2, Sch., SI 1998/646 Reg.9, SI 1999/767 Reg.2, Reg.3, Sch.
Reg.5, amended: SI 1996/583 Reg.3, Sch, SI 1997/559 Reg.2, Sch., SI 1998/491 Reg.2, Sch., SI 1999/767 Reg.2, Reg.3, Sch.
Reg.6, amended: SI 1999/767 Reg.2
Reg.8, amended: SI 1996/583 Reg.3, Sch, SI 1997/559 Reg.2, Sch., SI 1998/491 Reg.2, Sch., SI 1999/767 Reg.3, Sch.
Reg.8, applied: SI 1997/559 Reg.3, SI 1998/491 Reg.3, SI 1999/767 Reg.3
Sch.1, amended: SI 1996/583 Reg.3, Sch, SI 1997/559 Reg.2, Sch., SI 1998/491 Reg.2, Sch., SI 1999/767 Reg.3, Sch.
Sch.1, applied: SI 1997/559 Reg.3, SI 1998/491 Reg.3, SI 1999/767 Reg.3

422. Housing (Scotland) Superannuation Fund Regulations 1989
applied: SI 1998/364 Reg.4, Reg.6, Reg.19, Sch.2 para.2, Sch.2 para.5, Sch.4 para.8
referred to: SI 1998/364 Reg.3, Reg.10, Sch.2 para.4, Sch.2 para.6

424. Harbours Works (Assessment of Environmental Effects) (No.2) Regulations 1989
revoked (in part) SI 1999/3445 Reg.1
Reg.4, amended: SI 1996/1946 Reg.3
Reg.4, referred to: SI 1999/3445 Reg.1
Reg.4, revoked (in part): SI 1999/3445 Reg.1
Reg.5, amended: SI 1996/1946 Reg.3
Reg.5, revoked (in part): SI 1999/3445 Reg.1
Reg.7, amended: SI 1996/1946 Reg.3
Reg.7, revoked (in part): SI 1999/3445 Reg.1
Reg.8, amended: SI 1996/1946 Reg.3
Reg.8, revoked (in part): SI 1999/3445 Reg.1

425. Sea Fish Industry Authority (Levy) Regulations 1988 Confirmatory Order 1989
revoked: SI 1996/160 Art.3

428. European Parliamentary Elections (Welsh Forms) Order 1989
Art.3, amended: SI 1999/1402 Art.4
Art.4, amended: SI 1999/1402 Art.5

NO.

428. European Parliamentary Elections (Welsh Forms) Order 1989—*cont.*
Art.5, amended: SI 1999/1402 Art.5
Sch.1 Form 1, amended: SI 1999/1402 Art.6
Sch.1 Form 2, amended: SI 1999/1402 Art.6
Sch.1 Form 3, amended: SI 1999/1402 Art.6
Sch.1 Form 4, amended: SI 1999/1402 Art.6
Sch.1 Form 5, amended: SI 1999/1402 Art.6
Sch.1 Form 6, amended: SI 1999/1402 Art.6
Sch.2 Form 3, amended: SI 1999/1402 Art.7
Sch.2 Form 4, revoked: SI 1999/1402 Art.2
Sch.2 Form 5, amended: SI 1999/1402 Art.7
Sch.2 Form 6, amended: SI 1999/1402 Art.7

429. Representation of the People (Welsh Forms) Order 1989
Sch.1 Form 3, referred to: 1997 c.61 Sch.3 Table 5

433. Grant-aided Colleges (Scotland) Grant Regulations 1989
applied: SI 1998/1644 Art.5, SI 1998/2208 Art.5, SI 1999/442 Art.5

437. Public Trustee (Fees) (Amendment) Order 1989
revoked: SI 1999/855 Art.32, Sch.

438. Community Charge (Administration and Enforcement) Regulations 1989
applied: SI 1996/1880 Art.32
Part III, applied: SI 1996/1880 Art.37
Reg.4, see *Ellis v Lambeth LBC* Times, September 28, 1999 (CA), Swinton Thomas, L.J.
Reg.22, applied: SI 1996/1880 Art.36
Reg.26, applied: SI 1996/1880 Art.38
Reg.27, amended: SI 1996/1880 Art.47
Reg.31, see *R. v Cannock Justices Ex p. Ireland* [1996] R.A. 463 (CA), Henry, L.J.
Reg.31, applied: SI 1996/1880 Art.40
Reg.32, applied: SI 1996/1880 Art.41, Art.46
Reg.41, see *R. v Clerk to the South Cheshire Justices Ex p. Bold* (1996) 160 J.P. Rep. 1080 (CA), Nourse, L.J.; see *R. v Derwentside Magistrates Court Ex p. Gallimore* [1997] R.V.R. 123 (QBD), Harrison, J.; see *R. v Leeds Justices Ex p. Kennett* [1996] 36 R.V.R. 53 (QBD), Owen, J.; see *R. v Newcastle upon Tyne Justices Ex p. Devine* [1998] R.A. 97 (QBD), Latham, J.
Reg.44, applied: SI 1996/1880 Art.44
Reg.46, amended: SI 1996/2405 Reg.2
Reg.47, amended: SI 1996/675 Art.2, Sch para.8, SI 1996/1880 Art.47
Reg.52, amended: SI 1996/1880 Art.47
Sch.1, applied: SI 1996/1880 Art.35
Sch.3, amended: SI 1996/1880 Art.46
Sch.5, applied: SI 1996/1880 Art.42

439. Valuation and Community Charge Tribunals Regulations 1989
amended: SI 1997/75 Reg.2
Reg.3, substituted: SI 1997/2954 Reg.2
Reg.4, applied: SI 1997/2954 Reg.3
Reg.4, referred to: SI 1997/75 Reg.4, SI 1997/2954 Reg.3
Reg.4, substituted: SI 1996/43, SI 1997/75 Reg.3
Reg.6, amended: SI 1997/75 Reg.3
Reg.6, applied: SI 1997/75 Reg.4, SI 1997/2954 Reg.3
Sch.1, substituted: SI 1996/43, SI 1997/75 Reg.3, SI 1997/2954 Reg.2, Sch.1

440. Valuation and Community Charge Tribunals (Transfer of Jurisdiction) Regulations 1989
Reg.5, applied: SI 1997/1612 Reg.139
Sch.1, applied: SI 1997/1612 Reg.139

NO.

448. Meat (Sterilisation and Staining) Regulations (Northern Ireland) 1989
applied: SI 1996/1633 (NI.12) Art.11

465. Banking Act (Exempt Transactions) (Amendment) Regulations 1989
revoked: SI 1997/817 Reg.16

469. Personal Equity Plan Regulations 1989
Reg.2, amended: SI 1996/846 Reg.3, SI 1997/1716 Reg.3, SI 1998/1869 Reg.3
Reg.4, amended: SI 1996/1355 Reg.3, Reg.4, SI 1997/511 Reg.3, SI 1997/1716 Reg.4, SI 1998/1869 Reg.4
Reg.4A, amended: SI 1997/511 Reg.4
Reg.5, amended: SI 1997/1716 Reg.5
Reg.6, amended: SI 1996/846 Reg.4, SI 1997/1716 Reg.6
Reg.6A, amended: SI 1997/1716 Reg.7
Reg.6B, amended: SI 1996/846 Reg.5, SI 1997/1716 Reg.8
Reg.8, amended: SI 1998/1869 Reg.5
Reg.9, revoked: SI 1998/1869 Reg.6
Reg.10, revoked: SI 1998/1869 Reg.6
Reg.10A, added: SI 1996/846 Reg.6
Reg.10A, revoked: SI 1998/1869 Reg.6
Reg.16, amended: SI 1996/846 Reg.7, SI 1997/1716 Reg.9
Reg.16, revoked (in part): SI 1998/1869 Reg.7
Reg.17, amended: SI 1996/846 Reg.8, SI 1997/1716 Reg.10, SI 1998/1869 Reg.8
Reg.17A, referred to: SI 1996/846 Reg.9
Reg.19, amended: SI 1996/846 Reg.10, SI 1997/1716 Reg.11
Reg.19, revoked (in part): SI 1998/1869 Reg.9
Reg.24, amended (in part): SI 1998/1869 Reg.10
Reg.24A, amended: SI 1997/511 Reg.5, SI 1997/1716 Reg.12, SI 1998/1869 Reg.11
Reg.27, amended: SI 1996/846 Reg.11, SI 1997/1716 Reg.13, SI 1998/1869 Reg.12, Reg.13
Reg.28, amended: SI 1996/846 Reg.12

474. North and Western and North Wales Sea Fisheries District (Variation) Order 1989
revoked: SI 1999/1043 Art.5

477. Pensions Increase (Review) Order 1989
applied: SI 1997/634 Art.3, SI 1998/503 Art.3, Art.4, SI 1999/522 Art.3

490. Laganside Development (Northern Ireland) Order 1989
Art.19, substituted: SI 1999/662 (NI.6) Art.59
Sch.1 para.14, revoked: SI 1996/1297 (NI.7) Art.23, Sch.5

500. Personal and Occupational Pension Schemes (Miscellaneous Amendments) Regulations 1989
Reg.2, revoked: SI 1996/1172 Sch.2
Reg.4, revoked: SI 1997/470 Reg.20, Sch.3

505. Civil Legal Aid (Scotland) Amendment Regulations 1989
revoked: SI 1996/2444 Reg.3, Sch.1

506. Advice and Assistance (Scotland) Amendment Regulations 1989
revoked: SI 1996/2447 Reg.3, Sch.1

507. Community Charge (Deductions from Income Support) (Scotland) Regulations 1989
applied: SI 1999/991 Reg.27, Sch.2 para.9
Reg.1, amended: SI 1996/2344 Reg.2, SI 1998/563 Reg.3, SI 1999/2860 Art.3, Sch.5 para.1, SI 1999/3178 Art.3, Sch.10 para.1

NO.

507. Community Charge (Deductions from Income Support) (Scotland) Regulations 1989—*cont.*
Reg.2, amended: SI 1996/2344 Reg.3, SI 1999/2860 Art.3, Sch.5 para.2, SI 1999/3178 Art.3, Sch.10 para.2
Reg.2, revoked (in part): SI 1999/3178 Art.3, Sch.10 para.2
Reg.2A, added: SI 1996/2344 Reg.4
Reg.2A, amended: SI 1999/2860 Art.3, Sch.5 para.3
Reg.2A, revoked: SI 1999/3178 Art.3, Sch.10 para.3
Reg.3, amended: SI 1999/2860 Art.3, Sch.5 para.4
Reg.3, substituted: SI 1999/3178 Art.3, Sch.10 para.3
Reg.4, amended: SI 1996/2344 Reg.5, SI 1999/3178 Art.3, Sch.10 para.4
Reg.5, substituted: SI 1999/2860 Art.3, Sch.5 para.5, SI 1999/3178 Art.3, Sch.10 para.5
Reg.6, revoked: SI 1999/2860 Art.3, Sch.5 para.6
Reg.6, substituted: SI 1999/3178 Art.3, Sch.10 para.5
Reg.7, revoked: SI 1999/2860 Art.3, Sch.5 para.6, SI 1999/3178 Art.3, Sch.10 para.6
Reg.8, revoked: SI 1999/2860 Art.3, Sch.5 para.6, SI 1999/3178 Art.3, Sch.10 para.6
Reg.9, revoked: SI 1999/2860 Art.3, Sch.5 para.6, SI 1999/3178 Art.3, Sch.10 para.6
Reg.10, revoked: SI 1999/2860 Art.3, Sch.5 para.6, SI 1999/3178 Art.3, Sch.10 para.6
Reg.11, revoked: SI 1999/2860 Art.3, Sch.5 para.6, SI 1999/3178 Art.3, Sch.10 para.6
Sch.1, revoked: SI 1999/2860 Art.3, Sch.5 para.7, SI 1999/3178 Art.3, Sch.10 para.6
Sch.2, revoked: SI 1999/2860 Art.3, Sch.5 para.7, SI 1999/3178 Art.3, Sch.10 para.6

508. Offshore Installations (Safety Zones) Order 1989
revoked: SI 1997/735 Art.3, Sch.2

513. Housing (Right to Buy) (Maximum Discount) Order 1989
applied: SI 1998/2997 Art.5, SI 1999/292 Art.5
revoked (in part): SI 1998/2997 Art.6, SI 1999/292 Art.6

524. Welfare Food Amendment Regulations 1989
revoked: SI 1996/1434 Reg.23, Sch.7

532. Redundancy Payments (Local Government) (Modification) (Amendment) Order 1989
revoked: SI 1999/2277 Art.4, Sch.3

534. Income Support (General) Amendment Regulations 1989
Sch.1 para.6, revoked: SI 1996/206 Reg.28, Sch.3

549. Civil Legal Aid (Matrimonial Proceedings) Regulations 1989
revoked: 1999 c.22 s.106, Sch.15 Part I

550. Legal Advice and Assistance (Scope) Regulations 1989
amended: SI 1997/1731 Reg.3, SI 1998/2831 Reg.3, SI 1999/3377 Reg.4
Reg.2, amended: SI 1999/3377 Reg.5
Reg.3, substituted: SI 1999/3377 Reg.6
Reg.4, amended: SI 1999/3377 Reg.6
Reg.4A, added: SI 1997/1731 Reg.4
Reg.7, amended: SI 1997/997 Reg.3, SI 1998/2831 Reg.4, Reg.5
Reg.8A, added: SI 1998/2831 Reg.6
Reg.9, amended: SI 1997/997 Reg.4
Reg.9, revoked (in part): SI 1999/3377 Reg.9
Sch.2, amended: SI 1997/1078 Reg.4

NO.

550. Legal Advice and Assistance (Scope) Regulations 1989—*cont.*
Sch.2, applied: SI 1997/1078 Reg.4
Sch. para.2, amended: SI 1997/997 Reg.5
Sch. para.2, revoked (in part): SI 1999/3377 Reg.9
Sch.2 para.11, amended: SI 1997/1078 Reg.4

567. Merchant Shipping (Loading and Stability Assessment of Ro-Ro Passenger Ships) (Non-United Kingdom Ships) Regulations 1989
revoked: SI 1998/2514 Reg.1

602. National Health Service (General Dental Services) (Scotland) Amendment Regulations 1989
revoked: SI 1996/177 Reg.38, Sch.8

607. Housing Benefit (Subsidy) Order 1989
Art.3, applied: SI 1996/1217 Art.11, SI 1997/1004 Art.11

615. Road Traffic (Carriage of Explosives) Regulations 1989
applied: SI 1996/1350 Reg.6
revoked: SI 1996/2093 Reg.34

633. European Parliamentary Elections (Amendment) Regulations 1989
revoked: SI 1999/1214 Reg.20, Sch.5
Reg.2, revoked: SI 1999/1214 Reg.20, Sch.5

635. Electricity at Work Regulations 1989
Reg.3, amended: SI 1999/2024 Reg.48, Sch.5 Part II
Reg.19, amended: SI 1996/192 Reg.20, SI 1999/2550 Reg.3
Reg.31, substituted: SI 1997/1993 Reg.2

638. European Economic Interest Grouping Regulations 1989
referred to: SI 1999/268 Reg.3

661. Processed Animal Protein Order 1989
revoked: SI 1999/646 Art.35, Sch.6 Part I

670. Town and Country Planning (Control of Advertisements) Regulations 1989
Reg.8, see *Barking and Dagenham LBC v Mills & Allen Ltd* [1997] 3 P.L.R. 1 (QBD), Simon Brown, L.J.

671. Southern Sea Fisheries District Order 1989
Art.2, amended: SI 1997/1306 Art.2
Sch.1, substituted: SI 1997/1306 Art.2, Sch.

677. Matrimonial and Family Proceedings (Northern Ireland) Order 1989
Art.21, substituted: SI 1999/3147 (NI.11) Art.74, Sch.9 para.2
Art.22, amended: SI 1999/3147 (NI.11) Art.20
Art.25, amended: SI 1999/3147 (NI.11) Art.20, Art.74, Art.76, Sch.9 para.3, Sch.10 Part II
Art.26, substituted: SI 1998/1071 (NI.6) Art.41, Sch.3
Art.41, revoked: SI 1998/1071 (NI.6) Art.41, Sch.5
Part IV, applied: 1999 c.30 s.23, s.28, s.48, SI 1999/3147 (NI.11) Art.21, Art.25, Art.45
Sch.1, applied: SI 1998/1071 (NI.6) Art.41, Sch.4 para.3
Sch.1, revoked: SI 1998/1071 (NI.6) Art.41, Sch.5

728. Low Voltage Electrical Equipment (Safety) Regulations 1989
see *Drummond-Rees v Dorset CC (Trading Standards Department)* (1998) 162 J.P. 651 (QBD), Hooper, J.
applied: SI 1998/2306 Reg.10, Sch.1

762. Motor Vehicles (Driving Licences) (Amendment) (No.2) Regulations 1989
revoked: SI 1996/2824 Reg.2, Sch.1

NO.

768. Food Labelling (Amendment) Regulations 1989
revoked: SI 1996/1499 Reg.49, Sch.9
802. Local Government Superannuation (Scotland) Amendment Regulations 1989
applied: SI 1998/364 Reg.4, Reg.6, Reg.19, Sch.2 para.2, Sch.2 para.5, Sch.4 para.8
referred to: SI 1998/364 Reg.3, Reg.10, Sch.2 para.4, Sch.2 para.6
Reg.30, revoked: SI 1998/192 Reg.52, Sch.2
Reg.31, revoked: SI 1998/192 Reg.52, Sch.2
809. Food Labelling (Scotland) Amendment Regulations 1989
revoked: SI 1996/1499 Reg.49, Sch.9
811. Teachers' Superannuation (Amendment) (No.2) Regulations 1989
applied: SI 1997/3001 Reg.H12, Sch.15 para.2
revoked: SI 1997/3001 Reg.H12, Sch.14
835. Bure Valley Railway Light Railway Order 1989
Art.14, amended: SI 1996/362 Art.5, Sch.4
846. Food (Northern Ireland) Order 1989
revoked: SI 1996/1633 (NI.12) Art.11, Sch Art.17, referred to: 1999 c.28 s.40, Sch.5 para.42
Art.36, applied: SI 1997/1830 Sch.5 Part I
Art.38, applied: SI 1997/1830 Sch.5 Part I
851. National Health Service (General Dental Services) (Scotland) Amendment (No. 2) Regulations 1989
revoked: SI 1996/177 Reg.38, Sch.8
854. Firearms Rules 1989
revoked: SI 1998/1941 r.12, Sch.6
r.3, see *R. v Chelmsford Crown Court Ex p. Farrer* Times, November 5, 1999 (QBD), Hooper, J.
r.3, revoked: SI 1998/1941 r.12, Sch.6
r.4, see *R. v Chelmsford Crown Court Ex p. Farrer* Times, November 5, 1999 (QBD), Hooper, J.
r.4, revoked: SI 1998/1941 r.12, Sch.6
Sch.1 Part II, revoked: SI 1998/1941 r.12, Sch.6
869. Consumer Credit (Exempt Agreements) Order 1989
Art.3, see *Hatfield v Hiscock* [1998] C.C.L.R. 68 (CC) (Southampton), H.H.J. Burford Q.C.
Art.4, applied: SI 1998/1944 Art.3
Art.4, substituted: SI 1998/1944 Art.2, SI 1999/1956 Art.4
Sch.1 Part I, amended: SI 1996/3081 Art.2
Sch.1 Part III, amended: SI 1996/1445 Art.2
Sch.1 Part III, substituted: SI 1996/3081 Art.2
Sch.1 Part IV, amended: SI 1996/1445 Art.2
872. Social Security (Unemployment, Sickness and Invalidity Benefit) Amendment Regulations 1989
Reg.2, revoked (in part): SI 1996/1345 Reg.27, Sch.
880. Stock Transfer (Gilt-Edged Securities) (Exempt Transfer) Regulations 1989
Reg.2, amended: SI 1999/1210 Reg.2
887. Offshore Installations (Safety Zones) (No.2) Order 1989
revoked: SI 1997/735 Art.2, Sch.2
889. Firearms (Scotland) Rules 1989
revoked: SI 1998/1941 r.12, Sch.6
Sch.1 Part II, revoked: SI 1998/1941 r.12, Sch.6
901. Education (Modification of Enactments Relating to Employment) Order 1989
revoked: SI 1998/218 Art.1

NO.

948. Special Hospitals Service Authority (Establishment and Constitution) Order 1989
revoked: SI 1996/490 Art.2
949. Special Hospitals Service Authority (Functions and Membership) Regulations 1989
revoked: SI 1996/489 Reg.17
950. European Economic Interest Grouping (Fees) Regulations 1989
revoked: SI 1999/268 Reg.4
Reg.2, revoked: SI 1999/268 Reg.4
Sch., revoked: SI 1999/268 Reg.4
954. Education (School Curriculum and Related Information) Regulations 1989
applied: SI 1999/2257 Sch. para.21
967. Local Government Superannuation (Scotland) Amendment (No.2) Regulations 1989
applied: SI 1998/364 Reg.4, Reg.6, Reg.19, Sch.2 para.2, Sch.2 para.5, Sch.4 para.8
referred to: SI 1998/364 Reg.3, Reg.10, Sch.2 para.4, Sch.2 para.6
970. Magistrates' Courts (Remands in Custody) Order 1989
Art.2, amended: SI 1997/35 Art.2
971. Offshore Installations (Safety Representatives and Safety Committees) Regulations 1989
Reg.23, amended: SI 1999/3242 Reg.29, Sch.2
1020. Act of Adjournal (Consolidation Amendment No.2) (Forms of Warrant for Execution and Charge for Payment on Fine or Other Financial Penalty) 1989
revoked: SI 1996/513 Sch.2 r.3, Sch.3
1029. Offshore Installations (Emergency Pipe-line Valve) Regulations 1989
revoked: SI 1996/825 Reg.31, Sch.6 Part I
1034. Family Credit and Income Support (General) Amendment Regulations 1989
Reg.6, revoked: SI 1996/206 Reg.28, Sch.3
Reg.10, revoked: SI 1996/206 Reg.28, Sch.3
1058. Non-Domestic Rating (Collection and Enforcement) (Local Lists) Regulations 1989
applied: SI 1996/1880 Art.49
Part II, applied: SI 1996/1880 Art.51, Art.54
Reg.2, amended: SI 1996/675 Art.2, Sch para.9
Reg.5, see *Encon Insulation (Nottingham) Ltd v Nottingham City Council* [1999] R.A. 382 (QBD), David Pannick Q.C.
Reg.13, see *R. v Warrington Justices Ex p. Shone* (1996) 72 P. & C.R. D7 (QBD), Brooke, J.
Reg.13, amended: SI 1998/3089 Reg.3
Reg.14, amended: SI 1998/3089 Reg.4
Reg.15, see *R. v Epping Magistrates Ex p. Howard and Leach* [1997] R.A. 258 (QBD), Turner, J.
Reg.16, amended: SI 1998/3089 Reg.5
Reg.21, amended: SI 1996/1880 Art.61
Reg.23, amended: SI 1996/1880 Art.61
Sch.3, applied: SI 1996/1880 Art.58
Sch.3 para.1, amended: SI 1998/3089 Reg.6, Sch.2
Sch.3 para.2, amended: SI 1998/3089 Reg.6
Sch.3 para.2A, added: SI 1998/3089 Reg.6
Sch.4, added: SI 1998/3089 Reg.5, Sch.1
1060. Non-Domestic Rating (Miscellaneous Provisions) Regulations 1989
Reg.1, amended: SI 1996/619 Art.3
Reg.6, referred to: SI 1999/3453 Reg.3

NO.

1061. Unichem Limited (Allotment of Shares) Order 1989
revoked: SI 1997/1530 Art.2

1087. Town and Country Planning (Determination of Appeals by Appointed Persons) (Amendment) Regulations 1989
revoked: SI 1997/420 Reg.6, Sch

1120. Local Authorities' Traffic Orders (Procedure) (England and Wales) Regulations 1989
see *R. v Camden LBC Ex p. Cran* (1996) 94 L.G.R. 8 (QBD), McCullough, J.
revoked: SI 1996/2489 Reg.2
Reg.6, applied: SI 1996/2489 Reg.2
Reg.16, applied: SI 1996/2489 Reg.2

1125. Consumer Credit (Advertisements) Regulations 1989
see *Coventry CC v Lazarus* (1996) 160 J.P. 188 (QBD), Potts, J.
Reg.1, amended: SI 1999/3177 Reg.5
Sch.1 Part II, amended: SI 1999/2725 Reg.7
Sch.1 Part III, amended: SI 1999/2725 Reg.7
Sch.2 Part II, amended: SI 1999/2725 Reg.7
Sch.2 Part III, amended: SI 1999/2725 Reg.7
Sch.3 para.3, amended: SI 1999/3177 Reg.5
Sch.3 para.4, amended: SI 1999/3177 Reg.5
Sch.3 para.5, revoked: SI 1999/3177 Reg.5
Sch.3 para.6, revoked: SI 1999/3177 Reg.5

1126. Consumer Credit (Quotations) Regulations 1989
revoked: SI 1997/211 Reg.1

1129. Copyright Tribunal Rules 1989
r.48, see *AEI Rediffusion Music Ltd v Phonographic Performance Ltd (Costs)* [1999] E.M.L.R. 129 (Ch D), Neuberger, J.; see *AEI Rediffusion Music Ltd v Phonographic Performance Ltd (Costs)* [1999] 2 All E.R. 299 (CA), Mummery, L.J.

1130. Design Right (Proceedings before Comptroller) Rules 1989
r.4, amended: SI 1999/3195 r.3
r.5, amended: SI 1999/3195 r.4
r.18, amended: SI 1999/3195 r.5
r.20, amended: SI 1999/3195 r.6
r.21, amended: SI 1999/3195 r.7

1132. Value Added Tax (General) (Amendment) Regulations 1989
Reg.23, see *BJ Rice and Associates v Customs and Excise Commissioners* Times, February 14, 1996 (CA), Staughton, L.J.

1139. Education (Reorganisation in Inner London) (Compensation) Regulations 1989
Reg.1, amended: SI 1996/1935 Reg.3, Reg.4
Reg.8, applied: SI 1996/1935 Reg.7
Reg.9, amended: SI 1996/1935 Reg.5, Reg.7
Reg.11, amended: SI 1996/1935 Reg.6

1140. Non-Contentious Probate Fees (Amendment) Order 1989
revoked: SI 1999/688 Art.6 (with savings), Sch.2 (with savings)

1141. Health and Safety (Miscellaneous Modifications) Regulations 1989
revoked: SI 1998/2307 Reg.17, Sch.2

1147. Water Supply (Water Quality) Regulations 1989
Reg.23, amended: SI 1996/3001 Reg.8
Reg.23A, added: SI 1999/1524 Reg.2
Reg.23B, added: SI 1999/1524 Reg.2
Reg.28, amended: SI 1999/1524 Reg.2
Reg.29, amended: SI 1999/1524 Reg.2
Sch.2 Table B, applied: SI 1998/994 Sch.4 Part I
Sch.2 Table C, applied: SI 1998/994 Sch.4 Part I

NO.

1148. Surface Waters (Classification) Regulations 1989
revoked: SI 1996/3001 Reg.8

1151. Control of Pollution (Consents for Discharges etc.) (Secretary of State Functions) Regulations 1989
revoked: SI 1996/2971 Reg.18
Reg.2, applied: SI 1996/2909 Art.4
Reg.2, referred to: SI 1996/2971 Reg.18
Reg.2, revoked: SI 1996/2971 Reg.18
Reg.3, applied: SI 1996/2909 Art.4
Reg.3, referred to: SI 1996/2971 Reg.18
Reg.3, revoked: SI 1996/2971 Reg.18
Reg.4, applied: SI 1996/2909 Art.4
Reg.4, referred to: SI 1996/2971 Reg.18
Reg.4, revoked: SI 1996/2971 Reg.18
Reg.5, applied: SI 1996/2909 Art.4
Reg.5, referred to: SI 1996/2971 Reg.18
Reg.5, revoked: SI 1996/2971 Reg.18
Reg.6, applied: SI 1996/2909 Art.4
Reg.6, referred to: SI 1996/2971 Reg.18
Reg.6, revoked: SI 1996/2971 Reg.18
Reg.7, applied: SI 1996/2909 Art.4
Reg.7, referred to: SI 1996/2971 Reg.18
Reg.7, revoked: SI 1996/2971 Reg.18

1157. Control of Pollution (Discharges by the National Rivers Authority) Regulations 1989
applied: SI 1996/2909 Art.4
referred to: SI 1996/2971 Reg.18
revoked: SI 1996/2971 Reg.18

1159. Water Supply and Sewerage Services (Customer Service Standards) Regulations 1989
Reg.7AA, added: SI 1996/3065 Reg.2

1160. Control of Pollution (Registers) Regulations 1989
applied: SI 1996/2971 Reg.15
revoked: SI 1996/2971 Reg.18

1162. Water Appointment (Monopolies and Mergers Commission) Regulations 1989
revoked: SI 1999/3088 Reg.2

1180. Town and Country Planning (Cardiff Bay Urban Development) Special Development Order 1989
Art.2, amended: SI 1996/525 Sch para.12
Art.6, amended: SI 1996/525 Sch para.12

1181. Education (National Curriculum) (Temporary Exceptions for Individual Pupils) Regulations 1989
amended: SI 1999/2267 Reg.7
revoked (in part): SI 1999/1815 Reg.2 (with savings)
Reg.6, amended: SI 1999/2267 Reg.7
Reg.9, amended: SI 1999/2267 Reg.7
Reg.11, amended: SI 1999/2267 Reg.7
Reg.13, amended: SI 1999/2267 Reg.7

1212. Copyright (Librarians and Archivists) (Copying of Copyright Material) Regulations 1989
Sch.1 Part A, applied: SI 1996/2967 Reg.35
Sch.1 para.4, amended: SI 1999/1042 Art.3, Sch.1 para.15

1263. Sludge (Use in Agriculture) Regulations 1989
Reg.7, amended: SI 1996/593 Reg.3, Sch.2 para.5, SI 1996/973 Reg.2, Sch para.9
Reg.8, amended: SI 1996/593 Reg.3, Sch.2 para.5, SI 1996/973 Reg.2, Sch para.9
Sch.2 para.2, amended: SI 1996/593 Reg.3, Sch.2 para.5, SI 1996/973 Reg.2, Sch para.9

1276. Banks (Administration Proceedings) Order 1989
Sch., amended: SI 1998/1129 Art.2, Sch.1 para.9

1277. Education (School Premises) (Amendment) Regulations 1989
revoked: SI 1996/360 Sch.1

1284. Sea Fish (Specified Sea Area) (Regulation of Nets and Prohibition of Fishing Methods) Order 1989
Art.2, amended: SI 1999/74 Art.2
Art.3, amended: SI 1999/74 Art.2

1287. Education (Grant-Maintained Schools) (Finance) Regulations 1989
applied: SI 1996/889 Reg.3, SI 1998/799 Reg.3
referred to: SI 1997/996 Reg.3

1288. Education (Pre-Scheme Financial Statements) (Amendment) Regulations 1989
revoked: SI 1999/711 Reg.9, Sch.2

1297. Taxes (Interest Rate) Regulations 1989
Reg.2, amended: SI 1998/3176 Reg.3, Reg.4
Reg.3, amended: SI 1997/2707 Reg.2, SI 1998/310 Reg.2, SI 1999/2438 Reg.3
Reg.3, substituted: SI 1996/3187 Reg.2
Reg.3A, amended: SI 1998/3176 Reg.5
Reg.3AA, added: SI 1996/3187 Reg.2
Reg.3AA, amended: SI 1999/2637 Reg.3
Reg.3AA, revoked (in part): SI 1999/2438 Reg.4
Reg.3AB, added: SI 1996/3187 Reg.2
Reg.3AB, amended: SI 1999/2438 Reg.5
Reg.3AC, added: SI 1999/2637 Reg.4
Reg.3B, amended: SI 1998/3176 Reg.7
Reg.3BA, added: SI 1998/3176 Reg.8
Reg.3BB, added: SI 1998/3176 Reg.8
Reg.3BB, amended: SI 1999/1928 Reg.3
Reg.3ZA, added: SI 1998/3176 Reg.6
Reg.3ZB, added: SI 1998/3176 Reg.6
Reg.5, amended: SI 1996/54 Reg.2, SI 1996/1321 Art.2, SI 1996/2644 Reg.2, SI 1997/1681 Reg.2, SI 1999/419 Reg.2

1299. Income Tax (Stock Lending) Regulations 1989
revoked: SI 1997/987 Reg.2 (with savings), Sch.1 (with savings)
Reg.2, amended: SI 1996/1228 Reg.3, Reg.4
Reg.2, revoked: SI 1997/987 Reg.2 (with savings), Sch.1 (with savings)
Reg.3B, amended: SI 1996/1228 Reg.5
Reg.3B, revoked: SI 1997/987 Reg.2 (with savings), Sch.1 (with savings)
Reg.3C, revoked: SI 1997/987 Reg.2 (with savings), Sch.1 (with savings)
Reg.4, revoked: SI 1997/987 Reg.2 (with savings), Sch.1 (with savings)
Reg.4, substituted: SI 1996/1228 Reg.6
Reg.6, revoked (in part): SI 1996/1228 Reg.7
Reg.6A, revoked: SI 1997/987 Reg.2 (with savings), Sch.1 (with savings)
Reg.6B, revoked: SI 1997/987 Reg.2 (with savings), Sch.1 (with savings)
Reg.7, revoked: SI 1996/1228 Reg.7
Reg.8, revoked: SI 1996/1228 Reg.7
Reg.9, revoked: SI 1997/987 Reg.2 (with savings), Sch.1 (with savings)

1305. Merseyside Development Corporation (Vesting of Land) (General) Order 1989
revoked: SI 1998/769 Art.3, Sch.

1306. Outer Space Act 1986 (Fees) Regulations 1989
Reg.3, amended: SI 1998/2032 Reg.2

1319. Education (Teachers) Regulations 1989
referred to: SI 1999/2817 Reg.2, Sch.1 para.8
Reg.14, applied: SI 1999/2166 Reg.2, Sch.1 para 6, SI 1999/2817 Reg.2, Sch.1 para.6
Reg.15, applied: SI 1999/2166 Reg.2, Sch.1 para 1, SI 1999/2817 Reg.2, Sch.1 para.1
Reg.16, applied: SI 1999/2166 Reg.2, Sch.1 para 2, SI 1999/2817 Reg.2, Sch.1 para.2
Sch.2 para.2, applied: SI 1999/2166 Reg.10, Sch.2 para.2
Sch.3 para.2, applied: SI 1999/2166 Reg.2, Sch.1 para 4, SI 1999/2817 Reg.2, Reg.10, Sch.1 para.4, Sch.2 para.2
Sch.6, applied: SI 1999/2166 Reg.2, Sch.1 para 6, SI 1999/2817 Reg.2, Sch.1 para.6

1321. Community Charge Benefits (General) Regulations 1989
Reg.58, applied: SI 1996/1217 Art.19
Reg.60, applied: SI 1996/1217 Art.17, Art.18, Art.19, SI 1998/562 Art.19
Reg.60, referred to: SI 1997/1004 Art.18, Art.19, SI 1998/562 Art.18
Reg.63, applied: SI 1996/1217 Art.18

1322. Community Charge Benefits (Transitional) Order 1989
Art.2, applied: SI 1996/1217 Art.11, SI 1997/1004 Art.11, SI 1998/562 Art.19

1323. Income Support (General) Amendment No.2 Regulations 1989
Reg.4, revoked: SI 1996/206 Reg.28, Sch.3
Reg.5, revoked: SI 1996/206 Reg.28, Sch.3
Reg.6, revoked: SI 1996/206 Reg.28, Sch.3
Reg.7, revoked: SI 1996/206 Reg.28, Sch.3

1324. Social Security (Unemployment, Sickness and Invalidity Benefit) Amendment No.2 Regulations 1989
Reg.3, revoked: SI 1996/1345 Reg.27, Sch.
Reg.4, revoked: SI 1996/1345 Reg.27, Sch.
Reg.5, revoked: SI 1996/1345 Reg.27, Sch.
Reg.6, revoked: SI 1996/1345 Reg.27, Sch.
Reg.7, revoked: SI 1996/1345 Reg.27, Sch.
Reg.9, revoked: SI 1996/1345 Reg.27, Sch.
Reg.10, revoked: SI 1996/1345 Reg.27, Sch.

1330. Visiting Forces and International Headquarters (Application of Law) (Amendment) Order 1989
revoked: SI 1999/1736 Art.19, Sch.9

1339. Limitation (Northern Ireland) Order 1989
applied: SI 1997/2778 (NI.19) Art.45, SI 1998/1071 (NI.6) Art.17
Art.2, amended: 1996 c.23 Sch.3 para.52
Art.6, amended: 1996 c.31 s.6
Art.7, amended: SI 1997/1180 (NI.9) Art.8
Art.48, amended: 1996 c.31 s.6
Art.51, substituted: 1996 c.31 s.6
Art.72, revoked: 1996 c.23 Sch.4
Sch.3 para.1, revoked: 1996 c.23 Sch.4
Sch.3 para.13, revoked: SI 1998/1071 (NI.6) Art.41, Sch.5
Sch.3 para.17, revoked: SI 1998/1071 (NI.6) Art.41, Sch.5
Sch.3 para.53, amended: 1996 c.23 Sch.3 para.52

1341. Police and Criminal Evidence (Northern Ireland) Order 1989
amended: SI 1996/1296 Art.16
applied: SI 1996/716 Art.16, 1998 c.32 s.56, SI 1998/1504 (NI.9) Art.6, SI 1998/1531 Reg.4
referred to: SI 1999/1261 Reg.4, SI 1999/2821 Reg.4, SI 1999/2822 Reg.4

NO.

1989—cont.

1341. Police and Criminal Evidence (Northern Ireland) Order 1989—*cont.*

Art.2, amended: SI 1997/2983 (NI.21) Art.13, Sch.1 para.6, SI 1998/1504 (NI.9) Art.65, Sch.5 para.32, Sch.6

Art.2, referred to: SI 1998/1504 (NI.9) Art.65, Sch.6

Art.4, amended: 1996 c.22 Sch.6 para.12

Art.7, amended: 1998 c.32 s.74, Sch.4 para.18

Art.10, amended: SI 1996/1296 Art.16, 1999 c.33 s.169, Sch.14 para.90

Art.10, applied: 1996 c.49 s.7, 1997 c.43 Sch.1 para.9

Art.12, applied: SI 1996/696 Reg.8

Art.13, applied: SI 1996/696 Reg.8

Art.14, applied: SI 1996/696 Reg.8

Art.17, applied: SI 1996/3151 Sch.2 para.11

Art.18, applied: SI 1996/3151 Sch.2 para.11

Art.19, amended: SI 1998/1504 (NI.9) Art.65, Sch.5 para.33

Art.22, applied: SI 1996/3151 Sch.2 para.11

Art.23, applied: SI 1996/1299 (NI.9) Art.52, SI 1996/3151 Sch.2 para.11

Art.24, amended: 1998 c.32 s.74, Sch.4 para.18, 1999 c.33 s.169, Sch.14 para.90

Art.24, applied: SI 1996/1299 (NI.9) Art.52

Art.26, amended: SI 1996/3160 (NI.24) Art.55, SI 1997/1180 (NI.9) Art.4, SI 1997/2572 Art.16, SI 1997/2592 Art.12, SI 1998/1071 (NI.6) Art.26

Art.26, applied: SI 1996/2721 Reg.11, SI 1997/2572 Art.16, SI 1997/2592 Art.12, SI 1998/1065 Art.12, SI 1998/1531 Reg.4, SI 1998/1752 Art.18, SI 1999/1261 Reg.4, SI 1999/1516 Reg.9, SI 1999/2821 Reg.4, SI 1999/2822 Reg.4, SI 1999/3133 Art.8

Art.30, amended: 1996 c.22 Sch.6 para.13

Art.38, amended: SI 1998/1504 (NI.9) Art.65, Sch.6

Art.38, revoked (in part): SI 1998/1504 (NI.9) Art.65, Sch.6

Art.39, amended: SI 1998/1504 (NI.9) Art.65, Sch.5 para.34

Art.50, amended: 1998 c.32 s.74, Sch.4 para.18

Art.52, amended: SI 1998/1504 (NI.9) Art.65, Sch.5 para.35

Art.53, amended: SI 1996/1299 (NI.9) Art.57, Sch.3 para.10

Art.54, amended: 1996 c.22 Sch.6 para.14

Art.54, revoked (in part): 1996 c.22 Sch.7 Part II

Art.56, amended: 1998 c.32 s.74, Sch.4 para.18

Art.57, amended: SI 1996/1299 (NI.9) Art.57, Sch.3 para.11

Art.57, applied: SI 1998/1504 (NI.9) Art.10

Art.58, revoked: SI 1998/1504 (NI.9) Art.65, Sch.6

Art.59, amended: SI 1996/1299 (NI.9) Art.57, Sch.3 para.12

Art.60, amended: 1998 c.9 s.7, Sch.1 para.2

Art.61, amended: 1996 c.22 s.48, Sch.6 para.15, 1999 c.33 s.169, Sch.14 para.90

Art.62, amended: SI 1996/1320 (NI.10) Sch.3 para.35

Art.63A, amended: 1996 c.25 Sch.4 para.27

Art.66, amended: 1996 c.46 Sch.1 para.110

Art.66, applied: SI 1996/1299 (NI.9) Sch.2 para.8

Art.67, amended: SI 1997/2983 (NI.21) Art.13, Sch.1 para.6, SI 1999/2789 (NI.8) Art.40, Sch.3

Art.68, revoked: SI 1999/2789 (NI.8) Art.37, Art.40, Sch.3

1341. Police and Criminal Evidence (Northern Ireland) Order 1989—*cont.*

Art.70, amended: 1996 c.46 Sch.6 para.15, SI 1998/1504 (NI.9) Art.65, Sch.5 para.36

Art.73, revoked: SI 1996/3160 (NI.24) Sch.7

Art.74, amended: 1996 c.22 Sch.6 para.16

Art.76, amended: 1996 c.22 Sch.6 para.17

Art.78, amended: SI 1999/2789 (NI.8) Art.40, Sch.1 para.3

Art.79, amended: SI 1999/2789 (NI.8) Art.40, Sch.1 para.3, Sch.3

Art.79, revoked (in part): SI 1999/2789 (NI.8) Art.40, Sch.1 para.3, Sch.3

Art.79A, added: SI 1999/2789 (NI.8) Art.40, Sch.1 para.3

Art.81, amended: 1996 c.25 Sch.4 para.25, SI 1998/1504 (NI.9) Art.65, Sch.5 para.37

Art.81, referred to: SI 1999/2789 (NI.8) Art.40, Sch.2 para.2

Art.81, revoked: SI 1999/2789 (NI.8) Art.40, Sch.3

Art.81A, amended: 1996 c.25 Sch.4 para.25, SI 1998/1504 (NI.9) Art.65, Sch.5 para.38

Art.81A, referred to: SI 1999/2789 (NI.8) Art.40, Sch.2 para.2

Art.81A, revoked: SI 1999/2789 (NI.8) Art.40, Sch.3

Art.81B, revoked: SI 1999/2789 (NI.8) Art.40, Sch.3

Art.82, revoked: 1998 c.32 s.74, Sch.6

Art.83, revoked: 1998 c.32 s.74, Sch.6

Art.84, amended: 1998 c.32 s.74, Sch.4 para.18

Art.87, amended: SI 1996/1299 (NI.9) Art.57, Sch.3 para.13

Part III, amended: SI 1996/1296 Art.16

Sch.1, amended: SI 1996/1296 Art.16

Sch.2, revoked (in part): 1998 c.2 s.18, Sch.4, SI 1998/1504 (NI.9) Art.65, Sch.6

Sch.3, revoked: SI 1999/2789 (NI.8) Art.40, Sch.3

Sch.5 Part II, amended: SI 1996/1320 (NI.10) Sch.3 para.36

Sch.6 para.6, revoked (in part): SI 1998/1504 (NI.9) Art.65, Sch.6

Sch.6 para.16, revoked (in part): SI 1999/2789 (NI.8) Art.40, Sch.3

1342. Social Security (Northern Ireland) Order 1989

referred to: 1998 c.47 s.87

Sch.4 para.22, revoked (in part): SI 1997/1183 (NI.12) Art.31, Sch.4

Sch.5 para.5, applied: SI 1996/1919 (NI.16) Art.111

Sch.5 para.15, revoked: SI 1996/1919 (NI.16) Art.257, Sch.3

1344. Treatment of Offenders (Northern Ireland) Order 1989

Art.3, revoked: SI 1996/3160 (NI.24) Sch.7

Art.4, revoked: SI 1998/1504 (NI.9) Art.65, Sch.6

Art.5, revoked: SI 1998/1504 (NI.9) Art.65, Sch.6

Art.6, revoked: SI 1998/1504 (NI.9) Art.65, Sch.6

Art.10, revoked: SI 1996/3160 (NI.24) Sch.7

Art.11, applied: SI 1996/1320 (NI.10) Art.28

Art.11, revoked: SI 1996/3160 (NI.24) Sch.7

Sch.1 para.2, revoked: SI 1996/3160 (NI.24) Sch.7

Sch.1 para.3, revoked: SI 1996/3160 (NI.24) Sch.7

Sch.1 para.4, revoked: SI 1996/3160 (NI.24) Sch.7

NO.

1344. Treatment of Offenders (Northern Ireland) Order 1989—*cont.*
Sch.1 para.5, revoked: SI 1996/3160 (NI.24) Sch.7
Sch.1 para.6, revoked: SI 1996/3160 (NI.24) Sch.7
Sch.1 para.7, revoked: SI 1996/3160 (NI.24) Sch.7
Sch.1 para.8, revoked: SI 1996/3160 (NI.24) Sch.7
Sch.1 para.15, revoked: SI 1998/1504 (NI.9) Art.65, Sch.6
Sch.1 para.16, revoked: SI 1998/1504 (NI.9) Art.65, Sch.6
Sch.1 para.17, revoked: SI 1998/1504 (NI.9) Art.65, Sch.6
Sch.1 para.18, revoked: SI 1998/1504 (NI.9) Art.65, Sch.6
Sch.1 para.19, revoked: SI 1998/1504 (NI.9) Art.65, Sch.6
Sch.1 para.22, revoked: SI 1996/3160 (NI.24) Sch.7
Sch.1 para.23, revoked: SI 1996/3160 (NI.24) Sch.7
Sch.1 para.26, revoked: SI 1998/1504 (NI.9) Art.65, Sch.6
Sch.1 para.27, revoked: SI 1996/3160 (NI.24) Sch.7

1352. Education (Financial Delegation to Schools) (Mandatory Exceptions) Regulations 1989
applied: SI 1996/395 Reg.3

1355. Cider and Perry Regulations 1989
Reg.11, amended: SI 1996/2287 Reg.2, SI 1997/659 Reg.2
Reg.12, amended: SI 1996/2287 Reg.2
Reg.12A, added: SI 1996/2287 Reg.2
Reg.13, amended: SI 1996/2287 Reg.2, SI 1997/659 Reg.2
Reg.23, amended: SI 1996/2287 Reg.2, SI 1997/659 Reg.2

1356. Wine and Made-wine Regulations 1989
Reg.11, amended: SI 1996/2752 Reg.2, SI 1997/658 Reg.2
Reg.12, amended: SI 1996/2752 Reg.2
Reg.12A, added: SI 1996/2752 Reg.2
Reg.13, amended: SI 1996/2752 Reg.2, SI 1997/658 Reg.2
Reg.14, amended: SI 1997/658 Reg.2
Reg.23, amended: SI 1996/2752 Reg.2

1389. Black Country Development Corporation (Vesting of Land) (Borough of Walsall) Order 1989
revoked: SI 1998/769 Art.3, Sch.

1390. Black Country Development Corporation (Vesting of Land) (General) Order 1989
revoked: SI 1998/769 Art.3, Sch.

1391. London Docklands Development Corporation (Vesting of Land) (Port of London Authority and London Borough of Newham) Order 1989
revoked: SI 1998/769 Art.3, Sch.

1392. London Docklands Development Corporation (Vesting of Land) (Thames Water Authority) Order 1989
revoked: SI 1998/769 Art.3, Sch.

1393. Merseyside Development Corporation (Vesting of Land) (Transport Land) Order 1989
revoked: SI 1998/769 Art.3, Sch.

1394. Sheffield Development Corporation (Vesting of Land) (British Railways Board) Order 1989
revoked: SI 1998/769 Art.3, Sch.

NO.

1395. Black Country Development Corporation (Vesting of Land) (British Railways Board) Order 1989
revoked: SI 1998/769 Art.3, Sch.

1396. Black Country Development Corporation (Vesting of Land) (Central Electricity Generating Board) Order 1989
revoked: SI 1998/769 Art.3, Sch.

1403. Leeds Development Corporation (Vesting of Land) (British Railways Board) Order 1989
revoked: SI 1998/769 Art.3, Sch.

1404. Leeds Development Corporation (Vesting of Land) (General) Order 1989
revoked: SI 1998/769 Art.3, Sch.

1405. Tyne and Wear Development Corporation (Vesting of Land) (Port of Tyne Authority and British Railways Board) Order 1989
revoked: SI 1998/769 Art.3, Sch.

1406. Tyne and Wear Development Corporation (Vesting of Land) (Various Local Authorities) Order 1989
revoked: SI 1998/769 Art.3, Sch.

1489. Aerodromes (Designation) (Facilities for Consultation) Order 1989
revoked: SI 1996/1392 Art.3

1490. Civil Legal Aid (Scotland) (Fees) Regulations 1989
Reg.5, amended: SI 1999/1042 Art.3, Sch.1 para.16
Reg.10, amended: SI 1999/1042 Art.3, Sch.1 para.16
Sch.1 Table, amended: SI 1997/689 Reg.3
Sch.2 Table, amended: SI 1997/689 Reg.4
Sch.3, amended: SI 1997/689 Reg.5
Sch.3 para.6, substituted: SI 1997/689 Reg.5

1491. Criminal Legal Aid (Scotland) (Fees) Regulations 1989
applied: SI 1999/491 Reg.5
Reg.2, amended: SI 1999/1042 Art.3, Sch.1 para.17
Reg.3, amended: SI 1999/491 Reg.6
Reg.8, amended: SI 1997/719 Reg.4
Sch.1, amended: SI 1999/1042 Art.3, Sch.1 para.17
Sch.1 para.5, substituted: SI 1997/719 Reg.5
Sch.1 para.6, amended: SI 1999/1042 Art.3, Sch.1 para.17
Sch.1 para.6, revoked: SI 1997/719 Reg.5

1492. Advice and Assistance (Scotland) Amendment (No.2) Regulations 1989
revoked: SI 1996/2447 Reg.3, Sch.1

1503. Education (School Government) Regulations 1989
referred to: SI 1998/2763 Reg.3, SI 1999/362 Reg.4
Reg.9, amended: SI 1996/2050 Reg.3
Reg.10, amended: SI 1996/2050 Reg.4
Reg.13, amended: SI 1996/2050 Reg.5
Reg.14, amended: SI 1996/2050 Reg.6
Reg.23, amended: SI 1996/2050 Reg.7
Sch. para.2, amended: SI 1996/2050 Reg.8, SI 1999/711 Reg.7
Sch. para.3, amended: SI 1996/2050 Reg.8
Sch. para.4, amended: SI 1996/2050 Reg.8
Sch. para.7, amended: SI 1996/2050 Reg.8

1588. Local Government (Direct Labour Organisations) (Competition) Regulations 1989
Reg.7A, added: SI 1997/561 Reg.2
Reg.7B, added: SI 1997/2756 Reg.2

NO.

1588. Local Government (Direct Labour Organisations) (Competition) Regulations 1989—*cont.*
Reg.8, amended: SI 1997/561 Reg.2, SI 1997/2756 Reg.2, SI 1998/1805 Reg.2
Reg.9A, added: SI 1997/561 Reg.2
Reg.9B, added: SI 1997/2756 Reg.2
Reg.9C, added: SI 1998/1805 Reg.2

1611. Special Hospitals Service Authority (Functions and Membership) Amendment Regulations 1989
revoked: SI 1996/489 Reg.17

1612. Motor Vehicles (Driving Licences) (Amendment) (No.3) Regulations 1989
revoked: SI 1996/2824 Reg.2, Sch.1

1625. Bodmin Moor Railway Centre Light Railway Order 1989
Art.10, amended: SI 1996/362 Art.5, Sch.4

1628. Assured and Protected Tenancies (Lettings to Students) (Amendment) Regulations 1989
revoked: SI 1998/1967 Reg.6, Sch.3

1641. Personal and Occupational Pension Schemes (Miscellaneous Amendments) (No.2) Regulations 1989
Reg.3, revoked: SI 1996/1655 Reg.12, Sch.4

1642. Social Security (Abolition of Earnings Rule) (Consequential) Regulations 1989
Reg.3, revoked: SI 1996/2745 Reg.18, Sch.4

1671. Offshore Installations and Pipeline Works (First-Aid) Regulations 1989
Reg.7, amended: SI 1999/3242 Reg.25

1672. Offshore Installations (Operational Safety, Health and Welfare and Life-Saving Appliances) (Revocations) Regulations 1989
revoked: SI 1998/2306 Reg.39, Sch.4

1690. Social Security Benefit (Dependency and Computation of Earnings) Amendment Regulations 1989
Reg.3, revoked: SI 1996/2745 Reg.18, Sch.4
Reg.4, amended: SI 1996/2745 Reg.15

1716. M32 Motorway (Hambrook Interchange to Lower Ashley Road Interchange) and Connecting Roads Scheme 1989
Sch. Part II, amended: SI 1999/1416 para.1

1790. Noise at Work Regulations 1989
referred to: SI 1998/2306 Reg.12
Reg.2, amended: SI 1999/2024 Reg.48, Sch.5 Part II
Reg.3, substituted: SI 1997/1993 Reg.3
Reg.9, amended: SI 1996/341 Reg.8, Sch.3 Part II

1796. Road Vehicles Lighting Regulations 1989
applied: SI 1997/1639 Reg.3, SI 1999/854 Art.3, Sch. para.1
Reg.7, applied: SI 1996/2095 Sch.2 para.9
Reg.7, referred to: SI 1996/2093 Reg.4
Reg.9B, added: SI 1996/3016 Reg.3
Reg.11, applied: SI 1996/3013 Sch.2 Item 6
Reg.12, applied: SI 1996/3013 Sch.2 Item 6
Reg.13, applied: SI 1996/3013 Sch.2 Item 6
Reg.14, applied: SI 1996/3013 Sch.2 Item 6
Reg.15, applied: SI 1996/3013 Sch.2 Item 6
Reg.16, applied: SI 1996/3013 Sch.2 Item 6
Reg.17, applied: SI 1996/3013 Sch.2 Item 6
Reg.18, applied: SI 1996/3013 Sch.2 Item 6
Reg.19, applied: SI 1996/3013 Sch.2 Item 6
Reg.20, applied: SI 1996/3013 Sch.2 Item 6

1798. Merchant Shipping (Distress Signals and Prevention of Collisions) Regulations 1989
revoked: SI 1996/75 Reg.1

NO.

1815. London Government Reorganisation (Pensions etc.) Order 1989
Art.7, revoked (in part): SI 1996/1680 Reg.49, Sch.5
Sch.1 para.1, amended: 1999 c.29 s.403
Sch.1 para.1, applied: 1999 c.29 s.403
Sch.1 para.2, amended: 1999 c.29 s.403
Sch.1 para.2, applied: 1999 c.29 s.403

1833. Cholsey and Wallingford Light Railway Order 1989
Art.9, amended: SI 1996/362 Art.5, Sch.4

1849. Town and Country Planning (Simplified Planning Zones) (Excluded Development) Order 1989
Art.2, amended: SI 1996/525 Sch para.10

1851. Offshore Installations (Safety Zones) (No.3) Order 1989
revoked: SI 1997/735 Reg.3, Sch.2

1852. Medicines (Prescription Only, Pharmacy and General Sale) Amendment Order 1989
Art.2, revoked: SI 1997/1830 Art.16
Art.3, revoked: SI 1997/1830 Art.16
Art.4, revoked: SI 1997/1830 Art.16
Art.5, revoked: SI 1997/1830 Art.16
Art.6, revoked: SI 1997/1830 Art.16
Sch.1, revoked: SI 1997/1830 Art.16
Sch.2, revoked: SI 1997/1830 Art.16

1880. Carriage of Passengers and their Luggage by Sea (United Kingdom Carriers) (Amendment) Order 1989
revoked: SI 1998/2917 Art.2

1903. Health and Safety (Enforcing Authority) Regulations 1989
applied: SI 1996/1513 Reg.10, SI 1996/1647 Reg.2
referred to: SI 1996/890 Reg.6, SI 1996/2094 Reg.8
revoked: SI 1998/494 Reg.7, Sch.3
Reg.2, amended: SI 1996/1592 Reg.34, Sch.9 para.4, SI 1997/553 Reg.11
Reg.2, revoked: SI 1998/494 Reg.7, Sch.3
Reg.3, amended: SI 1997/553 Reg.11
Reg.3, referred to: SI 1996/2092 Reg.19, SI 1996/2093 Reg.30
Reg.3, revoked: SI 1998/494 Reg.7, Sch.3
Sch.1 para.1, revoked: SI 1998/494 Reg.7, Sch.3

1941. Cowes Harbour Revision Order 1989
Art.2, amended: SI 1996/362 Art.5, Sch.4

1952. Insurance Companies (Accounts and Statements) (Amendment) Regulations 1989
revoked: SI 1996/943 Reg.35, Sch.7

1958. Northern Ireland (Emergency Provisions) Act 1991 (Amendment) Order 1989
revoked: 1996 c.22 Sch.7 Part II

1976. Borough of Warrington (Electoral Arrangements) Order 1989
applied: SI 1996/1863 Art.7

1996. Turks and Caicos Islands (Territorial Sea) Order 1989
Sch., substituted: SI 1998/1260 Art.2

1999. Licensing and Clubs (Amendment) (Northern Ireland) Order 1989
revoked: SI 1996/3159 (NI.23) Sch.9

2000. Judicial Committee (Fees) Order 1989
revoked: SI 1996/3170 Art.2

2005. Collision Regulations (Seaplanes) Order 1989
revoked: SI 1996/75 Reg.1

NO.

2009. **Financial Services (Disclosure of Information) (Designated Authorities) (No.6) Order 1989**
Art.2, amended: SI 1999/506 Art.27

2011. **Bristol Development Corporation (Vesting of Land) (British Railways Board) Order 1989**
revoked: SI 1998/769 Art.3, Sch.

2037. **Education (Areas to which Pupils and Students Belong) Regulations 1989**
revoked: SI 1996/615 Reg.11

2057. **Motor Cars (Driving Instruction) Regulations 1989**
Reg.2, amended: SI 1996/1983 Reg.3, SI 1998/2247 Reg.3
Reg.3, revoked (in part): SI 1998/2247 Reg.4
Reg.4, amended: SI 1998/2247 Reg.5
Reg.7, amended: SI 1996/1983 Reg.4, SI 1998/2247 Reg.6
Reg.8, amended: SI 1998/2247 Reg.7
Reg.9, amended: SI 1998/2247 Reg.8
Reg.9, revoked (in part): SI 1998/2247 Reg.8
Reg.9A, added: SI 1997/650 Reg.3
Reg.9A, revoked: SI 1998/2247 Reg.9
Reg.11, substituted: SI 1998/2247 Reg.10
Reg.12, amended: SI 1998/2247 Reg.11
Reg.12, substituted: SI 1996/1983 Reg.5
Reg.13, amended: SI 1996/1983 Reg.6, SI 1997/650 Reg.4
Reg.14, amended: SI 1998/2247 Reg.12
Reg.14, substituted: SI 1996/1983 Reg.7
Reg.15, amended: SI 1998/2247 Reg.13
Reg.16, amended: SI 1996/1983 Reg.8, SI 1998/2247 Reg.14
Reg.16A, added: SI 1996/1983 Reg.9
Sch.1, substituted: SI 1998/2247 Reg.15, Sch.
Sch.2, amended: SI 1996/1983 Reg.10
Sch.2, substituted: SI 1998/2247 Reg.15, Sch.
Sch.3, amended: SI 1996/1983 Reg.11
Sch.3, substituted: SI 1998/2247 Reg.15, Sch.
Sch.4, substituted: SI 1998/2247 Reg.15, Sch.
Sch.5, added: SI 1998/2247 Reg.15, Sch.

2058. **Goods Vehicles (Authorisation of International Journeys) (Fees) (Amendment) Regulations 1989**
revoked: SI 1996/131 Reg.4, Sch.2

2062. **Civil Aviation (Investigation of Air Accidents) Regulations 1989**
revoked: SI 1996/2798 Reg.19

2094. **Church Representation Rules (Amendment) (No.1) Resolution 1989**
referred to: SI 1998/319, SI 1999/2112

2095. **Church Representation Rules (Amendment) (No.2) Resolution 1989**
referred to: SI 1998/319, SI 1999/2112

2107. **Human Organ Transplants (Establishment of Relationship) Regulations 1989**
revoked: SI 1998/1428 Reg.3

2122. **Social Security (Unemployment, Sickness and Invalidity Benefit) Amendment No.3 Regulations 1989**
revoked: SI 1996/1345 Reg.27, Sch.

2123. **Social Security Benefit (Computation of Earnings) Amendment Regulations 1989**
revoked: SI 1996/2745 Reg.18, Sch.4

2127. **Rules of Procedure (Army) (Amendment) Rules 1989**
revoked: SI 1997/169 r.90, Sch.7

2128. **Police and Criminal Evidence Act 1984 Codes of Practice (Armed Forces) Order 1989**
revoked: SI 1997/17 Art.3

NO.

2129. **Rules of Procedure (Air Force) (Amendment) Rules 1989**
revoked: SI 1997/171 r.90, Sch.7

2130. **Standing Civilian Courts (Amendment) Order 1989**
revoked: SI 1997/172 Art.93, Sch.5

2141. **Prison (Amendment) (No.2) Rules 1989**
revoked: SI 1999/728 r.85 (with savings), Sch. (with savings)

2169. **Pressure Systems and Transportable Gas Containers Regulations 1989**
applied: SI 1996/825 Reg.4, SI 1996/2095 Sch.2 para.4
referred to: SI 1996/2089 Reg.2
Reg.2, amended: SI 1996/2092 Reg.21, Sch.6 para.2, SI 1999/2024 Reg.48, Sch.5 Part II
Reg.3, amended: SI 1996/2092 Reg.21, Sch.6 para.3
Reg.4, amended: SI 1996/2092 Reg.21, Sch.6 para.4
Reg.16, applied: SI 1996/2092 Sch.8 para.3
Reg.16, revoked: SI 1996/2092 Reg.21, Sch.6 para.5
Reg.17, revoked: SI 1996/2092 Reg.21, Sch.6 para.5
Reg.18, revoked: SI 1996/2092 Reg.21, Sch.6 para.5
Reg.19, revoked: SI 1996/2092 Reg.21, Sch.6 para.5
Reg.20, revoked: SI 1996/2092 Reg.21, Sch.6 para.5
Reg.21, revoked: SI 1996/2092 Reg.21, Sch.6 para.5
Reg.22, revoked: SI 1996/2092 Reg.21, Sch.6 para.5
Reg.24, amended: SI 1996/2092 Reg.21, Sch.6 para.6
Sch.1, revoked (in part): SI 1996/2092 Reg.21, Sch.6 para.7
Sch.2, revoked (in part): SI 1996/2092 Reg.21, Sch.6 para.7
Sch.2 Part I, amended: SI 1996/1656 Reg.22, Sch.2 Part II, SI 1996/2092 Reg.21, Sch.6 para.8, SI 1997/2776 Reg.19, Sch.2 para.2, SI 1999/303 Reg.3, Sch.2 para.1
Sch.2 Part II, amended: SI 1996/2092 Reg.21, Sch.6 para.9
Sch.2 Part II, revoked (in part): SI 1999/303 Reg.3, Sch.2 para.2
Sch.5, amended: SI 1996/2092 Reg.21, Sch.6 para.10
Sch.6 Part IV, revoked (in part): SI 1999/1736 Art.19, Sch.9

2183. **Goods Vehicles (Operators' Licences) (Temporary Use in Great Britain) (Amendment) Regulations 1989**
revoked: SI 1996/2186 Reg.2, Sch.1

2184. **Goods Vehicles (Authorisation of International Journeys) (Fees) (Amendment) (No.2) Regulations 1989**
revoked: SI 1996/131 Reg.4

2195. **Pyramid Selling Schemes Regulations 1989**
referred to: SI 1997/30 Reg.1

2203. **Town and Country Planning (Central Manchester Urban Development Area) Special Development Order 1989**
revoked: SI 1996/232 Art.2

2204. **Town and Country Planning (Sheffield Urban Development Area) Special Development Order 1989**
revoked: SI 1997/13 Art.2

NO.

NO.

1989—cont.

1989—cont.

2209. Construction (Head Protection) Regulations 1989
referred to: SI 1998/2306 Reg.12
Reg.2, amended: SI 1997/2776 Reg.19, Sch.2 para.3

2233. Cosmetic Products (Safety) Regulations 1989
revoked: SI 1996/2925 Sch.9
Reg.2, amended: SI 1996/1446 Reg.2
Sch.1, amended: SI 1996/1446 Reg.2
Sch.2 Part II, revoked (in part): SI 1996/1446 Reg.2
Sch.4 Part II, amended: SI 1996/1446 Reg.2
Sch.4 Part II, revoked (in part): SI 1996/1446 Reg.2
Sch.5 Part I, amended: SI 1996/1446 Reg.2
Sch.5 Part II, amended: SI 1996/1446 Reg.2

2277. Apple and Pear Research Council Order 1989
referred to: SI 1999/672 Art.2, Sch.1

2307. Inshore Fishing (Prohibition of Fishing and Fishing Methods) (Scotland) Order 1989
Art.2, amended: SI 1996/1475 Art.2
Art.3, amended: SI 1996/1475 Art.2
Art.4, amended: SI 1996/1475 Art.2
Art.5, amended: SI 1996/1475 Art.2
Art.6, amended: SI 1996/1475 Art.2
Art.7, amended: SI 1996/1475 Art.2
Art.8, amended: SI 1996/1475 Art.2
Art.8, revoked: SI 1999/751 Art.2
Art.8A, amended: SI 1996/1475 Art.2
Sch.1, amended: SI 1996/1475 Art.2
Sch.2, amended: SI 1996/1475 Art.2
Sch.3, amended: SI 1996/1475 Art.2

2321. Caseins and Caseinates (Amendment) Regulations 1989
Reg.8, revoked: SI 1996/1499 Reg.49, Sch.9

2325. Medicines (Exemptions from Licences) (Intermediate Medicated Feeding Stuffs) Order 1989
revoked: SI 1998/1048 Reg.2, Sch.1
Art.3, revoked: SI 1998/1048 Reg.2, Sch.1

2390. Supply of Beer (Tied Estate) Order 1989
see *Bavarian Lager Co Ltd v Commission of the European Communities (T309/97)* [1999] 3 C.M.L.R. 544 (CFI) (Fourth Chamber), Moura Ramos (President)
Art.2, see *Plummer v Tibsco Ltd* [1999] E.G.C.S. 140 (Ch D), Neuberger, J.
Art.7, see *Plummer v Tibsco Ltd* Times, December 1, 1999 (Ch D), Neuberger, J.
Art.7, amended: SI 1997/1740 Art.2

2395. Air Navigation (Overseas Territories) Order 1989
Art.36, substituted: SI 1997/1746 Art.2
Sch.14 Reg.17, substituted: SI 1997/1746 Art.2

2396. Brunei (Appeals) Order 1989
Art.2, amended: SI 1998/255 Art.2
Art.2, revoked (in part): SI 1998/255 Art.2

2398. Continental Shelf (Designation of Additional Areas) Order 1989
referred to: SI 1999/2031

2404. Companies (Northern Ireland) Order 1989
Art.3, amended: 1999 c.23 s.67, Sch.4 para.18
Art.10, applied: SI 1996/1632 (NI.11) Sch.3 para.22
Art.23, amended: 1999 c.23 s.59, Sch.3 para.22
Part II, applied: SI 1996/1632 (NI.11) Sch.3 para.9, Sch.3 para.21, 1997 c.50 s.91, Sch.2 para.3

2405. Insolvency (Northern Ireland) Order 1989
referred to: SI 1996/1299 (NI.9) Sch.4 para.3, 1998 c.47 Sch.3 para.23
Art.2, amended: 1999 c.23 s.67, Sch.4 para.19
Art.2, applied: 1997 c.32 Sch.6
Art.3, applied: SI 1997/2778 (NI.19) Art.68
Art.5, applied: SI 1998/1806 Art.2
Art.11, referred to: SI 1999/3147 (NI.11) Art.13
Art.12, applied: SI 1998/1806 Art.2
Art.14, applied: 1997 c.32 Sch.6
Art.15, applied: 1997 c.32 Sch.6
Art.16, applied: 1997 c.32 Sch.6
Art.19, applied: 1997 c.32 Sch.6
Art.21, applied: 1997 c.32 Sch.6
Art.21, revoked (in part): 1997 c.32 Sch.6
Art.22, applied: 1997 c.32 Sch.6
Art.22, revoked (in part): 1997 c.32 Sch.6
Art.23, revoked (in part): 1997 c.32 Sch.6
Art.24, revoked (in part): 1997 c.32 Sch.6
Art.25, referred to: 1997 c.32 Sch.6
Art.26, applied: 1997 c.32 Sch.6
Art.27, applied: 1997 c.32 Sch.6
Art.28, amended: 1997 c.32 Sch.6
Art.28, revoked (in part): 1997 c.32 Sch.6
Art.29, applied: 1997 c.32 Sch.6
Art.31, revoked (in part): 1997 c.32 Sch.6
Art.35, applied: 1997 c.32 Sch.6
Art.36, applied: 1997 c.32 Sch.6
Art.37, applied: 1997 c.32 Sch.6
Art.39, applied: 1997 c.32 Sch.6
Art.42, applied: SI 1996/1632 (NI.11) Sch.3 para.1
Art.48, referred to: 1997 c.32 Sch.6
Art.49, applied: 1997 c.32 Sch.6
Art.50, revoked: 1997 c.32 Sch.6
Art.52, revoked: 1997 c.32 Sch.6
Art.53, revoked: 1997 c.32 Sch.6
Art.54, revoked: 1997 c.32 Sch.6
Art.55, revoked: 1997 c.32 Sch.6
Art.56, revoked: 1997 c.32 Sch.6
Art.57, revoked: 1997 c.32 Sch.6
Art.58, revoked: 1997 c.32 Sch.6
Art.59, revoked: 1997 c.32 Sch.6
Art.75, applied: SI 1997/274 (NI.1) Art.12
Art.87, applied: 1997 c.32 Sch.7 para.8
Art.104, applied: SI 1996/1632 (NI.11) Sch.3 para.24
Art.105, applied: SI 1998/1806 Art.2
Art.112, applied: SI 1996/1632 (NI.11) Sch.3 para.14
Art.113, applied: SI 1996/1632 (NI.11) Sch.3 para.13, Sch.3 para.15, Sch.3 para.16, Sch.3 para.17
Art.114, applied: SI 1996/1632 (NI.11) Sch.3 para.18
Art.115, applied: SI 1996/1632 (NI.11) Sch.3 para.1
Art.117, applied: SI 1996/1632 (NI.11) Sch.3 para.4, Sch.3 para.5
Art.120, applied: 1997 c.32 Sch.7 para.8
Art.135, applied: SI 1996/1632 (NI.11) Sch.3 para.19
Art.148, applied: SI 1996/1632 (NI.11) Sch.3 para.10
Art.151, applied: SI 1997/2778 (NI.19) Art.68
Art.152, referred to: SI 1999/662 (NI.6) Art.35
Art.177, referred to: 1997 c.32 Sch.6
Art.178, referred to: 1997 c.32 Sch.6
Art.197, amended: SI 1996/275 (NI.2) Art.71, Sch.6
Art.226, applied: SI 1998/1806 Art.2
Art.238, applied: SI 1998/1806 Art.2

NO.

2405. Insolvency (Northern Ireland) Order
1989—*cont.*
Art.253, applied: SI 1996/1632 (NI.11) Sch.3
para.12
Art.254, applied: SI 1996/1299 (NI.9) Art.37, SI
1996/1632 (NI.11) Sch.3 para.8
Art.255, amended: SI 1996/1299 (NI.9) Art.57,
Sch.3 para.14
Art.259, applied: SI 1996/1299 (NI.9) Art.37, SI
1996/1632 (NI.11) Sch.3 para.1
Art.259, referred to: SI 1996/1299 (NI.9) Sch.4
para.2
Art.261, applied: SI 1996/1632 (NI.11) Sch.3
para.12
Art.262, applied: SI 1996/1632 (NI.11) Sch.3
para.14
Art.263, applied: SI 1996/1632 (NI.11) Sch.3
para.13, Sch.3 para.15, Sch.3 para.16, Sch.3
para.17
Art.264, applied: SI 1996/1632 (NI.11) Sch.3
para.12
Art.268, applied: SI 1996/1632 (NI.11) Sch.3
para.5
Art.269, applied: SI 1996/1632 (NI.11) Sch.3
para.4
Art.272, applied: SI 1996/1632 (NI.11) Sch.3
para.10
Art.273, applied: SI 1996/1632 (NI.11) Sch.3
para.6, Sch.3 para.7
Art.274, applied: 1997 c.32 Sch.7 para.8
Art.280, applied: SI 1996/1299 (NI.9) Art.37
Art.280, referred to: SI 1998/2003 Reg.13, SI
1998/2026 Reg.13, SI 1999/496 Reg.28, SI
1999/1001 Reg.17
Art.281, applied: SI 1996/1299 (NI.9) Art.37
Art.283, amended: SI 1999/3147 (NI.11) Art.17,
Sch.2 para.1
Art.283, referred to: SI 1998/2003 Reg.13, SI
1998/2026 Reg.13, SI 1999/496 Reg.28, SI
1999/1001 Reg.17
Art.285, applied: SI 1996/1632 (NI.11) Sch.3
para.12
Art.288, referred to: SI 1999/662 (NI.6) Art.35
Art.306, applied: SI 1996/1632 (NI.11) Sch.3
para.12
Art.309, amended: SI 1998/1071 (NI.6) Art.41,
Sch.3
Art.309, applied: SI 1997/1179 (NI.8) Art.49
Art.310, amended: SI 1998/1071 (NI.6) Art.41,
Sch.3
Art.312, applied: SI 1996/1299 (NI.9) Art.37
Art.312, referred to: SI 1996/1299 (NI.9) Sch.4
para.2
Art.315A, substituted: SI 1999/3147 (NI.11)
Art.15
Art.315B, substituted: SI 1999/3147 (NI.11)
Art.15
Art.315C, substituted: SI 1999/3147 (NI.11)
Art.15
Art.315D, added: SI 1999/3147 (NI.11) Art.74,
Sch.9 para.54
Art.315E, added: SI 1999/3147 (NI.11) Art.74,
Sch.9 para.54
Art.315F, added: SI 1999/3147 (NI.11) Art.74,
Sch.9 para.54
Art.319, applied: SI 1996/1919 (NI.16) Art.229
Art.320A, added: 1996 c.23 Sch.3 para.53
Art.334, applied: SI 1996/1632 (NI.11) Sch.3
para.12
Art.335, applied: SI 1996/1632 (NI.11) Sch.3
para.14
Art.341, applied: SI 1997/2778 (NI.19) Art.68

NO.

2405. Insolvency (Northern Ireland) Order
1989—*cont.*
Art.343, amended: SI 1996/275 (NI.2) Art.71,
Sch.6
Art.253, applied: SI 1996/1632 (NI.11) Sch.3
para.12
Art.346, amended: 1996 c.8 Sch.5 para.12
Art.346, applied: SI 1996/1299 (NI.9) Art.5
Art.350, referred to: SI 1996/275 (NI.2) Art.44
Art.359, applied: SI 1996/1919 (NI.16) Art.229,
1997 c.32 Sch.6
Art.361, applied: 1997 c.32 Sch.6
Art.362, applied: 1997 c.32 Sch.6
Art.364, applied: SI 1997/274 (NI.1) Art.12
Art.365, applied: SI 1996/1919 (NI.16) Art.201,
Art.228, SI 1997/2778 (NI.19) Art.68
Art.366, amended: 1998 c.11 s.23, Sch.5
para.40
Art.367, applied: SI 1996/1299 (NI.9) Art.37
Art.367, referred to: SI 1996/1299 (NI.9) Sch.4
para.2
Art.373, applied: 1997 c.32 Sch.6
Art.375, amended: 1999 c.23 s.59, Sch.3
para.23
Art.378, applied: 1997 c.32 Sch.6
Art.380, revoked: SI 1996/1919 (NI.16) Art.257,
Sch.3
Part I, applied: 1997 c.32 Sch.6
Part II, applied: SI 1996/1527 Reg.47, SI 1996/
1919 (NI.16) Art.201, Art.228, Art.232, 1997
c.32 Sch.6, SI 1998/1806 Art.2
Part III, applied: 1997 c.32 Sch.6, SI 1997/274
(NI.1) Art.12, SI 1998/1806 Art.2
Part IV, applied: 1997 c.32 Sch.6, SI 1997/274
(NI.1) Art.12
Part V, applied: 1997 c.32 Sch.7 para.8, SI
1997/274 (NI.1) Art.12
Part VI, applied: 1997 c.32 Sch.7 para.8, SI
1997/274 (NI.1) Art.12
Part VII, applied: SI 1996/1919 (NI.16) Art.232,
1997 c.32 Sch.6
Part VIII, applied: SI 1998/1806 Art.2, SI 1999/
662 (NI.6) Art.9, Sch.1 para.8
Part VIII Ch.I, applied: SI 1996/3158 (NI.22)
Art.28
Part VIII Ch.II, applied: SI 1996/1527 Reg.47, SI
1996/3158 (NI.22) Art.28
Part IX, applied: SI 1996/1299 (NI.9) Art.37, SI
1997/274 (NI.1) Art.12, SI 1999/662 (NI.6)
Art.9, Sch.1 para.8
Part X, applied: SI 1999/662 (NI.6) Art.9, Sch.1
para.8
Part XI, applied: 1997 c.32 Sch.6
Part XII, applied: 1997 c.32 Sch.6
Sch.1 para.17, applied: 1997 c.32 Sch.6
Sch.2 para.7, amended: SI 1997/1179 (NI.8)
Art.53, Sch.4 para.5
Sch.3 para.10, amended: SI 1997/1179 (NI.8)
Art.53, Sch.4 para.5
Sch.4 para.3B, added: 1996 c.8 Sch.5 para.12
Sch.4 para.5, amended: 1997 c.16 Sch.2 para.6
Sch.4 para.5, referred to: 1997 c.16 Sch.18 Part
II
Sch.4 para.5, revoked (in part): 1997 c.16
Sch.18 Part II
Sch.4 para.13, amended: SI 1996/1919 (NI.16)
Art.255, Sch.1
Sch.7, applied: 1997 c.32 Sch.6
Sch.9 para.66, revoked: 1996 c.23 Sch.4
Sch.9 para.68, revoked: SI 1996/1919 (NI.16)
Art.257, Sch.3
Sch.9 para.88, revoked: SI 1996/1919 (NI.16)
Art.257, Sch.3

NO.

NO.

1989—cont.

2405. Insolvency (Northern Ireland) Order 1989—*cont.*

Sch.9 para.89, revoked: SI 1996/1919 (NI.16) Art.257, Sch.3

Sch.9 para.90, revoked: SI 1996/1919 (NI.16) Art.257, Sch.3

2406. Education Reform (Northern Ireland) Order 1989

applied: SI 1998/1759 (NI.13) Art.40, Sch.2 para.3

referred to: SI 1997/866 (NI.5) Art.2

Art.2, applied: SI 1997/1772 (NI.15) Art.2

Art.2, revoked (in part): SI 1998/1759 (NI.13) Art.91, Sch.6 Part II

Art.3, applied: SI 1997/1772 (NI.15) Art.4

Art.5, amended: SI 1996/274 (NI.1) Art.34

Art.6, referred to: SI 1998/1759 (NI.13) Art.11, Art.12

Art.7, amended: SI 1996/274 (NI.1) Art.35, SI 1998/1759 (NI.13) Art.10, Art.91, Sch.5 Part I

Art.7, applied: SI 1998/1759 (NI.13) Art.77

Art.7, referred to: SI 1998/1759 (NI.13) Art.74

Art.8, amended: SI 1998/1759 (NI.13) Art.91, Sch.5 Part I

Art.8, applied: SI 1998/1759 (NI.13) Art.77

Art.9, amended: SI 1996/274 (NI.1) Art.35

Art.9, revoked: SI 1998/1759 (NI.13) Art.91, Sch.6 Part I

Art.10, amended: SI 1998/1759 (NI.13) Art.91, Sch.5 Part I

Art.11, revoked (in part): SI 1998/1759 (NI.13) Art.91, Sch.6 Part I

Art.12, amended: SI 1996/274 (NI.1) Art.25

Art.13, amended: SI 1998/1759 (NI.13) Art.91, Sch.5 Part I

Art.13, revoked (in part): SI 1996/274 (NI.1) Art.44, Sch.6 Part I

Art.16, amended: SI 1996/274 (NI.1) Art.43, Sch.5 Part I

Art.17, amended: SI 1996/274 (NI.1) Art.43, Sch.5 Part I

Art.17A, revoked: SI 1998/1759 (NI.13) Art.91, Sch.6 Part I

Art.18, referred to: SI 1998/1759 (NI.13) Art.91, Sch.6 Part I

Art.18, revoked: SI 1998/1759 (NI.13) Art.91, Sch.6 Part I

Art.19, referred to: SI 1998/1759 (NI.13) Art.91, Sch.6 Part I

Art.19, revoked: SI 1998/1759 (NI.13) Art.91, Sch.6 Part I

Art.20, referred to: SI 1998/1759 (NI.13) Art.91, Sch.6 Part I

Art.20, revoked: SI 1998/1759 (NI.13) Art.91, Sch.6 Part I

Art.21, referred to: SI 1998/1759 (NI.13) Art.91, Sch.6 Part I

Art.21, revoked: SI 1998/1759 (NI.13) Art.91, Sch.6 Part I

Art.22, referred to: SI 1998/1759 (NI.13) Art.91, Sch.6 Part I

Art.22, revoked: SI 1998/1759 (NI.13) Art.91, Sch.6 Part I

Art.23, referred to: SI 1998/1759 (NI.13) Art.91, Sch.6 Part I

Art.23, revoked: SI 1998/1759 (NI.13) Art.91, Sch.6 Part I

Art.24, referred to: SI 1998/1759 (NI.13) Art.91, Sch.6 Part I

Art.24, revoked: SI 1998/1759 (NI.13) Art.91, Sch.6 Part I

Art.25, referred to: SI 1998/1759 (NI.13) Art.91, Sch.6 Part I

1989—cont.

2406. Education Reform (Northern Ireland) Order 1989—*cont.*

Art.25, revoked: SI 1998/1759 (NI.13) Art.91, Sch.6 Part I

Art.26, referred to: SI 1998/1759 (NI.13) Art.91, Sch.6 Part I

Art.26, revoked: SI 1998/1759 (NI.13) Art.91, Sch.6 Part I

Art.27, referred to: SI 1998/1759 (NI.13) Art.91, Sch.6 Part I

Art.30, revoked: SI 1996/274 (NI.1) Art.44, Sch.6 Part II

Art.31, amended: SI 1996/274 (NI.1) Art.43, Sch.5 Part I

Art.33, amended: SI 1996/274 (NI.1) Art.43, Sch.5 Part II, SI 1997/1772 (NI.15) Art.25, Sch.4

Art.34, amended: SI 1997/1772 (NI.15) Art.25, Sch.4, SI 1998/1759 (NI.13) Art.91, Sch.5 Part I

Art.34, referred to: SI 1998/1759 (NI.13) Art.91, Sch.6 Part I

Art.34, revoked (in part): SI 1997/1772 (NI.15) Art.25, Sch.4, Sch.5, SI 1998/1759 (NI.13) Art.91, Sch.6 Part I

Art.35, amended: SI 1997/866 (NI.5) Art.8

Art.35, applied: SI 1998/1759 (NI.13) Art.89

Art.35, revoked (in part): SI 1997/1772 (NI.15) Art.25, Sch.4, Sch.5, SI 1998/1759 (NI.13) Art.91, Sch.6 Part I

Art.36, amended: SI 1996/274 (NI.1) Art.43, Sch.5 Part I

Art.39, amended: SI 1996/274 (NI.1) Art.43, Sch.5 Part II

Art.41, amended: SI 1996/274 (NI.1) Art.43, Sch.5 Part II

Art.43, amended: SI 1996/274 (NI.1) Art.43, Sch.5 Part I

Art.44, revoked: SI 1996/274 (NI.1) Art.44, Sch.6 Part I

Art.46, amended: SI 1997/1772 (NI.15) Art.25, Sch.4

Art.46, referred to: SI 1998/1759 (NI.13) Art.91, Sch.6 Part II

Art.49, amended: SI 1998/1759 (NI.13) Art.91, Sch.5 Part I

Art.59, amended: SI 1996/1919 (NI.16) Art.255, Sch.1

Art.60, amended: SI 1997/866 (NI.5) Art.25, SI 1998/1759 (NI.13) Art.91, Sch.5 Part I

Art.60, referred to: SI 1998/1759 (NI.13) Art.91, Sch.6 Part II

Art.62, amended: SI 1997/866 (NI.5) Art.25

Art.62, referred to: SI 1998/1759 (NI.13) Art.91, Sch.6 Part II

Art.65, revoked: SI 1998/1759 (NI.13) Art.91, Sch.6 Part II

Art.66, applied: SI 1998/1759 (NI.13) Art.14

Art.68, revoked (in part): SI 1998/1759 (NI.13) Art.20

Art.68, revoked (in part): SI 1998/1759 (NI.13) Art.91, Sch.6 Part I

Art.69, amended: SI 1996/274 (NI.1) Art.36

Art.69, revoked (in part): SI 1996/274 (NI.1) Art.44, Sch.6 Part II

Art.71, amended: SI 1996/274 (NI.1) Art.37

Art.71, revoked (in part): SI 1996/274 (NI.1) Art.37, Art.44, Sch.6 Part II

Art.73, amended: SI 1996/274 (NI.1) Art.43, Sch.5 Part II

Art.77, amended: SI 1997/866 (NI.5) Art.25

Art.77, referred to: SI 1998/1759 (NI.13) Art.91, Sch.6 Part II

NO.

1989—cont.

2406. Education Reform (Northern Ireland) Order 1989—*cont.*
Art.77, revoked: SI 1998/1759 (NI.13) Art.91, Sch.6 Part II
Art.78, revoked: SI 1998/1759 (NI.13) Art.91, Sch.6 Part II
Art.81, revoked: SI 1998/1759 (NI.13) Art.91, Sch.6 Part II
Art.82, amended: SI 1998/1759 (NI.13) Art.91, Sch.5 Part II
Art.85, revoked: SI 1998/1759 (NI.13) Art.91, Sch.5 Part II, Sch.6 Part II
Art.87, amended: SI 1996/274 (NI.1) Art.43, Sch.5 Part II
Art.90, revoked (in part): SI 1998/1759 (NI.13) Art.20, Art.91, Sch.6
Art.93, amended: SI 1996/274 (NI.1) Art.43, Sch.5 Part II
Art.99, amended: SI 1996/274 (NI.1) Art.43, Sch.5 Part II
Art.105, amended: SI 1996/274 (NI.1) Art.38
Art.105, revoked (in part): SI 1996/274 (NI.1) Art.44, Sch.6 Part II
Art.119A, applied: SI 1997/1772 (NI.15) Art.10, Sch.2 para.18
Art.122, amended: SI 1996/274 (NI.1) Art.43, Sch.5 Part II
Art.124, referred to: SI 1998/1759 (NI.13) Art.91, Sch.6 Part I
Art.124, revoked (in part): SI 1997/1772 (NI.15) Art.25, Sch.4, Sch.5, SI 1998/1759 (NI.13) Art.91, Sch.6 Part I
Art.125, amended: SI 1998/1759 (NI.13) Art.15, Art.91, Sch.5 Part II
Art.125, applied: SI 1996/274 (NI.1) Art.8
Art.125, revoked (in part): SI 1997/1772 (NI.15) Art.25, Sch.4, Sch.5
Art.126, revoked (in part): SI 1996/274 (NI.1) Art.44, Sch.6 Part II, SI 1997/1772 (NI.15) Art.25, Sch.4, Sch.5
Art.130, amended: SI 1997/866 (NI.5) Art.23
Art.131, amended: 1999 c.10 s.1, Sch.1 para.6
Art.136A, added: SI 1998/1759 (NI.13) Art.84
Art.137, amended: SI 1997/866 (NI.5) Art.23, SI 1998/1759 (NI.13) Art.84
Art.138, revoked (in part): SI 1997/1772 (NI.15) Art.25, Sch.4, Sch.5
Art.143, substituted: SI 1998/1759 (NI.13) Art.43
Art.146, revoked (in part): SI 1996/274 (NI.1) Art.44, Sch.6 Part I
Art.147, revoked: SI 1997/1772 (NI.15) Art.25, Sch.4, Sch.5
Art.148, amended: SI 1997/1772 (NI.15) Art.25, Sch.4
Art.148, revoked (in part): SI 1997/1772 (NI.15) Art.25, Sch.4, Sch.5
Art.149, revoked (in part): SI 1997/1772 (NI.15) Art.25, Sch.4
Art.151, amended: SI 1998/1759 (NI.13) Art.91, Sch.5 Part II
Art.151, revoked (in part): SI 1997/1772 (NI.15) Art.25, Sch.4, Sch.5
Art.153, substituted: SI 1998/1759 (NI.13) Art.43
Art.155, revoked: SI 1996/274 (NI.1) Art.44, Sch.6 Part I
Art.157, revoked: SI 1998/1759 (NI.13) Art.91, Sch.6 Part I
Art.164, amended: SI 1998/1759 (NI.13) Art.91, Sch.5 Part I, Sch.6 Part II
Part III, applied: SI 1998/1759 (NI.13) Art.62, Art.64
Part IV, applied: SI 1997/866 (NI.5) Art.19

1989—cont.

2406. Education Reform (Northern Ireland) Order 1989—*cont.*
Part IV, revoked: SI 1997/866 (NI.5) Sch
Part V, revoked: SI 1998/1759 (NI.13) Art.91, Sch.6 Part II
Part VI, applied: SI 1996/274 (NI.1) Sch.4 para.2
Part VII, applied: SI 1996/274 (NI.1) Art.41, SI 1997/1772 (NI.15) Art.2, Art.10
Part VII, referred to: SI 1997/1772 (NI.15) Sch.2 para.20
Part VII, revoked: SI 1997/1772 (NI.15) Art.25, Sch.4, Sch.5
Part VIII Ch.II, referred to: SI 1998/1759 (NI.13) Art.72
Sch.1, amended: SI 1996/274 (NI.1) Art.35
Sch.2, substituted: SI 1996/274 (NI.1) Art.35
Sch.3, referred to: SI 1998/1759 (NI.13) Art.91, Sch.6 Part I
Sch.3, revoked: SI 1998/1759 (NI.13) Art.91, Sch.6 Part I
Sch.4, referred to: SI 1998/1759 (NI.13) Art.91, Sch.6 Part II
Sch.4, revoked: SI 1998/1759 (NI.13) Art.91, Sch.6 Part II
Sch.6 para.2, amended: SI 1998/1759 (NI.13) Art.91, Sch.5 Part I
Sch.6 para.3, revoked: SI 1998/1759 (NI.13) Art.91, Sch.5 Part II, Sch.6 Part II
Sch.7, revoked: SI 1997/1772 (NI.15) Art.25, Sch.4, Sch.5
Sch.8 para.11, amended: SI 1998/1759 (NI.13) Art.91, Sch.5 Part I
Sch.9, amended: SI 1998/1759 (NI.13) Art.91, Sch.6 Part I
Sch.9, revoked (in part): SI 1996/274 (NI.1) Art.44, Sch.6 Part I, Sch.6 Part II, SI 1996/1297 (NI.7) Art.23, Sch.5, SI 1996/1919 (NI.16) Art.257, Sch.3, SI 1997/1772 (NI.15) Art.25, Sch.5, SI 1998/1759 (NI.13) Art.91, Sch.6 Part II

2413. Youth Service (Northern Ireland) Order 1989
Sch. para.9, revoked: SI 1996/1297 (NI.7) Art.23, Sch.5

2428. Portland Harbour Fishery Order 1989
referred to: SI 1999/3049
Art.1, amended: SI 1999/3049 Art.2
Art.2, amended: SI 1999/3049 Art.2
Art.8, amended: SI 1996/362 Art.5, Sch.4

2431. Veterinary Surgeons and Veterinary Practitioners (Registration) (Amendment) Regulations Order of Council 1989
revoked: SI 1999/2846 Sch. Reg.22
Sch. para.2, revoked: SI 1999/2846 Sch. Reg.22
Sch. para.3, revoked: SI 1999/2846 Sch. Reg.22
Sch. para.4, revoked: SI 1999/2846 Sch. Reg.22
Sch. para.5, revoked: SI 1999/2846 Sch. Reg.22

2433. Sports Grounds and Sporting Events (Designation) (Scotland) Amendment Order 1989
revoked: SI 1998/2314 Art.3, Sch.3

2434. Safety of Sports Grounds (Designation) (Scotland) Order 1989
revoked: SI 1998/1601 Art.3, Sch.2

2442. Medicines (Intermediate Medicated Feedingstuffs) Order 1989
revoked: SI 1998/1048 Reg.2 (with savings), Sch.1 (with savings)

NO.

2454. Town and Country Planning (Liverpool and Wirral Urban Development Area) Special Development Order 1989
revoked: SI 1998/84 Art.2, Sch.

2474. Electricity Generators (Rateable Values) Order 1989
Art.3, see *Coventry & Solihull Waste Disposal Co Ltd v Russell (Valuation Officer)* Times, June 11, 1998 (CA), Waller, L.J.; see *Coventry and Solihull Waste Disposal Co Ltd v Russell (Valuation Officer)* [1999] 1 W.L.R. 2093 (HL), Lord Hope of Craighead
Art.4, see *Coventry and Solihull Waste Disposal Co Ltd v Russell (Valuation Officer)* [1999] 1 W.L.R. 2093 (HL), Lord Hope of Craighead

2480. Human Organ Transplants (Unrelated Persons) Regulations 1989
Reg.2, referred to: SI 1999/1319 Sch.

1990

British Railways Board Ammanford Level Crossing Order 1990
revoked: SI 1997/2466 Art.2

Home Guard War Widows Special Payments Regulations 1990
applied: SI 1996/2890 Sch.3 para.40

Lewisham (Waiting and Loading Restriction) Consolidation Order 1990
revoked (in part): SI 1997/2014 Art.11, SI 1999/81 Art.10

Lewisham (Waiting and Loading Restriction) Order 1990
revoked (in part): SI 1997/258 Art.11, SI 1998/1835 Art.10, SI 1998/2745 Art.11

Naval and Marine Pay and Pensions (Special War Widows Payment) Order 1990
applied: SI 1996/2890 Sch.3 para.40

1. Caseins and Caseinates (Scotland) Amendment Regulations 1990
Reg.8, revoked: SI 1996/1499 Reg.49, Sch.9

3. Welfare Food Amendment Regulations 1990
revoked: SI 1996/1434 Reg.23, Sch.7

13. Electrical Equipment for Explosive Atmospheres (Certification) Regulations 1990
revoked: SI 1996/192 Reg.1, Sch.1
Reg.2, amended: SI 1998/81 Reg.2, SI 1999/2550 Reg.2
Reg.12, amended: SI 1998/81 Reg.2
Reg.12, substituted: SI 1999/2550 Reg.2
Reg.12A, added: SI 1998/81 Reg.2
Reg.12A, amended: SI 1998/1469 Reg.2

18. Stock Transfer (Substitution of Forms) Order 1990
Sch., amended: SI 1996/1571 Art.3

20. Banking Act 1987 (Exempt Transactions) (Amendment) Regulations 1990
revoked: SI 1997/817 Reg.16

85. Registration of Births, Deaths, Marriages, etc. (Prescription of Forms) (Scotland) Amendment Regulations 1990
revoked: SI 1997/2348 Reg.30, Sch.27

90. Social Security (Refunds) (Repayment of Contractual Maternity Pay) Regulations (Northern Ireland) 1990
Reg.2, applied: SI 1999/671 Art.3, Sch.2
Reg.3, applied: SI 1999/671 Art.3, Sch.2

119. Water Supply (Water Quality) (Scotland) Regulations 1990
Reg.23, amended: SI 1996/3047 Reg.16
Reg.23, revoked (in part): SI 1996/3047 Reg.16
Sch.2 Table B, applied: SI 1998/994 Sch.4 Part I
Sch.2 Table C, applied: SI 1998/994 Sch.4 Part I

NO.

121. Surface Waters (Classification) (Scotland) Regulations 1990
revoked: SI 1996/3047 Reg.16

124. Education (Inner London Education Authority) (Property Transfer) Order 1990
Art.2, amended: SI 1996/584 Art.2
Art.2, applied: SI 1997/860 Art.2
Art.2, revoked (in part): SI 1997/860 Art.2

125. Local Government (Compensation for Premature Retirement) (Scotland) Amendment Regulations 1990
revoked: SI 1998/192 Reg.52, Sch.2

126. Surface Water (Dangerous Substances) (Classification) (Scotland) Regulations 1990
Sch.1, amended: SI 1998/1344 Reg.6
Sch.2, amended: SI 1998/1344 Reg.6

140. Coroners' Records (Fees for Copies) (Amendment) Rules 1990
revoked: SI 1997/2544 r.4

144. Driving Licences (Community Driving Licence) Regulations 1990
Sch.1 para.4, revoked (in part): SI 1998/1420 Reg.17, Sch.
Sch.1 para.5, revoked (in part): SI 1998/1420 Reg.17, Sch.
Sch.2 para.26, revoked (in part): SI 1998/1420 Reg.17, Sch.
Sch.2 para.27, revoked (in part): SI 1998/1420 Reg.17, Sch.
Sch.3 para.3, revoked (in part): SI 1998/1420 Reg.17, Sch.

145. Non-Domestic Rating (Collection and Enforcement) (Miscellaneous Provisions) Regulations 1990
Part II, applied: SI 1996/1880 Art.51
Reg.3, applied: SI 1996/1880 Art.51, Art.57

200. Official Secrets Act 1989 (Prescription) Order 1990
Sch.2, amended: SI 1999/1042 Art.3, Sch.1 para.18, SI 1999/1351 Art.17

216. Offshore Installations (Safety Zones) Order 1990
revoked: SI 1997/735 Art.3, Sch.2

244. Health Service Commissioner for England (Special Hospitals Service Authority) Order 1990
revoked: SI 1996/717 Art.2

246. Employment (Miscellaneous Provisions) (Northern Ireland) Order 1990
Art.13A, added: SI 1997/869 (NI.6) Art.73, Sch.2 para.5
Art.14, revoked: SI 1996/1919 (NI.16) Art.257, Sch.3
Art.15, revoked: SI 1996/1919 (NI.16) Art.257, Sch.3
Art.16, revoked: SI 1996/1919 (NI.16) Art.257, Sch.3
Art.17, revoked: SI 1996/1919 (NI.16) Art.257, Sch.3
Sch.3 Part I, revoked (in part): SI 1997/2779 (NI.20) Sch.3
Sch.4 para.1, revoked: SI 1996/1919 (NI.16) Art.257, Sch.3
Sch.4 para.2, revoked: SI 1996/1919 (NI.16) Art.257, Sch.3
Sch.4 para.3, revoked: SI 1996/1919 (NI.16) Art.257, Sch.3
Sch.4 para.4, revoked: SI 1996/1919 (NI.16) Art.257, Sch.3

NO.

246. Employment (Miscellaneous Provisions) (Northern Ireland) Order 1990—*cont.*
Sch.7 para.2, revoked: SI 1996/1919 (NI.16) Art.257, Sch.3
Sch.7 para.3, revoked: SI 1996/1919 (NI.16) Art.257, Sch.3
Sch.7 para.4, revoked: SI 1996/1919 (NI.16) Art.257, Sch.3

247. Health and Personal Social Services (Special Agencies) (Northern Ireland) Order 1990
Sch. para.6, amended: SI 1996/1919 (NI.16) Art.255, Sch.1
Sch. para.9, revoked (in part): SI 1996/1297 (NI.7) Art.23, Sch.5, SI 1996/1298 (NI.8) Art.21, Sch.6

251. Collision Regulations (Seaplanes) (Amendment) Order 1990
revoked: SI 1996/75 Reg.1

256. Social Security (Industrial Injuries) (Regular Employment) Regulations 1990
Reg.1, amended: SI 1996/425 Reg.6
Reg.2, amended: SI 1996/425 Reg.6

266. Fossil Fuel Levy Regulations 1990
Reg.2, revoked (in part): SI 1998/1828 Reg.3
Reg.12, amended: SI 1998/1828 Reg.4
Reg.19, amended: SI 1998/1828 Reg.5
Reg.20, amended: SI 1998/1828 Reg.6
Reg.21, amended: SI 1998/1828 Reg.7
Reg.22, amended: SI 1998/1828 Reg.8
Reg.30, amended: SI 1996/1309 Reg.3
Reg.32, amended: SI 1998/1828 Reg.9
Sch.1, substituted: SI 1998/1828 Reg.10
Sch.2, substituted: SI 1996/1309 Reg.4, SI 1998/1828 Reg.10
Sch.3, substituted: SI 1998/1828 Reg.10
Sch.4 Part I, amended: SI 1998/1828 Reg.11

293. Community Charges and Non-Domestic Rating (Demand Notices) (Wales) Regulations 1990
revoked: SI 1996/619 Art.12

304. Dangerous Substances (Notification and Marking of Sites) Regulations 1990
Reg.2, amended: SI 1996/341 Reg.8, Sch.3 Part II, SI 1996/2092 Reg.21
Reg.5, amended: SI 1996/341 Reg.8, Sch.3 Part II
Reg.6, amended: SI 1996/341 Reg.8, Sch.3 Part II

305. Potteries etc. (Modifications) Regulations 1990
revoked: SI 1998/543 Reg.14, Sch.3

322. Social Security (Recoupment) Regulations 1990
Reg.2, amended: SI 1996/672 Reg.5, SI 1996/1345 Reg.24

353. Education (School Financial Statements) (Prescribed Particulars etc.) Regulations 1990
applied: SI 1996/381 Reg.3, SI 1999/451 Reg.3, SI 1999/486 Reg.3

361. Education (Areas to which Pupils and Students Belong) (Amendment) Regulations 1990
revoked: SI 1996/615 Reg.11

364. Merchant Shipping (Light Dues) Regulations 1990
revoked: SI 1997/562 Reg.2, Sch.1

365. Merchant Shipping (Load Line) (Exemption) (Amendment) Order 1990
revoked: SI 1998/2241 Reg.3

NO.

367. Town and Country Planning (Assessment of Environmental Effects) (Amendment) Regulations 1990
revoked: SI 1999/293 Reg.34, Sch.5

380. Act of Sederunt (Copyright, Designs and Patents) 1990
amended: SI 1996/238 Reg.2
revoked: SI 1999/929 r.1.3, Sch.2
r.1, amended: SI 1996/238 Reg.2
r.1, revoked: SI 1999/929 r.1.3, Sch.2
r.2, amended: SI 1996/238 Reg.2
r.2, revoked: SI 1999/929 r.1.3, Sch.2
r.3, amended: SI 1996/238 Reg.2
r.3, revoked: SI 1999/929 r.1.3, Sch.2

388. Assistance for Minor Works to Dwellings Regulations 1990
applied: SI 1996/2842 Art.8
revoked: SI 1996/2842 Art.7, Sch Part I

396. Rent Officers (Additional Functions) (Scotland) Order 1990
applied: SI 1996/1217 Sch.6 para.8
Art.5, applied: SI 1997/1004 Art.8
Sch.1 para.1, applied: SI 1997/1004 Art.8
Sch.1 para.1, referred to: SI 1997/1004 Art.8
Sch.1 para.2, applied: SI 1996/1217 Sch.6 para.2, Sch.6 para.3, Sch.6 para.8
Sch.3 para.1, applied: SI 1996/1217 Sch.6 para.8

422. Local Government Superannuation (Scotland) Amendment Regulations 1990
applied: SI 1998/364 Reg.4, Reg.6, Reg.19, Sch.2 para.2, Sch.2 para.5, Sch.4 para.8
referred to: SI 1998/364 Reg.3, Reg.10, Sch.2 para.4, Sch.2 para.6
Reg.29, revoked: SI 1998/192 Reg.52, Sch.2
Reg.30, revoked: SI 1998/192 Reg.52, Sch.2

426. Local Authorities (Capital Finance) (Approved Investments) Regulations 1990
Reg.1, amended: SI 1997/319 Reg.161, SI 1999/1852 Reg.9
Reg.1, applied: SI 1997/319 Reg.62
Reg.2, amended: SI 1999/1852 Reg.2
Reg.2, applied: SI 1997/319 Reg.62
Sch. Part II, referred to: SI 1996/263 Reg.16
Sch. para.30, added: SI 1996/568 Reg.16

428. Rent Officers (Additional Functions) Order 1990
applied: SI 1996/1217 Sch.6 para.8
Art.5, applied: SI 1996/1217 Art.8, SI 1997/1004 Art.8
Sch.1 para.1, applied: SI 1996/1217 Art.8, SI 1997/1004 Art.8
Sch.1 para.1, referred to: SI 1997/1004 Art.8
Sch.1 para.2, applied: SI 1996/1217 Sch.6 para.2, Sch.6 para.3, Sch.6 para.8
Sch.3 para.1, applied: SI 1996/1217 Sch.6 para.8

432. Local Authorities (Capital Finance) Regulations 1990
applied: SI 1997/319 Reg.35
referred to: SI 1997/319 Reg.163
revoked: SI 1997/319 Reg.162 (with savings), Sch.3 (with savings)
Reg.6, amended: SI 1996/568 Reg.3, SI 1996/633 Art.8, SI 1996/910 Art.10
Reg.7, amended: SI 1996/568 Reg.4, SI 1996/910 Art.11, SI 1996/2121 Reg.3, SI 1996/2539 Reg.3
Reg.7, applied: SI 1997/319 Reg.32, Reg.50
Reg.7A, added: SI 1996/568 Reg.5
Reg.7A, revoked: SI 1996/2539 Reg.3
Reg.7B, added: SI 1996/568 Reg.5
Reg.7B, amended: SI 1996/2539 Reg.4

NO.

432. Local Authorities (Capital Finance) Regulations 1990—*cont.*
Reg.7C, added: SI 1996/2539 Reg.4
Reg.7D, added: SI 1996/2539 Reg.4
Reg.7E, added: SI 1996/2539 Reg.4
Reg.13, amended: SI 1996/568 Reg.6
Reg.14, amended: SI 1996/568 Reg.7, SI 1996/2121 Reg.4
Reg.15, amended: SI 1996/568 Reg.9
Reg.18, amended: SI 1996/2121 Reg.5
Reg.18, substituted: SI 1996/568 Reg.10
Reg.19D, amended: SI 1996/2121 Reg.6
Reg.20, amended: SI 1996/568 Reg.12, SI 1996/2121 Reg.7, SI 1996/2539 Reg.5
Reg.22A, added: SI 1996/2539 Reg.6
Reg.26, amended: SI 1996/568 Reg.13
Reg.26, applied: SI 1996/910 Art.9, SI 1997/319 Reg.153
Reg.26B, amended: SI 1996/568 Reg.14
Reg.27, amended: SI 1996/910 Art.10
Sch.1 Part I, amended: SI 1996/568 Reg.8
Sch.2, substituted: SI 1996/568 Reg.11
Sch.3 para.6, added: SI 1996/568 Reg.15
Sch.3 para.7, added: SI 1996/568 Reg.15
Sch.5, applied: SI 1996/910 Art.9
Sch.5 Part II, referred to: SI 1997/319 Reg.163
Sch.5 Part III, referred to: SI 1997/319 Reg.163
Sch.5 para.3, applied: SI 1997/319 Reg.139, Reg.140
Sch.5 para.5, applied: SI 1997/319 Reg.139, Reg.140
Sch.5 para.8, applied: SI 1997/319 Reg.151
Sch.6, applied: SI 1996/910 Art.9
Sch.6 Part IV, referred to: SI 1997/319 Reg.163
Sch.6 para.7, referred to: SI 1997/319 Reg.163

434. References to Rating (Housing) Regulations 1990
Sch. para.29, see *R. v London Rent Assessment Panel Ex p. Cadogan Estates Ltd* [1997] 34 E.G. 88 (QBD), Kay, J.

435. Accounts and Audit (Amendment) Regulations 1990
revoked (in part): SI 1996/590 Reg.3

442. Electricity and Pipe-line Works (Assessment of Environmental Effects) Regulations 1990
amended: SI 1999/1756 Art.2, Sch. para.20
applied: SI 1999/1750 Art.2, Sch.1
Reg.2, amended: SI 1997/629 Reg.2
Reg.3, amended: SI 1996/422 Reg.2
Reg.4, amended: SI 1996/422 Reg.3
Reg.8, amended: SI 1996/422 Reg.4
Reg.9, amended: SI 1996/422 Reg.5
Reg.10A, added: SI 1996/422 Reg.6

455. Electricity (Application for Consent) Regulations 1990
applied: SI 1999/1750 Art.2, Sch.1

479. Employment Tribunals (Interest) Order 1990
applied: SI 1996/2803 Reg.8

483. Pensions Increase (Review) Order 1990
applied: SI 1997/634 Art.3, SI 1998/503 Art.3, Art.4, SI 1999/522 Art.3

495. National Health Service (Optical Charges and Payments) Amendment Regulations 1990
revoked: SI 1997/818 Reg.24, Sch.4

504. National Health Service (Optical Charges and Payments) (Scotland) Amendment Regulations 1990
revoked: SI 1998/642 Reg.24, Sch.4

NO.

526. Electricity Act 1989 (Consequential Modifications of Subordinate Legislation) Order 1990
Art.2, revoked (in part): SI 1999/1892 Reg.18 (with savings)
Sch., revoked (in part): SI 1999/1892 Reg.18 (with savings)

528. Electricity Generating Stations and Overhead Lines (Inquiries Procedure) Rules 1990
r.2, amended: SI 1997/712 r.2
r.11, amended: SI 1997/712 r.2
r.11, revoked (in part): SI 1997/712 r.2

531. Justices of the Peace Act 1979 (Amendment) Order 1990
revoked: 1997 c.25 s.73, Sch.6 Part II

536. Social Security (Refunds) (Repayment of Contractual Maternity Pay) Regulations 1990
Reg.2, applied: 1999 c.2 s.1, Sch.2
Reg.3, applied: 1999 c.2 s.1, Sch.2

545. Community Charges (Deductions from Income Support) (No.2) Regulations 1990
applied: SI 1999/991 Reg.27, Sch.2 para.9
Reg.1, amended: SI 1996/2344 Reg.6, SI 1998/563 Reg.3, SI 1999/2860 Art.3, Sch.6 para.1, SI 1999/3178 Art.3, Sch.11 para.1
Reg.2, amended: SI 1996/2344 Reg.7, SI 1999/2860 Art.3, Sch.6 para.2, SI 1999/3178 Art.3, Sch.11 para.2
Reg.2, revoked (in part): SI 1999/3178 Art.3, Sch.11 para.2
Reg.2A, added: SI 1996/2344 Reg.8
Reg.2A, amended: SI 1999/2860 Art.3, Sch.6 para.3
Reg.2A, revoked: SI 1999/3178 Art.3, Sch.11 para.3
Reg.3, amended: SI 1999/2860 Art.3, Sch.6 para.4
Reg.3, substituted: SI 1999/3178 Art.3, Sch.11 para.3
Reg.4, amended: SI 1996/2344 Reg.9, SI 1999/3178 Art.3, Sch.11 para.4
Reg.5, substituted: SI 1999/2860 Art.3, Sch.6 para.5, SI 1999/3178 Art.3, Sch.11 para.5
Reg.6, revoked: SI 1999/2860 Art.3, Sch.6 para.6
Reg.6, substituted: SI 1999/3178 Art.3, Sch.11 para.5
Reg.7, revoked: SI 1999/2860 Art.3, Sch.6 para.6, SI 1999/3178 Art.3, Sch.11 para.6
Reg.8, revoked: SI 1999/2860 Art.3, Sch.6 para.6, SI 1999/3178 Art.3, Sch.11 para.6
Reg.9, revoked: SI 1999/2860 Art.3, Sch.6 para.6, SI 1999/3178 Art.3, Sch.11 para.6
Reg.10, revoked: SI 1999/2860 Art.3, Sch.6 para.6, SI 1999/3178 Art.3, Sch.11 para.6
Reg.11, revoked: SI 1999/2860 Art.3, Sch.6 para.6, SI 1999/3178 Art.3, Sch.11 para.6
Sch.1, revoked: SI 1999/2860 Art.3, Sch.6 para.7, SI 1999/3178 Art.3, Sch.11 para.6
Sch.2, revoked: SI 1999/2860 Art.3, Sch.6 para.7, SI 1999/3178 Art.3, Sch.11 para.6

547. Income Support (General) Amendment Regulations 1990
Reg.9, revoked: SI 1996/206 Reg.28, Sch.3
Reg.15, revoked: SI 1996/206 Reg.28, Sch.3
Reg.16, revoked: SI 1996/206 Reg.28, Sch.3

549. Education (Grant-Maintained Schools) (Finance) Regulations 1990
applied: SI 1996/889 Reg.3, SI 1997/599 Reg.3, SI 1998/799 Reg.3
referred to: 1996 c.56 Sch.39 para.33, SI 1997/996 Reg.3

NO.

549. Education (Grant-Maintained Schools) (Finance) Regulations 1990—*cont.*
Reg.13, applied: SI 1997/599 Reg.3

563. Town and Country Planning (Fees for Applications and Deemed Applications) (Scotland) Regulations 1990
revoked (in part): SI 1997/10 Reg.15

567. Medicines (Exemption from Licences) (Intermediate Medicated Feedingstuffs) (Amendment) Order 1990
revoked: SI 1998/1048 Reg.2, Sch.1

571. Welfare Food Amendment (No.2) Regulations 1990
revoked: SI 1996/1434 Reg.23, Sch.7

572. Companies (Forms) (Amendment) Regulations 1990
Sch.2 Form 224, revoked: SI 1996/594 Reg.3
Sch.2 Form 225, revoked (in part): SI 1996/594 Reg.3
Sch.2 Form 701, revoked (in part): SI 1996/594 Reg.3

586. Retirement Benefits Schemes (Tax Relief on Contributions) (Disapplication of Earnings Cap) Regulations 1990
amended: SI 1996/3113 Reg.4
Reg.2, amended: SI 1996/3113 Reg.3
Reg.6, added: SI 1996/3113 Reg.5

593. Companies (Northern Ireland) Order 1990
referred to: 1998 c.47 Sch.3 para.23
Art.28, revoked: 1997 c.24 Sch.3 para.2
Sch.10 para.30, revoked (in part): 1997 c.16 Sch.18 Part VI
Sch.14 para.8, amended: SI 1999/506 Art.41
Sch.14 para.9, substituted: 1998 c.41 Sch.2 para.3

594. Licensing (Northern Ireland) Order 1990
applied: SI 1996/3159 (NI.23) Art.5
referred to: SI 1996/3158 (NI.22) Art.7
revoked: SI 1996/3158 (NI.22) Sch.13
Art.12, applied: SI 1996/3158 (NI.22) Art.2
Art.12, referred to: SI 1996/3158 (NI.22) Art.5
Art.12, revoked: SI 1996/3158 (NI.22) Sch.13
Art.28, applied: SI 1996/3158 (NI.22) Sch.12 para.2
Art.28, revoked: SI 1996/3158 (NI.22) Sch.13
Art.29, applied: SI 1996/3158 (NI.22) Sch.12 para.2
Art.29, revoked: SI 1996/3158 (NI.22) Sch.13
Art.30, applied: SI 1996/3158 (NI.22) Sch.12 para.2
Art.30, revoked: SI 1996/3158 (NI.22) Sch.13
Sch.12 para.1, applied: SI 1996/3158 (NI.22) Sch.12 para.1
Sch.12 para.1, revoked: SI 1996/3158 (NI.22) Sch.13

607. Milk and Milk Products (Protection of Designations) Regulations 1990
Reg.5, revoked: SI 1996/1499 Reg.49, Sch.9

608. Non-Domestic Rating (Transitional Period) Regulations 1990
see *R. v Huelin Ex p. Murphy Ltd* [1999] R.V.R. 153 (QBD), Owen, J.

618. Plant Breeders' Rights (Fees) Regulations 1990
revoked: SI 1998/1021 Reg.7 (with savings), Sch.2 (with savings)
Reg.2, revoked: SI 1998/1021 Reg.7 (with savings), Sch.2 (with savings)
Reg.3, revoked: SI 1998/1021 Reg.7 (with savings), Sch.2 (with savings)
Reg.4, amended: SI 1997/382 Reg.2
Reg.4, revoked: SI 1998/1021 Reg.7 (with savings), Sch.2 (with savings)

NO.

618. Plant Breeders' Rights (Fees) Regulations 1990—*cont.*
Sch., revoked: SI 1998/1021 Reg.7 (with savings), Sch.2 (with savings)
Sch., substituted: SI 1997/382 Reg.2, Sch.
Sch. Part II, revoked: SI 1998/1021 Reg.7 (with savings), Sch.2 (with savings)
Sch. Part III, revoked: SI 1998/1021 Reg.7 (with savings), Sch.2 (with savings)
Sch. Part III, substituted: SI 1997/382 Reg.2, Sch.

631. Civil Legal Aid (Scotland) Amendment Regulations 1990
revoked: SI 1996/2444 Reg.3, Sch.1

632. Advice and Assistance (Scotland) Amendment Regulations 1990
revoked: SI 1996/2447 Reg.3, Sch.1

659. Merchant Shipping (Passenger Counting and Recording Systems) Regulations 1990
revoked: SI 1999/1869 Reg.2

660. Merchant Shipping (Emergency Information for Passengers) Regulations 1990
applied: SI 1996/3243 Sch Part I

687. European Parliamentary Elections (Amendment) Regulations 1990
revoked: SI 1999/1214 Reg.20, Sch.5

696. Financial Services Act 1986 (Listed Money Market Institutions and Miscellaneous Exemptions) Order 1990
Art.1, revoked (in part): SI 1997/816 Art.4
Art.2, revoked: SI 1997/816 Art.4

702. Public Trustee (Fees) (Amendment) Order 1990
revoked: SI 1999/855 Art.32, Sch.

703. Highways (Road Humps) Regulations 1990
referred to: SI 1996/1483 Reg.9
revoked: SI 1996/1483 Reg.8

718. Act of Adjournal (Consolidation Amendment No.2) (Drug Trafficking) 1990
revoked: SI 1996/513 Sch.2 r.3, Sch.3

719. Public Airport Companies (Capital Finance) Order 1990
revoked: SI 1996/604 Reg.5

720. Passenger Transport Executives (Capital Finance) Order 1990
Art.1, amended: SI 1996/3058 Art.2
Art.2, amended: SI 1997/253 Art.2, SI 1999/3310 Art.2
Art.2, revoked (in part): SI 1999/3310 Art.2
Art.3, amended: SI 1999/3310 Art.2
Art.3, revoked (in part): SI 1999/3310 Art.2
Art.4, amended: SI 1999/3310 Art.2
Art.5, amended: SI 1999/3310 Art.2

730. Football Spectators (Designation of Enforcing Authority) Order 1990
revoked: SI 1999/2459 Art.2

767. Local Authorities (Borrowing) Regulations 1990
Reg.7, amended: SI 1998/1129 Art.2, Sch.1 para.10

776. Local Government Finance (Repeals, Savings and Consequential Amendments) Order 1990
Sch.3 para.13, revoked: 1998 c.43 s.1, Sch.1 Part IV

778. Local Authorities (Capital Finance) (Consequential Amendments) Order 1990
Sch. para.2, revoked: 1996 c.52 Sch.19 Part IX

785. Housing Benefit (Subsidy) Order 1990
Art.3, applied: SI 1996/1217 Art.11, SI 1998/562 Art.19

1990—cont.

791. **Meters (Approval of Pattern or Construction and Method of Installation) Regulations 1990**
revoked: SI 1998/1565 Reg.12

792. **Meters (Certification) Regulations 1990**
revoked: SI 1998/1566 Reg.12

795. **Sunderland (Hylton Riverside and South-wick) Enterprise Zone (Designation) Order 1990**
referred to: SI 1998/576

803. **Town and Country Planning (Compensation for Restrictions on Mineral Working) (Amendment) Regulations 1990**
revoked: SI 1997/1111 Reg.8

816. **Milk and Milk Products (Designations) (Scotland) Regulations 1990**
Reg.5, revoked: SI 1996/1499 Reg.49, Sch.9

817. **Docks and Harbours (Rateable Values) (Scotland) Order 1990**
applied: SI 1997/452 Reg.6, SI 1998/519 Reg.6, SI 1999/276 Reg.6
referred to: SI 1996/103 Reg.6

830. **Housing (Management of Houses in Multiple Occupation) Regulations 1990**
see *Jacques v Liverpool City Council* (1996) 72 P. & C.R. D19 (QBD), McKinnon, J.

842. **Motor Vehicles (Driving Licences) (Amendment) Regulations 1990**
revoked: SI 1996/2824 Reg.2, Sch.1

851. **Local Government Officers (Political Restrictions) Regulations 1990**
see *Ahmed v United Kingdom* [1999] I.R.L.R. 188 (ECHR), R Bernhardt (President)
Sch. para.1, amended: SI 1998/3116 Reg.2, SI 1999/715 Reg.2, SI 1999/1665 Reg.2
Sch. para.1A, added: SI 1998/3116 Reg.2
Sch. para.1B, added: SI 1999/715 Reg.2
Sch. para.1C, added: SI 1999/715 Reg.2
Sch. para.2A, added: SI 1998/3116 Reg.2
Sch. para.2B, added: SI 1999/715 Reg.2
Sch. para.2C, added: SI 1999/715 Reg.2
Sch. para.2D, added: SI 1999/1665 Reg.2

862. **Redundancy Payments (Local Government) (Modification) (Amendment) Order 1990**
revoked: SI 1999/2277 Art.4, Sch.3

879. **Copyright (Certification of Licensing Scheme for Educational Recording of Broadcasts and Cable Programmes) (Educational Recording Agency Limited) Order 1990**
applied: SI 1999/3452
referred to: SI 1998/203
Sch. para.4, amended: SI 1996/191 Art.2, SI 1998/203 Art.2, SI 1999/3452 Art.2
Sch. para.10, amended: SI 1996/191 Art.2, SI 1998/203 Art.2, SI 1999/3452 Art.2

892. **Merchant Shipping (Passenger Ship Construction and Survey) (Amendment) Regulations 1990**
revoked: SI 1998/2514 Reg.1

896. **Offshore Installations (Safety Zones) (No.2) Order 1990**
revoked: SI 1997/735 Art.3, Sch.2

897. **Offshore Installations (Safety Zones) (No.3) Order 1990**
revoked: SI 1997/735 Art.3, Sch.2

958. **Seed Potatoes (Fees) Regulations 1990**
revoked: SI 1998/1228 Reg.4

1990—cont.

973. **Offshore Installations (Safety Zones) (No.4) Order 1990**
revoked: SI 1997/735 Art.3, Sch.2

996. **Diving Operations at Work (Amendment) Regulations 1990**
revoked: SI 1997/2776 Reg.18

1013. **Nitrate Sensitive Areas (Designation) Order 1990**
applied: SI 1996/3142 Reg.6, Reg.10

1017. **Police (Discipline) (Senior Officers) (Scotland) Regulations 1990**
revoked: SI 1996/1645 Reg.31 (with savings)

1018. **Banking Act 1987 (Exempt Transactions) (Amendment No.2) Regulations 1990**
revoked: SI 1997/817 Reg.16

1019. **Housing (Change of Landlord) (Payment of Disposal Cost by Instalments) Regulations 1990**
Reg.3, amended: SI 1996/184 Reg.2, SI 1996/1269 Reg.2, SI 1996/2228 Reg.2, SI 1997/328 Reg.2, SI 1997/1621 Reg.2, SI 1997/2001 Reg.2, SI 1998/265 Reg.2, SI 1998/2082 Reg.2
Reg.3, applied: SI 1997/319 Reg.6

1037. **Advice and Assistance (Scotland) Amendment (No.2) Regulations 1990**
revoked: SI 1996/2447 Reg.3, Sch.1

1085. **Education (Recognised Awards) (Amendment) Order 1990**
revoked: SI 1996/2564 Art.3, Sch.

1106. **Offshore Installations (Safety Zones) (No.5) Order 1990**
revoked: SI 1997/735 Art.3, Sch.2

1115. **Motor Vehicles (Driving Licences) (Amendment) (No.2) Regulations 1990**
revoked: SI 1996/2824 Reg.2, Sch.1

1141. **Personal and Occupational Pension Schemes (Miscellaneous Amendments) Regulations 1990**
Reg.2, revoked: SI 1997/358 Reg.7, Sch
Reg.6, revoked: SI 1996/1172 Sch.2
Reg.8, revoked: SI 1997/470 Reg.20, Sch.3

1142. **Personal and Occupational Pension Schemes (Miscellaneous Amendments) (No.2) Regulations 1990**
Reg.2, revoked: SI 1996/1172 Sch.2
Reg.5, revoked: SI 1996/1847 Reg.21, Sch.3
Reg.7, revoked: SI 1996/1537 Reg.18, Sch.

1143. **Personal and Occupational Pension Schemes (Perpetuities) Regulations 1990**
Reg.5, amended: SI 1996/2131 Reg.3

1156. **Bass (Specified Areas) (Prohibition of Fishing) Order 1990**
Art.2, amended: SI 1999/75 Art.2
Sch., substituted: SI 1999/75 Art.2, Sch.

1169. **Pleasure Craft (Arrival and Report) Regulations 1990**
revoked: SI 1996/1406 Reg.7

1181. **Insurance Companies (Credit Insurance) Regulations 1990**
Reg.6, revoked: SI 1996/943 Reg.35, Sch.7

1189. **Housing Renovation etc. Grants (Reduction of Grant) Regulations 1990**
Reg.10, applied: SI 1996/2890 Reg.13
Reg.11, applied: SI 1996/2890 Reg.13

1191. **Goods Vehicles (Operators' Licences) (Temporary Use in Great Britain) (Amendment) Regulations 1990**
revoked: SI 1996/2186 Reg.2, Sch.1

NO.

1199. Drug Trafficking Offences Act 1986 (Designated Countries and Territories) Order 1990
revoked: SI 1996/2880 Art.10
Sch.3, revoked: SI 1996/2880 Art.10

1200. Industrial Training (Northern Ireland) Order 1990
Art.3, revoked (in part): SI 1996/1919 (NI.16)
Art.257, Sch.3

1201. Trial of the Pyx (Amendment) Order 1990
revoked: SI 1998/1764 Art.16, Sch.3

1202. New Forest (Confirmation of the Byelaws of the Verderers of the New Forest) Order 1990
revoked: SI 1999/2134 Art.3

1211. Stock Transfer (Gilt-Edged Securities) (Exempt Transfer) Regulations 1990
Reg.2, amended: SI 1999/1210 Reg.2

1241. London Docklands Development Corporation (Vesting of Land) (London Borough of Southwark) Order 1990
revoked: SI 1998/769 Art.3, Sch.

1273. Local Authorities (Capital Finance) (Amendment) Regulations 1990
revoked: SI 1997/319 Reg.162, Sch.3

1276. Corn Returns (Scotland) (Variation) Regulations 1990
revoked: SI 1997/1873 Reg.5

1284. Local Government Superannuation (Scotland) (No.2) Regulations 1990
applied: SI 1998/364 Reg.4, Reg.6, Reg.19, Sch.2 para.2, Sch.2 para.5, Sch.4 para.8
referred to: SI 1998/364 Reg.3, Reg.10, Sch.2 para.4, Sch.2 para.6

1310. Nursing Homes Registration (Scotland) Regulations 1990
Sch.2, substituted: SI 1998/661 Reg.2

1316. Home-Grown Cereals Authority Levy (Variation) Scheme (Approval) Order 1990
applied: SI 1996/1577
referred to: SI 1996/2843, SI 1996/2843 Sch. para.2

1317. Home-Grown Cereals Authority Oilseeds Levy Scheme (Approval) Order 1990
applied: SI 1996/1454, SI 1997/1337
referred to: SI 1998/1314

1330. Family Health Services Authorities (Membership and Procedure) Regulations 1990
revoked: SI 1996/707 Reg.17, Sch.4 Part I

1331. Regional and District Health Authorities (Membership and Procedure) Regulations 1990
revoked: SI 1996/707 Reg.17, Sch.4 Part I

1333. Insurance Companies (Amendment) Regulations 1990
see *Credit Lyonnais v New Hampshire Insurance Co* [1997] 1 Lloyd's Rep. 191 (QBD), Barbara Dohmann Q.C.
Reg.3, revoked (in part): SI 1996/943 Reg.35, Sch.7
Reg.11, revoked (in part): SI 1996/943 Reg.35, Sch.7

1349. War Pensions Committees Regulations 1990
Sch.1, amended: SI 1996/1790 Reg.2

1351. Corn Returns (Variation) Regulations 1990
revoked: SI 1997/1873 Reg.5

1360. Land Registration (Matrimonial Homes) Rules 1990
revoked: SI 1997/1964 r.11

1375. Community Health Councils (Amendment) Regulations 1990
revoked: SI 1996/640 Reg.23

NO.

1380. Health and Safety (Training for Employment) Regulations 1990
applied: SI 1996/1513 Reg.10

1382. Lands Tribunal (Amendment) Rules 1990
revoked: SI 1996/1022 r.57, Sch.2

1396. Motor Vehicles (Driving Licences) (Amendment) (No.3) Regulations 1990
revoked: SI 1996/2824 Reg.2, Sch.1

1407. National Health Service (Appointment of Consultants) Amendment Regulations 1990
revoked: SI 1996/701 Art.10

1432. Education (Reorganisation in Inner London) (Redundancy Payments) (Amendment) Order 1990
revoked: SI 1999/2277 Art.4, Sch.3

1448. Police and Criminal Evidence Act 1984 (Application to Armed Forces) (Amendment) Order 1990
revoked: SI 1997/15 Art.3

1457. Register of Patent Agents Rules 1990
amended: SI 1999/983 r.2

1458. Register of Trade Mark Agents Rules 1990
amended: SI 1999/983 r.3

1460. Supreme Court Fees (Amendment) Order 1990
revoked: SI 1999/687 Art.8 (with savings), Sch.2 (with savings)

1484. Local Government Act 1988 (Defined Activities) (Competition and Specified Periods) (Scotland) Regulations 1990
Reg.4, amended: SI 1996/917 Reg.4

1485. Local Government Act 1988 (Defined Activities) (Exemptions) (Scotland) Amendment Order 1990
revoked: SI 1997/198 Art.11

1487. Social Security (Unemployment, Sickness and Invalidity Benefit) Regulations 1990
revoked: SI 1996/1345 Reg.27, Sch.

1500. Highways (Road Humps) (Amendment) Regulations 1990
revoked: SI 1996/1483 Reg.8

1504. Companies (No.2) (Northern Ireland) Order 1990
referred to: 1998 c.47 Sch.3 para.23
Art.93, amended: 1998 c.11 s.23, Sch.5 para.50
Art.98, amended: 1998 c.11 s.23, Sch.5 para.51
Sch.3 para.1, revoked: SI 1996/725 (NI.5) Sch.4
Sch.3 para.7, revoked: SI 1996/275 (NI.2) Art.71, Sch.8

1506. Education (Student Loans) (Northern Ireland) Order 1990
applied: SI 1997/817 Reg.11, SI 1998/2026 Reg.3, SI 1999/1001 Reg.4
referred to: SI 1998/2003 Reg.3, SI 1999/496 Reg.4
revoked: SI 1998/1760 (NI.14) Art.9, Sch.
Art.3, amended: SI 1996/274 (NI.1) Art.43, Sch.5 Part II, SI 1996/1918 (NI.15) Art.3, Sch para.2, SI 1997/1772 Art.25, Sch.4
Art.3, applied: SI 1996/207 Reg.103, Reg.136, SI 1996/2890 Reg.46, SI 1998/258 (NI.1) Art.5
Art.3, revoked: SI 1998/1760 (NI.14) Art.9, Sch.
Art.3A, added: SI 1998/258 (NI.1) Art.3
Art.3A, revoked: SI 1998/1760 (NI.14) Art.9, Sch.
Sch.2 para.1, amended: SI 1996/274 (NI.1) Art.43, Sch.5 Part II, SI 1996/1918 (NI.15) Sch para.2, SI 1998/258 (NI.1) Art.4

NO.

1506. Education (Student Loans) (Northern Ireland) Order 1990—*cont.*

Sch.2 para.1, revoked: SI 1998/1760 (NI.14) Art.9, Sch.

Sch.2 para.2, amended: SI 1996/274 (NI.1) Art.43, Sch.5 Part II, SI 1996/1918 (NI.15) Sch para.2, Sch para.3

Sch.2 para.2, revoked: SI 1998/1760 (NI.14) Art.9, Sch.

Sch.2 para.3, amended: SI 1996/1918 (NI.15) Sch para.2

Sch.2 para.3, applied: SI 1998/258 (NI.1) Art.5

Sch.2 para.3, revoked: SI 1998/1760 (NI.14) Art.9, Sch.

Sch.2 para.3, substituted: SI 1998/258 (NI.1) Art.5

Sch.2 para.3A, added: SI 1996/1918 (NI.15) Sch para.3

Sch.2 para.3A, amended: SI 1998/258 (NI.1) Art.5

Sch.2 para.3A, revoked: SI 1998/1760 (NI.14) Art.9, Sch.

Sch.2 para.4, amended: SI 1996/1918 (NI.15) Sch para.3, SI 1998/261 (NI.2) Art.5

Sch.2 para.4, revoked: SI 1998/1760 (NI.14) Art.9, Sch.

Sch.2 para.5, amended: SI 1996/1918 (NI.15) Sch para.3

Sch.2 para.5, revoked: SI 1998/1760 (NI.14) Art.9, Sch.

1507. European Convention on Extradition Order 1990

applied: SI 1996/2875 Art.2

Art.2, amended: SI 1996/2875 Art.2, SI 1997/1759 Art.2

Art.4, revoked: SI 1996/2875 Art.2

Sch.1, amended: SI 1996/2596 Art.2

Sch.2 Part I, amended: SI 1997/1759 Art.2, SI 1997/2596 Art.2, SI 1998/259 Art.2, SI 1999/2035 Art.2

Sch.3 Part 1, added: SI 1999/2035 Art.2

Sch.3 Part 1A, added: SI 1998/259 Art.2

Sch.3 Part 1AA, added: SI 1999/2035 Art.2

Sch.3 Part 1B, amended: SI 1998/259 Art.2

Sch.3 Part 1C, amended: SI 1998/259 Art.2

Sch.3 Part 3A, added: SI 1997/2596 Art.2

Sch.3 Part 11A, added: SI 1997/2596 Art.2

Sch.3 Part 13A, added: SI 1997/1759 Art.2

Sch.3 Part 13B, added: SI 1998/259 Art.2

Sch.3 Part 16A, added: SI 1998/259 Art.2

Sch.3 Part 21, added: SI 1999/2035 Art.2

Sch.4, see *R. v Governor of Brixton Prison Ex p. Cuoghi* [1998] 1 W.L.R. 1513 (QBD), Kennedy, L.J.

Sch.5, amended: SI 1999/2035 Art.2

Sch.5 Part 6, added: SI 1997/2596 Art.2, SI 1998/259 Art.2

Sch.5 Part 8, added: SI 1999/2035 Art.2

1511. Social Security (Northern Ireland) Order 1990

Art.17, amended: SI 1996/2879 (NI.21) Art.3

Art.17, referred to: SI 1999/659 (NI.3) Art.5

Sch.1 para.6, revoked: SI 1997/1183 (NI.12) Art.31, Sch.4

1514. Air Navigation (Noise Certification) Order 1990

Art.4, amended: SI 1999/1452 Reg.2

Art.5, revoked (in part): SI 1999/1452 Reg.2

Art.6, revoked (in part): SI 1999/1452 Reg.2

Sch.1 Part I, revoked (in part): SI 1999/1452 Reg.2

Sch.1 Part II, revoked: SI 1999/1452 Reg.2

NO.

1514. Air Navigation (Noise Certification) Order 1990—*cont.*

Sch.1 Part III, revoked: SI 1999/1452 Reg.2

Sch.1 Part IV, revoked: SI 1999/1452 Reg.2

Sch.1 Part VI, revoked: SI 1999/1452 Reg.2

1519. Planning (Listed Buildings and Conservation Areas) Regulations 1990

Reg.7, amended: SI 1996/525 Sch para.13

Reg.9, applied: SI 1996/1243 Sch.5 para.12

Reg.13, amended: SI 1996/525 Sch para.13

Sch.1 Part II, amended: SI 1996/525 Sch para.13

Sch.1 Part II, applied: SI 1996/1243 Sch.5 para.12

1525. Authorities for London Post-Graduate Teaching Hospitals (Constitution) Order 1990

revoked: SI 1996/511 Art.11

1526. London Post-Graduate Teaching Hospitals Regulations 1990

revoked: SI 1996/512 Reg.2

1529. Banking Act 1987 (Exempt Transactions) (Amendment No.3) Regulations 1990

referred to: SI 1997/817 Reg.16

1530. Occupational Pension Schemes (Transitional Provisions and Savings) Regulations 1990

revoked: SI 1996/2156 Reg.15 (with savings)

1532. Assured Tenancies and Agricultural Occupancies (Forms) (Amendment) Regulations 1990

revoked: SI 1997/194 Reg.4

1541. Life Assurance (Apportionment of Receipts of Participating Funds) (Applicable Percentage) Order 1990

Art.3, amended: SI 1998/2920 Art.3

Art.3, applied: SI 1998/2920 Art.1

1549. Social Security Benefits (Student Loans and Miscellaneous Amendments) Regulations 1990

Reg.5, revoked (in part): SI 1996/206 Reg.28, Sch.3

Reg.6, revoked: SI 1996/1345 Reg.27, Sch.

1553. Local Government (Committees and Political Groups) Regulations 1990

Reg.4, amended: SI 1998/1918 Reg.3

Reg.5, amended: SI 1999/500 Reg.2

Reg.16A, amended: SI 1998/1918 Reg.4

Reg.16B, added: SI 1998/1918 Reg.4

Reg.16B, amended: SI 1999/500 Reg.2

Sch., substituted: SI 1998/1918 Reg.3, Sch.

1564. Local Government Act 1988 (Defined Activities) (Competition) (England) Regulations 1990

Reg.3, applied: SI 1996/823 Reg.2

Reg.3, revoked: SI 1997/2747 Reg.2, Sch.

1567. London Docklands Development Corporation (Planning Functions) Order 1990

applied: SI 1996/2986 Art.6, SI 1996/3148 Art.6, SI 1997/1738 Art.6, SI 1997/2946 Art.3

revoked: SI 1997/2946 Art.2

1568. Merseyside Development Corporation (Planning Functions) Order 1990

revoked: SI 1998/84 Art.2, Sch.

1634. Gas (Alternative Method of Charge) Regulations 1990

applied: SI 1996/439 Reg.4

1640. Export of Goods (Control) (Iraq and Kuwait Sanctions) Order 1990

Art.3, amended: SI 1999/1776 Art.2

NO.

1643. Anglian Regional Flood Defence Committee Order 1990
revoked: SI 1996/1618 Art.3

1647. Wessex Regional Flood Defence Committee Order 1990
revoked: SI 1996/1615 Art.3

1651. Iraq and Kuwait (United Nations Sanctions) Order 1990
Art.1, amended: SI 1998/3163 Art.2
Art.6, amended: SI 1998/3163 Art.2
Art.7, amended: SI 1998/3163 Art.2
Art.8, amended: SI 1998/3163 Art.2
Sch. para.1, amended: SI 1998/3163 Art.2
Sch. para.2, amended: SI 1998/3163 Art.2
Sch. para.3, amended: SI 1998/3163 Art.2
Sch. para.4, amended: SI 1998/3163 Art.2

1652. Iraq and Kuwait (United Nations Sanctions) (Dependent Territories) Order 1990
Art.3, amended: SI 1997/1175 Art.2

1657. Income-related Benefits Amendment Regulations 1990
Reg.5, revoked (in part): SI 1996/206 Reg.28, Sch.3

1668. Import and Export (Plant Health Fees) (Forestry) (Great Britain) Order 1990
revoked: SI 1996/2291 Reg.3

1695. Building Societies (Transfer of Business) (Amendment) Regulations 1990
revoked: SI 1998/212 Reg.10

1712. Thames Regional Flood Defence Committee Order 1990
Art.2, revoked (in part): SI 1997/1363 Art.3
Sch., revoked: SI 1997/1363 Art.3

1719. Prescription Pricing Authority Regulations 1990
Reg.1, amended: SI 1996/707 Reg.17, Sch.5 para.3
Reg.8A, added: SI 1998/1576 Reg.2
Reg.9, amended: SI 1996/707 Reg.17, Sch.5 para.3
Reg.10, revoked: SI 1996/707 Reg.17
Sch., substituted: SI 1996/707 Reg.17, Sch.5 para.3

1730. Housing (Prescribed Forms) (No.2) Regulations 1990
Reg.2, amended: SI 1997/872 Sch.1 para.1, Sch.1 para.2
Sch. Form 1, amended: SI 1997/1903 Reg.2, Sch. para.1
Sch. Form 2, amended: SI 1997/1903 Reg.2, Sch. para.1
Sch. Form 3, amended: SI 1997/1903 Reg.2, Sch. para.1
Sch. Form 4, amended: SI 1997/1903 Reg.2, Sch. para.2
Sch. Form 5, amended: SI 1997/1903 Reg.2, Sch. para.2
Sch. Form 6, amended: SI 1997/872 Sch.2 para.1
Sch. Form 7, amended: SI 1997/872 Sch.2 para.2
Sch. Form 8, amended: SI 1997/872 Sch.2 para.3
Sch. Form 9, amended: SI 1997/872 Sch.2 para.4
Sch. Form 10, amended: SI 1997/872 Sch.2 para.5
Sch. Form 10A, added: SI 1997/872 Sch.2 para.6
Sch. Form 13, amended: SI 1997/1903 Reg.2, Sch. para.3
Sch. Form 14, amended: SI 1997/1903 Reg.2, Sch. para.4

NO.

1730. Housing (Prescribed Forms) (No.2) Regulations 1990—*cont.*
Sch. Form 19, amended: SI 1997/1903 Reg.2, Sch. para.5
Sch. Form 20, amended: SI 1997/1903 Reg.2, Sch. para.6
Sch. Form 21, amended: SI 1997/1903 Reg.2, Sch. para.7
Sch. Form 27, amended: SI 1997/872 Sch.2 para.7
Sch. Form 28, amended: SI 1997/872 Sch.2 para.8
Sch. Form 29, amended: SI 1997/872 Sch.2 para.9
Sch. Form 34, amended: SI 1997/872 Sch.2 para.10
Sch. Form 35, amended: SI 1997/872 Sch.2 para.11
Sch. Form 37, amended: SI 1997/872 Sch.2 para.12

1758. Regional and District Health Authorities (Membership and Procedure) Amendment Regulations 1990
revoked: SI 1996/707 Reg.17, Sch.4 Part I

1762. Prison (Amendment) Rules 1990
revoked: SI 1999/728 r.85 (with savings), Sch. (with savings)

1764. County Court (Amendment No.3) Rules 1990
r.17, see *Tarry v Humberclyde Finance Ltd* [1996] 1 W.L.R. 611 (CA), Sir Thomas Bingham, M.R.

1766. Companies (Forms Amendment No.2 and Company's Type and Business Activities) Regulations 1990
Reg.2, amended: SI 1996/1105 Reg.2
Reg.5, amended: SI 1996/1105 Reg.2
Reg.5, applied: SI 1996/1105 Reg.2
Sch.3 Part II, substituted: SI 1996/1105 Reg.2

1772. National Health Service (General Dental Services) (Miscellaneous Amendments) (Scotland) Regulations 1990
revoked (in part): SI 1996/177 Reg.38, Sch.8
Reg.6, revoked: SI 1997/174 Reg.18, Sch
Reg.7, revoked: SI 1997/174 Reg.18, Sch
Reg.9, revoked: SI 1997/174 Reg.18, Sch

1777. Income Support (Liable Relatives) Regulations 1990
Reg.3, applied: SI 1997/291 r.6.4

1812. Cosmetic Products (Safety) (Amendment) Regulations 1990
revoked: SI 1996/2925 Sch.9

1825. Assured and Protected Tenancies (Lettings to Students) (Amendment) Regulations 1990
revoked: SI 1998/1967 Reg.6, Sch.3

1828. Zebra Pedestrian Crossings (Amendment) Regulations 1990
revoked: SI 1997/2400 Reg.2

1855. Authorities for London Post-Graduate Teaching Hospitals (Constitution) Amendment Order 1990
revoked: SI 1996/511 Art.11

1867. Bovine Animals (Identification, Marking and Breeding Records) Order 1990
applied: SI 1997/1901 Reg.3, SI 1998/871 Reg.29
revoked: SI 1997/1901 Reg.10
Art.9, applied: SI 1996/3241 Reg.13
Art.9, revoked: SI 1997/1901 Reg.10

1904. Non-Domestic Rating (Payment of Interest) Regulations 1990
Reg.4, amended: SI 1998/1129 Art.3, Sch.2

NO.

1905. Special Hospitals Service Authority (Establishment and Constitution) Amendment Order 1990
revoked: SI 1996/490 Art.2

1940. National Health Service (General Dental Services) (Miscellaneous Amendments) (Scotland) (No.2) Regulations 1990
revoked: SI 1996/177 Reg.38, Sch.8

1989. Education (Grant) Regulations 1990
Reg.5, revoked (in part): SI 1998/86 Reg.2, Sch.1
Reg.6A, added: SI 1997/678 Reg.3
Reg.6B, added: SI 1997/2961 Reg.3
Reg.18, amended: SI 1997/678 Reg.4

2012. Welfare Food Amendment (No.3) Regulations 1990
revoked: SI 1996/1434 Reg.23, Sch.7

2021. Occupational Pension Schemes (Modification) Regulations 1990
applied: SI 1997/664 Art.6
Reg.2, revoked: SI 1996/2156 Reg.15 (with savings)
Reg.3, revoked: SI 1996/2156 Reg.15 (with savings)

2024. National Health Service Trusts (Membership and Procedure) Regulations 1990
Reg.1, amended: SI 1996/1755 Reg.2, SI 1998/646 Reg.10
Reg.2, substituted: SI 1998/1975 Reg.2
Reg.3, substituted: SI 1996/1755 Reg.2
Reg.7, amended: SI 1996/1755 Reg.2
Reg.8, amended: SI 1996/1755 Reg.2
Reg.9, amended: SI 1996/1755 Reg.2, SI 1997/2990 Reg.2
Reg.11, amended: SI 1997/2990 Reg.2, SI 1998/646 Reg.10, SI 1998/1975 Reg.3, SI 1999/945 Reg.2
Reg.11, revoked (in part): SI 1997/2990 Reg.2
Reg.12, amended: SI 1996/1755 Reg.2

2035. Overhead Lines (Exemption) Regulations 1990
applied: SI 1999/1750 Art.2, Sch.1

2075. Occupational Pension Schemes (Independent Trustee) Regulations 1990
revoked: SI 1997/252 Reg.9
Reg.4, revoked: SI 1997/252 Reg.9

2101. Retirement Benefits Schemes (Continuation of Rights of Members of Approved Schemes) Regulations 1990
amended: SI 1996/3114 Reg.4
applied: SI 1997/1612 Sch.4 para.7, SI 1998/366 Sch.4 para.7
Reg.2, amended: SI 1996/3114 Reg.3
Reg.3, amended: SI 1996/3114 Reg.5
Reg.3A, added: SI 1996/3114 Reg.6
Reg.3A, amended: SI 1996/3233 Reg.2
Reg.3B, added: SI 1996/3114 Reg.6
Reg.7AA, added: SI 1999/1963 Reg.3

2106. Act of Adjournal (Consolidation Amendment No.2) (Miscellaneous) 1990
revoked: SI 1996/513 Sch.2 r.3, Sch.3

2117. Offshore Installations (Safety Zones) (No.6) Order 1990
revoked: SI 1997/735 Art.3, Sch.2

2128. Merchant Shipping (Load Line) (Amendment) Rules 1990
referred to: SI 1998/1609 Reg.5, Reg.6, Sch.
revoked: SI 1998/2241 Reg.3

NO.

2145. Civil Aviation Act 1982 (Jersey) (Amendment) Order 1990
Sch.1 para.14, amended: SI 1998/748 Art.2
Sch.1 para.14, revoked (in part): SI 1998/748 Art.2
Sch.1 para.28, amended: SI 1998/748 Art.3

2164. Nursing Homes and Mental Nursing Homes (Amendment) Regulations 1990
revoked: SI 1998/902 Reg.4

2179. Building Standards (Scotland) Regulations 1990
applied: SI 1997/1872 Reg.2
Reg.2, amended: SI 1996/2251 Reg.2, SI 1997/2157 Reg.2, SSI 1999/173 Reg.2
Reg.11, amended: SSI 1999/173 Reg.2
Reg.13, amended: SSI 1999/173 Reg.2
Reg.14, substituted: SSI 1999/173 Reg.2
Reg.15, substituted: SSI 1999/173 Reg.2
Reg.16, amended: SSI 1999/173 Reg.2
Reg.17, amended: SSI 1999/173 Reg.2
Reg.18, amended: SSI 1999/173 Reg.2
Reg.22, amended: SI 1997/2157 Reg.2
Reg.23, revoked (in part): SI 1997/2157 Reg.2
Reg.24, amended: SSI 1999/173 Reg.2
Reg.25, amended: SI 1996/2251 Reg.2
Reg.25, substituted: SSI 1999/173 Reg.2
Reg.25A, added: SSI 1999/173 Reg.2
Reg.26A, added: SSI 1999/173 Reg.2
Reg.29, amended: SSI 1999/173 Reg.2
Reg.32, substituted: SSI 1999/173 Reg.2
Reg.33, revoked: SSI 1999/173 Reg.2
Sch.1, substituted: SI 1996/2251 Reg.2, Sch.1, SSI 1999/173 Reg.2, Sch.1
Sch.1 Class 8, amended: SI 1997/2157 Reg.2
Sch.2, amended: SI 1997/2157 Reg.2
Sch.2, substituted: SI 1996/2251 Reg.2, Sch.2, SSI 1999/173 Reg.2, Sch.2
Sch.4, substituted: SSI 1999/173 Reg.2, Sch.3
Sch.5 para.1, amended: SI 1996/2251 Reg.2
Sch.5 para.1A, added: SSI 1999/173 Reg.2
Sch.5 para.3, revoked: SI 1996/2251 Reg.2
Sch.5 para.3A, added: SI 1996/2251 Reg.2
Sch.5 para.4, amended: SI 1996/2251 Reg.2

2208. Social Security (Miscellaneous Provisions) Amendment Regulations 1990
Reg.5, revoked: SI 1996/2745 Reg.18, Sch.4
Reg.6, revoked: SI 1996/2745 Reg.18, Sch.4

2230. National Health Service (Local Health Councils) (Scotland) Regulations 1990
Reg.6, amended: SI 1997/2289 Reg.6

2231. Income Tax (Building Societies) (Dividends and Interest) Regulations 1990
Reg.2, amended: SI 1996/223 Reg.3
Reg.4, amended: SI 1996/223 Reg.4, Reg.5
Reg.11, amended: SI 1996/223 Reg.6, Reg.7

2236. Land Registration (Solicitor to HM Land Registry) Regulations 1990
revoked: SI 1997/713 Reg.1

2238. Act of Sederunt (Applications under the Social Security Act 1986) 1990
revoked: SI 1997/291 r.1.4, Sch.2

2276. Statutory Nuisance (Appeals) Regulations 1990
Reg.2, see *Budd v Colchester BC* [1997] Env. L.R. 128 (QBD), Schiemann, L.J.; see *R. v Mid Sussex Justices Ex p. Mid Sussex DC* [1996] E.G.C.S. 34 (QBD), Hidden, J.; see *Sterling Homes (Midlands) Ltd v Birmingham City Council* [1996] Env. L.R. (QBD), McCullough, J.

NO.

2278. **Register of Occupational and Personal Pension Schemes Regulations 1990**
applied: SI 1997/371 Reg.3, Reg.8
revoked: SI 1997/371 Reg.9, Sch.

2324. **Income Support (General and Transitional) Amendment Regulations 1990**
Reg.3, revoked: SI 1996/206 Reg.28, Sch.3

2325. **Control of Industrial Major Accident Hazards (Amendment) Regulations 1990**
revoked: SI 1999/743 Reg.24

2334. **Motor Vehicles (Driving Licences) (Amendment) (No.5) Regulations 1990**
revoked: SI 1996/2824 Reg.2, Sch.1

2345. **Oil Pollution (Compulsory Insurance) (Amendment) (No.2) Regulations 1990**
revoked: SI 1997/1820 Reg.2

2351. **Education (School Premises) (Amendment) Regulations 1990**
revoked: SI 1996/360 Sch.1

2360. **Public Lending Right Scheme 1982 (Commencement of Variations) Order 1990**
Appendix.2 Art.14A, amended: SI 1999/1042 Art.3, Sch.1 para.19
Sch.1 para.5, amended: SI 1999/1042 Art.3, Sch.1 para.19

2361. **Tax-exempt Special Savings Account Regulations 1990**
Reg.7, amended: SI 1996/844 Reg.3
Reg.11, amended: SI 1996/844 Reg.4

2365. **Goods Vehicles (Authorisation of International Journeys) (Fees) (Amendment) Regulations 1990**
revoked: SI 1996/131 Reg.4, Sch.2

2377. **Electrical Equipment for Explosive Atmospheres (Certification) (Amendment) Regulations 1990**
revoked: SI 1996/192 Reg.1, Sch.1

2380. **Local Government (Compensation for Redundancy and Premature Retirement) (Amendment) Regulations 1990**
revoked: SI 1996/1680 Reg.49, Sch.5

2384. **Patent Rules 1990**
r.80, see *Rhone-Poulenc Sante's European Patent, Re* [1996] R.P.C. 125 (PO), L Lewis

2385. **Motor Vehicles (Driving Licences) (Amendment) (No.6) Regulations 1990**
revoked: SI 1998/20 Reg.27

2389. **Broadcasting (Local Delivery Services) Order 1990**
revoked: SI 1998/1240 Art.3

2401. **Anglian Harbours National Health Service Trust (Establishment) Order 1990**
revoked: SI 1997/1987 Art.2

2405. **Central Middlesex Hospital National Health Service Trust (Establishment) Order 1990**
revoked: SI 1999/914 Art.2

2408. **Cornwall and Isles of Scilly Mental Handicap National Health Service Trust (Establishment) Order 1990**
revoked: SI 1999/634 Art.2
Art.1, amended: SI 1996/1768 Art.2
Art.1, revoked: SI 1999/634 Art.2
Art.2, amended: SI 1996/1768 Art.2
Art.2, revoked: SI 1999/634 Art.2

2410. **Croydon Community National Health Service Trust (Establishment) Order 1990**
Art.1, amended: SI 1999/3164 Art.2
Art.2, amended: SI 1999/3164 Art.2

2414. **Epsom Health Care National Health Service Trust (Establishment) Order 1990**
revoked: SI 1999/849 Art.2

NO.

2416. **Freeman Group of Hospitals National Health Service Trust (Establishment) Order 1990**
revoked: SI 1998/831 Art.2

2418. **Hillingdon Hospital National Health Service Trust (Establishment) Order 1990**
Art.3, amended: SI 1999/1769 Art.2

2422. **Lifecare National Health Service Trust (Establishment) Order 1990**
revoked: SI 1999/423 Art.2

2433. **Northumbria Ambulance Service National Health Service Trust (Establishment) Order 1990**
revoked: SI 1999/796 Art.2

2435. **Royal Free Hampstead National Health Service Trust (Establishment) Order 1990**
Art.3, amended: SI 1996/871 Art.2

2441. **Royal National Throat, Nose and Ear Hospital National Health Service Trust (Establishment) Order 1990**
revoked: SI 1996/886 Art.2

2442. **Royal Surrey County and St Luke's Hospitals National Health Service Trust (Establishment) Order 1990**
Art.1, amended: SI 1996/2860 Art.2
Art.2, amended: SI 1996/2860 Art.2

2443. **Rugby National Health Service Trust (Establishment) Order 1990**
revoked: SI 1998/813 Art.2

2444. **South Devon Health Care National Health Service Trust (Establishment) Order 1990**
Art.3, amended: SI 1996/999 Art.2

2445. **Southend Health Care Services NHS Trust (Establishment) Order 1990**
Art.1, amended: SI 1997/2938 Art.2
Art.2, amended: SI 1997/2938 Art.2

2446. **St Helens and Knowsley Hospital Services National Health Service Trust (Establishment) Order 1990**
Art.1, amended: SI 1999/632 Art.2
Art.3, substituted: SI 1999/632 Art.2

2447. **St Helier National Health Service Trust (Establishment) Order 1990**
revoked: SI 1999/849 Art.2

2457. **Stock Transfer (Gilt-Edged Securities) (Exempt Transfer) (No.2) Regulations 1990**
Reg.2, amended: SI 1999/1210 Reg.2

2463. **Food Safety (Sampling and Qualifications) Regulations 1990**
Reg.2, amended: SI 1999/1603 Reg.9
Sch.1, amended: SI 1997/1729 Reg.35, SI 1998/1376 Reg.13, SI 1999/1603 Reg.9, SI 1999/1540 Reg.20
Sch.1, revoked: SI 1999/1540 Reg.20 (in part

2468. **Local Government Act 1988 (Defined Activities) (Specified Periods) (Inner London) Regulations 1990**
revoked: SI 1997/2747 Reg.2, Sch.

2474. **Town and Country Planning (Fees for Applications and Deemed Applications) (Scotland) Amendment Regulations 1990**
revoked (in part): SI 1997/10 Reg.15

2485. **Legal Services Ombudsman (Jurisdiction) Order 1990**
Art.3, amended: SI 1998/935 Art.2
Sch. Part I, amended: SI 1998/935 Art.3, SI 1999/2905 Art.2
Sch. Part II, amended: SI 1998/935 Art.3

2486. **Food Safety Act 1990 (Consequential Modifications) (England and Wales) Order 1990**
Art.20, referred to: 1999 c.28 s.40, Sch.5 para.22

207

NO.

2487. Food Safety Act 1990 (Consequential Modifications) (No.2) (Great Britain) Order 1990
Art.3, revoked (in part): SI 1999/1540 Reg.21, Sch.4

2488. Food Labelling (Amendment) Regulations 1990
revoked: SI 1996/1499 Reg.49, Sch.9

2489. Food Labelling (Amendment) (Irradiated Food) Regulations 1990
revoked: SI 1996/1499 Reg.49, Sch.9

2497. National Health Service (General Dental Services) (Scotland) Amendment Regulations 1990
revoked: SI 1996/177 Reg.38, Sch.8

2504. Radioactive Substances (Appeals) Regulations 1990
Reg.4, amended: SI 1996/973 Reg.2, Sch para.10

2505. Food Labelling (Amendment) (Irradiated Food) (Scotland) Regulations 1990
revoked: SI 1996/1499 Reg.49, Sch.9

2506. Food Labelling (Scotland) Amendment Regulations 1990
revoked: SI 1996/1499 Reg.49, Sch.9

2507. Milk and Dairies (Scotland) Regulations 1990
Reg.2, amended: SI 1998/2424 Reg.10

2508. Milk Labelling (Scotland) Amendment Regulations 1990
revoked: SI 1996/1499 Reg.49, Sch.9

2552. Income Tax (Stock Lending) (Amendment) Regulations 1990
revoked: SI 1997/987 Reg.2 (with savings), Sch.1 (with savings)

2570. Companies (Revision of Defective Accounts and Report) Regulations 1990
Reg.6, amended: SI 1996/315 Reg.3
Reg.7, amended: SI 1996/315 Reg.3
Reg.9, amended: SI 1996/315 Reg.4
Reg.10, amended: SI 1996/315 Reg.5
Reg.13A, added: SI 1996/315 Reg.6
Reg.16, amended: SI 1996/315 Reg.7

2583. National Health Service (Appointment of Consultants) (Wales) Amendment Regulations 1990
revoked: SI 1996/1313 Reg.10

2588. Criminal Justice (Confiscation) (Northern Ireland) Order 1990
applied: SI 1996/1299 (NI.9) Art.6
revoked (in part): SI 1996/1299 (NI.9) Art.57, Sch.5
Art.2, applied: SI 1996/1299 (NI.9) Sch.4 para.1
Art.3, applied: SI 1996/1299 (NI.9) Sch.4 para.1
Art.4, applied: SI 1996/1299 (NI.9) Sch.4 para.1
Art.5, applied: SI 1996/1299 (NI.9) Sch.4 para.1
Art.6, applied: SI 1996/1299 (NI.9) Sch.4 para.1
Art.7, applied: SI 1996/1299 (NI.9) Sch.4 para.1
Art.8, applied: SI 1996/1299 (NI.9) Sch.4 para.1
Art.9, applied: SI 1996/1299 (NI.9) Sch.4 para.1
Art.10, applied: SI 1996/1299 (NI.9) Sch.4 para.1
Art.11, applied: SI 1996/1299 (NI.9) Sch.4 para.1
Art.12, applied: SI 1996/1299 (NI.9) Sch.4 para.1
Art.13, applied: SI 1996/1299 (NI.9) Sch.4 para.1
Art.14, applied: SI 1996/1299 (NI.9) Art.31, Sch.4 para.1
Art.14, referred to: SI 1996/1299 (NI.9) Art.34

NO.

2588. Criminal Justice (Confiscation) (Northern Ireland) Order 1990—*cont.*
Art.15, applied: SI 1996/1299 (NI.9) Sch.4 para.1
Art.16, applied: SI 1996/1299 (NI.9) Sch.4 para.1
Art.17, applied: SI 1996/1299 (NI.9) Sch.4 para.1
Art.18, applied: SI 1996/1299 (NI.9) Sch.4 para.1
Art.19, applied: SI 1996/1299 (NI.9) Sch.4 para.1
Art.20, applied: SI 1996/1299 (NI.9) Sch.4 para.1
Art.21, applied: SI 1996/1299 (NI.9) Sch.4 para.1
Art.22, applied: SI 1996/1299 (NI.9) Sch.4 para.1
Art.23, applied: SI 1996/1299 (NI.9) Sch.4 para.1
Art.24, applied: SI 1996/1299 (NI.9) Sch.4 para.1
Art.25, applied: SI 1996/1299 (NI.9) Sch.4 para.1
Art.26, applied: SI 1996/1299 (NI.9) Sch.4 para.1
Art.27, applied: SI 1996/1299 (NI.9) Sch.4 para.1
Art.28, applied: SI 1996/1299 (NI.9) Sch.4 para.1
Art.34, applied: SI 1996/1299 (NI.9) Sch.4 para.1

2602. Merchant Shipping (IBC Code) (Amendment) Regulations 1990
revoked: SI 1996/3010 Reg.1

2603. Merchant Shipping (BCH Code) (Amendment) Regulations 1990
revoked: SI 1996/3010 Reg.1

2604. Merchant Shipping (Control of Pollution by Noxious Liquid Substances in Bulk) (Amendment) Regulations 1990
revoked: SI 1996/3010 Reg.1

2605. Merchant Shipping (Dangerous Goods and Marine Pollutants) Regulations 1990
applied: SI 1996/3243 Sch Part I
revoked: SI 1997/2367 Reg.1

2611. Motor Vehicles (Driving Licences) (Heavy Goods and Public Service Vehicles) Regulations 1990
revoked: SI 1997/669 Reg.2

2612. Motor Vehicles (Driving Licences) (Large Goods and Passenger-Carrying Vehicles) Regulations 1990
revoked: SI 1996/2824 Reg.2, Sch.1
Reg.3, amended: SI 1996/212 Reg.3
Reg.3, revoked: SI 1996/2824 Reg.2, Sch.1
Reg.12A, revoked (in part): SI 1996/212 Reg.4, SI 1996/2824 Reg.2, Sch.1
Reg.15, revoked: SI 1996/2824 Reg.2, Sch.1
Reg.15, substituted: SI 1996/212 Reg.5
Reg.15A, added: SI 1996/212 Reg.5
Reg.15A, revoked: SI 1996/2824 Reg.2, Sch.1
Reg.15B, added: SI 1996/212 Reg.5
Reg.15B, revoked: SI 1996/2824 Reg.2, Sch.1
Reg.15C, added: SI 1996/212 Reg.5
Reg.15C, revoked: SI 1996/2824 Reg.2, Sch.1
Reg.18, amended: SI 1996/212 Reg.6
Reg.18, revoked: SI 1996/2824 Reg.2, Sch.1
Reg.21, revoked: SI 1996/2824 Reg.2, Sch.1
Reg.21, substituted: SI 1996/212 Reg.7

2615. Quick-frozen Foodstuffs Regulations 1990
Reg.2, amended: SI 1996/1499 Reg.49

NO.

1990—cont.

2623. Road Humps (Scotland) Regulations 1990
referred to: SI 1998/1448 Reg.8
revoked: SI 1998/1448 Reg.1 (with saving)

2628. Welfare of Animals at Markets Order 1990
Art.5, see *Davidson v Strong* [1998] C.O.D. 3
(QBD), Moses, J.
Art.20, see *Davidson v Strong* [1998] C.O.D. 3
(QBD), Moses, J.

**2647. Welsh Health Common Services Authority
Constitution Order 1990**
revoked: SI 1999/804 Art.2

**2648. Welsh Health Common Services Authority
Regulations 1990**
applied: SI 1996/707 Reg.17, Sch.4 Part II
revoked: SI 1999/806 Reg.2
Reg.5, amended: SI 1996/707 Reg.17, Sch.5
para.5, SI 1997/2991 Reg.3, Sch. para.1
Reg.5, revoked: SI 1999/806 Reg.2

1991

**Bexley (Waiting and Loading Restriction)
Order 1991**
revoked (in part): SI 1996/2726 Art.10, SI 1996/
2728 Art.10

**Croydon (Waiting and Loading Restriction)
Order No.20 1991**
revoked (in part): SI 1997/1211 Art.10, SI 1997/
2133 Art.11, SI 1999/414 Art.10

**Croydon (Waiting and Loading Restriction)
Order No.27 1991**
revoked (in part): SI 1997/1211 Art.10, SI 1997/
2133 Art.11, SI 1999/414 Art.10

**Croydon (Waiting and Loading Restriction)
Order No.34 1991**
revoked (in part): SI 1997/1211 Art.10, SI 1997/
2133 Art.11, SI 1999/414 Art.10

**Grampian Regional Council Milne's Insti-
tution Trust Scheme 1991**
amended: SI 1996/478 Sch

Midlothian Educational Trust Scheme 1991
para.8, referred to: SI 1996/630 Sch.2 Part II
para.20, applied: SI 1996/630 Sch.2 Part II
para.21, applied: SI 1996/630 Sch.2 Part II
para.25, applied: SI 1996/630 Sch.2 Part II

**3. Apple Orchard Grubbing Up Regulations
1991**
applied: SI 1998/1131 Reg.4
revoked: SI 1998/1131 Reg.3 (with savings)
Reg.2, revoked: SI 1998/1131 Reg.3 (with
savings)
Reg.5, revoked: SI 1998/1131 Reg.3 (with
savings)
Reg.7, revoked: SI 1998/1131 Reg.3 (with
savings)
Reg.8, revoked: SI 1998/1131 Reg.3 (with
savings)
Reg.8A, revoked: SI 1998/1131 Reg.3 (with
savings)
Reg.8B, revoked: SI 1998/1131 Reg.3 (with
savings)
Reg.9, revoked: SI 1998/1131 Reg.3 (with
savings)
Reg.10, revoked: SI 1998/1131 Reg.3 (with
savings)
Reg.10A, revoked: SI 1998/1131 Reg.3 (with
savings)
Reg.10B, revoked: SI 1998/1131 Reg.3 (with
savings)

NO.

1991—cont.

**3. Apple Orchard Grubbing Up Regulations
1991**—*cont.*
Reg.10C, revoked: SI 1998/1131 Reg.3 (with
savings)
Reg.13, revoked: SI 1998/1131 Reg.3 (with
savings)

**5. Food Protection (Emergency Prohibitions)
(Radioactivity in Sheep) (Wales) Order
1991**
revoked (in part): SI 1996/26 Art.2
Art.6, amended: SI 1998/72 Art.2
Sch.1, applied: SI 1998/72
Sch.1, revoked (in part): SI 1998/72 Art.2, Sch.
Part I, Sch. Part II
Sch.1 para.2, substituted: SI 1996/26 Art.2,
Sch. Part II, SI 1998/72 Art.2, Sch. Part III
Sch.1 para.11, substituted: SI 1998/72 Art.2,
Sch. Part IV

**5. Meat Inspection (Amendment) Regulations
(Northern Ireland) 1991**
applied: SI 1996/1633 (NI.12) Art.11

**6. Food Protection (Emergency Prohibitions)
(Radioactivity in Sheep) (England) Order
1991**
revoked (in part): SI 1996/62

**19. Act of Adjournal (Consolidation Amend-
ment) (Extradition Rules and Backing of
Irish Warrants) 1991**
revoked: SI 1996/513 Sch.2 r.3, Sch.3

**20. Food Protection (Emergency Prohibitions)
(Radioactivity in Sheep) Order 1991**
amended: SI 1999/80 Art.2
revoked (in part): SI 1996/31 Art.2, SI 1997/62
Art.2, SI 1998/82 Art.2, Sch.1
Sch.1 Part I, amended: SI 1996/31 Art.2, SI
1997/62 Art.2
Sch.1 Part I, revoked (in part): SI 1997/62 Art.2
Sch.1 Part II, amended: SI 1997/62 Art.2, Sch.2,
SI 1998/82 Art.2, Sch.2 para.1, Sch.2 para.2,
Sch.2 para.3, SI 1999/80 Art.2, Sch.2 para.1,
Sch.2 para.2

**29. Banking Act 1987 (Exempt Transactions)
(Amendment) Regulations 1991**
revoked: SI 1997/817 Reg.16

**53. General Medical Council (Registration
(Fees) (Amendment) Regulations) Order
1991**
revoked: SI 1999/3189 Art.2
Sch., revoked: SI 1999/3189 Art.2, Sch. Reg.2

**65. Merchant Shipping (Pilot Boats) Regu-
lations 1991**
applied: SI 1996/3243 Sch Part I
revoked: SI 1998/1609 Reg.1

**78. Local Government Superannuation (Scot-
land) Amendment Regulations 1991**
applied: SI 1998/364 Reg.4, Reg.6, Reg.19,
Sch.2 para.2, Sch.2 para.5, Sch.4 para.8
referred to: SI 1998/364 Reg.3, Reg.10, Sch.2
para.4, Sch.2 para.6

**118. Community Charges and Non-Domestic
Rating (Demand Notices) (Wales) (Amendment) Regulations 1991**
revoked: SI 1996/619 Art.12

**141. Non-Domestic Rating (Collection and
Enforcement) (Local Lists) (Amendment
and Miscellaneous Provision) Regulations 1991**
applied: SI 1996/1880 Art.60

**158. Building Standards (Relaxation by Local
Authorities) (Scotland) Regulations 1991**
applied: SI 1997/1872 Reg.3
revoked: SI 1997/1872 Reg.3

1991—cont.

158. Slaughterhouse (Hygiene) (Amendment) Regulations (Northern Ireland) 1991
applied: SI 1996/1633 (NI.12) Art.11

160. Building (Forms) (Scotland) Regulations 1991
Sch. Form 8, amended: SI 1997/2157 Reg.4

167. Occupational Pension Schemes (Preservation of Benefit) Regulations 1991
applied: SI 1997/786 Reg.3, Sch.1 para.3
Reg.1, amended: SI 1996/2131 Reg.2
Reg.5, revoked (in part): SI 1996/2131 Reg.2
Reg.6, amended: SI 1997/786 Reg.3, Sch.1 para.3
Reg.6, applied: SI 1996/1847 Reg.8
Reg.7, revoked (in part): SI 1996/2131 Reg.2
Reg.9, amended: SI 1996/2131 Reg.2, SI 1997/786 Reg.3, Sch.1 para.3
Reg.9, applied: SI 1997/784 Reg.6
Reg.11A, added: SI 1996/2131 Reg.2
Reg.12, amended: SI 1996/2131 Reg.2, SI 1997/786 Reg.3, Sch.1 para.3, SI 1999/2543 Reg.2
Reg.12, applied: SI 1996/1216 Reg.20, SI 1996/1462 Reg.9, SI 1996/3126 Reg.6
Reg.13, amended: SI 1996/2131 Reg.2
Reg.14, applied: SI 1996/2131 Reg.4
Reg.14, revoked (in part): SI 1996/2131 Reg.2
Reg.14A, added: SI 1996/2131 Reg.2
Reg.16, amended: SI 1996/2131 Reg.2
Reg.18, revoked: SI 1996/2131 Reg.2
Reg.20, amended: SI 1996/2131 Reg.2
Reg.24, revoked (in part): SI 1996/2131 Reg.2
Reg.25, revoked (in part): SI 1996/2131 Reg.2
Reg.26, revoked: SI 1996/2131 Reg.2
Reg.27, amended: SI 1996/2131 Reg.2
Reg.27A, added: SI 1996/2131 Reg.2
Reg.27B, added: SI 1996/2131 Reg.2
Reg.28, revoked: SI 1997/784 Reg.12, Sch.2
Sch.1, revoked (in part): SI 1997/784 Reg.12, Sch.2
Sch.1 para.2, revoked: SI 1996/1847 Reg.21, Sch.3
Sch.1 para.3, revoked: SI 1996/1655 Reg.12, Sch.4

183. British Nationality (Fees) (Amendment) Regulations 1991
revoked: SI 1996/444 Reg.1

185. Rates and Precepts (Final Adjustments) Order 1991
Art.2, amended: SI 1999/2629 Art.2
Art.3, amended: SI 1999/2629 Art.3
Art.3, applied: SI 1996/910 Art.13
Art.4, applied: SI 1996/910 Art.13

187. European Communities (Designation) Order 1991
revoked: SI 1996/1912 Art.3

194. Health and Personal Social Services (Northern Ireland) Order 1991
Art.7, amended: SI 1996/1919 (NI.16) Art.255, Sch.1
Art.8, amended: SI 1997/1177 (NI.7) Art.32, Sch.2
Art.8, applied: SI 1997/1177 (NI.7) Art.17
Art.8A, added: SI 1997/1177 (NI.7) Art.30
Art.9, applied: SI 1997/1177 (NI.7) Art.11
Art.10, amended: SI 1997/1177 (NI.7) Art.32, Sch.2
Art.12, amended: SI 1996/1919 (NI.16) Art.255, Sch.1
Art.12, revoked (in part): SI 1996/1919 (NI.16) Art.257, Sch.3

1991—cont.

194. Health and Personal Social Services (Northern Ireland) Order 1991—*cont.*
Art.17, amended: SI 1997/1177 (NI.7) Art.32, Sch.2
Art.17, applied: SI 1997/1177 (NI.7) Art.19
Art.18, amended: SI 1997/1177 (NI.7) Art.32, Sch.2
Art.21, amended: SI 1997/1177 (NI.7) Art.32, Sch.2
Art.31, amended (in part): SI 1997/1177 (NI.7) Art.32, Sch.3
Sch.5, revoked (in part): SI 1996/1919 (NI.16) Art.257, Sch.3
Sch.5 Part I, revoked (in part): SI 1996/1298 (NI.8) Art.21, Sch.6
Sch.5 Part II, revoked (in part): SI 1996/1297 (NI.7) Art.23, Sch.5

196. Redundancy Fund (Abolition) (Northern Ireland) Order 1991
revoked: SI 1996/1919 (NI.16) Art.257, Sch.3

197. Road Traffic (Amendment) (Northern Ireland) Order 1991
Art.8, revoked: SI 1996/1320 (NI.10) Sch.4
Part III, applied: SI 1996/1320 (NI.10) Art.96
Sch.4 para.2, revoked: SI 1996/1320 (NI.10) Sch.4
Sch.4 para.6, revoked (in part): SI 1996/1320 (NI.10) Sch.4
Sch.4 para.10, revoked: SI 1996/1320 (NI.10) Sch.4

207. Offshore Installations (Safety Zones) Order 1991
revoked: SI 1997/735 Art.3, Sch.2

232. Local Government Act 1988 (Defined Activities) (Competition) (Wales) Regulations 1991
amended: SI 1996/265 Reg.4
Reg.5, revoked: SI 1997/2747 Reg.2, Sch.

233. Assured and Protected Tenancies (Lettings to Students) (Amendment) Regulations 1991
revoked: SI 1998/1967 Reg.6, Sch.3

236. Income Support (General) Amendment Regulations 1991
Reg.2, revoked (in part): SI 1996/206 Reg.28, Sch.3
Reg.3, revoked: SI 1996/206 Reg.28, Sch.3
Reg.4, revoked: SI 1996/206 Reg.28, Sch.3
Reg.6, revoked: SI 1996/206 Reg.28, Sch.3
Reg.8, revoked: SI 1996/206 Reg.28, Sch.3
Reg.10, revoked: SI 1996/206 Reg.28, Sch.3
Reg.11, revoked: SI 1996/206 Reg.28, Sch.3

275. Community Health Councils (Amendment) Regulations 1991
revoked: SI 1996/640 Reg.23

288. Traffic Areas (Reorganisation) Order 1991
Sch.1, amended: SI 1999/1204 Art.3

308. Offshore Installations (Well Control) (Amendment) Regulations 1991
revoked: SI 1996/913 Reg.27, Sch.3

324. Control of Pollution (Silage, Slurry and Agricultural Fuel Oil) Regulations 1991
Reg.2, amended: SI 1997/547 Reg.2
Reg.3, amended: SI 1997/547 Reg.2
Reg.7, revoked (in part): SI 1996/2044 Reg.2, SI 1997/547 Reg.2 (with savings)
Reg.8, amended: SI 1997/547 Reg.2
Reg.8, revoked (in part): SI 1997/547 Reg.2
Reg.9, amended: SI 1997/547 Reg.2
Reg.10, amended: SI 1997/547 Reg.2
Sch.1 para.6, amended: SI 1997/547 Reg.2
Sch.2 para.5, amended: SI 1997/547 Reg.2

NO.

324. Control of Pollution (Silage, Slurry and Agri-cultural Fuel Oil) Regulations 1991—*cont.*
Sch.2 para.7, amended: SI 1997/547 Reg.2
Sch.3 para.7, amended: SI 1997/547 Reg.2

329. Regional and District Health Authorities (Membership and Procedure) Amendment Regulations 1991
revoked: SI 1996/707 Reg.17, Sch.4 Part I

344. Local Government and Housing Act 1989 (Commencement No.11 and Savings) Order 1991
Sch. para.2, amended: SI 1996/974 Art.2, Sch.1 para.8

346. Control of Pollution (Silage, Slurry and Agri-cultural Fuel Oil) (Scotland) Regulations 1991
Reg.1, amended: SI 1996/973 Reg.2, Sch para.12
Reg.8, amended: SI 1996/973 Reg.2, Sch para.12
Reg.9, amended: SI 1996/973 Reg.2, Sch para.12
Reg.10, amended: SI 1996/973 Reg.2, Sch para.12

351. Local Authorities (Members' Allowances) Regulations 1991
Reg.3, amended: SI 1996/469 Reg.2
Reg.5, amended: SI 1996/469 Reg.2
Reg.10, amended: SI 1996/469 Reg.2
Reg.17, amended: SI 1996/469 Reg.4, SI 1997/589 Reg.2, SI 1998/556 Reg.2, SI 1999/1086 Reg.2
Reg.18, amended: SI 1996/469 Reg.4, SI 1997/589 Reg.2, SI 1998/557 Reg.2, SI 1999/1087 Reg.2
Reg.24, amended: SI 1996/469 Reg.2

353. Education (Grant-Maintained Schools) (Finance) Regulations 1991
applied: SI 1996/889 Reg.3, SI 1998/799 Reg.3
referred to: SI 1997/996 Reg.3

358. National Health Service Trusts (Consul-tation before Establishment) (Scotland) Regulations 1991
applied: SI 1998/2709, SI 1998/2710, SI 1998/2711, SI 1998/2712, SI 1998/2713, SI 1998/2714, SI 1998/2715, SI 1998/2716, SI 1998/2717, SI 1998/2718, SI 1998/2719, SI 1998/2720, SI 1998/2721, SI 1998/2722, SI 1998/2723, SI 1998/2724, SI 1998/2725, SI 1998/2728, SI 1998/2729, SI 1998/2730, SI 1998/2731, SI 1998/2732, SI 1998/2733, SI 1998/2734, SI 1998/2735

364. Insolvency Rules (Northern Ireland) 1991
r.4, applied: SI 1996/1632 (NI.11) Sch.3 para.3, Sch.3 para.8, Sch.3 para.11, Sch.3 para.14
r.6, applied: SI 1996/1632 (NI.11) Sch.3 para.3, Sch.3 para.8, Sch.3 para.11, Sch.3 para.14
r.7.52, applied: SI 1996/1632 (NI.11) Sch.3 para.20

381. Passenger and Goods Vehicles (Recording Equipment) Regulations 1991
revoked: SI 1996/941 Reg.2

387. Enterprise (Scotland) Consequential Amendments Order 1991
Art.6, revoked (in part): SI 1996/1345 Reg.27, Sch.
Art.9, revoked (in part): SI 1996/206 Reg.28, Sch.3
Sch., revoked (in part): SI 1996/206 Reg.28, Sch.3

NO.

406. National Health Service (Vocational Train-ing) Amendment Regulations 1991
revoked: SI 1997/2817 Reg.20, Sch.5

407. United Kingdom Transplant Support Service Authority (Establishment and Consti-tution) Order 1991
Art.2, referred to: SI 1999/1319 Sch.
Art.8, added: SI 1998/1577 Art.8

408. United Kingdom Transplant Support Service Authority Regulations 1991
applied: SI 1996/707 Reg.17, Sch.4 Part II
Reg.8, amended: SI 1996/707 Reg.17, Sch.5 para.5, SI 1997/2991 Reg.3, Sch. para.2

411. Education (Publication of Proposals for Reduction in Standard Numbers) Regu-lations 1991
revoked (in part): SI 1999/1671 Reg.13, SI 1999/2213 Reg.19 (with savings)
Reg.2, revoked (in part): SI 1999/1671 Reg.13

423. Public Airport Companies (Capital Finance) (Amendment) Order 1991
revoked: SI 1996/604 Reg.5

434. Community Charges and Non-Domestic Rating (Demand Notices) (Wales) (Amend-ment) (No.2) Regulations 1991
revoked: SI 1996/619 Art.12

436. Wireless Telegraphy (Television Licence Fees) Regulations 1991
revoked: SI 1997/290 Reg.1, Sch
Sch.2, see SI 1996/379 Reg.2
Sch.2, revoked: SI 1997/290 Reg.1, Sch
Sch.3, amended: SI 1996/379 Reg.2, SI 1996/1772 Reg.2
Sch.3, revoked: SI 1997/290 Reg.1, Sch

447. Cosmetic Products (Safety) (Amendment) Regulations 1991
revoked: SI 1996/2925 Sch.9

460. Abortion (Scotland) Regulations 1991
Reg.4, amended: SI 1999/1042 Art.5, Sch.3 Part II
Reg.5, amended: SI 1999/1042 Art.5, Sch.3 Part II

472. Environmental Protection (Prescribed Pro-cesses and Substances) Regulations 1991
Reg.3, amended: SI 1998/767 Reg.2
Reg.3, applied: SI 1996/2678 Sch para.3, Sch para.4
Reg.3, referred to: SI 1996/2678 Sch para.2
Sch.1, see *R. v Secretary of State for the Environment Ex p. Torridge DC* [1997] Env. L.R. 557 (QBD), McCullough, J.
Sch.1 Part A, amended: SI 1998/767 Reg.2
Sch.2 para.4A, added: SI 1998/767 Reg.2
Sch.2 para.8A, added: SI 1998/767 Reg.2

481. National Health Service (Remuneration and Conditions of Service) Regulations 1991
Reg.1, amended: SI 1998/564 Reg.2
Reg.2, amended: SI 1998/564 Reg.3

485. Motor Vehicles (Driving Licences) (Amend-ment) Regulations 1991
revoked: SI 1996/2824 Reg.2, Sch.1

487. Merchant Shipping (Light Dues) (Amend-ment) Regulations 1991
revoked: SI 1997/562 Reg.2, Sch.1

497. Education (London Residuary Body) (Prop-erty Transfer) Order 1991
applied: SI 1997/1990 Art.2

500. Local Authorities (Capital Finance) (Amend-ment) Regulations 1991
revoked: SI 1997/319 Reg.162, Sch.3

NO.

507. **Environmental Protection (Applications, Appeals and Registers) Regulations 1991**
Reg.2, amended: SI 1996/667 Reg.2, Sch
Reg.3, amended: SI 1996/667 Reg.2, Sch
Reg.4, amended: SI 1996/667 Reg.2, Sch, SI 1996/2678 Reg.2
Reg.5, amended: SI 1996/667 Reg.2, Sch
Reg.6A, added: SI 1996/2678 Reg.2
Reg.10, applied: SI 1996/2678 Sch para.1
Reg.11, amended: SI 1996/667 Reg.2, Sch
Reg.13, amended: SI 1996/667 Reg.2, Sch
Reg.15, amended: SI 1996/979 Reg.2
Reg.15, substituted: SI 1996/667 Reg.2, Sch
Reg.15A, added: SI 1996/667 Reg.2, Sch
Reg.16, substituted: SI 1996/667 Reg.2, Sch
Reg.17, substituted: SI 1996/667 Reg.2, Sch

511. **Cambridgeshire (Coroners' Districts) (Amendment) Order 1991**
revoked: SI 1999/1325 Art.4

515. **Motor Vehicles (Driving Licences) (Large Goods and Passenger-Carrying Vehicles) (Amendment) Regulations 1991**
revoked: SI 1996/2824 Reg.2, Sch.1

534. **National Health Service (Optical Charges and Payments) (Miscellaneous Amendments) (Scotland) Regulations 1991**
revoked (in part): SI 1998/642 Reg.24, Sch.4

535. **National Health Service Trusts (Membership and Procedure) (Scotland) Regulations 1991**
applied: SI 1999/726 Art.5, Sch. Part III
Reg.2, substituted: SI 1999/1133 Reg.2
Reg.8, revoked (in part): SI 1998/1458 Reg.2, SI 1999/1133 Reg.3

537. **National Health Service (Remuneration and Conditions of Service) (Scotland) Regulations 1991**
applied: SI 1999/686 Art.5, Sch. Part III, SI 1999/726 Art.5, Sch. Part III
Reg.8, referred to: SI 1999/726 Art.5, Sch. Part III

554. **National Health Service Functions (Directions to Authorities and Administration Arrangements) Regulations 1991**
revoked: SI 1996/708 Reg.6, Sch.2

556. **National Health Service (Indicative Amounts) Regulations 1991**
revoked: SI 1997/980 Reg.4

567. **Advice and Assistance (Scotland) Amendment Regulations 1991**
revoked: SI 1996/2447 Reg.3, Sch.1

569. **National Health Service (General Dental Services) (Miscellaneous Amendments) (Scotland) Regulations 1991**
revoked (in part): SI 1996/177 Reg.38, Sch.8

576. **National Health Service (Vocational Training) (Scotland) Amendment Regulations 1991**
revoked: SI 1998/5 Reg.19, Sch.4

578. **Clinical Standards Advisory Group Regulations 1991**
applied: SI 1999/672 Art.2, Sch.1

583. **National Health Service (Optical Charges and Payments) (Miscellaneous Amendments) Regulations 1991**
revoked (in part): SI 1997/818 Reg.24, Sch.4

584. **National Health Service Superannuation, Premature Retirement and Injury Benefits (Amendment) Regulations 1991**
see *Thomas v Pensions Ombudsman* [1996] O.P.L.R. 161 (QBD), Carnwath, J.

NO.

585. **Welfare Food Amendment Regulations 1991**
revoked: SI 1996/1434 Reg.23, Sch.7

587. **Housing Benefit and Community Charge Benefit (Subsidy) Order 1991**
Art.3, applied: SI 1998/562 Art.19
Art.4, applied: SI 1996/1217 Art.11, SI 1997/1004 Art.11, SI 1998/562 Art.19
Art.15, applied: SI 1996/1217 Art.19, SI 1998/562 Art.19
Art.15, referred to: SI 1997/1004 Art.19

588. **Personal and Occupational Pension Schemes (Pensions Ombudsman) Regulations 1991**
see *Westminster City Council v Haywood* [1996] 3 W.L.R. 563 (Ch D), Robert Walker, J.
revoked: SI 1996/2475 Reg.7
Reg.2A, added: SI 1996/1271 Reg.2
Reg.2A, revoked: SI 1996/2475 Reg.7

633. **Medicines (Exemptions from Licences and Animal Test Certificates) (Amendment) Order 1991**
revoked (in part): SI 1996/2195 Art.2, SI 1996/2197 Art.2

638. **Merchant Shipping (Distress Signals and Prevention of Collisions) (Amendment) Regulations 1991**
revoked: SI 1996/75 Reg.1

650. **Offshore Installations (Safety Zones) (No.2) Order 1991**
revoked: SI 1997/735 Art.3, Sch.2

675. **Patent Office (Address) Rules 1991**
revoked: SI 1999/1993 r.2

680. **Submarine Pipe-lines (Inspectors and Safety) (Amendment) Regulations 1991**
Reg.3, revoked: SI 1996/825 Reg.31, Sch.6 Part I

684. **Pensions Increase (Review) Order 1991**
applied: SI 1997/634 Art.3, SI 1998/503 Art.3, Art.4, SI 1999/522 Art.3

695. **District of Welwyn Hatfield (Electoral Arrangements) Order 1991**
revoked: SI 1998/2560 Art.6

702. **Building Societies (Designated Capital Resources) (Permanent Interest Bearing Shares) Order 1991**
Art.2, amended: SI 1998/1129 Art.2, Sch.1 para.11

721. **Cornwall (Coroners' Districts) (Amendment) Order 1991**
revoked: SI 1996/2403 Art.4

724. **High Court and County Courts Jurisdiction Order 1991**
amended: SI 1999/1014 Art.3
Art.2, amended: SI 1996/3141 Art.2
Art.4, amended: SI 1999/1014 Art.4
Art.4A, revoked: SI 1999/1014 Art.5
Art.5, amended: SI 1999/1014 Art.6
Art.7, see *Practice Direction (No.3 of 1995) (Transfer of Chancery Work to the Central London County Court)* [1996] 1 W.L.R. 76 (Ch D), Sir Richard Scott, V.C.
Art.7, revoked: SI 1999/1014 Art.7
Art.8, see *Practice Direction (QBD: County Court Order: Enforcement) (No.2)* [1998] 1 W.L.R. 1557 (QBD), RL Turner
Art.8, amended: SI 1996/3141 Art.3, SI 1999/1014 Art.8
Art.8A, amended: SI 1996/3141 Art.4
Art.9, substituted: SI 1999/1014 Art.9
Art.10, revoked: SI 1999/1014 Art.10
Art.12, revoked (in part): SI 1999/1014 Art.11

1991—cont.

724. High Court and County Courts Jurisdiction Order 1991—*cont.*
Sch. Part I, revoked (in part): 1998 c.18 s.54, Sch.5

725. National Health Service Contracts (Dispute Resolution) Regulations 1991
revoked: SI 1996/623 Reg.4

745. Civil Legal Aid (Scotland) Amendment Regulations 1991
revoked: SI 1996/2444 Reg.3, Sch.1

755. European Communities (Designation) (No.2) Order 1991
revoked (in part): SI 1999/2788 Art.4, Sch.3

757. European Bank for Reconstruction and Development (Immunities and Privileges) Order 1991
Art.12A, added: SI 1999/2034 Art.2, Sch.

761. Financial Provisions (Northern Ireland) Order 1991
Sch.1 para.6, revoked: SI 1998/749 (NI.4) Art.9, Sch.

762. Food Safety (Northern Ireland) Order 1991
applied: SI 1996/3158 (NI.22) Art.73, Art.75, SI 1997/2778 (NI.19) Art.33, 1999 c.28 s.14, s.18, s.31, s.41, Sch.3 para.8
Art.2, amended: SI 1996/1633 (NI.12) Art.3, Art.7, 1999 c.28 s.40, Sch.5 para.29, Sch.6
Art.2, referred to: SI 1999/2109 Reg.2
Art.2, revoked (in part): SI 1996/1633 (NI.12) Art.11, Sch
Art.8, amended: 1999 c.28 s.40, Sch.5 para.27, Sch.5 para.28
Art.8, referred to: 1999 c.28 s.26
Art.8, revoked (in part): 1996 c.23 Sch.4
Art.10, amended: 1999 c.28 s.40, Sch.5 para.28
Art.10, referred to: 1999 c.28 s.26
Art.11, amended: 1999 c.28 s.40, Sch.5 para.27, Sch.5 para.28
Art.11, referred to: 1999 c.28 s.26
Art.11, revoked (in part): 1996 c.23 Sch.4
Art.12, amended: 1999 c.28 s.40, Sch.5 para.27, Sch.5 para.30
Art.12, applied: 1999 c.28 s.17, s.18, Sch.3 para.9
Art.12, revoked (in part): SI 1996/1633 (NI.12) Art.11, Sch
Art.15, amended: 1999 c.28 s.40, Sch.5 para.27
Art.15, applied: SI 1996/1633 (NI.12) Art.11
Art.16, amended: 1999 c.28 s.40, Sch.5 para.27
Art.17, amended: SI 1996/1633 (NI.12) Art.4, 1999 c.28 s.40, Sch.5 para.27
Art.18, amended: SI 1996/1633 (NI.12) Art.5, 1999 c.28 s.40, Sch.5 para.27, Sch.5 para.28
Art.18, referred to: 1999 c.28 s.26
Art.22, amended: SI 1996/1633 (NI.12) Art.6, 1999 c.28 s.40, Sch.5 para.28
Art.22, referred to: 1999 c.28 s.26
Art.22, revoked (in part): SI 1996/1633 (NI.12) Art.11, Sch
Art.24, revoked: 1999 c.28 s.40, Sch.5 para.31, Sch.6
Art.25, amended: 1999 c.28 s.40, Sch.5 para.32, Sch.6
Art.25, referred to: 1999 c.28 s.26
Art.26, amended: SI 1996/1633 (NI.12) Art.3, Art.7, 1999 c.28 s.40, Sch.5 para.33
Art.26, applied: 1999 c.28 s.18, Sch.3 para.10
Art.26, referred to: 1999 c.28 s.14
Art.26, revoked (in part): SI 1996/1633 (NI.12) Art.11, Sch.
Art.27, amended: SI 1996/1633 (NI.12) Art.7
Art.27, revoked (in part): 1999 c.28 s.40, Sch.5 para.34, Sch.6

1991—cont.

762. Food Safety (Northern Ireland) Order 1991—*cont.*
Art.30, referred to: SI 1999/2109 Reg.2
Art.31, amended: 1999 c.28 s.40, Sch.5 para.35
Art.31, referred to: SI 1999/2109 Reg.2
Art.33, amended: 1999 c.28 s.40, Sch.5 para.28
Art.37, amended: SI 1996/1633 (NI.12) Art.7, 1999 c.28 s.40, Sch.5 para.28
Art.39, amended: SI 1996/1633 (NI.12) Art.8, 1999 c.28 s.40, Sch.5 para.27, Sch.5 para.36
Art.39, applied: 1999 c.28 s.18, Sch.3 para.11
Art.40, amended: 1999 c.28 s.40, Sch.5 para.37
Art.40, applied: 1999 c.28 s.18, Sch.3 para.12
Art.41, amended: SI 1996/1633 (NI.12) Art.9, 1999 c.28 s.40, Sch.5 para.27, Sch.5 para.38
Art.41, applied: 1999 c.28 s.18, Sch.3 para.13
Art.42, amended: 1999 c.28 s.40, Sch.5 para.28
Art.44, amended: 1999 c.28 s.40, Sch.5 para.27, Sch.5 para.28, Sch.5 para.39
Art.45, amended: 1999 c.28 s.40, Sch.5 para.28
Art.46, revoked: SI 1996/1633 (NI.12) Art.4
Art.47, amended: 1999 c.28 s.40, Sch.5 para.27, Sch.5 para.40
Art.47, applied: 1999 c.28 s.18, Sch.3 para.14
Art.49, amended: 1999 c.28 s.40, Sch.5 para.28, SI 1999/1736 Art.12, Sch.6
Art.49, applied: SI 1999/1736 Art.12, Sch.6
Art.51, amended: 1999 c.28 s.40, Sch.5 para.27
Part II, referred to: 1999 c.28 s.26
Sch.1, amended: 1999 c.28 s.40, Sch.5 para.28
Sch.1, referred to: 1999 c.28 s.26
Sch.1 para.2, amended: 1999 c.28 s.40, Sch.5 para.41
Sch.1 para.3, amended: SI 1996/1633 (NI.12) Art.10, 1999 c.28 s.40, Sch.5 para.41
Sch.1 para.6A, added: 1999 c.28 s.40, Sch.5 para.41
Sch.1 para.7, amended: 1999 c.28 s.40, Sch.5 para.41
Sch.3 para.5, revoked: 1999 c.28 s.40, Sch.5 para.42, Sch.6

767. Social Security (Norway) Order 1991
Sch., amended: SI 1996/1928 Art.2, Sch.1

768. Collision Regulations (Seaplanes) (Amendment) Order 1991
revoked: SI 1996/75 Reg.1

773. Vehicle Inspectorate Trading Fund Order 1991
applied: SI 1997/668

777. Agricultural, Fishery and Aquaculture Products (Improvement Grant) Regulations 1991
Reg.3, amended: SI 1999/1820 Art.4, Sch.2 para.146

809. Health Boards (Membership and Procedure) (No.2) Regulations 1991
applied: SI 1999/686 Art.5, Sch. Part III, SI 1999/726 Art.5, Sch. Part III
Reg.6, referred to: SI 1999/726 Art.5, Sch. Part III
Reg.6, revoked (in part): SI 1998/1459 Reg.2, SI 1999/1132 Reg.2

818. Redundancy Payments (Local Government) (Modification) (Amendment) Order 1991
revoked: SI 1999/2277 Art.4, Sch.3

824. European Communities (Recognition of Professional Qualifications) Regulations 1991
Reg.6, applied: SI 1996/2374 Reg.16
Sch.1, applied: SI 1996/2374 Reg.4, Reg.9
Sch.1 Part II, applied: SI 1996/2374 Reg.24
Sch.3, referred to: SI 1996/2374 Reg.16

NO.

NO.

1991—cont.

1991—cont.

834. **Education (Fees and Awards, Allowances and Bursaries) (Scotland) Amendment Regulations 1991**
Reg.2, revoked: SI 1997/93 Reg.14, Sch.4

847. **Act of Adjournal (Consolidation Amendment No.1) 1991**
revoked: SI 1996/513 Sch.2 r.3, Sch.3

859. **Estate Agents (Provision of Information) Regulations 1991**
see *Harwood (t/a RSBS Group) v Smith* [1998] 1 E.G.L.R. 5 (CA), Hobhouse, L.J.

872. **Gaming Clubs (Multiple Bingo) (Amendment) Regulations 1991**
revoked: SI 1998/2151 Reg.3

875. **Buying Agency Trading Fund Order 1991**
Art.4, amended: SI 1996/1080 Art.2

880. **Financial Markets and Insolvency Regulations 1991**
Reg.7, amended: SI 1999/1209 Reg.3
Reg.12, amended: SI 1999/1209 Reg.3

881. **Broadcasting (Channel 3 Transmission and Shared Distribution Costs) Order 1991**
amended: SI 1996/3067

887. **Community Charges (Demand Notices) (Additional Provisions) (Wales) Regulations 1991**
revoked: SI 1996/619 Art.12

890. **Arrangements for Placement of Children (General) Regulations 1991**
Reg.2, amended: SI 1997/649 Reg.3

895. **Review of Children's Cases Regulations 1991**
Reg.13A, added: SI 1997/649 Reg.4

910. **Foster Placement (Children) Regulations 1991**
Reg.1, amended: SI 1997/2308 Reg.3
Reg.3, amended: SI 1997/2308 Reg.3
Sch.1 para.9, substituted: SI 1997/2308 Reg.3
Sch.4, added: SI 1997/2308 Reg.3, Sch.
Sch.4 para.2, amended: SI 1999/2768 Reg.2
Sch.4 para.9, amended: SI 1999/2768 Reg.2
Sch.4 para.13, amended: SI 1999/2768 Reg.2
Sch.4 para.14, revoked: SI 1999/2768 Reg.2

933. **North Tyneside Steam Railway Light Railway Order 1991**
Art.12, amended: SI 1996/362 Art.5, Sch.4

939. **Vaccine Damage Payments Act 1979 Statutory Sum Order 1991**
revoked: SI 1998/1587 Art.3

952. **Adopted Persons (Contact Register) (Fees) Rules 1991**
r.2, amended: SI 1998/615 r.2

962. **Medicines (Products Other Than Veterinary Drugs) (Prescription Only) Amendment Order 1991**
revoked: SI 1997/1830 Art.16, Sch.6

964. **Education (London Residuary Body) (Property Transfer) (No.2) Order 1991**
applied: SI 1997/1990 Art.2

968. **Employment Protection Code of Practice (Time Off) Order 1991**
referred to: SI 1998/46

973. **Fertilisers (Sampling and Analysis) Regulations 1991**
revoked: SI 1996/1342 Reg.9

981. **Petroleum (Production) (Landward Areas) Regulations 1991**
Sch.3, referred to: 1998 c.17 Sch.1 para.25, SI 1999/160 Sch.12 para.1, Sch.13 para.1
Sch.5, referred to: 1998 c.17 Sch.1 para.26, SI 1999/160 Sch.13 para.1

981. **Petroleum (Production) (Landward Areas) Regulations 1991**—*cont.*
Sch.6, referred to: 1998 c.17 Sch.1 para.27, SI 1999/160 Sch.14 para.1
Sch.6 cl.15, referred to: SI 1996/913 Reg.18

982. **Houses in Multiple Occupation (Charges for Registration Schemes) Regulations 1991**
revoked: SI 1998/1812 Reg.5 (with savings)

1031. **Savings Certificates Regulations 1991**
Reg.3, referred to: SI 1998/1449 Art.3, Sch. para.7
Reg.4, referred to: SI 1998/1449 Art.3, Sch. para.7
Reg.6, referred to: SI 1998/1449 Art.3, Sch. para.7
Reg.7, referred to: SI 1998/1449 Art.3, Sch. para.7
Reg.21, referred to: SI 1998/1449 Art.3, Sch. para.7
Reg.31, amended: SI 1997/1859 Reg.2
Reg.31, referred to: SI 1998/1449 Art.3, Sch. para.7

1034. **Education (Particulars of Independent Schools) (Amendment) Regulations 1991**
revoked: SI 1997/2918 Reg.3

1043. **Litter (Statutory Undertakers) (Designation and Relevant Land) Order 1991**
Art.1, amended: SI 1999/1443 Art.4
Art.2, amended: SI 1999/1443 Art.4

1094. **Civil Legal Aid (Financial Conditions) (Scotland) Regulations 1991**
revoked: SI 1996/1012 Reg.6

1102. **Health Promotion Authority for Wales Constitution Order 1991**
revoked: SI 1999/807 Art.2
Art.5, applied: SI 1997/327 Reg.3
Art.5, referred to: SI 1997/327 Reg.2, Reg.3
Art.5, substituted: SI 1997/326 Art.2

1103. **Health Promotion Authority for Wales Regulations 1991**
applied: SI 1996/707 Reg.17, Sch.4 Part II
revoked: SI 1997/327 Reg.6
Reg.3, amended: SI 1996/707 Reg.17, Sch.5 para.6
Reg.3, revoked: SI 1997/327 Reg.6

1106. **Montrose (Pilotage) Harbour Revision Order 1991**
Art.2, amended: SSI 1999/200 Art.8
Art.19, revoked: SSI 1999/200 Art.8

1121. **Motor Vehicles (Driving Licences) (Amendment) (No.2) Regulations 1991**
revoked: SI 1996/2824 Reg.2, Sch.1

1122. **Motor Vehicles (Driving Licences) (Large Goods and Passenger-Carrying Vehicles) (Amendment) (No.2) Regulations 1991**
revoked: SI 1996/2824 Reg.2, Sch.1

1142. **Data Protection Registration Fee Order 1991**
revoked: 1998 c.29 Sch.16 Part II

1145. **Stock Transfer (Gilt-Edged Securities) (Exempt Transfer) Regulations 1991**
Reg.2, amended: SI 1999/1210 Reg.2

1155. **Specified Diseases (Notification) Order 1991**
revoked: SI 1996/2628 Art.8, Sch.2
Art.3, revoked: SI 1996/2628 Art.8, Sch.2
Art.5, revoked: SI 1996/2628 Art.8, Sch.2

1176. **Broadcasting (Restrictions on the Holding of Licences) Order 1991**
revoked: SI 1996/2120 Sch.2
Art.2, revoked: 1996 c.55 Sch.11 Part II
Art.16, amended: SI 1999/122 Art.2
Art.16, revoked (in part): SI 1999/122 Art.2
Part II, revoked: 1996 c.55 Sch.11 Part II

NO.

1991—cont.

1176. Broadcasting (Restrictions on the Holding of Licences) Order 1991—*cont.*
Part III, revoked: 1996 c.55 Sch.11 Part II
Part IV, revoked: 1996 c.55 Sch.11 Part II

1184. County Courts (Interest on Judgment Debts) Order 1991
Art.1, amended: SI 1998/2400 Art.2
Art.5, substituted: SI 1996/2516 Art.2

1206. Companies (Fees) Regulations 1991
Sch., amended: SI 1996/1444 Reg.3, SI 1998/3088 Reg.3
Sch., referred to: SI 1996/1444 Reg.4

1209. Common Investment Scheme 1991
applied: SI 1999/551 para.5
para.2, amended: SI 1999/551 para.9
para.3, amended: SI 1999/551 para.8
para.5, amended: SI 1999/551 para.8
para.6, revoked: SI 1999/551 para.8
Sch.1, applied: SI 1999/551 para.3
Sch.1 para.8A, added: SI 1999/551 para.9
Sch.2, amended: SI 1999/551 para.8
Sch.3 para.2, amended: SI 1999/551 para.8
Sch.3 para.4, amended: SI 1999/551 para.8

1220. Planning (Northern Ireland) Order 1991
applied: SI 1999/1736 Art.11, SI 1999/3145 Art.2
referred to: SI 1996/275 (NI.2) Art.51, SI 1996/725 (NI.5) Sch.2 para.12, SI 1996/3158 (NI.22) Art.84, SI 1997/276 (NI.2) Art.35, SI 1997/2778 (NI.19) Art.8, Art.31, SI 1999/660 (NI.4) Art.2, SI 1999/2450 Sch.4 para.4.3
Art.2, amended: SI 1996/275 (NI.2) Art.71, Sch.6, SI 1999/660 (NI.4) Art.8, Sch. para.2
Art.3, amended: SI 1999/660 (NI.4) Art.8, Sch. para.3
Art.3, referred to: SI 1999/660 (NI.4) Art.3
Art.4, amended: SI 1999/660 (NI.4) Art.8, Sch. para.4
Art.20, applied: SI 1996/275 (NI.2) Art.47
Art.21, applied: SI 1996/275 (NI.2) Art.47
Art.22, amended: SI 1996/275 (NI.2) Art.71, Sch.6
Art.22, applied: SI 1996/275 (NI.2) Art.47
Art.23, applied: SI 1996/275 (NI.2) Art.47
Art.24, applied: SI 1996/275 (NI.2) Art.47
Art.26, amended: SI 1997/1772 (NI.15) Art.25, Sch.4
Art.31, see *FA Wellworth & Co Ltd's Application, Re* [1996] N.I. 509 (CA (NI)), Sir Brian Hutton, L.C.J.
Art.31, applied: SI 1999/662 (NI.6) Art.9, Sch.1 para.3
Art.40, referred to: 1998 c.41 Sch.3 para.1
Art.54, amended: SI 1998/2795 (NI.18) Art.6, Sch.1 para.22
Art.62, amended: SI 1998/2795 (NI.18) Art.6, Sch.1 para.22
Art.63, amended: SI 1998/2795 (NI.18) Art.6, Sch.1 para.23
Art.86, amended: SI 1999/660 (NI.4) Art.8, Sch. para.5
Art.100, amended: SI 1997/276 (NI.2) Art.75, Sch.8 para.9
Art.110, amended: SI 1999/663 Art.2, Sch.1 para.25
Art.110, referred to: SI 1996/1298 (NI.8) Sch.3
Art.111, applied: SI 1997/2777 (NI.18) Sch.2 para.1, Sch.2 para.2, Sch.2 para.3, Sch.2 para.4, SI 1997/2778 (NI.19) Sch.2 para.1
Art.118, applied: SI 1999/1736 Art.11, SI 1999/3145 Art.2
Part IV, applied: SI 1996/275 (NI.2) Sch.2 para.2

NO.

1991—cont.

1220. Planning (Northern Ireland) Order 1991—*cont.*
Part XII, applied: SI 1999/3145 Art.2
Sch.5, amended: 1997 c.14 Sch para.7
Sch.5, revoked (in part): SI 1996/3158 (NI.22) Sch.13, SI 1996/3159 (NI.23) Sch.9, SI 1997/276 (NI.2) Art.75, Sch.9, SI 1997/2778 (NI.19) Art.83, Sch.6

1243. European Parliamentary Elections (Amendment) Regulations 1991
revoked: SI 1999/1214 Reg.20, Sch.5

1246. Cable (Excepted Programmes) Order 1991
revoked: 1996 c.55 Sch.11 Part II, SI 1996/2120 Sch.1

1247. Family Proceedings Rules 1991
see *Practice Direction (Ancillary Relief Procedure: Pilot Scheme)* [1996] 2 F.L.R. 368 (Fam Div), Sir Stephen Brown; see *Practice Direction (Family Proceedings: Financial Dispute Resolution)* [1997] 1 W.L.R. 1069 (Fam Div), Sir Stephen Brown
amended: SI 1999/3491 r.3
applied: SI 1996/1674 r.3
Part III, applied: SI 1999/3491 r.20
r.1.2, amended: SI 1997/1056 r.6, SI 1999/3491 r.4
r.1.2, referred to: SI 1999/1012 r.3
r.1.3, amended: SI 1999/1012 r.3
r.1.3, referred to: SI 1999/1012 r.3
r.1.4, referred to: SI 1999/1012 r.3
r.2, see *T v T (Consent Order: Procedure to Set Aside)* [1996] 2 F.L.R. 640 (Fam Div), Richard Anelay Q.C.; see *T v T (Joinder of Third Parties)* [1996] 2 F.L.R. 357 (Fam Div), Wilson, J.
r.2.9, amended: SI 1997/1893 r.10
r.2.28, amended: SI 1997/1056 r.2
r.2.29, amended: SI 1997/1893 r.11
r.2.31, revoked: SI 1997/1056 r.3
r.2.36, amended: SI 1997/1893 r.12
r.2.40, amended: SI 1997/1893 r.13
r.2.45, amended: SI 1999/3491 r.5
r.2.45, revoked (in part): SI 1999/3491 r.5
r.2.51A, added: SI 1999/3491 r.6
r.2.51B, added: SI 1999/3491 r.6
r.2.52, applied: SI 1999/3491 r.20
r.2.53, amended: SI 1999/3491 r.7
r.2.53, applied: SI 1999/3491 r.20
r.2.54, amended: SI 1999/3491 r.7
r.2.54, applied: SI 1999/3491 r.20
r.2.55, applied: SI 1999/3491 r.20
r.2.55, revoked: SI 1999/3491 r.8
r.2.56, applied: SI 1999/3491 r.20
r.2.56, revoked: SI 1999/3491 r.8
r.2.57, applied: SI 1999/3491 r.20
r.2.58, applied: SI 1999/3491 r.20
r.2.58, revoked: SI 1999/3491 r.8
r.2.59, amended: SI 1999/3491 r.9
r.2.59, applied: SI 1999/3491 r.20
r.2.59, revoked (in part): SI 1999/3491 r.9
r.2.60, applied: SI 1999/3491 r.20
r.2.60, substituted: SI 1999/3491 r.10
r.2.61, amended: SI 1996/1674 r.4
r.2.61, applied: SI 1999/3491 r.20
r.2.61A, added: SI 1999/3491 r.11
r.2.61B, added: SI 1999/3491 r.11
r.2.61C, added: SI 1999/3491 r.11
r.2.61D, added: SI 1999/3491 r.11
r.2.61E, added: SI 1999/3491 r.11
r.2.61F, added: SI 1999/3491 r.11
r.2.62, amended: SI 1999/3491 r.12
r.2.62, applied: SI 1999/3491 r.20
r.2.62, revoked (in part): SI 1999/3491 r.12

NO.

1991—cont.

1247. Family Proceedings Rules 1991—*cont.*
r.2.63, applied: SI 1999/3491 r.20
r.2.63, revoked: SI 1999/3491 r.13
r.2.64, see *Wicks v Wicks* [1999] Fam. 65 (CA), Ward, L.J.
r.2.64, amended: SI 1999/3491 r.14
r.2.64, applied: SI 1999/3491 r.20
r.2.65, applied: SI 1999/3491 r.20
r.2.66, amended: SI 1999/3491 r.15
r.2.66, applied: SI 1999/3491 r.20
r.2.67, amended: SI 1999/3491 r.16
r.2.67, applied: SI 1999/3491 r.20
r.2.68, applied: SI 1999/3491 r.20
r.2.69, applied: SI 1999/3491 r.20
r.2.69, substituted: SI 1999/3491 r.17
r.2.69A, added: SI 1999/3491 r.17
r.2.69B, added: SI 1999/3491 r.17
r.2.69C, added: SI 1999/3491 r.17
r.2.69D, added: SI 1999/3491 r.17
r.2.69E, added: SI 1999/3491 r.17
r.2.69F, added: SI 1999/3491 r.17
r.2.70, added: SI 1996/1674 r.5
r.2.70, amended: SI 1996/1778 r.2, SI 1997/637 r.2, SI 1999/3491 r.18
r.2.70, applied: SI 1996/1676 Reg.4, Reg.8, Reg.11, SI 1999/3491 r.20
r.2.70, revoked (in part): SI 1999/3491 r.18
r.2.71, added: SI 1997/1056 r.4
r.2.71, revoked: SI 1999/3491 r.19
r.2.72, added: SI 1997/1056 r.4
r.2.72, revoked: SI 1999/3491 r.19
r.2.73, added: SI 1997/1056 r.4
r.2.73, revoked: SI 1999/3491 r.19
r.2.74, added: SI 1997/1056 r.4
r.2.74, revoked: SI 1999/3491 r.19
r.2.75, added: SI 1997/1056 r.4
r.2.75, revoked: SI 1999/3491 r.19
r.2.76, added: SI 1997/1056 r.4
r.2.76, revoked: SI 1999/3491 r.19
r.2.77, added: SI 1997/1056 r.4
r.2.77, revoked: SI 1999/3491 r.19
r.3, amended: SI 1996/816 r.4
r.3.1, amended: SI 1999/3491 r.21
r.3.8, substituted: SI 1997/1893 r.2
r.3.9, substituted: SI 1997/1893 r.2
r.3.9A, added: SI 1997/1893 r.2
r.3.10, substituted: SI 1997/1893 r.2
r.3.13, amended: SI 1997/1056 r.7, SI 1997/1893 r.14
r.4, see *A (Care Order: Discharge Application by Child), Re* [1996] 1 F.L.R. 599 (Fam Div), Thorpe, J.; see *A (Criminal Proceedings: Disclosure), Re* [1996] 1 F.L.R. 221 (CA), Butler-Sloss, L.J.; see *G (Minor) (Social Worker: Disclosure), Re* [1996] 1 W.L.R. 1407 (CA), Butler Sloss, L.J.; see *P-B (A Minor) (Child Cases: Hearings in Open Court), Re* [1997] 1 All E.R. 58 (CA), Butler-Sloss, L.J.; see *W (Minors) (Social Worker: Disclosure), Re* [1998] 2 All E.R. 801 (CA), Butler-Sloss, L.J.
r.4.8, see *X (Care: Notice of Proceedings), Re* [1996] 1 F.L.R. 186 (Fam Div), Stuart-White, J.
r.4.16, see *P-B (Children Act: Open Court), Re* [1996] Fam. Law 606 (CA), Butler-Sloss, L.J.
r.4.23, see *A (Disclosure of Medical Records to the GMC), Re* [1998] 2 F.L.R. 641 (Fam Div), Cazalet, J.; see *A County Council v W (Disclosure)* [1997] 1 F.L.R. 574 (Fam Div); see *W (Minors) (Social Worker: Disclosure), Re* [1998] 2 All E.R. 801 (CA), Butler-Sloss, L.J.

1991—cont.

1247. Family Proceedings Rules 1991—*cont.*
r.4.23, amended: SI 1997/1056 r.8
r.4.24, amended: SI 1997/1893 r.3
r.4.24A, added: SI 1997/1893 r.4
r.4.27, amended: SI 1997/1893 r.15
r.6.2, amended: SI 1997/1893 r.16
r.7, see *Hackshaw v Hackshaw* [1999] 2 F.L.R. 876 (Fam Div), Wilson, J.
r.7, amended: SI 1996/816 r.5, r.6, r.7, r.8
r.7.2, amended: SI 1997/1893 r.5, r.17
r.7.7, amended: SI 1997/1056 r.7
r.7.20, amended: SI 1997/1893 r.18
r.7.28, see *Hackshaw v Hackshaw* [1999] 2 F.L.R. 876 (Fam Div), Wilson, J.
r.8, see *A v A (Costs Appeal)* [1996] 1 F.L.R. 14 (Fam Div), Singer, J.; see *Hackshaw v Hackshaw* [1999] 2 F.L.R. 876 (Fam Div), Wilson, J.; see *Ritchie v Ritchie* [1996] 1 F.L.R. 898 (CA), Bennett, J.
r.8.1, see *K v D* [1998] 1 F.L.R. 700 (CC) (Birmingham), Judge D Hamilton
r.8.1, amended: SI 1997/1893 r.6
r.8.1A, added: SI 1997/1893 r.7
r.8.2, see *Hackshaw v Hackshaw* [1999] 2 F.L.R. 876 (Fam Div), Wilson, J.
r.9.2A, amended: SI 1997/1893 r.19
r.10.15, see *S v S (Judgment in Chambers: Disclosure)* [1997] 1 W.L.R. 1621 (Fam Div), Wilson, J.
r.10.20, see *A (Disclosure of Medical Records to the GMC), Re* [1998] 2 F.L.R. 641 (Fam Div), Cazalet, J.; see *S v S (Judgment in Chambers: Disclosure)* [1997] 1 W.L.R. 1621 (Fam Div), Wilson, J.
r.14, see *M (Terminating Appointment of Guardian Ad Litem), Re* [1999] 2 F.L.R. 717 (Fam Div), Kirkwood, J.
Appendix.1, amended: SI 1997/1893 r.8, Sch.2
Appendix.1 para.3, amended: SI 1998/1901 r.3
Appendix.1 Form C11, substituted: SI 1997/1893 r.8, Sch.1
Appendix.1 Form C23, substituted: SI 1997/1893 r.8, Sch.1
Appendix.1 Form C33, substituted: SI 1997/1893 r.8, Sch.1
Appendix.1 Form FL401, added: SI 1997/1893 r.8, Sch.3
Appendix.1 Form FL402, added: SI 1997/1893 r.8, Sch.3
Appendix.1 Form FL403, added: SI 1997/1893 r.8, Sch.3
Appendix.1 Form FL404, added: SI 1997/1893 r.8, Sch.3
Appendix.1 Form FL405, added: SI 1997/1893 r.8, Sch.3
Appendix.1 Form FL406, added: SI 1997/1893 r.8, Sch.3
Appendix.1 Form FL407, added: SI 1997/1893 r.8, Sch.3
Appendix.1 Form FL408, added: SI 1997/1893 r.8, Sch.3
Appendix.1 Form FL409, added: SI 1997/1893 r.8, Sch.3
Appendix.1 Form FL410, added: SI 1997/1893 r.8, Sch.3
Appendix.1 Form FL411, added: SI 1997/1893 r.8, Sch.3
Appendix.1 Form FL412, added: SI 1997/1893 r.8, Sch.3
Appendix.1 Form FL413, added: SI 1997/1893 r.8, Sch.3

1991—cont.

1247. Family Proceedings Rules 1991—*cont.*
Appendix.1 Form FL414, added: SI 1997/1893 r.8, Sch.3
Appendix.1 Form FL415, added: SI 1997/1893 r.8, Sch.3
Appendix.1 Form FL416, added: SI 1997/1893 r.8, Sch.3
Appendix.1 Form FL417, added: SI 1997/1893 r.8, Sch.3
Appendix.1 Form M1, substituted: SI 1997/637 r.3, Sch
Appendix.1 Form M5, amended: SI 1996/816 r.3
Appendix.1 Form M9, amended: SI 1996/816 r.3
Appendix.1 Form M10, amended: SI 1996/816 r.3
Appendix.1 Form M11, revoked: SI 1999/3491 r.22
Appendix.1 Form M12, revoked: SI 1999/3491 r.22
Appendix.1 Form M13, revoked: SI 1999/3491 r.22
Appendix.1 Form M14, revoked: SI 1999/3491 r.22
Appendix.1 Form M15, revoked: SI 1999/3491 r.22
Appendix.1 Form M18, revoked: SI 1997/1893 r.20
Appendix.1A Form A, added: SI 1997/1056 r.5, Sch
Appendix.1A Form A, substituted: SI 1999/3491 r.23
Appendix.1A Form B, added: SI 1997/1056 r.5, Sch
Appendix.1A Form B, substituted: SI 1999/3491 r.23
Appendix.1A Form C, added: SI 1997/1056 r.5, Sch
Appendix.1A Form C, substituted: SI 1999/3491 r.23
Appendix.1A Form D, added: SI 1997/1056 r.5, Sch
Appendix.1A Form D, substituted: SI 1999/3491 r.23
Appendix.1A Form E, added: SI 1997/1056 r.5, Sch
Appendix.1A Form E, substituted: SI 1999/3491 r.23
Appendix.1A Form F, added: SI 1997/1056 r.5, Sch
Appendix.1A Form F, substituted: SI 1999/3491 r.23
Appendix.1A Form G, substituted: SI 1999/3491 r.23
Appendix.1A Form H, substituted: SI 1999/3491 r.23
Appendix.1A Form I, substituted: SI 1999/3491 r.23

1259. Companies (Forms) (No.2) Regulations 1991
Sch.2 Form 363b, revoked: SI 1999/2356 Reg.3 (with saving)
Sch.2 Form 363s, revoked: SI 1999/2356 Reg.3 (with saving)

1260. Registration of Births, Still-births and Deaths (Prescription of Errors) (Scotland) Regulations 1991
revoked: SI 1997/1782 Reg.3

1991—cont.

1282. Smoke Control Areas (Authorised Fuels) Regulations 1991
Sch.1 para.1A, added: SI 1998/2154 Reg.2
Sch.1 para.1B, added: SI 1998/3096 Reg.2
Sch.1 para.1C, added: SI 1998/3096 Reg.2
Sch.1 para.4B, substituted: SI 1998/2154 Reg.2
Sch.1 para.4C, added: SI 1996/1145 Reg.2
Sch.1 para.4C, amended: SI 1998/3096 Reg.2
Sch.1 para.4C, referred to: SI 1998/3096 Reg.3
Sch.1 para.6, amended: SI 1996/1145 Reg.2
Sch.1 para.8, amended: SI 1996/1145 Reg.2
Sch.1 para.8AA, added: SI 1998/3096 Reg.2
Sch.1 para.12AAA, added: SI 1996/1145 Reg.2
Sch.1 para.12AAB, added: SI 1996/1145 Reg.2
Sch.1 para.12AB, added: SI 1997/2658 Reg.2
Sch.1 para.13B, referred to: SI 1998/2154 Reg.3
Sch.1 para.13B, revoked: SI 1998/2154 Reg.2
Sch.1 para.13BB, added: SI 1996/1145 Reg.2
Sch.1 para.14, amended: SI 1996/1145 Reg.2
Sch.1 para.14A, added: SI 1998/2154 Reg.2
Sch.1 para.15, amended: SI 1997/2658 Reg.2
Sch.1 para.16, referred to: SI 1998/3096 Reg.3
Sch.1 para.16, revoked: SI 1998/3096 Reg.2 (with savings)
Sch.1 para.16B, added: SI 1998/2154 Reg.2
Sch.1 para.17B, added: SI 1996/1145 Reg.2
Sch.1 para.18A, added: SI 1996/1145 Reg.2
Sch.1 para.18B, added: SI 1997/2658 Reg.2

1284. Fruit Juices and Fruit Nectars (England, Wales and Scotland) (Amendment) Regulations 1991
Reg.3, revoked (in part): SI 1996/1499 Reg.49, Sch.9
Reg.4, revoked (in part): SI 1996/1499 Reg.49, Sch.9

1298. Merchant Shipping (Load Lines) (Exemption) (Amendment) Order 1991
revoked: SI 1998/2241 Reg.3

1300. Merchant Shipping (Life-Saving Appliances) (Amendment) Regulations 1991
referred to: SI 1998/1609 Reg.5, Reg.6, Sch.
revoked: SI 1999/2721 Reg.1

1302. Home-Grown Cereals Authority Levy (Variation) Scheme (Approval) Order 1991
referred to: SI 1996/2843, SI 1996/2843 Sch. para.2

1304. Police Pensions (Additional Voluntary Contributions) Regulations 1991
applied: SI 1999/1750 Art.2, Sch.1

1324. Street Litter Control Notices Order 1991
Art.2, amended: SI 1997/632 Art.2

1325. Litter Control Areas Order 1991
Art.2, amended: SI 1997/633 Art.2
Art.2, applied: SI 1996/1243 Sch.5 para.13

1347. National Health Service Trusts (Consultation on Dissolution) Regulations 1991
revoked: SI 1996/653 Reg.3

1349. National Health Service (General Dental Services) (Scotland) Amendment Regulations 1991
revoked: SI 1996/177 Reg.38, Sch.8

1382. Price Marking Order 1991
revoked: SI 1999/3042 Art.2
Art.3, revoked: SI 1999/3042 Art.2
Art.4, revoked: SI 1999/3042 Art.2
Art.5, revoked: SI 1999/3042 Art.2
Art.6, revoked: SI 1999/3042 Art.2
Art.8, revoked: SI 1999/3042 Art.2
Art.12, revoked: SI 1999/3042 Art.2
Sch.1 Part I, revoked: SI 1999/3042 Art.2
Sch.2 Part I, revoked: SI 1999/3042 Art.2

NO.

1991—cont.

1382. Price Marking Order 1991—*cont.*
Sch.2 Part II, revoked: SI 1999/3042 Art.2
Sch.2 Part III, revoked: SI 1999/3042 Art.2
Sch.4 Part I, revoked: SI 1999/3042 Art.2
Sch.4 Part II, revoked: SI 1999/3042 Art.2
Sch.5, revoked: SI 1999/3042 Art.2

1395. Family Proceedings Courts (Children Act 1989) Rules 1991
see *K (Care Proceedings: Joinder of Father), Re* [1999] 2 F.L.R. 408 (Fam Div), Holman, J.
Appendix.1 Form C11, substituted: SI 1997/1895 r.7, Sch.
Appendix.1 Form C23, substituted: SI 1997/1895 r.7, Sch.
Appendix.1 Form C33, substituted: SI 1997/1895 r.7, Sch.
r.14, applied: SI 1999/2784 Sch. para.40
r.21, see *P (Minors) (Contact: Discretion), Re* [1998] 2 F.L.R. 696 (Fam Div), Wilson, J.; see *T v W (Contact: Reasons for Refusing Leave)* [1996] 2 F.L.R. 473 (Fam Div), Connell, J.
r.23, see *C (Minors) (Guardian Ad Litem: Disclosure of Report), Re* [1996] 1 F.L.R. 61 (Fam Div), Sir Stephen Brown
r.23, amended: SI 1997/1895 r.2
r.25, amended: SI 1997/1895 r.3
r.25A, added: SI 1997/1895 r.4
r.28, applied: SI 1999/2784 Sch. para.41
r.31, amended: SI 1997/1895 r.5
r.33, applied: SI 1999/2784 Sch. para.42
r.33B, added: SI 1997/1895 r.6

1397. Act of Sederunt (Messengers-at-Arms and Sheriff Officers Rules) 1991
r.2, amended: SI 1998/2636 r.2
r.7, amended: SI 1998/2636 r.2
r.8, amended: SI 1998/2636 r.2
r.10, amended: SI 1998/2636 r.2
r.11, amended: SI 1998/2636 r.2
r.17, amended: SI 1998/2636 r.2
r.18, amended: SI 1998/2636 r.2
r.21, applied: SI 1999/678 Sch.
r.22, applied: SI 1999/678 Sch.
r.23, applied: SI 1999/678 Sch.
r.24, applied: SI 1999/678 Sch.
r.28, amended: SI 1998/2636 r.2

1402. Erskine Bridge Tolls Extension Order 1991
referred to: SI 1996/1370

1407. Savings Certificates (Children's Bonus Bonds) Regulations 1991
Reg.3, referred to: SI 1998/1449 Art.3, Sch. para.8
Reg.6, referred to: SI 1998/1449 Art.3, Sch. para.8
Reg.7, referred to: SI 1998/1449 Art.3, Sch. para.8
Reg.18, referred to: SI 1998/1449 Art.3, Sch. para.8
Reg.28, amended: SI 1997/1860 Reg.2
Reg.28, referred to: SI 1998/1449 Art.3, Sch. para.8

1408. Broadcasting (Independent Productions) Order 1991
Art.2, amended: SI 1999/1820 Art.4, Sch.2 para.147

1409. Water (Compulsory Works Powers) (Notice) Regulations 1991
revoked: SI 1999/221 Reg.3

1462. Cinemas (Northern Ireland) Order 1991
Art.8, amended: SI 1998/2795 (NI.18) Art.6, Sch.1 para.24

NO.

1991—cont.

1463. Criminal Justice (International Co-operation) Act 1990 (Enforcement of Overseas Forfeiture Orders) Order 1991
Art.2, amended: SI 1997/1317 Art.2
Art.12, amended: SI 1996/2878 Art.2
Sch.1, amended: SI 1996/2878 Art.3, SI 1997/1317 Art.4, SI 1997/2977 Art.2
Sch.2, amended: SI 1996/2878 Art.4, SI 1997/1317 Art.5, SI 1997/2977 Art.3
Sch.3, amended: SI 1996/2878 Art.5, SI 1997/1317 Art.6, SI 1997/2977 Art.4

1464. Criminal Justice (International Co-operation) Act 1990 (Enforcement of Overseas Forfeiture Orders) (Northern Ireland) Order 1991
Art.2, amended: SI 1997/1317 Art.3
Art.12, amended: SI 1996/2878 Art.2
Sch.1, amended: SI 1996/2878 Art.3, SI 1997/1317 Art.4, SI 1997/2977 Art.2
Sch.2, amended: SI 1996/2878 Art.4, SI 1997/1317 Art.5, SI 1997/2977 Art.3
Sch.3, amended: SI 1996/2878 Art.5, SI 1997/1317 Art.6, SI 1997/2977 Art.4

1467. Confiscation of the Proceeds of Drug Trafficking (Designated Countries and Territories) (Scotland) Order 1991
Sch.1, revoked: SI 1999/673 Art.11
Sch.3, revoked: SI 1999/673 Art.11
Sch.3 Appendix, revoked: SI 1999/673 Art.11

1468. Criminal Justice (International Co-operation) Act 1990 (Enforcement of Overseas Orders) (Scotland) Order 1991
revoked: SI 1999/675 Art.11
Art.2, revoked: SI 1999/675 Art.11
Art.3, revoked: SI 1999/675 Art.11
Art.21, revoked: SI 1999/675 Art.11
Sch.1, revoked: SI 1999/675 Art.11
Sch.2, revoked: SI 1999/675 Art.11

1476. Food Safety (Exports) Regulations 1991
Sch.1 Part I, amended: SI 1998/2424 Reg.9, Sch.
Sch.1 Part I, revoked (in part): SI 1996/1499 Reg.49, Sch.9
Sch.1 Part II, revoked (in part): SI 1999/1540 Reg.21, Sch.4
Sch.2, amended: SI 1998/2424 Reg.9, Sch.
Sch.2, revoked (in part): SI 1996/1499 Reg.49, Sch.9

1487. Advisory Committee on Hazardous Substances Order 1991
Art.2, referred to: SI 1999/1319 Sch.

1505. Children (Secure Accommodation) Regulations 1991
Reg.10, see *AS (Secure Accommodation Order), Re* [1999] F.L.R. 103 (Fam Div), Bracewell, J.

1506. Children's Homes Regulations 1991
Reg.2, amended: SI 1996/692 Reg.2
Reg.5, amended: SI 1997/2308 Reg.4
Reg.17, amended: SI 1996/692 Reg.3
Sch.2 para.18, amended: SI 1998/646 Reg.11

1511. Education (School Teacher Appraisal) Regulations 1991
applied: SI 1999/2888 Reg.1
revoked (in part): SI 1999/2888 Reg.1
Reg.2, amended: SI 1999/2261 Reg.3
Reg.2, revoked (in part): SI 1999/2888 Reg.1
Reg.2A, added: SI 1999/2261 Reg.4
Reg.2A, revoked (in part): SI 1999/2888 Reg.1
Reg.7, amended: SI 1999/2261 Reg.5
Reg.7, revoked (in part): SI 1999/2888 Reg.1
Reg.8, amended: SI 1999/2261 Reg.6
Reg.8, revoked (in part): SI 1999/2888 Reg.1

NO.

1511. Education (School Teacher Appraisal) Regulations 1991—*cont.*
Reg.11, amended: SI 1999/2261 Reg.7
Reg.11, revoked (in part): SI 1999/2888 Reg.1
Reg.13, amended: SI 1999/2261 Reg.8
Reg.13, revoked (in part): SI 1999/2888 Reg.1
Reg.14, amended: SI 1999/2261 Reg.9
Reg.14, revoked (in part): SI 1999/2888 Reg.1

1518. Building Societies Act 1986 (Continuance of section 41) Order 1991
revoked: SI 1996/1844 Art.3

1522. Students' Allowances (Scotland) Regulations 1991
applied: SI 1996/1623 Art.3, SI 1996/1754 Sch.1 para.5, SI 1998/217 Art.2
revoked: SI 1996/1754 Reg.7, Sch.3
Sch.1, applied: SI 1996/1812 Reg.4, SI 1997/1675 Reg.4
Sch.1, revoked: SI 1996/1754 Reg.7, Sch.3

1537. Seed Potatoes (Fees) (Amendment) Regulations 1991
revoked: SI 1998/1228 Reg.4

1539. Public Works Loans (Fees) (Amendment) Regulations 1991
Reg.3, amended: SI 1997/985 Reg.2

1541. Motor Vehicles (Driving Licences) (Large Goods and Passenger-Carrying Vehicles) (Amendment) (No.3) Regulations 1991
revoked: SI 1996/2824 Reg.2, Sch.1

1559. Income Support (General) Amendment No.4 Regulations 1991
applied: SI 1998/217 Art.2, SI 1999/779 Art.2, Sch.
applied: SI 1996/1623 Art.3
Reg.13, revoked: SI 1996/206 Reg.28, Sch.3
Reg.14, revoked: SI 1996/206 Reg.28, Sch.3
Reg.22, referred to: SI 1996/207 Reg.51
Reg.24, amended: SI 1996/206 Reg.30

1565. Football (Offences) (Designation of Football Matches) Order 1991
revoked: SI 1999/2462 Art.2

1609. Bathing Waters (Classification) Regulations 1991
Sch.1 para.3, amended: SI 1996/973 Reg.2, Sch para.13

1614. Retirement Benefits Schemes (Restrictions on Discretion to Approve) (Small Self-administered Schemes) Regulations 1991
Reg.2, amended: SI 1998/728 Reg.3
Reg.4, amended: SI 1998/728 Reg.4, Reg.5, SI 1998/1315 Reg.3
Reg.5, amended: SI 1998/728 Reg.6, Reg.7
Reg.5, referred to: SI 1998/729 Reg.4
Reg.7, amended: SI 1998/728 Reg.8, SI 1998/1315 Reg.4, Reg.5
Reg.9, amended: SI 1998/1315 Reg.6
Reg.9, referred to: SI 1998/729 Reg.5
Reg.9, substituted: SI 1998/728 Reg.9
Reg.10, revoked: SI 1998/728 Reg.10

1620. Construction Products Regulations 1991
applied: SI 1998/2306 Reg.10, Sch.1
referred to: SI 1997/831 Reg.3

1624. Controlled Waste (Registration of Carriers and Seizure of Vehicles) Regulations 1991
Reg.3, amended: SI 1996/593 Reg.3, Sch.2 para.9
Reg.4, amended: SI 1998/605 Reg.2
Reg.14, amended: SI 1996/593 Reg.3, Sch.2 para.9
Sch.1, amended: SI 1996/972 Reg.22
Sch.2, revoked: SI 1998/605 Reg.2

NO.

1630. Farm and Conservation Grant Regulations 1991
applied: SI 1999/672 Art.2, Sch.1

1641. North Hull Housing Action Trust (Area and Constitution) Order 1991
revoked: SI 1998/2871 Art.7

1672. Civil Aviation Authority Regulations 1991
Reg.21, revoked (in part): SI 1996/1494 Reg.2

1673. Police (Discipline) (Amendment) Regulations 1991
revoked: SI 1999/730 Reg.2 (with saving)

1677. Children (Allocation of Proceedings) Order 1991
Art.6, amended: SI 1998/2166 Art.2
Art.9, amended: SI 1997/1897 Art.2
Art.11, amended: SI 1997/1897 Art.3
Art.19, see *S (Appeal from Principal Registry: Procedure), Re* [1997] 2 F.L.R. 856 (Fam Div), Cazalet, J.
Art.20, substituted: SI 1997/1897 Art.4
Sch.1, amended: SI 1997/1897 Art.5, SI 1999/524 Art.2
Sch.1, referred to: SI 1997/1896 Art.2
Sch.2, amended: SI 1997/1897 Art.6
Sch.2, referred to: SI 1997/1896 Art.2

1680. National Health Service (Optical Charges and Payments) Amendment Regulations 1991
revoked: SI 1997/818 Reg.24, Sch.4

1694. International Organisations (Miscellaneous Exemptions) Order 1991
revoked: SI 1997/168 Art.4

1699. Extradition (Aviation Security) Order 1991
revoked: SI 1997/1760 Art.4

1700. Extradition (Designated Commonwealth Countries) Order 1991
Sch.1, amended: SI 1996/279 Art.2, SI 1997/1761 Art.2

1701. Extradition (Drug Trafficking) Order 1991
revoked: SI 1997/1762 Art.4

1702. Extradition (Torture) Order 1991
revoked: SI 1997/1769 Art.4
Sch.5, revoked: SI 1997/1769 Art.4

1707. Access to Personal Files and Medical Reports (Northern Ireland) Order 1991
Art.4, amended: 1998 c.29 Sch.15 para.14
Art.6, amended: 1998 c.29 Sch.15 para.15
Part II, referred to: 1998 c.29 Sch.14 para.19
Part II, revoked: 1998 c.29 Sch.16 Part II
Sch., revoked: 1998 c.29 Sch.16 Part II

1709. Broadcasting Act 1990 (Guernsey) (No.2) Order 1991
Sch. para.29A, added: SI 1999/1314 Art.3
Sch. para.29B, added: SI 1999/1314 Art.3

1710. Broadcasting Act 1990 (Jersey) (No.2) Order 1991
Sch. para.29A, added: SI 1999/1315 Art.3
Sch. para.29B, added: SI 1999/1315 Art.3

1713. Fair Employment (Amendment) (Northern Ireland) Order 1991
revoked: SI 1998/3162 (NI.21) Art.105, Sch.5

1714. Genetically Modified Organisms (Northern Ireland) Order 1991
Art.2, amended: 1999 c.28 s.18, Sch.3 para.20
Art.5, amended: 1999 c.28 s.18, Sch.3 para.19
Art.8, amended: 1999 c.28 s.18, Sch.3 para.19
Art.22, substituted: 1999 c.28 s.18, Sch.3 para.20

1720. Extradition (Protection of Nuclear Material) Order 1991
revoked: SI 1997/1765 Art.4

NO.

1731. National Health Service (Optical Charges and Payments) (Scotland) Amendment Regulations 1991
revoked: SI 1998/642 Reg.24, Sch.4

1738. Free Zone (Liverpool) Designation Order 1991
amended: SI 1999/3122 Art.2
Art.2, referred to: SI 1999/3122 Art.3

1740. Free Zone (Southampton) Designation Order 1991
amended: SI 1996/2615 Art.2

1744. Dangerous Dogs Compensation and Exemption Schemes Order 1991
Art.4, amended: 1997 c.53 s.4
Art.6, amended: 1997 c.53 s.4
Art.9, amended: 1997 c.53 s.4, SI 1997/1152 Art.2
Part III, amended: 1997 c.53 s.4

1745. Montrose Harbour Revision Order 1991
Art.2, amended: SSI 1999/200 Art.8
Art.4, amended: SSI 1999/200 Art.4
Art.5, amended: SSI 1999/200 Art.4
Art.5, revoked (in part): SSI 1999/200 Art.4
Art.7, amended: SSI 1999/200 Art.4

1773. Swansea Bay Port Health Authority Order 1991
Art.1, amended: SI 1996/409 Art.2
Art.2, amended: SI 1996/409 Art.2, SI 1998/1604 Art.2
Sch.1, amended: SI 1998/1604 Art.2
Sch.2, substituted: SI 1998/1604 Art.2

1787. Education (London Residuary Body) (Property Transfer) (No.3) Order 1991
applied: SI 1997/1990 Art.2

1797. Merchant Shipping (Light Dues) (Amendment) (No.2) Regulations 1991
revoked: SI 1997/562 Reg.2, Sch.1

1819. Merchant Shipping (Certification of Deck Officers and Marine Engineer Officers) (Amendment) Regulations 1991
revoked: SI 1997/348 Reg.1

1832. Family Proceedings (Costs) Rules 1991
revoked: SI 1999/1012 r.4
r.2, revoked: SI 1999/1012 r.4

1877. County Court Appeals Order 1991
Art.3, see *Yui Tong Man v Mahmood* (1997) 74 P. & C.R. 320 (CA), Leggatt, L.J.

1890. Education (Financial Delegation for Primary Schools) Regulations 1991
revoked: 1996 c.56 Sch.38 Part III

1892. Gaming (Records of Cheques) (Amendment) Regulations 1991
revoked: SI 1997/1072 Reg.8

1904. Civil Legal Aid (Scotland) Amendment (No.2) Regulations 1991
revoked: SI 1996/2444 Reg.3, Sch.1

1916. Act of Adjournal (Consolidation Amendment No.2) (Evidence of Children) 1991
revoked: SI 1996/513 Sch.2 r.3, Sch.3

1920. Act of Sederunt (Proceedings in the Sheriff Court under the Debtors (Scotland) Act 1987) (Amendment) 1991
para.2, amended: SI 1996/2709 r.3, Sch.2

1922. Offshore Installations (Safety Zones) (No.3) Order 1991
revoked: SI 1997/735 Art.3, Sch.2

1924. Legal Aid Act 1988 (Children Act 1989) Order 1991
revoked: 1999 c.22 s.106, Sch.15 Part I

1961. Police (Promotion) (Amendment) Regulations 1991
revoked: SI 1996/1685 Reg.8, Sch.3

NO.

1991. Family Proceedings Courts (Matrimonial Proceedings etc.) Rules 1991
Part II, amended: SI 1997/1894 r.2
r.2, amended: SI 1997/1894 r.3, r.4
r.3, amended: SI 1997/1894 r.5, r.6, r.7
r.3, revoked (in part): SI 1997/1894 r.8
r.3A, added: SI 1997/1894 r.9
r.4, amended: SI 1997/1894 r.10
r.6, applied: SI 1999/2784 Sch. para.40
r.7, amended: SI 1997/1894 r.11
r.8, amended: SI 1997/1894 r.12
r.9, amended: SI 1997/1894 r.11
r.10, amended: SI 1997/1894 r.11
r.11, amended: SI 1997/1894 r.13
r.12, amended: SI 1997/1894 r.11
r.12A, added: SI 1997/1894 r.14
r.12B, added: SI 1997/1894 r.14
r.13, amended: SI 1997/1894 r.11
r.14, amended: SI 1997/1894 r.11
r.16, amended: SI 1997/1894 r.11
r.16, applied: SI 1999/2784 Sch. para.44
r.20, substituted: SI 1997/1894 r.15
r.21, substituted: SI 1997/1894 r.15
r.24, substituted: SI 1997/1894 r.16
r.25, substituted: SI 1997/1894 r.17
Sch.1 Form FL401, added: SI 1997/1894 r.18, Sch.1, Sch.2
Sch.1 Form FL402, added: SI 1997/1894 r.18, Sch.1, Sch.2
Sch.1 Form FL403, added: SI 1997/1894 r.18, Sch.1, Sch.2
Sch.1 Form FL404, added: SI 1997/1894 r.18, Sch.1, Sch.2
Sch.1 Form FL405, added: SI 1997/1894 r.18, Sch.1, Sch.2
Sch.1 Form FL406, added: SI 1997/1894 r.18, Sch.1, Sch.2
Sch.1 Form FL407, added: SI 1997/1894 r.18, Sch.1, Sch.2
Sch.1 Form FL408, added: SI 1997/1894 r.18, Sch.1, Sch.2
Sch.1 Form FL409, added: SI 1997/1894 r.18, Sch.1, Sch.2
Sch.1 Form FL410, added: SI 1997/1894 r.18, Sch.1, Sch.2
Sch.1 Form FL411, added: SI 1997/1894 r.18, Sch.1, Sch.2
Sch.1 Form FL412, added: SI 1997/1894 r.18, Sch.1, Sch.2
Sch.1 Form FL413, added: SI 1997/1894 r.18, Sch.1, Sch.2
Sch.1 Form FL414, added: SI 1997/1894 r.18, Sch.1, Sch.2
Sch.1 Form FL415, added: SI 1997/1894 r.18, Sch.1, Sch.2
Sch.1 Form FL416, added: SI 1997/1894 r.18, Sch.1, Sch.2
Sch.1 Form FL417, added: SI 1997/1894 r.18, Sch.1, Sch.2
Sch.1 Form FL418, added: SI 1997/1894 r.18, Sch.1, Sch.2
Sch.1 Form FL419, added: SI 1997/1894 r.18, Sch.1, Sch.2
Sch.1 Form FL420, added: SI 1997/1894 r.18, Sch.1, Sch.2
Sch.1 Form FL421, added: SI 1997/1894 r.18, Sch.1, Sch.2
Sch.1 Form FL422, added: SI 1997/1894 r.18, Sch.1, Sch.2
Sch.1 Form MAT 8, revoked: SI 1997/1894 r.18
Sch.1 Form MAT 10, revoked: SI 1997/1894 r.18

NO.

1991—cont.

1991. Family Proceedings Courts (Matrimonial Proceedings etc.) Rules 1991—*cont.*
Sch.1 Form MAT 11, revoked: SI 1997/1894 r.18
Sch.1 Form MAT 12, revoked: SI 1997/1894 r.18
Sch.1 Form MAT 13, revoked: SI 1997/1894 r.18

1997. Companies Act 1989 (Eligibility for Appointment as Company Auditor) (Consequential Amendments) Regulations 1991
Sch. para.69, revoked: 1999 c.22 s.106, Sch.15 Part I

2001. National Health Service Supplies Authority (Establishment and Constitution) Order 1991
Art.7, added: SI 1998/1577 Art.7

2002. National Health Service Supplies Authority Regulations 1991
applied: SI 1996/707 Reg.17, Sch.4 Part II
Reg.5, amended: SI 1996/707 Reg.17, Sch.5 para.7, SI 1997/2991 Reg.3, Sch. para.3

2036. Civil Legal Aid (General) (Amendment) (No.2) Regulations 1991
Reg.3, revoked: 1999 c.22 s.106, Sch.15 Part I

2038. Legal Aid in Family Proceedings (Remuneration) Regulations 1991
Reg.2, amended: SI 1996/650 Reg.2, SI 1997/2394 Reg.2
Reg.3, amended: SI 1996/650 Reg.2, SI 1997/2394 Reg.3, Reg.4
Sch.1, substituted: SI 1996/650 Reg.2, Sch.1
Sch.1 Part I, amended: SI 1996/1555 Reg.2
Sch.1A, added: SI 1996/650 Reg.2, Sch.1
Sch.1A Part I, amended: SI 1996/1555 Reg.2
Sch.2, substituted: SI 1996/650 Reg.2, Sch.2
Sch.2 Part I, amended: SI 1996/1555 Reg.2
Sch.2 Part V, amended: SI 1996/1555 Reg.2
Sch.2 para.10, amended: SI 1997/2394 Reg.5
Sch.2A, added: SI 1996/650 Reg.2, Sch.2
Sch.2A Part I, amended: SI 1996/1555 Reg.2
Sch.2A Part V, amended: SI 1996/1555 Reg.2
Sch.2A para.10, amended: SI 1997/2394 Reg.6

2041. Regional and District Health Authorities (Membership and Procedure) Amendment (No.2) Regulations 1991
revoked: SI 1996/707 Reg.17, Sch.4 Part I

2047. Gaming (Records of Cheques) (Scotland) (Amendment) Regulations 1991
revoked: SI 1997/1072 Reg.8

2050. Children (Private Arrangements for Fostering) Regulations 1991
Reg.2, amended: SI 1998/646 Reg.12

2051. Guardians Ad Litem and Reporting Officers (Panels) Regulations 1991
see *R. v Legal Aid Board Ex p. W (Children)* Times, November 25, 1999 (QBD), Scott Baker, J.
Reg.1, amended: SI 1997/1662 Reg.2
Reg.3, amended: SI 1997/1662 Reg.2
Reg.4, amended: SI 1997/1662 Reg.2
Reg.4A, added: SI 1997/1662 Reg.2
Reg.4A, referred to: SI 1997/1662 Reg.3
Reg.5, amended: SI 1997/1662 Reg.2
Reg.5, referred to: SI 1997/1662 Reg.3
Reg.6, amended: SI 1997/1662 Reg.2
Reg.6, referred to: SI 1997/1662 Reg.3
Reg.6A, added: SI 1997/1662 Reg.2
Reg.8, amended: SI 1997/1662 Reg.2
Reg.9, amended: SI 1997/1662 Reg.2
Reg.13, added: SI 1997/1662 Reg.2

NO.

1991—cont.

2051. Guardians Ad Litem and Reporting Officers (Panels) Regulations 1991—*cont.*
Sch.1, amended: SI 1996/858 Art.2, SI 1997/1662 Reg.2
Sch.2 para.1, amended: SI 1997/1662 Reg.2

2076. Child Minding and Day Care (Registration and Inspection Fees) Regulations 1991
Reg.3, amended: SI 1996/3180 Reg.2
Reg.4, amended: SI 1996/3180 Reg.2

2094. Disqualification for Caring for Children Regulations 1991
Sch. para.1, amended: SI 1997/2308 Reg.5, Sch.

2097. Packaging of Explosives for Carriage Regulations 1991
applied: SI 1996/2089 Reg.10, Reg.11
Reg.2, amended: SI 1996/2092 Reg.21, SI 1999/303 Reg.4, Sch.3 para.1
Reg.3, amended: SI 1999/303 Reg.4, Sch.3 para.2
Reg.13, amended: SI 1999/303 Reg.4, Sch.3 para.3
Sch.1 Part I, amended: SI 1999/303 Reg.4, Sch.3 para.4

2114. Family Proceedings Fees Order 1991
revoked: SI 1999/690 Art.7 (with savings), Sch.2 (with savings)
Art.1, amended: SI 1996/3190 Art.3
Art.1, revoked: SI 1999/690 Art.7 (with savings), Sch.2 (with savings)
Art.3, amended: SI 1997/1080 Art.2, SI 1997/2671 Art.2
Art.3, revoked: SI 1999/690 Art.7 (with savings), Sch.2 (with savings)
Art.3, substituted: SI 1996/3190 Art.4, SI 1997/788 Art.2
Art.4, amended: SI 1996/3190 Art.5
Art.4, revoked: SI 1999/690 Art.7 (with savings), Sch.2 (with savings)
Art.4, substituted: SI 1997/788 Art.2
Art.5, added: SI 1996/3190 Art.6
Art.5, revoked: SI 1999/690 Art.7 (with savings), Sch.2 (with savings)
Sch., amended: SI 1996/3190 Art.7, Art.8, Art.9, Art.10, Art.11, Art.12, Art.13, SI 1997/1899 Art.2
Sch., revoked: SI 1999/690 Art.7 (with savings), Sch.2 (with savings)

2168. Banking Act 1987 (Exempt Transactions) (Amendment No.2) Regulations 1991
revoked: SI 1997/817 Reg.16

2176. Betting, Gaming and Lotteries Act 1963 (Variation of Fees) (No.2) Order 1991
revoked: SI 1997/42 Art.3

2188. Broadcasting (Local Delivery Services) (Amendment) Order 1991
revoked: SI 1998/1240 Art.3

2194. Kirklees Light Railway Order 1991
Art.14, amended: SI 1996/362 Art.5, Sch.4

2197. Fertilisers Regulations 1991
amended: SI 1998/2024 Reg.5, Reg.6, Sch.1 Part I, Sch.1 Part II
applied: SI 1998/2024 Reg.8
Reg.1, amended: SI 1998/2024 Reg.3
Reg.1A, added: SI 1998/2024 Reg.4
Sch.1 Table, amended: SI 1997/1543 Reg.3, Sch.1, Sch.2, SI 1998/2024 Reg.7, Sch.2
Sch.1 Table, applied: SI 1996/1342 Reg.6

2205. Act of Sederunt (Rules for the Registration of Custody Orders of the Sheriff Court) (Amendment) 1991
revoked: SI 1997/291 r.1.4, Sch.2

NO.

1991—cont.

2206. Seed Potatoes Regulations 1991
Sch.1, applied: SI 1997/2092 Art.5
Sch.4 para.3, substituted: SI 1997/1474 Reg.2

2210. Grimsby and Louth Light Railway Order 1991
Art.12, amended: SI 1996/362 Art.5, Sch.4

2214. Act of Sederunt (Proceedings in the Sheriff Court under Model Law on International Commercial Arbitration) 1991
revoked: SI 1999/929 r.1.3, Sch.2

2242. Beef Carcase (Classification) Regulations 1991
Reg.2, amended: SI 1998/12 Reg.2
Sch.1, amended: SI 1998/12 Reg.2
Sch.2 para.2, amended: SI 1998/12 Reg.2
Sch.5 Part I, amended: SI 1998/12 Reg.2
Sch.5 Part II, amended: SI 1998/12 Reg.2
Sch.5 Part III, amended: SI 1998/12 Reg.2

2244. A406 London North Circular Trunk Road (East London River Crossing (A13 to A2) No.2 Bridge) Order 1991
revoked: SI 1997/842 Art.2

2245. A406 London North Circular Trunk Road (East London River Crossing (A13 to A2) Slip Roads) Order 1991
revoked: SI 1997/842 Art.2

2246. Bovine Spongiform Encephalopathy Order 1991
amended: SI 1996/962 Art.2
revoked: SI 1996/2007 Art.21
Art.4, revoked: SI 1996/2007 Art.21
Art.5, revoked: SI 1996/2007 Art.21
Art.12A, added: SI 1996/962 Art.2
Art.12A, revoked: SI 1996/2007 Art.21
Sch., revoked: SI 1996/2007 Art.21

2273. Occupational Pension Schemes (Miscellaneous Amendments) Regulations 1991
Reg.2, revoked: SI 1996/1172 Sch.2

2281. A41 London-Birmingham Trunk Road (East of Aylesbury to West of Tring) Detrunking Order 1991
Sch., substituted: SI 1996/2667 Art.2, Sch.

2285. Water (Prevention of Pollution) (Code of Practice) Order 1991
applied: SI 1996/3142 Sch.3 para.2
revoked: SI 1998/3084 Art.3

2294. Social Security (Contributions) (Northern Ireland) Order 1991
referred to: SI 1998/1506 (NI.10) Art.62

2307. Education (Polytechnics and Colleges Funding Council) (Prescribed Expenditure) Regulations 1991
Reg.2, amended: SI 1996/1680 Sch.4 para.1

2318. Allington National Health Service Trust (Establishment) Order 1991
revoked: SI 1999/850 Art.2

2319. Ashford Hospitals National Health Service Trust (Establishment) Order 1991
revoked: SI 1998/800 Art.2

2328. Bath Mental Health Care National Health Service Trust (Establishment) Order 1991
Art.1, amended: SI 1999/891 Art.2
Art.2, amended: SI 1999/891 Art.2
Art.4, amended: SI 1999/891 Art.3

2330. Bradford Community Health National Health Service Trust (Establishment) Order 1991
Art.3, substituted: SI 1998/1543 Art.2

2332. Central Sheffield University Hospitals National Health Service Trust (Establishment) Order 1991
Art.3, substituted: SI 1999/887 Art.2

NO.

1991—cont.

2334. Income Support (General) Amendment No.6 Regulations 1991
applied: SI 1996/1623 Art.3, SI 1998/217 Art.2, SI 1999/779 Art.2, Sch.
Reg.4, applied: SI 1996/207 Sch.1 para.15
Reg.5, applied: SI 1996/207 Sch.1 para.15
Reg.6, amended: SI 1996/206 Reg.31
Reg.6, applied: SI 1996/207 Sch.1 para.15

2335. Cleveland Ambulance National Health Service Trust (Establishment) Order 1991
revoked: SI 1999/799 Art.2
Art.4, revoked: SI 1999/799 Art.2

2338. Doncaster Healthcare National Health Service Trust (Establishment) Order 1991
Art.1, amended: SI 1999/2656 Art.2
Art.2, amended: SI 1999/2656 Art.2
Art.3, substituted: SI 1999/2656 Art.3

2342. East Birmingham Hospital National Health Service Trust (Establishment) Order 1991
revoked: SI 1996/882 Art.2

2345. Essex Ambulance Service National Health Service Trust (Establishment) Order 1991
Art.4, amended: SI 1996/2602 Art.2

2346. Essex Rivers Healthcare National Health Service Trust (Establishment) Order 1991
Art.3, amended: SI 1996/993 Art.2

2349. Frenchay Healthcare National Health Service Trust (Establishment) Order 1991
revoked: SI 1999/626 Art.2
Art.3, revoked: SI 1999/626 Art.2
Art.3, substituted: SI 1998/193 Art.2, SI 1998/2993 Art.2
Sch., added: SI 1998/193 Art.2, Sch., SI 1998/2993 Art.2, Sch.
Sch., revoked: SI 1999/626 Art.2

2353. Harefield Hospital National Health Service Trust (Establishment) Order 1991
revoked: SI 1998/783 Art.2

2358. Herefordshire Community Health National Health Service Trust (Establishment) Order 1991
Art.3, substituted: SI 1998/2948 Art.2

2361. Horizon National Health Service Trust (Establishment) Order 1991
Art.4, amended: SI 1997/1376 Art.2
Art.4, substituted: SI 1997/1483 Art.2

2364. Lancaster Acute Hospitals National Health Service Trust (Establishment) Order 1991
revoked: SI 1998/817 Art.2

2365. Lancaster Priority Services National Health Service Trust (Establishment) Order 1991
revoked: SI 1998/815 Art.2

2367. Luton and Dunstable Hospital National Health Service Trust (Establishment) Order 1991
Art.3, substituted: SI 1999/1218 Art.2

2368. Maidstone Priority Care National Health Service Trust (Establishment) Order 1991
revoked: SI 1997/418 Art.2

2369. Mersey Regional Ambulance Service National Health Service Trust (Establishment) Order 1991
Art.4, amended: SI 1997/2690 Art.2

2370. Mid Essex Hospital Services National Health Service Trust (Establishment) Order 1991
Art.4, amended: SI 1998/2116 Art.2

2373. Mulberry National Health Service Trust (Establishment) Order 1991
revoked: SI 1999/790 Art.2

2377. North Tees Health National Health Service Trust (Establishment) Order 1991
revoked: SI 1999/800 Art.2

2378. **Northallerton Health Services National Health Service Trust (Establishment) Order 1991**
Art.3, substituted: SI 1998/323 Art.2

2383. **Optimum Health Services National Health Service Trust (Establishment) Order 1991**
revoked: SI 1999/900 Art.2

2384. **Parkside National Health Service Trust (Establishment) Order 1991**
Art.3, amended: SI 1999/908 Art.3

2396. **St Peter's Hospital National Health Service Trust (Establishment) Order 1991**
revoked: SI 1998/800 Art.2

2400. **South Bedfordshire Community Health Care National Health Service Trust (Establishment) Order 1991**
revoked: SI 1999/894 Art.2

2401. **South Downs Health National Health Service Trust (Establishment) Order 1991**
Art.3, substituted: SI 1999/1052 Art.2

2402. **South Tees Acute Hospitals National Health Service Trust (Establishment) Order 1991**
Art.1, amended: SI 1998/2950 Art.2
Art.3, substituted: SI 1998/2950 Art.2

2403. **South Warwickshire Health Care National Health Service Trust (Establishment) Order 1991**
revoked: SI 1998/516 Art.2

2404. **South Yorkshire Metropolitan Ambulance and Paramedic Service National Health Service Trust (Establishment) Order 1991**
Art.4, amended: SI 1997/2767 Art.2

2405. **Southend Community Care Services National Health Service Trust (Establishment) Order 1991**
Art.3, substituted: SI 1999/1169 Art.2

2406. **Southmead Health Services National Health Service Trust (Establishment) Order 1991**
revoked: SI 1999/626 Art.2

2407. **Southport and Formby National Health Service Trust (Establishment) Order 1991**
revoked: SI 1999/889 Art.2

2408. **Staffordshire Ambulance Service National Health Service Trust (Establishment) Order 1991**
Art.4, amended: SI 1997/2788 Art.2

2409. **Thameslink Healthcare Services National Health Service Trust (Establishment) Order 1991**
revoked: SI 1998/807 Art.2

2411. **Walton Centre for Neurology and Neurosurgery National Health Service Trust (Establishment) Order 1991**
Art.3, amended: SI 1996/982 Art.2

2412. **Wellhouse National Health Service Trust (Establishment) Order 1991**
revoked: SI 1999/893 Art.2
Art.3, amended: SI 1996/992 Art.2
Art.3, revoked: SI 1999/893 Art.2

2413. **West Lambeth Community Care National Health Service Trust (Establishment) Order 1991**
revoked: SI 1999/900 Art.2
Art.1, amended: SI 1996/1769 Art.2
Art.1, revoked: SI 1999/900 Art.2
Art.2, amended: SI 1996/1769 Art.2
Art.2, revoked: SI 1999/900 Art.2

2414. **Weston Park Hospital National Health Service Trust (Establishment) Order 1991**
revoked: SI 1999/886 Art.2

2416. **Wiltshire Health Care National Health Service Trust (Establishment) Order 1991**
revoked: SI 1999/1771 Art.2

2437. **Rules of the Air Regulations 1991**
revoked: SI 1996/1393 Reg.3, Sch.2

2465. **National Health Service (Optical Charges and Payments) Amendment (No.2) Regulations 1991**
revoked: SI 1997/818 Reg.24, Sch.4

2486. **Imported Food and Feedingstuffs (Safeguards against Cholera) Regulations 1991**
revoked: SI 1996/1547 Reg.6, Sch.4

2487. **National Health Service (Optical Charges and Payments) (Scotland) Amendment (No.2) Regulations 1991**
revoked: SI 1998/642 Reg.24, Sch.4

2492. **Motor Vehicles (Driving Licences) (Large Goods and Passenger-Carrying Vehicles) (Amendment) (No.4) Regulations 1991**
revoked: SI 1996/2824 Reg.2, Sch.1

2493. **Motor Vehicles (Driving Licences) (Amendment) (No.3) Regulations 1991**
revoked: SI 1996/2824 Reg.2, Sch.1

2496. **Betting, Gaming and Lotteries Act 1963 (Variation of Fees) (Scotland) (No.2) Order 1991**
revoked: SI 1997/77 Art.3

2523. **Import and Export (Plant Health Fees) (Forestry) (Great Britain) (Amendment) Order 1991**
revoked: SI 1996/2291 Reg.3

2539. **Control of Pollution (Radioactive Waste) (Scotland) Regulations 1991**
Sch., amended: SI 1996/973 Reg.2, Sch para.14

2567. **Education (National Curriculum) (Modern Foreign Languages) Order 1991**
Sch., amended: SI 1999/2214 Art.2

2580. **Building Societies (Liquid Asset) Regulations 1991**
Sch. Part III, amended: SI 1998/1129 Art.2, Sch.1 para.12

2628. **Child Support (Northern Ireland) Order 1991**
amended: 1999 c.10 s.2, Sch.2 para.17
applied: SI 1998/1506 (NI.10) Art.4, Art.17
referred to: 1998 c.47 s.87
Art.2, amended: SI 1998/1506 (NI.10) Art.78, Sch.6 para.5, Sch.7, 1999 c.10 s.1, Sch.1 para.6
Art.6, amended: SI 1998/1506 (NI.10) Art.78, Sch.6 para.6, Sch.7
Art.7, amended: SI 1998/1506 (NI.10) Art.78, Sch.6 para.7, Sch.7
Art.9, amended: SI 1998/1506 (NI.10) Art.78, Sch.6 para.8, Sch.7, 1999 c.10 s.19, Sch.6
Art.10, amended: SI 1998/1506 (NI.10) Art.78, Sch.6 para.9
Art.12, amended: SI 1998/1506 (NI.10) Art.78, Sch.6 para.10
Art.13, amended: SI 1998/1506 (NI.10) Art.78, Sch.6 para.11
Art.14, amended: SI 1998/1506 (NI.10) Art.78, Sch.6 para.12
Art.15, applied: SI 1998/1506 (NI.10) Art.3, SI 1999/680 Art.2, Sch. Part I
Art.15, revoked: SI 1998/1506 (NI.10) Art.78, Sch.6 para.13, Sch.7
Art.16, amended: SI 1998/1506 (NI.10) Art.78, Sch.6 para.14, Sch.7
Art.16, revoked (in part): SI 1998/1506 (NI.10) Art.78, Sch.6 para.14, Sch.7

1991—cont.

2628. Child Support (Northern Ireland) Order 1991—*cont.*

Art.17, amended: SI 1998/1506 (NI.10) Art.78, Sch.6 para.15, Sch.7

Art.18, substituted: SI 1998/1506 (NI.10) Art.40

Art.19, substituted: SI 1998/1506 (NI.10) Art.41

Art.20, revoked: SI 1998/1506 (NI.10) Art.41

Art.21, revoked: SI 1998/1506 (NI.10) Art.41

Art.22, applied: SI 1998/1506 (NI.10) Art.5, Sch.1 para.4

Art.22, substituted: SI 1998/1506 (NI.10) Art.42

Art.23, applied: SI 1998/1506 (NI.10) Art.5

Art.23, referred to: SI 1996/1298 (NI.8) Sch.3

Art.23, revoked: SI 1998/1506 (NI.10) Art.42

Art.25, amended: SI 1998/1506 (NI.10) Art.78, Sch.6 para.16

Art.25, revoked (in part): SI 1998/1506 (NI.10) Art.78, Sch.6 para.16, Sch.7

Art.27, amended: SI 1998/1506 (NI.10) Art.78, Sch.6 para.17

Art.28, amended: SI 1998/1506 (NI.10) Art.78, Sch.6 para.18

Art.28A, amended: SI 1998/1506 (NI.10) Art.78, Sch.6 para.19

Art.28B, amended: SI 1998/1506 (NI.10) Art.78, Sch.6 para.20

Art.28B, revoked (in part): SI 1998/1506 (NI.10) Art.78, Sch.6 para.20, Sch.7

Art.28D, amended: SI 1998/1506 (NI.10) Art.78, Sch.6 para.21

Art.28F, amended: SI 1998/1506 (NI.10) Art.78, Sch.6 para.22

Art.28G, revoked (in part): SI 1998/1506 (NI.10) Art.78, Sch.6 para.23, Sch.7

Art.28H, substituted: SI 1998/1506 (NI.10) Art.78, Sch.6 para.24

Art.28ZA, added: SI 1998/1506 (NI.10) Art.43

Art.28ZB, added: SI 1998/1506 (NI.10) Art.43

Art.28ZC, added: SI 1998/1506 (NI.10) Art.44

Art.28ZD, added: SI 1998/1506 (NI.10) Art.44

Art.40, amended: SI 1998/1506 (NI.10) Art.78, Sch.6 para.25

Art.41, amended: SI 1998/1506 (NI.10) Art.78, Sch.6 para.26

Art.42, amended: SI 1998/1506 (NI.10) Art.78, Sch.6 para.27

Art.43, amended: SI 1998/1506 (NI.10) Art.78, Sch.6 para.28, Sch.7, 1999 c.10 s.19, Sch.6

Art.43A, added: SI 1998/1506 (NI.10) Art.78, Sch.6 para.29

Art.43B, added: SI 1998/1506 (NI.10) Art.78, Sch.6 para.29

Art.44, amended: 1999 c.10 s.1, Sch.1 para.6

Art.46, amended: SI 1998/1506 (NI.10) Art.78, Sch.6 para.30

Art.47, amended: SI 1998/1506 (NI.10) Art.78, Sch.6 para.31

Art.49, revoked (in part): 1998 c.47 s.87, s.100, Sch.15

Sch.1 para.8, amended: SI 1998/1506 (NI.10) Art.78, Sch.6 para.32

Sch.1 para.9, amended: SI 1998/1506 (NI.10) Art.78, Sch.6 para.32

Sch.1 para.13, amended: SI 1998/1506 (NI.10) Art.78, Sch.6 para.32

Sch.1 para.15, amended: SI 1998/1506 (NI.10) Art.78, Sch.6 para.32

Sch.1 para.16, amended: SI 1998/1506 (NI.10) Art.78, Sch.6 para.32

Sch.2, revoked: SI 1998/1506 (NI.10) Art.78, Sch.6 para.33, Sch.7

Sch.3, revoked: SI 1998/1506 (NI.10) Art.78, Sch.6 para.34, Sch.7

1991—cont.

2628. Child Support (Northern Ireland) Order 1991—*cont.*

Sch.3 para.3, applied: SI 1999/680 Art.2, Sch. Part I

Sch.4 para.1, amended: SI 1998/1506 (NI.10) Art.78, Sch.6 para.35

Sch.4 para.2, substituted: SI 1998/1506 (NI.10) Art.78, Sch.6 para.35

Sch.4 para.3, amended: SI 1998/1506 (NI.10) Art.78, Sch.6 para.35

Sch.4 para.3A, amended: SI 1998/1506 (NI.10) Art.78, Sch.6 para.35

Sch.4A para.1, amended: SI 1998/1506 (NI.10) Art.78, Sch.6 para.36, Sch.7

Sch.4A para.2, amended: SI 1998/1506 (NI.10) Art.78, Sch.6 para.36

Sch.4A para.4, amended: SI 1998/1506 (NI.10) Art.78, Sch.6 para.36, Sch.7

Sch.4A para.6, revoked: SI 1998/1506 (NI.10) Art.78, Sch.6 para.36, Sch.7

Sch.4A para.8, amended: SI 1998/1506 (NI.10) Art.78, Sch.6 para.36

Sch.4A para.9, amended: SI 1998/1506 (NI.10) Art.78, Sch.6 para.36

Sch.4C, added: SI 1998/1506 (NI.10) Art.78, Sch.6 para.37

Sch.5 para.1, revoked: SI 1998/1506 (NI.10) Art.78, Sch.7

2630. Immigration (Isle of Man) Order 1991

Sch.1 Part I, amended: SI 1997/275 Art.3

2638. Conservation of Seals (Common Seals) (Shetland Islands Area) Order 1991

revoked: SI 1998/923 Art.2

2646. Goods Vehicles (Authorisation of International Journeys) (Fees) (Amendment) Regulations 1991

revoked: SI 1996/131 Reg.4, Sch.2

2667. Magistrates' Courts (Remands in Custody) Order 1991

Art.2, amended: SI 1997/35 Art.2

2669. Offshore Installations (Safety Zones) (No.4) Order 1991

revoked: SI 1997/735 Art.3, Sch.2

2676. Act of Adjournal (Consolidation Amendment No.3) 1991

revoked: SI 1996/513 Sch.2 r.3, Sch.3

2677. Act of Adjournal (Consolidation Amendment No.4) (Supervised Attendance Orders) 1991

revoked: SI 1996/513 Sch.2 r.3, Sch.3

2680. Public Works Contracts Regulations 1991

applied: 1999 c.29 s.356

referred to: 1999 c.29 s.358

Reg.2, amended: SI 1996/2911 Reg.35, SI 1999/1042 Art.3, Sch.1 para.20

Reg.3, amended: SI 1996/974 Art.2, Sch.1 para.9, SI 1999/1042 Art.3, Sch.1 para.20

Reg.4, amended: SI 1996/2911 Reg.35

Reg.6, amended: SI 1996/2911 Reg.35

Reg.29, amended: SI 1999/1820 Art.4, Sch.2 para.148

2694. Goods Vehicles (Authorisation of International Journeys) (Fees) (Amendment) (No. 2) Regulations 1991

revoked: SI 1996/131 Reg.4, Sch.2

2696. Goods Vehicles (Operators' Licences) (Temporary Use in Great Britain) (Amendment) Regulations 1991

revoked: SI 1996/2186 Reg.2, Sch.1

2697. Pembrokeshire National Health Service Trust (Establishment) Order 1991

revoked: SI 1997/877 Art.2

NO.

2720. Armed Forces (Compensation Limits) Order 1991
revoked: SI 1996/1420 Art.3

2736. Insurance Companies (Accounts and Statements) (Amendment) Regulations 1991
revoked: SI 1996/943 Reg.35, Sch.7

2737. Naval Courts-Martial General Orders (Royal Navy) 1991
revoked: SI 1997/170 r.79

2740. Social Security (Attendance Allowance) Regulations 1991
amended: SI 1996/30 Reg.2
Reg.1A, added: SI 1997/2676 Reg.2
Reg.2, amended: SI 1998/563 Reg.18
Reg.4, revoked: SI 1997/793 Reg.19
Reg.6, amended: SI 1999/1326 Reg.3
Reg.7A, amended: SI 1999/2860 Art.3, Sch.8 para.1
Reg.8, amended: SI 1996/1345 Reg.10, SI 1999/2860 Art.3, Sch.8 para.1
Reg.8C, added: SI 1997/1839 Reg.2
Reg.8C, revoked: SI 1999/2860 Art.3, Sch.8 para.2
Reg.8D, added: SI 1997/1839 Reg.2
Reg.8D, revoked: SI 1999/2860 Art.3, Sch.8 para.2
Reg.8E, added: SI 1997/1839 Reg.2
Reg.8E, revoked: SI 1999/2860 Art.3, Sch.8 para.2

2742. Disability Living Allowance and Disability Working Allowance (Consequential Provisions) Regulations 1991
Reg.11, revoked (in part): SI 1996/206 Reg.28, Sch.3

2748. Electrically, Hydraulically and Oil-Electrically Operated Lifts (Components) (EEC Requirements) Regulations 1991
revoked: SI 1997/831 Reg.1

2749. Simple Pressure Vessels (Safety) Regulations 1991
applied: SI 1998/2306 Reg.10, Sch.1

2765. Town and Country Planning (Fees for Applications and Deemed Applications) (Scotland) Amendment Regulations 1991
revoked (in part): SI 1997/10 Reg.15

2768. Building Regulations 1991
see *Parlett v Kerrier DC* Independent, October 6, 1997 (C.S.) (QBD), Scott Baker, J.
applied: SI 1998/2561 Reg.4, Reg.5, Reg.6, SI 1998/3129 Reg.4, Reg.5, Reg.10, SI 1999/77 Reg.5, SI 1999/3410 Reg.4
Reg.2, amended: SI 1999/77 Reg.3
Reg.7, substituted: SI 1999/77 Reg.4
Reg.13A, applied: SI 1998/3129 Reg.4, Reg.10
Reg.14, applied: SI 1998/2561 Reg.4
Sch.1 Part B, substituted: SI 1999/3410 Reg.3
Sch.1 Part B1, substituted: SI 1999/3410 Reg.3
Sch.1 Part B2, substituted: SI 1999/3410 Reg.3
Sch.1 Part B3, substituted: SI 1999/3410 Reg.3
Sch.1 Part B4, substituted: SI 1999/3410 Reg.3
Sch.1 Part B5, substituted: SI 1999/3410 Reg.3
Sch.1 Part D, applied: SI 1998/3129 Reg.6
Sch.1 Part G, applied: SI 1998/3129 Reg.6
Sch.1 Part K, substituted: SI 1997/1904 Reg.3
Sch.1 Part M, substituted: SI 1998/2561 Reg.3
Sch.1 Part N, substituted: SI 1997/1904 Reg.4
Sch.1 para.B3, applied: SI 1996/428 Sch.1 para.5

NO.

2778. Education (London Residuary Body) (Property Transfer) (No.4) Order 1991
applied: SI 1997/1990 Art.2
Art.4, amended: SI 1998/1239 Art.2

2786. Rules of Procedure (Air Force) (Amendment) Rules 1991
revoked: SI 1997/171 r.90, Sch.7

2787. Rules of Procedure (Army) (Amendment) Rules 1991
revoked: SI 1997/169 r.90, Sch.7

2794. Town and Country Planning (Development Plan) Regulations 1991
see *Miller v Wycombe DC* [1997] J.P.L. 951 (CA), Pill, L.J.
applied: SI 1999/3280 Reg.45
revoked (in part): SI 1999/3280 Reg.45
Reg.2, amended: SI 1997/531 Reg.3, SI 1999/981 Reg.5
Reg.2, revoked (in part): SI 1999/3280 Reg.45
Reg.9, amended: SI 1997/531 Reg.4, SI 1999/981 Reg.5
Reg.9, revoked (in part): SI 1999/3280 Reg.45
Reg.10, amended: SI 1997/531 Reg.5
Reg.10, revoked (in part): SI 1999/3280 Reg.45
Reg.16, see *Modern Homes (Whitworth) Ltd v Lancashire CC* Times, May 14, 1998 (QBD), Nigel Macleod Q.C.; see *Peel Investments (North) Ltd v Rossendale BC* (1997) 73 P. & C.R. 191 (QBD), Ognall, J.
Reg.16, amended: SI 1997/531 Reg.6
Reg.16, revoked (in part): SI 1999/3280 Reg.45
Reg.17, see *Modern Homes (Whitworth) Ltd v Lancashire CC* Times, May 14, 1998 (QBD), Nigel Macleod Q.C.
Reg.17, revoked (in part): SI 1999/3280 Reg.45
Reg.18, amended: SI 1997/531 Reg.7
Reg.18, revoked (in part): SI 1999/3280 Reg.45
Reg.33, see *Cooper v Secretary of State for the Environment* (1996) 71 P. & C.R. 529 (QBD), Lockhart-Mummery Q.C.
Reg.33, revoked (in part): SI 1999/3280 Reg.45
Reg.35, amended: SI 1997/531 Reg.8
Reg.35, revoked (in part): SI 1999/3280 Reg.45
Sch., revoked (in part): SI 1999/3280 Reg.45
Sch., substituted: SI 1997/531 Reg.9, Sch.

2812. Peak Rail Light Railway Order 1991
Art.12, amended: SI 1996/362 Art.5, Sch.4

2814. Anthrax Order 1991
Art.2, amended: SI 1996/1855 Art.2
Art.10, amended: SI 1996/1855 Art.2
Sch.1 Part II, amended: SI 1996/1855 Art.2

2824. Fertilisers (Sampling and Analysis) (Amendment) Regulations 1991
revoked: SI 1996/1342 Reg.9

2825. Food Premises (Registration) Regulations 1991
Reg.1, amended: SI 1996/1499 Reg.49
Reg.3, amended: SI 1997/723 Reg.2, SI 1998/994 Reg.58
Reg.7, amended: SI 1997/723 Reg.2

2826. Electrical Equipment for Explosive Atmospheres (Certification) (Amendment) (No. 2) Regulations 1991
revoked: SI 1996/192 Reg.1, Sch.1

2828. Scottish Seed Potato Development Council (Amendment) Order 1991
revoked: SI 1997/2092 Art.9

2839. Environmental Protection (Duty of Care) Regulations 1991
referred to: SI 1996/1528 Art.8
Reg.2, amended: SI 1996/972 Reg.23

NO.

1991—cont.

2843. Animals, Meat and Meat Products (Examination for Residues and Maximum Residue Limits) Regulations 1991
revoked: SI 1997/1729 Reg.36, Sch.2
Sch.1, amended: SI 1996/374
Sch.1, revoked: SI 1997/1729 Reg.36, Sch.2

2873. Criminal Justice Act 1988 (Designated Countries and Territories) Order 1991
see *United States v Montgomery* Times, August 24, 1998 (CA), Stuart-Smith, L.J.
Art.5, amended: SI 1996/2877 Art.2
Sch.1, amended: SI 1996/278 Art.2, SI 1996/2877 Art.3, Sch.1, SI 1997/1316 Art.2, SI 1997/2976 Art.2, SI 1999/282 Art.2
Sch.2 para.2, substituted: SI 1996/2877 Art.4, Sch.2 para.1
Sch.2 para.4, substituted: SI 1996/2877 Art.4, Sch.2 para.2
Sch.2 para.5, amended: SI 1996/2877 Art.4, Sch.2 para.3
Sch.2 para.7, amended: SI 1996/2877 Art.4, Sch.2 para.4
Sch.2 para.14, amended: SI 1996/2877 Art.4, Sch.2 para.5
Sch.2 para.20, substituted: SI 1996/2877 Art.4, Sch.2 para.6
Sch.2 para.21, amended: SI 1996/278 Art.3, SI 1996/2877 Art.4, Sch.2 para.7, Sch.2 para.8, SI 1997/1316 Art.3, SI 1997/2976 Art.3, SI 1999/282 Art.3
Sch.2 para.23, substituted: SI 1996/2877 Art.4, Sch.2 para.9
Sch.3, amended: SI 1997/1316 Art.4, SI 1997/2976 Art.4, SI 1999/282 Art.4

2877. Double Taxation Relief (Taxes on Income) (Denmark) Order 1991
Sch., referred to: SI 1996/3165 Art.2

2878. Double Taxation Relief (Taxes on Income) (Finland) Order 1991
Sch., referred to: SI 1996/3166 Art.2

2887. Disability Working Allowance (General) Regulations 1991
applied: SI 1996/1623 Art.3, SI 1996/2545 Reg.10, SI 1998/217 Art.2, SI 1999/779 Art.2, Sch.
referred to: SI 1999/2566 Reg.2
Reg.2, amended: SI 1996/1345 Reg.7, SI 1996/1944 Reg.13, Sch. para.1, SI 1996/3137 Reg.2, SI 1998/563 Reg.5, SI 1998/2825 Reg.12, SI 1999/2165 Reg.2, SI 1999/2487 Reg.14, Reg.26, Sch.2, SI 1999/3156 Reg.12
Reg.2A, added: SI 1997/2676 Reg.5
Reg.2A, amended: SI 1999/2487 Reg.26, Sch.2
Reg.4, amended: SI 1999/2487 Reg.26
Reg.5, amended: SI 1996/30 Reg.5, SI 1998/563 Reg.18, SI 1999/2487 Reg.26, Sch.1, Sch.2
Reg.6, amended: SI 1998/2825 Reg.13, SI 1999/2165 Reg.4, SI 1999/2487 Reg.26, Sch.2, SI 1999/3156 Reg.13
Reg.6A, amended: SI 1999/2487 Reg.26, Sch.2
Reg.7, amended: SI 1996/1345 Reg.7
Reg.7A, amended: SI 1999/2487 Reg.26, Sch.2
Reg.8, amended: SI 1996/1345 Reg.7, SI 1999/2487 Reg.26, Sch.2
Reg.8, applied: SI 1996/2545 Reg.10
Reg.14, amended: SI 1999/2487 Reg.15
Reg.15, amended: SI 1996/599 Art.17, SI 1997/2793 Reg.2, SI 1999/2487 Reg.26, Sch.2
Reg.15, revoked (in part): SI 1999/2487 Reg.16

NO.

1991—cont.

2887. Disability Working Allowance (General) Regulations 1991—*cont.*
Reg.15A, amended: SI 1996/1008 Art.2, Sch para.10, SI 1996/2545 Reg.7, SI 1997/2793 Reg.2, SI 1999/714 Reg.5, SI 1999/2487 Reg.17
Reg.16, amended: SI 1996/1944 Reg.3, SI 1996/3137 Reg.2, SI 1999/2487 Reg.26
Reg.18, amended: SI 1996/3137 Reg.2
Reg.20, amended: SI 1996/3137 Reg.2
Reg.21, amended: SI 1999/1509 Reg.2, SI 1999/2487 Reg.26
Reg.24, amended: SI 1999/2165 Reg.4
Reg.25, amended: SI 1999/2487 Reg.26
Reg.28, amended: SI 1997/65 Reg.3
Reg.29, amended: SI 1997/2197 Reg.2, Reg.7, SI 1997/2863 Reg.17, SI 1998/563 Reg.6, SI 1998/2117 Reg.2, SI 1998/2825 Reg.14, SI 1999/2487 Reg.26, Sch.2, SI 1999/3156 Reg.14
Reg.31, amended: SI 1999/2487 Reg.26, Sch.2
Reg.32, amended: SI 1999/2487 Reg.26, Sch.2
Reg.34, amended: SI 1998/1174 Reg.7, SI 1999/3156 Reg.18
Reg.37, amended: SI 1997/2197 Reg.2, SI 1997/2863 Reg.17, SI 1998/2117 Reg.3, SI 1998/2825 Reg.15, SI 1999/2487 Reg.26, Sch.2, SI 1999/3156 Reg.15
Reg.38, amended: SI 1999/2487 Reg.26, Sch.1, Sch.2
Reg.39, amended: SI 1998/2250 Reg.2
Reg.41, amended: SI 1998/563 Reg.4, SI 1999/1935 Reg.7
Reg.42, amended: SI 1996/1759 Reg.2, SI 1997/1671 Reg.2, SI 1998/1379 Reg.2, SI 1999/1935 Reg.7
Reg.45, amended: SI 1996/462 Reg.8
Reg.46, amended: SI 1999/1935 Reg.7
Reg.47, amended: SI 1996/462 Reg.9, SI 1999/1935 Reg.7
Reg.48, amended: SI 1996/462 Reg.10, SI 1999/1935 Reg.7
Reg.48A, added: SI 1998/563 Reg.4
Reg.48A, amended: SI 1999/1935 Reg.7
Reg.51, amended: SI 1996/599 Art.17, SI 1996/2545 Reg.8, SI 1997/543 Art.17, SI 1998/470 Art.17, SI 1999/264 Art.17, SI 1999/2487 Reg.18, Reg.26, Sch.2
Reg.51, applied: SI 1996/2890 Sch.3 para.54
Reg.51A, added: SI 1999/2487 Reg.17
Reg.51A, amended: SI 1999/2487 Reg.19, Reg.26, Sch.2
Reg.52, amended: SI 1996/599 Art.17, SI 1997/543 Art.17, SI 1998/470 Art.17, SI 1999/264 Art.17, SI 1999/2487 Reg.20, Reg.26, Sch.2
Reg.53, amended: SI 1999/2487 Reg.21, Reg.26, Sch.2
Reg.54, amended: SI 1999/2487 Reg.26, Sch.2
Reg.55, amended: SI 1996/1345 Reg.7, SI 1999/2487 Reg.26, Sch.1, Sch.2
Reg.56, amended: SI 1996/1944 Reg.3, SI 1999/2487 Reg.26, Reg.27, Sch.1, Sch.2
Reg.56A, amended: SI 1999/1510 Art.5
Reg.56A, revoked (in part): SI 1999/1510 Art.5, SI 1999/2487 Reg.22 (rem.)
Reg.57, amended: SI 1999/2487 Reg.26, Sch.1, Sch.2
Sch.1 para.22, amended: SI 1999/2487 Reg.23, Reg.26, Sch.2
Sch.1 para.24, amended: SI 1999/2487 Reg.26
Sch.3 para.3, amended: SI 1996/1345 Reg.7
Sch.3 para.5, amended: SI 1996/1345 Reg.7

1991—cont.

2887. Disability Working Allowance (General) Regulations 1991—*cont.*

Sch.3 para.9, amended: SI 1997/2197 Reg.7, SI 1999/1677 Reg.2

Sch.3 para.11, amended: SI 1997/2863 Reg.17

Sch.3 para.12, amended: SI 1996/462 Reg.8

Sch.3 para.13, amended: SI 1999/2487 Reg.24

Sch.3 para.19, amended: SI 1996/599 Art.17

Sch.3 para.22, amended: SI 1998/563 Reg.7

Sch.3 para.24, substituted: SI 1998/563 Reg.7

Sch.3 para.25A, added: SI 1998/1173 Reg.3

Sch.3 para.29, amended: SI 1996/462 Reg.8

Sch.3 para.46, amended: SI 1999/2487 Reg.26, Sch.1

Sch.3 para.54, amended: SI 1996/1944 Reg.13, Sch. para.5

Sch.3 para.55, added: SI 1997/65 Reg.2

Sch.3 para.56, added: SI 1997/65 Reg.2

Sch.3 para.57, amended: SI 1997/2863 Reg.17

Sch.3 para.57, substituted: SI 1998/1174 Reg.7

Sch.3 para.58, amended: SI 1997/2863 Reg.17

Sch.3 para.59, added: SI 1998/1174 Reg.7, SI 1999/2487 Reg.24

Sch.3 para.59, amended: SI 1999/3156 Reg.18

Sch.3 para.60, added: SI 1998/2117 Reg.4

Sch.3 para.61, amended: SI 1998/2825 Reg.16, SI 1999/3156 Reg.16

Sch.3 para.62, amended: SI 1998/2825 Reg.16, SI 1999/3156 Reg.16

Sch.3 para.63, added: SI 1999/2165 Reg.4

Sch.4 para.6, amended: SI 1998/1174 Reg.7, SI 1999/3156 Reg.18

Sch.4 para.8, amended: SI 1996/1345 Reg.7, SI 1996/1944 Reg.13, Sch. para.7

Sch.4 para.45, amended: SI 1997/2197 Reg.7

Sch.4 para.46, amended: SI 1997/2197 Reg.7

Sch.4 para.48, added: SI 1996/3195 Reg.15

Sch.4 para.49, added: SI 1996/1345 Reg.7

Sch.4 para.51, amended: SI 1997/2863 Reg.17

Sch.4 para.51, substituted: SI 1998/1174 Reg.7

Sch.4 para.52, amended: SI 1997/2863 Reg.17

Sch.4 para.53, added: SI 1998/1174 Reg.7

Sch.4 para.53, amended: SI 1999/3156 Reg.18

Sch.4 para.54, added: SI 1998/2117 Reg.5

Sch.4 para.55, amended: SI 1998/2825 Reg.17, SI 1999/3156 Reg.17

Sch.4 para.56, amended: SI 1998/2825 Reg.17, SI 1999/3156 Reg.17

Sch.4 para.57, added: SI 1999/2165 Reg.4

Sch.5, amended: SI 1996/599 Art.17, Sch.3, SI 1997/543 Art.17, Sch.3, SI 1997/806 Reg.4, SI 1999/2487 Reg.25, Reg.26, Sch.2

Sch.5 para.1, amended: SI 1998/470 Art.17, Sch.3, SI 1999/264 Art.17, Sch.3

Sch.5 para.2, amended: SI 1998/470 Art.17, Sch.3, SI 1999/264 Art.17, Sch.3

Sch.5 para.2A, amended: SI 1998/470 Art.17, Sch.3, SI 1999/264 Art.17, Sch.3

Sch.5 para.2A, applied: SI 1996/2890 Sch.3 para.54

Sch.5 para.3, amended: SI 1998/470 Art.17, Sch.3, SI 1998/1541 Reg.3, SI 1999/264 Art.17, Sch.3

Sch.5 para.3, substituted: SI 1996/2545 Reg.9

Sch.5 para.4, amended: SI 1998/470 Art.17, Sch.3, SI 1999/264 Art.17, Sch.3

Sch.5 para.4, substituted: SI 1996/2545 Reg.9

Sch.5 para.5, amended: SI 1998/470 Art.17, Sch.3, SI 1999/264 Art.17, Sch.3

2890. Social Security (Disability Living Allowance) Regulations 1991

Reg.1, amended: SI 1999/2860 Art.3, Sch.7 para.1

Reg.1A, added: SI 1997/2676 Reg.4

Reg.2, amended: SI 1996/30 Reg.4, SI 1998/563 Reg.18, SI 1999/2860 Art.3, Sch.7 para.2

Reg.3, amended: SI 1997/349 Reg.2

Reg.4, amended: SI 1996/599 Art.12, SI 1997/543 Art.12, SI 1998/470 Art.12, SI 1999/264 Art.12

Reg.5, revoked: SI 1997/793 Reg.19

Reg.5A, added: SI 1997/1839 Reg.3

Reg.5A, revoked: SI 1999/2860 Art.3, Sch.7 para.3

Reg.5B, added: SI 1997/1839 Reg.3

Reg.5B, revoked: SI 1999/2860 Art.3, Sch.7 para.3

Reg.5C, added: SI 1997/1839 Reg.3

Reg.5C, revoked: SI 1999/2860 Art.3, Sch.7 para.3

Reg.8, amended: SI 1999/1326 Reg.4

Reg.9A, amended: SI 1999/2860 Art.3, Sch.7 para.4

Reg.10, amended: SI 1996/1345 Reg.17

Reg.12, see *M (A Child) v Chief Adjudication Officer* Times, November 11, 1999 (CA), Simon Brown, L.J.

Reg.12A, added: SI 1996/1436 Reg.2

Reg.12A, amended: SI 1999/1326 Reg.4

Reg.12B, added: SI 1996/1436 Reg.2

Reg.12B, amended: SI 1996/1767 Reg.2

Reg.12C, added: SI 1996/1436 Reg.2

Reg.13, applied: SI 1999/991 Reg.27, Sch.2 para.18

Reg.25, see *M (A Child) v Chief Adjudication Officer* Times, November 11, 1999 (CA), Simon Brown, L.J.

Sch.1 para.1, amended: SI 1999/2860 Art.3, Sch.7 para.5

Sch.1 para.2, amended: SI 1999/2860 Art.3, Sch.7 para.5

Sch.1 para.3, amended: SI 1999/2860 Art.3, Sch.7 para.5

Sch.1 para.5, amended: SI 1999/2860 Art.3, Sch.7 para.5

Sch.1 para.6, amended: SI 1999/2860 Art.3, Sch.7 para.5

Sch.1 para.7, amended: SI 1999/2860 Art.3, Sch.7 para.5

Sch.2, applied: SI 1999/991 Reg.27, Sch.2 para.18

2891. Social Security (Introduction of Disability Living Allowance) Regulations 1991

applied: SI 1999/2860 Art.4, Sch.16 para.10

2892. Smoke Control Areas (Exempted Fireplaces) Order 1991

Sch. Condition 2, amended: SI 1996/1108 Art.3

2898. South Ayrshire Hospitals National Health Service Trust (Establishment) Order 1991

revoked: SI 1999/1070 Art.2, Sch.2

2899. Forresterhill Hospitals National Health Service Trust (Establishment) Order 1991

revoked: SI 1999/1070 Art.2, Sch.2

2905. Planning and Compensation Act 1991 (Commencement No.5 and Transitional Provisions) Order 1991

see *William Boyer (Transport) Ltd v Secretary of State for the Environment* [1996] 1 P.L.R. 103 (CA), Evans, L.J.

NO.

1991—cont.

2913. Milford Port Health Authority Order 1991
Art.1, amended: SI 1997/143 Art.2
Art.2, amended: SI 1997/143 Art.2
Art.2, revoked (in part): SI 1997/143 Art.2
Art.3, revoked: SI 1997/143 Art.2
Art.4, revoked: SI 1997/143 Art.2
Art.5, revoked: SI 1997/143 Art.2
Art.6, revoked: SI 1997/143 Art.2
Art.7, amended: SI 1997/143 Art.2
Art.8, amended: SI 1997/143 Art.2
Art.9, revoked: SI 1997/143 Art.2
Art.10, revoked: SI 1997/143 Art.2
Sch.1, revoked: SI 1997/143 Art.2
Sch.2, amended: SI 1997/143 Art.2

2926. Rochdale Healthcare National Health Service Trust (Establishment) Order 1991
Art.3, amended: SI 1996/991 Art.2

2934. Imported Food and Feedingstuffs (Safeguards against Cholera) (Amendment) Regulations 1991
revoked: SI 1996/1547 Reg.6, Sch.4

1992

Camden and Westminster (Bus Lane) (No.2) Traffic Order 1992
amended: SI 1996/2165 Art.6
revoked (in part): SI 1998/3206 Art.6

3. Merchant Shipping (Radio Installations) Regulations 1992
applied: SI 1996/3243 Reg.5, Sch Part I, SI 1999/2029 Art.5, Art.6, Sch.1 Reg.36
referred to: SI 1996/3243 Sch Part II, SI 1998/1609 Reg.5, Reg.6, Sch.
revoked: SI 1998/2070 Reg.1
Reg.1, revoked: SI 1998/2070 Reg.1
Reg.2, amended: SI 1996/3188 Reg.17
Reg.2, revoked: SI 1998/2070 Reg.1
Reg.16, applied: SI 1997/348 Reg.9
Reg.16, revoked: SI 1998/2070 Reg.1

16. National Health Service (General Dental Services) (Miscellaneous Amendments) (Scotland) Regulations 1992
revoked: SI 1996/177 Reg.38, Sch.8

33. Medicines (Veterinary Drugs) (Pharmacy and Merchants' List) Order 1992
revoked: SI 1998/1044 Art.9, Sch.
Art.2, revoked: SI 1998/1044 Art.9, Sch.
Art.3, revoked: SI 1998/1044 Art.9, Sch.
Art.4, revoked: SI 1998/1044 Art.9, Sch.
Art.6, revoked: SI 1998/1044 Art.9, Sch.
Art.8, applied: SI 1998/1046 Reg.35
Art.8, revoked: SI 1998/1044 Art.9, Sch.
Art.9, revoked: SI 1998/1044 Art.9, Sch.
Art.11, revoked: SI 1998/1044 Art.9, Sch.
Art.13, revoked: SI 1998/1044 Art.9, Sch.
Art.16, revoked: SI 1998/1044 Art.9, Sch.
Sch.1, revoked: SI 1998/1044 Art.9, Sch.
Sch.1, substituted: SI 1996/3034 Art.2, Sch., SI 1997/2892 Art.2, Sch.
Sch.2, revoked: SI 1998/1044 Art.9, Sch.
Sch.2, substituted: SI 1996/3034 Art.2, Sch., SI 1997/2892 Art.2, Sch.
Sch.3, revoked: SI 1998/1044 Art.9, Sch.
Sch.3, substituted: SI 1996/3034 Art.2, Sch., SI 1997/2892 Art.2, Sch.
Sch.4, revoked: SI 1998/1044 Art.9, Sch.
Sch.4, substituted: SI 1996/3034 Art.2, Sch., SI 1997/2892 Art.2, Sch.
Sch.5, revoked: SI 1998/1044 Art.9, Sch.
Sch.5, substituted: SI 1996/3034 Art.2, Sch., SI 1997/2892 Art.2, Sch.

NO.

1992—cont.

42. Taxes (Relief for Gifts) (Designated Educational Establishments) Regulations 1992
Sch. Part I, revoked (in part): SI 1998/86 Reg.2, Sch.1

46. Opencast Coal (Rate of Interest on Compensation) Order 1992
Art.2, amended: SI 1998/1129 Art.3, Sch.2

51. Environmentally Sensitive Areas (West Penwith) Designation (Amendment) Order 1992
revoked: SI 1997/1444 Art.6 (with saving)

52. Environmentally Sensitive Areas (South Downs) Designation Order 1992
revoked: SI 1997/1443 Art.6 (with saving), SI 1997/1456 Reg.2 (with saving)
Art.2, amended: SI 1996/3104 Reg.2, SI 1997/1443 Sch.8 para.2
Art.5, amended: SI 1996/3104 Reg.2
Art.5A, added: SI 1996/3104 Reg.2
Art.5B, added: SI 1996/3104 Reg.2
Art.5C, added: SI 1996/3104 Reg.2
Art.6, amended: SI 1996/924 Art.2, SI 1997/1443 Sch.8 para.3, SI 1998/1297 Art.6
Art.7, applied: SI 1997/1443 Art.6
Sch.2 para.1, amended: SI 1996/3104 Reg.3

53. Environmentally Sensitive Areas (Somerset Levels and Moors) Designation Order 1992
revoked: SI 1997/1442 Art.6 (with saving), SI 1997/1456 Reg.2 (with saving)
Art.2, amended: SI 1996/3104 Reg.2, SI 1997/1442 Sch.11 para.2
Art.5, amended: SI 1996/3104 Reg.2
Art.5A, added: SI 1996/3104 Reg.2
Art.5B, added: SI 1996/3104 Reg.2
Art.5C, added: SI 1996/3104 Reg.2
Art.6, amended: SI 1997/1442 Sch.11 para.3, SI 1998/1298 Art.5
Art.9, applied: SI 1997/1442 Art.6

54. Environmentally Sensitive Areas (The Broads) Designation Order 1992
revoked: SI 1997/1440 Art.6 (with saving), SI 1997/1456 Reg.2 (with saving)
Art.2, amended: SI 1996/3104 Reg.2, SI 1997/1440 Sch.10 para.2
Art.5, amended: SI 1996/3104 Reg.2
Art.5A, added: SI 1996/3104 Reg.2
Art.5B, added: SI 1996/3104 Reg.2
Art.5C, added: SI 1996/3104 Reg.2
Art.6, amended: SI 1996/921 Art.2, SI 1997/1440 Sch.10 para.3, SI 1998/1299 Art.5
Art.7, applied: SI 1997/1440 Art.6
Sch.4 para.1, amended: SI 1996/3104 Reg.3

55. Environmentally Sensitive Areas (Pennine Dales) Designation Order 1992
revoked: SI 1997/1441 Art.6 (with saving), SI 1997/1456 Reg.2 (with saving)
Art.2, amended: SI 1996/923 Art.2, SI 1996/3104 Reg.2, SI 1997/1441 Sch.9 para.2
Art.5, amended: SI 1996/3104 Reg.2
Art.5A, added: SI 1996/3104 Reg.2
Art.5B, added: SI 1996/3104 Reg.2
Art.5C, added: SI 1996/3104 Reg.2
Art.6, amended: SI 1996/923 Art.2, SI 1997/1441 Sch.9 para.3, SI 1998/1300 Art.5
Art.7, applied: SI 1997/1441 Art.6
Sch.3, revoked: SI 1996/923 Art.2

1992—cont.

1992—cont.

64. **Veterinary Surgeons and Veterinary Practitioners (Registration) (Amendment) Regulations Order of Council 1992**
revoked: SI 1996/437 Art.3
Art.3, revoked: SI 1996/437 Sch
Art.4, revoked: SI 1996/437 Sch
Sch., revoked (in part): SI 1996/437 Sch

72. **Smoke Control Areas (Authorised Fuels) (Amendment) Regulations 1992**
Reg.2, revoked (in part): SI 1998/2154 Reg.3, SI 1998/3096 Reg.3

73. **Local Government (Publication of Information about Unused and Underused Land) (England) Regulations 1992**
revoked: SI 1996/585

78. **Disability Working Allowance (General) Regulations (Northern Ireland) 1992**
Reg.2, amended: SI 1999/2488 Reg.14, Reg.26, Sch.2, SI 1999/3188 Reg.4
Reg.2A, amended: SI 1999/2488 Reg.26, Sch.2
Reg.4, amended: SI 1999/2488 Reg.26
Reg.5, amended: SI 1999/2488 Reg.26, Sch.1, SI 1999/2588 Sch.2
Reg.6, amended: SI 1999/2488 Reg.26, Sch.2, SI 1999/3188 Reg.5
Reg.6A, amended: SI 1999/2488 Reg.26, Sch.2
Reg.7A, amended: SI 1999/2488 Reg.26, Sch.2
Reg.8, amended: SI 1999/2488 Reg.26, Sch.2
Reg.14, amended: SI 1999/2488 Reg.15
Reg.15, amended: SI 1999/2488 Reg.16
Reg.15, revoked (in part): SI 1999/2488 Reg.16
Reg.15A, amended: SI 1999/2488 Reg.17
Reg.16, amended: SI 1999/2488 Reg.26
Reg.21, amended: SI 1999/2488 Reg.26
Reg.22, amended: SI 1999/2488 Reg.26
Reg.25, amended: SI 1999/2488 Reg.26
Reg.29, amended: SI 1999/2488 Reg.26, Sch.2, SI 1999/3188 Reg.6
Reg.30, amended: SI 1999/2488 Reg.26, Sch.2
Reg.31, amended: SI 1999/2488 Reg.26, Sch.2
Reg.32, amended: SI 1999/2488 Reg.26, Sch.2
Reg.34, amended: SI 1999/3188 Reg.10
Reg.37, amended: SI 1999/2488 Reg.26, Sch.2, SI 1999/3188 Reg.7
Reg.38, amended: SI 1999/2488 Reg.26, Sch.1, Sch.2
Reg.51, amended: SI 1999/2488 Reg.18, Reg.26, Sch.2
Reg.51A, added: SI 1999/2488 Reg.17
Reg.51A, amended: SI 1999/2488 Reg.19, Reg.26, Sch.2
Reg.52, amended: SI 1999/2488 Reg.20
Reg.53, amended: SI 1999/2488 Reg.21, Reg.26, Sch.2
Reg.54, amended: SI 1999/2488 Reg.26, Sch.2
Reg.55, amended: SI 1999/2488 Reg.26, Sch.1, Sch.2
Reg.56, amended: SI 1999/2488 Reg.26, Reg.27, Sch.1, Sch.2
Reg.56A, revoked: SI 1999/2488 Reg.22
Reg.57, amended: SI 1999/2488 Reg.26, Sch.1, Sch.2
Sch.1 para.22, amended: SI 1999/2488 Reg.23, Reg.26, Sch.2
Sch.1 para.24, amended: SI 1999/2488 Reg.26
Sch.3 para.13, amended: SI 1999/2488 Reg.24
Sch.3 para.47, amended: SI 1999/2488 Reg.26, Sch.1
Sch.3 para.58, amended: SI 1999/3188 Reg.10
Sch.3 para.59, added: SI 1999/2488 Reg.24
Sch.3 para.63, amended: SI 1999/3188 Reg.8
Sch.3 para.64, amended: SI 1999/3188 Reg.8
Sch.4 para.6, amended: SI 1999/3188 Reg.10

78. **Disability Working Allowance (General) Regulations (Northern Ireland) 1992**—*cont.*
Sch.4 para.11, amended: SI 1999/2488 Reg.26, Sch.2
Sch.4 para.51, amended: SI 1999/3188 Reg.10
Sch.4 para.56, amended: SI 1999/3188 Reg.9
Sch.4 para.57, amended: SI 1999/3188 Reg.9
Sch.5, amended: SI 1999/2488 Reg.25, Reg.26, Sch.2

79. **Offshore Installations (Safety Zones) Order 1992**
revoked: SI 1997/735 Art.3, Sch.2

79. **Pressure Vessels (Verification) Regulations (Northern Ireland) 1992**
Reg.10, amended: SI 1999/2001 Reg.29

89. **Revenue Support Grant (Specified Bodies) Regulations 1992**
Reg.3, amended: SI 1998/2995 Reg.2
Reg.3, revoked (in part): SI 1998/2995 Reg.2

96. **Community Charges and Non-Domestic Rating (Demand Notices) (Wales) (Amendment) Regulations 1992**
revoked: SI 1996/619 Art.12

98. **Merchant Shipping (Prevention of Oil Pollution) (Amendment) Regulations 1992**
revoked: SI 1996/2154 Reg.1

110. **Education (Financial Delegation for Primary Schools) (Amendment) Regulations 1992**
revoked: 1996 c.56 Sch.38 Part III

122. **Land Registration (Open Register) Rules 1991 1992**
r.1, amended: SI 1999/2097 r.2, Sch.3 para.1
r.4, amended: SI 1999/2097 r.2, Sch.3 para.2
r.4A, amended: SI 1997/1710 Sch.3 Part II, SI 1999/2097 r.2, Sch.3 para.3
r.4A, applied: SI 1997/178 Sch.3 Part II, SI 1998/3199 Sch.3 Part II
r.4A, referred to: SI 1999/2254 Sch.3 Part II
r.9, amended: SI 1999/2097 r.2, Sch.3 para.4
r.14, amended: SI 1997/1964 r.10
Sch.1, applied: SI 1996/187 Art.10
Sch.1 Form 112A, applied: SI 1997/178 Art.10, SI 1997/1710 Art.10, SI 1998/3199 Art.10, SI 1999/2254 Art.10
Sch.1 Form 112B, applied: SI 1997/178 Art.10, SI 1997/1710 Art.10, SI 1998/3199 Art.10, SI 1999/2254 Art.10
Sch.1 Form 112C, applied: SI 1997/178 Art.10, SI 1997/1710 Art.10, SI 1998/3199 Art.10, SI 1999/2254 Art.10

129. **Firemen's Pension Scheme Order 1992**
applied: SI 1999/1750 Art.2, Sch.1
Sch.1 Part II, amended: SI 1998/1010 Sch. para.3
Sch.2, applied: SI 1996/2912 Sch para.25, SI 1996/2916 Sch para.25, SI 1996/2917 Sch para.25, SI 1996/2918 Sch para.25, SI 1996/2919 Sch para.25, SI 1996/2920 Sch para.25, SI 1996/2921 Sch para.25, SI 1996/2922 Sch para.25, SI 1996/2923 Sch para.25, SI 1996/2924 Sch para.25, SI 1997/2695 Sch. para.25, SI 1997/2696 Sch. para.25, SI 1997/2697 Sch. para.25, SI 1997/2698 Sch. para.25, SI 1997/2699 Sch. para.25, SI 1997/2700 Sch. para.25, SI 1997/2701 Sch. para.25, SI 1997/2702 Sch. para.25, SI 1997/2760 Sch. para.25, SI 1997/2761 Sch. para.25
Sch.2 r.A15, amended: SI 1997/2309 Art.2, Sch. para.1
Sch.2 r.F1, amended: SI 1997/2851 Art.2, Sch. para.1

NO.

NO.

129. **Firemen's Pension Scheme Order 1992**—*cont.*
    Sch.2 r.F6A, added: SI 1997/2851 Art.2, Sch. para.2
    Sch.2 r.F6B, added: SI 1997/2851 Art.2, Sch. para.2
    Sch.2 r.G3, amended: SI 1997/2851 Art.2, Sch. para.3
    Sch.2 r.H2, amended: SI 1997/2309 Art.2, Sch. para.2
    Sch.2 r.J1, amended: SI 1998/1010 Sch. para.1
    Sch.2 r.J2, amended: SI 1998/1010 Sch. para.2
    Sch.9 Part I, amended: SI 1997/2309 Art.2, Sch. para.4
    Sch.9 para.1, amended: SI 1997/2309 Art.2, Sch. para.5
    Sch.9 para.2, amended: SI 1997/2309 Art.2, Sch. para.6
    Sch.9 para.2A, added: SI 1997/2309 Art.2, Sch. para.7
    Sch.9 para.3, substituted: SI 1997/2309 Art.2, Sch. para.8
    Sch.9 para.4, amended: SI 1997/2309 Art.2, Sch. para.9
    Sch.9 para.5, substituted: SI 1997/2309 Art.2, Sch. para.10
    Sch.9 para.6, substituted: SI 1997/2309 Art.2, Sch. para.10
    Sch.9 para.7, amended: SI 1997/2309 Art.2, Sch. para.11
    Sch.9 para.8, amended: SI 1997/2309 Art.2, Sch. para.12

135. **Merchant Shipping (Cargo Ship Construction and Survey) Regulations 1984 (Amendment) Regulations 1992**
    revoked: SI 1997/1509 Reg.1

157. **State Scheme Premiums (Actuarial Tables) Regulations (Northern Ireland) 1992**
    applied: SI 1999/671 Art.3, Sch.2

166. **Motor Vehicles (Driving Licences) (Large Goods and Passenger-Carrying Vehicles) (Amendment) Regulations 1992**
    revoked: SI 1996/2824 Reg.2, Sch.1

168. **Lawnmowers (Harmonisation of Noise Emission Standards) Regulations 1992**
    applied: SI 1998/2306 Reg.10, Sch.1

172. **Local Government Superannuation (Amendment) Regulations 1992**
    revoked: SI 1996/1680 Reg.49, Sch.5

194. **Local Land Charges (Amendment) Rules 1992**
    revoked: SI 1998/1190 r.3

195. **Lifting Plant and Equipment (Records of Test and Examination etc.) Regulations 1992**
    revoked: SI 1998/2307 Reg.17, Sch.2

196. **Public Airport Companies (Capital Finance) (Second Amendment) Order 1992**
    revoked: SI 1996/604 Reg.5

198. **Pensions Increase (Review) Order 1992**
    applied: SI 1997/634 Art.3, SI 1998/503 Art.3, Art.4, SI 1999/522 Art.3

223. **Town and Country Planning (General Permitted Development) (Scotland) Order 1992**
    Art.2, amended: SI 1996/3023 Art.2, SI 1997/1871 Art.2, SI 1997/3060 Art.2, SSI 1999/1 Reg.47
    Art.3, amended: SI 1996/252 Art.2, Sch., SI 1997/1871 Art.3, SSI 1999/1 Reg.47
    Art.3, applied: 1998 c.iii s.64, SSI 1999/1 Reg.64, Sch.7
    Art.3, referred to: SI 1999/1672 Reg.5, SSI 1999/1 Reg.22

223. **Town and Country Planning (General Permitted Development) (Scotland) Order 1992**—*cont.*
    Art.3, revoked (in part): SSI 1999/1 Reg.47, Reg.64, Sch.7
    Art.4, referred to: SI 1999/1672 Reg.5
    Art.5, referred to: SI 1999/1672 Reg.5
    Sch.1, applied: SI 1997/10 Reg.13, SSI 1999/1 Reg.22
    Sch.1, referred to: SI 1997/10 Reg.5, SSI 1999/43 Reg.3
    Sch.1 Part 1, amended: SI 1996/3023 Art.3
    Sch.1 Part 3, amended: SI 1997/3060 Art.3, Art.4, Art.5, Art.6
    Sch.1 Part 6, revoked (in part): SI 1997/3060 Art.7
    Sch.1 Part 11, applied: 1998 c.iii s.64
    Sch.1 Part 12, amended: SI 1996/3023 Art.4, SSI 1999/1 Reg.47
    Sch.1 Part 13, amended: SI 1996/252 Art.2, Sch., SI 1996/3023 Art.5, SI 1997/3060 Art.8
    Sch.1 Class 18, applied: SI 1997/10 Reg.5, Sch.1 Table I, Sch.1 Table II
    Sch.1 Part 20, amended: SI 1998/1226 Art.2
    Sch.1 Part 20, referred to: SI 1999/2450 Sch.4 para.3.6, Sch.4 para.4.2, Sch.4 para.5.5
    Sch.1 Part 21, amended: SI 1998/1226 Art.3
    Sch.1 Part 25, added: SI 1996/1266 Art.2
    Sch.2, referred to: SSI 1999/43 Reg.3

224. **Town and Country Planning (General Development Procedure) (Scotland) Order 1992**
    Art.2, amended: SI 1996/252 Art.2, Sch, SI 1996/467 Art.2, SI 1997/749 Art.2
    Art.9, applied: SSI 1999/1 Reg.13, Sch.5, Sch.6
    Art.12, amended: SI 1996/467 Art.3
    Art.15, amended: SI 1996/467 Art.4, SI 1997/749 Art.3
    Art.16, substituted: SSI 1999/1 Reg.47
    Art.23, amended: SI 1996/467 Art.5, SI 1997/749 Art.4
    Art.23, revoked (in part): SI 1997/749 Art.4
    Sch.5 para.3, applied: SSI 1999/1 Reg.7

230. **Civil Aviation Act 1982 (Guernsey) Order 1992**
    applied: SI 1998/1503

231. **Electricity (Northern Ireland) Order 1992**
    referred to: SI 1996/275 (NI.2) Art.44
    Art.3, amended: SR 1999/250 Reg.4
    Art.3, referred to: SI 1999/2450 Sch.4 para.9.3
    Art.3, revoked (in part): SI 1999/506 Art.42
    Art.6, applied: 1998 c.41 s.54, Sch.10 para.7
    Art.7, applied: SI 1999/680 Art.2, Sch. Part I
    Art.10, applied: SI 1996/2911 Sch.1 Part D, 1997 c.58 s.2
    Art.10, referred to: SI 1999/662 (NI.6) Art.20
    Art.11A, added: SR 1999/250 Reg.5
    Art.15, amended: 1998 c.41 s.54, Sch.10 para.17, SI 1999/506 Art.42
    Art.15, applied: 1998 c.41 s.45, Sch.7 para.2
    Art.16, amended: SI 1999/506 Art.42
    Art.16, referred to: 1998 c.41 s.74, Sch.13 para.40
    Art.16, revoked (in part): 1998 c.41 s.54, s.74, Sch.10 para.17, Sch.14 Part II
    Art.17, amended: SI 1999/506 Art.42
    Art.18, amended: 1998 c.41 s.54, s.74, Sch.10 para.17, Sch.14 Part II
    Art.18, revoked (in part): 1998 c.41 s.54, s.74, Sch.10 para.17, Sch.14 Part II
    Art.18A, added: SR 1999/250 Reg.6
    Art.28, amended: 1998 c.41 s.54, Sch.10 para.17
    Art.39, amended: SR 1999/250 Reg.7

NO.

231. Electricity (Northern Ireland) Order 1992—*cont.*

Art.46, amended: 1998 c.41 s.54, s.74, Sch.10 para.7, Sch.10 para.17, Sch.14 Part II, SI 1999/506 Art.42

Art.46, applied: 1998 c.41 s.74, Sch.13 para.35

Art.46, revoked (in part): 1998 c.41 s.54, s.74, Sch.10 para.7, Sch.14 Part II

Art.53, amended: SI 1999/506 Art.42

Art.57, revoked (in part): SI 1996/1919 (NI.16) Art.257, Sch.3

Art.61, amended: SI 1996/275 (NI.2) Art.71, Sch.6, 1998 c.41 s.54, Sch.10 para.17, SI 1999/506 Art.42, SI 1999/662 (NI.6) Art.63, Sch.7

Art.61, revoked (in part): 1998 c.41 s.54, s.74, Sch.10 para.17, Sch.14 Part II

Part II, referred to: SI 1996/725 (NI.5) Art.4

Sch.1 para.7, revoked: SI 1996/1298 (NI.8) Art.21, Sch.6

Sch.4 para.2, amended: SI 1997/276 (NI.2) Art.75, Sch.8 para.10

Sch.5 para.2, referred to: SI 1999/662 (NI.6) Art.20

Sch.5 para.12, amended: SI 1999/662 (NI.6) Art.63, Sch.7

Sch.7 para.13, amended: SI 1997/2984 (NI.22) Art.9

Sch.12 para.5, referred to: SI 1996/725 (NI.5) Art.4

Sch.12 para.16, revoked: 1998 c.41 s.54, s.74, Sch.10 para.17, Sch.14 Part II

Sch.12 para.18, revoked: SI 1997/2778 (NI.19) Art.83, Sch.6

235. Tourism (Northern Ireland) Order 1992

Art.12, amended: SI 1996/3158 (NI.22) Sch.11 para.9

Art.12, applied: SI 1996/3158 (NI.22) Art.2, Art.11, Art.46

Art.13, applied: SI 1996/3158 (NI.22) Art.2, Art.11, Art.13

Art.13, referred to: SI 1996/3158 (NI.22) Art.17

Art.27, revoked: SI 1996/3158 (NI.22) Sch.13

Sch.2, revoked: SI 1996/3158 (NI.22) Sch.13

Sch.3, revoked (in part): SI 1996/3158 (NI.22) Sch.13

236. European Parliamentary Constituencies (Scotland) (Miscellaneous Changes) Order 1992

revoked: SI 1996/1926 Art.3

246. Occupational Pension Schemes (Investment of Scheme's Resources) Regulations 1992

revoked: SI 1996/3127 Reg.13, Sch.

Reg.5, applied: SI 1996/1536 Reg.6, SI 1996/3127 Reg.7

Reg.5, revoked: SI 1996/3127 Reg.13, Sch.

Reg.6, revoked: SI 1996/1655 Reg.12, Sch.4, SI 1996/3127 Reg.13, Sch.

247. Social Security (Miscellaneous Provisions) Amendment Regulations 1992

Reg.4, revoked (in part): SI 1996/1345 Reg.27, Sch.

264. River Tay Salmon Fishery District (Baits and Lures) Regulations 1992

revoked: SI 1999/376 Reg.4

269. Hill Livestock (Compensatory Allowances) Regulations 1992

applied: SI 1996/1500 Reg.3

NO.

272. Act of Sederunt (Judicial Factors Rules) 1992

r.2, amended: SI 1997/206 r.3

r.3, amended: SI 1996/2167 r.3, SI 1997/206 r.4

r.4, amended: SI 1997/206 r.5

r.6, amended: SI 1997/206 r.6

r.9, applied: SI 1996/2446 r.12, SI 1999/929 r.3.9.11

r.10, applied: SI 1996/2446 r.12, SI 1999/929 r.3.9.11

r.11, applied: SI 1996/2446 r.12, SI 1999/929 r.3.9.11

r.12, applied: SI 1996/2446 r.12, SI 1999/929 r.3.9.11

r.15, amended: SI 1997/206 r.7, SI 1997/2533 r.2

Sch. Form 8, added: SI 1997/206 r.8, Sch.

280. Teachers' Superannuation (Scotland) Regulations 1992

applied: SI 1996/2809 Reg.2, SI 1997/676 Reg.41, SI 1998/718 Reg.26, SI 1999/446 Reg.23, SI 1999/1750 Art.2, Sch.1

Part G, substituted: SI 1997/676 Reg.27, Sch.1

Reg.B2, applied: SI 1996/2317 Reg.7, Reg.8, Reg.9, Reg.16, SI 1999/446 Reg.22

Reg.B2, referred to: SI 1996/2317 Reg.3, SI 1999/446 Reg.22

Reg.B2, substituted: SI 1999/446 Reg.3

Reg.B4, amended: SI 1997/676 Reg.3, SI 1999/446 Reg.4

Reg.B5, amended: SI 1997/676 Reg.4

Reg.B6, applied: SI 1996/2317 Reg.7, Reg.8, Reg.9, Reg.16, Sch.2 para.3

Reg.B6, referred to: SI 1996/2317 Reg.3

Reg.C1, revoked (in part): SI 1998/718 Reg.3

Reg.C1A, added: SI 1998/718 Reg.4

Reg.C2, amended: SI 1998/718 Reg.5

Reg.C2A, added: SI 1999/446 Reg.5

Reg.C2A, referred to: SI 1999/446 Reg.22

Reg.C3, amended: SI 1997/676 Reg.5

Reg.C8, amended: SI 1997/676 Reg.6

Reg.C8A, amended: SI 1999/446 Reg.6

Reg.C10, amended: SI 1997/676 Reg.7

Reg.C11, amended: SI 1997/676 Reg.8

Reg.C13, amended: SI 1997/676 Reg.9

Reg.C14, amended: SI 1999/446 Reg.7

Reg.C14, referred to: SI 1999/446 Reg.22

Reg.D3, amended: SI 1997/676 Reg.10

Reg.E1, amended: SI 1998/718 Reg.6

Reg.E2, substituted: SI 1998/718 Reg.7

Reg.E5, amended: SI 1997/676 Reg.11

Reg.E5, applied: SI 1996/2317 Reg.6

Reg.E6, amended: SI 1997/676 Reg.12

Reg.E6, applied: SI 1996/2317 Reg.5

Reg.E7, amended: SI 1997/676 Reg.13

Reg.E7, applied: SI 1996/2317 Reg.5

Reg.E7, substituted: SI 1999/446 Reg.8

Reg.E10, amended: SI 1997/676 Reg.14, SI 1999/1820 Art.4, Sch.2 para.149

Reg.E11, amended: SI 1997/676 Reg.15

Reg.E12, applied: SI 1996/2317 Reg.6, Sch.4 para.2

Reg.E14, amended: SI 1997/676 Reg.16

Reg.E14A, added: SI 1997/676 Reg.17

Reg.E14A, amended: SI 1998/718 Reg.8

Reg.E15, amended: SI 1997/676 Reg.18

Reg.E16, amended: SI 1997/676 Reg.19

Reg.E18, amended: SI 1998/718 Reg.9

Reg.E18A, added: SI 1997/676 Reg.20

Reg.E19, amended: SI 1997/676 Reg.21, SI 1999/446 Reg.9

Reg.E19, referred to: SI 1997/676 Reg.40

Reg.E20, amended: SI 1997/676 Reg.22, SI 1999/446 Reg.10

NO.

NO.

1992—cont.

280. Teachers' Superannuation (Scotland) Regulations 1992—*cont.*
Reg.E20, referred to: SI 1997/676 Reg.40
Reg.E22, amended: SI 1999/446 Reg.11
Reg.E23, amended: SI 1997/676 Reg.23, SI 1999/446 Reg.12
Reg.E23, applied: SI 1996/2317 Reg.7, Reg.10
Reg.E23, referred to: SI 1997/676 Reg.40
Reg.E24, amended: SI 1997/676 Reg.24
Reg.E24, referred to: SI 1997/676 Reg.40
Reg.E25, amended: SI 1999/446 Reg.13
Reg.E25, applied: SI 1996/2317 Reg.8, Reg.9
Reg.E26, amended: SI 1998/718 Reg.10
Reg.E29, amended: SI 1999/446 Reg.14
Reg.E29, substituted: SI 1998/718 Reg.11
Reg.E31A, added: SI 1997/676 Reg.25
Reg.E31A, amended: SI 1998/718 Reg.12, SI 1998/1129 Art.3, Sch.2
Reg.E31A, revoked (in part): SI 1998/718 Reg.12
Reg.E31A, substituted: SI 1999/446 Reg.15
Reg.F1, amended: SI 1998/718 Reg.13
Reg.F1, referred to: SI 1996/2317 Reg.14
Reg.F3, amended: SI 1997/676 Reg.26
Reg.G1, substituted: SI 1997/676 Reg.27, Sch.1
Reg.G2, substituted: SI 1997/676 Reg.27, Sch.1
Reg.G3, substituted: SI 1997/676 Reg.27, Sch.1
Reg.G4, substituted: SI 1997/676 Reg.27, Sch.1
Reg.G5, substituted: SI 1997/676 Reg.27, Sch.1
Reg.G6, substituted: SI 1997/676 Reg.27, Sch.1
Reg.G7, added: SI 1997/676 Reg.27, Sch.1
Reg.G7, amended: SI 1998/718 Reg.14
Reg.G8, added: SI 1997/676 Reg.27, Sch.1
Reg.G9, added: SI 1997/676 Reg.27, Sch.1
Reg.G9A, added: SI 1998/718 Reg.15
Reg.G9B, added: SI 1999/446 Reg.16
Reg.G9B, referred to: SI 1999/446 Reg.22
Reg.G10, added: SI 1997/676 Reg.27, Sch.1
Reg.G10, amended: SI 1998/718 Reg.16, SI 1999/446 Reg.17
Reg.H1, substituted: SI 1998/718 Reg.17
Reg.H2, amended: SI 1997/676 Reg.28
Reg.H3, amended: SI 1999/446 Reg.18
Reg.H4A, added: SI 1999/446 Reg.19
Reg.H6, amended: SI 1997/676 Reg.29
Sch.1, amended: SI 1997/676 Reg.30, SI 1998/718 Reg.18, SI 1999/446 Reg.20
Sch.2 para.5C, added: SI 1998/1644 Art.9, Sch. para.2
Sch.2 para.5D, added: SI 1998/2208 Art.9, Sch. para.2
Sch.2 para.5E, added: SI 1999/442 Art.9, Sch. para.2
Sch.4 Table 1, substituted: SI 1998/718 Reg.19, Sch.
Sch.4 Table 2, substituted: SI 1998/718 Reg.19, Sch.
Sch.4 Table 3, substituted: SI 1998/718 Reg.20, Sch.
Sch.4 Table 4, substituted: SI 1998/718 Reg.21, Sch.
Sch.4 Table 5, substituted: SI 1998/718 Reg.21, Sch.
Sch.4 para.2, amended: SI 1997/676 Reg.31
Sch.4 para.5, amended: SI 1997/676 Reg.31
Sch.4 para.9, amended: SI 1999/446 Reg.21
Sch.4 para.13, amended: SI 1997/676 Reg.31

1992—cont.

280. Teachers' Superannuation (Scotland) Regulations 1992—*cont.*
Sch.5 para.6, amended: SI 1997/676 Reg.32
Sch.5 para.6, revoked (in part): SI 1997/676 Reg.32
Sch.6 para.10, amended: SI 1997/676 Reg.33
Sch.6 para.10, revoked (in part): SI 1997/676 Reg.33
Sch.7 para.1, amended: SI 1997/676 Reg.34
Sch.7 para.1, revoked (in part): SI 1997/676 Reg.34
Sch.7 para.1A, added: SI 1997/676 Reg.34
Sch.7 para.1B, added: SI 1997/676 Reg.34
Sch.7 para.1C, added: SI 1997/676 Reg.34
Sch.7 para.1D, added: SI 1997/676 Reg.34
Sch.7 para.2, amended: SI 1997/676 Reg.34
Sch.7 para.3, added: SI 1998/718 Reg.22
Sch.7 para.3, revoked: SI 1997/676 Reg.34
Sch.8 para.25, added: SI 1997/676 Reg.35
Sch.9 Part V, added: SI 1997/676 Reg.28, Sch.2
Sch.9 para.22, added: SI 1997/676 Reg.28, Sch.2
Sch.9 para.23, added: SI 1997/676 Reg.28, Sch.2
Sch.9 para.24, added: SI 1997/676 Reg.28, Sch.2
Sch.9 para.25, added: SI 1997/676 Reg.28, Sch.2
Sch.9 para.26, added: SI 1997/676 Reg.28, Sch.2
Sch.9A, added: SI 1997/676 Reg.36, Sch.3
Sch.9A Table 1, amended: SI 1998/718 Reg.23
Sch.10 para.1, amended: SI 1997/676 Reg.37
Sch.10 para.5, amended: SI 1997/676 Reg.37
Sch.10 para.9, amended: SI 1997/676 Reg.37
Sch.11 para.1, amended: SI 1998/718 Reg.24
Sch.11 para.4, amended: SI 1998/718 Reg.24
Sch.11 para.12, amended: SI 1997/676 Reg.38
Sch.11 para.13, amended: SI 1997/676 Reg.38
Sch.11 para.13A, added: SI 1997/676 Reg.38
Sch.11 para.14, amended: SI 1998/718 Reg.25
Sch.11 para.14, revoked (in part): SI 1998/718 Reg.25
Sch.12 para.1, amended: SI 1997/676 Reg.39
Sch.12 para.2, amended: SI 1997/676 Reg.39

300. Social Security Benefit (Computation of Earnings) Amendment Regulations 1992
revoked: SI 1996/2745 Reg.18, Sch.4

301. Environmentally Sensitive Areas (Pennine Dales) Designation (Amendment) Order 1992
revoked: SI 1997/1441 Art.6 (with saving)

333. Criminal Justice Act 1991 (Commencement No.3) Order 1992
Art.2, revoked (in part): SI 1999/1280 Art.2
Sch.3, revoked: SI 1999/1280 Art.2

348. Inner London Probation Area Order 1992
Art.4, amended: SI 1998/3266 Art.2

353. Wireless Telegraphy (Television Licence Fees) (Amendment) Regulations 1992
revoked: SI 1997/290 Reg.1, Sch

359. Building Societies (Accounts and Related Provisions) Regulations 1992
referred to: SI 1998/504 Reg.12
revoked: SI 1998/504 Reg.13
Reg.9, revoked: SI 1998/504 Reg.13
Reg.10, revoked: SI 1998/504 Reg.13
Sch.5 para.5, revoked: SI 1998/504 Reg.13
Sch.5 para.12, revoked: SI 1998/504 Reg.13
Sch.5 para.13, revoked: SI 1998/504 Reg.13
Sch.5 para.15, revoked: SI 1998/504 Reg.13
Sch.5 para.15A, revoked: SI 1998/504 Reg.13

NO.

1992—cont.

359. Building Societies (Accounts and Related Provisions) Regulations 1992—cont.
Sch.8 para.9, revoked: SI 1998/504 Reg.13
Sch.9 para.3, revoked: SI 1998/504 Reg.13
Sch.9 para.3A, revoked: SI 1998/504 Reg.13
Sch.10, revoked: SI 1998/504 Reg.13

368. Regional and District Health Authorities (Membership and Procedure) Amendment Regulations 1992
revoked: SI 1996/707 Reg.17, Sch.4 Part I

373. Advice and Assistance (Scotland) Amendment Regulations 1992
revoked: SI 1996/2447 Reg.3, Sch.1

395. Water (Prevention of Pollution) (Code of Practice) (Scotland) Order 1992
applied: SI 1996/3142 Sch.3 para.2
revoked: SI 1997/1584 Art.3

404. National Health Service (Optical Charges and Payments) (Miscellaneous Amendments) Regulations 1992
revoked (in part): SI 1997/818 Reg.24, Sch.4

433. Erskine Bridge Tolls Order 1992
applied: SSI 1999/116 Art.2

434. National Health Service (Service Committees and Tribunal) (Scotland) Regulations 1992
applied: SI 1996/177 Sch.1 para.26
Part II, amended: SI 1996/938 Reg.3
Part II, applied: SI 1996/177 Sch.1 para.2
Reg.1, amended: SI 1998/1424 Reg.2, SSI 1999/53 Reg.3
Reg.2, amended: SI 1996/938 Reg.3, SSI 1999/53 Reg.4
Reg.3, amended: SI 1996/938 Reg.3, SSI 1999/53 Reg.5
Reg.4, amended: SI 1996/938 Reg.3, SSI 1999/53 Reg.6
Reg.5, amended: SI 1996/938 Reg.3, SSI 1999/53 Reg.7
Reg.6, amended: SI 1996/938 Reg.3, SSI 1999/53 Reg.8
Reg.7, amended: SI 1996/938 Reg.3, SSI 1999/53 Reg.9
Reg.8, amended: SI 1996/938 Reg.3, SSI 1999/53 Reg.2
Reg.8, applied: SI 1996/177 Reg.25, Reg.31
Reg.9, amended: SI 1996/938 Reg.3, SSI 1999/53 Reg.10
Reg.10, amended: SI 1996/938 Reg.3, SSI 1999/53 Reg.2
Reg.11, amended: SI 1996/938 Reg.3, SSI 1999/53 Reg.2
Reg.12, amended: SI 1996/938 Reg.3
Reg.13, amended: SI 1996/938 Reg.3
Reg.14, amended: SI 1996/938 Reg.3
Reg.15, amended: SI 1996/938 Reg.3
Reg.16, amended: SSI 1999/53 Reg.11
Reg.17, amended: SSI 1999/53 Reg.2
Reg.18, amended: SSI 1999/53 Reg.2
Reg.19, amended: SSI 1999/53 Reg.2
Reg.20, added: SSI 1999/53 Reg.20
Reg.21, amended: SI 1998/657 Reg.2, SI 1998/1424 Reg.3, SSI 1999/53 Reg.2
Reg.24, amended: SI 1998/657 Reg.3, SI 1998/1424 Reg.4
Reg.25A, amended: SSI 1999/53 Reg.12
Reg.26, amended: SSI 1999/53 Reg.2
Reg.27, amended: SSI 1999/53 Reg.13
Reg.29, amended: SSI 1999/53 Reg.2
Reg.30, amended: SSI 1999/53 Reg.2
Reg.34, amended: SSI 1999/53 Reg.2
Reg.35, amended: SSI 1999/53 Reg.2

NO.

1992—cont.

434. National Health Service (Service Committees and Tribunal) (Scotland) Regulations 1992—cont.
Reg.37, amended: SSI 1999/53 Reg.2
Reg.38, amended: SI 1998/657 Reg.4, SSI 1999/53 Reg.2
Reg.41, amended: SI 1998/657 Reg.5, SSI 1999/53 Reg.2
Reg.43, amended: SI 1998/657 Reg.6
Reg.43B, added: SI 1998/657 Reg.7
Reg.43B, amended: SSI 1999/53 Reg.14
Reg.44, amended: SI 1998/1424 Reg.5, SSI 1999/53 Reg.2
Reg.46, amended: SI 1996/938 Reg.4, SSI 1999/53 Reg.15
Sch.1, substituted: SI 1996/938 Reg.5, Sch
Sch.1 para.1, amended: SI 1998/1424 Reg.6
Sch.1 para.3, amended: SI 1998/1424 Reg.6
Sch.1 para.6, amended: SSI 1999/53 Reg.16
Sch.1 para.8, amended: SI 1998/1424 Reg.6, SSI 1999/53 Reg.16
Sch.1A, added: SI 1996/938 Reg.5, Sch
Sch.1A para.1, amended: SSI 1999/53 Reg.17
Sch.1A para.2, amended: SSI 1999/53 Reg.17
Sch.1A para.3, amended: SSI 1999/53 Reg.17
Sch.1A para.4, amended: SSI 1999/53 Reg.17
Sch.1A para.5, amended: SSI 1999/53 Reg.17
Sch.1A para.6, amended: SSI 1999/53 Reg.17
Sch.1A para.7, amended: SSI 1999/53 Reg.17
Sch.1A para.8, amended: SI 1998/1424 Reg.7
Sch.1A para.9, amended: SI 1998/1424 Reg.7, SSI 1999/53 Reg.17
Sch.1B, added: SI 1996/938 Reg.5, Sch
Sch.3, amended: SSI 1999/53 Reg.18
Sch.4 Form 1, amended: SI 1998/657 Reg.8, SSI 1999/53 Reg.19
Sch.4 Form 2, amended: SI 1998/657 Reg.8, SSI 1999/53 Reg.19
Sch.4 Form 3, amended: SI 1998/657 Reg.8, SSI 1999/53 Reg.19
Sch.4 Form 4, amended: SSI 1999/53 Reg.19
Sch.4 Form 5, amended: SI 1998/657 Reg.8, SSI 1999/53 Reg.19
Sch.4 Form 6, amended: SI 1998/657 Reg.8, SSI 1999/53 Reg.19
Sch.4 Form 7, amended: SSI 1999/53 Reg.19
Sch.4 Form 8, amended: SI 1998/657 Reg.8
Sch.4 Form 9, amended: SI 1998/657 Reg.8

448. Planning (Control of Advertisements) Regulations (Northern Ireland) 1992
applied: SI 1996/1220 Art.3
Reg.2, amended: SI 1998/1126 Art.6, Sch.3, SI 1998/1287 Art.3, Sch.2
Reg.2, applied: SI 1996/1220 Art.3, Sch.2, SI 1998/1126 Art.6, Sch.3, SI 1998/1287 Art.3, Sch.2
Reg.4, amended: SI 1998/1126 Art.6, Sch.3, SI 1998/1287 Art.3, Sch.2
Reg.4, applied: SI 1996/1220 Art.3, Sch.2, SI 1998/1126 Art.6, Sch.3, SI 1998/1287 Art.3, Sch.2
Sch.1, amended: SI 1998/1126 Art.6, Sch.3, SI 1998/1287 Art.3, Sch.2
Sch.1, applied: SI 1996/1220 Art.3, Sch.2, SI 1998/1126 Art.6, Sch.3, SI 1998/1287 Art.3, Sch.2
Sch.2, amended: SI 1998/1287 Art.3, Sch.2
Sch.2, applied: SI 1998/1287 Art.3, Sch.2
Sch.2 Class F, amended: SI 1998/1126 Art.6, Sch.3
Sch.2 Class F, applied: SI 1996/1220 Art.3, Sch.2, SI 1998/1126 Art.6, Sch.3

NO.

462. **Environmental Protection (Waste Recycling Payments) Regulations 1992**
Reg.2, see *R. v North Yorkshire CC Ex p. Scarborough BC* [1999] Env. L.R. 768 (QBD), Collins, J.
Sch., substituted: SI 1996/634 Reg.6, SI 1997/351 Reg.3, SI 1998/607 Reg.2, SI 1999/546 Reg.2

468. **Income Support (General) Amendment Regulations 1992**
Reg.3, revoked (in part): SI 1996/206 Reg.28, Sch.3
Sch. para.6, revoked: SI 1996/206 Reg.28, Sch.3
Sch. para.7, revoked: SI 1996/206 Reg.28, Sch.3

472. **Merchant Shipping (Light Dues) (Amendment) Regulations 1992**
revoked: SI 1997/562 Reg.2, Sch.1

483. **Home Energy Efficiency Grants Regulations 1992**
applied: SI 1997/790 Reg.14
revoked: SI 1997/790 Reg.14, Sch.2
Reg.3, amended: SI 1996/587 Reg.4
Reg.3, revoked: SI 1997/790 Reg.14, Sch.2
Reg.4, amended: SI 1996/587 Reg.5
Reg.4, referred to: SI 1996/587 Reg.11
Reg.4, revoked: SI 1997/790 Reg.14, Sch.2
Reg.7, amended: SI 1996/587 Reg.6
Reg.7, revoked: SI 1997/790 Reg.14, Sch.2
Reg.8, amended: SI 1996/587 Reg.7
Reg.8, revoked: SI 1997/790 Reg.14, Sch.2
Reg.9, amended: SI 1996/587 Reg.8
Reg.9, revoked: SI 1997/790 Reg.14, Sch.2
Reg.10, amended: SI 1996/587 Reg.9
Reg.10, revoked: SI 1997/790 Reg.14, Sch.2
Reg.13, amended: SI 1996/587 Reg.10
Reg.13, revoked: SI 1997/790 Reg.14, Sch.2

502. **Local Authorities (Capital Finance) (Amendment) Regulations 1992**
revoked: SI 1997/319 Reg.162, Sch.3

514. **Prison (Amendment) Rules 1992**
revoked: SI 1999/728 r.85 (with savings), Sch. (with savings)

515. **Assured and Protected Tenancies (Lettings to Students) (Amendment) Regulations 1992**
revoked: SI 1998/1967 Reg.6, Sch.3

527. **Criminal Legal Aid (Scotland) Amendment Regulations 1992**
revoked: SI 1996/2555 Reg.3, Sch.

531. **National Health Service (Optical Charges and Payments) (Miscellaneous Amendments) (Scotland) Regulations 1992**
revoked (in part): SI 1998/642 Reg.24, Sch.4

535. **Manual Handling Operations Regulations (Northern Ireland) 1992**
referred to: SI 1998/2857 Reg.3

538. **Motor Vehicles (Driving Licences) (Large Goods and Passenger-Carrying Vehicles) (Amendment) (No.2) Regulations 1992**
revoked: SI 1996/2824 Reg.2, Sch.1

539. **Motor Vehicles (Driving Licences) (Amendment) Regulations 1992**
revoked: SI 1996/2824 Reg.2, Sch.1

548. **Council Tax (Discount Disregards) Order 1992**
Art.3, amended: SI 1996/636 Art.2, SI 1996/3143 Art.2, SI 1997/656 Art.4
Sch.1 para.1, amended: SI 1998/291 Art.3
Sch.1 para.3, amended: SI 1996/636 Art.2

NO.

549. **Council Tax (Chargeable Dwellings) Order 1992**
see *Butterfield v Ulm* (1997) 73 P. & C.R. 289 (QBD), Macpherson, J.
Art.2, amended: SI 1997/656 Art.2

550. **Council Tax (Situation and Valuation of Dwellings) Regulations 1992**
see *R. v East Sussex Valuation Tribunal Ex p. Silverstone* [1996] 36 R.V.R. 203 (QBD), Carnwath, J.
Reg.7, see *Atkinson v Cumbria Valuation Tribunal* (1997) 74 P. & C.R. 280 (QBD), Jowitt, J.

551. **Council Tax (Liability for Owners) Regulations 1992**
see *Pearson v Haringey LBC* [1998] R.V.R. 252 (QBD), Collins, J.
Reg.1, amended: SI 1997/74 Art.2, Sch para.12
Reg.2, see *Hayes v Humberside Valuation Tribunal* [1998] R.A. 37 (CA), Kennedy, L.J.

552. **Council Tax (Additional Provisions for Discount Disregards) Regulations 1992**
Reg.3, amended: SI 1997/657 Reg.2
Sch. para.1, amended: SI 1998/294 Reg.2
Sch. para.3, amended: SI 1996/637 Reg.2

553. **Council Tax (Contents of Valuation Lists) Regulations 1992**
Reg.1, amended: SI 1996/619 Art.7

554. **Council Tax (Reductions for Disabilities) Regulations 1992**
Reg.3, revoked (in part): SI 1999/1004 Reg.2
Reg.4, amended: SI 1999/1004 Reg.2

555. **Education (Grant-Maintained Schools) (Finance) Regulations 1992**
applied: SI 1996/889 Reg.3, SI 1998/799 Reg.3
referred to: SI 1997/996 Reg.3

558. **Council Tax (Exempt Dwellings) Order 1992**
Art.2, amended: SI 1997/74 Art.2, Sch para.13, SI 1997/656 Art.3, SI 1998/291 Art.2
Art.3, amended: SI 1999/536 Art.2, SI 1999/1522 Art.2
Art.3 Class V, added: SI 1997/656 Art.3

569. **Income Tax (Dividend Manufacturing) Regulations 1992**
revoked: SI 1997/987 Reg.3 (with savings)
Reg.20, applied: SI 1997/993 Reg.7
Reg.20, revoked: SI 1997/987 Reg.3 (with savings)

570. **Stamp Duty and Stamp Duty Reserve Tax (Investment Exchanges and Clearing Houses) Regulations 1992**
revoked (in part): SI 1997/2429 Reg.6

572. **Income Tax (Stock Lending) (Amendment) Regulations 1992**
revoked: SI 1997/987 Reg.2 (with savings), Sch.1 (with savings)

575. **Private Water Supplies (Scotland) Regulations 1992**
Reg.2, amended: SI 1998/1856 Reg.3, Reg.8
Reg.6, amended: SI 1998/1856 Reg.8
Reg.7, amended: SI 1998/1856 Reg.8
Reg.8, amended: SI 1998/1856 Reg.8
Reg.9, amended: SI 1998/1856 Reg.8
Reg.12, amended: SI 1998/1856 Reg.8
Reg.13, amended: SI 1998/1856 Reg.8
Reg.14, amended: SI 1998/1856 Reg.8
Reg.15, amended: SI 1998/1856 Reg.8
Reg.16, amended: SI 1998/1856 Reg.8
Reg.17, amended: SI 1998/1856 Reg.8
Reg.18, amended: SI 1998/1856 Reg.8
Reg.19, amended: SI 1998/1856 Reg.8
Reg.20, amended: SI 1998/1856 Reg.8
Reg.21, substituted: SI 1998/1856 Reg.4

NO.

NO.

1992—cont.

575. Private Water Supplies (Scotland) Regulations 1992—*cont.*
Reg.22, amended: SI 1998/1856 Reg.5, Reg.8
Sch.2, amended: SI 1998/1856 Reg.6
Sch.3 Part I, amended: SI 1998/1856 Reg.7, Reg.8

580. Nursing and Midwifery Student Allowances (Scotland) Regulations 1992
applied: SI 1996/1812 Reg.4, SI 1997/1675 Reg.4, SI 1998/211 Reg.4, SI 1998/2026 Reg.3, SI 1999/1001 Reg.4
referred to: SI 1998/2003 Reg.3, SI 1999/496 Reg.4

584. Birmingham Heartlands Development Corporation (Area and Constitution) Order 1992
Art.2, revoked: SI 1998/769 Art.2
Art.3, revoked: SI 1998/769 Art.2

587. Education (London Residuary Body) (Property Transfer) Order 1992
applied: SI 1997/1990 Art.2
Art.4, amended: SI 1997/1990 Art.5, SI 1998/723 Art.3
Art.4, applied: SI 1998/723 Art.2
Art.4, revoked (in part): SI 1996/2082 Art.2
Art.7, amended: SI 1997/860 Art.3
Sch.4, added: SI 1997/860 Art.3, Sch.

588. Controlled Waste Regulations 1992
Sch.3 para.18, amended: SI 1996/972 Reg.24

608. Diving Operations at Work (Amendment) Regulations 1992
revoked: SI 1997/2776 Reg.18

612. Local Authorities (Calculation of Council Tax Base) Regulations 1992
Reg.1, amended: SI 1999/3437 Reg.3
Reg.2, amended: SI 1999/3437 Reg.4
Reg.4, amended: SI 1999/3123 Reg.2
Reg.5A, added: SI 1999/3123 Reg.2
Reg.7, amended: SI 1999/3437 Reg.5
Reg.8, amended: SI 1999/3437 Reg.6
Reg.10, amended: SI 1999/3437 Reg.7

613. Council Tax (Administration and Enforcement) Regulations 1992
see *R. v Hackney LBC Ex p. Adebiri* [1999] 39 R.V.R. 24 (QBD), Kay, J.
Reg.2, applied: SI 1996/1880 Art.16
Reg.10, applied: SI 1996/1880 Art.10
Reg.18, amended: SI 1997/393 Reg.3
Reg.23, amended: SI 1997/393 Reg.4
Reg.23, referred to: SI 1996/1880 Art.18
Reg.31, referred to: SI 1996/1880 Art.20
Reg.32, amended: SI 1996/1880 Art.30, SI 1999/534 Reg.3
Reg.35, amended: SI 1998/295 Reg.3
Reg.36, applied: SI 1996/1880 Art.22
Reg.37, amended: SI 1998/295 Reg.4
Reg.37, applied: SI 1996/1880 Art.23, Art.29
Reg.42, amended: SI 1998/295 Reg.4, SI 1999/534 Reg.4
Reg.44, applied: SI 1996/1880 Art.24
Reg.45, amended: SI 1998/295 Reg.6, Reg.7
Reg.45A, added: SI 1998/295 Reg.7
Reg.50, applied: SI 1996/1880 Art.27
Reg.52, amended: SI 1996/2405 Reg.2
Reg.53, amended: SI 1996/675 Art.2, Sch para.10, SI 1996/1880 Art.30
Reg.57, amended: SI 1996/1880 Art.30
Sch.3, amended: SI 1996/1880 Art.29, SI 1999/534 Reg.4
Sch.4, substituted: SI 1998/295 Reg.5, Sch.
Sch.5, applied: SI 1996/1880 Art.25
Sch.5 para.1, amended: SI 1998/295 Reg.8

1992—cont.

613. Council Tax (Administration and Enforcement) Regulations 1992—*cont.*
Sch.5 para.2, amended: SI 1998/295 Reg.8
Sch.5 para.2A, added: SI 1998/295 Reg.8

618. Local Authorities (Members' Interests) Regulations 1992
Reg.2, amended: SI 1996/974 Art.2, Sch.1 para.10, SI 1996/1215 Reg.3, SI 1998/1003 Reg.3
Reg.3, amended: SI 1996/1215 Reg.4, SI 1998/1003 Reg.4
Reg.4, amended: SI 1996/1215 Reg.5
Reg.5, amended: SI 1996/1215 Reg.5
Sch., amended: SI 1996/1215 Reg.5

621. Birmingham Heartlands Development Corporation (Planning Functions) Order 1992
revoked: SI 1998/84 Art.2, Sch.

635. National Health Service (General Medical Services) Regulations 1992
see *R. v Secretary of State for Health Ex p. Pfizer Ltd* [1999] 3 C.M.L.R. 875 (QBD), Collins, J.
applied: SI 1998/668 Reg.4
Part III, applied: SI 1998/668 Reg.3
Part III, substituted: SI 1998/2838 Reg.5, Sch.1
Reg.2, amended: SI 1997/2468 Reg.3, SI 1998/682 Reg.3, Reg.10, SI 1998/2838 Reg.2, SI 1999/326 Reg.2
Reg.4, amended: SI 1996/702 Reg.2, SI 1998/682 Reg.8, SI 1998/2838 Reg.3
Reg.5, amended: SI 1998/682 Reg.8
Reg.5, applied: SI 1996/706 Reg.8
Reg.5, revoked: SI 1998/2838 Reg.5
Reg.5A, added: SI 1998/682 Reg.8
Reg.6, amended: SI 1998/2838 Reg.4
Reg.8, amended: SI 1997/730 Reg.4, SI 1997/2468 Reg.3
Reg.10, substituted: SI 1998/2838 Reg.5, Sch.1
Reg.11, substituted: SI 1998/2838 Reg.5, Sch.1
Reg.12, amended: SI 1998/682 Reg.7
Reg.12, substituted: SI 1998/2838 Reg.5, Sch.1
Reg.12A, amended: SI 1998/682 Reg.7
Reg.12A, revoked: SI 1998/2838 Reg.5, Sch.1
Reg.13, amended: SI 1998/682 Reg.7
Reg.13, substituted: SI 1998/2838 Reg.5, Sch.1
Reg.14, amended: SI 1998/682 Reg.7
Reg.14, substituted: SI 1998/2838 Reg.5, Sch.1
Reg.14A, added: SI 1998/682 Reg.7
Reg.14A, revoked: SI 1998/2838 Reg.5, Sch.1
Reg.15, substituted: SI 1998/2838 Reg.5, Sch.1
Reg.16, substituted: SI 1998/2838 Reg.5, Sch.1
Reg.17, substituted: SI 1998/2838 Reg.5, Sch.1
Reg.18, substituted: SI 1998/2838 Reg.5, Sch.1
Reg.18A, added: SI 1998/2838 Reg.5, Sch.1
Reg.18B, added: SI 1998/2838 Reg.5, Sch.1
Reg.18C, added: SI 1998/2838 Reg.5, Sch.1
Reg.18D, added: SI 1998/2838 Reg.5, Sch.1
Reg.18E, added: SI 1998/2838 Reg.5, Sch.1
Reg.18F, added: SI 1998/2838 Reg.5, Sch.1
Reg.18G, added: SI 1998/2838 Reg.5, Sch.1
Reg.18H, added: SI 1998/2838 Reg.5, Sch.1
Reg.18I, added: SI 1998/2838 Reg.5, Sch.1
Reg.18J, added: SI 1998/2838 Reg.5, Sch.1
Reg.18K, added: SI 1998/2838 Reg.5, Sch.1
Reg.18L, added: SI 1998/2838 Reg.5, Sch.1
Reg.19, amended: SI 1998/682 Reg.3
Reg.20, revoked: SI 1998/682 Reg.3
Reg.21, revoked: SI 1998/682 Reg.3
Reg.22, amended: SI 1998/682 Reg.3
Reg.22, revoked (in part): SI 1998/682 Reg.3
Reg.23, amended: SI 1997/730 Reg.2
Reg.23, applied: SI 1998/668 Reg.8

NO.

635. **National Health Service (General Medical Services) Regulations 1992**—*cont.*
Reg.24, amended: SI 1996/702 Reg.3
Reg.24, applied: SI 1998/668 Reg.2, Reg.4
Reg.25, amended: SI 1998/682 Reg.3, SI 1998/2838 Reg.6
Reg.25, revoked (in part): SI 1998/2838 Reg.6
Reg.26, substituted: SI 1998/682 Reg.3
Reg.27, amended: SI 1998/682 Reg.9
Reg.29, amended: SI 1998/682 Reg.9, Reg.11
Reg.30, amended: SI 1998/682 Reg.9
Reg.31, amended: SI 1998/682 Reg.3
Reg.32, amended: SI 1998/682 Reg.9
Reg.33, amended: SI 1998/682 Reg.3
Reg.34, amended: SI 1997/2468 Reg.2
Reg.34, applied: SI 1996/706 Reg.22, SI 1999/2541 Reg.8
Reg.34B, added: SI 1997/2468 Reg.2
Reg.35, amended: SI 1996/702 Reg.4, SI 1997/2468 Reg.2
Reg.40, added: SI 1998/2838 Reg.5
Sch.2, applied: SI 1998/665 Reg.3
Sch.2 para.1, amended: SI 1996/702 Reg.5, SI 1997/730 Reg.3, SI 1997/2468 Reg.3
Sch.2 para.4, amended: SI 1996/702 Reg.5, SI 1998/682 Reg.4, Reg.9
Sch.2 para.5, amended: SI 1998/682 Reg.4
Sch.2 para.6, amended: SI 1998/682 Reg.4
Sch.2 para.7, amended: SI 1998/682 Reg.4
Sch.2 para.9, amended: SI 1998/682 Reg.4
Sch.2 para.9A, applied: SI 1998/668 Reg.4
Sch.2 para.11, amended: SI 1998/682 Reg.12
Sch.2 para.13, amended: SI 1998/682 Reg.4
Sch.2 para.14, amended: SI 1998/682 Reg.4
Sch.2 para.16, amended: SI 1998/682 Reg.4
Sch.2 para.18, amended: SI 1996/702 Reg.5
Sch.2 para.18A, added: SI 1996/702 Reg.5
Sch.2 para.18A, amended: SI 1998/682 Reg.9
Sch.2 para.18B, added: SI 1996/702 Reg.5
Sch.2 para.18C, added: SI 1996/702 Reg.5
Sch.2 para.19, amended: SI 1998/682 Reg.6
Sch.2 para.20, amended: SI 1997/730 Reg.3, SI 1998/682 Reg.6
Sch.2 para.22, amended: SI 1998/682 Reg.6, Reg.9, Reg.12
Sch.2 para.22, substituted: SI 1997/730 Reg.3
Sch.2 para.22A, amended: SI 1997/2468 Reg.3, SI 1998/1664 Reg.4
Sch.2 para.22A, substituted: SI 1997/730 Reg.3
Sch.2 para.23, amended: SI 1998/682 Reg.9
Sch.2 para.26, amended: SI 1998/682 Reg.6
Sch.2 para.28A, added: SI 1999/326 Reg.3
Sch.2 para.32, amended: SI 1998/682 Reg.9, SI 1998/2838 Reg.7
Sch.2 para.33, amended: SI 1998/682 Reg.9
Sch.2 para.47A, applied: SI 1999/2541 Reg.12
Sch.2 para.47B, applied: SI 1999/2541 Reg.12
Sch.2 para.48, substituted: SI 1998/682 Reg.12
Sch.2 para.49A, added: SI 1996/702 Reg.5
Sch.2 para.49B, added: SI 1996/702 Reg.8
Sch.2 para.50, amended: SI 1997/730 Reg.5
Sch.3 Part I, substituted: SI 1998/2838 Reg.8, Sch.2
Sch.3 Part II, substituted: SI 1998/2838 Reg.8, Sch.2
Sch.3 Part III, substituted: SI 1998/2838 Reg.8, Sch.2
Sch.3 Part IIIA, revoked: SI 1998/2838 Reg.8, Sch.2
Sch.3 Part IIIB, revoked: SI 1998/2838 Reg.8, Sch.2
Sch.3 Part IIIC, revoked: SI 1998/2838 Reg.8, Sch.2

NO.

635. **National Health Service (General Medical Services) Regulations 1992**—*cont.*
Sch.3 Part IIID, revoked: SI 1998/2838 Reg.8, Sch.2
Sch.3 Part IV, revoked: SI 1998/2838 Reg.8, Sch.2
Sch.3 Part V, revoked: SI 1998/2838 Reg.8, Sch.2
Sch.3 Part VI, revoked: SI 1998/2838 Reg.8, Sch.2
Sch.3 para.19, amended: SI 1997/2468 Reg.3
Sch.3 para.20, amended: SI 1997/2468 Reg.3
Sch.5 Part I, amended: SI 1998/682 Reg.9
Sch.5 Part II, amended: SI 1998/682 Reg.5
Sch.7A, added: SI 1997/2468 Reg.2, Sch.
Sch.10, amended: SI 1997/981 Reg.2
Sch.11, amended: SI 1997/981 Reg.2, SI 1999/1627 Reg.2
Sch.12 para.9A, added: SI 1996/702 Reg.6
Sch.12 para.9A, amended: SI 1998/682 Reg.13
Sch.12 para.21, added: SI 1998/1664 Reg.4
Sch.13, amended: SI 1996/702 Reg.7
Sch.13 para.4, amended: SI 1997/730 Reg.5, SI 1998/682 Reg.14

637. **Welfare Food Amendment Regulations 1992**
revoked: SI 1996/1434 Reg.23, Sch.7

641. **National Health Service (General Dental Services) (Scotland) Amendment Regulations 1992**
revoked: SI 1996/177 Reg.38, Sch.8

656. **Planning (Hazardous Substances) Regulations 1992**
Reg.2, amended: SI 1999/981 Reg.3
Reg.3, amended: SI 1999/981 Reg.3
Reg.3, revoked (in part): SI 1999/981 Reg.3
Reg.4, amended: SI 1996/252 Art.2, Sch
Reg.4, substituted: SI 1999/981 Reg.3
Reg.10, amended: SI 1996/252 Art.2, Sch, SI 1999/981 Reg.3
Reg.16, amended: SI 1999/981 Reg.3
Sch.1, substituted: SI 1999/981 Reg.3, Sch.1
Sch.2 Form 1, substituted: SI 1999/981 Reg.3, Sch.2
Sch.2 Form 2, substituted: SI 1999/981 Reg.3, Sch.2
Sch.2 Form 8, substituted: SI 1999/981 Reg.3, Sch.2
Sch.3, amended: SI 1999/981 Reg.3

659. **National Health Service Functions (Administration Arrangements and Amendment of Directions) Regulations 1992**
revoked: SI 1996/708 Reg.6, Sch.2

661. **National Health Service (General Dental Services) Regulations 1992**
Part III, revoked: SI 1998/2222 Reg.4
Reg.2, amended: SI 1998/1648 Reg.3
Reg.4, amended: SI 1998/1648 Reg.4
Reg.5, amended: SI 1998/1648 Reg.5
Reg.5A, amended: SI 1998/1648 Reg.6, SI 1998/2224 Reg.3
Reg.8, amended: SI 1998/2224 Reg.3
Reg.20, amended: SI 1998/2224 Reg.3
Reg.22, amended: SI 1996/704 Reg.6
Reg.28, amended: SI 1996/704 Reg.6
Reg.29, amended: SI 1996/704 Reg.3
Reg.30A, added: SI 1996/704 Reg.4
Sch.1 para.2, amended: SI 1996/704 Reg.7
Sch.1 para.4, amended: SI 1996/2051 Reg.2
Sch.1 para.5, amended: SI 1996/2051 Reg.2
Sch.1 para.7, amended: SI 1998/2224 Reg.3
Sch.1 para.8, amended: SI 1996/2051 Reg.2
Sch.1 para.9, amended: SI 1996/2051 Reg.2

NO.

1992—cont.

661. National Health Service (General Dental Services) Regulations 1992—*cont.*
Sch.1 para.11, amended: SI 1998/1648 Reg.7
Sch.1 para.11A, added: SI 1998/1648 Reg.7
Sch.1 para.12, amended: SI 1998/2224 Reg.3
Sch.1 para.14, amended: SI 1998/2224 Reg.3
Sch.1 para.18, amended: SI 1998/2224 Reg.3
Sch.1 para.27, amended: SI 1996/704 Reg.7
Sch.1 para.31, substituted: SI 1996/704 Reg.7
Sch.1 para.31A, added: SI 1996/704 Reg.5
Sch.1 para.31B, added: SI 1996/704 Reg.5
Sch.1 para.31C, added: SI 1996/704 Reg.5
Sch.1 para.31D, added: SI 1998/1648 Reg.7
Sch.2 Part I, amended: SI 1998/1648 Reg.8
Sch.4 Part II, amended: SI 1998/1648 Reg.9

662. National Health Service (Pharmaceutical Services) Regulations 1992
see *R. v Maldon DC Ex p. Pattani* [1999] P.L.C.R. 1 (CA), Henry, L.J.; see *R. v North Staffordshire HA Ex p. Worthington* [1997] C.O.D. 272 (QBD), Schiemann, L.J.; see *R. v North York Family Health Services Authority Ex p. Wilson* (1996) 8 Admin. L.R. 613 (QBD), Carnwath, J.
Reg.2, amended: SI 1996/698 Reg.2, Reg.8, Reg.10, SI 1998/681 Reg.2, SI 1998/2224 Reg.2, SI 1999/696 Reg.2
Reg.4, see *R. v Family Health Services Appeal Authority Ex p. Boots the Chemist Ltd* (1997) 33 B.M.L.R. 1 (QBD), Tucker, J.; see *R. v Family Health Services Appeal Authority Ex p. E Moss Ltd* (1999) 48 B.M.L.R. 204 (CA), Beldam, L.J.; see *R. v Family Health Services Appeal Authority Ex p. Tesco Stores Ltd* [1999] Lloyd's Rep. Med. 377 (QBD), Maurice Kay, J.; see *R. v Humberside Family Health Services Authority Ex p. Moore* (1996) 30 B.M.L.R. 68 (QBD), Potts, J.; see *R. v North Yorkshire Family Health Services Authority Ex p. Wilson* (1997) 33 B.M.L.R. 12 (QBD) Carnwath, J.; see *R. v Yorkshire RHA Ex p. Baker* (1997) 35 B.M.L.R. 118 (QBD), Sir Louis Blom-Cooper Q.C.; see *R. v Yorkshire RHA Ex p. Suri* (1996) 30 B.M.L.R. 78 (CA), Russell, L.J.
Reg.6, amended: SI 1998/681 Reg.3
Reg.9, amended: SI 1998/681 Reg.4
Reg.11, amended: SI 1998/681 Reg.5
Reg.11B, added: SI 1999/696 Reg.9
Reg.12, see *R. v North Yorkshire Family Health Services Authority Ex p. Wilson* (1997) 33 B.M.L.R. 12 (QBD), Carnwath, J.
Reg.12, amended: SI 1998/681 Reg.6
Reg.13, amended: SI 1998/681 Reg.7
Reg.16, amended: SI 1996/698 Reg.9
Reg.16, revoked: SI 1999/696 Reg.3
Reg.16A, amended: SI 1996/698 Reg.9
Reg.17, amended: SI 1996/698 Reg.3, SI 1999/696 Reg.4
Reg.18, amended: SI 1999/696 Reg.5
Reg.18A, added: SI 1996/698 Reg.4
Reg.18B, added: SI 1999/696 Reg.6
Reg.19, amended: SI 1998/681 Reg.8
Reg.20, amended: SI 1998/681 Reg.9, SI 1999/696 Reg.7
Reg.21A, added: SI 1998/681 Reg.10
Reg.21B, added: SI 1998/681 Reg.11
Reg.21C, added: SI 1998/681 Reg.11
Reg.22, amended: SI 1998/681 Reg.12
Reg.24, amended: SI 1996/698 Reg.10
Sch.2 para.2, amended: SI 1996/698 Reg.10
Sch.2 para.2A, added: SI 1999/696 Reg.8

NO.

1992—cont.

662. National Health Service (Pharmaceutical Services) Regulations 1992—*cont.*
Sch.2 para.3, amended: SI 1996/698 Reg.11, SI 1999/696 Reg.8, SI 1999/2563 Reg.2
Sch.2 para.4, amended: SI 1996/698 Reg.11, SI 1999/696 Reg.8
Sch.2 para.5, amended: SI 1996/698 Reg.5
Sch.2 para.8, amended: SI 1996/698 Reg.9
Sch.2 para.8A, added: SI 1996/698 Reg.11
Sch.2 para.10A, added: SI 1996/698 Reg.6
Sch.2 para.10A, amended: SI 1999/696 Reg.8
Sch.2 para.11B, amended: SI 1999/2563 Reg.3
Sch.2 para.13, amended: SI 1998/681 Reg.13
Sch.2 para.14, added: SI 1996/698 Reg.7
Sch.2 para.15, added: SI 1998/681 Reg.13

663. Community Charges (Administration and Enforcement) (Attachment of Earnings Order) (Wales) Regulations 1992
Sch., amended: SI 1996/1880 Art.46

664. National Health Service (Service Committees and Tribunal) Regulations 1992
Part II, applied: SI 1996/2915 Sch.2 para.5
Reg.2, amended: SI 1996/703 Reg.3, SI 1998/674 Reg.2
Reg.3, substituted: SI 1996/703 Reg.4
Reg.4, amended: SI 1998/674 Reg.3
Reg.4, substituted: SI 1996/703 Reg.4
Reg.5, substituted: SI 1996/703 Reg.4
Reg.6, substituted: SI 1996/703 Reg.4
Reg.7, substituted: SI 1996/703 Reg.4
Reg.8, substituted: SI 1996/703 Reg.4
Reg.9, substituted: SI 1996/703 Reg.4
Reg.10, substituted: SI 1996/703 Reg.4
Reg.11, substituted: SI 1996/703 Reg.4
Reg.12, substituted: SI 1996/703 Reg.4
Reg.13, substituted: SI 1996/703 Reg.4
Reg.14, substituted: SI 1996/703 Reg.4
Reg.16, amended: SI 1996/703 Reg.5
Reg.17, amended: SI 1996/703 Reg.6
Reg.19, revoked: SI 1996/704 Reg.4
Reg.20, amended: SI 1998/674 Reg.4
Reg.21, amended: SI 1998/674 Reg.5
Reg.24, amended: SI 1998/674 Reg.6
Reg.26, amended: SI 1998/674 Reg.7
Reg.28, substituted: SI 1998/674 Reg.8
Reg.29, amended: SI 1998/674 Reg.9
Reg.31, amended: SI 1998/674 Reg.10
Reg.31B, added: SI 1998/674 Reg.11
Reg.32, amended: SI 1996/703 Reg.7
Reg.33, amended: SI 1996/703 Reg.8
Reg.35, amended: SI 1998/674 Reg.12
Reg.35, revoked (in part): SI 1996/703 Reg.9
Reg.36, amended: SI 1996/703 Reg.10
Reg.37, substituted: SI 1996/703 Reg.11
Sch.2, substituted: SI 1996/703 Reg.12
Sch.3, revoked: SI 1996/703 Reg.16
Sch.4, substituted: SI 1996/703 Reg.13
Sch.5, amended: SI 1996/703 Reg.14
Sch.6, revoked: SI 1996/703 Reg.16
Sch.8 Part I, amended: SI 1998/674 Reg.13
Sch.8 Part II, amended: SI 1998/674 Reg.13
Sch.9 para.1, amended: SI 1998/674 Reg.14
Sch.9 para.2, amended: SI 1998/674 Reg.14

666. Town and Country Planning (Control of Advertisements) Regulations 1992
see *Havering LBC v Network Sites Ltd* [1998] 1 P.L.R. 103 (QBD), Schiemann, L.J.; see *Torridge DC v Jarrad* Times, April 13, 1998 (QBD), Pill, L.J.; see *Wyatt v Jarrad* [1998] 2 P.L.R. 81 (QBD), Pill, L.J.
amended: SI 1999/450 Art.150
applied: 1997 c.61 Sch.3 para.3, SI 1998/746 Art.4, SI 1999/450 Art.150

NO.

1992—cont.

666. Town and Country Planning (Control of Advertisements) Regulations 1992—*cont.*
Reg.2, amended: SI 1996/252 Art.2, Sch, SI 1996/525 Sch para.14
Reg.6, see *Wandsworth LBC v Mills & Allen Ltd* (1998) 76 P. & C.R. 214 (QBD), G Moriarty Q.C.
Reg.8, see *Chequepoint UK Ltd v Secretary of State for the Environment* (1996) 72 P. & C.R. 415 (QBD), Gerald Moriarty Q.C.; see *O'Brien v Croydon LBC* (1999) 77 P. & C.R. 126 (QBD), Simon Brown, L.J.
Reg.9A, added: SI 1999/1810 Reg.3
Reg.11, amended: SI 1999/1810 Reg.6
Reg.12, amended: SI 1996/525 Sch para.14
Reg.13A, added: SI 1999/1810 Reg.4
Reg.15, applied: SI 1997/420 Reg.3
Reg.24, amended: SI 1999/1810 Reg.5
Sch.3 Class 13, see *Westminster City Council v Moran* [1999] J.P.L. 41 (QBD), Simon Brown, L.J.

707. European Communities (Designation) Order 1992
revoked: SI 1996/266 Art.3

711. Gas Appliances (Safety) Regulations 1992
applied: SI 1998/2306 Reg.10, Sch.1

723. European Parliamentary Elections (Amendment) Regulations 1992
revoked: SI 1997/874 Reg.3

724. Public Trustee (Fees) (Amendment) Order 1992
revoked: SI 1999/855 Art.32, Sch.

734. Vocational Training (Public Financial Assistance and Disentitlement to Tax Relief) Regulations 1992
Reg.2, amended: SI 1997/635 Reg.2
Reg.3, amended: SI 1996/3049 Reg.3
Reg.5, amended: SI 1996/3049 Reg.4

739. Housing Benefit and Community Charge Benefit (Subsidy) Order 1992
Art.4, applied: SI 1996/1217 Art.11, SI 1997/1004 Art.11, SI 1998/562 Art.19
Art.16, applied: SI 1996/1217 Art.19, SI 1998/562 Art.19
Art.16, referred to: SI 1997/1004 Art.19

742. Road Traffic (Carriage of Dangerous Substances in Packages etc.) Regulations 1992
applied: SI 1996/2095 Reg.28
revoked: SI 1996/2095 Reg.29

743. Road Traffic (Carriage of Dangerous Substances in Road Tankers and Tank Containers) Regulations 1992
applied: SI 1996/2095 Reg.28
referred to: SI 1996/2095 Sch.12 Part III
revoked: SI 1996/2095 Reg.29

744. Road Traffic (Training of Drivers of Vehicles Carrying Dangerous Goods) Regulations 1992
revoked: SI 1996/2094 Reg.13
Reg.4, applied: SI 1996/2094 Reg.11
Reg.4, revoked: SI 1996/2094 Reg.13
Reg.5, applied: SI 1996/2094 Reg.5, Reg.11
Reg.5, revoked: SI 1996/2094 Reg.13

746. Vocational Training (Tax Relief) Regulations 1992
Reg.2, amended: SI 1997/661 Reg.3
Reg.3, amended: SI 1996/1185 Reg.3, SI 1997/661 Reg.4
Reg.4A, added: SI 1996/1185 Reg.4
Reg.8, amended: SI 1997/661 Reg.5
Reg.10, amended: SI 1997/661 Reg.5

NO.

1992—cont.

746. Vocational Training (Tax Relief) Regulations 1992—*cont.*
Reg.11A, added: SI 1997/661 Reg.6
Reg.13, amended: SI 1996/1185 Reg.5
Reg.13, substituted: SI 1997/661 Reg.7
Reg.14, amended: SI 1997/661 Reg.8

751. Gaming Act (Variation of Monetary Limits) (Scotland) Order 1992
revoked: SI 1999/1260 Art.5, Sch.

752. Advice and Assistance (Scotland) Amendment (No.2) Regulations 1992
revoked: SI 1996/2447 Reg.3, Sch.1

753. Civil Legal Aid (Scotland) Amendment Regulations 1992
revoked: SI 1996/2444 Reg.3, Sch.1

796. State Scheme Premiums (Actuarial Tables) Regulations 1992
applied: 1999 c.2 s.1, Sch.2

798. Act of Sederunt (Coal Mining Subsidence Act 1991) 1992
revoked: SI 1999/929 r.1.3, Sch.2

800. Forresterhill Hospitals National Health Service Trust (Establishment) Order 1992
revoked: SI 1999/1070 Art.2, Sch.2

801. South Ayrshire Hospitals National Health Service Trust (Establishment) Order 1992
revoked: SI 1999/1070 Art.2, Sch.2

807. Industrial Relations (Northern Ireland) Order 1992
applied: SI 1999/2790 (NI.9) Art.24
Art.11A, amended: SI 1999/2790 (NI.9) Art.27
Art.13C, amended: SI 1999/2790 (NI.9) Art.28, Art.40, Sch.6 para.2, Sch.9 Part 7
Art.13C, revoked (in part): SI 1999/2790 (NI.9) Art.40, Sch.9 Part 7
Art.37, amended: SI 1999/2790 (NI.9) Art.28, Sch.6 para.3
Art.69, applied: SI 1999/680 Art.2, Sch. Part I
Art.70, amended: SI 1999/2790 (NI.9) Art.28, Art.40, Sch.6 para.4, Sch.9 Part 7
Art.70A, added: SI 1999/2790 (NI.9) Art.28, Sch.6 para.5
Art.70B, added: SI 1999/2790 (NI.9) Art.28, Sch.6 para.5
Art.83, amended: SI 1999/2790 (NI.9) Art.26, Art.40, Sch.9 Part 5
Art.84, amended: 1996 c.23 Sch.3 para.57
Art.84A, added: SI 1998/1265 (NI.8) Art.8
Art.84B, added: SI 1998/1265 (NI.8) Art.16, Sch.1 para.2
Art.90, amended: SI 1996/1919 (NI.16) Art.255, Sch.1
Art.91, referred to: SI 1996/1298 (NI.8) Sch.3
Art.91, substituted: SI 1999/2790 (NI.9) Art.25
Art.91A, added: SI 1999/2790 (NI.9) Art.25
Art.92, amended: 1996 c.23 Sch.3 para.57
Art.92, substituted: SI 1999/2790 (NI.9) Art.25
Art.92A, added: SI 1999/2790 (NI.9) Art.25
Art.96, referred to: SI 1996/1921 (NI.18) Art.12
Art.98, revoked: SI 1996/1919 (NI.16) Art.257, Sch.3
Art.99, revoked: SI 1996/1919 (NI.16) Art.257, Sch.3
Art.100, revoked: SI 1996/1921 (NI.18) Art.28, Sch.3
Art.105A, revoked (in part): SI 1996/1921 (NI.18) Art.28, Sch.3
Art.106, revoked: SI 1998/3162 (NI.21) Art.105, Sch.5
Art.107, amended: SI 1998/1265 (NI.8) Art.16, Sch.1 para.3
Art.108, revoked: SI 1996/1919 (NI.16) Art.257, Sch.3

NO.

807. **Industrial Relations (Northern Ireland) Order 1992**—*cont.*
Sch.5, revoked: SI 1996/1919 (NI.16) Art.257, Sch.3
Sch.5 para.6, revoked (in part): SI 1996/1921 (NI.18) Art.28, Sch.3
Sch.6, revoked: SI 1996/1919 (NI.16) Art.257, Sch.3

810. **Local Government (Miscellaneous Provisions) (Northern Ireland) Order 1992**
Art.18, amended: SI 1996/1919 (NI.16) Art.255, Sch.1
Art.19, amended: SI 1997/869 (NI.6) Art.73, Sch.2 para.6
Art.20, amended: SI 1998/3162 (NI.21) Art.105, Sch.3
Art.20A, added: SI 1997/869 (NI.6) Art.73, Sch.2 para.6
Sch.1 para.1, amended: SI 1997/2778 (NI.19) Art.83, Sch.5 para.6

833. **European Parliamentary Elections (Northern Ireland) (Amendment) Regulations 1992**
revoked: SI 1997/969 Reg.3

905. **Farm Woodland Premium Scheme 1992**
para.2, amended: SI 1997/829 para.16, Sch.3 para.1
para.3, revoked (in part): SI 1997/829 para.16, Sch.3 para.2
para.5, amended: SI 1997/829 para.16, Sch.3 para.3
para.7A, added: SI 1997/829 para.16, Sch.3 para.4
para.8, amended: SI 1997/829 para.16, Sch.3 para.5
para.9, amended: SI 1997/829 para.16, Sch.3 para.6
para.9, revoked (in part): SI 1997/829 para.16, Sch.3 para.6
para.13, amended: SI 1997/829 para.16, Sch.3 para.7
Sch.1, substituted: SI 1997/829 para.16, Sch.3 para.8

935. **Community Charges and Non-Domestic Rating (Demand Notices) (Wales) (Amendment) (No.2) Regulations 1992**
revoked: SI 1996/619 Art.12

995. **Shetland Islands Area (Electoral Arrangements) Order 1992**
revoked: SI 1999/104 Art.4

1025. **Designation of Institutions of Higher Education (Scotland) Order 1992**
Sch. para.3, revoked: SI 1998/192 Reg.52, Sch.2

1069. **Trade Marks and Service Marks (Fees) Rules 1992**
applied: SI 1996/1942 r.5

1076. **Act of Sederunt (Adoption of Children) (Amendment) 1992**
revoked: SI 1997/291 r.1.4, Sch.2

1077. **Act of Sederunt (Applications under Part III of the Criminal Justice (International Cooperation) Act 1990) 1992**
revoked: SI 1999/929 r.1.3, Sch.2

1084. **Sea Fishing (Enforcement of Community Conservation Measures) (Amendment) (No.2) Order 1992**
revoked: SI 1997/1949 Art.16, Sch.2

1113. **Cholsey and Wallingford Light Railway (Extension and Amendment) Order 1992**
Art.12, amended: SI 1996/362 Art.5, Sch.4

NO.

1121. **Social Security Commissioners Procedure (Amendment) Regulations 1992**
revoked (in part): SI 1999/1495 Reg.2

1136. **Harwich Parkeston Quay Harbour Revision Order 1992**
applied: SI 1996/2037 Sch

1215. **Road Traffic (Temporary Restrictions) (Procedure) Regulations 1992**
applied: SI 1999/1750 Art.2, Sch.1

1220. **Local Government Superannuation (Reserve Forces) (Scotland) Regulations 1992**
applied: SI 1998/364 Reg.4, Reg.6, Reg.19, Sch.2 para.2, Sch.2 para.5, Sch.4 para.8
referred to: SI 1998/364 Reg.3, Reg.10, Sch.2 para.4, Sch.2 para.6

1227. **Legal Aid in Contempt of Court Proceedings (Scotland) Regulations 1992**
Reg.2, amended: SI 1996/2550 Reg.3
Reg.7A, added: SI 1996/2550 Reg.4

1228. **Legal Aid in Contempt of Court Proceedings (Scotland) (Fees) Regulations 1992**
Sch.1 para.5, substituted: SI 1997/718 Reg.3
Sch.1 para.6, substituted: SI 1997/718 Reg.3

1267. **Brechin and Bridge of Dun Light Railway Order 1992**
Art.11, amended: SI 1996/362 Art.5, Sch.4

1285. **Road Vehicles (Prohibition) Regulations 1992**
Reg.7, amended: SI 1997/83 Reg.3
Reg.8, amended: SI 1997/83 Reg.4

1312. **Social Security (Australia) Order 1992**
Sch., amended: SI 1996/1928 Art.2, Sch.1

1315. **Transfer of Functions (Financial Services) Order 1992**
applied: SI 1996/1669 Reg.13
referred to: SI 1996/2827 Reg.73
Art.4, applied: SI 1997/2781 Art.2
Sch.1 para.6, applied: SI 1997/2781 Art.2, SI 1998/2842 Art.2, Sch. para.64
Sch.1 para.7, applied: SI 1997/2781 Art.2, SI 1998/2842 Art.2, Sch. para.64
Sch.1 para.8, applied: SI 1997/2781 Art.2, SI 1998/2842 Art.2, Sch. para.64
Sch.1 para.10, applied: SI 1997/2781 Art.2, SI 1998/2842 Art.2, Sch. para.64
Sch.1 para.18, applied: SI 1997/2781 Art.2
Sch.1 para.19, applied: SI 1997/2781 Art.2
Sch.1 para.23, applied: SI 1997/2781 Art.2
Sch.1 para.26, applied: SI 1997/2781 Art.2
Sch.2 para.1, applied: SI 1997/2781 Art.2, SI 1998/2842 Art.2, Sch. para.64
Sch.2 para.2, applied: SI 1997/2781 Art.2, SI 1998/2842 Art.2, Sch. para.64
Sch.2 para.4, applied: SI 1997/2781 Art.2
Sch.2 para.6, applied: SI 1997/2781 Art.2, SI 1998/2842 Art.2, Sch. para.64

1318. **Motor Vehicles (Driving Licences) (Amendment) (No.2) Regulations 1992**
revoked: SI 1996/2824 Reg.2, Sch.1

1332. **Council Tax (Administration and Enforcement) (Scotland) Regulations 1992**
Reg.1, amended: SI 1996/430 Reg.3
Reg.3, revoked (in part): SI 1996/430 Reg.4
Reg.6, revoked: SI 1996/430 Reg.5
Reg.9, amended: SI 1996/430 Reg.6, SI 1997/728 Art.4
Reg.10, revoked (in part): SI 1996/430 Reg.7
Reg.12, revoked (in part): SI 1996/430 Reg.8
Reg.17, amended: SI 1996/430 Reg.9
Reg.17, applied: SI 1997/362 Art.8, SI 1998/634 Art.8

1992—cont.

1332. Council Tax (Administration and Enforcement) (Scotland) Regulations 1992—*cont.*
Reg.17, referred to: SI 1996/325 Art.8
Reg.17, revoked (in part): SI 1996/430 Reg.9
Reg.18, revoked (in part): SI 1996/430 Reg.10
Reg.20, applied: SI 1996/325 Art.10, SI 1997/362 Art.10, SI 1998/634 Art.10
Reg.20, revoked (in part): SI 1996/430 Reg.11
Reg.21, applied: SI 1997/362 Art.10, SI 1998/634 Art.10
Reg.22, applied: SI 1997/362 Art.10, SI 1998/634 Art.10
Reg.22, revoked (in part): SI 1996/430 Reg.12
Reg.23, applied: SI 1996/325 Art.10, SI 1997/362 Art.10, SI 1998/634 Art.10
Reg.23, revoked (in part): SI 1996/430 Reg.13
Reg.24, applied: SI 1996/325 Art.10, SI 1997/362 Art.10, SI 1998/634 Art.10
Reg.24, revoked (in part): SI 1996/430 Reg.14
Reg.25, applied: SI 1996/325 Art.10, SI 1997/362 Art.10, SI 1998/634 Art.10
Reg.26, revoked (in part): SI 1996/430 Reg.15
Reg.27, applied: SI 1996/325 Art.10, SI 1997/362 Art.10, SI 1998/634 Art.10
Reg.27, revoked (in part): SI 1996/430 Reg.16
Reg.28, amended: SI 1996/430 Reg.17
Reg.28A, added: SI 1996/430 Reg.18
Reg.28A, revoked (in part): SI 1996/430 Reg.4
Reg.30, amended: SI 1996/430 Reg.19
Sch.1, applied: SI 1996/325 Art.10, SI 1997/362 Art.10, SI 1998/634 Art.10
Sch.1 para.5, revoked (in part): SI 1996/430 Reg.20
Sch.1 para.6, revoked (in part): SI 1996/430 Reg.20
Sch.2 para.3, amended: SI 1996/430 Reg.21
Sch.2 para.5, amended: SI 1996/746 Reg.5
Sch.2 para.5, revoked: SI 1996/430 Reg.21
Sch.2 para.8, amended: SI 1996/746 Reg.5
Sch.2 para.8, revoked: SI 1996/430 Reg.21
Sch.2 para.10, amended: SI 1996/746 Reg.5

1333. Council Tax (Exempt Dwellings) (Scotland) Order 1992
revoked: SI 1997/728 Art.5, Sch.2
Art.2, amended: SI 1996/580 Art.6
Art.2, revoked: SI 1997/728 Art.5, Sch.2
Sch. para.9, amended: SI 1996/580 Art.6
Sch. para.9, revoked: SI 1997/728 Art.5, Sch.2

1334. Council Tax (Dwellings) (Scotland) Regulations 1992
Reg.2, referred to: SI 1997/728 Sch.1 para.20

1335. Council Tax (Reductions for Disabilities) (Scotland) Regulations 1992
Reg.1, amended: SI 1996/580 Art.7
Reg.3, amended: SI 1996/580 Art.7, SI 1999/756 Reg.2
Reg.3, revoked (in part): SI 1999/756 Reg.2
Reg.4, amended: SI 1996/580 Art.7, SI 1999/756 Reg.3

1348. Education Transfer Council (Transfers under the Education Reform Act 1988) Regulations 1992
referred to: SI 1999/2323 Art.22

1356. Motor Vehicles (Driving Licences) (Large Goods and Passenger-Carrying Vehicles) (Amendment) (No.3) Regulations 1992
revoked: SI 1996/2824 Reg.2, Sch.1

1357. Food (Lot Marking) Regulations 1992
applied: SI 1996/1499 Reg.23
revoked: SI 1996/1502 Reg.7

1992—cont.

1365. Army Terms of Service Regulations 1992
applied: SI 1999/1610 Reg.3, SI 1999/2764 Reg.3
Reg.3, amended: SI 1996/2973 Reg.2
Reg.4A, added: SI 1996/2973 Reg.2
Reg.4A, amended: SI 1999/1610 Reg.2
Reg.4B, added: SI 1996/2973 Reg.2
Reg.5, amended: SI 1999/2764 Reg.2
Reg.7, revoked: SI 1999/1610 Reg.2
Reg.7A, added: SI 1999/1610 Reg.2
Reg.7A, amended: SI 1999/2764 Reg.2
Reg.8, revoked: SI 1999/1610 Reg.2
Reg.9, revoked (in part): SI 1999/1610 Reg.2
Reg.10, amended: SI 1999/1610 Reg.2, SI 1999/2764 Reg.2
Reg.10A, added: SI 1996/2973 Reg.2
Reg.11, amended: SI 1996/2973 Reg.2
Sch., amended: SI 1996/2973 Reg.2

1372. London Priority Route Order 1992
Sch. para.13, amended: SI 1997/1011 Art.2, Sch.
Sch. para.27, amended: SI 1997/1011 Art.2, Sch.
Sch. para.64, amended: SI 1997/1011 Art.2, Sch.
Sch. para.65, amended: SI 1997/1011 Art.2, Sch.
Sch. para.77, amended: SI 1997/1011 Art.2, Sch.
Sch. para.110, amended: SI 1997/1011 Art.2, Sch.

1386. Sea Fish Industry Authority (Levy) (Amendment) Regulations 1992 Confirmatory Order 1992
revoked: SI 1996/160 Art.3

1408. Council Tax (Discounts) (Scotland) Order 1992
Art.4, amended: SI 1997/586 Art.2
Art.5, amended: SI 1998/341 Art.2
Art.6, amended: SI 1997/586 Art.3

1409. Council Tax (Discounts) (Scotland) Regulations 1992
Reg.1, amended: SI 1996/580 Art.8
Reg.2, amended: SI 1997/587 Reg.2, SI 1998/340 Reg.2
Sch. para.3, referred to: SI 1997/728 Sch.1 para.10

1421. Harbour Works (Assessment of Environmental Effects) Regulations 1992
revoked: SI 1996/1946 Reg.1

1423. Ayr Road Route (M77) (City of Glasgow District Boundary - Malletsheugh) Special Road and Connecting Road Scheme 1992
applied: SI 1996/2863 Reg.1

1429. Offshore Installations (Safety Zones) (No.2) Order 1992
revoked: SI 1997/735 Art.3, Sch.2

1478. Hovercraft (Fees) Regulations 1992
revoked: SI 1997/320 Reg.2

1489. Act of Adjournal (Consolidation Amendment) (Criminal Justice International Co-operation Act 1990) 1992
revoked: SI 1996/513 Sch.2 r.3, Sch.3

1492. Town and Country Planning General Regulations 1992
Reg.2, amended: SI 1999/1892 Reg.17
Reg.3, applied: SI 1999/293 Reg.3
Reg.4, applied: SI 1999/293 Reg.3
Reg.9A, added: SI 1998/2800 Reg.2
Reg.9B, added: SI 1998/2800 Reg.2
Reg.11, amended: SI 1999/1892 Reg.17
Reg.11A, added: SI 1999/1892 Reg.17

NO.

1492. **Town and Country Planning General Regulations 1992**—*cont.*
Reg.12, amended: SI 1996/525 Sch para.15
Reg.12, applied: SI 1996/1243 Sch.5 para.15
Reg.14, amended: SI 1997/3006 Reg.2

1494. **Town and Country Planning (Assessment of Environmental Effects) (Amendment) Regulations 1992**
revoked: SI 1999/293 Reg.34, Sch.5

1501. **Invergarry-Kyle of Lochalsh Trunk Road (A87) Extension (Skye Bridge Crossing) Toll Order 1992**
Art.2, amended: SSI 1999/196 Art.2
Art.4, substituted: SSI 1999/196 Art.2
Art.5, revoked: SSI 1999/196 Art.2
Art.6, revoked: SSI 1999/196 Art.2
Sch.1, substituted: SSI 1999/196 Art.2, Sch.
Sch.1 Table, substituted: SI 1997/2941 Art.2
Sch.2, revoked: SSI 1999/196 Art.2

1507. **Food Safety (Fishery Products) (Derogations) Regulations 1992**
applied: SI 1996/3124 Reg.10, Sch.2 para.1
revoked: SI 1998/994 Reg.59, Sch.5
Reg.2, revoked: SI 1998/994 Reg.59, Sch.5
Sch., revoked: SI 1998/994 Reg.59, Sch.5

1508. **Food Safety (Live Bivalve Molluscs) (Derogations) Regulations 1992**
applied: SI 1996/3124 Reg.10, Sch.2 para.2
revoked: SI 1998/994 Reg.59, Sch.5
Reg.2, revoked: SI 1998/994 Reg.59, Sch.5
Sch., revoked: SI 1998/994 Reg.59, Sch.5

1520. **Medicines (Medicated Animal Feeding Stuffs) (No.2) Regulations 1992**
revoked: SI 1998/1048 Reg.2, Sch.1
Reg.2, revoked: SI 1998/1048 Reg.2, Sch.1
Reg.3, applied: SI 1998/1046 Reg.35
Reg.3, revoked: SI 1998/1048 Reg.2, Sch.1
Reg.4, revoked: SI 1998/1048 Reg.2, Sch.1
Reg.6, revoked: SI 1998/1048 Reg.2, Sch.1
Reg.8, revoked: SI 1998/1048 Reg.2, Sch.1
Reg.9, revoked: SI 1998/1048 Reg.2, Sch.1
Sch.2, revoked: SI 1998/1048 Reg.2, Sch.1
Sch.3, revoked: SI 1998/1048 Reg.2, Sch.1
Sch.3, substituted: SI 1996/769 Reg.2, SI 1997/638 Reg.2, Sch.

1525. **Cosmetic Products (Safety) (Amendment) Regulations 1992**
revoked: SI 1996/2925 Sch.9

1527. **Reservoirs (Panel of Civil Engineers) (Applications and Fees) Regulations 1992**
Reg.2, amended: SI 1998/2403 Reg.2

1528. **National Health Service (General Dental Services) (Scotland) Amendment (No.2) Regulations 1992**
revoked: SI 1996/177 Reg.38, Sch.8

1530. **Community Charges and Non-Domestic Rating (Demand Notices) (Wales) (Amendment) (No.3) Regulations 1992**
revoked: SI 1996/619 Art.12

1531. **Occupational and Personal Pension Schemes (Miscellaneous Amendments) Regulations 1992**
Reg.2, revoked: SI 1996/1172 Sch.2
Reg.3, revoked: SI 1997/784 Reg.12, Sch.2
Reg.4, revoked: SI 1996/1655 Reg.12, Sch.4
Reg.5, revoked: SI 1996/1655 Reg.12, Sch.4
Reg.6, revoked: SI 1996/1655 Reg.12, Sch.4
Reg.7, revoked: SI 1996/1655 Reg.12, Sch.4
Reg.8, revoked: SI 1996/1655 Reg.12, Sch.4
Reg.9, revoked: SI 1996/1655 Reg.12, Sch.4
Reg.10, revoked: SI 1996/1655 Reg.12, Sch.4
Reg.11, revoked: SI 1996/1655 Reg.12, Sch.4
Reg.12, revoked: SI 1996/1655 Reg.12, Sch.4

NO.

1531. **Occupational and Personal Pension Schemes (Miscellaneous Amendments) Regulations 1992**—*cont.*
Reg.13, revoked: SI 1996/1655 Reg.12, Sch.4
Reg.14, revoked: SI 1996/1655 Reg.12, Sch.4
Reg.15, revoked: SI 1996/1655 Reg.12, Sch.4
Reg.16, revoked: SI 1996/1655 Reg.12, Sch.4
Reg.17, revoked: SI 1996/1655 Reg.12, Sch.4
Reg.25, revoked: SI 1996/1537 Reg.18, Sch.
Reg.26, revoked: SI 1996/1537 Reg.18, Sch.
Reg.32, revoked: SI 1997/371 Reg.9, Sch.
Reg.33, revoked: SI 1997/371 Reg.9, Sch.

1534. **Medicines (Products Other Than Veterinary Drugs) (Prescription Only) Amendment Order 1992**
revoked: SI 1997/1830 Art.16, Sch.6

1548. **Education (National Curriculum) (Foundation Subjects at Key Stage 4) Order 1992**
revoked: 1996 c.56 Sch.38 Part III

1554. **Sports Grounds and Football (Amendment of Various Orders) Order 1992**
Art.2, revoked (in part): SI 1999/2462 Art.2

1556. **Public Order (Football Exclusion) (Amendment) Order 1992**
revoked: SI 1999/2460 Art.2

1564. **Merchant Shipping (Safe Manning Document) Regulations 1992**
applied: SI 1996/3243 Sch Part I
revoked: SI 1997/1320 Reg.1
Reg.1, referred to: SI 1997/1320 Reg.5
Reg.1, revoked: SI 1997/1320 Reg.1

1581. **Merchant Shipping (Navigational Warnings) (Amendment) Regulations 1992**
revoked: SI 1996/1815 Reg.1

1582. **Merchant Shipping (Signals of Distress) Rules 1992**
revoked: SI 1996/75 Reg.1

1586. **Civil Legal Aid (Financial Conditions) (Scotland) Regulations 1992**
revoked: SI 1996/1012 Reg.6

1588. **Advice and Assistance (Assistance by Way of Representation) (Scotland) Amendment Regulations 1992**
revoked: SI 1997/3070 Reg.2, Sch.
Reg.3, revoked: SI 1997/3070 Reg.2, Sch.

1597. **Transfer of Colleges of Further Education (Scotland) Order 1992**
Sch.2 para.1, revoked: SI 1998/192 Reg.52, Sch.2

1601. **Imported Food (Bivalve Molluscs and Marine Gastropods from Japan) Regulations 1992**
revoked: SI 1996/1547 Reg.6, Sch.4

1611. **Building Societies (Designated Capital Resources) Order 1992**
Art.4, revoked: SI 1996/2989 Art.2
Art.7, amended: SI 1996/2989 Art.2

1618. **Local Authorities (Capital Finance) (Amendment) (No.2) Regulations 1992**
revoked: SI 1997/319 Reg.162, Sch.3

1626. **Local Government Act 1988 (Defined Activities) (Exemption) (Small Schools) Order 1992**
revoked: SI 1997/2748 Art.3 (with saving)

1643. **Rating Lists (Valuation Date) Order 1992**
revoked: SI 1998/93 Art.3

1655. **Friendly Societies (Modification of the Corporation Tax Acts) Regulations 1992**
revoked: SI 1997/473 Reg.54 (with savings)
Reg.2, amended: SI 1997/471 Reg.3
Reg.4, amended: SI 1997/471 Reg.4
Reg.4A, added: SI 1997/471 Reg.5
Reg.5, amended: SI 1997/471 Reg.6

NO.

1655. **Friendly Societies (Modification of the Corporation Tax Acts) Regulations 1992**—*cont.*
Reg.7, referred to: SI 1996/21 Reg.7
Reg.7, revoked: SI 1997/473 Reg.54 (with savings)
Reg.18, amended: SI 1997/471 Reg.7
Reg.18AA, added: SI 1997/471 Reg.8

1670. **Criminal Justice Act 1991 (Notice of Transfer) Regulations 1992**
Reg.3, amended: SI 1998/461 Reg.2
Reg.3A, added: SI 1998/461 Reg.2
Reg.4, amended: SI 1998/461 Reg.2
Sch. Form 1, amended: SI 1997/738 Reg.2
Sch. Form 2, amended: SI 1997/738 Reg.2, SI 1998/461 Reg.2

1675. **Road Works (Qualifications of Supervisors and Operatives) (Scotland) Regulations 1992**
applied: SI 1996/2374 Sch.1 Part III

1676. **Road Works (Inspection Fees) (Scotland) Regulations 1992**
Reg.3, amended: SI 1998/1029 Reg.2

1687. **Street Works (Qualifications of Supervisors and Operatives) Regulations 1992**
applied: SI 1996/2374 Sch.1 Part III

1688. **Street Works (Inspection Fees) Regulations 1992**
Reg.3, amended: SI 1998/978 Reg.2
Reg.3, applied: SI 1999/2106 Art.2, Sch.2 para.6

1689. **Street Works (Reinstatement) Regulations 1992**
Reg.3, applied: SI 1999/2106 Art.2, Sch.2 para.7
Reg.10, applied: SI 1999/2106 Art.2, Sch.2 para.7

1690. **Street Works (Sharing of Costs of Works) Regulations 1992**
applied: SI 1999/2106 Art.2, Sch.2 para.8

1691. **Street Works (Maintenance) Regulations 1992**
Reg.3, applied: SI 1999/2106 Art.2, Sch.2 para.9
Reg.4, applied: SI 1999/2106 Art.2, Sch.2 para.4

1703. **Housing (Right to Buy) (Prescribed Persons) Order 1992**
Sch.1, amended: SI 1996/2651 Art.2

1725. **Housing (Northern Ireland) Order 1992**
referred to: SI 1999/3147 (NI.11) Art.70

1726. **Licensing (Validation) (Northern Ireland) Order 1992**
revoked: SI 1996/3158 (NI.22) Sch.13

1728. **Offshore, and Pipelines, Safety (Northern Ireland) Order 1992**
Art.3, referred to: 1998 c.17 Sch.3 para.11
Art.3, revoked (in part): 1998 c.17 s.51, Sch.5 Part II
Art.4, amended: SI 1996/275 (NI.2) Art.71, Sch.6
Art.5, revoked (in part): SI 1996/275 (NI.2) Art.71, Sch.8, 1998 c.17 s.51, Sch.5 Part II

1729. **Summer Time Order 1992**
revoked: SI 1997/2982 Art.6

1730. **Crown Office (Forms and Proclamations Rules) Order 1992**
Part II, amended: SI 1996/276 Art.2
Sch. Part II, amended: SI 1996/739 Art.7, Sch.1 para.13

NO.

1733. **Confiscation of the Proceeds of Drug Trafficking (Designated Countries and Territories) (Scotland) Amendment Order 1992**
revoked: SI 1999/673 Art.11

1734. **Criminal Justice (International Co-operation) Act 1990 (Enforcement of Overseas Forfeiture Orders) (Scotland) Amendment Order 1992**
revoked: SI 1999/675 Art.11

1736. **Merchant Shipping (Categorisation of Registries of Overseas Territories) Order 1992**
Sch., amended: SI 1996/280 Art.2

1741. **Council Tax (Administration and Enforcement) (Attachment of Earnings Order) (Wales) Regulations 1992**
Sch., amended: SI 1996/1880 Art.29

1757. **Motor Vehicles (Driving Licences) (Amendment) (No.3) Regulations 1992**
revoked: SI 1996/2824 Reg.2, Sch.1

1761. **Motor Vehicles (Driving Licences) (Large Goods and Passenger-Carrying Vehicles) (Amendment) (No.4) Regulations 1992**
revoked: SI 1996/2824 Reg.2, Sch.1

1812. **Child Support (Information, Evidence and Disclosure) Regulations 1992**
Reg.2, amended: SI 1996/1945 Reg.7, SI 1999/1510 Art.6
Reg.3, amended: SI 1996/1945 Reg.8, SI 1998/58 Reg.32, SI 1999/977 Reg.4, SI 1999/1510 Art.7
Reg.3A, substituted: SI 1999/1510 Art.8
Reg.5, amended: SI 1999/1510 Art.9
Reg.5, revoked (in part): SI 1999/1510 Art.9
Reg.6, amended: SI 1999/1510 Art.10
Reg.8, amended: SI 1996/2907 Reg.63, SI 1998/58 Reg.33, SI 1999/1510 Art.11
Reg.9, revoked: SI 1999/977 Reg.4
Reg.9A, amended: SI 1996/2907 Reg.64, SI 1998/58 Reg.34, SI 1999/977 Reg.4, SI 1999/1510 Art.12
Reg.10, amended: SI 1996/2907 Reg.65
Reg.10, revoked: SI 1999/1510 Art.13
Reg.10A, amended: SI 1996/2907 Reg.66
Reg.10A, revoked: SI 1999/1510 Art.13

1813. **Child Support (Maintenance Assessment Procedure) Regulations 1992**
applied: SI 1996/1623 Art.3, SI 1998/217 Art.2, SI 1999/779 Art.2, Sch.
Part V, substituted: SI 1999/1047 Reg.16
Part VA, added: SI 1998/2799 Reg.2
Part VI, substituted: SI 1999/1047 Reg.16
Part VII, substituted: SI 1999/1047 Reg.16
Reg.1, amended: SI 1996/1345 Reg.5, SI 1996/3196 Reg.5, SI 1999/1047 Reg.2, SI 1999/2566 Reg.5
Reg.3, amended: SI 1999/1047 Reg.3
Reg.7, amended: SI 1999/1047 Reg.4
Reg.8, amended: SI 1999/1047 Reg.5
Reg.8, applied: SI 1996/635 Reg.10
Reg.8, referred to: SI 1996/2907 Reg.10, SI 1999/1510 Art.48
Reg.8A, amended: SI 1998/58 Reg.35, SI 1999/1047 Reg.6
Reg.8B, amended: SI 1998/2799 Reg.2
Reg.8B, revoked: SI 1999/1047 Reg.7
Reg.8C, amended: SI 1999/1047 Reg.8
Reg.8D, amended: SI 1996/1345 Reg.5, SI 1996/3196 Reg.6, SI 1998/58 Reg.36, SI 1999/1047 Reg.9
Reg.8D, revoked (in part): SI 1999/1047 Reg.9
Reg.9, amended: SI 1998/58 Reg.37, SI 1998/2799 Reg.2

NO.

1813. Child Support (Maintenance Assessment Procedure) Regulations 1992—*cont.*
Reg.9, substituted: SI 1999/1047 Reg.10
Reg.9A, amended: SI 1998/2799 Reg.2
Reg.9A, revoked: SI 1999/1047 Reg.10
Reg.10, amended: SI 1996/2907 Reg.67, SI 1998/2799 Reg.2, SI 1999/1047 Reg.11
Reg.10, revoked (in part): SI 1999/1047 Reg.11
Reg.10A, added: SI 1998/58 Reg.38
Reg.10A, amended: SI 1999/1047 Reg.12
Reg.11, amended: SI 1998/2799 Reg.2
Reg.11, revoked: SI 1999/1047 Reg.13
Reg.12, revoked: SI 1999/1047 Reg.13
Reg.13, revoked: SI 1999/1047 Reg.13
Reg.14, revoked: SI 1999/1047 Reg.13
Reg.15, revoked: SI 1999/1047 Reg.13
Reg.15A, amended: SI 1996/1945 Reg.9
Reg.15A, revoked: SI 1999/1047 Reg.13
Reg.16, amended: SI 1999/1047 Reg.14
Reg.16A, substituted: SI 1999/1047 Reg.15
Reg.17, amended: SI 1996/1345 Reg.5, SI 1998/58 Reg.39, SI 1998/2799 Reg.2
Reg.17, applied: SI 1999/1510 Art.48
Reg.17, substituted: SI 1999/1047 Reg.16
Reg.18, substituted: SI 1999/1047 Reg.16
Reg.18A, added: SI 1998/2799 Reg.2
Reg.18B, added: SI 1998/2799 Reg.2
Reg.18C, added: SI 1998/2799 Reg.2
Reg.18D, added: SI 1998/2799 Reg.2
Reg.19, substituted: SI 1999/1047 Reg.16
Reg.20, amended: SI 1996/3196 Reg.7
Reg.20, applied: SI 1996/2907 Reg.11
Reg.20, substituted: SI 1999/1047 Reg.16
Reg.21, applied: SI 1996/2907 Reg.11
Reg.21, substituted: SI 1999/1047 Reg.16
Reg.22, applied: SI 1996/2907 Reg.11
Reg.22, substituted: SI 1999/1047 Reg.16
Reg.23, substituted: SI 1999/1047 Reg.16
Reg.24, substituted: SI 1999/1047 Reg.16
Reg.25, revoked: SI 1999/1047 Reg.16
Reg.26, revoked: SI 1999/1047 Reg.16
Reg.27, revoked: SI 1999/1047 Reg.16
Reg.28, revoked: SI 1999/1047 Reg.16
Reg.29, revoked: SI 1999/1047 Reg.16
Reg.30, amended: SI 1999/1047 Reg.17
Reg.30A, amended: SI 1996/3196 Reg.8, SI 1998/58 Reg.40, SI 1999/1047 Reg.18
Reg.31, amended: SI 1996/1945 Reg.10
Reg.31, revoked: SI 1999/1047 Reg.19
Reg.31A, revoked: SI 1999/1047 Reg.19
Reg.31B, revoked: SI 1999/1047 Reg.19
Reg.31C, amended: SI 1996/1945 Reg.11
Reg.31C, revoked: SI 1999/1047 Reg.19
Reg.32, amended: SI 1999/1047 Reg.20
Reg.32A, amended: SI 1999/1047 Reg.21
Reg.32B, amended: SI 1999/1047 Reg.22
Reg.33, amended: SI 1996/1945 Reg.12, SI 1999/1047 Reg.23
Reg.33, applied: SI 1996/1945 Reg.25
Reg.35, amended: SI 1996/1945 Reg.13
Reg.35, applied: SI 1996/1945 Reg.25
Reg.35, substituted: SI 1999/1047 Reg.24
Reg.35A, amended: SI 1996/1345 Reg.5, SI 1999/1047 Reg.25
Reg.36, amended: SI 1996/1345 Reg.5, SI 1996/1945 Reg.14, SI 1999/1047 Reg.26
Reg.36, applied: SI 1996/1945 Reg.25
Reg.37, amended: SI 1996/1345 Reg.5, SI 1996/2538 Reg.6
Reg.38, amended: SI 1996/1945 Reg.15, SI 1999/1047 Reg.27
Reg.39, amended: SI 1996/1945 Reg.16
Reg.40A, amended: SI 1996/2538 Reg.6

NO.

1813. Child Support (Maintenance Assessment Procedure) Regulations 1992—*cont.*
Reg.40A, applied: SI 1996/3196 Reg.16
Reg.40A, revoked: SI 1996/3196 Reg.9
Reg.40ZA, added: SI 1996/1345 Reg.5
Reg.41, substituted: SI 1999/1047 Reg.28
Reg.42, revoked: SI 1999/1047 Reg.28
Reg.43, revoked: SI 1999/1047 Reg.28
Reg.44, revoked: SI 1999/1047 Reg.28
Reg.45, revoked: SI 1999/1047 Reg.28
Reg.46, revoked: SI 1999/1047 Reg.28
Reg.47, amended: SI 1996/1345 Reg.5, SI 1996/1945 Reg.17, SI 1999/1047 Reg.29
Reg.47, applied: SI 1996/1945 Reg.25
Reg.49, substituted: SI 1999/1047 Reg.30
Reg.49A, applied: SI 1996/3196 Reg.16
Reg.49A, revoked: SI 1996/3196 Reg.9
Reg.52, revoked: SI 1999/1047 Reg.31
Reg.53, applied: SI 1996/2907 Reg.4
Reg.54, revoked: SI 1999/1047 Reg.31
Reg.55, revoked: SI 1999/1047 Reg.31
Reg.56, revoked: SI 1999/1047 Reg.31
Reg.57, revoked: SI 1999/1047 Reg.31
Sch.1 para.1, amended: SI 1996/1345 Reg.5, SI 1999/977 Reg.5
Sch.1 para.4, amended: SI 1999/977 Reg.5, SI 1999/1047 Reg.32
Sch.1 para.6, amended: SI 1999/977 Reg.5
Sch.2 para.3, amended: SI 1999/1047 Reg.33
Sch.2 para.4, amended: SI 1999/1047 Reg.33
Sch.2 para.6, amended: SI 1998/58 Reg.41

1814. Council Tax Benefit (General) Regulations 1992
see *R. v Doncaster MBC Ex p. Nortrop* (1996) 28 H.L.R. 862 (QBD), Brooke, J.
applied: SI 1996/1623 Art.3, SI 1997/261 Reg.4, SI 1998/214 Reg.6, SI 1998/217 Art.2, SI 1998/266 Reg.4, SI 1999/259 Reg.6, SI 1999/347 Reg.4, SI 1999/779 Art.2, Sch.
Part V, applied: SI 1997/791 Reg.24, SI 1997/1909 Reg.24
Reg.2, amended: SI 1996/194 Reg.8, SI 1996/1510 Reg.24, SI 1996/1944 Reg.2, Reg.13, Sch. para.1, Sch. para.2, SI 1997/1841 Reg.2, SI 1998/563 Reg.5, SI 1998/2825 Reg.12, SI 1999/1539 Reg.6, SI 1999/2165 Reg.2, SI 1999/2566 Reg.2, Sch.2 Part III, SI 1999/3156 Reg.12, SI 1999/3178 Art.3, Sch.7 para.1
Reg.2A, added: SI 1997/2676 Reg.3
Reg.2A, revoked: SI 1999/920 Reg.2
Reg.4, amended: SI 1996/1510 Reg.25, SI 1998/2825 Reg.13, SI 1999/2165 Reg.3, SI 1999/3156 Reg.13
Reg.4A, amended: SI 1996/30 Reg.3, SI 1996/1510 Reg.26, SI 1996/1944 Reg.2, SI 1996/2006 Reg.3, SI 1996/2432 Reg.2, SI 1998/563 Reg.18
Reg.4A, referred to: SI 1996/30 Reg.12, SI 1997/1004 Art.17
Reg.4B, amended: SI 1998/563 Reg.8
Reg.4D, added: SI 1996/2432 Reg.3
Reg.4D, applied: SI 1996/2890 Sch.3 para.49, Sch.4 para.45
Reg.5, amended: SI 1996/1510 Reg.27
Reg.5, applied: SI 1996/2545 Reg.10
Reg.8, amended: SI 1996/599 Art.22, SI 1996/2432 Reg.7, SI 1997/543 Art.22, SI 1998/470 Art.22, SI 1999/264 Art.22
Reg.9, amended: SI 1996/599 Art.22, SI 1996/2432 Reg.7, SI 1997/543 Art.22, SI 1998/470 Art.22, SI 1999/264 Art.22

1992—cont.

1814. Council Tax Benefit (General) Regulations 1992—*cont.*

Reg.10, amended: SI 1996/599 Art.22, SI 1996/ 1803 Reg.22, SI 1996/2432 Reg.7, SI 1997/ 543 Art.22, SI 1998/470 Art.22, SI 1999/264 Art.22

Reg.12, amended: SI 1996/1510 Reg.28

Reg.13, amended: SI 1996/599 Art.22, SI 1997/ 2793 Reg.2, SI 1999/920 Reg.3

Reg.13A, amended: SI 1996/1008 Art.2, Sch para.11, SI 1997/2793 Reg.2, SI 1999/920 Reg.4

Reg.13A, applied: SI 1996/2745 Sch.2 para.8

Reg.16, amended: SI 1996/1510 Reg.29

Reg.19, amended: SI 1999/1509 Reg.2

Reg.21, amended: SI 1999/2165 Reg.3

Reg.21A, amended: SI 1996/2545 Reg.3

Reg.24, amended: SI 1996/1510 Reg.30

Reg.25, amended: SI 1997/65 Reg.3

Reg.26, amended: SI 1996/1510 Reg.31, SI 1996/1803 Reg.23, SI 1997/2197 Reg.7, SI 1997/2863 Reg.17, SI 1998/563 Reg.6, SI 1998/2164 Reg.2, SI 1998/2825 Reg.14, SI 1999/2640 Reg.2, SI 1999/3156 Reg.14

Reg.31, amended: SI 1998/1174 Reg.7, SI 1999/3156 Reg.18

Reg.34, amended: SI 1997/2197 Reg.7, SI 1997/2863 Reg.17, SI 1998/2164 Reg.3, SI 1998/2825 Reg.15, SI 1999/2640 Reg.2, SI 1999/3156 Reg.15

Reg.35, amended: SI 1996/1510 Reg.32, SI 1996/1944 Reg.2, Reg.13, Sch. para.4, SI 1999/2566 Reg.2, Sch.2 Part I, Sch.2 Part II

Reg.36, amended: SI 1998/2250 Reg.2

Reg.38, amended: SI 1996/1944 Reg.2, SI 1997/791 Reg.24, SI 1997/1909 Reg.24, SI 1998/563 Reg.4, SI 1998/1274 Reg.10, SI 1999/1935 Reg.4

Reg.38, applied: SI 1997/791 Reg.24

Reg.40, amended: SI 1996/1510 Reg.33, SI 1996/1803 Reg.24, SI 1996/1944 Reg.2, SI 1997/1790 Reg.2, SI 1998/766 Reg.3

Reg.42, amended: SI 1996/1759 Reg.2, SI 1996/1944 Reg.2, SI 1997/1671 Reg.2, SI 1998/1379 Reg.2, SI 1999/1935 Reg.4

Reg.43, amended: SI 1996/1944 Reg.2

Reg.44, amended: SI 1996/1944 Reg.2

Reg.45, amended: SI 1996/462 Reg.8

Reg.46, amended: SI 1999/1935 Reg.4

Reg.47, amended: SI 1996/462 Reg.9, SI 1999/ 1935 Reg.4

Reg.48, amended: SI 1996/462 Reg.10, SI 1999/1935 Reg.4

Reg.48A, added: SI 1998/563 Reg.4

Reg.48A, amended: SI 1999/1935 Reg.4

Reg.51, amended: SI 1996/194 Reg.9, SI 1997/65 Reg.15, SI 1997/1841 Reg.2

Reg.51, applied: SI 1996/1217 Art.19, SI 1997/ 1004 Art.19, SI 1998/562 Art.19

Reg.52, amended: SI 1996/599 Art.22, SI 1996/ 1510 Reg.34, SI 1996/2518 Reg.2, SI 1997/ 543 Art.22, SI 1998/470 Art.22, SI 1999/264 Art.22

Reg.53A, added: SI 1996/194 Reg.10

Reg.53A, amended: SI 1999/2556 Reg.4

Reg.54, applied: SI 1996/1217 Art.19, SI 1997/ 1004 Art.19, SI 1998/562 Art.19

Reg.57, amended: SI 1996/1510 Reg.35

Reg.57, applied: SI 1996/1217 Art.18, SI 1998/ 562 Art.18

Reg.57, referred to: SI 1997/1004 Art.18

Reg.58, amended: SI 1996/1510 Reg.36

1992—cont.

1814. Council Tax Benefit (General) Regulations 1992—*cont.*

Reg.59, amended: SI 1996/1510 Reg.37

Reg.62, amended: SI 1996/462 Reg.5, SI 1996/ 1510 Reg.38, SI 1996/2432 Reg.7, SI 1999/ 1539 Reg.7, SI 1999/2556 Reg.4

Reg.62, applied: SI 1996/1217 Art.17, Art.18, Art.19, SI 1997/1004 Art.17, SI 1998/562 Art.14, Art.19

Reg.62, referred to: SI 1997/1004 Art.18, Art.19, SI 1998/562 Art.18

Reg.62A, added: SI 1999/1539 Reg.8

Reg.63, amended: SI 1996/2432 Reg.7

Reg.65, amended: SI 1996/1510 Reg.39, SI 1999/1539 Reg.9

Reg.65, applied: SI 1996/1217 Art.18

Reg.66, amended: SI 1996/194 Reg.11, SI 1996/1510 Reg.40, SI 1996/2432 Reg.7, SI 1999/2556 Reg.4

Reg.66, applied: SI 1997/1004 Sch.2 para.8, SI 1998/562 Sch.2 para.5

Reg.69, referred to: SI 1996/548 Art.2, SI 1996/ 549 Art.2

Reg.70, applied: SI 1998/214 Reg.8, SI 1998/ 266 Reg.5, SI 1999/259 Reg.8, SI 1999/347 Reg.5

Reg.70, referred to: SI 1996/309 Reg.4, SI 1996/548 Art.2, SI 1996/549 Art.2, SI 1997/ 215 Reg.8, SI 1997/261 Reg.5

Reg.71, applied: SI 1996/176 Reg.10, SI 1996/ 309 Reg.6, SI 1997/215 Reg.10, SI 1997/261 Reg.7, SI 1998/214 Reg.10, SI 1998/266 Reg.7, SI 1999/259 Reg.10, SI 1999/347 Reg.7

Reg.72, applied: SI 1996/176 Reg.10, SI 1996/ 309 Reg.6, SI 1997/215 Reg.10, SI 1997/261 Reg.7, SI 1998/214 Reg.10, SI 1998/266 Reg.7, SI 1999/259 Reg.10, SI 1999/347 Reg.7

Reg.80, amended: SI 1996/1510 Reg.41, SI 1999/3178 Art.3, Sch.7 para.2

Reg.81A, added: SI 1997/2434 Reg.5

Reg.83, see *R. v South Hams DC Ex p. Ash* Times, May 27, 1999 (QBD), Moses, J.

Reg.84, see *R. v South Hams DC Ex p. Ash* Times, May 27, 1999 (QBD), Moses, J.

Reg.84, amended: SI 1997/65 Reg.11

Reg.91, amended: SI 1996/1510 Reg.42

Reg.92, amended: SI 1996/194 Reg.12, SI 1996/1510 Reg.43

Reg.93, amended: SI 1996/1510 Reg.44

Reg.95, added: SI 1996/194 Reg.13

Reg.95, amended: SI 1999/2556 Reg.4

Sch.1 Part I, amended: SI 1996/599 Art.22, Sch.11, SI 1997/543 Art.22, Sch.11

Sch.1 Part II, amended: SI 1996/599 Art.22, SI 1996/1803 Reg.25, SI 1997/543 Art.22

Sch.1 Part III, amended: SI 1996/599 Art.22, SI 1996/1803 Reg.25, SI 1997/543 Art.22

Sch.1 Part III, revoked (in part): SI 1996/1803 Reg.25

Sch.1 Part IV, amended: SI 1996/599 Art.22, Sch.12, SI 1996/1803 Reg.25, SI 1997/543 Art.22, Sch.12

Sch.1 para.1, amended: SI 1998/470 Art.22, Sch.11, SI 1999/264 Art.22, Sch.11

Sch.1 para.2, amended: SI 1996/2545 Reg.2, SI 1997/543 Art.22, SI 1998/470 Art.22, Sch.11, SI 1998/1541 Reg.2, SI 1999/264 Art.22, Sch.11, SI 1999/2555 Reg.2

Sch.1 para.3, amended: SI 1997/1790 Reg.3, SI 1998/470 Art.22, SI 1998/766 Reg.4, SI 1999/264 Art.22

NO.

1992—cont.

1814. Council Tax Benefit (General) Regulations 1992—*cont.*

Sch.1 para.11, amended: SI 1998/2231 Reg.8

Sch.1 para.11, applied: SI 1996/2745 Sch.2 para.8

Sch.1 para.13, amended: SI 1998/2231 Reg.8, SI 1999/2566 Reg.2, Sch.2 Part II

Sch.1 para.15, amended: SI 1998/470 Art.22, SI 1999/264 Art.22

Sch.1 para.19, amended: SI 1998/470 Art.22, Sch.12, SI 1999/264 Art.22, Sch.11

Sch. A1, added: SI 1996/2432 Reg.6

Sch. A1 para.9, amended: SI 1997/852 Reg.2

Sch.2 Part I, amended: SI 1996/599 Art.22

Sch.2 Table, amended: SI 1997/1841 Reg.2

Sch.2 para.1, amended: SI 1996/1510 Reg.45, SI 1997/543 Art.22, SI 1997/1841 Reg.2

Sch.3 para.4, amended: SI 1996/1803 Reg.26

Sch.3 para.4, substituted: SI 1997/1790 Reg.4, SI 1998/766 Reg.5

Sch.3 para.10, amended: SI 1996/1510 Reg.46

Sch.3 para.16, added: SI 1999/920 Reg.6

Sch.3 para.16, amended: SI 1999/2566 Reg.2, Sch.2 Part IV

Sch.4 para.4, amended: SI 1996/1510 Reg.47

Sch.4 para.6, amended: SI 1996/1510 Reg.47

Sch.4 para.10, amended: SI 1997/2197 Reg.7, SI 1999/1677 Reg.2

Sch.4 para.11, amended: SI 1997/2863 Reg.17

Sch.4 para.13, amended: SI 1996/462 Reg.8

Sch.4 para.17, amended: SI 1999/1935 Reg.4

Sch.4 para.18, amended: SI 1999/1935 Reg.4

Sch.4 para.20, amended: SI 1996/599 Art.22

Sch.4 para.24, amended: SI 1998/563 Reg.7

Sch.4 para.26, substituted: SI 1998/563 Reg.7

Sch.4 para.29, substituted: SI 1998/1173 Reg.2

Sch.4 para.34, amended: SI 1996/462 Reg.8, SI 1998/563 Reg.7

Sch.4 para.36, amended: SI 1996/2432 Reg.4

Sch.4 para.40, amended: SI 1996/1510 Reg.47

Sch.4 para.46, amended: SI 1996/1803 Reg.27

Sch.4 para.51, amended: SI 1996/1510 Reg.47

Sch.4 para.56, amended: SI 1999/920 Reg.6, SI 1999/2566 Reg.2, Sch.2 Part II, Sch.2 Part IV

Sch.4 para.56, substituted: SI 1996/462 Reg.4

Sch.4 para.57, amended: SI 1999/920 Reg.6, SI 1999/2566 Reg.2, Sch.2 Part I

Sch.4 para.57, substituted: SI 1996/462 Reg.4

Sch.4 para.58, added: SI 1996/1803 Reg.27

Sch.4 para.59, amended: SI 1996/1944 Reg.13, Sch. para.6

Sch.4 para.60, added: SI 1996/2432 Reg.4

Sch.4 para.61, added: SI 1996/2432 Reg.4

Sch.4 para.62, added: SI 1997/65 Reg.2

Sch.4 para.63, added: SI 1997/65 Reg.2

Sch.4 para.64, amended: SI 1997/2863 Reg.17

Sch.4 para.64, substituted: SI 1998/1174 Reg.7

Sch.4 para.65, amended: SI 1997/2863 Reg.17

Sch.4 para.66, added: SI 1998/1174 Reg.7

Sch.4 para.66, amended: SI 1999/3156 Reg.18

Sch.4 para.67, added: SI 1998/2164 Reg.4

Sch.4 para.68, amended: SI 1998/2825 Reg.16, SI 1999/3156 Reg.16

Sch.4 para.69, amended: SI 1998/2825 Reg.16, SI 1999/3156 Reg.16

Sch.4 para.70, added: SI 1999/2165 Reg.3

Sch.5 para.5, amended: SI 1996/1510 Reg.48

Sch.5 para.7, amended: SI 1998/1174 Reg.7, SI 1999/3156 Reg.18

Sch.5 para.8, amended: SI 1996/1510 Reg.48, SI 1996/1944 Reg.13, Sch. para.7

NO.

1992—cont.

1814. Council Tax Benefit (General) Regulations 1992—*cont.*

Sch.5 para.34, amended: SI 1996/2432 Reg.5

Sch.5 para.46, amended: SI 1997/2197 Reg.7

Sch.5 para.47, amended: SI 1997/2197 Reg.7

Sch.5 para.49, added: SI 1996/1510 Reg.48

Sch.5 para.50, added: SI 1996/2432 Reg.5, SI 1996/3195 Reg.15

Sch.5 para.51, added: SI 1996/2432 Reg.5

Sch.5 para.53, amended: SI 1997/2863 Reg.17

Sch.5 para.53, substituted: SI 1998/1174 Reg.7

Sch.5 para.54, amended: SI 1997/2863 Reg.17

Sch.5 para.55, added: SI 1998/1174 Reg.7

Sch.5 para.55, amended: SI 1999/3156 Reg.18

Sch.5 para.56, added: SI 1998/2164 Reg.5

Sch.5 para.57, amended: SI 1998/2825 Reg.17, SI 1999/3156 Reg.17

Sch.5 para.58, amended: SI 1998/2825 Reg.17, SI 1999/3156 Reg.17

Sch.5 para.59, added: SI 1999/2165 Reg.3

Sch.5A, added: SI 1996/194 Reg.14

Sch.5A para.2, amended: SI 1996/1510 Reg.49, SI 1996/1803 Reg.28, SI 1997/1790 Reg.5, SI 1998/766 Reg.6, SI 1999/2556 Reg.4

Sch.5A para.3, amended: SI 1996/1510 Reg.49

Sch.5A para.6, amended: SI 1999/2556 Reg.4

Sch.5A para.7, amended: SI 1999/2556 Reg.4

Sch.5A para.8, amended: SI 1996/1510 Reg.49, SI 1999/2556 Reg.4

Sch.6 para.9, amended: SI 1996/1510 Reg.50

Sch.6 para.10, amended: SI 1996/1510 Reg.50

Sch.6 para.12, amended: SI 1996/1510 Reg.50

Sch.6 para.13, amended: SI 1996/1510 Reg.50

1815. Child Support (Maintenance Assessments and Special Cases) Regulations 1992

see *AMS v Child Support Officer* [1998] 1 F.L.R. 955 (CA), Simon Brown, L.J.

amended: SI 1999/2566 Reg.2, Sch.2 Part I, Sch.2 Part II

applied: SI 1996/1623 Art.3, SI 1998/217 Art.2, SI 1999/779 Art.2, Sch.

referred to: SI 1999/1510 Art.48

Reg.1, amended: SI 1996/1345 Reg.6, SI 1996/1803 Reg.7, SI 1996/1945 Reg.18, SI 1996/2907 Reg.68, SI 1996/3196 Reg.10, SI 1998/58 Reg.42, SI 1999/977 Reg.6, SI 1999/1510 Art.14, SI 1999/2566 Reg.2, Sch.2 Part III

Reg.1, referred to: SI 1999/1510 Art.48

Reg.2, amended: SI 1998/58 Reg.43, SI 1999/1510 Art.15

Reg.3, amended: SI 1996/1803 Reg.8, SI 1998/58 Reg.44

Reg.4, amended: SI 1996/1803 Reg.9

Reg.5, applied: SI 1996/2907 Reg.41

Reg.6, amended: SI 1996/1803 Reg.10, SI 1998/58 Reg.45

Reg.7, amended: SI 1996/1345 Reg.6, SI 1999/977 Reg.6, SI 1999/1510 Art.16

Reg.7, applied: SI 1996/635 Reg.18, SI 1996/2907 Reg.18

Reg.7, referred to: SI 1996/2907 Reg.24

Reg.8, referred to: SI 1996/2907 Reg.24

Reg.9, amended: SI 1996/1945 Reg.19, SI 1996/2907 Reg.68, SI 1998/58 Reg.46, Reg.47

Reg.9, applied: SI 1996/635 Reg.18, Reg.29, Reg.37, Reg.39, SI 1996/1803 Reg.11, SI 1996/2907 Reg.18, Reg.28, Reg.29, Reg.37, Reg.39, Reg.40, Reg.42

Reg.9, revoked (in part): SI 1998/58 Reg.47

NO.

1815. Child Support (Maintenance Assessments and Special Cases) Regulations 1992—*cont.*

Reg.10, applied: SI 1996/635 Reg.29, Reg.37, SI 1996/2907 Reg.28, Reg.29, Reg.37, Reg.39, Reg.40

Reg.10A, added: SI 1996/3196 Reg.11

Reg.10A, amended: SI 1999/1510 Art.16, SI 1999/2566 Reg.2, Sch.2 Part I, Sch.2 Part II

Reg.11, amended: SI 1996/1803 Reg.12, SI 1996/1945 Reg.20, SI 1998/58 Reg.48, Reg.49

Reg.11, applied: SI 1996/2907 Reg.38, Reg.40

Reg.11, revoked (in part): SI 1998/58 Reg.49

Reg.12, amended: SI 1996/1945 Reg.21, SI 1996/3196 Reg.12

Reg.13, amended: SI 1996/481 Reg.2

Reg.13, applied: SI 1996/635 Reg.39

Reg.14, applied: SI 1996/2907 Reg.40

Reg.15, amended: SI 1998/58 Reg.50

Reg.16, amended: SI 1998/58 Reg.51

Reg.16, applied: SI 1996/1945 Reg.25

Reg.16, substituted: SI 1996/1945 Reg.22

Reg.17, applied: SI 1996/1945 Reg.25

Reg.18, applied: SI 1996/1945 Reg.25, SI 1996/2907 Reg.26, Reg.40

Reg.19, amended: SI 1996/1803 Reg.13, SI 1996/1945 Reg.23, SI 1999/977 Reg.6, SI 1999/1510 Art.17

Reg.19, applied: SI 1996/1945 Reg.25

Reg.19, revoked (in part): SI 1998/58 Reg.52

Reg.20, amended: SI 1999/1510 Art.16

Reg.20, applied: SI 1996/635 Reg.14

Reg.20, referred to: SI 1996/2907 Reg.14

Reg.22, amended: SI 1996/2907 Reg.68, SI 1998/58 Reg.53, SI 1999/1510 Art.18

Reg.22, applied: SI 1996/635 Reg.42, SI 1996/2907 Reg.43

Reg.23, amended: SI 1996/1803 Reg.14

Reg.26, amended: SI 1996/1803 Reg.15, SI 1998/58 Reg.54

Reg.28, amended: SI 1996/1345 Reg.6, SI 1996/1803 Reg.16, SI 1998/58 Reg.55

Sch.1, amended: SI 1999/1510 Art.46

Sch.1 para.1, amended: SI 1996/1945 Reg.24, SI 1996/3196 Reg.13, SI 1998/58 Reg.56

Sch.1 para.2, amended: SI 1996/3196 Reg.13, SI 1999/1510 Art.19, SI 1999/2566 Reg.2, Sch.2 Part I, Sch.2 Part II

Sch.1 para.2A, added: SI 1999/977 Reg.6

Sch.1 para.2B, added: SI 1999/977 Reg.6

Sch.1 para.2C, added: SI 1999/977 Reg.6

Sch.1 para.3, amended: SI 1996/3196 Reg.13, SI 1998/58 Reg.56, SI 1999/977 Reg.6

Sch.1 para.5, amended: SI 1996/3196 Reg.13, SI 1999/977 Reg.6, SI 1999/1510 Art.19, SI 1999/2566 Reg.2, Sch.2 Part I, Sch.2 Part II

Sch.1 para.5A, added: SI 1999/977 Reg.6

Sch.1 para.6, amended: SI 1996/1345 Reg.6

Sch.1 para.7, amended: SI 1996/1345 Reg.6, SI 1996/1803 Reg.17, SI 1996/1945 Reg.24, SI 1999/977 Reg.6, SI 1999/2566 Reg.2, Sch.2 Part I

Sch.1 para.9A, added: SI 1999/977 Reg.6

Sch.1 para.14A, added: SI 1996/1945 Reg.24

Sch.1 para.15, amended: SI 1996/1945 Reg.24, SI 1998/58 Reg.56

Sch.1 para.16, amended: SI 1999/1510 Art.19

Sch.1 para.20, amended: SI 1996/1803 Reg.17, SI 1998/58 Reg.56

Sch.1 para.22, amended: SI 1996/1345 Reg.6, SI 1999/977 Reg.6

Sch.1 para.23, amended: SI 1998/58 Reg.56

NO.

1815. Child Support (Maintenance Assessments and Special Cases) Regulations 1992—*cont.*

Sch.1 para.26, amended: SI 1999/1510 Art.19

Sch.1 para.27, amended: SI 1999/1510 Art.19

Sch.1 para.28, amended: SI 1996/1345 Reg.6, SI 1996/1803 Reg.17

Sch.1 para.30, amended: SI 1999/1510 Art.19

Sch.1 para.31, amended: SI 1999/1510 Art.19

Sch.2 para.15, amended: SI 1996/1345 Reg.6

Sch.2 para.19, amended: SI 1996/481 Reg.3

Sch.2 para.20, amended: SI 1996/481 Reg.3

Sch.2 para.25, amended: SI 1998/58 Reg.57, SI 1999/977 Reg.6

Sch.2 para.39, amended: SI 1996/1345 Reg.6

Sch.2 para.44, amended: SI 1998/58 Reg.57

Sch.2 para.48C, added: SI 1996/3196 Reg.14

Sch.2 para.49, amended: SI 1996/1345 Reg.6

Sch.3 para.1, amended: SI 1996/3196 Reg.15, SI 1998/58 Reg.58

Sch.3 para.2, amended: SI 1999/1510 Art.20

Sch.3 para.3, amended: SI 1996/3196 Reg.15, SI 1998/58 Reg.58

Sch.3 para.3, referred to: SI 1996/2907 Reg.16

Sch.3 para.4, amended: SI 1996/3196 Reg.15

Sch.3A para.1, see *Secretary of State for Social Security v Henderson* [1999] 1 F.L.R. 496 (CA), Simon Brown, L.J.

Sch.3A para.1, amended: SI 1999/977 Reg.6

Sch.3A para.2, amended: SI 1999/1510 Art.21

Sch.3A para.3, substituted: SI 1999/1510 Art.21

Sch.3A para.4, amended: SI 1999/977 Reg.6

Sch.3A para.5, amended: SI 1999/977 Reg.6

Sch.3A para.6, amended: SI 1999/977 Reg.6

Sch.3A para.11, amended: SI 1999/977 Reg.6

Sch.3B para.1, amended: SI 1999/1510 Art.22

Sch.3B para.4, amended: SI 1999/1510 Art.22

Sch.3B para.8, amended: SI 1999/1510 Art.22

Sch.3B para.10, amended: SI 1999/1510 Art.22

Sch.3B para.15, amended: SI 1999/1510 Art.22

Sch.3B para.17, amended: SI 1999/1510 Art.22

Sch.4, amended: SI 1999/2566 Reg.2, Sch.2 Part II

Sch.5 para.1, revoked: SI 1999/1510 Art.23

Sch.5 para.2, revoked: SI 1999/1510 Art.23

Sch.5 para.3, revoked: SI 1999/1510 Art.23

Sch.5 para.3A, revoked: SI 1999/1510 Art.23

Sch.5 para.4, revoked: SI 1999/1510 Art.23

Sch.5 para.5, revoked: SI 1999/1510 Art.23

Sch.5 para.6, revoked: SI 1999/1510 Art.23

Sch.5 para.7, revoked: SI 1999/1510 Art.23

Sch.5 para.7A, revoked: SI 1999/1510 Art.23

Sch.5 para.8, revoked: SI 1999/1510 Art.23

1816. Child Support (Arrears, Interest and Adjustment of Maintenance Assessments) Regulations 1992

Reg.3, amended: SI 1999/1510 Art.24

Reg.4, amended: SI 1999/1510 Art.25

Reg.6, amended: SI 1998/1129 Art.3, Sch.2

Reg.7, amended: SI 1996/1345 Reg.3

Reg.8, amended: SI 1996/1345 Reg.3

Reg.10, amended: SI 1996/2907 Reg.62, SI 1998/2799 Reg.3, SI 1999/1510 Art.26

Reg.10A, amended: SI 1996/1345 Reg.3

Reg.11, amended: SI 1999/1510 Art.27

Reg.12, substituted: SI 1999/1510 Art.28

Reg.13, substituted: SI 1999/1510 Art.28

Reg.14, substituted: SI 1999/1510 Art.28

Reg.15, substituted: SI 1999/1510 Art.28

Reg.16, added: SI 1999/1510 Art.28

Reg.17, added: SI 1999/1510 Art.28

1829. Parole Board (Transfer of Functions) Order 1992
revoked: SI 1998/3218 Art.4
Art.3, revoked: SI 1998/3218 Art.4

1837. Assistance for Minor Works to Dwellings (Lead Pipes) Order 1992
applied: SI 1996/2842 Art.8
revoked: SI 1996/2842 Art.7, Sch Part I

1845. Assistance for Minor Works to Dwellings (Amendment) Regulations 1992
applied: SI 1996/2842 Art.8
revoked: SI 1996/2842 Art.7, Sch Part I

1878. Act of Sederunt (Fees of Witnesses and Shorthand Writers in the Sheriff Court) 1992
Sch.1 para.1, amended: SI 1999/188 Art.2, Sch.
Sch.1 para.2, amended: SI 1999/188 Art.2, Sch.
Sch.1 para.3, amended: SI 1999/188 Art.2, Sch.
Sch.1 para.4, amended: SI 1999/188 Art.2, Sch.
Sch.1 para.6, amended: SI 1999/188 Art.2, Sch.
Sch.2, amended: SI 1996/767 r.2
Sch.2, substituted: SI 1997/1118 para.2, Sch.
Sch.2 Table, amended: SI 1999/613 r.2, Sch.
Sch.2 para.1, amended: SI 1998/999 para.2, Sch.
Sch.2 para.4, amended: SI 1998/999 para.2, Sch.
Sch.2 para.5, amended: SI 1998/999 para.2, Sch.

1919. Environmentally Sensitive Areas (Loch Lomond) Designation Order 1992
Art.2, amended: SI 1996/3082 Reg.3
Art.5B, added: SI 1996/3082 Reg.4
Art.5B, amended: SI 1996/3082 Reg.6
Art.5C, added: SI 1996/3082 Reg.6

1920. Environmentally Sensitive Areas (Breadalbane) Designation Order 1992
Art.2, amended: SI 1996/3082 Reg.3
Art.5A, added: SI 1996/3082 Reg.4
Art.5B, added: SI 1996/3082 Reg.4
Art.5B, amended: SI 1996/3082 Reg.6
Art.5C, added: SI 1996/3082 Reg.6
Sch., amended: SI 1996/738 Art.2

1951. Town and Country Planning (Fees for Applications and Deemed Applications) (Scotland) Amendment Regulations 1992
revoked (in part): SI 1997/10 Reg.15

1966. Lay Representatives (Rights of Audience) Order 1992
revoked: SI 1999/1225 Art.2

1971. Flavourings in Food Regulations 1992
Reg.2, amended: SI 1996/1499 Reg.49
Reg.12, revoked: SI 1996/1499 Reg.49, Sch.9
Sch.3 Part I, amended: SI 1996/1499 Reg.49

1974. Salmon (Definition of Methods of Net Fishing and Construction of Nets) (Scotland) Regulations 1992
Part II, applied: SI 1999/1380 Art.3, Sch.2 para.1, SI 1999/1381 Art.3, Sch.2 para.1, SI 1999/1382 Art.3, Sch.2 para.1

1978. Food Additives Labelling Regulations 1992
amended: SI 1999/1136 Reg.14
Reg.2, amended: SI 1996/1499 Reg.49
Reg.6A, added: SI 1999/1136 Reg.14
Reg.8, revoked (in part): SI 1996/1499 Reg.49, Sch.9
Reg.9, revoked (in part): SI 1996/1499 Reg.49, Sch.9
Sch.1 Part II, referred to: SI 1999/982 Reg.3
Sch.1 para.s, revoked: SI 1999/1136 Reg.14
Sch.1 para.t, amended: SI 1999/1136 Reg.14
Sch.3 Part I, amended: SI 1996/1499 Reg.49

1989. Child Support (Collection and Enforcement) Regulations 1992
Reg.4, applied: SI 1996/207 Reg.128
Reg.8, amended: SI 1996/1945 Reg.3, SI 1999/977 Reg.2
Reg.11, amended: SI 1996/1945 Reg.4, SI 1998/2799 Reg.3, SI 1999/1510 Art.29
Reg.12, amended: SI 1998/58 Reg.6
Reg.25, amended: SI 1999/977 Reg.2

2007. Residential Care Homes (Amendment) Regulations 1992
revoked: SI 1998/902 Reg.4

2008. Wireless Telegraphy (Cordless Telephone Apparatus) (Exemption) Regulations 1992
revoked: SI 1996/316 Reg.2, Sch.1

2009. Wireless Telegraphy (Cordless Telephone Apparatus) (Restriction and Marking) Order 1992
revoked: SI 1999/2934 Art.2

2038. Town and Country Planning (Inquiries Procedure) Rules 1992
r.11, see *Barnett v Secretary of State for the Environment* [1996] E.G.C.S. 6 (QBD), R Purchas Q.C.
r.21, amended: SI 1996/525 Sch para.16

2039. Town and Country Planning Appeals (Determination by Inspectors) (Inquiries Procedure) Rules 1992
see *Tandridge DC v Secretary of State for the Environment and The Church of Jesus Christ of Latter Day Saints* (1996) 72 P. & C.R. 83 (QBD), Gerald Moriarty Q.C.

2051. Management of Health and Safety at Work Regulations 1992
applied: SI 1996/341 Reg.4, SI 1996/551 Sch.1 para.5, SI 1997/1840 Reg.7, SI 1999/3242 Reg.29
referred to: SI 1997/2962 Reg.3
revoked: SI 1999/3242 Reg.29
Reg.1, amended: SI 1997/135 Reg.2, SI 1997/1840 Reg.8
Reg.1, referred to: SI 1997/1840 Reg.9
Reg.1, revoked: SI 1999/3242 Reg.29
Reg.2, referred to: SI 1997/1840 Reg.9
Reg.2, revoked: SI 1999/3242 Reg.29
Reg.2, substituted: SI 1997/135 Reg.2
Reg.3, amended: SI 1997/135 Reg.2, SI 1997/1840 Reg.8
Reg.3, applied: SI 1996/341 Reg.4, SI 1996/551 Sch.1 para.5, SI 1998/1833 Reg.6, SI 1999/2024 Reg.7
Reg.3, referred to: SI 1997/1840 Reg.9, SI 1998/543 Reg.5, SI 1999/3232 Reg.7
Reg.3, revoked: SI 1999/3242 Reg.29
Reg.4, referred to: SI 1997/1840 Reg.9
Reg.4, revoked: SI 1999/3242 Reg.29
Reg.5, applied: SI 1999/2024 Reg.43
Reg.5, revoked: SI 1999/3242 Reg.29
Reg.6, amended: SI 1997/1840 Reg.8
Reg.6, applied: SI 1996/1513 Reg.3
Reg.6, referred to: SI 1997/1840 Reg.9
Reg.6, revoked: SI 1999/3242 Reg.29
Reg.7, applied: SI 1996/1513 Reg.3
Reg.7, referred to: SI 1997/1840 Reg.9
Reg.7, revoked: SI 1999/3242 Reg.29
Reg.8, amended: SI 1997/1840 Reg.8
Reg.8, referred to: SI 1997/1840 Reg.9
Reg.8, revoked: SI 1999/3242 Reg.29
Reg.8, substituted: SI 1997/135 Reg.2
Reg.9, amended: SI 1997/1840 Reg.8

NO.

2051. Management of Health and Safety at Work Regulations 1992—*cont.*
Reg.9, referred to: SI 1997/1840 Reg.9
Reg.9, revoked: SI 1999/3242 Reg.29
Reg.10, amended: SI 1997/1840 Reg.8
Reg.10, referred to: SI 1997/1840 Reg.9
Reg.10, revoked: SI 1999/3242 Reg.29
Reg.11, referred to: SI 1997/1840 Reg.9
Reg.11, revoked: SI 1999/3242 Reg.29
Reg.13A, revoked: SI 1999/3242 Reg.29
Reg.13B, revoked: SI 1999/3242 Reg.29
Reg.13C, revoked: SI 1999/3242 Reg.29
Reg.13D, added: SI 1997/135 Reg.2
Reg.13D, revoked: SI 1999/3242 Reg.29
Reg.14, revoked: SI 1999/3242 Reg.29
Reg.15, amended: SI 1997/135 Reg.2
Reg.15, revoked: SI 1999/3242 Reg.29

2070. Magistrates' Courts (Notice of Transfer) (Children's Evidence) Rules 1992
amended: SI 1997/709 r.2
r.5, revoked: SI 1997/709 r.2
r.6, amended: SI 1997/709 r.2
Sch.2 Form 4, revoked: SI 1997/709 r.2

2071. Magistrates' Courts (Children and Young Persons) Rules 1992
r.4, amended: SI 1998/2167 r.5
r.28, substituted: SI 1999/1343 r.2
Sch.2 Form 12, amended: SI 1999/1343 r.2
Sch.2 Form 14, amended: SI 1999/1343 r.2
Sch.2 Form 20, amended: SI 1999/1343 r.2
Sch.2 Form 29, amended: SI 1997/2420 r.4
Sch.2 Form 31, amended: SI 1997/2420 r.5
Sch.2 Form 42, amended: SI 1997/2420 r.5
Sch.2 Form 43, amended: SI 1997/2420 r.6
Sch.2 Form 44, amended: SI 1997/2420 r.6
Sch.2 Form 46, amended: SI 1997/2420 r.7
Sch.2 Form 47, amended: SI 1997/2420 r.8

2074. Income Tax (Manufactured Interest) Regulations 1992
revoked: SI 1997/987 Reg.4 (with savings), Sch.2 (with savings)
Part V, revoked: SI 1997/987 Reg.4 (with savings), Sch.2 (with savings)
Part V, substituted: SI 1996/1227 Reg.10
Reg.2, amended: SI 1996/1227 Reg.3
Reg.2, revoked: SI 1997/987 Reg.4 (with savings), Sch.2 (with savings)
Reg.2A, revoked: SI 1996/1227 Reg.4
Reg.3, amended: SI 1996/1227 Reg.5
Reg.3, revoked: SI 1997/987 Reg.4 (with savings), Sch.2 (with savings)
Reg.6, revoked: SI 1996/1227 Reg.6
Reg.7, revoked: SI 1996/1227 Reg.6
Reg.8, revoked: SI 1997/987 Reg.4 (with savings), Sch.2 (with savings)
Reg.9, amended: SI 1996/1227 Reg.7
Reg.9, revoked: SI 1997/987 Reg.4 (with savings), Sch.2 (with savings)
Reg.10, amended: SI 1996/1227 Reg.8
Reg.10, revoked: SI 1997/987 Reg.4 (with savings), Sch.2 (with savings)
Reg.12, amended: SI 1996/1227 Reg.9
Reg.12, revoked: SI 1997/987 Reg.4 (with savings), Sch.2 (with savings)

2080. Prison (Amendment) (No.2) Rules 1992
revoked: SI 1999/728 r.85 (with savings), Sch. (with savings)

2082. Charities (Scheme for the Transfer of Assets) (Scotland) Regulations 1992
applied: SI 1999/678 Sch.

NO.

2087. Wireless Telegraphy Apparatus Approval and Test Fees Order 1992
revoked: SI 1997/3050 Art.2 (with savings)

2111. Organic Products Regulations 1992
Reg.2, amended: SI 1997/166 Reg.3
Reg.3A, added: SI 1997/166 Reg.4
Reg.6, amended: SI 1997/166 Reg.5
Sch., substituted: SI 1997/166 Reg.6, Sch.

2159. Nurses, Midwives and Health Visitors (Electoral Scheme) Rules 1992
applied: 1997 c.24 s.1
Appendix.II, amended: SI 1997/746 Sch. para.2
r.1, amended: SI 1997/746 Sch. para.2
r.1, revoked (in part): SI 1997/746 Sch. para.2
r.5, amended: SI 1997/746 Sch. para.2
r.6, amended: SI 1997/746 Sch. para.2
r.8, amended: SI 1997/746 Sch. para.2
r.14, amended: SI 1997/746 Sch. para.2

2165. Charities Accounts (Scotland) Regulations 1992
Reg.9, applied: SI 1999/678 Sch.

2182. Fines (Deductions from Income Support) Regulations 1992
applied: SI 1999/991 Reg.27, Sch.2 para.8, SI 1999/2784 Sch. para.35, Sch. para.36
Reg.1, amended: SI 1996/2344 Reg.10, SI 1998/563 Reg.3, SI 1999/2860 Art.3, Sch.9 para.1, SI 1999/3178 Art.3, Sch.12 para.1
Reg.2, amended: SI 1996/2344 Reg.11
Reg.4, amended: SI 1996/2344 Reg.12, SI 1997/827 Reg.8, SI 1999/2860 Art.3, Sch.9 para.2, Sch.9 para.3
Reg.4, referred to: SI 1999/991 Reg.27, Sch.2 para.8
Reg.4, substituted: SI 1999/3178 Art.3, Sch.12 para.2
Reg.5, amended: SI 1999/2860 Art.3, Sch.9 para.4
Reg.5, revoked: SI 1999/3178 Art.3, Sch.12 para.2
Reg.6, amended: SI 1996/2344 Reg.13, SI 1999/2860 Art.3, Sch.9 para.5
Reg.6, revoked: SI 1999/3178 Art.3, Sch.12 para.2
Reg.6A, added: SI 1996/2344 Reg.14
Reg.6A, amended: SI 1999/2860 Art.3, Sch.9 para.5
Reg.6A, revoked: SI 1999/3178 Art.3, Sch.12 para.2
Reg.7, amended: SI 1996/2344 Reg.15, SI 1999/2860 Art.3, Sch.9 para.6, SI 1999/3178 Art.3, Sch.12 para.3
Reg.9, substituted: SI 1999/2860 Art.3, Sch.9 para.7, SI 1999/3178 Art.3, Sch.12 para.4
Reg.10, revoked: SI 1999/2860 Art.3, Sch.9 para.8
Reg.10, substituted: SI 1999/3178 Art.3, Sch.12 para.4
Reg.11, revoked: SI 1999/2860 Art.3, Sch.9 para.8, SI 1999/3178 Art.3, Sch.12 para.5
Reg.12, revoked: SI 1999/2860 Art.3, Sch.9 para.8, SI 1999/3178 Art.3, Sch.12 para.5
Reg.13, revoked: SI 1999/2860 Art.3, Sch.9 para.8, SI 1999/3178 Art.3, Sch.12 para.5
Reg.14, revoked: SI 1999/2860 Art.3, Sch.9 para.8, SI 1999/3178 Art.3, Sch.12 para.5
Reg.15, revoked: SI 1999/2860 Art.3, Sch.9 para.8, SI 1999/3178 Art.3, Sch.12 para.5
Sch.1, revoked: SI 1999/2860 Art.3, Sch.9 para.9, SI 1999/3178 Art.3, Sch.12 para.5
Sch.2, revoked: SI 1999/2860 Art.3, Sch.9 para.9, SI 1999/3178 Art.3, Sch.12 para.5

NO.

2182. Fines (Deductions from Income Support) Regulations 1992—*cont.*
Sch.3, amended: SI 1996/2344 Reg.16

2184. Non-Domestic Rating (Payment of Interest) (Scotland) Regulations 1992
applied: SI 1996/3070 Sch.1 para.9
Reg.4, amended: SI 1998/1129 Art.3, Sch.2
Reg.4, applied: SI 1996/3070 Sch.1 para.9

2186. Registration of Births, Still-births, Deaths and Marriages (Prescription of Forms) (Scotland) Amendment (No.2) Regulations 1992
revoked: SI 1997/2348 Reg.30, Sch.27

2257. Education (London Residuary Body) (Transfer of Functions and Property) (No.2) Order 1992
Art.1, amended: SI 1997/1990 Art.4, SI 1998/1129 Art.3, Sch.2
Art.13, amended: SI 1997/1990 Art.4

2314. Offshore Installations (Safety Zones) (No.3) Order 1992
revoked: SI 1997/735 Art.3, Sch.2

2326. Insurance Companies (Pension Business) (Transitional Provisions) Regulations 1992
Reg.1, amended: SI 1996/1 Reg.3
Reg.2, amended: SI 1996/1 Reg.4
Reg.4, amended: SI 1996/1 Reg.5, SI 1997/2865 Reg.3
Reg.5, amended: SI 1996/1 Reg.6, SI 1997/2865 Reg.4
Reg.6, amended: SI 1997/2865 Reg.5

2337. South Ayrshire Hospitals National Health Service Trust (Appointment of Trustees) Order 1992
revoked: SI 1999/1134 Art.3, Sch.2

2339. Aberdeen Royal Hospitals National Health Trust (Appointment of Trustees) Order 1992
revoked: SI 1999/1134 Art.3, Sch.2

2357. Merchant Shipping (Passenger Ships of Classes IV, V VI and VI(A) - Bridge Visibility) Regulations 1992
Reg.1, amended: SI 1998/1419 Reg.3

2358. Merchant Shipping (Passenger Ship Construction and Survey) (Amendment) Regulations 1992
revoked: SI 1998/2514 Reg.1

2359. Merchant Shipping (Life-Saving Appliances for Passenger Ships of Classes III to VI(A)) Regulations 1992
applied: SI 1996/3243 Sch Part I
referred to: SI 1998/1609 Reg.5, Reg.6, Sch.
revoked: SI 1999/2723 Reg.1

2360. Merchant Shipping (Fire Protection) (Amendment) Regulations 1992
revoked: SI 1998/1012 Reg.1
Reg.1, revoked: SI 1998/1012 Reg.1

2364. Imported Food and Feedingstuffs (Safeguards against Cholera) (Amendment) Regulations 1992
revoked: SI 1996/1547 Reg.6, Sch.4

2372. Electromagnetic Compatibility Regulations 1992
applied: SI 1998/2306 Reg.10, Sch.1
Reg.6, amended: SI 1999/1957 Reg.3, Sch.1 para.7

2373. Electromagnetic Compatibility (Wireless Telegraphy Apparatus) Certification and Test Fees Regulations 1992
revoked: SI 1997/3051 Reg.2 (with savings)

NO.

2383. United Kingdom Ecolabelling Board Regulations 1992
applied: SI 1997/1941 Sch.3 para.15
referred to: SI 1996/600 Sch.5 para.15, SI 1996/601 Sch.5 para.15, SI 1997/1624 Sch.5 para.15
revoked: SI 1999/931 Reg.10

2414. Town and Country Planning (Simplified Planning Zones) Regulations 1992
Reg.22, revoked: SI 1999/293 Reg.34, Sch.5

2423. Telecommunications Terminal Equipment Regulations 1992
applied: SI 1999/2450 Sch.1 para.20.8
referred to: SI 1998/1580 Reg.21

2428. Local Authorities (Funds) (England) Regulations 1992
Reg.2, amended: SI 1999/3459 Reg.4
Reg.3, amended: SI 1999/3459 Reg.5
Reg.8, amended: SI 1998/1129 Art.3, Sch.2
Reg.12, amended: SI 1999/3459 Reg.6
Sch.2 para.6, amended: SI 1999/3459 Reg.7

2432. Local Government (Compensation for Premature Retirement) (Amendment) Regulations 1992
revoked: SI 1996/1680 Reg.49, Sch.5

2465. Southport and Formby Community Health Services National Health Service Trust (Establishment) Order 1992
revoked: SI 1999/889 Art.2

2467. Wigan and Leigh Health Services National Health Service Trust (Establishment) Order 1992
Art.3, substituted: SI 1999/2307 Art.2

2468. West Lancashire National Health Service Trust (Establishment) Order 1992
revoked: SI 1999/889 Art.2

2471. West Lindsey National Health Service Trust (Establishment) Order 1992
revoked: SI 1999/637 Art.2
Art.4, revoked: SI 1999/637 Art.2

2472. Leicester General Hospital National Health Service Trust (Establishment) Order 1992
revoked: SI 1999/3036 Art.2

2475. Nottinghamshire Ambulance Service National Health Service Trust (Establishment) Order 1992
revoked: SI 1999/791 Art.2

2476. Derby City General Hospital National Health Service Trust (Establishment) Order 1992
revoked: SI 1998/850 Art.2

2477. Central Nottinghamshire Healthcare National Health Service Trust (Establishment) Order 1992
Art.3, amended: SI 1996/2588 Art.2
Art.3, substituted: SI 1999/422 Art.2

2478. Queen's Medical Centre, Nottingham, University Hospital National Health Service Trust (Establishment) Order 1992
Art.3, substituted: SI 1998/2947 Art.2

2482. Rotherham Priority Health Services National Health Service Trust (Establishment) Order 1992
Art.3, substituted: SI 1998/1172 Art.2

2483. Leicester Royal Infirmary National Health Service Trust (Establishment) Order 1992
revoked: SI 1999/3036 Art.2

2485. South Lincolnshire Community and Mental Health Services National Health Service Trust (Establishment) Order 1992
Art.1, amended: SI 1999/792 Art.2
Art.2, amended: SI 1999/792 Art.2
Art.3, substituted: SI 1999/792 Art.4

NO.

2485. **South Lincolnshire Community and Mental Health Services National Health Service Trust (Establishment) Order 1992**—*cont.*
Art.4, amended: SI 1997/1186 Art.2, SI 1999/792 Art.5

2486. **Glenfield Hospital National Health Service Trust (Establishment) Order 1992**
revoked: SI 1999/3036 Art.2

2488. **Humberside Ambulance Service National Health Service Trust (Establishment) Order 1992**
revoked: SI 1999/799 Art.2
Art.4, revoked: SI 1999/799 Art.2

2489. **North Yorkshire Ambulance Service National Health Service Trust (Establishment) Order 1992**
revoked: SI 1999/799 Art.2

2490. **Pinderfields Hospitals National Health Service Trust (Establishment) Order 1992**
revoked: SI 1997/583 Art.2

2491. **Pontefract Hospitals National Health Service Trust (Establishment) Order 1992**
revoked: SI 1997/581 Art.2

2492. **Scunthorpe Community Health Care National Health Service Trust (Establishment) Order 1992**
revoked: SI 1999/2655 Art.2

2493. **West Yorkshire Metropolitan Ambulance Service National Health Service Trust (Establishment) Order 1992**
Art.4, amended: SI 1997/1400 Art.2

2496. **Grimsby Health National Health Service Trust (Establishment) Order 1992**
Art.1, amended: SI 1996/2034 Art.2
Art.2, amended: SI 1996/2034 Art.2

2497. **Leeds Community and Mental Health Services Teaching National Health Service Trust (Establishment) Order 1992**
Art.3, amended: SI 1998/2478 Art.2
Art.3, substituted: SI 1998/322 Art.2

2498. **Calderdale Healthcare National Health Service Trust (Establishment) Order 1992**
Art.3, amended: SI 1997/835 Art.2

2499. **Royal Hull Hospital's National Health Service Trust (Establishment) Order 1992**
revoked: SI 1999/2674 Art.2
Art.4, revoked: SI 1999/2674 Art.2

2500. **East Yorkshire Hospitals National Health Service Trust (Establishment) Order 1992**
revoked: SI 1999/2674 Art.2
Art.3, revoked: SI 1999/2674 Art.2
Art.3, substituted: SI 1998/2485 Art.2

2502. **Isle of Wight Community Healthcare National Health Service Trust (Establishment) Order 1992**
revoked: SI 1996/2766 Art.2

2507. **St Mary's Hospital National Health Service Trust (Establishment) Order 1992**
revoked: SI 1996/2767 Art.2

2509. **Southampton University Hospitals National Health Service Trust (Establishment) Order 1992**
Art.4, amended: SI 1999/884 Art.4

2511. **Enfield Community Care National Health Service Trust (Establishment) Order 1992**
Art.3, substituted: SI 1998/1280 Art.2

2516. **Chase Farm Hospitals National Health Service Trust (Establishment) Order 1992**
revoked: SI 1999/893 Art.2

2517. **Redbridge Health Care National Health Service Trust (Establishment) Order 1992**
Art.3, substituted: SI 1999/2085 Art.2

NO.

2518. **Royal London Homeopathic National Health Service Trust (Establishment) Order 1992**
revoked: SI 1999/909 Art.2

2521. **Crawley Horsham National Health Service Trust (Establishment) Order 1992**
revoked: SI 1998/692 Art.2

2522. **East Surrey Hospital and Community Healthcare National Health Service Trust (Establishment) Order 1992**
revoked: SI 1998/692 Art.2
Art.2, revoked: SI 1998/692 Art.2

2523. **Richmond, Twickenham and Roehampton Healthcare National Health Service Trust (Establishment) Order 1992**
revoked: SI 1999/793 Art.2

2524. **Merton and Sutton Community National Health Service Trust (Establishment) Order 1992**
revoked: SI 1999/793 Art.2

2527. **Gloucestershire Royal National Health Service Trust (Establishment) Order 1992**
Art.3, amended: SI 1996/986 Art.2

2528. **Thanet Health Care National Health Service Trust (Establishment) Order 1992**
revoked: SI 1999/897 Art.2

2529. **Canterbury and Thanet Community Healthcare National Health Service Trust (Establishment) Order 1992**
Art.1, amended: SI 1998/845 Art.2
Art.2, amended: SI 1998/845 Art.2
Art.3, substituted: SI 1998/845 Art.3

2530. **Queen Mary's Sidcup National Health Service Trust (Establishment) Order 1992**
Art.3, amended: SI 1998/1341 Art.2

2532. **Kent and Canterbury Hospitals National Health Service Trust (Establishment) Order 1992**
revoked: SI 1999/897 Art.2

2533. **Greenwich Healthcare National Health Service Trust (Establishment) Order 1992**
Art.3, substituted: SI 1998/1417 Art.2
Sch., added: SI 1998/1417 Art.2, Sch.

2535. **Bromley Hospitals National Health Service Trust (Establishment) Order 1992**
Art.3, substituted: SI 1998/1171 Art.2, SI 1998/2486 Art.2
Sch., added: SI 1998/1171 Art.2, Sch.

2537. **Northwick Park Hospital National Health Service Trust (Establishment) Order 1992**
revoked: SI 1999/914 Art.2
Art.3, substituted: SI 1998/754 Art.2

2538. **Bedfordshire and Hertfordshire Ambulance and Paramedic Service National Health Service Trust (Establishment) Order 1992**
Art.4, amended: SI 1997/2 Art.2

2539. **West London Healthcare National Health Service Trust (Establishment) Order 1992**
revoked: SI 1998/2964 Art.2

2541. **Riverside Mental Health National Health Service Trust (Establishment) Order 1992**
revoked: SI 1998/2964 Art.2

2544. **South Cumbria Community and Mental Health National Health Service Trust (Establishment) Order 1992**
revoked: SI 1998/819 Art.2

2545. **Durham County Ambulance Service National Health Service Trust (Establishment) Order 1992**
revoked: SI 1999/796 Art.2
Art.4, revoked: SI 1999/796 Art.2

NO.

2546. Cumbria Ambulance Service National Health Service Trust (Establishment) Order 1992
Art.4, amended: SI 1998/1213 Art.2

2547. South West Durham Mental Health National Health Service Trust (Establishment) Order 1992
revoked: SI 1996/876 Art.2

2548. Westmorland Hospitals National Health Service Trust (Establishment) Order 1992
revoked: SI 1998/818 Art.2

2550. Gateshead Hospitals National Health Service Trust (Establishment) Order 1992
revoked: SI 1998/824 Art.2

2551. South Tees Community and Mental Health National Health Service Trust (Establishment) Order 1992
revoked: SI 1999/800 Art.2

2552. North Warwickshire National Health Service Trust (Establishment) Order 1992
Art.3, amended: SI 1998/814 Art.2

2555. South Worcestershire Community National Health Service Trust (Establishment) Order 1992
revoked: SI 1996/884 Art.2

2557. Shropshire's Mental Health National Health Service Trust (Establishment) Order 1992
revoked: SI 1998/518 Art.2

2560. Kidderminster Health Care National Health Service Trust (Establishment) Order 1992
revoked: SI 1999/3471 Art.2

2564. North East Worcestershire Community Health National Health Service Trust (Establishment) Order 1992
revoked: SI 1996/885 Art.2

2569. James Paget Hospital NHS Trust (Establishment) Order 1992
amended: SI 1997/1724 Art.2
Art.1, amended: SI 1997/1724 Art.2
Art.2, amended: SI 1997/1724 Art.2

2571. Lifespan Health Care Cambridge National Health Service Trust (Establishment) Order 1992
Art.3, substituted: SI 1998/957 Art.2

2573. Mid Anglia Community Health National Health Service Trust (Establishment) Order 1992
revoked: SI 1999/850 Art.2

2576. Horton General Hospital National Health Service Trust (Establishment) Order 1992
revoked: SI 1998/806 Art.2

2580. Radcliffe Infirmary National Health Service Trust (Establishment) Order 1992
revoked: SI 1999/1414 Art.2

2582. East Berkshire Community Health National Health Service Trust (Establishment) Order 1992
Art.3, substituted: SI 1998/1733 Art.2

2583. East Suffolk Local Health Services National Health Service Trust (Establishment) Order 1992
revoked: SI 1999/850 Art.2

2584. Southampton Community Health Services National Health Service Trust (Establishment) Order 1992
Art.3, substituted: SI 1998/3098 Art.2
Sch., added: SI 1998/3098 Art.2, Sch.

2585. West Middlesex University Hospital National Health Service Trust (Establishment) Order 1992
Art.3, amended: SI 1996/985 Art.2

NO.

2587. Bedford and Shires Health and Care National Health Service Trust (Establishment) Order 1992
revoked: SI 1999/894 Art.2

2588. Avalon, Somerset, National Health Service Trust (Establishment) Order 1992
Art.1, amended: SI 1999/3050 Art.2
Art.2, amended: SI 1999/3050 Art.2

2596. Food (Forces Exemptions) (Revocations) Regulations 1992
Sch. Part I, revoked (in part): SI 1996/1499 Reg.49, Sch.9
Sch. Part II, revoked (in part): SI 1996/1499 Reg.49, Sch.9
Sch. Part III, revoked (in part): SI 1999/1540 Reg.21, Sch.4

2597. Food Safety (Amendment) (Metrication) Regulations 1992
Reg.9, revoked: SI 1996/1499 Reg.49, Sch.9

2599. Swansea and Lliw Valley Youth Court Panel Order 1992
revoked: SI 1996/463 Sch.1 para.3

2633. Sea Fish Licensing Order 1992
applied: SI 1999/1512 Art.2, Sch.1 para.1, Sch.2 para.1
Art.2, amended: SI 1999/1820 Art.4, Sch.2 para.150
Art.3, amended: SI 1999/1820 Art.4, Sch.2 para.150

2640. Child Support Commissioners (Procedure) Regulations 1992
revoked (in part): SI 1999/1305 Reg.2
Reg.1, amended: SI 1997/955 Reg.10, SI 1997/802 Reg.2
Reg.1, revoked (in part): SI 1999/1305 Reg.2
Reg.2, amended: SI 1997/955 Reg.11
Reg.2, revoked (in part): SI 1999/1305 Reg.2
Reg.3, amended: SI 1997/955 Reg.12, SI 1997/802 Reg.3, Reg.4
Reg.3, revoked (in part): SI 1999/1305 Reg.2
Reg.5, amended: SI 1997/955 Reg.13
Reg.5, revoked (in part): SI 1999/1305 Reg.2
Reg.9, amended: SI 1997/802 Reg.5
Reg.9, revoked (in part): SI 1999/1305 Reg.2
Reg.22, revoked (in part): SI 1999/1305 Reg.2
Reg.22, substituted: SI 1997/802 Reg.6
Reg.23A, added: SI 1996/243 Reg.2
Reg.23A, revoked (in part): SI 1999/1305 Reg.2

2641. Child Support Appeal Tribunals (Procedure) Regulations 1992
applied: SI 1999/1510 Art.48
referred to: SI 1999/1510 Art.48
revoked: SI 1999/991 Reg.59 (with savings), Sch.4 (with savings)
Reg.1, amended: SI 1996/2907 Reg.52, SI 1998/58 Reg.2
Reg.2, substituted: SI 1996/3196 Reg.2
Reg.3, amended: SI 1996/2450 Reg.14, SI 1996/2907 Reg.53, SI 1996/3196 Reg.3, SI 1997/827 Reg.9, SI 1998/58 Reg.3, SI 1999/1510 Art.48
Reg.3, applied: SI 1996/2450 Reg.22, SI 1999/1510 Art.48
Reg.4, applied: SI 1999/1510 Art.48
Reg.5, amended: SI 1996/2450 Reg.15, SI 1996/2907 Reg.54, SI 1998/58 Reg.4
Reg.5, applied: SI 1999/1510 Art.48
Reg.6, amended: SI 1996/2450 Reg.16, SI 1996/2907 Reg.55
Reg.6, applied: SI 1996/2450 Reg.22, SI 1999/1510 Art.48
Reg.7, amended: SI 1996/2450 Reg.17, SI 1996/2907 Reg.56

NO.

2641. **Child Support Appeal Tribunals (Procedure) Regulations 1992**—*cont.*
Reg.7, applied: SI 1999/1510 Art.48
Reg.8, amended: SI 1996/2450 Reg.18
Reg.8, applied: SI 1999/1510 Art.48
Reg.9, applied: SI 1999/1510 Art.48
Reg.10, amended: SI 1996/2907 Reg.57
Reg.10, applied: SI 1999/1510 Art.48
Reg.11, amended: SI 1996/2450 Reg.11, SI 1996/2907 Reg.58, SI 1998/58 Reg.5
Reg.11, applied: SI 1996/2450 Reg.22, SI 1999/1510 Art.48
Reg.11, referred to: SI 1999/1510 Art.48
Reg.11A, added: SI 1996/2907 Reg.59
Reg.11B, added: SI 1996/2907 Reg.59
Reg.12, applied: SI 1999/1510 Art.48
Reg.13, amended: SI 1996/182 Reg.3, SI 1996/2450 Reg.20, SI 1996/2907 Reg.60
Reg.13, applied: SI 1999/1510 Art.48
Reg.14, amended: SI 1996/2907 Reg.61
Reg.14, applied: SI 1999/1510 Art.48
Reg.15, amended: SI 1996/2450 Reg.21, SI 1999/1510 Art.48
Reg.15, applied: SI 1999/1510 Art.48
Reg.17, referred to: SI 1999/1510 Art.48
Reg.17, substituted: SI 1996/1945 Reg.2

2644. **Child Support Act 1991 (Commencement No.3 and Transitional Provisions) Order 1992**
Sch. Part II, amended: SI 1999/1510 Art.30

2645. **Child Support (Maintenance Arrangements and Jurisdiction) Regulations 1992**
Reg.3, amended: SI 1999/1510 Art.31
Reg.4, amended: SI 1999/1510 Art.31
Reg.5, amended: SI 1999/1510 Art.31
Reg.7, amended: SI 1999/1510 Art.31
Reg.8, amended: SI 1999/1510 Art.31
Reg.8, applied: SI 1996/2907 Reg.35

2655. **International Organisations (Miscellaneous Exemptions) Order 1992**
revoked: SI 1997/168 Art.4

2656. **Scottish Land Court Rules 1992**
Sch. r.60, amended: SI 1999/1820 Art.4, Sch.2 para.151

2677. **Sheep Annual Premium Regulations 1992**
applied: SI 1996/1500 Reg.9, SI 1999/672 Art.2, Sch.1, SI 1999/3315 Reg.4, SSI 1999/187 Reg.14
Reg.3, amended: SI 1997/2500 Reg.2
Reg.3, applied: SI 1997/2844 Reg.4
Reg.4, revoked (in part): SI 1996/49 Reg.2
Reg.5, amended: SI 1996/49 Reg.2

2730. **Gwent Community Health National Health Service Trust (Establishment) Order 1992**
revoked: SI 1999/1120 Art.2, Sch.2
Art.4, revoked: SI 1999/1120 Art.2, Sch.2

2731. **Wrexham Maelor Hospital National Health Service Trust (Establishment) Order 1992**
revoked: SI 1999/1120 Art.2, Sch.2

2732. **Glan Clwyd District General Hospital National Health Service Trust (Establishment) Order 1992**
revoked: SI 1999/1120 Art.2, Sch.2

2733. **Glan Hafren National Health Service Trust (Establishment) Order 1992**
revoked: SI 1996/256 Art.2

2734. **Llanelli Dinefwr National Health Service Trust (Establishment) Order 1992**
revoked: SI 1999/1120 Art.2, Sch.2

2736. **Swansea National Health Service Trust (Establishment) Order 1992**
revoked: SI 1999/1120 Art.2, Sch.2

NO.

2737. **Llandough Hospital National Health Service Trust (Establishment) Order 1992**
revoked: SI 1999/1120 Art.2, Sch.2
Art.2, revoked: SI 1999/1120 Art.2, Sch.2
Art.3, revoked: SI 1999/1120 Art.2, Sch.2
Art.3, substituted: SI 1998/770 Art.2

2738. **Bridgend and District National Health Service Trust (Establishment) Order 1992**
revoked: SI 1996/255 Art.2

2739. **Gofal Cymuned Clwydian Community Care National Health Service Trust (Establishment) Order 1992**
revoked: SI 1999/1120 Art.2, Sch.2

2740. **South and East Wales Ambulance National Health Service Trust (Establishment) Order 1992**
revoked: SI 1998/679 Art.2
Art.4, revoked: SI 1998/679 Art.2
Art.4, substituted: SI 1996/2288 Art.2

2742. **Carmarthen and District National Health Service Trust (Establishment) Order 1992**
revoked: SI 1999/1120 Art.2, Sch.2

2762. **County Court Fees (Amendment) Order 1992**
revoked: SI 1999/689 Art.8 (with savings), Sch.2 (with savings)

2789. **Transport Levying Bodies Regulations 1992**
Reg.2, amended: SI 1997/165 Reg.3, Reg.4

2790. **Statistics of Trade (Customs and Excise) Regulations 1992**
Reg.1, amended: SI 1997/2864 Reg.3
Reg.3, amended: SI 1996/2968 Reg.4, SI 1997/2864 Reg.4, SI 1998/2973 Reg.2, SI 1999/3269 Reg.2
Reg.4A, revoked: SI 1997/2864 Reg.5
Reg.5, amended: SI 1997/2864 Reg.6
Reg.6, amended: SI 1997/2864 Reg.7
Reg.6, revoked (in part): SI 1997/2864 Reg.7

2793. **Manual Handling Operations Regulations 1992**
referred to: SI 1998/2857 Reg.3

2796. **Council Tax (Exempt Dwellings) (Scotland) Amendment Order 1992**
revoked: SI 1997/728 Art.5, Sch.2

2804. **Income Support (General) Amendment (No.3) Regulations 1992**
revoked: SI 1996/206 Reg.28, Sch.3

2819. **Local Authorities (Capital Finance) (Amendment) (No.3) Regulations 1992**
revoked: SI 1997/319 Reg.162, Sch.3

2821. **Firearms (Scotland) Amendment Rules 1992**
revoked: SI 1998/1941 r.12, Sch.6

2824. **Firearms (Amendment) Rules 1992**
revoked: SI 1998/1941 r.12, Sch.6

2852. **Offshore Installations (Safety Zones) (No.4) Order 1992**
revoked: SI 1997/735 Art.3, Sch.2

2871. **European Communities (Definition of Treaties) (Europe Agreement establishing an Association between the European Communities and their Member States and the Republic of Hungary) Order 1992**
referred to: SI 1996/2911 Sch.2

2872. **European Communities (Definition of Treaties) (Europe Agreement establishing an Association between the European Communities and their Member States and the Republic of Poland) Order 1992**
referred to: SI 1996/2911 Sch.2

2882. **Faculty Jurisdiction Rules 1992**
applied: SI 1996/3085 Sch. Table I
r.30, see *All Saints Church, Ecclesall, Re* Times, June 8, 1998 (Cons Ct), David McClean Q.C.

NO.

2885. Offshore Installations (Safety Case) Regulations 1992

Reg.2, amended: SI 1996/913 Sch.2 para.2, Sch.2 para.3, Sch.2 para.4, Sch.2 para.5, SI 1997/2776 Reg.19, Sch.2 para.4
Reg.8, amended: SI 1996/913 Sch.2 para.6
Reg.11, amended: SI 1996/913 Sch.2 para.7
Reg.13A, added: SI 1996/913 Sch.2 para.8
Reg.15, amended: SI 1996/913 Sch.2 para.9, Sch.2 para.10
Reg.15A, added: SI 1996/913 Sch.2 para.11
Reg.15B, added: SI 1996/913 Sch.2 para.11
Reg.15C, added: SI 1996/913 Sch.2 para.11
Reg.15D, added: SI 1996/913 Sch.2 para.11
Reg.15E, added: SI 1996/913 Sch.2 para.11
Sch.2, amended: SI 1996/913 Reg.26
Sch.2 para.9A, added: SI 1996/913 Sch.2 para.12
Sch.3 para.7A, added: SI 1996/913 Sch.2 para.13
Sch.6, amended: SI 1996/913 Sch.2 para.14
Sch.6A, added: SI 1996/913 Sch.2 para.15
Sch.9, added: SI 1996/913 Sch.2 para.16

2890. Insurance Companies (Amendment) Regulations 1992

Reg.17, revoked (in part): SI 1996/943 Reg.35, Sch.7

2902. Transport and Works (Applications and Objections Procedure) Rules 1992

applied: SI 1996/2714, SI 1997/264, SI 1997/1266, SI 1997/1688, SI 1997/2232, SI 1997/2262, SI 1998/1936, SI 1998/2919, SI 1999/50, SI 1999/217, SI 1999/537, SI 1999/1306, SI 1999/1555, SI 1999/1664, SI 1999/2129, SI 1999/2336, SI 1999/2400, SI 1999/2587, SI 1999/2981
referred to: SI 1997/2465, SI 1997/2466, SI 1998/3269
r.2, amended: SI 1996/252 Art.2, Sch
Sch.2, amended: SI 1997/1744 Art.2, Sch. para.4
Sch.2, applied: SI 1997/1744 Art.2, Sch. para.4
Sch.5, amended: SI 1997/1744 Art.2, Sch. para.4
Sch.5, applied: SI 1997/1744 Art.2, Sch. para.4

2903. Levying Bodies (General) Regulations 1992

Reg.10, amended: SI 1998/1129 Art.3, Sch.2

2905. National Health Service Trusts (Consultation on Dissolution) Amendment Regulations 1992

revoked: SI 1996/653 Reg.3

2913. Social Security (Unemployment, Sickness and Invalidity Benefit) Amendment Regulations 1992

revoked: SI 1996/1345 Reg.27, Sch.

2929. Local Authorities (Funds) (Wales) Regulations 1992

Reg.8, amended: SI 1998/1129 Art.3, Sch.2

2932. Provision and Use of Work Equipment Regulations 1992

revoked: SI 1998/2306 Reg.39, Sch.4
Reg.2, see *Kelly v First Engineering Ltd* 1999 S.C.L.R. 1025 (OH), Lord Abernethy
Reg.5, see *English v North Lanarkshire Council* 1999 S.C.L.R. 310 (OH), Lord Reed
Reg.6, see *Kelly v First Engineering Ltd* 1999 S.C.L.R. 1025 (OH), Lord Abernethy
Reg.8, see *English v North Lanarkshire Council* 1999 S.C.L.R. 310 (OH), Lord Reed

NO.

2932. Provision and Use of Work Equipment Regulations 1992—*cont.*

Reg.9, see *English v North Lanarkshire Council* 1999 S.C.L.R. 310 (OH), Lord Reed
Reg.10, applied: SI 1996/192 Reg.21, SI 1997/831 Reg.24
Reg.10, revoked: SI 1998/2306 Reg.39, Sch.4
Reg.11, see *English v North Lanarkshire Council* 1999 S.C.L.R. 310 (OH), Lord Reed
Sch.1, applied: SI 1997/831 Reg.24
Sch.1, revoked: SI 1998/2306 Reg.39, Sch.4
Sch.1 para.1, revoked: SI 1998/2306 Reg.39, Sch.4
Sch.1 para.25, revoked: SI 1998/2306 Reg.39, Sch.4
Sch.1 para.28, revoked: SI 1998/2306 Reg.39, Sch.4
Sch.1 para.29, revoked: SI 1998/2306 Reg.39, Sch.4
Sch.1 para.31, amended: SI 1996/3039 Reg.2
Sch.1 para.31, revoked: SI 1998/2306 Reg.39, Sch.4
Sch.1 para.33, revoked: SI 1998/2306 Reg.39, Sch.4
Sch.1 para.36, revoked: SI 1998/2306 Reg.39, Sch.4
Sch.1 para.37, added: SI 1996/192 Reg.21
Sch.1 para.37, revoked: SI 1998/2306 Reg.39, Sch.4
Sch.1 para.38, added: SI 1997/831 Reg.24
Sch.1 para.38, revoked: SI 1998/2306 Reg.39, Sch.4

2937. Medicines (Products Other Than Veterinary Drugs) (Prescription Only) Amendment (No.2) Order 1992

revoked: SI 1997/1830 Art.16, Sch.6

2957. River Roach Oyster Fishery Order 1992

Art.9, amended: SI 1996/362 Art.5, Sch.4

2964. Act of Sederunt (Proceedings in the Sheriff Court under the Debtors (Scotland) Act 1987) (Amendment) 1992

revoked: SI 1996/2709 r.3, Sch.2

2966. Personal Protective Equipment at Work Regulations 1992

referred to: SI 1999/2205 Reg.3
Reg.3, amended: SI 1999/3232 Reg.41, Sch.9 para.3
Reg.4, amended: SI 1999/860 Reg.4
Sch.1, amended: SI 1996/3039 Reg.2
Sch.2 Part VI, revoked: SI 1999/3232 Reg.41

2977. National Assistance (Assessment of Resources) Regulations 1992

see *R. v Sefton MBC Ex p. Help the Aged* [1997] 4 All E.R. 532 (CA), Lord Woolf, M.R.; see *R. v Somerset CC Ex p. Harcombe* (1997) 37 B.M.L.R. 1 (QBD), Forbes, J.; see *Yule v South Lanarkshire Council* 1998 S.L.T. 490 (OH), Lord Philip
Reg.2, amended: SI 1996/602 Reg.2, SI 1997/485 Reg.2, SI 1998/1730 Reg.2
Reg.20, amended: SI 1996/602 Reg.2
Reg.23, amended: SI 1998/1730 Reg.3
Reg.25, see *Yule v South Lanarkshire Council (No.2)* 1999 S.C.L.R. 985 (OH), Lord Philip
Reg.25, amended: SI 1998/497 Reg.2
Reg.28, substituted: SI 1996/602 Reg.2
Reg.29, amended: SI 1998/1730 Reg.4
Sch.3 para.10A, added: SI 1996/602 Reg.2
Sch.3 para.10A, amended: SI 1997/485 Reg.2
Sch.4, see *R. v Somerset CC Ex p. Harcombe* (1997) 37 B.M.L.R. 1 (QBD), Forbes, J.
Sch.4 para.1, amended: SI 1998/1730 Reg.5

NO.

1992—cont.

2977. National Assistance (Assessment of Resources) Regulations 1992—*cont.*
Sch.4 para.5, amended: SI 1998/1730 Reg.5
Sch.4 para.19, added: SI 1998/497 Reg.3

2985. Street Works (Registers, Notices, Directions and Designations) Regulations 1992
Reg.3, applied: SI 1999/1048 Reg.3, SI 1999/2106 Art.2, Sch.2 para.10
Reg.5, applied: SI 1999/2106 Art.2, Sch.2 para.10
Reg.7, applied: SI 1999/2106 Art.2, Sch.2 para.10
Reg.8, applied: SI 1999/2106 Art.2, Sch.2 para.10
Reg.11, applied: SI 1999/2106 Art.2, Sch.2 para.10
Reg.12, applied: SI 1999/2106 Art.2, Sch.2 para.10
Reg.13, applied: SI 1999/2106 Art.2, Sch.2 para.10
Sch.1 Part IIA, added: SI 1999/1049 Reg.2
Sch.1 para.8A, added: SI 1999/1049 Reg.2
Sch.1 para.13, substituted: SI 1999/1049 Reg.2

2991. Road Works (Registers, Notices, Directions, and Designations) (Scotland) Regulations 1992
Reg.3, amended: SI 1997/1505 Reg.2
Reg.3 Table, amended: SI 1997/1505 Reg.2
Reg.13, amended: SI 1997/1505 Reg.2
Sch.3, added: SI 1997/1505 Reg.2
Sch.3, amended: SI 1998/2254 Reg.2

2992. Licensing of Air Carriers Regulations 1992
referred to: SI 1996/2199 Reg.28
Reg.11, revoked (in part): SI 1998/1751 Art.5

3004. Workplace (Health, Safety and Welfare) Regulations 1992
Reg.2, amended: SI 1999/2024 Reg.48, Sch.5 Part II
Reg.3, amended: SI 1996/1592 Reg.34, Sch.9 para.5

3014. Drink-Drive Offenders (Designation of Areas) Order 1992
revoked: SI 1997/2913 Art.2

3023. Council Tax (Prescribed Class of Dwellings) (Wales) Regulations 1992
Reg.3, amended: SI 1998/105 Reg.7

3025. Local Government Superannuation (Scotland) Amendment Regulations 1992
applied: SI 1998/364 Reg.4, Reg.6, Reg.19, Sch.2 para.2, Sch.2 para.5, Sch.4 para.8
referred to: SI 1998/364 Reg.3, Reg.10, Sch.2 para.4, Sch.2 para.6

3027. Bass (Specified Areas) (Prohibition of Fishing) (Variation) Order 1992
revoked: SI 1999/75 Art.3

3036. Motor Vehicles (Compulsory Insurance) Regulations 1992
see *R. v Secretary of State for Transport Ex p. National Insurance Guarantee Corp Plc* Times, June 3, 1996 (QBD), Popplewell, J.

3038. Wash Fishery Order 1992
Art.16, amended: SI 1996/362 Art.5, Sch.4

3045. Horses (Zootechnical Standards) Regulations 1992
applied: SI 1997/2789 Art.3

3046. National Health Service (Superannuation, Premature Retirement and Injury Benefits) (Scotland) Amendment Regulations 1992
Reg.17, revoked: SI 1998/1594 Reg.24, Sch.
Reg.18, revoked: SI 1998/1594 Reg.24, Sch.
Reg.19, revoked: SI 1998/1594 Reg.24, Sch.
Reg.20, revoked: SI 1998/1594 Reg.24, Sch.
Reg.21, revoked: SI 1998/1594 Reg.24, Sch.

NO.

1992—cont.

3056. Public Airport Companies (Capital Finance) (Third Amendment) Order 1992
revoked: SI 1996/604 Reg.5

3060. Railway Regulations 1992
revoked: SI 1998/1340 Reg.2
Reg.2, revoked: SI 1998/1340 Reg.2
Reg.4, revoked: SI 1998/1340 Reg.2
Reg.6, revoked: SI 1998/1340 Reg.2
Reg.8, revoked: SI 1998/1340 Reg.2
Reg.9, revoked: SI 1998/1340 Reg.2
Reg.14, revoked: SI 1998/1340 Reg.2
Reg.15, revoked: SI 1998/1340 Reg.2
Sch.1 r.1, revoked: SI 1998/1340 Reg.2
Sch.1 r.2, revoked: SI 1998/1340 Reg.2
Sch.1 r.3, revoked: SI 1998/1340 Reg.2
Sch.1 r.4, revoked: SI 1998/1340 Reg.2
Sch.1 r.5, revoked: SI 1998/1340 Reg.2

3061. Non-Domestic Rating Contributions (Scotland) Regulations 1992
revoked: SI 1996/3070 Reg.10, Sch.4
Reg.2, revoked: SI 1996/3070 Reg.10, Sch.4
Sch.1 para.9, revoked: SI 1996/3070 Reg.10, Sch.4
Sch.1 para.10, revoked: SI 1996/3070 Reg.10, Sch.4
Sch.2 para.2, revoked: SI 1996/3070 Reg.10, Sch.4
Sch.2 para.3, revoked: SI 1996/3070 Reg.10, Sch.4
Sch.3 para.3, revoked: SI 1996/3070 Reg.10, Sch.4

3067. Asbestos (Prohibitions) Regulations 1992
Reg.2, amended: SI 1999/2373 Reg.2
Reg.3, substituted: SI 1999/2373 Reg.2
Reg.4, amended: SI 1999/2373 Reg.2
Reg.5, amended: SI 1999/2373 Reg.2
Reg.7, substituted: SI 1999/2373 Reg.2
Reg.8, amended: SI 1999/2373 Reg.2
Sch., substituted: SI 1999/2373 Reg.2, Sch.
Sch. para.1, amended: SI 1999/2977 Reg.2
Sch. para.2, amended: SI 1999/2977 Reg.2
Sch. para.9, amended: SI 1999/2977 Reg.2

3073. Supply of Machinery (Safety) Regulations 1992
applied: SI 1998/2306 Reg.10, Sch.1

3077. Goods Vehicles (Community Authorisations) Regulations 1992
Reg.15, revoked: SI 1996/2186 Reg.2, Sch.1

3081. Medicines (Veterinary Drugs) (Pharmacy and Merchants' List) (Amendment) Order 1992
revoked: SI 1998/1044 Art.9, Sch.

3082. Non-Domestic Rating Contributions (England) Regulations 1992
Reg.6, amended: SI 1996/561 Reg.2
Sch.1 Part II, amended: SI 1996/3245 Reg.3, SI 1997/3031 Reg.3, SI 1998/3038 Reg.3
Sch.1 Part II, substituted: SI 1999/3275 Reg.3
Sch.1 para.1, amended: SI 1996/3245 Reg.3, SI 1997/3031 Reg.3, SI 1998/3038 Reg.3, SI 1999/3275 Reg.3
Sch.1 para.3, amended: SI 1997/3031 Reg.4
Sch.1 para.4, amended: SI 1996/3245 Reg.3, SI 1997/3031 Reg.3, SI 1998/3038 Reg.3, SI 1999/3275 Reg.3
Sch.2 Part II, substituted: SI 1999/3275 Reg.5
Sch.2 para.2, amended: SI 1996/3245 Reg.4, SI 1997/3031 Reg.5, SI 1998/3038 Reg.4, SI 1999/3275 Reg.4

NO.

3082. Non-Domestic Rating Contributions (England) Regulations 1992—*cont.*

Sch.2 para.8, amended: SI 1996/3245 Reg.4, SI 1997/3031 Reg.5, SI 1998/3038 Reg.4, SI 1999/3275 Reg.4

3089. Motor Vehicles (Driving Licences) (Large Goods and Passenger-Carrying Vehicles) (Amendment) (No.5) Regulations 1992

revoked: SI 1996/2824 Reg.2, Sch.1

3090. Motor Vehicles (Driving Licences) (Amendment) (No.4) Regulations 1992

revoked: SI 1996/2824 Reg.2, Sch.1

3094. Child Support Fees Regulations 1992

Reg.1, amended: SI 1996/1945 Reg.5

Reg.3, amended: SI 1996/1345 Reg.4, SI 1996/1945 Reg.6, SI 1996/3196 Reg.4, SI 1999/977 Reg.3

3107. Motor Vehicles (EC Type Approval) Regulations 1992

applied: SI 1997/564 Reg.13, SI 1998/2051 Reg.19

Reg.2, amended: SI 1997/1501 Reg.3

Reg.2, revoked: SI 1998/2051 Reg.2, Sch.3

Reg.3, revoked: SI 1998/2051 Reg.2, Sch.3

Reg.4, revoked: SI 1998/2051 Reg.2, Sch.3

Reg.5, revoked: SI 1998/2051 Reg.2, Sch.3

Reg.6, revoked: SI 1998/2051 Reg.2, Sch.3

Reg.7, revoked: SI 1998/2051 Reg.2, Sch.3

Reg.8, revoked: SI 1998/2051 Reg.2, Sch.3

Reg.9, revoked: SI 1998/2051 Reg.2, Sch.3

Reg.10, amended: SI 1997/1501 Reg.4

Reg.10, revoked: SI 1998/2051 Reg.2, Sch.3

Reg.10A, added: SI 1997/1501 Reg.5

Reg.10A, revoked: SI 1998/2051 Reg.2, Sch.3

Reg.11, revoked: SI 1998/2051 Reg.2, Sch.3

Reg.12, amended: SI 1997/1501 Reg.6

Reg.12, revoked: SI 1998/2051 Reg.2, Sch.3

Reg.13, revoked: SI 1998/2051 Reg.2, Sch.3

Reg.14, revoked: SI 1998/2051 Reg.2, Sch.3

Reg.15, revoked: SI 1998/2051 Reg.2, Sch.3

Reg.17, revoked: SI 1998/2051 Reg.2, Sch.3

Reg.18, revoked: SI 1998/2051 Reg.2, Sch.3

Sch.1, revoked: SI 1998/2051 Reg.2, Sch.3

Sch.1 Item 1, revoked: SI 1998/2051 Reg.2, Sch.3

Sch.1 Item 1, substituted: SI 1997/191 Reg.2

Sch.1 Item 2, revoked: SI 1998/2051 Reg.2, Sch.3

Sch.1 Item 2, substituted: SI 1997/191 Reg.2

Sch.1 Item 10, revoked: SI 1998/2051 Reg.2, Sch.3

Sch.1 Item 10, substituted: SI 1997/191 Reg.2

Sch.1 Item 11, revoked: SI 1998/2051 Reg.2, Sch.3

Sch.1 Item 11, substituted: SI 1997/191 Reg.2

Sch.1 Item 13, revoked: SI 1998/2051 Reg.2, Sch.3

Sch.1 Item 13, substituted: SI 1997/191 Reg.2

Sch.1 Item 15, revoked: SI 1998/2051 Reg.2, Sch.3

Sch.1 Item 15, substituted: SI 1997/191 Reg.2

Sch.1 Item 19, revoked: SI 1998/2051 Reg.2, Sch.3

Sch.1 Item 19, substituted: SI 1997/191 Reg.2

Sch.1 Item 27, revoked: SI 1998/2051 Reg.2, Sch.3

Sch.1 Item 27, substituted: SI 1997/191 Reg.2

Sch.1 Item 31, revoked: SI 1998/2051 Reg.2, Sch.3

Sch.1 Item 31, substituted: SI 1997/191 Reg.2

Sch.1 Item 39, revoked: SI 1998/2051 Reg.2, Sch.3

NO.

3107. Motor Vehicles (EC Type Approval) Regulations 1992—*cont.*

Sch.1 Item 39, substituted: SI 1997/191 Reg.2

Sch.1 Item 40, revoked: SI 1998/2051 Reg.2, Sch.3

Sch.1 Item 40, substituted: SI 1997/191 Reg.2

Sch.1 Item 41, revoked: SI 1998/2051 Reg.2, Sch.3

Sch.1 Item 41, substituted: SI 1997/191 Reg.2

Sch.1 Item 44, revoked: SI 1998/2051 Reg.2, Sch.3

Sch.1 Item 44, substituted: SI 1997/191 Reg.2

Sch.1 Item 49, revoked: SI 1998/2051 Reg.2, Sch.3

Sch.1 Item 49, substituted: SI 1997/191 Reg.2

Sch.1 Item 54, revoked: SI 1998/2051 Reg.2, Sch.3

Sch.1 Item 54, substituted: SI 1997/191 Reg.2

Sch.1A, added: SI 1997/1501 Reg.7, Sch.

Sch.1A, revoked: SI 1998/2051 Reg.2, Sch.3

Sch.3, revoked: SI 1998/2051 Reg.2, Sch.3

3121. Value Added Tax (Place of Supply of Services) Order 1992

Art.14, amended: SI 1996/2992 Art.2

Art.15, amended: SI 1996/2992 Art.2

Art.17, amended: SI 1997/1524 Art.3

Art.17, substituted: SI 1998/763 Art.3

Art.18, amended: SI 1997/1524 Art.4

Art.18, substituted: SI 1998/763 Art.4

Art.19, added: SI 1997/1524 Art.5

Art.19, revoked: SI 1998/763 Art.5

Art.20, added: SI 1997/1524 Art.5

Art.20, revoked: SI 1998/763 Art.5

Art.21, added: SI 1997/1524 Art.5

3122. Value Added Tax (Cars) Order 1992

Art.2, amended: SI 1998/759 Art.3, SI 1999/2832 Art.3

Art.4A, amended: SI 1999/2832 Art.4

Art.5, amended: SI 1999/2832 Art.5, Art.6, Art.7

Art.6, revoked: SI 1999/2832 Art.8

Art.6A, revoked: SI 1999/2832 Art.8

Art.7, amended: SI 1999/2832 Art.9

Art.8, see *Peugeot Motor Co Plc v Customs and Excise Commissioners* [1998] B.V.C. 2111 (V & DT), David Demack (Chairman)

Art.8, amended: SI 1997/1615 Art.3, Art.4, SI 1998/759 Art.4, SI 1999/2832 Art.10

3123. Value Added Tax (Input Tax) (Specified Supplies) Order 1992

revoked: SI 1999/3121 Art.5

3135. Excise Goods (Holding, Movement, Warehousing and REDS) Regulations 1992

Reg.2, amended: SI 1999/1278 Reg.23, SI 1999/1565 Reg.27

Reg.4, referred to: SI 1998/202 Reg.3

Reg.4, revoked (in part): SI 1999/1278 Reg.23

Reg.5, referred to: SI 1998/202 Reg.3

Reg.6, referred to: SI 1998/202 Reg.3

Reg.8, referred to: SI 1998/202 Reg.3

Reg.8, revoked (in part): SI 1999/1278 Reg.23

Reg.9, see *R. v Hayward (John Victor)* Times, July 13, 1998 (CA (Crim Div)), Judge, L.J.

Reg.9, referred to: SI 1998/202 Reg.3

Reg.10, see *R. v Hayward (John Victor)* Times, July 13, 1998 (CA (Crim Div)), Judge, L.J.

Reg.10, referred to: SI 1998/202 Reg.3

Reg.11, referred to: SI 1998/202 Reg.3

Reg.14, applied: SI 1999/1565 Reg.21

3137. Town and Country Planning (Fees for Applications and Deemed Applications) (Scotland) Amendment (No.2) Regulations 1992

revoked (in part): SI 1997/10 Reg.15

NO.

1992—cont.

3139. Personal Protective Equipment (EC Directive) Regulations 1992
amended: SI 1996/3039 Reg.2
applied: SI 1998/543 Reg.6, SI 1998/2306 Reg.10, Sch.1, SI 1999/437 Reg.7, SI 1999/3232 Reg.9
referred to: SI 1999/2024 Reg.21

3143. Milk and Dairies (Standardisation and Importation) Regulations 1992
Reg.2, revoked: SI 1998/2424 Reg.9, Sch.

3145. Plastic Materials and Articles in Contact with Food Regulations 1992
revoked: SI 1998/1376 Reg.14
Reg.2, amended: SI 1996/694 Reg.2, SI 1996/2817 Reg.2
Reg.2, revoked: SI 1998/1376 Reg.14
Reg.5, amended: SI 1996/2817 Reg.2
Reg.5, applied: SI 1998/1376 Reg.3
Reg.5, revoked: SI 1998/1376 Reg.14
Reg.6, revoked: SI 1998/1376 Reg.14
Reg.13, revoked: SI 1998/1376 Reg.14
Reg.14, added: SI 1996/694 Reg.2
Reg.14, revoked: SI 1998/1376 Reg.14
Reg.14A, added: SI 1996/2817 Reg.2
Reg.14A, revoked: SI 1998/1376 Reg.14
Reg.15, added: SI 1996/694 Reg.2
Reg.15, revoked: SI 1998/1376 Reg.14
Sch.1, revoked: SI 1998/1376 Reg.14
Sch.1 Part I, amended: SI 1996/694 Reg.2, SI 1996/2817 Reg.2, Sch.1, Sch.2, Sch.3
Sch.1 Part I, revoked: SI 1998/1376 Reg.14
Sch.2, added: SI 1996/694 Reg.2
Sch.2, revoked: SI 1998/1376 Reg.14
Sch.3, added: SI 1996/694 Reg.2
Sch.3, revoked: SI 1998/1376 Reg.14
Sch.3 Part I, amended: SI 1996/2817 Reg.2, Sch.4
Sch.3 Part I, revoked: SI 1998/1376 Reg.14

3146. Active Implantable Medical Devices Regulations 1992
applied: SI 1998/2306 Reg.10, Sch.1

3150. Revenue Traders (Accounts and Records) Regulations 1992
Reg.10, added: SI 1998/62 Reg.2
Reg.11, added: SI 1998/62 Reg.2
Reg.12, added: SI 1998/62 Reg.2
Reg.13, added: SI 1998/62 Reg.2
Reg.14, added: SI 1998/62 Reg.2
Reg.15, added: SI 1998/62 Reg.2
Reg.16, added: SI 1998/62 Reg.2
Reg.17, added: SI 1998/62 Reg.2

3152. Excise Duties (Deferred Payment) Regulations 1992
Reg.6, amended: SI 1996/2537 Reg.15
Reg.6, applied: SI 1996/2537 Reg.7
Reg.11, amended: SI 1996/2537 Reg.15

3155. Excise Duties (Personal Reliefs) Order 1992
Art.4, revoked: SI 1999/1617 Art.2
Art.5, see *R. v Customs and Excise Commissioners Ex p. Mortimer* [1998] 3 All E.R. 229 (QBD), Lord Bingham of Cornhill, L.C.J.; see *R. v Travers (Kelvin)* [1998] Crim. L.R. 655 (CA (Crim Div)) Waller, L.J.
Art.5, amended: SI 1999/1617 Art.3

3159. Specified Diseases (Notification and Slaughter) Order 1992
Art.3, revoked: SI 1996/2628 Art.8, Sch.2
Sch.1, revoked: SI 1996/2628 Art.8, Sch.2

NO.

1992—cont.

3162. Patents (Supplementary Protection Certificate for Medicinal Products) Rules 1992
revoked: SI 1997/64 r.12

3163. Food Safety (Fishery Products) Regulations 1992
applied: SI 1996/3124 Reg.10, Sch.2 para.1
revoked: SI 1998/994 Reg.59, Sch.5
Reg.2, revoked: SI 1998/994 Reg.59, Sch.5
Reg.3, revoked: SI 1998/994 Reg.59, Sch.5
Reg.5, revoked: SI 1998/994 Reg.59, Sch.5
Reg.6, revoked: SI 1998/994 Reg.59, Sch.5
Reg.9, revoked: SI 1998/994 Reg.59, Sch.5
Reg.11, revoked: SI 1998/994 Reg.59, Sch.5
Reg.11A, revoked: SI 1998/994 Reg.59, Sch.5
Reg.13, revoked: SI 1998/994 Reg.59, Sch.5
Reg.14, revoked: SI 1998/994 Reg.59, Sch.5
Reg.15, revoked: SI 1998/994 Reg.59, Sch.5
Reg.16, revoked: SI 1998/994 Reg.59, Sch.5
Reg.18, revoked: SI 1998/994 Reg.59, Sch.5
Reg.20, revoked: SI 1998/994 Reg.59, Sch.5
Reg.21, revoked: SI 1998/994 Reg.59, Sch.5
Reg.22, revoked: SI 1998/994 Reg.59, Sch.5
Reg.23, revoked: SI 1998/994 Reg.59, Sch.5
Reg.24, revoked: SI 1998/994 Reg.59, Sch.5
Sch.1 Part I, revoked: SI 1998/994 Reg.59, Sch.5
Sch.1 Part II, amended: SI 1996/1547 Reg.2, Sch.1
Sch.1 Part II, revoked: SI 1998/994 Reg.59, Sch.5
Sch.3, amended: SI 1996/1499 Reg.49
Sch.3, revoked: SI 1998/994 Reg.59, Sch.5
Sch.5, revoked: SI 1998/994 Reg.59, Sch.5

3164. Food Safety (Live Bivalve Molluscs and Other Shellfish) Regulations 1992
see *Bowden v South West Water Services Ltd* [1999] Eu. L.R. 573 (CA), Beldam, L.J.; see *Bowden v South West Water Services Ltd* [1998] Env. L.R. 445 (QBD), Carnwath, J.
applied: SI 1996/3124 Reg.10, Sch.2 para.2
revoked: SI 1998/994 Reg.59, Sch.5
Reg.2, revoked: SI 1998/994 Reg.59, Sch.5
Reg.3, revoked: SI 1998/994 Reg.59, Sch.5
Reg.6, see *R. v Stone (Michael James Roy)* [1998] Env. L.R. 618 (CA (Crim Div)), Henry, L.J.
Reg.6, revoked: SI 1998/994 Reg.59, Sch.5
Reg.7, revoked: SI 1998/994 Reg.59, Sch.5
Reg.9, revoked: SI 1998/994 Reg.59, Sch.5
Reg.10, revoked: SI 1998/994 Reg.59, Sch.5
Reg.11, revoked: SI 1998/994 Reg.59, Sch.5
Reg.11A, revoked: SI 1998/994 Reg.59, Sch.5
Reg.12, revoked: SI 1998/994 Reg.59, Sch.5
Reg.14, revoked: SI 1998/994 Reg.59, Sch.5
Reg.15, revoked: SI 1998/994 Reg.59, Sch.5
Reg.18, see *R. v Stone (Michael James Roy)* [1998] Env. L.R. 618 (CA (Crim Div)), Henry, L.J.
Reg.18, revoked: SI 1998/994 Reg.59, Sch.5
Reg.19, revoked: SI 1998/994 Reg.59, Sch.5
Reg.22, revoked: SI 1998/994 Reg.59, Sch.5
Sch.1 para.1, amended: SI 1996/1499 Reg.49
Sch.1 para.1, revoked: SI 1998/994 Reg.59, Sch.5
Sch.1 para.4, revoked: SI 1998/994 Reg.59, Sch.5
Sch.3 Part 2, revoked: SI 1998/994 Reg.59, Sch.5
Sch.6 para.3, revoked: SI 1998/994 Reg.59, Sch.5
Sch.9 para.1, revoked: SI 1998/994 Reg.59, Sch.5

NO.

3164. Food Safety (Live Bivalve Molluscs and Other Shellfish) Regulations 1992—*cont.*
Sch.9 para.2, revoked: SI 1998/994 Reg.59, Sch.5
Sch.9 para.5, revoked: SI 1998/994 Reg.59, Sch.5

3165. Food Safety (Fishery Products on Fishing Vessels) Regulations 1992
applied: SI 1996/3124 Reg.10, Sch.2 para.1
revoked: SI 1998/994 Reg.59, Sch.5
Reg.2, amended: SI 1996/1547 Reg.3
Reg.2, revoked: SI 1998/994 Reg.59, Sch.5
Reg.7, revoked: SI 1998/994 Reg.59, Sch.5
Sch. Part I, revoked: SI 1998/994 Reg.59, Sch.5

3172. Employers' Liability (Compulsory Insurance) Exemption (Amendment) Regulations 1992
revoked: SI 1998/2573 Reg.10, Sch.3

3179. Overseas Companies and Credit and Financial Institutions (Branch Disclosure) Regulations 1992
see *Saab v Saudi American Bank* [1998] 1 W.L.R. 937 (QBD), Tuckey, J.

3200. Extradition (Hijacking) Order 1992
revoked: SI 1997/1763 Art.4

3204. Registered Homes (Northern Ireland) Order 1992
Art.7, referred to: SI 1996/1298 (NI.8) Sch.3
Art.32, amended: 1997 c.24 s.23, Sch.4 para.5
Art.33, amended: 1996 c.23 Sch.3 para.58

3217. Genetically Modified Organisms (Contained Use) Regulations 1992
applied: SI 1996/2791 Reg.15, Sch.12, SI 1997/2505 Reg.15, Sch.12, SI 1999/645 Reg.17, Sch.14
referred to: SI 1999/437 Sch.3 Part I
Reg.2, amended: SI 1996/967 Reg.2, Sch.1 para.2
Reg.2, applied: SI 1996/1106 Reg.3
Reg.3, applied: SI 1996/1106 Reg.3
Reg.6, amended: SI 1998/1548 Reg.2
Reg.8, applied: SI 1997/2505 Sch.12, SI 1999/645 Reg.17, Sch.14
Reg.9, applied: SI 1997/2505 Sch.12, SI 1999/645 Reg.17, Sch.14
Sch.1 Part II, applied: SI 1996/1106 Reg.3
Sch.1 Part III, applied: SI 1996/1106 Reg.3

3218. Banking Coordination (Second Council Directive) Regulations 1992
applied: 1998 c.11 Sch.2 para.1, SI 1998/1870 Reg.14
referred to: 1998 c.11 s.17, s.21
Reg.2, amended: SI 1996/1669 Reg.23, Sch.5 para.10, 1998 c.11 s.23, Sch.5 para.22, SI 1999/2094 Reg.2
Reg.2B, added: SI 1999/2094 Reg.2
Reg.2C, added: SI 1999/2094 Reg.2
Reg.3, amended: SI 1999/2094 Reg.2
Reg.4, amended: SI 1999/2094 Reg.2
Reg.8, amended: 1998 c.11 s.23, Sch.5 para.23
Reg.9, amended: 1998 c.11 s.23, Sch.5 para.23
Reg.10, amended: 1998 c.11 s.23, Sch.5 para.23
Reg.11, amended: 1998 c.11 s.23, Sch.5 para.24
Reg.12, amended: 1998 c.11 s.23, Sch.5 para.25
Reg.13A, amended: 1998 c.11 s.23, Sch.5 para.25
Reg.14, substituted: 1998 c.11 s.23, Sch.5 para.26
Reg.20, amended: 1998 c.11 s.23, Sch.5 para.27

NO.

3218. Banking Coordination (Second Council Directive) Regulations 1992—*cont.*
Reg.23, amended: 1998 c.11 s.23, Sch.5 para.27
Reg.38, referred to: 1998 c.11 s.36
Reg.39, referred to: 1998 c.11 s.36
Reg.40, referred to: 1998 c.11 s.36
Reg.41, referred to: 1998 c.11 s.36
Reg.42, referred to: 1998 c.11 s.36
Reg.48, amended: 1998 c.11 s.23, Sch.5 para.27
Reg.58, amended: 1998 c.11 s.23, Sch.5 para.27
Reg.62, amended: 1998 c.11 s.23, Sch.5 para.28
Reg.76, revoked (in part): 1998 c.11 s.43, Sch.9 Part II
Reg.82, applied: SI 1997/817 Sch.1
Sch.2, amended: 1998 c.11 s.23, Sch.5 para.29
Sch.3, amended: 1998 c.11 s.23, Sch.5 para.29
Sch.4 para.1, revoked (in part): 1998 c.11 s.23, s.43, Sch.5 para.30, Sch.9 Part II
Sch.5, amended: 1998 c.11 s.23, Sch.5 para.31
Sch.6, amended: 1998 c.11 s.23, Sch.5 para.31
Sch.7, amended: 1998 c.11 s.23, Sch.5 para.31
Sch.8, amended: 1998 c.11 s.23, Sch.5 para.32
Sch.8 para. 8, referred to: SI 1999/2094 Reg.3
Sch.8 para. 9, referred to: SI 1999/2094 Reg.3
Sch.8 para. 10, referred to: SI 1999/2094 Reg.3
Sch.9 para.19, amended: 1998 c.11 s.23, Sch.5 para.33
Sch.10 para.8, revoked (in part): 1998 c.11 s.43, Sch.9 Part II
Sch.10 para.15, revoked: 1998 c.29 Sch.16 Part II
Sch.10 para.23, revoked: SI 1997/816 Art.5
Sch.10 para.31, revoked (in part): 1998 c.11 s.43, Sch.9 Part II
Sch.10 para.33, amended: 1998 c.11 s.23, Sch.5 para.34
Sch.10 para.40, amended: 1998 c.11 s.23, Sch.5 para.34
Sch.10 para.40, revoked: 1998 c.29 Sch.16 Part II
Sch.11 para.4, amended: 1998 c.11 s.23, Sch.5 para.35
Sch.11 para.5, amended: 1998 c.11 s.23, Sch.5 para.35

3222. Value Added Tax (Input Tax) Order 1992
see *Customs and Excise Commissioners v British Telecommunications Plc* [1997] S.T.C. 475 (QBD), Dyson, J.; see *Customs and Excise Commissioners v BRS Automotive Ltd* [1997] S.T.C. 336 (QBD), Sedley, J.
Art.2, amended: SI 1999/2930 Art.3, SI 1999/3118 Art.3
Art.4, revoked: SI 1999/2930 Art.4
Art.5, see *BMW (GB) Ltd v Customs and Excise Commissioners* [1997] S.T.C. 824 (QBD), Keene, J.; see *Customs and Excise Commissioners v Kilroy Television Co Ltd* [1997] S.T.C. 901 (QBD), Carnwath, J.
Art.5, amended: SI 1999/2930 Art.5
Art.5, revoked (in part): SI 1999/2930 Art.5
Art.7, see *Customs and Excise Commissioners v British Telecommunications Plc (1997)* [1998] S.T.C. 544 (CA), Nourse, L.J.; see *Customs and Excise Commissioners v BRS Automotive Ltd* [1998] S.T.C. 1210 (CA), Pill, L.J.; see *Royscot Leasing Ltd v Customs and Excise Commissioners* Independent, July 22, 1996 (C.S.) (QBD), Turner, J.

NO.

3222. Value Added Tax (Input Tax) Order 1992— *cont.*
Art.7, amended: SI 1998/2767 Art.2, SI 1999/ 2930 Art.6
Art.7, revoked (in part): SI 1999/2930 Art.6

3230. Transport and Works (Descriptions of Works Interfering with Navigation) Order 1992
Art.2, amended: SI 1997/2906 Art.2
Art.3, amended: SI 1997/2906 Art.3

3231. Transport and Works (Guided Transport Modes) Order 1992
Art.3, amended: SI 1997/1951 Art.2

3236. Aflatoxins in Nuts, Nut Products, Dried Figs and Dried Fig Products Regulations 1992
revoked: SI 1999/1603 Reg.10
Reg.2, amended: SI 1996/1499 Reg.49
Reg.2, revoked: SI 1999/1603 Reg.10

3238. Non-Domestic Rating Contributions (Wales) Regulations 1992
Sch.1 para.3, amended: SI 1997/3003 Reg.3
Sch.1 para.4, amended: SI 1996/619 Art.4, SI 1999/3439 Reg.2
Sch.2 para.2, amended: SI 1996/3018 Reg.2, SI 1997/3003 Reg.4, SI 1998/2962 Reg.2, SI 1999/3439 Reg.2
Sch.2 para.8, amended: SI 1996/3018 Reg.2, SI 1997/3003 Reg.4, SI 1998/2962 Reg.2
Sch.4, substituted: SI 1996/3018 Reg.2, Sch., SI 1997/3003 Reg.4, Sch., SI 1998/2962 Reg.2, Sch., SI 1999/3439 Reg.2, Sch.

3240. Environmental Information Regulations 1992
applied: SI 1999/672 Art.2, Sch.1, SI 1999/743 Sch.8 para.20
referred to: SI 1997/189 Reg.9
Reg.3, applied: SI 1999/1676 Sch.5 para.12
Reg.3, referred to: SI 1996/600 Sch.5 para.15, SI 1996/601 Sch.5 para.15, SI 1997/1624 Sch.5 para.15, SI 1999/1517 Reg.12, Sch.4 para.12
Reg.4, amended: SI 1998/1447 Reg.2
Reg.4, applied: SI 1999/293 Reg.12, SI 1999/ 2228 Reg.12
Reg.4, referred to: SI 1999/367 Reg.7, SI 1999/ 1783 Reg.9, SI 1999/2892 Reg.14, SSI 1999/1 Reg.12, SSI 1999/43 Reg.12
Reg.4, revoked (in part): SI 1998/1447 Reg.2

3256. Act of Sederunt (Commissary Court Books) 1992
para.3, amended: SI 1996/3144 para.2
para.3, revoked (in part): SI 1996/3144 para.2
para.4, amended: SI 1996/3144 para.2
para.5, amended: SI 1996/3144 para.2
para.6, amended: SI 1996/3144 para.2

3257. Local Authorities (Capital Finance) (Amendment) (No.4) Regulations 1992
revoked: SI 1997/319 Reg.162, Sch.3

3279. Utilities Supply and Works Contracts Regulations 1992
revoked: SI 1996/2911 Reg.34
Sch.2, see *R. v HM Treasury Ex p. British Telecommunications Plc (C392/93)* [1996] Q.B. 615 (ECJ), G C Rodriguez Iglesias (President)

3280. Genetically Modified Organisms (Deliberate Release) Regulations 1992
applied: SI 1996/1106 Reg.3
Reg.10, amended: SI 1997/1900 Reg.2
Sch.2, substituted: SI 1997/1900 Reg.2, Sch.

NO.

3281. Driving Licences (Designation of Relevant External Law) Order 1992
revoked: SI 1996/3206 Art.3

3288. Package Travel, Package Holidays and Package Tours Regulations 1992
referred to: 1998 c.46 s.30, Sch.5 s.C7
Reg.7, amended: SI 1998/1208 Reg.5
Sch.1 para.5, amended: SI 1998/1208 Reg.4

3298. Products of Animal Origin (Import and Export) Regulations 1992
revoked: SI 1996/3124 Reg.42, Sch.7
Part II, applied: SI 1996/2265 Reg.3
Part II, revoked: SI 1996/3124 Reg.42, Sch.7
Reg.1, revoked: SI 1996/3124 Reg.42, Sch.7
Reg.5, amended: SI 1996/2265 Reg.9
Reg.5, revoked: SI 1996/3124 Reg.42, Sch.7
Reg.7, revoked: SI 1996/3124 Reg.42, Sch.7
Reg.10, revoked: SI 1996/3124 Reg.42, Sch.7
Reg.15, applied: SI 1996/2265 Reg.3
Reg.15, revoked: SI 1996/3124 Reg.42, Sch.7
Sch.3, applied: SI 1996/2265 Reg.3
Sch.3, revoked: SI 1996/3124 Reg.42, Sch.7

3299. Products of Animal Origin (Third Country Imports) (Charges) Regulations 1992
revoked: SI 1996/3124 Reg.42, Sch.7

3300. Fish Health Regulations 1992
applied: SI 1996/3124 Reg.10, Sch.2 para.3
referred to: SI 1998/994 Reg.44
revoked: SI 1997/1881 Reg.24
Reg.7, see *Booker Aquaculture Ltd (t/a Marine Harvest McConnell) v Secretary of State for Scotland* [1999] Eu L.R. 54 (OH), Lord Cameron of Lochbroom
Reg.14, amended: SI 1996/3124 Reg.41, Sch.6 para.3
Reg.14, revoked: SI 1997/1881 Reg.24
Reg.16, amended: SI 1996/3124 Reg.41, Sch.6 para.3
Reg.16, revoked: SI 1997/1881 Reg.24

3301. Shellfish and Specified Fish (Third Country Imports) Order 1992
applied: SI 1998/190 Reg.34, Sch.6
referred to: SI 1998/190 Reg.34, Sch.6, SI 1998/ 994 Reg.44

3303. Animal By-Products Order 1992
applied: SI 1998/871 Reg.7, Reg.20, SI 1999/ 646 Art.34
revoked: SI 1999/646 Art.35, Sch.6 Part I
Art.3, amended: SI 1996/827 Art.2, SI 1997/ 2894 Art.2
Art.3, revoked: SI 1999/646 Art.35, Sch.6 Part I
Art.4, amended: SI 1996/827 Art.3
Art.4, revoked: SI 1999/646 Art.35, Sch.6 Part I
Art.5, amended: SI 1996/827 Art.4
Art.5, revoked: SI 1999/646 Art.35, Sch.6 Part I
Art.5, substituted: SI 1997/2894 Art.2
Art.6, amended: SI 1996/827 Art.5
Art.6, revoked: SI 1999/646 Art.35, Sch.6 Part I
Art.6, substituted: SI 1997/2894 Art.2
Art.6A, added: SI 1997/2894 Art.2
Art.6A, revoked: SI 1999/646 Art.35, Sch.6 Part I
Art.6B, added: SI 1997/2894 Art.2
Art.6B, revoked: SI 1999/646 Art.35, Sch.6 Part I
Art.8, revoked (in part): SI 1997/2894 Art.2, SI 1999/646 Art.35 (rem.), Sch.6 Part I (rem.)
Art.9, amended: SI 1996/827 Art.6
Art.9, revoked: SI 1999/646 Art.35, Sch.6 Part I
Art.10, amended: SI 1996/827 Art.7
Art.10, revoked: SI 1999/646 Art.35, Sch.6 Part I
Art.12, revoked: SI 1999/646 Art.35, Sch.6 Part I

NO.

1992—cont.

3303. Animal By-Products Order 1992—*cont.*
Art.12, substituted: SI 1996/827 Art.8
Art.13, amended: SI 1996/827 Art.9
Art.13, revoked: SI 1999/646 Art.35, Sch.6 Part I
Sch.1 Part II, referred to: SI 1997/2959 Reg.8
Sch.1 Part II, revoked: SI 1999/646 Art.35, Sch.6 Part I
Sch.4 para.6, amended: SI 1996/827 Art.10
Sch.4 para.6, revoked: SI 1999/646 Art.35, Sch.6 Part I
Sch.4 para.9, added: SI 1996/827 Art.10
Sch.4 para.9, revoked: SI 1999/646 Art.35, Sch.6 Part I

3307. Orkney Islands Area (Electoral Arrangements) Order 1992
revoked: SI 1999/103 Art.4

3308. Monklands and Bellshill Hospitals National Health Service Trust (Establishment) Order 1992
revoked: SI 1999/1070 Art.2, Sch.2
Art.1, amended: SI 1998/922 Art.2
Art.1, revoked: SI 1999/1070 Art.2, Sch.2
Art.2, amended: SI 1998/922 Art.3
Art.2, revoked: SI 1999/1070 Art.2, Sch.2
Art.3, amended: SI 1998/922 Art.4
Art.3, revoked: SI 1999/1070 Art.2, Sch.2

3309. Moray Health Services National Health Service Trust (Establishment) Order 1992
revoked: SI 1999/1070 Art.2, Sch.2

3310. West Lothian National Health Service Trust (Establishment) Order 1992
revoked: SI 1999/1070 Art.2, Sch.2

3311. North Ayrshire and Arran National Health Service Trust (Establishment) Order 1992
revoked: SI 1999/1070 Art.2, Sch.2

3312. Ayrshire and Arran Community Health Care National Health Service Trust (Establishment) Order 1992
revoked: SI 1999/1070 Art.2, Sch.2
Art.2, revoked: SI 1999/1070 Art.2, Sch.2
Art.2, substituted: SI 1996/1681 Art.2

3313. Caithness and Sutherland National Health Service Trust (Establishment) Order 1992
revoked: SI 1999/1070 Art.2, Sch.2

3314. Southern General Hospital National Health Service Trust (Establishment) Order 1992
revoked: SI 1999/1070 Art.2, Sch.2

3315. Grampian National Health Service Trust (Establishment) Order 1992
revoked: SI 1999/1070 Art.2, Sch.2

3316. Royal Alexandra Hospital National Health Service Trust (Establishment) Order 1992
revoked: SI 1999/1070 Art.2, Sch.2

3317. Victoria Infirmary National Health Service Trust (Establishment) Order 1992
revoked: SI 1999/1070 Art.2, Sch.2

3318. Stirling Royal Infirmary National Health Service Trust (Establishment) Order 1992
revoked: SI 1999/1070 Art.2, Sch.2

3319. Raigmore Hospital National Health Service Trust (Establishment) Order 1992
revoked: SI 1999/1070 Art.2, Sch.2

3320. Dundee Teaching Hospitals National Health Service Trust (Establishment) Order 1992
revoked: SI 1999/1070 Art.2, Sch.2
Art.3, revoked: SI 1999/1070 Art.2, Sch.2
Art.3, substituted: SI 1997/2948 Art.2

3324. Mink Keeping Order 1992
applied: SI 1997/2750

NO.

1993

Camden (Waiting and Loading Restriction) (No.2) Order 1993
amended: SI 1996/216 Art.11
revoked (in part): SI 1996/1136 Art.11, SI 1996/1137 Art.11, SI 1996/1222 Art.5, SI 1997/208 Art.11, SI 1997/2002 Art.10, SI 1997/2326 Art.10, SI 1998/1105 Art.10

Camden (Waiting and Loading Restriction) (Special Parking Area) Order 1993
amended: SI 1996/1078 Art.5, SI 1996/1135 Art.5
revoked (in part): SI 1996/1222 Art.5, SI 1996/2155 Art.11

Croydon (Waiting and Loading Restriction) Order No.23 1993
revoked (in part): SI 1997/1211 Art.10, SI 1997/2133 Art.11, SI 1999/414 Art.10

Education (Significant Variation of Schemes for Financing Schools) Order 1993
revoked: SI 1999/711 Reg.9, Sch.2

Hammersmith & Fulham (Waiting and Loading Restriction) Order 1993
referred to: SI 1997/2657 Art.10
revoked (in part): SI 1997/2657 Art.10, SI 1997/2785 Art.11, SI 1999/1147 Art.10

Hammersmith & Fulham (Waiting and Loading Restrictions) (Special Parking Area) Order 1993
revoked (in part): SI 1999/1264 Art.10

Vacancy in See Committees Regulations 1993
applied: SI 1996/3084 Appendix para.4, SI 1997/1890 Appendix para.4, SI 1998/1712 Appendix para.4, SI 1999/2108 Appendix para.4

3. London Borough of Redbridge Waiting and Loading Restriction Consolidation Order 1993
revoked (in part): SI 1996/1624 Art.10, SI 1996/1892 Art.10, SI 1996/1893 Art.10, SI 1999/2804 Art.10, SI 1999/2805 Art.10

9. Rail Crossing Extinguishment and Diversion Orders Regulations 1993
Sch.1 Form 1, amended: SI 1996/252 Art.2, Sch
Sch.1 Form 2, amended: SI 1996/252 Art.2, Sch

15. Genetically Modified Organisms (Contained Use) Regulations 1993
revoked: SI 1996/1106 Reg.1

19. Provision and Use of Work Equipment Regulations (Northern Ireland) 1993
Reg.10, applied: SI 1997/831 Reg.24
Sch.1, applied: SI 1997/831 Reg.24
Sch.1 para.19, amended: SI 1996/3039 Reg.2
Sch.1 para.24, added: SI 1997/831 Reg.24

20. Personal Protective Equipment at Work Regulations (Northern Ireland) 1993
referred to: SI 1999/2205 Reg.3
Sch. para.1, amended: SI 1996/3039 Reg.2

21. Wireless Telegraphy Apparatus (Land Mobile-Satellite Service) (Low Bit Rate Data) (Exemption) Regulations 1993
revoked: SI 1999/930 Reg.2, Sch.1

28. Warrington Hospital National Health Service Trust (Establishment) Order 1993
Art.3, substituted: SI 1999/58 Art.2

34. North West London Mental Health National Health Service Trust (Establishment) Order 1993
revoked: SI 1998/2964 Art.2

NO.

69. Merchant Shipping (Navigational Equipment) Regulations 1993
applied: SI 1996/3243 Reg.5, Sch Part I
referred to: SI 1996/3243 Sch Part I, SI 1998/2771 Reg.4, Reg.5, Sch.1, Sch.2
Reg.2, amended: SI 1996/3188 Reg.17
Reg.3, applied: SI 1998/2070 Reg.8
Reg.10, amended: SI 1999/1957 Reg.3, Sch.1 para.6

72. Education (Training Grants) Regulations 1993
referred to: 1996 c.56 Sch.39 para.43

82. Environmentally Sensitive Areas (North Kent Marshes) Designation Order 1993
amended: SI 1998/2176 Art.3
applied: SI 1998/2176 Art.3
referred to: SI 1998/1295 Reg.3, Reg.4
Art.2, amended: SI 1996/3104 Reg.2, SI 1998/1304 Art.4
Art.4, substituted: SI 1998/1304 Art.5
Art.4A, revoked: SI 1998/1304 Art.9
Art.5, amended: SI 1996/3104 Reg.2
Art.5, substituted: SI 1998/1304 Art.6
Art.5A, added: SI 1996/3104 Reg.2
Art.5B, added: SI 1996/3104 Reg.2
Art.5C, added: SI 1996/3104 Reg.2
Art.6, amended: SI 1997/1453 Art.4
Art.6, revoked: SI 1998/1304 Art.9
Sch.1, substituted: SI 1998/1304 Art.7, Sch.1
Sch.1A, revoked: SI 1998/1304 Art.9
Sch.2, substituted: SI 1998/1304 Art.8, Sch.2
Sch.2 Part I, amended: SI 1999/1366 Art.3
Sch.3, amended: SI 1996/3104 Reg.3
Sch.3, revoked: SI 1998/1304 Art.9
Sch.4, revoked: SI 1998/1304 Art.9
Sch.4 para.3, amended: SI 1997/1453 Art.5
Sch.4 para.3, revoked: SI 1998/1304 Art.9
Sch.4 para.7, revoked: SI 1998/1304 Art.9

83. Environmentally Sensitive Areas (Exmoor) Designation Order 1993
amended: SI 1998/2174 Art.3
applied: SI 1998/2174 Art.3
referred to: SI 1998/1295 Reg.3, Reg.4
Art.2, amended: SI 1996/3104 Reg.2, SI 1998/1302 Art.4
Art.4, substituted: SI 1998/1302 Art.5
Art.4A, revoked: SI 1998/1302 Art.9
Art.5, amended: SI 1996/3104 Reg.2
Art.5, substituted: SI 1998/1302 Art.6
Art.5A, added: SI 1996/3104 Reg.2
Art.5B, added: SI 1996/3104 Reg.2
Art.5C, added: SI 1996/3104 Reg.2
Art.6, amended: SI 1997/1451 Art.4
Art.6, revoked: SI 1998/1302 Art.9
Sch.1, amended: SI 1998/2174 Art.4
Sch.1, substituted: SI 1998/1302 Art.7, Sch.1
Sch.1A, revoked: SI 1998/1302 Art.9
Sch.2, substituted: SI 1998/1302 Art.8, Sch.2
Sch.2 Part I, amended: SI 1998/2174 Art.5, SI 1999/1371 Art.3
Sch.4, revoked: SI 1998/1302 Art.9
Sch.5, revoked: SI 1998/1302 Art.9
Sch.5 para.7, revoked: SI 1998/1302 Art.9
Sch.5 para.8, added: SI 1997/1451 Art.5
Sch.5 para.8, revoked: SI 1998/1302 Art.9

84. Environmentally Sensitive Areas (Avon Valley) Designation Order 1993
amended: SI 1998/2172 Art.3
applied: SI 1998/2172 Art.3
referred to: SI 1998/1295 Reg.3, Reg.4

NO.

84. Environmentally Sensitive Areas (Avon Valley) Designation Order 1993—*cont.*
Art.2, amended: SI 1996/3104 Reg.2, SI 1998/1307 Art.4
Art.4, substituted: SI 1998/1307 Art.5
Art.4A, revoked: SI 1998/1307 Art.9
Art.5, amended: SI 1996/3104 Reg.2
Art.5, substituted: SI 1998/1307 Art.6
Art.5A, added: SI 1996/3104 Reg.2
Art.5B, added: SI 1996/3104 Reg.2
Art.5C, added: SI 1996/3104 Reg.2
Art.6, amended: SI 1997/1450 Art.4
Art.6, revoked: SI 1998/1307 Art.9
Sch.1, substituted: SI 1998/1307 Art.7, Sch.1
Sch.1A, revoked: SI 1998/1307 Art.9
Sch.2, substituted: SI 1998/1307 Art.8, Sch.2
Sch.2 Part I, amended: SI 1999/1368 Art.3
Sch.3, amended: SI 1996/3104 Reg.3
Sch.3, revoked: SI 1998/1307 Art.9
Sch.4, revoked: SI 1998/1307 Art.9
Sch.4 para.3, revoked: SI 1998/1307 Art.9
Sch.4 para.3, substituted: SI 1997/1450 Art.5
Sch.4 para.3A, added: SI 1997/1450 Art.5
Sch.4 para.3A, revoked: SI 1998/1307 Art.9
Sch.4 para.7, revoked: SI 1998/1307 Art.9
Sch.4 para.8, added: SI 1997/1450 Art.5
Sch.4 para.8, revoked: SI 1998/1307 Art.9

85. Environmentally Sensitive Areas (Lake District) Designation Order 1993
amended: SI 1998/2177 Art.3
applied: SI 1998/2177 Art.3
referred to: SI 1998/1295 Reg.3, Reg.4
Art.2, amended: SI 1996/3104 Reg.2, SI 1998/1301 Art.4
Art.3, amended: SI 1998/1301 Art.5
Art.4, substituted: SI 1998/1301 Art.6
Art.4A, revoked: SI 1998/1301 Art.10
Art.5, amended: SI 1996/3104 Reg.2
Art.5, substituted: SI 1998/1301 Art.7
Art.5A, added: SI 1996/3104 Reg.2
Art.5B, added: SI 1996/3104 Reg.2
Art.5C, added: SI 1996/3104 Reg.2
Art.6, amended: SI 1997/1452 Art.4
Art.6, revoked: SI 1998/1301 Art.10
Sch.1, substituted: SI 1998/1301 Art.8, Sch.1
Sch.1A, revoked: SI 1998/1301 Art.10
Sch.2, substituted: SI 1998/1301 Art.9, Sch.2
Sch.2 Part I, amended: SI 1999/1363 Art.4
Sch.4, revoked: SI 1998/1301 Art.10
Sch.5, revoked: SI 1998/1301 Art.10
Sch.5 para.7, revoked: SI 1998/1301 Art.10
Sch.5 para.8, added: SI 1997/1452 Art.5
Sch.5 para.8, revoked: SI 1998/1301 Art.10

86. Environmentally Sensitive Areas (South Wessex Downs) Designation Order 1993
amended: SI 1998/2175 Art.3
applied: SI 1998/2175 Art.3
referred to: SI 1998/1295 Reg.3, Reg.4
Art.2, amended: SI 1996/3104 Reg.2, SI 1998/1309 Art.4
Art.3, amended: SI 1998/1309 Art.5
Art.4, substituted: SI 1998/1309 Art.6
Art.4A, revoked: SI 1998/1309 Art.10
Art.5, amended: SI 1996/3104 Reg.2
Art.5, substituted: SI 1998/1309 Art.5
Art.5A, added: SI 1996/3104 Reg.2
Art.5B, added: SI 1996/3104 Reg.2
Art.5C, added: SI 1996/3104 Reg.2
Art.6, amended: SI 1997/1454 Art.4
Art.6, revoked: SI 1998/1309 Art.10
Sch.1, substituted: SI 1998/1309 Art.8, Sch.1
Sch.1A, revoked: SI 1998/1309 Art.10

NO.

86. **Environmentally Sensitive Areas (South Wessex Downs) Designation Order 1993** *—cont.*
Sch.2, substituted: SI 1998/1309 Art.9, Sch.2
Sch.2 Part I, amended: SI 1999/1370 Art.4
Sch.2 Part II, amended: SI 1999/1370 Art.5
Sch.2 para.2, amended: SI 1996/3104 Reg.3
Sch.3, revoked: SI 1998/1309 Art.10
Sch.3 para.4, revoked: SI 1998/1309 Art.10
Sch.3 para.5, revoked: SI 1998/1309 Art.10
Sch.3 para.5, substituted: SI 1997/1454 Art.5
Sch.3 para.5A, added: SI 1997/1454 Art.5
Sch.3 para.5A, revoked: SI 1998/1309 Art.10
Sch.3 para.7, revoked: SI 1998/1309 Art.10

87. **Environmentally Sensitive Areas (South West Peak) Designation Order 1993**
referred to: SI 1998/1295 Reg.3, Reg.4
Art.2, amended: SI 1996/3104 Reg.2, SI 1998/1305 Art.4
Art.4, substituted: SI 1998/1305 Art.5
Art.4A, revoked: SI 1998/1305 Art.9
Art.5, amended: SI 1996/3104 Reg.2
Art.5, substituted: SI 1998/1305 Art.6
Art.5A, added: SI 1996/3104 Reg.2
Art.5B, added: SI 1996/3104 Reg.2
Art.5C, added: SI 1996/3104 Reg.2
Art.6, amended: SI 1997/1455 Art.4
Art.6, revoked: SI 1998/1305 Art.9
Sch.1, substituted: SI 1998/1305 Art.7, Sch.1
Sch.1A, revoked: SI 1998/1305 Art.9
Sch.2, substituted: SI 1998/1305 Art.8, Sch.2
Sch.4, revoked: SI 1998/1305 Art.9
Sch.5, revoked: SI 1998/1305 Art.9
Sch.5 para.8, revoked: SI 1998/1305 Art.9
Sch.5 para.9, added: SI 1997/1455 Art.5
Sch.5 para.9, revoked: SI 1998/1305 Art.9

113. **Education (School Financial Statements) (Prescribed Particulars etc.) Regulations 1993**
applied: SI 1996/381 Reg.3, SI 1999/451 Reg.3, SI 1999/486 Reg.3

114. **Teachers' Superannuation (Amendment) Regulations 1993**
applied: SI 1997/3001 Reg.H12, Sch.15 para.2
revoked: SI 1997/3001 Reg.H12, Sch.14

122. **East Birmingham Hospital National Health Service Trust (Change of Name) Order 1993**
revoked: SI 1996/882 Art.2

123. **Teddington Memorial Hospital National Health Service Trust (Establishment) Order 1993**
Art.1, amended: SI 1999/795 Art.2, Art.4
Art.2, amended: SI 1999/795 Art.2
Art.3, substituted: SI 1999/795 Art.4

167. **Spring Traps Approval (Scotland) (Variation) Order 1993**
revoked: SI 1996/2202 Art.3

178. **Local Government Act 1988 (Defined Activities) (Specified Periods) (Scotland) Amendment Regulations 1993**
revoked: SI 1996/917 Reg.5

191. **Council Tax and Non-Domestic Rating (Demand Notices) (England) Regulations 1993**
Reg.1, amended: SI 1998/47 Reg.2
Reg.1, referred to: SI 1996/1880 Art.74
Reg.2, referred to: SI 1996/1880 Art.74
Reg.3, amended: SI 1998/47 Reg.2
Reg.3, referred to: SI 1996/1880 Art.65, Art.74
Sch.1, referred to: SI 1996/1880 Art.65
Sch.1 para.13, amended: SI 1997/394 Reg.3
Sch.1 para.16, amended: SI 1997/394 Reg.4

NO.

191. **Council Tax and Non-Domestic Rating (Demand Notices) (England) Regulations 1993**—*cont.*
Sch.2 Part I, amended: SI 1997/394 Reg.6
Sch.2 Part IA, added: SI 1998/47 Reg.2
Sch.2 Part II, amended: SI 1997/394 Reg.6
Sch.2 Part II, referred to: SI 1996/1880 Art.65
Sch.2 para.5, amended: SI 1997/394 Reg.5
Sch.3 Part I, amended: SI 1996/263 Reg.13, SI 1996/504 Reg.2
Sch.3 Part I, referred to: SI 1996/1880 Art.65
Sch.3 Part II, amended: SI 1996/504 Reg.2
Sch.3 Part II, referred to: SI 1996/1880 Art.65

202. **Local Authorities (Standing Orders) Regulations 1993**
referred to: SI 1996/1243 Sch.7 para.8
Reg.1, applied: SI 1996/1243 Sch.5 para.5
Reg.2, applied: SI 1996/1243 Sch.5 para.5
Reg.2, referred to: SI 1996/1243 Sch.7 para.10
Reg.4, applied: SI 1996/1243 Sch.5 para.5, Sch.7 para.10
Sch.1 Part I, applied: SI 1996/1243 Sch.7 para.10
Sch.1 Part II para.3, applied: SI 1996/1243 Sch.7 para.10
Sch.2, applied: SI 1997/2416 Reg.2, SI 1998/1002 Reg.2
Sch.2 para.2, applied: SI 1996/1243 Sch.5 para.5

208. **Coal and Other Safety-Lamp Mines (Explosives) Regulations 1993**
Reg.5, amended: SI 1996/2093 Reg.33

230. **Academic Awards and Distinctions (Queen Margaret College) (Scotland) Order of Council 1993**
applied: SI 1998/1148 Art.4
revoked: SI 1998/1148 Art.3

244. **Criminal Justice Act 1988 (Application to Service Courts) (Evidence through Television Links) Order 1993**
revoked: SI 1996/2592 Art.3

251. **Police (Promotion) (Scotland) Amendment Regulations 1993**
revoked: SI 1996/221 Reg.10, Sch.2

252. **Non-Domestic Rating (Demand Notices) (Wales) Regulations 1993**
Reg.1, amended: SI 1996/1880 Art.75
Reg.2, amended: SI 1996/311 Reg.2, SI 1996/1880 Art.75
Reg.9, amended: SI 1996/311 Reg.2
Sch.1, referred to: SI 1996/1880 Art.66
Sch.1 para.2, amended: SI 1996/311 Reg.3
Sch.1 para.5, amended: SI 1998/155 Reg.2
Sch.1 para.5, revoked (in part): SI 1997/356 Reg.2
Sch.2 Part I, amended: SI 1996/311 Reg.2, SI 1997/356 Reg.2, SI 1998/155 Reg.2
Sch.2 Part I, referred to: SI 1996/1880 Art.66
Sch.2 Part II, amended: SI 1996/311 Reg.2, SI 1997/356 Reg.2, SI 1998/155 Reg.2
Sch.2 Part II, referred to: SI 1996/1880 Art.66
Sch.3 Part I, amended: SI 1996/311 Reg.2
Sch.3 Part I, referred to: SI 1996/1880 Art.66

254. **Rules of the Air (Amendment) Regulations 1993**
revoked: SI 1996/1393 Reg.3, Sch.2

255. **Council Tax (Demand Notices) (Wales) Regulations 1993**
Reg.1, amended: SI 1996/1880 Art.75
Reg.2, amended: SI 1996/310 Reg.2, Reg.3, SI 1996/1880 Art.75
Reg.6, amended: SI 1996/310 Reg.2
Sch.1, applied: SI 1997/357 Reg.2

NO.

1993—cont.

255. Council Tax (Demand Notices) (Wales) Regulations 1993—*cont.*
Sch.1, referred to: SI 1996/1880 Art.66
Sch.1 para.6, amended: SI 1996/310 Reg.3, SI 1997/357 Reg.2, SI 1998/267 Reg.2, SI 1999/348 Reg.2
Sch.1 para.13, amended: SI 1996/310 Reg.3
Sch.1 para.13A, added: SI 1997/357 Reg.2, SI 1998/267 Reg.2, SI 1999/348 Reg.2
Sch.2 Part I, amended: SI 1996/310 Reg.2, SI 1996 310 Reg.3, SI 1997/357 Reg.2, SI 1998/267 Reg.2, SI 1999/348 Reg.2
Sch.2 Part I, applied: SI 1997/357 Reg.2
Sch.2 Part I, referred to: SI 1996/1880 Art.66
Sch.2 para.6, amended: SI 1996/310 Reg.2, Reg.3
Sch.2 para.8, amended: SI 1996/310 Reg.2
Sch.2 para.11, amended: SI 1996/310 Reg.3
Sch.2 para.12, amended: SI 1996/310 Reg.3
Sch.2 para.13, amended: SI 1996/310 Reg.2, Reg.3
Sch.2 para.15, amended: SI 1996/310 Reg.3

259. Warwickshire Ambulance Service National Health Service Trust (Establishment) Order 1993
Art.3, substituted: SI 1998/2949 Art.2

276. River Tay Catchment Area Protection (Renewal) Order 1993
Art.4, amended: SI 1996/58 Art.2

278. Planning (General Development) Order (Northern Ireland) 1993
Part 17, referred to: SI 1999/2450 Sch.4 para.3.6, Sch.4 para.4.2, Sch.4 para.5.5

290. Council Tax (Alteration of Lists and Appeals) Regulations 1993
Reg.2, amended: SI 1996/619 Art.8
Reg.4, see *R. v East Sussex Valuation Tribunal Ex p. Silverstone* [1996] 36 R.V.R. 203 (QBD), Carnwath, J.
Reg.14, amended: SI 1996/619 Art.8
Reg.15, amended: SI 1996/619 Art.8

291. Non-Domestic Rating (Alteration of Lists and Appeals) Regulations 1993
Part VI, applied: SI 1999/3379 Reg.37, SI 1999/3454 Reg.12
Reg.4B, amended: SI 1996/619 Art.5
Reg.13, applied: SI 1999/3379 Reg.13
Reg.18, amended: SI 1996/619 Art.5

293. A65 Trunk Road (Manor Park Improvement) Order 1993
revoked: SI 1998/1206 Art.1

294. A65 Trunk Road (Denton Bridge to Black Bull Farm) (Detrunking) Order 1993
revoked: SI 1998/1207 Art.1

302. Mines (Shafts and Winding) Regulations 1993
applied: SI 1998/2306 Reg.6
referred to: SI 1998/2307 Reg.9

315. Income-related Benefits Schemes (Miscellaneous Amendments) Regulations 1993
Reg.5, revoked: SI 1996/206 Reg.28, Sch.3

323. Town and Country Planning (Hazardous Substances) (Scotland) Regulations 1993
Reg.4, amended: SI 1996/252 Art.2
Reg.11, amended: SI 1996/252 Art.2, Sch

345. Council Tax (Exempt Dwellings) (Scotland) Amendment Order 1993
revoked: SI 1997/728 Art.5, Sch.2

352. St George's Healthcare National Health Service Trust (Establishment) Order 1993
Art.3, substituted: SI 1999/1168 Art.2

NO.

1993—cont.

355. Council Tax (Alteration of Lists and Appeals) (Scotland) Regulations 1993
Part IV, applied: SI 1996/325 Art.12, SI 1997/362 Art.12, SI 1998/634 Art.12
Reg.2, amended: SI 1996/580 Art.9
Reg.3, amended: SI 1996/580 Art.9
Reg.21, amended: SI 1996/580 Art.9
Reg.25, amended: SI 1996/580 Art.9

384. Offshore Safety (Repeals and Modifications) Regulations (Northern Ireland) 1993
applied: 1998 c.17 s.12
Reg.4, revoked (in part): 1998 c.17 s.51, Sch.5 Part II

407. Local Authorities (Recovery of Costs for Public Path Orders) Regulations 1993
Reg.2, amended: SI 1996/1978 Reg.3
Reg.4, revoked (in part): SI 1996/1978 Reg.3

418. National Health Service (Optical Charges and Payments) Amendment Regulations 1993
revoked: SI 1997/818 Reg.24, Sch.4

429. Seeds (Fees) (Amendment) Regulations 1993
revoked: SI 1996/1486 Reg.3

445. Environmental Protection (Waste Recycling Payments) (Amendment) Regulations 1993
revoked: SI 1997/351 Reg.4

455. Environmentally Sensitive Areas (Breckland) Designation Order 1993
referred to: SI 1998/1295 Reg.3, Reg.4
Art.2, amended: SI 1996/3104 Reg.2, SI 1998/1306 Art.4
Art.3, amended: SI 1998/1306 Art.5
Art.4, substituted: SI 1998/1306 Art.6
Art.4A, revoked: SI 1998/1306 Art.10
Art.5, amended: SI 1996/3104 Reg.2
Art.5, substituted: SI 1998/1306 Art.7
Art.5A, added: SI 1996/3104 Reg.2
Art.5B, added: SI 1996/3104 Reg.2
Art.5C, added: SI 1996/3104 Reg.2
Art.6, amended: SI 1997/1445 Art.4
Art.6, revoked: SI 1998/1306 Art.10
Art.7, revoked: SI 1998/1306 Art.10
Sch.1, substituted: SI 1998/1306 Art.8, Sch.1
Sch.2, amended: SI 1996/3104 Reg.3
Sch.2, substituted: SI 1998/1306 Art.9, Sch.2
Sch.2 para.1, amended: SI 1997/1364 Art.3
Sch.3, revoked: SI 1998/1306 Art.10
Sch.4, revoked: SI 1998/1306 Art.10
Sch.5, revoked: SI 1998/1306 Art.10
Sch.6, revoked: SI 1998/1306 Art.10
Sch.6A, revoked: SI 1998/1306 Art.10
Sch.7 para.4, substituted: SI 1997/1445 Art.5
Sch.7 para.4A, added: SI 1997/1445 Art.5

456. Environmentally Sensitive Areas (Clun) Designation Order 1993
referred to: SI 1998/1295 Reg.3, Reg.4
Art.2, amended: SI 1996/3104 Reg.2, SI 1998/1311 Art.4
Art.4, substituted: SI 1998/1311 Art.5
Art.4A, revoked: SI 1998/1311 Art.9
Art.5, amended: SI 1996/3104 Reg.2
Art.5, substituted: SI 1998/1311 Art.6
Art.5A, added: SI 1996/3104 Reg.2
Art.5B, added: SI 1996/3104 Reg.2
Art.5C, added: SI 1996/3104 Reg.2
Art.6, amended: SI 1997/1446 Art.4
Art.6, revoked: SI 1998/1311 Art.9
Sch.1, amended: SI 1999/1369 Art.4
Sch.1, substituted: SI 1998/1311 Art.7, Sch.1
Sch.1A, revoked: SI 1998/1311 Art.9

NO.

456. **Environmentally Sensitive Areas (Clun) Designation Order 1993**—*cont.*
Sch.2, substituted: SI 1998/1311 Art.8, Sch.2
Sch.2 Item 1, amended: SI 1999/1369 Art.5
Sch.2 Item 3, amended: SI 1999/1369 Art.5
Sch.3, revoked: SI 1998/1311 Art.9
Sch.4, revoked: SI 1998/1311 Art.9
Sch.5, revoked: SI 1998/1311 Art.9
Sch.5 para.1, amended: SI 1996/3104 Reg.3
Sch.7, revoked: SI 1998/1311 Art.9
Sch.8, revoked: SI 1998/1311 Art.9
Sch.8 para.5, revoked: SI 1998/1311 Art.9
Sch.8 para.5, substituted: SI 1997/1446 Art.5
Sch.8 para.5A, added: SI 1997/1446 Art.5
Sch.8 para.5A, revoked: SI 1998/1311 Art.9
Sch.8 para.9, revoked: SI 1998/1311 Art.9

457. **Environmentally Sensitive Areas (North Peak) Designation Order 1993**
amended: SI 1998/2173 Art.3
applied: SI 1998/2173 Art.3
referred to: SI 1998/1295 Reg.3, Reg.4
Art.2, amended: SI 1996/3104 Reg.2, SI 1998/1303 Art.4
Art.3, amended: SI 1998/1303 Art.5
Art.4, substituted: SI 1998/1303 Art.6
Art.4A, revoked: SI 1998/1303 Art.10
Art.5, amended: SI 1996/3104 Reg.2
Art.5, substituted: SI 1998/1303 Art.7
Art.5A, added: SI 1996/3104 Reg.2
Art.5B, added: SI 1996/3104 Reg.2
Art.5C, added: SI 1996/3104 Reg.2
Art.6, amended: SI 1997/1447 Art.4
Art.6, revoked: SI 1998/1303 Art.10
Sch.1, substituted: SI 1998/1303 Art.8, Sch.1
Sch.1A, revoked: SI 1998/1303 Art.10
Sch.2, substituted: SI 1998/1303 Art.9, Sch.2
Sch.2 Part I, amended: SI 1999/1367 Art.3
Sch.4, revoked: SI 1998/1303 Art.10
Sch.4 para.2, revoked: SI 1998/1303 Art.10
Sch.4 para.2, substituted: SI 1997/1447 Art.5
Sch.4 para.2A, added: SI 1997/1447 Art.5
Sch.4 para.2A, revoked: SI 1998/1303 Art.10
Sch.4 para.5, revoked: SI 1998/1303 Art.10
Sch.4 para.10, revoked: SI 1998/1303 Art.10

458. **Environmentally Sensitive Areas (Suffolk River Valleys) Designation Order 1993**
referred to: SI 1998/1295 Reg.3, Reg.4
Art.2, amended: SI 1996/3104 Reg.2, SI 1998/1310 Art.4
Art.3, amended: SI 1998/1310 Art.5
Art.4, substituted: SI 1998/1310 Art.6
Art.4A, revoked: SI 1998/1310 Art.10
Art.5, amended: SI 1996/3104 Reg.2
Art.5, substituted: SI 1998/1310 Art.7
Art.5A, added: SI 1996/3104 Reg.2
Art.5B, added: SI 1996/3104 Reg.2
Art.5C, added: SI 1996/3104 Reg.2
Art.6, amended: SI 1997/1448 Art.4
Art.6, revoked: SI 1998/1310 Art.10
Sch.1, substituted: SI 1998/1310 Art.8, Sch.1
Sch.1A, revoked: SI 1998/1310 Art.10
Sch.2, substituted: SI 1998/1310 Art.9, Sch.2
Sch.2 Item 1, amended: SI 1999/1372 Art.3
Sch.2 Item 8, amended: SI 1999/1372 Art.3
Sch.3, revoked: SI 1998/1310 Art.10
Sch.4, amended: SI 1996/3104 Reg.3
Sch.4, revoked: SI 1998/1310 Art.10
Sch.5, revoked: SI 1998/1310 Art.10
Sch.6, revoked: SI 1998/1310 Art.10
Sch.6 para.3, revoked: SI 1998/1310 Art.10
Sch.6 para.3, substituted: SI 1997/1448 Art.5
Sch.6 para.3A, added: SI 1997/1448 Art.5

NO.

458. **Environmentally Sensitive Areas (Suffolk River Valleys) Designation Order 1993**—*cont.*
Sch.6 para.3A, revoked: SI 1998/1310 Art.10
Sch.6 para.10, revoked: SI 1998/1310 Art.10
Sch.6 para.11, added: SI 1997/1448 Art.5
Sch.6 para.11, revoked: SI 1998/1310 Art.10

459. **Environmentally Sensitive Areas (Test Valley) Designation Order 1993**
amended: SI 1998/2178 Art.3
applied: SI 1998/2178 Art.3
referred to: SI 1998/1295 Reg.3, Reg.4
Art.2, amended: SI 1996/3104 Reg.2, SI 1998/1308 Art.4
Art.3, amended: SI 1998/1308 Art.5
Art.4, substituted: SI 1998/1308 Art.6
Art.4A, revoked: SI 1998/1308 Art.10
Art.5, amended: SI 1996/3104 Reg.2
Art.5, substituted: SI 1998/1308 Art.7
Art.5A, added: SI 1996/3104 Reg.2
Art.5B, added: SI 1996/3104 Reg.2
Art.5C, added: SI 1996/3104 Reg.2
Art.6, amended: SI 1997/1449 Art.4
Art.6, revoked: SI 1998/1308 Art.10
Sch.1, substituted: SI 1998/1308 Art.8, Sch.1
Sch.1A, revoked: SI 1998/1308 Art.10
Sch.2, amended: SI 1996/3104 Reg.3
Sch.2, substituted: SI 1998/1308 Art.9, Sch.2
Sch.2 Part I, amended: SI 1999/1365 Art.3
Sch.3, revoked: SI 1998/1308 Art.10
Sch.3 para.2, revoked: SI 1998/1308 Art.10
Sch.3 para.2, substituted: SI 1997/1449 Art.5
Sch.3 para.2A, added: SI 1997/1449 Art.5
Sch.3 para.2A, revoked: SI 1998/1308 Art.10
Sch.3 para.4, revoked: SI 1998/1308 Art.10
Sch.3 para.9, revoked: SI 1998/1308 Art.10
Sch.3 para.10, added: SI 1997/1449 Art.5
Sch.3 para.10, revoked: SI 1998/1308 Art.10

460. **Environmentally Sensitive Areas (Pennine Dales) Designation (Amendment) Order 1993**
revoked: SI 1997/1441 Art.6 (with saving)

475. **Merchant Shipping (Light Dues) (Amendment) Regulations 1993**
revoked: SI 1997/562 Reg.2, Sch.1

476. **Wireless Telegraphy (Television Licence Fees) (Amendment) Regulations 1993**
revoked: SI 1997/290 Reg.1, Sch

481. **Education (Prescribed Courses of Higher Education) (Wales) Regulations 1993**
amended: SI 1998/1970 Reg.2
Reg.1, amended: SI 1998/1970 Reg.2
Reg.2, amended: SI 1998/1970 Reg.2
Reg.3, amended: SI 1998/1970 Reg.2

486. **Bankruptcy Fees (Scotland) Regulations 1993**
Reg.2, amended: SI 1999/752 Reg.3
Sch., substituted: SI 1999/752 Reg.4

487. **Registered Housing Associations (Accounting Requirements) (Scotland) Order 1993**
revoked: SI 1999/1073 Art.1 (with saving)

488. **National Health Service (Fund-Holding Practices) (Scotland) Regulations 1993**
revoked: SI 1997/1014 Reg.24, Sch.3
Reg.1, amended: SI 1996/748 Reg.2
Reg.8, substituted: SI 1996/748 Reg.3
Reg.9, amended: SI 1996/748 Reg.4
Reg.10, amended: SI 1996/748 Reg.5
Reg.10, revoked (in part): SI 1996/748 Reg.5
Reg.16, amended: SI 1996/748 Reg.6
Reg.17, amended: SI 1996/748 Reg.7
Reg.19, amended: SI 1996/748 Reg.8
Reg.19A, amended: SI 1996/748 Reg.9

NO.

488. National Health Service (Fund-Holding Practices) (Scotland) Regulations 1993—*cont.*
Reg.20, amended: SI 1996/748 Reg.10
Sch.1 para.5, amended: SI 1996/748 Reg.11
Sch.2 para.4, added: SI 1996/748 Reg.12
Sch.2 para.5, added: SI 1996/748 Reg.12
Sch.2 para.13, added: SI 1996/748 Reg.12

490. Jordanhill College of Education (Closure) (Scotland) Order 1993
Sch. para.1, revoked: SI 1998/192 Reg.52, Sch.2

494. Council Tax (Deductions from Income Support) Regulations 1993
applied: SI 1999/991 Reg.27, Sch.2 para.9
Reg.1, amended: SI 1996/2344 Reg.17, SI 1998/563 Reg.3, SI 1999/2860 Art.3, Sch.10 para.1, SI 1999/3178 Art.3, Sch.13 para.1
Reg.2, amended: SI 1996/2344 Reg.18
Reg.3, amended: SI 1996/712 Art.2, SI 1996/2344 Reg.19
Reg.4, amended: SI 1996/2344 Reg.20
Reg.5, amended: SI 1996/2344 Reg.21, SI 1997/827 Reg.8, SI 1999/2860 Art.3, Sch.10 para.2, Sch.10 para.3
Reg.5, substituted: SI 1999/3178 Art.3, Sch.13 para.2
Reg.6, amended: SI 1999/2860 Art.3, Sch.10 para.4
Reg.6, revoked: SI 1999/3178 Art.3, Sch.13 para.2
Reg.7, amended: SI 1996/2344 Reg.22, SI 1999/2860 Art.3, Sch.10 para.5
Reg.7, revoked: SI 1999/3178 Art.3, Sch.13 para.2
Reg.7A, added: SI 1996/2344 Reg.23
Reg.7A, amended: SI 1999/2860 Art.3, Sch.10 para.5
Reg.7A, revoked: SI 1999/3178 Art.3, Sch.13 para.2
Reg.8, amended: SI 1996/2344 Reg.24, SI 1999/2860 Art.3, Sch.10 para.6, SI 1999/3178 Art.3, Sch.13 para.3
Reg.10, substituted: SI 1999/2860 Art.3, Sch.10 para.7, SI 1999/3178 Art.3, Sch.13 para.4
Reg.11, revoked: SI 1999/2860 Art.3, Sch.10 para.8
Reg.11, substituted: SI 1999/3178 Art.3, Sch.13 para.4
Reg.12, revoked: SI 1999/2860 Art.3, Sch.10 para.8, SI 1999/3178 Art.3, Sch.13 para.5
Reg.13, revoked: SI 1999/2860 Art.3, Sch.10 para.8, SI 1999/3178 Art.3, Sch.13 para.5
Reg.14, revoked: SI 1999/2860 Art.3, Sch.10 para.8, SI 1999/3178 Art.3, Sch.13 para.5
Reg.15, revoked: SI 1999/2860 Art.3, Sch.10 para.8, SI 1999/3178 Art.3, Sch.13 para.5
Reg.16, revoked: SI 1999/2860 Art.3, Sch.10 para.8, SI 1999/3178 Art.3, Sch.13 para.5
Sch.1, revoked: SI 1999/2860 Art.3, Sch.10 para.9, SI 1999/3178 Art.3, Sch.13 para.5
Sch.2, revoked: SI 1999/2860 Art.3, Sch.10 para.9, SI 1999/3178 Art.3, Sch.13 para.5

516. Prison (Amendment) Rules 1993
revoked: SI 1999/728 r.85 (with savings), Sch. (with savings)

519. Occupational and Personal Pension Schemes (Miscellaneous Amendments) Regulations 1993
Reg.2, revoked: SI 1996/1172 Sch.2
Reg.5, revoked: SI 1997/470 Reg.20, Sch.3

NO.

520. Local Authorities (Capital Finance) (Amendment) Regulations 1993
revoked: SI 1997/319 Reg.162, Sch.3

523. National Health Service (Dental Services) (Miscellaneous Amendments) (Scotland) Regulations 1993
revoked (in part): SI 1996/177 Reg.38, Sch.8
Reg.2, revoked: SI 1997/174 Reg.18, Sch
Reg.3, revoked: SI 1997/174 Reg.18, Sch

524. National Health Service (Optical Charges and Payments) (Scotland) Amendment Regulations 1993
revoked: SI 1998/642 Reg.24, Sch.4

525. Education (Fees and Awards) (Scotland) Amendment Regulations 1993
revoked: SI 1997/93 Reg.14, Sch.4

533. Advice and Assistance (Scotland) Amendment Regulations 1993
revoked: SI 1996/2447 Reg.3, Sch.1

534. Legal Aid (Scotland) (Children) Amendment Regulations 1993
revoked: SI 1997/690 Reg.12 (with savings)

535. Civil Legal Aid (Scotland) Amendment Regulations 1993
revoked: SI 1996/2444 Reg.3, Sch.1

541. Statistics of Trade (Customs and Excise) (Amendment) Regulations 1993
Reg.3, revoked: SI 1997/2864 Reg.8
Reg.4, revoked: SI 1997/2864 Reg.8
Reg.5, revoked: SI 1997/2864 Reg.8
Reg.6, revoked: SI 1997/2864 Reg.8

543. Education (Teachers) Regulations 1993
amended: SI 1999/711 Reg.2, Sch.1
applied: SI 1997/2679 Reg.6, SI 1999/2166 Reg.2, Sch.1 para.7, SI 1999/2817 Reg.2, Sch.1 para.7
referred to: SI 1999/2817 Reg.2, Sch.1 para.8
Reg.2, revoked (in part): SI 1999/2166 Reg.2, Sch.1 Part I, SI 1999/2817 Reg.2, Sch.1 Part I
Reg.3, amended: SI 1997/2679 Reg.2
Reg.3, revoked (in part): SI 1999/2166 Reg.2, Sch.1 Part I, SI 1999/2817 Reg.2, Sch.1 Part I
Reg.3A, revoked: SI 1997/2679 Reg.3
Reg.4, revoked (in part): SI 1999/2166 Reg.2, Sch.1 Part I, SI 1999/2817 Reg.2, Sch.1 Part I
Reg.6, revoked (in part): SI 1999/2166 Reg.2, Sch.1 Part I, SI 1999/2817 Reg.2, Sch.1 Part I
Reg.7, amended: SI 1998/1584 Reg.3
Reg.8, amended: SI 1997/543 Reg.2
Reg.8, revoked (in part): SI 1999/2166 Reg.2, Sch.1 Part I, SI 1999/2817 Reg.2, Sch.1 Part I
Reg.9, revoked (in part): SI 1999/2166 Reg.2, Sch.1 Part I, SI 1999/2817 Reg.2, Sch.1 Part I
Reg.10, applied: SI 1997/3001 Reg.E4
Reg.10A, added: SI 1998/1584 Reg.3
Reg.11, amended: SI 1998/1584 Reg.3
Reg.12, amended: SI 1998/1584 Reg.4
Reg.12, revoked (in part): SI 1999/2166 Reg.2, Sch.1 Part I, SI 1999/2817 Reg.2, Sch.1 Part I
Reg.12A, added: SI 1998/1584 Reg.4
Reg.13, revoked (in part): SI 1999/2166 Reg.2, Sch.1 Part I, SI 1999/2817 Reg.2, Sch.1 Part I
Reg.14, applied: SI 1999/2166 Reg.2, Sch.1 para 1, SI 1999/2817 Reg.2, Sch.1 para.1
Reg.14, revoked (in part): SI 1999/2166 Reg.2, Sch.1 Part I, SI 1999/2817 Reg.2, Sch.1 Part I
Reg.15, applied: SI 1999/2166 Reg.2, Sch.1 para 2, SI 1999/2817 Reg.2, Sch.1 para.2
Reg.15, revoked (in part): SI 1999/2166 Reg.2, Sch.1 Part I, SI 1999/2817 Reg.2, Sch.1 Part I
Reg.16, revoked (in part): SI 1999/2166 Reg.2, Sch.1 Part I, SI 1999/2817 Reg.2, Sch.1 Part I

NO.

NO.

1993—cont.

1993—cont.

543. Education (Teachers) Regulations 1993— *cont.*

Reg.17, revoked (in part): SI 1999/2166 Reg.2, Sch.1 Part I, SI 1999/2817 Reg.2, Sch.1 Part I

Sch.1 para.2, revoked (in part): SI 1999/2166 Reg.2, Sch.1 Part I, SI 1999/2817 Reg.2, Sch.1 Part I

Sch.1 para.3, revoked (in part): SI 1999/2166 Reg.2, Sch.1 Part I, SI 1999/2817 Reg.2, Sch.1 Part I

Sch.1 para.4, revoked (in part): SI 1999/2166 Reg.2, Sch.1 Part I, SI 1999/2817 Reg.2, Sch.1 Part I

Sch.1 para.5, revoked (in part): SI 1999/2166 Reg.2, Sch.1 Part I, SI 1999/2817 Reg.2, Sch.1 Part I

Sch.1 para.6, revoked (in part): SI 1999/2166 Reg.2, Sch.1 Part I, SI 1999/2817 Reg.2, Sch.1 Part I

Sch.1 para.7, revoked (in part): SI 1999/2166 Reg.2, Sch.1 Part I, SI 1999/2817 Reg.2, Sch.1 Part I

Sch.2, revoked: SI 1999/2166 Reg.2, Sch.1 Part I

Sch.2, substituted: SI 1997/2679 Reg.4, Sch.1

Sch.2 Part II, revoked (in part): SI 1999/2817 Reg.2, Sch.1 Part I

Sch.2 Part III, revoked (in part): SI 1999/2817 Reg.2, Sch.1 Part I

Sch.2 para.2, applied: SI 1999/2166 Reg.10, Sch.2 para 2, SI 1999/2817 Reg.10, Sch.2 para.2

Sch.2 para.2, revoked (in part): SI 1999/2817 Reg.2, Sch.1 Part I

Sch.2 para.3, applied: SI 1997/2679 Reg.6, SI 1999/2817 Reg.3, Reg.10, Reg.11, Reg.12, Reg.13, Sch.3 para.8

Sch.2 para.3, revoked (in part): SI 1999/2817 Reg.2, Sch.1 Part I

Sch.2 para.3A, added: SI 1996/1603 Reg.2

Sch.2 para.3A, revoked (in part): SI 1999/2817 Reg.2, Sch.1 Part I

Sch.3, applied: SI 1999/2166 Reg.10, Sch.3 para 1, SI 1999/2817 Reg.3, Reg.10, Sch.3 para.1

Sch.3, revoked (in part): SI 1999/2166 Reg.2, Sch.1 Part I, SI 1999/2817 Reg.2, Sch.1 Part I

Sch.3, substituted: SI 1997/2679 Reg.5, Sch.2

Sch.3 para.1, revoked (in part): SI 1999/2817 Reg.2, Sch.1 Part I

Sch.3 para.2, amended: SI 1997/543 Reg.3

Sch.3 para.2, revoked (in part): SI 1999/2817 Reg.2, Sch.1 Part I

Sch.3 para.3, applied: SI 1999/2166 Reg.2, Sch.1 para 5, SI 1999/2817 Reg.2, Sch.1 para.5

Sch.3 para.3, revoked (in part): SI 1999/2817 Reg.2, Sch.1 Part I

553. Housing Renovation etc. Grants (Grant Limit) Order 1993

applied: SI 1996/2842 Art.8

revoked: SI 1996/2842 Art.7, Sch Part I

554. Assistance for Minor Works to Dwellings (Amendment) Order 1993

applied: SI 1996/2842 Art.8

revoked: SI 1996/2842 Art.7, Sch Part I

559. Further and Higher Education Act 1992 (Consequential Amendments) Regulations 1993

Reg.6, revoked: SI 1998/1967 Reg.6, Sch.3

567. National Health Service (Fund-Holding Practices) Regulations 1993

revoked: SI 1996/706 Reg.28

substituted: SI 1996/706

Reg.1, revoked: SI 1996/706 Reg.28

Reg.3, revoked: SI 1996/706 Reg.28

Reg.9, revoked: SI 1996/706 Reg.28

Reg.13, revoked: SI 1996/706 Reg.28

Reg.18A, revoked: SI 1996/706 Reg.28

568. Education (Grant-Maintained Schools) (Finance) Regulations 1993

applied: SI 1996/889 Reg.3, SI 1998/799 Reg.3

referred to: SI 1997/996 Reg.3

569. Education (Grants) (Travellers and Displaced Persons) Regulations 1993

Reg.2, amended: SI 1999/606 Reg.12

Reg.5, amended: SI 1999/606 Reg.12

573. Regional and District Health Authorities (Membership and Procedure) Amendment Regulations 1993

revoked: SI 1996/707 Reg.17, Sch.4 Part I

578. Qualifications of Directors of Social Work (Scotland) Amendment Regulations 1993

revoked: SI 1996/515 Reg.4

585. National Blood Authority (Establishment and Constitution) Order 1993

Art.8, added: SI 1998/1577 Art.6

586. National Blood Authority Regulations 1993

applied: SI 1996/707 Reg.17, Sch.4 Part II

Reg.6, amended: SI 1996/707 Reg.17, Sch.5 para.8, SI 1997/2991 Reg.3, Sch. para.4

592. Social Security (Northern Ireland) Order 1993

Art.4, amended: SI 1996/1919 (NI.16) Art.255, Sch.1, SI 1999/671 Art.4, Sch.3 para.52

Art.4, revoked (in part): SI 1999/671 Art.4, Art.24, Sch.3 para.52, Sch.9 Part I

593. Reciprocal Enforcement of Maintenance Orders (Hague Convention Countries) Order 1993

Sch.1, amended: SI 1999/1318 Art.2

Sch.2 para.5, amended: SI 1999/1318 Art.3

Sch.2 para.5, revoked (in part): SI 1999/1318 Art.3

Sch.2 para.6, amended: SI 1999/1318 Art.3

Sch.2 para.9, amended: SI 1999/1318 Art.3

Sch.2 para.9, revoked (in part): SI 1999/1318 Art.9

Sch.3, amended: SI 1999/1318 Art.4, Art.5, Art.6, Art.7

Sch.3, revoked (in part): SI 1999/1318 Art.4, Art.7

599. Continental Shelf (Designation of Additional Areas) Order 1993

referred to: SI 1999/2031

600. Appropriation (Northern Ireland) Order 1993

revoked: SI 1996/1917 (NI.14) Art.2, Sch.2

609. Further Education (Attribution of Surpluses and Deficits) Regulations 1993

amended: SI 1996/1766 Reg.4

applied: SI 1996/1766 Reg.3

610. Veterinary Surgeons and Veterinary Practitioners (Registration) (Amendment) Regulations Order of Council 1993

revoked: SI 1996/437 Art.3

619. Public Trustee (Fees) (Amendment) Order 1993

revoked: SI 1999/855 Art.32, Sch.

265

NO.

1993—cont.

621. Children (Admissibility of Hearsay Evidence) Order 1993
see *J (A Minor) (Expert Evidence: Hearsay), Re* [1999] 2 F.L.R. 661 (Fam Div), Cazalet, J.; see *R. v Stratford Youth Court Exp. S* [1998] 1 W.L.R. 1758 (QBD), Schiemann, L.J.

625. Education (Listed Bodies) Order 1993
revoked: SI 1997/54 Art.3

626. Education (Recognised Bodies) Order 1993
revoked: SI 1997/1 Art.3

629. National Board for Nursing, Midwifery and Health Visiting for England (Constitution and Administration) Order 1993
Art.12, amended: SI 1997/1963 Art.2
Art.12, revoked (in part): SI 1997/1963 Art.2, SI 1999/766 Art.2 (rem.)

654. Assured Tenancies and Agricultural Occupancies (Forms) (Amendment) Regulations 1993
revoked: SI 1997/194 Reg.4

722. Social Security (Industrial Injuries) (Dependency) (Permitted Earnings Limits) Order 1993
revoked: SI 1996/671 Art.3

728. Rules of the Air (Second Amendment) Regulations 1993
revoked: SI 1996/1393 Reg.3, Sch.2

743. Income Tax (Sub-contractors in the Construction Industry) Regulations 1993
Part IIA, added: SI 1998/2622 Reg.13
Reg.2, amended: SI 1998/2622 Reg.3, SI 1999/2159 Reg.3
Reg.3, substituted: SI 1998/2622 Reg.4
Reg.3A, added: SI 1998/2622 Reg.4
Reg.5, revoked: SI 1998/2622 Reg.5
Reg.6, revoked: SI 1998/2622 Reg.6
Reg.7, amended: SI 1998/2622 Reg.7
Reg.7A, added: SI 1998/2622 Reg.8
Reg.7B, added: SI 1998/2622 Reg.8
Reg.7C, added: SI 1998/2622 Reg.8
Reg.7D, added: SI 1998/2622 Reg.8
Reg.7E, added: SI 1998/2622 Reg.8
Reg.7F, added: SI 1998/2622 Reg.8
Reg.9, amended: SI 1999/825 Reg.2
Reg.10, amended: SI 1996/981 Reg.3
Reg.11, revoked: SI 1998/2622 Reg.9
Reg.13, amended: SI 1996/981 Reg.4, SI 1998/2622 Reg.10
Reg.17, amended: SI 1996/981 Reg.5
Reg.18, amended: SI 1996/981 Reg.4
Reg.20, revoked: SI 1998/2622 Reg.11 (with savings)
Reg.20A, added: SI 1998/2622 Reg.12
Reg.20B, added: SI 1998/2622 Reg.13
Reg.21A, added: SI 1998/2622 Reg.14
Reg.21B, added: SI 1998/2622 Reg.14
Reg.21C, added: SI 1998/2622 Reg.14
Reg.21C, amended: SI 1999/2159 Reg.4
Reg.21D, added: SI 1998/2622 Reg.14
Reg.21D, amended: SI 1999/2159 Reg.5
Reg.21E, added: SI 1998/2622 Reg.14
Reg.21E, amended: SI 1999/2159 Reg.6
Reg.22, amended: SI 1998/2622 Reg.15
Reg.22, revoked (in part): SI 1998/2622 Reg.15
Reg.23, amended: SI 1998/2622 Reg.16
Reg.23, revoked (in part): SI 1998/2622 Reg.16
Reg.23A, added: SI 1998/2622 Reg.17
Reg.23A, amended: SI 1999/2159 Reg.7
Reg.23B, added: SI 1998/2622 Reg.17
Reg.24, amended: SI 1998/2622 Reg.18
Reg.24, revoked (in part): SI 1998/2622 Reg.18
Reg.25, amended: SI 1998/2622 Reg.19
Reg.26, substituted: SI 1998/2622 Reg.20
Reg.28, amended: SI 1998/2622 Reg.21

NO.

1993—cont.

743. Income Tax (Sub-contractors in the Construction Industry) Regulations 1993—cont.
Reg.29, amended: SI 1998/2622 Reg.22
Reg.29, revoked (in part): SI 1998/2622 Reg.22
Reg.30, revoked: SI 1998/2622 Reg.23
Reg.32, revoked: SI 1998/2622 Reg.24
Reg.33, amended: SI 1998/2622 Reg.25
Reg.35, substituted: SI 1998/2622 Reg.26
Reg.36, revoked: SI 1998/2622 Reg.27
Reg.37, revoked: SI 1998/2622 Reg.28
Reg.37A, added: SI 1998/2622 Reg.29
Reg.38, amended: SI 1998/2622 Reg.30
Reg.38, revoked (in part): SI 1998/2622 Reg.30
Reg.39, revoked: SI 1998/2622 Reg.31
Reg.40, revoked: SI 1998/2622 Reg.32
Reg.40A, added: SI 1998/2622 Reg.33
Reg.41, amended: SI 1998/2622 Reg.34, SI 1999/2159 Reg.8
Reg.44A, added: SI 1998/2622 Reg.35
Reg.45, revoked (in part): SI 1998/2622 Reg.36
Sch.1, amended: SI 1999/2159 Reg.10
Sch.1, substituted: SI 1998/2622 Reg.38
Sch. A1, added: SI 1998/2622 Reg.37
Sch. A1, amended: SI 1999/2159 Reg.9
Sch.2, substituted: SI 1998/2622 Reg.38

744. Income Tax (Employments) Regulations 1993
applied: SI 1996/2631 Reg.3, SI 1999/3219 Reg.3
Part VI Ch.V, added: SI 1996/2631 Reg.4
Reg.2, amended: SI 1998/2484 Reg.3, SI 1999/2155 Reg.8
Reg.5, amended: SI 1996/1312 Reg.3
Reg.6, amended: SI 1998/2484 Reg.4
Reg.7, amended: SI 1999/2155 Reg.3
Reg.7, revoked (in part): SI 1996/1312 Reg.4
Reg.9, amended: SI 1996/1312 Reg.5
Reg.10, amended: SI 1999/2155 Reg.4, Reg.15, Reg.20
Reg.11, amended: SI 1996/1312 Reg.6
Reg.12, amended: SI 1999/2155 Reg.4, Reg.16, Reg.21
Reg.13, amended: SI 1999/2155 Reg.5, Reg.17, Reg.22
Reg.20, referred to: SI 1999/3219 Reg.3
Reg.23, amended: SI 1996/804 Reg.3, SI 1998/2484 Reg.5
Reg.24, amended: SI 1998/2484 Reg.6
Reg.25, amended: SI 1996/804 Reg.4, SI 1998/2484 Reg.7
Reg.26, amended: SI 1996/804 Reg.5, SI 1998/2484 Reg.8
Reg.27, amended: SI 1996/804 Reg.6, SI 1998/2484 Reg.9
Reg.28, amended: SI 1998/2484 Reg.10, SI 1999/2155 Reg.6
Reg.29, amended: SI 1996/2554 Reg.3, SI 1999/2155 Reg.9
Reg.30, amended: SI 1996/2554 Reg.4, SI 1998/2484 Reg.11, SI 1999/2155 Reg.10
Reg.32, amended: SI 1999/2155 Reg.11
Reg.34, amended: SI 1996/804 Reg.7, SI 1998/2484 Reg.12
Reg.37, amended: SI 1996/804 Reg.8, SI 1998/2484 Reg.13
Reg.38, applied: SI 1999/3219 Reg.6
Reg.39, applied: SI 1999/3219 Reg.6
Reg.41, amended: SI 1999/824 Reg.2
Reg.42, amended: SI 1996/980 Reg.3
Reg.43, amended: SI 1998/2484 Reg.14
Reg.43, applied: SI 1999/3219 Reg.6
Reg.46, amended: SI 1998/2484 Reg.15

NO.

744. Income Tax (Employments) Regulations 1993—*cont.*
Reg.46A, amended: SI 1998/2484 Reg.18
Reg.46AA, amended: SI 1996/1312 Reg.7, SI 1998/2484 Reg.16
Reg.46AB, amended: SI 1998/2484 Reg.17
Reg.46ZA, added: SI 1999/70 Reg.3
Reg.48, amended: SI 1996/980 Reg.4
Reg.49, see *R. v Inland Revenue Commissioners Ex p. McVeigh* [1996] S.T.C. 91 (QBD), May, J.
Reg.49, amended: SI 1996/1312 Reg.8, SI 1999/2155 Reg.7
Reg.52, amended: SI 1996/980 Reg.5
Reg.53, amended: SI 1996/980 Reg.4, SI 1996/1312 Reg.9
Reg.53A, added: SI 1996/1312 Reg.10
Reg.55, amended: SI 1998/2484 Reg.19
Reg.59, amended: SI 1997/214 Reg.3, Reg.4
Reg.63, amended: SI 1996/1312 Reg.11
Reg.68, amended: SI 1996/1312 Reg.12
Reg.80A, added: SI 1996/2631 Reg.4
Reg.80A, amended: SI 1998/2484 Reg.20
Reg.80B, added: SI 1996/2631 Reg.4
Reg.80C, added: SI 1996/2631 Reg.4
Reg.80D, added: SI 1996/2631 Reg.4
Reg.80E, added: SI 1996/2631 Reg.4
Reg.80F, added: SI 1996/2631 Reg.4
Reg.80F, amended: SI 1999/2155 Reg.12
Reg.80G, added: SI 1996/2631 Reg.4
Reg.80H, added: SI 1996/2631 Reg.4
Reg.80J, added: SI 1996/2631 Reg.4
Reg.80K, added: SI 1996/2631 Reg.4
Reg.80L, added: SI 1996/2631 Reg.4
Reg.80M, added: SI 1996/2631 Reg.4
Reg.80N, added: SI 1996/2631 Reg.4
Reg.80ZA, added: SI 1998/1891 Reg.8
Reg.81, amended: SI 1996/2381 Reg.3
Reg.83, amended: SI 1996/2381 Reg.4
Reg.84, amended: SI 1996/804 Reg.9, SI 1998/2484 Reg.21, SI 1999/2155 Reg.13
Reg.88, amended: SI 1996/804 Reg.10, SI 1996/1312 Reg.12
Reg.89, amended: SI 1996/804 Reg.11
Reg.91, amended: SI 1996/804 Reg.12, SI 1998/2484 Reg.22
Reg.92, amended: SI 1996/804 Reg.13
Reg.98C, amended: SI 1999/2155 Reg.14, Reg.23
Reg.98C, revoked (in part): SI 1999/2155 Reg.18
Reg.98E, amended: SI 1996/804 Reg.14, SI 1998/2484 Reg.23
Reg.98F, amended: SI 1999/2155 Reg.19, Reg.24
Reg.98F, revoked (in part): SI 1999/2155 Reg.19
Reg.99, substituted: SI 1996/1312 Reg.13
Reg.100, revoked (in part): SI 1996/1312 Reg.19
Reg.101, amended: SI 1996/1312 Reg.14
Reg.101A, added: SI 1996/1312 Reg.15
Reg.102, revoked (in part): SI 1996/1312 Reg.16
Reg.103, revoked (in part): SI 1996/1312 Reg.19
Reg.104, amended: SI 1996/1312 Reg.17
Reg.104, revoked (in part): SI 1996/1312 Reg.17
Reg.105, revoked (in part): SI 1996/1312 Reg.18

NO.

751. Medicines Control Agency Trading Fund Order 1993
Sch.1 para.2A, added: SI 1997/805 Art.2
779. Pensions Increase (Review) Order 1993
applied: SI 1997/634 Art.3, SI 1998/503 Art.3, Art.4, SI 1999/522 Art.3
784. Redundancy Payments (Local Government) (Modification) (Amendment) Order 1993
revoked: SI 1999/2277 Art.4, Sch.3
798. Measuring Instruments (EEC Requirements) (Fees) Regulations 1993
revoked: SI 1998/1177 Reg.1
Sch.2 para.1, amended: SI 1996/690 Reg.2, SI 1997/630 Reg.2
Sch.2 para.1, revoked: SI 1998/1177 Reg.1
Sch.3 para.1, amended: SI 1996/690 Reg.2, SI 1997/630 Reg.2
Sch.3 para.1, revoked: SI 1998/1177 Reg.1
Sch.4, revoked: SI 1998/1177 Reg.1
Sch.4 para.3, amended: SI 1996/690 Reg.2
Sch.4 para.3, revoked: SI 1998/1177 Reg.1
Sch.5 para.1, amended: SI 1996/690 Reg.2, SI 1997/630 Reg.2
Sch.5 para.1, revoked: SI 1998/1177 Reg.1
Sch.6 para.1, amended: SI 1996/690 Reg.2, SI 1997/630 Reg.2
Sch.6 para.1, revoked: SI 1998/1177 Reg.1
811. Walsgrave Hospitals National Health Service Trust (Establishment) Order 1993
Art.3, amended: SI 1998/812 Art.2
Art.4, amended: SI 1998/3082 Art.2, SI 1999/1392 Art.2
813. Cornwall Healthcare National Health Service Trust (Establishment) Order 1993
Art.3, substituted: SI 1999/633 Art.2
Art.4, amended: SI 1999/885 Art.2
818. Civil Legal Aid (Scotland) Amendment (No.2) Regulations 1993
revoked: SI 1996/2444 Reg.3, Sch.1
819. Advice and Assistance (Scotland) Amendment (No.2) Regulations 1993
revoked: SI 1996/2447 Reg.3, Sch.1
848. Local Government (Direct Service Organisations) (Competition) Regulations 1993
applied: SI 1997/2747 Reg.2
Reg.1, amended: SI 1996/1680 Sch.4 para.2
Reg.2, revoked: SI 1997/2747 Reg.2, Sch.
Reg.3, revoked: SI 1997/2747 Reg.2, Sch.
Reg.4, revoked (in part): SI 1997/2747 Reg.2, Sch.
Reg.5, revoked: SI 1997/2747 Reg.2, Sch.
Reg.6, revoked: SI 1997/2747 Reg.2, Sch.
Reg.7, revoked: SI 1997/2747 Reg.2, Sch.
Reg.8, revoked: SI 1997/2747 Reg.2, Sch.
Reg.9, revoked: SI 1997/2747 Reg.2, Sch.
Reg.10, revoked: SI 1997/2747 Reg.2, Sch.
Reg.11, revoked: SI 1997/2747 Reg.2, Sch.
Reg.12, amended: SI 1996/1680 Sch.4 para.2
Reg.12, revoked: SI 1997/2747 Reg.2, Sch.
Reg.13, revoked: SI 1997/2747 Reg.2, Sch.
Reg.14, revoked: SI 1997/2747 Reg.2, Sch.
Reg.14A, revoked: SI 1997/2747 Reg.2, Sch.
Reg.15, see *South Lanarkshire Council v Secretary of State for Scotland (1997)* 1998 S.L.T. 445 (OH), Lord Cameron of Lochbroom
Sch., revoked: SI 1997/2747 Reg.2, Sch.
891. A1 Trunk Road (Islington) Red Route Traffic Order 1993
revoked (in part): SI 1999/1484 Art.5
Art.2, revoked (in part): SI 1999/1484 Art.5

NO.

NO.

1993—cont.

891. A1 Trunk Road (Islington) Red Route Traffic Order 1993—*cont.*

Art.4, amended: SI 1997/202 Art.3, SI 1999/2745 Art.3

Art.4, revoked (in part): SI 1999/1484 Art.5

Art.7, amended: SI 1998/77 Art.7, SI 1999/1475 Art.6, Art.7

Art.7, revoked (in part): SI 1999/1484 Art.5

Part VI, added: SI 1997/202 Art.4

Part VI, revoked (in part): SI 1999/1484 Art.5

Part VII, added: SI 1997/202 Art.4

Part VII, revoked (in part): SI 1999/1484 Art.5

Part VIII, added: SI 1997/202 Art.4

Part VIII, revoked (in part): SI 1999/1484 Art.5

Sch.1 Part I, amended: SI 1999/2745 Art.4

Sch.1 Part I, revoked: SI 1999 1484 Art.5

Sch.1 Item 7, amended: SI 1999/2745 Art.5

Sch.1 Item 7, revoked: SI 1999 1484 Art.5

Sch.2 Part I, amended: SI 1999/2745 Art.6

Sch.2 Part I, revoked: SI 1999 1484 Art.5

Sch.2 Part II, amended: SI 1999/2745 Art.7

Sch.2 Part II, revoked: SI 1999 1484 Art.5

Sch.2 Part III, amended: SI 1999/2745 Art.8

Sch.2 Part III, revoked: SI 1999 1484 Art.5

Sch.2 Part IV, amended: SI 1999/2745 Art.9

Sch.2 Part IV, revoked: SI 1999 1484 Art.5

Sch.2 Part V, amended: SI 1999/2745 Art.10

Sch.2 Part V, revoked: SI 1999 1484 Art.5

Sch.2 Part VI, amended: SI 1999/2745 Art.11

Sch.2 Part VI, revoked: SI 1999 1484 Art.5

Sch.2 Part VII, amended: SI 1999/2745 Art.12

Sch.2 Part VII, revoked: SI 1999 1484 Art.5

Sch.2 para.1, revoked (in part): SI 1999/1484 Art.5

Sch.2 para.4A, added: SI 1999/273 Art.3

Sch.2 para.4A, revoked (in part): SI 1999/1484 Art.5

Sch.2 para.6, revoked (in part): SI 1999/1484 Art.5

Sch.2 para.6A, revoked (in part): SI 1999/1484 Art.5

Sch.2 para.7A, revoked (in part): SI 1999/1484 Art.5

Sch.2 para.7B, revoked (in part): SI 1999/1484 Art.5

Sch.2 para.7B, substituted: SI 1996/1881 Art.2

Sch.2 para.7C, revoked (in part): SI 1999/1484 Art.5

Sch.2 para.7C, substituted: SI 1996/1881 Art.2

Sch.2 para.7D, added: SI 1996/1881 Art.2

Sch.2 para.7D, revoked (in part): SI 1999/1484 Art.5

Sch.2 para.11, added: SI 1997/202 Art.4

Sch.2 para.11, revoked (in part): SI 1999/1484 Art.5

Sch.2 para.12, added: SI 1997/202 Art.4

Sch.2 para.12, revoked (in part): SI 1999/1484 Art.5

Sch.2 para.13, added: SI 1997/202 Art.4

Sch.2 para.13, revoked (in part): SI 1999/1484 Art.5

Sch.2 para.14, added: SI 1997/202 Art.4

Sch.2 para.14, revoked (in part): SI 1999/1484 Art.5

Sch.2 para.15, added: SI 1997/202 Art.4

Sch.2 para.15, revoked (in part): SI 1999/1484 Art.5

Sch.2 para.16, added: SI 1997/202 Art.4

Sch.2 para.16, revoked (in part): SI 1999/1484 Art.5

Sch.2 para.16, substituted: SI 1999/273 Art.3

Sch.2 para.17, added: SI 1997/202 Art.4

Sch.2 para.17, revoked (in part): SI 1999/1484 Art.5

1993—cont.

891. A1 Trunk Road (Islington) Red Route Traffic Order 1993—*cont.*

Sch.2 para.18, added: SI 1997/202 Art.4

Sch.2 para.18, revoked (in part): SI 1999/1484 Art.5

Sch.2 para.19, added: SI 1997/202 Art.4

Sch.2 para.19, revoked (in part): SI 1999/1484 Art.5

Sch.2 para.20, added: SI 1997/202 Art.4

Sch.2 para.20, revoked (in part): SI 1999/1484 Art.5

Sch.2 para.21, added: SI 1997/202 Art.4

Sch.2 para.21, revoked (in part): SI 1999/1484 Art.5

Sch.2 para.22, added: SI 1997/202 Art.4

Sch.2 para.22, amended: SI 1999/273 Art.3

Sch.2 para.22, revoked (in part): SI 1999/1484 Art.5

Sch.2 para.23, added: SI 1997/202 Art.4

Sch.2 para.23, revoked (in part): SI 1999/1484 Art.5

Sch.2 para.24, added: SI 1997/202 Art.4

Sch.2 para.24, revoked (in part): SI 1999/1484 Art.5

Sch.3 Part I, amended: SI 1999/2745 Art.13

Sch.3 Part I, revoked: SI 1999 1484 Art.5

Sch.3 Part II, amended: SI 1999/2745 Art.14

Sch.3 Part II, revoked: SI 1999 1484 Art.5

Sch.3 Part III, amended: SI 1999/2745 Art.15

Sch.3 Part III, revoked: SI 1999 1484 Art.5

Sch.3 Part IV, amended: SI 1999/2745 Art.16

Sch.3 Part IV, revoked: SI 1999 1484 Art.5

Sch.3 Part V, amended: SI 1999/2745 Art.17

Sch.3 Part V, revoked: SI 1999 1484 Art.5

Sch.3 Part VII, amended: SI 1999/2745 Art.18

Sch.3 Part VII, revoked: SI 1999 1484 Art.5

Sch.3 para.3, revoked (in part): SI 1999/1484 Art.5

Sch.3 para.5, revoked (in part): SI 1999/1484 Art.5

Sch.3 para.6A, revoked (in part): SI 1999/1484 Art.5

Sch.3 para.6B, revoked (in part): SI 1999/1484 Art.5

Sch.3 para.6B, substituted: SI 1996/1881 Art.3

Sch.3 para.6C, added: SI 1996/1881 Art.3

Sch.3 para.6C, revoked (in part): SI 1999/1484 Art.5

Sch.3 para.10A, added: SI 1997/2783 Art.5

Sch.3 para.10A, revoked (in part): SI 1999/1484 Art.5

Sch.3 para.11, revoked (in part): SI 1999/1484 Art.5

Sch.3 para.11, substituted: SI 1999/273 Art.4

Sch.3 para.14, revoked (in part): SI 1999/1484 Art.5

Sch.3 para.14, substituted: SI 1999/273 Art.4

Sch.3 para.15, revoked (in part): SI 1999/1484 Art.5

Sch.3 para.15, substituted: SI 1997/202 Art.5

Sch.3 para.16, revoked (in part): SI 1999/1484 Art.5

Sch.3 para.16, substituted: SI 1997/202 Art.5

Sch.3 para.17, revoked (in part): SI 1999/1484 Art.5

Sch.3 para.17, substituted: SI 1997/202 Art.5

Sch.3 para.17A, added: SI 1997/202 Art.5

Sch.3 para.17A, revoked (in part): SI 1999/1484 Art.5

Sch.3 para.19, revoked (in part): SI 1999/1484 Art.5

Sch.3 para.19, substituted: SI 1997/202 Art.5, SI 1999/273 Art.4

NO.

891. A1 Trunk Road (Islington) Red Route Traffic Order 1993—*cont.*

Sch.3 para.19A, added: SI 1997/202 Art.5
Sch.3 para.19A, revoked (in part): SI 1999/1484 Art.5
Sch.3 para.19A, substituted: SI 1999/273 Art.4
Sch.3 para.20, revoked (in part): SI 1999/1484 Art.5
Sch.3 para.20, substituted: SI 1999/273 Art.4
Sch.3 para.21, revoked: SI 1999/273 Art.4
Sch.3 para.23, revoked (in part): SI 1999/1484 Art.5
Sch.3 para.23, substituted: SI 1997/202 Art.5
Sch.3 para.25, revoked (in part): SI 1999/1484 Art.5
Sch.3 para.25, substituted: SI 1999/273 Art.4
Sch.3 para.26A, revoked (in part): SI 1999/1484 Art.5
Sch.3 para.32A, revoked (in part): SI 1999/1484 Art.5
Sch.3 para.34, revoked (in part): SI 1999/1484 Art.5
Sch.3 para.34, substituted: SI 1999/273 Art.4
Sch.3 para.38, revoked (in part): SI 1999/1484 Art.5
Sch.3 para.38, substituted: SI 1999/273 Art.4
Sch.3 para.40, revoked (in part): SI 1999/1484 Art.5
Sch.3 para.40, substituted: SI 1999/273 Art.4
Sch.3 para.47, revoked (in part): SI 1999/1484 Art.5
Sch.3 para.47, substituted: SI 1999/273 Art.4
Sch.3 para.49, revoked: SI 1997/2783 Art.3
Sch.3 para.50, revoked (in part): SI 1999/1484 Art.5
Sch.3 para.50, substituted: SI 1997/202 Art.5, SI 1997/2783 Art.4
Sch.3 para.51A, added: SI 1997/2783 Art.6
Sch.3 para.51A, revoked (in part): SI 1999/1484 Art.5
Sch.3 para.55, revoked (in part): SI 1999/1484 Art.5
Sch.3 para.55, substituted: SI 1997/202 Art.5
Sch.3 para.56, revoked (in part): SI 1999/1484 Art.5
Sch.3 para.56, substituted: SI 1997/202 Art.5
Sch.3 para.57, revoked: SI 1997/202 Art.5
Sch.3 para.58, revoked (in part): SI 1999/1484 Art.5
Sch.3 para.58, substituted: SI 1997/202 Art.5
Sch.3 para.59, revoked: SI 1997/202 Art.5
Sch.3 para.60, revoked (in part): SI 1999/1484 Art.5
Sch.3 para.60, substituted: SI 1997/202 Art.5
Sch.3 para.60A, added: SI 1997/202 Art.5
Sch.3 para.60A, revoked (in part): SI 1999/1484 Art.5
Sch.4, amended: SI 1998/77 Art.3, Art.5, SI 1999/1475 Art.3
Sch.4, revoked (in part): SI 1999/1484 Art.5
Sch.4 para.2, revoked (in part): SI 1999/1484 Art.5
Sch.4 para.2, substituted: SI 1999/273 Art.5
Sch.4 para.2A, added: SI 1999/273 Art.5
Sch.4 para.2A, revoked (in part): SI 1999/1484 Art.5
Sch.4 para.5, revoked (in part): SI 1999/1484 Art.5
Sch.4 para.5, substituted: SI 1999/273 Art.5
Sch.4 para.19, revoked (in part): SI 1999/1484 Art.5
Sch.4 para.19, substituted: SI 1996/99 Art.6, SI 1997/202 Art.6, SI 1999/273 Art.5

NO.

891. A1 Trunk Road (Islington) Red Route Traffic Order 1993—*cont.*

Sch.4 para.21, revoked (in part): SI 1999/1484 Art.5
Sch.4 para.21, substituted: SI 1999/273 Art.5
Sch.4 para.22, revoked (in part): SI 1999/1484 Art.5
Sch.4 para.22, substituted: SI 1999/273 Art.5
Sch.4 para.23, revoked (in part): SI 1999/1484 Art.5
Sch.4 para.23, substituted: SI 1996/99 Art.6, SI 1997/202 Art.6
Sch.4 para.24, revoked (in part): SI 1999/1484 Art.5
Sch.4 para.24, substituted: SI 1999/273 Art.5
Sch.4 para.26, revoked (in part): SI 1999/1484 Art.5
Sch.4 para.29, amended: SI 1999/273 Art.5
Sch.4 para.29, revoked (in part): SI 1999/1484 Art.5
Sch.4 para.30, revoked (in part): SI 1999/1484 Art.5
Sch.4 para.30, substituted: SI 1999/273 Art.5
Sch.4 para.33, revoked (in part): SI 1999/1484 Art.5
Sch.4 para.33, substituted: SI 1999/273 Art.5
Sch.4 para.34, revoked (in part): SI 1999/1484 Art.5
Sch.4 para.34, substituted: SI 1996/99 Art.6, SI 1997/202 Art.6
Sch.4 para.36, revoked: SI 1999/273 Art.5
Sch.4 para.37, revoked (in part): SI 1999/1484 Art.5
Sch.4 para.37, substituted: SI 1999/273 Art.5
Sch.4 para.38, revoked (in part): SI 1999/1484 Art.5
Sch.4 para.38, substituted: SI 1999/273 Art.5
Sch.4 para.39, revoked (in part): SI 1999/1484 Art.5
Sch.4 para.39, substituted: SI 1999/273 Art.5
Sch.4 para.40, revoked (in part): SI 1999/1484 Art.5
Sch.4 para.41, revoked (in part): SI 1999/1484 Art.5
Sch.4 para.42, revoked (in part): SI 1999/1484 Art.5
Sch.4 para.45, revoked (in part): SI 1999/1484 Art.5
Sch.4 para.45, substituted: SI 1996/99 Art.6, SI 1997/202 Art.6
Sch.4 para.48, revoked (in part): SI 1999/1484 Art.5
Sch.4 para.48, substituted: SI 1999/273 Art.5
Sch.4 para.49, revoked (in part): SI 1999/1484 Art.5
Sch.4 para.49, substituted: SI 1998/77 Art.4, SI 1999/1475 Art.4
Sch.4 para.52A, added: SI 1999/273 Art.5
Sch.4 para.52A, revoked (in part): SI 1999/1484 Art.5
Sch.4 para.55, revoked (in part): SI 1999/1484 Art.5
Sch.4 para.55, substituted: SI 1999/273 Art.5
Sch.4 para.56, revoked (in part): SI 1999/1484 Art.5
Sch.4 para.56, substituted: SI 1999/273 Art.5
Sch.4 para.57, revoked (in part): SI 1999/1484 Art.5
Sch.4 para.57, substituted: SI 1999/273 Art.5
Sch.4 para.59, revoked (in part): SI 1999/1484 Art.5
Sch.4 para.59, substituted: SI 1999/273 Art.5

NO.

1993—cont.

891. A1 Trunk Road (Islington) Red Route Traffic Order 1993—*cont.*

Sch.4 para.61, revoked (in part): SI 1999/1484 Art.5

Sch.4 para.61, substituted: SI 1999/273 Art.5

Sch.4 para.62, revoked (in part): SI 1999/1484 Art.5

Sch.4 para.62, substituted: SI 1999/273 Art.5

Sch.4 para.63, revoked (in part): SI 1999/1484 Art.5

Sch.4 para.63, substituted: SI 1999/273 Art.5

Sch.4 para.64, revoked (in part): SI 1999/1484 Art.5

Sch.4 para.64, substituted: SI 1999/273 Art.5

Sch.4 para.65, revoked (in part): SI 1999/1484 Art.5

Sch.4 para.65, substituted: SI 1999/273 Art.5

Sch.4 para.66, added: SI 1998/77 Art.5, SI 1999/1475 Art.5

Sch.4 para.66, revoked (in part): SI 1999/1484 Art.5

893. Nurses, Midwives and Health Visitors (Professional Conduct) Rules 1993

see *Balamoody v United Kingdom Central Council For Nursing, Midwifery and Health Visiting* Independent, June 15, 1998 (C.S.) (QBD), Pill, L.J.

r.2, amended: SI 1998/1103 Sch. r.2

r.18, amended: SI 1998/1103 Sch. r.2

r.22, amended: SI 1998/1103 Sch. r.2

r.22, revoked (in part): SI 1998/1103 Sch. r.2

r.49, amended: SI 1998/1103 Sch. r.2

r.49, revoked (in part): SI 1998/1103 Sch. r.2

895. A1 Trunk Road (Islington) (Bus Lanes) Red Route Traffic Order 1993

revoked (in part): SI 1997/445 Art.5

896. A1 Trunk Road (Haringey) Red Route Traffic Order 1993

Art.4, amended: SI 1996/98 Art.3, SI 1997/201 Art.3, SI 1999/2806 Art.3

Sch.1, amended: SI 1999/2806 Art.4

Sch.2, amended: SI 1998/56 Art.3, Art.4

Sch.2 Part I, amended: SI 1999/2806 Art.5

Sch.2 Part II, amended: SI 1999/2806 Art.5, Art.6

Sch.2 para.1, substituted: SI 1996/98 Art.4, SI 1997/201 Art.4

Sch.2 para.1A, added: SI 1996/98 Art.4, SI 1997/201 Art.4

Sch.2 para.7, added: SI 1996/98 Art.4, SI 1997/201 Art.4

Sch.2 para.7, substituted: SI 1999/143 Art.3

Sch.3, amended: SI 1999/2806 Art.7

Sch.3 para.1, amended: SI 1996/98 Art.5, SI 1997/201 Art.5

Sch.3 para.2, amended: SI 1996/98 Art.5

Sch.4 para.3, substituted: SI 1996/98 Art.6, SI 1997/201 Art.6

Sch.4 para.6, amended: SI 1999/143 Art.4

Sch.4 para.7, substituted: SI 1996/98 Art.6, SI 1997/201 Art.6, SI 1999/143 Art.4

Sch.4 para.9, substituted: SI 1996/98 Art.6, SI 1997/201 Art.6, SI 1999/143 Art.4

Sch.4 para.9A, added: SI 1996/98 Art.6, SI 1997/201 Art.6

Sch.4 para.11, substituted: SI 1996/98 Art.6, SI 1997/201 Art.6

Sch.4 para.12, amended: SI 1996/98 Art.5, SI 1997/201 Art.6

Sch.4 para.13, substituted: SI 1999/143 Art.4

Sch.4 para.14, revoked: SI 1999/143 Art.4

Sch.4 para.15, substituted: SI 1996/98 Art.6, SI 1997/201 Art.6, SI 1999/143 Art.4

NO.

1993—cont.

896. A1 Trunk Road (Haringey) Red Route Traffic Order 1993—*cont.*

Sch.4 para.16, revoked: SI 1999/143 Art.4

Sch.4 para.17, substituted: SI 1999/143 Art.4

897. A1 Trunk Road (Haringey) (Bus Lanes) Red Route Traffic Order 1993

revoked (in part): SI 1997/449 Art.5

Art.2, amended: SI 1996/589 Art.2, SI 1996/591 Art.2

Art.5, amended: SI 1996/589 Art.2, SI 1996/591 Art.2

Art.8, amended: SI 1996/589 Art.2, SI 1996/591 Art.2

911. Plymouth Development Corporation (Area and Constitution) Order 1993

Art.2, revoked: SI 1998/769 Art.2

Art.3, revoked: SI 1998/769 Art.2

920. Act of Sederunt (Child Support Rules) 1993

r.2, see *Secretary of State for Social Security v Love* 1996 S.L.T. (Sh Ct) 78; see *Secretary of State for Social Security v Nicol* 1996 S.L.T. (Sh Ct) 34

921. Act of Sederunt (Bankruptcy Rules) 1993

revoked: SI 1996/2507 para.3

935. Housing Benefit and Community Charge Benefit (Subsidy) (No.2) Order 1993

Art.4, applied: SI 1996/1217 Art.11, SI 1997/1004 Art.11, SI 1998/562 Art.19

Art.16, applied: SI 1996/1217 Art.19, SI 1998/562 Art.19

Art.16, referred to: SI 1997/1004 Art.19

942. Copyright (Application to Other Countries) Order 1993

revoked: SI 1999/1751 Art.8, Sch.6

Art.3, revoked: SI 1999/1751 Art.8, Sch.6

Art.4, revoked: SI 1999/1751 Art.8, Sch.6

Sch.1, revoked: SI 1999/1751 Art.8, Sch.6

Sch.2, revoked: SI 1999/1751 Art.8, Sch.6

Sch.3, revoked: SI 1999/1751 Art.8, Sch.6

Sch.4 para.1, revoked: SI 1999/1751 Art.8, Sch.6

Sch.4 para.2, revoked: SI 1999/1751 Art.8, Sch.6

Sch.4 para.3, revoked: SI 1999/1751 Art.8, Sch.6

Sch.4 para.4, revoked: SI 1999/1751 Art.8, Sch.6

946. Insurance Companies (Accounts and Statements) (Amendment) Regulations 1993

revoked: SI 1996/943 Reg.35, Sch.7

947. Patents (Supplementary Protection Certificate for Medicinal Products) (Amendment) Rules 1993

revoked: SI 1997/64 r.12

948. Chessington Computer Centre Trading Fund Order 1993

revoked: SI 1996/1995 Art.2

954. Financial Services Act 1986 (Overseas Investment Exchanges and Overseas Clearing Houses) (Periodical Fees) Regulations 1993

revoked: SI 1999/1576 Reg.3

972. Advice and Assistance (Assistance by Way of Representation) (Scotland) Amendment Regulations 1993

revoked: SI 1997/3070 Reg.2, Sch.

984. Building Societies (Prescribed Contracts) Order 1993

Sch. Part IV, substituted: SI 1996/1605 Art.2, Sch.

NO.

1993—cont.

990. Animals, Meat and Meat Products (Examination for Residues and Maximum Residue Limits) (Amendment) Regulations 1993
revoked: SI 1997/1729 Reg.36, Sch.2

994. National Health Service (Appointment of Consultants) (Scotland) Regulations 1993
applied: SI 1999/686 Art.5, Sch. Part III, SI 1999/726 Art.5, Sch. Part III

996. Environmentally Sensitive Areas (Central Southern Uplands) Designation Order 1993
Art.2, amended: SI 1996/1969 Art.2, SI 1996/3082 Reg.3
Art.5A, added: SI 1996/3082 Reg.4
Art.5B, added: SI 1996/3082 Reg.4
Art.5B, amended: SI 1996/3082 Reg.6
Art.5C, added: SI 1996/3082 Reg.6
Art.6, amended: SI 1996/1969 Art.3
Art.7, amended: SI 1996/1969 Art.4
Sch., amended: SI 1996/1969 Art.5

997. Environmentally Sensitive Areas (Western Southern Uplands) Designation Order 1993
Art.2, amended: SI 1996/1968 Art.2, SI 1996/3082 Reg.3
Art.5A, added: SI 1996/3082 Reg.4
Art.5B, added: SI 1996/3082 Reg.4
Art.5B, amended: SI 1996/3082 Reg.6
Art.5C, added: SI 1996/3082 Reg.6
Art.6, amended: SI 1996/1968 Art.3
Art.7, amended: SI 1996/1968 Art.4
Sch. para.5, amended: SI 1996/1968 Art.5
Sch. para.10, amended: SI 1996/1968 Art.5

1038. Town and Country Planning (Use Classes) (Scotland) Amendment Order 1993
revoked: SI 1997/3061 Art.5

1072. Merchant Shipping (Vessels in Commercial Use for Sport and Pleasure) Regulations 1993
applied: SI 1996/3243 Sch Part I
referred to: SI 1998/1609 Reg.5, Reg.6, Sch.
revoked: SI 1998/2771 Reg.1 (with savings)
Reg.3, referred to: SI 1997/1320 Reg.3, SI 1998/2771 Reg.1
Reg.16, referred to: SI 1997/1320 Reg.3
Sch.2, referred to: SI 1998/2771 Reg.1

1073. Aviation Security (Air Cargo Agents) Regulations 1993
Reg.8, amended: SI 1998/1152 Reg.2
Reg.10, amended: SI 1996/1607 Reg.2, SI 1998/1152 Reg.2

1075. Plymouth Development Corporation (Planning Functions) Order 1993
revoked: SI 1998/84 Art.2, Sch.

1083. Peak Light Railway Order 1993
Art.11, amended: SI 1996/362 Art.5, Sch.4

1098. Local Government Staff Commission (England) Order 1993
revoked: SI 1998/898 Art.3

1105. Welfare Food Amendment Regulations 1993
revoked: SI 1996/1434 Reg.23, Sch.7

1126. Moray Health Services National Health Service Trust (Appointment of Trustees) Order 1993
revoked: SI 1999/1134 Art.3, Sch.2

1127. Royal Scottish National Hospital and Community National Health Service Trust (Appointment of Trustees) Order 1993
revoked: SI 1999/1134 Art.3, Sch.2

1128. Royal Alexandra National Health Service Trust (Appointment of Trustees) Order 1993
revoked: SI 1999/1134 Art.3, Sch.2

NO.

1993—cont.

1129. Raigmore Hospital National Health Service Trust (Appointment of Trustees) Order 1993
revoked: SI 1999/1134 Art.3, Sch.2

1130. Grampian Healthcare National Health Service Trust (Appointment of Trustees) Order 1993
revoked: SI 1999/1134 Art.3, Sch.2

1131. Dundee Teaching Hospitals National Health Service Trust (Appointment of Trustees) Order 1993
revoked: SI 1999/1134 Art.3, Sch.2

1132. Caithness and Sutherland National Health Service Trust (Appointment of Trustees) Order 1993
revoked: SI 1999/1134 Art.3, Sch.2

1133. Southern General Hospital National Health Service Trust (Appointment of Trustees) Order 1993
revoked: SI 1999/1134 Art.3, Sch.2

1134. Stirling Royal Infirmary National Health Service Trust (Appointment of Trustees) Order 1993
revoked: SI 1999/1134 Art.3, Sch.2

1135. Victoria Infirmary National Health Service Trust (Appointment of Trustees) Order 1993
revoked: SI 1999/1134 Art.3, Sch.2

1136. West Lothian National Health Service Trust (Appointment of Trustees) Order 1993
revoked: SI 1999/1134 Art.3, Sch.2

1138. North Ayrshire and Arran National Health Service Trust (Appointment of Trustees) Order 1993
revoked: SI 1999/1134 Art.3, Sch.2

1139. Monklands and Bellshill Hospitals National Health Service Trust (Appointment of Trustees) Order 1993
revoked: SI 1999/1134 Art.3, Sch.2

1140. Ayrshire and Arran Community Healthcare National Health Service Trust (Appointment of Trustees) Order 1993
revoked: SI 1999/1134 Art.3, Sch.2

1148. Greater London and Surrey (County and London Borough Boundaries) (No.3) Order 1993
see *R. v Secretary of State for the Environment Ex p. Sutton LBC* [1997] C.O.D. 308 (CA), Pill, L.J.

1155. Control of Pollution (Registers) (Scotland) Regulations 1993
Reg.2, amended: SI 1996/973 Reg.2, Sch para.15
Reg.3, amended: SI 1996/973 Reg.2, Sch para.15
Reg.6, amended: SI 1996/973 Reg.2, Sch para.15
Reg.8, amended: SI 1996/973 Reg.2, Sch para.15

1193. Electricity (Standards of Performance) Regulations 1993
Reg.2, amended: SI 1998/1547 Reg.2
Reg.5, amended: SI 1998/1547 Reg.3
Reg.9A, added: SI 1998/1547 Reg.4
Reg.10, amended: SI 1998/1547 Reg.5
Reg.11, amended: SI 1998/1547 Reg.6
Reg.13, amended: SI 1998/1547 Reg.7
Reg.14, amended: SI 1998/1547 Reg.8
Reg.16, substituted: SI 1998/1547 Reg.9
Sch. Part I, added: SI 1998/1547 Reg.10, Sch.

NO.

1993—cont.

1193. Electricity (Standards of Performance) Regulations 1993—*cont.*
Sch. Part II, added: SI 1998/1547 Reg.10, Sch.
Sch.1, revoked: SI 1998/1547 Reg.10
Sch.2, revoked: SI 1998/1547 Reg.10
Sch.3, revoked: SI 1998/1547 Reg.10
Sch.4, revoked: SI 1998/1547 Reg.10
Sch.5, revoked: SI 1998/1547 Reg.10
Sch.6, revoked: SI 1998/1547 Reg.10
Sch.7, revoked: SI 1998/1547 Reg.10
Sch.8, revoked: SI 1998/1547 Reg.10
Sch.9, revoked: SI 1998/1547 Reg.10
Sch.10, revoked: SI 1998/1547 Reg.10
Sch.11, revoked: SI 1998/1547 Reg.10
Sch.12, revoked: SI 1998/1547 Reg.10
Sch.13, revoked: SI 1998/1547 Reg.10
Sch.14, revoked: SI 1998/1547 Reg.10

1202. Road Traffic (Parking Adjudicators) (London) Regulations 1993
Reg.2, amended: SI 1999/1205 Reg.3
Reg.3, amended: SI 1999/1205 Reg.4
Reg.4, amended: SI 1999/1205 Reg.5
Reg.6, amended: SI 1999/1205 Reg.6
Reg.9, amended: SI 1999/1205 Reg.7
Reg.11, amended: SI 1999/1205 Reg.8
Reg.14, amended: SI 1999/1205 Reg.9
Reg.18, substituted: SI 1999/1205 Reg.10
Reg.19, amended: SI 1999/1205 Reg.11

1210. Environmentally Sensitive Areas (Ynys Mon) Designation Order 1993
Art.2, amended: SI 1996/3077 Reg.2, SI 1997/975 Art.2
Art.5, amended: SI 1996/3077 Reg.2
Art.5A, added: SI 1996/3077 Reg.2
Art.5B, added: SI 1996/3077 Reg.2
Art.5C, added: SI 1996/3077 Reg.2
Art.6, amended: SI 1997/975 Art.2
Art.6, revoked (in part): SI 1997/975 Art.2
Art.7, added: SI 1999/1175 Art.2
Sch.2 para.2, substituted: SI 1997/975 Art.2
Sch.4 para.6, amended: SI 1997/975 Art.2
Sch.4 para.10, added: SI 1997/975 Art.2
Sch.4 para.11, added: SI 1997/975 Art.2

1211. Environmentally Sensitive Areas (Radnor) Designation Order 1993
Art.2, amended: SI 1996/3077 Reg.2, SI 1997/976 Art.2
Art.5, amended: SI 1996/3077 Reg.2
Art.5A, added: SI 1996/3077 Reg.2
Art.5B, added: SI 1996/3077 Reg.2
Art.5C, added: SI 1996/3077 Reg.2
Art.6, amended: SI 1997/976 Art.2
Art.6, revoked (in part): SI 1997/976 Art.2
Art.7, added: SI 1999/1175 Art.2
Sch.2 para.2, substituted: SI 1997/976 Art.2
Sch.4 para.6, amended: SI 1997/976 Art.2
Sch.4 para.10, added: SI 1997/975 Art.2
Sch.4 para.11, added: SI 1997/975 Art.2

1213. Merchant Shipping (Local Passenger Vessels) (Masters' Licences and Hours, Manning and Training) Regulations 1993
Part II, applied: SI 1996/3243 Sch Part V

1221. Motor Vehicles (EC Type Approval) (Amendment) Regulations 1993
revoked: SI 1998/2051 Reg.2, Sch.3

1241. South West Regional Flood Defence Committee Order 1993
revoked: SI 1998/1640 Art.3

1244. Iraq (United Nations) (Sequestration of Assets) Order 1993
Art.2, amended: SI 1998/1129 Art.3, Sch.2

NO.

1993—cont.

1250. Access to Health Records (Northern Ireland) Order 1993
Art.2, amended: SI 1997/1177 (NI.7) Art.32, Sch.2
Art.2, revoked (in part): 1998 c.29 Sch.16 Part II
Art.3, amended: SI 1997/1177 (NI.7) Art.32, Sch.2
Art.3, revoked (in part): 1998 c.29 Sch.16 Part II
Art.4, amended: 1998 c.29 Sch.15 para.17
Art.5, amended: 1998 c.29 Sch.15 para.18
Art.5, referred to: 1998 c.29 Sch.14 para.18
Art.5, revoked (in part): 1998 c.29 Sch.16 Part II
Art.6, revoked (in part): 1998 c.29 Sch.16 Part II
Art.7, amended: 1998 c.29 Sch.15 para.19
Art.7, revoked (in part): 1998 c.29 Sch.16 Part II
Art.8, referred to: 1998 c.29 Sch.14 para.18
Art.10, referred to: 1998 c.29 Sch.14 para.18

1252. Financial Provisions (Northern Ireland) Order 1993
Art.8, amended: SI 1998/749 (NI.4) Art.7
Art.8, revoked (in part): 1998 c.47 s.100, Sch.15

1283. Plant Health (Forestry) (Great Britain) Order 1993
Art.2, amended: SI 1996/751 Art.3
Art.21, applied: SI 1997/1160 Reg.6
Art.22, applied: SI 1997/1160 Reg.6
Art.24, amended: SI 1998/2206 Art.2
Art.28A, added: SI 1996/751 Art.3
Sch.1, amended: SI 1998/3109 Art.3
Sch.4 Part A, amended: SI 1998/3109 Art.3
Sch.4 Part B, amended: SI 1996/751 Art.5
Sch.4 Part C, amended: SI 1996/751 Art.5
Sch.5 Part B, amended: SI 1996/751 Art.6
Sch.6, amended: SI 1996/751 Art.7
Sch.7, amended: SI 1996/751 Art.8

1317. Integrated Administration and Control Systems Regulations 1993
applied: SI 1999/672 Art.2, Sch.1
Reg.2, amended: SI 1997/1148 Reg.3, SI 1999/1820 Art.4, Sch.2 para.152
Reg.2A, added: SI 1997/1148 Reg.4
Reg.4A, applied: SI 1996/3142 Reg.15
Reg.6, amended: SI 1997/1148 Reg.5
Reg.6A, added: SI 1999/1820 Art.4, Sch.2 para.152
Reg.8, amended: SI 1997/1148 Reg.6
Reg.8, revoked (in part): SI 1997/1148 Reg.6

1320. Plant Health (Great Britain) Order 1993
amended: SI 1996/25 Art.2
applied: SI 1996/2563 Reg.5, SI 1997/2441 Reg.5
referred to: SI 1996/26 Reg.1
Art.2, amended: SI 1996/25 Art.3, SI 1997/2907 Art.2
Art.4, amended: SI 1996/1165 Art.3
Art.8, amended: SI 1999/2726 Art.2, SSI 1999/129 Art.3
Art.12, applied: SI 1999/1801 Reg.12
Art.15, referred to: SI 1999/1801 Reg.7
Art.17, amended: SI 1999/2726 Art.2, SSI 1999/129 Art.4
Art.18, amended: SI 1999/2126 Art.2, SI 1999/2641 Art.2, SSI 1999/22 Art.2
Art.20, applied: SI 1998/201 Reg.5
Art.20, referred to: SI 1999/1801 Reg.8
Art.21, applied: SI 1998/201 Reg.5
Art.22, applied: SI 1996/2563 Reg.5, SI 1997/1160 Reg.6, SI 1997/2441 Reg.5, SI 1998/201 Reg.5
Art.23, applied: SI 1996/2563 Reg.5, SI 1997/1160 Reg.6, SI 1997/2441 Reg.5, SI 1998/201 Reg.5

NO.

1320. Plant Health (Great Britain) Order 1993— cont.

Art.23A, added: SI 1999/2126 Art.2, SI 1999/2641 Art.2, SSI 1999/22 Art.3

Art.24, applied: SI 1996/2563 Reg.5, SI 1997/2441 Reg.5, SI 1998/201 Reg.5

Art.25, amended: SI 1998/2245 Art.2

Art.25, applied: SI 1996/2563 Reg.5, Reg.6, SI 1997/2441 Reg.5, Reg.6, SI 1998/201 Reg.5

Art.30A, added: SI 1996/25 Art.4

Sch.1 Part A, amended: SI 1996/3242 Art.3, SI 1998/1121 Art.2, SSI 1999/22 Art.4, SI 1999/2126 Art.2, SI 1999/2641 Art.2

Sch.1 Part B, amended: SI 1996/1165 Art.4

Sch.2 Part A, amended: SI 1998/1121 Art.2

Sch.2 Part B, amended: SI 1996/25 Art.5, SI 1996/1165 Art.5

Sch.3 Part A, amended: SI 1997/1145 Art.2, SI 1998/1121 Art.2

Sch.3 Part B, amended: SI 1996/1165 Art.6

Sch.4 Part A, amended: SI 1996/25 Art.6, SI 1996/3242 Art.4, SI 1998/349 Art.2, SI 1998/1121 Art.2, SI 1999/2126 Art.2, SI 1999/2641 Art.2, SSI 1999/22 Art.4

Sch.4 Part A, referred to: SI 1998/201 Reg.3

Sch.4 Part B, amended: SI 1996/25 Art.7, SI 1996/1165 Art.7, SI 1998/1121 Art.2

Sch.5 Part A, amended: SI 1998/1121 Art.2

Sch.5 Part AI, amended: SI 1996/25 Art.8

Sch.5 Part AII, amended: SI 1996/1165 Art.8

Sch.5 Part B, amended: SI 1996/3242 Art.5, SI 1998/349 Art.2, SI 1998/1121 Art.2

Sch.5 Part BII, amended: SI 1996/1165 Art.8

Sch.6, applied: SI 1999/1801 Reg.8

Sch.8, amended: SI 1996/25 Art.9, SI 1996/1165 Art.9

Sch.13A, added: SI 1999/2126 Art.2, Sch., SI 1999/2641 Art.2, Sch., SSI 1999/22 Art.5, Sch.

Sch.16, amended: SI 1996/25 Art.10, SI 1996/1165 Art.10, SI 1996/3242 Art.6, SI 1997/1145 Art.2, SI 1997/2907 Art.2, SI 1998/349 Art.2, SI 1998/1121 Art.2, SI 1999/2126 Art.2, SI 1999/2641 Art.2, SSI 1999/22 Art.6

1339. Local Government (Committees) (Amendment) Regulations 1993

Reg.2, revoked: SI 1999/500 Reg.3

Sch.1, revoked: SI 1999/500 Reg.3

1354. Civil Legal Aid (Scope) Regulations 1993

revoked: 1999 c.22 s.106, Sch.15 Part I

1369. National Health Service (Fund-Holding Practices) (Scotland) Amendment Regulations 1993

revoked: SI 1997/1014 Reg.24, Sch.3

1406. Offshore Installations (Safety Zones) Order 1993

revoked: SI 1997/735 Art.3, Sch.2

1409. Aeroplane Noise (Limitation on Operation of Aeroplanes) Regulations 1993

revoked: SI 1999/1452 Reg.2

1412. Sports Grounds and Sporting Events (Designation) (Scotland) Amendment Order 1993

revoked: SI 1998/2314 Art.3, Sch.3

1416. Goods Vehicles (Operators' Licences) (Temporary Use in Great Britain) (Amendment) Regulations 1993

revoked: SI 1996/2186 Reg.2, Sch.1

NO.

1441. Suckler Cow Premium Regulations 1993

applied: SI 1996/1500 Reg.9, SI 1999/672 Art.2, Sch.1, SI 1999/3315 Reg.4, SSI 1999/187 Reg.14

Reg.3, amended: SI 1996/1488 Reg.2, SI 1997/249 Reg.2

Reg.3, applied: SI 1997/2844 Reg.4

Reg.4, amended: SI 1997/1901 Reg.10, SI 1998/871 Reg.36

1461. Road Traffic Act 1991 (Commencement No.6 and Transitional Provisions) Order 1993

Art.1, revoked (in part): SI 1998/967 Art.3, Sch.

Art.3, revoked (in part): SI 1998/967 Art.3, Sch.

Art.4, revoked (in part): SI 1998/967 Art.3, Sch.

Art.5, revoked (in part): SI 1998/967 Art.3, Sch.

Art.6, revoked: SI 1998/967 Art.3, Sch.

1474. Road Traffic (Special Parking Areas) (London Borough of Wandsworth) Order 1993

Sch. para.31, substituted: SI 1998/575 Art.2, Sch. para.1

Sch. para.38, substituted: SI 1998/575 Art.2, Sch. para.2

Sch. para.48, substituted: SI 1998/575 Art.2, Sch. para.3

Sch. para.52, amended: SI 1998/575 Art.2, Sch. para.4

Sch. para.57, substituted: SI 1998/575 Art.2, Sch. para.5

Sch. para.60, substituted: SI 1998/575 Art.2, Sch. para.6

Sch. para.62, amended: SI 1998/575 Art.2, Sch. para.7

Sch. para.73, substituted: SI 1998/575 Art.2, Sch. para.8

Sch. para.74, substituted: SI 1998/575 Art.2, Sch. para.9

Sch. para.255A, added: SI 1998/575 Art.2, Sch. para.10

Sch. para.257, substituted: SI 1998/575 Art.2, Sch. para.11

Sch. para.265, substituted: SI 1998/575 Art.2, Sch. para.12

Sch. para.277, substituted: SI 1998/575 Art.2, Sch. para.13

Sch. para.280, substituted: SI 1998/575 Art.2, Sch. para.14

Sch. para.288, substituted: SI 1998/575 Art.2, Sch. para.15

Sch. para.289, substituted: SI 1998/575 Art.2, Sch. para.16

1500. Local Authorities' Traffic Orders (Procedure) (England and Wales) (Amendment) Regulations 1993

revoked: SI 1996/2489 Reg.2

1507. Value Added Tax (Supply of Services) Order 1993

Art.6, amended: SI 1998/762 Art.3

Art.7, amended: SI 1998/762 Art.4

Art.8, added: SI 1998/762 Art.5

Art.9, added: SI 1998/762 Art.5

1520. Egg Products Regulations 1993

applied: SI 1996/3124 Reg.10, Sch.2 para.4

Sch.10 para.1, amended: SI 1996/1499 Reg.49

1539. Cosmetic Products (Safety) (Amendment) Regulations 1993

revoked: SI 1996/2925 Sch.9

1567. Family Law (Northern Ireland) Order 1993

Art.14, revoked: SI 1998/1071 (NI.6) Art.41, Sch.5

1573. Child Abduction and Custody (Parties to Conventions) (Amendment) (No.2) Order 1993

revoked: SI 1996/2595 Art.2

NO.

1993—cont.

1574. Extradition (Hijacking) (Amendment) Order 1993
revoked: SI 1997/1763 Art.4

1591. Wireless Telegraphy (Short Range Devices) (Exemption) Regulations 1993
revoked: SI 1999/930 Reg.2, Sch.1
Reg.1, amended: SI 1997/1996 Reg.3
Reg.3, amended: SI 1997/1996 Reg.4, Reg.5
Reg.4, amended: SI 1997/1996 Reg.6
Reg.5, substituted: SI 1997/1996 Reg.7
Sch.1, amended: SI 1997/1996 Reg.8
Sch.1 para.1, amended: SI 1997/1996 Reg.8
Sch.1 para.3, amended: SI 1997/1996 Reg.8
Sch.1 para.14, amended: SI 1997/1996 Reg.8
Sch.1 para.15, amended: SI 1997/1996 Reg.8
Sch.1 para.17, added: SI 1997/1996 Reg.8
Sch.1 para.18, added: SI 1997/1996 Reg.8
Sch.2, added: SI 1997/1996 Reg.9

1593. Local Government Superannuation (Scotland) Amendment Regulations 1993
applied: SI 1998/364 Reg.4, Reg.6, Reg.19, Sch.2 para.2, Sch.2 para.5, Sch.4 para.8
referred to: SI 1998/364 Reg.3, Reg.10, Sch.2 para.4, Sch.2 para.6
Reg.29, revoked: SI 1998/192 Reg.52, Sch.2

1595. Severn Bridge Regulations 1993
revoked: SI 1996/1316 Reg.2

1602. Motor Vehicles (Driving Licences) (Amendment) Regulations 1993
revoked: SI 1996/2824 Reg.2, Sch.1

1603. Motor Vehicles (Driving Licences) (Large Goods and Passenger-Carrying Vehicles) (Amendment) Regulations 1993
revoked: SI 1996/2824 Reg.2, Sch.1

1607. Swanage Light Railway (Extension) Order 1993
Art.13, amended: SI 1996/362 Art.5, Sch.4

1622. Air Navigation (General) Regulations 1993
Reg.18, amended: SI 1997/881 Reg.2
Reg.18A, added: SI 1999/1324 Reg.2

1625. Right to Purchase (Prescribed Persons) (Scotland) Order 1993
Art.2, amended: SI 1998/1275 Art.2

1626. Sheep Annual Premium and Suckler Cow Premium Quotas Regulations 1993
see *R. v Ministry of Agriculture, Fisheries and Food Ex p. National Union of Farmers* [1996] C.O.D. 94 (QBD), Macpherson of Cluny, J.
revoked: SI 1997/2844 Reg.16
Reg.2, amended: SI 1996/1939 Reg.2
Reg.2, applied: SI 1997/2844 Sch.3 Part I
Reg.2, revoked: SI 1997/2844 Reg.16
Reg.5, amended: SI 1996/1939 Reg.2
Reg.5, revoked: SI 1997/2844 Reg.16
Reg.7, revoked: SI 1997/2844 Reg.16
Reg.7, substituted: SI 1996/1939 Reg.2
Reg.10, revoked: SI 1997/2844 Reg.16
Reg.13A, amended: SI 1996/1939 Reg.2
Reg.13A, revoked: SI 1996/48 Reg.11, SI 1997/2844 Reg.16
Reg.13B, added: SI 1996/1939 Reg.2
Reg.13B, revoked: SI 1997/2844 Reg.16
Reg.14, revoked: SI 1997/2844 Reg.16
Reg.15A, revoked: SI 1997/2844 Reg.16
Sch.2, revoked: SI 1997/2844 Reg.16
Sch.2 Part II, amended: SI 1996/1939 Reg.2
Sch.2 Part II, revoked: SI 1997/2844 Reg.16
Sch.2 Part V, revoked: SI 1996/48 Reg.11, SI 1997/2844 Reg.16
Sch.3, amended: SI 1996/1939 Reg.2
Sch.3, revoked: SI 1997/2844 Reg.16
Sch.3 para.9, revoked: SI 1997/2844 Reg.16

NO.

1993—cont.

1626. Sheep Annual Premium and Suckler Cow Premium Quotas Regulations 1993—cont.
Sch.4, revoked: SI 1997/2844 Reg.16

1641. Import (Plant Health Fees) (England and Wales) Order 1993
revoked: SI 1996/26 Reg.2

1642. Plant Passport (Plant Health Fees) (England and Wales) Regulations 1993
Sch., substituted: SI 1997/1961 Reg.2, Sch.

1651. Tunbridge Wells and Eridge Light Railway Order 1993
Art.8, amended: SI 1996/362 Art.5, Sch.4

1656. Immigration (Restricted Right of Appeal Against Deportation) (Exemption) Order 1993
applied: 1999 c.33 s.169, Sch.15 para.11
Art.2, amended: SI 1996/2145 Art.2

1658. Extraction Solvents in Food Regulations 1993
referred to: SI 1996/1499 Reg.4
Reg.4, amended: SI 1998/2257 Reg.2
Reg.9, added: SI 1998/2257 Reg.2
Sch.1 Part I, amended: SI 1998/2257 Reg.2
Sch.2, substituted: SI 1998/2257 Reg.2, Sch.
Sch.3, amended: SI 1998/2257 Reg.2

1661. Asylum Appeals (Procedure) Rules 1993
see *R. v Secretary of State for the Home Department Ex p. Abdi* Times, February 17, 1996 (HL), Lord Lloyd of Berwick
revoked: SI 1996/2070 r.1
r.22, see *R. v Immigration Appeal Tribunal Ex p. Jeyeanthan* [1998] Imm. A.R. 369 (QBD), Sedley, J.
r.22, revoked: SI 1996/2070 r.1

1662. Immigration Appeals (Procedure) Rules 1993
r.5, see *R. v Secretary of State for the Home Department Ex p. Singh (Manvinder)* [1996] Imm. A.R. 41 (QBD), Carnwath, J.

1664. Offshore Installations (Safety Zones) (No.2) Order 1993
revoked: SI 1997/735 Art.3, Sch.2

1678. Immigration (Transit Visa) Order 1993
Art.2, amended: SI 1998/55 Art.2, SI 1998/1014 Art.3
Sch., substituted: SI 1996/2065 Art.2, SI 1998/1014 Art.2, SI 1998/2483 Art.2, Sch., SI 1999/3086 Art.2, Sch.

1679. Income Support (General) Amendment No.3 Regulations 1993
Reg.4, applied: SI 1996/207 Reg.87

1680. Merchant Shipping (Prevention of Oil Pollution) (Amendment) Regulations 1993
revoked: SI 1996/2154 Reg.1

1681. Merchant Shipping (Prevention of Pollution by Garbage) (Amendment) Regulations 1993
revoked: SI 1998/1377 Reg.1

1691. Football Spectators (Designation of Football Matches in England and Wales) Order 1993
revoked: SI 1999/2461 Art.2

1734. Beef Special Premium Regulations 1993
revoked: SI 1996/3241 Reg.22

1746. Chemicals (Hazard Information and Packaging) Regulations 1993
applied: SI 1996/2092 Reg.20

1754. Social Security (Unemployment, Sickness and Invalidity Benefit) Amendment Regulations 1993
Reg.3, revoked: SI 1996/1345 Reg.27, Sch.

NO.

1774. Civil Defence (General Local Authority Functions) (Scotland) Regulations 1993
Reg.2, substituted: SI 1996/739 Art.7, Sch.1 para.14
Reg.4, substituted: SI 1996/739 Art.7, Sch.1 para.14
Reg.5, revoked: SI 1996/739 Art.7, Sch.1 para.14

1782. Continental Shelf (Designation of Additional Areas) Order 1993
referred to: SI 1999/2031

1787. United Nations Arms Embargoes (Liberia, Somalia and the Former Yugoslavia) Order 1993
Art.2, amended: SI 1996/1629 Art.2, SI 1998/1501 Art.2
Art.3, amended: SI 1996/1629 Art.3, SI 1997/273 Art.2
Art.7, amended: SI 1997/273 Art.2
Art.8, amended: SI 1996/1629 Art.4, SI 1997/273 Art.2, SI 1998/1501 Art.3
Art.10, amended: SI 1997/273 Art.2
Sch. para.4, amended: SI 1996/1629 Art.4, SI 1998/1501 Art.3

1788. Appropriation (No.2) (Northern Ireland) Order 1993
revoked: SI 1996/1917 (NI.14) Art.2, Sch.2

1806. Confiscation of the Proceeds of Drug Trafficking (Designated Countries and Territories) (Scotland) Amendment Order 1993
revoked: SI 1999/675 Art.11

1807. Criminal Justice (International Co-operation) Act 1990 (Enforcement of Overseas Forfeiture Orders) (Scotland) Amendment Order 1993
revoked: SI 1999/675 Art.11

1812. Civil Defence (General Local Authority Functions) Regulations 1993
Reg.4, amended: SI 1996/330 Reg.3

1813. Channel Tunnel (International Arrangements) Order 1993
Art.4, amended: SI 1996/2283 Art.2
Art.7, amended: SI 1996/2283 Art.2
Sch.1, amended: SI 1996/2283 Art.2

1814. Local Government Superannuation (Part-time Employees) Regulations 1993
revoked: SI 1996/1680 Reg.49, Sch.5

1823. Offshore Safety (Repeals and Modifications) Regulations 1993
applied: 1998 c.17 s.12
Reg.3, referred to: SI 1997/2703
Reg.4, revoked (in part): 1998 c.17 s.51, Sch.5 Part II

1849. Highways (Traffic Calming) Regulations 1993
applied: SI 1998/1936 Art.8, SI 1999/1026 Reg.11
revoked: SI 1999/1026 Reg.10 (with saving)

1890. Medicines (Products Other Than Veterinary Drugs) (Prescription Only) Amendment Order 1993
revoked: SI 1997/1830 Art.16, Sch.6

1893. Offshore Installations (Safety Zones) (No.3) Order 1993
revoked: SI 1997/735 Art.3, Sch.2

1897. Management and Administration of Safety and Health at Mines Regulations 1993
Reg.2, referred to: SI 1999/2024 Reg.3
Reg.35, applied: SI 1999/2463 Reg.6
Reg.40, amended: SI 1996/1592 Reg.34, Sch.9 para.6
Reg.41, referred to: SI 1997/2703

NO.

1933. Money Laundering Regulations 1993
amended: SI 1997/316 Reg.28, SI 1997/317 Reg.26
applied: SI 1996/1299 (NI.9) Sch.2 para.3, SI 1997/316 Reg.28, SI 1997/317 Reg.26
referred to: 1998 c.46 s.30, Sch.5 s.A5, 1998 c.47 Sch.3 para.25
Reg.8, amended: SI 1998/1129 Art.2, Sch.1 para.13
Reg.15, amended: SI 1998/1129 Art.2, Sch.1 para.13

1955. Act of Adjournal (Consolidation Amendment) (Courses for Drink-drive Offenders) 1993
revoked: SI 1996/513 Sch.2 r.3, Sch.3

1956. Act of Sederunt (Sheriff Court Ordinary Cause Rules) 1993
amended: SI 1996/2167 r.2, Sch
applied: SI 1997/687 Sch.1 Table
Ch.33 Part II, applied: SI 1996/125 Art.3
Form G13, see *Stewart v Callaghan* 1996 S.L.T. 12 (Sh Ct)
r.33.20, see *McGrath v McGrath* 1999 S.L.T. (Sh Ct) 90 (Sh Pr), EF Bowen Q.C., Sheriff Principal
r.33.22A, see *Ross v Ross* 1999 S.C.L.R. 1112 (Sh Pr), EF Bowen Q.C., Sheriff Principal
r.33.22A, applied: SI 1996/2444 Reg.18
r.33.29, applied: SI 1997/687 Sch.1 Table
r.36.14, applied: SI 1996/207 Sch.8 para.43
r.128, applied: SI 1996/207 Sch.8 para.43

1957. Double Taxation Relief (Taxes on Income) (General) (Manufactured Overseas Dividends) Regulations 1993
amended: SI 1996/2654 Reg.2

1975. Education Act 1993 (Commencement No.1 and Transitional Provisions) Order 1993
Sch.2 para.4, referred to: 1996 c.56 Sch.39 para.30

1982. Education (School Inspection) (Wales) (No.2) Regulations 1993
amended: SI 1996/2087 Reg.2
revoked: SI 1998/1866 Reg.1, Sch.
Reg.7, amended: SI 1997/1833 Reg.2
Reg.7, revoked: SI 1998/1866 Reg.1, Sch.
Reg.7, substituted: SI 1996/1934 Reg.2
Reg.8, revoked: SI 1998/1866 Reg.1, Sch.

1986. Education (School Inspection) (No.2) Regulations 1993
revoked: SI 1997/1966 Reg.1, Sch. Part I
Reg.4, amended: SI 1996/2087 Reg.2
Reg.4, revoked: SI 1997/1966 Reg.1, Sch. Part I
Reg.4, substituted: SI 1996/3099 Reg.2, SI 1997/995 Reg.2
Reg.7, revoked: SI 1997/1966 Reg.1, Sch. Part I
Reg.7, substituted: SI 1996/1737 Reg.2

1987. Education (Further Education in Schools) Regulations 1993
revoked: SI 1999/1867 Reg.3

1994. Merchant Shipping (Load Lines) Act 1967 (Unregistered Ships) Order 1993
referred to: SI 1998/1609 Reg.5, Reg.6, Sch.
revoked: SI 1998/2241 Reg.3

2001. Value Added Tax (Payments on Account) Order 1993
Art.2, amended: SI 1996/1196 Art.3
Art.8, amended: SI 1996/1196 Art.4
Art.9, amended: SI 1996/1196 Art.5
Art.10, revoked: SI 1996/1196 Art.6
Art.11, amended: SI 1996/1196 Art.7

NO.

2001. Value Added Tax (Payments on Account) Order 1993—*cont.*
Art.12, amended: SI 1996/1196 Art.8
Art.12A, added: SI 1996/1196 Art.10
Art.13, amended: SI 1996/1196 Art.9
Art.14, amended: SI 1996/1196 Art.9
Art.15, amended: SI 1996/1196 Art.9
Art.17, amended: SI 1996/1196 Art.11

2003. Income Tax (Stock Lending) (Amendment) Regulations 1993
revoked: SI 1997/987 Reg.2 (with savings), Sch.1 (with savings)

2004. Income Tax (Manufactured Overseas Dividends) Regulations 1993
Reg.2, amended: SI 1996/1229 Reg.3, SI 1996/2643 Reg.3
Reg.2A, amended: SI 1997/988 Reg.3
Reg.2A, revoked (in part): SI 1997/988 Reg.3
Reg.2B, added: SI 1996/2643 Reg.4
Reg.2B, amended: SI 1997/987 Reg.8
Reg.4, amended: SI 1996/1229 Reg.4, SI 1996/2643 Reg.5, SI 1997/988 Reg.4
Reg.5, amended: SI 1996/1229 Reg.4, SI 1996/2643 Reg.6
Reg.6A, added: SI 1996/2643 Reg.7
Reg.7, amended: SI 1996/1229 Reg.4, SI 1996/2643 Reg.8, SI 1997/988 Reg.5
Reg.7A, added: SI 1996/2643 Reg.9
Reg.7A, revoked: SI 1997/987 Reg.8
Reg.9, amended: SI 1996/1229 Reg.5, SI 1996/2643 Reg.10, SI 1997/988 Reg.6
Reg.9A, added: SI 1997/988 Reg.7
Reg.10, amended: SI 1996/2643 Reg.11, SI 1997/988 Reg.8
Reg.11, amended: SI 1996/1229 Reg.6, SI 1997/988 Reg.9
Reg.12, amended: SI 1996/1229 Reg.7, SI 1996/2643 Reg.12
Reg.12, revoked (in part): SI 1997/2706 Reg.2
Reg.13, amended: SI 1996/1229 Reg.8
Reg.13, revoked: SI 1996/2643 Reg.13
Reg.15, amended: SI 1996/2643 Reg.14
Reg.16, revoked: SI 1997/987 Reg.8 (with savings)
Reg.16, substituted: SI 1996/1229 Reg.9

2005. Cereal Seeds Regulations 1993
Reg.3, amended: SI 1999/1860 Reg.3, SI 1999/2196 Reg.2
Reg.5, amended: SI 1999/1860 Reg.3
Reg.6, amended: SI 1999/1860 Reg.3
Reg.6, referred to: SI 1999/1860 Reg.4
Reg.6A, added: SI 1999/1860 Reg.3
Reg.6A, referred to: SI 1999/1860 Reg.4
Reg.8A, added: SI 1999/1860 Reg.3
Reg.9, amended: SI 1999/1860 Reg.3
Reg.9A, added: SI 1999/1860 Reg.3
Sch.2A, added: SI 1999/1860 Reg.3
Sch.2A para.2, referred to: SI 1999/1860 Reg.4
Sch.3A, added: SI 1999/1860 Reg.3
Sch.4 Part I, amended: SI 1999/1860 Reg.3, SI 1999/2196 Reg.2
Sch.4 Part I, referred to: SI 1999/1860 Reg.4
Sch.4 Part II, amended: SI 1999/2196 Reg.2
Sch.6, amended: SI 1997/616 Reg.4

2006. Beet Seeds Regulations 1993
Reg.3, amended: SI 1997/616 Reg.4, SI 1999/1861 Reg.3
Reg.5, amended: SI 1997/616 Reg.4, SI 1999/1861 Reg.3
Reg.6, amended: SI 1999/1861 Reg.3
Reg.6, referred to: SI 1999/1861 Reg.4
Reg.6A, added: SI 1999/1861 Reg.3

NO.

2006. Beet Seeds Regulations 1993—*cont.*
Reg.6A, referred to: SI 1999/1861 Reg.4
Reg.8, amended: SI 1997/616 Reg.4
Reg.8A, added: SI 1999/1861 Reg.3
Reg.9, amended: SI 1997/616 Reg.4, SI 1999/1861 Reg.3
Reg.9A, added: SI 1999/1861 Reg.3
Sch.2A, added: SI 1999/1861 Reg.3
Sch.2A para.2, referred to: SI 1999/1861 Reg.4
Sch.3A, added: SI 1999/1861 Reg.3
Sch.4 Part I, amended: SI 1999/1861 Reg.3
Sch.4 Part I, referred to: SI 1999/1861 Reg.4
Sch.6, amended: SI 1997/616 Reg.4

2007. Oil and Fibre Plant Seeds Regulations 1993
Reg.3, amended: SI 1999/1862 Reg.3
Reg.5, amended: SI 1997/616 Reg.2, Reg.4
Reg.5, amended: SI 1999/1862 Reg.3
Reg.6, amended: SI 1999/1862 Reg.3
Reg.6, referred to: SI 1999/1862 Reg.4
Reg.6A, added: SI 1999/1862 Reg.3
Reg.6A, referred to: SI 1999/1862 Reg.4
Reg.8A, added: SI 1999/1862 Reg.3
Reg.9, amended: SI 1997/616 Reg.2, SI 1999/1862 Reg.3
Reg.9A, added: SI 1999/1862 Reg.3
Sch.2A, added: SI 1999/1862 Reg.3
Sch.2A para.2, referred to: SI 1999/1862 Reg.4
Sch.3A, added: SI 1999/1862 Reg.3
Sch.4 Part I, amended: SI 1999/1862 Reg.3
Sch.4 Part I, referred to: SI 1999/1862 Reg.4
Sch.5 Part I, amended: SI 1996/1451 Reg.2
Sch.5 Part II, amended: SI 1996/1451 Reg.2
Sch.6, amended: SI 1997/616 Reg.4
Sch.6 Part IV, added: SI 1997/616 Reg.2

2008. Vegetable Seeds Regulations 1993
Reg.3, amended: SI 1999/1863 Reg.3
Reg.5, amended: SI 1999/1863 Reg.3
Reg.6, amended: SI 1999/1863 Reg.3
Reg.6, referred to: SI 1999/1863 Reg.4
Reg.6A, added: SI 1999/1863 Reg.3
Reg.6A, referred to: SI 1999/1863 Reg.4
Reg.8A, added: SI 1999/1863 Reg.3
Reg.9, amended: SI 1999/1863 Reg.3
Reg.9A, added: SI 1999/1863 Reg.3
Sch.2A, added: SI 1999/1863 Reg.3
Sch.2A para.2, referred to: SI 1999/1863 Reg.4
Sch.3A, added: SI 1999/1863 Reg.3
Sch.4 Part I, amended: SI 1999/1863 Reg.3
Sch.4 Part I, referred to: SI 1999/1863 Reg.4
Sch.5 Part I, amended: SI 1996/1452 Reg.2
Sch.5 Part II, amended: SI 1996/1452 Reg.2
Sch.6, amended: SI 1997/616 Reg.4

2009. Fodder Plant Seeds Regulations 1993
Reg.3, amended: SI 1997/616 Reg.4, SI 1999/1864 Reg.3
Reg.5, amended: SI 1997/616 Reg.4, SI 1999/1864 Reg.3
Reg.6, amended: SI 1999/1864 Reg.3
Reg.6, referred to: SI 1999/1864 Reg.4
Reg.6A, added: SI 1999/1864 Reg.4
Reg.6A, referred to: SI 1999/1864 Reg.4
Reg.8, amended: SI 1997/616 Reg.4
Reg.8A, added: SI 1999/1864 Reg.4
Reg.9, amended: SI 1997/616 Reg.4, SI 1999/1864 Reg.3
Reg.9, revoked (in part): SI 1997/616 Reg.3
Reg.9A, added: SI 1999/1864 Reg.4
Sch.2A, added: SI 1999/1864 Reg.4
Sch.2A para.2, referred to: SI 1999/1864 Reg.4
Sch.3A, added: SI 1999/1864 Reg.4
Sch.4 Part I, amended: SI 1999/1864 Reg.3

1993—cont.

2009. Fodder Plant Seeds Regulations 1993—*cont.*
Sch.4 Part I, referred to: SI 1999/1864 Reg.4
Sch.5 Part I, amended: SI 1996/1453 Reg.2
Sch.5 Part II, amended: SI 1996/1453 Reg.2
Sch.6, amended: SI 1997/616 Reg.4
Sch.6 Part IV, amended: SI 1997/616 Reg.3

2013. Local Government Superannuation (Scotland) Amendment (No.2) Regulations 1993
applied: SI 1998/364 Reg.4, Reg.6, Reg.19, Sch.2 para.2, Sch.2 para.5, Sch.4 para.8
referred to: SI 1998/364 Reg.3, Reg.10, Sch.2 para.4, Sch.2 para.6

2014. Local Authorities (Capital Finance) (Amendment) (No.2) Regulations 1993
revoked: SI 1997/319 Reg.162, Sch.3

2072. Enforcement of Road Traffic Debts (Certificated Bailiffs) Regulations 1993
Sch.1 para.2, amended: SI 1998/1351 Reg.2
Sch.1 para.4, amended: SI 1998/1351 Reg.2

2073. Road Traffic Debts Order 1993
Art.2, applied: SI 1997/3058 Reg.11
Art.3, referred to: SI 1997/3058 Reg.11

2120. Goods Vehicles (Operators' Licences) (Temporary Use in Great Britain) (Amendment) (No.2) Regulations 1993
revoked: SI 1996/2186 Reg.2, Sch.1

2135. Edinburgh Assay Office (Amendment) Order 1993
referred to: 1996 c.i Sch.

2153. Manchester, Liverpool Road (Castlefield Properties Limited) Light Railway Order 1993
Art.8, amended: SI 1996/362 Art.5, Sch.4

2154. East Kent Light Railway Order 1993
Art.7, amended: SI 1996/362 Art.5, Sch.4

2155. Mental Health (Nurses) Amendment Order 1993
revoked: SI 1998/2625 Art.3

2198. Motor Vehicles (EC Type Approval) (Amendment) (No.2) Regulations 1993
revoked: SI 1998/2051 Reg.2, Sch.3

2205. Wireless Telegraphy (Television Licence Fees) (Amendment) (No.2) Regulations 1993
revoked: SI 1997/290 Reg.1, Sch

2210. Dental Vocational Training Authority Regulations 1993
applied: SI 1996/707 Reg.17, Sch.4 Part II
Reg.5, amended: SI 1996/707 Reg.17, Sch.5 para.9, SI 1997/2991 Reg.3, Sch. para.5
Reg.8, added: SI 1998/1576 Reg.3

2224. National Health Service (General Dental Services) (Scotland) Amendment Regulations 1993
revoked: SI 1996/177 Reg.38, Sch.8

2225. Parole Board (Scotland) Rules 1993
r.2, amended: SI 1997/2317 r.2, r.3, SI 1999/1116 r.2
r.4, amended: SI 1999/1116 r.3
r.5, amended: SI 1997/2317 r.4
r.6, substituted: SI 1998/1904 r.2
r.7, substituted: SI 1998/1904 r.2
r.8, amended: SI 1998/1904 r.3
r.8, revoked (in part): SI 1998/1904 r.3
r.14, amended: SI 1997/2317 r.5, SI 1998/1904 r.4
r.15, amended: SI 1998/1904 r.5, r.6
r.17, amended: SI 1999/1116 r.4
r.25, amended: SI 1997/2317 r.6

1993—cont.

2229. Road Traffic Act 1991 (Commencement No.7 and Transitional Provisions) Order 1993
Art.6, revoked: SI 1998/967 Art.3, Sch.

2237. Road Traffic (Special Parking Areas) (London Boroughs of Bromley, Hammersmith and Fulham and Lewisham) (London Borough of Wandsworth) (Amendment) Order 1993
Sch.2 para.2, substituted: SI 1997/3056 Art.2

2241. Housing (Preservation of Right to Buy) Regulations 1993
Sch.5A, substituted: SI 1999/1213 Reg.2, Sch.

2254. Public Trusts (Reorganisation) (Scotland) (No.2) Regulations 1993
applied: SI 1999/678 Sch.

2255. Fish Health (Amendment) Regulations 1993
revoked: SI 1997/1881 Reg.24

2330. Telecommunications (Leased Lines) Regulations 1993
revoked: SI 1997/2932 Reg.15
Reg.2, revoked: SI 1997/2932 Reg.15
Sch.2, revoked: SI 1997/2932 Reg.15

2345. Environmentally Sensitive Areas (Cairngorms Straths) Designation Order 1993
Art.2, amended: SI 1996/1963 Art.2, SI 1996/3082 Reg.3
Art.5A, amended: SI 1996/3082 Reg.4
Art.5B, added: SI 1996/3082 Reg.4
Art.5B, amended: SI 1996/3082 Reg.6
Art.5C, added: SI 1996/3082 Reg.6
Art.6, amended: SI 1996/1963 Art.3
Art.7, amended: SI 1996/1963 Art.4
Sch. para.10, amended: SI 1996/1963 Art.5

2358. Medicines (Applications for Grant of Product Licences - Products for Human Use) Regulations 1993
Reg.1, amended: SI 1997/654 Reg.17
Sch.1 para.17, amended: SI 1997/654 Reg.17

2379. Ionising Radiations (Outside Workers) Regulations 1993
applied: SI 1999/3232 Reg.39
revoked: SI 1999/3232 Reg.41
Reg.2, amended: SI 1999/2024 Reg.48, Sch.5 Part II
Reg.2, revoked: SI 1999/3232 Reg.41

2390. Assured and Protected Tenancies (Lettings to Students) (Amendment) Regulations 1993
revoked: SI 1998/1967 Reg.6, Sch.3

2391. Act of Adjournal (Consolidation Amendment No.2) (Miscellaneous) 1993
revoked: SI 1996/513 Sch.2 r.3, Sch.3

2408. Rent Assessment Committee (England and Wales) (Leasehold Valuation Tribunal) Regulations 1993
Reg.2, amended: SI 1996/2305 Reg.2, SI 1997/1854 Reg.3
Reg.3, amended: SI 1997/1854 Reg.4
Reg.4A, added: SI 1997/1854 Reg.5
Reg.4B, added: SI 1997/1854 Reg.5
Reg.4C, added: SI 1997/1854 Reg.5
Reg.4D, added: SI 1997/1854 Reg.5
Reg.4E, added: SI 1997/1854 Reg.5
Reg.4F, added: SI 1997/1854 Reg.5
Reg.4G, added: SI 1997/1854 Reg.5
Reg.4H, added: SI 1997/1854 Reg.5
Reg.5, amended: SI 1997/1854 Reg.6
Reg.11A, added: SI 1997/1854 Reg.7

1993—cont.

2408. Rent Assessment Committee (England and Wales) (Leasehold Valuation Tribunal) Regulations 1993—*cont.*
Reg.11B, added: SI 1997/1854 Reg.7
Reg.14A, added: SI 1997/1854 Reg.8
Sch.1, amended: SI 1996/2305 Reg.2
Sch.1 para.19, amended: SI 1997/74 Art.2, Sch para.11

2409. Leasehold Reform (Notices) (Amendment) Regulations 1993
revoked: SI 1997/640 Reg.4 (with savings)

2479. Offshore Installations (Safety Zones) (No.4) Order 1993
revoked: SI 1997/735 Art.3, Sch.2

2499. Smoke Control Areas (Authorised Fuels) Regulations 1993
Reg.2, revoked: SI 1998/2154 Reg.3

2513. Teachers' (Superannuation and Compensation for Premature Retirement) (Scotland) Amendment Regulations 1993
Reg.18, revoked: SI 1996/2317 Reg.20, Sch.5
Reg.19, revoked: SI 1996/2317 Reg.20, Sch.5
Reg.20, revoked: SI 1996/2317 Reg.20, Sch.5
Reg.21, revoked: SI 1996/2317 Reg.20, Sch.5

2542. Northern Birmingham Community Health National Health Service Trust Establishment Order 1993
revoked: SI 1999/3466 Art.2

2543. South Birmingham Community Health National Health Service Trust (Establishment) Order 1993
revoked: SI 1999/3466 Art.2
Art.1, revoked: SI 1999/3466 Art.2
Art.2, revoked: SI 1999/3466 Art.2

2544. Churchill John Radcliffe National Health Service Trust (Establishment) Order 1993
Art.1, amended: SI 1998/1227 Art.2
Art.2, amended: SI 1998/1227 Art.2

2546. Derbyshire Ambulance Service National Health Service Trust (Establishment) Order 1993
revoked: SI 1999/791 Art.2

2547. Derbyshire Royal Infirmary National Health Service Trust (Establishment) Order 1993
revoked: SI 1998/849 Art.2

2549. East Wiltshire Health Care National Health Service Trust (Establishment) Order 1993
revoked: SI 1999/1771 Art.2

2550. East Yorkshire Community Healthcare National Health Service Trust (Establishment) Order 1993
revoked: SI 1999/2687 Art.2
Art.3, revoked: SI 1999/2687 Art.2
Art.3, substituted: SI 1996/1002 Art.2

2552. Hereford Hospitals National Health Service Trust (Establishment) Order 1993
Art.3, amended: SI 1996/990 Art.2

2553. Hereford and Worcester Ambulance Service National Health Service Trust (Establishment) Order 1993
Art.3, substituted: SI 1998/2841 Art.2

2554. Hull and Holderness Community Health National Health Service Trust (Establishment) Order 1993
revoked: SI 1999/2687 Art.2
Art.3, amended: SI 1996/988 Art.2
Art.3, revoked: SI 1999/2687 Art.2

2558. Leicestershire Ambulance and Paramedic Service National Health Service Trust (Establishment) Order 1993
revoked: SI 1999/791 Art.2
Art.4, amended: SI 1997/1325 Art.2

1993—cont.

2558. Leicestershire Ambulance and Paramedic Service National Health Service Trust (Establishment) Order 1993—*cont.*
Art.4, revoked: SI 1999/791 Art.2
Art.4, substituted: SI 1997/1482 Art.2

2559. Leicestershire Mental Health Service National Health Service Trust (Establishment) Order 1993
revoked: SI 1998/3068 Art.2

2566. Oxfordshire Mental Healthcare National Health Service Trust (Establishment) Order 1993
Art.3, substituted: SI 1998/1285 Art.2
Sch., added: SI 1998/1285 Art.2, Sch.

2578. Wandsworth Community Health National Health Service Trust (Establishment) Order 1993
revoked: SI 1999/793 Art.2

2580. South Warwickshire Mental Health National Health Service Trust (Establishment) Order 1993
revoked: SI 1998/516 Art.2

2582. Worcester Royal Infirmary National Health Service Trust (Establishment) Order 1993
revoked: SI 1999/3471 Art.2
Art.3, amended: SI 1997/836 Art.2
Art.3, revoked: SI 1999/3471 Art.2

2589. Chichester Priority Care Services National Health Service Trust (Establishment) Order 1993
Art.1, amended: SI 1998/2923 Art.2
Art.2, amended: SI 1998/2923 Art.2
Art.3, substituted: SI 1998/321 Art.2
Sch., added: SI 1998/321 Art.2, Sch.

2591. Hartlepool Community Care National Health Service Trust (Dissolution) Order 1993
revoked: SI 1996/887 Art.2

2592. Blackburn, Hyndburn and Ribble Valley Health Care National Health Service Trust (Establishment) Order 1993
Art.3, substituted: SI 1999/2308 Art.2

2593. Northumberland Community Health National Health Service Trust (Establishment) Order 1993
revoked: SI 1998/825 Art.2

2600. Greater Manchester Ambulance Service National Health Service Trust (Establishment) Order 1993
Art.4, amended: SI 1997/2518 Art.2

2603. Darlington Memorial Hospital National Health Service Trust (Establishment) Order 1993
revoked: SI 1998/833 Art.2

2607. Wirral Community Healthcare National Health Service Trust (Establishment) Order 1993
revoked: SI 1997/834 Art.2

2609. North Downs Community Health National Health Service Trust (Establishment) Order 1993
revoked: SI 1998/502 Art.2

2610. South Durham Health Care National Health Service Trust (Establishment) Order 1993
revoked: SI 1996/880 Art.2

2612. Community Health Care: North Durham National Health Service Trust (Establishment) Order 1993
revoked: SI 1998/822 Art.2
Art.3, revoked: SI 1998/822 Art.2

2613. Kingston and District Community National Health Service Trust (Establishment) Order 1993
Art.3, amended: SI 1997/1002 Art.2

1993—cont.

2614. North Durham Acute Hospitals National Health Service Trust (Establishment) Order 1993
revoked: SI 1998/830 Art.2
Art.3, amended: SI 1996/984 Art.2
Art.3, revoked: SI 1998/830 Art.2

2616. Bishop Auckland Hospitals National Health Service Trust (Establishment) Order 1993
revoked: SI 1998/823 Art.2
Art.3, amended: SI 1996/989 Art.2
Art.3, revoked: SI 1998/823 Art.2

2617. Carlisle Hospitals National Health Service Trust (Establishment) Order 1993
Art.3, amended: SI 1997/837 Art.2

2618. Cheviot and Wansbeck National Health Service Trust (Establishment) Order 1993
revoked: SI 1998/825 Art.2

2620. West Cheshire National Health Service Trust (Establishment) Order 1993
revoked: SI 1997/832 Art.2

2621. South Kent Community Healthcare National Health Service Trust (Establishment) Order 1993
revoked: SI 1998/846 Art.2

2624. North Tyneside Healthcare National Health Service Trust (Establishment) Order 1993
revoked: SI 1998/825 Art.2

2627. Hartlepool and Peterlee Hospitals National Health Service Trust (Dissolution) Order 1993
revoked: SI 1996/879 Art.2

2628. Stockport Healthcare National Health Service Trust (Establishment) Order 1993
Art.3, substituted: SI 1998/2310 Art.2

2630. Shropshire's Community Health Service National Health Service Trust (Establishment) Order 1993
revoked: SI 1998/515 Art.2

2631. Hill Livestock (Compensatory Allowances) Regulations 1993
applied: SI 1996/1500 Reg.3

2633. South East London Mental Health National Health Service Trust (Establishment) Order 1993
revoked: SI 1999/900 Art.2
Art.3, revoked: SI 1999/900 Art.2
Art.4, revoked: SI 1999/900 Art.2

2635. North Staffordshire Combined Healthcare National Health Service Trust (Establishment) Order 1993
Art.3, amended: SI 1999/640 Art.2
Art.3, substituted: SI 1998/2972 Art.2
Sch., added: SI 1998/2972 Sch.

2636. Lincoln District Healthcare National Health Service Trust (Establishment) Order 1993
Art.3, substituted: SI 1999/363 Art.2

2637. Swindon and Marlborough National Health Service Trust (Establishment) Order 1993
Art.3, amended: SI 1996/987 Art.2, SI 1999/630 Art.2

2638. Louth and District Healthcare National Health Service Trust (Establishment) Order 1993
revoked: SI 1996/877 Art.2

2639. North Kent Healthcare National Health Service Trust (Establishment) Order 1993
revoked: SI 1998/807 Art.2
Art.3, revoked: SI 1998/807 Art.2

2640. Medway National Health Service Trust (Establishment) Order 1993
Art.3, substituted: SI 1999/11 Art.2

1993—cont.

2642. Dartford and Gravesham National Health Service Trust (Establishment) Order 1993
Art.3, amended: SI 1996/994 Art.2

2661. European Communities (Designation) (No.3) Order 1993
revoked (in part): SI 1997/2563 Art.3, SI 1999/2788 Art.4, Sch.3

2668. Industrial Relations (Northern Ireland) Order 1993
Art.2, revoked (in part): SI 1996/1919 (NI.16) Art.257, Sch.3
Art.3, revoked: SI 1996/1919 (NI.16) Art.257, Sch.3
Art.4, revoked: SI 1996/1919 (NI.16) Art.257, Sch.3
Art.5, revoked: SI 1996/1919 (NI.16) Art.257, Sch.3
Art.6, revoked: SI 1996/1919 (NI.16) Art.257, Sch.3
Art.7, revoked: SI 1996/1919 (NI.16) Art.257, Sch.3
Art.8, revoked: SI 1996/1919 (NI.16) Art.257, Sch.3
Art.9, amended: 1996 c.14 Sch.10 para.27
Art.9, revoked (in part): SI 1996/1919 (NI.16) Art.257, Sch.3, SI 1996/1921 (NI.18) Art.28, Sch.3
Art.10, amended: 1996 c.46 s.27
Art.10, referred to: SI 1996/1919 (NI.16) Sch.2 para.12, SI 1996/1921 (NI.18) Sch.2 para.8
Art.10, revoked: SI 1996/1919 (NI.16) Art.257, Sch.3
Art.12, revoked: SI 1996/1919 (NI.16) Art.257, Sch.3
Art.13, revoked: SI 1996/1919 (NI.16) Art.257, Sch.3
Art.14, revoked: SI 1996/1921 (NI.18) Art.28, Sch.3
Art.15, revoked: SI 1996/1921 (NI.18) Art.28, Sch.3
Art.16, revoked (in part): SI 1996/1919 (NI.16) Art.257, Sch.3
Art.17, revoked: SI 1996/1921 (NI.18) Art.28, Sch.3
Art.18, revoked (in part): SI 1996/1919 (NI.16) Art.257, Sch.3
Sch.1, revoked: SI 1996/1919 (NI.16) Art.257, Sch.3
Sch.2, revoked: SI 1996/1919 (NI.16) Art.257, Sch.3
Sch.3, revoked: SI 1996/1919 (NI.16) Art.257, Sch.3
Sch.4 para.2, revoked: SI 1996/1919 (NI.16) Art.257, Sch.3
Sch.4 para.3, revoked: SI 1996/1919 (NI.16) Art.257, Sch.3
Sch.5 para.1, revoked: SI 1996/1921 (NI.18) Art.28, Sch.3
Sch.5 para.2, revoked: SI 1996/1919 (NI.16) Art.257, Sch.3, SI 1996/1921 (NI.18) Art.28, Sch.3
Sch.5 para.3, revoked: SI 1996/1919 (NI.16) Art.257, Sch.3, SI 1996/1921 (NI.18) Art.28, Sch.3
Sch.5 para.4, revoked: SI 1996/1921 (NI.18) Art.28, Sch.3
Sch.5 para.5, revoked: SI 1996/1919 (NI.16) Art.257, Sch.3
Sch.5 para.7, revoked: SI 1996/1919 (NI.16) Art.257, Sch.3
Sch.6, revoked: SI 1996/1919 (NI.16) Art.257, Sch.3

NO.

NO.

1993—cont.

2668. Industrial Relations (Northern Ireland) Order 1993—*cont.*

Sch.6 Art.56, revoked: SI 1996/1921 (NI.18) Art.28, Sch.3

Sch.6 Art.59, revoked: SI 1996/1921 (NI.18) Art.28, Sch.3

Sch.7, revoked: SI 1996/1919 (NI.16) Art.257, Sch.3

Sch.7 para.2, referred to: SI 1996/1919 (NI.16) Sch.2 para.7

Sch.8, revoked: SI 1996/1919 (NI.16) Art.257, Sch.3

2687. Employment Tribunals (Constitution and Rules of Procedure) Regulations 1993

see *Lewisham & Guys Mental Health NHS Trust v Andrews* [1999] I.R.L.R. 407 (EAT), Morison, J.; see *Selkent Bus Co Ltd v Moore* [1996] I.C.R. 836 (EAT), Mummery, J.; see *Tsangacos v Amalgamated Chemicals Ltd* [1997] I.R.L.R. 4 (EAT), Morison, J.

applied: SI 1997/407 Art.9, SI 1997/408 Art.9, SI 1998/726 Art.9, SI 1998/727 Art.9, SI 1999/158 Art.9, SI 1999/159 Art.9

referred to: SI 1996/101 Art.9, SI 1996/102 Art.9, SI 1999/743 Reg.22

Reg.2, amended: SI 1996/1757 Reg.2

Reg.6, amended: SI 1996/1757 Reg.3

Reg.8, applied: SI 1999/743 Reg.18

Reg.9, substituted: SI 1996/1757 Reg.4

Sch.1, see *Bewry v Cumbria CC* Times, November 17, 1998 (CA), Peter Gibson, L.J.; see *Eurobell (Holdings) Plc v Barker* Times, November 12, 1997 (EAT), Morison, J.; see *R. v London (North) Industrial Tribunal Ex p. Associated Newspapers Ltd* [1998] I.C.R. 1212 (QBD), Keene, J.; see *Sutcliffe v Big C's Marine* [1998] I.C.R. 913 (EAT), Morison, J.

Sch.1 r.1, amended: SI 1996/1757 Reg.5

Sch.1 r.3, see *Sutcliffe v Big C's Marine* [1998] I.C.R. 913 (EAT), Morison, J.

Sch.1 r.3, amended: SI 1996/1757 Reg.6, Reg.7

Sch.1 r.3, revoked (in part): SI 1996/1757 Reg.8

Sch.1 r.6, see *Sutcliffe v Big C's Marine* [1998] I.C.R. 913 (EAT), Morison, J.

Sch.1 r.7, amended: SI 1996/1757 Reg.9, Reg.10

Sch.1 r.9, see *Eurobell (Holdings) Plc v Barker* [1998] I.C.R. 299 (EAT), Morison, J.; see *Gulson v Zurich Insurance Co* [1998] I.R.L.R. 118 (EAT), Kirkwood, J.; see *Mensah v East Hertfordshire NHS Trust* [1998] I.R.L.R. 531 (CA), Peter Gibson, L.J.

Sch.1 r.10, amended: SI 1996/1757 Reg.11

Sch.1 r.10, revoked (in part): SI 1996/1757 Reg.12

Sch.1 r.13, see *Sutcliffe v Big C's Marine* [1998] I.C.R. 913 (EAT), Morison, J.

Sch.1 r.13, amended: SI 1996/1757 Reg.13, Reg.14

Sch.1 r.13.1, see *Eurobell (Holdings) Plc v Barker* [1998] I.C.R. 299 (EAT), Morison, J.

Sch.1 r.14, see *Associated Newspapers Ltd v London (North) Industrial Tribunal* [1998] I.R.L.R. 569 (QBD), Keene, J.; see *M v Vincent* [1998] I.C.R. 73 (EAT), Morison, J.; see *R. v London (North) Industrial Tribunal Ex p. Associated Newspapers Ltd* [1998] I.C.R. 1212 (QBD), Keene, J.; see *X v Z Ltd* [1998] I.C.R. 43 (CA), Staughton, L.J.

Sch.1 r.14, amended: SI 1996/1757 Reg.15

Sch.1 r.17, see *Affleck v Newcastle Mind* [1999] I.C.R. 852 (EAT), Morison, J.

2687. Employment Tribunals (Constitution and Rules of Procedure) Regulations 1993—*cont.*

Sch.1 r.19A, added: SI 1996/1757 Reg.16

Sch.1 r.20, amended: SI 1996/1757 Reg.17, Reg.18, Reg.19, Reg.20

Sch.2 r.8A, amended: SI 1996/1757 Reg.21, Reg.22, Reg.23

Sch.2 r.9, amended: SI 1996/1757 Reg.24

Sch.2 r.10, amended: SI 1996/1757 Reg.25

Sch.2 r.12, amended: SI 1996/1757 Reg.26

Sch.2 r.13, amended: SI 1996/1757 Reg.27, Reg.28, Reg.29

Sch.2 r.20, amended: SI 1996/1757 Reg.30, Reg.31, Reg.32, Reg.33

Sch.3 r.14, amended: SI 1996/1757 Reg.34

Sch.4, applied: SI 1999/743 Reg.18

2688. Employment Tribunals (Constitution and Rules of Procedure) (Scotland) Regulations 1993

applied: SI 1996/1360 Reg.13, SI 1997/407 Art.9, SI 1997/408 Art.9, SI 1998/726 Art.9, SI 1998/727 Art.9, SI 1999/158 Art.9, SI 1999/159 Art.9

referred to: SI 1996/101 Art.9, SI 1996/102 Art.9, SI 1999/743 Reg.22

Reg.8, applied: SI 1999/743 Reg.18

Reg.9, substituted: SI 1996/1758 Reg.2

Sch.1 r.1, amended: SI 1996/1758 Reg.3

Sch.1 r.3, amended: SI 1996/1758 Reg.4, Reg.5

Sch.1 r.3, revoked (in part): SI 1996/1758 Reg.6

Sch.1 r.7, amended: SI 1996/1758 Reg.7, Reg.8

Sch.1 r.10, amended: SI 1996/1758 Reg.9

Sch.1 r.10, revoked (in part): SI 1996/1758 Reg.10

Sch.1 r.13, amended: SI 1996/1758 Reg.11, Reg.12

Sch.1 r.14, amended: SI 1996/1758 Reg.13

Sch.1 r.19A, added: SI 1996/1758 Reg.14

Sch.1 r.20, amended: SI 1996/1758 Reg.15, Reg.16

Sch.2 r.8A, amended: SI 1996/1758 Reg.17, Reg.18, Reg.19

Sch.2 r.9, amended: SI 1996/1758 Reg.20

Sch.2 r.10, amended: SI 1996/1758 Reg.21

Sch.2 r.12, amended: SI 1996/1758 Reg.22

Sch.2 r.13, amended: SI 1996/1758 Reg.23, Reg.24, Reg.25

Sch.2 r.20, amended: SI 1996/1758 Reg.26, Reg.27

Sch.3 r.14, amended: SI 1996/1758 Reg.28

Sch.4, applied: SI 1999/743 Reg.18

2690. Surviving Spouse (Scotland) Order 1993

revoked: SI 1999/445 Art.3

2709. Education (No.2) Act 1986 (Amendment) Order 1993

revoked: 1996 c.56 Sch.38 Part III

2711. Housing Renovation etc. Grants (Grant Limit) (Amendment) Order 1993

applied: SI 1996/2842 Art.8

revoked: SI 1996/2842 Art.7, Sch Part I

2731. Food Labelling (Scotland) Amendment Regulations 1993

revoked: SI 1996/1499 Reg.49, Sch.9

2755. Copyright (Certification of Licensing Scheme for Educational Recording of Broadcasts) (Open University Educational Enterprises Limited) Order 1993

Sch. para.5, amended: SI 1996/190 Art.2

NO.

1993—cont.

2759. Food Labelling (Amendment) Regulations 1993
revoked: SI 1996/1499 Reg.49, Sch.9

2767. Environmentally Sensitive Areas (Central Borders) Designation Order 1993
Art.2, amended: SI 1996/1964 Art.2, SI 1996/3082 Reg.3
Art.5A, added: SI 1996/3082 Reg.4
Art.5B, added: SI 1996/3082 Reg.4
Art.5B, amended: SI 1996/3082 Reg.6
Art.5C, added: SI 1996/3082 Reg.6
Art.7, amended: SI 1996/1964 Art.3
Sch. para.10, amended: SI 1996/1964 Art.4

2768. Environmentally Sensitive Areas (Stewartry) Designation Order 1993
Art.2, amended: SI 1996/1967 Art.2, SI 1996/3082 Reg.3
Art.5A, added: SI 1996/3082 Reg.4
Art.5B, added: SI 1996/3082 Reg.4
Art.5B, amended: SI 1996/3082 Reg.6
Art.5C, added: SI 1996/3082 Reg.6
Art.7, amended: SI 1996/1967 Art.3
Sch. para.10, amended: SI 1996/1967 Art.4

2775. Plant Breeders' Rights (Amendment) Regulations 1993
applied: SI 1998/1027 Reg.22
revoked: SI 1998/1027 Reg.21 (with savings), Sch.2 (with savings)

2783. Local Government Superannuation (South Yorkshire Transport Limited) Regulations 1993
Reg.1, amended: SI 1997/1613 Reg.27, Sch.3 para.4
Reg.2, amended: SI 1997/1613 Reg.27, Sch.3 para.4
Reg.5, amended: SI 1997/1613 Reg.27, Sch.3 para.4
Reg.5, revoked (in part): SI 1997/1613 Reg.27, Sch.3 para.4

2788. Northern Ireland (Emergency Provisions) Act 1991 (Codes of Practice) (No.2) Order 1993
revoked: SI 1996/1698 Art.4

2798. Sex Discrimination and Equal Pay (Remedies) Regulations 1993
revoked: SI 1996/2803 Reg.1
Sch. para.1, revoked (in part): 1996 c.18 Sch.3 Part II, SI 1996/2803 Reg.1
Sch. para.2, revoked: 1996 c.18 Sch.3 Part II, SI 1996/2803 Reg.1

2799. Home Energy Efficiency Grants (Amendment) Regulations 1993
revoked: SI 1997/790 Reg.14, Sch.2

2803. Road Traffic Act 1991 (Commencement No.8 and Transitional Provisions) Order 1993
Art.5, revoked: SI 1998/967 Art.3, Sch.

2807. Libya (United Nations Sanctions) Order 1993
Art.12, amended: SI 1998/1129 Art.3, Sch.2

2810. Education and Libraries (Northern Ireland) Order 1993
applied: SI 1998/1759 (NI.13) Art.40, Sch.2 para.3
referred to: SI 1997/866 (NI.5) Art.2
Art.1, revoked: SI 1997/1772 (NI.15) Art.25, Sch.5
Art.7, applied: SI 1997/1772 (NI.15) Art.10, Sch.2 para.8
Art.20, referred to: SI 1998/1759 (NI.13) Sch.4 para.1
Art.21, amended: SI 1998/3162 (NI.21) Art.105, Sch.3
Art.26, revoked: SI 1997/1772 (NI.15) Art.25, Sch.4, Sch.5

NO.

1993—cont.

2810. Education and Libraries (Northern Ireland) Order 1993—*cont.*
Art.27, applied: SI 1996/274 (NI.1) Art.41
Art.27, revoked: SI 1997/1772 (NI.15) Art.25, Sch.4, Sch.5
Art.28, revoked (in part): SI 1998/1759 (NI.13) Art.91, Sch.6 Part II
Art.30, amended: SI 1997/1772 (NI.15) Art.25, Sch.4
Art.30, applied: SI 1998/1760 (NI.14) Art.7
Art.30, revoked (in part): SI 1997/1772 (NI.15) Art.25, Sch.4, Sch.5
Art.31, revoked (in part): SI 1997/1772 (NI.15) Art.25, Sch.4, Sch.5, SI 1998/1759 (NI.13) Art.91, Sch.6 Part II
Art.32, referred to: SI 1998/1759 (NI.13) Art.72
Art.32, revoked (in part): SI 1998/1759 (NI.13) Art.91, Sch.6 Part I
Art.33, revoked: SI 1997/1772 (NI.15) Art.25, Sch.4, Sch.5
Art.34, revoked: SI 1998/1759 (NI.13) Art.91, Sch.6 Part I
Art.35, revoked (in part): SI 1997/866 (NI.5) Sch, SI 1998/1759 (NI.13) Art.91, Sch.6 Part I
Art.36, revoked (in part): SI 1996/274 (NI.1) Art.44, Sch.6 Part I, SI 1998/1759 (NI.13) Art.91, Sch.6 Part I
Art.40, revoked: SI 1998/1759 (NI.13) Art.91, Sch.6 Part I
Art.41, revoked: SI 1998/1759 (NI.13) Art.91, Sch.6 Part I
Art.45, revoked: SI 1996/274 (NI.1) Art.35, Art.44, Sch.6 Part II
Art.46, revoked: SI 1998/1759 (NI.13) Art.91, Sch.6 Part I
Part II, applied: SI 1997/1772 (NI.15) Art.10, Sch.2 para.8
Sch.1 para.2, revoked (in part): SI 1997/1772 (NI.15) Art.25, Sch.4, Sch.5
Sch.3, revoked: SI 1996/274 (NI.1) Art.44, Sch.6 Part II
Sch.4, revoked (in part): SI 1996/1297 (NI.7) Art.23, Sch.5, SI 1996/1919 (NI.16) Art.257, Sch.3
Sch.4 Part I, revoked (in part): SI 1998/1759 (NI.13) Art.91, Sch.6 Part I
Sch.4 Part II, revoked (in part): SI 1996/274 (NI.1) Art.44, Sch.6 Part I, Art.44, Sch.6 Part II, SI 1997/866 (NI.5) Sch, SI 1997/1772 (NI.15) Art.25, Sch.5, SI 1998/1760 (NI.14) Art.9, Sch., SI 1998/1759 (NI.13) Art.91, Sch.6 Part I, Sch.6 Part II

2827. Education (No.2) Act 1986 (Amendment) (No.2) Order 1993
revoked: 1996 c.56 Sch.38 Part III

2828. Education (Recognised Awards) (Richmond College) Order 1993
revoked: SI 1996/2564 Art.3, Sch.

2834. Mid Glamorgan Ambulance National Health Service Trust (Establishment) Order 1993
revoked: SI 1998/671 Art.2

2835. Derwen National Health Service Trust (Establishment) Order 1993
revoked: SI 1997/875 Art.2

2836. North Wales Ambulance National Health Service Trust (Establishment) Order 1993
revoked: SI 1998/670 Art.2

2837. Rhondda Healthcare National Health Service Trust (Establishment) Order 1993
revoked: SI 1999/1120 Art.2, Sch.2

NO.

2838. Velindre National Health Service Trust (Establishment) Order 1993
  Art.2, substituted: SI 1999/826 Art.2
  Art.3, substituted: SI 1999/826 Art.2

2839. Gwynedd Community Health National Health Service Trust (Establishment) Order 1993
  revoked: SI 1999/1120 Art.2, Sch.2

2840. Nevill Hall and District National Health Service Trust (Establishment) Order 1993
  revoked: SI 1999/1120 Art.2, Sch.2
  Art.3, revoked: SI 1999/1120 Art.2, Sch.2
  Art.3, substituted: SI 1997/2605 Art.2

2841. Gwynedd Hospitals National Health Service Trust (Establishment) Order 1993
  revoked: SI 1999/1120 Art.2, Sch.2

2846. Redundant Churches Fund Order 1993
  revoked: SI 1996/3086 Art.5

2854. Employment Appeal Tribunal Rules 1993
  r.3, see *Practice Direction (Employment Appeal Tribunal: Procedure)* [1996] I.C.R. 422 (EAT), Mummery, J.
  r.14, applied: SI 1999/901 Art.5, Sch.
  r.16, applied: SI 1999/901 Art.5, Sch.
  r.23A, added: SI 1996/3216 r.2
  r.31, see *Persson v Matra Marconi Space UK Ltd* Times, December 10, 1996 (CA), Mummery, L.J.

2856. Mid Essex Community and Mental Health National Health Service Trust (Establishment) Order 1993
  Art.4, amended: SI 1996/3012 Art.2

2875. Public Airport Companies (Capital Finance) (Fourth Amendment) Order 1993
  revoked: SI 1996/604 Reg.5

2890. Local Government (Compensation for Premature Retirement) (Amendment) Regulations 1993
  revoked: SI 1996/1680 Reg.49, Sch.5

2908. Western Isles Islands Council (Brevig) Harbour Empowerment Order 1993
  applied: SI 1997/209 Art.15
  Art.34, applied: SI 1997/209 Art.15
  Part II, applied: SI 1997/209 Art.15
  Part III, applied: SI 1997/209 Art.15

2914. Education (Mandatory Awards) (No.2) Regulations 1993
  Reg.25, applied: SI 1998/1166 Reg.6, SI 1999/1494 Reg.6
  Reg.25, referred to: SI 1997/431 Reg.6

2919. Firearms (Amendment) Act 1988 (Firearms Consultative Committee) Order 1993
  Art.2, amended: SI 1996/3272 Art.2

2926. Dundee Healthcare National Health Service Trust (Establishment) Order 1993
  revoked: SI 1999/1070 Art.2, Sch.2

2927. Falkirk and District Royal Infirmary National Health Service Trust (Establishment) Order 1993
  revoked: SI 1999/1070 Art.2, Sch.2

2928. Hairmyres and Stonehouse Hospitals National Health Service Trust (Establishment) Order 1993
  revoked: SI 1999/1070 Art.2, Sch.2
  Art.3, revoked: SI 1999/1070 Art.2, Sch.2
  Art.3, substituted: SI 1998/804 Art.2

2929. Law Hospital National Health Service Trust (Establishment) Order 1993
  revoked: SI 1999/1070 Art.2, Sch.2
  Art.3, amended: SI 1998/926 Art.2
  Art.3, revoked: SI 1999/1070 Art.2, Sch.2

NO.

2930. Perth and Kinross National Health Service Trust (Establishment) Order 1993
  revoked: SI 1999/1070 Art.2, Sch.2

2931. East and Midlothian National Health Service Trust (Establishment) Order 1993
  revoked: SI 1999/1070 Art.2, Sch.2

2932. Royal Infirmary of Edinburgh National Health Service Trust (Establishment) Order 1993
  revoked: SI 1999/1070 Art.2, Sch.2
  Art.3, revoked: SI 1999/1070 Art.2, Sch.2
  Art.3, substituted: SI 1998/1841 Art.2

2933. Western General Hospitals National Health Service Trust (Establishment) Order 1993
  revoked: SI 1999/1070 Art.2, Sch.2

2935. Glasgow Community and Mental Health Services National Health Service Trust (Establishment) Order 1993
  revoked: SI 1999/1070 Art.2, Sch.2
  Art.2, revoked: SI 1999/1070 Art.2, Sch.2

2936. Edinburgh Sick Children's National Health Service Trust (Establishment) Order 1993
  revoked: SI 1999/1070 Art.2, Sch.2

2937. Fife Healthcare National Health Service Trust (Establishment) Order 1993
  revoked: SI 1999/1070 Art.2, Sch.2

2938. Edinburgh Healthcare National Health Service Trust (Establishment) Order 1993
  revoked: SI 1999/1070 Art.2, Sch.2
  Art.3, revoked: SI 1999/1070 Art.2, Sch.2
  Art.3, substituted: SI 1998/2802 Art.2

2956. Animals (Scientific Procedures) Act (Fees) Order 1993
  revoked: SI 1996/3091 Art.1

2957. Sheriff Court Fees Amendment (No.2) Order 1993
  revoked: SI 1997/687 Art.11, Sch.2
  Art.2, revoked: SI 1996/628 Art.3

2968. Education (School Inspection) (Wales) (No.2) (Amendment) Regulations 1993
  revoked: SI 1996/1934 Reg.3, SI 1998/1866 Reg.1, Sch.

2969. Scottish College of Textiles (Scotland) Order of Council 1993
  revoked: SI 1998/2208 Art.8

2973. Education (School Inspection) (No.2) (Amendment) Regulations 1993
  revoked: SI 1997/1966 Reg.1, Sch. Part I
  Reg.2, revoked: SI 1997/1966 Reg.1, Sch. Part I

2974. Port of Bristol Harbour Revision Order 1993
  Art.4, amended: SI 1998/1209 Art.15
  Art.4, applied: SI 1998/1209 Art.15
  Art.5, amended: SI 1998/1209 Art.15
  Art.5, applied: SI 1998/1209 Art.15
  Art.6, amended: SI 1998/1209 Art.15
  Art.6, applied: SI 1998/1209 Art.15
  Art.7, amended: SI 1998/1209 Art.15
  Art.7, applied: SI 1998/1209 Art.15

3016. Retirement Benefits Schemes (Restriction on Discretion to Approve) (Additional Voluntary Contributions) Regulations 1993
  applied: SI 1996/1582 Reg.3
  Reg.4, amended: SI 1999/1964 Reg.3
  Reg.5, amended: SI 1999/1964 Reg.4
  Reg.5, applied: SI 1996/2156 Reg.10, SI 1997/1612 Reg.85, SI 1998/366 Reg.84, SI 1998/1451 Reg.13, SI 1999/1082 Art.R1, Sch.6 para.11
  Reg.6, amended: SI 1999/1964 Reg.5
  Reg.6, applied: SI 1997/1612 Reg.85, SI 1998/366 Reg.84, SI 1998/1451 Reg.13, SI 1999/1082 Art.R1, Sch.6 para.11

NO.

1993—cont.

3018. Inverclyde Royal National Health Service Trust (Establishment) Order 1993
revoked: SI 1999/1070 Art.2, Sch.2

3019. Kirkcaldy Acute Hospitals National Health Service Trust (Establishment) Order 1993
revoked: SI 1999/1070 Art.2, Sch.2

3020. Queen Margaret Hospital National Health Service Trust (Establishment) Order 1993
revoked: SI 1999/1070 Art.2, Sch.2

3021. Stobhill National Health Service Trust (Establishment) Order 1993
revoked: SI 1999/1070 Art.2, Sch.2

3022. Angus National Health Service Trust (Establishment) Order 1993
revoked: SI 1999/1070 Art.2, Sch.2

3023. Glasgow Royal Infirmary University National Health Service Trust (Establishment) Order 1993
revoked: SI 1999/1070 Art.2, Sch.2

3024. Renfrewshire Healthcare National Health Service Trust (Establishment) Amendment Order 1993
revoked: SI 1999/1070 Art.2, Sch.2
Art.3, revoked: SI 1999/1070 Art.2, Sch.2
Art.3, substituted: SI 1999/999 Art.2

3025. West Glasgow Hospitals University National Health Service Trust (Establishment) Order 1993
revoked: SI 1999/1070 Art.2, Sch.2
Art.3, revoked: SI 1999/1070 Art.2, Sch.2
Art.3, substituted: SI 1996/324 Art.2

3026. Highland Communities National Health Service Trust (Establishment) Order 1993
revoked: SI 1999/1070 Art.2, Sch.2
Art.3, revoked: SI 1999/1070 Art.2, Sch.2
Art.3, substituted: SI 1999/366 Art.2

3029. Trade Marks and Service Marks (Fees) (Amendment) Rules 1993
applied: SI 1996/1942 r.5

3044. Local Government Superannuation (Scotland) Amendment (No.3) Regulations 1993
applied: SI 1998/364 Reg.4, Reg.6, Reg.19, Sch.2 para.2, Sch.2 para.5, Sch.4 para.8
referred to: SI 1998/364 Reg.3, Reg.10, Sch.2 para.4, Sch.2 para.6

3050. Notification of New Substances Regulations 1993
applied: SI 1996/2791 Sch.13, SI 1997/2505 Reg.16, Sch.13, SI 1999/645 Reg.18, Sch.15
Reg.2, amended: SI 1997/654 Reg.18
Reg.3, amended: SI 1999/3232 Reg.41, Sch.9 para.4
Reg.4, amended: SI 1997/654 Reg.18
Reg.4, applied: SI 1997/2505 Sch.13, SI 1999/645 Reg.18, Sch.15
Reg.5, amended: SI 1997/654 Reg.18
Reg.5, applied: SI 1997/2505 Sch.13, SI 1999/645 Reg.18, Sch.15
Reg.6, applied: SI 1997/2505 Sch.13, SI 1999/645 Reg.18, Sch.15
Reg.14, amended: SI 1997/654 Reg.18
Reg.14, revoked (in part): SI 1997/654 Reg.18
Reg.23, applied: SI 1997/2505 Sch.13

3053. Commercial Agents (Council Directive) Regulations 1993
see *AMB Imballaggi Plastici SRL v Pacflex Ltd* [1999] 2 All E.R. (Comm) 249 (CA), Waller, L.J.; see *Ingmar (GB) Ltd v Eaton Leonard Technologies Inc* [1999] Eu L.R. 88 (CA), Peter Gibson, L.J.; see *Roy v MR Pearlman Ltd* Times, May 13, 1999 (OH), Lord Hamilton

NO.

1993—cont.

3053. Commercial Agents (Council Directive) Regulations 1993—*cont.*
referred to: 1998 c.46 s.30, Sch.5 s.C7
Reg.1, amended: SI 1998/2868 Reg.2
Reg.2, amended: SI 1998/2868 Reg.2
Reg.7, see *Roy v MR Pearlman Ltd* 1999 S.C. 459 (OH), Lord Hamilton
Reg.8, see *Roy v MR Pearlman Ltd* 1999 S.C. 459 (OH), Lord Hamilton
Reg.17, see *Duffen v FRA BO SpA* [1999] E.C.C. 58 (CA), Otton, L.J.; see *Moore v Piretta PTA Ltd* [1999] 1 All E.R. 174 (QBD), John Mitting Q.C.; see *Page v Combined Shipping & Trading Co Ltd* [1997] 3 All E.R. 656 (CA), Staughton, L.J.; see *Roy v MR Pearlman Ltd* 1999 S.C. 459 (OH), Lord Hamilton
Reg.17, amended: SI 1998/2868 Reg.2
Reg.18, see *Moore v Piretta PTA Ltd* [1999] 1 All E.R. 174 (QBD), John Mitting Q.C.

3054. Local Authorities (Capital Finance) (Amendment) (No.3) Regulations 1993
revoked: SI 1997/319 Reg.162, Sch.3

3057. National Health Service Trusts (Consultation on Dissolution) (Scotland) Regulations 1993
applied: SI 1998/2709, SI 1998/2710, SI 1998/2711, SI 1998/2712, SI 1998/2713, SI 1998/2714, SI 1998/2715, SI 1998/2716, SI 1998/2717, SI 1998/2718, SI 1998/2719, SI 1998/2720, SI 1998/2721, SI 1998/2722, SI 1998/2723, SI 1998/2724, SI 1998/2725, SI 1998/2728, SI 1998/2729, SI 1998/2730, SI 1998/2731, SI 1998/2732, SI 1998/2733, SI 1998/2734, SI 1998/2735

3059. Non-Domestic Rating Contributions (Scotland) Amendment Regulations 1993
revoked: SI 1996/3070 Reg.10, Sch.4

3070. Education (Publication of Schemes for Financing Schools) Regulations 1993
revoked: SI 1999/711 Reg.9, Sch.2

3074. Personal Protective Equipment (EC Directive) (Amendment) Regulations 1993
Sch., amended: SI 1996/3039 Reg.2

3075. Prison (Amendment) (No.2) Rules 1993
revoked: SI 1999/728 r.85 (with savings), Sch. (with savings)

3080. Act of Sederunt (Fees of Solicitors in the Sheriff Court) (Amendment and Further Provisions) 1993
Sch.1, applied: SI 1998/2675 para.3, SSI 1999/149 para.3
Sch.1 Table, amended: SI 1996/236 Reg.2, Sch., SI 1998/2675 para.2, Sch., SSI 1999/149 para.2, Sch.
Sch.1 para.5, amended: SI 1998/2675 para.2
Sch.1 para.6, amended: SI 1998/2675 para.2
Sch.1 para.11, amended: SI 1998/2675 para.2
Sch.1 para.14, amended: SI 1998/2675 para.2

3100. Credit Unions (Authorised Investments) Order 1993
Art.4, amended: SI 1997/2646 Reg.7
Sch. para.6, added: SI 1997/2646 Reg.7

3102. Education (Grant-Maintained Schools) (Initial Governing Instruments) Regulations 1993
Sch.1 para.25, amended: SI 1996/2049 Reg.2
Sch.1 para.35, amended: SI 1996/2049 Reg.2
Sch.1 para.41, amended: SI 1996/2049 Reg.2
Sch.1 para.43, revoked (in part): SI 1999/703 Reg.8
Sch.1 para.43, substituted: SI 1996/2049 Reg.2

NO.

NO.

3102. Education (Grant-Maintained Schools) (Initial Governing Instruments) Regulations 1993—*cont.*
Sch.2 Art.1, amended: SI 1996/2049 Reg.3
Sch.2 Art.7, amended: SI 1996/2049 Reg.3
Sch.2 Art.8, amended: SI 1996/2049 Reg.3
Sch.2 Art.13, amended: SI 1996/2049 Reg.3
Sch.2 Art.19, amended: SI 1996/2049 Reg.3
Sch.1 Appendix 1, amended: SI 1996/2049 Reg.2
Sch.1 Appendix 2, amended: SI 1996/2049 Reg.2
Sch.1 Appendix 3, amended: SI 1996/2049 Reg.2
Sch.1 Appendix 3, revoked (in part): SI 1999/703 Reg.8
Sch.2 Appendix 2, amended: SI 1996/2049 Reg.3

3104. Education (Application of Financing Schemes to Special Schools) Regulations 1993
revoked: SI 1999/711 Reg.9, Sch.2

3106. Education Act 1993 (Commencement No.2 and Transitional Provisions) Order 1993
Art.8, applied: 1996 c.56 Sch.39 para.24
Art.9, applied: 1996 c.56 Sch.39 para.24

3108. Local Government (Compensation for Premature Retirement) (Amendment) (No.2) Regulations 1993
revoked: SI 1996/1680 Reg.49, Sch.5

3112. Friendly Societies (Provisional Repayments for Exempt Business) Regulations 1993
revoked (in part): SI 1999/622 Reg.13
Reg.2, amended: SI 1997/474 Reg.3
Reg.2, revoked (in part): SI 1999/622 Reg.13
Reg.4, amended: SI 1996/21 Reg.5, SI 1997/474 Reg.4, Reg.5
Reg.4, revoked (in part): SI 1999/622 Reg.13
Reg.5, amended: SI 1996/21 Reg.6
Reg.5, revoked (in part): SI 1999/622 Reg.13
Reg.5A, added: SI 1996/21 Reg.7
Reg.5A, amended: SI 1997/475 Reg.4
Reg.5A, revoked (in part): SI 1999/622 Reg.13
Reg.5B, added: SI 1996/21 Reg.7
Reg.5B, revoked (in part): SI 1999/622 Reg.13
Reg.6, amended: SI 1996/21 Reg.8
Reg.6, revoked (in part): SI 1999/622 Reg.13
Reg.7, amended: SI 1996/21 Reg.9
Reg.7, revoked (in part): SI 1999/622 Reg.13

3113. Education (Publication of School Proposals and Notices) Regulations 1993
revoked (in part): SI 1999/1671 Reg.13, SI 1999/2213 Reg.19 (with savings)

3127. Insurance Companies (Switzerland) Regulations 1993
Reg.6, revoked: SI 1996/943 Reg.35, Sch.7

3136. Environmentally Sensitive Areas (Argyll Islands) Designation Order 1993
Art.2, amended: SI 1996/1966 Art.2, SI 1996/3082 Reg.3
Art.5A, added: SI 1996/3082 Reg.5
Art.5B, added: SI 1996/3082 Reg.5
Art.5B, amended: SI 1996/3082 Reg.6
Art.5C, added: SI 1996/3082 Reg.6
Art.7, amended: SI 1996/1966 Art.3
Sch. para.12, amended: SI 1996/1966 Art.4

3138. Merchant Shipping (Registration of Ships) Regulations 1993
applied: SI 1996/197 Art.4, SI 1996/3243 Sch Part I
Reg.1, amended: SI 1998/1915 Reg.3, SI 1998/2976 Reg.3, SI 1999/3206 Reg.3
Reg.7, amended: SI 1998/2976 Reg.4

3138. Merchant Shipping (Registration of Ships) Regulations 1993—*cont.*
Reg.12, amended: SI 1998/2976 Reg.5
Reg.20, amended: SI 1998/2976 Reg.6
Reg.28, amended: SI 1998/2976 Reg.7, SI 1999/3206 Reg.4
Reg.29, amended: SI 1998/1915 Reg.4, Reg.5, SI 1998/2976 Reg.8, SI 1999/3206 Reg.5
Reg.29A, added: SI 1999/3206 Reg.6
Reg.29B, added: SI 1999/3206 Reg.6
Reg.31, amended: SI 1999/3206 Reg.7
Reg.34, amended: SI 1998/2976 Reg.9
Reg.39, amended: SI 1998/2976 Reg.10
Reg.40, amended: SI 1999/3206 Reg.8
Reg.41, substituted: SI 1998/2976 Reg.11
Reg.42, amended: SI 1998/1915 Reg.6, SI 1999/3206 Reg.9
Reg.42, applied: SI 1996/3243 Sch Part VII, Sch Part VIII
Reg.50, amended: SI 1999/3206 Reg.10
Reg.51, amended: SI 1999/3206 Reg.11
Reg.56, amended: SI 1998/1915 Reg.7, Reg.8, SI 1998/2976 Reg.12, SI 1999/3206 Reg.12
Reg.72A, added: SI 1998/2976 Reg.13
Reg.77, amended: SI 1999/3206 Reg.13
Reg.79, amended: SI 1999/3206 Reg.14
Reg.80, amended: SI 1999/3206 Reg.15
Reg.82, amended: SI 1998/2976 Reg.14
Reg.83, amended: SI 1998/2976 Reg.15
Reg.87, amended: SI 1998/2976 Reg.16, SI 1999/3206 Reg.16
Reg.89, amended: SI 1998/2976 Reg.17
Reg.98, amended: SI 1998/2976 Reg.18
Reg.99, amended: SI 1998/2976 Reg.19
Reg.101, amended: SI 1998/2976 Reg.20, SI 1999/3206 Reg.17
Reg.106, substituted: SI 1999/3206 Reg.18
Reg.112, amended: SI 1999/3206 Reg.19
Reg.113A, added: SI 1998/2976 Reg.21
Reg.114, amended: SI 1999/3206 Reg.20
Reg.115, amended: SI 1998/2976 Reg.22
Reg.116, substituted: SI 1998/2976 Reg.23
Reg.116A, added: SI 1998/2976 Reg.24
Reg.118, amended: SI 1998/2976 Reg.25
Reg.119, amended: SI 1998/2976 Reg.26
Reg.121, revoked: SI 1998/2976 Reg.27
Sch.2 Part 1, amended: SI 1998/2976 Reg.28
Sch.2 Part 2, amended: SI 1999/3206 Reg.21
Sch.3 para.5, amended: SI 1999/3206 Reg.22
Sch.3 para.7, amended: SI 1998/2976 Reg.29
Sch.4 para.4, amended: SI 1998/2976 Reg.30
Sch.4 para.5, amended: SI 1999/3206 Reg.23
Sch.4 para.6, amended: SI 1999/3206 Reg.24
Sch.5 para.1, amended: SI 1998/2976 Reg.31
Sch.5 para.2, amended: SI 1998/2976 Reg.31, SI 1999/3206 Reg.25
Sch.5 para.3, amended: SI 1998/2976 Reg.31, SI 1999/3206 Reg.26

3144. Child Abduction and Custody (Parties to Conventions) Order 1993
revoked: SI 1996/2595 Art.2
Sch., revoked: SI 1996/2595 Art.2
Sch., substituted: SI 1996/269 Art.4

3146. Criminal Justice (Confiscation) (Northern Ireland) Order 1993
revoked: SI 1996/1299 (NI.9) Art.57, Sch.5

3149. Environmentally Sensitive Areas (Machair of the Uists and Benbecula, Barra and Vatersay) Designation Order 1993
Art.2, amended: SI 1996/1962 Art.2, SI 1996/3082 Reg.3
Art.5A, added: SI 1996/3082 Reg.5

NO.

3149. **Environmentally Sensitive Areas (Machair of the Uists and Benbecula, Barra and Vatersay) Designation Order 1993**—*cont.*
Art.5B, added: SI 1996/3082 Reg.5
Art.5B, amended: SI 1996/3082 Reg.6
Art.5C, added: SI 1996/3082 Reg.6
Art.6, amended: SI 1996/1962 Art.3
Art.7, amended: SI 1996/1962 Art.4
Art.8, amended: SI 1996/1962 Art.5
Art.9, amended: SI 1996/1962 Art.6
Sch. Part I, amended: SI 1996/1962 Art.7
Sch. Part II, amended: SI 1996/1962 Art.7

3150. **Environmentally Sensitive Areas (Shetland Islands) Designation Order 1993**
Art.2, amended: SI 1996/1965 Art.2, SI 1996/3082 Reg.3
Art.5A, added: SI 1996/3082 Reg.5
Art.5B, added: SI 1996/3082 Reg.5
Art.5B, amended: SI 1996/3082 Reg.6
Art.5C, added: SI 1996/3082 Reg.6
Art.6, amended: SI 1996/1965 Art.3
Art.7, amended: SI 1996/1965 Art.4
Art.8, amended: SI 1996/1965 Art.5
Art.9, amended: SI 1996/1965 Art.6
Sch. Part I, amended: SI 1996/1965 Art.7
Sch. Part II, amended: SI 1996/1965 Art.7

3151. **Registration of Births, Deaths and Marriages (Fees) (Scotland) Order 1993**
revoked: SI 1997/717 Art.3

3152. **Marriage Fees (Scotland) Regulations 1993**
revoked: SI 1996/572 Reg.3

3153. **Registration of Births, Deaths, Marriages and Divorces (Fees) (Scotland) Regulations 1993**
revoked: SI 1997/716 Reg.7
Reg.5, amended: SI 1996/574 Reg.3
Reg.5, revoked: SI 1997/716 Reg.7
Sch.1, amended: SI 1996/574 Reg.4, Reg.5
Sch.1, revoked: SI 1997/716 Reg.7

3154. **Maximum Number of Judges (Scotland) Order 1993**
revoked: SSI 1999/158 Art.3

3155. **Criminal Justice (International Co-operation) Act 1990 (Enforcement of Overseas Forfeiture Orders) (Scotland) Amendment (No.2) Order 1993**
revoked: SI 1999/675 Art.11

3156. **Confiscation of the Proceeds of Drug Trafficking (Designated Countries and Territories) (Scotland) Amendment (No.2) Order 1993**
revoked: SI 1999/673 Art.11

3159. **Environment and Safety Information (Northern Ireland) Order 1993**
Art.5, amended: SI 1998/2795 (NI.18) Art.6, Sch.1 para.25, Sch.2
Sch.1, amended: 1998 c.47 s.99, Sch.13 para.13
Sch.2, revoked: SI 1998/2795 (NI.18) Art.6, Sch.1 para.25, Sch.2

3160. **Roads (Northern Ireland) Order 1993**
Art.2, amended: SI 1996/275 (NI.2) Art.71, Sch.6
Art.5, amended: SI 1997/276 (NI.2) Art.75, Sch.8 para.11
Art.20, applied: SI 1996/1320 (NI.10) Art.23, Sch.1 Part II
Art.23, applied: SI 1999/2450 Sch.4 para.16.2
Art.24, amended: SI 1997/276 (NI.2) Art.75, Sch.8 para.12
Art.25, amended: SI 1997/276 (NI.2) Art.75, Sch.8 para.13
Art.33, amended: SR 1999/89 Reg.3

NO.

3160. **Roads (Northern Ireland) Order 1993**—*cont.*
Art.45, referred to: SI 1999/662 (NI.6) Art.10
Art.47, referred to: SI 1999/662 (NI.6) Art.10
Art.65, amended: SI 1997/276 (NI.2) Art.75, Sch.8 para.14
Art.65A, added: SI 1997/276 (NI.2) Art.64
Art.110, amended: SI 1997/276 (NI.2) Art.75, Sch.8 para.15
Art.110, applied: SI 1997/276 (NI.2) Art.10
Art.131, amended: 1996 c.23 Sch.3 para.60
Art.132, revoked: SI 1997/276 (NI.2) Art.75, Sch.9
Sch.4 para.3, amended: 1996 c.23 Sch.3 para.60

3161. **Merchant Shipping (Fire Protection) (Non-United Kingdom) (Non-SOLAS Ships) (Amendment) Rules 1993**
revoked: SI 1998/1012 Reg.1

3162. **Merchant Shipping (Fire Appliances) (Amendment) Regulations 1993**
revoked: SI 1998/1012 Reg.1

3163. **Merchant Shipping (Fire Protection) (Amendment) Regulations 1993**
revoked: SI 1998/1012 Reg.1

3164. **Merchant Shipping (Fire Protection) (Ships built before 25th May 1980) (Amendment) Regulations 1993**
revoked: SI 1998/1012 Reg.1

3165. **Water and Sewerage Services (Amendment) (Northern Ireland) Order 1993**
Art.16, revoked: SI 1999/662 (NI.6) Art.63, Sch.8 Part II
Art.17, revoked: SI 1999/662 (NI.6) Art.63, Sch.8 Part II

3170. **Town and Country Planning (Fees for Applications and Deemed Applications) (Amendment) Regulations 1993**
Reg.3, revoked: SI 1997/37 Reg.6
Reg.4, revoked: SI 1997/37 Reg.6
Reg.5, revoked: SI 1997/37 Reg.6
Reg.6, revoked: SI 1997/37 Reg.6
Reg.7, revoked: SI 1997/37 Reg.6

3182. **Education (Individual Pupils' Achievements) (Information) Regulations 1993**
revoked: SI 1997/1368 Reg.2
Reg.3, amended: SI 1996/1146 Reg.8, Sch.2 para.1, Sch.2 para.2, Sch.2 para.3
Reg.3, revoked: SI 1997/1368 Reg.2
Reg.4, amended: SI 1996/1146 Reg.2
Reg.4, revoked: SI 1997/1368 Reg.2
Reg.6, amended: SI 1996/1146 Reg.3
Reg.6, revoked: SI 1997/1368 Reg.2
Sch.1 para.1, amended: SI 1996/1146 Reg.4
Sch.1 para.1, revoked: SI 1997/1368 Reg.2
Sch.1 para.4, amended: SI 1996/1146 Reg.8, Sch.2 para.1
Sch.1 para.4, revoked: SI 1997/1368 Reg.2
Sch.1 para.5, amended: SI 1996/1146 Reg.8, Sch.2 para.4
Sch.1 para.5, revoked: SI 1997/1368 Reg.2
Sch.2 para.1, amended: SI 1996/1146 Reg.5
Sch.2 para.1, revoked: SI 1997/1368 Reg.2
Sch.2A para.1, amended: SI 1996/1146 Reg.6
Sch.2A para.1, revoked: SI 1997/1368 Reg.2
Sch.2A para.2, amended: SI 1996/1146 Reg.6
Sch.2A para.2, revoked: SI 1997/1368 Reg.2
Sch.3, revoked: SI 1997/1368 Reg.2
Sch.3, substituted: SI 1996/1146 Reg.7

NO.

1993—cont.

3184. **Education (European Economic Area) (Scotland) Regulations 1993**
revoked (in part): SI 1997/93 Reg.14, Sch.4
Reg.3, revoked: SI 1996/1754 Reg.7, Sch.3

3185. **Liquor Licensing (Fees) (Scotland) Order 1993**
revoked: SI 1997/1721 Art.3

3186. **Advice and Assistance (Assistance by Way of Representation) (Scotland) Amendment (No.2) Regulations 1993**
revoked: SI 1997/3070 Reg.2, Sch.

3191. **Supreme Court Fees (Amendment) Order 1993**
revoked: SI 1999/687 Art.8 (with savings), Sch.2 (with savings)

3199. **Broadcasting (Restrictions on the Holding of Licences) (Amendment) Order 1993**
revoked: 1996 c.55 Sch.11 Part II, SI 1996/2120 Sch.2

3211. **Town and Country Planning (Fees for Applications and Deemed Applications) (Scotland) Amendment Regulations 1993**
revoked (in part): SI 1997/10 Reg.15

3216. **Upper Spey and Associated Waters Protection (Renewal) Order 1993**
Art.4, amended: SI 1996/57

3223. **Lotteries Regulations 1993**
Reg.6, revoked: SI 1996/1306 Reg.2

3227. **Utilities Supply and Works Contracts (Amendment) Regulations 1993**
revoked: SI 1996/2911 Reg.34

3228. **Public Services Contracts Regulations 1993**
see *R. v Secretary of State for the Environment Ex p. Harrow LBC* (1997) 29 H.L.R. 1 (QBD), Judge, J.
applied: 1999 c.29 s.356
referred to: 1999 c.29 s.358
Reg.2, amended: SI 1996/2911 Reg.35, SI 1999/1042 Art.3, Sch.1 para.21
Reg.3, amended: SI 1996/974 Art.2, Sch.1 para.11, SI 1999/1042 Art.3, Sch.1 para.21
Reg.4, amended: SI 1996/2911 Reg.35
Reg.28, amended: SI 1999/1820 Art.4, Sch.2 para.153
Reg.29, amended: SI 1996/2911 Reg.35
Reg.32, see *Matra Communications SAS v Home Office* [1999] 1 W.L.R. 1646 (CA), Buxton, L.J.; see *R. v Tower Hamlets LBC Ex p. Luck (t/a G Luck Arboricultural and Horticultural Services)* (1999) 15 Const. L.J. 235 (CA), Simon Brown, L.J.

3231. **Merchant Shipping (Musters and Training) (Amendment) Regulations 1993**
revoked: SI 1999/2722 Reg.1

3232. **Merchant Shipping (Pilot Ladders and Hoists) (Amendment) Regulations 1993**
revoked: SI 1999/17 Reg.2

3238. **Road Traffic Act 1991 (Commencement No.9 and Transitional Provisions) Order 1993**
Art.5, revoked: SI 1998/967 Art.3, Sch.

3240. **Act of Sederunt (Sheriff Court Summary Application Rules) 1993**
revoked: SI 1999/929 r.1.3, Sch.2

3249. **Importation of Bees (Amendment) Order 1993**
revoked: SI 1997/310 Art.8, Sch

3250. **Specified Animal Pathogens Order 1993**
revoked: SI 1998/463 Art.9
Art.5, revoked: SI 1998/463 Art.9

NO.

1993—cont.

3252. **Parliamentary Pension Scheme (Additional Voluntary Contributions) Regulations 1993**
Reg.2, amended: SI 1999/780 Reg.3
Reg.5, amended: SI 1999/780 Reg.4
Reg.12, substituted: SI 1999/780 Reg.5

3253. **Parliamentary Pensions (Consolidation and Amendment) Regulations 1993**
Reg.E2, amended: SI 1996/2406 Reg.3
Reg.F2, amended: SI 1996/2406 Reg.4, Reg.5
Reg.F4, amended: SI 1996/2406 Reg.4, Reg.5
Reg.L1, amended: SI 1996/2406 Reg.7
Reg.L2, referred to: SI 1996/2406 Reg.8
Reg.N2, applied: SI 1996/1493 Sch. para.5
Reg.N3, applied: SI 1996/1493 Sch. para.5
Reg.N5, applied: SI 1996/1493 Sch. para.5
Sch.1 para.1, amended: SI 1999/2100 Reg.2, Sch. para.1
Sch.1 para.2, substituted: SI 1999/2100 Reg.2, Sch. para.2
Sch.1 para.2A, added: SI 1999/2100 Reg.2, Sch. para.3
Sch.1 para.5, substituted: SI 1999/2100 Reg.2, Sch. para.4

3256. **Medicines (Products Other Than Veterinary Drugs) (Prescription Only) Amendment (No.2) Order 1993**
revoked: SI 1997/1830 Art.16, Sch.6

3276. **Land Registration (Official Searches) Rules 1993**
r.14, amended: SI 1997/1710 Sch.3 Part III
r.14, applied: SI 1998/3199 Sch.3 Part III
r.14, referred to: SI 1999/2254 Sch.3 Part III

1994

A2 Greenwich (Waiting and Loading Restriction) Order 1994
revoked (in part): SI 1997/21 Art.10

Barnet (Waiting and Loading Restrictions) (Priority Routes and Side Roads) Order 1994
revoked (in part): SI 1996/815 Art.10, SI 1996/818 Art.10, SI 1996/819 Art.10, SI 1996/820 Art.10, SI 1996/821 Art.10, SI 1997/1608 Art.10, SI 1997/2489 Art.10, SI 1999/553 Art.11, SI 1999/555 Art.11

Barnet (Waiting and Loading Restrictions) (Special Parking Areas) Order 1994
revoked (in part): SI 1996/815 Art.10, SI 1996/818 Art.10, SI 1996/819 Art.10, SI 1996/820 Art.10, SI 1996/821 Art.10, SI 1997/1608 Art.10, SI 1997/2489 Art.10

County Borough of Caerphilly Electoral Arrangements Order 1994
Sch., revoked: SI 1998/3135 Art.2

Ecclesiastical Exemption (Listed Buildings and Conservation Areas) Order 1994
Art.4, referred to: 1999 m.2 s.1
Art.5, applied: 1999 m.1 s.16

Education (Significant Variation of Schemes for Financing Schools) (Amendment) Order 1994
revoked: SI 1999/711 Reg.9, Sch.2

Enfield (Restriction of Waiting on Bus Stops) (Priority Routes and Side Roads) Order 1994
revoked: SI 1996/2543 Art.10

Enfield (Waiting and Loading Restriction) (Priority Routes and Side Roads) Order 1994
revoked (in part): SI 1996/2543 Art.10

1994—cont.

Greenwich (Waiting and Loading Restriction) Order 1994
revoked (in part): SI 1996/2727 Art.10

Haringey (Waiting and Loading Restriction) (Special Parking Area) (No.1) Order 1994
revoked (in part): SI 1998/2184 Art.11, SI 1999/553 Art.11, SI 1999/555 Art.11, SI 1999/2635 Art.11

Hillingdon (Waiting and Loading Restrictions) (Consolidation) Order 1994
revoked (in part): SI 1996/1163 Art.10, SI 1997/1507 Art.10

Kensington & Chelsea (Waiting and Loading Restriction) (No.2) Order 1994
revoked (in part): SI 1997/2785 Art.11, SI 1999/1147 Art.10

Kensington & Chelsea (Waiting and Loading Restrictions) (Special Parking Area) Order 1994
revoked (in part): SI 1999/1264 Art.10

Kingston Upon Thames (Waiting and Loading Restriction) (No.1) Traffic Order 1994
revoked (in part): SI 1996/2332 Art.10, SI 1996/2339 Art.10

London Borough of Greenwich (Waiting and Loading Restriction) Order 1994
revoked (in part): SI 1997/139 Art.11, SI 1998/382 Art.10

Naval and Marine Pay and Pensions (Disablement Awards) Order 1994
revoked: SI 1996/1638 Art.4, Sch.3

Naval and Marine Pay and Pensions (Widows Attributable Pensions) Order 1994
revoked: SI 1996/1638 Art.4, Sch.3

Newham (Waiting and Loading Restriction) (Proposed Priority Route) Order 1994
revoked (in part): SI 1997/465 Art.10

11. **London Borough of Richmond upon Thames (Waiting and Loading Restrictions) Order 1994**
amended: SI 1996/264 Art.11
revoked (in part): SI 1996/2164 Art.10, SI 1996/3152 Art.10, SI 1997/1824 Art.10

70. **General Optical Council (Testing of Sight by Persons Training as Ophthalmic Opticians) Rules Order of Council 1994**
Sch. r.4, amended: SI 1999/2897 Sch. r.2

81. **Road Traffic Act 1991 (Commencement No.10 and Transitional Provisions) Order 1994**
Art.6, revoked: SI 1998/967 Art.3, Sch.

105. **Medicines (Homeopathic Medicinal Products for Human Use) Regulations 1994**
Part II, applied: SI 1997/321 Sch.1 Part II, SI 1997/1469 Sch.5 Part II, SI 1998/2428 Sch.5 Part II
Reg.1, amended: SI 1996/482 Reg.2, SI 1998/574 Reg.2
Reg.1, referred to: SI 1999/2109 Reg.2
Reg.11, amended: SI 1998/574 Reg.2
Reg.14, amended: SI 1999/566 Reg.2
Reg.14, substituted: SI 1998/574 Reg.2
Reg.15, amended: SI 1998/574 Reg.2
Sch.2, substituted: SI 1996/482 Reg.3
Sch.2 Table, amended: SI 1998/574 Reg.2, SI 1999/566 Reg.2
Sch.4, amended: SI 1996/482 Reg.4

107. **Glasgow Community and Mental Health Services National Health Service Trust (Change of Name) (Establishment) Order 1994**
revoked: SI 1999/1070 Art.2, Sch.2

1994—cont.

116. **Driving Licences (Designation of Relevant External Law) Order 1994**
revoked: SI 1996/3206 Art.3

118. **Control of Industrial Major Accident Hazards (Amendment) Regulations 1994**
revoked: SI 1999/743 Reg.24

129. **Fertilisers (Sampling and Analysis) (Amendment) Regulations 1994**
revoked: SI 1996/1342 Reg.9

131. **National Health Service (Optical Charges and Payments) Amendment Regulations 1994**
revoked: SI 1997/818 Reg.24, Sch.4

132. **Friendly Societies (Auditors) Order 1994**
Art.2, amended: SI 1996/1669 Sch.4 para.4
Art.3, amended: SI 1996/1669 Sch.4 para.4

133. **Secure Tenants of Local Housing Authorities (Right to Repair) Regulations 1994**
Reg.3, amended: SI 1997/73 Reg.2
Reg.5, amended: SI 1997/73 Reg.2
Reg.7, amended: SI 1997/73 Reg.2

145. **National Health Service (Optical Charges and Payments) (Scotland) Amendment Regulations 1994**
revoked: SI 1998/642 Reg.24, Sch.4

156. **Education (Grant) (Henrietta Barnett School) Regulations 1994**
Reg.2, amended: SI 1996/205 Reg.2

157. **Railways and other Transport Systems (Approval of Works, Plant and Equipment) Regulations 1994**
applied: SI 1997/553 Reg.10, SI 1997/1688 Art.11, SI 1997/2232 Art.9
referred to: SI 1998/3269 Art.42

161. **South Manchester University Hospitals National Health Service Trust (Establishment) Order 1994**
Art.3, amended: SI 1996/983 Art.2

162. **Dudley Priority Health National Health Service Trust (Establishment) Order 1994**
Art.3, substituted: SI 1998/2667 Art.2

164. **Salford Royal Hospitals National Health Service Trust (Establishment) Order 1994**
Art.3, substituted: SI 1999/2176 Art.2

165. **Mid-Sussex National Health Service Trust (Establishment) Order 1994**
Art.3, substituted: SI 1999/199 Art.2

169. **Alexandra Health Care National Health Service Trust (Establishment) Order 1994**
revoked: SI 1999/3471 Art.2

170. **Coventry Healthcare National Health Service Trust (Establishment) Order 1994**
Art.3, substituted: SI 1998/1170 Art.2

171. **South Birmingham Mental Health National Health Service Trust (Establishment) Order 1994**
Art.3, substituted: SI 1999/1169 Art.2

172. **Sandwell Healthcare National Health Service Trust (Establishment) Order 1994**
Art.3, substituted: SI 1999/62 Art.2

173. **Northern Birmingham Mental Health Service Trust (Establishment) Order 1994**
Art.3, substituted: SI 1999/2955 Art.2

174. **Weald of Kent Community National Health Service Trust (Establishment) Order 1994**
revoked: SI 1997/417 Art.2

175. **South Kent Hospitals National Health Service Trust (Establishment) Order 1994**
revoked: SI 1999/897 Art.2

1994—cont.

176. **Maternity Allowance and Statutory Maternity Pay Regulations (Northern Ireland) 1994**
Reg.2, revoked (in part): SI 1999/3147 (NI.11) Art.76, Sch.10 Part V
Reg.6, revoked (in part): SI 1999/3147 (NI.11) Art.76, Sch.10 Part V

176. **Norfolk and Norwich Health Care National Health Service Trust (Establishment) Order 1994**
Art.3, amended: SI 1996/1001 Art.2

179. **Furness Hospitals National Health Service Trust (Establishment) Order 1994**
revoked: SI 1998/820 Art.2

181. **East Surrey Learning Disability and Mental Health Service National Health Service Trust (Establishment) Order 1994**
revoked: SI 1998/652 Art.2
Art.1, revoked: SI 1998/652 Art.2
Art.2, revoked: SI 1998/652 Art.2

183. **Bexley Community Health National Health Service Trust (Establishment) Order 1994**
Art.3, amended: SI 1996/1000 Art.2

184. **Heathlands Mental Health National Health Service Trust (Establishment) Order 1994**
revoked: SI 1998/502 Art.2

185. **Mancunian Community Health National Health Service Trust (Establishment) Order 1994**
Art.3, substituted: SI 1999/631 Art.2

187. **Insider Dealing (Securities and Regulated Markets) Order 1994**
Art.10, amended: SI 1996/1561 Art.3
Sch., amended: SI 1996/1561 Art.4

196. **Gateshead Healthcare National Health Service Trust (Establishment) Order 1994**
revoked: SI 1998/826 Art.2

199. **Environmental Protection (Non-Refillable Refrigerant Containers) Regulations 1994**
Reg.7, amended: SI 1996/506 Reg.14

222. **Education (Teachers) (Amendment) Regulations 1994**
Reg.2, revoked: SI 1997/2679 Reg.7, Sch.3

227. **Child Support (Miscellaneous Amendments and Transitional Provisions) Regulations 1994**
Reg.6, amended: SI 1999/1510 Art.32
Reg.10, amended: SI 1999/1510 Art.33
Reg.11, substituted: SI 1999/1510 Art.34
Reg.12, substituted: SI 1999/1510 Art.35
Reg.13, revoked: SI 1999/1510 Art.36
Reg.14, revoked: SI 1999/1510 Art.36

228. **Legal Aid in Civil Proceedings (Remuneration) Regulations 1994**
Reg.2, amended: SI 1996/645 Reg.2, SI 1999/3098 Reg.3
Reg.4, amended: SI 1996/645 Reg.2, SI 1999/3098 Reg.4, Reg.5
Sch., substituted: SI 1996/645 Reg.2

237. **Railways (Safety Case) Regulations 1994**
Reg.2, amended: SI 1996/1592 Reg.34, Sch.9 para.7, SI 1999/2024 Reg.48, Sch.5 Part II
Reg.4, applied: SI 1998/1340 Reg.13
Sch.1 para.6, amended: SI 1999/3242 Reg.29, Sch.2

238. **Environmentally Sensitive Areas (Clwydian Range) Designation Order 1994**
Art.2, amended: SI 1996/3077 Reg.2, SI 1997/973 Art.2
Art.5, amended: SI 1996/3077 Reg.2
Art.5A, added: SI 1996/3077 Reg.2
Art.5B, added: SI 1996/3077 Reg.2
Art.5C, added: SI 1996/3077 Reg.2

1994—cont.

238. **Environmentally Sensitive Areas (Clwydian Range) Designation Order 1994**—*cont.*
Art.6, amended: SI 1997/973 Art.2
Art.6, revoked (in part): SI 1997/973 Art.2
Art.7, added: SI 1999/1175 Art.2
Sch.4 para.6, amended: SI 1997/973 Art.2

239. **Environmentally Sensitive Areas (Preseli) Designation Order 1994**
Art.2, amended: SI 1996/3077 Reg.2, SI 1997/974 Art.2
Art.5, amended: SI 1996/3077 Reg.2
Art.5A, added: SI 1996/3077 Reg.2
Art.5B, added: SI 1996/3077 Reg.2
Art.5C, added: SI 1996/3077 Reg.2
Art.6, amended: SI 1997/974 Art.2, SI 1997/2868 Art.2
Art.6, revoked (in part): SI 1997/974 Art.2
Art.7, added: SI 1999/1175 Art.2
Sch.4 para.6, amended: SI 1997/974 Art.2

263. **Copyright (Application to Other Countries) (Amendment) Order 1994**
revoked: SI 1999/1751 Art.8, Sch.6

271. **Statutory Maternity Pay (Compensation of Employers) and Miscellaneous Amendment Regulations (Northern Ireland) 1994**
Reg.6, applied: SI 1999/671 Art.3, Sch.2

277. **Education (Financial Delegation to Schools) (Mandatory Exceptions) Regulations 1994**
revoked (in part): SI 1996/395 Reg.3

284. **National Health Service (Functions of Family Health Services in London) Regulations 1994**
revoked: SI 1996/654 Reg.3

288. **Solicitors (Disciplinary Proceedings) Rules 1994**
r.16, see *Solicitor, Re* Times, March 18, 1996 (QBD), Lord Taylor of Gosforth, C.J.
r.30, see *Solicitor, Re* Times, March 18, 1996 (QBD), Lord Taylor of Gosforth, C.J.

299. **Railways (Safety Critical Work) Regulations 1994**
Reg.2, amended: SI 1996/1592 Reg.34, Sch.9 para.8, SI 1999/2024 Reg.48, Sch.5 Part II

305. **Veterinary Surgeons and Veterinary Practitioners (Registration) (Amendment) Regulations Order of Council 1994**
revoked: SI 1996/437 Art.3

307. **Royal Hospital of St Bartholomew, the Royal London Hospital and London Chest Hospital National Health Service Trust (Establishment) Order 1994**
Art.1, amended: SI 1999/1823 Art.2
Art.2, amended: SI 1999/1823 Art.2

316. **East Glamorgan National Health Service Trust (Establishment) Order 1994**
revoked: SI 1999/1120 Art.2, Sch.2
Art.3, revoked: SI 1999/1120 Art.2, Sch.2
Art.3, substituted: SI 1998/2034 Art.2

317. **Morriston Hospital National Health Service Trust (Establishment) Order 1994**
revoked: SI 1999/1120 Art.2, Sch.2

323. **Education (School Financial Statements) (Prescribed Particulars etc.) Regulations 1994**
applied: SI 1996/381 Reg.3, SI 1999/451 Reg.3, SI 1999/486 Reg.3
revoked (in part): SI 1996/381 Reg.3

326. **Inshore Fishing (Prohibition of Fishing and Fishing Methods) (Scotland) Amendment Order 1994**
Art.2, revoked: SI 1999/751 Art.3

NO.

338. Local Government, Planning and Land Act 1980 (Competition) (Wales) Regulations 1994
referred to: SI 1997/999 Reg.12

339. Local Government Act 1988 (Defined Activities) (Exemptions) (Wales) Order 1994
referred to: SI 1997/528 Art.3
Art.4, amended: SI 1996/3179 Art.3, SI 1997/1698 Art.2, SI 1998/2188 Art.2
Art.4, revoked (in part): SI 1998/2188 Art.2
Art.5, added: SI 1998/2188 Art.2
Sch., substituted: SI 1996/3179 Art.4, SI 1998/2188 Art.2, Sch.

342. European Parliamentary Elections (Changes to the Franchise and Qualification of Representatives) Regulations 1994
Reg.4, revoked (in part): 1999 c.1 s.3, Sch.3 para.4, Sch.4
Reg.5, revoked: SI 1999/1214 Reg.20, Sch.5
Reg.7, amended: 1999 c.1 s.3, Sch.3 para.4
Reg.9, amended: 1999 c.1 s.3, Sch.3 para.4
Reg.15, revoked: SI 1999/1214 Reg.20, Sch.5

372. Offshore Installations (Safety Zones) Order 1994
revoked: SI 1997/735 Art.3, Sch.2

379. Maternity (Compulsory Leave) Regulations (Northern Ireland) 1994
revoked: SI 1999/2790 (NI.9) Art.40, Sch.9 Part 2

391. Act of Sederunt (Fees of Messengers-at-Arms) 1994
Sch.1 Table, substituted: SI 1996/2855 r.2, Sch., SI 1997/2825 para.2, Sch., SI 1998/2668 para.2, Sch., SSI 1999/151 para.2, Sch.

392. Act of Sederunt (Fees of Sheriff Officers) 1994
Sch.1 Table, substituted: SI 1996/2858 r.2, Sch., SI 1997/2824 para.2, Sch., SI 1998/2669 para.2, Sch., SSI 1999/151 para.2, Sch.

402. Royal Brompton Hospital National Health Service Trust (Establishment) Order 1994
revoked: SI 1998/783 Art.2

404. Bethlem and Maudsley National Health Service Trust (Establishment) Order 1994
revoked: SI 1999/900 Art.2

426. Airports (Northern Ireland) Order 1994
Art.19, amended: SI 1996/1919 (NI.16) Art.255, Sch.1
Art.27, amended: SI 1999/506 Art.43
Art.35, amended: 1998 c.41 s.74, Sch.12 para.20
Art.36, referred to: 1998 c.41 s.74, Sch.13 para.40
Art.36, revoked (in part): 1998 c.41 s.74, Sch.12 para.20, Sch.14 Part II
Art.45, amended: 1998 c.41 s.74, Sch.12 para.20, Sch.14 Part II
Art.45, revoked (in part): 1998 c.41 s.74, Sch.12 para.20, Sch.14 Part II
Art.47, amended: 1998 c.41 s.74, Sch.12 para.20, Sch.14 Part II
Art.49, amended: SI 1996/275 (NI.2) Art.71, Sch.6, SI 1996/2199 Reg.29, SI 1999/506 Art.43
Part IV, referred to: SI 1996/275 (NI.2) Art.44, SI 1996/2199 Reg.28
Sch.9 para.5, revoked: 1998 c.41 s.74, Sch.12 para.20, Sch.14 Part II

428. European Parliamentary Constituencies (Wales) Order 1994
applied: 1998 c.38 s.2, Sch.1 para.2

NO.

429. Health and Personal Social Services (Northern Ireland) Order 1994
referred to: SI 1996/3160 (NI.24) Art.2
Sch.1, revoked (in part): SI 1996/274 (NI.1) Art.44, Sch.6 Part I, 1998 c.29 Sch.16 Part II, SI 1998/1504 (NI.9) Art.65, Sch.6

440. Ozone Monitoring and Information Regulations 1994
applied: SI 1999/672 Art.2, Sch.1

449. Auditors (Insurance Companies Act 1982) Regulations 1994
Reg.2, amended: SI 1996/1669 Sch.4 para.5
Reg.3, amended: SI 1996/1669 Sch.4 para.5

451. Sea Fishing (Enforcement of Community Control Measures) Order 1994
Art.2, amended: SI 1996/2 Art.3
Art.3, amended: SI 1996/2 Art.4
Art.4, amended: SI 1996/2 Art.5
Art.5, amended: SI 1996/2 Art.6
Art.6, amended: SI 1996/2 Art.7
Art.8, amended: SI 1996/2 Art.8
Art.10, amended: SI 1996/2 Art.9
Art.12, amended: SI 1996/2 Art.10
Sch., amended: SI 1996/2 Art.11, Sch.

453. Broadcasting (Foreign Satellite Programmes) (Specified Countries) Order 1994
applied: SI 1997/1682 Reg.5
Sch., referred to: SI 1997/1682 Reg.5

454. Broadcasting (Prescribed Countries) Order 1994
revoked: SI 1996/904 Art.3

495. National Health Service (Optical Charges and Payments) Amendment (No.2) Regulations 1994
revoked: SI 1997/818 Reg.24, Sch.4

501. Return of Cultural Objects Regulations 1994
Reg.2, amended: SI 1997/1719 Reg.2
Sch., amended: SI 1997/1719 Reg.2

507. Education Act 1993 (Commencement No.3 and Transitional Provisions) Order 1994
Sch.3 para.5, applied: 1996 c.56 Sch.39 para.35

517. Transport Systems (Approval of Works, Plant and Equipment) Regulations 1994
applied: SI 1996/937 Art.16

520. Employers' Liability (Compulsory Insurance) Exemption (Amendment) Regulations 1994
revoked: SI 1998/2573 Reg.10, Sch.3

522. Environmental Protection (Waste Recycling Payments) (Amendment) Regulations 1994
Reg.2, revoked (in part): SI 1997/351 Reg.4

523. Housing Benefit and Council Tax Benefit (Subsidy) Order 1994
Art.4, applied: SI 1996/1217 Art.11, SI 1997/1004 Art.11, SI 1998/562 Art.19
Art.11, applied: SI 1996/1217 Art.10, SI 1997/1004 Art.10, SI 1998/562 Art.18
Art.19, applied: SI 1996/1217 Art.18, Art.19, SI 1997/1004 Art.18, SI 1998/562 Art.18, Art.19
Art.19, referred to: SI 1997/1004 Art.19

524. Accountants (Banking Act 1987) Regulations 1994
Reg.2, amended: SI 1996/1669 Sch.4 para.1, SI 1998/1129 Art.2, Sch.1 para.14
Reg.3, amended: SI 1996/1669 Sch.4 para.1, SI 1998/1129 Art.2, Sch.1 para.14

525. Building Societies (Auditors) Order 1994
Art.2, amended: SI 1996/1669 Sch.4 para.2
Art.3, amended: SI 1996/1669 Sch.4 para.2

1994—cont.

526. **Auditors (Financial Services Act 1986) Rules 1994**
r.2, amended: SI 1996/1669 Sch.4 para.3
r.3, amended: SI 1996/1669 Sch.4 para.3

527. **Income-related Benefits Schemes (Miscellaneous Amendments) Regulations 1994**
Reg.7, revoked: SI 1996/206 Reg.28, Sch.3
Reg.21, see *Swaddling v Adjudication Officer (C90/97)* [1999] All E.R. (EC) 217 (ECJ) (Fifth Chamber), P Jann (President)

528. **Local Government Finance (Scotland) Order 1994**
Art.2, revoked: SI 1996/755 Art.7
Sch.1, revoked: SI 1996/755 Art.7

531. **Local Government Superannuation (Scotland) Amendment Regulations 1994**
applied: SI 1998/364 Reg.4, Reg.6, Reg.19, Sch.2 para.2, Sch.2 para.5, Sch.4 para.8
referred to: SI 1998/364 Reg.3, Reg.10, Sch.2 para.4, Sch.2 para.6

537. **Education (Particulars of Independent Schools) (Amendment) Regulations 1994**
revoked: SI 1997/2918 Reg.3

553. **Local Authorities (Capital Finance) (Amendment) Regulations 1994**
revoked: SI 1997/319 Reg.162, Sch.3

558. **Medicines (Products Other Than Veterinary Drugs) (Prescription Only) Amendment Order 1994**
revoked: SI 1997/1830 Art.16, Sch.6

565. **Housing Renovation etc. Grants (Prescribed Forms and Particulars) Regulations 1994**
applied: SI 1996/2842 Art.8
revoked: SI 1996/2842 Art.7, Sch Part I
Sch.1 Form 1, amended: SI 1996/1332 Reg.2, Sch.1
Sch.1 Form 1, revoked: SI 1996/2842 Art.7, Sch Part I
Sch.1 Form 2, amended: SI 1996/1332 Reg.2, Sch.2
Sch.1 Form 2, revoked: SI 1996/2842 Art.7, Sch Part I
Sch.1 Form 3, amended: SI 1996/1332 Reg.2, Sch.3
Sch.1 Form 3, revoked: SI 1996/2842 Art.7, Sch Part I

570. **Channel Tunnel (Security) Order 1994**
amended: 1998 c.9 s.2
Art.4, applied: 1996 c.22 Sch.1 para.21
Art.5, applied: 1996 c.22 Sch.1 para.21
Sch.3 para.1, revoked: 1996 c.22 Sch.7 Part II

573. **Railways (London Regional Transport) (Exemptions) Order 1994**
referred to: 1999 c.29 s.198
Art.2, amended: 1999 c.29 s.198

586. **National Board for Nursing, Midwifery and Health Visiting for England (Constitution and Administration) Amendment Order 1994**
revoked: SI 1997/1963 Art.3

590. **National Health Service Functions (Directions to Authorities and Administration Arrangements) Amendment Regulations 1994**
revoked: SI 1996/708 Reg.6, Sch.2

595. **Wireless Telegraphy (Television Licence Fees) (Amendment) Regulations 1994**
revoked: SI 1997/290 Reg.1, Sch

1994—cont.

599. **Medicines (Veterinary Drugs) (Pharmacy and Merchants' List) (Amendment) Order 1994**
revoked: SI 1998/1044 Art.9, Sch.

600. **Crown Office Fees Order 1994**
revoked: SI 1999/692 Art.3

602. **Microbiological Research Authority Regulations 1994**
Reg.1, amended: SI 1996/707 Reg.17, Sch.5 para.10
Reg.3, amended: SI 1996/707 Reg.17, Sch.5 para.10
Reg.5, amended: SI 1996/707 Reg.17, Sch.5 para.10
Reg.6, substituted: SI 1996/707 Reg.17, Sch.5 para.10
Reg.8, added: SI 1998/1576 Reg.4

607. **Railways (Alternative Closure Procedure) Order 1994**
Art.2, amended: SI 1999/3113 Art.2
Sch., amended: SI 1999/3113 Art.2

608. **Railways (Amendment) Regulations 1994**
revoked: SI 1998/1340 Reg.2

610. **Education (Grant-Maintained Schools) (Finance) (Wales) Regulations 1994**
applied: SI 1997/599 Reg.3
Reg.23, applied: SI 1997/599 Reg.3

617. **Motor Vehicles (EC Type Approval) (Amendment) Regulations 1994**
revoked: SI 1998/2051 Reg.2, Sch.3

623. **Parliamentary Elections (Returning Officers) (Scotland) Order 1994**
revoked: SI 1996/753 Reg.3

628. **Council Tax (Exempt Dwellings) (Scotland) Amendment Order 1994**
revoked: SI 1997/728 Art.5, Sch.2

635. **National Health Service (Optical Charges and Payments) (Scotland) Amendment (No.2) Regulations 1994**
revoked: SI 1998/642 Reg.24, Sch.4

637. **Home Energy Efficiency Grants (Amendment) Regulations 1994**
revoked: SI 1997/790 Reg.14, Sch.2

638. **Motor Vehicles (Driving Licences) (Amendment) Regulations 1994**
revoked: SI 1996/2824 Reg.2, Sch.1

639. **Motor Vehicles (Driving Licences) (Large Goods and Passenger-Carrying Vehicles) (Amendment) Regulations 1994**
revoked: SI 1996/2824 Reg.2, Sch.1

640. **National Health Service (Fund-Holding Practices) Amendment Regulations 1994**
revoked: SI 1996/706 Reg.28

648. **Housing Renovation etc. Grants (Reduction of Grant) Regulations 1994**
applied: SI 1996/1623 Art.3, SI 1996/2842 Art.8
revoked: SI 1996/2842 Art.7, Sch Part I
Reg.2, amended: SI 1996/1008 Art.2, Sch para.12, SI 1996/1331 Reg.3
Reg.2, revoked: SI 1996/2842 Art.7, Sch Part I
Reg.5, amended: SI 1996/1331 Reg.4
Reg.5, revoked: SI 1996/2842 Art.7, Sch Part I
Reg.10, amended: SI 1996/1331 Reg.5
Reg.10, applied: SI 1996/2890 Reg.13
Reg.10, revoked: SI 1996/2842 Art.7, Sch Part I
Reg.11, applied: SI 1996/2890 Reg.13
Reg.16A, amended: SI 1996/1008 Art.2, Sch para.12, SI 1996/1331 Reg.6
Reg.16A, revoked: SI 1996/2842 Art.7, Sch Part I
Reg.24, amended: SI 1996/1331 Reg.7
Reg.24, revoked: SI 1996/2842 Art.7, Sch Part I
Reg.28, amended: SI 1996/1331 Reg.8

NO.

1994—cont.

648. Housing Renovation etc. Grants (Reduction of Grant) Regulations 1994—*cont.*
Reg.28, revoked: SI 1996/2842 Art.7, Sch Part I
Reg.32, amended: SI 1996/1331 Reg.9
Reg.32, revoked: SI 1996/2842 Art.7, Sch Part I
Reg.35, amended: SI 1996/1331 Reg.10
Reg.35, revoked: SI 1996/2842 Art.7, Sch Part I
Reg.36, amended: SI 1996/1331 Reg.11
Reg.36, revoked: SI 1996/2842 Art.7, Sch Part I
Reg.38, amended: SI 1996/1331 Reg.12
Reg.38, revoked: SI 1996/2842 Art.7, Sch Part I
Reg.40, amended: SI 1996/1331 Reg.13
Reg.40, revoked: SI 1996/2842 Art.7, Sch Part I
Sch.1 Part IV, revoked: SI 1996/2842 Art.7, Sch Part I
Sch.1 Part IV, substituted: SI 1996/1331 Reg.14
Sch.1 para.1, revoked: SI 1996/2842 Art.7, Sch Part I
Sch.1 para.1, substituted: SI 1996/1331 Reg.14
Sch.1 para.2, revoked: SI 1996/2842 Art.7, Sch Part I
Sch.1 para.2, substituted: SI 1996/1331 Reg.14
Sch.1 para.3, amended: SI 1996/1331 Reg.14
Sch.1 para.3, revoked: SI 1996/2842 Art.7, Sch Part I
Sch.1 para.12, amended: SI 1996/1331 Reg.14
Sch.1 para.12, revoked: SI 1996/2842 Art.7, Sch Part I
Sch.3 para.2, amended: SI 1996/1331 Reg.15
Sch.3 para.2, revoked: SI 1996/2842 Art.7, Sch Part I
Sch.3 para.12, revoked: SI 1996/1331 Reg.15, SI 1996/2842 Art.7, Sch Part I
Sch.3 para.14, revoked: SI 1996/2842 Art.7, Sch Part I
Sch.3 para.14, substituted: SI 1996/1331 Reg.15
Sch.3 para.51, amended: SI 1996/1331 Reg.15
Sch.3 para.51, revoked: SI 1996/2842 Art.7, Sch Part I
Sch.3 para.55, added: SI 1996/1331 Reg.15
Sch.3 para.55, revoked: SI 1996/2842 Art.7, Sch Part I
Sch.3 para.56, added: SI 1996/1331 Reg.15
Sch.3 para.56, revoked: SI 1996/2842 Art.7, Sch Part I
Sch.4 para.7, revoked: SI 1996/2842 Art.7, Sch Part I
Sch.4 para.7, substituted: SI 1996/1331 Reg.16
Sch.4 para.29A, added: SI 1996/1331 Reg.16
Sch.4 para.29A, revoked: SI 1996/2842 Art.7, Sch Part I
Sch.4 para.30, amended: SI 1996/1331 Reg.16
Sch.4 para.30, revoked: SI 1996/2842 Art.7, Sch Part I

650. Education (Payment for Special Educational Needs Supplies) Regulations 1994
revoked: SI 1999/710 Reg.3 (with savings)
Reg.2, revoked: SI 1999/710 Reg.3 (with savings)

651. Education (Special Educational Needs) (Approval of Independent Schools) Regulations 1994
Reg.2, amended: SI 1998/417 Reg.2
Reg.5, see *R. v Secretary of State for Education and Employment Ex p. McCarthy* Times, July 24, 1996 (QBD), Hidden, J.
Sch.1 para.2, substituted: SI 1998/417 Reg.4
Sch.1 para.4, substituted: SI 1998/417 Reg.5
Sch.1 para.10, amended: SI 1998/417 Reg.6
Sch.2 para.3, revoked: SI 1998/417 Reg.8
Sch.2 para.5, substituted: SI 1998/417 Reg.9

NO.

1994—cont.

651. Education (Special Educational Needs) (Approval of Independent Schools) Regulations 1994—*cont.*
Sch.2 para.10, amended: SI 1998/417 Reg.10, Reg.11

652. Education (Special Schools) Regulations 1994
revoked (in part): SI 1999/2257 Reg.1

653. Education (Grant-Maintained Special Schools) Regulations 1994
applied: SI 1998/1969 Reg.18
Reg.4, amended: SI 1996/111 Reg.2
Reg.17, revoked: SI 1996/2303 Reg.3
Reg.20, amended: SI 1996/2303 Reg.2
Reg.23, amended: SI 1997/996 Reg.62
Reg.33, applied: SI 1999/2323 Art.16
Reg.41, substituted: SI 1997/2175 Reg.2
Reg.42, applied: SI 1999/2323 Art.19
Reg.42, revoked (in part): SI 1996/360 Sch.1
Sch., applied: SI 1999/2323 Art.19
Sch. Part II, applied: SI 1999/101 Sch.4 para.3

669. Carriage of Dangerous Goods by Road and Rail (Classification, Packaging and Labelling) Regulations 1994
applied: SI 1996/2092 Reg.20
revoked: SI 1996/2092 Reg.21

670. Carriage of Dangerous Goods by Rail Regulations 1994
applied: SI 1996/2089 Reg.33, SI 1996/2090 Reg.9, Reg.44
revoked: SI 1996/2089 Reg.34

672. Dairy Produce Quotas Regulations 1994
revoked: SI 1997/733 Reg.35
Reg.7, see *Harries v Barclays Bank Plc* [1997] B.P.I.R. 667 (CA), Morritt, L.J.
Reg.13, amended: SI 1997/250 Reg.2
Reg.15, amended: SI 1996/2657 Reg.2
Reg.18, amended: SI 1997/250 Reg.2

673. Bovine Spongiform Encephalopathy Compensation Order 1994
revoked (in part): SI 1996/3184 Art.5
Art.2, amended: SI 1996/1351 Art.2
Art.2, revoked (in part): SI 1996/3184 Art.5
Art.4, amended: SI 1996/1351 Art.2
Art.4, revoked (in part): SI 1996/3184 Art.5
Sch., amended: SI 1996/1351 Art.2
Sch., revoked (in part): SI 1996/3184 Art.5

675. Plant Breeders' Rights (Fees) (Amendment) Regulations 1994
revoked: SI 1998/1021 Reg.7 (with savings), Sch.2 (with savings)

676. Seeds (National Lists of Varieties) (Fees) Regulations 1994
Reg.3, amended: SI 1997/383 Reg.2
Sch.1, substituted: SI 1997/383 Reg.2, Sch., SI 1998/1022 Reg.2, Sch., SI 1999/1090 Reg.2, Sch.
Sch.2, substituted: SI 1997/383 Reg.2, Sch., SI 1998/1022 Reg.2, Sch., SI 1999/1090 Reg.2, Sch.
Sch.3, substituted: SI 1997/383 Reg.2, Sch., SI 1998/1022 Reg.2, Sch., SI 1999/1090 Reg.2, Sch.
Sch.4, substituted: SI 1997/383 Reg.2, Sch., SI 1998/1022 Reg.2, Sch., SI 1999/1090 Reg.2, Sch.
Sch.5, substituted: SI 1997/383 Reg.2, Sch., SI 1998/1022 Reg.2, Sch., SI 1999/1090 Reg.2, Sch.

677. Town and Country Planning (Assessment of Environmental Effects) (Amendment) Regulations 1994
revoked: SI 1999/293 Reg.34, Sch.5

NO.

682. National Health Service (Regional and District Health Authorities) (Miscellaneous Amendments) Regulations 1994
revoked: SI 1996/707 Reg.17, Sch.4 Part I

691. Bowes Extension Light Railway Order 1994
Art.9, amended: SI 1996/362 Art.5, Sch.4

692. Education (No.2) Act 1986 (Amendment) Order 1994
revoked: 1996 c.56 Sch.38 Part III

693. Housing Renovation etc. Grants (Prescribed Forms and Particulars) (Welsh Forms and Particulars) Regulations 1994
applied: SI 1996/2842 Art.8
revoked: SI 1996/2842 Art.7, Sch Part I
Sch.1 Form 1, amended: SI 1996/1378 Reg.2, Sch.1
Sch.1 Form 1, revoked: SI 1996/2842 Art.7, Sch Part I
Sch.1 Form 2, amended: SI 1996/1378 Reg.2, Sch.2
Sch.1 Form 2, revoked: SI 1996/2842 Art.7, Sch Part I
Sch.1 Form 3, amended: SI 1996/1378 Reg.2, Sch.3
Sch.1 Form 3, revoked: SI 1996/2842 Art.7, Sch Part I

707. Environmentally Sensitive Areas (Blackdown Hills) Designation Order 1994
referred to: SI 1999/2231 Reg.3, Reg.4
Art.2, amended: SI 1996/2106 Art.2, SI 1996/3104 Reg.2, SI 1999/2233 Art.4
Art.3, amended: SI 1999/2233 Art.5
Art.4, substituted: SI 1999/2233 Art.6
Art.5, substituted: SI 1999/2233 Art.7
Art.6, amended: SI 1996/3104 Reg.2
Art.6, revoked: SI 1999/2233 Art.10
Art.6A, added: SI 1996/3104 Reg.2
Art.6B, added: SI 1996/3104 Reg.2
Art.6C, added: SI 1996/3104 Reg.2
Art.7, amended: SI 1996/2106 Art.2
Art.7, revoked: SI 1999/2233 Art.10
Sch.1, substituted: SI 1999/2233 Art.8, Sch.1
Sch.1 para.1, amended: SI 1996/2106 Art.2
Sch.1 para.4, amended: SI 1996/2106 Art.2
Sch.2, substituted: SI 1999/2233 Art.9, Sch.2
Sch.3, revoked: SI 1999/2233 Art.10
Sch.4, revoked: SI 1996/2106 Art.2, SI 1999/2233 Art.10
Sch.5, amended: SI 1996/2106 Art.2
Sch.5, revoked: SI 1999/2233 Art.10
Sch.6, revoked: SI 1999/2233 Art.10
Sch.6 para.1, amended: SI 1996/2106 Art.2
Sch.6 para.3, substituted: SI 1996/2106 Art.2
Sch.6 para.8, added: SI 1996/2106 Art.2
Sch.6 para.9, added: SI 1996/2106 Art.2
Sch.6 para.10, added: SI 1996/2106 Art.2

708. Environmentally Sensitive Areas (Cotswold Hills) Designation Order 1994
referred to: SI 1999/2231 Reg.3, Reg.4
Art.2, amended: SI 1996/3104 Reg.2, SI 1999/2234 Art.4
Art.3, amended: SI 1999/2234 Art.5
Art.4, substituted: SI 1999/2234 Art.6
Art.5, substituted: SI 1999/2234 Art.7
Art.6, amended: SI 1996/3104 Reg.2
Art.6, revoked: SI 1999/2234 Art.10
Art.6A, added: SI 1996/3104 Reg.2
Art.6B, added: SI 1996/3104 Reg.2
Art.6C, added: SI 1996/3104 Reg.2
Art.7, amended: SI 1996/2107 Art.2, SI 1998/1800 Art.2

NO.

708. Environmentally Sensitive Areas (Cotswold Hills) Designation Order 1994—*cont.*
Art.7, revoked: SI 1999/2234 Art.10
Sch.1, substituted: SI 1999/2234 Art.8, Sch.1
Sch.1 para.1, amended: SI 1996/2107 Art.2
Sch.2, substituted: SI 1999/2234 Art.9, Sch.2
Sch.3, amended: SI 1996/2107 Art.2
Sch.3, revoked: SI 1999/2234 Art.10
Sch.4, revoked: SI 1999/2234 Art.10
Sch.5, revoked: SI 1999/2234 Art.10
Sch.5 para.2, amended: SI 1996/2107 Art.2
Sch.5 para.3, substituted: SI 1996/2107 Art.2
Sch.5 para.4, substituted: SI 1996/2107 Art.2
Sch.5 para.9, added: SI 1996/2107 Art.2

709. Environmentally Sensitive Areas (Shropshire Hills) Designation Order 1994
referred to: SI 1999/2231 Reg.3, Reg.4
Art.2, amended: SI 1996/2109 Art.2, SI 1996/3104 Reg.2, SI 1999/2235 Art.4
Art.4, substituted: SI 1999/2235 Art.5
Art.5, substituted: SI 1999/2235 Art.6
Art.6, amended: SI 1996/3104 Reg.2
Art.6, revoked: SI 1999/2235 Art.9
Art.6A, added: SI 1996/3104 Reg.2
Art.6B, added: SI 1996/3104 Reg.2
Art.6C, added: SI 1996/3104 Reg.2
Art.7, amended: SI 1996/2109 Art.2
Art.7, revoked: SI 1999/2235 Art.9
Sch.1, substituted: SI 1999/2235 Art.7, Sch.1
Sch.1 para.1, amended: SI 1996/2109 Art.2
Sch.1 para.4, amended: SI 1996/2109 Art.2
Sch.2, substituted: SI 1999/2235 Art.8, Sch.2
Sch.3, revoked: SI 1999/2235 Art.9
Sch.4, revoked: SI 1996/2109 Art.2, SI 1999/2235 Art.9
Sch.5, revoked: SI 1999/2235 Art.9
Sch.6, revoked: SI 1999/2235 Art.9
Sch.6 para.1, amended: SI 1996/2109 Art.2
Sch.6 para.2, substituted: SI 1996/2109 Art.2

710. Environmentally Sensitive Areas (Dartmoor) Designation Order 1994
referred to: SI 1999/2231 Reg.3, Reg.4
Art.2, amended: SI 1996/2110 Art.2, SI 1996/3104 Reg.2, SI 1999/2236 Art.4
Art.4, substituted: SI 1999/2236 Art.5
Art.5, substituted: SI 1999/2236 Art.6
Art.6, amended: SI 1996/3104 Reg.2
Art.6, revoked: SI 1999/2236 Art.9
Art.6A, added: SI 1996/3104 Reg.2
Art.6B, added: SI 1996/3104 Reg.2
Art.6C, added: SI 1996/3104 Reg.2
Art.7, amended: SI 1996/2110 Art.2
Art.7, revoked: SI 1999/2236 Art.9
Sch.1, substituted: SI 1999/2236 Art.7, Sch.1
Sch.1 para.1, amended: SI 1996/2110 Art.2
Sch.1 para.5, amended: SI 1996/2110 Art.2
Sch.2, substituted: SI 1999/2236 Art.8, Sch.2
Sch.3, revoked: SI 1999/2236 Art.9
Sch.4, amended: SI 1996/2110 Art.2
Sch.4, revoked: SI 1999/2236 Art.9
Sch.5, revoked: SI 1996/2110 Art.2, SI 1999/2236 Art.9
Sch.6, amended: SI 1996/2110 Art.2
Sch.6, revoked: SI 1999/2236 Art.9
Sch.7, revoked: SI 1999/2236 Art.9
Sch.8, revoked: SI 1999/2236 Art.9
Sch.8 para.4, amended: SI 1996/2110 Art.2
Sch.8 para.7, added: SI 1996/2110 Art.2
Sch.8 para.8, added: SI 1996/2110 Art.2

NO.

711. **Environmentally Sensitive Areas (Essex Coast) Designation Order 1994**
referred to: SI 1999/2231 Reg.3, Reg.4
Art.2, amended: SI 1996/3104 Reg.2, SI 1999/2232 Art.4
Art.3, amended: SI 1999/2232 Art.5
Art.4, substituted: SI 1999/2232 Art.6
Art.5, substituted: SI 1999/2232 Art.7
Art.6, amended: SI 1996/3104 Reg.2
Art.6, revoked: SI 1999/2232 Art.10
Art.6A, added: SI 1996/3104 Reg.2
Art.6B, added: SI 1996/3104 Reg.2
Art.6C, added: SI 1996/3104 Reg.2
Art.7, amended: SI 1996/2108 Art.2
Art.7, revoked: SI 1999/2232 Art.10
Sch.1, substituted: SI 1999/2232 Art.8, Sch.1
Sch.2, substituted: SI 1999/2232 Art.9, Sch.2
Sch.3, amended: SI 1996/2108 Art.2
Sch.3, revoked: SI 1999/2232 Art.10
Sch.4, amended: SI 1996/2108 Art.2
Sch.4, revoked: SI 1999/2232 Art.10
Sch.5, amended: SI 1996/2108 Art.2
Sch.5, revoked: SI 1999/2232 Art.10

712. **Environmentally Sensitive Areas (Upper Thames Tributaries) Designation Order 1994**
referred to: SI 1999/2231 Reg.3, Reg.4
Art.2, amended: SI 1996/3104 Reg.2, SI 1999/2237 Art.4
Art.3, amended: SI 1999/2237 Art.5
Art.4, substituted: SI 1999/2237 Art.6
Art.5, substituted: SI 1999/2237 Art.7
Art.6, amended: SI 1996/3104 Reg.2
Art.6, revoked: SI 1999/2237 Art.10
Art.6A, added: SI 1996/3104 Reg.2
Art.6B, added: SI 1996/3104 Reg.2
Art.6C, added: SI 1996/3104 Reg.2
Art.7, amended: SI 1996/2105 Art.2, SI 1998/1803 Art.2
Art.7, revoked: SI 1999/2237 Art.10
Sch.1, substituted: SI 1999/2237 Art.8, Sch.1
Sch.1 para.1, amended: SI 1996/2105 Art.2
Sch.2, substituted: SI 1999/2237 Art.9, Sch.2
Sch.3, revoked: SI 1999/2237 Art.10
Sch.4, amended: SI 1996/2105 Art.2
Sch.4, revoked: SI 1999/2237 Art.10
Sch.5, revoked: SI 1999/2237 Art.10
Sch.6, revoked: SI 1999/2237 Art.10
Sch.6 para.2, amended: SI 1996/2105 Art.2
Sch.6 para.7, substituted: SI 1996/2105 Art.2

714. **Public Trustee (Fees) (Amendment) Order 1994**
revoked: SI 1999/855 Art.32, Sch.

717. **Education (Registered Inspectors of Schools Appeal Tribunal) (Procedure) Regulations 1994**
revoked: SI 1999/265 Reg.1

729. **General Optical Council (Registration and Enrolment (Amendment) Rules) Order of Council 1994**
revoked: SI 1996/3021, SI 1996/3021 Sch para.3

743. **Drinking Water in Containers Regulations 1994**
referred to: SI 1999/1540 Reg.18
revoked: SI 1999/1540 Reg.21, Sch.4
Reg.3, revoked: SI 1999/1540 Reg.21, Sch.4

747. **Representation of the People (Variation of Limits of Candidates' Election Expenses) Order 1994**
revoked: SI 1997/879 Art.9

NO.

748. **European Parliamentary Elections (Amendment) Regulations 1994**
revoked: SI 1999/1214 Reg.20, Sch.5
Reg.2, revoked: SI 1997/874 Reg.3, SI 1999/1214 Reg.20, Sch.5

749. **Building Societies (Undated Subordinated Debt) Order 1994**
Art.2, amended: SI 1998/1129 Art.2, Sch.1 para.15
Sch.2 para.3, amended: SI 1998/1129 Art.2, Sch.1 para.15

758. **European Communities (Definition of Treaties) (Europe Agreement establishing an Association between the European Communities and their Member States and the Republic of Bulgaria) Order 1994**
referred to: SI 1996/2911 Sch.2

759. **European Communities (Definition of Treaties) (Europe Agreement establishing an Association between the European Communities and their Member States and the Czech Republic) Order 1994**
referred to: SI 1996/2911 Sch.2

760. **European Communities (Definition of Treaties) (Europe Agreement establishing an Association between the European Communities and their Member States and Romania) Order 1994**
referred to: SI 1996/2911 Sch.2

761. **European Communities (Definition of Treaties) (Europe Agreement establishing an Association between the European Communities and their Member States and the Slovak Republic) Order 1994**
referred to: SI 1996/2911 Sch.2

762. **Appropriation (Northern Ireland) Order 1994**
revoked: SI 1997/1754 (NI.13) Art.6, Sch.2

763. **Local Elections (Variation of Limits of Candidates' Election Expenses) (Northern Ireland) Order 1994**
revoked: SI 1997/868 Art.3

764. **Northern Ireland (Emergency Provisions) Act 1991 (Guernsey) Order 1994**
revoked: 1996 c.22 Sch.7 Part II

765. **Social Security (Contributions) (Northern Ireland) Order 1994**
Art.3, revoked: SI 1998/1506 (NI.10) Art.78, Sch.7

776. **Pensions Increase (Review) Order 1994**
applied: SI 1997/634 Art.3, SI 1998/503 Art.3, Art.4, SI 1999/522 Art.3

781. **Housing Benefit and Council Tax Benefit (Subsidy) Regulations 1994**
applied: SI 1996/1314 Reg.4
Reg.1, amended: SI 1996/1314 Reg.2
Sch. para.12, substituted: SI 1996/1314 Reg.3
Sch. para.13, substituted: SI 1996/1314 Reg.3
Sch. para.16, substituted: SI 1996/1314 Reg.3

782. **European Parliamentary Elections (Northern Ireland) (Amendment) Regulations 1994**
Reg.2, revoked (in part): SI 1999/1268 Reg.8

804. **Food Labelling (Amendment) Regulations 1994**
revoked: SI 1996/1499 Reg.49, Sch.9

848. **Harrow and Hillingdon Healthcare National Health Service Trust (Establishment) Order 1994**
Art.3, substituted: SI 1998/1992 Art.2

1994—cont.

849. **Royal Victoria Infirmary and Associated Hospitals National Health Service Trust (Establishment) Order 1994**
revoked: SI 1998/831 Art.2

850. **University College London National Health Service Trust (Establishment) Order 1994**
revoked: SI 1996/881 Art.2

852. **Mount Vernon and Watford Hospitals National Health Service Trust (Establishment) Order 1994**
Art.3, amended: SI 1999/1768 Art.2

867. **Local Government Changes for England Regulations 1994**
applied: SI 1996/1867 Art.20
Reg.1, amended: SI 1996/611 Reg.2
Reg.2, amended: SI 1996/330 Reg.2
Reg.4, applied: SI 1996/263 Reg.18
Reg.5, amended: SI 1996/611 Reg.2
Reg.7, amended: SI 1996/330 Reg.2
Reg.15, amended: SI 1996/330 Reg.2
Reg.23, revoked: SI 1996/611 Reg.2
Reg.25, amended: SI 1996/330 Reg.2
Reg.27, applied: SI 1996/1879 Art.9
Reg.27A, added: SI 1996/330 Reg.2
Sch. para.2, referred to: SI 1996/1876 Art.11

895. **Occupational Pension Schemes (Deficiency on Winding Up etc.) Regulations 1994**
revoked: SI 1996/3128 Reg.13 (with savings)
Reg.2, amended: SI 1996/5 Reg.2
Reg.2, revoked: SI 1996/3128 Reg.13 (with savings)

929. **Environmentally Sensitive Areas (The Broads) Designation (Amendment) (No.2) Order 1994**
revoked: SI 1997/1440 Art.6 (with saving)

930. **Environmentally Sensitive Areas (Pennine Dales) Designation (Amendment) (No.2) Order 1994**
revoked: SI 1997/1441 Art.6 (with saving)

931. **Environmentally Sensitive Areas (South Downs) Designation (Amendment) (No.2) Order 1994**
revoked: SI 1997/1443 Art.6 (with saving)

932. **Environmentally Sensitive Areas (Somerset Levels and Moors) Designation (Amendment) (No.2) Order 1994**
revoked: SI 1997/1442 Art.6 (with saving)

933. **Environmentally Sensitive Areas (West Penwith) Designation (Amendment) (No.2) Order 1994**
revoked: SI 1997/1444 Art.6 (with saving)

938. **Education (Grant-Maintained Schools) (Finance) Regulations 1994**
applied: SI 1996/889 Reg.3, SI 1998/799 Reg.3

948. **Local Government Superannuation (Greater Manchester Buses Limited) Regulations 1994**
Reg.2, amended: SI 1997/1613 Reg.27, Sch.3 para.5
Reg.4, amended: SI 1997/1613 Reg.27, Sch.3 para.5

959. **Education (Individual Pupils' Achievements) (Information) (Wales) Regulations 1994**
revoked: SI 1996/382 Reg.1

960. **Food Labelling (Scotland) Amendment Regulations 1994**
revoked: SI 1996/1499 Reg.49, Sch.9

963. **Local Government Superannuation (Greater Manchester Buses North Limited) Regulations 1994**
Reg.2, amended: SI 1997/1613 Reg.27, Sch.3 para.6

1994—cont.

1000. **Advice and Assistance (Assistance by Way of Representation) (Scotland) Amendment Regulations 1994**
revoked: SI 1997/3070 Reg.2, Sch.

1001. **Criminal Legal Aid (Scotland) (Prescribed Proceedings) Regulations 1994**
revoked: SI 1997/3069 Reg.2, Sch.
Reg.3, amended: SI 1996/1009 Reg.3
Reg.3, revoked: SI 1997/3069 Reg.2, Sch.

1017. **Legal Aid (Scotland) (Children) Amendment Regulations 1994**
revoked: SI 1997/690 Reg.12 (with savings)

1044. **Parliamentary Elections (Returning Officers' Charges) Order 1994**
revoked: SI 1997/1034 Art.1

1047. **Education (Special Educational Needs) Regulations 1994**
Reg.6, applied: SI 1999/1780 Reg.13, SI 1999/2212 Reg.19
Reg.11, applied: SI 1996/710 Reg.10
Reg.13, see *L v Clarke* [1998] E.L.R. 129 (QBD), Laws, J.
Reg.14, applied: SI 1996/710 Reg.10, Reg.12, Reg.13
Reg.14, referred to: SI 1996/710 Reg.11

1048. **Education (Special Educational Needs) (Information) Regulations 1994**
revoked (in part): SI 1999/1442 Reg.7, SI 1999/2506 Reg.1
Reg.2, applied: SI 1996/2585 Sch.2 para.6, SI 1997/1832 Sch.2 para.6, SI 1998/2526 Reg.8, Sch.2 para.6
Reg.2, referred to: SI 1999/1812 Reg.10, Sch.3 para.6
Reg.2, revoked (in part): SI 1999/1442 Reg.7, SI 1999/2506 Reg.1
Reg.3, applied: SI 1996/2585 Sch.2 para.6, SI 1997/1832 Sch.2 para.6, SI 1998/2526 Reg.8, Sch.2 para.6
Reg.3, referred to: SI 1999/1812 Reg.10, Sch.3 para.6
Reg.3, revoked (in part): SI 1999/1442 Reg.7, SI 1999/2506 Reg.1
Reg.4, applied: SI 1996/2585 Sch.2 para.6, SI 1997/1832 Sch.2 para.6, SI 1998/2526 Reg.8, Sch.2 para.6
Reg.4, referred to: SI 1999/1812 Reg.10, Sch.3 para.6
Reg.4, revoked (in part): SI 1999/1442 Reg.7, SI 1999/2506 Reg.1

1049. **Civil Legal Aid (Scotland) Amendment Regulations 1994**
revoked: SI 1996/2444 Reg.3, Sch.1

1050. **Criminal Legal Aid (Scotland) Amendment Regulations 1994**
revoked: SI 1996/2555 Reg.3, Sch.

1056. **Waste Management Licensing Regulations 1994**
see *Lilley v Secretary of State for the Environment and North Yorkshire CC* [1996] 1 P.L.R. 28 (QBD), Sir Graham Eyre Q.C.; see *Mayer Parry Recycling Ltd v Environment Agency* [1999] 1 C.M.L.R. 963 (Ch D), Carnwath, J.; see *R. v Bolton MBC Ex p. Kirkman* [1998] Env. L.R. 719 (CA), Schiemann, L.J.; see *R. v Vale of Glamorgan Ex p. James* [1996] Env. L.R. 102 (QBD), Popplewell, L.J.
applied: SI 1999/672 Art.2, Sch.1
Reg.1, amended: SI 1996/972 Reg.25, Sch.3
Reg.3, amended: SI 1996/972 Reg.25, Sch.3

NO.

1056. Waste Management Licensing Regulations 1994—*cont.*
Reg.3, applied: SI 1997/351 Reg.2
Reg.4, amended: SI 1996/634 Reg.2, SI 1996/916 Reg.2
Reg.4, applied: SI 1996/634 Reg.4
Reg.4 Table 1, substituted: SI 1997/2203 Reg.2
Reg.5, amended: SI 1996/634 Reg.2
Reg.5, applied: SI 1996/634 Reg.5
Reg.8, amended: SI 1996/593 Reg.3, Sch.2 para.10
Reg.10, amended: SI 1996/593 Reg.3, Sch.2 para.10, SI 1996/972 Reg.25, Sch.3, SI 1996/973 Reg.2, Sch para.17
Reg.12, amended: SI 1996/634 Reg.2
Reg.15, see *Guthrie, Petitioner* [1998] Env. L.R. 128 (OH), Lord Johnston; see *R. v Vale of Glamorgan BC Ex p. James* [1997] Env. L.R. 195 (CA), Hirst, L.J.
Reg.16, applied: SI 1996/972 Reg.15
Reg.17, see *Environment Agency v Short* [1999] E.H.L.R. 3 (QBD), Bell, J.; see *London Waste Regulation Authority v Drinkwater Sabey Ltd* [1997] Env. L.R. 137 (QBD), Smith, J.; see *North Yorkshire CC v Boyne* [1997] Env. L.R. 91 (QBD), Pill, L.J.
Reg.17, amended: SI 1996/972 Reg.25, Sch.3
Reg.17, applied: SI 1996/972 Reg.17
Reg.18, amended: SI 1996/593 Reg.3, Sch.2 para.10, SI 1996/634 Reg.2, SI 1998/606 Reg.2
Reg.40, see *North Yorkshire CC v Boyne* [1997] Env. L.R. 91 (QBD), Pill, L.J.
Sch.3, see *London Waste Regulation Authority v Drinkwater Sabey Ltd* [1997] Env. L.R. 137 (QBD), Smith, J.
Sch.3 para.3, amended: SI 1996/972 Reg.25, Sch.3
Sch.3 para.17, amended: SI 1996/1279 Reg.2
Sch.3 para.18, amended: SI 1996/972 Reg.25, Sch.3
Sch.3 para.19, see *Environment Agency v Short* [1999] E.H.L.R. 3 (QBD), Bell, J.
Sch.3 para.28, substituted: SI 1996/972 Reg.25, Sch.3
Sch.3 para.43, amended: SI 1996/634 Reg.2
Sch.3 para.45, amended: SI 1996/634 Reg.2, SI 1998/606 Reg.2
Sch.4 para.1, amended: SI 1996/593 Reg.3, Sch.2 para.10, SI 1996/973 Reg.2, Sch para.17
Sch.4 para.2, amended: SI 1996/593 Reg.3, Sch.2 para.10
Sch.4 para.3, amended: SI 1996/593 Reg.3, Sch.2 para.10, SI 1996/973 Reg.2, Sch para.17, SI 1998/2746 Reg.17
Sch.4 para.6, see *Guthrie, Petitioner* [1998] Env. L.R. 128 (OH), Lord Johnston
Sch.4 para.6, amended: SI 1996/593 Reg.3, Sch.2 para.10
Sch.4 para.9, amended: SI 1996/972 Reg.25, Sch.3
Sch.4 para.12, amended: SI 1996/593 Reg.3, Sch.2 para.10
Sch.4 para.13, amended: SI 1996/593 Reg.3, Sch.2 para.10, SI 1996/972 Reg.25, Sch.3
Sch.4 para.14, amended: SI 1996/972 Reg.25, Sch.3
Sch.5 Part II, amended: SI 1996/972 Reg.25, Sch.3
Sch.5 Part II, revoked: SI 1998/606 Reg.2
Sch.5 Part III, amended: SI 1996/972 Reg.25, Sch.3

NO.

1056. Waste Management Licensing Regulations 1994—*cont.*
Sch.5 Part III, revoked: SI 1998/606 Reg.2
Sch.5 para.3, amended: SI 1998/606 Reg.2

1058. Teachers' Superannuation (Amendment) Regulations 1994
applied: SI 1997/3001 Reg.H12, Sch.15 para.2
revoked: SI 1997/3001 Reg.H12, Sch.14

1059. Teachers (Compensation for Redundancy and Premature Retirement) (Amendment) Regulations 1994
revoked: SI 1997/311 Reg.28

1061. Advice and Assistance (Scotland) Amendment Regulations 1994
revoked: SI 1996/2447 Reg.3, Sch.1

1062. Occupational and Personal Pension Schemes (Consequential Amendments) Regulations 1994
Reg.2, revoked (in part): SI 1996/1172 Sch.2, SI 1996/1537 Reg.18, Sch., SI 1997/358 Reg.7, Sch., SI 1997/371 Reg.9, Sch., SI 1997/470 Reg.20, Sch.3, SI 1997/784 Reg.12, Sch.2
Sch.2 para.1, revoked (in part): SI 1997/358 Reg.7, Sch
Sch.2 para.3, revoked (in part): SI 1997/358 Reg.7, Sch
Sch.2 para.4, revoked: SI 1996/1172 Sch.2
Sch.2 para.5, revoked: SI 1996/1462 Reg.14, Sch.3
Sch.2 para.6, revoked (in part): SI 1997/784 Reg.12, Sch.2
Sch.2 para.7, revoked: SI 1996/1847 Reg.21, Sch.3
Sch.2 para.8, revoked: SI 1996/1655 Reg.12, Sch.4
Sch.2 para.10, revoked: SI 1996/1172 Sch.2
Sch.2 para.19, revoked: SI 1996/1537 Reg.18, Sch.
Sch.2 para.20, revoked: SI 1996/1461 Reg.7, Sch.1
Sch.2 para.21, revoked (in part): SI 1997/470 Reg.20, Sch.3
Sch.2 para.28, revoked (in part): SI 1997/371 Reg.9, Sch.
Sch.2 para.32, revoked: SI 1996/2475 Reg.7
Sch.2 para.33, revoked: SI 1996/3127 Reg.13, Sch.

1065. European Convention on Cinematographic Co-production Order 1994
Sch., amended: SI 1996/2600 Art.2, SI 1996/3169 Art.2, SI 1997/870 Art.2, SI 1997/1319 Art.2, SI 1997/1743 Art.2, SI 1999/3131 Art.2

1084. Education (Special Schools Conducted by Education Associations) Regulations 1994
Reg.8, revoked (in part): SI 1996/360 Sch.1

1104. Merchant Shipping (Radio) (Fishing Vessels) (Amendment) Rules 1994
revoked (in part): SI 1999/3210 Reg.2

1137. Transfrontier Shipment of Waste Regulations 1994
Reg.6, amended: SI 1996/593 Reg.3, Sch.2 para.
Reg.9, amended: SI 1996/593 Reg.3, Sch.2 para.
Reg.18, revoked (in part): SI 1996/972 Reg.26

1170. National Lottery (Revocation of Licenses) Procedure Regulations 1994
revoked: SI 1999/137 Reg.2

NO.

1994—cont.

1191. Export of Goods (Control) Order 1994
applied: SI 1998/1530 Art.2, SI 1998/1752 Art.5, SI 1998/1757 Art.5
referred to: SI 1996/2721 Reg.14
Art.1, amended: SI 1996/2663 Art.2
Art.3, amended: SI 1996/2663 Art.2, SI 1997/323 Art.2, SI 1997/2464 Art.2, SI 1997/2758 Art.2, Art.3, SI 1998/1530 Art.3, SI 1999/63 Art.3, SI 1999/1777 Art.2
Art.3, applied: SI 1997/2464 Art.2, SI 1998/1530 Art.3
Art.3B, amended: SI 1996/1341 Art.2, SI 1996/2663 Art.2, SI 1997/2758 Art.4, Sch.1
Art.3B, revoked (in part): SI 1999/63 Art.2
Art.4, amended: SI 1997/2464 Art.2, SI 1998/1530 Art.3
Art.4, applied: SI 1997/2464 Art.2, SI 1998/1530 Art.3
Art.5, amended: SI 1997/2464 Art.2, SI 1998/1530 Art.3, SI 1999/1777 Art.2
Art.5, applied: SI 1997/2464 Art.2, SI 1998/1530 Art.3
Art.6, amended: SI 1997/2464 Art.2, SI 1998/1530 Art.3
Art.6, applied: SI 1997/2464 Art.2, SI 1998/1530 Art.3
Art.7, amended: SI 1997/2464 Art.2, SI 1998/1530 Art.3
Art.7, applied: SI 1997/2464 Art.2, SI 1998/1530 Art.3
Art.8, amended: SI 1997/2464 Art.2, SI 1998/1530 Art.3
Art.8, applied: SI 1997/2464 Art.2, SI 1998/1530 Art.3
Sch.1 Part I, amended: SI 1996/1341 Art.2, SI 1997/2758 Art.5, Art.6, Sch.2, SI 1999/63 Art.4, SI 1999/1777 Art.3, SI 1999/3411 Art.2
Sch.1 Part I, revoked (in part): SI 1996/2663, SI 1999/63 Art.2
Sch.1 Part II, revoked: SI 1996/2663 Art.2
Sch.1 Part III, amended: SI 1996/1124 Reg.2, SI 1997/1008 Art.2, SI 1997/2758 Art.7, SI 1999/63 Art.5, SI 1999/1777 Art.4
Sch.1 Part III, applied: SI 1996/1736 Reg.4, SI 1997/2592 Sch.1, SI 1998/1530 Art.3, SI 1999/2610 Art.2
Sch.1 Part III, revoked (in part): SI 1997/2758 Art.7
Sch.1 Part III, substituted: SI 1996/2663 Art.2, Sch.1
Sch.3, amended: SI 1997/323 Art.3, SI 1997/2464 Art.3, SI 1997/2758 Art.8, SI 1999/335 Art.2, SI 1999/2609 Art.1

1192. HMSO Trading Fund (Amendment) Order 1994
referred to: SI 1996/2483
revoked: SI 1996/2483 Art.2

1210. Isle of Wight (Structural Change) Order 1994
Art.5, revoked (in part): SI 1999/2393 Art.12

1212. Income Tax (Employments) (Notional Payments) Regulations 1994
Reg.2, amended: SI 1998/1891 Reg.3
Reg.3, amended: SI 1996/2969 Reg.2, SI 1998/1891 Reg.4
Reg.3A, added: SI 1998/1891 Reg.5
Reg.3B, added: SI 1998/1891 Reg.5
Reg.7, amended: SI 1998/1891 Reg.6
Reg.8, amended: SI 1998/1891 Reg.6
Reg.8A, added: SI 1998/1891 Reg.7
Reg.12A, added: SI 1998/1891 Reg.8

NO.

1994—cont.

1230. Maternity Allowance and Statutory Maternity Pay Regulations 1994
referred to: SI 1999/3309 Art.2
Reg.2, revoked (in part): 1999 c.30 s.88, Sch.13 Part V
Reg.6, revoked (in part): 1999 c.30 s.88, Sch.13 Part V

1256. Education (Information as to Provision of Education) (England) Regulations 1994
revoked: SI 1999/1066 Reg.5

1262. Regional and District Health Authorities (Membership and Procedure) Amendment Regulations 1994
revoked: SI 1996/707 Reg.17, Sch.4 Part I

1291. Habitat (Water Fringe) Regulations 1994
applied: SI 1996/3142 Reg.6, SI 1997/2844 Sch.3 Part I, Sch.4 para.3
Reg.2, amended: SI 1996/1480 Reg.4, SI 1996/3106 Reg.2
Reg.3, amended: SI 1996/1480 Reg.5, SI 1996/3106 Reg.2
Reg.4, amended: SI 1996/1480 Reg.6, SI 1996/3106 Reg.2
Reg.4A, added: SI 1999/3160 Reg.3
Reg.5, amended: SI 1996/3106 Reg.2
Reg.6, amended: SI 1996/3106 Reg.2
Reg.7, amended: SI 1996/1480 Reg.7, SI 1996/3106 Reg.2
Reg.7A, added: SI 1996/1480 Reg.8
Reg.7A, amended: SI 1996/3106 Reg.2
Reg.8, amended: SI 1996/3106 Reg.2
Reg.8, substituted: SI 1996/1480 Reg.9
Reg.10, amended: SI 1996/1480 Reg.10
Reg.10, substituted: SI 1996/3106 Reg.2
Reg.10A, added: SI 1996/3106 Reg.2
Reg.10B, added: SI 1996/3106 Reg.2
Sch.2 para.1, substituted: SI 1996/1480 Reg.11
Sch.5, amended: SI 1996/1480 Reg.11
Sch.5 para.1, substituted: SI 1996/1480 Reg.11
Sch.5 para.11, amended: SI 1996/1480 Reg.11
Sch.5 para.12, amended: SI 1996/1480 Reg.11
Sch.5 para.16, substituted: SI 1996/1480 Reg.11
Sch.5 para.20, added: SI 1996/1480 Reg.11
Sch.6, amended: SI 1996/1480 Reg.11
Sch.6 para.2, substituted: SI 1996/1480 Reg.11
Sch.6 para.13, amended: SI 1996/1480 Reg.11
Sch.6 para.14, amended: SI 1996/1480 Reg.11
Sch.6 para.18, added: SI 1996/1480 Reg.11

1292. Habitat (Former Set-Aside Land) Regulations 1994
applied: SI 1996/3142 Reg.6
Reg.2, amended: SI 1996/3107 Reg.2
Reg.6, amended: SI 1996/3107 Reg.2
Reg.7, amended: SI 1996/1478 Reg.2, SI 1996/3107 Reg.2
Reg.10, substituted: SI 1996/3107 Reg.2
Reg.10A, added: SI 1996/3107 Reg.2
Reg.10B, added: SI 1996/3107 Reg.2

1293. Habitat (Salt-Marsh) Regulations 1994
applied: SI 1996/3142 Reg.6, SI 1997/2844 Sch.3 Part I, Sch.4 para.3
Reg.2, amended: SI 1996/3108 Reg.2
Reg.4A, added: SI 1999/3161 Reg.3
Reg.5, amended: SI 1996/3108 Reg.2
Reg.6, amended: SI 1996/3108 Reg.2
Reg.7, amended: SI 1996/1479 Reg.2, SI 1996/3108 Reg.2
Reg.7A, amended: SI 1996/1479 Reg.2, SI 1996/3108 Reg.2
Reg.10, substituted: SI 1996/3108 Reg.2
Reg.10A, added: SI 1996/3108 Reg.2
Reg.10B, added: SI 1996/3108 Reg.2

1994—cont.

1293. Habitat (Salt-Marsh) Regulations 1994—
cont.
Sch. para.1, amended: SI 1996/1479 Reg.2

1331. Lydney and Parkend Light Railway (Extension and Amendment) Order 1994
Art.11, amended: SI 1996/362 Art.5, Sch.4

1371. Edinburgh-Berwick Upon Tweed Trunk Road (A1) Old Craighall Roundabout to East of Haddington Special Road Scheme 1994
applied: SI 1996/2448 Reg.1

1372. Edinburgh-Berwick Upon Tweed Trunk Road (A1) Old Craighall Roundabout to East of Haddington Special Road Scheme (No.2) 1994
applied: SI 1996/2448 Reg.1

1379. European Parliamentary Elections (Returning Officers' Charges) Order 1994
revoked: SI 1999/1378 Art.1

1382. Hovercraft (Fees) Regulations 1994
revoked: SI 1997/320 Reg.2

1383. Merchant Shipping (Ro-Ro Passenger Ship Survivability) (No.2) Regulations 1994
revoked: SI 1997/647 Reg.1

1404. Marketing Development Scheme (Specification of Activities) Order 1994
para.2, amended: SI 1997/2674 Art.3

1409. Guarantee Payments (Exemption) (No.29) Order 1994
revoked: SI 1996/2132 Art.3

1410. Free Zone (Southampton) Designation (Variation) Order 1994
amended: SI 1996/2615 Art.2

1412. European Parliamentary Elections (Returning Officer's Charges) (Northern Ireland) Order 1994
revoked: SI 1999/1342 Art.1

1413. Parliamentary Elections (Returning Officer's Charges) (Northern Ireland) Order 1994
revoked: SI 1997/774 Art.1

1417. Redundancy Payments (Local Government) (Modification) (Amendment) Order 1994
revoked: SI 1999/2277 Art.4, Sch.3

1420. Education (School Performance Information) (England) Regulations 1994
revoked (in part): SI 1996/2577 Reg.4
Sch.1 para.2, amended: SI 1996/1596 Reg.2
Sch.1 para.2B, amended: SI 1996/1596 Reg.2
Sch.1 para.4, amended: SI 1996/1596 Reg.2
Sch.2 para.3, substituted: SI 1996/1596 Reg.2
Sch.2 para.4, substituted: SI 1996/1596 Reg.2
Sch.2 para.7, amended: SI 1996/1596 Reg.2
Sch.2 para.7A, added: SI 1996/1596 Reg.2

1421. Education (School Information) (England) Regulations 1994
revoked: SI 1996/2585 Reg.2
Reg.8, applied: SI 1996/2585 Reg.15
Reg.8, revoked: SI 1996/2585 Reg.2

1432. Railway Pensions (Protection and Designation of Schemes) Order 1994
Art.6, see *South West Trains Ltd v Wightman* [1997] O.P.L.R. 249 (Ch D), Neuberger, J.

1433. Railways Pension Scheme Order 1994
see *South West Trains Ltd v Wightman* [1997] O.P.L.R. 249 (Ch D), Neuberger, J.

1441. Plant Health Fees (Scotland) Order 1994
revoked: SI 1996/1784 Reg.5

1443. Act of Sederunt (Rules of the Court of Session) 1994
Sch.2 Ch.1, amended: SI 1999/1386 r.2
Sch.2 r.1.3, amended: SI 1996/2587 r.2

1994—cont.

1443. Act of Sederunt (Rules of the Court of Session) 1994—*cont.*
Sch.2 r.1.4, added: SI 1999/1386 r.2
Sch.2 r.3.6A, added: SI 1998/2637 r.2
Sch.2 r.3.6A, amended: SI 1999/1386 r.2
Sch.2 r.4.2, amended: SI 1997/1720 r.2, SI 1997/3059 r.2
Sch.2 r.4.3, amended: SI 1997/1720 r.3
Sch.2 r.4.7, amended: SI 1996/1756 para.2
Sch.2 r.4.7, revoked (in part): SI 1996/1756 para.2
Sch.2 Ch.6, referred to: SI 1998/890 r.4
Sch.2 r.6.2, amended: SI 1998/890 r.2
Sch.2 r.6.3, substituted: SI 1998/890 r.2
Sch.2 r.7.7, applied: SI 1996/2444 Reg.41
Sch.2 Ch.11, amended: SI 1997/2692 r.2
Sch.2 Ch.11, applied: SI 1997/2692 r.5
Sch.2 r.11.1, amended: SI 1997/2692 r.2
Sch.2 r.13.10, amended: SI 1998/890 r.2
Sch.2 r.14.2, amended: SI 1996/1756 para.2
Sch.2 r.14.2, revoked (in part): SI 1996/1756 para.2
Sch.2 r.14.3, referred to: SI 1998/890 r.4
Sch.2 r.14.3, revoked (in part): SI 1998/890 r.2
Sch.2 r.14.5, amended: SI 1996/2168 r.2
Sch.2 r.14.7, amended: SI 1996/1756 para.2
Sch.2 r.16.1, applied: SI 1997/688 Sch.1 Table
Sch.2 r.16.4, amended: SI 1997/1720 r.4
Sch.2 r.16.15, amended: SI 1998/2637 r.2
Sch.2 Ch.22, referred to: SI 1998/890 r.4
Sch.2 r.22.1, substituted: SI 1998/890 r.2
Sch.2 r.22.2, amended: SSI 1999/109 para.2
Sch.2 r.22.2, substituted: SI 1998/890 r.2
Sch.2 r.22.3, amended: SI 1998/890 r.2
Sch.2 r.22.3, substituted: SI 1998/890 r.2
Sch.2 r.24.2, amended: SI 1999/1386 r.2
Sch.2 Ch.25A, added: SI 1999/1345 r.2
Sch.2 r.25A.1, added: SI 1999/1345 r.2
Sch.2 r.25A.2, added: SI 1999/1345 r.2
Sch.2 r.25A.3, added: SI 1999/1345 r.2
Sch.2 r.25A.4, added: SI 1999/1345 r.2
Sch.2 r.25A.5, added: SI 1999/1345 r.2
Sch.2 r.25A.6, added: SI 1999/1345 r.2
Sch.2 r.25A.7, added: SI 1999/1345 r.2
Sch.2 r.25A.8, added: SI 1999/1345 r.2
Sch.2 r.25A.9, added: SI 1999/1345 r.2
Sch.2 r.25A.10, added: SI 1999/1345 r.2
Sch.2 r.25A.11, added: SI 1999/1345 r.2
Sch.2 r.25A.12, added: SI 1999/1345 r.2
Sch.2 r.28A.1, added: SI 1996/2168 r.2
Sch.2 r.28A.2, added: SI 1996/2168 r.2
Sch.2 r.28A.2, revoked (in part): SI 1997/1050 r.2
Sch.2 r.30.2, amended: SI 1996/2168 r.2
Sch.2 r.30.3, amended: SI 1997/1050 r.2
Sch.2 Ch.34A, applied: SI 1996/2769 r.3
Sch.2 Ch.34A, revoked: SI 1996/2769 r.2
Sch.2 r.34A.1, added: SI 1996/2168 r.2
Sch.2 r.34A.2, added: SI 1996/2168 r.2
Sch.2 r.34A.3, added: SI 1996/2168 r.2
Sch.2 r.34A.4, added: SI 1996/2168 r.2
Sch.2 r.34A.5, added: SI 1996/2168 r.2
Sch.2 r.34A.6, see *Taylor v Marshalls Food Group (No.2)* 1998 S.L.T. 1022 (1 Div), Lord Rodger L.P., Lord Allanbridge, Lord Coulsfield
Sch.2 r.34A.6, added: SI 1996/2168 r.2
Sch.2 r.35.2, applied: SI 1999/901 Art.5, Sch.
Sch.2 r.35.3, substituted: SI 1996/2168 r.2
Sch.2 r.35.3A, added: SI 1996/2168 r.2
Sch.2 r.36.4, amended: SI 1996/2168 r.2
Sch.2 r.36.6, revoked: SI 1996/2168 r.2

NO.

NO.

1994—cont.

1994—cont.

1443. Act of Sederunt (Rules of the Court of Session) 1994—*cont.*

Sch.2 r.36.7, amended: SI 1997/1050 r.2

Sch.2 r.37, see *McGee v Matthew Hall* 1996 S.L.T. 399 (OH)

Sch.2 r.37.2, amended: SI 1999/1386 r.2

Sch.2 r.37.4, amended: SI 1998/890 r.2

Sch.2 r.37.5A, added: SI 1998/890 r.2

Sch.2 Ch.38, amended: SI 1997/2692 r.3

Sch.2 Ch.38, applied: SI 1997/2692 r.5

Sch.2 r.38.4, amended: SI 1998/890 r.2

Sch.2 r.38.7A, added: SI 1997/2692 r.3

Sch.2 r.38.13, amended: SI 1997/2692 r.3

Sch.2 r.38.19, amended: SI 1997/2692 r.3

Sch.2 Ch.40, amended: SI 1997/2692 r.4

Sch.2 Ch.40, applied: SI 1997/2692 r.5

Sch.2 r.40, see *McInnes v Lawrence* 1996 S.C.L.R. 169 (IH)

Sch.2 r.40.1, amended: SI 1996/1756 para.2, SI 1996/2587 r.2

Sch.2 r.40.1, revoked (in part): SI 1996/1756 para.2

Sch.2 r.40.4, amended: SI 1996/2587 r.2

Sch.2 r.40.7A, added: SI 1997/2692 r.4

Sch.2 r.40.9, amended: SI 1997/2692 r.4

Sch.2 r.40.11, amended: SI 1997/2692 r.4

Sch.2 r.40.12, amended: SI 1996/1756 para.2

Sch.2 r.40.17, amended: SI 1997/2692 r.4

Sch.2 r.40.20, added: SI 1996/2587 r.2

Sch.2 Ch.41, applied: SI 1998/2637 r.3

Sch.2 Ch.41, substituted: SI 1998/2637 r.2

Sch.2 r.41.1, amended: SI 1996/1756 para.2

Sch.2 r.41.2, amended: SI 1996/1756 para.2

Sch.2 r.41.2, revoked (in part): SI 1996/1756 para.2

Sch.2 r.41.5, amended: SI 1996/1756 para.2

Sch.2 r.41.20, amended: SI 1996/1756 para.2

Sch.2 r.41.20, revoked (in part): SI 1996/1756 para.2

Sch.2 r.41.21, amended: SI 1996/1756 para.2

Sch.2 r.41.23, amended: SSI 1999/192 para.2

Sch.2 r.41.25, amended: SSI 1999/192 para.2

Sch.2 r.41.28, substituted: SI 1998/2637 r.2

Sch.2 r.41.29, substituted: SI 1998/2637 r.2

Sch.2 r.41.30, substituted: SI 1998/2637 r.2

Sch.2 r.41.31, substituted: SI 1998/2637 r.2

Sch.2 r.41.32, substituted: SI 1998/2637 r.2

Sch.2 r.41.33, substituted: SI 1998/2637 r.2

Sch.2 r.41.41, amended: SI 1997/1050 r.2

Sch.2 r.41.44, added: SI 1996/2168 r.2

Sch.2 r.41.45, added: SI 1996/2168 r.2

Sch.2 Ch.42, amended: SI 1998/2674 r.2, SSI 1999/166 para.2, Sch.

Sch.2 Ch.42, applied: SI 1998/2674 r.3, SSI 1999/166 para.3

Sch.2 r.42.1, see *Fane v Murray* 1996 S.C.L.R. 323 (IH)

Sch.2 r.42.1, amended: SI 1996/1756 para.2, SI 1998/890 r.2

Sch.2 r.42.4, amended: SI 1996/1756 para.2

Sch.2 r.42.11, revoked: SI 1998/2674 r.2

Sch.2 r.42.13, amended: SI 1996/1756 para.2, SI 1998/890 r.2

Sch.2 r.42.13, revoked (in part): SI 1996/1756 para.2

Sch.2 r.42.14, amended: SSI 1999/109 para.2

Sch.2 r.42.16, amended: SI 1996/237 Reg.2, Sch., SI 1996/754 r.2, SI 1997/1260 r.2, SI 1998/993 r.2, Sch., SI 1998/2674 r.2, Sch., SI 1999/187 r.2, Sch., SI 1999/615 r.2, Sch., SSI 1999/166 para.2, Sch.

Sch.2 Ch.43, revoked: SI 1996/2587 r.2

1443. Act of Sederunt (Rules of the Court of Session) 1994—*cont.*

Sch.2 Ch.43A, added: SI 1997/1527 r.2

Sch.2 r.43.15, applied: SI 1996/207 Sch.8 para.43, SI 1996/2890 Sch.4 para.47

Sch.2 r.43.29, added: SI 1996/2168 r.2

Sch.2 r.43.30, added: SI 1996/2168 r.2

Sch.2 r.43.31, added: SI 1996/2168 r.2

Sch.2 r.43A.1, added: SI 1997/1527 r.2

Sch.2 r.43A.2, added: SI 1997/1527 r.2

Sch.2 r.45A.1, added: SI 1996/2168 r.2

Sch.2 r.45A.2, added: SI 1996/2168 r.2

Sch.2 r.45A.3, added: SI 1996/2168 r.2

Sch.2 r.45A.4, added: SI 1996/2168 r.2

Sch.2 r.46.9, amended: SI 1996/1756 para.2

Sch.2 Ch.49, added: SI 1996/2587 r.2, SI 1997/1720 r.5

Sch.2 Ch.49, amended: SI 1996/2587 r.2

Sch.2 Ch.49, applied: SI 1996/125 Art.3

Sch.2 r.49.1, amended: SI 1996/2587 r.2

Sch.2 r.49.3, amended: SI 1996/2587 r.2

Sch.2 r.49.8, amended: SI 1996/1756 para.2, SI 1996/2587 r.2

Sch.2 r.49.8, revoked (in part): SI 1996/1756 para.2

Sch.2 r.49.10, amended: SI 1996/2587 r.2

Sch.2 r.49.11, amended: SI 1996/2587 r.2

Sch.2 r.49.15, substituted: SI 1996/2587 r.2

Sch.2 r.49.20, substituted: SI 1996/2587 r.2

Sch.2 r.49.21, revoked: SI 1996/2587 r.2

Sch.2 r.49.22, amended: SI 1996/2587 r.2

Sch.2 r.49.23, amended: SI 1996/1756 para.2, SI 1996/2587 r.2

Sch.2 r.49.23, revoked (in part): SI 1996/1756 para.2

Sch.2 r.49.25, amended: SI 1996/2587 r.2

Sch.2 r.49.26, amended: SI 1996/2587 r.2

Sch.2 r.49.27, amended: SI 1996/2587 r.2

Sch.2 r.49.27A, added: SSI 1999/109 para.2

Sch.2 r.49.28, amended: SI 1996/2587 r.2

Sch.2 r.49.31, amended: SI 1996/2587 r.2

Sch.2 r.49.35, amended: SI 1996/2587 r.2

Sch.2 r.49.36, amended: SI 1996/2587 r.2

Sch.2 r.49.37, revoked: SI 1996/2587 r.2

Sch.2 r.49.38, revoked: SI 1996/2587 r.2

Sch.2 r.49.39, revoked: SI 1996/2587 r.2

Sch.2 r.49.40, amended: SI 1997/1050 r.2

Sch.2 r.49.40, substituted: SI 1996/2587 r.2

Sch.2 r.49.41, amended: SI 1996/2587 r.2

Sch.2 r.49.42, amended: SI 1996/2587 r.2

Sch.2 r.49.49, amended: SI 1996/1756 para.2

Sch.2 r.49.53, amended: SI 1996/1756 para.2

Sch.2 r.49.58, substituted: SI 1996/2587 r.2

Sch.2 r.49.59, amended: SI 1996/2587 r.2

Sch.2 r.49.60, applied: SI 1999/901 Art.5, Sch.

Sch.2 r.49.60, revoked (in part): SI 1998/890 r.2

Sch.2 r.49.60, substituted: SI 1996/2587 r.2

Sch.2 r.49.61, amended: SI 1996/2587 r.2

Sch.2 r.49.62, revoked: SI 1996/2587 r.2

Sch.2 r.49.63, amended: SI 1996/2587 r.2

Sch.2 r.49.76, applied: SI 1997/688 Sch.1 Table

Sch.2 r.49.81, revoked (in part): SI 1996/1756 para.2

Sch.2 r.49.85, added: SI 1996/2587 r.2

Sch.2 r.49.86, added: SI 1996/2587 r.2

Sch.2 r.49.87, added: SI 1996/2587 r.2

Sch.2 r.49.88, added: SI 1996/2587 r.2

Sch.2 r.49.88, amended: SI 1997/1050 r.2

Sch.2 r.49.89, added: SI 1997/1720 r.5

Sch.2 r.50.2, amended: SI 1999/1386 r.2

Sch.2 r.50.2, revoked (in part): SI 1999/1386 r.2

Sch.2 r.50.3, revoked: SI 1999/1386 r.2

1994—cont.

1443. Act of Sederunt (Rules of the Court of Session) 1994—*cont.*

Sch.2 r.52.1, applied: SI 1999/901 Art.5, Sch.

Sch.2 Ch.53, see *Bell v Fiddes* 1996 S.L.T. 51 (OH)

Sch.2 r.53.2, see *Saunders, Petitioner* 1999 S.C. 564 (OH), Lord MacLean

Sch.2 Ch.55, applied: SI 1999/1785 r.3

Sch.2 r.55.1, amended: SI 1996/1756 para.2

Sch.2 r.55.1, revoked (in part): SI 1996/1756 para.2

Sch.2 r.55.2, amended: SI 1999/1785 r.2

Sch.2 r.55.2A, added: SI 1999/1785 r.2

Sch.2 r.55.3, amended: SI 1996/1756 para.2, SI 1999/1785 r.2

Sch.2 r.55.4, amended: SI 1999/1785 r.2

Sch.2 r.55.14, amended: SI 1999/1785 r.2

Sch.2 r.55.15, amended: SI 1999/1785 r.2

Sch.2 r.55.16, amended: SI 1999/1785 r.2

Sch.2 r.55.17, amended: SI 1996/1756 para.2

Sch.2 r.55.17, revoked (in part): SI 1996/1756 para.2

Sch.2 r.55.19, amended: SI 1999/1785 r.2

Sch.2 Ch.58, see *Bell v Fiddes* 1996 S.L.T. 51 (OH)

Sch.2 r.58.3, see *Saunders, Petitioner* 1999 S.C. 564 (OH), Lord MacLean

Sch.2 r.59.1, amended: SI 1996/1756 para.2, SI 1997/1050 r.2, SI 1998/890 r.2, SSI 1999/109 para.2

Sch.2 Ch.60, see *Bell v Fiddes* 1996 S.L.T. 51 (OH)

Sch.2 Ch.61, amended: SI 1997/1720 r.6

Sch.2 Ch.61, referred to: SI 1998/890 r.3

Sch.2 r.61.1, amended: SI 1997/1720 r.6

Sch.2 r.61.2, amended: SI 1998/890 r.3

Sch.2 r.61.2, substituted: SI 1997/1720 r.6

Sch.2 r.61.5, amended: SI 1997/1720 r.6

Sch.2 r.61.13, amended: SI 1997/1720 r.6

Sch.2 r.61.14, amended: SI 1997/1720 r.6

Sch.2 r.61.14, applied: SI 1997/688 Sch.1 Table

Sch.2 Ch.62, amended: SI 1999/1220 r.2

Sch.2 r.62.8, amended: SI 1996/2168 r.2

Sch.2 r.62.15, amended: SI 1996/2168 r.2

Sch.2 r.62.18, amended: SI 1998/2637 r.2, SI 1999/1281 r.2

Sch.2 r.62.22, amended: SI 1996/2168 r.2

Sch.2 r.62.32, amended: SI 1996/2168 r.2

Sch.2 r.62.37, amended: SI 1996/2168 r.2

Sch.2 r.62.40, amended: SI 1996/2168 r.2

Sch.2 r.62.41, amended: SI 1996/1756 para.2

Sch.2 r.62.46, amended: SI 1996/2168 r.2

Sch.2 r.62.47, amended: SI 1996/1756 para.2, SI 1996/2168 r.2, SI 1999/1220 r.2

Sch.2 r.62.47, revoked (in part): SI 1996/1756 para.2

Sch.2 r.62.48, amended: SI 1996/1756 para.2, SI 1996/2168 r.2, SI 1999/1220 r.2

Sch.2 r.62.48, revoked (in part): SI 1996/1756 para.2

Sch.2 r.62.49, amended: SI 1996/1756 para.2

Sch.2 r.62.50, amended: SI 1996/1756 para.2

Sch.2 r.62.51, amended: SI 1996/1756 para.2

Sch.2 r.62.51A, amended: SI 1999/1220 r.2

Sch.2 r.62.52, amended: SI 1996/1756 para.2, SI 1996/2168 r.2

Sch.2 r.62.53, amended: SI 1996/1756 para.2, SI 1996/2168 r.2

Sch.2 r.62.54, amended: SI 1996/1756 para.2

Sch.2 r.62.54, revoked (in part): SI 1996/1756 para.2

Sch.2 r.62.54, substituted: SI 1996/2168 r.2

1994—cont.

1443. Act of Sederunt (Rules of the Court of Session) 1994—*cont.*

Sch.2 r.62.58, amended: SI 1996/2168 r.2

Sch.2 r.62.61, added: SI 1996/2168 r.2

Sch.2 r.62.62, added: SI 1996/2168 r.2

Sch.2 r.62.63, added: SI 1996/2168 r.2

Sch.2 r.62.64, added: SI 1996/2168 r.2

Sch.2 r.62.65, added: SI 1996/2168 r.2

Sch.2 r.62.66, added: SI 1996/2168 r.2

Sch.2 r.63.10, amended: SI 1999/1386 r.2

Sch.2 r.63.10, applied: SI 1999/678 Sch.

Sch.2 r.65.1, amended: SI 1999/1282 r.2

Sch.2 r.65.2, amended: SI 1999/1281 r.2

Sch.2 r.65.3, amended: SI 1999/1281 r.2

Sch.2 r.66.3, revoked (in part): SI 1998/2637 r.2

Sch.2 Ch.67, amended: SI 1997/853 r.2

Sch.2 Ch.67, applied: SI 1997/853 r.4

Sch.2 r.67.1, amended: SI 1997/853 r.2

Sch.2 r.67.4, substituted: SI 1997/853 r.2

Sch.2 r.67.4A, added: SI 1997/853 r.2

Sch.2 r.67.5, amended: SI 1997/853 r.2

Sch.2 r.67.5A, added: SI 1997/853 r.2

Sch.2 r.67.6A, added: SI 1997/853 r.2

Sch.2 r.67.9, amended: SI 1997/853 r.2

Sch.2 r.67.11, amended: SI 1997/853 r.2

Sch.2 r.67.12, amended: SI 1997/853 r.2

Sch.2 r.67.13, amended: SI 1997/853 r.2

Sch.2 r.67.13A, added: SI 1997/853 r.2

Sch.2 r.67.14, amended: SI 1997/853 r.2

Sch.2 r.67.15A, added: SI 1997/853 r.2

Sch.2 r.67.17, substituted: SI 1997/853 r.2

Sch.2 r.67.18, amended: SI 1997/853 r.2

Sch.2 r.67.21, amended: SI 1997/853 r.2

Sch.2 r.67.24, amended: SI 1997/853 r.2, SI 1998/890 r.2

Sch.2 r.67.25, amended: SI 1997/853 r.2

Sch.2 r.67.25A, added: SI 1997/853 r.2

Sch.2 r.67.26, revoked: SI 1997/853 r.2

Sch.2 r.67.32, amended: SI 1997/853 r.2

Sch.2 r.68.2, amended: SI 1997/1050 r.2

Sch.2 r.69.1, amended: SI 1999/787 Art.97, Sch.8 para.3

Sch.2 r.69.5, amended: SI 1999/1386 r.2

Sch.2 r.69.9, amended: SI 1999/787 Art.97, Sch.8 para.3, SI 1999/1386 r.2

Sch.2 r.69.10, amended: SI 1999/787 Art.97, Sch.8 para.3

Sch.2 r.69.11, amended: SI 1999/1386 r.2

Sch.2 r.69.12, amended: SI 1999/1386 r.2

Sch.2 r.69.13, amended: SI 1999/1386 r.2

Sch.2 r.69.19, amended: SI 1999/787 Art.97, Sch.8 para.3, SI 1999/1386 r.2

Sch.2 r.69.20, amended: SI 1999/1386 r.2

Sch.2 r.69.21, amended: SI 1999/1386 r.2

Sch.2 r.69.23, amended: SI 1999/787 Art.97, Sch.8 para.3, SI 1999/1386 r.2

Sch.2 r.69.24, amended: SI 1999/787 Art.97, Sch.8 para.3, SI 1999/1386 r.2

Sch.2 r.69.25, amended: SI 1999/1386 r.2

Sch.2 r.69.26, amended: SI 1999/787 Art.97, Sch.8 para.3, SI 1999/1386 r.2

Sch.2 r.69.27, amended: SI 1999/787 Art.97, Sch.8 para.3

Sch.2 r.69.29, amended: SI 1999/787 Art.97, Sch.8 para.3, SI 1999/1386 r.2

Sch.2 r.69.30, amended: SI 1999/1386 r.2

Sch.2 r.70.1, amended: SI 1996/1756 para.2

Sch.2 r.70.5, amended: SI 1996/1756 para.2

Sch.2 r.70.5, revoked (in part): SI 1996/1756 para.2

Sch.2 r.70.6, amended: SI 1996/1756 para.2, SI 1998/890 r.2

NO.

1994—cont.

1443. Act of Sederunt (Rules of the Court of Session) 1994—*cont.*
Sch.2 r.70.8, amended: SI 1996/1756 para.2
Sch.2 r.70.9, amended: SI 1996/1756 para.2
Sch.2 r.70.9, revoked (in part): SI 1996/1756 para.2
Sch.2 r.70.10, amended: SI 1996/1756 para.2, SI 1998/890 r.2
Sch.2 r.70.12, amended: SI 1996/1756 para.2
Sch.2 r.70.13, amended: SI 1996/1756 para.2
Sch.2 Ch.71, amended: SI 1997/795 r.2
Sch.2 r.71.1, amended: SI 1997/795 r.2
Sch.2 r.71.2, amended: SI 1997/795 r.2
Sch.2 r.71.3, amended: SI 1997/795 r.2
Sch.2 r.71.4, amended: SI 1997/795 r.2
Sch.2 r.71.5, amended: SI 1997/795 r.2
Sch.2 r.71.6, amended: SI 1997/795 r.2
Sch.2 r.71.7, amended: SI 1997/795 r.2
Sch.2 r.71.8, amended: SI 1997/795 r.2
Sch.2 r.74.1, amended: SI 1996/1756 para.2
Sch.2 Ch.75, added: SI 1996/1756 para.2
Sch.2 Ch.75, amended: SI 1996/1756 para.2
Sch.2 r.75.1, amended: SI 1996/1756 para.2
Sch.2 r.75.4, amended: SI 1996/1756 para.2
Sch.2 r.75.5, added: SI 1996/1756 para.2
Sch.2 r.75.6, added: SI 1996/1756 para.2
Sch.2 r.75.7, added: SI 1996/1756 para.2
Sch.2 r.75.8, added: SI 1996/1756 para.2
Sch.2 Ch.76, amended: SI 1996/2168 r.2
Sch.2 r.76.1, amended: SI 1996/2168 r.2
Sch.2 r.76.3, amended: SI 1996/2168 r.2, SI 1999/1220 r.2
Sch.2 r.76.4, amended: SI 1996/2168 r.2, SI 1999/1220 r.2
Sch.2 r.76.5, amended: SI 1996/2168 r.2
Sch.2 r.76.6, amended: SI 1996/2168 r.2
Sch.2 r.76.7, amended: SI 1996/2168 r.2
Sch.2 r.76.8, amended: SI 1996/2168 r.2, SI 1998/890 r.2
Sch.2 r.76.9, amended: SI 1996/2168 r.2
Sch.2 r.76.14, amended: SI 1996/2168 r.2
Sch.2 r.76.15, amended: SI 1996/2168 r.2
Sch.2 r.76.16, amended: SI 1996/2168 r.2
Sch.2 r.76.17, amended: SI 1996/2168 r.2
Sch.2 r.76.18, revoked: SI 1996/2168 r.2
Sch.2 r.76.19, amended: SI 1996/2168 r.2
Sch.2 r.76.22, amended: SI 1996/2168 r.2
Sch.2 Ch.81, amended: SI 1997/854 r.2
Sch.2 Ch.81, applied: SI 1997/854 r.4
Sch.2 r.81.4, substituted: SI 1997/854 r.2
Sch.2 r.81.11, amended: SI 1997/854 r.2
Sch.2 r.81.13, revoked: SI 1997/854 r.2
Sch.2 r.81.18, amended: SI 1997/854 r.2
Sch.2 Annex, added: SI 1999/1281 r.2, Sch.2
Sch.2 Appendix, added: SI 1996/1756 para.2, Sch., SI 1996/2168 r.2, SI 1996/2587 r.2, SI 1997/853 r.3, Sch.1, Sch.2, SI 1997/1720 r.7, SI 1998/890 r.2, SI 1998/2637 r.2, Sch.
Sch.2 Appendix, amended: SI 1996/1756 para.2, SI 1996/2168 r.2, SI 1996/2587 r.2, SI 1997/853 r.3, SI 1997/854 r.3, SI 1997/1050 r.2, SI 1998/890 r.2, SI 1999/787 Art.97, Sch.8 para.3, SI 1999/1281 r.2, Sch.1, SI 1999/1345 r.2, SSI 1999/109 para.2, Sch.
Sch.2 Appendix, revoked (in part): SI 1996/1756 para.2, SI 1996/2769 r.2, SI 1996/2587 r.2, SI 1998/890 r.2
Sch.2 Appendix, substituted: SI 1996/1756 para.2, Sch., SI 1996/2168 r.2, SI 1996/2587 r.2, SI 1997/1050 r.2, Sch., SI 1998/2637 r.2, Sch.

NO.

1994—cont.

1444. Rules of the Air (Third Amendment) Regulations 1994
revoked: SI 1996/1393 Reg.3, Sch.2

1446. Trade Effluent (Asbestos) (Scotland) Regulations 1994
applied: SI 1999/901 Art.5, Sch.

1447. Diseases of Fish (Control) Regulations 1994
Reg.4, referred to: SI 1997/1881 Reg.3
Reg.5, referred to: SI 1997/1881 Reg.3
Reg.9, referred to: SI 1997/1881 Reg.3
Reg.10, referred to: SI 1997/1881 Reg.3

1448. Fish Health (Amendment) Regulations 1994
revoked: SI 1997/1881 Reg.24

1482. Road Traffic Act 1991 (Commencement No.11 and Transitional Provisions) Order 1994
Art.5, revoked: SI 1998/967 Art.3, Sch.

1484. Road Traffic Act 1991 (Commencement No.12 and Transitional Provisions) Order 1994
Art.3, revoked: SI 1998/967 Art.3, Sch.

1486. Flavourings in Food (Amendment) Regulations 1994
Reg.3, revoked: SI 1996/1499 Reg.49, Sch.9

1490. Road Traffic (Special Parking Area) (London Borough of Croydon) Order 1994
revoked: SI 1997/1342 Art.2
Sch., revoked: SI 1997/1342 Art.2

1492. Road Traffic (Special Parking Area) (London Borough of Haringey) Order 1994
Sch. para.3, substituted: SI 1997/3057 Art.2, Sch. para.1
Sch. para.64, revoked: SI 1997/3057 Art.2, Sch. para.2
Sch. para.76, revoked: SI 1997/3057 Art.2, Sch. para.3
Sch. para.77, revoked: SI 1997/3057 Art.2, Sch. para.3
Sch. para.78, revoked: SI 1997/3057 Art.2, Sch. para.3
Sch. para.79, revoked: SI 1997/3057 Art.2, Sch. para.3
Sch. para.80, revoked: SI 1997/3057 Art.2, Sch. para.3
Sch. para.81, revoked: SI 1997/3057 Art.2, Sch. para.3
Sch. para.82, revoked: SI 1997/3057 Art.2, Sch. para.3
Sch. para.83, revoked: SI 1997/3057 Art.2, Sch. para.3
Sch. para.84, revoked: SI 1997/3057 Art.2, Sch. para.3
Sch. para.85, revoked: SI 1997/3057 Art.2, Sch. para.3
Sch. para.86, revoked: SI 1997/3057 Art.2, Sch. para.3
Sch. para.87, revoked: SI 1997/3057 Art.2, Sch. para.3
Sch. para.88, revoked: SI 1997/3057 Art.2, Sch. para.3
Sch. para.89, revoked: SI 1997/3057 Art.2, Sch. para.3
Sch. para.90, revoked: SI 1997/3057 Art.2, Sch. para.3
Sch. para.91, revoked: SI 1997/3057 Art.2, Sch. para.3
Sch. para.92, revoked: SI 1997/3057 Art.2, Sch. para.3
Sch. para.93, revoked: SI 1997/3057 Art.2, Sch. para.3
Sch. para.94, revoked: SI 1997/3057 Art.2, Sch. para.3

NO.

1492. Road Traffic (Special Parking Area) (London Borough of Haringey) Order 1994—*cont.*
Sch. para.95, revoked: SI 1997/3057 Art.2, Sch. para.3
Sch. para.96, revoked: SI 1997/3057 Art.2, Sch. para.3
Sch. para.97, revoked: SI 1997/3057 Art.2, Sch. para.3
Sch. para.98, revoked: SI 1997/3057 Art.2, Sch. para.3
Sch. para.99, revoked: SI 1997/3057 Art.2, Sch. para.3
Sch. para.100, revoked: SI 1997/3057 Art.2, Sch. para.3
Sch. para.101, revoked: SI 1997/3057 Art.2, Sch. para.3
Sch. para.102, revoked: SI 1997/3057 Art.2, Sch. para.3
Sch. para.103, revoked: SI 1997/3057 Art.2, Sch. para.3
Sch. para.104, revoked: SI 1997/3057 Art.2, Sch. para.3
Sch. para.105, revoked: SI 1997/3057 Art.2, Sch. para.3
Sch. para.106, revoked: SI 1997/3057 Art.2, Sch. para.3
Sch. para.107, revoked: SI 1997/3057 Art.2, Sch. para.3
Sch. para.108, revoked: SI 1997/3057 Art.2, Sch. para.3
Sch. para.109, revoked: SI 1997/3057 Art.2, Sch. para.3
Sch. para.110, revoked: SI 1997/3057 Art.2, Sch. para.3
Sch. para.111, revoked: SI 1997/3057 Art.2, Sch. para.3
Sch. para.149, added: SI 1997/3057 Art.2, Sch. para.4
Sch. para.150, added: SI 1997/3057 Art.2, Sch. para.4
Sch. para.151, added: SI 1997/3057 Art.2, Sch. para.4
Sch. para.152, added: SI 1997/3057 Art.2, Sch. para.4
Sch. para.153, added: SI 1997/3057 Art.2, Sch. para.4
Sch. para.154, added: SI 1997/3057 Art.2, Sch. para.4
Sch. para.155, added: SI 1997/3057 Art.2, Sch. para.4
Sch. para.156, added: SI 1997/3057 Art.2, Sch. para.4
Sch. para.157, added: SI 1997/3057 Art.2, Sch. para.4
Sch. para.158, added: SI 1997/3057 Art.2, Sch. para.4
Sch. para.159, added: SI 1997/3057 Art.2, Sch. para.4
Sch. para.160, added: SI 1997/3057 Art.2, Sch. para.4
Sch. para.161, added: SI 1997/3057 Art.2, Sch. para.4
Sch. para.162, added: SI 1997/3057 Art.2, Sch. para.4
Sch. para.163, added: SI 1997/3057 Art.2, Sch. para.4
Sch. para.164, added: SI 1997/3057 Art.2, Sch. para.4
Sch. para.165, added: SI 1997/3057 Art.2, Sch. para.4
Sch. para.166, added: SI 1997/3057 Art.2, Sch. para.4

NO.

1492. Road Traffic (Special Parking Area) (London Borough of Haringey) Order 1994—*cont.*
Sch. para.167, added: SI 1997/3057 Art.2, Sch. para.4
Sch. para.168, added: SI 1997/3057 Art.2, Sch. para.4
Sch. para.169, added: SI 1997/3057 Art.2, Sch. para.4

1497. Road Traffic (Special Parking Area) (Royal Borough of Kingston upon Thames) Order 1994
revoked: SI 1996/3038 Art.2, Sch.1
Sch. para.10A, added: SI 1996/1110 Art.2
Sch. para.10A, revoked: SI 1996/3038 Art.2, Sch.1
Sch. para.25A, added: SI 1996/1110 Art.2
Sch. para.25A, revoked: SI 1996/3038 Art.2, Sch.1

1504. Road Traffic (Special Parking Area) (City of Westminster) Order 1994
Sch. Part II, amended: SI 1997/1369 Art.2
Sch. para.181A, added: SI 1996/2284 Art.2
Sch. para.191A, added: SI 1996/2284 Art.2
Sch. para.192A, added: SI 1996/2284 Art.2
Sch. para.193A, added: SI 1996/2284 Art.2

1506. Road Traffic (Special Parking Area) (London Borough of Newham) Order 1994
Sch. para.5, substituted: SI 1996/1112 Art.2, Sch para.1
Sch. para.6, substituted: SI 1996/1112 Art.2, Sch para.1
Sch. para.7, substituted: SI 1996/1112 Art.2, Sch para.1
Sch. para.8, substituted: SI 1996/1112 Art.2, Sch para.1
Sch. para.9, substituted: SI 1996/1112 Art.2, Sch para.1
Sch. para.10, substituted: SI 1996/1112 Art.2, Sch para.1
Sch. para.10A, substituted: SI 1996/1112 Art.2, Sch para.1
Sch. para.11, substituted: SI 1996/1112 Art.2, Sch para.1
Sch. para.12, substituted: SI 1996/1112 Art.2, Sch para.1
Sch. para.13, substituted: SI 1996/1112 Art.2, Sch para.1
Sch. para.14, substituted: SI 1996/1112 Art.2, Sch para.1
Sch. para.15, substituted: SI 1996/1112 Art.2, Sch para.1
Sch. para.16, substituted: SI 1996/1112 Art.2, Sch para.1
Sch. para.17, substituted: SI 1996/1112 Art.2, Sch para.1
Sch. para.18, substituted: SI 1996/1112 Art.2, Sch para.1
Sch. para.19, substituted: SI 1996/1112 Art.2, Sch para.1
Sch. para.20, substituted: SI 1996/1112 Art.2, Sch para.1
Sch. para.21, substituted: SI 1996/1112 Art.2, Sch para.1
Sch. para.22, substituted: SI 1996/1112 Art.2, Sch para.1
Sch. para.23, revoked: SI 1996/1112 Art.2, Sch para.2
Sch. para.24, substituted: SI 1996/1112 Art.2, Sch para.3
Sch. para.25, substituted: SI 1996/1112 Art.2, Sch para.3
Sch. para.26, substituted: SI 1996/1112 Art.2, Sch para.3

NO.

NO.

1994—cont.

1994—cont.

1506. Road Traffic (Special Parking Area) (London Borough of Newham) Order 1994—*cont.*
Sch. para.27, substituted: SI 1996/1112 Art.2, Sch para.3
Sch. para.28, substituted: SI 1996/1112 Art.2, Sch para.3
Sch. para.28A, substituted: SI 1996/1112 Art.2, Sch para.3
Sch. para.29, substituted: SI 1996/1112 Art.2, Sch para.3
Sch. para.29A, substituted: SI 1996/1112 Art.2, Sch para.3
Sch. para.30, substituted: SI 1996/1112 Art.2, Sch para.3
Sch. para.31, substituted: SI 1996/1112 Art.2, Sch para.3
Sch. para.32, revoked: SI 1996/1112 Art.2, Sch para.4
Sch. para.33, substituted: SI 1996/1112 Art.2, Sch para.5
Sch. para.34, substituted: SI 1996/1112 Art.2, Sch para.5
Sch. para.35, substituted: SI 1996/1112 Art.2, Sch para.5
Sch. para.36, substituted: SI 1996/1112 Art.2, Sch para.5
Sch. para.37, substituted: SI 1996/1112 Art.2, Sch para.5
Sch. para.38, substituted: SI 1996/1112 Art.2, Sch para.5
Sch. para.39, substituted: SI 1996/1112 Art.2, Sch para.5
Sch. para.40, substituted: SI 1996/1112 Art.2, Sch para.5
Sch. para.41, revoked: SI 1996/1112 Art.2, Sch para.6
Sch. para.42, substituted: SI 1996/1112 Art.2, Sch para.7
Sch. para.43, substituted: SI 1996/1112 Art.2, Sch para.7
Sch. para.43A, substituted: SI 1996/1112 Art.2, Sch para.7
Sch. para.44, substituted: SI 1996/1112 Art.2, Sch para.7
Sch. para.45, substituted: SI 1996/1112 Art.2, Sch para.7
Sch. para.46, substituted: SI 1996/1112 Art.2, Sch para.7
Sch. para.46A, substituted: SI 1996/1112 Art.2, Sch para.7
Sch. para.47, substituted: SI 1996/1112 Art.2, Sch para.7
Sch. para.48, substituted: SI 1996/1112 Art.2, Sch para.7
Sch. para.49, substituted: SI 1996/1112 Art.2, Sch para.7
Sch. para.50, substituted: SI 1996/1112 Art.2, Sch para.7
Sch. para.51, substituted: SI 1996/1112 Art.2, Sch para.7
Sch. para.52, substituted: SI 1996/1112 Art.2, Sch para.7
Sch. para.52A, substituted: SI 1996/1112 Art.2, Sch para.7
Sch. para.52B, substituted: SI 1996/1112 Art.2, Sch para.7

1507. Road Traffic (Special Parking Area) (London Borough of Sutton) Order 1994
revoked: SI 1998/1134 Art.2, Sch.1
Art.3, revoked: SI 1998/1134 Art.2, Sch.1

1509. Road Traffic (Special Parking Area) (London Borough of Redbridge) Order 1994
Sch. para.78A, added: SI 1998/3238 Art.2
Sch. para.79, revoked: SI 1996/3059 Art.2

1515. Insurance Companies (Accounts and Statements) (Amendment) Regulations 1994
revoked: SI 1996/943 Reg.35, Sch.7

1516. Insurance Companies Regulations 1994
applied: SI 1996/942 Reg.15, SI 1996/943 Reg.19, Reg.20
Part VIII, applied: SI 1996/943 Reg.4, Sch.6 para.8
Part IX, applied: SI 1996/943 Reg.4, Sch.6 para.8
Reg.2, amended: SI 1996/944 Reg.6
Reg.7, applied: SI 1996/943 Sch.6 para.3
Reg.9, applied: SI 1998/2842 Art.2, Sch. para.68
Reg.12, applied: SI 1998/2842 Art.2, Sch. para.68
Reg.13, applied: SI 1998/2842 Art.2, Sch. para.68
Reg.14, applied: SI 1998/2842 Art.2, Sch. para.68
Reg.23, amended: SI 1996/942 Reg.2
Reg.23, applied: SI 1996/943 Sch.6 para.10
Reg.27, applied: SI 1996/943 Sch.2 para.27, Sch.6 para.1
Reg.28, applied: SI 1996/943 Sch.6 para.1
Reg.29, applied: SI 1996/943 Sch.6 para.1
Reg.30, applied: SI 1996/943 Sch.6 para.1
Reg.31, applied: SI 1996/943 Sch.6 para.1
Reg.32, applied: SI 1996/943 Sch.6 para.1
Reg.32, referred to: SI 1996/943 Sch.2 para.27
Reg.44, amended: SI 1996/942 Reg.3, SI 1998/2996 Reg.2
Reg.45, applied: SI 1996/943 Reg.4, Sch.4 para.6
Reg.48, amended: SI 1996/942 Reg.5
Reg.51, amended: SI 1996/942 Reg.6
Reg.52, amended: SI 1996/942 Reg.7
Reg.55, amended: SI 1996/942 Reg.8
Reg.55, referred to: SI 1996/943 Reg.23
Reg.56, amended: SI 1996/942 Reg.9
Reg.56, referred to: SI 1996/943 Reg.23
Reg.59, applied: SI 1996/943 Reg.4
Reg.60, amended: SI 1996/942 Reg.10
Reg.61, amended: SI 1996/942 Reg.11
Reg.61, applied: SI 1996/943 Sch.1 para.12
Reg.64, applied: SI 1996/943 Sch.4 para.3, Sch.4 para.6
Reg.65, applied: SI 1996/943 Sch.4 para.6
Reg.66, applied: SI 1996/943 Sch.4 para.8
Reg.67, applied: SI 1996/943 Sch.4 para.8
Reg.68, applied: SI 1996/943 Sch.4 para.6, Sch.4 para.8
Reg.69, applied: SI 1996/943 Sch.4 para.8, Sch.4 para.21
Reg.70, applied: SI 1996/943 Sch.4 para.8
Reg.71, applied: SI 1996/943 Sch.4 para.8, Sch.4 para.9
Reg.72, applied: SI 1996/943 Sch.4 para.8
Reg.73, applied: SI 1996/943 Sch.4 para.6, Sch.4 para.8
Reg.74, applied: SI 1996/943 Sch.4 para.8
Reg.75, applied: SI 1996/943 Sch.4 para.7, Sch.4 para.8
Reg.76, applied: SI 1996/946 Sch.2 para.2, SI 1996/2991 Reg.13
Reg.76, revoked: SI 1996/946 Reg.14
Reg.77, applied: SI 1996/946 Sch.2 para.2
Reg.77, revoked: SI 1996/946 Reg.14

1994—cont.

1516. Insurance Companies Regulations 1994— cont.

Reg.78, applied: SI 1996/946 Sch.2 para.2, SI 1996/2991 Reg.13

Reg.78, revoked: SI 1996/946 Reg.14

Reg.80, applied: SI 1998/2842 Art.2, Sch. para.68

Reg.81, applied: SI 1998/2842 Art.2, Sch. para.68

Sch.3, applied: SI 1996/943 Sch.1 para.10

Sch.3, referred to: SI 1998/2842 Art.2, Sch. para.67

Sch.3 para.1, amended: SI 1996/942 Reg.12

Sch.4, applied: SI 1996/943 Sch.1 para.10

Sch.4, referred to: SI 1998/2842 Art.2, Sch. para.67

Sch.5, applied: SI 1996/943 Sch.1 para.10

Sch.10 Part I, applied: SI 1996/943 Sch.4 para.5

Sch.10 para.1, substituted: SI 1996/942 Reg.13

Sch.10 para.2, substituted: SI 1996/942 Reg.13

Sch.10 para.15, amended: SI 1996/942 Reg.13

Sch.10 para.15, referred to: SI 1996/943 Reg.23

Sch.10 para.15A, added: SI 1996/942 Reg.13

Sch.10 para.16, amended: SI 1996/942 Reg.13

Sch.12 Part I, amended: SI 1996/942 Reg.14

Sch.12 Part I, applied: SI 1996/943 Sch.1 para.11

Sch.12 Part II, amended: SI 1996/942 Reg.14

Sch.14, applied: SI 1996/946 Sch.2 para.2, SI 1996/2991 Reg.13

Sch.14, revoked: SI 1996/946 Reg.14

1519. Traffic Signs Regulations and General Directions 1994

applied: SI 1996/1786 Reg.9, SI 1996/2714 Art.54, SI 1997/1266 Art.42, SI 1997/2400 Reg.7, Reg.16, SI 1998/1448 Reg.6, SI 1998/1936 Art.46, SI 1999/1750 Art.2, Sch.1

Part I, applied: SI 1997/3053 Reg.5, SI 1999/1025 Reg.6, SI 1999/2359 Reg.2

Part I, referred to: SI 1999/1187 Reg.2

Part I Reg.4, referred to: SI 1998/883 Art.4

Part I Reg.33, see *Griffin v Mersey Regional Ambulance Service* [1998] P.I.Q.R. P34 (CA), Simon Brown, L.J.

Part I Reg.34, see *Griffin v Mersey Regional Ambulance Service* [1998] P.I.Q.R. P34 (CA), Simon Brown, L.J.

Part I Reg.41, applied: SI 1997/3053 Reg.17

Part I Reg.44, applied: SI 1997/3053 Reg.9, Reg.11

Part I Sch.2, applied: SI 1997/2400 Reg.9, Dir.2, SI 1997/3053 Reg.8

Part I Sch.4, applied: SI 1997/2400 Reg.9

Part I Sch.6, applied: SI 1996/1459 Art.3, SI 1996/1463 Art.3, SI 1997/2400 Reg.9, Sch.1 para.10, Sch.4 Part I

Part I Sch.8, applied: SI 1997/2400 Sch.2 para.3, Sch.3 para.2

Part I Sch.9, applied: SI 1997/2400 Sch.2 para.4

Part I Sch.12, applied: SI 1997/3053 Reg.11

Part I Sch.17, applied: SI 1997/3053 Reg.8

Part II Dir.4, applied: SI 1996/1088 Art.8, SI 1996/1163 Art.8, SI 1996/1459 Art.3, SI 1996/1463 Art.3

Part II Dir.4, referred to: SI 1996/41 Art.8, SI 1996/2165 Art.3

Part II Dir.14A, added: SI 1999/1723 Dir.2

Part II Dir.26, see *McKenzie v DPP* [1997] R.T.R. 175 (QBD), Newman, J.

Part II Dir.49, applied: SI 1999/672 Art.2, Sch.1

1994—cont.

1529. Cosmetic Products (Safety) (Amendment) Regulations 1994

revoked: SI 1996/2925 Sch.9

1531. Medicines (Medicated Animal Feedingstuffs) (Amendment) Regulations 1994

revoked: SI 1998/1048 Reg.2, Sch.1

1533. Reservoirs (Panels of Civil Engineers) (Application Fees) (Amendment) Regulations 1994

revoked: SI 1998/2403 Reg.3

1570. Motor Vehicles (EC Type Approval) (Amendment) (No.2) Regulations 1994

revoked: SI 1998/2051 Reg.2, Sch.3

1607. Central Scotland Healthcare National Health Service Trust (Establishment) Order 1994

revoked: SI 1999/1070 Art.2, Sch.2

1610. Feeding Stuffs (Sampling and Analysis) (Amendment) Regulations 1994

revoked: SI 1999/1663 Reg.10

1623. Employment Tribunals Extension of Jurisdiction (England and Wales) Order 1994

Art.3, see *Sarker v South Tees Acute Hospitals NHS Trust* [1997] I.C.R. 673 (EAT), Keene, J.

1632. Export of Goods (Control) Order 1994 (Amendment) Order 1994

Art.2, amended: SI 1996/2663 Art.3, Sch.2

1643. Visiting Forces and International Headquarters (Application of Law) (Amendment) Order 1994

revoked: SI 1999/1736 Art.19, Sch.9

1644. Confiscation of the Proceeds of Drug Trafficking (Designated Countries and Territories) (Scotland) Amendment Order 1994

revoked: SI 1999/673 Art.11

1645. Criminal Justice (International Co-operation) Act 1990 (Enforcement of Overseas Forfeiture Orders) (Scotland) Amendment Order 1994

revoked: SI 1999/675 Art.11

1646. Social Security (Cyprus) Order 1994

Sch., amended: SI 1996/1928 Art.2, Sch.1

1662. European Parliamentary (United Kingdom Representatives) Pensions (Consolidation and Amendment) Order 1994

Art.6, applied: SI 1996/1493 Art.7, Sch. para.6

Art.6, substituted: SI 1996/1493 Art.3

Art.7, amended: SI 1996/1493 Art.4

Art.16, amended: SI 1996/1493 Art.6

Art.16, applied: SI 1996/1493 Art.7

Art.17, applied: SI 1996/1493 Art.7

Art.30A, added: SI 1997/1291 Art.3

Sch.7 para.8, applied: SI 1996/1493 Sch. para.6

1680. Sea Fishing (Enforcement of Community Conservation Measures) (Amendment) (No.6) Order 1994

revoked: SI 1997/1949 Art.16, Sch.2

1696. Insurance Companies (Third Insurance Directives) Regulations 1994

Sch.8 para.8, revoked: 1998 c.29 Sch.16 Part II

Sch.8 para.21, revoked: 1996 c.22 Sch.7 Part II

1697. Education (Amount to follow Permanently Excluded Pupil) Regulations 1994

revoked: SI 1997/680 Reg.4

1701. Organic Aid (Scotland) Regulations 1994

applied: SI 1996/3083 Reg.2

referred to: SSI 1999/107 Reg.3

Reg.2, amended: SI 1996/3083 Reg.3, SSI 1999/107 Reg.4

Reg.4, amended: SI 1996/3083 Reg.4

Reg.6, amended: SI 1996/3083 Reg.5

Reg.7, amended: SI 1996/3083 Reg.6

NO.

1994—cont.

1701. Organic Aid (Scotland) Regulations 1994— *cont.*
Reg.9, amended: SI 1996/3083 Reg.7
Reg.10, amended: SSI 1999/107 Reg.5
Reg.10, substituted: SI 1996/3083 Reg.8
Reg.12, amended: SI 1996/3083 Reg.9
Reg.12A, added: SI 1996/3083 Reg.10
Reg.12B, added: SI 1996/3083 Reg.10
Sch., substituted: SSI 1999/107 Reg.6, Sch.
Sch. para.4, revoked: SI 1996/3083 Reg.11

1715. Duncan of Jordanstone College of Art (Closure) (Scotland) Regulations 1994
Sch. para.1, revoked: SI 1998/192 Reg.52, Sch.2

1721. Organic Farming (Aid) Regulations 1994
applied: SI 1997/2844 Sch.3 Part I, SI 1999/590 Reg.9, Reg.13, SI 1999/672 Art.2, Sch.1, SI 1999/2611 Reg.9, Reg.13, Reg.22
referred to: SI 1999/590 Reg.13, Reg.21, SI 1999/2611 Reg.13
Reg.2, amended: SI 1996/3109 Reg.2, SI 1998/1606 Reg.4
Reg.3, amended: SI 1998/1606 Reg.5
Reg.4, amended: SI 1996/3109 Reg.2
Reg.5, amended: SI 1996/3109 Reg.2
Reg.5, applied: SI 1999/2611 Reg.13
Reg.5, referred to: SI 1999/590 Reg.13
Reg.6, amended: SI 1996/3109 Reg.2
Reg.7, amended: SI 1996/3109 Reg.2
Reg.8, amended: SI 1996/3109 Reg.2
Reg.9, substituted: SI 1996/3109 Reg.2, SI 1998/1606 Reg.6
Reg.11, substituted: SI 1996/3109 Reg.2
Reg.11A, added: SI 1996/3109 Reg.2
Reg.11B, added: SI 1996/3109 Reg.2

1729. Nitrate Sensitive Areas Regulations 1994
applied: SI 1996/3142 Reg.6, Reg.10, SI 1997/2844 Sch.3 Part I, Sch.4 para.3, SI 1998/2138 Reg.2
Reg.2, amended: SI 1996/3105 Reg.2, SI 1997/990 Reg.2
Reg.4, amended: SI 1996/3105 Reg.2
Reg.5, amended: SI 1998/2138 Reg.6
Reg.7, amended: SI 1998/2138 Reg.7
Reg.7, applied: SI 1998/2138 Reg.2
Reg.8, amended: SI 1998/2138 Reg.8
Reg.11, amended: SI 1996/3105 Reg.2, SI 1998/2138 Reg.9
Reg.12, amended: SI 1996/3105 Reg.2
Reg.13, amended: SI 1996/3105 Reg.2
Reg.15, substituted: SI 1996/3105 Reg.2
Reg.15A, added: SI 1996/3105 Reg.2
Reg.15B, added: SI 1996/3105 Reg.2
Sch.2, amended: SI 1998/2138 Reg.10
Sch.3, amended: SI 1998/2138 Reg.11
Sch.4, amended: SI 1998/2138 Reg.12
Sch.5, amended: SI 1998/2138 Reg.13
Sch.6, amended: SI 1998/2138 Reg.14
Sch.6 para.4, amended: SI 1998/79 Reg.2
Sch.6 para.6B, amended: SI 1997/990 Reg.2, SI 1998/79 Reg.2

1734. Aeroplane Noise (Limitation on Operation of Aeroplanes) (Amendment) Regulations 1994
revoked: SI 1999/1452 Reg.2

1737. Aircraft Operators (Accounts and Records) Regulations 1994
Reg.9, added: SI 1998/63 Reg.2
Reg.10, added: SI 1998/63 Reg.2
Reg.11, added: SI 1998/63 Reg.2
Reg.12, added: SI 1998/63 Reg.2
Reg.13, added: SI 1998/63 Reg.2

NO.

1994—cont.

1737. Aircraft Operators (Accounts and Records) Regulations 1994—*cont.*
Reg.14, added: SI 1998/63 Reg.2
Reg.15, added: SI 1998/63 Reg.2
Reg.16, added: SI 1998/63 Reg.2

1748. Race Relations (Interest on Awards) Regulations 1994
revoked: SI 1996/2803 Reg.1

1751. Protected Rights (Transfer Payment) Amendment Regulations 1994
revoked: SI 1996/1461 Reg.7, Sch.1

1757. Drug Trafficking Offences Act 1986 (Crown Servants and Regulators etc.) Regulations 1994
Reg.4, amended: SI 1998/1129 Art.2, Sch.1 para.16

1758. Prevention of Terrorism (Temporary Provisions) Act 1989 (Crown Servants and Regulators etc.) Regulations 1994
Reg.4, amended: SI 1998/1129 Art.2, Sch.1 para.17

1760. Northern Ireland (Emergency Provisions) Act 1991 (Crown Servants and Regulators etc.) Regulations 1994
Reg.4, amended: SI 1998/1129 Art.2, Sch.1 para.18

1761. Wirral Tramway Light Railway Order 1994
applied: SI 1999/1306 Art.22, Sch.1
Art.22, amended: SI 1996/362 Art.5, Sch.4

1769. Act of Adjournal (Consolidation Amendment) (Miscellaneous) 1994
revoked: SI 1996/513 Sch.2 r.3, Sch.3

1774. Insurance Premium Tax Regulations 1994
Part IVA, added: SI 1998/60 Reg.2
Reg.2, amended: SI 1997/1157 Reg.3
Reg.4A, added: SI 1997/1157 Reg.4
Reg.5, amended: SI 1997/1157 Reg.5
Reg.6A, added: SI 1997/1157 Reg.6
Reg.11, amended: SI 1997/1157 Reg.7
Reg.16, amended: SI 1997/1157 Reg.8
Reg.17, amended: SI 1997/1157 Reg.9
Reg.18, amended: SI 1997/1157 Reg.10
Reg.19, amended: SI 1997/1157 Reg.11
Reg.19A, added: SI 1998/60 Reg.2
Reg.19B, added: SI 1998/60 Reg.2
Reg.19C, added: SI 1998/60 Reg.2
Reg.19D, added: SI 1998/60 Reg.2
Reg.19E, added: SI 1998/60 Reg.2
Reg.19F, added: SI 1998/60 Reg.2
Reg.19G, added: SI 1998/60 Reg.2
Reg.19H, added: SI 1998/60 Reg.2
Reg.29, amended: SI 1997/1157 Reg.12
Reg.30, amended: SI 1997/1157 Reg.13
Reg.31, amended: SI 1997/1157 Reg.14
Reg.42, amended: SI 1996/2099 Reg.4
Reg.42, revoked: SI 1997/1431 Reg.3, Sch.3
Reg.A42, added: SI 1996/2099 Reg.3
Reg.43, amended: SI 1996/2099 Reg.4
Sch.1 Form 1, substituted: SI 1997/1157 Reg.15, Sch.
Sch.1 Form 4, substituted: SI 1997/1157 Reg.15, Sch.
Sch.1 Form 5, substituted: SI 1997/1157 Reg.15, Sch.
Sch.1 Form 6, substituted: SI 1997/1157 Reg.15, Sch.

1778. Lerwick Harbour Revision Order 1994
revoked: SI 1999/1170 Art.24

1806. Notification of Existing Substances (Enforcement) Regulations 1994
Reg.4, amended: SI 1996/1373 Art.2
Reg.5, amended: SI 1996/1373 Art.2

NO.

1806. **Notification of Existing Substances (Enforcement) Regulations 1994**—*cont.*
Reg.7, amended: SI 1996/1373 Art.2

1807. **Income-related Benefits Schemes (Miscellaneous Amendments) (No.3) Regulations 1994**
see *Nessa v Chief Adjudication Officer* [1998] 2 All E.R. 728 (CA), Sir Christopher Staughton; see *Nessa v Chief Adjudication Officer* [1999] 1 W.L.R. 1937 (HL), Lord Slynn of Hadley

1811. **Special Commissioners (Jurisdiction and Procedure) Regulations 1994**
applied: 1997 c.58 Sch.2 para.11
Reg.2, amended: SI 1999/3292 Reg.3
Reg.18, amended: SI 1999/3292 Reg.4
Reg.22, amended: SI 1999/3292 Reg.5
Reg.23, substituted: SI 1999/3292 Reg.6

1812. **General Commissioners (Jurisdiction and Procedure) Regulations 1994**
applied: SI 1999/3219 Reg.8
Reg.10, see *Johnson v Blackpool General Commissioners* [1997] S.T.C. 1202 (CA), Morritt, L.J.; see *McKinney (Inspector of Taxes) v Hagans Caravans (Manufacturing) Ltd* [1997] S.T.C. 1023 (CA (NI)), Carswell, L.C.J; see *Phipps v Income Tax General Commissioners for New Forest West* [1997] S.T.C. 797 (Ch D), Lightman, J.
Reg.16, amended: SI 1999/3293 Reg.3
Reg.18, amended: SI 1999/3293 Reg.4
Reg.19, substituted: SI 1999/3293 Reg.5
Reg.20, amended: SI 1999/3293 Reg.6
Reg.22, see *McKinney (Inspector of Taxes) v Hagans Caravans (Manufacturing) Ltd* [1997] S.T.C. 1023 (CA (NI)), Carswell, L.C.J.

1814. **Education (National Curriculum) (Foundation Subjects at Key Stage 4) Order 1994**
revoked: 1996 c.56 Sch.38 Part III

1819. **Insurance Premium Tax (Prescribed Rates of Interest) Order 1994**
Art.2, amended: SI 1996/166 Art.2

1820. **Air Passenger Duty (Prescribed Rates of Interest) (Amendment) Order 1994**
Art.2, amended: SI 1996/164 Art.2

1831. **Authorities for London Post-Graduate Teaching Hospitals (Abolition) Order 1994**
Art.1, revoked (in part): SI 1996/511 Art.11
Art.2, revoked (in part): SI 1996/511 Art.11

1836. **Offshore Installations (Safety Zones) (No.2) Order 1994**
revoked: SI 1997/735 Art.3, Sch.2

1838. **Passenger and Goods Vehicles (Recording Equipment) Regulations 1994**
revoked: SI 1996/941 Reg.2

1862. **Motor Vehicles (Driving Licences) (Amendment) (No.2) Regulations 1994**
revoked: SI 1996/2824 Reg.2, Sch.1

1882. **Statutory Maternity Pay (Compensation of Employers) and Miscellaneous Amendment Regulations 1994**
Reg.3, amended: SI 1996/668 Reg.2, SI 1997/574 Reg.2, SI 1998/522 Reg.2, SI 1999/363 Reg.2
Reg.3, applied: 1999 c.2 s.1, Sch.2
Reg.6, applied: 1999 c.2 s.1, Sch.2

1885. **Local Authorities (Charges for Land Searches) Regulations 1994**
Reg.1, amended: SI 1996/525 Sch para.17

1886. **Gas Safety (Installation and Use) Regulations 1994**
Reg.1, amended: SI 1996/550 Art.3
Reg.1, revoked: SI 1998/2451 Reg.41

NO.

1886. **Gas Safety (Installation and Use) Regulations 1994**—*cont.*
Reg.2, amended: SI 1996/252 Art.2, Sch., SI 1996/550 Art.4, Art.5, Art.6, Art.7
Reg.2, applied: SI 1996/551 Sch.3 Part I para.3
Reg.2, revoked: SI 1998/2451 Reg.41
Reg.3, amended: SI 1996/550 Art.8, Art.9
Reg.3, revoked: SI 1998/2451 Reg.41
Reg.6, amended: SI 1996/550 Art.10
Reg.6, revoked: SI 1998/2451 Reg.41
Reg.8, amended: SI 1996/550 Art.11
Reg.8, revoked: SI 1998/2451 Reg.41
Reg.9, amended: SI 1996/550 Art.12
Reg.9, revoked: SI 1998/2451 Reg.41
Reg.11, amended: SI 1996/550 Art.13
Reg.11, revoked: SI 1998/2451 Reg.41
Reg.14, amended: SI 1996/550 Art.14, Art.15, Art.16
Reg.14, revoked: SI 1998/2451 Reg.41
Reg.18, amended: SI 1996/550 Art.17
Reg.18, revoked: SI 1998/2451 Reg.41
Reg.26, amended: SI 1996/550 Art.18
Reg.26, revoked: SI 1998/2451 Reg.41
Reg.34, amended: SI 1996/550 Art.19, Art.20
Reg.34, revoked: SI 1998/2451 Reg.41
Reg.35, revoked: SI 1998/2451 Reg.41
Reg.35, substituted: SI 1996/550 Art.21
Reg.35A, added: SI 1996/550 Art.21
Reg.35A, amended: SI 1996/2541 Reg.2
Reg.35A, revoked: SI 1998/2451 Reg.41
Reg.36, amended: SI 1996/252 Art.2, Sch, SI 1996/551 Reg.12
Reg.36, revoked: SI 1998/2451 Reg.41
Reg.37, amended: SI 1996/550 Art.22
Reg.37, revoked: SI 1998/2451 Reg.41

1887. **European Communities (Designation) (No.3) Order 1994**
revoked (in part): SI 1999/2788 Art.4, Sch.3

1890. **European Molecular Biology Laboratory (Immunities and Privileges) Order 1994**
Art.12A, added: SI 1999/2034 Art.2, Sch.

1891. **Agriculture (Miscellaneous Provisions) (Northern Ireland) Order 1994**
Art.16, revoked: SI 1999/662 (NI.6) Art.63, Sch.8 Part I

1892. **Appropriation (No.2) (Northern Ireland) Order 1994**
revoked: SI 1997/1754 (NI.13) Art.6, Sch.2

1894. **Civil Service (Management Functions) (Northern Ireland) Order 1994**
Art.3, amended: 1998 c.47 s.99, Sch.13 para.14
Art.4, amended: SI 1999/283 (NI.1) Art.9, Sch.2

1895. **Immigration (European Economic Area) Order 1994**
applied: 1997 c.68 Sch.2 para.5
referred to: 1999 c.33 s.80
Art.5, see *Secretary of State for Social Security v Remilien* [1997] 1 W.L.R. 1640 (HL), Lord Hoffmann
Art.6, see *R. v Westminster City Council Ex p. Castelli* Times, February 27, 1996 (CA), Evans, L.J.; see *R. v Westminster City Council Ex p. Castelli (No.2)* (1996) 28 H.L.R. 616 (CA), Evans, L.J.
Art.6, amended: SI 1997/2981 Art.2
Art.12, amended: SI 1997/2981 Art.2
Art.15, see *Secretary of State for Social Security v Remilien* [1997] 1 W.L.R. 1640 (HL), Lord Hoffmann
Art.15, applied: 1997 c.68 s.2
Art.18, see *Boukssid (Fatima) v Secretary of State for the Home Department* [1998] 2 F.L.R. 200 (CA), Stuart-Smith, L.J.

NO.

1994—cont.

1895. Immigration (European Economic Area) Order 1994—*cont.*
Art.18, applied: 1997 c.68 s.2
Art.20, referred to: 1997 c.68 s.2

1896. Litter (Northern Ireland) Order 1994
Art.2, amended: SI 1997/1772 (NI.15) Art.25, Sch.4
Art.7, applied: SI 1997/276 (NI.2) Art.7
Art.8, amended: SI 1997/276 (NI.2) Art.75, Sch.8 para.16
Art.17, amended: SI 1997/2778 (NI.19) Art.83, Sch.5 para.7

1898. Social Security (Incapacity for Work) (Northern Ireland) Order 1994
applied: SI 1996/1927 Sch, SI 1997/871 Sch.1, SI 1998/1506 (NI.10) Art.4
referred to: 1998 c.47 s.87
Art.8, revoked (in part): SI 1998/1506 (NI.10) Art.78, Sch.7
Art.11, revoked: SI 1999/3147 (NI.11) Art.76, Sch.10 Part IV
Sch.1 para.11, revoked: SI 1998/1506 (NI.10) Art.78, Sch.7
Sch.1 para.18, revoked: SI 1999/3147 (NI.11) Art.76, Sch.10 Part IV
Sch.1 para.45, revoked: SI 1998/1506 (NI.10) · Art.78, Sch.7
Sch.1 para.47, revoked: SI 1998/1506 (NI.10) Art.78, Sch.7
Sch.1 para.52, revoked: SI 1998/1506 (NI.10) Art.78, Sch.7
Sch.1 para.53, revoked: SI 1996/1919 (NI.16) Art.257, Sch.3
Sch.2, revoked (in part): SI 1999/3147 (NI.11) Art.76, Sch.10 Part IV

1910. Special Educational Needs Tribunal Regulations 1994
applied: SI 1996/710 Reg.16
Reg.41, see *R. v Special Educational Needs Tribunal Ex p. Brophy* [1997] E.L.R. 291 (QBD), Carnwath, J.

1922. Monopoly References (Alteration of Exclusions) Order 1994
revoked: SI 1998/2253 Art.3

1931. Prisons and Young Offenders Institutions (Scotland) Rules 1994
amended: SI 1998/2251 Art.16
applied: SI 1998/2251 Art.16
Part 2A, added: SI 1998/1589 r.7
Part 2A, applied: SI 1998/1589 r.61
Part 13, referred to: SI 1998/2251 Art.16
Part 16, referred to: SI 1996/32 r.57, SI 1998/2251 Art.16
r.2, amended: SI 1998/1589 r.2
r.2, substituted: SI 1999/374 r.2
r.2A, added: SI 1999/374 r.2
r.2B, added: SI 1999/374 r.2
r.3, amended: SI 1996/32 r.2, SI 1997/2007 r.2, SI 1998/1589 r.3, SI 1998/2504 r.2, SI 1999/374 r.3
r.7, amended: SI 1999/374 r.4
r.8, amended: SI 1998/1589 r.4
r.9, amended: SI 1999/374 r.5
r.10, amended: SI 1996/32 r.3, SI 1998/1589 r.5
r.12, amended: SI 1996/32 r.4
r.12, applied: SI 1998/1589 r.61
r.12, revoked: SI 1998/1589 r.6
r.14A, added: SI 1998/1589 r.7
r.14B, added: SI 1998/1589 r.7
r.14C, added: SI 1998/1589 r.7
r.14C, amended: SI 1999/374 r.6
r.14D, added: SI 1998/1589 r.7

NO.

1994—cont.

1931. Prisons and Young Offenders Institutions (Scotland) Rules 1994—*cont.*
r.14D, amended: SI 1999/374 r.7
r.14E, added: SI 1998/1589 r.7
r.15, amended: SI 1999/374 r.8
r.16, amended: SI 1999/374 r.9
r.17, amended: SI 1998/1589 r.8, SI 1999/374 r.10
r.18, amended: SI 1999/374 r.11
r.19, amended: SI 1999/374 r.12
r.21, amended: SI 1996/32 r.5, SI 1998/1589 r.9, SI 1999/374 r.13
r.22, amended: SI 1998/1589 r.10
r.23, revoked: SI 1998/1589 r.11
r.24, substituted: SI 1998/1589 r.12
r.25, substituted: SI 1998/1589 r.13
r.26, substituted: SI 1998/1589 r.14
r.27, amended: SI 1996/32 r.6, SI 1998/1589 r.15
r.27, revoked (in part): SI 1998/1589 r.15
r.28, substituted: SI 1998/1589 r.16
r.29, amended: SI 1998/1589 r.17
r.30, substituted: SI 1996/32 r.7
r.31, amended: SI 1998/1589 r.18, SI 1999/374 r.14
r.32, amended: SI 1998/1589 r.19
r.34, referred to: SI 1996/32 r.57
r.36, referred to: SI 1996/32 r.57, SI 1998/2251 Art.16
r.37, referred to: SI 1996/32 r.57, SI 1998/2251 Art.16
r.38, amended: SI 1998/1589 r.20
r.38, referred to: SI 1998/2251 Art.16
r.40, amended: SI 1996/32 r.8
r.40, referred to: SI 1996/32 r.57
r.42, referred to: SI 1996/32 r.57
r.45, amended: SI 1998/1589 r.21
r.48, referred to: SI 1996/32 r.57
r.49, amended: SI 1999/374 r.15
r.51, amended: SI 1998/1589 r.22
r.52, amended: SI 1998/1589 r.23
r.54, referred to: SI 1996/32 r.57
r.55, amended: SI 1998/1589 r.24, SI 1999/374 r.15
r.55, referred to: SI 1996/32 r.57
r.56, amended: SI 1996/32 r.9, SI 1998/1589 r.25, SI 1999/374 r.17
r.57, amended: SI 1998/1589 r.26
r.58, amended: SI 1998/1589 r.27
r.61, amended: SI 1999/374 r.13
r.62, amended: SI 1999/374 r.19
r.62A, added: SI 1998/1589 r.28
r.62A, amended: SI 1999/1820 Art.4, Sch.2 para.154
r.62B, added: SI 1998/1589 r.28
r.62B, amended: SI 1999/1351 Art.17
r.62C, added: SI 1998/1589 r.28
r.62D, added: SI 1998/1589 r.28
r.62E, added: SI 1999/374 r.20
r.63, amended: SI 1996/32 r.10
r.63, substituted: SI 1998/1589 r.29
r.64, amended: SI 1996/32 r.11, SI 1999/374 r.21
r.67, amended: SI 1996/32 r.12
r.68, amended: SI 1998/1589 r.30
r.69, amended: SI 1996/32 r.13
r.71, referred to: SI 1998/2251 Art.16
r.73, amended: SI 1999/374 r.22
r.75, amended: SI 1998/1589 r.31, SI 1999/374 r.23
r.75, referred to: SI 1996/32 r.52
r.75, substituted: SI 1996/32 r.14

NO.

1994—cont.

1931. Prisons and Young Offenders Institutions (Scotland) Rules 1994—*cont.*
r.76, amended: SI 1996/32 r.15
r.80, amended: SI 1996/32 r.16, SI 1998/1589 r.32
r.80, revoked (in part): SI 1998/1589 r.32
r.81, amended: SI 1998/1589 r.33
r.83, amended: SI 1998/1589 r.34
r.84, amended: SI 1998/1589 r.35
r.85, amended: SI 1998/1589 r.36
r.85A, added: SI 1998/1589 r.37
r.86, amended: SI 1999/374 r.24
r.86, substituted: SI 1996/32 r.17, SI 1998/1589 r.38
r.86A, added: SI 1998/1589 r.38
r.86A, amended: SI 1999/374 r.25
r.86B, added: SI 1998/1589 r.38
r.86B, amended: SI 1999/374 r.26
r.86C, added: SI 1999/374 r.27
r.87, amended: SI 1996/32 r.18
r.88, amended: SI 1996/32 r.19
r.88A, added: SI 1996/32 r.20
r.88B, added: SI 1998/1589 r.39
r.91, amended: SI 1996/32 r.21
r.92, substituted: SI 1998/1589 r.40
r.93, amended: SI 1996/32 r.22
r.95, amended: SI 1996/32 r.23
r.96, amended: SI 1996/32 r.24
r.97, amended: SI 1997/2007 r.3, SI 1998/1589 r.41
r.98, amended: SI 1996/32 r.25, SI 1997/2007 r.4, SI 1998/1589 r.42
r.99, amended: SI 1998/1589 r.43
r.100, amended: SI 1996/32 r.26, SI 1998/1589 r.44
r.100, substituted: SI 1998/2504 r.3
r.100A, added: SI 1998/2504 r.3
r.101A, added: SI 1996/32 r.27
r.102, substituted: SI 1997/2007 r.5
r.104, amended: SI 1996/32 r.28
r.104, referred to: SI 1998/2251 Art.16
r.105, amended: SI 1996/32 r.29
r.105, referred to: SI 1998/2251 Art.16
r.106, amended: SI 1996/32 r.30
r.106, referred to: SI 1998/2251 Art.16
r.107, amended: SI 1996/32 r.31
r.107, referred to: SI 1998/2251 Art.16
r.108, amended: SI 1996/32 r.32
r.108, referred to: SI 1998/2251 Art.16
r.108A, added: SI 1996/32 r.33
r.108A, amended: SI 1998/1589 r.45
r.109, amended: SI 1996/32 r.34
r.109, referred to: SI 1996/32 r.57, SI 1998/2251 Art.16
r.110, amended: SI 1996/32 r.35, SI 1999/374 r.28
r.110, referred to: SI 1998/2251 Art.16
r.111, substituted: SI 1996/32 r.36
r.112, referred to: SI 1996/32 r.57
r.112, substituted: SI 1996/32 r.37
r.112A, added: SI 1996/32 r.38
r.113, substituted: SI 1996/32 r.39
r.115, amended: SI 1998/1589 r.46, SI 1999/374 r.29
r.115, referred to: SI 1996/32 r.57
r.118, substituted: SI 1998/1589 r.47
r.119A, added: SI 1998/1589 r.48
r.120, amended: SI 1996/32 r.40
r.120, referred to: SI 1996/32 r.57
r.120, substituted: SI 1998/1589 r.49
r.120A, added: SI 1996/32 r.41
r.121, amended: SI 1996/32 r.42

NO.

1994—cont.

1931. Prisons and Young Offenders Institutions (Scotland) Rules 1994—*cont.*
r.121, referred to: SI 1996/32 r.57
r.122, amended: SI 1999/374 r.30
r.123, substituted: SI 1996/32 r.43
r.123A, added: SI 1996/32 r.44
r.123A, amended: SI 1998/1589 r.50
r.124, amended: SI 1996/32 r.45, SI 1999/374 r.31
r.126, amended: SI 1996/32 r.46
r.130, amended: SI 1996/32 r.47, SI 1998/1589 r.51, SI 1999/374 r.32
r.132, substituted: SI 1998/1589 r.52
r.132A, added: SI 1998/1589 r.53
r.133, amended: SI 1996/32 r.48
r.133, referred to: SI 1996/32 r.57
r.133A, added: SI 1998/1589 r.54
r.134, amended: SI 1996/32 r.49
r.135, referred to: SI 1996/32 r.57
r.136, referred to: SI 1996/32 r.57
r.139, referred to: SI 1996/32 r.57
r.140A, added: SI 1996/32 r.50
r.140A, referred to: SI 1996/32 r.52
r.141, amended: SI 1996/32 r.51, SI 1998/1589 r.55
Sch.1, referred to: SI 1996/32 r.57
Sch.1, revoked: SI 1998/1589 r.56
Sch.2, amended: SI 1996/32 r.53
Sch.2, revoked: SI 1998/1589 r.57
Sch.3, referred to: SI 1996/32 r.57
Sch.3, substituted: SI 1996/32 r.54, Sch.1
Sch.3 para.(i), amended: SI 1998/1589 r.58
Sch.3 para.(t), amended: SI 1999/374 r.33
Sch.3 para.(v), amended: SI 1998/1589 r.58
Sch.4, amended: SI 1998/1589 r.59, SI 1999/374 r.34
Sch.4, referred to: SI 1996/32 r.57
Sch.4, substituted: SI 1996/32 r.55, Sch.2
Sch.4A, added: SI 1996/32 r.56, Sch.3
Sch.4A, amended: SI 1998/1589 r.60, SI 1999/374 r.35
Sch.4A, referred to: SI 1996/32 r.52

1932. Medicines (Advertising) Regulations 1994
Reg.2, amended: SI 1999/267 Reg.2
Reg.3A, added: SI 1999/267 Reg.3
Reg.4, amended: SI 1999/267 Reg.4
Reg.6, amended: SI 1996/1552 Reg.2
Reg.12, substituted: SI 1999/267 Reg.5
Reg.14, amended: SI 1999/267 Reg.6
Reg.20, amended: SI 1999/267 Reg.7
Reg.23, amended: SI 1999/267 Reg.8
Sch.1, amended: SI 1996/1552 Reg.2
Sch.2, amended: SI 1999/267 Reg.9

1933. Monitoring of Advertising Regulations 1994
Reg.2, amended: SI 1999/267 Reg.10
Reg.3, amended: SI 1999/267 Reg.11
Reg.12, added: SI 1999/267 Reg.12
Reg.13, added: SI 1999/267 Reg.12
Sch., added: SI 1999/267 Reg.13
Sch. para.7, amended: SI 1999/784 Reg.2

1936. County Court Fees (Amendment) Order 1994
revoked: SI 1999/689 Art.8 (with savings), Sch.2 (with savings)

1953. Police (Promotion) (Scotland) Amendment Regulations 1994
revoked: SI 1996/221 Reg.10, Sch.2

1974. Land Registration Fees Order 1994
revoked: SI 1996/187 Art.1

1981. Friendly Societies (Insurance Business) Regulations 1994
Reg.9, applied: SI 1997/741 Sch.2, SI 1998/673 Reg.5, Sch.2 para.35, SI 1999/736 Sch.2 para.35

NO.

NO.

1994—cont.

1994—cont.

1981. Friendly Societies (Insurance Business) Regulations 1994—*cont.*

Reg.10, applied: SI 1997/741 Sch.2, SI 1998/673 Reg.5, Sch.2 para.35, SI 1999/736 Sch.2 para.35

Reg.11, applied: SI 1997/741 Sch.2, SI 1998/673 Reg.5, Sch.2 para.35, SI 1999/736 Sch.2 para.35

Reg.16, substituted: SI 1998/3034 Reg.3

Reg.17, amended: SI 1996/3008 Reg.2

Reg.18, amended: SI 1996/3008 Reg.3

Reg.19, amended: SI 1996/3008 Reg.4, Reg.5

Reg.20, amended: SI 1996/3008 Reg.6

Reg.22, amended: SI 1996/3008 Reg.7

Reg.22A, added: SI 1996/3008 Reg.8

Reg.23, substituted: SI 1996/3008 Reg.9

Reg.26, substituted: SI 1996/3008 Reg.10

Reg.27, substituted: SI 1996/3008 Reg.11

Reg.28, substituted: SI 1996/3008 Reg.12

Reg.30, substituted: SI 1996/3008 Reg.13

Reg.31, amended: SI 1997/966 Reg.2

Reg.31, substituted: SI 1996/3008 Reg.14

Reg.32, substituted: SI 1996/3008 Reg.15

Reg.33, amended: SI 1996/3008 Reg.16

Reg.36, substituted: SI 1996/3008 Reg.17

Reg.37, substituted: SI 1996/3008 Reg.18

Reg.38, amended: SI 1996/3008 Reg.19

Reg.43, amended: SI 1996/3008 Reg.20

Reg.45, amended: SI 1996/3008 Reg.21

Reg.51, amended: SI 1996/3008 Reg.22

Reg.51, applied: SI 1996/3008 Reg.28

Reg.53, amended: SI 1996/3008 Reg.23

Reg.55, applied: SI 1997/741 Sch.2, SI 1998/673 Reg.5, Sch.2 para.34, SI 1999/736 Sch.2 para.34

Reg.55, revoked: SI 1997/2849 Reg.6

Reg.56, amended: SI 1996/3008 Reg.24, SI 1997/2849 Reg.6

Reg.56, applied: SI 1997/741 Sch.2, SI 1998/673 Reg.5, Sch.2 para.34

Reg.57, applied: SI 1997/741 Sch.2, SI 1998/673 Reg.5, Sch.2 para.34, SI 1999/736 Sch.2 para.34

Reg.58, amended: SI 1997/2849 Reg.6

Sch.2 para.1, amended: SI 1996/3008 Reg.25

Sch.5, substituted: SI 1996/3008 Reg.26, Sch.1

Sch.6, substituted: SI 1996/3008 Reg.27, Sch.2

1983. Friendly Societies (Accounts and Related Provisions) Regulations 1994

applied: SI 1996/614 Sch.1 para.2, Sch.1 para.3, SI 1997/741 Sch.1 para.2, Sch.1 para.3, SI 1998/673 Reg.3, Sch.1 para.2, Sch.1 para.3, Sch.1 para.4, SI 1999/736 Sch.1 para.2, Sch.1 para.3, Sch.1 para.4

Sch.1 Part I, applied: SI 1997/741 Sch.1 para.2, SI 1998/673 Reg.3, Sch.1 para.2, SI 1999/736 Sch.1 para.2

Sch.7 Part I, applied: SI 1996/614 Sch.1 para.3, SI 1997/741 Sch.1 para.3, Sch.1 para.4, SI 1998/673 Reg.3, Sch.1 para.3, Sch.1 para.4, SI 1999/736 Sch.1 para.3, Sch.1 para.4

1985. Pesticides (Maximum Residue Levels in Crops, Food and Feeding Stuffs) Regulations 1994

Reg.2, amended: SI 1998/2922 Reg.3

Reg.2, revoked (in part): SI 1999/3483 Reg.7, Sch.4

Reg.5, amended: SI 1998/2922 Reg.4

Reg.5, revoked (in part): SI 1999/3483 Reg.7, Sch.4

Reg.7, amended: SI 1998/2922 Reg.5

Reg.7, revoked (in part): SI 1999/3483 Reg.7, Sch.4

1985. Pesticides (Maximum Residue Levels in Crops, Food and Feeding Stuffs) Regulations 1994—*cont.*

Sch.1, amended: SI 1996/1487 Reg.3, SI 1997/567 Reg.3, SI 1999/1109 Reg.3, Sch.1

Sch.1, revoked (in part): SI 1999/3483 Reg.7, Sch.4

Sch.2 Part 1, amended: SI 1996/1487 Reg.4, SI 1997/567 Reg.4, SI 1999/1109 Reg.4, Sch.2

Sch.2 Part 1, revoked (in part): SI 1999/3483 Reg.7, Sch.4

Sch.2 Part 2, amended: SI 1996/1487 Reg.5, Reg.6, Reg.7, Reg.8, SI 1997/567 Reg.5, Reg.6, SI 1999/1109 Reg.5, Reg.6, Sch.3, Sch.4

Sch.2 Part 2, revoked (in part): SI 1999/3483 Reg.7, Sch.4

Sch.3, amended: SI 1996/1487 Reg.9, SI 1999/1109 Reg.7

Sch.3, revoked (in part): SI 1999/3483 Reg.7, Sch.4

2004. Welfare Food Amendment Regulations 1994

revoked: SI 1996/1434 Reg.23, Sch.7

2009. Ecclesiastical Judges and Legal Officers (Fees) Order 1994

applied: SI 1997/1890 Appendix para.4

2012. Environmental Assessment (Scotland) Amendment Regulations 1994

Sch. para.1, applied: SSI 1999/1 Reg.64, Sch.7

Sch. para.1, revoked: SSI 1999/1 Reg.64, Sch.7

Sch. para.2, applied: SSI 1999/1 Reg.64, Sch.7

Sch. para.2, revoked: SSI 1999/1 Reg.64, Sch.7

Sch. para.3, applied: SSI 1999/1 Reg.64, Sch.7

Sch. para.3, revoked: SSI 1999/1 Reg.64, Sch.7

Sch. para.4, applied: SSI 1999/1 Reg.64, Sch.7

Sch. para.4, revoked: SSI 1999/1 Reg.64, Sch.7

Sch. para.5, applied: SSI 1999/1 Reg.64, Sch.7

Sch. para.5, revoked: SSI 1999/1 Reg.64, Sch.7

Sch. para.6, applied: SSI 1999/1 Reg.64, Sch.7

Sch. para.6, revoked: SSI 1999/1 Reg.64, Sch.7

Sch. para.7, applied: SSI 1999/1 Reg.64, Sch.7

Sch. para.7, revoked: SSI 1999/1 Reg.64, Sch.7

Sch. para.8, applied: SSI 1999/1 Reg.64, Sch.7

Sch. para.8, revoked: SSI 1999/1 Reg.64, Sch.7

Sch. para.9, applied: SSI 1999/1 Reg.64, Sch.7

Sch. para.9, revoked: SSI 1999/1 Reg.64, Sch.7

Sch. para.14, applied: SSI 1999/1 Reg.64, Sch.7

Sch. para.14, revoked: SSI 1999/1 Reg.64, Sch.7

Sch. para.15, applied: SSI 1999/1 Reg.64, Sch.7

Sch. para.15, revoked: SSI 1999/1 Reg.64, Sch.7

Sch. para.16, applied: SSI 1999/1 Reg.64, Sch.7

Sch. para.16, revoked: SSI 1999/1 Reg.64, Sch.7

Sch. para.17, applied: SSI 1999/1 Reg.64, Sch.7

Sch. para.17, revoked: SSI 1999/1 Reg.64, Sch.7

Sch. para.18, applied: SSI 1999/1 Reg.64, Sch.7

1994—cont.

2012. Environmental Assessment (Scotland) Amendment Regulations 1994—*cont.*
Sch. para.18, revoked: SSI 1999/1 Reg.64, Sch.7
Sch. para.19, applied: SSI 1999/1 Reg.64, Sch.7
Sch. para.19, revoked: SSI 1999/1 Reg.64, Sch.7
Sch. para.20, applied: SSI 1999/1 Reg.64, Sch.7
Sch. para.20, revoked: SSI 1999/1 Reg.64, Sch.7
Sch. para.21, applied: SSI 1999/1 Reg.64, Sch.7
Sch. para.21, revoked: SSI 1999/1 Reg.64, Sch.7
Sch. para.22, applied: SSI 1999/1 Reg.64, Sch.7
Sch. para.22, revoked: SSI 1999/1 Reg.64, Sch.7
Sch. para.23, applied: SSI 1999/1 Reg.64, Sch.7
Sch. para.23, revoked: SSI 1999/1 Reg.64, Sch.7
Sch. para.26, applied: SSI 1999/1 Reg.64, Sch.7
Sch. para.26, revoked: SSI 1999/1 Reg.64, Sch.7

2013. Merchant Shipping (Accident Investigation and Reporting) Regulations 1994
see *M/V Derbyshire, The* Times, October 28, 1999 (QBD (Adm Ct)), Colman, J.
applied: SI 1997/2962 Reg.16
revoked: SI 1999/2567 Reg.1

2014. Merchant Shipping (Safety Officials and Reporting of Accidents and Dangerous Occurrences) (Amendment) Regulations 1994
revoked: SI 1997/2962 Reg.1

2016. Education (Bursaries for Teacher Training) Regulations 1994
revoked (in part): SI 1999/2162 Art.2, SI 1999/2816 Reg.1
Reg.1, revoked (in part): SI 1999/2162 Art.2, SI 1999/2816 Reg.1

2020. Building (Prescribed Fees) Regulations 1994
applied: SI 1998/3129 Reg.14
revoked: SI 1998/3129 Reg.16

2022. General Medical Council (Constitution of Fitness to Practise Committees) (Amendment) Rules Order of Council 1994
revoked: SI 1996/2125 Sch. para.16, Sch.2
r.1, revoked (in part): SI 1996/2125 Sch. para.16, Sch. Sch.1

2031. Dartford-Thurrock Crossing Regulations 1994
revoked: SI 1998/1908 Reg.11, Sch.
Reg.4, revoked: SI 1998/1908 Reg.11, Sch.
Reg.5, revoked: SI 1998/1908 Reg.11, Sch.
Reg.11, revoked: SI 1998/1908 Reg.11, Sch.

2032. Railway Heritage Scheme Order 1994
revoked: SI 1997/39 Art.3

2038. Education Act 1993 (Commencement No.5 and Transitional Provisions) Order 1994
Sch.4 para.2, applied: 1996 c.56 Sch.39 para.34
Sch.4 para.4, applied: 1996 c.56 Sch.39 para.34

1994—cont.

2082. Merchant Shipping (IBC Code) (Amendment) Regulations 1994
revoked: SI 1996/3010 Reg.1

2084. Merchant Shipping (BCH Code) (Amendment) Regulations 1994
revoked: SI 1996/3010 Reg.1

2085. Merchant Shipping (Prevention of Oil Pollution) (Amendment) Regulations 1994
revoked: SI 1996/2154 Reg.1

2092. Education (No.2) Act 1986 (Amendment) (No.2) Order 1994
revoked: 1996 c.56 Sch.38 Part III

2103. Education (Pupil Referral Units) (Application of Enactments) Regulations 1994
Reg.2, applied: SI 1996/951 Art.2
Sch.1 Part I, amended: SI 1996/2087 Reg.2
Sch.1 Part II, amended: SI 1996/2087 Reg.2
Sch.1 para.3A, substituted: SI 1997/1966 Reg.1, Sch. Part II
Sch.1 para.6, revoked: SI 1997/2679 Reg.7, Sch.3
Sch.1 para.8, substituted: SI 1997/1966 Reg.1, Sch. Part II
Sch.2 para.2, revoked: SI 1996/360 Sch.1
Sch.2 para.4, revoked: SI 1997/2679 Reg.7, Sch.3

2111. Education (Grant-Maintained Special Schools) (Finance) Regulations 1994
applied: SI 1996/889 Reg.3, SI 1998/799 Reg.3

2112. Education (National Curriculum) (Exceptions) Regulations 1994
revoked: SI 1996/2083 Reg.2
Reg.4, applied: SI 1996/2083 Reg.2
Reg.4, revoked: SI 1996/2083 Reg.2

2126. Welfare of Livestock Regulations 1994
Reg.2, amended: SI 1998/1709 Reg.2
Sch.2, substituted: SI 1998/1709 Reg.2

2127. Preserved Tuna and Bonito (Marketing Standards) Regulations 1994
Reg.2, amended: SI 1996/1008 Art.2, Sch para.13
Reg.6, revoked: SI 1996/1499 Reg.49, Sch.9

2138. Council Tax Benefit (Permitted Total) Order 1994
revoked: SI 1996/678 Art.4

2145. Compulsory Purchase of Land Regulations 1994
Sch. Form 1, amended: SI 1996/1008 Art.2, Sch para.14
Sch. Form 2, amended: SI 1996/1008 Art.2, Sch para.14
Sch. Form 3, amended: SI 1996/1008 Art.2, Sch para.14

2156. Education (Payment for Special Educational Needs Supplies) (Amendment) Regulations 1994
revoked: SI 1999/710 Reg.3 (with savings)

2206. Education (National Curriculum) (Exceptions) (Wales) Regulations 1994
revoked: SI 1996/2259 Reg.2

2231. Police (Scotland) Amendment (No.2) Regulations 1994
Sch., applied: SI 1996/1645 Reg.29
Sch. para.2, applied: SI 1996/1642 Reg.22, SI 1996/1645 Reg.29
Sch. para.3, applied: SI 1996/1642 Reg.22, SI 1996/1645 Reg.29
Sch. para.4, applied: SI 1996/1642 Reg.22, SI 1996/1645 Reg.29
Sch. para.5, applied: SI 1996/1642 Reg.22, SI 1996/1645 Reg.29
Sch. para.6, applied: SI 1996/1642 Reg.22, SI 1996/1645 Reg.29

NO.

2249. Marketing of Gas Oil (Sulphur Content) Regulations 1994

Reg.3, amended: SI 1996/1008 Art.2, Sch para.15

2250. Wireless Telegraphy (Short Range Devices) (Exemption) (Amendment) Regulations 1994

revoked: SI 1999/930 Reg.2, Sch.1

2251. Telecommunications (Leased Lines) (Amendment) Regulations 1994

revoked: SI 1997/2932 Reg.15

2295. Motor Fuel (Composition and Content) Regulations 1994

revoked: SI 1999/3107 Reg.18

2296. Local Government Act 1988 (Defined Activities) (Exemptions) (England and Wales) (Amendment) Order 1994

revoked (in part): SI 1997/176 Art.4, SI 1997/934 Art.6, Sch.2

2297. Local Government Act 1988 (Competition) (Housing Management) (England) Regulations 1994

Reg.2, amended: SI 1997/2732 Reg.5

Reg.3, amended: SI 1996/154, SI 1997/2734 Reg.3

2318. Income Tax (Authorised Unit Trusts) (Interest Distributions) Regulations 1994

Reg.2, amended: SI 1997/1154 Reg.28

Reg.4, amended: SI 1997/1154 Reg.28

Reg.5, amended: SI 1997/1154 Reg.28

Reg.6, amended: SI 1997/1154 Reg.28

Reg.7, amended: SI 1997/1154 Reg.28

Reg.8, amended: SI 1997/1154 Reg.28

Reg.9, amended: SI 1997/1154 Reg.28

2325. Civil Aviation (Canadian Navigation Services) Regulations 1994

revoked: SI 1996/688 Reg.3, Sch.1

Reg.4, revoked: SI 1996/688 Reg.3, Sch.1

Reg.4, substituted: SI 1996/22 Reg.2

2326. Personal Protective Equipment (EC Directive) (Amendment) Regulations 1994

Reg.4, amended: SI 1996/3039 Reg.2

Sch., amended: SI 1996/3039 Reg.2

2328. General Product Safety Regulations 1994

see *R. v Liverpool City Council Ex p. Baby Products Association* Times, December 1, 1999 (QBD), Lord Bingham of Cornhill, L.C.J.

referred to: SI 1999/1820 Art.2, Sch.1 Part I

Reg.7, see *R. v Newcastle upon Tyne Magistrates Court Ex p. Poundstretcher Ltd* [1998] C.O.D. 256 (QBD), Dyson, L.J.

Reg.13, see *Coventry City Council v Padgett Brothers (A to Z) Ltd* Times, February 24, 1998 (QBD), Poole, J.

Reg.15, see *Coventry City Council v Padgett Brothers (A to Z) Ltd* Times, February 24, 1998 (QBD), Poole, J.

2329. Thames Estuary Cockle Fishery Order 1994

Art.12, amended: SI 1996/362 Art.5, Sch.4

2330. Education (School Information) (Wales) Regulations 1994

revoked: SI 1997/1832 Reg.2

Reg.3, amended: SI 1996/1936 Reg.2

Reg.3, revoked: SI 1997/1832 Reg.2

Reg.9A, added: SI 1996/1936 Reg.3

Reg.9A, revoked: SI 1997/1832 Reg.2

Sch.2 para.10A, added: SI 1996/1936 Reg.4

Sch.2 para.10A, revoked: SI 1997/1832 Reg.2

Sch.2 para.17, revoked: SI 1997/1832 Reg.2

Sch.2 para.17, substituted: SI 1996/1936 Reg.5

NO.

2330. Education (School Information) (Wales) Regulations 1994—*cont.*

Sch.2 para.17A, revoked: SI 1997/1832 Reg.2

Sch.2 para.17A, substituted: SI 1996/1936 Reg.6

Sch.2 para.18, revoked: SI 1997/1832 Reg.2

Sch.2 para.18, substituted: SI 1996/1936 Reg.7

Sch.2 para.18A, added: SI 1996/1936 Reg.8

Sch.2 para.18A, revoked: SI 1997/1832 Reg.2

Sch.2 para.18B, added: SI 1996/1936 Reg.8

Sch.2 para.18B, revoked: SI 1997/1832 Reg.2

Sch.2 para.18C, added: SI 1996/1936 Reg.8

Sch.2 para.18C, revoked: SI 1997/1832 Reg.2

Sch.2 para.21, amended: SI 1996/1936 Reg.9

Sch.2 para.21, revoked: SI 1997/1832 Reg.2

2349. Countryside Access Regulations 1994

applied: SI 1999/672 Art.2, Sch.1

Reg.2, amended: SI 1996/3111 Reg.2

Reg.3, substituted: SI 1996/3111 Reg.2

Reg.7, amended: SI 1996/3111 Reg.2

Reg.8, amended: SI 1996/3111 Reg.2

Reg.11, substituted: SI 1996/3111 Reg.2

Reg.11A, added: SI 1996/3111 Reg.2

Reg.11B, added: SI 1996/3111 Reg.2

Reg.13, added: SI 1999/1174 Reg.3

Reg.14, added: SI 1999/2197 Reg.3

2387. Education (School Information) (England) (Amendment) Regulations 1994

revoked: SI 1996/2585 Reg.2

2421. Insolvent Partnerships Order 1994

Art.6, applied: SI 1998/1806 Art.2

Art.7, amended: SI 1996/1308 Art.2

Art.7, applied: SI 1998/1806 Art.2

Art.8, applied: SI 1998/1806 Art.2

Art.9, applied: SI 1998/1806 Art.2

Art.10, applied: SI 1998/1806 Art.2

Sch.2, see *HS Smith & Sons, Re* Times, January 6, 1999 (Ch D), Park, J.

2448. Dairy Produce Quotas (Amendment) Regulations 1994

revoked: SI 1997/733 Reg.35

2459. Building Societies (Accounts and Related Provisions) (Amendment) Regulations 1994

revoked: SI 1998/504 Reg.13

2464. Merchant Shipping (Gas Carriers) Regulations 1994

applied: SI 1996/3243 Sch Part I

2465. Animals, Meat and Meat Products (Examination for Residues and Maximum Residue Limits) (Amendment) Regulations 1994

revoked: SI 1997/1729 Reg.36, Sch.2

2479. Maternity (Compulsory Leave) Regulations 1994

referred to: SI 1999/2830 Art.2, Sch.2 Part II

revoked: 1999 c.26 s.44, Sch.9 Part 2

2485. Central Scotland Healthcare National Health Service Trust (Appointment of Trustees) Order 1994

revoked: SI 1999/1134 Art.3, Sch.2

2488. Roads (Traffic Calming) (Scotland) Regulations 1994

applied: SI 1999/1750 Art.2, Sch.1

Reg.7, substituted: SI 1999/1000 Reg.3

2518. Export of Goods (Control) Order 1994 (Amendment No.2) Order 1994

revoked: SI 1996/2633 Art.3, Sch.2

2524. Salmon (Fish Passes and Screens) (Scotland) Regulations 1994

applied: SI 1999/1380 Art.3, Sch.2 para.2, SI 1999/1381 Art.3, Sch.2 para.2, SI 1999/1382 Art.3, Sch.2 para.2

1994—cont.

2567. Coal Industry Act 1994 (Consequential Modifications of Subordinate Legislation) Order 1994
Art.2, revoked (in part): SI 1997/1111 Reg.8, SI 1998/2914 Reg.8
Sch., revoked (in part): SI 1997/1111 Reg.8, SI 1998/2914 Reg.8

2578. London Docklands Development Corporation (Alteration of Boundaries) Order 1994
applied: SI 1997/2946 Art.6
Art.4, revoked: SI 1997/2946 Art.6
Art.6, revoked (in part): SI 1997/2946 Art.6

2581. Trade Marks and Service Marks (Fees) (Amendment) Rules 1994
applied: SI 1996/1942 r.5

2583. Trade Marks Rules 1994
applied: SI 1996/714 Art.32, SI 1996/1908 Reg.11, SI 1998/1776 r.3
referred to: SI 1996/1942 r.3, SI 1998/1776 r.2
r.5, amended: SI 1996/714 Art.3
r.5, applied: SI 1998/1776 r.3, Sch.
r.5, substituted: SI 1998/925 r.4
r.6, see *POSTPERFECT Trade Mark, Re* [1998] R.P.C. 255, Geoffrey Hobbs Q.C.
r.6, amended: SI 1996/714 Art.3
r.7, amended: SI 1996/714 Art.3
r.8, amended: SI 1996/714 Art.3
r.8, applied: SI 1998/1776 r.3, Sch.
r.10, amended: SI 1996/714 Art.3
r.11, amended: SI 1996/714 Art.3, SI 1998/925 r.5
r.13, applied: SI 1996/714 Art.10, SI 1998/1776 r.3, Sch.
r.13, substituted: SI 1998/925 r.6
r.14, applied: SI 1996/714 Art.10
r.18, amended: SI 1998/925 r.7
r.18, applied: SI 1998/1776 r.3, Sch.
r.19, see *DUCATI Trade Mark* [1998] R.P.C. 227 (TMR), SJ Probert; see *Interlego AG's Trade Mark Applications, Re* [1998] R.P.C. 69 (Ch D), Neuberger, J.
r.19, applied: SI 1998/1776 r.3, Sch.
r.20, amended: SI 1998/925 r.8
r.20, applied: SI 1998/1776 r.3, Sch.
r.21, applied: SI 1998/1776 r.3, Sch.
r.22, applied: SI 1998/1776 r.3, Sch.
r.23, amended: SI 1998/925 r.9
r.23, applied: SI 1998/1776 r.3, Sch.
r.25, applied: SI 1998/1776 r.3, Sch.
r.26, applied: SI 1998/1776 r.3, Sch.
r.27, substituted: SI 1998/925 r.10
r.28, applied: SI 1998/1776 r.3, Sch.
r.29, amended: SI 1998/925 r.11
r.29, applied: SI 1998/1776 r.3, Sch.
r.30, applied: SI 1998/1776 r.3, Sch.
r.31, applied: SI 1996/714 Art.13, SI 1996/1908 Reg.3, SI 1998/1776 r.3, Sch.
r.33, amended: SI 1998/925 r.12
r.35, applied: SI 1998/1776 r.3, Sch.
r.37, applied: SI 1998/1776 r.3, Sch.
r.39, amended: SI 1998/925 r.13
r.39, applied: SI 1998/1776 r.3, Sch.
r.41, applied: SI 1998/1776 r.3, Sch.
r.42, applied: SI 1998/1776 r.3, Sch.
r.44, amended: SI 1998/925 r.14
r.44, applied: SI 1996/714 Art.25
r.45, applied: SI 1996/714 Art.25
r.56, amended: SI 1998/925 r.15
r.56, applied: SI 1998/1776 r.3, Sch.

1994—cont.

2583. Trade Marks Rules 1994—*cont.*
r.60, see *DUCATI Trade Mark* [1998] R.P.C. 227 (TMR), SJ Probert
r.60, substituted: SI 1998/925 r.16
r.62, amended: SI 1998/925 r.17
r.62, applied: SI 1998/1776 r.3, Sch.
r.68, revoked: SI 1998/925 r.18
Sch.2, revoked: SI 1998/925 r.18
Sch.3, applied: SI 1998/1776 r.3, Sch.
Sch.4, applied: SI 1998/1776 r.3, Sch.
Sch.4 Class 7, substituted: SI 1998/925 r.19

2584. Trade Marks (Fees) Rules 1994
revoked: SI 1996/1942 r.5

2587. National Health Service (Optical Charges and Payments) (Scotland) Amendment (No.3) Regulations 1994
revoked: SI 1998/642 Reg.24, Sch.4

2594. Police and Magistrates' Courts Act 1994 (Commencement No.3 and Transitional Provisions) Order 1994
revoked: 1997 c.25 s.73, Sch.6 Part II

2616. Solicitors (Non-Contentious Business) Remuneration Order 1994
see *C v C (Costs: Non-Contentious Business)* [1997] 2 F.L.R. 22 (CC), King, J.
applied: SI 1996/3084 Appendix para.1, Appendix para.4, SI 1996/3085 Sch. Table VI, SI 1997/1890 Appendix para.1, Appendix para.4, SI 1998/1712 Appendix para.1, Appendix para.4, SI 1999/2108 Appendix para.1, Appendix para.4
Art.4, see *Riley v Dibb Lupton Alsop* (1997) 147 N.L.J. 1422 (QBD), Sedley, J.
Art.14, see *Riley v Dibb Lupton Alsop* (1997) 147 N.L.J. 1422 (QBD), Sedley, J.

2619. National Health Service (Optical Charges and Payments) Amendment (No.3) Regulations 1994
revoked: SI 1997/818 Reg.24, Sch.4

2625. Trade Marks (Customs) Regulations 1994
applied: SI 1996/714 Art.16, SI 1996/1908 Reg.6

2627. Spongiform Encephalopathy (Miscellaneous Amendments) Order 1994
Art.3, revoked: SI 1996/2628 Art.8, Sch.2

2678. Police (Secretary of State's Objectives) Order 1994
revoked: SI 1998/216 Art.2

2690. East Birmingham Hospital National Health Service Trust (Establishment) Amendment Order 1994
revoked: SI 1996/882 Art.2

2710. Habitats (Scotland) Regulations 1994
applied: SI 1996/3142 Reg.6, SI 1997/330 Reg.7, SI 1997/2844 Sch.3 Part I, Sch.4 para.3
revoked: SI 1996/3035 Reg.9 (with savings)
Reg.2, amended: SI 1996/3035 Reg.3
Reg.2, revoked: SI 1996/3035 Reg.9 (with savings)
Reg.3, amended: SI 1996/3035 Reg.4
Reg.3, revoked: SI 1996/3035 Reg.9 (with savings)
Reg.9, amended: SI 1996/3035 Reg.5
Reg.9, revoked: SI 1996/3035 Reg.9 (with savings)
Reg.10, amended: SI 1996/3035 Reg.6
Reg.10, revoked: SI 1996/3035 Reg.9 (with savings)
Reg.12, amended: SI 1996/3035 Reg.7
Reg.12, revoked: SI 1996/3035 Reg.9 (with savings)

NO.

NO.

2710. **Habitats (Scotland) Regulations 1994**—*cont.*
Reg.12A, added: SI 1996/3035 Reg.8
Reg.12A, revoked: SI 1996/3035 Reg.9 (with savings)
Reg.12B, added: SI 1996/3035 Reg.8
Reg.12B, revoked: SI 1996/3035 Reg.9 (with savings)
Reg.12C, added: SI 1996/3035 Reg.8
Reg.12C, revoked: SI 1996/3035 Reg.9 (with savings)

2711. **Export of Goods (Control) Order 1994 (Amendment No.3) Order 1994**
Art.2, amended: SI 1996/2663 Art.3, Sch.2

2716. **Conservation (Natural Habitats etc.) Regulations 1994**
applied: SI 1999/672 Art.2, Sch.1
Reg.2, amended: SI 1997/3055 Reg.2
Reg.3, amended: SI 1997/3055 Reg.2
Reg.5, amended: SI 1996/525 Sch para.18, SI 1996/973 Reg.2, Sch para.18
Reg.6, amended: SI 1996/525 Sch para.18, SI 1999/1820 Art.4, Sch.2 para.155
Reg.6, applied: SI 1996/1243 Sch.5 para.14
Reg.7, applied: SI 1996/3142 Reg.6
Reg.8, applied: SI 1999/916 Reg.7
Reg.8, referred to: SI 1999/916 Reg.7
Reg.10, applied: SI 1996/3142 Reg.6
Reg.40, amended: SI 1996/525 Sch para.18
Reg.48, see *WWF UK Ltd v Secretary of State for Scotland* [1999] 1 C.M.L.R. 1021 (IH), Lord Nimmo Smith
Reg.50, applied: SI 1997/1266 Sch.3 para.2
Reg.51, applied: SI 1997/1266 Sch.3 para.2
Reg.55, amended: SI 1996/525 Sch para.18
Reg.71, applied: SI 1997/1266 Sch.3 para.2
Reg.71, referred to: SI 1999/672 Art.2, Sch.1
Reg.72, applied: SI 1997/1266 Sch.3 para.2
Reg.72, referred to: SI 1999/672 Art.2, Sch.1
Reg.73, referred to: SI 1999/672 Art.2, Sch.1
Reg.74, referred to: SI 1999/672 Art.2, Sch.1
Reg.75, referred to: SI 1999/672 Art.2, Sch.1
Reg.76, referred to: SI 1999/672 Art.2, Sch.1
Reg.77, referred to: SI 1999/672 Art.2, Sch.1
Reg.78, referred to: SI 1999/672 Art.2, Sch.1

2731. **Apple Orchard Grubbing Up (Amendment) Regulations 1994**
applied: SI 1998/1131 Reg.4
revoked: SI 1998/1131 Reg.3 (with savings)

2732. **Education (No.2) Act 1986 (Amendment) (No.3) Order 1994**
revoked: 1996 c.56 Sch.38 Part III

2740. **Hill Livestock (Compensatory Allowances) Regulations 1994**
amended: SI 1996/27 Reg.2
applied: SI 1996/1500 Reg.3, SI 1999/672 Art.2, Sch.1, SI 1999/3316 Reg.5, SSI 1999/187 Reg.5
revoked (in part): SI 1996/1500 Reg.18
Reg.2, amended: SI 1996/27 Reg.2
Reg.3, amended: SI 1996/28 Reg.2
Reg.5, amended: SI 1996/27 Reg.2

2762. **Brucellosis (England and Wales) (Amendment) Order 1994**
revoked: SI 1997/758 Art.24, Sch.2

2765. **Housing Renovation etc. Grants (Prescribed Forms and Particulars) (Welsh Forms and Particulars) (Amendment) Regulations 1994**
applied: SI 1996/2842 Art.8
revoked: SI 1996/2842 Art.7, Sch Part I

2768. **Legal Aid (Scope) Regulations 1994**
Reg.2, revoked: 1999 c.22 s.106, Sch.15 Part I

2770. **Brucellosis (Scotland) (Amendment) Order 1994**
revoked: SI 1997/758 Art.24, Sch.2

2774. **Teachers' Superannuation (Amendment) (No.2) Regulations 1994**
applied: SI 1997/3001 Reg.H12, Sch.15 para.2
revoked: SI 1997/3001 Reg.H12, Sch.14

2782. **Food Safety (Live Bivalve Molluscs and Other Shellfish) (Import Conditions and Miscellaneous Amendments) Regulations 1994**
revoked: SI 1998/994 Reg.59, Sch.5
Reg.2, amended: SI 1996/3124 Reg.41, Sch.6 para.4
Reg.2, revoked: SI 1998/994 Reg.59, Sch.5
Reg.3, amended: SI 1996/1547 Reg.4, Sch.2 para.1
Reg.3, revoked: SI 1998/994 Reg.59, Sch.5
Sch.1 para.1, amended: SI 1996/1547 Reg.4, Sch.2 para.2
Sch.1 para.1, revoked: SI 1998/994 Reg.59, Sch.5
Sch.1 para.2, added: SI 1996/1547 Reg.4, Sch.2 para.3
Sch.1 para.2, revoked: SI 1998/994 Reg.59, Sch.5
Sch.1 para.3, added: SI 1996/1547 Reg.4, Sch.2 para.3
Sch.1 para.3, revoked: SI 1998/994 Reg.59, Sch.5
Sch.1 para.4, added: SI 1996/1547 Reg.4, Sch.2 para.3
Sch.1 para.4, revoked: SI 1998/994 Reg.59, Sch.5
Sch.4 para.13, revoked (in part): SI 1996/1499 Reg.49, Sch.9, SI 1998/994 Reg.59, Sch.5

2783. **Food Safety (Fishery Products) (Import Conditions and Miscellaneous Amendments) Regulations 1994**
revoked: SI 1998/994 Reg.59, Sch.5
Reg.2, amended: SI 1996/1547 Reg.5, Sch.3 para.1, SI 1996/3124 Reg.41, Sch.6 para.5
Reg.2, revoked: SI 1998/994 Reg.59, Sch.5
Reg.3, amended: SI 1996/1547 Reg.5, Sch.3 para.2
Reg.3, revoked: SI 1998/994 Reg.59, Sch.5
Reg.4, amended: SI 1996/1547 Reg.5, Sch.3 para.3
Reg.4, revoked: SI 1998/994 Reg.59, Sch.5
Reg.5, revoked: SI 1998/994 Reg.59, Sch.5
Reg.6, revoked: SI 1998/994 Reg.59, Sch.5
Reg.7, revoked: SI 1998/994 Reg.59, Sch.5
Reg.8, revoked: SI 1998/994 Reg.59, Sch.5
Reg.9, revoked: SI 1996/1547 Reg.6, Sch.4, SI 1998/994 Reg.59, Sch.5
Reg.11, revoked: SI 1996/1547 Reg.6, Sch.4, SI 1998/994 Reg.59, Sch.5
Reg.14, revoked: SI 1996/3124 Reg.42, Sch.7, SI 1998/994 Reg.59, Sch.5
Sch.1 para.1, amended: SI 1996/1547 Reg.5, Sch.3 para.4
Sch.1 para.1, revoked: SI 1998/994 Reg.59, Sch.5
Sch.1 para.2, amended: SI 1996/1547 Reg.5, Sch.3 para.4
Sch.1 para.2, revoked: SI 1998/994 Reg.59, Sch.5
Sch.1 para.3, amended: SI 1996/1547 Reg.5, Sch.3 para.4

NO.

1994—cont.

2783. Food Safety (Fishery Products) (Import Conditions and Miscellaneous Amendments) Regulations 1994—*cont.*

Sch.1 para.3, revoked: SI 1998/994 Reg.59, Sch.5

Sch.1 para.4, amended: SI 1996/1547 Reg.5, Sch.3 para.4

Sch.1 para.4, revoked: SI 1998/994 Reg.59, Sch.5

Sch.1 para.5, amended: SI 1996/1547 Reg.5, Sch.3 para.4

Sch.1 para.5, revoked: SI 1998/994 Reg.59, Sch.5

Sch.1 para.6, amended: SI 1996/1547 Reg.5, Sch.3 para.4

Sch.1 para.6, revoked: SI 1998/994 Reg.59, Sch.5

Sch.1 para.7, revoked: SI 1996/1547 Reg.5, Sch.3 para.4, SI 1998/994 Reg.59, Sch.5

Sch.1 para.8, amended: SI 1996/1547 Reg.5, Sch.3 para.4

Sch.1 para.8, revoked: SI 1998/994 Reg.59, Sch.5

Sch.1 para.9, amended: SI 1996/1547 Reg.5, Sch.3 para.4

Sch.1 para.9, revoked: SI 1998/994 Reg.59, Sch.5

Sch.1 para.10, amended: SI 1996/1547 Reg.5, Sch.3 para.4

Sch.1 para.10, revoked: SI 1998/994 Reg.59, Sch.5

Sch.1 para.11, amended: SI 1996/1547 Reg.5, Sch.3 para.4

Sch.1 para.11, revoked: SI 1998/994 Reg.59, Sch.5

Sch.1 para.12, amended: SI 1996/1547 Reg.5, Sch.3 para.4

Sch.1 para.12, revoked: SI 1998/994 Reg.59, Sch.5

Sch.1 para.13, added: SI 1996/1547 Reg.5, Sch.3 para.5

Sch.1 para.13, revoked: SI 1998/994 Reg.59, Sch.5

Sch.1 para.14, added: SI 1996/1547 Reg.5, Sch.3 para.5

Sch.1 para.14, revoked: SI 1998/994 Reg.59, Sch.5

Sch.1 para.15, added: SI 1996/1547 Reg.5, Sch.3 para.5

Sch.1 para.15, revoked: SI 1998/994 Reg.59, Sch.5

Sch.1 para.16, added: SI 1996/1547 Reg.5, Sch.3 para.5

Sch.1 para.16, revoked: SI 1998/994 Reg.59, Sch.5

Sch.1 para.17, added: SI 1996/1547 Reg.5, Sch.3 para.5

Sch.1 para.17, revoked: SI 1998/994 Reg.59, Sch.5

Sch.1 para.18, added: SI 1996/1547 Reg.5, Sch.3 para.5

Sch.1 para.18, revoked: SI 1998/994 Reg.59, Sch.5

Sch.1 para.19, added: SI 1996/1547 Reg.5, Sch.3 para.5

Sch.1 para.19, revoked: SI 1998/994 Reg.59, Sch.5

Sch.2, amended: SI 1996/1547 Reg.5, Sch.3 para.6

Sch.2, revoked: SI 1998/994 Reg.59, Sch.5

Sch.2 para.5, amended: SI 1996/1547 Reg.5, Sch.3 para.6

NO.

1994—cont.

2783. Food Safety (Fishery Products) (Import Conditions and Miscellaneous Amendments) Regulations 1994—*cont.*

Sch.2 para.5, revoked: SI 1998/994 Reg.59, Sch.5

Sch.4, revoked: SI 1996/1547 Reg.6, Sch.4, SI 1998/994 Reg.59, Sch.5

Sch.7, revoked: SI 1996/3124 Reg.42, Sch.7, SI 1998/994 Reg.59, Sch.5

2795. Criminal Justice (Northern Ireland) Order 1994

Art.2, revoked (in part): 1999 c.23 s.67, Sch.6

Art.3, revoked (in part): SI 1998/1504 (NI.9) Art.65, Sch.6

Art.11, amended: 1997 c.30 s.3

Art.11, applied: SI 1996/1299 (NI.9) Art.12, Art.25, SI 1996/3160 (NI.24) Art.4, Art.10, Art.13, 1998 c.32 s.31

Art.11, referred to: SI 1996/1299 (NI.9) Art.5, SI 1996/3160 (NI.24) Art.11

Art.11, revoked (in part): 1998 c.32 s.74, Sch.6

Art.12, amended: 1998 c.32 s.74, Sch.4 para.19

Art.12, applied: 1998 c.32 s.31

Art.14, amended: SI 1996/1299 (NI.9) Art.57, Sch.3 para.16, SI 1998/1504 Art.65, Sch.5 para.41

Art.14, applied: SI 1996/1299 (NI.9) Art.12, Art.17, SI 1996/3160 (NI.24) Art.4, Art.10, Art.13, SI 1997/1183 (NI.12) Sch.1 para.2

Art.14, referred to: SI 1996/1299 (NI.9) Art.12, SI 1996/3160 (NI.24) Art.11

Art.16, amended: SI 1996/1299 (NI.9) Art.57, Sch.3 para.17

Art.18, revoked (in part): 1999 c.23 s.67, Sch.6

Art.19, revoked: 1999 c.23 s.48, s.67, Sch.2 para.15, Sch.6

Art.20, revoked: 1999 c.23 s.48, s.67, Sch.2 para.15, Sch.6

Art.21, revoked: 1999 c.23 s.48, s.67, Sch.2 para.15, Sch.6

Art.22, revoked: 1999 c.23 s.48, s.67, Sch.2 para.15, Sch.6

Art.23, revoked: 1999 c.23 s.48, s.67, Sch.2 para.15, Sch.6

Art.24, revoked: 1999 c.23 s.48, s.67, Sch.2 para.15, Sch.6

Sch.1, revoked (in part): SI 1996/3160 (NI.24) Sch.7

Sch.2 para.1, revoked: SI 1996/3160 (NI.24) Sch.7

Sch.2 para.2, revoked: SI 1996/3160 (NI.24) Sch.7

Sch.2 para.5, revoked: SI 1998/1504 (NI.9) Art.65, Sch.6

Sch.2 para.6, revoked: SI 1996/3160 (NI.24) Sch.7

Sch.2 para.17, revoked: SI 1996/1299 (NI.9) Art.57, Sch.5

Sch.2 para.18, revoked: SI 1996/1299 (NI.9) Art.57, Sch.5

2798. Summer Time Order 1994

revoked: SI 1997/2982 Art.6

2802. Social Security (Jersey and Guernsey) Order 1994

Sch., amended: SI 1996/1928 Art.2, Sch.1

2804. Parental Orders (Human Fertilisation and Embryology) (Scotland) Regulations 1994

Sch.1, applied: SI 1997/291 r.2.55, r.2.56, r.2.59

Sch.1 para.15, applied: SI 1997/291

NO.

2805. Act of Sederunt (Sheriff Court Parental Orders (Human Fertilisation and Embryology) Rules) 1994
revoked: SI 1997/291 r.1.4, Sch.2

2811. Magistrates' Courts Committees (Constitution) Regulations 1994
applied: SI 1996/1024 Art.5, SI 1998/1175 Art.5, Sch. para.5, SI 1998/1176 Art.5, Sch. para.5, SI 1998/1432 Art.5, Sch. para.5, SI 1998/2664 Art.5, Sch. para.5, SI 1998/2769 Art.5, Sch. para.5, SI 1998/2707 Art.5, Sch. para.5, SI 1999/1609 Art.5, Sch. para.5, SI 1999/1705 Art.5, Sch. para.5, SI 1999/2209 Art.5, Sch. para.5, SI 1999/2426 Art.5, Sch. para.5, SI 1999/2542 Art.5, Sch. para.5
referred to: SI 1999/2395 Reg.3
revoked: SI 1999/2395 Reg.3 (with savings)
Reg.2, referred to: SI 1996/1024 Art.5, SI 1998/1175 Art.5, Sch. para.5, SI 1998/1176 Art.5, Sch. para.5, SI 1998/1432 Art.5, Sch. para.5, SI 1998/1492 Art.5, Sch. para.5, SI 1998/2664 Art.5, Sch. para.5, SI 1998/2707 Art.5, Sch. para.5, SI 1998/3133 Art.5, Sch. para.5, SI 1999/523 Art.5, Sch. para.5, SI 1999/1609 Art.5, Sch. para.5, SI 1999/1705 Art.5, Sch. para.5, SI 1999/2209 Art.5, Sch. para.5, SI 1999/2426 Art.5, Sch. para.5, SI 1999/2542 Art.5, Sch. para.5
Reg.2, revoked: SI 1999/2395 Reg.3 (with savings)
Reg.3, referred to: SI 1998/1175 Art.5, Sch. para.5, SI 1998/1176 Art.5, Sch. para.5, SI 1998/1432 Art.5, Sch. para.5, SI 1998/1492 Art.5, Sch. para.5, SI 1998/2664 Art.5, Sch. para.5, SI 1998/2707 Art.5, Sch. para.5, SI 1998/3133 Art.5, Sch. para.5, SI 1999/523 Art.5, Sch. para.5, SI 1999/1609 Art.5, Sch. para.5, SI 1999/1705 Art.5, Sch. para.5, SI 1999/2209 Art.5, Sch. para.5, SI 1999/2426 Art.5, Sch. para.5, SI 1999/2542 Art.5, Sch. para.5
Reg.3, revoked: SI 1999/2395 Reg.3 (with savings)
Reg.5, amended: SI 1999/2426 Art.5, Sch. para.2, Sch. para.4
Reg.5, applied: SI 1996/1024 Art.4, SI 1998/1175 Art.5, Sch. para.4, SI 1998/1176 Art.5, Sch. para.4, SI 1998/1432 Art.5, Sch. para.4, SI 1998/1492 Art.5, Sch. para.4, SI 1998/2664 Art.5, Sch. para.4, SI 1998/2707 Art.5, Sch. para.4, SI 1998/2769 Art.5, Sch. para.4, SI 1998/3133 Art.5, Sch. para.4, SI 1999/523 Art.5, Sch. para.4, SI 1999/1609 Art.5, Sch. para.4, SI 1999/1705 Art.5, Sch. para.4, SI 1999/2209 Art.5, Sch. para.4, SI 1999/2426 Art.5, Sch. para.4, SI 1999/2542 Art.5, Sch. para.4
Reg.5, referred to: SI 1996/1024 Art.2, Art.4, SI 1998/1175 Art.5, Sch. para.2, Sch. para.4, SI 1998/1176 Art.5, Sch. para.2, Sch. para.4, SI 1998/1432 Art.5, Sch. para.2, Sch. para.4, SI 1998/1492 Art.5, Sch. para.4, SI 1998/2664 Art.5, Sch. para.2, Sch. para.4, SI 1998/2707 Art.5, Sch. para.2, Sch. para.4, SI 1998/2769 Art.5, Sch. para.2, Sch. para.4, SI 1998/3133 Art.5, Sch. para.2, Sch. para.4, SI 1999/523 Art.5, Sch. para.2, Sch. para.4, SI 1999/1609 Art.5, Sch. para.2, Sch. para.4, SI 1999/1705 Art.5, Sch. para.2, Sch. para.4, SI 1999/2209 Art.5, Sch. para.2, Sch. para.4, SI 1999/2542 Art.5, Sch. para.2, Sch. para.4
Reg.5, revoked: SI 1999/2395 Reg.3 (with savings)

NO.

2811. Magistrates' Courts Committees (Constitution) Regulations 1994—*cont.*
Reg.6, referred to: SI 1996/1024 Art.5, SI 1998/1175 Art.5, Sch. para.5, SI 1998/1176 Art.5, Sch. para.5, SI 1998/1432 Art.5, Sch. para.5, SI 1998/1492 Art.5, Sch. para.5, SI 1998/2664 Art.5, Sch. para.5, SI 1998/2707 Art.5, Sch. para.5, SI 1998/2769 Art.5, Sch. para.5, SI 1998/3133 Art.5, Sch. para.2, Sch. para.5, SI 1999/523 Art.5, Sch. para.5, SI 1999/1609 Art.5, Sch. para.5, SI 1999/1705 Art.5, Sch. para.5, SI 1999/2209 Art.5, Sch. para.5, SI 1999/2426 Art.5, Sch. para.5, SI 1999/2542 Art.5, Sch. para.5
Reg.6, revoked: SI 1999/2395 Reg.3 (with savings)
Reg.7, amended: SI 1998/1175 Art.5, Sch. para.5, SI 1998/1176 Art.5, Sch. para.5, SI 1998/1432 Art.5, Sch. para.5, SI 1998/2664 Art.5, Sch. para.5, SI 1998/2707 Art.5, Sch. para.5, SI 1999/2426 Art.5, Sch. para.5
Reg.7, applied: SI 1996/1024 Art.5, SI 1998/1175 Art.5, Sch. para.5, SI 1998/1176 Art.5, Sch. para.5, SI 1998/1432 Art.5, Sch. para.5, SI 1998/1492 Art.5, Sch. para.5, SI 1998/2664 Art.5, Sch. para.5, SI 1998/2707 Art.5, Sch. para.5, SI 1998/2769 Art.5, Sch. para.5, SI 1998/3133 Art.5, Sch. para.5, SI 1999/523 Art.5, Sch. para.5, SI 1999/1609 Art.5, Sch. para.5, SI 1999/1705 Art.5, Sch. para.5, SI 1999/2209 Art.5, Sch. para.5, SI 1999/2542 Art.5, Sch. para.5
Reg.7, revoked: SI 1999/2395 Reg.3 (with savings)
Reg.8, applied: SI 1998/1492 Art.5, Sch. para.5, SI 1998/3133 Art.5, Sch. para.5, SI 1999/523 Art.5, Sch. para.5, SI 1999/1609 Art.5, Sch. para.5, SI 1999/1705 Art.5, Sch. para.5
Reg.8, referred to: SI 1998/1175 Art.5, Sch. para.5, SI 1998/1176 Art.5, Sch. para.5, SI 1998/1432 Art.5, Sch. para.5, SI 1998/2664 Art.5, Sch. para.5, SI 1998/2707 Art.5, Sch. para.5, SI 1998/2769 Art.5, Sch. para.5, SI 1998/3133 Art.5, Sch. para.2, SI 1999/2209 Art.5, Sch. para.5, SI 1999/2426 Art.5, Sch. para.5, SI 1999/2542 Art.5, Sch. para.5
Reg.8, revoked: SI 1999/2395 Reg.3 (with savings)
Reg.10, applied: SI 1996/1024 Art.5, Art.6, SI 1998/1492 Art.5, Sch. para.5, SI 1998/3133 Art.5, Sch. para.5, SI 1999/523 Art.5, Sch. para.5, SI 1999/1609 Art.5, Sch. para.5, SI 1999/1705 Art.5, Sch. para.6
Reg.10, referred to: SI 1998/1175 Art.5, Sch. para.5, Sch. para.6, SI 1998/1176 Art.5, Sch. para.5, Sch. para.6, SI 1998/1432 Art.5, Sch. para.5, Sch. para.6, SI 1998/1492 Art.5, Sch. para.5, Sch. para.6, SI 1998/2664 Art.5, Sch. para.5, Sch. para.6, SI 1998/2707 Art.5, Sch. para.5, Sch. para.6, SI 1998/2769 Art.5, Sch. para.5, Sch. para.6, SI 1998/3133 Art.5, Sch. para.6, SI 1999/523 Art.5, Sch. para.6, SI 1999/1609 Art.5, Sch. para.6, SI 1999/2209 Art.5, Sch. para.5, Sch. para.6, SI 1999/2426 Art.5, Sch. para.5, Sch. para.6, SI 1999/2542 Art.5, Sch. para.5
Reg.10, revoked: SI 1999/2395 Reg.3 (with savings)
Reg.11, applied: SI 1996/1024 Art.5, SI 1998/1175 Art.5, Sch. para.5, SI 1998/1176 Art.5, Sch. para.5, SI 1998/1432 Art.5, Sch. para.5, SI 1998/1492 Art.5, Sch. para.5, SI 1998/3133 Art.5, Sch. para.5, SI 1999/523 Art.5, Sch. para.5, SI 1999/2426 Art.5, Sch. para.5

NO.

1994—cont.

2811. Magistrates' Courts Committees (Constitution) Regulations 1994—*cont.*
Reg.11, referred to: SI 1999/1609 Art.5, Sch. para.5
Reg.11, revoked: SI 1999/2395 Reg.3 (with savings)
Reg.14, applied: SI 1996/1024 Art.5
Reg.14, referred to: SI 1996/1024 Art.5, SI 1998/1175 Art.5, Sch. para.5, SI 1998/1176 Art.5, Sch. para.5, SI 1998/1432 Art.5, Sch. para.5, SI 1998/1492 Art.5, Sch. para.5, SI 1998/2664 Art.5, Sch. para.5, SI 1998/2707 Art.5, Sch. para.5, SI 1998/3133 Art.5, Sch. para.5, SI 1999/523 Art.5, Sch. para.5, SI 1999/1609 Art.5, Sch. para.5, SI 1999/1705 Art.5, Sch. para.5, SI 1999/2209 Art.5, Sch. para.5, SI 1999/2542 Art.5, Sch. para.5
Reg.14, revoked: SI 1999/2395 Reg.3 (with savings)
Reg.15, referred to: SI 1996/1024 Art.5, SI 1998/1175 Art.5, Sch. para.5, SI 1998/1176 Art.5, Sch. para.5, SI 1998/1432 Art.5, Sch. para.5, SI 1998/2664 Art.5, Sch. para.5, SI 1998/2707 Art.5, Sch. para.5, SI 1998/2769 Art.5, Sch. para.5, SI 1998/3133 Art.5, Sch. para.5, SI 1999/523 Art.5, Sch. para.5, SI 1999/1609 Art.5, Sch. para.5, SI 1999/1705 Art.5, Sch. para.5, SI 1999/2209 Art.5, Sch. para.5, SI 1999/2426 Art.5, Sch. para.5, SI 1999/2542 Art.5, Sch. para.5
Reg.15, revoked: SI 1999/2395 Reg.3 (with savings)
Reg.16, referred to: SI 1996/1024 Art.5, SI 1998/1175 Art.5, Sch. para.5, SI 1998/1176 Art.5, Sch. para.5, SI 1998/1432 Art.5, Sch. para.5, SI 1998/2664 Art.5, Sch. para.5, SI 1998/2707 Art.5, Sch. para.5, SI 1998/2769 Art.5, Sch. para.5, SI 1998/3133 Art.5, Sch. para.5, SI 1999/523 Art.5, Sch. para.5, SI 1999/1609 Art.5, Sch. para.5, SI 1999/1705 Art.5, Sch. para.5, SI 1999/2209 Art.5, Sch. para.5, SI 1999/2426 Art.5, Sch. para.5, SI 1999/2542 Art.5, Sch. para.5
Reg.16, revoked: SI 1999/2395 Reg.3 (with savings)
Sch.2, applied: SI 1996/1024 Art.5
Sch.2, referred to: SI 1998/1175 Art.5, Sch. para.5, SI 1998/1176 Art.5, Sch. para.5, SI 1998/1432 Art.5, Sch. para.5, SI 1998/1492 Art.5, Sch. para.5, SI 1998/2664 Art.5, Sch. para.5, SI 1998/2707 Art.5, Sch. para.5, SI 1998/2769 Art.5, Sch. para.5, SI 1998/3133 Art.5, Sch. para.5, SI 1999/523 Art.5, Sch. para.5, SI 1999/1609 Art.5, Sch. para.5, SI 1999/1705 Art.5, Sch. para.5, SI 1999/2209 Art.5, Sch. para.5, SI 1999/2426 Art.5, Sch. para.5, SI 1999/2542 Art.5, Sch. para.5
Sch.2, revoked: SI 1999/2395 Reg.3 (with savings)
Sch.3, referred to: SI 1996/1024 Art.5, SI 1998/1175 Art.5, Sch. para.5, SI 1998/1176 Art.5, Sch. para.5, SI 1998/1432 Art.5, Sch. para.5, SI 1998/1492 Art.5, Sch. para.5, SI 1998/2664 Art.5, Sch. para.5, SI 1998/2707 Art.5, Sch. para.5, SI 1998/2769 Art.5, Sch. para.5, SI 1998/3133 Art.5, Sch. para.5, SI 1999/523 Art.5, Sch. para.5, SI 1999/1609 Art.5, Sch. para.5, SI 1999/1705 Art.5, Sch. para.5, SI 1999/2209 Art.5, Sch. para.5, SI 1999/2426 Art.5, Sch. para.5, SI 1999/2542 Art.5, Sch. para.5
Sch.3, revoked: SI 1999/2395 Reg.3 (with savings)

NO.

1994—cont.

2825. Local Government Changes for England (Finance) Regulations 1994
applied: SI 1996/1867 Art.15, SI 1996/1879 Art.6
Reg.49, applied: SI 1997/165 Reg.3
Reg.54A, amended: SI 1996/563 Reg.2

2841. Urban Waste Water Treatment (England and Wales) Regulations 1994
see *R. v Secretary of State for the Environment Ex p. Kingston Upon Hull City Council* [1996] Env. L.R. 248 (QBD), Harrison, J.

2842. Urban Waste Water Treatment (Scotland) Regulations 1994
Reg.2, amended: SI 1996/973 Reg.2, Sch para.19
Reg.3, amended: SI 1996/973 Reg.2, Sch para.19
Reg.4, amended: SI 1996/973 Reg.2, Sch para.19
Reg.5, amended: SI 1996/973 Reg.2, Sch para.19
Reg.6, amended: SI 1996/973 Reg.2, Sch para.19
Reg.11, amended: SI 1996/973 Reg.2, Sch para.19
Reg.12, amended: SI 1996/973 Reg.2, Sch para.19
Sch.3 Part II, amended: SI 1996/973 Reg.2, Sch para.19

2844. Dangerous Substances and Preparations (Safety) (Consolidation) Regulations 1994
Reg.1, amended: SI 1996/2635 Reg.2
Reg.2, amended: SI 1999/2084 Reg.2
Reg.2A, added: SI 1996/2635 Reg.2
Reg.3, amended: SI 1996/2635 Reg.2
Reg.3A, added: SI 1999/2084 Reg.2
Reg.6A, added: SI 1996/2635 Reg.2
Reg.6B, added: SI 1996/2635 Reg.2
Reg.6C, added: SI 1996/2635 Reg.2
Reg.6D, added: SI 1996/2635 Reg.2
Sch., amended: SI 1996/2635 Reg.2
Sch.2, added: SI 1996/2635 Reg.2, Sch
Sch.2, substituted: SI 1999/3193 Reg.2, Sch.

2865. Management of Health and Safety at Work (Amendment) Regulations 1994
revoked: SI 1999/3242 Reg.29

2876. Teachers' Superannuation (Amendment) (No.3) Regulations 1994
applied: SI 1997/3001 Reg.H12, Sch.15 para.2
revoked: SI 1997/3001 Reg.H12, Sch.14

2887. A13 Trunk Road (Tower Hamlets) (Bus Lanes) Traffic Order 1994
revoked (in part): SI 1999/3051 Art.6

2898. Free Zone (Port of Sheerness) Designation Order 1994
Art.2, amended: SI 1997/994 Art.2

2919. Dairy Produce Quotas (Amendment) (No.2) Regulations 1994
revoked: SI 1997/733 Reg.35

2924. Teachers' Superannuation (Additional Voluntary Contributions) Regulations 1994
applied: SI 1997/3001 Sch.3 para.2
referred to: SI 1997/3001 Reg.B3
Reg.2, amended: SI 1997/3001 Reg.H11
Reg.7, amended: SI 1997/3001 Reg.H11
Reg.8, amended: SI 1997/3001 Reg.H11
Reg.11, amended: SI 1997/3001 Reg.H11
Reg.12, amended: SI 1997/3001 Reg.H11
Reg.15, amended: SI 1997/3001 Reg.H11
Reg.16, amended: SI 1997/3001 Reg.H11
Reg.20, revoked (in part): SI 1997/3001 Reg.H11

NO.

2924. Teachers' Superannuation (Additional Voluntary Contributions) Regulations 1994— *cont.*
Sch. para.3, amended: SI 1997/3001 Reg.H11
Sch. para.4, amended: SI 1997/3001 Reg.H11
Sch. para.5, amended: SI 1997/3001 Reg.H11
Sch. para.11, amended: SI 1997/3001 Reg.H11
Sch. para.12, amended: SI 1997/3001 Reg.H11

2930. Suspension from Work (on Maternity Grounds) Order 1994
Art.1, amended: SI 1999/3242 Reg.29, Sch.2
Art.2, amended: SI 1999/3242 Reg.29, Sch.2

2945. Social Security (Incapacity Benefit - Increases for Dependants) Regulations 1994
Reg.3, amended: SI 1999/2422 Art.3, Sch.9
Reg.5, revoked: SI 1996/2745 Reg.18, Sch.4
Reg.10, amended: SI 1996/1345 Reg.19
Reg.15, revoked (in part): SI 1996/1345 Reg.27, Sch.

2946. Social Security (Incapacity Benefit) Regulations 1994
Reg.2A, added: SI 1997/2676 Reg.9
Reg.4, amended: SI 1999/2226 Reg.2
Reg.5A, added: SI 1998/2231 Reg.2
Reg.8, amended: SI 1996/670 Reg.6, SI 1997/576 Reg.6, SI 1998/563 Reg.6, SI 1999/858 Reg.5
Reg.10, amended: SI 1996/599 Art.14, SI 1997/543 Art.14, SI 1998/470 Art.14, SI 1999/264 Art.14

2957. Education (Chief Inspector of Schools in Wales) Order 1994
revoked: SI 1996/3172 Art.3

2958. Local Government Staff Commission (Scotland) Order 1994
revoked: SI 1997/672 Art.3

2965. Diseases of Animals (Approved Disinfectants) (Amendment) Order 1994
revoked: SI 1997/2347 Art.3

2987. Medicines (Restrictions on the Administration of Veterinary Medicinal Products) Regulations 1994
Reg.2, amended: SI 1997/322 Reg.37, Sch.6
Reg.2, substituted: SI 1997/2884 Reg.3
Reg.3, amended: SI 1997/322 Reg.37, Sch.6
Reg.3, substituted: SI 1997/2884 Reg.3
Reg.4, applied: SI 1997/1729 Reg.6
Reg.4, substituted: SI 1997/2884 Reg.3
Reg.5, amended: SI 1997/322 Reg.37, Sch.6
Reg.5, applied: SI 1997/1729 Reg.6
Reg.5, substituted: SI 1997/2884 Reg.3
Reg.13, revoked: SI 1997/1729 Reg.36, Sch.2

2994. Scottish Ambulance Service National Health Service Trust (Establishment) Order 1994
revoked: SI 1999/653 Art.2

2995. Glasgow Dental Hospital and School National Health Service Trust (Establishment) Order 1994
revoked: SI 1999/1070 Art.2, Sch.2

2996. Argyll and Bute National Health Service Trust (Establishment) Order 1994
revoked: SI 1999/1070 Art.2, Sch.2

2997. Borders Community Health Services National Health Service Trust (Establishment) Order 1994
revoked: SI 1999/1070 Art.2, Sch.2

2999. Dumfries and Galloway Community Health National Health Service Trust (Establishment) Order 1994
revoked: SI 1999/1070 Art.2, Sch.2

NO.

3000. Lanarkshire Healthcare National Health Service Trust (Establishment) Order 1994
revoked: SI 1999/1070 Art.2, Sch.2

3001. Lomond Healthcare National Health Service Trust (Establishment) Order 1994
revoked: SI 1999/1070 Art.2, Sch.2

3005. A1 Trunk Road (Haringey) (Bus Lanes) Red Route Traffic Order 1993 Variation Order 1994
revoked (in part): SI 1997/449 Art.5

3007. A1 Trunk Road (Islington) (Bus Lanes) Red Route Traffic Order 1993 Variation Order 1994
revoked (in part): SI 1997/445 Art.5

3016. Medicines (Products Other Than Veterinary Drugs) (Prescription Only) Amendment (No.2) Order 1994
revoked: SI 1997/1830 Art.16, Sch.6

3017. Medical Devices Regulations 1994
applied: SI 1998/2306 Reg.10, Sch.1

3018. Accounts and Audit (Amendment) Regulations 1994
revoked (in part): SI 1996/590 Reg.3

3022. Firearms (Amendment) Rules 1994
revoked: SI 1998/1941 r.12, Sch.6

3024. Charitable Institutions (Fund-Raising) Regulations 1994
Reg.1, amended: SI 1998/1129 Art.3, Sch.2

3025. Local Government (Compensation for Redundancy) Regulations 1994
Part II, applied: SI 1996/330 Reg.12
Part II, revoked: SI 1996/1680 Reg.49, Sch.5
Part III, applied: SI 1996/330 Reg.12, SI 1996/1680 Reg.32, Reg.39
Part III, referred to: SI 1996/532 Art.3
Reg.2, amended: SI 1996/456 Reg.2, SI 1996/1680 Sch.4 para.3, SI 1997/1613 Reg.27, Sch.3 para.7, SI 1997/2059 Reg.2
Reg.3, amended: SI 1996/456 Reg.3
Reg.4, amended: SI 1996/456 Reg.3
Reg.5, substituted: SI 1996/456 Reg.4
Reg.6, amended: SI 1996/456 Reg.6, SI 1996/1680 Sch.4 para.3, SI 1997/2059 Reg.2
Reg.6, substituted: SI 1996/456 Reg.4
Reg.7, amended: SI 1997/2059 Reg.2
Reg.7, applied: SI 1997/2059 Reg.3
Reg.7, substituted: SI 1996/456 Reg.4
Reg.8, substituted: SI 1996/456 Reg.4
Reg.9, amended: SI 1997/1613 Reg.27, Sch.3 para.8
Reg.9, applied: SI 1997/1612 Reg.26
Reg.9, substituted: SI 1996/456 Reg.4
Reg.10, amended: SI 1996/1680 Sch.4 para.3
Reg.10, substituted: SI 1996/456 Reg.4
Reg.11, substituted: SI 1996/456 Reg.4
Reg.12, amended: SI 1996/1680 Sch.4 para.3
Reg.12, substituted: SI 1996/456 Reg.4
Reg.15, amended: SI 1996/1680 Reg.49, Sch.5
Reg.15, applied: SI 1997/1612 Reg.26
Reg.16, amended: SI 1996/1680 Reg.49, Sch.5
Reg.17, revoked: SI 1996/1680 Reg.49, Sch.5
Sch., added: SI 1996/456 Reg.5

3026. Local Government Superannuation (Amendment) Regulations 1994
Reg.10, amended: SI 1997/1613 Reg.27, Sch.3 para.9

3038. National Health Service (Service Committees and Tribunal) (Scotland) Amendment Regulations 1994
Reg.20, revoked: SI 1996/938 Reg.7

NO.

1994—cont.

3042. Education (Fees and Awards) Regulations 1994
revoked: SI 1997/1972 Reg.8
Reg.2, amended: SI 1996/1640 Reg.3
Reg.2, revoked: SI 1997/1972 Reg.8
Sch.1 para.7, revoked: SI 1997/1972 Reg.8
Sch.1 para.7, substituted: SI 1996/1640 Reg.4
Sch.1 para.8, amended: SI 1996/1640 Reg.5
Sch.1 para.8, revoked: SI 1997/1972 Reg.8
Sch.2 para.2, revoked: SI 1997/1972 Reg.8
Sch.2 para.2, substituted: SI 1996/1640 Reg.6

3044. Education (Mandatory Awards) Regulations 1994
Reg.7, see *R. v Shropshire CC Ex p. Jones* [1997] E.L.R. 357 (QBD), Carnwath, J.
Reg.11, see *R. v Shropshire CC Ex p. Jones* [1997] E.L.R. 357 (QBD), Carnwath, J.
Reg.12, see *R. v Shropshire CC Ex p. Jones* [1997] E.L.R. 357 (QBD), Carnwath, J.
Reg.25, applied: SI 1998/1166 Reg.6, SI 1999/1494 Reg.6
Reg.25, referred to: SI 1997/431 Reg.6

3045. Education (Student Loans) Regulations 1994
referred to: SI 1996/1812 Reg.7
revoked: SI 1996/1812 Reg.2

3046. Court of Protection Rules 1994
r.9, amended: SI 1999/2504 r.3
r.21, amended: SI 1999/2504 r.4
r.79, amended: SI 1999/2504 r.5
r.80, amended: SI 1999/2504 r.6
r.82, substituted: SI 1999/2504 r.7
r.89, substituted: SI 1999/2504 r.8
r.93, see *Hughes (Deceased), Re* Times, January 8, 1999 (Ch D), Judge Weeks Q.C.
Appendix.Table 1, amended: SI 1999/2504 r.9
Appendix.Table 2, amended: SI 1999/2504 r.9
Appendix.para.1, amended: SI 1999/2504 r.9
Appendix.para.4, substituted: SI 1999/2504 r.9
Appendix.para.7, amended: SI 1999/2504 r.9

3047. Court of Protection (Enduring Powers of Attorney) Rules 1994
Sch.2, amended: SI 1999/2505 r.2

3049. Merchant Shipping (Liability of Shipowners and Others) (Rate of Interest) Order 1994
revoked: SI 1998/1795 Art.2

3050. Medicines (Products Other Than Veterinary Drugs) (Prescription Only) Amendment (No.3) Order 1994
revoked: SI 1997/1830 Art.16, Sch.6

3055. Civil Aviation (Joint Financing) Regulations 1994
revoked: SI 1997/2937 Reg.3, Sch.1
Reg.4, amended: SI 1996/3032 Reg.2
Reg.4, revoked: SI 1997/2937 Reg.3, Sch.1
Reg.15, amended: SI 1996/3032 Reg.2
Reg.15, revoked: SI 1997/2937 Reg.3, Sch.1

3068. Local Government (Compensation for Redundancy) (Scotland) Regulations 1994
applied: SI 1998/192 Reg.52
revoked: SI 1998/192 Reg.52, Sch.2
Reg.3, amended: SI 1996/1360 Reg.15
Reg.3, revoked: SI 1998/192 Reg.52, Sch.2

3082. Meat Products (Hygiene) Regulations 1994
applied: SI 1996/3124 Reg.3, Reg.10, Sch.2 para.5, SI 1999/646 Art.33
Reg.2, amended: SI 1996/1499 Reg.49, SI 1999/683 Reg.2
Reg.2, applied: SI 1997/2964 Sch.1
Reg.4, amended: SI 1999/683 Reg.2
Reg.10, amended: SI 1999/683 Reg.2

NO.

1994—cont.

3082. Meat Products (Hygiene) Regulations 1994 —cont.
Reg.14, amended: SI 1999/683 Reg.2
Sch.1 Part I, amended: SI 1999/683 Reg.2
Sch.1 Part IIA, amended: SI 1999/683 Reg.2
Sch.2 Part III, amended: SI 1999/683 Reg.2
Sch.2 Part V, amended: SI 1999/683 Reg.2
Sch.2 Part VI, amended: SI 1999/683 Reg.2
Sch.2 Part VII, amended: SI 1999/683 Reg.2
Sch.2 Part VIII, amended: SI 1999/683 Reg.2
Sch.2 Part IX, amended: SI 1999/683 Reg.2
Sch.5 Part IIA, amended: SI 1999/683 Reg.2
Sch.5 Part IIB, amended: SI 1999/683 Reg.2

3085. Set-Aside Access (Scotland) Regulations 1994
applied: SI 1997/330 Reg.7
revoked: SI 1996/3037 Reg.7 (with savings)
Reg.2, amended: SI 1996/3037 Reg.3
Reg.7, amended: SI 1996/3037 Reg.4
Reg.11, amended: SI 1996/3037 Reg.5
Reg.11A, added: SI 1996/3037 Reg.6

3086. Act of Sederunt (Proceedings in the Sheriff Court under the Debtors (Scotland) Act 1987) (Amendment) 1994
revoked: SI 1996/2709 r.3, Sch.2

3096. Highlands and Islands Agricultural Programme Regulations 1994
Reg.2, amended: SI 1999/647 Reg.3
Reg.5, applied: SI 1999/647 Reg.2
Reg.6, amended: SI 1999/647 Reg.4
Reg.8, amended: SI 1999/647 Reg.5
Reg.9, amended: SI 1999/647 Reg.6
Sch., substituted: SI 1999/647 Reg.7, Sch.

3099. Habitat (Broadleaved Woodland) (Wales) Regulations 1994
applied: SI 1996/3142 Reg.6, SI 1997/2844 Sch.3 Part I, Sch.4 para.3, SI 1999/672 Art.2, Sch.1
Reg.2, amended: SI 1996/3075 Reg.2
Reg.3, amended: SI 1996/3075 Reg.2
Reg.5, amended: SI 1996/3075 Reg.2
Reg.6, amended: SI 1996/3075 Reg.2
Reg.7, amended: SI 1996/3075 Reg.2
Reg.10, substituted: SI 1996/3075 Reg.2
Reg.10A, added: SI 1996/3075 Reg.2
Reg.10B, added: SI 1996/3075 Reg.2
Reg.12, added: SI 1999/1176 Reg.14, Sch.6

3100. Habitat (Water Fringe) (Wales) Regulations 1994
applied: SI 1996/3142 Reg.6, SI 1997/2844 Sch.3 Part I, Sch.4 para.3, SI 1999/672 Art.2, Sch.1
Reg.2, amended: SI 1996/3073 Reg.2
Reg.3, amended: SI 1996/3073 Reg.2
Reg.5, amended: SI 1996/3073 Reg.2
Reg.6, amended: SI 1996/3073 Reg.2
Reg.7, amended: SI 1996/3073 Reg.2
Reg.10, substituted: SI 1996/3073 Reg.2
Reg.10A, added: SI 1996/3073 Reg.2
Reg.10B, added: SI 1996/3073 Reg.2
Reg.12, added: SI 1999/1176 Reg.14, Sch.6

3101. Habitat (Coastal Belt) (Wales) Regulations 1994
applied: SI 1996/3142 Reg.6, SI 1997/2844 Sch.3 Part I, Sch.4 para.3, SI 1999/672 Art.2, Sch.1
Reg.2, amended: SI 1996/3074 Reg.2
Reg.3, amended: SI 1996/3074 Reg.2
Reg.5, amended: SI 1996/3074 Reg.2
Reg.6, amended: SI 1996/3074 Reg.2
Reg.7, amended: SI 1996/3074 Reg.2
Reg.10, substituted: SI 1996/3074 Reg.2

NO.

3101. Habitat (Coastal Belt) (Wales) Regulations 1994—*cont.*
Reg.10A, added: SI 1996/3074 Reg.2
Reg.10B, added: SI 1996/3074 Reg.2
Reg.12, added: SI 1999/1176 Reg.14, Sch.6

3102. Habitat (Species-Rich Grassland) (Wales) Regulations 1994
applied: SI 1996/3142 Reg.6, SI 1997/2844 Sch.3 Part I, Sch.4 para.3, SI 1999/672 Art.2, Sch.1
Reg.2, amended: SI 1996/3072 Reg.2
Reg.3, amended: SI 1996/3072 Reg.2
Reg.5, amended: SI 1996/3072 Reg.2
Reg.6, amended: SI 1996/3072 Reg.2
Reg.7, amended: SI 1996/3072 Reg.2
Reg.10, substituted: SI 1996/3072 Reg.2
Reg.10A, added: SI 1996/3072 Reg.2
Reg.10B, added: SI 1996/3072 Reg.2
Reg.12, added: SI 1999/1176 Reg.14, Sch.6

3117. Motor Vehicle Tyres (Safety) Regulations 1994
Reg.1, amended: SI 1997/815 Reg.2
Reg.11, amended: SI 1996/3227 Reg.2

3118. Church Representation Rules (Amendment) Resolution 1994
referred to: SI 1998/319, SI 1999/2112

3121. Central Rating Lists Regulations 1994
Reg.4, applied: SI 1997/968 Reg.4
Reg.5, amended: SI 1996/620 Reg.2
Sch. Part 2, added: SI 1996/620 Reg.2
Sch. Part 6, amended: SI 1996/620 Reg.2

3123. Non-Domestic Rating (Railways, Telecommunication and Canals) Regulations 1994
revoked (in part): SI 1999/3453 Reg.7
Reg.3, amended: SI 1999/3453 Reg.6
Reg.3, applied: SI 1999/3453 Reg.3, Sch. Part 4
Reg.3, revoked (in part): SI 1999/3453 Reg.6, Reg.7
Reg.4, applied: SI 1999/3453 Reg.3, Sch. Part 5
Reg.5, applied: SI 1999/3453 Reg.3, Sch. Part 1
Reg.5, revoked (in part): SI 1999/3453 Reg.7

3130. Vocational Training for General Medical Practice (European Requirements) Regulations 1994
applied: SI 1997/2817 Reg.3, SI 1998/5 Reg.3
Part III, revoked (in part): SI 1997/2817 Reg.20, Sch.5, SI 1998/5 Reg.19, Sch.4
Reg.5, amended: SI 1998/669 Reg.4

3131. Beef Special Premium (Amendment) Regulations 1994
revoked: SI 1996/3241 Reg.22

3133. Insurance Companies (Amendment No.2) Regulations 1994
Reg.18, revoked: SI 1996/943 Reg.35, Sch.7
Reg.19, revoked: SI 1996/943 Reg.35, Sch.7
Reg.20, revoked: SI 1996/943 Reg.35, Sch.7
Reg.21, revoked: SI 1996/943 Reg.35, Sch.7

3140. Construction (Design and Management) Regulations 1994
Reg.2, amended: SI 1996/1592 Reg.34, Sch.9 para.9
Reg.2, referred to: SI 1996/1656 Reg.3, SI 1998/2451 Reg.2
Reg.3, referred to: SI 1996/1656 Reg.3
Reg.7, applied: SI 1998/494 Sch.2 para.4
Reg.16, amended: SI 1999/3242 Reg.29, Sch.2
Reg.17, amended: SI 1999/3242 Reg.29, Sch.2
Reg.19, amended: SI 1999/3242 Reg.29, Sch.2
Reg.24, revoked (in part): SI 1998/494 Reg.7, Sch.3

NO.

3141. Diseases of Poultry Order 1994
Art.3, amended: SI 1997/150 Art.2
Art.5A, added: SI 1997/150 Art.2

3142. Marketing Authorisations for Veterinary Medicinal Products Regulations 1994
applied: SI 1997/968 Art.4, SI 1998/2428 Reg.15, SI 1999/3142 Art.2
referred to: SI 1996/2194 Sch.1 Part I, 1998 c.46 s.30, Sch.5 s.J4, SI 1998/463 Art.5, SI 1999/1540 Reg.3
Reg.1, amended: SI 1997/654 Reg.19, SI 1999/3142 Art.5, Sch. para.2
Reg.5, referred to: SI 1998/2428 Sch.7 para.4
Reg.6, amended: SI 1998/1048 Reg.3, Sch.2 para.2
Reg.12, applied: SI 1997/1469 Reg.15
Sch.1 para.3, amended: SI 1997/654 Reg.19
Sch.2 para.1, amended: SI 1997/654 Reg.19
Sch.5 para.13, revoked: SI 1999/1540 Reg.21, Sch.4
Sch.5 para.23, revoked: SI 1997/1729 Reg.36, Sch.2
Sch.5 para.32, revoked: SI 1997/2884 Reg.4

3143. Medicines (Veterinary Drugs) (Renewal Applications for Licences and Animal Test Certificates) Regulations 1994
revoked (in part): SI 1996/2194 Reg.6, Sch.3

3144. Medicines for Human Use (Marketing Authorisations etc.) Regulations 1994
see *R. v Wilson (Paul)* [1998] 1 Cr. App. R. (S.) 364 (CA (Crim Div)), Sachs, J.
referred to: 1998 c.46 s.30, Sch.5 s.J4, SI 1998/463 Art.5, SI 1999/1540 Reg.3
Reg.1, referred to: SI 1999/2109 Reg.2
Reg.11, amended: SI 1998/3105 Reg.2
Sch.3 para.11, amended: SI 1998/3105 Reg.5
Sch.3 para.12, amended: SI 1998/3105 Reg.5
Sch.5 para.5, amended: SI 1998/3105 Reg.3
Sch.5A, added: SI 1998/3105 Reg.4
Sch.7 para.11, revoked: SI 1996/1499 Reg.49, Sch.9
Sch.7 para.12, revoked: SI 1999/1540 Reg.21, Sch.4
Sch.7 para.19, revoked: SI 1999/1540 Reg.21, Sch.4
Sch.7 para.22, revoked: SI 1997/2884 Reg.4

3146. Non-Domestic Rating Contributions (Scotland) Amendment Regulations 1994
revoked: SI 1996/3070 Reg.10, Sch.4
Reg.6, revoked: SI 1996/3070 Reg.10, Sch.4

3148. Education (European Community Enlargement) (Scotland) Regulations 1994
revoked (in part): SI 1997/93 Reg.14, Sch.4
Reg.3, revoked: SI 1996/1754 Reg.7, Sch.3

3151. Registration of Births, Still-births, Deaths and Marriages (Prescription of Forms) (Scotland) Amendment Regulations 1994
revoked: SI 1997/2348 Reg.30, Sch.27
Reg.5, revoked: SI 1997/512 Reg.5, SI 1997/2348 Reg.30, Sch.27
Sch.2, revoked: SI 1997/512 Reg.5, SI 1997/2348 Reg.30, Sch.27

3159. Unfair Terms in Consumer Contracts Regulations 1994
see *Falco Finance Ltd v Gough* (1999) 17 Tr. L.R. 526 (CC) (Macclesfield), Judge Elystan Morgan
applied: 1996 c.23 s.89
revoked: SI 1999/2083 Reg.2
Reg.3, revoked: SI 1999/2083 Reg.2

NO.

3164. Local Government Act 1988 (Competition) (Legal Services) (England) Regulations 1994

Reg.2, amended: SI 1997/175 Reg.6, SI 1997/2732 Reg.7

Reg.3, amended: SI 1997/175 Reg.6, SI 1997/2732 Reg.7

3165. Local Government Act 1988 (Defined Activities) (Competition) (Supervision of Parking, Management of Vehicles and Security Work) (England) Regulations 1994

Reg.2, amended: SI 1997/561 Reg.3

Reg.2, revoked (in part): SI 1997/175 Reg.8

Reg.3, revoked: SI 1997/2747 Reg.2, Sch.

3166. Local Government Act 1988 (Competition) (Construction and Property Services) (England) Regulations 1994

Reg.2, amended: SI 1997/175 Reg.3, SI 1997/2732 Reg.3

Reg.3, amended: SI 1997/175 Reg.3, SI 1997/2732 Reg.3

3167. Local Government Changes for England (Direct Labour and Service Organisations) Regulations 1994

Reg.2, amended: SI 1996/1882 Reg.2

3169. Medicines (Veterinary Drugs) (Pharmacy and Merchants' List) (Amendment No.2) Order 1994

revoked: SI 1998/1044 Art.9, Sch.

3170. Council Tax (Reduction of Liability) (Scotland) Regulations 1994

Reg.6, revoked (in part): SI 1996/746 Reg.6

3171. General Medical Council (Constitution of Fitness to Practise Committees) (Amendment No.2) Rules Order of Council 1994

revoked: SI 1996/2125 Sch. para.16, Sch.2

3172. Broadcasting (Unlicensed Television Services) Exemption Order 1994

revoked: SI 1999/2628 Art.2

3177. Black Country Mental Health National Health Service Trust (Establishment) Order 1994

Art.3, substituted: SI 1998/1187 Art.2

3178. Pathfinder National Health Service Trust (Establishment) Order 1994

Art.1, amended: SI 1999/1384 Art.2

Art.2, amended: SI 1999/1384 Art.2

3181. Homerton Hospital National Health Service Trust (Establishment) Order 1994

Art.3, substituted: SI 1998/3192 Art.2

Art.4, amended: SI 1998/3192 Art.3

3182. Birmingham Children's Hospital National Health Service Trust (Establishment) Order 1994

Art.3, amended: SI 1999/370 Art.2

3183. St James and Seacroft University Hospitals National Health Service Trust (Establishment) Order 1994

revoked: SI 1998/839 Art.2

3185. Fosse Health, Leicestershire Community National Health Service Trust (Establishment) Order 1994

revoked: SI 1998/3068 Art.2

3186. United Leeds Teaching Hospitals National Health Service Trust (Establishment) Order 1994

revoked: SI 1998/838 Art.2

3187. Air Navigation (Dangerous Goods) Regulations 1994

Reg.3, amended: SI 1996/3100 Reg.2, SI 1997/2666 Reg.2, SI 1998/2536 Reg.2

NO.

3195. Prison (Amendment) Rules 1994

revoked: SI 1999/728 r.85 (with savings), Sch. (with savings)

3198. Firearms (Scotland) Amendment Rules 1994

revoked: SI 1998/1941 r.12, Sch.6

3211. Double Taxation Relief (Taxes on Income) (Kazakhstan) Order 1994

Sch., referred to: SI 1998/2567 Art.2

Sch. Art.11, amended: SI 1998/2567 Sch. Art.I

Sch. Art.25, amended: SI 1998/2567 Sch. Art.II

3226. Exchange Gains and Losses (Transitional Provisions) Regulations 1994

Reg.1, amended: SI 1996/1349 Reg.3

Reg.6, amended: SI 1996/1349 Reg.4

Reg.10, amended: SI 1996/1349 Reg.5

Reg.13, amended: SI 1996/1349 Reg.6

Reg.14, amended: SI 1996/1349 Reg.7

Reg.14, revoked (in part): SI 1996/1349 Reg.7

Reg.15, amended: SI 1996/1349 Reg.8

Reg.18, amended: SI 1996/1349 Reg.9

3227. Exchange Gains and Losses (Alternative Method of Calculation of Gain or Loss) Regulations 1994

Reg.4, amended: SI 1996/1347 Reg.3

Reg.5, amended: SI 1996/1347 Reg.4

Reg.10, amended: SI 1996/1347 Reg.5

Reg.11, amended: SI 1996/1347 Reg.6

3228. Exchange Gains and Losses (Deferral of Gains and Losses) Regulations 1994

Reg.2, amended: SI 1996/1348 Reg.3

Reg.2, referred to: SI 1998/3177 Reg.7

Reg.4, amended: SI 1996/1348 Reg.4

3230. Local Currency Elections Regulations 1994

applied: SI 1998/3177 Reg.43, Reg.44

Reg.3, amended: SI 1998/3177 Reg.45

Reg.3, applied: SI 1998/3177 Reg.43

Reg.4, applied: SI 1998/3177 Reg.43, Reg.44

Reg.5, amended: SI 1998/3177 Reg.42

Reg.6, amended: SI 1998/3177 Reg.42

Reg.8, amended: SI 1998/3177 Reg.46

Reg.9, amended: SI 1998/3177 Reg.47

3231. Exchange Gains and Losses (Insurance Companies) Regulations 1994

Reg.1, amended: SI 1996/673 Reg.3

Reg.5A, added: SI 1996/1485 Reg.3

Reg.6, revoked: SI 1996/673 Reg.5

Reg.7, added: SI 1996/673 Reg.4

Reg.7, amended: SI 1997/1155 Reg.3, Reg.4, Reg.5

Reg.8, added: SI 1996/673 Reg.4

Reg.8, amended: SI 1996/1485 Reg.4

Reg.8A, added: SI 1996/1485 Reg.5

Reg.9, added: SI 1996/673 Reg.4

Reg.10, added: SI 1996/673 Reg.4

Reg.11, added: SI 1996/673 Reg.4

Reg.12, added: SI 1996/673 Reg.4

3246. Control of Substances Hazardous to Health Regulations 1994

applied: SI 1996/2791 Reg.3, Sch.6, SI 1997/2505 Reg.3, Sch.6, SI 1999/645 Reg.3, Reg.7, Sch.6

referred to: SI 1998/2306 Reg.12

revoked: SI 1999/437 Reg.18

Reg.2, amended: SI 1996/2001 Reg.3, SI 1996/3138 Reg.2

Reg.2, revoked: SI 1999/437 Reg.18

Reg.5, amended: SI 1996/2001 Reg.3

Reg.5, revoked: SI 1999/437 Reg.18

Reg.13, amended: SI 1996/3138 Reg.2

Reg.13, revoked: SI 1999/437 Reg.18

Reg.15, amended: SI 1996/3138 Reg.2

Reg.15, revoked: SI 1999/437 Reg.18

Sch.1, amended: SI 1998/1357 Reg.2

NO.

NO.

1994—cont.

1994—cont.

3246. Control of Substances Hazardous to Health Regulations 1994—*cont.*
Sch.1, revoked: SI 1999/437 Reg.18
Sch.1, substituted: SI 1996/3138 Reg.2, Sch.
Sch.2, amended: SI 1996/3138 Reg.2
Sch.2, revoked: SI 1999/437 Reg.18
Sch.2, substituted: SI 1998/1357 Reg.2, Sch.
Sch.4, amended: SI 1996/3138 Reg.2
Sch.4, revoked: SI 1999/437 Reg.18
Sch.5, amended: SI 1996/3138 Reg.2
Sch.5, revoked: SI 1999/437 Reg.18
Sch.6, amended: SI 1996/3138 Reg.2
Sch.6, revoked: SI 1999/437 Reg.18
Sch.8, amended: SI 1998/1357 Reg.2
Sch.8, revoked: SI 1999/437 Reg.18

3247. Chemicals (Hazard Information and Packaging for Supply) Regulations 1994
applied: SI 1999/197 Reg.4, SI 1999/3165 Reg.5
Reg.2, amended: SI 1996/1092 Reg.3, SI 1997/1460 Reg.3, Sch. para.1, SI 1999/3165 Reg.3
Reg.3, amended: SI 1996/1092 Reg.3, SI 1997/1460 Reg.3, Sch. para.2, SI 1999/3232 Reg.41, Sch.9 para.5
Reg.3, revoked (in part): SI 1997/1460 Reg.3, Sch. para.2
Reg.4, amended: SI 1996/1092 Reg.3
Reg.4, substituted: SI 1997/1460 Reg.3, Sch. para.3, SI 1998/3106 Reg.2, SI 1999/197 Reg.3, SI 1999/3165 Reg.4
Reg.5, amended: SI 1997/1460 Reg.3, Sch. para.4
Reg.5, applied: SI 1999/743 Sch.1 Part.3
Reg.5, referred to: SI 1996/825 Sch.2 para.10
Reg.9, amended: SI 1996/1092 Reg.3, SI 1996/2092 Reg.21, SI 1997/1460 Reg.3, Sch. para.5
Reg.9, applied: SI 1996/2092 Reg.9, Reg.10, Reg.11
Reg.11, applied: SI 1996/2092 Reg.11
Reg.12, amended: SI 1996/1092 Reg.3, SI 1997/1460 Reg.3, Sch. para.6
Reg.16, amended: SI 1996/1092 Reg.3, SI 1997/1460 Reg.3, Sch. para.7
Reg.18, amended: SI 1996/1092 Reg.3
Reg.19, revoked (in part): SI 1998/494 Reg.7, Sch.3
Sch.3 Part I, amended: SI 1997/1460 Reg.3, Sch. para.8
Sch.3 Part II, amended: SI 1996/1092 Reg.3, Sch.1, SI 1997/1460 Reg.3, Sch. para.8
Sch.4 para.2, amended: SI 1997/1460 Reg.3, Sch. para.9
Sch.6 Part I, amended: SI 1997/1460 Reg.3, Sch. para.10
Sch.6 Part II, amended: SI 1997/1460 Reg.3, Sch. para.10
Sch.6 Part III, added: SI 1996/1092 Reg.3, Sch.2
Sch.6 Part III, substituted: SI 1999/3194 Reg.2, Sch.

3249. Welfare of Animals During Transport Order 1994
revoked: SI 1997/1480 Art.22, Sch.12 Part II
Art.1, revoked: SI 1997/1480 Art.22, Sch.12 Part II
Art.7, revoked: SI 1997/1480 Art.22, Sch.12 Part II
Art.13, revoked: SI 1997/1480 Art.22, Sch.12 Part II

3255. Local Government (Transitional Election Arrangements) (Scotland) Order 1994
revoked: SI 1996/739 Art.8, Sch.3

3260. Electrical Equipment (Safety) Regulations 1994
applied: SI 1997/1941 Sch.3 para.15, SI 1998/2306 Reg.10, Sch.1
referred to: SI 1996/600 Sch.5 para.15, SI 1996/601 Sch.5 para.15, SI 1997/1624 Sch.5 para.15, SI 1999/1517 Reg.12, Sch.4 para.12, SI 1999/1676 Sch.5 para.12

3262. Police and Magistrates' Courts Act 1994 (Commencement No.5 and Transitional Provisions) Order 1994
Art.9, applied: SI 1997/319 Reg.24, Reg.160

3263. Highways (Inquiries Procedure) Rules 1994
r.2, amended: SI 1996/525 Sch para.19

3265. Court of Session etc. Fees Amendment Order 1994
revoked: SI 1996/514 Art.3

3266. High Court of the Justiciary Fees Amendment Order 1994
Art.2, revoked: SI 1996/516 Art.3

3269. Town and Country Planning (Fees for Applications and Deemed Applications) (Scotland) Amendment Regulations 1994
revoked (in part): SI 1997/10 Reg.15

3279. Non-Domestic Rating (Chargeable Amounts) Regulations 1994
Part VII, added: SI 1996/3214 Reg.12
Reg.1, amended: SI 1996/3214 Reg.5
Reg.4, amended: SI 1996/911 Reg.2, SI 1996/3214 Reg.6
Reg.6, amended: SI 1996/911 Reg.2
Reg.7, amended: SI 1996/911 Reg.2
Reg.7, applied: SI 1999/3379 Reg.5
Reg.8, amended: SI 1996/911 Reg.2, SI 1996/3214 Reg.3
Reg.8, applied: SI 1999/3379 Reg.5
Reg.9, amended: SI 1996/911 Reg.2
Reg.10, amended: SI 1997/3017 Reg.2
Reg.10, applied: SI 1999/3379 Reg.5, Reg.17, Reg.21
Reg.10, referred to: SI 1999/3379 Reg.6, Reg.17, Reg.20
Reg.10A, added: SI 1996/911 Reg.2
Reg.11, amended: SI 1996/911 Reg.2, SI 1996/3214 Reg.7
Reg.11, applied: SI 1999/3379 Reg.5, Reg.17, Reg.21
Reg.11, referred to: SI 1999/3379 Reg.5, Reg.17, Reg.21
Reg.12, amended: SI 1996/911 Reg.2
Reg.13, amended: SI 1996/911 Reg.2
Reg.21, applied: SI 1999/3379 Reg.21
Reg.23, applied: SI 1999/3379 Reg.21
Reg.24, amended: SI 1996/911 Reg.2, SI 1996/3214 Reg.8
Reg.25, applied: SI 1999/3379 Reg.21
Reg.25, referred to: SI 1999/3379 Reg.17, Reg.20
Reg.26, applied: SI 1999/3379 Reg.17
Reg.26, referred to: SI 1999/3379 Reg.17, Reg.21
Reg.32, amended: SI 1996/911 Reg.2
Reg.37, added: SI 1996/3214 Reg.12
Reg.38, added: SI 1996/3214 Reg.12
Reg.38, amended: SI 1997/960 Reg.2
Reg.39, added: SI 1996/3214 Reg.12
Reg.39, amended: SI 1997/960 Reg.2
Sch.1 para.3, amended: SI 1996/3214 Reg.9
Sch.2, applied: SI 1999/3379 Reg.5

NO.

1994—cont.

3279. Non-Domestic Rating (Chargeable Amounts) Regulations 1994—*cont.*
Sch.2, referred to: SI 1999/3379 Reg.5
Sch.2 para.5, amended: SI 1997/3017 Reg.3
Sch.2 para.6, amended: SI 1997/3017 Reg.3
Sch.2 para.7, amended: SI 1996/3214 Reg.10
Sch.2 para.8, amended: SI 1996/3214 Reg.11
Sch.2 para.9, amended: SI 1997/3017 Reg.3
Sch.2A, added: SI 1996/911 Reg.2
Sch.2A para.1, amended: SI 1996/3214 Reg.12

3282. Electricity Supply Industry (Rateable Values) Order 1994
Art.8B, amended: SI 1996/912 Art.2
Art.8C, added: SI 1996/912 Art.2
Art.8D, added: SI 1996/912 Art.2
Part IA, applied: SI 1999/3379 Sch.4 para.9

3283. British Gas Plc (Rateable Values) Order 1994
Art.2, amended: SI 1997/224 Art.2, SI 1997/961 Art.2
Art.5, amended: SI 1997/224 Art.2

3284. Railways (Rateable Values) Order 1994
Art.2, amended: SI 1999/1003 Art.4
Art.5, amended: SI 1999/1003 Art.3
Art.6, amended: SI 1999/1003 Art.4
Art.6, revoked (in part): SI 1999/1003 Art.4
Art.7, revoked: SI 1999/1003 Art.4

3285. Water Undertakers (Rateable Values) Order 1994
Art.5, amended: SI 1996/912 Art.3
Art.11, amended: SI 1996/912 Art.3

3301. Employers' Liability (Compulsory Insurance) General (Amendment) Regulations 1994
revoked: SI 1998/2573 Reg.10, Sch.3

1995

Barking (Waiting and Loading Restriction) Order 1995
revoked (in part): SI 1996/1896 Art.10
Croydon (Waiting and Loading Restriction) Order No.12 1995
revoked (in part): SI 1997/2133 Art.11, SI 1999/414 Art.10

1. National Health Service (Optical Charges and Payments) (Scotland) Amendment Regulations 1995
revoked: SI 1998/642 Reg.24, Sch.4

11. Pigs (Records, Identification and Movement) Order 1995
Art.3, revoked: SI 1999/437 Reg.18

12. Bovine Animals (Records, Identification and Movement) Order 1995
applied: SI 1996/1500 Reg.9, SI 1996/1686 Art.6, Art.12, SI 1997/1901 Reg.3, SI 1998/871 Reg.11, Reg.29, SI 1999/672 Art.2, Sch.1
Art.5, applied: SI 1996/1500 Reg.12, SI 1996/3241 Reg.13
Art.5, revoked (in part): SI 1997/1901 Reg.10, SI 1998/871 Reg.36, Sch.3
Art.6, applied: SI 1996/1686 Art.17
Art.6, substituted: SI 1996/1686 Art.17
Art.7, revoked (in part): SI 1996/1686 Art.17, SI 1997/1901 Reg.10, SI 1998/871 Reg.36, Sch.3
Art.8, referred to: SI 1996/3241 Reg.3
Art.8, revoked (in part): SI 1997/1901 Reg.10, SI 1998/871 Reg.36, Sch.3
Art.9, referred to: SI 1996/3241 Reg.3
Art.9, revoked: SI 1998/871 Reg.36, Sch.3

NO.

1995—cont.

12. Bovine Animals (Records, Identification and Movement) Order 1995—*cont.*
Art.10, referred to: SI 1996/3241 Reg.3
Art.10, revoked: SI 1998/871 Reg.36, Sch.3
Art.11, referred to: SI 1996/3241 Reg.3
Art.11, revoked: SI 1998/871 Reg.36, Sch.3
Art.11A, added: SI 1996/1686 Art.17
Art.12, referred to: SI 1996/3241 Reg.3
Art.12, revoked: SI 1997/1901 Reg.10, SI 1998/871 Reg.36, Sch.3
Art.13, referred to: SI 1996/3241 Reg.3
Art.13, revoked: SI 1998/871 Reg.36, Sch.3
Art.14, referred to: SI 1996/3241 Reg.3
Art.14, revoked: SI 1998/871 Reg.36, Sch.3
Art.15, revoked: SI 1998/871 Reg.36, Sch.3
Sch.2, revoked: SI 1997/1901 Reg.10, SI 1998/871 Reg.36, Sch.3

13. Enzootic Bovine Leukosis (Amendment) Order 1995
revoked: SI 1997/757 Art.15, Sch.3

14. Beef Special Premium (Amendment) Regulations 1995
revoked: SI 1996/3241 Reg.22

31. Credit Unions (Authorised Investments) Regulations (Northern Ireland) 1995
Reg.3, amended: SI 1997/2646 Reg.7

31. Employment Protection (Part-time Employees) Regulations 1995
see *Hammersmith and Fulham LBC v Jesuthasan* [1998] I.R.L.R. 372 (CA), Mummery, L.J.
revoked: 1996 c.18 Sch.3 Part II

34. National Health Service (Optical Charges and Payments) Amendment Regulations 1995
revoked: SI 1997/818 Reg.24, Sch.4

35. Occupational and Personal Pension Schemes (Miscellaneous Amendments) Regulations 1995
Reg.2, revoked: SI 1996/1172 Sch.2
Reg.3, revoked: SI 1997/784 Reg.12, Sch.2
Reg.4, revoked: SI 1996/1172 Sch.2
Reg.6, revoked: SI 1996/1537 Reg.18, Sch.
Reg.7, revoked: SI 1997/470 Reg.20, Sch.3

40. Apple Orchard Grubbing Up (Amendment) Regulations 1995
applied: SI 1998/1131 Reg.4
revoked: SI 1998/1131 Reg.3 (with savings)

42. Police and Magistrates' Courts Act 1994 (Commencement No.6 and Transitional Provisions) Order 1995
revoked: 1997 c.25 s.73, Sch.6 Part II

46. Employment Protection (Part-time Employees) Regulations (Northern Ireland) 1995
revoked: SI 1996/1919 (NI.16) Art.257

49. Home Energy Efficiency Grants (Amendment) Regulations 1995
revoked: SI 1997/790 Reg.14, Sch.2

51. Control of Substances Hazardous to Health Regulations (Northern Ireland) 1995
Reg.11, applied: SI 1996/1919 (NI.16) Art.96

54. Education (National Curriculum) (Attainment Targets and Programmes of Study in History) (England) Order 1995
revoked: SI 1998/1988 Art.2

55. Education (National Curriculum) (Attainment Targets and Programmes of Study in Geography) (England) Order 1995
revoked: SI 1998/1989 Art.2

1995—cont.

56. Education (National Curriculum) (Attainment Targets and Programmes of Study in Technology) Order 1995
    revoked (in part): SI 1998/1890 Art.2, SI 1998/1986 Art.2

58. Education (National Curriculum) (Attainment Targets and Programmes of Study in Art) (England) Order 1995
    revoked: SI 1998/1990 Art.2

59. Education (National Curriculum) (Attainment Targets and Programmes of Study in Music) (England) Order 1995
    revoked: SI 1998/1991 Art.2

60. Education (National Curriculum) (Attainment Targets and Programmes of Study in Physical Education) Order 1995
    revoked (in part): SI 1998/1887 Art.2, SI 1998/1987 Art.2

69. Education (National Curriculum) (Attainment Targets and Programmes of Study in Welsh) Order 1995
    Art.5, amended: SI 1998/2576 Art.2
    Sch.5, amended: SI 1998/2576 Art.2

69. Statutory Sick Pay Percentage Threshold Order (Northern Ireland) 1995
    Art.4, applied: SI 1999/671 Art.3, Sch.2

70. Education (National Curriculum) (Attainment Targets and Programmes of Study in Music) (Wales) Order 1995
    revoked: SI 1998/1889 Art.2

71. Education (National Curriculum) (Attainment Targets and Programmes of Study in Art) (Wales) Order 1995
    revoked: SI 1998/1886 Art.2

72. Education (National Curriculum) (Attainment Targets and Programmes of Study in Geography) (Wales) Order 1995
    revoked: SI 1998/1885 Art.2

73. Education (National Curriculum) (Attainment Targets and Programmes of Study in History) (Wales) Order 1995
    revoked: SI 1998/1888 Art.2

77. Infant Formula and Follow-on Formula Regulations 1995
    Reg.1, amended: SI 1997/451 Reg.2
    Reg.2, applied: SI 1997/451 Reg.3
    Reg.3, amended: SI 1997/451 Reg.2
    Reg.3, applied: SI 1997/451 Reg.3
    Reg.5, amended: SI 1997/451 Reg.2
    Reg.5, applied: SI 1997/451 Reg.3
    Reg.6, amended: SI 1997/451 Reg.2
    Reg.6, applied: SI 1997/451 Reg.3
    Reg.7, applied: SI 1997/451 Reg.3
    Reg.12, amended: SI 1997/451 Reg.2
    Reg.13, amended: SI 1997/451 Reg.2
    Reg.14, amended: SI 1997/451 Reg.2
    Reg.14A, added: SI 1997/451 Reg.2
    Reg.22, amended: SI 1997/451 Reg.2
    Reg.22, applied: SI 1997/451 Reg.3
    Reg.25, revoked: SI 1996/1499 Reg.49, Sch.9
    Sch.1, amended: SI 1997/451 Reg.2
    Sch.1 para.3, amended: SI 1997/451 Reg.2
    Sch.1 para.5, amended: SI 1997/451 Reg.2
    Sch.1 para.6, amended: SI 1997/451 Reg.2
    Sch.1 para.7, added: SI 1997/451 Reg.2
    Sch.2 para.2, amended: SI 1997/451 Reg.2
    Sch.2 para.3, amended: SI 1997/451 Reg.2
    Sch.2 para.7, added: SI 1997/451 Reg.2
    Sch.3, amended: SI 1997/451 Reg.2
    Sch.4, amended: SI 1997/451 Reg.2
    Sch.8, added: SI 1997/451 Reg.2

1995—cont.

100. Hill Livestock (Compensatory Allowances) (Amendment) Regulations 1995
     revoked (in part): SI 1996/1500 Reg.18

122. Gaming (Bingo) Act (Variation of Monetary Limit) Order 1995
     revoked: SI 1998/2153 Art.3

124. A205 Trunk Road (Richmond and Wandsworth) Red Route Experimental Traffic Order 1995
     revoked: SI 1996/2164 Art.10
     Sch.2C, amended: SI 1996/217 Art.2
     Sch.2C, revoked: SI 1996/2164 Art.10
     Sch.4, amended: SI 1996/217 Art.2
     Sch.4, revoked: SI 1996/2164 Art.10

125. A205 Trunk Road (Hounslow) Red Route (Bus Lanes) Experimental Traffic Order 1995
     revoked: SI 1996/2335 Art.5

126. A205 Trunk Road (Hounslow) Red Route Experimental Traffic Order 1995
     revoked (in part): SI 1996/2336 Art.10

131. Welfare of Animals During Transport (Amendment) Order 1995
     revoked: SI 1997/1480 Art.22, Sch.12 Part II

132. Lyon Court and Office Fees (Variation) Order 1995
     revoked: SI 1996/413

136. Bovine Offal (Prohibition) (Amendment) Regulations (Northern Ireland) 1995
     applied: SI 1996/1633 (NI.12) Art.11

137. Police (Scotland) Amendment Regulations 1995
     Reg.4, revoked: SI 1996/3232 Reg.13

141. West Wales Ambulance National Health Service Trust (Establishment) Order 1995
     revoked: SI 1998/677 Art.2

142. Cardiff Community Healthcare National Health Service Trust (Establishment) Order 1995
     revoked: SI 1999/1120 Art.2, Sch.2
     Art.3, revoked: SI 1999/1120 Art.2, Sch.2
     Art.3, substituted: SI 1998/2033 Art.2

143. University Dental Hospital National Health Service Trust (Establishment) Order 1995
     revoked: SI 1999/1120 Art.2, Sch.2

157. Merchant Shipping (Hours of Work) Regulations 1995
     revoked: SI 1997/1320 Reg.1

164. Valuation Timetable (Scotland) Order 1995
     Sch., amended: SI 1997/1781 Art.2

171. Friendly Societies (Taxation of Transfers of Business) Regulations 1995
     revoked: SI 1997/473 Reg.54 (with savings)
     Reg.4, amended: SI 1997/472 Reg.3
     Reg.4A, added: SI 1997/472 Reg.4

178. Education (Financial Delegation to Schools) (Mandatory Exceptions) Regulations 1995
     revoked: SI 1999/711 Reg.9, Sch.2
     Reg.1, amended: SI 1996/395 Reg.2
     Reg.1, revoked: SI 1999/711 Reg.9, Sch.2
     Reg.3, amended: SI 1996/395 Reg.2
     Reg.3, revoked: SI 1999/711 Reg.9, Sch.2

197. Road Traffic (Northern Ireland) Order 1995
     Part III, applied: SI 1999/2920 Reg.15

201. Public Supply Contracts Regulations 1995
     applied: 1999 c.29 s.356
     referred to: 1999 c.29 s.358
     Reg.2, amended: SI 1996/2911 Reg.35, SI 1999/1042 Art.3, Sch.1 para.22
     Reg.3, amended: SI 1999/1042 Art.3, Sch.1 para.22
     Reg.4, amended: SI 1996/2911 Reg.35

NO.

201. Public Supply Contracts Regulations 1995— *cont.*
Reg.6, amended: SI 1996/2911 Reg.35
Reg.26, applied: SI 1999/1820 Art.4, Sch.2 para.156
Sch.1, amended: SI 1997/1744 Art.2, Sch. para.5, SI 1999/506 Art.35, SI 1999/1042 Art.3, Art.4, Sch.1 para.22, Sch.2 para.13, SI 1999/1351 Art.17
Sch.1, applied: SI 1997/1744 Art.2, Sch. para.5

202. Financial Services Act 1986 (Miscellaneous Exemptions) Order 1995
Art.3, substituted: SI 1999/3085 Art.2

204. Toys (Safety) Regulations 1995
see *R. v Newcastle upon Tyne Magistrates Court Ex p. Poundstretcher Ltd* [1998] C.O.D. 256 (QBD), Dyson, L.J.

207. Veterinary Surgeons and Veterinary Practitioners (Registration) (Amendment) Regulations Order of Council 1995
revoked: SI 1996/437 Art.3
Art.2, revoked: SI 1996/437 Sch
Art.3, revoked: SI 1996/437 Sch
Art.4, revoked: SI 1996/437 Sch
Sch., revoked (in part): SI 1996/437 Sch

208. Education (School Financial Statements) (Prescribed Particulars etc.) Regulations 1995
applied: SI 1999/451 Reg.3, SI 1999/486 Reg.3
revoked (in part): SI 1999/451 Reg.3, SI 1999/486 Reg.3
Reg.1, amended: SI 1996/381 Reg.2
Reg.1, revoked (in part): SI 1999/486 Reg.3
Reg.3, applied: SI 1996/889 Sch.3 para.6, SI 1997/956 Sch.1 para.4, Sch.1 para.5, SI 1997/996 Sch.1 para.6, Sch.1 para.7, Sch.1 para.8, SI 1998/798 Sch.1 para.3, Sch.1 para.4, SI 1998/799 Sch.1 para.3, Sch.1 para.4, Sch.1 para.5
Reg.3, referred to: SI 1998/799 Sch.3 para.2
Reg.3, revoked (in part): SI 1999/486 Reg.3
Reg.4, applied: SI 1996/537 Reg.15, SI 1996/889 Reg.28, Reg.45, SI 1997/599 Reg.18, SI 1997/956 Reg.16, SI 1997/996 Reg.30, Reg.50
Reg.4, revoked (in part): SI 1999/486 Reg.3
Reg.6, amended: SI 1996/381 Reg.2
Reg.6, revoked (in part): SI 1999/486 Reg.3
Sch.1, amended: SI 1996/381 Reg.2
Sch.1, applied: SI 1996/537 Reg.15, SI 1996/889 Reg.45, Sch.1 para.6, SI 1997/599 Reg.18, SI 1997/956 Sch.1 para.4, Sch.1 para.5, SI 1997/996 Reg.50, Sch.1 para.6, Sch.1 para.7, Sch.1 para.8, SI 1998/798 Sch.1 para.3, Sch.1 para.4, SI 1998/799 Sch.1 para.3, Sch.1 para.4, Sch.1 para.5
Sch.1, referred to: SI 1998/799 Sch.3 para.2
Sch.1, revoked (in part): SI 1999/486 Reg.3
Sch.2, amended: SI 1996/381 Reg.2
Sch.2, revoked (in part): SI 1999/486 Reg.3

214. Local Government Superannuation (Scotland) Amendment Regulations 1995
applied: SI 1998/364 Reg.4, Reg.6, Reg.19, Sch.2 para.2, Sch.2 para.5, Sch.4 para.8
referred to: SI 1998/364 Reg.3, Reg.10, Sch.2 para.4, Sch.2 para.6

215. Police Regulations 1995
Reg.4, amended: SI 1996/699 Reg.2
Reg.5A, added: SI 1998/493 Reg.2
Reg.14, see *R. v Chief Constable of Greater Manchester Ex p. Lainton* Independent, June 28, 1999 (C.S.) (QBD), Jackson, J.

NO.

215. Police Regulations 1995—*cont.*
Reg.14, amended: SI 1996/699 Reg.3
Reg.14, revoked (in part): SI 1998/493 Reg.2
Reg.15, revoked (in part): SI 1998/493 Reg.2
Reg.16A, added: SI 1996/699 Reg.9
Reg.17, amended: SI 1999/732 Reg.23
Reg.36, substituted: SI 1996/699 Reg.4
Reg.36A, added: SI 1996/699 Reg.4
Reg.39, amended: SI 1996/699 Reg.5
Reg.40, amended: SI 1996/699 Reg.6
Reg.46A, added: SI 1996/699 Reg.7
Reg.47, amended: SI 1996/699 Reg.8
Sch.1 para.12, revoked: SI 1996/699 Reg.9
Sch.6 para.1, amended: SI 1996/699 Reg.10
Sch.6 para.3, amended: SI 1996/699 Reg.11
Sch.6 para.4, amended: SI 1999/732 Reg.22
Sch.6 para.4, applied: SI 1999/730 Reg.37
Sch.10 para.1, amended: SI 1996/699 Reg.12

225. Insolvent Partnerships Order (Northern Ireland) 1995
Art.6, applied: SI 1998/1806 Art.2
Art.7, applied: SI 1998/1806 Art.2
Art.8, applied: SI 1998/1806 Art.2
Art.9, applied: SI 1998/1806 Art.2
Art.10, applied: SI 1998/1806 Art.2

235. Billing Authorities (Anticipation of Precepts) (Amendment) Regulations 1995
Reg.3, amended: SI 1998/119 Reg.5
Reg.3, applied: SI 1998/119 Reg.5

238. Overseas Service (Pensions Supplement) Regulations 1995
Reg.6, amended: SI 1996/1476 Reg.2
Reg.18, amended: SI 1996/1476 Reg.3
Reg.19, amended: SI 1999/735 Reg.2
Reg.19A, added: SI 1996/1476 Reg.4
Reg.20, amended: SI 1996/1476 Reg.5
Reg.22, amended: SI 1999/735 Reg.3
Sch.2 para.11, substituted: SI 1996/1476 Reg.6
Sch.3, amended: SI 1999/735 Reg.4

254. Dairy Produce Quotas (Amendment) Regulations 1995
revoked: SI 1997/733 Reg.35

263. Health and Safety at Work etc. Act 1974 (Application outside Great Britain) Order 1995
applied: SI 1996/341 Reg.3, SI 1996/825 Reg.4, SI 1997/2776 Reg.3, SI 1998/543 Reg.13, SI 1998/2306 Reg.3, SI 1998/2307 Reg.3, SI 1999/3232 Reg.38, SI 1999/3242 Reg.23
Art.4, applied: SI 1996/913 Reg.3
Art.4, referred to: SI 1997/1713 Reg.8, SI 1999/437 Reg.15
Art.5, applied: SI 1996/913 Reg.3
Art.5, referred to: SI 1997/1713 Reg.8
Art.6, applied: SI 1996/825 Reg.4
Art.6, referred to: SI 1997/1713 Reg.8, SI 1999/437 Reg.15
Art.7, referred to: SI 1997/1713 Reg.8
Art.8, applied: SI 1996/1592 Reg.32, SI 1997/1713 Reg.8, SI 1999/437 Reg.15

271. Dual-Use and Related Goods (Export Control) Regulations 1995
applied: SI 1996/2721 Reg.15
revoked: SI 1996/2721 Sch.1
Reg.1, amended: SI 1996/1124 Reg.2
Reg.1, applied: SI 1996/1736 Reg.2
Reg.1, revoked: SI 1996/2721 Sch.1
Reg.3, amended: SI 1996/1124 Reg.2
Reg.3, applied: SI 1996/1736 Reg.2
Reg.3, revoked: SI 1996/2721 Sch.1
Reg.11, revoked: SI 1996/2721 Sch.1

NO.

271. Dual-Use and Related Goods (Export Control) Regulations 1995—*cont.*
Reg.12, revoked: SI 1996/2721 Sch.1
Reg.13, revoked: SI 1996/2721 Sch.1
Reg.14, amended: SI 1996/1124 Reg.2
Reg.14, applied: SI 1996/1736 Reg.2
Reg.14, revoked: SI 1996/2721 Sch.1
Sch.1, amended: SI 1996/1124 Reg.2, Sch, SI 1996/1736 Reg.2, Sch. para.1, Sch. para.2
Sch.1, applied: SI 1996/1736 Reg.4
Sch.1, revoked: SI 1996/2721 Sch.1
Sch.2, amended: SI 1996/1124 Reg.2, SI 1996/1736 Reg.2
Sch.2, applied: SI 1996/1736 Reg.4
Sch.2, revoked: SI 1996/2721 Sch.1
Sch.3, amended: SI 1996/1736 Reg.3
Sch.3, applied: SI 1996/1736 Reg.4
Sch.3, revoked: SI 1996/2721 Sch.1

278. Insolvency of Employer (Excluded Classes) Regulations 1995
revoked: 1996 c.18 Sch.3 Part II

288. Waste Management Licensing (Amendment etc.) Regulations 1995
Reg.4, amended: SI 1996/634 Reg.3
Reg.4, applied: SI 1996/634 Reg.5

300. National Health Service Pension Scheme Regulations 1995
applied: SI 1996/701 Art.5, SI 1996/1313 Reg.5, SI 1997/311 Reg.6, SI 1997/1613 Reg.23
referred to: SI 1996/1680 Reg.32, SI 1997/3001 Sch.10 para.34, Sch.10 para.38
Part Q, applied: SI 1997/3001 Sch.10 para.36
Reg.A2, amended: SI 1997/1888 Reg.3, SI 1998/666 Reg.3, SI 1998/2216 Reg.3
Reg.B2, amended: SI 1998/2216 Reg.4
Reg.B5, added: SI 1997/80 Reg.3
Reg.C1, amended: SI 1997/80 Reg.4
Reg.D1, amended: SI 1998/2216 Reg.5
Reg.E2, amended: SI 1998/666 Reg.4
Reg.E3, amended: SI 1997/1888 Reg.4, SI 1998/666 Reg.5, SI 1998/2216 Reg.6
Reg.E4, amended: SI 1997/1888 Reg.5, SI 1998/666 Reg.6, SI 1998/2216 Reg.7
Reg.L4, amended: SI 1998/666 Reg.7
Reg.M3, amended: SI 1997/80 Reg.5
Reg.N1, added: SI 1997/80 Reg.6
Reg.N3A, added: SI 1997/80 Reg.6
Reg.Q1, amended: SI 1998/666 Reg.8
Reg.Q1, applied: SI 1997/3001 Sch.10 para.36
Reg.R2, applied: SI 1997/3001 Sch.10 para.37
Reg.R3, applied: SI 1997/3001 Sch.10 para.37
Reg.R4, amended: SI 1998/666 Reg.9
Reg.R5, amended: SI 1997/1888 Reg.6
Reg.R8, amended: SI 1998/666 Reg.9
Reg.R11, added: SI 1998/666 Reg.9
Reg.R11, substituted: SI 1998/2216 Reg.8
Reg.S1, amended: SI 1998/666 Reg.10
Reg.S2, amended: SI 1998/666 Reg.11
Sch.2 para.1, amended: SI 1997/1888 Reg.7
Sch.2 para.3, amended: SI 1998/666 Reg.12
Sch.2 para.6, amended: SI 1998/666 Reg.12, SI 1998/2216 Reg.9
Sch.2 para.19, amended: SI 1998/666 Reg.12, SI 1998/2216 Reg.9

307. Scottish Land Court (Fees) Order 1995
revoked: SI 1996/680 Art.4

308. Lands Tribunal for Scotland (Amendment) (Fees) Rules 1995
revoked: SI 1996/519 r.3

NO.

310. Social Security (Incapacity Benefit) (Transitional) Regulations 1995
Reg.11, amended: SI 1996/3207 Reg.3
Reg.17, amended: SI 1996/3207 Reg.3
Reg.17B, added: SI 1998/2231 Reg.3
Reg.18, amended: SI 1996/599 Art.15, SI 1996/3207 Reg.3, SI 1997/543 Art.15, SI 1998/470 Art.15, SI 1999/264 Art.15
Reg.23, amended: SI 1998/2231 Reg.3
Reg.24, amended: SI 1998/2231 Reg.3
Reg.25, amended: SI 1998/2231 Reg.3
Reg.28, amended: SI 1998/2231 Reg.3
Reg.31, amended: SI 1996/3207 Reg.3, SI 1998/2231 Reg.3, SI 1999/3109 Reg.7
Reg.32, amended: SI 1999/3109 Reg.7

311. Social Security (Incapacity for Work) (General) Regulations 1995
amended: SI 1999/1088 Reg.3
applied: SI 1999/1088 Reg.3, Reg.7
Part II Ch.V, revoked: SI 1999/2422 Art.3, Sch.10 para.3
Part III, amended: SI 1999/3109 Reg.3
Reg.2, amended: SI 1996/3207 Reg.2, SI 1999/2422 Art.3, Sch.10 para.1, SI 1999/2860 Art.3, Sch.11 para.1, SI 1999/3109 Reg.2
Reg.6, amended: SI 1996/1345 Reg.20, SI 1999/3109 Reg.2
Reg.7, amended: SI 1999/3109 Reg.2
Reg.8, amended: SI 1999/3109 Reg.2
Reg.8, referred to: SI 1999/991 Reg.19
Reg.10, amended: SI 1996/3207 Reg.2, SI 1997/1009 Reg.2, SI 1999/3109 Reg.2
Reg.10, referred to: SI 1999/991 Reg.7
Reg.13, amended: SI 1996/3207 Reg.2
Reg.13A, added: SI 1998/2231 Reg.4
Reg.13A, amended: SI 1999/3109 Reg.2
Reg.14, amended: SI 1999/3109 Reg.2
Reg.16, amended: SI 1996/3207 Reg.2, SI 1999/3109 Reg.2
Reg.16, referred to: SI 1999/1088 Reg.4
Reg.17, amended: SI 1996/484 Reg.2, SI 1997/546 Reg.2, SI 1998/407 Reg.2, SI 1998/2231 Reg.4, SI 1999/862 Reg.3, SI 1999/2860 Art.3, Sch.11 para.2
Reg.17A, amended: SI 1996/1345 Reg.20, SI 1999/3109 Reg.2
Reg.18, amended: SI 1996/3207 Reg.2, SI 1999/2422 Art.3, Sch.10 para.2
Reg.19, revoked: SI 1999/991 Reg.59 (with savings), Sch.4 (in savings), SI 1999/2422 Art.3, Sch.10 para.3
Reg.20, revoked: SI 1999/991 Reg.59 (with savings), Sch.4 (in savings), SI 1999/2422 Art.3, Sch.10 para.3
Reg.21, revoked: SI 1999/991 Reg.59 (with savings), Sch.4 (in savings), SI 1999/2422 Art.3, Sch.10 para.3
Reg.22, revoked: SI 1999/991 Reg.59 (with savings), Sch.4 (in savings), SI 1999/2422 Art.3, Sch.10 para.3
Reg.24, substituted: SI 1999/3109 Reg.3
Reg.25, amended: SI 1996/3207 Reg.2, SI 1999/3109 Reg.3
Reg.26, amended: SI 1996/3207 Reg.2
Reg.27, amended: SI 1999/3109 Reg.3
Reg.27, substituted: SI 1996/3207 Reg.2
Reg.28, amended: SI 1996/3207 Reg.2, SI 1999/3109 Reg.3
Reg.28, applied: SI 1999/3109 Reg.4
Sch. Part I, amended: SI 1996/3207 Reg.2
Sch. Part II, amended: SI 1996/3207 Reg.2

NO.

321. **Gaming Act (Variation of Fees) Order 1995**
referred to: SI 1998/456 Art.2
revoked: SI 1998/456 Art.3
322. **Gaming (Bingo) Act (Fees) (Amendment) Order 1995**
revoked: SI 1998/454 Art.3
323. **Lotteries (Gaming Board Fees) Order 1995**
revoked: SI 1996/468 Art.9
335. **A3 Trunk Road (Wandsworth) Red Route (Clearway) Experimental Traffic Order 1995**
revoked (in part): SI 1996/2338 Art.10
336. **A3 Trunk Road (Merton) Red Route Experimental Traffic Order 1995**
revoked (in part): SI 1996/2334 Art.10
337. **A3 Trunk Road (Kingston Upon Thames) Red Route (Clearway) Experimental Traffic Order 1995**
revoked (in part): SI 1996/2339 Art.10
338. **A3 Trunk Road (Merton) Red Route (Clearway) Experimental Traffic Order 1995**
revoked (in part): SI 1996/2333 Art.10
339. **A3 Trunk Road (Kingston Upon Thames) Red Route Experimental Traffic Order 1995**
revoked (in part): SI 1996/2332 Art.10
340. **Local Government (Compensation for Redundancy or Premature Retirement on Reorganisation) (Scotland) Regulations 1995**
Part II, referred to: SI 1998/192 Reg.34
Reg.2, amended: SI 1997/720 Reg.2
Reg.5, applied: SI 1998/192 Reg.8
Reg.7, referred to: SI 1998/366 Reg.25
Reg.11, applied: SI 1998/366 Reg.25
Reg.13, revoked: SI 1998/192 Reg.52, Sch.2
Reg.14, revoked: SI 1998/192 Reg.52, Sch.2
342. **Employment Protection (Increase of Limits) Order (Northern Ireland) 1995**
Art.4, referred to: SI 1996/1919 (NI.16) Sch.2 para.8
351. **Lloyd's Underwriters (Tax) Regulations 1995**
amended: SI 1997/2681 Reg.3
applied: SI 1997/2681 Reg.3
Reg.2, amended: SI 1996/781 Reg.3
352. **Lloyd's Underwriters (Tax) (1992-93 to 1996-97) Regulations 1995**
Reg.2, amended: SI 1996/782 Reg.3
Reg.10A, added: SI 1996/782 Reg.4
356. **Milk Development Council Order 1995**
applied: SI 1999/672 Art.2, Sch.1, SI 1999/1747 Art.3, Sch.17 para.3
Art.3, referred to: SI 1999/1319 Sch.
Art.9, applied: SI 1997/2893 Reg.4
360. **Plastic Materials and Articles in Contact with Food (Amendment) Regulations 1995**
revoked: SI 1998/1376 Reg.14
361. **Meat (Hygiene, Inspection and Examinations for Residues) (Charges) Regulations 1995**
revoked: SI 1998/2095 Reg.5
Reg.2, amended: SI 1997/1729 Reg.35, SI 1997/2893 Art.6
Reg.2, revoked: SI 1998/2095 Reg.5
Reg.4, revoked (in part): SI 1997/2893 Reg.6, SI 1998/2095 Reg.5
Reg.8, revoked: SI 1997/2893 Reg.6
Reg.9, revoked: SI 1998/2095 Reg.5
Sch.1 Part II, revoked: SI 1997/2893 Reg.6
Sch.2 para.a, revoked: SI 1998/2095 Reg.5
Sch.2 para.b, revoked: SI 1998/2095 Reg.5
Sch.3, revoked: SI 1998/2095 Reg.5

NO.

362. **Agricultural Processing and Marketing Grant Regulations 1995**
applied: SI 1999/672 Art.2, Sch.1
Reg.3, amended: SI 1999/1820 Art.4, Sch.2 para.157
365. **National Health Service Superannuation Scheme (Scotland) Regulations 1995**
applied: SI 1996/2809 Reg.2, SI 1998/364 Reg.22, SI 1998/1451 Reg.4, Reg.10, Reg.11, Sch. para.14, Sch. para.15, SI 1999/1750 Art.2, Sch.1
Part H, applied: SI 1998/1451 Reg.11
Reg.A2, amended: SI 1997/1916 Reg.3, SI 1998/1593 Reg.3, SI 1999/443 Reg.3
Reg.B1, substituted: SI 1997/1434 Reg.3
Reg.B2, amended: SI 1999/443 Reg.4
Reg.B3, applied: SI 1998/1451 Reg.6
Reg.B4, applied: SI 1998/1451 Reg.6
Reg.B5, applied: SI 1998/1451 Reg.9
Reg.B6, added: SI 1997/1434 Reg.4
Reg.B6, applied: SI 1998/1451 Reg.9
Reg.C1, amended: SI 1997/1434 Reg.5
Reg.C2, amended: SI 1997/1916 Reg.4
Reg.C4, amended: SI 1997/1916 Reg.5
Reg.D1, amended: SI 1999/443 Reg.5
Reg.D1, referred to: SI 1998/1451 Reg.3, Reg.6
Reg.E1, applied: SI 1998/1451 Reg.6, Reg.15, Sch. para.8, Sch. para.9
Reg.E2, amended: SI 1998/1593 Reg.4
Reg.E2, applied: SI 1998/1451 Reg.6, Reg.15, Sch. para.12
Reg.E3, amended: SI 1997/1916 Reg.6, SI 1998/1593 Reg.5, SI 1999/443 Reg.6
Reg.E3, applied: SI 1998/1451 Reg.6, Reg.15, Sch. para.13
Reg.E4, amended: SI 1997/1916 Reg.7, SI 1998/1593 Reg.6, SI 1999/443 Reg.7
Reg.E4, applied: SI 1998/1451 Reg.6, Reg.15, Sch. para.13
Reg.E5, applied: SI 1998/1451 Reg.6, Reg.15, Sch. para.13
Reg.E6, applied: SI 1998/1451 Reg.6, Reg.15, Sch. para.10
Reg.E9, applied: SI 1998/1451 Reg.14
Reg.F2, amended: SI 1998/1593 Reg.7
Reg.F5, applied: SI 1998/1451 Reg.15
Reg.L4, amended: SI 1998/1593 Reg.8
Reg.M1, applied: SI 1998/1451 Reg.10
Reg.M3, amended: SI 1997/1434 Reg.6
Reg.N1, amended: SI 1997/1434 Reg.7
Reg.N3A, added: SI 1997/1434 Reg.8
Reg.N3A, applied: SI 1998/1451 Reg.9
Reg.Q1, amended: SI 1998/1593 Reg.9, SI 1999/443 Reg.8
Reg.R2, applied: SI 1998/1451 Sch. para.11
Reg.R3, applied: SI 1998/1451 Sch. para.11
Reg.R4, amended: SI 1998/1593 Reg.10
Reg.R7, amended: SI 1998/1593 Reg.11
Reg.R8, amended: SI 1998/1593 Reg.12
Reg.R13, added: SI 1998/1593 Reg.13
Reg.R13, substituted: SI 1999/443 Reg.9
Reg.S1, amended: SI 1998/1593 Reg.14
Reg.S2, amended: SI 1997/1434 Reg.9, SI 1998/1593 Reg.15
Reg.T5, applied: SI 1998/1451 Reg.19, SI 1998/1594 Reg.4
Reg.T6, applied: SI 1998/1451 Reg.20, SI 1998/1594 Reg.4
Reg.U2, amended: SI 1997/1434 Reg.10

NO.

365. National Health Service Superannuation Scheme (Scotland) Regulations 1995— *cont.*
Sch.1 Part I, amended: SI 1997/1916 Reg.8
Sch.1 para.1, amended: SI 1999/443 Reg.10
Sch.1 para.3, amended: SI 1998/1593 Reg.16
Sch.1 para.6, amended: SI 1998/1593 Reg.16, SI 1999/443 Reg.10
Sch.1 para.18, amended: SI 1998/1593 Reg.16, SI 1999/443 Reg.10

366. Mines and Quarries (Rateable Values) (Scotland) Order 1995
applied: SI 1997/452 Reg.6, SI 1998/519 Reg.6, SI 1999/276 Reg.6
referred to: SI 1996/103 Reg.6

368. British Gas Plc (Rateable Values) (Scotland) Order 1995
Art.3, referred to: SI 1996/103 Reg.13
Art.5, amended: SI 1997/1048 Art.3
Art.6, amended: SI 1997/1048 Art.4

369. Electricity Generation Lands (Rateable Values) (Scotland) Order 1995
Art.3, referred to: SI 1996/103 Reg.13

370. Electricity Transmission Lands (Rateable Values) (Scotland) Order 1995
Art.3, referred to: SI 1996/103 Reg.13

371. Electricity Generators (Rateable Values) (Scotland) Order 1995
applied: SI 1997/452 Reg.6, SI 1998/519 Reg.6, SI 1999/276 Reg.6
referred to: SI 1996/103 Reg.6

372. Electricity Generators (Aluminium) (Rateable Values) (Scotland) Order 1995
applied: SI 1997/452 Reg.6, SI 1998/519 Reg.6, SI 1999/276 Reg.6
referred to: SI 1996/103 Reg.6

373. Electricity Distribution Lands (Rateable Values) (Scotland) Order 1995
Art.3, referred to: SI 1996/103 Reg.13

391. Local Government Finance (Scotland) Order 1995
Art.2, revoked: SI 1996/755 Art.7
Art.4, revoked: SI 1996/755 Art.7
Art.5, revoked: SI 1996/755 Art.7
Sch.1, revoked: SI 1996/755 Art.7

392. Revenue Support Grant (Scotland) Order 1995
Art.3, revoked: SI 1996/756 Art.4
Art.4, revoked: SI 1996/756 Art.4
Sch., revoked: SI 1996/756 Art.4

401. Local Government Residuary Body (England) Order 1995
Art.2, amended: SI 1997/732 Art.2
Art.15, referred to: SI 1997/2842
Art.19, amended: SI 1997/732 Art.2
Art.20, amended: SI 1997/732 Art.2
Art.21, amended: SI 1997/732 Art.2
Art.24, amended: SI 1998/1129 Art.3, Sch.2
Art.25, amended: SI 1997/732 Art.2
Art.27, referred to: SI 1999/2890
Part II, revoked: SI 1999/2890 Art.4
Part III, referred to: SI 1999/2890 Art.3

402. Local Government Changes for England (Property Transfer and Transitional Payments) Regulations 1995
applied: SI 1997/319 Reg.24, Reg.160
Part III, applied: SI 1996/1867 Art.15, SI 1996/1879 Art.6
Part III, referred to: SI 1996/710 Reg.17
Reg.2, amended: SI 1996/Reg.2
Reg.5, amended: SI 1996/312 Reg.2, SI 1996/330 Reg.10

NO.

402. Local Government Changes for England (Property Transfer and Transitional Payments) Regulations 1995—*cont.*
Reg.6, amended: SI 1996/312 Reg.2, SI 1996/330 Reg.10
Reg.6, applied: SI 1996/1867 Art.15, SI 1996/1879 Art.6, SI 1997/2842 Art.1
Reg.7, amended: SI 1996/330 Reg.10
Reg.8, amended: SI 1996/312 Reg.2, SI 1996/330 Reg.10
Reg.9, amended: SI 1996/330 Reg.10
Reg.10, amended: SI 1996/330 Reg.10
Reg.18, amended: SI 1998/1129 Art.3, Sch.2
Reg.19, amended: SI 1996/312 Reg.2, SI 1996/2825 Reg.2
Reg.21, amended: SI 1996/2825 Reg.2
Sch. para.1, amended: SI 1996/2825 Reg.2
Sch. para.4, amended: SI 1996/2825 Reg.2
Sch. para.4A, added: SI 1996/2825 Reg.2
Sch. para.4B, added: SI 1996/2825 Reg.2
Sch. para.5A, added: SI 1996/2825 Reg.2
Sch. para.5B, added: SI 1996/2825 Reg.2
Sch. para.6A, amended: SI 1996/2825 Reg.2

414. Marketing of Ornamental Plant Material Regulations (Northern Ireland) 1995
revoked: SR 1999/502 Reg.15

414. National Health Service (Pharmaceutical Services) (Scotland) Regulations 1995
Reg.2, amended: SI 1996/840 Reg.2, Reg.7, SI 1996/1504 Reg.3, SI 1998/2224 Reg.8, SSI 1999/57 Reg.3
Reg.3, amended: SSI 1999/57 Reg.4
Reg.5, amended: SSI 1999/57 Reg.5
Reg.5, revoked (in part): SI 1997/696 Reg.2
Reg.6, amended: SSI 1999/57 Reg.2
Reg.7, amended: SI 1996/840 Reg.3, SSI 1999/57 Reg.2
Reg.8, amended: SSI 1999/57 Reg.2
Reg.9, amended: SI 1997/696 Reg.3, SSI 1999/57 Reg.2
Reg.9A, added: SI 1996/840 Reg.4
Reg.11, amended: SI 1997/696 Reg.4, SSI 1999/57 Reg.2
Sch.1 para.1, amended: SI 1996/1504 Reg.3, SI 1997/696 Reg.5, SSI 1999/57 Reg.6
Sch.1 para.2, amended: SI 1996/840 Reg.7, SSI 1999/57 Reg.6
Sch.1 para.3, amended: SI 1996/1504 Reg.3, SI 1998/3031 Reg.2
Sch.1 para.4, amended: SSI 1999/57 Reg.6
Sch.1 para.5, amended: SI 1996/840 Reg.5, SSI 1999/57 Reg.6
Sch.1 para.6, amended: SSI 1999/57 Reg.6
Sch.1 para.7, amended: SSI 1999/57 Reg.6
Sch.1 para.8, amended: SSI 1999/57 Reg.6
Sch.1 para.9, amended: SSI 1999/57 Reg.6
Sch.1 para.9A, added: SI 1996/840 Reg.6
Sch.1 para.9B, added: SI 1996/840 Reg.6
Sch.1 para.9B, amended: SSI 1999/57 Reg.6
Sch.1 para.11, amended: SSI 1999/57 Reg.6
Sch.2 Form A, amended: SI 1997/696 Reg.6, SSI 1999/57 Reg.7
Sch.2 Form A (MR), amended: SSI 1999/57 Reg.8
Sch.2 Form B, amended: SSI 1999/57 Reg.9, Reg.10
Sch.2 Form C, amended: SSI 1999/57 Reg.11
Sch.2 Form D, amended: SSI 1999/57 Reg.12
Sch.3, amended: SSI 1999/57 Reg.13
Sch.3 para.1, amended: SSI 1999/57 Reg.13
Sch.3 para.2, amended: SSI 1999/57 Reg.13
Sch.3 para.3, amended: SSI 1999/57 Reg.13
Sch.3 para.4, amended: SSI 1999/57 Reg.13

NO.

414. National Health Service (Pharmaceutical Services) (Scotland) Regulations 1995— *cont.*

Sch.4 para.1, amended: SSI 1999/57 Reg.14
Sch.4 para.2, amended: SSI 1999/57 Reg.14
Sch.4 para.3, amended: SSI 1999/57 Reg.14
Sch.4 para.6, amended: SSI 1999/57 Reg.14
Sch.4 para.7, amended: SSI 1999/57 Reg.14
Sch.4 para.9, amended: SSI 1999/57 Reg.14
Sch.4 para.10, amended: SSI 1999/57 Reg.14
Sch.4 para.11, amended: SSI 1999/57 Reg.14
Sch.4 para.15, amended: SSI 1999/57 Reg.14

416. National Health Service (General Medical Services) (Scotland) Regulations 1995

applied: SI 1998/659 Reg.4
Part III, applied: SI 1998/659 Reg.3
Reg.2, amended: SI 1996/1504 Reg.2, SI 1997/943 Reg.2, SI 1998/4 Reg.2, SI 1998/660 Reg.2, Reg.7, SI 1999/749 Reg.2, SSI 1999/54 Reg.3
Reg.4, amended: SI 1996/842 Reg.2, SSI 1999/54 Reg.4
Reg.5, amended: SSI 1999/54 Reg.2
Reg.6, amended: SI 1997/943 Reg.3, SI 1998/4 Reg.2, SSI 1999/54 Reg.5
Reg.7, amended: SSI 1999/54 Reg.2
Reg.8, amended: SSI 1999/54 Reg.2
Reg.9, amended: SSI 1999/54 Reg.2
Reg.10, amended: SSI 1999/54 Reg.6
Reg.11, amended: SSI 1999/54 Reg.7
Reg.12, amended: SSI 1999/54 Reg.8
Reg.14, amended: SSI 1999/54 Reg.2
Reg.16, amended: SSI 1999/54 Reg.9
Reg.17, amended: SSI 1999/54 Reg.2
Reg.19, revoked: SI 1998/660 Reg.2
Reg.20, revoked: SI 1998/660 Reg.2
Reg.21, amended: SI 1996/842 Reg.3, SSI 1999/54 Reg.10
Reg.21, applied: SI 1998/659 Reg.2, Reg.4
Reg.22, amended: SSI 1999/54 Reg.11
Reg.22, revoked (in part): SI 1998/660 Reg.2
Reg.23, amended: SSI 1999/54 Reg.2
Reg.24, amended: SI 1998/660 Reg.2, SSI 1999/54 Reg.2
Reg.25, amended: SSI 1999/54 Reg.12
Reg.25, applied: SI 1998/659 Reg.8
Reg.26, amended: SSI 1999/54 Reg.13
Reg.26, substituted: SI 1998/660 Reg.2
Reg.27, amended: SI 1998/660 Reg.2, SSI 1999/54 Reg.2
Reg.28, amended: SI 1998/660 Reg.6, SSI 1999/54 Reg.14
Reg.29, amended: SSI 1999/54 Reg.2
Reg.30, amended: SSI 1999/54 Reg.2
Reg.31, amended: SI 1998/660 Reg.2, SSI 1999/54 Reg.2
Reg.31, substituted: SI 1997/943 Reg.4
Reg.32, amended: SSI 1999/54 Reg.15
Reg.33, amended: SSI 1999/54 Reg.2
Reg.34, amended: SSI 1999/54 Reg.2
Reg.35, amended: SI 1998/1600 Reg.2, SI 1999/749 Reg.2, SSI 1999/54 Reg.16
Reg.35A, amended: SI 1999/749 Reg.2
Reg.35B, added: SI 1998/1600 Reg.2
Reg.35B, amended: SI 1999/749 Reg.2, SSI 1999/54 Reg.17
Reg.36, amended: SI 1998/1600 Reg.2, SI 1999/749 Reg.2, SSI 1999/54 Reg.2
Reg.37, amended: SSI 1999/54 Reg.2
Reg.38, amended: SSI 1999/54 Reg.2
Sch.1, amended: SSI 1999/54 Reg.18
Sch.1, applied: SI 1998/665 Reg.3
Sch.1 para.1, amended: SI 1996/1504 Reg.2, SI 1997/943 Reg.5

NO.

416. National Health Service (General Medical Services) (Scotland) Regulations 1995— *cont.*

Sch.1 para.4, amended: SI 1996/842 Reg.4, SI 1998/660 Reg.3
Sch.1 para.5, amended: SI 1998/660 Reg.3
Sch.1 para.7, amended: SI 1998/660 Reg.3
Sch.1 para.9, amended: SI 1998/660 Reg.3
Sch.1 para.9, applied: SI 1998/659 Reg.4
Sch.1 para.9A, added: SI 1997/943 Reg.5
Sch.1 para.9B, added: SI 1997/943 Reg.5
Sch.1 para.11, revoked (in part): SI 1997/943 Reg.5
Sch.1 para.12A, added: SI 1996/842 Reg.4
Sch.1 para.12A, amended: SI 1999/749 Reg.2
Sch.1 para.12A, applied: SI 1997/1014 Sch.2 para.13
Sch.1 para.12B, added: SI 1996/842 Reg.4
Sch.1 para.12B, applied: SI 1997/1014 Sch.2 para.13
Sch.1 para.13, amended: SI 1998/660 Reg.3
Sch.1 para.14, amended: SI 1998/660 Reg.3
Sch.1 para.16, amended: SI 1998/660 Reg.3
Sch.1 para.17A, added: SI 1996/842 Reg.4
Sch.1 para.17A, amended: SI 1998/660 Reg.6
Sch.1 para.17B, added: SI 1996/842 Reg.4
Sch.1 para.18, amended: SI 1997/943 Reg.5, SI 1998/660 Reg.5
Sch.1 para.19, amended: SI 1998/660 Reg.5, Reg.6, Reg.8
Sch.1 para.19, substituted: SI 1997/943 Reg.5
Sch.1 para.20, amended: SI 1998/4 Reg.2, SI 1998/1667 Reg.4
Sch.1 para.20, substituted: SI 1997/943 Reg.5
Sch.1 para.20A, added: SI 1998/660 Reg.6
Sch.1 para.29, amended: SI 1996/1504 Reg.2
Sch.1 para.29A, added: SI 1996/1504 Reg.2
Sch.1 para.29B, added: SI 1999/1620 Reg.2
Sch.1 para.29B, amended: SSI 1999/54 Reg.18
Sch.1 para.32, revoked: SI 1999/1057 Reg.2
Sch.1 para.34, substituted: SI 1998/660 Reg.8
Sch.1 para.35, amended: SI 1997/943 Reg.5
Sch.1 para.36, referred to: SI 1997/1014 Sch.2 para.12
Sch.2 Part I, amended: SSI 1999/54 Reg.19
Sch.2 Part II, amended: SSI 1999/54 Reg.19
Sch.2 Part III, amended: SSI 1999/54 Reg.19
Sch.3 para.1, amended: SSI 1999/54 Reg.20
Sch.3 para.3, amended: SSI 1999/54 Reg.20
Sch.4 para.18, amended: SI 1996/842 Reg.4
Sch.4A, added: SI 1997/943 Reg.6, Sch.
Sch.4A para.3, amended: SI 1998/660 Reg.4
Sch.5 para.9A, added: SI 1996/842 Reg.5
Sch.5 para.22, added: SI 1998/1667 Reg.4
Sch.6 para.7, amended: SSI 1999/54 Reg.21
Sch.7 para.1, amended: SSI 1999/54 Reg.22
Sch.7 para.4, amended: SI 1997/943 Reg.7
Sch.7 para.5, added: SI 1996/842 Reg.6
Sch.8A, added: SI 1998/1600 Reg.2, Sch.
Sch.8A, amended: SSI 1999/54 Reg.23
Sch.10, amended: SI 1997/1473 Reg.2
Sch.11, amended: SI 1997/1473 Reg.3, SI 1999/1620 Reg.3, SSI 1999/54 Reg.24

417. Collective Redundancies and Transfer of Undertakings (Amendment) Regulations (Northern Ireland) 1995

revoked: SI 1996/1919 (NI.16) Art.257
Reg.7, revoked (in part): SI 1996/1919 (NI.16) Art.257, SI 1996/1921 (NI.18) Art.28
Reg.8, revoked (in part): SI 1996/1919 (NI.16) Art.257, SI 1996/1921 (NI.18) Art.28
Reg.9, revoked (in part): SI 1996/1919 (NI.16) Art.257, SI 1996/1921 (NI.18) Art.28

NO.

417. Town and Country Planning (Environmental Assessment and Permitted Development) Regulations 1995
applied: SI 1999/672 Art.2, Sch.1
revoked: SI 1999/293 Reg.34, Sch.5
Reg.2, amended: SI 1999/107 Reg.4
Reg.2, applied: SI 1999/107 Reg.4
Reg.2, revoked: SI 1999/293 Reg.34, Sch.5
Reg.3, amended: SI 1999/107 Reg.4
Reg.3, applied: SI 1999/107 Reg.4
Reg.3, revoked: SI 1999/293 Reg.34, Sch.5
Reg.4, amended: SI 1999/107 Reg.4
Reg.4, applied: SI 1999/107 Reg.4
Reg.4, revoked: SI 1999/293 Reg.34, Sch.5
Reg.6, amended: SI 1999/107 Reg.4
Reg.6, applied: SI 1999/107 Reg.4
Reg.6, revoked: SI 1999/293 Reg.34, Sch.5

418. Town and Country Planning (General Permitted Development) Order 1995
see *Thames Heliport Plc v Tower Hamlets LBC* (1997) 74 P. & C.R. 164 (CA), Schiemann, L.J.
referred to: 1996 c.61 s.9, 1998 c.ii s.11, SI 1999/403 Art.16, SI 1999/1892 Reg.2, Sch. Art.5
Art.1, amended: SI 1996/252 Art.2, Sch, SI 1996/528 Art.2
Art.1, revoked (in part): SI 1999/1661 Art.6
Art.3, amended: SI 1996/252 Art.2, Sch, SI 1999/293 Reg.35, SI 1999/1783 Reg.15
Art.3, applied: SI 1997/1160 Reg.6, 1998 c.iv s.40
Art.3, referred to: SI 1999/293 Reg.22, SI 1999/1672 Reg.4
Art.3, revoked (in part): SI 1999/293 Reg.34, Sch.5
Art.4, see *Historic Buildings and Monuments Commission for England v Secretary of State for the Environment* [1997] 3 P.L.R. 8 (QBD), Judge Moriarty Q.C.
Art.4, amended: SI 1996/528 Art.2
Art.4, referred to: SI 1999/1672 Reg.4
Art.5, referred to: SI 1999/1672 Reg.4
Sch.1 Part 1, amended: SI 1996/528 Art.2
Sch.1 Part 1, revoked: SI 1999/1661 Art.6
Sch.1 Part 3, amended: SI 1996/528 Art.2
Sch.1 Part 11, amended: SI 1996/528 Art.2
Sch.2, see *R. v Staffordshire Moorlands DC Ex p. Bartlam* [1998] P.L.C.R. 385 (CA (Crim Div)), Nourse, L.J.; see *Shepherd v Secretary of State for the Environment* (1998) 76 P. & C.R. 74 (CA), Buxton, L.J.
Sch.2, applied: SI 1999/293 Reg.22
Sch.2 Part 4, amended: SI 1997/366 Art.2
Sch.2 Part 6, applied: SI 1997/1440 Sch.1 para.2, SI 1997/1441 Sch.1 para.1, SI 1997/1442 Sch.1 para.1, SI 1997/1443 Sch.1 para.3, SI 1997/1444 Sch.1 para.1
Sch.2 Part 7, applied: SI 1997/1440 Sch.1 para.2, SI 1997/1441 Sch.1 para.1, SI 1997/1442 Sch.1 para.1, SI 1997/1443 Sch.1 para.3, SI 1997/1444 Sch.1 para.1
Sch.2 Part 1, amended: SI 1998/462 Art.2, SI 1999/1661 Art.2
Sch.2 Part 7, referred to: SI 1999/2228 Reg.3
Sch.2 Part 11, applied: 1998 c.iv s.40
Sch.2 Part 13, amended: SI 1999/293 Reg.35
Sch.2 Part 17, amended: SI 1996/252 Art.2, Sch, SI 1996/528 Art.2
Sch.2 Part 24, amended: SI 1998/462 Art.3, SI 1999/1661 Art.3
Sch.2 Part 24, referred to: SI 1999/2450 Sch.4 para.3.6, Sch.4 para.4.2, Sch.4 para.5.5

NO.

418. Town and Country Planning (General Permitted Development) Order 1995—*cont.*
Sch.2 Part 24A, see *R. v Staffordshire Moorlands DC Ex p. Bartlam* (1999) 77 P. & C.R. 210 (CA (Crim Div)), Nourse, L.J.
Sch.2 Part 25, amended: SI 1998/462 Art.4, SI 1999/1661 Art.4

419. Town and Country Planning (General Development Procedure) Order 1995
referred to: SI 1997/858 Art.3
Art.5, amended: SI 1996/525 Sch para.20
Art.8, amended: SI 1999/293 Reg.35
Art.8, applied: SI 1999/293 Reg.17
Art.10, amended: SI 1996/525 Sch para.20, SI 1996/1817 Art.2, Art.3, SI 1997/858 Art.2, SI 1999/266 Art.8, SI 1999/981 Reg.6
Art.10, applied: SI 1999/266 Art.8
Art.13, amended: SI 1996/525 Sch para.20
Art.14, amended: SI 1999/293 Reg.35
Art.20, see *R. v Secretary of State for the Environment, Transport and the Regions Ex p. Bath and North East Somerset DC* Times, January 28, 1999 (QBD), Christopher Lockhart-Mummery Q.C.
Art.20, applied: SI 1999/293 Reg.3
Art.24, see *R. v Flintshire CC Ex p. Somerfield Stores Ltd* [1998] P.L.C.R. 336 (QBD), Carnwath, J.
Art.25, amended: SI 1996/525 Sch para.20
Art.25, applied: SI 1999/293 Reg.7
Sch.1 Part 2, amended: SI 1996/525 Sch para.20, SI 1996/1243 Sch.5 para.16

421. Bristol City Docks Harbour Revision Order 1995
Art.7, applied: SI 1998/1209 Art.5
Art.8, applied: SI 1998/1209 Art.5
Art.9, applied: SI 1998/1209 Art.5
Art.10, applied: SI 1998/1209 Art.5
Art.11, applied: SI 1998/1209 Art.5
Art.12, applied: SI 1998/1209 Art.5

441. Dual-Use and Related Goods (Export Control) (Suspension) Regulations 1995
applied: SI 1996/2721 Reg.15
revoked: SI 1996/2721 Sch.1

443. National Assistance (Sums for Personal Requirements) Regulations 1995
revoked: SI 1996/391

444. National Health Service (Dental Charges) Amendment Regulations 1995
revoked: SI 1996/389 Reg.3

449. Medical Devices (Consultation Requirements) (Fees) Regulations 1995
Reg.3, amended: SI 1996/622 Reg.2, SI 1998/574 Reg.3, SI 1999/566 Reg.3

451. Feeding Stuffs Regulations (Northern Ireland) 1995
applied: SI 1999/2325 Reg.7
Reg.22, revoked: SI 1999/2325 Reg.15

457. Specified Bovine Offal (Treatment and Disposal) Regulations (Northern Ireland) 1995
applied: SI 1996/1633 (NI.12) Art.11

470. Housing Support Grant (Scotland) Order 1995
Art.2, amended: SI 1996/814 Art.2
Art.3, amended: SI 1996/814 Art.2

470. Mechanically Recovered Meat Regulations (Northern Ireland) 1995
applied: SI 1996/1633 (NI.12) Art.11

NO.

476. **Environmental Protection (Waste Recycling Payments) (Amendment) Regulations 1995**
revoked: SI 1997/351 Reg.4

482. **Disability Working Allowance and Income Support (General) Amendment Regulations 1995**
Reg.6, revoked: SI 1996/206 Reg.28, Sch.3
Reg.7, revoked: SI 1996/206 Reg.28, Sch.3
Reg.8, revoked: SI 1996/206 Reg.28, Sch.3
Reg.9, revoked: SI 1996/206 Reg.28, Sch.3
Reg.14, revoked: SI 1996/206 Reg.28, Sch.3
Reg.15, revoked: SI 1996/206 Reg.28, Sch.3
Reg.19, amended: SI 1999/2422 Art.3, Sch.11

483. **Certification Officer (Amendment of Fees) Regulations 1995**
revoked: SI 1996/651 Reg.8

490. **Antarctic Regulations 1995**
applied: SI 1997/2966 Art.2, SI 1997/2967 Art.2, SI 1997/2968 Art.2
Reg.1, amended: SI 1997/2966 Art.2, Sch. para.1, SI 1997/2967 Art.2, Sch. para.1, SI 1997/2968 Art.2, Sch. para.1
Reg.2, amended: SI 1997/2966 Art.2, Sch. para.2, SI 1997/2967 Art.2, Sch. para.2, SI 1997/2968 Art.2, Sch. para.2
Reg.4, amended: SI 1997/2966 Art.2, Sch. para.3
Reg.9, amended: SI 1997/2966 Art.2, Sch. para.4, SI 1997/2967 Art.2, Sch. para.4, SI 1997/2968 Art.2, Sch. para.3
Reg.17, amended: SI 1997/2966 Art.2, Sch. para.5, SI 1997/2967 Art.2, Sch. para.4
Reg.18, amended: SI 1997/2966 Art.2, Sch. para.6, SI 1997/2967 Art.2, Sch. para.5, SI 1997/2968 Art.2, Sch. para.4, SI 1998/1007 Reg.2
Reg.19, amended: SI 1997/2966 Art.2, Sch. para.7, SI 1997/2967 Art.2, Sch. para.6, SI 1997/2968 Art.2, Sch. para.5
Reg.20, amended: SI 1997/2966 Art.2, Sch. para.8, SI 1997/2967 Art.2, Sch. para.7, SI 1997/2968 Art.2, Sch. para.6
Sch.1, amended: SI 1998/1007 Reg.3
Sch.2, amended: SI 1998/1007 Reg.3

493. **Avon (Structural Change) Order 1995**
referred to: SI 1996/656 Art.2
Art.8, revoked: SI 1998/2699 Art.4
Art.9, revoked (in part): SI 1998/2700 Art.6, SI 1998/2701 Art.14
Art.13, revoked: 1996 c.16 Sch.9 Part III
Sch.1, revoked: SI 1998/2700 Art.6
Sch.2, amended: SI 1996/446 Art.9
Sch.2, revoked: SI 1998/2701 Art.14

494. **Offshore Installations (Safety Zones) Order 1995**
revoked: SI 1997/735 Art.3, Sch.2

497. **Civil Aviation (Navigation Services Charges) Regulations 1995**
revoked: SI 1998/532 Reg.3, Sch.1
Reg.2, amended: SI 1996/689 Reg.2
Reg.2, revoked: SI 1998/532 Reg.3, Sch.1
Reg.2 Table, revoked: SI 1998/532 Reg.3, Sch.1
Reg.2 Table, substituted: SI 1997/667 Reg.2
Reg.6, amended: SI 1996/689 Reg.2, SI 1997/667 Reg.2
Reg.6, revoked: SI 1998/532 Reg.3, Sch.1
Reg.7, amended: SI 1996/689 Reg.2, SI 1997/667 Reg.2
Reg.7, revoked: SI 1998/532 Reg.3, Sch.1

NO.

501. **Education (Grants for Education Support and Training) (Wales) Regulations 1995**
revoked: SI 1996/334 Reg.12

512. **Statutory Sick Pay Percentage Threshold Order 1995**
Art.4, applied: 1999 c.2 s.1, Sch.2

516. **Income-related Benefits Schemes (Miscellaneous Amendments) Regulations 1995**
Reg.28, applied: SI 1996/207 Reg.87

520. **Local Government Changes for England (Staff) Regulations 1995**
Reg.3, applied: SI 1996/3118 Art.5, SI 1997/3067 Art.5
Reg.4, applied: SI 1996/3118 Art.5, SI 1997/3067 Art.5
Reg.5, applied: SI 1996/330 Reg.12, SI 1996/3118 Art.5, SI 1997/3067 Art.5

522. **Education (Individual Pupils' Achievements) (Information) (Wales) (Amendment) Regulations 1995**
revoked: SI 1996/382 Reg.1

524. **Occupational and Personal Pension Schemes (Levy) Regulations 1995**
applied: SI 1997/666 Reg.12, Reg.14
revoked: SI 1997/666 Reg.14

525. **Merchant Shipping (Light Dues) (Amendment) Regulations 1995**
revoked: SI 1997/562 Reg.2, Sch.1

531. **Local Government Changes for England (Housing Benefit and Council Tax Benefit) Regulations 1995**
Reg.2, amended: SI 1996/547 Reg.2
Reg.3, amended: SI 1996/547 Reg.2
Reg.5, added: SI 1996/547 Reg.2

532. **Education (School Financial Statements) (Prescribed Particulars etc.) (Amendment) Regulations 1995**
revoked: SI 1996/381 Reg.3

539. **Fresh Meat (Hygiene and Inspection) Regulations 1995**
applied: SI 1996/963 Art.26, SI 1996/1192 Art.26, SI 1996/1743 Reg.6, SI 1996/1941 Art.26, SI 1996/2264 Art.11, SI 1996/2999 Reg.6, SI 1996/3124 Reg.3, Reg.10, Sch.2 para.6, SI 1997/617 Art.28, SI 1997/1986 Reg.6, SI 1997/2959 Reg.12, SI 1997/2965 Reg.17, Reg.31, SI 1999/646 Art.33, SI 1999/680 Art.2, Sch. Part I, SI 1999/1103 Reg.10, Reg.11, SSI 1999/186 Reg.10
referred to: SI 1996/2005 Reg.6
Reg.2, applied: SI 1997/2964 Sch.1
Reg.2, referred to: SI 1999/1103 Reg.10
Reg.4, amended: SI 1996/2235 Art.10
Reg.5, amended: SI 1996/2235 Art.10
Reg.7, amended: SI 1996/1148 Reg.2, SI 1997/2074 Reg.2
Reg.7, revoked (in part): SI 1997/2074 Reg.2
Reg.8, applied: SI 1996/1686 Art.10, SI 1998/190 Reg.12, SSI 1999/186 Reg.10
Reg.18, applied: SI 1996/2097 Reg.4
Reg.18, referred to: SI 1996/2097 Reg.3
Sch.9 para.1, amended: SI 1997/1729 Reg.35

540. **Poultry Meat, Farmed Game Bird Meat and Rabbit Meat (Hygiene and Inspection) Regulations 1995**
see *R. v Altaf (Mohammed)* [1999] E.H.L.R. Dig. 204 (CA (Crim Div)), Mantle L.J.
applied: SI 1996/3124 Reg.3, Reg.10, Sch.2 para.7, SI 1999/646 Art.33, SI 1999/680 Art.2, Sch. Part I
Reg.8, applied: SI 1998/190 Reg.12
Sch.9 para.5, amended: SI 1997/1729 Reg.35

NO.

1995—cont.

548. **Non-Domestic Rates (Levying) (Scotland) Regulations 1995**
revoked: SI 1996/103 Reg.30
Part II, referred to: SI 1996/103 Reg.11
Part III, referred to: SI 1996/103 Reg.6, Reg.11, Reg.23
Part IV, referred to: SI 1996/103 Reg.11
Reg.7, referred to: SI 1996/103 Reg.6, Reg.23

553. **Local Authorities (Members' Allowances) (Amendment) Regulations 1995**
Reg.5, revoked (in part): SI 1998/556 Reg.3, SI 1998/557 Reg.3

559. **Social Security Benefits Up-rating Order 1995**
revoked: SI 1996/599 Art.24

571. **Gaming Act (Variation of Fees) (Scotland) Order 1995**
referred to: SI 1998/456 Art.2
revoked: SI 1998/456 Art.3

572. **Valuation Appeal Committee (Procedure in Appeals under the Valuation Acts) (Scotland) Regulations 1995**
Reg.2, amended: SI 1996/580 Art.10
Reg.8, amended: SI 1996/580 Art.10

580. **Social Security Benefits Up-rating Regulations 1995**
revoked: SI 1996/670 Reg.7
Reg.1, revoked: SI 1996/670 Reg.7
Reg.3, revoked: SI 1996/670 Reg.7
Reg.4, revoked: SI 1996/670 Reg.7
Reg.5, revoked: SI 1996/670 Reg.7
Reg.6, revoked: SI 1996/670 Reg.7
Reg.7, revoked: SI 1996/670 Reg.7
Reg.8, revoked: SI 1996/670 Reg.7

581. **Social Security (Industrial Injuries) (Dependency) (Permitted Earnings Limits) Order 1995**
revoked: SI 1996/671 Art.3

587. **Education (Grant-Maintained Schools) (Finance) (Wales) Regulations 1995**
applied: SI 1997/599 Reg.3
revoked: SI 1996/537 Reg.3
Reg.5, applied: SI 1996/537 Reg.6
Reg.6, applied: SI 1996/537 Reg.6
Reg.7, applied: SI 1996/537 Reg.6
Reg.13, applied: SI 1996/537 Reg.6
Reg.23, applied: SI 1997/599 Reg.3

598. **Council Tax (Exempt Dwellings) (Scotland) Amendment Order 1995**
revoked: SI 1997/728 Art.5, Sch.2

600. **Humberside (Structural Change) Order 1995**
referred to: SI 1996/658 Art.2, Art.3
Art.11, revoked: 1996 c.16 Sch.9 Part III

601. **Teacher Training Agency (Additional Functions) Order 1995**
revoked: SI 1997/2678 Art.1

602. **Education (Teachers) (Amendment) Regulations 1995**
revoked: SI 1997/2679 Reg.7, Sch.3

603. **Education (Bursaries for Teacher Training) (Amendment) Regulations 1995**
revoked (in part): SI 1999/2162 Art.2, SI 1999/2816 Reg.1

605. **Education (Grants for Education Support and Training) (England) Regulations 1995**
revoked: SI 1996/734 Reg.12
Reg.8, applied: SI 1996/235 Reg.8
Reg.8, revoked: SI 1996/734 Reg.12
Reg.9, applied: SI 1996/235 Reg.9
Reg.9, revoked: SI 1996/734 Reg.12

NO.

1995—cont.

606. **Plant Breeders' Rights (Fees) (Amendment) Regulations 1995**
revoked: SI 1998/1021 Reg.7 (with savings), Sch.2 (with savings)

610. **North Yorkshire (District of York) (Structural and Boundary Changes) Order 1995**
referred to: SI 1996/659 Art.3
Art.12, revoked: 1996 c.16 Sch.9 Part III

614. **Animal By-Products (Identification) Regulations 1995**
applied: SI 1998/871 Reg.7, Reg.20
Reg.3, amended: SI 1997/2073 Reg.2

615. **Common Agricultural Policy (Wine) Regulations 1995**
revoked: SI 1996/696 Reg.2

617. **Road Traffic (Special Parking Area) (Royal Borough of Kingston upon Thames) (Amendment) Order 1995**
revoked: SI 1996/3038 Art.2, Sch.1

618. **Road Traffic (Special Parking Area) (London Borough of Sutton) (Amendment) Order 1995**
revoked: SI 1998/1134 Art.2, Sch.1

621. **Family Health Services Appeal Authority (Establishment and Constitution) Order 1995**
Art.8, added: SI 1998/1577 Art.3

622. **Family Health Services Appeal Authority Regulations 1995**
Reg.5, amended: SI 1997/2991 Reg.3, Sch. para.6
Reg.7, amended: SI 1997/2991 Reg.3, Sch. para.6
Reg.12, revoked (in part): SI 1996/708 Reg.6, Sch.2

629. **Education (Payment for Special Educational Needs Supplies) (Amendment) Regulations 1995**
revoked: SI 1999/710 Reg.3 (with savings)

632. **Judicial Pensions (Miscellaneous) Regulations 1995**
Part II, substituted: SI 1996/2893 Reg.3
Reg.3, substituted: SI 1996/2893 Reg.3
Reg.4, substituted: SI 1996/2893 Reg.3
Reg.4A, added: SI 1997/1687 Reg.4
Reg.4B, added: SI 1997/1687 Reg.4
Reg.5, revoked (in part): SI 1997/1687 Reg.5
Reg.5, substituted: SI 1996/2893 Reg.3
Reg.6, revoked (in part): SI 1997/1687 Reg.6
Reg.6, substituted: SI 1996/2893 Reg.3

636. **Judicial Pensions (Transfer Between Judicial Pension Schemes) Regulations 1995**
applied: SI 1998/1219 Reg.16
referred to: SI 1996/52 Reg.9
Reg.4, applied: SI 1998/1219 Reg.12
Reg.5, applied: SI 1998/1219 Reg.12
Reg.6, amended: SI 1998/2527 Reg.2
Reg.6, applied: SI 1998/1219 Reg.12

638. **Judicial Pensions (Contributions) Regulations 1995**
referred to: SI 1998/1219 Reg.4
revoked: SI 1998/1219 Reg.3 (with savings)
Reg.3, revoked: SI 1998/1219 Reg.3 (with savings)
Reg.4, revoked: SI 1998/1219 Reg.3 (with savings)
Reg.5, revoked: SI 1998/1219 Reg.3 (with savings)
Reg.6, revoked: SI 1998/1219 Reg.3 (with savings)

NO.

638. Judicial Pensions (Contributions) Regulations 1995—*cont.*
Reg.7, revoked: SI 1998/1219 Reg.3 (with savings)
Reg.8, revoked: SI 1998/1219 Reg.3 (with savings)

639. Judicial Pensions (Additional Voluntary Contributions) Regulations 1995
applied: SI 1998/1219 Reg.11
Reg.2, amended: SI 1996/52 Reg.3, Reg.4, Reg.5, Reg.6, Reg.7
Reg.3, amended: SI 1996/52 Reg.8
Reg.4, amended: SI 1996/52 Reg.9, Reg.10, Reg.11, Reg.12, Reg.13, Reg.14, Reg.15
Sch.2, substituted: SI 1996/52 Reg.16

646. Registration of Births, Deaths, Marriages and Divorces (Fees) (Scotland) Amendment Regulations 1995
revoked: SI 1997/716 Reg.7
Reg.4, revoked: SI 1996/574 Reg.6, SI 1997/716 Reg.7

647. Police (Discipline) (Miscellaneous Amendments) (Scotland) Regulations 1995
revoked: SI 1996/1642 Reg.25, Sch.2

650. Defence Evaluation and Research Agency Trading Fund (Amendment) Order 1995
Art.3, revoked (in part): SI 1996/1447 Art.2

655. Wireless Telegraphy (Television Licence Fees) (Amendment) Regulations 1995
revoked: SI 1997/290 Reg.1, Sch

677. Local Government, Planning and Land Act 1980 (Competition) (Scotland) Regulations 1995
revoked: SI 1996/2935 Reg.10
Reg.7, amended: SI 1996/2936 Reg.2
Reg.7, revoked: SI 1996/2935 Reg.10
Reg.7, substituted: SI 1997/1439 Reg.2
Reg.8, amended: SI 1996/2936 Reg.2
Reg.8, revoked: SI 1996/2935 Reg.10, SI 1997/1439 Reg.2
Reg.9, amended: SI 1996/2936 Reg.2, SI 1997/1439 Reg.3
Reg.9, revoked (in part): SI 1996/2935 Reg.10, SI 1997/1439 Reg.3

678. Local Government (Exemption from Competition) (Scotland) Order 1995
Art.3, amended: SI 1999/937 Art.2
Art.7, amended: SI 1997/1438 Art.2, SI 1998/1421 Art.2, SI 1999/937 Art.3
Sch.2, amended: SI 1997/1438 Art.3, SI 1998/1421 Art.3, SI 1999/937 Art.4

685. Police and Magistrates' Courts Act 1994 (Commencement No.8 and Transitional Provisions) Order 1995
revoked: 1997 c.25 s.73, Sch.6 Part II
Art.6, applied: 1997 c.25 s.73, Sch.4 para.16
Art.6, revoked: 1997 c.25 s.73, Sch.6 Part II

686. Justices' Chief Executives and Justices' Clerks (Appointment) Regulations 1995
revoked: SI 1999/2397 Reg.3

688. Insurance (Fees) Regulations 1995
revoked: SI 1996/546 Reg.2

691. National Health Service (Optical Charges and Payments) Amendment (No.2) Regulations 1995
revoked: SI 1997/818 Reg.24, Sch.4

692. National Health Service (Functions of Family Health Services Authorities) (Prescribing Incentive Schemes) Regulations 1995
revoked: SI 1998/632 Reg.3

NO.

693. National Health Service (Fund-Holding Practices) Amendment Regulations 1995
revoked: SI 1996/706 Reg.28

700. Friendly Societies (General Charge and Fees) Regulations 1995
revoked: SI 1996/614 Reg.7

705. National Health Service (Optical Charges and Payments) (Scotland) Amendment (No.2) Regulations 1995
revoked: SI 1998/642 Reg.24, Sch.4

707. Common Police Services (Scotland) Order 1995
applied: SI 1996/745 Art.4
revoked: SI 1996/745 Art.4

708. Pensions Increase (Review) Order 1995
applied: SI 1997/634 Art.3, SI 1998/503 Art.3, Art.4, SI 1999/522 Art.3

711. Building Societies (General Charge and Fees) Regulations 1995
revoked: SI 1996/609 Reg.11

712. Industrial and Provident Societies (Credit Unions) (Amendment of Fees) Regulations 1995
revoked: SI 1996/612 Reg.3

713. Industrial and Provident Societies (Amendment of Fees) Regulations 1995
revoked: SI 1996/613 Reg.4

731. Welfare of Animals (Slaughter or Killing) Regulations 1995
applied: SI 1999/672 Art.2, Sch.1
referred to: SI 1998/2095
Reg.7, amended: SI 1999/1820 Art.4, Sch.2 para.158
Reg.14, amended: SI 1999/400 Reg.2
Reg.22, amended: SI 1999/400 Reg.2
Sch.12 para.8, substituted: SI 1999/400 Reg.2

734. Companies (Welsh Language Forms and Documents) (Amendment) Regulations 1995
Sch. Form 288b CYM, revoked: SI 1999/2357 Reg.3 (with saving)
Sch. Form 363 CYM, revoked: SI 1999/2357 Reg.3 (with saving)

736. Companies (Forms) (Amendment) Regulations 1995
Sch.2 Form 288b, revoked (in part): SI 1999/2356 Reg.3 (with saving)
Sch.2 Form 363a, revoked (in part): SI 1999/2356 Reg.3 (with saving)

738. Offshore Installations and Pipeline Works (Management and Administration) Regulations 1995
applied: SI 1996/551 Reg.6
referred to: SI 1998/2573
Reg.3, referred to: SI 1998/494 Reg.3

739. European Parliamentary (United Kingdom Representatives) Pensions (Additional Voluntary Contributions Scheme) (No.2) Order 1995
Art.2, amended: SI 1999/2101 Art.3
Art.5, amended: SI 1999/2101 Art.4
Sch.2 para.3, amended: SI 1999/2101 Art.5

741. Law Hospital National Health Service Trust (Establishment) Amendment Order 1995
revoked: SI 1999/1070 Art.2, Sch.2

742. Royal Infirmary of Edinburgh National Health Service Trust (Establishment) Amendment Order 1995
revoked: SI 1998/1841 Art.3

NO.

1995—cont.

743. **Offshore Installations (Prevention of Fire and Explosion, and Emergency Response) Regulations 1995**
Reg.11, applied: SI 1996/341 Reg.4
750. **Local Government (Superannuation and Compensation for Premature Retirement) (Scotland) Amendment Regulations 1995**
applied: SI 1998/364 Reg.4, Reg.6, Reg.19, Sch.2 para.2, Sch.2 para.5, Sch.4 para.8
referred to: SI 1998/364 Reg.3, Reg.10, Sch.2 para.4, Sch.2 para.6
Reg.2, amended: SI 1998/192 Reg.52, Sch.2
Reg.3, revoked: SI 1998/192 Reg.52, Sch.2
751. **European Communities (Designation) (No.2) Order 1995**
revoked: SI 1996/266 Art.3
752. **Intelligence Services Act 1994 (Dependent Territories) Order 1995**
Sch., amended: SI 1996/2876 Art.2
754. **Appropriation (Northern Ireland) Order 1995**
revoked: SI 1998/1758 (NI.12) Art.6, Sch.2
755. **Children (Northern Ireland) Order 1995**
applied: 1996 c.14 Sch.1 para.2, SI 1996/3267 Reg.5, 1998 c.29 Sch.12 para.6, SI 1998/1071 (NI.6) Art.3, SI 1998/1504 (NI.9) Art.43
referred to: 1999 c.23 s.50
Art.2, amended: SI 1996/274 (NI.1) Art.43, Sch.5 Part I, SI 1996/3160 (NI.24) Sch.5 para.17, SI 1998/1071 (NI.6) Art.29, SI 1998/1504 (NI.9) Art.65, Sch.5 para.42, Sch.6, 1999 c.10 s.1, Sch.1 para.6
Art.8, amended: SI 1998/1071 (NI.6) Art.41, Sch.3
Art.8, revoked (in part): SI 1998/1071 (NI.6) Art.41, Sch.5
Art.12A, added: SI 1998/1071 (NI.6) Art.28
Art.18, applied: SI 1998/1504 (NI.9) Art.43, 1999 c.10 s.1, Sch.1 para.6
Art.24, amended: 1999 c.10 s.1, Sch.1 para.6
Art.25, applied: SI 1998/1504 (NI.9) Art.10
Art.33, applied: SI 1996/3267 Reg.3
Art.39, amended: 1999 c.10 s.1, Sch.1 para.6
Art.46, revoked (in part): SI 1996/274 (NI.1) Art.43, Sch.5 Part I, Art.44, Sch.6 Part I
Art.47, amended: SI 1996/274 (NI.1) Art.43, Sch.5 Part I
Art.50, amended: SI 1998/1504 (NI.9) Art.65, Sch.6
Art.50, applied: SI 1996/3267 Sch.3
Art.50, referred to: SI 1996/3267 Sch.5
Art.55, applied: SI 1996/3267 Sch.3
Art.55, referred to: SI 1996/3267 Sch.5
Art.57, applied: SI 1998/1071 (NI.6) Art.25, Art.27
Art.57A, added: SI 1998/1071 (NI.6) Art.29
Art.57A, applied: SI 1998/1071 (NI.6) Art.25, Art.27
Art.58, amended: SI 1998/1071 (NI.6) Art.29
Art.63, applied: SI 1998/1071 (NI.6) Art.20, Art.25, Art.27
Art.63A, added: SI 1998/1071 (NI.6) Art.29
Art.63A, applied: SI 1998/1071 (NI.6) Art.20, Art.25, Art.27
Art.64, amended: SI 1998/1071 (NI.6) Art.29
Art.70, amended: SI 1998/1504 (NI.9) Art.65, Sch.5 para.43
Art.74, amended: SI 1998/1504 (NI.9) Art.65, Sch.5 para.44
Art.107, amended: SI 1998/1504 (NI.9) Art.65, Sch.5 para.45
Art.108, applied: 1997 c.50 s.115
Art.118, applied: 1997 c.50 s.115
Art.165, applied: SI 1998/1071 (NI.6) Art.34

NO.

1995—cont.

755. **Children (Northern Ireland) Order 1995—** *cont.*
Art.169, amended: SI 1997/2983 (NI.21) Art.13, Sch.1 para.8
Art.169, applied: SI 1997/2983 (NI.21) Art.6
Art.169, referred to: SI 1998/1504 (NI.9) Art.19
Part V, applied: SI 1998/1504 (NI.9) Art.10
Sch.1 para.2, applied: SI 1998/1071 (NI.6) Art.13, Art.14
Sch.2 para.4, amended: SI 1996/274 (NI.1) Art.43, Sch.5 Part I
Sch.4 para.4, amended: SI 1998/1504 (NI.9) Art.65, Sch.5 para.46
Sch.8 para.35, revoked: SI 1998/2857 Reg.1
Sch.9 para.26, revoked: SI 1998/1504 (NI.9) Art.65, Sch.6
Sch.9 para.27, revoked: SI 1998/1504 (NI.9) Art.65, Sch.6
Sch.9 para.28, revoked: SI 1998/1504 (NI.9) Art.65, Sch.6
Sch.9 para.29, revoked: SI 1998/1504 (NI.9) Art.65, Sch.6
Sch.9 para.30, revoked: SI 1998/1504 (NI.9) Art.65, Sch.6
Sch.9 para.31, revoked: SI 1998/1504 (NI.9) Art.65, Sch.6
Sch.9 para.32, revoked: SI 1998/1504 (NI.9) Art.65, Sch.6
Sch.9 para.33, revoked: SI 1998/1504 (NI.9) Art.65, Sch.6
Sch.9 para.34, revoked: SI 1998/1504 (NI.9) Art.65, Sch.6
Sch.9 para.35, revoked: SI 1998/1504 (NI.9) Art.65, Sch.6
Sch.9 para.36, revoked: SI 1998/1504 (NI.9) Art.65, Sch.6
Sch.9 para.37, revoked: SI 1998/1504 (NI.9) Art.65, Sch.6
Sch.9 para.39, revoked: SI 1998/1504 (NI.9) Art.65, Sch.6
Sch.9 para.40, revoked: SI 1998/1504 (NI.9) Art.65, Sch.6
Sch.9 para.41, revoked: SI 1998/1504 (NI.9) Art.65, Sch.6
Sch.9 para.42, revoked: SI 1998/1504 (NI.9) Art.65, Sch.6
Sch.9 para.43, revoked: SI 1998/1504 (NI.9) Art.65, Sch.6
Sch.9 para.44, revoked: SI 1998/1504 (NI.9) Art.65, Sch.6
Sch.9 para.45, revoked: SI 1998/1504 (NI.9) Art.65, Sch.6
Sch.9 para.46, revoked: SI 1998/1504 (NI.9) Art.65, Sch.6
Sch.9 para.47, revoked: SI 1998/1504 (NI.9) Art.65, Sch.6
Sch.9 para.48, revoked: SI 1998/1504 (NI.9) Art.65, Sch.6
Sch.9 para.49, revoked: SI 1998/1504 (NI.9) Art.65, Sch.6
Sch.9 para.50, revoked: SI 1998/1504 (NI.9) Art.65, Sch.6
Sch.9 para.51, revoked: SI 1998/1504 (NI.9) Art.65, Sch.6
Sch.9 para.52, revoked: SI 1998/1504 (NI.9) Art.65, Sch.6
Sch.9 para.55, revoked: SI 1998/1504 (NI.9) Art.65, Sch.6
Sch.9 para.56, revoked: SI 1998/1504 (NI.9) Art.65, Sch.6
Sch.9 para.57, revoked: SI 1998/1504 (NI.9) Art.65, Sch.6

NO.

755. **Children (Northern Ireland) Order 1995—** *cont.*
Sch.9 para.118, revoked: SI 1998/1504 (NI.9) Art.65, Sch.6
Sch.9 para.177, revoked: 1998 c.29 Sch.16 Part II
Sch.9 para.191, revoked: 1998 c.29 Sch.16 Part II

757. **Children's Evidence (Northern Ireland) Order 1995**
Art.3, revoked: SI 1998/1504 (NI.9) Art.65, Sch.6
Art.4, amended: SI 1999/2789 (NI.8) Art.40, Sch.1 para.4
Art.4, applied: SI 1996/1141 (NI.6) Art.5
Art.5, revoked: SI 1999/2789 (NI.8) Art.40, Sch.3
Sch.1 para.3, amended: 1996 c.25 Sch.4 para.18
Sch.1 para.4, referred to: SI 1999/2789 (NI.8) Art.29
Sch.1 para.5, amended: 1996 c.25 Sch.4 para.18
Sch.2 para.2, revoked: SI 1998/1504 (NI.9) Art.65, Sch.6
Sch.2 para.3, revoked: SI 1998/1504 (NI.9) Art.65, Sch.6
Sch.2 para.6, revoked: 1996 c.25 Sch.4 para.36
Sch.2 para.11, revoked: SI 1999/2789 (NI.8) Art.40, Sch.3

758. **Fair Employment (Amendment) (Northern Ireland) Order 1995**
revoked: SI 1998/3162 (NI.21) Art.105, Sch.5

764. **Double Taxation Relief (Taxes on Income) (Republic of Ireland) Order 1995**
Sch., referred to: SI 1998/3151 Art.2

767. **Social Security (Reciprocal Agreements) Order 1995**
Sch.2, amended: SI 1996/1927 Art.3, SI 1997/871 Art.3, SI 1997/1778 Art.3
Sch.3, amended: SI 1997/1778 Art.3

769. **Glan-y-Mor National Health Service Trust (Establishment) Order 1995**
revoked: SI 1999/1120 Art.2, Sch.2

770. **University Hospital of Wales Healthcare National Health Service Trust (Establishment) Order 1995**
revoked: SI 1999/1120 Art.2, Sch.2

789. **Local Government (Application of Enactments) (Scotland) Order 1995**
revoked: SI 1996/739 Art.8, Sch.3

798. **Local Government Changes for England (Capital Finance) Regulations 1995**
Reg.10, amended: SI 1996/2826 Reg.3
Reg.11, amended: SI 1996/2826 Reg.4
Reg.14, amended: SI 1996/2826 Reg.5
Reg.15, amended: SI 1996/2826 Reg.6
Reg.19, amended: SI 1996/2826 Reg.7

799. **Medicines (Medicated Animal Feedingstuffs) (Amendment) Regulations 1995**
revoked: SI 1998/1048 Reg.2, Sch.1

817. **Local Government (Compensation for Redundancy and Premature Retirement) (Amendment) Regulations 1995**
revoked: SI 1996/1680 Reg.49, Sch.5

829. **Social Security (Incapacity Benefit) (Consequential and Transitional Amendments and Savings) Regulations 1995**
Reg.12, revoked: SI 1996/2745 Reg.18, Sch.4
Reg.17, revoked (in part): SI 1996/1345 Reg.27, Sch.

NO.

830. **Elections (Welsh Forms) Order 1995**
Art.3, revoked: SI 1999/1402 Art.2

838. **Housing Renovation etc. Grants (Reduction of Grant) (Amendment) Regulations 1995**
applied: SI 1996/2842 Art.8
revoked: SI 1996/2842 Art.7, Sch Part I

839. **Housing Renovation etc. Grants (Prescribed Forms and Particulars) (Amendment) Regulations 1995**
applied: SI 1996/2842 Art.8
revoked: SI 1996/2842 Art.7, Sch Part I

840. **Local Government (Education Administration) (Compensation for Redundancy or Premature Retirement on Reorganisation) (Scotland) Regulations 1995**
Reg.2, amended: SI 1997/720 Reg.2

842. **Newham Community Health Services National Health Service Trust (Establishment) Order 1995**
Art.3, substituted: SI 1999/1773 Art.2

848. **Surrey Heartlands National Health Service Trust (Establishment) Order 1995**
revoked: SI 1998/652 Art.2

849. **Local Authorities (Companies) Order 1995**
Art.12, amended: SI 1996/621 Art.3
Art.14, amended: SI 1996/621 Art.4
Art.14, applied: SI 1997/319 Reg.129
Art.16, amended: SI 1996/621 Art.5

850. **Local Authorities (Capital Finance and Approved Investments) (Amendment) Regulations 1995**
revoked (in part): SI 1997/319 Reg.162, Sch.3

857. **Housing Renovation etc. Grants (Prescribed Forms and Particulars) (Welsh Forms and Particulars) (Amendment) Regulations 1995**
applied: SI 1996/2842 Art.8
revoked: SI 1996/2842 Art.7, Sch Part I

866. **National Health Service (Injury Benefits) Regulations 1995**
applied: SI 1997/2205 Reg.2
Reg.2, amended: SI 1997/646 Reg.3, SI 1998/667 Reg.2, SI 1998/2217 Reg.3
Reg.3, amended: SI 1998/667 Reg.3, SI 1998/2217 Reg.4
Reg.4, amended: SI 1997/646 Reg.4, SI 1998/667 Reg.4
Reg.4A, added: SI 1997/646 Reg.5
Reg.4A, amended: SI 1998/667 Reg.5, SI 1998/2217 Reg.5

872. **Housing Benefit and Council Tax Benefit (Subsidy) Order 1995**
applied: SI 1996/1217 Sch.6 para.8
Art.4, applied: SI 1996/1217 Art.11, SI 1997/1004 Art.11, SI 1998/562 Art.19
Art.6, applied: SI 1996/1217 Art.6
Art.11, applied: SI 1996/1217 Art.10, SI 1997/1004 Art.10, SI 1998/562 Art.18
Art.19, applied: SI 1996/1217 Art.18, Art.19, SI 1997/1004 Art.18, SI 1998/562 Art.18, Art.19
Art.19, referred to: SI 1997/1004 Art.19
Sch.1, applied: SI 1996/1217 Sch.2 para.3
Sch.2, applied: SI 1996/1217 Sch.2 para.3

886. **Fish Health (Amendment) Regulations 1995**
revoked: SI 1997/1881 Reg.24

887. **Plant Protection Products Regulations 1995**
applied: SI 1997/189 Reg.5, Reg.6, Sch.1 para.2, Sch.2 para.1, Sch.3 para.1, SI 1999/3430 Reg.1
Reg.2, amended: SI 1996/1940 Reg.2, SI 1997/7 Reg.3, SI 1997/2499 Reg.3, SI 1998/2760 Reg.2, SI 1999/1228 Reg.2, SI 1999/3430 Reg.2

NO.

887. **Plant Protection Products Regulations 1995**
—cont.
Reg.5, applied: SI 1996/2089 Reg.2, SI 1996/
2094 Sch.2 Part I, SI 1996/2095 Sch.2 para.7,
SI 1996/3142 Sch.2 para.20
Reg.5, referred to: SI 1999/257 Reg.3, Sch.1
para.1
Reg.7, applied: SI 1996/3142 Sch.2 para.20
Reg.8, applied: SI 1996/3142 Sch.2 para.20
Reg.11, applied: SI 1996/3142 Sch.2 para.20
Reg.13, applied: SI 1997/189 Reg.5, Reg.6
Reg.20, amended: SI 1997/7 Reg.4
Reg.21, amended: SI 1997/7 Reg.5
Reg.22, amended: SI 1997/7 Reg.6
Reg.24, amended: SI 1997/7 Reg.7
Reg.27, amended: SI 1997/7 Reg.8
Sch.2 para.1, applied: SI 1997/189 Sch.1
para.2
Sch.2 para.6, amended: SI 1997/7 Reg.9
Sch.2 para.6, applied: SI 1997/189 Sch.1
para.2
Sch.3 para.1A, added: SI 1997/2499 Reg.4
Sch.3 para.1B, added: SI 1997/2499 Reg.4
Sch.3 para.1C, added: SI 1997/2499 Reg.4
Sch.3 para.8, substituted: SI 1997/2499 Reg.5

888. **Plant Protection Products (Fees) Regulations 1995**
Reg.2, amended: SI 1998/2760 Reg.2, SI 1999/
1228 Reg.3, SI 1999/3430 Reg.3
Sch., substituted: SI 1997/884 Reg.2, Sch.

891. **Heather Moorland (Livestock Extensification) (Scotland) Regulations 1995**
applied: SI 1997/330 Reg.7
referred to: SI 1997/330 Sch.4 Part IV
revoked: SI 1996/3036 Reg.9 (with savings)
Reg.2, amended: SI 1996/3036 Reg.3
Reg.3, amended: SI 1996/3036 Reg.4
Reg.10, amended: SI 1996/3036 Reg.5
Reg.11, amended: SI 1996/3036 Reg.6
Reg.13, amended: SI 1996/3036 Reg.7
Reg.13A, added: SI 1996/3036 Reg.8
Reg.13B, added: SI 1996/3036 Reg.8
Reg.13C, added: SI 1996/3036 Reg.8

903. **Education (School Curriculum and Assessment Authority) (Transfer of Functions) Order 1995**
Art.4, referred to: 1996 c.56 Sch.39 para.36

904. **Moorland (Livestock Extensification) Regulations 1995**
Reg.2, amended: SI 1996/2393 Reg.2, SI 1996/
3110 Reg.2
Reg.3, amended: SI 1996/2393 Reg.2
Reg.4, amended: SI 1996/2393 Reg.2
Reg.5, amended: SI 1996/2393 Reg.2, SI 1999/
2361 Reg.2
Reg.7, amended: SI 1996/2393 Reg.2, SI 1996/
3110 Reg.2
Reg.8, amended: SI 1996/2393 Reg.2, SI 1996/
3110 Reg.2
Reg.8, revoked (in part): SI 1996/2393 Reg.2
Reg.9, amended: SI 1996/2393 Reg.2
Reg.10, substituted: SI 1996/3110 Reg.2
Reg.10A, added: SI 1996/3110 Reg.2
Reg.10B, added: SI 1996/3110 Reg.2

907. **Third Country Fishing (Enforcement) Order 1995**
revoked (in part): SI 1996/1036 Art.13

908. **Sea Fishing (Enforcement of Community Quota Measures) Order 1995**
revoked: SI 1996/247 Art.13

NO.

909. **Electricity (Class Exemptions from the Requirement for a Licence) (No.2) Order 1995**
revoked: SI 1997/989 Art.5

912. **Local Authorities etc. (Allowances) (Scotland) Regulations 1995**
Reg.20, amended: SI 1997/1631 Reg.3, SI
1998/3219 Reg.3
Reg.21, amended: SI 1997/1631 Reg.4, SI
1998/3219 Reg.4
Sch.2, amended: SI 1997/1631 Reg.5, SI 1998/
3219 Reg.5

918. **Llandough Hospital National Health Service Trust (Change of Name) Order 1995**
revoked: SI 1999/1120 Art.2, Sch.2

924. **Education (Individual Pupils' Achievements) (Information) (Amendment) Regulations 1995**
revoked: SI 1997/1368 Reg.2

925. **Motor Vehicles (Type Approval and Approval Marks) (Fees) Regulations 1995**
revoked: SI 1996/958 Reg.2

926. **Gaming Act (Variation of Monetary Limits) Order 1995**
revoked: SI 1999/1260 Art.5, Sch.
Art.2, revoked: SI 1998/962 Art.4, SI 1999/1260
Art.5, Sch.
Art.3, revoked: SI 1998/962 Art.4, SI 1999/1260
Art.5, Sch.
Art.4, revoked: SI 1997/1828 Art.3, SI 1999/
1260 Art.5, Sch.

927. **Gaming Clubs (Hours and Charges) (Amendment) Regulations 1995**
revoked: SI 1996/1109 Reg.3

928. **Amusements with Prizes (Variation of Monetary Limits) Order 1995**
revoked: SI 1997/2080 Art.3

929. **Railtrack Plc (Rateable Values) (Scotland) Order 1995**
Art.3, referred to: SI 1996/103 Reg.13

930. **British Railways Board (Rateable Values) (Scotland) Order 1995**
revoked: SI 1998/947 Art.9
Art.3, applied: SI 1997/452 Reg.13
Art.3, referred to: SI 1996/103 Reg.13
Art.3, revoked: SI 1998/947 Art.9

936. **Education (Grant-Maintained and Grant-Maintained Special Schools) (Finance) Regulations 1995**
applied: SI 1998/799 Reg.3
revoked: SI 1996/889 Reg.3
Reg.6, see *R. v Funding Agency for Schools Ex
p. Bromley LBC* Times, January 16, 1996
(QBD), Schiemann, L.J.
Reg.6, revoked: SI 1996/889 Reg.3
Reg.10, applied: SI 1996/889 Reg.43
Reg.11, applied: SI 1996/889 Reg.43
Reg.15, applied: SI 1996/889 Reg.42, SI 1997/
996 Reg.25, Reg.45, SI 1998/799 Reg.25
Reg.15, referred to: SI 1997/996 Reg.25, SI
1998/799 Reg.25
Reg.16, applied: SI 1996/889 Reg.42, SI 1997/
996 Reg.25, Reg.45, SI 1998/799 Reg.25
Reg.30, applied: SI 1996/889 Reg.42, SI 1997/
996 Reg.25, Reg.45, SI 1998/799 Reg.25
Sch.1, applied: SI 1996/889 Sch.1 para.6

948. **Legal Aid in Contempt Proceedings (Remuneration) Regulations 1995**
Reg.6, amended: SI 1996/643 Reg.2

NO.

1995—cont.

958. Value Added Tax (Treatment of Transactions) Order 1995
Art.2, substituted: SI 1999/3119 Art.3

971. Justices of the Peace (Size and Chairmanship of Bench) Rules 1995
r.2, amended: SI 1999/2396 r.3
r.4, amended: SI 1999/2396 r.3
r.15, amended: SI 1999/2396 r.3
r.16, amended: SI 1999/2396 r.3
r.17, amended: SI 1999/2396 r.3

972. Merchant Shipping (Employment of Young Persons) Regulations 1995
revoked: SI 1998/2411 Reg.1

983. Prison (Amendment) Rules 1995
see *R. v Secretary of State for the Home Department Ex p. Hargreaves* [1997] 1 W.L.R. 906 (CA), Hirst, L.J.
revoked: SI 1999/728 r.85 (with saving), Sch. (with saving)

991. Public Record Office (Fees) Regulations 1995
revoked: SI 1996/575 Reg.3

993. Hyde Park and The Regent's Park (Vehicle Parking) Regulations 1995
Reg.2, amended: SI 1999/392 Reg.2
Reg.3, substituted: SI 1999/392 Reg.2
Reg.4, substituted: SI 1999/392 Reg.2
Reg.6, substituted: SI 1999/392 Reg.2
Reg.8, revoked (in part): SI 1999/392 Reg.2

1014. Measuring Equipment (Liquid Fuel and Lubricants) Regulations 1995
Reg.1, amended: SI 1998/2218 Reg.3
Reg.2, amended: SI 1998/2218 Reg.3
Reg.10A, added: SI 1998/2218 Reg.3
Reg.11, revoked: SI 1998/2218 Reg.3
Reg.12, substituted: SI 1998/2218 Reg.3
Reg.17, amended: SI 1998/2218 Reg.3
Reg.19, amended: SI 1998/2218 Reg.3

1019. Local Government Pension Scheme Regulations 1995
amended: SI 1996/184 Reg.2, SI 1996/185 Reg.2, Reg.3
applied: SI 1996/1428 Reg.29, SI 1996/1680 Reg.17, Reg.29, Reg.31, Reg.39, SI 1997/218 Reg.5, SI 1997/311 Reg.6, SI 1997/578 Reg.17, SI 1997/956 Sch.4 para.2, SI 1997/996 Sch.9 para.2, SI 1997/1612 Reg.48, Reg.94, Reg.107, Reg.110, Reg.111, Reg.115, SI 1997/1613 Reg.19, SI 1997/3001 Reg.B1, 1998 c.18 Sch.2 para.1, SI 1998/798 Sch.4 para.2, SI 1998/799 Sch.6 para.2
referred to: SI 1997/1612 Reg.117, Reg.119, SI 1997/3001 Reg.B4, SI 1998/568 Reg.3
Part D, applied: SI 1996/1680 Reg.11, Reg.17, Reg.36, Sch.3 para.9
Part F, applied: SI 1996/1680 Reg.20, Sch.3 para.9
Part G, applied: SI 1996/1680 Sch.3 para.9
Part J, applied: SI 1997/329 Reg.6
Part J, revoked: SI 1997/1613 Reg.29
Part K, amended: SI 1997/954 Reg.4
Part K, applied: SI 1996/2180 Reg.3, SI 1997/1613 Reg.25
Part K, revoked: SI 1997/1613 Reg.29
Part L, revoked: SI 1997/1613 Reg.29
Reg.B2, amended: SI 1997/954 Reg.2
Reg.B2, applied: SI 1996/1680 Reg.32, SI 1997/311 Reg.6
Reg.B7, applied: SI 1996/1680 Reg.33
Reg.B10, amended: SI 1996/1428 Reg.2
Reg.B10, applied: SI 1996/1680 Reg.7

NO.

1995—cont.

1019. Local Government Pension Scheme Regulations 1995—*cont.*
Reg.B10, referred to: SI 1996/1680 Reg.39
Reg.B12, applied: SI 1996/1680 Reg.7, Reg.39, SI 1997/1613 Reg.3
Reg.B12, referred to: SI 1996/1680 Reg. 40, SI 1997/1613 Reg.3
Reg.B13, amended: SI 1997/954 Reg.3
Reg.B14, applied: SI 1997/1613 Reg.7
Reg.B14, referred to: SI 1997/1613 Reg.11
Reg.B18, amended: SI 1996/1680 Sch.4 para.4, SI 1997/218 Reg.3
Reg.B18, applied: SI 1996/1680 Reg.8, SI 1997/218 Reg.5
Reg.B19, amended: SI 1996/1680 Sch.4 para.4
Reg.B19, applied: SI 1997/218 Reg.5
Reg.C1, amended: SI 1997/218 Reg.2
Reg.C1, revoked: SI 1997/1613 Reg.29
Reg.C2, amended: SI 1996/1428 Reg.3
Reg.C4, applied: SI 1997/578 Reg.16, SI 1997/1612 Reg.87
Reg.C5, applied: SI 1997/1612 Reg.87, SI 1997/1613 Reg.11
Reg.C5, referred to: SI 1997/1613 Reg.11
Reg.C6, applied: SI 1997/1612 Reg.87, SI 1997/1613 Reg.11
Reg.C6, referred to: SI 1997/1613 Reg.11
Reg.C7, applied: SI 1997/1612 Reg.87, SI 1997/1613 Reg.11
Reg.C7, referred to: SI 1997/1613 Reg.11
Reg.C9, applied: SI 1997/1612 Reg.87, SI 1997/1613 Reg.11, Sch.2 para.9
Reg.C9, referred to: SI 1997/1613 Reg.11, Reg.23, Sch.2 para.9
Reg.C10, amended: SI 1996/1428 Reg.4
Reg.C13, applied: SI 1997/1612 Reg.87, SI 1997/1613 Reg.8, Sch.2 para.9
Reg.C13, referred to: SI 1997/1613 Reg.9
Reg.C14, applied: SI 1997/1612 Reg.87
Reg.C14, referred to: SI 1997/1613 Reg.9
Reg.C21, applied: SI 1997/1612 Reg.115
Reg.C21, revoked: SI 1997/1613 Reg.29
Reg.C21A, added: SI 1996/1428 Reg.5
Reg.C24, applied: SI 1997/1613 Reg.14
Reg.D1, applied: SI 1996/1680 Reg.36
Reg.D2, applied: SI 1996/1680 Reg.18
Reg.D4, amended: SI 1996/1428 Reg.6
Reg.D5, applied: SI 1996/1680 Reg.16
Reg.D6, applied: SI 1996/1680 Reg.6, Reg.9, Reg.10, Reg.11, Reg.16, Reg.19, Reg.42
Reg.D7, amended: SI 1997/578 Reg.2, SI 1998/530 Reg.2
Reg.D7, applied: SI 1996/1680 Reg.16, Reg.21, Reg.25
Reg.D8, amended: SI 1997/1613 Reg.27, Sch.3 para.10
Reg.D8, applied: SI 1997/1612 Reg.6, Reg.88
Reg.D9, applied: SI 1996/1680 Reg.16
Reg.D11, amended: SI 1997/578 Reg.3
Reg.D11, applied: SI 1997/2467 Reg.4
Reg.D11A, added: SI 1996/1428 Reg.7
Reg.D12, amended: SI 1997/1613 Reg.27, Sch.3 para.11
Reg.D12, applied: SI 1997/1612 Reg.32, Reg.116, Sch.3, SI 1997/1613 Sch.2 para.6, Sch.2 para.7, Sch.4 para.5
Reg.D13, amended: SI 1996/1428 Reg.8
Reg.D14, amended: SI 1996/1680 Reg.19
Reg.D14, referred to: SI 1996/1680 Reg.19
Reg.D15, amended: SI 1997/1613 Reg.27, Sch.3 para.12
Reg.D17, amended: SI 1997/1613 Reg.27, Sch.3 para.13

NO.

1995—cont.

1019. Local Government Pension Scheme Regulations 1995—*cont.*

Reg.D21, amended: SI 1997/1613 Reg.27, Sch.3 para.14

Reg.E1, amended: SI 1996/1428 Reg.9, Reg.10

Reg.E2, amended: SI 1996/1428 Reg.10

Reg.E3, amended: SI 1996/1428 Reg.10, SI 1997/1613 Reg.27, Sch.3 para.15

Reg.E4, amended: SI 1996/1428 Reg.10, SI 1997/1613 Reg.27, Sch.3 para.15

Reg.E6, amended: SI 1997/1613 Reg.27, Sch.3 para.16

Reg.E7, amended: SI 1997/578 Reg.4

Reg.E8, added: SI 1996/1428 Reg.11

Reg.E8, substituted: SI 1997/578 Reg.5

Reg.F1, amended: SI 1997/1613 Reg.27, Sch.3 para.17

Reg.F2, amended: SI 1997/1613 Reg.27, Sch.3 para.18

Reg.F4, amended: SI 1997/1613 Reg.27, Sch.3 para.19

Reg.F5, amended: SI 1997/1613 Reg.27, Sch.3 para.20

Reg.F6, applied: SI 1996/1680 Reg.20

Reg.F7, amended: SI 1997/1613 Reg.27, Sch.3 para.21

Reg.F8, applied: SI 1996/1680 Reg.20

Reg.F10, amended: SI 1997/1613 Reg.27, Sch.3 para.22

Reg.F11, amended: SI 1997/1613 Reg.27, Sch.3 para.23, SI 1998/2118 Reg.7

Reg.G3, amended: SI 1997/578 Reg.6, SI 1997/1613 Reg.27, Sch.3 para.24

Reg.G3, applied: SI 1996/1680 Reg.24

Reg.G4, applied: SI 1996/1680 Reg.22

Reg.G5, applied: SI 1996/1680 Reg.24

Reg.G6, amended: SI 1997/1613 Reg.27, Sch.3 para.25

Reg.G6, applied: SI 1996/1680 Reg.24

Reg.G7, amended: SI 1997/1613 Reg.27, Sch.3 para.25

Reg.G7, applied: SI 1996/1680 Reg.22

Reg.G10, applied: SI 1996/1680 Reg.25

Reg.G11, applied: SI 1996/1680 Reg.26

Reg.G12, amended: SI 1997/1613 Reg.27, Sch.3 para.26

Reg.H1, amended: SI 1997/329 Reg.3, SI 1997/578 Reg.7

Reg.H1, revoked: SI 1997/1613 Reg.29

Reg.H3, revoked: SI 1997/1613 Reg.29

Reg.H4, amended: SI 1997/578 Reg.8

Reg.H4, revoked: SI 1997/1613 Reg.29

Reg.H5, revoked: SI 1997/1613 Reg.29

Reg.H6, revoked: SI 1997/1613 Reg.29

Reg.H7, revoked: SI 1997/1613 Reg.29

Reg.J1, amended: SI 1997/329 Reg.2, SI 1997/578 Reg.9

Reg.J2, amended: SI 1996/1428 Reg.12

Reg.J4, amended: SI 1997/329 Reg.2

Reg.J5, applied: SI 1997/329 Reg.6

Reg.J6, added: SI 1997/329 Reg.2

Reg.J7, added: SI 1997/329 Reg.2

Reg.J8, added: SI 1997/329 Reg.2

Reg.J9, added: SI 1997/329 Reg.2

Reg.J10, added: SI 1997/329 Reg.2

Reg.J11, added: SI 1997/329 Reg.2

Reg.K1, amended: SI 1998/530 Reg.3

Reg.K2, applied: SI 1996/2180 Reg.3

Reg.K7, applied: SI 1997/1612 Reg.116

Reg.K8, amended: SI 1998/530 Reg.3

Reg.K9A, added: SI 1998/530 Reg.3

NO.

1995—cont.

1019. Local Government Pension Scheme Regulations 1995—*cont.*

Reg.K12, applied: SI 1996/1613 Reg.25

Reg.K13, amended: SI 1998/530 Reg.3

Reg.K13, applied: SI 1996/1613 Reg.23

Reg.K14, amended: SI 1997/954 Reg.4, SI 1998/530 Reg.3

Reg.K15A, added: SI 1997/954 Reg.4

Reg.K15A, substituted: SI 1998/530 Reg.3

Reg.K16, applied: SI 1996/711 Reg.6

Reg.K17, applied: SI 1996/1613 Reg.17

Reg.K21, applied: SI 1996/1680 Reg.40

Reg.K21, referred to: SI 1996/711 Reg.7

Reg.K24, amended: SI 1996/1428 Reg.13, SI 1997/2467 Reg.3

Reg.K24, applied: SI 1997/2467 Reg.3

Reg.K25A, amended: SI 1996/1428 Reg.14

Reg.K29, added: SI 1997/954 Reg.4

Reg.L1, referred to: SI 1996/1883 Art.4

Reg.L4, applied: SI 1997/1613 Reg.4

Reg.L4, referred to: SI 1997/1612 Reg.81

Reg.L4, revoked: SI 1998/1831 Reg.13

Reg.L5, applied: SI 1997/1613 Reg.4

Reg.L5, revoked: SI 1998/1831 Reg.13

Reg.L6, applied: SI 1997/1613 Reg.4

Reg.L6, revoked: SI 1998/1831 Reg.13

Reg.L7, applied: SI 1997/1613 Reg.4

Reg.L7, revoked: SI 1998/1831 Reg.13

Reg.L8, applied: SI 1997/1613 Reg.4

Reg.L8, revoked: SI 1998/1831 Reg.13

Reg.L11, amended: SI 1996/1428 Reg.15

Reg.L11, applied: SI 1996/711 Reg.8

Reg.L12, applied: SI 1996/711 Reg.8, SI 1996/1428 Reg.27

Reg.L12, referred to: SI 1996/1428 Reg.27

Reg.L13, applied: SI 1997/1613 Reg.16, Reg.20

Reg.L13, referred to: SI 1996/1428 Reg.27, SI 1997/218 Reg.4, SI 1997/1613 Reg.20

Reg.L15, applied: SI 1997/1613 Reg.21

Reg.L21, amended: SI 1996/711 Reg.3

Reg.M4, revoked: SI 1997/1613 Reg.29

Reg.M5, amended: SI 1997/329 Reg.4, SI 1998/530 Reg.4

Reg.M5, revoked: SI 1997/1613 Reg.29

Reg.M6, amended: SI 1997/329 Reg.4

Reg.M6, revoked: SI 1997/1613 Reg.29

Sch. A1, amended: SI 1996/711 Reg.4, SI 1996/1428 Reg.16, SI 1997/1613 Reg.27, Sch.3 para.27, SI 1998/1129 Art.3, Sch.2

Sch. B1, amended: SI 1996/1428 Reg.17

Sch. B1 Part I, amended: SI 1996/711 Reg.3

Sch. B1 Part II, amended: SI 1997/578 Reg.10

Sch. B3 para.5, applied: SI 1997/2467 Reg.2

Sch. B6, applied: SI 1996/2180 Reg.3

Sch. B6 Part II, applied: SI 1996/1680 Reg.6, Reg.8

Sch. B6 para.4, amended: SI 1997/1613 Reg.27, Sch.3 para.28

Sch. B6 para.4, applied: SI 1996/1680 Reg.17

Sch. C1, revoked: SI 1997/1613 Reg.29

Sch. C1 Part II, revoked: SI 1997/1613 Reg.29

Sch. C1 Part III, amended: SI 1996/185 Reg.2, Reg.3, SI 1997/578 Reg.11

Sch. C1 Part III, revoked: SI 1997/1613 Reg.29

Sch. C2 para.7, amended: SI 1996/1428 Reg.18

Sch. C3, amended: SI 1996/1428 Reg.19

Sch. C4, referred to: SI 1997/1612 Sch.4 para.7

Sch. C4 para.16, amended: SI 1996/1428 Reg.20

Sch. C5 Part III, applied: SI 1997/1613 Sch.2 para.8

NO.

1019. Local Government Pension Scheme Regulations 1995—*cont.*

Sch. C5 para.1, amended: SI 1997/578 Reg.12, SI 1997/954 Reg.5

Sch. C5 para.4, amended: SI 1996/1428 Reg.21

Sch. C5 para.8, amended: SI 1997/578 Reg.12

Sch. C5 para.9, amended: SI 1997/578 Reg.12

Sch. C5 para.9A, added: SI 1997/578 Reg.12

Sch. C6 para.1, applied: SI 1997/1613 Reg.12, Reg.15

Sch. D1 para.2, applied: SI 1996/1680 Reg.7

Sch. D1 para.3, applied: SI 1996/1680 Reg.7

Sch. D1 para.4, amended: SI 1996/1428 Reg.22

Sch. D1 para.4, applied: SI 1996/1680 Reg.7

Sch. D1 para.4, referred to: SI 1996/1680 Reg.36

Sch. D1 para.5, applied: SI 1996/1680 Reg.7

Sch. D1 para.6, referred to: SI 1996/1680 Reg.7

Sch. D1 para.9, amended: SI 1997/578 Reg.13

Sch. D3 para.4, amended: SI 1996/1428 Reg.23, SI 1997/578 Reg.14

Sch. D5, applied: SI 1997/1613 Sch.2

Sch. D5 Part I, applied: SI 1997/1613 Sch.2 para.3

Sch. D5 Part II, applied: SI 1997/1612 Reg.126, SI 1997/1613 Sch.2 para.4

Sch. D5 Part IV, applied: SI 1997/1612 Reg.126

Sch. D5 Part IV, referred to: SI 1997/1613 Sch.2 para.5

Sch. D5 para.1, referred to: SI 1996/1680 Reg.16

Sch. D5 para.5, applied: SI 1996/1680 Reg.16

Sch. D5 para.10, amended: SI 1996/1428 Reg.24

Sch. D5 para.10, applied: SI 1997/1613 Sch.2 para.5

Sch. D5 para.17, referred to: SI 1997/1613 Sch.2 para.5

Sch. D5 para.18, referred to: SI 1997/1613 Sch.2 para.5

Sch. D6, referred to: SI 1997/3001 Reg.E9

Sch. F1 para.1, referred to: SI 1997/1613 Reg.9

Sch. F1 para.2, applied: SI 1996/1680 Sch.3 para.9

Sch. F1 para.2, referred to: SI 1997/1613 Reg.9

Sch. F1 para.3, applied: SI 1996/1680 Sch.3 para.9

Sch. K1, revoked: SI 1997/1613 Reg.29

Sch. K2, added: SI 1997/954 Reg.6

Sch. K2, revoked: SI 1997/1613 Reg.29

Sch. K2 para.3, amended: SI 1998/530 Reg.3

Sch. K2 para.5, substituted: SI 1998/530 Reg.3

Sch. L1, revoked: SI 1997/1613 Reg.29

Sch. M2 para.2, amended: SI 1997/329 Reg.5, SI 1998/530 Reg.4

Sch. M2 para.4, amended: SI 1997/329 Reg.5, SI 1998/530 Reg.4

Sch. M2 para.6, applied: SI 1997/1612 Sch.6 para.7

Sch. M2 para.9, added: SI 1996/711 Reg.5

Sch. M2 para.9, amended: SI 1996/1428 Reg.25, SI 1997/578 Reg.15, SI 1998/568 Reg.2

Sch. M2 para.9, applied: SI 1996/711 Reg.6

Sch. M2 para.10, added: SI 1997/598 Reg.2

Sch. M2 para.10, amended: SI 1998/530 Reg.5

Sch. M2 para.10, referred to: SI 1997/1613 Reg.23

Sch. M3 para.3, applied: SI 1997/1612 Sch.6 para.2

NO.

1019. Local Government Pension Scheme Regulations 1995—*cont.*

Sch. M4, applied: SI 1996/1680 Reg.49

Sch. M4 para.2, applied: SI 1997/1613 Sch.4 para.2

Sch. M4 para.12, applied: SI 1997/1613 Sch.4 para.4

Sch. M4 para.14A, added: SI 1996/1428 Reg.26

Sch. M4 para.15, applied: SI 1997/1613 Sch.4 para.5

Sch. M4 para.20, applied: SI 1997/1613 Sch.4 para.6

1020. Gaming Act (Variation of Monetary Limits) (Scotland) Order 1995

revoked: SI 1999/1260 Art.5, Sch.

Art.2, revoked: SI 1998/962 Art.4, SI 1999/1260 Art.5, Sch.

Art.3, revoked: SI 1998/962 Art.4, SI 1999/1260 Art.5, Sch.

Art.4, revoked: SI 1997/1828 Art.3, SI 1999/1260 Art.5, Sch., Art.5, Sch.

1021. Amusements with Prizes (Variation of Monetary Limits) (Scotland) Order 1995

revoked: SI 1997/2080 Art.3

1022. Gaming Clubs (Hours and Charges) (Scotland) Amendment Regulations 1995

revoked: SI 1996/1144 Reg.3

1030. Antarctic Act 1994 (Overseas Territories) Order 1995

Sch.2, amended: SI 1996/2593 Art.2

1032. United Nations Arms Embargoes (Dependent Territories) Order 1995

Art.2, amended: SI 1998/1502 Art.2

Art.3, amended: SI 1997/272 Art.2

Art.4, amended: SI 1997/272 Art.2

Art.8, amended: SI 1997/272 Art.2

Art.9, amended: SI 1997/272 Art.2, SI 1998/1502 Art.3

Art.11, amended: SI 1997/272 Art.2

Sch.3 para.4, amended: SI 1998/1502 Art.3

1033. Antarctic Act 1994 (Guernsey) Order 1995

applied: SI 1997/2966

1034. Antarctic Act 1994 (Jersey) Order 1995

applied: SI 1997/2967

1035. Antarctic Act 1994 (Isle of Man) Order 1995

applied: SI 1997/2968

1037. Parliamentary Constituencies (Scotland) Order 1995

referred to: SI 1996/1926 Art.2

1045. Child Support and Income Support (Amendment) Regulations 1995

Reg.63, amended: SI 1999/1510 Art.37

Reg.63, revoked (in part): SI 1999/1510 Art.37

Reg.64, amended: SI 1999/1510 Art.38

1046. Excise Goods (Drawback) Regulations 1995

applied: SI 1999/1565 Reg.22

Reg.5, revoked (in part): SI 1999/1565 Reg.22

Reg.6, revoked (in part): SI 1999/1565 Reg.22

Reg.7, revoked (in part): SI 1999/1565 Reg.22

Reg.8, revoked (in part): SI 1999/1565 Reg.22

Reg.9, revoked (in part): SI 1999/1565 Reg.22

Reg.10, revoked (in part): SI 1999/1565 Reg.22

Reg.11, revoked (in part): SI 1999/1565 Reg.22

Reg.12, revoked (in part): SI 1999/1565 Reg.22

Reg.12A, added: SI 1999/1565 Reg.22

Reg.14, applied: SI 1999/1565 Reg.21

Sch.1, revoked (in part): SI 1999/1565 Reg.22

Sch.2, revoked (in part): SI 1999/1565 Reg.22

NO.

1053. Personal and Occupational Pension Schemes (Pensions Ombudsman) (Procedure) Rules 1995
see *Legal & General Assurance Society Ltd v Pensions Ombudsman* Times, December 7, 1999 (Ch D), Lightman, J.
r.1, amended: SI 1996/2638 r.2
r.2, amended: SI 1996/2638 r.2
r.15A, added: SI 1996/2638 r.2

1054. Civil Aviation (Air Travel Organisers' Licensing) Regulations 1995
Reg.1, amended: SI 1997/2912 Reg.2
Reg.3, amended: SI 1996/1390 Reg.2, SI 1997/2912 Reg.2
Reg.4, amended: SI 1996/1390 Reg.2, SI 1997/2912 Reg.2
Reg.4, revoked (in part): SI 1997/2912 Reg.2

1057. Police Cadets (Scotland) Amendment Regulations 1995
revoked: SI 1997/2791 Reg.6

1065. Civil Legal Aid (Scotland) Amendment Regulations 1995
revoked: SI 1996/2444 Reg.3, Sch.1

1066. Advice and Assistance (Scotland) Amendment Regulations 1995
revoked: SI 1996/2447 Reg.3, Sch.1

1081. Wireless Telegraphy (Short Range Devices) (Exemption) (Amendment) Regulations 1995
revoked: SI 1999/930 Reg.2, Sch.1

1086. Dairy Products (Hygiene) Regulations 1995
applied: SI 1996/3124 Reg.10, Sch.2 para.8
Reg.2, amended: SI 1996/1699 Reg.3, SI 1998/2424 Reg.10
Reg.3, substituted: SI 1996/1699 Reg.4
Reg.6, amended: SI 1996/1699 Reg.5
Reg.16, amended: SI 1996/1699 Reg.6
Reg.21, amended: SI 1996/1699 Reg.7
Reg.22, amended: SI 1996/1699 Reg.8
Reg.24, revoked (in part): SI 1996/1499 Reg.49, Sch.9, SI 1998/2424 Reg.9, Sch.
Sch.1 Part IA, amended: SI 1996/1699 Reg.9
Sch.3 para.1, amended: SI 1997/1729 Reg.35
Sch.4 Part III, amended: SI 1996/1699 Reg.10
Sch.6 Part I, amended: SI 1996/1699 Reg.11
Sch.6 Part II, amended: SI 1996/1699 Reg.11
Sch.6 Part III, amended: SI 1996/1699 Reg.11
Sch.6 Part IV, amended: SI 1996/1699 Reg.11
Sch.10 Part I, amended: SI 1996/1499 Reg.49
Sch.10 Part II, amended: SI 1996/1499 Reg.49, SI 1996/1699 Reg.12
Sch.11 para.4, revoked: SI 1996/1699 Reg.13
Sch.13, revoked: SI 1996/1499 Reg.49, Sch.9

1092. Charities (Trustee Investments Act 1961) Order 1995
revoked: SI 1996/1268

1116. Medicines (Products for Human Use - Fees) Regulations 1995
Reg.2, amended: SI 1996/683 Reg.2
Reg.6, amended: SI 1996/683 Reg.3, Sch., SI 1998/574 Reg.5, Sch., SI 1999/566 Reg.4, Sch.
Reg.10, amended: SI 1996/683 Reg.3, Sch., SI 1998/574 Reg.5, Sch., SI 1999/566 Reg.4, Sch.
Reg.14, amended: SI 1996/683 Reg.4
Sch.1 Part I, amended: SI 1996/683 Reg.6
Sch.1 Part II, amended: SI 1996/683 Reg.3, Reg.5, Sch, SI 1998/574 Reg.4, Reg.5, Sch., SI 1999/566 Reg.4, Sch.
Sch.1 Part III, amended: SI 1996/683 Reg.3, Reg.5, Sch, SI 1998/574 Reg.4, Reg.5, Sch., SI 1999/566 Reg.4, Sch.

NO.

1116. Medicines (Products for Human Use - Fees) Regulations 1995—*cont.*
Sch.2 para.2, amended: SI 1996/683 Reg.3, Sch., SI 1998/574 Reg.5, Sch., SI 1999/566 Reg.4, Sch.
Sch.2 para.5, amended: SI 1998/574 Reg.4, SI 1999/566 Reg.4, Sch.
Sch.3 Part I, amended: SI 1996/683 Reg.6, SI 1998/574 Reg.4
Sch.3 Part II, amended: SI 1998/574 Reg.4
Sch.3 Part III, amended: SI 1996/683 Reg.6, Sch., SI 1998/574 Reg.4, Reg.5, Sch., SI 1999/566 Reg.4, Sch.
Sch.3 Part IV, amended: SI 1996/683 Reg.2
Sch.5 para.3, amended: SI 1996/683 Reg.7
Sch.5 para.4A, added: SI 1996/683 Reg.7
Sch.5 para.6, amended: SI 1996/683 Reg.7
Sch.5 para.7, added: SI 1996/683 Reg.7

1142. Returning Officers (Parliamentary Constituencies) (Wales) Order 1995
revoked: SI 1996/897 Art.3

1143. Welfare Food (Amendment) Regulations 1995
revoked: SI 1996/1434 Reg.23, Sch.7

1151. Dual-Use and Related Goods (Export Control) (Suspension No.2) Regulations 1995
applied: SI 1996/2721 Reg.15
revoked: SI 1996/2721 Sch.1

1157. Redundancy Payments (Local Government) (Modification) (Amendment) Order 1995
revoked: SI 1999/2277 Art.4, Sch.3

1159. Moorland (Livestock Extensification) (Wales) Regulations 1995
applied: SI 1999/672 Art.2, Sch.1
Reg.2, amended: SI 1996/2449 Reg.2, SI 1996/3076 Reg.2
Reg.3, amended: SI 1996/2449 Reg.2
Reg.7, amended: SI 1996/3076 Reg.2
Reg.8, amended: SI 1996/2449 Reg.2, SI 1996/3076 Reg.2
Reg.9, amended: SI 1996/2449 Reg.2
Reg.10, substituted: SI 1996/3076 Reg.2
Reg.10A, added: SI 1996/3076 Reg.2
Reg.10B, added: SI 1996/3076 Reg.2
Reg.12, added: SI 1999/1176 Reg.15

1162. Motor Vehicles (Driving Licences) (Large Goods and Passenger-Carrying Vehicles) (Amendment) Regulations 1995
revoked: SI 1996/2824 Reg.2, Sch.1

1186. Electrical Equipment for Explosive Atmospheres (Certification) (Amendment) Regulations 1995
revoked: SI 1996/192 Reg.1, Sch.1

1200. Motor Vehicles (Driving Licences) (Amendment) Regulations 1995
revoked: SI 1996/2824 Reg.2, Sch.1

1210. Merchant Shipping (Survey and Certification) Regulations 1995
applied: SI 1996/3243 Reg.5, Sch Part I
referred to: SI 1996/3243 Sch Part I, SI 1998/1609 Reg.5, Reg.6, Sch., SI 1998/2771 Reg.4, Sch.1
Reg.1, amended: SI 1996/2418 Reg.2
Reg.2, amended: SI 1996/3188 Reg.17
Reg.3, amended: SI 1996/2418 Reg.2
Reg.6, amended: SI 1996/2418 Reg.2
Reg.7, referred to: SI 1999/1644 Reg.4
Reg.11, amended: SI 1996/2418 Reg.2
Reg.13, amended: SI 1996/2418 Reg.2
Reg.15, amended: SI 1996/2418 Reg.2
Reg.21, amended: SI 1996/2418 Reg.2

NO.

1995—cont.

1219. Advice and Assistance (Assistance by Way of Representation) (Scotland) Amendment Regulations 1995
revoked: SI 1997/3070 Reg.2, Sch.

1220. Advice and Assistance (Financial Conditions) (Scotland) Regulations 1995
revoked: SI 1996/1010 Reg.6

1221. Civil Legal Aid (Financial Conditions) (Scotland) Regulations 1995
revoked: SI 1996/1012 Reg.6

1222. Criminal Legal Aid (Scotland) (Prescribed Proceedings) Amendment Regulations 1995
revoked: SI 1997/3069 Reg.2, Sch.

1239. Pipe-lines (Inquiries Procedure) Rules 1995
r.10, amended: SI 1996/1008 Art.2, Sch para.16, SI 1997/712 r.3
r.10, revoked (in part): SI 1997/712 r.3

1240. Education (Mandatory Awards) (Amendment) Regulations 1995
see *B v B (Adult Student: Liability to Support)* [1998] 1 F.L.R. 373 (CA), Thorpe, L.J.

1241. Education (Fees and Awards) (Amendment) Regulations 1995
revoked: SI 1997/1972 Reg.8

1266. Financial Services Act 1986 (Investment Advertisements) (Exemptions) Order 1995
revoked: SI 1996/1586 Art.19

1268. Value Added Tax (Special Provisions) Order 1995
Art.2, amended: SI 1998/760 Art.3, SI 1999/2831 Art.2, SI 1999/3120 Art.3
Art.5, amended: SI 1998/760 Art.4
Art.12, amended: SI 1997/1616 Art.3, SI 1998/760 Art.5, Art.6
Art.13, amended: SI 1999/3120 Art.4

1271. Education (Fees and Awards) (Scotland) Amendment Regulations 1995
revoked: SI 1997/93 Reg.14, Sch.4

1273. Parole Board (Scotland) Rules 1995
r.6, substituted: SI 1998/1904 r.2
r.7, substituted: SI 1998/1904 r.2
r.8, amended: SI 1998/1904 r.3
r.8, revoked (in part): SI 1998/1904 r.3
r.13, amended: SI 1998/1904 r.4
r.14, amended: SI 1998/1904 r.5, r.6

1283. Income Tax (Stock Lending) (Amendment) Regulations 1995
revoked: SI 1997/987 Reg.2 (with savings), Sch.1 (with savings)

1295. Child Abduction and Custody (Parties to Conventions) (Amendment) (No. 3) Order 1995
revoked: SI 1996/269 Art.2

1300. Northampton and Lamport Light Railway Order 1995
Art.9, amended: SI 1996/362 Art.5, Sch.4

1331. Wireless Telegraphy (Licence Charges) Regulations 1995
revoked: SI 1999/1774 Reg.2, Sch.1
Reg.3, amended: SI 1997/1006 Reg.2, SI 1997/1885 Reg.2, SI 1998/1567 Reg.2
Reg.3, revoked (in part): SI 1998/460 Reg.3, SI 1999/1774 Reg.2, Sch.1
Reg.4, amended: SI 1997/1885 Reg.2
Reg.4, revoked: SI 1999/1774 Reg.2, Sch.1
Reg.5, amended: SI 1998/1567 Reg.2
Reg.5, revoked: SI 1999/1774 Reg.2, Sch.1
Sch.2, revoked: SI 1999/1774 Reg.2, Sch.1
Sch.2, substituted: SI 1998/460 Reg.3, Sch.1
Sch.3, amended: SI 1996/1464 Reg.2, Sch.1
Sch.3, revoked: SI 1999/1774 Reg.2, Sch.1

NO.

1995—cont.

1331. Wireless Telegraphy (Licence Charges) Regulations 1995—*cont.*
Sch.4, amended: SI 1996/1464 Reg.2, Sch.2, SI 1997/1006 Reg.2, Sch., SI 1997/1885 Reg.2, Sch., SI 1998/1567 Reg.2, Sch. Part I, Sch. Part II
Sch.4, revoked: SI 1999/1774 Reg.2, Sch.1
Sch.4, substituted: SI 1998/460 Reg.3, Sch.2

1333. Road Traffic (Special Parking Area) (Royal Borough of Kingston upon Thames) (Amendment No.2) Order 1995
revoked: SI 1996/3038 Art.2, Sch.1

1334. Road Traffic (Special Parking Area) (London Borough of Sutton) (Amendment No.2) Order 1995
revoked: SI 1998/1134 Art.2, Sch.1

1336. Local Government (Direct Service Organisations) (Competition) (Amendment) Regulations 1995
Reg.4, revoked: SI 1997/2747 Reg.2, Sch.
Reg.5, revoked: SI 1997/2747 Reg.2, Sch.
Reg.7, revoked: SI 1997/2747 Reg.2, Sch.
Reg.8, revoked: SI 1997/2747 Reg.2, Sch.
Reg.9, revoked: SI 1997/2747 Reg.2, Sch.
Reg.10, revoked: SI 1997/2747 Reg.2, Sch.

1372. Dairy Products (Hygiene) (Scotland) Regulations 1995
applied: SI 1996/3124 Reg.10, Sch.2 para.9
Reg.2, amended: SI 1996/2465 Reg.3, SI 1998/2424 Reg.10
Reg.3, amended: SI 1996/2465 Reg.4
Reg.6, amended: SI 1996/2465 Reg.5
Reg.8, amended: SI 1996/2465 Reg.6
Reg.18, amended: SI 1996/2465 Reg.7
Reg.22, amended: SI 1996/2465 Reg.8
Reg.24, revoked (in part): SI 1996/1499 Reg.49, Sch.9, SI 1998/2424 Reg.9, Sch.
Sch.1 Part 1A, amended: SI 1996/2465 Reg.9
Sch.3 para.1, amended: SI 1997/1729 Reg.35
Sch.4 Part III, amended: SI 1996/2465 Reg.10
Sch.6 Part I, amended: SI 1996/2465 Reg.11
Sch.6 Part II, amended: SI 1996/2465 Reg.11
Sch.6 Part III, amended: SI 1996/2465 Reg.11
Sch.6 Part IV, amended: SI 1996/2465 Reg.11
Sch.10 Part I, amended: SI 1996/1499 Reg.49
Sch.10 Part II, amended: SI 1996/1499 Reg.49, SI 1996/2465 Reg.12
Sch.11 para.4, revoked: SI 1996/2465 Reg.13

1376. Measuring Instruments (EC Requirements) (Fees) (Amendment) Regulations 1995
revoked: SI 1998/1177 Reg.1

1384. Medicines (Products Other Than Veterinary Drugs) (Prescription Only) Amendment Order 1995
revoked: SI 1997/1830 Art.16, Sch.6

1412. Feeding Stuffs Regulations 1995
applied: SI 1999/2325 Reg.7
Reg.2, amended: SI 1996/1260 Reg.3, SI 1998/104 Reg.3, Reg.4, SI 1999/1528 Reg.3
Reg.10, substituted: SI 1996/1260 Reg.4
Reg.14, amended: SI 1998/104 Reg.4
Reg.15, amended: SI 1996/1260 Reg.5, SI 1999/1528 Reg.4
Reg.15, revoked (in part): SI 1999/1528 Reg.4
Reg.22, amended: SI 1996/1260 Reg.6
Reg.22, revoked: SI 1999/2325 Reg.15
Sch.1 para.6A, added: SI 1998/104 Reg.6
Sch.1 para.6B, added: SI 1998/104 Reg.6
Sch.1 para.19A, added: SI 1998/104 Reg.6
Sch.1 para.19B, added: SI 1998/104 Reg.6
Sch.3 Part C, amended: SI 1996/1260 Reg.7
Sch.4 Part II, amended: SI 1996/1260 Reg.8
Sch.4 Part VI, amended: SI 1996/1260 Reg.8

NO.

1412. Feeding Stuffs Regulations 1995—*cont.*
Sch.4 Part XI, added: SI 1998/104 Reg.7, Sch.1
Sch.4 Table, amended: SI 1998/2072 Reg.3
Sch.5, referred to: SI 1999/1663 Reg.6, Sch.2
Part I
Sch.5 Part I, amended: SI 1996/1260 Reg.9, SI
1998/2072 Reg.4, SI 1999/1528 Reg.5
Sch.5 Part II, amended: SI 1998/2072 Reg.4
Sch.5 Part II, substituted: SI 1999/1528 Reg.5,
Sch.
Sch.6 Part II, substituted: SI 1998/104 Reg.8,
Sch.2
Sch.7, amended: SI 1996/1260 Reg.10

1424. Dual-Use and Related Goods (Export Control) (Amendment) Regulations 1995
applied: SI 1996/2721 Reg.15
revoked: SI 1996/2721 Sch.1
Reg.3, revoked: SI 1996/2721 Sch.1

1425. Public Trustee (Fees) (Amendment) Order 1995
revoked: SI 1999/855 Art.32, Sch.

1429. Merchant Shipping (Certification of Deck and Marine Engineer Officers) (Amendment) Regulations 1995
revoked: SI 1997/348 Reg.1

1430. Counterfeit and Pirated Goods (Customs) Regulations 1995
revoked: SI 1999/1601 Reg.9

1435. Petroleum (Production) (Seaward Areas) (Amendment) Regulations 1995
referred to: 1998 c.17 Sch.1 para.20, Sch.1
para.21, Sch.1 para.24, SI 1999/160 Sch.9
para.1, Sch.10 para.1, Sch.11 para.1

1436. Petroleum (Production) (Landward Areas) Regulations 1995
Sch.3 cl.17, referred to: SI 1996/913 Reg.18

1442. Credit Institutions (Protection of Depositors) Regulations 1995
Reg.2, amended: SI 1998/1129 Art.2, Sch.1
para.19, SI 1999/2094 Reg.4
Reg.3, amended: SI 1998/1129 Art.2, Sch.1
para.19
Reg.9, amended: SI 1998/1129 Art.2, Sch.1
para.19
Reg.17, amended: SI 1998/1129 Art.2, Sch.1
para.19
Reg.19, amended: SI 1998/1129 Art.2, Sch.1
para.19
Reg.41, referred to: SI 1997/2668 Art.2, Sch.
Part I
Reg.41, revoked (in part): 1997 c.32 Sch.9
Reg.46, amended: SI 1998/1129 Art.2, Sch.1
para.19
Reg.49, amended: SI 1998/1129 Art.2, Sch.1
para.19

1447. Counterfeit and Pirated Goods (Consequential Provisions) Regulations 1995
revoked: SI 1999/1618 Reg.9

1455. Vehicle Excise (Design Weight Certificate) Regulations 1995
see *Department of Transport v Caird Environmental Services Ltd* [1999] R.T.R. 137 (QBD),
Pill, L.J.

1475. Police (Discipline) (Amendment) Regulations 1995
revoked: SI 1999/730 Reg.2 (with saving)

1476. Roads (Transitional Powers) (Scotland) Order 1995
referred to: SI 1996/682 Art.19
Sch.2, amended: SI 1996/496 Art.2

NO.

1478. Cosmetic Products (Safety) (Amendment) Regulations 1995
revoked: SI 1996/2925 Sch.9
Reg.2, revoked: SI 1996/2925 Sch.9

1481. Hill Livestock (Compensatory Allowances) (Amendment) (No.2) Regulations 1995
revoked (in part): SI 1996/1500 Reg.18

1483. Pesticides (Maximum Residue Levels in Crops, Food and Feeding Stuffs) (Amendment) Regulations 1995
revoked (in part): SI 1999/3483 Reg.7, Sch.4

1513. Motor Cycle (EC Type Approval) Regulations 1995
applied: SI 1999/2920 Reg.26
revoked: SI 1999/2920 Reg.2
Sch., amended: SI 1997/2282 Reg.2
Sch., revoked: SI 1999/2920 Reg.2
Sch. Item 11, added: SI 1997/2282 Reg.2
Sch. Item 11, revoked: SI 1999/2920 Reg.2

1526. Local Authorities (Capital Finance) (Amendment) Regulations 1995
revoked: SI 1997/319 Reg.162, Sch.3

1527. Fraserburgh Harbour Revision Order 1995
Art.17, amended: SSI 1999/40 Art.16

1536. Financial Services Act 1986 (Investment Advertisements) (Exemptions) (No.2) Order 1995
Art.8, amended: SI 1999/1820 Art.4, Sch.2
para.159
Art.15, applied: SI 1997/817 Reg.14

1537. Public Offers of Securities Regulations 1995
Reg.2, amended: SI 1999/734 Reg.2
Reg.7, amended: SI 1999/734 Reg.2, SI 1999/
1146 Reg.2
Reg.8, amended: SI 1999/734 Reg.2
Reg.8, referred to: SI 1999/727 Art.2
Reg.13, amended: SI 1999/734 Reg.2
Sch.1 para.10, amended: SI 1999/734 Reg.2
Sch.1 para.45, amended: SI 1999/734 Reg.2
Sch.4 para.8, revoked (in part): SI 1999/734
Reg.2
Sch.4 para.11, revoked: SI 1999/734 Reg.2
Sch.5 para.1, revoked (in part): SI 1999/734
Reg.2

1544. Eggs (Marketing Standards) Regulations 1995
applied: SI 1999/672 Art.2, Sch.1
Reg.4, amended: SI 1996/1725 Reg.3
Reg.7A, added: SI 1996/1725 Reg.4
Reg.10, substituted: SI 1997/1414 Reg.3
Sch. para.2, amended: SI 1996/1725 Reg.5, SI
1997/1414 Reg.4, SI 1998/1665 Reg.2

1561. Education (School Performance Information) (England) (Amendment) Regulations 1995
revoked: SI 1996/2577 Reg.4
Reg.2, revoked: SI 1996/2577 Reg.4
Reg.3, revoked: SI 1996/2577 Reg.4
Reg.4, revoked: SI 1996/2577 Reg.4
Reg.5, revoked: SI 1996/2577 Reg.4
Reg.6, revoked: SI 1996/2577 Reg.4
Reg.7, revoked: SI 1996/2577 Reg.4
Reg.8, revoked: SI 1996/2577 Reg.4
Reg.9, revoked: SI 1996/2577 Reg.4

1571. National Health Service (Fund-Holding Practices) (Scotland) Amendment Regulations 1995
revoked: SI 1997/1014 Reg.24, Sch.3

1576. Fisheries and Aquaculture Structures (Grants) Regulations 1995
Reg.2, amended: SI 1998/1365 Reg.3
Reg.7, amended: SI 1999/1820 Art.4, Sch.2
para.160

1995—cont.

1596. **Act of Sederunt (Registration Appeal Court) 1995**
revoked: SI 1997/379 para.2

1598. **Prison (Amendment) (No.2) Rules 1995**
revoked: SI 1999/728 r.85 (with savings), Sch. (with savings)
r.2, revoked: SI 1999/728 r.85 (with savings), Sch. (with savings)

1610. **Fishing Vessels (Decommissioning) Scheme 1995**
applied: SI 1996/1242 para.3

1612. **Personal Pension Schemes (Appropriate Schemes) Amendment Regulations 1995**
Reg.2, revoked: SI 1997/470 Reg.20, Sch.3

1615. **Parliamentary Commissioner Order 1995**
referred to: SI 1999/1290 Art.4
Art.2, amended: 1998 c.38 s.152, Sch.18 Part I

1616. **Child Abduction and Custody (Parties to Conventions) (Amendment) (No.4) Order 1995**
revoked: SI 1996/269 Art.2

1617. **Consular Fees Order 1995**
revoked: SI 1996/1915 Art.4
Sch. Part II, revoked: SI 1996/1915 Art.4

1625. **Historic Monuments and Archaeological Objects (Northern Ireland) Order 1995**
referred to: SI 1999/2450 Sch.4 para.4.3
applied: SI 1999/3145 Art.3
Art.37, applied: SI 1999/3145 Art.3
Art.42, amended: 1996 c.24 s.14, SI 1998/261 (NI.2) Art.15, Sch.3
Sch.3 para.2, revoked: 1997 c.14 Sch para.8

1626. **Parliamentary Constituencies (England) Order 1995**
Sch., amended: SI 1996/1922 Art.2, Art.3, SI 1998/3152 Art.2, Art.3, Art.4, Sch.

1629. **Gas Appliances (Safety) Regulations 1995**
applied: SI 1998/2306 Reg.10, Sch.1

1642. **Rent Officers (Additional Functions) Order 1995**
applied: SI 1996/1217 Sch.6 para.8, SI 1997/1004 Art.8, Sch.6 para.8, SI 1998/562 Sch.4 para.3
revoked: SI 1997/1984 Art.9
Art.2, revoked: SI 1997/1984 Art.9
Art.5, amended: SI 1996/959 Art.3, SI 1997/1000 Art.2
Art.5, revoked: SI 1997/1984 Art.9
Art.6, amended: SI 1997/1984 Art.8
Art.6, revoked: SI 1997/1984 Art.9
Art.7, revoked: SI 1997/1984 Art.9
Sch.1 Part I, revoked: SI 1997/1984 Art.9
Sch.1 Part II, amended: SI 1996/959 Art.5
Sch.1 Part II, revoked: SI 1997/1984 Art.9
Sch.1 Part III, amended: SI 1996/959 Art.6
Sch.1 Part III, revoked: SI 1997/1984 Art.9
Sch.1 para.2, see *R. v Swale BC Ex p. Marchant* [1999] 1 F.L.R. 1087 (QBD), Kay, J.; see *R. v Swale BC Ex p. Marchant* Times, November 17, 1999 (CA), Potter, L.J.
Sch.1 para.2, applied: SI 1996/1217 Sch.6 para.2, Sch.6 para.3
Sch.1 para.2, referred to: SI 1997/1004 Sch.6 para.2, Sch.6 para.3
Sch.1 para.2, revoked: SI 1997/1984 Art.9
Sch.1 para.4A, added: SI 1996/959 Art.4
Sch.1 para.4A, revoked: SI 1997/1984 Art.9
Sch.3 para.1, amended: SI 1997/1000 Art.2
Sch.3 para.1, applied: SI 1996/1217 Sch.6 para.8, SI 1997/1004 Sch.6 para.8
Sch.3 para.1, revoked: SI 1997/1984 Art.9

1995—cont.

1643. **Rent Officers (Additional Functions) (Scotland) Order 1995**
applied: SI 1996/1217 Sch.6 para.8, SI 1997/1004 Art.8, Sch.6 para.8, SI 1998/562 Sch.4 para.3
revoked: SI 1997/1995 Art.9, Sch.5
Art.5, amended: SI 1996/975 Art.3, SI 1997/1003 Art.2
Art.5, revoked: SI 1997/1995 Art.9, Sch.5
Art.6, amended: SI 1997/1995 Art.8
Art.6, revoked: SI 1997/1995 Art.9, Sch.5
Sch.1 Part I, amended: SI 1996/975 Art.4
Sch.1 Part I, revoked: SI 1997/1995 Art.9, Sch.5
Sch.1 Part III, amended: SI 1996/975 Art.5
Sch.1 Part III, revoked: SI 1997/1995 Art.9, Sch.5
Sch.1 Part IV, amended: SI 1996/975 Art.6
Sch.1 Part IV, revoked: SI 1997/1995 Art.9, Sch.5
Sch.1 para.2, applied: SI 1996/1217 Sch.6 para.2, Sch.6 para.3
Sch.1 para.2, referred to: SI 1997/1004 Sch.6 para.2, Sch.6 para.3
Sch.1 para.2, revoked: SI 1997/1995 Art.9, Sch.5
Sch.1 para.4, revoked: SI 1997/1995 Art.9, Sch.5
Sch.1 para.7, revoked: SI 1997/1995 Art.9, Sch.5
Sch.1 para.9, revoked: SI 1997/1995 Art.9, Sch.5
Sch.3 para.1, amended: SI 1997/1003 Art.3
Sch.3 para.1, applied: SI 1996/1217 Sch.6 para.8, SI 1997/1004 Sch.6 para.8
Sch.3 para.1, revoked: SI 1997/1995 Art.9, Sch.5

1644. **Housing Benefit (General) Amendment Regulations 1995**
applied: SI 1999/2734 Reg.13
Reg.10, amended: SI 1996/1944 Reg.10, SI 1996/2432 Reg.14, SI 1998/563 Reg.17, SI 1998/2231 Reg.11, SI 1999/2734 Reg.10
Reg.10, applied: SI 1997/852 Reg.4

1645. **National Lottery Charities Board (Increase in Membership) Order 1995**
revoked: SI 1999/1878 Art.2

1666. **Value Added Tax (Input Tax) (Amendment) (No.3) Order 1995**
see *Customs and Excise Commissioners v BRS Automotive Ltd* [1997] S.T.C. 336 (QBD), Sedley, J.

1674. **Conditional Fee Agreements Order 1995**
see *Bevan Ashford v Geoff Yeandle (Contractors) Ltd (In Liquidation)* [1999] Ch. 239 (Ch D), Sir Richard Scott, V.C.
revoked: SI 1998/1860 Art.2

1675. **Conditional Fee Agreements Regulations 1995**
see *Bevan Ashford v Geoff Yeandle (Contractors) Ltd (In Liquidation)* [1998] 3 W.L.R. 172 (Ch D), Sir Richard Scott, V.C.

1677. **Severn Bridge (Amendment) Regulations 1995**
revoked: SI 1996/1316 Reg.2

1692. **A12 Trunk Road (Redbridge) (No.1) Red Route Experimental Traffic Order 1995**
revoked: SI 1996/1624 Art.10

1693. **A316 Trunk Road (Hounslow) Red Route Traffic Order 1995**
Art.2, amended: SI 1999/272 Art.2, Sch. Part A
Art.9, amended: SI 1999/272 Art.2, Sch. Part A

1995—cont.

1694. A316 Trunk Road (Richmond) (No.1) Red Route Experimental Traffic Order 1995
revoked (in part): SI 1996/3052 Art.10

1695. A12 Trunk Road (Redbridge) Red Route Experimental Traffic Order 1995
revoked (in part): SI 1996/1893 Art.10

1697. A316 Trunk Road (Richmond) Red Route (Clearway) Traffic Order 1995
Art.2, amended: SI 1999/272 Art.2, Sch. Part B
Art.9, amended: SI 1999/272 Art.2, Sch. Part B

1698. A316 Trunk Road (Hounslow) Red Route (Clearway) Traffic Order 1995
Art.2, amended: SI 1999/272 Art.2, Sch. Part B
Art.9, amended: SI 1999/272 Art.2, Sch. Part B
Sch.2, amended: SI 1997/549 Art.3
Sch.2 Item 1, added: SI 1997/549 Art.4

1699. A406 Trunk Road (Newham and Barking and Dagenham) Red Route Experimental Traffic Order 1995
revoked (in part): SI 1996/1895 Art.10

1700. A13 Trunk Road (Barking and Dagenham) Red Route Experimental Traffic Order 1995
revoked (in part): SI 1996/1896 Art.10

1701. A13 Trunk Road (Newham) Red Route Experimental Traffic Order 1995
revoked (in part): SI 1997/465 Art.10

1702. A10 Trunk Road (Haringey) Red Route Experimental Traffic Order 1995
revoked (in part): SI 1997/464 Art.10

1703. A13 Trunk Road (Havering) Red Route Experimental Traffic Order 1995
revoked (in part): SI 1996/1894 Art.10

1705. Education (Grants for Education Support and Training) (England) (Amendment) Regulations 1995
revoked: SI 1996/734 Reg.12

1712. St Mary's Music School (Aided Places) Regulations 1995
Reg.2, amended: SI 1996/1807 Reg.2
Sch.1 para.1, amended: SI 1996/1640 Reg.2
Sch.1 para.10, amended: SI 1996/1807 Reg.3, SI 1997/1640 Reg.2, SI 1998/1498 Reg.2, SI 1999/1060 Reg.2
Sch.1 para.13, amended: SI 1996/1807 Reg.3, SI 1997/1640 Reg.2, SI 1998/1498 Reg.2, SI 1999/1060 Reg.2
Sch.1 para.14, amended: SI 1996/1807 Reg.3, SI 1997/1640 Reg.2, SI 1998/1498 Reg.2
Sch.1 para.17, amended: SI 1997/1640 Reg.2
Sch.1 para.18, amended: SI 1996/1807 Reg.3, SI 1997/1640 Reg.2, SI 1998/1498 Reg.2, SI 1999/1060 Reg.2
Sch.1 para.21, amended: SI 1996/1807 Reg.3
Sch.1 para.22, amended: SI 1996/1807 Reg.3, SI 1997/1640 Reg.2
Sch.1 para.24, amended: SI 1996/1807 Reg.3, SI 1997/1640 Reg.2, SI 1998/1498 Reg.2, SI 1999/1060 Reg.2

1713. Education (Assisted Places) (Scotland) Regulations 1995
Part VA, added: SI 1997/2773 Reg.2
Reg.2, amended: SI 1996/1808 Reg.2, SI 1997/1641 Reg.2
Reg.5, amended: SI 1996/1808 Reg.2
Reg.9, amended: SI 1996/1808 Reg.2, SI 1997/1641 Reg.2, SI 1998/1497 Reg.2, SI 1999/1059 Reg.2

1995—cont.

1713. Education (Assisted Places) (Scotland) Regulations 1995—*cont.*
Reg.13, amended: SI 1996/1808 Reg.2, SI 1997/1641 Reg.2, SI 1998/1497 Reg.2, SI 1999/1059 Reg.2
Reg.15, amended: SI 1996/1808 Reg.2, SI 1997/1641 Reg.2, SI 1998/1497 Reg.2, SI 1999/1059 Reg.2
Reg.16, amended: SI 1996/1808 Reg.2, SI 1997/1641 Reg.2, SI 1998/1497 Reg.2, SI 1999/1059 Reg.2
Reg.17, amended: SI 1996/1808 Reg.2, SI 1997/1641 Reg.2, SI 1998/1497 Reg.2, SI 1999/1059 Reg.2
Reg.18, amended: SI 1997/1641 Reg.2
Reg.23A, added: SI 1997/2773 Reg.2
Reg.23B, added: SI 1997/2773 Reg.2
Reg.23C, added: SI 1998/1994 Reg.2
Reg.24, revoked: SI 1997/1641 Reg.2
Sch.2, substituted: SI 1996/1808 Reg.2, SI 1997/1641 Reg.2, SI 1998/1497 Reg.2, SI 1999/1059 Reg.2

1730. Insurance Companies (Taxation of Reinsurance Business) Regulations 1995
Reg.3, amended: SI 1996/1621 Reg.3
Reg.5, amended: SI 1996/1621 Reg.4
Reg.11, amended: SI 1996/1621 Reg.5

1738. Arable Area Payments Regulations 1995
applied: SI 1996/1593 Reg.4
revoked: SI 1996/3142 Reg.20
Reg.2, amended: SI 1996/1482 Reg.2
Reg.2, revoked: SI 1996/3142 Reg.20
Reg.5, amended: SI 1996/1482 Reg.2
Reg.5, revoked: SI 1996/3142 Reg.20
Reg.5A, amended: SI 1996/1482 Reg.2
Reg.5A, revoked: SI 1996/3142 Reg.20
Reg.8, revoked: SI 1996/3142 Reg.20
Reg.9, revoked: SI 1996/3142 Reg.20
Reg.10, revoked: SI 1996/3142 Reg.20
Reg.10, substituted: SI 1996/1482 Reg.2
Reg.10A, revoked: SI 1996/3142 Reg.20
Reg.11, revoked: SI 1996/3142 Reg.20
Reg.13, amended: SI 1996/1482 Reg.2
Reg.13, revoked: SI 1996/3142 Reg.20
Reg.15, applied: SI 1996/1593 Reg.5
Reg.15, revoked: SI 1996/3142 Reg.20
Reg.18, revoked: SI 1996/3142 Reg.20
Sch.1, revoked: SI 1996/3142 Reg.20
Sch.1 Part I, amended: SI 1996/1482 Reg.2
Sch.1 Part I, revoked: SI 1996/3142 Reg.20
Sch.1 Part II, amended: SI 1996/1482 Reg.2
Sch.1 Part II, revoked: SI 1996/3142 Reg.20
Sch.2, applied: SI 1996/1593 Reg.4
Sch.2, revoked: SI 1996/3142 Reg.20
Sch.2 Part A, amended: SI 1996/1482 Reg.2
Sch.2 Part A, revoked: SI 1996/3142 Reg.20
Sch.2 Part B, amended: SI 1996/1482 Reg.2
Sch.2 Part B, revoked: SI 1996/3142 Reg.20
Sch.3 para.1A, added: SI 1996/1482 Reg.2
Sch.3 para.1A, revoked: SI 1996/3142 Reg.20

1739. Education Authority Bursaries (Scotland) Regulations 1995
applied: SI 1996/1623 Art.3, SI 1998/217 Art.2, SI 1999/779 Art.2, Sch.
Reg.2, amended: SI 1997/1049 Reg.2
Sch.1 para.1, amended: SI 1997/1049 Reg.2
Sch.1 para.2, substituted: SI 1997/1049 Reg.2
Sch.1 para.2A, added: SI 1997/1049 Reg.2
Sch.1 para.2B, added: SI 1997/1049 Reg.2
Sch.1 para.3, amended: SI 1997/1049 Reg.2
Sch.1 para.3A, added: SI 1997/1049 Reg.2
Sch.2 para.2, amended: SI 1997/1049 Reg.2

NO.

NO.

1995—cont.

1742. Social Security Benefits (Miscellaneous Amendments) Regulations 1995
Reg.2, revoked (in part): SI 1996/1345 Reg.27, Sch.

1743. Education (School Teachers' Pay and Conditions) (No.2) Order 1995
amended: SI 1996/1003 Art.3
revoked: SI 1996/1816 Art.1

1747. Cleveland (Further Provision) Order 1995
referred to: SI 1996/657 Art.2
Art.4, revoked: 1996 c.16 Sch.9 Part III

1748. Local Government Changes for England (Miscellaneous Provision) Regulations 1995
Reg.8, amended: SI 1996/330 Reg.3
Reg.9, amended: 1997 c.23 s.8
Reg.9, revoked: 1997 c.23 s.8

1763. Food Safety (General Food Hygiene) Regulations 1995
Reg.2, amended: SI 1997/2537 Reg.10, Sch.2 para.1, SI 1999/1360 Reg.2, SI 1999/1540 Reg.20
Reg.2, revoked (in part): SI 1999/1540 Reg.20
Reg.3, amended: SI 1996/1699 Reg.14, SI 1996/2465 Reg.14, SI 1998/994 Reg.58
Reg.3, revoked (in part): SI 1998/994 Reg.58
Sch.1 Ch.IV, amended: SI 1997/2537 Reg.10, Sch.2 para.2, Sch.2 para.3, Sch.2 para.4, SI 1999/1360 Reg.3, Reg.4
Sch.2 para.3, revoked: SI 1998/994 Reg.59, Sch.5
Sch.2 para.4, revoked: SI 1998/994 Reg.59, Sch.5
Sch.2 para.5, revoked: SI 1998/994 Reg.59, Sch.5
Sch.2 para.6, revoked: SI 1998/994 Reg.59, Sch.5
Sch.2 para.7, revoked: SI 1998/994 Reg.59, Sch.5

1769. Buckinghamshire (Borough of Milton Keynes) (Structural Change) Order 1995
applied: SI 1997/479 Art.1
Art.2, amended: SI 1996/446 Art.8
Art.5, revoked: 1996 c.16 Sch.9 Part III
Sch.1, amended: SI 1996/446 Art.8

1770. East Sussex (Boroughs of Brighton and Hove) (Structural Change) Order 1995
applied: SI 1997/461 Art.1
Art.7, revoked: 1996 c.16 Sch.9 Part III

1771. Dorset (Boroughs of Poole and Bournemouth) (Structural Change) Order 1995
applied: SI 1997/458 Art.1
Art.5, revoked: 1996 c.16 Sch.9 Part III
Art.8, referred to: SI 1997/497 Art.2

1772. Durham (Borough of Darlington) (Structural Change) Order 1995
applied: SI 1997/460 Art.1
Art.5, revoked: 1996 c.16 Sch.9 Part III
Art.8, referred to: SI 1997/498 Art.2

1773. Derbyshire (City of Derby) (Structural Change) Order 1995
applied: SI 1997/459 Art.1
Art.5, revoked: 1996 c.16 Sch.9 Part III
Art.8, referred to: SI 1997/496 Art.2

1774. Wiltshire (Borough of Thamesdown) (Structural Change) Order 1995
applied: SI 1997/456 Art.1
Part III, revoked: SI 1999/2927 Art.9
Art.5, revoked: 1996 c.16 Sch.9 Part III
Art.8, referred to: SI 1997/493 Art.2

1995—cont.

1775. Hampshire (Cities of Portsmouth and Southampton) (Structural Change) Order 1995
applied: SI 1997/468 Art.1
Art.5, revoked: 1996 c.16 Sch.9 Part III
Art.8, referred to: SI 1997/489 Art.2, Art.3

1776. Bedfordshire (Borough of Luton) (Structural Change) Order 1995
applied: SI 1997/478 Art.1
Art.4, amended: SI 1996/446 Art.7
Art.5, revoked: 1996 c.16 Sch.9 Part III
Art.8, referred to: SI 1997/494 Art.2

1779. Staffordshire (City of Stoke-on-Trent) (Structural and Boundary Changes) Order 1995
applied: SI 1997/469 Art.1
Art.3, referred to: SI 1997/492 Art.2
Art.7, revoked: 1996 c.16 Sch.9 Part III

1780. Training for Work (Miscellaneous Provisions) Order 1995
amended: SI 1998/1426 Art.2
referred to: SI 1998/1426
Sch., substituted: SI 1998/1426 Art.2, Sch.

1801. Social Security (Adjudication) Regulations 1995
revoked: SI 1999/991 Reg.59 (with savings), Sch.4 (with savings)
Part I, applied: SI 1996/207 Reg.42
Part I, revoked: SI 1999/991 Reg.59 (with savings), Sch.4 (with savings)
Part II, applied: SI 1996/207 Reg.42
Part II, revoked: SI 1999/991 Reg.59 (with savings), Sch.4 (with savings)
Part IV s.B, revoked: SI 1999/991 Reg.59 (with savings), Sch.4 (with savings)
Part IV s.B, substituted: SI 1996/1518 Reg.2
Reg.1, amended: SI 1996/1518 Reg.2, SI 1996/2450 Reg.2, SI 1997/955 Reg.2
Reg.1, revoked: SI 1999/991 Reg.59 (with savings), Sch.4 (with savings)
Reg.2, amended: SI 1996/2450 Reg.3
Reg.2, revoked: SI 1999/991 Reg.59 (with savings), Sch.4 (with savings)
Reg.3, amended: SI 1996/182 Reg.2, SI 1996/2450 Reg.4, SI 1999/1958 Art.5, Sch.12 para.12, SI 1999/2422 Art.4, Sch.14 para.5, Sch.14 para.12, Sch.14 para.17, SI 1999/2739 Art.3, Sch.2 para.5, Sch.2 para.12, SI 1999/2860 Art.4, Sch.16 para.5, Sch.16 para.13, SI 1999/3178 Art.4, Sch.22 para.4, Sch.22 para.11
Reg.3, applied: SI 1996/2450 Reg.22, SI 1999/1958 Art.5, Sch.12 para.12, SI 1999/2422 Art.4, Sch.14 para.5, Sch.14 para.12, SI 1999/2739 Art.3, Sch.2 para.5, Sch.2 para.12, SI 1999/2860 Art.4, Sch.16 para.5, Sch.16 para.13, SI 1999/3178 Art.4, Sch.22 para.4, Sch.22 para.11
Reg.3, referred to: SI 1999/2422 Art.4, Sch.14 para.17, SI 1999/2739 Art.3, Sch.2 para.5
Reg.3, revoked: SI 1999/991 Reg.59 (with savings), Sch.4 (with savings)
Reg.4, amended: SI 1996/2450 Reg.5
Reg.4, revoked: SI 1999/991 Reg.59 (with savings), Sch.4 (with savings)
Reg.5, amended: SI 1996/2450 Reg.6
Reg.5, revoked: SI 1999/991 Reg.59 (with savings), Sch.4 (with savings)
Reg.6, amended: SI 1996/2450 Reg.7
Reg.6, revoked: SI 1999/991 Reg.59 (with savings), Sch.4 (with savings)
Reg.7, amended: SI 1996/2450 Reg.8

NO.

1801. Social Security (Adjudication) Regulations 1995—*cont.*

Reg.7, applied: SI 1996/2450 Reg.22, SI 1999/1958 Art.5, Sch.12 para.8, SI 1999/2422 Art.4, Sch.14 para.8, SI 1999/2739 Art.3, Sch.2 para.8, SI 1999/2860 Art.4, Sch.16 para.8, SI 1999/3178 Art.4, Sch.22 para.7

Reg.7, revoked: SI 1999/991 Reg.59 (with savings), Sch.4 (with savings)

Reg.10, amended: SI 1996/2450 Reg.9, SI 1999/1958 Art.5, Sch.12 para.12, SI 1999/2422 Art.4, Sch.14 para.12, SI 1999/2739 Art.3, Sch.2 para.12, SI 1999/2860 Art.4, Sch.16 para.13, SI 1999/3178 Art.4, Sch.22 para.11

Reg.10, applied: SI 1999/1958 Art.5, Sch.12 para.12, SI 1999/2422 Art.4, Sch.14 para.12, SI 1999/2739 Art.3, Sch.2 para.12, SI 1999/2860 Art.4, Sch.16 para.13, SI 1999/3178 Art.4, Sch.22 para.11

Reg.10, referred to: SI 1999/2860 Art.4, Sch.16 para.13

Reg.10, revoked: SI 1999/991 Reg.59 (with savings), Sch.4 (with savings)

Reg.20, revoked: SI 1999/776 Reg.4

Reg.21, revoked: SI 1999/991 Reg.59 (with savings), Sch.4 (with savings)

Reg.22, amended: SI 1996/2450 Reg.10

Reg.22, applied: SI 1996/207 Reg.42, SI 1996/2450 Reg.22, SI 1999/2422 Art.4, Sch.14 para.7, SI 1999/2739 Art.3, Sch.2 para.7, SI 1999/2860 Art.4, Sch.16 para.7, SI 1999/3178 Art.4, Sch.22 para.6

Reg.22, referred to: SI 1999/1958 Art.5, Sch.12 para.7, SI 1999/2739 Art.3, Sch.2 para.7, SI 1999/2860 Art.4, Sch.16 para.7

Reg.22, revoked: SI 1999/991 Reg.59 (with savings), Sch.4 (with savings)

Reg.23, amended: SI 1996/182 Reg.2, SI 1996/2450 Reg.11

Reg.23, applied: SI 1996/207 Reg.42

Reg.23, revoked: SI 1999/991 Reg.59 (with savings), Sch.4 (with savings)

Reg.24, amended: SI 1997/955 Reg.3, SI 1999/2422 Art.4, Sch.14 para.17

Reg.24, applied: SI 1996/207 Reg.42

Reg.24, referred to: SI 1999/2422 Art.4, Sch.14 para.17

Reg.24, revoked: SI 1999/991 Reg.59 (with savings), Sch.4 (with savings)

Reg.29, amended: SI 1996/182 Reg.2, SI 1996/2450 Reg.12

Reg.29, applied: SI 1996/2450 Reg.22, SI 1999/2739 Art.3, Sch.2 para.7, SI 1999/2860 Art.4, Sch.16 para.7

Reg.29, referred to: SI 1999/2739 Art.3, Sch.2 para.7, SI 1999/2860 Art.4, Sch.16 para.7

Reg.29, revoked: SI 1999/991 Reg.59 (with savings), Sch.4 (with savings)

Reg.32, amended: SI 1997/955 Reg.4

Reg.32, revoked: SI 1999/991 Reg.59 (with savings), Sch.4 (with savings)

Reg.36, revoked: SI 1999/991 Reg.59 (with savings), Sch.4 (with savings)

Reg.38, amended: SI 1996/182 Reg.2, SI 1996/2450 Reg.13

Reg.38, applied: SI 1996/2450 Reg.22, SI 1999/2422 Art.4, Sch.14 para.7, SI 1999/2860 Art.4, Sch.16 para.7

Reg.38, referred to: SI 1999/2860 Art.4, Sch.16 para.7

Reg.38, revoked: SI 1999/991 Reg.59 (with savings), Sch.4 (with savings)

NO.

1801. Social Security (Adjudication) Regulations 1995—*cont.*

Reg.39, amended: SI 1997/955 Reg.5

Reg.39, revoked: SI 1999/991 Reg.59 (with savings), Sch.4 (with savings)

Reg.40, revoked: SI 1999/991 Reg.59 (with savings), Sch.4 (with savings)

Reg.44, revoked: SI 1999/991 Reg.59 (with savings), Sch.4 (with savings)

Reg.45, revoked: SI 1999/991 Reg.59 (with savings), Sch.4 (with savings)

Reg.46, amended: SI 1997/810 Reg.2

Reg.46, revoked: SI 1999/991 Reg.59 (with savings), Sch.4 (with savings)

Reg.47, amended: SI 1997/810 Reg.3

Reg.47, revoked: SI 1999/991 Reg.59 (with savings), Sch.4 (with savings)

Reg.48A, added: SI 1997/810 Reg.4

Reg.48A, revoked: SI 1999/991 Reg.59 (with savings), Sch.4 (with savings)

Reg.51, revoked: SI 1999/991 Reg.59 (with savings), Sch.4 (with savings)

Reg.52, amended: SI 1997/793 Reg.8

Reg.52, revoked: SI 1999/991 Reg.59 (with savings), Sch.4 (with savings)

Reg.57, amended: SI 1997/793 Reg.9

Reg.57, revoked: SI 1999/991 Reg.59 (with savings), Sch.4 (with savings)

Reg.59, amended: SI 1996/425 Reg.2, SI 1996/1518 Reg.2, SI 1996/1803 Reg.2, SI 1997/793 Reg.10, SI 1997/2290 Reg.2, Reg.7

Reg.59, applied: SI 1997/793 Reg.20, SI 1997/2290 Reg.7

Reg.59, revoked (in part): SI 1997/793 Reg.10, SI 1999/991 Reg.59 (with savings), Sch.4 (with savings)

Reg.59A, added: SI 1999/1302 Reg.2

Reg.59A, revoked: SI 1999/991 Reg.59 (with savings), Sch.4 (with savings)

Reg.60, amended: SI 1996/425 Reg.2, SI 1997/793 Reg.11

Reg.60, revoked: SI 1999/991 Reg.59 (with savings), Sch.4 (with savings)

Reg.62, amended: SI 1997/793 Reg.12

Reg.62, revoked: SI 1999/991 Reg.59 (with savings), Sch.4 (with savings)

Reg.63, amended: SI 1996/1518 Reg.2, SI 1996/2306 Reg.8, SI 1997/793 Reg.13, SI 1997/2290 Reg.3, SI 1997/2305 Reg.4

Reg.63, revoked: SI 1999/991 Reg.59 (with savings), Sch.4 (with savings)

Reg.63A, added: SI 1996/1518 Reg.2

Reg.63A, amended: SI 1996/2306 Reg.9, SI 1996/2659 Reg.2, SI 1997/793 Reg.14, SI 1997/2290 Reg.4, SI 1997/2305 Reg.4

Reg.63A, revoked (in part): SI 1997/793 Reg.14, SI 1999/991 Reg.59 (with savings), Sch.4 (with savings)

Reg.63B, added: SI 1997/2305 Reg.4

Reg.63B, revoked: SI 1999/991 Reg.59 (with savings), Sch.4 (with savings)

Reg.64, revoked: SI 1999/991 Reg.59 (with savings), Sch.4 (with savings)

Reg.65, amended: SI 1997/793 Reg.15

Reg.65, revoked: SI 1999/991 Reg.59 (with savings), Sch.4 (with savings)

Reg.66, amended: SI 1997/65 Reg.16, SI 1997/793 Reg.16

Reg.66, revoked: SI 1999/991 Reg.59 (with savings), Sch.4 (with savings)

Reg.67, amended: SI 1997/793 Reg.17

1995—cont.

1801. Social Security (Adjudication) Regulations 1995—*cont.*
Reg.67, revoked (in part): SI 1997/793 Reg.17, SI 1999/991 Reg.59 (with savings), Sch.4 (with savings)
Reg.67A, added: SI 1997/1839 Reg.4
Reg.67A, revoked: SI 1999/991 Reg.59 (with savings), Sch.4 (with savings)
Reg.68, revoked: SI 1999/991 Reg.59 (with savings), Sch.4 (with savings)
Reg.69, revoked: SI 1999/991 Reg.59 (with savings), Sch.4 (with savings)
Sch.2, amended: SI 1999/2422 Art.4, Sch.14 para.17
Sch.2, referred to: SI 1999/2422 Art.4, Sch.14 para.17
Sch.2 para.7, amended: SI 1997/955 Reg.6
Sch.2 para.7, revoked: SI 1999/991 Reg.59 (with savings), Sch.4 (with savings)
Sch.2 para.8, amended: SI 1997/955 Reg.6
Sch.2 para.8, revoked: SI 1999/991 Reg.59 (with savings), Sch.4 (with savings)
Sch.2 para.9, amended: SI 1997/955 Reg.6
Sch.2 para.9, revoked: SI 1999/991 Reg.59 (with savings), Sch.4 (with savings)

1802. Merchant Shipping and Fishing Vessels (Medical Stores) Regulations 1995
referred to: SI 1998/2771 Reg.5, Sch.2
Reg.4, amended: SI 1996/2821 Reg.2

1803. Merchant Shipping (Ships' Doctors) Regulations 1995
applied: SI 1996/3243 Sch Part III

1875. Act of Adjournal (Consolidation Amendment) (Supervised Release Orders) 1995
revoked: SI 1996/513 r.3, Sch.2
para.2, revoked: SI 1996/513 r.3, Sch.2

1876. Act of Sederunt (Proceedings in the Sheriff Court under the Debtors (Scotland) Act 1987) (Amendment) 1995
revoked: SI 1996/2709 r.3, Sch.2

1878. Local Government (Transitional Provisions) (Scotland) Order 1995
revoked: SI 1996/739 Art.8, Sch.3

1879. Aberdeen and Grampian Tourist Board Scheme Order 1995
Sch. para.8, amended: SI 1998/496 Sch. para.2

1880. Angus and City of Dundee Tourist Board Scheme Order 1995
Sch. para.8, amended: SI 1998/496 Sch. para.2

1881. Argyll, the Isles, Loch Lomond, Stirling and Trossachs Tourist Board Scheme Order 1995
Sch. para.8, amended: SI 1998/496 Sch. para.2

1882. Ayrshire and Arran Tourist Board Scheme Order 1995
Sch. para.8, amended: SI 1998/496 Sch. para.2

1883. Dumfries and Galloway Tourist Board Scheme Order 1995
Sch. para.8, amended: SI 1998/496 Sch. para.2

1884. Edinburgh and Lothians Tourist Board Scheme Order 1995
Sch. para.8, referred to: SI 1998/496 Sch. para.2

1885. Greater Glasgow and Clyde Valley Tourist Board Scheme Order 1995
Sch. para.8, amended: SI 1998/496 Sch. para.2

1886. Highlands of Scotland Tourist Board Scheme Order 1995
Sch. para.8, amended: SI 1998/496 Sch. para.2

1887. Kingdom of Fife Tourist Board Scheme Order 1995
Sch. para.8, amended: SI 1998/496 Sch. para.2

1995—cont.

1888. Orkney Tourist Board Scheme Order 1995
Sch. para.8, amended: SI 1998/496 Sch. para.2

1889. Perthshire Tourist Board Scheme Order 1995
Sch. para.8, amended: SI 1998/496 Sch. para.2

1890. Scottish Borders Tourist Board Scheme Order 1995
Sch. para.8, amended: SI 1998/496 Sch. para.2

1891. Shetland Tourist Board Scheme Order 1995
Sch. para.8, amended: SI 1998/496 Sch. para.2

1892. Western Isles Tourist Board Scheme Order 1995
Sch. para.8, amended: SI 1998/496 Sch. para.2

1893. Merchant Shipping (Fees) Regulations 1995
revoked: SI 1996/3243 Reg.2
Reg.2, revoked: SI 1996/3243 Reg.2
Reg.4, amended: SI 1996/2632 Reg.2
Reg.4, revoked: SI 1996/3243 Reg.2
Reg.5, revoked: SI 1996/3243 Reg.2
Sch.1 Part I, amended: SI 1996/2632 Reg.2
Sch.1 Part I, revoked: SI 1996/3243 Reg.2

1904. Education (School Performance Information) (Wales) Regulations 1995
revoked: SI 1997/1633 Reg.2
Reg.2, revoked: SI 1997/1633 Reg.2
Reg.3, amended: SI 1996/1665 Reg.2
Reg.3, revoked: SI 1997/1633 Reg.2
Sch.1 para.15, amended: SI 1996/1665 Reg.3
Sch.1 para.15, revoked: SI 1997/1633 Reg.2
Sch.2 para.5, added: SI 1996/1665 Reg.4
Sch.2 para.5, revoked: SI 1997/1633 Reg.2
Sch.2 para.6, added: SI 1996/1665 Reg.4
Sch.2 para.6, revoked: SI 1997/1633 Reg.2

1907. Non-automatic Weighing Instruments (EEC Requirements) Regulations 1995
Reg.2, amended: SI 1997/3035 Reg.2
Reg.3, amended: SI 1997/3035 Reg.2
Reg.8, amended: SI 1997/3035 Reg.2
Reg.9, applied: SI 1998/1177 Reg.5, Sch.4 para.1, Sch.4 para.3
Reg.10, applied: SI 1998/1177 Reg.6, Sch.5 para.1
Reg.11, amended: SI 1997/3035 Reg.2
Reg.12, amended: SI 1997/3035 Reg.2
Reg.12, applied: SI 1998/1177 Reg.7, Sch.6 para.1
Reg.13, amended: SI 1997/3035 Reg.2
Reg.14, amended: SI 1997/3035 Reg.2
Reg.16, substituted: SI 1997/3035 Reg.2
Reg.17, amended: SI 1997/3035 Reg.2
Reg.20, revoked: SI 1997/3035 Reg.2
Reg.21, amended: SI 1997/3035 Reg.2
Reg.22, amended: SI 1997/3035 Reg.2
Reg.22, revoked (in part): SI 1997/3035 Reg.2
Reg.23, amended: SI 1997/3035 Reg.2
Reg.26, substituted: SI 1997/3035 Reg.2
Reg.26A, added: SI 1997/3035 Reg.2
Reg.27A, added: SI 1997/3035 Reg.2
Reg.28, substituted: SI 1998/2994 Reg.2
Reg.29, substituted: SI 1998/2994 Reg.2
Reg.30, substituted: SI 1998/2994 Reg.2
Reg.31, substituted: SI 1998/2994 Reg.2
Reg.32, substituted: SI 1998/2994 Reg.2
Reg.33, substituted: SI 1998/2994 Reg.2
Reg.34, substituted: SI 1998/2994 Reg.2
Reg.35, substituted: SI 1998/2994 Reg.2
Reg.36, substituted: SI 1998/2994 Reg.2
Reg.37, substituted: SI 1998/2994 Reg.2

1995—cont.

1907. Non-automatic Weighing Instruments (EEC Requirements) Regulations 1995—cont.
Reg.38, amended: SI 1997/3035 Reg.2
Reg.40, amended: SI 1997/3035 Reg.2

1924. Broadcasting (Restrictions on the Holding of Licences) (Amendment) Order 1995
revoked: 1996 c.55 Sch.11 Part II, SI 1996/2120 Sch.2

1928. Specified Bovine Offal Order 1995
revoked: SI 1996/963 Art.27

1945. Fees in the Registers of Scotland Order 1995
Art.2, amended: SI 1999/1085 Art.2
Sch. Part I, amended: SI 1999/1085 Art.3
Sch. Part II, amended: SI 1999/1085 Art.4
Sch. Part XII, amended: SI 1999/1085 Art.5

1948. Local Government Elections (Changes to the Franchise and Qualification of Members) Regulations 1995
Sch.2 para.27, revoked: SI 1999/1214 Reg.20, Sch.5

1953. Employment Protection (Increase of Limits) Order 1995
revoked: SI 1998/924 Art.2
Art.2, revoked: SI 1998/924 Art.2
Art.3, applied: 1996 c.18 Sch.2 para.8
Art.3, revoked: SI 1998/924 Art.2

1954. Housing Benefit (Permitted Totals) Order 1995
revoked: SI 1996/677 Art.6
Art.4, revoked: SI 1996/677 Art.6
Art.4A, revoked: SI 1996/677 Art.6

1956. Offshore Installations (Safety Zones) (No.4) Order 1995
revoked: SI 1997/735 Art.3, Sch.2

1959. Legal Officers (Annual Fees) Order 1995
revoked: SI 1996/3084 Art.3
Art.3, revoked: SI 1996/3084 Art.3
Sch. Table I, revoked: SI 1996/3084 Art.3
Sch. Table I, substituted: SI 1996/3084 Sch. Table I
Sch. Table II, revoked: SI 1996/3084 Art.3
Sch. Table II, substituted: SI 1996/3084 Sch. Table II

1960. Parochial Fees Order 1995
revoked: SI 1996/1994 Art.4

1961. Ecclesiastical Judges and Legal Officers (Fees) Order 1995
applied: SI 1996/3085 Sch. Table VI
revoked: SI 1996/3085 Art.2
Art.2, revoked: SI 1996/3085 Art.2

1969. Appropriation (No.2) (Northern Ireland) Order 1995
revoked: SI 1998/1758 (NI.12) Art.6, Sch.2

1970. Air Navigation (No.2) Order 1995
referred to: SI 1998/2284 Reg.3
Art.3, amended: SI 1998/753 Art.2
Art.4, amended: SI 1996/1301 Art.2
Art.8, amended: SI 1999/1123 Art.3
Art.10, amended: SI 1998/753 Art.2
Art.15, amended: SI 1999/1123 Art.3
Art.20, amended: SI 1996/1301 Art.2, SI 1998/ 753 Art.2
Art.21, amended: SI 1996/1301 Art.2, SI 1998/ 753 Art.2, SI 1999/1123 Art.3, SI 1999/2059 Art.3
Art.22, substituted: SI 1999/2059 Art.3
Art.22A, added: SI 1999/2059 Art.3
Art.22B, added: SI 1999/2059 Art.3
Art.22C, added: SI 1999/2059 Art.3
Art.22D, added: SI 1999/2059 Art.3
Art.23, amended: SI 1999/2059 Art.3
Art.25, amended: SI 1999/2059 Art.3
Art.32A, added: SI 1998/753 Art.2

1995—cont.

1970. Air Navigation (No.2) Order 1995—cont.
Art.34, substituted: SI 1997/287 Art.2
Art.41, amended: SI 1999/1123 Art.3
Art.41, revoked (in part): SI 1998/753 Art.2
Art.42, substituted: SI 1997/287 Art.2
Art.44A, added: SI 1999/1123 Art.4
Art.48, applied: SI 1996/1393 Sch.1 r.5
Art.50, applied: SI 1996/1393 Sch.1 r.5
Art.51, amended: SI 1997/287 Art.2
Art.54, amended: SI 1996/1301 Art.2
Art.55, see *R. v Whitehouse (Neil)* Times, December 10, 1999 (CA), Pill, L.J.
Art.59, amended: SI 1996/1301 Art.2
Art.59A, added: SI 1999/2059 Art.4
Art.61, applied: SI 1996/1393 Sch.1 r.5
Art.61, substituted: SI 1999/1123 Art.5
Art.62, amended: SI 1999/1123 Art.6
Art.68, amended: SI 1996/1301 Art.2
Art.74, applied: SI 1996/1393 Sch.1 r.31
Art.75, amended: SI 1999/1123 Art.5
Art.76A, added: SI 1996/1301 Art.2
Art.83, amended: SI 1998/753 Art.2
Art.84, amended: SI 1996/1301 Art.2
Art.87, amended: SI 1999/1123 Art.7
Art.88, amended: SI 1999/1123 Art.7
Art.89, amended: SI 1999/1123 Art.7
Art.102, see *H5 Air Service Norway AS v Civil Aviation Authority* [1998] 1 Lloyd's Rep. 364 (CA), Evans, L.J.
Art.102, referred to: SI 1999/2018 Reg.3, SI 1999/3166 Reg.4
Art.106, amended: SI 1996/1301 Art.2, SI 1999/ 1123 Art.8
Art.111, amended: SI 1996/1301 Art.2, SI 1999/ 1123 Art.10
Art.113, amended: SI 1996/1301 Art.2
Art.115, amended: SI 1999/1123 Art.6
Art.117, amended: SI 1999/1123 Art.7
Art.118, amended: SI 1996/1301 Art.2, SI 1997/ 287 Art.2, SI 1998/753 Art.2, SI 1999/1123 Art.3, Art.5, Art.7, SI 1999/2059 Art.3
Art.118, revoked (in part): SI 1996/1301 Art.2
Art.119, amended: SI 1996/1301 Art.2, SI 1999/ 1123 Art.5
Art.121, substituted: SI 1996/1301 Art.2
Sch.4 para.4, amended: SI 1996/1301 Art.2
Sch.4 para.4, revoked (in part): SI 1996/1301 Art.2
Sch.4 para.5, amended: SI 1998/753 Art.2
Sch.5 para.2, amended: SI 1996/1301 Art.2
Sch.5 para.2, substituted: SI 1998/753 Art.2, SI 1999/1123 Art.4
Sch.5 para.4, amended: SI 1999/1123 Art.4
Sch.6 para.1, amended: SI 1998/753 Art.2
Sch.7, amended: SI 1997/287 Art.2
Sch.8, substituted: SI 1999/2059 Art.3
Sch.8 Part A, amended: SI 1996/1301 Art.2, SI 1998/753 Art.2
Sch.8 Part B, amended: SI 1996/1301 Art.2, SI 1998/753 Art.2
Sch.9 para.2, amended: SI 1997/287 Art.2
Sch.10 Part A, amended: SI 1999/1123 Art.4
Sch.10 Part B, amended: SI 1997/287 Art.2
Sch.11, amended: SI 1997/287 Art.2, SI 1998/ 753 Art.2
Sch.12 Part A, amended: SI 1996/1301 Art.2, SI 1997/287 Art.2, SI 1998/753 Art.2, SI 1999/ 1123 Art.4, Art.5, Art.9, SI 1999/2059 Art.4
Sch.12 Part B, amended: SI 1999/2059 Art.4

NO.

1995—cont.

1973. Local Government Act 1988 (Defined Activities) (Cleaning of Police Buildings) (England and Wales) Regulations 1995
Reg.5, revoked: SI 1997/2747 Reg.2, Sch.

1979. Venture Capital Trust Regulations 1995
Part III Ch.II, revoked: SI 1999/819 Reg.4
Reg.2, amended: SI 1999/819 Reg.3
Reg.10, revoked: SI 1999/819 Reg.4
Reg.11, revoked: SI 1999/819 Reg.4
Reg.12, revoked: SI 1999/819 Reg.4
Reg.13, revoked: SI 1999/819 Reg.4
Reg.14, revoked: SI 1999/819 Reg.4
Reg.15, revoked: SI 1999/819 Reg.4
Reg.16, revoked: SI 1999/819 Reg.4
Reg.17, revoked: SI 1999/819 Reg.4
Reg.18, revoked: SI 1999/819 Reg.4
Reg.19, revoked: SI 1999/819 Reg.4
Reg.20, revoked: SI 1999/819 Reg.4
Reg.21, revoked: SI 1999/819 Reg.4
Reg.21A, added: SI 1999/819 Reg.5
Reg.22, amended: SI 1999/819 Reg.6

1980. Trade Union and Labour Relations (Northern Ireland) Order 1995
applied: SI 1999/2790 (NI.9) Art.24
referred to: SI 1999/2790 (NI.9) Art.12, Art.21
Art.2, amended: SI 1996/1919 (NI.16) Art.255, Sch.1
Art.2, revoked (in part): SI 1996/1919 (NI.16) Art.257, Sch.3
Art.3, amended: SI 1999/2790 (NI.9) Art.28, Art.40, Sch.6 para.7, Sch.9 Part 7
Art.4, amended: SI 1999/2790 (NI.9) Art.28, Art.40, Sch.6 para.8, Sch.9 Part 7
Art.5, amended: SI 1999/2790 (NI.9) Art.28, Art.40, Sch.6 para.9, Sch.9 Part 7
Art.6, amended: SI 1999/2790 (NI.9) Art.28, Sch.6 para.10
Art.6, revoked (in part): SI 1999/2790 (NI.9) Art.28, Art.40, Sch.6 para.10, Sch.9 Part 7
Art.21, amended: SI 1999/2790 (NI.9) Art.28, Art.40, Sch.6 para.11, Sch.9 Part 7
Art.22, amended: SI 1999/2790 (NI.9) Art.28, Art.40, Sch.6 para.12, Sch.9 Part 3
Art.23, amended: SI 1999/2790 (NI.9) Art.28, Sch.6 para.13
Art.23, revoked (in part): SI 1999/2790 (NI.9) Art.28, Art.40, Sch.6 para.13, Sch.9 Part 7
Art.31, applied: SI 1996/1921 (NI.18) Art.20
Art.32, amended: SI 1999/2790 (NI.9) Art.40, Sch.9 Part 6
Art.34, amended: SI 1996/1919 (NI.16) Art.255, Sch.1
Art.35, amended: SI 1996/1919 (NI.16) Art.255, Sch.1
Art.35, applied: SI 1996/1921 (NI.18) Art.20, SI 1999/691 (NI.5) Art.4
Art.35, substituted: SI 1999/661 (NI.5) Art.3
Art.36, amended: SI 1996/1919 (NI.16) Art.255, Sch.1, SI 1999/691 (NI.5) Art.3
Art.38, applied: SI 1996/1921 (NI.18) Art.20
Art.40, amended: SI 1996/1919 (NI.16) Art.255, Sch.1
Art.40, referred to: SI 1999/2790 (NI.9) Art.33
Art.42, revoked: SI 1996/1919 (NI.16) Art.257, Sch.3
Art.43, revoked: SI 1996/1919 (NI.16) Art.257, Sch.3
Art.44A, added: SI 1999/2790 (NI.9) Art.3
Art.44B, added: SI 1999/2790 (NI.9) Art.7
Art.44C, added: SI 1999/2790 (NI.9) Art.7
Art.46A, added: SI 1999/2790 (NI.9) Art.28, Sch.6 para.14
Art.54, amended: SI 1999/2790 (NI.9) Art.28, Art.40, Sch.6 para.15, Sch.9 Part 7

NO.

1995—cont.

1980. Trade Union and Labour Relations (Northern Ireland) Order 1995—*cont.*
Art.55, amended: SI 1999/2790 (NI.9) Art.28, Art.40, Sch.6 para.16, Sch.9 Part 7
Art.56, amended: SI 1999/2790 (NI.9) Art.28, Sch.6 para.17
Art.56, revoked (in part): SI 1999/2790 (NI.9) Art.28, Art.40, Sch.6 para.17, Sch.9 Part 7
Art.57, amended: SI 1999/2790 (NI.9) Art.28, Sch.6 para.18
Art.61, substituted: SI 1998/1265 (NI.8) Art.7
Art.62, amended: SI 1996/1919 (NI.16) Art.255, Sch.1
Art.62, referred to: SI 1998/1265 (NI.8) Art.16, Sch.2
Art.62, revoked: SI 1998/1265 (NI.8) Art.16, Sch.2
Art.69, amended: SI 1999/2790 (NI.9) Art.40, Sch.9 Part 7
Art.72, amended: SI 1999/2790 (NI.9) Art.28, Sch.6 para.19
Art.84, amended: SI 1999/2790 (NI.9) Art.28, Sch.6 para.20
Art.85, amended: SI 1999/2790 (NI.9) Art.40, Sch.9 Part 7
Art.90, amended: SI 1999/2790 (NI.9) Art.28, Sch.6 para.21
Art.90A, added: SI 1999/2790 (NI.9) Art.28, Sch.6 para.22
Art.90B, added: SI 1999/2790 (NI.9) Art.28, Sch.6 para.22
Art.104, amended: SI 1999/2790 (NI.9) Art.6, Art.40, Sch.3 para.2, Sch.9 Part 1
Art.105, amended: SI 1999/2790 (NI.9) Art.6, Sch.3 para.3
Art.108, revoked (in part): SI 1999/2790 (NI.9) Art.6, Art.40, Sch.3 para.4, Sch.9 Part 1
Art.109, substituted: SI 1999/2790 (NI.9) Art.6, Sch.3 para.5
Art.109A, added: SI 1999/2790 (NI.9) Art.6, Sch.3 para.5
Art.110, amended: SI 1999/2790 (NI.9) Art.6, Sch.3 para.6
Art.111, amended: SI 1999/2790 (NI.9) Art.6, Sch.3 para.7
Art.115A, added: SI 1999/2790 (NI.9) Art.6, Sch.3 para.8
Art.115B, added: SI 1999/2790 (NI.9) Art.6, Sch.3 para.9
Art.117, amended: SI 1999/2790 (NI.9) Art.6, Sch.3 para.10
Art.118, amended: SI 1999/2790 (NI.9) Art.6, Art.40, Sch.3 para.11, Sch.9 Part 1
Art.121, revoked: SI 1999/2790 (NI.9) Art.27, Art.40, Sch.9 Part 6
Art.122, revoked: SI 1999/2790 (NI.9) Art.27, Art.40, Sch.9 Part 6
Art.129, amended: SI 1999/2790 (NI.9) Art.6, Sch.3 para.6
Art.136, revoked: SI 1996/1919 (NI.16) Art.257, Sch.3
Art.138, revoked (in part): SI 1999/2790 (NI.9) Art.40, Sch.9 Part 5
Art.141, amended: SI 1996/1919 (NI.16) Art.255, Sch.1, SI 1998/1265 (NI.8) Art.16, Sch.1 para.4
Art.144, amended: SI 1997/1177 (NI.7) Art.32, Sch.2
Art.145, referred to: 1998 c.32 s.56
Art.146, amended: SI 1996/1921 (NI.18) Art.26, Sch.1 para.11, SI 1998/1265 (NI.8) Art.9, Art.10, Art.11, Art.16, Sch.1 para.5

NO.

1980. Trade Union and Labour Relations (Northern Ireland) Order 1995—*cont.*
Art.148, revoked: SI 1996/1921 (NI.18) Art.28, Sch.3
Art.149, amended: SI 1999/2790 (NI.9) Art.7, Art.28, Sch.6 para.23
Part IVA, added: SI 1999/2790 (NI.9) Art.3
Part VIA, added: SI 1999/2790 (NI.9) Art.28, Sch.6 para.22
Part VII, revoked: SI 1999/2790 (NI.9) Art.27, Art.40, Sch.9 Part 6
Part IX, revoked: SI 1999/2790 (NI.9) Art.27, Art.40, Sch.9 Part 6
Sch.1, revoked: SI 1996/1919 (NI.16) Art.257, Sch.3
Sch.1A, added: SI 1999/2790 (NI.9) Art.3, Sch.1
Sch.1A para.163, revoked: SI 1999/2790 (NI.9) Art.40, Sch.9 Part 3
Sch.2, revoked (in part): SI 1996/1297 (NI.7) Art.23, Sch.5, SI 1996/1919 (NI.16) Art.257, Sch.3, SI 1999/2790 (NI.9) Art.40, Sch.9 Part 6
Sch.2 Art.56, revoked: SI 1996/1921 (NI.18) Art.28, Sch.3
Sch.2 Art.80, revoked: SI 1996/1921 (NI.18) Art.28, Sch.3

1982. Local Authorities (Capital Finance and Approved Investments) (Amendment No.2) Regulations 1995
revoked (in part): SI 1997/319 Reg.162, Sch.3

1985. Local Government Pension Scheme (Local Government Reorganisation in Wales) Regulations 1995
applied: SI 1997/1613 Reg.4, Reg.19, Sch.2 para.2
referred to: SI 1996/532 Art.3, SI 1997/1613 Reg.3, Sch.2 para.6
Reg.1, amended: SI 1996/1428 Reg.28, SI 1997/1613 Reg.27, Sch.3 para.29, SI 1998/1831 Reg.13, Sch.2 para.1
Reg.3, amended: SI 1997/1613 Reg.27, Sch.3 para.30, SI 1998/1831 Reg.13, Sch.2 para.2
Reg.3, applied: SI 1997/1612 Sch.5
Reg.4, amended: SI 1997/1613 Reg.27, Sch.3 para.31
Reg.5, amended: SI 1997/1613 Reg.27, Sch.3 para.32
Reg.6, amended: SI 1997/1613 Reg.27, Sch.3 para.33

1987. Legal Advice and Assistance (Scope) (Amendment) Regulations 1995
revoked: SI 1997/997 Reg.6

1996. A1400 Trunk Road (Redbridge) Red Route Experimental Traffic Order 1995
revoked (in part): SI 1996/1892 Art.10

2004. Teachers' Superannuation (Amendment) Regulations 1995
applied: SI 1997/3001 Reg.H12, Sch.15 para.2
revoked: SI 1997/3001 Reg.H12, Sch.14

2005. Mines Miscellaneous Health and Safety Provisions Regulations 1995
Reg.2, amended: SI 1999/3242 Reg.29, Sch.2
Reg.4, amended: SI 1999/2463 Reg.17, SI 1999/3242 Reg.26, Reg.29, Sch.2
Reg.4, revoked (in part): SI 1999/3242 Reg.26

2006. Local Government (Publication of Staffing Information) (England) Regulations 1995
revoked: SI 1999/1267 Reg.2

NO.

2016. Education (Assisted Places) Regulations 1995
see *R. v Cobham Hall School Ex p. G* [1998] Ed. C.R. 79 (QBD), Dyson, J.
Part II, applied: SI 1997/1968 Reg.18, Reg.20
Reg.2, applied: SI 1997/1968 Reg.18, Reg.20
Reg.5, amended: SI 1996/2113 Reg.3
Reg.11, amended: SI 1996/2113 Reg.4
Reg.19, amended: SI 1996/2113 Reg.5
Reg.19, applied: SI 1997/1968 Reg.18
Reg.21, amended: SI 1996/2113 Reg.6
Reg.21, applied: SI 1997/1968 Reg.4
Sch.2 para.1, amended: SI 1996/2113 Reg.7
Sch.2 para.2, substituted: SI 1996/2113 Reg.7

2017. Education (Assisted Places) (Incidental Expenses) Regulations 1995
see *R. v Cobham Hall School Ex p. S* [1998] E.L.R. 389 (QBD), Dyson, J.
amended: SI 1996/2035 Reg.2
Reg.3, amended: SI 1996/2035 Reg.3
Reg.5, amended: SI 1996/2035 Reg.4
Reg.7, amended: SI 1996/2035 Reg.5
Reg.8, amended: SI 1996/2035 Reg.5
Reg.11, amended: SI 1996/2035 Reg.6

2018. Education (Grants) (Music, Ballet and Choir Schools) Regulations 1995
amended: SI 1996/2036 Reg.2
Reg.3, amended: SI 1996/2036 Reg.3
Sch.1, amended: SI 1996/2036 Reg.4
Sch.1 para.7, amended: SI 1997/1967 Reg.2
Sch.1 para.8, amended: SI 1997/1967 Reg.2, SI 1998/1583 Reg.3, SI 1999/1503 Reg.2
Sch.1 para.8, revoked (in part): SI 1997/1967 Reg.2
Sch.1 para.13, amended: SI 1996/2036 Reg.4, SI 1997/1967 Reg.2, SI 1998/1583 Reg.3, SI 1999/1503 Reg.2
Sch.1 para.14, amended: SI 1996/2036 Reg.4, SI 1997/1967 Reg.2, SI 1998/1583 Reg.3, SI 1999/1503 Reg.2
Sch.1 para.15, substituted: SI 1997/1967 Reg.2
Sch.1 para.16, substituted: SI 1997/1967 Reg.2
Sch.1 para.17, amended: SI 1996/2036 Reg.4, SI 1997/1967 Reg.2, SI 1998/1583 Reg.3
Sch.1 para.17, substituted: SI 1999/1503 Reg.2
Sch.1 para.19, amended: SI 1996/2036 Reg.4, SI 1997/1967 Reg.2, SI 1998/1583 Reg.3, SI 1999/1503 Reg.2
Sch.1 para.24, amended: SI 1996/2036 Reg.4
Sch.2 para.3, substituted: SI 1996/2036 Reg.5
Sch.2 para.12, amended: SI 1997/1967 Reg.3
Sch.3, amended: SI 1996/2036 Reg.6, SI 1998/1583 Reg.4

2036. Quarries Miscellaneous Health and Safety Provisions Regulations 1995
revoked: SI 1999/2024 Reg.48, Sch.5 Part I
Reg.2, amended: SI 1999/3242 Reg.29, Sch.2
Reg.4, amended: SI 1999/3242 Reg.29, Sch.2

2038. Borehole Sites and Operations Regulations 1995
applied: SI 1996/551 Reg.6
referred to: SI 1996/913 Reg.17
Reg.7, amended: SI 1999/2463 Reg.17, SI 1999/3242 Reg.29, Sch.2

2049. Financial Markets and Insolvency (Money Markets) Regulations 1995
referred to: SI 1998/27
Reg.2, amended: SI 1998/27 Reg.2, SI 1998/1129 Art.2, Sch.1 para.20
Reg.7, amended: SI 1998/1129 Art.2, Sch.1 para.20
Reg.8, amended: SI 1998/1129 Art.2, Sch.1 para.20

NO.

2049. Financial Markets and Insolvency (Money Markets) Regulations 1995—*cont.*
Reg.9, amended: SI 1998/1129 Art.2, Sch.1 para.20
Reg.10, amended: SI 1998/1129 Art.2, Sch.1 para.20
Reg.11, amended: SI 1998/1129 Art.2, Sch.1 para.20
Reg.12, amended: SI 1998/1129 Art.2, Sch.1 para.20
Reg.13, amended: SI 1998/1129 Art.2, Sch.1 para.20
Reg.14, amended: SI 1998/1129 Art.2, Sch.1 para.20
Reg.15, amended: SI 1998/1129 Art.2, Sch.1 para.20
Reg.16, amended: SI 1998/1129 Art.2, Sch.1 para.20
Reg.17, amended: SI 1998/1129 Art.2, Sch.1 para.20
Reg.18, amended: SI 1998/1129 Art.2, Sch.1 para.20
Reg.19, amended: SI 1998/1129 Art.2, Sch.1 para.20
Reg.27, amended: SI 1998/1129 Art.2, Sch.1 para.20
Reg.28, amended: SI 1998/1129 Art.2, Sch.1 para.20
Reg.29, revoked: SI 1998/1129 Art.2 (with savings), Sch.1 para.20 (with savings)

2052. Income Tax (Manufactured Dividends) (Tradepoint) Regulations 1995
revoked: SI 1997/987 Reg.6 (with savings)

2056. Charities (Dormant Accounts) (Scotland) Regulations 1995
Reg.2A, added: SI 1997/964 Reg.2
Reg.7, amended: SI 1997/964 Reg.2
Reg.7A, added: SI 1997/964 Reg.4
Reg.9, amended: SI 1997/964 Reg.5

2059. Dartford-Thurrock Crossing Tolls Order 1995
revoked: SI 1996/2046 Art.3

2060. Dartford-Thurrock Crossing (Amendment) Regulations 1995
revoked: SI 1998/1908 Reg.11, Sch.
Reg.2 Part I, revoked: SI 1998/1908 Reg.11, Sch.
Reg.2 Part I, substituted: SI 1996/2047 Reg.2
Reg.2 Part II, revoked: SI 1998/1908 Reg.11, Sch.
Reg.2 Part II, substituted: SI 1996/2047 Reg.2
Reg.3, amended: SI 1996/2047 Reg.3
Reg.3, revoked: SI 1998/1908 Reg.11, Sch.
Reg.4 Table, revoked: SI 1998/1908 Reg.11, Sch.
Reg.4 Table, substituted: SI 1996/2047 Reg.4

2061. Returning Officers (Parliamentary Constituencies) (England) Order 1995
Art.4A, added: SI 1996/898 Art.2
Sch.1, amended: SI 1996/898 Art.3, SI 1997/537 Art.2
Sch.2A, added: SI 1996/898 Art.4
Sch.2A, amended: SI 1997/537 Art.3
Sch.3, added: SI 1996/898 Art.5
Sch.3, amended: SI 1999/950 Art.2

2065. Education (Further Education Institutions Information) (England) Regulations 1995
Part III, revoked: SI 1998/2220 Reg.7
Reg.2, amended: SI 1998/2220 Reg.3, Reg.4
Reg.5, amended: SI 1998/2220 Reg.4, Reg.5
Reg.6, amended: SI 1997/2173 Reg.2, SI 1998/2220 Reg.6

NO.

2065. Education (Further Education Institutions Information) (England) Regulations 1995—*cont.*
Reg.7, revoked: SI 1998/2220 Reg.7
Reg.8, revoked: SI 1998/2220 Reg.7
Sch. para.2, revoked (in part): SI 1998/2220 Reg.8
Sch. para.3, revoked (in part): SI 1998/2220 Reg.8
Sch. para.4, revoked (in part): SI 1998/2220 Reg.8
Sch. para.5, revoked (in part): SI 1998/2220 Reg.8
Sch. para.6, revoked (in part): SI 1998/2220 Reg.8
Sch. para.7, revoked (in part): SI 1998/2220 Reg.8
Sch. para.8, revoked (in part): SI 1998/2220 Reg.8
Sch. para.9, revoked (in part): SI 1998/2220 Reg.8
Sch. para.10, amended: SI 1998/2220 Reg.8
Sch. para.10, revoked (in part): SI 1998/2220 Reg.8
Sch. para.11, amended: SI 1998/2220 Reg.8, SI 1999/2578 Reg.2
Sch. para.11, revoked (in part): SI 1998/2220 Reg.8

2070. Education (School Information) (Wales) (Amendment) Regulations 1995
revoked: SI 1997/1832 Reg.2

2071. Education (National Curriculum) (Assessment Arrangements for the Core Subjects) (Key Stage 1) (England) Order 1995
applied: SI 1997/514 Sch. para.2, SI 1997/2176 Art.3, SI 1998/656 Sch. para.6
revoked: SI 1999/1236 Art.2, Sch.
Art.3, amended: SI 1997/2176 Art.2
Art.3, revoked: SI 1999/1236 Art.2, Sch.
Art.4, amended: SI 1996/2114 Art.2
Art.4, revoked: SI 1999/1236 Art.2, Sch.
Art.5, amended: SI 1996/2114 Art.2
Art.5, applied: SI 1996/2577 Sch.1 para.1, SI 1998/1929 Sch.1 para.1, SI 1999/1178 Reg.5, Reg.6, Sch.1 para.1
Art.5, revoked: SI 1999/1236 Art.2, Sch.
Art.6, amended: SI 1997/1931 Art.3
Art.6, applied: SI 1996/734 Sch para.2, SI 1997/514 Sch. para.2, SI 1998/656 Sch. para.6
Art.6, revoked: SI 1999/1236 Art.2, Sch.
Art.7, applied: SI 1997/1368 Reg.4, Sch.1 para.1
Art.7, revoked: SI 1999/1236 Art.2, Sch.

2072. Education (National Curriculum) (Assessment Arrangements for the Core Subjects) (Key Stage 2) (England) Order 1995
applied: SI 1996/734 Sch para.2, Sch para.3, SI 1997/1368 Reg.4, SI 1997/2176 Art.3, SI 1999/1236 Art.7
revoked: SI 1999/2188 Art.2
Art.3, amended: SI 1996/2115 Art.2, SI 1997/2176 Art.2
Art.3, revoked: SI 1999/2188 Art.2
Art.4, amended: SI 1996/2115 Art.2
Art.4, revoked: SI 1999/2188 Art.2
Art.5, applied: SI 1997/1368 Sch.1 para.1, SI 1999/1178 Reg.13
Art.5, revoked: SI 1999/2188 Art.2
Art.5, substituted: SI 1996/2115 Art.2
Art.9, amended: SI 1996/2115 Art.2
Art.9, revoked: SI 1999/2188 Art.2

NO.

2073. Education (National Curriculum) (Assessment Arrangements for the Core Subjects) (Key Stage 3) (England) Order 1995
applied: SI 1996/734 Sch para.2
revoked: SI 1996/2116 Art.2

2074. Local Government Act 1988 (Security Work) (Exemption) (England) Order 1995
Art.2, amended: SI 1997/176 Art.3

2075. Motor Vehicles (Driving Licences) (Large Goods and Passenger-Carrying Vehicles) (Amendment) (No.2) Regulations 1995
revoked: SI 1996/2824 Reg.2, Sch.1

2076. Motor Vehicles (Driving Licences) (Amendment) (No.2) Regulations 1995
revoked: SI 1996/2824 Reg.2, Sch.1

2089. Education (Pupil Registration) Regulations 1995
applied: SI 1997/1832 Sch.2 para.26, SI 1998/1969 Reg.6, Reg.9
referred to: SI 1998/2876 Reg.4, SI 1999/1439 Reg.15, SI 1999/1811 Reg.7
Reg.2, amended: SI 1999/2267 Reg.8
Reg.7, amended: SI 1997/2624 Reg.3
Reg.8, revoked (in part): SI 1997/2624 Reg.4
Reg.9, amended: SI 1997/2624 Reg.5
Reg.10, amended: SI 1997/2624 Reg.6

2093. Patents Rules 1995
applied: SI 1996/2972 r.2, r.3, SI 1998/1778 r.3
referred to: SI 1998/1778 r.2
r.2, amended: SI 1999/1092 r.3
r.6, amended: SI 1999/1092 r.4, SI 1999/3197 r.4
r.7, amended: SI 1999/3197 r.3, r.5
r.8, amended: SI 1999/3197 r.3, r.6
r.12, amended: SI 1999/3197 r.3
r.13, amended: SI 1999/3197 r.3
r.14, amended: SI 1999/3197 r.3, r.7
r.22, amended: SI 1999/1092 r.5
r.24, see *Luk Lamellan und Kupplungsbau GmbH's Application (No.2), Re* [1997] R.P.C. 104 (Pat Ct), Nigel Pumfrey Q.C.
r.24, amended: SI 1999/1092 r.6, SI 1999/3197 r.8
r.24, revoked (in part): SI 1999/3197 r.8
r.25, amended: SI 1999/3197 r.9
r.32, amended: SI 1999/3197 r.10
r.38, amended: SI 1999/3197 r.11
r.39, amended: SI 1999/3197 r.12
r.40, amended: SI 1999/3197 r.3
r.41, applied: SI 1996/2972 Sch Part A, SI 1998/1778 r.3, Sch. Part A
r.43, amended: SI 1999/3197 r.3, r.13
r.44, amended: SI 1999/3197 r.14
r.46, amended: SI 1999/3197 r.15
r.48, applied: SI 1998/1778 r.3, Sch. Part A
r.49, amended: SI 1999/1092 r.7
r.49, applied: SI 1996/2972 Sch Part A, SI 1998/1778 r.3, Sch. Part A
r.53, applied: SI 1996/2972 Sch Part A, SI 1998/1778 r.3, Sch. Part A
r.54, amended: SI 1999/3197 r.3, r.16
r.58, amended: SI 1999/3197 r.3
r.59, amended: SI 1999/3197 r.3
r.62, amended: SI 1999/3197 r.3
r.68, applied: SI 1999/1899 Reg.12
r.68, substituted: SI 1999/1899 Reg.9
r.70, applied: SI 1999/1899 Reg.12
r.70, substituted: SI 1999/1899 Reg.10
r.71, amended: SI 1999/1899 Reg.11, SI 1999/3197 r.3
r.71, applied: SI 1999/1899 Reg.12
r.72, amended: SI 1999/3197 r.3
r.73, amended: SI 1999/3197 r.3

NO.

2093. Patents Rules 1995—*cont.*
r.74, amended: SI 1999/3197 r.3
r.75, amended: SI 1999/3197 r.3
r.78, amended: SI 1999/1092 r.8
r.79, applied: SI 1996/2972 Sch Part A, SI 1998/1778 r.3, Sch. Part A
r.79, revoked (in part): SI 1999/1092 r.9
r.81, applied: SI 1996/2972 Sch Part A, SI 1998/1778 r.3, Sch. Part A
r.85, amended: SI 1999/1092 r.10, SI 1999/3197 r.17
r.85, applied: SI 1996/2972 Sch Part A, SI 1998/1778 r.3, Sch. Part A
r.86, applied: SI 1996/2972 Sch Part A, SI 1998/1778 r.3, Sch. Part A
r.88, amended: SI 1999/3197 r.18
r.93, applied: SI 1996/2972 Sch Part A, SI 1998/1778 r.3, Sch. Part A
r.98, amended: SI 1999/1092 r.11
r.99, amended: SI 1999/1092 r.12
r.100, see *Luk Lamellan und Kupplungsbau GmbH's Application (No.2), Re* [1997] R.P.C. 104 (Pat Ct), Nigel Pumfrey Q.C.
r.102, amended: SI 1999/1092 r.13
r.103, amended: SI 1999/3197 r.19
r.104A, added: SI 1999/3197 r.20
r.110, see *Luk Lamellan und Kupplungsbau GmbH's Application (No.2), Re* [1997] R.P.C. 104 (Pat Ct), Nigel Pumfrey Q.C.
r.110, amended: SI 1999/1092 r.14, SI 1999/3197 r.21
r.110, applied: SI 1996/2972 Sch Part A, SI 1998/1778 r.3, Sch. Part A
r.115, substituted: SI 1999/1092 r.15
r.118, amended: SI 1999/1092 r.16
r.118, applied: SI 1996/2972 Sch Part A, SI 1998/1778 r.3, Sch. Part A
r.119, amended: SI 1999/1092 r.17
Sch.1, amended: SI 1999/1092 r.18
Sch.1 Form 12/77, substituted: SI 1999/3197 r.22, Sch.
Sch.3, revoked: SI 1999/3197 r.23

2101. Local Government Act 1988 (Competition) (Personnel Services) (England) Regulations 1995
Reg.2, amended: SI 1997/175 Reg.7, SI 1997/2732 Reg.8
Reg.3, amended: SI 1997/175 Reg.7, SI 1997/2732 Reg.8

2125. Agricultural Holdings (Units of Production) Order 1995
revoked: SI 1996/2163 Art.3

2144. Civil Aviation (Canadian Navigation Services) (Amendment) Regulations 1995
revoked: SI 1996/688 Reg.3, Sch.1

2145. Swansea Bay Mussel Fishery Order 1995
Art.6, amended: SI 1996/362 Art.5, Sch.4

2148. Wild Game Meat (Hygiene and Inspection) Regulations 1995
applied: SI 1996/3124 Reg.3, Reg.10, Sch.2 para.10, SI 1999/646 Art.33, SI 1999/680 Art.2, Sch. Part I

2164. Patents (Fees) Rules 1995
revoked: SI 1996/2972 r.1

2181. Goods Vehicles (Licensing of Operators) Act 1995 (Commencement and Transitional Provisions) Order 1995
referred to: SI 1996/2186 Reg.31

NO.

2192. Social Security (Unemployment, Sickness and Invalidity Benefit) Amendment Regulations 1995
revoked: SI 1996/1345 Reg.27, Sch.

2193. Conon Salmon Fishery District Designation Order 1995
revoked: SI 1999/1381 Art.1

2194. Alness Salmon Fishery District Designation Order 1995
revoked: SI 1999/1381 Art.1

2195. Land Drainage Improvement Works (Assessment of Environmental Effects) (Amendment) Regulations 1995
revoked: SI 1999/1783 Reg.15

2200. Food Safety (Temperature Control) Regulations 1995
Reg.2, amended: SI 1996/1499 Reg.49, SI 1998/1398 Reg.18
Reg.3, amended: SI 1998/994 Reg.58
Reg.3, revoked (in part): SI 1998/994 Reg.58

2202. Rural Development Grants (Agriculture) (No.2) Regulations 1995
Reg.2, amended: SI 1996/2394 Reg.2
Reg.5, amended: SI 1996/2394 Reg.2
Reg.11, amended: SI 1996/2394 Reg.2
Sch. para.1, amended: SI 1996/2394 Reg.2
Sch. para.2, amended: SI 1996/2394 Reg.2
Sch. para.10, added: SI 1996/2394 Reg.2

2207. Education (National Curriculum) (Assessment Arrangements for English, Welsh, Mathematics and Science) (Key Stage 1) (Wales) Order 1995
revoked: SI 1997/2011 Art.2
Art.4, applied: SI 1997/390 Sch para.2
Art.4, revoked: SI 1997/2011 Art.2
Art.5, applied: SI 1997/390 Sch para.2
Art.5, revoked: SI 1997/2011 Art.2
Art.6, applied: SI 1997/390 Sch para.2
Art.6, revoked: SI 1997/2011 Art.2
Art.7, applied: SI 1997/390 Sch para.2
Art.7, revoked: SI 1997/2011 Art.2
Art.8, applied: SI 1997/390 Sch para.2
Art.8, revoked: SI 1997/2011 Art.2
Art.9, applied: SI 1997/390 Sch para.2
Art.9, revoked: SI 1997/2011 Art.2
Art.10, applied: SI 1997/390 Sch para.2
Art.10, revoked: SI 1997/2011 Art.2
Art.11, applied: SI 1997/390 Sch para.2
Art.11, revoked: SI 1997/2011 Art.2

2208. Education (National Curriculum) (Assessment Arrangements for English, Welsh, Mathematics and Science) (Key Stage 2) (Wales) Order 1995
revoked: SI 1997/2009 Art.2
Art.4, applied: SI 1997/390 Sch para.2
Art.4, revoked: SI 1997/2009 Art.2
Art.5, applied: SI 1997/390 Sch para.2
Art.5, revoked: SI 1997/2009 Art.2
Art.6, applied: SI 1997/390 Sch para.2
Art.6, revoked: SI 1997/2009 Art.2
Art.7, applied: SI 1997/390 Sch para.2
Art.7, revoked: SI 1997/2009 Art.2
Art.8, applied: SI 1997/390 Sch para.2
Art.8, revoked: SI 1997/2009 Art.2
Art.9, applied: SI 1997/390 Sch para.2
Art.9, revoked: SI 1997/2009 Art.2

2209. Education (National Curriculum) (Assessment Arrangements for English, Welsh, Mathematics and Science) (Key Stage 3) (Wales) Order 1995
revoked: SI 1996/2337 Art.2

NO.

2245. A13 Trunk Road (Tower Hamlets) Red Route Experimental Traffic Order 1995
revoked (in part): SI 1996/1891 Art.10

2246. A406 Trunk Road (Enfield) Red Route Experimental Traffic Order 1995
revoked (in part): SI 1996/2543 Art.10

2249. Local Government Pension Scheme (Pensionable Remuneration Amendment) Regulations 1995
applied: SI 1997/1613 Reg.4, Reg.19, Sch.2 para.2
referred to: SI 1997/1613 Reg.3, Sch.2 para.6

2258. Town and Country Planning (Environmental Assessment and Unauthorised Development) Regulations 1995
applied: SI 1999/672 Art.2, Sch.1
referred to: SI 1997/420 Reg.4
revoked: SI 1999/293 Reg.34, Sch.5

2259. Town and Country Planning (Determination of Appeals by Appointed Persons) (Prescribed Classes) (Amendment) Regulations 1995
revoked: SI 1997/420 Reg.6, Sch

2262. Acquisition of Land (Rate of Interest after Entry) Regulations 1995
Reg.2, amended: SI 1998/1129 Art.3, Sch.2

2287. Income Support (General) Amendment and Transitional Regulations 1995
Reg.3, applied: SI 1996/207 Sch.2 para.18

2288. Gaming Act (Variation of Monetary Limits) (No.2) Order 1995
Art.2, revoked: SI 1997/2079 Art.4
Sch., revoked (in part): SI 1997/2079 Art.4

2303. Income-related Benefits Schemes and Social Security (Claims and Payments) (Miscellaneous Amendments) Regulations 1995
Reg.6, revoked (in part): SI 1996/206 Reg.28, Sch.3
Reg.7, applied: SI 1996/1217 Art.8, SI 1997/1004 Art.8
Reg.7, referred to: SI 1997/1004 Art.8

2306. Residuary Body for Wales (Levies) Regulations 1995
revoked: SI 1996/2900 Reg.11
Reg.9, amended: SI 1998/1129 Art.3, Sch.2

2307. National Health Service (Optical Charges and Payments) Amendment (No.3) Regulations 1995
revoked: SI 1997/818 Reg.24, Sch.4
Reg.2, revoked: SI 1997/818 Reg.24, Sch.4

2320. Criminal Legal Aid (Scotland) Amendment Regulations 1995
revoked: SI 1996/2555 Reg.3, Sch.

2328. Motor Vehicles (EC Type Approval) (Amendment) Regulations 1995
revoked: SI 1998/2051 Reg.2, Sch.3
Reg.2, revoked: SI 1998/2051 Reg.2, Sch.3

2351. Customs Reviews and Appeals (Binding Tariff Information) Regulations 1995
revoked: SI 1997/534 Reg.7

2352. National Health Service (Travelling Expenses and Remission of Charges) Amendment No.2 Regulations 1995
revoked: SI 1996/410 Reg.11
Reg.2, revoked: SI 1996/410 Reg.11

2360. Gaming Act (Variation of Monetary Limits) (Scotland) (No.2) Order 1995
Art.2, revoked: SI 1997/2079 Art.4
Sch., revoked (in part): SI 1997/2079 Art.4

NO.

2361. **Rent Officers (Additional Functions) (Scotland) Amendment Order 1995**
revoked: SI 1997/1995 Art.9, Sch.5

2363. **Offshore Installations (Safety Zones) (No.5) Order 1995**
revoked: SI 1997/735 Art.3, Sch.2

2364. **Medicines (Products for Animal Use - Fees) Regulations 1995**
revoked: SI 1997/1469 Reg.21
Reg.2, amended: SI 1996/2196 Reg.3
Reg.2, revoked: SI 1997/1469 Reg.21
Sch.1 Part I, amended: SI 1996/2196 Reg.4
Sch.1 Part I, revoked: SI 1997/1469 Reg.21
Sch.1 Part II, amended: SI 1996/2196 Reg.5
Sch.1 Part II, revoked: SI 1997/1469 Reg.21
Sch.1 Part IV, amended: SI 1996/2196 Reg.6
Sch.1 Part IV, revoked: SI 1997/1469 Reg.21
Sch.1 Part V, amended: SI 1996/2196 Reg.7
Sch.1 Part V, revoked: SI 1997/1469 Reg.21

2365. **Rent Officers (Additional Functions) (Amendment) Order 1995**
revoked: SI 1997/1984 Art.9
Art.2, revoked: SI 1997/1984 Art.9
Art.3, revoked: SI 1997/1984 Art.9

2369. **National Health Service (Optical Charges and Payments) (Scotland) Amendment (No.3) Regulations 1995**
revoked: SI 1998/642 Reg.24, Sch.4

2374. **Betting and Gaming Duties Act 1981 (Monetary Amounts) Order 1995**
Art.4, revoked (in part): SI 1996/1422 Art.2, SI 1998/1839 Art.2
Art.5, revoked (in part): SI 1997/1714 Art.3

2381. **National Health Service (Travelling Expenses and Remission of Charges) (Scotland) Amendment (No.2) Regulations 1995**
revoked: SI 1996/429 Reg.11

2396. **Veterinary Surgeons (Examination of Commonwealth and Foreign Candidates) (Amendment) Regulations Order of Council 1995**
revoked: SI 1998/271 Art.2
Art.1, revoked: SI 1998/271 Art.2
Art.2, revoked: SI 1998/271 Art.2
Sch., revoked: SI 1998/271 Art.2, Sch. Reg.3

2428. **Animals and Animal Products (Import and Export) Regulations 1995**
amended: SI 1997/1881 Reg.17
applied: SI 1997/310 Art.4, SI 1997/1881 Reg.17
revoked: SI 1998/190 Reg.35
Part II, applied: SI 1996/2265 Reg.3, SI 1997/389 Reg.6
Part II, revoked: SI 1998/190 Reg.35
Part III, applied: SI 1997/639 Reg.3
Part III, revoked: SI 1998/190 Reg.35
Reg.1, amended: SI 1996/1008 Art.2, Sch para.17
Reg.1, revoked: SI 1998/190 Reg.35
Reg.5, amended: SI 1997/389 Reg.13
Reg.5, revoked: SI 1998/190 Reg.35
Reg.6, amended: SI 1996/2265 Reg.9
Reg.6, revoked (in part): SI 1997/389 Reg.13, SI 1998/190 Reg.35
Reg.10, amended: SI 1996/1111 Reg.2
Reg.10, applied: SI 1997/1881 Reg.15
Reg.10, revoked: SI 1998/190 Reg.35
Reg.12, revoked: SI 1998/190 Reg.35
Reg.17, revoked: SI 1998/190 Reg.35
Reg.33, revoked: SI 1998/190 Reg.35
Reg.34, revoked: SI 1998/190 Reg.35

NO.

2428. **Animals and Animal Products (Import and Export) Regulations 1995**—*cont.*
Sch.2, revoked: SI 1998/190 Reg.35
Sch.2, substituted: SI 1996/1111 Reg.3, Sch.1
Sch.3, applied: SI 1996/2265 Reg.3
Sch.3, revoked: SI 1998/190 Reg.35
Sch.3, substituted: SI 1996/1111 Reg.3, Sch.2
Sch.5, revoked: SI 1998/190 Reg.35
Sch.5, substituted: SI 1996/1111 Reg.3, Sch.3
Sch.6, revoked: SI 1998/190 Reg.35
Sch.6, substituted: SI 1996/1111 Reg.3, Sch.3

2437. **Third Country Fishing (Enforcement) (Amendment) Order 1995**
revoked: SI 1996/1036 Art.13

2443. **A20 Trunk Road (Greenwich) Red Route Experimental Traffic Order 1995**
revoked: SI 1996/2727 Art.10
Art.2, revoked: SI 1996/2727 Art.10
Art.8, revoked: SI 1996/2727 Art.10

2444. **A2 Trunk Road (Bexley) Red Route Experimental Traffic Order 1995**
revoked: SI 1996/2726 Art.10
Art.2, revoked: SI 1996/2726 Art.10
Art.8, revoked: SI 1996/2726 Art.10

2445. **A20 Trunk Road (Bexley and Bromley) Red Route Experimental Traffic Order 1995**
revoked: SI 1996/2728 Art.10
Art.2, revoked: SI 1996/2728 Art.10
Art.8, revoked: SI 1996/2728 Art.10

2478. **Bovine Embryo (Collection, Production and Transfer) Regulations 1995**
Reg.21, amended: SI 1996/3124 Reg.41, Sch.6 para.7

2480. **Education (School Information) (England) (Amendment) Regulations 1995**
revoked: SI 1996/2585 Reg.2

2484. **Local Government Act 1988 (Defined Activities) (Specified Periods) (England) Regulations 1995**
revoked: SI 1997/2747 Reg.2, Sch.
Reg.3, revoked: SI 1997/2747 Reg.2, Sch.
Reg.4, revoked: SI 1997/2747 Reg.2, Sch.

2487. **Medical Devices Fees Regulations 1995**
Reg.6, amended: SI 1997/694 Reg.3
Sch. Table, amended: SI 1997/694 Reg.2

2498. **Merchant Shipping (Reporting Requirements for Ships Carrying Dangerous or Polluting Goods) Regulations 1995**
applied: SI 1996/2154 Reg.33, SI 1999/2029 Art.5, Art.6, Sch.1 Reg.35
Reg.2, amended: SI 1999/2121 Reg.2
Reg.3, amended: SI 1999/2121 Reg.3
Reg.5, amended: SI 1999/2121 Reg.4
Reg.6, amended: SI 1999/2121 Reg.5
Reg.9, amended: SI 1999/2121 Reg.6
Reg.12, amended: SI 1999/2121 Reg.7
Reg.15, amended: SI 1999/2121 Reg.8
Reg.15, revoked (in part): SI 1999/2121 Reg.8

2499. **Local Authorities (Property Transfer) (Scotland) Order 1995**
see *Stirling Council v Local Government Property Commission (Scotland)* 1998 S.L.T. 1396 (OH), Lord Bonomy
applied: SI 1996/682 Sch.2
referred to: SI 1996/682 Art.19
revoked: SI 1997/2880 Art.3
Art.1, revoked: SI 1997/2880 Art.3
Art.7A, added: SI 1996/578 Art.2
Art.7A, revoked: SI 1997/2880 Art.3
Art.10, revoked: SI 1997/2880 Art.3

NO.

2500. Local Government Property Commission (Scotland) Order 1995
referred to: SI 1997/2880 Art.2
revoked: SI 1997/2880 Art.3

2501. Low Moor Tramway Light Railway Order 1995
Art.10, amended: SI 1996/362 Art.5, Sch.4

2507. Motorways Traffic (Scotland) Regulations 1995
referred to: SI 1997/3053 Reg.18
Reg.3, amended: SI 1996/2664 Reg.3
Sch., added: SI 1996/2664 Reg.3

2517. Police (Discipline) (Amendment No.2) Regulations 1995
revoked: SI 1999/730 Reg.2 (with saving)

2518. Value Added Tax Regulations 1995
Part VA, added: SI 1998/59 Reg.2
Part VII, substituted: SI 1996/542 Art.3
Part XIX, amended: 1999 c.16 s.15
Part XIXA, added: SI 1997/1086 Reg.16
Part XVI (A), added: SI 1996/1250 Reg.13
Part XVIII, revoked: SI 1997/1086 Reg.9
Reg.2, amended: SI 1996/1250 Reg.4
Reg.6, amended: SI 1997/1086 Reg.3
Reg.9, amended: SI 1996/1250 Reg.5
Reg.13, amended: SI 1996/1250 Reg.6
Reg.14, amended: SI 1996/1250 Reg.7
Reg.21, revoked (in part): SI 1996/210 Reg.3
Reg.22, amended: SI 1996/210 Reg.4
Reg.22, revoked (in part): SI 1996/210 Reg.5, Reg.6
Reg.23, amended: SI 1996/210 Reg.7
Reg.24, amended: SI 1999/3114 Reg.3
Reg.29, see *BICC Plc v Customs and Excise Commissioners* [1998] B.V.C. 2120 (V & DT), Stephen Oliver Q.C. (Chairman)
Reg.29, amended: SI 1997/1086 Reg.4
Reg.31, amended: SI 1996/1250 Reg.8
Reg.31A, added: SI 1999/3114 Reg.4
Reg.31B, added: SI 1999/3114 Reg.4
Reg.31C, added: SI 1999/3114 Reg.4
Reg.33A, added: SI 1999/3114 Reg.5
Reg.33B, added: SI 1999/3114 Reg.5
Reg.34, amended: SI 1997/1086 Reg.5
Reg.38, amended: SI 1997/1086 Reg.6
Reg.40, substituted: SI 1996/1250 Reg.9
Reg.40A, added: SI 1996/1198 Reg.3
Reg.41, revoked (in part): SI 1996/1250 Reg.10
Reg.43, amended: SI 1996/1250 Reg.11
Reg.43A, added: SI 1998/59 Reg.2
Reg.43A, amended: SI 1999/438 Reg.3
Reg.43B, added: SI 1998/59 Reg.2
Reg.43B, amended: SI 1999/438 Reg.3, Reg.4
Reg.43C, added: SI 1998/59 Reg.2
Reg.43C, amended: SI 1999/438 Reg.3, Reg.5
Reg.43D, added: SI 1998/59 Reg.2
Reg.43D, amended: SI 1999/438 Reg.3, Reg.6
Reg.43E, added: SI 1998/59 Reg.2
Reg.43E, amended: SI 1999/438 Reg.3
Reg.43F, added: SI 1998/59 Reg.2
Reg.43F, amended: SI 1999/438 Reg.3, Reg.7
Reg.43G, added: SI 1998/59 Reg.2
Reg.43G, amended: SI 1999/438 Reg.3, Reg.8
Reg.43H, added: SI 1998/59 Reg.2
Reg.43H, amended: SI 1999/438 Reg.3, Reg.9
Reg.46A, added: SI 1996/1198 Reg.4
Reg.58, substituted: SI 1997/1614 Reg.3
Reg.59, amended: SI 1997/1614 Reg.4
Reg.60, substituted: SI 1997/1614 Reg.5
Reg.61, substituted: SI 1997/1614 Reg.6
Reg.62, substituted: SI 1997/1614 Reg.7
Reg.63, amended: SI 1997/1614 Reg.8

NO.

2518. Value Added Tax Regulations 1995—*cont.*
Reg.64, substituted: SI 1997/1614 Reg.9
Reg.67, see *United Norwest Co-Operative Ltd v Customs and Excise Commissioners* [1998] S.T.C. 1065 (QBD), Dyson, J.
Reg.70, revoked: SI 1997/2437 Reg.2
Reg.73, revoked: SI 1997/2437 Reg.2
Reg.74, revoked: SI 1997/2437 Reg.2
Reg.82, amended: SI 1997/1523 Art.4
Reg.82, applied: SI 1997/1523 Art.4
Reg.89, amended: SI 1997/2887 Reg.3
Reg.90, amended: SI 1997/1525 Reg.3, SI 1997/2887 Reg.4, SI 1998/765 Reg.2
Reg.90A, added: SI 1997/1525 Reg.4
Reg.90B, added: SI 1997/1525 Reg.4
Reg.93, substituted: SI 1997/2887 Reg.5, SI 1999/1374 Reg.2
Reg.94, amended: SI 1997/1525 Reg.5
Reg.94A, added: SI 1999/599 Reg.3
Reg.99, amended: SI 1999/3114 Reg.6
Reg.99, referred to: SI 1999/599 Reg.1
Reg.101, revoked (in part): SI 1996/1250 Reg.14
Reg.102, see *Kwik-Fit (GB) Ltd v Customs and Excise Commissioners* 1998 S.C. 139 (Ex Div), Lord McCluskey
Reg.103, amended: SI 1999/3114 Reg.7
Reg.103A, added: SI 1999/3114 Reg.8
Reg.105, revoked: SI 1999/599 Reg.4
Reg.107, amended: SI 1999/599 Reg.5
Reg.110, substituted: SI 1999/3114 Reg.9
Reg.111, amended: SI 1997/1086 Reg.7
Reg.112, amended: SI 1999/3114 Reg.10
Reg.113, amended: SI 1997/1614 Reg.10
Reg.114, amended: SI 1997/1614 Reg.11
Reg.114, revoked (in part): SI 1997/1614 Reg.11
Reg.115, amended: SI 1997/1086 Reg.8, SI 1997/1614 Reg.12, SI 1999/599 Reg.6
Reg.116, amended: SI 1997/1614 Reg.13
Reg.117, amended: SI 1996/210 Reg.8, SI 1999/438 Reg.10
Reg.117, revoked (in part): SI 1996/210 Reg.9, SI 1999/438 Reg.10
Reg.127, revoked: SI 1999/438 Reg.11
Reg.130, amended: SI 1999/438 Reg.12
Reg.145A, added: SI 1996/1250 Reg.13
Reg.145B, added: SI 1996/1250 Reg.13
Reg.145C, added: SI 1996/1250 Reg.13
Reg.145D, added: SI 1996/1250 Reg.13
Reg.145E, added: SI 1996/1250 Reg.13
Reg.145F, added: SI 1996/1250 Reg.13
Reg.145G, added: SI 1996/1250 Reg.13
Reg.145H, added: SI 1996/1250 Reg.13
Reg.145I, added: SI 1996/1250 Reg.13
Reg.145J, added: SI 1996/1250 Reg.13
Reg.156, revoked: SI 1997/1086 Reg.9
Reg.157, revoked: SI 1997/1086 Reg.9
Reg.158, revoked: SI 1997/1086 Reg.9
Reg.159, revoked: SI 1997/1086 Reg.9
Reg.160, revoked: SI 1997/1086 Reg.9
Reg.161, revoked: SI 1997/1086 Reg.9
Reg.162, revoked: SI 1997/1086 Reg.9
Reg.163, revoked: SI 1997/1086 Reg.9
Reg.164, revoked: SI 1997/1086 Reg.9
Reg.165A, added: SI 1997/1086 Reg.10
Reg.166, amended: SI 1997/1086 Reg.11
Reg.166A, added: SI 1997/1086 Reg.12
Reg.168, amended: SI 1997/1086 Reg.13
Reg.172, amended: SI 1996/2960 Reg.2, SI 1997/1086 Reg.14

NO.

1995—cont.

2518. Value Added Tax Regulations 1995—*cont.*
Reg.172A, added: SI 1997/1086 Reg.15
Reg.172B, added: SI 1997/1086 Reg.15
Reg.172C, added: SI 1997/1086 Reg.16
Reg.172D, added: SI 1997/1086 Reg.16
Reg.172E, added: SI 1997/1086 Reg.16
Reg.212, amended: SI 1996/2098 Reg.3
Reg.212, revoked: SI 1997/1431 Reg.3, Sch.3
Reg.A212, added: SI 1996/2098 Reg.3
Reg.213, amended: SI 1996/2098 Reg.3
s.165, amended: SI 1999/3029 Reg.3
s.171, amended: SI 1999/3029 Reg.4
s.171, referred to: 1999 c.16 s.15
Sch.1 Form 17, added: SI 1996/1250 Reg.15, Sch.1
Sch.1 Form 18, added: SI 1996/1250 Reg.15, Sch.1
Sch.1A, added: SI 1996/1250 Reg.16, Sch.2

2519. A2 Trunk Road (Bexley) Red Route (Clearway) Traffic Order 1995
Art.2, amended: SI 1999/272 Art.2, Sch. Part B
Art.9, amended: SI 1999/272 Art.2, Sch. Part B

2520. A2 Trunk Road (Greenwich) Red Route (Clearway) Traffic Order 1995
Art.2, amended: SI 1999/272 Art.2, Sch. Part B
Art.9, amended: SI 1999/272 Art.2, Sch. Part B

2521. A10 Trunk Road (Enfield) Red Route (Clearway) Traffic Order 1995
Art.2, amended: SI 1999/272 Art.2, Sch. Part B
Art.9, amended: SI 1999/272 Art.2, Sch. Part B

2522. A12 Trunk Road (Havering) Red Route (Clearway) Traffic Order 1995
Art.2, amended: SI 1999/272 Art.2, Sch. Part B
Art.9, amended: SI 1999/272 Art.2, Sch. Part B

2523. A12 Trunk Road (Redbridge and Barking & Dagenham) Red Route (Clearway) Traffic Order 1995
Art.2, amended: SI 1999/272 Art.2, Sch. Part B
Art.9, amended: SI 1999/272 Art.2, Sch. Part B

2524. A13 Trunk Road (Barking & Dagenham and Newham) Red Route (Clearway) Traffic Order 1995
Art.2, amended: SI 1999/272 Art.2, Sch. Part B
Art.9, amended: SI 1999/272 Art.2, Sch. Part B

2525. A13 Trunk Road (Havering) Red Route (Clearway) Traffic Order 1995
Art.2, amended: SI 1999/272 Art.2, Sch. Part B
Art.9, amended: SI 1999/272 Art.2, Sch. Part B

2526. A13 Trunk Road (Newham) Red Route (Clearway) Traffic Order 1995
Art.2, amended: SI 1999/272 Art.2, Sch. Part B
Art.9, amended: SI 1999/272 Art.2, Sch. Part B

2527. A20 Trunk Road (Bexley and Bromley) Red Route (Clearway) Traffic Order 1995
Art.2, amended: SI 1999/272 Art.2, Sch. Part B
Art.9, amended: SI 1999/272 Art.2, Sch. Part B

2528. A20 Trunk Road (Greenwich) Red Route (Clearway) Traffic Order 1995
Art.2, amended: SI 1999/272 Art.2, Sch. Part B
Art.9, amended: SI 1999/272 Art.2, Sch. Part B
Sch.2, revoked (in part): SI 1996/2727 Art.10

2529. A102 Trunk Road (Greenwich) Red Route (Clearway) Traffic Order 1995
Art.2, amended: SI 1999/272 Art.2, Sch. Part B
Art.9, amended: SI 1999/272 Art.2, Sch. Part B

2530. A102 Trunk Road (Tower Hamlets) Red Route (Clearway) Traffic Order 1995
Art.2, amended: SI 1999/272 Art.2, Sch. Part B
Art.9, amended: SI 1999/272 Art.2, Sch. Part B

NO.

1995—cont.

2531. A127 Trunk Road (Havering) Red Route (Clearway) Traffic Order 1995
Art.2, amended: SI 1999/272 Art.2, Sch. Part B
Art.9, amended: SI 1999/272 Art.2, Sch. Part B

2532. A406 Trunk Road (Enfield) Red Route (Clearway) Traffic Order 1995
Art.2, amended: SI 1999/272 Art.2, Sch. Part B
Art.9, amended: SI 1999/272 Art.2, Sch. Part B
Sch.3A, amended: SI 1996/2792 Art.2

2533. A406 Trunk Road (Redbridge) Red Route (Clearway) Traffic Order 1995
Art.2, amended: SI 1999/272 Art.2, Sch. Part B
Art.9, amended: SI 1999/272 Art.2, Sch. Part B

2534. A406 Trunk Road (Newham, Redbridge, Barking & Dagenham) Red Route (Clearway) Traffic Order 1995
Art.2, amended: SI 1999/272 Art.2, Sch. Part B
Art.9, amended: SI 1999/272 Art.2, Sch. Part B

2535. A406 Trunk Road (Waltham Forest) Red Route (Clearway) Traffic Order 1995
Art.2, amended: SI 1999/272 Art.2, Sch. Part B
Art.9, amended: SI 1999/272 Art.2, Sch. Part B

2536. A1400 Trunk Road (Redbridge) Red Route (Clearway) Traffic Order 1995
Art.2, amended: SI 1999/272 Art.2, Sch. Part B
Art.9, amended: SI 1999/272 Art.2, Sch. Part B

2559. Social Security (Effect of Family Credit on Earnings Factors) Regulations 1995
Reg.2, amended: SI 1999/2566 Reg.2, Sch.2 Part I, Sch.2 Part II

2561. Local Authorities (Calculation of Council Tax Base) (Wales) Regulations 1995
Reg.4, amended: SI 1999/2935 Reg.2
Reg.5, applied: SI 1999/2935 Reg.2

2562. Local Authorities (Precepts) (Wales) Regulations 1995
applied: SI 1996/2914 Art.10
Reg.5, amended: SI 1996/2914 Art.10, SI 1999/1289 Art.8
Reg.8, amended: SI 1998/1129 Art.3, Sch.2
Sch. Part II, amended: SI 1996/2914 Art.10, SI 1999/1289 Art.8

2587. Collective Redundancies and Transfer of Undertakings (Protection of Employment) (Amendment) Regulations 1995
see *R. v Secretary of State for Trade and Industry Ex p. UNISON* [1996] I.R.L.R. 438 (QBD), Otton, L.J.
applied: 1996 c.18 Sch.2 para.10
Reg.12, revoked (in part): 1996 c.17 Sch.3 Part II, 1996 c.18 Sch.3 Part II
Reg.13, revoked (in part): 1996 c.17 Sch.3 Part II, 1996 c.18 Sch.3 Part II
Reg.14, revoked (in part): 1996 c.17 Sch.3 Part II, 1996 c.18 Sch.3 Part II

2588. Wireless Telegraphy (Citizens' Band and Amateur Apparatus) (Various Provisions) (Amendment) Order 1995
revoked: SI 1998/2531 Art.2
Art.4, revoked: SI 1998/2531 Art.2
Art.5, revoked: SI 1998/2531 Art.2
Art.7, revoked: SI 1998/2531 Art.2
Sch.1, revoked: SI 1998/2531 Art.2

2589. Valuation Joint Boards (Scotland) Order 1995
applied: SI 1996/682 Art.18

2607. Measuring Instruments (EC Requirements) (Electrical Energy Meters) Regulations 1995
Reg.3, referred to: SI 1998/1565 Reg.3

NO.

NO.

2702. Child Support (Northern Ireland) Order 1995 —cont.

Sch.3 para.6, revoked: SI 1998/1506 (NI.10) Art.78, Sch.7

Sch.3 para.7, revoked (in part): SI 1998/1506 (NI.10) Art.78, Sch.7

Sch.3 para.14, revoked: SI 1998/1506 (NI.10) Art.78, Sch.7

2705. Jobseekers (Northern Ireland) Order 1995

applied: SI 1996/1927 Sch, 1997 c.16 s.110, SI 1997/932 Reg.2, 1998 c.29 s.56, SI 1998/1506 (NI.10) Art.4, Art.9, Art.12, Art.28, SI 1999/671 Art.8, SI 1999/1027 Reg.3

referred to: 1998 c.47 s.87, 1999 c.33 s.115, s.123, SI 1999/3147 (NI.11) Art.69

Art.2, amended: SI 1998/1506 (NI.10) Art.78, Sch.6 para.101, Sch.7, SI 1999/671 Art.4, Sch.3 para.53, SI 1999/3147 (NI.11) Art.56, Sch.7 para.2

Art.3, amended: SI 1999/3147 (NI.11) Art.56, Art.76, Sch.7 para.3, Sch.10 Part V

Art.4, amended: SI 1998/1506 (NI.10) Art.78, Sch.6 para.102, SI 1999/3147 (NI.11) Art.56, Sch.7 para.4

Art.5, amended: SI 1999/3147 (NI.11) Art.56, Sch.7 para.5

Art.5A, added: SI 1999/3147 (NI.11) Art.56, Sch.7 para.5

Art.5B, added: SI 1999/3147 (NI.11) Art.56, Sch.7 para.5

Art.6, amended: SI 1999/3147 (NI.11) Art.56, Art.67, Sch.7 para.6, Sch.8 para.27

Art.6A, added: SI 1999/3147 (NI.11) Art.56, Sch.7 para.7

Art.8, amended: SI 1998/1506 (NI.10) Art.78, Sch.6 para.103, Sch.7

Art.9, amended: SI 1998/1506 (NI.10) Art.78, Sch.6 para.104, Sch.7

Art.10, amended: SI 1999/3147 (NI.11) Art.56, Art.67, Sch.7 para.8, Sch.8 para.27

Art.11, amended: SI 1998/1506 (NI.10) Art.78, Sch.6 para.105, SI 1999/3147 (NI.11) Art.56, Sch.7 para.9

Art.11, applied: SI 1998/1506 (NI.10) Sch.3 para.8

Art.11, revoked (in part): SI 1998/1506 (NI.10) Art.78, Sch.6 para.105, Sch.7

Art.12, amended: SI 1998/1506 (NI.10) Art.78, Sch.6 para.106

Art.12, applied: SI 1998/1506 (NI.10) Sch.3 para.8

Art.12, revoked (in part): SI 1998/1506 (NI.10) Art.78, Sch.6 para.106, Sch.7

Art.13, revoked: SI 1998/1506 (NI.10) Art.78, Sch.6 para.107, Sch.7

Art.15, amended: SI 1999/3147 (NI.11) Art.56, Sch.7 para.10

Art.16, amended: SI 1996/1919 (NI.16) Art.255, Sch.1

Art.17A, added: SI 1999/3147 (NI.11) Art.56, Sch.7 para.11

Art.18, amended: SI 1998/1506 (NI.10) Art.78, Sch.6 para.108

Art.18, applied: SI 1998/1506 (NI.10) Sch.2 para.1

Art.19, amended: SI 1998/1506 (NI.10) Art.78, Sch.2 para.1, Sch.6 para.109, SI 1999/3147 (NI.11) Art.56, Art.67, Sch.7 para.12, Sch.8 para.27

Art.21, amended: SI 1996/1919 (NI.16) Art.255, Sch.1, SI 1998/1506 (NI.10) Art.78, Sch.6 para.110, SI 1999/3147 (NI.11) Art.56, Sch.7 para.13

NO.

2705. Jobseekers (Northern Ireland) Order 1995— cont.

Art.21, applied: SI 1997/932 Reg.4, SI 1998/1506 (NI.10) Sch.3 para.3, SI 1999/3147 (NI.11) Art.57

Art.21, referred to: SI 1997/932 Reg.5

Art.22, amended: SI 1998/1506 (NI.10) Art.77, Art.78, Sch.5 para.9, Sch.6 para.111, SI 1999/3147 (NI.11) Art.67, Sch.8 para.27

Art.22, applied: SI 1999/3147 (NI.11) Art.57

Art.22A, added: SI 1999/3147 (NI.11) Art.56, Sch.7 para.14

Art.22A, applied: SI 1999/3147 (NI.11) Art.57

Art.22B, added: SI 1999/3147 (NI.11) Art.56, Sch.7 para.14

Art.22B, applied: SI 1999/3147 (NI.11) Art.57

Art.28, applied: SI 1996/2890 Sch.4 para.49

Art.29, amended: SI 1999/671 Art.3, Art.4, Art.24, Sch.1 para.79, Sch.3 para.54, Sch.9 Part I

Art.29, applied: SI 1998/1506 (NI.10) Sch.3 para.24, SI 1999/671 Art.7

Art.30, revoked: SI 1998/1506 (NI.10) Art.78, Sch.7

Art.31, amended: 1999 c.10 s.1, Sch.1 para.6

Art.32, amended: SI 1998/1506 (NI.10) Art.78, Sch.6 para.112, SI 1999/3147 (NI.11) Art.56, Sch.7 para.15

Art.35, revoked (in part): SI 1997/1182 (NI.11) Art.19, Sch.2

Art.36, amended: SI 1999/671 Art.4, Sch.3 para.55

Art.37, amended: SI 1998/1506 (NI.10) Art.78, Sch.6 para.113, SI 1999/671 Art.4, Sch.3 para.56, SI 1999/3147 (NI.11) Art.67, Sch.8 para.27

Art.38, amended: SI 1999/671 Art.3, Sch.1 para.80

Art.38, amended: SI 1999/671 Art.4, Sch.3 para.57

Sch.1 para.6, amended: SI 1996/1919 (NI.16) Art.255, Sch.1

Sch.1 para.8A, added: SI 1999/3147 (NI.11) Art.56, Sch.7 para.16

Sch.1 para.9, amended: SI 1999/3147 (NI.11) Art.56, Sch.7 para.16

Sch.1 para.9A, added: SI 1999/3147 (NI.11) Art.56, Sch.7 para.16

Sch.1 para.9B, added: SI 1999/3147 (NI.11) Art.56, Sch.7 para.16

Sch.1 para.9C, added: SI 1999/3147 (NI.11) Art.56, Sch.7 para.16

Sch.1 para.9D, added: SI 1999/3147 (NI.11) Art.56, Sch.7 para.16

Sch.1 para.10, amended: SI 1998/1506 (NI.10) Art.77, Art.78, Sch.5 para.5, Sch.6 para.114, SI 1999/3147 (NI.11) Art.56, Art.67, Sch.7 para.16, Sch.8 para.27

Sch.2 para.1, referred to: SI 1996/1921 (NI.18) Sch.2 para.7

Sch.2 para.1, revoked: SI 1996/1921 (NI.18) Art.28, Sch.3

Sch.2 para.4, revoked (in part): SI 1998/1506 (NI.10) Art.78, Sch.7

Sch.2 para.24, revoked: SI 1998/1506 (NI.10) Art.78, Sch.7

Sch.2 para.25, revoked: SI 1998/1506 (NI.10) Art.78, Sch.7

Sch.2 para.26, revoked: SI 1998/1506 (NI.10) Art.78, Sch.7

Sch.2 para.27, revoked: SI 1998/1506 (NI.10) Art.78, Sch.7

NO.

2705. Jobseekers (Northern Ireland) Order 1995— *cont.*
 Sch.2 para.28, revoked: SI 1998/1506 (NI.10) Art.78, Sch.7
 Sch.2 para.29, revoked: SI 1998/1506 (NI.10) Art.78, Sch.7
 Sch.2 para.30, revoked: SI 1998/1506 (NI.10) Art.78, Sch.7
 Sch.2 para.35, revoked: SI 1997/1183 (NI.12) Art.31, Sch.4
 Sch.2 para.37, revoked: SI 1997/1183 (NI.12) Art.31, Sch.4
 Sch.2 para.39, revoked: SI 1998/1506 (NI.10) Art.78, Sch.7
 Sch.2 para.40, revoked: 1997 c.47 s.22, Sch.2
 Sch.2 para.43, revoked: SI 1997/1182 (NI.11) Art.19, Sch.2
 Sch.2 para.46, revoked: SI 1999/663 Art.2, Sch.2
 Sch.2 para.47, revoked: SI 1999/663 Art.2, Sch.2

2713. Civil Aviation (Canadian Navigation Services) (Second Amendment) Regulations 1995
 revoked: SI 1996/688 Reg.3, Sch.1

2724. Charities (Accounts and Reports) Regulations 1995
 Sch.2 Part III, amended: SI 1998/1129 Art.3, Sch.2

2743. A1 Trunk Road (Islington) Red Route Traffic Order 1993 Experimental Variation Order 1995
 revoked: SI 1996/1881 Art.5

2744. A205 Trunk Road (Richmond and Wandsworth) Red Route Experimental Traffic Order 1995 Amendment Order 1995
 revoked: SI 1996/2164 Art.10

2746. A205 Trunk Road (Upper Richmond Road West) Red Route (Prescribed Route No.1) Experimental Traffic Order 1995
 revoked: SI 1997/200 Art.5

2766. Local Government (Application of Enactments) (Scotland) (No.2) Order 1995
 revoked: SI 1996/739 Art.8, Sch.3

2778. Hill Livestock (Compensatory Allowances) (Amendment) (No.3) Regulations 1995
 revoked (in part): SI 1996/1500 Reg.18

2780. Arable Area Payments (Amendment) Regulations 1995
 revoked: SI 1996/3142 Reg.20
 Reg.2, revoked: SI 1996/3142 Reg.20

2791. Acquisition of Land (Rate of Interest after Entry) (Scotland) Regulations 1995
 Reg.2, amended: SI 1998/1129 Art.3, Sch.2

2793. Housing Benefit (Permitted Totals) and Council Tax Benefit (Permitted Total) (Pensions for War Widows) Amendment Order 1995
 revoked: SI 1996/678 Art.4
 Art.4, revoked: SI 1996/678 Art.4

2795. Offshore Installations (Safety Zones) (No.6) Order 1995
 revoked: SI 1997/735 Art.3, Sch.2

2797. Gwent Community Health National Health Service Trust (Establishment) Amendment Order 1995
 revoked: SI 1999/1120 Art.2, Sch.2
 Art.2, revoked: SI 1999/1120 Art.2, Sch.2

2801. National Health Service Litigation Authority Regulations 1995
 Reg.1, amended: SI 1998/646 Reg.13
 Reg.5, amended: SI 1997/2991 Reg.3, Sch. para.7

NO.

2801. National Health Service Litigation Authority Regulations 1995—*cont.*
 Reg.7, amended: SI 1997/2991 Reg.3, Sch. para.7
 Reg.12, revoked: SI 1996/708 Reg.6, Sch.2
 Reg.16, added: SI 1998/1576 Reg.5
 Sch. para.5, amended: SI 1996/968 Reg.2

2803. National Park Authorities (Wales) Order 1995
 applied: SI 1996/532 Art.17
 Sch.5 para.2A, added: SI 1996/534 Art.3, Sch Part I
 Sch.5 para.2B, added: SI 1996/534 Art.3, Sch Part I
 Sch.5 para.2C, added: SI 1996/534 Art.3, Sch Part I
 Sch.5 para.2D, added: SI 1996/534 Art.3, Sch Part I
 Sch.5 para.2E, added: SI 1996/1224 Art.2
 Sch.5 para.6, referred to: SI 1996/1215 Reg.4
 Sch.5 para.11, added: SI 1996/534 Art.3, Sch Part II
 Sch.5 para.12, added: SI 1996/534 Art.3, Sch Part II
 Sch.5 para.13, added: SI 1996/534 Art.3, Sch Part II
 Sch.5 para.14, added: SI 1996/534 Art.3, Sch Part II
 Sch.5 para.15, added: SI 1996/534 Art.3, Sch Part II
 Sch.5 para.16, added: SI 1996/534 Art.3, Sch Part II
 Sch.5 para.16, revoked: SI 1997/633 Art.3
 Sch.5 para.17, added: SI 1996/534 Art.3, Sch Part II
 Sch.5 para.18, added: SI 1996/534 Art.3, Sch Part II
 Sch.5 para.19, added: SI 1996/534 Art.3, Sch Part II
 Sch.5 para.20, added: SI 1996/534 Art.3, Sch Part II
 Sch.5 para.21, added: SI 1996/534 Art.3, Sch Part II
 Sch.5 para.22, added: SI 1996/1224 Art.2

2813. Local Government Act 1988 (Competition) (Information Technology) (England) Regulations 1995
 Reg.2, amended: SI 1997/175 Reg.5, SI 1997/2732 Reg.6
 Reg.3, amended: SI 1997/175 Reg.5, SI 1997/2732 Reg.6

2814. Teachers' Superannuation (Additional Voluntary Contributions) (Scotland) Regulations 1995
 applied: SI 1999/1750 Art.2, Sch.1

2823. Housing (Change of Landlord) (Payment of Disposal Cost by Instalments) (Amendment No.2) Regulations 1995
 revoked: SI 1996/184 Reg.3

2837. Local Government Reorganisation (Compensation for Loss of Remuneration) Regulations 1995
 Reg.2, amended: SI 1996/660 Reg.2
 Reg.4, amended: SI 1996/660 Reg.3, SI 1996/1680 Sch.4 para.5
 Reg.8, amended: SI 1996/660 Reg.4, SI 1996/1680 Sch.4 para.5

2840. Curfew Order (Responsible Officer) (Berkshire, Greater Manchester and Norfolk) Order 1995
 revoked: SI 1997/2351 Art.5
 Art.5, revoked: SI 1997/2351 Art.5

NO.

2865. **Local Government (Compensation for Reduction of Remuneration on Reorganisation) (Scotland) Regulations 1995**
applied: SI 1998/364 Reg.4, Reg.6, Reg.19, Sch.2 para.2, Sch.2 para.5, Sch.4 para.8
referred to: SI 1998/364 Reg.3, Reg.10, Sch.2 para.4, Sch.2 para.6, SI 1998/366 Reg.12
Reg.2, amended: SI 1997/720 Reg.2

2867. **Parliamentary Pensions (Amendment) Regulations 1995**
Reg.5, amended: SI 1996/2406 Reg.6

2869. **Goods Vehicles (Licensing of Operators) Regulations 1995**
amended: SI 1996/2186 Reg.31
Reg.4, amended: SI 1996/2186 Sch.6 Part I
Reg.7, amended: SI 1996/2186 Sch.6 Part II
Reg.8, amended: SI 1996/2186 Sch.6 Part II
Reg.9, amended: SI 1996/2186 Sch.6 Part II
Reg.10, amended: SI 1996/2186 Sch.6 Part II
Reg.11, amended: SI 1996/2186 Sch.6 Part II
Reg.12, amended: SI 1996/2186 Sch.6 Part II
Reg.13, amended: SI 1996/2186 Sch.6 Part II
Reg.14, amended: SI 1996/2186 Sch.6 Part II
Reg.15, amended: SI 1996/2186 Sch.6 Part II
Reg.16, amended: SI 1996/2186 Sch.6 Part II
Reg.17, amended: SI 1996/2186 Sch.6 Part II
Reg.18, amended: SI 1996/2186 Sch.6 Part II
Reg.19, amended: SI 1996/2186 Sch.6 Part II
Reg.21, amended: SI 1996/2186 Sch.6 Part II
Reg.22, amended: SI 1996/2186 Sch.6 Part II
Reg.23, amended: SI 1996/2186 Sch.6 Part II
Reg.26, amended: SI 1996/2186 Sch.6 Part II
Reg.28, amended: SI 1996/2186 Sch.6 Part II
Reg.29, amended: SI 1996/2186 Sch.6 Part II
Reg.31, amended: SI 1996/2186 Sch.6 Part II
Reg.33, amended: SI 1996/2186 Sch.6 Part II
Reg.36, amended: SI 1996/2186 Sch.6 Part II

2870. **Escape and Rescue from Mines Regulations 1995**
Reg.2, amended: SI 1999/3242 Reg.29, Sch.2
Reg.4, amended: SI 1999/3242 Reg.29, Sch.2

2874. **Seed Potatoes Originating in the Netherlands (Notification) (Scotland) Order 1995**
revoked: SI 1996/2563 Reg.2

2889. **Local Government Changes for England (Collection Fund Surpluses and Deficits) Regulations 1995**
Reg.3, amended: SI 1996/2177 Reg.2
Reg.5, amended: SI 1996/2177 Reg.3

2895. **Local Government Changes for England (Payments to Designated Authorities) (Minimum Revenue Provisions) Regulations 1995**
Reg.7, amended: SI 1998/1129 Art.3, Sch.2
Reg.9, revoked: SI 1998/1937 Reg.12

2896. **Sporting Grounds and Sporting Events (Designation) (Scotland) Amendment Order 1995**
revoked: SI 1998/2314 Art.3, Sch.3
Art.2, revoked: SI 1998/2314 Art.3, Sch.3

2907. **Child Support Commissioners (Procedure) (Amendment) Regulations 1995**
revoked: SI 1996/243 Reg.3

2908. **Public Service Vehicles (Operators' Licences) Regulations 1995**
Reg.25, referred to: SI 1999/1205 Art.7, Sch. para.5

2911. **Products of Animal Origin (Import and Export) (Amendment) Regulations 1995**
revoked: SI 1996/3124 Reg.42, Sch.7
Reg.2, revoked: SI 1996/3124 Reg.42, Sch.7

NO.

2912. **Registered Designs Rules 1995**
applied: SI 1998/1777 r.3
referred to: SI 1998/1777 r.2
r.2, amended: SI 1999/3196 r.3
r.4, applied: SI 1998/1777 r.3
r.5, amended: SI 1999/3196 r.4
r.17, amended: SI 1999/3196 r.5
r.18, amended: SI 1999/3196 r.6
r.19, substituted: SI 1999/3196 r.7
r.23, amended: SI 1999/3196 r.8
r.28, amended: SI 1999/3196 r.9
r.31, applied: SI 1998/1777 r.3, Sch.
r.32, amended: SI 1999/3196 r.10
r.38, amended: SI 1999/3196 r.11
r.42, applied: SI 1998/1777 r.3, Sch.
r.45, applied: SI 1998/1777 r.3, Sch.
r.48, amended: SI 1999/3196 r.12
r.57, amended: SI 1999/3196 r.13
r.59, amended: SI 1999/3196 r.14
r.62, amended: SI 1999/3196 r.15
r.63, amended: SI 1999/3196 r.16
r.64A, added: SI 1999/3196 r.17
r.67, amended: SI 1999/3196 r.18
r.73, applied: SI 1998/1777 r.3, Sch.
r.74, amended: SI 1999/3196 r.19
r.75, amended: SI 1999/3196 r.20
Sch.2, revoked: SI 1999/3196 r.21

2913. **Registered Designs (Fees) (No.2) Rules 1995**
revoked: SI 1998/1777 r.1
r.1, revoked: SI 1998/1777 r.1
r.2, revoked: SI 1998/1777 r.1

2916. **Local Government Act 1988 (Competition) (Financial Services) (England) Regulations 1995**
Reg.2, amended: SI 1997/175 Reg.4, SI 1997/2732 Reg.4
Reg.2, revoked (in part): SI 1997/2732 Reg.9
Reg.3, amended: SI 1997/175 Reg.4, SI 1997/2732 Reg.4

2922. **Animal Health Orders (Divisional Veterinary Manager Amendment) Order 1995**
Sch.1 Part I, revoked (in part): SI 1996/2628 Art.8, Sch.2

2930. **Road Traffic (Special Parking Area) (London Borough of Croydon) (Amendment) Order 1995**
revoked: SI 1997/1342 Art.2
Art.2, revoked: SI 1997/1342 Art.2

2946. **Statistics of Trade (Customs and Excise) (Amendment) Regulations 1995**
revoked: SI 1996/2968 Reg.2
Reg.2, revoked: SI 1996/2968 Reg.2
Reg.4, revoked: SI 1996/2968 Reg.2

2947. **Plant Breeders' Rights (Fees) (Amendment) (No.2) Regulations 1995**
revoked: SI 1998/1021 Reg.7 (with savings), Sch.2 (with savings)
Reg.2, revoked: SI 1998/1021 Reg.7 (with savings), Sch.2 (with savings)

2950. **Environment Act 1995 (Commencement No.4 and Saving Provisions) Order 1995**
Art.3, revoked (in part): SI 1996/2560 Art.3

2953. **Local Government Pension Scheme (Augmentation) Regulations 1995**
applied: SI 1997/1613 Reg.4, Reg.19, Sch.2 para.2
referred to: SI 1997/1613 Reg.3, Sch.2 para.6
Reg.3, amended: SI 1996/1680 Sch.4 para.6

NO.

2961. Judicial Pensions (Contributions) (Amendment) Regulations 1995
referred to: SI 1998/1219 Reg.4
revoked: SI 1998/1219 Reg.3 (with savings)
Reg.3, revoked: SI 1998/1219 Reg.3 (with savings)
Reg.4, revoked: SI 1998/1219 Reg.3 (with savings)
Reg.5, revoked: SI 1998/1219 Reg.3 (with savings)
Reg.6, revoked: SI 1998/1219 Reg.3 (with savings)
Reg.7, revoked: SI 1998/1219 Reg.3 (with savings)
Reg.8, revoked: SI 1998/1219 Reg.3 (with savings)
Reg.9, revoked: SI 1998/1219 Reg.3 (with savings)
Reg.10, revoked: SI 1998/1219 Reg.3 (with savings)
Reg.11, revoked: SI 1998/1219 Reg.3 (with savings)
Reg.12, revoked: SI 1998/1219 Reg.3 (with savings)
Reg.13, revoked: SI 1998/1219 Reg.3 (with savings)
Reg.14, revoked: SI 1998/1219 Reg.3 (with savings)
Reg.15, revoked: SI 1998/1219 Reg.3 (with savings)
Reg.16, revoked: SI 1998/1219 Reg.3 (with savings)
Reg.17, revoked: SI 1998/1219 Reg.3 (with savings)
Reg.18, revoked: SI 1998/1219 Reg.3 (with savings)
Reg.19, revoked: SI 1998/1219 Reg.3 (with savings)
Reg.20, revoked: SI 1998/1219 Reg.3 (with savings)
Reg.21, revoked: SI 1998/1219 Reg.3 (with savings)
Reg.22, revoked: SI 1998/1219 Reg.3 (with savings)

2962. Land Registration (District Registries) Order 1995
substituted: SI 1997/1534 Art.1

2984. Ministerial and other Salaries Order 1995
revoked: SI 1996/1913 Art.1

2987. Copyright (Application to other Countries) (Amendment) Order 1995
revoked: SI 1999/1751 Art.8, Sch.6
Art.2, revoked: SI 1999/1751 Art.8, Sch.6
Art.3, revoked: SI 1999/1751 Art.8, Sch.6

2990. Performances (Reciprocal Protection) (Convention Countries) Order 1995
revoked: SI 1999/1752 Art.4
Art.4, revoked: SI 1999/1752 Art.4

2991. Financial Provisions (Northern Ireland) Order 1995
Art.7, revoked: SI 1998/749 (NI.4) Art.9, Sch.

2992. Parliamentary Constituencies (Northern Ireland) Order 1995
applied: 1996 c.11 Sch.1 para.2

2993. Police (Amendment) (Northern Ireland) Order 1995
applied: 1997 c.50 s.39
Art.2, referred to: SR 1999/176 Art.3
Art.2, revoked (in part): 1998 c.32 s.74, Sch.6
Art.9, revoked (in part): 1996 c.22 Sch.7 Part II
Part III, revoked: 1998 c.32 s.74, Sch.6
Part IV, referred to: SR 1999/176 Art.3

NO.

2993. Police (Amendment) (Northern Ireland) Order 1995—*cont.*
Part IV, revoked: 1998 c.32 s.74, Sch.6
Sch.1, revoked (in part): 1998 c.32 s.74, Sch.6, SI 1998/1504 (NI.9) Art.65, Sch.6

2994. Road Traffic (Northern Ireland) Order 1995
amended: SI 1998/1074 (NI.7) Art.7
Art.2, amended: SI 1996/1320 (NI.10) Sch.3 para.24, SI 1997/276 (NI.2) Art.75, Sch.8 para.17, Sch.8 para.21
Art.3, referred to: SI 1997/276 (NI.2) Art.68
Art.4, amended: SI 1996/1320 (NI.10) Sch.3 para.25
Art.5, amended: SI 1996/1320 (NI.10) Sch.3 para.26, SI 1997/276 (NI.2) Art.75, Sch.8 para.22
Art.6, amended: SI 1996/1320 (NI.10) Sch.3 para.27
Art.7, amended: SI 1996/1320 (NI.10) Sch.3 para.28
Art.8, referred to: SI 1997/276 (NI.2) Art.69
Art.9, applied: SI 1996/1320 (NI.10) Art.26, Art.41, Art.50, Sch.1 Part I
Art.10, applied: SI 1996/1320 (NI.10) Art.26, Art.41, Art.50, Sch.1 Part I
Art.12, applied: SI 1996/1320 (NI.10) Art.26, Sch.1 Part I
Art.14, applied: SI 1996/1320 (NI.10) Art.18, Art.26, Art.35, Art.36, Art.50, Sch.1 Part I
Art.15, applied: SI 1996/1320 (NI.10) Art.9, Art.18, Art.26, Art.35, Art.36, Art.50, Sch.1 Part I
Art.16, applied: SI 1996/1320 (NI.10) Art.9, Art.18, Art.26, Art.35, Art.36, Art.50, Sch.1 Part I
Art.17, amended: SI 1996/1320 (NI.10) Sch.3 para.29
Art.17, applied: SI 1996/1320 (NI.10) Art.18, Sch.1 Part I
Art.18, amended: 1996 c.25 Sch.4 para.26
Art.18, applied: SI 1996/1320 (NI.10) Art.9, Art.18, Art.26, Art.35, Art.36, Art.50, Sch.1 Part I
Art.19, applied: SI 1996/1320 (NI.10) Art.18
Art.20, applied: SI 1996/1320 (NI.10) Art.18
Art.21, applied: SI 1996/1320 (NI.10) Art.18
Art.23, applied: SI 1996/1320 (NI.10) Sch.1 Part I
Art.24, applied: SI 1996/1320 (NI.10) Sch.1 Part I
Art.25, amended: 1999 c.10 s.1, Sch.1 para.6
Art.26, applied: SI 1996/1320 (NI.10) Sch.1 Part I
Art.27, applied: SI 1996/1320 (NI.10) Sch.1 Part I
Art.28, applied: SI 1996/1320 (NI.10) Sch.1 Part I
Art.29, applied: SI 1996/1320 (NI.10) Sch.1 Part I
Art.30, applied: SI 1996/1320 (NI.10) Sch.1 Part I
Art.32, amended: SI 1996/1320 (NI.10) Sch.3 para.30
Art.32, applied: SI 1996/1320 (NI.10) Sch.1 Part I
Art.33, applied: SI 1996/1320 (NI.10) Sch.1 Part I
Art.34, applied: SI 1996/1320 (NI.10) Sch.1 Part I
Art.35, applied: SI 1996/1320 (NI.10) Art.36, Sch.1 Part I
Art.36, amended: SI 1997/276 (NI.2) Art.75, Sch.8 para.23

1995—cont.

2994. Road Traffic (Northern Ireland) Order 1995— *cont.*

Art.36, applied: SI 1996/1320 (NI.10) Sch.1 Part I

Art.37, applied: SI 1996/1320 (NI.10) Sch.1 Part I

Art.38, applied: SI 1996/1320 (NI.10) Sch.1 Part I

Art.39, applied: SI 1996/1320 (NI.10) Sch.1 Part I

Art.40, applied: SI 1996/1320 (NI.10) Sch.1 Part I

Art.41, applied: SI 1996/1320 (NI.10) Sch.1 Part I

Art.42, applied: SI 1996/1320 (NI.10) Art.26, Sch.1 Part I

Art.43, applied: SI 1996/1320 (NI.10) Art.26, Sch.1 Part I

Art.44, applied: SI 1996/1320 (NI.10) Sch.1 Part I

Art.45, applied: SI 1996/1320 (NI.10) Sch.1 Part I

Art.46, applied: SI 1996/1320 (NI.10) Sch.1 Part I

Art.47, applied: SI 1996/1320 (NI.10) Sch.1 Part I

Art.48, applied: SI 1996/1320 (NI.10) Sch.1 Part I

Art.49, amended: SI 1996/1320 (NI.10) Sch.3 para.31

Art.49, applied: SI 1996/1320 (NI.10) Art.23, Sch.1 Part I

Art.49, referred to: SI 1997/276 (NI.2) Art.44

Art.49, substituted: SI 1997/276 (NI.2) Art.75, Sch.8 para.18

Art.50, amended: SI 1997/276 (NI.2) Art.61

Art.50, applied: SI 1997/276 (NI.2) Art.7

Art.50, referred to: SI 1997/276 (NI.2) Art.44

Art.50, substituted: SI 1997/276 (NI.2) Art.75, Sch.8 para.19

Art.54, applied: SI 1996/1320 (NI.10) Art.17, Art.20, Art.53, Sch.1 Part I, SI 1997/276 (NI.2) Art.66

Art.56, applied: SI 1996/1320 (NI.10) Art.20, Art.53, Sch.1 Part I, SI 1997/276 (NI.2) Art.66

Art.57, applied: SI 1996/1320 (NI.10) Art.20, Sch.1 Part I, SI 1997/276 (NI.2) Art.66

Art.58, applied: SI 1996/1320 (NI.10) Art.20, Sch.1 Part I, SI 1997/276 (NI.2) Art.66

Art.61, applied: SI 1998/3094 Reg.14

Art.63, applied: SI 1996/1320 (NI.10) Sch.1 Part I

Art.64, amended: SI 1997/2984 (NI.22) Art.7

Art.65, applied: SI 1996/1320 (NI.10) Sch.1 Part I, SI 1998/3094 Reg.14

Art.67, applied: SI 1996/1320 (NI.10) Sch.1 Part I

Art.69, applied: SI 1996/1320 (NI.10) Sch.1 Part I

Art.70, applied: SI 1996/1320 (NI.10) Sch.1 Part I

Art.71, applied: SI 1996/1320 (NI.10) Sch.1 Part I

Art.74, applied: SI 1996/1320 (NI.10) Art.8

Art.75, applied: SI 1996/1320 (NI.10) Sch.1 Part I

Art.76, amended: SI 1997/276 (NI.2) Art.75, Sch.8 para.20

Art.76, applied: SI 1996/1320 (NI.10) Sch.1 Part I

Art.76, referred to: SI 1999/1736 Art.9

Art.77, referred to: SI 1999/1736 Art.9

1995—cont.

2994. Road Traffic (Northern Ireland) Order 1995— *cont.*

Art.78, referred to: SI 1999/1736 Art.9

Art.79, applied: SI 1996/1320 (NI.10) Art.20

Art.79, referred to: SI 1999/1736 Art.9

Art.80, applied: SI 1996/1320 (NI.10) Sch.1 Part I

Art.80, referred to: SI 1999/1736 Art.9

Art.81, referred to: SI 1999/1736 Art.9

Art.82, applied: SI 1996/1320 (NI.10) Art.17, Sch.1 Part I

Art.82, referred to: SI 1999/1736 Art.9

Art.83, applied: SI 1996/1320 (NI.10) Sch.1 Part I

Art.84, applied: SI 1996/1320 (NI.10) Sch.1 Part I

Art.85, applied: SI 1996/1320 (NI.10) Sch.1 Part I

Art.86, applied: SI 1996/1320 (NI.10) Sch.1 Part I

Art.88, applied: SI 1996/1320 (NI.10) Sch.1 Part I

Art.90, applied: SI 1996/1320 (NI.10) Sch.1 Part I

Art.93, revoked: SI 1997/276 (NI.2) Art.75, Sch.9

Art.94, revoked: SI 1996/1320 (NI.10) Sch.4

Art.95, revoked: SI 1996/1320 (NI.10) Sch.4

Art.96, revoked: SI 1996/1320 (NI.10) Sch.4

Art.97, revoked: SI 1996/1320 (NI.10) Sch.4

Art.98, revoked (in part): SI 1996/1320 (NI.10) Sch.4

Art.100, revoked: SI 1996/1320 (NI.10) Sch.4

Art.101, revoked: SI 1996/1320 (NI.10) Sch.4

Art.102, revoked: SI 1996/1320 (NI.10) Sch.4

Art.103, revoked: SI 1996/1320 (NI.10) Sch.4

Art.104, revoked: SI 1996/1320 (NI.10) Sch.4

Art.105, amended: SI 1996/1320 (NI.10) Sch.3 para.32

Art.106, revoked (in part): SI 1996/1320 (NI.10) Sch.4

Art.109, revoked (in part): SI 1997/276 (NI.2) Art.75, Sch.9

Part III, applied: SI 1996/1320 (NI.10) Art.20

Sch.1 para.4, applied: SI 1996/1320 (NI.10) Sch.1 Part I

Sch.2, revoked: SI 1996/1320 (NI.10) Sch.4

Sch.3 Part I, revoked (in part): SI 1998/1074 (NI.7) Art.13, Sch.4

Sch.3 para.10, revoked (in part): SI 1997/276 (NI.2) Art.75, Sch.9

Sch.3 para.11, revoked: SI 1996/1320 (NI.10) Sch.4

Sch.3 para.12, revoked (in part): SI 1997/276 (NI.2) Art.75, Sch.9

Sch.3 para.21, revoked: SI 1996/1320 (NI.10) Sch.4

Sch.3 para.22, amended: SI 1996/1320 (NI.10) Sch.3 para.33

Sch.3 para.22, referred to: SI 1997/276 (NI.2) Art.1

Sch.3 para.22, revoked: SI 1997/276 (NI.2) Art.75, Sch.9

Sch.3 para.23, revoked: SI 1996/1320 (NI.10) Sch.4

Sch.3 para.24, revoked: SI 1996/1320 (NI.10) Sch.4

Sch.3 para.25, revoked: SI 1996/1320 (NI.10) Sch.4

Sch.3 para.26, revoked: SI 1996/1320 (NI.10) Sch.4

Sch.3 para.32, revoked: SI 1996/1320 (NI.10) Sch.4

NO.

1995—cont.

2996. Local Government Act 1988 (Defined Activities, Exemptions) (Wales) (Amendment) Order 1995
revoked: SI 1996/3179 Art.5
Art.3, revoked: SI 1996/3179 Art.5

3000. Goods Vehicles (Licensing of Operators) (Fees) Regulations 1995
referred to: SI 1996/2186 Reg.31

3018. Seed Potatoes Originating in the Netherlands Order 1995
revoked: SI 1996/2563 Reg.2

3019. National Park Authorities (Levies) (Wales) Regulations 1995
Reg.3, amended: SI 1996/2913 Reg.3
Reg.6, amended: SI 1996/2913 Reg.3
Reg.7, amended: SI 1996/2913 Reg.3
Reg.9, amended: SI 1998/1129 Art.3, Sch.2
Reg.10, substituted: SI 1996/2913 Reg.3

3025. Police Grant (Scotland) (Amendment) Order 1995
revoked: SI 1996/780 Art.7, Sch.2

3029. Medicines (Pharmacies) (Applications for Registration and Fees) Amendment Regulations 1995
revoked: SI 1996/3054 Reg.3
Reg.2, revoked: SI 1996/3054 Reg.3
Reg.3, revoked: SI 1996/3054 Reg.3

3036. Manufactured Payments and Transfer of Securities (Tax Relief) Regulations 1995
Reg.3, amended: SI 1998/1871 Reg.24
Reg.4, amended: SI 1998/1871 Reg.24

3041. Value Added Tax (Tax Free Shops) Order 1995
revoked: SI 1999/1642 Art.3

3060. Export of Goods (Control) (Amendment) Order 1995
revoked: SI 1997/2758 Art.1

3065. Building Societies (Accounts and Related Provisions) (Amendment) Regulations 1995
revoked: SI 1998/504 Reg.13
Reg.2, revoked: SI 1998/504 Reg.13

3069. Act of Sederunt (Lands Valuation Appeal Court) 1995
revoked: SI 1996/2856 r.2

3093. National Health Service (General Medical Services) Amendment (No.2) Regulations 1995
Sch.10, see *R. v Secretary of State for Health Ex p. RP Scherer Ltd* [1998] Eu L.R. 1 (QBD), Judge, J.

3098. London Docklands Development Corporation (Alteration of Boundaries) Order 1995
applied: SI 1997/2946 Art.6
Art.4, revoked: SI 1997/2946 Art.6
Art.8, revoked (in part): SI 1997/2946 Art.6

3106. Local Government (Registration Service in Wales) Order 1995
amended: SI 1996/2914 Art.15, SI 1996/2915 Art.11
referred to: SI 1996/532 Art.3

3113. Special Educational Needs Tribunal Regulations 1995
applied: SI 1996/710 Reg.16
Reg.7, see *R. v Special Educational Needs Tribunal Ex p. J* [1997] E.L.R. 237 (QBD), Tucker, J.
Reg.8, see *Lucy v Kensington and Chelsea RLBC* [1997] E.L.R. 155 (QBD), Dyson, J.

NO.

1995—cont.

3113. Special Educational Needs Tribunal Regulations 1995—*cont.*
Reg.28, see *L v Salford City Council* [1998] E.L.R. 28 (QBD), Tucker, J.
Reg.29, see *Duncan v Bedfordshire CC* [1997] E.L.R. 299 (QBD), Dyson, J.
Reg.33, see *C v Lambeth LBC* [1999] Ed. C.R. 933 (QBD), Keene, J.
Reg.36, see *Ealing LBC v White* [1999] E.L.R. 150 (CA), Butler-Sloss, L.J.
Reg.41, see *R. v Special Educational Needs Tribunal Ex p. J* [1997] E.L.R. 237 (QBD), Tucker, J.

3114. Local Government Changes for England (Local Management of Schools) Regulations 1995
revoked: SI 1999/711 Reg.9, Sch.2

3116. Spreadable Fats (Marketing Standards) Regulations 1995
revoked (in part): SI 1999/2457 Reg.9, Sch.2, SSI 1999/34 Reg.9, Sch.2
Reg.2, amended: SI 1998/452 Reg.3, SI 1998/2538 Reg.3, SI 1999/540 Reg.2
Reg.2, revoked (in part): SI 1999/2457 Reg.9, Sch.2, SSI 1999/34 Reg.9, Sch.2
Reg.3, amended: SI 1998/452 Reg.4
Reg.3, revoked (in part): SI 1999/2457 Reg.9, Sch.2, SSI 1999/34 Reg.9, Sch.2
Reg.7, amended: SI 1998/452 Reg.5
Reg.7, revoked (in part): SI 1999/2457 Reg.9, Sch.2, SSI 1999/34 Reg.9, Sch.2
Reg.8, revoked (in part): SI 1999/2457 Reg.9, Sch.2, SSI 1999/34 Reg.9, Sch.2
Reg.8, substituted: SI 1998/452 Reg.6
Reg.9, revoked (in part): SI 1999/2457 Reg.9, Sch.2, SSI 1999/34 Reg.9, Sch.2
Sch.1, revoked (in part): SI 1999/2457 Reg.9, Sch.2, SSI 1999/34 Reg.9, Sch.2
Sch.1, substituted: SI 1998/452 Reg.7, Sch.
Sch.1 para.2, amended: SI 1998/2538 Reg.4
Sch.1 para.2, revoked (in part): SI 1999/2457 Reg.9, Sch.2, SSI 1999/34 Reg.9, Sch.2

3118. Local Government Act 1988 (Defined Activities) (Specified Periods) (England) (Amendment) Regulations 1995
revoked: SI 1997/2747 Reg.2, Sch.
Reg.2, revoked: SI 1997/2747 Reg.2, Sch.

3123. Sweeteners in Food Regulations 1995
amended: SI 1999/982 Reg.2
applied: SI 1996/1499 Reg.34
Reg.2, amended: SI 1997/814 Reg.2
Reg.3, amended: SI 1996/1477 Reg.2, SI 1997/814 Reg.2
Reg.5, amended: SI 1997/814 Reg.2
Reg.5A, added: SI 1997/814 Reg.2
Reg.11, amended: SI 1997/814 Reg.2
Reg.11, revoked (in part): SI 1997/814 Reg.2
Sch.1, substituted: SI 1997/814 Reg.2, Sch.

3128. Merchant Shipping (Port State Control) Regulations 1995
amended: SI 1998/1433 Reg.3
Part I, applied: SI 1996/3243 Sch Part I
Reg.2, amended: SI 1998/1433 Reg.4, Reg.5, SI 1998/2198 Reg.3, Reg.4, Reg.5
Reg.5, amended: SI 1998/2198 Reg.6
Reg.9A, added: SI 1998/1433 Reg.6
Reg.10, applied: SI 1997/1320 Reg.16
Reg.11, applied: SI 1997/1320 Reg.16
Reg.12, applied: SI 1997/1320 Reg.16
Reg.14, amended: SI 1998/1433 Reg.7
Reg.15, amended: SI 1998/2198 Reg.7
Reg.18, amended: SI 1998/1433 Reg.8

1995—cont.

1995—cont.

3138. **A4 Trunk Road (Hillingdon and Hounslow) Red Route Experimental Traffic Order 1995**
revoked (in part): SI 1997/1507 Art.10

3139. **A40 Trunk Road (Ealing) Red Route (Clearway) Traffic Order 1995**
Art.2, amended: SI 1999/272 Art.2, Sch. Part B
Art.4, amended: SI 1999/12 Art.4
Art.7, amended: SI 1999/12 Art.5
Art.9, amended: SI 1999/272 Art.2, Sch. Part B
Sch.1 Item 2, amended: SI 1999/12 Art.3
Sch.3A, added: SI 1999/12 Art.6

3140. **A40 Trunk Road (Ealing) Red Route Traffic Order 1995**
Art.2, amended: SI 1999/272 Art.2, Sch. Part A
Art.9, amended: SI 1999/272 Art.2, Sch. Part A
Sch.1 Item 4, added: SI 1999/13 Art.3
Sch.2B, amended: SI 1999/13 Art.5
Sch.4 Item 4, added: SI 1999/13 Art.6
Sch.4 Item 5, added: SI 1999/13 Art.6
Sch.4 Item 6, added: SI 1999/13 Art.6

3141. **A406 Trunk Road (Ealing) Red Route (Clearway) Traffic Order 1995**
Art.2, amended: SI 1999/272 Art.2, Sch. Part B
Art.9, amended: SI 1999/272 Art.2, Sch. Part B

3142. **A406 Trunk Road (Brent) Red Route (Clearway) Traffic Order 1995**
Art.2, amended: SI 1999/272 Art.2, Sch. Part B
Art.9, amended: SI 1999/272 Art.2, Sch. Part B

3143. **A406 Trunk Road (Brent) Red Route Experimental Traffic Order 1995**
revoked (in part): SI 1997/1223 Art.10
Art.2, revoked (in part): SI 1997/1223 Art.10
Art.8, revoked (in part): SI 1997/1223 Art.10

3144. **A406 Trunk Road (Brent) Red Route (Prescribed Route) Experimental Traffic Order 1995**
revoked: SI 1997/1224 Art.5

3148. **Rent Officers (Additional Functions) (Amendment No.2) Order 1995**
revoked: SI 1997/1984 Art.9
Art.2, revoked: SI 1997/1984 Art.9

3156. **Marriage (Prescription of Forms) (Scotland) Amendment Regulations 1995**
revoked: SI 1997/2349 Reg.9
Reg.3, revoked: SI 1997/2349 Reg.9
Reg.4, revoked: SI 1997/2349 Reg.9
Reg.5, revoked: SI 1997/2349 Reg.9

3157. **Registration of Births, Still-births, Deaths and Marriages (Prescription of Forms) (Scotland) Amendment Regulations 1995**
revoked: SI 1997/2348 Reg.30, Sch.27
Reg.3, revoked: SI 1997/2348 Reg.30, Sch.27
Reg.4, revoked: SI 1997/2348 Reg.30, Sch.27
Reg.5, revoked: SI 1997/2348 Reg.30, Sch.27
Reg.6, revoked: SI 1997/2348 Reg.30, Sch.27

3160. **Civil Aviation (Route Charges for Navigation Services) Regulations 1995**
revoked: SI 1997/2920 Reg.2, Sch.1
Reg.5, amended: SI 1996/1495 Reg.2, SI 1996/3089 Reg.2
Reg.5, revoked: SI 1997/2920 Reg.2, Sch.1
Reg.8, revoked: SI 1997/2920 Reg.2, Sch.1
Reg.8, substituted: SI 1996/3089 Reg.2
Reg.20, added: SI 1996/3089 Reg.2
Reg.20, revoked: SI 1997/2920 Reg.2, Sch.1
Sch.2, revoked: SI 1997/2920 Reg.2, Sch.1
Sch.2, substituted: SI 1996/1495 Reg.2, SI 1996/3089 Reg.2, SI 1997/1653 Reg.2
Sch.3, revoked: SI 1997/2920 Reg.2, Sch.1

3160. **Civil Aviation (Route Charges for Navigation Services) Regulations 1995—cont.**
Sch.3, substituted: SI 1996/1495 Reg.2, SI 1996/3089 Reg.2, SI 1997/1653 Reg.2

3161. **Civil Aviation (Joint Financing) (Amendment) Regulations 1995**
revoked: SI 1997/2937 Reg.3, Sch.1
Reg.2, revoked: SI 1997/2937 Reg.3, Sch.1

3162. **Registration of Births, Deaths and Marriages (Fees) Order 1995**
revoked: SI 1996/3152 Art.3

3163. **Reporting of Injuries, Diseases and Dangerous Occurrences Regulations 1995**
applied: SI 1999/743 Reg.15, SI 1999/2024 Reg.40
referred to: SI 1996/913 Reg.9
Reg.2, amended: SI 1997/2776 Reg.19, Sch.2 para.5, SI 1999/437 Reg.18, SI 1999/2024 Reg.48, Sch.5 Part II
Reg.6, applied: SI 1996/551 Reg.7
Reg.7, applied: SI 1996/1513 Reg.5
Sch.2 Part I, amended: SI 1996/2092 Reg.21, SI 1997/2776 Reg.19, Sch.2 para.5
Sch.2 para.8, amended: SI 1999/3232 Reg.41, Sch.9 para.6
Sch.2 para.43, amended: SI 1999/2024 Reg.48, Sch.5 Part II
Sch.2 para.45, amended: SI 1999/2024 Reg.48, Sch.5 Part II
Sch.2 para.46, amended: SI 1999/2024 Reg.48, Sch.5 Part II
Sch.2 para.59, amended: SI 1996/2089 Reg.34
Sch.2 para.72, amended: SI 1999/2244 Reg.7
Sch.5 para.1, amended: SI 1999/2024 Reg.48, Sch.5 Part II
Sch.5 para.4, amended: SI 1999/2024 Reg.48, Sch.5 Part II
Sch.5 para.5, amended: SI 1999/2024 Reg.48, Sch.5 Part II

3164. **A40 Trunk Road (Hillingdon) Red Route (Clearway) Traffic Order 1995**
Art.2, amended: SI 1999/272 Art.2, Sch. Part B
Art.9, amended: SI 1999/272 Art.2, Sch. Part B

3166. **A41 Trunk Road (Baker Street) Red Route (Prohibited Turn) (No.1) Experimental Traffic Order 1995**
revoked: SI 1997/1222 Art.4

3167. **A41 Trunk Road (Westminster) Red Route (Bus Lane) Experimental Traffic Order 1995**
revoked: SI 1996/2165 Art.7

3174. **Medicines (Products Other Than Veterinary Drugs) (Prescription Only) Amendment (No.2) Order 1995**
revoked: SI 1997/1830 Art.16, Sch.6
Art.2, revoked: SI 1997/1830 Art.16, Sch.6
Art.3, revoked: SI 1997/1830 Art.16, Sch.6
Art.4, revoked: SI 1997/1830 Art.16, Sch.6
Art.5, revoked: SI 1997/1830 Art.16, Sch.6

3177. **Non-Domestic Rating Contributions (Scotland) Amendment Regulations 1995**
revoked: SI 1996/3070 Reg.10, Sch.4
Reg.3, revoked: SI 1996/3070 Reg.10, Sch.4
Reg.4, revoked: SI 1996/3070 Reg.10, Sch.4
Reg.5, revoked: SI 1996/3070 Reg.10, Sch.4
Reg.6, revoked: SI 1996/3070 Reg.10, Sch.4
Reg.7, revoked: SI 1996/3070 Reg.10, Sch.4

3185. **Rent Officers (Additional Functions) (Scotland) (Amendment No.2) Order 1995**
revoked: SI 1997/1995 Art.9, Sch.5

NO.

3187. Miscellaneous Food Additives Regulations 1995
Reg.2, amended: SI 1997/1413 Reg.3, SI 1999/1136 Reg.3
Reg.2, referred to: SI 1999/982 Reg.3
Reg.3, amended: SI 1999/1136 Reg.4
Reg.4, amended: SI 1997/1413 Reg.4
Reg.8, amended: SI 1997/1413 Reg.5
Reg.9, amended: SI 1997/1413 Reg.6
Reg.11, amended: SI 1997/1413 Reg.7, SI 1999/1136 Reg.5
Sch.1, amended: SI 1997/1413 Reg.8, SI 1999/1136 Reg.6
Sch.2, amended: SI 1997/1413 Reg.9
Sch.2 Part A, amended: SI 1999/1136 Reg.7
Sch.2 Part B, amended: SI 1999/1136 Reg.7
Sch.2 Part C, amended: SI 1999/1136 Reg.7
Sch.2 Part D, amended: SI 1999/1136 Reg.7
Sch.3, amended: SI 1997/1413 Reg.10
Sch.3, substituted: SI 1999/1136 Reg.8, Sch.1
Sch.4, amended: SI 1999/1136 Reg.9
Sch.5, amended: SI 1999/1136 Reg.10, Sch.2
Sch.5, revoked (in part): SI 1997/1413 Reg.11, Sch.
Sch.6, amended: SI 1999/1136 Reg.11
Sch.7, substituted: SI 1999/1136 Reg.12, Sch.3
Sch.8, amended: SI 1999/1136 Reg.13
Sch.8 Part 1, amended: SI 1999/1136 Reg.13
Sch.8 Part 2, amended: SI 1999/1136 Reg.13
Sch.8 Part 3, amended: SI 1999/1136 Reg.13
Sch.8 Part 4, amended: SI 1999/1136 Reg.13

3193. Medicines (Veterinary Drugs) (Pharmacy and Merchants' List) (Amendment) Order 1995
revoked: SI 1998/1044 Art.9, Sch.

3200. National Health Service (General Dental Services) (Scotland) Amendment Regulations 1995
revoked: SI 1996/177 Reg.38, Sch.8
Reg.2, revoked: SI 1996/177 Reg.38
Reg.3, revoked: SI 1996/177 Reg.38
Reg.4, revoked: SI 1996/177 Reg.38
Reg.5, revoked: SI 1996/177 Reg.38
Reg.6, revoked: SI 1996/177 Reg.38
Reg.7, revoked: SI 1996/177 Reg.38
Reg.8, revoked: SI 1996/177 Reg.38
Reg.9, revoked: SI 1996/177 Reg.38

3201. National Health Service (Service Committees and Tribunal) (Scotland) Amendment Regulations 1995
Reg.12, revoked (in part): SSI 1999/53 Reg.21

3202. Bread and Flour Regulations 1995
revoked: SI 1998/141 Reg.12, Sch.4
Reg.2, amended: SI 1996/1499 Reg.49, SI 1996/1501 Reg.2
Reg.2, revoked: SI 1998/141 Reg.12, Sch.4
Reg.3, amended: SI 1996/1501 Reg.2
Reg.3, revoked: SI 1998/141 Reg.12, Sch.4
Reg.4, applied: SI 1996/1499 Reg.18
Reg.4, revoked: SI 1998/141 Reg.12, Sch.4
Reg.5, amended: SI 1996/1501 Reg.2
Reg.5, revoked: SI 1998/141 Reg.12, Sch.4
Reg.10, amended: SI 1996/1501 Reg.2
Reg.10, revoked: SI 1998/141 Reg.12, Sch.4
Sch.3, amended: SI 1996/1501 Reg.2
Sch.3, revoked: SI 1998/141 Reg.12, Sch.4

3205. Minced Meat and Meat Preparations (Hygiene) Regulations 1995
applied: SI 1996/3124 Reg.3, Reg.10, Sch.2 para.11, SI 1999/646 Art.33
Reg.2, amended: SI 1996/3124 Reg.41, Sch.6 para.8
Reg.2, applied: SI 1997/2964 Sch.1

NO.

3208. European Specialist Medical Qualifications Order 1995
Art.2, amended: SI 1997/2928 Reg.2, SI 1999/1373 Reg.2, SI 1999/3154 Reg.2
Art.3, applied: SI 1998/5 Reg.8
Art.6, amended: SI 1997/2928 Reg.2
Art.7, applied: SI 1997/2817 Reg.8, SI 1998/5 Reg.8
Art.8, applied: SI 1996/701 Art.4, SI 1996/1313 Reg.4
Art.12, amended: SI 1997/2928 Reg.2
Sch.1 Part I, amended: SI 1997/2928 Reg.2
Sch.1 Part I, applied: SI 1998/5 Reg.8
Sch.2 Part I, amended: SI 1997/2928 Reg.2, SI 1999/1373 Reg.2, SI 1999/3154 Reg.2
Sch.2 Part II, amended: SI 1997/2928 Reg.2, SI 1999/1373 Reg.2

3210. Street Works (Northern Ireland) Order 1995
applied: SI 1999/2450 Sch.4 para.2
Art.13, applied: SI 1999/2450 Sch.4 para.10.1
Sch.3, revoked (in part): SI 1996/275 (NI.2) Art.71, Sch.8
Sch.3 para.8, revoked: SI 1997/276 (NI.2) Art.75, Sch.9

3211. Polygamous Marriages (Northern Ireland) Order 1995
Sch. para.2, revoked: SI 1998/1071 (NI.6) Art.41, Sch.5

3213. Pensions (Northern Ireland) Order 1995
referred to: 1998 c.47 s.87, SI 1999/3147 (NI.11) Art.75
Art.3, amended: SI 1999/3147 (NI.11) Art.17, Art.74, Art.76, Sch.2 para.7, Sch.9 para.33, Sch.10 Part III
Art.3, applied: 1998 c.36 s.92, Sch.15 para.7, SI 1999/3147 (NI.11) Art.4, Art.8, Sch.1 para.1
Art.4, applied: 1998 c.36 s.92, Sch.15 para.7, SI 1999/3147 (NI.11) Art.8, Sch.1 para.1
Art.5, applied: SI 1999/3147 (NI.11) Art.8, Sch.1 para.1
Art.6, applied: SI 1999/3147 (NI.11) Art.8, Sch.1 para.1
Art.7, applied: SI 1999/3147 (NI.11) Art.8, Sch.1 para.1
Art.8, amended: SI 1999/3147 (NI.11) Art.17, Art.76, Sch.2 para.8, Sch.10 Part I
Art.8, applied: SI 1999/3147 (NI.11) Art.8, Sch.1 para.1
Art.9, applied: SI 1999/3147 (NI.11) Art.8, Sch.1 para.1
Art.10, amended: SI 1999/3147 (NI.11) Art.17, Sch.2 para.9
Art.10, applied: SI 1999/3147 (NI.11) Art.4, Art.5, Art.8, Art.30, Sch.1 para.1
Art.11, applied: SI 1999/3147 (NI.11) Art.8, Sch.1 para.1
Art.13, applied: SI 1999/3147 (NI.11) Art.8, Sch.1 para.1
Art.15, applied: SI 1999/3147 (NI.11) Art.8, Sch.1 para.1
Art.16, amended: SI 1999/3147 (NI.11) Art.74, Sch.9 para.34
Art.17, amended: SI 1999/3147 (NI.11) Art.74, Sch.9 para.35
Art.18, amended: SI 1999/3147 (NI.11) Art.74, Sch.9 para.36
Art.20, amended: SI 1999/3147 (NI.11) Art.74, Sch.9 para.37
Art.21, amended: SI 1999/3147 (NI.11) Art.74, Sch.9 para.38

NO.

3213. Pensions (Northern Ireland) Order 1995—
cont.

Art.22, applied: SI 1997/371 Reg.6

Art.27, applied: SI 1999/3147 (NI.11) Art.8, Sch.1 para.1

Art.28, applied: SI 1999/3147 (NI.11) Art.8, Sch.1 para.1

Art.29, applied: 1998 c.36 s.92, Sch.15 para.7, SI 1999/3147 (NI.11) Art.8, Sch.1 para.1

Art.30, applied: SI 1999/3147 (NI.11) Art.8, Sch.1 para.1

Art.31, applied: SI 1999/3147 (NI.11) Art.8, Sch.1 para.1

Art.32, applied: SI 1999/3147 (NI.11) Art.8, Sch.1 para.1

Art.33, applied: SI 1999/3147 (NI.11) Art.8, Sch.1 para.1

Art.34, applied: SI 1999/3147 (NI.11) Art.8, Sch.1 para.1

Art.35, applied: SI 1999/3147 (NI.11) Art.8, Sch.1 para.1

Art.36, applied: SI 1999/3147 (NI.11) Art.8, Sch.1 para.1

Art.38, amended: SI 1999/3147 (NI.11) Art.74, Art.76, Sch.9 para.39, Sch.10 Part III

Art.41, applied: SI 1999/3147 (NI.11) Art.8, Sch.1 para.1

Art.42, referred to: SI 1996/1919 (NI.16) Sch.2 para.11

Art.42, revoked: SI 1996/1919 (NI.16) Art.257, Sch.3

Art.43, referred to: SI 1996/1919 (NI.16) Sch.2 para.11

Art.43, revoked: SI 1996/1919 (NI.16) Art.257, Sch.3

Art.44, referred to: SI 1996/1919 (NI.16) Sch.2 para.11

Art.44, revoked: SI 1996/1919 (NI.16) Art.257, Sch.3

Art.45, referred to: SI 1996/1919 (NI.16) Sch.2 para.11

Art.45, revoked: SI 1996/1919 (NI.16) Art.257, Sch.3

Art.46, referred to: SI 1996/1919 (NI.16) Sch.2 para.11

Art.46, revoked: SI 1996/1919 (NI.16) Art.257, Sch.3

Art.47, applied: SI 1999/3147 (NI.11) Art.8, Sch.1 para.1

Art.48, applied: SI 1999/3147 (NI.11) Art.8, Sch.1 para.1

Art.49, amended: SI 1999/3147 (NI.11) Art.11, Art.17, Sch.2 para.10

Art.49, applied: SI 1999/3147 (NI.11) Art.8, Sch.1 para.1

Art.50, applied: SI 1999/3147 (NI.11) Art.8, Sch.1 para.1

Art.51, amended: SI 1999/3147 (NI.11) Art.74, Sch.9 para.40

Art.53, amended: SI 1999/3147 (NI.11) Art.74, Sch.9 para.41

Art.54, amended: SI 1999/3147 (NI.11) Art.17, Sch.2 para.11

Art.56, amended: SI 1999/3147 (NI.11) Art.32, Sch.5 para.8

Art.56, referred to: SI 1999/3147 (NI.11) Art.35

Art.58, amended: SI 1999/3147 (NI.11) Art.17, Art.76, Sch.2 para.12, Sch.10 Part I

Art.59, amended: SI 1999/3147 (NI.11) Art.17, Sch.2 para.12

Art.67, amended: SI 1999/3147 (NI.11) Art.74, Sch.9 para.42

NO.

3213. Pensions (Northern Ireland) Order 1995—
cont.

Art.68, applied: SI 1999/3147 (NI.11) Art.8, Art.74, Sch.1 para.1, Sch.9 para.43

Art.73, amended: SI 1999/3147 (NI.11) Art.35, Art.74, Sch.9 para.44

Art.74, applied: SI 1999/3147 (NI.11) Art.74, Sch.9 para.45

Art.77, amended: SI 1999/3147 (NI.11) Art.17, Sch.2 para.13

Art.78, applied: SI 1997/724 Reg.9, Reg.16, Reg.24

Art.79, amended: SI 1999/3147 (NI.11) Art.16

Art.79, applied: SI 1999/3147 (NI.11) Art.8, Sch.1 para.1

Art.80, applied: SI 1999/3147 (NI.11) Art.8, Sch.1 para.1

Art.81, amended: SI 1999/3147 (NI.11) Art.16, Art.76, Sch.10 Part I

Art.81, applied: SI 1999/3147 (NI.11) Art.8, Sch.1 para.1

Art.82, applied: SI 1999/3147 (NI.11) Art.8, Sch.1 para.1

Art.83, applied: SI 1999/3147 (NI.11) Art.8, Sch.1 para.1

Art.84, applied: SI 1999/3147 (NI.11) Art.8, Sch.1 para.1

Art.86, amended: SI 1999/3147 (NI.11) Art.11

Art.89, amended: SI 1999/3147 (NI.11) Art.74, Sch.9 para.46

Art.89, applied: SI 1999/3147 (NI.11) Art.8, Sch.1 para.1

Art.89, referred to: SI 1999/3147 (NI.11) Art.41

Art.89, revoked (in part): SI 1999/3147 (NI.11) Art.76, Sch.10 Part I

Art.90, amended: SI 1999/3147 (NI.11) Art.74, Art.76, Sch.9 para.47, Sch.10 Part I

Art.90, applied: SI 1999/3147 (NI.11) Art.8, Sch.1 para.1

Art.90, revoked (in part): SI 1999/3147 (NI.11) Art.14

Art.91, amended: SI 1999/3147 (NI.11) Art.74, Sch.9 para.48

Art.92, applied: SI 1999/3147 (NI.11) Art.8, Sch.1 para.1

Art.93, revoked: SI 1999/3147 (NI.11) Art.76, Sch.10 Part I

Art.94, applied: SI 1999/3147 (NI.11) Art.8, Sch.1 para.1

Art.96, applied: SI 1999/3147 (NI.11) Art.8, Sch.1 para.2

Art.96, referred to: SI 1999/3147 (NI.11) Art.6

Art.97, amended: SI 1999/3147 (NI.11) Art.74, Sch.9 para.49

Art.97, applied: SI 1999/3147 (NI.11) Art.8, Sch.1 para.2, Sch.1 para.3

Art.97, referred to: SI 1999/3147 (NI.11) Art.6

Art.98, amended: SI 1999/3147 (NI.11) Art.6, Art.8, Sch.1 para.2

Art.98, applied: SI 1999/3147 (NI.11) Art.6, Art.8, Sch.1 para.2, Sch.1 para.3

Art.99, amended: SI 1999/3147 (NI.11) Art.6

Art.99, applied: SI 1999/3147 (NI.11) Art.6

Art.100, amended: SI 1999/3147 (NI.11) Art.6

Art.100, applied: SI 1999/3147 (NI.11) Art.6

Art.101, amended: SI 1999/3147 (NI.11) Art.6

Art.101, applied: SI 1999/3147 (NI.11) Art.6

Art.105, amended: 1998 c.11 s.23, Sch.5 para.72, SI 1999/671 Art.3, Sch.1 para.81

Art.106, amended: SI 1999/671 Art.3, Sch.1 para.82

Art.106, applied: SI 1999/3147 (NI.11) Art.8, Sch.1 para.1

NO.

1995—cont.

3213. Pensions (Northern Ireland) Order 1995— *cont.*

Art.108, applied: SI 1999/3147 (NI.11) Art.8, Sch.1 para.1

Art.108, referred to: SI 1999/3147 (NI.11) Art.8, Sch.1 para.2

Art.109, referred to: SI 1999/3147 (NI.11) Art.8, Sch.1 para.2

Art.113, referred to: SI 1999/3147 (NI.11) Art.8, Sch.1 para.2

Art.114, applied: SI 1999/3147 (NI.11) Art.8, Sch.1 para.1

Art.121, amended: SI 1999/3147 (NI.11) Art.8, Art.17, Art.74, Sch.1 para.1, Sch.2 para.14, Sch.9 para.50

Art.121, applied: SI 1999/3147 (NI.11) Art.8, Sch.1 para.1

Art.122, applied: SI 1999/3147 (NI.11) Art.8, Sch.1 para.1

Art.125, amended: SI 1999/3147 (NI.11) Art.67, Sch.8 para.18

Art.134, revoked (in part): SI 1998/1506 (NI.10) Art.78, Sch.7

Art.139, amended: SI 1999/3147 (NI.11) Art.76, Sch.10 Part I

Art.162, amended: SI 1999/3147 (NI.11) Art.74, Sch.9 para.51

Sch.1 para.1, revoked: SI 1996/1919 (NI.16) Art.257, Sch.3

Sch.1 para.2, revoked: SI 1996/1919 (NI.16) Art.257, Sch.3

Sch.1 para.3, revoked: SI 1996/1919 (NI.16) Art.257, Sch.3

Sch.1 para.4, revoked: SI 1996/1919 (NI.16) Art.257, Sch.3

Sch.1 para.5, revoked: SI 1996/1919 (NI.16) Art.257, Sch.3

Sch.1 para.6, revoked: SI 1996/1919 (NI.16) Art.257, Sch.3

Sch.1 para.7, revoked: SI 1996/1919 (NI.16) Art.257, Sch.3

Sch.1 para.9, revoked: SI 1996/1919 (NI.16) Art.257, Sch.3

Sch.1 para.37, revoked (in part): SI 1999/3147 (NI.11) Art.76, Sch.10 Part III

Sch.2 para.1, applied: SI 1996/275 (NI.2) Art.5

Sch.3 para.12, revoked (in part): SI 1999/671 Art.24, Sch.9 Part I

Sch.3 para.14, revoked (in part): SI 1999/671 Art.24, Sch.9 Part I

Sch.3 para.15, revoked: SI 1999/671 Art.24, Sch.9 Part I

Sch.3 para.60, revoked: SI 1998/1506 (NI.10) Art.78, Sch.7

3219. Income Tax (Stock Lending) (Amendment No.2) Regulations 1995

revoked: SI 1997/987 Reg.2 (with savings), Sch.1 (with savings)

Reg.3, revoked: SI 1997/987 Reg.2 (with savings), Sch.1 (with savings)

Reg.4, revoked: SI 1997/987 Reg.2 (with savings), Sch.1 (with savings)

Reg.5, revoked: SI 1997/987 Reg.2 (with savings), Sch.1 (with savings)

Reg.6, revoked: SI 1997/987 Reg.2 (with savings), Sch.1 (with savings)

Reg.7, revoked: SI 1997/987 Reg.2 (with savings), Sch.1 (with savings)

Reg.8, revoked: SI 1997/987 Reg.2 (with savings), Sch.1 (with savings)

Reg.9, revoked: SI 1997/987 Reg.2 (with savings), Sch.1 (with savings)

NO.

1995—cont.

3219. Income Tax (Stock Lending) (Amendment No.2) Regulations 1995—*cont.*

Reg.10, revoked: SI 1997/987 Reg.2 (with savings), Sch.1 (with savings)

Reg.11, revoked: SI 1997/987 Reg.2 (with savings), Sch.1 (with savings)

Reg.12, revoked: SI 1997/987 Reg.2 (with savings), Sch.1 (with savings)

3221. Income Tax (Manufactured Interest) (Amendment) Regulations 1995

revoked: SI 1997/987 Reg.4 (with savings), Sch.2 (with savings)

Reg.3, revoked: SI 1997/987 Reg.4 (with savings), Sch.2 (with savings)

Reg.4, revoked: SI 1997/987 Reg.4 (with savings), Sch.2 (with savings)

Reg.5, revoked: SI 1997/987 Reg.4 (with savings), Sch.2 (with savings)

Reg.6, revoked: SI 1997/987 Reg.4 (with savings), Sch.2 (with savings)

Reg.7, revoked: SI 1997/987 Reg.4 (with savings), Sch.2 (with savings)

Reg.8, revoked: SI 1997/987 Reg.4 (with savings), Sch.2 (with savings)

3223. Insurance Companies (Gilt-Edged Securities) (Periodic Accounting for Tax on Interest) Regulations 1995

revoked (in part): SI 1999/623 Reg.10

Reg.3, revoked (in part): SI 1999/623 Reg.10

Reg.5, revoked (in part): SI 1999/623 Reg.10

Reg.6, amended: SI 1996/1180 Reg.3, SI 1997/987 Reg.7

Reg.6, referred to: SI 1996/21 Reg.3

Reg.6, revoked (in part): SI 1999/623 Reg.10

Reg.7, amended: SI 1996/1180 Reg.4

Reg.7, revoked (in part): SI 1999/623 Reg.10

Reg.8, amended: SI 1996/1180 Reg.5

Reg.8, revoked (in part): SI 1999/623 Reg.10

Reg.10, revoked (in part): SI 1999/623 Reg.10

3224. Gilt-Edged Securities (Periodic Accounting for Tax on Interest) Regulations 1995

referred to: SI 1999/623 Reg.3, SI 1999/624 Reg.3

Reg.2, amended: SI 1997/987 Reg.7, SI 1999/620 Reg.2

Reg.9, amended: SI 1996/1181 Reg.3, Reg.4, Reg.5

Reg.13, amended: SI 1996/1181 Reg.6

Reg.14, amended: SI 1996/1181 Reg.6

Reg.16, amended: SI 1996/1015 Reg.2

Reg.19, amended: SI 1996/1015 Reg.2

Reg.20, amended: SI 1996/1015 Reg.2

3225. Lloyd's Underwriters (Gilt-Edged Securities) (Periodic Accounting for Tax on Interest) Regulations 1995

Reg.2, amended: SI 1997/987 Reg.7

Reg.5, amended: SI 1996/1182 Reg.3, Reg.4, Reg.5

Reg.7, amended: SI 1996/1182 Reg.6

Reg.8, amended: SI 1996/1014 Reg.2

Reg.11, amended: SI 1996/1014 Reg.2

Reg.12, amended: SI 1996/1014 Reg.2

3228. Jobseekers Act 1995 (Commencement No.1) Order 1995

Art.2, amended: SI 1996/1126 Art.3

3233. Deregulation (Building Societies) Order 1995

Art.5, see *Gyoury v Northern Rock Building Society* [1997] E.G.C.S. 56 (Ch D), Carnwath, J.

NO.

NO.

3237. Insurance Companies (Overseas Life Assurance Business) (Compliance) Regulations 1995
Reg.2, amended: SI 1998/1872 Reg.2, SI 1999/2839 Reg.3
Reg.3, revoked: SI 1999/2839 Reg.4
Reg.3A, added: SI 1997/481 Reg.2
Reg.5, amended: SI 1999/2839 Reg.5
Reg.7, amended: SI 1999/2839 Reg.6
Reg.7, revoked (in part): SI 1999/2839 Reg.6
Reg.7A, added: SI 1999/2839 Reg.7
Reg.8, amended: SI 1999/2839 Reg.8
Reg.8, revoked (in part): SI 1999/2839 Reg.8
Reg.9, amended: SI 1999/2839 Reg.9
Reg.10, amended: SI 1999/2839 Reg.10
Reg.10A, added: SI 1999/2839 Reg.11
Reg.11, amended: SI 1999/2839 Reg.12
Reg.13, amended: SI 1999/2839 Reg.13
Reg.14, amended: SI 1999/2839 Reg.14
Reg.14A, amended: SI 1999/2839 Reg.15
Reg.15, amended: SI 1999/2839 Reg.16
Reg.16, amended: SI 1999/2839 Reg.17
Reg.16A, added: SI 1999/2839 Reg.18
Reg.17, revoked: SI 1999/2839 Reg.4
Reg.18, amended: SI 1999/2839 Reg.19
Reg.18A, added: SI 1999/2839 Reg.20
Reg.19, amended: SI 1999/2839 Reg.21
Reg.20, revoked: SI 1999/2839 Reg.4

3240. Cheese and Cream Regulations 1995
applied: SI 1996/1499 Reg.50
revoked: SI 1996/1499 Reg.49, Sch.9

3243. Church Representation Rules (Amendment) Resolution 1995
referred to: SI 1998/319, SI 1999/2112

3246. Specified Bovine Offal (Amendment) Order 1995
revoked: SI 1996/963 Art.27

3248. Insurance Companies (Amendment) Regulations 1995
Reg.21, applied: SI 1996/942 Reg.15

3249. Export of Goods (Control) (Amendment No.2) Order 1995
revoked: SI 1999/63 Art.2
Art.3, amended: SI 1996/2663 Art.3, Sch.2
Art.3, revoked: SI 1999/63 Art.2
Art.4, revoked: SI 1997/2758 Art.1

3252. Water Undertakings (Rateable Values) (Scotland) (No.2) Order 1995
Art.3, referred to: SI 1996/103 Reg.13

3254. Severn Bridges Tolls Order 1995
revoked: SI 1996/3212 Art.3
Art.3, revoked: SI 1996/3212 Art.3

3261. Child Support (Miscellaneous Amendments) (No.2) Regulations 1995
Reg.56, substituted: SI 1999/1510 Art.39
Reg.57, amended: SI 1999/1510 Art.40
Reg.57, revoked (in part): SI 1999/1510 Art.40

3263. Child Support (Compensation for Recipients of Family Credit and Disability Working Allowance) Regulation 1995
revoked: SI 1999/2566 Reg.6 (with saving)
Reg.1, revoked: SI 1999/2566 Reg.6 (with saving)
Reg.2, revoked: SI 1999/2566 Reg.6 (with saving)
Reg.5, amended: SI 1999/1510 Art.41
Reg.5, revoked: SI 1999/2566 Reg.6 (with saving)

3271. Financial Services Act 1986 (Investment Services) (Extension of Scope of Act) Order 1995
Art.6, revoked (in part): SI 1996/2996 Art.2

3272. Uncertificated Securities Regulations 1995
Reg.3, amended: SI 1996/2827 Reg.75, Sch.8 Part II
Reg.19, amended: SI 1996/2827 Reg.75, Sch.8 Part II
Reg.22, applied: SI 1996/2827 Reg.44
Reg.23, referred to: SI 1996/2827 Sch.4 para.2
Reg.25, applied: SI 1996/1469 Reg.5
Reg.27, referred to: SI 1996/2827 Sch.5 para.3
Sch.2 para.5, amended: SI 1999/506 Art.36

3273. Financial Services Act 1986 (EEA Regulated Markets) (Exemption) Order 1995
see *Securities and Investments Board v Scandex Capital Management A/S* [1998] 1 W.L.R. 712 (CA), Millet L.J.

3275. Investment Services Regulations 1995
referred to: SI 1996/1669 Reg.9, Reg.10, 1998 c.11 s.21
Reg.2, amended: SI 1996/1669 Reg.23, Sch.5 para.11, 1998 c.11 s.23, Sch.5 para.45
Reg.2, applied: SI 1996/1883 Art.9
Reg.8, revoked (in part): 1998 c.11 s.43, Sch.9 Part II
Reg.13, revoked: 1998 c.11 s.43, Sch.9 Part II
Reg.14, revoked: 1998 c.11 s.43, Sch.9 Part II
Reg.17, amended: 1998 c.11 s.23, Sch.5 para.45
Reg.18, amended: 1998 c.11 s.23, Sch.5 para.45
Reg.26, amended: 1998 c.11 s.23, s.25, Sch.5 para.45
Reg.26, revoked (in part): 1998 c.11 s.43, Sch.9 Part II
Reg.42, amended: 1998 c.11 s.23, Sch.5 para.45
Reg.44, amended: 1998 c.11 s.23, Sch.5 para.45
Reg.46, amended: 1998 c.11 s.23, Sch.5 para.45
Reg.48, amended: SI 1996/1669 Reg.11
Reg.54, amended: 1998 c.11 s.23, Sch.5 para.45
Reg.56, amended: 1998 c.11 s.23, Sch.5 para.45
Sch.3 para.1, revoked (in part): 1998 c.11 s.43, Sch.9 Part II
Sch.3 para.3, revoked (in part): 1998 c.11 s.43, Sch.9 Part II
Sch.3 para.4, revoked (in part): 1998 c.11 s.43, Sch.9 Part II
Sch.3 para.5, revoked (in part): 1998 c.11 s.43, Sch.9 Part II
Sch.3 para.6, revoked: 1998 c.11 s.43, Sch.9 Part II
Sch.6 para.1, revoked (in part): 1998 c.11 s.43, Sch.9 Part II
Sch.6 para.2, revoked (in part): 1998 c.11 s.43, Sch.9 Part II
Sch.6 para.3, revoked (in part): 1998 c.11 s.43, Sch.9 Part II
Sch.6 para.4, amended: 1998 c.11 s.23, Sch.5 para.45
Sch.6 para.4, revoked (in part): 1998 c.11 s.43, Sch.9 Part II
Sch.6 para.5, revoked (in part): 1998 c.11 s.43, Sch.9 Part II
Sch.6 para.6, revoked (in part): 1998 c.11 s.43, Sch.9 Part II
Sch.6 para.7, amended: 1998 c.11 s.23, Sch.5 para.45
Sch.6 para.7, revoked (in part): 1998 c.11 s.43, Sch.9 Part II

NO.

3275. Investment Services Regulations 1995— *cont.*

Sch.6 para.8, amended: 1998 c.11 s.23, Sch.5 para.45

Sch.6 para.9, revoked: 1998 c.11 s.43, Sch.9 Part II

Sch.8 para.5a, added: SI 1996/1669 Reg.11, Sch.2

Sch.8 para.5b, added: SI 1996/1669 Reg.11, Sch.2

Sch.8 para.6, substituted: SI 1996/1669 Reg.11, Sch.2

Sch.10 para.3, revoked: 1998 c.29 Sch.16 Part II

Sch.10 para.15, revoked: 1998 c.29 Sch.16 Part II

3276. Jobseeker's Allowance (Transitional Provisions) Regulations 1995

applied: SI 1996/1307 Reg.6

revoked: SI 1996/2567 Reg.22

Reg.1, amended: SI 1996/1515 Reg.2, SI 1996/2538 Reg.3

Reg.2, amended: SI 1996/2519 Reg.2

Reg.3, amended: SI 1996/1515 Reg.3, SI 1996/2519 Reg.2

Reg.5, amended: SI 1996/1515 Reg.5

Reg.5A, added: SI 1996/2519 Reg.2

Reg.5A, amended: SI 1996/2538 Reg.3

Reg.6, amended: SI 1996/1515 Reg.6

Reg.7, amended: SI 1996/1515 Reg.7, SI 1996/2519 Reg.2

Reg.8, amended: SI 1996/1515 Reg.8, SI 1996/2519 Reg.2

Reg.9, amended: SI 1996/1515 Reg.9, SI 1996/2519 Reg.2

Reg.9, applied: SI 1996/2890 Sch.3 para.50

Reg.9A, added: SI 1996/1515 Reg.10

Reg.11, amended: SI 1996/1515 Reg.11, SI 1996/2519 Reg.2

Reg.13, amended: SI 1996/1515 Reg.12

Reg.14, amended: SI 1996/1515 Reg.13, SI 1996/2538 Reg.3

Reg.15, amended: SI 1996/1515 Reg.15

Reg.16, amended: SI 1996/1515 Reg.16

Reg.18, added: SI 1996/1515 Reg.14

Reg.19, added: SI 1996/1515 Reg.14

3280. National Health Service (Fund-Holding Practices) (Functions of Family Health Services Authorities) Regulations 1995

revoked: SI 1996/706 Reg.28

3294. Local Government (Superannuation and Compensation for Redundancy or Premature Retirement) (Scotland) Amendment Regulations 1995

applied: SI 1998/364 Reg.4, Reg.6, Reg.19, Sch.2 para.2, Sch.2 para.5, Sch.4 para.8

referred to: SI 1998/364 Reg.3, Reg.10, Sch.2 para.4, Sch.2 para.6

Reg.11, revoked: SI 1998/192 Reg.52, Sch.2

3295. Rural Diversification Programme (Scotland) Regulations 1995

Reg.2, amended: SI 1999/651 Reg.3

Reg.3, amended: SI 1999/651 Reg.4

Reg.4, applied: SI 1999/651 Reg.2

Reg.5, amended: SI 1999/651 Reg.5

Reg.7, amended: SI 1997/722 Reg.2, SI 1999/651 Reg.6

Reg.8, amended: SI 1999/651 Reg.7

Sch.2, substituted: SI 1997/722 Reg.3, Sch, SI 1999/651 Reg.8, Sch.

NO.

3297. Duration of Copyright and Rights in Performances Regulations 1995

Reg.15, applied: SI 1996/2967 Reg.19

Reg.16, applied: SI 1996/2967 Reg.19

Reg.19, applied: SI 1996/2967 Reg.19

3298. Dual-Use and Related Goods (Export Control) (Amendment No.2) Regulations 1995

applied: SI 1996/2721 Reg.15

revoked: SI 1996/2721 Sch.1

Reg.2, revoked: SI 1996/2721 Sch.1

3320. Income Support (General) Amendment Regulations 1995

revoked: SI 1996/909 Reg.3

Reg.1, revoked: SI 1996/909 Reg.3

Reg.2, revoked: SI 1996/909 Reg.3

3321. Education (Mandatory Awards) Regulations 1995

see *B v B (Adult Student: Liability to Support)* [1998] 1 F.L.R. 373 (CA), Thorpe, L.J.

applied: SI 1996/1623 Art.3

revoked: SI 1997/431 Reg.6

Reg.2, amended: SI 1996/2088 Reg.3

Reg.2, revoked: SI 1997/431 Reg.6

Reg.3, amended: SI 1996/2088 Reg.4

Reg.3, revoked: SI 1997/431 Reg.6

Reg.4, revoked: SI 1997/431 Reg.6

Reg.6, revoked: SI 1997/431 Reg.6

Reg.9, amended: SI 1996/2088 Reg.5

Reg.9, revoked: SI 1997/431 Reg.6

Reg.10, amended: SI 1996/2088 Reg.6

Reg.10, revoked: SI 1997/431 Reg.6

Reg.12, amended: SI 1996/2088 Reg.7

Reg.12, revoked: SI 1997/431 Reg.6

Reg.13, amended: SI 1996/2088 Reg.8

Reg.13, revoked: SI 1997/431 Reg.6

Reg.17, applied: SI 1996/2890 Reg.43

Reg.17, revoked: SI 1997/431 Reg.6

Reg.25, amended: SI 1996/2088 Reg.9

Reg.25, revoked: SI 1997/431 Reg.6

Sch.2 para.7, applied: SI 1996/2890 Reg.43

Sch.2 para.7, revoked: SI 1997/431 Reg.6

Sch.3, revoked: SI 1997/431 Reg.6

Sch.5, revoked: SI 1997/431 Reg.6

Sch.5 para.1, referred to: SI 1996/1944 Reg.8

Sch.5 para.1, revoked: SI 1997/431 Reg.6

3325. Olympics Association Right (Infringement Proceedings) Regulations 1995

applied: SI 1998/3132 r.49

Reg.3, applied: SI 1999/929 r.3.5.2

Reg.5, applied: SI 1999/929 r.3.5.2, r.3.5.3

1996

Kensington & Chelsea (Waiting and Loading Restrictions) (Special Parking Area) (Amendment No.14) Order 1996

revoked (in part): SI 1999/1264 Art.10

11. Social Security (Persons from Abroad) (Miscellaneous Amendments) Regulations (Northern Ireland) 1996

Reg.4, amended: 1996 c.49 Sch.1 para.8

Reg.5, amended: 1996 c.49 Sch.1 para.9

Reg.11, amended: 1996 c.49 Sch.1 para.10

21. Friendly Societies (Gilt-Edged Securities) (Periodic Accounting for Tax on Interest) Regulations 1996

revoked (in part): SI 1999/624 Reg.9

Reg.3, revoked (in part): SI 1999/624 Reg.9

Reg.5, revoked (in part): SI 1999/624 Reg.9

Reg.6, revoked (in part): SI 1999/624 Reg.9

Reg.7, amended: SI 1997/475 Reg.4

Reg.7, revoked (in part): SI 1999/624 Reg.9

NO.

21. **Friendly Societies (Gilt-Edged Securities) (Periodic Accounting for Tax on Interest) Regulations 1996**—*cont.*
    Reg.8, revoked (in part): SI 1999/624 Reg.9
    Reg.9, revoked (in part): SI 1999/624 Reg.9
22. **Civil Aviation (Canadian Navigation Services) (Third Amendment) Regulations 1996**
    revoked: SI 1996/688 Reg.3, Sch.1
    Reg.2, revoked: SI 1996/688 Reg.3, Sch.1
27. **Hill Livestock (Compensatory Allowances) (Amendment) Regulations 1996**
    revoked (in part): SI 1996/1500 Reg.18
28. **Sheep and Goats (Records, Identification and Movement) Order 1996**
    applied: SI 1996/1500 Reg.9, SI 1999/3315 Reg.4, SSI 1999/187 Reg.14
    Art.4, applied: SI 1996/1500 Reg.12
    Art.5, applied: SI 1996/49 Reg.2, SSI 1999/187 Reg.17
    Art.5, referred to: SI 1999/3316 Reg.15
30. **Employer's Contributions Reimbursement Regulations (Northern Ireland) 1996**
    Reg.1, revoked (in part): SI 1999/671 Art.24, Sch.9 Part II
    Reg.7, applied: SI 1999/671 Art.3, Sch.2
    Reg.8, applied: SI 1999/671 Art.3, Sch.2
    Reg.9, applied: SI 1999/671 Art.3, Sch.2
30. **Social Security (Persons from Abroad) Miscellaneous Amendments Regulations 1996**
    see *R. v Adjudication Officer Ex p. B* Times, July 27, 1998 (QBD), Sedley, J.; see *R. v Secretary of State for Social Security Ex p. Joint Council for the Welfare of Immigrants* [1997] 1 W.L.R. 275 (CA), Simon Brown, L.J.; see *R. v Secretary of State for Social Security Ex p. Tamenene* [1997] C.O.D. 288 (QBD), Potts, J.
    Reg.3, amended: 1996 c.49 Sch.1 para.4
    Reg.4, see *R. v Chief Adjudication Officer Ex p. B* [1999] 1 W.L.R. 1695 (CA), Peter Gibson, L.J.
    Reg.7, amended: 1996 c.49 Sch.1 para.3
    Reg.8, see *R. v Secretary of State for Social Security Ex p. Vijeikis* [1998] C.O.D. 49 (QBD), Judge Hague Q.C.
    Reg.8, amended: 1996 c.49 Sch.1 para.2
    Reg.12, see *R. v Chief Adjudication Officer Ex p. B* [1999] 1 W.L.R. 1695 (CA), Peter Gibson, L.J.; see *R. v Secretary of State for Social Security Ex p. Vijeikis* [1998] C.O.D. 49 (QBD), Judge Hague Q.C.
    Reg.12, amended: 1996 c.49 Sch.1 para.5, SI 1999/2422 Art.3, Sch.12
    Reg.12, referred to: SI 1999/3056 Reg.7
41. **A41 Trunk Road (Barnet) Red Route (No.1) Experimental Traffic Order 1996**
    revoked: SI 1997/467 Art.10
    Art.5, revoked: SI 1997/467 Art.10
    Art.8, revoked: SI 1997/467 Art.10
    Art.11, revoked: SI 1997/467 Art.10
42. **A41 Trunk Road (Barnet) Red Route (No.2) Experimental Traffic Order 1996**
    revoked: SI 1997/1210 Art.10
    Art.11, revoked: SI 1997/1210 Art.10
47. **Spreadable Fats (Marketing Standards) Regulations (Northern Ireland) 1996**
    revoked: SR 1999/383 Reg.9, Sch.2
50. **Miscellaneous Food Additives Regulations (Northern Ireland) 1996**
    referred to: 1996 c.56 Sch.40 para.10

NO.

56. **Local Government Reorganisation (Wales) (Council Tax Reduction Scheme) Order 1996**
    referred to: SI 1999/2262 Reg.4
63. **A30 Trunk Road (Hounslow and Hillingdon) Red Route (Clearway) Traffic Order 1996**
    amended: SI 1996/215 Art.5
    Art.2, amended: SI 1999/272 Art.2, Sch. Part B
    Art.9, amended: SI 1999/272 Art.2, Sch. Part B
    Sch.2 Item 1, substituted: SI 1997/548 Art.3
    Sch.2 Item 2, substituted: SI 1997/548 Art.3
    Sch.2 Item 3, substituted: SI 1997/548 Art.3
    Sch.2 Item 4, substituted: SI 1997/548 Art.3
    Sch.2 Item 5, substituted: SI 1997/548 Art.3
    Sch.2 Item 6, substituted: SI 1997/548 Art.3
    Sch.2 Item 7, substituted: SI 1997/548 Art.3
    Sch.2 Item 8, substituted: SI 1997/548 Art.3
    Sch.2 Item 9, added: SI 1997/548 Art.3
    Sch.3A Item 1, revoked: SI 1997/548 Art.4
81. **Diseases of Animals (Importation of Bird Products) Order (Northern Ireland) 1996**
    referred to: SI 1997/322 Reg.36
90. **London Ambulance Service National Health Service Trust (Establishment) Order 1996**
    Art.3, substituted: SI 1998/2837 Art.2
97. **Offshore Installations (Safety Zones) Order 1996**
    revoked: SI 1997/735 Art.3, Sch.2
98. **A1 Trunk Road (Haringey) Red Route Traffic Order 1993 Experimental Variation Order 1996**
    revoked: SI 1997/201 Art.7
    Art.3, revoked: SI 1997/201 Art.7
    Art.4, revoked: SI 1997/201 Art.7
    Art.5, revoked: SI 1997/201 Art.7
    Art.6, revoked: SI 1997/201 Art.7
99. **A1 Trunk Road (Islington) Red Route Traffic Order 1993 Experimental Variation No.3 Order 1996**
    revoked: SI 1997/202 Art.7
    Art.3, revoked: SI 1997/202 Art.7
    Art.4, revoked: SI 1997/202 Art.7
    Art.5, revoked: SI 1997/202 Art.7
    Art.6, revoked: SI 1997/202 Art.7
99. **Child Support Commissioners (Procedure) (Amendment) Regulations (Northern Ireland) 1996**
    revoked: SR 1999/226
103. **Non-Domestic Rates (Levying) (Scotland) Regulations 1996**
    revoked: SI 1997/452 Reg.26
    Part II, applied: SI 1997/452 Reg.11
    Part II, revoked: SI 1997/452 Reg.26
    Part IV, applied: SI 1997/452 Reg.6, Reg.11
    Part IV, referred to: SI 1997/452 Reg.18
    Part IV, revoked: SI 1997/452 Reg.26
    Part V, applied: SI 1997/452 Reg.11
    Part V, revoked: SI 1997/452 Reg.26
    Reg.6, revoked: SI 1997/452 Reg.26
    Reg.7, applied: SI 1997/452 Reg.6
    Reg.7, referred to: SI 1997/452 Reg.18
    Reg.7, revoked: SI 1997/452 Reg.26
    Reg.11, revoked: SI 1997/452 Reg.26
    Reg.12, revoked: SI 1997/452 Reg.26
    Reg.13, revoked: SI 1997/452 Reg.26
    Reg.23, revoked: SI 1997/452 Reg.26
    Reg.27, revoked: SI 1997/452 Reg.26
    Reg.28, revoked: SI 1997/452 Reg.26
    Reg.30, revoked: SI 1997/452 Reg.26

NO.

107. Vehicle Excise Duty (Immobilisation, Removal and Disposal of Vehicles) Regulations 1996
revoked: SI 1997/2439 Reg.1
Reg.5, revoked: SI 1997/2439 Reg.1
Reg.8, amended: SI 1997/565 Reg.3
Reg.8, revoked: SI 1997/2439 Reg.1
Reg.9, revoked: SI 1997/2439 Reg.1
Reg.11, amended: SI 1997/565 Reg.4
Reg.11, revoked: SI 1997/2439 Reg.1
Reg.16, revoked: SI 1997/2439 Reg.1
Sch.2, revoked: SI 1997/2439 Reg.1
Sch.2, substituted: SI 1997/565 Reg.5, Sch

119. Health and Safety (Safety Signs and Signals) Regulations (Northern Ireland) 1996
amended: SR 1999/150 Reg.2, Sch.

160. Sea Fish Industry Authority (Levy) Regulations 1995 Confirmation Order 1996
Sch., substituted: SI 1999/837 Sch. para.3

176. Local Government Changes for England (Council Tax) (Transitional Reduction) Regulations 1996
applied: SI 1998/214 Reg.11
revoked (in part): SI 1999/259 Reg.11
Reg.2, amended: SI 1997/215 Reg.11, Sch.4 para.1
Reg.2, applied: SI 1999/259 Reg.11
Reg.2, revoked (in part): SI 1999/259 Reg.11
Reg.3, amended: SI 1997/215 Reg.11, Sch.4 para.2, SI 1998/214 Reg.11, Sch.4 para.1
Reg.3, revoked (in part): SI 1999/259 Reg.11
Reg.4, revoked (in part): SI 1999/259 Reg.11
Reg.10, revoked (in part): SI 1999/259 Reg.11
Sch.1, applied: SI 1999/259 Reg.11
Sch.1, revoked (in part): SI 1999/259 Reg.11
Sch.1 para.3, applied: SI 1999/259 Sch. Part I
Sch.1 para.3, revoked (in part): SI 1999/259 Reg.11
Sch.2 para.1, amended: SI 1996/333 Reg.2, SI 1997/215 Reg.11, Sch.4 para.3, SI 1998/214 Reg.11, Sch.4 para.2
Sch.2 para.1, revoked (in part): SI 1999/259 Reg.11
Sch.2 para.1A, added: SI 1996/333 Reg.2
Sch.2 para.1A, revoked (in part): SI 1999/259 Reg.11
Sch.2 para.2, amended: SI 1996/333 Reg.2
Sch.2 para.2, revoked (in part): SI 1999/259 Reg.11
Sch.3, applied: SI 1999/259 Reg.11
Sch.3, revoked (in part): SI 1999/259 Reg.11
Sch.3 Part 1, applied: SI 1999/259 Sch. Part I
Sch.3 Part 1, revoked (in part): SI 1999/259 Reg.11
Sch.3 Part 2, applied: SI 1999/259 Sch. Part I
Sch.3 Part 2, revoked (in part): SI 1999/259 Reg.11
Sch.3 Part 4, applied: SI 1999/259 Sch. Part I
Sch.3 Part 4, revoked (in part): SI 1999/259 Reg.11

177. National Health Service (General Dental Services) (Scotland) Regulations 1996
applied: SI 1997/174 Reg.17
Part III, revoked: SI 1998/2259 Reg.4
Reg.2, amended: SI 1998/1663 Reg.3, SI 1999/724 Reg.2, SSI 1999/51 Reg.3
Reg.3, amended: SSI 1999/51 Reg.2
Reg.4, amended: SI 1998/1663 Reg.4, SI 1999/724 Reg.3, SSI 1999/51 Reg.4
Reg.5, amended: SSI 1999/51 Reg.2
Reg.6, amended: SI 1996/2060 Reg.2, SI 1998/1663 Reg.5, SI 1998/2224 Reg.4, SSI 1999/51 Reg.2

NO.

177. National Health Service (General Dental Services) (Scotland) Regulations 1996—*cont.*
Reg.9, amended: SSI 1999/51 Reg.5
Reg.10, amended: SSI 1999/51 Reg.2
Reg.11, amended: SI 1998/2224 Reg.4, SSI 1999/51 Reg.2
Reg.12, amended: SSI 1999/51 Reg.2
Reg.12, revoked (in part): SI 1999/724 Reg.4
Reg.13, amended: SSI 1999/51 Reg.2
Reg.14, amended: SSI 1999/51 Reg.2
Reg.15, amended: SSI 1999/51 Reg.2
Reg.16, amended: SSI 1999/51 Reg.2
Reg.17, amended: SSI 1999/51 Reg.6
Reg.18, amended: SI 1999/724 Reg.5, SSI 1999/51 Reg.7
Reg.19, amended: SI 1999/724 Reg.6, SSI 1999/51 Reg.8
Reg.23, amended: SI 1998/2224 Reg.4, SI 1999/724 Reg.7, SSI 1999/51 Reg.9
Reg.24, amended: SSI 1999/51 Reg.2
Reg.25, amended: SI 1996/2060 Reg.2, SI 1999/724 Reg.8, SSI 1999/51 Reg.2
Reg.27, amended: SSI 1999/51 Reg.2
Reg.28, amended: SSI 1999/51 Reg.2
Reg.29, amended: SI 1999/724 Reg.9, SSI 1999/51 Reg.2
Reg.30, amended: SI 1999/724 Reg.10, SSI 1999/51 Reg.2
Reg.31, amended: SI 1999/724 Reg.11, SSI 1999/51 Reg.10
Reg.32, amended: SI 1999/724 Reg.12
Reg.33, amended: SI 1996/841 Reg.3
Reg.34A, added: SI 1996/841 Reg.4
Reg.34A, amended: SSI 1999/51 Reg.11
Reg.35, amended: SSI 1999/51 Reg.12
Reg.35, amended: SSI 1999/51 Reg.2
Reg.36, amended: SSI 1999/51 Reg.2
Sch.1 para.2, amended: SI 1996/841 Reg.6, SSI 1999/51 Reg.13
Sch.1 para.4, amended: SI 1996/2060 Reg.2, SSI 1999/51 Reg.13
Sch.1 para.5, amended: SI 1996/2060 Reg.2, SSI 1999/51 Reg.13
Sch.1 para.7, amended: SI 1998/2224 Reg.4
Sch.1 para.8, amended: SI 1996/2060 Reg.2, SSI 1999/51 Reg.13
Sch.1 para.9, amended: SI 1996/2060 Reg.2, SSI 1999/51 Reg.13
Sch.1 para.11, amended: SI 1998/1663 Reg.6, SSI 1999/51 Reg.13
Sch.1 para.11A, added: SI 1998/1663 Reg.6
Sch.1 para.11A, amended: SSI 1999/51 Reg.13
Sch.1 para.12, amended: SI 1998/2224 Reg.4
Sch.1 para.13, amended: SSI 1999/51 Reg.13
Sch.1 para.14, amended: SI 1998/2224 Reg.4
Sch.1 para.15, amended: SSI 1999/51 Reg.13
Sch.1 para.17, revoked (in part): SI 1998/1663 Reg.6
Sch.1 para.18, amended: SI 1998/2224 Reg.4
Sch.1 para.25, amended: SSI 1999/51 Reg.13
Sch.1 para.27, amended: SSI 1999/51 Reg.13
Sch.1 para.31, amended: SI 1996/2060 Reg.2, SSI 1999/51 Reg.13
Sch.1 para.31, substituted: SI 1996/841 Reg.6
Sch.1 para.31A, added: SI 1996/841 Reg.5
Sch.1 para.31A, amended: SI 1996/2060 Reg.2, SSI 1999/51 Reg.13
Sch.1 para.31B, added: SI 1996/841 Reg.5
Sch.1 para.31B, amended: SSI 1999/51 Reg.13
Sch.1 para.31C, added: SI 1996/841 Reg.5
Sch.1 para.31C, amended: SI 1996/2060 Reg.2, SSI 1999/51 Reg.13
Sch.1 para.31D, added: SI 1998/1663 Reg.6

NO.

177. National Health Service (General Dental Services) (Scotland) Regulations 1996—*cont.*
Sch.1 para.31D, amended: SSI 1999/51 Reg.13
Sch.1 para.32, amended: SSI 1999/51 Reg.13
Sch.1 para.33, amended: SSI 1999/51 Reg.13
Sch.1 para.35, amended: SSI 1999/51 Reg.13
Sch.1 para.39, amended: SI 1999/724 Reg.13, SSI 1999/51 Reg.13
Sch.1 para.40, amended: SI 1999/724 Reg.13, SSI 1999/51 Reg.13
Sch.1 para.41, amended: SI 1999/724 Reg.13, SSI 1999/51 Reg.13
Sch.1 para.42, amended: SI 1999/724 Reg.13, SSI 1999/51 Reg.13
Sch.1 para.43, amended: SI 1999/724 Reg.13, SSI 1999/51 Reg.13
Sch.1 para.44, amended: SI 1999/724 Reg.13, SSI 1999/51 Reg.13
Sch.1 para.45, amended: SI 1999/724 Reg.13
Sch.2 para.9, amended: SSI 1999/51 Reg.14
Sch.2 para.10, amended: SSI 1999/51 Reg.14
Sch.2 para.16, added: SI 1998/1663 Reg.7
Sch.2 para.17, added: SI 1998/1663 Reg.7
Sch.4 Part II, amended: SI 1998/1663 Reg.8
Sch.6, amended: SSI 1999/51 Reg.15
Sch.6 para.2, amended: SI 1999/724 Reg.14, SSI 1999/51 Reg.15

182. Social Security (Adjudication) and Child Support Amendment Regulations 1996
Reg.2, revoked: SI 1999/991 Reg.59 (with savings), Sch.4 (with savings)

184. Housing (Change of Landlord) (Payment of Disposal Cost by Instalments) (Amendment) Regulations 1996
revoked: SI 1996/1269 Reg.3

185. Local Government Pension Scheme (Appropriate Pension Fund) Regulations 1996
applied: SI 1997/1613 Reg.4, Reg.19, Sch.2 para.2
referred to: SI 1997/1613 Reg.3, Sch.2 para.6

187. Land Registration Fees Order 1996
revoked: SI 1997/178 Art.1

188. Social Security (Additional Pension) (Contributions Paid in Error) Regulations (Northern Ireland) 1996
applied: SI 1999/671 Art.3, Sch.2

192. Equipment and Protective Systems Intended for Use in Potentially Explosive Atmospheres Regulations 1996
applied: SI 1998/2306 Reg.10, Sch.1
Sch.1, amended: SI 1998/81 Reg.3

193. Social Security (Back to Work Bonus) Regulations 1996
revoked: SI 1996/2570 Reg.28
Reg.1, amended: SI 1996/2538 Reg.4
Reg.2, amended: SI 1996/1511 Reg.3
Reg.3, amended: SI 1996/1511 Reg.4
Reg.4, amended: SI 1996/1511 Reg.5, Reg.23, Sch.
Reg.5, amended: SI 1996/2538 Reg.4
Reg.7, amended: SI 1996/1511 Reg.6, Reg.23, Sch., SI 1996/2538 Reg.4
Reg.8, amended: SI 1996/1511 Reg.7, Reg.23, Sch.
Reg.9, amended: SI 1996/1511 Reg.8
Reg.10, amended: SI 1996/1511 Reg.9
Reg.11, amended: SI 1996/1511 Reg.10
Reg.12, amended: SI 1996/1511 Reg.11, Reg.23, Sch.
Reg.14, amended: SI 1996/1511 Reg.12
Reg.15, amended: SI 1996/1511 Reg.13, SI 1996/2538 Reg.4

NO.

193. Social Security (Back to Work Bonus) Regulations 1996—*cont.*
Reg.16, amended: SI 1996/1511 Reg.14
Reg.17, amended: SI 1996/2538 Reg.4
Reg.18, revoked: SI 1996/1511 Reg.15
Reg.19, amended: SI 1996/1511 Reg.16
Reg.20, amended: SI 1996/1511 Reg.17, Reg.23, Sch.
Reg.21, amended: SI 1996/1511 Reg.18, SI 1996/2538 Reg.4
Reg.23, amended: SI 1996/1511 Reg.19, Reg.23, Sch.
Reg.25, amended: SI 1996/1511 Reg.20
Reg.25A, added: SI 1996/1511 Reg.21
Reg.25B, added: SI 1996/1511 Reg.21
Reg.26, amended: SI 1996/1511 Reg.22, Reg.23, Sch.

195. Employer's Contributions Re-imbursement Regulations 1996
Reg.1, revoked (in part): 1999 c.2 s.26, Sch.10 Part II
Reg.5, amended: SI 1999/286 Reg.2
Reg.6, amended: SI 1999/286 Reg.2
Reg.7, applied: 1999 c.2 s.1, Sch.2
Reg.8, applied: 1999 c.2 s.1, Sch.2
Reg.9, applied: 1999 c.2 s.1, Sch.2

206. Income Support (General) (Jobseeker's Allowance Consequential Amendments) Regulations 1996
Reg.32, amended: SI 1996/1944 Reg.12

207. Jobseeker's Allowance Regulations 1996
amended: SI 1997/1909 Reg.4
applied: SI 1996/1623 Art.3, SI 1997/791 Reg.26, SI 1997/1909 Reg.26, SI 1998/217 Art.2, SI 1999/779 Art.2, Sch.
referred to: SI 1998/1541 Reg.1
Ch.IVA, added: SI 1998/1174 Reg.3
Part II Ch. IV, applied: SI 1999/991 Reg.27, Sch.2 para.19
Part V, referred to: SI 1998/2825 Reg.7
Part IX, applied: SI 1996/2570 Reg.5
Part X, applied: SI 1996/2570 Reg.5
Part XI, applied: SI 1996/2570 Reg.8
Reg.1, amended: SI 1996/1516 Reg.2, Reg.20, Sch. Part II, SI 1996/2538 Reg.2, SI 1997/65 Reg.4, SI 1997/454 Reg.2, SI 1998/563 Reg.5, SI 1998/1274 Reg.2, SI 1998/2231 Reg.14, SI 1998/2825 Reg.12, SI 1999/2566 Reg.2, Sch.2 Part III, SI 1999/3156 Reg.12
Reg.1, applied: SI 1997/791 Reg.3
Reg.2, amended: SI 1999/2165 Reg.2
Reg.2, applied: SI 1997/984 Reg.6
Reg.2A, added: SI 1997/2676 Reg.12
Reg.3, amended: SI 1997/2863 Reg.2
Reg.3, applied: SI 1997/984 Reg.6
Reg.4, amended: SI 1996/2538 Reg.2, SI 1997/2863 Reg.3, SI 1998/1274 Reg.3
Reg.4, referred to: SI 1997/984 Reg.6
Reg.6, referred to: SI 1997/791 Reg.6, Reg.7, SI 1997/1909 Reg.6, Reg.7
Reg.7, referred to: SI 1997/791 Reg.6, Reg.7, SI 1997/1909 Reg.6, Reg.7
Reg.11, amended: SI 1996/1517 Reg.3, SI 1999/3087 Reg.2
Reg.11, applied: SI 1997/791 Reg.23, Reg.25, SI 1997/1909 Reg.23, Reg.25
Reg.11, referred to: SI 1997/791 Reg.22, SI 1997/1909 Reg.22
Reg.12, amended: SI 1996/1517 Reg.4
Reg.13, applied: SI 1997/791 Reg.6, Reg.9, SI 1997/1909 Reg.6, Reg.9
Reg.13, referred to: SI 1997/791 Reg.7, SI 1997/1909 Reg.7

NO.

207. Jobseeker's Allowance Regulations 1996—
cont.

Reg.14, amended: SI 1996/1517 Reg.5, SI 1997/563 Reg.2, SI 1997/982 Reg.4, SI 1999/3087 Reg.3

Reg.15, amended: SI 1997/563 Reg.3, SI 1998/2825 Reg.8, SI 1999/3156 Reg.8

Reg.15, applied: SI 1999/991 Reg.27, Sch.2 para.19

Reg.15, referred to: SI 1997/791 Reg.13, SI 1997/1909 Reg.13

Reg.17, amended: SI 1996/1517 Reg.6

Reg.17A, added: SI 1998/1274 Reg.4

Reg.17A, amended: SI 1998/2874 Reg.2, SI 1999/3083 Reg.2

Reg.18, applied: SI 1997/791 Reg.23, Reg.25, SI 1997/1909 Reg.23, Reg.25

Reg.18, referred to: SI 1997/791 Reg.22, SI 1997/1909 Reg.22

Reg.18A, added: SI 1997/563 Reg.4

Reg.18A, amended: SI 1999/3087 Reg.4

Reg.19, amended: SI 1996/1517 Reg.7, SI 1997/563 Reg.5, SI 1998/1274 Reg.5, SI 1999/3087 Reg.5

Reg.21A, added: SI 1998/1274 Reg.6

Reg.23, amended: SI 1999/3108 Reg.18, Sch.3 para.1

Reg.23, applied: SI 1996/1307 Reg.3, SI 1996/2567 Reg.20, Reg.21, SI 1997/791 Reg.3, Reg.5, Reg.22, Reg.23, SI 1997/982 Reg.3, SI 1997/983 Reg.3, SI 1997/984 Reg.3, SI 1997/1909 Reg.3, Reg.5, Reg.22, Reg.23, SI 1998/2825 Reg.3, Reg.4, Reg.5, SI 1999/3156 Reg.3, Reg.4, Reg.5

Reg.23, referred to: SI 1997/791 Reg.22

Reg.24, amended: SI 1996/1517 Reg.8, SI 1999/3108 Reg.18, Sch.3 para.1

Reg.24, applied: SI 1996/2567 Reg.21, SI 1999/991 Reg.27, Sch.2 para.19

Reg.25, amended: SI 1999/530 Reg.2

Reg.26, amended: SI 1996/1516 Reg.8, Sch. Part I, SI 1996/1517 Reg.9

Reg.26, applied: SI 1996/2567 Reg.21

Reg.31, amended: SI 1999/2860 Art.3, Sch.12 para.1, Sch.12 para.2

Reg.32, amended: SI 1999/2860 Art.3, Sch.12 para.2, Sch.12 para.3

Reg.33, amended: SI 1999/2860 Art.3, Sch.12 para.2

Reg.34, amended: SI 1996/1516 Reg.3

Reg.35, amended: SI 1999/2860 Art.3, Sch.12 para.2

Reg.36, amended: SI 1996/1517 Reg.10

Reg.39, amended: SI 1999/2860 Art.3, Sch.12 para.2

Reg.40, amended: SI 1999/2860 Art.3, Sch.12 para.2

Reg.41, revoked: SI 1999/2860 Art.3, Sch.12 para.4

Reg.42, amended: SI 1997/454 Reg.2

Reg.42, revoked: SI 1999/2860 Art.3, Sch.12 para.4

Reg.43, revoked: SI 1999/2860 Art.3, Sch.12 para.4

Reg.44, revoked: SI 1999/2860 Art.3, Sch.12 para.4

Reg.45, revoked: SI 1999/2860 Art.3, Sch.12 para.4

Reg.46, amended: SI 1998/71 Reg.2

Reg.47, amended: SI 1996/1517 Reg.14, SI 1996/2538 Reg.2, SI 1999/714 Reg.2, SI 1999/2226 Reg.3

NO.

207. Jobseeker's Allowance Regulations 1996—
cont.

Reg.47A, added: SI 1996/2538 Reg.2

Reg.47A, amended: SI 1997/2677 Reg.2, SI 1998/563 Reg.16

Reg.48, amended: SI 1996/1517 Reg.15, SI 1996/2538 Reg.2, SI 1997/454 Reg.2, SI 1997/2863 Reg.4

Reg.48, applied: SI 1997/791 Reg.3, SI 1997/1909 Reg.3

Reg.49, amended: SI 1996/1517 Reg.16

Reg.51, amended: SI 1996/1516 Reg.9, Reg.20, Sch. Part II, SI 1997/454 Reg.2, SI 1999/2860 Art.3, Sch.12 para.5

Reg.52, amended: SI 1996/1516 Reg.20, Sch. Part II, SI 1999/2556 Reg.3

Reg.53, amended: SI 1996/1516 Reg.20, Sch. Part II, SI 1998/2825 Reg.13, SI 1999/2165 Reg.7, SI 1999/3156 Reg.13

Reg.54, amended: SI 1997/2863 Reg.5

Reg.54, applied: SI 1999/991 Reg.15

Reg.55, amended: SI 1996/1517 Reg.17, SI 1999/2860 Art.3, Sch.12 para.2

Reg.57, amended: SI 1996/1516 Reg.4, SI 1996/1517 Reg.11, SI 1998/1698 Reg.2

Reg.63, amended: SI 1997/827 Reg.2

Reg.63, applied: SI 1999/991 Reg.7

Reg.65A, added: SI 1996/1517 Reg.12

Reg.66, amended: SI 1996/1516 Reg.8, Sch. Part I

Reg.67, amended: SI 1996/1517 Reg.13

Reg.68, amended: SI 1997/827 Reg.3, SI 1999/2860 Art.3, Sch.12 para.2

Reg.69, amended: SI 1997/982 Reg.5, SI 1997/983 Reg.4, SI 1997/984 Reg.4, SI 1997/2863 Reg.6, SI 1998/2825 Reg.6, SI 1999/2677 Reg.5

Reg.69, applied: SI 1996/1307 Reg.6, SI 1999/991 Reg.7

Reg.70, amended: SI 1999/2860 Art.3, Sch.12 para.2

Reg.71, amended: SI 1996/1516 Reg.5

Reg.72, amended: SI 1997/454 Reg.2, SI 1997/791 Reg.21, SI 1997/1909 Reg.21, SI 1998/1274 Reg.7

Reg.72, applied: SI 1997/791 Reg.20, SI 1997/1909 Reg.20

Reg.72, referred to: SI 1997/791 Reg.21, SI 1997/1909 Reg.21

Reg.73, amended: SI 1996/1516 Reg.6, SI 1997/2863 Reg.7, SI 1998/1274 Reg.8

Reg.73, applied: SI 1996/1307 Reg.5, SI 1997/791 Reg.19, SI 1997/982 Reg.6, SI 1997/983 Reg.5, SI 1997/984 Reg.5, SI 1997/1909 Reg.19, SI 1999/3156 Reg.9

Reg.73, referred to: SI 1998/2825 Reg.9

Reg.74A, added: SI 1996/1516 Reg.7

Reg.75, amended: SI 1997/367 Reg.2, SI 1997/454 Reg.2, SI 1998/1174 Reg.3, SI 1998/1274 Reg.9, SI 1998/1698 Reg.3, Reg.4

Reg.75, applied: SI 1996/1307 Reg.4

Reg.75, referred to: SI 1998/2825 Reg.6

Reg.75, revoked (in part): SI 1998/1698 Reg.3

Reg.75, substituted: SI 1997/2863 Reg.8

Reg.76, applied: SI 1996/940 Reg.3, SI 1996/2545 Reg.10

Reg.77, applied: SI 1996/940 Reg.4

Reg.78, amended: SI 1996/1516 Reg.20, Sch. Part II, SI 1996/1517 Reg.18

Reg.78, applied: SI 1996/940 Reg.5

Reg.79, amended: SI 1997/543 Art.23, SI 1998/470 Art.23, SI 1999/264 Art.23

NO.

207. Jobseeker's Allowance Regulations 1996— *cont.*

Reg.79, applied: SI 1996/1345 Reg.12, Reg.19

Reg.80, amended: SI 1997/454 Reg.2

Reg.81, amended: SI 1996/1517 Reg.19, SI 1997/454 Reg.2

Reg.83, amended: SI 1998/470 Art.24, SI 1999/264 Art.24

Reg.83, applied: SI 1997/543 Art.24, SI 1998/2825 Reg.10, SI 1999/3156 Reg.10

Reg.84, amended: SI 1996/1516 Reg.20, Sch. Part II, SI 1997/543 Art.24, SI 1998/470 Art.24, SI 1999/264 Art.24

Reg.84, applied: SI 1998/2825 Reg.10, SI 1999/3156 Reg.10

Reg.85, amended: SI 1996/1516 Reg.10, Reg.20, Sch. Part II, SI 1996/2538 Reg.2, SI 1997/454 Reg.2, SI 1997/543 Art.24, SI 1998/470 Art.24, SI 1998/563 Reg.8, Reg.18, SI 1999/264 Art.24

Reg.85, applied: SI 1998/19 Reg.2, SI 1998/2825 Reg.10, SI 1999/3156 Reg.10

Reg.86, applied: SI 1998/19 Reg.2, SI 1998/2825 Reg.10, SI 1999/3156 Reg.10

Reg.87, amended: SI 1996/1516 Reg.20, Sch. Part II, SI 1996/1517 Reg.20

Reg.87, applied: SI 1999/991 Reg.14

Reg.87A, added: SI 1996/1517 Reg.21

Reg.88, amended: SI 1996/1516 Reg.20, Sch. Part II

Reg.88A, added: SI 1998/1174 Reg.3

Reg.94, amended: SI 1997/65 Reg.5, SI 1998/563 Reg.12, SI 1999/2860 Art.3, Sch.12 para.2

Reg.97, amended: SI 1997/65 Reg.6, SI 1997/454 Reg.2

Reg.98, amended: SI 1996/1517 Reg.22, SI 1997/454 Reg.2, SI 1999/1509 Reg.2

Reg.99, applied: SI 1996/2570 Reg.8

Reg.100, amended: SI 1999/2165 Reg.7

Reg.101, amended: SI 1999/2860 Art.3, Sch.12 para.2

Reg.101, applied: SI 1996/2570 Reg.8

Reg.102A, added: SI 1998/1174 Reg.3

Reg.102A, amended: SI 1999/3156 Reg.18

Reg.102B, added: SI 1998/1174 Reg.3

Reg.102C, added: SI 1998/1174 Reg.3

Reg.102D, added: SI 1998/1174 Reg.3

Reg.103, amended: SI 1996/1517 Reg.23, SI 1997/65 Reg.7, SI 1997/454 Reg.2

Reg.104, amended: SI 1997/65 Reg.3, SI 1999/2860 Art.3, Sch.12 para.5

Reg.105, amended: SI 1996/1803 Reg.42, SI 1997/2197 Reg.6, Reg.7, SI 1997/2863 Reg.9, SI 1998/563 Reg.6, SI 1998/2117 Reg.2, SI 1998/2825 Reg.14, SI 1999/2566 Reg.2, Sch.2 Part I, Sch.2 Part II, SI 1999/2640 Reg.2, SI 1999/2860 Art.3, Sch.12 para.2, Sch.12 para.6, SI 1999/3156 Reg.14, SI 1999/3324 Reg.3

Reg.106, amended: SI 1999/2860 Art.3, Sch.12 para.5

Reg.107, substituted: SI 1996/1516 Reg.11

Reg.110, amended: SI 1998/563 Reg.14

Reg.111, amended: SI 1999/2860 Art.3, Sch.12 para.5

Reg.113, amended: SI 1997/2197 Reg.6, SI 1997/2863 Reg.10, SI 1998/2117 Reg.3, SI 1998/2825 Reg.15, SI 1999/2640 Reg.2, SI 1999/3156 Reg.15

Reg.115, amended: SI 1998/2250 Reg.2

Reg.116, amended: SI 1996/1516 Reg.12, SI 1997/65 Reg.8, SI 1997/2197 Reg.7

NO.

207. Jobseeker's Allowance Regulations 1996— *cont.*

Reg.121, amended: SI 1996/1803 Reg.43

Reg.129, amended: SI 1996/2538 Reg.2

Reg.130, amended: SI 1998/563 Reg.4, SI 1999/1935 Reg.2

Reg.131, amended: SI 1996/1516 Reg.20, Sch. Part II, SI 1996/1517 Reg.24, SI 1997/1671 Reg.2, SI 1998/1379 Reg.2, SI 1999/1935 Reg.2

Reg.135, amended: SI 1999/1935 Reg.2

Reg.136, amended: SI 1999/1935 Reg.2

Reg.136, referred to: SI 1999/991 Reg.6

Reg.137, amended: SI 1999/1935 Reg.2

Reg.137A, added: SI 1998/563 Reg.4

Reg.137A, amended: SI 1999/1935 Reg.2

Reg.139, amended: SI 1999/2860 Art.3, Sch.12 para.2

Reg.140, amended: SI 1996/1516 Reg.13, Reg.20, Sch. Part II, SI 1996/1517 Reg.25, SI 1997/2863 Reg.11, SI 1999/2860 Art.3, Sch.12 para.2

Reg.140A, added: SI 1997/2863 Reg.12

Reg.140A, amended: SI 1999/2860 Art.3, Sch.12 para.7

Reg.141, amended: SI 1996/1517 Reg.26, SI 1996/2538 Reg.2, SI 1998/71 Reg.3, SI 1999/2860 Art.3, Sch.12 para.2, Sch.12 para.8

Reg.142, amended: SI 1996/1517 Reg.27, SI 1996/2538 Reg.2, SI 1999/2860 Art.3, Sch.12 para.9

Reg.144, amended: SI 1996/1516 Reg.14

Reg.145, amended: SI 1996/1516 Reg.15, SI 1996/1517 Reg.28, SI 1997/543 Art.24, Sch.17, SI 1998/470 Art.24, Sch.17, SI 1999/264 Art.24, Sch.17

Reg.145, applied: SI 1998/2825 Reg.10, SI 1999/3156 Reg.10

Reg.145, revoked (in part): SI 1996/1516 Reg.15

Reg.146, amended: SI 1999/2860 Art.3, Sch.12 para.9

Reg.147, amended: SI 1996/1516 Reg.10, SI 1999/2860 Art.3, Sch.12 para.2

Reg.147, applied: SI 1996/2570 Reg.5

Reg.148, amended: SI 1997/543 Art.24, Sch.17, SI 1998/470 Art.24, Sch.17, SI 1999/264 Art.24, Sch.17

Reg.148, applied: SI 1998/2825 Reg.10, SI 1999/3156 Reg.10

Reg.149, amended: SI 1996/1516 Reg.20, Sch. Part II, SI 1998/563 Reg.19

Reg.151, amended: SI 1996/1516 Reg.16

Reg.161, amended: SI 1996/1516 Reg.17

Reg.163, amended: SI 1996/1516 Reg.20, Sch. Part II, SI 1999/2860 Art.3, Sch.12 para.2

Reg.166, amended: SI 1996/1516 Reg.20, Sch. Part II

Reg.170, amended: SI 1998/1698 Reg.5

Reg.171, amended: SI 1996/1516 Reg.20, Sch. Part II

Reg.172, amended: SI 1997/543 Art.25, SI 1998/470 Art.25, SI 1999/264 Art.25

Sch.1 Part I, amended: SI 1997/543 Art.24, Sch.13

Sch.1 Part II, amended: SI 1996/1803 Reg.44, SI 1997/543 Art.24

Sch.1 Part III, amended: SI 1996/1803 Reg.44, SI 1997/543 Art.24

Sch.1 Part III, revoked (in part): SI 1996/1803 Reg.44

Sch.1 Part IV, amended: SI 1996/1803 Reg.44, SI 1997/543 Art.24, Sch.14

NO.

1996—cont.

207. Jobseeker's Allowance Regulations 1996— *cont.*

Sch.1 para.1, amended: SI 1996/1516 Reg.18, Reg.20, Sch. Part II, SI 1998/470 Art.24, Sch.13, SI 1999/264 Art.24, Sch.13

Sch.1 para.2, amended: SI 1996/2545 Reg.2, SI 1997/543 Art.24, SI 1998/470 Art.24, Sch.13, SI 1998/1541 Reg.2, SI 1999/264 Art.24, Sch.13, SI 1999/2555 Reg.2

Sch.1 para.3, amended: SI 1997/2197 Reg.7, SI 1998/470 Art.24, Sch.13, SI 1999/264 Art.24, Sch.13

Sch.1 para.3, applied: SI 1998/19 Reg.2

Sch.1 para.4, amended: SI 1997/1790 Reg.13, SI 1998/470 Art.24, SI 1998/766 Reg.14, SI 1999/264 Art.24

Sch.1 para.4, applied: SI 1998/1581 Reg.4

Sch.1 para.8, amended: SI 1996/2538 Reg.2

Sch.1 para.10, applied: SI 1998/19 Reg.2, SI 1998/1581 Reg.4

Sch.1 para.11, applied: SI 1998/19 Reg.2

Sch.1 para.12, amended: SI 1996/2538 Reg.2, SI 1998/2231 Reg.14

Sch.1 para.12, applied: SI 1998/19 Reg.2, SI 1998/1581 Reg.4

Sch.1 para.13, applied: SI 1998/1581 Reg.4

Sch.1 para.14, amended: SI 1996/1516 Reg.20, Sch. Part II, SI 1999/2566 Reg.2, Sch.2 Part II

Sch.1 para.20, amended: SI 1996/1516 Reg.20, Sch. Part II, SI 1998/470 Art.24, Sch.14, SI 1999/264 Art.24, Sch.14

Sch.2, applied: SI 1999/991 Reg.7

Sch.2 para.1, amended: SI 1996/1516 Reg.20, Sch. Part II

Sch.2 para.1A, added: SI 1997/2305 Reg.3

Sch.2 para.2, amended: SI 1996/1516 Reg.20, Sch. Part II

Sch.2 para.3, amended: SI 1996/1516 Reg.20, Sch. Part II

Sch.2 para.4, amended: SI 1996/1517 Reg.29, SI 1996/2538 Reg.2, SI 1997/2863 Reg.13

Sch.2 para.5, amended: SI 1997/543 Art.24, Sch.17, SI 1998/470 Art.24, Sch.17, SI 1999/264 Art.24, Sch.17

Sch.2 para.6, amended: SI 1997/543 Art.24, Sch.17, SI 1997/2305 Reg.3, SI 1998/470 Art.24, Sch.17, SI 1999/264 Art.24, Sch.17

Sch.2 para.6, applied: SI 1999/991 Reg.7

Sch.2 para.7, amended: SI 1996/1516 Reg.20, Sch. Part II, SI 1997/543 Art.24, Sch.17, SI 1997/2305 Reg.3, SI 1998/470 Art.24, Sch.17, SI 1999/264 Art.24, Sch.17

Sch.2 para.7, applied: SI 1999/991 Reg.7

Sch.2 para.8, applied: SI 1999/991 Reg.7

Sch.2 para.9, amended: SI 1997/543 Art.24, Sch.17, SI 1998/470 Art.24, Sch.17, SI 1999/264 Art.24, Sch.17

Sch.2 para.10, amended: SI 1996/1516 Reg.20, Sch. Part II, SI 1997/543 Art.24, Sch.17, SI 1998/470 Art.24, Sch.17, SI 1999/264 Art.24, Sch.17

Sch.2 para.11, amended: SI 1996/1517 Reg.29, SI 1997/543 Art.24, Sch.17, SI 1998/470 Art.24, Sch.17, SI 1999/264 Art.24, Sch.17

Sch.2 para.12, amended: SI 1999/2860 Art.3, Sch.12 para.5, Sch.12 para.11

Sch.2 para.13, amended: SI 1996/1516 Reg.20, Sch. Part II, SI 1996/1517 Reg.29, SI 1996/2538 Reg.2, SI 1997/827 Reg.4, SI 1997/2863 Reg.13, SI 1998/2231 Reg.14, SI

1996—cont.

207. Jobseeker's Allowance Regulations 1996— *cont.*

Sch.2 para.13, amended:—*cont.* 1999/714 Reg.2, SI 1999/1921 Reg.2, SI 1999/2860 Art.3, Sch.12 para.5, Sch.12 para.10, Sch.12 para.11

Sch.2 para.14, applied: SI 1999/991 Reg.7

Sch.2 para.15, applied: SI 1999/991 Reg.7

Sch.2 para.17, amended: SI 1996/1517 Reg.29, SI 1996/2518 Reg.4, SI 1996/2538 Reg.2, SI 1997/543 Art.24, SI 1997/827 Reg.4, SI 1998/470 Art.24, SI 1999/2860 Art.3, Sch.12 para.2

Sch.2 para.18, amended: SI 1996/1517 Reg.29

Sch.3, amended: SI 1997/454 Reg.2

Sch.4, amended: SI 1997/543 Art.24

Sch.4 para.1, amended: SI 1997/543 Art.24, SI 1998/470 Art.24, SI 1999/264 Art.24

Sch.4 para.2, amended: SI 1997/543 Art.24, Sch.15 Part II, SI 1998/470 Art.24, Sch.15 Part II, SI 1999/264 Art.24, Sch.15 Part II

Sch.4 para.5, amended: SI 1997/543 Art.24, Sch.15 Part I, SI 1998/470 Art.24, Sch.15 Part I, SI 1999/264 Art.24, Sch.15 Part I

Sch.4 para.6, amended: SI 1997/543 Art.24, Sch.15 Part I, SI 1998/470 Art.24, Sch.15 Part I, SI 1999/264 Art.24, Sch.15 Part I

Sch.4 para.8, amended: SI 1996/1516 Reg.20, Sch. Part II

Sch.4 para.9, amended: SI 1997/543 Art.24, Sch.15 Part I, SI 1998/470 Art.24, Sch.15 Part I, SI 1999/264 Art.24, Sch.15 Part I

Sch.4 para.10, amended: SI 1996/1516 Reg.20, Sch. Part II, SI 1999/2860 Art.3, Sch.12 para.2

Sch.4 para.11, amended: SI 1997/543 Art.24, Sch.15 Part I, SI 1998/470 Art.24, Sch.15 Part I, SI 1999/264 Art.24, Sch.15 Part I

Sch.5 para.1, amended: SI 1996/1516 Reg.20, Sch. Part II, SI 1997/543 Art.24, Sch.16 Part I, SI 1998/470 Art.24, Sch.16 Part I, SI 1999/264 Art.24, Sch.16 Part I

Sch.5 para.2, amended: SI 1996/1516 Reg.20, Sch. Part II, SI 1997/543 Art.24, Sch.16 Part I, SI 1999/264 Art.24, Sch.16 Part I

Sch.5 para.3, applied: SI 1998/19 Reg.2

Sch.5 para.4, amended: SI 1997/543 Art.24, Sch.16 Part II, SI 1998/470 Art.24, Sch.16 Part II, SI 1999/264 Art.24, Sch.16 Part II

Sch.5 para.5, applied: SI 1998/19 Reg.2

Sch.5 para.6, applied: SI 1998/19 Reg.2

Sch.5 para.7, amended: SI 1996/2538 Reg.2, SI 1997/543 Art.24, Sch.16 Part I, SI 1998/470 Art.24, Sch.16 Part I, SI 1999/264 Art.24, Sch.16 Part I

Sch.5 para.8, amended: SI 1996/1516 Reg.20, Sch. Part II, SI 1997/543 Art.24, Sch.16 Part I, SI 1998/470 Art.24, Sch.16 Part I, SI 1999/264 Art.24, Sch.16 Part I

Sch.5 para.9, amended: SI 1996/1803 Reg.45, SI 1997/543 Art.24, Sch.16 Part I, SI 1998/470 Art.24, Sch.16 Part I, SI 1999/264 Art.24, Sch.16 Part I

Sch.5 para.11, amended: SI 1996/1516 Reg.20, Sch. Part II, SI 1997/454 Reg.2

Sch.5 para.13, amended: SI 1996/1516 Reg.20, Sch. Part II, SI 1996/2538 Reg.2

Sch.5 para.14, amended: SI 1996/1516 Reg.20, Sch. Part II, SI 1997/543 Art.24, Sch.16 Part II, SI 1998/470 Art.24, Sch.16 Part II, SI 1999/264 Art.24, Sch.16 Part II

NO.

207. Jobseeker's Allowance Regulations 1996— cont.

Sch.5 para.15, amended: SI 1996/1516 Reg.20, Sch. Part II, SI 1997/543 Art.24, Sch.16 Part I, SI 1998/470 Art.24, Sch.16 Part I, SI 1999/264 Art.24, Sch.16 Part I

Sch.5 para.15, applied: SI 1998/19 Reg.2

Sch.5 para.16, amended: SI 1997/543 Art.24, Sch.16 Part II, SI 1998/470 Art.24, Sch.16 Part II, SI 1999/264 Art.24, Sch.16 Part II

Sch.5 para.17, amended: SI 1996/1516 Reg.20, Sch. Part II, SI 1996/1517 Reg.30, SI 1997/543 Art.24, Sch.16 Part I, SI 1998/470 Art.24, Sch.16 Part I, SI 1999/264 Art.24, Sch.16 Part I

Sch.6 para.1, amended: SI 1996/1516 Reg.20, Sch. Part II, SI 1996/1517 Reg.31

Sch.6 para.2, amended: SI 1996/1517 Reg.31

Sch.6 para.5, applied: SI 1996/2570 Reg.8

Sch.6 para.6, amended: SI 1996/1803 Reg.46

Sch.6 para.6, applied: SI 1996/2570 Reg.8

Sch.6 para.6, substituted: SI 1997/1790 Reg.14, SI 1998/766 Reg.15

Sch.6 para.7, applied: SI 1996/2570 Reg.8

Sch.6 para.8, applied: SI 1996/2570 Reg.8

Sch.6 para.9, applied: SI 1996/2570 Reg.8

Sch.6 para.10, applied: SI 1996/2570 Reg.8

Sch.6 para.11, amended: SI 1996/1516 Reg.19

Sch.6 para.11, applied: SI 1996/2570 Reg.8

Sch.7 para.12, amended: SI 1997/2197 Reg.7, SI 1999/1677 Reg.2

Sch.7 para.14, amended: SI 1997/2863 Reg.14

Sch.7 para.16A, added: SI 1996/1517 Reg.32

Sch.7 para.16A, amended: SI 1997/65 Reg.2

Sch.7 para.23, amended: SI 1996/1516 Reg.20, Sch. Part II

Sch.7 para.26, amended: SI 1998/563 Reg.7

Sch.7 para.28, substituted: SI 1998/563 Reg.7

Sch.7 para.30, referred to: SI 1999/991 Reg.7

Sch.7 para.31, amended: SI 1998/1173 Reg.5

Sch.7 para.31, referred to: SI 1999/991 Reg.7

Sch.7 para.31A, added: SI 1998/1173 Reg.5

Sch.7 para.38, amended: SI 1997/454 Reg.2

Sch.7 para.56, added: SI 1997/65 Reg.2

Sch.7 para.57, added: SI 1997/65 Reg.2

Sch.7 para.58, added: SI 1997/65 Reg.2

Sch.7 para.59, added: SI 1997/65 Reg.2

Sch.7 para.59, amended: SI 1999/1935 Reg.2

Sch.7 para.60, added: SI 1997/2863 Reg.14

Sch.7 para.60, substituted: SI 1998/1174 Reg.4

Sch.7 para.61, added: SI 1997/2863 Reg.14

Sch.7 para.62, amended: SI 1999/3156 Reg.18

Sch.7 para.62, substituted: SI 1998/1174 Reg.4

Sch.7 para.63, added: SI 1998/563 Reg.13

Sch.7 para.63, substituted: SI 1998/2117 Reg.4

Sch.7 para.64, added: SI 1998/2117 Reg.6

Sch.7 para.65, amended: SI 1998/2825 Reg.16, SI 1999/3156 Reg.16

Sch.7 para.66, amended: SI 1998/2825 Reg.16, SI 1999/3156 Reg.16

Sch.7 para.67, added: SI 1999/2165 Reg.7

Sch.8 para.11, amended: SI 1998/1174 Reg.5, SI 1999/3156 Reg.18

Sch.8 para.12, amended: SI 1996/2538 Reg.2

Sch.8 para.42, amended: SI 1997/2197 Reg.7

Sch.8 para.43, amended: SI 1997/2197 Reg.7

Sch.8 para.45, added: SI 1997/2863 Reg.15

Sch.8 para.45, substituted: SI 1998/1174 Reg.5

Sch.8 para.46, added: SI 1997/2863 Reg.15

Sch.8 para.47, amended: SI 1999/3156 Reg.18

Sch.8 para.47, substituted: SI 1998/1174 Reg.5

Sch.8 para.48, added: SI 1998/2117 Reg.5

NO.

207. Jobseeker's Allowance Regulations 1996— cont.

Sch.8 para.49, amended: SI 1998/2825 Reg.17, SI 1999/3156 Reg.17

Sch.8 para.50, amended: SI 1998/2825 Reg.17, SI 1999/3156 Reg.17

Sch.8 para.51, added: SI 1999/2165 Reg.7

211. Motor Vehicles (Driving Licences) (Amendment) Regulations 1996

revoked: SI 1996/2824 Reg.2, Sch.1

Reg.3, revoked: SI 1996/2824 Reg.2, Sch.1

Reg.4, revoked: SI 1996/2824 Reg.2, Sch.1

Reg.5, revoked: SI 1996/2824 Reg.2, Sch.1

Reg.6, revoked: SI 1996/2824 Reg.2, Sch.1

Reg.7, revoked: SI 1996/2824 Reg.2, Sch.1

Reg.8, revoked: SI 1996/2824 Reg.2, Sch.1

212. Motor Vehicles (Driving Licences) (Large Goods and Passenger Carrying Vehicles) (Amendment) Regulations 1996

revoked: SI 1996/2824 Reg.2, Sch.1

Reg.3, revoked: SI 1996/2824 Reg.2, Sch.1

Reg.4, revoked: SI 1996/2824 Reg.2, Sch.1

Reg.5, revoked: SI 1996/2824 Reg.2, Sch.1

Reg.6, revoked: SI 1996/2824 Reg.2, Sch.1

Reg.7, revoked: SI 1996/2824 Reg.2, Sch.1

217. A205 Trunk Road (Richmond and Wandsworth) Red Route Experimental Traffic Order 1995 (Amendment No.1) Order 1996

revoked: SI 1996/2164 Art.10

Art.2, revoked: SI 1996/2164 Art.10

228. Offshore Installations and Wells (Design and Construction, etc.) Regulations (Northern Ireland) 1996

amended: SR 1999/150 Reg.2, Sch.

230. Hill Livestock (Compensatory Allowances) Regulations (Northern Ireland) 1996

revoked: SR 1999/497 Reg.15 (with savings)

232. Central Manchester Development Corporation (Planning Functions) Order 1996

Art.4, applied: SI 1996/233 Art.2

235. Education (Grants for Education Support and Training: Nursery Education) (England) Regulations 1996

referred to: SI 1996/889 Reg.23

revoked: SI 1998/656 Reg.12

Reg.6, amended: SI 1997/514 Reg.12

Reg.6, revoked: SI 1998/656 Reg.12

Reg.8, revoked: SI 1998/656 Reg.12

Reg.9, revoked: SI 1998/656 Reg.12

243. Child Support Commissioners (Procedure) (Amendment) Regulations 1996

revoked (in part): SI 1999/1305 Reg.2

Reg.2, revoked (in part): SI 1999/1305 Reg.2

Reg.3, revoked (in part): SI 1999/1305 Reg.2

244. Carriage by Air (Sterling Equivalents) Order 1996

revoked: SI 1999/2881 Art.2

Art.2, revoked: SI 1999/2881 Art.2

Art.3, revoked: SI 1999/2881 Art.2

247. Sea Fishing (Enforcement of Community Quota Measures) Order 1996

revoked: SI 1997/883 Art.13 (with savings)

Art.2, amended: SI 1996/2433 Art.3

Art.2, revoked: SI 1997/883 Art.13 (with savings)

Art.5, revoked: SI 1997/883 Art.13 (with savings)

Art.13, revoked: SI 1997/883 Art.13 (with savings)

Sch., revoked: SI 1997/883 Art.13 (with savings)

Sch., substituted: SI 1996/2433 Art.4, Sch.

1996—cont.

251. National Health Service (Clinical Negligence Scheme) Regulations 1996
referred to: SI 1999/873 Reg.4, SI 1999/874 Reg.4
Reg.1, amended: SI 1997/527 Reg.2
Reg.3, amended: SI 1997/527 Reg.3
Reg.9, amended: SI 1997/527 Reg.4, SI 1999/1274 Reg.2
Reg.9A, added: SI 1999/1274 Reg.3

257. Bridgend and District National Health Service Trust (Establishment) Order 1996
revoked: SI 1999/1120 Art.2, Sch.2

258. Glan Hafren National Health Service Trust (Establishment) Order 1996
revoked: SI 1999/1120 Art.2, Sch.2
Art.3, revoked: SI 1999/1120 Art.2, Sch.2
Art.3, substituted: SI 1997/1225 Art.2

263. Charter Trustees Regulations 1996
Reg.5, amended: SI 1996/610 Reg.2
Reg.6, referred to: SI 1998/582 Art.6
Reg.7, amended: SI 1996/610 Reg.2
Reg.7, applied: SI 1998/582 Art.6
Reg.8, applied: SI 1998/582 Art.6
Reg.9, applied: SI 1998/582 Art.6
Reg.10, applied: SI 1998/582 Art.6
Reg.11, applied: SI 1998/582 Art.6
Reg.11A, added: SI 1996/610 Reg.2
Reg.12, applied: SI 1998/582 Art.6
Reg.13, amended: SI 1996/610 Reg.2
Reg.13, applied: SI 1998/582 Art.5, Art.6
Reg.14, applied: SI 1998/582 Art.6
Reg.15, applied: SI 1998/582 Art.6
Reg.16, applied: SI 1998/582 Art.6
Reg.17, applied: SI 1998/582 Art.6
Reg.18, applied: SI 1998/582 Art.6
Reg.18, revoked: SI 1999/545 Reg.17

264. A316 Trunk Road (Richmond) (No.2) Red Route Experimental Traffic Order 1996
revoked (in part): SI 1997/1824 Art.10
Art.11, revoked (in part): SI 1997/1824 Art.10

265. Local Government Act 1988 (Defined Activities) (Specified Periods) (Wales) Regulations 1996
revoked: SI 1997/2747 Reg.2, Sch.
Reg.4, revoked: SI 1997/2747 Reg.2, Sch.
Reg.5, revoked: SI 1997/2747 Reg.2, Sch.

266. European Communities (Designation) Order 1996
revoked (in part): SI 1999/2788 Art.4, Sch.3
Art.3, revoked (in part): SI 1999/2788 Art.4, Sch.3

269. Child Abduction and Custody (Parties to Conventions) (Amendment) Order 1996
revoked: SI 1996/2595 Art.2
Art.2, revoked: SI 1996/2595 Art.2
Art.3, revoked: SI 1996/2595 Art.2
Art.4, revoked: SI 1996/2595 Art.2

272. International Tribunal for the Law of the Sea (Immunities and Privileges) Order 1996
referred to: 1997 c.28 s.28

274. Education (Northern Ireland) Order 1996
applied: SI 1998/1759 (NI.13) Art.40, Sch.2 para.3
Art.1, referred to: SI 1997/866 (NI.5) Art.1
Art.16, referred to: SI 1997/866 (NI.5) Art.18, SI 1998/1759 (NI.13) Art.8, Art.22
Art.24, amended: SI 1997/866 (NI.5) Art.26
Art.24, referred to: SI 1997/866 (NI.5) Art.1
Art.35, revoked (in part): SI 1998/1759 (NI.13) Art.91, Sch.6 Part I
Art.38, revoked: SI 1997/1772 (NI.15) Art.25, Sch.4, Sch.5

1996—cont.

274. Education (Northern Ireland) Order 1996— *cont.*
Art.39, amended: SI 1998/1759 (NI.13) Art.91, Sch.5 Part II
Art.41, revoked: SI 1997/1772 (NI.15) Art.25, Sch.4, Sch.5
Art.42, applied: SI 1998/1759 (NI.13) Art.24, Art.28
Art.42, referred to: SI 1997/866 (NI.5) Art.10
Sch.2 para.6, amended: SI 1998/1759 (NI.13) Art.85
Sch.5 Part I, revoked (in part): SI 1997/866 (NI.5) Sch
Sch.5 Part II, revoked (in part): SI 1997/866 (NI.5) Sch., SI 1997/1772 (NI.15) Art.25, Sch.5, SI 1998/1760 (NI.14) Art.9, Sch.

275. Gas (Northern Ireland) Order 1996
Art.5, amended: 1998 c.41 s.54, Sch.10 para.8
Art.15, amended: 1998 c.41 s.54, Sch.10 para.18, SI 1999/506 Art.44
Art.16, amended: SI 1999/506 Art.44
Art.16, referred to: 1998 c.41 s.74, Sch.13 para.40
Art.16, revoked (in part): 1998 c.41 s.54, s.74, Sch.10 para.18, Sch.14 Part II
Art.17, amended: SI 1999/506 Art.44
Art.18, amended: 1998 c.41 s.54, s.74, Sch.10 para.18, Sch.14 Part II
Art.18, revoked (in part): 1998 c.41 s.54, s.74, Sch.10 para.18, Sch.14 Part II
Art.19, amended: 1998 c.41 s.54, s.74, Sch.10 para.18, Sch.14 Part II
Art.23, amended: 1998 c.41 s.54, s.74, Sch.10 para.8, Sch.14 Part II, SI 1999/506 Art.44
Art.23, applied: 1998 c.41 s.74, Sch.13 para.35
Art.23, revoked (in part): 1998 c.41 s.54, s.74, Sch.10 para.8, Sch.14 Part II
Art.41, applied: 1998 c.41 s.74, Sch.13 para.32, Sch.13 para.33
Art.44, amended: 1998 c.41 s.54, Sch.10 para.18, SI 1999/506 Art.44, SI 1999/662 (NI.6) Art.63, Sch.7
Art.44, revoked (in part): 1998 c.41 s.54, s.74, Sch.10 para.18, Sch.14 Part II
Sch.1 para.7, revoked: SI 1996/1298 (NI.8) Art.21, Sch.6
Sch.6, revoked (in part): SI 1997/2778 (NI.19) Art.83, Sch.6

275. Motor Vehicles (Construction and Use) (Amendment) Regulations (Northern Ireland) 1996
revoked: SR 1999/454 Reg.126, Sch.19

285. A1 Trunk Road (Barnet) (50 mph Speed Limit) Order 1996
revoked (in part): SI 1999/1203 Art.5
Art.3, revoked (in part): SI 1999/1203 Art.5

293. Fossil Fuel Levy (Scotland) Regulations 1996
Reg.25, amended: SI 1996/1512 Reg.2

316. Wireless Telegraphy (Cordless Telephone Apparatus) (Exemption) Regulations 1996
revoked: SI 1999/930 Reg.2, Sch.1
Reg.2, revoked: SI 1999/930 Reg.2, Sch.1
Reg.4, revoked: SI 1999/930 Reg.2, Sch.1
Sch.1, revoked: SI 1999/930 Reg.2, Sch.1

324. West Glasgow Hospitals University National Health Service Trust (Establishment) (Amendment) Order 1996
revoked: SI 1999/1070 Art.2, Sch.2
Art.2, revoked: SI 1999/1070 Art.2, Sch.2

NO.

NO.

325. **Magistrates' Courts (Children and Young Persons) (Amendment) Rules (Northern Ireland) 1996**
revoked: SR 1999/7 r.2, Sch.2

325. **Water Services Charges (Billing and Collection) (Scotland) Order 1996**
referred to: SI 1996/326 Reg.2

326. **Domestic Sewerage Charges (Reduction) (Scotland) Regulations 1996**
referred to: SI 1996/325 Art.9

330. **Curriculum (Programmes of Study and Attainment Target in Home Economics at Key Stages 3 and 4) Order (Northern Ireland) 1996**
revoked: SR 1999/269 Art.2 (with saving)

330. **Local Government Changes for England (Miscellaneous Provision) Regulations 1996**
Part V, applied: SI 1996/1867 Art.15, SI 1996/1879 Art.6
Reg.12, amended: SI 1996/1680 Sch.4 para.7

333. **Local Government Changes for England (Council Tax) (Transitional Reduction) (Amendment) Regulations 1996**
revoked: SI 1999/259 Reg.11
Reg.2, revoked: SI 1999/259 Reg.11

334. **Education (Grants for Education Support and Training) (Wales) Regulations 1996**
revoked: SI 1997/390 Reg.12
Reg.6, revoked: SI 1997/390 Reg.12
Reg.12, revoked: SI 1997/390 Reg.12

338. **Curriculum (Programmes of Study and Attainment Target in Technology and Design at Key Stages 3 and 4) Order (Northern Ireland) 1996**
revoked: SR 1999/270 Art.2 (with saving)

341. **Health and Safety (Safety Signs and Signals) Regulations 1996**
Reg.2, amended: SI 1996/2092 Reg.21
Reg.4, amended: SI 1999/3242 Reg.29, Sch.2

342. **Local Authorities (Goods and Services) (Public Bodies) (Trunk Roads) Order 1996**
Art.2, amended: SI 1997/849 Art.2
Art.5, amended: SI 1997/849 Art.2
Art.7, referred to: SI 1996/1814 Art.5

348. **Restrictive Trade Practices (Non-notifiable Agreements) (Turnover Threshold) Order 1996**
Art.3, amended: SI 1997/2944 Art.2

355. **Social Security (Adjudication) (Amendment) Regulations (Northern Ireland) 1996**
revoked: SR 1999/162 Reg.59, Sch.3

360. **Education (School Premises) Regulations 1996**
revoked: SI 1999/2 Reg.25 (with savings)
Sch.1, revoked: SI 1999/2 Reg.25 (with savings)
Sch.2 para.3, applied: SI 1999/2 Reg.26
Sch.2 para.3, referred to: SI 1999/2 Reg.26
Sch.2 para.3, revoked: SI 1999/2 Reg.25 (with savings)
Sch.2 para.4, applied: SI 1999/2 Reg.26
Sch.2 para.4, referred to: SI 1999/2 Reg.26
Sch.2 para.4, revoked: SI 1999/2 Reg.25 (with savings)
Sch.2 para.5, applied: SI 1999/2 Reg.26
Sch.2 para.5, referred to: SI 1999/2 Reg.26
Sch.2 para.5, revoked: SI 1999/2 Reg.25 (with savings)

372. **Redundancy Payments (Local Government) (Modification) (Amendment) Order 1996**
revoked: SI 1999/2277 Art.4, Sch.3
Art.2, revoked: SI 1999/2277 Art.4, Sch.3

374. **Animals, Meat and Meat Products (Examination for Residues and Maximum Residue Limits) (Amendment) Regulations 1996**
revoked: SI 1997/1729 Reg.36, Sch.2
Reg.2, revoked: SI 1997/1729 Reg.36, Sch.2

379. **Wireless Telegraphy (Television Licence Fees) (Amendment) Regulations 1996**
revoked: SI 1997/290 Reg.1, Sch
Reg.2, revoked: SI 1997/290 Reg.1, Sch

381. **Education (School Financial Statements) (Prescribed Particulars etc.) (Amendment and Revocation) Regulations 1996**
revoked (in part): SI 1999/451 Reg.3
Reg.3, revoked (in part): SI 1999/451 Reg.3

382. **Education (Individual Pupils' Achievements) (Information) (Wales) Regulations 1996**
revoked: SI 1997/573 Reg.1
Reg.1, revoked: SI 1997/573 Reg.1

389. **National Health Service (Dental Charges) Amendment Regulations 1996**
revoked: SI 1997/558 Reg.3
Reg.2, revoked: SI 1997/558 Reg.3
Reg.3, revoked: SI 1997/558 Reg.3
Reg.4, revoked: SI 1997/558 Reg.3

391. **National Assistance (Sums for Personal Requirements) Regulations 1996**
revoked: SI 1997/486 Reg.3
Reg.3, revoked: SI 1997/486 Reg.3

395. **Education (Financial Delegation to Schools) (Mandatory Exceptions) (Revocation and Amendment) Regulations 1996**
revoked: SI 1999/711 Reg.9, Sch.2
Reg.2, revoked: SI 1999/711 Reg.9, Sch.2
Reg.3, revoked: SI 1999/711 Reg.9, Sch.2

401. **University College London Hospitals National Health Service Trust (Establishment) Order 1996**
Art.3, substituted: SI 1999/2372 Art.2

414. **Local Government Superannuation (Scotland) Amendment Regulations 1996**
applied: SI 1998/364 Reg.4, Reg.6, Reg.19, Sch.2 para.2, Sch.2 para.5, Sch.4 para.8
referred to: SI 1998/364 Reg.3, Reg.10, Sch.2 para.4, Sch.2 para.6

425. **Social Security (Industrial Injuries and Diseases) (Miscellaneous Amendments) Regulations 1996**
Reg.2, revoked: SI 1999/991 Reg.59 (with savings), Sch.4 (with savings)

428. **Noise Insulation (Railways and Other Guided Transport Systems) Regulations 1996**
Reg.9, amended: SI 1998/1701 Reg.2

433. **National Health Service (Appointment of Consultants) (Wales) Continuation and Transitional Provisions Order 1996**
revoked: SI 1996/1313 Reg.10
Art.3, revoked: SI 1996/1313 Reg.10
Art.4, revoked: SI 1996/1313 Reg.10

433. **Social Security (Contributions) (Amendment No.5) Regulations (Northern Ireland) 1996**
revoked (in part): SR 1999/117 Reg.13

437. **Veterinary Surgeons and Veterinary Practitioners (Registration) (Amendment) Regulations Order of Council 1996**
revoked: SI 1998/270 Art.2
Art.3, revoked: SI 1998/270 Art.2
Sch., revoked: SI 1998/270 Art.2, Sch. Reg.6

NO.

1996—cont.

439. **Gas (Calculation of Thermal Energy) Regulations 1996**
Reg.2, amended: SI 1997/937 Reg.3, Reg.4
Reg.3, amended: SI 1997/937 Reg.5
Reg.4, amended: SI 1997/937 Reg.6
Reg.4A, added: SI 1997/937 Reg.7
Reg.5, amended: SI 1997/937 Reg.8
Reg.6, amended: SI 1997/937 Reg.9
Reg.10, amended: SI 1997/937 Reg.10
Reg.13, amended: SI 1997/937 Reg.11
Sch. Part I, amended: SI 1997/937 Reg.12

444. **British Nationality (Fees) Regulations 1996**
Reg.2, amended: SI 1997/1328 Reg.2
Reg.3, amended: SI 1997/1328 Reg.2
Sch., amended: SI 1997/1328 Reg.2

448. **Food Protection (Emergency Prohibitions) (Oil and Chemical Pollution of Fish and Plants) Order 1996**
amended: SI 1996/1712 Art.2
applied: SI 1996/2649
referred to: SI 1996/448 Sch, SI 1997/1481 Sch. Part I
revoked (in part): SI 1996/1213 Art.2, SI 1996/1319 Art.3, SI 1996/1712 Art.2, SI 1996/1957 Art.2, SI 1996/2649 Art.2, SI 1997/239 Art.2, SI 1997/1481 Art.2, SI 1997/2206 Art.2
Art.3, revoked (in part): SI 1996/1319 Art.2, SI 1997/1481 Art.2, SI 1997/2206 Art.2
Sch., amended: SI 1996/2355 Art.2
Sch., applied: SI 1996/1213, SI 1997/1481
Sch., referred to: SI 1996/1319, SI 1996/1712, SI 1996/1957, SI 1996/2355, SI 1997/239, SI 1997/2206
Sch., revoked (in part): SI 1996/1319 Art.2, SI 1996/2355 Art.2, SI 1997/1481 Art.2, SI 1997/2206 Art.2

456. **Local Government (Compensation for Redundancy) (Amendment) Regulations 1996**
Reg.3, revoked: SI 1996/1680 Reg.49, Sch.5
Reg.7, applied: SI 1996/1680 Sch.3 para.10

456. **Plant Protection Products (Amendment) Regulations (Northern Ireland) 1996**
revoked: SR 1999/282 Reg.3

457. **Social Security (Adjudication) and Child Support (Amendment No.2) Regulations (Northern Ireland) 1996**
revoked: SR 1999/162 Reg.59, Sch.3

458. **Assured and Protected Tenancies (Lettings to Students) (Amendment) Regulations 1996**
revoked: SI 1998/1967 Reg.6, Sch.3
Reg.2, revoked: SI 1998/1967 Reg.6, Sch.3

462. **Motor Vehicles (Construction and Use) (Amendment No.2) Regulations (Northern Ireland) 1996**
revoked: SR 1999/454 Reg.126, Sch.19

468. **Lotteries (Gaming Board Fees) Order 1996**
revoked: SI 1997/1783 Art.9
Art.3, revoked: SI 1997/1783 Art.9
Art.4, revoked: SI 1997/1783 Art.9
Art.5, revoked: SI 1997/1783 Art.9
Art.6, revoked: SI 1997/1783 Art.9
Art.7, revoked: SI 1997/1783 Art.9
Art.8, revoked: SI 1997/1783 Art.9
Art.9, revoked: SI 1997/1783 Art.9

469. **Local Authorities (Members' Allowances) (Amendment) Regulations 1996**
Reg.4, revoked (in part): SI 1998/556 Reg.3, SI 1998/557 Reg.3

NO.

1996—cont.

473. **National Health Service (Optical Charges and Payments) (Scotland) Amendment Regulations 1996**
revoked: SI 1998/642 Reg.24, Sch.4
Reg.2, revoked: SI 1998/642 Reg.24, Sch.4
Reg.3, revoked: SI 1998/642 Reg.24, Sch.4
Reg.4, revoked: SI 1998/642 Reg.24, Sch.4
Sch., revoked: SI 1998/642 Reg.24, Sch.4

488. **Authorities for the Ashworth, Broadmoor and Rampton Hospitals (Establishment and Constitution) Order 1996**
Art.6, added: SI 1998/1577 Art.2

489. **Ashworth, Broadmoor and Rampton Hospital Authorities (Functions and Membership) Regulations 1996**
Reg.1, amended: SI 1998/646 Reg.14
Reg.7, amended: SI 1997/2991 Reg.3, Sch. para.8
Reg.8, amended: SI 1997/2991 Reg.3, Sch. para.8

493. **Occupational Pension Schemes (Contracting Out) Regulations (Northern Ireland) 1996**
applied: SI 1999/671 Art.3, Sch.2
Reg.23, referred to: SI 1999/671 Art.3, Sch.2
Reg.78, referred to: 1999 c.30 s.81, Sch.11 para.36

498. **Financial Services Act 1986 (Gas Industry Exemption) Order 1996**
revoked: SI 1999/2586 Art.6
Art.1, amended: SI 1996/1197 Art.2
Art.1, revoked: SI 1999/2586 Art.6
Art.2, revoked: SI 1999/2586 Art.6

498. **Hill Livestock (Compensatory Allowances) (Amendment) Regulations (Northern Ireland) 1996**
revoked: SR 1999/497 Reg.15 (with savings)

499. **Social Security (Adjudication) (Amendment No.2) Regulations (Northern Ireland) 1996**
revoked: SR 1999/162 Reg.59, Sch.3

500. **Road Traffic Act 1991 (Amendment of Schedule 3) (England and Wales) Order 1996**
Art.2, referred to: SI 1998/2018 Art.2

501. **Local Government Reorganisation (Wales) (Staff) Order 1996**
Art.5, referred to: SI 1996/905 Art.4, SI 1996/1214 Art.3
Sch. Part 7, amended: SI 1996/905 Art.4

507. **Leicestershire (City of Leicester and District of Rutland) (Structural Change) Order 1996**
applied: SI 1997/476 Art.1
Art.5, revoked: 1996 c.16 Sch.9 Part III
Art.8, referred to: SI 1997/490 Art.2, Art.3

510. **Construction (Health, Safety and Welfare) Regulations (Northern Ireland) 1996**
amended: SR 1999/150 Reg.2, Sch.

510. **Mental Health Review Tribunals (Regions) Order 1996**
revoked: SI 1998/1460 Art.4
Art.2, revoked: SI 1998/1460 Art.4
Art.3, revoked: SI 1998/1460 Art.4

513. **Act of Adjournal (Criminal Procedure Rules) 1996**
Sch.2 Ch.1, amended: SI 1999/1387 r.2
Sch.2 r.1.4, added: SI 1999/1387 r.2
Sch.2 r.3.5A, added: SI 1999/1387 r.2
Sch.2 r.8.1A, added: SI 1999/78 r.2
Sch.2 r.8.1B, added: SI 1999/78 r.2

NO.   NO.

1996—cont.

513. Act of Adjournal (Criminal Procedure Rules) 1996—*cont.*
Sch.2 r.11.2, amended: SI 1996/2147 r.2
Sch.2 r.15.12A, added: SI 1997/1834 r.2
Sch.2 r.15.13, amended: SI 1997/1788 r.2
Sch.2 r.15.14, added: SI 1996/2147 r.2
Sch.2 r.18.4, amended: SI 1997/63 r.2
Sch.2 r.19.10A, added: SI 1997/1834 r.2
Sch.2 r.19.17, amended: SI 1997/1788 r.2
Sch.2 r.19.18, added: SI 1996/2147 r.2
Sch.2 r.20.1, revoked: SI 1999/1387 r.2
Sch.2 r.20.3A, added: SI 1997/2082 r.2
Sch.2 r.20.10A, added: SI 1997/1526 r.2
Sch.2 r.20.10B, added: SI 1997/1526 r.2
Sch.2 r.20.12A, added: SI 1998/1842 r.2
Sch.2 r.20.12B, added: SSI 1999/191 para.2
Sch.2 Ch.22, amended: SI 1997/1834 r.2
Sch.2 r.22.1, amended: SI 1997/1834 r.2
Sch.2 r.22.2, amended: SI 1997/1834 r.2
Sch.2 r.27.4, added: SI 1997/63 r.2
Sch.2 r.27.4, amended: SI 1997/1788 r.2
Sch.2 r.27.5, added: SI 1997/2082 r.2
Sch.2 r.31.1, amended: SI 1999/1282 r.2
Sch.2 r.31.1, applied: SI 1997/3070 Reg.6
Sch.2 r.31.5, amended: SI 1999/1282 r.2
Sch.2 r.31.7, amended: SI 1996/2147 r.2
Sch.2 Ch.37A, added: SI 1997/2081 r.2
Sch.2 r.37A, added: SI 1997/2081 r.2
Sch.2 r.37.1, added: SI 1996/2147 r.2
Sch.2 r.37.2, amended: SI 1996/2147 r.2
Sch.2 r.37.4, added: SI 1997/2653 r.2
Sch.2 r.37.5, added: SI 1997/2653 r.2
Sch.2 Ch.38, added: SI 1997/1834 r.2, SI 1997/2653 r.2
Sch.2 r.38.1, added: SI 1997/2653 r.2
Sch.2 r.38.2, added: SI 1997/2653 r.2
Sch.2 r.38.3, added: SI 1997/2653 r.2
Sch.2 Ch.40, added: SI 1999/1346 r.2
Sch.2 r.40.1, added: SI 1999/1346 r.2
Sch.2 r.40.2, added: SI 1999/1346 r.2
Sch.2 r.40.3, added: SI 1999/1346 r.2
Sch.2 r.40.4, added: SI 1999/1346 r.2
Sch.2 r.40.5, added: SI 1999/1346 r.2
Sch.2 r.40.6, added: SI 1999/1346 r.2
Sch.2 r.40.7, added: SI 1999/1346 r.2
Sch.2 r.40.8, added: SI 1999/1346 r.2
Sch.2 r.40.9, added: SI 1999/1346 r.2
Sch.2 r.40.10, added: SI 1999/1346 r.2
Sch.2 r.40.11, added: SI 1999/1346 r.2
Sch.2 r.40.12, added: SI 1999/1346 r.2
Sch.2 Annex, added: SI 1999/1282 r.2, Sch.2
Sch.2 Appendix, amended: SI 1996/2147 r.2, SI 1997/63 r.2, Sch., SI 1997/1526 r.2, Sch., SI 1997/1788 r.2, SI 1997/1834 r.2, SI 1997/2081 r.2, Sch., SI 1997/2082 r.2, Sch.1, Sch.2, Sch.3, SI 1997/2653 r.2, Sch., SI 1998/1842 r.2, Sch., SI 1999/1282 r.2, Sch.1, SI 1999/1346 r.2
Sch.2 Appendix, revoked (in part): SI 1999/1387 r.2
Sch.2 Appendix.Form 20.12B, added: SSI 1999/191 para.2, Sch.I

514. Court of Session etc. Fees Amendment Order 1996
revoked: SI 1997/688 Art.6, Sch.2
Art.2, revoked: SI 1997/688 Art.6, Sch.2
Art.3, revoked: SI 1997/688 Art.6, Sch.2

516. High Court of Justiciary Fees Amendment Order 1996
Art.2, revoked: SI 1999/753 Art.3

1996—cont.

529. Rural Development Grants (Agriculture) (Wales) Regulations 1996
applied: SI 1999/672 Art.2, Sch.1
Reg.2, amended: SI 1997/568 Reg.2
Reg.5, amended: SI 1997/568 Reg.2
Reg.11, amended: SI 1997/568 Reg.2
Sch. para.1, amended: SI 1997/568 Reg.2
Sch. para.2, amended: SI 1997/568 Reg.2
Sch. para.5, added: SI 1997/568 Reg.2

532. Local Government Reorganisation (Wales) (Property etc.) Order 1996
applied: SI 1996/2819 Sch., SI 1997/262 Sch., SI 1997/319 Reg.24, Reg.160
Art.22, applied: SI 1997/540 Art.4
Art.22, referred to: SI 1998/2859 Art.3
Sch.2, amended: SI 1996/906 Art.2
Sch.3 Part I, amended: SI 1996/906 Art.2
Sch.3 Part I, revoked (in part): SI 1996/906 Art.2

534. National Park Authorities (Wales) (Amendment) Order 1996
Sch. para.2, amended: SI 1997/633 Art.3

536. Motor Vehicles (Driving Licences) (Amendment) (No.2) Regulations 1996
revoked: SI 1996/2824 Reg.2, Sch.1
Reg.2, revoked: SI 1996/2824 Reg.2, Sch.1

537. Education (Grant-Maintained and Grant-Maintained Special Schools) (Finance) (Wales) Regulations 1996
applied: SI 1997/599 Reg.3
revoked: SI 1997/599 Reg.3
Reg.3, revoked: SI 1997/599 Reg.3
Reg.4, amended: SI 1996/1911 Reg.2
Reg.4, revoked: SI 1997/599 Reg.3
Reg.4A, added: SI 1996/1911 Reg.2
Reg.4A, revoked: SI 1997/599 Reg.3
Reg.5, applied: SI 1997/599 Reg.6
Reg.5, revoked: SI 1997/599 Reg.3
Reg.6, applied: SI 1997/599 Reg.6
Reg.6, revoked: SI 1997/599 Reg.3
Reg.7, applied: SI 1997/599 Reg.6
Reg.10, revoked: SI 1997/599 Reg.3
Reg.11, revoked: SI 1997/599 Reg.3
Reg.13, applied: SI 1997/599 Reg.6
Reg.15, revoked: SI 1997/599 Reg.3
Reg.19, revoked: SI 1997/599 Reg.3
Reg.22, revoked: SI 1997/599 Reg.3
Reg.23, applied: SI 1997/599 Reg.3
Reg.23, revoked: SI 1997/599 Reg.3
Sch.2 para.2, revoked: SI 1997/599 Reg.3
Sch.5 para.2, amended: SI 1996/1334 Reg.2
Sch.5 para.2, revoked: SI 1997/599 Reg.3

538. Regional Flood Defence Committee (Welsh Region) Order 1996
added: SI 1996/1007 Art.2
referred to: SI 1996/1007
Art.3, added: SI 1996/1007 Art.2

546. Insurance (Fees) Regulations 1996
revoked: SI 1997/653 Reg.2
Reg.2, revoked: SI 1997/653 Reg.2
Reg.4, revoked: SI 1997/653 Reg.2
Reg.7, revoked: SI 1997/653 Reg.2
Reg.9, revoked: SI 1997/653 Reg.2
Reg.10, revoked: SI 1997/653 Reg.2

550. Gas Safety (Installation and Use) (Amendment) Regulations 1996
revoked: SI 1998/2451 Reg.41
Reg.3, revoked: SI 1998/2451 Reg.41
Reg.4, revoked: SI 1998/2451 Reg.41
Reg.5, revoked: SI 1998/2451 Reg.41
Reg.6, revoked: SI 1998/2451 Reg.41
Reg.7, revoked: SI 1998/2451 Reg.41
Reg.8, revoked: SI 1998/2451 Reg.41

1996—cont.

550. Gas Safety (Installation and Use) (Amendment) Regulations 1996—*cont.*
Reg.9, revoked: SI 1998/2451 Reg.41
Reg.10, revoked: SI 1998/2451 Reg.41
Reg.11, revoked: SI 1998/2451 Reg.41
Reg.12, revoked: SI 1998/2451 Reg.41
Reg.13, revoked: SI 1998/2451 Reg.41
Reg.14, revoked: SI 1998/2451 Reg.41
Reg.15, revoked: SI 1998/2451 Reg.41
Reg.16, revoked: SI 1998/2451 Reg.41
Reg.17, revoked: SI 1998/2451 Reg.41
Reg.18, revoked: SI 1998/2451 Reg.41
Reg.19, revoked: SI 1998/2451 Reg.41
Reg.20, revoked: SI 1998/2451 Reg.41
Reg.21, revoked: SI 1998/2451 Reg.41
Reg.22, revoked: SI 1998/2451 Reg.41

551. Gas Safety (Management) Regulations 1996
Reg.2, applied: SI 1998/2451 Reg.37
Reg.2, referred to: SI 1996/2535 Reg.3
Sch.1 para.5, amended: SI 1999/3242 Reg.29, Sch.2

568. Local Authorities (Capital Finance and Approved Investments) (Amendment) Regulations 1996
revoked (in part): SI 1997/319 Reg.162, Sch.3
Reg.1, revoked: SI 1997/319 Reg.162, Sch.3
Reg.2, revoked: SI 1997/319 Reg.162, Sch.3
Reg.3, revoked: SI 1997/319 Reg.162, Sch.3
Reg.4, revoked: SI 1997/319 Reg.162, Sch.3
Reg.5, revoked: SI 1997/319 Reg.162, Sch.3
Reg.6, revoked: SI 1997/319 Reg.162, Sch.3
Reg.7, revoked: SI 1997/319 Reg.162, Sch.3
Reg.8, revoked: SI 1997/319 Reg.162, Sch.3
Reg.9, revoked: SI 1997/319 Reg.162, Sch.3
Reg.10, revoked: SI 1997/319 Reg.162, Sch.3
Reg.11, revoked: SI 1997/319 Reg.162, Sch.3
Reg.12, revoked: SI 1997/319 Reg.162, Sch.3
Reg.13, revoked: SI 1997/319 Reg.162, Sch.3
Reg.14, revoked: SI 1997/319 Reg.162, Sch.3
Reg.15, revoked: SI 1997/319 Reg.162 (with savings)

572. Marriage Fees (Scotland) Regulations 1996
revoked: SI 1998/643 Reg.8
Reg.2, revoked: SI 1998/643 Reg.8
Reg.3, revoked: SI 1998/643 Reg.8

573. Gaming (Bingo) (Amendment) Regulations (Northern Ireland) 1996
revoked: SR 1999/5 Reg.4

574. Registration of Births, Deaths, Marriages and Divorces (Fees) (Scotland) Amendment Regulations 1996
revoked: SI 1997/716 Reg.7
Reg.3, revoked: SI 1997/716 Reg.7
Reg.4, revoked: SI 1997/716 Reg.7
Reg.5, revoked: SI 1997/716 Reg.7
Reg.6, revoked: SI 1997/716 Reg.7

575. Public Record Office (Fees) Regulations 1996
revoked: SI 1997/400 Reg.3
Reg.3, revoked: SI 1997/400 Reg.3

578. Local Authorities (Property Transfer) (Scotland) Amendment Order 1996
revoked: SI 1997/2880 Art.3
Art.2, revoked: SI 1997/2880 Art.3

580. Rating, Valuation and Council Tax (Miscellaneous Provisions) (Scotland) Order 1996
Art.6, revoked: SI 1997/728 Art.5, Sch.2

1996—cont.

582. National Health Service (Optical Charges and Payments) Amendment Regulations 1996
revoked: SI 1997/818 Reg.24, Sch.4
Reg.2, revoked: SI 1997/818 Reg.24, Sch.4
Reg.3, revoked: SI 1997/818 Reg.24, Sch.4
Reg.4, revoked: SI 1997/818 Reg.24, Sch.4
Sch., revoked: SI 1997/818 Reg.24, Sch.4

587. Home Energy Efficiency Grants (Amendment) Regulations 1996
revoked: SI 1997/790 Reg.14, Sch.2
Reg.4, revoked: SI 1997/790 Reg.14, Sch.2
Reg.5, revoked: SI 1997/790 Reg.14, Sch.2
Reg.6, revoked: SI 1997/790 Reg.14, Sch.2
Reg.7, revoked: SI 1997/790 Reg.14, Sch.2
Reg.8, revoked: SI 1997/790 Reg.14, Sch.2
Reg.9, revoked: SI 1997/790 Reg.14, Sch.2
Reg.10, revoked: SI 1997/790 Reg.14, Sch.2
Reg.11, revoked: SI 1997/790 Reg.14, Sch.2

589. A1 Trunk Road (Islington) (Bus Lanes) Red Route Experimental Order 1996
revoked (in part): SI 1997/445 Art.5
Art.2, revoked (in part): SI 1997/445 Art.5

590. Accounts and Audit Regulations 1996
referred to: SI 1996/1243 Sch.7 para.8
Reg.10, revoked: SI 1997/2747 Reg.2, Sch.
Sch., revoked: SI 1997/2747 Reg.2, Sch.

591. A1 Trunk Road (Haringey) (Bus Lanes) Red Route Experimental Order 1996
revoked (in part): SI 1997/449 Art.5

593. Environment Act 1995 (Consequential Amendments) Regulations 1996
referred to: SI 1999/672 Art.2, Sch.1
Sch.1 para.19, revoked: 1996 c.18 Sch.3 Part II

599. Social Security Benefits Up-rating Order 1996
revoked: SI 1997/543 Art.27

600. Energy Information (Washing Machines) Regulations 1996
Reg.2, amended: SI 1997/803 Reg.2
Reg.3, amended: SI 1997/803 Reg.2

604. Public Airport Companies (Capital Finance) Order 1996
Art.1, amended: SI 1999/554 Art.2
Sch., revoked: SI 1999/554 Art.2
Sch.1, added: SI 1999/554 Art.2
Sch.1, revoked (in part): SI 1999/2125 Art.2
Sch.2, added: SI 1999/554 Art.2
Sch.2, revoked (in part): SI 1999/2125 Art.2

609. Building Societies (General Charge and Fees) Regulations 1996
revoked: SI 1997/740 Reg.11
Reg.3, revoked: SI 1997/740 Reg.11
Reg.5, revoked: SI 1997/740 Reg.11
Reg.6, revoked: SI 1997/740 Reg.11
Reg.7, revoked: SI 1997/740 Reg.11
Reg.8, revoked: SI 1997/740 Reg.11
Reg.11, revoked: SI 1997/740 Reg.11
Sch.1, revoked: SI 1997/740 Reg.11

612. Industrial and Provident Societies (Credit Unions) (Amendment of Fees) Regulations 1996
revoked: SI 1997/742 Reg.3
Reg.2, revoked: SI 1997/742 Reg.3
Reg.3, revoked: SI 1997/742 Reg.3

613. Industrial and Provident Societies (Amendment of Fees) Regulations 1996
revoked: SI 1997/743 Reg.4
Reg.2, revoked: SI 1997/743 Reg.4
Reg.3, revoked: SI 1997/743 Reg.4
Reg.4, revoked: SI 1997/743 Reg.4

NO.

1996—cont.

613. **Road Humps (Amendment) Regulations (Northern Ireland) 1996**
revoked: SR 1999/101

614. **Friendly Societies (General Charge and Fees) Regulations 1996**
revoked: SI 1997/741 Reg.7
Reg.5, revoked: SI 1997/741 Reg.7
Reg.7, revoked: SI 1997/741 Reg.7
Sch.1 para.2, revoked: SI 1997/741 Reg.7
Sch.1 para.3, revoked: SI 1997/741 Reg.7
Sch.2, revoked: SI 1997/741 Reg.7
Sch.2 para.5, revoked: SI 1997/741 Reg.7
Sch.2 para.5, substituted: SI 1996/3094 Reg.3

615. **Education (Areas to which Pupils and Students Belong) Regulations 1996**
Reg.3, substituted: SI 1997/597 Reg.2
Reg.8, applied: SI 1996/710 Reg.20, SI 1998/1166 Reg.8
Reg.8, referred to: SI 1999/1494 Reg.8

618. **Contracting Out (Transfer and Transfer Payment) Regulations (Northern Ireland) 1996**
referred to: SI 1999/3147 (NI.11) Art.32, Sch.5 para.6

620. **Central Rating Lists (Amendment) Regulations 1996**
revoked (in part): SI 1999/3453 Reg.7
Reg.2, revoked (in part): SI 1999/3453 Reg.7

622. **Medical Devices (Consultation Requirements) (Fees) Amendment Regulations 1996**
revoked: SI 1998/574 Reg.6
Reg.2, revoked: SI 1998/574 Reg.6

624. **Health Authorities (England) Establishment Order 1996**
Sch., amended: SI 1999/616 Art.2, Art.3, Art.4

627. **Criminal Legal Aid (Scotland) Amendment Regulations 1996**
revoked: SI 1996/2555 Reg.3, Sch.
Reg.3, revoked: SI 1996/2555 Reg.3, Sch.
Reg.4, revoked: SI 1996/2555 Reg.3, Sch.

628. **Sheriff Court Fees Amendment Order 1996**
revoked: SI 1997/687 Art.11, Sch.2
Art.2, revoked: SI 1997/687 Art.11, Sch.2
Art.3, revoked: SI 1997/687 Art.11, Sch.2
Sch., revoked: SI 1997/687 Art.11, Sch.2

633. **Local Government Reorganisation (Wales) (Capital Finance) Order 1996**
Art.1, amended: SI 1996/1366 Art.2

634. **Waste Management Regulations 1996**
Reg.6, revoked: SI 1997/351 Reg.4

635. **Child Support Departure Direction (Anticipatory Applications) Regulations 1996**
applied: SI 1996/2907 Reg.47
revoked: SI 1996/2907 Reg.51
Reg.2, revoked: SI 1996/2907 Reg.51
Reg.7, revoked: SI 1996/2907 Reg.51
Reg.8, revoked: SI 1996/2907 Reg.51
Reg.10, revoked: SI 1996/2907 Reg.51
Reg.11, revoked: SI 1996/2907 Reg.51
Reg.12, revoked: SI 1996/2907 Reg.51
Reg.13, revoked: SI 1996/2907 Reg.51
Reg.14, revoked: SI 1996/2907 Reg.51
Reg.15, revoked: SI 1996/2907 Reg.51
Reg.16, revoked: SI 1996/2907 Reg.51
Reg.17, revoked: SI 1996/2907 Reg.51
Reg.18, revoked: SI 1996/2907 Reg.51
Reg.19, revoked: SI 1996/2907 Reg.51
Reg.21, revoked: SI 1996/2907 Reg.51
Reg.22, revoked: SI 1996/2907 Reg.51
Reg.23, revoked: SI 1996/2907 Reg.51
Reg.24, revoked: SI 1996/2907 Reg.51
Reg.25, revoked: SI 1996/2907 Reg.51

NO.

1996—cont.

635. **Child Support Departure Direction (Anticipatory Applications) Regulations 1996—** *cont.*
Reg.26, revoked: SI 1996/2907 Reg.51
Reg.27, revoked: SI 1996/2907 Reg.51
Reg.28, revoked: SI 1996/2907 Reg.51
Reg.29, revoked: SI 1996/2907 Reg.51
Reg.31, revoked: SI 1996/2907 Reg.51
Reg.32, revoked: SI 1996/2907 Reg.51
Reg.35, revoked: SI 1996/2907 Reg.51
Reg.36, revoked: SI 1996/2907 Reg.51
Reg.37, revoked: SI 1996/2907 Reg.51
Reg.38, revoked: SI 1996/2907 Reg.51
Reg.39, revoked: SI 1996/2907 Reg.51
Reg.40, revoked: SI 1996/2907 Reg.51
Reg.41, revoked: SI 1996/2907 Reg.51
Reg.42, revoked: SI 1996/2907 Reg.51

640. **Community Health Councils Regulations 1996**
Reg.18, see *R. v North and East Devon HA Ex p. Pow* (1998) 39 B.M.L.R. 77 (QBD), Moses, J.
Reg.18, amended: SI 1997/2289 Reg.5, SI 1999/2906 Reg.2
Reg.18, referred to: SI 1999/2337 Reg.6

651. **Certification Officer (Amendment of Fees) Regulations 1996**
revoked: SI 1997/677 Reg.8
Reg.2, revoked: SI 1997/677 Reg.8
Reg.3, revoked: SI 1997/677 Reg.8
Reg.4, revoked: SI 1997/677 Reg.8
Reg.5, revoked: SI 1997/677 Reg.8
Reg.6, revoked: SI 1997/677 Reg.8
Reg.7, revoked: SI 1997/677 Reg.8
Reg.8, revoked: SI 1997/677 Reg.8

653. **National Health Service Trusts (Consultation on Establishment and Dissolution) Regulations 1996**
referred to: SI 1999/2337 Reg.6
Reg.2, referred to: SI 1999/2337 Reg.6

658. **Humberside (Coroners) Order 1996**
amended: SI 1996/787 Art.2
Art.3, amended: SI 1996/787 Art.2
Art.4, amended: SI 1996/787 Art.2

661. **Coroners' Districts (Wales) Order 1996**
applied: SI 1996/662 Art.2
Art.2, amended: SI 1996/2914 Art.14
Art.2, applied: SI 1996/2915 Art.10

666. **Regional Health Authorities (Transfer of Trust Property) Order 1996**
Sch.7 Part II, amended: SI 1996/969 Art.2

670. **Social Security Benefits Up-rating Regulations 1996**
revoked: SI 1997/576 Reg.7
Reg.2, revoked: SI 1997/576 Reg.7
Reg.3, revoked: SI 1997/576 Reg.7
Reg.4, revoked: SI 1997/576 Reg.7
Reg.5, revoked: SI 1997/576 Reg.7
Reg.6, revoked: SI 1997/576 Reg.7
Reg.7, revoked: SI 1997/576 Reg.7

671. **Social Security (Industrial Injuries) (Dependency) (Permitted Earnings Limits) Order 1996**
revoked: SI 1998/520 Art.3
Art.2, revoked: SI 1998/520 Art.3
Art.3, revoked: SI 1998/520 Art.3

674. **Local Government Changes for England (Magistrates' Courts) Regulations 1996**
referred to: SI 1996/675 Art.1
Reg.3, amended: SI 1996/674 Reg.4
Sch. para.1, revoked: 1997 c.25 s.73, Sch.6 Part II
Sch. para.2, revoked (in part): 1999 c.22 s.106, Sch.15 Part V(1)

NO.

674. Local Government Changes for England (Magistrates' Courts) Regulations 1996—cont.
Sch. para.4, revoked (in part): 1997 c.25 s.73, Sch.6 Part II
Sch. para.5, revoked: 1999 c.22 s.106, Sch.15 Part V(1)

675. Magistrates' Courts (Wales) (Consequences of Local Government Changes) Order 1996
referred to: SI 1996/676 Art.1
Sch. Part II, revoked (in part): 1999 c.22 s.106, Sch.15 Part V(1)
Sch. para.1, revoked: 1997 c.25 s.73, Sch.6 Part II

676. Commission Areas (Gwent, Mid Glamorgan and South Glamorgan) Order 1996
revoked: 1997 c.25 s.73, Sch.6 Part II
Art.1, revoked: 1997 c.25 s.73, Sch.6 Part II
Art.2, revoked: 1997 c.25 s.73, Sch.6 Part II

677. Housing Benefit (Permitted Totals) Order 1996
Art.2, amended: SI 1998/566 Art.2
Art.4, amended: SI 1996/2326 Art.4
Art.5, amended: SI 1998/566 Art.3
Sch., added: SI 1998/566 Art.2, Sch.1
Sch., substituted: SI 1999/642 Art.2, Sch.

681. Accounts Commission (Scotland) Regulations 1996
Reg.4, applied: SI 1996/682 Art.20

686. National Health Service (Existing Liabilities Scheme) Regulations 1996
referred to: SI 1999/873 Reg.4, SI 1999/874 Reg.4
Reg.1, amended: SI 1997/526 Reg.3
Reg.6, amended: SI 1997/526 Reg.3, SI 1999/1275 Reg.2
Reg.6A, added: SI 1999/1275 Reg.3

688. Civil Aviation (Canadian Navigation Services) Regulations 1996
revoked: SI 1998/2575 Reg.3, Sch.1
Reg.2, revoked: SI 1998/2575 Reg.3, Sch.1
Reg.2, substituted: SI 1996/2540 Reg.2
Reg.3, revoked: SI 1998/2575 Reg.3, Sch.1
Reg.4, revoked: SI 1998/2575 Reg.3, Sch.1
Reg.4, substituted: SI 1996/2540 Reg.2, SI 1998/205 Reg.2
Reg.13, revoked: SI 1998/2575 Reg.3, Sch.1
Reg.15, revoked: SI 1998/2575 Reg.3, Sch.1
Reg.15, substituted: SI 1996/2540 Reg.2
Sch.1, revoked: SI 1998/2575 Reg.3, Sch.1

689. Civil Aviation (Navigation Services Charges) (Amendment) Regulations 1996
revoked: SI 1998/532 Reg.3, Sch.1
Reg.2, revoked: SI 1998/532 Reg.3, Sch.1

690. Measuring Instruments (EEC Requirements) (Fees) (Amendment) Regulations 1996
revoked: SI 1998/1177 Reg.1
Reg.2, revoked: SI 1998/1177 Reg.1

694. Plastic Materials and Articles in Contact with Food (Amendment) Regulations 1996
revoked: SI 1998/1376 Reg.14
Reg.2, revoked: SI 1998/1376 Reg.14

695. Countryside Stewardship Regulations 1996
revoked: SI 1998/1327 Reg.2, Sch.2
Reg.1, amended: SI 1996/1481 Reg.2
Reg.1, revoked: SI 1998/1327 Reg.2, Sch.2
Reg.2, amended: SI 1996/3123 Reg.2, SI 1997/1827 Reg.2
Reg.2, revoked: SI 1998/1327 Reg.2, Sch.2
Reg.3, amended: SI 1996/3123 Reg.2, SI 1997/1827 Reg.2
Reg.3, revoked: SI 1998/1327 Reg.2, Sch.2

NO.

695. Countryside Stewardship Regulations 1996—cont.
Reg.5, amended: SI 1996/3123 Reg.2
Reg.5, revoked: SI 1998/1327 Reg.2, Sch.2
Reg.9, revoked: SI 1998/1327 Reg.2, Sch.2
Reg.9, substituted: SI 1996/3123 Reg.2
Reg.10, added: SI 1996/3123 Reg.2
Reg.10, revoked: SI 1998/1327 Reg.2, Sch.2
Reg.11, added: SI 1996/3123 Reg.2
Reg.11, revoked: SI 1998/1327 Reg.2, Sch.2
Reg.12, added: SI 1996/3123 Reg.2
Reg.12, revoked: SI 1998/1327 Reg.2, Sch.2
Sch., revoked: SI 1998/1327 Reg.2, Sch.2
Sch., substituted: SI 1997/1827 Reg.2, Sch.

696. Common Agricultural Policy (Wine) Regulations 1996
applied: SI 1999/672 Art.2, Sch.1
Reg.2, amended: SI 1997/542 Reg.3
Reg.3, referred to: SI 1999/672 Art.2, Sch.1
Reg.5A, added: SI 1997/542 Reg.4
Reg.11, amended: SI 1998/453 Reg.3
Sch.1 Item 4, revoked: SI 1997/542 Reg.5
Sch.1 Item 5, revoked: SI 1997/542 Reg.5
Sch.1 Item 6, revoked: SI 1997/542 Reg.5
Sch.1 Item 9, amended: SI 1999/482 Reg.3
Sch.1 Item 13, amended: SI 1998/453 Reg.4
Sch.1 Item 14, amended: SI 1997/542 Reg.5, SI 1998/453 Reg.4, SI 1999/482 Reg.3
Sch.1 Item 15, amended: SI 1998/453 Reg.4, SI 1999/482 Reg.3
Sch.1 Item 19, amended: SI 1997/542 Reg.5, SI 1999/482 Reg.3
Sch.1 Item 24, amended: SI 1997/542 Reg.5, SI 1999/482 Reg.3
Sch.1 Item 26, amended: SI 1997/542 Reg.5, SI 1998/453 Reg.4, SI 1999/482 Reg.3
Sch.1 Item 27, amended: SI 1997/542 Reg.5
Sch.1 Item 28, revoked: SI 1997/542 Reg.5
Sch.1 Item 29, amended: SI 1997/542 Reg.5, SI 1998/453 Reg.4, SI 1999/482 Reg.3
Sch.1 Item 33, amended: SI 1998/453 Reg.4
Sch.1 Item 34, amended: SI 1998/453 Reg.4, SI 1999/482 Reg.3
Sch.1 Item 35, amended: SI 1997/542 Reg.5
Sch.1 Item 37, amended: SI 1998/453 Reg.4
Sch.1 Item 38, amended: SI 1997/542 Reg.5, SI 1998/453 Reg.4, SI 1999/482 Reg.3
Sch.1 Item 40, amended: SI 1997/542 Reg.5
Sch.1 Item 41, revoked: SI 1997/542 Reg.5
Sch.1 Item 45, amended: SI 1997/542 Reg.5, SI 1998/453 Reg.4, SI 1999/482 Reg.3
Sch.1 Item 46, amended: SI 1997/542 Reg.5
Sch.1 Item 47, amended: SI 1997/542 Reg.5
Sch.1 Item 52, amended: SI 1999/482 Reg.3
Sch.1 Item 55, amended: SI 1997/542 Reg.5
Sch.1 Item 56, added: SI 1997/542 Reg.5
Sch.1 Item 56, amended: SI 1998/453 Reg.4
Sch.1 Item 57, added: SI 1999/482 Reg.3
Sch.2 Part I, amended: SI 1997/542 Reg.6, SI 1998/453 Reg.5, SI 1999/482 Reg.4
Sch.2 Part II, amended: SI 1997/542 Reg.7, SI 1999/482 Reg.5
Sch.2 Part III, amended: SI 1997/542 Reg.8, SI 1998/453 Reg.6, SI 1999/482 Reg.6
Sch.2 Part IV, amended: SI 1997/542 Reg.9, SI 1998/453 Reg.7, SI 1999/482 Reg.7
Sch.2 Part V, amended: SI 1997/542 Reg.10, SI 1998/453 Reg.8, SI 1999/482 Reg.8
Sch.2 Part VIII, amended: SI 1998/453 Reg.9
Sch.3, amended: SI 1997/542 Reg.11, SI 1998/453 Reg.10, SI 1999/482 Reg.9
Sch.3A, added: SI 1997/542 Reg.12

NO.

NO.

696. Common Agricultural Policy (Wine) Regulations 1996—*cont.*
Sch.4 Part I, substituted: SI 1997/542 Reg.13, SI 1998/453 Reg.11
Sch.4 Part II, amended: SI 1998/453 Reg.12
Sch.5, amended: SI 1998/453 Reg.13
Sch.6 para.7, amended: SI 1997/542 Reg.14

697. Diseases of Animals (Approved Disinfectants) (Amendment) Order 1996
revoked: SI 1997/2347 Art.3
Art.2, revoked: SI 1997/2347 Art.3

706. National Health Service (Fund-Holding Practices) Regulations 1996
applied: SI 1996/708 Reg.3
Part IV, added: SI 1997/747 Reg.9
Part VII, amended: SI 1997/747 Reg.15
Reg.1, amended: SI 1997/747 Reg.2, SI 1998/693 Reg.2, Reg.12, SI 1999/261 Reg.2, Reg.9
Reg.2, revoked: SI 1999/261 Reg.28
Reg.2, substituted: SI 1997/747 Reg.3
Reg.3, amended: SI 1997/747 Reg.4, SI 1998/693 Reg.3, SI 1999/261 Reg.10
Reg.3, applied: SI 1997/1678 Reg.7, SI 1999/261 Reg.31
Reg.3, revoked (in part): SI 1999/261 Reg.3, Reg.10
Reg.5, amended: SI 1997/747 Reg.5, SI 1997/1678 Reg.2, SI 1998/693 Reg.9, SI 1999/261 Reg.4, Reg.11
Reg.7, amended: SI 1997/747 Reg.6, SI 1999/261 Reg.12
Reg.7, revoked (in part): SI 1999/261 Reg.12
Reg.8, revoked: SI 1999/261 Reg.28
Reg.9, amended: SI 1997/747 Reg.7, SI 1998/693 Reg.4, SI 1999/261 Reg.13
Reg.9, applied: SI 1999/261 Reg.29, SI 1999/2541 Reg.8
Reg.9, revoked (in part): SI 1999/261 Reg.13
Reg.10, amended: SI 1997/747 Reg.8
Reg.10, revoked: SI 1999/261 Reg.8
Reg.10A, added: SI 1998/693 Reg.12
Reg.10A, revoked: SI 1999/261 Reg.8
Reg.11, amended: SI 1999/261 Reg.14
Reg.11, applied: SI 1999/261 Reg.9
Reg.11, revoked (in part): SI 1999/261 Reg.14
Reg.12, amended: SI 1998/693 Reg.13, SI 1999/261 Reg.15
Reg.12, applied: SI 1999/261 Reg.33
Reg.13, amended: SI 1997/747 Reg.10, SI 1999/261 Reg.5, Reg.16
Reg.13, applied: SI 1999/2541 Reg.9
Reg.14, amended: SI 1999/261 Reg.6
Reg.14, applied: SI 1999/2541 Reg.9
Reg.15, applied: SI 1999/2541 Reg.9
Reg.16, applied: SI 1999/2541 Reg.9
Reg.17, applied: SI 1999/2541 Reg.8
Reg.17, referred to: SI 1999/261 Reg.33
Reg.18, amended: SI 1997/1678 Reg.3, SI 1998/693 Reg.12, SI 1999/261 Reg.7
Reg.18, applied: SI 1999/2541 Reg.14
Reg.18, referred to: SI 1999/2541 Reg.14
Reg.19, amended: SI 1998/693 Reg.5
Reg.19, revoked: SI 1999/261 Reg.28
Reg.20, amended: SI 1997/747 Reg.11, SI 1997/1678 Reg.4, SI 1999/261 Reg.17
Reg.20, revoked (in part): SI 1999/261 Reg.17
Reg.21, amended: SI 1997/747 Reg.12
Reg.21, revoked (in part): SI 1999/261 Reg.18
Reg.22, amended: SI 1997/747 Reg.13, SI 1998/693 Reg.6
Reg.22, revoked: SI 1999/261 Reg.28

706. National Health Service (Fund-Holding Practices) Regulations 1996—*cont.*
Reg.23, amended: SI 1998/693 Reg.10, SI 1999/261 Reg.19
Reg.23, revoked (in part): SI 1999/261 Reg.19
Reg.24, amended: SI 1998/693 Reg.20
Reg.24, applied: SI 1999/261 Reg.29
Reg.24, revoked (in part): SI 1999/261 Reg. 20
Reg.24A, added: SI 1999/261 Reg.21
Reg.25, amended: SI 1997/747 Reg.14, SI 1997/1678 Reg.5, SI 1998/693 Reg.10, Reg.11, SI 1999/261 Reg.22
Reg.25, applied: SI 1998/693 Reg.11, SI 1999/261 Reg.29, SI 1999/2541 Reg.6, Reg.15
Reg.25, referred to: SI 1999/2541 Reg.15
Reg.25, revoked (in part): SI 1999/261 Reg.22
Reg.25A, added: SI 1998/693 Reg.10
Reg.25A, amended: SI 1999/261 Reg.23
Reg.25A, applied: SI 1999/261 Reg.29
Reg.26, amended: SI 1998/693 Reg.26
Reg.26, applied: SI 1999/2541 Reg.16
Reg.27, amended: SI 1997/1678 Reg.6
Sch.1, amended: SI 1997/747 Reg.16
Sch.1 para.1, revoked: SI 1999/261 Reg.25
Sch.1 para.1, substituted: SI 1997/747 Reg.16
Sch.1 para.6, added: SI 1998/693 Reg.7
Sch.1 para.6, amended: SI 1999/261 Reg.25
Sch.2, amended: SI 1997/747 Reg.17
Sch.2 para.1, amended: SI 1997/747 Reg.17
Sch.2 para.1, revoked: SI 1999/261 Reg.26
Sch.2 para.2, amended: SI 1997/747 Reg.17
Sch.2 para.2, revoked: SI 1999/261 Reg.26
Sch.2 para.5, amended: SI 1999/261 Reg.26
Sch.2 para.15, added: SI 1998/693 Reg.8
Sch.2 para.15, amended: SI 1999/261 Reg.26
Sch.2 para.16, added: SI 1999/261 Reg.26
Sch.2 para.17, added: SI 1999/261 Reg.26
Sch.3, added: SI 1999/261 Reg.27, Sch.

707. Health Authorities (Membership and Procedure) Regulations 1996
amended: SI 1997/327 Reg.4
Reg.1, amended: SI 1998/646 Reg.15, SI 1998/2621 Reg.2, SI 1999/1901 Reg.2
Reg.7, applied: SI 1997/327 Reg.4
Reg.8, amended: SI 1997/2991 Reg.2
Reg.8, applied: SI 1997/327 Reg.4
Reg.9, applied: SI 1997/327 Reg.4
Reg.10, amended: SI 1997/327 Reg.4, SI 1997/2991 Reg.2, SI 1998/646 Reg.15
Reg.10, applied: SI 1997/327 Reg.4
Reg.10, revoked (in part): SI 1997/2991 Reg.2
Reg.11, applied: SI 1997/327 Reg.4
Reg.12, applied: SI 1997/327 Reg.4
Reg.13, applied: SI 1997/327 Reg.4
Reg.14, amended: SI 1998/2621 Reg.2, SI 1999/1901 Reg.2
Reg.14, applied: SI 1997/327 Reg.4
Reg.15, applied: SI 1997/327 Reg.4
Reg.16, amended: SI 1998/646 Reg.15
Reg.16, applied: SI 1997/327 Reg.4
Sch.2, amended: SI 1997/2991 Reg.2, SI 1999/946 Reg.2
Sch.3, applied: SI 1997/327 Reg.4

708. National Health Service (Functions of Health Authorities and Administration Arrangements) Regulations 1996
Reg.2, amended: SI 1998/646 Reg.16, SI 1999/628 Reg.2, SI 1999/1902 Reg.2
Reg.3, amended: SI 1999/628 Reg.2
Reg.3A, added: SI 1999/628 Reg.2
Reg.3A, amended: SI 1999/1902 Reg.2
Reg.5, amended: SI 1998/646 Reg.16

NO.

709. Health Authorities Act 1995 (Transitional Provisions) Order 1996
referred to: SI 1996/703 Reg.15, 1999 c.8 s.44
Art.2, amended: SI 1996/971 Art.2
Art.4, amended: SI 1996/971 Art.2
Art.5, applied: SI 1996/2285 Reg.2
Art.9, applied: SI 1996/2285 Reg.2
Art.10, applied: SI 1996/2285 Reg.2
Art.12, amended: SI 1996/2310 Art.2, SI 1996/3019 Art.2
Art.13, amended: SI 1996/971 Art.2
Art.14, amended: SI 1996/971 Art.2
Art.15, amended: SI 1996/971 Art.2
Art.16, added: SI 1996/971 Art.2
Art.17, added: SI 1996/971 Art.2
Art.18, added: SI 1996/971 Art.2
Art.19, added: SI 1996/971 Art.2
Art.20, added: SI 1996/971 Art.2
Sch.1 Part III, referred to: 1999 c.8 s.44
Sch.1 Part IV, referred to: 1999 c.8 s.44
Sch.2 Part III, referred to: 1999 c.8 s.44
Sch.2 Part IV, referred to: 1999 c.8 s.44
Sch.3, amended: SI 1996/971 Art.2

710. Local Government Changes for England (Education) (Miscellaneous Provisions) Regulations 1996
Reg.19, revoked: 1996 c.56 Sch.38 Part III

711. Local Government Pension Scheme (Environment Agency) Regulations 1996
applied: SI 1997/1613 Reg.4, Reg.19, Sch.2 para.2
referred to: SI 1997/1613 Reg.3, Sch.2 para.6
Reg.1, amended: SI 1997/1613 Reg.27, Sch.3 para.34
Reg.2, amended: SI 1997/1613 Reg.27, Sch.3 para.35
Reg.2, applied: SI 1997/1612 Reg.91, Reg.144
Reg.6, amended: SI 1997/1613 Reg.27, Sch.3 para.36
Reg.8, amended: SI 1997/1613 Reg.27, Sch.3 para.37

714. Trade Marks (International Registration) Order 1996
applied: SI 1996/715, SI 1998/1776 r.3
referred to: SI 1996/715, SI 1996/1942 r.3, SI 1998/1776 r.2
Art.6, applied: SI 1998/1776 r.3, Sch.
Art.6, referred to: SI 1996/715 Sch
Art.10, applied: SI 1998/1776 r.3, Sch.
Art.10, referred to: SI 1996/715 Sch
Art.13, applied: SI 1998/1776 r.3, Sch.
Art.13, referred to: SI 1996/715 Sch
Art.15, applied: SI 1998/1776 r.3, Sch.
Art.15, referred to: SI 1996/715 Sch
Art.19, applied: SI 1998/1776 r.3, Sch.
Art.19, referred to: SI 1996/715 Sch
Art.20, applied: SI 1998/1776 r.3, Sch.
Art.20, referred to: SI 1996/715 Sch
Art.21, applied: SI 1998/1776 r.3, Sch.
Art.21, referred to: SI 1996/715 Sch
Art.22, applied: SI 1998/1776 r.3, Sch.
Art.22, referred to: SI 1996/715 Sch
Art.25, applied: SI 1998/1776 r.3, Sch.
Art.25, referred to: SI 1996/715 Sch
Art.31, applied: SI 1998/1776 r.3, Sch.
Art.31, referred to: SI 1996/715 Sch

715. Trade Marks (International Registration) (Fees) Rules 1996
revoked: SI 1996/1942 r.5
r.2, revoked: SI 1996/1942 r.5
r.3, revoked: SI 1996/1942 r.5
Sch., revoked: SI 1996/1942 r.5

NO.

716. United Nations (International Tribunal) (Former Yugoslavia) Order 1996
amended: SI 1997/1753 Art.3
applied: SI 1997/1753 Art.3
Art.11, substituted: SI 1998/1755 Art.2, Sch.1
Art.12, substituted: SI 1998/1755 Art.2, Sch.1
Art.13, substituted: SI 1998/1755 Art.2, Sch.1
Art.22, amended: SI 1997/1752 Art.2

721. Appropriation (Northern Ireland) Order 1996
revoked: SI 1999/1742 (NI.7) Art.6, Sch.2
Art.2, revoked: SI 1999/1742 (NI.7) Art.6, Sch.2

725. Business Tenancies (Northern Ireland) Order 1996
referred to: 1998 c.v s.14, 1999 c.33 s.149, 1999 c.iv s.15
Art.2, amended: SI 1997/1179 (NI.8) Art.53, Sch.4 para.6
Art.4, revoked (in part): SI 1997/1179 (NI.8) Art.53, Sch.5
Art.6, amended: SI 1997/1179 (NI.8) Art.53, Sch.4 para.6
Art.8, amended: SI 1997/1179 (NI.8) Art.53, Sch.4 para.6
Art.18, amended: SI 1996/3158 (NI.22) Sch.11 para.10

734. Education (Grants for Education Support and Training) (England) Regulations 1996
revoked: SI 1997/514 Reg.13
Reg.2, amended: SI 1996/3066 Reg.3
Reg.2, revoked: SI 1997/514 Reg.13
Reg.2A, added: SI 1996/3066 Reg.4
Reg.2A, revoked: SI 1997/514 Reg.13
Reg.5, amended: SI 1996/3066 Reg.5
Reg.5, revoked: SI 1997/514 Reg.13
Reg.6, amended: SI 1996/3066 Reg.6
Reg.6, revoked: SI 1997/514 Reg.13
Reg.12, revoked: SI 1997/514 Reg.13
Sch. para.2, revoked: SI 1997/514 Reg.13
Sch. para.3, revoked: SI 1997/514 Reg.13
Sch. para.7, revoked: SI 1997/514 Reg.13
Sch. para.14A, added: SI 1996/3066 Reg.7
Sch. para.14A, revoked: SI 1997/514 Reg.13
Sch. para.17, added: SI 1996/3066 Reg.7
Sch. para.17, revoked: SI 1997/514 Reg.13

743. Mental Health (Prescribed Forms) (Scotland) Regulations 1996
Sch.2 Form 22, applied: SI 1996/2149 r.9
Sch.2 Form 22, referred to: SI 1999/929 r.3.8.9

745. Common Police Services (Scotland) Order 1996
revoked: SI 1997/695 Art.4 (with savings)
Art.2, referred to: SI 1996/780 Reg.4
Art.2, revoked: SI 1997/695 Art.4 (with savings)
Art.3, referred to: SI 1996/780 Reg.4
Art.3, revoked: SI 1997/695 Art.4 (with savings)
Art.4, revoked: SI 1997/695 Art.4 (with savings)

748. National Health Service (Fund-Holding Practices) (Scotland) Amendment Regulations 1996
revoked: SI 1997/1014 Reg.24, Sch.3
Reg.2, revoked: SI 1997/1014 Reg.24, Sch.3
Reg.3, revoked: SI 1997/1014 Reg.24, Sch.3
Reg.4, revoked: SI 1997/1014 Reg.24, Sch.3
Reg.5, revoked: SI 1997/1014 Reg.24, Sch.3
Reg.6, revoked: SI 1997/1014 Reg.24, Sch.3
Reg.7, revoked: SI 1997/1014 Reg.24, Sch.3
Reg.8, revoked: SI 1997/1014 Reg.24, Sch.3
Reg.9, revoked: SI 1997/1014 Reg.24, Sch.3
Reg.10, revoked: SI 1997/1014 Reg.24, Sch.3
Reg.11, revoked: SI 1997/1014 Reg.24, Sch.3

NO.

748. **National Health Service (Fund-Holding Practices) (Scotland) Amendment Regulations 1996**—*cont.*
Reg.12, revoked: SI 1997/1014 Reg.24, Sch.3

752. **Gas (Extent of Domestic Supply Licences) Order 1996**
Art.3, amended: SI 1996/3275 Art.2
Art.4, amended: SI 1996/3275 Art.2
Art.4, revoked: SI 1997/826 Art.7
Art.5, amended: SI 1996/3275 Art.2
Art.5, revoked: SI 1997/826 Art.7
Art.6, amended: SI 1996/3275 Art.2
Art.6, revoked: SI 1997/826 Art.7

755. **Local Government Finance (Scotland) Order 1996**
Art.2, revoked: SI 1997/938 Art.6
Sch.1, revoked (in part): SI 1997/938 Art.6

756. **Revenue Support Grant (Scotland) Order 1996**
revoked: SI 1997/939 Art.4
Art.4, revoked: SI 1997/939 Art.4

767. **Act of Sederunt (Fees of Shorthand Writers in the Sheriff Court) (Amendment) 1996**
para.2 Table, applied: SI 1997/1118 para.3

769. **Medicines (Medicated Animal Feeding Stuffs) (Amendment) Regulations 1996**
revoked: SI 1998/1048 Reg.2, Sch.1
Reg.2, revoked: SI 1998/1048 Reg.2, Sch.1

770. **Local Government Act 1988 (Defined Activities) (Exemptions) (England and Wales) Order 1996**
Art.3, amended: SI 1998/1380 Art.3
Art.4, amended: SI 1998/1380 Art.3

772. **Adventure Activities Licensing Regulations 1996**
applied: SI 1996/1647 Reg.2
Reg.7, amended: SI 1996/1647 Reg.3

773. **Hydrographic Office Trading Fund Order 1996**
Art.4, amended: SI 1997/1428 Art.2
Sch.2, referred to: SI 1997/1428

776. **Personal and Occupational Pension Schemes (Miscellaneous Amendments) Regulations 1996**
Reg.2, revoked: SI 1996/1172 Sch.2
Reg.3, revoked: SI 1996/1537 Reg.18, Sch.
Reg.6, revoked: SI 1997/470 Reg.20, Sch.3

780. **Police Grant (Scotland) Order 1996**
revoked: SI 1997/721 Art.7 (with savings)
Art.3, revoked: SI 1997/721 Art.7 (with savings)
Art.4, revoked: SI 1997/721 Art.7 (with savings)
Art.6, revoked: SI 1997/721 Art.7 (with savings)
Art.7, revoked: SI 1997/721 Art.7 (with savings)
Sch.2, revoked: SI 1997/721 Art.7 (with savings)

800. **Pensions Increase (Review) Order 1996**
applied: SI 1997/634 Art.3, SI 1998/503 Art.3, Art.4, SI 1999/522 Art.3

811. **Advice and Assistance (Scotland) Amendment Regulations 1996**
revoked: SI 1996/2447 Reg.3, Sch.1
Reg.3, revoked: SI 1996/2447 Reg.3, Sch.1
Reg.4, revoked: SI 1996/2447 Reg.3, Sch.1
Reg.5, revoked: SI 1996/2447 Reg.3, Sch.1
Reg.6, revoked: SI 1996/2447 Reg.3, Sch.1

812. **Civil Legal Aid (Scotland) Amendment Regulations 1996**
revoked: SI 1996/2444 Reg.3, Sch.1
Reg.3, revoked: SI 1996/2444 Reg.3, Sch.1
Reg.4, revoked: SI 1996/2444 Reg.3, Sch.1
Reg.5, revoked: SI 1996/2444 Reg.3, Sch.1

NO.

815. **A41 Trunk Road (Barnet) Red Route (Clearway) (No.1) Traffic Order 1996**
Art.2, amended: SI 1999/272 Art.2, Sch. Part B
Art.9, amended: SI 1999/272 Art.2, Sch. Part B

817. **A41 Trunk Road (Barnet) Red Route (Clearway) (No.2) Traffic Order 1996**
Art.2, amended: SI 1999/272 Art.2, Sch. Part B
Art.9, amended: SI 1999/272 Art.2, Sch. Part B
Sch.2 Table, amended: SI 1997/554 Art.2

818. **A41 Trunk Road (Barnet) Red Route (Clearway) (No.3) Traffic Order 1996**
Art.2, amended: SI 1999/272 Art.2, Sch. Part B
Art.9, amended: SI 1999/272 Art.2, Sch. Part B

819. **A1 Trunk Road (Barnet) Red Route (Clearway) Traffic Order 1996**
Art.2, amended: SI 1999/272 Art.2, Sch. Part B
Art.9, amended: SI 1999/272 Art.2, Sch. Part B
Sch.1 Table 1, substituted: SI 1997/2299 Art.3
Sch.2 Item 13, revoked: SI 1999/997 Art.3
Sch.2 Item 14, revoked: SI 1998/3127 Art.3
Sch.2 Item 15, revoked: SI 1998/3127 Art.3

820. **A406 Trunk Road (Barnet) Red Route (Clearway) Traffic Order 1996**
Art.2, amended: SI 1999/272 Art.2, Sch. Part B
Art.4, amended: SI 1997/1513 Art.3
Art.7, amended: SI 1997/1513 Art.4
Art.9, amended: SI 1999/272 Art.2, Sch. Part B
Sch.2 Item 1, amended: SI 1997/1513 Art.5
Sch.2 Item 2, amended: SI 1997/1513 Art.5
Sch.2 Item 3, amended: SI 1997/1513 Art.5
Sch.2 Item 4, amended: SI 1997/1513 Art.5
Sch.2 Item 5, amended: SI 1997/1513 Art.5
Sch.2 Item 6, amended: SI 1997/1513 Art.5
Sch.2 Item 7, amended: SI 1997/1513 Art.5
Sch.2 Item 8, amended: SI 1997/1513 Art.5
Sch.2 Item 8, revoked: SI 1997/1513 Art.6
Sch.2 Item 9, amended: SI 1997/1513 Art.5
Sch.2 Item 9, revoked: SI 1997/1513 Art.6
Sch.2 Item 10, amended: SI 1997/1513 Art.5
Sch.2 Item 11, amended: SI 1997/1513 Art.5
Sch.2 Item 12, amended: SI 1997/1513 Art.5
Sch.2 Item 13, added: SI 1997/1513 Art.7
Sch.2 Item 14, added: SI 1997/1513 Art.7
Sch.2 Item 15, added: SI 1997/1513 Art.7
Sch.2 Item 15, revoked: SI 1999/1359 Art.3
Sch.2 Item 16, added: SI 1997/1513 Art.7
Sch.2 Item 16, revoked: SI 1999/1359 Art.3
Sch.2 Item 17, added: SI 1997/1513 Art.7
Sch.2 Item 17, revoked: SI 1999/1359 Art.3
Sch.2 Item 18, added: SI 1997/1513 Art.7
Sch.2 Item 18, revoked: SI 1999/1359 Art.3
Sch.3A, added: SI 1997/1513 Art.8
Sch.3A Item 1, substituted: SI 1999/1359 Art.4

821. **A406 Trunk Road (Barnet) Red Route Experimental Traffic Order 1996**
revoked (in part): SI 1997/1608 Art.10

823. **Local Government Act 1988 (Defined Activities) (Specified Period) (Redbridge London Borough Council) Regulations 1996**
revoked: SI 1997/2747 Reg.2, Sch.
Reg.2, revoked: SI 1997/2747 Reg.2, Sch.

825. **Pipelines Safety Regulations 1996**
Reg.3, applied: SI 1998/494 Sch.2 para.11

826. **Diseases of Animals (Waste Food) (Amendment) Order 1996**
revoked: SI 1999/646 Art.35, Sch.6 Part I
Art.2, revoked: SI 1999/646 Art.35, Sch.6 Part I

827. **Animal By-Products (Amendment) Order 1996**
revoked: SI 1999/646 Art.35, Sch.6 Part I
Art.2, revoked: SI 1999/646 Art.35, Sch.6 Part I
Art.3, revoked: SI 1999/646 Art.35, Sch.6 Part I

NO.

827. Animal By-Products (Amendment) Order 1996—*cont.*
Art.4, revoked: SI 1999/646 Art.35, Sch.6 Part I
Art.5, revoked: SI 1999/646 Art.35, Sch.6 Part I
Art.6, revoked: SI 1999/646 Art.35, Sch.6 Part I
Art.7, revoked: SI 1999/646 Art.35, Sch.6 Part I
Art.8, revoked: SI 1999/646 Art.35, Sch.6 Part I
Art.9, revoked: SI 1999/646 Art.35, Sch.6 Part I
Art.10, revoked: SI 1999/646 Art.35, Sch.6 Part I

845. Trustee Investments (Division of Trust Fund) Order 1996
referred to: SI 1996/1268 Art.1

848. Deregulation (Corn Returns Act 1882) Order 1996
referred to: SI 1999/672 Art.2, Sch.1

850. Offshore Installations (Safety Zones) (No.2) Order 1996
revoked: SI 1997/735 Art.3, Sch.2

856. Food Protection (Emergency Prohibitions) (Oil and Chemical Pollution of Salmon and Migratory Trout) Order 1996
applied: SI 1996/1212
revoked: SI 1996/1212 Art.2

858. Contracting Out (Functions in Relation to the provision of Guardians Ad Litem and Reporting Officers Panels) Order 1996
revoked: SI 1997/1652 Art.3
Art.2, revoked: SI 1997/1652 Art.3

873. Hartlepool and East Durham National Health Service Trust (Establishment) Order 1996
revoked: SI 1999/800 Art.2

874. Worcestershire Community Healthcare National Health Service Trust (Establishment) Order 1996
revoked: SI 1999/3471 Art.2

875. South Durham National Health Service Trust (Establishment) Order 1996
revoked: SI 1998/828 Art.2

888. Protection of Water Against Agricultural Nitrate Pollution (England and Wales) Regulations 1996
applied: SI 1999/672 Art.2, Sch.1
referred to: SI 1999/672 Art.2, Sch.1
Reg.5, revoked: SI 1998/1202 Reg.9

889. Education (Grant-Maintained and Grant-Maintained Special Schools) (Finance) Regulations 1996
applied: SI 1997/996 Reg.48, Sch.5 para.16A
revoked: SI 1997/996 Reg.3
Reg.3, revoked: SI 1997/996 Reg.3
Reg.6, applied: SI 1997/996 Reg.7
Reg.6, revoked: SI 1997/996 Reg.3
Reg.7, applied: SI 1997/996 Reg.7
Reg.7, revoked: SI 1997/996 Reg.3
Reg.8, applied: SI 1997/996 Reg.10, Reg.48
Reg.8, revoked: SI 1997/996 Reg.3
Reg.9, applied: SI 1997/996 Reg.48
Reg.9, revoked: SI 1997/996 Reg.3
Reg.10, applied: SI 1997/996 Reg.48
Reg.10, revoked: SI 1997/996 Reg.3
Reg.11, applied: SI 1997/996 Reg.48
Reg.11, revoked: SI 1997/996 Reg.3
Reg.12, applied: SI 1997/996 Reg.7
Reg.12, revoked: SI 1997/996 Reg.3
Reg.13, revoked: SI 1997/996 Reg.3
Reg.14, revoked: SI 1997/996 Reg.3
Reg.16, applied: SI 1997/996 Reg.10
Reg.16, revoked: SI 1997/996 Reg.3
Reg.18, applied: SI 1997/996 Reg.48
Reg.18, revoked: SI 1997/996 Reg.3
Reg.19, applied: SI 1997/996 Reg.7
Reg.19, revoked: SI 1997/996 Reg.3

NO.

889. Education (Grant-Maintained and Grant-Maintained Special Schools) (Finance) Regulations 1996—*cont.*
Reg.20, revoked: SI 1997/996 Reg.3
Reg.21, revoked: SI 1997/996 Reg.3
Reg.22, applied: SI 1997/996 Reg.48
Reg.22, revoked: SI 1997/996 Reg.3
Reg.23, applied: SI 1997/996 Reg.48
Reg.23, revoked: SI 1997/996 Reg.3
Reg.24, revoked: SI 1997/996 Reg.3
Reg.25, applied: SI 1997/996 Reg.25, Reg.45, SI 1998/799 Reg.25
Reg.25, referred to: SI 1997/996 Reg.25, SI 1998/799 Reg.25
Reg.25, revoked: SI 1997/996 Reg.3
Reg.26, applied: SI 1997/996 Reg.25, Reg.45, SI 1998/799 Reg.25
Reg.26, revoked: SI 1997/996 Reg.3
Reg.28, revoked: SI 1997/996 Reg.3
Reg.30, revoked: SI 1997/996 Reg.3
Reg.31, revoked: SI 1997/996 Reg.3
Reg.36, revoked: SI 1997/996 Reg.3
Reg.37, revoked: SI 1997/996 Reg.3
Reg.38, revoked: SI 1997/996 Reg.3
Reg.40, applied: SI 1997/996 Sch.5 para.16A
Reg.40, revoked: SI 1997/996 Reg.3
Reg.42, applied: SI 1997/996 Reg.25, Reg.45, SI 1998/799 Reg.25
Reg.42, revoked: SI 1997/996 Reg.3
Reg.43, applied: SI 1997/996 Reg.48, Sch.5 para.16A
Reg.43, revoked: SI 1997/996 Reg.3
Reg.45, applied: SI 1997/996 Sch.5 para.16A, Sch.5 para.16B
Reg.45, revoked: SI 1997/996 Reg.3
Reg.55, revoked: SI 1997/996 Reg.3
Reg.56, revoked: SI 1997/996 Reg.3
Sch.1 para 6, revoked: SI 1997/996 Reg.3
Sch.2 para 2, revoked: SI 1997/996 Reg.3
Sch.7 para 2, revoked: SI 1997/996 Reg.3

892. Prevention of Terrorism (Exclusion Orders) Regulations 1996
see *Vitol Energy (Bermuda) Ltd v Pisco Shipping Co Ltd* [1998] 1 Lloyd's Rep. 509 (CA), Hirst, L.J.

904. Broadcasting (Prescribed Countries) Order 1996
revoked: SI 1997/1682 Reg.6
Art.2, revoked: SI 1997/1682 Reg.6
Art.3, revoked: SI 1997/1682 Reg.6

905. Local Government Reorganisation (Wales) (Staff) (No.2) Order 1996
Art.5, referred to: SI 1996/1214 Art.3

909. Income Support (General) Amendment (No.2) Regulations 1996
revoked: SI 1996/1363 (with savings)

910. Local Government Reorganisation (Wales) (Capital Finance and Miscellaneous Provisions) Order 1996
Art.3, amended: SI 1996/1366 Art.3
Art.4, amended: SI 1999/1782 Art.2
Sch.3, added: SI 1999/1782 Art.2

913. Offshore Installations and Wells (Design and Construction, etc.) Regulations 1996
Sch.1 para.67, revoked: SI 1997/1993 Reg.4

916. Waste Management Licensing (Scotland) Regulations 1996
Reg.2, applied: SI 1997/257 Reg.2

920. Environmentally Sensitive Areas (Somerset Levels and Moors) Designation (Amendment) Order 1996
revoked: SI 1997/1442 Art.6 (with saving)

NO.

921. Environmentally Sensitive Areas (The Broads) Designation (Amendment) Order 1996
revoked: SI 1997/1440 Art.6 (with saving)

922. Environmentally Sensitive Areas (West Penwith) Designation (Amendment) Order 1996
revoked: SI 1997/1444 Art.6 (with saving)

923. Environmentally Sensitive Areas (Pennine Dales) Designation (Amendment) Order 1996
revoked: SI 1997/1441 Art.6 (with saving)

924. Environmentally Sensitive Areas (South Downs) Designation (Amendment) Order 1996
revoked: SI 1997/1443 Art.6 (with saving)

943. Insurance Companies (Accounts and Statements) Regulations 1996
referred to: SI 1996/2991 Reg.5
Reg.4, amended: SI 1997/2911 Reg.2
Reg.6, amended: SI 1997/2911 Reg.3
Reg.12, amended: SI 1998/2996 Reg.3
Sch.1 Form 9, amended: SI 1997/2911 Reg.5
Sch.1 Form 13, amended: SI 1997/2911 Reg.5, SI 1998/2996 Reg.5
Sch.1 Form 14, substituted: SI 1997/2911 Reg.5, Sch.
Sch.1 para.14, amended: SI 1997/2911 Reg.4
Sch.1 para.17, amended: SI 1998/2996 Reg.4
Sch.2 para.3, amended: SI 1998/2996 Reg.6
Sch.2 para.5, amended: SI 1998/2996 Reg.7
Sch.2 para.11, amended: SI 1997/2911 Reg.6
Sch.2 para.13, amended: SI 1997/2911 Reg.6
Sch.2 para.17, amended: SI 1997/2911 Reg.6
Sch.2 para.19, amended: SI 1997/2911 Reg.7
Sch.2 Form 20, substituted: SI 1997/2911 Reg.10, Sch.
Sch.2 para.20, amended: SI 1997/2911 Reg.8
Sch.2 Form 24, amended: SI 1997/2911 Reg.10
Sch.2 para.24, amended: SI 1997/2911 Reg.9
Sch.2 Form 28, amended: SI 1997/2911 Reg.10
Sch.2 Form 29, amended: SI 1997/2911 Reg.10
Sch.2 Form 30, amended: SI 1997/2911 Reg.10
Sch.2 Form 32, amended: SI 1997/2911 Reg.10
Sch.2 Form 33, amended: SI 1997/2911 Reg.10, SI 1998/2996 Reg.8
Sch.2 Form 34, amended: SI 1997/2911 Reg.10, SI 1998/2996 Reg.8
Sch.2 Form 35, amended: SI 1997/2911 Reg.10
Sch.2 Form 36, amended: SI 1997/2911 Reg.10, SI 1998/2996 Reg.8
Sch.2 Form 37, amended: SI 1997/2911 Reg.10
Sch.2 Form 38, amended: SI 1997/2911 Reg.10
Sch.2 Form 39, amended: SI 1997/2911 Reg.10
Sch.3 para.2, amended: SI 1997/2911 Reg.11
Sch.4 para.7, amended: SI 1997/2911 Reg.12
Sch.4 para.15, amended: SI 1997/2911 Reg.13
Sch.4 para.19, amended: SI 1997/2911 Reg.14
Sch.4 para.20, amended: SI 1997/2911 Reg.15, SI 1998/2996 Reg.9
Sch.4 para.21, amended: SI 1997/2911 Reg.16
Sch.4 Form 47, amended: SI 1997/2911 Reg.17
Sch.4 Form 48, amended: SI 1997/2911 Reg.17
Sch.4 Form 49, amended: SI 1997/2911 Reg.17
Sch.4 Form 51, amended: SI 1997/2911 Reg.17
Sch.4 Form 52, amended: SI 1997/2911 Reg.17
Sch.4 Form 53, amended: SI 1997/2911 Reg.17
Sch.4 Form 54, amended: SI 1997/2911 Reg.17
Sch.4 Form 55, amended: SI 1997/2911 Reg.17
Sch.4 Form 56, amended: SI 1997/2911 Reg.17
Sch.4 Form 57, substituted: SI 1997/2911 Reg.17, Sch.
Sch.4 Form 60, amended: SI 1998/2996 Reg.10

NO.

943. Insurance Companies (Accounts and Statements) Regulations 1996—*cont.*
Sch.5 para.4, amended: SI 1997/2911 Reg.18
Sch.6 para.1, amended: SI 1997/2911 Reg.19
Sch.6 para.10, amended: SI 1997/2911 Reg.20

946. Insurance Companies (Reserves) Regulations 1996
referred to: SI 1996/943 Reg.16
Reg.2, amended: SI 1998/2996 Reg.11
Sch.2 para.2, referred to: SI 1996/2991 Reg.12

951. Deregulation (Length of the School Day) Order 1996
revoked: 1996 c.56 Sch.38 Part III
Art.2, revoked: 1996 c.56 Sch.38 Part III
Art.4, revoked: 1996 c.56 Sch.38 Part III
Art.5, revoked: 1996 c.56 Sch.38 Part III

958. Motor Vehicles (Type Approval and Approval Marks) (Fees) Regulations 1996
revoked: SI 1997/564 Reg.2
Reg.2, revoked: SI 1997/564 Reg.2

959. Rent Officers (Additional Functions) (Amendment) Order 1996
revoked: SI 1997/1984 Art.9
Art.3, revoked: SI 1997/1984 Art.9
Art.4, revoked: SI 1997/1984 Art.9
Art.5, revoked: SI 1997/1984 Art.9
Art.6, revoked: SI 1997/1984 Art.9

961. Beef (Emergency Control) Order 1996
revoked: SI 1996/1742 Art.2
Art.1, amended: SI 1996/1043 Art.2, SI 1996/1166 Art.2
Art.1, revoked: SI 1996/1742 Art.2
Art.2, amended: SI 1996/1043 Art.2, SI 1996/1091 Art.2, SI 1996/1166 Art.2
Art.2, revoked: SI 1996/1742 Art.2
Sch., added: SI 1996/1091 Art.2
Sch., revoked: SI 1996/1742 Art.2

962. Bovine Spongiform Encephalopathy (Amendment) Order 1996
revoked: SI 1996/2007 Art.21
Art.2, revoked: SI 1996/2007 Art.21

963. Specified Bovine Material Order 1996
revoked: SI 1996/1192 Art.27
Art.18, revoked: SI 1996/1192 Art.27
Art.21, revoked: SI 1996/1192 Art.27
Art.26, revoked: SI 1996/1192 Art.27
Art.27, revoked: SI 1996/1192 Art.27

965. Housing Benefit (General) Amendment Regulations 1996
Reg.1, amended: SI 1996/1944 Reg.11

972. Special Waste Regulations 1996
applied: SI 1999/672 Art.2, Sch.1
Reg.1, amended: SI 1996/2019 Reg.2, Sch. para.2
Reg.2, applied: SI 1997/257 Reg.2, SI 1997/648 Sch.3 para.3
Reg.2, substituted: SI 1996/2019 Reg.2, Sch. para.3
Reg.4, amended: SI 1996/2019 Reg.2, Sch. para.4
Reg.8, amended: SI 1996/2019 Reg.2, Sch. para.5
Reg.14, amended: SI 1996/2019 Reg.2, Sch. para.6
Reg.20, amended: SI 1997/251 Reg.2
Reg.20A, added: SI 1997/251 Reg.2
Sch.2 Part IV, added: SI 1996/2019 Reg.2, Sch. para.7

973. Environment Act 1995 (Consequential and Transitional Provisions) (Scotland) Regulations 1996
Sch. para.4, revoked: 1996 c.18 Sch.3 Part II

1996—cont.

975. **Rent Officers (Additional Functions) (Scotland) Amendment Order 1996**
revoked: SI 1997/1995 Art.9, Sch.5
Art.3, revoked: SI 1997/1995 Art.9, Sch.5
Art.4, revoked: SI 1997/1995 Art.9, Sch.5
Art.5, revoked: SI 1997/1995 Art.9, Sch.5
Art.6, revoked: SI 1997/1995 Art.9, Sch.5

1003. **Education (School Teachers' Pay and Conditions) Order 1996**
revoked: SI 1996/1816 Art.1

1004. **Registers of Scotland Executive Agency Trading Fund Order 1996**
applied: SI 1999/441 Art.22
referred to: SI 1999/441 Art.22

1005. **Sheriff Court Districts (Alteration of Boundaries) Order 1996**
Art.2, amended: SI 1996/2192 Art.2
Sch.1, amended: SI 1996/2192 Art.2

1009. **Criminal Legal Aid (Scotland) (Prescribed Proceedings) Amendment Regulations 1996**
revoked: SI 1997/3069 Reg.2, Sch.
Reg.3, revoked: SI 1997/3069 Reg.2, Sch.

1010. **Advice and Assistance (Financial Conditions) (Scotland) Regulations 1996**
revoked: SI 1997/1113 (with savings)
Reg.3, revoked: SI 1997/1113 (with savings)
Reg.4, revoked: SI 1997/1113 (with savings)
Reg.5, revoked: SI 1997/1113 (with savings)
Reg.6, revoked: SI 1997/1113 (with savings)

1011. **Advice and Assistance (Assistance by Way of Representation) (Scotland) Amendment Regulations 1996**
revoked: SI 1997/3070 Reg.2, Sch.
Reg.3, revoked: SI 1997/3070 Reg.2, Sch.
Reg.4, revoked: SI 1997/3070 Reg.2, Sch.
Reg.5, revoked: SI 1997/3070 Reg.2, Sch.

1012. **Civil Legal Aid (Financial Conditions) (Scotland) Regulations 1996**
Reg.3, revoked: SI 1997/1112 (with savings)
Reg.5, revoked: SI 1997/1112 (with savings)

1022. **Lands Tribunal Rules 1996**
Part IIA, added: SI 1997/1965 r.4
r.5A, added: SI 1997/1965 r.4
r.5B, added: SI 1997/1965 r.4
r.5C, added: SI 1997/1965 r.4
r.5D, added: SI 1997/1965 r.4
r.5E, added: SI 1997/1965 r.4
r.5F, added: SI 1997/1965 r.4
r.5G, added: SI 1997/1965 r.4
r.5H, added: SI 1997/1965 r.4
r.6, amended: SI 1997/1965 r.5, r.6, r.7
r.26, applied: SI 1997/1965 r.12
r.26, substituted: SI 1997/1965 r.8
r.26A, added: SI 1997/1965 r.8
r.26A, applied: SI 1997/1965 r.12
r.29A, added: SI 1998/22 r.3
r.32, amended: SI 1998/22 r.4
r.32, applied: SI 1997/1965 r.12
r.32, substituted: SI 1997/1965 r.9
r.45, see *Rees-Davies (Personal Representatives of Rees-Davies (WR) (Deceased)) v Westminster City Council* [1998] R.V.R. 219 (CA), Otton, L.J.
r.46, see *Rees-Davies (Personal Representatives of Rees-Davies (WR) (Deceased)) v Westminster City Council* [1998] R.V.R. 219 (CA), Otton, L.J.
r.46, amended: SI 1997/1965 r.10
r.50, amended: SI 1997/1965 r.11

1996—cont.

1022. **Lands Tribunal Rules 1996**—*cont.*
r.52, see *Stanford Marsh Ltd v Secretary of State for the Environment* [1997] 37 R.V.R. 34 (Lands Tr), PH Clarke, FRICS

1035. **Fishing Boats (Specified Countries) Designation Order 1996**
Sch.2, substituted: SI 1997/1630 Art.2, Sch.

1036. **Third Country Fishing (Enforcement) Order 1996**
revoked: SI 1997/931 Art.13 (with savings)
Art.5, revoked: SI 1997/931 Art.13 (with savings)
Art.13, revoked: SI 1997/931 Art.13 (with savings)

1043. **Beef (Emergency Control) (Amendment) Order 1996**
revoked: SI 1996/1742 Art.2
Art.2, revoked: SI 1996/1742 Art.2

1055. **Social Security (Reduced Rates of Class 1 Contributions and Rebates) (Money Purchase Contracted-out Schemes) Order 1996**
Art.2, amended: SI 1998/945 Art.3
Sch. Table, amended: SI 1998/945 Art.3

1056. **Social Security (Minimum Contributions to Appropriate Personal Pension Schemes) Order 1996**
Art.2, amended: SI 1998/944 Art.3
Sch. Table, amended: SI 1998/944 Art.3

1088. **A406 Trunk Road (Ealing and Hounslow) Red Route Experimental Traffic Order 1996**
revoked (in part): SI 1997/2386 Art.10

1089. **A406 Trunk Road (North Circular Road, Ealing) Red Route (Prescribed Routes and Turns No.1) Experimental Traffic Order 1996**
revoked: SI 1997/2003 Art.5

1090. **A406 Trunk Road (North Circular Road, Hounslow) Red Route (Prescribed Route No.1) Experimental Traffic Order 1996**
revoked: SI 1997/2401 Art.5

1091. **Beef (Emergency Control) (Amendment) (No.2) Order 1996**
revoked: SI 1996/1742 Art.2
Art.2, revoked: SI 1996/1742 Art.2

1104. **Prohibition of Keeping of Live Fish (Crayfish) Order 1996**
Sch., substituted: SI 1996/1374 Art.2, Sch.

1106. **Genetically Modified Organisms (Risk Assessment) (Records and Exemptions) Regulations 1996**
Reg.3, amended: SI 1997/1900 Reg.3

1108. **Smoke Control Areas (Exempted Fireplaces) Order 1996**
Sch., amended: SI 1999/1515 Art.3, SSI 1999/58 Art.3

1109. **Gaming Clubs (Hours and Charges) (Amendment) Regulations 1996**
revoked: SI 1998/961 Reg.4
Reg.2, revoked: SI 1998/961 Reg.4
Reg.3, revoked: SI 1998/961 Reg.4

1110. **Road Traffic (Special Parking Area) (Royal Borough of Kingston upon Thames) (Amendment) Order 1996**
revoked: SI 1996/3038 Art.2, Sch.1
Art.2, revoked: SI 1996/3038 Art.2, Sch.1

1111. **Animals and Animal Products (Import and Export) (Amendment) Regulations 1996**
revoked: SI 1998/190 Reg.35
Reg.2, revoked: SI 1998/190 Reg.35

1996—cont.

1996—cont.

1111. Animals and Animal Products (Import and Export) (Amendment) Regulations 1996— *cont.*
Reg.3, revoked: SI 1998/190 Reg.35
Sch.1, revoked: SI 1998/190 Reg.35
Sch.2, revoked: SI 1998/190 Reg.35
Sch.3, revoked: SI 1998/190 Reg.35

1124. Dual-Use and Related Goods (Export Control) (Amendment) Regulations 1996
applied: SI 1996/2721 Reg.15
revoked: SI 1996/2721 Sch.1
Reg.2, revoked: SI 1996/2721 Sch.1
Sch., revoked: SI 1996/2721 Sch.1

1125. Fertilisers (Mammalian Meat and Bone Meal) Regulations 1996
referred to: SI 1996/2007 Art.14, SI 1996/3183 Art.15
revoked: SI 1998/954 Reg.5
Reg.2, amended: SI 1996/2473 Reg.2
Reg.2, revoked: SI 1998/954 Reg.5

1134. A406 Trunk Road (North Circular Road, Ealing) Red Route (Prescribed Turns No.2) Experimental Traffic Order 1996
revoked: SI 1997/2013 Art.5

1136. A501 Trunk Road (Camden and Islington) Red Route Experimental Traffic Order 1996
revoked (in part): SI 1997/2326 Art.10

1137. A501 Trunk Road (Camden, Islington and Westminster) Red Route Experimental Traffic Order 1996
revoked (in part): SI 1997/2002 Art.10

1138. Hong Kong (Overseas Public Servants) (Retirement and Compensation) Order 1996
applied: SI 1996/1139 Art.5

1141. Juries (Northern Ireland) Order 1996
amended: SI 1996/1298 (NI.8) Art.21, Sch.5
Sch.2, amended: 1997 c.50 s.134, Sch.9 para.91, 1998 c.32 s.74, Sch.4 para.21, SI 1998/1504 (NI.9) Art.65, Sch.5 para.49
Sch.3, amended: SI 1996/1298 (NI.8) Art.21, Sch.5, SI 1999/1042 Art.3, Sch.1 para.23

1143. Merchant Shipping (Liability and Compensation for Oil Pollution Damage) (Transitional Provisions) Order 1996
applied: SI 1997/2598 Art.5, SI 1998/260 Art.5
revoked: SI 1997/2566 Art.2
Art.1, amended: SI 1997/2598 Art.5, Sch.2 para.1, SI 1998/260 Art.5, Sch.2 para.1
Art.1, revoked: SI 1997/2566 Art.2
Art.2, amended: SI 1997/2578 Art.2, Sch., SI 1997/2598 Art.5, Sch.2 para.2, SI 1998/260 Art.5, Sch.2 para.2
Art.2, applied: SI 1997/2578 Art.2, Sch.
Art.2, revoked: SI 1997/2566 Art.2
Art.3, amended: SI 1997/2578 Art.2, Sch., SI 1997/2598 Art.5, Sch.2 para.3, SI 1998/260 Art.5, Sch.2 para.3
Art.3, applied: SI 1997/2578 Art.2, Sch.
Art.3, revoked: SI 1997/2566 Art.2
Art.4, amended: SI 1997/2578 Art.2, Sch., SI 1997/2598 Art.5, Sch.2 para.4, SI 1998/260 Art.5, Sch.2 para.4
Art.4, applied: SI 1997/2578 Art.2, Sch.
Art.4, revoked: SI 1997/2566 Art.2
Art.5, amended: SI 1997/2578 Art.2, Sch.
Art.5, applied: SI 1997/2578 Art.2, Sch.
Art.5, revoked: SI 1997/2566 Art.2
Art.6, amended: SI 1997/2578 Art.2, Sch.
Art.6, applied: SI 1997/2578 Art.2, Sch.
Art.6, revoked: SI 1997/2566 Art.2
Sch.1, amended: SI 1997/2578 Art.2, Sch.

1143. Merchant Shipping (Liability and Compensation for Oil Pollution Damage) (Transitional Provisions) Order 1996—*cont.*
Sch.1, applied: SI 1997/2578 Art.2, Sch.
Sch.2, amended: SI 1997/2578 Art.2, Sch.
Sch.2, applied: SI 1997/2578 Art.2, Sch.
Sch.2, revoked: SI 1997/2566 Art.2
Sch.2 Part A, amended: SI 1997/2598 Art.5, Sch.2 para.5, Sch.2 para.6, Sch.2 para.7, Sch.2 para.8, SI 1998/260 Art.5, Sch.2 para.5, Sch.2 para.6, Sch.2 para.7, Sch.2 para.8
Sch.2 Part A, revoked: SI 1997/2566 Art.2
Sch.2 Part B, amended: SI 1997/2598 Art.5, Sch.2 para.9, Sch.2 para.10, Sch.2 para.11, SI 1998/260 Art.5, Sch.2 para.9, Sch.2 para.10, Sch.2 para.11
Sch.2 Part B, revoked: SI 1997/2566 Art.2
Sch.3, amended: SI 1997/2578 Art.2, Sch.
Sch.3, applied: SI 1997/2578 Art.2, Sch.
Sch.3, revoked: SI 1997/2566 Art.2
Sch.3, substituted: SI 1997/2598 Art.5, Sch.2 para.12, SI 1998/260 Art.5, Sch.2 para.12

1144. Gaming Clubs (Hours and Charges) (Scotland) Amendment Regulations 1996
revoked: SI 1998/961 Reg.4
Reg.2, revoked (in part): SI 1997/942 Reg.4, SI 1998/961 Reg.4
Reg.3, revoked: SI 1998/961 Reg.4

1146. Education (Individual Pupils' Achievements) (Information) (Amendment) Regulations 1996
revoked: SI 1997/1368 Reg.2
Reg.2, revoked: SI 1997/1368 Reg.2
Reg.3, revoked: SI 1997/1368 Reg.2
Reg.4, revoked: SI 1997/1368 Reg.2
Reg.5, revoked: SI 1997/1368 Reg.2
Reg.6, revoked: SI 1997/1368 Reg.2
Reg.7, revoked: SI 1997/1368 Reg.2
Reg.8, revoked: SI 1997/1368 Reg.2
Sch.2 para.1, revoked: SI 1997/1368 Reg.2
Sch.2 para.2, revoked: SI 1997/1368 Reg.2
Sch.2 para.3, revoked: SI 1997/1368 Reg.2
Sch.2 para.4, revoked: SI 1997/1368 Reg.2

1163. A4 Trunk Road (Hillingdon) Red Route (Clearway) Traffic Order 1996
Art.2, amended: SI 1999/272 Art.2, Sch. Part B
Art.9, amended: SI 1999/272 Art.2, Sch. Part B
Sch.2, substituted: SI 1998/2611 Art.3
Sch.2 Item 5, substituted: SI 1997/2385 Art.3, SI 1998/2611 Art.3
Sch.3A, revoked: SI 1998/2611 Art.4

1166. Beef (Emergency Control) (Amendment) (No.3) Order 1996
revoked: SI 1996/1742 Art.2
Art.2, revoked: SI 1996/1742 Art.2

1170. A4 Trunk Road (Hounslow) Red Route (Clearway) Traffic Order 1996
Art.2, amended: SI 1999/272 Art.2, Sch. Part B
Art.9, amended: SI 1999/272 Art.2, Sch. Part B
Sch.2 Table, substituted: SI 1997/550 Art.3, Sch, SI 1998/1642 Art.3, Sch., SI 1998/2545 Art.3, Sch.
Sch.3A, amended: SI 1998/2545 Art.5
Sch.3D, amended: SI 1998/2545 Art.4
Sch.4B, amended: SI 1998/2545 Art.6

1171. Road Traffic (Permitted Parking Area and Special Parking Area) (County of Hampshire, City of Winchester) Order 1996
applied: SI 1999/1918 Reg.20
referred to: SI 1999/1918
Sch.1 para.5, substituted: SI 1999/132 Art.3
Sch.1 para.6A, added: SI 1996/2017 Art.2

NO.

1171. **Road Traffic (Permitted Parking Area and Special Parking Area) (County of Hampshire, City of Winchester) Order 1996—** *cont.*

Sch.1 para.7, amended: SI 1999/132 Art.4

Sch.1 para.8, amended: SI 1999/132 Art.5

Sch.1 para.8, revoked (in part): SI 1999/132 Art.5

1172. **Occupational Pension Schemes (Contracting Out) Regulations 1996**

applied: SI 1997/786 Reg.3, Sch.1 para.4, 1999 c.2 s.1, Sch.2

Part II, applied: SI 1997/38 Reg.2, Reg.3

Part III, amended: SI 1996/1977 Reg.3

Part IV, amended: SI 1996/1977 Reg.3

Part V, amended: SI 1996/1977 Reg.3

Part V, applied: SI 1997/784 Reg.8

Part VII, amended: SI 1996/1977 Reg.3

Reg.1, amended: SI 1997/786 Reg.3, Sch.1 para.4, SI 1999/3198 Reg.3

Reg.1, referred to: SI 1997/1612 Reg.118, SI 1998/366 Reg.118

Reg.2, amended: SI 1997/786 Reg.3, Sch.1 para.4

Reg.3, amended: SI 1996/1977 Reg.3, SI 1997/786 Reg.3, Sch.1 para.4

Reg.6, amended: SI 1996/1977 Reg.3

Reg.6, revoked (in part): SI 1997/786 Reg.3, Reg.4, Sch.1 para.4, Sch.2

Reg.7, amended: SI 1997/786 Reg.3, Sch.1 para.4

Reg.9, amended: SI 1996/1977 Reg.3, SI 1997/786 Reg.3, Sch.1 para.4

Reg.10, amended: SI 1996/1977 Reg.3

Reg.12, amended: SI 1999/3198 Reg.3

Reg.16, amended: SI 1996/1977 Reg.3

Reg.23, referred to: 1999 c.2 s.1, Sch.2

Reg.37, applied: SI 1996/1537 Reg.3

Reg.39, amended: SI 1997/819 Reg.3

Reg.42, amended: SI 1997/786 Reg.3, Sch.1 para.4

Reg.45, amended: SI 1997/819 Reg.3

Reg.46, amended: SI 1997/819 Reg.3

Reg.48, amended: SI 1997/786 Reg.3, Sch.1 para.4, SI 1999/3198 Reg.3

Reg.49, amended: SI 1996/1977 Reg.3

Reg.50A, added: SI 1998/1397 Reg.5

Reg.52, amended: SI 1997/786 Reg.3, Sch.1 para.4

Reg.54, applied: SI 1997/1612 Reg.92, SI 1998/366 Reg.91

Reg.55, amended: SI 1997/786 Reg.3, Sch.1 para.4

Reg.60, amended: SI 1997/786 Reg.3, Sch.1 para.4

Reg.61, referred to: 1999 c.2 s.1, Sch.2

Reg.70, amended: SI 1996/1977 Reg.3

Reg.71, amended: SI 1996/1977 Reg.3

Reg.72, amended: SI 1996/1977 Reg.3, SI 1997/786 Reg.3, Sch.1 para.4

Reg.72, revoked (in part): SI 1997/786 Reg.3, Reg.4, Sch.1 para.4, Sch.2

Reg.76A, added: SI 1996/1577 Reg.2

Reg.76A, amended: SI 1997/819 Reg.3, SI 1997/786 Reg.3, Sch.1 para.4, SI 1997/3038 Reg.2

Reg.76B, added: SI 1997/786 Reg.3, Sch.1 para.4

Reg.77, referred to: 1999 c.30 s.81, Sch.11 para.35

NO.

1180. **Insurance Companies (Gilt-Edged Securities) (Periodic Accounting for Tax on Interest) (Amendment) Regulations 1996**

revoked (in part): SI 1999/623 Reg.10

Reg.3, revoked (in part): SI 1999/623 Reg.10

Reg.4, revoked (in part): SI 1999/623 Reg.10

Reg.5, revoked (in part): SI 1999/623 Reg.10

1191. **A303 Trunk Road (Sparkford to Ilchester Improvement and Slip Roads) Order 1996**

applied: SI 1996/1190 Art.2

Art.2, applied: SI 1996/1190 Art.2

1192. **Specified Bovine Material (No.2) Order 1996**

revoked: SI 1996/1941 Art.27 (with saving)

Art.18, revoked: SI 1996/1941 Art.27 (with saving)

Art.21, revoked: SI 1996/1941 Art.27 (with saving)

Art.26, revoked: SI 1996/1941 Art.27 (with saving)

Art.27, revoked: SI 1996/1941 Art.27 (with saving)

Sch.2, revoked: SI 1996/1941 Art.27 (with saving)

1194. **Offshore Installations (Safety Zones) (No.3) Order 1996**

revoked: SI 1997/735 Art.3, Sch.2

1199. **Children's Hearings (Scotland) Amendment Rules 1996**

revoked: SI 1997/692 r.2

r.2, revoked: SI 1997/692 r.2

1216. **Occupational Pension Schemes (Member-nominated Trustees and Directors) Regulations 1996**

applied: SI 1997/786 Reg.3, Sch.1 para.5

Reg.2, amended: SI 1997/786 Reg.3, Sch.1 para.5, SI 1999/3198 Reg.7

Reg.2, revoked (in part): SI 1997/786 Reg.4, Sch.2

Reg.3, substituted: SI 1997/786 Reg.3, Sch.1 para.5

Reg.4, revoked (in part): SI 1997/786 Reg.3, Reg.4, Sch.1 para.5, Sch.2

Reg.5, revoked (in part): SI 1997/786 Reg.3, Reg.4, Sch.1 para.5, Sch.2

Reg.6, amended: SI 1997/786 Reg.3, Sch.1 para.5

Reg.6, revoked (in part): SI 1997/786 Reg.3, Reg.4, Sch.1 para.5, Sch.2

Reg.9, amended: SI 1997/786 Reg.3, Sch.1 para.5

Reg.10, amended: SI 1999/3198 Reg.7

Reg.13, amended: SI 1997/786 Reg.3, Sch.1 para.5

Reg.15, amended: SI 1997/786 Reg.3, Sch.1 para.5

Reg.16, amended: SI 1999/3198 Reg.7

Reg.18, amended: SI 1997/3038 Reg.3

Reg.20, amended: SI 1997/786 Reg.3, Sch.1 para.5

Reg.23, amended: SI 1997/786 Reg.3, Sch.1 para.5

Sch.1 para.6, amended: SI 1997/786 Reg.3, Sch.1 para.5

Sch.1 para.6, revoked (in part): SI 1997/786 Reg.4, Sch.2

Sch.1 para.8, amended: SI 1997/786 Reg.3, Sch.1 para.5

Sch.2 para.2, amended: SI 1997/786 Reg.3, Sch.1 para.5

Sch.3 para.1, amended: SI 1997/786 Reg.3, Sch.1 para.5

Sch.3 para.2, amended: SI 1997/786 Reg.3, Sch.1 para.5, SI 1999/3198 Reg.7

NO.

1216. **Occupational Pension Schemes (Member-nominated Trustees and Directors) Regulations 1996**—*cont.*
Sch.3 para.3, amended: SI 1997/786 Reg.3, Sch.1 para.5, SI 1999/3198 Reg.7
Sch.3 para.8, substituted: SI 1997/786 Reg.3, Sch.1 para.5

1217. **Housing Benefit and Council Tax Benefit (Subsidy) Order 1996**
applied: SI 1997/1004 Sch.6 para.8
Art.4, applied: SI 1997/1004 Art.11, SI 1998/562 Art.19
Art.11, applied: SI 1997/1004 Art.10, SI 1998/562 Art.18
Art.19, applied: SI 1997/1004 Art.18, SI 1998/562 Art.18, Art.19
Art.19, referred to: SI 1997/1004 Art.19
Sch.2, applied: SI 1997/1004 Sch.2 para.13
Sch.6 para.6, applied: SI 1998/562 Art.19

1220. **Elections (Northern Ireland) Order 1996**
Art.3, applied: SI 1996/1408, SI 1996/1408 Art.2
Sch.1, applied: SI 1996/1408, SI 1996/1408 Art.2

1226. **Income Tax (Unapproved Manufactured Payments) Regulations 1996**
revoked: SI 1997/987 Reg.5 (with savings)
Reg.2, revoked: SI 1997/987 Reg.5 (with savings)

1227. **Income Tax (Manufactured Interest) (Amendment) Regulations 1996**
revoked: SI 1997/987 Reg.4 (with savings), Sch.2 (with savings)
Reg.3, revoked: SI 1997/987 Reg.4 (with savings), Sch.2 (with savings)
Reg.4, revoked: SI 1997/987 Reg.4 (with savings), Sch.2 (with savings)
Reg.5, revoked: SI 1997/987 Reg.4 (with savings), Sch.2 (with savings)
Reg.6, revoked: SI 1997/987 Reg.4 (with savings), Sch.2 (with savings)
Reg.7, revoked: SI 1997/987 Reg.4 (with savings), Sch.2 (with savings)
Reg.8, revoked: SI 1997/987 Reg.4 (with savings), Sch.2 (with savings)
Reg.9, revoked: SI 1997/987 Reg.4 (with savings), Sch.2 (with savings)
Reg.10, revoked: SI 1997/987 Reg.4 (with savings), Sch.2 (with savings)

1228. **Income Tax (Stock Lending) (Amendment) Regulations 1996**
revoked: SI 1997/987 Reg.2 (with savings), Sch.1 (with savings)
Reg.3, revoked: SI 1997/987 Reg.2 (with savings), Sch.1 (with savings)
Reg.4, revoked: SI 1997/987 Reg.2 (with savings), Sch.1 (with savings)
Reg.5, revoked: SI 1997/987 Reg.2 (with savings), Sch.1 (with savings)
Reg.6, revoked: SI 1997/987 Reg.2 (with savings), Sch.1 (with savings)
Reg.7, revoked: SI 1997/987 Reg.2 (with savings), Sch.1 (with savings)

1230. **A35 Trunk Road (Chideock Morecombelake Bypass) Order 1996**
revoked: SI 1999/1725 Art.2

1241. **Local Government (Superannuation and Compensation for Premature Retirement) (Scotland) Amendment Regulations 1996**
applied: SI 1998/364 Reg.4, Reg.6, Reg.19, Sch.2 para.2, Sch.2 para.5, Sch.4 para.8
referred to: SI 1998/364 Reg.3, Reg.10, Sch.2 para.4, Sch.2 para.6
Reg.3, revoked: SI 1998/192 Reg.52, Sch.2

NO.

1242. **Fishing Vessels (Decommissioning) Scheme 1996**
referred to: SI 1997/1924 para.3

1243. **National Park Authorities (England) Order 1996**
Art.15, applied: SI 1997/319 Reg.24, Reg.34
Sch.5 para.13, revoked: SI 1997/633 Art.4
Sch.7 para.10, amended: SI 1996/2546 Art.2

1245. **Social Security (Additional Pension) (Contributions Paid in Error) Regulations 1996**
amended: 1999 c.2 s.1, Sch.2

1252. **Income Support (Pilot Scheme) Regulations 1996**
applied: SI 1996/1307 Reg.6
revoked: SI 1997/984 Reg.1
Reg.3, revoked: SI 1997/984 Reg.1
Reg.5, revoked: SI 1997/984 Reg.1

1259. **Motor Vehicles (Driving Licences) (Amendment) (No.3) Regulations 1996**
revoked: SI 1996/2824 Reg.2, Sch.1
Reg.3, revoked: SI 1996/2824 Reg.2, Sch.1
Reg.4, revoked: SI 1996/2824 Reg.2, Sch.1
Reg.5, revoked: SI 1996/2824 Reg.2, Sch.1
Reg.6, revoked: SI 1996/2824 Reg.2, Sch.1
Reg.7, revoked: SI 1996/2824 Reg.2, Sch.1
Reg.8, revoked: SI 1996/2824 Reg.2, Sch.1
Reg.9, revoked: SI 1996/2824 Reg.2, Sch.1
Reg.10, revoked: SI 1996/2824 Reg.2, Sch.1
Reg.11, revoked: SI 1996/2824 Reg.2, Sch.1
Sch.1, revoked: SI 1996/2824 Reg.2, Sch.1
Sch.2, revoked: SI 1996/2824 Reg.2, Sch.1
Sch.3, revoked: SI 1996/2824 Reg.2, Sch.1
Sch.4, revoked: SI 1996/2824 Reg.2, Sch.1

1269. **Housing (Change of Landlord) (Payment of Disposal Cost by Instalments) (Amendment No.2) Regulations 1996**
revoked: SI 1996/2228 Reg.3

1270. **Occupational Pension Schemes (Internal Dispute Resolution Procedures) Regulations 1996**
Reg.5, amended: SI 1999/3198 Reg.6
Reg.7, amended: SI 1999/3198 Reg.6

1271. **Personal and Occupational Pension Schemes (Pensions Ombudsman) Amendment Regulations 1996**
revoked: SI 1996/2475 Reg.7
Reg.2, revoked: SI 1996/2475 Reg.7

1294. **Hong Kong (Overseas Public Servants) (Pension Supplements) Order 1996**
applied: SI 1999/666
Art.2, amended: SI 1998/1066 Art.2, SI 1999/666 Art.2
Sch., amended: SI 1999/666 Art.3
Sch. Head G, substituted: SI 1998/1066 Art.3, Sch.
Sch. Head I1, amended: SI 1998/1066 Art.3
Sch. Head I2, amended: SI 1998/1066 Art.3

1295. **International Oil Pollution Compensation Fund 1992 (Immunities and Privileges) Order 1996**
Art.12A, added: SI 1999/2034 Art.2, Sch.

1296. **United Nations (International Tribunal) (Rwanda) Order 1996**
amended: SI 1997/1753 Art.3
applied: SI 1997/1753 Art.3
Art.22, amended: SI 1997/1751 Art.2
Sch. Art.10, substituted: SI 1998/1755 Art.3, Sch.2
Sch. Art.11, substituted: SI 1998/1755 Art.3, Sch.2
Sch. Art.12, substituted: SI 1998/1755 Art.3, Sch.2

NO.

1297. Commissioner for Complaints (Northern Ireland) Order 1996

Art.2, amended: SI 1997/1758 (NI.14) Art.4, Sch. para.2

Art.5A, added: SI 1997/1758 (NI.14) Art.4, Sch. para.3

Art.6, amended: SI 1997/1758 (NI.14) Art.4, Sch. para.4

Art.7, substituted: SI 1997/1758 (NI.14) Art.3

Art.8, substituted: SI 1997/1758 (NI.14) Art.3

Art.9, amended: 1998 c.47 s.99, Sch.13 para.17

Art.9, referred to: 1998 c.47 s.78

Art.9, substituted: SI 1997/1758 (NI.14) Art.3

Art.10, amended: SI 1997/1758 (NI.14) Art.4, Sch. para.5

Art.10A, added: SI 1997/1758 (NI.14) Art.4

Art.11, amended: SI 1997/1758 (NI.14) Art.4, Sch. para.6

Art.12, amended: SI 1997/1758 (NI.14) Art.4, Sch. para.7

Art.14, amended: SI 1997/1758 (NI.14) Art.4, Sch. para.8

Art.15, substituted: SI 1997/1758 (NI.14) Art.4, Sch. para.9

Art.21, amended: SI 1997/1758 (NI.14) Art.6

Art.23, revoked (in part): 1998 c.47 s.100, Sch.15

Sch.2, amended: SI 1997/869 (NI.6) Art.73, Sch.2 para.7, 1998 c.47 s.73, Sch.8 para.11, SI 1998/261 (NI.2) Art.15, Sch.3, SI 1998/2795 (NI.18) Art.6, Sch.1 para.26

Sch.2, applied: 1998 c.47 s.76, s.77

Sch.2, referred to: SI 1999/2204 Art.3

Sch.2, revoked (in part): 1998 c.47 s.100, Sch.15, SI 1998/261 (NI.2) Art.15, Sch.4, SI 1999/2790 (NI.9) Art.40, Sch.9 Part 6

Sch.3 para.3, revoked: SI 1997/1758 (NI.14) Art.7

Sch.4, revoked: 1998 c.47 s.100, Sch.15

1298. Ombudsman (Northern Ireland) Order 1996

Art.3, revoked (in part): 1998 c.47 s.100, Sch.15

Art.10, amended: 1998 c.47 s.99, Sch.13 para.18

Art.10, referred to: 1998 c.47 s.78

Art.14, amended: SI 1999/663 Art.2, Sch.1 para.26

Sch.2, amended: SI 1999/283 (NI.1) Art.9, Sch.2, SI 1999/859 Art.4, Art.8, Art.11, Art.14, Art.17, Art.20, Sch.2 para.5

Sch.2, applied: 1998 c.47 s.76, s.77

Sch.2, revoked (in part): SI 1999/283 (NI.1) Art.9, Sch.2, Sch.3

Sch.3, amended: SI 1996/1921 (NI.18) Art.26, Sch.1 para.13, SI 1998/1506 (NI.10) Art.78, Sch.6 para.115, Sch.7, SI 1998/3162 (NI.21) Art.105, Sch.3

Sch.5, revoked (in part): 1998 c.47 s.100, Sch.15

1299. Proceeds of Crime (Northern Ireland) Order 1996

applied: SI 1998/752 Art.3, Art.4

referred to: SI 1998/752 Art.1

Art.8, applied: SI 1998/752 Art.3

Art.13, amended: SI 1998/1504 (NI.9) Art.65, Sch.5 para.50

Art.35, applied: SI 1998/752 Art.3

Art.50, referred to: 1998 c.35 s.14

Art.51, referred to: 1998 c.35 s.14

Art.54, referred to: 1998 c.35 s.14

Sch.2, referred to: 1998 c.35 s.14

NO.

1299. Proceeds of Crime (Northern Ireland) Order 1996—*cont.*

Sch.2 para.6, amended: 1999 c.23 s.59, Sch.3 para.26

1307. Jobseeker's Allowance (Pilot Scheme) Regulations 1996

revoked: SI 1997/984 Reg.1

Reg.3, revoked: SI 1997/984 Reg.1

Reg.4, revoked: SI 1997/984 Reg.1

Reg.5, revoked: SI 1997/984 Reg.1

Reg.6, revoked: SI 1997/984 Reg.1

Sch., amended: SI 1996/1856 Reg.2

Sch., revoked: SI 1997/984 Reg.1

1320. Road Traffic Offenders (Northern Ireland) Order 1996

amended: SI 1998/1074 (NI.7) Art.7

Art.2, amended: SI 1997/276 (NI.2) Art.75, Sch.8 para.24

Art.5, amended: SI 1997/276 (NI.2) Art.75, Sch.8 para.25

Art.10, amended: SI 1998/1074 (NI.7) Art.13, Sch.3 para.5

Art.11, applied: SI 1998/1074 (NI.7) Sch.1 para.3

Art.15, amended: SI 1997/276 (NI.2) Art.75, Sch.8 para.26

Art.16, amended: SI 1997/2983 (NI.21) Art.13, Sch.1 para.9

Art.20, applied: SI 1997/276 (NI.2) Art.66

Art.20, referred to: SI 1997/276 (NI.2) Art.66

Art.23, amended: SI 1997/276 (NI.2) Art.75, Sch.8 para.27, SR 1999/435 Art.2

Art.30, applied: SI 1998/1074 (NI.7) Art.4

Art.31, applied: SI 1998/1074 (NI.7) Art.4

Art.41, applied: SI 1998/1074 (NI.7) Art.6, Art.9, Sch.1 para.10

Art.49, referred to: SI 1998/1074 (NI.7) Art.4

Art.52, amended: SI 1998/1074 (NI.7) Art.13, Sch.3 para.6

Art.57, revoked (in part): SI 1998/1074 (NI.7) Sch.2 para.6

Art.60, applied: SI 1998/1074 (NI.7) Art.4, Sch.1 para.3

Art.63, amended: SI 1998/1074 (NI.7) Art.13, Sch.3 para.7

Art.63, applied: SI 1998/1074 (NI.7) Art.4, Sch.1 para.7

Art.80, applied: SI 1998/1074 (NI.7) Art.4, Sch.1 para.3

Art.82, amended: SI 1998/1074 (NI.7) Art.13, Sch.3 para.8

Art.82, applied: SI 1998/1074 (NI.7) Art.4, Sch.1 para.7

Art.90, amended: SI 1997/276 (NI.2) Art.75, Sch.8 para.28

Art.90, applied: SI 1997/276 (NI.2) Art.44

Sch.1, revoked (in part): SI 1997/276 (NI.2) Art.75, Sch.9

Sch.1 Part I, amended: SI 1997/276 (NI.2) Art.61, Sch.7, Sch.8 para.29, SI 1998/1074 (NI.7) Art.13, Sch.2 para.7, Sch.3 para.9, SI 1999/2920 Reg.19, Sch.2 para.9

Sch.3 Part I, revoked (in part): SI 1998/1074 (NI.7) Art.13, Sch.4

Sch.3 para.13, revoked: SI 1997/276 (NI.2) Art.75, Sch.9

Sch.3 para.21, amended: SI 1998/1074 (NI.7) Art.13, Sch.3 para.10

Sch.3 para.31, revoked: SI 1997/276 (NI.2) Art.75, Sch.9

Sch.3 para.33, revoked: SI 1997/276 (NI.2) Art.75, Sch.9

NO.

1320. **Road Traffic Offenders (Northern Ireland) Order 1996**—*cont.*
Sch.4, revoked (in part): SI 1997/276 (NI.2) Art.75, Sch.9

1331. **Housing Renovation etc. Grants (Reduction of Grant) (Amendment) Regulations 1996**
applied: SI 1996/2842 Art.8
revoked: SI 1996/2842 Art.7, Sch Part I

1332. **Housing Renovation etc. Grants (Prescribed Forms and Particulars) (Amendment) Regulations 1996**
applied: SI 1996/2842 Art.8
revoked: SI 1996/2842 Art.7, Sch Part I
Reg.2, revoked: SI 1996/2842 Art.7, Sch Part I
Sch.1, revoked: SI 1996/2842 Art.7, Sch Part I
Sch.2, revoked: SI 1996/2842 Art.7, Sch Part I
Sch.3, revoked: SI 1996/2842 Art.7, Sch Part I

1334. **Education (Grant-Maintained and Grant-Maintained Special Schools) (Finance) (Wales) (Amendment) Regulations 1996**
revoked: SI 1997/599 Reg.3
Reg.2, revoked: SI 1997/599 Reg.3

1341. **Export of Goods (Control) (Amendment) Order 1996**
revoked: SI 1997/2758 Art.1
Art.2, revoked: SI 1997/2758 Art.1
Art.3, revoked: SI 1997/2758 Art.1

1343. **A501 Trunk Road (Camden and Islington) Red Route (Bus Lanes) Experimental Traffic Order 1996**
revoked (in part): SI 1997/445 Art.5, SI 1997/463 Art.5

1344. **A501 Trunk Road (Camden) Red Route (Bus Lane) (No.1) Experimental Traffic Order 1996**
revoked (in part): SI 1997/463 Art.5

1345. **Social Security and Child Support (Jobseeker's Allowance) (Consequential Amendments) Regulations 1996**
referred to: SI 1996/2519 Reg.1
Reg.11, revoked: SI 1996/2745 Reg.18, Sch.4

1350. **Radioactive Material (Road Transport) (Great Britain) Regulations 1996**
applied: SI 1996/2094 Reg.3
referred to: SI 1996/2090 Sch.13 para.20

1351. **Bovine Spongiform Encephalopathy Compensation (Amendment) Order 1996**
revoked (in part): SI 1996/3184 Art.5
Art.2, revoked (in part): SI 1996/3184 Art.5

1353. **Recreational Craft Regulations 1996**
Reg.15, amended: SI 1998/116 Reg.2

1360. **Compensation for Redundancy or Premature Retirement (Scottish Environment Protection Agency and River Purification Boards Transitional Arrangements) (Scotland) Regulations 1996**
Reg.14, revoked: SI 1998/192 Reg.52, Sch.2
Reg.15, revoked: SI 1998/192 Reg.52, Sch.2

1363. **Income Support (General) (Standard Interest Rate Amendment) Regulations 1996**
revoked: SI 1996/1889 Reg.3 (with savings)

1378. **Housing Renovation etc. Grants (Prescribed Forms and Particulars) (Welsh Forms and Particulars) (Amendment) Regulations 1996**
applied: SI 1996/2842 Art.8
revoked: SI 1996/2842 Art.7, Sch Part I
Reg.2, revoked: SI 1996/2842 Art.7, Sch Part I
Sch.1, revoked: SI 1996/2842 Art.7, Sch Part I
Sch.2, revoked: SI 1996/2842 Art.7, Sch Part I
Sch.3, revoked: SI 1996/2842 Art.7, Sch Part I

NO.

1388. **Rules of Procedure (Army) (Amendment) Rules 1996**
revoked: SI 1997/169 r.90, Sch.7
r.2, revoked: SI 1997/169 r.90, Sch.7
Sch. para.1, revoked: SI 1997/169 r.90, Sch.7
Sch. para.2, revoked: SI 1997/169 r.90, Sch.7
Sch. para.3, revoked: SI 1997/169 r.90, Sch.7
Sch. para.4, revoked: SI 1997/169 r.90, Sch.7
Sch. para.5, revoked: SI 1997/169 r.90, Sch.7
Sch. para.6, revoked: SI 1997/169 r.90, Sch.7
Sch. para.7, revoked: SI 1997/169 r.90, Sch.7
Sch. para.8, revoked: SI 1997/169 r.90, Sch.7
Sch. para.9, revoked: SI 1997/169 r.90, Sch.7
Sch. para.10, revoked: SI 1997/169 r.90, Sch.7
Sch. para.11, revoked: SI 1997/169 r.90, Sch.7

1389. **Rules of Procedure (Air Force) (Amendment) Rules 1996**
revoked: SI 1997/171 r.90, Sch.7
r.2, revoked: SI 1997/171 r.90, Sch.7
Sch. para.1, revoked: SI 1997/171 r.90, Sch.7
Sch. para.2, revoked: SI 1997/171 r.90, Sch.7
Sch. para.3, revoked: SI 1997/171 r.90, Sch.7
Sch. para.4, revoked: SI 1997/171 r.90, Sch.7
Sch. para.5, revoked: SI 1997/171 r.90, Sch.7
Sch. para.6, revoked: SI 1997/171 r.90, Sch.7
Sch. para.7, revoked: SI 1997/171 r.90, Sch.7
Sch. para.8, revoked: SI 1997/171 r.90, Sch.7
Sch. para.9, revoked: SI 1997/171 r.90, Sch.7
Sch. para.10, revoked: SI 1997/171 r.90, Sch.7

1393. **Rules of the Air Regulations 1996**
referred to: SI 1997/2920 Reg.7, SI 1999/3260 Reg.7
r.5, amended: SI 1999/1323 Reg.2
r.20, amended: SI 1999/1323 Reg.2
r.36, amended: SI 1999/1323 Reg.2
r.39, amended: SI 1999/1323 Reg.2

1422. **Amusement Machine Licence Duty (Small-prize Machines) Order 1996**
revoked: SI 1998/2207 Art.2
Art.2, revoked: SI 1998/2207 Art.2
Art.3, revoked: SI 1998/2207 Art.2

1428. **Local Government Pension Scheme (Amendment) Regulations 1996**
applied: SI 1997/1613 Reg.4, Reg.19, Sch.2 para.2
referred to: SI 1997/1613 Reg.3, Sch.2 para.6

1434. **Welfare Food Regulations 1996**
applied: SI 1999/672 Art.2, Sch.1, SI 1999/1512 Art.2, Sch.3 para.1, Sch.3 para.2, SI 1999/1750 Art.5, Sch.4 para.3
Reg.2, amended: SI 1999/2561 Reg.2
Reg.6, amended: SI 1997/857 Reg.2
Reg.6, referred to: SI 1999/672 Art.2, Sch.1
Reg.7, amended: SI 1997/857 Reg.3, SI 1998/691 Reg.2, SI 1999/2561 Reg.3
Reg.8, amended: SI 1999/2561 Reg.4
Reg.8, referred to: SI 1999/672 Art.2, Sch.1
Reg.10, amended: SI 1999/2561 Reg.5
Reg.12, applied: SI 1999/1512 Art.2, Sch.2 para.10, SI 1999/1750 Art.2, Sch.1
Reg.12, referred to: SI 1999/672 Art.2, Sch.1
Reg.13, referred to: SI 1999/672 Art.2, Sch.1
Reg.15, applied: SI 1999/1512 Art.2, Sch.2 para.10, SI 1999/1750 Art.2, Sch.1
Reg.15, referred to: SI 1999/672 Art.2, Sch.1
Reg.16, applied: SI 1999/1512 Art.2, Sch.2 para.11, SI 1999/1750 Art.2, Sch.1
Reg.20, applied: SI 1999/1512 Art.2, Sch.2 para.11, SI 1999/1750 Art.2, Sch.1

NO.

1435. **Personal Pension Schemes (Appropriate Schemes and Disclosure of Information) (Miscellaneous Amendments) Regulations 1996**
Reg.2, revoked: SI 1997/470 Reg.20, Sch.3

1446. **Cosmetic Products (Safety) (Amendment) Regulations 1996**
revoked: SI 1996/2925 Sch.9
Reg.2, revoked: SI 1996/2925 Sch.9

1459. **A10 Trunk Road (Enfield and Haringey) Red Route (Bus Lanes) (No.1) Traffic Order 1996**
revoked (in part): SI 1997/449 Art.5, SI 1997/450 Art.5

1461. **Protected Rights (Transfer Payment) Regulations 1996**
amended: SI 1996/1977 Reg.4
applied: SI 1997/786 Reg.3, Sch.1 para.6
Reg.1, amended: SI 1997/786 Reg.3, Sch.1 para.6, SI 1999/3198 Reg.13
Reg.2, applied: SI 1996/1847 Reg.12
Reg.4, amended: SI 1997/786 Reg.3, Sch.1 para.6

1462. **Contracting Out (Transfer and Transfer Payment) Regulations 1996**
amended: SI 1996/1977 Reg.4
applied: SI 1997/786 Reg.3, Sch.1 para.7
referred to: 1999 c.30 s.35, Sch.5 para.6
Reg.1, amended: SI 1997/786 Reg.3, Sch.1 para.7, SI 1999/3198 Reg.2
Reg.2, applied: SI 1996/1847 Reg.12
Reg.3, applied: SI 1997/784 Reg.3
Reg.5, applied: SI 1997/784 Reg.3
Reg.6, amended: SI 1997/786 Reg.3, Sch.1 para.7
Reg.6, applied: SI 1997/784 Reg.3
Reg.7, amended: SI 1997/786 Reg.3, Sch.1 para.7
Reg.7, applied: SI 1996/1847 Reg.12
Reg.7, revoked (in part): SI 1997/786 Reg.4, Sch.2
Reg.8, amended: SI 1997/786 Reg.3, Sch.1 para.7
Reg.11, applied: SI 1996/1847 Reg.12
Reg.13, amended: SI 1997/786 Reg.3, Sch.1 para.7
Reg.13A, added: SI 1997/786 Reg.3, Sch.1 para.7
Sch.2 para.1, substituted: SI 1997/786 Reg.3, Sch.1 para.7
Sch.2 para.4, amended: SI 1997/786 Reg.3, Sch.1 para.7
Sch.2 para.6, substituted: SI 1997/786 Reg.3, Sch.1 para.7
Sch.2 para.9, revoked: SI 1997/786 Reg.3, Reg.4, Sch.1 para.7, Sch.2

1463. **A10 Trunk Road (Enfield) Red Route (Bus Lanes) (No.2) Traffic Order 1996**
revoked (in part): SI 1997/450 Art.5

1464. **Wireless Telegraphy (Licence Charges) (Amendment) Regulations 1996**
revoked: SI 1999/1774 Reg.2, Sch.1
Reg.2, revoked: SI 1999/1774 Reg.2, Sch.1
Sch.1, revoked: SI 1999/1774 Reg.2, Sch.1
Sch.2, revoked: SI 1999/1774 Reg.2, Sch.1

1474. **Disability Discrimination Act 1995 (Commencement No.3 and Saving and Transitional Provisions) Order 1996**
Art.3, applied: SI 1997/536 Art.4

1475. **Inshore Fishing (Prohibition of Fishing and Fishing Methods) (Scotland) Amendment Order 1996**
Art.2, revoked (in part): SI 1999/751 Art.3

NO.

1481. **Countryside Stewardship (Amendment) (Extension to the Isles of Scilly) Regulations 1996**
revoked: SI 1998/1327 Reg.2, Sch.2
Reg.2, revoked: SI 1998/1327 Reg.2, Sch.2

1482. **Arable Area Payments (Amendment) Regulations 1996**
revoked: SI 1996/3142 Reg.20
Reg.2, revoked: SI 1996/3142 Reg.20

1483. **Highways (Road Humps) Regulations 1996**
applied: SI 1999/1025 Reg.9
revoked: SI 1999/1025 Reg.8 (with saving)
Reg.3, revoked: SI 1999/1025 Reg.8 (with saving)
Reg.4, revoked: SI 1999/1025 Reg.8 (with saving)
Reg.8, revoked: SI 1999/1025 Reg.8 (with saving)
Reg.9, revoked: SI 1999/1025 Reg.8 (with saving)

1487. **Pesticides (Maximum Residue Levels in Crops, Food and Feeding Stuffs) (Amendment) Regulations 1996**
revoked (in part): SI 1999/3483 Reg.7, Sch.4
Reg.3, revoked (in part): SI 1999/3483 Reg.7, Sch.4
Reg.4, revoked (in part): SI 1999/3483 Reg.7, Sch.4
Reg.5, revoked (in part): SI 1999/3483 Reg.7, Sch.4
Reg.6, revoked (in part): SI 1999/3483 Reg.7, Sch.4
Reg.7, revoked (in part): SI 1999/3483 Reg.7, Sch.4
Reg.8, revoked (in part): SI 1999/3483 Reg.7, Sch.4
Reg.9, revoked (in part): SI 1999/3483 Reg.7, Sch.4

1492. **Offshore Installations (Safety Zones) (No.4) Order 1996**
revoked: SI 1997/735 Art.3, Sch.2

1495. **Civil Aviation (Route Charges for Navigation Services) (Amendment) Regulations 1996**
revoked: SI 1997/2920 Reg.2, Sch.1
Reg.2, revoked: SI 1997/2920 Reg.2, Sch.1

1499. **Food Labelling Regulations 1996**
see *Hackney LBC v Cedar Trading Ltd* [1999] E.T.M.R. 801 (QBD), Kennedy, L.J.
amended: SI 1999/1136 Reg.14
applied: SI 1998/994 Sch.3 Ch.IV
referred to: SI 1998/994 Sch.2 Ch.X, Sch.3 Ch.VII
Reg.2, amended: SI 1998/141 Reg.11, SI 1998/1398 Reg.3, SI 1998/2424 Reg.10, SI 1999/747 Reg.3, SI 1999/1483 Reg.3, SI 1999/1540 Reg.20
Reg.3, amended: SI 1998/1398 Reg.4, SI 1999/747 Reg.4, SI 1999/1483 Reg.4
Reg.4, amended: SI 1998/1398 Reg.5
Reg.5, amended: SI 1998/1398 Reg.6
Reg.6, amended: SI 1998/1398 Reg.7
Reg.14, amended: SI 1999/1136 Reg.14
Reg.14, applied: SI 1998/141 Reg.5
Reg.17, referred to: SI 1998/141 Reg.5
Reg.18, amended: SI 1998/1398 Reg.8
Reg.19, amended: SI 1999/1483 Reg.5
Reg.19, substituted: SI 1998/1398 Reg.9
Reg.23, amended: SI 1998/1398 Reg.10
Reg.23, applied: SI 1998/141 Reg.5
Reg.26, amended: SI 1999/747 Reg.5, SI 1999/1483 Reg.6
Reg.34, referred to: SI 1999/982 Reg.3
Reg.35, amended: SI 1999/747 Reg.6

NO.

1996—cont.

1499. Food Labelling Regulations 1996—*cont.*
Reg.36, amended: SI 1999/747 Reg.7
Reg.36, applied: SI 1998/141 Reg.5
Reg.38, amended: SI 1999/747 Reg.8, SI 1999/1540 Reg.19
Reg.38, applied: SI 1999/1540 Reg.19
Reg.42, amended: SI 1998/1398 Reg.11
Reg.44, amended: SI 1999/747 Reg.9
Reg.47, amended: SI 1998/1398 Reg.12, SI 1999/747 Reg.10
Reg.48, substituted: SI 1999/747 Reg.11
Reg.49, revoked (in part): SI 1998/141 Reg.12, Sch.4, SI 1999/1603 Reg.10
Reg.50, amended: SI 1998/1398 Reg.13, SI 1999/747 Reg.12, SI 1999/1136 Reg.14, SI 1999/1483 Reg.7
Sch. A1, added: SI 1998/1398 Reg.14, Sch.
Sch.3, amended: SI 1998/1398 Reg.15
Sch.4, amended: SI 1998/1398 Reg.16
Sch.6 Part II, amended: SI 1998/1398 Reg.17
Sch.6 Part II, referred to: SI 1997/2182 Reg.3
Sch.8 Part 1, referred to: SI 1999/982 Reg.3

1500. Hill Livestock (Compensatory Allowances) Regulations 1996
applied: SI 1996/2163 Sch. para.1, SI 1997/1962 Sch., SI 1999/672 Art.2, Sch.1, SI 1999/2230 Art.2, Sch., SI 1999/3316 Reg.5, SSI 1999/187 Reg.5
revoked: SI 1999/3316 Reg.18 (with saving), SSI 1999/187 Reg.23 (with savings), Sch.2 (with savings)
Reg.2, amended: SI 1997/33 Reg.2, SI 1998/206 Reg.2, SI 1999/375 Reg.2
Reg.2, revoked: SI 1999/3316 Reg.18 (with saving), SSI 1999/187 Reg.23 (with savings), Sch.2 (with savings)
Reg.3, amended: SI 1997/33 Reg.2, SI 1998/206 Reg.2, SI 1999/375 Reg.2
Reg.3, revoked (in part): SI 1999/3316 Reg.18 (with saving), SI 1998/206 Reg.2, SSI 1999/187 Reg.23 (with savings), Sch.2 (with savings)
Reg.4, amended: SI 1997/33 Reg.2
Reg.4, referred to: SI 1999/3316 Reg.7, SSI 1999/187 Reg.7, Reg.8
Reg.4, revoked: SI 1999/3316 Reg.18 (with saving), SSI 1999/187 Reg.23 (with savings), Sch.2 (with savings)
Reg.5, amended: SI 1997/33 Reg.2
Reg.5, referred to: SI 1999/3316 Reg.8
Reg.5, revoked: SI 1999/3316 Reg.18 (with saving), SSI 1999/187 Reg.23 (with savings), Sch.2 (with savings)
Reg.6, amended: SI 1997/33 Reg.2
Reg.6, revoked: SI 1999/3316 Reg.18 (with saving), SSI 1999/187 Reg.23 (with savings), Sch.2 (with savings)
Reg.9, amended: SI 1998/206 Reg.2, SI 1999/375 Reg.2
Reg.9, revoked: SI 1999/3316 Reg.18 (with saving) SSI 1999 187 Reg.23 (with savings), SSI 1999/187 Sch.2 (with savings)
Reg.12, amended: SI 1998/206 Reg.2, SI 1999/375 Reg.2
Reg.12, revoked: SI 1999/3316 Reg.18 (with saving), SSI 1999/187 Reg.23 (with savings), Sch.2 (with savings)
Reg.14, referred to: SI 1999/3316 Reg.18
Reg.14, revoked: SI 1999/3316 Reg.18 (with saving)
Reg.16, revoked: SI 1999/3316 Reg.18 (with saving), SSI 1999/187 Reg.23 (with savings), Sch.2 (with savings)

NO.

1996—cont.

1500. Hill Livestock (Compensatory Allowances) Regulations 1996—*cont.*
Reg.18, revoked: SI 1999/3316 Reg.18 (with saving), SSI 1999/187 Reg.23 (with savings), Sch.2 (with savings)

1501. Bread and Flour (Amendment) Regulations 1996
revoked: SI 1998/141 Reg.12, Sch.4
Reg.2, revoked: SI 1998/141 Reg.12, Sch.4

1502. Food (Lot Marking) Regulations 1996
applied: SI 1998/994 Sch.3 Ch.IV

1511. Social Security (Back to Work Bonus) (Amendment) Regulations 1996
revoked: SI 1996/2570 Reg.28

1513. Health and Safety (Consultation with Employees) Regulations 1996
applied: SI 1999/101 Reg.4, Reg.5, Sch.1 para.35, Sch.2 para.38
Reg.3, amended: SI 1997/1840 Reg.21, SI 1999/3242 Reg.29, Sch.2

1514. Medicines (Products Other Than Veterinary Drugs) (Prescription Only) Amendment Order 1996
revoked: SI 1997/1830 Art.16, Sch.6
Art.2, revoked: SI 1997/1830 Art.16, Sch.6
Art.3, revoked: SI 1997/1830 Art.16, Sch.6
Art.4, revoked: SI 1997/1830 Art.16, Sch.6
Art.5, revoked: SI 1997/1830 Art.16, Sch.6
Art.6, revoked: SI 1997/1830 Art.16, Sch.6

1515. Jobseeker's Allowance (Transitional Provisions) (Amendment) Regulations 1996
referred to: SI 1996/2519 Reg.1
revoked: SI 1996/2567 Reg.22
Reg.5, substituted: SI 1996/2378 Reg.2

1517. Jobseeker's Allowance and Income Support (General) (Amendment) Regulations 1996
Reg.27, revoked: SI 1996/2538 Reg.7

1518. Social Security (Adjudication) Amendment Regulations 1996
revoked: SI 1999/991 Reg.59 (with savings), Sch.4 (with savings)
Reg.2, revoked: SI 1999/991 Reg.59 (with savings), Sch.4 (with savings)

1527. Landfill Tax Regulations 1996
Reg.14A, added: SI 1998/61 Reg.2
Reg.14B, added: SI 1998/61 Reg.2
Reg.14C, added: SI 1998/61 Reg.2
Reg.14D, added: SI 1998/61 Reg.2
Reg.14E, added: SI 1998/61 Reg.2
Reg.14F, added: SI 1998/61 Reg.2
Reg.14G, added: SI 1998/61 Reg.2
Reg.14H, added: SI 1998/61 Reg.2
Reg.30, amended: SI 1999/3270 Reg.3
Reg.31, amended: SI 1999/3270 Reg.4
Reg.31, revoked (in part): SI 1999/3270 Reg.4
Reg.32, amended: SI 1999/3270 Reg.5
Reg.33, amended: SI 1999/3270 Reg.6
Reg.33A, added: SI 1999/3270 Reg.7
Reg.34, amended: SI 1999/3270 Reg.8
Reg.34, revoked (in part): SI 1999/3270 Reg.8
Reg.35, amended: SI 1999/3270 Reg.9
Reg.35, revoked (in part): SI 1999/3270 Reg.9
Reg.36, amended: SI 1999/3270 Reg.10
Reg.48, amended: SI 1996/2100 Reg.4
Reg.48, revoked: SI 1997/1431 Reg.3, Sch.3
Reg.A48, added: SI 1996/2100 Reg.4
Reg.49, amended: SI 1996/2100 Reg.4

1530. Criminal Justice and Public Order Act 1994 (Commencement No.9) Order 1996
revoked: SI 1996/1608 Art.3

1996—cont.
1536. **Occupational Pension Schemes (Minimum Funding Requirement and Actuarial Valuations) Regulations 1996**
applied: SI 1996/3126 Reg.13, SI 1997/786 Reg.3, Sch.1 para.8
Reg.3, amended: SI 1996/3128 Reg.3
Reg.3, applied: SI 1996/3128 Reg.3, SI 1997/665 Reg.5
Reg.4, amended: SI 1996/3128 Reg.3
Reg.4, applied: SI 1996/3128 Reg.3, SI 1997/665 Reg.5
Reg.5, amended: SI 1996/3128 Reg.3
Reg.5, applied: SI 1996/3128 Reg.3, SI 1997/665 Reg.5
Reg.6, amended: SI 1996/3127 Reg.12, SI 1996/3128 Reg.3, SI 1997/786 Reg.3, Sch.1 para.8
Reg.6, applied: SI 1996/3128 Reg.3, Reg.5, Reg.6, SI 1997/665 Reg.5
Reg.7, amended: SI 1996/3126 Reg.4, SI 1996/3128 Reg.3, SI 1997/786 Reg.3, Sch.1 para.8
Reg.7, applied: SI 1996/3126 Reg.4, SI 1996/3128 Reg.3, SI 1997/665 Reg.5
Reg.8, amended: SI 1996/3126 Reg.4, SI 1996/3128 Reg.3
Reg.8, applied: SI 1996/3126 Reg.4, SI 1996/3128 Reg.3, SI 1997/665 Reg.5
Reg.9, applied: SI 1997/665 Reg.5
Reg.10, amended: SI 1997/786 Reg.3, Sch.1 para.8
Reg.16, amended: SI 1999/3198 Reg.8
Reg.16, applied: SI 1996/3126 Reg.3
Reg.17, amended: SI 1997/786 Reg.3, Sch.1 para.8
Reg.20, amended: SI 1997/786 Reg.3, Sch.1 para.8
Reg.23, amended: SI 1999/3198 Reg.8
Reg.25, amended: SI 1997/786 Reg.3, Sch.1 para.8
Reg.28, amended: SI 1997/786 Reg.3, Sch.1 para.8, SI 1997/3038 Reg.4
Reg.29, amended: SI 1997/3038 Reg.4
Reg.30, amended: SI 1997/786 Reg.3, Sch.1 para.8
Reg.30, applied: SI 1997/664 Art.7
Sch.2 para.5, added: SI 1997/786 Reg.3, Sch.1 para.8
Sch.2 para.6, added: SI 1997/786 Reg.3, Sch.1 para.8
Sch.4 para.1, amended: SI 1997/786 Reg.3, Sch.1 para.8
Sch.5 para.1, amended: SI 1997/786 Reg.3, Sch.1 para.8
Sch.5 para.1, applied: SI 1996/3126 Reg.12
Sch.5 para.2, amended: SI 1997/786 Reg.3, Sch.1 para.8
Sch.5 para.2, revoked (in part): SI 1997/786 Reg.4, Sch.2
Sch.5 para.7, added: SI 1997/3038 Reg.4
1537. **Personal and Occupational Pension Schemes (Protected Rights) Regulations 1996**
amended: 1999 c.2 s.1, Sch.2
applied: SI 1997/786 Reg.3, Sch.1 para.9
Reg.1, amended: SI 1997/786 Reg.3, Sch.1 para.9, SI 1999/3198 Reg.12
Reg.3, amended: SI 1997/786 Reg.3, Sch.1 para.9
Reg.3, applied: SI 1997/470 Reg.2
Reg.4, referred to: 1999 c.2 s.1, Sch.2

1996—cont.
1547. **Food Safety (Fishery Products and Live Bivalve Molluscs and Other Shellfish) (Miscellaneous Amendments) Regulations 1996**
revoked: SI 1998/994 Reg.59, Sch.5
Reg.2, revoked: SI 1998/994 Reg.59, Sch.5
Reg.3, revoked: SI 1998/994 Reg.59, Sch.5
Reg.4, revoked: SI 1998/994 Reg.59, Sch.5
Reg.5, revoked: SI 1998/994 Reg.59, Sch.5
Reg.6, revoked: SI 1998/994 Reg.59, Sch.5
Sch.1, revoked: SI 1998/994 Reg.59, Sch.5
Sch.2 para.1, revoked: SI 1998/994 Reg.59, Sch.5
Sch.2 para.2, revoked: SI 1998/994 Reg.59, Sch.5
Sch.2 para.3, revoked: SI 1998/994 Reg.59, Sch.5
Sch.3 para.1, revoked: SI 1998/994 Reg.59, Sch.5
Sch.3 para.2, revoked: SI 1998/994 Reg.59, Sch.5
Sch.3 para.3, revoked: SI 1998/994 Reg.59, Sch.5
Sch.3 para.4, revoked: SI 1998/994 Reg.59, Sch.5
Sch.3 para.5, revoked: SI 1998/994 Reg.59, Sch.5
Sch.3 para.6, revoked: SI 1998/994 Reg.59, Sch.5
Sch.4, revoked: SI 1998/994 Reg.59, Sch.5
1557. **Education (Recognised Awards) (Richmond College) Order 1996**
revoked: SI 1996/2564 Art.3, Sch.
Art.2, revoked: SI 1996/2564 Art.3, Sch.
1564. **Protection of Water Against Agricultural Nitrate Pollution (Scotland) Regulations 1996**
Reg.5, revoked: SI 1998/2927 Reg.9
1583. **Capital Gains Tax (Pension Funds Pooling Schemes) Regulations 1996**
applied: SI 1996/1585 Reg.4
1584. **Stamp Duty and Stamp Duty Reserve Tax (Pension Funds Pooling Schemes) Regulations 1996**
applied: SI 1996/1585 Reg.4
1586. **Financial Services Act 1986 (Investment Advertisements) (Exemptions) Order 1996**
Art.10, substituted: SI 1997/963 Art.3
Art.11, amended: SI 1997/963 Art.4, SI 1999/1820 Art.4, Sch.2 para.161
Sch.1 Part I, amended: SI 1997/963 Art.5
1592. **Construction (Health, Safety and Welfare) Regulations 1996**
Reg.19, applied: SI 1996/1656 Reg.13
Reg.20, amended: SI 1999/3242 Reg.27
Reg.20, applied: SI 1996/1656 Reg.13
Reg.21, applied: SI 1996/1656 Reg.14
Reg.22, applied: SI 1996/1656 Reg.18
Reg.25, applied: SI 1996/1656 Reg.13
Reg.27, revoked: SI 1998/2306 Reg.39, Sch.4
Reg.29, applied: SI 1998/2306 Reg.6
Sch.9 para.3, revoked: SI 1998/2307 Reg.17, Sch.2
Sch.9 para.4, revoked: SI 1998/494 Reg.7, Sch.3
1596. **Education (School Performance Information) (England) (Amendment) Regulations 1996**
revoked: SI 1996/2577 Reg.4
Reg.2, revoked: SI 1996/2577 Reg.4

NO.

1603. Education (Teachers) (Amendment) Regulations 1996
revoked: SI 1997/2679 Reg.7, Sch.3
Reg.2, revoked: SI 1997/2679 Reg.7, Sch.3

1615. Wessex Regional Flood Defence Committee Order 1996
revoked: SI 1997/1364 Art.3
Art.1, revoked: SI 1997/1364 Art.3
Art.3, revoked: SI 1997/1364 Art.3

1616. Severn-Trent Regional Flood Defence Committee Order 1996
revoked: SI 1997/1361 Art.3
Art.1, revoked: SI 1997/1361 Art.3
Art.3, revoked: SI 1997/1361 Art.3

1617. Northumbria Regional Flood Defence Committee Order 1996
revoked: SI 1997/1360 Art.3
Art.1, revoked: SI 1997/1360 Art.3
Art.3, revoked: SI 1997/1360 Art.3

1618. Anglian Regional Flood Defence Committee Order 1996
revoked: SI 1997/1359 Art.3
Art.1, revoked: SI 1997/1359 Art.3
Art.3, revoked: SI 1997/1359 Art.3

1624. A12 Trunk Road (Redbridge) (No.1) Red Route Traffic Order 1996
Art.2, amended: SI 1999/272 Art.2, Sch. Part A
Art.9, amended: SI 1999/272 Art.2, Sch. Part A
Sch.2A Item 7, added: SI 1997/87 Art.2, SI 1998/26 Art.2

1625. A501 Trunk Road (Euston Road, Camden) Red Route (Prescribed Routes) Experimental Traffic Order 1996
revoked: SI 1998/15 Art.5

1628. Territorial Sea (Amendment) Order 1996
revoked: SI 1998/2564 Art.4
Art.2, revoked: SI 1998/2564 Art.4
Art.4, revoked: SI 1998/2564 Art.4

1632. Deregulation and Contracting Out (Northern Ireland) Order 1996
Art.13, applied: SI 1996/1633 (NI.12) Art.7
Art.14, applied: SI 1996/1633 (NI.12) Art.7
Art.15, applied: SI 1996/1633 (NI.12) Art.7
Art.17, amended: SI 1997/1183 (NI.12) Art.31, Sch.3 para.12, SI 1998/1506 (NI.10) Art.78, Sch.6 para.116, SI 1999/3147 (NI.11) Art.74, Sch.9 para.60
Sch.2 para.5A, added: SI 1999/3147 (NI.11) Art.74, Sch.9 para.61
Sch.5 para.5, revoked: SI 1997/1182 (NI.11) Art.19, Sch.2

1633. Food Safety (Amendment) (Northern Ireland) Order 1996
Art.3, revoked (in part): 1999 c.28 s.40, Sch.6
Art.7, revoked (in part): 1999 c.28 s.40, Sch.6
Art.8, revoked: 1999 c.28 s.40, Sch.6
Art.9, revoked: 1999 c.28 s.40, Sch.6

1640. Education (Fees and Awards) (Amendment) Regulations 1996
revoked: SI 1997/1972 Reg.8
Reg.3, revoked: SI 1997/1972 Reg.8
Reg.4, revoked: SI 1997/1972 Reg.8
Reg.5, revoked: SI 1997/1972 Reg.8
Reg.6, revoked: SI 1997/1972 Reg.8

1642. Police (Conduct) (Scotland) Regulations 1996
Reg.2, amended: SI 1999/1072 Reg.2
Reg.6, amended: SI 1999/1072 Reg.3
Reg.6, revoked (in part): SI 1999/1072 Reg.3
Reg.7, amended: SI 1999/1072 Reg.4
Reg.7A, added: SI 1999/1072 Reg.5
Reg.13, amended: SI 1999/1072 Reg.6
Reg.15, substituted: SI 1999/1072 Reg.7

NO.

1642. Police (Conduct) (Scotland) Regulations 1996—*cont.*
Reg.16, amended: SI 1999/1072 Reg.8
Reg.20, amended: SI 1999/1072 Reg.9
Reg.21, amended: SI 1999/1072 Reg.10

1645. Police (Conduct) (Senior Officers) (Scotland) Regulations 1996
referred to: SI 1999/1074 Reg.31
revoked: SI 1999/1074 Reg.31 (with savings)
Reg.2, referred to: SI 1999/1074 Reg.31
Reg.2, revoked: SI 1999/1074 Reg.31 (with savings)
Reg.7, revoked: SI 1999/1074 Reg.31 (with savings)
Reg.16, revoked: SI 1999/1074 Reg.31 (with savings)
Reg.22, revoked: SI 1999/1074 Reg.31 (with savings)
Reg.29, revoked: SI 1999/1074 Reg.31 (with savings)
Reg.31, referred to: SI 1999/1074 Reg.31
Reg.31, revoked: SI 1999/1074 Reg.31 (with savings)
Sch.1 para.2, revoked: SI 1999/1074 Reg.31 (with savings)
Sch.1 para.13, referred to: SI 1999/1074 Reg.31
Sch.1 para.13, revoked: SI 1999/1074 Reg.31 (with savings)

1646. Police and Magistrates' Courts Act 1994 (Commencement No.10 and Savings) (Scotland) Order 1996
Art.1, applied: SI 1996/1642 Reg.25, SI 1996/1645 Reg.31

1654. Income Tax (Payments on Account) Regulations 1996
Reg.4, amended: SI 1997/2491 Reg.2

1655. Occupational Pension Schemes (Disclosure of Information) Regulations 1996
applied: SI 1997/786 Reg.3, Sch.1 para.10, SI 1999/3198 Reg.15
referred to: SI 1999/3198 Reg.15
Reg.1, amended: SI 1997/786 Reg.3, Sch.1 para.10
Reg.1, revoked (in part): SI 1997/786 Reg.3, Reg.4, Sch.1 para.10, Sch.2
Reg.2, amended: SI 1997/786 Reg.3, Sch.1 para.10
Reg.4, amended: SI 1997/819 Reg.4, SI 1997/3038 Reg.6
Reg.5, amended: SI 1997/786 Reg.3, Sch.1 para.10, SI 1997/3038 Reg.6, SI 1999/3198 Reg.5
Reg.5, revoked (in part): SI 1997/786 Reg.3, Reg.4, Sch.1 para.10, Sch.2
Reg.6, amended: SI 1997/786 Reg.3, Sch.1 para.10
Reg.11, amended: SI 1997/786 Reg.3, Sch.1 para.10, SI 1999/3198 Reg.5
Sch.1 para.12A, added: SI 1997/786 Reg.3, Sch.1 para.10
Sch.1 para.26, amended: SI 1999/3198 Reg.5
Sch.1 para.26, applied: SI 1999/3198 Reg.15
Sch.2 para.6A, added: SI 1997/786 Reg.3, Sch.1 para.10
Sch.3 para.16, substituted: SI 1997/786 Reg.3, Sch.1 para.10

1656. Work in Compressed Air Regulations 1996
applied: SI 1996/2791 Sch.6, SI 1997/2505 Reg.7, Sch.6, SI 1999/645 Reg.7, Sch.6
Reg.3, amended: SI 1997/2776 Reg.19, Sch.2 para.6

NO.

1663. Prison (Amendment) Rules 1996
revoked: SI 1999/728 r.85 (with savings), Sch. (with savings)
r.2, revoked: SI 1999/728 r.85 (with savings), Sch. (with savings)
r.3, revoked: SI 1999/728 r.85 (with savings), Sch. (with savings)
Sch. para.1, revoked: SI 1999/728 r.85 (with savings), Sch. (with savings)
Sch. para.2, revoked: SI 1999/728 r.85 (with savings), Sch. (with savings)
Sch. para.3, revoked: SI 1999/728 r.85 (with savings), Sch. (with savings)
Sch. para.4, revoked: SI 1999/728 r.85 (with savings), Sch. (with savings)
Sch. para.5, revoked: SI 1999/728 r.85 (with savings), Sch. (with savings)

1665. Education (School Performance Information) (Wales) (Amendment) Regulations 1996
revoked: SI 1997/1633 Reg.2
Reg.2, revoked: SI 1997/1633 Reg.2
Reg.3, revoked: SI 1997/1633 Reg.2
Reg.4, revoked: SI 1997/1633 Reg.2

1669. Financial Institutions (Prudential Supervision) Regulations 1996
Reg.1, amended: SI 1998/1129 Art.2, Sch.1 para.21
Reg.5, referred to: 1998 c.11 s.36
Reg.9, amended: SI 1998/1129 Art.2, Sch.1 para.21
Reg.21, applied: SI 1998/2842 Art.2, Sch. para.69
Sch.4 para.1, amended: SI 1998/1129 Art.2, Sch.1 para.21

1674. Family Proceedings (Amendment) (No.2) Rules 1996
r.3, applied: SI 1996/1675 Art.4

1676. Divorce etc. (Pensions) Regulations 1996
Reg.3, amended: SI 1997/636 Reg.3
Reg.4, amended: SI 1997/636 Reg.4
Reg.6, amended: SI 1997/636 Reg.5
Reg.8A, added: SI 1997/636 Reg.6
Reg.10A, added: SI 1997/636 Reg.7

1678. Deregulation (Model Appeal Provisions) Order 1996
applied: SI 1999/678 Sch.
Sch. Ch.1, applied: SI 1996/3030 Art.2
Sch. r.1, amended: SI 1996/3030 Sch. para.1
Sch. r.6, amended: SI 1996/3030 Sch. para.2
Sch. r.6, applied: SI 1999/1750 Art.2, Sch.1
Sch. r.23, amended: SI 1996/3030 Sch. para.3
Sch. r.29, amended: SI 1996/3030 Sch. para.4
Sch. r.30, amended: SI 1996/3030 Sch. para.5
Sch. r.31, amended: SI 1996/3030 Sch. para.6
Sch. r.32, amended: SI 1996/3030 Sch. para.7
Sch. r.33, amended: SI 1996/3030 Sch. para.8
Sch. r.33, applied: SI 1999/1750 Art.2, Sch.1

1680. Local Government (Discretionary Payments) Regulations 1996
amended: SI 1999/711 Reg.2, Sch.1
referred to: SI 1998/559 Reg.3
referred to: SI 1999/2311 Reg.4
Part III, applied: SI 1997/1612 Reg.143
Part VI, applied: SI 1997/1612 Reg.27
Reg.2, amended: SI 1997/1613 Reg.27, Sch.3 para.38, SI 1999/502 Reg.3, SI 1999/2311 Reg.2
Reg.5, amended: SI 1997/1613 Reg.27, Sch.3 para.43
Reg.6, amended: SI 1997/1613 Reg.27, Sch.3 para.40

NO.

1680. Local Government (Discretionary Payments) Regulations 1996—*cont.*
Reg.7, amended: SI 1997/1613 Reg.27, Sch.3 para.41
Reg.8, amended: SI 1997/1613 Reg.27, Sch.3 para.42, SI 1998/559 Reg.2, SI 1999/502 Reg.8
Reg.8, applied: SI 1997/1612 Reg.52
Reg.9, amended: SI 1997/1613 Reg.27, Sch.3 para.43
Reg.10, amended: SI 1997/1613 Reg.27, Sch.3 para.43
Reg.11, amended: SI 1997/1613 Reg.27, Sch.3 para.44, SI 1998/559 Reg.2
Reg.16, amended: SI 1997/1613 Reg.27, Sch.3 para.45
Reg.17, amended: SI 1997/1613 Reg.27, Sch.3 para.46
Reg.18, amended: SI 1997/1613 Reg.27, Sch.3 para.47
Reg.19, amended: SI 1997/1613 Reg.27, Sch.3 para.48
Reg.20, amended: SI 1997/1613 Reg.27, Sch.3 para.49, SI 1998/559 Reg.2
Reg.21, amended: SI 1997/1613 Reg.27, Sch.3 para.50
Reg.22, amended: SI 1997/1613 Reg.27, Sch.3 para.51
Reg.24, amended: SI 1997/1613 Reg.27, Sch.3 para.52
Reg.25, amended: SI 1997/1613 Reg.27, Sch.3 para.53
Reg.26, amended: SI 1997/1613 Reg.27, Sch.3 para.54
Reg.31, amended: SI 1998/559 Reg.2
Reg.32, amended: SI 1999/502 Reg.5
Reg.33, amended: SI 1997/1613 Reg.27, Sch.3 para.55
Reg.36, amended: SI 1997/1613 Reg.27, Sch.3 para.56
Reg.39, amended: SI 1997/1613 Reg.27, Sch.3 para.57
Reg.40, amended: SI 1997/1613 Reg.27, Sch.3 para.58
Reg.42, amended: SI 1997/1613 Reg.27, Sch.3 para.59
Reg.44, amended: SI 1998/559 Reg.2
Reg.46A, added: SI 1999/502 Reg.6
Reg.48, revoked (in part): SI 1997/2747 Reg.2, Sch.
Sch.1 Table, substituted: SI 1998/559 Reg.2
Sch.2 Part IV, added: SI 1998/559 Reg.2
Sch.2 para.2, amended: SI 1999/2311 Reg.3
Sch.2 para.2, revoked (in part): SI 1999/2311 Reg.3
Sch.2 para.4, amended: SI 1998/559 Reg.2, SI 1999/2311 Reg.3
Sch.2 para.5, amended: SI 1999/2311 Reg.3
Sch.2 para.7, revoked (in part): SI 1999/2311 Reg.3
Sch.2 para.8, amended: SI 1999/2311 Reg.3
Sch.3 para.9, amended: SI 1997/1613 Reg.27, Sch.3 para.60
Sch.4 para.2, revoked: SI 1997/2747 Reg.2, Sch.

1681. Ayrshire and Arran Community Health Care National Health Service Trust (Establishment) Amendment Order 1996
revoked: SI 1999/1070 Art.2, Sch.2
Art.2, revoked: SI 1999/1070 Art.2, Sch.2

NO.

1686. Cattle Passports Order 1996
revoked: SI 1998/871 Reg.36 (with savings), Sch.3 (with savings)
Art.6, revoked: SI 1998/871 Reg.36 (with savings), Sch.3 (with savings)
Art.10, revoked: SI 1998/871 Reg.36 (with savings), Sch.3 (with savings)
Art.12, revoked: SI 1998/871 Reg.36 (with savings), Sch.3 (with savings)
Art.13, applied: SI 1996/2255 Art.2
Art.13, revoked: SI 1998/871 Reg.36 (with savings), Sch.3 (with savings)
Art.17, revoked: SI 1998/871 Reg.36 (with savings), Sch.3 (with savings)

1715. Occupational Pension Schemes (Scheme Administration) Regulations 1996
applied: SI 1997/786 Reg.3, Sch.1 para.11
Reg.1, amended: SI 1997/786 Reg.3, Sch.1 para.11
Reg.3, amended: SI 1997/786 Reg.3, Sch.1 para.11, SI 1998/1494 Reg.2
Reg.5, amended: SI 1997/819 Reg.5, SI 1997/3038 Reg.7, SI 1999/3198 Reg.10
Reg.7, amended: SI 1997/819 Reg.5
Reg.11, amended: SI 1999/3198 Reg.10
Reg.17, amended: SI 1997/786 Reg.3, Sch.1 para.11
Reg.19, amended: SI 1999/3198 Reg.10
Reg.21, amended: SI 1999/3198 Reg.10

1736. Dual-Use and Related Goods (Export Control) (Amendment No.2) Regulations 1996
applied: SI 1996/2721 Reg.15
revoked: SI 1996/2721 Sch.1
Reg.2, revoked: SI 1996/2721 Sch.1
Reg.3, revoked: SI 1996/2721 Sch.1
Reg.4, revoked: SI 1996/2721 Sch.1
Sch. para.1, revoked: SI 1996/2721 Sch.1
Sch. para.2, revoked: SI 1996/2721 Sch.1

1737. Education (School Inspection) (No.2) (Amendment) Regulations 1996
revoked: SI 1997/1966 Reg.1, Sch. Part I
Reg.2, revoked: SI 1997/1966 Reg.1, Sch. Part I
Reg.3, revoked: SI 1997/1966 Reg.1, Sch. Part I

1743. Fresh Meat (Beef Controls) Regulations 1996
revoked: SI 1996/2097 Reg.8
Reg.5, revoked: SI 1996/2097 Reg.8
Reg.6, revoked: SI 1996/2097 Reg.8

1754. Students' Allowances (Scotland) Regulations 1996
applied: SI 1998/2026 Reg.7, SI 1999/1001 Reg.10, Reg.14, SI 1999/1131 Sch.1 para.8
revoked: SI 1999/1131 Reg.7 (with savings)
Reg.3, revoked: SI 1999/1131 Reg.7 (with savings)
Reg.4, applied: SI 1999/1001 Reg.11
Reg.4, revoked: SI 1999/1131 Reg.7 (with savings)
Reg.7, revoked: SI 1999/1131 Reg.7 (with savings)
Sch.1 para.1, amended: SI 1997/1049 Reg.3
Sch.1 para.1, revoked: SI 1999/1131 Reg.7 (with savings)
Sch.1 para.2, revoked: SI 1999/1131 Reg.7 (with savings)
Sch.1 para.2, substituted: SI 1997/1049 Reg.3
Sch.1 para.2A, added: SI 1997/1049 Reg.3
Sch.1 para.2A, revoked: SI 1999/1131 Reg.7 (with savings)
Sch.1 para.2B, added: SI 1997/1049 Reg.3
Sch.1 para.2B, revoked: SI 1999/1131 Reg.7 (with savings)
Sch.1 para.3, amended: SI 1997/1049 Reg.3

NO.

1754. Students' Allowances (Scotland) Regulations 1996—*cont.*
Sch.1 para.3, revoked: SI 1999/1131 Reg.7 (with savings)
Sch.1 para.3A, added: SI 1997/1049 Reg.3
Sch.1 para.3A, revoked: SI 1999/1131 Reg.7 (with savings)
Sch.1 para.5, revoked: SI 1999/1131 Reg.7 (with savings)
Sch.2 para.2, amended: SI 1997/1049 Reg.3
Sch.2 para.2, revoked: SI 1999/1131 Reg.7 (with savings)
Sch.2 para.3, revoked: SI 1999/1131 Reg.7 (with savings)
Sch.3, revoked: SI 1999/1131 Reg.7 (with savings)

1772. Wireless Telegraphy (Television Licence Fees) (Amendment) (No.2) Regulations 1996
revoked: SI 1997/290 Reg.1, Sch
Reg.2, revoked: SI 1997/290 Reg.1, Sch

1778. Family Proceedings (Amendment) (No.3) Rules 1996
revoked: SI 1997/637 r.4
r.2, revoked: SI 1997/637 r.4

1780. Income Tax (Paying and Collecting Agents) Regulations 1996
Reg.2, amended: SI 1997/2705 Reg.3, Reg.4, Reg.5
Reg.2A, added: SI 1997/2705 Reg.6
Reg.2B, added: SI 1997/2705 Reg.6
Reg.2B, amended: SI 1999/823 Reg.2
Reg.2C, added: SI 1997/2705 Reg.6
Reg.2D, added: SI 1997/2705 Reg.6
Reg.2E, added: SI 1997/2705 Reg.6
Reg.2F, added: SI 1997/2705 Reg.6
Reg.2G, added: SI 1997/2705 Reg.6
Reg.2H, added: SI 1997/2705 Reg.6
Reg.2J, added: SI 1997/2705 Reg.6
Reg.2K, added: SI 1997/2705 Reg.6
Reg.2L, added: SI 1997/2705 Reg.6
Reg.2M, added: SI 1997/2705 Reg.6
Reg.2N, added: SI 1997/2705 Reg.6
Reg.3A, added: SI 1997/2705 Reg.7
Reg.4, amended: SI 1997/2705 Reg.8
Reg.6, amended: SI 1997/2705 Reg.9
Reg.6A, added: SI 1997/2705 Reg.10
Reg.6B, added: SI 1997/2705 Reg.10
Reg.8A, added: SI 1997/2705 Reg.11
Reg.8B, added: SI 1997/2705 Reg.11
Reg.8C, added: SI 1997/2705 Reg.11
Reg.10, amended: SI 1997/2705 Reg.12
Reg.14, amended: SI 1997/2705 Reg.13
Reg.15, amended: SI 1997/2705 Reg.12
Reg.16, amended: SI 1997/2705 Reg.12

1783. Grants for Pre-School Education (Scotland) Regulations 1996
Reg.3, amended: SI 1997/715 Reg.2

1803. Child Benefit, Child Support and Social Security (Miscellaneous Amendments) Regulations 1996
Reg.2, revoked: SI 1997/793 Reg.19
Reg.49, substituted: SI 1999/1510 Art.42

1812. Education (Student Loans) Regulations 1996
referred to: SI 1997/1675 Reg.7
revoked: SI 1997/1675 Reg.2
Reg.2, revoked: SI 1997/1675 Reg.2
Reg.4, revoked: SI 1997/1675 Reg.2
Reg.5, revoked: SI 1997/1675 Reg.2
Reg.7, revoked: SI 1997/1675 Reg.2
Reg.11, revoked: SI 1997/1675 Reg.2

NO.

1996—cont.

1754. Students' Allowances (Scotland) Regulations 1996
Reg.13, revoked: SI 1997/1675 Reg.2
Sch. para.1, revoked: SI 1997/1675 Reg.2
Sch. para.2, revoked: SI 1997/1675 Reg.2

1816. Education (School Teachers' Pay and Conditions) (No.2) Order 1996
revoked: SI 1997/1789 Art.1
Art.1, revoked: SI 1997/1789 Art.1
Art.2, revoked: SI 1997/1789 Art.1

1826. Manufactured Overseas Dividends (French Indemnity Payments) Regulations 1996
Reg.3, amended: SI 1996/2642 Reg.2
Reg.4, amended: SI 1996/2642 Reg.2

1841. A13 Trunk Road (Tower Hamlets) Red Route (No.2) Experimental Traffic Order 1996
revoked (in part): SI 1997/466 Art.10

1847. Occupational Pension Schemes (Transfer Values) Regulations 1996
applied: SI 1997/786 Reg.3, Sch.1 para.12
Reg.1, amended: SI 1997/786 Reg.3, Sch.1 para.12, SI 1997/1613 Reg.27, Sch.3 para.61
Reg.1A, added: SI 1997/786 Reg.3, Sch.1 para.12
Reg.2, referred to: SI 1997/1612 Reg.116, SI 1998/366 Reg.116
Reg.3, applied: SI 1997/1612 Reg.116, SI 1998/366 Reg.116
Reg.4, applied: SI 1997/1612 Reg.116, SI 1998/366 Reg.116
Reg.5, applied: SI 1997/1612 Reg.116, SI 1998/366 Reg.116
Reg.7, amended: SI 1996/3126 Reg.3, SI 1997/786 Reg.3, Sch.1 para.12
Reg.7, applied: SI 1996/3126 Reg.3
Reg.7, revoked (in part): SI 1997/786 Reg.4, Sch.2
Reg.8, amended: SI 1996/3126 Reg.3
Reg.8, applied: SI 1996/3126 Reg.3
Reg.10, applied: SI 1997/1612 Reg.116
Reg.10, referred to: SI 1998/366 Reg.116
Reg.12, amended: SI 1997/786 Reg.3, Sch.1 para.12
Reg.12, applied: SI 1997/784 Reg.3
Reg.18, applied: SI 1997/1612 Reg.116, SI 1998/366 Reg.116

1853. Pensions Act 1995 (Commencement No.6) Order 1996
Art.1, amended: SI 1996/2150 Art.2

1856. Jobseeker's Allowance (Pilot Scheme) (Amendment) Regulations 1996
revoked: SI 1997/984 Reg.1
Reg.2, revoked: SI 1997/984 Reg.1

1862. Offshore Installations (Safety Zones) (No.5) Order 1996
applied: SI 1996/2304 Art.3
revoked: SI 1997/735 Art.3, Sch.2
Sch., amended: SI 1996/2304 Art.3

1863. Cheshire (Boroughs of Halton and Warrington) (Structural Change) Order 1996
referred to: SI 1998/446 Art.1
Art.6, referred to: SI 1998/356 Art.2
Art.7, revoked (in part): SI 1997/779 Art.3, SI 1997/781 Art.4

1865. Devon (City of Plymouth and Borough of Torbay) (Structural Change) Order 1996
referred to: SI 1998/451 Art.1
Art.6, referred to: SI 1998/355 Art.2, Art.3

1866. Shropshire (District of The Wrekin) (Structural Change) Order 1996
referred to: SI 1998/448 Art.1
Art.6, referred to: SI 1998/363 Art.3
Art.7, revoked: SI 1997/780 Art.4

NO.

1996—cont.

1867. Hereford and Worcester (Structural, Boundary and Electoral Changes) Order 1996
referred to: SI 1998/444 Art.1, SI 1998/582
Art.4, referred to: SI 1998/359 Art.3
Art.5, referred to: SI 1998/359 Art.2
Art.13, applied: SI 1998/582 Art.5

1868. Lancashire (Boroughs of Blackburn and Blackpool) (Structural Change) Order 1996
referred to: SI 1998/445 Art.1
Art.6, referred to: SI 1998/360 Art.2, Art.3
Art.7, revoked (in part): SI 1997/783 Art.3

1875. Essex (Boroughs of Colchester, Southend-on-Sea and Thurrock and District of Tendring) (Structural, Boundary and Electoral Changes) Order 1996
referred to: SI 1998/442 Art.1
Art.6, referred to: SI 1998/357 Art.2, Art.3

1876. Kent (Borough of Gillingham and City of Rochester upon Medway) (Structural Change) Order 1996
referred to: SI 1998/449 Art.1
Art.5, referred to: SI 1998/358 Art.2
Art.9, revoked: SI 1997/776 Art.4
Art.10, revoked: SI 1997/776 Art.4

1877. Nottinghamshire (City of Nottingham) (Structural Change) Order 1996
referred to: SI 1998/447 Art.1
Art.6, referred to: SI 1998/361 Art.2

1878. Cambridgeshire (City of Peterborough) (Structural, Boundary and Electoral Changes) Order 1996
referred to: SI 1998/443 Art.1
Art.3, referred to: SI 1998/362 Art.2
Art.4, amended: SI 1997/777 Art.9
Art.8, revoked: SI 1997/777 Art.9
Art.9, revoked: SI 1997/777 Art.9
Art.10, amended: SI 1997/777 Art.9

1879. Berkshire (Structural Change) Order 1996
referred to: SI 1998/450 Art.1
Art.2, referred to: SI 1998/1641 Art.2

1887. Food Protection (Emergency Prohibitions) (Paralytic Shellfish Poisoning) Order 1996
revoked: SI 1996/2466 Art.2
Art.3, revoked: SI 1996/2466 Art.2

1889. Income Support (General) (Standard Interest Rate Amendment) (No.2) Regulations 1996
revoked: SI 1996/2903 Reg.3
Reg.2, revoked: SI 1996/2903 Reg.3
Reg.3, revoked: SI 1996/2903 Reg.3

1891. A13 Trunk Road (Tower Hamlets) Red Route Traffic Order 1996
Art.2, amended: SI 1999/272 Art.2, Sch. Part A
Art.9, amended: SI 1999/272 Art.2, Sch. Part A

1892. A1400 Trunk Road (Redbridge) Red Route Traffic Order 1996
Art.2, amended: SI 1999/272 Art.2, Sch. Part A
Art.9, amended: SI 1999/272 Art.2, Sch. Part A
Sch.2B Table, amended: SI 1998/30 Art.4
Sch.3A Item 2, revoked: SI 1998/30 Art.3
Sch.4 Item 2, amended: SI 1998/30 Art.5
Sch.4 Item 3, amended: SI 1998/30 Art.6

1893. A12 Trunk Road (Redbridge) Red Route Traffic Order 1996
Art.2, amended: SI 1999/272 Art.2, Sch. Part A
Art.9, amended: SI 1999/272 Art.2, Sch. Part A
Sch.2B Table, amended: SI 1998/29 Art.3
Sch.2B Item 1, added: SI 1997/1632 Art.3

NO.

NO.

1996—cont.

1996—cont.

1893. A12 Trunk Road (Redbridge) Red Route Traffic Order 1996—*cont.*
Sch.3A Item 2, amended: SI 1998/29 Art.4
Sch.3A Item 3, added: SI 1997/1632 Art.4
Sch.4 Table, amended: SI 1997/1632 Art.6
Sch.4 Item 1, substituted: SI 1997/1632 Art.5

1894. A13 Trunk Road (Havering) Red Route Traffic Order 1996
Art.2, amended: SI 1999/272 Art.2, Sch. Part A
Art.9, amended: SI 1999/272 Art.2, Sch. Part A

1895. A406 Trunk Road (Newham and Barking and Dagenham) Red Route Traffic Order 1996
Art.2, amended: SI 1999/272 Art.2, Sch. Part A
Art.9, amended: SI 1999/272 Art.2, Sch. Part A

1896. A13 Trunk Road (Barking and Dagenham) Red Route Traffic Order 1996
Art.2, amended: SI 1999/272 Art.2, Sch. Part A
Art.9, amended: SI 1999/272 Art.2, Sch. Part A

1901. Divorce etc. (Pensions) (Scotland) Regulations 1996
Reg.2, amended: SI 1997/745 Reg.3
Reg.3, amended: SI 1997/745 Reg.4
Reg.4, amended: SI 1997/745 Reg.5
Reg.5, amended: SI 1997/745 Reg.6
Reg.8A, added: SI 1997/745 Reg.7
Reg.9, amended: SI 1997/745 Reg.8

1911. Education (Grant-Maintained and Grant-Maintained Special Schools) (Finance) (Wales) (Amendment) (No.2) Regulations 1996
revoked: SI 1997/599 Reg.3
Reg.2, revoked: SI 1997/599 Reg.3

1915. Consular Fees Order 1996
revoked: SI 1997/1314 Art.4
Art.3, revoked: SI 1997/1314 Art.4
Art.4, revoked: SI 1997/1314 Art.4

1917. Appropriation (No.2) (Northern Ireland) Order 1996
revoked: SI 1999/1742 (NI.7) Art.6, Sch.2
Art.2, revoked: SI 1999/1742 (NI.7) Art.6, Sch.2
Sch.2, revoked: SI 1999/1742 (NI.7) Art.6, Sch.2

1918. Education (Student Loans) (Northern Ireland) Order 1996
revoked: SI 1998/1760 (NI.14) Art.9, Sch.
Art.3, revoked: SI 1998/1760 (NI.14) Art.9, Sch.
Sch. para.2, revoked: SI 1998/1760 (NI.14) Art.9, Sch.
Sch. para.3, revoked (in part): SI 1998/258 (NI.1) Art.6, SI 1998/1760 (NI.14) Art.9, Sch.

1919. Employment Rights (Northern Ireland) Order 1996
applied: 1998 c.39 s.24, SI 1999/671 Art.22, SI 1999/2038 Art.3, SI 1999/2790 (NI.9) Art.24
referred to: SI 1997/274 (NI.1) Art.3, 1998 c.47 s.98, SI 1998/2574 Art.3, SI 1998/3162 (NI.21) Art.85, 1999 c.10 s.16, SI 1999/2790 (NI.9) Art.21
Part I Ch.III, referred to: SI 1997/2779 (NI.20) Sch.2 para.1
Part I Ch.IV, applied: SI 1999/2790 (NI.9) Art.13, SI 1999/3323 Reg.26
Part IV, applied: 1998 c.39 s.18
Part V, applied: SI 1996/1921 (NI.18) Art.18
Part VA, added: SI 1998/1763 (NI.17) Art.3
Part VI Ch.I, applied: SI 1999/2790 (NI.9) Art.16
Part VI, applied: SI 1996/1921 (NI.18) Art.18, Art.20
Part VII, applied: SI 1996/1921 (NI.18) Art.18, Art.20
Part VIII, applied: SI 1996/1921 (NI.18) Art.18, Art.20

1919. Employment Rights (Northern Ireland) Order 1996—*cont.*
Part IX, substituted: SI 1999/2790 (NI.9) Art.9, Sch.4 Part I
Part XI, applied: SI 1996/1921 (NI.18) Art.18, Art.20, SI 1997/2779 (NI.20) Sch.2 para.10, Sch.2 para.11, Sch.2 para.12, SI 1998/3162 (NI.21) Art.85, SI 1999/2790 (NI.9) Art.14, Art.20, SI 1999/3323 Reg.28
Part XI, referred to: SI 1997/2779 (NI.20) Sch.2 para.1, 1998 c.39 s.23, 1999 c.10 s.7, Sch.3 para.1
Part XI Ch.II, referred to: SI 1999/2790 (NI.9) Art.14
Art.2, added: 1999 c.10 s.7, Sch.3 para.4
Art.2, amended: SI 1998/1763 (NI.17) Art.4, SI 1999/2790 (NI.9) Art.40, Sch.9 Part 2
Art.3, amended: SI 1998/1763 (NI.17) Art.4
Art.3, applied: 1998 c.39 s.24
Art.5, applied: SI 1998/3162 (NI.21) Art.48
Art.8, amended: SI 1999/2790 (NI.9) Art.11, Art.40, Sch.4 para.1, Sch.9 Part 2
Art.8, applied: SI 1997/2779 (NI.20) Sch.2 para.2
Art.8, revoked (in part): SI 1999/2790 (NI.9) Art.40, Sch.9 Part 2
Art.11, amended: SI 1998/1506 (NI.10) Art.78, Sch.6 para.117, SI 1999/671 Art.17, Sch.6 para.15
Art.12, referred to: SI 1996/1919 (NI.16) Art.142
Art.15, amended: SI 1998/1265 (NI.8) Art.16, Sch.1 para.7, Sch.2
Art.15, applied: SI 1997/869 (NI.6) Art.73, Sch.2 para.8, SI 1997/2779 (NI.20) Sch.2 para.2
Art.15, revoked (in part): SI 1998/1265 (NI.8) Art.16, SI 1998/Sch.1 para.7, SI 1998/1265 Sch.2
Art.21, amended: SI 1998/1761 (NI.15) Art.5, Sch. para.1, SI 1999/2790 (NI.9) Art.11, Sch.4 para.2
Art.22, amended: SI 1998/1265 (NI.8) Art.16, Sch.1 para.8
Art.22, revoked (in part): SI 1999/2790 (NI.9) Art.40, Sch.9 Part 2
Art.23, applied: SI 1999/2790 (NI.9) Art.13
Art.23, referred to: SI 1999/2790 (NI.9) Art.33
Art.23, revoked (in part): SI 1999/2790 (NI.9) Art.35, Art.40, Sch.9 Part 2, Sch.9 Part 10
Art.26, applied: SI 1996/1921 (NI.18) Art.20
Art.27, applied: SI 1996/1921 (NI.18) Art.20
Art.40, applied: SI 1996/1921 (NI.18) Art.20, 1998 c.39 s.12
Art.43, applied: 1998 c.39 s.12
Art.44, applied: 1998 c.39 s.12
Art.45, applied: SI 1996/1921 (NI.18) Art.20
Art.45, referred to: 1998 c.39 s.20
Art.47, applied: SI 1996/1921 (NI.18) Art.20
Art.50, applied: SI 1996/1921 (NI.18) Art.20
Art.53, applied: SI 1996/1921 (NI.18) Art.20
Art.55, amended: SI 1998/1265 (NI.8) Art.16, Sch.1 para.9
Art.55, applied: SI 1996/1921 (NI.18) Art.6, 1998 c.39 s.28
Art.55, referred to: 1998 c.39 s.20
Art.60, applied: SI 1996/1921 (NI.18) Art.20
Art.63, amended: SI 1999/2790 (NI.9) Art.34
Art.63, referred to: SI 1999/2790 (NI.9) Art.33
Art.67A, added: SI 1998/1763 (NI.17) Art.3
Art.67A, applied: SI 1999/3323 Reg.28, Reg.31
Art.67A, referred to: SI 1999/3323 Reg.23
Art.67B, added: SI 1998/1763 (NI.17) Art.3
Art.67C, added: SI 1998/1763 (NI.17) Art.3

1996—cont.

1919. **Employment Rights (Northern Ireland) Order 1996**—*cont.*

Art.67D, added: SI 1998/1763 (NI.17) Art.3
Art.67E, added: SI 1998/1763 (NI.17) Art.3
Art.67F, added: SI 1998/1763 (NI.17) Art.3
Art.67G, added: SI 1998/1763 (NI.17) Art.3
Art.67H, added: SI 1998/1763 (NI.17) Art.3
Art.67J, added: SI 1998/1763 (NI.17) Art.3
Art.67K, added: SI 1998/1763 (NI.17) Art.3
Art.67L, added: SI 1998/1763 (NI.17) Art.3
Art.68, amended: SI 1999/2790 (NI.9) Art.20, Art.40, Sch.9 Part 3
Art.68, referred to: SI 1997/2779 (NI.20) Sch.2 para.10
Art.68A, amended: SI 1999/2790 (NI.9) Art.20, Art.40, Sch.9 Part 3
Art.69, amended: SI 1999/2790 (NI.9) Art.20, Art.40, Sch.9 Part 3, SI 1999/3147 (NI.11) Art.17, Sch.2 para.15
Art.69, applied: SI 1999/3147 (NI.11) Art.8
Art.69, referred to: SI 1997/2779 (NI.20) Sch.2 para.10
Art.70, amended: SI 1999/2790 (NI.9) Art.20, Art.40, Sch.9 Part 3, SR 1999/432 Reg.4
Art.70, referred to: SI 1997/2779 (NI.20) Sch.2 para.10
Art.70A, added: SI 1998/1761 (NI.15) Art.5, Sch. para.2
Art.70A, amended: SI 1999/2790 (NI.9) Art.20, Art.40, Sch.9 Part 3
Art.70B, added: SI 1998/1763 (NI.17) Art.5
Art.70B, amended: SI 1999/2790 (NI.9) Art.20, Art.40, Sch.9 Part 3
Art.70C, added: SI 1999/2790 (NI.9) Art.11, Sch.4 para.3
Art.71, amended: SI 1997/2779 (NI.20) Sch.2 para.10, SI 1998/1761 (NI.15) Art.5, Sch. para.3, SI 1998/1763 (NI.17) Art.6, 1999 c.10 s.7, Sch.3 para.2, SI 1999/2790 (NI.9) Art.11, Sch.4 para.4, SI 1999/3323 Reg.32
Art.71, applied: 1998 c.39 s.24, 1999 c.10 s.7, Sch.3 para.2, SI 1999/2790 (NI.9) Art.14, SI 1999/3323 Reg.32
Art.71, referred to: 1998 c.39 s.24, 1999 c.10 s.7, Sch.3 para.2, SI 1999/3323 Reg.32
Art.72, amended: SI 1997/2779 (NI.20) Sch.2 para.10, SI 1998/1763 (NI.17) Art.7, 1999 c.10 s.7, Sch.3 para.2
Art.72, applied: 1998 c.39 s.24, 1999 c.10 s.7, Sch.3 para.2
Art.72A, added: SI 1997/1774 (NI.16) Art.5
Art.72A, applied: SI 1997/1774 (NI.16) Art.7
Art.73, amended: SI 1999/2790 (NI.9) Art.4, Sch.2 para.2
Art.74, amended: SI 1999/2790 (NI.9) Art.4, Sch.2 para.3
Art.74, applied: SI 1996/1921 (NI.18) Art.12
Art.75, amended: SI 1999/2790 (NI.9) Art.4, Sch.2 para.4
Art.76, amended: SI 1999/2790 (NI.9) Art.4, Sch.2 para.5
Art.77, amended: SI 1999/2790 (NI.9) Art.4, Sch.2 para.6
Art.78, amended: SI 1998/1759 (NI.13) Art.91, Sch.5 Part II
Art.85A, added: SI 1999/2790 (NI.9) Art.10, Sch.4 Part II
Art.85B, added: SI 1999/2790 (NI.9) Art.10, Sch.4 Part II
Art.86, amended: SI 1998/1761 (NI.15) Art.5, Sch. para.4, SI 1999/3147 (NI.11) Art.17, Sch.2 para.15

1996—cont.

1919. **Employment Rights (Northern Ireland) Order 1996**—*cont.*

Art.86, applied: SI 1999/3147 (NI.11) Art.8
Art.89, amended: SR 1999/432 Reg.5
Art.90, referred to: SI 1999/3323 Reg.26
Art.91A, added: SI 1998/1761 (NI.15) Art.3
Art.91B, added: SI 1998/1761 (NI.15) Art.3
Art.91C, added: SI 1998/1761 (NI.15) Art.3
Art.92, amended: SR 1999/432 Reg.6
Art.92, applied: SI 1999/2790 (NI.9) Art.12
Art.93, applied: SI 1999/2790 (NI.9) Art.12
Art.95, applied: SI 1999/2790 (NI.9) Art.12
Art.103, substituted: SI 1999/2790 (NI.9) Art.9, Sch.4 Part I
Art.104, substituted: SI 1999/2790 (NI.9) Art.9, Sch.4 Part I
Art.105, substituted: SI 1999/2790 (NI.9) Art.9, Sch.4 Part I
Art.106, substituted: SI 1999/2790 (NI.9) Art.9, Sch.4 Part I
Art.107, substituted: SI 1999/2790 (NI.9) Art.9, Sch.4 Part I
Art.108, substituted: SI 1999/2790 (NI.9) Art.9, Sch.4 Part I
Art.109, substituted: SI 1999/2790 (NI.9) Art.9, Sch.4 Part I
Art.110, substituted: SI 1999/2790 (NI.9) Art.9, Sch.4 Part I
Art.111, applied: SI 1997/2779 (NI.20) Sch.2 para.3
Art.111, substituted: SI 1999/2790 (NI.9) Art.9, Sch.4 Part I
Art.112, substituted: SI 1999/2790 (NI.9) Art.9, Sch.4 Part I
Art.120, amended: SI 1999/2790 (NI.9) Art.11, Sch.4 para.5
Art.121, amended: SI 1999/2790 (NI.9) Art.11, Sch.4 para.5
Art.124, amended: SI 1999/2790 (NI.9) Art.11, Sch.4 para.6, SR 1999/277 Art.3
Art.124, applied: SI 1996/1921 (NI.18) Art.20
Art.125, applied: SI 1996/1921 (NI.18) Art.18
Art.127, amended: SI 1999/2790 (NI.9) Art.40, Sch.9 Part 2
Art.128, applied: SI 1997/2779 (NI.20) Sch.2 para.1, Sch.2 para.3
Art.128, revoked: SI 1999/2790 (NI.9) Art.40, Sch.9 Part 2
Art.129, referred to: SI 1998/2574 Art.3
Art.129, revoked (in part): SI 1999/2790 (NI.9) Art.40, Sch.9 Part 2
Art.130, amended: SI 1999/2790 (NI.9) Art.11, Sch.4 para.7
Art.130, revoked (in part): SI 1999/2790 (NI.9) Art.40, Sch.9 Part 2
Art.131, applied: SI 1996/1921 (NI.18) Art.12, SI 1999/2790 (NI.9) Art.20
Art.131, substituted: SI 1999/2790 (NI.9) Art.11, Sch.4 para.8
Art.132, applied: SI 1996/1921 (NI.18) Art.12
Art.133, amended: SI 1999/3147 (NI.11) Art.17, Sch.2 para.15
Art.133, applied: SI 1999/3147 (NI.11) Art.8
Art.134, amended: SR 1999/432 Reg.7
Art.134, applied: SI 1996/1921 (NI.18) Art.12
Art.134A, added: SI 1998/1763 (NI.17) Art.8
Art.135, amended: SI 1997/2779 (NI.20) Sch.2 para.15, SI 1998/1761 (NI.15) Art.5, Sch. para.5
Art.135, applied: SI 1999/2790 (NI.9) Art.20
Art.135A, added: 1998 c.39 s.26
Art.135B, added: 1999 c.10 s.7, Sch.3 para.4

NO.

NO.

1996—cont.

1996—cont.

1919. Employment Rights (Northern Ireland) Order 1996—*cont.*

Art.137, amended: 1998 c.39 s.26, SI 1998/1763 (NI.17) Art.9, 1999 c.10 s.7, Sch.3 para.4, SI 1999/2790 (NI.9) Art.18, Sch.5 para.2, SI 1999/3323 Reg.30

Art.137, applied: SI 1996/1921 (NI.18) Art.12

Art.137, revoked (in part): SI 1999/2790 (NI.9) Art.40, Sch.9 Part 2

Art.140, amended: 1998 c.39 s.26, SI 1998/1763 (NI.17) Art.10, 1999 c.10 s.7, Sch.3 para.4, SI 1999/2790 (NI.9) Art.18, Sch.5 para.3, SR 1999/277 Art.4, Art.5, SI 1999/3323 Reg.30

Art.140, referred to: SI 1997/2779 (NI.20) Sch.2 para.13, SI 1999/2790 (NI.9) Art.14

Art.140, revoked (in part): SI 1999/2790 (NI.9) Art.40, Sch.9 Part 2

Art.141, amended: 1998 c.39 s.26, SI 1998/1763 (NI.17) Art.10, 1999 c.10 s.7, Sch.3 para.4, SI 1999/2790 (NI.9) Art.18, Sch.5 para.3, SI 1999/3323 Reg.30

Art.141, referred to: SI 1997/2779 (NI.20) Sch.2 para.13, SI 1999/2790 (NI.9) Art.14

Art.141, revoked (in part): SI 1999/2790 (NI.9) Art.40, Sch.9 Part 2

Art.142, amended: 1998 c.39 s.26, SI 1998/1265 (NI.8) Art.13

Art.142, revoked (in part): 1998 c.39 s.53, Sch.3

Art.143, amended: SI 1998/1763 (NI.17) Art.11, SI 1999/2790 (NI.9) Art.11, Sch.4 para.9, Sch.4 para.10

Art.143, revoked (in part): SI 1999/2790 (NI.9) Art.40, Sch.9 Part 2

Art.144, amended: SI 1999/2790 (NI.9) Art.11, Art.18, Sch.4 para.9, Sch.4 para.11, Sch.5 para.4, Sch.5 para.5

Art.144, revoked (in part): SI 1999/2790 (NI.9) Art.40, Sch.9 Part 2

Art.144A, added: SI 1999/2790 (NI.9) Art.18, Sch.5 para.6

Art.145, applied: SI 1996/1921 (NI.18) Art.9, Art.11, Art.12, Art.15, Art.20, SI 1997/1774 (NI.16) Art.7

Art.146, amended: SI 1998/1265 (NI.8) Art.16, Sch.1 para.10, SI 1998/1763 (NI.17) Art.12, SI 1999/2790 (NI.9) Art.40, Sch.9 Part 11

Art.148, revoked (in part): SI 1999/2790 (NI.9) Art.40, Sch.9 Part 2

Art.149, revoked (in part): SI 1999/2790 (NI.9) Art.40, Sch.9 Part 2

Art.151, amended: SI 1997/869 (NI.6) Art.73, Sch.2 para.8, SI 1998/1265 (NI.8) Art.15, SI 1998/1763 (NI.17) Art.12, SI 1998/1265 (NI.8) Art.16, Sch.1 para.11, Sch.2, SI 1998/3162 (NI.21) Art.105, Sch.3, SI 1999/2790 (NI.9) Art.32, Art.40, Sch.9 Part 10, Sch.9 Part 11, SR 1999/402 Reg.3

Art.151, revoked (in part): SI 1999/2790 (NI.9) Art.32, Art.40, Sch.9 Part 2

Art.152, amended: SI 1998/1265 (NI.8) Art.16, Sch.1 para.12, SI 1998/1763 (NI.17) Art.12, SI 1999/2790 (NI.9) Art.11, Art.40, Sch.4 para.12, Sch.9 Part 11

Art.152, revoked (in part): SI 1999/2790 (NI.9) Art.32, Art.40, Sch.9 Part 10

Art.153, applied: 1998 c.39 s.24

Art.153, revoked (in part): SI 1999/2790 (NI.9) Art.40, Sch.9 Part 2

Art.154, referred to: SI 1999/2790 (NI.9) Art.33

Art.154, revoked (in part): SI 1999/2790 (NI.9) Art.35, Art.40, Sch.9 Part 10

1919. Employment Rights (Northern Ireland) Order 1996—*cont.*

Art.156, amended: SI 1998/1265 (NI.8) Art.16, Sch.1 para.13

Art.157, amended: SI 1998/1265 (NI.8) Art.16, Sch.1 para.14

Art.157, applied: 1998 c.39 s.24

Art.158, amended: SI 1999/2790 (NI.9) Art.33, Art.36, SR 1999/402 Reg.3

Art.158, applied: 1998 c.39 s.24

Art.158, referred to: SI 1999/2790 (NI.9) Art.33

Art.158, revoked (in part): SI 1999/2790 (NI.9) Art.35, Art.40, Sch.9 Part 10

Art.159, revoked: SI 1999/2790 (NI.9) Art.32, Art.40, Sch.9 Part 10

Art.160, amended: SI 1997/869 (NI.6) Art.73, Sch.2 para.8, SI 1998/1265 (NI.8) Art.15, Art.16, Sch.2, SI 1998/3162 (NI.21) Art.105, Sch.3

Art.162, revoked: SI 1999/2790 (NI.9) Art.40, Sch.9 Part 2

Art.162A, added: SI 1998/1265 (NI.8) Art.14

Art.162A, referred to: SI 1999/2790 (NI.9) Art.13

Art.162B, added: SI 1998/1763 (NI.17) Art.12

Art.162B, revoked: SI 1999/2790 (NI.9) Art.36, Art.40, Sch.9 Part 11

Art.163, amended: SI 1998/1763 (NI.17) Art.13, SI 1999/2790 (NI.9) Art.8

Art.163, applied: SI 1996/1921 (NI.18) Art.6, SI 1999/2790 (NI.9) Art.14

Art.164, amended: SI 1998/1763 (NI.17) Art.13, SI 1999/2790 (NI.9) Art.8

Art.164, applied: SI 1999/2790 (NI.9) Art.14

Art.165, applied: SI 1999/2790 (NI.9) Art.14

Art.166, applied: SI 1996/1921 (NI.18) Art.6, SI 1999/2790 (NI.9) Art.14

Art.167, applied: SI 1996/1921 (NI.18) Art.6, SI 1999/2790 (NI.9) Art.14

Art.169A, added: SI 1997/1774 (NI.16) Art.6

Art.169A, applied: SI 1997/1774 (NI.16) Art.7

Art.172, revoked: SI 1999/2790 (NI.9) Art.40, Sch.9 Part 2

Art.180, revoked (in part): SI 1999/2790 (NI.9) Art.40, Sch.9 Part 2

Art.181, revoked (in part): SI 1999/2790 (NI.9) Art.40, Sch.9 Part 2

Art.191, revoked (in part): SI 1999/2790 (NI.9) Art.40, Sch.9 Part 2

Art.192, revoked (in part): SI 1999/2790 (NI.9) Art.40, Sch.9 Part 2

Art.197, revoked (in part): SI 1999/2790 (NI.9) Art.40, Sch.9 Part 2

Art.198, applied: SI 1996/1921 (NI.18) Art.9

Art.201, amended: SI 1998/1265 (NI.8) Art.12, Art.16, Sch.2

Art.202, referred to: 1998 c.47 Sch.2 para.10

Art.203, amended: SI 1998/1265 (NI.8) Art.12, Art.16, Sch.2

Art.216, amended: SR 1999/432 Reg.8

Art.216, applied: SI 1996/1921 (NI.18) Art.20

Art.216A, added: SR 1999/432 Reg.9

Art.217, amended: SR 1999/432 Reg.10

Art.217, applied: SI 1996/1921 (NI.18) Art.18

Art.218, applied: SI 1996/1921 (NI.18) Art.20

Art.220, applied: SI 1996/1921 (NI.18) Art.18

Art.224, amended: SR 1999/432 Reg.11

Art.227, referred to: 1998 c.47 Sch.2 para.10

Art.229, amended: SI 1998/1265 (NI.8) Art.13

Art.231, referred to: SI 1999/2790 (NI.9) Art.33

Art.231, revoked (in part): SI 1999/2790 (NI.9) Art.35, Art.40, Sch.9 Part 10

Art.233, applied: SI 1996/1921 (NI.18) Art.6

NO.

1919. Employment Rights (Northern Ireland) Order 1996—*cont.*

Art.234, referred to: 1998 c.47 Sch.2 para.10

Art.236, applied: 1998 c.47 s.44

Art.237, amended: SI 1999/2790 (NI.9) Art.11, Sch.4 para.13

Art.238, amended: SI 1998/1763 (NI.17) Art.14

Art.238, substituted: SI 1999/2790 (NI.9) Art.38, Sch.8 para.1

Art.239, amended: SI 1998/1763 (NI.17) Art.15, SI 1999/2790 (NI.9) Art.40, Sch.9 Part 2

Art.239, applied: SI 1997/2779 (NI.20) Sch.2 para.10

Art.239, revoked (in part): SI 1999/2790 (NI.9) Art.40, Sch.9 Part 2

Art.239, substituted: SI 1999/2790 (NI.9) Art.31

Art.240, amended: SI 1999/2790 (NI.9) Art.40, Sch.9 Part 3

Art.240, applied: SI 1997/2779 (NI.20) Sch.2 para.11, 1998 c.39 s.23, 1999 c.10 s.7, Sch.3 para.1

Art.240, referred to: SI 1999/2790 (NI.9) Art.20

Art.240, revoked (in part): SI 1999/2790 (NI.9) Art.20, Art.40, Sch.9 Part 3

Art.242, amended: SI 1999/2790 (NI.9) Art.31, Art.40, Sch.9 Part 2, Sch.9 Part 9

Art.242, revoked (in part): SI 1999/2790 (NI.9) Art.40, Sch.9 Part 2

Art.243, amended: SI 1997/1774 (NI.16) Art.8, SI 1998/1763 (NI.17) Art.16, SI 1999/2790 (NI.9) Art.11, Art.40, Sch.4 para.14, Sch.9 Part 2

Art.243, referred to: 1998 c.32 s.56

Art.244, amended: SI 1999/2790 (NI.9) Art.11, Sch.4 para.15

Art.245, amended: SI 1998/1265 (NI.8) Art.9, Art.10, Art.11, Art.16, Sch.1 para.15, Sch.2, SI 1999/2790 (NI.9) Art.40, Sch.9 Part 3

Art.245, applied: SI 1999/2790 (NI.9) Art.16

Art.245, referred to: SI 1997/2779 (NI.20) Sch.2 para.14

Art.246, revoked (in part): SI 1999/2790 (NI.9) Art.40, Sch.9 Part 9

Art.247, amended: SI 1998/1763 (NI.17) Art.17

Art.247, applied: SI 1999/2790 (NI.9) Art.12

Art.248, applied: SI 1997/2779 (NI.20) Sch.2 para.10

Art.249, applied: SI 1997/2779 (NI.20) Sch.2 para.10

Art.250, amended: SI 1999/2790 (NI.9) Art.40, Sch.9 Part 9

Art.250, applied: SI 1999/2790 (NI.9) Art.24

Art.250, revoked (in part): SI 1999/2790 (NI.9) Art.24, Art.40, Sch.9 Part 2, Sch.9 Part 4

Art.251, amended: SI 1999/2790 (NI.9) Art.11, Art.40, Sch.4 para.16, Sch.9 Part 2, Sch.9 Part 10

Art.252, referred to: 1998 c.47 Sch.2 para.10

Sch.1, amended: 1999 c.30 s.88, Sch.13 Part VII

Sch.1, revoked (in part): SI 1998/1265 (NI.8) Art.16, Sch.2, SI 1998/1759 (NI.13) Art.91, Sch.6 Part II, SI 1998/3162 (NI.21) Art.105, Sch.5, SI 1999/661 (NI.5) Art.5

Sch.2 para.13, revoked: SI 1998/1265 (NI.8) Art.16, Sch.2

1921. Industrial Tribunals (Northern Ireland) Order 1996

referred to: 1998 c.47 s.98

Art.5, amended: SI 1999/663 Art.2, Sch.1 para.27

NO.

1921. Industrial Tribunals (Northern Ireland) Order 1996—*cont.*

Art.6, amended: 1998 c.39 s.27, SI 1998/1265 (NI.8) Art.4, Art.5, Art.6, Art.16, Sch.1 para.16, Sch.2, SI 1998/3162 (NI.21) Art.105, Sch.3

Art.6, revoked (in part): SI 1999/2790 (NI.9) Art.38, Art.40, Sch.8 para.2, Sch.9 Part 12

Art.7, amended: SI 1998/1265 (NI.8) Art.16, Sch.1 para.17, Sch.2

Art.9, amended: SI 1998/1265 (NI.8) Art.3, Art.16, Sch.1 para.18, Sch.2

Art.9, revoked (in part): SI 1998/1265 (NI.8) Art.16, Sch.2

Art.11, amended: SI 1998/1265 (NI.8) Art.16, Sch.1 para.19, SI 1998/3162 (NI.21) Art.105, Sch.3

Art.11, referred to: SI 1998/3162 (NI.21) Art.85

Art.12, referred to: SI 1996/1919 (NI.16) Art.142

Art.12, substituted: SI 1999/2790 (NI.9) Art.38, Sch.8 para.3

Art.12A, added: SI 1999/2790 (NI.9) Art.38, Sch.8 para.3

Art.12B, added: SI 1999/2790 (NI.9) Art.38, Sch.8 para.3

Art.15, amended: SI 1999/2790 (NI.9) Art.40, Sch.9 Part 2

Art.16, applied: SI 1998/3162 (NI.21) Art.85

Art.17, applied: SI 1998/3162 (NI.21) Art.85

Art.18, amended: SI 1998/1506 (NI.10) Art.78, Sch.6 para.118, Sch.7

Art.20, amended: SI 1997/869 (NI.6) Art.73, Sch.2 para.10, 1998 c.39 s.30, SI 1998/1265 (NI.8) Art.12, Art.16, Sch.1 para.20, SI 1999/3323 Reg.33

Art.20, applied: SI 1996/1919 (NI.16) Art.15, SI 1997/2779 (NI.20) Sch.2 para.10, Sch.2 para.14, SI 1999/2790 (NI.9) Art.16

Art.20, referred to: 1998 c.39 s.49, SI 1999/3323 Art.41

Art.22, applied: SI 1998/3162 (NI.21) Art.85

Art.25, amended: SI 1999/663 Art.2, Sch.1 para.27, Sch.2

Sch.1 para.2, revoked: SI 1998/3162 (NI.21) Art.105, Sch.5

Sch.1 para.4, revoked: SI 1998/3162 (NI.21) Art.105, Sch.5

Sch.1 para.7, revoked: SI 1998/3162 (NI.21) Art.105, Sch.5

Sch.1 para.8, revoked: SI 1998/1506 (NI.10) Art.78, Sch.7

1924. Maximum Number of Stipendiary Magistrates Order 1996

revoked: 1997 c.25 s.73, Sch.6 Part II

Art.2, revoked: 1997 c.25 s.73, Sch.6 Part II

1926. European Parliamentary Constituencies (Scotland) Order 1996

applied: 1998 c.46, 1998 c.46 Sch.1 para.2

1934. Education (School Inspection) (Wales) (No.2) (Amendment) Regulations 1996

revoked: SI 1998/1866 Reg.1, Sch.

Reg.2, revoked: SI 1998/1866 Reg.1, Sch.

Reg.3, revoked: SI 1998/1866 Reg.1, Sch.

1936. Education (School Information) (Wales) (Amendment) Regulations 1996

revoked: SI 1997/1832 Reg.2

Reg.2, revoked: SI 1997/1832 Reg.2

Reg.3, revoked: SI 1997/1832 Reg.2

Reg.4, revoked: SI 1997/1832 Reg.2

Reg.5, revoked: SI 1997/1832 Reg.2

Reg.6, revoked: SI 1997/1832 Reg.2

Reg.7, revoked: SI 1997/1832 Reg.2

Reg.8, revoked: SI 1997/1832 Reg.2

1996—cont.

1936. Education (School Information) (Wales) (Amendment) Regulations 1996—cont.
Reg.9, revoked: SI 1997/1832 Reg.2

1940. Plant Protection Products (Amendment) Regulations 1996
revoked: SI 1999/1228 Reg.4
Reg.2, revoked: SI 1999/1228 Reg.4

1941. Specified Bovine Material (No.3) Order 1996
revoked: SI 1997/617 Art.29 (with saving)
Art.2, amended: SI 1996/3185 Art.2
Art.2, revoked: SI 1997/617 Art.29 (with saving)
Art.3, amended: SI 1996/3268 Art.2
Art.3, revoked: SI 1997/617 Art.29 (with saving)
Art.10, applied: SI 1996/2264 Art.6
Art.10, revoked: SI 1997/617 Art.29 (with saving)
Art.11, amended: SI 1996/2264 Art.10
Art.11, revoked: SI 1997/617 Art.29 (with saving)
Art.16, applied: SI 1996/2264 Art.10
Art.16, revoked: SI 1997/617 Art.29 (with saving)
Art.17, applied: SI 1996/2264 Art.10
Art.17, revoked: SI 1997/617 Art.29 (with saving)
Art.18, amended: SI 1996/2264 Art.10, SI 1996/3268 Art.2
Art.18, applied: SI 1996/2264 Art.10
Art.18, revoked: SI 1997/617 Art.29 (with saving)
Art.20, amended: SI 1996/2264 Art.10
Art.20, applied: SI 1996/2264 Art.10
Art.20, revoked: SI 1997/617 Art.29 (with saving)
Art.21, applied: SI 1996/2264 Art.10
Art.21, revoked: SI 1997/617 Art.29 (with saving)
Art.24, applied: SI 1996/2264 Art.10
Art.24, revoked: SI 1997/617 Art.29 (with saving)
Art.25, applied: SI 1996/2264 Art.10
Art.25, revoked: SI 1997/617 Art.29 (with saving)
Art.26, revoked: SI 1997/617 Art.29 (with saving)
Art.27, revoked: SI 1997/617 Art.29 (with saving)

1942. Trade Marks (Fees) Rules 1996
revoked: SI 1998/1776 r.5 (with savings)
r.3, revoked: SI 1998/1776 r.5 (with savings)
r.5, revoked: SI 1998/1776 r.5 (with savings)

1945. Child Support (Miscellaneous Amendments) Regulations 1996
Reg.25, amended: SI 1996/2378 Reg.3, SI 1999/1510 Art.43

1946. Harbour Works (Assessment of Environmental Effects) (Amendment) Regulations 1996
revoked (in part): SI 1999/3445 Reg.1
Reg.1, revoked (in part): SI 1999/3445 Reg.1
Reg.2, revoked (in part): SI 1999/3445 Reg.1
Reg.3, revoked (in part): SI 1999/3445 Reg.1

1974. Driving Licences (Community Driving Licence) Regulations 1996
referred to: SI 1998/1946 Art.2, Art.3
Sch.1 para.3, revoked (in part): SI 1998/1420 Reg.17, Sch.
Sch.1 para.7, revoked (in part): SI 1998/1420 Reg.17, Sch.

1996—cont.

1975. Occupational Pension Schemes (Requirement to obtain Audited Accounts and a Statement from the Auditor) Regulations 1996
applied: SI 1997/786 Reg.3, Sch.1 para.13
Reg.1, amended: SI 1997/786 Reg.3, Sch.1 para.13
Reg.4, amended: SI 1997/786 Reg.3, Sch.1 para.13
Sch. para.2, amended: SI 1997/786 Reg.3, Sch.1 para.13
Sch. para.5, substituted: SI 1997/3038 Reg.8
Sch. para.6, amended: SI 1997/786 Reg.3, Sch.1 para.13

1977. Occupational Pension Schemes (Mixed Benefit Contracted Out Schemes) Regulations 1996
Reg.3, amended: 1999 c.2 s.1, Sch.2

1982. Housing Accommodation and Homelessness (Persons Subject to Immigration Control) Order 1996
Art.2, amended: SI 1998/139 Art.2
Art.3, amended: SI 1998/139 Art.3, SI 1999/723 Art.2, SI 1999/3057 Art.2, SI 1999/3465 Art.2
Art.4, amended: SI 1997/628 Art.3, SI 1999/723 Art.3

1994. Parochial Fees Order 1996
revoked: SI 1997/1891 Art.4
Art.1, revoked: SI 1997/1891 Art.4
Art.4, revoked: SI 1997/1891 Art.4

1997. Motor Vehicles (Driving Licences) (Amendment) (No.4) Regulations 1996
revoked: SI 1996/2824 Reg.2, Sch.1
Reg.2, revoked: SI 1996/2824 Reg.2, Sch.1

2005. Beef (Marketing Payment) Regulations 1996
applied: SI 1997/1986 Reg.3
referred to: SI 1996/2999 Reg.3
Reg.9, substituted: SI 1996/2561 Reg.2

2007. Bovine Spongiform Encephalopathy Order 1996
revoked: SI 1996/3183 Art.23
Art.4, amended: SI 1996/2458 Art.2
Art.4, revoked: SI 1996/3183 Art.23
Art.9, revoked: SI 1996/3183 Art.23
Art.10, revoked: SI 1996/3183 Art.23
Art.13, amended: SI 1996/2458 Art.2
Art.13, revoked: SI 1996/3183 Art.23
Art.14, revoked: SI 1996/3183 Art.23
Art.15, amended: SI 1996/2458 Art.2
Art.15, revoked: SI 1996/3183 Art.23
Art.16, amended: SI 1996/2458 Art.2
Art.16, revoked: SI 1996/3183 Art.23
Art.21, revoked: SI 1996/3183 Art.23

2046. Dartford-Thurrock Crossing Tolls Order 1996
revoked: SI 1997/1914 Art.3
Art.3, revoked: SI 1997/1914 Art.3

2047. Dartford-Thurrock Crossing (Amendment) Regulations 1996
revoked: SI 1998/1908 Reg.11, Sch.
Reg.2, revoked: SI 1998/1908 Reg.11, Sch.
Reg.2 Table, amended: SI 1997/1915 Reg.2
Reg.2 Table, revoked: SI 1998/1908 Reg.11, Sch.
Reg.3, amended: SI 1997/1915 Reg.3
Reg.3, revoked: SI 1998/1908 Reg.11, Sch.
Reg.4, revoked: SI 1998/1908 Reg.11, Sch.
Reg.4 Table, revoked: SI 1998/1908 Reg.11, Sch.
Reg.4 Table, substituted: SI 1997/1915 Reg.4

1996—cont.

2065. Immigration (Transit Visa) (Amendment) Order 1996
revoked: SI 1998/1014 Art.4
Art.2, revoked: SI 1998/1014 Art.4

2070. Asylum Appeals (Procedure) Rules 1996
see *Meflah v Secretary of State for the Home Department* [1997] Imm. A.R. 555 (IAT), Professor DC Jackson (Chairman); see *Susikanth v Secretary of State for the Home Department* [1998] Imm. A.R. 96 (CA), Hobhouse, L.J.
r.2, see *R. v Immigration Appeal Tribunal Ex p. S* [1998] Imm. A.R. 252 (QBD), Sullivan, J.
r.13, see *R. v Immigration Appeal Tribunal Ex p. Mubassir* [1998] Imm. A.R. 304 (QBD), Laws, J.
r.14, see *R. v Immigration Appeal Tribunal Ex p. Mubassir* [1998] Imm. A.R. 304 (QBD), Laws, J.
r.23, see *R. v Immigration Appeal Tribunal Ex p. S* [1998] Imm. A.R. 252 (QBD), Sullivan, J.
r.24, see *R. v Immigration Appeal Tribunal Ex p. S* [1998] Imm. A.R. 252 (QBD), Sullivan, J.
r.27, see *Macharia v Secretary of State for the Home Department* Times, November 25, 1999 (CA), Peter Gibson, L.J.
r.32, see *R. v Secretary of State for the Home Department Ex p. Singh* [1998] I.N.L.R. 608 (CA), Sir Patrick Russell
r.35, see *R. v Immigration Appeal Tribunal Ex p. Ali (Mohammed Sarif)* [1998] I.N.L.R. 526 (QBD), Carnwath, J.; see *R. v Immigration Appeal Tribunal Ex p. S* [1998] Imm. A.R. 252 (QBD), Sullivan, J.
r.42, see *R. v Secretary of State for the Home Department Ex p. Saleem* [1999] I.N.L.R. 621 (QBD), Hooper, J.

2075. Health and Safety at Work etc. Act 1974 (Application to Environmentally Hazardous Substances) Regulations 1996
Reg.2, amended: SI 1999/40 Reg.2

2086. Nursery Education Regulations 1996
revoked (in part): SI 1998/655 Reg.2, SI 1999/1441 Reg.5
Reg.2, amended: SI 1996/3117 Reg.3
Reg.2, revoked (in part): SI 1999/1441 Reg.5
Reg.3, amended: SI 1996/3117 Reg.4
Reg.3, revoked (in part): SI 1999/1441 Reg.5
Reg.4, revoked (in part): SI 1997/2006 Reg.3, SI 1999/1441 Reg.5
Reg.4A, revoked (in part): SI 1999/1441 Reg.5
Reg.4B, added: SI 1997/2006 Reg.3
Reg.4B, revoked (in part): SI 1999/1441 Reg.5
Reg.4C, added: SI 1997/2006 Reg.3
Reg.4C, revoked (in part): SI 1999/1441 Reg.5
Reg.5, revoked (in part): SI 1997/2006 Reg.4, SI 1999/1441 Reg.5
Reg.6, revoked (in part): SI 1999/1441 Reg.5
Reg.7, amended: SI 1996/3117 Reg.5, SI 1997/2006 Reg.5
Reg.7, revoked (in part): SI 1999/1441 Reg.5
Reg.8, added: SI 1996/3117 Reg.6
Reg.8, revoked (in part): SI 1999/1441 Reg.5
Sch., added: SI 1997/2006 Reg.6, Sch.
Sch., revoked (in part): SI 1999/1441 Reg.5

2088. Education (Mandatory Awards) (Amendment) Regulations 1996
revoked: SI 1997/431 Reg.6
Reg.3, revoked: SI 1997/431 Reg.6
Reg.4, revoked: SI 1997/431 Reg.6
Reg.5, revoked: SI 1997/431 Reg.6
Reg.6, revoked: SI 1997/431 Reg.6
Reg.7, revoked: SI 1997/431 Reg.6

1996—cont.

2088. Education (Mandatory Awards) (Amendment) Regulations 1996—*cont.*
Reg.8, revoked: SI 1997/431 Reg.6
Reg.9, revoked: SI 1997/431 Reg.6

2089. Carriage of Dangerous Goods by Rail Regulations 1996
Reg.1, amended: SI 1999/303 Reg.5, Sch.4 para.1, SI 1999/2024 Reg.48, Sch.5 Part II
Reg.2, amended: SI 1998/2885 Reg.4, SI 1999/303 Reg.5, Sch.4 para.2
Reg.3, amended: SI 1999/303 Reg.5, Sch.4 para.3
Reg.5, amended: SI 1999/303 Reg.5, Sch.4 para.4
Reg.7, amended: SI 1999/303 Reg.5, Sch.4 para.5, Sch.4 para.6
Reg.8, amended: SI 1999/303 Reg.5, Sch.4 para.7
Reg.9, amended: SI 1998/2885 Reg.4, SI 1999/303 Reg.5, Sch.4 para.8
Reg.11, amended: SI 1999/303 Reg.5, Sch.4 para.9
Reg.12, amended: SI 1999/303 Reg.5, Sch.4 para.10
Reg.18, amended: SI 1999/303 Reg.5, Sch.4 para.11
Reg.24, amended: SI 1999/303 Reg.5, Sch.4 para.12
Reg.25, amended: SI 1999/303 Reg.5, Sch.4 para.13
Reg.28, amended: SI 1999/303 Reg.5, Sch.4 para.14
Reg.29A, added: SI 1999/303 Reg.5, Sch.4 para.15
Reg.30, amended: SI 1999/303 Reg.5, Sch.4 para.16
Reg.31, amended: SI 1999/303 Reg.5, Sch.4 para.17
Reg.32, amended: SI 1999/303 Reg.5, Sch.4 para.18
Reg.32, referred to: SI 1996/2090 Reg.9
Sch.1, amended: SI 1998/2885 Reg.4
Sch.1 para.1, amended: SI 1999/303 Reg.5, Sch.4 para.19
Sch.2 para.1, amended: SI 1999/303 Reg.5, Sch.4 para.20
Sch.2 para.2, amended: SI 1999/303 Reg.5, Sch.4 para.20
Sch.2 para.3, amended: SI 1999/303 Reg.5, Sch.4 para.20
Sch.2 para.4, amended: SI 1999/303 Reg.5, Sch.4 para.20
Sch.2 para.5, amended: SI 1999/303 Reg.5, Sch.4 para.20
Sch.2 para.7, amended: SI 1999/303 Reg.5, Sch.4 para.20
Sch.2 para.8, substituted: SI 1999/303 Reg.5, Sch.4 para.20
Sch.3 para.2, amended: SI 1999/303 Reg.5, Sch.4 para.21
Sch.3 para.4, amended: SI 1999/303 Reg.5, Sch.4 para.21
Sch.3 para.6, amended: SI 1999/303 Reg.5, Sch.4 para.21
Sch.3 para.7, amended: SI 1999/303 Reg.5, Sch.4 para.21
Sch.3 para.8, amended: SI 1999/303 Reg.5, Sch.4 para.21
Sch.3 para.9, amended: SI 1999/303 Reg.5, Sch.4 para.21

1996—cont.

2089. Carriage of Dangerous Goods by Rail Regulations 1996—*cont.*

Sch.3 para.10, revoked (in part): SI 1999/303 Reg.5, Sch.4 para.21

Sch.3 para.11, amended: SI 1999/303 Reg.5, Sch.4 para.21

Sch.3A, added: SI 1999/303 Reg.5, Sch.4 para.22

Sch.5 para.1, amended: SI 1999/303 Reg.5, Sch.4 para.23

Sch.5 para.5, amended: SI 1999/303 Reg.5, Sch.4 para.23

Sch.5 para.5A, added: SI 1999/303 Reg.5, Sch.4 para.23

Sch.5 para.9, amended: SI 1999/303 Reg.5, Sch.4 para.23

Sch.6 Table, revoked: SI 1999/303 Reg.5, Sch.4 para.24

Sch.6 para.1, substituted: SI 1999/303 Reg.5, Sch.4 para.24

Sch.6 para.2, substituted: SI 1999/303 Reg.5, Sch.4 para.24

Sch.6 para.3, added: SI 1999/303 Reg.5, Sch.4 para.24

Sch.6 para.4, added: SI 1999/303 Reg.5, Sch.4 para.24

Sch.7, substituted: SI 1999/303 Reg.5, Sch.4 para.25

Sch.9, amended: SI 1999/303 Reg.5, Sch.4 para.26

2090. Packaging, Labelling and Carriage of Radio-active Material by Rail Regulations 1996

Reg.1, amended: SI 1999/303 Reg.6, Sch.5 para.1, SI 1999/2024 Reg.48, Sch.5 Part II

Reg.1, referred to: SI 1999/257 Reg.3, Reg.4, Sch.1 para.2

Reg.2, amended: SI 1999/303 Reg.6, Sch.5 para.2

Reg.3, amended: SI 1999/303 Reg.6, Sch.5 para.3

Reg.9, amended: SI 1999/303 Reg.6, Sch.5 para.4

Reg.18, amended: SI 1999/303 Reg.6, Sch.5 para.5

Reg.21, amended: SI 1999/303 Reg.6, Sch.5 para.6

Reg.24, amended: SI 1999/303 Reg.6, Sch.5 para.7

Reg.27, amended: SI 1999/303 Reg.6, Sch.5 para.8

Reg.38, amended: SI 1999/303 Reg.6, Sch.5 para.9

Reg.41, amended: SI 1999/303 Reg.6, Sch.5 para.10

Reg.42, amended: SI 1999/303 Reg.6, Sch.5 para.11

Reg.43, amended: SI 1999/303 Reg.6, Sch.5 para.12

Sch.10A, added: SI 1999/303 Reg.6, Sch.5 para.13

Sch.13 Part III, amended: SI 1999/303 Reg.6, Sch.5 para.15

Sch.13 para.13, substituted: SI 1999/303 Reg.6, Sch.5 para.14

Sch.13 para.13A, added: SI 1999/303 Reg.6, Sch.5 para.14

Sch.13 para.14, amended: SI 1999/303 Reg.6, Sch.5 para.14

Sch.13 para.15, amended: SI 1999/303 Reg.6, Sch.5 para.14

Sch.13 para.16, amended: SI 1999/303 Reg.6, Sch.5 para.14

1996—cont.

2090. Packaging, Labelling and Carriage of Radio-active Material by Rail Regulations 1996— *cont.*

Sch.13 para.17, amended: SI 1999/303 Reg.6, Sch.5 para.14

Sch.13 para.18, amended: SI 1999/303 Reg.6, Sch.5 para.24

Sch.14 para.1, amended: SI 1999/3232 Reg.41, Sch.9 para.7

Sch.14 para.2, amended: SI 1999/303 Reg.6, Sch.5 para.16

2092. Carriage of Dangerous Goods (Classification, Packaging and Labelling) and Use of Transportable Pressure Receptacles Regulations 1996

applied: SI 1996/2089 Reg.10, Reg.11, SI 1996/2095 Reg.13, Reg.18, Sch.2 para.7

Reg.1, amended: SI 1998/2885 Reg.5

Reg.2, amended: SI 1999/303 Reg.7, Sch.6 para.1, SI 1999/2024 Reg.48, Sch.5 Part II

Reg.2, applied: SI 1997/648 Sch.3 para.3

Reg.3, amended: SI 1998/2885 Reg.5, SI 1999/257 Reg.11, SI 1999/303 Reg.7, Sch.6 para.2

Reg.4, amended: SI 1999/257 Reg.11, SI 1999/303 Reg.7, Sch.6 para.3

Reg.4, applied: SI 1996/2089 Reg.3, SI 1996/2095 Reg.5

Reg.5, amended: SI 1999/303 Reg.7, Sch.6 para.4

Reg.8, amended: SI 1999/303 Reg.7, Sch.6 para.5

Reg.8, applied: SI 1997/648 Sch.3 para.3

Reg.9, applied: SI 1997/648 Sch.3 para.3

Reg.10, applied: SI 1997/648 Sch.3 para.3

Reg.11, applied: SI 1996/2095 Sch.2 para.7

Reg.13, amended: SI 1999/303 Reg.7, Sch.6 para.6

Reg.14, amended: SI 1999/257 Reg.11

Reg.18, amended: SI 1999/303 Reg.7, Sch.6 para.7

Reg.19, amended: SI 1999/257 Reg.11, SI 1999/303 Reg.7, Sch.6 para.8

Reg.21, amended: SI 1998/2885 Reg.5

Sch.1, amended: SI 1999/303 Reg.7, Sch.6 para.9

Sch.3, applied: SI 1999/257 Reg.7

Sch.3 Table, substituted: SI 1999/303 Reg.7, Sch.6 para.10

Sch.8, amended: SI 1998/2885 Reg.5

Sch.8 para.3, amended: SI 1998/2885 Reg.5

Sch.8 para.4, amended: SI 1998/2885 Reg.5

Sch.8 para.5, amended: SI 1998/2885 Reg.5

Sch.9 para.3, amended: SI 1999/303 Reg.7, Sch.6 para.11

2093. Carriage of Explosives by Road Regulations 1996

applied: SI 1996/2089 Reg.2, SI 1996/2094 Reg.3

Reg.2, amended: SI 1999/303 Reg.8, Sch.7 para.1

Reg.3, amended: SI 1999/303 Reg.8, Sch.7 para.2

Reg.5, applied: SI 1996/2090 Reg.28

Reg.7, amended: SI 1999/303 Reg.8, Sch.7 para.3

Reg.11, amended: SI 1999/303 Reg.8, Sch.7 para.4

Reg.14, amended: SI 1999/303 Reg.8, Sch.7 para.5

Reg.15, amended: SI 1999/303 Reg.8, Sch.7 para.6

Reg.17, amended: SI 1999/303 Reg.8, Sch.7 para.7

1996—cont.

2093. Carriage of Explosives by Road Regulations 1996—*cont.*

Reg.20, amended: SI 1999/303 Reg.8, Sch.7 para.8

Reg.21, amended: SI 1999/303 Reg.8, Sch.7 para.9

Reg.22A, added: SI 1999/303 Reg.8, Sch.7 para.10

Reg.25, amended: SI 1999/303 Reg.8, Sch.7 para.11

Reg.29, amended: SI 1999/303 Reg.8, Sch.7 para.12

Reg.31, amended: SI 1999/303 Reg.8, Sch.7 para.13

Sch.1, amended: SI 1999/303 Reg.8, Sch.7 para.14

Sch.1 Part II, amended: SI 1999/303 Reg.8, Sch.7 para.14

Sch.1 Part II, referred to: SI 1996/2094 Sch.2 Part II

Sch.1 Part III, amended: SI 1999/303 Reg.8, Sch.7 para.14

Sch.2 para.3, amended: SI 1999/303 Reg.8, Sch.7 para.15

Sch.3 para.7, added: SI 1999/303 Reg.8, Sch.7 para.16

Sch.4 para.2, amended: SI 1999/303 Reg.8, Sch.7 para.17

Sch.4 para.3, amended: SI 1999/303 Reg.8, Sch.7 para.17

Sch.4 para.4, amended: SI 1999/303 Reg.8, Sch.7 para.17

Sch.4 para.5, amended: SI 1999/303 Reg.8, Sch.7 para.17

Sch.4 para.6, amended: SI 1999/303 Reg.8, Sch.7 para.17

Sch.4 para.7, amended: SI 1999/257 Reg.13, SI 1999/303 Reg.8, Sch.7 para.17

Sch.5 para.1, amended: SI 1999/303 Reg.8, Sch.7 para.18

Sch.5 para.8, amended: SI 1999/303 Reg.8, Sch.7 para.18

Sch.5 para.11, amended: SI 1999/303 Reg.8, Sch.7 para.18

Sch.5 para.12, amended: SI 1999/303 Reg.8, Sch.7 para.18

Sch.5 para.13, substituted: SI 1999/303 Reg.8, Sch.7 para.18

Sch.5 para.15, referred to: SI 1999/257 Reg.3, Reg.4, Sch.1 para.2

Sch.5 para.15, substituted: SI 1999/303 Reg.8, Sch.7 para.19

Sch.6 Part I, amended: SI 1999/303 Reg.8, Sch.7 para.20

Sch.6 Part II, amended: SI 1999/303 Reg.8, Sch.7 para.21

Sch.6 Part III, added: SI 1999/303 Reg.8, Sch.7 para.22

Sch.8 para.1, amended: SI 1999/303 Reg.8, Sch.7 para.1

Sch.8 para.3, substituted: SI 1999/303 Reg.8, Sch.7 para.23

Sch.8 para.8, substituted: SI 1999/303 Reg.8, Sch.7 para.23

2094. Carriage of Dangerous Goods by Road (Driver Training) Regulations 1996

applied: SI 1996/2791 Sch.11, SI 1999/645 Reg.13, Reg.14, Sch.11, Sch.12

Reg.2, amended: SI 1999/303 Reg.9, Sch.8 para.1

Reg.3, amended: SI 1999/303 Reg.9, Sch.8 para.2

1996—cont.

2094. Carriage of Dangerous Goods by Road (Driver Training) Regulations 1996—*cont.*

Reg.4, amended: SI 1999/303 Reg.9, Sch.8 para.3

Reg.4, applied: SI 1996/2791 Reg.13, SI 1997/2505 Reg.13, Sch.11, SI 1999/645 Reg.13, Reg.14

Reg.9, amended: SI 1999/303 Reg.9, Sch.8 para.4

Reg.10, amended: SI 1999/303 Reg.9, Sch.8 para.5

Sch.1, amended: SI 1999/303 Reg.9, Sch.8 para.6

Sch.2 Part II, amended: SI 1999/303 Reg.9, Sch.8 para.7

Sch.3 para.1, amended: SI 1999/303 Reg.9, Sch.8 para.8

Sch.3 para.2, amended: SI 1999/303 Reg.9, Sch.8 para.8

Sch.3 para.3, substituted: SI 1999/303 Reg.9, Sch.8 para.8

Sch.3 para.4, added: SI 1999/303 Reg.9, Sch.8 para.8

Sch.3 para.5, added: SI 1999/303 Reg.9, Sch.8 para.5

Sch.4, revoked: SI 1999/303 Reg.9, Sch.8 para.9

2095. Carriage of Dangerous Goods by Road Regulations 1996

applied: SI 1996/2089 Reg.2, SI 1996/2094 Reg.3

Reg.2, amended: SI 1999/257 Reg.12, SI 1999/303 Reg.10, Sch.9 para.1, Sch.9 para.2

Reg.3, referred to: SI 1996/2094 Sch.2 Part I

Reg.5, amended: SI 1999/303 Reg.10, Sch.9 para.3

Reg.8, amended: SI 1999/303 Reg.10, Sch.9 para.4

Reg.9, amended: SI 1999/303 Reg.10, Sch.9 para.5

Reg.10, amended: SI 1999/303 Reg.10, Sch.9 para.6

Reg.11, amended: SI 1998/2885 Reg.6

Reg.12, amended: SI 1999/303 Reg.10, Sch.9 para.7

Reg.13, amended: SI 1999/303 Reg.10, Sch.9 para.8

Reg.14, amended: SI 1999/303 Reg.10, Sch.9 para.9

Reg.17, amended: SI 1999/303 Reg.10, Sch.9 para.10

Reg.18, amended: SI 1999/303 Reg.10, Sch.9 para.11

Reg.23, amended: SI 1999/303 Reg.10, Sch.9 para.12

Reg.24, amended: SI 1999/303 Reg.10, Sch.9 para.13

Reg.25, amended: SI 1999/303 Reg.10, Sch.9 para.14

Reg.25A, added: SI 1999/303 Reg.10, Sch.9 para.15

Reg.26, amended: SI 1999/303 Reg.10, Sch.9 para.16

Reg.27, amended: SI 1999/303 Reg.10, Sch.9 para.17

Sch.1 Table 1, amended: SI 1999/257 Reg.12, SI 1999/303 Reg.10, Sch.9 para.18

Sch.1 Table 2, amended: SI 1999/257 Reg.12

Sch.1 Table 2, referred to: SI 1999/257 Reg.3, Reg.4, Sch.1 para.2

Sch.2 para.2, amended: SI 1999/303 Reg.10, Sch.9 para.19

1996—cont.

2095. Carriage of Dangerous Goods by Road Regulations 1996—cont.

Sch.2 para.3, amended: SI 1999/303 Reg.10, Sch.9 para.19

Sch.2 para.3A, added: SI 1999/303 Reg.10, Sch.9 para.19

Sch.2 para.8, substituted: SI 1999/257 Reg.12

Sch.3, amended: SI 1998/2885 Reg.6

Sch.4, amended: SI 1999/303 Reg.10, Sch.9 para.20

Sch.4 Part II, added: SI 1999/303 Reg.10, Sch.9 para.20

Sch.4 para.3, amended: SI 1999/303 Reg.10, Sch.9 para.20

Sch.4 para.7A, added: SI 1999/303 Reg.10, Sch.9 para.20

Sch.4 para.8, amended: SI 1999/303 Reg.10, Sch.9 para.20

Sch.4 para.11, added: SI 1999/303 Reg.10, Sch.9 para.20

Sch.4 para.12, added: SI 1999/303 Reg.10, Sch.9 para.20

Sch.4 para.13, added: SI 1999/303 Reg.10, Sch.9 para.20

Sch.4 para.14, added: SI 1999/303 Reg.10, Sch.9 para.20

Sch.4 para.15, added: SI 1999/303 Reg.10, Sch.9 para.20

Sch.4 para.16, added: SI 1999/303 Reg.10, Sch.9 para.20

Sch.4 para.17, added: SI 1999/303 Reg.10, Sch.9 para.20

Sch.5 para.3, revoked (in part): SI 1999/303 Reg.10, Sch.9 para.21

Sch.5 para.7, amended: SI 1999/303 Reg.10, Sch.9 para.21

Sch.5 para.13, revoked: SI 1999/303 Reg.10, Sch.9 para.21

Sch.5 para.15, revoked: SI 1999/303 Reg.10, Sch.9 para.21

Sch.5 para.17, substituted: SI 1999/303 Reg.10, Sch.9 para.21

Sch.5 para.17A, added: SI 1999/303 Reg.10, Sch.9 para.21

Sch.5 para.19, added: SI 1999/303 Reg.10, Sch.9 para.21

Sch.6 para.3, revoked (in part): SI 1999/303 Reg.10, Sch.9 para.22

Sch.6 para.9, revoked: SI 1999/303 Reg.10, Sch.9 para.22

Sch.6 para.12, revoked: SI 1999/303 Reg.10, Sch.9 para.22

Sch.6 para.13, amended: SI 1999/303 Reg.10, Sch.9 para.22

Sch.6 para.15, revoked: SI 1999/303 Reg.10, Sch.9 para.22

Sch.6 para.16, amended: SI 1999/303 Reg.10, Sch.9 para.22

Sch.6 para.17, revoked: SI 1999/303 Reg.10, Sch.9 para.22

Sch.6 para.19, substituted: SI 1999/303 Reg.10, Sch.9 para.22

Sch.6 para.20, added: SI 1999/303 Reg.10, Sch.9 para.22

Sch.7, amended: SI 1999/303 Reg.10, Sch.9 para.23

Sch.7 Part II, added: SI 1999/303 Reg.10, Sch.9 para.23

Sch.7 para.1, amended: SI 1999/303 Reg.10, Sch.9 para.23

Sch.7 para.8, revoked: SI 1999/303 Reg.10, Sch.9 para.23

1996—cont.

2095. Carriage of Dangerous Goods by Road Regulations 1996—cont.

Sch.7 para.14, added: SI 1999/303 Reg.10, Sch.9 para.23

Sch.7 para.15, added: SI 1999/303 Reg.10, Sch.9 para.23

Sch.9A, added: SI 1999/303 Reg.10, Sch.9 para.24

Sch.10, amended: SI 1999/303 Reg.10, Sch.9 para.25

Sch.10 para.11, amended: SI 1998/2885 Reg.6

Sch.10 para.17, amended: SI 1999/303 Reg.10, Sch.9 para.25

Sch.10 para.25, added: SI 1999/303 Reg.10, Sch.9 para.25

Sch.11 para.1, amended: SI 1999/303 Reg.10, Sch.9 para.26

Sch.11 para.16, amended: SI 1999/303 Reg.10, Sch.9 para.26

Sch.11 para.18, amended: SI 1999/303 Reg.10, Sch.9 para.26

2097. Fresh Meat (Beef Controls) (No.2) Regulations 1996

Reg.2, amended: SI 1996/2522 Reg.2

Sch.1 Part I, amended: SI 1996/2522 Reg.2

Sch.1 Part II, amended: SI 1996/2522 Reg.2

2114. Education (National Curriculum) (Assessment Arrangements for the Core Subjects) (Key Stage 1) (England) (Amendment) Order 1996

revoked: SI 1999/1236 Art.2, Sch.

Art.2, revoked: SI 1999/1236 Art.2, Sch.

2115. Education (National Curriculum) (Assessment Arrangements for the Core Subjects) (Key Stage 2) (England) (Amendment) Order 1996

revoked: SI 1999/2188 Art.2

Art.2, revoked: SI 1999/2188 Art.2

2116. Education (National Curriculum) (Key Stage 3 Assessment Arrangements) (England) Order 1996

applied: SI 1997/1368 Reg.4, SI 1997/2176 Art.3

revoked: SI 1999/2189 Art.2

Art.2, revoked: SI 1999/2189 Art.2

Art.3, amended: SI 1997/2176 Art.2

Art.3, revoked: SI 1999/2189 Art.2

Art.5, applied: SI 1997/514 Sch. para.2

Art.5, revoked: SI 1999/2189 Art.2

Art.6, applied: SI 1997/514 Sch. para.2

Art.6, revoked: SI 1999/2189 Art.2

Art.7, applied: SI 1997/514 Sch. para.2

Art.7, revoked: SI 1999/2189 Art.2

Art.8, applied: SI 1997/514 Sch. para.2

Art.8, revoked: SI 1999/2189 Art.2

Art.9, applied: SI 1997/514 Sch. para.2

Art.9, revoked: SI 1999/2189 Art.2

Art.10, applied: SI 1999/1178 Reg.13

Art.10, revoked: SI 1999/2189 Art.2

2121. Local Authorities (Capital Finance) (Amendment No.2) Regulations 1996

revoked: SI 1997/319 Reg.162, Sch.3

Reg.3, revoked: SI 1997/319 Reg.162, Sch.3

Reg.4, revoked: SI 1997/319 Reg.162, Sch.3

Reg.5, revoked: SI 1997/319 Reg.162, Sch.3

Reg.6, revoked: SI 1997/319 Reg.162, Sch.3

Reg.7, revoked: SI 1997/319 Reg.162, Sch.3

2128. Merchant Shipping (Prevention of Pollution) (Limits) Regulations 1996

Sch.2 para.1, amended: SI 1997/506 Reg.2

2149. Act of Sederunt (Mental Health Rules) 1996

revoked: SI 1999/929 r.1.3, Sch.2

r.1, revoked: SI 1999/929 r.1.3, Sch.2

2149. **Act of Sederunt (Mental Health Rules) 1996**
—*cont.*
r.2, revoked: SI 1999/929 r.1.3, Sch.2
r.3, revoked: SI 1999/929 r.1.3, Sch.2
r.5, revoked: SI 1999/929 r.1.3, Sch.2
r.9, revoked: SI 1999/929 r.1.3, Sch.2
r.11, revoked: SI 1999/929 r.1.3, Sch.2

2154. **Merchant Shipping (Prevention of Oil Pollution) Regulations 1996**
applied: SI 1996/3243 Sch Part I
Reg.1, amended: SI 1999/1957 Reg.3, Sch.1 para.5
Reg.7, amended: SI 1997/1910 Reg.3
Reg.8, amended: SI 1997/1910 Reg.4
Reg.14, amended: SI 1997/1910 Reg.5
Reg.16, amended: SI 1997/1910 Reg.6
Reg.32, amended: SI 1997/1910 Reg.7
Reg.36, amended: SI 1997/1910 Reg.8
Reg.37, amended: SI 1997/1910 Reg.9

2155. **A501 Trunk Road (Camden and Westminster) Red Route Experimental Traffic Order 1996**
revoked (in part): SI 1998/78 Art.10

2156. **Occupational Pension Schemes (Payments to Employers) Regulations 1996**
applied: SI 1997/786 Reg.3, Sch.1 para.14
Reg.12, amended: SI 1997/786 Reg.3, Sch.1 para.14
Reg.13, amended: SI 1997/786 Reg.3, Sch.1 para.14
Reg.13, revoked (in part): SI 1997/786 Reg.4, Sch.2
Reg.14, amended: SI 1997/2559 Reg.2

2163. **Agricultural Holdings (Units of Production) Order 1996**
revoked: SI 1997/1962 Art.3
Art.2, revoked: SI 1997/1962 Art.3
Art.3, revoked: SI 1997/1962 Art.3
Sch. para.1, revoked: SI 1997/1962 Art.3

2164. **A205 Trunk Road (Richmond and Wandsworth) Red Route Traffic Order 1996**
Art.2, amended: SI 1999/272 Art.2, Sch. Part A
Art.9, amended: SI 1999/272 Art.2, Sch. Part A

2165. **A41 Trunk Road (Camden and Westminster) Red Route (Bus Lanes) Experimental Traffic Order 1996**
revoked: SI 1997/446 Art.5
Art.3, revoked: SI 1997/446 Art.5
Art.6, revoked: SI 1997/446 Art.5
Art.7, revoked: SI 1997/446 Art.5

2166. **A41 Trunk Road (Westminster) Red Route Experimental Traffic Order 1996**
revoked: SI 1998/76 Art.10
Art.5, revoked: SI 1998/76 Art.10
Art.9, revoked: SI 1998/76 Art.10
Art.11, revoked: SI 1998/76 Art.10

2168. **Act of Sederunt (Rules of the Court of Session Amendment No.4) (Miscellaneous) 1996**
r.2, see *Taylor v Marshalls Food Group (No.2)* 1998 S.L.T. 1022 (1 Div), Lord Rodger L.P., Lord Allanbridge, Lord Coulsfield

2180. **Local Government Pension Scheme (Crown Prosecution Service) (Transfer of Pension Rights) Regulations 1996**
applied: SI 1997/1613 Reg.4, Reg.19, Sch.2 para.2
referred to: SI 1997/1613 Reg.3, Sch.2 para.6

2182. **Contracting Out of Functions (Court Staff) Order 1996**
revoked: SI 1999/1013 Art.3
Art.2, revoked: SI 1999/1013 Art.3
Art.3, amended: SI 1996/3096 Art.2

2182. **Contracting Out of Functions (Court Staff) Order 1996**—*cont.*
Art.3, revoked: SI 1999/1013 Art.3
Art.4, revoked: SI 1999/1013 Art.3

2185. **Advanced Television Services (Industrial Property Rights) Regulations 1996**
revoked: SI 1996/3151 Reg.2

2196. **Medicines (Products for Animal Use - Fees) (Amendment) Regulations 1996**
revoked: SI 1997/1469 Reg.21
Reg.3, revoked: SI 1997/1469 Reg.21
Reg.4, revoked: SI 1997/1469 Reg.21
Reg.5, revoked: SI 1997/1469 Reg.21
Reg.6, revoked: SI 1997/1469 Reg.21

2198. **Assured and Protected Tenancies (Lettings to Students) (Amendment) (No.2) Regulations 1996**
revoked: SI 1998/1967 Reg.6, Sch.3
Reg.2, revoked: SI 1998/1967 Reg.6, Sch.3

2199. **EC Competition Law (Articles 88 and 89) Enforcement Regulations 1996**
Reg.2, amended: SI 1999/506 Art.37
Reg.2, revoked (in part): SI 1999/506 Art.37
Reg.4, amended: SI 1999/506 Art.37
Reg.5, amended: SI 1999/506 Art.37
Reg.9, amended: SI 1999/506 Art.37
Reg.10, amended: SI 1999/506 Art.37
Reg.11, amended: SI 1999/506 Art.37
Reg.12, amended: SI 1999/506 Art.37
Reg.13, amended: SI 1999/506 Art.37
Reg.14, amended: SI 1999/506 Art.37
Reg.15, amended: SI 1999/506 Art.37
Reg.16, amended: SI 1999/506 Art.37
Reg.17, amended: SI 1999/506 Art.37
Reg.18, amended: SI 1999/506 Art.37
Reg.19, amended: SI 1999/506 Art.37
Reg.20, amended: SI 1999/506 Art.37
Reg.21, amended: SI 1999/506 Art.37
Reg.25, amended: SI 1999/506 Art.37
Reg.28, amended: SI 1999/506 Art.37
Reg.30, amended: SI 1999/506 Art.37

2203. **Children (Scotland) Act 1995 (Commencement No.2 and Transitional Provisions) Order 1996**
Art.5A, added: SI 1997/137 Art.2
Sch. Table, amended: SI 1996/2708 Art.2

2228. **Housing (Change of Landlord) (Payment of Disposal Cost by Instalments) (Amendment No.3) Regulations 1996**
revoked: SI 1997/328 Reg.3
Reg.2, revoked: SI 1997/328 Reg.3
Reg.3, revoked: SI 1997/328 Reg.3

2247. **Education (Transfer of Functions Relating to Grant-Maintained Schools) Order 1996**
revoked: SI 1997/294 Art.2
Art.2, revoked: SI 1997/294 Art.2

2255. **Cattle Passports (Fees) Order 1996**
revoked: SI 1998/871 Reg.36, Sch.3
Art.2, revoked: SI 1998/871 Reg.36, Sch.3

2264. **Heads of Sheep and Goats Order 1996**
revoked: SI 1997/2964 Art.18
Art.6, revoked: SI 1997/2964 Art.18
Art.10, revoked: SI 1997/2964 Art.18
Art.11, revoked: SI 1997/2964 Art.18
Art.12, revoked: SI 1997/2964 Art.18

2265. **Bovine Products (Despatch to other Member States) Regulations 1996**
revoked: SI 1997/389 Reg.14
Reg.3, revoked: SI 1997/389 Reg.14
Reg.3A, added: SI 1996/3000 Reg.2
Reg.3A, revoked: SI 1997/389 Reg.14
Reg.3B, added: SI 1996/3000 Reg.2
Reg.3B, revoked: SI 1997/389 Reg.14

NO.

NO.

1996—cont.

1996—cont.

2265. Bovine Products (Despatch to other Member States) Regulations 1996—*cont.*
Reg.7, revoked: SI 1997/389 Reg.14
Reg.9, revoked: SI 1997/389 Reg.14

2269. Teachers' Superannuation (Amendment) Regulations 1996
applied: SI 1997/3001 Reg.H12, Sch.15 para.2
revoked: SI 1997/3001 Reg.H12, Sch.14
Reg.3, applied: SI 1997/3001 Reg.H12, Sch.15 para.2
Reg.3, revoked: SI 1997/3001 Reg.H12, Sch.14
Reg.4, applied: SI 1997/3001 Reg.H12, Sch.15 para.2
Reg.4, revoked: SI 1997/3001 Reg.H12, Sch.14
Reg.5, applied: SI 1997/3001 Reg.H12, Sch.15 para.2
Reg.5, revoked: SI 1997/3001 Reg.H12, Sch.14
Reg.6, applied: SI 1997/3001 Reg.H12, Sch.15 para.2
Reg.6, revoked: SI 1997/3001 Reg.H12, Sch.14
Reg.7, applied: SI 1997/3001 Reg.H12, Sch.15 para.2
Reg.7, revoked: SI 1997/3001 Reg.H12, Sch.14
Reg.8, applied: SI 1997/3001 Reg.H12, Sch.15 para.2
Reg.8, revoked: SI 1997/3001 Reg.H12, Sch.14
Reg.9, applied: SI 1997/3001 Reg.H12, Sch.15 para.2
Reg.9, revoked: SI 1997/3001 Reg.H12, Sch.14
Reg.10, applied: SI 1997/3001 Reg.H12, Sch.15 para.2
Reg.10, revoked: SI 1997/3001 Reg.H12, Sch.14
Reg.11, applied: SI 1997/3001 Reg.H12, Sch.15 para.2
Reg.11, revoked: SI 1997/3001 Reg.H12, Sch.14
Reg.12, applied: SI 1997/3001 Reg.H12, Sch.15 para.2
Reg.12, revoked: SI 1997/3001 Reg.H12, Sch.14
Reg.13, applied: SI 1997/3001 Reg.H12, Sch.15 para.2
Reg.13, revoked: SI 1997/3001 Reg.H12, Sch.14
Reg.14, applied: SI 1997/3001 Reg.H12, Sch.15 para.2
Reg.14, revoked: SI 1997/3001 Reg.H12, Sch.14
Reg.15, applied: SI 1997/3001 Reg.H12, Sch.15 para.2
Reg.15, revoked: SI 1997/3001 Reg.H12, Sch.14
Reg.16, applied: SI 1997/3001 Reg.H12, Sch.15 para.2
Reg.16, revoked: SI 1997/3001 Reg.H12, Sch.14
Reg.17, applied: SI 1997/3001 Reg.H12, Sch.15 para.2
Reg.17, revoked: SI 1997/3001 Reg.H12, Sch.14
Reg.18, applied: SI 1997/3001 Reg.H12, Sch.15 para.2
Reg.18, revoked: SI 1997/3001 Reg.H12, Sch.14
Reg.19, applied: SI 1997/3001 Reg.H12, Sch.15 para.2
Reg.19, revoked: SI 1997/3001 Reg.H12, Sch.14
Reg.20, applied: SI 1997/3001 Reg.H12, Sch.15 para.2
Reg.20, revoked: SI 1997/3001 Reg.H12, Sch.14

2269. Teachers' Superannuation (Amendment) Regulations 1996—*cont.*
Reg.21, applied: SI 1997/3001 Reg.H12, Sch.15 para.2
Reg.21, revoked: SI 1997/3001 Reg.H12, Sch.14
Reg.22, applied: SI 1997/3001 Reg.H12, Sch.15 para.2
Reg.22, revoked: SI 1997/3001 Reg.H12, Sch.14
Reg.23, applied: SI 1997/3001 Reg.H12, Sch.15 para.2
Reg.23, revoked: SI 1997/3001 Reg.H12, Sch.14
Reg.24, applied: SI 1997/3001 Reg.H12, Sch.15 para.2
Reg.24, revoked: SI 1997/3001 Reg.H12, Sch.14
Reg.25, applied: SI 1997/3001 Reg.H12, Sch.15 para.2
Reg.25, revoked: SI 1997/3001 Reg.H12, Sch.14
Reg.26, applied: SI 1997/3001 Reg.H12, Sch.15 para.2
Reg.26, revoked: SI 1997/3001 Reg.H12, Sch.14

2288. South and East Wales Ambulance National Health Service Trust (Establishment) (Amendment) Order 1996
revoked: SI 1998/679 Art.2
Art.2, revoked: SI 1998/679 Art.2

2291. Plant Health (Fees) (Forestry) (Great Britain) Regulations 1996
Reg.1, amended: SI 1997/655 Reg.3, SI 1999/783 Reg.2
Reg.2, amended: SI 1997/655 Reg.4
Sch.1, amended: SI 1997/655 Reg.5
Sch.3, added: SI 1997/655 Reg.6, Sch.
Sch.3, substituted: SI 1999/783 Reg.2, Sch.

2304. Offshore Installations (Safety Zones) (No.6) Order 1996
revoked: SI 1997/735 Art.3, Sch.2

2306. Social Security (Claims and Payments and Adjudication) Amendment Regulations 1996
Reg.8, revoked: SI 1999/991 Reg.59 (with savings), Sch.4 (with savings)
Reg.9, revoked: SI 1999/991 Reg.59 (with savings), Sch.4 (with savings)

2317. Teachers (Compensation for Premature Retirement and Redundancy) (Scotland) Regulations 1996
applied: SI 1999/1750 Art.2, Sch.1
Part IIIA, added: SI 1997/675 Reg.7
Part IIIB, added: SI 1997/675 Reg.7
Reg.2, amended: SI 1997/675 Reg.3
Reg.3, amended: SI 1997/675 Reg.4
Reg.5, amended: SI 1997/675 Reg.5
Reg.16, amended: SI 1997/675 Reg.6
Reg.16A, added: SI 1997/675 Reg.7
Reg.16B, added: SI 1997/675 Reg.7
Reg.16B, amended: SI 1998/719 Reg.2
Reg.16C, added: SI 1997/675 Reg.7
Reg.16D, added: SI 1997/675 Reg.7
Reg.16E, added: SI 1997/675 Reg.7
Reg.16F, added: SI 1997/675 Reg.7
Reg.16G, added: SI 1997/675 Reg.7
Reg.17, amended: SI 1997/675 Reg.8
Reg.18, amended: SI 1997/675 Reg.9
Reg.19, amended: SI 1997/675 Reg.10
Reg.19A, added: SI 1997/675 Reg.11
Sch.1, amended: SI 1999/442 Art.9, Sch. para.1

NO.

2444. Civil Legal Aid (Scotland) Regulations 1996 *—cont.*

Sch.3 r.8, amended: SI 1997/727 Reg.7
Sch.3 r.15, amended: SI 1998/725 Reg.4

2445. Act of Sederunt (Sheriff Court Ordinary Cause Rules Amendment) (Miscellaneous) 1996

para.2, revoked: SI 1996/2586 r.2

2446. Act of Sederunt (Proceeds of Crime Rules) 1996

revoked: SI 1999/929 r.1.3, Sch.2
r.2, revoked: SI 1999/929 r.1.3, Sch.2
r.3, revoked: SI 1999/929 r.1.3, Sch.2
r.4, revoked: SI 1999/929 r.1.3, Sch.2
r.5, revoked: SI 1999/929 r.1.3, Sch.2
r.6, revoked: SI 1999/929 r.1.3, Sch.2
r.8, revoked: SI 1999/929 r.1.3, Sch.2
r.9, revoked: SI 1999/929 r.1.3, Sch.2
r.10, revoked: SI 1999/929 r.1.3, Sch.2
r.12, revoked: SI 1999/929 r.1.3, Sch.2
r.15, revoked: SI 1999/929 r.1.3, Sch.2
r.16, revoked: SI 1999/929 r.1.3, Sch.2
r.17, revoked: SI 1999/929 r.1.3, Sch.2
r.18, revoked: SI 1999/929 r.1.3, Sch.2

2447. Advice and Assistance (Scotland) (Consolidation and Amendment) Regulations 1996

Reg.9, referred to: SI 1998/1938 Reg.4
Reg.11, referred to: SI 1998/1938 Reg.4
Reg.16, amended: SI 1998/724 Reg.3
Reg.17, applied: SI 1998/1938 Reg.4
Reg.17, referred to: SI 1998/1938 Reg.4
Reg.18, referred to: SI 1998/1938 Reg.4
Reg.19, referred to: SI 1998/1938 Reg.4
Reg.21, applied: SI 1998/1938 Reg.4
Reg.21, substituted: SI 1998/724 Reg.4
Sch.2 para.1, amended: SI 1998/724 Reg.5
Sch.2 para.5, amended: SI 1997/726 Reg.5
Sch.2 para.6, amended: SI 1998/724 Reg.5
Sch.2 para.7, amended: SI 1997/726 Reg.5
Sch.2 para.7, substituted: SI 1998/724 Reg.5
Sch.2 para.10, amended: SI 1998/724 Reg.5
Sch.3 Part I, amended: SI 1997/726 Reg.6
Sch.3 Part II, amended: SI 1997/726 Reg.6
Sch.3 para.3, substituted: SI 1997/726 Reg.6

2450. Social Security (Adjudication) and Child Support Amendment (No.2) Regulations 1996

Reg.2, revoked: SI 1999/991 Reg.59 (with savings), Sch.4 (with savings)
Reg.3, revoked: SI 1999/991 Reg.59 (with savings), Sch.4 (with savings)
Reg.4, revoked: SI 1999/991 Reg.59 (with savings), Sch.4 (with savings)
Reg.5, revoked: SI 1999/991 Reg.59 (with savings), Sch.4 (with savings)
Reg.6, revoked: SI 1999/991 Reg.59 (with savings), Sch.4 (with savings)
Reg.7, revoked: SI 1999/991 Reg.59 (with savings), Sch.4 (with savings)
Reg.8, revoked: SI 1999/991 Reg.59 (with savings), Sch.4 (with savings)
Reg.9, revoked: SI 1999/991 Reg.59 (with savings), Sch.4 (with savings)
Reg.10, revoked: SI 1999/991 Reg.59 (with savings), Sch.4 (with savings)
Reg.11, revoked: SI 1999/991 Reg.59 (with savings), Sch.4 (with savings)
Reg.12, revoked: SI 1999/991 Reg.59 (with savings), Sch.4 (with savings)
Reg.13, revoked: SI 1999/991 Reg.59 (with savings), Sch.4 (with savings)

NO.

2458. Bovine Spongiform Encephalopathy (Amendment) Order 1996

revoked: SI 1996/3183 Art.23
Art.2, revoked: SI 1996/3183 Art.23

2473. Fertilisers (Mammalian Meat and Bone Meal) (Amendment) Regulations 1996

revoked: SI 1998/954 Reg.5
Reg.2, revoked: SI 1998/954 Reg.5

2475. Personal and Occupational Pension Schemes (Pensions Ombudsman) Regulations 1996

applied: SI 1997/786 Reg.3, Sch.1 para.15
Reg.1, amended: SI 1997/786 Reg.3, Sch.1 para.15
Reg.1A, added: SI 1997/3038 Reg.9
Reg.6, amended: SI 1998/1129 Art.3, Sch.2
Reg.7, amended: SI 1997/786 Reg.3, Sch.1 para.15

2479. Housing (Right to Buy) (Priority of Charges) Order 1996

revoked: SI 1997/945 Art.3
Art.2, revoked: SI 1997/945 Art.3

2482. Urban Waste Water Treatment (Scotland) Regulations 1996

Reg.14, applied: SI 1999/901 Art.5, Sch.

2503. Chemical Weapons (Notification) Regulations 1996

Reg.1, amended: SI 1996/2669 Reg.2

2517. Occupational Pension Schemes (Modification of Schemes) Regulations 1996

Reg.1, amended: SI 1999/3198 Reg.9
Reg.2A, added: SI 1997/786 Reg.3, Sch.1 para.16
Reg.6, substituted: SI 1999/3198 Reg.9
Reg.8, amended: SI 1997/786 Reg.3, Sch.1 para.16

2519. Social Security (Jobseeker's Allowance and Payments on Account) (Miscellaneous Amendments) Regulations 1996

Reg.2, revoked: SI 1996/2567 Reg.22

2538. Social Security and Child Support (Jobseeker's Allowance) (Miscellaneous Amendments) Regulations 1996

Reg.2, revoked (in part): SI 1997/454 Reg.9
Reg.3, revoked: SI 1996/2567 Reg.22
Reg.4, revoked: SI 1996/2570 Reg.28

2539. Local Authorities (Capital Finance) (Amendment No.3) Regulations 1996

revoked: SI 1997/319 Reg.162, Sch.3
Reg.3, revoked: SI 1997/319 Reg.162, Sch.3
Reg.4, revoked: SI 1997/319 Reg.162, Sch.3
Reg.5, revoked: SI 1997/319 Reg.162, Sch.3
Reg.6, revoked: SI 1997/319 Reg.162, Sch.3

2540. Civil Aviation (Canadian Navigation Services) (Amendment) Regulations 1996

revoked: SI 1998/2575 Reg.3, Sch.1
Reg.2, revoked: SI 1998/2575 Reg.3, Sch.1

2541. Gas Safety (Installation and Use) (Amendment) (No.2) Regulations 1996

revoked: SI 1998/2451 Reg.41
Reg.2, revoked: SI 1998/2451 Reg.41

2543. A406 Trunk Road (Enfield) Red Route Traffic Order 1996

Art.2, amended: SI 1999/272 Art.2, Sch. Part A
Art.9, amended: SI 1999/272 Art.2, Sch. Part A

2545. Income-related Benefits and Jobseeker's Allowance (Personal Allowances for Children and Young Persons) (Amendment) Regulations 1996

Reg.1, amended: SI 1997/806 Reg.5
Reg.10, amended: SI 1997/806 Reg.5
Reg.10, applied: SI 1997/543 Art.18, Art.21, Art.22, Art.24, SI 1998/470 Art.16, Art.17
Reg.10, referred to: SI 1998/470 Art.21

NO.

NO.

1996—cont.

1996—cont.

2555. Criminal Legal Aid (Scotland) Regulations 1996
amended: SI 1998/1938 Reg.5
Reg.2, amended: SI 1999/1042 Art.3, Sch.1 para.25
Reg.4, amended: SI 1999/1042 Art.3, Sch.1 para.25
Reg.14, amended: SI 1999/1042 Art.3, Sch.1 para.25
Reg.17, referred to: SI 1999/491 Reg.4
Reg.18, applied: SI 1998/1938 Reg.5
Sch., revoked: SI 1996/627

2556. National Health Service (Optical Charges and Payments) (Scotland) Amendment (No.3) Regulations 1996
revoked: SI 1998/642 Reg.24, Sch.4
Reg.2, revoked: SI 1998/642 Reg.24, Sch.4

2558. Registration of Marriages (Amendment) Regulations 1996
Reg.3, revoked: SI 1999/1621 Reg.10, Sch.3

2563. Potatoes Originating in the Netherlands Regulations 1996
revoked: SI 1997/2441 Reg.2
Reg.2, revoked: SI 1997/2441 Reg.2
Reg.5, revoked: SI 1997/2441 Reg.2
Reg.6, revoked: SI 1997/2441 Reg.2

2567. Jobseeker's Allowance (Transitional Provisions) Regulations 1996
applied: SI 1998/217 Art.2, SI 1999/779 Art.2, Sch.
Reg.3, amended: SI 1997/454 Reg.4
Reg.7, applied: SI 1999/991 Reg.7
Reg.8, amended: SI 1997/454 Reg.4, SI 1997/2677 Reg.3
Reg.9, amended: SI 1997/454 Reg.4
Reg.10, amended: SI 1997/454 Reg.4

2570. Social Security (Back to Work Bonus) (No.2) Regulations 1996
applied: SI 1998/217 Art.2, SI 1999/779 Art.2, Sch.
Reg.5, amended: SI 1997/454 Reg.3, SI 1999/2860 Art.3, Sch.14 para.1, SI 1999/3178 Art.3, Sch.15 para.1
Reg.8, amended: SI 1999/2860 Art.3, Sch.14 para.1, Sch.14 para.2, SI 1999/3178 Art.3, Sch.15 para.1, Sch.15 para.2
Reg.9, amended: SI 1999/2860 Art.3, Sch.14 para.3, SI 1999/3178 Art.3, Sch.15 para.3
Reg.13, amended: SI 1997/454 Reg.3
Reg.18, amended: SI 1997/454 Reg.3
Reg.19, amended: SI 1997/454 Reg.3
Reg.21, amended: SI 1999/2566 Reg.2, Sch.2 Part I, Sch.2 Part II
Reg.25, amended: SI 1999/2860 Art.3, Sch.14 para.1, SI 1999/3178 Art.3, Sch.15 para.1

2574. National Health Service (Optical Charges and Payments) Amendment (No.3) Regulations 1996
revoked: SI 1997/818 Reg.24, Sch.4
Reg.2, revoked: SI 1997/818 Reg.24, Sch.4

2577. Education (School Performance Information) (England) Regulations 1996
revoked: SI 1998/1929 Reg.4 (with savings)
Reg.2, amended: SI 1997/2060 Reg.2, SI 1997/2364 Reg.2, SI 1997/2816 Reg.2
Reg.2, revoked: SI 1998/1929 Reg.4 (with savings)
Reg.4, revoked: SI 1998/1929 Reg.4 (with savings)
Reg.12, revoked: SI 1998/1929 Reg.4 (with savings)
Reg.13, added: SI 1997/2816 Reg.2

2577. Education (School Performance Information) (England) Regulations 1996—cont.
Reg.13, revoked: SI 1998/1929 Reg.4 (with savings)
Sch.1 para.1, revoked: SI 1998/1929 Reg.4 (with savings)
Sch.1 para.2, revoked: SI 1998/1929 Reg.4 (with savings)
Sch.1 para.3, revoked: SI 1998/1929 Reg.4 (with savings)
Sch.2 para.1, revoked: SI 1998/1929 Reg.4 (with savings)
Sch.2 para.1, substituted: SI 1997/2364 Reg.3
Sch.2 para.2, revoked: SI 1998/1929 Reg.4 (with savings)
Sch.2 para.2, substituted: SI 1997/2364 Reg.3
Sch.2 para.3, revoked: SI 1998/1929 Reg.4 (with savings)
Sch.2 para.3, substituted: SI 1997/2364 Reg.3
Sch.2 para.4, revoked: SI 1998/1929 Reg.4 (with savings)
Sch.2 para.4, substituted: SI 1997/2364 Reg.3
Sch.2 para.5, revoked: SI 1998/1929 Reg.4 (with savings)
Sch.2 para.5, substituted: SI 1997/2364 Reg.3
Sch.2 para.6, revoked: SI 1997/2364 Reg.3
Sch.3 para.2A, added: SI 1997/2060 Reg.2
Sch.3 para.2A, revoked: SI 1998/1929 Reg.4 (with savings)
Sch.3 para.3, amended: SI 1997/2060 Reg.2
Sch.3 para.3, revoked: SI 1998/1929 Reg.4 (with savings)
Sch.3 para.4A, added: SI 1997/2060 Reg.2
Sch.3 para.4A, revoked: SI 1998/1929 Reg.4 (with savings)
Sch.3 para.4B, added: SI 1997/2060 Reg.2
Sch.3 para.4B, revoked: SI 1998/1929 Reg.4 (with savings)
Sch.3 para.4C, added: SI 1997/2060 Reg.2
Sch.3 para.4C, revoked: SI 1998/1929 Reg.4 (with savings)
Sch.3 para.4D, added: SI 1997/2060 Reg.2
Sch.3 para.4D, revoked: SI 1998/1929 Reg.4 (with savings)
Sch.3 para.10, added: SI 1997/2060 Reg.2
Sch.3 para.10, revoked: SI 1998/1929 Reg.4 (with savings)
Sch.3 para.11, added: SI 1997/2060 Reg.2
Sch.3 para.11, revoked: SI 1998/1929 Reg.4 (with savings)
Sch.5 para.5, revoked: SI 1998/1929 Reg.4 (with savings)
Sch.5 para.6, revoked: SI 1998/1929 Reg.4 (with savings)
Sch.6 para.5, revoked: SI 1998/1929 Reg.4 (with savings)
Sch.6 para.6, revoked: SI 1998/1929 Reg.4 (with savings)
Sch.7, added: SI 1997/2816 Reg.3, Sch.1
Sch.7, revoked: SI 1998/1929 Reg.4 (with savings)

2585. Education (School Information) (England) Regulations 1996
revoked: SI 1998/2526 Reg.2
Reg.2, revoked: SI 1998/2526 Reg.2
Reg.7, revoked: SI 1998/2526 Reg.2
Reg.8, referred to: SI 1998/2526 Reg.15
Reg.12, revoked: SI 1998/2526 Reg.2
Reg.15, revoked: SI 1998/2526 Reg.2
Sch.1 para.18, revoked: SI 1998/2526 Reg.2
Sch.2, referred to: SI 1998/2526 Reg.15
Sch.2 para.6, revoked: SI 1998/2526 Reg.2

NO.

1996—cont.

2585. **Education (School Information) (England) Regulations 1996**—*cont.*
Sch.2 para.8, revoked: SI 1998/2526 Reg.2
Sch.2 para.11, revoked: SI 1998/2526 Reg.2
Sch.2 para.12, revoked: SI 1998/2526 Reg.2
Sch.2 para.16, revoked: SI 1998/2526 Reg.2
Sch.2 para.17, revoked: SI 1998/2526 Reg.2
Sch.2 para.18, revoked: SI 1998/2526 Reg.2
Sch.2 para.21, revoked: SI 1998/2526 Reg.2

2595. **Child Abduction and Custody (Parties to Conventions) (Amendment) (No.2) Order 1996**
revoked: SI 1996/2874 Art.2
Art.2, revoked: SI 1996/2874 Art.2
Art.3, revoked: SI 1996/2874 Art.2
Sch., revoked: SI 1996/2874 Art.2

2628. **Specified Diseases (Notification) Order 1996**
Sch.1 Part I, amended: SI 1998/1645 Art.12

2632. **Merchant Shipping (Fees) (Amendment) Regulations 1996**
revoked: SI 1996/3243 Reg.2
Reg.2, revoked: SI 1996/3243 Reg.2

2641. **River Forth Salmon Fishery District (Baits and Lures) Regulations 1996**
revoked: SSI 1999/188 Reg.4
Reg.2, revoked: SSI 1999/188 Reg.4

2650. **Road Traffic (Permitted Parking Areas and Special Parking Areas) (City of Oxford and Parish of North Hinksey) Order 1996**
applied: SI 1999/1918 Reg.20
referred to: SI 1999/1918
Sch.2 para.5, substituted: SI 1999/1668 Art.3
Sch.2 para.8, amended: SI 1999/1668 Art.4
Sch.2 para.9, amended: SI 1999/1668 Art.5
Sch.2 para.9, revoked (in part): SI 1999/1668 Art.5

2653. **Sports Grounds and Sporting Events (Designation) (Scotland) Amendment Order 1996**
revoked: SI 1998/2314 Art.3, Sch.3
Art.2, revoked: SI 1998/2314 Art.3, Sch.3

2657. **Dairy Produce Quotas (Amendment) Regulations 1996**
revoked: SI 1997/733 Reg.35
Reg.2, revoked: SI 1997/733 Reg.35

2659. **Social Security (Adjudication) Amendment (No.2) Regulations 1996**
revoked: SI 1999/991 Reg.59 (with savings), Sch.4 (with savings)
Reg.2, revoked: SI 1999/991 Reg.59 (with savings), Sch.4 (with savings)

2663. **Export of Goods (Control) (Amendment No.2) Order 1996**
Art.2, revoked (in part): SI 1997/2758 Art.1, SI 1999/63 Art.2
Sch.2 para.4, revoked: SI 1999/63 Art.2

2677. **Endangered Species (Import and Export) Act 1976 (Amendment) Order 1996**
revoked: SI 1996/2684 Reg.7
Art.2, revoked: SI 1996/2684 Reg.7
Art.3, revoked: SI 1996/2684 Reg.7
Art.4, revoked: SI 1996/2684 Reg.7
Art.5, revoked: SI 1996/2684 Reg.7

2687. **A41 Trunk Road (Camden and Westminster) Red Route (Bus Lanes) (No.2) Experimental Traffic Order 1996**
revoked: SI 1997/203 Art.6
Art.4, revoked: SI 1997/203 Art.6

2688. **A41 Trunk Road (Westminster) Red Route (No.2) Experimental Traffic Order 1996**
applied: SI 1996/2687 Art.4
revoked: SI 1998/938 Art.10

NO.

1996—cont.

2688. **A41 Trunk Road (Westminster) Red Route (No.2) Experimental Traffic Order 1996**—*cont.*
Art.5, revoked: SI 1998/938 Art.10
Art.9, revoked: SI 1998/938 Art.10
Art.11, revoked: SI 1998/938 Art.10

2714. **Greater Manchester (Light Rapid Transit System) (Eccles Extension) Order 1996**
Art.20, applied: SI 1997/1266 Art.35, SI 1998/1936 Art.39
Art.35, applied: SI 1997/1266 Art.35, SI 1998/1936 Art.39
Art.36, amended: SI 1997/1266 Art.43
Art.36, applied: SI 1997/1266 Art.35, SI 1998/1936 Art.39
Art.37, applied: SI 1997/1266 Art.35, SI 1998/1936 Art.39
Art.38, applied: SI 1997/1266 Art.35, SI 1998/1936 Art.39
Art.40, applied: SI 1997/1266 Art.35, SI 1998/1936 Art.39
Art.41, applied: SI 1997/1266 Art.35, SI 1998/1936 Art.39
Art.42, applied: SI 1997/1266 Art.35, SI 1998/1936 Art.39
Art.43, applied: SI 1997/1266 Art.35, SI 1998/1936 Art.39
Art.44, amended: SI 1997/1266 Art.35
Art.44, applied: SI 1997/1266 Art.35, SI 1998/1936 Art.39
Art.44, revoked (in part): SI 1997/1266 Art.43
Art.45, applied: SI 1997/1266 Art.35, SI 1998/1936 Art.39
Art.46, applied: SI 1997/1266 Art.35, SI 1998/1936 Art.39
Art.47, applied: SI 1997/1266 Art.35, SI 1998/1936 Art.39
Art.51, applied: SI 1998/1936 Art.39

2721. **Dual-Use and Related Goods (Export Control) Regulations 1996**
applied: SI 1998/1752 Art.5, SI 1998/1757 Art.5
Reg.2, amended: SI 1997/1007 Reg.2, SI 1997/1694 Reg.2, SI 1998/272 Reg.2, SI 1998/899 Reg.2, SI 1999/984 Reg.3, SI 1999/1778 Reg.2
Reg.4, amended: SI 1999/1778 Reg.3
Reg.5, amended: SI 1997/324 Reg.2
Reg.8, amended: SI 1999/1778 Reg.4
Sch.2, amended: SI 1997/324 Reg.3, SI 1997/2759 Reg.3, Reg.4, Reg.5, Reg.7, Reg.8, Reg.9, SI 1999/984 Reg.4, SI 1999/1778 Reg.5, SI 1999/2091 Reg.2
Sch.2, revoked (in part): SI 1997/1694 Reg.3, SI 1997/2759 Reg.6, SI 1998/272 Reg.3
Sch.2 para.5, amended: SI 1997/2759 Reg.2

2726. **A2 Trunk Road (Bexley) Red Route Traffic Order 1996**
Art.2, amended: SI 1999/272 Art.2, Sch. Part A
Art.9, amended: SI 1999/272 Art.2, Sch. Part A
Sch.3B Item 2A, added: SI 1998/1809 Art.3
Sch.3B Item 2B, added: SI 1998/1809 Art.3
Sch.3B Item 2C, added: SI 1998/1809 Art.3
Sch.3B Item 3A, added: SI 1998/1809 Art.3
Sch.3B Item 4A, added: SI 1998/1809 Art.3
Sch.3B Item 8A, added: SI 1998/1809 Art.3
Sch.3B Item 8B, added: SI 1998/1809 Art.3
Sch.3B Item 8C, added: SI 1998/1809 Art.3
Sch.3B Item 9A, added: SI 1998/1809 Art.3

2727. **A20 Trunk Road (Greenwich) Red Route Traffic Order 1996**
Art.2, amended: SI 1999/272 Art.2, Sch. Part A
Art.9, amended: SI 1999/272 Art.2, Sch. Part A

NO.

2727. **A20 Trunk Road (Greenwich) Red Route Traffic Order 1996**—*cont.*
Sch.2A Item 1, substituted: SI 1999/342 Art.3
2728. **A20 Trunk Road (Bexley and Bromley) Red Route Traffic Order 1996**
Art.2, amended: SI 1999/272 Art.2, Sch. Part A
Art.9, amended: SI 1999/272 Art.2, Sch. Part A
2745. **Social Security Benefit (Computation of Earnings) Regulations 1996**
amended: SI 1999/2422 Art.3, Sch.13 para.1, SI 1999/2860 Art.3, Sch.15 para.1, SI 1999/3178 Art.3, Sch.16 para.1
applied: SI 1998/470 Art.6, SI 1999/1088 Reg.4
Reg.2, amended: SI 1999/2422 Art.3, Sch.13 para.2, SI 1999/2860 Art.3, Sch.15 para.2, SI 1999/3178 Art.3, Sch.16 para.2
Reg.2, referred to: SI 1999/264 Art.6
Reg.4, amended: SI 1999/2422 Art.3, Sch.13 para.3, SI 1999/2860 Art.3, Sch.15 para.3, SI 1999/3178 Art.3, Sch.16 para.3
Reg.6, amended: SI 1999/2422 Art.3, Sch.13 para.4, SI 1999/2860 Art.3, Sch.15 para.4, SI 1999/3178 Art.3, Sch.16 para.4
Reg.7, applied: SI 1997/543 Art.6, SI 1999/264 Art.6
Reg.13, amended: SI 1999/2422 Art.3, Sch.13 para.5, SI 1999/2860 Art.3, Sch.15 para.5, SI 1999/3178 Art.3, Sch.16 para.5
Reg.14, amended: SI 1999/2422 Art.3, Sch.13 para.6, SI 1999/2860 Art.3, Sch.15 para.6, SI 1999/3178 Art.3, Sch.16 para.6
Reg.16, revoked: SI 1999/2422 Art.3, Sch.13 para.7, SI 1999/2860 Art.3, Sch.15 para.7, SI 1999/3178 Art.3, Sch.16 para.7
2753. **Allocation of Housing Regulations 1996**
Reg.1, amended: SI 1996/3122 Reg.9
Reg.4, amended: SI 1997/631 Reg.2, SI 1999/2135 Reg.2
Reg.5, amended: SI 1999/2135 Reg.3
Reg.6, amended: SI 1997/631 Reg.3, SI 1997/2046 Reg.2
2754. **Homelessness Regulations 1996**
Reg.3, amended: SI 1997/631 Reg.4, SI 1999/2135 Reg.4
Reg.4, amended: SI 1997/631 Reg.5, SI 1997/2046 Reg.3, SI 1999/2135 Reg.5
2760. **Independent Analogue Broadcasters (Reservation of Digital Capacity) Order 1996**
Art.1, amended: SI 1999/1996 Art.2
Art.9, substituted: SI 1999/1996 Art.3
2777. **Teachers (Compensation for Redundancy and Premature Retirement) (Amendment) Regulations 1996**
applied: SI 1997/311 Reg.17
referred to: SI 1997/311 Reg.16
revoked: SI 1997/311 Reg.28
2791. **Health and Safety (Fees) Regulations 1996**
revoked: SI 1997/2505 Reg.17
Reg.3, revoked: SI 1997/2505 Reg.17
Reg.4, revoked: SI 1997/2505 Reg.17
Reg.5, revoked: SI 1997/2505 Reg.17
Reg.6, revoked: SI 1997/2505 Reg.17
Reg.7, revoked: SI 1997/2505 Reg.17
Reg.8, revoked: SI 1997/2505 Reg.17
Reg.9, revoked: SI 1997/2505 Reg.17
Reg.10, revoked: SI 1997/2505 Reg.17
Reg.11, revoked: SI 1997/2505 Reg.17
Reg.12, revoked: SI 1997/2505 Reg.17
Reg.13, revoked: SI 1997/2505 Reg.17
Reg.15, revoked: SI 1997/2505 Reg.17
Reg.16, revoked: SI 1997/2505 Reg.17
Reg.17, revoked: SI 1997/2505 Reg.17
Sch.3, revoked: SI 1997/2505 Reg.17

NO.

2791. **Health and Safety (Fees) Regulations 1996**—*cont.*
Sch.4, revoked: SI 1997/2505 Reg.17
Sch.5, revoked: SI 1997/2505 Reg.17
Sch.6, revoked: SI 1997/2505 Reg.17
Sch.7, revoked: SI 1997/2505 Reg.17
Sch.8, revoked: SI 1997/2505 Reg.17
Sch.9 Part I, revoked: SI 1997/2505 Reg.17
Sch.9 Part II, revoked: SI 1997/2505 Reg.17
Sch.9 Part V, revoked: SI 1997/2505 Reg.17
Sch.9 Part VI, revoked: SI 1997/2505 Reg.17
Sch.10, revoked: SI 1997/2505 Reg.17
Sch.11, revoked: SI 1997/2505 Reg.17
Sch.12, revoked: SI 1997/2505 Reg.17
Sch.13, revoked: SI 1997/2505 Reg.17
2794. **National Park Authorities (Levies) (England) Regulations 1996**
Reg.4, amended: SI 1996/2976 Reg.2
Reg.8, amended: SI 1998/1129 Art.3, Sch.2
2795. **Gas Act 1986 (Exemptions) (No.4) Order 1996**
Art.1, amended: SI 1999/3026 Art.2
2798. **Civil Aviation (Investigation of Air Accidents and Incidents) Regulations 1996**
Reg.1, amended: SI 1998/1503 Art.2, Sch. para.1
Reg.2, amended: SI 1998/1503 Art.2, Sch. para.2
Reg.3, amended: SI 1998/1503 Art.2, Sch. para.3
Reg.5, amended: SI 1998/1503 Art.2, Sch. para.4
Reg.6, amended: SI 1998/1503 Art.2, Sch. para.5
Reg.7, amended: SI 1998/1503 Art.2, Sch. para.6
Reg.8, amended: SI 1998/1503 Art.2, Sch. para.7
Reg.8, revoked (in part): SI 1998/1503 Art.2, Sch. para.7
Reg.9, amended: SI 1998/1503 Art.2, Sch. para.8
Reg.9, revoked (in part): SI 1998/1503 Art.2, Sch. para.8
Reg.11, amended: SI 1998/1503 Art.2, Sch. para.9
Reg.11, revoked (in part): SI 1998/1503 Art.2, Sch. para.9
Reg.12, amended: SI 1998/1503 Art.2, Sch. para.10
Reg.13, amended: SI 1998/1503 Art.2, Sch. para.11
Reg.14, amended: SI 1998/1503 Art.2, Sch. para.12
Reg.17, amended: SI 1998/1503 Art.2, Sch. para.13
Reg.18, amended: SI 1998/1503 Art.2, Sch. para.14
Reg.19, revoked: SI 1998/1503 Art.2, Sch. para.15
2809. **Local Government, Teachers' and National Health Service (Scotland) Pension Schemes (Provision of Information and Administrative Expenses etc.) Regulations 1996**
Reg.2, amended: SI 1998/364 Sch.3 para.2
Reg.3, amended: SI 1998/364 Sch.3 para.2
2817. **Plastic Materials and Articles in Contact with Food (Amendment) (No.2) Regulations 1996**
revoked: SI 1998/1376 Reg.14
Reg.2, revoked: SI 1998/1376 Reg.14

NO.

2817. Plastic Materials and Articles in Contact with Food (Amendment) (No.2) Regulations 1996—*cont.*
Sch.1, revoked: SI 1998/1376 Reg.14
Sch.2, revoked: SI 1998/1376 Reg.14
Sch.3, revoked: SI 1998/1376 Reg.14
Sch.4, revoked: SI 1998/1376 Reg.14

2824. Motor Vehicles (Driving Licences) Regulations 1996
revoked: SI 1999/2864 Reg.2, Sch.1
Reg.2, revoked: SI 1999/2864 Reg.2, Sch.1
Reg.3, amended: SI 1997/669 Reg.4, SI 1997/846 Reg.3, SI 1997/2915 Reg.3, SI 1998/20 Reg.3
Reg.3, revoked: SI 1999/2864 Reg.2, Sch.1
Reg.4, amended: SI 1997/669 Art.5
Reg.4, revoked: SI 1999/2864 Reg.2, Sch.1
Reg.5, amended: SI 1997/669 Reg.6
Reg.5, revoked: SI 1999/2864 Reg.2, Sch.1
Reg.6, amended: SI 1997/2915 Reg.4
Reg.6, revoked: SI 1999/2864 Reg.2, Sch.1
Reg.6, substituted: SI 1997/669 Reg.7, Sch.1
Reg.7, amended: SI 1997/669 Reg.8, SI 1997/2915 Reg.5, SI 1998/20 Reg.4
Reg.7, revoked: SI 1999/2864 Reg.2, Sch.1
Reg.8, amended: SI 1998/20 Reg.5
Reg.8, revoked: SI 1999/2864 Reg.2, Sch.1
Reg.10, amended: SI 1997/669 Reg.9, SI 1998/20 Reg.6
Reg.10, revoked: SI 1999/2864 Reg.2, Sch.1
Reg.11, revoked: SI 1999/2864 Reg.2, Sch.1
Reg.13, amended: SI 1997/669 Reg.10, SI 1999/617 Reg.3
Reg.13, revoked (in part): SI 1999/617 Reg.3, SI 1999/2864 Reg.2 (rem.), Sch.1 (rem.)
Reg.13A, added: SI 1999/617 Reg.4
Reg.13A, revoked: SI 1999/2864 Reg.2, Sch.1
Reg.14, revoked: SI 1999/2864 Reg.2, Sch.1
Reg.15, amended: SI 1997/669 Reg.11, SI 1998/20 Reg.7
Reg.15, revoked: SI 1999/2864 Reg.2, Sch.1
Reg.16, revoked: SI 1999/2864 Reg.2, Sch.1
Reg.17, amended: SI 1997/669 Reg.12
Reg.17, revoked: SI 1999/2864 Reg.2, Sch.1
Reg.18, revoked: SI 1999/2864 Reg.2, Sch.1
Reg.18, substituted: SI 1998/1229 Reg.2
Reg.21, amended: SI 1997/669 Reg.13, SI 1998/2038 Reg.3
Reg.21, revoked: SI 1999/2864 Reg.2, Sch.1
Reg.22, amended: SI 1997/669 Reg.14, SI 1998/2038 Reg.4
Reg.22, revoked: SI 1999/2864 Reg.2, Sch.1
Reg.23, amended: SI 1997/669 Reg.15, SI 1998/20 Reg.8
Reg.23, revoked: SI 1999/2864 Reg.2, Sch.1
Reg.26A, added: SI 1997/2070 Reg.3
Reg.26A, revoked: SI 1999/2864 Reg.2, Sch.1
Reg.27, amended: SI 1997/669 Reg.16, SI 1998/528 Reg.3
Reg.27, revoked: SI 1999/2864 Reg.2, Sch.1
Reg.28, amended: SI 1997/669 Reg.17, SI 1997/2070 Reg.4
Reg.28, revoked: SI 1999/2864 Reg.2, Sch.1
Reg.29, amended: SI 1997/669 Reg.18, SI 1997/2070 Reg.5
Reg.29, revoked: SI 1999/2864 Reg.2, Sch.1
Reg.30, amended: SI 1997/669 Reg.19, SI 1997/2070 Reg.5
Reg.30, revoked: SI 1999/2864 Reg.2, Sch.1
Reg.30A, added: SI 1997/2070 Reg.6
Reg.30A, revoked: SI 1999/2864 Reg.2, Sch.1
Reg.31, amended: SI 1999/72 Reg.3, SI 1999/617 Reg.5

NO.

2824. Motor Vehicles (Driving Licences) Regulations 1996—*cont.*
Reg.31, revoked: SI 1999/2864 Reg.2, Sch.1
Reg.31, substituted: SI 1997/2070 Reg.7
Reg.32, revoked: SI 1999/2864 Reg.2, Sch.1
Reg.33, amended: SI 1997/669 Reg.20, SI 1999/617 Reg.5
Reg.33, revoked: SI 1999/2864 Reg.2, Sch.1
Reg.34, amended: SI 1997/669 Reg.21, SI 1997/2070 Reg.8, SI 1998/20 Reg.9
Reg.34, revoked: SI 1999/2864 Reg.2, Sch.1
Reg.35, amended: SI 1997/669 Reg.22
Reg.35, revoked: SI 1999/2864 Reg.2, Sch.1
Reg.36, amended: SI 1997/669 Reg.23, SI 1999/617 Reg.7
Reg.36, revoked: SI 1999/2864 Reg.2, Sch.1
Reg.37, amended: SI 1997/669 Reg.24
Reg.37, revoked: SI 1999/2864 Reg.2, Sch.1
Reg.39, amended: SI 1997/669 Reg.25
Reg.39, revoked: SI 1999/2864 Reg.2, Sch.1
Reg.40, amended: SI 1997/669 Reg.26
Reg.40, revoked: SI 1999/2864 Reg.2, Sch.1
Reg.42, amended: SI 1997/669 Reg.27, SI 1998/20 Reg.10
Reg.42, revoked: SI 1999/2864 Reg.2, Sch.1
Reg.43, amended: SI 1997/669 Reg.28, SI 1998/20 Reg.11
Reg.43, revoked: SI 1999/2864 Reg.2, Sch.1
Reg.44, amended: SI 1997/2070 Reg.9
Reg.44, revoked: SI 1999/2864 Reg.2, Sch.1
Reg.45, amended: SI 1997/669 Reg.29, SI 1998/528 Reg.3, SI 1998/2038 Reg.5
Reg.45, revoked (in part): SI 1997/2070 Reg.10, SI 1999/2864 Reg.2, Sch.1
Reg.46, amended: SI 1997/669 Reg.30
Reg.46, revoked: SI 1999/2864 Reg.2, Sch.1
Reg.47, amended: SI 1997/669 Reg.31
Reg.47, revoked: SI 1999/2864 Reg.2, Sch.1
Reg.48, amended: SI 1997/669 Reg.32
Reg.48, revoked: SI 1999/2864 Reg.2, Sch.1
Reg.49, revoked: SI 1999/2864 Reg.2, Sch.1
Reg.50, revoked: SI 1999/2864 Reg.2, Sch.1
Reg.51, amended: SI 1997/669 Reg.33
Reg.51, revoked: SI 1999/2864 Reg.2, Sch.1
Reg.52, revoked: SI 1999/2864 Reg.2, Sch.1
Reg.52, substituted: SI 1998/20 Reg.12
Reg.53, revoked: SI 1999/2864 Reg.2, Sch.1
Reg.53, substituted: SI 1998/20 Reg.13
Reg.54, revoked: SI 1999/2864 Reg.2, Sch.1
Reg.55, amended: SI 1997/669 Reg.34, SI 1998/20 Reg.14
Reg.55, revoked: SI 1999/2864 Reg.2, Sch.1
Reg.56, amended: SI 1997/669 Reg.35
Reg.56, revoked: SI 1999/2864 Reg.2, Sch.1
Reg.56, substituted: SI 1998/20 Reg.15
Reg.56A, added: SI 1998/20 Reg.15
Reg.56A, revoked: SI 1999/2864 Reg.2, Sch.1
Reg.57, amended: SI 1997/669 Reg.36, SI 1998/20 Reg.16
Reg.57, revoked: SI 1999/2864 Reg.2, Sch.1
Reg.58, amended: SI 1997/669 Reg.37, SI 1998/20 Reg.17
Reg.58, revoked: SI 1999/2864 Reg.2, Sch.1
Reg.59, amended: SI 1997/669 Reg.38
Reg.59, revoked: SI 1999/2864 Reg.2, Sch.1
Reg.60, amended: SI 1997/669 Reg.39, SI 1998/20 Reg.18
Reg.60, revoked: SI 1999/2864 Reg.2, Sch.1
Reg.60A, added: SI 1998/20 Reg.19
Reg.60A, revoked: SI 1999/2864 Reg.2, Sch.1
Reg.62, amended: SI 1997/669 Reg.40, SI 1998/20 Reg.20

NO.

2824. Motor Vehicles (Driving Licences) Regulations 1996—*cont.*
Reg.62, revoked: SI 1999/2864 Reg.2, Sch.1
Reg.63, amended: SI 1997/256 Reg.2, SI 1997/669 Reg.41, SI 1998/20 Reg.21
Reg.63, revoked: SI 1999/2864 Reg.2, Sch.1
Reg.64, amended: SI 1997/669 Reg.42
Reg.64, revoked: SI 1999/2864 Reg.2, Sch.1
Reg.65, amended: SI 1997/669 Reg.43, SI 1997/2915 Reg.6
Reg.65, revoked: SI 1999/2864 Reg.2, Sch.1
Reg.66, revoked: SI 1999/2864 Reg.2, Sch.1
Reg.67, revoked: SI 1999/2864 Reg.2, Sch.1
Reg.68, amended: SI 1997/669 Reg.44, SI 1998/2038 Reg.6, SI 1999/617 Reg.8
Reg.68, revoked: SI 1999/2864 Reg.2, Sch.1
Reg.69, amended: SI 1997/669 Reg.45
Reg.69, revoked: SI 1999/2864 Reg.2, Sch.1
Reg.69A, added: SI 1999/72 Reg.6
Reg.69A, revoked: SI 1999/2864 Reg.2, Sch.1
Reg.70, amended: SI 1996/3198 Reg.2
Reg.70, revoked: SI 1999/2864 Reg.2, Sch.1
Reg.71A, added: SI 1997/669 Reg.46
Reg.71A, revoked: SI 1999/2864 Reg.2, Sch.1
Reg.72, amended: SI 1997/669 Reg.47
Reg.72, revoked: SI 1999/2864 Reg.2, Sch.1
Reg.73, revoked: SI 1999/2864 Reg.2, Sch.1
Reg.73, substituted: SI 1997/2915 Reg.7
Reg.74, amended: SI 1997/669 Reg.48, SI 1998/20 Reg.22
Reg.74, revoked: SI 1999/2864 Reg.2, Sch.1
Reg.75, revoked: SI 1999/2864 Reg.2, Sch.1
Reg.76, revoked: SI 1999/2864 Reg.2, Sch.1
Reg.77, revoked: SI 1999/2864 Reg.2, Sch.1
Sch.1, revoked: SI 1999/2864 Reg.2, Sch.1
Sch.2, amended: SI 1997/669 Reg.49, SI 1998/20 Reg.23
Sch.2, revoked: SI 1999/2864 Reg.2, Sch.1
Sch.3, revoked: SI 1999/2864 Reg.2, Sch.1
Sch.3, substituted: SI 1998/1229 Reg.2, Sch.
Sch.3 Part I, amended: SI 1997/669 Reg.50
Sch.3 Part I, revoked: SI 1999/2864 Reg.2, Sch.1
Sch.3 Part I, substituted: SI 1998/1229 Reg.2, Sch., SI 1999/72 Reg.4, Sch.1
Sch.3 Part II, amended: SI 1997/669 Reg.50
Sch.3 Part II, revoked: SI 1999/2864 Reg.2, Sch.1
Sch.3 Part II, substituted: SI 1998/1229 Reg.2, Sch.
Sch.5, revoked: SI 1999/2864 Reg.2, Sch.1
Sch.5, substituted: SI 1997/669 Reg.51, Sch.2, SI 1998/528 Reg.3
Sch.5 Table, applied: SI 1999/72 Reg.7
Sch.5 Table, revoked: SI 1999/2864 Reg.2, Sch.1
Sch.5 Table, substituted: SI 1999/72 Reg.5, Sch.2
Sch.6, amended: SI 1997/669 Reg.52
Sch.6, revoked: SI 1999/2864 Reg.2, Sch.1
Sch.6 para.2, amended: SI 1998/20 Reg.24, SI 1999/1820 Art.4, Sch.2 para.162
Sch.6 para.2, revoked: SI 1999/2864 Reg.2, Sch.1
Sch.7 Part 3, revoked: SI 1999/2864 Reg.2, Sch.1
Sch.7 Part 3, substituted: SI 1999/617 Reg.9, Sch.
Sch.7 Part 4, revoked: SI 1999/2864 Reg.2, Sch.1
Sch.7 Part 4, substituted: SI 1999/617 Reg.9, Sch.

NO.

2824. Motor Vehicles (Driving Licences) Regulations 1996—*cont.*
Sch.8 Part I, amended: SI 1997/669 Reg.53
Sch.8 Part I, revoked: SI 1999/2864 Reg.2, Sch.1
Sch.8 Part III, amended: SI 1997/669 Reg.53
Sch.8 Part III, revoked: SI 1999/2864 Reg.2, Sch.1
Sch.8 Part IV, amended: SI 1997/669 Reg.53
Sch.8 Part IV, revoked: SI 1999/2864 Reg.2, Sch.1
Sch.11, amended: SI 1998/20 Reg.25
Sch.11, revoked: SI 1999/2864 Reg.2, Sch.1
Sch.12 Part I, amended: SI 1998/20 Reg.26
Sch.12 Part I, revoked: SI 1999/2864 Reg.2, Sch.1
Sch.13, revoked: SI 1999/2864 Reg.2, Sch.1
Sch.13, substituted: SI 1997/669 Reg.54, Sch.3

2827. Open-Ended Investment Companies (Investment Companies with Variable Capital) Regulations 1996
Reg.65, applied: SI 1998/3087 Sch.
Sch.8 para.3, revoked: 1998 c.29 Sch.16 Part II
Sch.8 para.26, revoked: 1998 c.29 Sch.16 Part II

2856. Act of Sederunt (Lands Valuation Appeal Court) 1996
revoked: SI 1997/378 para.2
r.2, revoked: SI 1997/378 para.2

2859. Offshore Installations (Safety Zones) (No.7) Order 1996
revoked: SI 1997/735 Art.3, Sch.2

2874. Child Abduction and Custody (Parties to Conventions) (Amendment) (No.3) Order 1996
revoked: SI 1997/1747 Art.2
Art.2, revoked: SI 1997/1747 Art.2
Art.3, revoked: SI 1997/1747 Art.2
Sch., revoked: SI 1997/1747 Art.2

2880. Drug Trafficking Act 1994 (Designated Countries and Territories) Order 1996
Appendix., amended: SI 1997/1318 Art.3, SI 1997/2980 Art.5
Sch.1, amended: SI 1997/1318 Art.2, SI 1997/2980 Art.2
Sch.2 para.8, amended: SI 1997/2980 Art.3
Sch.3, amended: SI 1997/2980 Art.4

2882. Naval, Military and Air Forces etc. (Disablement and Death) Service Pensions Amendment (No.3) Order 1996
Art.10, revoked: SI 1997/286 Art.11

2887. Home Repair Assistance Regulations 1996
Sch. I Part I, amended: SI 1996/3119 Reg.2
Sch. I Part III, amended: SI 1998/2998 Reg.3

2890. Housing Renewal Grants Regulations 1996
applied: SI 1997/977 Reg.9, SI 1997/2764 Reg.5, SI 1998/217 Art.2, SI 1999/779 Art.2, Sch.
Part II, amended: SI 1997/2764 Reg.6
Reg.2, amended: SI 1997/2764 Reg.6, SI 1998/808 Reg.3, SI 1999/1523 Reg.3, SI 1999/2568 Reg.3, SI 1999/3468 Reg.3
Reg.3, revoked: SI 1997/2764 Reg.6
Reg.4, revoked: SI 1997/2764 Reg.6
Reg.5, amended: SI 1997/2764 Reg.6
Reg.5, revoked (in part): SI 1997/2764 Reg.6
Reg.5, substituted: SI 1997/977 Reg.3
Reg.7, amended: SI 1998/808 Reg.4, SI 1999/1523 Reg.4
Reg.10, amended: SI 1996/3119 Reg.3, SI 1998/808 Reg.5

NO.

1996—cont.

2890. Housing Renewal Grants Regulations 1996
—*cont.*

Reg.12, amended: SI 1997/977 Reg.4, SI 1997/ 2764 Reg.6, SI 1998/808 Reg.6, SI 1999/ 1523 Reg.5

Reg.12, revoked (in part): SI 1997/2764 Reg.6

Reg.13, amended: SI 1998/808 Reg.7

Reg.13, revoked: SI 1997/2764 Reg.6

Reg.18, amended: SI 1998/808 Reg.8

Reg.19, amended: SI 1997/977 Reg.5, SI 1998/ 808 Reg.9, SI 1999/2568 Reg.4, SI 1999/ 3468 Reg.4

Reg.25, amended: SI 1999/2568 Reg.5, SI 1999/3468 Reg.5

Reg.26, amended: SI 1998/808 Reg.10

Reg.27, amended: SI 1998/808 Reg.11, SI 1999/2568 Reg.5, SI 1999/3468 Reg.5

Reg.29, amended: SI 1998/808 Reg.12

Reg.30, substituted: SI 1998/808 Reg.13

Reg.31, amended: SI 1997/2764 Reg.6, SI 1998/808 Reg.14, SI 1999/1523 Reg.6

Reg.31, revoked (in part): SI 1997/2764 Reg.6

Reg.35, amended: SI 1999/1523 Reg.7

Reg.38, amended: SI 1998/808 Reg.15, SI 1999/1523 Reg.8

Reg.39, amended: SI 1999/1523 Reg.9

Reg.40, amended: SI 1997/2764 Reg.6

Reg.41, amended: SI 1999/1523 Reg.10

Reg.43, amended: SI 1998/808 Reg.16, SI 1999/1523 Reg.11

Reg.47A, added: SI 1999/1523 Reg.12

Reg.48, revoked: SI 1997/2764 Reg.6

Sch.1 Part IV, substituted: SI 1997/977 Reg.6

Sch.1 para.1, amended: SI 1998/808 Reg.17, SI 1999/1523 Reg.13

Sch.1 para.1, substituted: SI 1997/977 Reg.6

Sch.1 para.2, amended: SI 1997/977 Reg.9, SI 1998/808 Reg.17, SI 1999/1523 Reg.13

Sch.1 para.2, substituted: SI 1997/977 Reg.6

Sch.1 para.3, amended: SI 1997/977 Reg.6, SI 1998/808 Reg.21

Sch.1 para.3, substituted: SI 1998/808 Reg.17, SI 1999/1523 Reg.13

Sch.1 para.4, amended: SI 1997/977 Reg.6

Sch.1 para.7, revoked: SI 1997/977 Reg.6

Sch.1 para.8, referred to: SI 1998/808 Reg.21

Sch.1 para.9, referred to: SI 1998/808 Reg.21

Sch.1 para.10, referred to: SI 1998/808 Reg.21

Sch.1 para.11, referred to: SI 1998/808 Reg.21

Sch.1 para.18, amended: SI 1998/808 Reg.17, SI 1999/1523 Reg.13

Sch.1 para.18, substituted: SI 1997/977 Reg.6

Sch.2 para.4, amended: SI 1997/977 Reg.7

Sch.2 para.4, substituted: SI 1998/808 Reg.18

Sch.2 para.18, added: SI 1999/2568 Reg.6, SI 1999/3468 Reg.6

Sch.3 para.6, amended: SI 1996/3119 Reg.3

Sch.3 para.10, amended: SI 1998/808 Reg.19

Sch.3 para.11, amended: SI 1998/808 Reg.19

Sch.3 para.22, amended: SI 1999/1523 Reg.14

Sch.3 para.24, substituted: SI 1999/1523 Reg.14

Sch.3 para.26, substituted: SI 1999/1523 Reg.14

Sch.3 para.31, amended: SI 1997/977 Reg.8, SI 1999/1523 Reg.14

Sch.3 para.45, amended: SI 1997/977 Reg.8

Sch.3 para.54, amended: SI 1999/2568 Reg.7, SI 1999/3468 Reg.7

Sch.3 para.55, amended: SI 1999/2568 Reg.7, SI 1999/3468 Reg.7

Sch.3 para.59, added: SI 1998/808 Reg.19

Sch.3 para.60, added: SI 1998/808 Reg.19

NO.

1996—cont.

2890. Housing Renewal Grants Regulations 1996
—*cont.*

Sch.3 para.61, added: SI 1998/808 Reg.19

Sch.3 para.61, substituted: SI 1999/1523 Reg.14

Sch.3 para.62, added: SI 1998/808 Reg.19

Sch.3 para.63, added: SI 1999/1523 Reg.14

Sch.3 para.64, added: SI 1999/1523 Reg.14

Sch.3 para.65, added: SI 1999/1523 Reg.14

Sch.3 para.66, added: SI 1999/1523 Reg.14

Sch.4 para.1, substituted: SI 1997/2764 Reg.6

Sch.4 para.4, amended: SI 1997/2764 Reg.6

Sch.4 para.8, amended: SI 1999/1523 Reg.15

Sch.4 para.46, amended: SI 1998/808 Reg.20

Sch.4 para.47, amended: SI 1998/808 Reg.20

Sch.4 para.52, added: SI 1998/808 Reg.20

Sch.4 para.52, substituted: SI 1999/1523 Reg.15

Sch.4 para.53, added: SI 1998/808 Reg.20

Sch.4 para.54, added: SI 1999/1523 Reg.15

Sch.4 para.55, added: SI 1999/1523 Reg.15

Sch.4 para.56, added: SI 1999/1523 Reg.15

Sch.4 para.57, added: SI 1999/1523 Reg.15

2891. Housing Renewal Grants (Prescribed Form and Particulars) Regulations 1996

Reg.2, applied: SI 1998/1113 Reg.2

Sch., amended: SI 1996/3119 Reg.4, SI 1997/ 978 Reg.2, Sch.

Sch. Form, amended: SI 1998/809 Reg.2, Sch., SI 1999/1607 Reg.2, Sch., SI 1999/2624 Reg.2, Sch.

Sch.1 Form, amended: SI 1999/3470 Reg.2, Sch.1

2892. Rules of the Supreme Court (Amendment) 1996

see *Vitol Energy (Bermuda) Ltd v Pisco Shipping Co Ltd* [1998] C.L.C. 362 (CA), Hirst, L.J.

2894. Law Reform (Miscellaneous Provisions) (Scotland) Act 1990 (Commencement No.13) Order 1996

amended: SI 1996/2966 Art.2

Art.3, amended: SI 1996/2966 Art.2

2900. Residuary Body for Wales (Levies) Regulations 1996

Reg.9, amended: SI 1998/1129 Art.3, Sch.2

2903. Income Support (General) (Standard Interest Rate Amendment) (No.3) Regulations 1996

revoked: SI 1997/944 Reg.3 (with savings)

Reg.2, revoked: SI 1997/944 Reg.3 (with savings)

Reg.3, revoked: SI 1997/944 Reg.3 (with savings)

2907. Child Support Departure Direction and Consequential Amendments Regulations 1996

Reg.1, amended: SI 1999/1047 Reg.34

Reg.4, revoked (in part): SI 1999/1047 Reg.35

Reg.6, amended: SI 1999/1047 Reg.36

Reg.8, amended: SI 1998/58 Reg.7, SI 1999/ 1047 Reg.37

Reg.8, revoked (in part): SI 1999/1047 Reg.37

Reg.8A, added: SI 1999/1047 Reg.38

Reg.9, amended: SI 1999/2566 Reg.2, Sch.2 Part I, Sch.2 Part II

Reg.9, substituted: SI 1998/58 Reg.8

Reg.11, amended: SI 1998/58 Reg.9

Reg.11, revoked: SI 1999/1047 Reg.39

Reg.11A, added: SI 1998/58 Reg.10

Reg.11A, amended: SI 1998/2799 Reg.3

Reg.11A, substituted: SI 1999/1047 Reg.40

Reg.12, amended: SI 1999/2566 Reg.2, Sch.2 Part I, Sch.2 Part II

NO.

1996—cont.

2907. Child Support Departure Direction and Consequential Amendments Regulations 1996—cont.

Reg.14, amended: SI 1999/1047 Reg.41
Reg.15, amended: SI 1998/58 Reg.11, SI 1999/1047 Reg.42
Reg.17, amended: SI 1998/58 Reg.12
Reg.17, revoked (in part): SI 1998/58 Reg.12
Reg.18, amended: SI 1998/58 Reg.13, Reg.14
Reg.18, revoked (in part): SI 1998/58 Reg.13
Reg.22, amended: SI 1998/58 Reg.15
Reg.23, revoked (in part): SI 1998/58 Reg.16
Reg.25, amended: SI 1998/58 Reg.17
Reg.32, amended: SI 1998/58 Reg.18, SI 1999/1047 Reg.43
Reg.32, revoked (in part): SI 1999/1047 Reg.43
Reg.32A, added: SI 1999/1047 Reg.44
Reg.32B, added: SI 1999/1047 Reg.44
Reg.32C, added: SI 1999/1047 Reg.44
Reg.32D, added: SI 1999/1047 Reg.44
Reg.32E, added: SI 1999/1047 Reg.44
Reg.32F, added: SI 1999/1047 Reg.44
Reg.32G, added: SI 1999/1047 Reg.44
Reg.33, amended: SI 1998/2799 Reg.3
Reg.33, revoked: SI 1999/1047 Reg.45
Reg.34, revoked: SI 1999/1047 Reg.45
Reg.34A, added: SI 1998/58 Reg.19
Reg.34A, amended: SI 1999/1047 Reg.46
Reg.35, amended: SI 1999/1047 Reg.47
Reg.37, amended: SI 1998/58 Reg.20
Reg.39, amended: SI 1998/58 Reg.21
Reg.40, amended: SI 1998/58 Reg.22
Reg.41, amended: SI 1998/58 Reg.23, SI 1998/2799 Reg.3, SI 1999/1047 Reg.48
Reg.41, revoked (in part): SI 1998/58 Reg.23
Reg.42, amended: SI 1998/58 Reg.24, SI 1999/1047 Reg.49
Reg.42A, added: SI 1998/58 Reg.25
Reg.43, amended: SI 1998/58 Reg.26
Reg.44, amended: SI 1998/58 Reg.27, SI 1999/1047 Reg.50
Reg.46, amended: SI 1998/58 Reg.28
Reg.46A, added: SI 1998/58 Reg.29
Reg.46A, amended: SI 1999/1047 Reg.51
Reg.47, amended: SI 1999/1047 Reg.52
Reg.50, amended: SI 1999/1047 Reg.53
Reg.68, revoked (in part): SI 1998/58 Reg.30
Sch. para.4, amended: SI 1998/58 Reg.31
Sch. para.5, revoked: SI 1998/58 Reg.31
Sch. Table, amended: SI 1998/58 Reg.31

2911. Utilities Contracts Regulations 1996
applied: 1999 c.29 s.356
referred to: 1999 c.29 s.358

2925. Cosmetic Products (Safety) Regulations 1996
Reg.1, amended: SI 1997/2914 Reg.2
Reg.2, amended: SI 1997/2914 Reg.2, SI 1998/1727 Reg.2, SI 1999/1552 Reg.2
Reg.4, amended: SI 1997/2914 Reg.2, SI 1998/1727 Reg.2
Reg.5, amended: SI 1998/1727 Reg.2
Reg.7, amended: SI 1997/2914 Reg.2
Reg.8, amended: SI 1997/2914 Reg.2
Sch.1, amended: SI 1997/2914 Reg.2, SI 1999/1552 Reg.2
Sch.4 Part I, amended: SI 1997/2914 Reg.2, SI 1998/1727 Reg.2, SI 1999/1552 Reg.2
Sch.4 Part II, amended: SI 1997/2914 Reg.2, SI 1999/1552 Reg.2
Sch.4 Part II, revoked (in part): SI 1999/1552 Reg.2
Sch.5 Part I, amended: SI 1997/2914 Reg.2, SI 1999/1552 Reg.2

NO.

1996—cont.

2925. Cosmetic Products (Safety) Regulations 1996—cont.

Sch.5 Part II, amended: SI 1997/2914 Reg.2, SI 1999/1552 Reg.2
Sch.5 Part II, revoked (in part): SI 1999/1552 Reg.2
Sch.5A, added: SI 1998/1727 Reg.2

2935. Local Government, Planning and Land Act 1980 (Competition) (Scotland) Regulations 1996
revoked: SI 1997/1439 Reg.4
Reg.3, revoked: SI 1997/1439 Reg.4
Reg.5, revoked: SI 1997/1439 Reg.4
Reg.6, revoked: SI 1997/1439 Reg.4
Reg.7, revoked: SI 1997/1439 Reg.4
Reg.9, revoked: SI 1997/1439 Reg.4
Reg.10, revoked: SI 1997/1439 Reg.4

2936. Local Government, Planning and Land Act 1980 (Competition) (Scotland) Amendment Regulations 1996
revoked: SI 1996/2935 Reg.10
Reg.2, revoked: SI 1996/2935 Reg.10, SI 1997/1439 Reg.4
Reg.3, revoked: SI 1997/1439 Reg.4
Reg.4, revoked (in part): SI 1996/2935 Reg.10, SI 1997/1439 Reg.4

2946. Petroleum (Production) (Seaward Areas) (Amendment) Regulations 1996
referred to: SI 1999/160 Sch.10 para.1

2968. Statistics of Trade (Customs and Excise) (Amendment) Regulations 1996
revoked: SI 1997/2864 Reg.9
Reg.2, revoked: SI 1997/2864 Reg.9
Reg.4, revoked: SI 1997/2864 Reg.9

2971. Control of Pollution (Applications, Appeals and Registers) Regulations 1996
applied: SI 1997/1626 Art.3, SI 1998/1649 Reg.2, Reg.3
Reg.1, amended: SI 1998/1649 Reg.3
Reg.3, amended: SI 1998/1649 Reg.2
Reg.3, referred to: SI 1998/1649 Reg.2
Reg.5, amended: SI 1998/1649 Reg.2
Reg.10, amended: SI 1998/1649 Reg.3
Reg.11, amended: SI 1998/1649 Reg.3
Reg.15, amended: SI 1999/1006 Reg.8
Reg.16, amended: SI 1998/1649 Reg.2, SI 1999/1006 Reg.8

2972. Patents (Fees) Rules 1996
revoked: SI 1998/1778 r.1
r.1, revoked: SI 1998/1778 r.1
r.2, revoked: SI 1998/1778 r.1
r.3, revoked: SI 1998/1778 r.1
Sch. Part A, revoked: SI 1998/1778 r.1
Sch. Part B, revoked: SI 1998/1778 r.1

2986. London Docklands Development Corporation (Alteration of Boundaries) (Surrey Docks) Order 1996
applied: SI 1997/2946 Art.6
Art.4, revoked: SI 1997/2946 Art.6
Art.8, revoked (in part): SI 1997/2946 Art.6

2987. Disability Discrimination Code of Practice (Goods, Services, Facilities and Premises) Order 1996
see *Rose v Bouchet* 1999 S.C.L.R. 1004 (Sh Pr), CGB Nicholson Q.C., Sheriff Principal
referred to: SI 1999/1992 Art.3

2991. Insurance Companies (Reserves) (Tax) Regulations 1996
Reg.8, amended: SI 1999/1408 Reg.7
Reg.8A, added: SI 1999/1408 Reg.7
Reg.8B, added: SI 1999/1408 Reg.7

NO.

NO.

1996—cont.

1996—cont.

2999. Beef (Marketing Payment) (No.2) Regulations 1996
applied: SI 1997/1986 Reg.3
Reg.3, amended: SI 1997/195 Reg.2
Reg.4, amended: SI 1997/195 Reg.2

3010. Merchant Shipping (Dangerous or Noxious Liquid Substances in Bulk) Regulations 1996
Reg.14, amended: SI 1998/1153 Reg.2
Reg.15, amended: SI 1998/1153 Reg.2

3013. Motor Vehicles (Approval) Regulations 1996
Part II, applied: SI 1997/1459 Reg.3
Part III, applied: SI 1997/1459 Reg.3
Reg.2, amended: SI 1998/1008 Reg.3
Reg.3, amended: SI 1998/1008 Reg.4, SI 1999/2082 Reg.3, SI 1999/3226 Reg.3
Reg.4, amended: SI 1997/1366 Reg.3, SI 1998/1008 Reg.5
Reg.5, amended: SI 1998/1008 Reg.6, SI 1999/2082 Reg.4, SI 1999/3226 Reg.4
Reg.6, amended: SI 1997/1366 Reg.4, SI 1998/1008 Reg.7
Reg.7, amended: SI 1997/1366 Reg.5
Reg.7, applied: SI 1997/1459 Reg.4, Reg.5
Reg.10, applied: SI 1997/1459 Reg.7
Reg.11, applied: SI 1997/1459 Reg.4, Reg.7
Reg.12, amended: SI 1998/1008 Reg.8, SI 1999/2082 Reg.5, SI 1999/3226 Reg.5
Reg.12A, added: SI 1997/1366 Reg.6
Reg.12A, applied: SI 1997/1459 Reg.9
Reg.14, amended: SI 1997/1366 Reg.7, SI 1997/2934 Reg.2, SI 1998/1008 Reg.9
Sch.1 para.1, amended: SI 1999/3226 Reg.6
Sch.1 para.1, revoked (in part): SI 1999/3226 Reg.6
Sch.1 para.1A, added: SI 1999/2082 Reg.6
Sch.1 para.1B, added: SI 1999/3226 Reg.6
Sch.1 para.4, added: SI 1998/1008 Reg.10, Sch.1
Sch.2 Item 2, amended: SI 1998/1008 Reg.11, Sch.2 para.1
Sch.2 Item 3, amended: SI 1998/1008 Reg.11, Sch.2 para.2
Sch.2 Item 4, amended: SI 1998/1008 Reg.11, Sch.2 para.3
Sch.2 Item 6, amended: SI 1998/1008 Reg.11, Sch.2 para.4
Sch.2 Item 6, applied: SI 1997/1459 Reg.5
Sch.2 Item 7, amended: SI 1998/1008 Reg.11, Sch.2 para.5
Sch.2 Item 8, applied: SI 1997/1459 Reg.5
Sch.2 Item 10, amended: SI 1998/1008 Reg.11, Sch.2 para.6
Sch.2 Item 12, amended: SI 1998/1008 Reg.11, Sch.2 para.7
Sch.2 Item 14, amended: SI 1998/1008 Reg.11, Sch.2 para.8
Sch.2 Item 15, amended: SI 1998/1008 Reg.11, Sch.2 para.9
Sch.2 Item 16, amended: SI 1998/1008 Reg.11, Sch.2 para.10
Sch.2 Item 17, amended: SI 1998/1008 Reg.11, Sch.2 para.11
Sch.2 Item 17, applied: SI 1997/1459 Reg.5
Sch.2 Item 18, amended: SI 1998/1008 Reg.11, Sch.2 para.12
Sch.2 Item 18, applied: SI 1997/1459 Reg.5
Sch.2 Item 19, amended: SI 1998/1008 Reg.11, Sch.2 para.13
Sch.2 Item 20, applied: SI 1997/1459 Reg.5
Sch.2 Item 21, applied: SI 1997/1459 Reg.5
Sch.2 Item 22, applied: SI 1997/1459 Reg.5
Sch.2 Table, applied: SI 1997/1459 Reg.5

3013. Motor Vehicles (Approval) Regulations 1996
—cont.
Sch.3 Item 1, amended: SI 1998/1008 Reg.11, Sch.3 para.1
Sch.3 Item 4, amended: SI 1998/1008 Reg.11, Sch.3 para.2
Sch.3 Item 5, amended: SI 1998/1008 Reg.11, Sch.3 para.3
Sch.3 Item 6, applied: SI 1997/1459 Reg.5
Sch.3 Table, applied: SI 1997/1459 Reg.5

3014. Motor Vehicles (Type Approval for Goods Vehicles) (Great Britain) (Amendment) (No.2) Regulations 1996
Reg.7, amended: SI 1997/1365 Reg.2

3015. Motor Vehicles (Type Approval) (Great Britain) (Amendment) (No.2) Regulations 1996
Reg.8, amended: SI 1997/1367 Reg.2

3017. Road Vehicles (Construction and Use) (Amendment) (No.6) Regulations 1996
Reg.4, amended: SI 1997/1458 Reg.2

3021. General Optical Council (Registration and Enrolment (Amendment) Rules) Order of Council 1996
revoked: SI 1998/73, SI 1998/73 Sch. para.3
Sch. para.2, revoked: SI 1998/73, SI 1998/73 Sch. para.3
Sch. para.3, revoked: SI 1998/73, SI 1998/73 Sch. para.3

3032. Civil Aviation (Joint Financing) (Second Amendment) Regulations 1996
revoked: SI 1997/2937 Reg.3, Sch.1
Reg.2, revoked: SI 1997/2937 Reg.3, Sch.1

3034. Medicines (Veterinary Drugs) (Pharmacy and Merchants' List) (Amendment) Order 1996
revoked: SI 1998/1044 Art.9, Sch.
Art.2, revoked: SI 1998/1044 Art.9, Sch.
Sch., revoked: SI 1998/1044 Art.9, Sch.

3038. Road Traffic (Special Parking Area) (Royal Borough of Kingston upon Thames) Order 1996
Sch.2 para.21, amended: SI 1998/273 Art.2

3051. A23 Trunk Road (Croydon) Red Route (Clearway) Traffic Order 1996
Art.2, amended: SI 1999/272 Art.2, Sch. Part B
Art.9, amended: SI 1999/272 Art.2, Sch. Part B

3052. A316 Trunk Road (Richmond) (No.1) Red Route Traffic Order 1996
Art.2, amended: SI 1999/272 Art.2, Sch. Part A
Art.9, amended: SI 1999/272 Art.2, Sch. Part A

3054. Medicines (Pharmacies) (Applications for Registration and Fees) Amendment Regulations 1996
revoked: SI 1997/2876 Reg.3
Reg.2, revoked: SI 1997/2876 Reg.3
Reg.3, revoked: SI 1997/2876 Reg.3

3066. Education (Grants for Education Support and Training) (England) (Amendment) Regulations 1996
revoked: SI 1997/514 Reg.13
Reg.3, revoked: SI 1997/514 Reg.13
Reg.4, revoked: SI 1997/514 Reg.13
Reg.5, revoked: SI 1997/514 Reg.13
Reg.6, revoked: SI 1997/514 Reg.13
Reg.7, revoked: SI 1997/514 Reg.13

3070. Non-Domestic Rating Contributions (Scotland) Regulations 1996
Reg.2, amended: SI 1997/2867 Reg.2
Sch.1 para.2, amended: SI 1997/2867 Reg.3
Sch.1 para.2, substituted: SSI 1999/153 Reg.2
Sch.1 para.6A, added: SI 1997/2867 Reg.3
Sch.1 para.6B, added: SI 1997/2867 Reg.3

1996—cont.

3070. Non-Domestic Rating Contributions (Scotland) Regulations 1996—*cont.*
Sch.1 para.6C, added: SI 1997/2867 Reg.3
Sch.1 para.6C, revoked: SI 1998/2957 Reg.2
Sch.1 para.7, amended: SSI 1999/153 Reg.3
Sch.1 para.7A, added: SSI 1999/153 Reg.4
Sch.1 para.8, added: SSI 1999/153 Reg.5
Sch.1 para.8A, added: SSI 1999/153 Reg.6
Sch.2 para.1, amended: SI 1997/2867 Reg.4
Sch.2 para.2, revoked (in part): SI 1997/2867 Reg.4
Sch.2 para.4, amended: SI 1997/2867 Reg.4

3079. Grants for Pre-school Education (Pre-scribed Children) (Scotland) Order 1996
Art.2, amended: SI 1999/79 Art.2

3084. Legal Officers (Annual Fees) Order 1996
revoked: SI 1997/1890 Art.3
Art.2, revoked: SI 1997/1890 Art.3
Art.3, revoked: SI 1997/1890 Art.3
Sch. Table I, revoked: SI 1997/1890 Art.3
Sch. Table I, substituted: SI 1997/1890 Sch. Table I
Sch. Table II, revoked: SI 1997/1890 Art.3
Sch. Table II, substituted: SI 1997/1890 Sch. Table II
Appendix.para.1, revoked: SI 1997/1890 Art.3
Appendix.para.4, revoked: SI 1997/1890 Art.3

3085. Ecclesiastical Judges and Legal Officers (Fees) Order 1996
revoked: SI 1997/1889 Art.2
Art.2, revoked: SI 1997/1889 Art.2
Art.3, revoked: SI 1997/1889 Art.2
Sch. Table I, revoked: SI 1997/1889 Art.2
Sch. Table I, substituted: SI 1997/1889 Art.1, Sch
Sch. Table II, revoked: SI 1997/1889 Art.2
Sch. Table II, substituted: SI 1997/1889 Art.1, Sch.
Sch. Table III, revoked: SI 1997/1889 Art.2
Sch. Table III, substituted: SI 1997/1889 Art.1, Sch.
Sch. Table IV, revoked: SI 1997/1889 Art.2
Sch. Table IV, substituted: SI 1997/1889 Art.1, Sch.
Sch. Table V, revoked: SI 1997/1889 Art.2
Sch. Table V, substituted: SI 1997/1889 Art.1, Sch.
Sch. Table VI, revoked: SI 1997/1889 Art.2
Sch. Table VI, substituted: SI 1997/1889 Art.1, Sch.
Sch. Table VII, revoked: SI 1997/1889 Art.2
Sch. Table VII, substituted: SI 1997/1889 Art.1, Sch.

3089. Civil Aviation (Route Charges for Navigation Services) (Second Amendment) Regulations 1996
revoked: SI 1997/2920 Reg.2, Sch.1
Reg.2, revoked: SI 1997/2920 Reg.2, Sch.1

3096. Contracting Out of Functions (Court Staff) (Amendment) Order 1996
revoked: SI 1999/1013 Art.3
Art.2, revoked: SI 1999/1013 Art.3

3099. Education (School Inspection) (No.2) (Amendment) (No.2) Regulations 1996
revoked: SI 1997/995 Reg.1
Reg.2, revoked: SI 1997/995 Reg.1

3101. Nurses, Midwives and Health Visitors Act 1979 (Amendment) Regulations 1996
referred to: SI 1996/3103
revoked: 1997 c.24 s.23, Sch.6

1996—cont.

3104. Environmentally Sensitive Areas (England) Designation Orders (Amendment) Regulations 1996
Reg.2, revoked (in part): SI 1998/1295 Reg.3, Reg.4, SI 1999/2231 Reg.3, Reg.4
Reg.3, revoked (in part): SI 1998/1295 Reg.3
Sch. Part II, referred to: SI 1998/1295 Reg.3, Reg.4

3117. Nursery Education (Amendment) Regulations 1996
revoked (in part): SI 1999/1441 Reg.5
Reg.3, revoked (in part): SI 1999/1441 Reg.5
Reg.4, revoked (in part): SI 1999/1441 Reg.5
Reg.5, revoked (in part): SI 1999/1441 Reg.5
Reg.6, revoked (in part): SI 1999/1441 Reg.5

3121. Industrial and Provident Societies (Forms and Procedure) Regulations 1996
Reg.12, applied: SI 1999/740 Sch. para.14

3122. Allocation of Housing and Homelessness (Review Procedures and Amendment) Regulations 1996
Reg.2, revoked: SI 1999/71 Reg.10 (with savings)
Reg.3, revoked: SI 1999/71 Reg.10 (with savings)
Reg.4, revoked: SI 1999/71 Reg.10 (with savings)
Reg.5, revoked: SI 1999/71 Reg.10 (with savings)
Reg.6, amended: SI 1997/631 Reg.6
Reg.6, revoked: SI 1999/71 Reg.10 (with savings)
Reg.7, revoked: SI 1999/71 Reg.10 (with savings)
Reg.8, amended: SI 1997/631 Reg.6
Reg.8, revoked: SI 1999/71 Reg.10 (with savings)

3123. Countryside Stewardship (Amendment) (No.2) Regulations 1996
revoked: SI 1998/1327 Reg.2, Sch.2
Reg.2, revoked: SI 1998/1327 Reg.2, Sch.2

3124. Products of Animal Origin (Import and Export) Regulations 1996
amended: SI 1997/1881 Reg.17
applied: SI 1997/1881 Reg.17, SI 1998/994 Reg.56, SI 1999/221 Reg.4
referred to: SI 1999/1103 Reg.4
Part II, applied: SI 1997/389 Reg.6, SI 1997/1905 Reg.3
Part III, applied: SI 1998/1135 Reg.3, SI 1999/1103 Reg.5
Reg.1, amended: SI 1997/3023 Reg.3, SI 1998/994 Reg.58
Reg.2, amended: SI 1999/221 Reg.2
Reg.5, applied: SI 1996/3125 Reg.14
Reg.6, amended: SI 1997/3023 Reg.4
Reg.13, applied: SI 1996/3125 Reg.14, SI 1997/1881 Reg.15
Reg.20, amended: SI 1997/3023 Reg.3
Reg.21, amended: SI 1998/994 Reg.58
Reg.22, amended: SI 1998/994 Reg.58
Reg.23, amended: SI 1998/994 Reg.58
Reg.24, amended: SI 1998/994 Reg.58
Reg.25, amended: SI 1998/994 Reg.58
Reg.25, applied: SI 1996/3125 Reg.14
Reg.30, substituted: SI 1997/3023 Reg.5
Reg.30A, added: SI 1997/3023 Reg.6
Sch.1 para.1, substituted: SI 1997/3023 Reg.7
Sch.1 para.1A, added: SI 1997/3023 Reg.7
Sch.1 para.1B, added: SI 1997/3023 Reg.7
Sch.1 para.4A, added: SI 1997/3023 Reg.7
Sch.1 para.4B, added: SI 1997/3023 Reg.7
Sch.1 para.5, substituted: SI 1997/3023 Reg.7

NO.

3124. Products of Animal Origin (Import and Export) Regulations 1996—*cont.*
Sch.2 para.1, substituted: SI 1998/994 Reg.58
Sch.2 para.2, substituted: SI 1998/994 Reg.58
Sch.2 para.3, substituted: SI 1998/994 Reg.58
Sch.2 para.4, substituted: SI 1998/994 Reg.58
Sch.2 para.5, amended: SI 1999/683 Reg.3
Sch.4, substituted: SI 1997/3023 Reg.8, Sch.1
Sch.4A, added: SI 1997/3023 Reg.9, Sch.2
Sch.4B, added: SI 1997/3023 Reg.9, Sch.2
Sch.4C, added: SI 1997/3023 Reg.9, Sch.2
Sch.6 para.4, revoked: SI 1998/994 Reg.59, Sch.5
Sch.6 para.5, revoked: SI 1998/994 Reg.59, Sch.5

3126. Occupational Pension Schemes (Winding Up) Regulations 1996
applied: SI 1997/784 Reg.8
Reg.2, applied: SI 1997/664 Art.11, SI 1997/785 Reg.2
Reg.3, amended: SI 1999/3198 Reg.11
Reg.12, amended: SI 1997/786 Reg.3, Sch.1 para.17

3127. Occupational Pension Schemes (Investment) Regulations 1996
Part III, amended: SI 1999/1849 Reg.2
Reg.1A, added: SI 1997/819 Reg.6
Reg.2, amended: SI 1999/1849 Reg.2
Reg.6, amended: SI 1997/819 Reg.6, SI 1999/1849 Reg.2
Reg.6, applied: SI 1997/785 Reg.8
Reg.7, amended: SI 1997/819 Reg.6
Reg.9, amended: SI 1997/786 Reg.3, Sch.1 para.18
Reg.11A, added: SI 1999/1849 Reg.2

3128. Occupational Pension Schemes (Deficiency on Winding Up etc.) Regulations 1996
applied: SI 1997/786 Reg.3, Sch.1 para.19
Reg.2, amended: SI 1997/786 Reg.3, Sch.1 para.19, SI 1997/3038 Reg.5
Reg.4, amended: SI 1997/786 Reg.3, Sch.1 para.19
Reg.5, amended: SI 1999/3198 Reg.4
Reg.6, amended: SI 1999/3198 Reg.4
Sch.2 para.4, revoked: SI 1997/786 Reg.3, Reg.4, Sch.1 para.19, Sch.2

3138. Control of Substances Hazardous to Health (Amendment) Regulations 1996
revoked: SI 1999/437 Reg.18
Reg.2, revoked: SI 1999/437 Reg.18
Sch., amended: SI 1997/11 Reg.2
Sch., revoked: SI 1999/437 Reg.18

3139. Offshore Installations (Safety Zones) (No.8) Order 1996
revoked: SI 1997/735 Art.3, Sch.2

3142. Arable Area Payments Regulations 1996
amended: SI 1998/3169 Reg.4
applied: SI 1999/672 Art.2, Sch.1
Reg.2, amended: SI 1997/2969 Reg.4, SI 1998/3169 Reg.3, SI 1999/8 Reg.2
Reg.6, amended: SI 1998/3169 Reg.3
Reg.7, revoked: SI 1998/3169 Reg.3
Reg.9, amended: SI 1997/2969 Reg.5
Reg.11, amended: SI 1997/2969 Reg.6, Reg.8
Reg.11A, added: SI 1998/3169 Reg.3
Reg.12, amended: SI 1997/2969 Reg.7, Reg.8
Reg.13, amended: SI 1998/3169 Reg.3
Reg.14, amended: SI 1997/2969 Reg.8
Reg.19, see *R. v Northallerton Magistrates Court Ex p. Dove* (1999) 163 J.P. 657 (QBD), Lord Bingham of Cornhill, L.C.J.
Sch.1, revoked: SI 1998/3169 Reg.3

NO.

3142. Arable Area Payments Regulations 1996—*cont.*
Sch.1 Part I, amended: SI 1997/2969 Reg.9
Sch.1 Part I, revoked: SI 1998/3169 Reg.3
Sch.1 Part II, amended: SI 1997/2969 Reg.9
Sch.1 Part II, revoked: SI 1998/3169 Reg.3
Sch.2 Part A, amended: SI 1998/3169 Reg.3
Sch.2 Part B, amended: SI 1998/3169 Reg.3
Sch.2 para.1, amended: SI 1997/2969 Reg.10
Sch.2 para.11, amended: SI 1997/2969 Reg.10
Sch.2 para.13, amended: SI 1997/2969 Reg.10
Sch.2 para.14, amended: SI 1997/2969 Reg.10
Sch.2 para.18, amended: SI 1997/2969 Reg.10
Sch.2 para.23, amended: SI 1997/2969 Reg.10
Sch.2 para.25, amended: SI 1997/2969 Reg.10
Sch.3 para.2, amended: SI 1997/2969 Reg.11
Sch.3 para.3, amended: SI 1997/2969 Reg.12

3148. London Docklands Development Corporation (Alteration of Boundaries) (Limehouse and Wapping) Order 1996
applied: SI 1997/2946 Art.6
Art.4, revoked: SI 1997/2946 Art.6
Art.8, revoked (in part): SI 1997/2946 Art.6

3151. Advanced Television Services Regulations 1996
Reg.11, applied: SI 1997/1856 Art.2
Sch.1, substituted: SI 1996/3197 Reg.3
Sch.2, substituted: SI 1996/3197 Reg.4

3152. Registration of Births, Deaths and Marriages (Fees) Order 1996
revoked: SI 1997/2939 Art.3
Art.3, revoked: SI 1997/2939 Art.3
Sch., revoked: SI 1997/2939 Art.3

3153. United Nations Arms Embargoes (Somalia, Liberia and Rwanda) (Isle of Man) Order 1996
Art.2, amended: SI 1998/1508 Art.2
Art.3, amended: SI 1997/280 Art.2
Art.7, amended: SI 1997/280 Art.2
Art.8, amended: SI 1997/280 Art.2, SI 1998/1508 Art.3
Art.10, amended: SI 1997/280 Art.2
Sch. para.4, amended: SI 1998/1508 Art.3

3154. United Nations Arms Embargoes (Somalia, Liberia and Rwanda) (Channel Islands) Order 1996
Art.2, amended: SI 1998/1507 Art.2
Art.3, amended: SI 1997/279 Art.2
Art.7, amended: SI 1997/279 Art.2, SI 1998/1507 Art.3
Art.8, amended: SI 1997/279 Art.2, SI 1998/1507 Art.4
Art.10, amended: SI 1997/279 Art.2
Sch. para.4, amended: SI 1998/1507 Art.4

3157. European Police Office (Legal Capacities) Order 1996
revoked: SI 1997/2973 Art.2

3158. Licensing (Northern Ireland) Order 1996
applied: SI 1996/3159 (NI.23) Art.5, Art.8, Art.21, SI 1999/3145 Art.7
Art.5, referred to: SI 1999/3144 (NI.10) Art.4
Art.30, applied: SI 1996/3159 (NI.23) Art.3, SI 1999/3144 (NI.10) Art.6
Art.42, referred to: SI 1999/3144 (NI.10) Art.4
Art.43, referred to: SI 1999/3144 (NI.10) Art.4
Art.44, referred to: SI 1999/3144 (NI.10) Art.4
Art.45, referred to: SI 1999/3144 (NI.10) Art.4
Art.47, referred to: SI 1999/3144 (NI.10) Art.4
Art.84, amended: SI 1999/1736 Art.12, Sch.6
Art.84, applied: SI 1999/1736 Art.12, Sch.6
Sch.11 para.1, revoked: SI 1996/3160 (NI.24) Sch.7

NO.

3159. Registration of Clubs (Northern Ireland) Order 1996
applied: SI 1996/3158 (NI.22) Art.78
referred to: SI 1996/3158 (NI.22) Art.67, Art.68
Art.5, referred to: SI 1999/3144 (NI.10) Art.9
Art.24, referred to: SI 1999/3144 (NI.10) Art.8
Art.26, referred to: SI 1999/3144 (NI.10) Art.8, Art.9

3160. Criminal Justice (Northern Ireland) Order 1996
amended: 1997 c.43 Sch.1 para.12, Sch.1 para.13
Part II, applied: SI 1998/2839 (NI.20) Art.8
Part II, referred to: SI 1998/2839 (NI.20) Art.2
Art.2, amended: SI 1998/1504 (NI.9) Art.65, Sch.5 para.51, Sch.6, SI 1998/2839 (NI.20) Art.11, Sch. para.13
Art.4, applied: SI 1998/2839 (NI.20) Art.6
Art.6, referred to: 1999 c.23 s.2
Art.7, amended: SI 1998/1504 (NI.9) Art.65, Sch.5 para.52
Art.9, amended: SI 1998/1504 (NI.9) Art.65, Sch.6, SI 1998/2839 (NI.20) Art.11, Sch. para.14
Art.17, amended: SI 1998/2839 (NI.20) Art.11, Sch. para.15
Art.18, amended: SI 1998/1504 (NI.9) Art.65, Sch.5 para.53
Art.19, amended: SI 1998/2839 (NI.20) Art.11, Sch. para.16
Art.19, referred to: SI 1998/2839 (NI.20) Art.10
Art.20, amended: SI 1998/1504 (NI.9) Art.65, Sch.6
Art.26, amended: SI 1998/2798 Art.2, Sch.1 para.8, Sch.1 para.9, Sch.1 para.10
Art.26, applied: 1997 c.43 Sch.1 para.12, Sch.1 para.13, SI 1997/1776 Art.2, Sch.1 para.8, Sch.1 para.9, Sch.1 para.10, SI 1998/2798 Art.2, Sch.1 para.8, Sch.1 para.9, Sch.1 para.10, SI 1999/1748 Art.8, Sch.4 para.2
Art.27, amended: SI 1998/2798 Art.2, Sch.1 para.8, Sch.1 para.9, Sch.1 para.10
Art.27, applied: 1997 c.43 Sch.1 para.12, Sch.1 para.13, SI 1997/1776 Art.2, Sch.1 para.8, Sch.1 para.9, Sch.1 para.10, SI 1998/2798 Art.2, Sch.1 para.8, Sch.1 para.9, Sch.1 para.10, SI 1999/1748 Art.8, Sch.4 para.2
Art.28, amended: SI 1998/2798 Art.2, Sch.1 para.8, Sch.1 para.9, Sch.1 para.10
Art.28, applied: 1997 c.43 Sch.1 para.12, Sch.1 para.13, SI 1997/1776 Art.2, Sch.1 para.8, Sch.1 para.9, Sch.1 para.10, SI 1998/2798 Art.2, Sch.1 para.8, Sch.1 para.9, Sch.1 para.10, SI 1999/1748 Art.8, Sch.4 para.2
Art.29, amended: SI 1998/1504 (NI.9) Art.65, Sch.5 para.54
Art.30, amended: SI 1998/1504 (NI.9) Art.65, Sch.5 para.55
Art.31, amended: SI 1998/1504 (NI.9) Art.65, Sch.5 para.56
Art.34, amended: SI 1998/1504 (NI.9) Art.65, Sch.5 para.57
Art.37, applied: SI 1998/1504 (NI.9) Art.39
Art.38, amended: SI 1997/277 (NI.3) Art.5
Art.42, revoked (in part): 1998 c.40 s.9, Sch.1 para.10, Sch.2 Part II
Art.43, amended: 1998 c.40 s.9, Sch.1 para.10, Sch.2 Part II
Art.47, amended: SI 1999/2789 (NI.8) Art.40, Sch.1 para.5

NO.

3160. Criminal Justice (Northern Ireland) Order 1996—*cont.*
Sch.1 para.5, amended: SI 1998/2839 (NI.20) Art.11, Sch. para.17
Sch.2, applied: SI 1998/1504 (NI.9) Art.37, SI 1998/2839 (NI.20) Art.11
Sch.2, referred to: SI 1998/2839 (NI.20) Art.11
Sch.2 para.1, amended: SI 1998/2839 (NI.20) Art.11, Sch. para.2
Sch.2 para.2, amended: SI 1998/2839 (NI.20) Art.11, Sch. para.3
Sch.2 para.3, amended: SI 1998/1504 (NI.9) Art.65, Sch.5 para.58
Sch.2 para.4, amended: SI 1998/1504 (NI.9) Art.65, Sch.5 para.58, SI 1998/2839 (NI.20) Art.11, Sch. para.4
Sch.2 para.5, amended: SI 1998/2839 (NI.20) Art.11, Sch. para.5
Sch.2 para.7, amended: SI 1998/2839 (NI.20) Art.11, Sch. para.6
Sch.2 para.8, amended: SI 1998/2839 (NI.20) Art.11, Sch. para.7
Sch.2 para.9, amended: SI 1998/2839 (NI.20) Art.11, Sch. para.8
Sch.2 para.11, amended: SI 1998/1504 (NI.9) Art.65, Sch.5 para.58
Sch.2 para.12, amended: SI 1998/2839 (NI.20) Art.11, Sch. para.9
Sch.2 para.14A, added: SI 1998/2839 (NI.20) Art.11, Sch. para.10
Sch.2 para.16, amended: SI 1998/2839 (NI.20) Art.11, Sch. para.11
Sch.2 para.18, amended: SI 1998/1504 (NI.9) Art.65, Sch.5 para.58, SI 1998/2839 (NI.20) Art.11, Sch. para.12
Sch.5 para.3, revoked: SI 1998/1504 (NI.9) Art.65, Sch.6
Sch.7, revoked (in part): SI 1998/1504 (NI.9) Art.65, Sch.6

3172. Education (Chief Inspector of Schools in Wales) Order 1996
revoked: SI 1997/288 Art.3
Art.3, revoked: SI 1997/288 Art.3

3179. Local Government Act 1988 (Defined Activities) (Exemptions) (Wales) (Amendment) Order 1996
revoked: SI 1998/2188 Art.3
Art.3, revoked: SI 1998/2188 Art.3
Art.4, revoked: SI 1998/2188 Art.3
Art.5, revoked: SI 1998/2188 Art.3

3183. Bovine Spongiform Encephalopathy (No.2) Order 1996
Art.4, amended: SI 1998/3071 Art.2, SI 1999/646 Art.35, Sch.6 Part II, SI 1999/921 Art.2
Art.6, amended: SI 1999/921 Art.2
Art.7, applied: SI 1996/3184 Art.4
Art.8, amended: SI 1999/921 Art.2
Art.10, amended: SI 1997/2387 Art.2
Art.16, amended: SI 1999/921 Art.2
Sch. Form F, amended: SI 1997/2387 Art.2
Sch. Form G, amended: SI 1997/2387 Art.2

3184. Bovine Spongiform Encephalopathy Compensation Order 1996
applied: SI 1998/3070 Reg.5
Art.3, amended: SI 1997/2365 Art.2
Art.4, amended: SI 1997/2365 Art.2
Sch.2 para.3, substituted: SI 1997/2365 Art.2

3185. Specified Bovine Material (No.3) (Amendment) Order 1996
revoked: SI 1997/617 Art.29
Art.2, revoked: SI 1997/617 Art.29

NO.

1996—cont.

3188. Merchant Shipping (High-Speed Craft) Regulations 1996
applied: SI 1996/3243 Sch Part I, SI 1998/2514 Reg.3, SI 1998/2515 Reg.3, SI 1999/1957 Reg.4
referred to: SI 1997/1509 Reg.4, SI 1998/1011 Reg.1, SI 1998/1012 Reg.1, SI 1998/2070 Reg.3, SI 1999/2722 Reg.3
Reg.4, amended: SI 1999/1957 Reg.3, Sch.1 para.4
Reg.4, applied: SI 1997/647 Reg.6

3189. County Court Fees (Amendment) Order 1996
revoked: SI 1999/689 Art.8 (with savings), Sch.2 (with savings)
Art.3, revoked: SI 1997/787 Art.3, SI 1999/689 Art.8 (with savings), Sch.2 (with savings)
Art.4, revoked: SI 1999/689 Art.8 (with savings), Sch.2 (with savings)
Art.5, revoked: SI 1999/689 Art.8 (with savings), Sch.2 (with savings)
Art.6, revoked: SI 1999/689 Art.8 (with savings), Sch.2 (with savings)
Art.7, revoked: SI 1999/689 Art.8 (with savings), Sch.2 (with savings)
Art.8, revoked: SI 1999/689 Art.8 (with savings), Sch.2 (with savings)
Art.9, revoked: SI 1999/689 Art.8 (with savings), Sch.2 (with savings)
Art.10, revoked: SI 1999/689 Art.8 (with savings), Sch.2 (with savings)
Art.11, revoked: SI 1999/689 Art.8 (with savings), Sch.2 (with savings)

3190. Family Proceedings Fees (Amendment) Order 1996
revoked: SI 1999/690 Art.7 (with savings), Sch.2 (with savings)
Art.3, revoked: SI 1999/690 Art.7 (with savings), Sch.2 (with savings)
Art.4, revoked: SI 1997/788 Art.3
Art.5, revoked: SI 1997/788 Art.3, SI 1999/690 Art.7 (with savings), Sch.2 (with savings)
Art.6, revoked: SI 1999/690 Art.7 (with savings), Sch.2 (with savings)
Art.7, revoked: SI 1999/690 Art.7 (with savings), Sch.2 (with savings)
Art.8, revoked: SI 1999/690 Art.7 (with savings), Sch.2 (with savings)
Art.9, revoked: SI 1999/690 Art.7 (with savings), Sch.2 (with savings)
Art.10, revoked: SI 1999/690 Art.7 (with savings), Sch.2 (with savings)
Art.11, revoked: SI 1999/690 Art.7 (with savings), Sch.2 (with savings)
Art.12, revoked: SI 1999/690 Art.7 (with savings), Sch.2 (with savings)
Art.13, revoked: SI 1999/690 Art.7 (with savings), Sch.2 (with savings)

3191. Supreme Court Fees (Amendment) Order 1996
revoked: SI 1999/687 Art.8 (with savings), Sch.2 (with savings)
Art.3, see *R. v Lord Chancellor Ex p. Witham* [1998] Q.B. 575 (QBD), Laws, J
Art.3, revoked: SI 1999/687 Art.8 (with savings), Sch.2 (with savings)
Art.4, revoked: SI 1999/687 Art.8 (with savings), Sch.2 (with savings)
Art.5, revoked: SI 1999/687 Art.8 (with savings), Sch.2 (with savings)
Art.6, revoked: SI 1999/687 Art.8 (with savings), Sch.2 (with savings)
Art.7, revoked: SI 1999/687 Art.8 (with savings), Sch.2 (with savings)

NO.

1996—cont.

3191. Supreme Court Fees (Amendment) Order 1996—*cont.*
Art.8, revoked: SI 1999/687 Art.8 (with savings), Sch.2 (with savings)
Art.9, revoked: SI 1999/687 Art.8 (with savings), Sch.2 (with savings)
Art.10, revoked: SI 1999/687 Art.8 (with savings), Sch.2 (with savings)

3193. Medicines (Products Other Than Veterinary Drugs) (Prescription Only) Amendment (No.2) Order 1996
revoked: SI 1997/1830 Art.16, Sch.6
Art.2, revoked: SI 1997/1830 Art.16, Sch.6
Art.3, revoked: SI 1997/1830 Art.16, Sch.6
Art.4, revoked: SI 1997/1830 Art.16, Sch.6
Art.5, revoked: SI 1997/1830 Art.16, Sch.6
Sch., revoked: SI 1997/1830 Art.16, Sch.6

3195. Social Security (Child Maintenance Bonus) Regulations 1996
Reg.1, amended: SI 1997/454 Reg.8, SI 1998/563 Reg.2
Reg.3, amended: SI 1997/454 Reg.8, SI 1998/563 Reg.2
Reg.4, amended: SI 1997/454 Reg.8, SI 1998/563 Reg.2
Reg.5, amended: SI 1997/454 Reg.8
Reg.6, amended: SI 1997/454 Reg.8
Reg.7, amended: SI 1997/454 Reg.8
Reg.10, amended: SI 1997/454 Reg.8, SI 1998/563 Reg.2
Reg.10, revoked (in part): SI 1998/563 Reg.2
Reg.14, amended: SI 1999/2566 Reg.2, Sch.2 Part I, Sch.2 Part II
Reg.15, amended: SI 1997/454 Reg.8
Reg.16, amended: SI 1997/454 Reg.8

3196. Child Support (Miscellaneous Amendments) (No.2) Regulations 1996
Reg.16, amended: SI 1999/1510 Art.44

3200. Fireworks (Safety) Regulations 1996
revoked: SI 1997/2294 Reg.1

3201. Children (Scotland) Act 1995 (Commencement No.3) Order 1996
Art.3, amended: SI 1997/744 Art.2
Art.4, added: SI 1997/744 Art.3

3204. Homelessness (Suitability of Accommodation) Order 1996
Art.3, added: SI 1997/1741 Art.2

3208. Amusements with Prizes (Variation of Monetary Limits) Order 1996
revoked: SI 1999/1259 Art.3, Sch.
Art.2, revoked: SI 1999/1259 Art.3, Sch.
Art.3, revoked: SI 1999/1259 Art.3, Sch.

3211. Unfair Arbitration Agreements (Specified Amount) Order 1996
revoked: SI 1999/2167 Art.2
Art.2, revoked: SI 1999/2167 Art.2

3212. Severn Bridges Tolls Order 1996
revoked: SI 1997/2947 Art.3
Art.1, revoked: SI 1997/2947 Art.3
Art.2, revoked: SI 1997/2947 Art.3
Art.3, revoked: SI 1997/2947 Art.3

3215. High Court and County Courts (Allocation of Arbitration Proceedings) Order 1996
Art.5, amended: SI 1999/1010 Art.2

3218. County Court (Amendment No.3) Rules 1996
r.3, revoked: SI 1998/1899 r.5

3219. Rules of the Supreme Court (Amendment No.2) 1996
amended: SI 1997/415 r.9
r.1, amended: SI 1997/415 r.9
r.9, revoked: SI 1998/1898 r.20

NO.

1996—cont.

3241. Beef Special Premium Regulations 1996
Reg.2, amended: SI 1999/1179 Reg.4
Reg.2A, added: SI 1999/1179 Reg.5
Reg.3, amended: SI 1999/1179 Reg.6
Reg.4, amended: SI 1999/1179 Reg.7
Reg.5, amended: SI 1999/1179 Reg.8
Reg.5A, added: SI 1999/1179 Reg.9
Reg.6, amended: SI 1999/1179 Reg.10
Reg.13, amended: SI 1997/1901 Reg.10, SI 1998/871 Reg.36
Reg.18, amended: SI 1999/1179 Reg.11

3243. Merchant Shipping (Fees) Regulations 1996
Part XIA, added: SI 1997/1820 Reg.5
Sch. Part I, amended: SI 1998/531 Reg.2, SI 1998/1609 Reg.2, SI 1999/1063 Reg.2
Sch. Part VII, amended: SI 1998/531 Reg.2
Sch. Part VIII, amended: SI 1998/531 Reg.2
Sch. Part XII, amended: SI 1998/531 Reg.2
Sch. Part XIII, added: SI 1997/3018 Reg.15
Sch. para.2, amended: SI 1999/1923 Reg.2
Sch. Table, amended: SI 1999/1923 Reg.2

3253. A23 Trunk Road (Croydon) Red Route (Prescribed Route No.2) Experimental Traffic Order 1996
revoked: SI 1998/25 Art.5

3254. A205 Trunk Road (Wandsworth and Richmond) Red Route Experimental Traffic Order 1996
revoked (in part): SI 1998/1462 Art.10

3255. Secure Accommodation (Scotland) Regulations 1996
applied: SI 1996/3261 r.5, r.15, r.16, r.18, r.26
Reg.3, applied: SI 1997/691 Reg.2
Reg.7, applied: SI 1996/3261 r.6

3256. Residential Establishments - Child Care (Scotland) Regulations 1996
Part II, applied: SI 1996/3255 Reg.4, SI 1996/3259 Reg.10

3261. Children's Hearings (Scotland) Rules 1996
r.21, applied: SI 1996/3260 Reg.3

3262. Arrangements to Look After Children (Scotland) Regulations 1996
Reg.3, referred to: SI 1997/744 Art.6
Reg.9, referred to: SI 1997/744 Art.6

3263. Fostering of Children (Scotland) Regulations 1996
Reg.7, applied: SI 1997/691 Reg.3
Reg.10, applied: SI 1996/3259 Reg.10
Reg.15, applied: SI 1996/3261 r.20

3266. Adoption Agencies (Scotland) Regulations 1996
Reg.12, applied: SI 1996/3257 Reg.3
Reg.24, applied: SI 1996/3257 Reg.8

3268. Specified Bovine Material (No.3) (Amendment) (No.2) Order 1996
revoked: SI 1997/617 Art.29
Art.2, revoked: SI 1997/617 Art.29

3273. Amusements with Prizes (Variation of Monetary Limits) (Scotland) Order 1996
revoked: SI 1999/1259 Art.3, Sch.
Art.2, revoked: SI 1999/1259 Art.3, Sch.
Art.3, revoked: SI 1999/1259 Art.3, Sch.

3274. Housing Accommodation and Homelessness (Persons Subject to Immigration Control) Order (Northern Ireland) 1996
revoked: SI 1998/1004 Art.2
Art.3, revoked: SI 1998/1004 Art.2
Art.4, revoked: SI 1998/1004 Art.2

NO.

1997

Veterinary Surgeons and Veterinary Practitioners (Registration) (Amendment) Regulations 1997
revoked: SI 1999/2846 Sch. Reg.22

1. Education (Recognised Bodies) Order 1997
revoked: SI 1999/833 Art.3
Art.3, revoked: SI 1999/833 Art.3

7. Occupational Pension Schemes (Contracting Out) (Transitional) Regulations (Northern Ireland) 1997
applied: SI 1999/671 Art.3, Sch.2

9. Channel Tunnel Rail Link (Nomination) Order 1997
revoked: SI 1999/391 Art.4
Art.3, revoked: SI 1999/391 Art.4

11. Control of Substances Hazardous to Health (Amendment) Regulations 1997
revoked: SI 1999/437 Reg.18
Reg.2, revoked: SI 1999/437 Reg.18

13. Hill Livestock (Compensatory Allowances) (Amendment) Regulations (Northern Ireland) 1997
revoked: SR 1999/497 Reg.15 (with savings)

14. Rules of Procedure (Air Force) (Amendment No.2) Rules 1997
revoked: SI 1997/171 r.90, Sch.7
r.2, revoked: SI 1997/171 r.90, Sch.7

18. Rules of Procedure (Army) (Amendment No.2) Rules 1997
revoked: SI 1997/169 r.90, Sch.7
r.2, revoked: SI 1997/169 r.90, Sch.7

19. Merchant Shipping (Carriage of Cargoes) Regulations 1997
revoked: SI 1999/336 Reg.1
Reg.1, revoked: SI 1999/336 Reg.1
Reg.2, amended: SI 1997/2366 Reg.3
Reg.2, revoked: SI 1999/336 Reg.1
Reg.3, amended: SI 1997/2366 Reg.4
Reg.3, revoked (in part): SI 1997/2366 Reg.4, SI 1999/336 Reg.1 (rem.)
Reg.4, amended: SI 1997/2366 Reg.5
Reg.4, revoked: SI 1999/336 Reg.1
Reg.5, amended: SI 1997/2366 Reg.6
Reg.5, revoked: SI 1999/336 Reg.1
Reg.6, amended: SI 1997/2366 Reg.7
Reg.6, revoked: SI 1999/336 Reg.1
Reg.9, revoked: SI 1999/336 Reg.1
Reg.12, revoked: SI 1999/336 Reg.1

21. A2 Trunk Road (Greenwich) Red Route (Clearway) Traffic Order 1997
Art.2, amended: SI 1999/272 Art.2, Sch. Part B
Art.9, amended: SI 1999/272 Art.2, Sch. Part B

22. Water Undertakers (Extension of Byelaws) Order 1997
revoked: SI 1998/2398 Art.3
Art.2, revoked: SI 1998/2398 Art.3

31. Trading Schemes (Exclusion) Regulations 1997
Reg.3, amended: SI 1997/1887 Reg.2

33. Hill Livestock (Compensatory Allowances) (Amendment) Regulations 1997
revoked: SI 1999/3316 Reg.18 (with saving), SSI 1999/187 Reg.23 (with savings), Sch.2 (with savings)
Reg.2, revoked: SI 1999/3316 Reg.18 (with saving), SSI 1999/187 Reg.23 (with savings), Sch.2 (with savings)

38. Occupational Pension Schemes (Contracting Out) Transitional Regulations 1997
amended: 1999 c.2 s.1, Sch.2

1997—cont.

39. **Personal and Occupational Pension Schemes (Pensions Ombudsman) Regulations (Northern Ireland) 1997**
Reg.6, amended: SI 1998/1129 Art.3, Sch.2

54. **Education (Listed Bodies) Order 1997**
revoked: SI 1999/834 Art.3
Art.2, revoked: SI 1999/834 Art.3
Art.3, revoked: SI 1999/834 Art.3
Sch. Part I, amended: SI 1998/876 Art.2
Sch. Part I, revoked: SI 1999/834 Art.3

56. **Personal and Occupational Pensions Schemes (Protected Rights) Regulations (Northern Ireland) 1997**
applied: SI 1999/671 Art.3, Sch.2
Reg.4, referred to: SI 1999/671 Art.3, Sch.2

56. **Road Traffic (Permitted Parking Area and Special Parking Area) (County of Buckinghamshire) (High Wycombe Town Centre) Order 1997**
applied: SI 1999/1918 Reg.20
referred to: SI 1999/1918
Sch.3 para.5, substituted: SI 1999/1667 Art.3
Sch.3 para.8, amended: SI 1999/1667 Art.4

65. **Income-related Benefits and Jobseeker's Allowance (Miscellaneous Amendments) Regulations 1997**
Reg.16, revoked: SI 1999/991 Reg.59 (with savings), Sch.4 (with savings)

87. **A12 Trunk Road (Redbridge) (No.1) Red Route Traffic Order 1996 Experimental Variation Order 1997**
revoked: SI 1998/26 Art.3
Art.2, revoked: SI 1998/26 Art.3

88. **A312 Trunk Road (Hounslow) Red Route (Clearway) Traffic Order 1997**
Art.2, amended: SI 1999/272 Art.2, Sch. Part B
Art.9, amended: SI 1999/272 Art.2, Sch. Part B

93. **Education (Fees and Awards) (Scotland) Regulations 1997**
referred to: SI 1997/2008 Reg.2
Reg.6, amended: SI 1997/2008 Reg.3, SI 1998/2324 Reg.2
Reg.6A, added: SI 1998/2324 Reg.2
Reg.9, amended: SI 1997/2008 Reg.3
Reg.12, amended: SI 1997/2008 Reg.3
Sch.1, applied: SI 1997/2008 Reg.5
Sch.1 para.3A, added: SI 1997/2008 Reg.5
Sch.1 para.4, revoked: SI 1997/2008 Reg.3
Sch.1 para.6, amended: SI 1997/2008 Reg.4
Sch.1 para.6, applied: SI 1997/2008 Reg.4

95. **Occupational Pension Schemes (Mixed Benefit Contracted-out Schemes) Regulations (Northern Ireland) 1997**
Reg.3, applied: SI 1999/671 Art.3, Sch.2

123. **A41 Trunk Road (Camden) Red Route (Bus Lanes) Experimental Traffic Order 1997**
revoked: SI 1998/381 Art.5
Art.4, revoked: SI 1998/381 Art.5

124. **Local Government Act 1988 (Security Work) (Exemption) (Wales) Order 1997**
Art.2, amended: SI 1997/2648 Art.3

125. **Local Government Act 1988 (Competition) (Information Technology Services) (Wales) Regulations 1997**
Reg.2, amended: SI 1997/2649 Reg.6
Reg.3, amended: SI 1998/2192 Reg.2, Sch.

126. **Local Government Act 1988 (Competition) (Legal Services) (Wales) Regulations 1997**
Reg.2, amended: SI 1997/1699 Reg.5, SI 1997/2649 Reg.7
Reg.3, amended: SI 1997/1699 Reg.5, SI 1998/2192 Reg.2, Sch.

1997—cont.

127. **Local Government Act 1988 (Competition) (Construction and Property Services) (Wales) Regulations 1997**
Reg.2, amended: SI 1997/1699 Reg.2, SI 1997/2649 Reg.3
Reg.3, amended: SI 1997/1699 Reg.2, SI 1998/2192 Reg.2, Sch.

128. **Local Government Act 1988 (Competition) (Supervision of Parking, Management of Vehicles and Security Work) (Wales) Regulations 1997**
Reg.2, amended: SI 1998/2192 Reg.2, Sch.
Reg.2, substituted: SI 1997/1699 Reg.6
Reg.3, revoked: SI 1997/2747 Reg.2, Sch.

129. **Local Government Act 1988 (Competition) (Personnel Services) (Wales) Regulations 1997**
Reg.2, amended: SI 1997/2649 Reg.8
Reg.3, amended: SI 1998/2192 Reg.2, Sch.

130. **Local Government Act 1988 (Competition) (Financial Services) (Wales) Regulations 1997**
Reg.2, amended: SI 1997/1699 Reg.3, SI 1997/2649 Reg.4
Reg.3, amended: SI 1997/1699 Reg.3, SI 1998/2192 Reg.2, Sch.

135. **Health and Safety (Young Persons) Regulations 1997**
referred to: SI 1998/2411 Reg.3
revoked: SI 1999/3242 Reg.29
Reg.2, revoked: SI 1999/3242 Reg.29
Reg.3, revoked: SI 1999/3242 Reg.29
Sch. Part I, revoked: SI 1999/3242 Reg.29
Sch. Part II, revoked: SI 1999/3242 Reg.29

139. **A205 Trunk Road (Greenwich) Red Route Experimental Traffic Order 1997**
revoked (in part): SI 1998/382 Art.10
Art.5, revoked (in part): SI 1998/382 Art.10
Art.9, revoked (in part): SI 1998/382 Art.10
Art.11, revoked (in part): SI 1998/382 Art.10
Sch.4 Item 14, substituted: SI 1998/979 Art.3

139. **Personal Pension Schemes (Appropriate Schemes) Regulations (Northern Ireland) 1997**
applied: SI 1999/671 Art.3, Sch.2

140. **Occupational and Personal Pension Schemes (Contracting Out etc.: Review of Determinations) Regulations (Northern Ireland) 1997**
applied: SI 1999/671 Art.3, Sch.2

164. **Social Security (Adjudication) (Amendment) Regulations (Northern Ireland) 1997**
revoked: SR 1999/162 Reg.59, Sch.3

169. **Motor Vehicles (Construction and Use) (Amendment) Regulations (Northern Ireland) 1997**
revoked: SR 1999/454 Reg.126, Sch.19

172. **Standing Civilian Courts Order 1997**
Art.16, applied: SI 1997/169 Sch.6 Part II, SI 1997/171 Sch.6 Part II
Art.17, applied: SI 1997/169 Sch.6 Part II, SI 1997/171 Sch.6 Part II

174. **Scottish Dental Practice Board Regulations 1997**
Reg.2, amended: SSI 1999/52 Reg.3
Reg.8, amended: SSI 1999/52 Reg.4
Reg.10, amended: SSI 1999/52 Reg.5

175. **Local Government Act 1988 (Competition) (England) Regulations 1997**
revoked: SI 1997/2732 Reg.9
Reg.3, revoked: SI 1997/2732 Reg.9
Reg.4, revoked: SI 1997/2732 Reg.9
Reg.5, revoked: SI 1997/2732 Reg.9

1997—cont.

175. **Local Government Act 1988 (Competition) (England) Regulations 1997**—*cont.*
Reg.6, revoked: SI 1997/2732 Reg.9
Reg.7, revoked: SI 1997/2732 Reg.9
Reg.8, revoked: SI 1997/2732 Reg.9

176. **Local Government Act 1988 (Defined Activities) (Housing Management and Security Work) (Exemptions) (England) Order 1997**
Art.2, amended: SI 1997/2733 Art.2
Art.3, revoked: SI 1997/2733 Art.2
Art.4, amended: SI 1997/2733 Art.2

178. **Land Registration Fees Order 1997**
substituted: SI 1997/1710 Art.1

189. **Plant Protection Products (Basic Conditions) Regulations 1997**
Reg.5, applied: SI 1999/1512 Art.2, Sch.2 para.12
Reg.6, applied: SI 1999/1512 Art.2, Sch.2 para.13
Reg.7, applied: SI 1999/1512 Art.2, Sch.2 para.14
Sch.1, applied: SI 1999/1512 Art.2, Sch.2 para.14
Sch.2, applied: SI 1999/1512 Art.2, Sch.2 para.14
Sch.3, applied: SI 1999/1512 Art.2, Sch.2 para.14
Sch.4, applied: SI 1999/1512 Art.2, Sch.2 para.14

191. **Motor Vehicles (EC Type Approval) (Amendment) Regulations 1997**
revoked: SI 1998/2051 Reg.2, Sch.3
Reg.2, revoked: SI 1998/2051 Reg.2, Sch.3

192. **Pensions (1995 Order) (Commencement No.8) Order (Northern Ireland) 1997**
referred to: 1999 c.30 s.81, Sch.11 para.34
Art.4, applied: SI 1999/671 Art.3, Sch.2
Art.13, applied: SI 1999/671 Art.3, Sch.2

193. **Pipelines Safety Regulations (Northern Ireland) 1997**
amended: SR 1999/150 Reg.2, Sch.

194. **Assured Tenancies and Agricultural Occupancies (Forms) Regulations 1997**
Reg.2, see *Tadema Holdings Ltd v Ferguson* [1999] E.G.C.S. 138 (CA), Peter Gibson, L.J.

194. **Gas Safety (Installation and Use) Regulations (Northern Ireland) 1997**
amended: SR 1999/150 Reg.2, Sch.

195. **Gas Safety (Management) Regulations (Northern Ireland) 1997**
amended: SR 1999/150 Reg.2, Sch.

197. **Local Government Act 1988 (Competition) (Scotland) Regulations 1997**
Reg.4, amended: SI 1997/1436 Reg.2, SI 1998/1422 Reg.2, SI 1999/947 Reg.2
Reg.5, revoked: SI 1997/1436 Reg.3
Reg.6, amended: SI 1997/1436 Reg.4, SI 1998/1422 Reg.3, SI 1999/947 Reg.3
Sch.6, amended: SI 1997/1436 Reg.5, SI 1998/1422 Reg.4, SI 1999/947 Reg.4

203. **City of Westminster (A41 Trunk Road) Red Route (Bus Lanes) Experimental Traffic Order 1997**
revoked (in part): SI 1997/2743 Art.5
Art.4, revoked (in part): SI 1997/2743 Art.5
Art.6, revoked (in part): SI 1997/2743 Art.5

208. **A41 Trunk Road (Camden) Red Route Experimental (No.2) Traffic Order 1997**
revoked (in part): SI 1997/2132 Art.5, SI 1997/2301 Art.5, SI 1997/2786 Art.5, SI 1997/3042 Art.5, SI 1998/383 Art.5, SI 1998/866 Art.5, SI 1998/1105 Art.10, SI 1998/1949 Art.5, SI 1998/1950 Art.5

1997—cont.

208. **A41 Trunk Road (Camden) Red Route Experimental (No.2) Traffic Order 1997**—*cont.*
Art.5, revoked (in part): SI 1997/2132 Art.5, SI 1997/3042 Art.5, SI 1998/1105 Art.10
Art.9, revoked (in part): SI 1997/2132 Art.5, SI 1997/3042 Art.5, SI 1998/1105 Art.10
Art.11, revoked (in part): SI 1997/2132 Art.5, SI 1997/3042 Art.5, SI 1998/1105 Art.10
Sch.1 Item 6, added: SI 1997/1607 Art.3
Sch.1 Item 6, revoked (in part): SI 1997/2132 Art.5, SI 1997/3042 Art.5, SI 1998/1105 Art.10
Sch.2B Item 32, revoked (in part): SI 1997/1607 Art.4, SI 1997/2132 Art.5, SI 1997/3042 Art.5, SI 1998/1105 Art.10
Sch.2D Item 1, added: SI 1997/1607 Art.5
Sch.2D Item 1, revoked (in part): SI 1997/2132 Art.5, SI 1997/3042 Art.5, SI 1998/1105 Art.10
Sch.3A Item 5, added: SI 1997/1607 Art.6
Sch.3A Item 5, revoked (in part): SI 1997/2132 Art.5, SI 1997/3042 Art.5, SI 1998/1105 Art.10
Sch.3A Item 6, added: SI 1997/1607 Art.6
Sch.3A Item 6, revoked (in part): SI 1997/2132 Art.5, SI 1997/3042 Art.5, SI 1998/1105 Art.10
Sch.3B Item 11, revoked (in part): SI 1997/2132 Art.5, SI 1997/3042 Art.5, SI 1998/1105 Art.10
Sch.3B Item 11, substituted: SI 1997/1514 Art.3
Sch.3B Item 15, revoked (in part): SI 1997/1607 Art.7, SI 1997/2132 Art.5, SI 1997/3042 Art.5, SI 1998/1105 Art.10
Sch.4 Item 14, revoked (in part): SI 1997/2132 Art.5, SI 1997/3042 Art.5, SI 1998/1105 Art.10
Sch.4 Item 14, substituted: SI 1997/1514 Art.4
Sch.4 Item 15, revoked (in part): SI 1997/2132 Art.5, SI 1997/3042 Art.5, SI 1998/1105 Art.10
Sch.4 Item 15, substituted: SI 1997/1514 Art.5
Sch.4 Item 46, added: SI 1997/1607 Art.8
Sch.4 Item 46, revoked (in part): SI 1997/2132 Art.5, SI 1997/3042 Art.5, SI 1998/1105 Art.10
Sch.4 Item 47, added: SI 1997/1607 Art.8
Sch.4 Item 47, revoked (in part): SI 1997/2132 Art.5, SI 1997/3042 Art.5, SI 1998/1105 Art.10

215. **Local Government Changes for England (Council Tax) (Transitional Reduction) Regulations 1997**
applied: SI 1998/214 Reg.11
revoked (in part): SI 1999/259 Reg.11
Reg.2, amended: SI 1998/214 Reg.11, Sch.5 para.1
Reg.2, applied: SI 1999/259 Reg.11
Reg.2, revoked (in part): SI 1999/259 Reg.11
Reg.3, amended: SI 1998/214 Reg.11, Sch.5 para.2
Reg.3, revoked (in part): SI 1999/259 Reg.11
Reg.4, revoked (in part): SI 1999/259 Reg.11
Reg.8, revoked (in part): SI 1999/259 Reg.11
Reg.10, revoked (in part): SI 1999/259 Reg.11
Reg.11, revoked (in part): SI 1999/259 Reg.11
Sch.1, applied: SI 1999/259 Reg.11
Sch.1, revoked (in part): SI 1999/259 Reg.11
Sch.1 para.3, applied: SI 1999/259 Sch.Part II
Sch.1 para.3, revoked (in part): SI 1999/259 Reg.11
Sch.1 para.4, revoked (in part): SI 1999/259 Reg.11

NO.

1997—cont.

215. Local Government Changes for England (Council Tax) (Transitional Reduction) Regulations 1997—*cont.*
Sch.2, applied: SI 1999/259 Reg.11
Sch.2, revoked (in part): SI 1999/259 Reg.11
Sch.2 Part 1, applied: SI 1999/259 Sch.Part II
Sch.2 Part 1, revoked (in part): SI 1999/259 Reg.11
Sch.2 Part 3, applied: SI 1999/259 Sch.Part II
Sch.2 Part 3, revoked (in part): SI 1999/259 Reg.11
Sch.3 para.1, amended: SI 1998/214 Reg.11, Sch.5 para.3
Sch.3 para.1, revoked (in part): SI 1999/259 Reg.11
Sch.3 para.2, revoked (in part): SI 1999/259 Reg.11
Sch.3 para.3, revoked (in part): SI 1999/259 Reg.11
Sch.4 para.1, revoked (in part): SI 1999/259 Reg.11
Sch.4 para.2, revoked (in part): SI 1999/259 Reg.11
Sch.4 para.3, revoked (in part): SI 1999/259 Reg.11

218. Local Government Pension Scheme (London Boroughs Children's Regional Planning Committee) Regulations 1997
applied: SI 1997/1613 Reg.4, Reg.19, Sch.2 para.2
referred to: SI 1997/1613 Reg.3, Sch.2 para.6

229. Health and Safety (Enforcing Authority) Regulations (Northern Ireland) 1997
revoked: SR 1999/90

229. Houses in Multiple Occupation (Fees for Registration Schemes) Order 1997
applied: SI 1998/1812 Reg.4
Art.2A, added: SI 1998/1813 Art.2
Art.3, substituted: SI 1998/1813 Art.2

235. Public Order (Prescribed Form) Regulations (Northern Ireland) 1997
revoked: SI 1998/395 Reg.3

247. Carriage of Dangerous Goods (Classification, Packaging and Labelling) and Use of Transportable Pressure Receptacles Regulations (Northern Ireland) 1997
amended: SR 1999/150 Reg.2, Sch.

248. Carriage of Dangerous Goods by Road Regulations (Northern Ireland) 1997
amended: SR 1999/150 Reg.2, Sch.

249. Carriage of Dangerous Goods by Road (Driver Training) Regulations (Northern Ireland) 1997
amended: SR 1999/150 Reg.2, Sch.

250. Dairy Produce Quotas (Amendment) Regulations 1997
revoked: SI 1997/733 Reg.35
Reg.2, revoked: SI 1997/733 Reg.35

251. Open-Ended Investment Companies (Investment Companies with Variable Capital) Regulations (Northern Ireland) 1997
referred to: 1998 c.47 Sch.3 para.23

252. Occupational Pension Schemes (Independent Trustee) Regulations 1997
Reg.2, amended: SI 1997/3038 Reg.10

256. Motor Vehicles (Driving Licences) (Amendment) Regulations 1997
revoked: SI 1999/2864 Reg.2, Sch.1
Reg.2, revoked: SI 1999/2864 Reg.2, Sch.1

NO.

1997—cont.

258. A205 Trunk Road (Lewisham) Red Route Experimental Traffic Order 1997
revoked (in part): SI 1998/1835 Art.10
Sch.2B Item 2, substituted: SI 1997/3066 Art.3
Sch.3B Item 1A, added: SI 1997/3066 Art.4
Sch.4 Item 7, substituted: SI 1997/3066 Art.5
Sch.4 Item 8, substituted: SI 1997/3066 Art.6
Sch.4 Item 12, revoked: SI 1997/3066 Art.8
Sch.4 Item 13, substituted: SI 1997/3066 Art.7
Sch.4 Item 19, revoked: SI 1997/3066 Art.8

258. Child Support Commissioners (Procedure) (Amendment) Regulations (Northern Ireland) 1997
revoked: SR 1999/226

266. Potato Industry Development Council Order 1997
applied: SI 1999/672 Art.2, Sch.1, SI 1999/1747 Art.3, Sch.4 para.3
Art.2, amended: SI 1999/1413 Art.3
Art.3, referred to: SI 1999/1319 Sch.
Art.6, amended: SI 1999/1413 Art.4
Art.7, amended: SI 1999/1413 Art.5
Art.8, amended: SI 1999/1413 Art.6
Art.9, amended: SI 1999/1413 Art.7
Art.9, revoked (in part): SI 1999/1413 Art.7
Art.13, added: SI 1999/1413 Art.8

268. Continental Shelf (Designation of Areas) Order 1997
referred to: SI 1999/2031, SI 1999/2031 Art.2, Sch.

276. Road Traffic Regulation (Northern Ireland) Order 1997
Art.44, amended: 1998 c.32 s.74, Sch.4 para.23
Art.61, revoked (in part): SI 1997/276 (NI.2)
Art.75, Sch.9

290. Wireless Telegraphy (Television Licence Fees) Regulations 1997
amended: SI 1999/765 Reg.2
Sch.2, amended: SI 1998/558 Reg.2
Sch.2 Part II, amended: SI 1999/765 Reg.2
Sch.2 Part II, revoked (in part): SI 1999/765 Reg.2
Sch.3, amended: SI 1999/765 Reg.2, Sch.
Sch.3 Item 1, amended: SI 1998/558 Reg.2
Sch.3 Item 2, substituted: SI 1998/558 Reg.2, Sch.
Sch.3 Item 3, amended: SI 1998/558 Reg.2

291. Act of Sederunt (Child Care and Maintenance Rules) 1997
r.3.59, amended: SI 1998/1993 r.2, SI 1998/2130 r.2

306. Reserve Forces Act 1996 (Transitional, Consequential and Saving Provisions) Regulations 1997
Reg.6, revoked: SI 1998/3086 Reg.11, Sch. para.8
Reg.8, revoked: SI 1998/3086 Reg.11, Sch. para.8

311. Teachers (Compensation for Redundancy and Premature Retirement) Regulations 1997
Part III, referred to: SI 1997/3001 Reg.E4
Reg.2, amended: SI 1998/2256 Reg.3, SI 1999/608 Reg.3
Reg.3, amended: SI 1998/2256 Reg.4, SI 1999/608 Reg.4
Reg.3, applied: SI 1999/608 Reg.9
Reg.3, revoked (in part): SI 1999/608 Reg.4
Reg.4, amended: SI 1998/2256 Reg.5
Reg.4, applied: SI 1997/3001 Reg.E4
Reg.5, amended: SI 1999/608 Reg.5
Reg.5, applied: SI 1999/608 Reg.9, SI 1999/638 Reg.7

NO.

311. Teachers (Compensation for Redundancy and Premature Retirement) Regulations 1997—*cont.*

Reg.6, amended: SI 1998/2256 Reg.6, SI 1999/608 Reg.5

Reg.6, applied: SI 1999/608 Reg.9, SI 1999/638 Reg.7

Reg.7, amended: SI 1998/2256 Reg.7

Reg.7, applied: SI 1999/608 Reg.9

Reg.7, referred to: SI 1997/3001 Reg.E9

Reg.8, amended: SI 1998/2256 Reg.20

Reg.8, applied: SI 1998/2256 Reg.20

Reg.8, substituted: SI 1998/2256 Reg.8

Reg.9, substituted: SI 1998/2256 Reg.9

Reg.10, amended: SI 1998/2256 Reg.10

Reg.12, amended: SI 1998/2256 Reg.11

Reg.12, applied: SI 1999/608 Reg.9

Reg.13, amended: SI 1998/2256 Reg.12

Reg.14, amended: SI 1998/2256 Reg.13

Reg.15, amended: SI 1998/2256 Reg.14

Reg.20, amended: SI 1998/2256 Reg.15, Reg.21, SI 1999/608 Reg.6

Reg.20, applied: SI 1998/2256 Reg.21

Reg.21, amended: SI 1998/2256 Reg.16

Reg.22, amended: SI 1998/2256 Reg.17

Reg.22, applied: SI 1999/608 Reg.9

Reg.22, revoked (in part): SI 1999/608 Reg.7

Reg.26, applied: SI 1999/608 Reg.9

Sch.1, amended: SI 1998/2256 Reg.18, SI 1999/608 Reg.8

Sch.2 para.1, amended: SI 1998/2256 Reg.19

312. Teachers' Superannuation (Amendment) Regulations 1997

applied: SI 1997/3001 Reg.H12, Sch.15 para.2

revoked: SI 1997/3001 Reg.H12, Sch.14

Reg.3, applied: SI 1997/3001 Reg.H12, Sch.15 para.2

Reg.3, revoked: SI 1997/3001 Reg.H12, Sch.14

Reg.4, applied: SI 1997/3001 Reg.H12, Sch.15 para.2

Reg.4, revoked: SI 1997/3001 Reg.H12, Sch.14

Reg.5, applied: SI 1997/3001 Reg.H12, Sch.15 para.2

Reg.5, revoked: SI 1997/3001 Reg.H12, Sch.14

Reg.6, applied: SI 1997/3001 Reg.H12, Sch.15 para.2

Reg.6, revoked: SI 1997/3001 Reg.H12, Sch.14

Reg.7, applied: SI 1997/3001 Reg.H12, Sch.15 para.2

Reg.7, revoked: SI 1997/3001 Reg.H12, Sch.14

Reg.8, applied: SI 1997/3001 Reg.H12, Sch.15 para.2

Reg.8, revoked: SI 1997/3001 Reg.H12, Sch.14

Reg.9, applied: SI 1997/3001 Reg.H12, Sch.15 para.2

Reg.9, revoked: SI 1997/3001 Reg.H12, Sch.14

Reg.10, applied: SI 1997/3001 Reg.H12, Sch.15 para.2

Reg.10, revoked: SI 1997/3001 Reg.H12, Sch.14

Reg.11, applied: SI 1997/3001 Reg.H12, Sch.15 para.2

Reg.11, revoked: SI 1997/3001 Reg.H12, Sch.14

Reg.12, applied: SI 1997/3001 Reg.H12, Sch.15 para.2

Reg.12, revoked: SI 1997/3001 Reg.H12, Sch.14

Reg.13, applied: SI 1997/3001 Reg.H12, Sch.15 para.2

Reg.13, revoked: SI 1997/3001 Reg.H12, Sch.14

NO.

312. Teachers' Superannuation (Amendment) Regulations 1997—*cont.*

Reg.14, applied: SI 1997/3001 Reg.H12, Sch.15 para.2

Reg.14, revoked: SI 1997/3001 Reg.H12, Sch.14

Reg.15, applied: SI 1997/3001 Reg.H12, Sch.15 para.2

Reg.15, revoked: SI 1997/3001 Reg.H12, Sch.14

Reg.16, applied: SI 1997/3001 Reg.H12, Sch.15 para.2

Reg.16, revoked: SI 1997/3001 Reg.H12, Sch.14

Reg.17, applied: SI 1997/3001 Reg.H12, Sch.15 para.2

Reg.17, revoked: SI 1997/3001 Reg.H12, Sch.14

Reg.18, applied: SI 1997/3001 Reg.H12, Sch.15 para.2

Reg.18, revoked: SI 1997/3001 Reg.H12, Sch.14

Reg.19, applied: SI 1997/3001 Reg.H12, Sch.15 para.2

Reg.19, revoked: SI 1997/3001 Reg.H12, Sch.14

Reg.20, applied: SI 1997/3001 Reg.H12, Sch.15 para.2

Reg.20, revoked: SI 1997/3001 Reg.H12, Sch.14

Reg.21, applied: SI 1997/3001 Reg.H12, Sch.15 para.2

Reg.21, revoked: SI 1997/3001 Reg.H12, Sch.14

Reg.22, applied: SI 1997/3001 Reg.H12, Sch.15 para.2

Reg.22, revoked: SI 1997/3001 Reg.H12, Sch.14

Reg.23, applied: SI 1997/3001 Reg.H12, Sch.15 para.2

Reg.23, revoked: SI 1997/3001 Reg.H12, Sch.14

Sch.1, applied: SI 1997/3001 Reg.H12, Sch.15 para.2

Sch.1, referred to: SI 1999/607 Reg.9

Sch.1, revoked: SI 1997/3001 Reg.H12, Sch.14

Sch.2, applied: SI 1997/3001 Reg.H12, Sch.15 para.2

Sch.2, revoked: SI 1997/3001 Reg.H12, Sch.14

Sch.3, applied: SI 1997/3001 Reg.H12, Sch.15 para.2

Sch.3, revoked: SI 1997/3001 Reg.H12, Sch.14

Sch.4, applied: SI 1997/3001 Reg.H12, Sch.15 para.2

Sch.4, revoked: SI 1997/3001 Reg.H12, Sch.14

316. Independent Qualified Conveyancers (Scotland) Regulations 1997

Reg.2, amended: SI 1998/1129 Art.3, Sch.2

317. Executry Practitioners (Scotland) Regulations 1997

Reg.2, amended: SI 1998/1129 Art.3, Sch.2

319. Local Authorities (Capital Finance) Regulations 1997

Reg.3, amended: SI 1999/1852 Reg.3

Reg.8A, added: SI 1998/1937 Reg.3

Reg.13, amended: SI 1998/371 Reg.3

Reg.16, amended: SI 1997/848 Reg.3, SI 1999/1852 Reg.4

Reg.16, applied: SI 1999/101 Reg.4, Reg.5, Sch.1 para.17, Sch.2 para.24, SI 1999/2212 Reg.10

Reg.16, referred to: SI 1999/101 Reg.15, Sch.3 para.17, SI 1999/2213 Reg.9

NO.

NO.

1997—cont.

319. Local Authorities (Capital Finance) Regulations 1997—cont.
Reg.16, revoked (in part): SI 1999/1852 Reg.4
Reg.16, substituted: SI 1998/371 Reg.4
Reg.24, amended: SI 1998/602 Reg.2
Reg.31, amended: SI 1999/1852 Reg.5
Reg.32A, added: SI 1999/1852 Reg.6
Reg.40, amended: SI 1997/848 Reg.4
Reg.40, substituted: SI 1999/3423 Reg.2
Reg.58A, added: SI 1998/1937 Reg.4
Reg.60, revoked: SI 1998/1937 Reg.12
Reg.64, amended: SI 1998/1937 Reg.5
Reg.64A, added: SI 1998/1937 Reg.6
Reg.65, amended: SI 1998/1937 Reg.7
Reg.66, amended: SI 1998/1937 Reg.8
Reg.66, revoked (in part): SI 1998/1937 Reg.8
Reg.66A, added: SI 1998/1937 Reg.9
Reg.68A, added: SI 1998/1937 Reg.10
Reg.70, revoked: SI 1998/1937 Reg.12
Reg.71, revoked: SI 1998/1937 Reg.12
Reg.73, revoked: SI 1998/1937 Reg.12
Reg.74, revoked: SI 1998/1937 Reg.12
Reg.75, revoked: SI 1998/1937 Reg.12
Reg.86, amended: SI 1997/848 Reg.5
Reg.87, amended: SI 1998/371 Reg.5
Reg.96, amended: SI 1999/1852 Reg.7
Reg.104, amended: SI 1999/501 Reg.3
Reg.104A, added: SI 1999/501 Reg.4
Reg.109, amended: SI 1999/1852 Reg.8
Reg.112, amended: SI 1997/848 Reg.6
Reg.130, amended: SI 1998/371 Reg.6
Reg.136, amended: SI 1998/371 Reg.6
Reg.138, amended: SI 1998/1937 Reg.11
Reg.153, amended: SI 1998/371 Reg.6

321. Registration of Homeopathic Veterinary Medicinal Products (Fees) Regulations 1997
revoked: SI 1997/1469 Reg.21
Sch.1 Part II, revoked: SI 1997/1469 Reg.21

322. Registration of Homeopathic Veterinary Medicinal Products Regulations 1997
applied: SI 1997/1349 Art.2, SI 1999/3142 Art.2
Reg.2, amended: SI 1999/3142 Art.5, Sch. para.3
Reg.2, referred to: SI 1998/2428 Reg.14
Reg.37, revoked: SI 1997/2884 Reg.4
Sch.6, revoked: SI 1997/2884 Reg.4

326. Health Promotion Authority for Wales Constitution (Amendment) Order 1997
revoked: SI 1999/807 Art.2
Art.2, revoked: SI 1999/807 Art.2

327. Health Promotion Authority for Wales Regulations 1997
revoked: SI 1999/805 Reg.2
Reg.2, revoked: SI 1999/805 Reg.2
Reg.3, revoked: SI 1999/805 Reg.2
Reg.4, revoked: SI 1999/805 Reg.2
Reg.6, revoked: SI 1999/805 Reg.2

328. Housing (Change of Landlord) (Payment of Disposal Cost by Instalments) (Amendment) Regulations 1997
revoked: SI 1997/1621 Reg.3 (with savings)
Reg.2, revoked: SI 1997/1621 Reg.3 (with savings)
Reg.3, revoked: SI 1997/1621 Reg.3 (with savings)

329. Local Government Pension Scheme (Internal Dispute Resolution Procedure) Regulations 1997
applied: SI 1997/1613 Reg.4, Reg.19, Sch.2 para.2
referred to: SI 1997/1613 Reg.3, Sch.2 para.6

1997—cont.

347. Merchant Shipping (Section 63 Inquiries) Rules 1997
r.5, applied: SI 1999/678 Sch., SI 1999/1750 Art.2, Sch.1

348. Merchant Shipping (Training and Certification) Regulations 1997
applied: SI 1997/1320 Reg.4
referred to: SI 1998/1609 Reg.5, Reg.6, Sch., SI 1998/2771 Reg.4, Reg.5, Sch.1, Sch.2
Reg.2, amended: SI 1997/1911 Reg.2
Reg.3, amended: SI 1997/1911 Reg.2
Reg.5, amended: SI 1997/1911 Reg.2

351. Waste Management (Miscellaneous Provisions) Regulations 1997
Reg.3, revoked: SI 1998/607 Reg.3

358. Occupational and Personal Pension Schemes (Contracting Out etc.: Review of Determinations) Regulations 1997
amended: 1999 c.2 s.1, Sch.2
applied: SI 1999/527 Art.4

362. Water Services Charges (Billing and Collection) (Scotland) Order 1997
applied: SI 1997/363 Reg.2

363. Domestic Sewerage Charges (Reduction) (Scotland) Regulations 1997
applied: SI 1997/362 Art.9

368. Education (Teachers) (Amendment) Regulations 1997
revoked (in part): SI 1999/2166 Reg.2, Sch.1 Part I, SI 1999/2817 Reg.2, Sch.1 Part I
Reg.2, revoked (in part): SI 1999/2166 Reg.2, Sch.1 Part I, SI 1999/2817 Reg.2, Sch.1 Part I
Reg.3, revoked (in part): SI 1999/2166 Reg.2, Sch.1 Part I, SI 1997/2679 Reg.7, Sch.3, SI 1999/2817 Reg.2, Sch.1 Part I

371. Motor Vehicles (Construction and Use) (Amendment No.2) Regulations (Northern Ireland) 1997
revoked: SR 1999/454 Reg.126, Sch.19

371. Register of Occupational and Personal Pension Schemes Regulations 1997
Reg.1, see *Bus Employees Pension Trustees Ltd v Harrod* [1999] 3 W.L.R. 1260 (Ch D), Sir Richard Scott, V.C.
Reg.1, amended: SI 1998/600 Reg.3
Reg.3, amended: SI 1997/3038 Reg.11, SI 1998/600 Reg.3
Reg.4, amended: SI 1997/1405 Reg.2, SI 1998/600 Reg.3
Reg.5, amended: SI 1998/600 Reg.3
Reg.8, amended: SI 1997/1405 Reg.2, SI 1998/600 Reg.3

382. Plant Breeders' Rights (Fees) (Amendment) Regulations 1997
revoked: SI 1998/1021 Reg.7 (with savings), Sch.2 (with savings)
Reg.2, revoked: SI 1998/1021 Reg.7 (with savings), Sch.2 (with savings)
Sch., revoked: SI 1998/1021 Reg.7 (with savings), Sch.2 (with savings)

387. Health and Safety (Young Persons) Regulations (Northern Ireland) 1997
referred to: SI 1998/2411 Reg.3

389. Bovine Products (Production and Despatch) Regulations 1997
revoked: SI 1997/1905 Reg.20
Reg.3, referred to: SI 1997/617 Art.6
Reg.3, revoked: SI 1997/1905 Reg.20
Reg.6, revoked: SI 1997/1905 Reg.20
Reg.10, revoked: SI 1997/1905 Reg.20
Reg.13, revoked: SI 1997/1905 Reg.20
Reg.14, revoked: SI 1997/1905 Reg.20

NO.

NO.

390. **Education (Grants for Education Support and Training) (Wales) Regulations 1997**
revoked: SI 1998/392 Reg.12
Reg.2, amended: SI 1997/2395 Reg.3
Reg.2, revoked: SI 1998/392 Reg.12
Reg.5, amended: SI 1997/2395 Reg.4
Reg.5, revoked: SI 1998/392 Reg.12
Reg.6, amended: SI 1997/2395 Reg.5
Reg.6, revoked: SI 1998/392 Reg.12
Reg.12, revoked: SI 1998/392 Reg.12
Sch.1 para.1, revoked: SI 1998/392 Reg.12
Sch. para.2, revoked: SI 1998/392 Reg.12
Sch. para.10, revoked: SI 1998/392 Reg.12
Sch. para.21, added: SI 1997/2395 Reg.6
Sch., amended: SI 1998/392 Reg.12

400. **Public Record Office (Fees) Regulations 1997**
revoked: SI 1998/599 Reg.3
Reg.3, revoked: SI 1998/599 Reg.3

401. **Explosives (Fireworks) Regulations (Northern Ireland) 1997**
revoked: SR 1999/392 Reg.14

403. **Economic Regulation of Airports (Expenses of the Monopolies and Mergers Commission) Regulations 1997**
Reg.2, amended: SI 1999/506 Art.38
Sch., amended: SI 1999/506 Art.38

405. **Lloyd's Underwriters (Double Taxation Relief) Regulations 1997**
amended: SI 1997/2681 Reg.3
applied: SI 1997/2681 Reg.3

421. **South East Water Limited (Extension of Byelaws) Order 1997**
revoked: SI 1998/2398 Art.3
Art.2, revoked: SI 1998/2398 Art.3

426. **Child Support Commissioners (Procedure) (Amendment No.2) Regulations (Northern Ireland) 1997**
revoked: SR 1999/226

427. **Social Security Commissioners Procedure (Amendment) Regulations (Northern Ireland) 1997**
revoked: SR 1999/225

430. **Social Security (Recovery of Benefits) (Appeals) Regulations (Northern Ireland) 1997**
revoked: SR 1999/162 Reg.59, Sch.3

431. **Education (Mandatory Awards) Regulations 1997**
applied: SI 1998/217 Art.2
referred to: SI 1998/1166 Reg.6
revoked: SI 1998/1166 Reg.6
Reg.3, revoked: SI 1998/1166 Reg.6
Reg.4, amended: SI 1997/1693 Reg.3
Reg.4, revoked: SI 1998/1166 Reg.6
Reg.6, revoked: SI 1998/1166 Reg.6
Reg.7, revoked: SI 1998/1166 Reg.6
Reg.8, revoked: SI 1998/1166 Reg.6
Reg.9, revoked: SI 1998/1166 Reg.6
Reg.10, amended: SI 1997/1693 Reg.4
Reg.10, revoked: SI 1998/1166 Reg.6
Reg.12, revoked: SI 1998/1166 Reg.6
Reg.20, amended: SI 1997/1693 Reg.5
Reg.20, revoked: SI 1998/1166 Reg.6
Reg.22, amended: SI 1997/1693 Reg.6
Reg.22, revoked: SI 1998/1166 Reg.6
Reg.23, amended: SI 1997/1693 Reg.7, SI 1998/162 Reg.2
Reg.23, revoked: SI 1998/1166 Reg.6
Sch.1, amended: SI 1997/1693 Reg.8

431. **Education (Mandatory Awards) Regulations 1997**—*cont.*
Sch.1, revoked: SI 1998/1166 Reg.6
Sch.2 para.16, revoked: SI 1998/1166 Reg.6
Sch.3 para.1, revoked: SI 1998/1166 Reg.6
Sch.3 para.3, revoked: SI 1998/1166 Reg.6
Sch.3 para.5, revoked: SI 1998/1166 Reg.6
Sch.3 para.6, amended: SI 1997/1693 Reg.9
Sch.3 para.6, revoked: SI 1998/1166 Reg.6

445. **London Borough of Islington (Trunk Roads) Red Route (Bus Lanes) Traffic Order 1997**
revoked (in part): SI 1999/1476 Art.6
Art.4, revoked (in part): SI 1999/1476 Art.6
Art.5, revoked (in part): SI 1999/1476 Art.6
Sch. Item 8, revoked: SI 1997/2784 Art.6

449. **London Borough of Haringey (Trunk Roads) Red Route (Bus Lanes) Traffic Order 1997**
revoked (in part): SI 1999/3254 Art.6
Art.4, revoked (in part): SI 1999/3254 Art.6
Art.5, revoked (in part): SI 1999/3254 Art.6
Sch. Item 2, amended: SI 1998/867 Art.3
Sch. Item 2, revoked (in part): SI 1999/3254 Art.6
Sch. Item 3, amended: SI 1998/867 Art.4
Sch. Item 3, revoked (in part): SI 1999/3254 Art.6

452. **Non-Domestic Rates (Levying) (Scotland) Regulations 1997**
revoked: SI 1998/519 Reg.21
Part II, applied: SI 1998/519 Reg.11
Part II, revoked: SI 1998/519 Reg.21
Part IV, applied: SI 1998/519 Reg.6, Reg.11
Part IV, referred to: SI 1998/519 Reg.13
Part IV, revoked: SI 1998/519 Reg.21
Part VI, referred to: SI 1998/519 Reg.11
Part VI, revoked: SI 1998/519 Reg.21
Reg.6, revoked: SI 1998/519 Reg.21
Reg.7, applied: SI 1998/519 Reg.6
Reg.7, referred to: SI 1998/519 Reg.13
Reg.7, revoked: SI 1998/519 Reg.21
Reg.11, revoked: SI 1998/519 Reg.21
Reg.12, revoked: SI 1998/519 Reg.21
Reg.13, revoked: SI 1998/519 Reg.21
Reg.18, revoked: SI 1998/519 Reg.21
Reg.22, revoked: SI 1998/519 Reg.21
Reg.23, revoked: SI 1998/519 Reg.21
Reg.24, revoked: SI 1998/519 Reg.21
Reg.25, revoked: SI 1998/519 Reg.21
Reg.26, revoked: SI 1998/519 Reg.21

455. **Local Government Act 1988 (Defined Activities) (Exemption) (Lichfield District Council) Order 1997**
revoked: SI 1998/2955 Art.3

455. **Reporting of Injuries, Diseases and Dangerous Occurrences Regulations (Northern Ireland) 1997**
amended: SR 1999/150 Reg.2, Sch.

463. **London Borough of Camden (Trunk Roads) Red Route (Bus Lanes) Traffic Order 1997**
revoked (in part): SI 1997/2682 Art.3
Art.4, revoked (in part): SI 1997/2682 Art.3
Art.5, revoked (in part): SI 1997/2682 Art.3

464. **A10 Trunk Road (Haringey) Red Route Traffic Order 1997**
Art.2, amended: SI 1999/272 Art.2, Sch. Part A
Art.9, amended: SI 1999/272 Art.2, Sch. Part A
Sch.2B, amended: SI 1998/57 Art.5
Sch.3A Item 1, substituted: SI 1998/57 Art.3
Sch.3A Item 2, substituted: SI 1998/57 Art.4

NO.

465. **A13 Trunk Road (Newham) Red Route Traffic Order 1997**
Art.2, amended: SI 1999/272 Art.2, Sch. Part A
Art.9, amended: SI 1999/272 Art.2, Sch. Part A
466. **A13 Trunk Road (Tower Hamlets) Red Route Traffic Order 1997**
Art.2, amended: SI 1999/272 Art.2, Sch. Part A
Art.9, amended: SI 1999/272 Art.2, Sch. Part A
467. **A41 Trunk Road (Barnet) Red Route Traffic Order 1997**
Art.2, amended: SI 1999/272 Art.2, Sch. Part A
Art.9, amended: SI 1999/272 Art.2, Sch. Part A
Sch.2B Item 6, amended: SI 1999/3222 Art.4
Sch.2B Item 13, amended: SI 1999/3222 Art.3
Sch.2B Table, substituted: SI 1997/1257 Art.3, Sch.
Sch.2C Item 2, substituted: SI 1997/1257 Art.4
Sch.3B Item 1, substituted: SI 1997/1257 Art.5
Sch.4 Item 4, substituted: SI 1997/1257 Art.8
Sch.4 Item 7, substituted: SI 1997/1257 Art.9
Sch.4 Item 8, substituted: SI 1997/1257 Art.10
Sch.4 Item 15, amended: SI 1999/3222 Art.5
Sch.4 Item 17, amended: SI 1999/3222 Art.6
Sch.4 Item 18, revoked: SI 1999/3222 Art.7
Sch.4 Item 20, added: SI 1997/1257 Art.6
Sch.4 Item 21, added: SI 1997/1257 Art.7
470. **Personal Pension Schemes (Appropriate Schemes) Regulations 1997**
amended: 1999 c.2 s.1, Sch.2
Reg.10, amended: SI 1997/3038 Reg.12
473. **Friendly Societies (Modification of the Corporation Tax Acts) Regulations 1997**
Reg.2, amended: SI 1998/1871 Reg.25
Reg.13A, added: SI 1999/2636 Reg.3
Reg.13B, added: SI 1999/2636 Reg.3
Reg.16, revoked: SI 1997/2877 Reg.3
Reg.19A, added: SI 1998/1871 Reg.25
Reg.20A, added: SI 1998/1871 Reg.25
Reg.21, revoked (in part): SI 1997/2877 Reg.4
Reg.30B, added: SI 1999/2636 Reg.4
Reg.31, added: SI 1998/1871 Reg.25
Reg.53, amended: SI 1999/2636 Reg.5
Reg.53A, added: SI 1997/2877 Reg.5
Reg.53B, added: SI 1999/2636 Reg.7
Reg.53ZA, added: SI 1999/2636 Reg.6
474. **Friendly Societies (Provisional Repayments for Exempt Business) (Amendment) Regulations 1997**
revoked (in part): SI 1999/622 Reg.13
Reg.3, revoked (in part): SI 1999/622 Reg.13
Reg.4, revoked (in part): SI 1999/622 Reg.13
Reg.5, revoked (in part): SI 1999/622 Reg.13
475. **Friendly Societies (Gilt-Edged Securities) (Periodic Accounting for Tax on Interest) (Amendment) Regulations 1997**
revoked (in part): SI 1999/624 Reg.9
Reg.4, revoked (in part): SI 1999/624 Reg.9
478. **Potatoes Originating in the Netherlands (Notification) Regulations (Northern Ireland) 1997**
revoked: SR 1999/1
486. **Hill Livestock (Compensatory Allowances) (Amendment) Regulations (Northern Ireland) 1997**
revoked: SR 1999/497 Reg.15 (with savings)
486. **National Assistance (Sums for Personal Requirements) Regulations 1997**
revoked: SI 1998/498 Reg.3
Reg.2, revoked: SI 1998/498 Reg.3
Reg.3, revoked: SI 1998/498 Reg.3

NO.

512. **Registration of Births, Still-births, Deaths and Marriages (Prescription of Forms) (Scotland) Amendment Regulations 1997**
revoked: SI 1997/2348 Reg.30, Sch.27
Reg.2, revoked: SI 1997/2348 Reg.30, Sch.27
Reg.3, revoked: SI 1997/2348 Reg.30, Sch.27
Reg.4, revoked: SI 1997/2348 Reg.30, Sch.27
Reg.5, revoked: SI 1997/2348 Reg.30, Sch.27
Sch.1, revoked: SI 1997/2348 Reg.30, Sch.27
Sch.2, revoked: SI 1997/2348 Reg.30, Sch.27
514. **Education (Grants for Education Support and Training) (England) Regulations 1997**
revoked: SI 1998/656 Reg.12
Reg.2, amended: SI 1997/2174 Reg.3
Reg.2, revoked: SI 1998/656 Reg.12
Reg.5, amended: SI 1997/2174 Reg.4, SI 1998/80 Reg.3
Reg.5, revoked: SI 1998/656 Reg.12
Reg.6, amended: SI 1997/2174 Reg.5
Reg.6, revoked: SI 1998/656 Reg.12
Reg.11, amended: SI 1998/80 Reg.4
Reg.11, revoked: SI 1998/656 Reg.12
Reg.12, revoked: SI 1998/656 Reg.12
Reg.13, revoked: SI 1998/656 Reg.12
Sch. para.2, revoked: SI 1998/656 Reg.12
Sch. para.16, revoked: SI 1998/656 Reg.12
Sch. para.20, added: SI 1997/2174 Reg.6
Sch. para.20, revoked: SI 1998/656 Reg.12
Sch. para.21, added: SI 1997/2174 Reg.6
Sch. para.21, revoked: SI 1998/656 Reg.12
Sch. para.22, added: SI 1997/2174 Reg.6
Sch. para.22, revoked: SI 1998/656 Reg.12
Sch. para.23, added: SI 1998/80 Reg.5
Sch. para.23, revoked: SI 1998/656 Reg.12
518. **Motor Vehicles (Construction and Use) (Amendment No.3) Regulations (Northern Ireland) 1997**
revoked: SR 1999/454 Reg.126, Sch.19
528. **Local Government Act 1988 (Direct Service Organisations) (Accounts etc.) (Extension) (Wales) Order 1997**
Art.3, amended: SI 1997/1702 Reg.2, SI 1998/2190 Art.2
528. **Section 2(1)(a) of the Petroleum Act 1987 (Modification) Regulations (Northern Ireland) 1997**
revoked: 1998 c.17 s.51, Sch.5 Part II
529. **Merchant Shipping (Minimum Standards of Safety Communications) Regulations 1997**
Reg.2, amended: SI 1999/1704 Reg.3, Reg.4
Reg.5, substituted: SI 1999/1704 Reg.5
530. **Magistrates' Courts (Children and Young Persons) (Amendment) Rules (Northern Ireland) 1997**
revoked: SR 1999/7 r.2, Sch.2
531. **Town and Country Planning (Development Plan) (Amendment) Regulations 1997**
revoked (in part): SI 1999/3280 Reg.45
Reg.3, revoked (in part): SI 1999/3280 Reg.45
Reg.4, revoked (in part): SI 1999/3280 Reg.45
Reg.5, revoked (in part): SI 1999/3280 Reg.45
Reg.6, revoked (in part): SI 1999/3280 Reg.45
Reg.7, revoked (in part): SI 1999/3280 Reg.45
Reg.8, revoked (in part): SI 1999/3280 Reg.45
Reg.9, revoked (in part): SI 1999/3280 Reg.45
Sch., revoked (in part): SI 1999/3280 Reg.45
532. **Local Government Act 1988 (Defined Activities) (Exemptions) (London Boroughs of Newham and Southwark) Order 1997**
Art.2, revoked: SI 1998/579 Art.3

1997—cont.

533. Local Government Act 1988 (Defined Activities) (Exemption) (London Borough of Brent) Order 1997
revoked: SI 1998/579 Art.3

543. Social Security Benefits Up-rating Order 1997
applied: SI 1997/576 Reg.3
referred to: SI 1997/576 Reg.2
revoked: SI 1998/470 Art.27
Art.3, revoked: SI 1998/470 Art.27
Art.4, revoked: SI 1998/470 Art.27
Art.5, revoked: SI 1998/470 Art.27
Art.6, revoked: SI 1998/470 Art.27
Art.7, revoked: SI 1998/470 Art.27
Art.8, revoked: SI 1998/470 Art.27
Art.9, revoked: SI 1998/470 Art.27
Art.10, revoked: SI 1998/470 Art.27
Art.11, revoked: SI 1998/470 Art.27
Art.12, revoked: SI 1998/470 Art.27
Art.13, revoked: SI 1998/470 Art.27
Art.14, revoked: SI 1998/470 Art.27
Art.15, revoked: SI 1998/470 Art.27
Art.16, revoked: SI 1998/470 Art.27
Art.17, revoked: SI 1998/470 Art.27
Art.18, revoked: SI 1998/470 Art.27
Art.19, revoked: SI 1998/470 Art.27
Art.20, revoked: SI 1998/470 Art.27
Art.21, revoked: SI 1998/470 Art.27
Art.22, revoked: SI 1998/470 Art.27
Art.23, revoked: SI 1998/470 Art.27
Art.24, revoked: SI 1998/470 Art.27
Art.25, revoked: SI 1998/470 Art.27
Art.27, revoked: SI 1998/470 Art.27
Sch.1, revoked: SI 1998/470 Art.27
Sch.2, revoked: SI 1998/470 Art.27
Sch.3, revoked: SI 1998/470 Art.27
Sch.4, revoked: SI 1998/470 Art.27
Sch.5, revoked: SI 1998/470 Art.27
Sch.6 Part I, revoked: SI 1998/470 Art.27
Sch.6 Part II, revoked: SI 1998/470 Art.27
Sch.7 Part I, revoked: SI 1998/470 Art.27
Sch.7 Part II, revoked: SI 1998/470 Art.27
Sch.8, revoked: SI 1998/470 Art.27
Sch.9, revoked: SI 1998/470 Art.27
Sch.10, revoked: SI 1998/470 Art.27
Sch.11, revoked: SI 1998/470 Art.27
Sch.12, revoked: SI 1998/470 Art.27
Sch.13, revoked: SI 1998/470 Art.27
Sch.14, revoked: SI 1998/470 Art.27
Sch.15 Part I, revoked: SI 1998/470 Art.27
Sch.15 Part II, revoked: SI 1998/470 Art.27
Sch.16 Part I, revoked: SI 1998/470 Art.27
Sch.16 Part II, revoked: SI 1998/470 Art.27
Sch.17, revoked: SI 1998/470 Art.27

550. A4 Trunk Road (Hounslow) Red Route (Clearway) Traffic Order 1996 Experimental Variation Order 1997
revoked: SI 1998/1642 Art.4
Art.3, revoked: SI 1998/1642 Art.4
Sch., revoked: SI 1998/1642 Art.4

553. Bovine Spongiform Encephalopathy Order (Northern Ireland) 1997
revoked: SR 1999/322 Art.17

553. Railway Safety (Miscellaneous Provisions) Regulations 1997
Reg.2, amended: SI 1999/2024 Reg.48, Sch.5 Part II
Reg.11, revoked: SI 1998/494 Reg.7, Sch.3

555. A205 Trunk Road (Lewisham) Red Route (Bus Lanes) Experimental Traffic Order 1997
revoked (in part): SI 1998/884 Art.5

1997—cont.

558. National Health Service (Dental Charges) Amendment Regulations 1997
revoked: SI 1998/490 Reg.3
Reg.2, revoked: SI 1998/490 Reg.3
Reg.3, revoked: SI 1998/490 Reg.3
Reg.4, revoked: SI 1998/490 Reg.3

562. Merchant Shipping (Light Dues) Regulations 1997
Sch.2 Part IV, amended: SI 1998/495 Reg.2

564. Motor Vehicles (Type Approval and Approval Marks) (Fees) Regulations 1997
revoked: SI 1999/2149 Reg.2
Reg.2, revoked: SI 1999/2149 Reg.2
Reg.7, revoked: SI 1999/2149 Reg.2
Reg.10, revoked: SI 1999/2149 Reg.2
Reg.13, revoked: SI 1999/2149 Reg.2
Reg.16, revoked: SI 1999/2149 Reg.2
Sch.1 Part II, revoked: SI 1999/2149 Reg.2
Sch.2, revoked: SI 1999/2149 Reg.2
Sch.3, revoked: SI 1999/2149 Reg.2
Sch.4, revoked: SI 1999/2149 Reg.2
Sch.5 Part I, revoked: SI 1999/2149 Reg.2
Sch.5 Part II, revoked: SI 1999/2149 Reg.2

565. Vehicle Excise Duty (Immobilisation, Removal and Disposal of Vehicles) (Amendment) Regulations 1997
revoked: SI 1997/2439 Reg.1
Reg.3, revoked: SI 1997/2439 Reg.1
Reg.4, revoked: SI 1997/2439 Reg.1
Reg.5, revoked: SI 1997/2439 Reg.1
Sch., revoked: SI 1997/2439 Reg.1

567. Pesticides (Maximum Residue Levels in Crops, Food and Feeding Stuffs) (Amendment) Regulations 1997
revoked (in part): SI 1999/3483 Reg.7, Sch.4
Reg.3, revoked (in part): SI 1999/3483 Reg.7, Sch.4
Reg.4, revoked (in part): SI 1999/3483 Reg.7, Sch.4
Reg.5, revoked (in part): SI 1999/3483 Reg.7, Sch.4
Reg.6, revoked (in part): SI 1999/3483 Reg.7, Sch.4

573. Education (Individual Pupils' Achievements) (Information) (Wales) Regulations 1997
Reg.2, amended: SI 1997/2709 Reg.3, SI 1999/1497 Reg.2
Sch.1 para.1, amended: SI 1997/2709 Reg.4
Sch.1 para.1, revoked (in part): SI 1997/2709 Reg.4
Sch.2 para.1, amended: SI 1997/2709 Reg.5
Sch.2 para.2, amended: SI 1997/2709 Reg.5
Sch.2 para.3, amended: SI 1997/2709 Reg.5
Sch.3 para.1, amended: SI 1997/2709 Reg.6
Sch.3 para.2, amended: SI 1998/2705 Reg.2

576. Social Security Benefits Up-rating Regulations 1997
revoked: SI 1998/563 Reg.7
Reg.2, revoked: SI 1998/563 Reg.7
Reg.3, revoked: SI 1998/563 Reg.7
Reg.4, revoked: SI 1998/563 Reg.7
Reg.5, revoked: SI 1998/563 Reg.7
Reg.6, revoked: SI 1998/563 Reg.7
Reg.7, revoked: SI 1998/563 Reg.7

577. Social Security (Industrial Injuries) (Dependency) (Permitted Earnings Limits) Order 1997
revoked: SI 1998/520 Art.3
Art.2, revoked: SI 1998/520 Art.3

NO.

578. Local Government Pension Scheme (Amendment) Regulations 1997
applied: SI 1997/1613 Reg.4, Reg.19, Sch.2 para.2
referred to: SI 1997/1613 Reg.3, Sch.2 para.6

589. Local Authorities (Members' Allowances) (Amendment) Regulations 1997
revoked (in part): SI 1998/556 Reg.3, SI 1998/557 Reg.3
Reg.2, revoked (in part): SI 1998/556 Reg.3, SI 1998/557 Reg.3

598. Local Government Pension Scheme (Transfers from the National Health Service Pension Scheme for England and Wales) Regulations 1997
applied: SI 1997/1613 Reg.4, Reg.19, Sch.2 para.2
referred to: SI 1997/1613 Reg.3, Sch.2 para.6

599. Education (Grant-Maintained and Grant-Maintained Special Schools) (Finance) (Wales) Regulations 1997
revoked: SI 1999/440 Reg.3
Reg.3, revoked: SI 1999/440 Reg.3
Reg.5, revoked: SI 1999/440 Reg.3
Reg.6, revoked: SI 1999/440 Reg.3
Reg.7, revoked: SI 1999/440 Reg.3
Reg.10, amended: SI 1998/391 Reg.2
Reg.10, revoked: SI 1999/440 Reg.3
Reg.11, revoked: SI 1999/440 Reg.3
Reg.13, amended: SI 1998/391 Reg.3
Reg.13, revoked: SI 1999/440 Reg.3
Reg.18, revoked: SI 1999/440 Reg.3
Reg.20, revoked: SI 1999/440 Reg.3
Reg.23, revoked: SI 1999/440 Reg.3
Reg.24, revoked: SI 1999/440 Reg.3
Sch.1 para.2, revoked: SI 1999/440 Reg.3
Sch.1 para.2, substituted: SI 1998/391 Reg.4
Sch.1 para.2A, added: SI 1998/391 Reg.4
Sch.1 para.2A, revoked: SI 1999/440 Reg.3
Sch.1 para.2B, added: SI 1998/391 Reg.4
Sch.1 para.2B, revoked: SI 1999/440 Reg.3
Sch.2 para.2, revoked: SI 1999/440 Reg.3
Sch.3 para.1, revoked: SI 1999/440 Reg.3
Sch.5 para.2, revoked: SI 1999/440 Reg.3

617. Specified Bovine Material Order 1997
applied: SI 1997/2965 Reg.32
revoked: SI 1997/2964 Art.18
Art.6, revoked: SI 1997/2964 Art.18
Art.19, applied: SI 1997/813 Reg.6
Art.19, revoked: SI 1997/2964 Art.18
Art.20, revoked: SI 1997/2964 Art.18
Art.23, revoked: SI 1997/2964 Art.18
Art.28, revoked: SI 1997/2964 Art.18
Art.29, revoked: SI 1997/2964 Art.18
Sch.2, revoked: SI 1997/2964 Art.18

620. Housing (Right to Acquire or Enfranchise) (Designated Rural Areas in the West Midlands) Order 1997
referred to: SI 1997/2792 Art.2

621. Housing (Right to Acquire or Enfranchise) (Designated Rural Areas in the South West) Order 1997
referred to: SI 1997/2792 Art.2
Sch.2 Part V, revoked (in part): SI 1999/1307 Art.3

622. Housing (Right to Acquire or Enfranchise) (Designated Rural Areas in the North West and Merseyside) Order 1997
referred to: SI 1997/2792 Art.2

NO.

623. Housing (Right to Acquire or Enfranchise) (Designated Rural Areas in the East) Order 1997
referred to: SI 1997/2792 Art.2
Sch.1 Part III, revoked (in part): SI 1999/1307 Art.3
Sch.2 Part VI, revoked (in part): SI 1999/1307 Art.3

624. Housing (Right to Acquire or Enfranchise) (Designated Rural Areas in the North East) Order 1997
referred to: SI 1997/2792 Art.2
Sch.1 Part IX, revoked (in part): SI 1999/1307 Art.3
Sch.2 Part VI, revoked (in part): SI 1999/1307 Art.3

625. Housing (Right to Acquire or Enfranchise) (Designated Rural Areas in the South East) Order 1997
referred to: SI 1997/2792 Art.2

626. Housing (Right to Acquire) (Discount) Order 1997
revoked: SI 1998/2014 Art.3
Art.2, revoked: SI 1998/2014 Art.3

630. Measuring Instruments (EEC Requirements) (Fees) (Amendment) Regulations 1997
revoked: SI 1998/1177 Reg.1
Reg.2, revoked: SI 1998/1177 Reg.1

631. Allocation of Housing and Homelessness (Amendment) Regulations 1997
Reg.1, amended: SI 1999/71 Reg.10

634. Pensions Increase (Review) Order 1997
applied: SI 1998/503 Art.3, Art.4, SI 1999/522 Art.3

638. Medicines (Medicated Animal Feeding Stuffs) (Amendment) Regulations 1997
revoked: SI 1998/1048 Reg.2, Sch.1
Reg.2, revoked: SI 1998/1048 Reg.2, Sch.1
Sch., revoked: SI 1998/1048 Reg.2, Sch.1

647. Merchant Shipping (Ro-Ro Passenger Ship Survivability) Regulations 1997
applied: SI 1998/2514 Reg.44

648. Producer Responsibility Obligations (Packaging Waste) Regulations 1997
Reg.2, amended: SI 1999/3447 Reg.2, Reg.3
Reg.3, amended: SI 1999/3447 Reg.2
Reg.4, amended: SI 1999/3447 Reg.2
Reg.4, revoked (in part): SI 1999/3447 Reg.2
Reg.6, amended: SI 1999/3447 Reg.2
Reg.8, amended: SI 1999/3447 Reg.2
Reg.9, amended: SI 1999/3447 Reg.2
Reg.12, amended: SI 1999/3447 Reg.2, Reg.3
Reg.12, applied: SI 1999/1512 Art.2, Sch.1 para.8
Reg.13, amended: SI 1999/3447 Reg.3
Reg.14, amended: SI 1999/3447 Reg.2
Reg.15, amended: SI 1999/3447 Reg.2
Reg.17, applied: SI 1999/1512 Art.2, Sch.1 para.9
Reg.17, amended: SI 1999/3447 Reg.3
Reg.18, applied: SI 1999/1512 Art.2, Sch.1 para.10
Reg.19, applied: SI 1999/1512 Art.2, Sch.1 para.11
Reg.20, applied: SI 1999/1512 Art.2, Sch.1 para.12
Reg.22, amended: SI 1999/3447 Reg.2
Reg.24, amended: SI 1999/3447 Reg.2
Reg.25, amended: SI 1999/3447 Reg.2
Reg.25A, added: SI 1999/3447 Reg.2
Reg.31, revoked: SI 1999/3447 Reg.3
Reg.32, revoked: SI 1999/3447 Reg.3
Reg.33, revoked: SI 1999/3447 Reg.3

NO.

648. Producer Responsibility Obligations (Packaging Waste) Regulations 1997—*cont.*
Reg.34, amended: SI 1999/3447 Reg.2, Reg.3
Reg.34, revoked (in part): SI 1999/3447 Reg.3
Sch.1 Table, amended: SI 1999/3447 Reg.2
Sch.1 para.1, amended: SI 1999/3447 Reg.2
Sch.1 para.1, revoked (in part): SI 1999/3447 Reg.2
Sch.1 para.2, amended: SI 1999/3447 Reg.2
Sch.1 para.2, revoked (in part): SI 1999/3447 Reg.2
Sch.1 para.3, amended: SI 1999/3447 Reg.2
Sch.1 para.4, amended: SI 1999/3447 Reg.2
Sch.2 para.2, amended: SI 1999/3447 Reg.2
Sch.2 para.3, amended: SI 1999/3447 Reg.2
Sch.2 para.4, amended: SI 1999/1361 Reg.2
Sch.2 para.5, amended: SI 1999/1361 Reg.2
Sch.2 para.6, substituted: SI 1999/3447 Reg.2
Sch.2 para.7, added: SI 1999/3447 Reg.2
Sch.3 Part I, amended: SI 1999/3447 Reg.2
Sch.3 Part III, amended: SI 1999/3447 Reg.2
Sch.4 Part II, revoked: SI 1999/3447 Reg.2
Sch.5, applied: SI 1999/1512 Art.2, Sch.1 para.11

653. Insurance (Fees) Regulations 1997
revoked: SI 1998/612 Reg.2
Reg.2, revoked: SI 1998/612 Reg.2
Reg.4, revoked: SI 1998/612 Reg.2
Reg.5, revoked: SI 1998/612 Reg.2
Reg.6, revoked: SI 1998/612 Reg.2
Reg.7, revoked: SI 1998/612 Reg.2
Reg.8, revoked: SI 1998/612 Reg.2
Reg.9, revoked: SI 1998/612 Reg.2
Reg.10, revoked: SI 1998/612 Reg.2

654. Good Laboratory Practice Regulations 1997
revoked: SI 1999/3106 Reg.17
Reg.6, applied: SI 1999/3106 Reg.6
Reg.6, revoked: SI 1999/3106 Reg.17
Reg.17, revoked: SI 1999/3106 Reg.17
Reg.18, revoked: SI 1999/3106 Reg.17
Reg.19, revoked: SI 1999/3106 Reg.17

664. Pensions Act 1995 (Commencement No.10) Order 1997
referred to: 1999 c.30 s.81, Sch.11 para.33
Art.4, amended: 1999 c.2 s.1, Sch.2
Art.4, referred to: SI 1999/527 Art.2, Sch.2
Art.13, amended: 1999 c.2 s.1, Sch.2

665. Occupational Pension Schemes (Pensions Compensation Provisions) Regulations 1997
Reg.1, amended: SI 1998/1129 Art.3, Sch.2
Reg.2, referred to: SI 1997/666 Reg.5

666. Occupational and Personal Pension Schemes (Levy) Regulations 1997
Reg.1, amended: SI 1998/600 Reg.2
Reg.2, amended: SI 1998/600 Reg.2
Reg.2, revoked (in part): SI 1998/600 Reg.2
Reg.3, amended: SI 1998/600 Reg.2
Reg.4, amended: SI 1998/600 Reg.2
Reg.4, revoked (in part): SI 1998/600 Reg.2
Reg.5, amended: SI 1998/600 Reg.2
Reg.5, revoked (in part): SI 1998/600 Reg.2
Reg.7, amended: SI 1998/600 Reg.2
Reg.7, revoked (in part): SI 1998/600 Reg.2
Reg.11, amended: SI 1998/600 Reg.2
Sch., substituted: SI 1998/600 Reg.2, Sch.
Sch. Part I, amended: SI 1999/682 Reg.2

667. Civil Aviation (Navigation Services Charges) (Second Amendment) Regulations 1997
revoked: SI 1998/532 Reg.3, Sch.1
Reg.2, revoked: SI 1998/532 Reg.3, Sch.1

NO.

669. Motor Vehicles (Driving Licences) (Amendment) (No.2) Regulations 1997
revoked: SI 1999/2864 Reg.2, Sch.1
Reg.2, revoked: SI 1999/2864 Reg.2, Sch.1
Reg.4, revoked (in part): SI 1997/846 Reg.2, SI 1999/2864 Reg.2, Sch.1
Reg.5, revoked: SI 1999/2864 Reg.2, Sch.1
Reg.6, revoked: SI 1999/2864 Reg.2, Sch.1
Reg.7, revoked: SI 1999/2864 Reg.2, Sch.1
Reg.8, revoked: SI 1999/2864 Reg.2, Sch.1
Reg.9, revoked: SI 1999/2864 Reg.2, Sch.1
Reg.10, revoked: SI 1999/2864 Reg.2, Sch.1
Reg.11, revoked: SI 1999/2864 Reg.2, Sch.1
Reg.12, revoked: SI 1999/2864 Reg.2, Sch.1
Reg.13, revoked: SI 1999/2864 Reg.2, Sch.1
Reg.14, revoked: SI 1999/2864 Reg.2, Sch.1
Reg.15, revoked: SI 1999/2864 Reg.2, Sch.1
Reg.16, revoked: SI 1999/2864 Reg.2, Sch.1
Reg.17, revoked: SI 1999/2864 Reg.2, Sch.1
Reg.18, revoked: SI 1999/2864 Reg.2, Sch.1
Reg.19, revoked: SI 1999/2864 Reg.2, Sch.1
Reg.20, revoked: SI 1999/2864 Reg.2, Sch.1
Reg.21, revoked: SI 1999/2864 Reg.2, Sch.1
Reg.22, revoked: SI 1999/2864 Reg.2, Sch.1
Reg.23, revoked: SI 1999/2864 Reg.2, Sch.1
Reg.24, revoked: SI 1999/2864 Reg.2, Sch.1
Reg.25, revoked: SI 1999/2864 Reg.2, Sch.1
Reg.26, revoked: SI 1999/2864 Reg.2, Sch.1
Reg.27, revoked: SI 1999/2864 Reg.2, Sch.1
Reg.28, revoked: SI 1999/2864 Reg.2, Sch.1
Reg.29, revoked: SI 1999/2864 Reg.2, Sch.1
Reg.30, revoked: SI 1999/2864 Reg.2, Sch.1
Reg.31, revoked: SI 1999/2864 Reg.2, Sch.1
Reg.32, revoked: SI 1999/2864 Reg.2, Sch.1
Reg.33, revoked: SI 1999/2864 Reg.2, Sch.1
Reg.34, revoked: SI 1999/2864 Reg.2, Sch.1
Reg.35, revoked: SI 1999/2864 Reg.2, Sch.1
Reg.36, revoked: SI 1999/2864 Reg.2, Sch.1
Reg.37, revoked: SI 1999/2864 Reg.2, Sch.1
Reg.38, revoked: SI 1999/2864 Reg.2, Sch.1
Reg.39, revoked: SI 1999/2864 Reg.2, Sch.1
Reg.40, revoked: SI 1999/2864 Reg.2, Sch.1
Reg.41, revoked: SI 1999/2864 Reg.2, Sch.1
Reg.42, revoked: SI 1999/2864 Reg.2, Sch.1
Reg.43, revoked: SI 1999/2864 Reg.2, Sch.1
Reg.44, revoked: SI 1999/2864 Reg.2, Sch.1
Reg.45, revoked: SI 1999/2864 Reg.2, Sch.1
Reg.46, revoked: SI 1999/2864 Reg.2, Sch.1
Reg.47, revoked: SI 1999/2864 Reg.2, Sch.1
Reg.48, revoked: SI 1999/2864 Reg.2, Sch.1
Reg.49, revoked: SI 1999/2864 Reg.2, Sch.1
Reg.50, revoked: SI 1999/2864 Reg.2, Sch.1
Reg.51, revoked: SI 1999/2864 Reg.2, Sch.1
Reg.52, revoked: SI 1999/2864 Reg.2, Sch.1
Reg.53, revoked: SI 1999/2864 Reg.2, Sch.1
Reg.54, revoked: SI 1999/2864 Reg.2, Sch.1
Sch.1, revoked: SI 1999/2864 Reg.2, Sch.1
Sch.2, revoked: SI 1999/2864 Reg.2, Sch.1
Sch.3, revoked: SI 1999/2864 Reg.2, Sch.1

673. Council Tax (Dwellings) (Scotland) Regulations 1997
Reg.2, referred to: SI 1997/728 Sch.1 para.24

674. Local Government Superannuation (Scotland) Amendment Regulations 1997
applied: SI 1998/364 Reg.4, Reg.6, Reg.19, Sch.2 para.2, Sch.2 para.5, Sch.4 para.8
referred to: SI 1998/364 Reg.3, Reg.10, Sch.2 para.4, Sch.2 para.6

680. Education (Amount to Follow Permanently Excluded Pupil) Regulations 1997
revoked: SI 1999/495 Reg.5 (with saving)
Reg.2, revoked: SI 1999/495 Reg.5 (with saving)

NO.

NO.

1997—cont.

1997—cont.

680. Education (Amount to Follow Permanently Excluded Pupil) Regulations 1997—*cont.*
Reg.3, revoked: SI 1999/495 Reg.5 (with saving)
Reg.4, revoked: SI 1999/495 Reg.5 (with saving)

684. Criminal Procedure and Investigations Act 1996 (Defence Disclosure Time Limits) Regulations 1997
Reg.3, applied: SI 1997/698 r.8, SI 1997/703 r.8
Reg.4, applied: SI 1997/698 r.8, SI 1997/703 r.8

687. Sheriff Court Fees Order 1997
Art.9, amended: SI 1999/754 Art.2
Sch.1 Table, substituted: SI 1999/754 Art.2, Sch.

688. Court of Session etc. Fees Order 1997
Art.4, amended: SI 1999/755 Art.2
Art.5A, added: SI 1999/755 Art.2
Art.5B, added: SI 1999/755
Sch.1 Table, substituted: SI 1999/755 Art.2

695. Common Police Services (Scotland) Order 1997
Art.2, applied: SI 1997/721 Art.4
Art.3, applied: SI 1997/721 Art.4

699. Crown Court (Criminal Procedure and Investigations Act 1996) (Confidentiality) Rules 1997
r.6, amended: SI 1999/598 r.3

710. Justices' Clerks (Amendment) Rules 1997
revoked: SI 1999/2784 r.4
r.3, revoked: SI 1999/2784 r.4
r.4, revoked: SI 1999/2784 r.4

716. Registration of Births, Deaths, Marriages and Divorces (Fees) (Scotland) Regulations 1997
revoked: SI 1998/643 Reg.8
Reg.2, amended: SI 1997/1680 Reg.3
Reg.3, revoked: SI 1998/643 Reg.8
Reg.5, revoked: SI 1998/643 Reg.8
Reg.6, revoked: SI 1998/643 Reg.8
Reg.7, revoked: SI 1998/643 Reg.8
Sch.1, amended: SI 1997/1680 Reg.4, Reg.5, Reg.6, Reg.7, Reg.8
Sch.1, revoked: SI 1998/643 Reg.8
Sch.2, revoked: SI 1998/643 Reg.8

722. Rural Diversification Programme (Scotland) Amendment Regulations 1997
revoked: SI 1999/651 Reg.9
Reg.2, revoked: SI 1999/651 Reg.9
Reg.3, revoked: SI 1999/651 Reg.9
Sch., revoked: SI 1999/651 Reg.9

728. Council Tax (Exempt Dwellings) (Scotland) Order 1997
Art.2, amended: SSI 1999/140 Art.2
Sch.1 para.2, substituted: SSI 1999/140 Art.2
Sch.1 para.10, amended: SI 1999/757 Art.2
Sch.1 para.11, amended: SI 1998/561 Art.2

733. Dairy Produce Quotas Regulations 1997
applied: SI 1999/672 Art.2, Sch.1
Reg.6, amended: SI 1997/1093 Reg.2
Reg.11, amended: SI 1997/1093 Reg.2
Reg.28A, added: SI 1998/2880 Reg.5

735. Offshore Installations (Safety Zones) Order 1997
Sch.1, revoked (in part): SI 1998/608 Art.3, SI 1999/547 Art.3

736. Severn Trent Water Limited (Extension of Byelaws) Order 1997
revoked: SI 1998/2399 Art.3

740. Building Societies (General Charge and Fees) Regulations 1997
revoked: SI 1998/675 Reg.11
Reg.3, revoked: SI 1998/675 Reg.11
Reg.4, revoked: SI 1998/675 Reg.11
Reg.5, revoked: SI 1998/675 Reg.11
Reg.6, revoked: SI 1998/675 Reg.11
Reg.7, revoked: SI 1998/675 Reg.11
Reg.8, revoked: SI 1998/675 Reg.11
Reg.11, revoked: SI 1998/675 Reg.11
Sch.1 para.3, revoked: SI 1998/675 Reg.11

741. Friendly Societies (General Charge and Fees) Regulations 1997
revoked: SI 1998/673 Reg.7
Reg.5, revoked: SI 1998/673 Reg.7
Reg.7, revoked: SI 1998/673 Reg.7
Sch.1 para.2, revoked: SI 1998/673 Reg.7
Sch.1 para.3, revoked: SI 1998/673 Reg.7
Sch.1 para.4, revoked: SI 1998/673 Reg.7
Sch.2, revoked: SI 1998/673 Reg.7

742. Industrial and Provident Societies (Credit Unions) (Amendment of Fees) Regulations 1997
revoked: SI 1998/672 Reg.3
Reg.2, revoked: SI 1998/672 Reg.3
Reg.3, revoked: SI 1998/672 Reg.3

743. Industrial and Provident Societies (Amendment of Fees) Regulations 1997
revoked: SI 1998/676 Reg.4
Reg.2, revoked: SI 1998/676 Reg.4
Reg.3, revoked: SI 1998/676 Reg.4
Reg.4, revoked: SI 1998/676 Reg.4

750. Town and Country Planning Appeals (Determination by Appointed Person) (Inquiries Procedure) (Scotland) Rules 1997
r.3, amended: SI 1998/2312 r.3
r.7, amended: SI 1998/2312 r.4
r.7, revoked (in part): SI 1998/2312 r.4
r.8, amended: SI 1998/2312 r.5
r.8, revoked (in part): SI 1998/2312 r.5
r.9, amended: SI 1998/2312 r.6
r.9, revoked (in part): SI 1998/2312 r.6
r.10A, added: SI 1998/2312 r.7
r.11, amended: SI 1998/2312 r.8
r.12, amended: SI 1998/2312 r.9
r.12, revoked (in part): SI 1998/2312 r.9
r.14, amended: SI 1998/2312 r.10
r.14, applied: SI 1998/2312 r.14
r.15, amended: SI 1998/2312 r.11
r.18, amended: SI 1998/2312 r.12
r.19, amended: SI 1998/2312 r.13

755. Education (School Teachers' Pay and Conditions) Order 1997
revoked: SI 1997/1789 Art.1

784. Occupational Pension Schemes (Discharge of Liability) Regulations 1997
Reg.1, amended: SI 1999/3198 Reg.14
Reg.4, amended: SI 1999/3198 Reg.14
Reg.11, amended: SI 1999/3198 Reg.14

785. Occupational Pension Schemes (Assignment, Forfeiture, Bankruptcy etc.) Regulations 1997
Reg.8, amended: SI 1999/1849 Reg.3

786. Personal and Occupational Pension Schemes (Miscellaneous Amendments) Regulations 1997
Reg.4, referred to: 1999 c.30 s.81, Sch.11 para.35

787. County Court Fees (Amendment) Order 1997
revoked: SI 1999/689 Art.8 (with savings), Sch.2 (with savings)
Art.2, revoked: SI 1999/689 Art.8 (with savings), Sch.2 (with savings)

1997—cont.

787. County Court Fees (Amendment) Order 1997
—cont.
Art.3, revoked: SI 1999/689 Art.8 (with savings), Sch.2 (with savings)

788. Family Proceedings Fees (Amendment) Order 1997
revoked: SI 1999/690 Art.7 (with savings), Sch.2 (with savings)
Art.2, revoked: SI 1999/690 Art.7 (with savings), Sch.2 (with savings)
Art.3, revoked: SI 1999/690 Art.7 (with savings), Sch.2 (with savings)

790. Home Energy Efficiency Scheme Regulations 1997
Reg.5, amended: SI 1999/1018 Reg.3
Reg.6, amended: SI 1999/1018 Reg.4
Reg.7, amended: SI 1999/1018 Reg.5

793. Social Security (Miscellaneous Amendments) (No.2) Regulations 1997
Reg.1, revoked (in part): SI 1999/991 Reg.59 (with savings), Sch.4 (with savings)
Reg.8, revoked: SI 1999/991 Reg.59 (with savings), Sch.4 (with savings)
Reg.9, revoked: SI 1999/991 Reg.59 (with savings), Sch.4 (with savings)
Reg.10, revoked: SI 1999/991 Reg.59 (with savings), Sch.4 (with savings)
Reg.11, revoked: SI 1999/991 Reg.59 (with savings), Sch.4 (with savings)
Reg.12, revoked: SI 1999/991 Reg.59 (with savings), Sch.4 (with savings)
Reg.13, revoked: SI 1999/991 Reg.59 (with savings), Sch.4 (with savings)
Reg.14, revoked: SI 1999/991 Reg.59 (with savings), Sch.4 (with savings)
Reg.15, revoked: SI 1999/991 Reg.59 (with savings), Sch.4 (with savings)
Reg.16, revoked: SI 1999/991 Reg.59 (with savings), Sch.4 (with savings)
Reg.17, revoked: SI 1999/991 Reg.59 (with savings), Sch.4 (with savings)

796. Town and Country Planning (Inquiries Procedure) (Scotland) Rules 1997
r.3, amended: SI 1998/2311 r.3
r.7, amended: SI 1998/2311 r.4
r.7, revoked (in part): SI 1998/2311 r.4
r.8, amended: SI 1998/2311 r.5
r.8, revoked (in part): SI 1998/2311 r.5
r.9, amended: SI 1998/2311 r.6
r.9, revoked (in part): SI 1998/2311 r.6
r.10A, added: SI 1998/2311 r.7
r.12, amended: SI 1998/2311 r.8
r.13, amended: SI 1998/2311 r.9
r.13, revoked (in part): SI 1998/2311 r.9
r.15, amended: SI 1998/2311 r.10
r.15, applied: SI 1998/2311 r.13
r.16, amended: SI 1998/2311 r.11
r.19, amended: SI 1998/2311 r.12

802. Child Support Commissioners (Procedure) (Amendment) Regulations 1997
revoked (in part): SI 1999/1305 Reg.2
Reg.2, revoked (in part): SI 1999/1305 Reg.2
Reg.3, revoked (in part): SI 1999/1305 Reg.2
Reg.4, revoked (in part): SI 1999/1305 Reg.2
Reg.5, revoked (in part): SI 1999/1305 Reg.2
Reg.6, revoked (in part): SI 1999/1305 Reg.2

810. Social Security (Industrial Injuries) (Miscellaneous Amendments) Regulations 1997
Reg.2, revoked: SI 1999/991 Reg.59 (with savings), Sch.4 (with savings)
Reg.3, revoked: SI 1999/991 Reg.59 (with savings), Sch.4 (with savings)

1997—cont.

810. Social Security (Industrial Injuries) (Miscellaneous Amendments) Regulations 1997
—cont.
Reg.4, revoked: SI 1999/991 Reg.59 (with savings), Sch.4 (with savings)

817. Banking Act 1987 (Exempt Transactions) Regulations 1997
Reg.14, amended: SI 1997/1866 Reg.2

818. National Health Service (Optical Charges and Payments) Regulations 1997
Reg.1, amended: SI 1997/2488 Reg.2, SI 1999/609 Reg.2, SI 1999/2562 Reg.2, SI 1999/2841 Reg.2
Reg.8, amended: SI 1999/609 Reg.3, SI 1999/2562 Reg.2
Reg.9, amended: SI 1999/609 Reg.4
Reg.11, substituted: SI 1999/609 Reg.5
Reg.12, amended: SI 1999/609 Reg.6
Reg.12, applied: SI 1998/499 Reg.4
Reg.13, amended: SI 1999/609 Reg.7
Reg.17, applied: SI 1998/499 Reg.4
Reg.19, amended: SI 1998/499 Reg.2, SI 1999/609 Reg.8
Reg.20, amended: SI 1999/609 Reg.9
Sch.1, amended: SI 1998/499 Reg.3
Sch.1, substituted: SI 1999/609 Reg.10, Sch. Part I
Sch.2 para.1, amended: SI 1998/499 Reg.3, SI 1999/609 Reg.10, Reg.11
Sch.2 para.1, revoked (in part): SI 1999/609 Reg.11
Sch.2 para.2, amended: SI 1998/499 Reg.3, SI 1999/609 Reg.10
Sch.3, substituted: SI 1998/499 Reg.3, Sch., SI 1999/609 Reg.10, Sch. Part II

831. Lifts Regulations 1997
applied: SI 1998/2306 Reg.10, Sch.1

846. Motor Vehicles (Driving Licences) (Amendment) (No.3) Regulations 1997
revoked: SI 1999/2864 Reg.2, Sch.1
Reg.2, revoked: SI 1999/2864 Reg.2, Sch.1
Reg.3, revoked: SI 1999/2864 Reg.2, Sch.1

848. Local Authorities (Capital Finance) (Amendment) Regulations 1997
Reg.4, revoked: SI 1999/3423 Reg.3

852. Housing Benefit and Council Tax Benefit (General) Amendment Regulations 1997
applied: SI 1999/2734 Reg.13
Reg.3, amended: SI 1997/1975 Reg.2
Reg.3, referred to: SI 1999/2734 Reg.11
Reg.3, revoked (in part): SI 1997/1975 Reg.2
Reg.4, amended: SI 1997/1975 Reg.2, SI 1998/2231 Reg.12
Reg.4, applied: SI 1999/2734 Reg.11
Reg.4, referred to: SI 1999/2734 Reg.11

866. Education (Northern Ireland) Order 1997
applied: SI 1998/1759 (NI.13) Art.40, Sch.2 para.3
Art.2, revoked (in part): SI 1997/1772 (NI.15) Art.25, Sch.5
Art.12, amended: SI 1998/1759 (NI.13) Art.16
Art.15, applied: SI 1998/1759 (NI.13) Art.22, Art.27, Art.31
Art.18, amended: SI 1998/1759 (NI.13) Art.91, Sch.5 Part I
Art.18, applied: SI 1998/1759 (NI.13) Art.17
Art.25, revoked (in part): SI 1998/1759 (NI.13) Art.91, Sch.6 Part II
Part II, revoked: SI 1998/1759 (NI.13) Art.91, Sch.6 Part I

NO.

869. Race Relations (Northern Ireland) Order 1997

referred to: SI 1998/3162 (NI.21) Art.85, SI 1999/2204 Art.3

Part II, applied: SI 1998/3162 (NI.21) Art.85

Art.2, amended: 1998 c.47 s.99, Sch.13 para.19

Art.5, amended: SI 1998/3162 (NI.21) Art.105, Sch.3

Art.17, amended: 1998 c.32 s.74, Sch.4 para.24

Art.18, amended: SI 1997/1772 (NI.15) Art.25, Sch.4

Art.36A, added: SI 1998/3162 (NI.21) Art.97

Art.41, applied: SI 1998/3162 (NI.21) Art.105, Sch.4 para.4

Art.41, revoked (in part): SI 1998/3162 (NI.21) Art.105, Sch.4 para.4

Art.41, substituted: SI 1998/3162 (NI.21) Art.98

Art.41A, added: SI 1998/3162 (NI.21) Art.98

Art.41A, applied: SI 1998/3162 (NI.21) Art.105, Sch.4 para.4

Art.41A, revoked (in part): SI 1998/3162 (NI.21) Art.105, Sch.4 para.4

Art.42, revoked (in part): 1998 c.47 s.99, s.100, Sch.13 para.19, Sch.15

Art.52, amended: SI 1998/3162 (NI.21) Art.105, Sch.3

Art.52, referred to: SI 1998/3162 (NI.21) Art.85

Art.66, amended: SI 1998/3162 (NI.21) Art.98, Art.105, Sch.5

Art.66, revoked (in part): SI 1998/3162 (NI.21) Art.105, Sch.5

Art.68, amended: SI 1998/1265 (NI.8) Art.9, Art.10, Art.11, Art.16, Sch.1 para.21

Art.69, amended: 1998 c.17 Sch.4 para.41

Sch.1, revoked: 1998 c.47 s.99, s.100, Sch.13 para.19, Sch.15

Sch.1 para.1, revoked: 1998 c.47 s.99, s.100, Sch.13 para.19, Sch.15

Sch.1 para.15, revoked: 1998 c.47 s.99, s.100, Sch.13 para.19, Sch.15

Sch.2, revoked (in part): SI 1998/3162 (NI.21) Art.105, Sch.5

Sch.2 para.1, revoked: 1998 c.47 s.100, Sch.15

Sch.2 para.7, revoked: 1998 c.47 s.100, Sch.15

Sch.2 para.8, revoked (in part): SI 1998/1265 (NI.8) Art.16, Sch.2, SI 1999/2790 (NI.9) Art.40, Sch.9 Part 10

874. European Parliamentary Elections (Amendment) Regulations 1997

revoked: SI 1999/1214 Reg.20, Sch.5

Reg.2, revoked: SI 1999/1214 Reg.20, Sch.5

Reg.3, revoked: SI 1999/1214 Reg.20, Sch.5

883. Sea Fishing (Enforcement of Community Quota Measures) Order 1997

revoked: SI 1998/268 Art.14

Art.5, revoked: SI 1998/268 Art.14

Art.13, revoked: SI 1998/268 Art.14

931. Third Country Fishing (Enforcement) Order 1997

revoked: SI 1998/269 Art.13

Art.5, revoked: SI 1998/269 Art.13

Art.13, revoked: SI 1998/269 Art.13

Sch. para.1, amended: SI 1997/1629 Art.2

Sch. para.1, revoked: SI 1998/269 Art.13

Sch. para.2, amended: SI 1997/1629 Art.2

Sch. para.2, revoked: SI 1998/269 Art.13

934. Local Government Act 1988 (Defined Activities) (Housing Management) (Exemptions) (Wales) Order 1997

Art.3, amended: SI 1997/2648 Art.2

Art.5, amended: SI 1997/1701 Art.2, SI 1998/2189 Art.2

NO.

935. Local Government Act 1988 (Competition) (Housing Management) (Wales) Regulations 1997

Reg.2, amended: SI 1997/2649 Reg.5

Reg.3, amended: SI 1997/1699 Reg.4, SI 1997/2649 Reg.5, SI 1998/2192 Reg.2, Sch.

Sch., revoked: SI 1997/1699 Reg.4

938. Local Government Finance (Scotland) Order 1997

Art.2, revoked: SI 1998/1082 Art.5

Sch.1, revoked (in part): SI 1998/1082 Art.5

939. Revenue Support Grant (Scotland) Order 1997

Art.3, revoked: SI 1998/1083 Art.3

Sch., revoked (in part): SI 1998/1083 Art.3

940. Housing Support Grant (Scotland) Order 1997

Art.2, amended: SI 1998/873 Art.2

Art.3, amended: SI 1998/873 Art.2

944. Income Support (General) (Standard Interest Rate Amendment) Regulations 1997

revoked: SI 1997/2055 Reg.3 (with saving)

946. Occupational Pension Schemes (Age-related Payments) Regulations 1997

Reg.4, amended: SI 1997/3038 Reg.13

Reg.7, amended: SI 1997/3038 Reg.13

950. Deregulation (Casinos) Order 1997

Art.5, revoked: SI 1999/2136 Art.4

954. Local Government Pension Scheme (Provision of Information, Administrative Expenses and Restitution) Regulations 1997

Reg.3, amended: SI 1999/1212 Reg.25

Reg.3, substituted: SI 1997/1613 Art.27, Sch.3 para.62

Reg.4, amended: SI 1997/1613 Art.27, Sch.3 para.62

Reg.5, amended: SI 1997/1613 Art.27, Sch.3 para.62

Reg.6, amended: SI 1997/1613 Art.27, Sch.3 para.62

955. Social Security (Adjudication) and Commissioners Procedure and Child Support Commissioners (Procedure) Amendment Regulations 1997

revoked (in part): SI 1999/1305 Reg.2, SI 1999/1495 Reg.2

Reg.1, amended: SI 1999/991 Reg.59, Sch.4

Reg.1, revoked (in part): SI 1999/1305 Reg.2, SI 1999/1495 Reg.2

Reg.2, revoked (in part): SI 1999/991 Reg.59 (with savings), Sch.4 (with savings), SI 1999/1305 Reg.2, SI 1999/1495 Reg.2

Reg.3, revoked (in part): SI 1999/991 Reg.59 (with savings), Sch.4 (with savings), SI 1999/1305 Reg.2, SI 1999/1495 Reg.2

Reg.4, revoked (in part): SI 1999/991 Reg.59 (with savings), Sch.4 (with savings), SI 1999/1305 Reg.2, SI 1999/1495 Reg.2

Reg.5, revoked (in part): SI 1999/991 Reg.59 (with savings), Sch.4 (with savings), SI 1999/1305 Reg.2, SI 1999/1495 Reg.2

Reg.6, revoked (in part): SI 1999/991 Reg.59 (with savings), Sch.4 (with savings), SI 1999/1305 Reg.2, SI 1999/1495 Reg.2

Reg.7, revoked (in part): SI 1999/1305 Reg.2, SI 1999/1495 Reg.2

Reg.8, revoked (in part): SI 1999/1305 Reg.2, SI 1999/1495 Reg.2

Reg.9, revoked (in part): SI 1999/1305 Reg.2, SI 1999/1495 Reg.2

Reg.10, revoked (in part): SI 1999/1305 Reg.2, SI 1999/1495 Reg.2

1997—cont.

955. Social Security (Adjudication) and Commissioners Procedure and Child Support Commissioners (Procedure) Amendment Regulations 1997—*cont.*
Reg.11, revoked (in part): SI 1999/1305 Reg.2, SI 1999/1495 Reg.2
Reg.12, revoked (in part): SI 1999/1305 Reg.2, SI 1999/1495 Reg.2
Reg.13, revoked (in part): SI 1999/1305 Reg.2, SI 1999/1495 Reg.2

956. Education (New Grant-Maintained Schools) (Finance) Regulations 1997
revoked: SI 1998/798 Reg.3 (with savings)

980. National Health Service (Indicative Amounts) Regulations 1997
Reg.1, amended: SI 1999/1606 Reg.2
Reg.2, amended: SI 1999/1606 Reg.2

987. Stock Lending and Manufactured Payments (Revocations and Amendments) Regulations 1997
Reg.7, revoked (in part): SI 1999/623 Reg.10

993. Manufactured Dividends (Tax) Regulations 1997
Reg.2, amended: SI 1999/621 Reg.2

995. Education (School Inspection) (No.2) (Amendment) Regulations 1997
revoked: SI 1997/1966 Reg.1, Sch. Part I
Reg.1, revoked: SI 1997/1966 Reg.1, Sch. Part I
Reg.2, revoked: SI 1997/1966 Reg.1, Sch. Part I

996. Education (Grant-Maintained and Grant-Maintained Special Schools) (Finance) Regulations 1997
applied: SI 1998/799 Reg.3, Sch.2 para.2
revoked: SI 1998/799 Reg.3 (with savings)
Part II, applied: SI 1998/799 Sch.2 para.2
Part III, applied: SI 1998/799 Sch.2 para.2
Reg.5, applied: SI 1998/799 Sch.2 para.2
Reg.6, applied: SI 1998/799 Reg.7, Sch.2 para.2
Reg.7, applied: SI 1998/799 Reg.7, Sch.2 para.2
Reg.8, applied: SI 1998/799 Sch.2 para.2
Reg.9, referred to: SI 1998/799 Sch.2 para.2
Reg.10, applied: SI 1998/799 Sch.2 para.2
Reg.11, applied: SI 1998/799 Sch.2 para.2
Reg.12, applied: SI 1998/799 Reg.7, Sch.2 para.2
Reg.13, referred to: SI 1998/799 Sch.2 para.2
Reg.14, referred to: SI 1998/799 Sch.2 para.2
Reg.15, applied: SI 1998/799 Sch.2 para.2
Reg.15, referred to: SI 1998/799 Sch.2 para.2
Reg.17, referred to: SI 1998/799 Sch.2 para.2
Reg.18, referred to: SI 1998/799 Sch.2 para.2
Reg.19, applied: SI 1998/799 Reg.7, Sch.2 para.2
Reg.20, applied: SI 1998/799 Sch.2 para.2
Reg.20, referred to: SI 1998/799 Sch.2 para.2
Reg.21, referred to: SI 1998/799 Sch.2 para.2
Reg.22, applied: SI 1998/799 Sch.2 para.2
Reg.22, referred to: SI 1998/799 Sch.2 para.2, Sch.2 para.3
Reg.23, applied: SI 1998/799 Sch.2 para.2
Reg.24, referred to: SI 1998/799 Sch.2 para.2
Reg.25, applied: SI 1998/799 Reg.25
Reg.25, referred to: SI 1998/799 Reg.25, Sch.2 para.2
Reg.26, applied: SI 1998/799 Reg.25
Reg.26, referred to: SI 1998/799 Sch.2 para.2
Reg.27, referred to: SI 1998/799 Sch.2 para.2
Reg.28, referred to: SI 1998/799 Sch.2 para.2
Reg.31, referred to: SI 1998/799 Sch.2 para.2
Reg.32, applied: SI 1998/799 Sch.2 para.2
Reg.33, applied: SI 1998/799 Sch.2 para.2

1997—cont.

996. Education (Grant-Maintained and Grant-Maintained Special Schools) (Finance) Regulations 1997—*cont.*
Reg.43, applied: SI 1998/799 Sch.2 para.2
Reg.44, applied: SI 1998/799 Sch.2 para.2
Reg.45, applied: SI 1998/799 Reg.25
Reg.45, referred to: SI 1998/799 Sch.2 para.2
Reg.46, referred to: SI 1998/799 Sch.2 para.2
Reg.47, referred to: SI 1998/799 Sch.2 para.2
Reg.50, applied: SI 1998/799 Sch.2 para.2
Reg.50, referred to: SI 1998/799 Sch.2 para.3
Reg.52, applied: SI 1998/799 Sch.2 para.2
Reg.53, applied: SI 1998/799 Sch.2 para.2
Reg.57, applied: SI 1998/799 Sch.2 para.2
Sch.9 para.2, applied: SI 1998/799 Sch.2 para.2

999. Local Authorities (Direct Labour Organisations) (Competition) (Wales) Regulations 1997
Reg.3, amended: SI 1997/1697 Reg.2, SI 1998/2193 Reg.2, SI 1999/1084 Reg.3
Reg.4, amended: SI 1997/2756 Reg.3
Reg.6, amended: SI 1997/2756 Reg.3
Reg.8A, added: SI 1997/2756 Reg.3
Reg.9, amended: SI 1997/2756 Reg.3, SI 1998/537 Reg.2
Reg.10A, added: SI 1997/2756 Reg.3
Reg.10B, added: SI 1998/537 Reg.2

1000. Rent Officers (Additional Functions) (Amendment) Order 1997
revoked: SI 1997/1984 Art.9
Art.2, revoked: SI 1997/1984 Art.9

1003. Rent Officers (Additional Functions) (Scotland) Amendment Order 1997
revoked: SI 1997/1995 Art.9, Sch.5
Art.2, revoked: SI 1997/1995 Art.9, Sch.5
Art.3, revoked: SI 1997/1995 Art.9, Sch.5

1004. Housing Benefit and Council Tax Benefit (Subsidy) Order 1997
Art.4, applied: SI 1998/562 Art.19
Art.6, applied: SI 1998/562 Art.15
Art.11, applied: SI 1998/562 Art.18
Art.19, applied: SI 1998/562 Art.18, Art.19
Sch.4 para.17, applied: SI 1998/562 Art.23
Sch.6 para.6, applied: SI 1998/562 Art.23
Sch.6 para.13, applied: SI 1998/562 Art.23

1006. Wireless Telegraphy (Licence Charges) (Amendment) Regulations 1997
revoked: SI 1999/1774 Reg.2, Sch.1
Reg.2, revoked: SI 1999/1774 Reg.2, Sch.1
Sch., revoked: SI 1999/1774 Reg.2, Sch.1

1007. Dual-Use and Related Goods (Export Control) (Amendment No.2) Regulations 1997
revoked: SI 1999/984 Reg.2
Reg.2, revoked: SI 1999/984 Reg.2

1013. National Health Service (Optical Charges and Payments) (Scotland) Amendment Regulations 1997
revoked: SI 1998/642 Reg.24, Sch.4
Reg.2, revoked: SI 1998/642 Reg.24, Sch.4
Reg.3, revoked: SI 1998/642 Reg.24, Sch.4
Reg.4, revoked: SI 1998/642 Reg.24, Sch.4
Reg.5, revoked: SI 1998/642 Reg.24, Sch.4
Reg.6, revoked: SI 1998/642 Reg.24, Sch.4
Reg.7, revoked: SI 1998/642 Reg.24, Sch.4
Reg.8, revoked: SI 1998/642 Reg.24, Sch.4
Reg.9, revoked: SI 1998/642 Reg.24, Sch.4
Reg.10, revoked: SI 1998/642 Reg.24, Sch.4
Reg.11, revoked: SI 1998/642 Reg.24, Sch.4
Reg.12, revoked: SI 1998/642 Reg.24, Sch.4
Sch., revoked: SI 1998/642 Reg.24, Sch.4

NO.

1997—cont.

1014. National Health Service (Fund-Holding Practices) (Scotland) Regulations 1997
Reg.1, amended: SI 1998/658 Reg.2, SI 1999/365 Reg.2, Reg.8
Reg.2, amended: SI 1998/658 Reg.3
Reg.2, revoked (in part): SI 1999/365 Reg.3, Reg.9
Reg.3, amended: SI 1999/365 Reg.10
Reg.6, amended: SI 1999/365 Reg.11
Reg.7, revoked: SI 1999/365 Reg.23
Reg.8, amended: SI 1998/658 Reg.4, SI 1999/365 Reg.12
Reg.8, applied: SI 1999/365 Reg.24
Reg.8, revoked (in part): SI 1998/658 Reg.9, SI 1999/365 Reg.12
Reg.9, amended: SI 1998/658 Reg.10
Reg.9, revoked: SI 1999/365 Reg.7
Reg.10, revoked (in part): SI 1998/658 Reg.11
Reg.11, amended: SI 1998/658 Reg.12, SI 1999/365 Reg.13
Reg.11, applied: SI 1999/365 Reg.28
Reg.12, amended: SI 1999/365 Reg.4, Reg.14
Reg.12, applied: SSI 1999/56 Art.7
Reg.13, amended: SI 1999/365 Reg.5
Reg.13, applied: SSI 1999/56 Art.7
Reg.13, revoked (in part): SI 1999/365 Reg.5
Reg.14, applied: SSI 1999/56 Art.7
Reg.14, referred to: SI 1999/365 Reg.28
Reg.16, amended: SI 1998/658 Reg.13
Reg.17, amended: SI 1998/658 Reg.5
Reg.17, revoked: SI 1999/365 Reg.23
Reg.18, amended: SI 1999/365 Reg.15
Reg.18, revoked (in part): SI 1999/365 Reg.15
Reg.19, amended: SI 1999/365 Reg.16
Reg.19, revoked (in part): SI 1999/365 Reg.16
Reg.19A, added: SI 1999/365 Reg.17
Reg.20, amended: SI 1998/658 Reg.6
Reg.20, applied: SSI 1999/56 Art.6
Reg.21, amended: SI 1999/365 Reg.18
Reg.21, revoked (in part): SI 1999/365 Reg.18
Reg.22, amended: SI 1998/658 Reg.14, SI 1999/365 Reg.6
Reg.22, applied: SSI 1999/56 Art.6
Reg.22, referred to: SSI 1999/56 Art.4
Reg.23, amended: SI 1999/365 Reg.19
Reg.23, applied: SI 1999/365 Reg.24, SSI 1999/56 Art.8
Sch.1 para.1, revoked: SI 1999/365 Reg.20
Sch.1 para.3, amended: SI 1998/658 Reg.15
Sch.1 para.5, added: SI 1998/658 Reg.7
Sch.1 para.5, amended: SI 1999/365 Reg.20
Sch.2 para.1, revoked: SI 1999/365 Reg.21
Sch.2 para.3, amended: SI 1999/365 Reg.21
Sch.2 para.14, added: SI 1998/658 Reg.8
Sch.2 para.14, amended: SI 1999/365 Reg.21
Sch.2 para.15, added: SI 1999/365 Reg.21
Sch.2 para.16, added: SI 1999/365 Reg.21
Sch.4, added: SI 1999/365 Reg.22, Sch.

1016. Air Passenger Duty and other Indirect Taxes (Interest Rate) Regulations 1997
revoked: SI 1998/1461 Reg.3
Reg.2, revoked: SI 1998/1461 Reg.3
Reg.3, revoked: SI 1998/1461 Reg.3

1053. Criminal Procedure and Investigations Act 1996 (Preparatory Hearings) (Interlocutory Appeals) Rules 1997
r.10, amended: SI 1999/598 r.4
r.12, amended: SI 1999/598 r.4

1056. Family Proceedings (Amendment No.2) Rules 1997
see *Practice Direction (Family Proceedings: Financial Dispute Resolution)* [1997] 1 W.L.R. 1069 (Fam Div), Sir Stephen Brown

NO.

1997—cont.

1078. Legal Aid (Mediation in Family Matters) Regulations 1997
Reg.1, amended: SI 1999/2576 Reg.4, SI 1999/2738 Reg.4
Reg.2, amended: SI 1999/2576 Reg.5, SI 1999/2738 Reg.6
Reg.2, applied: SI 1999/2738 Reg.3
Reg.3, amended: SI 1998/900 Reg.3, SI 1999/816 Reg.2
Reg.4, amended: SI 1998/900 Reg.3, SI 1999/2576 Reg.6, SI 1999/2738 Reg.7

1080. Family Proceedings Fees (Amendment) (No.2) Order 1997
revoked: SI 1999/690 Art.7 (with savings), Sch.2 (with savings)
Art.2, revoked: SI 1999/690 Art.7 (with savings), Sch.2 (with savings)

1112. Civil Legal Aid (Financial Conditions) (Scotland) Regulations 1997
revoked: SI 1998/970 Reg.5 (with savings)

1113. Advice and Assistance (Financial Conditions) (Scotland) Regulations 1997
revoked: SI 1998/971 Reg.6 (with savings)

1118. Act of Sederunt (Fees of Shorthand Writers in the Sheriff Court) (Amendment) 1997
Sch. para.4, amended: SI 1997/1265 para.2

1143. Local Government Superannuation (Scottish Environment Protection Agency) (Scotland) Regulations 1997
applied: SI 1998/364 Reg.4, Reg.6, Reg.19, Sch.2 para.2, Sch.2 para.5, Sch.4 para.8
referred to: SI 1998/364 Reg.3, Reg.10, Sch.2 para.4, Sch.2 para.6
Reg.1, amended: SI 1998/364 Sch.3 para.3
Reg.5, amended: SI 1998/364 Sch.3 para.3

1154. Open-Ended Investment Companies (Tax) Regulations 1997
Reg.3, substituted: SI 1997/1715 Reg.3
Reg.5, amended: SI 1997/1715 Reg.4
Reg.7, amended: SI 1997/1715 Reg.5
Reg.11, amended: SI 1997/1715 Reg.6

1156. Stamp Duty and Stamp Duty Reserve Tax (Open-Ended Investment Companies) Regulations 1997
Reg.2, amended: SI 1999/3261 Reg.3
Reg.3, substituted: SI 1999/3261 Reg.4
Reg.4, substituted: SI 1999/3261 Reg.5
Reg.4A, added: SI 1999/3261 Reg.5
Reg.4B, added: SI 1999/3261 Reg.5
Reg.5, amended: SI 1999/3261 Reg.6
Reg.6, revoked: SI 1999/3261 Reg.7
Reg.9, amended: SI 1999/1467 Reg.3
Reg.9, revoked (in part): SI 1999/1467 Reg.3
Reg.10, amended: SI 1999/1467 Reg.4

1180. Protection from Harassment (Northern Ireland) Order 1997
Art.4, referred to: SI 1998/1071 (NI.6) Art.26
Art.4, revoked (in part): SI 1998/1071 (NI.6) Art.41, Sch.5

1181. Public Order (Amendment) (Northern Ireland) Order 1997
revoked: 1998 c.2 s.18, Sch.4
Art.1, revoked: 1998 c.2 s.18, Sch.4
Art.2, revoked: 1998 c.2 s.18, Sch.4
Art.3, revoked: 1998 c.2 s.18, Sch.4
Art.4, revoked: 1998 c.2 s.18, Sch.4

1182. Social Security Administration (Fraud) (Northern Ireland) Order 1997
Art.16, revoked: SI 1998/1506 (NI.10) Art.78, Sch.7
Art.17, revoked: SI 1998/1506 (NI.10) Art.78, Sch.7

NO.

1997—cont.

1182. Social Security Administration (Fraud) (Northern Ireland) Order 1997—cont.
Sch.1 para.1, revoked: SI 1998/1506 (NI.10) Art.78, Sch.7

1183. Social Security (Recovery of Benefits) (Northern Ireland) Order 1997
applied: SI 1998/1506 (NI.10) Art.4, Art.12, Art.28
referred to: 1998 c.47 s.87
Art.2, amended: SI 1998/1506 (NI.10) Art.78, Sch.6 para.119
Art.3, referred to: 1999 c.10 s.2, Sch.2 para.18
Art.12, amended: SI 1998/1506 (NI.10) Art.78, Sch.6 para.120, Sch.7
Art.13, amended: SI 1998/1506 (NI.10) Art.78, Sch.6 para.121, Sch.7
Art.13, applied: SI 1998/1506 (NI.10) Art.5
Art.13, revoked (in part): SI 1998/1506 (NI.10) Art.78, Sch.6 para.121, Sch.7
Art.14, amended: SI 1998/1506 (NI.10) Art.78, Sch.6 para.122, Sch.7
Art.14, revoked (in part): SI 1998/1506 (NI.10) Art.78, Sch.6 para.122, Sch.7
Art.15, amended: SI 1998/1506 (NI.10) Art.78, Sch.6 para.123, Sch.7
Art.15, revoked (in part): SI 1998/1506 (NI.10) Art.78, Sch.7
Sch.2, amended: 1999 c.10 s.2, s.19, Sch.2 para.18, Sch.6
Sch.3, amended: SI 1998/1506 (NI.10) Art.78, Sch.7
Sch.3 para.4, revoked (in part): SI 1998/1506 (NI.10) Art.78, Sch.7

1210. A41 Trunk Road (Barnet) Red Route (No.2) Traffic Order 1997
Art.2, amended: SI 1999/272 Art.2, Sch. Part A
Art.9, amended: SI 1999/272 Art.2, Sch. Part A

1211. A23 Trunk Road (Croydon) Red Route Traffic Order 1997
Art.2, amended: SI 1999/272 Art.2, Sch. Part A
Art.9, amended: SI 1999/272 Art.2, Sch. Part A
Art.10, amended: SI 1997/2749 Art.3, Art.4
Art.10, revoked (in part): SI 1997/2749 Art.5
Sch.2B Table, amended: SI 1997/2749 Art.6
Sch.2D Table, revoked (in part): SI 1997/2749 Art.7
Sch.3B Table, amended: SI 1997/2749 Art.8
Sch.4 Table, revoked (in part): SI 1997/2749 Art.9

1223. A406 Trunk Road (Brent) Red Route Traffic Order 1997
Art.2, amended: SI 1999/272 Art.2, Sch. Part A
Art.9, amended: SI 1999/272 Art.2, Sch. Part A

1225. Glan Hafren National Health Service Trust (Establishment) Amendment Order 1997
revoked: SI 1999/1120 Art.2, Sch.2
Art.2, revoked: SI 1999/1120 Art.2, Sch.2

1266. Greater Manchester (Light Rapid Transit System) (Airport Extension) Order 1997
amended: SI 1999/217 Art.3, Sch.
applied: SI 1999/217 Art.3
referred to: SI 1999/217 Art.3
Sch.4, amended: SI 1999/217 Art.3

1314. Consular Fees Order 1997
revoked: SI 1998/257 Art.4
Art.3, revoked: SI 1998/257 Art.4
Art.4, revoked: SI 1998/257 Art.4
Sch. para.9, revoked: SI 1998/257 Art.4
Sch. para.25, revoked: SI 1998/257 Art.4
Sch. para.27, revoked: SI 1998/257 Art.4
Sch. para.49, revoked: SI 1998/257 Art.4

NO.

1997—cont.

1320. Merchant Shipping (Safe Manning, Hours of Work and Watchkeeping) Regulations 1997
referred to: SI 1998/1609 Reg.5, Reg.6, Sch., SI 1998/2771 Reg.4, Sch.1
Reg.2, amended: SI 1997/1911 Reg.3
Reg.3, amended: SI 1997/1911 Reg.3
Reg.9, applied: SI 1998/2411 Reg.6
Reg.16, amended: SI 1997/1911 Reg.3
Reg.17, amended: SI 1997/1911 Reg.3

1335. Novel Foods and Novel Food Ingredients Regulations 1997
Reg.3, substituted: SI 1999/1756 Art.2, Sch. para.21
Reg.6, amended: SI 1999/3182 Reg.2

1336. Novel Foods and Novel Food Ingredients (Fees) Regulations 1997
Reg.3, amended: SI 1999/1756 Art.2, Sch. para.22

1359. Anglian Regional Flood Defence Committee Order 1997
revoked: SI 1998/1636 Art.3
Art.3, revoked: SI 1998/1636 Art.3

1361. Severn Trent Regional Flood Defence Committee Order 1997
revoked: SI 1998/1638 Art.3
Art.3, revoked: SI 1998/1638 Art.3

1362. Southern Regional Flood Defence Committee Order 1997
revoked: SI 1998/1639 Art.3
Art.3, revoked: SI 1998/1639 Art.3

1363. Thames Regional Flood Defence Committee Order 1997
revoked: SI 1998/1641 Art.3
Art.3, revoked: SI 1998/1641 Art.3

1368. Education (Individual Pupils' Achievements) (Information) Regulations 1997
Reg.3, amended: SI 1998/877 Reg.2, SI 1999/2937 Reg.3
Reg.4, amended: SI 1998/877 Reg.3
Reg.4, revoked (in part): SI 1998/877 Reg.3
Reg.8, amended: SI 1999/2937 Reg.3
Sch.1 para.2, amended: SI 1998/877 Reg.4
Sch.2 para.3, amended: SI 1998/877 Reg.5

1372. Control of Trade in Endangered Species (Enforcement) Regulations 1997
Reg.9, see *R. v Marylebone Magistrates Court Ex p. Amdrell Ltd (t/a Get Stuffed Ltd)* (1998) 162 J.P. 719 (QBD), Rose, L.J.

1373. Local Government Superannuation (Scotland) Amendment (No.2) Regulations 1997
applied: SI 1998/364 Reg.4, Reg.6, Reg.19, Sch.2 para.2, Sch.2 para.5, Sch.4 para.8
referred to: SI 1998/364 Reg.3, Reg.10, Sch.2 para.4, Sch.2 para.6

1377. Police Act 1997 (Commencement No.1 and Transitional Provisions) Order 1997
Art.3, revoked (in part): SI 1997/2390 Art.8

1410. Northern Ireland (Entry to Negotiations, etc.) Act 1996 (Revival of Section 3) Order 1997
revoked: SI 1998/1127 Art.3
Art.2, revoked: SI 1998/1127 Art.3

1435. Local Government Superannuation (Scotland) Amendment (No.3) Regulations 1997
applied: SI 1998/364 Reg.4, Reg.6, Reg.19, Sch.2 para.2, Sch.2 para.5, Sch.4 para.8, SI 1999/1750 Art.2, Sch.1
referred to: SI 1998/364 Reg.3, Reg.10, Sch.2 para.4, Sch.2 para.6

1436. Local Government Act 1988 (Competition) (Scotland) Amendment Regulations 1997
revoked: SI 1998/1422 Reg.5
Reg.2, revoked: SI 1998/1422 Reg.5

NO.

1997—cont.

1436. Local Government Act 1988 (Competition) (Scotland) Amendment Regulations 1997 —cont.
Reg.3, revoked: SI 1998/1422 Reg.5
Reg.4, revoked: SI 1998/1422 Reg.5
Reg.5, revoked: SI 1998/1422 Reg.5

1438. Local Government (Exemption from Competition) (Scotland) Amendment Order 1997
revoked: SI 1998/1421 Art.4
Art.2, revoked: SI 1998/1421 Art.4
Art.3, revoked: SI 1998/1421 Art.4

1440. Environmentally Sensitive Areas (The Broads) Designation Order 1997
Art.6, referred to: SI 1998/1299 Art.5
Sch.9 Part I, substituted: SI 1998/1299 Art.4
Sch.9 Part II, substituted: SI 1998/1299 Art.4

1441. Environmentally Sensitive Areas (Pennine Dales) Designation Order 1997
Art.6, referred to: SI 1998/1300 Art.5
Sch.8 Part II, amended: SI 1998/1300 Art.4

1442. Environmentally Sensitive Areas (Somerset Levels and Moors) Designation Order 1997
Art.6, referred to: SI 1998/1298 Art.5
Sch.10 Part II, amended: SI 1998/1298 Art.4

1443. Environmentally Sensitive Areas (South Downs) Designation Order 1997
Art.6, referred to: SI 1998/1297 Art.6
Sch.7 Part I, substituted: SI 1998/1297 Art.4
Sch.7 Part II, amended: SI 1998/1297 Art.5

1444. Environmentally Sensitive Areas (West Penwith) Designation Order 1997
Art.6, referred to: SI 1998/1296 Art.6
Sch.6 Part I, amended: SI 1998/1296 Art.4
Sch.6 Part II, amended: SI 1998/1296 Art.5

1468. Education Act 1997 (Commencement No.2 and Transitional Provisions) Order 1997
referred to: SI 1997/2140

1469. Medicines (Products for Animal Use - Fees) Regulations 1997
applied: SI 1998/2428 Reg.22
revoked: SI 1998/2428 Reg.21
Reg.15, revoked: SI 1998/2428 Reg.21
Reg.21, revoked: SI 1998/2428 Reg.21
Sch.1 Part I, revoked: SI 1998/2428 Reg.21
Sch.2 para.2, revoked: SI 1998/2428 Reg.21
Sch.3 para.3, revoked: SI 1998/1048 Reg.3, Sch.2 para.3
Sch.5 Part II, revoked: SI 1998/2428 Reg.21
Sch.7 para.4, revoked: SI 1998/2428 Reg.21

1480. Welfare of Animals (Transport) Order 1997
Art.21A, added: SI 1999/1622 Art.2

1489. Education (Individual Performance Information) (Identification of Individual Pupils) Regulations 1997
revoked: SI 1998/1834 Reg.1
Reg.2, revoked: SI 1998/1834 Reg.1

1499. Contaminants in Food Regulations 1997
Reg.2, amended: SI 1999/1603 Reg.3, SI 1999/3221 Reg.2, SSI 1999/171 Reg.2
Reg.3, amended: SI 1999/1603 Reg.4
Reg.4, amended: SI 1999/1603 Reg.5
Reg.4A, added: SI 1999/1603 Reg.6
Reg.5A, added: SI 1999/1603 Reg.7
Reg.6, amended: SI 1999/1603 Reg.8

1501. Motor Vehicles (EC Type Approval) (Amendment) (No.2) Regulations 1997
revoked: SI 1998/2051 Reg.2, Sch.3
Reg.3, revoked: SI 1998/2051 Reg.2, Sch.3
Reg.4, revoked: SI 1998/2051 Reg.2, Sch.3
Reg.5, revoked: SI 1998/2051 Reg.2, Sch.3
Reg.6, revoked: SI 1998/2051 Reg.2, Sch.3
Reg.7, revoked: SI 1998/2051 Reg.2, Sch.3

NO.

1997—cont.

1501. Motor Vehicles (EC Type Approval) (Amendment) (No.2) Regulations 1997—cont.
Sch., revoked: SI 1998/2051 Reg.2, Sch.3

1507. A4 Trunk Road (Hillingdon and Hounslow) Red Route Traffic Order 1997
Art.2, amended: SI 1999/272 Art.2, Sch. Part A
Art.9, amended: SI 1999/272 Art.2, Sch. Part A
Sch.2B Item 1, added: SI 1999/2346 Art.3
Sch.2B Item 2, added: SI 1999/2346 Art.3
Sch.2B Item 3, added: SI 1999/2346 Art.3
Sch.2B Item 3, revoked: SI 1999/2346 Art.3
Sch.2B Item 4, revoked: SI 1999/2346 Art.3
Sch.3B, amended: SI 1999/2346 Art.4
Sch.3B Item 1, revoked: SI 1999/2346 Art.4
Sch.3B Item 2, revoked: SI 1999/2346 Art.4

1508. Merchant Shipping (Crew Accommodation) Regulations 1997
referred to: SI 1998/1609 Reg.5, Reg.6, Sch., SI 1998/2771 Reg.4, Reg.5, Sch.1, Sch.2

1509. Merchant Shipping (Cargo Ship Construction) Regulations 1997
applied: SI 1998/2070 Reg.17, SI 1999/2721 Reg.34, Reg.71, Reg.74
referred to: SI 1998/1609 Reg.5, Reg.6, Sch., SI 1998/2771 Reg.4, Sch.1
Part III, amended: SI 1999/643 Reg.5
Reg.4, amended: SI 1999/643 Reg.3
Reg.12A, added: SI 1999/643 Reg.4
Reg.14, amended: SI 1999/643 Reg.5
Reg.14, revoked (in part): SI 1999/643 Reg.5
Reg.15, amended: SI 1999/643 Reg.6
Reg.16, amended: SI 1999/643 Reg.7
Reg.22, amended: SI 1999/643 Reg.8
Reg.23, applied: SI 1998/1011 Reg.25, SI 1998/1012 Reg.31
Reg.27, amended: SI 1999/643 Reg.9
Reg.28, amended: SI 1999/643 Reg.10
Reg.47, amended: SI 1999/643 Reg.11
Reg.48, applied: SI 1998/1012 Reg.48
Reg.49, amended: SI 1999/643 Reg.12
Reg.54A, added: SI 1999/643 Reg.13
Reg.54B, added: SI 1999/643 Reg.13
Reg.54C, added: SI 1999/643 Reg.13
Reg.58, substituted: SI 1999/643 Reg.14

1510. Merchant Shipping (Tonnage) Regulations 1997
Part IIA, added: SI 1998/1916 Reg.2
Reg.2, amended: SI 1998/1916 Reg.2, SI 1999/3206 Reg.27
Reg.12A, added: SI 1998/1916 Reg.2
Reg.12B, added: SI 1998/1916 Reg.2
Reg.12C, added: SI 1998/1916 Reg.2
Reg.12D, added: SI 1998/1916 Reg.2
Reg.12E, added: SI 1998/1916 Reg.2
Reg.16, amended: SI 1998/1916 Reg.2

1514. A41 Trunk Road (Camden) Red Route Experimental (No.2) Traffic Order 1997 Variation Order 1997
revoked: SI 1998/1105 Art.10
Art.3, revoked: SI 1998/1105 Art.10
Art.4, revoked: SI 1998/1105 Art.10
Art.5, revoked: SI 1998/1105 Art.10

1515. A406 Trunk Road (Hanger Lane, Ealing) Red Route (Prohibited Turns) Experimental Traffic Order 1997
revoked: SI 1998/1919 Art.5

1528. Protection of Wrecks (Designation) Order 1997
revoked: SI 1998/1650 Art.3
Art.2, revoked: SI 1998/1650 Art.3
Art.3, revoked: SI 1998/1650 Art.3

1997—cont.

1534. Land Registration (District Registries) Order 1997
revoked: SI 1998/140 Art.1
Art.1, revoked: SI 1998/140 Art.1

1535. Firearms (Amendment) Act 1997 (Commencement) (No.2) Order 1997
Art.4, substituted: SI 1997/1536 Art.2
Art.4A, added: SI 1997/1536 Art.2

1565. Food Protection (Emergency Prohibitions) (Paralytic Shellfish Poisoning) Order 1997
revoked (in part): SI 1997/1739 Art.2, SI 1997/1978 Art.2
Art.3, revoked (in part): SI 1997/1739 Art.2, SI 1997/1978 Art.2

1579. Transfer of Prisoners (Isle of Man) Order 1997
referred to: SI 1997/1776, SI 1998/2798

1585. Police Act 1997 (Provisions in relation to the NCIS Service Authority) (No.1) Order 1997
revoked: SI 1998/633 Art.A3
Sch. para.1, amended: SI 1997/2391 Art.4
Sch. para.1, revoked: SI 1998/633 Art.A3

1604. Horserace Betting Levy (Bookmakers' Committee) Regulations 1997
revoked: SI 1999/1468 Reg.8
Reg.8, revoked: SI 1999/1468 Reg.8

1607. A41 Trunk Road (Camden) Red Route Experimental (No.2) Traffic Order 1997 Variation (No.2) Order 1997
revoked: SI 1998/1105 Art.10
Art.3, revoked: SI 1998/1105 Art.10
Art.4, revoked: SI 1998/1105 Art.10
Art.5, revoked: SI 1998/1105 Art.10
Art.6, revoked: SI 1998/1105 Art.10
Art.7, revoked: SI 1998/1105 Art.10
Art.8, revoked: SI 1998/1105 Art.10

1608. A406 Trunk Road (Barnet) Red Route Traffic Order 1997
Art.2, amended: SI 1999/272 Art.2, Sch. Part A
Art.9, amended: SI 1999/272 Art.2, Sch. Part A

1612. Local Government Pension Scheme Regulations 1997
applied: SI 1997/1613 Reg.12, Reg.14, SI 1997/3001 Reg.B1, SI 1998/1238 Reg.35, SI 1998/1831 Reg.5, SI 1999/1212 Reg.23, SI 1999/3438 Reg.9, Reg.10
referred to: SI 1997/3001 Reg.B4
Part II, referred to: SI 1997/1613 Reg.4, Sch.2 para.2
Part III, referred to: SI 1997/1613 Reg.4, Sch.2 para.2
Part IV, applied: SI 1997/1613 Reg.4, Sch.2 para.2
Part V, referred to: SI 1997/1613 Reg.4, Sch.2 para.2
Reg.4, amended: SI 1998/1238 Reg.3
Reg.4, revoked (in part): SI 1999/1212 Reg.3
Reg.5, amended: SI 1999/1212 Reg.4
Reg.5, Substituted: SI 1999/3438 Reg.3
Reg.6, amended: SI 1998/1238 Reg.4, SI 1999/1212 Reg.5, SI 1999/3438 Reg.4
Reg.9, amended: SI 1999/1212 Reg.6
Reg.9, applied: SI 1997/1613 Reg.6, Reg.7, Reg.8, Reg.10, Reg.11, Reg.12, Reg.13, Sch.2 para.6
Reg.9, referred to: SI 1997/1613 Reg.9, Reg.17, Reg.24
Reg.10, amended: SI 1998/1238 Reg.5
Reg.13, amended: SI 1997/1613 Reg.22, SI 1998/1238 Reg.6, SI 1999/1212 Reg.7
Reg.13, applied: SI 1997/1613 Reg.22
Reg.13, revoked (in part): SI 1998/1238 Reg.6

1997—cont.

1612. Local Government Pension Scheme Regulations 1997—*cont.*
Reg.14, amended: SI 1998/1238 Reg.7
Reg.16, amended: SI 1998/1238 Reg.8
Reg.16, referred to: SI 1997/1613 Reg.16, Reg.17
Reg.19, applied: SI 1997/1613 Reg.24
Reg.20, amended: SI 1998/1238 Reg.9, SI 1999/1212 Reg.8
Reg.20, applied: SI 1997/1613 Reg.18
Reg.20, referred to: SI 1997/1613 Reg.13
Reg.21, amended: SI 1998/1238 Reg.10
Reg.22, amended: SI 1998/1238 Reg.11
Reg.23, amended: SI 1998/1238 Reg.12
Reg.25, applied: SI 1997/1613 Reg.18, Reg.24
Reg.25A, added: SI 1999/1212 Reg.9
Reg.26, applied: SI 1997/1613 Reg.18
Reg.27, amended: SI 1999/1212 Reg.10
Reg.27, applied: SI 1997/1613 Reg.8, Reg.18
Reg.28, amended: SI 1998/1238 Reg.13
Reg.29, applied: SI 1997/1613 Reg.18, Sch.2 para.4, Sch.2 para.5
Reg.29, referred to: SI 1997/1613 Sch.2 para.5, Sch.2 para.6, Sch.2 para.8
Reg.31, amended: SI 1997/1613 Reg.22, Reg.23, SI 1998/1238 Reg.14
Reg.31, applied: SI 1997/1613 Reg.18, Reg.22
Reg.31, referred to: SI 1997/1613 Reg.24
Reg.32, amended: SI 1998/1238 Reg.15, SI 1999/3438 Reg.5
Reg.32, applied: SI 1997/1613 Sch.2 para.7, Sch.2 para.9
Reg.32, referred to: SI 1997/1613 Sch.2 para.6, Sch.2 para.8
Reg.34, applied: SI 1997/1613 Reg.18
Reg.38, amended: SI 1998/1238 Reg.16, SI 1999/1212 Reg.11
Reg.38, applied: SI 1997/1613 Reg.18
Reg.39, applied: SI 1997/1613 Sch.2 para.5
Reg.41, applied: SI 1997/1613 Reg.24
Reg.42, amended: SI 1998/1238 Reg.17
Reg.42, applied: SI 1997/1613 Reg.18
Reg.45, amended: SI 1998/1238 Reg.18
Reg.45, applied: SI 1997/1613 Reg.18
Reg.46, amended: SI 1998/1238 Reg.19
Reg.46, applied: SI 1997/1613 Reg.18
Reg.48, applied: SI 1997/1613 Sch.2 para.5
Reg.49, applied: SI 1997/1613 Reg.4
Reg.50, applied: SI 1997/1613 Reg.4
Reg.52, amended: SI 1999/1212 Reg.12
Reg.53, amended: SI 1998/1238 Reg.20
Reg.53, applied: SI 1997/1613 Reg.4
Reg.55, applied: SI 1997/1613 Sch.2 para.9
Reg.55, referred to: SI 1997/1613 Reg.15
Reg.55, revoked (in part): SI 1998/1238 Reg.21
Reg.57, referred to: SI 1997/1613 Reg.23
Reg.60, amended: SI 1998/1238 Reg.22, SI 1999/1212 Reg.13
Reg.61, applied: SI 1998/1831 Reg.5
Reg.68, applied: SI 1998/1831 Reg.5
Reg.78, amended: SI 1999/1212 Reg.14, SI 1999/3438 Reg.6
Reg.79, applied: SI 1997/1613 Reg.21, SI 1998/1831 Reg.5
Reg.80, applied: SI 1998/1831 Reg.5
Reg.82, amended: SI 1998/1238 Reg.23
Reg.82, applied: SI 1998/1831 Reg.5
Reg.82, revoked (in part): SI 1998/1238 Reg.23
Reg.87, amended: SI 1998/1238 Reg.24
Reg.87, applied: SI 1997/1613 Reg.18, Reg.24
Reg.88, amended: SI 1998/1238 Reg.25
Reg.89, amended: SI 1998/1238 Reg.26

NO.

1997—cont.

1612. Local Government Pension Scheme Regulations 1997—*cont.*
Reg.93, referred to: SI 1997/1613 Sch.4 para.8
Reg.94, amended: SI 1998/1238 Reg.27
Reg.97, amended: SI 1998/1238 Reg.28, SI 1999/1212 Reg.15
Reg.106, amended: SI 1998/1238 Reg.29
Reg.109, amended: SI 1998/1238 Reg.30
Reg.109, applied: SI 1997/1613 Sch.2 para.3
Reg.109, referred to: SI 1997/1613 Reg.22
Reg.110, applied: SI 1997/1613 Sch.2 para.3
Reg.110, referred to: SI 1997/1613 Reg.22
Reg.111, amended: SI 1998/1238 Reg.31
Reg.116, referred to: SI 1997/1613 Reg.25
Reg.119, referred to: SI 1997/1613 Reg.13
Reg.122A, amended: SI 1998/2118 Reg.8
Reg.123, applied: SI 1997/1613 Reg.23
Reg.123, referred to: SI 1997/1613 Reg.18
Reg.127, amended: SI 1999/1212 Reg.16
Reg.128, amended: SI 1999/1212 Reg.17
Reg.133, amended: SI 1998/1238 Reg.32, SI 1999/1212 Reg.18
Reg.134, amended: SI 1999/1212 Reg.19
Reg.135, amended: SI 1999/1212 Reg.20
Reg.142, referred to: SI 1997/3001 Reg.E9
Sch.1, amended: SI 1998/1129 Art.3, Sch.2, SI 1998/1238 Reg.33, SI 1999/1212 Reg.21
Sch.2, amended: SI 1999/1212 Reg.22
Sch.2, applied: SI 1997/1613 Sch.4 para.6
Sch.2A, added: SI 1999/3438 Reg.7, Sch.
Sch.4, amended: SI 1998/1238 Reg.34, Sch. para.1, Sch. para.2
Sch.4, applied: SI 1997/1613 Reg.13, Sch.2 para.8
Sch.4 para.1, amended: SI 1998/1238 Reg.34, Sch. para.3, Sch. para.4, Sch. para.5, Sch. para.6, Sch. para.7, SI 1999/3438 Reg.8
Sch.4 para.2, amended: SI 1998/1238 Reg.34, Sch. para.8, Sch. para.10, Sch. para.11, Sch. para.12, Sch. para.13, Sch. para.14, Sch. para.15, Sch. para.16, Sch. para.17, Sch. para.18
Sch.4 para.2, revoked (in part): SI 1998/1238 Reg.34, Sch. para.9
Sch.4 para.3, amended: SI 1998/1238 Reg.34, Sch. para.19
Sch.4 para.4, amended: SI 1998/1238 Reg.34, Sch. para.20, Sch. para.21, Sch. para.22, Sch. para.24, Sch. para.25
Sch.4 para.4, referred to: SI 1998/1238 Reg.34, Sch. para.2
Sch.4 para.4, revoked (in part): SI 1998/1238 Reg.34, Sch. para.23
Sch.4 para.5, substituted: SI 1998/1238 Reg.34, Sch. para.26
Sch.4 para.6, amended: SI 1998/1238 Reg.34, Sch. para.27
Sch.4 para.7, amended: SI 1998/1238 Reg.34, Sch. para.28
Sch.4 para.8, amended: SI 1998/1238 Reg.34, Sch. para.29, Sch. para.30, Sch. para.31, Sch. para.32
Sch.4 para.8, referred to: SI 1998/1238 Reg.34, Sch. para.2
Sch.4 para.9, amended: SI 1998/1238 Reg.34, Sch. para.33
Sch.5, applied: SI 1998/1831 Reg.5
Sch.5 Part III, applied: SI 1997/1613 Reg.19
1613. Local Government Pension Scheme (Transitional Provisions) Regulations 1997
applied: SI 1997/1612 Reg.9, Reg.42, Reg.145, SI 1997/3001 Reg.B1, SI 1998/1831 Reg.5

NO.

1997—cont.

1613. Local Government Pension Scheme (Transitional Provisions) Regulations 1997—*cont.*
referred to: SI 1997/1612 Reg.117
Reg.2, amended: SI 1998/1831 Reg.13, Sch.2 para.3
Reg.8, amended: SI 1998/2118 Reg.3
Reg.9, amended: SI 1998/2118 Reg.4
Reg.15, revoked (in part): SI 1998/2118 Reg.5
Reg.19, applied: SI 1997/1612 Reg.74
Reg.21, applied: SI 1998/1831 Reg.5
Reg.22, amended: SI 1999/1212 Reg.24
Reg.23, amended: SI 1998/2118 Reg.6
Sch.2 para.1, amended: SI 1999/1212 Reg.24
Sch.2 para.4, amended: SI 1999/1212 Reg.24
Sch.2 para.5, amended: SI 1999/1212 Reg.24
Sch.2 para.8, amended: SI 1999/1212 Reg.24
Sch.3 para.23, revoked: SI 1998/2118 Reg.7
1621. Housing (Change of Landlord) (Payment of Disposal Cost by Instalments) (Amendment) (No.2) Regulations 1997
revoked: SI 1997/2001 Reg.3
Reg.2, revoked: SI 1997/2001 Reg.3
Reg.3, revoked: SI 1997/2001 Reg.3
1625. Education (Disability Statements for Local Education Authorities) (England) Regulations 1997
Reg.3, amended: SI 1998/1339 Reg.2
Reg.3, applied: SI 1998/1339 Reg.2
1629. Third Country Fishing (Enforcement) (Amendment) Order 1997
revoked: SI 1998/269 Art.13
Art.2, revoked: SI 1998/269 Art.13
1631. Local Authorities etc. (Allowances) (Scotland) Amendment Regulations 1997
revoked: SI 1998/3219 Reg.6
Reg.3, revoked: SI 1998/3219 Reg.6
Reg.4, revoked: SI 1998/3219 Reg.6
Reg.5, revoked: SI 1998/3219 Reg.6
1633. Education (School Performance Information) (Wales) Regulations 1997
revoked: SI 1998/1867 Reg.2
Reg.2, revoked: SI 1998/1867 Reg.2
Sch.1 Part I, applied: SI 1997/1832 Sch.2 para.16
Sch.1 Part I, revoked: SI 1998/1867 Reg.2
Sch.1 Part II, applied: SI 1997/1832 Sch.2 para.16
Sch.1 Part II, revoked: SI 1998/1867 Reg.2
Sch.1 Part III, applied: SI 1997/1832 Sch.2 para.16
Sch.1 Part III, revoked: SI 1998/1867 Reg.2
Sch.1 para.2, referred to: SI 1997/1832 Sch.2 para.23
Sch.1 para.2, revoked: SI 1998/1867 Reg.2
Sch.1 para.10, referred to: SI 1997/1832 Sch.2 para.23
Sch.1 para.10, revoked: SI 1998/1867 Reg.2
Sch.1 para.15, referred to: SI 1997/1832 Sch.2 para.23
Sch.1 para.15, revoked: SI 1998/1867 Reg.2
Sch.2, applied: SI 1997/1832 Sch.2 para.16
Sch.2, revoked: SI 1998/1867 Reg.2
Sch.2 para.4, referred to: SI 1997/1832 Sch.2 para.23
Sch.2 para.4, revoked: SI 1998/1867 Reg.2
Sch.3 para.6, revoked: SI 1998/1867 Reg.2
1638. Grants for School Education (Early Intervention and Alternatives to Exclusion) (Scotland) Regulations 1997
revoked: SI 1998/3051 Reg.6 (with saving)

NO.

1639. **Royal Parks and Other Open Spaces Regulations 1997**
Reg.3, applied: SI 1999/904 Art.3, Sch. para.5
Reg.4, applied: SI 1999/904 Art.3, Sch. para.5

1653. **Civil Aviation (Route Charges for Navigation Services) (Third Amendment) Regulations 1997**
revoked: SI 1997/2920 Reg.2, Sch.1
Reg.2, revoked: SI 1997/2920 Reg.2, Sch.1

1666. **Local Government Act 1988 (Defined Activities) (Exemption) (Craven, Kerrier and Mid-Devon District Councils and Middlesbrough Borough Council) Order 1997**
Art.2, revoked (in part): SI 1998/580 Art.3

1675. **Education (Student Loans) Regulations 1997**
revoked: SI 1998/211 Reg.2
Reg.2, revoked: SI 1998/211 Reg.2
Reg.4, revoked: SI 1998/211 Reg.2
Reg.5, revoked: SI 1998/211 Reg.2
Reg.7, revoked: SI 1998/211 Reg.2
Reg.13, revoked: SI 1998/211 Reg.2
Sch. para.1, revoked: SI 1998/211 Reg.2
Sch. para.4A, added: SI 1997/2919 Reg.2
Sch. para.4A, revoked: SI 1998/211 Reg.2

1678. **National Health Service (Fund-Holding Practices) Amendment (No.2) Regulations 1997**
Reg.7, amended: SI 1998/693 Reg.14

1680. **Registration of Births, Deaths, Marriages and Divorces (Fees) (Scotland) Amendment Regulations 1997**
revoked: SI 1998/643 Reg.8
Reg.3, revoked: SI 1998/643 Reg.8
Reg.4, revoked: SI 1998/643 Reg.8
Reg.5, revoked: SI 1998/643 Reg.8
Reg.6, revoked: SI 1998/643 Reg.8
Reg.7, revoked: SI 1998/643 Reg.8
Reg.8, revoked: SI 1998/643 Reg.8

1682. **Satellite Television Service Regulations 1997**
Sch. para.1, revoked (in part): SI 1998/3196 Reg.4
Sch. para.3, revoked: SI 1998/3196 Reg.4
Sch. para.14, revoked (in part): SI 1998/3196 Reg.4

1693. **Education (Mandatory Awards) (Amendment) Regulations 1997**
revoked: SI 1998/1166 Reg.6
Reg.3, revoked: SI 1998/1166 Reg.6
Reg.4, revoked: SI 1998/1166 Reg.6
Reg.5, revoked: SI 1998/1166 Reg.6
Reg.6, revoked: SI 1998/1166 Reg.6
Reg.7, revoked: SI 1998/1166 Reg.6
Reg.8, revoked: SI 1998/1166 Reg.6
Reg.9, revoked: SI 1998/1166 Reg.6

1694. **Dual-Use and Related Goods (Export Control) (Amendment No.3) Regulations 1997**
Reg.2, revoked: SI 1999/984 Reg.2

1697. **Local Authorities (Direct Labour Organisations) (Competition) (Wales) (Amendment) Regulations 1997**
revoked: SI 1998/2193 Reg.3
Reg.2, revoked: SI 1998/2193 Reg.3

1699. **Local Government Act 1988 (Competition) (Wales) Regulations 1997**
Reg.2, revoked (in part): SI 1997/2649 Reg.9, SI 1998/2192 Reg.3
Reg.3, revoked (in part): SI 1997/2649 Reg.9, SI 1998/2192 Reg.3
Reg.4, revoked (in part): SI 1998/2192 Reg.3
Reg.5, revoked (in part): SI 1997/2649 Reg.9, SI 1998/2192 Reg.3

NO.

1700. **Local Government Act 1988 (Defined Activities) (Works Contracts) (Exemptions) (Wales) Order 1997**
Sch., substituted: SI 1998/2191 Art.2, Sch.

1701. **Local Government Act 1988 (Defined Activities) (Housing Management) (Exemptions) (Wales) (Amendment) Order 1997**
revoked: SI 1998/2189 Art.3
Art.2, revoked: SI 1998/2189 Art.3

1702. **Local Government Act 1988 (Direct Service Organisations) (Accounts etc.) (Extension) (Wales) (Amendment) Order 1997**
revoked: SI 1998/2190 Art.3
Art.2, revoked: SI 1998/2190 Art.3

1713. **Confined Spaces Regulations 1997**
Reg.1, amended: SI 1997/2776 Reg.19, Sch.2 para.7
Reg.2, amended: SI 1997/2776 Reg.19, Sch.2 para.7

1714. **Betting and Gaming Duties Act 1981 (Bingo Prize Limit) Order 1997**
Art.1, revoked: SI 1999/3205 Art.3
Art.2, revoked: SI 1999/3205 Art.3
Art.3, revoked: SI 1999/3205 Art.3

1720. **Act of Sederunt (Rules of the Court of Session Amendment No.7) (Judicial Factors) 1997**
referred to: SI 1998/890 r.3
r.6, amended: SI 1998/890 r.3

1738. **London Docklands Development Corporation (Alteration of Boundaries) Order 1997**
applied: SI 1997/2946 Art.6
Art.4, revoked: SI 1997/2946 Art.6
Art.8, revoked (in part): SI 1997/2946 Art.6

1747. **Child Abduction and Custody (Parties to Conventions) (Amendment) Order 1997**
revoked: SI 1997/2575 Art.2
Art.2, revoked: SI 1997/2575 Art.2
Art.3, revoked: SI 1997/2575 Art.2
Sch., revoked: SI 1997/2575 Art.2

1772. **Further Education (Northern Ireland) Order 1997**
applied: SI 1998/1759 (NI.13) Art.40, Sch.2 para.3
referred to: SI 1998/1760 (NI.14) Art.7, SI 1998/3162 (NI.21) Art.27
Art.5, applied: SI 1998/1760 (NI.14) Art.7
Art.5, referred to: SI 1998/3162 (NI.21) Art.27
Art.14, amended: SI 1998/1759 (NI.13) Art.83
Sch.1, referred to: SI 1999/584 Reg.12
Sch.4, amended: SI 1998/1759 (NI.13) Art.91, Sch.6 Part I
Sch.4, revoked (in part): SI 1998/1759 (NI.13) Art.91, Sch.6 Part II, SI 1998/3162 (NI.21) Art.105, Sch.5

1774. **Police (Health and Safety) (Northern Ireland) Order 1997**
Art.7, amended: 1998 c.32 s.74, Sch.4 para.25

1775. **Transfer of Prisoners (Isle of Man) (No.2) Order 1997**
Art.2, amended: SI 1998/2797 Art.2
Sch. para.7, amended: SI 1998/2797 Art.2
Sch. para.9, revoked: SI 1998/2797 Art.3

1776. **Transfer of Prisoners (Restricted Transfers) (Channel Islands and Isle of Man) Order 1997**
revoked: SI 1998/2798 Art.5
Art.2, revoked: SI 1998/2798 Art.5
Art.3, revoked: SI 1998/2798 Art.5

1997—cont.

1776. Transfer of Prisoners (Restricted Transfers) (Channel Islands and Isle of Man) Order 1997—*cont.*
Sch.1 para.2, revoked: SI 1998/2798 Art.5
Sch.1 para.3, revoked: SI 1998/2798 Art.5
Sch.1 para.4, revoked: SI 1998/2798 Art.5
Sch.1 para.5, revoked: SI 1998/2798 Art.5
Sch.1 para.6, revoked: SI 1998/2798 Art.5
Sch.1 para.7, revoked: SI 1998/2798 Art.5
Sch.1 para.8, revoked: SI 1998/2798 Art.5
Sch.1 para.9, revoked: SI 1998/2798 Art.5
Sch.1 para.10, revoked: SI 1998/2798 Art.5
Sch.1 para.11, revoked: SI 1998/2798 Art.5
Sch.1 para.12, revoked: SI 1998/2798 Art.5
Sch.1 para.13, revoked: SI 1998/2798 Art.5
Sch.1 para.14, revoked: SI 1998/2798 Art.5
Sch.1 para.15, revoked: SI 1998/2798 Art.5
Sch.1 para.16, revoked: SI 1998/2798 Art.5
Sch.1 para.17, revoked: SI 1998/2798 Art.5
Sch.1 para.18, revoked: SI 1998/2798 Art.5
Sch.1 para.19, revoked: SI 1998/2798 Art.5
Sch.2 para.2, revoked: SI 1998/2798 Art.5
Sch.2 para.3, revoked: SI 1998/2798 Art.5
Sch.2 para.4, revoked: SI 1998/2798 Art.5
Sch.2 para.5, revoked: SI 1998/2798 Art.5
Sch.2 para.6, revoked: SI 1998/2798 Art.5
Sch.2 para.7, revoked: SI 1998/2798 Art.5

1783. Lotteries (Gaming Board Fees) Order 1997
revoked: SI 1998/455 Art.9
Art.3, revoked: SI 1998/455 Art.9
Art.4, revoked: SI 1998/455 Art.9
Art.5, revoked: SI 1998/455 Art.9
Art.6, revoked: SI 1998/455 Art.9
Art.7, revoked: SI 1998/455 Art.9
Art.8, revoked: SI 1998/455 Art.9
Art.9, revoked: SI 1998/455 Art.9

1787. Sports Grounds and Sporting Events (Designation) (Scotland) Amendment Order 1997
revoked: SI 1998/2314 Art.3, Sch.3
Art.2, revoked: SI 1998/2314 Art.3, Sch.3

1789. Education (School Teachers' Pay and Conditions) (No.2) Order 1997
revoked: SI 1998/1884 Art.1
Art.1, revoked: SI 1998/1884 Art.1

1790. Social Security (Lone Parents) (Amendment) Regulations 1997
revoked: SI 1998/766 Reg.2
Reg.2, revoked: SI 1998/766 Reg.2
Reg.3, revoked: SI 1998/766 Reg.2
Reg.4, revoked: SI 1998/766 Reg.2
Reg.5, revoked: SI 1998/766 Reg.2
Reg.6, revoked: SI 1998/766 Reg.2
Reg.7, revoked: SI 1998/766 Reg.2
Reg.8, revoked: SI 1998/766 Reg.2
Reg.9, revoked: SI 1998/766 Reg.2
Reg.10, revoked: SI 1998/766 Reg.2
Reg.11, revoked: SI 1998/766 Reg.2
Reg.12, revoked: SI 1998/766 Reg.2
Reg.13, revoked: SI 1998/766 Reg.2
Reg.14, revoked: SI 1998/766 Reg.2

1821. National Health Service (Pilot Schemes: Financial Assistance for Preparatory Work) Regulations 1997
revoked: SI 1998/1330 Reg.5, Sch.1
Reg.2, amended: SI 1997/3021 Reg.2
Reg.2, applied: SI 1998/1330 Reg.4
Reg.2, revoked: SI 1998/1330 Reg.5, Sch.1
Reg.3, amended: SI 1997/2289 Reg.4, SI 1997/3021 Reg.2
Reg.3, revoked: SI 1998/1330 Reg.5, Sch.1
Reg.4, added: SI 1997/3021 Reg.2
Reg.4, applied: SI 1998/1330 Reg.4

1997—cont.

1821. National Health Service (Pilot Schemes: Financial Assistance for Preparatory Work) Regulations 1997—*cont.*
Reg.4, revoked: SI 1998/1330 Reg.5, Sch.1
Reg.5, added: SI 1997/3021 Reg.2
Reg.5, revoked: SI 1998/1330 Reg.5, Sch.1
Reg.6, added: SI 1997/3021 Reg.2
Reg.6, applied: SI 1998/1330 Reg.4
Reg.6, revoked: SI 1998/1330 Reg.5, Sch.1
Reg.7, added: SI 1997/3021 Reg.2
Reg.7, revoked: SI 1998/1330 Reg.5, Sch.1

1824. A316 Trunk Road (Richmond) Red Route Traffic Order 1997
Art.2, amended: SI 1999/272 Art.2, Sch. Part A
Art.9, amended: SI 1999/272 Art.2, Sch. Part A

1827. Countryside Stewardship (Amendment) Regulations 1997
revoked: SI 1998/1327 Reg.2, Sch.2
Reg.2, revoked: SI 1998/1327 Reg.2, Sch.2
Sch., revoked: SI 1998/1327 Reg.2, Sch.2

1828. Gaming Act (Variation of Monetary Limits) Order 1997
revoked: SI 1999/1260 Art.5, Sch.
Art.2, revoked: SI 1999/1260 Art.5, Sch.
Art.3, revoked: SI 1999/1260 Art.5, Sch.

1830. Prescription Only Medicines (Human Use) Order 1997
Art.3, amended: SI 1998/108 Art.2
Art.8, amended: SI 1998/2081 Art.2
Sch.1, amended: SI 1997/2044 Art.2, Sch.1, SI 1998/108 Art.3, SI 1998/1178 Art.2, SI 1998/2081 Art.3, Sch., SI 1999/1044 Art.2, SI 1999/3463 Art.2
Sch.3, amended: SI 1998/108 Art.4
Sch.5 Part I, amended: SI 1998/108 Art.5, Sch., SI 1998/2081 Art.4
Sch.5 Part II, amended: SI 1998/2081 Art.4
Sch.5 Part III, amended: SI 1998/108 Art.5, SI 1998/1178 Art.3

1832. Education (School Information) (Wales) Regulations 1997
revoked: SI 1999/1812 Reg.2
Part IIA, added: SI 1999/127 Reg.4
Part IIA, revoked: SI 1999/1812 Reg.2
Part III, referred to: SI 1999/2242 Reg.42
Part IIIA, added: SI 1999/127 Reg.5
Part IIIA, revoked: SI 1999/1812 Reg.2
Reg.2, revoked: SI 1999/1812 Reg.2
Reg.3, amended: SI 1998/2697 Reg.2, SI 1999/127 Reg.3
Reg.3, revoked: SI 1999/1812 Reg.2
Reg.6, revoked: SI 1999/1812 Reg.2
Reg.6A, added: SI 1999/127 Reg.4
Reg.6A, revoked: SI 1999/1812 Reg.2
Reg.6B, added: SI 1999/127 Reg.4
Reg.6B, revoked: SI 1999/1812 Reg.2
Reg.6C, added: SI 1999/127 Reg.4
Reg.6C, revoked: SI 1999/1812 Reg.2
Reg.9, revoked: SI 1999/1812 Reg.2
Reg.9A, added: SI 1999/127 Reg.5
Reg.9A, revoked: SI 1999/1812 Reg.2
Sch.1A, added: SI 1999/127 Reg.6
Sch.1A, revoked: SI 1999/1812 Reg.2
Sch.1 para.6, revoked: SI 1999/1812 Reg.2
Sch.1 para.14, revoked: SI 1999/1812 Reg.2
Sch.1 para.20, revoked: SI 1999/1812 Reg.2
Sch.1 para.23, revoked: SI 1999/1812 Reg.2
Sch.2 para.5, revoked: SI 1999/1812 Reg.2
Sch.2 para.6, revoked: SI 1999/1812 Reg.2
Sch.2 para.8, revoked: SI 1999/1812 Reg.2
Sch.2 para.12, revoked: SI 1999/1812 Reg.2
Sch.2 para.13, revoked: SI 1999/1812 Reg.2
Sch.2 para.16, amended: SI 1998/2697 Reg.3

1997—cont.

1832. Education (School Information) (Wales) Regulations 1997—*cont.*
Sch.2 para.16, revoked: SI 1999/1812 Reg.2
Sch.2 para.17, revoked: SI 1999/1812 Reg.2
Sch.2 para.18, revoked: SI 1999/1812 Reg.2
Sch.2 para.19, revoked: SI 1999/1812 Reg.2
Sch.2 para.20, revoked: SI 1999/1812 Reg.2
Sch.2 para.23, revoked: SI 1998/2697 Reg.3, SI 1999/1812 Reg.2
Sch.2 para.26, revoked: SI 1999/1812 Reg.2

1833. Education (School Inspection) (Wales) (No.2) (Amendment) Regulations 1997
revoked: SI 1998/1866 Reg.1, Sch.
Reg.2, revoked: SI 1998/1866 Reg.1, Sch.

1839. Social Security (Attendance Allowance and Disability Living Allowance) (Miscellaneous Amendments) Regulations 1997
Reg.1, amended: SI 1999/991 Reg.59, Sch.4
Reg.4, revoked: SI 1999/991 Reg.59 (with savings), Sch.4 (with savings)

1840. Fire Precautions (Workplace) Regulations 1997
applied: SI 1999/677 Art.5
Part II, applied: SI 1999/3242 Reg.3, Reg.7, Reg.11, Reg.12
Part II, referred to: SI 1999/3242 Reg.11, Reg.12
Part III, revoked: SI 1999/3242 Reg.29
Part IV, amended: SI 1999/1877 Reg.17, Sch.
Reg.2, amended: SI 1999/1877 Reg.4, SI 1999/3242 Reg.29, Sch.2
Reg.3, amended: SI 1999/1877 Reg.5
Reg.3, revoked (in part): SI 1999/1877 Reg.5
Reg.4, amended: SI 1999/1877 Reg.6
Reg.4, referred to: SI 1999/3242 Reg.10
Reg.9, amended: SI 1999/1877 Reg.7, Reg.17, Sch., SI 1999/3242 Reg.29, Sch.2
Reg.9, referred to: SI 1999/3242 Reg.28
Reg.10, amended: SI 1999/1877 Reg.17, Sch.
Reg.10, revoked (in part): SI 1999/1877 Reg.8
Reg.11, amended: SI 1999/1877 Reg.9, Reg.17, Sch.
Reg.12, amended: SI 1999/1877 Reg.10, Reg.17, Sch.
Reg.13, amended: SI 1999/1877 Reg.11, Reg.17, Sch.
Reg.13, referred to: SI 1999/1877 Reg.18
Reg.13, revoked (in part): SI 1999/1877 Reg.11
Reg.14, amended: SI 1999/1877 Reg.12, Reg.17, Sch.
Reg.14, revoked (in part): SI 1999/1877 Reg.12
Reg.15, amended: SI 1999/1877 Reg.17, Sch.
Reg.15, referred to: SI 1999/1877 Reg.18
Reg.16, referred to: SI 1999/1877 Reg.18
Reg.16, revoked: SI 1999/1877 Reg.13
Reg.17, amended: SI 1999/1877 Reg.14
Reg.17A, added: SI 1999/1877 Reg.15
Reg.18, amended: SI 1999/1877 Reg.16
Reg.18, applied: SI 1999/677 Art.5

1841. Council Tax Benefit (General) Amendment Regulations 1997
Reg.3, added: SI 1998/911 Reg.2
Reg.3, amended: SI 1998/2231 Reg.9

1842. Wireless Telegraphy (Control of Interference from Videosenders) Order 1997
revoked: SI 1998/722 Art.2

1848. Thames Valley (Police Authority) Order 1997
applied: SI 1997/2293 Art.2

1851. Housing Act 1996 (Commencement No.11 and Savings) Order 1997
Sch. para.1, referred to: SI 1998/1768 Art.2

1997—cont.

1870. Environmental Assessment (Scotland) Amendment Regulations 1997
Reg.4, applied: SSI 1999/1 Reg.64, Sch.7
Reg.4, revoked: SSI 1999/1 Reg.64, Sch.7
Reg.5, applied: SSI 1999/1 Reg.64, Sch.7
Reg.5, revoked: SSI 1999/1 Reg.64, Sch.7
Reg.6, applied: SSI 1999/1 Reg.64, Sch.7
Reg.6, revoked: SSI 1999/1 Reg.64, Sch.7
Reg.7, applied: SSI 1999/1 Reg.64, Sch.7
Reg.7, revoked: SSI 1999/1 Reg.64, Sch.7
Reg.8, applied: SSI 1999/1 Reg.64, Sch.7
Reg.8, revoked: SSI 1999/1 Reg.64, Sch.7
Reg.9, applied: SSI 1999/1 Reg.64, Sch.7
Reg.9, revoked: SSI 1999/1 Reg.64, Sch.7
Reg.10, applied: SSI 1999/1 Reg.64, Sch.7
Reg.10, revoked: SSI 1999/1 Reg.64, Sch.7
Reg.11, applied: SSI 1999/1 Reg.64, Sch.7
Reg.11, revoked: SSI 1999/1 Reg.64, Sch.7
Reg.12, applied: SSI 1999/1 Reg.64, Sch.7
Reg.12, revoked: SSI 1999/1 Reg.64, Sch.7
Reg.13, applied: SSI 1999/1 Reg.64, Sch.7
Reg.13, revoked: SSI 1999/1 Reg.64, Sch.7
Reg.14, applied: SSI 1999/1 Reg.64, Sch.7
Reg.14, revoked: SSI 1999/1 Reg.64, Sch.7
Reg.15, applied: SSI 1999/1 Reg.64, Sch.7
Reg.15, revoked: SSI 1999/1 Reg.64, Sch.7
Reg.16, applied: SSI 1999/1 Reg.64, Sch.7
Reg.16, revoked: SSI 1999/1 Reg.64, Sch.7
Reg.17, applied: SSI 1999/1 Reg.64, Sch.7
Reg.17, revoked: SSI 1999/1 Reg.64, Sch.7
Reg.18, applied: SSI 1999/1 Reg.64, Sch.7
Reg.18, revoked: SSI 1999/1 Reg.64, Sch.7
Reg.19, applied: SSI 1999/1 Reg.64, Sch.7
Reg.19, revoked: SSI 1999/1 Reg.64, Sch.7
Reg.20, applied: SSI 1999/1 Reg.64, Sch.7
Reg.20, revoked: SSI 1999/1 Reg.64, Sch.7
Reg.21, applied: SSI 1999/1 Reg.64, Sch.7
Reg.21, revoked: SSI 1999/1 Reg.64, Sch.7
Reg.22, applied: SSI 1999/1 Reg.64, Sch.7
Reg.22, revoked: SSI 1999/1 Reg.64, Sch.7
Reg.23, applied: SSI 1999/1 Reg.64, Sch.7
Reg.23, revoked: SSI 1999/1 Reg.64, Sch.7
Reg.24, applied: SSI 1999/1 Reg.64, Sch.7
Reg.24, revoked: SSI 1999/1 Reg.64, Sch.7
Reg.25, applied: SSI 1999/1 Reg.64, Sch.7
Reg.25, revoked: SSI 1999/1 Reg.64, Sch.7
Reg.26, applied: SSI 1999/1 Reg.64, Sch.7
Reg.26, revoked: SSI 1999/1 Reg.64, Sch.7
Reg.27, applied: SSI 1999/1 Reg.64, Sch.7
Reg.27, revoked: SSI 1999/1 Reg.64, Sch.7
Reg.28, applied: SSI 1999/1 Reg.64, Sch.7
Reg.28, revoked: SSI 1999/1 Reg.64, Sch.7
Reg.29, applied: SSI 1999/1 Reg.64, Sch.7
Reg.29, revoked: SSI 1999/1 Reg.64, Sch.7
Reg.30, applied: SSI 1999/1 Reg.64, Sch.7
Reg.30, revoked: SSI 1999/1 Reg.64, Sch.7
Reg.31, applied: SSI 1999/1 Reg.64, Sch.7
Reg.31, revoked: SSI 1999/1 Reg.64, Sch.7
Reg.32, applied: SSI 1999/1 Reg.64, Sch.7
Reg.32, revoked: SSI 1999/1 Reg.64, Sch.7
Reg.33, applied: SSI 1999/1 Reg.64, Sch.7
Reg.33, revoked: SSI 1999/1 Reg.64, Sch.7
Reg.34, applied: SSI 1999/1 Reg.64, Sch.7
Reg.34, revoked: SSI 1999/1 Reg.64, Sch.7

1885. Wireless Telegraphy (Licence Charges) (Amendment No.2) Regulations 1997
revoked: SI 1999/1774 Reg.2, Sch.1
Reg.2, revoked: SI 1999/1774 Reg.2, Sch.1
Sch., revoked: SI 1999/1774 Reg.2, Sch.1

1997—cont.

1886. Telecommunications (Voice Telephony) Regulations 1997
Reg.1, amended: SI 1998/1580 Reg.3
Reg.2, amended: SI 1998/1580 Reg.3
Reg.3, amended: SI 1998/1580 Reg.3
Reg.4, revoked: SI 1998/1580 Reg.4
Reg.5, revoked: SI 1998/1580 Reg.4
Reg.6, revoked: SI 1998/1580 Reg.4
Reg.7, revoked: SI 1998/1580 Reg.4
Reg.8, revoked: SI 1998/1580 Reg.4
Reg.9, amended: SI 1998/1580 Reg.3
Sch.1, amended: SI 1998/1580 Reg.4
Sch.1, revoked (in part): SI 1998/1580 Reg.4
Sch.2, revoked: SI 1998/1580 Reg.4
Sch.3, revoked: SI 1998/1580 Reg.4
Sch.4, revoked: SI 1998/1580 Reg.4

1889. Ecclesiastical Judges and Legal Officers (Fees) Order 1997
revoked: SI 1998/1711 Art.2
Art.1, revoked: SI 1998/1711 Art.2
Art.2, revoked: SI 1998/1711 Art.2
Art.3, revoked: SI 1998/1711 Art.2
Sch., revoked: SI 1998/1711 Art.2
Sch. Table I, revoked: SI 1998/1711 Art.2
Sch. Table I, substituted: SI 1998/1711 Art.1, Sch.
Sch. Table II, revoked: SI 1998/1711 Art.2
Sch. Table II, substituted: SI 1998/1711 Art.1, Sch.
Sch. Table III, revoked: SI 1998/1711 Art.2
Sch. Table III, substituted: SI 1998/1711 Art.1, Sch.
Sch. Table IV, revoked: SI 1998/1711 Art.2
Sch. Table IV, substituted: SI 1998/1711 Art.1, Sch.
Sch. Table V, revoked: SI 1998/1711 Art.2
Sch. Table V, substituted: SI 1998/1711 Art.1, Sch.
Sch. Table VI, revoked: SI 1998/1711 Art.2
Sch. Table VI, substituted: SI 1998/1711 Art.1, Sch.
Sch. Table VII, revoked: SI 1998/1711 Art.2
Sch. Table VII, substituted: SI 1998/1711 Art.1, Sch.

1890. Legal Officers (Annual Fees) Order 1997
revoked: SI 1998/1712 Art.3
Appendix.para.1, revoked: SI 1998/1712 Art.3
Appendix.para.4, revoked: SI 1998/1712 Art.3
Art.2, revoked: SI 1998/1712 Art.3
Art.3, revoked: SI 1998/1712 Art.3
Sch. Table I, revoked: SI 1998/1712 Art.3
Sch. Table I, substituted: SI 1998/1712 Sch. Table I
Sch. Table II, revoked: SI 1998/1712 Art.3
Sch. Table II, substituted: SI 1998/1712 Sch. Table II

1891. Parochial Fees Order 1997
revoked: SI 1998/1714 Art.4
Art.1, revoked: SI 1998/1714 Art.4
Art.4, revoked: SI 1998/1714 Art.4
Sch. Part I, revoked: SI 1998/1714 Art.4
Sch. Part II, revoked: SI 1998/1714 Art.4

1898. Family Law Act 1996 (Modifications of Enactments) Order 1997
Art.3, revoked: 1999 c.22 s.106, Sch.15 Part V(8)

1899. Family Proceedings Fees (Amendment) (No.3) Order 1997
revoked: SI 1999/690 Art.7 (with savings), Sch.2 (with savings)
Art.2, revoked: SI 1999/690 Art.7 (with savings), Sch.2 (with savings)

1997—cont.

1901. Cattle Identification (Enforcement) Regulations 1997
revoked: SI 1998/871 Reg.36, Sch.3
Reg.3, revoked: SI 1998/871 Reg.36, Sch.3
Reg.10, revoked: SI 1998/871 Reg.36, Sch.3

1905. Bovines and Bovine Products (Despatch Prohibition and Production Restriction) Regulations 1997
revoked: SI 1998/1135 Reg.21
Reg.3, revoked: SI 1998/1135 Reg.21
Reg.16, revoked: SI 1998/1135 Reg.21
Reg.20, revoked: SI 1998/1135 Reg.21

1908. Police (Property) Regulations 1997
applied: SI 1999/269 Reg.3

1911. Merchant Shipping (Training, Certification and Safe Manning) (Amendment) Regulations 1997
referred to: SI 1998/1609 Reg.5, Reg.6, Sch.

1914. Dartford-Thurrock Crossing Tolls Order 1997
revoked: SI 1998/1907 Art.3
Art.3, revoked: SI 1998/1907 Art.3
Sch., revoked: SI 1998/1907 Art.3

1915. Dartford-Thurrock Crossing (Amendment) Regulations 1997
revoked: SI 1998/1908 Reg.11, Sch.
Reg.2, revoked: SI 1998/1908 Reg.11, Sch.
Reg.3, revoked: SI 1998/1908 Reg.11, Sch.
Reg.4, revoked: SI 1998/1908 Reg.11, Sch.

1930. Police Act 1997 (Commencement No.3 and Transitional Provisions) Order 1997
Art.4, referred to: SI 1997/2390 Art.3

1931. Education (National Curriculum) (Assessment Arrangements for the Core Subjects) (Key Stage 1) (England) (Amendment) Order 1997
revoked: SI 1999/1236 Art.2, Sch.
Art.3, revoked: SI 1999/1236 Art.2, Sch.

1940. Local Government Act 1988 (Defined Activities) (Exemption) (Christchurch Borough Council) Order 1997
revoked: SI 1998/2862 Art.3

1949. Sea Fishing (Enforcement of Community Conservation Measures) Order 1997
Art.2, amended: SI 1998/268 Art.13, SI 1999/424 Art.13
Art.3, see *Unity FR 165 Ltd v Ministry of Agriculture, Fisheries and Food* Times, January 20, 1999 (QBD), Buxton, L.J.
Art.10, amended: SI 1997/2841 Art.2
Art.11, amended: SI 1997/2841 Art.2

1954. Nursery Education (Amendment) Regulations 1997
revoked (in part): SI 1999/1441 Reg.5
Reg.2, revoked (in part): SI 1999/1441 Reg.5

1962. Agricultural Holdings (Units of Production) Order 1997
revoked: SI 1998/2025 Art.3
Art.3, revoked: SI 1998/2025 Art.3
Sch., revoked: SI 1998/2025 Art.3

1963. National Board for Nursing, Midwifery and Health Visiting for England (Constitution and Administration) Amendment Order 1997
revoked: SI 1999/766 Art.3
Art.2, revoked: SI 1999/766 Art.3
Art.3, revoked: SI 1999/766 Art.3

1966. Education (School Inspection) Regulations 1997
Reg.5, amended: SI 1999/601 Reg.3, SI 1999/2545 Reg.2
Reg.5, revoked (in part): SI 1999/2545 Reg.2

NO.

1966. **Education (School Inspection) Regulations 1997**—*cont.*
Reg.6, amended: SI 1999/2545 Reg.2
Reg.7, amended: SI 1999/601 Reg.4
Reg.12, amended: SI 1999/2545 Reg.2
Reg.13, amended: SI 1999/2545 Reg.2
Reg.13, revoked (in part): SI 1999/601 Reg.5, SI 1999/2545 Reg.2

1968. **Education (Assisted Places) Regulations 1997**
Reg.2, applied: SI 1997/1969 Reg.1
Reg.3, applied: SI 1997/1969 Reg.1
Reg.4, amended: SI 1998/1726 Reg.3, SI 1998/1966 Reg.3
Reg.5, revoked: SI 1998/1726 Reg.4
Reg.6, amended: SI 1998/1726 Reg.5, SI 1998/1966 Reg.4
Reg.9, applied: SI 1997/1969 Reg.11
Reg.10, amended: SI 1998/1726 Reg.6, SI 1999/1504 Reg.2
Reg.10, applied: SI 1997/1969 Reg.11
Reg.11, revoked (in part): SI 1998/1726 Reg.7
Reg.12, applied: SI 1997/1969 Reg.11
Reg.13, applied: SI 1997/1969 Reg.11
Reg.14, applied: SI 1997/1969 Reg.11
Reg.15, applied: SI 1997/1969 Reg.11
Reg.16, amended: SI 1998/1726 Reg.8
Reg.16, applied: SI 1997/1969 Reg.10
Reg.17, applied: SI 1997/1969 Reg.13
Reg.18, applied: SI 1997/1969 Reg.13
Reg.19, amended: SI 1998/1726 Reg.9, SI 1998/1966 Reg.5, Reg.6
Reg.19, revoked (in part): SI 1998/1966 Reg.6
Reg.19A, added: SI 1998/1966 Reg.7
Reg.19B, added: SI 1998/1966 Reg.8
Sch.1, applied: SI 1997/1969 Reg.11
Sch.2 para.1, amended: SI 1998/1726 Reg.10, SI 1999/1504 Reg.2
Sch.2 para.2, amended: SI 1998/1726 Reg.11, SI 1999/1504 Reg.2

1969. **Education (Assisted Places) (Incidental Expenses) Regulations 1997**
Reg.1, amended: SI 1998/1585 Reg.3
Reg.2, amended: SI 1998/1585 Reg.4
Reg.2, substituted: SI 1999/1505 Reg.2
Reg.4, amended: SI 1998/1585 Reg.5, SI 1999/1505 Reg.2
Reg.9, amended: SI 1998/1585 Reg.6

1971. **Nursery Education (Amendment) Regulations 1997**
revoked: SI 1997/2006 Reg.2

1972. **Education (Fees and Awards) Regulations 1997**
Reg.2, amended: SI 1998/1965 Reg.3, SI 1999/229 Reg.5
Reg.4, revoked (in part): SI 1998/1965 Reg.4
Reg.5, amended: SI 1999/229 Reg.5
Reg.8, amended: SI 1998/1965 Reg.5
Sch. para.3, amended: SI 1998/1965 Reg.6
Sch. para.7, amended: SI 1998/1965 Reg.6
Sch. para.8, amended: SI 1998/1965 Reg.6

1974. **Housing Benefit (General) Amendment (No.2) Regulations 1997**
Reg.3, amended: SI 1998/1732 Reg.2, SI 1999/2734 Reg.12

1984. **Rent Officers (Housing Benefit Functions) Order 1997**
applied: SI 1998/562 Sch.4 para.3

1995. **Rent Officers (Housing Benefit Functions) (Scotland) Order 1997**
applied: SI 1998/562 Sch.4 para.3

NO.

1996. **Wireless Telegraphy (Short Range Devices) (Exemption) (Amendment) Regulations 1997**
revoked: SI 1999/930 Reg.2, Sch.1
Reg.3, revoked: SI 1999/930 Reg.2, Sch.1
Reg.4, revoked: SI 1999/930 Reg.2, Sch.1
Reg.5, revoked: SI 1999/930 Reg.2, Sch.1
Reg.6, revoked: SI 1999/930 Reg.2, Sch.1
Reg.7, revoked: SI 1999/930 Reg.2, Sch.1
Reg.8, revoked: SI 1999/930 Reg.2, Sch.1
Reg.9, revoked: SI 1999/930 Reg.2, Sch.1

2001. **Housing (Change of Landlord) (Payment of Disposal Cost by Instalments) (Amendment) (No.3) Regulations 1997**
revoked: SI 1998/265 Reg.3
Reg.2, revoked: SI 1998/265 Reg.3
Reg.3, revoked: SI 1998/265 Reg.3

2002. **A501 Trunk Road (Camden, Islington and Westminster) Red Route Traffic Order 1997**
revoked (in part): SI 1997/2682 Art.5
Art.2, amended: SI 1999/272 Art.2, Sch. Part A
Art.5, revoked (in part): SI 1997/2682 Art.5
Art.8, revoked (in part): SI 1997/2682 Art.5
Art.9, amended: SI 1999/272 Art.2, Sch. Part A
Art.9, revoked (in part): SI 1997/2682 Art.5
Art.10, revoked (in part): SI 1997/2682 Art.5

2009. **Education (National Curriculum) (Assessment Arrangements for English, Welsh, Mathematics and Science) (Key Stage 2) (Wales) Order 1997**
Art.4, applied: SI 1998/392 Sch. para.2, SI 1999/521 Sch.para.2
Art.5, amended: SI 1998/1977 Art.2
Art.5, applied: SI 1998/392 Sch. para.2, SI 1999/521 Sch.para.2
Art.6, applied: SI 1998/392 Sch. para.2, SI 1999/521 Sch.para.2
Art.7, applied: SI 1998/392 Sch. para.2, SI 1999/521 Sch.para.2
Art.8, applied: SI 1998/392 Sch. para.2, SI 1999/521 Sch.para.2
Art.9, applied: SI 1998/392 Sch. para.2, SI 1999/521 Sch.para.2

2010. **Education (National Curriculum) (Key Stage 3 Assessment Arrangements) (Wales) Order 1997**
Art.4, applied: SI 1998/392 Sch. para.2, SI 1999/521 Sch. para.2
Art.5, applied: SI 1998/392 Sch. para.2, SI 1999/521 Sch. para.2
Art.6, applied: SI 1998/392 Sch. para.2, SI 1999/521 Sch. para.2
Art.7, applied: SI 1998/392 Sch. para.2, SI 1999/521 Sch. para.2
Art.8, applied: SI 1998/392 Sch. para.2, SI 1999/521 Sch. para.2
Art.9, applied: SI 1998/392 Sch. para.2, SI 1999/521 Sch. para.2
Art.10, amended: SI 1998/1976 Art.2
Art.10, applied: SI 1998/392 Sch. para.2, SI 1999/521 Sch. para.2
Art.11, applied: SI 1998/392 Sch. para.2, SI 1999/521 Sch. para.2
Art.12, applied: SI 1998/392 Sch. para.2, SI 1999/521 Sch. para.2

2011. **Education (National Curriculum) (Assessment Arrangements for English, Welsh, Mathematics and Science) (Key Stage 1) (Wales) Order 1997**
Art.4, applied: SI 1998/392 Sch. para.2, SI 1999/521 Sch. para.2

NO.

1997—cont.

2011. Education (National Curriculum) (Assessment Arrangements for English, Welsh, Mathematics and Science) (Key Stage 1) (Wales) Order 1997—*cont.*
Art.5, applied: SI 1998/392 Sch. para.2, SI 1999/521 Sch. para.2
Art.6, applied: SI 1998/392 Sch. para.2, SI 1999/521 Sch. para.2
Art.7, applied: SI 1998/392 Sch. para.2, SI 1999/521 Sch. para.2
Art.8, applied: SI 1998/392 Sch. para.2, SI 1999/521 Sch. para.2
Art.9, applied: SI 1998/392 Sch. para.2, SI 1999/521 Sch. para.2

2012. A205 Trunk Road (Lewisham) Red Route (Cycle Lane) Experimental Traffic Order 1997
revoked: SI 1998/1106 Art.5
Art.4, revoked: SI 1998/1106 Art.5

2014. A205 Trunk Road (Lewisham) Red Route Experimental Traffic Order 1997
revoked: SI 1999/81 Art.10
Art.5, revoked: SI 1999/81 Art.10
Art.8, revoked: SI 1999/81 Art.10
Art.9, revoked: SI 1999/81 Art.10
Art.11, revoked: SI 1999/81 Art.10

2042. Processed Cereal-based Foods and Baby Foods for Infants and Young Children Regulations 1997
Reg.1, amended: SI 1999/275 Reg.2
Reg.5A, added: SI 1999/275 Reg.2
Reg.6, amended: SI 1999/275 Reg.2
Reg.8, amended: SI 1999/275 Reg.2
Sch.2 para.1.3a, added: SI 1999/275 Reg.2
Sch.2 para.1.4a, added: SI 1999/275 Reg.2
Sch.2 para.1.4b, added: SI 1999/275 Reg.2
Sch.6, added: SI 1999/275 Reg.2, Sch.

2050. A23 Trunk Road (Croydon) Red Route (Prohibited Turns) Experimental Traffic Order 1997
revoked: SI 1997/2134

2055. Income Support (General) (Standard Interest Rate Amendment) (No.2) Regulations 1997
revoked: SI 1997/2604 Reg.3 (with savings)
Reg.1, revoked: SI 1997/2604 Reg.3 (with savings)
Reg.2, revoked: SI 1997/2604 Reg.3 (with savings)
Reg.3, revoked: SI 1997/2604 Reg.3 (with savings)

2060. Education (School Performance Information) (England) (Amendment) Regulations 1997
revoked: SI 1998/1929 Reg.4
Reg.2, revoked: SI 1998/1929 Reg.4

2070. Motor Vehicles (Driving Licences) (Amendment) (No.4) Regulations 1997
revoked: SI 1999/2864 Reg.2, Sch.1
Reg.3, revoked: SI 1999/2864 Reg.2, Sch.1
Reg.4, revoked: SI 1999/2864 Reg.2, Sch.1
Reg.5, revoked: SI 1999/2864 Reg.2, Sch.1
Reg.6, revoked: SI 1999/2864 Reg.2, Sch.1
Reg.7, revoked: SI 1999/2864 Reg.2, Sch.1
Reg.8, revoked: SI 1999/2864 Reg.2, Sch.1
Reg.9, revoked: SI 1999/2864 Reg.2, Sch.1
Reg.10, revoked: SI 1999/2864 Reg.2, Sch.1

2071. A23 Trunk Road (Croydon) Red Route Experimental Traffic Order 1997
revoked: SI 1997/2133 Art.11
Art.7, amended: SI 1998/1706 Art.4, Art.5
Art.7, revoked (in part): SI 1998/1706 Art.3
Sch.2C(I), amended: SI 1998/1706 Art.12

NO.

1997—cont.

2071. A23 Trunk Road (Croydon) Red Route Experimental Traffic Order 1997—*cont.*
Sch.2C(II), added: SI 1998/1706 Art.13
Sch.2A Item 1, amended: SI 1998/1706 Art.6
Sch.2B Item 8A, amended: SI 1998/1706 Art.7
Sch.2B Item 15, amended: SI 1998/1706 Art.8
Sch.2B Item 15A, amended: SI 1998/1706 Art.9
Sch.2B Item 16, revoked: SI 1998/1706 Art.10
Sch.2B Item 17, amended: SI 1998/1706 Art.11
Sch.3A Item 2, revoked: SI 1998/1706 Art.14
Sch.4 Item 5, amended: SI 1998/1706 Art.15
Sch.4 Item 43, amended: SI 1998/1706 Art.16
Sch.4 Item 44, revoked: SI 1998/1706 Art.17
Sch.4 Item 64, amended: SI 1998/1706 Art.18
Sch.4 Item 82, amended: SI 1998/1706 Art.19
Sch.4 Item 82A, amended: SI 1998/1706 Art.20

2078. Road Traffic (Permitted Parking Area and Special Parking Area) (County of Kent) (Borough of Maidstone) Order 1997
applied: SI 1999/1918 Reg.20
referred to: SI 1999/1918
Art.3, revoked: SI 1999/639 Art.3
Art.4, amended: SI 1999/639 Art.3
Sch.1, revoked: SI 1999/639 Art.3
Sch.1 para.7, amended: SI 1999/130 Art.4
Sch.1 para.7, revoked: SI 1999/639 Art.3
Sch.2, revoked: SI 1999/639 Art.3
Sch.3 para.5, substituted: SI 1999/130 Art.3

2079. Gaming Act (Variation of Monetary Limits) (No.2) Order 1997
Art.2, revoked: SI 1998/2152 Art.4

2080. Amusements with Prizes (Variation of Monetary Limits) Order 1997
revoked: SI 1999/1259 Art.3, Sch.
Art.2, revoked: SI 1999/1259 Art.3, Sch.
Art.3, revoked: SI 1999/1259 Art.3, Sch.

2133. A23 Trunk Road (Croydon) Red Route (No.2) Experimental Traffic Order 1997
revoked (in part): SI 1999/414 Art.10
Art.5, revoked (in part): SI 1999/414 Art.10
Art.8, revoked (in part): SI 1999/414 Art.10
Art.9, revoked (in part): SI 1999/414 Art.10
Art.11, revoked (in part): SI 1999/414 Art.10

2134. A23 Trunk Road (Croydon) Red Route (Prohibited Turns) (No.2) Experimental Traffic Order 1997
revoked: SI 1998/1278 Art.6
Art.6, revoked: SI 1998/1278 Art.6

2137. Wireless Telegraphy (Network User Stations) (Exemption) Regulations 1997
revoked: SI 1999/930 Reg.2, Sch.1
Reg.3, revoked: SI 1999/930 Reg.2, Sch.1

2173. Education (Further Education Institutions Information) (England) (Amendment) Regulations 1997
revoked: SI 1998/2220 Reg.9
Reg.2, revoked: SI 1998/2220 Reg.9

2174. Education (Grants for Education Support and Training) (England) (Amendment) Regulations 1997
revoked: SI 1998/656 Reg.12
Reg.3, revoked: SI 1998/656 Reg.12
Reg.4, revoked: SI 1998/656 Reg.12
Reg.5, revoked: SI 1998/656 Reg.12
Reg.6, revoked: SI 1998/656 Reg.12

2176. Education (National Curriculum) (Assessment Arrangements for Key Stages 1, 2 and 3) (England) (Amendment) Order 1997
revoked (in part): SI 1999/1236 Art.2, Sch., SI 1999/2188 Art.2 (rem.)
Art.2, revoked (in part): SI 1999/1236 Art.2, Sch., SI 1999/2188 Art.2 (rem.)

NO.

2176. Education (National Curriculum) (Assessment Arrangements for Key Stages 1, 2 and 3) (England) (Amendment) Order 1997 —cont.
Art.3, revoked (in part): SI 1999/1236 Art.2, Sch., SI 1999/2188 Art.2 (rem.)

2196. Gaming Duty Regulations 1997
Reg.5, amended: SI 1998/2055 Reg.4, SI 1999/2489 Reg.4

2204. Registration of Marriages (Amendment) Regulations 1997
Reg.3, revoked: SI 1999/1621 Reg.10, Sch.3

2205. Social Security (Recovery of Benefits) Regulations 1997
Reg.12, amended: SI 1999/3178 Art.3, Sch.17

2237. Social Security (Recovery of Benefits) (Appeals) Regulations 1997
revoked: SI 1999/991 Reg.59 (with savings), Sch.4 (with savings)
Reg.1, revoked: SI 1999/991 Reg.59 (with savings), Sch.4 (with savings)
Reg.2, amended: SI 1999/3178 Art.4, Sch.21 para.1, Sch.21 para.6
Reg.2, applied: SI 1999/3178 Art.4, Sch.21 para.1, Sch.21 para.6
Reg.2, revoked: SI 1999/991 Reg.59 (with savings), Sch.4 (with savings)
Reg.3, revoked: SI 1999/991 Reg.59 (with savings), Sch.4 (with savings)
Reg.4, applied: SI 1999/3178 Art.4, Sch.21 para.3
Reg.5, revoked: SI 1999/991 Reg.59 (with savings), Sch.4 (with savings)
Reg.7, revoked: SI 1999/991 Reg.59 (with savings), Sch.4 (with savings)
Reg.11, amended: SI 1999/3178 Art.4, Sch.21 para.6
Reg.11, applied: SI 1999/3178 Art.4, Sch.21 para.6
Reg.12, applied: SI 1999/3178 Art.4, Sch.21 para.6
Reg.13, revoked: SI 1999/991 Reg.59 (with savings), Sch.4 (with savings)

2238. Food (Pistachios from Iran) (Emergency Control) Order 1997
Art.2, amended: SI 1997/3046 Art.2

2239. Social Security (Claims and Payments and Adjudication) Amendment Regulations 1997
revoked: SI 1997/2290 Reg.8

2259. Local Government Act 1988 (Defined Activities) (Exemption) (Brent London Borough Council and Harrogate Borough Council) Order 1997
revoked: SI 1998/579 Art.3

2282. Motor Cycle (EC Type Approval) (Amendment) Regulations 1997
revoked: SI 1999/2920 Reg.2
Reg.2, revoked: SI 1999/2920 Reg.2

2283. National Crime Squad Service Authority (Levying) Order 1997
Art.13, amended: SI 1998/3259 Art.2
Art.13, revoked (in part): SI 1998/3259 Art.2
Art.14, amended: SI 1998/1129 Art.3, Sch.2
Sch., substituted: SI 1998/3259 Art.2

2284. NCIS Service Authority (Levying) Order 1997
Art.13, amended: SI 1998/3258 Art.2
Art.13, revoked (in part): SI 1998/3258 Art.2
Art.14, amended: SI 1998/1129 Art.3, Sch.2
Sch., substituted: SI 1998/3258 Art.2

NO.

2289. National Heath Service (Proposals for Pilot Schemes) and (Miscellaneous Amendments) Regulations 1997
Reg.2, amended: SI 1998/3 Reg.2
Reg.3, amended: SI 1998/3 Reg.2
Reg.4, revoked: SI 1998/1330 Reg.5, Sch.1

2300. A1 Trunk Road (Barnet) Red Route Traffic Order 1997
Art.2, amended: SI 1999/272 Art.2, Sch. Part A
Art.9, amended: SI 1999/272 Art.2, Sch. Part A

2304. Road Traffic (Permitted Parking Area and Special Parking Area) (County of Hertfordshire) (Borough of Watford) Order 1997
applied: SI 1999/1918 Reg.20
referred to: SI 1999/1918
Sch.1 para.5, substituted: SI 1999/1669 Art.3

2305. Social Security (Miscellaneous Amendments) (No.4) Regulations 1997
Reg.4, revoked: SI 1999/991 Reg.59 (with savings), Sch.4 (with savings)

2308. Children (Protection from Offenders) (Miscellaneous Amendments) Regulations 1997
see *A (Protection from Offenders Regulations), Re* [1999] 1 F.L.R. 697 (Fam Div), Hogg, J.; see *Lincolnshire CC v R-J (X Intervening)* [1998] 1 W.L.R. 1679 (Fam Div), Michael Horowitz Q.C.; see *R. v Secretary of State for Health Ex p. B* [1999] 1 F.L.R. 656 (QBD), Scott Baker, J.; see *R. v Secretary of State for Health Ex p. C (Minors)* Times, November 11, 1998 (QBD), Scott Baker, J.; see *RJ (Foster Placement), Re* [1999] 1 W.L.R. 581 (CA), Butler-Sloss, L.J.; see *RJ (Wardship), Re* [1999] 1 F.L.R. 618 (Fam Div), Cazalet, J.
Reg.3, see *RJ (Foster Placement), Re* [1998] 2 F.L.R. 110 (Fam Div), Sir Stephen Brown

2326. A501 Trunk Road (Camden and Islington) Red Route Traffic Order 1997
Art.2, amended: SI 1999/272 Art.2, Sch. Part A
Art.9, amended: SI 1999/272 Art.2, Sch. Part A

2347. Diseases of Animals (Approved Disinfectants) (Amendment) Order 1997
revoked: SI 1999/919 Art.3
Art.2, revoked: SI 1999/919 Art.3
Art.3, revoked: SI 1999/919 Art.3
Sch.1, revoked: SI 1999/919 Art.3
Sch.2, revoked: SI 1999/919 Art.3

2348. Registration of Births, Still-births, Deaths and Marriages (Prescription of Forms) (Scotland) Regulations 1997
Sch.2 Form, substituted: SSI 1999/104 Reg.2, Sch.1
Sch.6 Form, substituted: SSI 1999/104 Reg.3, Sch.2
Sch.10, substituted: SI 1998/2285 Reg.2, Sch.1
Sch.11, substituted: SI 1998/2285 Reg.3, Sch.2
Sch.21 Form, substituted: SSI 1999/104 Reg.4, Sch.3
Sch.22 Form, substituted: SSI 1999/104 Reg.5, Sch.4

2351. Curfew Order (Responsible Officer) Order 1997
revoked: SI 1999/3155 Art.6
Art.3, amended: SI 1999/10 Art.2
Art.3, revoked: SI 1999/3155 Art.6
Art.3A, added: SI 1999/10 Art.2
Art.3A, revoked: SI 1999/3155 Art.6
Art.4, amended: SI 1998/3067 Art.2
Art.4, revoked: SI 1999/3155 Art.6
Art.5, revoked: SI 1999/3155 Art.6

NO.

2364. **Education (School Performance Information) (England) (Amendment) (No.2) Regulations 1997**
revoked: SI 1998/1929 Reg.4
Reg.2, revoked: SI 1998/1929 Reg.4
Reg.3, revoked: SI 1998/1929 Reg.4

2366. **Merchant Shipping (Carriage of Cargoes) (Amendment) Regulations 1997**
revoked: SI 1999/336 Reg.1
Reg.3, revoked: SI 1999/336 Reg.1
Reg.4, revoked: SI 1999/336 Reg.1
Reg.5, revoked: SI 1999/336 Reg.1
Reg.6, revoked: SI 1999/336 Reg.1
Reg.7, revoked: SI 1999/336 Reg.1

2367. **Merchant Shipping (Dangerous Goods and Marine Pollutants) Regulations 1997**
applied: SI 1999/336 Reg.3

2386. **A406 Trunk Road (Ealing and Hounslow) Red Route Traffic Order 1997**
Art.2, amended: SI 1999/272 Art.2, Sch. Part A
Art.9, amended: SI 1999/272 Art.2, Sch. Part A

2389. **Airports (Groundhandling) Regulations 1997**
Reg.2, amended: SI 1998/2918 Reg.3
Reg.2, revoked (in part): SI 1998/2918 Reg.3
Reg.13, substituted: SI 1998/2918 Reg.4
Reg.14, amended: SI 1998/2918 Reg.5
Reg.21, substituted: SI 1998/2918 Reg.6
Reg.24, amended: SI 1998/2918 Reg.7
Reg.27, added: SI 1998/2918 Reg.8
Sch.1 para.1, amended: SI 1998/2918 Reg.9
Sch.1 para.3, amended: SI 1998/2918 Reg.9
Sch.1 para.5A, added: SI 1998/2918 Reg.9
Sch.1 para.7, amended: SI 1998/2918 Reg.9
Sch.1 para.11, substituted: SI 1998/2918 Reg.9
Sch.1 para.14, amended: SI 1998/2918 Reg.9
Sch.2 Part I, amended: SI 1998/2918 Reg.10
Sch.2 Part II, amended: SI 1998/2918 Reg.11
Sch.2 Part II, revoked (in part): SI 1998/2918 Reg.11

2390. **Police Act 1997 (Commencement No.4 and Transitional Provisions) Order 1997**
Art.4, revoked: SI 1998/354 Art.7
Art.5, revoked: SI 1998/354 Art.7
Art.6, revoked: SI 1998/354 Art.7
Art.7, revoked: SI 1998/354 Art.7

2391. **Police Act 1997 (Provisions in relation to the NCIS Service Authority) (No.2) Order 1997**
revoked: SI 1998/633 Art.A3
Art.4, revoked: SI 1998/633 Art.A3
Art.5, revoked: SI 1998/633 Art.A3
Art.12, revoked: SI 1998/633 Art.A3
Art.13, revoked: SI 1998/633 Art.A3
Art.14, revoked: SI 1998/633 Art.A3
Art.16, revoked: SI 1998/633 Art.A3

2395. **Education (Grants for Education Support and Training) (Wales) (Amendment) Regulations 1997**
revoked: SI 1998/392 Reg.12
Reg.3, revoked: SI 1998/392 Reg.12
Reg.4, revoked: SI 1998/392 Reg.12
Reg.5, revoked: SI 1998/392 Reg.12
Reg.6, revoked: SI 1998/392 Reg.12

2400. **Zebra, Pelican and Puffin Pedestrian Crossings Regulations and General Directions 1997**
applied: SI 1999/1750 Art.2, Sch.1
Dir.8, amended: SI 1998/901 Dir.2
Reg.24, applied: SI 1999/1851 Art.2
Sch.1 Part II, applied: SI 1999/1025 Reg.4

NO.

2402. **A205 Trunk Road (Hounslow) Red Route (Bus Lanes) Traffic Order 1997**
revoked: SI 1999/2127 Art.5
Art.4, revoked: SI 1999/2127 Art.5
Art.5, revoked: SI 1999/2127 Art.5

2435. **Housing Benefit (Recovery of Overpayments) Regulations 1997**
Reg.3, amended: SI 1998/2454 Reg.2

2439. **Vehicle Excise Duty (Immobilisation, Removal and Disposal of Vehicles) Regulations 1997**
Reg.2, amended: SI 1997/3063 Reg.3, SI 1998/1217 Reg.2, Sch. para.1
Reg.4, amended: SI 1997/3063 Reg.4
Reg.5, amended: SI 1997/3063 Reg.5, SI 1998/1217 Reg.2, Sch. para.2
Reg.9, amended: SI 1997/3063 Reg.6, SI 1998/1217 Reg.2, Sch. para.3
Reg.10, amended: SI 1999/35 Reg.2
Reg.17, amended: SI 1997/3063 Reg.7, SI 1998/1217 Reg.2, Sch. para.4

2440. **Education (Individual Performance Information) (Prescribed Bodies and Persons) Regulations 1997**
revoked: SI 1999/903 Reg.1
Reg.3, revoked: SI 1999/903 Reg.1

2441. **Potatoes Originating in the Netherlands Regulations 1997**
Reg.3, amended: SI 1998/3168 Reg.2
Reg.4, amended: SI 1998/3168 Reg.2
Reg.6, amended: SI 1998/3168 Reg.2

2453. **Oxleas National Health Service Trust (Transfer of Trust Property) Order 1997**
Art.1, amended: SI 1997/2691 Art.2

2454. **A205 Trunk Road (Lewisham) Red Route (Bus Lane) (No.2) Experimental Traffic Order 1997**
revoked: SI 1998/2502 Art.5
Art.4, revoked: SI 1998/2502 Art.5

2464. **Export of Goods (United Nations Sanctions) (Sierra Leone) Order 1997**
Art.2, revoked: SI 1997/3033 Art.2

2489. **A1 Trunk Road (Barnet) Red Route (Clearway) Traffic Order 1997**
Art.2, amended: SI 1999/272 Art.2, Sch. Part B
Art.9, amended: SI 1999/272 Art.2, Sch. Part B

2492. **National Health Service (Optical Charges and Payments) (Scotland) Amendment (No.2) Regulations 1997**
revoked: SI 1998/642 Reg.24, Sch.4
Reg.2, revoked: SI 1998/642 Reg.24, Sch.4

2505. **Health and Safety (Fees) Regulations 1997**
revoked: SI 1999/645 Reg.19
Reg.3, amended: SI 1999/437 Reg.18
Reg.3, revoked: SI 1999/645 Reg.19
Reg.4, revoked: SI 1999/645 Reg.19
Reg.5, revoked: SI 1999/645 Reg.19
Reg.6, revoked: SI 1999/645 Reg.19
Reg.7, revoked: SI 1999/645 Reg.19
Reg.8, revoked: SI 1999/645 Reg.19
Reg.9, revoked: SI 1999/645 Reg.19
Reg.10, revoked: SI 1999/645 Reg.19
Reg.11, revoked: SI 1999/645 Reg.19
Reg.12, revoked: SI 1999/645 Reg.19
Reg.13, revoked: SI 1999/645 Reg.19
Reg.13A, added: SI 1999/257 Reg.14
Reg.13A, revoked: SI 1999/645 Reg.19
Reg.13B, added: SI 1999/303 Reg.11, Sch.10 para.1
Reg.13B, revoked: SI 1999/645 Reg.19
Reg.15, revoked: SI 1999/645 Reg.19
Reg.16, revoked: SI 1999/645 Reg.19
Reg.17, revoked: SI 1999/645 Reg.19

NO.

2505. Health and Safety (Fees) Regulations 1997—
cont.
Sch.3, revoked: SI 1999/645 Reg.19
Sch.4, revoked: SI 1999/645 Reg.19
Sch.5, revoked: SI 1999/645 Reg.19
Sch.6, revoked: SI 1999/645 Reg.19
Sch.6 Table, amended: SI 1999/437 Reg.18
Sch.6 Table, revoked: SI 1999/645 Reg.19
Sch.7, revoked: SI 1999/645 Reg.19
Sch.8, revoked: SI 1999/645 Reg.19
Sch.9 Part I, revoked: SI 1999/645 Reg.19
Sch.9 Part II, revoked: SI 1999/645 Reg.19
Sch.9 Part V, revoked: SI 1999/645 Reg.19
Sch.9 Part VI, revoked: SI 1999/645 Reg.19
Sch.10, revoked: SI 1999/645 Reg.19
Sch.11, revoked: SI 1999/645 Reg.19
Sch.11A, added: SI 1999/257 Reg.14, Sch.5
Sch.11A, revoked: SI 1999/645 Reg.19
Sch.12, revoked: SI 1999/645 Reg.19
Sch.13, revoked: SI 1999/645 Reg.19
Sch.14, added: SI 1999/303 Reg.11, Sch.10
para.2
Sch.14, revoked: SI 1999/645 Reg.19

2509. Food Protection (Emergency Prohibitions) (Oil and Chemical Pollution of Fish) Order 1997
revoked (in part): SI 1997/2735 Art.2, SI 1998/314 Art.2 (rem.)
Art.3, revoked (in part): SI 1997/2735 Art.2, SI 1998/314 Art.2 (rem.)

2563. European Communities (Designation) (No.3) Order 1997
revoked (in part): SI 1999/2788 Art.4, Sch.3
Art.2, revoked (in part): SI 1999/2788 Art.4, Sch.3
Art.3, revoked (in part): SI 1999/2788 Art.4, Sch.3

2573. Angola (United Nations Sanctions) (Dependent Territories) Order 1997
Art.3, amended: SI 1998/1753 Art.21
Art.4, amended: SI 1998/1753 Art.21
Art.14, amended: SI 1998/1753 Art.21

2575. Child Abduction and Custody (Parties to Conventions) (Amendment) (No.2) Order 1997
revoked: SI 1998/256 Art.2
Art.2, revoked: SI 1998/256 Art.2
Art.3, revoked: SI 1998/256 Art.2
Sch., revoked: SI 1998/256 Art.2

2585. Merchant Shipping (Oil Pollution) (Pitcairn) Order 1997
Sch., amended: SI 1998/1067 Art.2

2587. Merchant Shipping (Oil Pollution) (Sovereign Base Areas) Order 1997
s.177, amended: SI 1998/1068 Art.2

2591. State Immunity (Merchant Shipping) Order 1997
see *Guiseppe di Vittorio (No.2), The* [1998] 1 Lloyd's Rep. 661 (QBD (Adm Ct)), Clarke, J.
revoked: SI 1999/668 Art.2
Art.2, revoked: SI 1999/668 Art.2
Art.3, revoked: SI 1999/668 Art.2
Art.4, revoked: SI 1999/668 Art.2

2592. Sierra Leone (United Nations Sanctions) Order 1997
revoked: SI 1998/1501 Art.4
Art.10, revoked: SI 1998/1501 Art.4
Art.12, revoked: SI 1998/1501 Art.4
Sch.1, revoked: SI 1998/1501 Art.4

2593. Sierra Leone (United Nations Sanctions) (Dependent Territories) Order 1997
revoked: SI 1998/1502 Art.4
Art.10, revoked: SI 1998/1502 Art.4

NO.

2599. Sierra Leone (United Nations Sanctions) (Channel Islands) Order 1997
revoked: SI 1998/1507 Art.5
Art.10, revoked: SI 1998/1507 Art.5

2600. Sierra Leone (United Nations Sanctions) (Isle of Man) Order 1997
revoked: SI 1998/1508 Art.4
Art.10, revoked: SI 1998/1508 Art.4

2604. Income Support (General) (Standard Interest Rate Amendment) (No.3) Regulations 1997
revoked: SI 1998/1128 Reg.3 (with savings)
Reg.1, revoked: SI 1998/1128 Reg.3 (with savings)
Reg.2, revoked: SI 1998/1128 Reg.3 (with savings)
Reg.3, revoked: SI 1998/1128 Reg.3 (with savings)

2605. Nevill Hall and District National Health Service Trust (Establishment) Amendment Order 1997
revoked: SI 1999/1120 Art.2, Sch.2
Art.2, revoked: SI 1999/1120 Art.2, Sch.2

2655. A316 Trunk Road (Hounslow) Red Route Experimental Traffic Order 1997
revoked: SI 1998/2615 Art.10
Art.5, revoked: SI 1998/2615 Art.10
Art.8, revoked: SI 1998/2615 Art.10
Art.9, revoked: SI 1998/2615 Art.10
Art.11, revoked: SI 1998/2615 Art.10

2656. A316 Trunk Road (Hounslow and Richmond) Red Route (Clearway) Traffic Order 1997
Art.2, amended: SI 1999/272 Art.2, Sch. Part B
Art.9, amended: SI 1999/272 Art.2, Sch. Part B

2657. A4 Trunk Road (Hounslow and Hammersmith & Fulham) Red Route (Clearway) Traffic Order 1997
Art.2, amended: SI 1999/272 Art.2, Sch. Part B
Art.9, amended: SI 1999/272 Art.2, Sch. Part B

2668. Building Societies Act 1997 (Commencement No.3) Order 1997
Art.2, applied: SI 1998/504 Reg.12
Sch. Part II, applied: SI 1998/504 Reg.12
Sch. Part II, referred to: SI 1997/2840 Art.3

2670. County Court Fees (Amendment) (No.2) Order 1997
revoked: SI 1999/689 Art.8 (with savings), Sch.2 (with savings)
Art.2, revoked: SI 1999/689 Art.8 (with savings), Sch.2 (with savings)

2671. Family Proceedings Fees (Amendment) (No.4) Order 1997
revoked: SI 1999/690 Art.7 (with savings), Sch.2 (with savings)
Art.2, revoked: SI 1999/690 Art.7 (with savings), Sch.2 (with savings)

2672. Supreme Court Fees (Amendment) Order 1997
revoked: SI 1999/687 Art.8 (with savings), Sch.2 (with savings)
Art.3, revoked: SI 1999/687 Art.8 (with savings), Sch.2 (with savings)
Art.4, revoked: SI 1999/687 Art.8 (with savings), Sch.2 (with savings)
Art.5, revoked: SI 1999/687 Art.8 (with savings), Sch.2 (with savings)

2673. Food Industry Development Scheme 1997
para.4, referred to: SI 1997/2674 Art.2

2679. Education (Teachers) (Amendment) (No.2) Regulations 1997
referred to: SI 1999/2166 Reg.2, Sch.1 para 7, SI 1999/2817 Reg.2, Sch.1 para.7

NO.

2679. Education (Teachers) (Amendment) (No.2) Regulations 1997—*cont.*

Reg.2, revoked (in part): SI 1999/2166 Reg.2, Sch.1 Part I, SI 1999/2817 Reg.2, Sch.1 Part I

Reg.3, revoked (in part): SI 1999/2166 Reg.2, Sch.1 Part I, SI 1999/2817 Reg.2, Sch.1 Part I

Reg.4, revoked (in part): SI 1999/2166 Reg.2, Sch.1 Part I, SI 1999/2817 Reg.2, Sch.1 Part I

Reg.5, revoked (in part): SI 1999/2166 Reg.2, Sch.1 Part I, SI 1999/2817 Reg.2, Sch.1 Part I

Reg.6, revoked (in part): SI 1999/2166 Reg.2, Sch.1 Part I, SI 1999/2817 Reg.2, Sch.1 Part I

Reg.7, revoked (in part): SI 1999/2166 Reg.2, Sch.1 Part I, SI 1999/2817 Reg.2, Sch.1 Part I

Sch.1, revoked: SI 1999/2166 Reg.2, Sch.1 Part I

Sch.2, revoked: SI 1999/2166 Reg.2, Sch.1 Part I

Sch.3, revoked: SI 1999/2166 Reg.2, Sch.1 Part I

2703. Section 7 of the Petroleum (Production) Act 1934 and Section 2(1)(a) of the Petroleum Act 1987 (Modification) Regulations 1997

revoked: 1998 c.17 s.51, Sch.5 Part II

Reg.2, revoked: 1998 c.17 s.51, Sch.5 Part II

Reg.3, revoked: 1998 c.17 s.51, Sch.5 Part II

2757. Sole, Plaice, etc. (Specified Sea Areas) (Prohibition of Fishing) Order 1997

revoked: SI 1997/2891 Art.4

Art.3, revoked: SI 1997/2891 Art.4

2758. Export of Goods (Control) (Amendment No.3) Order 1997

Art.1, revoked (in part): SI 1999/63 Art.2

2759. Dual-Use and Related Goods (Export Control) (Amendment No.4) Regulations 1997

Reg.4, revoked: SI 1998/272 Reg.3

Reg.5, amended: SI 1998/272 Reg.4

Reg.7, revoked: SI 1998/272 Reg.3

2777. Industrial Pollution Control (Northern Ireland) Order 1997

applied: SI 1999/662 (NI.6) Art.10

Art.7, amended: SI 1999/662 (NI.6) Art.63, Sch.7

Art.7, revoked (in part): SI 1997/2777 (NI.18) Art.35, Sch.5

Art.17, revoked (in part): SI 1997/2777 (NI.18) Art.35, Sch.5

Art.20, applied: SI 1999/662 (NI.6) Art.30

Art.23, referred to: SI 1999/662 (NI.6) Art.10

Art.27, applied: SI 1997/2778 (NI.19) Art.70

Art.28, amended: SI 1997/2778 (NI.19) Art.83, Sch.5 para.8, SI 1999/662 (NI.6) Art.63, Sch.7

Sch.4 para.5, revoked: SI 1999/662 (NI.6) Art.63, Sch.8 Part II

Sch.4 para.6, revoked: SI 1999/662 (NI.6) Art.63, Sch.8 Part II

Sch.4 para.7, revoked: SI 1999/662 (NI.6) Art.63, Sch.8 Part II

2778. Waste and Contaminated Land (Northern Ireland) Order 1997

applied: SI 1999/662 (NI.6) Art.10

Art.5, revoked (in part): SI 1997/2778 (NI.19) Art.83, Sch.6

Art.7, referred to: SI 1999/662 (NI.6) Art.18

Art.8, amended: SI 1998/2795 (NI.18) Art.6, Sch.1 para.27, SI 1999/662 (NI.6) Art.63, Sch.7

Art.10, amended: SI 1998/2795 (NI.18) Art.6, Sch.1 para.28

Art.23, revoked: SI 1997/2778 (NI.19) Art.83, Sch.6

NO.

2778. Waste and Contaminated Land (Northern Ireland) Order 1997—*cont.*

Art.37, revoked (in part): SI 1997/2778 (NI.19) Art.83, Sch.6

Art.43, revoked (in part): SI 1997/2778 (NI.19) Art.83, Sch.6

Art.49, amended: SI 1999/662 (NI.6) Art.63, Sch.7

Art.56A, added: SI 1999/662 (NI.6) Art.63, Sch.7

Art.60, amended: SI 1999/662 (NI.6) Art.63, Sch.7

Art.61, amended: SI 1999/662 (NI.6) Art.63, Sch.7

Art.70, amended: SI 1999/662 (NI.6) Art.63, Sch.7

Art.72, revoked (in part): SI 1997/2778 (NI.19) Art.83, Sch.6

2779. Shops (Sunday Trading &c.) (Northern Ireland) Order 1997

applied: SI 1999/2790 (NI.9) Art.24

Art.3, referred to: SI 1999/1736 Art.12, Sch.5

Art.4, referred to: SI 1999/1736 Art.12, Sch.5

Art.5, referred to: SI 1999/1736 Art.12, Sch.5

Art.6, referred to: SI 1999/1736 Art.12, Sch.5

Art.8, referred to: SI 1999/1736 Art.12, Sch.5

Art.9, referred to: SI 1999/1736 Art.12, Sch.5

Sch.2 para.1, revoked (in part): SI 1999/2790 (NI.9) Art.40, Sch.9 Part 2

Sch.2 para.3, amended: SI 1999/2790 (NI.9) Art.40, Sch.9 Part 2

Sch.2 para.9, amended: SI 1999/2790 (NI.9) Art.40, Sch.9 Part 2

Sch.2 para.9, revoked (in part): SI 1999/2790 (NI.9) Art.40, Sch.9 Part 2

Sch.2 para.10, amended: SI 1998/1761 (NI.15) Art.5, Sch. para.6, SI 1998/1763 (NI.17) Art.18

Sch.2 para.10, revoked (in part): SI 1999/2790 (NI.9) Art.40, Sch.9 Part 9

Sch.2 para.11, revoked (in part): SI 1999/2790 (NI.9) Art.20, Art.40, Sch.9 Part 3

Sch.2 para.13, amended: SI 1998/1265 (NI.8) Art.16, Sch.2

2785. A4 Trunk Road (Hammersmith & Fulham and Kensington & Chelsea) Red Route Experimental Traffic Order 1997

revoked (in part): SI 1999/1147 Art.10

Art.5, revoked (in part): SI 1999/1147 Art.10

Art.8, revoked (in part): SI 1999/1147 Art.10

Art.9, revoked (in part): SI 1999/1147 Art.10

Art.11, revoked (in part): SI 1999/1147 Art.10

Sch.2B Item 1, added: SI 1998/1951 Art.4

Sch.2B Item 1, revoked (in part): SI 1998/1951 Art.3, SI 1999/1147 Art.10

Sch.2B Item 2, added: SI 1998/1951 Art.4

Sch.2B Item 2, revoked (in part): SI 1998/1951 Art.3, SI 1999/1147 Art.10

Sch.2B Item 3, added: SI 1998/1951 Art.4

Sch.2B Item 3, revoked (in part): SI 1999/1147 Art.10

Sch.2B Item 4, added: SI 1998/1951 Art.4

Sch.2B Item 4, revoked (in part): SI 1999/1147 Art.10

Sch.3B Item 4, added: SI 1998/1951 Art.5

Sch.3B Item 4, revoked (in part): SI 1999/1147 Art.10

Sch.3B Item 5, added: SI 1998/1951 Art.5

Sch.3B Item 5, revoked (in part): SI 1999/1147 Art.10

Sch.3B Item 6, added: SI 1998/1951 Art.5

Sch.3B Item 6, revoked (in part): SI 1999/1147 Art.10

1997—cont.

2787. **National Health Service (Vocational Train-ing) Amendment Regulations 1997**
revoked: SI 1997/2817 Reg.20, Sch.5
Reg.2, revoked: SI 1997/2817 Reg.20, Sch.5
2789. **Horse Passports Order 1997**
Art.9, amended: SI 1998/2367 Art.2
2816. **Education (School Performance Infor-mation) (England) (Amendment) (No.3) Regulations 1997**
revoked: SI 1998/1929 Reg.4
Reg.2, revoked: SI 1998/1929 Reg.4
Reg.3, revoked: SI 1998/1929 Reg.4
Sch.1, revoked: SI 1998/1929 Reg.4
2817. **National Health Service (Vocational Training for General Medical Practice) Regulations 1997**
Reg.2, amended: SI 1998/669 Reg.2
Reg.6, applied: SI 1998/646 Reg.5
Reg.7, amended: SI 1998/669 Reg.2
Reg.7, revoked (in part): SI 1998/669 Reg.2
Reg.9, amended: SI 1998/669 Reg.2
Reg.12, applied: SI 1998/646 Reg.5
2844. **Sheep Annual Premium and Suckler Cow Premium Quotas Regulations 1997**
applied: SI 1999/672 Art.2, Sch.1
2847. **Relocation Grants (Form of Application) Regulations 1997**
Reg.2, referred to: SI 1999/2315 Reg.3
Sch., referred to: SI 1999/2315 Reg.3
Sch. Form, amended: SI 1998/810 Reg.2, Sch., SI 1999/1541 Reg.2, Sch., SI 1999/2625 Reg.2, Sch., SI 1999/3469 Reg.2, Sch.1
Sch. Form, revoked (in part): SI 1998/810 Reg.2, Sch.
2863. **Social Security Amendment (New Deal) Regulations 1997**
Reg.18, revoked: SI 1998/1174 Reg.8
2864. **Statistics of Trade (Customs and Excise) (Amendment) Regulations 1997**
Reg.4, revoked: SI 1998/2973 Reg.3
2876. **Medicines (Pharmacies) (Applications for Registration and Fees) Amendment Regu-lations 1997**
revoked: SI 1998/3085 Reg.3
Reg.2, revoked: SI 1998/3085 Reg.3
Reg.3, revoked: SI 1998/3085 Reg.3
2885. **Non-Domestic Rating (Rural Settlements) (Wales) Order 1997**
revoked: SI 1998/2963 Art.4
Art.2, revoked: SI 1998/2963 Art.4
Art.3, revoked: SI 1998/2963 Art.4
Sch. Part I, amended: SI 1998/390 Art.2
Sch. Part I, revoked: SI 1998/2963 Art.4
Sch. Part II, amended: SI 1998/390 Art.2
Sch. Part II, revoked: SI 1998/2963 Art.4
2892. **Medicines (Veterinary Drugs) (Pharmacy and Merchants' List) (Amendment) Order 1997**
revoked: SI 1998/1044 Art.9, Sch.
Art.2, revoked: SI 1998/1044 Art.9, Sch.
Sch., revoked: SI 1998/1044 Art.9, Sch.
2893. **Charges for Inspections and Controls Regu-lations 1997**
Reg.2, amended: SI 1998/2880 Reg.3
Reg.4, amended: SI 1998/2880 Reg.4
Reg.4, revoked (in part): SI 1998/2880 Reg.4
Sch., amended: SI 1998/2880 Reg.5
2894. **Animal By-Products (Amendment) Order 1997**
revoked: SI 1999/646 Art.35, Sch.6 Part I
Art.2, revoked: SI 1999/646 Art.35, Sch.6 Part I

1997—cont.

2915. **Motor Vehicles (Driving Licences) (Amend-ment) (No.5) Regulations 1997**
revoked: SI 1999/2864 Reg.2, Sch.1
Reg.3, revoked: SI 1999/2864 Reg.2, Sch.1
Reg.4, revoked: SI 1999/2864 Reg.2, Sch.1
Reg.5, revoked: SI 1999/2864 Reg.2, Sch.1
Reg.6, revoked: SI 1999/2864 Reg.2, Sch.1
Reg.7, revoked: SI 1999/2864 Reg.2, Sch.1
2919. **Education (Student Loans) (Amendment) Regulations 1997**
revoked: SI 1998/211 Reg.2
Reg.2, revoked: SI 1998/211 Reg.2
2920. **Civil Aviation (Route Charges for Navigation Services) Regulations 1997**
revoked: SI 1999/3260 Reg.2, Sch.1
Reg.2, revoked: SI 1999/3260 Reg.2, Sch.1
Reg.3, amended: SI 1998/2999 Reg.2
Reg.3, revoked: SI 1999/3260 Reg.2, Sch.1
Reg.5, amended: SI 1998/2999 Reg.2
Reg.5, revoked: SI 1999/3260 Reg.2, Sch.1
Reg.6, amended: SI 1998/2999 Reg.2
Reg.6, revoked: SI 1999/3260 Reg.2, Sch.1
Reg.7, amended: SI 1998/2999 Reg.2
Reg.7, revoked: SI 1999/3260 Reg.2, Sch.1
Reg.13, revoked: SI 1999/3260 Reg.2, Sch.1
Reg.16, revoked: SI 1999/3260 Reg.2, Sch.1
Reg.18, revoked: SI 1999/3260 Reg.2, Sch.1
Sch.1, revoked: SI 1999/3260 Reg.2, Sch.1
Sch.2, amended: SI 1999/1544 Reg.2, SI 1999/2276 Reg.2
Sch.2, revoked: SI 1999/3260 Reg.2, Sch.1
Sch.2, substituted: SI 1998/1537 Reg.2, SI 1998/2999 Reg.2
Sch.3 para.1, revoked: SI 1999/3260 Reg.2, Sch.1
2921. **A205 Trunk Road (Southwark) Red Route (Bus Lanes) Experimental Traffic Order 1997**
revoked: SI 1999/15 Art.5
Art.4, revoked: SI 1999/15 Art.5
2922. **A23 Trunk Road (Lambeth) Red Route Experimental Traffic Order 1997**
revoked (in part): SI 1999/1724 Art.10 (with saving)
Art.5, revoked (in part): SI 1999/1724 Art.10 (with saving)
Art.8, revoked (in part): SI 1999/1724 Art.10 (with saving)
Art.9, revoked (in part): SI 1999/1724 Art.10 (with saving)
Art.11, revoked (in part): SI 1999/1724 Art.10 (with saving)
2929. **National Health Service (Pilot Schemes-Health Service Bodies) Regulations 1997**
Reg.1, amended: SI 1998/1136 Reg.2
2931. **Telecommunications (Interconnection) Regulations 1997**
Reg.2, amended: SI 1999/3449 Reg.3
Reg.4, applied: SI 1999/2450 Sch.1 para.44.1, Sch.1 para.50.5
Reg.6, amended: SI 1999/3449 Reg.4, Reg.10
Reg.6, applied: SI 1999/2450 Sch.1 para.9.1, Sch.1 para.9.2, Sch.1 para.9.3, Sch.1 para.9.6, Sch.1 para.45.1, Sch.1 para.45.2, Sch.1 para.45.5, Sch.1 para.48.6, Sch.1 para.49.8
Reg.7, amended: SI 1999/3449 Reg.7
Reg.7, applied: SI 1999/2450 Sch.1 para.9.3, Sch.1 para.45.5, Sch.1 para.48.6
Reg.10, amended: SI 1999/3449 Reg.7
Reg.10, applied: SI 1999/2450 Sch.1 para.9.3, Sch.1 para.45.5, Sch.1 para.48.6

NO.

1997—cont.

2931. Telecommunications (Interconnection) Regulations 1997—cont.
Reg.11, amended: SI 1999/3449 Reg.6, SI 1999/3448 Reg.3
Reg.12A, added: SI 1999/3180 Reg.5
Reg.13, amended: SI 1999/3449 Reg.9
Reg.14A, added: SI 1999/3180 Reg.6
Reg.38A, added: SI 1999/3180 Reg.7
Sch.1 Part I, applied: SI 1999/2450 Sch.1 para.47.1
Sch.1 Part II, applied: SI 1999/2450 Sch.1 para.47.1
Sch.3 Part II, applied: SI 1998/1580 Reg.27
Sch.3 Part IV, applied: SI 1999/2450 Sch.1 para.33.4
Sch.5, applied: SI 1999/2450 Sch.1 para.39.1
Sch.7, added: SI 1999/3449 Reg.9, Sch.2
Sch.7, applied: SI 1999/3449 Reg.8

2932. Telecommunications (Open Network Provision and Leased Lines) Regulations 1997
Reg.8, applied: SI 1999/2450 Sch.1 para.55.1
Reg.12, applied: SI 1999/2450 Sch.1 para.55.15
Sch.2 para.A, applied: SI 1999/2450 Sch.1 para.55.3
Sch.2 para.B, applied: SI 1999/2450 Sch.1 para.55.3
Sch.2 para.C, applied: SI 1999/2450 Sch.1 para.55.3
Sch.3, applied: SI 1999/2450 Sch.1 para.55.12

2937. Civil Aviation (Joint Financing) Regulations 1997
Reg.4, amended: SI 1998/3000 Reg.2, SI 1999/3268 Reg.2
Reg.15, amended: SI 1998/3000 Reg.2, SI 1999/3268 Reg.2

2939. Registration of Births, Deaths and Marriages (Fees) Order 1997
revoked: SI 1998/3171 Art.3
Art.3, revoked: SI 1998/3171 Art.3
Sch., revoked: SI 1998/3171 Art.3

2941. Invergarry-Kyle of Lochalsh Trunk Road (A87) Extension (Skye Bridge Crossing) Toll Order (Variation) Order 1997
revoked: SSI 1999/196 Art.3
Art.2, revoked: SSI 1999/196 Art.3

2947. Severn Bridges Tolls Order 1997
revoked: SI 1998/2958 Art.3
Art.2, revoked: SI 1998/2958 Art.3
Art.3, revoked: SI 1998/2958 Art.3

2948. Dundee Teaching Hospitals National Health Service Trust (Establishment) Amendment Order 1997
revoked: SI 1999/1070 Art.2, Sch.2
Art.2, revoked: SI 1999/1070 Art.2, Sch.2

2959. Beef Bones Regulations 1997
revoked: SSI 1999/186 Reg.11
Reg.3, see *MacNeill v Sutherland* 1998 S.C.C.R. 474 (HCJ Appeal) High Court of Justiciary (Appeal), Lord Cullen L.J.C., Lord Coulsfield, Lord Abernethy
Reg.3, revoked: SSI 1999/186 Reg.11
Reg.3, substituted: SI 1999/3371 Reg.2, SI 1999/3464 Reg.2
Reg.4, substituted: SI 1999/3371 Reg.2, SI 1999/3464 Reg.2
Reg.5, substituted: SI 1999/3371 Reg.2, SI 1999/3464 Reg.2
Reg.6, revoked: SI 1999/3371 Reg.2
Reg.7, substituted: SI 1999/3371 Reg.2, SI 1999/3464 Reg.2

NO.

1997—cont.

2959. Beef Bones Regulations 1997—cont.
Reg.8, revoked: SI 1999/3371 Reg.2, SI 1999/3464 Reg.2, SSI 1999/186 Reg.11
Reg.8, substituted: SI 1999/3464 Reg.2
Reg.9, substituted: SI 1999/3371 Reg.2
Reg.10, revoked: SSI 1999/186 Reg.11
Reg.11, revoked: SSI 1999/186 Reg.11
Reg.12, revoked: SSI 1999/186 Reg.11

2962. Merchant Shipping and Fishing Vessels (Health and Safety at Work) Regulations 1997
Reg.2, amended: SI 1998/2411 Reg.17
Reg.3, amended: SI 1998/2411 Reg.17
Reg.4, amended: SI 1998/2411 Reg.17
Reg.5, amended: SI 1998/2411 Reg.17
Reg.7, applied: SI 1998/2857 Reg.5
Reg.8, applied: SI 1998/587 Art.2
Reg.9, applied: SI 1998/587 Art.2
Reg.11, referred to: SI 1998/2411 Reg.7
Reg.17, amended: SI 1998/2411 Reg.17
Reg.25, amended: SI 1998/2411 Reg.17

2964. Specified Risk Material Order 1997
referred to: SI 1999/646 Art.3, Art.7, Art.8
Art.10, applied: SI 1997/2965 Reg.5, Reg.21, Reg.24

2965. Specified Risk Material Regulations 1997
applied: SI 1997/2964 Art.8
referred to: SI 1999/646 Art.3, Art.7, Art.8
Reg.2, amended: SI 1998/2405 Reg.2
Reg.7, amended: SI 1997/3062 Reg.2, SI 1998/2405 Reg.2
Reg.10, amended: SI 1998/2405 Reg.2, SI 1999/539 Reg.5
Reg.16A, added: SI 1998/2405 Reg.2
Reg.17, amended: SI 1998/2405 Reg.2
Reg.18, amended: SI 1998/2405 Reg.2
Reg.19, amended: SI 1997/3062 Reg.2, SI 1998/2405 Reg.2
Reg.19A, added: SI 1998/2405 Reg.2
Reg.29, amended: SI 1998/2405 Reg.2
Reg.31A, added: SI 1999/539 Reg.5

2971. Secretary of State for the Environment, Transport and the Regions Order 1997
referred to: SI 1999/672 Art.2, Sch.1

2983. Civil Evidence (Northern Ireland) Order 1997
Art.1, amended: SI 1999/663 Art.2, Sch.1 para.28
Sch.1 para.4, revoked: SI 1999/2789 (NI.8) Art.40, Sch.3

3001. Teachers' Pensions Regulations 1997
applied: SI 1998/2255 Reg.17
Reg.A3, added: SI 1998/2255 Reg.3
Reg.A3, amended: SI 1999/607 Reg.3
Reg.B1, amended: SI 1998/2255 Reg.4
Reg.B1, applied: SI 1998/2255 Reg.15
Reg.B1, referred to: SI 1998/2255 Reg.15
Reg.C3A, added: SI 1998/2255 Reg.5
Reg.C3A, referred to: SI 1998/2255 Reg.15
Reg.C18, amended: SI 1998/2255 Reg.6
Reg.C18, referred to: SI 1998/2255 Reg.15
Reg.E1, amended: SI 1998/2255 Reg.7
Reg.E4, applied: SI 1999/2166 Reg.6, SI 1999/2817 Reg.6
Reg.E14, amended: SI 1998/2255 Reg.8, Reg.16
Reg.E14, applied: SI 1998/2255 Reg.16
Reg.E34, amended: SI 1998/1129 Art.3, Sch.2
Reg.G4, amended: SI 1999/607 Reg.4
Reg.G5, amended: SI 1999/607 Reg.5
Reg.G5, revoked (in part): SI 1998/2255 Reg.9
Reg.G8, amended: SI 1998/2255 Reg.10

NO.

NO.

1997—cont.

3001. **Teachers' Pensions Regulations 1997—**
cont.
Reg.G8, referred to: SI 1998/2255 Reg.15
Reg.H3, amended: SI 1998/2255 Reg.11
Sch.1, amended: SI 1998/2255 Reg.12, SI 1999/607 Reg.6
Sch.2 para.1, amended: SI 1998/2670 Reg.10
Sch.2 para.1, applied: SI 1998/2670 Reg.10
Sch.2 para.1A, added: SI 1998/2255 Reg.13
Sch.2 para.2, amended: SI 1999/607 Reg.7
Sch.2 para.3, amended: SI 1999/607 Reg.7
Sch.2 para.4, revoked: SI 1999/607 Reg.7
Sch.10 para.28A, added: SI 1998/2255 Reg.14
Sch.15 para.7, referred to: SI 1999/607 Reg.9
Sch.15 para.9, amended: SI 1999/607 Reg.8

3018. **Merchant Shipping (Port Waste Reception**
Facilities) Regulations 1997
Reg.15, amended: SI 1998/531 Reg.3

3021. **National Health Service (Pilot Schemes:**
Financial Assistance for Preparatory
Work) Amendment Regulations 1997
revoked: SI 1998/1330 Reg.5, Sch.1
Reg.2, revoked: SI 1998/1330 Reg.5, Sch.1

3025. **Road Vehicles (Statutory Off-Road Notifi-**
cation) Regulations 1997
Reg.5, amended: SI 1999/713 Reg.2
Reg.6, amended: SI 1999/713 Reg.2
Reg.8, added: SI 1999/713 Reg.2

3032. **Copyright and Rights in Databases Regu-**
lations 1997
Reg.14, amended: SI 1999/1042 Art.3, Sch.1
para.26
Sch.2 para.15, amended: SI 1999/506 Art.39

3038. **Personal and Occupational Pension**
Schemes (Miscellaneous Amendments)
(No.2) Regulations 1997
Reg.11, amended: SI 1998/600 Reg.4

3045. **A205 Trunk Road (Southwark) Red Route**
Experimental Traffic Order 1997
revoked (in part): SI 1999/1805 Art.10
Art.5, revoked (in part): SI 1999/1805 Art.10
Art.8, revoked (in part): SI 1999/1805 Art.10
Art.9, revoked (in part): SI 1999/1805 Art.10
Art.11, revoked (in part): SI 1999/1805 Art.10

3048. **Local Government Superannuation (Scot-**
land) Amendment (No.4) Regulations 1997
applied: SI 1998/364 Reg.4, Reg.6, Reg.19,
Sch.2 para.2, Sch.2 para.5, Sch.4 para.8
referred to: SI 1998/364 Reg.3, Reg.10, Sch.2
para.4, Sch.2 para.6

3054. **Sole, etc. (Specified Sea Areas) (Prohibition**
of Fishing) Order 1997
Art.2, amended: SI 1998/207 Art.2

3061. **Town and Country Planning (Use Classes)**
(Scotland) Order 1997
Art.3, amended: SSI 1999/1 Reg.47
Sch. Class 9, amended: SI 1998/1196 Art.2

3066. **A205 Trunk Road (Lewisham) Red Route**
Experimental Traffic Order 1997 Variation
Order 1997
revoked (in part): SI 1998/1835 Art.10

3069. **Criminal Legal Aid (Scotland) (Prescribed**
Proceedings) Regulations 1997
Reg.3, amended: SI 1998/969 Reg.2, SI 1999/
215 Reg.2

3070. **Advice and Assistance (Assistance by Way**
of Representation) (Scotland) Regu-
lations 1997
Reg.1, amended: SI 1998/972 Reg.2
Reg.4, amended: SI 1998/972 Reg.3, SI 1999/
214 Reg.2

1998

5. **National Health Service (Vocational Training**
for General Medical Practice) (Scotland)
Regulations 1998
Reg.2, amended: SI 1998/669 Reg.3
Reg.6, applied: SI 1998/646 Reg.5
Reg.7, revoked (in part): SI 1998/669 Reg.3
Reg.9, amended: SI 1998/669 Reg.3
Reg.12, applied: SI 1998/646 Reg.5

19. **Social Fund Winter Fuel Payment Regu-**
lations 1998
Reg.1, amended: SI 1998/1910 Reg.2, SI 1999/
1880 Reg.2, SI 1999/3178 Art.3, Sch.18
para.1
Reg.2, amended: SI 1998/1910 Reg.2
Reg.2, revoked (in part): SI 1998/1910 Reg.2
Reg.3, amended: SI 1998/1910 Reg.2, SI 1999/
1880 Reg.2
Reg.4, amended: SI 1999/3178 Art.3, Sch.18
para.2

20. **Motor Vehicles (Driving Licences) (Amend-**
ment) Regulations 1998
revoked: SI 1999/2864 Reg.2, Sch.1
Reg.3, revoked: SI 1999/2864 Reg.2, Sch.1
Reg.4, revoked: SI 1999/2864 Reg.2, Sch.1
Reg.5, revoked: SI 1999/2864 Reg.2, Sch.1
Reg.6, revoked: SI 1999/2864 Reg.2, Sch.1
Reg.7, revoked: SI 1999/2864 Reg.2, Sch.1
Reg.8, revoked: SI 1999/2864 Reg.2, Sch.1
Reg.9, revoked: SI 1999/2864 Reg.2, Sch.1
Reg.10, revoked: SI 1999/2864 Reg.2, Sch.1
Reg.11, revoked: SI 1999/2864 Reg.2, Sch.1
Reg.12, revoked: SI 1999/2864 Reg.2, Sch.1
Reg.13, revoked: SI 1999/2864 Reg.2, Sch.1
Reg.14, revoked: SI 1999/2864 Reg.2, Sch.1
Reg.15, revoked: SI 1999/2864 Reg.2, Sch.1
Reg.16, revoked: SI 1999/2864 Reg.2, Sch.1
Reg.17, revoked: SI 1999/2864 Reg.2, Sch.1
Reg.18, revoked: SI 1999/2864 Reg.2, Sch.1
Reg.20, revoked: SI 1999/2864 Reg.2, Sch.1
Reg.21, revoked: SI 1999/2864 Reg.2, Sch.1
Reg.22, revoked: SI 1999/2864 Reg.2, Sch.1
Reg.23, revoked: SI 1999/2864 Reg.2, Sch.1
Reg.24, revoked: SI 1999/2864 Reg.2, Sch.1
Reg.25, revoked: SI 1999/2864 Reg.2, Sch.1
Reg.26, revoked: SI 1999/2864 Reg.2, Sch.1
Reg.27, revoked: SI 1999/2864 Reg.2, Sch.1
Reg.60A, revoked: SI 1999/2864 Reg.2, Sch.1

23. **Prison (Amendment) Rules 1998**
revoked: SI 1999/728 r.85 (with savings), Sch.
(with savings)
r.2, revoked: SI 1999/728 r.85 (with savings),
Sch. (with savings)

34. **Hill Livestock (Compensatory Allowances)**
(Amendment) Regulations (Northern Ire-
land) 1998
revoked: SR 1999/497 Reg.15 (with savings)

54. **Social Security (Incapacity for Work) (Gen-**
eral) (Amendment) Regulations (Northern
Ireland) 1998
revoked: SR 1999/138 Reg.4

55. **Spreadable Fats (Marketing Standards)**
(Amendment) Regulations (Northern Ire-
land) 1998
revoked: SR 1999/383 Reg.9, Sch.2

58. **Child Support (Miscellaneous Amend-**
ments) Regulations 1998
Reg.59, substituted: SI 1999/1510 Art.45

62. **Statutory Maternity Pay (Compensation of**
Employers) (Amendment) Regulations
(Northern Ireland) 1998
revoked: SR 1999/65 Reg.3

1998—cont.

1998—cont.

63. Social Security Benefits Up-rating Regulations (Northern Ireland) 1998
revoked: SR 1999/139

64. Social Security (Industrial Injuries) (Dependency) (Permitted Earnings Limits) Order (Northern Ireland) 1998
revoked: SR 1999/94

69. Meat (Sterilisation and Staining) (Amendment) Regulations (Northern Ireland) 1998
revoked: SR 1999/418 Reg.15

71. Jobseeker's Allowance (Amendment) Regulations 1998
revoked: SI 1998/1174 Reg.2
Reg.2, revoked: SI 1998/1174 Reg.2
Reg.3, revoked: SI 1998/1174 Reg.2

72. Social Security (Contributions) (Amendment) Regulations (Northern Ireland) 1998
revoked: SR 1999/118 Sch.

73. General Optical Council (Registration and Enrolment (Amendment) Rules) Order of Council 1998
revoked: SI 1999/69, SI 1999/69 Sch. r.3
Sch., revoked: SI 1999/69, SI 1999/69 Sch. r.3
Sch. para.2, revoked: SI 1999/69, SI 1999/69 Sch. r.3
Sch. para.3, revoked: SI 1999/69, SI 1999/69 Sch. r.3

76. A41 Trunk Road (Westminster) Red Route Traffic Order 1998
Art.2, amended: SI 1999/272 Art.2, Sch. Part A
Art.9, amended: SI 1999/272 Art.2, Sch. Part A
Art.10, amended: SI 1998/2035 Art.3
Sch.3B Item 22, added: SI 1998/2035 Art.4
Sch.4 Item 9, amended: SI 1998/2035 Art.5
Sch.4 Item 13, revoked: SI 1998/2035 Art.7
Sch.4 Item 14, amended: SI 1998/2035 Art.6

78. A501 Trunk Road (Camden and Westminster) Red Route Traffic Order 1998
Art.2, amended: SI 1999/272 Art.2, Sch. Part A
Art.9, amended: SI 1999/272 Art.2, Sch. Part A

78. Employer's Liability (Compulsory Insurance) Exemption Regulations (Northern Ireland) 1998
revoked: SR 1999/448 Sch.3

80. Education (Grants for Education Support and Training) (England) (Amendment) Regulations 1998
revoked: SI 1998/656 Reg.12
Reg.3, revoked: SI 1998/656 Reg.12
Reg.4, revoked: SI 1998/656 Reg.12
Reg.5, revoked: SI 1998/656 Reg.12

84. Workmen's Compensation (Supplementation) (Amendment) Regulations (Northern Ireland) 1998
revoked: SR 1999/113

90. Legal Advice and Assistance (Amendment) Regulations (Northern Ireland) 1998
revoked: SR 1999/131

91. Legal Advice and Assistance (Financial Conditions) Regulations (Northern Ireland) 1998
revoked: SR 1999/130 Reg.2

92. Legal Aid (Financial Conditions) Regulations (Northern Ireland) 1998
revoked: SR 1999/132 (with saving)

109. National Crime Squad (Secretary of State's Objectives) Order 1998
revoked: SI 1999/821 Art.2

110. NCIS (Secretary of State's Objectives) Order 1998
revoked: SI 1999/882 Art.2

116. Motor Vehicles (Construction and Use) (Amendment) Regulations (Northern Ireland) 1998
revoked: SR 1999/454 Reg.126, Sch.19

118. London Borough of Lambeth (Trunk Roads) Red Route (Bus Lanes) Traffic Order 1998
revoked (in part): SI 1998/3128 Art.6
Art.4, revoked (in part): SI 1998/3128 Art.6
Art.5, revoked (in part): SI 1998/3128 Art.6

119. Local Government Finance (New Parishes) Regulations 1998
Reg.2, amended: SI 1998/3270 Reg.2
Reg.3, amended: SI 1998/3270 Reg.2, Reg.3
Reg.4, amended: SI 1998/3270 Reg.2
Reg.5, amended: SI 1998/3270 Reg.2, Reg.4
Reg.6, amended: SI 1998/3270 Reg.2, Reg.5

125. Health and Safety (Fees) Regulations (Northern Ireland) 1998
amended: SR 1999/150 Reg.2, Sch.

131. Carriage of Dangerous Goods by Rail Regulations (Northern Ireland) 1998
amended: SR 1999/150 Reg.2, Sch.

132. Packaging, Labelling and Carriage of Radioactive Material by Rail Regulations (Northern Ireland) 1998
amended: SR 1999/150 Reg.2, Sch.

135. Charges for Drugs and Appliances (Amendment No.2) Regulations (Northern Ireland) 1998
revoked (in part): SR 1999/166 Reg.5

140. Land Registration (District Registries) Order 1998
revoked: SI 1998/2974 Art.1
Art.1, revoked: SI 1998/2974 Art.1

141. Bread and Flour Regulations 1998
Reg.5, amended: SI 1999/1136 Reg.14
Sch.3, revoked: SI 1999/1136 Reg.14

155. Lands Tribunal (Salaries) Order (Northern Ireland) 1998
revoked: SR 1999/236

162. Education (Mandatory Awards) (Amendment) Regulations 1998
revoked: SI 1998/1166 Reg.6
Reg.2, revoked: SI 1998/1166 Reg.6

163. Bovines and Bovine Products (Trade) Regulations (Northern Ireland) 1998
applied: SI 1999/1103 Reg.4, Reg.5
referred to: SI 1998/1135 Reg.6, SI 1999/1103 Reg.4, Reg.6, Reg.9, Reg.15, Reg.17
revoked: SR 1999/308 Reg.25
Reg.3, referred to: SI 1998/1135 Reg.3
Reg.3, revoked: SR 1999/308 Reg.25
Reg.8, applied: SI 1998/1135 Reg.3
Reg.8, revoked: SR 1999/308 Reg.25
Sch.3, applied: SI 1998/1135 Reg.4
Sch.3, revoked: SR 1999/308 Reg.25
Sch.4, applied: SI 1998/1135 Reg.4
Sch.4, revoked: SR 1999/308 Reg.25

179. A205 Trunk Road (Southwark) Red Route (Prohibited Turns) Experimental Traffic Order 1998
revoked: SI 1999/142 Art.6

181. Salaries (Assembly Ombudsman and Commissioner for Complaints) Order (Northern Ireland) 1998
revoked: SR 1999/274 Art.2

NO.

1998—cont.

192. Local Government (Discretionary Payments and Injury Benefits) (Scotland) Regulations 1998
amended: SI 1998/364 Sch.3 para.4
applied: SI 1999/1750 Art.2, Sch.1
Part III, amended: SI 1998/366 Reg.136
Part VI, amended: SI 1998/366 Reg.26
Reg.2, amended: SI 1998/364 Sch.3 para.4
Reg.5, amended: SI 1998/364 Sch.3 para.4
Reg.6, amended: SI 1998/364 Sch.3 para.4
Reg.7, amended: SI 1998/364 Sch.3 para.4
Reg.8, amended: SI 1998/364 Sch.3 para.4
Reg.8, applied: SI 1998/366 Reg.51
Reg.9, amended: SI 1998/364 Sch.3 para.4
Reg.10, amended: SI 1998/364 Sch.3 para.4
Reg.11, amended: SI 1998/364 Sch.3 para.4
Reg.16, amended: SI 1998/364 Sch.3 para.4
Reg.17, amended: SI 1998/364 Sch.3 para.4
Reg.18, amended: SI 1998/364 Sch.3 para.4
Reg.19, amended: SI 1998/364 Sch.3 para.4
Reg.20, amended: SI 1998/364 Sch.3 para.4
Reg.21, amended: SI 1998/364 Sch.3 para.4
Reg.22, amended: SI 1998/364 Sch.3 para.4
Reg.24, amended: SI 1998/364 Sch.3 para.4
Reg.25, amended: SI 1998/364 Sch.3 para.4
Reg.26, amended: SI 1998/364 Sch.3 para.4
Reg.31, amended: SI 1998/364 Sch.3 para.4
Reg.37, amended: SI 1998/364 Sch.3 para.4
Reg.38, amended: SI 1998/364 Sch.3 para.4
Reg.41, amended: SI 1998/364 Sch.3 para.4
Reg.44, amended: SI 1998/364 Sch.3 para.4
Reg.45, amended: SI 1998/364 Sch.3 para.4
Reg.46, amended: SI 1998/364 Sch.3 para.4
Reg.48, amended: SI 1998/364 Sch.3 para.4

194. Horse Racing (Charges on Bookmakers) Order (Northern Ireland) 1998
revoked: SR 1999/231

201. Potatoes Originating in Egypt Regulations 1998
Reg.2, amended: SI 1998/3167 Reg.2
Reg.5A, added: SI 1998/3167 Reg.2
Reg.6, amended: SI 1998/3167 Reg.2

202. Excise Duty Point (External and Internal Community Transit Procedure) Regulations 1998
Reg.9, substituted: SI 1998/3110 Reg.2

205. Civil Aviation (Canadian Navigation Services) (Second Amendment) Regulations 1998
revoked: SI 1998/2575 Reg.3, Sch.1
Reg.2, revoked: SI 1998/2575 Reg.3, Sch.1

206. Hill Livestock (Compensatory Allowances) (Amendment) Regulations 1998
revoked: SI 1999/3316 Reg.18 (with saving), SSI 1999/187 Reg.23 (with savings), Sch.2 (with savings)
Reg.2, revoked: SI 1999/3316 Reg.18 (with saving), SSI 1999/187 Reg.23 (with savings), Sch.2 (with savings)

208. Occupational Pension Schemes (Contracting Out) (Amount Required for Restoring State Scheme Rights and Miscellaneous Amendment) Regulations (Northern Ireland) 1998
applied: SI 1999/671 Art.3, Sch.2
Reg.4, amended: SI 1999/3069 Reg.2
Sch.2, amended: SI 1999/3069 Reg.2

211. Education (Student Loans) Regulations 1998
Reg.3, amended: SI 1998/1676 Reg.3
Reg.4, amended: SI 1998/1676 Reg.4
Reg.6, amended: SI 1998/1676 Reg.5, SI 1999/1784 Reg.3

NO.

1998—cont.

211. Education (Student Loans) Regulations 1998—*cont.*
Reg.8, amended: SI 1998/2005 Reg.3
Sch.2 para.1, amended: SI 1999/1784 Reg.4
Sch.2 para.3, amended: SI 1999/1784 Reg.4
Sch.2 para.15, amended: SI 1998/1676 Reg.6

214. Local Government Changes for England (Council Tax) (Transitional Reduction) Regulations 1998
revoked (in part): SI 1999/259 Reg.11
Reg.2, applied: SI 1999/259 Reg.11
Reg.2, revoked (in part): SI 1999/259 Reg.11
Reg.4, revoked (in part): SI 1999/259 Reg.11
Reg.6, revoked (in part): SI 1999/259 Reg.11
Reg.8, revoked (in part): SI 1999/259 Reg.11
Reg.10, revoked (in part): SI 1999/259 Reg.11
Reg.11, revoked (in part): SI 1999/259 Reg.11
Sch.1, applied: SI 1999/259 Reg.11
Sch.1, revoked (in part): SI 1999/259 Reg.11
Sch.1 para.3, applied: SI 1999/259 Sch.Part III
Sch.1 para.3, revoked (in part): SI 1999/259 Reg.11
Sch.2, applied: SI 1999/259 Reg.11
Sch.2, revoked (in part): SI 1999/259 Reg.11
Sch.2 Part 1, applied: SI 1999/259 Sch.Part III
Sch.2 Part 1, revoked (in part): SI 1999/259 Reg.11
Sch.2 Part 2, applied: SI 1999/259 Sch.Part III
Sch.2 Part 2, revoked (in part): SI 1999/259 Reg.11
Sch.2 Part 4, applied: SI 1999/259 Sch.Part III
Sch.2 Part 4, revoked (in part): SI 1999/259 Reg.11
Sch.3 para.1, revoked (in part): SI 1999/259 Reg.11
Sch.3 para.2, revoked (in part): SI 1999/259 Reg.11
Sch.3 para.3, revoked (in part): SI 1999/259 Reg.11
Sch.4 para.1, revoked (in part): SI 1999/259 Reg.11
Sch.4 para.2, revoked (in part): SI 1999/259 Reg.11
Sch.5 para.1, revoked (in part): SI 1999/259 Reg.11
Sch.5 para.2, revoked (in part): SI 1999/259 Reg.11
Sch.5 para.3, revoked (in part): SI 1999/259 Reg.11

216. Police (Secretary of State's Objectives) Order 1998
revoked: SI 1999/543 Art.2
Art.2, revoked: SI 1999/543 Art.2
Art.3, revoked: SI 1999/543 Art.2

217. New Deal (Miscellaneous Provisions) Order 1998
referred to: SI 1998/1425
Art.1, amended: SI 1998/1425 Art.2
Art.2, substituted: SI 1998/1425 Art.2

218. Education (Modification of Enactments Relating to Employment) Order 1998
see *Lancashire CC v Mason* [1998] I.C.R. 907 (EAT), Judge Byrt Q.C.
revoked: SI 1999/2256 Art.1
Art.1, revoked: SI 1999/2256 Art.1
Art.2, amended: SI 1999/711 Reg.8
Art.2, revoked: SI 1999/2256 Art.1
Art.3, revoked: SI 1999/2256 Art.1
Art.4, revoked: SI 1999/2256 Art.1
Art.5, revoked: SI 1999/2256 Art.1
Art.6, revoked: SI 1999/2256 Art.1

1998—cont.

222. **Planning (General Development) (Amendment) Order (Northern Ireland) 1998**
referred to: SI 1999/2450 Sch.4 para.3.6, Sch.4 para.4.2, Sch.4 para.5.5

225. **Motor Vehicles (Construction and Use) (Amendment No.2) Regulations (Northern Ireland) 1998**
revoked: SR 1999/454 Reg.126, Sch.19

253. **Visiting Forces and International Headquarters (Application of Law) (Amendment) Order 1998**
revoked: SI 1999/1736 Art.19, Sch.9
Art.2, revoked: SI 1999/1736 Art.19, Sch.9

256. **Child Abduction and Custody (Parties to Conventions) (Amendment) Order 1998**
revoked: SI 1999/2030 Art.2
Art.2, revoked: SI 1999/2030 Art.2
Art.3, revoked: SI 1999/2030 Art.2
Sch., revoked: SI 1999/2030 Art.2

257. **Consular Fees Order 1998**
revoked: SI 1999/655 Art.4
Art.3, revoked: SI 1999/655 Art.4
Art.4, revoked: SI 1999/655 Art.4
Sch. para.9, revoked: SI 1999/655 Art.4
Sch. para.25, revoked: SI 1999/655 Art.4
Sch. para.27, revoked: SI 1999/655 Art.4
Sch. para.49, revoked: SI 1999/655 Art.4

258. **Education (Student Loans) (Northern Ireland) Order 1998**
revoked: SI 1998/1760 (NI.14) Art.9, Sch.
Art.1, revoked: SI 1998/1760 (NI.14) Art.9, Sch.
Art.2, revoked: SI 1998/1760 (NI.14) Art.9, Sch.
Art.3, revoked: SI 1998/1760 (NI.14) Art.9, Sch.
Art.4, revoked: SI 1998/1760 (NI.14) Art.9, Sch.
Art.5, revoked: SI 1998/1760 (NI.14) Art.9, Sch.
Art.6, revoked: SI 1998/1760 (NI.14) Art.9, Sch.

264. **Trial of the Pyx (Amendment) Order 1998**
revoked: SI 1998/1764 Art.16, Sch.3
Art.2, revoked: SI 1998/1764 Art.16, Sch.3

265. **Housing (Change of Landlord) (Payment of Disposal Cost by Instalments) (Amendment) Regulations 1998**
revoked: SI 1998/2082 Reg.3
Reg.2, revoked: SI 1998/2082 Reg.3
Reg.3, revoked: SI 1998/2082 Reg.3

267. **Occupational Pension Schemes (Validation of Rule Alterations) Regulations (Northern Ireland) 1998**
applied: SI 1999/671 Art.3, Sch.2

268. **Sea Fishing (Enforcement of Community Quota Measures) Order 1998**
revoked: SI 1999/424 Art.14
Art.5, revoked: SI 1999/424 Art.14
Art.13, revoked: SI 1999/424 Art.14
Art.14, revoked: SI 1999/424 Art.14

269. **Third Country Fishing (Enforcement) Order 1998**
revoked: SI 1999/425 Art.13
Art.5, revoked: SI 1999/425 Art.13
Art.13, revoked: SI 1999/425 Art.13

272. **Dual-Use and Related Goods (Export Control) (Amendment) Regulations 1998**
Reg.2, revoked: SI 1999/984 Reg.2

272. **Salaries (Comptroller and Auditor General) Order (Northern Ireland) 1998**
revoked: SR 1999/364 Art.2

273. **Students Awards Regulations (Northern Ireland) 1998**
revoked: SR 1999/351 Reg.2 (with saving)

281. **Control of Lead at Work Regulations (Northern Ireland) 1998**
amended: SR 1999/150 Reg.2, Sch.

1998—cont.

293. **Tuberculosis Control (Amendment) Order (Northern Ireland) 1998**
revoked: SR 1999/263 Sch.

295. **Council Tax (Administration and Enforcement) (Amendment) Regulations 1998**
revoked (in part): SI 1999/534 Reg.4
Reg.3, revoked (in part): SI 1999/534 Reg.4
Reg.4, amended: SI 1999/534 Reg.4
Reg.4, revoked (in part): SI 1999/534 Reg.4
Reg.5, revoked (in part): SI 1999/534 Reg.4
Reg.6, revoked (in part): SI 1999/534 Reg.4
Reg.7, revoked (in part): SI 1999/534 Reg.4
Reg.8, revoked (in part): SI 1999/534 Reg.4
Sch., revoked (in part): SI 1999/534 Reg.4

300. **Students Awards (Amendment) Regulations (Northern Ireland) 1998**
revoked: SR 1999/351 Reg.2 (with saving)

322. **Seeds (Fees) Regulations (Northern Ireland) 1998**
revoked: SR 1999/379 Reg.2

332. **Social Security (Contributions) (Amendment No.4) Regulations (Northern Ireland) 1998**
revoked: SR 1999/117 Reg.13

354. **Police Act 1997 (Commencement No.5 and Transitional Provisions) Order 1998**
Art.5, applied: SI 1998/633 Art.G10

364. **Local Government Pension Scheme (Transitional Provisions) (Scotland) Regulations 1998**
applied: SI 1998/366 Reg.8, Reg.41, Reg.137, SI 1998/2888 Reg.5, SI 1999/1750 Art.2, Sch.1
referred to: SI 1998/366 Reg.117
Reg.2, amended: SI 1998/2888 Reg.13, Sch.2 para.1
Reg.19, applied: SI 1998/366 Reg.73

366. **Local Government Pension Scheme (Scotland) Regulations 1998**
applied: SI 1998/364 Reg.10, Reg.12, Reg.13, Reg.14, Reg.18, Reg.19, Reg.21, Reg.22, Sch.2 para.5, Sch.4 para.2, SI 1998/2888 Reg.5, SI 1999/1750 Art.2, Sch.1
referred to: SI 1998/364 Sch.4 para.4, Sch.4 para.5
Part II, applied: SI 1998/364 Sch.2 para.2
Part II, referred to: SI 1998/364 Reg.4
Part III, applied: SI 1998/364 Sch.2 para.2
Part III, referred to: SI 1998/364 Reg.4
Part IV, applied: SI 1998/364 Reg.4
Part V, applied: SI 1998/364 Sch.2 para.2
Part V, referred to: SI 1998/364 Reg.4
Reg.8, applied: SI 1998/364 Reg.6, Reg.7, Reg.9, Reg.10, Reg.11, Reg.12, Reg.13, Sch.2 para.6
Reg.8, referred to: SI 1998/364 Reg.17
Reg.12, amended: SI 1998/364 Reg.21
Reg.15, referred to: SI 1998/364 Reg.16
Reg.19, applied: SI 1998/364 Reg.13, Reg.18
Reg.19, referred to: SI 1998/364 Reg.18
Reg.24, referred to: SI 1998/364 Reg.18
Reg.25, referred to: SI 1998/364 Reg.18
Reg.26, applied: SI 1998/364 Reg.8
Reg.26, referred to: SI 1998/364 Reg.18
Reg.28, applied: SI 1998/364 Reg.18, Sch.2 para.4, Sch.2 para.5, Sch.2 para.6
Reg.28, referred to: SI 1998/364 Reg.18, Sch.2 para.8
Reg.30, amended: SI 1998/364 Reg.21, Reg.22
Reg.30, referred to: SI 1998/364 Reg.18

NO.

1998—cont.

366. Local Government Pension Scheme (Scotland) Regulations 1998—*cont.*

Reg.31, applied: SI 1998/364 Sch.2 para.6, Sch.2 para.7, SI 1998/366 Sch.2 para.8, SI 1998/364 Sch.2 para.9

Reg.33, applied: SI 1998/364 Reg.18

Reg.33, referred to: SI 1998/364 Reg.18

Reg.37, applied: SI 1998/364 Reg.18

Reg.37, referred to: SI 1998/364 Reg.18

Reg.38, applied: SI 1998/364 Sch.2 para.5

Reg.41, applied: SI 1998/364 Reg.18

Reg.41, referred to: SI 1998/364 Reg.18

Reg.44, applied: SI 1998/364 Reg.18

Reg.44, referred to: SI 1998/364 Reg.18

Reg.45, applied: SI 1998/364 Reg.18

Reg.45, referred to: SI 1998/364 Reg.18

Reg.47, applied: SI 1998/364 Sch.2 para.5

Reg.48, applied: SI 1998/364 Reg.4, Sch.2 para.2

Reg.49, applied: SI 1998/364 Reg.4, Sch.2 para.2

Reg.52, applied: SI 1998/364 Reg.13

Reg.54, applied: SI 1998/364 Reg.15, Sch.2 para.9

Reg.54, referred to: SI 1998/364 Reg.15

Reg.56, applied: SI 1998/364 Reg.22

Reg.60, applied: SI 1998/2888 Reg.5

Reg.67, applied: SI 1998/2888 Reg.5

Reg.78, applied: SI 1998/2888 Reg.5

Reg.79, applied: SI 1998/2888 Reg.5

Reg.81, applied: SI 1998/2888 Reg.5

Reg.86, applied: SI 1998/364 Reg.18

Reg.86, referred to: SI 1998/364 Reg.18

Reg.92, referred to: SI 1998/364 Sch.4 para.8

Reg.109, applied: SI 1998/364 Reg.21, Sch.2 para.3

Reg.110, applied: SI 1998/364 Reg.21, Sch.2 para.3

Reg.119, applied: SI 1998/364 Reg.13

Reg.123, applied: SI 1998/364 Reg.18, Reg.22

Reg.130, amended: SI 1999/787 Art.97, Sch.8 para.2

Sch.1, amended: SI 1998/1129 Art.3, Sch.2

Sch.4, applied: SI 1998/364 Reg.13, Sch.2 para.8

Sch.5, applied: SI 1998/2888 Reg.5

375. Mines (Safety of Exit) Regulations (Northern Ireland) 1998

amended: SR 1999/150 Reg.2, Sch.

381. A41 Trunk Road (Camden) Red Route (Bus Lanes) Traffic Order 1998

revoked (in part): SI 1998/3206 Art.6

382. A205 Trunk Road (Greenwich) Red Route Traffic Order 1998

Art.2, amended: SI 1999/272 Art.2, Sch. Part A

Art.9, amended: SI 1999/272 Art.2, Sch. Part A

Sch.4 Item 14, substituted: SI 1999/996 Art.3

384. Spreadable Fats (Marketing Standards) (Amendment No.2) Regulations (Northern Ireland) 1998

revoked: SR 1999/383 Reg.9, Sch.2

391. Education (Grant-Maintained and Grant-Maintained Special Schools) (Finance) (Wales) (Amendment) Regulations 1998

revoked: SI 1999/440 Reg.3

Reg.2, revoked: SI 1999/440 Reg.3

Reg.3, revoked: SI 1999/440 Reg.3

Reg.4, revoked: SI 1999/440 Reg.3

NO.

1998—cont.

392. Education (Grants for Education Support and Training) (Wales) Regulations 1998

referred to: SI 1999/521 Reg.12

revoked: SI 1999/521 Reg.12

Reg.5, amended: SI 1998/1489 Reg.3

Reg.5, revoked: SI 1999/521 Reg.12

Reg.6, amended: SI 1998/1489 Reg.4

Reg.6, revoked: SI 1999/521 Reg.12

Reg.12, revoked: SI 1999/521 Reg.12

Sch. para.1, revoked: SI 1999/521 Reg.12

Sch. para.2, revoked: SI 1999/521 Reg.12

Sch. para.11, revoked: SI 1999/521 Reg.12

Sch. para.27, added: SI 1998/1489 Reg.5

Sch. para.27, revoked: SI 1999/521 Reg.12

Sch. para.28, added: SI 1998/1489 Reg.5

Sch. para.28, revoked: SI 1999/521 Reg.12

394. A205 Trunk Road (Lambeth) Red Route Experimental Traffic Order 1998

revoked (in part): SI 1999/2217 Art.10 (with savings)

Art.5, revoked (in part): SI 1999/2217 Art.10 (with savings)

Art.8, revoked (in part): SI 1999/2217 Art.10 (with savings)

Art.9, revoked (in part): SI 1999/2217 Art.10 (with savings)

Art.11, revoked (in part): SI 1999/2217 Art.10 (with savings)

403. Eel Fishing (Licence Duties) Regulations (Northern Ireland) 1998

revoked: SR 1999/487 Reg.3

407. Social Security (Incapacity for Work) (General) Amendment Regulations 1998

revoked: SI 1999/862 Reg.4

Reg.2, revoked: SI 1999/862 Reg.4

416. Social Security (Contributions) (Amendment No.5) Regulations (Northern Ireland) 1998

revoked (in part): SR 1999/117 Reg.13

417. Income Support (General) (Standard Interest Rate Amendment No.2) Regulations (Northern Ireland) 1998

revoked: SR 1999/35 Reg.3 (with saving)

421. Social Security (New Deal Pilot) Regulations (Northern Ireland) 1998

Reg.3, referred to: SI 1999/3188 Reg.3

Reg.4, referred to: SI 1999/3188 Reg.3

439. Hill Livestock (Compensatory Allowances) (Amendment) Regulations (Northern Ireland) 1998

revoked: SR 1999/497 Reg.15 (with savings)

449. Pre-School Education in Schools (Admissions Criteria) Regulations (Northern Ireland) 1998

revoked: SR 1999/419 Reg.5 (with saving)

452. Spreadable Fats (Marketing Standards) (Amendment) Regulations 1998

revoked (in part): SI 1999/2457 Reg.9, Sch.2, SSI 1999/34 Reg.9, Sch.2

Reg.3, revoked (in part): SI 1999/2457 Reg.9, Sch.2, SSI 1999/34 Reg.9, Sch.2

Reg.4, revoked (in part): SI 1999/2457 Reg.9, Sch.2, SSI 1999/34 Reg.9, Sch.2

Reg.5, revoked (in part): SI 1999/2457 Reg.9, Sch.2, SSI 1999/34 Reg.9, Sch.2

Reg.6, revoked (in part): SI 1999/2457 Reg.9, Sch.2, SSI 1999/34 Reg.9, Sch.2

Reg.7, revoked (in part): SI 1999/2457 Reg.9, Sch.2, SSI 1999/34 Reg.9, Sch.2

Sch., revoked (in part): SI 1999/2457 Reg.9, Sch.2, SSI 1999/34 Reg.9, Sch.2

NO.

NO.

1998—cont.

1998—cont.

455. Lotteries (Gaming Board Fees) Order 1998
revoked: SI 1999/436 Art.9
Art.3, revoked: SI 1999/436 Art.9
Art.4, revoked: SI 1999/436 Art.9
Art.5, revoked: SI 1999/436 Art.9
Art.6, revoked: SI 1999/436 Art.9
Art.7, revoked: SI 1999/436 Art.9
Art.8, revoked: SI 1999/436 Art.9
Art.9, revoked: SI 1999/436 Art.9

460. Wireless Telegraphy (Licence Charges) (Amendment) Regulations 1998
revoked: SI 1999/1774 Reg.2, Sch.1
Reg.3, revoked: SI 1999/1774 Reg.2, Sch.1
Sch.1, revoked: SI 1999/1774 Reg.2, Sch.1
Sch.2, revoked: SI 1999/1774 Reg.2, Sch.1

469. Social Security (Contributions) (Re-rating and National Insurance Fund Payments) Order 1998
referred to: SI 1998/524 Reg.1

470. Social Security Benefits Up-rating Order 1998
applied: SI 1998/521 Reg.3
referred to: SI 1998/521 Reg.2
revoked: SI 1999/264 Art.27
Art.1, revoked: SI 1999/264 Art.27
Art.3, revoked: SI 1999/264 Art.27
Art.4, revoked: SI 1999/264 Art.27
Art.5, revoked: SI 1999/264 Art.27
Art.6, revoked: SI 1999/264 Art.27
Art.7, revoked: SI 1999/264 Art.27
Art.8, revoked: SI 1999/264 Art.27
Art.9, revoked: SI 1999/264 Art.27
Art.10, revoked: SI 1999/264 Art.27
Art.11, revoked: SI 1999/264 Art.27
Art.12, revoked: SI 1999/264 Art.27
Art.13, revoked: SI 1999/264 Art.27
Art.14, revoked: SI 1999/264 Art.27
Art.15, revoked: SI 1999/264 Art.27
Art.16, revoked: SI 1999/264 Art.27
Art.17, revoked: SI 1999/264 Art.27
Art.18, referred to: SI 1998/563 Reg.1
Art.18, revoked: SI 1999/264 Art.27
Art.19, revoked: SI 1999/264 Art.27
Art.20, revoked: SI 1999/264 Art.27
Art.21, revoked: SI 1999/264 Art.27
Art.22, revoked: SI 1999/264 Art.27
Art.23, revoked: SI 1999/264 Art.27
Art.24, revoked: SI 1999/264 Art.27
Art.25, revoked: SI 1999/264 Art.27
Art.27, revoked: SI 1999/264 Art.27
Sch.1, revoked: SI 1999/264 Art.27
Sch.2, revoked: SI 1999/264 Art.27
Sch.3, revoked: SI 1999/264 Art.27
Sch.4, revoked: SI 1999/264 Art.27
Sch.5, revoked: SI 1999/264 Art.27
Sch.6 Part I, revoked: SI 1999/264 Art.27
Sch.6 Part II, revoked: SI 1999/264 Art.27
Sch.7, referred to: SI 1998/563 Reg.1
Sch.7, revoked: SI 1999/264 Art.27
Sch.7 Part I, revoked: SI 1999/264 Art.27
Sch.7 Part II, revoked: SI 1999/264 Art.27
Sch.8, revoked: SI 1999/264 Art.27
Sch.9, revoked: SI 1999/264 Art.27
Sch.10, revoked: SI 1999/264 Art.27
Sch.11, revoked: SI 1999/264 Art.27
Sch.12, revoked: SI 1999/264 Art.27
Sch.13, revoked: SI 1999/264 Art.27
Sch.14, revoked: SI 1999/264 Art.27
Sch.15 Part I, revoked: SI 1999/264 Art.27
Sch.15 Part II, revoked: SI 1999/264 Art.27
Sch.16 Part I, revoked: SI 1999/264 Art.27
Sch.16 Part II, revoked: SI 1999/264 Art.27
Sch.17, revoked: SI 1999/264 Art.27

473. Secure Training Centres (Escorts) Rules 1998
r.2, amended: SI 1998/1343 r.2

490. National Health Service (Dental Charges) Amendment Regulations 1998
revoked: SI 1999/544 Reg.3
Reg.2, revoked: SI 1999/544 Reg.3
Reg.3, revoked: SI 1999/544 Reg.3
Reg.4, revoked: SI 1999/544 Reg.3

494. Health and Safety (Enforcing Authority) Regulations 1998
applied: SI 1998/1833 Reg.28
referred to: SI 1999/743 Reg.20, SI 1999/2892 Reg.16
Reg.2, amended: SI 1999/2024 Reg.48, Sch.5 Part II, SI 1999/3232 Reg.41, Sch.9 para.8
Sch.2, amended: SI 1999/2024 Reg.48, Sch.5 Part II
Sch.2 para.4, amended: SI 1999/3232 Reg.41, Sch.9 para.8
Sch.2 para.5, amended: SI 1999/3232 Reg.41, Sch.9 para.8

498. National Assistance (Sums for Personal Requirements) Regulations 1998
revoked: SI 1999/549 Reg.3
Reg.2, revoked: SI 1999/549 Reg.3
Reg.3, revoked: SI 1999/549 Reg.3

503. Pensions Increase (Review) Order 1998
applied: SI 1999/522 Art.3

504. Building Societies (Accounts and Related Provisions) Regulations 1998
applied: SI 1999/248 Reg.4
Reg.2, amended: SI 1999/248 Reg.3, Sch. para.7
Reg.3, amended: SI 1999/248 Reg.3, Sch. para.8
Reg.4, amended: SI 1999/248 Reg.3, Sch. para.9
Reg.12, amended: SI 1999/248 Reg.3, Sch. para.10
Reg.12, applied: SI 1999/248 Reg.4
Sch.3, revoked: SI 1999/248 Reg.3, Sch. para.11
Sch.4 para.1, amended: SI 1999/248 Reg.3, Sch. para.12
Sch.4 para.2, amended: SI 1999/248 Reg.3, Sch. para.12
Sch.4 para.5, amended: SI 1999/248 Reg.3, Sch. para.12
Sch.5 para.1, amended: SI 1999/248 Reg.3, Sch. para.13
Sch.5 para.2, amended: SI 1999/248 Reg.3, Sch. para.13
Sch.6 para.3, amended: SI 1999/248 Reg.3, Sch. para.14
Sch.6 para.7, amended: SI 1999/248 Reg.3, Sch. para.14
Sch.6 para.11, amended: SI 1999/248 Reg.3, Sch. para.14
Sch.6 para.15, amended: SI 1999/248 Reg.3, Sch. para.14
Sch.6 para.18, amended: SI 1999/248 Reg.3, Sch. para.14
Sch.6 para.20, amended: SI 1999/248 Reg.3, Sch. para.14

519. Non-Domestic Rates (Levying) (Scotland) Regulations 1998
revoked: SI 1999/276 Reg.21
Part II, applied: SI 1999/276 Reg.11
Part II, revoked: SI 1999/276 Reg.21

NO.

1998—cont.

641. NCIS (Complaints) Regulations 1998
Part I, amended: SI 1999/1273 Reg.4
Part III, added: SI 1999/1273 Reg.5
Reg.2, amended: SI 1999/1273 Reg.3
Reg.7, applied: SI 1998/636 Reg.5
Reg.10, amended: SI 1999/1273 Reg.4
Reg.18, added: SI 1999/1273 Reg.5
Reg.19, added: SI 1999/1273 Reg.5
Reg.20, added: SI 1999/1273 Reg.5
Reg.21, added: SI 1999/1273 Reg.5
Reg.22, added: SI 1999/1273 Reg.5
Reg.23, added: SI 1999/1273 Reg.5
Reg.24, added: SI 1999/1273 Reg.5
Reg.25, added: SI 1999/1273 Reg.5
Reg.26, added: SI 1999/1273 Reg.5
Reg.27, added: SI 1999/1273 Reg.5
Reg.28, added: SI 1999/1273 Reg.5
Reg.29, added: SI 1999/1273 Reg.5

642. National Health Service (Optical Charges and Payments) (Scotland) Regulations 1998
Reg.1, amended: SI 1999/748 Reg.3, SSI 1999/64 Reg.3
Reg.2, amended: SSI 1999/64 Reg.4
Reg.8, amended: SI 1999/748 Reg.4, SSI 1999/64 Reg.5
Reg.8, applied: SSI 1999/64 Reg.10
Reg.9, amended: SI 1999/748 Reg.5
Reg.10, amended: SSI 1999/64 Reg.6
Reg.11, amended: SSI 1999/64 Reg.7
Reg.11, substituted: SI 1999/748 Reg.6
Reg.12, amended: SI 1999/748 Reg.7
Reg.13, amended: SI 1999/748 Reg.8
Reg.19, amended: SI 1999/748 Reg.9
Reg.20, amended: SI 1999/748 Reg.10
Reg.22, amended: SI 1999/748 Reg.11
Sch.1, amended: SSI 1999/64 Reg.8
Sch.1, substituted: SI 1999/748 Reg.12, Sch
Sch.2, substituted: SI 1999/748 Reg.12, Sch.
Sch.3 para.1, amended: SI 1999/748 Reg.12, Reg.13, SSI 1999/64 Reg.9
Sch.3 para.1, revoked (in part): SI 1999/748 Reg.13
Sch.3 para.2, amended: SI 1999/748 Reg.12

643. Births, Deaths, Marriages and Divorces (Fees) (Scotland) Regulations 1998
Sch.1 Part III, amended: SI 1998/3191 Reg.2
Sch.3, amended: SI 1998/3191 Reg.3

649. Scheme for Construction Contracts (England and Wales) Regulations 1998
Sch. Part I, see *Macob Civil Engineering Ltd v Morrison Construction Ltd* [1999] C.L.C. 739 (QBD (T&CC)), Dyson, J.

655. Nursery Education (England) Regulations 1998
Reg.1A, added: SI 1999/802 Reg.2
Reg.3, substituted: SI 1999/2130 Reg.2
Reg.4, amended: SI 1999/802 Reg.3
Sch., added: SI 1999/2130 Reg.3, Sch.

656. Education (Grants for Education Support and Training) (England) Regulations 1998
revoked: SI 1999/606 Reg.12
Reg.2, amended: SI 1998/1741 Reg.3, SI 1998/2698 Reg.3, SI 1999/252 Reg.3, SI 1999/447 Reg.3
Reg.2, revoked: SI 1999/606 Reg.12
Reg.5, amended: SI 1998/1741 Reg.4, SI 1998/2698 Reg.4, SI 1999/252 Reg.4
Reg.5, revoked: SI 1999/606 Reg.12
Reg.6, revoked: SI 1999/606 Reg.12
Reg.11, amended: SI 1998/1741 Reg.5, SI 1998/2698 Reg.5, SI 1999/252 Reg.5

NO.

1998—cont.

656. Education (Grants for Education Support and Training) (England) Regulations 1998 —cont.
Reg.11, revoked: SI 1999/606 Reg.12
Reg.12, revoked: SI 1999/606 Reg.12
Sch. para.5, revoked: SI 1999/606 Reg.12
Sch. para.5, substituted: SI 1998/1741 Reg.6
Sch. para.6, revoked: SI 1999/606 Reg.12
Sch. para.19, revoked: SI 1999/606 Reg.12
Sch. para.22, revoked: SI 1999/606 Reg.12
Sch. para.25, added: SI 1998/1741 Reg.6
Sch. para.25, revoked: SI 1999/606 Reg.12
Sch. para.26, added: SI 1998/1741 Reg.6
Sch. para.26, revoked: SI 1999/606 Reg.12
Sch. para.27, added: SI 1998/1741 Reg.6
Sch. para.27, revoked: SI 1999/606 Reg.12
Sch. para.28, added: SI 1998/1741 Reg.6
Sch. para.28, revoked: SI 1999/606 Reg.12
Sch. para.29, added: SI 1998/1741 Reg.6
Sch. para.29, revoked: SI 1999/606 Reg.12
Sch. para.30, added: SI 1998/1741 Reg.6
Sch. para.30, revoked: SI 1999/606 Reg.12
Sch. para.31, added: SI 1998/2698 Reg.6
Sch. para.31, revoked: SI 1999/606 Reg.12
Sch. para.32, added: SI 1998/2698 Reg.6
Sch. para.32, revoked: SI 1999/606 Reg.12
Sch. para.33, added: SI 1998/2698 Reg.6
Sch. para.33, revoked: SI 1999/606 Reg.12
Sch. para.34, added: SI 1999/252 Reg.6
Sch. para.34, revoked: SI 1999/606 Reg.12
Sch. para.35, added: SI 1999/252 Reg.6
Sch. para.35, revoked: SI 1999/606 Reg.12
Sch. para.35, substituted: SI 1999/447 Reg.4
Sch. para.36, added: SI 1999/252 Reg.6
Sch. para.36, revoked: SI 1999/606 Reg.12

668. National Health Service (Choice of Medical Practitioner) Regulations 1998
Reg.4, amended: SI 1999/3179 Reg.2
Reg.5, amended: SI 1999/3179 Reg.2

672. Industrial and Provident Societies (Credit Unions) (Amendment of Fees) Regulations 1998
revoked: SI 1999/739 Reg.3
Reg.2, revoked: SI 1999/739 Reg.3
Reg.3, revoked: SI 1999/739 Reg.3

673. Friendly Societies (General Charge and Fees) Regulations 1998
revoked: SI 1999/736 Reg.7
Reg.3, revoked: SI 1999/736 Reg.7
Reg.5, revoked: SI 1999/736 Reg.7
Reg.7, revoked: SI 1999/736 Reg.7
Sch.1 para.2, revoked: SI 1999/736 Reg.7
Sch.1 para.3, revoked: SI 1999/736 Reg.7
Sch.1 para.4, revoked: SI 1999/736 Reg.7
Sch.2 para.3, revoked: SI 1999/736 Reg.7
Sch.2 para.4, revoked: SI 1999/736 Reg.7
Sch.2 para.21, revoked: SI 1999/736 Reg.7
Sch.2 para.22, revoked: SI 1999/736 Reg.7
Sch.2 para.23, revoked: SI 1999/736 Reg.7
Sch.2 para.25, revoked: SI 1999/736 Reg.7
Sch.2 para.31, revoked: SI 1999/736 Reg.7
Sch.2 para.32, revoked: SI 1999/736 Reg.7
Sch.2 para.33, revoked: SI 1999/736 Reg.7
Sch.2 para.34, revoked: SI 1999/736 Reg.7
Sch.2 para.35, revoked: SI 1999/736 Reg.7

675. Building Societies (General Charge and Fees) Regulations 1998
revoked: SI 1999/738 Reg.11
Reg.3, revoked: SI 1999/738 Reg.11
Reg.5, revoked: SI 1999/738 Reg.11
Reg.6, revoked: SI 1999/738 Reg.11
Reg.7, revoked: SI 1999/738 Reg.11
Reg.8, revoked: SI 1999/738 Reg.11

NO.

675. Building Societies (General Charge and Fees) Regulations 1998—*cont.*
Reg.11, revoked: SI 1999/738 Reg.11

676. Industrial and Provident Societies (Amendment of Fees) Regulations 1998
revoked: SI 1999/740 Reg.4
Reg.2, revoked: SI 1999/740 Reg.4
Reğ.3, revoked: SI 1999/740 Reg.4
Reg.4, revoked: SI 1999/740 Reg.4

687. Scheme for Construction Contracts (Scotland) Regulations 1998
Reg.23, see *Allied London & Scottish Properties Plc v Riverbrae Construction Ltd* [1999] B.L.R. 346 (OH), Lord Kingarth

728. Retirement Benefits Schemes (Restriction on Discretion to Approve) (Small Self-administered Schemes) (Amendment) Regulations 1998
Reg.6, referred to: SI 1998/729 Reg.4
Reg.7, referred to: SI 1998/729 Reg.4
Reg.9, referred to: SI 1998/729 Reg.5

749. Financial Provisions (Northern Ireland) Order 1998
Art.7, revoked: 1998 c.47 s.100, Sch.15

770. Llandough Hospital and Community National Health Service Trust (Establishment) Amendment Order 1998
revoked: SI 1999/1120 Art.2, Sch.2
Art.2, revoked: SI 1999/1120 Art.2, Sch.2

798. Education (New Grant-Maintained Schools) (Finance) Regulations 1998
revoked: SI 1999/698 Reg.3
Reg.1, revoked: SI 1999/698 Reg.3
Reg.3, revoked: SI 1999/698 Reg.3
Reg.7, revoked: SI 1999/698 Reg.3
Reg.9, revoked: SI 1999/698 Reg.3
Reg.21, revoked: SI 1999/698 Reg.3
Reg.26, amended: SI 1999/532 Reg.5
Reg.26, revoked: SI 1999/698 Reg.3
Reg.29, amended: SI 1999/532 Reg.5
Reg.29, revoked: SI 1999/698 Reg.3
Reg.30, revoked: SI 1999/698 Reg.3
Sch.1 para.3, revoked: SI 1999/698 Reg.3
Sch.1 para.4, revoked: SI 1999/698 Reg.3
Sch.2 para.1, revoked: SI 1999/698 Reg.3
Sch.4 para.4, amended: SI 1999/532 Reg.5
Sch.4 para.4, revoked: SI 1999/698 Reg.3

799. Education (Grant-Maintained and Grant-Maintained Special Schools) (Finance) Regulations 1998
applied: SI 1999/101 Sch.4 para.3
revoked: SI 1999/698 Reg.3
Reg.1, revoked: SI 1999/698 Reg.3
Reg.3, revoked: SI 1999/698 Reg.3
Reg.4, applied: SI 1999/101 Sch.4 para.2
Reg.4, revoked: SI 1999/698 Reg.3
Reg.5, applied: SI 1999/101 Sch.4 para.7
Reg.5, revoked: SI 1999/698 Reg.3
Reg.6, applied: SI 1999/101 Sch.4 para.2
Reg.6, revoked: SI 1999/698 Reg.3
Reg.7, applied: SI 1999/101 Sch.4 para.2
Reg.7, revoked: SI 1999/698 Reg.3
Reğ.8, applied: SI 1999/101 Sch.4 para.2
Reg.8, revoked: SI 1999/698 Reg.3
Reg.9, applied: SI 1999/101 Sch.4 para.2
Reg.9, referred to: SI 1999/101 Reg.16
Reg.9, revoked: SI 1999/698 Reg.3
Reg.10, applied: SI 1999/101 Sch.4 para.3
Reg.10, referred to: SI 1999/101 Sch.4 para.2
Reg.10, revoked: SI 1999/698 Reg.3
Reg.11, applied: SI 1999/101 Sch.4 para.2
Reg.11, revoked: SI 1999/698 Reg.3

NO.

799. Education (Grant-Maintained and Grant-Maintained Special Schools) (Finance) Regulations 1998—*cont.*
Reg.12, applied: SI 1999/101 Sch.4 para.2
Reg.12, revoked: SI 1999/698 Reg.3
Reg.13, referred to: SI 1999/101 Sch.4 para.2
Reg.13, revoked: SI 1999/698 Reg.3
Reg.14, referred to: SI 1999/101 Sch.4 para.2
Reg.14, revoked: SI 1999/698 Reg.3
Reg.15, applied: SI 1999/101 Sch.4 para.2
Reg.15, revoked: SI 1999/698 Reg.3
Reg.17, applied: SI 1999/101 Sch.4 para.3
Reg.17, referred to: SI 1999/101 Sch.4 para.2
Reg.17, revoked: SI 1999/698 Reg.3
Reg.18, referred to: SI 1999/101 Sch.4 para.2
Reg.18, revoked: SI 1999/698 Reg.3
Reg.19, applied: SI 1999/101 Sch.4 para.2
Reg.19, revoked: SI 1999/698 Reg.3
Reg.20, applied: SI 1999/101 Sch.4 para.2
Reg.20, revoked: SI 1999/698 Reg.3
Reg.21, referred to: SI 1999/101 Sch.4 para.2
Reg.21, revoked: SI 1999/698 Reg.3
Reg.22, applied: SI 1999/101 Sch.4 para.2, Sch.4 para.3
Reg.22, referred to: SI 1999/101 Sch.4 para.2, Sch.4 para.4
Reg.22, revoked: SI 1999/698 Reg.3
Reg.23, applied: SI 1999/101 Sch.4 para.2
Reg.23, revoked: SI 1999/698 Reg.3
Reg.24, applied: SI 1999/101 Sch.4 para.3
Reg.24, referred to: SI 1999/101 Sch.4 para.2
Reg.24, revoked: SI 1999/698 Reg.3
Reg.25, applied: SI 1999/101 Sch.4 para.3
Reg.25, referred to: SI 1999/101 Sch.4 para.2
Reg.25, revoked: SI 1999/698 Reg.3
Reg.26, applied: SI 1999/101 Sch.4 para.3
Reg.26, referred to: SI 1999/101 Sch.4 para.2
Reg.26, revoked: SI 1999/698 Reg.3
Reg.27, referred to: SI 1999/101 Sch.4 para.2
Reg.27, revoked: SI 1999/698 Reg.3
Reg.28, referred to: SI 1999/101 Sch.4 para.2
Reg.28, revoked: SI 1999/698 Reg.3
Reg.31, referred to: SI 1999/101 Sch.4 para.2
Reg.31, revoked: SI 1999/698 Reg.3
Reg.32, applied: SI 1999/101 Sch.4 para.2
Reg.32, revoked: SI 1999/698 Reg.3
Reg.33, applied: SI 1999/101 Sch.4 para.2
Reg.33, revoked: SI 1999/698 Reg.3
Reg.38, amended: SI 1999/532 Reg.5
Reg.38, revoked: SI 1999/698 Reg.3
Reg.41, amended: SI 1999/532 Reg.5
Reg.41, revoked: SI 1999/698 Reg.3
Reg.42, revoked: SI 1999/698 Reg.3
Sch.1 para.3, revoked: SI 1999/698 Reg.3
Sch.1 para.4, revoked: SI 1999/698 Reg.3
Sch.1 para.5, revoked: SI 1999/698 Reg.3
Sch.2 para.2, revoked: SI 1999/698 Reg.3
Sch.2 para.3, revoked: SI 1999/698 Reg.3
Sch.3 para.2, revoked: SI 1999/698 Reg.3
Sch.4 para.1, revoked: SI 1999/698 Reg.3
Sch.4 para.4, amended: SI 1999/532 Reg.5
Sch.4 para.4, revoked: SI 1999/698 Reg.3
Sch.6 para.2, applied: SI 1999/698 Reg.5, Sch.2 para.1
Sch.6 para.2, revoked: SI 1999/698 Reg.3

804. Hairmyres and Stonehouse Hospitals National Health Service Trust (Establishment) Amendment Order 1998
revoked: SI 1999/1070 Art.2, Sch.2
Art.2, revoked: SI 1999/1070 Art.2, Sch.2

NO.

808. **Housing Renewal Grants (Amendment) Regulations 1998**
Reg.21, revoked (in part): SI 1999/1523 Reg.16

829. **Durham County Priority Services National Health Service Trust (Establishment) Order 1998**
Art.1, amended: SI 1999/60 Art.2

871. **Cattle Identification Regulations 1998**
applied: SI 1998/1796 Reg.6, SI 1999/672 Art.2, Sch.1, SSI 1999/187 Reg.14, SI 1999/3315 Reg.4
Reg.3, amended: SI 1998/2969 Reg.2
Reg.13, amended: SI 1998/2969 Reg.2
Reg.13, substituted: SI 1998/1796 Reg.17
Reg.18, substituted: SI 1998/1796 Reg.17
Reg.26, applied: SI 1998/1796 Reg.8
Reg.26, substituted: SI 1998/1796 Reg.17
Reg.27, applied: SI 1998/1796 Reg.8
Reg.27, referred to: SI 1998/1796 Reg.4
Reg.27, substituted: SI 1998/1796 Reg.17
Reg.29, amended: SI 1999/1339 Reg.2
Reg.29, referred to: SSI 1999/187 Reg.17, SI 1999/3316 Reg.15
Reg.31A, added: SI 1998/1796 Reg.17

876. **Education (Listed Bodies) (Amendment) Order 1998**
revoked: SI 1999/834 Art.3
Art.2, revoked: SI 1999/834 Art.3

883. **A205 Trunk Road (Lambeth) Red Route (Prohibition of Traffic) Experimental Traffic Order 1998**
revoked (in part): SI 1999/2348 Art.5
Art.4, revoked (in part): SI 1999/2348 Art.5

893. **Northern Ireland Arms Decommissioning Act 1997 (Amnesty Period) Order 1998**
revoked: SI 1999/454 Art.3
Art.2, revoked: SI 1999/454 Art.3

899. **Dual-Use and Related Goods (Export Control) (Amendment No.2) Regulations 1998**
revoked: SI 1999/984 Reg.2
Reg.2, revoked: SI 1999/984 Reg.2

903. **Education (School Teachers' Pay and Conditions) Order 1998**
revoked: SI 1998/1884 Art.1

922. **Monklands and Bellshill Hospitals National Health Service Trust (Establishment) (Change of Name and Amendment) Order 1998**
revoked: SI 1999/1070 Art.2, Sch.2

924. **Employment Rights (Increase of Limits) Order 1998**
revoked: SI 1999/3375 Art.2
Art.2, revoked: SI 1999/3375 Art.2
Art.3, revoked: SI 1999/3375 Art.2
Sch., revoked: SI 1999/3375 Art.2

926. **Law Hospital National Health Service Trust (Establishment) Amendment Order 1998**
revoked: SI 1999/1070 Art.2, Sch.2
Art.2, revoked: SI 1999/1070 Art.2, Sch.2

938. **A41 Trunk Road (Westminster) Red Route (No.2) Traffic Order 1998**
Art.2, amended: SI 1999/272 Art.2, Sch. Part A
Art.9, amended: SI 1999/272 Art.2, Sch. Part A

939. **A3 Trunk Road (Wandsworth) Red Route Experimental Traffic Order 1998**
revoked (in part): SI 1999/2344 Art.10
Art.5, revoked (in part): SI 1999/2344 Art.10
Art.8, revoked (in part): SI 1999/2344 Art.10
Art.9, revoked (in part): SI 1999/2344 Art.10
Art.11, revoked (in part): SI 1999/2344 Art.10

NO.

946. **Financial Assistance for Environmental Purposes (No.2) Order 1998**
revoked: SI 1998/1001 Art.3

947. **Railways (Rateable Values) (Scotland) Order 1998**
revoked: SI 1999/853 Art.9
Art.3, revoked: SI 1999/853 Art.9
Art.4, revoked: SI 1999/853 Art.9
Art.5, revoked: SI 1999/853 Art.9
Art.7, revoked: SI 1999/853 Art.9
Art.8, revoked: SI 1999/853 Art.9
Art.9, revoked: SI 1999/853 Art.9

955. **Fertilisers (Mammalian Meat and Bone Meal) (Conditions of Manufacture) Regulations 1998**
Reg.3, applied: SI 1998/954 Reg.4

961. **Gaming Clubs (Hours and Charges) (Amendment) Regulations 1998**
revoked: SI 1999/1258 Reg.4
Reg.2, revoked: SI 1999/1258 Reg.4
Reg.3, revoked: SI 1999/1258 Reg.4
Reg.4, revoked: SI 1999/1258 Reg.4

962. **Gaming Act (Variation of Monetary Limits) Order 1998**
revoked: SI 1999/1260 Art.5, Sch.
Art.2, revoked: SI 1999/1260 Art.5, Sch.
Art.3, revoked: SI 1999/1260 Art.5, Sch.
Art.4, revoked: SI 1999/1260 Art.5, Sch.

968. **Offshore Petroleum Production and Pipelines (Assessment of Environmental Effects) Regulations 1998**
applied: SI 1999/360 Reg.2
revoked: SI 1999/360 Reg.2 (with savings)
Reg.3, revoked: SI 1999/360 Reg.2 (with savings)
Reg.16, revoked: SI 1999/360 Reg.2 (with savings)

970. **Civil Legal Aid (Financial Conditions) (Scotland) Regulations 1998**
revoked: SI 1999/1019 Reg.5 (with savings)
Reg.3, revoked: SI 1999/1019 Reg.5 (with savings)
Reg.4, revoked: SI 1999/1019 Reg.5 (with savings)
Reg.5, revoked: SI 1999/1019 Reg.5 (with savings)

971. **Advice and Assistance (Financial Conditions) (Scotland) Regulations 1998**
revoked: SI 1999/1020 Reg.6 (with savings)
Reg.3, revoked: SI 1999/1020 Reg.6 (with savings)
Reg.4, revoked: SI 1999/1020 Reg.6 (with savings)
Reg.5, revoked: SI 1999/1020 Reg.6 (with savings)
Reg.6, revoked: SI 1999/1020 Reg.6 (with savings)

994. **Food Safety (Fishery Products and Live Shellfish) (Hygiene) Regulations 1998**
Part V, substituted: SI 1999/1585 Reg.6
Reg.2, amended: SI 1999/399 Reg.2, Reg.5, Sch. para.1, SI 1999/1585 Reg.2
Reg.19, amended: SI 1999/399 Reg.3, Reg.5, SI 1999/994 Sch. para.2
Reg.20, amended: SI 1999/1585 Reg.3
Reg.30, substituted: SI 1999/1585 Reg.4
Reg.38, amended: SI 1999/399 Reg.5, Sch. para.3
Reg.41, amended: SI 1999/1585 Reg.5
Reg.47, substituted: SI 1999/1585 Reg.6
Sch.2 Ch.II, amended: SI 1999/399 Reg.4, Sch.para.4, Sch.para.5

NO.

1998—cont.

994. Food Safety (Fishery Products and Live Shellfish) (Hygiene) Regulations 1998—
cont.
Sch.2 Ch.III, amended: SI 1999/399 Reg.4, Reg.5, Sch. para.5
Sch.2 Ch.IV, amended: SI 1999/399 Reg.4, Reg.5, Sch. para.5
Sch.2 Ch.V, amended: SI 1999/399 Reg.4
Sch.3 Ch.III, amended: SI 1999/1585 Reg.7
Sch.4A, added: SI 1999/1585 Reg.8, Sch.

1011. Merchant Shipping (Fire Protection: Small Ships) Regulations 1998
referred to: SI 1998/1609 Reg.5, Reg.6, Sch., SI 1998/2771 Reg.4, Reg.5, Sch.1, Sch.2
Reg.1, amended: SI 1999/992 Reg.29, Reg.30, SI 1999/1957 Reg.3, Sch.1 para.3
Reg.2, amended: SI 1999/992 Reg.31
Reg.25, amended: SI 1999/992 Reg.32
Reg.43, substituted: SI 1999/992 Reg.33

1012. Merchant Shipping (Fire Protection: Large Ships) Regulations 1998
applied: SI 1999/2721 Reg.71, Reg.72
referred to: SI 1998/1609 Reg.5, Reg.6, Sch., SI 1998/2771 Reg.4, Sch.1
Reg.1, amended: SI 1999/992 Reg.3, SI 1999/1957 Reg.3, Sch.1 para.2
Reg.2, amended: SI 1999/992 Reg.4
Reg.12, amended: SI 1999/992 Reg.5
Reg.16, amended: SI 1999/992 Reg.6
Reg.18, amended: SI 1999/992 Reg.7
Reg.25, amended: SI 1999/992 Reg.8
Reg.30, amended: SI 1999/992 Reg.9
Reg.34, substituted: SI 1999/992 Reg.10
Reg.37, amended: SI 1999/992 Reg.11
Reg.51, amended: SI 1999/992 Reg.12
Reg.53, amended: SI 1999/992 Reg.13
Reg.53A, added: SI 1999/992 Reg.14
Reg.57, amended: SI 1999/992 Reg.15, Reg.16
Reg.58, amended: SI 1999/992 Reg.17
Reg.60, amended: SI 1999/992 Reg.18
Reg.62, amended: SI 1999/992 Reg.19
Reg.65, amended: SI 1999/992 Reg.20
Reg.66, amended: SI 1999/992 Reg.21
Reg.68, amended: SI 1999/992 Reg.22
Reg.75, amended: SI 1999/992 Reg.23
Reg.77, amended: SI 1999/992 Reg.24
Reg.78, amended: SI 1999/992 Reg.25
Reg.80, amended: SI 1999/992 Reg.26
Reg.88, amended: SI 1999/992 Reg.27

1014. Immigration (Transit Visa) (Amendment No.2) Order 1998
Art.2, revoked: SI 1998/2483 Art.3
Sch., revoked: SI 1998/2483 Art.3

1020. General Osteopathic Council (Conditional Registration) Rules Order of Council 1998
Sch. r.3, amended: SI 1998/2695 Sch. r.2

1021. Plant Breeders' Rights (Fees) Regulations 1998
Sch.1, substituted: SI 1999/1089 Reg.2, Sch.

1024. Plant Breeders' Rights (Information Notices) Regulations 1998
applied: SI 1998/1023 Reg.2
Reg.3, amended: SI 1998/1023 Reg.2
Sch. Part I, amended: SI 1998/1023 Reg.2

1027. Plant Breeders' Rights Regulations 1998
Reg.3, amended: SI 1998/1021 Reg.6
Reg.3, applied: SI 1998/1021 Reg.6
Reg.14, amended: SI 1998/1021 Reg.6
Reg.14, applied: SI 1998/1021 Reg.6
Reg.16, amended: SI 1998/1021 Reg.6
Reg.16, applied: SI 1998/1021 Reg.6
Reg.18, amended: SI 1998/1021 Reg.6
Reg.18, applied: SI 1998/1021 Reg.6

NO.

1998—cont.

1027. Plant Breeders' Rights Regulations 1998— *cont.*
Reg.19, amended: SI 1998/1021 Reg.6
Reg.19, applied: SI 1998/1021 Reg.6
Reg.20, amended: SI 1998/1021 Reg.6
Reg.20, applied: SI 1998/1021 Reg.6

1046. Medicated Feedingstuffs Regulations 1998
applied: SI 1998/1047 Reg.15, SI 1999/1871 Reg.15
Reg.3, applied: SI 1998/1047 Reg.15, SI 1999/1871 Reg.15
Reg.3, referred to: SI 1999/1871 Reg.15
Reg.4, applied: SI 1998/1047 Reg.15
Reg.4, referred to: SI 1999/1871 Reg.15
Reg.43, referred to: SI 1998/1048 Reg.2

1047. Feedingstuffs (Zootechnical Products) Regulations 1998
applied: SI 1998/1046 Reg.35, SI 1998/1049 Reg.19, Reg.21, Reg.26, Reg.28, Reg.46, Reg.47
revoked: SI 1999/1871 Reg.1
Reg.10, applied: SI 1998/1046 Reg.35
Reg.10, revoked: SI 1999/1871 Reg.1
Reg.11, applied: SI 1998/1046 Reg.35
Reg.11, revoked: SI 1999/1871 Reg.1
Reg.12, applied: SI 1998/1046 Reg.35
Reg.12, revoked: SI 1999/1871 Reg.1
Reg.15, revoked: SI 1999/1871 Reg.1
Reg.51, applied: SI 1998/1049 Reg.47
Reg.51, revoked: SI 1999/1871 Reg.1
Reg.70, revoked: SI 1999/1871 Reg.1
Reg.74, referred to: SI 1998/1048 Reg.2
Reg.74, revoked: SI 1999/1871 Reg.1
Reg.75, revoked: SI 1999/1871 Reg.1

1049. Feeding Stuffs (Establishments and Intermediaries) Regulations 1998
referred to: SI 1999/1872 Reg.71
revoked: SI 1999/1872 Reg.1
Reg.19, revoked: SI 1999/1872 Reg.1
Reg.21, revoked: SI 1999/1872 Reg.1
Reg.26, revoked: SI 1999/1872 Reg.1
Reg.28, revoked: SI 1999/1872 Reg.1
Reg.46, revoked: SI 1999/1872 Reg.1
Reg.47, revoked: SI 1999/1872 Reg.1
Reg.83, revoked: SI 1999/1872 Reg.1
Reg.84, revoked: SI 1999/1872 Reg.1
Reg.89, revoked: SI 1999/1872 Reg.1
Reg.93, revoked: SI 1999/1872 Reg.1
Reg.96, revoked: SI 1999/1872 Reg.1

1064. Federal Republic of Yugoslavia (United Nations Sanctions) (Dependent Territories) Order 1998
Art.2, amended: SI 1999/280 Art.2, SI 1999/281 Art.2
Art.5A, added: SI 1999/280 Art.3, SI 1999/281 Art.3
Art.6, substituted: SI 1999/280 Art.4, SI 1999/281 Art.4
Art.12, amended: SI 1999/280 Art.5, Art.6, Art.7, SI 1999/281 Art.5

1066. Hong Kong (Overseas Public Servants) (Pension Supplements) (Amendment) Order 1998
referred to: SI 1999/666
Art.2, amended: SI 1999/666 Art.2
Sch., amended: SI 1999/666 Art.3

1069. Activity Centres (Young Persons' Safety) (Northern Ireland) Order 1998
amended: SI 1998/2795 (NI.18) Art.6, Sch.1 para.29
Art.3, amended: SI 1998/2795 (NI.18) Art.6, Sch.1 para.30

NO.

1998—cont.

1071. Family Homes and Domestic Violence (Northern Ireland) Order 1998
Art.1, amended: SI 1999/663 Art.2, Sch.1 para.29
Art.40, amended: SI 1999/663 Art.2, Sch.2

1072. Federal Republic of Yugoslavia (United Nations Sanctions) (Channel Islands) Order 1998
Art.2, amended: SI 1999/284 Art.2
Art.5A, added: SI 1999/284 Art.3
Art.6, substituted: SI 1999/284 Art.4
Art.12, amended: SI 1999/284 Art.5

1073. Federal Republic of Yugoslavia (United Nations Sanctions) (Isle of Man) Order 1998
Art.2, amended: SI 1999/285 Art.2
Art.5A, added: SI 1999/285 Art.3
Art.6, substituted: SI 1999/285 Art.4
Art.12, amended: SI 1999/285 Art.5

1082. Local Government Finance (Scotland) Order 1998
Art.2, revoked: SI 1999/364 Art.5
Sch.1, revoked (in part): SI 1999/364 Art.5

1105. A41 Trunk Road (Camden) Red Route Traffic Order 1998
Art.2, amended: SI 1999/272 Art.2, Sch. Part A
Art.9, amended: SI 1999/272 Art.2, Sch. Part A
Sch.2B Item 6A, added: SI 1998/3214 Art.3
Sch.2B Item 11, substituted: SI 1998/3214 Art.4
Sch.4 Item 14, substituted: SI 1998/3214 Art.5
Sch.4 Item 15, substituted: SI 1998/3214 Art.6
Sch.4 Item 33, substituted: SI 1998/3214 Art.7
Sch.4 Item 33A, added: SI 1998/3214 Art.8

1113. Housing Renewal Grants (Prescribed Form and Particulars) (Welsh Form and Particulars) Regulations 1998
Sch. Form, amended: SI 1999/2316 Reg.2, Sch., SI 1999/3470 Reg.2, Sch.2

1125. A205 Trunk Road (Wandsworth) Red Route (Clearway) Traffic Order 1998
Art.2, amended: SI 1999/272 Art.2, Sch. Part B
Art.9, amended: SI 1999/272 Art.2, Sch. Part B

1126. Northern Ireland Negotiations (Referendum) Order 1998
Art.6, applied: SI 1998/1286, SI 1998/1286 Art.2
Sch.2, applied: SI 1998/1286, SI 1998/1286 Art.2

1128. Income Support (General) (Standard Interest Rate Amendment) Regulations 1998
revoked: SI 1998/2878 Reg.3 (with savings)
Reg.1, revoked: SI 1998/2878 Reg.3 (with savings)
Reg.2, revoked: SI 1998/2878 Reg.3 (with savings)
Reg.3, revoked: SI 1998/2878 Reg.3 (with savings)

1135. Bovines and Bovine Products (Trade) Regulations 1998
referred to: SI 1999/1103 Reg.26
revoked: SI 1999/1103 Reg.26 (with savings)
Reg.3, revoked: SI 1999/1103 Reg.26 (with savings)
Reg.4, revoked: SI 1999/1103 Reg.26 (with savings)
Reg.6, revoked: SI 1999/1103 Reg.26 (with savings)
Reg.7, referred to: SI 1999/1103 Reg.9
Reg.7, revoked: SI 1999/1103 Reg.26 (with savings)
Reg.21, revoked: SI 1999/1103 Reg.26 (with savings)

NO.

1998—cont.

1150. A3 Trunk Road (Wandsworth) Red Route (Clearway) Traffic Order 1998
Art.2, amended: SI 1999/272 Art.2, Sch. Part B
Art.9, amended: SI 1999/272 Art.2, Sch. Part B

1166. Education (Mandatory Awards) Regulations 1998
applied: SI 1998/2004 Art.4, Art.7, SI 1999/779 Art.2, Sch.
revoked: SI 1999/1494 Reg.6 (with saving)
Reg.1, applied: SI 1998/2004 Art.7
Reg.1, revoked: SI 1999/1494 Reg.6 (with saving)
Reg.2, amended: SI 1998/1972 Reg.3
Reg.2, revoked: SI 1999/1494 Reg.6 (with saving)
Reg.6, amended: SI 1998/1972 Reg.4, Reg.5
Reg.6, revoked (in part): SI 1998/1972 Reg.5, SI 1999/1494 Reg.6 (with saving)
Reg.7, revoked: SI 1999/1494 Reg.6 (with saving)
Reg.8, revoked: SI 1999/1494 Reg.6 (with saving)
Reg.9, revoked: SI 1999/1494 Reg.6 (with saving)
Reg.10, revoked: SI 1999/1494 Reg.6 (with saving)
Reg.12, amended: SI 1998/1972 Reg.6
Reg.12, revoked: SI 1999/1494 Reg.6 (with saving)
Reg.13, revoked: SI 1999/1494 Reg.6 (with saving)
Reg.15, amended: SI 1999/1824 Reg.3
Reg.15, revoked: SI 1999/1494 Reg.6 (with saving)
Reg.23, revoked: SI 1999/1494 Reg.6 (with saving)
Sch.1 para.(b), amended: SI 1998/1972 Reg.7
Sch.1 para.(b), revoked: SI 1999/1494 Reg.6 (with saving)
Sch.2 para.15, revoked: SI 1999/1494 Reg.6 (with saving)
Sch.3 para.1, amended: SI 1999/1824 Reg.4
Sch.3 para.1, revoked: SI 1999/1494 Reg.6 (with saving)
Sch.3 para.6, amended: SI 1998/1972 Reg.8
Sch.3 para.6, revoked: SI 1999/1494 Reg.6 (with saving)
Sch.5 para.1, amended: SI 1999/1824 Reg.5
Sch.5 para.2, amended: SI 1999/1824 Reg.5

1175. Magistrates' Courts Committees (Merseyside) Amalgamation Order 1998
Sch. para.1, amended: SI 1998/1293 Art.2

1177. Measuring Instruments (EEC Requirements) (Fees) Regulations 1998
Reg.2, amended: SI 1999/861 Reg.2
Reg.5, amended: SI 1999/861 Reg.2
Sch.2 para.2, amended: SI 1999/861 Reg.2
Sch.4 para.2A, added: SI 1999/861 Reg.2

1195. Cod (Specified Sea Areas) (Prohibition of Fishing) Order 1998
revoked: SI 1998/2074 Art.2
Art.3, revoked: SI 1998/2074 Art.2

1202. Action Programme for Nitrate Vulnerable Zones (England and Wales) Regulations 1998
applied: SI 1999/672 Art.2, Sch.1

1216. Education (Grants to Aided and Special Agreement Schools) Regulations 1998
revoked: SI 1999/2020 Reg.7
Reg.3, revoked: SI 1999/2020 Reg.7
Reg.5, revoked: SI 1999/2020 Reg.7
Reg.6, applied: SI 1999/2020 Reg.7

NO.

1216. Education (Grants to Aided and Special Agreement Schools) Regulations 1998—cont.
Reg.6, revoked: SI 1999/2020 Reg.6

1224. Offshore Installations (Safety Zones) (No.2) Order 1998
Sch., revoked (in part): SI 1999/547 Art.3

1229. Motor Vehicles (Driving Licences) (Amendment) (No.3) Regulations 1998
revoked: SI 1999/2864 Reg.2, Sch.1
Reg.2, revoked: SI 1999/2864 Reg.2, Sch.1
Sch., revoked: SI 1999/2864 Reg.2, Sch.1

1265. Employment Rights (Dispute Resolution) (Northern Ireland) Order 1998
Art.15, revoked (in part): SI 1999/2790 (NI.9)
Art.32, Art.40, Sch.9 Part 10

1277. Food (Cheese) (Emergency Control) Order 1998
applied: SI 1998/1284
referred to: SI 1998/1673
Art.2, amended: SI 1998/1673 Art.2
Art.4, amended: SI 1998/1284 Art.2

1287. New Northern Ireland Assembly (Elections) Order 1998
Art.3, applied: SI 1998/1493, SI 1998/1493 Art.3
Sch.1, applied: SI 1998/1493, SI 1998/1493 Art.3

1296. Environmentally Sensitive Areas (West Penwith) Designation (Amendment) Order 1998
Art.7, amended: SI 1998/2232 Art.3

1301. Environmentally Sensitive Areas (Lake District) Designation (Amendment) Order 1998
Art.2, amended: SI 1998/2177 Art.3

1302. Environmentally Sensitive Areas (Exmoor) Designation (Amendment) Order 1998
Art.2, amended: SI 1998/2174 Art.3

1303. Environmentally Sensitive Areas (North Peak) Designation (Amendment) Order 1998
Art.2, amended: SI 1998/2173 Art.3

1304. Environmentally Sensitive Areas (North Kent Marshes) Designation (Amendment) Order 1998
Art.2, amended: SI 1998/2176 Art.3

1307. Environmentally Sensitive Areas (Avon Valley) Designation (Amendment) Order 1998
Art.2, amended: SI 1998/2172 Art.3

1308. Environmentally Sensitive Areas (Test Valley) Designation (Amendment) Order 1998
Art.2, amended: SI 1998/2178 Art.3

1309. Environmentally Sensitive Areas (South Wessex Downs) Designation (Amendment) Order 1998
Art.2, amended: SI 1998/2175 Art.3

1327. Countryside Stewardship Regulations 1998
Sch.1 Part I, amended: SI 1999/1177 Reg.4, Sch.1 Part I, Sch.1 Part II
Sch.1 Part II, amended: SI 1999/1177 Reg.5, Sch.2
Sch.1 Part III, amended: SI 1999/1177 Reg.6, Sch.2
Sch.1 Part IV, amended: SI 1999/1177 Reg.7

1340. Railways Regulations 1998
Reg.21, amended: SI 1998/1519 Reg.2

1342. Food Protection (Emergency Prohibitions) (Paralytic Shellfish Poisoning) Order 1998
revoked (in part): SI 1998/1801 Art.2, SI 1998/2045 Art.2, SI 1998/2119 Art.2 (rem.)
Art.3, revoked (in part): SI 1998/2045 Art.2, SI 1998/2119 Art.2 (rem.)

NO.

1357. Control of Substances Hazardous to Health (Amendment) Regulations 1998
revoked: SI 1999/437 Reg.18
Reg.2, revoked: SI 1999/437 Reg.18
Sch., revoked: SI 1999/437 Reg.18

1397. Occupational Pension Schemes (Contracting Out) (Amount Required for Restoring State Scheme Rights and Miscellaneous Amendment) Regulations 1998
amended: 1999 c.2 s.1, Sch.2
Reg.4, amended: SI 1999/3069 Reg.2
Sch.2, amended: SI 1999/3069 Reg.2

1421. Local Government (Exemption from Competition) (Scotland) Amendment Order 1998
revoked: SI 1999/937 Art.5
Art.2, revoked: SI 1999/937 Art.5
Art.3, revoked: SI 1999/937 Art.5
Art.4, revoked: SI 1999/937 Art.5

1422. Local Government Act 1988 (Competition) (Scotland) Amendment Regulations 1998
revoked: SI 1999/947 Reg.5
Reg.2, revoked: SI 1999/947 Reg.5
Reg.3, revoked: SI 1999/947 Reg.5
Reg.4, revoked: SI 1999/947 Reg.5
Reg.5, revoked: SI 1999/947 Reg.5

1448. Road Humps (Scotland) Regulations 1998
applied: SI 1999/1750 Art.2, Sch.1
Reg.7, substituted: SI 1999/1000 Reg.4

1451. National Health Service Superannuation Scheme (Scotland) (Additional Voluntary Contributions) Regulations 1998
applied: SI 1999/1750 Art.2, Sch.1

1462. A205 Trunk Road (Wandsworth and Richmond) Red Route Traffic Order 1998
Art.2, amended: SI 1999/272 Art.2, Sch. Part A
Art.9, amended: SI 1999/272 Art.2, Sch. Part A

1489. Education (Grants for Education Support and Training) (Wales) (Amendment) Regulations 1998
referred to: SI 1999/521 Reg.12
revoked: SI 1999/521 Reg.12
Reg.3, revoked: SI 1999/521 Reg.12
Reg.4, revoked: SI 1999/521 Reg.12
Reg.5, revoked: SI 1999/521 Reg.12

1504. Criminal Justice (Children) (Northern Ireland) Order 1998
Art.20, revoked: SI 1999/2789 (NI.8) Art.40, Sch.3
Art.22, revoked: 1999 c.23 s.67, Sch.6
Art.30A, added: SI 1998/2839 (NI.20) Art.4
Sch.5 para.9, revoked: SI 1999/2789 (NI.8) Art.40, Sch.3
Sch.5 para.31, revoked: SI 1999/2789 (NI.8) Art.40, Sch.3
Sch.5 para.37, revoked: SI 1999/2789 (NI.8) Art.40, Sch.3
Sch.5 para.38, revoked: SI 1999/2789 (NI.8) Art.40, Sch.3

1506. Social Security (Northern Ireland) Order 1998
applied: 1999 c.10 s.2, Sch.2 para.36
referred to: 1998 c.47 s.87
Art.3, applied: 1999 c.10 s.1, Sch.2 para.6, SI 1999/671 Art.17, Art.24, Sch.6 para.16, Sch.9 Part I, 1999 c.30 s.88, Sch.13 Part VII
Art.9, applied: 1999 c.10 s.2, Sch.2 para.6
Art.9, revoked (in part): SI 1999/671 Art.24, Sch.9 Part I
Art.10, applied: 1999 c.10 s.2, Sch.2 para.6
Art.11, amended: SI 1999/671 Art.17, Sch.6 para.17

1998—cont.

1506. Social Security (Northern Ireland) Order 1998—*cont.*

Art.11, referred to: 1999 c.10 s.10, Sch.4 para.3

Art.11, revoked (in part): SI 1999/671 Art.17, Art.24, Sch.6 para.11, Sch.9 Part I

Art.11A, added: SI 1999/671 Art.17, Sch.6 para.18

Art.12, applied: 1999 c.10 s.2, Sch.2 para.6

Art.13, amended: SI 1999/671 Art.17, Art.24, Sch.6 para.19, Sch.9 Part I

Art.13, applied: 1999 c.10 s.10, Sch.4 para.3

Art.13, referred to: 1999 c.10 s.2, Sch.2 para.37

Art.13, revoked (in part): SI 1999/671 Art.24, Sch.9 Part I

Art.14, amended: SI 1999/671 Art.17, Sch.6 para.20

Art.14, applied: 1999 c.10 s.10, Sch.4 para.3

Art.15, amended: SI 1999/671 Art.24, Sch.9 Part I

Art.15, applied: 1999 c.10 s.10, Sch.4 para.3

Art.15, revoked (in part): SI 1999/671 Art.17, Art.24, Sch.6 para.21, Sch.9 Part I

Art.16, revoked (in part): SI 1999/671 Art.17, Art.24, Sch.6 para.22, Sch.9 Part I

Art.18, amended: SI 1999/671 Art.17, Sch.6 para.23

Art.18, revoked (in part): SI 1999/671 Art.17, Art.24, Sch.6 para.23, Sch.9 Part I

Art.19, amended: SI 1999/671 Art.17, Art.24, Sch.6 para.24, Sch.9 Part I

Art.20, amended: SI 1999/671 Art.17, Art.24, Sch.6 para.25, Sch.9 Part I

Art.21, revoked (in part): SI 1999/671 Art.17, Art.24, Sch.6 para.26, Sch.9 Part I

Art.24A, added: SI 1999/671 Art.17, Sch.6 para.27

Art.27, referred to: 1999 c.10 s.2, Sch.2 para.19

Art.28, amended: SI 1999/671 Art.17, Sch.6 para.28

Art.39, amended: SI 1999/671 Art.17, Sch.6 para.29, SI 1999/3147 (NI.11) Art.56, Sch.7 para.17

Art.48, referred to: SI 1999/671 Art.24, Sch.7 para.4

Art.48, revoked: 1999 c.30 s.88, Sch.13 Part VII

Art.55, revoked: SI 1999/671 Art.24, Sch.9 Part I

Art.57, revoked (in part): SI 1999/671 Art.24, Sch.9 Part I

Art.58, revoked (in part): SI 1999/671 Art.24, Sch.9 Part I

Art.61, revoked (in part): 1999 c.30 s.88, Sch.13 Part VII

Art.73, revoked (in part): SI 1999/3147 (NI.11) Art.76, Sch.10 Part IV

Art.74, amended: 1999 c.10 s.2, Sch.2 para.22

Art.75, referred to: 1999 c.10 s.2, Sch.2 para.37, Sch.2 para.38

Art.77, revoked: SI 1998/1506 (NI.10) Art.78, Sch.7

Part II Ch.I, referred to: 1999 c.10 s.11

Part II Ch.II, amended: 1999 c.10 s.2, Sch.2 para.23

Part II Ch.II, applied: 1999 c.2 s.23, SI 1999/671 Art.16, SI 1999/3147 (NI.11) Art.49

Part II Ch.II, referred to: SI 1999/671 Art.14, Art.16

Sch.3 para.10, revoked: SI 1999/671 Art.17, Art.24, Sch.6 para.30, Sch.9 Part I

Sch.3 para.11, revoked: SI 1999/671 Art.17, Art.24, Sch.6 para.30, Sch.9 Part I

Sch.3 para.12, revoked: SI 1999/671 Art.17, Art.24, Sch.6 para.30, Sch.9 Part I

1998—cont.

1506. Social Security (Northern Ireland) Order 1998—*cont.*

Sch.3 para.13, revoked: SI 1999/671 Art.17, Art.24, Sch.6 para.30, Sch.9 Part I

Sch.3 para.14, revoked: SI 1999/671 Art.17, Art.24, Sch.6 para.30, Sch.9 Part I

Sch.3 para.15, revoked: SI 1999/671 Art.17, Art.24, Sch.6 para.30, Sch.9 Part I

Sch.3 para.16, applied: 1999 c.2 s.23, SI 1999/671 Art.7

Sch.3 para.17, applied: 1999 c.2 s.23, SI 1999/671 Art.7

Sch.3 para.18, revoked: SI 1999/671 Art.17, Art.24, Sch.6 para.30, Sch.9 Part I

Sch.3 para.19, revoked: SI 1999/671 Art.17, Art.24, Sch.6 para.30, Sch.9 Part I

Sch.3 para.20, revoked: SI 1999/671 Art.17, Art.24, Sch.6 para.30, Sch.9 Part I

Sch.3 para.21, revoked: SI 1999/671 Art.17, Art.24, Sch.6 para.30, Sch.9 Part I

Sch.3 para.22, revoked: SI 1999/671 Art.17, Art.24, Sch.6 para.30, Sch.9 Part I

Sch.3 para.23, revoked: SI 1999/671 Art.17, Art.24, Sch.6 para.30, Sch.9 Part I

Sch.3 para.24, revoked: SI 1999/671 Art.17, Art.24, Sch.6 para.30, Sch.9 Part I

Sch.3 para.25, revoked: SI 1999/671 Art.17, Art.24, Sch.6 para.30, Sch.9 Part I

Sch.3 para.26, revoked: SI 1999/671 Art.17, Art.24, Sch.6 para.30, Sch.9 Part I

Sch.3 para.27, revoked: SI 1999/671 Art.17, Art.24, Sch.6 para.30, Sch.9 Part I

Sch.3 para.28, revoked: SI 1999/671 Art.17, Art.24, Sch.6 para.30, Sch.9 Part I

Sch.3 para.29, revoked: SI 1999/671 Art.17, Art.24, Sch.6 para.30, Sch.9 Part I

Sch.5, revoked: SI 1998/1506 (NI.10) Art.78, Sch.7

Sch.5 para.1, revoked: SI 1998/1506 (NI.10) Art.78, Sch.7

Sch.5 para.2, revoked: SI 1998/1506 (NI.10) Art.78, Sch.7

Sch.5 para.3, revoked: SI 1998/1506 (NI.10) Art.78, Sch.7

Sch.5 para.4, revoked: SI 1998/1506 (NI.10) Art.78, Sch.7

Sch.5 para.5, revoked: SI 1998/1506 (NI.10) Art.78, Sch.7

Sch.5 para.6, revoked: SI 1998/1506 (NI.10) Art.78, Sch.7

Sch.5 para.7, revoked: SI 1998/1506 (NI.10) Art.78, Sch.7

Sch.5 para.8, revoked: SI 1998/1506 (NI.10) Art.78, Sch.7

Sch.5 para.9, revoked: SI 1998/1506 (NI.10) Art.78, Sch.7

Sch.6 para.39, revoked: 1999 c.30 s.88, Sch.13 Part VII

Sch.6 para.58, revoked (in part): SI 1999/671 Art.24, Sch.9 Part I

Sch.6 para.59, revoked: SI 1999/3147 (NI.11) Art.76, Sch.10 Part V

Sch.6 para.82, revoked: SI 1999/663 Art.2, Sch.2

Sch.6 para.83, revoked: SI 1999/663 Art.2, Sch.2

Sch.6 para.98, revoked (in part): SI 1999/671 Art.24, Sch.9 Part I

Sch.6 para.99, referred to: SI 1999/671 Art.15

Sch.6 para.100, revoked: SI 1999/671 Art.24, Sch.9 Part I

Sch.6 para.117, revoked: SI 1999/671 Art.24, Sch.9 Part I

NO.

1531. Federal Republic of Yugoslavia (Supply and Sale of Equipment) (Penalties and Licences) Regulations 1998
Reg.3, amended: SI 1999/1775 Reg.2

1532. Education (School Performance Targets) (England) Regulations 1998
applied: SI 1999/138 Reg.10
Reg.2, amended: SI 1999/2267 Reg.6
Reg.3, applied: SI 1999/138 Reg.13
Reg.4, applied: SI 1999/138 Reg.13

1537. Civil Aviation (Route Charges for Navigation Services) (Amendment) Regulations 1998
revoked: SI 1999/3260 Reg.2, Sch.1
Reg.2, revoked: SI 1999/3260 Reg.2, Sch.1

1539. Road Traffic (Permitted Parking Area and Special Parking Area) (City of Edinburgh) Designation Order 1998
referred to: SI 1998/2233 Reg.2

1544. Prison (Amendment) (No.2) Rules 1998
revoked: SI 1999/728 r.85 (with savings), Sch. (with savings)
r.2, revoked: SI 1999/728 r.85 (with savings), Sch. (with savings)
Sch. r.1, revoked: SI 1999/728 r.85 (with savings), Sch. (with savings)
Sch. r.2, revoked: SI 1999/728 r.85 (with savings), Sch. (with savings)
Sch. r.3, revoked: SI 1999/728 r.85 (with savings), Sch. (with savings)
Sch. r.4, revoked: SI 1999/728 r.85 (with savings), Sch. (with savings)
Sch. r.5, revoked: SI 1999/728 r.85 (with savings), Sch. (with savings)
Sch. r.6, revoked: SI 1999/728 r.85 (with savings), Sch. (with savings)
Sch. r.7, revoked: SI 1999/728 r.85 (with savings), Sch. (with savings)
Sch. r.8, revoked: SI 1999/728 r.85 (with savings), Sch. (with savings)
Sch. r.9, revoked: SI 1999/728 r.85 (with savings), Sch. (with savings)
Sch. r.10, revoked: SI 1999/728 r.85 (with savings), Sch. (with savings)

1551. Education (Baseline Assessment) (England) Regulations 1998
Reg.2, amended: SI 1999/2267 Reg.4
Sch. Part I, revoked: SI 1999/2267 Reg.4

1567. Wireless Telegraphy (Licence Charges) (Amendment No.2) Regulations 1998
revoked: SI 1999/1774 Reg.2, Sch.1
Reg.2, amended: SI 1998/1703 Reg.2
Reg.2, revoked: SI 1999/1774 Reg.2, Sch.1
Reg.3, added: SI 1998/2210 Reg.3
Reg.3, revoked: SI 1999/1774 Reg.2, Sch.1
Sch. Part I, revoked: SI 1999/1774 Reg.2, Sch.1
Sch. Part II, revoked: SI 1999/1774 Reg.2, Sch.1

1578. Homelessness (Decisions on Referrals) Order 1998
applied: SI 1999/71 Reg.7
Sch. para.3, applied: SI 1999/71 Reg.7

1580. Telecommunications (Open Network Provision) (Voice Telephony) Regulations 1998
applied: SI 1999/2450 Sch.1 para.32.1, Sch.1 para.35.5
Reg.2, amended: SI 1999/2093 Reg.3, Sch.1 para.4
Reg.6, applied: SI 1999/2450 Sch.1 para.51.1
Reg.10, amended: SI 1999/2093 Reg.3, Sch.1 para.5

NO.

1580. Telecommunications (Open Network Provision) (Voice Telephony) Regulations 1998—*cont.*
Reg.10, applied: SI 1999/2450 Sch.1 para.29.3
Reg.15, applied: SI 1999/2450 Sch.1 para.10.3
Reg.17, applied: SI 1999/2450 Sch.1 para.15.8
Reg.19, applied: SI 1999/2450 Sch.1 para.51.2, Sch.1 para.52.2, Sch.1 para.52.4
Reg.21, amended: SI 1999/2093 Reg.3, Sch.1 para.6, SI 1999/2450 Sch.1 para.20.2
Reg.21, referred to: SI 1999/2450 Sch.1 para.20.1
Reg.22, applied: SI 1999/2450 Sch.1 para.13.2
Reg.26, referred to: SI 1999/2450 Sch.1 para.53.2, Sch.1 para.53.5, Sch.1 para.53.6
Reg.27, applied: SI 1999/2450 Sch.1 para.54.1
Reg.31, applied: SI 1999/2450 Sch.1 para.54.11
Reg.34, applied: SI 1999/2450 Sch.1 para.2.4, Sch.1 para.4.2
Reg.37, applied: SI 1999/2450 Sch.1 para.32.1
Reg.40, revoked (in part): SI 1998/3170 Reg.3, Sch.1 para.2
Sch. I Part 2, applied: SI 1999/2450 Sch.1 para.52.5, Sch.1 para.52.6
Sch. I Part 3, applied: SI 1999/2450 Sch.1 para.52.6
Sch. II, referred to: SI 1999/2450 Sch.1 para.53.1
Sch. III, applied: SI 1999/2450 Sch.1 para.52.1
Sch. IV, applied: SI 1999/2450 Sch.1 para.54.2

1582. Food Protection (Emergency Prohibitions) (Paralytic Shellfish Poisoning) (No.2) Order 1998
revoked (in part): SI 1999/649 Art.2, SI 1999/1067 Art.2 (rem.)
Art.3, revoked (in part): SI 1999/649 Art.2, SI 1999/1067 Art.2 (rem.)

1584. Education (Teachers) (Amendment) Regulations 1998
revoked (in part): SI 1999/2817 Reg.2, Sch.1 Part I
Reg.3, revoked (in part): SI 1999/2817 Reg.2, Sch.1 Part I
Reg.4, revoked: SI 1999/2166 Reg.2, Sch.1 Part I

1589. Prisons and Young Offenders Institutions (Scotland) Amendment Rules 1998
r.31, revoked (in part): SI 1999/374 r.36

1594. National Health Service (Scotland) (Injury Benefits) Regulations 1998
applied: SI 1999/1750 Art.2, Sch.1
Reg.2, amended: SI 1999/444 Reg.3, SSI 1999/195 Reg.3
Reg.3, amended: SI 1999/444 Reg.4
Reg.4A, added: SSI 1999/195 Reg.4

1642. A4 Trunk Road (Hounslow) Red Route (Clearway) Traffic Order 1996 Variation Order 1998
revoked: SI 1998/2545 Art.7
Art.3, revoked: SI 1998/2545 Art.7
Art.4, revoked: SI 1998/2545 Art.7
Sch., revoked: SI 1998/2545 Art.7

1643. Federal Republic of Yugoslavia and Serbia (Freezing of Funds) Regulations 1998
revoked: SI 1999/1786 Reg.6
Reg.4, amended: SI 1998/1873 Reg.6
Reg.4, revoked: SI 1999/1786 Reg.6

1645. Sheep and Goats Spongiform Encephalopathy Order 1998
Art.4, applied: SI 1998/1646 Reg.3
Art.7, applied: SI 1998/1646 Reg.3

NO.

1998—cont.

1646. Sheep and Goats Spongiform Encephalopathy Regulations 1998
Reg.3, applied: SI 1998/1645 Art.4

1659. Sports Grounds and Sporting Events (Designation) (Scotland) Amendment Order 1998
revoked: SI 1998/2314 Art.3, Sch.3
Art.3, revoked: SI 1998/2314 Art.3, Sch.3
Art.4, revoked: SI 1998/2314 Art.3, Sch.3

1703. Wireless Telegraphy (Licence Charges) (Amendment No.3) Regulations 1998
revoked: SI 1999/1774 Reg.2, Sch.1
Reg.2, revoked: SI 1999/1774 Reg.2, Sch.1

1705. A205 Trunk Road (Lewisham) Red Route (Prescribed Route) Experimental Traffic Order 1998
revoked: SI 1999/1706 Art.5
Art.6, revoked: SI 1999/1706 Art.5

1706. A23 Trunk Road (Croydon) Red Route (No.2) Experimental Traffic Order 1997 Variation Order 1998
revoked (in part): SI 1999/414 Art.10
Art.3, revoked (in part): SI 1999/414 Art.10
Art.4, revoked (in part): SI 1999/414 Art.10
Art.5, revoked (in part): SI 1999/414 Art.10
Art.6, revoked (in part): SI 1999/414 Art.10
Art.7, revoked (in part): SI 1999/414 Art.10
Art.8, revoked (in part): SI 1999/414 Art.10
Art.9, revoked (in part): SI 1999/414 Art.10
Art.10, revoked (in part): SI 1999/414 Art.10
Art.11, revoked (in part): SI 1999/414 Art.10
Art.12, revoked (in part): SI 1999/414 Art.10
Art.13, revoked (in part): SI 1999/414 Art.10
Art.14, revoked (in part): SI 1999/414 Art.10
Art.15, revoked (in part): SI 1999/414 Art.10
Art.16, revoked (in part): SI 1999/414 Art.10
Art.17, revoked (in part): SI 1999/414 Art.10
Art.18, revoked (in part): SI 1999/414 Art.10
Art.19, revoked (in part): SI 1999/414 Art.10
Art.20, revoked (in part): SI 1999/414 Art.10

1708. M4 Motorway (Hillingdon and Hounslow) (Speed Limits) Regulations 1998
Sch. para.6A, added: SI 1999/167 Reg.2

1711. Ecclesiastical Judges and Legal Officers (Fees) Order 1998
revoked: SI 1999/2110 Art.2 (with saving)
Art.1, amended: SI 1999/2110 Art.6, Sch.2 para.1
Art.1, revoked: SI 1999/2110 Art.2 (with saving)
Art.2, revoked: SI 1999/2110 Art.2 (with saving)
Art.3, revoked: SI 1999/2110 Art.2 (with saving)
Art.4, amended: SI 1999/2110 Art.6, Sch.2 para.2
Art.4, revoked: SI 1999/2110 Art.2 (with saving)
Sch., revoked: SI 1999/2110 Art.2 (with saving)
Sch. Table I, amended: SI 1999/2110 Art.6, Sch.2 para.3
Sch. Table I, revoked: SI 1999/2110 Art.2 (with saving)
Sch. Table I, substituted: SI 1999/2110 Art.1, Sch.1
Sch. Table II, revoked: SI 1999/2110 Art.2 (with saving)
Sch. Table II, substituted: SI 1999/2110 Art.1, Sch.1
Sch. Table III, revoked: SI 1999/2110 Art.2 (with saving)
Sch. Table III, substituted: SI 1999/2110 Art.1, Sch.1
Sch. Table IV, revoked: SI 1999/2110 Art.2 (with saving)
Sch. Table IV, substituted: SI 1999/2110 Art.1, Sch.1

NO.

1998—cont.

1711. Ecclesiastical Judges and Legal Officers (Fees) Order 1998—cont.
Sch. Table V, revoked: SI 1999/2110 Art.2 (with saving)
Sch. Table V, substituted: SI 1999/2110 Art.1, Sch.1
Sch. Table VI, revoked: SI 1999/2110 Art.2 (with saving)
Sch. Table VI, substituted: SI 1999/2110 Art.1, Sch.1
Sch. Table VII, revoked: SI 1999/2110 Art.2 (with saving)
Sch. Table VII, substituted: SI 1999/2110 Art.1, Sch.1

1712. Legal Officers (Annual Fees) Order 1998
revoked: SI 1999/2108 Art.3
Appendix.para.1, revoked: SI 1999/2108 Art.3
Appendix.para.4, revoked: SI 1999/2108 Art.3
Art.2, revoked: SI 1999/2108 Art.3
Art.3, revoked: SI 1999/2108 Art.3
Sch. Table I, revoked: SI 1999/2108 Art.3
Sch. Table I, substituted: SI 1999/2108 Sch. Table I
Sch. Table II, revoked: SI 1999/2108 Art.3
Sch. Table II, substituted: SI 1999/2108 Sch. Table II

1714. Parochial Fees Order 1998
revoked: SI 1999/2113 Art.4
Art.1, revoked: SI 1999/2113 Art.4
Art.4, revoked: SI 1999/2113 Art.4
Sch. Part I, revoked: SI 1999/2113 Art.4
Sch. Part II, revoked: SI 1999/2113 Art.4

1715. National Institutions of the Church of England (Transfer of Functions) Order 1998
applied: SI 1999/2113

1726. Education (Assisted Places) (Amendment) Regulations 1998
Reg.9, revoked: SI 1998/1966 Reg.9

1728. Social Security (Categorisation of Earners) Amendment Regulations 1998
Reg.5, revoked: SI 1999/3 Reg.2

1731. Environmental Assessment (Forestry) Regulations 1998
applied: SSI 1999/43 Reg.25
referred to: SI 1999/2228 Reg.25
revoked (in part): SI 1999/2228 Reg.25 (with savings), SSI 1999/43 Reg.25
Reg.3, applied: SSI 1999/43 Reg.25
Reg.3, referred to: SI 1999/2228 Reg.25
Reg.3, revoked (in part): SI 1999/2228 Reg.25 (with savings), SSI 1999/43 Reg.25
Reg.4, applied: SSI 1999/43 Reg.25
Reg.4, referred to: SI 1999/2228 Reg.25
Reg.4, revoked (in part): SI 1999/2228 Reg.25 (with savings), SSI 1999/43 Reg.25
Reg.6, applied: SSI 1999/43 Reg.25
Reg.6, referred to: SI 1999/2228 Reg.25
Reg.6, revoked (in part): SI 1999/2228 Reg.25 (with savings), SSI 1999/43 Reg.25
Reg.7, applied: SSI 1999/43 Reg.25
Reg.7, referred to: SI 1999/2228 Reg.25
Reg.7, revoked (in part): SI 1999/2228 Reg.25 (with savings), SSI 1999/43 Reg.25
Reg.8, applied: SSI 1999/43 Reg.25
Reg.8, revoked (in part): SI 1999/2228 Reg.25 (with savings), SSI 1999/43 Reg.25
Reg.13, applied: SSI 1999/43 Reg.25
Reg.13, referred to: SI 1999/2228 Reg.25
Reg.13, revoked (in part): SI 1999/2228 Reg.25 (with savings), SSI 1999/43 Reg.25
Reg.16, applied: SSI 1999/43 Reg.25

NO.

1998—cont.

1731. Environmental Assessment (Forestry) Regulations 1998—*cont.*
Reg.16, revoked (in part): SI 1999/2228 Reg.25 (with savings), SSI 1999/43 Reg.25
Reg.20, revoked (in part): SI 1999/2228 Reg.25 (with savings), SSI 1999/43 Reg.25

1741. Education (Grants for Education Support and Training) (England) Regulations 1998 (Amendment) Regulations 1998
revoked: SI 1999/606 Reg.12
Reg.3, revoked: SI 1999/606 Reg.12
Reg.4, revoked: SI 1999/606 Reg.12
Reg.5, revoked: SI 1999/606 Reg.12
Reg.6, revoked: SI 1999/606 Reg.12

1760. Education (Student Support) (Northern Ireland) Order 1998
applied: SI 1999/1001 Reg.4
Art.3, applied: SI 1999/3219 Reg.7

1763. Public Interest Disclosure (Northern Ireland) Order 1998
Art.1, revoked (in part): SI 1999/2790 (NI.9) Art.40, Sch.9 Part 11
Art.12, revoked: SI 1999/2790 (NI.9) Art.40, Sch.9 Part 11
Art.14, revoked: SI 1999/2790 (NI.9) Art.40, Sch.9 Part 12

1778. Patents (Fees) Rules 1998
Sch. Part A, amended: SI 1999/1093 r.3, r.4

1795. Merchant Shipping (Liability of Shipowners and Others) (Rate of Interest) Order 1998
revoked: SI 1999/1922 Art.2
Art.2, revoked: SI 1999/1922 Art.2
Art.3, revoked: SI 1999/1922 Art.2

1802. Restriction of Liberty Order (Scotland) Regulations 1998
Reg.2, amended: SI 1999/144 Reg.3
Sch.2 para.4, added: SI 1999/144 Reg.3

1831. Local Government Pension Scheme (Management and Investment of Funds) Regulations 1998
Reg.2, amended: SI 1999/3259 Reg.3
Reg.7, amended: SI 1999/3259 Reg.4
Reg.9A, added: SI 1999/3259 Reg.5
Sch.1 Part III, amended: SI 1999/3259 Reg.6
Sch.1 para.9, substituted: SI 1999/3259 Reg.6
Sch.1 para.9A, substituted: SI 1999/3259 Reg.6
Sch.1 para.9B, substituted: SI 1999/3259 Reg.6
Sch.1 para.14, amended: SI 1999/3259 Reg.6

1833. Working Time Regulations 1998
Reg.4, see *Barber v RJB Mining (UK) Ltd* [1999] I.R.L.R. 308 (QBD), Gage, J.
Reg.4, amended: SI 1999/3372 Reg.3
Reg.5, amended: SI 1999/3372 Reg.3
Reg.5, revoked (in part): SI 1999/3372 Reg.3
Reg.6, amended: SI 1999/3242 Reg.29, Sch.2
Reg.20, amended: SI 1999/3372 Reg.4
Reg.35A, added: SI 1999/3372 Reg.5

1834. Education (Individual Performance Information) (Identification of Individual Pupils) Regulations 1998
revoked: SI 1999/903 Reg.1
Reg.1, revoked: SI 1999/903 Reg.1
Reg.2, revoked: SI 1999/903 Reg.1

1835. A205 Trunk Road (Lewisham) Red Route Traffic Order 1998
Art.2, amended: SI 1999/272 Art.2, Sch. Part A
Art.9, amended: SI 1999/272 Art.2, Sch. Part A
Sch.2B Item 2, substituted: SI 1999/3224 Art.3

1841. Royal Infirmary of Edinburgh National Health Service Trust (Establishment) Amendment Order 1998
revoked: SI 1999/1070 Art.2, Sch.2

NO.

1998—cont.

1841. Royal Infirmary of Edinburgh National Health Service Trust (Establishment) Amendment Order 1998—*cont.*
Art.2, revoked: SI 1999/1070 Art.2, Sch.2
Art.3, revoked: SI 1999/1070 Art.2, Sch.2

1846. Occupational Pension Schemes (Validation of Rule Alterations) Regulations 1998
Reg.2, amended: 1999 c.2 s.1, Sch.2

1866. Education (School Inspection) (Wales) Regulations 1998
amended: SI 1999/711 Reg.2, Sch.1
Reg.5, amended: SI 1999/1440 Reg.3
Reg.5, revoked (in part): SI 1999/1440 Reg.3
Reg.6, amended: SI 1999/1440 Reg.4
Reg.12, amended: SI 1999/1440 Reg.5
Reg.13, revoked (in part): SI 1999/1440 Reg.6

1867. Education (School Performance Information) (Wales) Regulations 1998
Reg.3, amended: SI 1999/1470 Reg.3
Reg.4, amended: SI 1999/1470 Reg.4
Reg.4, referred to: SI 1999/1812 Reg.10, Sch.3 para.16
Reg.10, amended: SI 1999/1470 Reg.5
Sch.1 Part I, applied: SI 1999/1812 Reg.10, Sch.3 para.16
Sch.1 Part II, applied: SI 1999/1812 Reg.10, Sch.3 para.16
Sch.1 Part III, applied: SI 1999/1812 Reg.10, Sch.3 para.16
Sch.1 para.2, substituted: SI 1999/1470 Reg.6
Sch.1 para.4, amended: SI 1999/1470 Reg.7
Sch.2, applied: SI 1999/1812 Reg.10, Sch.3 para.16
Sch.2 para.1, substituted: SI 1999/1470 Reg.8
Sch.2 para.3, substituted: SI 1999/1470 Reg.9
Sch.3 para.4, amended: SI 1999/1470 Reg.10

1870. Individual Savings Account Regulations 1998
Reg.2, amended: SI 1998/3174 Reg.3
Reg.6, amended: SI 1998/3174 Reg.4
Reg.7, amended: SI 1998/3174 Reg.5
Reg.8, amended: SI 1998/3174 Reg.6
Reg.9, amended: SI 1998/3174 Reg.7
Reg.14, amended: SI 1998/3174 Reg.8
Reg.25, amended: SI 1998/3174 Reg.9
Reg.26, amended: SI 1998/3174 Reg.10
Reg.35, amended: SI 1998/3174 Reg.11
Reg.36, added: SI 1998/3174 Reg.12

1871. Individual Savings Account (Insurance Companies) Regulations 1998
Reg.25, amended: SI 1998/3174 Reg.13

1873. Republic of Serbia (Prohibition on Investment) Regulations 1998
revoked: SI 1999/1786 Reg.6
Reg.6, revoked: SI 1999/1786 Reg.6

1882. Northern Ireland (Sentences) Act 1998 (Specified Organisations) Order 1998
revoked: SI 1998/2869 Art.3
Art.2, revoked: SI 1998/2869 Art.3

1884. Education (School Teachers' Pay and Conditions) (No.2) Order 1998
revoked: SI 1999/2160 Art.1
Art.1, revoked: SI 1999/2160 Art.1

1907. Dartford-Thurrock Crossing Tolls Order 1998
revoked: SI 1999/2207 Art.3
Art.3, revoked: SI 1999/2207 Art.3
Sch., revoked: SI 1999/2207 Art.3

1908. Dartford-Thurrock Crossing Regulations 1998
Reg.4, amended: SI 1999/2208 Reg.2

NO.

NO.

1998—cont.

1929. Education (School Performance Information) (England) Regulations 1998
revoked: SI 1999/1178 Reg.4 (with savings)
Reg.2, amended: SI 1998/3260 Reg.2
Reg.2, revoked: SI 1999/1178 Reg.4 (with savings)
Reg.4, revoked: SI 1999/1178 Reg.4 (with savings)
Reg.11A, added: SI 1998/3260 Reg.3
Reg.11A, revoked: SI 1999/1178 Reg.4 (with savings)
Reg.12, amended: SI 1998/3260 Reg.4
Reg.12, revoked (in part): SI 1998/3260 Reg.4, SI 1999/1178 Reg.4 (with savings)
Sch.1 para.1, revoked: SI 1999/1178 Reg.4 (with savings)
Sch.1 para.2, revoked: SI 1999/1178 Reg.4 (with savings)
Sch.1 para.3, revoked: SI 1999/1178 Reg.4 (with savings)
Sch.2 para.3, revoked: SI 1999/1178 Reg.4 (with savings)
Sch.2 para.4, revoked: SI 1999/1178 Reg.4 (with savings)
Sch.2 para.5, revoked: SI 1999/1178 Reg.4 (with savings)
Sch.3 para.3, revoked: SI 1999/1178 Reg.4 (with savings)
Sch.3 para.4, revoked: SI 1999/1178 Reg.4 (with savings)
Sch.5 para.4, revoked: SI 1999/1178 Reg.4 (with savings)
Sch.5 para.5, revoked: SI 1999/1178 Reg.4 (with savings)
Sch.5 para.6, revoked: SI 1999/1178 Reg.4 (with savings)
Sch.5 para.7, revoked: SI 1999/1178 Reg.4 (with savings)
Sch.5 para.9, revoked: SI 1999/1178 Reg.4 (with savings)
Sch.6 para.5, revoked: SI 1999/1178 Reg.4 (with savings)
Sch.6 para.6, revoked: SI 1999/1178 Reg.4 (with savings)
Sch.8, added: SI 1998/3260 Reg.5, Sch.
Sch.8, revoked: SI 1999/1178 Reg.4 (with savings)

1941. Firearms Rules 1998
r.6, amended: SI 1999/1820 Art.4, Sch.2 para.164
Sch.2, amended: SI 1999/1820 Art.4, Sch.2 para.164

1944. Consumer Credit (Exempt Agreements) (Amendment) Order 1998
revoked (in part): SI 1999/1956 Art.2
Art.2, revoked (in part): SI 1999/1956 Art.2
Art.3, revoked (in part): SI 1999/1956 Art.2

1947. Education (Infant Class Sizes) (Transitional Provisions) Regulations 1998
Reg.1, applied: SI 1999/1016 Art.6, Sch.4 para.2
Reg.2, applied: SI 1999/1016 Art.6, Sch.4 para.2
Reg.3, applied: SI 1999/1016 Art.6, Sch.4 para.2
Reg.4, applied: SI 1999/1016 Art.6, Sch.4 para.2
Reg.4, referred to: SI 1998/1942 Sch. para.17, SI 1998/1971 Sch. para.20

1998—cont.

1948. Education Act 1996 (Infant Class Sizes) (Modification) Regulations 1998
referred to: SI 1999/1016 Art.6, Sch.4 para.2, Sch.4 para.6, Sch.4 para.7, Sch.4 para.8, Sch.4 para.10
Sch., referred to: SI 1998/1947 Reg.5

1951. A4 Trunk Road (Hammersmith & Fulham and Kensington & Chelsea) Red Route Experimental Traffic Order 1997 Variation Order 1998
revoked (in part): SI 1999/1147 Art.10
Art.3, revoked (in part): SI 1999/1147 Art.10
Art.4, revoked (in part): SI 1999/1147 Art.10
Art.5, revoked (in part): SI 1999/1147 Art.10

1953. Blackburn and Darwen Education Action Zone Order 1998
revoked: SI 1998/2085 Art.3
Art.3, revoked: SI 1998/2085 Art.3
Art.10, revoked: SI 1998/2085 Art.3

1957. East Middlesbrough Education Action Zone Order 1998
revoked: SI 1998/2450 Art.3
Art.3, revoked: SI 1998/2450 Art.3
Art.10, revoked: SI 1998/2450 Art.3

1958. Newcastle Education Action Zone Order 1998
revoked: SI 1998/2084 Art.3
Art.3, revoked: SI 1998/2084 Art.3
Art.10, revoked: SI 1998/2084 Art.3

1967. Assured and Protected Tenancies (Lettings to Students) Regulations 1998
Sch.2, amended: SI 1999/1803 Reg.2, SI 1999/2268 Reg.2

1969. Education (Allocation of Grant-Maintained and Grant-Maintained Special Schools to New Categories) Regulations 1998
applied: SI 1999/101 Sch.4 para.3

1972. Education (Mandatory Awards) Regulations 1998 (Amendment) Regulations 1998
revoked: SI 1999/1494 Reg.6 (with saving)
Reg.3, revoked: SI 1999/1494 Reg.6 (with saving)
Reg.4, revoked: SI 1999/1494 Reg.6 (with saving)
Reg.5, revoked: SI 1999/1494 Reg.6 (with saving)
Reg.6, revoked: SI 1999/1494 Reg.6 (with saving)
Reg.7, revoked: SI 1999/1494 Reg.6 (with saving)
Reg.8, revoked: SI 1999/1494 Reg.6 (with saving)

1993. Act of Sederunt (Child Care and Maintenance Rules) (Amendment) 1998
revoked: SI 1998/2130 r.3

2003. Education (Student Support) Regulations 1998
applied: SI 1999/496 Reg.3
revoked: SI 1999/496 Reg.3
Reg.3, revoked: SI 1999/496 Reg.3
Reg.4, revoked: SI 1999/496 Reg.3
Reg.6, revoked: SI 1999/496 Reg.3
Reg.7, revoked: SI 1999/496 Reg.3
Reg.11, applied: SI 1999/496 Reg.3
Reg.11, revoked: SI 1999/496 Reg.3
Reg.12, applied: SI 1999/496 Reg.3
Reg.12, revoked: SI 1999/496 Reg.3
Reg.13, applied: SI 1999/496 Reg.3
Reg.13, revoked: SI 1999/496 Reg.3
Reg.14, applied: SI 1999/496 Reg.3
Reg.14, revoked: SI 1999/496 Reg.3
Sch.1 para.1, revoked: SI 1999/496 Reg.3

NO.

2014. Housing (Right to Acquire) (Discount) Order 1998
revoked: SI 1999/1135 Art.3
Art.2, revoked: SI 1999/1135 Art.3
Art.3, revoked: SI 1999/1135 Art.3

2025. Agricultural Holdings (Units of Production) Order 1998
revoked (in part): SI 1999/2230 Art.3
Art.2, revoked (in part): SI 1999/2230 Art.3
Art.3, revoked (in part): SI 1999/2230 Art.3

2026. Education (Student Loans) (Scotland) Regulations 1998
applied: SI 1999/1001 Reg.3
revoked: SI 1999/1001 Reg.3
Reg.3, revoked: SI 1999/1001 Reg.3
Reg.6, revoked: SI 1999/1001 Reg.3
Reg.7, revoked: SI 1999/1001 Reg.3
Reg.11, applied: SI 1999/1001 Reg.3
Reg.11, revoked: SI 1999/1001 Reg.3
Reg.12, applied: SI 1999/1001 Reg.3
Reg.12, revoked: SI 1999/1001 Reg.3
Reg.13, applied: SI 1999/1001 Reg.3
Reg.13, revoked: SI 1999/1001 Reg.3
Reg.14, applied: SI 1999/1001 Reg.3
Reg.14, revoked: SI 1999/1001 Reg.3
Sch.1 para.1, revoked: SI 1999/1001 Reg.3

2033. Cardiff Community Healthcare National Health Service Trust (Establishment) Amendment Order 1998
revoked: SI 1999/1120 Art.2, Sch.2
Art.2, revoked: SI 1999/1120 Art.2, Sch.2

2034. East Glamorgan National Health Service Trust (Establishment) Amendment Order 1998
revoked: SI 1999/1120 Art.2, Sch.2
Art.2, revoked: SI 1999/1120 Art.2, Sch.2

2038. Motor Vehicles (Driving Licences) (Amendment) (No.4) Regulations 1998
revoked: SI 1999/2864 Reg.2, Sch.1
Reg.3, revoked: SI 1999/2864 Reg.2, Sch.1
Reg.4, revoked: SI 1999/2864 Reg.2, Sch.1
Reg.5, revoked: SI 1999/2864 Reg.2, Sch.1
Reg.6, revoked: SI 1999/2864 Reg.2, Sch.1

2051. Motor Vehicles (EC Type Approval) Regulations 1998
referred to: SI 1999/2149 Reg.9
Reg.15, amended: SI 1999/778 Reg.2
Sch.1 Table, amended: SI 1999/778 Reg.3
Sch.1 Item 5, amended: SI 1999/2324 Reg.2
Sch.1 Item 23, amended: SI 1999/2324 Reg.2
Sch.1 Item 25, amended: SI 1999/2324 Reg.2
Sch.1 Item 26, amended: SI 1999/2324 Reg.2
Sch.1 Item 28, amended: SI 1999/2324 Reg.2
Sch.1 Item 30, amended: SI 1999/2324 Reg.2

2070. Merchant Shipping (Radio Installations) Regulations 1998
applied: SI 1999/2721 Reg.34
referred to: SI 1998/2771 Reg.4, Reg.5, Sch.1, Sch.2
Reg.6, amended: SI 1999/1957 Reg.3, Sch.1 para.1

2171. A205 Trunk Road (Lewisham) Red Route (Bus Lanes) Experimental Traffic Order 1998
Sch. Item 1, amended: SI 1999/1707 Art.3
Sch. Item 2, amended: SI 1999/1707 Art.4
Sch. Item 3, amended: SI 1999/1707 Art.5
Sch. Item 4, amended: SI 1999/1707 Art.6
Sch. Item 5, amended: SI 1999/1707 Art.7

NO.

2193. Local Authorities (Direct Labour Organisations) (Competition) (Wales) (Amendment) Regulations 1998
revoked: SI 1999/1084 Reg.3
Reg.2, revoked: SI 1999/1084 Reg.3
Reg.3, revoked: SI 1999/1084 Reg.3

2196. Education (School Performance Targets) (Wales) Regulations 1998
applied: SI 1999/1439 Reg.16
revoked: SI 1999/1811 Reg.2

2210. Wireless Telegraphy (Licence Charges) (Channel Islands and Isle of Man) Regulations 1998
revoked: SI 1999/1774 Reg.2, Sch.1
Reg.3, revoked: SI 1999/1774 Reg.2, Sch.1

2212. School Standards and Framework Act 1998 (Commencement No.2 and Supplemental, Saving and Transitional Provisions) Order 1998
Art.4, amended: SI 1998/2459 Art.2
Sch.2, amended: SI 1998/2459 Art.2
Sch.2 para.4A, added: SI 1998/2459 Art.2
Sch.2 para.5, amended: SI 1999/1016 Art.7

2219. Education (Grammar School Designation) Order 1998
Sch., applied: SI 1999/2456 Art.2, Art.3

2241. Merchant Shipping (Load Line) Regulations 1998
applied: SI 1998/2647 Reg.3, SI 1999/1644 Reg.6
referred to: SI 1998/2771 Reg.4, Reg.5, Sch.1, Sch.2
Reg.32, applied: SI 1999/336 Reg.10
Reg.32, referred to: SI 1999/336 Reg.9

2259. National Health Service (Choice of Dental Practitioner) (Scotland) Regulations 1998
Reg.3, amended: SI 1998/3052 Reg.2

2284. Yugoslavia (Prohibition of Flights) Regulations 1998
revoked: SI 1999/2018 Reg.2
Reg.3, revoked: SI 1999/2018 Reg.2

2306. Provision and Use of Work Equipment Regulations 1998
Reg.4, amended: SI 1999/860 Reg.5
Sch.1, amended: SI 1999/2001 Reg.29

2327. Crime and Disorder Act 1998 (Commencement No.2 and Transitional Provisions) Order 1998
Art.3, amended: SI 1998/2412 Art.2
Art.4, amended: SI 1998/2906 Art.2
Art.4, revoked (in part): SI 1998/2906 Art.2

2405. Specified Risk Material (Amendment) Regulations 1998
Reg.1, amended: SI 1998/2431 Reg.2

2427. A205 Trunk Road (Lewisham) Red Route (Prohibited Turns) Experimental Traffic Order 1998
revoked (in part): SI 1999/2343 Art.5, SI 1999/2701 (rem.)

2428. Medicines (Products for Animal Use-Fees) Regulations 1998
Reg.12, amended: SI 1999/2512 Reg.2, Sch.
Reg.13, amended: SI 1999/2512 Reg.2, Sch.
Reg.14, amended: SI 1999/2512 Reg.2, Sch.
Reg.17, applied: SI 1999/2512 Reg.4
Sch.1 Part II, amended: SI 1999/2512 Reg.2, Sch.
Sch.1 Part III, amended: SI 1999/2512 Reg.2, Sch.
Sch.1 Part IV, amended: SI 1999/2512 Reg.2, Sch.
Sch.1 Part V, amended: SI 1999/2512 Reg.2, Sch.

NO.

1998—cont.

2428. Medicines (Products for Animal Use-Fees) Regulations 1998—cont.
Sch.3 Part II, amended: SI 1999/2512 Reg.3
Sch.3 Part III, amended: SI 1999/2512 Reg.3
Sch.5 Part II, amended: SI 1999/2512 Reg.2, Sch.
Sch.6, amended: SI 1999/2512 Reg.2, Sch.

2451. Gas Safety (Installation and Use) Regulations 1998
Reg.2, amended: SI 1999/2024 Reg.48, Sch.5 Part II

2452. Crime and Disorder Strategies (Prescribed Descriptions) Order 1998
Art.2, revoked (in part): SI 1998/2513 Art.2
Art.3, amended: SI 1998/2513 Art.2, SI 1999/483 Art.2

2456. Rail Vehicle Accessibility Regulations 1998
applied: SI 1998/2457 Sch. para.8
Reg.4, applied: SI 1999/520 Art.4, Art.5, Art.6
Reg.4, referred to: SI 1999/1448 Art.4, Art.5, SI 1999/1931 Art.4, Art.5, SI 1999/1932 Art.4, Art.5, SI 1999/2404 Art.4, Art.5, SI 1999/2547 Art.4, Art.5, SI 1999/2932 Art.4, Art.5
Reg.5, applied: SI 1999/1931 Art.6, SI 1999/1932 Art.6
Reg.5, referred to: SI 1999/1931 Art.4, Art.5, SI 1999/1932 Art.4, Art.5, SI 1999/2404 Art.4, Art.5, SI 1999/2547 Art.4, Art.5, Art.6
Reg.6, referred to: SI 1999/2404 Art.4, Art.5
Reg.8, referred to: SI 1999/1448 Art.4, Art.5
Reg.11, applied: SI 1999/520 Art.4, Art.5, Art.6
Reg.11, referred to: SI 1999/2404 Art.4, Art.5, SI 1999/2932 Art.4, Art.5
Reg.13, applied: SI 1999/520 Art.4, Art.5, SI 1999/1256 Art.3, SI 1999/1932 Art.7
Reg.13, referred to: SI 1999/1932 Art.4, Art.5, SI 1999/2404 Art.4, Art.5
Reg.16, applied: SI 1999/520 Art.4, Art.5
Reg.16, referred to: SI 1999/1448 Art.4, Art.5
Reg.20, referred to: SI 1999/2404 Art.4, Art.5

2479. Late Payment of Commercial Debts (Interest) Act 1998 (Commencement No.1) Order 1998
applied: SI 1998/2481 Reg.2
Sch.2, applied: SI 1999/1816 Art.2

2480. Late Payment of Commercial Debts (Rate of Interest) Order 1998
revoked: SI 1998/2765 Art.2
Art.3, revoked: SI 1998/2765 Art.2

2483. Immigration (Transit Visa) (Amendment No.3) Order 1998
revoked: SI 1999/3086 Art.3
Art.2, revoked: SI 1999/3086 Art.3
Art.3, revoked: SI 1999/3086 Art.3
Sch., revoked: SI 1999/3086 Art.3

2514. Merchant Shipping (Passenger Ship Construction: Ships of Classes I, II and II(A)) Regulations 1998
applied: SI 1999/2721 Reg.34, Reg.71, Reg.74
referred to: SI 1999/1869 Reg.5

2526. Education (School Information) (England) Regulations 1998
Part IIIA, added: SI 1999/251 Reg.4
Part IV, referred to: SI 1999/2163 Reg.42
Reg.3, amended: SI 1999/251 Reg.3, SI 1999/2267 Reg.5
Reg.7A, added: SI 1999/251 Reg.4
Reg.7B, added: SI 1999/251 Reg.4
Reg.7C, added: SI 1999/251 Reg.4
Reg.8, applied: SI 1999/2157 Reg.3, Sch. para.5, Sch. para.7, Sch. para.13
Reg.12, amended: SI 1999/2267 Reg.5
Reg.13A, added: SI 1999/251 Reg.5

NO.

1998—cont.

2526. Education (School Information) (England) Regulations 1998—cont.
Sch.1 para.4, amended: SI 1999/2267 Reg.5
Sch.1 para.14, amended: SI 1999/2267 Reg.5
Sch.1 para.15, amended: SI 1999/2267 Reg.5
Sch.1 para.17, amended: SI 1999/2267 Reg.5
Sch.1A, added: SI 1999/251 Reg.6
Sch.2 para.2, amended: SI 1999/2267 Reg.5
Sch.2 para.3, amended: SI 1999/2267 Reg.5
Sch.2 para.13, applied: SI 1999/2157 Reg.3, Sch. para.13
Sch.2 para.14, applied: SI 1999/2157 Reg.3, Sch. para.5
Sch.2 para.15, applied: SI 1999/2157 Reg.3, Sch. para.7

2535. Religious Character of Schools (Designation Procedure) Regulations 1998
applied: SI 1999/1814, SI 1999/2432
Reg.7, applied: SI 1999/2432 Art.5
Reg.9, amended: SI 1999/2243 Reg.62

2538. Spreadable Fats (Marketing Standards) (Amendment) (No.2) Regulations 1998
revoked (in part): SI 1999/2457 Reg.9, Sch.2, SSI 1999/34 Reg.9, Sch.2
Reg.3, revoked (in part): SI 1999/2457 Reg.9, Sch.2, SSI 1999/34 Reg.9, Sch.2
Reg.4, revoked (in part): SI 1999/2457 Reg.9, Sch.2, SSI 1999/34 Reg.9, Sch.2

2573. Employers' Liability (Compulsory Insurance) Regulations 1998
Sch.2 para.1, amended: SI 1999/1820 Art.4, Sch.2 para.165

2575. Civil Aviation (Canadian Navigation Services) Regulations 1998
Reg.4, amended: SI 1999/271 Reg.2, SI 1999/2458 Reg.2

2615. A316 Trunk Road (Hounslow) Red Route Traffic Order 1998
Art.2, amended: SI 1999/272 Art.2, Sch. Part A
Art.9, amended: SI 1999/272 Art.2, Sch. Part A

2668. Act of Sederunt (Fees of Messengers-at-Arms) 1998
Sch., amended: SI 1998/3256 para.2

2670. School Standards and Framework Act 1998 (Modification) Regulations 1998
Reg.2, referred to: SI 1998/3217 Reg.2, SI 1999/495 Reg.1

2697. Education (School Information) (Wales) (Amendment) Regulations 1998
revoked: SI 1999/1812 Reg.2
Reg.2, revoked: SI 1999/1812 Reg.2
Reg.3, revoked: SI 1999/1812 Reg.2

2698. Education (Grants for Education Support and Training) (England) Regulations 1998 (Amendment) (No.2) Regulations 1998
revoked: SI 1999/606 Reg.12
Reg.3, revoked: SI 1999/606 Reg.12
Reg.4, revoked: SI 1999/606 Reg.12
Reg.5, revoked: SI 1999/606 Reg.12
Reg.6, revoked: SI 1999/606 Reg.12

2707. Magistrates' Courts Committees (Northumbria) Amalgamation Order 1998
Sch. para.4, amended: SI 1998/3108 Art.3
Sch. para.5, amended: SI 1998/3108 Art.4
Sch. para.6, amended: SI 1998/3108 Art.5
Sch. para.9, amended: SI 1998/3108 Art.6

2709. Borders Primary Care National Health Service Trust (Establishment) Order 1998
Art.3, substituted: SSI 1999/92 Art.2
Art.4, amended: SSI 1999/92 Art.2

NO.
1998—cont.

2710. **Tayside Primary Care National Health Service Trust (Establishment) Order 1998**
Art.3, substituted: SI 1999/1875 Art.2, SSI 1999/83 Art.2
Art.4, amended: SSI 1999/83 Art.2

2711. **Lothian Primary Care National Health Service Trust (Establishment) Order 1998**
Art.3, substituted: SSI 1999/95 Art.2
Art.4, amended: SSI 1999/95 Art.2

2712. **Fife Primary Care National Health Service Trust (Establishment) Order 1998**
Art.3, substituted: SSI 1999/94 Art.2
Art.4, amended: SSI 1999/94 Art.2

2713. **Forth Valley Primary Care National Health Service Trust (Establishment) Order 1998**
Art.3, substituted: SSI 1999/164 Art.2
Art.4, amended: SSI 1999/164 Art.2

2714. **Dumfries and Galloway Primary Care National Health Service Trust (Establishment) Order 1998**
Art.3, substituted: SSI 1999/96 Art.2
Art.4, amended: SSI 1999/96 Art.2

2715. **Ayrshire and Arran Primary Care National Health Service Trust (Establishment) Order 1998**
Art.3, substituted: SSI 1999/165 Art.2
Art.4, amended: SSI 1999/165 Art.2

2716. **Argyll and Clyde Acute Hospitals National Health Service Trust (Establishment) Order 1998**
Art.3, substituted: SI 1999/1115 Art.2, SSI 1999/77 Art.2
Art.4, amended: SSI 1999/77 Art.2

2717. **Lothian University Hospitals National Health Service Trust (Establishment) Order 1998**
Art.3, substituted: SI 1999/1071 Art.3, SSI 1999/81 Art.2
Art.4, amended: SSI 1999/81 Art.2

2718. **Grampian University Hospitals National Health Service Trust (Establishment) Order 1998**
Art.3, substituted: SSI 1999/82 Art.2
Art.4, amended: SSI 1999/82 Art.2

2719. **Greater Glasgow Primary Care National Health Service Trust (Establishment) Order 1998**
Art.3, substituted: SSI 1999/87 Art.2
Art.4, amended: SSI 1999/87 Art.2

2720. **Grampian Primary Care National Health Service Trust (Establishment) Order 1998**
Art.3, substituted: SSI 1999/98 Art.2
Art.4, amended: SSI 1999/98 Art.2

2721. **Highland Primary Care National Health Service Trust (Establishment) Order 1998**
Art.3, substituted: SI 1999/1069 Art.2, SSI 1999/93 Art.2
Art.4, amended: SSI 1999/93 Art.2
Sch., added: SI 1999/1069 Art.2, Sch.

2722. **Highland Acute Hospitals National Health Service Trust (Establishment) Order 1998**
Art.3, substituted: SSI 1999/80 Art.2
Art.4, amended: SSI 1999/80 Art.2

2723. **Fife Acute Hospitals National Health Service Trust (Establishment) Order 1998**
Art.3, substituted: SSI 1999/89 Art.2, SSI 1999/198 Art.2
Art.4, amended: SSI 1999/89 Art.2, SSI 1999/198 Art.2

2724. **Lanarkshire Acute Hospitals National Health Service Trust (Establishment) Order 1998**
Art.3, substituted: SSI 1999/78 Art.2
Art.4, amended: SSI 1999/78 Art.2

NO.
1998—cont.

2725. **Forth Valley Acute Hospitals National Health Service Trust (Establishment) Order 1998**
Art.3, substituted: SSI 1999/79 Art.2
Art.4, amended: SSI 1999/79 Art.2

2728. **Tayside University Hospitals National Health Service Trust (Establishment) Order 1998**
Art.3, substituted: SSI 1999/84 Art.2
Art.4, amended: SSI 1999/84 Art.2

2729. **North Glasgow University Hospitals National Health Service Trust (Establishment) Order 1998**
Art.3, substituted: SSI 1999/86 Art.2
Art.4, amended: SSI 1999/86 Art.2

2730. **South Glasgow University Hospitals National Health Service Trust (Establishment) Order 1998**
Art.3, substituted: SSI 1999/85 Art.2
Art.4, amended: SSI 1999/85 Art.2

2731. **West Lothian Healthcare National Health Service Trust (Establishment) Order 1998**
Art.3, substituted: SSI 1999/91 Art.2
Art.4, amended: SSI 1999/91 Art.2

2733. **Renfrewshire and Inverclyde Primary Care National Health Service Trust (Establishment) Order 1998**
Art.3, substituted: SSI 1999/97 Art.2
Art.4, amended: SSI 1999/97 Art.2

2734. **Lomond and Argyll Primary Care National Health Service Trust (Establishment) Order 1998**
Art.3, substituted: SSI 1999/99 Art.2
Art.4, amended: SSI 1999/99 Art.2

2735. **Ayrshire and Arran Acute Hospitals National Health Service Trust (Establishment) Order 1998**
Art.3, substituted: SSI 1999/197 Art.2
Art.4, amended: SSI 1999/197 Art.2

2745. **A205 Trunk Road (Lewisham) Red Route Experimental Traffic Order 1998**
Sch.1 Item 3, substituted: SI 1999/1991 Art.3
Sch.1 Item 5, substituted: SI 1999/1991 Art.4
Sch.1 Item 5A, added: SI 1999/1991 Art.4
Sch.1 Item 5B, added: SI 1999/1991 Art.4
Sch.1 Item 5C, added: SI 1999/1991 Art.4
Sch.1 Item 5D, added: SI 1999/1991 Art.4
Sch.1 Item 5E, added: SI 1999/1991 Art.4
Sch.4 Item 6, substituted: SI 1999/1991 Art.5
Sch.4 Item 7, substituted: SI 1999/1991 Art.6
Sch.4 Item 8, revoked: SI 1999/1991 Art.7
Sch.4 Item 15, substituted: SI 1999/1991 Art.8
Sch.4 Item 17, substituted: SI 1999/1991 Art.9

2760. **Plant Protection Products (Amendment) Regulations 1998**
revoked: SI 1999/1228 Reg.4
Reg.2, revoked: SI 1999/1228 Reg.4
Reg.3, revoked: SI 1999/1228 Reg.4

2763. **Education (School Government) (Transition to New Framework) Regulations 1998**
amended: SI 1999/1287 Reg.6
applied: SI 1999/362 Reg.3, SI 1999/2242 Reg.38
referred to: SI 1999/362 Reg.57, SI 1999/2163 Reg.38
Reg.2, amended: SI 1999/362 Reg.61
Reg.6, amended: SI 1999/362 Reg.61
Reg.7, amended: SI 1999/362 Reg.61
Reg.10, amended: SI 1999/362 Reg.61
Reg.10, referred to: SI 1999/1287 Reg.6
Reg.12, amended: SI 1999/362 Reg.59, Reg.61

NO.

1998—cont.

2763. Education (School Government) (Transition to New Framework) Regulations 1998—
cont.

Reg.13, amended: SI 1999/2163 Reg.58, Sch.7 para.3, SI 1999/2242 Reg.58, Sch.8 para.3

Reg.13, applied: SI 1999/2163 Reg.14, Reg.58, Sch.7 para.4, SI 1999/2242 Reg.14

Reg.13, referred to: SI 1999/2163 Reg.58, Sch.7 para.4, SI 1999/2242 Reg.58, Sch.8 para.4

Reg.14, amended: SI 1999/362 Reg.61

Reg.16, amended: SI 1999/2163 Reg.58, Sch.7 para.10

Reg.16, revoked (in part): SI 1999/2163 Reg.58, Sch.7 para.10

Reg.18, applied: SI 1999/2163 Reg.58, Sch.7 para.1, SI 1999/2242 Reg.4, Reg.58, Sch.8 para.1

Reg.18, referred to: SI 1999/2163 Reg.4

Reg.19, amended: SI 1999/362 Reg.61

Reg.19, applied: SI 1999/2163 Reg.58, Sch.7 para.4, SI 1999/2242 Reg.58, Sch.8 para.7, SI 1999/2323 Art.5, Sch.7 para.2

Reg.19, referred to: SI 1999/2163 Reg.58, Sch.7 para.1, Sch.7 para.7, SI 1999/2242 Reg.58, Sch.8 para.1

Reg.20, amended: SI 1999/362 Reg.61

Reg.20, referred to: SI 1999/2163 Reg.14, Reg.58, Sch.7 para.4, SI 1999/2242 Reg.58, Sch.8 para.4

Reg.21, amended: SI 1999/1287 Reg.6

Reg.22, revoked (in part): SI 1999/2163 Reg.58, Sch.7 para.6, SI 1999/2242 Reg.58, Sch.8 para.6

Reg.23, amended: SI 1999/362 Reg.57

Reg.23, revoked (in part): SI 1999/2163 Reg.58, Sch.7 para.2, SI 1999/2242 Reg.58, Sch.8 para.2

Sch.1 para.1, amended: SI 1999/362 Reg.61

Sch.2, amended: SI 1999/1287 Reg.6

Sch.2 para.4, amended: SI 1999/1287 Reg.6

Sch.2 para.5, substituted: SI 1999/1287 Reg.6

Sch.3, revoked (in part): SI 1999/2163 Reg.58, Sch.7 para.10

Sch.5 para.1, amended: SI 1999/362 Reg.61

Sch.6, revoked (in part): SI 1999/2163 Reg.58, Sch.7 para.2, SI 1999/2242 Reg.58, Sch.8 para.2

Sch.6 para.3, amended: SI 1999/362 Reg.61

2769. Magistrates' Courts Committees (West Yorkshire) Amalgamation Order 1998

Sch. para.2, amended: SI 1999/152 Art.3

Sch. para.3, amended: SI 1999/152 Art.4

Sch. para.4, amended: SI 1999/152 Art.5

Sch. para.5, amended: SI 1999/152 Art.6

Sch. para.6, amended: SI 1999/152 Art.7

2780. Social Security Act 1998 (Commencement No.2) Order 1998

Art.3, referred to: SI 1999/1510 Art.48

2798. Transfer of Prisoners (Restricted Transfers) (Channel Islands and Isle of Man) Order 1998

Sch.1 para.2, amended: SI 1998/2798 Art.3, Sch.2 para.2, Sch.2 para.3

Sch.1 para.2, applied: SI 1998/2798 Art.3, Sch.2 para.3

Sch.1 para.3, amended: SI 1998/2798 Art.3, Sch.2 para.2, Sch.2 para.4

Sch.1 para.3, applied: SI 1998/2798 Art.3, Sch.2 para.4

Sch.1 para.4, amended: SI 1998/2798 Art.3, Sch.2 para.2, Sch.2 para.5

NO.

1998—cont.

2798. Transfer of Prisoners (Restricted Transfers) (Channel Islands and Isle of Man) Order 1998—*cont.*

Sch.1 para.4, applied: SI 1998/2798 Art.3, Sch.2 para.5

Sch.1 para.5, amended: SI 1998/2798 Art.3, Sch.2 para.6

Sch.1 para.5, applied: SI 1998/2798 Art.3, Sch.2 para.6, SI 1999/1748 Art.4, Sch.2 para.4

Sch.1 para.5, referred to: SI 1999/1748 Art.4, Art.8, Sch.2 para.4, Sch.3 para.3, Sch.3 para.7

Sch.1 para.6, amended: SI 1998/2798 Art.3, Sch.2 para.7

Sch.1 para.6, applied: SI 1998/2798 Art.3, Sch.2 para.7, SI 1999/1748 Art.4, Sch.2 para.4

Sch.1 para.6, referred to: SI 1999/1748 Art.4, Art.8, Sch.2 para.4, Sch.3 para.4, Sch.3 para.8

Sch.1 para.7, amended: SI 1998/2798 Art.3, Sch.2 para.8

Sch.1 para.7, applied: SI 1998/2798 Art.3, Sch.2 para.8, SI 1999/1748 Art.4, Sch.2 para.4

Sch.1 para.7, referred to: SI 1999/1748 Art.4, Art.8, Sch.2 para.4, Sch.3 para.3

Sch.1 para.12, referred to: SI 1999/1748 Art.8, Sch.4 para.4

Sch.1 para.15, referred to: SI 1999/1748 Art.8, Sch.4 para.5

Sch.1 para.18, referred to: SI 1999/1748 Art.8, Sch.4 para.3

2802. Edinburgh Healthcare National Health Service Trust (Establishment) Amendment Order 1998

revoked: SI 1999/1070 Art.2, Sch.2

Art.2, revoked: SI 1999/1070 Art.2, Sch.2

2825. Social Security (New Deal Pilot) Regulations 1998

applied: SI 1999/779 Art.2, Sch.

Reg.3, referred to: SI 1999/3156 Reg.19

Reg.4, referred to: SI 1999/3156 Reg.19

Reg.5, referred to: SI 1999/3156 Reg.19

Reg.11, amended: SI 1999/976 Reg.2

Reg.12, amended: SI 1999/976 Reg.2

Reg.14, amended: SI 1999/2554 Reg.3

Reg.16, amended: SI 1999/976 Reg.2

Reg.17, amended: SI 1999/976 Reg.2

Reg.18, added: SI 1999/976 Reg.2

2857. Merchant Shipping and Fishing Vessels (Manual Handling Operations) Regulations 1998

Reg.1, amended: SI 1999/2205 Reg.18

Reg.13, amended: SI 1999/2205 Reg.18

2869. Northern Ireland (Sentences) Act 1998 (Specified Organisations) (No.2) Order 1998

revoked: SI 1999/1152 Art.3

Art.2, revoked: SI 1999/1152 Art.3

Art.3, revoked: SI 1999/1152 Art.3

2876. Education (Grammar School Ballots) Regulations 1998

Reg.4, referred to: SI 1999/2103 Reg.5

Reg.6, amended: SI 1999/2102 Reg.3

Reg.6, applied: SI 1999/2102 Reg.3

Reg.7, referred to: SI 1999/2103 Reg.5

Reg.9, referred to: SI 1999/2103 Reg.5

Reg.10, applied: SI 1999/2103 Reg.4

Reg.18, amended: SI 1999/2103 Reg.6

Sch.2, amended: SI 1999/2102 Reg.3

Sch.2, applied: SI 1999/2102 Reg.3

NO.

1998—cont.

1998—cont.

2876. Education (Grammar School Ballots) Regulations 1998—cont.
Sch.3, amended: SI 1999/2102 Reg.3
Sch.3, applied: SI 1999/2102 Reg.3

2878. Income Support (General) (Standard Interest Rate Amendment) (No.2) Regulations 1998
revoked: SI 1999/123 Reg.3
Reg.1, revoked: SI 1999/123 Reg.3
Reg.2, revoked: SI 1999/123 Reg.3
Reg.3, revoked: SI 1999/123 Reg.3

2887. Scottish Further Education Funding Council (Establishment) (Scotland) Order 1998
Art.7, revoked (in part): SI 1999/1820 Art.4, Sch.2 para.166
Art.9, amended: SI 1999/1820 Art.4, Sch.2 para.166
Art.10, amended: SI 1999/1820 Art.4, Sch.2 para.166
Art.10, referred to: SI 1999/1820 Art.4, Sch.2 para.166

2922. Pesticides (Maximum Residue Levels in Crops, Food and Feeding Stuffs) (Amendment) Regulations 1998
revoked (in part): SI 1999/3483 Reg.7, Sch.4
Reg.3, revoked (in part): SI 1999/3483 Reg.7, Sch.4
Reg.4, revoked (in part): SI 1999/3483 Reg.7, Sch.4
Reg.5, revoked (in part): SI 1999/3483 Reg.7, Sch.4

2958. Severn Bridges Tolls Order 1998
revoked: SI 1999/3252 Art.3
Art.1, revoked: SI 1999/3252 Art.3
Art.3, revoked: SI 1999/3252 Art.3

2973. Statistics of Trade (Customs and Excise) (Amendment) Regulations 1998
revoked: SI 1999/3269 Reg.3
Reg.2, revoked: SI 1999/3269 Reg.3
Reg.3, revoked: SI 1999/3269 Reg.3

2999. Civil Aviation (Route Charges for Navigation Services) (Second Amendment) Regulations 1998
revoked: SI 1999/3260 Reg.2, Sch.1
Reg.2, revoked: SI 1999/3260 Reg.2, Sch.1

3049. Rules of the Supreme Court (Amendment No.2) 1998
r.3, see *Plumb v Ayres* Times, May 11, 1999 (CA), Brooke, L.J.

3067. Curfew Order (Responsible Officer) (Amendment) Order 1998
revoked: SI 1999/3155 Art.6
Art.2, revoked: SI 1999/3155 Art.6

3069. Leicestershire and Rutland Healthcare National Health Service Trust (Establishment) Order 1998
Art.2, amended: SI 1999/1825 Art.2

3085. Medicines (Pharmacies) (Applications for Registration and Fees) Amendment Regulations 1998
revoked: SI 1999/3295 Reg.3
Reg.2, revoked: SI 1999/3295 Reg.3
Reg.3, revoked: SI 1999/3295 Reg.3

3132. Civil Procedure Rules 1998
see *Breeze v John Stacey & Sons Ltd* Times, July 8, 1999 (CA), Peter Gibson, L.J.; see *Federal Bank of the Middle East v Hadkinson (Security for Costs) (No.2)* Times, December 7, 1999 (CA), Mummery, L.J.; see *Jones v Telford and Wrekin Council* Times, July 29, 1999 (CA), Lord Woolf, M.R.; see *Mars UK Ltd v Teknowledge Ltd (No.2)* [1999] 2 Costs

3132. Civil Procedure Rules 1998—cont.
see—cont.
L.R. 44 (Ch D), Jacob, J.; see *Matthews v Tarmac Bricks & Tiles Ltd* Times, July 1, 1999 (CA), Lord Woolf, M.R.; see *Practice Direction (CA: Consolidation: Notice of Consolidation)* [1999] 2 All E.R. 490 (CA), Lord Woolf, M.R.; see *Practice Directions (Civil Procedure Rules)* [1999] 1 W.L.R. 1124 (Sup Ct), Lord Bingham of Cornhill, L.C.J.; see *Practice Direction (Fam Div: Family Proceedings: Costs)* Times, May 4, 1999 (Fam Div), Lord Irvine of Lairg; see *R v Secretary of State for the Environment, Transport and the Regions Ex p. O'Byrne* Times, November 12, 1999 (QBD), Hooper, J.; see *RRH Tomlinssons (Trowbridge) Ltd v Secretary of State for the Environment, Transport and the Regions* [1999] 2 B.C.L.C. 760 (CA), Mummery L.J.; see *Shikari v Malik* Times, May 20, 1999 (CA), Henry, L.J.; see *St Albans Court Ltd v Daldorch Estates Ltd* Times, May 24, 1999 (Ch D), Arden, J.; see *Thermos Ltd v Aladdin Sales and Marketing Ltd* Independent, December 13, 1999 (C.S.) (Pat Ct), Jacob, J.
Part 3, see *Practice Direction (QBD: Vibration White Finger Actions) (No.3)* Times, August 5, 1999 (QBD), Lord Bingham of Cornhill, L.C.J.
Part 21, see *Beatham v Carlisle Hospitals NHS Trust* Times, May 20, 1999 (QBD), Buckley, J.
Part 25, amended: SI 1999/1008 r.8
Part 30, see *Practice Direction (QBD: Vibration White Finger Actions) (No.3)* Times, August 5, 1999 (QBD), Lord Bingham of Cornhill, L.C.J.
Part 36, see *Little v George Little Sebire & Co (Enhanced Interest)* Times, November 17, 1999 (QBD), David Foskett Q.C.
Part 43, applied: SI 1999/1012 r.4
Part 44, see *Practice Note (CA: Assessment of Costs)* [1999] 1 W.L.R. 871 (CA), Lord Woolf, M.R.
Part 44, applied: SI 1999/1012 r.4
Part 47, applied: SI 1999/1012 r.4
Part 48, applied: SI 1999/1012 r.4
Part 49, see *Practice Note (Ch D: Civil Procedure Rules)* Times, May 4, 1999 (Ch D), Neuberger, J.
r.1, see *Little v George Little Sebire & Co (Enhanced Interest)* Times, November 17, 1999 (QBD), David Foskett Q.C.; see *Morris v Banque Arab et Internationale d'Investissement SA* Times, December 23, 1999 (Ch D), Neuberger, J.; see *Natwest Lombard Factors Ltd v Arbis* Times, December 10, 1999 (Ch D), Hart, J.; see *North Holdings Ltd v Southern Tropics Ltd* [1999] 2 B.C.L.C. 625 (CA), Aldous, L.J.
r.1.1(e), see *Stephenson (SBJ) Ltd v Mandy* Times, July 21, 1999 (CA), Nourse, L.J.
r.1.1(2)(a), see *Maltez v Lewis* Times, May 4, 1999 (Ch D), Neuberger, J.
r.1.4(2), see *North Holdings Ltd v Southern Tropics Ltd* [1999] B.C.C. 746 (CA), Aldous, L.J.
r.2.1, amended: SI 1999/1008 r.3
r.3, see *Practice Note (Ch D: Civil Procedure Rules)* Times, May 4, 1999 (Ch D), Neuberger, J.
r.3.1, amended: SI 1999/1008 r.4
r.3.1(2)(a), see *Mealey Horgan Plc v Horgan* Times, July 6, 1999 (QBD), Buckley, J.

NO.

1998—cont.

3132. Civil Procedure Rules 1998—cont.

r.3.1(2)(c), see *Baron v Lovell* [1999] C.P.L.R. 630 (CA), Brooke, L.J.

r.3.1(2)(m), see *Mullan v Birmingham City Council* Times, July 29, 1999 (QBD), David Foskett Q.C.

r.3.3, see *Practice Direction (Ch D: Interim Applications to Chancery Division)* [1999] B.C.C. 846 (Ch D), Neuberger, J.

r.3.4(2)(c), see *Biguzzi v Rank Leisure Plc* [1999] 1 W.L.R. 1926 (CA), Lord Woolf, M.R.

r.6.6, see *Tadema Holdings Ltd v Ferguson* [1999] E.G.C.S. 138 (CA), Peter Gibson, L.J.

r.13.4, amended: SI 1999/1008 r.5

r.13.19, see *Morris v Banque Arab et Internationale d'Investissement SA* Times, December 23, 1999 (Ch D), Neuberger, J.

r.16.3, amended: SI 1999/1008 r.6

r.23.1, see *Cripps v Heritage Distribution Corp* Times, November 10, 1999 (CA), Kennedy, L.J.

r.24.2, see *Swain v Hillman* Times, November 4, 1999 (CA), Lord Woolf, M.R.

r.24.3, amended: SI 1999/1008 r.7

r.25.11, added: SI 1999/1008 r.8

r.27.14, amended: SI 1999/1008 r.9

r.29.3(2), see *Baron v Lovell* [1999] C.P.L.R. 630 (CA), Brooke, L.J.

r.32.1, see *Grobbelaar v Sun Newspapers Ltd* Times, August 12, 1999 (CA), Potter, L.J.

r.32.4, see *McPhilemy v Times Newspapers Ltd* [1999] 3 All E.R. 775 (CA), Lord Woolf, M.R.

r.32.10, see *Mealey Horgan Plc v Horgan* Times, July 6, 1999 (QBD), Buckley, J.

r.33.3, amended: SI 1999/1008 r.10

r.34, see *Harrison v Bloom Camillin* Independent, June 28, 1999 (C.S.) (Ch D), Neuberger, J.

r.34.13, amended: SI 1999/1008 r.11

r.34.14, amended: SI 1999/1008 r.11

r.36, see *Little v George Little Sebire & Co (Enhanced Interest)* Times, November 17, 1999 (QBD), David Foskett Q.C.

r.36.4, amended: SI 1999/1008 r.12

r.36.6, amended: SI 1999/1008 r.13

r.36.17, amended: SI 1999/1008 r.14

r.36.20, amended: SI 1999/1008 r.15

r.38, see *Stanway v Attorney General* Times, November 25, 1999 (Ch D), Lloyd, J.

r.42.2, amended: SI 1999/1008 r.16

r.43.2, amended: SI 1999/1012 r.4

r.44.3, see *Customs and Excise Commissioners v Anchor Foods Ltd (No.3)* Times, September 28, 1999 (Ch D), Neuberger, J.

r.44.3, referred to: SI 1999/1012 r.4

r.44.9, amended: SI 1999/1008 r.17

r.47.4, see *Practice Direction (Fam Div: Family Proceedings: Allocation of Costs)* [1999] 1 W.L.R. 1128 (Fam Div), Lord Irvine of Lairg

r.47.11, amended: SI 1999/1008 r.18

r.47.14, amended: SI 1999/1008 r.19

r.47.16, amended: SI 1999/1008 r.20

r.47.24, amended: SI 1999/1008 r.21

r.47.25, amended: SI 1999/1008 r.22

r.48, see *General Mediterranean Holdings SA v Patel* [1999] 3 All E.R. 673 (QBD (Comm Ct)), Toulson, J.

r.48.2, see *National Justice Compania Naviera SA v Prudential Assurance Co Ltd (The Ikarian Reefer) (No.2)* [1999] 2 All E.R. (Comm) 673 (CA), Waller, L.J.

r.48.4, amended: SI 1999/1008 r.23

r.48.8, amended: SI 1999/1008 r.24

NO.

1998—cont.

3132. Civil Procedure Rules 1998—cont.

r.48.10, amended: SI 1999/1008 r.25

r.59, see *Natwest Lombard Factors Ltd v Arbis* Times, December 10, 1999 (Ch D), Hart, J.

Sch.1, see *Clark v Chief Constable of Cleveland* Times, May 13, 1999 (CA), Roch, L.J.

Sch.1 Ord.11, amended: SI 1999/1008 r.26

Sch.1 Ord.17, amended: SI 1999/1008 r.27

Sch.1 Ord.30, amended: SI 1999/1008 r.28

Sch.1 Ord.31, amended: SI 1999/1008 r.29

Sch.1 Ord.44, amended: SI 1999/1008 r.30

Sch.1 Ord.48, amended: SI 1999/1008 r.31

Sch.1 Ord.52, amended: SI 1999/1008 r.32

Sch.1 Ord.53, amended: SI 1999/1008 r.33, r.63

Sch.1 Ord.54, amended: SI 1999/1008 r.62

Sch.1 Ord.55, amended: SI 1999/1008 r.34, r.62

Sch.1 Ord.56, amended: SI 1999/1008 r.62, r.63

Sch.1 Ord.57, amended: SI 1999/1008 r.35

Sch.1 Ord.58, amended: SI 1999/1008 r.36

Sch.1 Ord.59, amended: SI 1999/1008 r.37, r.62

Sch.1 Ord.59, referred to: SI 1999/2689 Art.3

Sch.1 Ord.71, amended: SI 1999/1008 r.38, r.62

Sch.1 Ord.77, amended: SI 1999/1008 r.39

Sch.1 Ord.79, amended: SI 1999/1008 r.40, r.62

Sch.1 Ord.79, revoked (in part): SI 1999/1008 r.41

Sch.1 Ord.81, amended: SI 1999/1008 r.42, r.43

Sch.1 Ord.82, amended: SI 1999/1008 r.44

Sch.1 Ord.91, amended: SI 1999/1008 r.45

Sch.1 Ord.93, amended: SI 1999/1008 r.46, r.62

Sch.1 Ord.94, amended: SI 1999/1008 r.47, r.48, r.63

Sch.1 Ord.95, amended: SI 1999/1008 r.49

Sch.1 Ord.96, amended: SI 1999/1008 r.50

Sch.1 Ord.97, amended: SI 1999/1008 r.51

Sch.1 Ord.97, revoked (in part): SI 1999/1008 r.51

Sch.1 Ord.98, amended: SI 1999/1008 r.52

Sch.1 Ord.99, revoked (in part): SI 1999/1008 r.53

Sch.1 Ord.101, amended: SI 1999/1008 r.54

Sch.1 Ord.106, amended: SI 1999/1008 r.62

Sch.1 Ord.109, amended: SI 1999/1008 r.55, r.62

Sch.1 Ord.110, amended: SI 1999/1008 r.56

Sch.1 Ord.112, amended: SI 1999/1008 r.57

Sch.1 Ord.113, amended: SI 1999/1008 r.58

Sch.1 Ord.114, amended: SI 1999/1008 r.59

Sch.1 Ord.115, amended: SI 1999/1008 r.60, r.62

Sch.1 Ord.116, added: SI 1999/1008 r.61, Appendix 1

Sch.2 Ord.6, amended: SI 1999/1008 r.64

Sch.2 Ord.13, amended: SI 1999/1008 r.65

Sch.2 Ord.24, amended: SI 1999/1008 r.66

Sch.2 Ord.27, amended: SI 1999/1008 r.67

Sch.2 Ord.28, amended: SI 1999/1008 r.68

Sch.2 Ord.42, amended: SI 1999/1008 r.69

Sch.2 Ord.43, amended: SI 1999/1008 r.70

Sch.2 Ord.43, revoked (in part): SI 1999/1008 r.70

Sch.2 Ord.48B, amended: SI 1999/1008 r.71

Sch.2 Ord.48D, added: SI 1999/1008 r.72, Appendix 2

NO.

3132. Civil Procedure Rules 1998—*cont.*
Sch.2 Ord.49, amended: SI 1999/1008 r.73
Sch.2 Ord.49, revoked (in part): SI 1999/1008 r.73

3160. County of Swansea (Electoral Arrangements) Order 1998
revoked: SI 1998/3261 Art.4

3162. Fair Employment and Treatment (Northern Ireland) Order 1998
Sch.3, revoked (in part): SI 1999/2790 (NI.9) Art.40, Sch.9 Part 10
Sch.4 para.6, referred to: SI 1999/2204 Art.2, Art.3

3170. Telecommunications (Data Protection and Privacy) (Direct Marketing) Regulations 1998
referred to: SI 1999/2093 Reg.34, Sch.3 para.5, SI 1999/2450 Sch.1 para.18.4
revoked: SI 1999/2093 Reg.3
Reg.3, revoked: SI 1999/2093 Reg.3
Reg.6, referred to: SI 1999/2450 Sch.1 para.17.4
Reg.7, referred to: SI 1999/2093 Reg.34, Sch.3 para.3
Reg.7, revoked: SI 1999/2093 Reg.3
Reg.9, applied: SI 1999/2093 Reg.34, Sch.3 para.3
Reg.9, referred to: SI 1999/2093 Reg.34, Sch.3 para.3
Reg.9, revoked: SI 1999/2093 Reg.3
Reg.10, amended: SI 1999/2093 Reg.3, Sch.1 Part I
Reg.10, referred to: SI 1999/2093 Reg.34, Sch.3 para.3
Reg.10, revoked: SI 1999/2093 Reg.3
Reg.13, applied: SI 1999/2093 Reg.34, Sch.3 para.4
Reg.13, referred to: SI 1999/2093 Reg.34, Sch.3 para.4
Reg.13, revoked: SI 1999/2093 Reg.3
Sch.1 para.1, revoked: SI 1999/2093 Reg.3
Sch.1 para.2, revoked: SI 1999/2093 Reg.3
Sch.2 para.1, revoked: SI 1999/2093 Reg.3
Sch.2 para.2, revoked: SI 1999/2093 Reg.3
Sch.2 para.3, revoked: SI 1999/2093 Reg.3
Sch.2 para.4, revoked: SI 1999/2093 Reg.3
Sch.2 para.5, revoked: SI 1999/2093 Reg.3
Sch.2 para.6, revoked: SI 1999/2093 Reg.3
Sch.2 para.7, revoked: SI 1999/2093 Reg.3

3171. Registration of Births, Deaths and Marriages (Fees) Order 1998
revoked: SI 1999/3311 Art.3
Art.2, revoked: SI 1999/3311 Art.3
Art.3, revoked: SI 1999/3311 Art.3
Sch., revoked: SI 1999/3311 Art.3
Sch., amended: SI 1999/1303 Art.2
Sch., revoked: SI 1999/3311 Art.3

3172. School Standards and Framework Act 1998 (Proposals under section 211 of the Education Act 1996) (Transitional Provisions) Regulations 1998
Reg.2, applied: SI 1999/2323 Art.17

3174. Individual Savings Account (Amendment) Regulations 1998
Reg.13, amended: SI 1998/1871 Reg.25

3175. Corporation Tax (Instalment Payments) Regulations 1998
applied: SI 1999/358 Reg.21
Reg.9, amended: SI 1999/1929 Reg.3
Reg.12, amended: SI 1999/1929 Reg.4

NO.

3199. Land Registration Fees Order 1998
revoked: SI 1999/2254 Art.1
Art.2, revoked: SI 1999/2254 Art.1
Art.4, revoked: SI 1999/2254 Art.1
Art.10, revoked: SI 1999/2254 Art.1
Art.14, revoked: SI 1999/2254 Art.1
Sch.3 Part I, revoked: SI 1999/2254 Art.1
Sch.3 Part II, revoked: SI 1999/2254 Art.1
Sch.3 Part III, revoked: SI 1999/2254 Art.1
Sch.3 Part IV, revoked: SI 1999/2254 Art.1
Sch.4, revoked: SI 1999/2254 Art.1

3207. Road Traffic (Permitted Parking Area and Special Parking Area) (Borough of Luton) Order 1998
applied: SI 1999/1918 Reg.20
referred to: SI 1999/1918
Sch.1 para.4, substituted: SI 1999/1666 Art.3

3212. A13 Trunk Road (Tower Hamlets) Red Route Experimental Traffic Order 1998
Sch.3A Item 4, substituted: SI 1999/1091 Art.3, SI 1999/1974 Art.3
Sch.3A Item 6, substituted: SI 1999/1091 Art.3
Sch.4 Item 8, substituted: SI 1999/1091 Art.4, SI 1999/1974 Art.4
Sch.4 Item 8A, added: SI 1999/1091 Art.5
Sch.4 Item 19, substituted: SI 1999/1091 Art.4, SI 1999/1974 Art.4
Sch.4 Item 19A, added: SI 1999/1091 Art.5

3237. Teaching and Higher Education Act 1998 (Commencement No.4 and Transitional Provisions) Order 1998
Art.3, referred to: SI 1999/1494 Reg.7
Art.4, referred to: SI 1999/1494 Reg.7

3260. Education (School Performance Information) (England) (Amendment) Regulations 1998
revoked: SI 1999/1178 Reg.4 (with savings)
Reg.2, revoked: SI 1999/1178 Reg.4 (with savings)
Reg.3, revoked: SI 1999/1178 Reg.4 (with savings)
Reg.4, revoked: SI 1999/1178 Reg.4 (with savings)
Reg.5, revoked: SI 1999/1178 Reg.4 (with savings)
Sch., revoked: SI 1999/1178 Reg.4 (with savings)

3315. Swansea (1999) National Health Service Trust (Establishment) Order 1998
Art.1, amended: SI 1999/1321 Art.2
Art.2, amended: SI 1999/1321 Art.2

9. Motor Vehicles (Construction and Use) (Amendment) Regulations (Northern Ireland) 1999
revoked: SR 1999/454 Reg.126, Sch.19

10. Curfew Order (Responsible Officer) (Amendment) Order 1999
revoked: SI 1999/3155 Art.6
Art.2, revoked: SI 1999/3155 Art.6

13. Confined Spaces Regulations (Northern Ireland) 1999
amended: SR 1999/150 Reg.2, Sch.

35. Income Support (General) (Standard Interest Rate Amendment) Regulations (Northern Ireland) 1999
revoked: SR 1999/70 Reg.3 (with saving)

NO.

1999—cont.

45. **Foyle Area (Licensing of Fishing Engines) (Amendment) Regulations 1999**
revoked: SR 1999/485 Reg.3

57. **Plant Protection Products (Amendment) Regulations (Northern Ireland) 1999**
revoked: SR 1999/282 Reg.3

68. **Hill Livestock (Compensatory Allowances) (Amendment) Regulations (Northern Ireland) 1999**
revoked: SR 1999/497 Reg.15 (with savings)

70. **Income Support (General) (Standard Interest Rate Amendment No.2) Regulations (Northern Ireland) 1999**
revoked: SR 1999/144 (with saving)

72. **Motor Vehicles (Driving Licences) (Amendment) Regulations 1999**
revoked: SI 1999/2864 Reg.2, Sch.1
Reg.3, revoked: SI 1999/2864 Reg.2, Sch.1
Reg.4, revoked: SI 1999/2864 Reg.2, Sch.1
Reg.5, revoked: SI 1999/2864 Reg.2, Sch.1
Reg.6, revoked: SI 1999/2864 Reg.2, Sch.1
Reg.7, revoked: SI 1999/2864 Reg.2, Sch.1
Sch.1, revoked: SI 1999/2864 Reg.2, Sch.1
Sch.2, revoked: SI 1999/2864 Reg.2, Sch.1

93. **Spreadable Fats (Marketing Standards) (Amendment) Regulations (Northern Ireland) 1999**
revoked: SR 1999/383 Reg.9, Sch.2

101. **Financing of Maintained Schools Regulations 1999**
Reg.11, applied: SI 1999/451 Reg.1
Reg.11, referred to: SI 1999/486 Reg.2
Sch.1 para.1, applied: SI 1999/138 Reg.17
Sch.1 para.2, applied: SI 1999/138 Reg.17
Sch.1 para.3, applied: SI 1999/138 Reg.17
Sch.1 para.4, applied: SI 1999/138 Reg.17
Sch.1 para.5, applied: SI 1999/138 Reg.17
Sch.1 para.6, applied: SI 1999/138 Reg.17
Sch.1 para.7, applied: SI 1999/138 Reg.17
Sch.1 para.8, applied: SI 1999/138 Reg.17
Sch.1 para.9, applied: SI 1999/138 Reg.17
Sch.1 para.10, applied: SI 1999/138 Reg.17
Sch.1 para.11, applied: SI 1999/138 Reg.17
Sch.1 para.12, applied: SI 1999/138 Reg.17
Sch.1 para.13, applied: SI 1999/138 Reg.17
Sch.1 para.14, applied: SI 1999/138 Reg.17
Sch.1 para.15, applied: SI 1999/138 Reg.17
Sch.1 para.16, applied: SI 1999/138 Reg.17
Sch.1 para.17, applied: SI 1999/138 Reg.17
Sch.1 para.18, applied: SI 1999/138 Reg.17
Sch.1 para.19, applied: SI 1999/138 Reg.17
Sch.1 para.20, applied: SI 1999/138 Reg.17
Sch.1 para.21, applied: SI 1999/138 Reg.17
Sch.1 para.22, applied: SI 1999/138 Reg.17
Sch.1 para.23, applied: SI 1999/138 Reg.17
Sch.1 para.24, applied: SI 1999/138 Reg.17
Sch.1 para.25, applied: SI 1999/138 Reg.17
Sch.1 para.26, applied: SI 1999/138 Reg.17
Sch.1 para.27, applied: SI 1999/138 Reg.17
Sch.1 para.28, applied: SI 1999/138 Reg.17
Sch.1 para.29, applied: SI 1999/138 Reg.17
Sch.1 para.30, applied: SI 1999/138 Reg.17
Sch.1 para.31, applied: SI 1999/138 Reg.17
Sch.1 para.32, applied: SI 1999/138 Reg.17
Sch.1 para.33, applied: SI 1999/138 Reg.17
Sch.1 para.34, applied: SI 1999/138 Reg.17
Sch.1 para.35, applied: SI 1999/138 Reg.17
Sch.1 para.36, applied: SI 1999/138 Reg.17
Sch.1 para.37, applied: SI 1999/138 Reg.17
Sch.1 para.38, applied: SI 1999/138 Reg.17
Sch.1 para.39, applied: SI 1999/138 Reg.17
Sch.1 para.40, applied: SI 1999/138 Reg.17

NO.

1999—cont.

101. **Financing of Maintained Schools Regulations 1999**—*cont.*
Sch.1 para.41, applied: SI 1999/138 Reg.17
Sch.2 para.1, referred to: SI 1999/1439 Reg.18
Sch.2 para.2, referred to: SI 1999/1439 Reg.18
Sch.2 para.3, referred to: SI 1999/1439 Reg.18
Sch.2 para.4, referred to: SI 1999/1439 Reg.18
Sch.2 para.5, referred to: SI 1999/1439 Reg.18
Sch.2 para.6, referred to: SI 1999/1439 Reg.18
Sch.2 para.7, referred to: SI 1999/1439 Reg.18
Sch.2 para.8, referred to: SI 1999/1439 Reg.18
Sch.2 para.9, referred to: SI 1999/1439 Reg.18
Sch.2 para.10, referred to: SI 1999/1439 Reg.18
Sch.2 para.11, referred to: SI 1999/1439 Reg.18
Sch.2 para.12, referred to: SI 1999/1439 Reg.18
Sch.2 para.13, referred to: SI 1999/1439 Reg.18
Sch.2 para.14, referred to: SI 1999/1439 Reg.18
Sch.2 para.15, referred to: SI 1999/1439 Reg.18
Sch.2 para.20, referred to: SI 1999/1439 Reg.18
Sch.2 para.21, referred to: SI 1999/1439 Reg.18
Sch.2 para.22, referred to: SI 1999/1439 Reg.18
Sch.2 para.23, referred to: SI 1999/1439 Reg.18

103. **Motor Vehicles (Construction and Use) (Amendment No.2) Regulations (Northern Ireland) 1999**
revoked: SR 1999/454 Reg.126, Sch.19

104. **Motor Vehicles (Construction and Use) (Amendment No.3) Regulations (Northern Ireland) 1999**
revoked: SR 1999/454 Reg.126, Sch.19

123. **Income Support (General) (Standard Interest Rate Amendment) Regulations 1999**
revoked: SI 1999/371 Reg.3 (with saving)
Reg.1, revoked: SI 1999/371 Reg.3 (with saving)
Reg.2, revoked: SI 1999/371 Reg.3 (with saving)
Reg.3, revoked: SI 1999/371 Reg.3 (with saving)

124. **Education (Relevant Areas for Consultation on Admission Arrangements) Regulations 1999**
applied: SI 1999/2666 Reg.4, SI 1999/2800 Reg.4

125. **Education (Objections to Admission Arrangements) Regulations 1999**
applied: SI 1999/2800 Reg.6
Reg.2, applied: SI 1999/2666 Reg.5
Reg.2, referred to: SI 1999/2800 Reg.5

127. **Education (School Information) (Wales) (Amendment) Regulations 1999**
revoked: SI 1999/1812 Reg.2
Reg.3, revoked: SI 1999/1812 Reg.2
Reg.4, revoked: SI 1999/1812 Reg.2
Reg.5, revoked: SI 1999/1812 Reg.2
Reg.6, revoked: SI 1999/1812 Reg.2

131. **Road Traffic (Permitted Parking Area and Special Parking Area) (City of Manchester) Order 1999**
applied: SI 1999/1918 Reg.20
referred to: SI 1999/1918

NO.

144. **Income Support (General) (Standard Interest Rate Amendment No.3) Regulations (Northern Ireland) 1999**
revoked: SR 1999/187 (with saving)
160. **Petroleum (Current Model Clauses) Order 1999**
Sch.2 Cl.35, substituted: SI 1999/160 Sch.2 para.3
Sch.2 Cl.40, amended: SI 1999/160 Sch.2 para.3, Sch.2 para.4
Sch.4 Cl.22, amended: SI 1999/160 Sch.4 para.3
Sch.4 Cl.23, amended: SI 1999/160 Sch.4 para.3
Sch.5 Cl.3, amended: SI 1999/160 Sch.5 para.7
Sch.5 Cl.3, revoked (in part): SI 1999/160 Sch.5 para.7
Sch.5 Cl.4, substituted: SI 1999/160 Sch.5 para.7
Sch.5 Cl.5, substituted: SI 1999/160 Sch.5 para.7
Sch.5 Cl.7, substituted: SI 1999/160 Sch.5 para.7
Sch.5 Cl.9, amended: SI 1999/160 Sch.5 para.7
Sch.5 Cl.14, substituted: SI 1999/160 Sch.5 para.7
Sch.5 Cl.22, amended: SI 1999/160 Sch.5 para.6
Sch.5 Cl.36, substituted: SI 1999/160 Sch.5 para.3
Sch.5 Cl.41, amended: SI 1999/160 Sch.5 para.3, Sch.5 para.4
Sch.6 Cl.35, substituted: SI 1999/160 Sch.6 para.3
Sch.6 Cl.40, amended: SI 1999/160 Sch.6 para.3, Sch.6 para.4
Sch.9 Cl.10, amended: SI 1999/160 Sch.9 para.6
Sch.9 Cl.10, revoked (in part): SI 1999/160 Sch.9 para.6
Sch.9 Cl.11, revoked: SI 1999/160 Sch.9 para.6
Sch.9 Cl.12, revoked: SI 1999/160 Sch.9 para.6
Sch.9 Cl.13, revoked: SI 1999/160 Sch.9 para.6
Sch.9 Cl.30, revoked: SI 1999/160 Sch.9 para.6
Sch.9 Cl.31, amended: SI 1999/160 Sch.9 para.6
Sch.9 Cl.32, amended: SI 1999/160 Sch.9 para.6
Sch.9 Cl.34, amended: SI 1999/160 Sch.9 para.6
Sch.9 Cl.38, substituted: SI 1999/160 Sch.9 para.3
Sch.9 Cl.42, amended: SI 1999/160 Sch.9 para.6
Sch.9 Cl.43, amended: SI 1999/160 Sch.9 para.3, Sch.9 para.4
Sch.10 Cl.38, substituted: SI 1999/160 Sch.10 para.3
Sch.10 Cl.43, amended: SI 1999/160 Sch.10 para.3, Sch.10 para.4
Sch.11 Cl.12, amended: SI 1999/160 Sch.11 para.3
Sch.11 Cl.13, amended: SI 1999/160 Sch.11 para.3
Sch.11 Cl.15, amended: SI 1999/160 Sch.11 para.3
Sch.11 Cl.21, amended: SI 1999/160 Sch.11 para.3
Sch.12 Cl.29, amended: SI 1999/160 Sch.12 para.3

NO.

162. **Social Security and Child Support (Decisions and Appeals) Regulations (Northern Ireland) 1999**
Reg.1, amended: SI 1999/2588 Reg.3, Reg.4
Reg.2, amended: SI 1999/2588 Reg.5
Reg.3, amended: SI 1999/2588 Reg.6
Reg.4, amended: SI 1999/2588 Reg.7
Reg.5, amended: SI 1999/2588 Reg.8
Reg.6, amended: SI 1999/2588 Reg.9
Reg.7, amended: SI 1999/2588 Reg.10
Reg.8, amended: SI 1999/2588 Reg.11
Reg.16, amended: SI 1999/2588 Reg.12
Reg.17, substituted: SI 1999/2588 Reg.13
Reg.18, substituted: SI 1999/2588 Reg.13
Reg.19, amended: SI 1999/2588 Reg.14
Reg.20, amended: SI 1999/2588 Reg.15
Reg.21, amended: SI 1999/2588 Reg.16
Reg.22, amended: SI 1999/2588 Reg.17
Reg.26, amended: SI 1999/2588 Reg.18
Reg.28, amended: SI 1999/2588 Reg.19
Reg.30, amended: SI 1999/2588 Reg.20
Reg.31, amended: SI 1999/2588 Reg.21
Reg.33, amended: SI 1999/2588 Reg.22
Reg.34, amended: SI 1999/2588 Reg.23
Reg.40, amended: SI 1999/2588 Reg.24
Reg.41, amended: SI 1999/2588 Reg.25
Reg.58, amended: SI 1999/2588 Reg.26
166. **Legal Aid (Prescribed Panels) Regulations 1999**
Reg.2, amended: SI 1999/3378 Reg.3
Reg.5, added: SI 1999/3378 Reg.4
Reg.6, added: SI 1999/3378 Reg.4
Reg.7, added: SI 1999/3378 Reg.4
Reg.8, added: SI 1999/3378 Reg.4
186. **Electricity (Standards of Performance) (Amendment) Regulations 1999**
revoked: SR 1999/331 Reg.1
187. **Income Support (General) (Standard Interest Rate Amendment No.4) Regulations (Northern Ireland) 1999**
revoked: SR 1999/239 (with saving)
220. **National Institute for Clinical Excellence (Establishment and Constitution) Order 1999**
Art.3, amended: SI 1999/2219 Art.2
Art.4, applied: SI 1999/260 Reg.7
Art.6, added: SI 1999/2219 Art.2
228. **Local Authorities (Alteration of Requisite Calculations) (England) Regulations 1999**
Sch., applied: SI 1999/2842 Reg.2
Sch. para.1, referred to: SI 1999/2842 Reg.2
229. **Local Education Authority (Post-Compulsory Education Awards) Regulations 1999**
Reg.4, referred to: SI 1999/2168 Reg.3
233. **Legal Aid in Criminal Cases (Statement of Means) Rules (Northern Ireland) 1999**
amended: SR 1999/241 r.2
235. **Motor Vehicles (Construction and Use) (Amendment No.4) Regulations (Northern Ireland) 1999**
revoked: SR 1999/454 Reg.126, Sch.19
252. **Education (Grants for Education Support and Training) (England) Regulations 1998 (Amendment) Regulations 1999**
revoked: SI 1999/606 Reg.12
Reg.3, revoked: SI 1999/606 Reg.12
Reg.4, revoked: SI 1999/606 Reg.12
Reg.5, revoked: SI 1999/606 Reg.12
Reg.6, revoked: SI 1999/606 Reg.12

NO.   NO.

255. **Food (Animals and Animal Products from Belgium) (Emergency Control) Order (Northern Ireland) 1999**
revoked: SR 1999/335 Art.6

257. **Transport of Dangerous Goods (Safety Advisers) Regulations 1999**
applied: SI 1999/645 Reg.15, Sch.13
Reg.2, amended: SI 1999/2024 Reg.48, Sch.5 Part II
Reg.7, applied: SI 1999/645 Reg.15

259. **Motor Vehicles (Construction and Use) (Amendment No.5) Regulations (Northern Ireland) 1999**
revoked: SR 1999/454 Reg.126, Sch.19

260. **National Institute for Clinical Excellence Regulations 1999**
Reg.1, amended: SI 1999/2218 Reg.2
Reg.4, amended: SI 1999/2218 Reg.2

261. **Animal Feedingstuffs from Belgium (Control) Regulations (Northern Ireland) 1999**
revoked: SR 1999/336 Reg.7

263. **Social Security (Contributions) (Re-rating and National Insurance Fund Payments) Order 1999**
referred to: SI 1999/361 Reg.1

264. **Social Security Benefits Up-rating Order 1999**
applied: SI 1999/858 Reg.3
Art.3, referred to: SI 1999/341 Art.1

270. **Scottish Parliament (Regional Returning Officers) (Scotland) Order 1999**
revoked: SI 1999/829 Art.1
Art.2, revoked: SI 1999/829 Art.1

279. **Motor Vehicles (Construction and Use) (Amendment No.6) Regulations (Northern Ireland) 1999**
revoked: SR 1999/454 Reg.126, Sch.19

283. **Departments (Northern Ireland) Order 1999**
Art.1, applied: SI 1999/660 (NI.4) Art.1

293. **Town and Country Planning (Environmental Impact Assessment) (England and Wales) Regulations 1999**
applied: SI 1999/672 Art.2, Sch.1
referred to: SI 1999/1672 Reg.4
Reg.6, referred to: SI 1999/1672 Reg.4
Reg.27, amended: SI 1999/293 Reg.26
Sch.1, referred to: SI 1999/2228 Reg.3
Sch.2 Table, referred to: SI 1999/2228 Reg.3

296. **Feeding Stuffs (Sampling and Analysis) Regulations (Northern Ireland) 1999**
Reg.3, amended: SI 1999/1871 Reg.76
Reg.3, applied: SI 1999/1871 Reg.76
Reg.3, amended: SI 1999/1872 Reg.98
Reg.3, applied: SI 1999/1872 Reg.98
Sch.1, applied: SI 1999/1872 Reg.98
Sch.1, amended: SI 1999/1871 Reg.76
Sch.1, applied: SI 1999/1871 Reg.76
Sch.1 Part II, applied: SI 1999/1872 Reg.98
Sch.1 Part II, amended: SI 1999/1871 Reg.76
Sch.1 Part II, applied: SI 1999/1871 Reg.76, SI 1999/2325 Reg.8
Sch.1 Part III, applied: SI 1999/1871 Reg.77
Sch.1 Part III, applied: SI 1999/1872 Reg.99
Sch.1 para.1, amended: SI 1999/1872 Reg.98
Sch.1 para.1, applied: SI 1999/1872 Reg.98
Sch.1 para.10, applied: SI 1999/1872 Reg.98
Sch.2 Part I, applied: SI 1999/1871 Reg.84
Sch.2 Part II, applied: SI 1999/1872 Reg.106

299. **Food (Animals and Animal Products from Belgium) (Emergency Control) (Amendment) Order (Northern Ireland) 1999**
revoked: SR 1999/335 Art.6

305. **Provision and Use of Work Equipment Regulations (Northern Ireland) 1999**
Sch.2, amended: SI 1999/2001 Reg.29

307. **Animal Feedingstuffs from Belgium (Control) (Amendment) Regulations (Northern Ireland) 1999**
revoked: SR 1999/336 Reg.7

335. **Food (Animals and Animal Products from Belgium) (Emergency Control) (No.2) Order (Northern Ireland) 1999**
revoked: SR 1999/357 Art.6

336. **Animal Feedingstuffs from Belgium (Control) (No.2) Regulations (Northern Ireland) 1999**
revoked: SR 1999/360 Reg.7

336. **Merchant Shipping (Carriage of Cargoes) Regulations 1999**
Reg.4, applied: SI 1999/1644 Reg.11
Reg.4, referred to: SI 1999/1644 Reg.11
Reg.10, applied: SI 1999/1644 Reg.10
Reg.13, applied: SI 1999/1644 Reg.11
Reg.14, applied: SI 1999/1644 Reg.11

357. **Food (Animals and Animal Products from Belgium) (Emergency Control) (No.3) Order (Northern Ireland) 1999**
revoked: SR 1999/420 Art.6

360. **Animal Feedingstuffs from Belgium (Control) (No.3) Regulations (Northern Ireland) 1999**
revoked: SR 1999/422 Reg.7

362. **Education (Transition to New Framework) (New Schools, Groups and Miscellaneous) Regulations 1999**
amended: SI 1999/1287 Reg.6
applied: SI 1999/2163 Reg.58, Sch.7 para.9, SI 1999/2242 Reg.38, Reg.58, Sch.8 para.9
referred to: SI 1999/2163 Reg.38, Reg.58, Sch.7 para.1, SI 1999/2242 Reg.58, Sch.8 para.1
Reg.6, applied: SI 1999/704 Reg.18, SI 1999/2800 Reg.8
Reg.6, referred to: SI 1999/704 Reg.11, Reg.17
Reg.7, applied: SI 1999/362 Reg.12, Reg.29, Reg.46, Sch.2 Part I, Sch.2 Part II, Sch.2 Part IV, Sch.2 Part V
Reg.8, applied: SI 1999/362 Reg.12, Reg.29, Reg.46, Sch.2 Part IV, Sch.2 Part V
Reg.9, applied: SI 1999/362 Reg.12, Reg.29, Reg.46, Sch.2 Part IV, Sch.2 Part V
Reg.12, referred to: SI 1999/1287 Reg.6
Reg.13, applied: SI 1999/2163 Reg.58, Sch.7 para.8, SI 1999/2242 Reg.58, Sch.8 para.8, SI 1999/2262 Reg.53, SI 1999/2323 Art.5, Sch.7 para.3
Reg.13, referred to: SI 1999/2243 Reg.3, Reg.4, Reg.25, Reg.29, Reg.48, Reg.53, SI 1999/2262 Reg.4, Reg.25, Reg.29, Reg.48
Reg.14, applied: SI 1999/2242 Reg.58, Sch.8 para.5
Reg.14, referred to: SI 1999/2163 Reg.58, Sch.7 para.5
Reg.16, amended: SI 1999/2163 Reg.58, Sch.7 para.10
Reg.16, revoked (in part): SI 1999/2163 Reg.58, Sch.7 para.10
Reg.19, amended: SI 1999/1287 Reg.6
Reg.20, revoked (in part): SI 1999/2163 Reg.58, Sch.7 para.6, SI 1999/2242 Reg.58, Sch.8 para.6
Reg.21, revoked (in part): SI 1999/2163 Reg.58, Sch.7 para.2, SI 1999/2242 Reg.58, Sch.8 para.2

NO.

362. Education (Transition to New Framework) (New Schools, Groups and Miscellaneous) Regulations 1999—*cont.*

Reg.26, applied: SI 1999/362 Reg.12, Reg.29, Reg.46, Sch.2 Part I, Sch.2 Part III, Sch.2 Part IV, Sch.2 Part V

Reg.27, applied: SI 1999/362 Reg.12, Reg.29, Reg.46, Sch.2 Part III, Sch.2 Part IV, Sch.2 Part V

Reg.30, applied: SI 1999/2163 Reg.58, Sch.7 para.4, SI 1999/2323 Art.5, Sch.7 para.5

Reg.33, amended: SI 1999/2163 Reg.58, Sch.7 para.3, SI 1999/2242 Reg.58, Sch.8 para.3

Reg.33, applied: SI 1999/362 Reg.12, Reg.29, Reg.46, Sch.2 Part III, Sch.2 Part IV, Sch.2 Part V, SI 1999/2163 Reg.14, Reg.58, Sch.7 para.4

Reg.33, referred to: SI 1999/362 Reg.12, Reg.29, Reg.46, Sch.2 Part III, Sch.2 Part IV, Sch.2 Part V

Reg.35, applied: SI 1999/2242 Reg.58, Sch.8 para.5

Reg.35, referred to: SI 1999/2163 Reg.58, Sch.7 para.5

Reg.36, amended: SI 1999/2163 Reg.58, Sch.7 para.10

Reg.36, revoked (in part): SI 1999/2163 Reg.58, Sch.7 para.10

Reg.39, revoked (in part): SI 1999/2163 Reg.58, Sch.7 para.6

Reg.40, revoked (in part): SI 1999/2163 Reg.58, Sch.7 para.2, SI 1999/2242 Reg.58, Sch.8 para.2

Reg.42, amended: SI 1999/2163 Reg.58, Sch.7 para.11, SI 1999/2242 Reg.58, Sch.8 para.10

Reg.42, applied: SI 1999/362 Reg.12, Reg.29, Reg.46, Sch.2 Part I, Sch.2 Part II, Sch.2 Part III, Sch.2 Part IV, Sch.2 Part V

Reg.43, applied: SI 1999/362 Reg.12, Reg.29, Reg.46, Sch.2 Part III, Sch.2 Part IV, Sch.2 Part V

Reg.46, referred to: SI 1999/1287 Reg.6

Reg.47, applied: SI 1999/2242 Reg.58, Sch.8 para.5

Reg.47, referred to: SI 1999/2163 Reg.58, Sch.7 para.5

Reg.49, applied: SI 1999/2163 Reg.58, Sch.7 para.9, SI 1999/2242 Reg.58, Sch.8 para.9

Reg.52, revoked (in part): SI 1999/2163 Reg.58, Sch.7 para.6, SI 1999/2242 Reg.58, Sch.8 para.6

Reg.53, revoked (in part): SI 1999/2163 Reg.58, Sch.7 para.2, SI 1999/2242 Reg.58, Sch.8 para.2

Reg.54, applied: SI 1999/3297 Reg.4

Reg.54, substituted: SI 1999/3297 Reg.3

Reg.54A, added: SI 1999/3297 Reg.3

Reg.54B, added: SI 1999/3297 Reg.3

Reg.54C, added: SI 1999/3297 Reg.3

Reg.57, amended: SI 1999/2163 Reg.58, Sch.7 para.4

Reg.57, applied: SI 1999/2163 Reg.14, SI 1999/2242 Reg.14

Sch.2, amended: SI 1999/1287 Reg.6

Sch.2 para.4, amended: SI 1999/1287 Reg.6

Sch.2 para.5, substituted: SI 1999/1287 Reg.6

Sch.3, revoked (in part): SI 1999/2163 Reg.58, Sch.7 para.10

Sch.6, revoked (in part): SI 1999/2163 Reg.58, Sch.7 para.2, SI 1999/2242 Reg.58, Sch.8 para.2

NO.

366. Highland Communities National Health Service Trust (Establishment) Amendment Order 1999

revoked: SI 1999/1070 Art.2, Sch.2

Art.2, revoked: SI 1999/1070 Art.2, Sch.2

367. Environmental Impact Assessment (Fish Farming in Marine Waters) Regulations 1999

referred to: SI 1999/3445 Reg.3

371. Income Support (General) (Standard Interest Rate Amendment) (No.2) Regulations 1999

revoked: SI 1999/907 Reg.3 (with saving)

Reg.2, revoked: SI 1999/907 Reg.3 (with saving)

Reg.3, revoked: SI 1999/907 Reg.3 (with saving)

375. Hill Livestock (Compensatory Allowances) (Amendment) Regulations 1999

revoked: SI 1999/3316 Reg.18 (with saving), SSI 1999/187 Reg.23 (with savings), Sch.2 (with savings)

Reg.2, revoked: SI 1999/3316 Reg.18 (with saving), SSI 1999/187 Reg.23 (with savings), Sch.2 (with savings)

399. Food Safety (Fishery Products and Live Shellfish) (Hygiene) Amendment Regulations 1999

Sch. para.5, amended: SI 1999/1585 Reg.9

406. Scottish Land Election Amendment Rules 1999

revoked: SI 1999/492 r.4

414. A23 Trunk Road (Croydon) Red Route Traffic Order 1999

Sch.2B Item 1, amended: SI 1999/3419 Art.3

Sch.2B Item 1A, added: SI 1999/3419 Art.3

Sch.2B Item 1B, added: SI 1999/3419 Art.3

Sch.2B Item 2A, added: SI 1999/3419 Art.3

Sch.2B Item 3A, added: SI 1999/3419 Art.3

Sch.2B Item 4, revoked: SI 1999/3419 Art.3

Sch.2B Item 11A, added: SI 1999/3419 Art.3

Sch.2B Item 12, amended: SI 1999/3419 Art.3

Sch.2B Item 16A, added: SI 1999/3419 Art.3

Sch.2B Item 16B, added: SI 1999/3419 Art.3

Sch.2B Item 20, amended: SI 1999/3419 Art.3

Sch.2B Item 23, amended: SI 1999/3419 Art.3

Sch.2B Item 23A, added: SI 1999/3419 Art.3

Sch.2B Item 23B, added: SI 1999/3419 Art.3

Sch.2B Item 24, revoked: SI 1999/3419 Art.3

Sch.2B Item 26, amended: SI 1999/3419 Art.3

Sch.2B Item 28, amended: SI 1999/3419 Art.3

Sch.2B Item 28A, added: SI 1999/3419 Art.3

Sch.2B Item 29, amended: SI 1999/3419 Art.3

Sch.2B Item 31, amended: SI 1999/3419 Art.3

Sch.2B Item 34, amended: SI 1999/3419 Art.3

Sch.2B Item 41A, added: SI 1999/3419 Art.3

Sch.3A Item 1, amended: SI 1999/3419 Art.4

Sch.3B Item 1, revoked: SI 1999/3419 Art.5

Sch.3B Item 2, amended: SI 1999/3419 Art.5

Sch.3B Item 2A, added: SI 1999/3419 Art.5

Sch.3B Item 5, amended: SI 1999/3419 Art.5

Sch.3B Item 5A, added: SI 1999/3419 Art.5

Sch.3B Item 7, amended: SI 1999/3419 Art.5

Sch.3B Item 8, revoked: SI 1999/3419 Art.5

Sch.3B Item 12, revoked: SI 1999/3419 Art.5

Sch.3B Item 13, revoked: SI 1999/3419 Art.5

Sch.3B Item 15, amended: SI 1999/3419 Art.5

Sch.3B Item 16, revoked: SI 1999/3419 Art.5

Sch.4 Item 4, amended: SI 1999/3419 Art.6

Sch.4 Item 5, amended: SI 1999/3419 Art.6

Sch.4 Item 7, amended: SI 1999/3419 Art.6

Sch.4 Item 8, revoked: SI 1999/3419 Art.6

Sch.4 Item 9, amended: SI 1999/3419 Art.6

NO.

1999—cont.

1999—cont.

414. A23 Trunk Road (Croydon) Red Route Traffic Order 1999—*cont.*
Sch.4 Item 13, amended: SI 1999/3419 Art.6
Sch.4 Item 14, amended: SI 1999/3419 Art.6
Sch.4 Item 18, amended: SI 1999/3419 Art.6
Sch.4 Item 19, amended: SI 1999/3419 Art.6
Sch.4 Item 23, revoked: SI 1999/3419 Art.6
Sch.4 Item 24, amended: SI 1999/3419 Art.6
Sch.4 Item 29, amended: SI 1999/3419 Art.6
Sch.4 Item 34, amended: SI 1999/3419 Art.6
Sch.4 Item 35, amended: SI 1999/3419 Art.6
Sch.4 Item 37, amended: SI 1999/3419 Art.6
Sch.4 Item 54, amended: SI 1999/3419 Art.6
Sch.4 Item 55, amended: SI 1999/3419 Art.6
Sch.4 Item 56, amended: SI 1999/3419 Art.6
Sch.4 Item 66, amended: SI 1999/3419 Art.6
Sch.4 Item 71, amended: SI 1999/3419 Art.6
Sch.4 Item 76, amended: SI 1999/3419 Art.6
Sch.4 Item 84, amended: SI 1999/3419 Art.6
Sch.4 Item 85, revoked: SI 1999/3419 Art.6

437. Control of Substances Hazardous to Health Regulations 1999
Sch.3 para.14, amended: SI 1999/1820 Art.4, Sch.2 para.167

441. Scotland Act 1998 (Transitory and Transitional Provisions) (Finance) Order 1999
Art.2, substituted: SI 1999/3273 Art.2
Art.24, revoked: SI 1999/1594 Art.4

447. Education (Grants for Education Support and Training) (England) Regulations 1998 (Amendment No.2) Regulations 1999
revoked: SI 1999/606 Reg.12
Reg.3, revoked: SI 1999/606 Reg.12
Reg.4, revoked: SI 1999/606 Reg.12

449. National Assembly for Wales (Disqualification) Order 1999
applied: SI 1999/450 Art.15, Art.158, Sch.5 para.9

450. National Assembly for Wales (Representation of the People) Order 1999
Art.14, applied: SI 1999/942 Sch. para.4, Sch. para.5, Sch. para.7, SI 1999/943 Art.3
Art.17, applied: SI 1999/942 Sch. para.10
Art.20, applied: SI 1999/942 Art.3
Sch.5 Appendix, amended: SI 1999/450 Art.14, Sch.4 para.21, Sch.4 para.22
Sch.5 para.25, amended: SI 1999/450 Art.14, Sch.4 para.5
Sch.5 para.29, amended: SI 1999/450 Art.14, Sch.4 para.6
Sch.5 para.33, amended: SI 1999/450 Art.14, Sch.4 para.7
Sch.5 para.34, amended: SI 1999/450 Art.14, Sch.4 para.8
Sch.5 para.35, amended: SI 1999/450 Art.14, Sch.4 para.9
Sch.5 para.40, amended: SI 1999/450 Art.14, Sch.4 para.10
Sch.5 para.42, amended: SI 1999/450 Art.14, Sch.4 para.11
Sch.5 para.43, amended: SI 1999/450 Art.14, Sch.4 para.12
Sch.5 para.44, amended: SI 1999/450 Art.14, Sch.4 para.13
Sch.5 para.45, amended: SI 1999/450 Art.14, Sch.4 para.14
Sch.5 para.47, amended: SI 1999/450 Art.14, Sch.4 para.15
Sch.5 para.48, amended: SI 1999/450 Art.14, Sch.4 para.16
Sch.5 para.49, amended: SI 1999/450 Art.14, Sch.4 para.17

450. National Assembly for Wales (Representation of the People) Order 1999—*cont.*
Sch.5 para.50, amended: SI 1999/450 Art.14, Sch.4 para.18
Sch.5 para.51, applied: SI 1999/942 Sch. para.7
Sch.5 para.52, applied: SI 1999/942 Sch. para.7
Sch.5 para.62, amended: SI 1999/450 Art.14, Sch.4 para.19
Sch.5 para.65, amended: SI 1999/450 Art.14, Sch.4 para.20

474. Social Security (New Deal Pilot) Regulations (Northern Ireland) 1999
Reg.2, applied: SI 1999/3188 Reg.3
Reg.3, applied: SI 1999/3188 Reg.3
Reg.4, applied: SI 1999/3188 Reg.3

491. Criminal Legal Aid (Fixed Payments) (Scotland) Regulations 1999
Reg.2, amended: SI 1999/1820 Art.4, Sch.2 para.168, SSI 1999/48 Reg.2
Sch.2, amended: SSI 1999/48 Reg.2

496. Education (Student Support) Regulations 1999
applied: SI 1999/2263 Reg.3, Reg.5, Reg.6, SI 1999/2270 Reg.3
referred to: SI 1999/603 Reg.3
Reg.4, amended: SI 1999/2266 Reg.3
Reg.4, referred to: SI 1999/603 Reg.2
Reg.6, referred to: SI 1999/603 Reg.2
Reg.8, applied: SI 1999/2270 Reg.5
Reg.9, applied: SI 1999/2270 Reg.5
Reg.10, amended: SI 1999/2266 Reg.4
Reg.10, referred to: SI 1999/603 Reg.2
Reg.11, amended: SI 1999/2266 Reg.5
Reg.12, amended: SI 1999/2266 Reg.6
Reg.12, revoked (in part): SI 1999/2266 Reg.6
Reg.15, amended: SI 1999/2266 Reg.7
Reg.15, applied: SI 1999/2270 Reg.7
Reg.16, amended: SI 1999/2266 Reg.8
Reg.18, amended: SI 1999/2266 Reg.9
Reg.19, amended: SI 1999/2266 Reg.10
Reg.20, amended: SI 1999/2266 Reg.11
Reg.21, amended: SI 1999/2270 Reg.9
Reg.24, amended: SI 1999/2266 Reg.12
Sch.1, applied: SI 1999/603 Reg.2
Sch.1 para.7, amended: SI 1999/2266 Reg.13
Sch.1 para.7, referred to: SI 1999/2270 Reg.3, Reg.6
Sch.2, referred to: SI 1999/2263 Reg.4
Sch.3, applied: SI 1999/2270 Reg.9
Sch.3 Part II, referred to: SI 1999/2270 Reg.9
Sch.3 para.1, amended: SI 1999/2266 Reg.14
Sch.3 para.3, amended: SI 1999/2266 Reg.14
Sch.3 para.4, amended: SI 1999/2270 Reg.9
Sch.3 para.6, amended: SI 1999/2266 Reg.14
Sch.3 para.8, amended: SI 1999/2270 Reg.9

520. Rail Vehicle Accessibility (Midland Metro T69 Vehicles) Exemption Order 1999
Art.5, amended: SI 1999/586 Art.2

527. Social Security Contributions (Transfer of Functions, etc.) Act 1999 (Commencement No.1 and Transitional Provisions) Order 1999
Art.4, referred to: SI 1999/978 Reg.2, SI 1999/3178 Art.2, Art.3

532. Education (Schedule 32 to the School Standards and Framework Act 1998) (England) Regulations 1999
Reg.2, referred to: SI 1999/531 Art.2

1999—cont.

540. Spreadable Fats (Marketing Standards) (Amendment) Regulations 1999
revoked (in part): SI 1999/2457 Reg.9, Sch.2, SSI 1999/34 Reg.9, Sch.2
Reg.2, revoked (in part): SI 1999/2457 Reg.9, Sch.2, SSI 1999/34 Reg.9, Sch.2

543. Police (Secretary of State's Objectives) Order 1999
revoked: SI 1999/1415 Art.2
Art.2, revoked: SI 1999/1415 Art.2
Art.3, revoked: SI 1999/1415 Art.2

547. Offshore Installations (Safety Zones) Order 1999
Sch.1, amended: SI 1999/2206 Art.3

584. National Minimum Wage Regulations 1999
applied: SI 1999/1128 Art.5, SI 1999/712
referred to: SI 1999/750

590. Organic Farming Regulations 1999
Reg.2, amended: SI 1999/2735 Reg.4
Reg.6A, added: SI 1999/2735 Reg.5
Reg.6A, amended: SI 1999/2933 Reg.4
Sch.3, added: SI 1999/2735 Reg.6, Sch.

604. Education (Transfer of Functions Concerning School Lunches) (England) Order 1999
revoked: SI 1999/2164 Art.5
Art.2, revoked: SI 1999/2164 Art.5
Art.3, revoked: SI 1999/2164 Art.5
Art.4, revoked: SI 1999/2164 Art.5

606. Education (Education Standards Etc. Grants) (England) Regulations 1999
Reg.2, amended: SI 1999/1955 Reg.3, SI 1999/3211 Reg.3
Reg.5, amended: SI 1999/1955 Reg.4, SI 1999/3211 Reg.4
Reg.11, amended: SI 1999/1955 Reg.5, SI 1999/3211 Reg.5
Sch.1 para.30, substituted: SI 1999/1955 Reg.6
Sch.1 para.36, added: SI 1999/1955 Reg.6
Sch.1 para.37, added: SI 1999/1955 Reg.6
Sch.1 para.38, added: SI 1999/1955 Reg.6
Sch.1 para.39, added: SI 1999/1955 Reg.6
Sch.1 para.40, added: SI 1999/3211 Reg.6
Sch.1 para.41, added: SI 1999/3211 Reg.6
Sch.1 para.42, added: SI 1999/3211 Reg.6
Sch.1 para.43, added: SI 1999/3211 Reg.6
Sch.1 para.44, added: SI 1999/3211 Reg.6
Sch.1 para.45, added: SI 1999/3211 Reg.6
Sch.1 para.46, added: SI 1999/3211 Reg.6
Sch.2, amended: SI 1999/1955 Reg.6

610. Education (Transfer of Functions Concerning School Lunches) (Wales) Order 1999
Art.2, referred to: SI 1999/1779 Art.3

616. Health Authorities (England) Establishment Order 1996 Amendment to the Cambridgeshire and Norfolk Health Authorities (Establishment etc.) Order 1999
Art.3, amended: SI 1999/1024 Art.2

617. Motor Vehicles (Driving Licences) (Amendment) (No.2) Regulations 1999
revoked: SI 1999/2864 Reg.2, Sch.1
Reg.3, revoked: SI 1999/2864 Reg.2, Sch.1
Reg.4, revoked: SI 1999/2864 Reg.2, Sch.1
Reg.5, revoked: SI 1999/2864 Reg.2, Sch.1
Reg.6, revoked: SI 1999/2864 Reg.2, Sch.1
Reg.7, revoked: SI 1999/2864 Reg.2, Sch.1
Reg.8, revoked: SI 1999/2864 Reg.2, Sch.1
Reg.9, revoked: SI 1999/2864 Reg.2, Sch.1
Sch., revoked: SI 1999/2864 Reg.2, Sch.1

1999—cont.

622. Friendly Societies (Provisional Repayments for Exempt Business) Regulations 1999
applied: SI 1999/624 Reg.4
referred to: SI 1999/624 Reg.1
Reg.8, amended: SI 1999/624 Reg.5
Reg.8A, added: SI 1999/624 Reg.6
Reg.9, amended: SI 1999/624 Reg.7
Reg.10, amended: SI 1999/624 Reg.8

623. Insurance Companies (Gilt-Edged Securities) (Periodic Accounting for Tax on Interest) Regulations 1999
referred to: SI 1999/624 Reg.1
Reg.6, referred to: SI 1999/624 Reg.3

645. Health and Safety (Fees) Regulations 1999
Reg.1, amended: SI 1999/2024 Reg.48, Sch.5 Part II
Reg.3, amended: SI 1999/3232 Reg.41, Sch.9 para.9
Reg.9, amended: SI 1999/3232 Reg.41, Sch.9 para.9
Reg.18A, added: SI 1999/2597 Reg.2, Sch.1
Reg.18B, added: SI 1999/2597 Reg.2, Sch.1
Reg.18C, added: SI 1999/2597 Reg.2, Sch.1
Reg.18D, added: SI 1999/2597 Reg.2, Sch.1
Sch.8, amended: SI 1999/3232 Reg.41, Sch.9 para.9
Sch.16, added: SI 1999/2597 Reg.2, Sch.2
Sch.17, added: SI 1999/2597 Reg.2, Sch.2
Sch.18, added: SI 1999/2597 Reg.2, Sch.2

655. Consular Fees Order 1999
revoked: SI 1999/3132 Art.4
Art.3, revoked: SI 1999/3132 Art.4
Art.4, revoked: SI 1999/3132 Art.4
Sch. para.9, revoked: SI 1999/3132 Art.4
Sch. para.25, revoked: SI 1999/3132 Art.4
Sch. para.27, revoked: SI 1999/3132 Art.4
Sch. para.49, revoked: SI 1999/3132 Art.4

662. Water (Northern Ireland) Order 1999
Art.3, amended: SI 1999/859 Art.24, Sch.6
Art.13, amended: SI 1999/859 Art.24, Sch.6
Art.39, applied: SI 1999/859 Sch.3
Art.40, applied: SI 1999/859 Sch.3
Art.41, applied: SI 1999/859 Sch.3
Art.42, applied: SI 1999/859 Sch.3
Art.43, amended: SI 1999/859 Art.5, Sch.4 para.4
Art.43, applied: SI 1999/859 Art.5, Sch.3, Sch.4 para.4
Art.43, revoked (in part): SI 1999/859 Art.5, Sch.4 para.4
Art.44, applied: SI 1999/859 Sch.3
Art.45, applied: SI 1999/859 Sch.3
Art.45, referred to: SI 1999/859 Art.5, Sch.4 para.4
Art.46, applied: SI 1999/859 Sch.3
Art.47, referred to: SI 1999/859 Sch.3
Art.48, amended: SI 1999/859 Art.5, Sch.4 para.4
Art.48, applied: SI 1999/859 Art.5, Sch.3, Sch.4 para.4
Art.49, applied: SI 1999/859 Sch.3
Art.49, referred to: SI 1999/859 Art.5, Sch.4 para.4
Art.50, applied: SI 1999/859 Sch.3
Art.51, applied: SI 1999/859 Sch.3
Art.52, applied: SI 1999/859 Sch.3
Art.53, referred to: SI 1999/859 Sch.3
Art.54, referred to: SI 1999/859 Sch.3
Art.55, referred to: SI 1999/859 Sch.3
Art.56, referred to: SI 1999/859 Sch.3
Part III, applied: SI 1999/859 Sch.3
Sch.1 para.2, amended: SI 1999/859 Art.24, Sch.6

NO.

662. Water (Northern Ireland) Order 1999—*cont.*
Sch.1 para.3, amended: SI 1999/859 Art.24, Sch.6
Sch.1 para.4, amended: SI 1999/859 Art.24, Sch.6
Sch.1 para.5, amended: SI 1999/859 Art.24, Sch.6
Sch.4, applied: SI 1999/859 Sch.3
Sch.5, applied: SI 1999/859 Sch.3

671. Social Security Contributions (Transfer of Functions, etc.) (Northern Ireland) Order 1999
Art.3, referred to: 1999 c.30 s.81, Sch.11 para.36
Art.7, applied: SI 1999/1027 Reg.3
Art.7, referred to: SI 1999/1027 Reg.5
Art.10, applied: SI 1999/1027 Reg.3
Art.15, referred to: 1999 c.30 s.81, Sch.11 para.26
Art.20, amended: 1999 c.30 s.81, Sch.11 para.38
Part III, referred to: SI 1999/1027 Reg.7, Reg.8, Reg.9, Reg.10, Reg.12
Sch.1 para.4, referred to: 1999 c.30 s.81, Sch.11 para.32
Sch.1 para.22, revoked (in part): 1999 c.30 s.88, Sch.13 Part VII
Sch.1 para.24, revoked (in part): 1999 c.30 s.88, Sch.13 Part VII
Sch.1 para.33, revoked (in part): 1999 c.30 s.88, Sch.13 Part VII
Sch.1 para.75, referred to: 1999 c.30 s.81, Sch.11 para.27
Sch.1 para.75, revoked (in part): 1999 c.30 s.88, Sch.13 Part VII
Sch.2, amended: 1999 c.30 s.81, Sch.11 para.34
Sch.2, referred to: 1999 c.30 s.81, Sch.11 para.36
Sch.3 para.3, revoked: 1999 c.30 s.88, Sch.13 Part VII
Sch.3 para.6, revoked: 1999 c.30 s.88, Sch.13 Part VII
Sch.3 para.7, revoked: 1999 c.30 s.88, Sch.13 Part VII
Sch.3 para.9, revoked: 1999 c.30 s.88, Sch.13 Part VII
Sch.3 para.10, revoked: 1999 c.30 s.88, Sch.13 Part VII
Sch.3 para.38, revoked (in part): 1999 c.30 s.88, Sch.13 Part VII
Sch.3 para.49, revoked (in part): 1999 c.30 s.88, Sch.13 Part VII
Sch.5 para.2, referred to: 1999 c.30 s.81, Sch.11 para.17
Sch.5 para.2, revoked (in part): 1999 c.30 s.88, Sch.13 Part VII
Sch.7 para.1, amended: 1999 c.30 s.81, Sch.11 para.38
Sch.7 para.2, amended: 1999 c.30 s.81, Sch.11 para.38
Sch.7 para.3, revoked: 1999 c.30 s.88, Sch.13 Part VII
Sch.7 para.4, revoked: 1999 c.30 s.88, Sch.13 Part VII

672. National Assembly for Wales (Transfer of Functions) Order 1999
applied: SI 1999/2242
referred to: SI 1999/2243
applied: 1999 c.28 s.40
Art.5, applied: SI 1999/2801 Reg.3

NO.

672. National Assembly for Wales (Transfer of Functions) Order 1999—*cont.*
Sch.1, amended: 1999 c.8 s.66
Sch.2, amended: 1999 c.8 s.66
Sch.2, applied: SI 1999/2801 Reg.3

674. Scotland Act 1998 (Transitory and Transitional Provisions) (Appropriations) Order 1999
Art.2, amended: SSI 1999/175 Art.2
Sch., substituted: SSI 1999/175 Art.2, Sch.

680. Scottish Parliament (Disqualification) Order 1999
Sch. Part I, amended: SI 1999/1351 Art.17

687. Supreme Court Fees Order 1999
Art.5, amended: SI 1999/2569 Art.4
Sch.1, amended: SI 1999/2569 Art.5

688. Non-Contentious Probate Fees Order 1999
Sch.1 Table, substituted: SI 1999/755 Sch.

689. County Court Fees Order 1999
Art.5, amended: SI 1999/2548 Art.3

690. Family Proceedings Fees Order 1999
Art.4, amended: SI 1999/2549 Art.3

691. Public Record Office (Fees) Regulations 1999
revoked: SI 1999/3298 Reg.3
Reg.3, revoked: SI 1999/3298 Reg.3
Sch. para.6.1, revoked (in part): SI 1999/1616 Reg.2, SI 1999/3298 Reg.3 (rem.)

695. National Health Service Information Authority (Establishment and Constitution) Order 1999
Art.4, applied: SI 1999/694 Reg.5

700. Education (School Organisation Committees) (England) Regulations 1999
applied: SI 1999/2212 Reg.14, SI 1999/2213 Reg.13, SI 1999/2259 Reg.6

701. Education (School Organisation Plans) (England) Regulations 1999
Reg.8, applied: SI 1999/1286 Reg.3
Reg.10, applied: SI 1999/1286 Reg.3
Reg.12, applied: SI 1999/1286 Reg.3
Reg.13, applied: SI 1999/1286 Reg.3

702. Education (References to Adjudicator) Regulations 1999
Reg.2, amended: SI 1999/1286 Reg.18

704. Education (Transition to New Framework) (School Organisation Proposals) Regulations 1999
Reg.8, applied: SI 1999/2243 Reg.4, SI 1999/2323 Art.17
Reg.8, referred to: SI 1999/2262 Reg.4
Reg.12, amended: SI 1999/1671 Reg.12, SI 1999/2213 Reg.18
Reg.12, applied: SI 1999/2800 Reg.8
Reg.13, applied: SI 1999/2163 Reg.58, Sch.7 para.8, SI 1999/2242 Reg.58, Sch.8 para.8, SI 1999/2243 Reg.8, SI 1999/2262 Reg.8, Reg.53, SI 1999/2323 Art.5, Sch.7 para.4
Reg.13, referred to: SI 1999/2243 Reg.3, Reg.4, Reg.25, Reg.29, Reg.48, Reg.53, SI 1999/2262 Reg.4, Reg.25, Reg.29, Reg.48
Reg.14, applied: SI 1999/2323 Art.17
Reg.19, applied: SI 1999/2212 Reg.17, SI 1999/2213 Reg.17
Reg.49, applied: SI 1999/2323 Art.5, Sch.7 para.6
Reg.50, applied: SI 1999/2323 Art.5, Sch.7 para.6
Sch., applied: SI 1999/2213 Reg.17
Sch., referred to: SI 1999/2212 Reg.17, SI 1999/2213 Reg.17, SI 1999/2259 Reg.10

NO.

1999—cont.

711. Education (References to Delegated Budgets and Revocation) Regulations 1999
revoked: SI 1999/2267 Reg.10
Reg.2, revoked: SI 1999/2267 Reg.10
Reg.3, revoked: SI 1999/2267 Reg.10
Reg.4, revoked: SI 1999/2267 Reg.10
Reg.5, applied: SI 1999/2267 Reg.10
Reg.5, revoked: SI 1999/2267 Reg.10
Reg.6, revoked: SI 1999/2267 Reg.10
Reg.7, revoked: SI 1999/2267 Reg.10
Reg.8, revoked: SI 1999/2267 Reg.10
Reg.9, revoked: SI 1999/2267 Reg.10
Sch.1, revoked: SI 1999/2267 Reg.10
Sch.2, revoked: SI 1999/2267 Reg.10

728. Prison Rules 1999
r.39, see *R. v Secretary of State for the Home Department Ex p. Daly* [1999] C.O.D. 388 (CA), Kennedy, L.J.

729. Young Offender Institution (Amendment) Rules 1999
revoked: SI 1999/962 r.2

730. Police (Conduct) Regulations 1999
referred to: SI 1999/818 r.5
Reg.12, substituted: SI 1999/730 Reg.39, Sch.2 para.2
Reg.13, substituted: SI 1999/730 Reg.39, Sch.2 para.2
Reg.15, substituted: SI 1999/730 Reg.39, Sch.2 para.3
Reg.16, substituted: SI 1999/730 Reg.39, Sch.2 para.3
Reg.17, amended: SI 1999/730 Reg.39, Sch.2 para.4
Reg.17, revoked (in part): SI 1999/730 Reg.39, Sch.2 para.4
Reg.18, substituted: SI 1999/730 Reg.39, Sch.2 para.5
Reg.19, revoked: SI 1999/730 Reg.39, Sch.2 para.6
Reg.20, amended: SI 1999/730 Reg.39, Sch.2 para.7
Reg.21, amended: SI 1999/730 Reg.39, Sch.2 para.8
Reg.22, substituted: SI 1999/730 Reg.39, Sch.2 para.9
Reg.23, amended: SI 1999/730 Reg.39, Sch.2 para.10
Reg.25, amended: SI 1999/730 Reg.39, Sch.2 para.11
Reg.26, amended: SI 1999/730 Reg.39, Sch.2 para.12
Reg.27, revoked: SI 1999/730 Reg.39, Sch.2 para.13
Reg.28, amended: SI 1999/730 Reg.39, Sch.2 para.14
Reg.29, amended: SI 1999/730 Reg.39, Sch.2 para.15
Reg.29, revoked (in part): SI 1999/730 Reg.39, Sch.2 para.15
Reg.30, amended: SI 1999/730 Reg.39, Sch.2 para.16
Reg.31, amended: SI 1999/730 Reg.39, Sch.2 para.17
Reg.32, amended: SI 1999/730 Reg.39, Sch.2 para.18
Reg.33, amended: SI 1999/730 Reg.39, Sch.2 para.19
Reg.34, amended: SI 1999/730 Reg.39, Sch.2 para.20
Reg.36, amended: SI 1999/730 Reg.39, Sch.2 para.21
Reg.37, revoked: SI 1999/730 Reg.39, Sch.2 para.22

NO.

1999—cont.

730. Police (Conduct) Regulations 1999—*cont.*
Reg.39, applied: SI 1999/818 r.5
Sch.1, referred to: SI 1999/731 Reg.11
Sch.2 Part II, referred to: SI 1999/818 r.5
Sch.2 para.22, revoked: SI 1999/730 Reg.37

731. Police (Conduct) (Senior Officers) Regulations 1999
referred to: SI 1999/818 r.5
Reg.11, amended: SI 1999/731 Reg.25, Sch. para.2
Reg.12, substituted: SI 1999/731 Reg.25, Sch. para.3
Reg.13, substituted: SI 1999/731 Reg.25, Sch. para.3
Reg.15, amended: SI 1999/731 Reg.25, Sch. para.4
Reg.16, amended: SI 1999/731 Reg.25, Sch. para.5
Reg.17, substituted: SI 1999/731 Reg.25, Sch. para.6
Reg.19, amended: SI 1999/731 Reg.25, Sch. para.7
Reg.21, amended: SI 1999/731 Reg.25, Sch. para.8
Reg.22, amended: SI 1999/731 Reg.25, Sch. para.9
Reg.25, applied: SI 1999/818 r.5
Sch. Part II, referred to: SI 1999/818 r.5

734. Public Offers of Securities (Amendment) Regulations 1999
Reg.2, revoked (in part): SI 1999/1146 Reg.4
Reg.4, revoked (in part): SI 1999/1146 Reg.4

743. Control of Major Accident Hazards Regulations 1999
Reg.22, amended: SI 1999/2597 Reg.3, Sch.3

755. Court of Session etc. Fees Amendment Order 1999
revoked (in part): SI 1999/2788 Art.4, Sch.3

768. Road Traffic (Permitted Parking Area and Special Parking Area) (City of Portsmouth) Order 1999
applied: SI 1999/1918 Reg.20
referred to: SI 1999/1918

786. Road Traffic (NHS Charges) (Reviews and Appeals) Regulations 1999
revoked (in part): SI 1999/1843 Reg.13
Reg.2, revoked (in part): SI 1999/1843 Reg.13
Reg.3, revoked (in part): SI 1999/1843 Reg.13
Reg.4, revoked (in part): SI 1999/1843 Reg.13
Reg.6, revoked (in part): SI 1999/1843 Reg.13
Reg.8, revoked (in part): SI 1999/1843 Reg.13
Reg.11, revoked (in part): SI 1999/1843 Reg.13
Reg.12, revoked (in part): SI 1999/1843 Reg.13

787. Scottish Parliament (Elections etc.) Order 1999
applied: SI 1999/1094 Art.2, Sch. Part C
Appendix.Form T, substituted: SI 1999/787 Art.13, Sch.5 para.21, Appendix Form AD
Art.13, applied: SI 1999/492 r.2
Art.15, applied: SI 1999/1094 Art.2, Art.3, Sch. Part C
Art.18, applied: SI 1999/1094, SI 1999/1094 Art.3
Art.18, referred to: SI 1999/1094 Art.2, SI 1999/1512 Art.2, Sch.1 para.4, SI 1999/1766
Art.20, applied: SI 1999/1512 Art.2, Sch.1 para.13
Art.23, applied: SI 1999/1512 Art.2, Sch.1 para.14
Art.39, applied: SI 1999/1512 Art.2, Sch.1 para.15

NO.

787. Scottish Parliament (Elections etc.) Order 1999—*cont.*

Art.40, applied: SI 1999/1512 Art.2, Sch.1 para.15

Art.47, applied: SI 1999/1512 Art.2, Sch.1 para.15

Art.49, applied: SI 1999/1512 Art.2, Sch.1 para.15

Art.55, applied: SI 1999/1512 Art.2, Sch.1 para.16

Art.57, applied: SI 1999/1512 Art.2, Sch.1 para.17

Art.83, referred to: SI 1999/1350 Sch. para.4

Sch.2, applied: SI 1999/787 Art.62, Art.63, Art.64

Sch.2, referred to: SI 1999/787 Art.12, Sch.4 para.20

Sch.2 r.2, applied: SI 1999/787 Art.89

Sch.2 r.7, referred to: SI 1999/787 Art.35

Sch.2 r.19, applied: SI 1999/787 Art.58

Sch.2 r.28, amended: SI 1999/787 Art.13, Sch.5 para.5

Sch.2 r.32, amended: SI 1999/787 Art.13, Sch.5 para.6

Sch.2 r.32, applied: SI 1999/787 Art.13, Sch.5 para.2

Sch.2 r.33, applied: SI 1999/787 Art.13, Sch.5 para.2

Sch.2 r.34, applied: SI 1999/787 Art.13, Sch.5 para.2

Sch.2 r.35, applied: SI 1999/787 Art.13, Sch.5 para.2

Sch.2 r.36, amended: SI 1999/787 Art.13, Sch.5 para.7

Sch.2 r.37, amended: SI 1999/787 Art.13, Sch.5 para.8

Sch.2 r.37, applied: SI 1999/787 Art.13, Sch.5 para.2

Sch.2 r.37, referred to: SI 1999/787 Art.13, Sch.5 para.21

Sch.2 r.38, amended: SI 1999/787 Art.13, Sch.5 para.9

Sch.2 r.39, applied: SI 1999/787 Art.13, Sch.5 para.2

Sch.2 r.40, applied: SI 1999/787 Art.13, Sch.5 para.2

Sch.2 r.41, applied: SI 1999/787 Art.13, Sch.5 para.2

Sch.2 r.43, amended: SI 1999/787 Art.13, Sch.5 para.10

Sch.2 r.45, amended: SI 1999/787 Art.13, Sch.5 para.11

Sch.2 r.46, amended: SI 1999/787 Art.13, Sch.5 para.12

Sch.2 r.47, amended: SI 1999/787 Art.13, Sch.5 para.13

Sch.2 r.48, amended: SI 1999/787 Art.13, Sch.5 para.14

Sch.2 r.50, amended: SI 1999/787 Art.13, Sch.5 para.15

Sch.2 r.51, amended: SI 1999/787 Art.13, Sch.5 para.16

Sch.2 r.52, amended: SI 1999/787 Art.13, Sch.5 para.17

Sch.2 r.53, amended: SI 1999/787 Art.13, Sch.5 para.18

Sch.2 r.53, applied: SI 1999/787 Art.12, Art.13, Sch.4 para.15, Sch.5 para.2

Sch.2 r.60, referred to: SI 1999/787 Art.85

Sch.2 r.64, referred to: SI 1999/787 Art.85

Sch.2 r.67, amended: SI 1999/787 Art.13, Sch.5 para.19

NO.

787. Scottish Parliament (Elections etc.) Order 1999—*cont.*

Sch.2 r.67, referred to: SI 1999/787 Art.12, Sch.4 para.20

Sch.2 r.70, amended: SI 1999/787 Art.13, Sch.5 para.20

Sch.4 para.20, applied: SI 1999/1512 Art.2, Sch.1 para.18

Sch.7 para.1, applied: SI 1999/1512 Art.2, Sch.1 para.19

859. North/South Co-operation (Implementation Bodies) (Northern Ireland) Order 1999

Art.3, amended: SI 1999/2062 Art.2

Art.14, amended: SI 1999/2062 Art.2

Sch.1A, added: SI 1999/2062 Art.2, Sch.

873. National Health Service (Liabilities to Third Parties Scheme) Regulations 1999

referred to: SI 1999/874 Reg.4

874. National Health Service (Property Expenses Scheme) Regulations 1999

referred to: SI 1999/873 Reg.4

896. East Kent Hospitals National Health Service Trust (Establishment) Order 1999

Art.4, amended: SI 1999/1858 Art.2

901. Scotland Act 1998 (General Transitory, Transitional and Savings Provisions) Order 1999

Art.9, amended: SI 1999/1334 Art.3

Art.13, added: SI 1999/1334 Art.4

907. Income Support (General) (Standard Interest Rate Amendment) (No.3) Regulations 1999

revoked: SI 1999/1153 Reg.3 (with saving)

Reg.1, revoked: SI 1999/1153 Reg.3 (with saving)

Reg.2, revoked: SI 1999/1153 Reg.3 (with saving)

Reg.3, revoked: SI 1999/1153 Reg.3 (with saving)

915. Water Protection Zone (River Dee Catchment) Designation Order 1999

applied: SI 1999/916 Reg.3

Art.6, applied: SI 1999/916 Reg.10, Reg.11, Reg.13

916. Water Protection Zone (River Dee Catchment) (Procedural and Other Provisions) Regulations 1999

Reg.5, applied: SI 1999/915 Art.7

917. Education (School Teachers' Pay and Conditions) Order 1999

revoked: SI 1999/2160 Art.1

Art.2, revoked: SI 1999/2160 Art.1

920. Housing Benefit and Council Tax Benefit (General) Amendment Regulations 1999

Sch., amended: SI 1999/1539 Reg.10

942. National Assembly for Wales (Returning Officers' Charges) Order 1999

Sch. para.4, referred to: SI 1999/943 Art.3

Sch. para.5, referred to: SI 1999/943 Art.3

Sch. para.7, referred to: SI 1999/943 Art.3

Sch. para.18, referred to: SI 1999/943 Art.3

977. Child Support (Miscellaneous Amendments) Regulations 1999

Reg.6, amended: SI 1999/1510 Art.46

Reg.7, substituted: SI 1999/1510 Art.47

981. Planning (Control of Major-Accident Hazards) Regulations 1999

Reg.5, revoked (in part): SI 1999/3280 Reg.45

NO.

991. Social Security and Child Support (Decisions and Appeals) Regulations 1999

Part III Ch.I, applied: SI 1999/1958 Art.5, Sch.12 para.13, SI 1999/2422 Art.4, Sch.14 para.13, SI 1999/2739 Art.3, Sch.2 para.13, SI 1999/2860 Art.4, Sch.16 para.14, SI 1999/3178 Art.4, Sch.22 para.12

Part V, referred to: SI 1999/2860 Art.4, Sch.16 para.6

Part V Ch.III, referred to: SI 1999/1958 Art.5, Sch.12 para.6, SI 1999/2422 Art.4, Sch.14 para.6, SI 1999/2739 Art.3, Sch.2 para.6, SI 1999/3178 Art.4, Sch.21 para.3, Sch.22 para.5

Reg.1, amended: SI 1999/1662 Art.3, SI 1999/1670 Reg.2, SI 1999/2570 Reg.3, Reg.4

Reg.1, referred to: SI 1999/2422 Art.4, Sch.14 para.16

Reg.2, amended: SI 1999/2570 Reg.5

Reg.3, amended: SI 1999/1623 Reg.2, SI 1999/1662 Art.3, SI 1999/2570 Reg.6, SI 1999/2677 Reg.6

Reg.3, referred to: SI 1999/2422 Art.4, Sch.14 para.5, SI 1999/2860 Art.4, Sch.16 para.5, SI 1999/3178 Art.4, Sch.22 para.4

Reg.4, amended: SI 1999/2570 Reg.7

Reg.5, amended: SI 1999/2570 Reg.8

Reg.6, amended: SI 1999/1623 Reg.3, SI 1999/2570 Reg.9, SI 1999/2677 Reg.7

Reg.7, amended: SI 1999/1623 Reg.4, SI 1999/2570 Reg.10, SI 1999/2677 Reg.8, SI 1999/3178 Art.3, Sch.19 para.1

Reg.7, referred to: SI 1999/2860 Art.4, Sch.16 para.3

Reg.7A, added: SI 1999/1623 Reg.5

Reg.8, amended: SI 1999/2570 Reg.11

Reg.8, applied: SI 1999/2860 Art.4, Sch.16 para.3

Reg.11A, added: SI 1999/1670 Reg.2

Reg.16, amended: SI 1999/2570 Reg.12

Reg.17, substituted: SI 1999/2570 Reg.13

Reg.18, substituted: SI 1999/2570 Reg.13

Reg.19, amended: SI 1999/2570 Reg.14

Reg.20, amended: SI 1999/1623 Reg.6, SI 1999/2570 Reg.15

Reg.21, amended: SI 1999/2570 Reg.16

Reg.22, amended: SI 1999/2570 Reg.17

Reg.25, amended: SI 1999/2570 Reg.18

Reg.26, amended: SI 1999/2570 Reg.19

Reg.28, amended: SI 1999/2570 Reg.20

Reg.30, amended: SI 1999/2570 Reg.21

Reg.31, amended: SI 1999/2570 Reg.22

Reg.33, amended: SI 1999/1662 Art.3, SI 1999/2570 Reg.23, SI 1999/2677 Reg.9

Reg.34, amended: SI 1999/2570 Reg.24

Reg.36, amended: SI 1999/1466 Reg.2

Reg.38A, added: SI 1999/1670 Reg.2

Reg.39, referred to: SI 1999/3178 Art.4, Sch.21 para.3

Reg.40, amended: SI 1999/2570 Reg.25

Reg.41, amended: SI 1999/1670 Reg.2, SI 1999/2570 Reg.26

Reg.41, revoked (in part): SI 1999/1670 Reg.2

Reg.46, applied: SI 1999/1510 Art.48, SI 1999/1958 Art.5, Sch.12 para.7, SI 1999/2739 Art.3, Sch.2 para.7, SI 1999/2860 Art.4, Sch.16 para.7, SI 1999/3178 Art.4, Sch.22 para.6

Reg.46, referred to: SI 1999/2422 Art.4, Sch.14 para.7

Reg.53, amended: SI 1999/2677 Reg.10

Reg.58, amended: SI 1999/2570 Reg.27

NO.

991. Social Security and Child Support (Decisions and Appeals) Regulations 1999—*cont.*

Reg.59, referred to: SI 1999/1958 Art.3, Art.5, Sch.12 para.5, Sch.12 para.12, SI 1999/2422 Art.4, Art.5, Sch.14 para.5, Sch.14 para.12, Sch.14 para.17, SI 1999/2739 Art.3, Sch.2 para.5, Sch.2 para.12, SI 1999/2860 Art.4, Art.5, Sch.16 para.5, Sch.16 para.13, SI 1999/3178 Art.4, Sch.21 para.1, Sch.21 para.6, Sch.22 para.4, Sch.22 para.11

Sch.2 para.8, amended: SI 1999/3178 Art.3, Sch.19 para.2

Sch.4, amended: SI 1999/1623 Reg.7

996. A205 Trunk Road (Greenwich) Red Route Traffic Order 1998 Variation Order 1999

revoked: SI 1999/1885 Art.2

Art.3, revoked: SI 1999/1885 Art.2

998. London Borough of Barnet (Trunk Roads) Red Route (Priority Traffic Lanes) Experimental Traffic Order 1999

revoked: SI 1999/3417 Art.2

Art.4, revoked: SI 1999/3417 Art.2

1001. Education (Student Loans) (Scotland) Regulations 1999

Reg.6, amended: SSI 1999/124 Reg.2

Reg.10, amended: SSI 1999/124 Reg.3

Reg.12, amended: SSI 1999/124 Reg.4

Reg.13, amended: SSI 1999/124 Reg.5

Reg.13, revoked (in part): SSI 1999/124 Reg.5

1005. Food Protection (Emergency Prohibitions) (Amnesic Shellfish Poisoning) Order 1999

revoked: SI 1999/1192 Art.2

Art.3, revoked: SI 1999/1192 Art.2

1012. Family Proceedings (Miscellaneous Amendments) Rules 1999

see *Practice Direction (Fam Div: Family Proceedings: Allocation of Costs)* [1999] 1 W.L.R. 1128 (Fam Div), Lord Irvine of Lairg

1016. School Standards and Framework Act 1998 (Commencement No.6 and Saving and Transitional Provisions) Order 1999

Sch.4, referred to: SI 1999/2323 Art.5, Sch.7 para.12

Sch.4 para.2, amended: SI 1999/2484 Art.2

Sch.4 para.11, amended: SI 1999/2484 Art.2

Sch.4 para.12, added: SI 1999/2484 Art.2

1053. Non-Road Mobile Machinery (Emission of Gaseous and Particulate Pollutants) Regulations 1999

Reg.8, applied: SI 1999/1054 Reg.3

Reg.9, applied: SI 1999/1054 Reg.4

Reg.10, applied: SI 1999/1054 Reg.3, Reg.4

1064. School Standards and Framework Act 1998 (Admissions and Standard Numbers) (Modification) Regulations 1999

Reg.9, referred to: SI 1999/2213 Reg.15, Reg.17

1065. Education (Induction Arrangements for School Teachers) (England) Regulations 1999

Reg.2, amended: SI 1999/2211 Reg.3

Reg.4, amended: SI 1999/2211 Reg.4

Sch.1 para.7, amended: SI 1999/2211 Reg.5

Sch.1 para.9, amended: SI 1999/2211 Reg.6

Sch.1 para.9, revoked (in part): SI 1999/2211 Reg.6

1066. Education (Information as to Provision of Education) (England) Regulations 1999

Sch., applied: SI 1999/2213 Reg.2

NO.

1081. Scotland Act 1998 (Transitory and Transitional Provisions) (Grants to Members and Officeholders) Order 1999
Art.J1, amended: SI 1999/1891 Art.3
Art.P1, amended: SI 1999/1891 Art.3
Art.4, amended: SI 1999/1891 Art.2
Sch.1 para.3, amended: SI 1999/1891 Art.3

1094. Scottish Parliamentary Elections (Returning Officers' Charges) Order 1999
Art.1, amended: SI 1999/1766 Art.2
Art.3, amended: SI 1999/1766 Art.2

1103. Bovines and Bovine Products (Trade) Regulations 1999
Reg.13, amended: SI 1999/1554 Reg.2

1109. Pesticides (Maximum Residue Levels in Crops, Food and Feeding Stuffs) (Amendment) Regulations 1999
revoked (in part): SI 1999/3483 Reg.7, Sch.4
Reg.3, revoked (in part): SI 1999/3483 Reg.7, Sch.4
Reg.4, revoked (in part): SI 1999/3483 Reg.7, Sch.4
Reg.5, revoked (in part): SI 1999/3483 Reg.7, Sch.4
Reg.6, revoked (in part): SI 1999/3483 Reg.7, Sch.4
Reg.7, revoked (in part): SI 1999/3483 Reg.7, Sch.4
Sch.1, revoked (in part): SI 1999/3483 Reg.7, Sch.4
Sch.2, revoked (in part): SI 1999/3483 Reg.7, Sch.4
Sch.3, revoked (in part): SI 1999/3483 Reg.7, Sch.4
Sch.4, revoked (in part): SI 1999/3483 Reg.7, Sch.4

1112. Road Traffic (Permitted Parking Area and Special Parking Area) (County of East Sussex) (Borough of Hastings) Order 1999
applied: SI 1999/1918 Reg.20
referred to: SI 1999/1918

1118. Cardiff and District Community National Health Service Trust (Establishment) Order 1999
revoked: SI 1999/3450 Art.2, Sch.
Art.3, revoked: SI 1999/3450 Art.2, Sch.
Art.4, revoked: SI 1999/3450 Art.2, Sch.
Art.6, revoked: SI 1999/3450 Art.2, Sch.

1119. University Hospital of Wales and Llandough National Health Service Trust (Establishment) Order 1999
revoked: SI 1999/3450 Art.2, Sch.

1135. Housing (Right to Acquire) (Discount) Order 1999
Art.2, amended: SI 1999/3028 Art.2

1148. Water Supply (Water Fittings) Regulations 1999
Reg.5, amended: SI 1999/1506 Reg.2
Reg.5, applied: SI 1999/3442 Reg.2
Reg.6, amended: SI 1999/1506 Reg.2
Reg.10, amended: SI 1999/1506 Reg.2
Sch.2 para.14, amended: SI 1999/1506 Reg.2
Sch.2 para.17, amended: SI 1999/1506 Reg.2

1153. Income Support (General) (Standard Interest Rate Amendment) (No.4) Regulations 1999
revoked: SI 1999/1411 Reg.3 (with savings)
Reg.1, revoked: SI 1999/1411 Reg.3 (with savings)
Reg.2, revoked: SI 1999/1411 Reg.3 (with savings)
Reg.3, revoked: SI 1999/1411 Reg.3 (with savings)

NO.

1176. Land in Care Scheme (Tir Gofal) (Wales) Regulations 1999
Reg.3, amended: SI 1999/3337 Reg.2
Reg.5, amended: SI 1999/3337 Reg.2
Reg.9A, added: SI 1999/3337 Reg.2
Reg.11, amended: SI 1999/2611 Reg.21

1178. Education (School Performance Information) (England) Regulations 1999
Reg.2, amended: SI 1999/2158 Reg.2, SI 1999/2937 Reg.2
Reg.11A, added: SI 1999/2158 Reg.2
Reg.11B, added: SI 1999/2937 Reg.2
Reg.14, amended: SI 1999/2387 Reg.2, SI 1999/2937 Reg.2
Reg.14, revoked (in part): SI 1999/2387 Reg.2
Sch.1 para.2, amended: SI 1999/2937 Reg.2
Sch.2 para.2, amended: SI 1999/2387 Reg.3
Sch.2 para.4, revoked (in part): SI 1999/2387 Reg.3
Sch.2 para.5, amended: SI 1999/2387 Reg.3
Sch.2 para.5, revoked (in part): SI 1999/2387 Reg.3
Sch.3 para.8, substituted: SI 1999/2158 Reg.2
Sch.3 para.8A, added: SI 1999/2158 Reg.2
Sch.3 para.9, amended: SI 1999/2158 Reg.2
Sch.5 para.10, added: SI 1999/2158 Reg.2
Sch.6 para.8, added: SI 1999/2387 Reg.4
Sch.8, substituted: SI 1999/2387 Reg.5, Sch.
Sch.9, added: SI 1999/2158 Reg.2, Sch.
Sch.10, added: SI 1999/2937 Reg.2, Sch.

1214. European Parliamentary Elections Regulations 1999
applied: SI 1999/1378 Sch. Part C
referred to: SI 1999/1377 Sch. Part C
Reg.3, referred to: SI 1999/1512 Art.2, Sch.1 para.3
Reg.6, applied: SI 1999/1378 Sch. Part B
Sch.1, referred to: SI 1999/1512 Art.2, Sch.1 para.3
Sch.1 Annex, applied: SI 1999/1402 Art.3

1228. Plant Protection Products (Amendment) Regulations 1999
revoked: SI 1999/3430 Reg.4
Reg.2, revoked: SI 1999/3430 Reg.4
Reg.3, revoked: SI 1999/3430 Reg.4
Reg.4, revoked: SI 1999/3430 Reg.4

1236. Education (National Curriculum) (Key Stage 1 Assessment Arrangements) (England) Order 1999
Art.4, amended: SI 1999/2187 Art.2
Art.7, amended: SI 1999/2187 Art.2

1261. Federal Republic of Yugoslavia (Supply, Sale and Export of Petroleum and Petroleum Products) (Penalties and Licences) Regulations 1999
revoked: SI 1999/1516 Reg.12
Reg.4, revoked: SI 1999/1516 Reg.12

1286. Education (Adjudicators Inquiry Procedure etc.) Regulations 1999
referred to: SI 1999/2213 Reg.12
Reg.15, referred to: SI 1999/2212 Reg.13

1288. Road Traffic (Permitted Parking Area and Special Parking Area) (County Borough of Neath Port Talbot) Order 1999
applied: SI 1999/1918 Reg.20
referred to: SI 1999/1918

1303. Registration of Births, Deaths and Marriages (Fees) (Amendment) Order 1999
revoked: SI 1999/3311 Art.3
Art.2, revoked: SI 1999/3311 Art.3

1999—cont.

1305. **Child Support Commissioners (Procedure) Regulations 1999**
applied: SI 1999/1510 Art.48
1351. **Scotland Act 1998 (Transitory and Transitional Provisions) (Complaints of Maladministration) Order 1999**
Art.17, amended: SI 1999/1595 Art.3
1415. **Police (Secretary of State's Objectives) (No.2) Order 1999**
revoked: SI 1999/3424 Art.2
Art.2, revoked: SI 1999/3424 Art.2
Art.3, revoked: SI 1999/3424 Art.2
1452. **Aeroplane Noise Regulations 1999**
Sch., revoked (in part): SI 1999/2253 Reg.2
1469. **Education (Schedule 32 to the School Standards and Framework Act 1998) (Wales) Regulations 1999**
referred to: SI 1999/1498 Art.2
1521. **Road Vehicles (Construction and Use) (Amendment) Regulations 1999**
Reg.3, amended: SI 1999/1959 Reg.2
1542. **Food (Animals and Animal Products from Belgium) (Emergency Control) Order 1999**
revoked (in part): SI 1999/2025 Reg.6, SSI 1999/14 Art.6
Art.1, amended: SI 1999/1763 Art.3
Art.1, revoked (in part): SI 1999/2025 Reg.6, SSI 1999/14 Art.6
Art.1A, added: SI 1999/1763 Art.4
Art.1A, revoked (in part): SI 1999/2025 Reg.6, SSI 1999/14 Art.6
Art.3, amended: SI 1999/1763 Art.5
Art.3, revoked (in part): SI 1999/2025 Reg.6, SSI 1999/14 Art.6
Art.4, amended: SI 1999/1763 Art.6
Art.4, revoked (in part): SI 1999/2025 Reg.6, SSI 1999/14 Art.6
1543. **Animal Feedingstuffs from Belgium (Control) Regulations 1999**
revoked (in part): SI 1999/2026 Reg.6, SSI 1999/15 Reg.6
Reg.1, amended: SI 1999/1764 Reg.3
Reg.1, revoked (in part): SI 1999/2026 Reg.6, SSI 1999/15 Reg.6
Reg.1A, added: SI 1999/1764 Reg.4
Reg.1A, revoked (in part): SI 1999/2026 Reg.6, SSI 1999/15 Reg.6
Reg.2, amended: SI 1999/1764 Reg.5
Reg.2, revoked (in part): SI 1999/2026 Reg.6, SSI 1999/15 Reg.6
Reg.3, amended: SI 1999/1764 Reg.6
Reg.3, revoked (in part): SI 1999/2026 Reg.6, SSI 1999/15 Reg.6
Reg.4, amended: SI 1999/1764 Reg.7
Reg.4, revoked (in part): SI 1999/2026 Reg.6, SSI 1999/15 Reg.6
1544. **Civil Aviation (Route Charges for Navigation Services) (Third Amendment) Regulations 1999**
revoked: SI 1999/1859 Reg.2
Reg.2, revoked: SI 1999/1859 Reg.2
1616. **Public Record Office (Fees) (Amendment) Regulations 1999**
revoked: SI 1999/3298 Reg.3
Reg.2, revoked: SI 1999/3298 Reg.3
1619. **General Teaching Council for Wales (Constitution) Regulations 1999**
Reg.2, amended: SI 1999/3185 Reg.3, Reg.4
Reg.4, substituted: SI 1999/3185 Reg.5
Reg.9, amended: SI 1999/3185 Reg.6

1999—cont.

1663. **Feeding Stuffs (Sampling and Analysis) Regulations 1999**
Reg.3, amended: SI 1999/1871 Reg.76, SI 1999/1872 Reg.98
Reg.3, applied: SI 1999/1871 Reg.76, SI 1999/1872 Reg.98
Reg.3, substituted: SI 1999/1871 Reg.93
Sch.1, applied: SI 1999/1871 Reg.76, SI 1999/1872 Reg.98
Sch.1, amended: SI 1999/1871 Reg.76
Sch.1 Part II, amended: SI 1999/1871 Reg.76
Sch.1 Part II, applied: SI 1999/1871 Reg.76, SI 1999/1872 Reg.98, SI 1999/2325 Reg.8
Sch.1 Part III, applied: SI 1999/1871 Reg.77, SI 1999/1872 Reg.99
Sch.1 para.1, amended: SI 1999/1872 Reg.98
Sch.1 para.1, applied: SI 1999/1872 Reg.98
Sch.1 para.10, applied: SI 1999/1872 Reg.98
Sch.2 Part I, applied: SI 1999/1871 Reg.84
Sch.2 Part II, applied: SI 1999/1872 Reg.106
1672. **Public Gas Transporter Pipe-Line Works (Environmental Impact Assessment) Regulations 1999**
Reg.2, amended: SSI 1999/1 Reg.47
Reg.5, amended: SSI 1999/1 Reg.47
1726. **General Teaching Council for England (Constitution) Regulations 1999**
Reg.12, amended: SI 1999/2019 Reg.2
1763. **Food (Animals and Animal Products from Belgium) (Emergency Control) (Amendment) Order 1999**
revoked (in part): SI 1999/2025 Reg.6, SSI 1999/14 Art.6
Art.3, revoked (in part): SI 1999/2025 Reg.6, SSI 1999/14 Art.6
Art.4, revoked (in part): SI 1999/2025 Reg.6, SSI 1999/14 Art.6
Art.5, revoked (in part): SI 1999/2025 Reg.6, SSI 1999/14 Art.6
Art.6, revoked (in part): SI 1999/2025 Reg.6, SSI 1999/14 Art.6
1764. **Animal Feedingstuffs from Belgium (Control) (Amendment) Regulations 1999**
revoked (in part): SI 1999/2026 Reg.6, SSI 1999/15 Reg.6
Reg.3, revoked (in part): SI 1999/2026 Reg.6, SSI 1999/15 Reg.6
Reg.4, revoked (in part): SI 1999/2026 Reg.6, SSI 1999/15 Reg.6
Reg.5, revoked (in part): SI 1999/2026 Reg.6, SSI 1999/15 Reg.6
Reg.6, revoked (in part): SI 1999/2026 Reg.6, SSI 1999/15 Reg.6
Reg.7, revoked (in part): SI 1999/2026 Reg.6, SSI 1999/15 Reg.6
1774. **Wireless Telegraphy (Licence Charges) Regulations 1999**
Sch.3 Part III, amended: SI 1999/3243 Reg.2
Sch.3 Part I, substituted: SI 1999/3243 Reg.2, Sch.1
Sch.4, substituted: SI 1999/3243 Reg.2, Sch.2
Sch.5 Part II, substituted: SI 1999/3243 Reg.2, Sch.3
Sch.6, amended: SI 1999/3243 Reg.2
1871. **Feedingstuffs (Zootechnical Products) Regulations 1999**
applied: SI 1999/1872 Reg.19, Reg.21, Reg.26, Reg.28
Reg.3, referred to: SI 1999/1872 Reg.53, Reg.54

NO.

1933. Postal Privilege (Suspension) Order 1999
revoked: SI 1999/2863 Art.2
Art.1, revoked: SI 1999/2863 Art.2
Art.2, revoked: SI 1999/2863 Art.2

1958. Social Security Act 1998 (Commencement No.8, and Savings and Consequential and Transitional Provisions) Order 1999
Art.3, amended: SI 1999/3178 Art.3, Sch.20 para.2
Art.4, revoked (in part): SI 1999/3178 Art.3, Sch.20 para.1
Sch.5, revoked: SI 1999/3178 Art.3, Sch.20 para.1
Sch.5 para.1, revoked: SI 1999/3178 Art.3, Sch.20 para.1
Sch.5 para.2, revoked: SI 1999/3178 Art.3, Sch.20 para.1
Sch.5 para.3, revoked: SI 1999/3178 Art.3, Sch.20 para.1
Sch.9, revoked: SI 1999/3178 Art.3, Sch.20 para.1
Sch.9 para.1, revoked: SI 1999/3178 Art.3, Sch.20 para.1
Sch.9 para.2, revoked: SI 1999/3178 Art.3, Sch.20 para.1
Sch.9 para.3, revoked: SI 1999/3178 Art.3, Sch.20 para.1
Sch.9 para.4, revoked: SI 1999/3178 Art.3, Sch.20 para.1
Sch.9 para.5, revoked: SI 1999/3178 Art.3, Sch.20 para.1
Sch.10, revoked: SI 1999/3178 Art.3, Sch.20 para.1
Sch.10 para.1, revoked: SI 1999/3178 Art.3, Sch.20 para.1
Sch.10 para.2, revoked: SI 1999/3178 Art.3, Sch.20 para.1
Sch.10 para.3, revoked: SI 1999/3178 Art.3, Sch.20 para.1
Sch.10 para.4, revoked: SI 1999/3178 Art.3, Sch.20 para.1
Sch.10 para.5, revoked: SI 1999/3178 Art.3, Sch.20 para.1
Sch.11, revoked: SI 1999/3178 Art.3, Sch.20 para.1

1985. Channel Tunnel Rail Link (Nomination) (London Underground Works) Order 1999
Art.2, amended: SI 1999/2198 Art.2

2018. Yugoslavia (Prohibition of Flights) Regulations 1999
revoked: SI 1999/3166 Reg.2
Reg.2, revoked: SI 1999/3166 Reg.2
Reg.3, revoked: SI 1999/3166 Reg.2

2024. Quarries Regulations 1999
Reg.2, amended: SI 1999/3242 Reg.29, Sch.2
Reg.7, amended: SI 1999/3242 Reg.29, Sch.2
Reg.43, amended: SI 1999/3242 Reg.29, Sch.2

2025. Food (Animals and Animal Products from Belgium) (Emergency Control) (England and Wales) Order 1999
revoked: SI 1999/2332 Reg.6
Art.2, applied: SI 1999/2026 Reg.2
Art.2, revoked: SI 1999/2332 Reg.6
Art.4, revoked: SI 1999/2332 Art.6
Art.5, revoked: SI 1999/2332 Art.6
Art.6, revoked: SI 1999/2332 Art.6

2026. Animal Feedingstuffs from Belgium (Control) (England and Wales) Regulations 1999
revoked: SI 1999/2333 Reg.6
Reg.2, revoked: SI 1999/2333 Reg.6
Reg.4, revoked: SI 1999/2333 Reg.6

NO.

2026. Animal Feedingstuffs from Belgium (Control) (England and Wales) Regulations 1999—*cont.*
Reg.5, revoked: SI 1999/2333 Reg.6
Reg.6, revoked: SI 1999/2333 Reg.6

2102. Education (Substituted Grammar Schools) Regulations 1999
applied: SI 1999/2456

2109. Medicines (Aristolochia) (Emergency Prohibition) Order 1999
revoked: SI 1999/2889 Art.3
Art.2, revoked: SI 1999/2889 Art.3

2150. Travel Documents (Refugees and Stateless Persons) (Fees) Regulations 1999
revoked: SI 1999/3339 Reg.5

2163. Education (School Government) (England) Regulations 1999
Part II, applied: SI 1999/2259 Reg.9
Reg.9, amended: SI 1999/2262 Reg.62
Reg.17, referred to: SI 1999/2262 Reg.25
Reg.18, applied: SI 1999/2262 Reg.25
Reg.19, applied: SI 1999/2262 Reg.25
Reg.20, referred to: SI 1999/2262 Reg.25
Reg.37, amended: SI 1999/2262 Reg.55
Sch.1, amended: SI 1999/2262 Reg.33
Sch.1, applied: SI 1999/2262 Reg.33
Sch.2, amended: SI 1999/2262 Reg.38
Sch.2, applied: SI 1999/2262 Reg.38
Sch.3, amended: SI 1999/2262 Reg.38
Sch.3, applied: SI 1999/2262 Reg.38
Sch.4, amended: SI 1999/2262 Reg.40
Sch.4, applied: SI 1999/2262 Reg.40
Sch.4, referred to: SI 1999/2262 Reg.38
Sch.5, amended: SI 1999/2262 Reg.24
Sch.5, applied: SI 1999/2262 Reg.24
Sch.5 para.1, amended: SI 1999/2262 Reg.24
Sch.5 para.3, referred to: SI 1999/2262 Reg.24
Sch.5 para.4, referred to: SI 1999/2262 Reg.24
Sch.5 para.9, referred to: SI 1999/2262 Reg.24
Sch.5 para.10, amended: SI 1999/2163 Reg.50
Sch.5 para.10, referred to: SI 1999/2262 Reg.24
Sch.5 para.10, revoked (in part): SI 1999/2163 Reg.50
Sch.5 para.13, referred to: SI 1999/2262 Reg.24
Sch.5 para.14, substituted: SI 1999/2262 Reg.24
Sch.5 para.16, substituted: SI 1999/2262 Reg.24

2242. Education (School Government) (Wales) Regulations 1999
Part II, applied: SI 1999/2633 Reg.8
Reg.17, applied: SI 1999/2243 Reg.25
Reg.18, applied: SI 1999/2243 Reg.25
Reg.19, applied: SI 1999/2243 Reg.25
Reg.20, applied: SI 1999/2243 Reg.25
Reg.37, amended: SI 1999/2243 Reg.55
Sch.1, amended: SI 1999/2243 Reg.33
Sch.1, applied: SI 1999/2243 Reg.33
Sch.2, amended: SI 1999/2243 Reg.38
Sch.2, applied: SI 1999/2243 Reg.38
Sch.3, amended: SI 1999/2243 Reg.38
Sch.3, applied: SI 1999/2243 Reg.38
Sch.4, applied: SI 1999/2243 Reg.38
Sch.4 para.1, amended: SI 1999/2243 Reg.38
Sch.4 para.2, amended: SI 1999/2243 Reg.38
Sch.4 para.3, amended: SI 1999/2243 Reg.38
Sch.5, amended: SI 1999/2243 Reg.40
Sch.5, applied: SI 1999/2243 Reg.40
Sch.5, referred to: SI 1999/2243 Reg.38
Sch.6, amended: SI 1999/2243 Reg.24
Sch.6, applied: SI 1999/2243 Reg.24

NO.

2242. Education (School Government) (Wales) Regulations 1999—*cont.*
Sch.6 para.1, amended: SI 1999/2243 Reg.24
Sch.6 para.3, referred to: SI 1999/2243 Reg.24
Sch.6 para.4, referred to: SI 1999/2243 Reg.24
Sch.6 para.10, referred to: SI 1999/2243 Reg.24
Sch.6 para.14, substituted: SI 1999/2243 Reg.24
Sch.6 para.16, substituted: SI 1999/2243 Reg.24

2264. Education (Grants) (Dance and Drama) (England) Regulations 1999
applied: SI 1999/2269 Art.2

2276. Civil Aviation (Route Charges for Navigation Services) (Fourth Amendment) Regulations 1999
revoked: SI 1999/3260 Reg.2, Sch.1
Reg.2, revoked: SI 1999/3260 Reg.2, Sch.1

2315. Relocation Grants (Form of Application) (Welsh Forms of Application) Regulations 1999
Sch. Form, amended: SI 1999/3469 Reg.2

2323. School Standards and Framework Act 1998 (Commencement No.7 and Saving and Transitional Provisions) Order 1999
Art.16, amended: SI 1999/2484 Art.3

2332. Food (Animals and Animal Products from Belgium) (Emergency Control) (England and Wales) (No.2) Order 1999
revoked: SI 1999/2798 Art.6
Art.2, applied: SI 1999/2333 Reg.2
Art.2, revoked: SI 1999/2798 Art.6
Art.4, revoked: SI 1999/2798 Art.6
Art.5, revoked: SI 1999/2798 Art.6
Art.6, revoked: SI 1999/2798 Art.6

2333. Animal Feedingstuffs from Belgium (Control) (England and Wales) (No.2) Regulations 1999
revoked: SI 1999/2799 Reg.6
Reg.2, revoked: SI 1999/2799 Reg.6
Reg.4, revoked: SI 1999/2799 Reg.6
Reg.5, revoked: SI 1999/2799 Reg.6
Reg.6, revoked: SI 1999/2799 Reg.6

2342. Health Act 1999 (Commencement No.2) Order 1999
referred to: SI 1999/2540 Art.2, Sch.1

2349. A40 Trunk Road (Ealing and Hammersmith & Fulham) Red Route Experimental Traffic Order 1999
Sch.2B Item 3, substituted: SI 1999/3416 Art.3
Sch.2B Item 11, substituted: SI 1999/3416 Art.4
Sch.4 Item 3, substituted: SI 1999/3416 Art.5
Sch.4 Item 9, substituted: SI 1999/3416 Art.6

2356. Companies (Forms) (Amendment) Regulations 1999
Sch. Form 88(2), revoked: SI 1999/2678 Reg.2

2357. Companies (Welsh Language Forms) (Amendment) Regulations 1999
Sch. Form 88(2)CYM, revoked: SI 1999/2679 Reg.2

2403. Administration of the Rent Officer Service (England) Order 1999
applied: SI 1999/2511 Reg.2

2422. Social Security Act 1998 (Commencement No.9, and Savings and Consequential and Transitional Provisions) Order 1999
Art.3, revoked (in part): SI 1999/3178 Art.3, Sch.20 para.1
Art.5, amended: SI 1999/3178 Art.3, Sch.20 para.2
Sch.2, revoked: SI 1999/3178 Art.3, Sch.20 para.1

NO.

2422. Social Security Act 1998 (Commencement No.9, and Savings and Consequential and Transitional Provisions) Order 1999— *cont.*
Sch.7, revoked: SI 1999/3178 Art.3, Sch.20 para.1
Sch.8, revoked: SI 1999/3178 Art.3, Sch.20 para.1
Sch.13, revoked: SI 1999/3178 Art.3, Sch.20 para.1

2450. Telecommunications (Licence Modification) (Standard Schedules) Regulations 1999
Sch.1 Part I, amended: SI 1999/2452 Reg.3, Sch.2 para.1, SI 1999/2453 Reg.3, Sch.2 para.1, Sch.2 para.2, SI 1999/2455 Reg.3, Sch.2 para.1, SI 1999/3448 Reg.4, Sch. Part I, SI 1999/3449 Reg.9, Sch.1
Sch.1 Part J, added: SI 1999/2452 Reg.3, Sch.2 para.14, SI 1999/2453 Reg.3, Sch.2 para.12, SI 1999/2455 Reg.3, Sch.2 para.7
Sch.1 para.1.3, added: SI 1999/2452 Reg.3, Sch.2 para.2
Sch.1 para.1.4, added: SI 1999/2452 Reg.3, Sch.2 para.2
Sch.1 para.1.5, added: SI 1999/2452 Reg.3, Sch.2 para.2
Sch.1 para.5, substituted: SI 1999/2452 Reg.3, Sch.2 para.3
Sch.1 para.5.1, substituted: SI 1999/2452 Reg.3, Sch.2 para.3
Sch.1 para.5.2, substituted: SI 1999/2452 Reg.3, Sch.2 para.3
Sch.1 para.5.3, substituted: SI 1999/2452 Reg.3, Sch.2 para.3
Sch.1 para.5.4, substituted: SI 1999/2452 Reg.3, Sch.2 para.3
Sch.1 para.5.5, substituted: SI 1999/2452 Reg.3, Sch.2 para.3
Sch.1 para.5.6, substituted: SI 1999/2452 Reg.3, Sch.2 para.3
Sch.1 para.7.2, amended: SI 1999/2452 Reg.3, Sch.2 para.4
Sch.1 para.7.6, added: SI 1999/2452 Reg.3, Sch.2 para.4
Sch.1 para.15.3, amended: SI 1999/2452 Reg.3, Sch.2 para.5
Sch.1 para.22.9, amended: SI 1999/2452 Reg.3, Sch.2 para.6
Sch.1 para.23, substituted: SI 1999/2452 Reg.3, Sch.2 para.7
Sch.1 para.23.1, substituted: SI 1999/2452 Reg.3, Sch.2 para.7
Sch.1 para.23.2, substituted: SI 1999/2452 Reg.3, Sch.2 para.7
Sch.1 para.23.3, substituted: SI 1999/2452 Reg.3, Sch.2 para.7
Sch.1 para.28, substituted: SI 1999/3449 Reg.9, Sch.1
Sch.1 para.34, referred to: SI 1999/2450 Sch.2 para.1
Sch.1 para.34.2, referred to: SI 1999/2450 Sch.2 para.1
Sch.1 para.34.3, referred to: SI 1999/2450 Sch.2 para.1
Sch.1 para.36, referred to: SI 1999/2450 Sch.2 para.1
Sch.1 para.38.1, substituted: SI 1999/2453 Reg.3, Sch.2 para.3, SI 1999/2455 Reg.3, Sch.2 para.2
Sch.1 para.40, amended: SI 1999/2453 Reg.3, Sch.2 para.4, SI 1999/2455 Reg.3, Sch.2 para.3

1999—cont.

1999—cont.

2450. **Telecommunications (Licence Modification) (Standard Schedules) Regulations 1999—** *cont.*

Sch.1 para.41, amended: SI 1999/2453 Reg.3, Sch.2 para.4, SI 1999/2455 Reg.3, Sch.2 para.3

Sch.1 para.42, amended: SI 1999/2453 Reg.3, Sch.2 para.4, SI 1999/2455 Reg.3, Sch.2 para.3

Sch.1 para.43.1, substituted: SI 1999/2453 Reg.3, Sch.2 para.5, SI 1999/2455 Reg.3, Sch.2 para.4

Sch.1 para.43.2, amended: SI 1999/2453 Reg.3, Sch.2 para.5, SI 1999/2455 Reg.3, Sch.2 para.4

Sch.1 para.46.1, amended: SI 1999/2452 Reg.3, Sch.2 para.8

Sch.1 para.46.2, amended: SI 1999/2453 Reg.3, Sch.2 para.6

Sch.1 para.46.3, amended: SI 1999/2453 Reg.3, Sch.2 para.6

Sch.1 para.47.1, amended: SI 1999/2453 Reg.3, Sch.2 para.7

Sch.1 para.47.2, amended: SI 1999/2453 Reg.3, Sch.2 para.7

Sch.1 para.47.4, amended: SI 1999/2453 Reg.3, Sch.2 para.7

Sch.1 para.47.5, amended: SI 1999/2453 Reg.3, Sch.2 para.7

Sch.1 para.47.6, amended: SI 1999/2453 Reg.3, Sch.2 para.7

Sch.1 para.47.8, amended: SI 1999/2453 Reg.3, Sch.2 para.7

Sch.1 para.48.3, amended: SI 1999/2452 Reg.3, Sch.2 para.9

Sch.1 para.48.3A, added: SI 1999/2452 Reg.3, Sch.2 para.9

Sch.1 para.50, amended: SI 1999/2453 Reg.3, Sch.2 para.8

Sch.1 para.50A, added: SI 1999/3448 Reg.4, Sch. Part II

Sch.1 para.56A, added: SI 1999/2452 Reg.3, Sch.2 para.10

Sch.1 para.56A.1, added: SI 1999/2452 Reg.3, Sch.2 para.10

Sch.1 para.56A.2, added: SI 1999/2452 Reg.3, Sch.2 para.10

Sch.1 para.56B, added: SI 1999/2452 Reg.3, Sch.2 para.10

Sch.1 para.56B.1, added: SI 1999/2452 Reg.3, Sch.2 para.10

Sch.1 para.56B.2, added: SI 1999/2452 Reg.3, Sch.2 para.10

Sch.1 para.56B.3, added: SI 1999/2452 Reg.3, Sch.2 para.10

Sch.1 para.56B.4, added: SI 1999/2452 Reg.3, Sch.2 para.10

Sch.1 para.56B.5, added: SI 1999/2452 Reg.3, Sch.2 para.10

Sch.1 para.57.1, amended: SI 1999/2452 Reg.3, Sch.2 para.11, SI 1999/2453 Reg.3, Sch.2 para.9, SI 1999/2455 Reg.3, Sch.2 para.5

Sch.1 para.57.2, added: SI 1999/2452 Reg.3, Sch.2 para.11

Sch.1 para.58.1, amended: SI 1999/2452 Reg.3, Sch.2 para.12

Sch.1 para.58.1, substituted: SI 1999/2453 Reg.3, Sch.2 para.10, SI 1999/2455 Reg.3, Sch.2 para.6

Sch.1 para.58.2, amended: SI 1999/2453 Reg.3, Sch.2 para.10, SI 1999/2455 Reg.3, Sch.2 para.6

2450. **Telecommunications (Licence Modification) (Standard Schedules) Regulations 1999—** *cont.*

Sch.1 para.58.7, added: SI 1999/2452 Reg.3, Sch.2 para.12

Sch.1 para.58.8, added: SI 1999/2452 Reg.3, Sch.2 para.12

Sch.1 para.62, amended: SI 1999/2453 Reg.3, Sch.2 para.11

Sch.1 para.64.8A, added: SI 1999/2452 Reg.3, Sch.2 para.13

Sch.1 para.65, added: SI 1999/2452 Reg.3, Sch.2 para.14, SI 1999/2453 Reg.3, Sch.2 para.12

Sch.1 para.65.1, added: SI 1999/2452 Reg.3, Sch.2 para.14, SI 1999/2453 Reg.3, Sch.2 para.12, SI 1999/2455 Reg.3, Sch.2 para.7

Sch.1 para.65.2, added: SI 1999/2452 Reg.3, Sch.2 para.14, SI 1999/2453 Reg.3, Sch.2 para.12, SI 1999/2455 Reg.3, Sch.2 para.7

Sch.1 para.65.3, added: SI 1999/2452 Reg.3, Sch.2 para.14, SI 1999/2453 Reg.3, Sch.2 para.12, SI 1999/2455 Reg.3, Sch.2 para.7

Sch.1 para.65.4, added: SI 1999/2453 Reg.3, Sch.2 para.12, SI 1999/2455 Reg.3, Sch.2 para.7

Sch.1 para.65.5, added: SI 1999/2453 Reg.3, Sch.2 para.12, SI 1999/2455 Reg.3, Sch.2 para.7

Sch.1 para.65.6, added: SI 1999/2453 Reg.3, Sch.2 para.12

Sch.1 para.65.7, added: SI 1999/2453 Reg.3, Sch.2 para.12

Sch.1 para.66, added: SI 1999/2452 Reg.3, Sch.2 para.14, SI 1999/2453 Reg.3, Sch.2 para.12

Sch.1 para.66.1, added: SI 1999/2452 Reg.3, Sch.2 para.14, SI 1999/2453 Reg.3, Sch.2 para.12, SI 1999/2455 Reg.3, Sch.2 para.7

Sch.1 para.66.2, added: SI 1999/2452 Reg.3, Sch.2 para.14, SI 1999/2455 Reg.3, Sch.2 para.7

Sch.1 para.66.3, added: SI 1999/2452 Reg.3, Sch.2 para.14, SI 1999/2455 Reg.3, Sch.2 para.7

Sch.1 para.66.4, added: SI 1999/2452 Reg.3, Sch.2 para.14

Sch.1 para.66.5, added: SI 1999/2452 Reg.3, Sch.2 para.14

Sch.1 para.67, added: SI 1999/2452 Reg.3, Sch.2 para.14, SI 1999/2453 Reg.3, Sch.2 para.12

Sch.1 para.67.1, added: SI 1999/2452 Reg.3, Sch.2 para.14, SI 1999/2453 Reg.3, Sch.2 para.12, SI 1999/2455 Reg.3, Sch.2 para.7

Sch.1 para.67.2, added: SI 1999/2453 Reg.3, Sch.2 para.12, SI 1999/2455 Reg.3, Sch.2 para.7

Sch.1 para.67.3, added: SI 1999/2453 Reg.3, Sch.2 para.12, SI 1999/2455 Reg.3, Sch.2 para.7

Sch.1 para.67.4, added: SI 1999/2455 Reg.3, Sch.2 para.7

Sch.1 para.68, added: SI 1999/2452 Reg.3, Sch.2 para.14, SI 1999/2453 Reg.3, Sch.2 para.12

Sch.1 para.68.1, added: SI 1999/2452 Reg.3, Sch.2 para.14, SI 1999/2453 Reg.3, Sch.2 para.12, SI 1999/2455 Reg.3, Sch.2 para.7

Sch.1 para.68.2, added: SI 1999/2452 Reg.3, Sch.2 para.14, SI 1999/2453 Reg.3, Sch.2 para.12, SI 1999/2455 Reg.3, Sch.2 para.7

NO.

NO.

1999—cont.

2450. Telecommunications (Licence Modification) (Standard Schedules) Regulations 1999— *cont.*

Sch.1 para.68.3, added: SI 1999/2452 Reg.3, Sch.2 para.14, SI 1999/2453 Reg.3, Sch.2 para.12, SI 1999/2455 Reg.3, Sch.2 para.7

Sch.1 para.68.4, added: SI 1999/2452 Reg.3, Sch.2 para.14, SI 1999/2453 Reg.3, Sch.2 para.12, SI 1999/2455 Reg.3, Sch.2 para.7

Sch.1 para.68.5, added: SI 1999/2452 Reg.3, Sch.2 para.14, SI 1999/2453 Reg.3, Sch.2 para.12

Sch.1 para.68.6, added: SI 1999/2452 Reg.3, Sch.2 para.14, SI 1999/2453 Reg.3, Sch.2 para.12

Sch.1 para.68.7, added: SI 1999/2452 Reg.3, Sch.2 para.14, SI 1999/2453 Reg.3, Sch.2 para.12

Sch.1 para.68.8, added: SI 1999/2452 Reg.3, Sch.2 para.14

Sch.1 para.69, added: SI 1999/2452 Reg.3, Sch.2 para.14, SI 1999/2453 Reg.3, Sch.2 para.12

Sch.1 para.69.1, added: SI 1999/2452 Reg.3, Sch.2 para.14, SI 1999/2453 Reg.3, Sch.2 para.12

Sch.1 para.69.2, added: SI 1999/2452 Reg.3, Sch.2 para.14, SI 1999/2453 Reg.3, Sch.2 para.12

Sch.1 para.69.3, added: SI 1999/2452 Reg.3, Sch.2 para.14, SI 1999/2453 Reg.3, Sch.2 para.12

Sch.1 para.69.4, added: SI 1999/2452 Reg.3, Sch.2 para.14, SI 1999/2453 Reg.3, Sch.2 para.12

Sch.1 para.69.5, added: SI 1999/2453 Reg.3, Sch.2 para.12

Sch.1 para.69.6, added: SI 1999/2453 Reg.3, Sch.2 para.12

Sch.1 para.69.7, added: SI 1999/2453 Reg.3, Sch.2 para.12

Sch.1 para.69.8, added: SI 1999/2453 Reg.3, Sch.2 para.12

Sch.1 para.69.9, added: SI 1999/2453 Reg.3, Sch.2 para.12

Sch.1 para.69.10, added: SI 1999/2453 Reg.3, Sch.2 para.12

Sch.1 para.69.11, added: SI 1999/2453 Reg.3, Sch.2 para.12

Sch.1 para.69.12, added: SI 1999/2453 Reg.3, Sch.2 para.12

Sch.1 para.69.13, added: SI 1999/2453 Reg.3, Sch.2 para.12

Sch.1 para.69.14, added: SI 1999/2453 Reg.3, Sch.2 para.12

Sch.1 para.69.15, added: SI 1999/2453 Reg.3, Sch.2 para.12

Sch.1 para.69.16, added: SI 1999/2453 Reg.3, Sch.2 para.12

Sch.1 para.69.17, added: SI 1999/2453 Reg.3, Sch.2 para.12

Sch.1 para.69.18, added: SI 1999/2453 Reg.3, Sch.2 para.12

Sch.1 para.69.19, added: SI 1999/2453 Reg.3, Sch.2 para.12

Sch.1 para.69.20, added: SI 1999/2453 Reg.3, Sch.2 para.12

Sch.1 para.69.21, added: SI 1999/2453 Reg.3, Sch.2 para.12

Sch.1 para.69.22, added: SI 1999/2453 Reg.3, Sch.2 para.12

Sch.1 para.69.23, added: SI 1999/2453 Reg.3, Sch.2 para.12

1999—cont.

2450. Telecommunications (Licence Modification) (Standard Schedules) Regulations 1999— *cont.*

Sch.1 para.69.24, added: SI 1999/2453 Reg.3, Sch.2 para.12

Sch.1 para.69.25, added: SI 1999/2453 Reg.3, Sch.2 para.12

Sch.1 para.70, added: SI 1999/2453 Reg.3, Sch.2 para.12

Sch.1 para.70.1, added: SI 1999/2453 Reg.3, Sch.2 para.12

Sch.1 para.70.2, added: SI 1999/2453 Reg.3, Sch.2 para.12

Sch.1 para.70.3, added: SI 1999/2453 Reg.3, Sch.2 para.12

Sch.1 para.70.4, added: SI 1999/2453 Reg.3, Sch.2 para.12

Sch.1 para.70.5, added: SI 1999/2453 Reg.3, Sch.2 para.12

Sch.1 para.70.6, added: SI 1999/2453 Reg.3, Sch.2 para.12

Sch.1 para.70.7, added: SI 1999/2453 Reg.3, Sch.2 para.12

Sch.1 para.70.8, added: SI 1999/2453 Reg.3, Sch.2 para.12

Sch.1 para.70.9, added: SI 1999/2453 Reg.3, Sch.2 para.12

Sch.1 para.70.10, added: SI 1999/2453 Reg.3, Sch.2 para.12

Sch.1 para.70.11, added: SI 1999/2453 Reg.3, Sch.2 para.12

Sch.1 para.70.12, added: SI 1999/2453 Reg.3, Sch.2 para.12

Sch.1 para.70.13, added: SI 1999/2453 Reg.3, Sch.2 para.12

Sch.1 para.70.14, added: SI 1999/2453 Reg.3, Sch.2 para.12

Sch.1 para.70.15, added: SI 1999/2453 Reg.3, Sch.2 para.12

Sch.1 para.70.16, added: SI 1999/2453 Reg.3, Sch.2 para.12

Sch.1 para.70.17, added: SI 1999/2453 Reg.3, Sch.2 para.12

Sch.1 para.70.18, added: SI 1999/2453 Reg.3, Sch.2 para.12

Sch.1 para.70.19, added: SI 1999/2453 Reg.3, Sch.2 para.12

Sch.1 para.71, added: SI 1999/2453 Reg.3, Sch.2 para.12

Sch.1 para.71.1, added: SI 1999/2453 Reg.3, Sch.2 para.12

Sch.1 para.71.2, added: SI 1999/2453 Reg.3, Sch.2 para.12

Sch.1 para.71.3, added: SI 1999/2453 Reg.3, Sch.2 para.12

Sch.1 para.71.4, added: SI 1999/2453 Reg.3, Sch.2 para.12

Sch.1 para.71.5, added: SI 1999/2453 Reg.3, Sch.2 para.12

Sch.1 para.71.6, added: SI 1999/2453 Reg.3, Sch.2 para.12

Sch.1 para.71.7, added: SI 1999/2453 Reg.3, Sch.2 para.12

Sch.1 para.71.8, added: SI 1999/2453 Reg.3, Sch.2 para.12

Sch.1 para.71.9, added: SI 1999/2453 Reg.3, Sch.2 para.12

Sch.1 para.71.10, added: SI 1999/2453 Reg.3, Sch.2 para.12

Sch.1 para.71.11, added: SI 1999/2453 Reg.3, Sch.2 para.12

Sch.1 para.71.12, added: SI 1999/2453 Reg.3, Sch.2 para.12

NO.

NO.

1999—cont.

1999—cont.

2450. Telecommunications (Licence Modification) (Standard Schedules) Regulations 1999— *cont.*

Sch.1 para.71.13, added: SI 1999/2453 Reg.3, Sch.2 para.12

Sch.1 para.71.14, added: SI 1999/2453 Reg.3, Sch.2 para.12

Sch.1 para.72, added: SI 1999/2453 Reg.3, Sch.2 para.12

Sch.1 para.72.1, added: SI 1999/2453 Reg.3, Sch.2 para.12

Sch.1 para.72.2, added: SI 1999/2453 Reg.3, Sch.2 para.12

Sch.1 para.72.3, added: SI 1999/2453 Reg.3, Sch.2 para.12

Sch.1 para.72.4, added: SI 1999/2453 Reg.3, Sch.2 para.12

Sch.1 para.72.5, added: SI 1999/2453 Reg.3, Sch.2 para.12

Sch.1 para.73, added: SI 1999/2453 Reg.3, Sch.2 para.12

Sch.1 para.73.1, added: SI 1999/2453 Reg.3, Sch.2 para.12

Sch.1 para.73.2, added: SI 1999/2453 Reg.3, Sch.2 para.12

Sch.1 para.73.3, added: SI 1999/2453 Reg.3, Sch.2 para.12

Sch.1 para.73.4, added: SI 1999/2453 Reg.3, Sch.2 para.12

Sch.1 para.73.5, added: SI 1999/2453 Reg.3, Sch.2 para.12

Sch.1 para.74, added: SI 1999/2453 Reg.3, Sch.2 para.12

Sch.1 para.74.1, added: SI 1999/2453 Reg.3, Sch.2 para.12

Sch.1 para.74.2, added: SI 1999/2453 Reg.3, Sch.2 para.12

Sch.1 para.74.3, added: SI 1999/2453 Reg.3, Sch.2 para.12

Sch.1 para.74.4, added: SI 1999/2453 Reg.3, Sch.2 para.12

Sch.1 para.74.5, added: SI 1999/2453 Reg.3, Sch.2 para.12

Sch.1 para.74.6, added: SI 1999/2453 Reg.3, Sch.2 para.12

Sch.1 para.75, added: SI 1999/2453 Reg.3, Sch.2 para.12

Sch.1 para.75.1, added: SI 1999/2453 Reg.3, Sch.2 para.12

Sch.1 para.75.2, added: SI 1999/2453 Reg.3, Sch.2 para.12

Sch.1 para.75.3, added: SI 1999/2453 Reg.3, Sch.2 para.12

Sch.1 para.75.4, added: SI 1999/2453 Reg.3, Sch.2 para.12

Sch.1 para.75.5, added: SI 1999/2453 Reg.3, Sch.2 para.12

Sch.1 para.75.6, added: SI 1999/2453 Reg.3, Sch.2 para.12

Sch.1 para.76, added: SI 1999/2453 Reg.3, Sch.2 para.12

Sch.1 para.76.1, added: SI 1999/2453 Reg.3, Sch.2 para.12

Sch.1 para.76.2, added: SI 1999/2453 Reg.3, Sch.2 para.12

Sch.1 para.76.3, added: SI 1999/2453 Reg.3, Sch.2 para.12

Sch.1 para.76.4, added: SI 1999/2453 Reg.3, Sch.2 para.12

Sch.1 para.76.5, added: SI 1999/2453 Reg.3, Sch.2 para.12

Sch.1 para.77, added: SI 1999/2453 Reg.3, Sch.2 para.12

2450. Telecommunications (Licence Modification) (Standard Schedules) Regulations 1999— *cont.*

Sch.1 para.77.1, added: SI 1999/2453 Reg.3, Sch.2 para.12

Sch.1 para.77.2, added: SI 1999/2453 Reg.3, Sch.2 para.12

Sch.1 para.77.3, added: SI 1999/2453 Reg.3, Sch.2 para.12

Sch.1 para.77.4, added: SI 1999/2453 Reg.3, Sch.2 para.12

Sch.1 para.77.5, added: SI 1999/2453 Reg.3, Sch.2 para.12

Sch.1 para.78, added: SI 1999/2453 Reg.3, Sch.2 para.12

Sch.1 para.78.1, added: SI 1999/2453 Reg.3, Sch.2 para.12

Sch.1 para.78.2, added: SI 1999/2453 Reg.3, Sch.2 para.12

Sch.1 para.78.3, added: SI 1999/2453 Reg.3, Sch.2 para.12

Sch.1 para.78.4, added: SI 1999/2453 Reg.3, Sch.2 para.12

Sch.1 para.78.5, added: SI 1999/2453 Reg.3, Sch.2 para.12

Sch.1 para.78.6, added: SI 1999/2453 Reg.3, Sch.2 para.12

Sch.1 para.78.7, added: SI 1999/2453 Reg.3, Sch.2 para.12

Sch.1 para.78.7A, added: SI 1999/2453 Reg.3, Sch.2 para.12

Sch.1 para.78.8, added: SI 1999/2453 Reg.3, Sch.2 para.12

Sch.1 para.78.9, added: SI 1999/2453 Reg.3, Sch.2 para.12

Sch.1 para.78.10, added: SI 1999/2453 Reg.3, Sch.2 para.12

Sch.1 para.78.11, added: SI 1999/2453 Reg.3, Sch.2 para.12

Sch.1 para.78.12, added: SI 1999/2453 Reg.3, Sch.2 para.12

Sch.1 para.78.13, added: SI 1999/2453 Reg.3, Sch.2 para.12

Sch.1 para.78.14, added: SI 1999/2453 Reg.3, Sch.2 para.12

Sch.1 para.78.15, added: SI 1999/2453 Reg.3, Sch.2 para.12

Sch.1 para.78.16, added: SI 1999/2453 Reg.3, Sch.2 para.12

Sch.1 para.78.17, added: SI 1999/2453 Reg.3, Sch.2 para.12

Sch.1 para.79, added: SI 1999/2453 Reg.3, Sch.2 para.12

Sch.1 para.79.1, added: SI 1999/2453 Reg.3, Sch.2 para.12

Sch.1 para.79.2, added: SI 1999/2453 Reg.3, Sch.2 para.12

Sch.1 para.79.3, added: SI 1999/2453 Reg.3, Sch.2 para.12

Sch.1 para.79.4, added: SI 1999/2453 Reg.3, Sch.2 para.12

Sch.1 para.79.5, added: SI 1999/2453 Reg.3, Sch.2 para.12

Sch.1 para.80, added: SI 1999/2453 Reg.3, Sch.2 para.12

Sch.1 para.80.1, added: SI 1999/2453 Reg.3, Sch.2 para.12

Sch.1 para.80.2, added: SI 1999/2453 Reg.3, Sch.2 para.12

Sch.1 para.80.3, added: SI 1999/2453 Reg.3, Sch.2 para.12

Sch.1 para.81, added: SI 1999/2453 Reg.3, Sch.2 para.12

NO.

1999—cont.

2450. Telecommunications (Licence Modification) (Standard Schedules) Regulations 1999— cont.
Sch.1 para.81.1, added: SI 1999/2453 Reg.3, Sch.2 para.12
Sch.1 para.81.2, added: SI 1999/2453 Reg.3, Sch.2 para.12
Sch.1 para.81.3, added: SI 1999/2453 Reg.3, Sch.2 para.12
Sch.1 para.81.4, added: SI 1999/2453 Reg.3, Sch.2 para.12
Sch.1 para.81.5, added: SI 1999/2453 Reg.3, Sch.2 para.12
Sch.1 para.82, added: SI 1999/2453 Reg.3, Sch.2 para.12
Sch.1 para.82.1, added: SI 1999/2453 Reg.3, Sch.2 para.12
Sch.1 para.82.2, added: SI 1999/2453 Reg.3, Sch.2 para.12
Sch.1 para.82.3, added: SI 1999/2453 Reg.3, Sch.2 para.12
Sch.1 para.82.4, added: SI 1999/2453 Reg.3, Sch.2 para.12
Sch.1 para.82.5, added: SI 1999/2453 Reg.3, Sch.2 para.12
Sch.3 para.3, referred to: SI 1999/2450 Sch.2 para.1

2560. Merger Reference (Universal Foods Corporation and Pointing Holdings Limited) (Interim Provision) Order 1999
revoked: SI 1999/3415 Art.2

2562. National Health Service (Optical Charges and Payments) and (General Ophthalmic Services) (Amendment) Regulations 1999
referred to: SI 1999/2841 Reg.4
Reg.3, amended: SI 1999/2714 Reg.2

2576. Legal Aid (Mediation in Family Matters) (Amendment) Regulations 1999
revoked: SI 1999/2738 Reg.4
Reg.3, revoked: SI 1999/2738 Reg.4
Reg.4, revoked: SI 1999/2738 Reg.4
Reg.5, revoked: SI 1999/2738 Reg.4
Reg.6, revoked: SI 1999/2738 Reg.4

2609. Export of Goods (Control) (Amendment No.4) Order 1999
Art.2, amended: SI 1999/2627

2611. Organic Farming (Wales) Regulations 1999
Reg.2, amended: SI 1999/2611 Reg.13
Reg.4, amended: SI 1999/2611 Reg.13
Reg.5, amended: SI 1999/2611 Reg.13
Reg.6, amended: SI 1999/3337 Reg.3
Reg.6A, added: SI 1999/3337 Reg.3

2714. National Health Service (General Ophthalmic Services) (Amendment) Regulations 1999
referred to: SI 1999/2841 Reg.4

2721. Merchant Shipping (Life-Saving Appliances for Ships Other than Ships of Classes III to VI(A)) Regulations 1999
applied: SI 1999/2722 Reg.2
Reg.54, applied: SI 1999/2722 Reg.10
Reg.75, applied: SI 1999/2722 Reg.10
Reg.84, applied: SI 1999/2722 Reg.10

2723. Merchant Shipping (Life-Saving Appliances for Passenger Ships of Classes III to VI(A)) Regulations 1999
applied: SI 1999/2722 Reg.2

2790. Employment Relations (Northern Ireland) Order 1999
Art.20, revoked (in part): SI 1999/2790 (NI.9) Art.40, Sch.9 Part 3

NO.

1999—cont.

2798. Food (Animals and Animal Products from Belgium) (Emergency Control) (England and Wales) (No.3) Order 1999
applied: SI 1999/2799
revoked: SI 1999/3421 Art.6
Art.4, applied: SI 1999/2798 Reg.2
Art.4, revoked: SI 1999/3421 Art.6
Art.5, revoked: SI 1999/3421 Art.6
Art.6, revoked: SI 1999/3421 Art.6

2799. Animal Feedingstuffs from Belgium (Control) (England and Wales) (No.3) Regulations 1999
revoked: SI 1999/3422 Reg.6
Reg.2, revoked: SI 1999/3422 Reg.6
Reg.4, revoked: SI 1999/3422 Reg.6
Reg.5, revoked: SI 1999/3422 Reg.6
Reg.6, revoked: SI 1999/3422 Reg.6

2817. Education (Teachers' Qualifications and Health Standards) (Wales) Regulations 1999
amended: SI 1999/2817 Reg.2, Sch.1 para.8

2846. Veterinary Surgeons and Veterinary Practitioners (Registration) Regulations Order of Council 1999
Sch. Sch, substituted: SI 1999/3461 Sch. Reg.2

2860. Social Security Act 1998 (Commencement No.11, and Savings and Consequential and Transitional Provisions) Order 1999
Art.3, revoked (in part): SI 1999/3178 Art.3, Sch.20 para.1
Art.5, amended: SI 1999/3178 Art.3, Sch.20 para.2
Sch.2, revoked: SI 1999/3178 Art.3, Sch.20 para.1
Sch.3, revoked: SI 1999/3178 Art.3, Sch.20 para.1
Sch.4, revoked: SI 1999/3178 Art.3, Sch.20 para.1
Sch.5, revoked: SI 1999/3178 Art.3, Sch.20 para.1
Sch.6, revoked: SI 1999/3178 Art.3, Sch.20 para.1
Sch.9, revoked: SI 1999/3178 Art.3, Sch.20 para.1
Sch.10, revoked: SI 1999/3178 Art.3, Sch.20 para.1
Sch.13, revoked: SI 1999/3178 Art.3, Sch.20 para.1
Sch.14, revoked: SI 1999/3178 Art.3, Sch.20 para.1
Sch.15, revoked: SI 1999/3178 Art.3, Sch.20 para.1

2864. Motor Vehicles (Driving Licences) Regulations 1999
Reg.40, amended: SI 1999/2864 Reg.41

2998. Fishing Vessels (EC Directive on Harmonised Safety Regime) Regulations 1999
Reg.2, amended: SI 1999/3210 Reg.2
Reg.11, amended: SI 1999/3210 Reg.2
Reg.14, amended: SI 1999/3210 Reg.2
Sch.3, amended: SI 1999/3210 Reg.2
Sch.3 Part I, added: SI 1999/3210 Reg.2
Sch.3 Part II, added: SI 1999/3210 Reg.2

3009. Petty Sessions Areas Order 1999
Sch. Part I, amended: SI 1999/3220 Art.2

3134. Afghanistan (United Nations Sanctions) (Channel Islands) Order 1999
Art.1, amended: SI 1999/3317 Art.2
Art.2, amended: SI 1999/3317 Art.3
Art.3, amended: SI 1999/3317 Art.4
Art.4, amended: SI 1999/3317 Art.5

NO.

1999—cont.

3135. Afghanistan (United Nations Sanctions) (Isle of Man) Order 1999
Art.3, amended: SI 1999/3318 Art.2
Sch. para.2, amended: SI 1999/3318 Art.3

3147. Welfare Reform and Pensions (Northern Ireland) Order 1999
Art.22, amended: SI 1999/3147 (NI.11) Art.74, Sch.9 para.52

NO.

1999—cont.

3315. Hill Livestock (Compensatory Allowances) (Enforcement) Regulations 1999
Reg.4, applied: SI 1999/3316 Reg.15
Reg.5, applied: SI 1999/3316 Reg.15

3436. Local Authorities (Funds) (England) (Amendment) Regulations 1999
revoked: SI 1999/3459 Reg.8

EUROPEAN LEGISLATION IMPLEMENTED BY STATUTORY INSTRUMENTS

The table below lists, in chronological order, the European legislation implemented by Statutory Instruments issued from 1996 to 1999.

Regulations	SIs
Council Reg. 136/66 ([1966] OJ 172/3025)	2410—Olive Oil (Marketing Standards) (Amendment) Regulations 1998
Council Reg. 805/68 ([1968] OJ L148/24)	249—Suckler Cow Premium (Amendment) Regulations 1997 1179—Beef Special Premium (Amendment) Regulations 1999 2844—Sheep Annual Premium and Suckler Cow Premium Quotas Regulations 1997
Council Reg. 351/79 ([1979] OJ L054/90)	696—Common Agricultural Policy (Wine) Regulations 1996
Council Reg. 357/79 ([1979] OJ L054/124)	696—Common Agricultural Policy (Wine) Regulations 1996
Council Reg. 1208/81 ([1981] OJ L123/3)	12—Beef Carcase (Classification) (Amendment) Regulations 1998
Council Reg. 3140/82 ([1982] OJ L331/7)	1110—Fish Producers' Organisations (Formation Grants) Regulations 1999
Council Reg. 3626/82 ([1982] OJ L384)	2684—Endangered Species (Import and Export) Act 1976 (Amendment) Regulations 1996
Council Reg. 1873/84 ([1984] OJ L176/6)	696—Common Agricultural Policy (Wine) Regulations 1996
Council Reg. 797/85 ([1985] OJ L93/43)	1500—Hill Livestock (Compensatory Allowances) Regulations 1996
Council Reg. 3805/85 ([1985] OJ L367/39)	696—Common Agricultural Policy (Wine) Regulations 1996
Council Reg. 2392/86 ([1986] OJ L208/1)	696—Common Agricultural Policy (Wine) Regulations 1996
Council Reg. 2930/86 ([1986] OJ L274/1)	1915—Merchant Shipping (Registration of Ships) (Tonnage Amendment) Regulations 1998 1916—Merchant Shipping (Tonnage) (Fishing Vessels) (Amendment) Regulations 1998 3206—Merchant Shipping (Registration of Ships, and Tonnage) (Amendment) Regulations 1999
Council Reg. 822/87 ([1987] OJ L084/1)	696—Common Agricultural Policy (Wine) Regulations 1996
Council Reg. 823/87 ([1987] OJ L084/59)	696—Common Agricultural Policy (Wine) Regulations 1996
Council Reg. 1898/87 ([1987] OJ L182/36)	452—Spreadable Fats (Marketing Standards) (Amendment) Regulations 1998
Council Reg. 2052/88 ([1988] OJ L185/9)	529—Rural Development Grants (Agriculture) (Wales) Regulations 1996 568—Rural Development Grants (Agriculture) (Wales) (Amendment) Regulations 1997 2394—Rural Development Grants (Agriculture) (Amendment) Regulations 1996

Council Reg. 4252/88 ([1988] OJ L373/59)	696—Common Agricultural Policy (Wine) Regulations 1996
Council Reg. 4253/88 ([1988] OJ L374/1)	529—Rural Development Grants (Agriculture) (Wales) Regulations 1996 568—Rural Development Grants (Agriculture) (Wales) (Amendment) Regulations 1997 2394—Rural Development Grants (Agriculture) (Amendment) Regulations 1996
Council Reg. 4256/88 ([1988] OJ L374/25)	529—Rural Development Grants (Agriculture) (Wales) Regulations 1996 568—Rural Development Grants (Agriculture) (Wales) (Amendment) Regulations 1997 2394—Rural Development Grants (Agriculture) (Amendment) Regulations 1996
Council Reg. 2048/89 ([1989] OJ L202/32)	696—Common Agricultural Policy (Wine) Regulations 1996
Council Reg. 2389/89 ([1989] OJ L232/1)	696—Common Agricultural Policy (Wine) Regulations 1996
Council Reg. 2390/89 ([1989] OJ L232/7)	696—Common Agricultural Policy (Wine) Regulations 1996
Council Reg. 2392/89 ([1989] OJ L232/13)	542—Common Agricultural Policy (Wine) (Amendment) Regulations 1997
Council Reg. 3013/89 ([1989] OJ L289/1)	2844—Sheep Annual Premium and Suckler Cow Premium Quotas Regulations 1997
Council Reg. 1907/90 ([1990] OJ L173/5)	1414—Eggs (Marketing Standards) (Amendment) Regulations 1997
Council Reg. 1601/91 ([1991] OJ L149/1)	696—Common Agricultural Policy (Wine) Regulations 1996
Council Reg. 2092/91 ([1991] OJ L198/1)	166—Organic Products (Amendment) Regulations 1997
Council Reg. 2328/91 ([1991] OJ L218/1)	33—Hill Livestock (Compensatory Allowances) (Amendment) Regulations 1997 1500—Hill Livestock (Compensatory Allowances) Regulations 1996
Council Reg. 3330/91 ([1991] OJ L316/1)	2968—Statistics of Trade (Customs and Excise) (Amendment) Regulations 1996
Council Reg. 3895/91 ([1991] OJ L368/1)	696—Common Agricultural Policy (Wine) Regulations 1996
Council Reg. 684/92 ([1992] OJ L74/1)	1322—Public Service Vehicles (Community Licences) Regulations 1999
Council Reg. 881/92 ([1992] OJ L095/1)	2186—Goods Vehicles (Licensing of Operators) (Temporary Use in Great Britain) Regulations 1996
Council Reg. 1765/92 ([1992] OJ L181/12)	1482—Arable Area Payments (Amendment) Regulations 1996 2969—Arable Area Payments (Amendment) Regulations 1997 3142—Arable Area Payments Regulations 1996 3169—Arable Area Payments (Amendment) Regulations 1998
Council Reg. 1768/92 ([1992] OJ L182/1)	64—Patents (Supplementary Protection Certificates) Rules 1997
Council Reg. 2066/92 ([1992] OJ L215/49)	249—Suckler Cow Premium (Amendment) Regulations 1997
Council Reg. 2078/92 ([1992] OJ L215/85)	79—Nitrate Sensitive Areas (Amendment) Regulations 1998

Council Reg. 2078/92 ([1992] OJ L215/85)—
cont.

330—Countryside Premium Scheme (Scotland) Regulations 1997

590—Organic Farming Regulations 1999

970—Environmentally Sensitive Areas (Cambrian Mountains) Designation (Amendment) Order 1997

971—Environmentally Sensitive Areas (Cambrian Mountains-Extension) Designation (Amendment) Order 1997

972—Environmentally Sensitive Areas (Lleyn Peninsula) Designation (Amendment) Order 1997

973—Environmentally Sensitive Areas (Clwydian Range) Designation (Amendment) Order 1997

974—Environmentally Sensitive Areas (Preseli) Designation (Amendment) Order 1997

975—Environmentally Sensitive Areas (Ynys Mon) Designation (Amendment) Order 1997

976—Environmentally Sensitive Areas (Radnor) Designation (Amendment) Order 1997

990—Nitrate Sensitive Areas (Amendment) Regulations 1997

1174—Countryside Access (Amendment) Regulations 1999

1176—Land in Care Scheme (Tir Gofal) (Wales) Regulations 1999

1327—Countryside Stewardship Regulations 1998

1440—Environmentally Sensitive Areas (The Broads) Designation Order 1997

1441—Environmentally Sensitive Areas (Pennine Dales) Designation Order 1997

1442—Environmentally Sensitive Areas (Somerset Levels and Moors) Designation Order 1997

1443—Environmentally Sensitive Areas (South Downs) Designation Order 1997

1444—Environmentally Sensitive Areas (West Penwith) Designation Order 1997

1456—Environmentally Sensitive Areas (England) Designation Orders (Revocation of Specified Provisions) Regulations 1997

1457—Agriculture Act 1986 (Amendment) Regulations 1997

1827—Countryside Stewardship (Amendment) Regulations 1997

2172—Environmentally Sensitive Areas (Avon Valley) Designation (Amendment) (No.2) Order 1998

2173—Environmentally Sensitive Areas (North Peak) Designation (Amendment) (No.2) Order 1998

2174—Environmentally Sensitive Areas (Exmoor) Designation (Amendment) (No.2) Order 1998

2175—Environmentally Sensitive Areas (South Wessex Downs) Designation (Amendment) (No.2) Order 1998

2176—Environmentally Sensitive Areas (North Kent Marshes) Designation (Amendment) (No.2) Order 1998

Council Reg. 2078/92 ([1992] OJ L215/85)—cont.

2177—Environmentally Sensitive Areas (Lake District) Designation (Amendment) (No.2) Order 1998
2178—Environmentally Sensitive Areas (Test Valley) Designation (Amendment) (No.2) Order 1998
2232—Environmentally Sensitive Areas (West Penwith) Designation (Amendment) (No.2) Order 1998
2868—Environmentally Sensitive Areas (Preseli) Designation (Amendment No.2) Order 1997
3035—Habitats (Scotland) Amendment Regulations 1996
3036—Heather Moorland (Livestock Extensification) (Scotland) Amendment Regulations 1996
3037—Set-Aside Access (Scotland) Amendment and Revocation Regulations 1996
3072—Habitat (Species-rich Grassland) (Wales) (Amendment) Regulations 1996
3073—Habitat (Water Fringe) (Wales) (Amendment) Regulations 1996
3074—Habitat (Coastal Belt) (Wales) (Amendment) Regulations 1996
3075—Habitat (Broadleaved Woodland) (Wales) (Amendment) Regulations 1996
3076—Moorland (Livestock Extensification) (Wales) (Amendment No.2) Regulations 1996
3077—Environmentally Sensitive Areas (Wales) Designation Orders (Amendment) Regulations 1996
3082—Environmentally Sensitive Areas (Scotland) Orders Amendment Regulations 1996
3083—Organic Aid (Scotland) Amendment Regulations 1996
3104—Environmentally Sensitive Areas (England) Designation Orders (Amendment) Regulations 1996
3106—Habitat (Water Fringe) (Amendment) (No.2) Regulations 1996
3107—Habitat (Former Set-Aside Land) (Amendment) (No.2) Regulations 1996
3108—Habitat (Salt-Marsh) (Amendment) (No.2) Regulations 1996
3109—Organic Farming (Aid) (Amendment) Regulations 1996
3110—Moorland (Livestock Extensification) (Amendment) (No.2) Regulations 1996
3111—Countryside Access (Amendment) Regulations 1996
3123—Countryside Stewardship (Amendment) (No.2) Regulations 1996

Council Reg. 2080/92 ([1992] OJ L215/96)

828—Farm Woodland (Amendment) Scheme 1997
829—Farm Woodland Premium Scheme 1997

Council Reg. 2083/92 ([1992] OJ L208/15)

166—Organic Products (Amendment) Regulations 1997

Council Reg. 2332/92 ([1992] OJ L231/1)

696—Common Agricultural Policy (Wine) Regulations 1996

Council Reg. 2333/92 ([1992] OJ L231/9)

696—Common Agricultural Policy (Wine) Regulations 1996

Council Reg. 2407/92 ([1992] OJ L240/1)	2245—Licensing of Air Carriers Regulations 1999
Council Reg. 2913/92 ([1992] OJ L302/1)	534—Customs Reviews and Appeals (Tariff and Origin) Regulations 1997
Council Reg. 3508/92 ([1992] OJ L355/1)	1148—Integrated Administration and Control System (Amendment) Regulations 1997 1500—Hill Livestock (Compensatory Allowances) Regulations 1996
Council Reg. 3759/92 ([1992] OJ L388/1)	1110—Fish Producers' Organisations (Formation Grants) Regulations 1999
Council Reg. 3950/92 ([1992] OJ L405/1)	250—Dairy Produce Quotas (Amendment) Regulations 1997 733—Dairy Produce Quotas Regulations 1997
Council Reg. 2081/93 ([1993] OJ L193/5)	529—Rural Development Grants (Agriculture) (Wales) Regulations 1996 2394—Rural Development Grants (Agriculture) (Amendment) Regulations 1996
Council Reg. 2082/93 ([1993] OJ L193/20)	529—Rural Development Grants (Agriculture) (Wales) Regulations 1996 2394—Rural Development Grants (Agriculture) (Amendment) Regulations 1996
Council Reg. 2085/93 ([1993] OJ L193/44)	529—Rural Development Grants (Agriculture) (Wales) Regulations 1996 2394—Rural Development Grants (Agriculture) (Amendment) Regulations 1996
Council Reg. 3118/93 ([1993] OJ L279/1)	2186—Goods Vehicles (Licensing of Operators) (Temporary Use in Great Britain) Regulations 1996
Council Reg. 3699/93 ([1993] OJ L346/1)	1365—Fisheries and Aquaculture Structure (Grants) Amendment Regulations 1998 1924—Fishing Vessels (Decommissioning) Scheme 1997
Council Reg. 40/94 ([1994] OJ L11/1)	1908—Community Trade Mark Regulations 1996
Council Reg. 2100/94 ([1994] OJ L227/1)	1023—Plant Breeders' Rights (Information Notices) (Extension to European Community Plant Variety Rights) Regulations 1998
Council Reg. 2991/94 ([1994] OJ L316/2)	383—Spreadable Fats (Marketing Standards) Regulations (Northern Ireland) 1999 2457—Spreadable Fats (Marketing Standards) (England) Regulations 1999
Council Reg. 3193/94 ([1994] OJ L337/11)	2394—Rural Development Grants (Agriculture) (Amendment) Regulations 1996
Council Reg. 3259/94 ([1994] OJ L339/11)	1915—Merchant Shipping (Registration of Ships) (Tonnage Amendment) Regulations 1998 1916—Merchant Shipping (Tonnage) (Fishing Vessels) (Amendment) Regulations 1998
Council Reg. 3295/94 ([1994] OJ L341/8)	1601—Goods Infringing Intellectual Property Rights (Customs) Regulations 1999 1618—Goods Infringing Intellectual Property Rights (Consequential Provisions) Regulations 1999

Council Reg. 3381/94 ([1994] OJ L367/1)	272—Dual-Use and Related Goods (Export Control) (Amendment) Regulations 1998 1008—Export of Goods (Control) (Amendment No.2) Order 1997 2721—Dual-Use and Related Goods (Export Control) Regulations 1996
Council Reg. 1935/95 ([1995] OJ L186/1)	166—Organic Products (Amendment) Regulations 1997
Council Reg. 2387/95 ([1995] OJ L244/50)	1500—Hill Livestock (Compensatory Allowances) Regulations 1996
Council Reg. 2719/95 ([1995] OJ L283/3)	1924—Fishing Vessels (Decommissioning) Scheme 1997
Council Reg. 3051/95 ([1995] OJ L320/14)	3022—Merchant Shipping (ISM Code) (Ro-Ro Passenger Ferries) Regulations 1997
Council Reg. 965/96 ([1996] OJ L131/1)	1924—Fishing Vessels (Decommissioning) Scheme 1997
Council Reg. 1357/96 ([1996] OJ L175/9)	195—Beef (Marketing Payment) (No.2) (Amendment) Regulations 1997 2999—Beef (Marketing Payment) (No.2) Regulations 1996
Council Reg. 1427/96 ([1996] OJ L184/3)	542—Common Agricultural Policy (Wine) (Amendment) Regulations 1997
Council Reg. 1484/96 ([1996] OJ L188/25)	3186—Selective Cull (Enforcement of Community Compensation Conditions) Regulations 1996
Council Reg. 1610/96 ([1996] OJ L198/30)	64—Patents (Supplementary Protection Certificates) Rules 1997 3120—Patents (Supplementary Protection Certificate for Plant Protection Products) Regulations 1996
Council Reg. 2222/96 ([1996] OJ L296/50)	3241—Beef Special Premium Regulations 1996
Council Reg. 2271/96 ([1996] OJ L309/1)	3171—Extraterritorial US Legislation (Sanctions against Cuba, Iran and Libya) (Protection of Trading Interests) Order 1996
Council Reg. 2443/96 ([1996] OJ L333/2)	249—Suckler Cow Premium (Amendment) Regulations 1997 1986—Veal (Marketing Payment) Regulations 1997
Council Reg. 82/97 ([1997] OJ L17/1)	534—Customs Reviews and Appeals (Tariff and Origin) Regulations 1997
Council Reg. 258/97 ([1997] OJ L43/1)	14—Genetically Modified Organisms (Contained Use) (Amendment) Regulations (Northern Ireland) 1999 1335—Novel Foods and Novel Food Ingredients Regulations 1997 1336—Novel Foods and Novel Food Ingredients (Fees) Regulations 1997 1548—Genetically Modified Organisms (Contained Use) (Amendment) Regulations 1998 1900—Genetically Modified Organisms (Deliberate Release and Risk Assessment - Amendment) Regulations 1997
Council Reg. 338/97 ([1997] OJ L61/1)	1372—Control of Trade in Endangered Species (Enforcement) Regulations 1997 1421—Control of Trade in Endangered Species (Fees) Regulations 1997
Council Reg. 390/97 ([1997] OJ L66/1)	883—Sea Fishing (Enforcement of Community Quota Measures) Order 1997

Council Reg. 391/97 ([1997] OJ L66/49)	931—Third Country Fishing (Enforcement) Order 1997 1629—Third Country Fishing (Enforcement) (Amendment) Order 1997
Council Reg. 393/97 ([1997] OJ L66/61)	931—Third Country Fishing (Enforcement) Order 1997 1629—Third Country Fishing (Enforcement) (Amendment) Order 1997
Council Reg. 820/97 ([1997] OJ L117/1)	616—Beef Labelling (Enforcement) Regulations 1998 871—Cattle Identification Regulations 1998 1339—Cattle Identification (Amendment) Regulations 1999 1796—Cattle Database Regulations 1998 1901—Cattle Identification (Enforcement) Regulations 1997 2969—Cattle Identification (Amendment) Regulations 1998
Council Reg. 894/97 ([1997] OJ L132/1)	1949—Sea Fishing (Enforcement of Community Conservation Measures) Order 1997
Council Reg. 950/97 ([1997] OJ L142/1)	375—Hill Livestock (Compensatory Allowances) (Amendment) Regulations 1999
Council Reg. 1103/97 ([1997] OJ L62/1)	2996—Insurance Companies (Amendment) Regulations 1998
Council Reg. 1255/97 ([1997] OJ L174/1)	2537—Welfare of Animals (Staging Points) Order 1998
Council Reg. 2200/97 ([1997] OJ L303/3)	1131—Apple and Pear Orchard Grubbing Up Regulations 1998
Council Reg. 2597/97 ([1997] OJ L351/13)	2424—Drinking Milk Regulations 1998
Council Reg. 11/98 ([1998] OJ L4/1)	1322—Public Service Vehicles (Community Licences) Regulations 1999
Council Reg. 12/98 ([1998] OJ L4/10)	3413—Road Transport (Passenger Vehicles Cabotage) Regulations 1999
Council Reg. 45/98 ([1998] OJ L12/1)	268—Sea Fishing (Enforcement of Community Quota Measures) Order 1998
Council Reg. 46/98 ([1998] OJ L12/50)	269—Third Country Fishing (Enforcement) Order 1998
Council Reg. 48/98 ([1998] OJ L12/62)	269—Third Country Fishing (Enforcement) Order 1998
Council Reg. 411/98 ([1998] OJ L52/8)	1622—Welfare of Animals (Transport) (Amendment) Order 1999
Council Reg. 850/98 ([1998] OJ L125/1)	74—Sea Fish (Specified Sea Area) (Regulation of Nets and Prohibition of Fishing Methods) (Variation) Order 1999
Council Reg. 926/98 ([1998] OJ L130/1)	1530—Export of Goods (Federal Republic of Yugoslavia) (Control) Order 1998 1531—Federal Republic of Yugoslavia (Supply and Sale of Equipment) (Penalties and Licences) Regulations 1998
Council Reg. 974/98 ([1998] OJ L139/1)	2996—Insurance Companies (Amendment) Regulations 1998
Council Reg. 1139/98 ([1998] OJ L159/4)	747—Food Labelling (Amendment) Regulations 1999
Council Reg. 1295/98 ([1998] OJ L178/33)	1643—Federal Republic of Yugoslavia and Serbia (Freezing of Funds) Regulations 1998

Council Reg. 1607/98 ([1998] OJ L209/16)	1873—Republic of Serbia (Prohibition on Investment) Regulations 1998
Council Reg. 1638/98 ([1998] OJ L210/32)	2410—Olive Oil (Marketing Standards) (Amendment) Regulations 1998
Council Reg. 1901/98 ([1998] OJ L 248/1)	2284—Yugoslavia (Prohibition of Flights) Regulations 1998
Council Reg. 2469/98 ([1998] OJ L312/19)	1110—Fish Producers' Organisations (Formation Grants) Regulations 1999
Council Reg. 2821/98 ([1998] OJ L351/4)	1871—Feedingstuffs (Zootechnical Products) Regulations 1999
Council Reg. 48/1999 ([1999] OJ L13/1)	424—Sea Fishing (Enforcement of Community Quota Measures) Order 1999
Council Reg. 50/1999 ([1999] OJ L13/59)	425—Third Country Fishing (Enforcement) Order 1999
Council Reg. 52/1999 ([1999] OJ L13/71)	425—Third Country Fishing (Enforcement) Order 1999
Council Reg. 241/1999 ([1999] OJ L271/1)	1601—Goods Infringing Intellectual Property Rights (Customs) Regulations 1999 1618—Goods Infringing Intellectual Property Rights (Consequential Provisions) Regulations 1999
Council Reg. 900/1999 ([1999] OJ L114/1)	1261—Federal Republic of Yugoslavia (Supply, Sale and Export of Petroleum and Petroleum Products) (Penalties and Licences) Regulations 1999 1516—Federal Republic of Yugoslavia (Supply, Sale and Export of Petroleum and Petroleum Products) (No.2) Regulations 1999
Council Reg. 1064/1999 ([1999] OJ L129/27)	2018—Yugoslavia (Prohibition of Flights) Regulations 1999
Council Reg. 1258/1999 ([1999] OJ L160/103)	2223—Paying Agency (National Assembly for Wales) Regulations 1999
Council Reg. 1294/1999 ([1999] OJ L153/63)	1786—Federal Republic of Yugoslavia (Freezing of Funds and Prohibition on Investment) Regulations 1999
Council Reg. 2111/1999 ([1999] OJ L258/12)	2821—Federal Republic of Yugoslavia (Supply, Sale and Export of Petroleum and Petroleum Products) (Penalties and Licences) (No.3) Regulations 1999
Council Reg. 2151/1999 ([1999] OJ L264/3)	3166—Yugoslavia (Prohibition of Flights) (No.2) Regulations 1999
Council Reg. 2158/1999 ([1999] OJ L265/1)	2822—Indonesia (Supply, Sale, Export and Shipment of Equipment) (Penalties and Licences) Regulations 1999
Commission Reg. 1135/70 ([1970] OJ L134/2)	696—Common Agricultural Policy (Wine) Regulations 1996
Commission Reg. 1618/70 ([1970] OJ L175/17)	696—Common Agricultural Policy (Wine) Regulations 1996
Commission Reg. 2314/72 ([1972] OJ L248/53)	696—Common Agricultural Policy (Wine) Regulations 1996
Commission Reg. 2247/73 ([1973] OJ L230/12)	696—Common Agricultural Policy (Wine) Regulations 1996
Commission Reg. 2805/73 ([1973] OJ L289/21)	696—Common Agricultural Policy (Wine) Regulations 1996
Commission Reg. 2152/75 ([1975] OJ L219/7)	696—Common Agricultural Policy (Wine) Regulations 1996

Commission Reg. 1972/78 ([1978] OJ L226/11)	696—Common Agricultural Policy (Wine) Regulations 1996
Commission Reg. 2903/79 ([1979] OJ L326/14)	696—Common Agricultural Policy (Wine) Regulations 1996
Commission Reg. 940/81 ([1981] OJ L096/10)	696—Common Agricultural Policy (Wine) Regulations 1996
Commission Reg. 3388/81 ([1981] OJ L341/19)	696—Common Agricultural Policy (Wine) Regulations 1996
Commission Reg. 3800/81 ([1981] OJ L381/1)	696—Common Agricultural Policy (Wine) Regulations 1996
Commission Reg. 1452/83 ([1983] OJ L149/5)	1110—Fish Producers' Organisations (Formation Grants) Regulations 1999
Commission Reg. 2394/84 ([1984] OJ L224/8)	696—Common Agricultural Policy (Wine) Regulations 1996
Commission Reg. 1907/85 ([1985] OJ L179/21)	696—Common Agricultural Policy (Wine) Regulations 1996
Commission Reg. 3590/85 ([1985] OJ L343/20)	696—Common Agricultural Policy (Wine) Regulations 1996
Commission Reg. 305/86 ([1986] OJ L038/13)	696—Common Agricultural Policy (Wine) Regulations 1996
Commission Reg. 1888/86 ([1986] OJ L163/19)	696—Common Agricultural Policy (Wine) Regulations 1996
Commission Reg. 2094/86 ([1986] OJ L180/17)	696—Common Agricultural Policy (Wine) Regulations 1996
Commission Reg. 649/87 ([1987] OJ L062/10)	696—Common Agricultural Policy (Wine) Regulations 1996
Commission Reg. 1381/87 ([1987] OJ L132/9)	3206—Merchant Shipping (Registration of Ships, and Tonnage) (Amendment) Regulations 1999
Commission Reg. 3929/87 ([1987] OJ L369/59)	696—Common Agricultural Policy (Wine) Regulations 1996
Commission Reg. 2202/89 ([1989] OJ L209/31)	696—Common Agricultural Policy (Wine) Regulations 1996
Commission Reg. 2240/89 ([1989] OJ L215/16)	696—Common Agricultural Policy (Wine) Regulations 1996
Commission Reg. 2676/90 ([1990] OJ L272/1)	696—Common Agricultural Policy (Wine) Regulations 1996
Commission Reg. 3201/90 ([1990] OJ L309/1)	696—Common Agricultural Policy (Wine) Regulations 1996
Commission Reg. 3302/90 ([1990] OJ L317/25)	696—Common Agricultural Policy (Wine) Regulations 1996
Commission Reg. 1274/91 ([1991] OJ L121/11)	1414—Eggs (Marketing Standards) (Amendment) Regulations 1997
Commission Reg. 3664/91 ([1991] OJ L348/53)	696—Common Agricultural Policy (Wine) Regulations 1996
Commission Reg. 3901/91 ([1991] OJ L368/15)	696—Common Agricultural Policy (Wine) Regulations 1996
Commission Reg. 94/92 ([1992] OJ L11/14)	166—Organic Products (Amendment) Regulations 1997
Commission Reg. 1535/92 ([1992] OJ L162/15)	166—Organic Products (Amendment) Regulations 1997
Commission Reg. 2009/92 ([1992] OJ L203/10)	696—Common Agricultural Policy (Wine) Regulations 1996
Commission Reg. 2256/92 ([1992] OJ L219/40)	2968—Statistics of Trade (Customs and Excise) (Amendment) Regulations 1996

Commission Reg. 3457/92 ([1992] OJ L350/56)	166—Organic Products (Amendment) Regulations 1997
Commission Reg. 3886/92 ([1992] OJ L391/20)	1179—Beef Special Premium (Amendment) Regulations 1999
Commission Reg. 3887/92 ([1992] OJ L391/36)	1148—Integrated Administration and Control System (Amendment) Regulations 1997
Commission Reg. 207/93 ([1993] OJ L25/5)	166—Organic Products (Amendment) Regulations 1997
Commission Reg. 334/93 ([1993] OJ L038/12)	1482—Arable Area Payments (Amendment) Regulations 1996 3142—Arable Area Payments Regulations 1996
Commission Reg. 536/93 ([1993] OJ L57/12)	250—Dairy Produce Quotas (Amendment) Regulations 1997 733—Dairy Produce Quotas Regulations 1997
Commission Reg. 586/93 ([1993] OJ L061/39)	696—Common Agricultural Policy (Wine) Regulations 1996
Commission Reg. 2238/93 ([1993] OJ L200/10)	696—Common Agricultural Policy (Wine) Regulations 1996
Commission Reg. 2454/93 ([1993] OJ L253/1)	534—Customs Reviews and Appeals (Tariff and Origin) Regulations 1997
Commission Reg. 2608/93 ([1993] OJ L239/10)	166—Organic Products (Amendment) Regulations 1997
Commission Reg. 2700/93 ([1993] OJ L245/99)	2500—Sheep Annual Premium (Amendment) Regulations 1997
Commission Reg. 3111/93 ([1993] OJ L278/48)	696—Common Agricultural Policy (Wine) Regulations 1996
Commission Reg. 122/94 ([1994] OJ L021/7)	696—Common Agricultural Policy (Wine) Regulations 1996
Commission Reg. 468/94 ([1994] OJ L59/1)	166—Organic Products (Amendment) Regulations 1997
Commission Reg. 762/94 ([1994] OJ L090/8)	1482—Arable Area Payments (Amendment) Regulations 1996 3142—Arable Area Payments Regulations 1996
Commission Reg. 792/94 ([1994] OJ L092/13)	2186—Goods Vehicles (Licensing of Operators) (Temporary Use in Great Britain) Regulations 1996
Commission Reg. 2381/94 ([1994] OJ L255/84)	166—Organic Products (Amendment) Regulations 1997
Commission Reg. 529/95 ([1995] OJ L54/10)	166—Organic Products (Amendment) Regulations 1997
Commission Reg. 554/95 ([1995] OJ L056/3)	696—Common Agricultural Policy (Wine) Regulations 1996
Commission Reg. 1201/95 ([1995] OJ L119/9)	166—Organic Products (Amendment) Regulations 1997
Commission Reg. 1202/95 ([1995] OJ L119/11)	166—Organic Products (Amendment) Regulations 1997
Commission Reg. 2387/95 ([1995] OJ L244/50)	33—Hill Livestock (Compensatory Allowances) (Amendment) Regulations 1997
Commission Reg. 2772/95 ([1995] OJ L288/35)	1327—Countryside Stewardship Regulations 1998 1440—Environmentally Sensitive Areas (The Broads) Designation Order 1997 1441—Environmentally Sensitive Areas (Pennine Dales) Designation Order 1997

Commission Reg. 2772/95 ([1995] OJ L288/35)—*cont.*	1442—Environmentally Sensitive Areas (Somerset Levels and Moors) Designation Order 1997 1443—Environmentally Sensitive Areas (South Downs) Designation Order 1997 1444—Environmentally Sensitive Areas (West Penwith) Designation Order 1997 1456—Environmentally Sensitive Areas (England) Designation Orders (Revocation of Specified Provisions) Regulations 1997 1457—Agriculture Act 1986 (Amendment) Regulations 1997 1827—Countryside Stewardship (Amendment) Regulations 1997
Commission Reg. 418/96 ([1996] OJ L59/10)	166—Organic Products (Amendment) Regulations 1997
Commission Reg. 522/96 ([1996] OJ L77/10)	166—Organic Products (Amendment) Regulations 1997
Commission Reg. 658/96 ([1996] OJ L091/46)	1482—Arable Area Payments (Amendment) Regulations 1996 3142—Arable Area Payments Regulations 1996
Commission Reg. 716/96 ([1996] OJ L99/14)	813—Bovine Hides Regulations 1997 1193—Bovine Animals (Enforcement of Community Purchase Scheme) Regulations 1996 3185—Specified Bovine Material (No.3) (Amendment) Order 1996
Commission Reg. 746/96 ([1996] OJ L102/19)	330—Countryside Premium Scheme (Scotland) Regulations 1997 590—Organic Farming Regulations 1999 1457—Agriculture Act 1986 (Amendment) Regulations 1997 2611—Organic Farming (Wales) Regulations 1999 3036—Heather Moorland (Livestock Extensification) (Scotland) Amendment Regulations 1996 3072—Habitat (Species-rich Grassland) (Wales) (Amendment) Regulations 1996 3073—Habitat (Water Fringe) (Wales) (Amendment) Regulations 1996 3074—Habitat (Coastal Belt) (Wales) (Amendment) Regulations 1996 3075—Habitat (Broadleaved Woodland) (Wales) (Amendment) Regulations 1996 3076—Moorland (Livestock Extensification) (Wales) (Amendment No.2) Regulations 1996 3077—Environmentally Sensitive Areas (Wales) Designation Orders (Amendment) Regulations 1996 3082—Environmentally Sensitive Areas (Scotland) Orders Amendment Regulations 1996 3083—Organic Aid (Scotland) Amendment Regulations 1996 3104—Environmentally Sensitive Areas (England) Designation Orders (Amendment) Regulations 1996 3106—Habitat (Water Fringe) (Amendment) (No.2) Regulations 1996 3107—Habitat (Former Set-Aside Land) (Amendment) (No.2) Regulations 1996

Commission Reg. 746/96 ([1996] OJ L102/19)—cont.	3108—Habitat (Salt-Marsh) (Amendment) (No.2) Regulations 1996 3109—Organic Farming (Aid) (Amendment) Regulations 1996 3110—Moorland (Livestock Extensification) (Amendment) (No.2) Regulations 1996 3111—Countryside Access (Amendment) Regulations 1996 3123—Countryside Stewardship (Amendment) (No.2) Regulations 1996
Commission Reg. 1091/96 ([1996] OJ L144/9)	258—Arable Area Payments (Grazing of Bovine Animals on Set-Aside Land) (Temporary Provisions) Regulations (Northern Ireland) 1996 1593—Arable Area Payments (Grazing of Bovine Animals on Set-Aside Land) (Temporary Provisions) Regulations 1996
Commission Reg. 1511/96 ([1996] OJ L189/91)	1414—Eggs (Marketing Standards) (Amendment) Regulations 1997
Commission Reg. 1526/96 ([1996] OJ L190/21)	2500—Sheep Annual Premium (Amendment) Regulations 1997
Commission Reg. 1962/96 ([1996] OJ L259/7)	1327—Countryside Stewardship Regulations 1998 1827—Countryside Stewardship (Amendment) Regulations 1997
Commission Reg. 2311/96 ([1996] OJ L313/9)	3241—Beef Special Premium Regulations 1996
Commission Reg. 12/97 ([1997] OJ L9/1)	534—Customs Reviews and Appeals (Tariff and Origin) Regulations 1997
Commission Reg. 194/97 ([1997] OJ L31/48)	1499—Contaminants in Food Regulations 1997 3221—Contaminants in Food (Amendment) (England and Wales) Regulations 1999
Commission Reg. 435/97 ([1997] OJ L67/2)	590—Organic Farming Regulations 1999 990—Nitrate Sensitive Areas (Amendment) Regulations 1997 1457—Agriculture Act 1986 (Amendment) Regulations 1997 2611—Organic Farming (Wales) Regulations 1999
Commission Reg. 577/97 ([1997] OJ L87/3)	383—Spreadable Fats (Marketing Standards) Regulations (Northern Ireland) 1999 2457—Spreadable Fats (Marketing Standards) (England) Regulations 1999
Commission Reg. 939/97 ([1997] OJ L140/9)	1372—Control of Trade in Endangered Species (Enforcement) Regulations 1997
Commission Reg. 1141/97 ([1997] OJ L165/7)	616—Beef Labelling (Enforcement) Regulations 1998
Commission Reg. 2502/97 ([1997] OJ L345/21)	1179—Beef Special Premium (Amendment) Regulations 1999
Commission Reg. 2628/97 ([1997] OJ L354/17)	871—Cattle Identification Regulations 1998
Commission Reg. 2629/97 ([1997] OJ L354/19)	871—Cattle Identification Regulations 1998 1796—Cattle Database Regulations 1998
Commission Reg. 505/98 ([1998] OJ L63/16)	1665—Eggs (Marketing Standards) (Amendment) Regulations 1998

Commission Reg. 623/98 ([1998] OJ L85/3)	2538—Spreadable Fats (Marketing Standards) (Amendment) (No.2) Regulations 1998
Commission Reg. 1298/98 ([1998] OJ L180/5)	540—Spreadable Fats (Marketing Standards) (Amendment) Regulations 1999 2538—Spreadable Fats (Marketing Standards) (Amendment) (No.2) Regulations 1998
Commission Reg. 1525/98 ([1998] OJ L201/43)	1603—Contaminants in Food (Amendment) Regulations 1999
Commission Reg. 2521/98 ([1998] OJ L315/12)	540—Spreadable Fats (Marketing Standards) (Amendment) Regulations 1999
Commission Reg. 2788/98 ([1998] OJ L347/31)	1871—Feedingstuffs (Zootechnical Products) Regulations 1999
Commission Reg. 2815/98 ([1998] OJ L349/56)	1513—Olive Oil (Designations of Origin) Regulations 1999
Commission Reg. 45/1999 ([1999] OJ L6/3)	1871—Feedingstuffs (Zootechnical Products) Regulations 1999
Commission Reg. 568/1999 ([1999] OJ L70/11)	2457—Spreadable Fats (Marketing Standards) (England) Regulations 1999
Commission Reg. 640/1999 ([1999] OJ L82/8)	1513—Olive Oil (Designations of Origin) Regulations 1999
Commission Reg. 864/1999 ([1999] OJ L108/16)	1603—Contaminants in Food (Amendment) Regulations 1999
Commission Reg. 1566/1999 ([1999] OJ L184/17)	3221—Contaminants in Food (Amendment) (England and Wales) Regulations 1999
Directives	**SIs**
Council Dir. 64/432 ([1964] OJ L121/1977)	757—Enzootic Bovine Leukosis Order 1997 758—Brucellosis Order 1997
Council Dir. 67/548 ([1967] OJ L196/1)	197—Chemicals (Hazard Information and Packaging for Supply) (Amendment) Regulations 459—Chemicals (Hazard Information and Packaging for Supply) (Amendment) Regulations (Northern Ireland) 1998 3106—Chemicals (Hazard Information and Packaging for Supply) (Amendment) Regulations 1998
Council Dir. 70/156 ([1970] OJ L42/1)	1501—Motor Vehicles (EC Type Approval) (Amendment) (No.2) Regulations 1997 2051—Motor Vehicles (EC Type Approval) Regulations 1998 3111—Road Vehicles (Authorised Weight) Regulations 1998
Council Dir. 70/157 ([1970] OJ L42/16)	58—Motor Vehicles (Designation of Approval Marks) (Amendment) Regulations 1997
Council Dir. 70/221 ([1970] OJ L76/23)	2051—Motor Vehicles (EC Type Approval) Regulations 1998
Council Dir. 70/524 ([1970] OJ L270/1)	259—Feeding Stuffs (Amendment) Regulations (Northern Ireland) 1996 1047—Feedingstuffs (Zootechnical Products) Regulations 1998 1871—Feedingstuffs (Zootechnical Products) Regulations 1999
Council Dir. 71/320 ([1971] OJ L202/37)	2978—Road Vehicles (Brake Linings Safety) Regulations 1999 3033—Road Vehicles (Construction and Use) (Amendment) (No.7) Regulations 1996
Council Dir. 72/245 ([1972] OJ L152/15)	58—Motor Vehicles (Designation of Approval Marks) (Amendment) Regulations 1997

Council Dir. 72/306 ([1972] OJ L190/1)	2051—Motor Vehicles (EC Type Approval) Regulations 1998
Council Dir. 72/461 ([1972] OJ L302/24)	3125—Fresh Meat (Import Conditions) Regulations 1996
Council Dir. 72/462 ([1972] OJ L302/28)	3125—Fresh Meat (Import Conditions) Regulations 1996
Council Dir. 73/239 ([1973] OJ L228/3)	1669—Financial Institutions (Prudential Supervision) Regulations 1996 3008—Friendly Societies (Insurance Business) (Amendment) Regulations 1996 3011—Insurance (Lloyd's) Regulations 1996
Council Dir. 74/61 ([1974] OJ L38/22)	58—Motor Vehicles (Designation of Approval Marks) (Amendment) Regulations 1997
Council Dir. 75/117 ([1975] OJ L45/19)	2803—Employment Tribunals (Interest on Awards in Discrimination Cases) Regulations 1996
Council Dir. 75/129 ([1975] OJ L48/29)	1925—Collective Redundancies and Transfer of Undertakings (Protection of Employment) (Amendment) Regulations 1999
Council Dir. 75/268 ([1975] OJ L128/1)	33—Hill Livestock (Compensatory Allowances) (Amendment) Regulations 1997 1500—Hill Livestock (Compensatory Allowances) Regulations 1996
Council Dir. 75/324 ([1975] OJ L147/40)	2421—Aerosol Dispensers (EEC Requirements) (Amendment) Regulations 1996
Council Dir. 75/440 ([1975] OJ L194/26)	3001—Surface Waters (Abstraction for Drinking Water) (Classification) Regulations 1996 3047—Surface Waters (Abstraction for Drinking Water) (Classification) (Scotland) Regulations 1996
Council Dir. 75/443 ([1975] OJ L196/1)	2051—Motor Vehicles (EC Type Approval) Regulations 1998
Council Dir. 76/116 ([1976] OJ L24/21)	1543—Fertilisers (Amendment) Regulations 1997
Council Dir. 76/207 ([1976] OJ L39/40)	2803—Employment Tribunals (Interest on Awards in Discrimination Cases) Regulations 1996
Council Dir. 76/464 ([1976] OJ L129/32)	250—Surface Waters (Dangerous Substances) (Classification) (Scotland) Regulations 1998
Council Dir. 76/756 ([1976] OJ L262/1)	2051—Motor Vehicles (EC Type Approval) Regulations 1998
Council Dir. 76/757 ([1976] OJ L262/32)	2051—Motor Vehicles (EC Type Approval) Regulations 1998
Council Dir. 76/758 ([1976] OJ L262/54)	2051—Motor Vehicles (EC Type Approval) Regulations 1998
Council Dir. 76/760 ([1976] OJ L262/85)	2051—Motor Vehicles (EC Type Approval) Regulations 1998
Council Dir. 76/768 ([1976] OJ L262/169)	2925—Cosmetic Products (Safety) Regulations 1996
Council Dir. 76/769 ([1976] OJ L262/201)	59—Marketing and Use of Dangerous Substances Regulations (Northern Ireland) 1999 437—Control of Substances Hazardous to Health Regulations 1999

Council Dir. 76/769 ([1976] OJ L262/201)—*cont.*	2084—Dangerous Substances and Preparations (Safety) (Consolidation) (Amendment) Regulations 1999 2373—Asbestos (Prohibitions) (Amendment) Regulations 1999 2635—Dangerous Substances and Preparations (Safety) (Consolidation) (Amendment) Regulations 1996
Council Dir. 77/91 ([1977] OJ L26/1)	2306—Companies (Membership of Holding Company) (Dealers in Securities) Regulations 1997 2770—Companies (Investment Companies) (Distribution of Profits) Regulations 1999
Council Dir. 77/93 ([1977] OJ L26/20)	25—Plant Health (Great Britain) (Amendment) Order 1996 655—Plant Health (Fees) (Forestry) (Great Britain) (Amendment) Regulations 1997 1145—Plant Health (Great Britain) (Amendment) Order 1997 1165—Plant Health (Great Britain) (Amendment) (No.2) Order 1996
Council Dir. 77/96 ([1977] OJ L26/67)	3125—Fresh Meat (Import Conditions) Regulations 1996
Council Dir. 77/99 ([1977] OJ L26/85)	683—Meat Products (Hygiene) (Amendment) Regulations 1999
Council Dir. 77/187 ([1977] OJ L61/62)	1925—Collective Redundancies and Transfer of Undertakings (Protection of Employment) (Amendment) Regulations 1999
Council Dir. 77/388 ([1977] OJ L145/1)	1250—Value Added Tax (Amendment) (No.3) Regulations 1996 1256—Value Added Tax (Cultural Services) Order 1996 1294—Value Added Tax (Osteopaths) Order 1998 1575—Value Added Tax (Chiropractors) Order 1999 2833—Value Added Tax (Supplies of Goods Where Input Tax Cannot Be Recovered) Order 1999 2834—Value Added Tax (Subscriptions to Trade Unions, Professional and other Public Interest Bodies) Order 1999 2992—Value Added Tax (Place of Supply of Services) (Amendment) Order 1996 3121—Value Added Tax (Input Tax) (Specified Supplies) Order 1999
Council Dir. 77/391 ([1977] OJ L145/44)	757—Enzootic Bovine Leukosis Order 1997 758—Brucellosis Order 1997
Council Dir. 77/452 ([1977] OJ L176/1)	3101—Nurses, Midwives and Health Visitors Act 1979 (Amendment) Regulations 1996 3102—European Nursing and Midwifery Qualifications Designation Order 1996
Council Dir. 77/453 ([1977] OJ L176/8)	3103—Nurses, Midwives and Health Visitors (Admission to the Register and Training) Amendment Rules Approval Order 1996
Council Dir. 77/539 ([1977] OJ L220/72)	2051—Motor Vehicles (EC Type Approval) Regulations 1998

Council Dir. 77/780 ([1977] OJ L322/30)

1669—Financial Institutions (Prudential Supervision) Regulations 1996
2094—Banking (Gibraltar) Regulations 1999

Council Dir. 78/610 ([1978] OJ L197/12)

437—Control of Substances Hazardous to Health Regulations 1999

Council Dir. 78/659 ([1978] OJ L222/1)

1331—Surface Waters (Fishlife) (Classification) Regulations 1997
2471—Surface Waters (Fishlife) (Classification) (Scotland) Regulations 1997

Council Dir. 78/686 ([1978] OJ L233/1)

811—European Primary and Specialist Dental Qualifications Regulations 1998

Council Dir. 78/687 ([1978] OJ L233/10)

811—European Primary and Specialist Dental Qualifications Regulations 1998

Council Dir. 78/1015 ([1978] OJ L349/21)

16—Road Vehicles (Construction and Use) (Amendment) Regulations 1996

Council Dir. 79/112 ([1979] OJ L33/1)

253—Food Labelling (Amendment) Regulations (Northern Ireland) 1998
747—Food Labelling (Amendment) Regulations 1999
1398—Food Labelling (Amendment) Regulations 1998
1483—Food Labelling (Amendment) (No.2) Regulations 1999
1499—Food Labelling Regulations 1996

Council Dir. 79/267 ([1979] OJ L063/1)

1669—Financial Institutions (Prudential Supervision) Regulations 1996
3008—Friendly Societies (Insurance Business) (Amendment) Regulations 1996

Council Dir. 79/269 ([1979] OJ L63/1)

3011—Insurance (Lloyd's) Regulations 1996

Council Dir. 79/869 ([1979] OJ L271/44)

3001—Surface Waters (Abstraction for Drinking Water) (Classification) Regulations 1996
3047—Surface Waters (Abstraction for Drinking Water) (Classification) (Scotland) Regulations 1996

Council Dir. 79/923 ([1979] OJ L281/47)

1332—Surface Waters (Shellfish) (Classification) Regulations 1997
2470—Surface Waters (Shellfish) (Classification) (Scotland) Regulations 1997

Council Dir. 80/51 ([1980] OJ L18/26)

1452—Aeroplane Noise Regulations 1999

Council Dir. 80/68 ([1980] OJ L20/43)

2746—Groundwater Regulations 1998

Council Dir. 80/154 ([1980] OJ L33/1)

3101—Nurses, Midwives and Health Visitors Act 1979 (Amendment) Regulations 1996
3102—European Nursing and Midwifery Qualifications Designation Order 1996

Council Dir. 80/155 ([1980] OJ L33/8)

3103—Nurses, Midwives and Health Visitors (Admission to the Register and Training) Amendment Rules Approval Order 1996

Council Dir. 80/181 ([1980] OJ L39/40)

1434—Welfare Food Regulations 1996

Council Dir. 80/777 ([1980] OJ L229/1)

1540—Natural Mineral Water, Spring Water and Bottled Drinking Water Regulations 1999

Council Dir. 80/778 ([1980] OJ L229/11)

1524—Water Supply (Water Quality) (Amendment) Regulations 1999

Council Dir. 80/778 ([1980] OJ L229/11)—*cont.*

1540—Natural Mineral Water, Spring Water and Bottled Drinking Water Regulations 1999

Council Dir. 80/1269 ([1980] OJ L375/46)

2051—Motor Vehicles (EC Type Approval) Regulations 1998

Council Dir. 81/851 ([1981] OJ L 317/1)

1044—Medicines (Exemptions for Merchants in Veterinary Drugs) Order 1998
2884—Medicines (Restrictions on the Administration of Veterinary Medicinal Products) Amendment Regulations 1997

Council Dir. 82/130 ([1982] OJ L59/10)

2550—Electrical Equipment for Explosive Atmospheres (Certification) (Amendment) Regulations 1999

Council Dir. 82/605 ([1982] OJ L247/12)

543—Control of Lead at Work Regulations 1998

Council Dir. 82/711 ([1982] OJ L297/26)

1376—Plastic Materials and Articles in Contact with Food Regulations 1998

Council Dir. 83/129 ([1983] OJ L091/30)

2686—Import of Seal Skins Regulations 1996

Council Dir. 83/189 ([1983] OJ L109/8)

3133—Road Vehicles (Construction and Use) (Amendment) (No.8) Regulations 1996

Council Dir. 83/206 ([1983] OJ L117/15)

1452—Aeroplane Noise Regulations 1999

Council Dir. 85/7 ([1985] OJ L2)

1499—Food Labelling Regulations 1996

Council Dir. 85/73 ([1985] OJ L32/14)

639—Animals (Third Country Imports) (Charges) Regulations 1997
2095—Meat (Hygiene and Inspection) (Charges) Regulations 1998
2893—Charges for Inspections and Controls Regulations 1997
3023—Products of Animal Origin (Import and Export) (Amendment) Regulations 1997

Council Dir. 85/337 ([1985] OJ L175/40)

107—Channel Tunnel Rail Link (Assessment of Environmental Effects) Regulations 1999
293—Town and Country Planning (Environmental Impact Assessment) (England and Wales) Regulations 1999
360—Offshore Petroleum Production and Pipelines (Assessment of Environmental Effects) Regulations 1999
415—Environmental Impact Assessment (Fish Farming in Marine Waters) Regulations (Northern Ireland) 1999
1672—Public Gas Transporter Pipe-Line Works (Environmental Impact Assessment) Regulations 1999
1731—Environmental Assessment (Forestry) Regulations 1998
1783—Environmental Impact Assessment (Land Drainage Improvement Works) Regulations 1999
1870—Environmental Assessment (Scotland) Amendment Regulations 1997
1871—Town and Country Planning (General Permitted Development) (Scotland) Amendment Order 1997
2226—Transport and Works (Assessment of Environmental Effects) Regulations 1998

Council Dir. 85/337 ([1998] OJ L175/40)—*cont.*	2228—Environmental Impact Assessment (Forestry) (England and Wales) Regulations 1999 2892—Nuclear Reactors (Environmental Impact Assessment for Decommissioning) Regulations 1999 3445—Harbour Works (Environmental Impact Assessment) Regulations 1999
Council Dir. 85/433 ([1985] OJ L253/37)	1405—Pharmaceutical Qualifications (Recognition) Regulations 1996
Council Dir. 85/444 ([1985] OJ L259)	2686—Import of Seal Skins Regulations 1996
Council Dir. 85/611 ([1985] OJ L375/3)	1669—Financial Institutions (Prudential Supervision) Regulations 1996
Council Dir. 86/197 ([1986] OJ L144)	1499—Food Labelling Regulations 1996
Council Dir. 86/609 ([1986] OJ L358/1)	1974—Animals (Scientific Procedures) Act 1986 (Amendment) Regulations 1998
Council Dir. 86/653 ([1986] OJ L382/17)	2868—Commercial Agents (Council Directive) (Amendment) Regulations 1998
Council Dir. 87/18 ([1987] OJ L15/29)	654—Good Laboratory Practice Regulations 1997 3106—Good Laboratory Practice Regulations 1999
Council Dir. 87/403 ([1987] OJ L220/44)	2051—Motor Vehicles (EC Type Approval) Regulations 1998
Council Dir. 88/182 ([1988] OJ L81/75)	3133—Road Vehicles (Construction and Use) (Amendment) (No.8) Regulations 1996
Council Dir. 88/320 ([1988] OJ L145/35)	654—Good Laboratory Practice Regulations 1997
Council Dir. 88/357 ([1988] OJ L172/1)	3008—Friendly Societies (Insurance Business) (Amendment) Regulations 1996 3011—Insurance (Lloyd's) Regulations 1996
Council Dir. 88/364 ([1988] OJ L179/44)	437—Control of Substances Hazardous to Health Regulations 1999
Council Dir. 89/39 ([1989] OJ L183/1)	2962—Merchant Shipping and Fishing Vessels (Health and Safety at Work) Regulations 1997
Council Dir. 89/48 ([1989] OJ L019/16)	2374—European Communities (Recognition of Professional Qualifications) (Second General System) Regulations 1996
Council Dir. 89/107 ([1989] OJ L40/27)	1413—Miscellaneous Food Additives (Amendment) Regulations 1997
Council Dir. 89/370 ([1989] OJ L163)	2686—Import of Seal Skins Regulations 1996
Council Dir. 89/391 ([1989] OJ L183/1)	1513—Health and Safety (Consultation with Employees) Regulations 1996 1840—Fire Precautions (Workplace) Regulations 1997 1877—Fire Precautions (Workplace) (Amendment) Regulations 1999
Council Dir. 89/395 ([1989] OJ L186)	1499—Food Labelling Regulations 1996 1502—Food (Lot Marking) Regulations 1996
Council Dir. 89/397 ([1989] OJ L186/23)	1499—Contaminants in Food Regulations 1997 2042—Processed Cereal-based Foods and Baby Foods for Infants and Young Children Regulations 1997

Council Dir. 89/398 ([1989] OJ L186/27)	1499—Food Labelling Regulations 1996
Council Dir. 89/552 ([1989] OJ L298/23)	1682—Satellite Television Service Regulations 1997
	3196—Television Broadcasting Regulations 1998
Council Dir. 89/594 ([1989] OJ L341/19)	3102—European Nursing and Midwifery Qualifications Designation Order 1996
	3103—Nurses, Midwives and Health Visitors (Admission to the Register and Training) Amendment Rules Approval Order 1996
Council Dir. 89/595 ([1989] OJ L341/30)	3103—Nurses, Midwives and Health Visitors (Admission to the Register and Training) Amendment Rules Approval Order 1996
Council Dir. 89/629 ([1989] OJ L363/27)	1452—Aeroplane Noise Regulations 1999
Council Dir. 89/646 ([1989] OJ L386/1)	1669—Financial Institutions (Prudential Supervision) Regulations 1996
	2094—Banking (Gibraltar) Regulations 1999
Council Dir. 89/654 ([1989] OJ L393/1)	1840—Fire Precautions (Workplace) Regulations 1997
	1877—Fire Precautions (Workplace) (Amendment) Regulations 1999
Council Dir. 89/655 ([1989] OJ L393/89)	2307—Lifting Operations and Lifting Equipment Regulations 1998
Council Dir. 89/656 ([1989] OJ L393/18)	2205—Merchant Shipping and Fishing Vessels (Personal Protective Equipment) Regulations 1999
Council Dir. 89/662 ([1989] OJ L395/13)	3124—Products of Animal Origin (Import and Export) Regulations 1996
Council Dir. 89/677 ([1989] OJ L398/19)	437—Control of Substances Hazardous to Health Regulations 1999
Council Dir. 89/686 ([1989] OJ L399/18)	3039—Personal Protective Equipment (EC Directive) (Amendment) Regulations 1996
Council Dir. 90/128 ([1990] OJ L372/14)	1376—Plastic Materials and Articles in Contact with Food Regulations 1998
Council Dir. 90/167 ([1990] OJ L92/42)	1046—Medicated Feedingstuffs Regulations 1998
Council Dir. 90/269 ([1990] OJ L156/9)	2857—Merchant Shipping and Fishing Vessels (Manual Handling Operations) Regulations 1998
Council Dir. 90/313 ([1990] OJ L158/56)	1447—Environmental Information (Amendment) Regulations 1998
Council Dir. 90/314 ([1990] OJ L158/59)	1208—Package Travel, Package Holidays and Package Tours (Amendment) Regulations 1998
Council Dir. 90/364 ([1990] OJ L180/26)	2981—Immigration (European Economic Area) (Amendment) Order 1997
Council Dir. 90/365 ([1990] OJ L180/28)	2981—Immigration (European Economic Area) (Amendment) Order 1997
Council Dir. 90/384 ([1990] OJ L258/1)	3035—Non-automatic Weighing Instruments (EEC Requirements) (Amendment) Regulations 1997
Council Dir. 90/387 ([1990] OJ L192/1)	2932—Telecommunications (Open Network Provision and Leased Lines) Regulations 1997
Council Dir. 90/394 ([1990] OJ L196/38)	437—Control of Substances Hazardous to Health Regulations 1999
	2001—Mines (Substances Hazardous to Health) Regulations 1996

Council Dir. 90/425 ([1990] OJ L224/29)

1941—Specified Bovine Material (No.3) Order 1996
2095—Meat (Hygiene and Inspection) (Charges) Regulations 1998

Council Dir. 90/427 ([1990] OJ L224/55)

2789—Horse Passports Order 1997

Council Dir. 90/496 ([1990] OJ L276/40)

1499—Food Labelling Regulations 1996

Council Dir. 90/619 ([1990] OJ L330/50)

3008—Friendly Societies (Insurance Business) (Amendment) Regulations 1996
3011—Insurance (Lloyd's) Regulations 1996

Council Dir. 90/641 ([1990] OJ L349/23)

3232—Ionising Radiations Regulations 1999

Council Dir. 90/667 ([1990] OJ L363/51)

646—Animal By-Products Order 1999
827—Animal By-Products (Amendment) Order 1996
1941—Specified Bovine Material (No.3) Order 1996

Council Dir. 90/675 ([1990] OJ L373/1)

2095—Meat (Hygiene and Inspection) (Charges) Regulations 1998
3023—Products of Animal Origin (Import and Export) (Amendment) Regulations 1997
3124—Products of Animal Origin (Import and Export) Regulations 1996

Council Dir. 90/679 ([1990] OJ L374/1)

437—Control of Substances Hazardous to Health Regulations 1999

Council Dir. 90/697 ([1990] OJ L374)

2001—Mines (Substances Hazardous to Health) Regulations 1996

Council Dir. 91/11 ([1992] OJ L65/32)

1502—Food (Lot Marking) Regulations 1996

Council Dir. 91/67 ([1991] OJ L46/1)

1881—Fish Health Regulations 1997

Council Dir. 91/72 ([1991] OJ L42)

1499—Food Labelling Regulations 1996

Council Dir. 91/238 ([1991] OJ L107/50)

1502—Food (Lot Marking) Regulations 1996

Council Dir. 91/383 ([1991] OJ L206/19)

2962—Merchant Shipping and Fishing Vessels (Health and Safety at Work) Regulations 1997

Council Dir. 91/414 ([1991] OJ L230/1)

7—Plant Protection Products (Amendment) Regulations 1997
189—Plant Protection Products (Basic Conditions) Regulations 1997
884—Plant Protection Products (Fees) (Amendment) Regulations 1997
1940—Plant Protection Products (Amendment) Regulations 1996
1940—Plant Protection Products (Amendment) Regulations 1996
2499—Plant Protection Products (Amendment) (No.2) Regulations 1997
2760—Plant Protection Products (Amendment) Regulations 1998

Council Dir. 91/422 ([1991] OJ L233/21)

3033—Road Vehicles (Construction and Use) (Amendment) (No.7) Regulations 1996

Council Dir. 91/439 ([1991] OJ L237/1)

357—Motor Cars (Driving Instruction) (Admission of Community Licence Holders) Regulations 1999
1259—Motor Vehicles (Driving Licences) (Amendment) (No.3) Regulations 1996
1974—Driving Licences (Community Driving Licence) Regulations 1996
2824—Motor Vehicles (Driving Licences) Regulations 1996

Council Dir. 91/439 ([1991] OJ L237/1)—*cont.*	3053—Motorways Traffic (England and Wales) (Amendment) Regulations 1996 3087—Community Bus (Amendment) Regulations 1996 3088—Minibus and Other Section 19 Permit Buses (Amendment) Regulations 1996
Council Dir. 91/440 ([1991] OJ L237/25)	1340—Railways Regulations 1998
Council Dir. 91/492 ([1991] OJ L268/1)	83—Food Safety (Fishery Products and Live Shellfish) (Hygiene) (Amendment) Regulations 1999
	399—Food Safety (Fishery Products and Live Shellfish) (Hygiene) Amendment Regulations 1999
	994—Food Safety (Fishery Products and Live Shellfish) (Hygiene) Regulations 1998
Council Dir. 91/493 ([1991] OJ L268/15)	994—Food Safety (Fishery Products and Live Shellfish) (Hygiene) Regulations 1998
Council Dir. 91/496 ([1991] OJ L268/56)	2095—Meat (Hygiene and Inspection) (Charges) Regulations 1998 3023—Products of Animal Origin (Import and Export) (Amendment) Regulations 1997
Council Dir. 91/628 ([1991] OJ L340/17)	1480—Welfare of Animals (Transport) Order 1997
Council Dir. 91/629 ([1991] OJ L240/28)	251—Welfare of Livestock (Amendment) Regulations (Northern Ireland) 1998 1709—Welfare of Livestock (Amendment) Regulations 1998
Council Dir. 91/676 ([1991] OJ L375/1)	1202—Action Programme for Nitrate Vulnerable Zones (England and Wales) Regulations 1998 1564—Protection of Water Against Agricultural Nitrate Pollution (Scotland) Regulations 1996
Council Dir. 91/689 ([1991] OJ L377/20)	972—Special Waste Regulations 1996 2019—Special Waste (Amendment) Regulations 1996
Council Dir. 92/5 ([1992] OJ L57/1)	683—Meat Products (Hygiene) (Amendment) Regulations 1999
Council Dir. 92/6 ([1992] OJ L57/27)	1340—Road Vehicles (Construction and Use) (Amendment) (No.3) Regulations 1997 2064—Road Vehicles (Construction and Use) (Amendment) (No.3) Regulations 1996
Council Dir. 92/12 ([1992] OJ L76/1)	1278—Warehousekeepers and Owners of Warehoused Goods Regulations 1999 1565—Excise Goods (Sales on Board Ships and Aircraft) Regulations 1999
Council Dir. 92/13 ([1992] OJ L76/14)	2911—Utilities Contracts Regulations 1996
Council Dir. 92/14 ([1992] OJ L76/21)	1452—Aeroplane Noise Regulations 1999
Council Dir. 92/24 ([1992] OJ L129/154)	1340—Road Vehicles (Construction and Use) (Amendment) (No.3) Regulations 1997
Council Dir. 92/27 ([1992] OJ L113/8)	3105—Medicines for Human Use (Marketing Authorisations etc.) Amendment Regulations 1998
Council Dir. 92/28 ([1992] OJ L113/13)	267—Medicine (Advertising and Monitoring of Advertising) Amendment Regulations 1999
Council Dir. 92/29 ([1992] OJ L113/19)	2821—Merchant Shipping and Fishing Vessels (Medical Stores) (Amendment) Regulations 1996

Council Dir. 92/43 ([1992]OJ L206/7)	3055—Conservation (Natural Habitats, &c.) (Amendment) Regulations 1997
Council Dir. 92/44 ([1992] OJ L165/27)	2932—Telecommunications (Open Network Provision and Leased Lines) Regulations 1997
Council Dir. 92/46 ([1992] OJ L268/1)	1699—Dairy Products (Hygiene) (Amendment) Regulations 1996
Council Dir. 92/49 ([1992] OJ L228/1)	944—Insurance Companies (Amendment No.2) Regulations 1996 1669—Financial Institutions (Prudential Supervision) Regulations 1996 3008—Friendly Societies (Insurance Business) (Amendment) Regulations 1996 3011—Insurance (Lloyd's) Regulations 1996
Council Dir. 92/51 ([1992] OJ L209/25)	2374—European Communities (Recognition of Professional Qualifications) (Second General System) Regulations 1996
Council Dir. 92/56 ([1992] OJ L245/3)	1925—Collective Redundancies and Transfer of Undertakings (Protection of Employment) (Amendment) Regulations 1999
Council Dir. 92/57 ([1992] OJ L245/6)	13—Confined Spaces Regulations (Northern Ireland) 1999 1592—Construction (Health, Safety and Welfare) Regulations 1996 1713—Confined Spaces Regulations 1997
Council Dir. 92/61 ([1992] OJ L225/72)	2920—Motor Cycles Etc. (EC Type Approval) Regulations 1999
Council Dir. 92/74 ([1992] OJ L297/12)	321—Registration of Homeopathic Veterinary Medicinal Products (Fees) Regulations 1997 322—Registration of Homeopathic Veterinary Medicinal Products Regulations 1997 1349—Medicines (Registered Homeopathic Veterinary Medicinal Products) (General Sale List) Order 1997 1350—Medicines (Pharmacy and General Sale-Exemption) (Amendment) Order 1997
Council Dir. 92/75 ([1992] OJ L297/16)	1517—Energy Information (Lamps) Regulations 1999 1624—Energy Information (Combined Washer-driers) Regulations 1997 1676—Energy Information (Dishwashers) Regulations 1999
Council Dir. 92/81 ([1992] OJ L316/12)	2537—Hydrocarbon Oil Duties (Marine Voyages Reliefs) Regulations 1996
Council Dir. 92/85 ([1992] OJ L348/1)	587—Suspension from Work on Maternity Grounds (Merchant Shipping and Fishing Vessels) Order 1998 2962—Merchant Shipping and Fishing Vessels (Health and Safety at Work) Regulations 1997
Council Dir. 92/91 ([1992] OJ L348/9)	913—Offshore Installations and Wells (Design and Construction, etc.) Regulations 1996
Council Dir. 92/94 ([1992] OJ L338/42)	2064—Road Vehicles (Construction and Use) (Amendment) (No.3) Regulations 1996
Council Dir. 92/96 ([1992] OJ L360/1)	944—Insurance Companies (Amendment No.2) Regulations 1996 1669—Financial Institutions (Prudential Supervision) Regulations 1996 3008—Friendly Societies (Insurance Business) (Amendment) Regulations 1996 3011—Insurance (Lloyd's) Regulations 1996

Council Dir. 92/97 ([1992] OJ L371/1)	58—Motor Vehicles (Designation of Approval Marks) (Amendment) Regulations 1997
Council Dir. 92/100 ([1992] OJ L346/61)	2967—Copyright and Related Rights Regulations 1996
Council Dir. 92/102 ([1992] OJ L355/32)	28—Sheep and Goats (Records, Identification and Movement) Order 1996
Council Dir. 92/104 ([1992] OJ L404/10)	2024—Quarries Regulations 1999
Council Dir. 92/118 ([1992] OJ L62/49)	157—Miscellaneous Products of Animal Origin (Import Conditions) Regulations 1999 3124—Products of Animal Origin (Import and Export) Regulations 1996
Council Dir. 93/7 ([1993] OJ L74/74)	1719—Return of Cultural Objects (Amendment) Regulations 1997
Council Dir. 93/13 ([1993] OJ L95/29)	2083—Unfair Terms in Consumer Contracts Regulations 1999 3211—Unfair Arbitration Agreements (Specified Amount) Order 1996
Council Dir. 93/14 ([1993] OJ L121/1)	3033—Road Vehicles (Construction and Use) (Amendment) (No.7) Regulations 1996
Council Dir. 93/16 ([1993] OJ L165/1)	5—National Health Service (Vocational Training for General Medical Practice) (Scotland) Regulations 1998 13—Medical Practitioners (Vocational Training) Regulations (Northern Ireland) 1998 1373—European Specialist Medical Qualifications Amendment Regulations 1999 1591—European Primary Medical Qualifications Regulations 1996 2928—European Specialist Medical Qualifications Amendment Regulations 1997
Council Dir. 93/22 ([1993] OJ L141/27)	1669—Financial Institutions (Prudential Supervision) Regulations 1996
Council Dir. 93/35 ([1993] OJ L151/32)	2925—Cosmetic Products (Safety) Regulations 1996
Council Dir. 93/38 ([1993] OJ L199/84)	2911—Utilities Contracts Regulations 1996
Council Dir. 93/43 ([1993] OJ L175/1)	1360—Food Safety (General Food Hygiene) (Amendment) Regulations 1999 2537—Imported Food Regulations 1997
Council Dir. 93/71 ([1993] OJ L221/27)	1940—Plant Protection Products (Amendment) Regulations 1996
Council Dir. 93/75 ([1993] OJ L247/19)	2121—Merchant Shipping (Reporting Requirements for Ships carrying Dangerous or Polluting Goods) (Amendment) Regulations 1999 2367—Merchant Shipping (Dangerous Goods and Marine Pollutants) Regulations 1997
Council Dir. 93/77 ([1993] OJ L244/23)	1413—Miscellaneous Food Additives (Amendment) Regulations 1997
Council Dir. 93/83 ([1993] OJ L248/15)	2967—Copyright and Related Rights Regulations 1996
Council Dir. 93/96 ([1993] OJ L317/59)	2981—Immigration (European Economic Area) (Amendment) Order 1997

Council Dir. 93/98 ([1993] OJ L290/9)	2967—Copyright and Related Rights Regulations 1996
Council Dir. 93/102 ([1993] OJ L291)	1499—Food Labelling Regulations 1996
Council Dir. 93/103 ([1993] OJ L307/1)	927—Fishing Vessels (Life-Saving Appliances) (Amendment) Regulations 1998 928—Fishing Vessels (Safety Provisions) (Amendment) Rules 1998 929—Merchant Shipping (Crew Accommodation) (Fishing Vessels) (Amendment) Regulations 1998
Council Dir. 93/104 ([1993] OJ L307/18)	1833—Working Time Regulations 1998 3372—Working Time Regulations 1999
Council Dir. 93/113 ([1993] OJ L334/17)	104—Feeding Stuffs (Amendment) Regulations 1998
Council Dir. 94/9 ([1994] OJ L100/1)	247—Equipment and Protective Systems Intended for Use in Potentially Explosive Atmospheres Regulations (Northern Ireland) 1996
Council Dir. 94/10 ([1994] OJ L100/30)	3133—Road Vehicles (Construction and Use) (Amendment) (No.8) Regulations 1996
Council Dir. 94/25 ([1994] OJ L164/15)	1353—Recreational Craft Regulations 1996
Council Dir. 94/33 ([1994] OJ L216/12)	135—Health and Safety (Young Persons) Regulations 1997 276—Children (Protection at Work) Regulations 1998 1833—Working Time Regulations 1998 2411—Merchant Shipping and Fishing Vessels (Health and Safety at Work) (Employment of Young Persons) Regulations 1998
Council Dir. 94/35 ([1994] OJ L237/3)	814—Sweeteners in Food (Amendment) Regulations 1997
Council Dir. 94/47 ([1994] OJ L280/83)	1081—Timeshare Regulations 1997
Council Dir. 94/55 ([1994] OJ L319/7)	303—Carriage of Dangerous Goods (Amendment) Regulations 1999 2075—Health and Safety at Work etc. Act 1974 (Application to Environmentally Hazardous Substances) Regulations 1996 2092—Carriage of Dangerous Goods (Classification, Packaging and Labelling) and Use of Transportable Pressure Receptacles Regulations 1996 2093—Carriage of Explosives by Road Regulations 1996 2094—Carriage of Dangerous Goods by Road (Driver Training) Regulations 1996 2095—Carriage of Dangerous Goods by Road Regulations 1996
Council Dir. 94/57 ([1994] OJ L319/20)	1509—Merchant Shipping (Cargo Ship Construction) Regulations 1997 2514—Merchant Shipping (Passenger Ship Construction: Ships of Classes I, II and II(A)) Regulations 1998 2515—Merchant Shipping (Passenger Ship Construction: Ships of Classes III to VI(A)) Regulations 1998 2908—Merchant Shipping (Ship Inspection and Survey Organisations) Regulations 1996

Council Dir. 94/58 ([1994] OJ L319/28)	529—Merchant Shipping (Minimum Standards of Safety Communications) Regulations 1997
	1704—Merchant Shipping (Minimum Standards of Safety Communications) (Amendment) Regulations 1999
Council Dir. 94/59 ([1994] OJ L315/18)	3125—Fresh Meat (Import Conditions) Regulations 1996
Council Dir. 94/60 ([1994] OJ L365/1)	1092—Chemicals (Hazard Information and Packaging for Supply) (Amendment) Regulations 1996
	2635—Dangerous Substances and Preparations (Safety) (Consolidation) (Amendment) Regulations 1996
	3244—Environmental Protection (Controls on Injurious Substances) Regulations 1999
Council Dir. 94/62 ([1994] OJ L365/10)	648—Producer Responsibility Obligations (Packaging Waste) Regulations 1997
	1165—Packaging (Essential Requirements) Regulations 1998
Council Dir. 94/63 ([1994] OJ L365/24)	268—Industrial Pollution Control (Prescribed Processes and Substances) (Amendment) Regulations (Northern Ireland) 1998
	2075—Health and Safety at Work etc. Act 1974 (Application to Environmentally Hazardous Substances) Regulations 1996
	2095—Carriage of Dangerous Goods by Road Regulations 1996
Council Dir. 94/67 ([1994] OJ L365/34)	767—Environmental Protection (Prescribed Processes and Substances) (Amendment) (Hazardous Waste Incineration) Regulations 1998
Council Dir. 94/69 ([1994] OJ L381/1)	1092—Chemicals (Hazard Information and Packaging for Supply) (Amendment) Regulations 1996
Council Dir. 94/79 ([1994] OJ L354/16)	1940—Plant Protection Products (Amendment) Regulations 1996
Council Dir. 95/1 ([1995] OJ L52/1)	2282—Motor Cycle (EC Type Approval) (Amendment) Regulations 1997
Council Dir. 95/2 ([1995] OJ L61/1)	1136—Miscellaneous Food Additives (Amendment) Regulations 1999
Council Dir. 95/7 ([1995] OJ L102/18)	1250—Value Added Tax (Amendment) (No.3) Regulations 1996
	2992—Value Added Tax (Place of Supply of Services) (Amendment) Order 1996
Council Dir. 95/18 ([1995] OJ L143/70)	1340—Railways Regulations 1998
Council Dir. 95/19 ([1995] OJ L143/75)	1340—Railways Regulations 1998
Council Dir. 95/26 ([1995] OJ L168/7)	1669—Financial Institutions (Prudential Supervision) Regulations 1996
Council Dir. 95/28 ([1995] OJ L281/1)	58—Motor Vehicles (Designation of Approval Marks) (Amendment) Regulations 1997
Council Dir. 95/29 ([1995] OJ L18/52)	1480—Welfare of Animals (Transport) Order 1997
Council Dir. 95/38 ([1995] OJ L197/14)	1487—Pesticides (Maximum Residue Levels in Crops, Food and Feeding Stuffs) (Amendment) Regulations 1996
Council Dir. 95/39 ([1995] OJ L197/29)	1487—Pesticides (Maximum Residue Levels in Crops, Food and Feeding Stuffs) (Amendment) Regulations 1996

Council Dir. 95/47 ([1995] OJ L281/51)

2185—Advanced Television Services (Industrial Property Rights) Regulations 1996
3151—Advanced Television Services Regulations 1996

Council Dir. 95/53 ([1995] OJ L265/17)

1663—Feeding Stuffs (Sampling and Analysis) Regulations 1999
1871—Feedingstuffs (Zootechnical Products) Regulations 1999
1872—Feeding Stuffs (Establishments and Intermediaries) Regulations 1999
2325—Feeding Stuffs (Enforcement) Regulations 1999

Council Dir. 95/61 ([1995] OJ L292/27)

1487—Pesticides (Maximum Residue Levels in Crops, Food and Feeding Stuffs) (Amendment) Regulations 1996

Council Dir. 95/62 ([1995] OJ L321/6)

1886—Telecommunications (Voice Telephony) Regulations 1997

Council Dir. 95/63 ([1995] OJ L335/28)

2307—Lifting Operations and Lifting Equipment Regulations 1998

Council Dir. 95/64 ([1995] OJ L320/25)

2330—Statistical Returns (Carriage of Goods and Passengers by Sea) Regulations 1997

Council Dir. 95/68 ([1995] OJ L332/10)

683—Meat Products (Hygiene) (Amendment) Regulations 1999

Council Dir. 95/69 ([1995] OJ L332/15)

1047—Feedingstuffs (Zootechnical Products) Regulations 1998
1049—Feeding Stuffs (Establishments and Intermediaries) Regulations 1998
1871—Feedingstuffs (Zootechnical Products) Regulations 1999
1872—Feeding Stuffs (Establishments and Intermediaries) Regulations 1999

Council Dir. 95/70 ([1995] OJ L332/33)

1881—Fish Health Regulations 1997

Council Dir. 96/1 ([1996] OJ L40/1)

191—Motor Vehicles (EC Type Approval) (Amendment) Regulations 1997

Council Dir. 96/9 ([1996] OJ L77/20)

3032—Copyright and Rights in Databases Regulations 1997

Council Dir. 96/16 ([1996] OJ L213/1)

831—Lifts Regulations 1997

Council Dir. 96/18 ([1996] OJ L76/21)

1451—Oil and Fibre Plant Seeds (Amendment) Regulations 1996

Council Dir. 96/22 ([1996] OJ L125/3)

1729—Animals and Animal Products (Examination for Residues and Maximum Residue Limits) Regulations 1997

Council Dir. 96/23 ([1996] OJ L125/10)

1729—Animals and Animal Products (Examination for Residues and Maximum Residue Limits) Regulations 1997
2893—Charges for Inspections and Controls Regulations 1997

Council Dir. 96/25 ([1996] OJ L125/35)

1528—Feeding Stuffs (Amendment) Regulations 1999

Council Dir. 96/27 ([1996] OJ L169/1)

191—Motor Vehicles (EC Type Approval) (Amendment) Regulations 1997

Council Dir. 96/29 ([1996] OJ L159/1)

3232—Ionising Radiations Regulations 1999

Council Dir. 96/32 ([1996] OJ L144/12)

567—Pesticides (Maximum Residue Levels in Crops, Food and Feeding Stuffs) (Amendment) Regulations 1997

Council Dir. 96/33 ([1996] OJ L144/35)	567—Pesticides (Maximum Residue Levels in Crops, Food and Feeding Stuffs) (Amendment) Regulations 1997
Council Dir. 96/34 ([1996] OJ L145/4)	3312—Maternity and Parental Leave etc. Regulations 1999
Council Dir. 96/35 ([1996] OJ L145/10)	257—Transport of Dangerous Goods (Safety Advisers) Regulations 1999
Council Dir. 96/43 ([1996] OJ L162/3)	639—Animals (Third Country Imports) (Charges) Regulations 1997 1585—Food Safety (Fishery Products and Live Shellfish) (Hygiene) Amendment (No.2) Regulations 1999 3023—Products of Animal Origin (Import and Export) (Amendment) Regulations 1997
Council Dir. 96/47 ([1996] OJ L235/1)	1420—Driving Licences (Community Driving Licence) Regulations 1998
Council Dir. 96/49 ([1996] OJ L235/25)	303—Carriage of Dangerous Goods (Amendment) Regulations 1999 2075—Health and Safety at Work etc. Act 1974 (Application to Environmentally Hazardous Substances) Regulations 1996 2089—Carriage of Dangerous Goods by Rail Regulations 1996 2090—Packaging, Labelling and Carriage of Radioactive Material by Rail Regulations 1996 2092—Carriage of Dangerous Goods (Classification, Packaging and Labelling) and Use of Transportable Pressure Receptacles Regulations 1996
Council Dir. 96/51 ([1996] OJ L235/39)	1049—Feeding Stuffs (Establishments and Intermediaries) Regulations 1998 1871—Feedingstuffs (Zootechnical Products) Regulations 1999 1872—Feeding Stuffs (Establishments and Intermediaries) Regulations 1999
Council Dir. 96/57 ([1996] OJ L236/36)	1941—Energy Efficiency (Refrigerators and Freezers) Regulations 1997
Council Dir. 96/58 ([1996] OJ L236/44)	3039—Personal Protective Equipment (EC Directive) (Amendment) Regulations 1996
Council Dir. 96/59 ([1996] OJ L243/31)	396—Environmental Protection Act 1990 (Extension of Section 140) Regulations 1999
Council Dir. 96/67 ([1996] OJ L272/36)	2389—Airports (Groundhandling) Regulations 1997
Council Dir. 96/69 ([1996] OJ L282/64)	191—Motor Vehicles (EC Type Approval) (Amendment) Regulations 1997
Council Dir. 96/71 ([1996] OJ L018/1)	3163—Equal Opportunities (Employment Legislation) (Territorial Limits) Regulations 1999
Council Dir. 96/72 ([1996] OJ L304/10)	616—Seeds (Miscellaneous Amendments) Regulations 1997 1474—Seed Potatoes (Amendment) Regulations 1997
Council Dir. 96/79 ([1996] OJ L18/7)	2051—Motor Vehicles (EC Type Approval) Regulations 1998
Council Dir. 96/82 ([1997] OJ L10/13)	743—Control of Major Accident Hazards Regulations 1999 981—Planning (Control of Major-Accident Hazards) Regulations 1999

Council Dir. 96/83 ([1997] OJ L48/16)

814—Sweeteners in Food (Amendment) Regulations 1997

Council Dir. 96/85 ([1996] OJ L86/4)

1413—Miscellaneous Food Additives (Amendment) Regulations 1997

Council Dir. 96/89 ([1996] OJ L338/85)

803—Energy Information (Washing Machines) (Amendment) Regulations 1997

Council Dir. 96/90 ([1996] OJ L13/24)

157—Miscellaneous Products of Animal Origin (Import Conditions) Regulations 1999

Council Dir. 96/98 ([1997] OJ L146/26)

1957—Merchant Shipping (Marine Equipment) Regulations 1999

Council Dir. 96/100 ([1996] OJ L60/59)

1719—Return of Cultural Objects (Amendment) Regulations 1997

Council Dir. 97/2 ([1997] OJ L25/24)

1709—Welfare of Livestock (Amendment) Regulations 1998

Council Dir. 97/4 ([1997] OJ L43/21)

253—Food Labelling (Amendment) Regulations (Northern Ireland) 1998
1398—Food Labelling (Amendment) Regulations 1998

Council Dir. 97/5 ([1997] OJ L 43/25)

1876—Cross-border Credit Transfers Regulations 1999

Council Dir. 97/9 ([1997] OJ L84/22)

2169—Investor Compensation Scheme Regulations 1998

Council Dir. 97/11 ([1997] OJ L73/5)

89—Roads (Environmental Impact Assessment) Regulations (Northern Ireland) 1999

293—Town and Country Planning (Environmental Impact Assessment) (England and Wales) Regulations 1999

360—Offshore Petroleum Production and Pipelines (Assessment of Environmental Effects) Regulations 1999

369—Highways (Assessment of Environmental Effects) Regulations 1999
415—Environmental Impact Assessment (Fish Farming in Marine Waters) Regulations (Northern Ireland) 1999

1672—Public Gas Transporter Pipe-Line Works (Environmental Impact Assessment) Regulations 1999
2226—Transport and Works (Assessment of Environmental Effects) Regulations 1998
2228—Environmental Impact Assessment (Forestry) (England and Wales) Regulations 1999
2892—Nuclear Reactors (Environmental Impact Assessment for Decommissioning) Regulations 1999

Council Dir. 97/13 ([1997] OJ L117/15)

2930—Telecommunications (Licensing) Regulations 1997
3180—Telecommunications (Appeals) Regulations 1999

2450—Telecommunications (Licence Modification) (Standard Schedules) Regulations 1999
2451—Telecommunications (Licence Modification) (Fixed Voice Telephony and International Facilities Operator Licences) Regulations 1999
2452—Telecommunications (Licence Modification) (Mobile Public Telecommunication Operators) Regulations 1999

Council Dir. 97/13 ([1997] OJ L117/15)—*cont.*	2453—Telecommunications (Licence Modification) (British Telecommunications Plc) Regulations 1999
	2454—Telecommunications (Licence Modification) (Cable and Local Delivery Operator Licences) Regulations 1999
	2455—Telecommunications (Licence Modification) (Kingston Communications (Hull) PLC) Regulations 1999
Council Dir. 97/16 ([1997] OJ L116/31)	545—Environmental Protection (Controls on Hexachloroethane) Regulations 1998
Council Dir. 97/18 ([1997] OJ L114/43)	2914—Cosmetic Products (Safety) (Amendment) Regulations 1997
Council Dir. 97/23 ([1997] OJ L181/1)	2001—Pressure Equipment Regulations 1999
Council Dir. 97/26 ([1997] OJ L150/41)	1420—Driving Licences (Community Driving Licence) Regulations 1998
Council Dir. 97/27 ([1997] OJ L233/1)	2051—Motor Vehicles (EC Type Approval) Regulations 1998
Council Dir. 97/33 ([1997] OJ L192/1)	2931—Telecommunications (Interconnection) Regulations 1997
Council Dir. 97/36 ([1997] OJ L202/60)	3196—Television Broadcasting Regulations 1998
Council Dir. 97/41 ([1997] OJ L184/33)	2922—Pesticides (Maximum Residue Levels in Crops, Food and Feeding Stuffs) (Amendment) Regulations 1998
Council Dir. 97/43 ([1997] OJ L180/22)	3232—Ionising Radiations Regulations 1999
Council Dir. 97/44 ([1997] OJ L206/62)	2982—Summer Time Order 1997
Council Dir. 97/45 ([1997] OJ L196/77)	2914—Cosmetic Products (Safety) (Amendment) Regulations 1997
Council Dir. 97/47 ([1997] OJ L211/45)	104—Feeding Stuffs (Amendment) Regulations 1998
Council Dir. 97/51 ([1997] OJ L295/23)	2932—Telecommunications (Open Network Provision and Leased Lines) Regulations 1997
	3180—Telecommunications (Appeals) Regulations 1999
Council Dir. 97/60 ([1997] OJ L331/7)	2257—Extraction Solvents in Food (Amendment) Regulations 1998
Council Dir. 97/61 ([1997] OJ L295/35)	83—Food Safety (Fishery Products and Live Shellfish) (Hygiene) (Amendment) Regulations 1999
	399—Food Safety (Fishery Products and Live Shellfish) (Hygiene) Amendment Regulations 1999
Council Dir. 97/63 ([1997] OJ L335/15)	2024—Fertilisers (Amendment) Regulations 1998
Council Dir. 97/66 ([1998] OJ L24/1)	3170—Telecommunications (Data Protection and Privacy) (Direct Marketing) Regulations 1998
	2093—Telecommunications (Data Protection and Privacy) Regulations 1999
Council Dir. 97/67 ([1997] OJ L15/14)	2107—Postal Services Regulations 1999
Council Dir. 97/68 ([1997] OJ L59/1)	1053—Non-Road Mobile Machinery (Emission of Gaseous and Particulate Pollutants) Regulations 1999
Council Dir. 97/70 ([1998] OJ L34/1)	2998—Fishing Vessels (EC Directive on Harmonised Safety Regime) Regulations 1999
	3210—Merchant Shipping (Radio) (Fishing Vessels) Regulations 1999

Council Dir. 97/74 ([1997] OJ L10/22)

3323—Transnational Information and Consultation of Employees Regulations 1999

Council Dir. 97/419 ([1997] OJ L178/1)

1694—Dual-Use and Related Goods (Export Control) (Amendment No.3) Regulations 1997

Council Dir. 98/3 ([1998] OJ L101/17)

3177—Consumer Credit (Total Charge for Credit, Agreements and Advertisements) (Amendment) Regulations 1999

Council Dir. 98/6 ([1998] OJ L180/27)

3042—Price Marking Order 1999

Council Dir. 98/10 ([1998] OJ L101/24)

1580—Telecommunications (Open Network Provision) (Voice Telephony) Regulations 1998

Council Dir. 98/12 ([1998] OJ L81/1)

2051—Motor Vehicles (EC Type Approval) Regulations 1998

Council Dir. 98/16 ([1998] OJ L209/50)

2072—Feeding Stuffs (Amendment) (No.2) Regulations 1998

Council Dir. 98/20 ([1998] OJ L107/4)

1452—Aeroplane Noise Regulations 1999

Council Dir. 98/25 ([1998] OJ L133/19)

1433—Merchant Shipping (Port State Control) (Amendment) Regulations 1998

Council Dir. 98/26 ([1998] OJ L166/45)

2979—Financial Markets and Insolvency (Settlement Finality) Regulations 1999

Council Dir. 98/35 ([1998] OJ L172/1)

1704—Merchant Shipping (Minimum Standards of Safety Communications) (Amendment) Regulations 1999
2722—Merchant Shipping (Musters, Training and Decision Support Systems) Regulations 1999

Council Dir. 98/41 ([1998] OJ L188/35)

1869—Merchant Shipping (Counting and Registration of Persons on Board Passenger Ships) Regulations 1999

Council Dir. 98/55 ([1998] OJ L125/65)

2121—Merchant Shipping (Reporting Requirements for Ships Carrying Dangerous or Polluting Goods) (Amendment) Regulations 1999

Council Dir. 98/56 ([1998] OJ L226/16)

1801—Marketing of Ornamental Plant Propagating Material Regulations 1999

Council Dir. 98/57 ([1998] OJ L235/1)

2126—Plant Health (Amendment) (England) Order 1999
2641—Plant Health (Amendment) (Wales) Order 1999

Council Dir. 98/61 ([1998] OJ L268/37)

3448—Telecommunications (Interconnection) (Carrier Pre-Selection) Regulations 1999

3449—Telecommunications (Interconnection) (Number Portability, etc.) Regulations 1999

Council Dir. 98/70 ([1998] OJ L350/58)

3107—Motor Fuel (Composition and Content) Regulations 1999

Council Dir. 98/76 ([1998] OJ L277/17)

2430—Goods Vehicle Operators (Qualifications) Regulations 1999
2431—Public Service Vehicle Operators (Qualifications) Regulations 1999

Council Dir. 98/80 ([1998] OJ L281/31)

3114—Value Added Tax (Amendment) (No.4) Regulations 1999
3115—Value Added Tax (Importation of Investment Gold) Relief Order 1999
3116—Value Added Tax (Investment Gold) Order 1999
3117—Value Added Tax (Terminal Markets) Order 1999

Council Dir. 98/80 ([1998] OJ L281/31)—*cont.*	3118—Value Added Tax (Input Tax) (Amendment) (No.2) Order 1999
	3120—Value Added Tax (Special Provisions) (Amendment) (No.2) Order 1999
	3121—Value Added Tax (Input Tax) (Specified Supplies) Order 1999
Council Dir. 1999/20 ([1999] OJ L80/20)	1871—Feedingstuffs (Zootechnical Products) Regulations 1999
	1872—Feeding Stuffs (Establishments and Intermediaries) Regulations 1999
	2325—Feeding Stuffs (Enforcement) Regulations 1999
Council Dir. 1999/29 ([1999] OJ L332/15)	1528—Feeding Stuffs (Amendment) Regulations 1999
Commission Dir. 71/250 ([1971] OJ L155/13)	1663—Feeding Stuffs (Sampling and Analysis) Regulations 1999
Commission Dir. 71/393 ([1971] OJ L279/7)	1663—Feeding Stuffs (Sampling and Analysis) Regulations 1999
Commission Dir. 72/199 ([1972] OJ L123/6)	1663—Feeding Stuffs (Sampling and Analysis) Regulations 1999
	1871—Feedingstuffs (Zootechnical Products) Regulations 1999
Commission Dir. 73/46 ([1973] OJ L83/21)	1663—Feeding Stuffs (Sampling and Analysis) Regulations 1999
Commission Dir. 73/47 ([1973] OJ L83/35)	1663—Feeding Stuffs (Sampling and Analysis) Regulations 1999
Commission Dir. 74/203 ([1974] OJ L108/7)	1663—Feeding Stuffs (Sampling and Analysis) Regulations 1999
	1871—Feedingstuffs (Zootechnical Products) Regulations 1999
Commission Dir. 76/371 ([1976] OJ L102/1)	1663—Feeding Stuffs (Sampling and Analysis) Regulations 1999
	1871—Feedingstuffs (Zootechnical Products) Regulations 1999
Commission Dir. 76/372 ([1976] OJ L102/8)	1663—Feeding Stuffs (Sampling and Analysis) Regulations 1999
Commission Dir. 77/535 ([1977] OJ L213/1)	1342—Fertilisers (Sampling and Analysis) Regulations 1996
Commission Dir. 78/633 ([1978] OJ L206/43)	1663—Feeding Stuffs (Sampling and Analysis) Regulations 1999
	1871—Feedingstuffs (Zootechnical Products) Regulations 1999
Commission Dir. 79/138 ([1979] OJ L39)	1342—Fertilisers (Sampling and Analysis) Regulations 1996
Commission Dir. 81/680 ([1981] OJ L246/32)	1663—Feeding Stuffs (Sampling and Analysis) Regulations 1999
	1871—Feedingstuffs (Zootechnical Products) Regulations 1999
Commission Dir. 81/715 ([1981] OJ L257/38)	1871—Feedingstuffs (Zootechnical Products) Regulations 1999
Commission Dir. 84/4 ([1984] OJ L15/28)	1663—Feeding Stuffs (Sampling and Analysis) Regulations 1999
	1871—Feedingstuffs (Zootechnical Products) Regulations 1999
Commission Dir. 84/425 ([1984] OJ L238/34)	1871—Feedingstuffs (Zootechnical Products) Regulations 1999

Commission Dir. 87/94 ([1987] OJ L38/1)	1342—Fertilisers (Sampling and Analysis) Regulations 1996
Commission Dir. 87/250 ([1987] OJ L113/57)	1499—Food Labelling Regulations 1996
Commission Dir. 87/566 ([1987] OJ L342)	1342—Fertilisers (Sampling and Analysis) Regulations 1996
Commission Dir. 88/126 ([1988] OJ L63)	1342—Fertilisers (Sampling and Analysis) Regulations 1996
Commission Dir. 89/491 ([1989] OJ L238/43)	58—Motor Vehicles (Designation of Approval Marks) (Amendment) Regulations 1997 191—Motor Vehicles (EC Type Approval) (Amendment) Regulations 1997
Commission Dir. 89/519 ([1989] OJ L265)	1342—Fertilisers (Sampling and Analysis) Regulations 1996
Commission Dir. 90/18 ([1990] OJ L11/37)	654—Good Laboratory Practice Regulations 1997
Commission Dir. 90/128 ([1990] OJ L75/19)	1376—Plastic Materials and Articles in Contact with Food Regulations 1998
Commission Dir. 92/89 ([1992] OJ L344/35)	1663—Feeding Stuffs (Sampling and Analysis) Regulations 1999
Commission Dir. 92/95 ([1992] OJ L327/54)	1663—Feeding Stuffs (Sampling and Analysis) Regulations 1999
Commission Dir. 92/562 ([1992] OJ L359/23)	646—Animal By-Products Order 1999
Commission Dir. 93/1 ([1993] OJ L113)	1342—Fertilisers (Sampling and Analysis) Regulations 1996
Commission Dir. 93/28 ([1993] OJ L179/8)	1663—Feeding Stuffs (Sampling and Analysis) Regulations 1999
Commission Dir. 93/70 ([1993] OJ L234/17)	1261—Medicines (Animal Feeding Stuffs) (Enforcement) (Amendment) Regulations 1996 1871—Feedingstuffs (Zootechnical Products) Regulations 1999
Commission Dir. 93/71 ([1993] OJ L221/27)	7—Plant Protection Products (Amendment) Regulations 1997
Commission Dir. 93/117 ([1993] OJ L329/54)	1261—Medicines (Animal Feeding Stuffs) (Enforcement) (Amendment) Regulations 1996 1871—Feedingstuffs (Zootechnical Products) Regulations 1999
Commission Dir. 94/1 ([1994] OJ L23/28)	2421—Aerosol Dispensers (EEC Requirements) (Amendment) Regulations 1996
Commission Dir. 94/14 ([1994] OJ L94/30)	1663—Feeding Stuffs (Sampling and Analysis) Regulations 1999
Commission Dir. 94/37 ([1994] OJ L194/65)	7—Plant Protection Products (Amendment) Regulations 1997
Commission Dir. 94/38 ([1994] OJ L217/8)	2374—European Communities (Recognition of Professional Qualifications) (Second General System) Regulations 1996
Commission Dir. 94/51 ([1994] OJ L297/29)	250—Genetically Modified Organisms (Contained Use) (Amendment) Regulations 1996
Commission Dir. 94/54 ([1994] OJ L300/14)	1499—Food Labelling Regulations 1996
Commission Dir. 94/79 ([1994] OJ L354/16)	7—Plant Protection Products (Amendment) Regulations 1997
Commission Dir. 95/2 ([1995] OJ L61/1)	1413—Miscellaneous Food Additives (Amendment) Regulations 1997
Commission Dir. 95/3 ([1995] OJ L41/44)	694—Plastic Materials and Articles in Contact with Food (Amendment) Regulations 1996
Commission Dir. 95/8 ([1995] OJ L86)	1342—Fertilisers (Sampling and Analysis) Regulations 1996

Commission Dir. 95/17 ([1995] OJ L140/26)	2925—Cosmetic Products (Safety) Regulations 1996
Commission Dir. 95/28 ([1995] OJ L281/1)	191—Motor Vehicles (EC Type Approval) (Amendment) Regulations 1997
Commission Dir. 95/31 ([1995] OJ L257/35)	982—Sweeteners in Food (Amendment) Regulations 1999
Commission Dir. 95/32 ([1995] OJ L178/20)	2925—Cosmetic Products (Safety) Regulations 1996
Commission Dir. 95/33 ([1995] OJ L167/17)	1260—Feeding Stuffs (Amendment) Regulations 1996
Commission Dir. 95/34 ([1995] OJ L167)	1446—Cosmetic Products (Safety) (Amendment) Regulations 1996
Commission Dir. 95/35 ([1995] OJ L172/6)	7—Plant Protection Products (Amendment) Regulations 1997
Commission Dir. 95/36 ([1995] OJ L172/8)	7—Plant Protection Products (Amendment) Regulations 1997
Commission Dir. 95/43 ([1995] OJ L184/21)	2374—European Communities (Recognition of Professional Qualifications) (Second General System) Regulations 1996
Commission Dir. 95/44 ([1995] OJ L184/34)	2907—Plant Health (Great Britain) (Amendment) (No.2) Order 1997
Commission Dir. 95/48 ([1995] OJ L233/73)	191—Motor Vehicles (EC Type Approval) (Amendment) Regulations 1997
Commission Dir. 95/54 ([1995] OJ L226/1)	58—Motor Vehicles (Designation of Approval Marks) (Amendment) Regulations 1997 191—Motor Vehicles (EC Type Approval) (Amendment) Regulations 1997
Commission Dir. 95/56 ([1995] OJ L286/1)	191—Motor Vehicles (EC Type Approval) (Amendment) Regulations 1997
Commission Dir. 95/65 ([1995] OJ L308/75)	25—Plant Health (Great Britain) (Amendment) Order 1996
Commission Dir. 95/66 ([1995] OJ L308/77)	25—Plant Health (Great Britain) (Amendment) Order 1996
Commission Dir. 95/96 ([1995] OJ L268/1)	58—Motor Vehicles (Designation of Approval Marks) (Amendment) Regulations 1997
Commission Dir. 96/3 ([1996] OJ L21/42)	2537—Imported Food Regulations 1997
Commission Dir. 96/4 ([1996] OJ L49/12)	451—Infant Formula and Follow-on Formula (Amendment) Regulations 1997
Commission Dir. 96/5 ([1996] OJ L49/17)	275—Processed Cereal-Based Foods and Baby Foods for Infants and Young Children (Amendment) Regulations 1999 2042—Processed Cereal-based Foods and Baby Foods for Infants and Young Children Regulations 1997
Commission Dir. 96/6 ([1996] OJ L49/29)	1260—Feeding Stuffs (Amendment) Regulations 1996
Commission Dir. 96/7 ([1996] OJ L51/45)	1260—Feeding Stuffs (Amendment) Regulations 1996
Commission Dir. 96/8 ([1996] OJ L55/22)	2182—Foods Intended for Use in Energy Restricted Diets for Weight Reduction Regulations 1997
Commission Dir. 96/11 ([1996] OJ L61/26)	2817—Plastic Materials and Articles in Contact with Food (Amendment) (No.2) Regulations 1996

Commission Dir. 96/12 ([1996] OJ L65/20)	7—Plant Protection Products (Amendment) Regulations 1997
Commission Dir. 96/14 ([1996] OJ L68/24)	249—Plant Health (Amendment No.2) Order (Northern Ireland) 1996 1165—Plant Health (Great Britain) (Amendment) (No.2) Order 1996
Commission Dir. 96/15 ([1996] OJ L70/35)	249—Plant Health (Amendment No.2) Order (Northern Ireland) 1996 1165—Plant Health (Great Britain) (Amendment) (No.2) Order 1996
Commission Dir. 96/18 ([1996] OJ L76/21)	1452—Vegetable Seeds (Amendment) Regulations 1996 1453—Fodder Plant Seeds (Amendment) Regulations 1996
Commission Dir. 96/20 ([1996] OJ L92/23)	191—Motor Vehicles (EC Type Approval) (Amendment) Regulations 1997
Commission Dir. 96/28 ([1996] OJ L140/30)	1543—Fertilisers (Amendment) Regulations 1997
Commission Dir. 96/36 ([1996] OJ L178/15)	191—Motor Vehicles (EC Type Approval) (Amendment) Regulations 1997
Commission Dir. 96/37 ([1996] OJ L186/28)	191—Motor Vehicles (EC Type Approval) (Amendment) Regulations 1997
Commission Dir. 96/38 ([1996] OJ L187/95)	191—Motor Vehicles (EC Type Approval) (Amendment) Regulations 1997
Commission Dir. 96/40 ([1996] OJ L196/8)	1433—Merchant Shipping (Port State Control) (Amendment) Regulations 1998
Commission Dir. 96/41 ([1996] OJ L198/36)	2925—Cosmetic Products (Safety) Regulations 1996
Commission Dir. 96/44 ([1996] OJ L210/25)	191—Motor Vehicles (EC Type Approval) (Amendment) Regulations 1997
Commission Dir. 96/45 ([1996] OJ L123/8)	2925—Cosmetic Products (Safety) Regulations 1996
Commission Dir. 96/46 ([1996] OJ L214/18)	7—Plant Protection Products (Amendment) Regulations 1997
Commission Dir. 96/55 ([1996] OJ L231/20)	437—Control of Substances Hazardous to Health Regulations 1999 1357—Control of Substances Hazardous to Health (Amendment) Regulations 1998
Commission Dir. 96/60 ([1996] OJ L266/1)	1624—Energy Information (Combined Washer-driers) Regulations 1997
Commission Dir. 96/64 ([1996] OJ L258/26)	191—Motor Vehicles (EC Type Approval) (Amendment) Regulations 1997
Commission Dir. 96/67 ([1996] OJ L272/36)	2918—Airports (Groundhandling) (Amendment) Regulations 1998
Commission Dir. 96/77 ([1996] OJ L339/1)	1136—Miscellaneous Food Additives (Amendment) Regulations 1999 1413—Miscellaneous Food Additives (Amendment) Regulations 1997
Commission Dir. 96/78 ([1996] OJ L321/20)	3242—Plant Health (Great Britain) (Amendment) (No.3) Order 1996
Commission Dir. 96/86 ([1996] OJ L335/43)	303—Carriage of Dangerous Goods (Amendment) Regulations 1999
Commission Dir. 96/87 ([1996] OJ L335/45)	303—Carriage of Dangerous Goods (Amendment) Regulations 1999
Commission Dir. 96/301 ([1996] OJ L115/47)	201—Potatoes Originating in Egypt Regulations 1998

Commission Dir. 96/385 ([1996] OJ L151/39)

3183—Bovine Spongiform Encephalopathy (No.2) Order 1996

Commission Dir. 96/449 ([1996] OJ L184/43)

955—Fertilisers (Mammalian Meat and Bone Meal) (Conditions of Manufacture) Regulations 1998

Commission Dir. 97/14 ([1997] OJ L87/17)

1145—Plant Health (Great Britain) (Amendment) Order 1997

Commission Dir. 97/17 ([1997] OJ L118/1)

1676—Energy Information (Dishwashers) Regulations 1999

Commission Dir. 97/19 ([1997] OJ L125/1)

2051—Motor Vehicles (EC Type Approval) Regulations 1998

Commission Dir. 97/20 ([1997] OJ L125/21)

2051—Motor Vehicles (EC Type Approval) Regulations 1998

Commission Dir. 97/21 ([1997] OJ L125/31)

2051—Motor Vehicles (EC Type Approval) Regulations 1998

Commission Dir. 97/28 ([1997] OJ L171/1)

2051—Motor Vehicles (EC Type Approval) Regulations 1998

Commission Dir. 97/29 ([1997] OJ L171/11)

2051—Motor Vehicles (EC Type Approval) Regulations 1998

Commission Dir. 97/30 ([1997] OJ L171/25)

2051—Motor Vehicles (EC Type Approval) Regulations 1998

Commission Dir. 97/31 ([1997] OJ L171/49)

2051—Motor Vehicles (EC Type Approval) Regulations 1998

Commission Dir. 97/32 ([1997] OJ L171/63)

2051—Motor Vehicles (EC Type Approval) Regulations 1998

Commission Dir. 97/35 ([1997] OJ L169/72)

1900—Genetically Modified Organisms (Deliberate Release and Risk Assessment - Amendment) Regulations 1997

Commission Dir. 97/37 ([1997] OJ L169/74)

1169—Textile Products (Indications of Fibre Content) (Amendment) Regulations 1998

Commission Dir. 97/39 ([1997] OJ L177/15)

2051—Motor Vehicles (EC Type Approval) Regulations 1998

Commission Dir. 97/46 ([1997] OJ L204/43)

2907—Plant Health (Great Britain) (Amendment) (No.2) Order 1997

Commission Dir. 97/53 ([1997] OJ L257/27)

81—Electrical Equipment for Explosive Atmospheres (Certification) (Amendment) Regulations 1998

Commission Dir. 97/64 ([1997] OJ L315/13)

2084—Dangerous Substances and Preparations (Safety) (Consolidation) (Amendment) Regulations 1999

Commission Dir. 97/69 ([1997] OJ L343/19)

3106—Chemicals (Hazard Information and Packaging for Supply) (Amendment) Regulations 1998

Commission Dir. 97/72 ([1997] OJ L351/55)

2072—Feeding Stuffs (Amendment) (No.2) Regulations 1998

Commission Dir. 98/1 ([1998] OJ L15/26)

1121—Plant Health (Great Britain) (Amendment) (No.2) Order 1998

Commission Dir. 98/2 ([1998] OJ L15/34)

1121—Plant Health (Great Britain) (Amendment) (No.2) Order 1998

Commission Dir. 98/3 ([1998] OJ L18/25)

2024—Fertilisers (Amendment) Regulations 1998

Commission Dir. 98/11 ([1998] OJ L71/1)

1517—Energy Information (Lamps) Regulations 1999

Commission Dir. 98/12 ([1998] OJ L81/1)

2978—Road Vehicles (Brake Linings Safety) Regulations 1999

Commission Dir. 98/14 ([1998] OJ L91/1)	2051—Motor Vehicles (EC Type Approval) Regulations 1998
Commission Dir. 98/16 ([1998] OJ L77/44)	1727—Cosmetic Products (Safety) (Amendment) Regulations 1998
Commission Dir. 98/21 ([1998] OJ L119/15)	1373—European Specialist Medical Qualifications Amendment Regulations 1999
Commission Dir. 98/22 ([1998] OJ L126/26)	2206—Plant Health (Forestry) (Great Britain) (Amendment) Order 1998
Commission Dir. 98/28 ([1998] OJ L140/10)	1360—Food Safety (General Food Hygiene) (Amendment) Regulations 1999
Commission Dir. 98/36 ([1998] OJ L167/23)	275—Processed Cereal-Based Foods and Baby Foods for Infants and Young Children (Amendment) Regulations 1999
Commission Dir. 98/42 ([1998] OJ L184/40)	2198—Merchant Shipping (Port State Control) (Amendment No.2) Regulations 1998
Commission Dir. 98/47 ([1998] OJ L191/50)	2760—Plant Protection Products (Amendment) Regulations 1998
Commission Dir. 98/51 ([1998] OJ L208/43)	1871—Feedingstuffs (Zootechnical Products) Regulations 1999 1872—Feeding Stuffs (Establishments and Intermediaries) Regulations 1999
Commission Dir. 98/53 ([1998] OJ L201/93)	1603—Contaminants in Food (Amendment) Regulations 1999
Commission Dir. 98/54 ([1998] OJ L208/49)	1663—Feeding Stuffs (Sampling and Analysis) Regulations 1999 1871—Feedingstuffs (Zootechnical Products) Regulations 1999
Commission Dir. 98/62 ([1998] OJ L253/20)	1552—Cosmetic Products (Safety) (Amendment) Regulations 1999
Commission Dir. 98/63 ([1998] OJ L253/24)	1373—European Specialist Medical Qualifications Amendment Regulations 1999
Commission Dir. 98/64 ([1998] OJ L257/14)	296—Feeding Stuffs (Sampling and Analysis) Regulations (Northern Ireland) 1999 1663—Feeding Stuffs (Sampling and Analysis) Regulations 1999 1871—Feedingstuffs (Zootechnical Products) Regulations 1999
Commission Dir. 98/65 ([1998] OJ L257/29)	2550—Electrical Equipment for Explosive Atmospheres (Certification) (Amendment) Regulations 1999
Commission Dir. 98/66 ([1998] OJ L257/35)	982—Sweeteners in Food (Amendment) Regulations 1999
Commission Dir. 98/68 ([1998] OJ L261/32)	2325—Feeding Stuffs (Enforcement) Regulations 1999
Commission Dir. 98/73 ([1998] OJ L305/1)	197—Chemicals (Hazard Information and Packaging for Supply) (Amendment) Regulations 1999
Commission Dir. 98/82 ([1998] OJ L290/25)	1109—Pesticides (Maximum Residue Levels in Crops, Food and Feeding Stuffs) (Amendment) Regulations 1999
Commission Dir. 98/85 ([1998] OJ L315/14)	1957—Merchant Shipping (Marine Equipment) Regulations 1999
Commission Dir. 98/86 ([1998] OJ L334/1)	1136—Miscellaneous Food Additives (Amendment) Regulations 1999

Commission Dir. 98/88 ([1998] OJ L318/45)	296—Feeding Stuffs (Sampling and Analysis) Regulations (Northern Ireland) 1999
	1663—Feeding Stuffs (Sampling and Analysis) Regulations 1999
Commission Dir. 98/98 ([1998] OJ L355/1)	3165—Chemicals (Hazard Information and Packaging for Supply) (Amendment) (No.2) Regulations 1999
Commission Dir. 98/272 ([1998] OJ L122/59)	1645—Sheep and Goats Spongiform Encephalopathy Order 1998
	1646—Sheep and Goats Spongiform Encephalopathy Regulations 1998
Commission Dir. 1999/7 ([1999] OJ L40/36)	2324—Motor Vehicles (EC Type Approval) (Amendment No.2) Regulations 1999
Commission Dir. 1999/8 ([1999] OJ L50/26)	2196—Cereal Seeds (Amendment) (England) Regulations 1999
Commission Dir. 1999/9 ([1999] OJ L56/46)	1676—Energy Information (Dishwashers) Regulations 1999
Commission Dir. 1999/10 ([1999] OJ L69/22)	1483—Food Labelling (Amendment) (No.2) Regulations 1999
Commission Dir. 1999/11 ([1999] OJ L77/8)	3106—Good Laboratory Practice Regulations 1999
Commission Dir. 1999/14 ([1999] OJ L97/1)	2324—Motor Vehicles (EC Type Approval) (Amendment No.2) Regulations 1999
Commission Dir. 1999/15 ([1999] OJ L97/14)	2324—Motor Vehicles (EC Type Approval) (Amendment No.2) Regulations 1999
Commission Dir. 1999/16 ([1999] OJ L97/33)	2324—Motor Vehicles (EC Type Approval) (Amendment No.2) Regulations 1999
Commission Dir. 1999/17 ([1999] OJ L97/45)	2324—Motor Vehicles (EC Type Approval) (Amendment No.2) Regulations 1999
Commission Dir. 1999/18 ([1999] OJ L97/82)	2324—Motor Vehicles (EC Type Approval) (Amendment No.2) Regulations 1999
Commission Dir. 1999/27 ([1999] OJ L118/36)	1663—Feeding Stuffs (Sampling and Analysis) Regulations 1999
	1871—Feedingstuffs (Zootechnical Products) Regulations 1999
Commission Dir. 1999/54 ([1999] OJ L142/30)	2196—Cereal Seeds (Amendment) (England) Regulations 1999
Commission Dir. 1999/73 ([1999] OJ L206/16)	3430—Plant Protection Products (Amendment) (No.2) Regulations 1999
Commission Dir. 1999/77 ([1999] OJ L207/18)	2373—Asbestos (Prohibitions) (Amendment) Regulations 1999
Commission Dir. 1999/80 ([1999] OJ L210/13)	3430—Plant Protection Products (Amendment) (No.2) Regulations 1999

Decisions	**SIs**
Council Decision 93/722 ([1993] OJ L337/11)	696—Common Agricultural Policy (Wine) Regulations 1996
Council Decision 93/723 ([1993] OJ L337/83)	696—Common Agricultural Policy (Wine) Regulations 1996
Council Decision 93/726 ([1993] OJ L337/177)	696—Common Agricultural Policy (Wine) Regulations 1996

Council Decision 94/15 ([1994] OJ L10/20)

1924—Fishing Vessels (Decommissioning) Scheme 1997

Council Decision 94/184 ([1994] OJ L86/1)

696—Common Agricultural Policy (Wine) Regulations 1996

Council Decision 94/942 ([1994] OJ L 367/1)

899—Dual-Use and Related Goods (Export Control) (Amendment No.2) Regulations 1998
984—Dual-use and Related Goods (Export Control) (Amendment) Regulations 1999
1007—Dual-Use and Related Goods (Export Control) (Amendment No.2) Regulations 1997
2721—Dual-Use and Related Goods (Export Control) Regulations 1996

Council Decision 95/1 ([1995] OJ L1/1)

33—Hill Livestock (Compensatory Allowances) (Amendment) Regulations 1997

Council Decision 96/613 ([1996] OJ L278/1)

1007—Dual-Use and Related Goods (Export Control) (Amendment No.2) Regulations 1997
2721—Dual-Use and Related Goods (Export Control) Regulations 1996

Council Decision 97/100 ([1997] OJ L34/1)

1007—Dual-Use and Related Goods (Export Control) (Amendment No.2) Regulations 1997
1008—Export of Goods (Control) (Amendment No.2) Order 1997

Council Decision 97/214 ([1997] OJ L86/33)

1523—Value Added Tax (Reverse Charge) (Anti-avoidance) Order 1997
1524—Value Added Tax (Place of Supply of Services) (Amendment) Order 1997

Council Decision 97/413 ([1997] OJ L175/27)

1924—Fishing Vessels (Decommissioning) Scheme 1997

Council Decision 98/232 ([1998] OJ L 92/1)

899—Dual-Use and Related Goods (Export Control) (Amendment No.2) Regulations 1998

Council Decision 98/256 ([1998] OJ L 113/32)

163—Bovines and Bovine Products (Trade) Regulations (Northern Ireland) 1998
1135—Bovines and Bovine Products (Trade) Regulations 1998

Council Decision 1999/193 ([1999] OJ L73/1)

984—Dual-use and Related Goods (Export Control) (Amendment) Regulations 1999

Commission Decision 92/562 ([1992] OJ L359/23)

826—Diseases of Animals (Waste Food) (Amendment) Order 1996
827—Animal By-Products (Amendment) Order 1996
1941—Specified Bovine Material (No.3) Order 1996

Commission Decision 92/593 ([1992] OJ L401/33)

1924—Fishing Vessels (Decommissioning) Scheme 1997

Commission Decision 93/623 ([1993] OJ L298/45)

2367—Horse Passports (Amendment) Order 1998
2789—Horse Passports Order 1997

Commission Decision 94/382 ([1994] OJ L172/25)

646—Animal By-Products Order 1999
826—Diseases of Animals (Waste Food) (Amendment) Order 1996
826—Diseases of Animals (Waste Food) (Amendment) Order 1996

Commission Decision 94/382 ([1994] OJ L172/25)—*cont.*	827—Animal By-Products (Amendment) Order 1996 827—Animal By-Products (Amendment) Order 1996 1941—Specified Bovine Material (No.3) Order 1996
Commission Decision 94/474 ([1994] OJ L194/96)	552—Specified Risk Material Regulations (Northern Ireland) 1997 882—Bovine Spongiform Encephalopathy (Feeding Stuffs and Surveillance) Regulations 1999 1941—Specified Bovine Material (No.3) Order 1996 2965—Specified Risk Material Regulations 1997
Commission Decision 95/29 ([1995] OJ L38/17)	646—Animal By-Products Order 1999 826—Diseases of Animals (Waste Food) (Amendment) Order 1996 827—Animal By-Products (Amendment) Order 1996 1941—Specified Bovine Material (No.3) Order 1996
Commission Decision 95/165 ([1995] OJ L108/84)	1699—Dairy Products (Hygiene) (Amendment) Regulations 1996
Commission Decision 95/274 ([1995] OJ L167/24)	1260—Feeding Stuffs (Amendment) Regulations 1996
Commission Decision 95/287 ([1995] OJ L181/40)	882—Bovine Spongiform Encephalopathy (Feeding Stuffs and Surveillance) Regulations 1999
Commission Decision 95/340 ([1995] OJ L200/38)	1699—Dairy Products (Hygiene) (Amendment) Regulations 1996
Commission Decision 95/506 ([1995] OJ L291)	2563—Potatoes Originating in the Netherlands Regulations 1996
Commission Decision 96/239 ([1996] OJ L78/47)	389—Bovine Products (Production and Despatch) Regulations 1997 1905—Bovines and Bovine Products (Despatch Prohibition and Production Restriction) Regulations 1997 2265—Bovine Products (Despatch to other Member States) Regulations 1996 3000—Bovine Products (Despatch to other Member States) (Amendment) Regulations 1996
Commission Decision 96/362 ([1996] OJ L139/17)	389—Bovine Products (Production and Despatch) Regulations 1997 1905—Bovines and Bovine Products (Despatch Prohibition and Production Restriction) Regulations 1997 2265—Bovine Products (Despatch to other Member States) Regulations 1996 3000—Bovine Products (Despatch to other Member States) (Amendment) Regulations 1996
Commission Decision 96/385 ([1996] OJ L151/39)	2387—Bovine Spongiform Encephalopathy (No.2) (Amendment) Order 1997 3186—Selective Cull (Enforcement of Community Compensation Conditions) Regulations 1996
Commission Decision 96/449 ([1996] OJ L184/43)	646—Animal By-Products Order 1999
Commission Decision 96/599 ([1996] OJ L265)	2563—Potatoes Originating in the Netherlands Regulations 1996

Commission Decision 97/89 ([1997] OJ L27/45)	330—Countryside Premium Scheme (Scotland) Regulations 1997
Commission Decision 97/125 ([1997] OJ L48/35)	616—Seeds (Miscellaneous Amendments) Regulations 1997
Commission Decision 97/613 ([1997] OJ L248/33)	2238—Food (Pistachios from Iran) (Emergency Control) Order 1997
Commission Decision 98/109 ([1998] OJ L27/47)	349—Plant Health (Great Britain) (Amendment) Order 1998
Commission Decision 98/256 ([1998] OJ L113/32)	1103—Bovines and Bovine Products (Trade) Regulations 1999
Commission Decision 98/503 ([1998] OJ L225/34)	3167—Potatoes Originating in Egypt (Amendment) Regulations 1998
Commission Decision 98/564 ([1998] OJ L273/37)	1103—Bovines and Bovine Products (Trade) Regulations 1999
Commission Decision 98/692 ([1998] OJ L328/28)	1103—Bovines and Bovine Products (Trade) Regulations 1999
Commission Decision 98/738 ([1998] OJ L354/62)	3168—Potatoes Originating in the Netherlands (Amendment) Regulations 1998
Commission Decision 1999/356 ([1999] OJ L139/32)	1800—Food (Peanuts from Egypt) (Emergency Control) Order 1999
Commission Decision 1999/363 ([1999] OJ L141/24)	1542—Food (Animals and Animal Products from Belgium) (Emergency Control) Order 1999 1543—Animal Feedingstuffs from Belgium (Control) Regulations 1999 1763—Food (Animals and Animal Products from Belgium) (Emergency Control) (Amendment) Order 1999 1764—Animal Feedingstuffs from Belgium (Control) (Amendment) Regulations 1999
Commission Decision 1999/389 ([1999] OJ L147/26)	1763—Food (Animals and Animal Products from Belgium) (Emergency Control) (Amendment) Order 1999 1764—Animal Feedingstuffs from Belgium (Control) (Amendment) Regulations 1999
Commission Decision 1999/390 ([1999] OJ L147/29)	1763—Food (Animals and Animal Products from Belgium) (Emergency Control) (Amendment) Order 1999 1764—Animal Feedingstuffs from Belgium (Control) (Amendment) Regulations 1999
Commission Decision 1999/419 ([1999] OJ L159/60)	1763—Food (Animals and Animal Products from Belgium) (Emergency Control) (Amendment) Order 1999 1764—Animal Feedingstuffs from Belgium (Control) (Amendment) Regulations 1999
Commission Decision 1999/449 ([1999] OJ L175/70)	2025—Food (Animals and Animal Products from Belgium) (Emergency Control) (England and Wales) Order 1999 2026—Animal Feedingstuffs from Belgium (Control) (England and Wales) Regulations 1999 2332—Food (Animals and Animal Products from Belgium) (Emergency Control) (England and Wales) (No.2) Order 1999 2333—Animal Feedingstuffs from Belgium (Control) (England and Wales) (No.2) Regulations 1999
Commission Decision 1999/551 ([1999] OJ L209/42)	2333—Animal Feedingstuffs from Belgium (Control) (England and Wales) (No.2) Regulations 1999

Commission Decision 1999/552 ([1999] OJ L209/42)	2332—Food (Animals and Animal Products from Belgium) (Emergency Control) (England and Wales) (No.2) Order 1999
Commission Decision 1999/640 ([1999] OJ L253/19)	2798—Food (Animals and Animal Products from Belgium) (Emergency Control) (England and Wales) (No.3) Order 1999
	2799—Animal Feedingstuffs from Belgium (Control) (England and Wales) (No.3) Regulations 1999
Commission Decision 1999/788 ([1999] OJ L310/62)	3421—Food (Animal Products from Belgium) (Emergency Control) (England and Wales) Order 1999
	3422—Animal Feedingstuffs from Belgium (Control) (England and Wales) (No.4) Regulations 1999

EUROPEAN LEGISLATION IMPLEMENTED BY SCOTTISH STATUTORY INSTRUMENTS

The table below lists, in chronological order, the European legislation implemented by Scottish Statutory Instruments issued in 1999.

Regulations	**SSIs**
Council Reg. 2991/94 ([1994] OJ L316/2)	34—Spreadable Fats (Marketing Standards) (Scotland) Regulations 1999
Commission Reg. 577/97 ([1997] OJ L87/3)	34—Spreadable Fats (Marketing Standards) (Scotland) Regulations 1999

Directives	**SSIs**
Council Dir. 77/93 ([1977] OJ L26/20)	22—Plant Health (Amendment) (Scotland) Order 1999
Council Dir. 85/337 ([1985] OJ L175/40)	1—Environmental Impact Assessment (Scotland) Regulations 1999
	43—Environmental Impact Assessment (Forestry) (Scotland) Regulations 1999
Council Dir. 97/11 ([1997] OJ L73/5)	1—Environmental Impact Assessment (Scotland) Regulations 1999
	43—Environmental Impact Assessment (Forestry) (Scotland) Regulations 1999
Council Dir. 98/57 ([1998] OJ L235/1)	22—Plant Health (Amendment) (Scotland) Order 1999

Decisions	**SSIs**
Commission Decision 1999/449 ([1999] OJ L175/70)	14—Food (Animals and Animal Products from Belgium) (Emergency Control) (Scotland) Order 1999
	15—Animal Feedingstuffs from Belgium (Control) (Scotland) Regulations 1999
	32—Food (Animals and Animal Products from Belgium) (Emergency Control) (No.2) (Scotland) Order 1999
	33—Animal Feedingstuffs from Belgium (Control) (No.2) (Scotland) Regulations 1999
Commission Decision 1999/551 ([1999] OJ L209/42)	32—Food (Animals and Animal Products from Belgium) (Emergency Control) (No.2) (Scotland) Order 1999
	33—Animal Feedingstuffs from Belgium (Control) (No.2) (Scotland) Regulations 1999